KT-466-260

Reader's Digest

REVERSE DICTIONARY

READER'S DIGEST REVERSE DICTIONARY

Text compiled by WordCraft Editing and Writing Limited

Edited and designed by
The Reader's Digest Association Limited, London

Printed in Italy

ISBN 0 276 49541 1

The typeface used for text in this book is
8 on 9pt Times Roman

Reader's Digest

REVERSE DICTIONARY

Published by

THE READER'S DIGEST ASSOCIATION LIMITED

London · New York · Montreal · Sydney

Contributors

EDITOR
John Ellison Kahn, MA, DPhil

CONSULTANT EDITOR
Robert Ilson, MA, PhD
Associate Director of The Survey of English Usage
Honorary Research Fellow, University College, London
Editor, International Journal of Lexicography

The publishers thank the following for their valuable editorial and lexicographic contributions to this book:

Faye Carney, MA

Sylvia Chalker, MA

Emily Driver, BA

Nicholas Jones, MA

Contents

Charts and illustrations

QUICK-REFERENCE FEATURES THAT PINPOINT THE WORD YOU NEED

Page numbers in **bold** figures indicate charts and tables
Page numbers in *italic* figures indicate illustrations

From the idea to the word

THE REVERSE DICTIONARY AND HOW IT WORKS

Everyone has experienced the frustration of mislaying a familiar word. You know what you want to say; you know that the precise word exists that would enable you to say it; and you know that you *know* this word ... but when you reach for it, it's not there. That's when the pantomime of exasperation begins: you snap your fingers, you frown, you rummage about in your mental attic, you say "It's on the tip of my tongue" or "What's that word — oh, *you* know." But the word, hovering just out of reach, continues to elude and tantalise you.

Psychologists studying this phenomenon compare it to being on the brink of a sneeze. Anticipation ... concentration ... and — frustration. What's needed, so to speak, is a pinch of snuff. The *Reverse Dictionary* provides one. It's a linguistic snuffbox, helping to release that pent-up sneeze. The relief it affords should be considerable.

Several angles of attack

The *Reverse Dictionary* is above all a word-finder. Its purpose is to identify the precise word for an idea that may be in your mind but that you can't express. You have the idea; the book provides the word. It does this by directing you from a familiar word connected with the idea to the elusive word you are looking for — from the word you know to the word you need.

The familiar "cue word" leads to the tricky "target word" in any of three different ways:

— by means of a definition leading you directly to the target word

— by referring you to a chart of terms on a particular subject, with the target word among them

— by referring you to an illustration on which the target word is pinpointed.

Suppose you are trying to recall or discover the name for the sculpture of a woman that serves as a column supporting the roof of a building in ancient Greece. Various words come to mind as possible cues — *woman*, say, or *sculpture*, or *column*. Look up any of these cue words, and it will lead you to the target word CARYATID. *Woman* takes you there by way of a definition, *sculpture* by way of a chart of sculpture terms, and *column* by way of an illustration.

Note the distinctive feature of this approach in each case: instead of starting with a headword and moving on to the definition, as in a conventional dictionary, the *Reverse Dictionary* starts with the definition, as it were, and leads from there to the word you are seeking — hence the title of the book.

Hitting the target

Most target words can be approached from several directions. First, you can look up any of several *synonyms*. If you're trying to remember the word TRAJECTORY, for instance, you'll find it if you look up **path** or **curve** ("curved flight path...") or **flight** ("flight path..."). Or you may approach the target word from its cluster of *associations* rather than its synonyms: a ball thrown through the air has a trajectory, so you might aim at the target word by looking up **ball** or **throw**. And since missiles too have trajectories, you could use the cue word **missile** to hit the target.

The linguistic side of the human mind works by lateral thinking as well as straight-line logical thinking, and many cue words have been selected to make provision for this. You can often approach a target word through its *collocations* — that is, through phrases in which it commonly occurs, phrases such as *connubial bliss*, *a sedentary job*, and *rancid butter*. You might accordingly look up the cue words **bliss**, **job**, and **butter** to find the respective target words CONNUBIAL, SEDENTARY, and RANCID.

A target word may even be cued by its *opposite* if that seems a promising approach. So the term RELEGATION could be found by looking up **promotion**, and LEVITY could be found by looking up **serious**.

Clearly it would be impracticable to provide every single possible approach to a target word, but the most promising and productive approaches will be there. If you don't find the cue word you want first time, just try again. "What's the word for that tiny Japanese tree — a sort of pot plant? ... oh, *you* know." You won't find the answer if you look up **tiny** – there are hundreds of tiny things, so **tiny** isn't really a useful cue word. But if you try again, and look up **miniature**, or **dwarf**, or simply **tree**, or **pot plant**, or the chart of **Japanese terms** ... you'll hit the target each time: BONSAI!

Enriching your vocabulary

The *Reverse Dictionary* is more than just a word-finder. It's a vocabulary-builder too. It sets out to extend your command of words — to bring into the centre of your working vocabulary those words that have up to now been only on its fringes. And it goes a step further — venturing beyond the fringes of the familiar, to give you access to the hinterland of the English language.

For the most part, the target words are moderately tricky, words at the level of TRAJECTORY, CONNUBIAL, and RELEGATION, or CORUSCATING, CRUSTACEAN, EUTHANASIA, ECLECTIC, PARSIMONIOUS, NONCHALANT, METAMORPHOSIS, EXUBERANT, PANACEA ...

But some target words seem to fall outside this middle range, and to be either very familiar or very obscure. This is often because the *meaning*, rather than the word, is under consideration. Take the terms STAR, CROWN, GLOVE BOX, and PEEL — extremely simple terms surely, and yet not so simple when it comes to connecting them with special meanings that you might have in mind. The term STAR can refer to the white spot on a horse's forehead (you'll find it at the cue word **horse**). The small, notched winding knob on an old-fashioned watch is a CROWN. The glove box in the dashboard of a car is not the only glove box — there's a laboratory GLOVE BOX too, the glass box with rubber gloves sealed into the side for handling dangerous radioactive or poisonous substances. And when a baker uses a long flat shovel to take bread or pies out of the oven, the implement that he's wielding is a PEEL.

Words you didn't know

Conversely, the words RETIARIUS, AUTOTOMY, ENTASIS, and ROWEL may be utterly unfamiliar to you. But you probably are familiar with their meanings — with the *ideas* underlying the words. A RETIARIUS was the gladiator in ancient Rome who went into the arena armed with a net and trident rather than a sword. When a lizard sheds its tail to escape an attacker, the process is known as AUTOTOMY. The slight bulge that makes a column on a Greek temple appear straight when viewed from below is called an ENTASIS. And the small toothed wheel on the end of the spur on a cowboy's boot is a ROWEL.

Sometimes even the idea, not just the word, may be unfamiliar to you, as with MOXIBUSTION perhaps, referring to a kind of alternative therapy that involves setting fire to herbs placed on the patient's skin.

There's a sprinkling of such complex terms spicing the text throughout — words you didn't know you didn't know.

Entertaining words

Some of these unfamiliar terms are just high-falutin synonyms for perfectly familiar words: ANTHROPOPHAGI for *cannibals*, or LYCANTHROPE for *werewolf*. Some are the unfamiliar technical terms for all-too-familiar realities. The romantic-sounding BORBORYGMUS refers to the less than romantic condition of tummy rumbling. The grandiose SINGULTUS refers to the humble hiccup. And the resonant STERNUTATION is simply — sneezing.

Such words would, of course, sound very pompous if used freely in conversation, and tend to be pretentious even in formal writing, but they're certainly worth *knowing*. And they're fun. This points to a third function of the *Reverse Dictionary*: providing enjoyment. Supplementing the book's value as a word-finder and a vocabulary-builder is its entertainment value. Many of the obscurer terms in the text have been included for sheer fun — swashbuckling, cheeky, invigorating, their claims are irresistible. A tightrope walker can be called a FUNAMBULIST, and a striptease artist an ECDYSIAST (the word *ecdysis* is the technical term for the sloughing of skin, as by a snake or insect). A DIASTEMA is a wide gap between the teeth, and a DEIPNOSOPHIST is an expert at dinner-table conversation. (Try dropping that casually into the conversation at the dinner table!)

Never at a loss for words

Finally, the book affords you an opportunity for some linguistic creativity of your own. Hundreds of the target words are word-elements rather than fully fledged words — prefixes, suffixes, and combining forms, mostly from Greek and Latin roots ... terms such as the fairly familiar ULTRA-, beyond-, and PSEUDC-, false-, and the less familiar -DENDRO-, referring to a tree (as in *rhododendron*), and -LATRY, meaning worship (as in *idolatry*). These are the materials on which you as wordsmith can get to work if the word you are groping for persists in eluding you. From the last two elements just mentioned, for instance, you could forge the term DENDROLATRY — that is, tree-worship, as practised by various pagan cultures in ancient times. Suppose you want to describe an insect or reptile that eats ants: look up **ant-** to find MYRMECO-, and **-eat-** to find -PHAGOUS — and there you have it, MYRMECOPHAGOUS. Or if you want to refer to a seven-sided coin, such as the British fifty-pence piece: **seven-** gives you HEPTA-, and **-sided** gives you -GON — yielding HEPTAGON.

So you can use the *Reverse Dictionary* inventively, as well as for reference. Use it for fun, as well as for illumination. Consider it a linguistic treasure-chest, as well as a linguistic snuffbox. Rummage among its pages from time to time to enjoy some of the coruscating jewels of the English vocabulary.

Happy browsing then — and successful sternutation.

The Editors

Part One

THE REVERSE DICTIONARY

a or **an** in English grammar, or equivalent word in other languages, introducing without strictly identifying the noun following it INDEFINITE ARTICLE
A-Z, or similar full range of a series GAMUT
abandon See **depart**, **give up**, **energy**, **enthusiasm**
abandoned child or baby, of unknown parentage FOUNDLING
abandoning or voluntary relinquishment of a claim, right, or privilege WAIVER
abbey See illustration, page 12
– abbey or cathedral in some cities MINSTER
– head of a convent, abbey, or similar kind of religious community SUPERIOR
abbot, bishop, or clergymen of similar standing PRELATE
abbreviate, cut short TRUNCATE
abbreviation consisting of initial letters, especially one, such as *BBC*, that unlike an acronym is pronounced as letters INITIALISM
– abbreviation in the form of a symbol or letter, such as &, representing an entire word or phrase LOGOGRAM, LOGOGRAPH
abdomen – abdomen's upper area, below the ribs HYPOCHONDRIUM
– membrane lining the abdominal cavity and covering most of the organs PERITONEUM
– network of nerves in the abdomen, spreading to the intestines and liver SOLAR PLEXUS
– relating to the abdomen COELIAC
abdominal, relating to the front of the body VENTRAL
– abdominal pain COLIC
Aberdeen – person born or living in Aberdeen ABERDONIAN
ability, inherent power, or skill FACULTY, CAPACITY, APTITUDE
– ability or character CALIBRE
– ability or expertise, especially in judging shrewdly ACUMEN
– ability not yet proved POTENTIAL
– extraordinary ability PROWESS
able See also **skilful**, **clever**, **expert**
– able, capable, suitably qualified COMPETENT, PROFICIENT
– extremely able, deft, expert ADROIT, ADEPT
abnormal See also **odd**
– abnormal, as in sexual behaviour DEVIANT
– abnormal, departing from the norm or convention ECCENTRIC, IDIOSYNCRATIC, OUTRÉ, ABERRANT
– abnormal, not natural, usual, or expected PRETERNATURAL
– abnormal, inconsistent, out of keeping, odd ANOMALOUS, INCONGRUOUS
– abnormal, through being corrupted PERVERTED
– abnormal sexual behaviour or act PERVERSION
abnormal- DYS-, PARA-
abnormality such as a disease or disturbed mental state PATHOLOGY
-abnormality- -OSIS, TERAT-, TERATO-
abolish See **destroy**, **get rid of**
abominable snowman YETI
Aboriginal terms See chart, and also **Australian terms**
abortion – bring on an abortion artificially, especially by the use of medical drugs INDUCE, TERMINATE
– emptying of the womb, especially for an abortion, by means of suction through a tube VACUUM ASPIRATION
about, concerning, regarding, relating to APROPOS OF
– about or approximately, as written before an uncertain date CIRCA
about- PERI-
about to happen IMMINENT, IMPENDING
about-turn, U-turn, reversal of attitude or policy VOLTE-FACE
above, term used to refer to an earlier part of a text SUPRA
– above, on top of SURMOUNTING
above- EPI-, HYPER-, SUPER-, SUPRA-, SUR-, TRANS-
abrasive mineral, aluminium oxide CORUNDUM, ALUMINA

ABORIGINAL TERMS

alcheringa/ dreamtime	mythical Golden Age of the past, or time of the creation of the natural world
bora	initiation ceremony for boys
boyla	witch doctor
bullroarer/ thunderstick	small wooden tile that booms when whirled about on a thong, used in religious ceremonies
bunyip	legendary monster haunting swamps and waterholes
churinga	sacred charm or amulet of stone; bullroarer
corroboree	ceremonial gathering and dance festival
didgeridoo	droning wind instrument with a long wooden tube
gunyah	shelter or hut, typically of branches and bark
lubra	Aboriginal woman or wife
nulla nulla	club or heavy stick
waddy	heavy wooden war club or throwing stick
walkabout	period of wandering in the bush, for spiritual renewal
woomera	hooked stick for launching spears or darts
wurley	shelter or hut, typically of branches, leaves and grass matting

abroad – person living abroad on money sent from home REMITTANCE MAN

abrupt in manner CURT

abscess – abnormal opening or passage between a hollow organ and the skin, as caused by an abscess FISTULA

absence or departure that is without permission or notification FRENCH LEAVE

– absence or opposite of something that is positive or real NEGATION

absent – while absent, although absent IN ABSENTIA

absent-minded, inattentive, daydreaming or distracted DISTRAIT, ABSTRACTED, PREOCCUPIED

– absent-minded through being excessively idealistic or romantic QUIXOTIC

– absent-mindedness, daydreaming WOOLGATHERING

absentee, especially from school or work TRUANT

abso-bloody-lutely – separation of the parts of a word by a word or words interposed, as in *abso-bloody-lutely* TMESIS

absolute, certain, without reservation, as a denial might be CATEGORICAL

– absolute, complete, utter outright RANK, UNADULTERATED, UNEQUIVOCAL, UNMITIGATED

– absolute, full, complete as a leader's powers might be PLENARY, PLENIPOTENTIARY

– absolute power, non-democratic rule, dictatorship or tyranny DESPOTISM, TOTALITARIANISM, AUTARCHY, AUTOCRACY

– absolute ruler who is enlightened, and well-disposed towards his subjects BENEVOLENT DESPOT

absolution granted or confession heard by a priest SHRIFT

– obtain or give absolution at confession SHRIVE

absorb, cause to become a full mem-

abbey buildings

ber, part, or participant INTEGRATE, ASSIMILATE, INCORPORATE
– absorb by or as if by swallowing INGEST
– absorbing gas or liquid POROUS
– process, unlike absorption, by which a thin film of substance accumulates on the surface of a solid ADSORPTION

absorbed See **interested**

absorption or gradual acquisition of something through exposure to it OSMOSIS

abstract, simplified, stylised, as a painting or design might be CONVENTIONALISED
– abstract, subtle, or complex, often excessively so METAPHYSICAL
– abstract or imaginary rather than actual NOTIONAL
– abstract sculpture CONSTRUCTION
– non-abstract, realistic as a painting might be FIGURATIVE
– treat an idea or abstraction as a real or concrete thing REIFY

absurd See also **ridiculous**
– absurd or apparently self-contradictory statement that is not necessarily untrue PARADOX
– following through an idea or principle to an absurd extreme REDUCTIO AD ABSURDUM

absurdity, gross misrepresentation, caricature TRAVESTY, CHARADE

abundance See **plenty**, **excess**

-abundant -ULENT

academic clothing, especially dark clothing worn on formal occasions at Oxford University SUBFUSC
– academic conference or discussion COLLOQUIUM
– academic retreat from everyday life, as a university is sometimes considered to be IVORY TOWER
– academic term, in the U.S. or Germany, typically forming half an academic year SEMESTER
– academic treatise or thesis, as for a higher degree DISSERTATION
– relating to two or more academic subjects or fields of study INTERDISCIPLINARY
– strips of white cloth on academic robes GENEVA BANDS

accelerated- TACH-, TACHY-, TACHEO-

accent See also **punctuation**, **pronunciation**, **speech**
– accent, vocabulary, and general form of a language used by a particular regional or social group DIALECT
– accent of a strong regional kind, especially Irish BROGUE
– accented, carrying the principal stress in a word TONIC
– throaty and harsh, as some accents or languages are GUTTURAL
– word in ancient Greek accented on the last syllable OXYTONE

accept, abide by, or reconcile oneself to a ruling, decision, or the like COMPLY WITH, ACCEDE TO, ACQUIESCE IN, RESIGN ONESELF TO

acceptable See also **mediocre**
– acceptable, effective, or sound, as an argument might be VALID
– acceptable to one's taste or ideas PALATABLE
– meet the required standards of acceptability PASS MUSTER
– model of behaviour, standard of acceptability, or the like NORM
– seemingly acceptable or valid, though often suspect PLAUSIBLE

acceptance as true, belief CREDENCE
– acceptance of an agreement or treaty ACCESSION
– acceptance or approval, as of a decision or course of action SANCTION, ENDORSEMENT

accepted widely, generally believed, time-honoured, as a theory or view might be RECEIVED

accepting, as of misfortune or unfair treatment, passive or submissive RESIGNED, ACQUIESCENT

accident, as caused by bad luck rather than negligence MISHAP
– accident or occurrence causing death FATALITY
– fatal accident not due to negligence or criminal intent MISADVENTURE
– tendency to make lucky discoveries by accident SERENDIPITY

accidental, unexpected or unplanned ADVENTITIOUS, FORTUITOUS
– accidental, chance, occurring randomly CONTINGENT, ALEATORY
– accidental, unintended, or impulsive UNPREMEDITATED
– accidental developments, or changes of fortune VICISSITUDES
– accidental yet unlawful killing MANSLAUGHTER

accidentally, unintentionally INADVERTENTLY, UNWITTINGLY

accommodation – assign accommodation to military officers or troops BILLET, QUARTER, CANTON

accompany or escort, especially a young unmarried woman, for protection and propriety CHAPERONE
– accompany troops, ships, or land vehicles for protection CONVOY
– accompanying, associated with, occurring together CONCOMITANT

accomplishment showing great skill TOUR DE FORCE

account, score, or recorded reckoning, as of accidents TALLY
– account, typically detailing the goods or services provided INVOICE
– alter a document or the like in order to deceive FALSIFY
– clearly described in vivid or exciting detail, as an account of an accident might be GRAPHIC
– examine, adjust, or certify accounts or other records AUDIT
– settling of a bill or account RECKONING

accounts book LEDGER

accuracy or strict adherence to the truth VERACITY
– demanding person, insisting on obedience, tidiness, accuracy, or the like STICKLER

accurate See also **precise**
– accurate or indisputably true statement, belief, principle, or the like VERITY

accusation See also **charge**
– accusation or a veiled criticism IMPUTATION
– accusations of a bitter, mutual kind RECRIMINATIONS
– acknowledgment of a telling point, argument, or accusation made against one TOUCHÉ
– false report or accusation, slander, slur ASPERSION
– reject or deny a claim or accusation REPUDIATE
– stop and confront a person, as with an accusation ACCOST

accuse, confront, or criticise TAX
– accuse of a crime, especially treason IMPEACH
– accuse of or charge with an offence or crime, especially before a court of law INDICT, ARRAIGN
– accuse or inform against DENOUNCE

accustomed to, used to HABITUATED, INURED, ACCLIMATISED, ATTUNED, WONT

aces – two aces, the lowest throw in playing dice AMBSACE

achieve or obtain, manage COMPASS, ENCOMPASS

achievement of a final stage or development, highpoint PINNACLE, ZENITH, MERIDIAN, SUMMIT
– achievement or success of a brilliant kind ÉCLAT
– achievement showing great skill or strength TOUR DE FORCE

acid See chart, page 14
– acid-alkali indicator PHENOLPHTHALEIN, LITMUS PAPER
– acid as used for etching on a printing plate MORDANT
– acid-like substance that dissolves anything, believed by alchemists to be discoverable ALKAHEST
– acid or other destructive chemical CORROSIVE
– able to react as both an acid and a base, as some chemicals are AMPHOTERIC, AMPHIPROTIC

– bottle for acids and other corrosive liquids CARBOY
– chemical compound that reacts with acids to form salts BASE
– soluble base that can neutralise an acid ALKALI

acidic or harsh, as in smell, manner, or effect ASTRINGENT

acknowledged, candidly admitted, self-confessed AVOWED

acorn – acorn's cup-like base, or other cup-shaped structure CUPULE
– acorns and beech nuts used as pig food MAST
– acorns and other pasturage for pigs, as in a forest PANNAGE

acrobat or entertainer who twists his limbs and body into abnormal positions CONTORTIONIST
– acrobat or gymnast specialising in turning somersaults or cartwheels TUMBLER
– acrobats' bar suspended from free-swinging ropes TRAPEZE

acronym – abbreviation consisting of initial letters, especially one, such as *BBC*, that unlike an acronym is pronounced as letters INITIALISM

across, from side to side, crossways TRANSVERSELY, ATHWART

across- DIA-, TRANS-

act or adventure, especially a noble or heroic one EXPLOIT
– act or behave in a specified way, conduct oneself COMPORT ONESELF

acting See also **drama**, **theatre**
– acting, especially excessively dramatic acting HISTRIONICS
– acting, provisional, being a temporary substitute for INTERIM, SURROGATE
– acting or speaking beyond the range of one's ability or expertise ULTRACREPIDARIAN
– acting profession, the stage, "boards", dramatics FOOTLIGHTS
– acting ruler during a monarch's illness, minority, or other disqualifying condition REGENT

acting-, in place of- PRO-

action aimed at resisting change or warding off likely defeat REARGUARD ACTION
– action taken to avoid likely trouble or problems EVASIVE ACTION
– behaviour or mental activity directed towards change or action, including desire, striving, and so on CONATION
– stimulation, impulse, or spur to action, drive or prompting MOTIVATION, INCENTIVE, INDUCEMENT

activate a mechanism by releasing a catch, trigger, or switch TRIP, ACTUATE

active See also **energetic**, **enthusiastic**
– active, lively, and vigorous, typically in spite of being old SPRY, SPRIGHTLY
– active, tireless, unfailingly energetic INDEFATIGABLE
– active, vigorous, and enthusiastic ANIMATED
– active in an excessive or uncontrolled way HYPERACTIVE, MANIC, HECTIC, FRENETIC
– actively promoting and committed to a moral or political cause ENGAGÉ
– inactive but still arousable, potentially active LATENT, DORMANT
– no longer active, as a volcano might be EXTINCT
– receiving or being subjected to an action rather than being active or taking the initiative PASSIVE

activity, amusement, or hobby, interesting pursuit DIVERSION, DISTRACTION, AVOCATION
– activity, such as spacewalking, outside the spacecraft while away from Earth EXTRAVEHICULAR ACTIVITY

actor in an old-fashioned masque or mime MUMMER
– actor or actress THESPIAN
– actor or actress who knows a role and can replace the regular actor or actress in an emergency UNDERSTUDY
– actor or comedian who overacts HAM
– actor or other performer having considerable experience, veteran artiste TROUPER
– actor who conveys ideas by the use of expression and gesture rather than words MIME
– actor who has a non-speaking

ACIDS

acetic acid	found in vinegar
amino acid	basis of proteins
ascorbic acid	vitamin C
carbolic acid/phenol	used in disinfectant soap
citric acid	found in lemons, oranges, grapefruit, limes and other citrus fruits
DNA/deoxyribonucleic acid	basis of chromosomes, and hence of genetic transmission
formic acid	naturally occurring in ants
hydrochloric acid/spirits of salt	found in dilute form in the digestive juices; wide industrial application
lactic acid	found in sour milk
malic acid	found in unripe apples and other fruit
nitric acid/aqua fortis	corrosive acid used in making explosives and rocket fuels
nitrohydrochloric acid/aqua regia	used for dissolving platinum and gold, and for testing metals
prussic acid/hydrocyanic acid	cyanide compound, a favourite poison of detective-story writers
RNA/ribonucleic acid	found in all living cells; essential for protein production
salicylic acid	basis of aspirin
sulphuric acid	highly dangerous and corrosive acid, with wide industrial application
tannic acid/tannin	used in tanning and clarifying wine and beer
tartaric acid	used in baking powder
uric acid	cause, when unregulated, of gout

role in a play or film, such as an extra or walk-on SUPERNUMERARY
– actor's cue to speak or enter CATCHWORD
– actor's first public appearance DEBUT
– actor's lengthy speech when alone on stage MONOLOGUE, SOLILOQUY
– laugh inappropriately on stage, as an actor might, or cause another actor to laugh CORPSE
– reappearance of an actor, cast, choir, or the like, to acknowledge applause CURTAIN CALL
– relating to an actor always cast in the same type of role TYPECAST

actress playing a young woman, especially a flirtatious lady's maid in a comedy or comic opera SOUBRETTE

actual See **real**

actually, really, in fact DE FACTO

acupuncture STYLOSTIXIS
– burning of leaf-down on the skin as a means of therapy, sometimes used as a supplement to acupuncture MOXIBUSTION

acute or piercing, as a pain might be LANCINATING

A.D. or Christian era as referred to by non-Christians COMMON ERA, C.E.

adapt See also **change**
– adapt, become integrated or absorbed ASSIMILATE
– adapt, familiarise, adjust to new circumstances ORIENTATE
– adapt or arrange a musical item for different instruments, voices, or the like TRANSCRIBE

adaptable, adjusting to changed conditions PLIABLE, VERSATILE
– adaptable or variable, as working hours might be FLEXIBLE

add, attach, or tack on AFFIX, ANNEX
– add or attach at the end APPEND, SUFFIX, SUBJOIN
– add to, complete, make perfect COMPLEMENT
– add to or aggravate an error or difficulty COMPOUND
– quantity that is added to another ADDEND
– quantity to which another is added AUGEND

added, supplementary, incidental rather than essential or belonging ADSCITITIOUS, ADVENTITIOUS, EXTRANEOUS, EXTRINSIC
– added clause, amendment, or qualification to a legal document, verdict, parliamentary bill, or the like RIDER
– added material at the end of a book, message, or the like AFTERTHOUGHT, POSTSCRIPT, APPENDIX, ANNEXE, SUPPLEMENT, ADDENDUM
– added or growing by a series of steps or additions CUMULATIVE
– added or related feature that is only incidental ADJUNCT

addiction See also **mania**
– addiction to alcohol or drugs DEPENDENCE

adding device, as used in Asia, operated by moving beads on rods ABACUS

addition bit by bit and a gradual increase, build-up ACCRETION
– addition or amendment to a will CODICIL
– addition or increase INCREMENT
– addition or newly acquired possession, as in a library or other collection ACCESSION
– addition or the total reached by it SUMMATION

additional, extra SUPPLEMENTARY, SUPERVENIENT
– additional, supplementary, or accompanying item, as to a motor car FITMENT, ACCESSORY
– additional charge or cost SURCHARGE
– additional or supplementary part, typically added to something more important APPENDAGE, APPURTENANCE, PENDANT
– additional proposition following from the proof of another proposition COROLLARY
– additional section at the end of a novel, piece of music, or the like CODA
– additional sum of money, such as a bonus or an increase in price PREMIUM

additional- EPI-

address See also **speech**
– address a book or other work specifically to a person or group as a mark of respect or affection DEDICATE
– address for postal deliveries that is different from the actual address of the person or business ACCOMMODATION ADDRESS
– address to an imaginary or absent person or a personified thing when digressing in a formal speech APOSTROPHE
– phrase used in the address on a letter that is to be kept at a particular post office for collection by the addressee GENERAL DELIVERY, POSTE RESTANTE

adequate See **mediocre**
– adequate but modest income or standard of living SUFFICIENCY, COMPETENCE

adjective or adverb in grammar MODIFIER, QUALIFIER
– adjective or descriptive term, often a scornful or disparaging one EPITHET
– degrees of comparison of adjectives and adverbs POSITIVE, COMPARATIVE, SUPERLATIVE
– referring or relating to an adjective typically directly in front of the noun, as in *the lonely child*, rather than separated from it by a verb ATTRIBUTIVE
– referring or relating to an adjective that is separated from the noun by a linking verb, as in *The child is lonely* PREDICATIVE
– word such as *the*, *six*, or *your*, that limits a noun and is placed before any descriptive adjectives DETERMINER

adjust See also **change**, **correct**, **improve**
– adjust, adapt, or tailor, as to improve or harmonise MODIFY, REGULATE
– adjust, alter, or tinker with, as to improve the relationship between corresponding parts of a machine ALIGN
– adjust, familiarise, adapt to new circumstances ORIENTATE
– adjust and correct, set right RECTIFY, REMEDY, REDRESS
– adjust organ pipes or a wind instrument to perfect the tone and pitch VOICE
– adjust to a new environment, harmonise ASSIMILATE

admiration See also **praise**
– admiration, great regard, high esteem APPROBATION, VENERATION
– deserving admiration, admirable COMMENDABLE, LAUDABLE, ESTIMABLE
– excessive admiration, doting devotion, hero-worship IDOLATRY

admire greatly, hold in very high esteem REVERE, IDOLISE

admired or beloved person, focus of attention CYNOSURE

admirers – group of ardent admirers CLAQUE

admission of guilt, acknowledgment of wrongdoing or sin PECCAVI, MEA CULPA
– admission qualifications, exams, or ceremony for a university or college MATRICULATION
– admission ritual or ceremony INITIATION

admit, confess, acknowledge AVOW, CONCEDE
– admit defeat in an election CONCEDE
– admitting of or permitting something, such as an interpretation SUSCEPTIBLE

adolescence in its early stages, in which adult reproductive charac-

teristics develop PUBERTY
adorn See **decorate**, **ornament**
adult insect IMAGO
adultery or other sexual unfaithfulness INFIDELITY
– adulterous, referring or relating to a spouse's sexual relationship outside marriage EXTRAMARITAL
– man who tolerates his wife's adultery WITTOL
– man whose wife has committed adultery CUCKOLD
– person cited in a divorce case as having committed adultery with the partner being sued CO-RESPONDENT
– tacit encouragement of a wrongful act, such as the adultery of one's spouse CONNIVANCE
advance arrival or announcer, forerunner, herald PREDECESSOR, PRECURSOR, HARBINGER
– advance explorer, reconnoitrer, scout OUTRIDER
– advance or intrusion into the time or territory of another INROAD, ENCROACHMENT, INCURSION, TRESPASS, INFRINGEMENT
– advance payment, as in a poker game or financial venture ANTE
– advance to a higher level or a more important role GRADUATE
– advancing by degrees or stages, as from one tone or colour to the next GRADATION
– sudden and dramatic advance or change QUANTUM LEAP, QUANTUM JUMP
advanced or clever beyond his years as a sophisticated child seems to be PRECOCIOUS
advantage, benefit, blessing BOON
– advantage of a temporary or uncertain kind TOEHOLD
– anything that can be turned to one's profit or advantage GRIST
– be of help or advantage AVAIL
– exploited person, person who is taken advantage of, dupe STOOGE, PATSY, CAT'S PAW
– have a specified effect, as to one's credit or advantage REDOUND
– person who exploits or takes advantage of another's generosity PARASITE, LEECH
– person who takes advantage of an opportunity, often unscrupulously OPPORTUNIST
– take advantage of an opportunity, turn something to advantage UTILISE, CAPITALISE ON
– take advantage of, especially selfishly and unjustly EXPLOIT
advantageous, favourable, healthy BENEFICIAL, BENIGN, BENIGNANT
adventure, deed, or feat, especially a noble or heroic one EXPLOIT
– adventure story CONTE
– mischievous adventure, spree, prank ESCAPADE, CAPER
adventurer, rogue PICARO, PICAROON
adventurous, flamboyant, daredevil, swaggering SWASHBUCKLING
adventurous spirit See **energy**
adverb or adjective in grammar MODIFIER, QUALIFIER
– degrees of comparison of adjectives and adverbs POSITIVE, COMPARATIVE, SUPERLATIVE
advertise a product by using one's name to recommend it ENDORSE
advertisement, notice, or leaflet distributed widely, handout HANDBILL, CIRCULAR, FLIER
– person who writes the text of advertisements COPYWRITER
– simple catchphrase, motto, or the like used repeatedly, as in advertisements SLOGAN
– simple, catchy tune or rhyme as used in advertisements JINGLE
– unauthorised sticking up of advertisements or other posters in public places FLYPOSTING
advertising and its philosophy MADISON AVENUE
– advertising and publicity language that is misleading or bewildering HOOPLA
– advertising display board HOARDING, BILLBOARD
– advertising or publicity campaign, or advertising in general PROMOTION
– advertising or publicity that is brash and sensational BALLYHOO, RAZZLE-DAZZLE, RAZZMATAZZ
– advertising or selling of an aggressive kind HARD SELL
– advertising pillar on a pavement MORRIS COLUMN
– advertising technique in film and television using flashed images, too quick to be consciously registered, supposedly to influence the viewer SUBLIMINAL ADVERTISING
advice, guidance COUNSEL
– advice or warning MONITION
– observer, as at a card game, offering uninvited comments or advice KIBITZER
– remedial, improving, beneficial, as advice might be SALUTARY
– seeking of or meeting for advice, as from a doctor or lawyer CONSULTATION
advisable, prudent JUDICIOUS, EXPEDIENT
adviser, assistant, right-hand man AIDE
– adviser or wise teacher MENTOR
– adviser to an editor or publisher on the suitability for publication of an academic article REFEREE
– advisers, unofficial yet influential, to a government or business leader KITCHEN CABINET
advocate See **barrister**
aerial, as for a radio ANTENNA
– aerial in the form of a straight metal rod, supported in the middle DIPOLE
– aerial manoeuvres in aerobatics SNAP ROLL, BARREL ROLL; WING-OVER, CHANDELLE
– directional aerial with several parallel elements, as used in radio astronomy and television reception YAGI
aeroplane See **aircraft**
aerosol – liquid or gas for dispersing substances, as in an aerosol DISPERSANT, PROPELLANT
affair, sexual relationship LIAISON
– referring or relating to a spouse's sexual relationship outside marriage EXTRAMARITAL, ADULTEROUS
affect See also **influence**
– have a favourable or unfavourable result or effect REDOUND
– affect, influence, serve as evidence MILITATE
affected See also **pompous**, **high-falutin**, **artificial**
– affected, over-dainty, over-refined, as in movement or behaviour MINCING, NIMINY-PIMINY
– affected, over-elegant, as manner or speech PRECIOUS, GENTEEL, LA-DI-DA
– affected, over-refined, over-elaborate, as with ideas or styles RECHERCHÉ
– affected readily or moved easily SUSCEPTIBLE
– affectedly pretty or fashionable CHICHI
-affected, -suffering -OTIC
affecting or touching POIGNANT, PATHETIC
affection See **liking**
– antagonise, alienate, lose the affection of ESTRANGE
afflicted, as by a disease or disaster STRICKEN
afraid See **frightened**
-afraid -PHOBE, -PHOBIA, -PHOBIC
Africa – bard or oral historian in a West African community GRIOT
– boss or employer in East Africa, or a respectful term of address BWANA
– charm, amulet, or fetish in West Africa, or its supposed supernatural powers JUJU
– brightly coloured cloth strip used as a garment in Africa KANGA, KENTE, KIKOI
– independence or freedom in

East Africa UHURU
– plantation or garden plot in East Africa SHAMBA
– region of northwest Africa between the Sahara and the Mediterranean MAGHREB
– shirt of a bright pullover style worn in West Africa DASHIKI
African – having tightly-curled hair on the head, as black Africans have ULOTRICHOUS
African lily AGAPANTHUS
after, later in time, following POSTERIOR, SUBSEQUENT
after – after the events, with retrospective effect EX POST FACTO
after- EPI-, POST-
afterbirth PLACENTA, SECUNDINES
aftereffects, complications, or condition following a disease SEQUELLA
afterlife – region or state in the afterlife between heaven and hell PURGATORY
– region or state in the afterlife for the souls of unbaptised babies and of just pre-Christians LIMBO
afternoon show, as of a theatrical performance MATINÉE
– afternoon sleep or rest, especially in hot countries SIESTA
– relating to the afternoon POSTMERIDIAN
again, audience's enthusiastic demand for a further performance, as by a musician ENCORE
– again and again, to a sickening extent AD NAUSEAM
again- ANA-, RE-
against one's interests, unfavourable ADVERSE
– vote or argument against CON
against- ANTI-, CONTRA-, COUNTER-, OB-
against the law ILLICIT, ILLEGAL, ILLEGITIMATE
age, historical period, era EPOCH
– age, long life LONGEVITY
– age according to years lived, in contrast to mental age, as used to assess IQ CHRONOLOGICAL AGE
– ageing, growing old SENESCENCE
– dominant outlook and spirit of a particular age ZEITGEIST
– period of being legally under age MINORITY, NONAGE
– person of the same age as another CONTEMPORARY
– retired or discharged because of old age or illness SUPERANNUATED
aged artificially, as some furniture or leather is DISTRESSED
agent, as of a university, in business matters SYNDIC
– agent, representative, or deputy MINISTER, PROXY, COMMISSARY, ASSIGNEE, VICAR
– agent in former times, as for conducting a case in court PROCTOR
– agent legally entitled to control or administer the property or funds of someone else TRUSTEE
– agent or go-between in a sexual relationship PIMP, PANDER, PANDERER, PROCURER
– agent or means mediating between people or things, go-between INTERMEDIARY
– agent or messenger sent on a mission, typically by a government or head of state EMISSARY
– agent or middleman in business dealings BROKER, FACTOR, JOBBER
– agent or representative, as at a conference DELEGATE
– agent secretly representing another FRONT, DUMMY
– agent who runs a landowner's estate STEWARD, BAILIFF
– agent's fee or percentage charged for successfully completed services COMMISSION
– appoint as one's agent, substitute, or representative DEPUTE
– deputy administrative officer or agent assisting a king, magistrate, or the like VICEGERENT
aggravate, worsen, or intensify something EXACERBATE
aggressive See also **hostile**
– aggressive, energetic, pushy, or go-getting COMBATIVE, ASSERTIVE
– aggressive and anti-social person, typically unstable and without conscience PSYCHOPATH, SOCIOPATH
– aggressively or ruthlessly seeking to increase one's own influence, wealth SELF-AGGRANDISING
– ferocious, aggressive person TARTAR
agitation of the mind or the feelings PERTURBATION, TUMULT
agony See **pain**
– occasion or place of great agony GETHSEMANE

AGES OF MAN

	PERSON AGED
quinquagenarian	50+
sexagenarian	60+
septuagenarian	70+
octogenarian	80+
nonagenarian	90+
centenarian	100+

agree, approve, or assent to a belief, opinion, or the like SUBSCRIBE, UNDERWRITE
– agree, correspond, match, be alike TALLY, ACCORD, COINCIDE, COMPORT, CHIME, HARMONISE, QUADRATE, SQUARE, EQUATE
– agree, in a haughty way, to do something DEIGN, CONDESCEND
– agree, share an opinion or conclusion CONCUR
– agree or consent to a request, comply with a demand, or the like ACCEDE, ACQUIESCE
– agree to the demands of an enemy for the sake of peace APPEASE
– make conflicting ideas, facts, or people agree or become compatible RECONCILE
agreeable See also **friendly**, **kind**
– agreeable, open to suggestion or ideas AMENABLE, RECEPTIVE
agreed to by everybody UNANIMOUS
agreeing, harmonious IN UNISON, IN CONCERT
– agreeing or assenting, as by answering yes AFFIRMATIVE
– agreeing with, conforming to PURSUANT TO
agreement, as between rival nations PACT, TREATY, ACCORD
– agreement, especially one by which creditors settle for partial payment of a debt COMPOSITION
– agreement, settlement, or compromise, as aimed at by an intermediary MEDIATION, ARBITRATION, CONCILIATION
– agreement by which wages are raised after a certain increase in the cost of living THRESHOLD AGREEMENT
– agreement or contract COMPACT, COVENANT
– agreement or harmony among parts, claims, or the like CONSISTENCY, COORDINATION, CONFORMITY, CONCORD, CONGRUITY, CONSONANCE, COMPATIBILITY
– agreement or informal understanding between countries or powers ENTENTE CORDIALE
– agreement that is general and widespread CONSENSUS
– acceptance of an agreement or treaty ACCESSION
– affecting or undertaken by two parties, as an agreement might be BIPARTITE, BILATERAL
– announce formally the rejection of an agreement DENOUNCE
– break an agreement, a contract, or the like INFRINGE, VIOLATE, RENEGE ON
– discuss terms, as of a contract, in the attempt to reach an agreement NEGOTIATE, PARLEY

– person or party that signs and is bound to a treaty or other agreement SIGNATORY
– require or lay down as a condition in an agreement or contract STIPULATE
– summary or memorandum of a meeting or agreement, used as the basis of a fully detailed text AIDE-MEMOIRE
– unspoken, implied, understood, as an informal agreement might be TACIT

agriculture See **farming**

aha!, exclamation of triumph on finding, solving, or discovering something EUREKA

aids or provisions, such as buildings and equipment, for a particular activity FACILITIES

aim, goal, desired objective, finishing point TERMINUS AD QUEM
– aim at or strive towards some goal, have an ambition ASPIRE

aimless, unsettled, drifting VAGABOND, VAGRANT

air – aerodynamics testing chamber for studying the effect of moving air speed on cars, aircraft, or the like WIND TUNNEL
– atmosphere of foul vapours or polluted air MIASMA
– bacterium or other organism that can live without air or free oxygen ANAEROBE
– bacterium or other organism that needs air or free oxygen to live AEROBE
– containing as much water vapour as possible, as humid air might SATURATED
– containing large amounts of water vapour, as moist air does, close, muggy HUMID
– death due to lack of air, suffocation ASPHYXIA
– fresh and pure air, as at the seaside OZONE
– low in density, thin, as the air of the upper atmosphere is or a gas might be RAREFIED
– pass fresh air through a room, mine, or the like VENTILATE
– relating to the air or other gases PNEUMATIC
– release air or gas from something, such as a tyre DEFLATE
– surrounding, in the immediate vicinity, as the air or temperature might be AMBIENT

-air- -AER-, -AERO-, ATMO-, PNEUM-, PNEUMO-, PNEUMATO-

air bed or inflatable rubber mattress, as used for floating on in swimming pools LILO

air bladder of a fish SOUND

air bubble BLEB

air conditioners – chemical used in refrigerators and air conditioners FREON
– air-conditioning channel DUCT

air cushion – support a severely burnt patient on a cushion of air LEVITATE

air-fare discount system APEX, PEX

air force See **military**, **services**

air-freshener or fumigating substance in the form of a small cone of an aromatic preparation that is set alight PASTILLE

air mail PAR AVION

air raid or similar intensive attack BLITZ

air-tight, firmly sealed HERMETIC

air traffic – exclusive right of a country to assign internal air traffic to its own carriers CABOTAGE

air turbulence caused by an aircraft WASH

air vent SPIRACLE

aircraft See illustration, and also **jet engine**
– aircraft, such as a balloon or dirigible, that is lighter than air AEROSTAT
– aircraft, train, or the like travelling empty DEADHEAD
– aircraft attack on enemy ground troops, typically a low-flying machine-gun attack STRAFE
– aircraft fuselage or car body in which the stress is taken mainly by the casing MONOCOQUE
– aircraft-launching device, as on an aircraft carrier CATAPULT
– aircraft that is heavier than air AERODYNE
– aircraft that is propelled by flapping wings ORNITHOPTER, ORTHOPTER
– aircraft with both a horizontal rotor and conventional propellers AUTOGYRO, GYROPLANE

aircraft

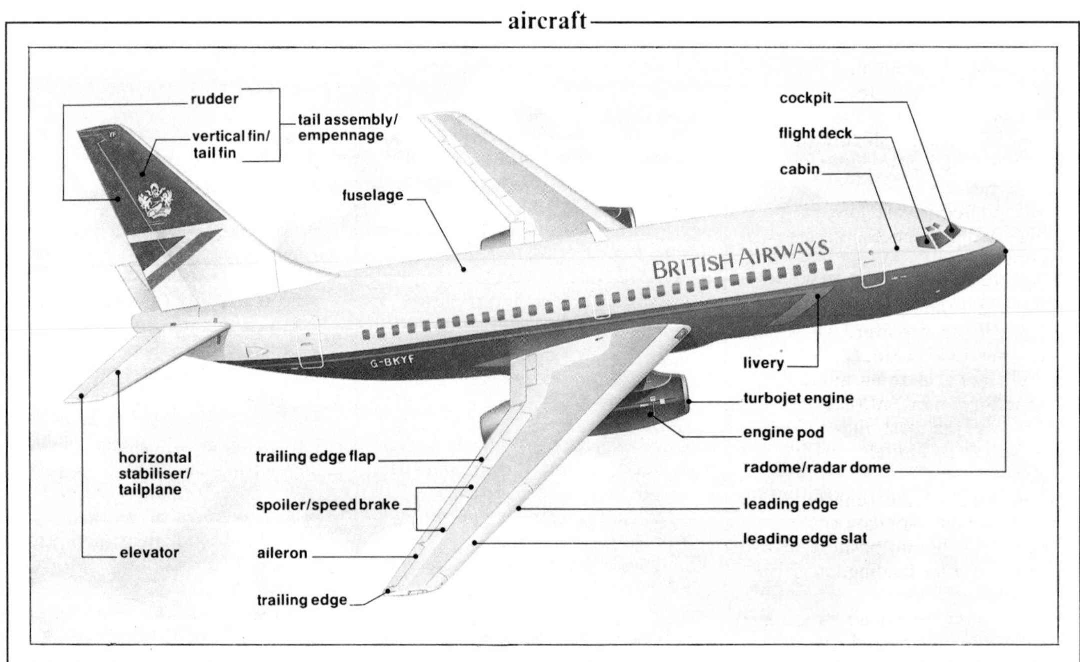

– aircraft that has its tailplane located in front of the main wings CANARD
– aircraft without a pilot, operated by remote control DRONE
– aircraft's "black box" or electronic recorder of technical details, used to establish the cause of a crash FLIGHT RECORDER
– aircraft's cockpit that can be ejected as a unit in an emergency CAPSULE
– aircraft's course or direction, especially when guided by radio VECTOR
– aircraft's flight path, typically circular, when awaiting clearance to land HOLDING PATTERN
– aircraft's load of cargo, passengers, bombs, or the like PAYLOAD
– aircraft's wing, tailplane, flap, or other surface affecting lift or stability in flight AEROFOIL
– aerodynamics testing chamber for studying the effect of moving air speed on cars, aircraft, or the like WIND TUNNEL
– air deflector, as on an aircraft's wing or a racing car, to increase drag and reduce the tendency to lift SPOILER
– arched or upwardly curved surface, as of a road or aircraft's wing CAMBER
– building for parking aircraft HANGAR
– circling an airport at different altitudes while waiting for landing clearance, as two or more aircraft might be STACKED
– explosive bang produced by the shock wave from an aircraft that is flying faster than the speed of sound SONIC BOOM
– fly an aircraft slightly into a crosswind to offset the drift it causes CRAB
– fly an aircraft very low, rising to avoid hedges, fences, and so on HEDGE HOP
– funnel-shaped target towed behind an aircraft DROGUE
– glide without power, as an aircraft might VOLPLANE
– instrument, as in an aircraft, for measuring altitude ALTIMETER
– land or run past the end of a runway, as an aircraft might OVERSHOOT
– land short of the runway, as an aircraft might UNDERSHOOT
– move slowly into position before takeoff or after landing, as aircraft do TAXI
– permission for an aircraft, ship, or the like to proceed, as after a customs inspection, traffic delay, or the like CLEARANCE
– referring to aircraft able to fly faster than the speed of sound SUPERSONIC
– referring to aircraft flying long distances non-stop LONG-HAUL
– seat in a military aircraft designed to hurl the pilot or crew member clear in an emergency EJECTION SEAT
– single raid or mission by a combat aircraft SORTIE
– spin or wobble in flight, as a missile or aircraft might YAW
– streamlined compartment, as for fuel or guns, on an aircraft POD
– sudden, steep, climbing turn made by an aircraft in order to ascend and change direction at the same time CHANDELLE
– take off quickly after an alert to intercept enemy aircraft SCRAMBLE
– tip or tilt sideways, as an aircraft does when turning BANK
– training device consisting of a model, machine, or system reproducing actual conditions, such as a model flight deck of an aircraft SIMULATOR
– transparent bubble-like cover of the cockpit of an aircraft CANOPY
– visible trail of condensed water vapour from the engine exhaust of an aircraft flying at high altitude VAPOUR TRAIL, CONDENSATION TRAIL, CONTRAIL

airfield – tapering cloth tube fixed to a pole to indicate wind direction, as at airfields WINDSOCK, WIND CORE, WIND SLEEVE, AIR SOCK, DROGUE

airport hall for passengers stopping temporarily, as for changing flights TRANSIT LOUNGE
– airport's forecourt for parked aircraft APRON
– conveyer-belt apparatus in the luggage-retrieval hall of an airport CAROUSEL
– open space for crowds, at an airport terminal, station, or other public place CONCOURSE
– rotating belt on floors, as in an airport, for transporting pedestrians and luggage MOVING PAVEMENT, WALKWAY, TRAVELATOR

airship of an early manoeuvrable kind DIRIGIBLE
– airship or balloon typically used as a barrage balloon BLIMP
– airship with a long oval body and rigid frame ZEPPELIN
– basket or cabin under a balloon or airship GONDOLA
– trailing rope on a balloon or airship, used for mooring or braking DRAGROPE

airstream behind a fast-moving aircraft or vehicle SLIPSTREAM

airy, light as air ETHEREAL
– airy, unrealistic VISIONARY

aisle, cloister, or similar covered area for walking AMBULATORY

alarm signal, typically sounded on a bell TOCSIN

alchemist, alchemist's distilling flask, an early form of retort ALEMBIC

alchemy See chart, page 20

alcohol See also **drink**
– alcohol of the basic kind as found in wines and spirits ETHANOL, ETHYL ALCOHOL
– alcohol of a poisonous kind, used as an antifreeze METHANOL
– alcohol or drug addiction DEPENDENCE
– alcohol solution of a medicinal substance TINCTURE
– add alcohol secretly to a drink SPIKE
– ban on the making, selling, and consuming of alcoholic drinks, as in the U.S. from 1920 to 1933 PROHIBITION
– bar or informal shop for the illicit sale of alcoholic drinks, especially during the Prohibition era in the U.S. SPEAKEASY
– bar or informal shop for the illicit sale of alcoholic drinks, especially in Ireland or southern Africa SHEBEEN
– blend or dilute whisky or other alcoholic spirits RECTIFY
– drink alcohol, in moderation or to excess INDULGE, IMBIBE
– leftover impure spirits from the distillation of alcoholic drinks, especially whisky FEINTS
– licensed purveyor of alcoholic spirits VICTUALLER
– lockable cage-like container for displaying decanters of alcoholic drinks TANTALUS
– make, sell, or transport goods illegally, especially alcohol during the Prohibition era in the U.S. BOOTLEG
– moderation in or shunning of the consumption of alcoholic drinks TEMPERANCE
– nausea-inducing substance added to methylated spirits or ethyl alcohol to make it unfit for drinking DENATURANT
– refraining from alcohol ABSTAINING, ABSTINENCE, TEETOTALISM
– valved tap on an inverted bottle of alcoholic spirits, as in a pub, releasing an exact tot measure OPTIC

alcoholic See also **drunk**
– alcoholic, addicted to or characterised by alcoholic drink BIBULOUS

ALCHEMY TERMS

alkahest	universal solvent, dissolving all substances
almagest	medieval textbook of techniques
arcanum	Nature's great secret, sought by alchemists
azoth	mercury considered as the basis of all metals; universal remedy of Paracelsus
elixir	substance able to convert base metals into silver or gold; universal remedy; substance maintaining life indefinitely
luna	silver
magistery	transmuting substance, such as the philosopher's stone
panacea	universal remedy, cure-all
philosopher's stone	stone or similar substance able to convert base metals into silver or gold
transmutation/ sublimation	conversion of base metals into silver or gold

alcoholic drink See **drinks, wines**
- alcoholic drink INTOXICANT, LIBATION, TINCTURE
- small drink of alcoholic spirits SNIFTER, SNORT
- small measure for alcoholic drinks JIGGER
- someone's favourite or usual alcoholic drink TIPPLE

alcoholism, craving for alcoholic drink DIPSOMANIA
- alcoholism treatment, a medical drug that causes nausea when one has an alcoholic drink ANTABUSE, DISULFIRAM
- liver disease or degeneration, typically irreversible, often due to alcoholism CIRRHOSIS
- severe mental disorder, sometimes accompanying alcoholism, involving tremors and hallucinations DELIRIUM TREMENS, D.T.'s

alert, watchful, on the lookout for danger VIGILANT, ON THE QUI VIVE, ARGUS-EYED
- take off quickly after an alert to intercept enemy aircraft SCRAMBLE

algae- PHYCO-

algebra – line drawn above two or more terms in algebra, linking them as a single unit VINCULUM
- algebraic system of symbolic logic BOOLEAN ALGEBRA

all- OMNI-, PAN-, PAN-, PANTO-

all agreeing, of one mind UNANIMOUS

all-embracing, as a view or survey might be PANOPTIC
- all-embracing, wide-ranging, liberal and broad-minded, as one's interests might be CATHOLIC

all-knowing OMNISCIENT

all-powerful OMNIPOTENT

all right, satisfactory, in good order HUNKY-DORY

all-rounder in learning, person who is learned in a variety of different subjects POLYMATH, POLYHISTOR, RENAISSANCE MAN

all the more so A FORTIORI

all together, as a whole, in a group EN BLOC, EN MASSE

allergy – allergy-induced skin rash, hives URTICARIA, UREDO
- substance that induces an allergy, ALLERGEN
- allergy test in which the allergens are applied to the skin by means of a surgical pad PATCH TEST
- allergic response to a medicine, pollen, or some other substance REACTION
- compound released in allergic reactions HISTAMINE
- medical drug used in the treatment of allergies ANTIHISTAMINE
- protein mixture in wheat flour, an occasional source of allergy in children GLUTEN
- sign, such as an allergy or dangerous side effect, that argues for the discontinuation of a medicine or treatment CONTRAINDICATION

alley between buildings GINNEL

alliance or union, typically temporary, of political parties or other groups COALITION

alligator – crocodile from tropical America, related to the alligator CAYMAN

allow, certify, or license something that meets a required standard ACCREDIT
- allow, enable, or permit AUTHORISE, EMPOWER, WARRANT
- allow oneself, in a haughty way, to do something DEIGN, CONDESCEND
- allow oneself to satisfy a whim or craving INDULGE
- allow or tolerate COUNTENANCE, SANCTION

allowance, salary, or similar regular payment or grant STIPEND
- allowance for a day's expenses PER DIEM
- allowance of money to an employee to cover incidental expenses or as an advance on pay SUBSISTENCE ALLOWANCE
- anticipate and make allowance for something unwanted or dangerous DISCOUNT, LEGISLATE FOR

alloy See **metal**
- alloy melted to fuse two metal parts SOLDER
- chief metal in an alloy MATRIX

almond biscuit MACAROON
- almond essence or flavouring RATAFIA
- almond-flavoured Italian liqueur AMARETTO
- almond paste, sweetened and used for sweets or icing MARZIPAN
- adjective for an almond AMYGDALATE
- loosen the skin of an almond by scalding BLANCH

almost or apparently, but not really QUASI-

almshouse – formerly a man living in an almshouse BEADSMAN, BEDESMAN

alone See also **lonely, unique**
- alone, cut off or remote from others of its kind ISOLATED, INSULATED, CLOISTERED, SEQUESTERED
- alone, or preferring to remain alone SOLITARY, SECLUDED
- person who lives alone, withdrawn in solitude RECLUSE, HERMIT

alone- MON-, MONO-

alongside, next to ADJACENT, CONTIGUOUS, ABUTTING, JUXTAPOSED, TANGENTIAL

alphabet See chart, and also **Greek alphabet, scripts, typefaces**
- alphabetic writing system ORTHOGRAPHY
- board displaying the alphabet, used in spiritualism sessions to register messages OUIJA BOARD
- code, as used by radio operators, for identifying letters of the alphabet, such as *Tango* standing for *T* PHONETIC ALPHABET
- series of notches cut into the

front edge of a dictionary or other book, as for easy alphabetical reference THUMB INDEX
– write or spell in the letters of another alphabet TRANSLITERATE

alpine house or hut CHALET

Alps – sing in a voice wavering between normal and falsetto, as among folk-singers in the Swiss Alps YODEL
– situated on, living on, or relating to the other side of the mountains, typically south of the Alps ULTRAMONTANE
– situated on, living on, or relating to this side of the mountains, typically north of the Alps CISMONTANE

also known as, under the assumed name of ALIAS

altar or chapel built specially for prayers or Mass for the benefactor's soul CHANTRY
– altar gift, offering of worship or thanksgiving OBLATION
– altar's canopy, either of fabric or of stone BALDACHIN, TESTER
– altar's covering or pulpit cloth ANTEPENDIUM
– altar's decorative hanging or tapestry FRONTAL, DOSSAL
– altar's platform or shelf, or the decoration for it PREDELLA
– altar's surrounding area or sanctuary in the Eastern Orthodox church BEMA
– cover or canopy over a high altar, supported upon four pillars CIBORIUM
– shelf or ledge above an altar, for the cross, lights, flowers, or the like RETABLE
– tapestry, sculpture, or other decoration behind an altar REREDOS

altar boy ACOLYTE

altarpiece painting or carving in three connected parts TRIPTYCH

alter See **change**
– alter a document or the like with the intent to deceive FALSIFY
– alteration or deliberate mutilation of a document so as to invalidate it SPOLIATION

alternate, proceed in a given order or sequence ROTATE

alternating back-and-forth movement RECIPROCATION

alternative medicine See **therapies**

-alternative medicine- -PATH-, -PATHY

alternatives – situation requiring a choice between two equal alternatives DILEMMA

aluminium – clayey mineral that is the chief ore of aluminium BAUXITE

always See **constant**, **permanent**

amateurish – person whose interest in something is amateurish or superficial DABBLER, DILETTANTE

amazed See **surprised**

amazing, wonderful, or extraordinary thing PRODIGY

ambassador See also **diplomat**
– ambassador from the Vatican NUNCIO
– ambassador or agent fully authorised to represent a foreign government PLENIPOTENTIARY
– document authorising an ambassador or other diplomat to act on behalf of his government LETTERS OF CREDENCE

ambiguity arising from grammatical form rather than from a word's meaning AMPHIBOLOGY
– ambiguity or multiple meaning in individual words POLYSEMY
– remove the ambiguity from, make clear DISAMBIGUATE

ambiguous or evasive, as an answer might be EQUIVOCAL
– ambiguous or evasive behaviour EQUIVOCATION, PREVARICATION, TEMPORISING, TERGIVERSATION
– ambiguous or obscure, as though spoken by an oracle DELPHIC

ambition, desire or striving for success and recognition ASPIRATION
– ambition of an excessive kind, delusions of grandeur FOLIE DE GRANDEUR
– excessive and unjustified, as someone's ambition might be OVERWEENING
– goal of one's ambitions MECCA
– ruin or thwart hopes, ambition, or the like BLIGHT

ALPHABETS AND WRITING SYSTEMS

cuneiform	ancient Middle Eastern script using wedge-shaped characters
Cyrillic	alphabet used in Russian and Bulgarian
Devanagari	syllabic script used in Sanskrit texts and Hindi and other Indian languages
futhark	alphabet of runes
Glagolitic	early Slavonic alphabet
hieroglyphics	ancient Egyptian picture writing
ideography	system of symbolic characters to represent entire words or ideas, as in Chinese
International Phonetic Alphabet (IPA)	standard set of letters and symbols, as used in dictionaries, to represent the sounds of all languages
kana	either of two Japanese syllabic scripts, hiragana or katakana
kanji	Japanese syllabary based on Chinese characters
Kufic	early Arabic script or alphabet
Linear A	ancient Cretan script, still undeciphered
Linear B	ancient script used in Crete and mainland Greece, deciphered in 1952
ogham	ancient angular Celtic alphabet and script, used mainly in Ireland
pictography	system of pictures to represent entire words or phrases, as in hieroglyphics
romaji	Roman alphabet as used to transliterate Japanese
Roman alphabet	standard alphabet of most western and central European languages
runes	ancient Germanic carved alphabetic script
syllabary	set of written characters, each representing a syllable

ambush AMBUSCADE
– ambush, lie in wait for and take by surprise WAYLAY
amendment, clause, or qualification added to a verdict, parliamentary bill, or the like RIDER
amends, atonement or reparation REDRESS, QUITTANCE, EXPIATION
– make amends, compensate or repay REIMBURSE, REQUITE, RECOUP, RECOMPENSE
America and Europe, and the West in general OCCIDENT
American black person considered excessively subservient to whites UNCLE TOM
– American girl fashionable around 1900 GIBSON GIRL
– American middle-class man, narrow-minded and self-satisfied BABBITT
– American nation or government personified UNCLE SAM
American Civil War – referring or relating to the period before the American Civil War ANTE-BELLUM
– referring or relating to the period following the American Civil War POST-BELLUM
American English terms See chart
American football – playing field in American football GRIDIRON
– session of continuous play in American football SCRIMMAGE
American Indian terms See chart
ammunition and weapons MUNITIONS, ORDNANCE
– ammunition box or horsedrawn vehicle formerly used to transport ammunition CAISSON
amoeba or similar tiny organism ANIMALCULE, PROTOZOAN
among- EPI-, INTER-
among other things INTER ALIA
amounting to, equivalent, equal in value or effect TANTAMOUNT
amphibian resembling a lizard in appearance SALAMANDER, AXOLOTL
– study of amphibians and reptiles HERPETOLOGY
amphitheatre – passageway to a bank of seats in a stadium or amphitheatre, as in the Colosseum in Rome VOMITORY

AMERICAN ENGLISH TERMS

billfold	wallet
bobby pin	hairgrip
collect call	reverse-charge call
cotton candy/ spun sugar	candy floss
decal/ decalcomania	transfer, transferable picture or design
derby	bowler hat
diaper	nappy
drapes	curtains
druggist	chemist, pharmacist
faucet	tap
fender	wing of a car
flashlight	battery-operated torch
furlough	leave of absence, as from military duty
hood	bonnet (of a car)
hope chest	bottom drawer, trunk for a trousseau
installment plan	hire purchase
intern	junior hospital doctor, houseman
kerosene	paraffin
longshoreman	docker, dockworker
mortician	undertaker, funeral director
muffler	car silencer
mutual fund	unit trust
odometer	mileometer
pacifier	baby's dummy
pari-mutuel	totalisator, the tote betting system
podiatrist	chiropodist
realtor	estate agent
rummage sale	jumble sale
rutabaga	swede, root vegetable
skillet	frying pan
slingshot	toy catapult
snap fastener	press stud
solitaire	card game of patience
sophomore	second-year student
suspenders	braces
thumbtack	drawing pin
tick-tack-toe	noughts and crosses
transom	fanlight
truck farm	market garden
trunk	boot of a car
tuxedo	dinner jacket; man's formal evening wear
unlisted	ex-directory
vest	waistcoat
veteran	ex-serviceman
zip code	postcode

amputation, either surgical or accidental AVULSION
– amputation or surgical excision ABLATION
– illusory limb, still felt as the source of pain even though the real limb has been amputated PHANTOM LIMB

amuse oneself or occupy oneself in a pleasurable activity DISPORT
– amuse or give pleasure to, as by telling stories REGALE

amusement See also **entertainment**
– amusement, recreation DIVERSION, DISTRACTION

amusing See **funny**

an or **a** in grammar, introducing without strictly identifying the noun following it INDEFINITE ARTICLE

anaemia in which bone marrow produces too few blood cells or other components APLASTIC ANAEMIA

anaesthetic – injection of anaesthetic into the lining of the spinal cord EPIDURAL
– gas commonly used as an anaesthetic LAUGHING GAS, NITROUS OXIDE
– local anaesthetic in common use NOVOCAIN, LIGNOCAINE
– poisonous chemical extract used as premedication before a general anaesthetic ATROPINE
– sedative given to a patient before a general anaesthetic PREMEDICATION
– semi-consciousness or drowsy pain-free state produced by certain anaesthetics TWILIGHT SLEEP
– volatile liquid formerly used as anaesthetic CHLOROFORM, ETHER

anal swelling and itching, piles HAEMORRHOIDS

analyse See also **examine**, **study**
– analyse in order to sort the good from the bad SIFT, WINNOW
– analyse or examine in fine detail DISSECT, ANATOMISE

analysis of a complex project, based on comparing various combinations of stages CRITICAL-PATH ANALYSIS
– analysis of complex information, plans, or the like, into simpler units, especially in an unsophisticated and misleading way REDUCTIONISM
– analysis or critical explanation of a text, especially of the Bible EXEGESIS
– analysis or interpretation of a literary work, theory, or the like EXPLICATION, EXPOSITION
– analysis or review of a recent event, game, failure, or the like POST-MORTEM

AMERICAN INDIAN TERMS

hogan	Navaho cabin of logs and mud
moccasin	soft leather shoe
papoose	baby or young child
potlatch	communal feast in north-west coastal regions, at which property is given away or destroyed
powwow	conference or ritual ceremony; medicine man
pueblo	communal residence or village in the southwestern U.S.
sachem, sagamore	tribal chief
squaw	woman or wife
tepee	cone-shaped tent
tomahawk	light axe
travois	sledge-like vehicle formerly used by the Plains Indians
wampum/peag	shell beads, used as money or decoration
wickiup	temporary hut of grass or reeds over a rough frame
wigwam	arching hut of branches, covered with bark, mats, or hides

– analysis or testing, especially of a precious metal ASSAY
– combining of separate elements into a coherent whole, the opposite process to analysis SYNTHESIS

ancestor PROGENITOR, PROCREATOR, FOREBEAR
– ancestor or forefather, especially the first or earliest ancestor as of a people PRIMOGENITOR
– ancestor or forerunner PRECURSOR, PREDECESSOR, ANTECEDENT
– descended from the same ancestor, though by different lines COLLATERAL
– family tree, or the study of someone's ancestors GENEALOGY, LINEAGE
– group of plants or animals with a common ancestor CLADE
– influenced by or derived from one's ancestors HEREDITARY
– reappearance in a plant or animal of long absent features that had been characteristic of an ancestor generation ATAVISM

ancestry, line of descent LINEAGE, DERIVATION, PEDIGREE

anchor – anchor cable HAWSER
– anchor used for manoeuvring a boat KEDGE
– anchor with several flukes, for mooring a small boat GRAPNEL
– opening in a ship's bow for the anchor cable HAWSE, HAWSEHOLE
– raise an anchor, as in preparation for sailing WEIGH, TRIP
– raised just clear of the bottom, as an anchor might be AWEIGH
– lowest part of an anchor, where the arms are fixed CROWN
– sea anchor DROGUE
– stone anchor KILLICK

anchovies – salad including chopped meat, anchovies, and eggs SALMAGUNDI

ancient, dating back to an earlier era ARCHAIC, ANCESTRAL
– ancient, going back beyond recorded history IMMEMORIAL
– ancient, no longer current, outmoded OBSOLETE, PASSÉ
– ancient, outmoded, or extremely old-fashioned ANTIQUATED
– ancient, primitive, prehistoric PRIMEVAL, PRISTINE
– ancient, stale, or unoriginal, as a joke might be HOARY, MUSTY
– ancient, stretching back to or as if back to the time before the Flood ANTEDILUVIAN
– ancient and respected VENERABLE
– ancient Egyptian writing system using pictures HIEROGLYPHICS
– ancient Middle Eastern writing system using wedge-shaped characters CUNEIFORM
– ancient objects, as of a bygone civilisation RELICS, ANTIQUITIES

– ancient times ANTIQUITY
– relating to the civilisation of ancient Greece and Rome, ancient China, or the like CLASSICAL
ancient- ARCHAEO-, PALAEO-
and – the sign & representing the word *and* AMPERSAND
– *and* or *but*, or similar conjunction joining words, phrases, or clauses of equal status in a sentence COORDINATING CONJUNCTION
– absence of conjunctions, especially *and*, in a phrase or sentence in which they could occur ASYNDETON
– repetition of *and* or other conjunctions for stylistic effect, as in *blood and sweat and tears* POLYSYNDETON
angel, chubby boy, or little cupid, as in paintings AMORETTO, PUTTO
– angel or similar non-physical being INTELLIGENCE
– appearance of a ghost, spirit, angel, or the like VISITATION

ANGELS

the nine orders or choirs of angels (in descending order)

seraphim
cherubim
thrones
dominations/dominions
virtues
powers
principalities
archangels
angels

anger See also **angry**
– anger greatly INCENSE, INFURIATE, OUTRAGE
– anger moderately, irritate, vex IRK, PIQUE, RANKLE
– anger to the point of bitterness or estrangement ANTAGONISE, ENVENOM, ALIENATE, EXACERBATE
– arousing strong feelings quickly, especially feelings of anger INCENDIARY, INFLAMMATORY
– calm or reduce someone's fear, anger, or the like ALLAY
– explode, burst out violently, as in anger ERUPT
– feeling of anger or distress arising from a sense of being injured or wronged GRIEVANCE
– feeling of anger or embarrassment due to disappointment or failure CHAGRIN
– feeling or display of anger, bitterness, or ill will ANIMOSITY, ACRIMONY, RANCOUR
– fit or tantrum, as of anger PAROXYSM, CONNIPTION
– indignation or outrage, feeling of anger or resentment UMBRAGE, HACKLES, DUDGEON
– irritability, moderate anger, ill temper ASPERITY
angle See also **geometry**
– angle, as of a star, from a fixed reference, usually due south on the horizon AZIMUTH
– angle added to another to produce a right angle COMPLEMENT
– angle at which light rays are first reflected by a surface, as of water or glass CRITICAL ANGLE
– angle between a leafstalk and the stem, between a branch and the trunk, or the like AXIL
– angle between lines or surfaces other than a right angle, or such a line or surface BEVEL, CANT
– angle between an aircraft's wing and a horizontal line DIHEDRAL ANGLE
– angle of 0.9°, one-hundredth of a right angle GRADE
– angle or degree of slope GRADIENT, INCLINATION
– angle or fork formed by branches, steps, trouser legs, or the like CROTCH
– angle or slope, as of a mast, theatre's stage, aircraft's wings, or cutting edge of a tool RAKE
– define an arc or angle by cutting or ending its lines SUBTEND
– instrument, used in navigation, for measuring the angles of stars and planets to determine the observer's position SEXTANT
– instrument used to measure and draw angles PROTRACTOR
– pointing or jutting outwards, as an angle might SALIENT
– triangular sheet of wood, metal, or plastic, used to construct certain angles quickly in geometry or technical drawing SET SQUARE
-angle- -CLIN-, CLINO-, -GON
Anglican EPISCOPAL
angling See **fishing**, **fishing terms**
Anglo-Saxon See **medieval terms**, **feudal system**
angry See also **anger**
– angry, or provoked IRATE, WRATHFUL, INDIGNANT, RILED
– angry criticism, expression of outrage FULMINATIONS, VITUPERATION, INVECTIVE
– angry in a snobbish way HOITY-TOITY
– angry mutual accusations RECRIMINATIONS
– angry or sulky frown SCOWL
– angry speech of denunciation HARANGUE, PHILIPPIC, JEREMIAD, TIRADE, DIATRIBE
– furious, intensely angry, seething, enraged APOPLECTIC, INCENSED, LIVID, RAMPAGEOUS
– glum, surly, or readily angered CURMUDGEONLY, QUERULOUS
– irritable, easily angered, peevish TETCHY, CHOLERIC, BILIOUS, FRACTIOUS, DYSPEPTIC
– irritable, ill-tempered, easily provoked into becoming very angry SPLENETIC, CANTANKEROUS, IRASCIBLE, ATRABILIOUS, BILIOUS
– moderately angry, displeased, crotchety DISGRUNTLED
– quick-tempered, easily angered VOLATILE, INFLAMMABLE
– unreasonably angry or discontented, snappish PETULANT
animal See chart, and also **bird** and other entries at specific classes, orders, and species
– animal, such as a horse or ox, used for pulling heavy loads DRAUGHT ANIMAL
– animal form of a basic single-celled type, typically microscopic, such as an amoeba PROTOZOAN
– animal-lover ZOOPHILE
– animal or plant bred from two varieties or species HYBRID
– animal or plant established in a region though not indigenous to it DENIZEN
– animal or plant in a very early stage of its development EMBRYO
– animal skin or hide removed from the carcass PELT
– animal that kills and eats prey PREDATOR
– animal that moves from one region to another MIGRANT
– animal-transmitted disease such as rabies or malaria ZOONOSIS
– animals collectively, especially of a given region FAUNA
– active during the day rather than at night, as most animals are DIURNAL
– active during the night, as some animals are NOCTURNAL
– belt or band encircling something, such as a stripe of colour on an animal's coat CINGULUM
– body of an animal, especially after being slaughtered and prepared for sale CARCASS
– book or collection, especially in medieval times, of moral fables based on animals BESTIARY
– cutting up or into the body of a living animal, especially for research VIVISECTION
– enclosure or tank for keeping or breeding animals or plants indoors VIVARIUM
– jaws and nose of an animal

ANIMAL TERMS						
ANIMAL	GROUP	MALE	FEMALE	YOUNG	RELATED ADJECTIVE	HOME OR MENAGERIE
ape	**shrewdness**				**simian, pongid**	
ass, donkey	**herd, drove, pace**	**jack, jackass dicky**	**jenny, she-ass**	**foal, colt (male), filly (female)**	**asinine**	
badger	**cete, colony**	**boar**	**sow**	**cub**	**meline**	**sett, set**
bear	**sloth**			**cub**	**ursine**	
boar	**sounder, herd, singular**	**boar**	**sow**	**piglet, squeaker, calf**	**porcine, suidian, suilline**	
cat	**clowder, cluster, glaring, dout/ destruction (of wild cats), litter/ kindle (of kittens)**	**tom, gib/gib-cat (usually castrated)**	**she-cat, queen, tabby, puss**	**kitten**	**feline**	**cattery, lair, den (wild cats)**
cattle	**herd, drove, team/yoke (oxen)**	**bull, ox (castrated)**	**cow**	**calf, stirk, bullock (male), heifer (female), steer (castrated male)**	**bovine, taurine (bulls)**	**barn, byre, stable, pasture**
deer	**herd, leash,parcel (hinds)**	**buck, stag, hart**	**doe, hind**	**fawn, calf, kid, pricket/brocket (male)**	**cervine**	
dog	**pack, kennel, litter**	**dog, hound**	**bitch**	**brocket, pup, whelp**	**canine**	**kennel**
elephant	**herd**	**bull**	**cow**	**calf**	**elephantine**	
ferret	**business, fesnying, cast**	**dog, buck, jack, hob**	**bitch, doe, jill**	**kit**	**musteline**	
fox	**skulk, lead**	**dog, vix**	**vixen**	**cub**	**vulpine**	**earth, lair**
frog	**army, colony**			**tadpole**	**ranine, batrachian, anuran, salientian**	
goat	**flock, herd, tribe**	**billy, buck**	**nanny, doe**	**kid, yearling**	**capric, hircine**	
hare	**drove, trace, down, husk, trip, leash**	**buck, jack**	**doe, puss**	**leveret**	**leporine**	**form**
horse	**herd, stable, harass, team, troop, race/rag/ rake (of colts)**	**stallion, horse, sire, stud, gelding (castrated)**	**mare, dam**	**foal, colt (male), filly (female)**	**equine**	**stable, paddock, stall, stud**
kangaroo	**troop, herd, mob**	**buck, boomer**	**doe, blue flier**	**joey**	**macropine**	
leopard	**leap, lepe**	**leopard**	**leopardess**	**cub**	**pardine**	
lion	**pride, sault, sowse, troop**	**lion**	**lioness**	**cub**	**leonine**	**den**
mole	**labour, movement, company**				**talpine**	**burrow, fortress, tunnel**
monkey	**troop, tribe, cartload**				**simian**	
mule	**barren, rake, pack, span**					
otter	**family, bevy**	**dog**	**bitch**	**cub**	**lutrine**	**holt, lodge**
pig	**herd, sounder, farrow (of piglets)**	**boar,hog (castrated)**	**sow, gilt**	**piglet, pigling, shoat, gilt (female)**	**porcíne**	**pen, sty**

continued

ANIMAL TERMS *continued*						
ANIMAL	GROUP	MALE	FEMALE	YOUNG	RELATED ADJECTIVE	HOME OR MENAGERIE
polecat	**chine**	**hob**	**jill**	**kit**	**mustelid, musteline**	
rabbit	**colony, bury, nest (of young)**	**buck**	**doe**	**nestling**	**oryctolagine**	**warren, burrow, cony-garth**
rat	**colony**	**buck**	**doe**	**nestling**	**murine**	
rhinoceros	**crash**	**bull**	**cow**	**calf**	**rhinocerotic**	
seal	**colony, crash, harem, bob, herd, pod, team**	**bull**	**cow**	**pup, cub**	**phocid, phocine**	
sheep	**flock, drove, trip, hurtle, down, fold**	**ram, tup, wether (castrated)**	**ewe**	**lamb, teg, hog**	**ovine**	**fold**
snake	**den, pit, nest**				**anguine, ophidian**	**nest**
squirrel				**nestling**	**sciurine**	**drey**
tiger	**ambush**	**tiger**	**tigress**	**cub**	**tigrine**	**lair**
walrus	**herd, pod**	**bull**	**cow**	**calf**	**odobenid**	
whale	**school, herd, gam, pod**	**bull**	**cow**	**calf**	**cetacean**	
wolf	**pack, herd, rout**	**dog, he-wolf**	**bitch, she-wolf**	**cub, whelp**	**lupine**	**lair, den**
zebra	**herd**	**stallion**	**mare**	**foal, colt (male), filly (female)**	**zebrine**	

SNOUT, MUZZLE
– kill an animal, especially a weak one, as to reduce a herd CULL
– learning process in young animals IMPRINTING
– light or coloured marking on an animal's coat FLASH
– plant-like animal ZOOPHYTE
– protective colouring of an animal, by which it resembles an unrelated animal that is poisonous or unpalatable to predators BATESIAN MIMICRY
– relating to animal diseases or injuries and the treatment of them VETERINARY
– reproduce or cause plants or animals to reproduce PROPAGATE
– small animals such as cockroaches or rats that are harmful or annoying to humans VERMIN
– spots on the skin of an animal MACULATIONS
– study of animal behaviour ETHOLOGY
– stuffing and preparing the skins of dead animals TAXIDERMY
– tame, train, or breed animals to live with and be of use to man DOMESTICATE
– use of animal forms or symbols, as in art ZOOMORPHISM

-animal- -ZO-, -ZOA, ZOO-, THERI-, THERIO-

ankle TARSUS
– ankle-bone TALUS
– ankle covering of cloth or leather, worn over the shoe GAITER, SPAT
– bony bump either side of the ankle MALLEOLUS
– metal fastening confining the wrists or ankles MANACLES, FETTERS, SHACKLES

annexation of Austria by Nazi Germany in 1938 ANSCHLUSS

anniversary See chart
– anniversary of a royal accession JUBILEE

announce, reveal, or disclose something private or secret DIVULGE
– announce news PROCLAIM, HERALD, BLAZON ABROAD
– announce or make known, often by subtle hints INTIMATE
– announce something publicly and officially, such as a law or doctrine PROMULGATE

announcement made officially to the press and public COMMUNIQUÉ, PROCLAMATION
– announcement of new information REVELATION, DISCLOSURE

annoy See **anger**, **angry**
– annoying, irritating IRKSOME, VEXATIOUS, PESTIFEROUS, PESTILENTIAL

annual publication listing information such as tide patterns and weather statistics ALMANAC
– annual payment of an allowance, dividends, or the like ANNUITY

anointing for ritual or healing purposes UNCTION
– mixture of oil and balsam used in sacramental anointing CHRISM

anorexia – illness, often combined with anorexia nervosa, in which compulsive eating is followed by bouts of self-induced vomiting BULIMIA, BULIMIA NERVOSA

answer, pay back in kind, respond with a counterattack RETALIATE
– answer, response REPLICATION
– answer, reply, quick retaliatory action or retort RIPOSTE, REJOINDER, REPARTEE
– answer or response, such as a chorus of disagreement ANTIPHON
– answer or statement that is very short or curt, specifically one of a single syllable MONOSYLLABLE
– answering and anticipation of an argument or objection before it has been stated PROLEPSIS
– deliberately vague or noncommital as an answer might be EVASIVE
– witty answer or retort that occurs to one only when it is too late ESPRIT D'ESCALIER

ant PISMIRE
– ant-eating MYRMECOPHAGOUS
– ant-like wood-eating insect TERMITE

– adjective for ants FORMIC
– practice among some species of ants of forcing ants from other species to do the work in their colony DULOSIS, HELOTISM
– study of ants MYRMECOLOGY
– swarm or teem, as if with ants FORMICATE
ant- MYRMEC-, MYRMECO-
anteater of tropical Asia and Africa, having scales, a long tail, and a sticky tongue PANGOLIN
anthem of France MARSEILLAISE
anthill, or ant-farm or colony kept in a glass box FORMICARY
– anthill-like nest built by a colony of termites TERMITARIUM
anthology, as of one author's works OMNIBUS
– anthology of literary extracts, as used for studying a foreign language CHRESTOMATHY
– anthology of varied writings MISCELLANY, COLLECTANEA
anti-aircraft guns or fire ACK-ACK, FLAK
anti-climax, disappointment, or failure following high expectations DAMP SQUIB
– anti-climax, especially from a high style to a low style BATHOS
anti-clockwise WIDDERSHINS, WITHERSHINS
anti-clockwise- LAEV-, LAEVO-, LEVO-
anti-communist drive in the U.S. in the 1950s McCARTHYISM
anti-establishment, attacking traditional ideas and institutions ICONOCLASTIC
anti-freeze chemical ETHYLENE GLYCOL
anti-intellectual, hostile to cultural pursuits and values PHILISTINE
– anti-intellectual, opposed to inquiry, reform, or new knowledge OBSCURANTIST
anti-knock – measure of petrol's anti-knock properties OCTANE NUMBER
anti-progressive, conservative, as in art or politics REACTIONARY
anti-social and aggressive person PSYCHOPATH, SOCIOPATH
anti-vivisectionist ZOOPHILE
antibody – antibody's destruction of bacteria LYSIS
anticipate and thereby make unnecessary OBVIATE, PRE-EMPT
– anticipation and answering of an argument or objection before it has been started PROLEPSIS
antidote to poison obtained from the blood or tissue of immunised animals SERUM
– supposed antidote against all poisons MITHRIDATE
antiques, curios, and objets d'art, or a cultivated liking for them VIRTU
– expert on antiques and other old objects ANTIQUARY
– relating to antiques and antiquities ANTIQUARIAN
antler – antler's flat section PALM
– branch of a deer's antler TINE
– falling off or shed, as leaves or antlers might be DECIDUOUS
anus See also **rectum**
– area between the anus and genitals in the human body PERINEUM
– circular or ring-like muscle constricting or relaxing a body passage, as in the anus SPHINCTER
– surgical construction of an opening between the colon and the surface of the abdomen to serve as an artificial anus COLOSTOMY
anus- PROCT-, PROCTO-
anxiety, feeling of evil or disaster FOREBODING, PREMONITION
– anxiety of a strong but unspecific kind ANGST
– anxiety or burden, such as a debt MILLSTONE
– free one's mind of a worry, grief, anxiety, guilt, or other burden DISBURDEN
– persistent or nagging, as a minor anxiety might be NIGGLING
anxious, concerned, or apprehensive SOLICITOUS
– anxious, fretful, very nervous or apprehensive OVERWROUGHT, PERTURBED, FRAUGHT, DISTRAUGHT

ANNIVERSARIES

GENERAL ANNIVERSARY	CELEBRATING
triennial	3 years
quinquennial	5 years
centenary	100 years
sesquicentennial	150 years
bicentenary	200 years
tercentenary/tricentennial	300 years
quatercentenary/quadricentennial	400 years
quincentenary	500 years
millennium	1000 years

WEDDING	CELEBRATING	WEDDING	CELEBRATING
cotton	1 year	**lace**	13
paper	2	**ivory**	14
leather	3	**crystal**	15
flower/fruit	4	**china**	20
wood	5	**silver**	25
iron/sugarcandy	6	**pearl**	30
wool	7	**coral**	35
bronze/electrical appliances	8	**ruby**	40
copper/pottery	9	**sapphire**	45
tin	10	**golden**	50
steel	11	**emerald**	55
silk and fine linen	12	**diamond**	60/65

– anxious, tense, nervous, in suspense ON TENTERHOOKS
apart, separately, in pieces, item by item PIECEMEAL
– apart or into pieces, as one might tear something ASUNDER
apart- DIA-
apathetic See **casual**, **indifferent**
ape, monkey, human, or related mammal PRIMATE
– ape, such as a gibbon or orang-utan PONGID
– ape-like in appearance or behaviour ANTHROPOID, SIMIAN
– large ape such as a chimpanzee or gorilla TROGLODYTE
– troop of apes SHREWDNESS
apeman See **prehistoric man**
aphrodisiac prepared from the crushed and dried bodies of a beetle CANTHARIDES, SPANISH FLY
Aphrodite – relating to the goddess Aphrodite PAPHIAN
apologetic, regretful DEPRECATORY
– apologetic, remorseful, self-reproaching CONTRITE, PENITENT, EXPIATORY
– apologetic or regretful, in a slightly cynical way, as a wry smile might be RUEFUL
apology – extremely humble, as an apology might be ABJECT
apparent, pretended, outward, as a given reason might be OSTENSIBLE
– apparent change in the position of an object when the observer changes position PARALLAX
– apparent focus of light rays, as in the image in a mirror VIRTUAL FOCUS
– apparent meaning PURPORT
– apparent rather than real, as a resemblance might be SUPERFICIAL
apparently, supposedly REPUTEDLY
– apparently genuine or sound, but not really so SPECIOUS
– apparently or almost, but not really QUASI-
appeal, attraction, or fascination ALLURE, CHARISMA
– appeal, aura of power or mystery MYSTIQUE
– appeal for, apply for, urge SOLICIT, INVOKE
– appeal or plead urgently, beg ENTREAT, BESEECH, ADJURE, IMPLORE, SUPPLICATE
– appeal to urgently or urge strongly EXHORT
– earnest appeal or passionate protest CRI DE COEUR
– person or party that appeals to a higher court to reverse a lower court's decision APPELLANT
appear or materialise, as a spirit might MANIFEST
– appear or claim to be or do something PURPORT, PROFESS
– appear or occur as an unexpected but important factor, as fate is said to do INTERVENE
appearance, especially a person's deceptive or suspect outward appearance FAÇADE
– appearance, expression, or manner MIEN, ASPECT, VISAGE
– appearance and character, as of a region PHYSIOGNOMY
– appearance of truth, likelihood VERISIMILITUDE
– appearance or aura acquired by age or association PATINA
– appearance or outward presentation SEMBLANCE, GUISE
– adopt or have the appearance of something else, often as a means of camouflage MIMIC, SIMULATE
– damaged in appearance, as by an accident or disease DEFORMED, MISSHAPEN, DISFIGURED
– give a deceptively acceptable or appealing appearance to GLOSS, VENEER
-appearance -PHANY
appendix VERMIFORM APPENDIX
– surgical removal of the appendix APPENDECTOMY
appetiser HORS D'OEUVRE, ANTIPASTO
– appetiser of a small open sandwich or spread biscuit CANAPÉ
appetising or attractive SUCCULENT, TOOTHSOME
– appetising or very appealing but unattainable TANTALISING
appetite – appetite-arousing drink before a meal APÉRITIF
– appetite for unnatural food, such as mud or chalk PICA
– having a huge appetite RAVENOUS, VORACIOUS
– increase appetite WHET
– indulge one's desires or appetites to the full SATE, SATIATE
– relating to the appetites ORECTIC
– unsatisfiable, as a desire or appetite might be INSATIABLE
applause See also **praise**
– applause or praise ACCLAIM, ACCOLADE
– applause that is prolonged and enthusiastic OVATION
– group of people hired, especially in former times, to applaud a play, concert, or the like CLAQUE
– reappearance on stage of a cast, choir, or the like, in acknowledgment of applause CURTAIN CALL
apple, pear, or related fleshy fruit whose seeds are in a large central capsule POME
– apple pulp remaining after the fruit has been crushed to extract the juice POMACE
– acid found in unripe fruit, especially apples MALIC ACID
– unripe apple CODLING
apple brandy CALVADOS
apple of one's eye, focus of attention, or beloved person CYNOSURE
applicable See **relevant**
application or practical side of a profession or field of study, as distinct from the theory PRAXIS
apply for, appeal for, urge SOLICIT, PETITION
appoint, choose for a task or position DESIGNATE, CONSTITUTE
– appoint as one's agent or representative DELEGATE, DEPUTE, COMMISSION
– appoint or elect a new member to a group by a decision of the existing group COOPT
– appoint to or recommend for an office or responsibility NOMINATE
appointment or meeting place, often secret RENDEZVOUS, ASSIGNATION, TRYST
apprentice – craftsman who is no longer apprenticed JOURNEYMAN
apprenticed, contracted as a trainee ARTICLED
approach, right to approach, or means of approaching ACCESS
– approach a problem, subject, or the like BROACH
– approach or come near or close to APPROXIMATE
– approach or intrude slowly on the property or rights of someone else, trespass ENCROACH
– approach or offer, as to initiate a relationship OVERTURE
– approach or stop in order to speak to ACCOST
– approach the same point from different directions CONVERGE
– based on past experience, as an approach to solving a problem might be HEURISTIC
appropriate See **suitable**, **relevant**
– appropriate, well-chosen, as a remark or compliment might be SEEMLY, OPPORTUNE, FELICITOUS
approval See also **praise**
– approval or praise, such as official endorsement COMMENDATION, PLAUDITS, APPROBATION
– official approval, as of a book, especially certified approval from a Roman Catholic censor NIHIL OBSTAT
approve See also **agree**, **allow**
– approve, agree, or assent to a belief, opinion, or the like SUBSCRIBE
– approve, support, or encourage COUNTENANCE
– approve or permit formally, confirm officially ENDORSE, RATIFY, SANCTION, VALIDATE

approximately or about, as written before an uncertain date CIRCA
apron, typically with a bib PINAFORE
apse, gallery, or bishop's throne in a church TRIBUNE
aquarium – tiny crustacean used as food for aquarium fish DAPHNIA
Arab See also **Islam**, **clothing**
– Arab headdress of a shawl held in place by a cord headband KAFFIYEH
– Arab peasants or farmworkers FELLAHIN
– Arab prince, chieftain, or high official EMIR, SHEIKH, SHERIF
– Arab warrior or commando, especially against Israel FEDAYEE
– Arabian trading boat, typically with a large lateen sail DHOW
– covered market in an Arab or Muslim town SOUK
– long hooded Arab cloak BURNOUS, JELLABA
– old quarter of an Arab town in North Africa KASBAH
arc of 90° QUADRANT
– draw a line, especially an arc or circle DESCRIBE
arch See illustration; also **bridge**
– arch built to reinforce a structure RELIEVING ARCH
– arch carrying the thrust of a vault towards a buttress FLYING BUTTRESS, ARC BOUTANT
– arch or frame made of crisscrossing sticks, on which vines or creepers are trained to grow TRELLIS
– arch or stretch over, bridge SPAN
– arch's highest section or point CROWN
– front part of a theatre stage, or the arch framing it PROSCENIUM
– referring or relating to a broad arch whose rise is less than half its width SURBASED
– supported from a higher point on one side than on the other, as an arch might be RAMPANT
– wall, pillar, or the like between two windows or arches TRUMEAU
archaeology See chart, page 30
archbishop METROPOLITAN, PRIMATE
– adjective relating to an archbishop ARCHIEPISCOPAL
archdeacon – adjective relating to an archdeacon ARCHIDIACONAL
– title of respect for an Anglican archdeacon VENERABLE
arched, curved, as horns might be ARCUATE
– arched building or passage ARCADE
– arched ceiling or roof, typically of stone or masonry VAULT
– arched or upwardly curved surface, as of a road CAMBER
– arched or vaulted structure, cave, room, or the like FORNIX
– arched recessed space, sometimes decorated with sculptures, above a doorway, as at the entrance of a medieval cathedral TYMPANUM

arch

BASIC ROUND ARCH

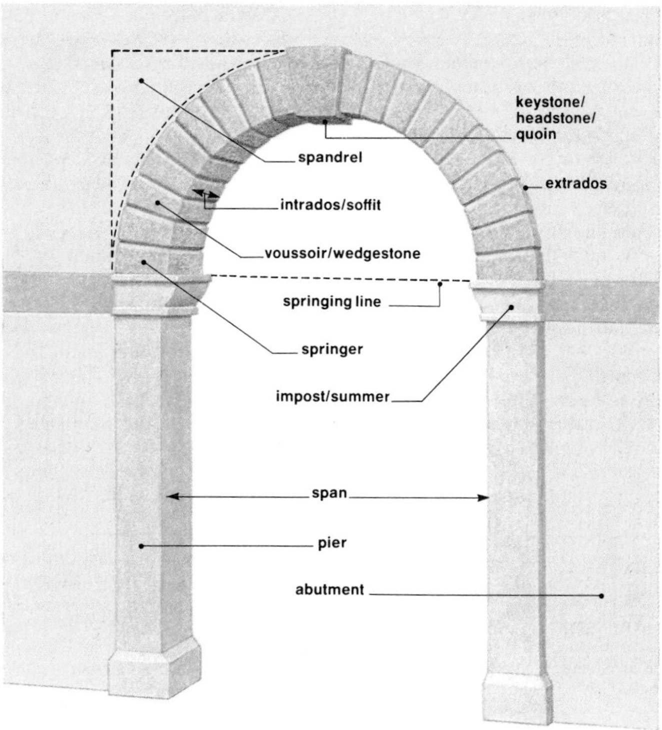

keystone/headstone/quoin
spandrel
extrados
intrados/soffit
voussoir/wedgestone
springing line
springer
impost/summer
span
pier
abutment

MAIN TYPES OF ARCH

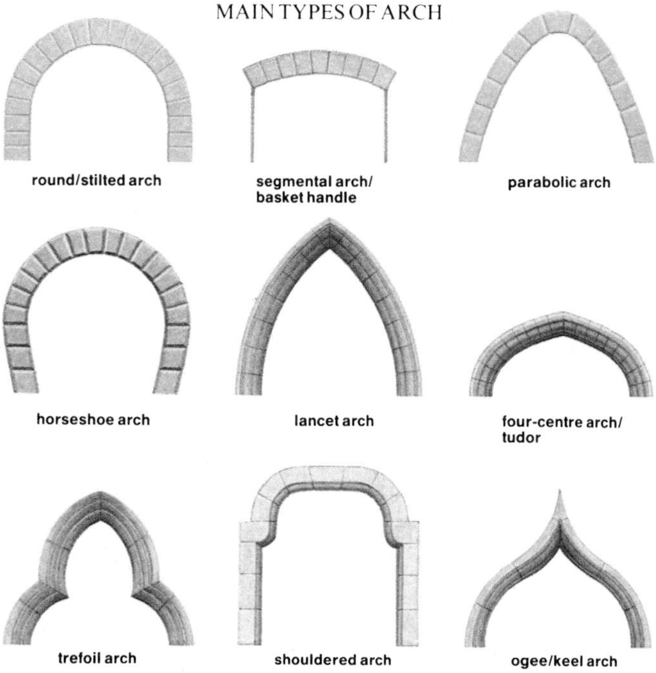

round/stilted arch
segmental arch/basket handle
parabolic arch
horseshoe arch
lancet arch
four-centre arch/tudor
trefoil arch
shouldered arch
ogee/keel arch

archery contest, boxing match, or other competition MAIN
– fan of archery TOXOPHILITE
– target in archery CLOUT

architecture See charts, pages 31 and 32, and also **arch**, **column**, **roof**
– architecture or other science of design ARCHITECTONICS
– architectural, relating to building or design or construction TECTONIC
– characteristic of a particular time or place, as local architecture would be VERNACULAR
– person skilled at drawing, especially of architectural or technical plans DRAUGHTSMAN

arctic, northerly HYPERBOREAN
– arctic or sub-arctic region between the perpetual snow and the tree line TUNDRA

area See also **region**
– area entirely within a larger area ENCLAVE
– area of land, stretch of territory or terrain EXPANSE, TRACT
– area of landed property, or any stretch of territory DEMESNE
– area or place where some particular event occurred, or where a play or novel is set LOCALE
– area served by a particular school or hospital CATCHMENT AREA
– area under someone's control, or sphere of someone's influence FIEFDOM, DOMAIN, DOMINION, REALM, PARISH, BAILIWICK
– area where an animal or plant normally lives HABITAT

arena, as for horse shows HIPPODROME
– arena, as for tournaments of chivalric combat LISTS
– arena, sports hall, or the like, with seating all the way round AMPHITHEATRE, CIRCUS, COLISEUM
– combatant, typically with a sword, in an arena in ancient Rome GLADIATOR

-arena -DROME

Argentine cowboy GAUCHO

arguable, still in dispute, open to debate MOOT

argue, protest, or object, typically in order to dissuade REMONSTRATE, EXPOSTULATE
– argue, quarrel, wrangle BICKER
– argue against, dispute, contradict or deny GAINSAY, REPUDIATE, OPPUGN, CONTROVERT
– argue against and disprove REFUTE, REBUT
– argue back, counter RETORT
– argue or object needlessly, split hairs QUIBBLE, CAVIL
– arguing, in open or complete disagreement AT LOGGERHEADS

argument See also **dispute**, **logic**, **reasoning**
– argument, clinching remark, or hostile gesture made when leaving PARTHIAN SHOT

ARCHAEOLOGY TERMS

barrow/tumulus	earth-covered burial mound	**megalith**	large stone used in construction
beehive tomb/ tholos	king's burial place, in the shape of a beehive	**menhir**	large free-standing stone or monolith
broch	round stone tower built in Scotland between 100 BC and AD 100	**Mesolithic**	Middle Stone Age
crannog	artificial island supporting buildings	**microlith**	very small and delicately worked flint
cromlech	circle of upright stones	**monolith**	single stone used as an upright in circles or avenues
dendrochronology	method of dating past events by analysis of tree rings	**Neolithic**	New Stone Age, when the hunting economy changed to a farming one
dene hole	vertical shaft which widens out into several chambers	**obelisk**	long, narrow shaft of stone
dolmen	chamber or tomb formed by two or more vertical stones supporting a horizontal one	**Palaeolithic**	Old Stone Age, which began two to three million years ago with the emergence of man as a toolmaking animal
Eolithic	earliest period of human culture, preceding the Palaeolithic	**palaeontology**	study of fossils and ancient forms of life
epigraphy	study of ancient inscriptions	**potsherd/sherd**	fragment of broken pottery found in an excavation
henge	circle of wooden or stone uprights enclosed by a bank of earth or stone	**radiocarbon dating/ carbon-14 dating**	dating objects by measuring in dead organic matter the radioactive isotope carbon-14 which decays at a constant rate
kitchen midden/ midden	mound of kitchen refuse left by Stone Age people	**sequence dating/ stratigraphy**	relative dating of objects by determining the layers in which they lie, the deepest layer being assumed to be the oldest
ley lines	straight lines linking hilltops, tumuli, church sites, and other hallowed places, sometimes appearing to correspond with prehistoric tracks	**stele**	upright slab or pillar, usually with an inscription or decorative carving
lynchet	man-made terrace on a hillside resulting from cultivation, probably in the Iron Age	**trilithon**	structure of two upright stones supporting a lintel stone

– argument, controversy, dispute, especially over a principle or belief POLEMIC
– argument, quarrel, heated disagreement ALTERCATION
– argument based less on reason than on references to one's opponent's personal affairs or qualities AD HOMINEM ARGUMENT
– argument in the form of an extended series of incomplete logical syllogisms SORITES
– argument of a spurious kind, put forward only to be knocked down at once MAN OF STRAW
– argument of a subtle philosophical or theological kind, as attempted by students QUODLIBET
– argument or conflict in which outsiders, often against their will, become involved CROSSFIRE
– argument or confrontation CONTRETEMPS
– argument or document presented for consideration SUBMISSION
– argument or quarrel involving a disturbance RUCTION, FRACAS
– argument or reasoning that is plausible but over-subtle, faulty, or deliberately deceptive CHOPLOGIC, CASUISTRY, SOPHISTRY
– argument or theme of a work, especially when used as the title LEMMA
– argument that is illogical or invalid, though not deliberately so PARALOGISM
– acknowledgment of a telling point, argument, or accusation made against one TOUCHÉ
– anticipation and answering of an argument or objection before it has been started PROLEPSIS
– arguing of an unfair or biased kind, selecting only favourable aspects SPECIAL PLEADING
– argumentation and logical disputing DIALECTIC
– base an argument on certain facts or suppositions PREDICATE
– based on reason and topical argument rather than on intuition DISCURSIVE
– disprove or weaken an argument, claim, or the like INVALIDATE, NULLIFY, VOID, VITIATE
– intended as a trap, treacherous, as a sneaky argument might be DEVIOUS, INSIDIOUS
– involved in an argument, scandal, or the like EMBROILED
– long and indirect, as a roundabout journey or argument might be CIRCUITOUS
– person who puts forward a contrary or unpopular view, for the sake of argument or provocation DEVIL'S ADVOCATE
– plausible but really false, as an argument or excuse might be SPECIOUS
– powerful and convincing, as an argument might be COGENT, COMPELLING, INCISIVE, TRENCHANT
– produce or cite an example, argument, or reason as evidence or proof ADDUCE
– proposition on which an argument is based or from which a conclusion can be drawn PREMISE
– proposition on which an argument is based, using incorrect assumptions FALSE PREMISE
– put forward a proposition or idea for the sake of argument POSTULATE, POSIT
– reasonable, plausible, or maintainable, against critical attack, as an argument might be TENABLE
– relating or given to argument, controversy, or logical dispute ERISTIC
– relating to argument from the general to the particular, from principles or causes to facts or effects DEDUCTIVE, A PRIORI
– relating to argument from the particular to the general, from facts or effects to principles and causes EMPIRICAL, INDUCTIVE, A POSTERIORI
– settle an argument decisively CLINCH
– settle an argument or differences COMPOSE, RECONCILE
– theory or proposition put forward and maintained by argument THESIS
– theory put forward for the sake

ARCHITECTURAL STYLES

Baroque	elaborate style developed in 17th-century Europe
Brutalism	stark modern style, without decoration
Byzantine	style marked by domes and minarets as in 5th-century Byzantium
Classical	formal, precise style based on Rome and Greece
Colonial	Georgian style of 17th and 18th-century English settlements in North America
Decorated	14th-century English Gothic style, using decorative mouldings and tracery
Early English	13th-century English Gothic style, with pointed arches and lancet windows
Flamboyant	15th and 16th-century French Gothic style
Gothic	13th to 15th-century style, with pointed windows and arches
Neo-classical	late 18th-century style reviving the precision and symmetry of Greece and Rome
Norman	late 11th and 12th-century style, introduced to England from Normandy
Palladian	18th-century style based on the Italian architect Andrea Palladio
Perpendicular	late Gothic style in England, with emphasis on vertical lines
Regency	style of 1811-20, using stucco, tall windows, and delicate iron balconies
Renaissance	style reviving Greek and Roman ideals in the 15th to 17th centuries
Rococo	profusely elaborate style developed in 18th-century Europe
Romanesque	European 9th to 12th-century style, represented by the Norman in Britain
Transitional	style of around 1100 in Europe, marked in Britain by a combination of Norman and Early English

of argument HYPOTHESIS, WORKING HYPOTHESIS
– undeniable, able to withstand attack, as a powerful argument might be IRREFUTABLE, INCONTROVERTIBLE, UNASSAILABLE
– unshakably strong, as an argument or legal case might be IRONCLAD, WATERTIGHT
– using the premise and conclusion to prove each other, as a faulty argument might CIRCULAR

aristocrat See **nobility**
aristocratic or dignified man GRAND SEIGNEUR, PATRICIAN
Aristotle – happiness or well-being, especially that produced, according to Aristotle's philosophy, by

ARCHITECTURE TERMS

arcade	roof supported by a series of arches
ashlar	masonry of smooth, squared stones
barge-board	sloping board, often carved, along a gable roof
barrel vault	continuous semicircular arched vault
bay	space between windows or pillars
boss	carved projection where ceiling ribs meet
buttress	brick or stone structure reinforcing a wall
campanile	detached bell tower
cartouche	decorative scrolled tablet, often inscribed
caryatid	supporting column in the form of a female figure
coffer/ coffering	sunken panel in a ceiling or vault
corbel	carved stone block used as a support
crenellations	indented battlements, as on a castle; square notchings or indentations as on a moulding
crocket	leaf-shaped ornament on Gothic pinnacles and gables
cruck	either of a pair of timbers joined to make a frame for a building
cupola	roof in the shape of a hemisphere
dado	lower part of an interior wall
engaged	partly sunk into a wall
entasis	bulge in a column, to counteract the optical illusion of concavity
exedra	alcove with a raised bench seat; apse or niche
façade	principal front of a building
fan vaulting	vaulting with curved ribs, resembling a fan
finial	ornament at the apex of a gable
flying buttress/ arc boutant	arch carrying the thrust of a vault towards a buttress
gable	triangular section of the end wall of a house
gargoyle	rainwater spout, often grotesquely carved
groin	curve formed at the intersection of two vaults
hammerbeam	bracket supporting the weight of a wooden arched roof
lantern	structure at the top of a building admitting light through open or glazed sides
lierne	supporting rib between the main ribs in a Gothic vault
loggia	roofed portico behind an open arcade
moulding	ornamental shaped strip of stone or wood, sometimes elaborately carved
ogive	diagonal rib of a Gothic vault
piano nobile	principal floor of a building
pilaster	rectangular column set into a wall for ornament
podium	continuous base under a building
quatrefoil	four-lobed ornamental opening in Gothic stonework
quoin	dressed stone at the corner of a wall
rustication	heavy stonework with a rough surface, used to give Renaissance buildings an impression of strength
saucer dome	shallow dome in the form of an inverted saucer
stoa	ancient Greek colonnade
strap-work	Early English stone ornament resembling interlaced straps
string course	projecting course running along the face of a building
stucco	fine plaster used on interior and exterior walls
stylobate	platform supporting a classical colonnade
swag	festoon of ornamental fruit or flowers
trabeated	having beams or lintels, rather than arches
tracery	ornamental stonework in the upper part of a Gothic window
transom	crossbar of stone or wood in a window
vault	arched roof of stone, brick, or concrete

an active and rational life EUDEMONIA
– relating to Aristotle's philosophy, Aristotelian PERIPATETIC

arithmetic – solve problems or make calculations by the use of arithmetic CIPHER

arithmetical and conversion table READY RECKONER
– arithmetical procedure using a series of steps, such as long division ALGORITHM
– arithmetical skills, basic competence in counting and numerical calculations NUMERACY

ark of the covenant – ark of the covenant's chamber or shrine within the Temple in ancient Israel HOLY OF HOLIES, SANCTUM SANCTORUM, ORACLE

arm – arm-like flexible projection near the mouth of an octopus, jellyfish, or the like TENTACLE
– arm or corresponding limb such as a flipper or wing BRACHIUM
– ancient measure of length, based on the length of the arm from fingertip to elbow CUBIT
– bind someone's arms to restrain him PINION
– relating to the arm, flipper, or wing BRACHIAL
– with hands on hips and elbows bent outwards, as one's arms might be AKIMBO

armband of black material, worn as a sign of mourning CREPE
– armband or identifying badge worn on the upper arm BRASSARD

armchair FAUTEUIL
– coverlet for the top of the back of an armchair or sofa ANTIMACASSAR

armour See illustration
– armour, weapons, and full equipment of a warrior PANOPLY
– armour-bearer, knight's squire ARMIGER

armour

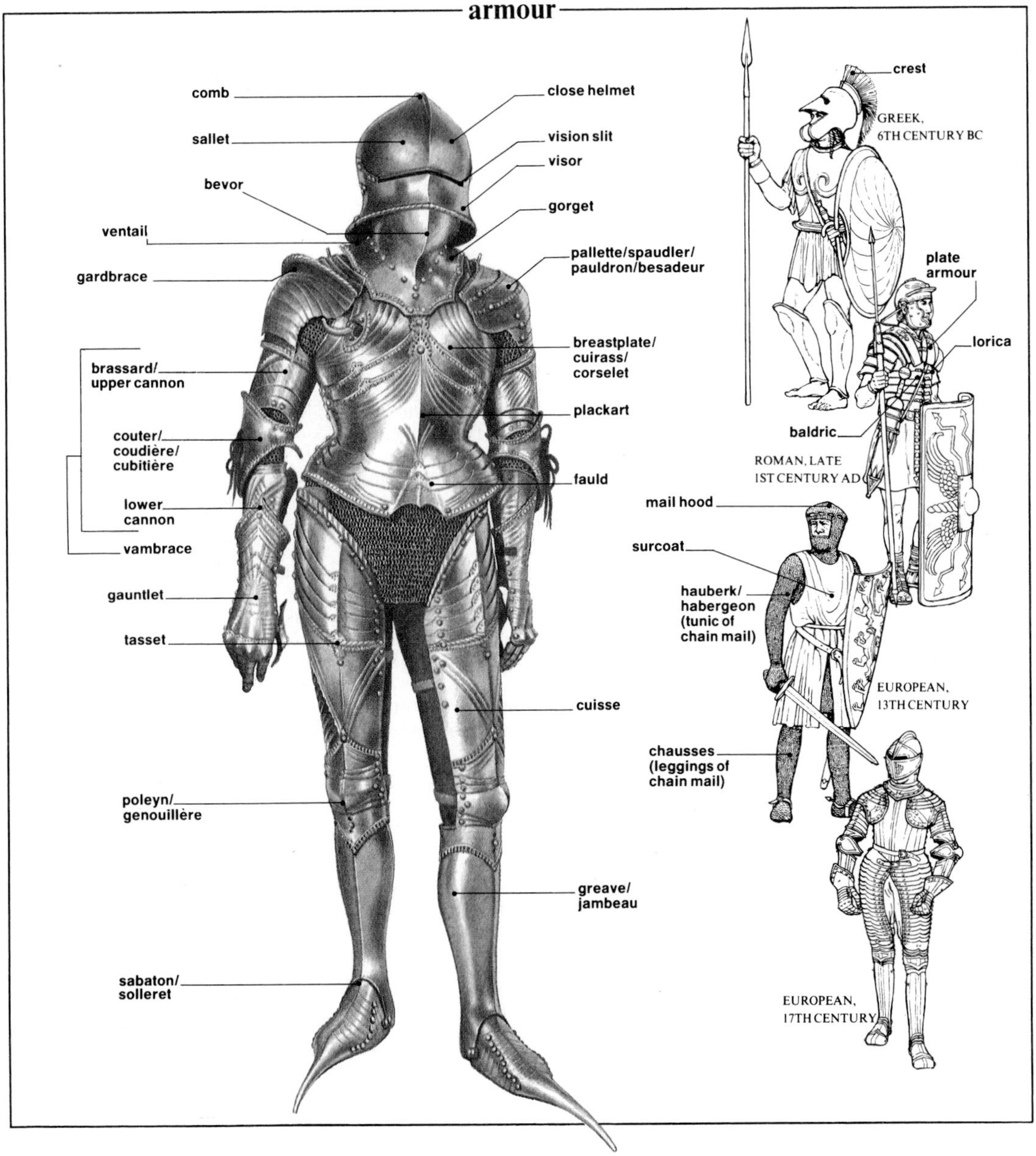

comb
sallet
bevor
ventail
gardbrace
brassard/
upper cannon
couter/
coudière/
cubitière
lower
cannon
vambrace
gauntlet
tasset
poleyn/
genouillère
sabaton/
solleret
close helmet
vision slit
visor
gorget
pallette/spaudler/
pauldron/besadeur
breastplate/
cuirass/
corselet
plackart
fauld
cuisse
greave/
jambeau
crest
GREEK,
6TH CENTURY BC
plate
armour
lorica
baldric
ROMAN, LATE
1ST CENTURY AD
mail hood
surcoat
hauberk/
habergeon
(tunic of
chain mail)
EUROPEAN,
13TH CENTURY
chausses
(leggings of
chain mail)
EUROPEAN,
17TH CENTURY

- armour for a horse's head CHAMFRON
- armour or ornamental covering on a horse BARD
- burrowing American mammal covered with armour-like scales ARMADILLO
- fastening consisting of a hook and loop, as formerly used on armour AGRAFFE
- pouch at the crotch of a suit of armour CODPIECE
- short tunic worn by a knight over his armour, and typically bearing his coat of arms TABARD

armpit AXILLA, OXTER
- relating to the armpit AXILLARY, ALAR
- swelling and inflammation of a lymph gland, especially in the armpit or groin BUBO

arms See **weapons**

army See also **military**, **services**
- army canteen or shop NAAFI
- army department in charge of food supplies and equipment COMMISSARIAT
- army of ordinary citizens rather than regular soldiers MILITIA
- army officer responsible for provisions, clothing, and the like QUARTERMASTER
- army officers who help to plan operations GENERAL STAFF
- army supplier in former times, often a camp follower selling provisions to soldiers SUTLER
- army's foot soldiers INFANTRY
- adjective for an army MILITARY, MARTIAL
- civilian, such as a pedlar or prostitute, who follows an army unit to provide unofficial services CAMP FOLLOWER
- dismiss with dishonour from the armed forces CASHIER
- front position or troops of an advancing army VANGUARD
- government by the army STRATOCRACY
- novice, inexperienced person, as in the armed forces ROOKIE
- plundering, pillaging, as an advancing army might be RAPACIOUS
- recruit forcibly into the army or navy PRESS, PRESS-GANG, IMPRESS
- release or exempt from active duty, as in the army, on the grounds of disability INVALID
- remove the army, military equipment, or military control from an area DEMILITARISE
- study of organising army personnel and equipment, especially the transport of them LOGISTICS

around- AMPH-, AMPHI-, CIRCUM-, EPI-, PERI-

arouse by suggestive or suspenseful stimulation TITILLATE
- arouse or summon a memory, answer, or the like EVOKE
- arouse someone's curiosity, interest, or the like PIQUE
- arousal, incentive, stimulus, or excitement FILLIP
- aroused or provoked very easily HAIR-TRIGGER
- arousing anger, curiosity, lust, or the like PROVOCATIVE
- arousing strong feelings quickly, especially anger INFLAMMATORY

arrange, organise, or construct with some overall effect in mind ORCHESTRATE
- arrange, set in order DISPOSE
- arrange in a corresponding or parallel relationship CORRELATE, COORDINATE
- arrange side by side, position together COLLOCATE
- arrange systematically DIGEST, CATALOGUE, CODIFY
- arrange things, such as computer data or pages of a book, in an appropriate layout or design FORMAT
- arranged, sponsored, or directed by UNDER THE AUSPICES OF, UNDER THE AEGIS OF
- arranging of any complicated project, especially one involving transport LOGISTICS

arrangement of parts CONFIGURATION, CONFORMATION, POSTURE
- arrangement or artistic organisation of the elements in a poem, painting, building plan, or the like ORDONNANCE
- arrangement or orderly display, as of troops ARRAY
- arrangement or sequence according to rank HIERARCHY
- arrangement to enable people with competing interests to continue working or living together MODUS VIVENDI
- lacking a planned order or arrangement RANDOM, HAPHAZARD, ARBITRARY

-arrangement- -TAX-, TAXO-, -TAXY, -TAXIS

arrest, seize, take into custody APPREHEND, NOBBLE
- arrest or confiscate with the backing of legal authority ATTACH
- arrest warrant or writ CAPIAS
- detention, being held under arrest or under guard CUSTODY
- immunity from arrest or punishment, as by taking refuge in a church or embassy SANCTUARY
- judicial writ authorising a search, arrest, or the like WARRANT

arrival, coming ADVENT

arrogance, haughtiness, or proud attitude HAUTEUR
- arrogance, typically leading to downfall HUBRIS
- downfall or undoing, typically just, as after arrogance NEMESIS

arrogant See also **pompous**, **cheeky**
- arrogant, boastful, and opinionated VAINGLORIOUS
- arrogant, disdainful or haughty, scornful SUPERCILIOUS
- arrogant, extremely forward or bold PRESUMPTUOUS
- arrogant, narrow-minded, and self-satisfied person PRIG
- arrogant, offhand, disregarding the feelings of others CAVALIER
- arrogant, overbearing IMPERIOUS, DOMINEERING, OVERWEENING, PEREMPTORY
- arrogant, pushy, high-handed, self-assertive BUMPTIOUS
- arrogant or presumptuous person, especially a newcomer to higher social status UPSTART

arrow for a crossbow QUARREL
- arrow-like, straight SAGITTAL
- arrow-maker FLETCHER
- arrow that is blunt and lacks a barb BUTT SHAFT
- arrow's feather VANE
- arrow's notch into which the bowstring fits NOCK
- barb or barbed head on an arrow, harpoon, or anchor arm FLUKE
- case for carrying arrows QUIVER
- feather or other flared tail giving stability to an arrow or dart FLIGHT
- fit an arrow with a feather FLEDGE, FLETCH
- simultaneous firing of a number of bullets, arrows, guns, or the like VOLLEY

arsonist INCENDIARY

art See chart, and also **arts**, **artist**, **painting**, **sculpture**
- art form or work in which many pieces of fabric, cloth, or the like are pasted on a surface COLLAGE
- art gallery or exhibition hall SALON
- art that is pretentious and vulgar KITSCH
- caretaker or keeper, as of an art collection CUSTODIAN
- category of art, films, or the like GENRE
- damaging or malicious destruction of public property, artistic works, or the like VANDALISM
- excessive sentimentality, as in art and music SCHMALTZ
- expert in wine, art, or the like, or a person having refined tastes CONNOISSEUR

– forefront of, or early participants in, an artistic trend, political movement, or the like AVANT-GARDE, VANGUARD
– great work of art **oeuvre**
– representation or conception of a work of art by a performance or adaptation of it INTERPRETATION
art exhibition covering many years of an artist's work RETROSPECTIVE
art lover, person who is sensitive to beauty AESTHETE
– art lover whose interest or knowledge is really amateurish or superficial DABBLER, DILETTANTE
artery just beneath the collarbone SUBCLAVIAN
– artery supplying blood to the head and neck CAROTID
– fatty deposit in an artery, restricting flow ATHEROMA
– hardening of the arteries SCLEROSIS
– main artery carrying blood from the heart AORTA
artichoke – inedible core or centre of an artichoke head CHOKE
article or booklet on some specialist subject MONOGRAPH
– article or essay outlining the life of someone in the news PROFILE
– article printed separately, after first appearing in a journal or book OFFPRINT
– agency selling cartoons, articles, and the like for publication in numerous newspapers SYNDICATE
– line under the title of a magazine or newspaper article giving

ART MOVEMENTS

Art Deco	decorative style of the 1920s and 1930s, marked by bold geometric shapes and the use of plastic and steel
Art Nouveau	decorative style of the 1890s, marked by tendril-like lines and swirling forms
Barbizon school	group of 19th-century French artists who delighted in landscape for its own sake
Baroque	ornate, dramatic style of the 17th and early 18th centuries
Bauhaus	20th-century German movement urging that the design of any object should be dictated by its function
Constructivism	form of non-representational, geometric art developed in Russia around 1920
Cubism	early 20th-century movement which distorted perspective and introduced multiple viewpoints
Dada	early 20th-century art movement which rejected conventions in favour of the irrational
de Stijl	20th-century Dutch movement ('The Style') which took abstraction to an extreme
Expressionism	early 20th-century movement in painting which rejected naturalism in favour of direct expression of the artist's feelings
Fauvism	early 20th-century movement in painting marked by bright, vibrant colours and bold brushwork
Futurism	early 20th-century Italian movement seeking to depict the energy of the machine age
Impressionism	19th-century French movement which concentrated on the immediate visual impact of a subject
Mannerism	16th-century Italian style marked by the idealisation of form and by extravagant effects
Neo-classicism	late 18th and early 19th-century movement marked by a revival of classical proportion and restraint
Op Art	form of art that exploits optical effects to create an impression of movement
Pointillism	movement based on the use of closely spaced dots of primary colour, blending from a distance to create a luminous quality
Pop Art	form of art that depicts everyday aspects of life, such as consumer goods and comic strips
Post-impressionism	movement in painting advancing from Impressionism towards compositions based on the arrangement of solid forms
Pre-Raphaelitism	English movement of the mid-19th century inspired by a romanticised vision of the Middle Ages and the style of painters before Raphael
Quattrocento	the 1400s, or 15th century, especially in Italian art
Realism	19th-century movement in many arts, directed or recording life objectively, with no idealisation
Romanticism	early 19th-century movement in the arts, emphasising individual emotions and free imagination
Surrealism	20th-century art movement that explored the world of fantasy, dreams, and the subconscious
Vorticism	English movement arising in 1914, marked by the expression of energy through abstract forms

the writer's name BY-LINE
– preliminary text or opening sentence or paragraph of a newspaper or magazine article STANDFIRST
– reject an article or report, as an editor might SPIKE

artificial, man-made SIMULATED, SYNTHETIC
– artificial, not natural, strained, unspontaneous CONTRIVED, FACTITIOUS, STUDIED, MANNERED
– artificial, substitute, or imitation ERSATZ
– artificial and sudden development or device introduced to resolve a tricky situation or plot DEUS EX MACHINA
– artificial human being ANDROID, HUMANOID
– artificial leg, eye, tooth, or other body part PROSTHESIS
– artificial or conventional rather than realistic STYLISED
– artificial sweetener, extracted from coal SACCHARIN
– artificial way of speaking, dressing, or behaving, in order to impress others AFFECTATION, PRETENTIOUSNESS
– artificially prepared, cultivated, fertilised, or the like in a laboratory environment rather than in a living organism IN VITRO

artillery ORDNANCE
– artillery bombardment CANNONADE, STONK
See also **gun**

artist – artist's complete works or output OEUVRE, CORPUS
– artist's studio ATELIER
– artists, writers, or other grouping whose aims or methods seem experimental, very daring, and ahead of their times AVANT-GARDE
– gathering of or reception for artists, celebrities, or the like SALON
– immature, early works of an artist or writer JUVENILIA

artistes in a group, especially a touring group TROUPE

artistic, literary, or cultural circle COTERIE, CLIQUE
– artistic incorruptibility, soundness of artistic values or standards INTEGRITY
– artistic or harmonious arrangement of parts, as in a painting COMPOSITION
– artistic or intellectual people, as a social class INTELLIGENTSIA
– artistic or literary person who lives in an unconventional way BOHEMIAN
– artistic rebirth or revival RENASCENCE, RENAISSANCE
– artistically impressive object, usually fairly small OBJET D'ART
– artistically impressive object that was not intended as a work of art OBJET TROUVÉ

artistry that displays outstanding technical ability, especially in playing a musical instrument VIRTUOSITY

arts or crafts, such as cabinetmaking or pottery, producing decorative objects or furniture DECORATIVE ARTS
– arts subjects and social sciences, as distinct from applied sciences and practical training LIBERAL ARTS, HUMANITIES
– arts such as film, painting, and sculpture, dealing with 3D representation PLASTIC ARTS
– fine arts BEAUX-ARTS

artwork illustrating a text GRAPHICS

as, in the role of QUA

as a whole, all together, in a group EN BLOC, EN MASSE

as good as, amounting to, equivalent in value or effect TANTAMOUNT

as such, in itself PER SE

ascribe See **assign**

asexual, developing or reproducing without sexual union and fertilisation AGAMIC, AGAMOGENETIC, PARTHENOGENETIC

ash or debris left by burnt coal or charcoal BREEZE
– consisting of ash, or resembling ash in texture or colour CINEROUS
– glowing or smouldering cinders, left with ash after burning EMBERS
– larger pieces of residue, left with ash after burning CLINKER
– partly burnt residue, left with ash after burning CINDERS

Ash Wednesday – recital of God's judgments on sinners, read in the Church of England on Ash Wednesday COMMINATION

ashamed or embarrassed ABASHED, OUT OF COUNTENANCE, DISCOMFITED
– ashamed or guilty-looking expression HANGDOG, SHAMEFACED, CRESTFALLEN
– deeply ashamed, humiliated MORTIFIED

ashes – place for keeping the ashes of a cremated body CINERARIUM

ASTROLOGY TERMS

ascendant	section of the zodiac rising above the eastern horizon at a given moment
aspect	relative positioning of planets or stars to one another or to the subject
combust	star or planet too close to the Sun to be visible
conjunction	overlapping or apparent meeting of two stars or planets
constellation	relative positioning of the planets or stars at the time of one's birth
cusp	division or transition between two houses or signs of the zodiac
descendant	point on the ecliptic opposite the ascendant
horoscope	relative positioning of the stars and planets at a given moment, or a diagram or forecast based on it
house/ mansion/sign	any of the 12 divisions of the heavens; sign of the zodiac in which a planet has its strongest influence
influence	ethereal force or fluid from the stars, affecting people's actions
nativity	horoscope based on the time of one's birth
quintile	relative positioning of two stars or planets 72° apart
trine	relative positioning of two stars or planets 120° apart
triplicity	group of three related signs of the zodiac
zodiac	imaginary band, representing the planets' paths, on the celestial sphere, divided into 12 sections or signs, each related to a constellation

– vase, especially one for storing ashes after cremation URN
– vault with niches for urns containing the ashes of the dead COLUMBARIUM

Asia – rainy season in south and southeast Asia MONSOON
– Asian countries, and the East in general ORIENT

ask for or demand, often officially and in writing, needed supplies or equipment REQUISITION
– ask for or request humbly or urgently, apply for PETITION, SOLICIT, SUPPLICATE
– ask or appeal to urgently, plead with or implore BESEECH, ENTREAT, EXHORT, ADJURE
– ask or demand insistently, press, urge IMPORTUNE
– ask questions of in a probing way, interrogate CATECHISE
– asked for or commanded by AT THE BEHEST OF
– asking, inquiring, always putting questions INQUISITIVE
– asking or begging humbly SUPPLIANT, SUPPLICANT

asleep, inactive, as during hibernation DORMANT

aspect or feature, as of someone's personality FACET

aspic, aspic-covered fish or meat dish, served cold GALANTINE

aspirin – aspirin-poisoning SALICYLISM
– pain reliever, alternative to aspirin PARACETAMOL, CODEINE

ass – ass-like **asinine**
– ass living wild in central Asia ONAGER

assemble See **gather**

assembly of churchmen, especially of the Anglican Church, for a conference SYNOD, CONVOCATION
– assembly of citizens in an ancient Greek city, or the marketplace where it met AGORA
– able to frame or alter a constitution, as a legislative assembly might be CONSTITUENT
– general assembly, meeting with all members present PLENUM
– summon an assembly, call a meeting, or the like CONVOKE, CONVENE

assertion that is arbitrary DOGMA, DICTUM, IPSE DIXIT

assertive, pushy, or insistent in manner STRIDENT

asset, such as a mine or oil well, whose value diminishes over the years WASTING ASSET
– assets easily convertible into cash LIQUID ASSETS
– business practice of buying a struggling company and selling off its assets bit by bit ASSET-STRIPPING
– convert property or assets into ready money LIQUIDATE, REALISE

assign or attach an error, guilt, or the like, credit with, pin or fasten on ASCRIBE, ATTRIBUTE, AFFIX, IMPUTE, PREDICATE
– assign or distribute, share out ALLOT, ALLOCATE, APPORTION
– assign work, duties, or powers to another DELEGATE, DEPUTE

assistance See also **help**
– assistance, especially financial support SUBVENTION
– assistance or relief in time of distress SUCCOUR

assistant or employee doing a variety of work FACTOTUM
– assistant or fellow worker COADJUTANT, COADJUTOR
– assistant or partner in some enterprise, especially a dubious scheme ACCOMPLICE, CONFEDERATE, COLLABORATOR
– assistant standing in temporarily for a superior DEPUTY
– assistant to a general or other senior officer AIDE-DE-CAMP, ADC

assisting or supplementing, secondary SUBSIDIARY, AUXILIARY

associate or socialise with CONSORT, FRATERNISE, HOB-NOB

association See also **group**
– association or loose relationship or membership AFFILIATION
– living together of two organisms in close or dependent association, especially when beneficial to both SYMBIOSIS
– associations and suggestions evoked by a word, rather than its literal meaning CONNOTATION

assume, put forward a proposition or idea for the sake of argument POSTULATE, POSIT, PREMISE
– assuming or demanding rights, intimacy, or other status to which one is not entitled PRESUMPTUOUS

assumed, hypothetical SUPPOSITITIOUS
– assumed, supposed, generally regarded as PUTATIVE

assumed name ALIAS
– in disguise or with an assumed name or appearance INCOGNITO

assurance, guarantee WARRANT, WARRANTY
– guarantee, give personal assurance for VOUCH FOR, ATTEST TO

assured See **confident**

asterisks – printing symbol of three asterisks arranged in a triangle, ⁂ or ⁂, to alert the reader to the passage following ASTERISM

asthma – snoring or whistling sound from the chest, as in asthma, caused by partial blocking of the air channels RHONCHUS

astonished See **surprised**

astrologer, sorcerer, or soothsayer, especially of ancient times MAGUS, CHALDEAN

astrology See chart, and also **zodiac**

astronaut from the USSR COSMONAUT
– astronaut's activity which takes place outside the spacecraft while away from Earth EXTRAVEHICULAR ACTIVITY
– astronaut's supply line or tether to the spacecraft during a space walk UMBILICAL CORD

astronomy See chart, page 38
– medieval textbook of astronomy or astrology ALMAGEST

at first sight, based on a first impression PRIMA FACIE

at once, without hesitation or delay, instantly, immediately INSTANTANEOUSLY, INSTANTER

atheist, or unbeliever with regard to a particular religion INFIDEL
– atheist or polytheist, especially from a nature-worshipping community HEATHEN, PAGAN
– atheist or sceptic who believes that man controls his own destiny HUMANIST
– atheist or sceptic who considers the existence of God to be unknowable AGNOSTIC
– atheist or sceptic who rejects religion as being contrary to reason RATIONALIST
– person without beliefs, such as an atheist NULLIFIDIAN

athletes – artificial hormone increasing muscle and bone growth, sometimes used by athletes ANABOLIC STEROID
– portico used by athletes for exercise in ancient Greece XYST

athlete's foot, ringworm, or similar fungal skin disease TINEA, DERMATOPHYTOSIS

athletics event in which each contestant has to compete in ten specific disciplines, such as long jump and shot putt DECATHLON

atmosphere See illustration, page 39
– atmosphere, thick or poisonous, as around a swamp MIASMA
– atmosphere based on feelings conveyed, often unconsciously, by one person or group to another VIBES
– atmosphere of a place, as of a restaurant or night-club AMBIANCE
– atmosphere of awe MYSTIQUE
– atmosphere of gloom PALL
– atmosphere or quality, typically romantic or splendid, surrounding a person or thing AURA, NIMBUS
– atmospheric, suggestive, or arousing memories, as an idea or

story might be EVOCATIVE
– cosy and cheerful, having a warm and friendly atmosphere GEMÜTLICH, CONGENIAL, AMIABLE
– heating of the Earth's atmosphere through increased absorption of solar radiation GREENHOUSE EFFECT
– low in density, thin, as the air of the upper atmosphere is or a gas might be RAREFIED
– sociable or festive, as a party atmosphere might be CONVIVIAL
atmospheric pressure – instrument for measuring atmospheric pressure BAROMETER
– line on a weather map linking places with the same atmospheric pressure ISOBAR
– unit of atmospheric pressure MILLIBAR

ASTRONOMY TERMS

aberration of starlight	apparent change in the position of a star
aphelion	point at which an object in solar orbit is farthest from the Sun
apogee	point at which an orbiting object is farthest from the Earth
armillary sphere	model with rings, used to show relationships among the circles on the celestial sphere
asteroid	minor planet in orbit round the Sun, 600 miles (1000km) or less in diameter
astrolabe	medieval instrument consisting of a graduated vertical circle with a movable arm, used to determine the altitude of celestial bodies
azimuth	horizontal bearing of a celestial object measured clockwise from a given direction
big bang theory	theory that the Universe came into being as the result of a gigantic explosion
black hole	object in space whose gravitational pull is so great that nothing, not even light, can escape from it
celestial sphere	imaginary sphere around the Earth on which celestial bodies are assumed to lie, for the purpose of finding or identifying their position
conjunction	occasion when two celestial bodies line up on the celestial sphere
Copernican theory/ heliocentric theory	belief that the Sun and not the Earth is the centre of the solar system
corona	faint halo of light around the Sun and Moon
cosmology	branch of astronomy that deals with the origin and evolution of the Universe
declination	angular measure of a star's position, measured in degrees north and south of the celestial equator
double star/ binary	pair of stars linked by mutual gravitational attraction
ecliptic	great circle on the celestial sphere representing the apparent annual path of the Sun relative to the stars
equinox	instant when the Sun lies directly overhead at the Equator
magnitude	measure of a celestial body's brightness, apparent or absolute
meteorite	chunk of rock or metal from space large enough to pass through the atmosphere of a planet without burning up and to reach the surface
nadir	point in the heavens diametrically opposite the zenith, or directly under an observer
nebula	cloud of dust and gas in a galaxy
nova	star that flares up suddenly in brightness to several times its normal magnitude
nutation	slight "nodding" of the Earth's axis
orrery	mechanical model of the solar system
perigee	point at which an orbiting object is closest to the Earth
perihelion	point at which an object in solar orbit is closest to the Sun
Ptolemaic theory/ geocentric theory	former view that the Earth is the centre of the Universe
pulsar	rapidly rotating star that sends out a regular flash of radiation
quasar	intensely brilliant object that may be the energetic nucleus of a distant galaxy
red shift	lengthening of the wavelength of light from a receding celestial body
singularity	point in space-time where there is an infinite density of matter
solstice	farthest point north or south of the Equator that the Sun reaches each year
steady-state theory	theory that the Universe has remained approximately the same throughout time
super nova	star exploding at the end of its life
syzygy	point in a celestial body's orbit at which it is either in opposition to or in conjunction with the Sun
zenith	point in the heavens directly above an observer

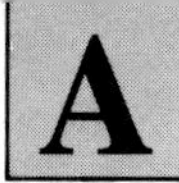

atmosphere

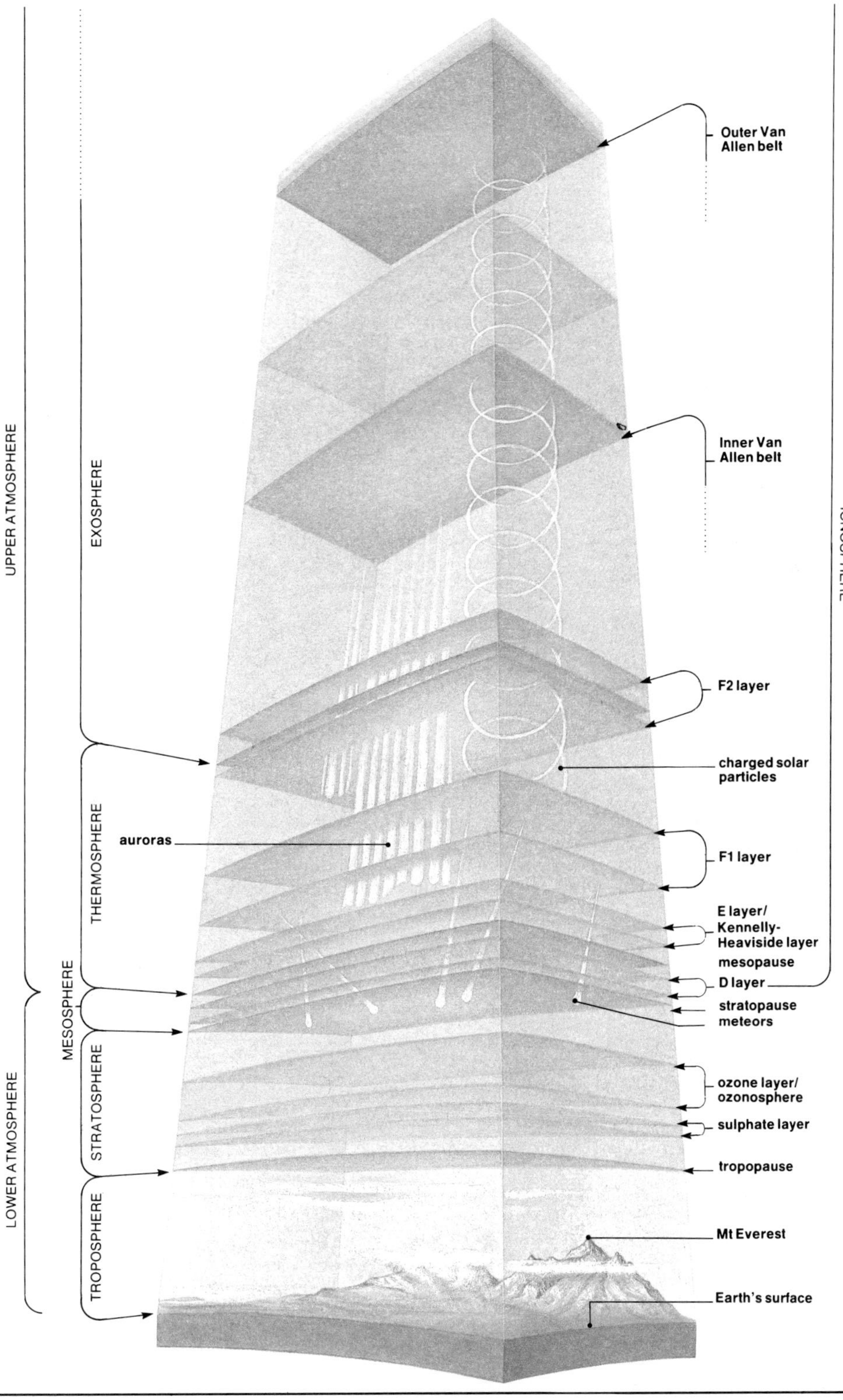

UPPER ATMOSPHERE

LOWER ATMOSPHERE

EXOSPHERE

THERMOSPHERE

MESOSPHERE

STRATOSPHERE

TROPOSPHERE

IONOSPHERE

Outer Van Allen belt

Inner Van Allen belt

F2 layer

charged solar particles

auroras

F1 layer

E layer/ Kennelly-Heaviside layer

mesopause

D layer

stratopause

meteors

ozone layer/ ozonosphere

sulphate layer

tropopause

Mt Everest

Earth's surface

atom See **subatomic particles, chemical**
– atom grouping of a chemical compound or element MOLECULE
– atom or group of atoms with one or more unpaired electrons RADICAL
– atom or group of atoms having an electric charge by gaining or losing one or more electrons ION
– atom with the same number of protons as another, but a different number of neutrons ISOTOPE
– atom's capacity to combine with other atoms VALENCY
– relating to atomic fusion at high temperatures, as in a hydrogen bomb THERMONUCLEAR
– splitting heavy atomic nuclei in a nuclear reaction FISSION

atomic accelerator, producing high-energy electron beams BETATRON
– atomic clock based on radiation frequency and used in defining the second CAESIUM CLOCK

-atomic accelerator -TRON

atomiser – convert a liquid to a fine spray, as by an atomiser NEBULISE

atonement, reparation or compensation REDRESS, AMENDS, EXPIATION, REDEMPTION
– making or needing atonement, especially for sacrilege PIACULAR

attach See **join**

attached at the base, without a stalk, as a leaf might be SESSILE

attachment, typically neurotic, to a person or thing FIXATION

attack See also **criticise**, **insult**
– attack, military raid, or invasion INCURSION, IRRUPTION
– attack an enemy in repeated raids HARASS, HARRY
– attack by surprise, as from an ambush WAYLAY
– attack enemy ground troops with bombs or machine-gun fire from low-flying aircraft STRAFE
– attack from all sides, or besiege BESET, BELEAGUER
– attack in revenge REPRISAL, RETALIATION
– attack of rage ACCESS
– attack on the opinions or beliefs of another POLEMIC
– attack or assault violently, as with blows to the body ASSAIL
– attack or burst of gunfire, rocket fire, or the like SALVO, FUSILLADE
– attack or minor manoeuvre to draw an enemy away from the planned main attack DIVERSION
– attack or raid by soldiers in a defensive position SORTIE, SALLY
– attack something that to the attacker seems powerful and threatening, but is in fact harmless TILT AT WINDMILLS
– attack with blows or criticism BELABOUR
– attack with gunfire from the side, raking the length of a troop formation or position ENFILADE
– act of scaling castle walls with ladders during a military attack ESCALADE
– drive back an attack REBUFF
– easily withstanding attack, criticism, or the like INVULNERABLE, IMPREGNABLE, UNASSAILABLE
– face the impact or main force of a blow, shock, or attack BEAR THE BRUNT OF
– fierce attack ONSLAUGHT
– harsh and scornful, as a criticism or verbal attack might be SCATHING, BLISTERING, WITHERING
– large-scale attack or assault, especially a military one OFFENSIVE
– position or foothold established in enemy territory during an attack BRIDGEHEAD
– short but intense military attack BLITZ, BLITZKRIEG
– sudden attack, raid, or military advance FORAY
– surprise attack COUP DE MAIN
– susceptible to danger, injury, or attack VULNERABLE

-attack, -seizure -LEPSY

attend or visit a place regularly HAUNT, FREQUENT

attendant or servant of a magician or scholar in medieval times FAMULUS
– attendants following an important person RETINUE, CORTÈGE

attention, public notice LIMELIGHT
– attracting attention through some striking feature CONSPICUOUS
– attracting little attention or publicity LOW-PROFILE, UNOBTRUSIVE, UNOSTENTATIOUS, INCONSPICUOUS
– focusing of one's gaze or attention firmly on something FIXATION
– rivet somebody's attention MESMERISE
– something that demands or diverts attention DISTRACTION

attentive, alert, watchful VIGILANT, ON THE QUI VIVE
– attentive or careful in a very conscientious way SOLICITOUS

attic, room just under a pitched roof GARRET

attitude, point of view STANDPOINT
– attitude or posture of the body BEARING, CARRIAGE, DEPORTMENT
– adopt exaggerated attitudes or behaviour for effect POSTURE
– having a specified attitude or inclination towards something DISPOSED, ORIENTATED
– offhand, disregarding the feelings of others, arrogant, as someone's attitude might be CAVALIER
– reversal or about-turn of attitude or policy VOLTE-FACE

attract, lure, tempt ENTICE

attraction, as between people or molecules AFFINITY
– move towards, as if drawn by an irresistible attraction GRAVITATE

-attraction to- -PHIL-, -PHILIA

attractive, fascinating, almost bewitching BEGUILING, CAPTIVATING, ALLURING, CHARISMATIC
– attractive, fetching, engaging COMELY, WINSOME
– attractive in a delicate or dainty way MINION
– attractive in a modest or unspectacular way, pleasing and presentable PREPOSSESSING, PERSONABLE
– attractive in a quaint or strikingly unusual way PICTURESQUE
– attractive in a vulgar way GARISH, TINSELLY, MERETRICIOUS
– attractive or appetising in a tempting way SUCCULENT, TOOTHSOME
– attractive or plausible in a superficial way GLOSSY, SPECIOUS
– attractive or striking in a slightly disturbing or provocative way PIQUANT
– person or thing that is strongly attractive LODESTONE
– strong sensual attractiveness, powerful personal presence or "chemistry" ANIMAL MAGNETISM

attribute See **assign**

auburn colour of hair, especially in a woman TITIAN, STRAWBERRY BLONDE

auction bidder whose task is illicitly to bid up the price for the seller BY-BIDDER
– auction in which the asking price is progressively lowered until a buyer accepts DUTCH AUCTION
– auctioneer's hammer GAVEL
– collection of varied items sold as a single lot in an auction JOB LOT
– lowest price acceptable at an auction RESERVE PRICE
– U.S. term for a public sale or auction VENDUE

audience figures, and hence popularity, as estimated for a given radio or television programme RATINGS
– part of the theatre in which the audience sits AUDITORIUM

aura of power or mystery MYSTIQUE
– aura or atmosphere, typically romantic or splendid, surrounding a person or thing NIMBUS

austerely self-disciplined, having great endurance SPARTAN

Australia and New Zealand from the point of view of Europe ANTIPODES

Australian terms See chart; also **Aboriginal terms** chart, page 11
Austria – political union imposed on Austria by Nazi Germany in 1938 ANSCHLUSS
author See also **writer**
– author who writes a memoir or book on behalf of somebody else GHOST WRITER
– author's right to fees on books borrowed from public libraries PUBLIC LENDING RIGHT, PLR
– adjective for an author AUCTORIAL
– complete works or output of an author OEUVRE, CORPUS
– definitive list, as of an author's works CANON
– immature or early works of an author JUVENILIA
– list of works by or about a particular author BIBLIOGRAPHY
– manuscript in the handwriting of its author HOLOGRAPH, AUTOGRAPH MANUSCRIPT
– relating to an unnamed author ANONYMOUS
– share of the proceeds paid to an author from the sales of his work ROYALTY
authorisation, official permission FIAT
– authorisation from the League of Nations for a country to adminis-

AUSTRALIAN TERMS

GENERAL

backblocks/ outback	remote country areas
billabong	waterhole in a drying river
bludge	to shirk; to scrounge; an easy task; a period of idleness
bombora	submerged reef, or the turbulent water above it
brumby	wild horse
chunder	vomit
cobber	mate, friend
Coolgardie safe	dampened box or cupboard for keeping food cool
digger	Australian soldier; Australian
dilly bag	bag of woven grass or reed fibre
dinkum	genuine; honestly
drongo	fool; worthless or clumsy person
furphy	unfounded rumour
galah	fool, dunce
glory box	bottom drawer, trunk for a trousseau
kelpie	sheepdog breed
larrikin	hooligan
the mallee	bush country
ocker	matey, unpolished Australian male
pavlova	meringue cake with fruit
sheila	woman
shiralee/ swag/bluey	tramp's bundle of belongings
skite	to boast
squatter/ pastoralist	large-scale sheep or cattle farmer
strine	broad Australian English
swagman	tramp, vagrant, or itinerant worker
tucker	food
waddy	club or stick
warrigal	dingo, or wild horse
wobble board	fibreboard sheet that booms when shaken, used as a musical instrument
wowser	puritan, killjoy, prude

PLANTS AND WILDLIFE

bandicoot	rat-like marsupial
barramundi	long edible lungfish
cassowary	large flightless bird
coolabah	eucalyptus tree on river banks
dingo	wild dog
echidna	burrowing, egg-laying mammal, the spiny anteater
emu	large flightless bird
eucalyptus	gum tree
galah	pink and grey cockatoo
goanna	monitor lizard
kookaburra/ laughing jackass	raucous kingfisher
kurrajong	evergreen tree
lorikeet	small, brightly coloured parrot
lyrebird	pheasant-like bird
platypus	egg-laying mammal with a broad bill and webbed feet
taipan	venomous snake
Tasmanian devil	small, fierce, flesh-eating marsupial
wombat	furry burrowing marsupial

ter a specific territory MANDATE
authorise See **allow**, **permit**
authorised or officially recognised, having credentials that are acceptable ACCREDITED
authoritarian non-democratic form of government, tyranny TOTALITARIANISM, DESPOTISM, ABSOLUTISM, AUTOCRACY, AUTARCHY
– authoritarian person, specifically an uncompromising military disciplinarian MARTINET
authoritative, commanding or controlling MAGISTERIAL
– authoritative, from the source of authority, as an official pronouncement might be EX CATHEDRA
– authoritative, reliable, and complete, as a history or biography might be DEFINITIVE
– authoritative but unsupported assertion DOGMA, DICTUM, IPSE DIXIT
– authoritative order from the tsar or other autocrat UKASE
authority See also **power**
– authority, complete control or power SUPREMACY
– authority, or its legal and territorial extent JURISDICTION
– authority, rule, control DOMINION, SOVEREIGNTY
– authority exercised in a fatherly way, typically generous and concerned but restricting individual responsibility PATERNALISM
– authority or complete freedom to act as one thinks best CARTE BLANCHE
– authority or government that was formerly in power but has now been replaced ANCIEN RÉGIME
– authority or influence of one state over another HEGEMONY
– area under someone's authority, or sphere of someone's influence FIEFDOM, DOMAIN, REALM, PARISH, BAILIWICK, AMBIT, REMIT
– explicit authority WRIT
– rejection of authority and all moral and social values NIHILISM
– rod or staff carried as an emblem of authority or office VERGE
– transfer of power from central government to regional or local authorities DEVOLUTION
authorship or origin PATERNITY
– of doubtful authorship or reliability, as a text or anecdote might be APOCRYPHAL
autobiography MEMOIRS
automatic and unthinking reaction KNEE-JERK REACTION
– automatic or predictable, as a reaction may be PAVLOVIAN
automatic doors – electronic device that reacts to changes in light intensity, as used in burglar alarms and automatic doors PHOTOELECTRIC CELL, PHOTOCELL, ELECTRIC EYE, MAGIC EYE
auxiliary- PARA-
available DISPOSABLE
– available readily ACCESSIBLE
– invent or devise using available resources IMPROVISE
average See **mediocre**
– average, commonest value or item in a set MODE, NORM
– average, middle value in a set of values MEDIAN
– average, sum total divided by the number of items in a set MEAN, ARITHMETIC MEAN
– average out, balance EQUATE
avocado dip, hors d'oeuvre, or salad, of Mexican origin GUACAMOLE
avoid, as by cunning or deceit EVADE
– avoid, ignore, or disregard BYPASS, CIRCUMVENT
– avoid, refuse, or be unwilling BAULK, SHRINK, JIB
– avoid committing oneself, speak cautiously HEDGE
– avoid or abstain from ESCHEW
– avoid or escape, especially by cunning ELUDE
– avoid or stave off a disaster, evil, or the like AVERT
– avoiding indicating any definite preference or purpose, as a cautious reply might NONCOMMITTAL
– avoiding of direct answers, evasiveness in discussion FENCING
– avoiding publicity INCONSPICUOUS, LOW-PROFILE, UNOBTRUSIVE, UNOSTENTATIOUS
– pretend to be ill or injured so as to avoid work or duty MALINGER
awaiting confirmation or completion, still unfinished PENDING
awake – state or period of remaining awake at night, as for guard duty or prayers VIGIL
– stay awake, be awake rather than asleep WATCH
award for work in the New York theatre TONY
– award or honour, as for bravery COMMENDATION, CITATION
– propose for an honour or award NOMINATE
aware, conscious, responsive to stimuli SENTIENT
– aware, informed, having knowledge COGNISANT, MINDFUL
away – carrying or conducting away from the brain, spinal cord, or other body part EFFERENT
away- CATA-
away from- AP-, APO-, EC-, EX-
awe – atmosphere of awe MYSTIQUE
awe-inspiring, exalted SUBLIME, AUGUST
– awe-inspiring NUMINOUS
awkward, bumbling, clumsy or ham-handed GAUCHE, MALADROIT, INEPT
– awkward, clumsy, gawky or lumbering, graceless in movement UNGAINLY, UNCOORDINATED, LUBBERLY
– awkward, difficult to move or use, as through being too heavy or unbalanced UNWIELDY, PONDEROUS, CUMBERSOME
– awkward or ill-at-ease teenager or young man or woman HOBBLEDEHOY
axe – blunt end of an axe, hammer, or the like POLL
– bundle of rods with an axe, carried as a symbol of the magistrates' authority in ancient Rome FASCES
– groove or notch made in wood by an axe or saw KERF
– handle of an axe or hatchet HELVE
– sacred double-headed axe in ancient Minoan culture LABYRIS
axle – axle-like spindle supporting wood on a lathe MANDREL
– axle pin holding the wheel in place LINCHPIN
– pivot of metal at the end of a wooden shaft or axle, as for a wheel to turn on GUDGEON

B

B.A. honours course or exam at Cambridge University TRIPOS
- B.A. or other bachelor's degree BACCALAUREATE

baby See also **birth**, **childbirth**, **offspring**, and **animal terms**
- baby born with a disorder of the red blood cells RHESUS BABY
- baby clothing and accessories LAYETTE
- baby of unknown parentage, found abandoned FOUNDLING
- baby or young animal that is still unweaned SUCKLING
- baby or young child, especially an Italian one BAMBINO, BAMBINA
- baby secretly substituted for another CHANGELING
- baby's cot or pram, usually made of basketwork and hooded BASSINET
- baby's dummy or teething ring PACIFIER
- baby's excrement expelled just after birth MECONIUM
- baby's pushchair STROLLER
- American-Indian baby carried on its mother's back PAPOOSE
- be pregnant, carry unborn babies GESTATE
- blood and tissue discharged normally after the birth of a baby AFTERBIRTH, SECUNDINES, LOCHIA
- bounce a baby affectionately up and down, especially on one's knees DANDLE
- cord or tube linking the baby in the womb to the mother's placenta UMBILICAL CORD
- covering of fine downy hair, as on a new-born baby or foetus LANUGO
- delivery of a baby feet or buttocks first BREECH BIRTH, BREECH DELIVERY
- delivery of a baby with medical tongs FORCEPS DELIVERY
- formation of a close relationship, usually between mother and baby BONDING
- get a baby or young animal off mother's milk and on to solid food WEAN
- human embryo of advanced development, prior to its birth as a baby FOETUS
- human product of conception during the first two months of pregnancy, before developing into the foetus and baby EMBRYO
- light wheeled frame supporting a baby learning to walk WALKER
- mass of tissue linking the unborn baby to the womb lining PLACENTA
- membrane surrounding an embryo, foetus, or unborn baby AMNION, CHORION
- nursery for babies or very young children, especially to enable parents to go to work CRÈCHE
- piece of the amniotic sac sometimes covering a baby's head at birth CAUL
- presence of two babies of different ages in the womb SUPERFETATION
- produce babies, reproduce PROCREATE
- producing many babies, very fertile PROLIFIC, PHILOPROGENITIVE
- referring to a baby born after the death of its father POSTHUMOUS
- relating to a baby less than one month old NEONATAL
- strips of cloth formerly wound around a newborn baby SWADDLING-CLOTHES
- study of the causes and development of abnormalities in unborn babies TERATOLOGY
- surgical cut into the uterus to deliver a baby CAESAREAN SECTION
- temperature-controlled container, as for premature babies INCUBATOR
- testing for the presence or position of a baby in the womb by prodding the uterus BALLOTTEMENT
- turning by hand the baby in the womb to aid delivery VERSION
- withdrawal by syringe of some of the fluid in a pregnant woman's womb, to monitor the health of the unborn baby AMNIOCENTESIS
- wrap a newborn baby tightly with clothes or narrow strips of cloth SWADDLE

-baby -LING

Babylonian temple tower, shaped like a pyramid ZIGGURAT

Bacchus – staff, typically decorated with leaves and tipped with a pine cone, carried by Bacchus and his followers THYRSUS

bachelor who has at last decided to get married BENEDICT
- bachelor's degree, such as B.A. or B.Sc. BACCALAUREATE
- desirable and worthy for marriage, as a rich bachelor might be considered ELIGIBLE

back away, retreat from a particular point RECEDE
- back away or shrink back, as through fear or pain RECOIL, FLINCH, WINCE, BLENCH
- back gate or side gate POSTERN
- back of the head OCCIPUT
- back or corresponding part of an organ or limb, such as the back of the hand DORSUM
- back of the neck NAPE, NUCHA
- back or upper surface of a body segment, as of an insect or lobster TERGUM
- back pain LUMBAGO
- back up or confirm an opinion or statement, as with additional evidence CORROBORATE, SUBSTANTIATE, VALIDATE
- adjective for the back DORSAL
- get back, regain RETRIEVE
- lying on one's back SUPINE
- position of one's back when sitting or standing POSTURE
- referring to the lower back and sides LUMBAR
- spring back, as a gun does on firing RECOIL
- wrench, sprain, or strain one's back, ankle, or the like RICK

back- ANA-, DORS-, DORSI-, DORSO-, NOT-, NOTO-, RETR-, RETRO-

back again- RE-

back-and-forth movement ALTERNATION, RECIPROCATION
- send or pass back and forth SHUTTLECOCK

back country, remote rural areas, the bush HINTERLAND, BOONDOCKS, BACKBLOCKS, OUTBACK, GRAMADOELAS, BUNDU

backbone See also **spine**, **bone**
- backbone, spine, or a cut of meat containing it CHINE
- any animal whose embryo has a notochord or primitive backbone CHORDATE

– having a backbone or spinal column VERTEBRATE
– having no backbone or spinal column INVERTEBRATE

backfire, return to the originator with damaging effect BOOMERANG, REBOUND

backgammon, or a variant form of it ACEY-DEUCY, SHESHBESH
– any of the 24 triangular partitions on a backgammon board POINT, FLÈCHE
– exposed single piece in backgammon BLOT
– win in backgammon achieved before the loser has borne off a single piece GAMMON, DOUBLE

background, conditions relating to and casting light on an event or statement CONTEXT
– background music accompanying a film or play INCIDENTAL MUSIC
– background music of a bland kind, as in waiting rooms MUZAK
– background of a design, as in lacework FOND
– background or early life of a person ANTECEDENTS
– forming part of the immediate background or environment, as the air temperature does AMBIENT
– in the background UNOBTRUSIVE, INCONSPICUOUS, LOW-PROFILE, UNOSTENTATIOUS

backless chair, as used by bishops FALDSTOOL

backward, mentally deficient RETARDED
– backward, reverse, unprogressive, going or bending backwards RETROGRADE, REGRESSIVE, RECESSIVE, RETROGRESSIVE
– backward flow of air or water, as from a propeller or a wave on the beach BACKWASH
– backward-looking, directed to the past RETROSPECTIVE
– backward pupils' lessons REMEDIAL CLASSES

backwards, to the rear, especially of a ship ASTERN
– word or words reading the same backwards as forwards PALINDROME

backwards- RETR-, RETRO-

backwoodsman or mountain dweller in the U.S. HILLBILLY

bacon See illustration, and also **pork**
– bacon or pork fat roasted with game or lean meat to keep it moist BARD
– salted and cured side of bacon FLITCH
– stale, decomposing, smelling off, as old butter or bacon fat might be RANCID
– thin slice of bacon or ham RASHER

bacteria colony, or growth of other microorganisms, as for medical research CULTURE
– bacteria's breeding place, focus of an infection NIDUS
– bacterium of a cylindrical or rod-like shape BACILLUS
– bacterium of a spherical shape COCCUS
– bacterium of a spiral shape SPIRILLUM
– bacterium or other organism that can live without air or free oxygen ANAEROBE
– bacterium or other organism that needs air or free oxygen to live AEROBE
– any of an order of thin, twisting bacteria, such as the one causing syphilis SPIROCHAETE
– capable of being decomposed by bacteria or by other biological processes as some packing materials are BIODEGRADABLE
– common bacterium, typically occurring clustered, often responsible for infection of wounds STAPHYLOCOCCUS
– common bacterium, typically occurring in chains, often responsible for throat and other infections STREPTOCOCCUS
– destruction of bacteria by an antibody LYSIS
– disease-producing bacteria, fungus, or the like PATHOGEN
– medicine for bacterial infection ANTIBIOTIC
– reflex movement, as by bacteria, in response to light or a similar stimulus TAXIS
– sewage tank in which solid waste is decomposed by bacteria SEPTIC TANK
– slimy bacterial mass, as formed in a sewage bed ZOOGLOEA

bad See also **disgusting**, **disobedient**, **evil**, **horrible**, **immoral**, **mediocre**, **rotten**, **rude**, **spiteful**
– bad, blameworthy, as someone's behaviour might be DISCREDITABLE, REPREHENSIBLE
– bad, contemptible, despicable, as a liar might be ABJECT
– bad, inappropriate, or improper, as a remark might be UNTIMELY, UNTOWARD, INFELICITOUS
– bad, off or bitter, as butter might be RANCID
– bad, rotten PUTRID
– bad, unwholesome, or undesirable atmosphere MALAISE
– bad and mean, base, as a betrayal might be SORDID, SQUALID, IGNOMINIOUS

bacon, gammon and ham

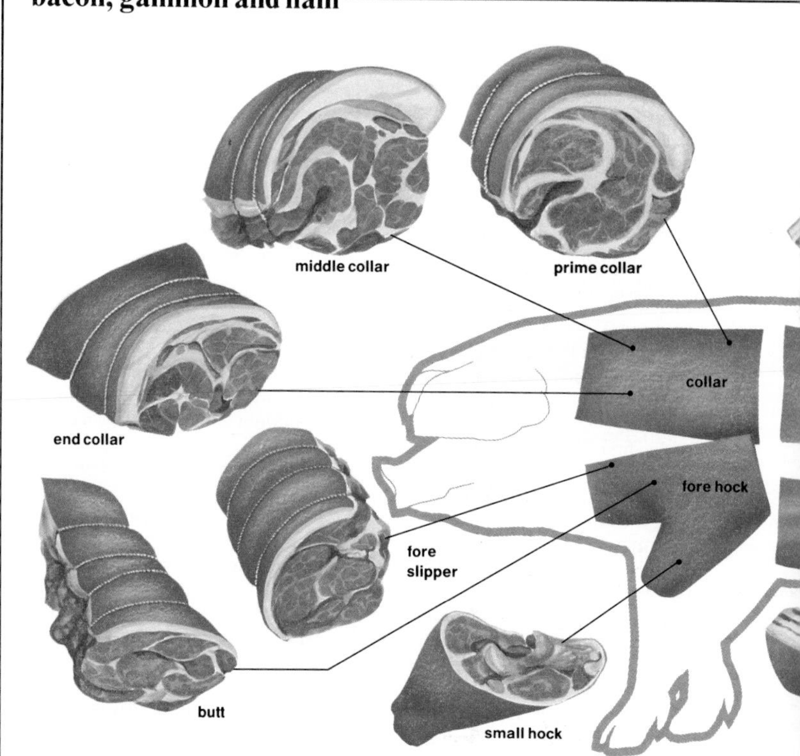

– bad beyond hope of improvement INCORRIGIBLE, UNREDEEMABLE
– disappointingly bad, woefully weak or inadequate, feeble MEAGRE, PALTRY
– extremely bad, appalling or disgraceful ATROCIOUS, ABOMINABLE, EXECRABLE
– glaringly bad or wrong, outrageous FLAGRANT, EGREGIOUS
– inferior, of poor quality, very bad or shoddy, as a performance might be ABYSMAL, LAMENTABLE, EXCRUCIATING, DEPLORABLE
– seedy or shady, having a bad reputation, undesirable DISREPUTABLE, UNSAVOURY, LOUCHE
– shockingly bad or evil DIABOLIC, FLAGITIOUS, HEINOUS, INIQUITOUS, NEFARIOUS, PERNICIOUS
– vile, extremely bad, hateful ODIOUS, OBNOXIOUS

bad- CACO-, DYS-, MAL-, MIS-

bad behaviour, bad deeds, misconduct MISDEMEANOURS, DELINQUENCY

bad breath HALITOSIS

bad luck, misfortune. MISADVENTURE, MISCHANCE, MISHAP, AMBSACE
– supposed bringer of bad luck JINX, JONAH, HOODOO

bad-mannered See **rude**

bad news – person who causes trouble or seems to herald bad news STORMY PETREL

bad person, rascal, rogue CHARLATAN, RAPSCALLION, SCALLYWAG, SCAPEGRACE, REPROBATE
– bad person, wretch or wrongdoer CAITIFF, MISCREANT

bad taste in painting and other arts KITSCH

bad-tempered See **angry**

badge PLAQUE
– badges or other official distinguishing symbols INSIGNIA

badger, or traditional name for a badger BROCK
– badger's burrow SETT
– group or colony of badgers CETE

badminton of an early style, or the racket used BATTLEDORE
– rounded cork with a cone of feathers used as the object of play in badminton SHUTTLECOCK

bag See also **case**, **handbag**, **suitcase**
– bag, often of canvas, with shoulder straps for carrying on the back RUCKSACK, HAVERSACK
– bag-like pouch, often filled with fluid, in a plant or animal SAC
– bag or basket of woven grass or bark in Australia DILLY BAG
– bag or bundle carried by a tramp or itinerant worker in Australia SWAG, SHIRALEE
– large cylindrical cloth bag closed by a drawstring DUFFEL BAG
– large light bag with two hinged compartments, used as hand luggage GLADSTONE BAG
– small bag, as for needle and thread, used by sailors DITTY BAG
– small bag, with a shoulder strap or straps, as used by schoolchildren for carrying books SATCHEL
– small bag or suitcase used as hand luggage VALISE

bagpipe music in the form of a series of martial or funeral variations PIBROCH
– bagpipe's bass drone BOURDON, BURDEN
– bagpipe's shrill piercing sound SKIRL
– pipe on bagpipes on which the melody is played CHANTER
– pipe on a set of bagpipes producing a single note DRONE

bail – hold a suspect on bail, or return him to prison, to await trial REMAND
– set someone free without bail, conditional on his abiding by an undertaking RELEASE SOMEONE ON HIS OWN RECOGNISANCE

bailiff's area of jurisdiction BAILIWICK

baker's long-handled shovel used for moving bread, pies, pizza, or the like in and out of an oven PEEL

bakery specialising in cakes and pastries PATISSERIE

baking and serving dish for individual portions, especially of egg dishes COCOTTE
– baking dish, typically of earthenware, in which patés are cooked and served TERRINE
– baking tin with a high rim that can be removed by releasing a clip SPRING-FORM MOULD

balance POISE
– balance, average out EQUATE
– balance, mix, or counteract and thereby make ineffective NEUTRALISE
– balance in metabolism, or in a society or personality HOMEOSTASIS
– balance of forces, state of stability EQUILIBRIUM, EQUIPOISE, STASIS
– balance of the body, dependent on mechanisms in the inner ear EQUILIBRIUM
– balance or equality of validity or effect EQUIPOLLENCE
– balance or oppose with equal force, offset EQUIPONDERATE, COUNTERVAIL
– balance or scale consisting of a

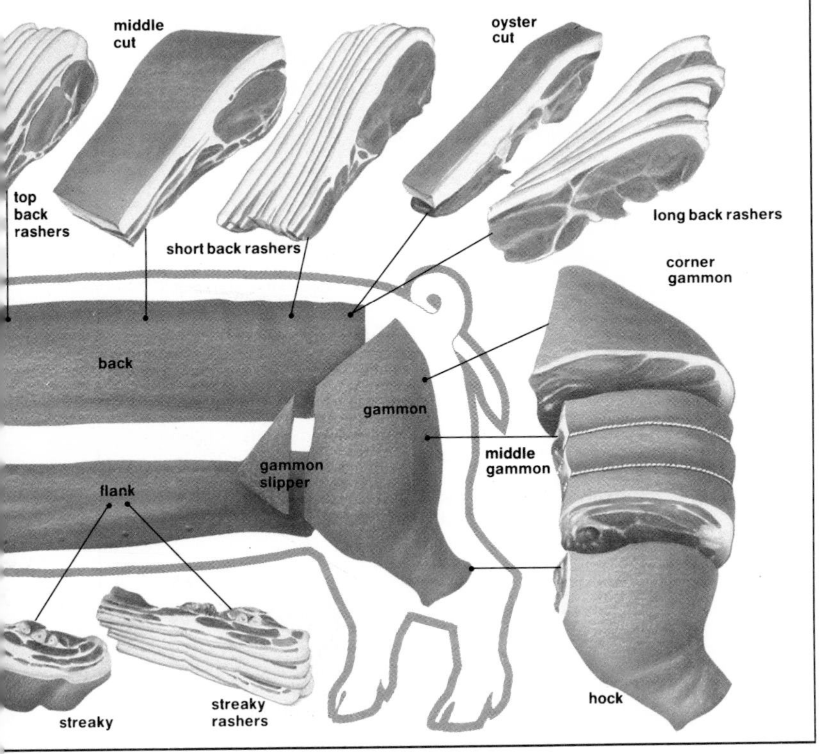

pivoted bar STEELYARD
– automatic movements and adjustments of the body to maintain balance COMPENSATION
– balanced and harmonious arrangement of parts SYMMETRY
– balanced very delicately, unstable PRECARIOUS
– set right, adjust, restore the balance REDRESS
-balance -STASIS
balcony in a U.S. theatre MEZZANINE
– balcony or verandah along the outside of the upper level of a building LOGGIA
– balcony, window or tower offering a wide view MIRADOR
– bracket or similar support, as for a balcony CANTILEVER
bald and smooth GLABROUS
– balding from the forehead backwards RECEDING
– baldness, as caused by a skin disease ALOPECIA
bald spot – wig or hairpiece covering a bald spot TOUPEE
ball at which masks are worn MASQUERADE, MASQUE
– ball of iron with four spikes, formerly used to slow down enemy troops CALTROP, CROWFOOT
– ball of yarn or thread CLEW
– ball or formal dance PROMENADE
– ball-shaped CONGLOBATE
– curved flight path of a missile, ball, or the like TRAJECTORY
– electrostatic generator in which the electric charge accumulates on a large hollow metal ball VAN DE GRAAFF GENERATOR
– gain possession of the ball by cutting off the pass, as in soccer or hockey INTERCEPT
– produce or become covered with small balls of fibre, as a woollen jumper might PILL
– strike a ball before it bounces VOLLEY
ballad – book of popular ballads, poems, religious homilies, or the like CHAPBOOK
ballerina's very short skirt TUTU
ballet See chart
– ballet-like body movements performed in a series as part of a Chinese form of exercise and mental training TAI CHI
– ballet-lover BALLETOMANE
balloon See also **airship**
– balloon, dirigible, or other lighter-than-air aircraft AEROSTAT
– balloon, filled with hydrogen, carrying weather-recording equip-

BALLET TERMS

arabesque	pose on one leg, with the other leg stretched out behind
attitude	pose similar to an arabesque, but with the raised leg bent at a right angle
ballon	leap with a floating quality
barre	wall-mounted exercise rail, at hip level
battement	loosening-up exercises at the barre
batterie/battu	leap during which the dancer beats his or her calves together sharply
bourrée/pas de bourrée	small steps on toe points
brisé, pas de brisé	leap from one leg, beating the legs together before landing on both feet
capriole/ cabriole	leap during which the dancer beats one leg against the other in midair
chassé, pas chassé	step taken by sliding the foot without raising the heel
ciseaux, pas ciseaux	leap with the legs wide apart in midair
corps de ballet	group of supporting dancers
coryphée	senior member of the corps de ballet
divertissement	self-contained short dance, often within a ballet or an opera
écarté	with arm and leg extended on the same side of the body
élevation	technique by which a dancer remains airborne during a movement: the ability to leap high and gracefully
entrechat	vertical jump in which a dancer changes leg positions after beating his or her calves together
fish dive	move in which the ballerina dives to be caught by her partner, with her head and shoulders just clear of the floor
fouetté	pirouette in which a dancer throws his or her raised leg out and in while spinning
glissade	slow sliding movement with knees bent and feet brought together between steps
jeté	leap from one leg to the other
pas de deux	dance for two
pas seul	solo dance
pirouette	spin on one foot with the other leg raised, straight or bent
plié	bending at the knees while standing
pointes, sur les pointes	dancing on the toes in blocked shoes
régisseur	director or producer of a ballet
répétiteur	person who coaches singers or ballet dancers
splits	move in which a dancer drops to the floor with the legs stretched to front and back in a straight line
stulchak	move in which a male dancer holds his partner above his head on one straight arm
tutu	classical ballet dress with hip-length bodice and short, frilled, net skirt

ment into the upper atmosphere BALLON SONDE, SOUNDING BALLOON
– balloon, often one of a series, holding up a cable or net that destroys or deters low-flying enemy aircraft BARRAGE BALLOON, BLIMP
– balloon-borne instrument used to collect and transmit information used for weather forecasting RADIOSONDE
– balloon pilot, or person flying in a lighter-than-air aircraft AERONAUT
– basket or cabin under a balloon or airship GONDOLA
– cord opening a panel on a balloon to release gas RIPCORD
– heavy material, such as sandbags, helping to stabilise a ship or balloon BALLAST
– system of ropes diverging from a single rope, as in the rigging of a balloon CROW'S-FOOT
– trailing rope on a balloon or airship, used for mooring or braking DRAGROPE

bamboo – Japanese martial art using wooden staves KENDO

ban See **prevent**, **prohibit**
– ban, prohibit, suppress PROSCRIBE, INTERDICT
– ban, reject, shun, or exclude from participation DEBAR, EXCOMMUNICATE, OSTRACISE, BLACKBALL

banana – banana-like starchy tropical fruit used in cooking PLANTAIN

band of black material, worn as a sign of mourning CREPE
– band of colour on an insect or plant FASCIA
– band of decoration, as along the top of a wall in a room FRIEZE
– band of metal or ribbon worn in the hair or round the neck FILLET
– band of musicians, especially jazz musicians COMBO
– band of musicians, group of dancers, or the like performing together ENSEMBLE
– band of musicians formerly playing at public processions or entertainments WAITS
– band of warriors, protesters, or the like COHORT
– bands of white cloth at the neck of some clerical or academic robes GENEVA BANDS
– narrow band, ribbon, velvet strip, or the like, worn in a woman's hair BANDEAU

bandage, wrap, or bind SWATHE, SWADDLE
– bandage-like device wound tight to stanch bleeding TOURNIQUET
– bandage or ointment applied to produce warmth CALEFACIENT
– bandage tied in a figure-of-eight pattern to immobilise a limb SPICA

bandit or robber BRIGAND

bang produced by the shock wave from an aircraft flying faster than the speed of sound SONIC BOOM

banish or exile DEPORT, PROSCRIBE
– banish or send to the country RUSTICATE
– banishment, shunning, or exclusion from a social group OSTRACISM
– banished, exiled, or living in a country other than one's homeland EXPATRIATE

banister – any of the supporting posts of a banister BALUSTER
– structure, such as a banister, consisting of a handrail and its supporting balusters BALUSTRADE
– supporting post at either end of a banister NEWEL POST

bank beside a drainage ditch DYKE
– bank annuities CONSOLS
– bank clerk TELLER
– bank of earth, as behind a trench, giving protection from the rear PARADOS
– bank of sand, stones, or the like, as a defence against enemy fire PARAPET, BULWARK, BREASTWORK
– bank or ridge bordering a river or irrigated field LEVEE
– banks' exchanging and cancelling of cheques, drafts, and the like, and the settling of remaining debts CLEARING
– centralised system for banks and post-office to transfer money GIRO
– drawing on one's bank account in excess of one's credit balance OVERDRAFT
– lowest rate of interest on bank loans PRIME RATE
– relating to or inhabiting a river bank RIPARIAN

banker or broker trading in shares or bonds for quick profits ARBITRAGEUR

banking and financial world in Britain THE CITY, LOMBARD STREET
– banking and financial world in New York, including the Stock Exchange WALL STREET

banknote or cheque that has been forged STUMER

bankrupt INSOLVENT
– person appointed by a court to take over and manage the property of a bankrupt, minor, defendant, or the like RECEIVER
– settlement by which creditors accept partial payment from a debtor about to go bankrupt COMPOSITION
– sheriff's officer who carries out a court's orders such as confiscating a bankrupt's property BAILIFF
– wind up a bankrupt business or estate LIQUIDATE

banned because, or as if because, blasphemous or cursed TABOO
– banned goods, obtainable only by smuggling CONTRABAND

banner See **flag**

banquet – luxurious or elaborate, as a banquet might be LUCULLAN
– person who proposes toasts and introduces speakers at a banquet TOASTMASTER
– silver wine vessel, with handles, that is drunk from in turn, as by guests at a banquet LOVING CUP

banter, frivolous style, speech, or the like PERSIFLAGE, RAILLERY

baptism, the Eucharist, or other church rite SACRAMENT
– baptism by pouring water on the head AFFUSION
– baptism by total submerging under the water IMMERSION
– mixture of oil and balsam used in sacramental anointing, as at baptism or confirmation CHRISM
– person, especially in the early days of Christianity, receiving instruction prior to baptism CATECHUMEN
– robe worn by a baby at baptism CHRISOM
– sprinkling of water, as at a baptism ASPERSION
– tank, font, building, or part of a church used for baptisms BAPTISTRY

bar in an inn or tavern TAPROOM
– bar inserted to fasten a loop or strap, or secure a knot TOGGLE
– bar of gold or other metal prepared for storage or transport INGOT
– bar of rolled steel with a U-shaped cross-section CHANNEL BAR
– bar on a studio wall at hip height used for ballet practice BARRE
– bar or frame of steel strengthening a car roof in case of accident ROLL BAR
– bar or informal shop for the illicit sale of alcoholic drinks, especially during the Prohibition period in the U.S. SPEAKEASY
– bar or informal shop for the illicit sale of alcoholic drinks, especially in Ireland or southern Africa SHEBEEN
– bar or rod supporting or bracing a structure by taking pressure down its length STRUT
– bar or small shabby café, especially in France ESTAMINET
– bar serving food as well as drinks BRASSERIE

– comfortable and often more expensive bar or part of a bar SALOON, LOUNGE BAR
– small separate bar or private room in a pub or inn SNUG
bar billiards BAGATELLE
bar diagram, as a statistical graph HISTOGRAM
barb or barbed head on an arrow, harpoon, or anchor arm FLUKE
barbecue of Japanese style, as used for cooking at table HIBACHI
– small brick of compressed charcoal or coal dust, used for fuel, as at barbecues BRIQUETTE
– South African term for a barbecue BRAAIVLEIS
barbed-wire fence or barrier of sharpened stakes FRAISE
– barrier of barbed wire or spikes CHEVAL-DE-FRISE, FRAISE
barber – relating to barbering or hairdressing TONSORIAL
bard or minstrel in ancient Scandinavia SKALD
bare- NUDI-
barefist boxer PUGILIST
barefooted, referring to those orders of monks and nuns that do not wear shoes DISCALCED
barest trace, tiny amount SEMBLANCE, MODICUM
bargain or haggle CHAFFER, NEGOTIATE, HORSETRADE, DICKER, HUCKSTER, PALTER
– secure a bargain finally and decisively CLINCH
barge, especially for carrying coal KEEL
– barge used for dumping by a dredger HOPPER
bark, rind, husk or similar outer layer CORTEX
– bark or tree from which quinine is derived CINCHONA
– cut a ring of bark from a tree trunk or branch to kill it or slow its growth RING-BARK, GIRDLE
– growing on or living in the bark of a tree CORTICOLOUS
barley – frame or floor on which barley is spread for malting COUCH
barn or cowshed BYRE
barnacles – immobile, rooted, fixed, as barnacles are SESSILE
barometer based on changes in slope of the lid of a partial-vacuum drum, according to variations in atmospheric pressure ANEROID BAROMETER
– vacuum formed at the top of an upright mercury-filled tube, as in a barometer TORRICELLIAN VACUUM
barracks or soldiers' quarters in a town, in former times CASERN
– barracks used in former times as temporary housing for slaves and convicts BARRACOON
barrel holding about 100 gallons PUNCHEON
– barrel holding 105 gallons PIPE
– barrel of about 54 gallons HOGSHEAD
– barrel of small size, typically for storing butter or cheese FIRKIN
– barrel or cask of large capacity, especially for beer or wine TUN
– barrel's projecting rim CHIME
– bulge of a barrel BILGE
– drawing off of beer or other liquid from a container such as a barrel, tapping DRAUGHT
– frame supporting a barrel that is lying on its side GANTRY
– hole in a cask or barrel for the passage of liquid BUNGHOLE
– mouth of a gun barrel MUZZLE
– person who makes or repairs barrels COOPER, HOOPER
– pierce a cask or barrel to draw off the liquid inside BROACH
– plug or bung in the vent of a cask or barrel SPIGOT, SPILE
– small barrel KILDERKIN, PIN
– wooden block, cradle, or wedge used to stop a barrel, wheel, or boat from rolling or sliding CHOCK
– wooden strip or plank forming part of a barrel, ship's hull, or the like STAVE
barrel organ or similar mechanical musical instrument HURDY-GURDY
barren, incapable of further reproduction, as a plant or animal might be EFFETE
barrier See also **fortification**
– barrier, consisting of a frame with spikes or barbed wire, against an enemy CHEVAL-DE-FRISE
– barrier floating on the water, as of logs or empty drums, to confine other logs, protect a harbour, or the iike BOOM
– barrier, such as a screen, curtain, or bank of earth TRAVERSE
– barrier of barbed wire or sharpened stakes FRAISE
– barrier or guarded line, as against a disease or hostile power CORDON SANITAIRE
– incapable of being overcome, as a barrier or obstacle might be INSUPERABLE, INSURMOUNTABLE
barrister, of senior rank, QC or KC SILK
– barrister of high rank in former times SERJEANT AT LAW
– barrister's additional fee, paid when a case takes more than one day in court REFRESHER
– barrister's training in the chambers of an established barrister PUPILLAGE
– barristers' set of rooms, as in the Inns of Court CHAMBERS
– expel a barrister from the Bar, preventing him from practising DISBAR
– instruct a barrister BRIEF
barrow – seller of food or goods from a barrow or market stall COSTERMONGER
base an argument on certain facts or suppositions PREDICATE
– base block or slab, as of a column, statue, vase, or trophy PLINTH, PEDESTAL
baseball – tap or prod the ball lightly with the bat in baseball rather than swinging at it BUNT
– U.S. term for the upper tiers of uncovered cheap seats at a baseball stadium BLEACHERS
based on or copied from an earlier example, unoriginal DERIVATIVE
basic See also **essence**, **essential**, **basis**
– basic nature or essence of something HYPOSTASIS, QUINTESSENCE
– basic or most important part of something ALPHA AND OMEGA
– basic principle believed to underlie a given thing QUINTESSENCE, ELIXIR
– basic principle or assumption, as in a philosophical argument AXIOM, PREMISE, POSTULATE
– basic principle or elementary stage of a skill or subject RUDIMENT
– basic support structure of society or an organisation, including transport, education, and health care INFRASTRUCTURE
basically, fundamentally AU FOND
basic- UR-
basin, typically set in the wall of a church for draining away the water used in ceremonial washing PISCINA, SACRARIUM
– basin for holy water at the entrance of a church STOUP, FONT
– basin or towel used in the ceremonial washing of the hands at Mass LAVABO
– low bathroom basin, used for washing one's private parts BIDET
basis, foundation, underlying principle SUBSTRATUM, ANLAGE, BEDROCK
– basis for judgment CANON, CRITERION
– basis or reason for an action, policy, or belief RATIONALE
– structure or conceptual system that is built on or developed from a basis or foundation SUPERSTRUCTURE
basket, small and rectangular, in which berries or other soft fruits are sold PUNNET

– basket as used for a variety of farm work SKEP
– basket of food and drink, or for laundry HAMPER
– basket of wood or wickerwork, for garden produce or shopping TRUG
– basket or cabin under a balloon or airship GONDOLA
– basket or similar carrier, as on a pack animal or bicycle PANNIER
– basket or trap for fish, lobsters, or the like, made of wickerwork CREEL
– basket used for catching fish COOP
– carved architectural ornament in the form of a basket of fruit CORBEIL
– dried leaves, straw, or the like prepared for weaving or basket-making CHIP
– fibre from palm leaves used for weaving baskets, mats, or the like RAFFIA
– plant shoots used to make baskets WICKER
– twig, or the willow bearing it, used in basketmaking OSIER

bastard, born out of wedlock, born of unmarried parents ILLEGITIMATE, MISBEGOTTEN, SPURIOUS, NATURAL, SUPPOSITITIOUS
– in heraldry, a band crossing the shield diagonally from the top right, typically indicating a bastard line BEND SINISTER

bat of a small, common, insect-eating kind PIPISTRELLE
– bat or related flying mammal CHIROPTERAN
– adjective for a bat VESPERTILIAN
– dialect term for the bat FLITTERMOUSE
– establishing of the position of an object, as by bats or dolphins, by means of high-frequency sound waves ECHOLOCATION
– wing-like membrane between the fore and hind limb of a bat, flying squirrel, or the like PATAGIUM

bath of small size for sitting but not lying in HIPBATH, SITZ BATH
– bath or hot tub, with underwater jets for massage JACUZZI
– bath tub covered at one end SLIPPER BATH
– lie or roll lazily about in mud, a hot bath, or the like WALLOW
– public baths, especially in ancient Greece and Rome THERMAE
– room for taking hot baths in ancient Rome CALDARIUM
– sponge-like, fibrous interior of the dishcloth gourd, used as a back-scrubber in the bath LOOFAH
– steam bath of Finnish origin, or the room or building used for it SAUNA
– take delight or sensual pleasure, as in a bath LUXURIATE, BASK, REVEL, INDULGE ONESELF, LANGUISH

bathing area in India formed by a flight of steps beside a river GHAT
– bathing beach LIDO
– relating to baths or bathing BALNEAL

bathroom fixture in the form of a low basin, for washing one's private parts BIDET
– bathroom or lavatory facilities at a military base or camp LATRINES, ABLUTIONS

batik – batik-like dyeing technique in which parts of the cloth are tied tightly to produce a mottled effect TIE-DYE

battery, as in a car ACCUMULATOR
– cables used to start a car by connecting its flat battery to another car's active battery JUMP LEADS
– condition of having two opposing physical properties at different points, as a magnet or battery has POLARITY
– conductor for the electric current into or out of the electrolyte in a battery ELECTRODE
– early battery-like device for the temporary storage of electric charge CAPACITOR, LEYDEN JAR
– ionising substance such as an acid or paste that conducts electricity in a battery ELECTROLYTE
– relating or referring to electric current produced by chemical action, as in a battery VOLTAIC, GALVANIC
– small projection for making connections at a battery terminal LUG

battery hens – hens kept in farmyards or fields, as distinct from battery hens FREE-RANGE HENS

battle formation of troops in close array PHALANX
– battle causing disaster and destruction ARMAGEDDON
– bravery, strength, or skill, as shown in battle PROWESS
– flag raised or waved on its pole as a rallying point for soldiers during a battle STANDARD
– minor or preliminary conflict, dispute, or battle SKIRMISH
– murderous, marked by widespread slaughter, as a bloody battle is INTERNECINE
– trial by combat or battle in medieval Britain WAGER OF BATTLE

battle cry, as formerly used by a Scottish clan SLOGAN

battlefield first-aid post DRESSING STATION

battlements See **castle**, **fortifications**
– battlements, as on a castle CRENELLATIONS

bay – bay-like body of sea water separated from the sea, as by coral reefs LAGOON
– bay or channel through which water flows inland ESTUARY
– bay or deep inlet from the sea SOUND
– bay or lake in Ireland LOUGH
– bay or lake in Scotland LOCH
– large expanse of sea partially enclosed by land, resembling a huge bay GULF
– small sheltered bay or inlet COVE
– wide bay, or the curve in the shoreline that forms it BIGHT

baying of the hounds when pursuing game QUESTING

bazaar or covered market in a Muslim country SOUK

BBC television information or viewdata service CEEFAX

be – verb such as *be* or *ring* that does not follow the usual pattern of inflections IRREGULAR VERB

beach for bathing LIDO
– beach or shore STRAND
– beach or shoreline covered with pebbles or stony gravel SHINGLE

beacon in the form of a flashing orange globe, indicating a pedestrian crossing on British roads BELISHA BEACON

bead at the end of each decade on the rosary, marking the point at which the Lord's prayer is said PATERNOSTER
– bead-like granules of cassava-root starch, used in milk puddings, as a thickener in soup, and the like TAPIOCA
– beads of shell formerly used as currency by North American Indians WAMPUM, PEAG
– string of beads, especially a small string of prayer beads CHAPLET
– string of beads used as an aid in counting prayers ROSARY

beak – bird's beak, insect's snout, projection at the front of a lobster's shell, or the like ROSTRUM
– either the upper or lower part of a bird's beak MANDIBLE
– waxy swelling around the nostrils at the base of the upper beak in the parrot and some other birds CERE

beam, block, stone slab, or the like set horizontally in a wall to distribute pressure, as over a door frame TEMPLATE
– beam between walls supporting a ceiling or roof JOIST
– beam in the frame of a vaulted

roof LAMELLA
– beam laid horizontally, as in building GIRDER
– beam or pillar driven into the ground, typically as part of a building's foundations PILE
– beam or similar projection fixed at only one end CANTILEVER
– beam or support along the top of a window or door frame LINTEL
– beam placed horizontally in a building, as for supporting a floor STRINGER, SUMMER
– hole or niche in a wall for supporting a beam COLUMBARIUM

bean, pea, or related pod-bearing plant LEGUME
– French bean or similar edible bean HARICOT, FLAGEOLET, FRIJOL

bean curd TOFU

bean sprouts – bean producing the bean sprouts used in salads and cooking MUNG BEAN

bear the impact or main force of a blow, shock, or attack BEAR THE BRUNT OF
– adjective for a bear URSINE
– group or family of bears SLOTH
– traditional name for a bear, as in children's stories BRUIN

-bear- -bearing -FER-, -FEROUS

beard – beard-like whiskers down each side of the face MUTTON-CHOPS, DUNDREARIES, SIDEBOARDS
– Australian term for a beard ZIFF
– former term for a beard or bearded man BEAVER
– short pointed beard GOATEE, VANDYKE BEARD, LOUIS NAPOLEON BEARD
– tip of a pointed beard PEAK

bearded POGIONATE
– bearded, as a plant or animal might be BARBATE

-bearer -PHORE, -PHOROUS

bearing, manner, behaviour DEMEANOUR, MIEN, COMPORTMENT
– bearing, method of carrying or holding oneself when walking DEPORTMENT, GAIT
– bearing live young rather than laying eggs VIVIPAROUS
– bearing more than one offspring at a time MULTIPAROUS
– bearing young by means of eggs that hatch outside the body OVIPAROUS
– bearing young by means of eggs that hatch within the female's body, as with some fish and reptiles OVOVIVIPAROUS
– horizontal bearing or alignment measured clockwise from a given direction AZIMUTH

bearings – finding one's bearings socially or spatially ORIENTATION
– having lost one's bearings, confused DISORIENTATED
– section of an axle or shaft covered or supported by a bearing JOURNAL

beast – adjective relating to a beast BESTIAL

beast- THERI-, THERIO-

beat See also **defeat**, **rhythm**
– beat abnormally fast, as the heart might PALPITATE
– beat in a regular rhythm, throb, as the heart does PULSATE
– beat or buffet with or as if with a club BASTE, BLUDGEON, CUDGEL, FUSTIGATE, BELABOUR
– beat or flog, often as a form of self-chastisement SCOURGE, FLAGELLATE
– beat or hit repeatedly, especially with the fists POMMEL, PUMMEL
– beat or strike heavily, as with the hand or a weapon SMITE
– beat or thrash with a stick DRUB, FLAIL, LAMBASTE

beef cuts

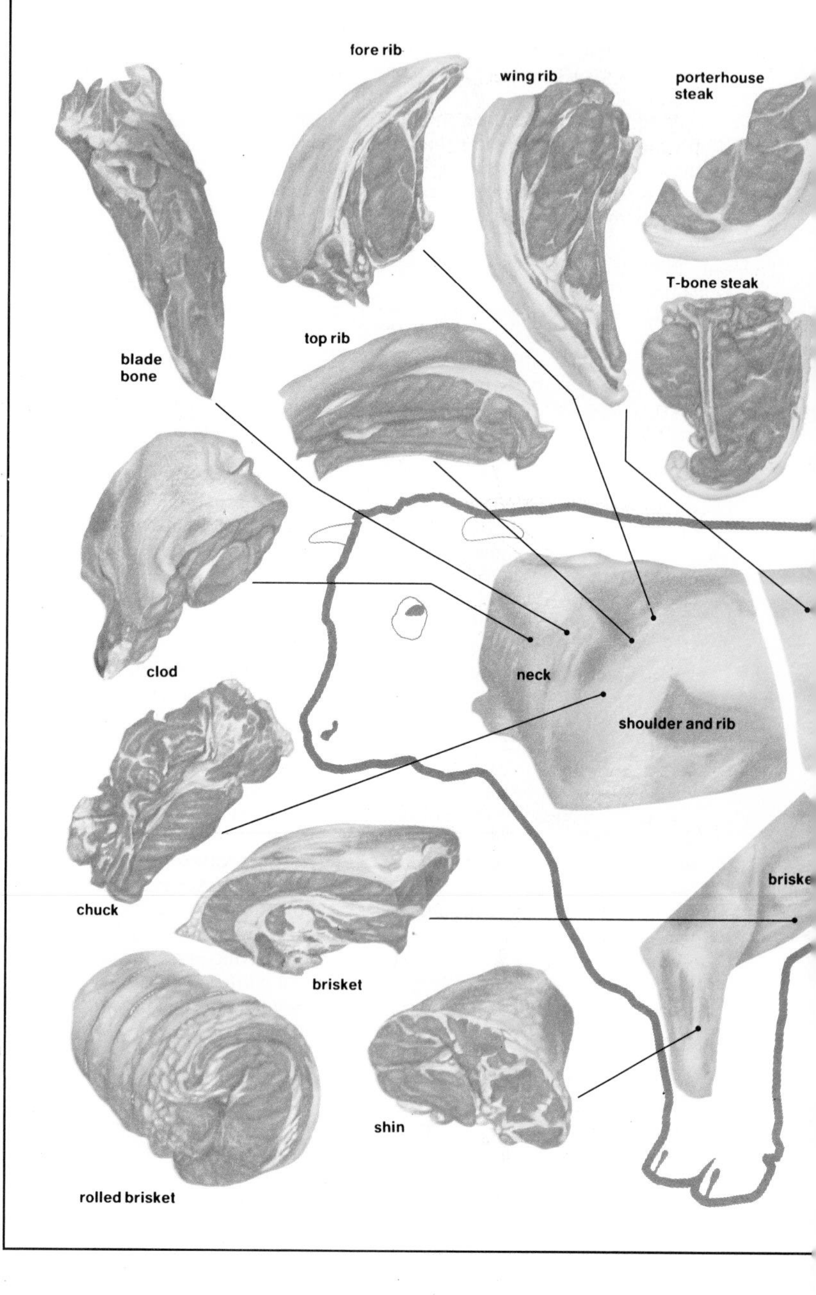

– beat with a whip to the point of stripping the skin from FLAY
– beating or striking of a surface, as by sound on the eardrum or by a stick on a drum PERCUSSION
– beating with a stick, especially on the soles of the feet, or the stick used BASTINADO
– punishment, as formerly in the army in which two lines of men beat an offender running between them GAUNTLET

beat about the bush, speak evasively, hedge EQUIVOCATE, TEMPORISE, PREVARICATE
beautiful See also **attractive**
– beautiful, gorgeous RAVISHING
– beautiful in a powerful sensual way, luscious VOLUPTUOUS
– beautiful or dignified, especially when massive STATUESQUE
– beautiful young man APOLLO, ADONIS, DEMIGOD
– delicately beautiful EXQUISITE

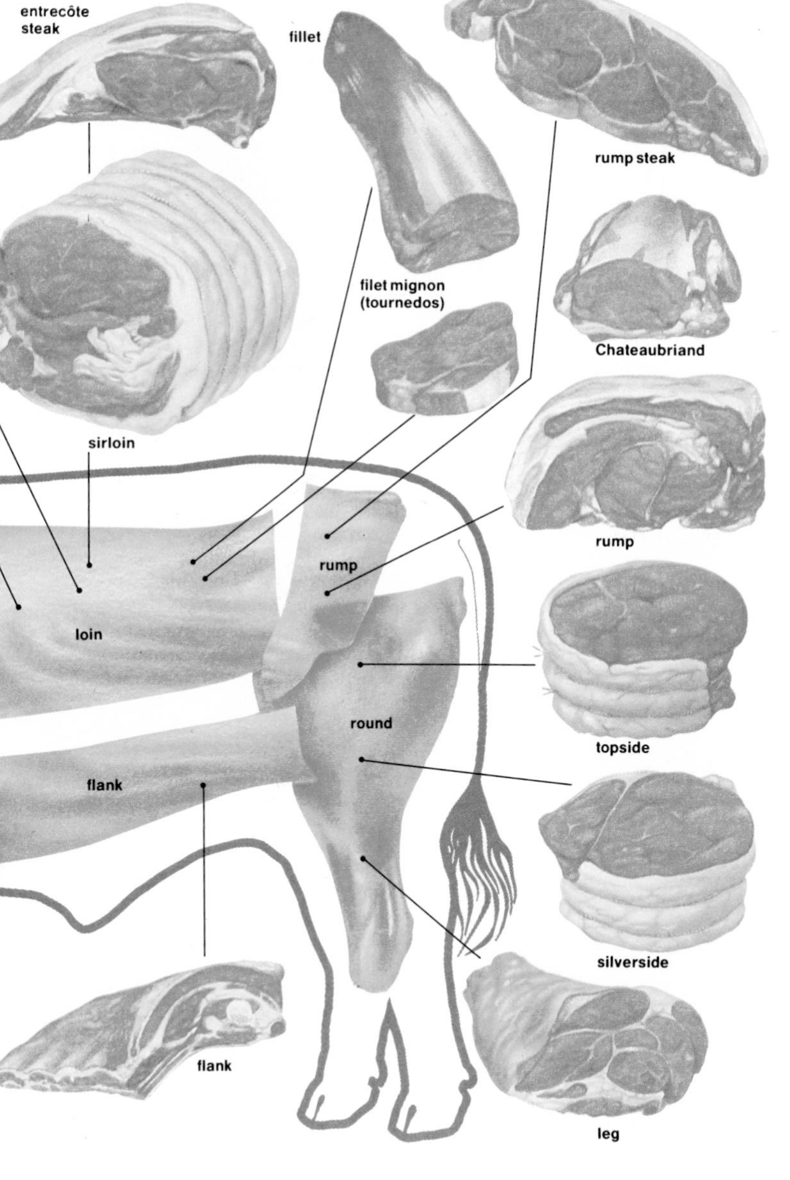

beautify See DECORATE
beauty PULCHRITUDE
– beauty arising from harmonious arrangement of parts SYMMETRY
– beauty parlour, stylish fashion store, or the like SALON
– lover of beauty AESTHETE
– relating to beauty or good taste AESTHETIC
– womanly beauty of a dangerously bewitching kind CIRCEAN
beauty- CALLI-
beaver's den or burrow LODGE
– rise to the surface to breathe, as beavers and otters do VENT
beaver hat CASTOR
become or grow WAX
-becoming -ESCENT
bed of canvas or string suspended at both ends HAMMOCK
– bed on castors that is low enough to be stored under another bed TRUCKLE BED, TRUNDLE BED
– bed-warmer, consisting of a covered metal pan filled with hot water or coals WARMING PAN
– canopy over a bed TESTER
– hard narrow bed, or straw-filled mattress PALLET, PALLIASSE
– reception held by a monarch just after getting out of bed LEVEE
– rest in bed for a woman just before or during childbirth CONFINEMENT, LYING-IN, ACCOUCHEMENT
– short decorative curtain hung along a pelmet, shelf, edge of the bed, or the like VALENCE
– simple, stretcher-like bed widely used in India CHARPOY
– unsprung mattress of Japanese style, used as a bed FUTON
bedbug or related insect CIMEX
bedroom or private sitting room of a woman BOUDOIR, BOWER
– bedroom or sleeping quarters for several people DORMITORY
bedsore DECUBITUS ULCER
bedspread, coverlet for a bed COUNTERPANE
– quilted bedspread DUVET, CONTINENTAL QUILT
– U.S. term for a quilted bedspread COMFORTER
bee – bee-eating APIVOROUS
– adjective for a bee APIAN
– having a sting, as a bee has ACULEATE
– male bee, doing no work except to fertilise the queen bee DRONE
– mixture of nectar and pollen fed by worker bees to the larvae BEEBREAD, AMBROSIA
– nourishing substance secreted by bees and fed to all larvae when very young ROYAL JELLY
beef See illustration
– double sirloin of beef BARON

– dried salted strips of meat, especially beef JERKY, CHARQUI, BILTONG
– streaks or mottling of fat on high-quality beef MARBLING
beehive or group of beehives APIARY
– beehive typically in the form of a straw dome SKEP
beekeeper APIARIST
beer See also **drink**
– beer barrel or wine cask of large capacity TUN
– beer mug in the shape of a man wearing a three-cornered hat TOBY JUG
– beer mug, typically made of pottery and having a lid, STEIN
– beer of a light, pale type with a strong flavour of hops PILSNER
– beer of a light, usually effervescent kind, typically brewed or stored for a relatively long time LAGER
– beer of poor quality SWIPES
– challenge a fellow student to drink a large amount of beer without stopping SCONCE
– clarifying of wine, beer, or the like, as by adding isinglass FINING
– clear wine, beer, or cider of its dregs, typically by siphoning RACK
– drawing off of beer or other liquid from a container such as a barrel DRAUGHT
– heat-treatment of milk, beer, and other liquids to destroy germs and regulate fermentation PASTEURISATION
beer brewing – fermentable pulp used in brewing beer MASH
– yeasty froth gathering at the surface of brewing beer or other fermenting malt liquors BARM
beer hall or German restaurant, originally in the cellar of a town hall RATSKELLER
beermats – collector of beermats TEGESTOLOGIST
beetle See **insect**
– beetle of a family including the dung beetles, treated as sacred in ancient Egypt SCARAB
– substance prepared from the crushed and dried bodies of a beetle, used as a counterirritant and aphrodisiac CANTHARIDES, SPANISH FLY
beetroot of a large, yellowish variety MANGEL-WURZEL
before, prior, earlier PRECEDING, ANTECEDENT, ANTERIOR
– before birth PRENATAL, ANTENATAL
– before noon, in the morning ANTEMERIDIAN
– before or in preparation for, introductory PRELIMINARY, PRELATORY, PREPARATORY
– anticipation and answering of an argument or objection before it has been started PROLEPSIS
– feeling of having undergone an experience that one is now having for the first time DÉJÀ VU
– person or thing that comes before another in time FORERUNNER, PRECURSOR, HERALD, HARBINGER
– person who goes before another in time, as in a job PREDECESSOR
– suggest or indicate beforehand, especially in a sinister way PORTEND, FORESHADOW, PRESAGE
before- ANTE-, FORE-, PRE-, PRO-
beg, apply for humbly or urgently PETITION, SOLICIT, SUPPLICATE
– beg or appeal to urgently, plead with or implore BESEECH, ENTREAT, EXHORT, ADJURE
– beg or demand insistently, press, urge SUE, IMPORTUNE
– beg or implore, typically by an oath CONJURE
– beg or plead on behalf of another INTERCEDE
– relating to begging or entreaty PRECATORY, SUPPLICATORY
– beggar-like guest or visitor who expects or accepts too much hospitality or generosity FREELOADER, SPONGER, SCROUNGER, CADGER, BLUDGER, SCHNORRER
– relating to beggars or begging MENDICANT
begging the question, fallacy of assuming in the premise the very conclusion to be proved PETITIO PRINCIPII
begin, commence, set out on EMBARK
– begin, introduce, or launch officially INAUGURATE
– begin, or urge others to begin, something bad, such as a plot FOMENT, INSTIGATE
– begin, originate, institute USHER IN, INITIATE
– begin or develop something new, pioneer INNOVATE
– begin or implement, set in motion, trigger ACTUATE
– begin the development or production of, give rise to ENGENDER, GERMINATE
– begin to discuss a subject BROACH
beginner, inexperienced person TENDERFOOT, GREENHORN, FLEDGLING
– beginner, learner, novice NEOPHYTE, TYRO, ABECEDARIAN
– beginner or novice, especially in a religious order NOVITIATE
– beginner's critical test in the form of a challenging problem PONS ASINORUM
beginning See also **origin**, **introduction**
– beginning, in a very early stage of development EMBRYONIC, INCHOATE, INCIPIENT
– beginning, just emerging or developing NASCENT
– beginning, origin, or creation of something GENESIS, CONCEPTION
– beginning, starting point, point of origin TERMINUS A QUO
– beginning of a course of action, career, or the like DEBUT
– beginning of a project or period OUTSET, INCEPTION
– beginning or emergence, as of a disease or problem ONSET
– beginning or introduction of something new INNOVATION
– dating from the beginning of time or history PRIMORDIAL
-beginning -ESCENT
behave in a way suggesting that others are one's inferiors CONDESCEND, DEIGN, PATRONISE
– behave in a way that departs from the norm DEVIATE
– behave or conduct oneself in a specified way COMPORT ONESELF, DEPORT ONESELF, ACQUIT ONESELF
– behaving badly, out of control, disobeying orders, rebellious RESTIVE, UNRULY, INSUBORDINATE
behaviour, conduct, manner DEMEANOUR, DEPORTMENT, MIEN
– behaviour in response to a stimulus that does not directly cause it but has come to be associated with it CONDITIONED RESPONSE
– behaviour modification, training, or learning process through adjustment of stimuli CONDITIONING
– behaviour of an exaggerated kind designed to conceal or make up for some defect or inadequacy COMPENSATION
– behaviour of an overemotional type MELODRAMA
– behaviour or mental activity directed towards change or action CONATION
– behaviour that is wild, intemperate, or overindulgent EXCESSES
– adopt exaggerated attitudes or behaviour for effect POSTURE
– artificial behaviour intended to impress others AFFECTATION, PRETENTIOUSNESS
– code of behaviour, etiquette PROTOCOL
– distinctive item of behaviour, peculiar trait or whim of a person IDIOSYNCRASY, ECCENTRICITY, FOIBLE, QUIRK, MANNERISM
– lapse or uncharacteristic piece of behaviour or thinking ABERRATION, BRAINSTORM

– model of behaviour, standard of acceptability, or the like NORM
– referring or relating to bad or inappropriate behaviour UNSEEMLY, INDECOROUS, UNBECOMING
– rough, noisy, and unrestrained, as children's behaviour might be BOISTEROUS
behead, cut off the head of DECAPITATE
– device for beheading, consisting of a heavy blade running between vertical posts GUILLOTINE
behind, at the rear POSTERIOR
– behind or to the rear of a ship ASTERN
behind- META-, POST-, RETR-, RETRO-
behind closed doors, as a court case might be IN CAMERA
being- ONTO-
belch or burp ERUCT
Belgian – Flemish-speaking Belgian FLEMING
– French-speaking Belgian WALLOON
belief See also **religion**, **philosophy**
– belief, acceptance as true CREDENCE
– belief, especially in a religious or ideological system, of a strict, unquestioningly literal, or passionate kind FUNDAMENTALISM
– belief, religious principle, body of teachings, or the like DOCTRINE, CREED
– belief, religious principle, or doctrine held very firmly DOGMA, ARTICLE OF FAITH
– belief differing from the orthodox view HERESY, HETERODOXY
– belief in the virtues of hard work WORK ETHIC
– belief or confident opinion PERSUASION, CONVICTION
– belief or doctrine, as of a religious or professional group TENET
– belief or opinion that is mistaken or misleading DELUSION
– belief-system and values of a society, especially as expressed in its arts MYTHOS
– beliefs or ideas as a system of thought IDEOLOGY
– belief that is uncritically accepted IDÉE REÇUE
– belief that violence, and especially war, is deeply wrong PACIFISM
– assent to a belief, opinion, or the like SUBSCRIBE, ESPOUSE
– declare a belief in something, especially in a religion PROFESS
– defence or formal justification, as of one's beliefs APOLOGIA
– disbeliever, sceptic, person without faith or beliefs NULLIFIDIAN
– established, fixed, firmly settled, as beliefs might be ENTRENCHED
– express personal belief TESTIFY
– justification, as for a belief WARRANT
– neurotic or false belief, that one is ill, or likely to become ill HYPOCHONDRIA, VALETUDINARIANISM
– recognition of others' rights to dissenting beliefs, especially on religion TOLERATION
– relating to belief DOXASTIC
– statement of beliefs or principles CREDO, CREED, TESTAMENT
believable or persuasive though not necessarily truthful, as an excuse or politician might be PLAUSIBLE
– believable or reliable CREDIBLE
believe – generally believed or accepted because of erudition or authority RECEIVED
– unwilling to believe or accept something SCEPTICAL, INCREDULOUS
believer in or follower of a particular doctrine, religion, or the like ADHERENT, VOTARY
believing something too easily, without sufficient evidence CREDULOUS, GULLIBLE
belittle, criticise openly, make light of DISPARAGE, DECRY, DEPRECIATE, DERIDE
bell at Lloyd's of London rung to announce news of an insured ship that has been missing LUTINE BELL
– bell-ringing, especially the art of musical ringing of church bells CAMPANOLOGY
– bell-ringing using all possible variations or bobs CHANGE-RINGING
– bell rung to indicate the time of the prayers commemorating the Annunciation ANGELUS
– bell-shaped, as some flowers are CAMPANULATE
– bell-shaped cover of plastic or glass, placed over young plants for protection CLOCHE
– bell-tower, especially one that is freestanding CAMPANILE
– bell-tower, or the part of it housing the church bells BELFRY
– bell used for sounding alarm signals TOCSIN
– bells played in a set, or a tune on these bells CARILLON, PEAL
– regulation requiring people to be indoors by a certain hour of night, or the times of or bell signalling this restriction CURFEW
– ringing or jingling of bells TINTINNABULATION
– solemn ringing of a bell, as at a funeral KNELL, TOLLING
– swinging metal bar inside a bell TONGUE, CLAPPER
– wooden block from which a bell hangs STOCK
bellflower CAMPANULA
belly of a mammal VENTER
– nerve network in the area of the belly, where one might be punched by an attacker SOLAR PLEXUS
belong as a necessary or rightful part PERTAIN, APPERTAIN
– belonging or existing as an essential part or characteristic INHERENT, INTRINSIC, INTEGRAL
belongings or personal property PARAPHERNALIA
below, under, especially beneath the Earth's surface NETHER
– below or later in the text INFRA
– below the threshold of consciousness or perception SUBLIMINAL
below- HYPO-, INFRA-, SUB-
belt fitted with cartridge pockets, worn across the chest BANDOLEER
– belt-like medical device worn to ease the pressure on a rupture TRUSS
– belt-like sash, wide and often pleated, worn with a dinner jacket CUMMERBUND
– belt or band encircling something, such as the ridge around the base of a tooth CINGULUM
– belt or girdle, as formerly worn by a bride CESTUS
– belt or sash crossing the chest from the shoulder, used for carrying a sword or bugle BALDRIC
– belt or sash worn round the waist, such as the cord on a monk's habit CINCTURE
– continuous moving belt carrying objects, as on a factory's assembly line CONVEYOR BELT
– military officer's wide belt supported by a diagonal strap passing over the right shoulder SAM BROWNE BELT
– ornamental belt presented as a trophy to a British boxing champion LONSDALE BELT
– put a belt around, or fasten with a belt GIRD
bench See also **furniture**
– high-backed wooden bench, typically with arms at the sides and a storage chest beneath SETTLE
– long upholstered bench against a wall BANQUETTE
– room, portico, or the like with a continuous bench, where people in ancient Greece and Rome would hold discussions EXEDRA
bend, curve, turn, or fold, as of a body part FLEXURE
– bend the knees, or kneel, as in worship GENUFLECT

– able to bend easily, or easy to bend SUPPLE, PLIANT, PLIABLE, FLEXIBLE, MALLEABLE, LITHE, LISSOM, LIMBER
– bending of a joint FLEXION
– bending or curving gracefully, as a winding road or the movements of a snake might be SINUOUS
– drive or travel successfully, as round a tight bend NEGOTIATE
– gentle bends in a river MEANDERS
– U-shaped bend in a river OXBOW
– warp, bend or crack, as a piece of wood might SPRING

bends, painful condition, as in deep-sea divers, following sudden change of pressure CAISSON DISEASE, DECOMPRESSION SICKNESS, AEROEMBOLISM

beneath- HYPO-, INFRA-, SUB-

beneath one's dignity INFRA DIG

benefactor or sponsor PATRON

beneficial, improving, correcting, as advice might be SALUTARY

benefit See also **advantage**
– benefit or bonus from a favour or investment DIVIDEND
– benefit or extra privilege from one's employment over and above one's salary or wages PERK, PERQUISITE, FRINGE BENEFIT

bent or twisted out of shape, as a face might be CONTORTED, WRY

benzene – organic compound such as benzene, containing only hydrogen and carbon HYDROCARBON

bequest or trust, or the income derived from it ENDOWMENT

berry See also **fruit**
– berry-bearing BACCIFEROUS
– berry-like, having the form, flavour, or texture of a berry BACCATE
– berry or fruit having a thick rind and segmented pulp, especially a citrus fruit HESPERIDIUM
– berry's small segment or division ACINUS, DRUPE
– berries used to flavour gin JUNIPER BERRIES
– clustered, formed of tightly packed parts, as the raspberry and mulberry are AGGREGATE
– small rectangular basket in which berries or other soft fruits are sold PUNNET

beside, next to, alongside ADJACENT, CONTIGUOUS, TANGENTIAL, ABUTTING, JUXTAPOSED, ADJOINING

beside- PARA-

besiege BELEAGUER

best, richest, most powerful, or the like within a given group ÉLITE
– best, supreme, foremost PEERLESS, UNSURPASSED, PARAMOUNT, PRE-EMINENT, NONPAREIL, PAR EXCELLENCE
– best of the best, very best CRÈME DE LA CRÈME
– best or most favourable OPTIMUM, OPTIMAL
– best part or detail HIGHLIGHT
– typical of the best of its kind VINTAGE

bet See also **gambling**, **horse racing**
– bet, gamble WAGER, PLEDGE
– bet on four or more successive races, the winnings each time becoming the stake on the next ACCUMULATOR, PARLAY
– bet-taker or card-dealer at a gambling table CROUPIER
– betting system in which the winners receive a share of the total amount bet TOTALISATOR, TOTE, PARI-MUTUEL
– betting technique of raising the stakes after each loss MARTINGALE
– better or gambler, especially on a horse race PUNTER
– balance a bet by taking other bets or precautions HEDGE
– risk everything on a single bet or chance GO NAP

betray or slander TRADUCE

betrayal, breach of trust PERFIDY

better, outdo, be superior to or greater than EXCEED, EXCEL
– get better after an illness RECUPERATE, CONVALESCE

bicycle

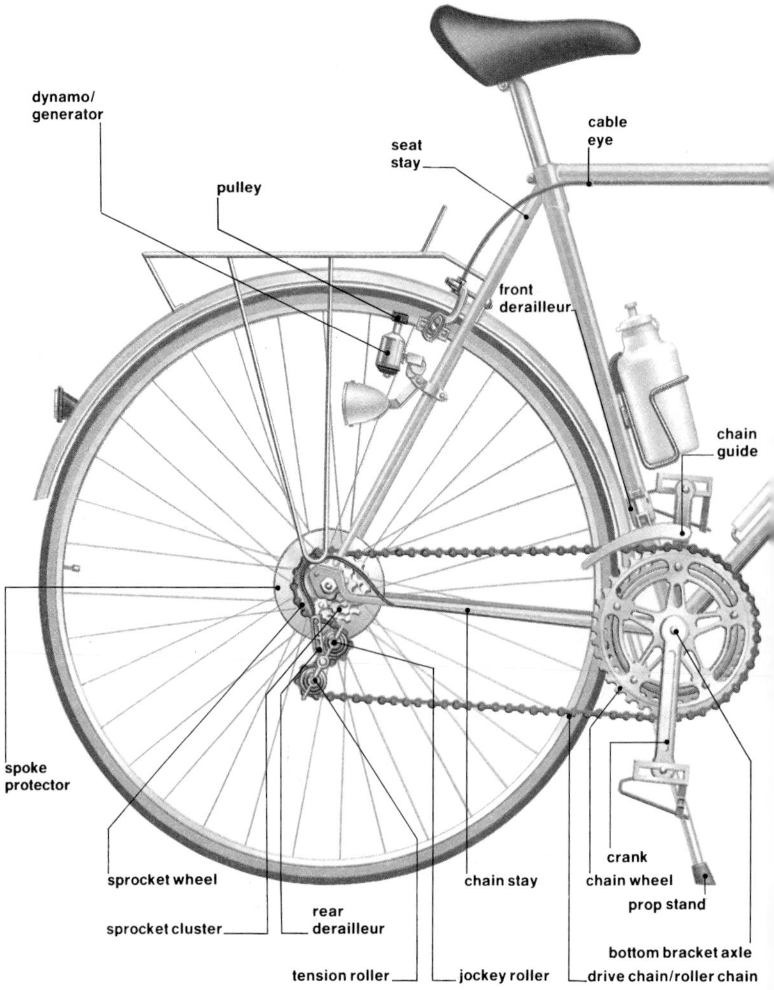

between, in the middle INTERMEDIATE, INTERVENING
between- INTER-
between ourselves, in confidence ENTRE NOUS
beware – schoolchildren's warning to beware CAVE!
bewitching, dangerously attractive or charming CIRCEAN
beyond one's authority, outside one's legal powers ULTRA VIRES
– acting or speaking beyond the range of one's ability or expertise ULTRACREPIDARIAN
– beyond reasonable limits, excessive, INORDINATE, IMMODERATE
– beyond the call of duty, overzealous SUPEREROGATORY
– beyond the limits of ordinary experience TRANSCENDENT
beyond- EXO-, HYPER-, META-, PARA-, SUPER-, SUPRA-, SUR-, TRANS-, ULTRA-
bias See **tendency**
– bias, prejudice, pre-formed judgment or preference PREDISPOSITION, PRECONCEPTION, PARTI PRIS
biased, favouring one particular view, especially a controversial one TENDENTIOUS
– biased, influenced by emotion or personal preference or involvement SUBJECTIVE
– biased, one-sided PARTIAL, PREDISPOSED, PARTISAN
– biased or prejudiced in an intolerant way BIGOTED
bible See also **scriptures**
– bible, as found in hotel rooms, distributed by an international organisation GIDEON BIBLE
– bible in an English translation of 1611 for use in the Anglican Church, the King James Bible AUTHORISED VERSION
– bible in an English translation of 1610 by Roman Catholic scholars DOUAY BIBLE
– bible in its Latin version by Saint Jerome, authorised by the Roman Catholic Church VULGATE
– bible or other book containing versions of a text in different languages POLYGLOT
– bible's first five, six, or seven books PENTATEUCH, HEXATEUCH, HEPTATEUCH
– biblical interpretation with a mystical emphasis, identifying spiritual symbols ANAGOGY
– critical analysis of a text, especially of the bible EXEGESIS
– disclosure of God's will or some religious truth, as through the bible REVELATION
– excessive reliance on the bible as a guide, or excessively literal interpretation of it BIBLIOLATRY
– fourteen books of the bible sometimes printed as an appendix to the Old Testament but which is excluded from the canon by Protestants APOCRYPHA
– God's promises to man, as revealed in the bible COVENANT
– literal belief in the bible as a divinely inspired and accurate historical account FUNDAMENTALISM
– officially recognised books of the bible CANON
– referring or relating to the first three biblical gospels SYNOPTIC
– study or methods of biblical interpretation HERMENEUTICS
– biblical founder or father of the human race or the Hebrew people PATRIARCH
bicycle See illustration
– bicycle for a small child, typically having two tiny extra supporting wheels FAIRY CYCLE
– bicycle-like vehicle with a single wheel UNICYCLE
– bicycle of an early design, propelled by pushing the feet along the ground VELOCIPEDE
– bicycle of an early kind with solid tyres BONESHAKER
– bicycle or motorcycle with high handlebars CHOPPER
– bicycle or tricycle for two or

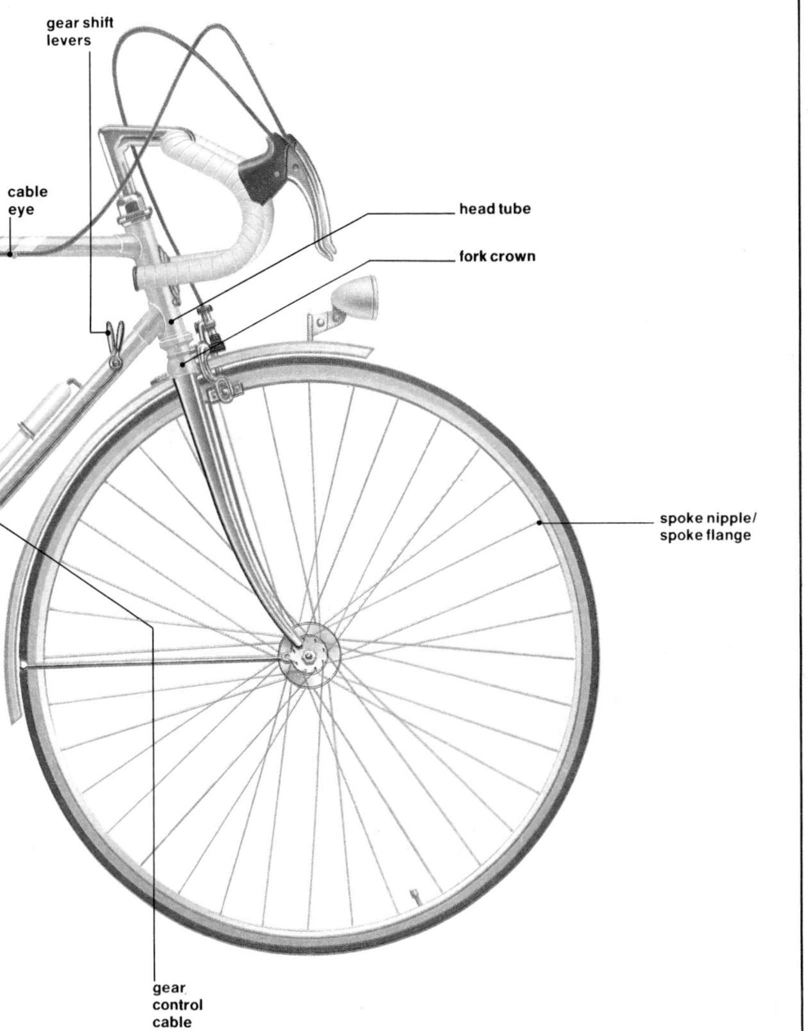

more riders seated one behind the other TANDEM
– bicycle-racing arena, typically with a banked track VELODROME
– bicycle's basket or bag, usually attached in a pair PANNIER
– airstream behind a fast-moving vehicle, such as a bicycle, car, or aircraft SLIPSTREAM
– small stabilising wheel attached to the back wheel of a child's bicycle FAIRY WHEEL, OUTRIDER

bid, offer to supply goods or labour at a specific rate or price TENDER

big See **large**, **huge**

Big Bang – hypothetical elemental matter, probably neutrons, according to the big-bang theory of the creation of the universe YLEM

big dipper, funfair elevated railway, providing a fast exciting ride ROLLER COASTER, SWITCHBACK

big-headed, self-important, boastful EGOTISTIC, VAINGLORIOUS, VAPOURING

big-hearted, forgiving, generous, noble MAGNANIMOUS

big toe HALLUX

big wheel, giant fairground wheel FERRIS WHEEL

bigoted or intolerant towards outsiders SECTARIAN

bikini bottom, topless swimming costume for a woman MONOKINI

bile- CHOLE-

bill, typically detailing the goods or services provided INVOICE
– added clause, amendment, or qualification to a verdict, parliamentary bill, or the like RIDER
– legislator who presents or supports a bill or motion SPONSOR
– list items one by one, as on a bill ITEMISE, ENUMERATE
– presentation of a bill to parliament READING
– settling of a bill or account RECKONING
– submit a bill for payment RENDER

billion U.S.-style, thousand million MILLIARD

bind See **join**
– bind a rope with a cord, or bind with a protective material in order to prevent fraying WHIP
– bind or fasten tightly by means of a coupling device SHACKLE, PINION
– bind or wrap SWATHE, SWADDLE
– binding together LIGATURE

binding – set of printed pages, typically 16 or 32, folded from a single sheet, for binding with others to form a book SIGNATURE, GATHER

bindweed or related plant CONVOLVULUS

bingo HOUSEY-HOUSEY
– bingo, especially as played by children LOTTO

biochemical catalyst in the form of a protein produced by living cells ENZYME

biography of saints, or over-admiring biography HAGIOGRAPHY
– of one's own life AUTOBIOGRAPHY, MEMOIRS
– biography that is very short POTTED BIOGRAPHY
– biographical article or essay, as in a newspaper PROFILE
– biographical film BIOPIC

biology See also **classification**
– biology of heredity in plants and animals GENETICS
– biological classification TAXONOMY
– biological degeneration, as opposed to evolution DEVOLUTION
– similarity of form or structure in biology ISOMORPHISM

biotechnology, study or application of biology and engineering in work ERGONOMICS

bird See illustration and chart, and also **feather**, **wing**
– bird, such as the ostrich, emu, or kiwi, that cannot fly RATITE
– bird of prey RAPTOR
– bird of prey's claw POUNCE, TALON
– bird of prey's swooping down on its victim STOOP
– bird or other animal, live or artificial, used to lure others into shooting range or capture DECOY
– bird still too young to leave the nest NESTLING
– bird that has just grown the feathers necessary for flying FLEDGLING
– bird's feathers PLUMAGE
– bird's stomach area, often containing grit, for breaking down food GIZZARD, VENTRICULUS

bird

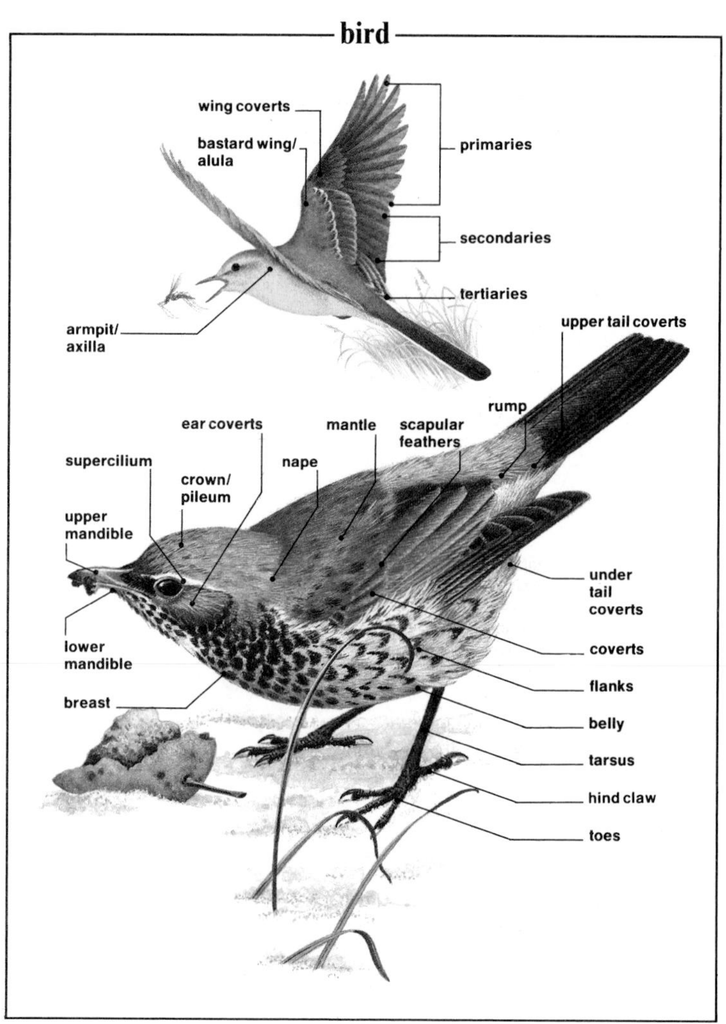

– bird's vocal organ in the lower part of the windpipe SYRINX
– bird's wing, specifically the rear section holding the flight feathers PINION
– active at twilight or before dawn, as some birds or other creatures are CREPUSCULAR
– adapted for running, as some birds or bones are CURSORIAL
– adjective relating to birds AVIAN, ORNITHIC
– band or distinctive patch of colour on the throat of a bird or other animal GORGET
– born blind and helpless, therefore requiring lengthy care in the nest, as some species of birds are NIDICOLOUS
– born fairly well-developed, and therefore able to leave the nest early, as some birds are NIDIFUGOUS
– clean the feathers with the beak, as a bird might PREEN
– cut or bind a bird's wings in order to restrain it PINION
– dip lightly into the water, as a bird might DAP
– dry internal shell of a squid-like shellfish, used in polishes and as a mineral supplement for a cage bird's diet CUTTLEBONE
– enclosure, such as a large cage, for live birds AVIARY
– excrete, as birds do MUTE
– feed and care for a baby bird until it leaves the nest FLEDGE
– fertiliser from coastal deposits of the dried dung of sea birds GUANO
– fledgling bird, especially a young pigeon SQUAB
– fold of skin hanging from the throat, as of some birds and lizards WATTLE
– huge and powerful bird of prey in Arabian legend ROC
– mass of undigested food, including bones, fur, and feathers, ejected by an owl or other bird of prey CAST, PELLET
– mythical bird that would burn itself every 500 years and rise rejuvenated from the ashes PHOENIX
– non-migratory, resident in one area only, as some birds are SEDENTARY
– opening for the digestive and genital tracts in birds, fish, and reptiles CLOACA
– pouch in a bird's gullet for storing or pre-digesting food CROP, CRAW
– relating or referring to a young bird still without flight feathers or not yet developed enough to fly CALLOW, UNFLEDGED
– relating or referring to the largest order of birds, the perching songbirds PASSERINE
– relating or referring to young birds that are naked and dependent when newly hatched ALTRICIAL
– scientific study of birds ORNITHOLOGY
– sticky substance spread to trap birds LIME, BIRDLIME

bird- ORNITHO-

bird-of-paradise flower STRELITZIA

birdwatcher whose main interest is in sighting as many rare species as possible TWITCHER
– birdwatcher's tent or hiding place HIDE, BLIND

Birmingham – person born or living in Birmingham BRUMMIE

birth See also **childbirth**
– birth, as of an idea or project GENESIS
– birth, or the circumstances of

BIRD GROUPS

birds in general	**flock, flight, volley, congregation, bevy, pod, volary, dissimulation; plump (of wild fowl); brood (of chicks)**	mallards	**sord, puddling (on water); flush, sute (on land)**
bitterns, cranes, herons	**sedge, siege**	nightingales	**match, watch**
choughs	**chattering, clattering**	owls	**stare, parliament**
coots	**covert, raft**	partridges	**covey**
crows	**murder, hover**	peafowl	**muster, pride, ostentation**
doves	**flight, dole, dule, prettying, pitying**	penguins	**rookery, colony**
ducks	**flush, team, plump (in flight); dopping (diving); baddling (on water)**	pheasants	**nye, bouquet**
eagles	**convocation**	pigeons	**flight, flock**
falcons	**cast**	plovers	**congregation, wing, leash**
finches	**trimming, trembling**	quails	**bevy, covey**
geese	**gaggle, nide, flock; skein (in flight)**	ravens	**unkindness**
goldfinches, hummingbirds	**charm, drum, chattering, troubling**	rooks	**parliament, building, clamour**
grouse	**covey**	snipe	**walk, wisp, whisper**
gulls	**colony**	sparrows	**host, quarrel, tribe**
hawks	**cast, leash**	starlings	**murmuration**
jays	**band, party**	swans	**herd, bevy, bank, wedge, game, squadron, whiteness**
lapwings	**desert, deceit**	teal	**spring, raft, coil, knob**
larks	**exaltation, bevy**	thrushes	**mutation**
magpies	**tittering, tiding**	turkeys	**flock, dole, dule, raft, raffle, rafter**
		wigeon	**company, bunch, knob, coil**
		woodcock	**fall, covey, plump**

one's birth NATIVITY
– birth or delivery of a baby feet or buttocks first BREECH BIRTH, BREECH DELIVERY
– birth or delivery of a baby requiring the use of medical tongs FORCEPS DELIVERY
– give birth, bear young, as sheep and goats do YEAN
– give birth to SPAWN, DROP
– give premature birth to a calf SLINK, SLIP
– giving birth by means of eggs that hatch outside the body OVIPAROUS
– giving birth by means of eggs that hatch within the female's body OVOVIVIPAROUS
– giving birth to live offspring rather than laying eggs VIVIPAROUS
– membranes and placenta expelled from the mother's uterus after the birth of a baby AFTERBIRTH, SECUNDINES, LOCHIA
– period of confinement of a woman at the time of giving birth LYING-IN, ACCOUCHEMENT
– piece of the amniotic sac sometimes covering a baby's head at birth CAUL
– present from birth, as a character trait might be INNATE
– referring to a condition or abnormality existing from birth but not hereditary CONGENITAL
– relating or belonging to the place of one's birth NATIVE
– relating to a baby during the first month after birth NEONATAL
– relating to birth NATAL
– relating to the time before birth or during pregnancy PRENATAL, ANTENATAL
– relating to the time just after birth or after giving birth POSTNATAL, POSTPARTUM
– relating to the time just before or after birth PERINATAL

-birth -GEN, -GENESIS, -GENOUS, -PAROUS

birthmark, mole, or other congenital skin blemish or growth NAEVUS
– birthmark, scar, spot, or rash on the skin MACULA, STIGMA

biscuit See chart, page 79

bisexual, having both male and female sex organs or characteristics HERMAPHRODITE, ANDROGYNOUS

bishop See also **clergyman**, **priest**
– bishop, abbot, or clergyman of similar standing PRELATE
– bishop assisting or subordinate to another bishop SUFFRAGAN
– bishop of an Eastern Orthodox church EPARCH
– bishop of high rank METROPOLITAN
– bishop of senior rank in the early Christian Church, or the Roman Catholic or various Orthodox Churches today PATRIARCH
– bishop of the highest rank in a region PRIMATE
– bishop or judge having direct judicial authority ORDINARY
– bishop's area of authority DIOCESE, SEE
– bishop's backless chair FALDSTOOL
– bishop's chief administrative officer, dealing with legal secular matters in the diocese CHANCELLOR
– bishop's hat, symbolic of his office or authority MITRE
– bishop's household helper or servant FAMILIAR
– bishop's junior or assistant bishop COADJUTOR
– bishop's letter to his diocese PASTORAL
– bishop's official chair or throne, or his office or diocese CATHEDRA
– bishop's official representative COMMISSARY
– bishop's permission for a clergyman to leave the diocese to work elsewhere EXEAT
– bishop's position, status, or term of office EPISCOPATE, EPISCOPACY
– bishop's staff, having a crook or cross at the top, carried as a symbol of office CROSIER
– bishop's throne in an apse TRIBUNE
– adjective for a bishop EPISCOPAL
– appoint someone as bishop or abbot MITRE
– clergy of the rank of bishop and above HIERARCHY
– clergyman in the Eastern Orthodox Church, ranking below a bishop ARCHIMANDRITE
– ordain a bishop CONSECRATE
– transfer a bishop to another diocese TRANSLATE

bit See **harness**

bit, limited amount MODICUM
– bit, portion SNIPPET, MOIETY
– bit, small or very modest amount DRIBLET, PITTANCE
– small bit or strand, such as a splinter or paring SLIVER
– tiny bit, extremely small amount IOTA, SCINTILLA, SMIDGEN
– tiny bit, merest hint SEMBLANCE, SOUPÇON, TINCTURE, VESTIGE

bite – performer who bites off the head of a live frog, mouse, chicken, or the like GEEK

biting or cutting, as wit can be CAUSTIC, MORDANT, PUNGENT, INCISIVE, ACERBIC

bits, fragments SMITHEREENS

bitter See also **biting**
– bitter juice of grapes, apples, or the like, formerly used in cookery VERJUICE
– bitter orange, as used for making marmalade SEVILLE ORANGE
– bitter, tart, sour-tasting ACERBIC, ACETOUS, ACIDULOUS
– bitter or harsh to the taste or smell ACRID, ASTRINGENT
– bitter or sharp in attitude, speech, or manner, caustic ACRIMONIOUS, RANCOROUS
– bitterly critical or condemnatory SCATHING, CAUSTIC, VITRIOLIC, VITUPERATIVE, VIRULENT
– cynical or pessimistic in a bitter or sarcastic way SARDONIC, JAUNDICED
– hurtful and bitter mutual accusations RECRIMINATIONS
– resentful, piqued, embittered AGGRIEVED

bitterness or some distressing cause of it WORMWOOD
– cause irritation or bitterness over a lengthy period of time FESTER, RANKLE

bitters, bitter tonic mixture used to flavour drinks ANGOSTURA BITTERS

black See also **colours**
– black American considered excessively servile to whites UNCLE TOM
– black and white in blotches, as a horse might be PIEBALD, PINTO
– black cultural pride or racial self-esteem NEGRITUDE
– black formal evening jacket for men TUXEDO, DINNER JACKET
– black nationalist cult member, venerating the former Ethiopian emperor Haile Selassie RASTAFARIAN
– black or coloured township in South Africa LOCATION
– black or white, of neutral colour ACHROMATIC
– blackish and glossy, pitch-like PICEOUS

black- MELAN-, MELANO-

black-and-white, as a photograph or television set might be MONOCHROME
– black-and-white portrait in the form of a shadow image or filled-in outline SILHOUETTE

black box, or electronic recorder of an aircraft's technical details, used to establish the cause of a crash FLIGHT RECORDER

black hole, hyper-dense region in space COLLAPSAR
– black hole's boundary EVENT HORIZON

black ice, thin coating of ice, as on a road GLAZE ICE

black magic based on worship of the

dead NECROLATRY
– black magic or supernatural arts THE OCCULT, DIABOLISM
– black-magic religious cult, of African origin, practised in Haiti VOODOO
– black-magic religious cult, of African origin, practised in the West Indies OBEAH, OBI
– man practising sorcery or black magic, male witch WARLOCK

Black Sea – relating to the Black Sea PONTIC

blackberry, dog rose, or similar prickly shrub or plant BRAMBLE

blackbird MERLE

blackcurrant syrup, cordial, or liqueur CASSIS

blackhead COMEDO

blacksmith – blacksmith's furnace FORGE
– blacksmith's hammer FULLER

bladder, especially the urinary bladder VESICA
– bladder-shaped AMPULLACEOUS
– bladder stone or gallstone CYSTOLITH
– surgical removal of the gall bladder or part of the urinary bladder CYSTECTOMY

bladder- CYST-, CYSTO-

blade of a knife, or similar sharp part of a tool BIT
– blade of a leaf or petal LAMINA
– blade of a skate or sledge RUNNER
– blade of a turbine, propeller, windmill, or the like VANE
– blade of an oar or paddle PALM
– blade on the hull of a boat that raises it when speeding HYDROFOIL
– implement having a wide-tipped and flexible blade SPATULA

blame See also **criticise**, **scold**
– blame for or prove involvement in a crime INCRIMINATE, INCULPATE
– blame oneself or others REPROACH
– consider or pronounce free of blame or guilt, or from responsibility ABSOLVE, EXONERATE, EXCULPATE, VINDICATE
– person or group made to bear the blame for faults or distress of others SCAPEGOAT, WHIPPING BOY

blameless, beyond reproach or doubt UNIMPEACHABLE

blameworthy, deserving of criticism REPREHENSIBLE, DEPLORABLE, DISCREDITABLE, HEINOUS
– blameworthy, and punishable for wrongdoing CULPABLE
– represent or try to represent a crime, fault, or the like as less serious or blameworthy, as by making certain excuses EXTENUATE

blank cut or punched from a sheet of metal BURR
– blank metal disc made ready for stamping into a coin FLAN

blanket – blanket-like cloak with a hole or slit in the middle for the head PONCHO
– woven with a loose, open texture like a blanket CELLULAR

blasphemy – misuse, desecration, or blasphemously disrespectful treatment of something sacred or regarded as sacred SACRILEGE, PROFANATION

bleach – oxygen in the form of O_3, used in bleaching OZONE
– watery chemical solution used as a disinfectant and bleaching agent JAVELLE WATER

bleeding See also **blood**
– bleeding, as from a wound HAEMORRHAGE
– hereditary disorder characterised by excessive or unstoppable bleeding HAEMOPHILIA
– point on the body where an artery can be pressed shut to stop the bleeding of a wound further on PRESSURE POINT
– stopping or slowing down bleeding ASTRINGENT, STYPTIC, HAEMOSTATIC

blend See **mix**
– blend, word formed by fusing elements from two separate words PORTMANTEAU WORD
– blend or combine MELD
– blend or dilute whisky or other alcoholic spirits RECTIFY

bless, make sacred or morally binding SANCTIFY, CONSECRATE, HALLOW

Bless you! – German equivalent of "Bless you!", said to someone who has sneezed GESUNDHEIT

blessedness or a state of serene, joyful happiness BEATITUDE, NIRVANA

blessing, act of blessing, blessedness, or invocation of God's blessing BENEDICTION, BENISON
– blessing, benefit BOON
– blessing or grace, as before meals BENEDICITE

blind – reading or printing system for the blind BRAILLE, MOON TYPE
– very short-sighted or nearly blind PURBLIND
– blindly committed to a theory, dogmatic DOCTRINAIRE

blind spot of the eye OPTIC DISC

blinds or shutter with horizontal adjustable slats JALOUSIE
– blinds that can be raised and lowered, and whose slats can be angled VENETIAN BLIND

blink or wink, especially involuntarily and repeatedly PALPEBRATE
– blink or wink NICTITATE

bliss – relating to the state of marriage, marital, as bliss might be CONNUBIAL

blissful or delightful ELYSIAN
– blissful state of freedom from care NIRVANA

blister BLEB, BULLA, VESICLE
– blister, boil, or inflammation filled with pus ABSCESS, PUSTULE
– blister-like sac or cavity in the body, normal or abnormal CYST
– blistering agent, such as mustard gas VESICANT
– clear watery fluid exuded by tissue, as in a blister SERUM

block See also **prevent**, **obstruct**
– block or ward off a blow, fencing thrust, or the like PARRY
– block or wedge placed under a wheel, log, or the like, to immobilise it on a slope SCOTCH
– blocked, overfull, clogged, as with blood or mucus CONGESTED
– blocking or deliberate exclusion of thoughts, desires, or the like from one's mind SUPPRESSION

block of flats or rented rooms, often in a slum area TENEMENT

blond and blue-eyed, and typically tall and long-headed in appearance NORDIC
– blond-haired TOWHEADED

blonde – pale silvery-blonde hair colour PLATINUM BLONDE

blood See chart, page 60, and also **heart**, **vein**, **artery**, **disease**, **bleeding**
– blood and tissue discharged normally after childbirth LOCHIA, AFTERBIRTH, SECUNDINES
– blood clot, air bubble, or the like drifting in the blood stream before becoming lodged EMBOLUS
– blood clot formed in a fixed position in a blood vessel or the heart THROMBUS
– blood from a wound, especially clotted blood GORE
– blood-letting by opening a vein PHLEBOTOMY, VENESECTION
– blood of the gods ICHOR
– blood poisoning PYAEMIA, SEPTICAEMIA, TOXAEMIA
– blood purifying organ below the stomach SPLEEN
– blood-red INCARNADINE
– blood relationship, or any close association CONSANGUINITY
– blood-sugar excess, as in diabetes HYPERGLYCAEMIA
– blood-sugar shortage, as in diabetes HYPOGLYCAEMIA
– accumulation of blood in a body part, caused by poor circulation HYPOSTASIS
– adjective for blood HAEMAL, HAEMATIC, HAEMIC

– artificial purifying of the blood, in cases of kidney failure HAEMODIALYSIS, RENAL DIALYSIS
– baby born with a disease that destroys its blood cells RHESUS BABY
– bandage or similar device wound tight to stanch a heavy flow of blood TOURNIQUET
– be soaked in or covered with blood WELTER
– become a soft, solidified mass, clot or curdle, as blood, milk, or other liquids might COAGULATE
– bloodthirsty, or characterised by blood or bloodshed SANGUINARY
– check or stop the flow of blood from a wound STANCH, STAUNCH
– fatty deposit on an artery wall, restricting the flow of blood ATHEROMA
– filled to excess with blood or other fluid ENGORGED
– former medical technique of attaching a glass cup to the skin by a partial vacuum, in order to draw blood to the surface CUPPING
– medical and scientific study of blood HAEMATOLOGY
– oxygenate blood VENTILATE
– patient receiving blood, tissue, a transplanted organ, or the like from a donor RECIPIENT
– person who gives blood for transfusion DONOR
– presence of nitrogen bubbles in the blood, or the resulting illness, caused by an abrupt reduction in atmospheric pressure AEROEMBOLISM, THE BENDS, DECOMPRESSION SICKNESS, CAISSON DISEASE
– referring to blood in the veins VENOUS
– salt solution of similar concentration to that in the blood, as used in a medical drip SALINE
– soapy substance found in tissue, blood, and bile CHOLESTEROL
– stage blood KENSINGTON GORE
– stopping or slowing down the flow of blood ASTRINGENT, STYPTIC, HAEMOSTATIC
– tissue death, or dead tissue, as due to a blood clot INFARCTION
– transfer by injection of blood, plasma, or the like into the blood stream TRANSFUSION
– unable to combine safely, as two types of blood in a transfusion might be INCOMPATIBLE
– watery liquid circulating like blood in the body, that purifies body tissue and produces antibodies LYMPH

-blood- -AEM-, -HAEM-, HAEMO-, HAEMATO-

-blood clot- -THROMB-, THROMBO-

blood feud, maintained by a cycle of revenge VENDETTA

blood pressure that is abnormally high HYPERTENSION
– blood pressure that is abnormally low HYPOTENSION
– instrument for measuring blood pressure SPHYGMOMANOMETER
– rotating cylinder on which a pen records changes in blood pressure, heartbeat, or the like KYMOGRAPH
– technique for regulating one's own heartbeat, blood pressure, or other apparently involuntary bodily functions BIOFEEDBACK

blood vessel of a very fine, thin-walled kind CAPILLARY
– blood vessel's outermost layer or covering ADVENTITIA
– air bubble, clot, or other body blocking a blood vessel, EMBOLUS
– blocked or obstructed, as a blood vessel might be OCCLUDED
– blocking of a blood vessel by a clot or air bubble EMBOLISM
– directed or conducting down or away from a centre, as some nerves and blood vessels are DEFERENT, EFFERENT
– network of nerves and blood vessels PLEXUS
– sac, bulge, or pouch in the weakened wall of a blood vessel ANEURYSM

blood vessel- ANGIO-, VAS-, VASO-

bloodhound's fleshy drooping upper lip FLEWS

bloodshed on a large scale, slaughter or massacre CARNAGE
– place or scene of bloodshed, or great destruction SHAMBLES

blooming process or period in plants ANTHESIS
– blooming twice or more during a season REMONTANT

blossom, bud, sprout, begin to grow BURGEON
– blossoming, blooming, or the time of bursting into flower EFFLORESCENCE, FLORESCENCE

BLOOD CONSTITUENTS AND CHEMICALS

albumin/ albumen	protein found in blood serum and in milk, egg white, and the like
complement/ alexin	substance in blood serum combining with antibodies to destroy bacteria, foreign cells, and the like
corpuscle	free-moving blood cell
erythrocyte	red corpuscle, in which oxygen is transported to the body's tissues
gamma globulin	protein, often an antibody, helping immunity
haemoglobin	red iron-containing protein in the red corpuscles, that transports oxygen to the body's tissues
insulin	protein hormone from the pancreas, controlling the level of sugar in the blood
leucocyte	any white corpuscle, with various defence and repair functions according to type
lymphocyte	common white corpuscle, with defence functions such as producing antibodies
phagocyte	cell, such as a white corpuscle, that envelopes and digests bacteria, tissue debris, and the like
plasma	yellowish liquid base containing the cells and platelets
platelet/ thrombocyte	tiny disc helping blood clotting
Rh factor/ rhesus factor	substance on the surface of red blood cells that reacts adversely to cells lacking it
serum	purified plasma, from which clotting agents have been removed
transferrin	blood protein transferring iron in the body

blouse See chart at **clothes**
– frills down the front of a blouse or shirt JABOT, RUFFLE
blow – ward off a blow, fencing thrust, or the like PARRY
blowhole of a whale or related marine mammal SPIRACLE
blowing or whispering sound heard through a stethoscope, typically due to blood flowing SOUFFLE
blown, dispersed as by wind, fanned WINNOWED
blue See **colours**
– blue in heraldry AZURE
– blue dye, used by ancient Britons to colour their skin WOAD
bluish, as a bruise might be LIVID
blunder See also **mistake**
– blunder made in one's speech, slip of the tongue LAPSUS LINGUAE
– blunder or laughable mistake HOWLER, BONER
– blunder or social mistake, such as a gauche or tactless remark GAFFE, FAUX PAS
blunt See **frank**, **rude**
– blunt or rounded at the tip, as a leaf or angle might be OBTUSE
blur, darken, make indistinct or dim OBFUSCATE
– blurred printed impressions, as caused by the paper's moving MACKLE
blushing or reddening of the skin ERUBESCENCE
board, typically heart-shaped and mounted on castors, that allegedly writes or spells out messages in spiritualism sessions PLANCHETTE
– board displaying the alphabet, used in spiritualism sessions to register messages OUIJA BOARD
– board forming the top rail of a fence or balustrade LEDGER BOARD
– board in an overlapping series, used especially to cover roofs or walls WEATHERBOARD, CLAPBOARD
– board made of thin sheets of wood glued together PLYWOOD
– board or boards laid to form a pathway DUCKBOARD
– board or signboard above the door or window of a shop FASCIA
– either of two advertising boards, suspended from a person's shoulders SANDWICH BOARD
board and lodging, as in a small French hotel, or the hotel itself PENSION
boast, congratulate or plume oneself, take pride in oneself PREEN
– boast or brag about, describe in a boastful way, extol VAUNT, EMBLAZON
– boaster, braggart, swaggerer GASCON, ROISTERER, BLUSTERER
– boastful, bragging, swanking or strutting THRASONICAL
– boastful, jumped-up, self-important man COCKALORUM
– boastful, self-important EGOTISTIC, VAINGLORIOUS, VAPOURING
– boastfulness, idle bluster, bravado BRAGGADOCIO, FANFARONADE, GASCONADE, RODOMONTADE
boat See chart, and also **ship**, **sailing**
– boat club's chairman COMMODORE
– boat-race or series of races for boats REGATTA
– boat's float, attached parallel on each side as stabiliser OUTRIGGER
– car tyre or similar bumper on the side of a boat for protection against collision FENDER
– deep, wide, and safe enough for ships or boats to sail on or through NAVIGABLE
– dragging or carrying of boats overland from one waterway to another PORTAGE
– line or edge at which the bottom and side of a boat meet CHINE
– make a boat watertight by packing the seams, as with tar CAULK
– move a boat by pulling on a rope attached to an anchor KEDGE
– peg or pin, especially one used as a boat's rowlock THOLE
– person who steers a boat or directs those rowing it, as in a race COXSWAIN, COX
– plate or place on the stern of a ship or boat bearing the vessel's name ESCUTCHEON
– responsive, easily manoeuvrable, as a boat might be YARE
– seat extending across a rowing boat THWART
– spaces at the front and back of a rowing boat SHEETS
– swivelling support for an oar on the side of a boat ROWLOCK
– upper edge of the side of a ship or boat GUNWALE, GUNNEL

BOATS

POWERED BY OAR, PEDAL, OR PADDLE

bumboat, **caïque**, **coble**, **coracle/currach**, **dinghy**, **felucca**, **gig**, **gondola**, **kayak**, **pedalo**, **pinnace**, **piragua/pirogue**, **punt**, **randan**, **sampan**, **scull**, **shallop**, **shell**, **skiff**, **umiak**, **wherry**

POWERED BY SAIL

caïque, **catamaran**, **coble**, **cutter**, **dhow**, **dinghy**, **felucca**, **gig**, **hoy**, **junk**, **lugger**, **nuggar**, **pink**, **pinnace**, **proa**, **sampan**, **shallop**, **skiff**, **sloop**, **smack**, **trimaran**, **wherry**

POWERED BY MOTOR

dory, **drifter**, **gig**, **hydrofoil/hydroplane**, **skiff**, **tender**, **trawler**, **vaporetto**, **vedette**

body See also **corpse**, **digestive system**, **organ**, **reproductive system**, and entries at various parts of the body
– body cavity, hollow, or channel, containing or conveying air, pus, blood, or the like SINUS
– body cavity, recess, sac, follicle, or the like CRYPT
– body cavity serving as an entrance VESTIBULE
– body cavity, tube, or pouch blocked at one end CUL-DE-SAC
– body channel of very small size, as in a bone CANALICULUS
– body channel DUCT, VAS
– body fluid in ancient and medieval medicine HUMOUR
– body movements performed very slowly and deliberately in a series as part of a Chinese form of exercise and mental training TAI CHI
– body of a dead animal or bird CARCASS
– body of a dead person, corpse CADAVER
– body opening ORIFICE
– body organs, especially those essential for maintaining life VITALS
– body part or organ, now degenerated or nonfunctioning, surviving from an earlier stage of development VESTIGE
– body processes and functions maintaining life METABOLISM
– body sense, awareness of one's body and its movements KINAESTHESIA
– body's make-up as an indication of health and strength CONSTITUTION
– body's structure or appearance, based on shape, size, and muscular development PHYSIQUE
– abnormal body sound, specifically a heart murmur BRUIT
– abnormal rift or gap in a body part or organ DIASTEMA
– adjective for the body CORPORAL
– affecting the entire body, as a

disease or poison might SYSTEMIC
– bodily defect or crippled condition, such as a hunchback DEFORMITY, DISFIGUREMENT
– building or room in which the bodies or bones of the dead were stored CHARNEL HOUSE
– corresponding in evolutionary origin but not in function, as body parts such as wings and arms are HOMOLOGOUS
– corresponding in function but not in evolutionary origin, as body parts such as gills and lungs are ANALOGOUS
– crossing-over of two structures in the body, such as the optic nerve fibres CHIASMA
– entertainer or acrobat who twists his limbs and body into abnormal positions CONTORTIONIST
– having bodily form INCARNATE
– having certain robot-like or electronically enhanced body parts or functions BIONIC
– having or referring to a heavy fat body or build, typically accompanied by an easygoing personality ENDOMORPHIC, PYKNIC
– having or referring to a strong and muscular body or build MESOMORPHIC
– having or referring to a thin weak body or build, typically accompanied by a nervous personality ECTOMORPHIC, LEPTOSOMIC
– lacking a body or lacking in reality INCORPOREAL, DISEMBODIED
– picture of the body, or a section of the body, without the skin, to illustrate the muscle structure ÉCORCHÉ
– rebirth in another body or form REINCARNATION
– relating to sexual and other appetites of the body SENSUAL, CARNAL
– relating to the front or lower surface of the body VENTRAL
– representative in bodily human form of an ideal or model EMBODIMENT, INCARNATION, AVATAR
– rhythm of bodily processes or functions that have a regular 24-hour cycle CIRCADIAN RHYTHM
– section of the body between hip and neck, trunk TORSO
– side of the body FLANK
– small body cavity or chamber, as in the heart VENTRICLE

bones

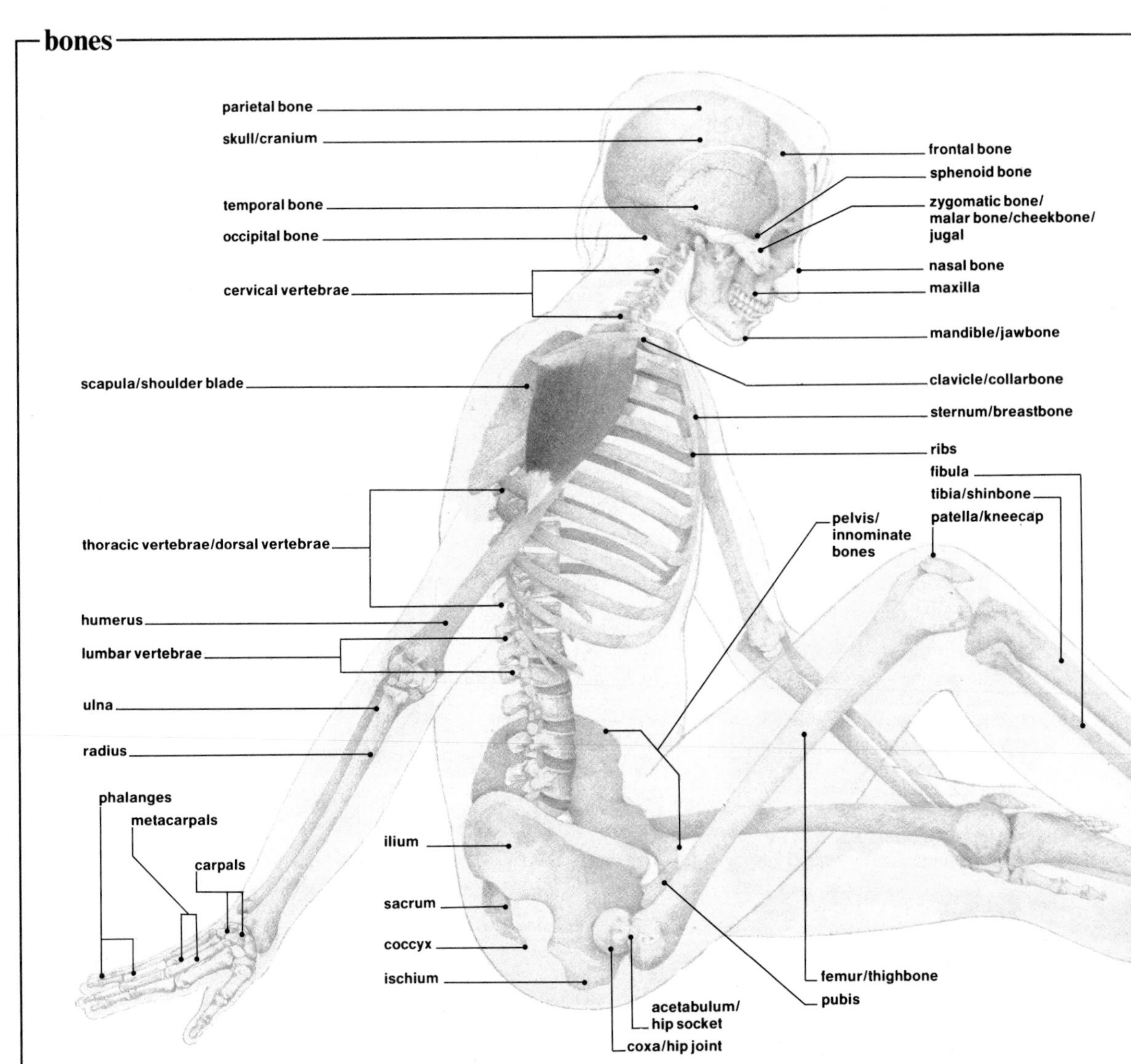

– wasting away of the body caused by lengthy disease TABES
– watery liquid that circulates in the body, purifies body tissues, and produces antibodies LYMPH

-body- SOMAT-, SOMATO-, -SOME, -OME

-body cavity- -COEL-, COELO-

body language – study of body language, such as gesture and facial expression, as a form of communication KINESICS

bodybuilding or exercise through contracting the muscles without changing their length or moving the limbs ISOMETRIC EXERCISE
– artificial hormone or drug, based on a ring of carbon atoms and increasing muscle and bone growth, sometimes used in bodybuilding ANABOLIC STEROID

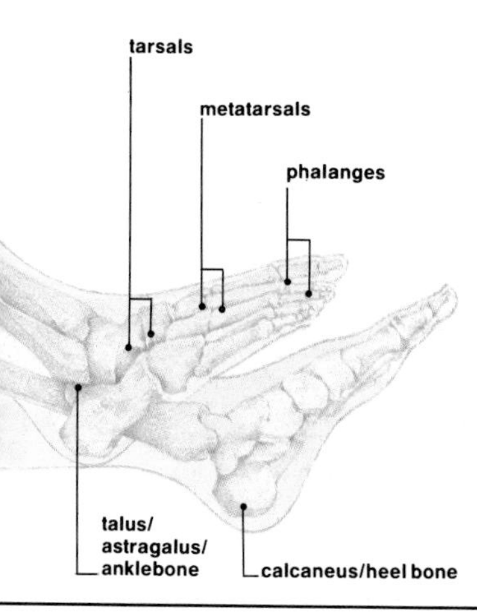

bodyguard for the sovereign, drawn from retired army officers GENTLEMAN-AT-ARMS
– corps of bodyguards PRAETORIAN GUARD

bog, marsh, swamp, or mire SLOUGH, QUAGMIRE, MORASS

boil, evaporate, and condense a liquid repeatedly, as when extracting substances REFLUX
– boil down and concentrate a liquid, or extract an essence from a liquid by boiling DECOCT
– boil food briefly, as to remove bitter flavour or prepare for freezing BLANCH
– boil partially PARBOIL
– pierce or cut, make an incision, as into a boil LANCE
– pus-filled channel, as from a boil ABSCESS, SINUS
– steep herbs, tea, or the like without boiling INFUSE
– technical name for a boil FURUNCLE

boiler – insulation material around a boiler LAGGING
– muddy deposit, as on a river bed or the inside of a boiler SLUDGE

bold See **brave**, **cheeky**

Bolshevik – Bolsheviks' liberal opponents before and after the Russian Revolution MENSHEVIKS

bolt, revolving axle, or the like, as in a lock or between two door handles SPINDLE
– bolt tightened by a peg-like crosspiece TOGGLE BOLT
– edge plate of a lock into which the bolt slots SELVAGE

bomb See also **missile**
– bomb fragments produced by an explosion SHRAPNEL
– bomb-like explosive device in a metal pipe, as for blasting a path through barbed wire BANGALORE TORPEDO
– bomb or machine-gun enemy ground troops from low-flying aircraft STRAFE
– bombing, blows, gunfire, or the like of a heavy and sustained kind BARRAGE
– aerial bomb scattering shrapnel widely CLUSTER BOMB, FRAGMENTATION BOMB
– atomic bomb, produced by the splitting of atomic nuclei FISSION BOMB
– explode, as a bomb might, or cause to explode DETONATE
– extremely heavy concentration of bombing or other military force on an enemy target SATURATION
– fire bomb designed to start a destructive fire INCENDIARY BOMB
– fire bomb that contains highly inflammable jellied petroleum NAPALM BOMB
– fire bomb or inflammable substance used in ancient sea warfare GREEK FIRE
– guiding or stabilising fin on a bomb or missile VANE
– hydrogen bomb or similar bomb produced by the fusion of light atomic nuclei FUSION BOMB, THERMONUCLEAR BOMB
– make a bomb inactive and harmless DEACTIVATE, DEFUSE
– nuclear bomb designed to kill people without destroying buildings, by releasing short-lived radiation NEUTRON BOMB, ENHANCED RADIATION BOMB
– petrol bomb or similar crude fire bomb thrown by hand, typically a fuel-filled bottle stoppered with a rag wick MOLOTOV COCKTAIL
– section of a bomb, missile, or the like containing the actual explosive or toxic material WARHEAD
– simultaneous or rapid discharge or release of several bombs or missiles SALVO
– small bell-shaped bomb used in former times, as for breaching a castle wall PETARD

bombard or shell heavily CRUMP
– bombardment, as by artillery fire CANNONADE, STONK

bond, tie, connection or link VINCULUM, LIGATURE, NEXUS
– bond, typically long-term and unsecured, issued by a company or government organisation DEBENTURE, DEBENTURE BOND

bone See illustration, and also **fractures**
– bone or tooth decay CARIES
– bone formation OSSIFICATION, OSTEOGENESIS
– bone of very small size, especially in the inner ear OSSICLE
– bone surgery or bone grafting OSTEOPLASTY
– break a bone into many pieces COMMINUTE
– breaking of a bone in surgery in order to reset it or correct a deformity OSTEOCLASIS
– brittleness or weakening of the bones OSTEOPOROSIS
– building or room in which the bodies or bones of the dead were stored CHARNEL HOUSE
– carved or engraved articles or ornaments of ivory, whalebone, or the like, typically made by sailors SCRIMSHAW
– container of the bones of a corpse, such as an urn or vault OSSUARY

– containing or consisting of bone OSSEOUS
– creak, rattle, or crackle, as diseased lungs or broken bones might CREPITATE
– creaking or grating sound of the rubbing of the two ends of a broken bone CREPITUS
– cutting or removal of part of a bone in surgery OSTEOTOMY
– displace a limb or organ, or put a bone out of joint DISLOCATE
– end of a long bone, fused to the shaft only late in the growth process EPIPHYSIS
– expert in ancient forms of life, as through the study of old bones and fossils PALAEONTOLOGIST
– having an enlarged head-like end, as some bones have CAPITATE
– head-like part, such as the end of a long bone or insect's antenna CAPITULUM
– hole or passageway in a bone through which nerves or blood vessels pass FORAMEN
– hollow or cavity in a bone, such as a sinus in the upper jawbone ANTRUM
– hollow or dimple-like pit in a bone or other body part FOSSA, FOVEA
– joining of broken bones, the edges of a wound, or the like COAPTATION
– knob on the end of a bone, as that fitting into a socket in a ball-and-socket joint CONDYLE
– medical specialist in bone diseases and disorders OSTEOLOGIST
– net-like, spongy, or porous in structure, as some bones are CANCELLATE
– projection or bump, especially on the end of a bone for attaching a muscle or tendon TUBEROSITY
– relating to bone OSTEAL
– remove the bones from a fish or cut of meat FILLET
– shaft of a long bone DIAPHYSIS
– surgeon specialising in bone and joint disorders ORTHOPAEDIC SURGEON
– surgical instrument for scraping bones XYSTER, RASPATORY
– technical term for a bone OS
– therapist skilled in manipulating bones, especially those of the spine OSTEOPATH
– thin ring or layer of bone LAMELLA, LAMINA
– tough band or strip of fibrous tissue connecting moving bones or cartilages, or supporting organs or muscles LIGAMENT
– tough tissue or gristle, as at the joints between bones CARTILAGE
– turn to bone, become hard or bony, as tissue might OSSIFY

bone- OSTE-, OSTEO-

bone marrow- MYEL-, MYELO-
– bone marrow MEDULLA

bonus, tip, or reward for services rendered BUCKSHEE, GRATUITY
– bonus or added benefit from one's job, such as a company car or free telephone calls PERK, PERQUISITE
– bonus or benefit, as derived from a favour or investment DIVIDEND
– bonus or similar additional sum of money, as added to a regular price, salary, or the like PREMIUM

bony, hardened SCLEROUS

book See chart, and also **scriptures**
– book, film, or the like, such as *Roots*, mixing fact and fiction FACTION
– book, film, or the like dealing with events earlier than those in the previous book, film, or the like PREQUEL
– book, film, or the like dealing with events following those in the previous book, film, or the like SEQUEL
– book, film, or the like that is well reviewed but fails to impress the public at large SUCCÈS D'ESTIME
– book, from surplus stock, sold off at a reduced price REMAINDER
– book, play, or the like written quickly and for money rather than intended as a serious work of art POTBOILER
– book, racehorse, or the like that achieves sudden success after an unpromising early phase SLEEPER
– book collection or catalogue BIBLIOTHECA
– book-collector or -lover BIBLIOPHILE
– book in which accounts are recorded in bookkeeping LEDGER
– book-learning, knowledge of a formal, unimaginative, drily detailed kind PEDANTRY
– book or document in the author's handwriting HOLOGRAPH
– book that is weighty in size or seriousness TOME
– book's additional material, collected at the end APPENDIX
– book's size, shape, layout, or design FORMAT
– books or magazines that are typically cheap and sensational or sentimental PULP
– books still kept in print by a publisher even though published a considerable time in the past BACKLIST
– address a book or other work specifically to a person or group as a mark of respect or affection DEDICATE
– blank leaf at the front or back of a book FLYLEAF
– censor or alter a book or other text by removing objectionable or obscene passages EXPURGATE
– classification or shelf number of a book in a library CALL NUMBER
– company or writer producing books to be marketed by a separate publisher PACKAGER
– concentrate intensely on a book PORE OVER
– decorative picture, vine-leaf design, or the like on a book's title page or at the beginning or end of a chapter VIGNETTE
– dedication written into a gift book INSCRIPTION
– description of the physical and technical features of a book COLLATION
– description or review for promotional purposes, as on the dust jacket of a book BLURB
– excessive interest in books BIBLIOLATRY
– extract the essentials of a book, report, or the like GUT
– hardback and cloth-covered, as a book might be CLOTHBOUND
– hardbacked, as a book might be CASED, CASEBOUND
– having the edges of the pages still unslit or untrimmed, as a book might UNCUT
– illustration at the front of a book, often opposite the title page FRONTISPIECE
– "into the middle of things", straight into the narrative or plot, as a book or play might begin IN MEDIAS RES
– leaf rapidly through files, the pages of a book, or the like RIFFLE
– left-hand, even-numbered page of a book VERSO
– library classification system for books and other publications DEWEY DECIMAL SYSTEM, LIBRARY OF CONGRESS CLASSIFICATION
– licence for the publication of a book, as by a bishop or censor IMPRIMATUR, NIHIL, OBSTAT
– list of corrections to a book, typically printed on a slip pasted at the front ERRATA, CORRIGENDA
– list of publishing details, such as dates and authorship, of editions of books BIBLIOGRAPHY
– material added to a book, article, or the like after the discovery of its omission ADDENDUM
– narrow decorative line pressed into a book cover, or the wheel

tool used to make it FILLET
– number assigned to a newly published book in keeping with an international book classification system ISBN
– passage copied from a book, speech, or the like, as for separate publication EXTRACT, EXCERPT
– produce the text of an anthology, dictionary, or other book by gathering the material from many sources COMPILE
– reading-stand for supporting a book or notes, as in a church or lecture hall LECTERN
– referring to a book published after the writer's death POSTHUMOUS
– review or criticism of a book, film, play, or the like CRITIQUE, COMPTE RENDU
– right-hand, odd-numbered page of a book RECTO
– scholarly comments, footnotes, variant readings, and so on in an edition of a book APPARATUS CRITICUS, CRITICAL APPARATUS
– section of a book, such as a dictionary, published separately FASCICLE, FASCICULE
– series of notches cut into the front edge of a dictionary or other book, for easy alphabetical reference THUMB INDEX
– set of all the leaves of a book before binding QUIRE
– stained or discoloured, as old books might be FOXED
– "the end", word used formerly to indicate the end of a book or manuscript EXPLICIT
– title, heading, or letter, typically illuminated in red in a manuscript or book RUBRIC
– white space between two postage stamps on a sheet, facing pages of a book, or the like GUTTER

book- BIBLIO-

book of changes, ancient Chinese book of philosophy and forecasts I CHING

bookbinding See illustration, page 66
– bookbinding tool for applying gold leaf PALLET
– cardboard as used in bookbinding PASTEBOARD
– check and order the sections of a book prior to binding COLLATE
– fine parchment of calfskin, lambskin, or kidskin, as used in bookbinding VELLUM

bookcase or press with a double face, as in a library RANGE

BOOKS

almagest	medieval textbook, as on astronomy or alchemy
almanac	annual compilation of lists and charts of varied information
annals	records and reports of a learned society, field of study, or the like
anthology	collection of writings, as by a single author or on a particular theme
armorial	book listing or illustrating coats of arms
Baedeker	guidebook, specifically a 19th-century tourist guidebook
bestiary	medieval collection of animal fables
breviary	prayer book and hymnal for Roman Catholic clergymen
cambist	manual of exchange rates and conversion charts for weights and measures
catechism	instruction manual containing a series of questions and answers, especially on Christianity
chapbook	booklet or pamphlet of popular poems, ballads, religious homilies, or the like
commonplace book	personal journal containing ideas, reflections, and quoted extracts
concordance	index recording all the occurrences in context of the words in a text
festschrift	book of essays by scholars and compiled as a tribute to a learned colleague
formulary	book of prayers; book listing medical drugs, pharmaceutical formulas, and the like
herbal	textbook on plants, especially useful plants
hornbook	elementary textbook introducing a subject, primer
incunabulum	book printed before 1501
lectionary	book of scriptural lessons for reading at religious services
lexicon	dictionary, especially of an ancient language
missal	prayer book, specifically for the Roman Catholic Mass
monograph	booklet or pamphlet on some specialist subject
omnibus	book assembling any related studies, or many writings by a single author
pharmacopoeia/ dispensatory	official manual listing and describing medical drugs and preparations
primer	introductory textbook, especially a language-teaching book
psalter	book of psalms for use in religious services
thesaurus	book presenting a specialised vocabulary
vade mecum	ready-reference manual, typically carried about constantly
variorum	edition of a text with notes by several scholars

bookish or scholarly people LITERATI
bookkeeping system in which all transactions are recorded as a debit in one account and a credit in another DOUBLE ENTRY
– book in which accounts are recorded in bookkeeping LEDGER
bookmaker See **horse-racing**
bookplates – "from the library of", used on bookplates before the owner's name EX LIBRIS
bookseller – specialising in old and rare books, as a bookseller might be ANTIQUARIAN
boot See also **shoe**
– large-headed nail protecting soles of boots HOBNAIL
– metal spikes fastened to a shoe or boot, as for mountaineering or walking on ice CRAMPONS
booty, loot, spoils, stolen property PLUNDER, PILLAGE
border See also **boundary**, **trimming**, **edge**
– border, especially the area of floor bordering a carpet, doorway, or the like SURROUND
– border area or outskirts PERIPHERY, PURLIEUS, PRECINCTS
– border marker TERMINUS
– border or frontier areas MARCHLANDS, MARCHES
– drapery forming a decorative

bookbinding

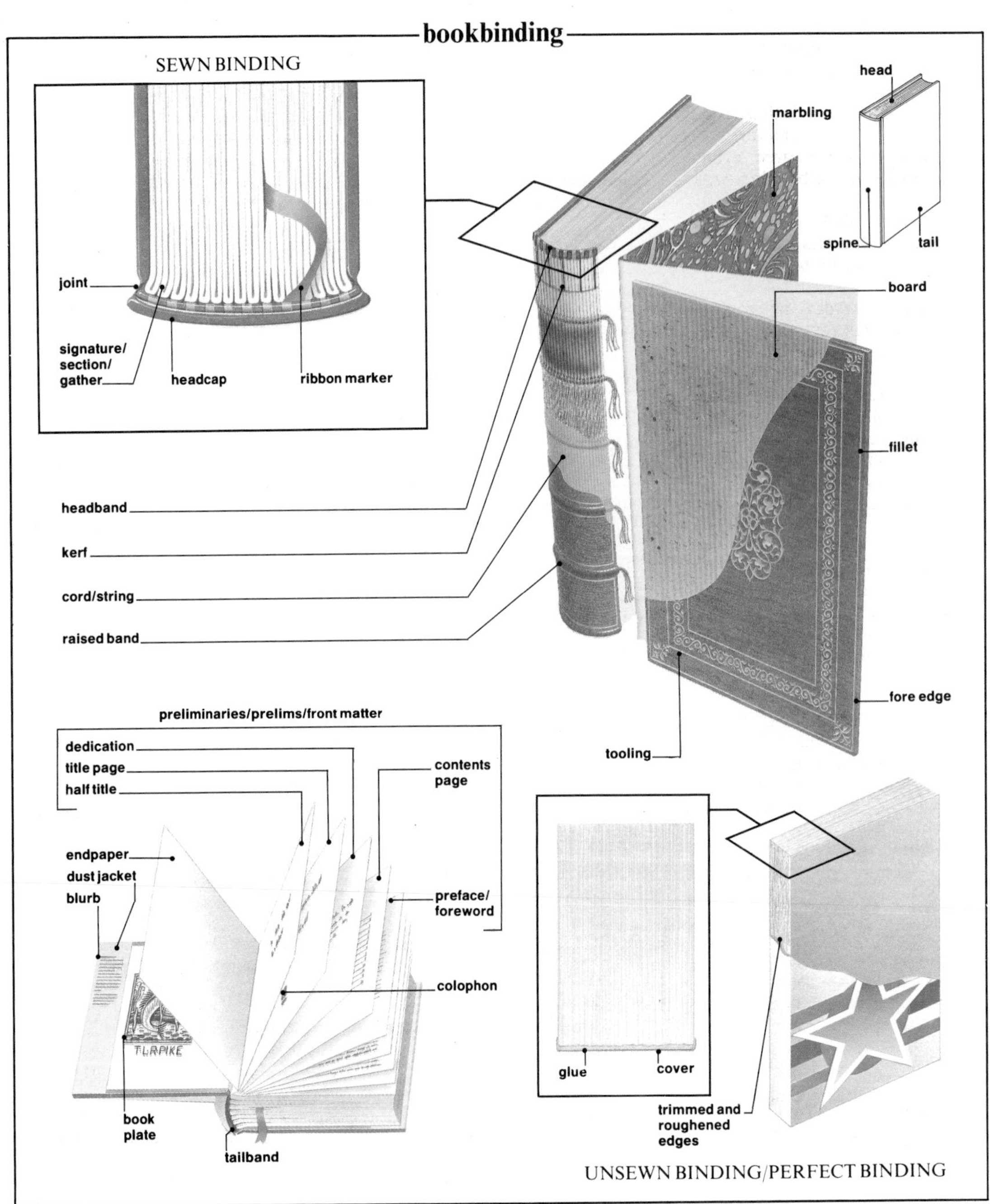

border, as along the edge of a bed or shelf VALANCE
– narrow border of a woven fabric to prevent unravelling SELVAGE

bordering, lying next to ADJACENT, ADJOINING, CONTIGUOUS, JUXTAPOSED, ABUTTING, TANGENTIAL

bore, become tiresome PALL
– bore or drill a well, mine-shaft or the like TREPAN
– boring tool AUGER, AWL

bored, uninterested or uncaring, indifferent APATHETIC
– bored or unenthusiastic because of overfamiliarity or overindulgence BLASÉ, JADED

boredom, depression, listlessness, or inactivity DOLDRUMS, ENNUI
– feeling of being tired of life, sense of desperate boredom TAEDIUM VITAE

boring See also **dull**
– boring, colourless or lifeless, as a textbook might be ARID, DESICCATED
– boring, everyday or commonplace, as a dull routine existence is HUMDRUM, QUOTIDIAN
– boring, tiresome, or annoying, as petty rules or a long-winded speech might be IRKSOME
– boring and seemingly never-ending INTERMINABLE
– boring or tiring work DRUDGERY
– boring periods of time or parts of a book, play, or film LONGUEURS
– boring through being too long or slow, wearisome TEDIOUS
– boring through being unvaried or repetitious, dreary and drab MONOTONOUS
– boring to the point of almost putting one to sleep, deadly dull STULTIFYING, STUPEFYING

born, used before the original surname when identifying a person who has changed name NÉ, NÉE
– born in wedlock, of married parents LEGITIMATE
– born out of wedlock, of unmarried parents, bastard ILLEGITIMATE, MISBEGOTTEN, SPURIOUS, NATURAL, SUPPOSITITIOUS
– just being born, beginning to develop, emerging NASCENT
– relating or belonging to the region where one was born NATIVE

borrowing of a word or phrase from another language by a literal translation of each element CALQUE, LOAN TRANSLATION
– borrowing or borrowed from a range of different sources ECLECTIC
– work, as of music, compiled by borrowing fragments or ideas from elsewhere PASTICCIO, PASTICHE

boss, employer, or sir, as used in East Africa as a respectful form of address BWANA
– boss, superior GAFFER

bossy See **dominating**

botany, study of plants PHYTOLOGY

both- AMBI-, AMPH-, AMPHI-, BI-

both sides – place or be placed on both sides of a divide STRADDLE

bother, inconvenience, put out INCOMMODE

bottle See chart, and also **wine**
– bottle, often in a protective box or basket, for acids and other corrosive liquids CARBOY
– bottle for wine or water at table CARAFE, DECANTER
– bottle or small dispenser for oil or vinegar, as used at table CRUET
– bottle top, as on beer and cold-drink bottles, with a crimped edge CROWN CAP
– bottle with only one surface, used as a mathematical brainteaser KLEIN BOTTLE
– bottle with more than one neck, used in a laboratory for bubbling gas through liquid WOULFE BOTTLE
– lockable cage-like container for displaying bottles or decanters of wine or spirits TANTALUS
– long narrow bottle or flask, sometimes covered in a straw casing DEMIJOHN
– narrow pitcher, or large bottle for wine or cider FLAGON
– small bottle, as for perfume, with a stopper FLACON
– small container, especially a tiny decorative bottle, for smelling salts VINAIGRETTE
– small container for medicine, poison, or other liquid, typically a tiny stoppered glass bottle VIAL, PHIAL
– squat two-handled bottle used in ancient Rome for storing wine, oil, or perfume AMPULLA

bottle gourd CALABASH

bottom layer SUBSTRATUM
– bottom part of a cycle, graph, or the like TROUGH

bounce or glance off a hard surface, as a bullet might RICOCHET
– bounce or jump back, as after a collision REBOUND, RECOIL
– bounce or skip, as over a stretch of water DAP
– pole, with a spring at the base, on which one can bounce along POGO STICK
– strike a ball before it bounces VOLLEY

boundary See also **border**, **trimming**, **edge**
– boundary, as of a geometric figure, sports field, or military position PERIMETER
– boundary, margin, or partition between the zones, distinct break DISCONTINUITY
– boundary, verge, or range COMPASS, CIRCUIT, BOURN, AMBIT
– boundary area, outskirts or outermost part PERIPHERY, PURLIEUS
– boundary between liquids, systems, phases, or the like INTERFACE
– boundary level above which something takes places or comes into effect THRESHOLD
– boundary line of an enclosed figure, especially a circle, or the length of it CIRCUMFERENCE
– boundary or boundary marker TERMINUS
– boundaries or limits, as of a budget or schedule PARAMETERS, CONSTRAINTS
– restrict, or establish the limits or boundaries of CIRCUMSCRIBE
– setting of boundaries between two areas, tasks, ideas, or the like DELIMITATION, DEMARCATION
– sharing a boundary, or having the same boundaries COTERMINOUS

bow, curtsy, or similar gesture of respect or submission OBEISANCE
– bow, kiss, or other gesture of greeting SALUTATION
– bow down or humble oneself, specifically by kneeling, as in worship GENUFLECT
– bow or lie down, as in worshipping or submission PROSTRATE
– bow very low, as in some Muslim societies, and touch one's forehead with the palm of one's right

BOTTLE SIZES

capacities expressed as multiples of the standard wine bottle holding 1.25 pints (0.7 litre)

NAME	SIZE
magnum	2x
flagon	3x
jeroboam/ double magnum	4x or 6x
methuselah/impériale	6x or 8x
salmanazar	12x
balthazar	16x
nebuchadnezzar	20x

hand SALAAM
– bow very low, in traditional Chinese fashion, touching the ground with one's forehead KOWTOW
– gesture of greeting or respect, as in India, by placing one's hands together out in front of one and bowing NAMASTE
– groove at either end of the bow for holding the string NOCK
– reappearance on stage of an actor, cast, choir, or the like, as to take a bow CURTAIN CALL

bow tie DICKY BOW

bowels – bulky fibre-rich food, such as bran, assisting bowel regularity ROUGHAGE
– medicine or other substance that stimulates the bowels and relieves constipation LAXATIVE, CATHARTIC, PURGATIVE
– remove the bowels or internal organs of DISEMBOWEL, EVISCERATE, EXENTERATE

bowl in which something is ground with a pestle MORTAR
– bowl or small cup with a handle PORRINGER
– bowl-shaped pan, used in Chinese cooking WOK
– broad, deep bowl, as used for serving soup TUREEN

bowler hat – U.S. term for a bowler hat DERBY

bowls – bowls-like game played in France, in which small metal balls are thrown at a target ball BOULES, PÉTANQUE
– ball rolled in bowls, a bowl WOOD
– characteristic of weight or shape that gives a bowl its swerve BIAS
– small white ball serving as the target in bowls JACK, MARK, KITTY
– uneven patch of the green in bowls RUB

box See also **container**
– box containing writing materials PAPETERIE
– box of large size and standard design for storing and transporting materials CONTAINER, SKIP
– box or small chest for jewellery or other valuables CASKET
– box such as a chest or strongbox for valuables COFFER
– box used by botanists for carrying plant specimens VASCULUM
– large box for ammunition CAISSON
– small box or tin, especially for storing tea CADDY
– small box with a perforated lid, containing perfume POUNCET BOX

boxer, especially a professional boxer PUGILIST
– boxer who guards with his left hand and leads with his right SOUTHPAW
– boxer who is clumsy or unsuccessful PALOOKA

boxing glove or hand-covering of leather loaded or studded with metal, worn by boxers in ancient Rome CESTUS
– code of rules in modern boxing QUEENSBERRY RULES
– lightest weight divisions in professional boxing FLYWEIGHT, BANTAMWEIGHT, FEATHERWEIGHT
– ornamental belt presented as a trophy to a British boxing champion LONSDALE BELT
– weight division just below heavyweight in boxing CRUISERWEIGHT
– wild swinging punch in boxing HAYMAKER

boy, especially a very young boy MANIKIN
– boy, lad, adolescent STRIPLING
– boy lover kept by a male homosexual CATAMITE
– boy or other person who gets the blame for other people's faults SCAPEGOAT, WHIPPING BOY
– boy roaming the streets URCHIN, WAIF, GAMIN, STREET ARAB, MUDLARK, GUTTERSNIPE
– awkward or gawky adolescent boy HOBBLEDEHOY

boyfriend BEAU

bracelet – relating to a bracelet ARMILLARY

braces – U.S. term for braces SUSPENDERS

bracket, usually of stone or brick, supporting a cornice, balcony, arch, or the like CORBEL, TRUSS, CANTILEVER
– bracket on a wall for holding a candle, torch, or the like SCONCE
– brackets or round brackets in punctuation PARENTHESES
– brackets that are arrow-shaped, < > ANGLE BRACKETS
– curly brackets { } BRACES
– ornamental bracket supporting a shelf or the like CONSOLE

braid, flat and narrow and forming zigzags, as used to trim clothing RICKRACK
– braid, metallic and plaited, as on the shoulder of a military uniform AIGUILLETTE
– braid, narrow and sometimes stiffened, used on clothes, curtains, and furniture GIMP, GUIMPE, GUIPURE
– braid or cord used for binding or trimming BOBBIN
– braid or looped cord used as a fastening, as formerly on military uniforms FROG
– braided cord on the left shoulder of a uniform FOURRAGÈRE
– gold or silver wire or braid used as a trimming, as on military uniforms BULLION FRINGE

Braille – reading and printing system for the blind, using raised letters, rather than dots as in Braille MOON TYPE

brain See illustration
– brain operation in which one or more of the nerve tracts in the frontal lobe are severed LOBOTOMY, PREFRONTAL LEUCOTOMY
– brain surgeon NEUROSURGEON
– brain's electrical wave form typical of a normal waking state BETA WAVE
– brain's electrical wave form typical of a resting or drowsy state ALPHA RHYTHM
– adjective for the brain CEREBRAL
– application of biology to engineering and electronics, especially of brain functions to computers BIONICS
– disorder of the brain's normal functioning, involving brief attacks of dislocation, convulsions, or unconsciousness EPILEPSY
– either half of the brain along a lengthwise divide HEMISPHERE
– figure of a man modelled with limbs and organs proportional in size to the areas of the brain controlling them HOMUNCULUS
– instrument recording the electrical impulses in the brain ELECTROENCEPHALOGRAPH, EEG
– irregular ridge between grooves on the surface of the brain GYRUS, CONVOLUTION
– jarring of the brain, typically causing brief unconsciousness and loss of bearings CONCUSSION
– membranes surrounding the brain and spinal cord MENINGES
– stroke that is often followed by paralysis, resulting from the bursting or blocking of a blood vessel in the brain APOPLEXY, CEREBRAL HAEMORRHAGE
– technical name for a brain ENCEPHALON
– therapy for treating psychiatric patients, in which an electric shock is administered to the brain ELECTROCONVULSIVE THERAPY, ECT
– tranquillising or pain-killing substance secreted by the brain ENDORPHIN

-brain- ENCEPHAL-, ENCEPHALO-, -CEREBR-, CEREBRO-, -PHREN-, PHRENO-

brain fever ENCEPHALITIS

brain-teaser in Zen Buddhism, designed to free the mind from the

constraints of logic KOAN

brake flap on an aeroplane's wing DECELERON
– brake on a wagon or carriage DRAG
– brakes operated by compressed fluid HYDRAULIC BRAKES
– braking rocket, used to slow down or reverse a spacecraft, or the like RETROROCKET, RETRO

bran or other fibre in the diet, assisting the regularity of bowel movement ROUGHAGE

branch, arrangement of branches, or branching process RAMIFICATION
– branch of knowledge, subject of study DISCIPLINE
– branching, forked FURCATE
– branching or repeated forking of a plant into two equal parts DICHOTOMY
– angle between a leafstalk and the stem, between a branch and the trunk, or the like AXIL
– bundle or cluster of leaves, branches, and the like FASCICLE, FASCICULE
– divide into several branches, as a plant stem might DELIQUESCE
– joint or branching point on a stem NODE
– having branches RAMATE, RAMOSE
– having spread-out branches arranged in pairs, as some trees have BRACHIATE
– spreading out widely, as branches might PATENT, PATULOUS
– stump remaining after a branch has broken off SNAG

brand mark as formerly on the skin of a slave or criminal STIGMA
– brand name or emblem MARQUE

brandy EAU DE VIE
– brandy, whisky, or other strong spirits AQUA VITAE
– brandy distilled from the left-over pulp of pressed grapes MARC
– brandy from France COGNAC, ARMAGNAC
– French apple brandy CALVADOS

brass – a brass-worker BRAZIER
– greenish coating forming on exposed copper, brass, or bronze objects VERDIGRIS, VERD ANTIQUE, AERUGO

brass instrument See **wind instrument**

brave in a dashing and sometimes daredevil way, very bold or daring AUDACIOUS, VENTURESOME
– brave in a spirited way, plucky FEISTY, DOUGHTY, METTLESOME
– brave in an honourable way, chivalrous and courageous, heroic GALLANT, VALIANT, VALOROUS
– fearless, extremely brave DAUNTLESS, INTREPID
– unshakably brave, unshrinking, resolute in the face of intimidation STALWART, UNDAUNTED, UNFLINCHING

bravery, strength, or skill, as shown in battle PROWESS
– bravery and enterprise, nerve GUMPTION
– bravery involving endurance and strong will FORTITUDE, TENACITY
– bravery or daring spirit, especially in chivalric adventures DERRING-DO, EMPRISE
– bravery that is confident or swaggering but probably false BRAVADO, BLUSTER, BRAGGADOCIO
– award or honour, as for bravery COMMENDATION

bread See also illustration, page 70

brain

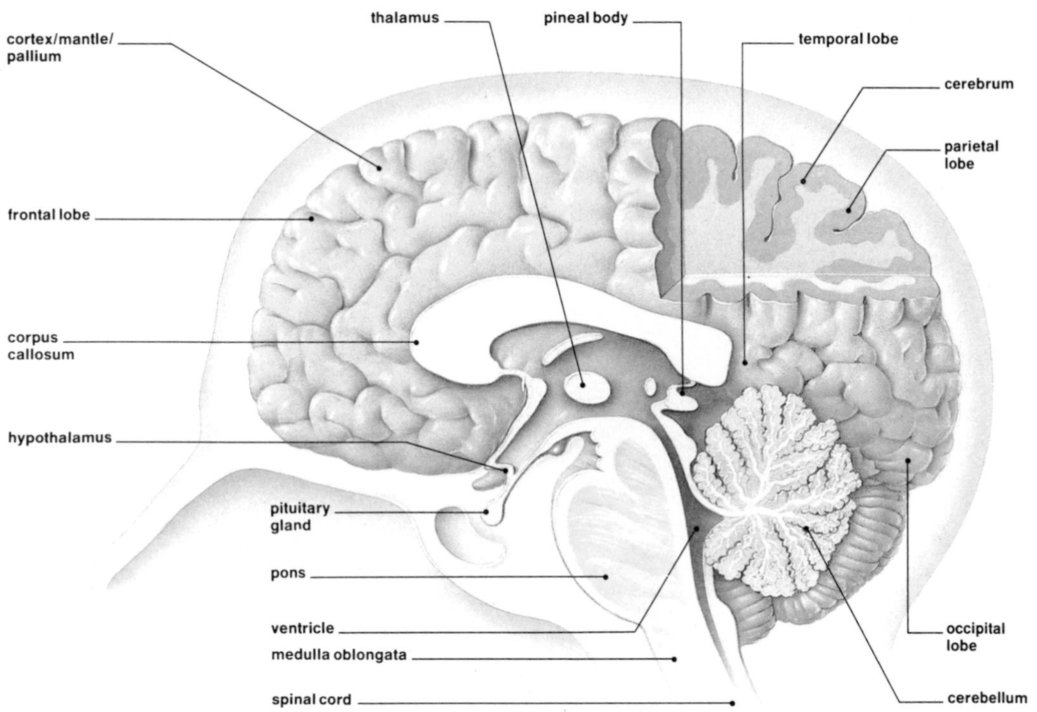

thalamus
pineal body
cortex/mantle/pallium
temporal lobe
cerebrum
parietal lobe
frontal lobe
corpus callosum
hypothalamus
pituitary gland
pons
ventricle
medulla oblongata
spinal cord
occipital lobe
cerebellum

– bread of malted rye and wheat flour, containing wholemeal kernels GRANARY BREAD
– bread or biscuit formerly on sailing ships HARDTACK, SHIP'S BISCUIT
– bread or wafer consecrated in the Eucharist HOST
– bread soaked or dunked in gravy, soup, milk, or the like BREWIS, SOP
– baker's long-handled shovel used for moving bread, pies, pizza, or the like in and out of an oven PEEL
– crusty end of a loaf of bread HEEL
– flat Indian breads CHAPATTI, ROTI, NAN, PARATHA, PURI
– flat oval Greek or Middle Eastern bread PITTA
– long, thin Italian breadsticks GRISSINI
– made of dough without yeast or other fermentation agent, as Passover bread is UNLEAVENED
– protein mixture in bread, cakes, and the like, avoided in certain diets GLUTEN
– rich Welsh bread containing mixed fruit BARA BRITH
– rich yeast bread of German origin containing dried fruit and nuts STOLLEN
– substance added to dough to aid fermentation, as in bread-making LEAVEN
– sweet Scottish bread containing dried fruit SELKIRK BANNOCK
– sweetened bread sliced and then crisped in an oven ZWIEBACK
– wedge of toast or fried bread, typically served as a garnish SIPPET

bread and wine consecrated and then consumed in commemoration of Jesus, or the Christian sacrament involved EUCHARIST
– coexistence of the consecrated Communion bread and wine with the body and blood of Christ, as understood by Anglicans CONSUBSTANTIATION
– conversion of the consecrated Communion bread and wine into the body and blood of Christ, as understood by Roman Catholics TRANSUBSTANTIATION

breadbasket – nerve network in the stomach, or "breadbasket", where one might be punched and winded SOLAR PLEXUS

breadcrumbs – coated with breadcrumbs and sometimes cheese, and then grilled or browned, as cauliflower might be AU GRATIN

break See also **destroy**, **cancel**, **gap**, **fracture**
– break a code, decode, translate DECIPHER, DECRYPT
– break apart or into parts, sever

bread

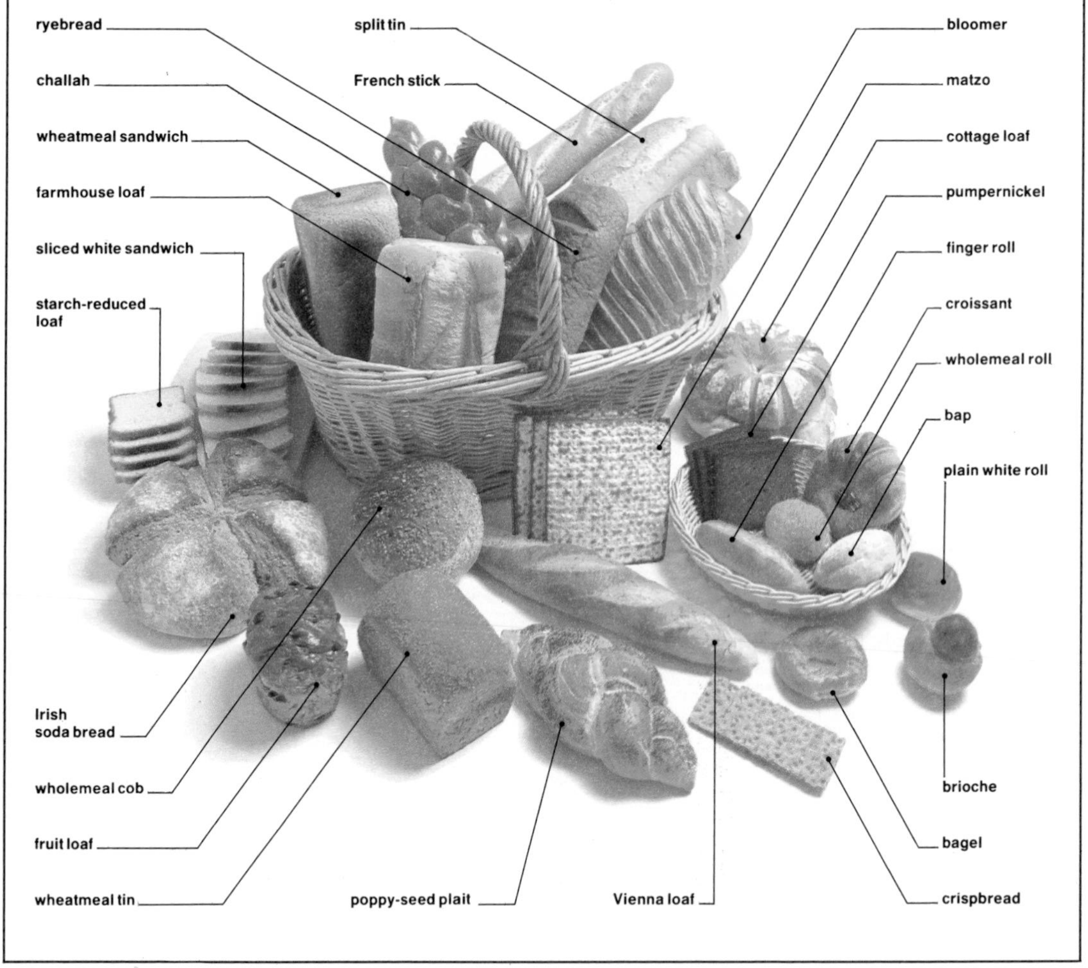

or fracture SUNDER, REAVE
– break away from an alliance, organisation, or the like SECEDE
– break by splitting CLEAVE, REND, RIFT
– break down into small or basic parts, crumble DECOMPOSE, DISINTEGRATE
– break down into tiny bits, reduce to a spray, powder, or the like ATOMISE, VAPORISE, PULVERISE
– break in continuity, such as a gap or interruption LACUNA, HIATUS
– break in proceedings, such as a pause or interval RECESS, RESPITE, INTERMISSION
– break in the metre or rhythm within a single line of verse CAESURA
– break open, burst open RUPTURE
– break or smash inwards, crush STAVE
– break out violently, explode, as in anger ERUPT
– break up a group or cease to function as a group DISBAND
– break up and loosen the surface of topsoil, a field, a road, or the like SCARIFY
– break up stone especially with a hammer SPALL
– breaking of a law or regulation VIOLATION, BREACH, INFRINGEMENT, TRANSGRESSION, INFRACTION, CONTRAVENTION
– breaking the law, especially by a public official MALFEASANCE, MALVERSATION
– person who breaks religious statues or sacred objects ICONOCLAST

break- FISSI-

breakable, brittle, fragile FRANGIBLE
– breakable, easily broken up or crumbled FRIABLE

breakfast food of cereals, nuts, raisins, and the like MUESLI

breakwater or jetty jutting into the sea to control erosion, protect a harbour, direct a current, or the like GROYNE, SPUR, MOLE

breast, udder, or teat DUG
– breast-examination by touch for a preliminary medical diagnosis PALPATION
– breast-examination by X-rays MAMMOGRAM, MAMMOGRAPHY
– breast-feeder of the child of another woman WET NURSE
– breast secretion of serum and white blood cells, lasting a few days after childbirth before the flow of milk begins COLOSTRUM
– abnormal enlargement of breasts in a man, as through hormone imbalance GYNAECOMASTIA
– adjective for a breast MAMMARY
– chemical polymer used in breast implants and other cosmetic surgery SILICONE
– darkish area, on a breast, surrounding the nipple AREOLA
– having or relating to full shapely breasts, busty PNEUMATIC
– line or hollow between a woman's breasts, as revealed by a low-cut dress CLEAVAGE
– produce milk, especially when breast-feeding LACTATE
– relating to the chest or breast PECTORAL
– surgical amputation of a breast MASTECTOMY
– surgical removal of a breast tumour without removing the whole breast LUMPECTOMY

breast- MAST-, MASTO-

breastbone STERNUM
– breastbone and its associated cartilages PLASTRON

breastplate as formerly worn under a coat of mail PLASTRON
– breastplate or item of armour protecting chest and back CUIRASS

breath that is bad-smelling HALITOSIS
– lozenge or pastille sucked in order to sweeten the breath CACHOU

breathe in INHALE
– breathe or sigh SUSPIRE
– breathe out EXHALE, EXPIRE

breathing RESPIRATION
– breathing at an abnormally decreased rate HYPOPNOEA
– breathing at an abnormally increased rate, as following exercise HYPERPNOEA, HYPERVENTILATION
– breathing difficulty, temporary inability to draw breath APNOEA
– breathing hole, as in a beetle's exoskeleton or behind a shark's eye SPIRACLE
– breathing with or relating to a heavy snoring noise STERTOROUS
– done with difficulty, as breathing might be LABOURED
– harsh vibrating sound in laboured breathing STRIDOR
– person who breathes heavily and noisily GRAMPUS
– relating to breathing or suction ASPIRATORY
– surgical cut or opening through the throat to help breathing TRACHEOTOMY
– unconsciousness or death resulting from restricted breathing and lack of oxygen, suffocation ASPHYXIATION

breathing- PNEUM-, PNEUMO-, PNEUMATO-, SPIRO-

breathing apparatus, for use under water, including an air cylinder and oxygen mask AQUALUNG

breathing space, pause, or rest, typically in the middle of something unpleasant RESPITE

breed, or cause plants or animals to breed PROPAGATE
– breed from two different varieties or species HYBRID
– breed or reproduce PROCREATE
– breed rapidly PULLULATE
– breeding place, as for bacteria NIDUS
– breeding record or family tree of a thoroughbred horse, dog, or other animal PEDIGREE
– deliberate modification of the gene structure, as in breeding improved plant or animal strains GENETIC ENGINEERING
– horses or other domestic animals kept for breeding STUD
– study of or attempts at improving the human race by selective breeding EUGENICS

brewing – chemistry of fermentation in brewing ZYMURGY
– fermentable pulp used in brewing beer MASH

bribe or payment made in an illicit or underhand way to secure a favour BACKHANDER
– bribe or small tip DOUCEUR
– bribe or threaten someone into committing a wrongful act, especially perjury SUBORN
– bribe paid to preserve secrecy HUSH MONEY
– bribery, as of disc jockeys, to promote a product PAYOLA
– fund used for bribing and other corrupt activities SLUSH FUND
– open to or marked by bribery, corrupt VENAL

bric-a-brac, showy but cheap finery TRUMPERY

brick laid parallel to the line of a wall STRETCHER
– brick laid perpendicular to the line of a wall HEADER
– brick of sun-dried clay, as used in Mexico ADOBE
– brick or small block of charcoal, ice cream or other substance BRIQUETTE
– brick tray, carried over the shoulder on a pole HOD
– bricks jutting out from a wall CORBELLING
– cement or thin mortar for filling cracks or seams, as between bricks or tiles POINTING, GROUTING
– horizontal row or layer of bricks, tiles, or the like COURSE
– notch or groove in a brick to make it lighter FROG

bricklayer's work bench BANKER

brickwork See illustration, page 73
– brickwork foundation of a building STEREOBATE

– brickwork or masonry used to fill in a wooden framework NOGGING

bride – bride's attendant who is herself married MATRON OF HONOUR
– bride's money or property handed over to her husband on their marriage DOWRY
– bride's special wardrobe assembled before her wedding TROUSSEAU

bridge – hand of 13 cards, especially in bridge or whist, in which no card is higher than a nine YARBOROUGH
– hand of 13 cards, especially in bridge or whist, in which no card is in trumps CHICANE
– match of three games in bridge or whist RUBBER
– trump a card in bridge or other card games RUFF

bridge See also illustration, page 74
– bridge, extend over SPAN
– bridge, typically supported by a series of arches, carrying a road or railway, as over a valley VIADUCT
– bridge above a road OVERPASS
– bridge-like, arched structure supporting a canal or water channel AQUEDUCT
– bridge or roadway hinged near a weighted end so as to be raised or lowered BASCULE
– bridge that can be raised to prevent access or allow vessels to pass DRAWBRIDGE
– bridge's supporting framework of beams, struts, or the like TRUSS, TRESTLE
– float for raising a sunken vessel or supporting a floating bridge PONTOON
– pillar or similar support at the meeting point of the spans of a bridge PIER
– relating to bridges PONTINE
– simple bridge, typically of stone slabs supported between piles of stones CLAPPER BRIDGE
– temporary steel bridge assembled from prefabricated parts BAILEY BRIDGE

bridle See **harness**
– bridle with an iron bit formerly used to silence scolding women BRANKS

brief See also **concise**, **short-lived**, **summary**
– brief and mechanical, as a glance or smile might be PERFUNCTORY
– brief and superficial, as an inspection might be CURSORY
– brief and unsympathetic treatment, curt consideration and dismissal SHORT SHRIFT
– brief appearance, in a film or play, of a famous actor or actress CAMEO ROLE
– brief or abrupt to the point of rudeness, very blunt or terse, curt BRUSQUE
– briefness, shortness BREVITY

briefcase for holding loose papers or official documents PORTFOLIO

bright See also **brilliant**
– bright, radiant, glossy or shiny LUSTROUS
– bright, striking, fresh, or lively VIVID
– bright in a dashing or showy way, glaring FLAMBOYANT
– bright through rubbing or polishing BURNISHED, FURBISHED
– brightened or beautified with colours, flowers, or the like EMBLAZONED
– unnaturally bright, flashy, gaudy GARISH, LURID

brilliance, as of a success or achievement ÉCLAT
– brilliance or outstanding technical ability, especially in playing a musical instrument VIRTUOSITY

brilliant, sparkling, glittering, as wit or a gemstone might be SCINTILLATING, CORUSCATING
– brilliant and successful act or decision MASTERSTROKE, COUP
– brilliant or dramatic display, as in a piano recital PYROTECHNICS
– brilliant or extremely successful person of very young age WHIZZ KID, WUNDERKIND, CHILD PRODIGY
– glowing intensely, brilliantly bright INCANDESCENT
– shining brilliantly, radiantly illuminated, dazzling RESPLENDENT, EFFULGENT

bring back to life, raise from the dead RESURRECT
– bring back to life, revive or reactivate RESUSCITATE, REANIMATE, REVITALISE, REVIVIFY, REGENERATE
– bring to light, draw out ELICIT
– bring up, train, foster NURTURE
– bring up or vomit partly digested food REGURGITATE

bristles – covered with tiny barbed hairs or bristles, as some plants and animals are BARBELLATE

bristling of the hair on the body, goose flesh HORRIPILATION

bristly- ECHINO-

Britain – poetic or old-fashioned term for Britain or England ALBION

British- ANGLO-

British Empire – former term for a large self-governing nation of the British Empire, such as Australia DOMINION

Britons – blue dye used by ancient Britons to colour their skin WOAD

brittleness or weakening of the bones, especially in elderly people OSTEOPOROSIS

broad, inclusive, wide-ranging COMPREHENSIVE, COMPENDIOUS
– broad-minded, forgiving, unresentful MAGNANIMOUS
– broad-minded, tolerant, having wide sympathies, especially regarding religion LATITUDINARIAN
– broad-minded or tolerant, especially in matters of sexual conduct PERMISSIVE
– broad-tipped or splay-tipped, as fingers or leaves might be SPATULATE

broad bean FAVA BEAN

broadcast See also **radio**, **television**
– broadcast announcements or linking items designed to avoid breaks between programmes CONTINUITY
– broadcast at the end of the day, typically a short religious programme EPILOGUE
– broadcast covering a week's episodes of a series that have previously been broadcast separately OMNIBUS EDITION
– broadcast live a concert, speech, or the like via a transmitter RELAY
– broadcast of a programme simultaneously on radio and television SIMULCAST
– broadcast that has been prerecorded TRANSCRIPTION
– broadcaster who coordinates many reports ANCHORMAN, ANCHORWOMAN
– broadcasting network GRID
– relating to broadcasting in which members of the general public rather than professionals make the programmes ACCESS

brochure from a university or other institution, detailing its main features PROSPECTUS

broken beyond repair, destroyed KAPUT
– broken bits, fragments, splinters SMITHEREENS
– broken down or worn out through age or overuse DECREPIT, DILAPIDATED
– broken fragments, scattered remains, rubble DEBRIS
– broken piece of glass, pottery, or other similarly brittle substance SHARD

broken leg – continuous stretching of a body part, as in treating a broken leg TRACTION

broker or banker trading in shares or bonds for quick profits ARBITRAGEUR

– brokerage of or speculation in stocks and shares AGIOTAGE

bronze – greenish coating forming on exposed copper, brass, or bronze objects VERDIGRIS, VERD ANTIQUE, AERUGO

– layer of oxide, usually green, forming naturally or artificially on a copper or bronze surface PATINA

-bronze- -CHALC-, CHALCO-

brooch, clasp, or other jewelled adornment in former times OUCH

– brooch, medal, or the like worn on the chest PECTORAL

– brooch worn as a membership badge PLAQUE

– medallion, on a brooch, ring, or the like, with a head in profile in raised relief CAMEO

broom of twigs BESOM

broth made in a casserole pot MARMITE

brothel BAGNIO, BAWDYHOUSE, BORDELLO

– brothel or other house where public order or decency is violated DISORDERLY HOUSE

– man who finds clients for a prostitute or brothel PIMP, PONCE

brother or sister SIBLING

– murder of a brother FRATRICIDE

brotherhood, fellowship, community FRATERNITY, SODALITY

brotherly FRATERNAL

brow – draw in and wrinkle the brow or forehead PURSE, PUCKER

brown See **colours**

– brown-haired and dark-eyed woman BRUNETTE

brown coal LIGNITE

browning – metal plate heated for browning puddings or other food SALAMANDER

bruise CONTUSION

– bluish, as bruised skin might be LIVID

brush for grooming or currying a horse DANDY-BRUSH

brutal, savage, beast-like BESTIAL

– brutally severe, extremely harsh, as repressive laws might be DRACONIAN

brutish, without truly human understanding or feelings INSENSATE, INSENSIBLE

bubble of air surrounding some water-dwelling insects PLASTRON

bubbling, as a carbonated drink is EFFERVESCENT

– bubbling with excitement or enthusiasm, full of high spirits EBULLIENT, EXUBERANT

bucket, basin, or large mug STOUP

– bucket of wood with one stave extended above the rim as a handle PIGGIN, PIPKIN

brickwork bonds

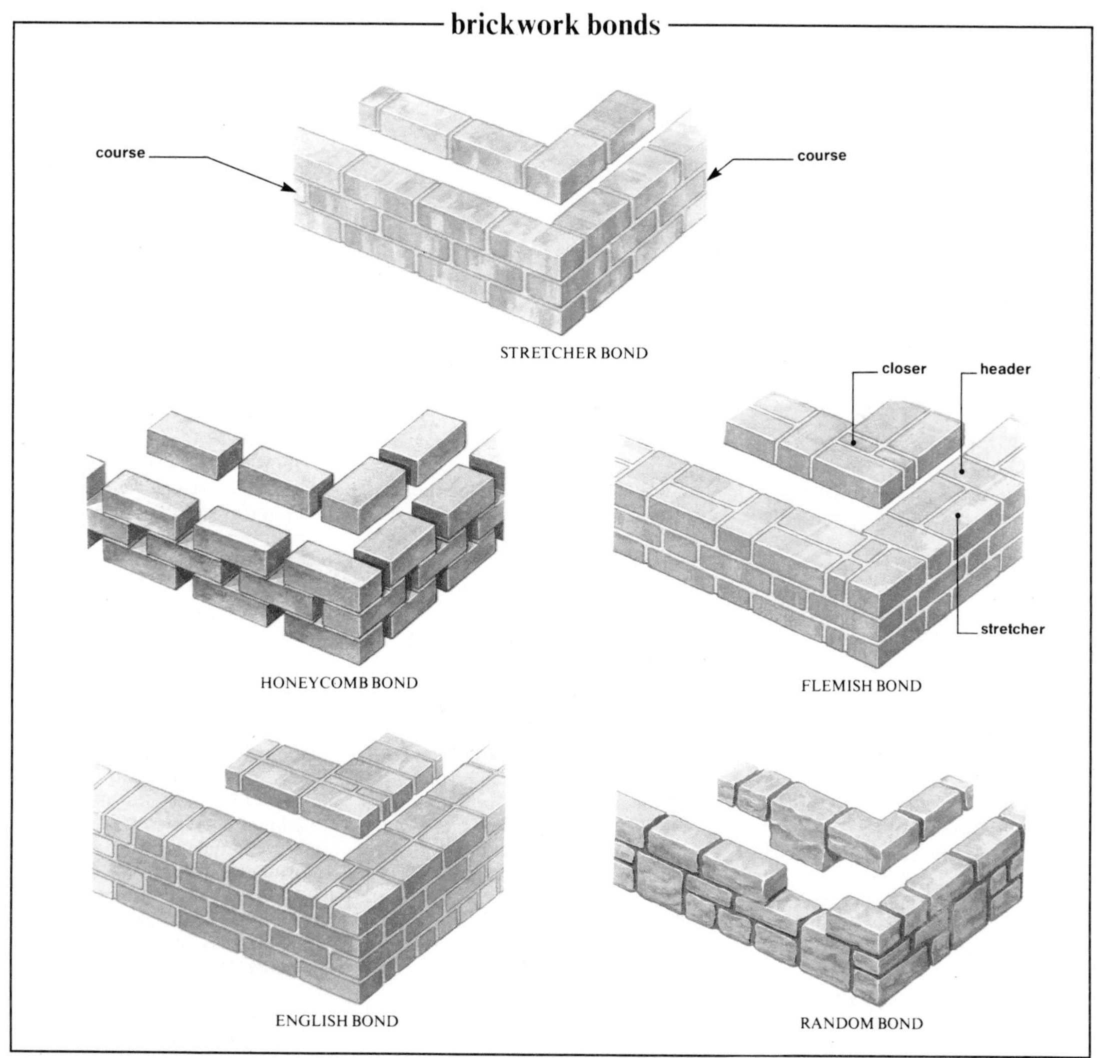

STRETCHER BOND

HONEYCOMB BOND

FLEMISH BOND

ENGLISH BOND

RANDOM BOND

bridges

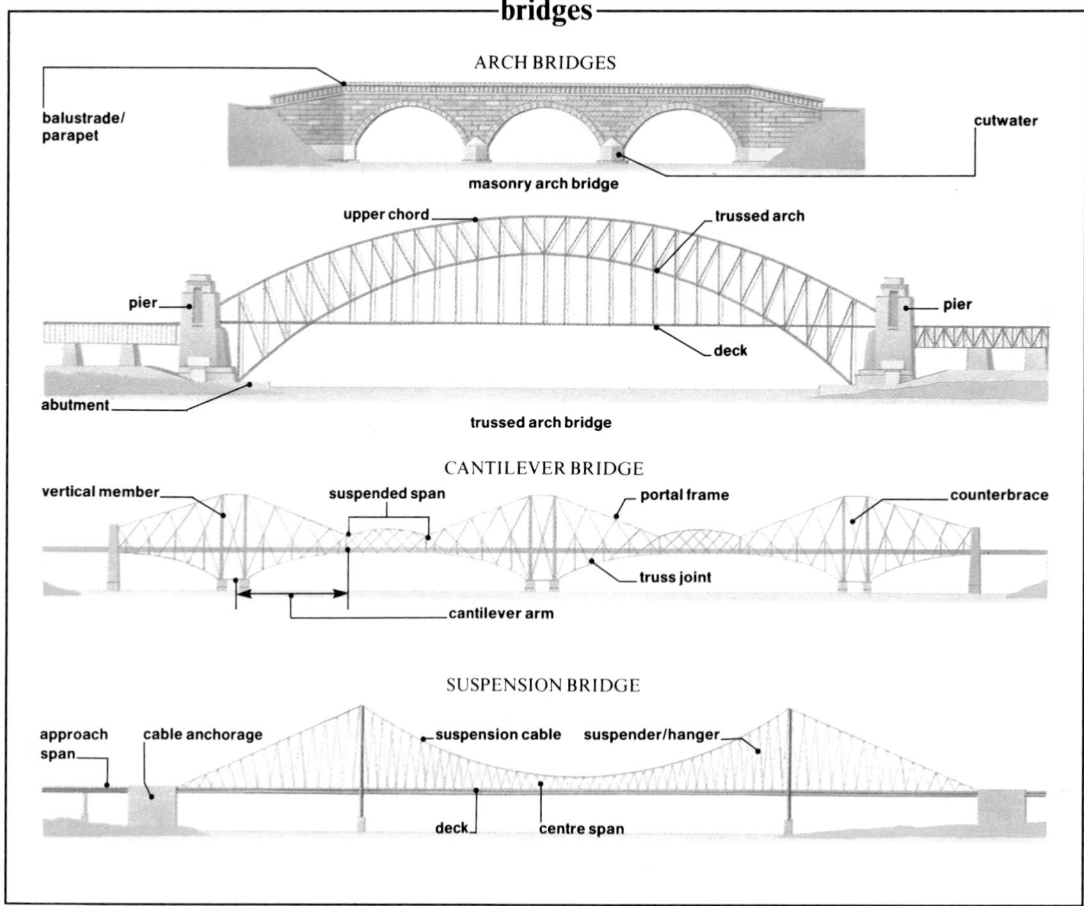

– bucket used in wells or mine shafts KIBBLE
– handle of a bucket, in the form of a hooped rod BAIL

buckle – buckle's metal prong CHAPE

bud, sprout, or shoot of a plant BURGEON, PULLULATE
– bud of a plant embryo, developing into the shoot PLUMULE
– multiplying by means of buds, shoots, or small bulbs rather than by seeds VIVIPAROUS

bud- BLASTO-

Buddhism See chart

Buddhist monastery in Tibet LAMASERY
– Buddhist shrine or Hindu temple, typically a multi-storeyed tapering tower PAGODA
– sacred language of Buddhists PALI

budget – limits or boundaries, as of a budget or schedule PARAMETERS, CONSTRAINTS

buffalo BISON
– hybrid cattle breed, a cross between a buffalo and domestic cow or bull CATALO

buffet – buffet-style meal of Swedish origin SMORGASBORD

bugle call at sunset when the flag is lowered RETREAT
– bugle call first thing in the morning REVEILLE
– bugle call or drumbeat signalling soldiers to return to their quarters in the evening TATTOO
– bugle call sounded at military funerals or to signal lights out in a military camp LAST POST, TAPS

build See **body**

builder specialising in building with stone MASON

building See also **house**, **architecture**, **foundations**, **roof**
– building, especially one that is large and imposing EDIFICE
– building with stone MASONRY
– building commemorating a nation's heroes PANTHEON
– building development, especially housing, along a road leading out of a town RIBBON DEVELOPMENT
– building labourer or similar unskilled worker NAVVY
– building of clay bricks or stone, typically of several storeys, used as a communal residence by American Indians in the southwestern U.S. PUEBLO
– building of rented flats, typically in a poor or slum area TENEMENT
– building of historical interest protected by law from alteration or demolition LISTED BUILDING
– building or room in former times housing bones or dead bodies CHARNEL HOUSE
– building or room, such as a private library, set aside for reading ATHENAEUM
– building structure, such as a wall or pillar, between two windows, arches, or the like TRUMEAU
– building workers who are self-employed and regarded as given to tax evasion THE LUMP
– building's basic framework of walls, floor, and roof FABRIC
– buildings, equipment, and other provisions for an activity FACILITIES
– buildings, land, and other immovable property REAL PROPERTY,

REAL ESTATE, REALTY
– buildings supervisor or maintenance officer CLERK OF THE WORKS
– added section of or near to a building ANNEXE, PAVILION
– beam laid horizontally, as in building GIRDER
– broken down, falling to pieces, as a shabby old building is DILAPIDATED
– circular, often domed, building or room ROTUNDA
– declare a building, park, or the like open at a special ceremony DEDICATE
– demolish a building or city, destroy down to the ground RAZE
– deserted and ruined, as an old building might be DERELICT
– destruction of disused buildings DEMOLITION
– estimating of building costs and materials QUANTITY SURVEYING
– front or face of a building FACADE, FRONTISPIECE
– foundation of a stone building STEREOBATE
– large and striking building or complex of buildings PILE
– large building for meetings, concerts, or the like AUDITORIUM
– movable platform on the outside walls of a building, as used by window cleaners GONDOLA
– non-functional and usually whimsical building erected purely for decorative purposes FOLLY
– person who climbs the outside of buildings, as for a prank or bet STEGOPHILIST
– ready-made standard unit used in constructing a building MODULE
– relating to building or construction TECTONIC
– restore a building to a former or better condition RENOVATE
– roundish building with tiers of seats surrounding an arena AMPHITHEATRE
– sinking of the ground or of a building SUBSIDENCE
– structural inspection of a building SURVEY

-building -ARIUM, -ORIUM

building material made of stone chips set in polished concrete slabs or tiles TERRAZZO
– building material of interlaced sticks plastered with mud or clay and horse manure WATTLE AND DAUB
– building material of large light blocks made of ash and cement BREEZE BLOCKS
– building material of overlapping boards used especially to cover roofs or walls WEATHERBOARDING, CLAPBOARDING
– building material of sun-dried clay bricks, as in Mexico ADOBE
– building material or stone, either a square block for walls or a thin slab for facings ASHLAR

build-up, slow increase through additions ACCRETION

built according to the buyer's specifications CUSTOM-BUILT
– built in sections in advance, prior to its assembly as cheap housing might be PREFABRICATED
– built shoddily JERRY-BUILT

bulb – bulb-like underground stem, as of the gladiolus CORM
– multiplying by means of buds, shoots, or small bulbs rather than by seeds VIVIPAROUS

bulging, protruding prominently outwards PROTUBERANT, CONVEX
– bulging-eyed, specifically as a result of excess thyroid hormone EXOPHTHALMIC
– bulging or swollen TUMESCENT, TUMID, TURGID, TUBEROUS

bulky fibre-rich food, assisting bowel regularity ROUGHAGE

bull – relating to a bull TAURINE
– bull's penis PIZZLE

bull- TAUR-, TAURO-
– monster, half man and half bull in Greek mythology MINOTAUR

bullet, shell, missile, rocket, or other object fired or hurled PROJECTILE
– bullet-belt worn across the chest from the shoulder BANDOLEER
– bullet leaving a trail of smoke or light which allows its path to be monitored TRACER BULLET
– bullet with a soft or hollow nose that spreads on impact to produce a gaping wound DUMDUM BULLET, SPREAD-ON-IMPACT BULLET
– diameter of the inside of a tube, the bore of a gun, or a bullet or shell CALIBRE
– former term for a cartridge, bullet, or box of cartridges CARTOUCHE
– groove, especially around a bullet CANNELURE

BUDDHIST TERMS

bonze	monk of the Mahayana school, active in China and Japan
bo tree/peepul	sacred fig tree, under which the Buddha attained enlightenment
Buddha	person who has achieved total spiritual enlightenment
Dalai Lama	traditional highest priest and ruler in Tibet and Mongolia
karma	sum of a person's total actions, determining his destiny in future lives; broadly, fate or destiny
lama	monk in Tibet or Mongolia
Mahayana	branch of Buddhism, as in Korea and Tibet, of a relatively liberal and evangelical kind
mandala	circular design symbolising the universe
mantra	sacred word or formula repeated, sometimes in one's head, during prayer or meditation
nirvana	release from the cycle of reincarnations into a state of blessedness
prajna	wisdom or enlightenment sought through contemplation
prayer wheel	wheel or cylinder with written prayers on or in it
stupa/tope	Buddhist shrine, typically dome-shaped
sutra	scriptural text, especially any supposed discourse by the Buddha
tantra	any text from a group of later mystical writings
Theravada/ Hinayana	branch of Buddhism, as in Sri Lanka and south-east Asia, of a fundamentalist and monastic kind
Zen	Mahayana school or sect favouring meditation and intuition rather than scripture as a means to enlightenment

– main explosive charge or gunpowder content of a bullet PROPELLANT
– rebound from a hard surface, as a bullet might RICOCHET
– simultaneous firing of a number of bullets, arrows, guns, or the like VOLLEY
– small explosive cap in the base of a bullet that detonates the main charge PRIMER, DETONATOR CAP, PERCUSSION CAP
– study of guns and bullets, shells, and so on BALLISTICS

bullfighting See chart
– pierce or stab with a horn or tusk, as in bullfighting GORE

bull's-eye, centre of a target BLANK
– bull's-eye of an archery target, or the target as a whole CLOUT

bully, oppress TYRANNISE
– bully, punish unfairly, or discriminate against VICTIMISE
– bully, threaten, or hector, as to persuade or discourage BROWBEAT
– bully or bulldoze into compliance DRAGOON, COERCE
– bully or frighten into submission INTIMIDATE
– bullying, overbearing IMPERIOUS, DOMINEERING, DESPOTIC
– bullying disciplinarian or authority MARTINET
– target of teasing, mockery, bullying, or the like BUTT

bump, bulge or similar projection PROTUBERANCE, PROTRUSION
– bump built across a road to limit the speed of vehicles SLEEPING POLICEMAN
– bump or knot on a tree or timber KNUR
– bump or tiny rounded projection, as on the tongue or the root of a hair PAPILLA
– small knob, bump, swelling, or lump NODULE, NODE

bumper – bumper's upright attachment, fitted in pairs to prevent interlocking with another vehicle's bumper OVERRIDER

bunch of flowers, often used as a small gift POSY

bundle of rods with an axe, carried as a symbol of the magistrates' authority in ancient Rome FASCES
– bundle of twigs, branches, or sticks FAGGOT
– small bundle or cluster FASCICLE

bung, plug STOPPLE, SPIGOT, SPILE

burden, handicap, or hinder ENCUMBER
– burden, obstacle, or impediment ENCUMBRANCE
– burden of anxiety, such as a debt MILLSTONE
– burden or responsibility ONUS

BULLFIGHTING TERMS

aficionado	fan or devotee of bullfights
banderilla	large decorated dart thrust into the bull's neck or shoulder
banderillero	assistant who inserts the banderillas
corrida	bullfight
matador	principal bullfighter who kills the bull
moment of truth	point at which the matador is poised to make the final thrust of the sword to kill the bull
muleta	small cape on a stick, used by the matador for luring the bull during his final series of passes
pase/pass	presenting or flourishing of the cape by the matador to manoeuvre the bull
picador	horseman who wounds and weakens the bull with a lance during the early stages
toreador	bullfighter, especially one on a horse
torero	bullfighter, especially a matador
veronica	pass in which the stationary matador slowly swings the cape away from the charging bull

burdensome, troublesome ONEROUS

bureaucracy or petty officialdom BEADLEDOM

bureaucrat or overzealous official APPARATCHIK
– bureaucratic jargon that is wordy and difficult to understand GOBBLEDEGOOK, OFFICIALESE

burglar – burglar's crowbar JEMMY

burglar alarm – electronic device that reacts to changes in light intensity, as used in burglar alarms and automatic doors PHOTOELECTRIC CELL, PHOTOCELL, ELECTRIC EYE, MAGIC EYE

burglary or large theft HEIST
– burglary or theft as formerly treated as a felony LARCENY

burial chamber, as beneath a church VAULT, CRYPT
– burial chamber or graveyard hidden underground CATACOMB, HYPOGEUM
– burial chamber, vault, or building in which the bones or bodies of the dead are stored CHARNEL HOUSE
– burial chamber or tomb, or an imposing building housing it MAUSOLEUM
– burial ground, especially a large and elaborate cemetery of an ancient city NECROPOLIS
– burial site or monument of standing stones from prehistoric times CROMLECH, DOLMEN
– burial vault, tomb, or grave SEPULCHRE, REPOSITORY
– cloth used to wrap a body for burial SHROUD, WINDING SHEET
– heap of earth or stones covering an ancient burial site BARROW, MOUND, TUMULUS

burn a corpse to ashes CREMATE
– burn flesh or tissue with a corrosive chemical or a very hot or very cold instrument, as in treating wounds CAUTERISE
– burn or cause to burn IGNITE, KINDLE
– burn or cause to burn fiercely or intensely DEFLAGRATE
– burn to ashes INCINERATE
– burn unevenly and drip wax down one side, as a candle might GUTTER
– burning, as of fuel COMBUSTION
– burning of a heretic at the stake as ordered by the Inquisition AUTO-DA-FÉ
– burning of buildings or other property deliberately, for criminal purposes ARSON
– burning of leaf-down on the skin as a form of therapy of Asian origin MOXIBUSTION
– burning or dissolving, as some chemicals are CAUSTIC, CORROSIVE
– burning readily, or catching fire easily INFLAMMABLE, FLAMMABLE
– burnt or charred substance CINDER, CLINKER

– dummy or crude image of a person, intended as an object of scorn or hatred, and sometimes burnt in public EFFIGY
– material that burns easily, such as twigs, used to get a fire going TINDER, KINDLING
– portable metal stand for burning coal or charcoal BRAZIER
– scab or layer of dead skin, as caused by a burn ESCHAR
– support a severely burnt patient on a cushion of air LEVITATE

burn- PYRO-
burner producing a hot gas flame, used for laboratory experiments BUNSEN BURNER
burnt offering HOLOCAUST
burp or belch ERUCT
burst in violently IRRUPT
– burst of cheering, applause, or the like SALVO
– burst of gunfire FUSILLADE, BARRAGE
– burst or break open RUPTURE
– burst or quick discharge of oaths, or the like VOLLEY
– burst or split open along the seam, as some seed capsules do DEHISCE
– bursting forth, as if into bloom EFFLORESCENCE

bury, place in a grave INHUME, INTER
– bury or imprison in or as if in a tomb ENTOMB

bus or large coach, as used for group outings CHARABANC
– bus station, or servicing area for buses or trains DEPOT

bush baby GALAGO
bushy mass, as of hair SHOCK
business See also **economics**
– business agent FACTOR
– business asset, such as goodwill, that has a value but no physical existence INTANGIBLE
– business association of various interests formed for some joint enterprise CONSORTIUM, SYNDICATE
– business association or grouping of companies, especially an illegal one, to monopolise manufacture or control prices CARTEL
– business corporation made up of many wide-ranging companies CONGLOMERATE
– business costs such as rent and rates, spread across all departments OVERHEADS, BURDEN, ONCOST
– business deal TRANSACTION
– business-like and practical, dealing with or relating to facts and actual circumstances rather than theories or ideals PRAGMATIC
– business or company controlling other businesses or companies HOLDING COMPANY
– business practice of buying a struggling company and selling off its assets bit by bit ASSET-STRIPPING
– business records of an organisation or society PROCEEDINGS
– business representative, as of a university SYNDIC
– business under another company's control SUBSIDIARY COMPANY
– business venture of a risky or daring kind FLIER
– business's most impressive or successful product FLAGSHIP
– business's owner or owner-manager PROPRIETOR
– authorisation given by a business enterprise to dealers to use its name and products FRANCHISE
– combining or uniting of separate businesses into a larger whole CONSOLIDATION
– exclusive control over some business activity MONOPOLY
– form a business into a registered company INCORPORATE
– "in or of the current month", as used in business correspondence INSTANT, INST.
– "in or of the next or following month", as used in business correspondence PROXIMO, PROX.
– "in or of the previous month", as used in business correspondence ULTIMO, ULT.
– launching or financing of a business venture by means of a share issue FLOTATION
– recruiting of business executives from other firms HEADHUNTING
– rules, or the document containing them, required for registering a business ARTICLES OF ASSOCIATION
– trademark, symbol, or emblem of a business company LOGO
– undertake a variety of activities or investments, as a large business might DIVERSIFY

businessman or -woman of great wealth and influence MAGNATE, TYCOON
– businessman or -woman undertaking ventures requiring risk and initiative ENTREPRENEUR

bust – short pillar with a stone bust on top, used as a boundary marker or architectural ornament in ancient Rome TERM, TERMINUS
bustle – woman's fashionable forward-tilting posture in the late 19th century, often enhanced by a bustle GRECIAN BEND
busy and persevering in carrying out one's duty, industrious SEDULOUS, ASSIDUOUS, DILIGENT
– busy in a bustling, energetic way VIBRANT
– busy in a feverish way HECTIC, FRANTIC

busybody or gossip QUIDNUNC
but, *and*, or similar conjunction joining words, phrases, or clauses of equal status in a sentence COORDINATING CONJUNCTION
– *but, however*, or other word expressing contrast or opposition ADVERSATIVE, DISJUNCTIVE

butcher's chopping knife CLEAVER
– butcher's frame from which animal carcasses are hung GAMBREL

butler or chief steward MAÎTRE D'HÔTEL, MAJOR-DOMO
butter, lard, or oil, as used to make crumbly biscuits or flaky pastry SHORTENING
– clarified butter from buffalo's milk, used in Indian cooking GHEE
– purify butter or fat by gentle heating CLARIFY
– relating to, resembling, or containing butter BUTYRACEOUS
– stale, decomposing, as old butter or bacon fat might be RANCID

buttercup RANUNCULUS
butterfly, moth, or related insect LEPIDOPTERAN
– expert in or collector of butterflies and moths LEPIDOPTERIST
– pupa of a moth or butterfly, often cased in a cocoon CHRYSALIS
– transformation, as of a caterpillar into a butterfly METAMORPHOSIS

buttocks, rump, posterior BREECH, FUNDAMENT, HAUNCHES, HUNKERS, NATES, DERRIÈRE, KEISTER
– development of large fatty deposits in the buttocks, as among the Bushmen STEATOPYGIA
– having beautiful or elegantly shaped buttocks CALLIPYGIAN

buttonhole flower BOUTONNIÈRE
buyer, purchaser VENDEE
– principle that the buyer bears the risk CAVEAT EMPTOR

buying and selling of a commodity in a risky but potentially very profitable way SPECULATION
– buying of currencies, shares, bonds, or the like for quick resale at a higher price ARBITRAGE

buzzing or ringing in the ear as a medical condition TINNITUS
– buzzing toy instrument activated by the player's humming KAZOO

by aeroplane, air mail PAR AVION
by chance, accidental, unplanned HAPHAZARD, FORTUITOUS, HAPLY
by definition, by its very nature IPSO FACTO
by heart BY ROTE
by right, legally DE JURE
by the way, in passing APROPOS, INCIDENTALLY, EN PASSANT

C

cabbage salad, finely shredded with mayonnaise COLESLAW
- cabbage with tightly packed crinkled leaves SAVOY
- shredded or chopped cabbage, salted and fermented in its own juice SAUERKRAUT

cabin, especially a large and comfortable private cabin, on a ship STATEROOM
- cabin or hut, typically crudely built and run-down SHANTY

cabinet or low chest of drawers, typically on short legs and richly ornamented COMMODE
- reorganisation of cabinet ministers undertaken by the Prime Minister RESHUFFLE
- cabinet minister's post or duty in the government PORTFOLIO
- unofficial yet powerful advisers to a government who are not members of the official cabinet KITCHEN CABINET

cable, suspended from pylons, of an electric railway, tram, or the like CATENARY
- cable-car, or transport system using such cars TELPHER
- cable-car, ski-lift cabin, or the like GONDOLA
- cable or rope for anchoring or towing a ship HAWSER
- cable or rope supporting a mast, radio tower, or the like GUY, STAY
- cable railway FUNICULAR
- cables used to start a car by connecting its flat battery to another car's active battery JUMP LEADS
- rotating drum on the deck of a ship around which ropes or cables are wound CAPSTAN

cactus or other plant that thrives in a very dry environment XEROPHYTE
- cactus or similar plant with fleshy, sap-conserving stems or leaves SUCCULENT
- Mexican cactus yielding a hallucinatory drug MESCAL, PEYOTE

café or small shabby bar, especially in France ESTAMINET

cafeteria See **restaurant**
- U.S. term for the cafeteria of a film company or radio studio COMMISSARY

caffeine or other drug, food, or drink that temporarily increases activity or efficiency STIMULANT

cage for moulting hawks MEW
- cage or container for small plants or animals TERRARIUM
- large cage for birds AVIARY

cake See chart, and also **dessert**
- cake decoration, consisting of the candied stem of an aromatic plant ANGELICA
- cakes, pastries, sweets, and other sweet items of prepared food CONFECTIONERY
- large rich cream cake GÂTEAU
- rich cakes and pastries, or a bakery selling them PATISSERIE

calculate and thereby ascertain COMPUTE, DETERMINE, CIPHER
- calculating device, as used in Asia, operated by moving beads on rods ABACUS
- calculating procedure using a series of steps ALGORITHM
- calculation of a rough-and-ready kind, based largely on guesswork DEAD RECKONING

calculations – aid to calculations, especially in the form of a table or list READY RECKONER

calculator – circuit in a calculator where figures are stored and computed ACCUMULATOR

calendar, with its system of leap years and new-style system of dates, introduced by Pope Gregory XIII GREGORIAN CALENDAR
- calendar in use before the current Gregorian calendar JULIAN CALENDAR
- calendar listing information such as tide patterns and weather statistics ALMANAC
- church calendar noting important religious events for each month MENOLOGY
- day falling roughly at the end of the first week of each month in the ancient Roman calendar NONES
- day falling roughly in the middle of each month in the ancient Roman calendar IDES
- first day of each month in the ancient Roman calendar CALENDS
- insertion of a day or days into the standard calendar to regularise it, as in leap years INTERCALATION, EMBOLISM

calf, especially a female calf, of about a year old STIRK
- calf or other baby domestic animal that is born prematurely SLINK
- hand-reared, as a calf might be CADE
- motherless calf DOGIE
- sterile female calf born as the twin of a male calf FREEMARTIN
- stomach lining of calves, or an extract of it used in cheesemaking RENNET

call, name, give a title or name to DESIGNATE, NOMINATE, STYLE, DUB
- call forth ELICIT, EVOKE
- call or address to an absent or dead person or personified thing APOSTROPHE
- call upon for help INVOKE
- ringing or inspiring, as a call to action might be CLARION

calling or strong inclination, as to a religious life VOCATION

calm, quiet, and passive SUBDUED, QUIESCENT
- calm, unemotional, expressionless IMPASSIVE, DISPASSIONATE
- calm and composed, self-possessed SEDATE
- calm and impassive in the endurance of pain or grief STOICAL
- calm and peaceful or quiet, typically in a dignified way TRANQUIL, SERENE
- calm and unexcitable in temperament or manner PLACID, IMPERTURBABLE
- calm and consistently even-tempered EQUABLE
- calm in the face of difficulties, accepting or resigned FATALISTIC, PHILOSOPHICAL
- calm or magically peaceful, as a childhood might be HALCYON
- calm state of restfulness, relaxation REPOSE
- calming, relaxing, soothing, as a medical drug might be SEDATIVE, ATARACTIC
- calming medicinal drug BROMIDE
- calmly detached, sober and distant STAID, ALOOF
- calmly indifferent, unemotional PHLEGMATIC
- coolness, calm self-control or poise COMPOSURE
- even-temperedness, calm self-possession EQUANIMITY

– imperturbable calm, unruffled temperament SANG-FROID
– interval of calm LULL
– pacify or calm, as by making concessions MOLLIFY, PLACATE, APPEASE, CONCILIATE
– reconcile, or calm an offended person or power PROPITIATE
– slacken, calm down, or simmer down, as a temper or raging storm might SUBSIDE, ABATE
– soothe, calm, or relieve ASSUAGE
– soothe, dispel, or calm someone's fears ALLAY, QUELL

Calvinist – referring to a Calvinist or Zwinglian church REFORMED

Cambridge resident, native, or graduate CANTABRIGIAN
– Cambridge university B.A. honours course or exam TRIPOS
– first-class honours graduate in the mathematics tripos at Cambridge WRANGLER

camel of an Arabian breed, having a single hump DROMEDARY
– camel with two humps, originating in central Asia BACTRIAN CAMEL

cameo or other ornament or sculpture in low relief ANAGLYPH
– design cut into the surface of a hard material, as opposed to a cameo INTAGLIO

camera See also **lens**, **photography**
– camera movement following a moving object or actor PAN
– camera movement towards or away from the subject ZOOM
– camera or projector for cinematic films CINEMATOGRAPH
– camera stand or support with three legs TRIPOD

CAKES AND BISCUITS

LARGE CAKES	
angel cake	light almond sponge
Battenberg cake	striped, coloured sponge layers covered in marzipan
Genoa cake	sponge cake, usually with cherries
kuchen	sugar-topped, yeast-dough coffee cake with fruit and nuts
lardy cake	sweet, bread-like cake with currants
panettone	Italian yeast cake
parkin	spiced, gingery cake
sachertorte	rich, iced chocolate cake with a jam filling, of Austrian origin
savarin	rich, ring-shaped yeast cake
simnel	traditional Easter fruit cake
torte	rich layer cake
SMALL CAKES AND BUNS	
Banbury cake	pastry cake filled with currants
brownies	flat chocolate squares with nuts
Chelsea bun	sugar-topped currant bun
drop scone/girdle cake/griddle cake	small, thick pancake
Eccles cake	sugar-topped, flaky pastry case with currant filling
frangipane	cream-filled, almond-flavoured pastry
madeleine	small sponge cake with a jam or coconut coating
maid of honour	custard tart flavoured with almond
millefeuille/napoleon	small flaky pastry filled with cream and jam
petit four	tiny, decoratively iced cake
popover	very light muffin
queen cake	iced sponge cake with currants, often heart-shaped
rum baba	yeast-leavened, rum-flavoured sponge cake
Sally Lunn	light tea cake
BISCUITS	
Bath Oliver	large round unsweetened biscuit, often eaten with cheese
brandy snap	sweet, very thin cylindrical ginger biscuit
farl	thin triangular Scottish biscuit, typically of oatmeal
flapjack	crunchy biscuit of oats and syrup
Florentine	rich biscuit of nuts and dried fruit with a chocolate backing
garibaldi	thin biscuit enclosing a layer of currants
gingersnap/gingernut	flat, brittle biscuit spiced with ginger
hardtack/ship's biscuit	hard unflavoured biscuit or bread formerly eaten by sailors
jumble/jumbal	light, crisp biscuit, typically with fruit or almonds and either ring-shaped or rolled-up
langue de chat	long, thin, finger-shaped sweet biscuit
macaroon	small, light, almond or coconut biscuit
oatcake	biscuit of baked oatmeal
pretzel	crisp salted biscuit, typically shaped like a loose knot
ratafia	small macaroon
shortbread	biscuit of flour, sugar and butter

– camera support consisting of a one-legged stand MONOPOD
– camera that produces a print a few seconds after taking the photograph POLAROID
– camera using a single lens to direct the image both onto the film and into the viewfinder SINGLE-LENS REFLEX CAMERA, SLR
– button on a camera pressed to take a photograph SHUTTER-RELEASE BUTTON
– disc in a camera with an adjustable opening to control the amount of light admitted through the lens DIAPHRAGM, STOP
– five-sided prism in an SLR camera that deflects the image into the viewfinder PENTAPRISM
– focusing device in a camera based on bringing together the images produced from two different angles RANGE FINDER
– lens or group of lenses producing the image in a camera or projector OBJECTIVE
– opening in a camera that is adjusted to limit the amount of light from the lense APERTURE
– short flexible syringe-operated wire used to operate a camera's shutter from a distance without shaking CABLE RELEASE

camouflage – defence mechanism of a vulnerable animal, whereby it closely resembles a dangerous or unpalatable species and so deters predators PROTECTIVE COLOURING, BATESIAN MIMICRY
– have a strong similarity or striking resemblance to something else, often as a means of camouflage MIMIC, SIMULATE
– referring or relating to the colouring of an animal that serves as camouflage APATETIC

camp – camp-follower or army shopkeeper in former times, who sold provisions to soldiers SUTLER
– camp for ox-wagon travellers OUTSPAN
– camp for temporary accommodation TRANSIT CAMP
– camp of a rough and temporary kind, as set up during a military operation BIVOUAC
– camp or temporary buildings for quartering troops CANTONMENT
– campsite services building LODGE
– campsite or inn for desert travellers CARAVANSERAI
– defensive camp, protected by wagons LAAGER
– small, portable camping stove, burning paraffin or oil PRIMUS

campaign for votes from people or a region in an election CANVASS
– campaign fervently in favour of a cause CRUSADE
– campaign of vindictive slander or obstructiveness VENDETTA
– campaigning for elections HUSTINGS
– catchphrase, motto, jingle, or the like used repeatedly, as in political campaigns SLOGAN, BANNER

Canada – financial centre of Canada, or financial interests BAY STREET

canal, channel, or small dam, or the gate or valve holding back or regulating the water SLUICE
– canal boat in Venice, propelled by a single oar GONDOLA
– dam in a river or canal to raise the water or regulate its flow WEIR
– manmade canal or water channel AQUEDUCT
– path along a canal or river, as used by horses pulling boats TOWPATH, BRIDLEPATH
– stretch of canal between two adjoining locks POUND
– uninterrupted stretch of water on a river or canal REACH

cancel, deprive of force or validity, make useless or ineffective NULLIFY, INVALIDATE, VITIATE, ANNUL
– cancel a claim, disown a belief, or the like RETRACT, RECANT, RENOUNCE, ABJURE, DISAVOW
– cancel a punishment REMIT
– cancel or abolish a law, ruling, or the like REPEAL, REVOKE, QUASH, ABROGATE, CASSATE
– cancel or erase, as by crossing through or obliterating DELETE, EFFACE, EXPUNGE
– cancel or reverse an order or command COUNTERMAND, RESCIND
– cancelling of common factors in a fraction, or converting a fraction to a decimal REDUCTION

cancer See also **tumour**
– cancer-causing CARCINOGENIC
– cancer-like, or skin cancer CANCROID
– cancer or malignant tumour CARCINOMA
– cancer treatment by means of drugs CHEMOTHERAPY
– cancer treatment by means of X-rays, injection of radioactive chemicals, and the like RADIOTHERAPY
– apparent decline in the severity of a disease such as cancer REMISSION
– cell used in cancer studies and biological research HE-LA CELL
– drug derived from peach pips, allegedly useful in cancer treatment LAETRILE
– fatal, certain to end in death, as an inoperable cancer is TERMINAL
– non-cancerous, controlled or unthreatening to life, as a tumour might be BENIGN
– protein produced in response to a virus and inhibiting its spread, used experimentally in cancer treatment INTERFERON
– spread of cancer cells from one part of the body to another METASTASIS
– spreading uncontrolled, and resistant to treatment, as a cancer tumour is MALIGNANT
– test for cancer of the cervix in women PAP TEST, SMEAR TEST

-cancer -OMA

candid See **frank**, **honest**

candle consisting of a reed pith coated in tallow RUSHLIGHT
– candle-holder of a large and branched design, usually hanging from the ceiling CHANDELIER
– candle lit and placed before a statue or shrine VIGIL LIGHT
– candle-maker or -seller CHANDLER
– candle of a very small or thin kind TAPER
– burn unevenly and drip wax down one side, as a candle might GUTTER
– extinguish a candle or trim the charred end of its wick SNUFF
– hard fatty substance extracted from beef or mutton fat, used in making candles TALLOW
– put out a flame, candle, or the like DOUSE, EXTINGUISH

candlestick attached to a handle or a bracket SCONCE
– candlestick of a large and ornamental kind FLAMBEAU
– candlestick with a spike for keeping the candle upright, or the spike itself PRICKET
– candlestick with many branches, typically attached to a wall or mirror GIRANDOLE
– candlestick with several arms CANDELABRUM
– candelabrum holding seven or nine candlesticks in Jewish tradition MENORAH
– stand or table for supporting torches or candlesticks TORCHÈRE

candy floss – U.S. term for candy floss SPUN SUGAR, COTTON CANDY

cane, ruler, or the like for beating children, especially on the hand FERULE
– cane from a tropical Asian palm, as used for wickerwork furniture and walking sticks RATTAN
– cane made from the stem of the rattan palm MALACCA CANE
– cane or short stick carried by army officers SWAGGER STICK

cannabis HEMP, INDIAN HEMP, HASHISH, MARIJUANA
canned Norwegian herring SILD
cannibals ANTHROPOPHAGI
– human flesh as eaten by cannibals LONG PIG
cannon firing shells at a steep angle HOWITZER
– cannon or machine-gun emplacement in the form of a low round concrete building PILLBOX
– cluster of small projectiles fired from cannons GRAPESHOT
– harness strapped to a soldier for hauling cannons BRICOLE
– pin on either side of a cannon, container, or the like enabling it to be pivoted on a supporting frame TRUNNION
– platform or mound along the wall of a fort, from which cannons are fired BARBETTE
– plug or cover for the muzzle of a cannon when not in use TAMPION
canoe – canoe's float, attached parallel to one or both sides for stabilisation OUTRIGGER
– Eskimo canoe KAYAK

CANONICAL HOURS

NAME OF PRAYER SERVICE	TIME ASSIGNED
matins, with lauds	dawn
prime	6am
terce	9am
sext	noon
nones	3pm
vespers	early evening
compline	just before bedtime

canonical hours See chart
canopy or other covering, as for a boat or wagon TILT
– canopy over a bed, altar, or the like TESTER
– canopy placed over an altar or dais, or used in church processions BALDACHIN
– canvas canopy over the entrance to a theatre, club, or the like as in the U.S. MARQUEE
canvas bed, suspended at both ends HAMMOCK
– canvas, tent-like cover for temporary exhibitions or the like MARQUEE
– canvas used as a waterproof covering TARPAULIN
cap See also **hat**
– cap as used in a toy pistol or in an ancient firearm, that explodes when struck PERCUSSION CAP
– cloth flap at the back of a cap, against sunburn HAVELOCK
– types of cap worn by Roman Catholic clergymen BIRETTA, CALOTTE, ZUCCHETTO
capable See **able**, **expert**
capital or principal sum of money, value of an estate, or the like, as distinct from the interest or income CORPUS
– capital provided for new business enterprises VENTURE CAPITAL
capital letter MAJUSCULE, UPPER-CASE LETTER
– letter of the alphabet that is not a capital letter MINUSCULE, LOWER-CASE LETTER
capital punishment – person who urges or favours getting rid of capital punishment ABOLITIONIST
– person who urges or favours the retaining of capital punishment RETENTIONIST
captive of a kidnapper or hijacker HOSTAGE
captivity, dependency, enslavement THRALL, THRALDOM
captured weapons and other spoils of victory TROPHY
car See illustration, page 83, and also **vehicles**
– car body COACHWORK
– car body or aircraft fuselage in which the stress is taken mainly by the casing MONOCOQUE
– car made before 1905 VETERAN CAR
– car made between 1905 and 1919 EDWARDIAN CAR
– car made between 1919 and 1930 VINTAGE CAR
– car of a very long and luxurious design LIMOUSINE
– car of an early type with a folding roof over the rear seat LANDAU
– car or other possession or project, expensive and inefficient, requiring more trouble than it is worth WHITE ELEPHANT
– car or other vehicle that is old, noisy, and run-down BONESHAKER, JALOPY, RATTLETRAP
– car radio device used for private radio communication between drivers CITIZENS' BAND RADIO
– car that is old-fashioned, especially a Model-T Ford TIN LIZZIE
– car whose roof can be folded back CONVERTIBLE, CABRIOLET
– car with a souped-up engine HOT ROD
– car with an upward-opening door at the rear HATCHBACK
– car with two doors COUPÉ
– air deflector, as on an aircraft's wing or a racing car, to increase drag and reduce the tendency to lift SPOILER
– airstream behind a fast-moving car or bicycle SLIPSTREAM
– board on small wheels or casters, for lying on when working under a car CREEPER, CRADLE
– brand name of a car MARQUE
– built according to the buyer's specifications, as a car might be CUSTOM-BUILT
– canvas roof of a car that opens by folding back DROP-HEAD
– closed car of a fairly large and standard design with two rows of seats SALOON, SEDAN
– decorative line painted along the side of a car or other vehicle COACH LINE, CARRIAGE LINE
– degree of stability of a car, as on wet roads ROADHOLDING
– flashing of all the indicators on a car, as to warn other motorists during a breakdown HAZARD WARNING SIGNAL
– footboard at the side of some old cars RUNNING BOARD
– framework of a car, to which the body is attached CHASSIS
– indicator, especially of an early kind in the form of a small arm, on the side of a car, that swung out and lit up TRAFFICATOR
– indoor light of a car COURTESY LIGHT
– loss in value, as of a car, as through age or wear DEPRECIATION
– luggage compartment or folding seat at the rear of some early motor cars DICKY, RUMBLE SEAT
– metal bar or frame strengthening a car roof in case of accident ROLL-BAR
– old fashioned term for an estate car SHOOTING BRAKE
– polish a car with wax SIMONISE
– process of or mechanism for igniting the fuel in an engine, as for starting a car IGNITION
– procession of cars or other motor vehicles MOTORCADE
– remove useful parts from a car, machine, or the like for repairing a similar model CANNIBALISE
– shock-reducing system in a car, including springs and shock absorbers SUSPENSION
– sports car or similar sleek high-speed car GRAN TURISMO, GT
– shafts, gears, and the like transmitting power from the engine to the car's wheels TRANSMISSION

– system of elastic cords joined at the centre, used for strapping down loads, as on a car roof SPIDER, OCTOPUS

car- AUTO-

car battery ACCUMULATOR

caravan – tinker or scrap-metal dealer living in a caravan, often taken for a Gypsy DIDICOY

-carbohydrate -OSE

carbon used in lead pencils and as a lubricant GRAPHITE, PLUMBAGO
– producing coal or carbon CARBONIFEROUS
– referring to carbon compounds in chemistry ORGANIC

carbon- ORGANO-

carbon paper – transfer a drawing without carbon paper by loosely shading or colouring its reverse side, and then tracing it onto a surface or paper underneath CALK

carbonated, producing or emitting small bubbles of gas, as with soda water or a sparkling cold drink EFFERVESCENT

carburettor – tube with a narrow throat, as in a carburettor, for providing suction VENTURI

card for brief display to an audience, especially as a visual aid in the classroom FLASHCARD
– card or disc that is spun or twirled to produce a merged image of the partial words or pictures on either side THAUMATROPE
– cards of a kind used in fortune-telling TAROT CARDS
– fortune-telling by means of a pack of tarot or playing cards CARTOMANCY

CARD GAMES

baccarat	**Newmarket**
beggar-my-neighbour	**old maid**
bezique	**ombre**
brag	**patience/solitaire**
bridge (auction, contract, duplicate)	**Pelmanism**
canasta	**pinochle**
chemin de fer	**piquet**
cribbage	**poker (stud p)**
écarté	**pontoon/twenty-one/vingt-et-un/blackjack**
euchre	**quadrille**
fantan	**racing demon**
faro	**rouge et noir**
gin/gin rummy	**rummy/gin rummy**
loo	**snap**
monte	**solo**
nap, napoleon	**speculation**
	whist

card games See chart, and also **gambling, bridge, poker**
– arrange playing cards secretly in a favourable order STACK
– card-dealer or bet-taker at a gambling table CROUPIER
– card that is the only one of its suit in a hand dealt SINGLETON
– cards not dealt out at the beginning of a game TALON, STOCK
– jack, queen, or king of any suit in a pack of cards COURT CARD
– observer, as at a card game, who offers uninvited comments or advice KIBITZER
– play a trump in card games RUFF
– shuffle playing cards by flicking through two piles with the thumbs RIFFLE
– the highest cards, especially in trumps HONOURS

cardboard as used in bookbinding PASTEBOARD
– cardboard to which a picture or photograph is pasted MOUNT

cardinal who handles the Pope's financial affairs, papal treasurer CAMERLINGO
– assembly of cardinals, presided over by the Pope CONSISTORY
– body or assembly of all the Roman Catholic cardinals, which elects and gives advice to the Pope COLLEGE OF CARDINALS, SACRED COLLEGE

care, safekeeping, or guardianship, as of a minor CUSTODY, TUTELAGE
– careful in providing for one's own interests, especially in being thrifty PROVIDENT
– child, senile person, or the like under the legal care of a guardian or court of law WARD
– put into the care of someone ENTRUST, CONSIGN, COMMIT, COMMEND
– relating or referring to spiritual care and guidance PASTORAL

care for, tend MINISTER

career, occupation, profession VOCATION, CALLING
– blossoming, emergence into prominence or success, as of a career EFFLORESCENCE
– person whose welfare is protected or career advanced by an influential patron PROTÉGÉ
– summary of one's education and career, as for job applications CURRICULUM VITAE, RÉSUMÉ
– test identifying a person's skills and potential, often used as an aid in career guidance APTITUDE TEST

carefree, indifferent, easygoing, or unconcerned NONCHALANT, INSOUCIANT, DEBONAIR, BLITHE

careful in showing concern for others SOLICITOUS
– careful or alert, on one's guard or on the lookout VIGILANT
– careful or conscientious in a painstaking way, attentive to detail SCRUPULOUS, PUNCTILIOUS, DILIGENT, ASSIDUOUS, SEDULOUS
– careful or precise to a fault METICULOUS, FASTIDIOUS
– careful or tactful, showing caution or good judgment DISCREET, PRUDENT, JUDICIOUS, POLITIC
– carefully or timidly GINGERLY
– carefully assessing the possible consequences of an action, wary or chary CIRCUMSPECT
– carefully avoiding indicating any definite preference or purpose, as an evasive reply would NONCOMMITTAL

careless, showing insufficient judgment IMPROVIDENT, IMPRUDENT, INJUDICIOUS
– careless, untidy, slapdash SLOVENLY, SLIPSHOD
– careless and rash, reckless or impulsive IMPETUOUS, PRECIPITATE, HARUM-SCARUM
– careless in a clumsy or irresponsible way, heedless or lax REMISS, NEGLIGENT, FECKLESS
– careless through inattentiveness INADVERTENT

caretaker of a church in former times OSTIARY
– caretaker or doorman of a building, especially of a block of flats JANITOR, CONCIÈRGE, PORTER
– caretaker or keeper, as of an art collection CUSTODIAN, CURATOR, CONSERVATOR
– caretaker's office LODGE
– U.S. term for a caretaker or porter SUPERINTENDENT

cargo list or inventory MANIFEST
– cargo or goods for delivery or disposal CONSIGNMENT
– cargo or wreckage remaining afloat after a ship has sunk FLOTSAM
– cargo thrown from a ship but marked by buoys for later recovery LAGAN
– cargo thrown overboard or washed ashore JETSAM
– large metal box of standard design for storing and transporting cargo CONTAINER
– load of cargo, passengers, bombs, or the like in an aircraft or spacecraft PAYLOAD
– stow cargo in a ship's hold STEEVE

caricature, crude and distorted imitation TRAVESTY

carnation, pink, or related flower DIANTHUS

carnival, holiday, feast FIESTA
– carnival celebrations held on Shrove Tuesday MARDI GRAS
– carnival or lively celebration JAMBOREE

carol – carol-singers WAITS
– carol sung at Christmas NOËL
– sing a part-song, such as a carol or round TROLL

carpentry See **joint**

carpet See also **rug**
– carpet of a flat-woven French type AUBUSSON
– carpet of English design or manufacture AXMINSTER, WILTON, KIDDERMINSTER
– coarse fabric or rough carpeting for covering a floor DRUGGET
– area bordering a carpet, doorway, or the like SURROUND
– edge, border, or fringe of a carpet, fabric, or the like finished so as to prevent unravelling SELVAGE
– long narrow carpet or tablecloth RUNNER
– long woolly nap, as on coarse cloth or a carpet SHAG
– soft raised velvety surface of a carpet PILE
– thick felt fabric laid under carpeting to increase insulation or resilience UNDERFELT

carriage, bearing, method of carrying or holding oneself when walking GAIT, DEPORTMENT

carriages See also **horse-drawn vehicles**
– carriage entrance into the courtyard of a large house PORTE-COCHÈRE
– carriage escort mounted on horseback OUTRIDER
– luggage compartment or folding seat at the rear of some carriages DICKY, RUMBLE SEAT

carrier, insect or other organism that transmits germs VECTOR

carry a sword or rifle diagonally across the body PORT
– carry lightly, as the wind carries the smell of flowers WAFT
– carrying or transportation, as of heavy supplies PORTAGE
– carrying something, such as nerve impulses, inwards or towards a centre, such as the brain AFFERENT
– carrying something, such as nerve impulses, outwards or away from a centre, such as the brain DEFERENT, EFFERENT

-carry- -FER-

carry out a plan, operate IMPLEMENT, EXECUTE
– carry out business TRANSACT

-carrying -PHORE, -PHOROUS

cart See **horse-drawn vehicle**, **wagon**
– open farm cart, or cart used during the French Revolution to transport condemned prisoners to the guillotine TUMBREL

Carthage – adjective for ancient Carthage PUNIC

-cartilage- -CHONDR-, CHONDRO-
– turn into cartilage CHONDRIFY

cartoon portrait CARICATURE
– process of filming a series of static drawings to give the impression of movement, as in a cartoon film ANIMATION
– outline, roughly oval-shaped, for the printed speech or thoughts of a character in a cartoon strip BALLOON
– single scene in a cartoon strip FRAME

cartridge – former term for a car-

car

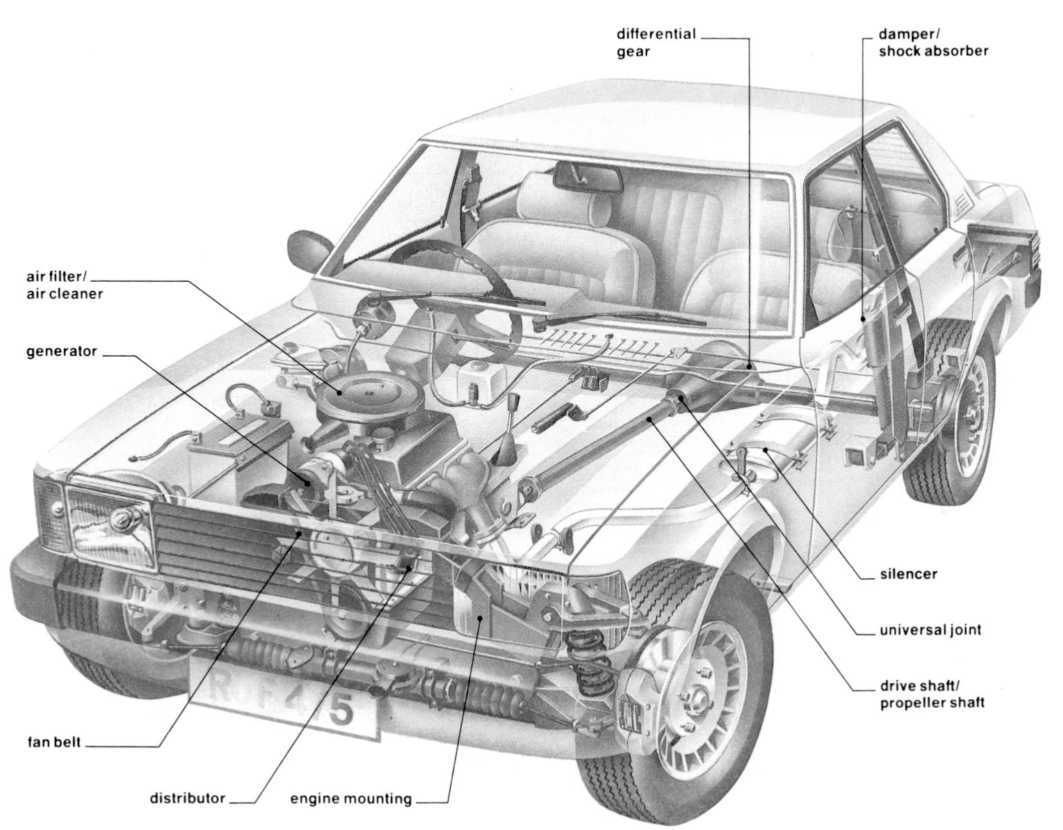

differential gear
damper/ shock absorber
air filter/ air cleaner
generator
silencer
universal joint
drive shaft/ propeller shaft
fan belt
distributor
engine mounting

tridge, bullet, or box of cartridges CARTOUCHE

carved architectural ornament in the form of a basket of fruit CORBEIL
– carved or engraved articles of ivory, whalebone, or the like, typically made by sailors SCRIMSHAW

Casablanca – old quarter of a North African town such as Casablanca KASBAH

case See also **bag**, **suitcase**
– case for carrying papers BRIEFCASE, ATTACHÉ CASE
– case for holding loose papers or official documents PORTFOLIO, DISPATCH BOX
– action or decision in a law court used as an example or justification when treating a later case similarly PRECEDENT
– handbag or small case used by women for carrying cosmetics or toiletries VANITY CASE
– mention or list a case, example, or the like, as to support an argument CITE
– unshakably strong, without loopholes, as a legal case might be IRONCLAD, WATERTIGHT

case history or full medical records of a patient ANAMNESIS

cash – having enough cash or assets to settle debts or run a business LIQUIDITY

cask See also **barrel**
– cask or small wooden barrel FIRKIN, KILDERKIN
– plug or bung in the vent of a cask SPIGOT, SPILE

casserole See **food**
– casserole pot MARMITE

cast of characters in a play DRAMATIS PERSONAE
– cast off or moult a dead outer skin, as snakes do SLOUGH
– cast out evil spirits or demons, or free a possessed person from them EXORCISE
– casting a spell, summoning a spirit INCANTATION, INVOCATION, CONJUNCTION

caste See also **Hinduism terms**
– member of the highest or priestly Hindu caste BRAHMAN
– "untouchable", member of the lowest classes in Hindu society, technically outside the caste system HARIJAN

castle See illustration, and also **fortification**
– castle-keeper or governor of a castle CASTELLAN, CHATELAIN, CHATELAINE, CONSTABLE
– castle-like, having turrets and battlements like a castle, or indentations resembling these CASTELLATED
– castle or manor house in France CHÂTEAU
– castle or stronghold protecting a town or city CITADEL
– back gate or door, as of a castle POSTERN
– embankment in front of a fort or castle, making attackers vulnerable to the defenders GLACIS, ESCARPMENT
– flat open area in front of a castle or other fortification, exposing the attackers to the defenders' fire ESPLANADE
– impossible to capture or enter forcibly, as a castle or fort might be IMPREGNABLE
– military governor or hereditary lord of a castle in medieval Germany BURGRAVE
– pathway between the moat and walls of a castle BERM
– slope formed, usually by rock debris, at the foot of a cliff, castle wall, or the like TALUS
– type or specific design of castle MOUND CASTLE, CONCENTRIC CASTLE, MOTTE-AND-BAILEY CASTLE

castrate, geld EMASCULATE, NEUTER
– castrated male chicken fattened for eating CAPON
– castrated male horse or other animal GELDING
– castrated male sheep WETHER
– castrated man, especially in former times, serving as a harem guard, court attendant, or the like EUNUCH
– pig castrated before reaching maturity BARROW
– pig or other male animal castrated after maturity STAG

casual, carefree, or unconcerned NONCHALANT, DEBONAIR, DÉGAGÉ,

castle

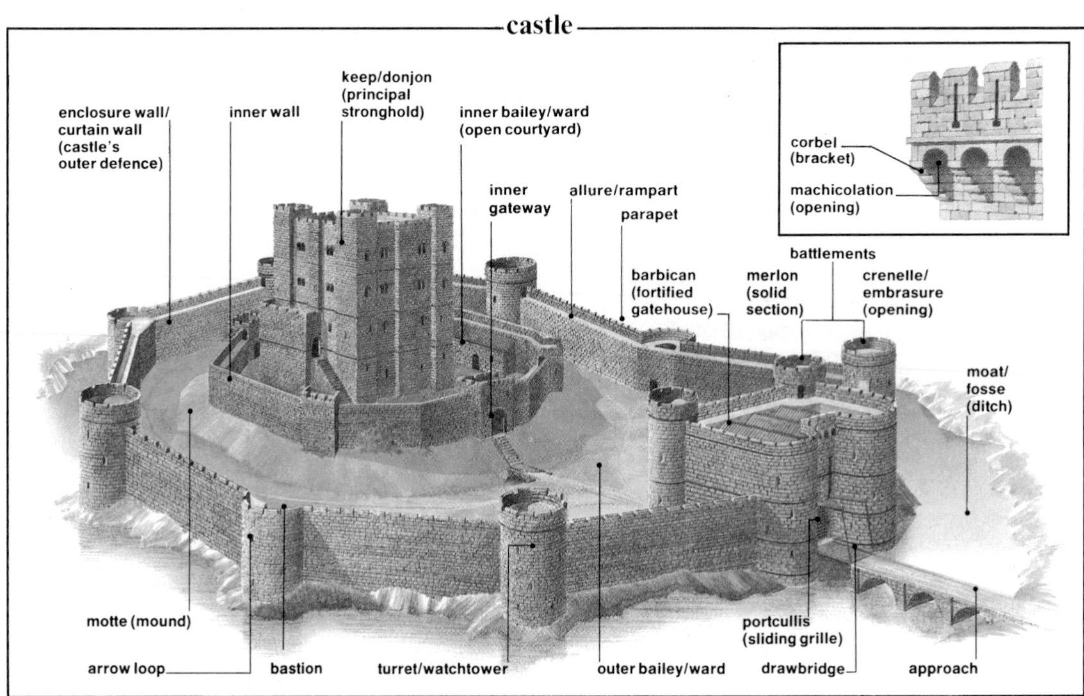

INSOUCIANT
– casual, disorganised HAPHAZARD, INDISCRIMINATE, LACKADAISICAL
– casual, offhand, or superficial, as a brief mechanical glance would be CURSORY, PERFUNCTORY
– casual, random, or unstructured, as a conversation might be DESULTORY
– casual, unimportant, or unplanned INCIDENTAL, UNPREMEDITATED
– chance, accidental, occurring casually or randomly CONTINGENT, ADVENTITIOUS, FORTUITOUS
– relating to or having casual sexual relationships with many partners PROMISCUOUS
– tendency to make casual finds of pleasing objects SERENDIPITY
– walk in a casual, leisurely, or aimless way, stroll SAUNTER, MEANDER, PROMENADE

casually, informally EN FAMILLE

cat, especially an old female cat, as in folk tales GRIMALKIN
– cat-like mammal secreting a fluid used as a fixative in perfume-making CIVET, ZIBET
– cat's whiskers or similar bristly hairs VIBRISSAE
– adjective for a cat FELINE
– brown or grey with darker streaks or spots, as a dog, cat, or cow might be BRINDLED
– informal term for a cat MOGGY
– shrill screech or cry, as of an excited cat CATERWAUL
– spotted forest cat of Central and South America OCELOT

catapult – catapult-like launcher of rocks or other heavy missiles, as used in ancient siege warfare BALLISTA, ONAGER, BRICOLE
– catapult or sling of large size, as used for hurling rocks, in medieval warfare TREBUCHET, MANGONEL

cataract – remove a cataract surgically by displacing the eye's lens downwards COUCH

catastrophe, great destruction, or devastating battle or conflict ARMAGEDDON

catch, capture, or arrest APPREHEND
– catch a disease, become infected with CONTRACT
– catch or tangle in or as if in a net ENMESH
– catch or tear clothing on a nail, wooden stump, or the like SNAG
– catch or trap ENSNARE

catch fire IGNITE

catching, spreading, communicable, as a disease or laughter might be INFECTIOUS, CONTAGIOUS

catchphrase, motto, jingle, or the like used repeatedly, as in advertising or political campaigns SLOGAN, BANNER

category – title of a category or class RUBRIC

cater for someone's unworthy wishes PANDER

caterpillar – creature resembling a caterpillar having two pairs of legs on each segment MILLIPEDE

cathedral or abbey in certain cities MINSTER
– cathedral surroundings or grounds PRECINCT, PURLIEU, CLOSE
– cathedral's canons as a group, or a meeting of them CHAPTER
– arched recess above a doorway, as at the entrance of a medieval cathedral TYMPANUM
– grotesque stone figure, as on a cathedral roof, often serving as a rainwater spout from a gutter GARGOYLE
– relating or belonging to a chapter of a cathedral CANONICAL

Catholic See chart at **Roman Catholic terms**

cat's eye or similar twinkling gemstone CHATOYANT

cattle See also **ox**
– cattle dealer or driver DROVER
– cattle round-up, as for branding or counting RODEO, DRIFT
– cattle stall CRIB
– adjective for cattle BOVINE
– any of various hoofed, cud-chewing mammals, such as cattle, sheep, and deer RUMINANT
– drive cattle with a sharpened or electrified rod GOAD
– enclosure for cattle in southern Africa KRAAL
– enclosure for cattle or horses CORRAL
– flap of loose skin or hide hanging under the throat of cattle or dogs DEWLAP
– headlong rush, as of startled cattle or horses or of a panic-stricken crowd STAMPEDE
– infectious bacterial disease of cattle and sheep ANTHRAX
– infectious cattle disease of various severe kinds MURRAIN
– infectious viral disease of cattle, causing internal ulcers, "cattle plague" RINDERPEST
– rack or manger for fodder for cattle or other farm animals CRATCH

cauliflower – coated with breadcrumbs and sometimes cheese, and then grilled or browned, as cauliflower might be AU GRATIN

cause, as of a disease AETIOLOGY
– cause, bring about, devise or produce ENCOMPASS, ENGENDER, PRECIPITATE
– cause, give rise to, prompt OCCASION, EFFECTUATE
– cause, provoke, stir up or promote INSTIGATE, FOMENT
– cause of a quarrel or war CASUS BELLI
– cause or principal source of some development MAINSPRING, FOUNTAINHEAD
– caused or developing outside the body or a body part EXOGENOUS
– caused or developing within the body or a body part ENDOGENOUS
– causing, promoting, contributing to, or favourable to a given result CONDUCIVE
– adopt or support a cause, faith, or ideal ESPOUSE
– belief or philosophy that everything follows inescapably from a cause or series of causes, and that there is no real free will DETERMINISM
– believer in or follower of a particular doctrine, cause, or the like ADHERENT
– defender or champion of a cause APOLOGIST
– energetically promoting a cause EVANGELISTIC
– person or thing that causes or provokes a change or event without itself being changed CATALYST
– self-generated, apparently uncaused SPONTANEOUS

-cause- -GEN-, -GENESIS, -GENOUS

-causing -FACIENT, -FIC, -OTIC

cautious See **careful**

cavalry horse CHARGER

cavalryman having an ornate uniform of Hungarian design HUSSAR

cave drawing, rock painting, or other ancient or prehistoric drawing or painting PICTOGRAPH
– cave-dweller or caveman TROGLODYTE
– cave of large size, or large chamber within a cave CAVERN
– cave or cavern, especially in a cliffside COVE
– icicle-like lime deposit hanging from the roof of a cave STALACTITE
– pillar or cone of lime deposit rising from the floor of a cave STALAGMITE
– small picturesque cave GROTTO
– study or exploration of caves SPELEOLOGY, SPELUNKING

caviar – caviar-producing fish STURGEON, BELUGA

cavity filled with gas or fluid, as in the body, plant tissue, or volcanic rock VESICLE
– cavity in the body, filled with fluid to reduce friction, as at joints BURSA

– cavity or blister-like sac in the body, either normal or abnormal CYST
– pitted with small cells or cavities, honeycombed FAVEOLATE
-cavity- -COEL-, COELO-
ceding or surrender of something, as of land, territory, or rights CESSION
ceiling, especially one decorated with paintings PLAFOND
– ceiling or roof or arched shape, typically of stone or masonry VAULT
– hanging sculpted ornament on a Gothic ceiling PENDANT
– inward curving surface between a ceiling and wall, or a concave moulding COVE, COVING
– light fixture, large and branched, usually hanging from the ceiling, holding many bulbs or candles CHANDELIER
– ornamental sunken panel in a ceiling, dome, or the like COFFER, LACUNA, CAISSON
celebrate noisily ROISTER, REVEL
– celebrate or glorify splendidly and showily EMBLAZON
– celebrate riotously in public MAFFICK
celebration See also **party**
– celebration, as of a triumph JUBILANCE, JUBILATION, EXULTATION
– celebration, typically an annual feast, at some schools and colleges GAUDY
– celebration of an anniversary JUBILEE
– celebration or festivity marked by heavy drinking and revelry WASSAIL, CAROUSAL, BACCHANAL
– celebration or pleasure outing, especially by public officials using public funds JUNKET
– noisy party or wild celebration SHINDIG
– solemn celebration or observance of an anniversary, such as a remembrance ceremony COMMEMORATION
– unrestrained licentious celebration, orgy, revelry SATURNALIA
celebrity or VIP PERSONAGE, DIGNITARY, LUMINARY
– treat someone as a celebrity LIONISE
celestial bodies See **astronomy**
cell biology CYTOLOGY
– cell division, as in a fertilised ovum CLEAVAGE, SEGMENTATION
– cell division in genetics MEIOSIS, MITOSIS
– cell tissue from which nails and teeth develop MATRIX
– cell used in cancer studies and biological research HE–LA CELL
– basic living matter in a plant or animal cell PROTOPLASM
– destruction or dissolving of a cell CYTOLYSIS
– fertilised egg or ovum, cell formed by the fusion of two reproductive cells ZYGOTE
– similarity of form or structure, as in different cells or crystals ISOMORPHISM
– sperm cell, male reproductive cell SPERMATOZOON
– sperm cell, ovum, or other cell that can combine to form a fertilised cell GAMETE
– splitting of a one-celled plant or animal as a means of reproduction FISSION
– tissue, typically a single layer of tightly packed cells, covering body organs and surfaces EPITHELIUM
– underground cell or dungeon whose door is in the ceiling OUBLIETTE
-cell- -CYT-, CYTO-, -CYTE, -BLAST, -PLAST
-cell material -PLASM
cell nucleus- KARY-, KARYO-
cellar – beer hall or German restaurant, originally in the cellar of a town hall RATSKELLAR
Celtic, relating to ancient Cornwall, Wales, Cumbria, and Brittany BRYTHONIC
– Celtic or Gaelic, or relating to a Gaelic speaker GOIDELIC
– Celtic people of the branch to which the Welsh, Cornish, and Bretons belong CYMRY
cement mixture or finish, as on a floor SCREED
– cement mixture or plaster used for coating walls PARGETING
– cement or mortar mixture for filling cracks or seams, as in brickwork or between tiles POINTING, GROUTING
– cement or other binding agent MATRIX
– cement that can set under water PORTLAND CEMENT
– tray, with a handle underneath, for carrying cement or plaster HAWK
– volcanic rock that can be ground for making cement TRASS
cemetery See also **burial**
– cemetery, burial place GOLGOTHA
– cemetery, especially a large and elaborate cemetery of an ancient city NECROPOLIS
censer THURIBLE
censor, remove from a text the parts considered indecent EXPURGATE, BOWDLERISE
– censor or ban, prohibit, suppress PROSCRIBE, INTERDICT
– censor or edit out BLUE-PENCIL
– censor the press, free speech, or the like MUZZLE
– licence for the publication of a book, as by a bishop or censor IMPRIMATUR, NIHIL OBSTAT
census – person who delivers and fetches census forms ENUMERATOR
centigrade CELSIUS
centipede – arthropod resembling a centipede having two pairs of legs on each segment MILLIPEDE
central heating – switching or controlling device for regulating temperature, as in a refrigerator or central-heating system THERMOSTAT
centralised, having or referring to a strongly centralised rather than federal government UNITARY
centre of a wheel or fan HUB
– centre of attention, interest, or action FOCUS
– centre of power, influence, or interest GANGLION
– centre or fundamental part around which others are grouped or from which development takes place NUCLEUS
– central or key component or participant LINCHPIN
– direct away from or move outwards and separate from a common centre DIVERGE
– direct towards, move towards, or meet at a common centre CONVERGE
– having a common centre, as two circles of different sizes might CONCENTRIC
– having different or offset centres, as two overlapping circles would ECCENTRIC
– moving or growing inwards, towards a centre or axis CENTRIPETAL, AFFERENT
– moving or growing outwards, away from a centre or axis CENTRIFUGAL, EFFERENT
– stone at Delphi thought by the ancient Greeks to mark the centre of the Earth OMPHALOS
centre- MES-, MESO-
ceramics See **pottery**
cereal See also **wheat**
– cereal fungus or disease ERGOT
– cereal grass producing edible glossy grains and a syrup SORGHUM
– cereal grass widely cultivated for grain and fodder MILLET
– cereal or breakfast food containing nuts, raisins, and the like MUESLI
– beat harvested cereal to separate the grain from the chaff THRESH, FLAIL
– expose harvested cereal to a cur-

rent of air to separate the grain from the chaff WINNOW

ceremony, custom, or ritual marking a change of status in a person's life RITE OF PASSAGE
– ceremony, formality, etiquette, propriety DECORUM, PROPRIETY
– ceremony at which a new monument, work of art, or the like, is formally displayed to the public for the first time UNVEILING
– ceremony conferring an office, award, or honour on a person INVESTITURE, INDUCTION
– ceremony or ritual of admission, as to membership of a group INITIATION
– ceremony or service honouring the memory of a person or event COMMEMORATION
– ceremonial military procession parading flags TROOPING THE COLOUR
– ceremonial parade of horses or cars, or similar colourful procession CAVALCADE
– celebrate a marriage, perform a ceremony, or the like with formal or religious rites SOLEMNISE
– formal opening ceremony, installation, or beginning INAUGURATION, DEDICATION, COMMENCEMENT
– garments worn by those officiating or assisting at a church service or ceremonial rite VESTMENTS

certain, absolute, without reservation or ambiguity, conclusive UNEQUIVOCAL, CATEGORICAL
– certain, incapable of failure or error INFALLIBLE
– certain, indisputable, without doubt INDUBITABLE, INCONTROVERTIBLE
– certain, proved beyond doubt, unquestionable APODICTIC
– certain, unyielding, refusing to budge ADAMANT
– certain means of accomplishing one's goal OPEN SESAME
– certain outcome, result that is definite or inevitable FOREGONE CONCLUSION
– certain to happen INEVITABLE

certainty, confident assurance CERTITUDE

certificate, voucher, or other formal document DOCKET
– certificate awarded for passing a course of study, or the course itself DIPLOMA
– certificate of entitlement, such as a share certificate SCRIP

certify, confirm, assure WARRANT
– certified or guaranteed as being up to a set standard ACCREDITED

Ceylonese, Sri Lankan belonging to the majority ethnic community SINGHALESE

chain, rope, or the like, as used for steadying a load or mooring an aerial GUY
– chain or clasp formerly worn by women at the waist, and used for holding keys, a handkerchief, or the like CHATELAINE
– chain together, link in a series CONCATENATE, CATENATE
– chains or confining bands around the ankles or wrists MANACLES, FETTERS, SHACKLES
– peg or crosspiece, attached to a rope, chain, or the like, used for fastening or to prevent slipping TOGGLE

chain of events – projected or possible chain of events SCENARIO

chain reaction KNOCK-ON EFFECT, DOMINO EFFECT

chain store MULTIPLE SHOP, MULTIPLE STORE

chair See also **furniture**
– chair, usually enclosed and carried on poles by a pair of footmen, used as a vehicle in former times SEDAN CHAIR
– chair to which wrongdoers or suspects were formerly tied, as for ducking or public mockery CUCKING-STOOL
– crosspiece linking and securing the legs of a chair STAVE, SALTIRE, STRETCHER
– fabric, padding, springs, and so on, as used in making a soft covering for chairs UPHOLSTERY
– single wooden slat, often decorated, as in the middle of the back of a chair SPLAT
– small swivelling wheel on each leg of an armchair, sofa, or the like, for easy moving CASTER
– upright sidepiece forming part of the back of a chair STILE

chairman of a meeting or synod MODERATOR
– chairman's hammer GAVEL

chalk ground for use in paint, polish, or putty WHITING
– chalky, containing or resembling calcium carbonate CALCAREOUS
– chalky crayon PASTEL
– process of becoming chalky or stony through the action of calcium salts CALCIFICATION

challenge, as to a duel THROW DOWN THE GAUNTLET
– challenge, criticise, attack as false IMPUGN
– challenge and rejection by the defendant, without having to give reasons, of certain proposed members of the jury in a criminal trial PEREMPTORY CHALLENGE
– challenge, or object such as a glove formerly thrown down to issue a challenge GAGE
– challenging problem or critical test for beginners PONS ASINORUM

chamber pot – chair containing a concealed chamber pot COMMODE
– empty one's chamber pot as a morning routine in prison SLOP OUT
– warning cry in former times, especially in Edinburgh, when emptying a chamber pot or other slops into the street GARDYLOO

Chamberlain – term given to Neville Chamberlain's policy of concessions to Hitler in the 1930s APPEASEMENT

champagne – sweetish rather than very dry, as a champagne might be SEC
– very dry, as a wine, especially champagne, might be BRUT

champion, leading supporter, as of a cult or doctrine GURU
– champion, supporter, upholder, as of a doctrine or cause ADVOCATE, PROPONENT

chance, accidental, occurring randomly CONTINGENT, ADVENTITIOUS, FORTUITOUS, HAPHAZARD
– chance, unexpected and unplanned, incidental or accidental UNPREMEDITATED, INADVERTENT
– chance of buying something such as a house before it is offered to others FIRST REFUSAL
– changes of fortune occurring by chance VICISSITUDES
– depending on or happening by chance or luck, random ARBITRARY, ALEATORY
– taking a chance, in the hope of success ON SPEC
– tendency to make fortunate finds by chance SERENDIPITY

chandelier, large and circular, hanging on a church ceiling CORONA
– chandelier, or any of its glass pendants LUSTRE
– chandelier illuminated with gas lights GASELIER

change, adjust, or tailor, as to improve or harmonise MODIFY, REGULATE
– change, convert, transform COMMUTE, MUTATE, TRANSMUTE
– change, vary, give variety to DIVERSIFY, VARIEGATE
– change in direction, attitude, policy, or results, as from bad to good TURNROUND, ABOUT-TURN, VOLTE-FACE, U-TURN
– change of mind on an impulse CAPRICE, WHIM
– change or adapt to new circumstances, accustom or accommodate

oneself to ACCLIMATISE, ORIENTATE
– change or adjust delicately, temper carefully, fine-tune MODULATE
– change or advance of a sudden, dramatic, and vast kind QUANTUM LEAP
– change or alter the tone or pitch of the voice INFLECT
– change or passing from one form or state to another TRANSITION
– change or reverse the ordering or relative position of two or more things TRANSPOSE
– change or swing, repeatedly or waveringly, from one state or action to another ALTERNATE, VACILLATE, FLUCTUATE, OSCILLATE
– change or switching of sounds or letters within a word, as in the development of *bird* from the earlier *brid* METATHESIS
– change or transformation of a spectacular kind TRANSFIGURATION, METAMORPHOSIS, TRANSMOGRIFICATION
– change or transformation of one substance into another, specifically of the Communion bread and wine into the body and blood of Christ TRANSUBSTANTIATION
– change or transition of an abrupt, discontinuous kind SALTATION
– change sides, defect, become a renegade TERGIVERSATE, APOSTATISE
– change slowly by degrees GRADUATE
– change that results in something new INNOVATION
– change the order or sequence of PERMUTE
– changes and development by slow or natural means, as of species, art, or social systems EVOLUTION
– changes in society, nature, or personal affairs VICISSITUDES
– constant change, instability FLUX
– not changing or ageing IMMUTABLE
– person or thing that provokes a change or event without itself being changed CATALYST
– relating to change or motion KINETIC
– sudden and violent disturbance, radical change UPHEAVAL
– sum of money used to provide change at the start of a business day FLOAT
– unprincipled person who changes his policies or opinions to serve his interests TRIMMER, TIMESERVER

-change- -TROP-, TROPO-, -TROPIC, -PLASIA, -PLASY

change of life, discontinuation of the menstrual cycle in women MENOPAUSE, CLIMACTERIC

changeable See **changing**

changeless, motionless, or producing no movement or change STATIC, IMMUTABLE

changes having been made as necessary MUTATIS MUTANDIS

changing, constantly altering, liable to change MUTABLE, LABILE
– changing, variable, shifting in shape, form, character, or mood PROTEAN
– changing constantly and rapidly, unpredictable QUICKSILVER, MERCURIAL, VOLATILE
– changing continually, disturbed, unstable TURBULENT, VERTIGINOUS
– changing course in speech or thought TANGENTIAL, DIGRESSIVE
– changing easily to new conditions, adaptable PLIABLE
– changing in colour, shimmering, as some fabrics do SHOT, IRIDESCENT, OPALESCENT, TAFFETA
– changing in lustre, twinkling, as a cat's eye or similar gemstone does CHATOYANT
– changing or inconsistent in affections or aims FICKLE
– changing or unpredictable in behaviour or attitude ERRATIC, SKITTISH, CAPRICIOUS, WHIMSICAL
– changing series or pattern of events KALEIDOSCOPE, CAVALCADE, CAROUSEL
– constant changing, unsteadiness, inconstancy LEVITY
– constantly changing or fickle person CHAMELEON

changing- TRANS-

changing money – fee or premium paid when changing money AGIO

channel, hollow, or cavity in the body, containing or conveying air, pus, blood, or the like SINUS
– channel, trench, or groove, as for drainpipes or electric wires CHASE
– channel connecting two large bodies of water STRAIT
– channel for excess water, as round the side of a dam SPILLWAY
– channel of a strong current of water RACE
– channel of very small size in the body, as in a bone CANALICULUS
– channel or bay extending inland from the sea, as to the mouth of a river ESTUARY, FIRTH, FIORD
– channel or ditch cut in the ground by rainwater or a stream GULLY
– channel or opening in the body MEATUS
– channel or pipe, as for rainwater or an electric cable CULVERT, CONDUIT
– channel or vessel in the body DUCT, VAS
– man-made water channel or chute, as for transporting logs FLUME
– relating to or containing channels for conveying blood, sap, or other biological fluids VASCULAR

chant of the medieval Church PLAINSONG
– chant or liturgical plainsong in the Roman Catholic Church GREGORIAN CHANT
– chant or recite in a half-musical tone INTONE, CANTILLATE
– chanting of ritual sounds or magic spells INCANTATION

chapel for seamen, or a Nonconformist chapel BETHEL
– chapel or altar built specially for prayers or Mass for the benefactor's soul CHANTRY

chaperone, especially an elderly woman DUENNA

chaplain or clergyman PADRE

character See also **personality**
– character, distinctive spirit, or value system of a particular culture, people, artistic movement, or the like ETHOS
– character or ability CALIBRE
– character or personality, characteristic thought or behaviour patterns of a person HUMOUR, DISPOSITION, TEMPERAMENT
– character written or printed slightly above another, as in ab^2 SUPERSCRIPT, SUPERIOR
– character written or printed slightly below another, as in H_2O SUBSCRIPT
– characters in a novel, play, or other literary work PERSONAE, DRAMATIS PERSONAE

characteristic, feature of personality TRAIT
– characteristic that makes up or compensates for faults or deficiencies, saving grace REDEEMING FEATURE, MITIGATING FACTOR
– characteristics, marks, or features of a very distinctive or important kind LINEAMENTS

charcoal grill of Japanese style, as used for cooking at table HIBACHI
– charcoal stick or drawing FUSAIN
– portable metal stand for burning coal or charcoal BRAZIER
– small brick of compressed charcoal or coal dust, used for fuel, as at barbecues BRIQUETTE

charge See also **accusation**
– charge formally with an offence or crime INDICT, ARRAIGN
– charge less than a rival in order

to secure a greater share of trade UNDERCUT
– additional charge or cost SURCHARGE
– clear of a charge or blame, declare innocent EXONERATE, EXCULPATE
– essential or most telling part of an accusation, charge, or complaint GRAVAMEN
– lay a charge against someone before a court PREFER
– obviously fabricated for base purposes, as a false charge or accusation might be TRUMPED-UP

charitable, concerned for others' welfare, humanitarian ALTRUISTIC, PHILANTHROPIC
– charitable, kindly, showing great goodwill BENEVOLENT, BENEFICENT
– charitable or generous in an ungrudging way BOUNTIFUL, MUNIFICENT
– charitable or religious gift or offering OBLATION, OFFERTORY

charity, Christian love, loving kindness, as distinct from erotic love AGAPE
– charity, small bribe, or tip, given in Eastern countries BAKSHEESH
– charity contribution, handout, or gift DONATION
– charity contribution that is small but considered generous WIDOW'S MITE
– charity or giving help, or a charitable gift BENEFACTION
– contribute or pledge a sum of money, as to a charity or for a telephone service SUBSCRIBE
– distributor of charity, alms giver, as on behalf of a church or royal household ALMONER
– formal agreement or pledge, as to pay a specified sum each year to a charity COVENANT
– person who receives charity, a favour, money from a will, or the like BENEFICIARY
– relating to charity ELEEMOSYNARY
– support a person or group undertaking a challenge on behalf of a charity SPONSOR

Charlemagne – relating to the life or times of Charlemagne or his Frankish dynasty CAROLINGIAN, CARLOVINGIAN

Charles – relating to the life or times of kings Charles I and II of England CAROLINE
– supporter of Charles I in the English Civil War CAVALIER, ROYALIST

charm, fetish, or amulet used in a West Indian form of witchcraft OBEAH, OBI
– charm, magic stone, or the like supposedly giving supernatural powers or protection TALISMAN, FETISH, JUJU
– charm, spell, or sorcerer in a Haitian religious cult VOODOO
– charm, win the confidence or affection of DISARM
– charm carried, usually around the neck, as a protection against evil or misfortune AMULET, PERIAPT
– charm or talisman in ancient Egypt in the form of a stone or earthenware beetle SCARAB
– charmed, spellbound ENRAPTURED, ENTRANCED, ENCHANTED, TRANSPORTED, RAVISHED
– charms, attractions, inducements, or appeal ALLURE, ENTICEMENTS, BLANDISHMENTS
– fixed formula of words recited as a prayer or charm PATERNOSTER
– magnetic personal charm and power of influence or inspiration CHARISMA
– strong personal charm and sensual attractiveness ANIMAL MAGNETISM

charming, fascinating, almost bewitching ALLURING, BEGUILING, CAPTIVATING
– charming in an insincere, overearnest way, currying favour UNCTUOUS, INGRATIATING
– charming or picturesque event or scene IDYLL
– charmingly simple and unsophisticated RUSTIC

chart or graph consisting of a series of bars whose lengths indicate quantities BAR GRAPH, BAR CHART
– chart or graph in the form of a circle with sectors of varying size representing the units PIE CHART

chatter, talk in an aimless, rambling, or incoherent manner PRATTLE, GIBBER, MAUNDER

cheap, priced at the manufacturer's bulk price, as distinct from retail WHOLESALE
– cheap and showy, and typically of poor quality, as imitation jewellery might be GAUDY, TAWDRY, BRUMMAGEM, GIMCRACK, CATCHPENNY
– cheap imitation, fake PINCHBECK
– cheaply sentimental MAUDLIN, MAWKISH

cheat, swindle, fleece, defraud COZEN, BEGUILE, BILK
– cheat, trick, dupe, or deceive HOODWINK, MULET, GULL, FLIMFLAM, GAMMON
– cheat by arranging playing cards secretly in a favourable order STACK
– cheat or betray by breaking an agreement DOUBLE-CROSS
– cheat or forgery, such as a counterfeit banknote STUMER
– cheat or trickster, con-man such as a quack MOUNTEBANK, CHARLATAN
– cheating, crafty scheming, or trickery JIGGERY-POKERY
– cheating or deception, especially the adoption of a false identity IMPOSTURE
– cheating or deception by trickery or lying DUPLICITY, CHICANERY
– achieve or acquire by trickery or cheating, wangle FINAGLE
– easily deceived, cheated, or duped CREDULOUS, GULLIBLE

check, keep tabs on, vet MONITOR
– check and confirm, prove correct or genuine VERIFY, VALIDATE, AUTHENTICATE, CORROBORATE, SUBSTANTIATE
– check off or tick off item by item TALLY
– check or stop a flow of blood or funds STANCH, STAUNCH
– checked pattern of coloured lines forming squares against a plain background TATTERSALL
– check shape or design on textiles HOUND'S-TOOTH CHECK

cheek of a rude or defiant kind, insolence, nerve GALL, EFFRONTERY, AUDACITY, TEMERITY
– cheek of a saucy, shameless, rather engaging kind, impudence CHUTZPAH

cheekbone JUGAL, MALAR, ZYGOMA, ZYGOMATIC BONE

cheeks or jaws JOWLS
– having rutted or hollow cheeks, as through exhaustion HAGGARD
– relating to the mouth or cheeks BUCCAL

cheeky, bold, saucy, sassy PERT, MALAPERT, IMPUDENT
– cheeky and uncooperative or unruly OBSTREPEROUS, STROPPY, BOLSHIE
– cheeky in an arrogant and disrespectful way PRESUMPTUOUS, BUMPTIOUS, INSOLENT
– cheeky in a defiant and contemptuous way BRAZEN
– cheeky or naughty child or young man JACKANAPES, WHELP

cheerful, confident, or optimistic SANGUINE
– cheerful and cosy, having a warm and friendly atmosphere GEMÜTLICH, CONGENIAL

cheese See chart, page 90
– cheese-like CASEOUS
– cheese puff GOUGÈRE
– coated with breadcrumbs and sometimes cheese, and then grilled

or browned, as cauliflower might be AU GRATIN
– container or frame used in cheesemaking CHESSEL
– dish of hot melted cheese and wine, eaten with pieces of bread or meat dipped into it FONDUE
– formation of cheese during the coagulation of milk CASEATION
– milk-protein that forms the basis of cheese CASEIN
– prepare, treat, or rectify something, such as cheese or photographic film, by a special method PROCESS
– stomach lining of calves, or an extract of it used in cheesemaking RENNET

chef of a very high standard or rank CORDON BLEU

chemical See chart of **chemistry terms**, pages 92-93
– chemical dissolving or wearing away, especially of metals CORROSION
– chemical secretion from glands, modifying the workings of a tissue or organ HORMONE
– burning or dissolving, as some chemicals are CAUSTIC, CORROSIVE

-chemical- -CHEM, CHEMO-

chemist temporarily replacing another LOCUM, LOCUM TENENS
– chemist who dispenses medical drugs PHARMACIST
– former term for a chemist or pharmacist APOTHECARY

chemistry See chart, pages 92-93
– misguided form of chemistry in the Middle Ages, seeking a cure-all medicine and a means of turning base metal into gold ALCHEMY

cheque or banknote that has been forged STUMER
– cheque stub or similar detachable record of a transaction, as on a receipt or postal order COUNTERFOIL
– date a cheque or other document earlier than the date of writing ANTEDATE
– date a cheque or other document later than the date of writing POSTDATE
– place one's signature on a document, the back of a cheque, or the like, as to indicate agreement, receipt, or transfer ENDORSE

chequered, mosaic-like TESSELLATED

cherry preserved in liqueur MARASCHINO CHERRY
– dark sour cherry MORELLO
– firm, sweet, heart-shaped cherry BIGARREAU
– pale sour cherry AMARELLE
– shiny sugar-coated cherry GLACÉ CHERRY
– sweet wild cherry GEAN, MAZZARD

cherry brandy KIRSCH

cherub or small boy in baroque paintings, sculptures, or reliefs PUTTO, AMORETTO

chess – drawn position in chess, in which any possible move by a player would place his king in check STALEMATE
– opening move or series of moves in chess, involving the sacrifice of a pawn or other piece for a positional advantage GAMBIT
– phrase used when touching a chesspiece to position it correctly rather than to make a move J'ADOUBE
– position in chess in which a player is forced to make a disadvantageous move ZUGZWANG
– referring to a chess piece exposed to capture EN PRISE
– winning position in chess, in which the opponent's king cannot escape CHECKMATE

chest, area of the body between the neck and abdomen THORAX
– crackling sound in the chest, as of pneumonia patients CREPITUS
– feeling of tightness or pressure, as in the chest CONSTRICTION
– relating to the chest or breast PECTORAL
– strongbox or chest, typically for storing valuables COFFER
– wooden trunk or chest, as for storing linen KIST

chest of drawers or low cabinet, typically on short legs and richly ornamented COMMODE

chestnuts preserved and coated in syrup MARRONS GLACÉS

chew, grind, or crush MASTICATE
– chew or munch impatiently or noisily CHAMP
– chew or nibble at repeatedly GNAW
– chew the cud RUMINATE
– chewing mixture in India, made

CHEESES

MEDIUM AND HARD CHEESE

British	Imported
Caerphilly	**Danbo** (Danish)
Cheddar	**Emmenthal** (Swiss)
Cheshire	**fetta/feta** (Greek)
Derby	**Gouda** (Dutch)
Double Gloucester	**Gruyère** (Swiss)
Dunlop	**Halumi** (Greek)
Lancashire	**Jarlsberg** (Norwegian)
Leicester	**Parmesan** (Italian)
Morven	**Pont l'Evêque** (French)
Orkney	**Port Salut** (French)
Wensleydale	**Saint Paulin** (French)
	Samsoe (Danish)
	Tilsit (German)

BLUE AND VEINED CHEESES

British	Imported
Blue Cheshire	**Bleu de Bresse** (French)
Red Windsor	**Danish blue** (Danish)

BLUE AND VEINED CHEESES *continued*

British	Imported
Sage Derby	**Dolce latte** (Italian)
Shropshire blue	**Gorgonzola** (Italian)
Stilton	**Roquefort** (French)

SOFT AND CREAM CHEESES

British	Imported
Caboc	**Bel paese** (Italian)
cottage cheese	**boursin/boursault** (French)
cream cheese	**Brie** (French)
Crowdie	**Camembert** (French)
curd cheese	**demi-sel** (French)
Limburger	**mozzarella** (Italian)
Lymeswold	**münster** (French)
	Petit Suisse (French)
	ricotta (Italian)
	vacherin (Swiss)

of betel nuts and leaves PAN
– chewing muscle MASSETER
– chewing tobacco in a wad QUID
– basic ingredient of chewing gum, gum from the sapodilla tree CHICLE

chewy and firm through being lightly cooked, as spaghetti might be AL DENTE

chick, young of a domestic fowl or related bird POULT

chicken See also **food**, **menu terms**
– chicken fat used in cooking SCHMALTZ
– chicken-rearing system involving confinement to cages for fast fattening or high production of eggs BATTERY
– chicken that is dressed, split open, and fried or grilled soon after slaughter SPATCHCOCK
– chicken's edible offal GIBLETS
– adjective for the domestic fowl or chicken GALLINACEOUS
– castrated male chicken fattened for eating CAPON
– disc of dark meat in the pelvic bone of a cooked chicken OYSTER
– tie up or skewer the wings or legs of a chicken or other fowl before cooking TRUSS
– very young chicken bred for eating POUSSIN

chickenpox VARICELLA

chickpea GARBANZO
– chickpea fritters or spicy delicacy of Middle Eastern origin FELAFEL
– chickpea paste, of Middle Eastern origin HUMMUS
– chickpeas, mung beans, or other seeds used for food in India GRAM

chief See **important**, **leader**, **main**
– chief, foremost, leading, supreme PARAMOUNT, PREDOMINANT, PRE-EMINENT, PREPONDERANT
– American Indian tribal chief SACHEM, SAGAMORE

chief- ARCH-

chief magistrate of a Scottish burgh PROVOST

child, especially a younger male child, in a family SCION
– child, grandchild, or more remote offspring DESCENDANT
– child, senile person, or the like under the legal protection of a guardian or court of law WARD
– child formerly thought to have been secretly exchanged for another by fairies CHANGELING
– child of unknown parentage, found abandoned FOUNDLING
– child or animal wandering about homeless WAIF
– child or baby, especially an Italian one BAMBINO
– child or worker who fails to achieve the results he is capable of UNDERACHIEVER
– child or young animal that is still unweaned SUCKLING
– child suffering from a mental illness involving a severe inability to relate to other people AUTISTIC CHILD
– child that is poor, dirty and ragged, or mischievous and cheeky URCHIN, RAGAMUFFIN
– child with exceptional powers or talents CHILD PRODIGY
– children and all the other descendants of a person POSTERITY, PROGENY, OFFSPRING
– bounce a child affectionately up and down, especially on one's knees DANDLE
– developing or maturing unusually early, as a clever or sophisticated child seems to do PRECOCIOUS
– guardianship, as of a minor child or a prisoner CUSTODY
– nursery for babies or very young children, especially to enable parents to go to work CRÈCHE
– produce children, reproduce PROCREATE
– producing many children PROLIFIC, PHILOPROGENITIVE
– referring to a child born after the death of the father POSTHUMOUS
– referring to a child in early adolescence, on the brink of sexual maturing PUBESCENT
– term used as an exemption or truce call, as in children's games PAX, SCRIBS, CREE, SKINCH, FAINS
– young child, youngster, young kid SHAVER, TYKE, NESTLING, NIPPER, SPROG

-child- -PAED-, PAEDO-

childbirth See also **birth**
– childbirth, act or process of giving birth PARTURITION
– blood and tissue discharged normally after childbirth AFTERBIRTH, SECUNDINES, LOCHIA
– custom in some cultures in which the husband too is put to bed while his wife is in labour or giving birth COUVADE
– hasten the onset of labour or childbirth, especially by the use of medicinal drugs INDUCE
– inducing contractions to bring on childbirth, as some drugs might OXYTOCIC
– occurring at or relating to the time just before or after birth PERINATAL
– relating to childbirth PUERPERAL
– relating to the care of women during pregnancy or after childbirth OBSTETRIC
– rest in bed for a woman just before or during childbirth CONFINEMENT, LYING-IN, ACCOUCHEMENT
– shortening or tensing of a muscle or organ, either voluntary or, as in childbirth, involuntary CONTRACTION
– toxic condition in a woman, involving convulsions and sometimes coma, shortly before childbirth ECLAMPSIA

-childbirth -PAROUS

childhood years important in one's development FORMATIVE YEARS

childish or immature, especially in being silly or impulsive PUERILE, JUVENILE, JEJUNE

chill or shivering attack, as preceding a fever RIGOR

chimney or similar opening for the escape of fumes, steam, or the like VENT
– hood-like cover on a chimney to control ventilation COWL, BONNET
– pipe or duct for hot air, smoke, or the like, as in a boiler or chimney FLUE
– sloping surround, as of cement, for draining away water from a chimney, or the like FLANCH

chin divided into two sides by a vertical indentation CLEFT CHIN
– chin that is squarish and jutting LANTERN JAW
– adjective for the chin GENIAL, MENTAL
– having a prominent chin because of a jutting jaw PROGNATHOUS
– having correctly positioned jaws, so that the chin is neither receding nor protruding ORTHOGNATHOUS

china See also **pottery**
– deliberate network of fine cracks in the glaze of a piece of pottery or china CRACKLING
– having a traditional blue-on-white pictorial design, as a china plate might WILLOW-PATTERN

China – ancient or poetic name for China CATHAY
– study of the language, culture, and history of China SINOLOGY

Chinese See also **menu terms**
– Chinese, Japanese, or person from any of various other East Asian countries ORIENTAL
– Chinese, the official national form of the language MANDARIN, GUOYU
– Chinese empire CELESTIAL EMPIRE
– Chinese form of exercise and mental training in which balletic body movements are performed slowly and deliberately TAI CHI

– Chinese gambling game based on guessing the number of counters, beans or coins hidden under a bowl FAN-TAN
– Chinese idol JOSS
– Chinese or Japanese figurine, usually in a grotesque, crouched position MAGOT
– Chinese or other language that distinguishes words by their pitch or by their intonation TONE LANGUAGE
– Chinese place of worship JOSS HOUSE
– Chinese public official, in imperial times MANDARIN
– Chinese puzzle consisting of a set of simple shapes for reassembling into different figures TANGRAM
– Chinese-style bow of former times, touching the ground with one's forehead KOWTOW
– Chinese-style pottery, ornaments, and decorative design generally CHINOISERIE
– Chinese-style therapy in which needles are inserted into the skin or body at given points ACUPUNCTURE
– Chinese symbol or character that represents a thing or idea rather than indicating its sound IDEOGRAM
– Chinese writing system, or other writing system resembling it, in which each word is represented by a single character or symbol LEXIGRAPHY
– active male force or principle in traditional Chinese philosophy YANG
– basic symbol or character, in Chinese or a similar writing system, that conveys a full meaning RADICAL
– bowl-shaped metal pan, as used in Chinese cooking for frying and the like WOK
– game of Chinese origin, played with small tiles bearing varied designs MAH-JONG
– passive female force or principle in traditional Chinese philosophy YIN
– pronunciation of the sound /r/ as /l/, as by Chinese people speaking English LALLATION
– strong colourless Chinese alcoholic drink distilled from grain MAO-TAI
– suit consisting of a loose jacket and trousers, as worn by Chinese women SAMFOO
– system of transcribing Chinese in the Roman alphabet PINYIN,

CHEMISTRY TERMS

alkali	soluble base, able to neutralise acids
allotrope	any of the different physical forms that an element may take, such as diamond and graphite in the case of carbon
amphoteric, amphiprotic	able to react as both an acid and a base
atomic number	number of protons in the atomic nucleus of an element
azeotropic mixture	mixture of liquids that cannot be separated by distillation
base	compound that reacts with an acid to form a salt
catalyst	substance that affects or speeds up a chemical reaction without itself being changed
chemical bond	force that holds atoms or ions together
colloid	mixture or suspension of very fine particles within a fluid, as with fog or paint
dopant	impurity added to a pure substance, such as a semiconductor, to alter its properties
efflorescence	process by which crystals are turned to powder by the loss of water
electrolysis	decomposition of a chemical compound by passing an electric current through it
electron	negatively charged particle orbiting the atomic nucleus
enzyme	protein of a kind produced by living cells and functioning as a biochemical catalyst
ester	organic compound, such as a fat, derived from the reaction of an acid with an alcohol
fractionation	separation of a mixture into its components on the basis of their different boiling points or different solubilities
halogen	any one of five non-metallic elements — fluorine, chlorine, bromine, iodine, and astatine
hydrocarbon	organic compound of hydrogen and carbon, such as benzene
hydrolysis	decomposition of a chemical compound by reaction with water
inert	chemically inactive, fully or almost fully unreactive, as some elements are
inhibitor	substance that slows down or stops a chemical reaction
inorganic	referring or relating to non-carbon compounds
ion	electrically charged atom, radical, or molecule
isomer	compound having the same elements and number of atoms as another, but with a different arrangement of the atoms and hence different properties
isotope	atom having the same number of protons in its nucleus as another atom of the same element, but a different number of neutrons

YALE, WADE-GILES, POSTAL
 – tight dress of Chinese design, with a slit skirt and high collar CHEONGSAM

Chinese- SINO-

Chinese restaurants – flavour-enhancer, as used in Chinese restaurants MONOSODIUM GLUTAMATE, MSG

chip See also **microchip**
 – chip, splinter, or break stone, especially with a hammer SPALL
 – chip or counter used in gambling JETTON

chirp – shrill grating chirp produced by a cricket or grasshopper STRIDULATION

chisel used for rough dressing of stone DROVE
 – handle of a chisel HELVE
 – shape or dress stone roughly with a broad chisel BOAST
 – sloping surface leading to the tip or cutting edge of a chisel, screwdriver, or other tool BEZEL

chivalrous man CHEVALIER
 – chivalrously and excessively idealistic, and hence impractical or absentminded QUIXOTIC

chocolate – chocolate-like substance or flavouring, made from an edible pod CAROB
 – chocolate strands used for sprinkling on cakes or desserts VERMICELLI

choice, act or instance of choosing OPTION
 – choice that is apparent rather than real, since there is no alternative HOBSON'S CHOICE
 – arising from or relating to free choice or a choice of one's own free will VOLUNTARY
 – optional, open to choice, as a course of study is ELECTIVE
 – power of choice, deliberate decision VOLITION
 – range of choices so wide as to make a decision very difficult EMBARRAS DE RICHESSES
 – right to act, or judge, power of choice DISCRETION
 – situation requiring a choice to be made between two equal and typically undesirable alternatives DILEMMA

choir, orchestra, or music society PHILHARMONIC
 – choir gallery LOFT
 – choir-leader, especially in ancient Athens CHORAGUS
 – choir-leader, lead singer, or soloist in a church or synagogue CANTOR, PRECENTOR
 – choir of four unaccompanied male voices BARBERSHOP QUARTET

latent heat	heat absorbed or released by a substance undergoing a change of state, as from ice to water	**radical**	atom or group of atoms with one or more unpaired electrons, acting as a unit in a compound
litmus paper	dyed paper that is turned red by acids but that remains, or reverts, to blue when treated with alkalis	**reagent**	substance used in analysing, measuring, or synthesising other substances in a chemical reaction
mass number	total number of protons and neutrons in the nucleus of an atom	**rectify**	refine, purify, or separate by means of distillation
molecule	group of atoms together as a stable entity	**reduction**	removal of oxygen from a compound or adding of hydrogen to it; reaction in which atoms, molecules, or the like gain electrons
noble gas	gas such as helium or neon that is almost inert or unreactive	**structural formula**	chemical formula detailing the arrangement of atoms and bonds within the molecule
neutron	electrically neutral particle in the atomic nucleus	**suspension**	mixture of undissolved particles within a fluid, as with muddy water
organic	referring or relating to carbon compounds	**syneresis**	slow release of the liquid from a gel, as in cheesemaking
osmosis	gradual passage of water or other solvent through a semi-permeable membrane until there is an equal concentration of solutions on either side	**synthesis**	chemical reaction in which a compound is built up from simpler units
oxidation	adding of oxygen to a compound or removal of hydrogen from it; reaction in which atoms, molecules, or the like gain electrons	**systematic name**	name of a chemical compound that conveys details of its atomic structure
periodic table	table of the chemical elements, grouping them in columns according to their properties	**titration**	procedure for determining the concentration of a solution by adding a standard reagent
polymer	compound, such as starch or polyethylene, formed of chains of repeated units of molecules	**trivial name**	common name for a chemical compound, giving no information about its components
proton	positively charged particle in the atomic nucleus	**valency**	power of an atom or group of atoms to combine with other atoms, represented by a number

– choir or chorus CHORALE
– choir or orchestra leader, as in 18th-century Germany KAPELLMEISTER
– choirboy or choir singer CHORISTER
– ledge on a choir-stall seat to lean against while standing MISERICORD
– procession of the choir and clergy out of the chancel at the end of a church service RECESSION
– situated on the north side of the choir in a church CANTORIAL
– small choir typically performing short light songs GLEE CLUB
– without instrumental accompaniment, as some choir music is A CAPPELLA

choke, gasp for breath GAG
– choke or strangle THROTTLE, ASPHYXIATE

choose as one's preference, single out, favour ELECT, PLUMP FOR
– choose between, distinguish, differentiate DISCRIMINATE
– choose from an assortment, pick out, select CULL
– choosing or chosen from a range of different sources ECLECTIC
– choosing or sorting by quality or to allocate scarce resources TRIAGE

chop – frilly paper covering adorning the end of a chop or cutlet PAPILLOTE, FRILL

chord played note by note in quick succession rather than simultaneously ARPEGGIO
– lowest note of a chord FUNDAMENTAL

chortle or similar word formed by fusing elements from two separate words PORTMANTEAU WORD, BLEND

chorus of a song or musical composition REFRAIN, BURDEN

chosen, optional, open to choice, as a course of study is ELECTIVE
– chosen freely rather than required or compelled VOLUNTARY
– chosen or choosing from a range of different sources ECLECTIC

Christ See **Jesus**
– Christ's salvation of man from sin REDEMPTION, DELIVERANCE

Christian See **clergymen**, **religion**
– Christian creed or profession of faith widely used in churches ATHENASIAN CREED, NICENE CREED
– Christian evangeliser full of enthusiasm HOT-GOSPELLER
– Christian group having doctrines and rites in common DENOMINATION, COMMUNION, CONFESSION
– Christian love, charity, loving kindness, as distinct from erotic love AGAPE
– Christian reform movement in 16th-century Europe that led to the emergence of the Protestant churches REFORMATION
– Christian sacrament commemorating the Last Supper by the consecration of bread and wine COMMUNION, EUCHARIST
– Christian studies THEOLOGY
– referring or relating to a person who has undergone a conversion to fervent Christianity BORN-AGAIN
– sacred Christian act, such as baptism, symbolising a spiritual reality and conferring grace SACRAMENT
– unintelligible ecstatic speech, as in some evangelical Christian services GLOSSOLALIA, GIFT OF TONGUES

Christian era or A.D. as referred to by non-Christians COMMON ERA, C.E.

Christianity, Judaism, Islam, or other religion based on belief in a single God MONOTHEISM
– formal statement of religious beliefs, confession of faith, especially in Christianity CREED
– question-and-answer examinations or instruction-book, particularly one on the basic principles of Christianity CATECHISM

Christmas buskers or carol-singers WAITS
– Christmas festival or season YULE, NATIVITY, NOËL

church See illustration, and also **altar**, **canonical hours**, **Communion**, **clergymen**, **Christian**, **prayer**
– church assembly, especially when illegal and held in secret CONVENTICLE
– church authority's release of someone from a vow or rule, or the document certifying it DISPENSATION
– church caretaker, often acting as bellringer and gravedigger as well SEXTON
– church conference or assembly of churchmen SYNOD, CONVOCATION
– church court or governing body, or a meeting of it CONSISTORY
– church endowment or estate of long standing PATRIMONY
– church land, typically granted to a clergyman as part of his benefice GLEBE
– church law or code of laws CANON
– church meeting of the parish committee or congregants VESTRY
– church of a monastery MINSTER
– church of any of various kinds, having more than one clergyman COLLEGIATE CHURCH
– church office or department dealing with legal matters, church records, and archives CHANCERY
– church officer in charge of the sacred vessels, vestments, and the like SACRISTAN
– church official in former times, with caretaking and ushering duties BEADLE
– church or cathedral used for special ceremonies among Roman Catholics BASILICA
– church or group having doctrines and rites in common DENOMINATION, COMMUNION, CONFESSION
– church or other place affording protection or refuge SANCTUARY
– church or place of prayer, especially a chapel in an institution or private home ORATORY
– church position, office, or job, together with its income LIVING, BENEFICE
– church position requiring little or no actual work in the parish SINECURE
– church service in the late afternoon or evening VESPERS
– church serving those living too far from the parish church CHAPEL OF EASE
– church surroundings or grounds, enclosed by a wall or other boundary PRECINCT
– church usher and attendant VERGER
– aisle around the east end of a church AMBULATORY
– alignment of a church so that the main altar is at the eastern end ORIENTATION
– anthem, biblical passage, or the like recited or sung as a response during a church service ANTIPHON
– any of various traditional, especially Eastern, Churches ORTHODOX CHURCH
– any place of worship that is not referred to as a church TABERNACLE
– area in a church where the nave and transept intersect CROSSING
– baptism, Communion, or sometimes any of various other church rites SACRAMENT
– basin set in the wall of a church for draining away the water used in ceremonial washing PISCINA, SACRARIUM
– bell tower detached from the main church building CAMPANILE
– calling on God's blessing, as at the end of a church service BENEDICTION
– candle lit by a worshipper and placed before a shrine or statue in

a church VIGIL LIGHT
– ceremonial garments worn by those officiating or assisting at a church service or rite VESTMENTS
– ceremony during a church service in which the priest washes his hands LAVABO
– chapel or porch at the entrance of a medieval church GALILEE
– chapel within a church, dedicated to the Virgin Mary LADY CHAPEL
– clergyman's salary or allowance paid by his church PREBEND
– corrupt buying and selling of church offices, relics, pardons, and the like SIMONY
– courtyard or colonnade in front of a church, palace or Roman house PARVIS, ATRIUM
– cut off from membership of a church or religion EXCOMMUNICATE
– desk at which the litany is recited in an Anglican church FALDSTOOL
– entrance hall at the west end of a church NARTHEX
– form of church service or public worship as officially prescribed LITURGY
– form or system of public worship in a church service LITURGY
– gallery forming an upper storey of a church, as above the aisles TRIFORIUM
– governing body of elders and pastors in some Reformed churches CLASSIS
– grotesque stone figure, as on the roof of a Gothic church, often serving as a waterspout from a gutter GARGOYLE
– ledge on a church-stall seat to lean against while standing MISERICORD, MISERERE
– make or declare something sacred, such as a church DEDICATE, CONSECRATE, SANCTIFY
– make something, such as a church, unfit for religious or ceremonial use, as by blasphemy or vandalism PROFANE, DESECRATE, DEFILE
– narrow spire, usually of wood, as on a church roof FLÈCHE
– non-compliance with the doctrines of an established church NONCONFORMITY, DISSENT
– ordinary members of a church, as distinct from the clergy LAITY, LAYMEN, LAY PEOPLE
– part of a church tower or steeple

church

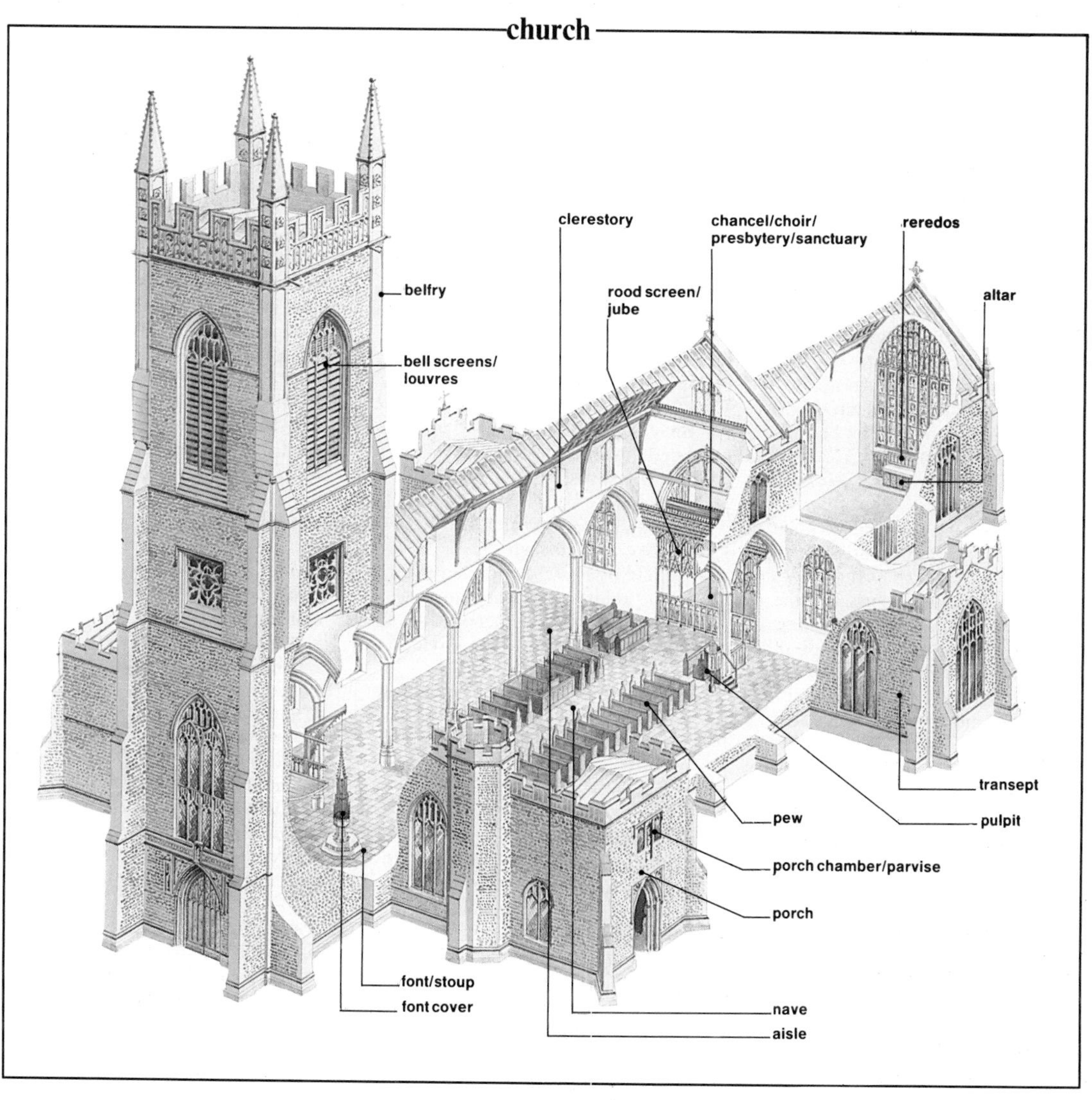

in which the bells are hung BELFRY
– platform or gallery in a church TRIBUNE
– prayer stool or kneeling bench in a church, with a shelf for elbows or books PRIE-DIEU
– procession of the choir and clergy out of the chancel at the end of a church service RECESSION
– promoting or relating to unity among the world's various churches ECUMENICAL
– rail or screen in a church, as for sectioning off a chapel PARCLOSE
– reading desk, as in a church for readings from the Bible LECTERN
– recess in the wall of a church, as for storing Communion vessels AMBRY, FENESTELLA
– relating to the church ECCLESIASTICAL
– room or annexe in a church where the sacred objects and vestments are stored SACRISTY, VESTRY, SACRARIUM
– rule or custom, as for the conducting of a church ceremony RUBRIC
– semicircular projecting side of a church, usually vaulted, typically at the east end APSE, CHEVET
– situated on the north side of the choir in a church CANTORIAL
– situated on the south side of the choir in a church DECANAL
– splitting into opposing factions, as within a church SCHISM
– spoiling or destruction of the sacred quality of a church, graveyard, or the like, as by blasphemy or vandalism DESECRATION, PROFANATION, VIOLATION, SACRILEGE, DEFILEMENT
– study of the lives and writings of the fathers of the early Christian church PATRISTICS, PATROLOGY
– tenth of one's yearly income or production donated as a tax or voluntarily to the church or other good cause TITHE
– underground chamber, such as a church vault CRYPT, UNDERCROFT
– unvarying parts of the Mass or church service ORDINARY, COMMON
– varying parts of the Mass or church service, according to the time, day, or feast PROPER
– verse or phrase, to be followed by the response, sung or recited by the leader of a church service VERSICLE
– verse or phrase sung or recited by the choir or congregation as a reply to the leader during a church service RESPONSE
– vow of faith and support by members of a church COVENANT

churchwarden – churchwarden's assistant, especially the person who takes the collection SIDESMAN

churchyard – churchyard's roofed gate, where the coffin is traditionally rested at the start of the burial service LICH GATE

-cide See **kill**

cider of a strong, rough brew, typically from south-west England SCRUMPY

cigar, typically with both ends cut square CHEROOT
– cigar case in which the humidity can be kept constant HUMIDOR
– cheap thin cigar STOGY
– dark strong cigar MADURO
– large, high-quality Cuban cigar HAVANA
– large cigar tapered at both ends PERFECTO
– long tapering cigar with blunt ends CORONA
– long thin cigar PANATELLA
– tobacco leaf around a cigar WRAPPER

cigarette of Indian origin, consisting of a rolled leaf secured with thread BEEDI
– breathe in cigarette or other tobacco smoke INHALE
– peppermint-flavoured, as some cigarettes are MENTHOLATED

cinema of an early kind in the U.S., charging five cents for admission NICKELODEON
– film library or repertory cinema CINEMATHEQUE
– toy producing simple cinematic images, consisting of a picture-lined cylinder revolving past a viewing slit ZOETROPE

cinema- CINE-

cinnamon stick QUILL

circle See also **geometry**
– circle of stone or wooden pillars, from prehistoric cultures HENGE
– circle rolling, either inside or outside, round a larger circle EPICYCLE
– circle round a point or axis, spin GYRATE
– circles, typically overlapping, used as a diagram representing mathematical or logical relations VENN DIAGRAM
– boundary line of an enclosed figure, especially a circle, or the length of it CIRCUMFERENCE
– draw a line, especially an arc or circle DESCRIBE
– draw a line or circle round CIRCUMSCRIBE
– having a common centre, as two circles of different size might CONCENTRIC
– having different centres, as two overlapping circles would ECCENTRIC
– imaginary half-circle joining the poles on the Earth's surface MERIDIAN
– shaped like a flattened or elongated circle ELLIPTICAL

circle- CYCL-, CYCLO-

circuit – electronic circuit formed on a microchip INTEGRATED CIRCUIT

circular band, as around the base of a tooth CINGULUM
– circular or ring-shaped figure, space, marking, part, or object ANNULUS
– circular design symbolising the universe, in Hindu and Buddhist art MANDALA
– circular painting, cameo, or medallion TONDO
– circular wall, especially one supporting a dome TAMBOUR

circular- GYRO-

circumference, as of a person's waist or a tree GIRTH

circumstances serving to make a crime, fault, or the like less serious or blameworthy EXTENUATING CIRCUMSTANCES, MITIGATING CIRCUMSTANCES

circus bar suspended from free-swinging ropes TRAPEZE
– circus horseback performer EQUESTRIAN, EQUESTRIENNE

citadel in ancient Greece ACROPOLIS

citizen, especially a middle-class citizen of a town in the Middle Ages BURGHER
– right of citizens to petition for a new law and get it voted on by the electorate INITIATIVE
– study of a citizen's rights and duties CIVICS

citizenship – foreigner having certain citizenship rights in his country of residence DENIZEN
– give voting rights or full citizenship rights to ENFRANCHISE
– grant citizenship to NATURALISE
– person having nationality, residence, or citizenship rights in the U.K., especially by virtue of a parent or grandparent born there PATRIAL

city See also **town**
– city, especially the chief city of a region METROPOLIS
– city, town, or other self-governing community MUNICIPALITY
– city area, inhabited by a poor or restricted minority group GHETTO
– city area, often closed to traffic, set apart for pedestrians and shopping PRECINCT
– city authorities CORPORATION
– city of vast extent, group of

towns fused into a single urban complex MEGALOPOLIS, CONURBATION
– city's electoral district, administrative division, or the like WARD
– adjective for a city CIVIC, MUNICIPAL, URBAN
– fortress or stronghold protecting a town or city CITADEL
– name of a city or other place used in a foreign language, such as *Florence* for *Firenze* EXONYM
– suburb or quarter of a city, especially a French-speaking city FAUBOURG

City of London trade association or guild LIVERY COMPANY

city-state in ancient Greece POLIS

civil servant of high rank and believed to have great political influence MANDARIN
– civil-service establishment in Britain WHITEHALL

civil war – mutually destructive or fatal, as civil war is INTERNECINE

civilian clothes, as distinct from military or other uniform MUFTI, CIVVIES

civilisation – relating to the civilisation of ancient Greece and Rome, or ancient China, or the like CLASSICAL

claim, usually false or unproven, to some right, title, skill, or the like PRETENSION
– claim as one's own without any right to do so APPROPRIATE, ARROGATE
– claim or appear to be or do something PURPORT, PROFESS
– claim or declare, typically without proving, merely state or maintain ALLEGE
– claim or declare, confidently or forcefully AFFIRM, ASSERT, AVER, AVOUCH, AVOW
– claim or declare, formally or earnestly ASSEVERATE
– claim or declare, to be true or existing, assume or put forward, as for the state of argument POSTULATE, PREMISE
– claim or declare, to belong to or be characteristic of someone or something PREDICATE
– disprove, weaken, or make ineffective an argument, claim, or the like INVALIDATE
– give up a claim or right voluntarily WAIVE, RELINQUISH
– having priority over, as one claim might have over another UNDERLIE
– reject or deny a claim or accusation REPUDIATE

clairvoyance – perception by means of a sixth sense, clairvoyance, telepathy, intuition, or the like EXTRASENSORY PERCEPTION, ESP, CRYPTAESTHESIA

clamp or vice used to hold a tool or workpiece, as in a drill or lathe CHUCK
– bent metal bar clamping stones or timber together, as in a wall CRAMP IRON, AGRAFFE

clan – group of related clans within a tribe PHRATRY

clarify a remark, idea, or the like by adding details AMPLIFY

clarinet – metal band securing the reed to the mouthpiece of a clarinet or saxophone LIGATURE

clasp or fastener hinged over a fixed staple, and typically secured with a padlock HASP

class given by a teacher to an individual student or a very small number of students TUTORIAL
– class in British schools, intermediate between two regular classes REMOVE
– class in school, specially designed for slow learners REMEDIAL CLASS
– class of manual labourers or industrial wage-earners, the working class generally PROLETARIAT
– class or category of art, films, or the like GENRE
– class-ridden, divided according to castes, classes, or the like, as a nation or society might be STRATIFIED
– class within society, especially any of the four major social divisions among Hindus CASTE
– alienated from one's social class, uprooted LUMPEN
– belonging to a higher or larger class or level of generality, as opposed to subordinate SUPERORDINATE
– level, such as a class or caste, within a society or series STRATUM
– title of a category or class RUBRIC

classically elegant in style, as poetry or drama might be AUGUSTAN

classification See chart
– classification, especially of plants and animals TAXONOMY
– classification, separation into groups or categories DISTRIBUTION
– classification according to rank or importance HIERARCHY
– classification of diseases NOSOLOGY
– classification of plants and animals in groups according to shared ancestry CLADISTICS
– classification or name of a group DENOMINATION, DESIGNATION
– classification system, such as the standard system of names for plants or chemicals NOMENCLATURE
– classification system for animals or plants using two Latin names indicating the genus and then the species BINOMIAL NOMENCLATURE, LINNAEAN NOMENCLATURE
– classification system such as a scale or series, or a step or stage within it GRADATION
– relating to a whole group, such as a genus in biological classification GENERIC
– species name as opposed to genus name in biological classification TRIVIAL NAME, SPECIFIC EPITHET

CLASSIFICATION

The main categories into which living things are divided, from the broadest to the most detailed

kingdom
phylum, division
class
order
(superfamily, stirps)
family
genus
species
(subspecies, stirps, variety, race, stock, strain, breed)
individual

classify, assign to a group or class CATEGORISE, PIGEONHOLE
– classify or include in a wider category or under a general heading or principle SUBSUME
– classify systematically DIGEST, CODIFY, CATALOGUE

clause, amendment, or qualification added to a legal document, verdict, parliamentary bill, or the like RIDER
– clause of equal status or parallel structure to another in a sentence, as distinct from a subordinate clause COORDINATE CLAUSE
– linking of phrases or clauses by means of punctuation rather than conjunctions PARATAXIS
– referring to a subordinate clause within a sentence EMBEDDED
– subordination of a clause in grammar, typically by means of a conjunction HYPOTAXIS

claw, nail, hoof, or similar part UNGUIS
– claw of a bird of prey TALON, POUNCE
– claw of a lobster, crab, scorpion, or the like PINCER, CHELA

clay, or a sun-dried brick made from

it, as in Mexico ADOBE
– clay as used in pottery ARGIL
– clay or brown earthy substance used as a pigment UMBER, SIENNA, BOLE
– clay used in filtering and decolouring FULLER'S EARTH
– brownish-red clay, or the pottery it is used to make TERRACOTTA
– china clay, used in ceramics and as a coating for paper KAOLIN, TERRA ALBA
– material made by firing clay or a similar substance, or an object made of such material CERAMIC
– moist clay used in making pottery or porcelain PASTE, PÂTE
– potter's wooden spatula used for mixing or moulding clay PALLET
– rock particles finer than sand but coarser than clay SILT
– stiff whitish English clay CLUNCH
– thinned clay used by a potter for coating or decorating SLIP

clay-pigeon shooting TRAPSHOOTING
– clay-pigeon shooting in which the targets are thrown at varying speeds and angles from traps on either side of the range SKEET

clean, thoroughly hygienic, free of all germs and infection SANITARY, SANITISED, DISINFECTED, ANTISEPTIC
– clean, repair, and restore something, such as a house REFURBISH
– cleaning or smoothing substance that scours and scrapes, such as pumice or emery ABRASIVE
– perfectly clean and pure, spotless and uncorrupted IMMACULATE, UNBLEMISHED, PRISTINE

clean slate, fresh start, need or chance to start again from scratch TABULA RASA

cleansing or purging, as of the digestive system CATHARTIC
– cleansing or scouring, as a cleaning powder might be ABSTERGENT
– chemical based cleansing substance as used for industrial and household cleaning DETERGENT

clear, as water or a literary style might be LIMPID
– clear, forceful, and crisp, as a remark might be INCISIVE, TRENCHANT, COGENT
– clear, fully expressed, as directions might be EXPLICIT
– clear, obvious, plain to see EVIDENT, PATENT, PALPABLE, MANIFEST
– clear, plain, unambiguous, not open to doubt UNEQUIVOCAL
– clear, transparent CRYSTALLINE, DIAPHANOUS
– clear and unavoidable, as destiny might be MANIFEST
– clear of a charge or blame, declare innocent ACQUIT, EXONERATE, EXCULPATE, ABSOLVE, VINDICATE
– clear or conclusive, beyond dispute, as a clear-cut victory is DECISIVE
– clear the throat loudly HAWK
– clearly, especially, extremely SIGNALLY, CONSPICUOUSLY
– clearly described in vivid or exciting detail GRAPHIC
– clearly expressed, easily understandable LUCID, LUMINOUS, PELLUCID, PERSPICUOUS
– clearness CLARITY
– make clear or comprehensible CLARIFY, ELUCIDATE
– make clear, remove the ambiguity from, clarify DISAMBIGUATE

clear-cut, well-defined, distinct, as a difference between two options might be TRENCHANT

clearing or open space in a wood or forest GLADE

clergy See also **church**
– belonging to the congregation or general public as opposed to the clergy, as a preacher might be LAY, SECULAR
– ordinary members of a church, as distinct from the clergy LAITY, LAYMEN, LAY PEOPLE
– organisation or grading according to rank or importance, as among the clergy HIERARCHY
– relating to clergymen or clergywomen CLERICAL

clergyman See chart, and also **church**, **priest**, and illustration of **clerical clothing**
– clergyman, priest ECCLESIASTIC
– clergyman holding a particular post INCUMBENT
– clergyman temporarily replacing the regular clergyman LOCUM, LOCUM TENENS
– clergyman who visits condemned convicts in the death cell ORDINARY

CLERGYMEN

archdeacon	clergyman with administrative responsibilities within a diocese
canon	member of a cathedral chapter
chancellor	priest serving as a bishop, legal officer or business manager
chaplain	clergyman who serves an individual or an institution, ship, regiment, college, or the like
curate	assistant to a parish priest
deacon	clergyman in the lowest stage of ordination, unqualified to perform certain sacraments
dean	cathedral administrator and head of the chapter of canons
metropolitan	bishop with authority over several dioceses; an archbishop or primate
padre	military chaplain
prebendary	canon, formerly having an endowed stipend
precentor	clergyman who directs choral services in a cathedral
prelate	high-ranking official such as a bishop or cardinal
primate	chief bishop or archbishop
prior	deputy head of a monastery, ranking below the abbot; head of any of various other religious communities
proctor	elected representative of the Anglican clergy in Convocation and the General Synod
provost	senior official in a cathedral of recent foundation
rural dean	clergyman with authority over a group of parishes
suffragan	assistant bishop in a diocese; bishop in relation to his archbishop

– clergyman's acceptance into the ministry, or the ceremony of admission ORDINATION
– clergyman's house, especially in Scotland MANSE
– clergyman's permission from the bishop to leave the diocese to work elsewhere EXEAT
– clergyman's privilege in the Middle Ages to be tried by a church court rather than a secular court BENEFIT OF CLERGY
– clergyman's salary or allowance, paid by his church PREBEND, STIPEND
– appoint a clergyman to a benefice COLLATE
– authorise to be a clergyman, invest into holy orders ORDAIN
– right to nominate a clergyman to a benefice PATRONAGE
– strip a clergyman of his status and rights in the church DEFROCK, UNFROCK
– theological school, especially as a training school for clergymen SEMINARY
– white neck-tabs on a clergyman's robes GENEVA BANDS

clerical clothing See illustration

clerk or official secretary SCRIBE, AMANUENSIS
– clerk or secretary in former times, especially one licensed to draft legal documents NOTARY

clever See also **skilful**, **sophisticated**
– clever, insightful, showing sensitive understanding or keen critical powers PERCEPTIVE, DISCERNING, PERCIPIENT, PENETRATING, PERSPICACIOUS
– clever, intelligent, quick at learning or at grasping new ideas RECEPTIVE, APT, GLEG
– clever, tactful, and usually cautious, as in dealings with others PRUDENT, POLITIC, JUDICIOUS
– clever, wise, showing sound judgment SAPIENT, SAGACIOUS
– clever and witty person, displaying a fine mind BEL ESPRIT
– clever in an inventive or cunning way INGENIOUS
– clever or capable in practical things, especially in difficult circumstances RESOURCEFUL
– clever or extremely successful person of very young age WHIZZ KID, WUNDERKIND, CHILD PRODIGY
– clever or shrewd, showing cunning and insight ASTUTE, CANNY
– clever or sophisticated beyond his years, as an advanced child seems to be PRECOCIOUS
– clever remark, witty saying BON MOT
– cleverness, insight, or good judgment ACUMEN
– cleverness, practical shrewdness, common sense GUMPTION
– cleverness of an imaginative or inventive kind INGENUITY

clever dick, wise guy WISEACRE

cliché, unoriginal and predictable remark, phrase, or thought PLATITUDE, COMMONPLACE, BROMIDE
– clichéd, unoriginal and overused, threadbare and uninspiring HACKNEYED, TRITE, BANAL, SHOPWORN
– clichéd and widespread saying or belief SHIBBOLETH
– clichéd moral lesson, sermon, or proverb HOMILY
– clichéd statement of an obvious truth TRUISM
– clichéd, especially pious formulas or the mindless repetition of them CANT
– pompous, moralising, and typically cliché-ridden SENTENTIOUS

clicking wooden shells operated in the hand, as by Spanish dancers, in time to the music CASTANETS

cliff, steep river bank, headland, or the like BLUFF
– cliff or cliff face, or peak of rock CRAG, PRECIPICE, SCAR
– cliff or high stretch of land above the sea HEADLAND, PROMONTORY
– cliff or steep slope, typically resulting from erosion or faulting ESCARPMENT
– cliffs in a line, as overlooking a river PALISADES
– descend, as from a cliff top or helicopter, by means of a supporting rope around one's body ABSEIL
– rock debris at the foot of a cliff TALUS

clerical clothing

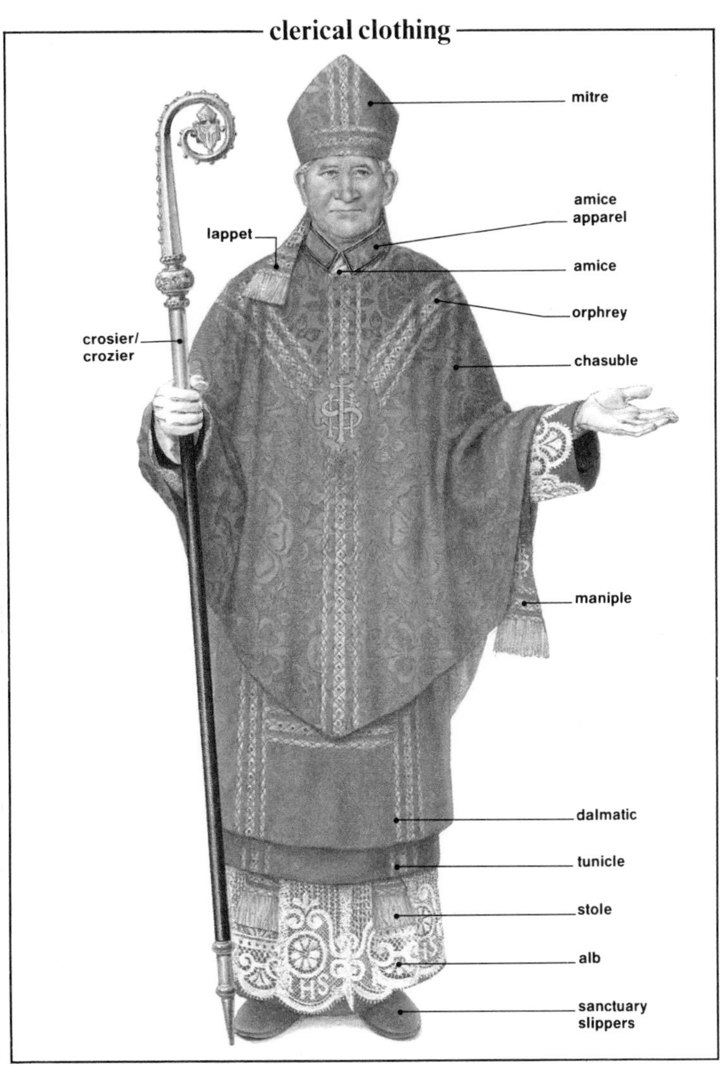

climate – adjust to a new climate or surroundings ACCLIMATISE
– having or referring to a mild climate TEMPERATE
– promoting or favourable to health or well-being, as a climate might be SALUBRIOUS
– referring to a climate having a relatively small range of temperature MARITIME, EQUABLE

climax, highest point CULMINATION, CRESCENDO
– climax of events in a story or play DENOUEMENT
– climax of sexual excitement ORGASM

climb awkwardly, as up a rocky slope CLAMBER, SCRAMBLE
– climb or scale a castle wall by means of a ladder, as during a military attack ESCALADE
– climb to the top of ASCEND, SURMOUNT
– person who climbs the outside of buildings, as for a prank or bet STEGOPHILIST

climbing plant or its stem BINE
– common climbing plant, twining around its support BINDWEED, CONVOLVULUS
– common woody climbing plant of tropical rain forests LIANA
– covered walk or arbour formed by a trellised roof carrying climbing plants PERGOLA
– twining shoot-like part, serving to attach a climbing plant to its support TENDRIL

clinging, sticking, or holding firmly TENACIOUS
– clinging or dependent person, parasite LEECH, LIMPET
– persistently clinging person or thing BURR

cloak See **clothes**
– woman's hooded cloak CAPUCHIN

clock made of imitation gold or gold-like alloy ORMOLU CLOCK
– clock mechanism, typically a ratchet system, for regulating the cogwheels and transmitting energy ESCAPEMENT
– clock of an ancient kind based on the dripping of water or mercury CLEPSYDRA
– clock of great accuracy, based on subatomic processes CAESIUM CLOCK
– clock or watch of a very precise kind, especially one used at sea CHRONOMETER
– clock or watch that can be primed to strike the hour or quarter-hour REPEATER
– clock's second hand SWEEP-SECOND HAND
– art of making watches or clocks, or the study of them HOROLOGY
– cone-shaped pulley or wheel with a spiralling groove, as in the mechanism of an early clock FUSEE
– device, as in a digital clock, that emits light when diodes are electrically stimulated LED
– display of symbols, as on a digital clock, produced by electrical stimulation of liquid crystals LCD
– glass or clear plastic cover over a watch or clock face CRYSTAL
– grandfather clock LONGCASE CLOCK
– referring to a watch or clock with changing numbers to indicate the time, rather than moving hands on a dial DIGITAL
– referring to a watch or clock with traditional hands and dial to indicate the time ANALOG
– swinging body freely suspended, as used for regulating a grandfather clock PENDULUM

clockwise- DEXTR-, DEXTRO-

clog See **shoe**

cloister, aisle, or similar covered area for walking AMBULATORY

close See also **end**, **stop**
– close at the end of a session, as the courts do ADJOURN
– close of the action of a play, usually in the form of a poem or speech EPILOGUE
– close to or next to ADJACENT, ADJOINING, CONTIGUOUS, ABUTTING
– close together, placed side by side, as for contrast JUXTAPOSED, APPOSED
– closely associated, very familiar or friendly INTIMATE
– closely linked CHEEK BY JOWL
– closeness in time or position PROPINQUITY, PROXIMITY, VICINITY
– closest relative or relatives NEXT OF KIN
– closing section of a speech, article, or the like, typically a summing-up PERORATION
– closing section of a play or novel, unwinding or resolving the plot DENOUEMENT

close to- EPI-

close watch or observation, especially on someone or something suspicious SURVEILLANCE

cloth See also **fabric**
– cloth, fabric, material TEXTILE
– cloth, padding, springs, and the like, as used in making a soft covering for furniture UPHOLSTERY
– cloth-dealer MERCER, DRAPER
– cloth left over after the rest of the roll has been sold REMNANT
– cloth or clothing arranged in folds, or a representation of it in sculpture or painting DRAPERY
– cloth scraps or fragments ODDMENTS, OFFCUTS
– cloth strip, brightly coloured, used as a man's garment in West Africa KENTE
– cloth strip, brightly coloured, used as a woman's garment in East Africa KANGA
– cloth strip, used as a flag or carrying a motto or slogan BANNER
– cloth strips or colourful streamers strung on a line for decoration BUNTING
– cloth strips, usually white, at the neck of some clerical or academic robes GENEVA BANDS
– cloth used to wrap a body for burial SHROUD, WINDING SHEET
– cut cloth to form a deeply indented edging VANDYKE
– diagonal cut across the grain of a piece of cloth BIAS
– frame for drying or stretching cloth during manufacture TENTER
– gathered strip of cloth or pleated ruffle sewn to a garment or curtain FLOUNCE
– knot or lump in yarn or cloth BURL, SLUB
– make or press fluted folds in a piece of fabric, as for a ruff QUILL
– picture or scene, as viewed through a slit, formed by lights shining through a series of translucent cloth sheets DIORAMA
– piece of cloth sewn at the edge of a garment, as for decoration or to prevent fraying FACING, LIST, SELVAGE
– press through which paper or cloth is rolled for a smooth or glossy finish CALENDER
– roll of cloth BOLT
– sample piece of cloth SWATCH
– thicken cloth by shrinking it or bulking it up through moisture, heat, and pressing FULL
– triangle or wedge of cloth, as in a skirt, umbrella, or sail GORE, GUSSET

clothes See chart, and also **shoes** and entries at various items of clothing
– clothes department or storeroom of a theatre, royal household, or the like WARDROBE
– clothes model, whether a woman or a life-size dummy MANNEQUIN
– clothes or accessories designed to be worn together COORDINATES
– clothes or personal belongings DUDS, TOGS
– clothes that are too expensive or ornate FRIPPERY, FROU-FROU, FAL-LAL
– clothing, clothes, outfit APPAREL, ATTIRE, GARB, GARMENTS, RAIMENT, HABILIMENTS

CLOTHES

DAYWEAR

Bermuda shorts	tight knee-length shorts
bolero	lady's very short jacket
chaps/ chaparejos	cowboy's seatless leather trousers
culottes	woman's trousers cut to resemble a skirt
dirndl	Tyrol-style dress with bodice and full skirt
dungarees	denim trousers, often with a bib front
fustanella	ceremonial white pleated skirt as worn by some Greek soldiers
gilet	woman's waistcoat
guernsey	knitted sweater
guimpe	blouse under a pinafore dress
halter	skimpy bodice tied behind the neck
jerkin	short jacket without sleeves or collar
jodhpurs	riding breeches, loose at the thighs
lederhosen	Austrian leather shorts with braces
leotard	tight sports garment from shoulder to thigh
muumuu	bright loose-fitting Hawaiian dress
Oxford bags	1920s-style baggy trousers
plus fours	men's baggy knickerbockers clasped below the knee
sloppy joe	long baggy sweater
trews	tight tartan trousers

COATS AND CLOAKS

afghan	sheepskin coat, often embroidered
anorak	padded waterproof jacket
Burberry	worsted trench coat
cagoule	light hooded raincoat
capote	long cloak
chesterfield	overcoat, typically with concealed buttons and a velvet collar
dolman	woman's cape-like cloak
domino	hooded robe worn at masked balls
duffle coat	short woollen coat, typically with a hood and toggles
Eton jacket	very short jacket with wide lapels
gaberdine	worsted raincoat
hacking jacket	riding jacket with slit sides or back
Inverness	loose overcoat with a removable cape
mantle	loose sleeveless cloak or overcoat
Norfolk jacket	man's jacket with a belt and box pleats
parka	hooded fur or cloth jacket
pelerine	woman's short cape
pelisse	long fur or fur-lined cloak
petersham	thick woollen overcoat
poncho	simple cloak of a large cloth with a hole for the head to pass through
raglan	coat or cloak with sleeves to the collar
reefer jacket	man's short double-breasted jacket
ulster	heavy overcoat, typically with a half-belt at the back

UNDERWEAR AND HOUSEWEAR

camisole	short negligee, or sleeveless underbodice
chemise/shift	woman's loose shirt-like undergarment
combinations	one-piece undergarment with sleeves and legs
corset, stays	tight supporting undergarment over the waist and hips
liberty bodice	buttoned sleeveless vest
negligee, peignoir	woman's light loose dressing gown
spencer	woman's short-sleeved vest

ACCESSORIES

bandanna	bright neckerchief or light scarf
boa	long stole or scarf, as of fur or feathers
cravat, ascot	man's small light knotted scarf
cummerbund	wide pleated sash for men, worn round the waist with a formal suit
dicky	bib-like detachable shirt front
fichu	woman's light triangular scarf
mantilla	lace shawl, as worn over the head and shoulders by Spanish women
stock	long white neckerchief worn with formal riding dress

continued

CLOTHES *continued*

CLERICAL AND RELIGIOUS	
alb	long white robe, as for Mass
amice	long white scarf tucked into the alb
cassock	black cloak
chasuble	long sleeveless vestment
cope	long outer cloak
cotta	short surplice, often sleeveless
cowl, capuche	monk's hood or hooded robe
dalmatic	wide-sleeved outer garment, as worn by Roman Catholic bishops
Geneva bands	pair of white cloth strips hanging from the collar
habit	dress or costume of a nun or friar
mozzetta	short hooded cloak for Roman Catholic bishops
rochet	tight-sleeved white surplice, as worn by bishops
scapular	monk's sleeveless cloak
soutane	black cloak worn by Roman Catholic priests
surplice	loose-flowing white outer robe, sometimes worn over a cassock
tippet	long stole
wimple	cloth covering the head and neck, worn by some nuns

AFRICAN AND ARABIC	
burka	long hooded cloak worn by Muslim women
burnous	long hooded Arabic cloak
caftan	long Arabic tunic with a sash belt
dashiki	loose tunic, as worn by African men
haik	Arab garment of a large cloth draped over the head and about the body
jellaba	long loose, hooded cloak, as worn by men in North Africa
kanga	bright cotton cloth draped about the body by women in East Africa
kanzu	long white tunic worn by men in East Africa
kente	bright toga worn in Ghana
yashmak	veil worn by Muslim women in public

ASIAN	
chador	garment worn by Muslim women covering the upper body and part of the face
cheongsam	tight Chinese dress with a high collar and slit skirt
choli	short-sleeved Indian blouse or bodice
dhoti	long skirt-like garment worn by Hindu men in India
khurta	long, loose, collarless Indian shirt
kimono	long, loose, formal Japanese robe, worn with a sash
lungi	loincloth, headdress or scarf worn by Indian men
samfoo	loose Chinese suit for women
sari	suit worn by Hindu women, consisting of a long cloth wound about the body
sarong	skirt-like Malay garment formed by a long bright cloth
shalwar	baggy trousers as worn in Pakistan
sherwani	Indian men's high-collared coat

HISTORICAL	
balmoral	woollen petticoat showing below the skirt
chiton	loose woollen tunic worn by men and women in ancient Greece
chlamys	man's short cloak in ancient Greece
codpiece	pouch in the crotch of men's breeches, 15th-16th century
crinoline	stiff petticoat, or hooped skirt
doublet	man's tight jacket, 15th-17th century
farthingale	hoop supporting a skirt, 16th century
frock coat, surtout	man's formal overcoat with skirts to the knee, 19th century
galligaskins	long loose breeches, 16th-17th century
himation	long loose cloak worn by men and women in ancient Greece
hose	breeches fastened to a doublet
mantua	loose gown revealing an underskirt, 17th-18th century
paletot	loose overcoat, 19th century
pallium, toga	cloak or robe in ancient Rome
peplos	woman's blouse or robe in ancient Greece

– clothing and accessories for a newborn baby LAYETTE
– clothing and sewing materials HABERDASHERY
– clothing for a member of a religious order HABIT
– clothing of a very smart or expensive kind FINERY, ARRAY, CAPARISON, REGALIA
– clothing of high fashion HAUTE COUTURE
– clothing or cloth arranged in loose folds, or a representation of it in art DRAPERY
– clothing or distinctive outfit or uniform of a group of servants, guild members, or the like LIVERY
– clothing or suit of clothes BIB AND TUCKER
– civilian clothes rather than military uniform CIVVIES, MUFTI
– designer, maker, and seller of fashionable clothing for women COUTURIER, MODISTE
– formal academic clothing, especially at Oxford SUBFUSC
– made-to-order, as a suit of clothes might be BESPOKE
– man of fashion, whose chief interest is in clothes and manners BEAU, BEAU BRUMMELL, DANDY, FOP, COCKSCOMB
– matching set of clothes, outfit ENSEMBLE
– men's leather shorts with braces, as part of traditional Tyrolean or Bavarian clothing LEDERHOSEN
– mourning clothes WEEDS
– person who enjoys wearing clothes designed for the opposite sex TRANSVESTITE, CROSS-DRESSER
– priest's official clothing CANONICALS, VESTMENTS
– put on one's hat or clothes DON
– referring to clothes, hairstyles, or the like suitable for people of either sex UNISEX
– referring to clothing of an aggressive style, characterised by black leather, studs, and chains BONDAGE
– relating to clothing, especially smart men's clothing SARTORIAL
– shabby, untidy, or old-fashioned, as a woman or her clothes might be DOWDY, FRUMPY
– strip of something, such as clothes, rights, or property DIVEST
– supplementary or additional item to basic clothing ACCESSORY
– take off one's hat or clothes DOFF
– tear or catch clothing on a nail, wooden stump, or the like SNAG

clotted cream DEVONSHIRE CREAM

cloud See illustration, page 104
– cloud of dust or gas in outer space NEBULA
– cloud or obscure something, as fog might OBNUBILATE, OBFUSCATE
– clouds broken and driven by high winds RACK
– cloudy, misty, hazy NEBULOUS
– cloudy luminous aura surrounding a god or goddess when visiting Earth NIMBUS
– cloudy with sediment, as river water might be TURBID
– covered with clouds, as the sky might be OVERCAST
– gathered in woolly masses, as clouds or dissolved particles might be FLOCCULENT
– sprinkle silver iodide or a similar chemical onto a cloud to produce rain SEED
– study of clouds NEPHOLOGY
– thin, wind-driven cloud SCUD

cloven, as a hoof might be, or having cloven hooves BISULCATE

clover leaf with four leaflets QUATREFOIL
– clover or similar plant whose leaves are made up of three leaflets TREFOIL, SHAMROCK
– three-leafed or with three leaflets, as the clover leaf TRIFOLIATE
– three-lobed ornamental figure, as in architecture, resembling a clover leaf TREFOIL

clown or fool in old comedies, especially one who mimics other characters ZANY
– amusing or irritating person given to clowning and ridiculous behaviour BUFFOON
– professional clown or fool in former times JESTER
– traditional clown, a clumsy shambling character with a wig and bulbous nose who ruins the tricks and gets water thrown over him AUGUSTE
– traditional clown character, a boastful and cowardly Spanish nobleman SCARAMOUCHE
– traditional clown character, a fat hunchbacked man with a beaked nose on which the puppet Punch is based PUNCHINELLO
– traditional clown character, a foolish or lecherous and badly dressed old man PANTALOON
– traditional clown in a black mask and diamond-patterned tights HARLEQUIN
– traditional clown in Spanish comedy GRACIOSO
– traditional French clown with a whitened face and conical hat popular in seaside shows PIERROT
– whitened with cosmetic paint, as a clown might be FARDED

club for elderly people DARBY-AND-JOAN CLUB
– club or short stick used by a policeman TRUNCHEON, NIGHTSTICK
– club or stick, or a beating with it, especially on the soles of the feet BASTINADO
– club-shaped, thickened at one end CLAVATE, CLAVIFORM
– club with a spiked metal head used in medieval battles MACE
– hit or batter with or as if with a club BASTE, FUSTIGATE
– local branch of a club or society CHAPTER
– short heavy club CUDGEL, BLUDGEON, BLACKJACK, LIFE PRESERVER
– small, weighted club for killing fish PRIEST
– vote against or veto someone, especially to membership of a club BLACKBALL
– wooden bottle-shaped club thrown or swung about in juggling and gymnastics INDIAN CLUB
– wooden club used by Australian Aborigines NULLA-NULLA, WADDY
– wooden club used in Ireland SHILLELAGH
– wooden club with a bulbous end used in Africa KNOBKERRIE

clump or tuft, as of grass or hair TUSSOCK, HASSOCK, TUFFET

clumsy, bumbling, ham-handed GAUCHE, INEPT, MALADROIT
– clumsy, jerky or graceless in movement, gawky or lumbering UNGAINLY, UNCOORDINATED, LUBBERLY, UNCOUTH
– clumsy and inelegant as a sentence might be CUMBERSOME
– clumsy person, oaf or lout, duffer CLODHOPPER, GALOOT, LUBBER, SCHLEMIEL, KLUTZ, PALOOKA, STUMBLEBUM, LUMMOX

cluster, mass CONGLOMERATE
– cluster of fruit or flowers at the end of a stalk TRUSS

clutching or retentive, as a good memory is TENACIOUS

coach or large bus, as used for group outings CHARABANC
– rider of the left front horse of a coach POSTILION

coal dust or waste, or inferior coal from a mine CULM
– coal miner, or coal ship COLLIER
– coal of a hard and heavy kind that burns slowly with a hot, clear flame ANTHRACITE
– coal of a poor peaty quality, "brown coal" LIGNITE
– coal of a soft and rich kind that burns with a smoky yellow flame BITUMINOUS COAL
– coal-producing CARBONIFEROUS
– coal that burns brightly and gives off much smoke CANNEL

– portable metal stand for burning coal or charcoal BRAZIER
– sloping channel or duct down which water, coal, parcels, or the like can be conveyed CHUTE
– small brick of compressed charcoal or coal dust, used for fuel, as at barbecues BRIQUETTE
– solid residue in ashes from burnt coal CLINKER
– thin seam of coal lying above a larger seam in a mine RIDER

cloud

cirrus (bad weather coming)

nimbostratus (rain imminent)

cirrocumulus (unsettled weather)

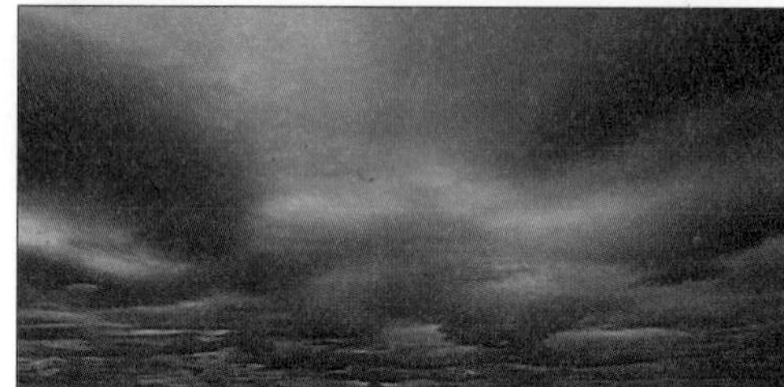
stratocumulus (dry but dull weather)

cirrostratus (showers or rain soon)

stratus (drizzle coming)

altocumulus (sunny periods)

cumulus/woolpack (sunny spells)

altostratus (rain likely)

cumulonimbus (showers and thunder)

coal mine COLLIERY
– methane-based gas, explosive when mixed with air, formed in coal mines FIREDAMP
– waste rocks and minerals from a coal mine SLAG

coarse See **rude**, **vulgar**

coast See also **geographical features**
– coast road, often built into the side of a cliff CORNICHE
– adjective for a coast LITTORAL
– organisation providing lighthouses, buoys, and other coastal safety measures TRINITY HOUSE

coat See **clothes**

coat food with flour, sugar, or the like, as by sprinkling DREDGE
– coat or cover a surface with grease, plaster, or mud DAUB
– coat or covering, such as a seed's coat INTEGUMENT
– coat with plaster or cement RENDER, PARGET
– coating, cover, or surrounding layer MANTLE
– coating, filler, or glaze, as for paper or walls, made of wax, clay, glue, resin, or the like SIZE
– coating, insulation, or facing material on the outside of a building, pipe, tank, or the like CLADDING
– mammal's coat PELAGE
– powdery coating as on plums and new coins BLOOM
– thin coating of plastic, wood, or the like LAMINATE, VENEER
– thin coating of substance on the surface of a solid ADSORPTION
– thin outer cover or coating, such as a membrane or film PELLICLE

coat of arms See also **heraldry**
– ideal or principle stated by a word or maxim, as on a coat of arms MOTTO
– knight's tunic bearing his coat of arms TABARD
– person entitled to a coat of arms ARMIGER
– relating to heraldry or coats of arms ARMORIAL
– shield, as in heraldry, bearing a coat of arms ESCUTCHEON
– study, devising, or awarding of coats of arms HERALDRY
– title or inscription, as on a coin or coat of arms LEGEND

cobra – king cobra HAMADRYAD

cobweb film or mesh floating in the air or found on foliage GOSSAMER

cock – cock's comb or similar outgrowth on an animal, seed, the skin, or the like CARUNCLE
– name for a cock CHANTICLEER
– young cockerel STAG

cockfight MAIN, SPAR
– metal spur on a gamecock's leg in cockfighting GAFF

cockpit – transparent cover of the cockpit of an aircraft CANOPY

cocktails See **drinks**

coconut biscuit MACAROON
– coconut-husk fibre, as used for ropes and matting COIR
– coconut meat, dried and prepared for oil extraction COPRA
– dried and shredded or powdered, as preserved coconut is DESICCATED

cocoon – pupa of a moth or butterfly, often encased in a cocoon CHRYSALIS

cod – young cod, codling SPRAG

code, as among children, formed by regular rearrangements of spoken words, as in turning *dog* into *ogday* PIG LATIN
– code, as used by radio operators, for identifying letters of the alphabet, such as *Tango* standing for *T* PHONETIC ALPHABET
– code of a simple kind, in which letters are substituted according to a key CIPHER
– code of laws, especially a digest of Roman law PANDECTS
– code or signalling system based on the position of two flags, one held in each hand SEMAPHORE
– coded writing or message CRYPTOGRAM
– deciphering of codes, secret writings, and the like CRYPTANALYSIS
– in ordinary language, not put in code EN CLAIR
– interpret or clarify a code, decode DECIPHER, DECRYPT
– put a text into code ENCIPHER
– study of codes, or the technique or process of coding messages CRYPTOGRAPHY, CRYPTOLOGY

coffee, tea, or other drink, food, or drug that temporarily increases activity or efficiency STIMULANT
– coffee brewed by steam or hot water under pressure ESPRESSO
– coffee cup of small size, or the strong black coffee drunk from it DEMITASSE
– coffee house or smoking room in former times DIVAN
– coffee of high quality MOCHA
– coffee with frothed milk CAPPUCCINO
– coffee with most of the caffeine removed DECAFFEINATED COFFEE
– coffeepot in which hot water filters through ground coffee held in a small perforated tray PERCOLATOR
– dregs or sediment, lees, such as coffee grounds GROUTS
– root product used as a coffee additive or substitute CHICORY
– stimulant substance in tea and coffee CAFFEINE

coffin carrier or attendant at a funeral PALLBEARER
– coffin of stone, typically having a sculpture or inscription SARCOPHAGUS
– platform or stand for a corpse or coffin, prior to burial BIER
– raised platform or table on which a coffin or corpse lies, as during a state funeral CATAFALQUE
– roofed gate of a churchyard, where the coffin is traditionally rested at the start of the burial service LICH GATE

cog – small cogwheel or gear-wheel which engages with a larger gear-wheel or toothed rack PINION
– toothed projection on a cog-wheel or cylinder, designed to engage a moving post SPROCKET

cohabiting LIVING TALLY

coil of thread, wool, rope, or yarn SKEIN, HANK
– coil or whirl, as of a spiral shell VOLUTION
– coil of wire producing a magnetic field when carrying an electric current, as used for activating switches SOLENOID
– coiled or ring-shaped, as the frond of a young fern might be CIRCINATE
– coiled or rolled up CONVOLUTE, CONVOLUTED

coin See also chart, page 106
– coin blank, plain metal disc ready for stamping as a coin PLANCHET, FLAN
– coin collector NUMISMATIST
– box in the British mint, in which new coins are kept for testing PYX
– coinage, minted money SPECIE
– circular inscription on a coin or medal CIRCUMSCRIPTION
– engraved metal block for punching or pressing a design, as onto coins DIE
– face or side of a coin bearing the main design, "heads" OBVERSE
– face or side of a coin bearing the secondary design, "tails" VERSO, REVERSE
– government revenue from the minting of coins, after the cost of metal and production has been subtracted SEIGNIORAGE
– grade or unit in a classification system, such as a coin of a specified value DENOMINATION
– grooves or ridges round the edge of a coin MILLING, REEDING, FLUTING, ENGRAILING
– roll of coins wrapped in paper ROULEAU
– space beneath the main design on the reverse of a coin, as used

for recording the date or place of minting EXERGUE
– specially minted coins given to poor people by the British king or queen on the Thursday before Easter MAUNDY MONEY
– study of coins, money, or medals NUMISMATICS
– title or inscription, as on a coin or coat of arms LEGEND

coincide, happen at the same time or place CONCUR
– coinciding, simultaneous occurrence CONJUNCTION
– coinciding or identical in range, size, meaning, or the like COTERMINOUS, CO-EXTENSIVE, CONGRUENT

coincidence of a supposedly significant kind, especially in Jungian philosophy SYNCHRONICITY

cold and clammy, as the skin of malaria patients is ALGID
– cold and sluggish in temperament SATURNINE
– cold-blooded, having a varying body temperature POIKILOTHERMIC
– cold drink with fizz CARBONATED DRINK
– cold remedy consisting of a hot sweet milk drink curdled with wine or beer POSSET
– cold remedy in the form of a preparation inhaled with steam FRIAR'S BALSAM
– coldly reserved ALOOF
– coldly simple, harsh or unadorned, austere, as furniture might be CLINICAL
– abnormally low body temperature, typically caused by exposure to the cold HYPOTHERMIA
– calmly indifferent, cold, stiff, unemotional IMPASSIVE, BLOODLESS, PHLEGMATIC
– cooling power of cold air based on wind speed and air temperature WIND-CHILL FACTOR
– freezing cold, icy HYPERBOREAN

cold- CRYO-, PSYCHRO-

collaborating, in partnership with, especially in some dubious enterprise IN CAHOOTS, COLLUDING

collapse See also **break**, **fall**
– collapse, cave in, as the ground might SUBSIDE
– collapse, fail or break down completely FOUNDER
– collapse in on itself, fold up CONCERTINA, TELESCOPE
– collapse inwards, crumple under external pressure IMPLODE

collar – collar-like piece of armour protecting the throat GORGET
– collar of a high, stiff, round style MANDARIN STYLE
– collar of a high and often tight-fitting style CHOKER, STOCK
– collar of a wide, deeply indented design VANDYKE
– collar or necklace, typically of twisted metal, worn in ancient times TORQUE
– ring on a dog's collar for attaching a leash TERRET
– stiff, upright collar worn in the 17th century REBATO, RABATO
– wide collar, often of lace, covering the shoulders and neckline BERTHA
– wide decorative collar of lace or fine fabric, as worn in the 16th and 17th centuries RUFF
– wide linen or lace collar worn flat on the shoulders by men in the 17th century FALLING BAND

collarbone CLAVICLE

colleague See **partner**

collect See **gather**

collection See also **group**, **crowd**
– collection, as of games or useful hints, grouped together COMPENDIUM
– collection or hoard of various things ACCUMULATION, STOCKPILE, ASSEMBLAGE, CONGLOMERATION
– collection of assorted writings, compiled from the works of one or more authors CHRESTOMATHY, ANTHOLOGY, COLLECTANEA, POT-POURRI, OMNIBUS, MISCELLANY
– collection of complete writings,

COINS

bezant	gold Byzantine coin; a solidus	**nickel**	US and Canadian five-cent piece
bob	old British shilling	**noble**	old British gold coin, one-third of a pound
dandiprat	small 16th-century English coin	**obol**	ancient Greek silver coin
denarius	ancient Roman silver coin	**rap**	counterfeit halfpenny in 18th-century Ireland
dime	US and Canadian ten-cent piece	**real**	old silver coin of Spain and Spanish America
doubloon	old Spanish gold coin	**sequin/ zecchino**	old coin of the Venetian Republic
ducat	old European gold coin	**sesterce/as**	ancient Roman coin, silver or bronze
florin	old British two-shilling coin	**solidus**	gold Byzantine coin
groat	old British silver fourpenny coin	**sou**	old French coin of low value
groschen	Austrian bronze coin, one-hundredth of a schilling; old silver German coin of varying value	**sovereign**	old British one pound coin
krugerrand	South African coin containing 1oz of pure gold	**stater**	ancient Greek coin
louis d'or	old French gold coin	**stiver**	old Dutch coin, one-twentieth of a guilder
moidore	old Portuguese gold coin	**taler/thaler**	old German, Swiss or Austrian silver coin
napoleon	old French gold coin	**tanner**	old British sixpence
		tickey	old South African threepenny piece

especially by a particular writer CORPUS, OEUVRE
– collection of unusual, foreign, or bizarre objects EXOTICA
– collection of varied items sold as a single lot JOB LOT
– collection or mixture of varied objects or elements CONGERIES, MOTLEY, FARRAGO
– church collection, offerings by the congregation OFFERTORY
– churchwarden's assistant, especially the person who takes the collection SIDESMAN

-collection -ANA, -IANA

collective farm in Israel KIBBUTZ
– collective farm in the USSR KOLKHOZ

collector or student of ancient art objects, pottery, jewellery, and the like ANTIQUARY
– collector of beer mats TEGESTOLOGIST
– collector of bookplates EX-LIBRIST
– collector of butterflies and moths LEPIDOPTERIST
– collector of coins, money, or medals NUMISMATIST
– collector of matchboxes, matchbox labels, and books of matches PHILLUMENIST
– collector of postcards DELTIOLOGIST
– collector of stamps, postmarks, and the like PHILATELIST
– collector or lover of fine books BIBLIOPHILE
– collector's items such as antiques and curios, or a cultivated liking for them VIRTU

college See also **university**
– college dining room HALL, REFECTORY
– college official who has nominal rights of inspection and arbitration VISITOR
– college or university education TERTIARY EDUCATION
– college or university official in charge of finances BURSAR
– college porter's office LODGE
– college principal or other administrative official WARDEN, RECTOR, PROVOST
– college reception clerk PORTER
– college steward who buys the provisions MANCIPLE
– college's annual feast GAUDY
– first-year student at a college or university FRESHER
– referring to non-resident students or to studies or activities outside the normal courses of a university or college EXTRAMURAL
– residence of the head of a college LODGE
– room in a college or university where students can buy food BUTTERY

colony or county whose ruler formerly had royal powers PALATINATE
– colonial representative, as formerly in a protected Indian State RESIDENT
– colonist or settler in a new region in former times PLANTER

Colosseum – passageway leading to a terrace of seats in a stadium, as in the Colosseum in Rome VOMITORY

colour See chart; also **heraldry**
– colour belonging to any of various groups considered capable of generating all colours PRIMARY COLOUR
– colour-changing lizard CHAMELEON
– colour of a light delicate tint PASTEL
– colour or shade HUE, TINT, TINCTURE

COLOURS

REDDISH-PURPLE

amaranth
burgundy
cerise
magenta
maroon
mauve
puce

PURPLISH-BLUE OR VIOLET

amethyst
aubergine
heliotrope

BLUE

azure
cerulean
gentian
indigo
lapis lazuli
sapphire
saxe blue
ultramarine

GREENISH-BLUE

aquamarine
cobalt blue
cyan
ice blue
Nile blue
teal
turquoise

GREEN

celadon
eau de nil
emerald
jade
Kendal green
Lincoln green
loden
terre-verte

YELLOWISH-GREEN

chartreuse
reseda
luteous

YELLOW OR BROWNISH-YELLOW

barium yellow
chamois
champagne
citrine
citron
fallow/fawn
flax
fulvous
gamboge
jonquil
maize
nankeen
ochre
old gold
saffron
topaz

REDDISH-YELLOW OR ORANGE

amber
apricot
coral
flamingo
peach
salmon
tea rose

RED

cardinal
carmine/crimson/cochineal
cherry
cinnabar
old rose
rubious
solferino
vermilion/vermiel

REDDISH-BROWN

auburn
brick
chestnut
ginger
henna
mahogany
oxblood
roan
rust/rubiginous/ferruginous
russet/rufous
sienna/raw sienna
sorrel
terracotta
titian

BROWN

bay
beaver
beige
biscuit
café au lait
cinnamon
dun
mocha
nutmeg
sandalwood
sepia
taupe
tawny
tortoiseshell
umber
walnut

GREY

battleship grey
charcoal grey
dove
nutria

BLACK

ebony
fuliginous
jet
raven
sable
subfuse

YELLOWISH-GREY OR OFF-WHITE

alabaster
bisque
ecru
eggshell
oyster
putty

– colour parts of cloth with dye while tying other parts tightly, producing a mottled effect TIE-DYE
– colour range, as of a painting or painter PALETTE
– coloured too brightly, over-ornamented, flashy, loud GAUDY, TAWDRY, GARISH, TECHNICOLOR
– colours, such as yellow and blue, that can be mixed to produce white or grey COMPLEMENTARY COLOURS

column

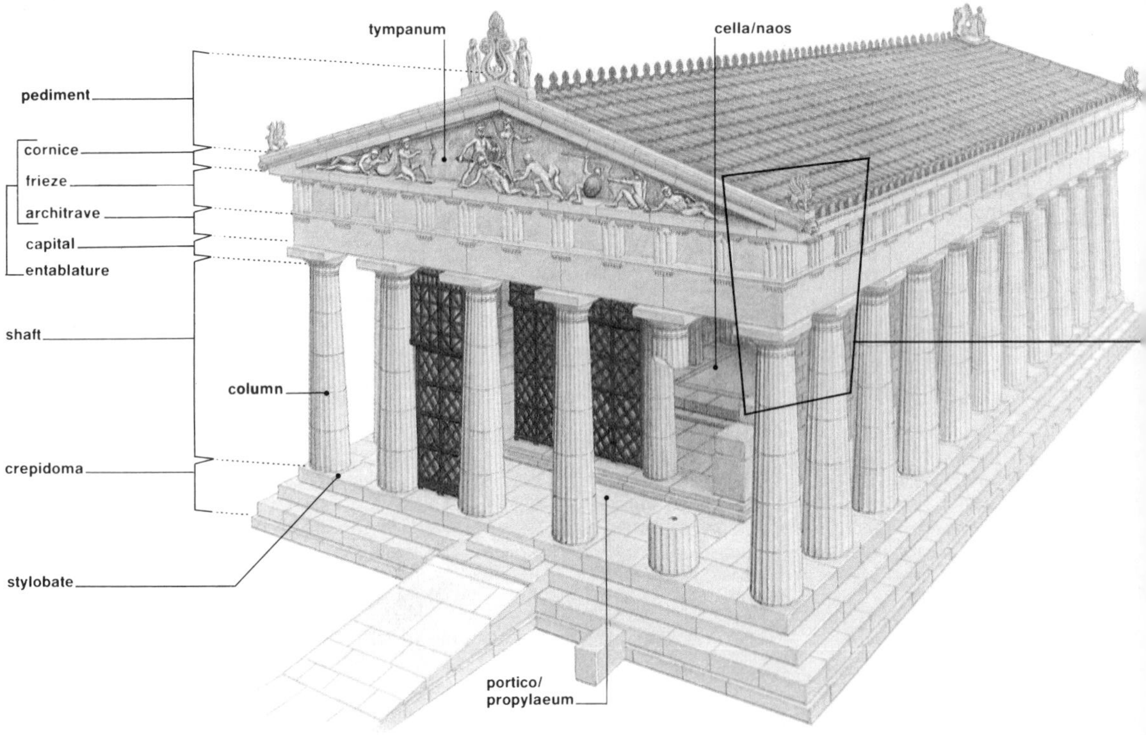

tympanum
cella/naos
pediment
cornice
frieze
architrave
capital
entablature
shaft
column
crepidoma
stylobate
portico/ propylaeum

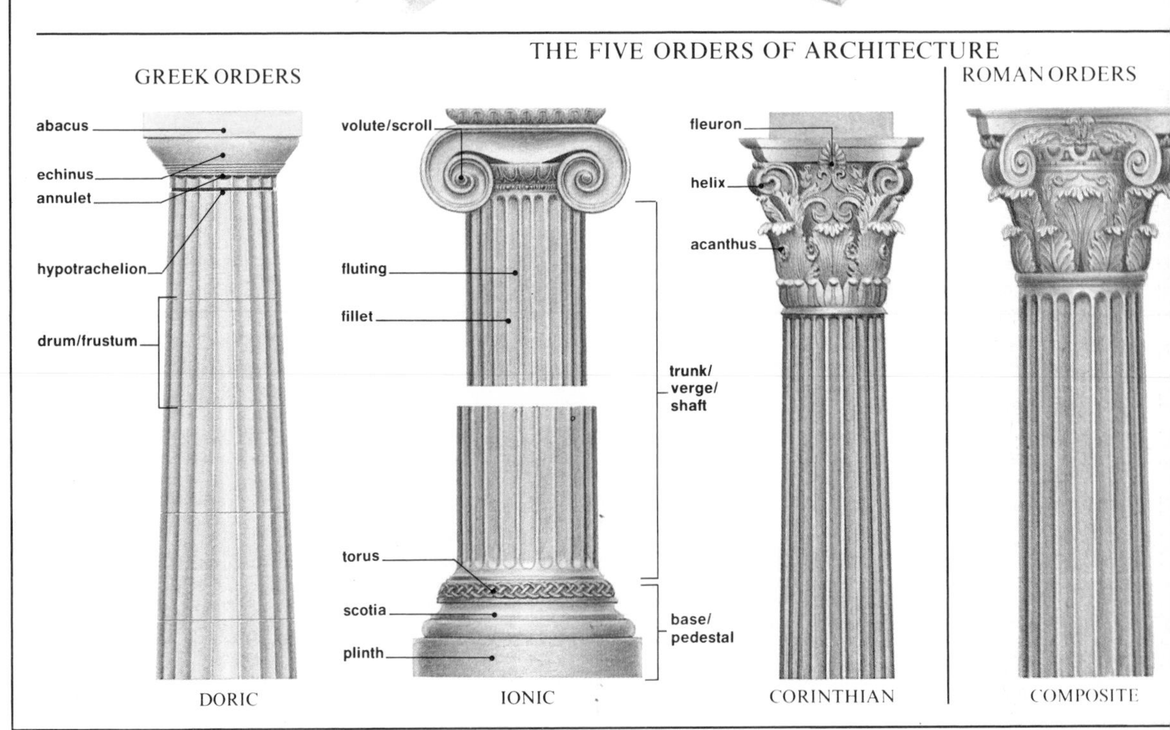

– band of colour on an insect or plant FASCIA
– changing pattern of colours KALEIDOSCOPE
– distinction or variation of a very fine or subtle kind, as of tone, colour, or meaning NUANCE
– having all the colours of the rainbow, multicoloured PRISMATIC
– having different colours, especially blotches of black and white, as a horse might PIEBALD, PINTO
– having or displaying a variety of colours MOTLEY, PIED, PARTI-COLOURED, VARICOLOURED, VARIEGATED, POLYCHROME
– maximum purity and vividness of a colour SATURATION
– pale shade or tinge of colour CAST
– range or image of the colours of the rainbow SPECTRUM
– relating to colour or colours CHROMATIC
– scale of colours MUNSELL SCALE
– scientific study of colour CHROMATICS
– sensation of colour evoked by a sound, or similar sensation of a sense different from the one stimulated SYNAESTHSIA
– shimmering or changing in colour, as some fabrics do SHOT, IRIDESCENT, OPALESCENT, TAFFETA
– spotted or streaked with different colours or tints MOTTLED
– spread across or through, as a colour might SUFFUSE

-colour- -CHROM-, CHROMO-

colour blindness in which all colours are a single hue MONOCHROMATISM
– partial colour blindness in which green and red are confused DALTONISM, PROTANOPIA
– partial colour blindness in which blue cannot be distinguished TRITANOPIA

colourful or noisy display, designed to impress or advertise RAZZLE-DAZZLE, RAZZMATAZZ

colouring chemical in the skin, hair, and eye MELANIN
– colouring matter, as for making paints or inks PIGMENT
– colouring or appearance that protects an animal by causing it to resemble an unrelated animal that is poisonous or unpalatable to predators BATESIAN MIMICRY
– colouring that protects or conceals an animal by camouflage CRYPTIC COLOURING
– referring or relating to the colouring of an animal that serves as camouflage APATETIC
– referring to the colouring of an animal that warns off predators by suggesting that it is poisonous or bad-tasting APOSEMATIC

colourless, or of neutral colour, such as black, white, or grey ACHROMATIC

colourless- LEUC-, LEUCO-, LEUKO-

column See illustration, and also **pillar**

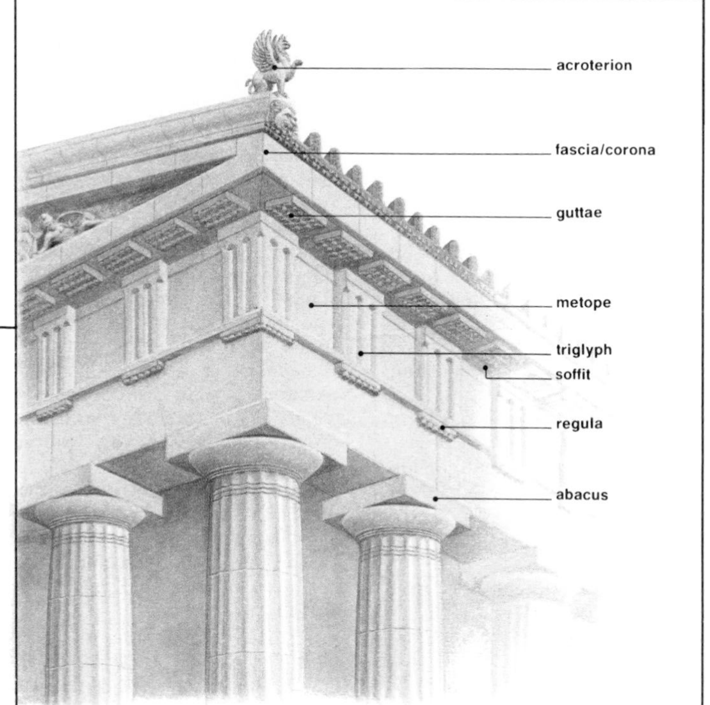

– column in classical architecture in the form of a statue of a man TELAMON, ATLAS
– column in classical architecture in the form of a statue of a woman CARYATID
– column or pillar on a pavement for the display of advertising posters MORRIS COLUMN
– column width or page width in printing MEASURE
– arranged in a table of rows and columns TABULAR
– building whose roof rests on rows of columns HYPOSTYLE
– covered walk with columns on one or both sides, as in ancient Greek buildings STOA
– having a row of columns on all sides PERIPTERAL
– presenting texts or data in columns side by side for comparison SYNOPTIC
– row of columns positioned at regular intervals COLONNADE
– row of columns surrounding a building or courtyard, or the area surrounded PERISTYLE
– slight bulge that makes a column appear straight when viewed from below ENTASIS
– style of classical architecture based on the type of column used ORDER

comb – comb-like, having protrusions resembling the teeth of a comb, as a perch's scales have CTENOID
– comb of a cock or similar outgrowth on an animal, seed, the skin, or the like CARUNCLE
– comb of steel for combing flax HACKLE
– comb the hair downwards near the roots in order to bulk it up BACKCOMB, TEASE

combat arena, as for chivalric tournaments LISTS
– combat between knights, with lances on horseback JOUST, TILTING MATCH
– trial by combat in former times WAGER OF BATTLE

combatant, typically armed with a sword, in an ancient Roman arena GLADIATOR
– combatant armed with a net and trident in an ancient Roman arena RETIARIUS

combination See also **collection**, **group**, **mixture**
– combination of businesses or interests formed for some joint enterprise SYNDICATE, CONSORTIUM
– combination of experiences, such as those that make up a relationship GESTALT
– combination or possible variation of numbers, elements or members PERMUTATION

combine See **join**, **mix**
– combine or arrange in correct order COLLOCATE
– combine or blend into a single unit INCORPORATE, MELD
– combined, planned or performed together, as an effort might be CONCERTED, COORDINATED
– combined action, as of medicines or muscles, producing a greater effect than the sum of the individual effects SYNERGISM
– combining and uniting of separate things, such as small businesses, into a larger whole CONSOLIDATION, AMALGAMATION
– combining of parts or elements to form a whole, or the whole so produced SYNTHESIS
– combining property of an atom or chemical group VALENCY

come before in time or order PRECEDE

come down, or behave as if coming down, to the level of others CONDESCEND, DEIGN, PATRONISE

come out, issue from a source EMANATE

come to pass, turn out, happen EVENTUATE, TRANSPIRE

comedian, joker, or prankster FARCEUR, BUFFOON
– comedian's partner or foil who supplies openings or cues for jokes FEED, STRAIGHT MAN, STOOGE

comedy See **satire**, **joke**, **drama**
– comedy of an unsubtle, energetic, farcical kind SLAPSTICK

comet – bright dense central part of the head of a comet NUCLEUS
– cloud around the nucleus of a comet COMA
– point furthest from the Sun in the orbit of a planet or comet APHELION
– point nearest to the Sun in the orbit of a planet or comet PERIHELION

comfort See also **calm**
– comfort, sympathy, or reassurance SOLACE, CONSOLATION
– comforting, soothing ANODYNE
– comforts, conveniences, pleasant and helpful features or services FACILITIES, AMENITIES
– relieve pain, grief, or the like in order to bring comfort ALLAY, ASSUAGE, ALLEVIATE, PALLIATE
– valued domestic comforts LARES ET PENATES

comfortable, easy, as a job might be CUSHY
– comfortable and cosy, snug GEMÜTLICH
– comfortable and spacious COMMODIOUS
– comfortable enough to live in, adequate HABITABLE
– comfortable place, land of plenty and contentment GOSHEN

comforter or sympathiser who causes only distress JOB'S COMFORTER

comic opera – male, usually bass, singer of comic opera roles BUFFO

coming, arrival ADVENT
– coming together, as of events CONFLUENCE, CONCOURSE

command See **order**

commanding, authoritative MAGISTERIAL

commandments – relating to Noah or his time, as the seven pre-Mosaic commandments do NOACHIAN

comment See also **remark**
– comment made in passing, incidental remark OBITER DICTUM
– comment on or discuss in detail EXPOUND, DESCANT, DISCOURSE
– comment or carefully considered observation, usually very critical ANIMADVERSION
– comments or notes written in the margin of a book ANNOTATIONS, MARGINALIA
– clear, crisp, and forceful, as a comment or argument might be TRENCHANT, COGENT
– cutting, penetrating, to the point, as a comment might be INCISIVE, MORDANT
– hurtfully indirect, cutting, as a comment might be BARBED
– throw in a comment by way of interruption INTERJECT, INTERPOSE

commentary, detailed explanation EXPOSITION, EXEGESIS
– commentary of an unseen narrator on events in a filmed programme VOICE-OVER
– commentary on a text, note of criticism or explanation ANNOTATION, GLOSS, SCHOLIUM
– formal commentary or treatise on a subject DISQUISITION

commerce See also **company**, **economics**
– adjective for trade or commerce MERCANTILE
– commercial activity, such as buying and selling, of a business TURNOVER

commit a crime, perform a hoax, make a blunder, or the like PERPETRATE
– commit oneself irrevocably to a particular course of action CROSS THE RUBICON
– commit oneself to a difficult task or risky project GRASP THE NETTLE

committed to and actively promoting a moral or political cause ENGAGÉ

committee set up for a particular purpose or occasion AD HOC COMMITTEE
– elect a new member to a committee or other group by a decision of the existing group COOPT
– number of persons required for a committee meeting, assembly, or the like QUORUM
common, shared, joint MUTUAL, RECIPROCAL
– common, standard, or constantly needed commodity STAPLE
– common and typically unsophisticated opinion, taste, or group of people LOWEST COMMON DENOMINATOR
– common name, as of a plant or animal, by contrast with a technical Latin name TRIVIAL NAME
– common opinion, general agreement or attitude CONSENSUS
– common or crude, having vulgar tastes PLEBEIAN
– common or deeply-rooted within a particular area or group ENDEMIC
– common or frequent, widespread PREVAILING, PREVALENT, PREDOMINANT, RIFE, REGNANT
– common or vulgar people, the masses or mob, rabble or riffraff HOI POLLOI, CANAILLE
– common people, especially lower-class working people PROLETARIAT
– common people of ancient Rome PLEBS
– common people or inhabitants COMMONALTY, POPULACE
– common speech of the people VERNACULAR, VULGATE, DEMOTIC
– commonest item in a numerical list MODE
– right to pasture animals on common land COMMONAGE
-common- -COEN-, COENO-
common-law husband TALLYMAN
common sense practical shrewdness GUMPTION, NOUS
commonsense rejection of commonsense observation in favour of abstract theory RATIONALISM
commonplace See **cliché**, **dull**
– commonplace or familiar theme, idea, or image in literature TOPOS
Commonwealth – former term for a large self-governing nation of the Commonwealth DOMINION
communicate, make known, reveal IMPART, DISCLOSE, DIVULGE
communication between two minds by a sixth sense TELEPATHY
– communication or contact, as between various sections of the armed forces LIAISON
– communication system sending telegrams through automatic exchanges TELEX
– characteristic way of thinking and feeling as a help or hindrance to communication with others WAVELENGTH
– referring to conversation, as about the weather, which expresses friendly feelings rather than to communicate ideas PHATIC
– study of gesture, facial expression, and the like as a form of communication KINESICS
– supplementing verbal communication, as voice qualities and gestures do PARALINGUISTIC
– unable to communicate with others INCOMMUNICADO
Communion given to a person in danger of death VIATICUM
– Communion service, especially in Eastern Churches LITURGY
– bell rung during the elevation of the Communion bread and wine in a Roman Catholic church SACRING BELL
– bread or wafer consecrated in the Communion HOST, SACRAMENT, EUCHARIST
– breaking of the bread by the priest at Communion FRACTION
– calling on the Holy Spirit to consecrate the Communion bread and wine EPICLESIS
– consecrated bread and wine at Communion SPECIES
– container for storing the Communion bread and wine, typically an ornamental box TABERNACLE
– container for the consecrated Communion wafers CIBORIUM, PYX, MONSTRANCE, OSTENSORY
– container for the water or wine at Communion CRUET, AMPULLA
– conversion of the consecrated Communion bread and wine into the body and blood of Christ TRANSUBSTANTIATION
– coexistence of the consecrated Communion bread and wine with the body and blood of Christ CONSUBSTANTIATION
– cup for the consecrated wine at Communion CHALICE
– kiss of peace at Communion, or the plate formerly used to convey it PAX
– lifting up of the Communion bread and wine for adoration by the congregation ELEVATION
– linen cloth for wiping the Communion chalice or the celebrant's lips PURIFICATOR
– linen square covering the Communion chalice PALL
– offering to God of the bread and wine of Communion OBLATION, OFFERTORY
– plate, typically of silver or gold, used for holding the bread at Communion PATEN
– priest officiating at Communion or some other religious ceremony or rite CELEBRANT, OFFICIANT
– table for the Communion bread and wine CREDENCE TABLE
– thin disc of unleavened bread used in Communion WAFER
– white linen cloth on which the bread and wine are placed for a Communion service CORPORAL
communist emblem HAMMER AND SICKLE
– communist or extreme radical BOLSHEVIK, BOLSHIE
– communist-party official in charge of political education and party loyalty COMMISSAR
– communist-party supporter who is not actually a member of it FELLOW TRAVELLER
– communist party's system of internal administration APPARAT
– persecution of suspected communist sympathisers in the U.S. in the 1950s MCCARTHYISM
community, brotherhood, fellowship FRATERNITY, SODALITY
– relating to neighbouring or rival communities SECTARIAN
companion, typically an older woman, for a young woman in public CHAPERONE, DUENNA
– companion or friend who is affectionate, reliable, and usually lively BOON COMPANION
– sociable or festive, as a party atmosphere or drinking companion might be JOVIAL, CONVIVIAL
companionship, comradely or brotherly spirit ESPIRIT DE CORPS, CAMARADERIE, FRATERNITY
company grouping or business association, especially an illegal one, to monopolise manufacture or control prices CARTEL, TRUST
– company of actors performing a variety of plays during a season REPERTORY COMPANY
– company or business having control of other businesses HOLDING COMPANY
– company producing books, TV films, or the like for another company PACKAGER
– company that is under another company's control SUBSIDIARY COMPANY
– company trademark, emblem, or symbol LOGO
– company's distinctive colour scheme on its vehicles, aircraft, or the like LIVERY
– company's rules, or the document containing them, required

for registration ARTICLES OF ASSOCIATION
– business association of various interests or companies formed for some joint enterprise CONSORTIUM, SYNDICATE
– business corporation made up of many wide-ranging companies CONGLOMERATE
– combining or uniting of separate businesses into a larger company CONSOLIDATION
– engage in a variety of activities or investments, as a large company might DIVERSIFY
– financing and launching of a company by means of a share issue FLOTATION
– form a business into a registered company INCORPORATE
– keep company or associate with in a friendly way CONSORT, FRATERNISE, HOBNOB

compared with, in relation to, regarding VIS-À-VIS

comparison or metaphor of a witty, far-fetched kind CONCEIT
– comparison showing the similarity between otherwise differing elements ANALOGY
– degrees of comparison of adjectives and adverbs POSITIVE, COMPARATIVE, SUPERLATIVE
– measure or standard used for comparison YARDSTICK
– placed side by side, as for comparison JUXTAPOSED
– so different or distinct that no comparison is possible DISPARATE
– standard of comparison in a statistical analysis or scientific experiment CONTROL
– unfair or offensive, as a discriminatory comparison would be INVIDIOUS

compass direction or course, as of an aircraft, especially when guided by radio VECTOR
– compass error due to variant local magnetic conditions DEVIATION
– compass-stand on a ship BINNACLE
– circle, often decorated, printed on a map, showing the points of the compass COMPASS ROSE
– device to keep a compass horizontal at sea GIMBALS
– four main compass points CARDINAL POINTS

compasses – measuring instrument resembling a pair of compasses, used for measuring angular distance SECTOR
– instrument resembling a pair of compasses, used in draughtsmanship for measuring or comparing lengths DIVIDERS
– pair of compasses for drawing large circles, or similar instrument for drawing ellipses TRAMMEL

compatible – make two apparently conflicting things consistent or compatible with each other RECONCILE

compensate for loss or damages INDEMNIFY, REIMBURSE, RECOMPENSE
– compensate for, offset, make up for COUNTERVAIL
– compensation, making good, repayment RESTITUTION, REPARATIONS, REDEMPTION, AMENDS, REDRESS

compete, struggle, or strive VIE, CONTEND
– compete with or rival, strive to equal or outdo EMULATE

competition See also **contest**
– competition, contest, or race in which the entire prize is awarded to the winner SWEEPSTAKE
– competition, of Welsh origin, for young musicians, actors, or the like EISTEDDFOD
– competition or tournament in which all the contestants compete against one another in turn, the "league" system ROUND ROBIN
– relating to competitions and competitors AGONISTIC

complain See also **protest**, **object**, **criticise**
– complain, fret, be disheartened or depressed REPINE
– complain, protest, or object earnestly REMONSTRATE, EXPOSTULATE
– complain at or regret sadly, lament BEWAIL
– complain or grumble at petty things, nitpick, raise trivial objections CAVIL, CARP
– complain or grumble in a whining way WHINGE, KVETCH, YAMMER
– complaining in a whining way, fretful or peevish QUERULOUS
– complaining noisily VOCIFEROUS

complaint, protest, or statement, as in diplomatic matters or to the public authorities DÉMARCHE
– complaint or protest, or the injustice giving rise to it GRIEVANCE
– complaint that is long and lamenting JEREMIAD
– complaints or appeals, as to an authority REPRESENTATIONS
– essential or most telling part of an acccusation, charge, or complaint GRAVAMEN
– official investigating citizens' complaints into government incompetence or unfairness OMBUDSMAN
– register a complaint LODGE

complement, additional or matching part PENDANT
– complement or counterpart OBVERSE

complete See also **end**, **stop**
– complete, absolute, unlimited, as the surrender of a warring nation might be UNCONDITIONAL
– complete, detailed, thorough, as a report might be COMPREHENSIVE, CIRCUMSTANTIAL, EXHAUSTIVE
– complete, reliable, and authoritative, as a history or biography might be DEFINITIVE
– complete, utter, absolute RANK, OUTRIGHT, UNMITIGATED
– complete and impressive display, defence, or the like PANOPLY
– completeness, fullness PLENITUDE, PLENUM
– completeness, unity, undivided or unbroken condition INTEGRITY
– steps towards the completion of a task or process INROADS
– time required to complete a process, especially in manufacturing or transport TURNROUND

complete- HOL-, HOLO-, TEL-, TELO-

completely- CATA-, PAN-

complex of unconscious emotions, in Freudian theory, affecting a young child, including sexual desire in the boy for his mother, and in the girl for her father OEDIPUS COMPLEX
– Oedipus complex in a young girl ELECTRA COMPLEX

complexion – pale sickly yellowish in colour or complexion SALLOW
– reddish in appearance or complexion, rosy, ruddy, or flushed FLORID
– referring to or having a reddish complexion SANGUINE

complicate, obscure, confuse OBFUSCATE

complicated See **difficult**
– complicated, complex, having many interrelated or entangled elements INTRICATE, INVOLUTED, RETICULAR
– complicated or devious, as intrigue often is LABYRINTHINE, BYZANTINE

complication, tangle, confusing factor CONVOLUTION
– complications, aftereffects, or condition following a disease SEQUELLA
– complications, unavoidable and usually undesirable consequences of an action or decision RAMIFICATIONS

compliment See **praise**

compliments, respects, courteous greetings DEVOIRS

composer – composer's work, typically numbered in sequence OPUS

– share of the proceeds paid to a composer from sales or performances of his work ROYALTY

compound, made up of several parts COMPOSITE

– breaking down of a chemical compound into its constituents ANALYSIS

– forming of a chemical compound from its constituents SYNTHESIS

compressed air – filled with or run by compressed air, as most tyres and some drills are PNEUMATIC

compromise, adapt oneself, or submit so as to fit in with current conditions as a way of gaining time TEMPORISE

– compromise between people with competing interests, allowing them to get on together MODUS VIVENDI

– compromising or insincere person adapting his actions and opinions to those currently accepted TIMESERVER

compulsion or force, as by threatening DURESS, COERCION, CONSTRAINT

– compulsion to talk, sometimes caused by mental illness LOGORRHOEA

compulsive, irrational and habitual, as a liar might be PATHOLOGICAL

compulsory, unavoidable, required OBLIGATORY, STATUTORY, MANDATORY, IMPERATIVE

– compulsory, done or required against one's will INVOLUNTARY

computer See also chart of **computer terms**, page 114

– computer-aided study of information flow and control systems in electronics, mechanics, and biology CYBERNETICS

– computer chip, tiny electronic circuit based on a semiconductor wafer SILICON CHIP

– application of biology to engineering and electronics, especially of brain functions to computers BIONICS

– capable of functioning together in an efficient way, as two linked computer parts should be COMPATIBLE

– computerised mathematical representation of a problem, system, or situation SIMULATION

comradely feeling, trust, and understanding between people RAPPORT, CAMARADERIE

conceal See **hidden**, **hide**

– conceal or cover up mistakes or wrongdoing WHITEWASH

– concealment of relevant information in order to mislead SUBREPTION

– steps taken to conceal misdeeds or actions in order to mislead SMOKE SCREEN

concentrate or thicken, as by boiling or evaporation INSPISSATE

– concentrated and exaggerated interest in a single idea or subject MONOMANIA

– concentrated extract or essence of something QUINTESSENCE

– concentrating intensely, deeply absorbed INTENT, ENGROSSED

– gradual evening out of differently concentrated solutions by transfer through the separating membrane OSMOSIS

– interruption, hindrance to concentration DISTRACTION

– measurement of the concentration of a solute by adding a chemical reagent to the solution TITRATION

– restore something to its natural state, such as dried food or concentrated lemon juice, as by adding water RECONSTITUTE

conception occurring in a female who has already conceived SUPERFETATION

concert building or theatre in ancient Greece and Rome ODEUM

– concert performance by a solo musician RECITAL

– payment or order for an advance purchase, as of concert tickets or issues of a magazine over a period of time SUBSCRIPTION

– producer or organiser of stage shows, concerts, or the like IMPRESARIO

concise See also **brief**, **summary**

– concise, clearly, and economically expressed, unelaborated and to the point SUCCINCT, TERSE, PITHY, SUMMARY, COMPENDIOUS

– concise, often to the point of obscurity, as a literary style might be ELLIPTICAL

– concise and elegant, as a prose style might be LAPIDARY

– concise in a wry or offhand way LACONIC

– concisely and cleverly expressed, pointed, typically with a witty twist or puzzle EPIGRAMMATIC, APHORISTIC, GNOMIC

– conciseness, terseness, as of speech or writing BREVITY

conclude See **end**, **stop**

concluding part of a formal speech or written discourse, typically a rhetorical summing-up PERORATION

– concluding part of the action in a play or novel, resolving or unravelling the plot DENOUEMENT

– concluding poem or speech following the end of the action of a play EPILOGUE

conclusion based on strict logical reasoning DEDUCTION, INFERENCE

– conclusion on the basis of evidence that is not or cannot ever be exhaustive GENERALISATION

– conclusion that is wrongly or illogically derived from the premises NON SEQUITUR

– proposition on which an argument is based or from which a conclusion can be drawn PREMISE

– reasonable or logical, as a conclusion might be LEGITIMATE

concrete See also **cement**

– concrete machine-gun emplacement PILLBOX

– concrete mixture or finish, as on a floor SCREED

– coarse gravel, sand, or stones, used in making concrete BALLAST, AGGREGATE

– slab of reinforced concrete laid on soft ground as part of a building's foundations RAFT

condemn See **criticise**

condense See **summary**

– condense or thicken, as by boiling or evaporation INSPISSATE

– condenser used in distillation, as for purifying chemicals RECTIFIER

condescend to do something DEIGN

– condescend to, treat graciously as though dealing with a subordinate PATRONISE

– condescending system of government or authority, typically caring but restricting individual responsibility PATERNALISM

condition See also **disease**

– condition of difficulty or distress PLIGHT, PREDICAMENT, QUANDARY, DILEMMA

– condition or restriction, as in an agreement or document PROVISO

– clause, typically beginning with *if* or *unless*, stating the condition in a conditional sentence or proposition PROTASIS, ANTECEDENT

– main clause, stating the conclusion or consequence, in a conditional sentence or proposition APODOSIS, CONSEQUENT

– prior condition for something, necessity or requirement PREREQUISITE, PRESUPPOSITION

– require or lay down as a condition in an agreement or contract STIPULATE

-condition -OSIS, -TUDE

conditional, depending CONTINGENT

conditioning, in psychology, based on associating a response with a reinforcing reward OPERANT CONDITIONING, INSTRUMENTAL CONDITIONING

– conditioning, in psychology, based on associating two stimuli and thereby eliciting a response from an originally unrelated stimulus CLASSICAL CONDITIONING, PAVLOVIAN CONDITIONING
conduct See **behave**
conductor, music teacher, leading musician, orchestra conductor or any artistic master MAESTRO
– conductor's stick for directing the orchestra BATON
– platform, as for a public speaker or music conductor ROSTRUM, DAIS, PODIUM
cone or cylinder with its top cut off at an angle UNGULA
– cone-shaped tied bundle, as of hay or straw COCK
– cone-shaped ornament or container CORNUCOPIA
– cone-shaped, resembling a cone on its tip TURBINATE
– cone-shaped roll of thread wound on a spindle COP
– cone-shaped starched headdress worn by women in the late Middle

COMPUTER TERMS

ALGOL	Algorithmic Oriented Language — an arithmetical computer language
analog computer	former type of computer operating with numbers represented by corresponding voltages, rotations, or other physical quantities
BASIC	Beginner's All-purpose Symbolic Instruction Code — a computer language
binary system	number system, as used by computers, representing all numbers as combinations of the digits 0 and 1
bit	smallest unit in a computer's memory
bug	fault in a computer system or program
byte	standard unit, equivalent to eight bits, used to measure a computer's memory
COBOL	Common Business Oriented Language — a computer language
CPU	Central Processing Unit — the core of a computer, performing the logical and arithmetical operations on the data
cursor	movable pointer on a VDU, typically a small square of light, indicating a specific position
dedicated	referring to a computer or program designed or set apart for a particular function
digital computer	computer operating with numbers represented by separate electronically expressed digits, typically in the binary system
disk	information storage device, consisting of a flat rotating circular disc with a magnetic coating
disk drive	device for "playing" a disk to transfer information to or from it
format	arrange data in a form that is usable by a computer
floppy disk/ diskette	thin flexible plastic disk, as used in home computers
FORTRAN	Formula Translation — an algebraic computer language
GIGO	Garbage In, Garbage Out — a formula serving as a reminder that a computer is only as good as its users
hacker	person who gains unauthorised access to a computer system
hardware	actual machinery or physical parts of a computer
interface	item of hardware or software that connects two other items of computing equipment
K/kilobyte	standard unit of measure for a computer's capacity, 1024 bytes
mainframe	large powerful computer; CPU
modem	modulator demodulator — device for transmitting computer data along telephone lines
mouse	small device rolled along the table top, used to move a cursor on a VDU
OCR	Optical Character Reader — device for "reading" printed texts and converting them into an electronic form usable by a computer
peripheral	item of hardware, such as a modem or disk drive, that is not specifically part of the CPU
pixel	basic unit of a computer graphics display on a VDU
program	set of directions or procedures that a computer follows to operate on data
RAM	Random Access Memory — set of data that may be changed or erased
ROM	Read Only Memory — set of data that cannot be changed or erased
scrolling	vertical movement of text on a VDU
software	set of programs, data, and the like essential to a computer system but not forming part of the actual machinery
user friendly	easy for a person to handle
VDU	Visual Display Unit — the screen, such as a cathode ray tube, displaying information from a computer

Ages CORNET
– base part or mid-section of a cone, pyramid, or other solid object FRUSTUM

conference of top officials SUMMIT
– conference or discussion, typically on a specialist academic or professional theme SYMPOSIUM, COLLOQUIUM
– conference or meeting for the exchange of information SEMINAR
– conference representative DELEGATE
– published records or transcripts of a conference, learned society's meetings, or the like PROCEEDINGS, TRANSACTIONS

confess, admit, acknowledge AVOW, CONCEDE
– confess or hear confession SHRIVE

confession heard or absolution granted by a priest SHRIFT
– confession of guilt, acknowledgment of wrongdoing or sin PECCAVI, MEA CULPA
– person who confesses his sins to a priest and submits to penance PENITENT

confetti – welcoming parade in the U.S., where paper strips are thrown like confetti TICKER-TAPE PARADE

confide or reveal one's thoughts or feelings UNBOSOM

confident, optimistic SANGUINE
– confident, poised, not embarrassed UNABASHED
– confident and optimistic spirits, as among soldiers MORALE
– confidence, self-assurance, poise APLOMB
– cause to lose confidence, discourage DISHEARTEN, DEMORALISE
– lose confidence momentarily, hesitate WAVER, FALTER
– shy, lacking in confidence or self-assertiveness DIFFIDENT, HALTING
– strengthen or revive something, such as a person's confidence BOLSTER

confidentially, between ourselves, in confidence ENTRE NOUS

confine, as in jail INCARCERATE
– confine, shackle, make fast or secure PINION

confirm See also **strengthen**
– confirm, assure WARRANT
– confirm a law, ruling, or the like, approve officially RATIFY, SANCTION, VALIDATE
– confirm as genuine, prove, bear out VOUCH FOR, ATTEST, VERIFY, AUTHENTICATE
– confirm as valid or just, uphold something, such as an objection in a court of law SUSTAIN
– confirm or back up an opinion or statement, as with additional evidence CORROBORATE, SUBSTANTIATE

confirmation – mixture of oil and balsam used in sacramental anointing, as at baptism or confirmation CHRISM

confiscate or arrest with the backing of legal authority ATTACH
– confiscate or hold in custody IMPOUND, EMBARGO
– confiscate or seize for military use COMMANDEER
– confiscate or seize property temporarily, especially a debtor's goods SEQUESTRATE
– confiscate or transfer the ownership of, especially for public use EXPROPRIATE
– sheriff's officer who carries out a court's orders, such as confiscating the property of a bankrupt BAILIFF

conflict See also **fight**, **hostile**, **dispute**
– conflict, inconsistency, lack of agreement, as between two claims DISPARITY, DISCREPANCY, DISSONANCE, INCONGRUITY
– conflict, strife, disharmony, infighting DISCORD, DISSENSION
– conflict between two rules or laws ANTINOMY
– conflict or argument within a larger dispute, often affecting outsiders CROSSFIRE
– conflict or disagreement within a group, nation, or the like FACTION
– belief or religion based on a conflict between the universal forces or principles, as of good and evil, or the light and the dark MANICHAEISM
– minor or preliminary conflict, dispute, or military encounter SKIRMISH
– referring to destructive conflict within a group INTERNECINE
– standstill in a conflict, resulting from equal strength or stubbornness STALEMATE, DEADLOCK

conflicting, differing, not in agreement, in dispute AT VARIANCE, AT LOGGERHEADS
– conflicting, inharmonious, incapable of working or living together INCOMPATIBLE, IRRECONCILABLE
– conflicting trend, tendency, or the like CROSSCURRENT

conformity – arbitrary standard that must be conformed to exactly PROCRUSTEAN BED

confront, accuse, or criticise TAX
– confront someone unexpectedly ACCOST, WAYLAY

confuse, embarrass, or fluster DISCONCERT, DISCOMFIT, DISCOUNTENANCE
– confuse, mistake one thing for another, treat two different things as the same CONFOUND
– confuse, obscure, complicate OBFUSCATE

confused, dazed, or dizzy WOOZY
– confused, disordered, or entangled, as a complicated state of affairs might be EMBROILED, TURBID
– confused, flustered, taken aback DISCOMBOBULATED
– confused, puzzled, mystified BEWILDERED, PERPLEXED, NONPLUSSED, FLUMMOXED, BEMUSED
– confused, stunned, or dazed, as by drink STUPEFIED, BEFUDDLED
– confused or disorganised, utterly chaotic HAYWIRE, SHAMBOLIC, ANARCHIC
– confused or entangled situation IMBROGLIO, PREDICAMENT, MORASS, QUAGMIRE
– confused or haphazard in structure, made up of a random mix of elements PROMISCUOUS
– confused or nonsensical speech or writing RIGMAROLE
– confused or uneasy through having lost one's bearings DISORIENTATED
– confused use of a word through mistaking it for a similar-sounding word MALAPROPISM
– confusedly, haphazardly, in a disordered way HELTER-SKELTER

confusing, maze-like place or thing, such as a crowded neighbourhood WARREN

confusion See also **mixture**, **nonsense**
– confusion, muddle, disorder HUGGER-MUGGER, HURLY-BURLY, SCHEMOZZLE
– confusion, stir, upheaval, fuss HULLABALOO, BROUHAHA, FURORE, KERFUFFLE
– confusion, uproar, utter chaos BEDLAM, PANDEMONIUM, MAYHEM, HAVOC
– burst of excitement, confusion, or activity FLURRY
– dismay or amazement that throws everything into confusion CONSTERNATION
– noisy confusion or upheaval COMMOTION, HUBBUB, TUMULT
– scene of confusion or noisy disorder BABEL, BEAR GARDEN
– sense of dizziness and confusion, as through fear of heights VERTIGO
– situation of utter confusion, hopeless mess SNAFU, SHAMBLES
– state of agitation, unrest, or confusion FERMENT, TURBULENCE,

TURMOIL, WELTER, PERTURBATION
– state of disorder or confusion DISARRAY, MAELSTROM, ANARCHY
– sudden violent disturbance, disruption, or confusion UPHEAVAL
congratulate oneself on something, plume oneself PIQUE, PREEN
congratulations FELICITATIONS
conjunction, such as *and* or *but*, joining words, phrases, or clauses of equal status in a sentence COORDINATING CONJUNCTION
– conjunction, such as *if* or *provided that*, introducing a supposition SUPPOSITIVE
– conjunction, such as *when* or *if*, joining clauses of unequal status in a sentence SUBORDINATING CONJUNCTION, SUBORDINATOR
– conjunctions, such as *neither* and *nor*, paired in a complementary grammatical relationship CORRELATIVE CONJUNCTIONS
– linking of phrases or clauses by means of punctuation rather than conjunctions PARATAXIS
– omission of conjunctions from a sentence ASYNDETON
– repetition of conjunctions for stylistic effect, as in *blood and sweat and tears* POLYSYNDETON
– serving to connect, as a conjunction does, or joined by a conjunction SYNDETIC
– subordination of a clause in grammar by means of a conjunction HYPOTAXIS
conjure up a spirit EVOKE
conjuring See **magician**
connect See also **join**
– connect, as two rooms might, through a shared door, passage, or the like COMMUNICATE
– connect, join, or fit neatly or harmoniously DOVETAIL
– connect in a series CONCATENATE, CATENATE
– connect with, be related to, belong to as a rightful part or function APPERTAIN
– connecting tie or bond LIGAMENT
connection or network of connections NEXUS
connoisseur, person appreciating fine food and wine, GOURMET, EPICURE, GASTRONOME
– connoisseur in the arts VIRTUOSO
– connoisseurs, experts in a particular subject or art COGNOSCENTI
conquer See also **defeat**
– conquer and subdue, force into subjection SUBJUGATE
– conquer or occupy territory, and incorporate it into another state or an empire ANNEX
conqueror, specifically any of the 16th-century Spanish conquerors of Mexico, Peru, and other regions in the New World CONQUISTADOR
conscience, guilty feeling, regret or remorse COMPUNCTION
– driven by conscience to rebuke oneself or others REPROACH
– pang of doubt, hesitation for reasons of conscience, principle, social unease, or the like MISGIVING, SCRUPLE, QUALM
– unscrupulous, not guided or restrained by conscience UNCONSCIONABLE
conscientious, active or industrious, persevering in one's duty SEDULOUS, ASSIDUOUS, DILIGENT
– conscientious in a rigorous, painstaking way SCRUPULOUS, PUNCTILIOUS, METICULOUS
conscious, aware, responsive to stimuli SENTIENT
– conscious, informed, having knowledge COGNISANT
– conscious or sane period between bouts of coma or insanity LUCID MOMENT
– attempted suspension of normal consciousness by writers and artists to bring out submerged ideas AUTOMATISM
– below or beyond the threshold of consciousness or perception SUBLIMINAL
consequences See **result**
conservative, anti-progressive, as in art or politics REACTIONARY
– conservative and pompous man, especially an officer or bureaucrat COLONEL BLIMP
– conservative and powerful group of people, directing or influencing social trends, artistic activity, or the like ESTABLISHMENT
– conservative element, as in a political party REARGUARD
– conservative or reactionary, as in politics HARD-HAT
– extreme conservative, stubbornly opposed to change DIEHARD
consider See **think**
consist of, be composed of COMPRISE
consistent See also **agree**, **regular**
– consistent, corresponding, in a harmonious or matching relationship COORDINATED, CONGRUOUS, CONSONANT
– consistent, in agreement CONFORMABLE, IN UNISON
– consistent, unchanging, regular and reliable UNDEVIATING, UNSWERVING, UNFALTERING, UNWAVERING, STEADFAST
– consistent, uniform, or unchanging, as through habit CHRONIC, INVETERATE, UNREGENERATE
– consistency or harmony, as between attitudes or claims CONCORD, CONCURRENCE
– fitting, living, or working together in a harmonious and consistent relationship COMPATIBLE
– make two apparently conflicting things consistent with each other RECONCILE
consolation, comfort, cheer SOLACE
conspicuous or exceptionally noticeable PROMINENT
– conspicuously or glaringly wrong or evil FLAGRANT, EGREGIOUS
conspiracy See also **plot**
– conspiracy or plot, or group of plotters CABAL, CONFEDERACY
– banded together in conspiracy IN CAHOOTS
– criminal conspiracy to cheat or injure a victim COVIN
constant See also **permanent**
– constant, continuing uninterruptedly, unceasing INCESSANT
– constant, long-lasting DURABLE, ABIDING, PERSISTENT
– constant, regular, even, unchanging INVARIABLE
– constant, unchanging, regular and reliable UNDEVIATING, STEADFAST, UNWAVERING, UNSWERVING, UNFALTERING
– constant, uniform, as through habit or compulsion CHRONIC, INVETERATE, UNREGENERATE
– constant, untiring, ceaseless UNFLAGGING, UNREMITTING
– constant or variable determining the form of a mathematical expression PARAMETER
constellation See chart, and also **zodiac**
– constellation or star-cluster ASTERISM

CONSTELLATIONS

Andromeda
Aquarius/ Water Bearer
Aquila/Eagle
Aries/Ram
Auriga/ Charioteer
Boötes/ Herdsman
Cancer/ Crab
Capricornus/ Goat
Cassiopeia
Cepheus
Cetus
Crux/Southern Cross
Cygnus/Swan
Draco/Dragon
Gemini/Twins
Leo/Lion
Libra/Scales
Orion
Pegasus/Flying Horse
Perseus
Pisces/Fish
Sagittarius/ Archer
Scorpius/ Scorpion
Taurus/Bull
Ursa Major/ Great Bear
Ursa Minor/ Little Bear
Virgo/Virgin

constipated or causing constipation COSTIVE
– medicine or other substance that stimulates the bowels and relieves constipation LAXATIVE, CATHARTIC, PURGATIVE

constituency – manipulation of the boundaries of an electoral constituency for party advantage GERRYMANDERING

constitution or statement of aims CHARTER

consume, use up EXPEND

consumption TUBERCULOSIS, TB, PHTHISIS

contact – spread by physical contact, as a disease might be CONTAGIOUS

contagious or infectious, as a disease might be COMMUNICABLE

contain, include, consist of COMPRISE
– contain, take in, or include INCORPORATE, ENCOMPASS
– contain or enclose something considered sacred ENSHRINE
– contained within, forming an integral part of IMPLICIT, INHERENT

-contain- -FER-

container See also **barrel**, **drink**, **jar**, **laboratory**
– container for holy water, oil, or wine AMPULLA, CRUSE
– container for molten metal CRUCIBLE
– container or cage for small plants or animals TERRARIUM
– container or chamber, as for a fluid RESERVOIR, RECEPTACLE, CISTERN
– container or shrine for sacred relics RELIQUARY
– container or small box, especially for tea CADDY
– flat metal container for carrying petrol JERRY CAN
– fuel container, such as a coal bin or petrol tank BUNKER
– large cylindrical container for liquids, towed by a ship DRACONE
– metal container for gas, chemicals, or the like CANISTER
– pressurised steam-heated container AUTOCLAVE
– small bottle or container with a perforated top VINAIGRETTE
– small container, such as a jewellery case CASKET

contemplative, thoughtful, meditative RUMINANT

contemporary, of the same age or period COETANEOUS, COEVAL

contempt or hatred ODIUM
– contempt or scorn DISDAIN
– contemptuous behaviour CONTUMELY
– show contempt or disrespect, belittle, slight DISPARAGE, DECRY, DEPRECIATE, COCK A SNOOK

contempt of court, as by failing to appear in court or disregarding a court order CONTUMACY

contest See also **competition**
– contest for superiority between two people, especially a hand-to-hand contest GRAPPLE
– competition, contest, lottery, or race in which the entry fees form the prize SWEEPSTAKE
– scratch from or fail to appear in a contest or match, thereby forfeiting it DEFAULT
– relating to contests AGONISTIC

context, network, or environment in which something develops MATRIX

continent – original single landmass that split up into the continents of today PANGAEA
– southern part of the Earth's original landmass or supercontinent Pangaea GONDWANALAND
– northern part of the Earth's original landmass or supercontinent Pangaea LAURASIA

continental quilt DUVET

continual See **constant**

continuation, development, something following SEQUEL
– continuation or uncontrollable repetition of an idea, spoken word, or the like PERSEVERATION

continue after a break RESUME
– continue despite discouragement, PERSIST, PERSEVERE
– continue in existence or manage to survive SUBSIST
– continue or persist in so as to complete PROSECUTE
– prolong; continue PERPETUATE

continuous or unbroken belief, course of action, or the like PERSEVERANCE, STEADFASTNESS
– continuous variation in form among members of a widespread species or population CLINE

contort the face into an expression of pain or disgust GRIMACE

contraceptive, especially a condom PREVENTATIVE, PROPHYLACTIC
– internal temporary contraceptive device CERVICAL CAP, DUTCH CAP, DIAPHRAGM
– semi-permanent internal contraceptive device, such as the coil INTRAUTERINE DEVICE, IUD
– sex involving withdrawal prior to ejaculation as a means of contraception COITUS INTERRUPTUS
– surgical cutting of the sperm ducts in the testes, as permanent contraception VASECTOMY

contract, binding agreement, treaty COVENANT, COMPACT
– contract, money, or the like held by a third party until certain conditions are fulfilled ESCROW
– contract to repay a debt after the death of a person whose heir the debtor is POST-OBIT
– amendment to a contract or other document ENDORSEMENT
– clause or amendment added to a contract or other document RIDER
– distinct section of a document, contract, law, or the like CLAUSE
– force or occurrence that unavoidably spoils one's plans or prevents the fulfilment of a contract FORCE MAJEURE
– make ineffective an argument, contract, or the like NULLIFY, INVALIDATE, VITIATE, VOID
– promise or action aimed at producing a legally binding contract CONSIDERATION
– require or lay down as a condition in a contract STIPULATE
– run out, as a contract or membership might EXPIRE
– spoken rather than written, as a contract might be ORAL, VERBAL

contracted as an apprentice or trainee ARTICLED
– contracted as a labourer for a specific period INDENTURED

contradict, dispute, deny, or call into question OPPUGN
– contradict, prove false, give the lie to BELIE, NEGATE

contradiction between two equally plausible statements PARADOX, ANTINOMY
– contradiction or incongruous phrase used as a figure of speech OXYMORON

contrary, opposing others' wishes or suggestions unreasonably PERVERSE, FROWARD

contrast, as of colour or shading, and the resulting emphasis RELIEF
– contrast as a literary or artistic technique CHIAROSCURO
– contrast or opposite ANTITHESIS
– contrasting person or thing FOIL
– placed side by side, as for contrast JUXTAPOSED

contribute or pledge a sum of money, as to a charity or for a telephone service SUBSCRIBE

contribution that is small but considered generous WIDOW'S MITE
– referring to a contribution made by an unknown or unnamed donor ANONYMOUS

control, direct, have or exercise authority PRESIDE
– control rule, power, or authority DOMINION, SOVEREIGNTY, JURISDICTION
– control and direct a force or energy HARNESS
– control events by careful manipulation STAGE-MANAGE

– control fully, dominate to the exclusion of all others MONOPOLISE
– control operation or project, as to prevent further damage HOLDING OPERATION
– control or care, as granted by a court CUSTODY
– control or direct in keeping with the standard rules REGULATE
– control or self-restraint, such as sexual restraint CONTINENCE
– controlling and constricting force, as of custom TYRANNY, STRANGLEHOLD
– controlling or steering position, as in government TILLER, HELM
– controlling power over a dependent state, typically over its foreign affairs SUZERAINTY
– leading position of power, influence, or control DOMINANCE, PRE-EMINENCE, ASCENDANCY
– loss of bodily power or control PALSY
– medicinal drug that controls by calming or suppressing emotions BROMIDE
– self-control in surprising or dangerous circumstances SANG FROID
– subject to one's control by restraining or subduing SUBJUGATE, SUBORDINATE
– supervise, oversee, have control over SUPERINTEND

controversy See **argument**, **dispute**
– notorious or controversial court case or other event that is hotly debated in public CAUSE CÉLÈBRE

convalescent home SANATORIUM

conveniences, comforts or services FACILITIES, AMENITIES

convenient, advantageous rather than fair or moral EXPEDIENT
– convenient, handy, occurring at a favourable time OPPORTUNE

convent, monastery, or other place of seclusion or retreat CLOISTER
– convent or monastery PRIORY
– head of a convent or other religious community SUPERIOR

conventional, coldly formal, or traditional in approach to art or the like ACADEMIC
– conventional, usually oversimplified image or opinion of someone or something STEREOTYPE
– conventional current, direction, or trend MAINSTREAM
– conventional medicine, as op-

COOKING TERMS

al dente	referring to pasta that is cooked but firm to the bite	**hull**	remove the leaves and stems of soft fruit
à point	referring to medium-cooked meat	**infuse**	steep in water or other liquid
au bleu	referring to very rare meat	**jardinière**	garnished with vegetables
bard	place fat or bacon on lean meat before roasting	**lard**	thread strips of fat through lean meat before roasting
bien cuit	referring to well-done meat	**liaison**	thickening agent such as cream, for sauces, soups, and the like
blanch	boil very briefly	**macedoine**	mixture of fruit or vegetables
bouchée	small puff-pastry case	**macerate**	soften by soaking in liquid
bouillon	stock or clear broth	**marinade**	blend of oil, wine or vinegar, herbs and spices used to tenderise and flavour meat, game, or poultry
bouquet garnis	bunch or small bag of herbs	**marinate**	steep in marinade
brulé	glazed with a caramelised sugar	**medallion**	small circular cut of meat or fish
chine	separate backbone from ribs in a joint of meat	**parboil**	boil briefly to cook food slightly
coddle	simmer eggs slowly	**purée**	mash or pulp fruit or vegetables, as by long cooking or in a blender
crème fraiche	cream that is mature but not sour	**roux**	mixture of fat and flour, used as base for sauce
crimp	gash or score meat for crisper cooking	**saignant**	referring to underdone meat
devilling	grilling or roasting with highly seasoned ingredients	**sauté**	fry lightly in a little fat
dredge	coat with flour or sugar	**shirr**	bake eggs that have been removed from their shells
en croute	in pastry	**soused**	pickled
farci	stuffed	**sweat**	cook vegetables or fruit slowly to release their juices
fines herbes	fresh, finely chopped mixture of parsley, chervil, tarragon and chives	**zest**	outer, coloured skin of citrus fruit
flambé	served or covered with flaming spirit		

posed to homeopathy ALLOPATHY
– conventional or artificial rather than realistic STYLISED
conventions of a social group, defining it and its values MORES
conversation, especially between two people or groups DIALOGUE
– conversation, exchange of views DISCOURSE, CONFABULATION, PARLEY
– conversation in private between two people TÊTE-À-TÊTE
– conversation monopolised by one speaker MONOLOGUE
– conversation or formal dialogue or interview COLLOQUY
– conversation or gossipy meeting GABFEST, CAUSERIE
– conversation of a playful and joking nature BADINAGE, BANTER
– conversation with sharp and witty retorts BACKCHAT, REPARTEE
– jumping about, disconnected, as conversation might be DESULTORY
– observation, as in a conversation, that departs from the main subject DIGRESSION, ASIDE, PARENTHESIS, EXCURSION, EXCURSUS
– person taking part in a conversation INTERLOCUTOR, COLLOCUTOR
– person who excels in conversations at the dinner table DEIPNOSOPHIST
– referring to conversation, as about the weather, which expresses friendly feelings rather than communicates ideas PHATIC
conversational, informal, as in casual spoken language COLLOQUIAL
conversion and arithmetical table READY RECKONER
– conversion chart or manual for exchange rates or weights and measures CAMBIST
convert See also **change**
– convert, especially a new convert, to a religion or doctrine PROSELYTE, NEOPHYTE
– convert from Judaism to Christianity in medieval Spain or Portugal MARRANO
– convert or channel a sexual urge or other instinctual energy into a socially or culturally more acceptable activity SUBLIMATE
– convert or desert, become a renegade TERGIVERSATE, APOSTATISE, RENEGE
– convert or transform something, such as base metal into gold COMMUTE
convict with special privileges, as for good behaviour TRUSTY
– ship a convict in former times overseas to a penal colony TRANSPORT
– temporary barracks for convicts or slaves in former times BARRACOON
convincing See **persuasive**
– convincing or the quality of being convincing CONVICTION
cook food, especially eggs, in water at just below boiling point CODDLE
cooker top HOB
cooking See charts, and also **menu terms** and entries at various types of food
– cooking, as of a particular style or region CUISINE, GASTRONOMY
– cooking of a high-class French style that cuts down on rich ingredients CUISINE MINCEUR
– cooking of high quality HAUTE CUISINE
– cooking stove of a large iron make, usually burning coal or wood, with one or more ovens RANGE
– cooking stove, small and portable, burning paraffin or kerosene PRIMUS
– metal stand or support, usually with three legs, especially for cooking pots or hot dishes TRIVET
– referring to food or cooking of a very high standard CORDON BLEU
– relating to cooking or the kitchen CULINARY
cool See **cold**, **calm**
cooling substance, as for operating a fridge or reducing a fever REFRIGERANT
coolness, calmness, self-possession, ability to remain unruffled when in danger or under stress SANG-FROID
cooperate, act together, combine CONCUR
– cooperate secretly, conspire CONNIVE
– cooperate in a treasonous way with the enemy forces occupying one's country COLLABORATE
– cooperate with, indulge, or give in to a person's whims or wishes GRATIFY, PANDER TO
– cooperating, capable of living, working, or functioning together in a harmonious or efficient way COMPATIBLE
– cooperating, working in conjunction IN TANDEM
– cooperation or obedience of a token or insincere kind LIP SERVICE
cooperative, helpful, or considerate OBLIGING, COMPLIANT, COMPLAISANT, ACCOMMODATING
– cooperative, readily influenceable MALLEABLE, PLIABLE, FLEXIBLE
– cooperative, submissive, easily controlled AMENABLE, BIDDABLE, TRACTABLE, DOCILE

COOKING UTENSILS

bain-marie	double saucepan, or large pan of hot water in which smaller pans are placed
brochette	small spit or skewer
casserole	ovenproof dish with a close-fitting lid
cocotte	small ovenproof dish
coquille	shell-shaped ovenproof dish
Dutch oven	large, heavy iron pan with a lid; three-sided metal oven used in front of an open fire; oven that cooks by means of preheated bricks
griddle	flat cooking surface, as used for drop scones
mandolin	vegetable slicer in the form of a wooden board and adjustable blade, used for fine-slicing vegetables
olla	wide-mouthed earthenware pot or jar
palette knife	knife with a flat, blunt, pliable blade
ramekin	individual ovenproof dish
terrine	earthenware pot
timbale	cup-shaped mould
wok	large, bowl-shaped metal pan used in Chinese cooking

– cooperative action of two or more muscles, medicines, or the like to produce a greater joint effect SYNERGISM
– cooperative business relationship, trade policy, exchange of commercial favours and privileges, and so on RECIPROCITY
– cooperative farm or settlement in Israel KIBBUTZ
– cooperative farm or settlement in the USSR KOLKHOZ
– cooperative or protective instinct or behaviour among animals, serving to benefit the species as a whole ALTRUISM
– cooperative relationship or close beneficial association between two or more different plants or animals SYMBIOSIS
– cooperative settlement in Israel, consisting of a group of small farms MOSHAV

coordination – lack of coordination, movement disability, caused by brain damage or disease APRAXIA, ATAXIA

cope, contend with or struggle to overcome GRAPPLE

copper – greenish coating forming on exposed copper, brass, or bronze objects VERDIGRIS, VERD ANTIQUE, AERUGO
– thin layer of oxide, usually green, forming naturally or artificially on a copper or bronze surface PATINA

-copper- -CHALC-, CHALCO-, CUPR-, CUPRI-, CUPRO-

copy See also **imitate**
– copy, often on a smaller scale, especially of a work of art REPLICA, REPRODUCTION
– copy in writing or typescript of court proceedings, a student's academic record, or the like TRANSCRIPT
– copy of a garment made up in cheap cloth as a basis for alterations TOILE
– copy or exact reproduction, as of a document FACSIMILE
– copy or forge something, especially money, for the purpose of fraud COUNTERFEIT
– copy someone else's ideas, writings, or the like and present them as one's own PLAGIARISE
– copy or model in reduced size MINIATURE
– copy or reproduce four times QUADRUPLICATE
– copy or reproduce three times TRIPLICATE
– copy or reproduce twice DUPLICATE
– copied from or based on an earlier example, unoriginal DERIVATIVE
– copying process, as in some photocopying machines XEROGRAPHY, XEROX
– exact genetic copy or duplicate, or group of genetically identical organisms, such as plants produced from cuttings CLONE
– instrument for copying which transfers a diagram by means of a lever system when the original is traced over PANTOGRAPH
– machine for copying, typically one in which a stencil is stretched over a rotating inked drum DUPLICATOR, MIMEOGRAPH, RONEO, CYCLOSTYLE
– make or be a copy of, reproduce REPLICATE
– neat and clean copy of a revised and corrected document FAIR COPY
– person who copied manuscripts in former times SCRIBE, SCRIVENER, AMANUENSIS
– separate multiple copies, continuous stationery, or the like into individual documents DECOLLATE

copyright – unauthorised use of someone else's idea, patent, copyright material, or the like PIRACY, PLAGIARISM

coral, sea anemone, or related aquatic creature, typically tube-like and tentacled POLYP
– coral or rock reef, parallel to the coastline and often forming a lagoon BARRIER REEF
– coral reef or small coral island chain, typically circular and forming a lagoon ATOLL

cord, twine, or rope used for tying or binding LASHING
– cord or narrow braid used for binding or trimming BOBBIN
– cord or tube linking a foetus to the mother's placenta UMBILICAL CORD
– decoratively braided cord, worn on the left shoulder, as on a military uniform FOURRAGÈRE
– cord worn round an Arab headdress to hold it in place AGAL

cordial or flavouring of pomegranate or redcurrant syrup GRENADINE

corduroy – rib or ridge on corduroy or a similar fabric, or the texture of such a fabric WALE

core of a speech, plot, or argument GIST, BURDEN, GRAVAMEN

cork, bung, plug STOPPLE
– cork or flat bung for a wide-mouthed bottle SHIVE
– corky, relating to or consisting of cork tissue SUBEROSE

corn, wart, or other small benign growth PAPILLOMA
– corn on the cob INDIAN CORN, MAIZE, MEALIE
– beat corn to separate the seed from the stems and husks THRESH, FLAIL
– gather leftover corn or other crops from a field after harvesting GLEAN
– treatment or care of the feet, as by cutting corns CHIROPODY

cornea- KERAT-, KERATO-

corner by a fireplace, often with seats facing each other INGLENOOK
– corner on the outside of a building CANT
– cut off the edge or corner of something BEVEL, CHAMFER

cornerstone of a building QUOIN, COIGN

coronation – cushioned stool for kneeling on during prayer, as by a sovereign at the coronation FALDSTOOL

coroner and public prosecutor in Scotland PROCURATOR FISCAL
– coroner's court finding of death without specifying the cause OPEN VERDICT
– coroner's investigation or inquiry into the cause of a death INQUEST

corpse, especially for medical research or dissection CADAVER
– corpse animated by a voodoo spell ZOMBIE
– corpse of an animal or bird CARCASS
– building or room in which corpses are stored prior to autopsy, burial, or the like MORTUARY, MORGUE
– building or room in which corpses or bones were stored in former times CHARNEL HOUSE
– cloth used to wrap a corpse for burial SHROUD, WINDING SHEET
– deep-freezing of a corpse, with the intention of reviving it in the future CRYONICS
– disposal of a corpse by burning it to ashes in a furnace CREMATION
– feeding on corpses or carrion NECROPHAGOUS
– medical examination or dissection of a corpse, usually to establish the cause of death POSTMORTEM, AUTOPSY, NECROPSY
– platform or stand for a corpse or coffin, prior to burial BIER
– preserve a corpse from decay by chemical treatment EMBALM
– raised platform or table on which a coffin or corpse lies, as during a state funeral CATAFALQUE
– remove a corpse from a grave EXHUME, DISINTER
– slang term for a corpse STIFF
– wax-coated cloth in which

corpses were formerly wrapped CERECLOTH, CEREMENT
corpse- NECR-, NECRO-
correct See also **improve**, **perfect**, **true**, **accurate**
– correct, proper, as it should be COMME IL FAUT
– correct, put someone right, rid someone of a mistaken idea DISABUSE
– correct, right and proper, acceptable or genuine PUKKA, KOSHER
– correct, set right, adjust RECTIFY, REMEDY, REDRESS
– correct all the time and in every case INFALLIBLE, UNERRING
– correct and improve a text by critical editing EMEND
– correct or applicable, as a sound argument is VALID
– capable of being corrected, or submitting to correction CORRIGIBLE
– confirm as existent, true, correct, or genuine ATTEST, CORROBORATE
– correcting, improving, beneficial, as advice might be SALUTARY
– correcting defects, faulty habits, or the like REMEDIAL
correct- ORTHO-
correction or allowance made for the variation in measurement or judgment due to human error PERSONAL EQUATION
– corrections and errors in a book, as listed on an inserted sheet of paper CORRIGENDA, ERRATA
– word written to instruct a typesetter or printer to ignore a correction STET
corrective action or punishment DISCIPLINARY ACTION
correspond See also **agree**
– correspond, agree, match, be alike TALLY
– correspond to, agree or harmonise with CONFORM WITH, COMPORT WITH
– corresponding in amount, level, or degree, proportionate, as one's salary might be with one's qualifications COMMENSURATE
– corresponding in evolutionary origin but not in function, as a human arm and a bird's wing are HOMOLOGOUS
– corresponding in function but not in evolutionary origin, as gills and lungs are ANALOGOUS
– corresponding person in another team or organisation COUNTERPART, OPPOSITE NUMBER, VIS-À-VIS
– corresponding with or agreeing with exactly COINCIDENT
correspondence, parallelism, or mutual relationship between two things CORRELATION
– correspondence, rule associating the members of one set with those of another MAPPING
– correspondence or harmony among parts, claims, or the like CONSISTENCY, CONGRUITY, CONSONANCE
– relationship of correspondence, equivalence, or identity between systems or parts of a system SYMMETRY
– mathematical variable related to another in always having a corresponding value FUNCTION
corresponding- COUNTER-
corrupt See also **immoral**
– corrupt, debase, impair or taint VITIATE, DEFILE
– corrupt, open to or marked by bribery VENAL
– corrupt, pervert, or undermine SUBVERT
– corrupt, twist from what is correct or proper, warp PERVERT
– corrupt or dirty place or situation AUGEAN STABLES
– corrupt or seduce someone, especially someone young and innocent DEBAUCH
– corrupt someone into wrongdoing, specifically by bribing to commit perjury SUBORN
– corrupted or decaying, as in morals or culture DECADENT
– corrupting, damaging, harmful, or evil PERNICIOUS, PESTIFEROUS, PESTILENT, NOXIOUS
corruption, decay, or evil, especially when spreading rampantly CANKER
– corruption, private profit derived from a public office JOBBERY, GRAFT
– fund used for bribing public officials and for other corrupt activities SLUSH FUND
– moral corruption, pervertedness DEPRAVITY
– relating or referring to a powerful and politically corrupt organisation in a U.S. city or state government TAMMANY
corset stiffened with strips of bone, plastic, or metal STAYS
– confine or bind with a tight-fitting garment such as a corset or strait-jacket TRUSS
– thin strip of wood, whalebone, or the like for stiffening a corset BUSK
cosmetics, make-up MAQUILLAGE
– black cosmetic powder used, especially in Asia, to darken the eyelids KOHL
– dark cosmetic preparation applied to the eyelashes MASCARA
– fat from sheep's wool, used in cosmetics and ointments LANOLIN
– small case for needles, make-up, or the like ÉTUI
Cossack captain HETMAN, ATAMAN
cost – additional cost or charge SURCHARGE
– cut back on costs ECONOMISE, RETRENCH
– pay, meet the costs or expenses DEFRAY
cost of living – pay agreement by which wages are raised after a certain increase in the cost of living THRESHOLD AGREEMENT
– rising in keeping with the cost of living, as one's earnings or pension might INDEX-LINKED
costume ball at which masks are worn MASQUERADE
– costume department or storeroom of a theatre, royal household, or the like WARDROBE
cosy, informal, and private, as a small nightclub might be INTIMATE
– cosy and cheerful, having a warm and friendly atmosphere GEMÜTLICH, CONGENIAL
cot or pram for a baby, usually made of basketwork and hooded BASSINET
– cot death SUDDEN INFANT DEATH SYNDROME
cottage that goes with a particular job TIED HOUSE
– farm worker or crofter in Scotland renting a cottage and smallholding COTTER
cotton or wool wadding used as stuffing for furniture or mattresses BATTING
– cotton-wool ball or similar piece of absorbent material used for cleaning, applying a lotion, or the like SWAB
– open and clean raw cotton or wool fibres by means of a spiked drum WILLOW
– seed pod of cotton, flax, or similar plants BOLL
– strengthen and improve cotton thread by chemical treatment MERCERISE
couch See **furniture**
cough TUSSIS
– cough mixture that eases the production and expulsion of phlegm or sputum EXPECTORANT
– cough-relieving, as a drug might be ANTITUSSIVE
– cough syrup LINCTUS
– cough up and spit out EXPECTORATE
council appointed to advise the British king or queen PRIVY COUNCIL
– relating to a council, especially a church council CONCILIAR

– senior member of a town council ALDERMAN
count, reckon TALLY
– count off or list one by one ENUMERATE
counter, quick retaliatory action or retort RIPOSTE
– counter or turn aside a fencing thrust, hostile question, or the like PARRY
counteract and thereby make ineffective NEUTRALISE
counteract- PARA-
counter-clockwise- LAEV-, LAEVO-, LEVO-
counterfeit See **fake**
– counterfeit banknote or cheque STUMER
counterpart, corresponding person VIS-À-VIS
– counterpart or complement OBVERSE
counterpoint, combination of two or more distinct melodic parts POLYPHONY
– counterpoint added above a basic musical theme DESCANT
counting individually, by head CAPITATION
– act or system of numbering or counting NUMERATION
country, usually small and neutral, lying between two powerful rival states BUFFER STATE
– country areas considered remote and undeveloped, the sticks, the bush HINTERLAND, BOONDOCKS, BACKVELD, BACKBLOCKS, OUTBACK, GRAMADOELAS, BUNDU
– country-dweller, unfamiliar with city ways BUMPKIN, YOKEL, BUSHWHACKER, BACKWOODSMAN
– country economically or politically dependent on a more powerful country CLIENT STATE
– country gentleman in medieval England FRANKLIN
– country house in Russia DACHA
– country scene or event of simple charm IDYLL
– country's authority or power of jurisdiction beyond its borders, as over its citizens living abroad EXTRATERRITORIALITY
– countryman, typically owning a small farm in former times YEOMAN
– desert one's country, political party, or the like, especially to join its opponent DEFECT
– expel a foreigner from a country DEPORT
– narrow strip of land, as for allowing an inland country access to the sea CORRIDOR
– open level country, such as a stretch of plain CHAMPAIGN
– part of a country that is isolated within a foreign country's territory EXCLAVE
– part of a foreign country entirely within a country's territory ENCLAVE
– person from the same country as another person COMPATRIOT
– person who has left or been driven from his native country and now lives in another EXPATRIATE, EXILE
– person who has lived or travelled in many countries and is free of national prejudices COSMOPOLITAN
– person who "takes to the hills", living a primitive country life, to escape the effects of an expected nuclear war SURVIVALIST
– relating to country life, country people, or farming RURAL, PASTORAL, BUCOLIC
– relating to open country or uncultivated fields CAMPESTRAL
– return someone or something to the country of origin REPATRIATE
– send or banish to the country RUSTICATE
county or colony whose ruler formerly had royal powers PALATINATE
– "county" in dress and manner TWEEDY
– officer of the Crown in an English or Welsh county SHERIFF
coupons – exchange coupons, vouchers, or the like for goods REDEEM
courage See **brave**, **bravery**
– summon up courage MUSTER
courgettes – Italian and U.S. term for courgettes ZUCCHINI
course just before the main course, or the main course itself, of a meal ENTRÉE
– course of study CURRICULUM, SYLLABUS
– course of study offered by a university or college to part-time students EXTENSION COURSE
– course of study reacquainting and updating people already familiar with a subject REFRESHER COURSE
– course or dish served between the main courses of a meal ENTREMETS
– course or general direction, as of someone's life TENOR
– learning unit with a training course or educational syllabus MODULE
– optional, open to choice, as a course of study might be ELECTIVE
course of action – projected or possible course of action SCENARIO
court See also **trial**
– court case arousing great public interest CAUSE CÉLÈBRE
– court case debated as a training exercise by law students MOOT
– court of appeal APPELLATE COURT
– court of justice, adjudicating board, or the like TRIBUNAL, FORUM
– court officer in former times who collected debts and pursued debtors BUM-BAILIFF
– court officer in the U.S. MARSHAL
– court official's call for attention OYEZ
– court or parliamentary meeting, series of meetings, or period for meeting SESSION
– court or tribunal that is secretive and harsh STAR CHAMBER
– court order directed at some lower court, official body, or the like MANDAMUS
– court order directing the addressee to do or stop doing a specified act WRIT, INJUNCTION
– court order for the imprisonment of a person COMMITTAL, MITTIMUS
– court order prohibiting something INTERDICT
– court without legal jurisdiction, operated by a mob, prisoners, or the like KANGAROO COURT
– court's adviser on a case in which he is not directly involved AMICUS CURIAE
– court's powers, duties, or knowledge in a case COGNISANCE
– applying or turning for help to a person or thing, such as the courts RECOURSE
– attempt to influence a court of law, as by bribes or threats EMBRACERY
– awaiting or undergoing a court hearing, in litigation IN CHANCERY
– break in proceedings or temporary ending of business, as between court sessions or during the parliamentary holiday RECESS
– bringing a lawsuit, pursuing a case in court LITIGATION
– child, senile person, or the like under the legal protection of a guardian or court of law WARD
– close at the end of a session, as the courts and parliament do ADJOURN
– courts of law and judges collectively JUDICATURE, JUDICIARY
– declare or give evidence under oath, as in a court of law TESTIFY
– deliberate giving of false evidence while under oath by a witness in court PERJURY

– division of the High Court of Justice dealing with equity cases CHANCERY
– doorkeeper in a court of law, parliament, or the like USHER
– duty lawyer's consultation with or hiring by the accused in the court building DOCK BRIEF
– evidence or declaration given in court by a witness under oath TESTIMONY
– failure to appear in court DEFAULT
– hold a suspect on bail, or return him to prison, as done by a court REMAND
– judge in a county court CIRCUIT JUDGE
– official summons to appear in court CITATION
– open central space in front of the judge's bench in a courtroom WELL
– person or group against whom a lawsuit or civil action is brought in court DEFENDANT
– person or group that sues another or brings a civil action in court PLAINTIFF
– privilege of clergymen in the Middle Ages to be tried by a church court rather than a secular court BENEFIT OF CLERGY
– promise or obligation, recorded in court, to appear in court, keep the peace, or the like BOND, RECOGNISANCE
– question a witness who was called by the opposing side in a court case CROSS-EXAMINE, CROSS-QUESTION
– question one's own witness in a court case EXAMINE-IN-CHIEF
– refer a case or decision to a lower court, committee, or the like REMIT
– refusal to appear in court or obey a court order, contempt of court CONTUMACY
– relating to a court hearing held in private, with the public excluded IN CAMERA
– relating to criminal law and court cases FORENSIC
– relating to the principles of law guiding a court rather than to court rules or procedures SUBSTANTIVE
– relating to the rules or procedures of a court rather than to principles of law ADJECTIVE
– sessions of the law courts in English and Welsh counties in former times ASSIZES
– still before a judge or court, and therefore not to be discussed in public SUB JUDICE
– summary of a court case DOCKET
– writ summoning someone to appear in court SUBPOENA, SUMMONS

courteous, gentlemanly, especially towards women CHIVALROUS
– courteous and respectful DEFERENTIAL

courtesy, politeness CIVILITY, COMITY
– courtesies, polite social gestures AMENITIES, PLEASANTRIES

courtyard in front of a church or within an ancient Roman house ATRIUM
– courtyard or colonnade in front of a church or palace PARVIS
– courtyard surrounded by cloisters GARTH
– open-air courtyard within a house PATIO

cousin – first cousin COUSIN-GERMAN
– separated by a specified number of generations, as distant cousins might be REMOVED

cover of velvet for a coffin or tomb PALL
– cover or front man, apparently but not really in charge of a dubious scheme MAN OF STRAW
– cover or shelter from the wind LEE
– cover up mistakes or wrongdoing WHITEWASH
– cover with a thin sheet of plastic wood, or the like LAMINATE
– cover with fog or clouds OBNUBILATE
– bell-shaped cover of plastic or glass, placed over young plants for protection CLOCHE
– covered walk around a quadrangle CLOISTERS
– covered walk or arbour formed by a trellised roof carrying climbing plants PERGOLA
– covering, as of canvas, as for a boat or wagon TILT
– covering, such as a seed's coat or an animal's skin INTEGUMENT
– covering or ornamental awning, as above a throne CANOPY
– covering or outer layer, as of the brain PALLIUM, MANTLE
– covering that is dark and oppressive, as of smoke PALL

cover charge in a restaurant COUVERT

coverlet for the top of the back of an armchair or sofa ANTIMACASSAR

cow, sheep, deer, or related hoofed, cud-chewing mammal RUMINANT
– cow on the verge of giving birth SPRINGER
– cow or bullock between one or two years old, yearling STIRK
– cow that is young and not yet breeding HEIFER
– cow that yields milk for human use MILCH COW
– cow's first milk produced after giving birth BEESTINGS, COLOSTRUM
– adjective for a cow BOVINE
– brown or grey with darker streaks or spots, as a dog, cat, or cow might be BRINDLED
– bushy tip of the tail of a cow or other animal SWITCH
– cowshed or barn BYRE
– frame of two upright bars securing a cow round the neck in a stall STANCHION
– not pregnant or not calving in a particular year, as a cow might be FARROW

cow's stomachs See **stomach**

cowardly, base or weak-willed, spineless PUSILLANIMOUS, DASTARDLY, LILY-LIVERED, NIDDERING, CRAVEN, RECREANT
– cowardly wretch POLTROON, CAITIFF

cowboy, especially one tending horses WRANGLER
– cowboy in South America GAUCHO
– cowboy or herdsman in the southwestern U.S VAQUERO
– cowboy working far from the main group or camp OUTRIDER
– cowboy's heavy leather trousers, without a seat, worn over ordinary trousers to protect the legs CHAPS
– display or contest of cowboy skills, such as lassoing and bronco riding RODEO
– small toothed wheel on the end of a cowboy's spur ROWEL

cower See **draw back**

cowpox VACCINIA

crab, lobster, prawn, or related creature having a segmented body, jointed limbs, and horny shell CRUSTACEAN
– crab, lobster, prawn, or related ten-legged crustacean DECAPOD
– crab family of crustaceans BRACHYURA
– crab-like CANCROID
– crab's pincer-like claw CHELA

crack See also **break**, **gap**
– deep crack or chasm, as in a glacier CREVASSE
– having a network of fine cracks, as a piece of glazed pottery might CRAZED
– narrow crack or split, as in a rock face CLEFT, CREVICE, FISSURE
– network of fine cracks made deliberately in the glaze of a piece of pottery CRACKLING
– network of small cracks in the paint or varnish of an old painting CRAQUELURE

crack- FISSI-

cracker – joke, verse, or proverb on

a slip of paper inside a paper cracker MOTTO

craftsman, skilled worker ARTISAN, ARTIFICER
- craftsman who is qualified but still employed by someone else JOURNEYMAN
- craftsman's work bench BANKER

crafty, scheming CALCULATING, CONNIVING

cramp or rigid muscular contraction, as in a fever RIGOR

crane on a ship, typically paired with another, for hoisting lifeboats, cargo, or the like DAVIT
- crane or other lifting apparatus HOIST
- crane or spar for stowing cargo in a ship's hold STEEVE
- crane with boom and cables for lifting heavy objects DERRICK
- crane's moving hoist or similar lifting machine CRAB
- bridge-like frame supporting a travelling crane, railway signals, or the like GANTRY
- move the jib of a crane LUFF
- pivoting arm or spar on a crane or derrick, used to guide or steady the load BOOM

crater formed by the toppling or collapse of a volcano's cone CALDERA

craving for unnatural food, such as mud or chalk, occurring sometimes in hysteria or during pregnancy PICA

crawl or lie face downwards, as in self-abasement or fear GROVEL

crayon made of chalky paste, or a picture made with such crayons PASTEL

craze or obsession MANIA

creak, rattle, or crackle, as diseased lungs or broken bones might CREPITATE

cream – rich, clotted cream DEVONSHIRE CREAM
- whipped cream, slightly sweetened CHANTILLY CREAM

crease, wrinkle, gather in folds, RUCK, PUCKER
- creased, ruffled RUMPLED

creation, as of an idea or project GENESIS, PROCREATION, INCEPTION

creative, original, or life-enhancing PROMETHEAN
- creative in a passionate and energetic way DIONYSIAC
- creative inspiration, especially a poetic impulse AFFLATUS

credit See **assign**
- have a specified effect, as to one's credit or advantage REDOUND

creditor – substitution of one person, especially a creditor, for another SUBROGATION

creed or profession of faith widely used in churches NICENE CREED, ATHANASIAN CREED

creeper See **climbing plant**
- growing along the ground as a vine or creeper might PROSTRATE

cremation site for Hindus at the top of a flight of riverside steps BURNING GHAT
- place for keeping the ashes of a cremated body CINERARIUM
- wood pile prepared for a funeral fire on which to cremate a corpse PYRE

Creole or dialect PATOIS
- simplified language of communication between two different language groups, sometimes developing into a Creole or mother tongue PIDGIN

crescent-shaped BICORN, BICUSPID, LUNATE, LUNULAR, LUNULATE
- crescent-shaped mark at the base of a fingernail LUNULA
- crescent-shaped object or design MENISCUS
- crescent-shaped object or structure, such as the outwork of a fort DEMILUNE

crest- LOPHO-

crested, as some birds are PILEATED

cricket See chart and illustration

cricket's shrill grating chirp STRIDULATION

crime, misconduct, or wrongdoing, especially by an official MALFEASANCE
- crime, offence, or wrongful act of a serious kind FELONY
- crime, offence, or wrongful act of a very minor kind MISDEMEANOUR, DELINQUENCY, VIOLATION
- crime association SYNDICATE
- crime of concealing information about treason or some other serious offence MISPRISION
- crime of forcing money or favours from someone by blackmail, violence, or the like EXTORTION
- crime of fraudulently appropriating or misusing someone else's property or funds entrusted to one's care EMBEZZLEMENT, DEFALCATION, PECULATION
- crime of having sexual relations with a girl who is not yet of the age of consent STATUTORY RAPE
- crime of kidnapping ABDUCTION
- "crime of passion", typically a murder provoked by sexual jealousy CRIME PASSIONEL
- crime of marrying a person or persons while still married to someone else BIGAMY, POLYGAMY
- crime of setting fire deliberately to property ARSON
- crime of theft LARCENY
- crime of treason, or offence against the dignity of a ruler LESE MAJESTY
- crime of trying to influence a judge or jury outside the usual courtroom procedures, as by bribes or threats EMBRACERY
- crime or offence in former times of stirring up quarrels or bringing groundless lawsuits repeatedly BARRATRY
- crime or offence of contempt of court, as by failing to appear in court or disregarding a court order CONTUMACY
- crime or offence of giving false evidence, especially in court while under oath PERJURY
- crime or offence of homelessness combined with public nuisance VAGRANCY
- crime or offence of sexual intercourse between two close relatives INCEST
- crime or sin TRANSGRESSION
- accuse formally of an offence or crime INDICT
- agree not to prosecute a crime or felony, as in return for a bribe COMPOUND
- attribute a crime or fault to someone IMPUTE
- being an accomplice to a crime, cruel deed, or the like COMPLICITY
- civilian arrogating crime-prevention and punitive powers to himself VIGILANTE
- clear someone of blame, a charge, or a crime, declare to be not guilty ACQUIT, EXONERATE, EXCULPATE, ABSOLVE, VINDICATE
- devise a dramatised version of a crime or historical event to gain a vivid idea of what actually took place RECONSTRUCT
- forgive or overlook an offence or crime CONDONE
- ignore or pretend ignorance of a crime, and thereby encourage it CONNIVE AT, WINK AT
- in the very act of committing a crime IN FLAGRANTE DELICTO, RED-HANDED
- involve in or prove involvement in a crime INCRIMINATE, INCULPATE
- law setting a time limit for prosecuting a crime or bringing a legal action STATUTE OF LIMITATIONS
- lessen or try to lessen the seriousness of a crime, by offering excuses EXTENUATE, MITIGATE
- monstrous or outrageous act, such as an abominable crime ENORMITY
- performing of a crime, sin, or the like COMMISSION, PERPETRATION

– person guilty of a crime or responsible for a mistake or accident CULPRIT
– person who encourages or helps another in the committing of a crime, either before or after, though not directly involved in it ACCESSORY, ACCESSARY
– person who helps another to commit a crime ACCOMPLICE
– plan or supervise a crime MASTERMIND
– plea that mental abnormality at the time of a crime reduces the culprit's responsibility DIMINISHED RESPONSIBILITY
– revealing of a scandal or crime, or the book, broadcast or the like in which it is reported EXPOSÉ
– tendency of former prisoners to revert to crime RECIDIVISM
– tricking or luring of someone as by the police, into crime, danger, or the like ENTRAPMENT
– wrongful act, other than a breach of contract, in civil law, in contrast to a crime TORT

criminal See also **evil**, **immoral**
– criminal, wrongdoer, or villain MISCREANT, MALEFACTOR, FELON

CRICKET TERMS

the Ashes	trophy for which England and Australia compete, or Test series between them
body-line	fast bowling directed straight at the batsman, to intimidate him
bouncer	fast ball pitched short so that it bounces high, to intimidate the batsman
bye	run scored from a ball which passes the wicket without touching the bat or batsman
chinaman	off-break bowled by a left-handed bowler to a right-handed batsman
dolly catch/ sitter	easy catch
follow-on	forced start to a team's second innings immediately after its first innings
full toss	ball which reaches the batsman without bouncing
googly	off-break disguised to resemble a leg-break
grub	ball bowled underarm along the ground
hat-trick	bowler's feat of dismissing three batsmen with consecutive balls
hook	stroke which hits a ball from the off-side of the wicket to the on-side
leg-break	ball that turns from leg to off on pitching
long hop	poorly bowled short-pitched ball
maiden over	over in which no runs are conceded
nightwatchman	non-specialist batsman sent in to play out time
no-ball	an unlawfully delivered ball
off-break	ball that turns from off to leg on pitching
shooter	ball that does not rise as expected
yorker	ball that pitches directly at the batsman's feet

FIELDING POSITIONS

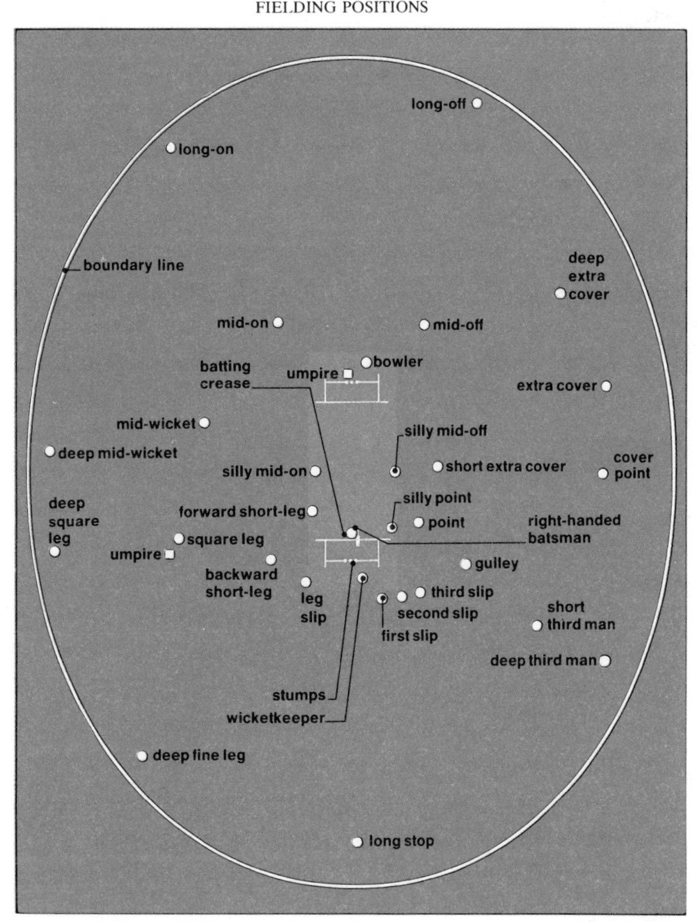

– criminal gangster, as in the Mafia MOBSTER
– criminal gangster or bandit, especially in mountainous country BRIGAND
– criminal gangster or hoodlum in Paris APACHE
– criminal or aggressive person with an antisocial personality disorder PSYCHOPATH, SOCIOPATH
– criminal or suspect who is on the run FUGITIVE
– criminal who informs to the police, especially on his fellow-criminals GRASS
– criminal who is reckless and desperate DESPERADO
– conditional release of a criminal from jail prior to the end of his prison term PAROLE
– handing over a criminal, fugitive, or the like to the authority or country where he is wanted EXTRADITION
– help a criminal to adjust to a conventional job or role within society REHABILITATE
– legal term for criminal intent MENS REA
– kit or method for creating a picture of a wanted criminal IDENTIKIT, PHOTOFIT
– loss of civil rights in former times, suffered by a convicted traitor, outlaw, or criminal under sentence of death ATTAINDER
– man serving as a respectable cover for some secret or criminal activity FRONT MAN
– person working for or running criminal business operations RACKETEER
– person who hunts criminals or dangerous animals for a financial reward BOUNTY HUNTER
– secret agent who joins a political or criminal group and tries to entrap it into punishable or discrediting activities AGENT PROVOCATEUR
– study of the punishment and treatment of criminals, especially prison management PENOLOGY
– unscrupulous and often criminal politician, lawyer, or the like SHYSTER

crippled condition or bodily defect, such as a hunchback DEFORMITY, DISFIGUREMENT

crisis, fit, spasm, frenzy PAROXYSM, SEIZURE, APOPLEXY, CONVULSION
– negotiation or the art of gaining an advantage by pressing a dispute towards a crisis without backing down BRINKMANSHIP
– remove the tension or danger from a situation or crisis DEFUSE

crosses

ankh/ansate · Avelian · botonné/preflée · Calvary · cardinal's · Celtic · Constantinian/monogram

crosslet · fitché · fleury · formé · fourché · Greek · Latin/passion

Lorraine · Maltese · moline · papal · patriarchal · pommé · potent/Jerusalem

quadrate · Russian · St Andrew's/saltire · St Anthony's/tau · St Peter's · swastika/fylfot/gammadion · Y cross

crisscross pattern, as on a map or framework GRID
- crisscross pattern or design TRACERY
- crisscrossed strips of wood or metal, as in a screen or window LATTICE
- crisscrossing sticks forming a frame, as for climbing plants TRELLIS

criterion, test, standard, or measure used for judgment or comparison YARDSTICK, TOUCHSTONE

critical, disapproving, judgmental CENSORIOUS, DYSLOGISTIC
- critical edition or revision of a text, incorporating the most plausible variant readings RECENSION
- critical in a nitpicking way, fault-finding CARPING, CAPTIOUS
- critical interpretation or analysis of a literary work, philosophical theory, or the like EXPLICATION, EXPOSITION
- critical period, stage, or event CLIMACTERIC, WATERSHED
- critical point beyond which a tense situation will erupt into war or violence FLASHPOINT
- critical success but a failure with the public at large, as a book or film might be SUCCÈS D'ESTIME

criticise See also **scold**, **insult**
- criticise, attack verbally BELABOUR, DECLAIM AGAINST
- criticise, challenge, attack as false IMPUGN
- criticise, punish, or scold severely CASTIGATE, CHASTISE
- criticise abusively or argue against passionately, rail against REVILE, VITUPERATE, INVEIGH AGAINST, EXCORIATE, FULMINATE AGAINST
- criticise in a belittling or dismissive way DECRY, DISPARAGE, DEPRECIATE, DEROGATE
- criticise mercilessly, pan, slate FLAY, CRUCIFY, PILLORY, SCARIFY
- criticise openly and earnestly, condemn CENSURE, REPREHEND
- criticise or disapprove of strongly DEPLORE, REPROBATE
- criticise, admonish, or explain in a priggish or preachy way MORALISE, SERMONISE
- criticise vehemently, condemn strongly DENOUNCE, EXECRATE
- criticising ignorantly, without the necessary knowledge or experience to warrant it ULTRACREPIDARIAN

criticism, disapproval STRICTURES, CENSURE, FLAK
- criticism or blunt critical remark BRICKBAT, BROADSIDE
- criticism or destruction of popular beliefs, cherished traditions, or the like ICONOCLASM
- criticism or fierce verbal attack launched maliciously HATCHET JOB
- criticism or rebuke for a misdeed or failing REPROOF
- criticism or review of a book, film, play, or the like CRITIQUE, APPRAISAL
- criticism or short review, especially of a book COMPTE RENDU
- criticism or veiled accusation IMPUTATION, ANIMADVERSION
- criticism that is petty and trifling CAVIL
- bitter or abusive criticism, or a speech or text containing it INVECTIVE, DIATRIBE, POLEMIC
- easily withstanding attack, criticism, or the like INVULNERABLE, IMPREGNABLE
- harsh and extremely scornful, as a criticism or verbal attack might be SCATHING, BLISTERING, WITHERING, VITRIOLIC, CAUSTIC
- idea, custom, institution, or person considered, unreasonably, to be beyond criticism SACRED COW
- long passionate speech of criticism HARANGUE, TIRADE, PHILIPPIC
- open condemnation, strong or abusive criticism DENUNCIATION, EXECRATION, VITUPERATION, OBLOQUY
- undergo severe criticism RUN THE GAUNTLET

critics – astonish someone or prove someone wrong, such as the critics CONFOUND

crocodile from tropical America, related to the alligator CAYMAN
- crocodile-like reptile with a narrow snout, found in India GAVIAL, GHARIAL

crop or commodity that is the major product of its kind grown in a region STAPLE
- crop or plant growing from seed that was not deliberately sown VOLUNTEER
- crop producing oil seed and fodder, with a distinctive yellow flower RAPE, COLZA
- cultivated soil, or its crop-bearing quality TILTH
- gather leftover corn or other crops from a field after harvesting GLEAN
- plant or grow crops in a fixed sequence ROTATE

crop-spraying – fly very low when crop-spraying, rising to avoid hedges, fences, and so on HEDGEHOP

croquet stick MALLET
- hit another player's ball with one's own in croquet, qualifying one to croquet it or drive it away ROQUET
- send another player's ball through a hoop in croquet PEEL
- small post in croquet that a ball must hit to end a game PEG

cross See **angry**, **anger**

cross See illustration
- cross-bearer, as in a religious procession CRUCIFER
- cross-bred, mixed in origin or make-up HYBRID
- cross or crucifix representing the cross on which Jesus died ROOD, HOLY ROOD
- cross or divide a line or space INTERSECT
- cross or intersect to form an X DECUSSATE
- cross out or erase written or printed words DELETE
- cross-shaped CRUCIATE, CRUCIFORM
- crossing over of two structures in the body, such as the optic nerve fibres in the brain CHIASMA
- horizontal beam or crossbar, as on a gallows or cross TRANSOM
- taking down of Jesus from the cross, or a painting or sculpture of this DEPOSITION

cross-country motorcycle racing SCRAMBLING, MOTOCROSS
- cross-country racing involving use of a compass and map-reading skills ORIENTEERING
- cross-country runner HARRIER

crossbow bolt or arrow QUARREL
- crossbow-like launcher of rocks or other heavy missiles, as used in ancient siege warfare BALLISTA

crossing at which predestrians themselves activate the traffic lights on the roadside PELICAN CROSSING

crosswise, diagonal, slanting CATER-CORNERED, OBLIQUE
- crosswise, lying across ATHWART, TRANSVERSE
- crosswise path, movement, line, building beam, or the like TRAVERSE

crow, both scavenging and predatory, with a black bill CARRION CROW
- adjective for a crow CORVINE

crowbar as used by burglars JEMMY

crowd, horde, or mob of people THRONG, MULTITUDE, CONCOURSE, RUCK
- crowd, large gathering or converging, as of people CONFLUENCE
- crowd together, assemble CONGREGATE
- crowded, containing a great multitude of inhabitants POPULOUS, TEEMING

– crowded, pressed together, tightly packed SERRIED
– crowds of moving people DROVES
– close-knit crowd of people PHALANX
– fear of crowds OCHLOPHOBIA, DEMOPHOBIA
– headlong rush, as of startled cattle or horses, or of a panic-stricken crowd STAMPEDE
– noisy and disorderly commotion of a crowd TUMULT
– overcrowded CONGESTED
– relating to a crowd, flock, or the like GREGARIOUS
– speechmaker who rouses a crowd to violent passions or actions RABBLE-ROUSER, DEMAGOGUE

crown DIADEM
– crown of small size, as worn by princes or noblemen as a sign of rank CORONET
– crown of the head PATE
– crown-shaped body part, such as the top of the head CORONA
– crowning of a king or queen CORONATION
– Pope's beehive-shaped three-tiered crown or hat TIARA

crucial time or event WATERSHED

crucifix representing the cross on which Jesus died ROOD, HOLY ROOD

Crucifixion as represented in sculpture CALVARY
– sufferings of Jesus prior to and during the Crucifixion PASSION

crude See also **rude**, **vulgar**
– crude, primitive, unsophisticated, basic RUDIMENTARY
– crude or uncouth RUSTIC

cruel, aggressively harsh TRUCULENT
– cruel, insensitive, heartless CALLOUS, INDURATE
– cruel and greedy, in a wolflike way LUPINE
– cruel in a perverted way, relishing the inflicting of pain SADISTIC
– cruel oppression or ill-treatment PERSECUTION
– cruel or frightful person OGRE
– cruel or greedy person HARPY
– cruel or extremely violent act, outrage ATROCITY, ENORMITY
– brutal, inhumanly cruel BESTIAL, FELL, FLAGITIOUS
– mercilessly cruel or grim, pitiless, unsparing REMORSELESS, IMPLACABLE, INEXORABLE

crumble, decay, turn to dust MOULDER AWAY
– crumbly FRIABLE

crumbs – coated with breadcrumbs and sometimes cheese, and then grilled or browned, as cauliflower might be AU GRATIN
– crumbed and fried, as a veal cutlet might be MILANESE

crumpet PIKELET

Crusades – Muslim at the time of the Crusades SARACEN

crush, grind, or pound into powder or small particles TRITURATE, PULVERISE, BRAY, COMMINUTE
– crush or put an end to something, such as a rumour or rebellion SCOTCH, SUPPRESS, SUBDUE, QUELL, QUASH, REPRESS
– crush or smash inwards STAVE
– crushing, stamping, or grinding implement, as in a mill PESTLE

crust forming in bottles of old wine, especially port, or a wine containing this crust BEESWING

cry and sob noisily BLUBBER
– cry from the heart, earnest appeal CRI DE COEUR
– cry of praise to God HOSANNA
– cry or wail with a loud keening howl ULULATE
– cry or screech, as of an excited cat CATERWAUL
– cry or whimper repeatedly YAMMER
– cry weakly or whimper MEWL
– cry out or shout loudly, especially in protest VOCIFERATE
– crying continually LACHRYMOSE

crypt, vault, underground chamber UNDERCROFT

crystal, quill, bristle, or similar needle-shaped natural object or part ACICULA, ACULEUS
– crystal that produces electric polarity when subjected to pressure PIEZOELECTRIC CRYSTAL
– crystal that branches into a tree-like structure DENDRITE
– add a crystal to a liquid to cause it to crystallise SEED
– any of the different physical forms, such as crystals, that an element may take ALLOTROPE
– between liquid and solid or crystal in structure or properties MESOMORPHIC, NEMATIC, SMECTIC
– capable of occurring in different forms, as crystals of a mineral might be POLYMORPHIC
– crystals of potassium permanganate, producing a purplish solution used as a disinfectant or snakebite treatment CONDY'S CRYSTALS
– instrument for measuring the angles of crystals GONIOMETER
– not possessing a distinct crystalline structure, as a rock or chemical might AMORPHOUS
– process by which crystals are turned to powder by loss of water EFFLORESCENCE
– regular geometric arrangement, as of the molecules in a crystal LATTICE
– rock cavity lined with crystals GEODE
– rock cavity or vein into which crystals project DRUSE
– similarity of form or structure, as in different cells or crystals ISOMORPHISM

crystal ball – see the future by gazing into a crystal ball SCRY

cub scouts' adult organiser AKELA

cube extended hypothetically into the fourth dimension TESSERACT

cuckold, man who tolerates his wife's infidelities WITTOL

cucumber – small cucumber, usually pickled GHERKIN

cud – cud-chewing, hoofed mammal, such as a cow, sheep, or deer RUMINANT
– chew the cud RUMINATE

cue for an actor or actress to speak or enter CATCHWORD

cult, aura of power or mystery MYSTIQUE, MYTHOS

cultivated, superior, and well-bred person PATRICIAN

cultivation of land for crops TILTH, TILLAGE
– cultivation of plants, especially flowers HORTICULTURE
– cultivation of plants without soil, using nutrients dissolved in water HYDROPONICS, AQUICULTURE

culture, including the classics and the arts, as distinct from the sciences HUMANITIES
– culture passed down over the generations HERITAGE
– change in culture through contact with another culture, usually more advanced ACCULTURATION
– declining or decaying, as in morals or culture DECADENT
– lacking in or hostile to cultural interests and values PHILISTINE
– place where different cultures meet and mix MELTING POT
– rebirth or revival of culture RENASCENCE, RENAISSANCE
– relating to a distinctive racial, religious, or cultural group within a society ETHNIC
– rootless, separated from one's homeland, social origins, familiar culture, or natural environment DERACINATED, DÉRACINÉ
– study of the culture of peoples, especially primitive peoples ETHNOLOGY

culture- ETHN-, ETHNO-

cultured or intellectual people INTELLIGENTSIA, COGNOSCENTI
– cultured or intellectual HIGHBROW

cunning, craftiness GUILE, WILES
– cunning, sly, or shrewd ARTFUL

– cunning in a shifty or calculating way DISINGENUOUS, DESIGNING
– cunning or opportunism in politics MACHIAVELLIANISM

cup, mug, or tankard STOUP
– cup for the consecrated wine at Mass CHALICE
– cup of small size, or the strong black coffee drunk from it DEMITASSE
– cup or platter used, according to medieval legend, by Jesus at the Last Supper GRAIL, HOLY GRAIL, SANGRAAL
– cup or small bowl with a handle PORRINGER
– cup or small can CANNIKIN
– cup or small metal pan PANNIKIN
– cup or small mug NOGGIN
– cup-shaped COTYLOID, CUPULATE
– cup-shaped flower CHALICE
– cup-shaped mould for jellies, small cakes, or the like DARIOLE

cupid, cherub, or small boy in baroque paintings, sculptures, or reliefs PUTTO, AMORETTO

curative, remedial THERAPEUTIC
– curative, restoring or promoting health SALUTARY

curdle CLABBER

curds – watery part of milk that can be separated from the solid curds WHEY, SERUM

cure, heal, treat medically PHYSIC
– cure-all, universal remedy, as sought by alchemists PANACEA, ELIXIR, CATHOLICON
– cure fish by smoking BLOAT
– cure in the form of a counteracting remedy, especially for poisoning ANTIDOTE
– cure or solution to a problem of doubtful effectiveness, quack remedy NOSTRUM
– curing, healing SANATIVE

curio or small trinket BIBELOT
– curios, antiques, and objets d'art, or a cultivated liking for them VIRTU

curiosity – arouse someone's curiosity, interest, or the like PIQUE

curious, prying, nosy INQUISITIVE
– impatient with curiosity AGOG

curl of hair or ringlet over the forehead LOVELOCK
– curly or spiral design or structure, as on a shell WHORL, VOLUTE
– pinch into tight curls, folds, or the like CRIMP

curling contest or game BONSPIEL
– broom or brush used in curling to smooth the path of the stone over the ice BESOM

currency See chart
– currency, money serving as a medium of exchange CIRCULATING MEDIUM, LEGAL TENDER
– currency equivalent, at the official rate of exchange PARITY
– currency exchanging or brokerage AGIOTAGE
– currency unit, or monetary unit used for purposes of accounting UNIT OF ACCOUNT
– allow a currency to find its real exchange value freely according to market forces FLOAT
– reduction by a government in the monetary or exchange value of a currency DEVALUATION
– referring or relating to paper currency that is not backed by gold FIDUCIARY

current, conventional direction, or trend MAINSTREAM
– current, conventional, or widespread PREVAILING, PREVALENT
– current and interesting or important, as news might be TOPICAL
– current in an electrical circuit that changes direction continually ALTERNATING CURRENT, AC
– current in an electrical circuit that flows in a single direction DIRECT CURRENT, DC
– current of water RACE
– current or backward pull of receding waves after breaking on the shore UNDERTOW
– current or dangerous eddy in a narrow channel, caused by the tides MAELSTROM
– current or swirl moving against the main current, often creating a miniature whirlpool EDDY

CURRENCY

austral	Argentina	**leu (100 bani)**	Romania
baht (100 satangs)	Thailand	**lev (100 stotinki)**	Bulgaria
balboa	Panama	**lira**	Italy, Malta, Turkey
bolívar	Venezuela	**markka (100 penniä)**	Finland
colón	Costa Rica	**peseta**	Spain
cruzado	Brazil	**peso**	Philippines, Mexico, Chile, Cuba, and others
dalasi (100 bututs)	Gambia	**quetzal**	Guatemala
dinar	Yugoslavia, Algeria, Kuwait and others	**rand**	South Africa
dirham	Morocco, United Arab Emirates	**rial**	Iran, Saudi Arabia, Yemen
dong (10 chao)	Vietnam	**ringgit**	Malaysia
drachma (100 lepta)	Greece	**rouble (100 kopeks)**	USSR
escudo	Cape Verde, Portugal	**rupee**	India, Pakistan and others
forint (100 fillér)	Hungary	**rupiah**	Indonesia
guilder/florin	Netherlands	**shekel**	Israel
koruna (100 haleru)	Czechoslovakia	**sucre**	Ecuador
krona	Sweden, Iceland	**won**	North Korea, South Korea
krone	Denmark, Norway	**yen**	Japan
kwacha	Malawi, Zambia	**yuan**	China
lek (100 quintars)	Albania	**zloty (100 groszy)**	Poland

– convert alternating current into direct current RECTIFY

current- RHEO-

curse EXECRATION, IMPRECATION

– curse of excommunication or damnation ANATHEMA

– curse or slanderous accusation MALEDICTION, DENUNCIATION, FULMINATION

curtain behind which women are screened, especially in India PURDAH

– curtain drawn up and outwards to produce a draped effect, especially on a stage TABLEAU CURTAIN

– curtain hung over a doorway PORTIÈRE

– gathered strip of material or ornamental pleated ruffle sewn to a garment or curtain FLOUNCE

– length of board or fabric along the top of a window, used to hide the curtain rod PELMET

– short decorative curtain hung along a pelmet, shelf, edge of the bed, or the like VALENCE

curtsy, bow, or similar gesture of respect or submission OBEISANCE

curve, bend, turn, or fold, as of a body part FLEXURE

– curve hypothetically formed by a uniform cable suspended from two points CATENARY

– curve on a geometric graph PARABOLA, HYPERBOLA

– curve or line enclosing a plane area in geometry PERIMETER

– curved surface, as of a road or aerofoil CAMBER

– curved, arched, as horns might be ARCUATE

– curved, scimitar-shaped, as some leaves are ACINACIFORM

– curved flight path of a missile, ball, or the like TRAJECTORY

– curved moulding, having an S-shape OGEE

– curved surface of a liquid MENISCUS

– curving gracefully, as a winding road or the movements of a snake might be SINUOUS

– curving inwards, as a mirror or lens might CONCAVE

– curving outwards, as a mirror or lens might CONVEX

– curving or turning line or shape, as of a whirlpool SPIRAL, HELIX, VOLUTE, WHORL

– draughtsman's plastic stencil having many curves FRENCH CURVE

– line approaching a curve, as on a graph, such that they will meet only at infinity ASYMPTOTE

– point of intersection of two arcs of a geometrical curve CUSP, SPINODE

– touch, without intersecting, as two adjoining curves in geometry might OSCULATE

cushion, as of a sofa or car seat SQUAB

– cushion for kneeling on or resting feet on, especially in church HASSOCK

– cushion of a large firm kind, used as a seat POUFFE

– cushion or long, cylindrical pillow that is typically hard, stiff, and narrow BOLSTER

– cushioned stool for kneeling on during prayer, as by a sovereign at the coronation FALDSTOOL

– silky plant fibre used for stuffing cushions, for soundproofing, and so on KAPOK

– strong cloth used to cover a mattress or cushion TICKING

custard slice, or similar cream-filled puff pastry MILLE-FEUILLE

custom, ceremony, or ritual marking a change of status in a person's life RITE OF PASSAGE

– custom, habit WONT, USAGE

– customs of a social group, defining it and its values MORES, PRAXIS

custom- NOMO-

customer buyer, reader, or the like PATRON, PUNTER

– customers or clients as a group, as of a restaurant or hairdresser CLIENTELE

– seek customers or support, especially in a forthright way TOUT

customs certificate authorising repayment of duty DEBENTURE

– customs label or receipt DOCKET

– customs list of a ship's cargo MANIFEST

– customs permit for the temporary importing of a car or other vehicle CARNET

– customs union ZOLLVEREIN

– seize at customs CONFISCATE, IMPOUND, EMBARGO

cut, as in surgery INCISION

– cut a groove in FLUTE, CHAMFER, CHASE

– cut a surface into wood, a slope, or the like, to form an angle other than a right angle BEVEL

– cut from a text, delete EXCISE

– cut from a text the parts considered indecent EXPURGATE, BOWDLERISE

– cut or divide a line or space, cross INTERSECT, TRANSECT, DECUSSATE

– cut or divide into two equal parts BISECT

– cut or lop top branches from a tree to promote lower and thicker growth POLLARD

– cut or scratch the skin slightly, as for vaccination SCARIFY

– cut or tear the flesh to form a jagged wound LACERATE

– cut or trim hair, grass, the edges of a photograph, or the like CROP

– cut small shavings from wood WHITTLE

– cut the hair, wool, or horns of POLL

– cut through an object, or the resulting piece or surface, revealing its inner structure CROSS-SECTION

– cut to pieces DISMEMBER

– cut up or open, as in surgery or laboratory examination DISSECT

– cutting, splitting, dividing SCISSION

– cutting up or into the body of a living animal, especially for research VIVISECTION

– pencil-like stick containing a chemical for stopping the bleeding from small cuts STYPTIC PENCIL

-cut- -TOM-, -TOME, -TOMY, -SECT

cut back on expenditure, economise RETRENCH, CURTAIL

cut off, seize, or stop something, such as a message, in its course INTERCEPT

– cut off from membership of a church or religion EXCOMMUNICATE

– cut off from outside influences CLOISTERED, HERMETIC, INSULATED, ISOLATED

cut short, abbreviate, or lop TRUNCATE

cutting, penetrating, to the point, as a remark might be INCISIVE, TRENCHANT, MORDANT, CAUSTIC

– cutting for planting or grafting SLIP, SCION

cuttings – tray of soil, usually covered, in which seeds or cuttings are grown PROPAGATOR

cycle of change in a system, involving a swing from one extreme to the other and then back OSCILLATION, PERIOD

– cycle or pattern of one's mental, physical, or emotional condition BIORHYTHM

– cycle-racing arena, typically with a banked track VELODROME

– cycling race in which two riders or teams try to overtake each other on a circular track PURSUIT

cylinder or cone with its top cut off at an angle UNGULA

– smooth worn-out engine cylinders by drilling, and fit slightly larger pistons REBORE

cymbals operated by a pedal in a pop or jazz group HI-HAT

cynical, unidealistic DISILLUSIONED, DISENCHANTED, DISABUSED

D

daddy-longlegs CRANEFLY
daffodil or related flower NARCISSUS
- crown-shaped part of the daffodil or similar flower CORONA

dagger worn in the stocking of a person wearing traditional Scottish Highland dress SKEAN-DHU, DIRK
daily DIURNAL
- daily, occurring every day, as attacks of malaria might be QUOTIDIAN
- daily allowance for expenses PER DIEM

dainty in an affected, over-refined way MINCING
daisy, dandelion, or related plant having compound flower heads COMPOSITE
- flower cluster in the form of a dense disc, as in the daisy CAPITULUM
- tiny disc flower or ray flower, usually in a cluster, as in the head of a daisy or other composite flower FLORET

dam in a river or canal to raise the water or regulate its flow WEIR
- dam used for generating electricity HYDROELECTRIC DAM
- dam wall or similar obstruction across a waterway BARRAGE
- channel for excess water, as round the side of a dam SPILLWAY
- channel or small dam, or the gate or valve holding back or regulating the water SLUICE

damage, as caused by war HAVOC, DEVASTATION
- damage, harm, disadvantage DETRIMENT, DISSERVICE
- damage, weaken, or disable IMPAIR, MAR, INCAPACITATE
- damage extensively, spoil or destroy, as grief or fire might RAVAGE, DEVASTATE
- damage or destroy, as through neglect BLIGHT
- damage or destroy personal or public property wantonly and maliciously VANDALISE
- damage or spoil, reduce to imperfection VITIATE
- damage severely or maim, as by removal of a limb or vital element MUTILATE
- damage the appearance or shape of DEFACE, DISFIGURE
- damage the reputation of, disgrace, dishonour DISCREDIT
- damage to a property caused by the tenant's neglect, or a list of the necessary repairs DILAPIDATIONS
- impossible to repair or make good, as devastating damage might be IRREPARABLE

damages – guilty party in a damages case TORTFEASOR
- fine or damages imposed by a court in former times AMERCEMENT
- succeed in a lawsuit, or gain compensation or damages through it RECOVER

damaging, harmful, or corrupting NOXIOUS, DELETERIOUS
- damaging or malicious destruction of public property, artistic works, or the like VANDALISM

damnation, hell PERDITION
- damnation curse ANATHEMA
- person doomed or predestined to damnation, in theology REPROBATE

damp, high in moisture content, as air might be HUMID
damper or mute for a musical instrument SORDINO
dance See chart, and also **ballet**
- dance of a rhythmical free-style kind, or a form of musical training using such movement EURHYTHMICS
- "dance of death" DANSE MACABRE
- dance popular in the 1920s and 1930s, held at teatime in the afternoon THÉ DANSANT
- dance step in ballroom dancing in which the couple are side by side FEATHER

DANCES

BALLROOM	HISTORICAL	FOLK	MODERN
beguine	**allemande**	**dashing white sergeant**	**body popping**
carioca	**bourrée**	**eightsome reel**	**boogie**
cha-cha	**chaconne**	**gigue/jig**	**bop**
foxtrot	**Charleston**	**Highland fling**	**break dancing**
Gay Gordons	**cotillion**	**hoe-down**	**frug**
hokey-cokey	**courante**	**hornpipe**	**go-go dancing**
Lambeth walk	**écossaise**	**morris dancing**	**jitterbug**
lancers	**galliard**	**Sir Roger de Coverley**	**jive**
mambo	**gavotte**	**strathspey**	**rock 'n' roll**
merengue	**minuet**	**strip the willow**	**salsa**
paso doble	**passacaglia**	**sword dance**	**shuffle**
Paul Jones	**passepied**		**twist**
polka	**pavane**		
quickstep	**quadrille**		
rumba	**rigadoon**		
samba	**sarabande**		
shimmy	**schottische**		
tango	**turkey trot**		
waltz	**volta**		

NATIONAL

bolero – Spanish	**habanera** – Cuban	**maxixe** – Brazilian
bossa nova – Brazilian	**haka** – Maori	**mazurka** – Polish
cachucha – Spanish	**hora** – Romanian/Israeli	**nautch** – Indian
czardas – Hungarian	**hula** – Polynesian	**polonaise** – Polish
fandango – Spanish	**kazatzka** – Russian	**saltarello** – Italian
farandole – French	**ländler** – Austrian	**seguidilla** – Spanish
flamenco – Spanish	**limbo** – Caribbean	**tambourin** – French
galop/galopade – German/French	**malaguena** – Spanish	**tarantella** – Italian
		zapateado – Spanish

– dance step in Eastern European folk dancing, in which the legs are kicked out alternately from a squatting position PRISIADKA
– dance step or series of dance steps PAS
– dancing or ballet as an art CHOREOGRAPHY
– figure in country dancing in which couples join hands and circle one another POUSSETTE
– figure in square or country dancing in which two dancers pass each other and then circle back to back DO-SI-DO
– girl or woman who is seldom invited to partner a man at a dance WALLFLOWER
– marching sequence during a square or country dance PROMENADE
– relating to dancing TERPSICHOREAN

dancer employed by a nightclub or dance hall to dance with the patrons for a fee each time TAXI DANCER
– dancer's close-fitting sleeveless garment LEOTARD
– supple and lithe, as the movements of a ballet dancer might be SINUOUS

dandelion, daisy, or related plant having compound flower heads COMPOSITE
– dandelion's tuft of fluff, helping to disperse the seeds PAPPUS

dandruff or similar scaling of the skin SCURF, FURFURES

dandy FOP

danger, threat, risk MENACE
– danger or risk associated with one's job or a specified activity OCCUPATIONAL HAZARD
– hidden danger or difficulty PITFALL
– in great danger, distress, or need IN EXTREMITY
– open to danger, attack, or criticism VULNERABLE, EXPOSED, SUSCEPTIBLE
– prevent or ward off danger, disaster, or the like AVERT
– put in danger IMPERIL, JEOPARDISE
– risk-taking of a foolhardy kind, disregard of danger TEMERITY

dangerous, corrupting, evil PERNICIOUS, PESTIFEROUS, PESTILENT
– dangerous, risky HAZARDOUS, PERILOUS
– dangerous and uncertain PARLOUS
– dangerous in a subtle or treacherous way INSIDIOUS
– dangerous or risky project, such as a new business undertaking, or the like VENTURE
– dangerous or threatening FORBIDDING
– dangerous or worrying experience, of short duration MAUVAIS QUART D'HEURE
– dangerous trouble spot or explosive situation TINDERBOX, POWDER KEG
– dangerous venture of a suicidally risky kind RUSSIAN ROULETTE
– dangerously attractive or charming, bewitching CIRCEAN
– glass box in which dangerous radioactive or toxic substances can be handled with protective gloves sealed into the side GLOVE BOX
– dangerously positioned, insecure, liable to failure or disaster PRECARIOUS
– caught between two equally dangerous alternatives BETWEEN SCYLLA AND CHARYBDIS

dare, risk, gamble, expose to danger HAZARD, VENTURE, BRAVE

daredevil, adventurous, flamboyant SWASHBUCKLING

dark, dim, gloomy, murky SOMBRE, TENEBROUS, FUNEREAL, CALIGINOUS
– dark, drab, dull, SUBFUSC
– dark, very gloomy CIMMERIAN, STYGIAN
– dark area, especially the darkest part of a shadow UMBRA
– dark-skinned or sunburnt in appearance SWARTHY
– darkish area, as during an eclipse, between areas of full shadow and full illumination PENUMBRA

dark- MELAN-, MELANO-, NYCT-, NYCTI-, NYCTO-

dark chamber in which the image of an outside view is projected onto a surface by a lens above or opposite CAMERA OBSCURA

darken, as with fog or clouds OBNUBILATE
– darken, blur, make indistinct or dim OBFUSCATE
– darkening or changing colour when exposed to light, as the glass or plastic in some sunglasses does PHOTOCHROMIC

dart or steel missile dropped from an aircraft, as in the First World War FLÈCHETTE
– feather or other flared tail giving stability to an arrow or dart FLIGHT
– line from which a darts player throws darts at the board OCHE

Darwin – theory of the gradual and natural development of species EVOLUTIONISM
– "survival of the fittest", as in the theory of Charles Darwin NATURAL SELECTION
– theory, going against strict Darwinian ideas of evolution, that acquired characteristics can be inherited LAMARCKISM, LYSENKOISM

dashboard FASCIA

date a cheque or other document earlier than the date of writing ANTEDATE
– date a cheque or other document later than the date of writing POSTDATE
– about or approximately, as written before an uncertain date CIRCA
– calculation of the dates of past events, or ordering of events according to their dates, or a list of such events CHRONOLOGY
– outmoded system of reckoning dates, replaced by the Gregorian calendar JULIAN CALENDAR
– present system of reckoning dates, on the basis of the Gregorian calendar NEW STYLE

dating, as of wood samples or of archaeological specimens, by measuring their radioactive carbon-14 content RADIOCARBON DATING, CARBON DATING
– dating method for rocks and minerals up to 1000 million years old RUBIDIUM-STRONTIUM DATING

daughter – adjective for a son or daughter FILIAL

dawn – poem, song, or tune suited to or dealing with dawn or the early morning AUBADE

day beginning a new season or payment quarter QUARTER DAY
– active during the day rather than at night, as most animals are DIURNAL
– days of fine weather, tranquillity, or prosperity HALCYON DAYS
– days of summer, hot and lazy, from mid-July to September DOG DAYS
– either of the two times during the year when day and night are of equal length all over the Earth EQUINOX
– either the longest or the shortest day of the year SOLSTICE
– relating to biological processes that have a regular cycle of a 24-hour day CIRCADIAN
– weekday that is not a feast day FERIA

daybreak, spring, or similar early part or beginning of something PRIME

daydream REVERIE
– daydreamer, typically a person who indulges in fantasies to compensate for his own inadequacies WALTER MITTY

– daydreaming, absent-mindedness WOOLGATHERING
dazed, confused, or dizzy WOOZY, STUPEFIED, GROGGY
– dazed, hypnotic, or dream-like state TRANCE
de, *von*, or similar preposition accompanying a title or surname, indicating noble rank NOBILIARY PARTICLE
deacon – office or status, or deacons collectively DIACONATE
– adjective for a deacon DIACONAL
dead See also **death**
– dead, invalid, or inoperative DEFUNCT
– dead, lifeless, not living INANIMATE
– dead as a species, having died out EXTINCT
– dead person THE DECEASED, DECEDENT
– conjuring up of the spirits of the dead as a supposed means of predicting or influencing the future NECROMANCY
– hymn, service, or piece of music for a dead person REQUIEM
– list of dead people, especially those who have died recently NECROLOGY
– pretend to be dead, asleep, or ignorant PLAY POSSUM
– speech or poem of praise or a written tribute, as for someone recently dead EULOGY, ELEGY
– speech or written obituary commemorating a dead person EPITAPH
dead- NECR-, NECRO-
dead animal – body of a dead animal or bird CARCASS
– flesh of a dead animal or bird CARRION
– hyena, vulture, insect, or the like that feeds on dead animals, rotting meat, or other decaying organic matter SCAVENGER
– stuffing and preparing the skins of dead animals for exhibiting TAXIDERMY
dead body See **corpse**
dead end CUL-DE-SAC
– dead end, deadlock IMPASSE
– dead end, road blocked at one end CLOSE
dead matter- SAPR-, SAPRO-
deaden, dull PETRIFY
deadlock, drawn contest, or unresolvable difficulty, blocking progress IMPASSE, STALEMATE
deadly, destructive LETHAL, FATAL, BANEFUL, PERNICIOUS, PESTILENT
deaf – sign language with the hands, as used by deaf and dumb people DACTYLOLOGY
-dealer -MONGER
dean – adjective for a dean DECANAL
Dear Sir or similar conventional opening words of a letter SALUTATION
death See also **dead**
– death DEMISE
– death, decay, or disintegration DISSOLUTION
– death as a relief or release from life QUIETUS
– death as personified in Greek mythology, or death-wish in Freudian theory THANATOS
– death-like or temporary dormant state of a living organism SUSPENDED ANIMATION
– death notice, as in a newspaper, often with a short biography of the deceased OBITUARY
– death of body tissue NECROSIS, GANGRENE, MORTIFICATION
– death of many people, specifically one million MEGADEATH
– death or an accident or occurrence causing death FATALITY
– death through accident rather than crime MISADVENTURE
– Death viewed as Father Time with his scythe GRIM REAPER
– apparition of a person supposedly appearing just before his death WRAITH
– at the point of death IN EXTREMIS, MORIBUND
– causing, able to cause, or relating to death LETHAL, FATAL
– deliberate causing of a painless death in order to relieve suffering, as from an incurable illness EUTHANASIA
– deprived or desolated, as by the death of a loved one BEREAVED, BEREFT
– fascinated by or preoccupied with death MORBID
– fatal, certain to end in death, as an inoperable cancer is TERMINAL
– hospital specialising in care for those near to death HOSPICE
– medical specialist and public official conducting inquests with a jury into deaths that may not have been due to natural causes CORONER
– medical specialist who conducts post-mortem examinations to establish the cause of death PATHOLOGIST
– occurring after death POST-MORTEM
– painful spasms, as on approaching death PANGS, THROES
– person excessively fascinated by death GHOUL
– premature, before the proper or allotted time, as an early death is UNTIMELY
– relating to death MORTAL, MORTUARY
– relating to the time after a person's death POSTHUMOUS, POST-OBIT
– reminder of inescapable death, such as a skull MEMENTO MORI
– reminiscent of death and its horrors MACABRE
– signal or omen of disaster or death KNELL
– starvation or exhaustion as a cause of death INANITION
– temporary rigidity, caused by chemical changes, of the muscles and joints of a dead body RIGOR MORTIS
death- NECR-, NECRO-
death penalty – cancellation or postponement of a punishment, such as the death penalty REPRIEVE, RESPITE
– person who urges or favours the ending of the death penalty ABOLITIONIST
– person who urges or favours the retaining of the death penalty RETENTIONIST
deathly, ghastly SEPULCHRAL, CHARNEL
– deathly pale, ill-looking CADAVEROUS
debate, discuss, or negotiate PARLEY
– debate, especially a formal and learned debate DISPUTATION
– debate on a legal topic conducted by law students MOOT
– ending of a debate, as in Parliament, and the immediate voting on the motion CLOSURE, CLOTURE
debauched man, rake, especially an ageing one ROUÉ
debt, financial obligation LIABILITY
– debt, such as rent, that remains unpaid ARREARS
– debt as recorded in the left-hand side of an account or bookkeeping ledger DEBIT
– debt collector, or his insistent demand for payment DUN
– debt collector and court officer who pursued debtors in former times BUM-BAILIFF
– adjust a debt and settle for a smaller amount than the claim COMPOUND
– bond or contract to repay a debt after the death of a person whose heir the debtor is POST-OBIT
– certificate or voucher acknowledging a debt DEBENTURE
– discharge, as from duty or debt QUIETUS, QUITTANCE
– fail to carry out a task, promise, or duty, especially to pay a debt DEFAULT, WELSH
– in debt and unable to pay it off

INSOLVENT, BANKRUPT
– in debt to, owing thanks to OBLIGED, INDEBTED, BEHOLDEN
– part-payment of a debt made as part of a series INSTALMENT
– pay off a debt or mortgage by instalments AMORTISE
– postponement or suspension of debt payments MORATORIUM
– reduce or revise a debt, payment, or the like COMMUTE
– refuse to acknowledge a debt REPUDIATE
– run away, especially when leaving unpaid debts behind LEVANT
– run up a debt INCUR, CONTRACT
– settle a debt, in law EXTINGUISH
– settle a debt or claim LIQUIDATE
– value of a property or business once all debts are taken into account EQUITY
– withhold the pay or seize the property of a debtor GARNISHEE, SEQUESTER

debtor – legal right to a debtor's property until he settles the debt LIEN
– sheriff's officer in medieval times who arrested debtors CATCHPOLE

decanters – lockable cage-like container for displaying decanters of wine or spirits TANTALUS

decay, crumble away, turn to dust MOULDER
– decay, evil, or corruption, especially when spreading rampantly CANKER
– decay and death of body tissue, limbs, or the like, typically through a failure of blood supply GANGRENE, NECROSIS, MORTIFICATION
– decay of teeth or bones CARIES
– decay or rot DECOMPOSE, FESTER, PUTREFY
– decay or waste away, as through disuse ATROPHY
– decayed organic matter that enriches the soil HUMUS
– decaying, falling to pieces, broken down, as a shabby old house is DILAPIDATED, DECREPIT
– decaying flesh of a dead animal CARRION
– decaying or rotting smell, as from a swamp or rubbish heap EFFLUVIUM
– hyena, vulture, insect, or the like that feeds on dead animals, rotting meat, or other decaying organic matter SCAVENGER

decaying matter- SAPR-, SAPRO-

deceive See also **cheat**
– deceive, pretend to be something or someone that one is not MASQUERADE, DISSEMBLE
– deceive or flatter with smooth, charming talk BLARNEY
– easily deceived, fooled, or duped CREDULOUS, GULLIBLE

deception, cheating, fraud DUPLICITY, CHICANERY
– deception, crafty scheme, or the like, as to conceal, escape, or evade something SUBTERFUGE
– deception or clever trickery SLEIGHT OF HAND, LEGERDEMAIN
– deception or fraud, as by assuming a false identity IMPOSTURE
– deceptions, tricks WILES

deceptive, apparently attractive, genuine, or sound, but not really so SPECIOUS
– deceptive, misleading, or imaginary ILLUSORY, FALLACIOUS
– deceptive or evasive, as an ambiguous reply might be EQUIVOCAL
– deceptive person or thing WILL-O'-THE-WISP, IGNIS FATUUS
– deceptive 3D painting technique that makes the objects look like real ones TROMPE L'OEIL
– deceptively attractive or superficially impressive outward appearance VENEER, GLOSS
– deceptively luxurious or abundant, sham or counterfeit, as a feast might be BARMECIDAL

decide See also **choose**
– decide when mediating, act as judge ARBITRATE, ADJUDICATE
– decided in advance PREDETERMINED

decimal fraction with a repeated and neverending pattern REPEATING DECIMAL, RECURRING DECIMAL, CIRCULATING DECIMAL
– decimal point RADIX POINT
– decimal system of numbers ALGORISM

decipher See also **code**
– deciphering of codes, secret writings, and the like CRYPTANALYSIS

decision, deliberate choice VOLITION
– decision, legal judgment, or the like used as an example or standard justification when treating later cases similarly PRECEDENT
– decision already taken, preconceived opinion, prejudice PARTI PRIS
– decision taken on a particular occasion or issue rather than as general policy AD HOC DECISION
– agree to, support, or subscribe to a decision UNDERWRITE
– analysis of the efficiency of a workforce, machine system, or the like, as an aid to decision-making OPERATIONAL RESEARCH
– backward, unprogressive, as a step or decision might be RETROGRADE
– coming to a decision according to one's own judgment rather than according to a set of rules DISCRETIONARY
– disallow or reverse something, such as a decision OVERRULE, RESCIND, INVALIDATE, OVERTURN, QUASH
– impossible to change, reverse, or take back, as a decision might be IRREVOCABLE
– overhasty or sudden, as a decision might be IMPETUOUS, IMPULSIVE, PRECIPITATE
– settle a dispute by an authoritative decision DETERMINE

decisive, definite, conclusive, as a refusal or victory might be CATEGORICAL, UNEQUIVOCAL
– decisive factor, telling argument or strategy TRUMP CARD, CLINCHER
– decisive vote cast by the chairman or presiding officer when the votes in an assembly are tied CASTING VOTE

deck above the main deck near the back of a ship POOP DECK
– deck or section of the upper deck, near the front of a ship FORECASTLE, FO'C'S'LE
– part of a ship's structure situated above the main deck SUPERSTRUCTURE
– stairway from a ship's upper deck to the cabins or deck below COMPANIONWAY

declaration in writing that is made under oath AFFIDAVIT
– make a declaration or state formally ENUNCIATE

declare See **claim**

decline See **lessen**
– decline or regress after apparently recovering from illness RELAPSE
– declining or decaying, as in culture or morals DECADENT

decode, interpret or clarify a code DECIPHER, DECRYPT

decompose – capable of being decomposed by bacteria or by other biological processes, as some materials are BIODEGRADABLE

decorate a surface by embedding ornamental pieces in it INLAY
– decorate food, as with cress or a slice of lemon GARNISH
– decorate in a gaudy or vulgar way BEDAUB, BEDIZEN
– decorate lavishly, as in luxurious clothing, deck out, adorn ARRAY, BEDECK, CAPARISON
– decorate metal by engraving or embossing CHASE, ENCHASE
– decorate metal by etching or inlaying wavy patterns DAMASCENE, DAMASK
– decorate splendidly, typically in

bright colours EMBLAZON

decoration, such as a trill added by a musician EMBELLISHMENT
- decoration formed by fastening small pieces of one material onto the surface of another material, such as wooden cuttings onto metal APPLIQUÉ
- decoration in the form of a chain or garland of flowers, ribbons, or the like suspended in a loop FESTOON
- decoration of coloured cloth strips or streamers strung on a line BUNTING
- decoration of thin bright threads or strips, as on a Christmas tree TINSEL
- decoration or ornamentation, as of buildings or clothing TRIM
- decorations and furniture of a place, or the style of decoration DÉCOR
- delicate and intricate decoration, especially ornamental work of gold or silver wire FILIGREE

decoy, informer, or police spy STOOL PIGEON

decrease See **lessen**
- decrease, deterioration, or deviation from a standard, custom, or the like DECLENSION, DECLINATION
- decrease, or the amount lost or wasted in a decrease DECREMENT, DIMINUTION
- decreasing output or reward, after a certain point, for each increase in input, effort, or production DIMINISHING RETURNS

decree, arbitrary command, or order FIAT
- taking effect, as a divorce decree might, on a specificed date unless the court is shown cause why it should not NISI

deduce, infer, work out, or prove by reasoning DERIVE
- deduce, or guess at from known information EXTRAPOLATE

deduction from a sum of money to be paid REBATE
- deductive reasoning, logical deduction SYNTHESIS
- inference of general truths from particular instances, as distinct from strict logical deduction INDUCTION
- pattern of deduction in which two premises generate a conclusion SYLLOGISM

deed or adventure, especially a noble or heroic one EXPLOIT, GEST
- deed showing right of ownership of a property TITLE DEED

deep, at or from a great depth PROFOUND
- deep, dark, and empty CAVERNOUS
- deep, wide, and safe enough for ships or boats to sail on or through NAVIGABLE
- deep-rooted, persistent, long-established, as a tendency might be INVETERATE
- deep-seated and hard to remove, as dirt or vices may be INGRAINED
- deepest, lowest, furthest down NETHERMOST
- deepest or lowest point, as of one's fortunes or of depression NADIR
- deeply-rooted or common within a particular area or group ENDEMIC
- period or state of deep thought BROWN STUDY, REVERIE
- extremely or immeasurably deep FATHOMLESS

deep- BATH-, BATHY-, BATHO-

deer, cow or other hoofed mammal, having two or four toes on each foot ARTIODACTYL
- deer-like African forest mammal, related to the giraffe OKAPI
- deer's flesh used as food VENISON
- deer's offal, as formerly given as food to hunt attendants UMBLES, NUMBLES
- deer's track or trail SLOT
- adjective relating to a deer CERVINE
- young male deer with unbranched antlers PRICKET

defeat, outperform, outshine, as in a competition ECLIPSE, EXCEL, SURPASS
- defeat oneself by being too ambitious OVERREACH
- defeat or overcome, as in battle VANQUISH
- defeat overwhelmingly, crush, trounce ANNIHILATE, DEVASTATE, PULVERISE, ROUT, CRUCIFY
- bring under control or force into submission, as after a defeat SUBJUGATE, SUBDUE

defect, as in a machine MALFUNCTION
- defect, change sides, become a renegade TERGIVERSATE, APOSTATISE

defence See also **protection**, **fortification**
- defence of any kind, as against oppression BULWARK, BASTION, OUTPOST, STRONGHOLD
- defence of life and property to be undertaken by civilians in time of war or natural disaster CIVIL DEFENCE
- defence or formal justification, as of one's beliefs APOLOGIA
- defence or fortification against enemy fire or observation DEFILADE
- defence or protection, specifically the embankment and walls of a fortification RAMPART
- defence policy or weapons, such as nuclear warheads, designed to discourage enemy attack DETERRENT
- defender or champion of a cause APOLOGIST

defendant in a divorce action RESPONDENT

defender of the faith, one of the titles of the British sovereign FIDEI DEFENSOR

defensible or maintainable, as a military or philosophical position might be TENABLE

defensive, jealously protective TERRITORIAL
- defensive bank, as behind a trench, giving protection from the rear PARADOS
- defensive bank of sand, stones, or the like, protecting against enemy fire PARAPET, BULWARK, BREASTWORK
- defensive barrier or fortress made of upright posts or stakes STOCKADE
- defensive barrier, such as a bank of earth, in front of a trench or rampart TRAVERSE
- defensive obstacle, consisting of a frame with spikes or barbed wire, against enemy troops or horses CHEVAL-DE-FRISE
- defensive shelter underground with a bank or gun emplacements above ground BUNKER
- defensive stronghold, usually a small and temporary fortification REDOUBT
- defensive trench or wall, within outer walls or fortifications RETRENCHMENT
- defensive wall or barricade for protection against explosions REVETMENT
- defensive wall surrounding a castle, town, or the like, or the area protected by it ENCEINTE

define, set the limits or boundaries of DELIMIT, DEMARCATE, CIRCUMSCRIBE
- defining or limiting factor, as of a budget or schedule PARAMETERS, CONSTRAINTS

definite, particular, individual SPECIFIC

definition by means of a direct example of the term defined OSTENSIVE DEFINITION
- by definition, by its very nature IPSO FACTO

degree awarded "with great praise" MAGNA CUM LAUDE
- degree awarded "with greatest

praise" SUMMA CUM LAUDE
– degree awarded "with praise" CUM LAUDE
– degree conferred on a student who was too ill to sit exams at the time AEGROTAT
– degree ranking below a doctorate in some European universities LICENTIATE
– awarded as an honour, as a degree might be HONORARY, HONORIS CAUSA
– present or bestow a degree or honour CONFER
– referring to a degree awarded even though the graduate is absent IN ABSENTIA
– research report, especially for a higher academic degree THESIS, DISSERTATION
– student about to receive a degree GRADUAND

degrees of comparison of adjectives and adverbs POSITIVE, COMPARATIVE, SUPERLATIVE

deity, saint, or other protecting power TUTELARY

delay See also **postpone**
– delay PROCRASTINATION, CUNCTATION
– delay, hinder, or obstruct as a deliberate strategy, as in cricket or parliamentary debate STONEWALL
– delay, lag, be late or slow in doing something TARRY, LOITER
– delay by holding back or preventing the departure of DETAIN
– delay decisions or draw out discussions as a way of gaining time TEMPORISE
– delay or block legislation, voting, or the like by means of lengthy speeches or other obstructive tactics FILIBUSTER
– delay or postponement, as of payments MORATORIUM
– delay or slow down the development or progress of something RETARD
– delayed, late in arriving TARDY
– delaying, wasting time, dawdling DILATORY
– cause a delay by being indecisive or disorganised DITHER, DILLY-DALLY, VACILLATE, SHILLY-SHALLY
– temporary delay, relief, or postponement, such as a stay of execution RESPITE, REPRIEVE

delegate or representative, as of the Pope LEGATE, EMISSARY

delete, erase, or obliterate something, such as a word EXPUNGE
– delete a passage from a text EXCISE
– delete words, passages, or the like from a text considered to be improper, objectionable, or obscene EXPURGATE, BOWDLERISE

deliberate, planned beforehand, as a murder might be PREMEDITATED
– deliberate decision, choice VOLITION

delicacy, precision, subtlety, as in negotiations NICETY
– delicacy or sensitivity, as in one's dealings with other people TACT
– delicacy or subtlety, as of painting style, negotiation technique, or tennis strokes FINESSE

delicate, light, insubstantial GOSSAMER
– delicate, sensitive, capable of or based on fine distinctions SUBTLE, EXQUISITE
– delicate, very refined ETHEREAL
– delicate or dainty in an affected way MINCING, NIMINY-PIMINY

delicious, especially when sweet and juicy LUSCIOUS
– delicious, tempting TOOTHSOME
– delicious drink NECTAR
– delicious food AMBROSIA
– delicious or delightful DELECTABLE, SCRUMPTIOUS

delight, great joy ECSTASY, RAPTURE, TRANSPORT, JUBILATION, EXULTATION, ELATION
– delight, please, afford satisfaction to GRATIFY
– delight in or satisfaction at others' misfortunes SCHADENFREUDE
– regard with cruel or smug delight GLOAT

delightful See also **attractive**, **charming**
– delightful or blissful ELYSIAN, IDYLLIC
– delightful or delicious DELECTABLE, SCRUMPTIOUS

delivery See also **birth**, **childbirth**
– delivery of a baby requiring the use of medical tongs FORCEPS DELIVERY

Delphi – prophecy, shrine, or priest of a prophetic god, as in ancient Delphi ORACLE

delusion, or wishful thinking MARE'S NEST
– delusions of grandeur FOLIE DE GRANDEUR
– delusions of grandeur or persecution PARANOIA

demand, require or lay down as a condition in an agreement or contract STIPULATE
– demand or request, often in writing and official, for needed supplies or equipment REQUISITION
– demand persistently IMPORTUNE, HECTOR

demanding, exacting, pressing, urgent EXIGENT
– demanding, exacting, requiring painstaking work or one's detailed attention NIGGLING
– demanding, strict, rigorous STRINGENT
– demanding, tiring, requiring great effort TAXING
– demanding and determined person, insisting on obedience, tidiness, accuracy, or the like STICKLER
– referring to or making insistent demands STRIDENT

demolish a building or city, destroy down to the ground RAZE

demon or evil spirit reputed to have sex with a sleeping man SUCCUBUS
– demon or evil spirit reputed to have sex with a sleeping woman INCUBUS
– demon that preys on corpses, in Muslim legend GHOUL
– drive out demons or evil spirits, or free a possessed person from them, as by religious rites EXORCISE
– person supposedly possessed by a demon DEMONIAC, ENERGUMEN
– summon a demon or spirit by means of a magic spell CONJURE

demonstrate See also **prove**
– demonstrate, indicate, signify BESPEAK, BETOKEN
– demonstrate or reveal, make evident MANIFEST, EVINCE
– demonstrated beyond doubt, indisputably certain APODICTIC
– demonstrating or showing directly, pointing out OSTENSIVE, DEICTIC

demonstration, political protest rally MANIFESTATION
– demonstration or protest outside a place of work, typically during a strike, as to discourage other workers or customers from entering PICKET
– placard or message-bearing cloth strip carried in a demonstration or procession BANNER

demonstrative emotionally GUSHING, EFFUSIVE

demotion, as to a lower division of a football league RELEGATION

denial of an allegation in a lawsuit TRAVERSE
– absolute, without reservation, as a denial might be CATEGORICAL

dental filling, as of gold or porcelain, cemented into a cavity INLAY
– dental plate with a false tooth or teeth permanently fixed to natural teeth BRIDGE, BRIDGEWORK
– mercury alloy, as used for dental fillings AMALGAM

dentist specialising in correcting the positioning of teeth ORTHODONTIST

– dentist's colleague specialising in scaling and polishing the teeth DENTAL HYGIENIST

dentistry concerned with diseases of the tissues and supporting structures surrounding the teeth PERIODONTICS
– rubbery latex substance used in electrical insulation and dentistry GUTTA-PERCHA

deny and disprove REFUTE, REBUT
– deny or contradict NEGATE, CONTROVERT, GAINSAY
– deny or reject without necessarily disproving REPUDIATE
– deny or withdraw a former statement or belief RECANT, RETRACT, RENOUNCE, FORSWEAR, ABJURE
– deny responsibility for or connection with DISAVOW, DISCLAIM, DISOWN

depart hastily, run away, or flee SKEDADDLE, SCARPER, VAMOOSE
– depart or flee secretly, as after committing a theft ABSCOND, DECAMP, ABSQUATULATE, HIGHTAIL
– depart or flee secretly with a lover, typically to get married ELOPE
– depart or withdraw, as from a dangerous area EVACUATE, VACATE
– departure, especially of a large number of people EXODUS
– departure from a convention, norm, standard, set path, or the like DIVERGENCE, DEVIATION
– departure or absence that is without permission or notification FRENCH LEAVE

department – administrative department of a large public or international organisation such as the United Nations SECRETARIAT

department store or large retail shop selling a wide range of goods EMPORIUM

dependency, captivity, enslavement THRALL, THRALDOM
– value or thing in a relationship of dependency with or close correspondence to another FUNCTION

dependent clinging person, parasite LEECH, LIMPET
– dependent, hinging on, conditional CONTINGENT, PROVISIONAL
– dependent relationship, typically that of living together, of two organisms, especially when beneficial to both SYMBIOSIS

deposit money EARNEST
– deposit of fine sandy sediment in or from a river SILT, ALLUVIUM
– deposit of rock fragments or similar debris left by wind, water, or glaciers SEDIMENT
– deposit of sediment in a river's tidal estuary WARP
– deposit or pledge given as security GAGE

depot or warehouse ENTREPÔT

depression MELANCHOLIA
– depression, boredom, or inactivity DOLDRUMS, ENNUI
– depression, state of deep despair SLOUGH OF DESPOND
– depression or hysteria, supposed in former times to be caused by gases produced within the body THE VAPOURS
– depression or unease MALAISE
– depression or withdrawn condition accompanying a nervous breakdown NEURASTHENIA

deprive of meaning, importance, or an essential part EVISCERATE
– deprive or strip of something, such as clothes, rights, or property DIVEST, DENUDE, DESPOIL
– deprive someone of something, seize or appropriate, as by way of punishment or in an emergency EXPROPRIATE, CONFISCATE, COMMANDEER

depth, as of feeling, meaning, or thinking PROFUNDITY
– depth appearance of various objects in different spatial relationships PERSPECTIVE
– establishing the depth of water by high-frequency sound waves ECHO SOUNDING, ASDIC, SONAR
– instrument for measuring the depth of water BATHOMETER
– measure the depth of, as with a weighted line SOUND, FATHOM, PLUMB

depth- BATH-, BATHO-, BATHY-

deputy See also **agent**, **substitute**
– deputy, representative of a superior official LIEUTENANT
– deputy, substitute, or stand-in VICAR, SURROGATE
– deputy administrative officer assisting a king, magistrate, or the like VICEGERENT
– deputy who does someone else's dirty work HATCHET MAN

Derby or any other of the five major British flat horseraces CLASSIC

derived from- AP-, APO-

Descartes – relating to Descartes' philosophy, mathematics, or methods CARTESIAN

descendant or offspring, especially male SCION
– descendants of a particular ancestor LINEAGE, POSTERITY

descend – descended from the same ancestor, though by different lines, as branches of a family might be COLLATERAL
– descended in a direct line from a particular ancestor LINEAL
– descended through the male line, related on the father's side AGNATE
– descending slope or downward tendency DECLENSION, DECLINATION, DECLINE, DECLIVITY
– descent, source, or origin DERIVATION
– relating to the female line of descent MATRILINEAL
– family tree or lineage, or study of descent and ancestors GENEALOGY
– relating to the male line of descent PATRILINEAL

describe or draw, either in broad or in precise detail DELINEATE, DEPICT
– describe or portray, characterise LIMN
– difficult to describe, lacking distinct individual features, uninteresting NONDESCRIPT

description – brief description or account of someone, as in a magazine article PROFILE, POTTED BIOGRAPHY, THUMBNAIL SKETCH, PEN-PORTRAIT
– precise description, list of components or details, plan, or proposal SPECIFICATION

desert, wilderness WASTE, WASTELAND
– desert-like area with eroded ridges and gullies BADLANDS
– desert one's country, political party, or the like, especially to join its opponent DEFECT
– desert or convert, become a renegade TERGIVERSATE, APOSTATISE
– desert rat JERBOA
– deserted, uninhabited DESOLATE
– deserter of a religion or cause RENEGADE, APOSTATE
– dry and infertile, as desert land might be ARID
– fertile area in a desert OASIS
– illusion or image of a non-present object, such as an oasis in a desert MIRAGE
– relating to an extremely dry habitat such as a desert XERIC
– travellers in a group or convoy, as through a desert CARAVAN

deserved and appropriate, as a punishment might be CONDIGN

design See also **pattern**
– design, typically stamped or gilded, on books or leather TOOLING
– design, usually circular, symbolising the universe, in Hindu and Buddhist art MANDALA
– design consisting of superimposed letters, as for an emblem MONOGRAM, CIPHER
– design made up of many other

designs or pictures overlapping or stuck side by side MONTAGE, COLLAGE
– design of modern style using industrial materials HIGH-TECH
– design or painting on a wall or ceiling MURAL
– design or picture made up of many small pieces of stone, tile, or glass MOSAIC
– design or purpose in Nature, or the study of or belief in it TELEOLOGY
– design or structure, as in architecture or music ARCHITECTONICS
– design or symbol, as on a flag or embroidery DEVICE, EMBLEM
– design produced by superimposing one pattern on another MOIRÉ PATTERN
– designed for aesthetic rather than realistic effect STYLISED
– designer, or craftsman who is highly skilled ARTIFICER
– background for a design, as in lacework FOND
– basic design or layout, as of a broadcast or diagram FORMAT
– make a design or pattern by embedding decorative pieces in a surface INLAY
– original design or model, on which later versions are based PROTOTYPE, ARCHETYPE
– repeated shape or theme in a design or composition LEITMOTIV, MOTIF
– simplified, abstract, stylised, as a painting or design might be CONVENTIONALISED

desirable but frustratingly inaccessible TANTALISING

desire See also **tendency**
– desire or look forward to eagerly RELISH
– desire or slight tendency, without any action taken to fulfil it VELLEITY
– desire something that belongs to someone else COVET
– desire that is compulsive and harmful, mania CACOETHES
– desire to achieve or succeed at something ASPIRATION
– behaviour or mental activity, such as desire, directed towards change or action CONATION
– deep or intense desire, longing, yearning, craving HANKERING, YEN
– exclusion or deliberate blocking of thoughts, desires, or the like from one's mind SUPPRESSION
– frenzy of frustrated desire for something unattainable NYMPHOLEPSY
– indulge one's desires or appetites to the full SATE, SATIATE
– indulge or yield to a whim, desire, or the like GRATIFY

DESSERTS AND PUDDINGS

baked Alaska	ice cream covered with baked meringue
Bakewell tart	open tart with almond-flavoured sponge over a layer of jam
baklava	paper-thin pastry with chopped nuts and honey
bavarois	fruit-flavoured or chocolate-flavoured egg custard with whipped cream
bombe	moulded ice cream
cassata	Neopolitan ice cream with candied fruit and nuts
charlotte	sponge cake or bread mould filled with fruit
compôte	dish of fresh or dried fruit in syrup
coupe	garnished ice cream
crème brûlée	dish of cream or custard with a caramelised sugar top
crêpe suzette	thin pancake with orange sauce, served with flaming spirit sauce
Eve's pudding	baked sponge pudding with a fruit base
flummery	custard, blancmange or similar soft, bland dessert
fool	cold pudding of crushed fruit mixed with cream or custard
frappé	fruit-flavoured water ice
frumenty	sweetened and spiced milk pudding of boiled wheat
granita	coarse water ice
halva	sweetmeat of ground sesame seed or semolina and chopped nuts, in syrup, lemon juice, or the like
junket	sweetened milk set with rennet
mela stregata	ball of ice cream flavoured with strega liqueur, and coated with chocolate
Nesselrode	frozen pudding with preserved fruit and chestnut purée
pandowdy	U.S. dessert of baked apple slices with a sweet crust
parfait	frozen pudding of cream, eggs, sugar, and flavouring
pavlova	meringue cake topped with whipped cream and fresh fruit, originating in Australia
profiteroles	small, cream-filled choux pastry rolls, usually with a chocolate sauce
sorbet	water ice of fruit juice or fruit purée
strudel	baked pastry consisting of fruit rolled in wafer-thin sheets of dough
sundae	ice cream with various toppings
syllabub	sweetened, thickened cream flavoured with sherry or wine and fruit juice
vacherin	meringue with cream and fresh fruit
zabaglione	beaten egg yolks with marsala wine and sugar
zuppa inglese	Italian trifle

– natural desire, tendency, or attraction APPETENCE
– relating to the desires ORECTIC
– something wished for, needed, or desired DESIDERATUM
– strong desire, especially sexual desire CONCUPISCENCE
– strong desire or greed, especially for money or material things CUPIDITY
– unsatisfiable, as an appetite or desire might be INSATIABLE

-desire -MANIA

desk See also **furniture**
– desk at which a person may kneel to pray PRIE-DIEU
– desk or panel containing the controls of a computer, lighting system, or the like CONSOLE
– rolltop desk's sliding front of wooden strips TAMBOUR
– set of drawers supporting a desk top PEDESTAL

despair, state of deep depression SLOUGH OF DESPOND
– despair or spiritual lethargy ACCIDIE

despise See **dislike**, **insult**
– despise or scorn DISDAIN, CONTEMN

despot See **dictator**
– despot or absolute ruler who is moderate, enlightened, and well-disposed towards his subjects BENEVOLENT DESPOT

dessert See chart, and also **cake**
– dessert, or light dish just before the dessert ENTREMETS

destination, purpose, goal, finishing point TERMINUS AD QUEM
– destination or goal BOURN

destine, decree ORDAIN

destiny See **fate**
– clear and unavoidable, as destiny might be MANIFEST

destroy, get rid of, or put an end to rules, practices, or the like ABOLISH
– destroy, ruin, or damage something, such as a plan SCUPPER, SCUTTLE
– destroy by taking to pieces DISMANTLE
– destroy completely, snuff out ANNIHILATE, EXTINGUISH, SPIFLICATE
– destroy a building or city, tear down to the ground DEMOLISH, RAZE
– destroy gradually, wear away CORRODE, ERODE
– destroy or eliminate something completely, such as vermin EXTERMINATE
– destroy or get rid of completely, stamp out ERADICATE, OBLITERATE, EXTIRPATE, EXPUNGE
– destroy or kill a large proportion of DECIMATE
– destroy or make ineffective an argument, contract, or the like ANNUL, NULLIFY, VOID, INVALIDATE, VITIATE
– destroy or obscure something, such as a memory EFFACE
– destroy the inside or power of GUT
– destroyed or completely ruined FOREDONE
– explode or be destroyed, either automatically or following a signal, as a misfired missile might SELF-DESTRUCT

-destroy- -PHAG-, PHAGO-, -PHAGOUS

destruction, as caused by a war HAVOC, DEVASTATION
– destruction and plunder DEPREDATION
– destruction by breaking up DISINTEGRATION, PULVERISATION, DISSOLUTION
– destruction by fire HOLOCAUST
– destruction of bacteria by an antibody LYSIS
– destruction of sacred objects or traditions ICONOCLASM
– destruction or attempted undermining, by secret activity, of a government or political system SUBVERSION
– destruction or damaging of property, as by enemy agents or dissatisfied workers SABOTAGE
– destruction or failure of some magnificent project or person GÖTTERDÄMMERUNG
– destruction or injury of a wanton or widespread kind MAYHEM
– destruction or just retribution, or an agent of it NEMESIS
– destruction or malicious damaging of public property, artistic works, or the like VANDALISM
– random, wilful, unprovoked, as mindless destruction is WANTON, GRATUITOUS
– sudden and violent change, upheaval, or destruction CATACLYSM

destructive, deadly, harmful LETHAL, FATAL, BANEFUL, PERNICIOUS, PESTILENT
– destructive, especially through plundering or robbery PREDATORY
– destructive, frenzied, or violent in behaviour RAMPAGING, ON THE RAMPAGE
– destructive effects, damage RAVAGES
– destructiveness of an unselective all-embracing kind NIHILISM

detach someone from old habits and pastimes and thereby encourage his independence WEAN

detail, individual item PARTICULAR
– detail, subtle point, fine distinction NICETY
– detail that is important only to a specialist, or that arises only from a strict ruling TECHNICALITY
– detail that is trivial, needless, or oversubtle QUIBBLE, NIGGLE
– clearly described in vivid or exciting detail GRAPHIC
– detailed, complete, thorough, as a report might be COMPREHENSIVE, CIRCUMSTANTIAL
– detailed analysis or criticism DISSECTION
– detailed and clearly expressed, as directions might be EXPLICIT
– details, particulars SPECIFICS, SPECIFICATIONS
– details that are precise or sometimes needlessly fussy MINUTIAE, TRIVIA
– excessive attention to small details of knowledge at the expense of deeper insight and understanding PEDANTRY
– improve or enliven a report or story by adding colourful, often false or unnecessary, details EMBELLISH, EMBROIDER
– over-concerned with details NIT-PICKING, HAIRSPLITTING, METICULOUS
– over-fussy detail, as of etiquette or protocol PUNCTILIO
– talk or write at length and in detail on a subject ELABORATE, EXPATIATE, ENLARGE, DILATE

detain or imprison, especially in wartime INTERN

detective, private eye SLEUTH, SHAMUS, GUMSHOE

detention, being held under arrest or under guard, as by the police CUSTODY

determined, fussy, or insistent person, making demands in the face of difficulties STICKLER
– determined, gritty, stubbornly persevering DOGGED, TENACIOUS
– determined, single-mindedly firm of purpose, staunch and unwavering RESOLUTE, STALWART, STEADFAST
– determined, unshakable, unyielding INDOMITABLE

detour for traffic DIVERSION

devastate, afflict severely SCOURGE

develop, help to grow, encourage the advancement of NURTURE, FOSTER
– develop, reproduce, breed PROPAGATE
– develop, stir up, or provoke troubles, or the like FOMENT
– develop buds or sprouts, or breed rapidly PULLULATE
– develop, enlarge, or expand a statement, speech, idea, or the like

AMPLIFY, ELABORATE
– develop or grow rapidly FLOURISH, BURGEON
– develop slowly or gradually, or cause to develop GERMINATE, INCUBATE, GESTATE

-develop -GEN, -GENESIS, -GENY

developing, just beginning or emerging NASCENT
– developing or caused outside the body or a body part EXOGENOUS
– developing or caused within the body or a body part ENDOGENOUS
– developing or maturing unusually early, as a bright, clever, or sophisticated child seems to do PRECOCIOUS
– developing or shaping one's personality FORMATIVE

-developing -PLASTIC

development by slow or natural means, as of species, art, or social systems EVOLUTION
– development of housing along a road leading out of a town RIBBON DEVELOPMENT
– development or evolution of a species, genus, language, custom, or the like PHYLOGENY
– development or evolution of an individual ONTOGENY
– in the earliest stage of growth or development EMBRYONIC, SEMINAL, GERMINAL
– something that nourishes or promotes growth or development NUTRIMENT

deviate briefly from the correct course, as a ship or aircraft might YAW

device adopted for an urgent purpose EXPEDIENT
– referring to any device or technique that encourages the learning process through independent investigation HEURISTIC

devil See **demon**
– devil worship, black magic, witchcraft, or the like DIABOLISM

devilish, hellish, demonic DIABOLIC, FIENDISH, SATANIC, INFERNAL

devil's advocate – official name in the Roman Catholic Church for the devil's advocate PROMOTER OF THE FAITH, FIDEI DEFENSOR

devise or perform a poem, play, melody, or the like, composing as one goes IMPROVISE

devote one's life or time fully to a specified cause or purpose CONSECRATE, DEDICATE
– devoted or dutiful, especially in one's religious observances, pious DEVOUT
– devoted to one's wife, especially in an excessive or fawning way UXORIOUS
– devotion, great respect, awe, as shown to God REVERENCE, VENERATION
– devotion or excessive admiration IDOLATRY, HERO-WORSHIP

diabetes – abnormally high sugar-level in the blood, as in diabetes HYPERGLYCAEMIA
– abnormally low sugar-level in the blood, as in diabetes HYPOGLYCAEMIA
– hormone regulating the blood sugar level, deficiency of which results in diabetes INSULIN

diacritical marks See **punctuation**

diagnosis by means of tapping the chest, back, or the like and assessing the sound produced PERCUSSION
– diagnostic sign identifying a disease STIGMA
– dye, radioactive substance, or the like, whose course can be monitored through a system, as used in medical diagnosis TRACER
– listening to body sounds, as through a stethoscope, for purposes of diagnosis AUSCULTATION

diagonal, crosswise CATER-CORNERED
– diagonal or crosswise route across a slope, as in skiing TRAVERSE
– diagonal punctuation mark, slash, as in *and/or* SOLIDUS, VIRGULE, OBLIQUE, SHILLING MARK

diagram explaining a series of operations, as in a computer program or industrial process FLOW CHART
– diagram or illustration of a machine or structure showing its parts separately EXPLODED VIEW
– diagram or model, as of an engine or building, with part of the wall or casing omitted or cut away to reveal the interior CUTAWAY
– diagram in the form of a circle divided into sectors, showing the proportions of the various parts PIE CHART
– diagram showing the relationships within an industrial process, electronic system, or the like by means of lines linking labelled rectangles BLOCK DIAGRAM

dial – referring to a watch, clock, or meter indicating readings by changing numbers rather than by moving hands on a dial DIGITAL
– referring to a watch, clock, or meter indicating readings by moving hands on a dial rather than by changing numbers ANALOG

dialect, especially a provincial dialect PATOIS
– line on a dialect map linking places using the same distinctive word or pronunciation ISOGLOSS

dialectic – final stage in the dialectical reasoning process of Hegel, through combining thesis and antithesis SYNTHESIS

dialogue, as in ancient Greek drama, in which alternate lines of verse are spoken by different characters STICHOMYTHIA
– dialogue in a literary composition COLLOQUY
– person taking part in a dialogue or discussion INTERLOCUTOR

diameter of the inside of a tube, the bore of a gun, or a bullet or shell CALIBRE

diamond See also **gemstone**
– diamond-bearing rock KIMBERLITE
– diamond-like in brilliance or hardness ADAMANTINE
– diamond-like mineral used as a gemstone ZIRCON
– diamond-like shape or geometrical figure LOZENGE, RHOMBUS
– diamond of poor quality, used for industrial purposes BORT, BORTZ
– diamond or other gemstone set by itself, as in a ring SOLITAIRE
– diamond that is unflawed and very large PARAGON
– any of the different physical forms that an element may take, such as diamond or graphite as forms of carbon ALLOTROPE
– artificial diamond made of paste or quartz RHINESTONE
– decorated with glass, sequins, or artificial jewels to produce a diamond-like glitter DIAMANTÉ
– headband or semicircle, typically decorated with diamonds or other jewels, worn by a woman on formal occasions TIARA
– brilliance of a diamond WATER
– relating to or resembling diamonds DIAMANTINE

diaphragm- PHREN-, PHRENO-

diarrhoea as experienced by tourists in hot countries, especially Mexico MONTEZUMA'S REVENGE
– discharge of body fluids in abnormally large quantities, as of watery faeces in diarrhoea FLUX
– inflammation of the lining of the stomach and intestines, causing diarrhoea GASTROENTERITIS

dice throw MAIN
– dice throw producing the lowest score, especially a throw of two with a pair of dice CRABS, AMBSACE
– group or setting of five objects arranged in a rectangle with one in the middle, as with the five on dice QUINCUNX

dictation – secretary or scribe who takes dictation or makes neat

copies of documents AMANUENSIS

dictator See also **ruler**, **bully**
- dictator or authoritarian ruler DESPOT, TYRANT, FÜHRER, AUTOCRAT, AUTARCH
- dictator, usually a military leader, in Spanish-speaking countries CAUDILLO
- dictator who is moderate, enlightened, and well-disposed towards his subjects BENEVOLENT DESPOT
- dictatorial person, specifically an authoritarian and uncompromising military disciplinarian MARTINET
- group of military officers ruling a country in a dictatorial way, especially after a coup d'état JUNTA
- dictatorial system aiming at total control TOTALITARIANISM, ABSOLUTISM
- subordinate dictator SATRAP

dictionary classifying synonyms and sometimes antonyms systematically THESAURUS
- dictionary compiler, editor, or expert LEXICOGRAPHER
- dictionary definition or explanation of a headword DEFINIENS
- dictionary headword that is the subject of the definition DEFINIENDUM
- dictionary of a small specialised kind, as for reference in a textbook LEXICON, GLOSSARY, VOCABULARY
- dictionary or listing of places GAZETTEER
- produce the text of an anthology, dictionary, or other book by gathering the material from many sources COMPILE
- quotation or reference used as an authority, as for a dictionary or legal argument CITATION
- series of notches cut into the front edge of a dictionary or other book, as for easy alphabetical reference THUMB INDEX
- word at the top of a page of a dictionary, telephone directory, or the like, indicating the alphabetical entries of that page CATCHWORD, GUIDE WORD, RUNNING HEAD
- word or phrase forming a main heading and fully explained or defined in a dictionary HEADWORD

die See also **dead**, **death**
- die, breathe one's last EXPIRE, PERISH
- "he died" or "she died", formal term used before the date of death OBIIT

diesel engine COMPRESSION-IGNITION ENGINE
- diesel fuel's performance rating CETANE NUMBER
- diesel oil used as fuel for road vehicles DERV

diet system based on cereals and organically grown vegetables MACROBIOTICS
- preparation taken to balance or improve the diet SUPPLEMENT
- protein mixture in wheat flour, avoided in certain diets GLUTEN
- study of the intake, assimilation, and value of food, especially in the human diet NUTRITION
- system of exercise, therapy, diet, or the like REGIMEN

difference See also **change**, **dispute**, **disagreement**
- difference, contrast, or opposite ANTITHESIS
- difference, variation, departure from the norm DEVIATION, DIVERGENCE, ECCENTRICITY
- difference in brightness, as of separate areas of a photograph or television picture CONTRAST
- difference or alteration of a very fine or subtle kind, such as a shade of meaning NUANCE
- difference or inconsistency, as in results, claims, reports, or the like DISCREPANCY

different, completely dissimilar, so distinct that no comparison is possible DISPARATE
- different, numerous and assorted, various SUNDRY, MISCELLANEOUS, DIVERSE, MANIFOLD
- different in an unexpected or inharmonious way HETEROGENEOUS, INCONGRUOUS
- having or displaying a variety of different colours MOTLEY, PIED, PARTICOLOURED, VARIEGATED, POLYCHROME
- slightly different from the standard form, spelling, pronunciation, or the like VARIANT

different- ALLO-, ANISO-, HETER-, HETERO-, VARI-, VARIO-, XENO-

different direction- DIA-

differentiate, distinguish, tell apart DISCRIMINATE
- differentiating, indicating or serving as a difference or distinction DIACRITICAL

difficult, mysterious, or secret, as sacred rites might be ARCANE, OCCULT, ESOTERIC
- difficult and painful route or course of action VIA DOLOROSA
- difficult or demanding, burdensome, as a task might be ONEROUS, EXIGENT, EXACTING
- difficult or very straining, as a task might be HERCULEAN
- difficult to accomplish, backbreaking, taking great effort ARDUOUS, STRENUOUS
- difficult to deal with or defeat, as a problem or opponent might be FORMIDABLE
- difficult to follow or unravel, extremely complicated or devious, as intrigue might be BYZANTINE, LABYRINTHINE, TORTUOUS
- difficult to hold, catch, remember, or the like ELUSIVE
- difficult to interpret, obscure or ambiguous, as a warning might be DELPHIC, ORACULAR
- difficult to solve or deal with, as a knotty problem would be INTRACTABLE, SCABROUS
- difficult to understand, complex ABSTRUSE, RECONDITE, IMPALPABLE
- difficult to understand, or disentangle, knotty, highly complicated INTRICATE, CONVOLUTED
- impossibly difficult to follow, baffling, beyond understanding INCOMPREHENSIBLE, UNINTELLIGIBLE, UNFATHOMABLE, OPAQUE

difficult- DYS-

difficulty, minor obstacle SNAG
- add to or aggravate an error or difficulty COMPOUND
- in very serious difficulty IN EXTREMIS
- overcome a difficulty or obstacle SURMOUNT
- painful difficulty, trying or distressing situation or experience ORDEAL, TRIBULATION
- serious difficulty or distress PLIGHT, PREDICAMENT, QUANDARY, STRAITS

dig, hollow out, as to make a hole or tunnel EXCAVATE
- dig up and remove a dead body from a grave EXHUME, DISINTER

digest, absorb, or incorporate something, such as food or facts ASSIMILATE

digestion See illustration, page 142
- milky fluid formed in the small intestine during digestion CHYLE
- relating to digestion PEPTIC
- relating to food, nutrition, or digestion ALIMENTARY

digital display of symbols, as on a watch, produced by electrical stimulation of liquid crystals LCD

dignified or aristocratic man GRAND SEIGNEUR
- dignified or beautiful, especially when formal, or massive STATUESQUE
- dignified or noble in appearance DISTINGUÉ

dignity – beneath one's dignity INFRA DIG
- challenge, attack, or spoil someone's dignity, honour, or the like IMPUGN

– do something below one's dignity DEIGN, CONDESCEND

– snobbishly standing on one's dignity HOITY-TOITY

digressive, changing course in speech or thought, as a comment might be TANGENTIAL

dilemma, situation of unresolvable conflict DOUBLE BIND

– dilemma or predicament QUANDARY

dilute, thin, or weaken a solution or other substance ATTENUATE

– dilute or add impurities to milk, wine, or the like ADULTERATE

dim, make faded, EFFACE

– dim or faint, as a weak light is WAN

diminish See **lessen**

dinghy or service boat towed or carried by a yacht, launch, or small ship TENDER

dining hall in a monastery REFECTORY, FRATER

dinner – just after dinner POSTPRANDIAL

– relating to dinner PRANDIAL

dinner jacket – U.S. term for a dinner jacket TUXEDO

dinner table – person who excels in conversations at the dinner table DEIPNOSOPHIST

dinosaur See illustration, page 144

– extinct dinosaur-like flying reptile PTERODACTYL

– heavy three-horned dinosaur of North America, with a large skull, bony collar, and powerful tail TRICERATOPS

– huge long-necked dinosaur once inhabiting all the continents BRONTOSAURUS

diocese, bishop's area of authority and jurisdiction SEE

Dionysus – staff, typically decorated with leaves and tipped with a pine cone, carried by Dionysus and his followers THYRSUS

dip lightly into the water, as a bird might DAP

diplomat of high rank, just beneath ambassador MINISTER

– diplomat of senior rank COUNSELLOR

– diplomat fully authorised to represent a foreign government PLENIPOTENTIARY

– diplomat representing a country's commercial interests and assisting its citizens abroad CONSUL

– diplomat standing in for an ambassador or minister CHARGÉ D'AFFAIRES

– diplomat who is unacceptable to a foreign government PERSONA NON GRATA

digestive system

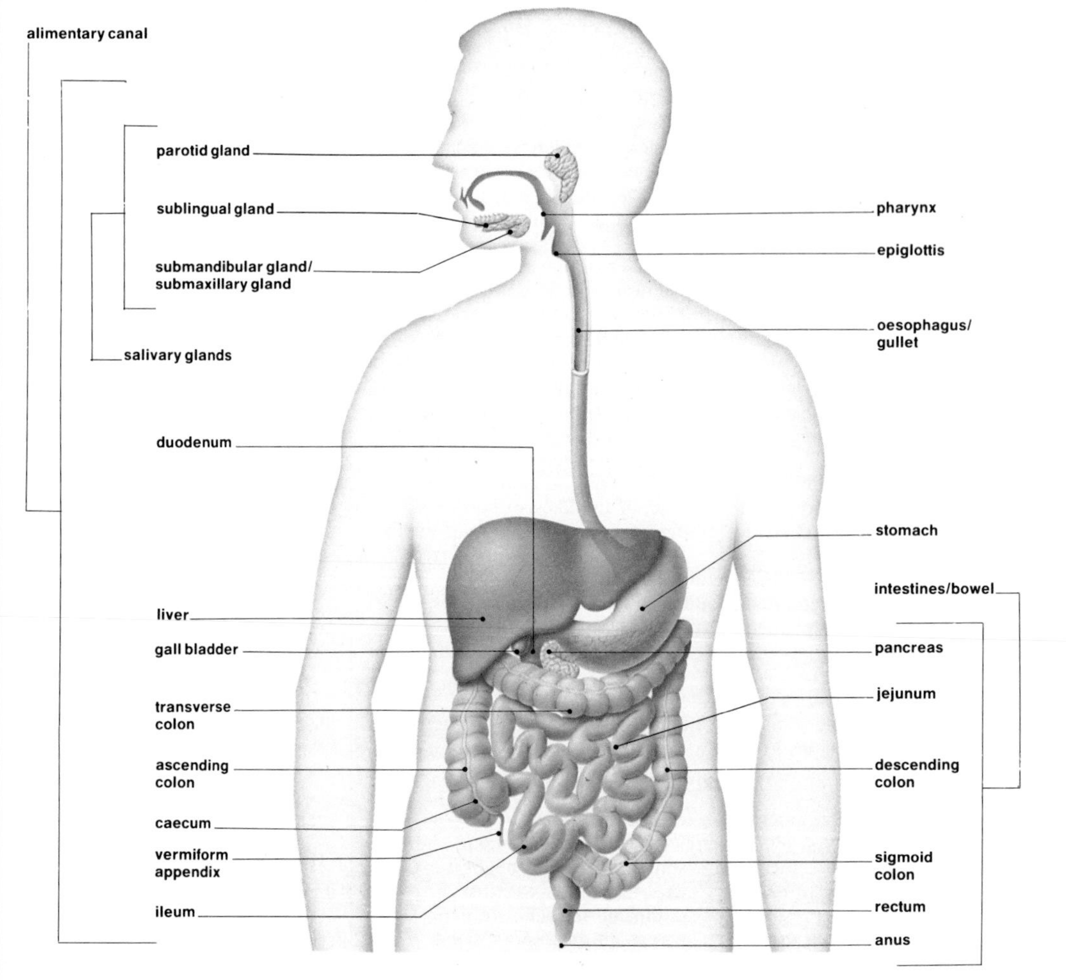

– diplomat's document of authorisation and introduction to a foreign government LETTERS OF CREDENCE
– diplomats' code of etiquette and official formalities PROTOCOL
– diplomatic agent sent on a special mission ENVOY, EMISSARY
– chief secretary of a diplomatic mission CHANCELLOR
– officially authorised, having acceptable credentials, as a diplomat might be ACCREDITED
– senior diplomatic representative in a protected state in former times RESIDENT
– senior diplomatic representative of one Commonwealth country serving in another HIGH COMMISSIONER
– technical expert assigned to a diplomatic mission ATTACHÉ

diplomatic immunity or similar exemption from the jurisdiction of one's country of residence EXTRATERRITORIALITY
– diplomatic in one's dealings with others, tactful and cautious PRUDENT, DISCREET, JUDICIOUS
– diplomatic initiative or step DÉMARCHE
– diplomatic mission ranking below an embassy in status LEGATION
– political section of a diplomatic mission CHANCELLORY, CHANCERY

direction, as of a ship or aircraft BEARING
– direction, conventional current, or trend MAINSTREAM
– direction, supervision, sponsorship AUSPICES, AEGIS
– direction or course, especially when guided by radio VECTOR
– direction or general movement, as of someone's life TENOR
– directional tendency of a plant's growth TROPISM
– approach from several different directions to meet at a point CONVERGE
– having lost one's sense of direction or bearings DISORIENTATED
– separate and move in different directions from a point DIVERGE

-direction- -TROP-, TROPO-, -TROPIC, -WARD, -WARDS, -WISE

director of a ballet or other theatrical work RÉGISSEUR
– director of a museum or public art gallery CURATOR

dirt – deep-seated, hard to remove, as dirt may be INGRAINED

dirty, run-down house or hut HOVEL
– dirty, soil, or spoil, as through adding impurities CONTAMINATE, POLLUTE, ADULTERATE
– dirty, spattered or smudged SPLODGED
– dirty, taint, stain or corrupt DEFILE, SULLY, TARNISH
– dirty all over, thoroughly soiled, covered or smeared with grime BEDAUBED, BEFOULED, BEMIRED, BESMIRCHED
– dirty and disgusting place CESSPOOL
– dirty and untidily dressed child RAGAMUFFIN
– dirty and untidy, as after being caught in the rain BEDRAGGLED
– dirty or corrupt place or situation AUGEAN STABLES
– dirty or seedy, as through neglect SQUALID, SLEAZY, SORDID
– extremely dirty, filthy, soiled by or as if by excrement FECULENT

disadvantage, disability, handicap, hindrance LIABILITY, DRAWBACK
– disadvantage, harm, damage DETRIMENT

disagreement See also **dispute**
– disagreement, as of political opinions DISSIDENCE, DISSENT
– disagreement, difference of opinion DISSENSION, VARIANCE
– disagreement or disharmony among parts, claims, statements or the like INCONSISTENCY, DISCREPANCY, IRRECONCILABILITY, DISPARITY, DISSONANCE, DISCORD, INCOMPATIBILITY, INCONGRUITY
– preposition used to acknowledge someone when disagreeing with his opinion, "despite the opinion of" PACE

disappear, by or as if by losing bodily form DEMATERIALISE
– disappear after breaking up or scattering DISPERSE, DISSIPATE
– disappear or fade, as hopes might WITHER
– disappear slowly, as mist might EVANESCE
– disappearance of a heavenly body during an eclipse OCCULTATION

disappointed, discontented, dissatisfied DISILLUSIONED, DISENCHANTED, DISABUSED

disappointing, unimpressive, failing to come up to expectations UNDERWHELMING
– disappointing outcome, failure, or anticlimax following high expectations ANTICLIMAX, BATHOS, DAMP SQUIB

disapprove See **complain**, **criticise**
– disapprove of, discourage, protest against DEPRECATE, LOOK ASKANCE AT, DISCOUNTENANCE
– disapproval DISAPPROBATION
– disapprove of strongly, condemn DEPLORE, REPREHEND, REPROBATE
– disapproving or unfavourable, as a particular sense or use of a word might be PEJORATIVE, DISPARAGING, DEPRECIATORY
– puritanically disapproving, self-righteous and usually hypocritical PHARISAICAL

disarmament – involving a single nation or faction operating on its own, as disarmament might UNILATERAL
– involving several nations or factions, as disarmament might MULTILATERAL

disaster, appalling mishap or destruction DEVASTATION, CALAMITY, CATASTROPHE
– disaster, event involving enormous destruction or disruption APOCALYPSE, CATACLYSM
– disaster, great destruction, or terrible battle or conflict ARMAGEDDON
– disaster about to happen, or the constant threat of disaster SWORD OF DAMOCLES
– disastrous collapse, failure, or defeat ROUT, DÉBÂCLE, FIASCO
– prevent or ward off danger, disaster, or the like AVERT

disbelief – feeling or expressing disbelief, doubting INCREDULOUS, SCEPTICAL

disbelieve or cast doubt on DISCREDIT
– disbeliever, sceptic, person without faith or beliefs NULLIFIDIAN

disc of metal PATEN, PLANCHET
– disc of shiny metal or plastic, used to ornament clothing, handbags, or the like SEQUIN
– disc of silicon or other semiconductor material, as used for integrated circuits WAFER
– disc or card that is spun or twirled to produce a merged image of the partial words or pictures on either side THAUMATROPE
– disc or wheel whose axis is off-centre and which converts rotary motion to reciprocating motion ECCENTRIC
– disc used as an ornament in architecture BEZANT

discharge, as from duty QUIETUS
– discharge of body fluids in abnormally large quantities, as of watery faeces in diarrhoea FLUX

-discharge -RRHOEA, -RRHAGIA

disciple, imitator, or follower who is markedly inferior to his master EPIGONE
– disciple or pupil of a guru CHELA

discipline one's body by self-denial or punishment MORTIFY
– discipline or punish in order to improve CHASTEN
– strict disciplinarian or person in authority MARTINET

discomfort, feeling of unease or anxiety DISQUIETUDE
disconnected, disordered, incoherent, as a report or story might be DISJOINTED
– disconnected, jumping about, as conversation might be DESULTORY
– abrupt, distinct, disconnected, and jerky in sound STACCATO
discontented, disappointed, and dissatisfied DISILLUSIONED, DISENCHANTED
– discontented, no longer feeling affection or loyalty ALIENATED, DISAFFECTED
– discontented, rebellious person MALCONTENT
discontinue parliament, or a similar body, without dissolving it PROROGUE
discontinuous, irregular, periodic INTERMITTENT
discount or partial refund, as on a bulk purchase REBATE
discourage, cause to lose confidence, morale, or hope DISPIRIT, DISHEARTEN, DEMORALISE, DAUNT
– discourage, disapprove of, dissuade DEPRECATE
– discourage or prevent someone from doing something, as by threatening DETER
discover or bring to light by careful searching or research FERRET OUT, UNEARTH
– discover or detect after conscientious effort DESCRY
– discover or prove definitely ASCERTAIN
– discover the meaning or secret of FATHOM
– exclamation of triumph on finding, solving, or discovering something EUREKA
discovery, or bright new idea TROUVAILLE
– helping or encouraging the process of learning or discovery HEURISTIC
– tendency to make lucky discoveries by accident SERENDIPITY
discriminate against, bully, or punish unfairly VICTIMISE
discus – discus-thrower or statue of one in ancient Greece and Rome DISCOBOLUS
discuss, exchange views, or consult PARLEY, CONFER, DISCOURSE
– discuss an issue freely, express openly, examine publicly VENTILATE
– discuss and investigate a subject thoroughly CANVASS
– discuss or comment on something at length DESCANT
– discuss or consider seriously and in detail DELIBERATE, MOOT
– discuss or converse earnestly CONFABULATE
– discuss terms, such as a contract, in the attempt to reach an agreement NEGOTIATE
– avoid or evade direct answers, refuse to discuss seriously FENCE, PREVARICATE, TEMPORISE, EQUIVOCATE
– begin to discuss a subject BROACH
discussion, as at a public meeting or in a magazine column FORUM
– discussion and logical disputing DIALECTIC
– discussion between two people, private conversation TÊTE-À-TÊTE
– discussion group or social clique CENACLE
– discussion or conference, as

dinosaurs

Brachiosaurus
Diplodocus
Coelophysis
Camptosaurus
Ankylosaurus
Hadrosaurus
Stegosaurus
Tyrannosaurus

among rival interest groups PALAVER, POWWOW, INDABA
– discussion or conference, typically on a specialist academic or professional theme SYMPOSIUM, COLLOQUIUM
– discussion or exchange of views DIALOGUE
– informal chat or discussion CAUSERIE
– person taking part in a conversation or discussion INTERLOCUTOR, COLLOCUTER

disdainful, haughty, scornful SUPERCILIOUS

disease See chart, page 147
– disease, illness AILMENT, MALADY
– disease, such as tuberculosis, that weakens, decays, or emaciates the body WASTING DISEASE
– disease-causing agent, germ PATHOGEN
– disease in which no organic change or cause is observable FUNCTIONAL DISEASE
– disease in which the structure of a body part or organ is affected ORGANIC DISEASE
– disease of a serious infectious kind, such as cholera or tuberculosis, that has to be reported to the health authorities NOTIFIABLE DISEASE
– disease resulting from one's job OCCUPATIONAL DISEASE
– disease that develops slowly or lasts a long time CHRONIC DISEASE
– disease that is sudden and severe, or that lasts only a short time ACUTE DISEASE
– disease that is very widespread EPIDEMIC, PANDEMIC
– disease transmitted by an animal, such as rabies or malaria ZOONOSIS
– diseased or infectious PESTIFEROUS, PESTILENT
– affecting the entire body, as a disease or poison might SYSTEMIC
– aftereffects, complications, or condition following a disease SEQUELLA
– branch of medicine dealing with classification of diseases NOSOLOGY
– catch a disease CONTRACT
– cause or origin of a disease, or study of such AETIOLOGY
– caused or developing outside the body or a body part, as some diseases are EXOGENOUS
– caused or developing within the body or a body part, as some diseases are ENDOGENOUS
– decline in the severity of a disease REMISSION
– decline in the severity of the symptoms of a disease over a long period LYSIS
– detention or isolation of a sick or possibly sick person or animal, to prevent the spread of disease QUARANTINE
– dormant or inactive, as a disease might be QUIESCENT
– forecast of the developmnt of a disease PROGNOSIS
– hospital for treating contagious diseases in former times LAZARET, LAZARETTO
– identification of a disease, injury, or problem DIAGNOSIS
– indication, especially as expressed by the patient, of a disease or disorder SYMPTOM
– insect or other organism that transmits disease-causing microorganisms VECTOR, CARRIER
– localised, restricted to a particular area or group, as a disease might be ENDEMIC
– medical testing for potential sufferers from a disease, carried out on a wide range of the population SCREENING
– preventing or protecting against something, especially disease PROPHYLACTIC
– protect against disease, as by injecting a vaccine INOCULATE, VACCINATE
– recurrence of a disease after a period of inactivity or improvement RELAPSE, RECRUDESCENCE
– referring to a disease or abnormality existing from birth but not hereditary CONGENITAL
– referring to a disease that strikes suddenly and fiercely FOUDROYANT
– relating or referring to physical diseases or disorders caused or aggravated by psychological factors such as stress PSYCHOSOMATIC
– relating to disease MORBID, PATHOLOGICAL
– relating to the early stage of an infection or disease before symptoms have been revealed SUBCLINICAL
– scientific study of disease PATHOLOGY
– spread of a disease from one part of the body to another METASTASIS
– spreading or progressing almost unnoticed, as a disease might be INSIDIOUS
– spreading uncontrolled, as a life-threatening disease might MALIGNANT, VIRULENT
– symptoms or signs jointly indicating or characterising a disease, abnormality, or the like SYNDROME
– tendency to contract a particular disease PREDISPOSITION
– tending to be affected by something adverse, such as a disease SUSCEPTIBLE
– transmittable, liable to be passed on, as many diseases are INFECTIOUS, COMMUNICABLE
– transmitted by physical contact, as a disease might be CONTAGIOUS
– unresponsive to treatment, as a disease might be REFRACTORY

-disease- NOS-, NOSO-, -PATH-, PATHO-, -PATHY, -OSIS

-diseased- DYS-, -OTIC

disembowel, remove the internal organs of EVISCERATE, EXENTERATE

disentangle, untangle, unravel UNSNARL

disgrace, as by deprivation of rank, status, office, or the like DEGRADATION
– disgrace, dishonour, bad reputation DISREPUTE, OBLOQUY
– disgrace, dishonour, damage the reputation of DISCREDIT
– disgrace of an extreme kind due especially to wickedness INFAMY, ODIUM
– disgrace or dishonour, shame or humiliation IGNOMINY, OPPROBIUM
– mark or sign of shame or disgrace STIGMA
– shun or banish a person in disgrace OSTRACISE

disguise oneself as someone else IMPERSONATE
– disguise or hide something, such as one's fear, feelings, or intentions DISSIMULATE, DISSEMBLE
– disguised enemy or threat within one's own ranks TROJAN HORSE, FIFTH COLUMN
– disguised or under a false name INCOGNITO

disgust, feeling of sheer loathing or distaste REVULSION
– disgust, sicken, or infuriate NAUSEATE, MAKE SOMEONE'S GORGE RISE
– disgust or extreme dislike, or the person or thing causing it AVERSION
– draw back, as in fear or disgust RECOIL, BLENCH

disgusting, appalling, horribly distasteful ABHORRENT
– disgusting, extremely distasteful or offensive, detestable REPULSIVE, REPUGNANT
– disgusting, offensive, foul, loathsome ABOMINABLE, ODIOUS
– disgusting, offensive to good taste FULSOME
– disgusting, sickening, gross NAUSEATING, REVOLTING
– disgusting or forbidding, repellent or fearsome REBARBATIVE
– disgusting or offensive, as a

foul smell is NOISOME
– disgustingly base, despicable SCURVY, SCROFULOUS
– disgustingly dirty or corrupt place CESSPOOL
– disgustingly often, repeatedly to a tiresome extent AD NAUSEAM

dish See also **cooking utensils**, **plate**, **menu terms**
– dish, typically of glass or plastic and fitted with a loose cover, as used in laboratories for growing bacteria cultures PETRI DISH
– dish just before the main dish, or the main dish itself, of a meal ENTRÉE
– dish or course served between the main courses of a meal ENTREMETS
– dish set on a hotplate or warmer, used to cook food or keep it warm CHAFING DISH
– dish that forms the main part of a meal PIÈCE DE RÉSISTANCE

dishonest, false, lying, deliberately misleading DECEITFUL, MENDACIOUS
– dishonest dealings, deception, sharp practice CHICANERY
– dishonestly or hypocritically appearing naïve, deceptively candid or sincere DISINGENUOUS
– dishonesty, deliberate deception, double dealing DUPLICITY
– speak or act in an evasive or dishonest way, so as to obscure the truth EQUIVOCATE, PREVARICATE

dishonour See **disgrace**
– dishonourable discharge, specifically from the armed forces CASHIERING

dishwashing – room off or recess in a kitchen for dishwashing, vegetable peeling, and the like SCULLERY

disillusioned or disappointed DISABUSED, DISENCHANTED

disinfect – fill a room or building with poisonous smoke to disinfect it, exterminate insects, and so on FUMIGATE
– watery chemical solution used as a disinfectant and bleaching agent JAVELLE WATER

disintegrate, separate, or soften by means of soaking MACERATE

dislike See also **hatred**
– dislike intensely, loathe ABHOR, ABOMINATE, EXECRATE
– dislike or displeasure DISTASTE
– arousing dislike or resentment, offensive INVIDIOUS
– extreme dislike or intense feeling of hostility or repulsion AVERSION, ANTIPATHY, REVULSION, REPUGNANCE
– indicating dislike or hostility, cold and unfriendly INIMICAL
– person or thing that one has a particular dislike of BÊTE NOIRE
– strong dislike or bitter enmity ANIMOSITY, ANIMUS
– strong or unreasonable dislike or prejudice SCUNNER

disloyal, unfaithful, characteristic of a deserter RECREANT, RENEGADE
– disloyalty, faithlessness, treachery PERFIDY, INFIDELITY

dismay or amazement that throws everything into confusion CONSTERNATION

dismissal, permission or order to leave NUNC DIMITTIS
– dismissal from a job, the sack, the push CONGÉ, HEAVE-HO
– dishonourable dismissal from the armed forces CASHIERING

disobedient towards central authority, rebellious or divisive DISSENTING, FACTIOUS
– conscientiously disobedient, refusing to submit to established authority RECUSANT
– openly disobedient towards lawful authority, rebellious MUTINOUS
– persistently disobedient or unruly, uncontrollable, resisting authority INSUBORDINATE, REFRACTORY, RESTIVE, TURBULENT
– stubbornly disobedient, or challenging or ignoring authority repeatedly DEFIANT, RECALCITRANT, CONTUMACIOUS, TRUCULENT
– stubbornly disobedient or uncooperative, firmly fixed in attitude or behaviour INTRANSIGENT
– tending to be disobedient or uncooperative CONTRARY, PERVERSE, FROWARD, WAYWARD

disobey a rule, break a law, defy a code of practice, or the like INFRINGE, VIOLATE, CONTRAVENE, TRANSGRESS
– disobey a ruling contemptuously, openly defy a convention, or the like FLOUT
– disobey or confront a person or authority boldly and unwaveringly OUTFACE

disorder See **confusion**, **disease**

disorganised See **confused**

disown or cast off a wife, husband, lover, or relative REPUDIATE

dispensary PHARMACY

displace a limb or organ, or put a bone out of joint DISLOCATE

display in a showy way BRANDISH
– display of symbols, as on a digital watch, produced by electrical stimulation of liquid crystals LCD
– display or symbol that is colourful, dramatic, or showy BLAZON, FLOURISH
– display stand or exhibition hall PAVILION
– complete and impressive display PANOPLY

dispose of, make unnecessary OBVIATE
– disposable, unnecessary, inessential EXPENDABLE

disprove, show to be false or invalid CONFUTE, REFUTE, REBUT
– disprove, weaken, or make ineffective an argument, claim, or the like INVALIDATE
– reject or deny without actually disproving REPUDIATE

dispute, contradict, deny, or call into question OPPUGN, GAINSAY, REPUDIATE, CONTROVERT
– dispute, controversy, argument, especially over a principle or belief POLEMIC
– dispute, difference of opinion DISSENSION, VARIANCE
– dispute, quarrel, heated disagreement CONTRETEMPS, ALTERCATION
– dispute or quarrel involving a noisy disturbance RUCTION
– causing disputes DIVISIVE
– come forward to mediate in a dispute INTERCEDE
– committee investigating or arbitrating a dispute, or the place where this is done TRIBUNAL
– go-between or judge in a dispute ARBITRATOR, MEDIATOR, HONEST BROKER, MODERATOR, INTERMEDIARY
– involved in a dispute, scandal, or the like EMBROILED
– minor or preliminary conflict, dispute, or military encounter SKIRMISH
– mutually destructive dispute INTERNECINE
– point still in dispute, not yet agreed MOOT POINT
– settle a dispute or difference between parties RECONCILE, COMPOSE, DETERMINE
– settle or attempt to settle a dispute between other people or groups MEDIATE, ARBITRATE, CONCILIATE
– settlement of a dispute by an impartial third party ARBITRATION, ADJUDICATION

disregard See **ignore**

disreputable, seedy or squalid, as a nightclub or café might be SORDID, SLEAZY
– disreputable, shady or shifty UNSAVOURY, LOUCHE

disrespect – treat disrespectfully, mess about TRIFLE WITH

dissatisfied, disappointed, stripped of one's illusions DISILLUSIONED, DISENCHANTED

– dissatisfied, peeved DISGRUNTLED
– dissatisfied, no longer feeling affection or loyalty ALIENATED, DISAFFECTED

dissidents – elimination of political opponents or dissidents PURGE

dissolve gradually, as some chemicals do, by absorbing water vapour from the air DELIQUESCE
– dissolve away soluble part, as from soil LEACH
– capable of being dissolved SOLUBLE
– containing as much dissolved substance as possible, as a solution might SATURATED
– impossible to solve or resolve a problem or dissolve a substance INSOLUBLE
– liquid in which a substance dissolves SOLVENT
– mixture of solid particles dispersed in but not dissolved in a liquid SUSPENSION, COLLOID
– substance that dissolves in a liquid SOLUTE

-dissolving- -LYS-, LYSO-, -LYSIS

distance See also **weights and measures**
– distance, division, unbridgeable gap GULF
– distance round the edge of a shape CIRCUMFERENCE
– distance or time between limits SPAN
– report or official communication sent over a distance DISPATCH

distance- TEL-, TELE-

distant See also **shy**, **stiff**
– distant and inaccessible place, or a fortified place or stronghold FASTNESS
– distant country areas, the sticks, the bush HINTERLAND, BOONDOCKS, BACKBLOCKS, OUTBACK, BEYOND THE BLACK STUMP, GRAMADOELAS, BUNDU
– distant region, goal, or ideal ULTIMA THULE
– fairly distant or remote from the centre OUTLYING

distillation, crystallisation, or other means of separating a mixture of chemicals into its components FRACTIONATION
– distillation flask as used by alchemists ALEMBIC

DISEASES, DISORDERS, AND CONDITIONS

BLOOD, HEART OR CIRCULATION

anaemia
aneurism
angina
atheroma
Buerger's disease
decompression sickness/caisson disease/bends
haemophilia
hypertension/high blood pressure
hypotension/low blood pressure
leukaemia
oedema/dropsy
pericarditis
phlebitis
Raynaud's syndrome
septicaemia/blood poisoning
tachycardia
toxaemia/blood poisoning

BONES OR JOINTS

bursitis/housemaid's knee
bursitis/tennis elbow
fibrositis
osteoarthritis
osteomyelitis
Paget's disease
Perthes' disease
scoliosis
synovitis

BRAIN OR NERVOUS SYSTEM

Alzheimer's disease
Bell's palsy
catalepsy
catatonia
delirium tremens (DTs)
dementia
Down's syndrome/mongolism
dyslexia
encephalitis
hydrocephalus/water on the brain
meningitis
motor neuron disease
multiple sclerosis
muscular dystrophy
myasthenia gravis
narcolepsy
Parkinson's disease
porphyria
rabies/hydrophobia
spina bifida
Sydenham's chorea/St Vitus' dance
trigeminal neuralgia/"tic douloureux"

DIGESTIVE OR URINARY SYSTEM

cirrhosis
coeliac disease
colitis
cystic fibrosis
diverticulitis
hepatitis
nephritis/Bright's disease
peritonitis
regional ileitis/Crohn's disease
schistosomiasis/bilharziasis
strangury
trichinosis
typhoid/enteric fever

EARS, EYES, OR MOUTH

blepharitis
conjunctivitis
gingivitis
glaucoma
labyrinthitis
mastoiditis
Ménière's disease
nystagmus
otitis
pyorrhoea
tinnitus
trachoma

GLANDS OR CELLS

Addison's disease
carcinoma/cancer
Cushing's disease or syndrome
Hodgkin's disease
scrofula/king's evil
thyrotoxicosis/Graves' disease/exophthalmic goitre

INFECTIOUS, VIRAL, OR PARASITIC DISEASES

AIDS (Acquired Immune Deficiency Syndrome)
anthrax
brucellosis
dengue fever
diphtheria
gonorrhoea
Lassa fever
leishmaniasis/dum dum fever/kala-azar
poliomyelitis/infantile paralysis
Q fever
rubella/German measles
rubeola/measles
tetanus/lockjaw
trypanosomiasis/sleeping sickness
variola/smallpox
yaws

MEN'S DISORDERS

balanitis
hydrocele
orchitis
prostatis

PSYCHIATRIC DISORDERS

amnesia
anorexia nervosa
autism
bulimia nervosa
schizophrenia

RESPIRATORY SYSTEM

emphysema
legionnaires' disease
mononucleosis/glandular fever
pleurisy
pneumoconiosis
psittacosis/parrot fever
quinsy
silicosis
tuberculosis/consumption/phthisis

SKIN

candidiasis/moniliasis/thrush
dermatitis
eczema
erysipelas/St Anthony's fire
herpes zoster/shingles
icthyosis
impetigo
lupus
miliaria rubra/prickly heat
myxoedema
psoriasis
rosacea
scabies
seborrhoea
tinea/ringworm
urticaria/nettlerash/hives

VITAMIN DEFICIENCY

beriberi
kwashiorkor
pellagra
rachitis/rickets
scurvy

WOMEN'S DISORDERS

amenorrhoea
eclampsia
endometriosis
mastitis
puerperal fever
salpingitis

– distillation flask with a long neck, formerly used in chemistry MATRAS
– glass vessel with a long, bent over neck, as used in a laboratory for distillation RETORT
– refine, separate, or purify in chemistry RECTIFY

distinct, individual DIVERSE
– distinct, separate, unconnected, individual DISCRETE, DISPARATE
– make or become distinct DIFFERENTIATE

distinction of a very fine or subtle kind, such as a shade of meaning NUANCE, NICETY, SUBTLETY
– making needless or oversubtle distinctions HAIRSPLITTING, QUIBBLING

distinctive quality or pattern of a piece of music, historical period, or the like TEXTURE

distinguishing, indicating or serving as a difference or distinction DIACRITICAL

distress call MAYDAY
– distress or cause of distress WORMWOOD
– distress, or great or prolonged suffering TRIBULATION
– distressing or affecting the emotions POIGNANT
– person who tries to give comfort but in fact causes only distress JOB'S COMFORTER

distribute in shares, assign proportionally, parcel out ALLOCATE, ADMEASURE, APPORTION, PRORATE
– distribute or deal out something, especially justice or punishment METE OUT, ALLOT, ADMINISTER, DISPENSE
– distribute throughout a speech, text, or the like, interlace INTERLARD, INTERSPERSE
– distribute widely, spread over a wide area DISPERSE, DIFFUSE, DISSEMINATE, PROPAGATE

disturb See also **confusion**
– disturb, confuse, embarrass, or unsettle DISCONCERT, DISCOMFIT
– disturb, inconvenience, annoy DISCOMMODE
– disturb, stir up ROIL, AGITATE
– disturb or interrupt the peace, someone's privacy, or the like VIOLATE
– disturb seriously, cause anxiety to, agitate PERTURB
– disturb the serenity of, make uneasy DISQUIET, DISCOMPOSE
– disturbed, agitated, as rushing water is TURBULENT
– disturbing, annoying, causing a nuisance VEXATIOUS
– make trouble, cause an uproar or disturbance RAISE CAIN
– sudden and violent disturbance, radical change UPHEAVAL

disuse, state of being out of use or practice DESUETUDE

ditch, as for drainage, typically with a raised bank alongside DYKE
– ditch or channel cut in the ground by water GULLY
– ditch or defensive moat FOSSE
– ditch or moat as a barrier, as in a garden HA-HA, SUNK FENCE
– ditch or water channel in South Africa SLOOT

dive down quickly and deep, as a whale or large fish might SOUND
– dive in which the diver bends double at the hips and then straightens out before entering the water JACKKNIFE
– dive in which the diver's back is arched and arms spread outwards SWALLOW DIVE
– dive involving a forward leap followed by a backward somersault GAINER
– diving position in which the body is bent double at the hips PIKE
– diving vessel for manned scientific observation in deep water at sea BATHYSCAPH, BATHYSPHERE

diver or underwater researcher AQUANAUT
– diver using a compressed-air breathing apparatus SCUBA DIVER
– diver's breathing apparatus, including an air cylinder and oxygen mask AQUALUNG
– diver's supply line or tether to the vessel UMBILICAL CORD
– painful condition, as in deep-sea divers, following sudden change of pressure THE BENDS, CAISSON DISEASE, DECOMPRESSION SICKNESS, AEROEMBOLISM

diverging from the point, changing course in speech or thought TANGENTIAL, DIGRESSIVE

divide See also **cut**, **separate**, **division**
– divide a territory into small warring states BALKANISE
– divide into steps or intervals, as for making measurements GRADUATE
– divide into two opposing positions or groups POLARISE
– divide or cut into two equal parts BISECT
– divide or separate into different classes, categories, sections, or the like COMPARTMENTALISE, PIGEONHOLE
– divide up, separate into sections PARTITION, DISMEMBER, SEGMENT, FRAGMENT
– divided, separated, split CLEFT, ASUNDER
– divided according to castes, classes, or the like, as a nation or society might be STRATIFIED
– divided along racial or sectarian lines SEGREGATED
– divided into two equal parts BINARY, BIPARTITE
– divided into two streams or parts, forked, branched BIFURCATE
– dividing an exact number of times, without remainder, into a larger quantity ALIQUOT
– number or a quantity by which another is divided DIVISOR, DENOMINATOR
– number or a quantity that is divided by another DIVIDEND, NUMERATOR

-divide -SECT

-dividing -KINESIS

divination See **fortune-telling**
– divining for water, ore, or the like by means of a rod or wand DOWSING, RHABDOMANCY

-divination -MANCY

divine, filled with a sense of divine influence or energy NUMINOUS
– divine manifestation, appearance of God or of a god to man THEOPHANY
– divine manifestation or revelation EPIPHANY
– divine word, God's self-revealing thought and will LOGOS
– communion with the divine, or meditation designed to achieve it MYSTICISM

division See also **divide**, **classification**, **boundary**
– division, partition, or membrane separating tissues or cavities, as between the nostrils SEPTUM
– division, separation, disconnection DISJUNCTION, PARTITION
– division, splitting, or cutting SCISSION, RUPTURE
– division into opposing factions, as within a church SCHISM
– division of cells in genetics MEIOSIS, MITOSIS
– division of overheads among the various departments of a business ALLOCATION
– division or classification into two parts, such as conflicting opinions DICHOTOMY
– division or group, as within a political party, typically dissenting from the larger group FACTION
– quantity or total produced by dividing one number by another QUOTIENT

division- SCHIZ-, SCHIZO-

divorce – final court ruling granting a divorce DECREE ABSOLUTE
– financial support given by one former spouse to the other after a

divorce ALIMONY, MAINTENANCE
– financial support given to a lover after separation, as is maintenance after divorce PALIMONY
– person against whom a divorce action is brought RESPONDENT
– person bringing a divorce action APPLICANT
– person cited in a divorce case as having committed adultery with the partner being sued CO-RESPONDENT
– preliminary and provisional court ruling, especially that in a divorce case DECREE NISI
– right of access to the children by a divorced or separated parent in U.S. law VISITATION

dizzy, confused, groggy, or dazed WOOZY
– dizziness, giddiness VERTIGO

DNA molecule's twin spiral structure DOUBLE HELIX

do without, avoid FORGO, FORBEAR, REFRAIN, ABSTAIN

dock – dock-worker in the U.S. LONGSHOREMAN
– dock-worker who boards ships to load and unload them STEVEDORE
– docking platform, pier, or the like at which ships can moor for loading or unloading WHARF
– docks for small boats MARINA

doctor especially one who is not a surgeon PHYSICIAN
– doctor, psychologist, or psychiatrist practising or studying the treatment of patients CLINICIAN
– doctor in the U.S. doing a term of specialised training RESIDENT
– doctor of the highest rank in a hospital CONSULTANT
– doctor of the second highest rank in hospital REGISTRAR
– doctor or other professional person pursuing his occupation PRACTITIONER
– doctor qualified as a specialist DIPLOMATE
– doctor specialising in heart diseases CARDIOLOGIST
– doctor temporarily replacing another LOCUM, LOCUM TENENS
– doctor's instrument for listening to sounds produced in the body STETHOSCOPE
– doctor's medical equipment and supplies ARMAMENTARIUM
– doctor's negligence or misconduct MALPRACTICE
– doctor's oath to observe professional ethics HIPPOCRATIC OATH
– doctor's small, portable radio receiver sounding a coded alert signal BLEEPER
– caused by the doctor or his treatment, as an illness might be IATROGENIC
– family doctor GENERAL PRACTITIONER, G.P.
– junior doctor undergoing hospital training HOUSEMAN, INTERN
– specialist in children's ailments PAEDIATRICIAN
– symbol, associated with doctors, of a winged staff with two snakes twined around it CADUCEUS

doctrine See also **philosophy**
– doctrine or principle, as of a religious or professional group TENET

document authorising a diplomat to act on behalf of his government LETTERS OF CREDENCE
– document certifying a contract or transfer of property DEED
– document in writing, warranted under oath as true AFFIDAVIT
– document of entitlement, such as a share certificate SCRIP
– document or argument presented for consideration SUBMISSION
– document or book in the author's handwriting HOLOGRAPH
– document in the form of a roll of parchment or paper SCROLL
– document or image sent or produced telegraphically as a facsimile FAX
– document or pamphlet containing a forceful declaration or rallying call TRACT
– document showing right of ownership of a property TITLE DEED
– document such as an official voucher or certificate DOCKET
– document in former times under a sovereign's seal, authorising imprisonment without trial LETTRE DE CACHET
– document's introductory statement or explanation PREAMBLE
– added clause, amendment, or qualification to a legal document, verdict, or the like RIDER
– addition to a document APPENDIX, ADDENDUM, ANNEXE, SUPPLEMENT, POSTSCRIPT, CODICIL
– alter a document, accounts, evidence, or the like in order to deceive FALSIFY
– amendment to, draft for, or supplement to a treaty or other such document PROTOCOL
– clean copy of a revised and corrected document FAIR COPY
– deliberate alteration or mutilation of a document so as to make it invalid SPOLIATION
– exact copy or reproduction, as of a document FACSIMILE
– file of documents on a particular person or subject DOSSIER
– formal document or statement, such as a royal warrant PRESENTS
– giving advice, as a discussion document might CONSULTATIVE
– legally enforced revealing of relevant documents by a party in a civil action DISCOVERY
– public document or deed CHARTER
– reservation or proviso, as in a legal document SALVO
– sign or endorse a document UNDERWRITE
– study of ancient or historical documents DIPLOMATICS
– transfer ownership of or sell documents, shares, or the like NEGOTIATE

-doer -TOR, -TRESS, -TRIX

dog, especially a mongrel, with a vicious nature CUR
– dog placed in a treadmill in former times to turn a roasting spit TURNSPIT
– dog's snout, or the small basket of wire or leather fitted over the snout of a dog or other animal to restrain it MUZZLE
– adjective for a dog CANINE
– brown or grey with darker streaks or spots, as a dog, cat, or cow might be BRINDLED
– disease affecting young dogs, a contagious viral fever DISTEMPER
– fear of dogs CYNOPHOBIA
– flap of a dog's ear LEATHER
– fleshy drooping upper lip of the bloodhound or similar dog FLEWS
– free a dog, hawk, or the like from restraint SLIP
– functionless rudimentary inner claw on a dog's foot DEWCLAW
– give birth to a young dog, wolf, or other canine WHELP
– group of dogs PACK, KENNEL
– half-wild or stray dog in Asia PYE DOG, PARIAH DOG
– highest point on the back of a horse or dog, between the shoulders WITHERS
– hindquarters or rump of a horse or dog CROUP
– knee joint in the hind leg of a horse or dog STIFLE
– long hair on the legs or tail of some horses or dogs FEATHERS
– loose fold of skin under the throat of a dog, ox, or the like DEWLAP
– section of the body of a horse or dog between the forequarters and hindquarters COUPLING
– three-headed dog in Greek myth that guards the entrance to the underworld CERBERUS

dog-sledge journey MUSH

dogmatic, pedantic, excessively precise or subtle SCHOLASTIC
– dogmatic, self-assured, arrogant,

overbearing PEREMPTORY
– dogmatic and unduly fussy about details PEDANTIC
– dogmatic and unsupported assertion DICTUM, IPSE DIXIT
– dogmatically and blindly committed to a theory, impractical DOCTRINAIRE
– speak in a pompous, dogmatic, or over-confident way PONTIFICATE, DOGMATISE

doh-re-mi – use of the *doh-re-mi* syllables to correspond to notes of the scale, as for voice training TONIC SOL FA, SOLFEGGIO, SOLMISATION

doll – magic intended to achieve an effect by some imitative ceremony or symbolic object, as in sticking pins into a doll SYMPATHETIC MAGIC
– model house like a doll's house, but large enough for children to play in WENDY HOUSE
– Russian set of wooden dolls, in which each except the largest is encased within another BABUSHKA, MATRIOSHKA

dolphin – dolphin-like sea mammal with a blunt snout GRAMPUS
– dolphin or related mammal with a beak-like snout BOTTLENOSE

dome formed of interlocking polygons GEODESIC DOME
– dome-shaped Buddhist shrine STUPA, TOPE
– dome-shaped roof or ceiling, or dome on a roof or larger dome CUPOLA
– dome-shaped room or building for projecting images of the stars and planets PLANETARIUM
– circular, often domed, building or room ROTUNDA
– circular or crescent-shaped opening in a domed roof LUNETTE
– circular wall, especially one supporting a dome TAMBOUR
– ornamental sunken panel in a ceiling, dome, or the like COFFER, LACUNA, CAISSON

domestic or unskilled work MENIAL WORK

dominate See also **bully**, **dictator**
– dominate or discourage by threats or bullying BROWBEAT
– dominate or force into submission by means of threats or by violence INTIMIDATE
– dominate to the exclusion of all others, control fully MONOPOLISE
– dominated by a nagging or wilful wife HENPECKED
– domination or mastery, as in the political or economic sphere PRE-EMINENCE, SUPREMACY, ASCENDANCY
– domination of one group or country over another HEGEMONY

dominating in an arrogantly assured way, lordly, overbearing IMPERIOUS, MAGISTERIAL, OVERWEENING, DOMINEERING

dominion or power over a dependent state, typically over its foreign affairs SUZERAINTY

donation that provides a source of income ENDOWMENT

done – something that is already done and unalterable, an unchangeable fact FAIT ACCOMPLI

donkey, especially one used as a pack animal BURRO
– informal term for a donkey MOKE

doom – prophet of doom whose warnings are ignored CASSANDRA

door, entrance, or gateway, typically large or impressive PORTAL
– door hinge consisting of two metal flaps linked with a stout pin BUTT HINGE
– door or window with slats LOUVRE
– door-to-door seller of goods HAWKER, PEDLAR
– doorway or entrance, or the plank or stone lying under a door THRESHOLD
– arched recess above a doorway, as at the entrance of a medieval cathedral TYMPANUM
– axle, revolving bolt, or the like, as in a lock or between two door handles SPINDLE
– back door or gate POSTERN
– central vertical strip separating the panels in a door MUNTIN
– crescent-shaped window or recess above a door LUNETTE
– decorative moulded frame around a door or window ARCHITRAVE
– decorative triangular recess or projection of stone or masonry above a door or window PEDIMENT, FRONTISPIECE, GABLE
– glass door, typically occurring in pairs, opening onto a garden or balcony FRENCH WINDOW
– horizontal beam or crossbar over a door LINTEL, TEMPLATE, TRANSOM
– one-way viewing hole or tiny window in a door, for identifying visitors PEEPHOLE, JUDAS
– opening in a wall, wider inside than out, for a door or window EMBRASURE
– shield-like plate covering a keyhole, surrounding a door handle, protecting a light switch, or the like ESCUTCHEON
– sloping or bevelled recess wall, as at a door or window SPLAY
– small door or gate, often forming part of a larger one WICKET
– upright post or strut of a door frame, window sash, or the like JAMB, STILE

doorkeeper in a court of law, parliament, or the like USHER

doorman at a hotel, theatre, or the like, dressed in a uniform COMMISSIONAIRE
– doorman or caretaker of a building, especially a block of flats JANITOR, CONCIÈRGE, SUPERINTENDENT, PORTER

dormant or inactive, as a disease might be QUIESCENT

dot-dot-dot or series of asterisks indicating the omission of words or letters in a text ELLIPSIS

dots, usually regularly arranged, on a patterned fabric POLKA DOTS
– dots placed above a vowel, as in *naïve* DIAERESIS, UMLAUT
– dotted, spotted, pockmarked, or the like PUNCTATE
– dotted or flecked, as with paint or natural colours STIPPLED

double, twofold DIPLOID, DUAL
– double, twofold, having two separate parts BINARY
– double or ghostly counterpart, sometimes haunting a person in legend DOPPELGÄNGER
– double vowel, speech sound in which a vowel changes in quality during the syllable, such as the *i*-sound in *sigh* DIPHTHONG
– doubled, forming a pair GEMINATE

double- AMPH-, AMPHI-, DI-, DIPL-, DIPLO-, ZYG-, ZYGO-

doubt or cast doubt on DISCREDIT
– doubt or worry leading to the withholding of full support or approval RESERVATION, QUALIFICATION
– doubting, disbelieving SCEPTICAL, INCREDULOUS
– doubts and uncertainties that discourage a projected action SCRUPLES
– express doubts or reluctance, protest or object DEMUR
– pang of doubt, a feeling of conscience or mistrust, or the like MISGIVING, QUALM
– persistent or nagging, as minor doubts might be NIGGLING
– state of doubt, perplexity or the like DILEMMA, QUANDARY

doubtful, hesitant, or uncertain WAVERING, IRRESOLUTE, INDECISIVE, VACILLATING
– doubtful, insecure, not certain to succeed PRECARIOUS
– doubtful, suspiciously vague, and

possibly insincere EQUIVOCAL, AMBIGUOUS
- doubtful, uncertain, or uncommitted AGNOSTIC
- of doubtful accuracy or authenticity, as a far-fetched or fanciful anecdote is APOCRYPHAL
- of doubtful quality, legality, or the like, or causing suspicions DUBIOUS, SUSPECT

dough – substance added to dough to aid fermentation, as in bread-making LEAVEN

doughnut – shape of a doughnut TORUS

dove – adjective for a dove COLUMBINE
- dovecote COLUMBARIUM

down feather PLUMULE

downfall or undoing, typically just retribution, as following pride or overconfidence NEMESIS

downward slope or tendency DECLINATION, DECLENSION
- downward stroke of the pen in handwriting MINIM

downwards- CATA-

dowry, woman's marriage portion DOT
- money or goods given, as a kind of reverse dowry in some societies, by the bridegroom's family to the bride's BRIDE PRICE, LOBOLA

drab, dusky, dull in colour SUBFUSC

dragon with wings and a serpent's tail, as in heraldry WYVERN
- adjective for a dragon DRACONIC

drain a body cavity of fluid by means of a suction device, as in surgery ASPIRATE
- drain or sewer, as under a road CULVERT, CONDUIT
- drainage pit, as in a mine SUMP
- kitchen utensil for rinsing or draining, consisting of a perforated bowl COLANDER
- pit or hole for sewage or waste from household drains CESSPOOL
- rubber suction cup with a long handle, used for clearing blocked drains and pipes PLUNGER, PLUMBER'S HELPER

drama See chart, pages 152-153, and also **theatre**

dramatic, relating to drama or acting THESPIAN
- dramatic or brilliant display, as in a piano recital PYROTECHNICS
- dramatic or over-emotional behaviour HISTRIONICS
- dramatic situation at the end of an episode of a serialised film, play, or the like CLIFFHANGER

drapery – ornamental loop of drapery, flowers, or the like FESTOON, SWAG
- short decorative skirt of drapery hung along a pelmet, shelf, edge of the bed, or the like VALENCE

draw a line, especially a circle or arc DESCRIBE
- draw attention away from, steal the show from UPSTAGE
- draw or derive pleasure, interest, or the like from a seemingly unpromising source EXTRACT
- draw or describe, either in broad or in precise detail DELINEATE
- draw or paint a picture of LIMN
- draw out, bring to light ELICIT
- drawing lots SORTITION
- drawn contest, deadlocked situation STALEMATE
- game, match, or the like played between two drawn or tied contestants to find a winner PLAY-OFF
- U.S. term for a draw, tie, or deadlock, especially in a sports event STANDOFF

draw back, as from pain or in fear, shy away WINCE, FLINCH, SHRINK, QUAIL, BLENCH, RECOIL, COWER
- draw back, as the tide might RECEDE
- draw back something, as a snail might draw in its horns RETRACT

drawer – set of drawers supporting a desk top PEDESTAL
- supporting strut along which a drawer slides RUNNER

drawing made to scale PROTRACTION
- drawing or diagram of a machine or structure showing its parts separately EXPLODED VIEW
- drawing or model, as of an engine or building, with part of the wall or casing omitted or cut away to reveal the interior CUTAWAY
- drawing or preliminary sketch, often full-size, for a tapestry, painting, mosaic, or the like CARTOON
- drawing to scale of an outside face of a building or structure ELEVATION
- drawings or writings, often witty or obscene, scribbled typically on walls in public places GRAFFITI
- art of drawing, as in architecture or engineering, according to mathematical rules of projection, technical drawing GRAPHICS
- person skilled at drawing, especially of architectural or technical plans DRAUGHTSMAN
- shading of a drawing with intersecting sets of parallel lines CROSS-HATCHING
- shading of fine lines in a drawing HATCHING
- sheet of wood, metal, or plastic, usually triangular, used to construct certain angles and lines quickly in technical drawing SET SQUARE
- sheet of wood, metal, or plastic with the outlines of various curves on it, used for drawing curves in technical drawing FRENCH CURVE
- shortening of lines in drawing or painting a scene, for apparent depth or distance FORESHORTENING, PERSPECTIVE
- transfer a drawing by loosely shading or colouring its reverse side, and then tracing it onto a surface or paper underneath CALK

-drawing -GRAM, -GRAPH

drawing pin – U.S. term for a drawing pin THUMBTACK

drawing room, as in a large French house, for receiving guests SALON

dream – dream-like, dazed, or hypnotic state TRANCE
- dream-like, distorted or irrational in a bizarre way SURREAL
- dream-like false perception or illusion HALLUCINATION
- dream-like succession of confusing images, as experienced in a fever PHANTASMAGORIA
- dream world, impractical realm of fantasy and imagination CLOUD-CUCKOO-LAND
- dreamy, lost in thought, moony and absent-minded ABSTRACTED, PREOCCUPIED
- adjective for dreams ONEIRIC
- movement of the eyeballs behind closed lids during the dreaming phase of sleep REM, RAPID EYE MOVEMENT
- relating or referring to dreams or hallucinations that are proved true by subsequent events or revelations VERIDICAL
- relating to dreams VISIONARY

dream- ONEIR-, ONEIRO-

dregs or other matter that settles at the bottom of a liquid SEDIMENT
- dregs or sediment of wine, cider, or the like LEES
- dregs or sediment, such as coffee grounds GROUTS
- clear wine, beer, or cider of its dregs, usually by siphoning RACK

dress See also **clothes**
- dress in or put on one's hat or clothes DON
- dress made up in cheap cloth as a basis for alterations or copies TOILE
- dress or tidy oneself very neatly PRIMP, PREEN, PRINK
- adoption of female dress and behaviour by a man EONISM, TRANSVESTISM
- dressed or equipped in a specified way ACCOUTRED
- gather fabric into decorative rows, as on a dress, often using elastic thread SHIRR

– insert or fill-in at the front of a low-cut dress GUIMPE
– low revealing neckline, or a dress or blouse with such a neckline DÉCOLLETAGE
– part of a dress or gown trailing behind the wearer TRAIN
– part of a dress or other garment that has been gathered into a puff POUFFE
– state of being undressed or partially dressed DISHABILLE, DÉSHABILLÉ
– waist or bodice of a dress CORSAGE

dress shirt's false front DICKY, PLASTRON

dressing, as of moist bread or meal heated and spread on a cloth, then applied to ease pain or inflammation POULTICE, CATAPLASM

dressing gown, light and loose-fitting, for a woman NEGLIGÉE, PEIGNOIR

dressing room, bedroom, or private sitting room of a woman BOUDOIR, BOWER

dressmaking or designing of high quality for women of fashion COUTURE, HAUTE COUTURE

dribble saliva from the mouth SLOBBER, DROOL, SLAVER

dried, cured, and salted strips of meat, especially beef JERKY, CHARQUI, BILTONG, BRESAOLA
– dried, demoisturised, as some preserved food is DEHYDRATED, DESICCATED
– dried up, shrivelled and wrinkled, as an old person's face might be WIZENED
– restore something to its natural state, such as dried food or concentrated lemon juice, as by adding water RECONSTITUTE
– traditional North American Indian food of cakes of pounded dried meat PEMMICAN

drift or float gently, as the smell of flowers does in the wind WAFT

drill – drill-like tool, as used in mining TREPAN
– drill worked by hand BRACE AND BIT
– drill's handle or brace, into which the bit is fixed BITSTOCK
– drill's socket in which the bit is held POD
– drilling or boring tool AUGER, AWL, WIMBLE
– equipment for a specified purpose, as for drilling or for extracting oil from a well RIG
– filled with or run by compressed air, as some drills are PNEUMATIC
– vice or clamp used to hold a tool or workpiece, as in a drill CHUCK

drink See chart, page 154, and also **alcohol**, **wine**, **tea**
– drink, apart from water BEVERAGE
– drink, as of beer, taken after

DRAMA TERMS

Absurd, theatre of the absurd	modern drama emphasising the cruelty and futility of modern life
alienation effect	deliberate effect, as in the plays of Brecht, of reducing the audience's involvement with the action of the play, as when an actor addresses them directly
anagnorisis	moment of recognition of the truth by the hero in classical tragedy which leads to the dénouement
black comedy	comedy with an underlying pessimism, typically dealing with grim or grotesque subjects
business	various incidental actions by an actor, as during a pause
catharsis	drama which figuratively cleanses the emotions of the audience
comedy of manners	play that satirises the faults of society
commedia dell'arte	comedy of a type developed in 16th-century Italy, placing stock characters in an improvised plot
corpse	to laugh on stage inappropriately, as an actor might when something goes wrong
coup de théâtre	sudden turn of events in a play; brilliant or astonishing piece of stagecraft
curtain call	reappearance on stage of an actor, cast, choir, or the like, to acknowledge applause
dénouement, catastrophe	solution, climax or unravelling of a plot
deus ex machina	god brought in to resolve a tricky situation in the plot in classical drama
dramatic irony	drama in which the meaning of the words are understood by the audience but not the characters
dramatis personae	list of a play's characters
dry	to forget one's lines while on stage, as a nervous actor might
duologue	play or scene in which only two actors have speaking parts
ensemble	entire cast of a play; specifically, the supporting actors
epilogue	concluding poem or speech following the end of the action of a play
epitasis	part of a play, especially a Greek tragedy, in which the plot moves towards its climax
figurant	minor character or walk-on part, typically without any speeches
Grand Guignol	short horrifying macabre play, or the style based on it
interlude, entr'acte, divertissement	short entertainment between the acts of a play
Kabuki	elaborate Japanese drama with music and dancing, in which all parts are played by men

spirits CHASER
– drink, food, or drug, such as caffeine, that temporarily increases activity or efficiency STIMULANT
– drink, or the act of drinking POTATION
– drink heavily, go on a drinking spree CAROUSE
– drink of the gods in Greek and Roman mythology NECTAR
– drink or swallow eagerly, gulp SWIG, SWILL, QUAFF
– drink someone's health or engage in riotous festive drinking WASSAIL
– drink someone's health, toast PLEDGE
– drink something, especially alcohol IMBIBE
– drinks machine or other vending machine DISPENSER
– add alcohol secretly to a drink SPIKE
– refraining from alcoholic drink TEETOTALISM, ABSTINENCE, TEMPERANCE
– sliver of citrus peel to decorate or flavour a drink TWIST
– small drink of alcoholic spirits SNIFTER, SNORT
– small mat or disc placed under a drink to protect the table top COASTER
– small thin stick for stirring or removing bubbles from a drink SWIZZLE STICK

drinkable, non-poisonous POTABLE

drinker, especially an excessive drinker, as of wine BIBBER, TIPPLER, WINE-BIBBER, TOPER
– heavy drinker, drunkard LUSH, SOAK, SOT, SOUSE, TOSSPOT

drinking fountain, or formerly, a water cask on a ship SCUTTLEBUTT
– drinking or act of swallowing, or the amount taken in DRAUGHT
– drinking party in ancient Greece, typically with music and conversation SYMPOSIUM
– drinking spree RAZZLE
– drinking vessel, especially for wine, with a stem GOBLET
– drinking vessel filled to the brim, as for a toast BUMPER
– drinking vessel holding two quarts POTTLE
– drinking vessel such as a flat leather flask formerly carried attached to one's belt COSTREL
– flask as used by soldiers for carrying drinking water CANTEEN
– glass drinking vessel, typically with a rounded bottom inside TUMBLER
– horn-shaped drinking vessel in ancient Greece RHYTON
– large cup-like drinking vessel with a wide mouth BEAKER
– large drinking bowl, typically of wood, in former times MAZER
– large drinking glass, usually with a short stem RUMMER

kitchen-sink drama	modern drama representing sordid domestic life
legitimate	referring to serious plays, as opposed to comedies, satirical revues, musicals, and the like
masque	spectacular entertainment of dance, music and drama, based on a mythical or allegorical theme, popular in English courts in the 16th and 17th centuries
melodrama	play characterised by sensational and highly emotional episodes and exaggerated vice and virtue, popular in the 19th century
method	type of acting, developed by Stanislavski, emphasising identification with the character
mime	play or scene acted out with gestures but no speech
miracle play, mystery play	medieval dramatisation of events from the Bible or the lives of the saints
mise en scène	stage setting, or the props and scenery used for it
monologue	long speech by a single actor
morality play	allegorical play of the 15th and 16th centuries, such as *Everyman*, in which the characters represent abstract virtues and vices
mummer	actor in a traditional folk drama or mime dealing with death and resurrection
Noh, No	classical Japanese drama, developed in the 14th century, representing legends and Buddhist themes with dance and song
peripeteia	sudden change in the course of events in a play; a twist in the plot
prologue	speech introducing the action of a play, or the character or actor delivering it
protagonist	principal character in a traditional play
protasis	introductory section of a play, especially a classical tragedy, introducing and developing the plot
repertory	presentation by a theatre company of a succession of plays, typically alternating, in a single season
soliloquy	monologue typically representing the character's unspoken thoughts
stichomythia	dialogue in Greek drama in which alternate lines of verse are spoken by different characters
tableau	stage scene in which the actors freeze briefly
tetralogy	group of four related dramas, especially a series of three tragedies and one satire in ancient Greece
unities	three principles of composition — unity of action, time, and place — requiring that a classical drama limit itself to a single plot-line, day and location

DRINKS

BEERS, CIDERS AND OTHER FERMENTED DRINKS

barley wine
bock
dortmunder
kumiss
kvass
mead
metheglin
münchener
perry
pilsener
pombe
porter
scrumpy

BEVERAGES AND SOFT DRINKS

camomile tea
float
grenadine
infusion
julep
maté/ Paraguay tea/ yerba maté
root beer
saloop
sarsaparilla
seltzer
tiger's milk
tisane

COCKTAILS AND LONG DRINKS

Bacardi
black velvet
Bloody Mary
Bronx
buck's fizz
caudle
cobbler
daiquiri
eggnog
frappé
gimlet
gin sling
glühwein
Harvey Wallbanger
highball
kir
Manhattan
margarita
martini
mint julep
negus
old-fashioned
orgeat
piña colada
planter's punch
posset
rickey
sangria
screwdriver
shandy
shrub
sidecar
snowball
stinger
syllabub/ sillabub
Tom Collins
wassail
whiskey sour
White Satin

SPIRITS AND LIQUEURS

absinthe
advocaat
amaretto
anisette
applejack
aquavit
aqua vitae
armagnac
arrack/arak
bourbon
calvados
crème de cacao
crème de cassis
crème de menthe
crème de noyau
curaçao
fine champagne
fior d'Alp
galliano
grappa
Hollands/geneva
kirsch/ kirschwasser
kümmel
mao-tai
maraschino
marc
mastika
mescal
mirabelle
negra
ouzo
pastis
poteau
pousse-café
raki
ratafia
redeye
sake
sambucca
schnapps
slivovitz
steinhager
strega
tequila
Tia Maria
van der Hum

– large drinking glass for sherry or port, or large glass for beer SCHOONER
– leather drinking vessel treated with tar or wax BLACKJACK
– large drinking vessel with a handle, used especially for beer TANKARD, POT
– small can or cup for drinking CANNIKIN
– treatment for drinking problems, a drug that causes nausea when one has an alcoholic drink ANTABUSE, DISULFIRAM

drip in or into a vein, as an injection or feeding drip might be INTRAVENOUS
– salt solution used in a medical drip SALINE

drive away or dispel a crowd, meeting, or the like DISPERSE, DISSIPATE, ROUT
– drive away or expel a person from his homeland BANISH, EXILE, EXPATRIATE
– drive away or expel someone foreign from a country DEPORT
– drive back or repel an attack REBUFF, REPULSE
– drive dangerously closely behind another vehicle TAILGATE
– drive or instinctive interest MOTIVATION
– drive or prod cattle with a sharpened or electrified rod GOAD
– drive or travel successfully, as round a tight bend NEGOTIATE
– drive out, throw out, force out, expel EJECT, OUST
– drive out an evil spirit, or free a possessed person from evil spirits, as by religious rites EXORCISE
– drive out or expel a tenant or squatter from a property EVICT
– driving or pushing forward PROPULSION
– irresistible and often irrational drive to perform a certain action COMPULSION

-driving away -FUGE

driving licence – record of a motoring offence on a driving licence ENDORSEMENT

drone of bagpipes BURDEN

droop from heat or exhaustion WILT
– drooping, as some flowers and buds are CERNUOUS
– drooping limply, flabby, lacking firmness FLACCID

drop See also **fall**
– drop-like or having drops GUTTATE
– drop of liquid, or very small amount DRIBLET

droplet of liquid GLOBULE

droppings, animal dung, especially that of animals being trailed or hunted SCATS

dropsy OEDEMA

drug See chart, and also **medicines, medical**
– drug, food, or drink, such as coffee, that temporarily increases activity or efficiency STIMULANT
– drug, often addictive and illegal, that typically dulls the senses or induces a deep sleep NARCOTIC
– drug, potion, or technique for forgetting pains and sorrows NEPENTHE
– drug, such as LSD, producing hallucinations or sensory distortion HALLUCINOGENIC DRUG, PSYCHEDELIC DRUG
– drug addiction, or a drugged state NARCOTISM
– drug-dealer PUSHER, PEDDLER
– drug-induced illusion HALLUCINATION
– drug-induced stupor or unconsciousness NARCOSIS
– drug or alcohol addiction DEPENDENCE
– drug or hormone, based on a ring of carbon atoms, sometimes used by bodybuilders and athletes STEROID
– drug slipped into a drink to make the drinker unconscious MICKEY FINN, KNOCKOUT DROPS
– drug that neutralises or counteracts the effects of another drug ANTAGONIST
– drugging, narcotic STUPEFACIENT
– drugs collectively, as used in the preparation of medicine PHARMACOPOEIA
– effect, especially an adverse one produced by a drug REACTION
– effective, powerful, or still active, as drugs or medicines might be POTENT
– inject drugs directly into a vein MAINLINE
– painful effects of giving up drugs WITHDRAWAL SYMPTOMS
– painful method of curing drug addiction by sudden and complete disuse COLD TURKEY
– person delivering messages, parcels, smuggled drugs, or the like on behalf of another COURIER
– plant with a forked root, formerly used as a narcotic drug MANDRAKE
– pleasant relaxed feeling, as from a drug BUZZ, HIGH

DRUGS OF ABUSE

HALLUCINOGENS

LSD/acid
magic mushroom/sacred mushroom
mescal/peyote
mescaline
STP

STIMULANTS

amphetamine/Benzedrine/benny/blue/purple heart/speed
amyl nitrite/popper
anabolic steroid
coca/cocaine/crack/snow/speedball
cubeb
doll/pop pill
upper

SEDATIVES OR NARCOTICS

barbiturate/doll/goofball
betel
bhang/cannabis/dagga/ganja/grass/hashish/Indian hemp/marijuana/pot/weed
downer
heroin
laudanum
morphine
narceine
opiate
opium
truth drug/Pentathol

drug- PHARMACO-, NARCO-
Druid circle of stone or wooden pillars HENGE
drum See also **percussion**
– drum, cymbal, xylophone, or related instrument that is struck to produce the sound PERCUSSION INSTRUMENT
– drum major's or majorette's stick that is spun and thrown into the air BATON
– drumhead, skin of a drum TYMPAN, VELLUM
– drummer in an orchestra, especially one who plays the kettledrums TYMPANIST
– any of the strings stretched over the lower skin of a small drum to produce a rattling sound SNARE
– big bass drum TAMBOUR
– deaden the sound of a drum MUFFLE
– narrow cylindrical drum beaten with the hands in Latin American music BONGO DRUM, CONGA DRUM, TIMBAL
– pair of small Indian drums that are beaten with the hands TABLA
– small drum played to accompany the fife TABOR
drumbeat DUB
– drumbeat in a regular, even rhythm TATTOO
– low and continuous drumbeat, softer than a drumroll RUFFLE
drunk INTOXICATED, INEBRIATED, STOTIOUS, PIXILATED, SHICKERED, NON COMPOS MENTIS
– drunk and confused or stupefied BEFUDDLED, BESOTTED
– drunk and tearfully sentimental MAUDLIN
– drunken, or addicted to alcohol BIBULOUS
– drunken, or having a hangover after drunkenness CRAPULENT
– drunken party, noisy festivity BACCHANAL, REVEL, CAROUSAL, WASSAIL, BACCHANALIA, RAZZLE
– tending to cause drunkenness HEADY, INTOXICATING
– slightly drunk, tiddly TIPSY, MELLOW, SQUIFFY
drunkard, heavy drinker LUSH, SOAK, SOT, SOUSE, TOPER, TOSSPOT, BIBBER
– habitual drunkard, alcoholic DIPSOMANIAC
dry See also **dried**, **dull**
– dry, as a wine might be SEC
– dry, as champagne might be BRUT
– dry, deprived of water or moisture DEHYDRATED
– dry, withered, shrivelled, as a dead leaf would be SERE
– dry or parched, as land might be ARID
– dry and over-precise, pedantic or dogmatic SCHOLASTIC
– dry by heating PARCH
– dry out, remove moisture from, as for preserving DESICCATE
– dry scrubland vegetation MAQUIS, CHAPARRAL
– dry up, as parched flowers might SHRIVEL, WITHER, SEAR
– drying device, squeezing water from wet laundry by pressing it between rollers WRINGER, MANGLE
– drying substance, as added to paints SICCATIVE
– relating to or of an extremely dry habitat XERIC
dry- XERO-
dry land, solid ground TERRA FIRMA
duck that feeds near the surface of the water or on land rather than deep underwater DABBLING DUCK
– bright coloured patch on a duck's wing SPECULUM
– flock of geese or wild ducks in flight SKEIN
– group or flock of ducks FLUSH, PLUMP
– webbed, as a duck's feet are PALMATE
– wild duck MALLARD, WIGEON
ducking – ducking-stool to which wrongdoers or suspects were formerly tied, as for ducking or public mockery CUCKING STOOL
duct, bodily vessel or channel VAS
duel between knights, with lances on horseback JOUST, TILTING MATCH
– duel over a point of honour AFFAIRE D'HONNEUR
duffel coat – peg or crosspiece, such as a duffel coat's button, used for fastening TOGGLE
duke – adjective for a duke DUCAL
– dukedom, territory ruled by a duke or duchess DUCHY
dull, boring periods of time or parts of a book, play, or film LONGUEURS
– dull, conventional, everyday, lacking in any striking features NONDESCRIPT, FACELESS, STEREOTYPED, IDENTIKIT
– dull, laborious, stodgy, plodding, as a speech might be PONDEROUS, PEDESTRIAN
– dull, lifeless, colourless, sterile, as a textbook might be ARID, PALLID, DESICCATED, LACKLUSTRE
– dull, narrow-minded, limited in outlook, unimaginative PAROCHIAL
– dull, ordinary, unoriginal, as a person's imagination or conversation might be MUNDANE, HUMDRUM, BANAL, PROSAIC, BOVINE
– dull, trite, or obvious remark PLATITUDE, COMMONPLACE, BROMIDE, TRUISM
– dull, unadventurous, lacking in zest or flavour INSIPID, BLAND, VAPID, ANODYNE
– dull and inactive, sluggish or stale STAGNANT
– dull and indistinct rather than acute, as a pain might be OBTUSE
– dull finish or surface, as of a non-glossy paint MATT
– dull in colour, drab SUBFUSC
– dull or mindless, as the expression on someone's face might be VACUOUS
– dull or purposeless task or way of life SQUIRREL CAGE
– dull or tiring routine work DRUDGERY
– dull to the point of almost sending one to sleep, extremely boring STULTIFYING, STUPEFYING
– dully austere, lacking in liveliness or decoration, as a room or report might be CLINICAL, ASEPTIC
– dully mechanical, purely functional or materialistic BANAUSIC
– dully routine, drearily repetitious TEDIOUS, MONOTONOUS
– lead a dull, passive life VEGETATE, STAGNATE
dumb or speechless because shy, em-

barrassed, or astonished TONGUE-TIED
– struck dumb, silent MUMCHANCE

dummy or crude image of a person, intended as an object of scorn or hatred, and sometimes burnt in public EFFIGY
– jointed dummy of a human figure, used as an artists' model LAY FIGURE, MANNEQUIN
– U.S. term for a baby's dummy COMFORTER, PACIFIER
– voice-production, especially by an entertainer, giving the impression that the sound originates in a dummy VENTRILOQUISM

dung See also **excrement**
– dung, excrement ORDURE
– dung-eating, as some beetles and flies are COPROPHAGOUS, SCATOPHAGOUS
– dung of sea birds, collected from dried deposits along the coast for use as a fertiliser GUANO
– dung or droppings, especially of animals being trailed or hunted SCATS
– containing or relating to dung STERCORACEOUS
– dunghill or rubbish heap MIDDEN

dung- COPRO-

dung beetle SCARAB

dungeon whose door is in the ceiling OUBLIETTE

duplicating machine typically based on a wax stencil stretched over a rotating inked cylinder MIMEOGRAPH, RONEO, CYCLOSTYLE

during- DIA-, INTRA-

dust speck MOTE
– crumble, decay, turn to dust MOULDER AWAY

dutiful, loyal, or enthusiastic to an excessive, foolish, uncritical, or dangerous degree GUNG HO
– dutiful, working attentively or applying oneself conscientiously to a task DILIGENT, ASSIDUOUS, SEDULOUS
– dutiful or conscientious in a very rigorous, careful, or painstaking way SCRUPULOUS, PUNCTILIOUS, METICULOUS
– dutiful or devoted, especially in religious observance, pious, DEVOUT
– dutiful or respectful, especially to one's elders and betters DEFERENTIAL
– dutifulness, devotion, or loyalty, especially towards one's parents and family PIETY

duty, honour, or respect, granted to someone or to a belief or cause HOMAGE
– duty, promise, contract, or the like demanding a certain course of action OBLIGATION
– duty or loyalty owed by a vassal to his feudal lord FEALTY
– duty or responsibility DEVOIR
– duty or responsibility, burdensome task, as to prove one's allegations ONUS
– duty or task that one has been specifically set to perform ASSIGNMENT
– duty payment, tax, or levy IMPOST
– duty schedule or system of taxes, especially on imports TARIFF
– duty to which a soldier may be specially assigned DETAIL
– assign work, duties, or powers to one's agent or subordinate DELEGATE, DEPUTE
– beyond the call of duty SUPEREROGATORY
– discharge, as from duty or debt QUIETUS
– failure or neglect in the performing of one's duty NEGLIGENCE, DERELICTION, DELINQUENCY
– financial or moral duty or obligation COMMITMENT
– free from responsibility, a duty, or the like EXONERATE, EXEMPT
– in proportion to the value of the goods, as a tax or duty might be AD VALOREM
– list of duties or register of the people to perform them ROSTER, ROTA
– perform official duties on a formal occasion, as a host or priest would OFFICIATE
– period or fixed amount of work or duty STINT
– referring to the duty or respect owed by sons and daughters to their parents FILIAL
– period or shift of duty on guard or on shipboard WATCH, TRICK
– person such as an actor or actress able and ready to take on the duties of another in an emergency UNDERSTUDY
– relating or referring to the religious duties of spiritual care and guidance PASTORAL
– relating to rights, duties, and similar ethical concepts DEONTIC
– release from guard duty, through the arrival of a replacement guard RELIEF
– required as a duty INCUMBENT, OBLIGATORY
– shirk work or duty, skive SCRIMSHANK

duvet CONTINENTAL QUILT

dwarf See **gnome**
– dwarf, in Greek mythology PYGMY
– dwarf tree or shrub produced by rigorous pruning, or the traditional Japanese art of producing such plants BONSAI
– bone condition that causes dwarfism ACHONDROPLASIA

dye See chart
– dye, radioactive substance, or the like, whose course can be monitored through a system, as used in medical diagnosis TRACER
– dye of a kind made fast by being oxidised once within the fibre to an insoluble form VAT DYE

DYES AND PIGMENTS

RED

alkanet
brazilin
carmine
carotene
chrome red
cinnabar
cochineal
Congo red
crocein
fuchsine/magenta
henna
jeweller's rouge
kermes
lake
madder
orcein
red arsenic
red lead/minium
red ochre
rhodamine
ruddle/reddle/raddle
vermilion/mercuric sulphide

BLUE/VIOLET

anil
cobalt blue
cyanine
gentian violet
indigo
mauveine/Perkin's mauve
orchil/cudbear
Prussian blue/iron blue
Tyrian purple
ultramarine
woad

YELLOW AND ORANGE

annatto
bistre
cadmium yellow
chrome yellow
flavin
fustic
Indian yellow
phosphine/chrysaniline yellow
safflower/dyer's thistle
saffron
weld/dyer's rocket
yellow ochre

GREEN

chrome green
sumach
terre-verte
viridian

BROWN

bistre
brown ochre
butternut
catechu/cachou/cutch
sienna
tannin/tannic acid
umber

BLACK

black iron oxide
boneblack
carbon black
lampblack
nigrosine

WHITE

Chinese white/zinc white
titanium white
white lead

– dye of red ochre, used for marking sheep RUDDLE
– dye parts of cloth while tying other parts tightly, producing a mottled effect TIE-DYE
– dye produced synthetically, especially from coal-tar compounds ANILINE DYE
– dye used by ancient Britons to colour their skin blue WOAD
– dyeing chemical, acting as a fixative MORDANT
– dyeing technique involving the use of wax to keep areas of the cloth undyed BATIK
– referring to a dye or colour that needs no fixative SUBSTANTIVE

dying See also **dead**, **death**
– dying, on the brink of death MORIBUND, IN EXTREMIS
– hospital specialising in care for the dying HOSPICE

dyke – stretch of low-lying land, especially in Holland, reclaimed from the sea and protected by dykes, POLDER

dynasty See chart

DYNASTIES

Abbassids	Arabic 8th-13th century
Achaemenid	Persian, 6th-4th century BC
Almoravides	Berber, 11th-12th century
Angevin	English, 12th-13th century
Árpád	Hungarian, 9th-14th century
Aviz	Portuguese, 14th-16th century
Bourbon	Franco-Spanish, from 16th century
Bragança	Portuguese, 17th-20th century
Capetian	French, 10th-14th century
Carolingian/ Carlovingian	Frankish, 8th-10th century
Chakkri	Siamese (Thai), from 18th century
Ch'in/Qin	Chinese, 3rd century BC
Ch'ing/Qing	Chinese 17th-20th century
Chou	Chinese, 11th-3rd century BC
Fatimids	North African, 10th-12th century
Franconian/ Salian	German, 11th-12th century
Habsburg/ Hapsburg	Holy Roman Empire and the Austro-Hungarian Empire, 13th-20th century
Han	Chinese, 3rd century BC to 3rd century AD
Hanoverian	Germano-British, 17th-20th century
Hohenstaufen	German, 12th-13th century
Hohenzollern	Brandenburg-Prussian, 15th-20th century
Hyksos	Egyptian, 17th-16th century BC
Lancaster	English, 15th century
Mameluke/ Mamluk	Egyptian, 13th-16th century
Merovingian	Frankish, 6th-8th century
Ming	Chinese, 14th-17th century
Mogul/ Moghul/ Mughal	Indian, 16th-19th century
Nasrid	Moorish (Granada), 13th-15th century
O'Neill/Uí Néill	Irish, 8th-10th century
Orange	Netherlands, from 19th century
Ottoman	Turkish, 14th-20th century
Pahlavi	Iranian, 20th century
Plantagenet	English, 12th-15th century
Ptolemaic	Egyptian, 4th-1st century BC
Qājar	Persian, 18th-20th century
Romanov	Russian, 17th-20th century
Safavid	Persian, 16th-18th century
Savoy	Italian, 19th-20th century
Seleucid	Hellenic, 4th-1st century BC
Seljuk	Turkish, 11th-13th century
Shang	Chinese *c* 16th century BC
Stewart/Stuart	Scottish, 14th-18th century
Sung	Chinese, 10th-13th century
Tang	Chinese, 7th-10th century
Tudor	English, 15th-17th century
Umayyad/ Ommiad	Arabian, 8th-11th century
Valois	French, 14th-16th century
Varangian	Russo-Scandinavian, 9th century
Windsor	British, 20th century
Wittelsbach	German, 14th-20th century
York	English, 15th century
Yuan	Mongol, 13th century
Zand	Persian, 18th century

E

each other – felt, owed, given, or done by two people or groups about or to each other MUTUAL, RECIPROCAL
eager See **enthusiastic**, **emotional**
– eager, hopeful, looking forward to EXPECTANT
– eager and willing SOLICITOUS
– eager or impatient with curiosity AGOG
– eager to please, cooperative COMPLIANT, COMPLAISANT, OBLIGING
– eager to please or obey in a fawning or excessive way SERVILE
– be eager for or excited at something SALIVATE
eagle – eagle-like, relating to an eagle AQUILINE
– eagle's nest built on a cliff or other high place EYRIE, AERIE
ear See illustration
– ear, nose, and throat specialist OTORHINOLARYNGOLOGIST
– ear-shaped AURICULATE
– ear-shaped part or extension on a body organ AURICLE
– buzzing or ringing in the ear as a medical condition TINNITUS
– clip part of an animal's ear, especially for identification CROP
– having drooping ears, as beagles might LOP-EARED
– relating to or hearing with both ears BINAURAL
– relating to or hearing with only one ear MONAURAL
– relating to the ear AURAL, AURICULAR, OTIC
– simple small metal ring worn in a pierced ear to prevent the hole from sealing up when earrings are not being worn SLEEPER
– small chamber in the inner ear important for bodily balance and coordination UTRICLE, SACCULE
– small structure in the inner ear that converts sound into nerve impulses to be transmitted to the brain ORGAN OF CORTI
-ear- -OT-, OTO-
eardrum, resonating membrane in the ear TYMPANIC MEMBRANE, TYMPANUM
earlier, previous, being before in time, rank, order, or the like PRECEDING, ANTECEDENT, ANTERIOR
– come earlier in time, precede ANTEDATE
– scene or passage in a novel, film, or the like that interrupts the main story line to revert to earlier events FLASHBACK
earlier- PRE-
earliest, first, or original PRIMEVAL, PRIMITIVE, PRIMAL, ARCHETYPAL
– earliest example or model, on which copies or later developments are based PROTOTYPE, ARCHETYPE
– relating to the earliest time or condition PRISTINE, PRIMORDIAL
earliest- PROTO-
early, immature works of a composer, writer, or the like JUVENILIA
– early, in the morning MATUTINAL
– early in development, in the earliest stage of growth EMBRYONIC, SEMINAL, GERMINAL, NASCENT
– early in development, just beginning INCHOATE, INCIPIENT
– act, use, pay, or produce too early, before the appropriate time ANTICIPATE
– developing or maturing unusually early, especially in intellectual ability PRECOCIOUS
– occurring too early PREMATURE, PREVIOUS, UNTIMELY
early- EO-
early show, as of a play MATINÉE
earn or obtain money in dubious ways HUSTLE
earring with a large stone surrounded by smaller ones GIRANDOLE
Earth See illustration, page 160, and also **atmosphere**
– heating of the Earth's atmosphere because of increased absorption of solar radiation GREENHOUSE EFFECT
– imaginary half-circle joining the poles on the Earth's surface MERIDIAN
– point in its orbit when the Moon or a satellite is farthest from the Earth APOGEE
– point in its orbit when the Moon or a satellite is nearest to the Earth PERIGEE
– regarding the Earth as the centre of the universe, as in early astronomy GEOCENTRIC
– relating to the Earth, earthly TERRESTRIAL, PLANETARY, TELLURIC
– relating to the Earth, earthly existence, or everyday life, as opposed to higher or more spiritual concerns MUNDANE, SUBLUNARY, TEMPORAL
– sail or fly completely around something, such as the Earth CIRCUMNAVIGATE
– spherical but flattened at the poles, as the Earth is OBLATE
– spin or turn on an axis, as the Earth does ROTATE
– study of the Earth's crust on the theory that it consists of giant sliding plates PLATE TECTONICS
– zone on the Earth's surface lying between the tropics TORRID ZONE
– zones on the Earth's surface lying between the polar regions and the tropics TEMPERATE ZONES
– zones on the Earth's surface lying within the polar regions FRIGID ZONES
earth- AGR-, AGRI-, AGRO-
Earth- GEO-
earthquake or series of tremors that follows the main shock of a large earthquake AFTERSHOCK
– area on the Earth's surface directly above the point of origin of an earthquake EPICENTRE
– energy of an earthquake at its source, as measured on the Richter scale MAGNITUDE
– instrument for detecting and measuring tremors of the Earth's crust as caused by earthquakes or explosions SEISMOGRAPH
– preliminary tremor of an earthquake FORESHOCK
– relating to an earthquake, large explosion, or other vibration of the Earth's crust SEISMIC
– scale registering the magnitude of an earthquake RICHTER SCALE
– study of earthquakes and other vibrations of the Earth's crust or mantle SEISMOLOGY
earthquake- SEISM-, SEISMO-
earthworm, leech, or other similarly segmented worm ANNELID
– coil of earth excreted by an earthworm CAST, CASTING
earwax CERUMEN
ease, help to bring about FACILITATE

– ease, make bearable PALLIATE
– ease of action or performance FACILITY
– easing of tension, as between nations DÉTENTE

Easter – adjective for Easter or the Passover PASCHAL

eastern Mediterranean countries LEVANT
– eastern temple or shrine, typically a tapering tower PAGODA
– Far Eastern regions ORIENT

Eastern Orthodox abbot, head of an Eastern Orthodox monastery HEGUMEN, ARCHIMANDRITE
– Eastern Orthodox bishop, or governor of an Eastern Orthodox diocese EPARCH
– Eastern Orthodox monk CALOYER
– Eastern Orthodox Churches' liturgical language OLD CHURCH SLAVONIC

easy See also **simple**
– easy, relating to basic knowledge, elementary RUDIMENTARY
– easy but very profitable work GRAVY TRAIN
– easy to obtain or to understand ACCESSIBLE
– easy to understand, clearly expressed PERSPICUOUS, LUCID, TRANSPARENT
– easy-to-beat opponent or easily accomplished task PUSHOVER
– computer term for easy to handle USER FRIENDLY
– something easy to achieve, or a certainty CINCH

eat See also **feeding**
– eat gluttonously or greedily, gorge GORMANDISE
– eat or swallow greedily and hastily DEVOUR
– eat or swallow INGEST
– eatable, fit to eat EDIBLE, COMESTIBLE, ESCULENT
– eating with a huge appetite RAVENOUS, VORACIOUS
– eating all kinds of food, both meat and plant foods OMNIVOROUS
– eating and drinking excessively, overindulgent, gluttonous INTEMPERATE, CRAPULENT
– eating meat occasionally or eating only meat, as lions and some other animals do CARNIVOROUS
– eating plants only, as many animals do HERBIVOROUS
– art of good eating or cooking GASTRONOMY
– full or over-full after eating SATIATED, SATED, GLUTTED
– person who enjoys food and eats abundantly TRENCHERMAN
– person who enjoys fine cooking or eating GOURMET
– person who enjoys good or excessive eating GOURMAND

-eat- -PHAG-, PHAGO-, -PHAGOUS, -VOROUS

ebb, flowing back REFLUX

eccentric gesture, quaint idea, or the like WHIMSY

echo – echo-like sound, heard by a

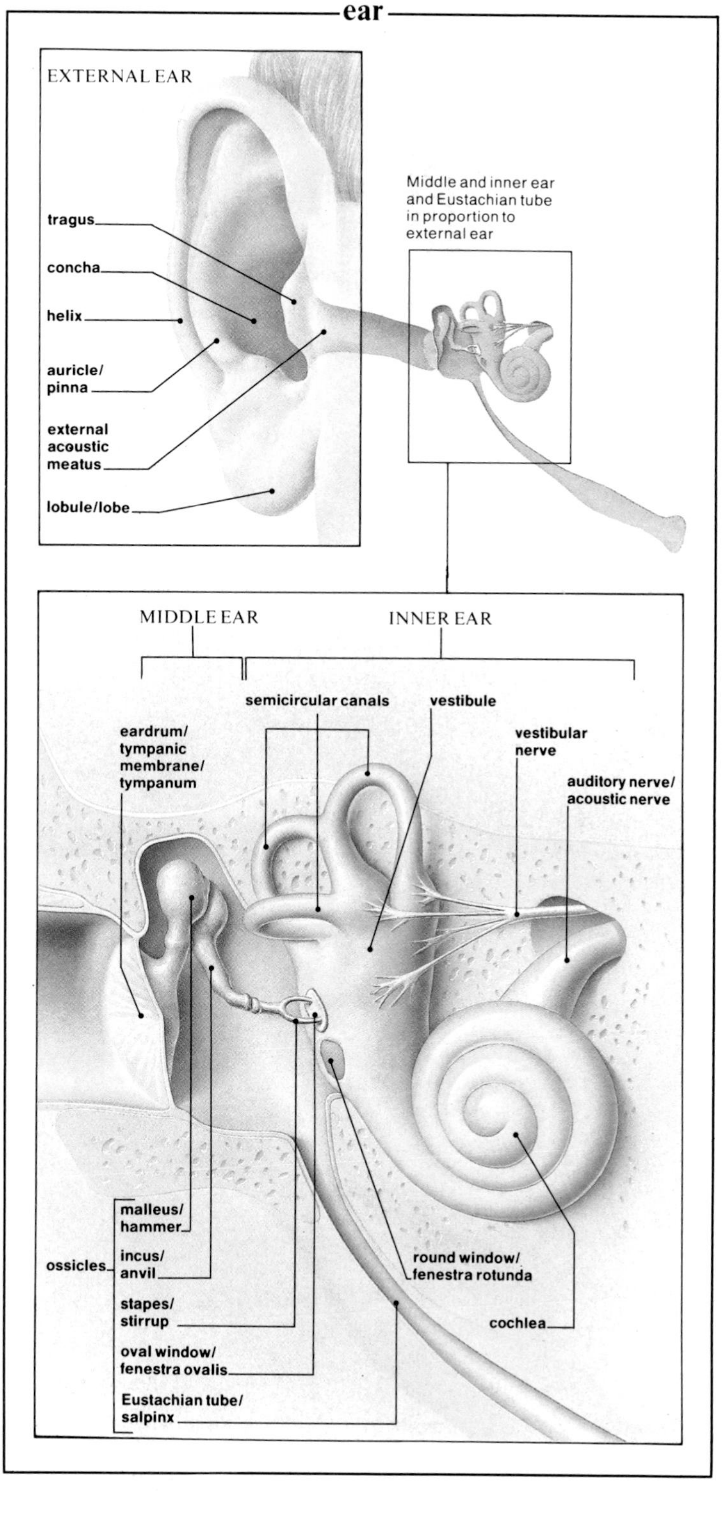

ear

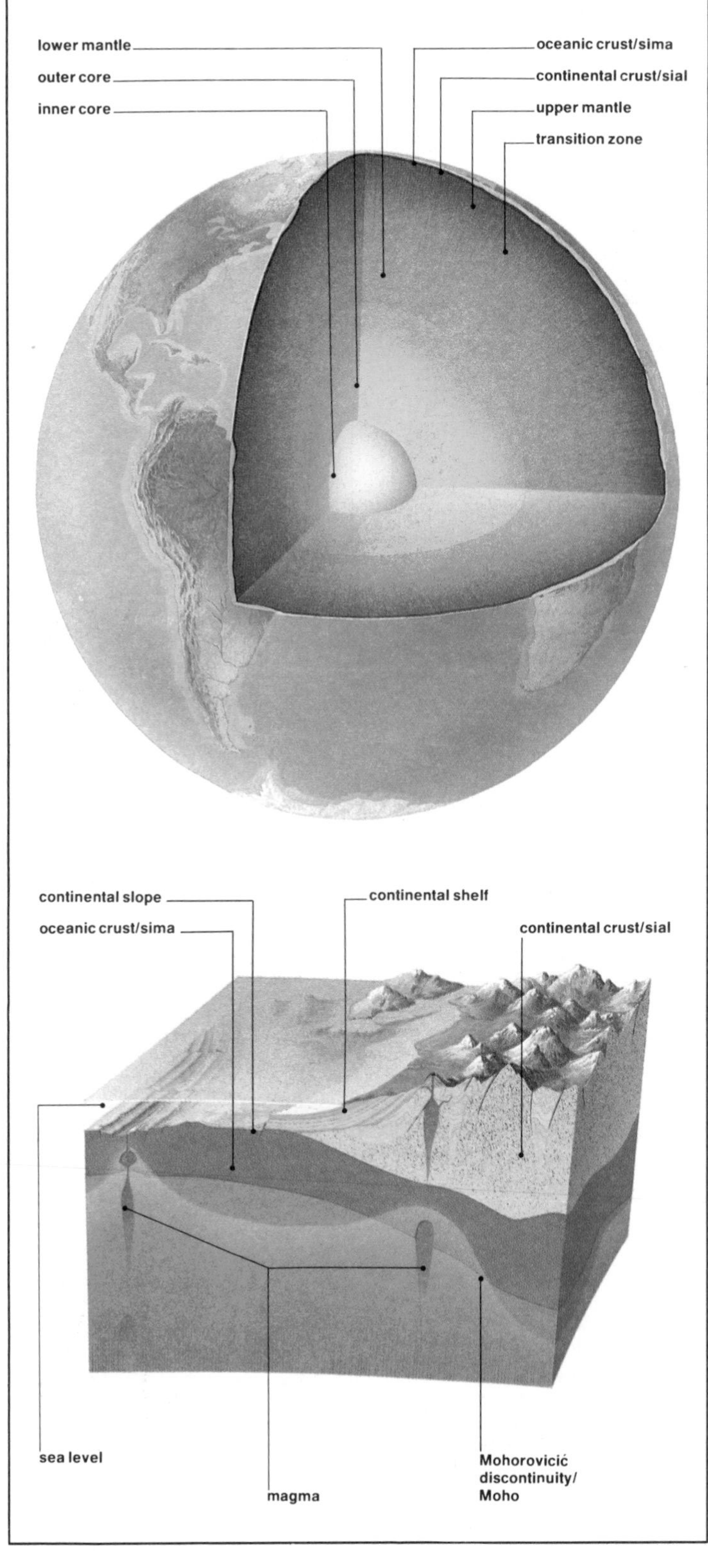

doctor tapping a patient's chest RESONANCE
– echo or ring with noise RESOUND, REVERBERATE
– echo sounder, used for detecting enemy submarines ASDIC

éclair pastry, made with eggs CHOUX PASTRY

eclipse, or disappearance of a heavenly body during an eclipse OCCULTATION
– eclipse in which a ring of the Sun remains visible around the silhouetted Moon ANNULAR ECLIPSE
– arrangement of three celestial bodies in a straight line, as of the Earth, Sun, and Moon during an eclipse SYZYGY
– close approach, but without eclipse, of two celestial bodies APPULSE
– huge column of burning gas rising from the Sun, visible during a total eclipse PROMINENCE
– partial shadow, as during an eclipse, between areas of full shadow and full illumination PENUMBRA
– region of full shadow cast on the Earth's surface during a total eclipse UMBRA

economic independence from the need for imports or aid AUTARKY
– economic system in Europe after the feudal system, based on increased foreign trade MERCANTILE SYSTEM, MERCANTILISM

economical See **thrifty**
– economical use of resources HUSBANDRY, CONSERVATION

economics See chart

economics – relating to the economics of large and complex systems, such as a whole country or region MACROECONOMICS

economise, cut back on expenses RETRENCH

ecstatic, highly enthusiastic or elated RHAPSODIC
– ecstatic, irrational DIONYSIAC
– ecstatic and usually unintelligible or nonsensical speech, as in some religious services, "gift of tongues" GLOSSOLALIA
– become enraptured or ecstatic SWOON

edge See also **border**, **boundary**, **trimming**
– edge, border, or fringe of a fabric, carpet, or the like finished so as to prevent unravelling SELVAGE
– edge, end, farthest point or part EXTREMITY
– edge, fringe, or boundary, as of a social group PERIPHERY
– edge or outer limits, as of one's authority or hearing PERIMETER

– edge or protecting rim, as on a wheel or beam, for strengthening, attaching, or the like FLANGE
– edging of tiny loops, as on ribbon or lace PICOTS
– edging or trimming, as for upholstery, consisting of a narrow tube of folded cloth, that often envelops a cord PIPING
– cut cloth to form a deeply indented edging VANDYKE
– cut off the edge or corner of BEVEL, CHAMFER
– drapery forming a decorative border, as along the edge of a bed or shelf VALANCE
– ornamental border or edging, as on a violin or building PURFLE
– ornamental strip of wood, metal, or the like, typically for edging BEADING

edible, suitable for eating ESCULENT, COMESTIBLE

edit, correct, or revise, especially by censoring or editing out some of the material BLUE-PENCIL
– edit or revise a text for publication REDACT

edition of a writer's works, together with accumulated notes and comments by many scholars VARIORUM
– edition or critical revision of a text, incorporating the most plausible variant readings RECENSION

educate, train, foster NURTURE
– educated, cultured, or intellectual people as a group or social class INTELLIGENTSIA, LITERATI, CLERISY
– educated, learned, scholarly LITERATE

education and the world of scholar-

ECONOMICS AND FINANCE TERMS

arbitrage	buying of shares, currencies and commodities for quick resale at a higher price
arbitrageur	speculator who buys up shares in companies threatened by takeover bids, to resell at a profit if the bid succeeds
asset-stripping	commercial practice of taking over a company and selling off its assets for a quick profit
bear	speculator who anticipates falling prices, and sells securities hoping to re-buy them later at a lower price
black economy	unofficial and technically illegal production and sale of goods and services, evading the tax system
blue chip	share considered safe and profitable through having a long record of reliability
bull	speculator who anticipates rising prices, and buys securities hoping to sell them later at a profit
cartel	agreement between producers or manufacturers to control output, prices and the like, often resulting in an illegal monopoly
collateral	property pledged as security for a loan
conglomerate	business corporation made up of many wide-ranging companies
consolidation	combining or uniting of separate businesses into a larger whole
consols, consolidated stock	interest-bearing British government stock, without a fixed redemption date
consortium, syndicate	business association of various interests formed for some joint enterprise
dawn raid	surprise attempt by a person or group to buy a large shareholding in a company, often at an inflated price, typically prior to a takeover bid
debenture, loan stock	fixed-interest security, typically long-term and guaranteed, issued by a company or government organisation
deflation	reduction in the level of prices and general economic activity, especially through a government policy of restricting the money supply
discount rate	rate of interest deducted in advance, as on a treasury bill
Dow Jones Index	daily average of prices on the New York Stock Exchange, based on the average price of a selected group of ordinary shares
equities, common stock	ordinary shares, as distinct from fixed-interest securities such as preference shares
fiscal year	accounting period of 12 months, such as the government's tax year
floating	referring to a currency whose exchange rate is determined solely by the forces of supply and demand, without government intervention
flotation	launching or financing of a business venture by means of a share issue
FT Index	daily average of prices on the London Stock Exchange, based on the average price of either 30 or 100 selected ordinary shares
futures	commodities or securities bought or sold at an agreed price for future delivery
gilts/gilt-edged securities	low-risk fixed-interest securities issued by the government
gross domestic product/GDP	total value of the goods and services produced in a country in one year, excluding income from investments abroad
gross national product/GNP	total value of the goods and services produced in a country in one year, including the net income from investments abroad

continued

ECONOMICS AND FINANCE TERMS *continued*			
intangible	business asset, such as goodwill, that has a value but no physical existence	**scrip issue/ bonus issue**	issue of new shares free to current shareholders in a company, in proportion to their existing shareholdings
laissez-faire	policy or practice of non-intervention by a government in economic activity	**securities**	stock certificates, bonds, or similar saleable evidence of ownership or entitlement used to guarantee an obligation; investments generally in the form of stock, shares and bonds
letter of credit	written authorisation by a banker for a named person to draw a stated sum from the addressee		
minimum lending rate/ MLR	rate of interest at which a central bank, especially the Bank of England, lends money to the rest of the banking system	**the Snake**	system agreed by members of the EEC to keep fluctuations in exchange rates within certain limits
monetarism	doctrine that a country's economy is best managed by keeping close control over the amount of money in circulation	**stag**	speculator who buys newly issued shares in the hope of selling them at a profit as soon as dealing opens
par value, nominal value	face value of a security	**stagflation**	combination of static or falling production with inflation in an economy
portfolio	investor's entire set of securities	**supply-side**	referring or relating to an economic doctrine that encourages tax reductions as a means of boosting investment and productivity
preference share	fixed-interest security, with dividends payable before any are assigned to ordinary shares		
promissory note, note of hand	written IOU or promise to repay a loan at a given time or on demand	**tontine**	finance or insurance scheme in which a member's shares or benefits pass on to the other members of the group, when he dies or defaults
recession	reduction in economic activity, less severe than a depression, at a generally prosperous time	**treasury bill**	bill of exchange or guaranteed IOU issued by the Treasury in return for money lent to the government
reflation	increase in general economic activity, especially through a government policy of easing the money supply	**underwriter**	person or company that guarantees the success of a share issue by undertaking to buy any securities left over
restrictive practices	trading agreements considered unfair to competitors or generally against the public interest	**unit trust, mutual fund**	finance and investment company that buys a variety of shares and sells units from the combined portfolio to the public
revaluation	increase in the official value or exchange rate of a country's currency, based on a formal government decision	**valorise**	raise or maintain artificially the value or price of a commodity, especially by deliberate government action
rights issue	issue of new shares to current shareholders, normally at a discount price and in proportion to their existing shareholdings	**white knight**	person or group that acts to rescue a company threatened by closure or takeover

ship and universities ACADEMIA
– education at university or college level TERTIARY EDUCATION
– education technique based on questioning assumptions and drawing out supposedly inborn knowledge SOCRATIC METHOD
– education technique for young children, based on play, self-expression, and initiative rather than discipline and control MONTESSORI METHOD
– relating to a method in education in which the learner is allowed or encouraged to discover things for himself HEURISTIC
– report or summary of a person's education and career, as for job applications CURRICULUM VITAE, RÉSUMÉ

EEC – EEC's pricing unit, independent of individual national currencies ECU

eel of a large sea-dwelling species or family CONGER, CONGER EEL
– eel-like creature with a jawless sucking mouth LAMPREY
– eel-like fish of a brightly coloured, tropical, sea-dwelling species MORAY
– eel-shaped ANGUILLIFORM
– eel that is split and then grilled or fried SPITCHCOCK
– young or undeveloped eel ELVER, GLASS EEL, LEPTOCEPHALUS

effect See also **result**
– effect that is a by-product or side-effect of some previous effect KNOCK-ON EFFECT
– have a favourable or unfavourable effect REDOUND
– positive effect on a patient's condition of an inactive substance taken by him in the belief that it is a medicine PLACEBO EFFECT

effective, sound, or acceptable, as an argument, title, or passport might be VALID
– effective or penetrating, as an argument might be TRENCHANT, INCISIVE, COGENT
effeminate EPICENE
– effeminate or homosexual CAMP
efficiency – analysis of the efficiency of a workforce, machine system, or the like, as an aid to policy-making OPERATIONAL RESEARCH
– modernise an industry, process, or the like, and increase its efficiency RATIONALISE
– plan or use with maximum efficiency OPTIMISE
effort, hard work, and conscientious attention to duty or tasks DILIGENCE, ASSIDUITY, SEDULOUSNESS, APPLICATION
– effort, labour, strenuous physical or mental endeavours TRAVAIL, EXERTIONS
– effort that is quick and intense BLITZ
– planned or performed together, combined, as an effort might be CONCERTED, COORDINATED
– requiring a great deal of effort ARDUOUS, STRENUOUS
effortless, flowing, or graceful FLUENT
– effortless, fluent FACILE
egg See illustration
– egg cell, unfertilised reproductive cell in female animals OVUM
– egg eaten raw, usually with Worcestershire sauce or vinegar, as a hangover remedy PRAIRIE OYSTER
– egg laid by hens kept in farmyards or fields rather than batteries FREE-RANGE EGG
– egg-laying mammal such as the platypus MONOTREME
– egg-laying tube in most insects and some fish OVIPOSITOR
– egg-producing gland OVARY
– egg-shaped OVAL, OVATE
– egg with a tough shell, typical of birds, insects, and reptiles CLEIDOIC EGG
– eggs of a fish, frog, or the like SPAWN
– bake eggs that have been removed from their shells SHIRR
– chicken-rearing system involving confinement to cages for fast fattening or high production of eggs BATTERY
– cook food, especially eggs, in water at just below boiling point CODDLE
– dish of fried or poached eggs with spinach EGGS FLORENTINE
– fertilisation of an egg cell by a sperm, the beginning of pregnancy CONCEPTION, IMPREGNATION
– fertilised egg or ovum ZYGOTE
– fluffy baked egg dish, either savoury or sweet SOUFFLÉ
– full of eggs or roe GRAVID
– keep eggs warm prior to hatching INCUBATE, BROOD
– mature, unfertilised female egg cell or male sperm GAMETE
– organism in a very early stage of its development, such as a fertilised egg EMBRYO
– ornamental jewelled egg made by a famous Russian goldsmith FABERGÉ EGG
– produce an egg cell or ovum OVULATE
– producing only one egg or offspring at a time UNIPAROUS
– rotten, as an egg might be ADDLED
– small dish for baking and serving individual portions, especially of egg dishes COCOTTE
-egg- -OO-, -OV-, OVI-, OVO-
egg white ALBUMEN
egg yolk VITELLUS, PARABLAST
egocentric, self-regarding, or in love with oneself NARCISSISTIC
Egypt – ancient water-raising device, as used in Egypt, consisting of a pivoted pole with a bucket and a counterweight SHADOOF
– building with columns supporting the roof, as in ancient Egyptian architecture HYPOSTYLE
– Egyptian Christian Church COPTIC CHURCH
– beetle of a family including the dung beetles, treated as sacred in ancient Egypt SCARAB
– jar used in ancient Egypt for holding a mummy's entrails CANOPIC JAR
– Ottoman viceroy in Egypt in former times KHEDIVE
– ruling caste in Egypt between the 13th and 16th centuries MAMELUKE
– script or hieroglyphics of a complex rounded form used by priests in ancient Egypt HIERATIC
– script or hieroglyphics of a simplified form, used by literate laymen in ancient Egypt DEMOTIC
– stone tablet providing the key to ancient Egyptian hieroglyphics ROSETTA STONE
– tapering four-sided stone pillar with a pyramidal top, of a kind used as a monument in ancient Egypt OBELISK
– tomb in ancient Egypt, of oblong shape with sloping sides and a flat roof MASTABA
– writing system using pictures in ancient Egypt HIEROGLYPHICS

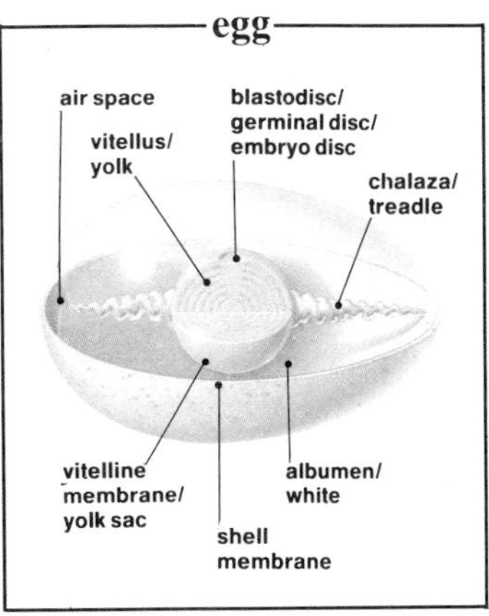

eight – eight-note pitch interval between the notes of music OCTAVE
– eight-sided figure OCTAGON
– eight singers or musicians, or a composition for such a group OCTET
eight- OCT-, OCTO-
eighty-year-old, or a person aged between 80 and 89 OCTOGENARIAN
elaborate See **high-falutin**, **showy**, **complicated**, **decorate**
elastic, extendable without breaking, stretchable EXTENSILE, DUCTILE
elbow one's way in a crowd JOSTLE
eldest or senior member of a group, society, diplomatic circle, or the like DOYEN, DOYENNE
– state of being the eldest child, or his right to inherit the title or entire estate PRIMOGENITURE
elect or appoint a new member to a group by a decision of the existing group COOPT
election See also **vote**
– election campaigning HUSTINGS
– election in the U.S. in which members of a political party or voters in a region choose their delegates or candidates PRIMARY
– election majority in which the winner fails to secure more than half of the total votes or seats RELATIVE MAJORITY, PLURALITY
– election majority in which the winner secures more than half of the total votes or seats ABSOLUTE MAJORITY
– election officer, who announces the number of votes and the result RETURNING OFFICER
– admit defeat in an election CONCEDE
– campaign for votes from people or a region in an election campaign CANVASS
– catchphrase, motto, jingle, or the like used repeatedly, as in advertising or elections SLOGAN

– list of people entitled to vote in an election ELECTORAL ROLL, ELECTORAL REGISTER
– person who checks or counts votes at an election SCRUTINEER, TELLER
– political party's declaration of its policies, as before an election MANIFESTO
– poll taken in a cross-section of society, especially to forecast election results GALLUP POLL
– referring or relating to an election system in which the candidate with most votes wins, whether with a simple or absolute majority FIRST-PAST-THE-POST
– representation of parties in an elective body according to the proportion of votes that they win in an election PROPORTIONAL REPRESENTATION
– study of, elections, and electoral systems PSEPHOLOGY
– support for a government's policies, as considered given by an election victory MANDATE
– withdraw official backing from someone, especially a sitting MP, as party candidate in an election DESELECT

electioneering by touring rural areas in the U.S. and making speeches there BARNSTORMING
– electioneering tour in which a politician briefly visits a series of small towns WHISTLE-STOP TOUR

electoral district, or the group of voters within it CONSTITUENCY
– electoral district in a town or city WARD
– electoral district in the U.S. PRECINCT
– electoral district under the controlling influence of one person or family, especially in England before the Reform Act of 1832 POCKET BOROUGH
– electoral district with very few voters, especially in England before 1832 ROTTEN BOROUGH
– manipulation of the boundaries of an electoral district for party advantage GERRYMANDERING

electricity See chart
– electric cables' supporting tower PYLON
– electric sparks or crackling, as produced by friction STATIC
– electrical element or coil in a hot-water tank IMMERSION HEATER
– electrical glow seen on a ship's mast, church spire, or the like during stormy weather ST. ELMO'S FIRE, CORPOSANT
– electrical or mechanical device or element forming part of a machine or circuit COMPONENT
– electrical plug connecting one or more other plugs to a socket ADAPTER
– electricity connection point, such

ELECTRICITY AND ELECTRONICS TERMS

alternating current/AC	current that changes direction continually
alternator	generator producing alternating current
ammeter	instrument that measures electric current
ampere/amp	unit of electric current
anode	positive electrode, as in a battery
armature	rotor, wound with wire coils, of an electric motor or generator; vibrating part of a loudspeaker, electric bell, or other electromagnetic device
band-pass filter	filter that blocks all signals except those within a selected frequency range
capacitance	ability to store electric charge; measure of this ability, the ratio of induced charge to potential difference
capacitor, condenser	circuit element used to store charge temporarily
cathode	negative electrode, as in a battery
cathode-ray tube	vacuum tube for focusing an electron beam onto a fluorescent screen, as in television sets and oscilloscopes
commutator	device, as on an electric motor or generator, for reversing the direction of a current, or converting alternating current into direct current
conductance, conductivity	property of transferring, or measure of the ability to transfer, electric current in a circuit
coulomb	unit of electrical charge
dielectric	nonconductor of electric current, insulator
diode	component with two terminals, typically allowing current to flow in only one direction
Dolby	system in a tape recorder, cassette player, or the like for reducing hiss and other unwanted noise
dynamo	generator, especially for direct current
electrode	conductor for an electric current, as in a battery or valve
electrolyte	solution that conducts electricity, as in a battery
farad	unit of electrical capacitance
Faraday cage	screen used to insulate apparatus from outside electrical interference
galvanic, voltaic	relating or referring to electric current produced by chemical action, as in a battery
galvanometer	instrument for detecting or measuring small electric currents
henry	unit of electrical inductance
impedance, reactance, resistance	property of opposing, or measure of the opposition to, the flow of current, especially alternating current, in a circuit
inductance	property of a circuit allowing electrical induction

as a wall socket OUTLET
– electricity produced from the energy of running water HYDRO-ELECTRICITY
– electricity supply failure OUTAGE
– frame on the roof of an electric train engine, tram, or trolleybus, collecting current from an overhead wire PANTOGRAPH
– network of power stations and cables for distributing electricity over a wide area GRID
– pipe or channel for electric wires or cables DUCT, CONDUIT
– prevent or reduce the transfer of electricity, sound, or heat INSULATE
– rubbery latex substance used in electrical insulation and dentistry GUTTA-PERCHA
– sudden increase in electric current SURGE
– therapy for treating psychiatric patients, in which an electric shock is administered to the brain ELECTROCONVULSIVE THERAPY, ECT

electron – atom or group of atoms having an electric charge through gaining or losing one or more electrons ION

electronics See chart
– electronic keyboard instrument capable of imitating various instruments and producing a wide range of musical sounds MOOG SYNTHESISER
– electronic keyboard instrument producing eerie musical sounds by means of varying frequencies in an oscillator ONDES MARTENOT
– electronic keyboard instrument using tape loops to imitate various orchestral instruments MELLOTRON

elegant, refined, exquisite, especially in an affected or pretentious way RECHERCHÉ
– elegant, sophisticated, or well-groomed, polished SOIGNÉ
– elegant and concise, as a prose style might be LAPIDARY
– elegant in an affected, over-refined way MINCING
– elegant or refined feature NICETY
– elegant or refined in manner, courtly, polished URBANE, GENTEEL
– luxurious and grand, extravagantly elegant LAVISH, SUMPTUOUS
– majestic, grand, elegantly formal STATELY, STATUESQUE

element, part of a whole COMPONENT, CONSTITUENT
– element, such as zinc, present in tiny quantities in an organism and essential for its full functioning or development TRACE ELEMENT
– any of the different physical forms, such as crystals, that an element may take ALLOTROPE
– gaseous chemical element, such as helium or neon, formerly con-

induction	generation of electrical charge or other form of energy in an object, typically by the use of a magnetic field set up by another object nearby
integrated circuit	electronic circuit with components connected in a single small package, as on a silicon chip
inverter	device for converting direct current into alternating current
joule	unit of work or energy
modulation	superimposing or combining of two waves, so that their frequency, amplitude, or the like vary in unison, as for transmitting a sound signal by means of a radio wave, such as frequency modulation, FM
ohm	unit of resistance
oscilloscope	instrument presenting varying signals in visible form as a graph or trace on the screen of a cathode-ray tube
piezoelectricity	electricity generated by crystals subjected to pressure
polarity	property of having either a positive or negative electric charge
potential difference	energy needed to move a unit quantity of electricity from one point to another
rectifier	device, such as a diode, for converting alternating current into direct current
resistor	component with a known resistance to electric current
rheostat	continuously variable resistor, typically with a sliding contact, used to regulate current, as in a lighting system
semiconductor	solid crystalline substance, such as silicon, with medium conductivity
siemens	unit of electrical conductance
solenoid	coil of wire producing a magnetic field when electrically charged, as used for activating switches
solid-state	based on semiconductors or microchips, as many modern appliances are
superconductor	substance that, typically at low temperatures, has almost no electrical resistance
transformer	device for changing the voltage of an alternating current without alteration of the frequency
tweeter	loudspeaker in a hi-fi system for reproducing chiefly high-pitched sounds
Van de Graaff generator	generator of high-voltage static electricity that accumulates on a large hollow metal ball
volt	unit of electric potential
watt	unit of power
Wheatstone bridge	instrument used to measure resistance
woofer	loudspeaker for reproducing chiefly low-pitched sounds

sidered incapable of chemical reaction INERT GAS, NOBLE GAS, RARE GAS
– table of the chemical elements arranged according to their atomic number and other properties PERIODIC TABLE

elementary, relating to basic knowledge, simple, basic RUDIMENTARY

elephant, hippopotamus, or similar thick-skinned mammal PACHYDERM
– elephant driver and keeper in India or the East Indies MAHOUT
– elephant or wild boar with impressive tusks TUSKER
– elephant's trunk or similar long flexible snout PROBOSCIS
– extinct prehistoric mammal resembling an elephant or mammoth MASTODON
– frenzied sexual excitement in male elephants and other large mammals MUSTH
– seat with a canopy on an elephant's back HOWDAH

eleven- HENDECA-

elf or fairy FAY
– mischievous elf, in Irish folklore, typically a cobbler with buried treasure LEPRECHAUN

eliminate, destroy, wipe out, erase EXPUNGE
– eliminate or exclude after careful sorting, sift out WINNOW OUT

elk WAPITI

ellipse – instrument used for drawing ellipses TRAMMEL

elusive or slippery LUBRICOUS
– elusive person or thing WILL-O'-THE-WISP, IGNIS FATUUS

embankment with two faces forming an outward-projecting angle in front of a fortification RAVELIN

embarrass cruelly, shame HUMILIATE, MORTIFY
– embarrass in a humbling or belittling way, put down or degrade DEMEAN, DEFLATE
– embarrass or annoy CHAGRIN, DISCOMFIT
– embarrass someone with a surprise move that puts him in an awkward position WRONG-FOOT
– embarrassed or ashamed ABASHED, DISCOUNTENANCED, OUT OF COUNTENANCE
– embarrassing or awkward situation or occurrence CONTRETEMPS

embassy See also **diplomat**
– diplomatic mission ranking below an embassy in status LEGATION
– political section of an embassy CHANCELLORY, CHANCERY

embezzle, misuse or misappropriate funds DEFALCATE, PECULATE

emblem, symbol, or trademark of a company LOGO
– emblems, badges, or other official distinguishing symbols INSIGNIA

embodied, having bodily or human form INCARNATE
– embodiment or incarnation of an idea or model AVATAR

embrace CLINCH

embroidery See illustration, and also **sewing**
– embroidery, needlework, or other decoration consisting of different materials pasted or sewn

embroidery stitches

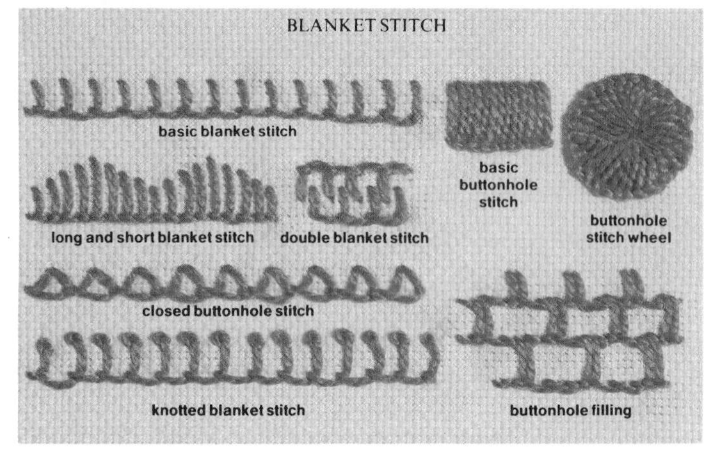

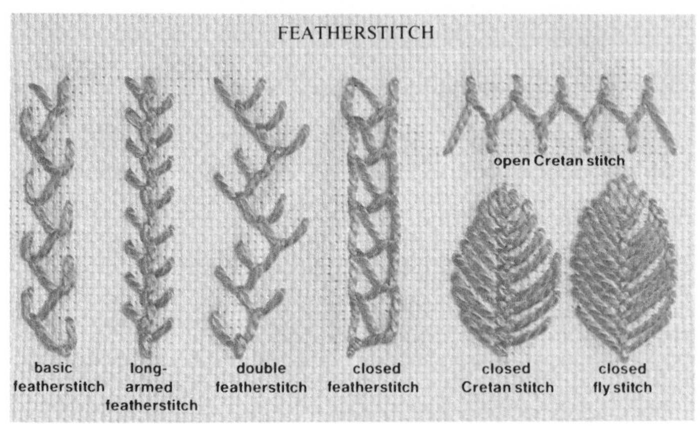

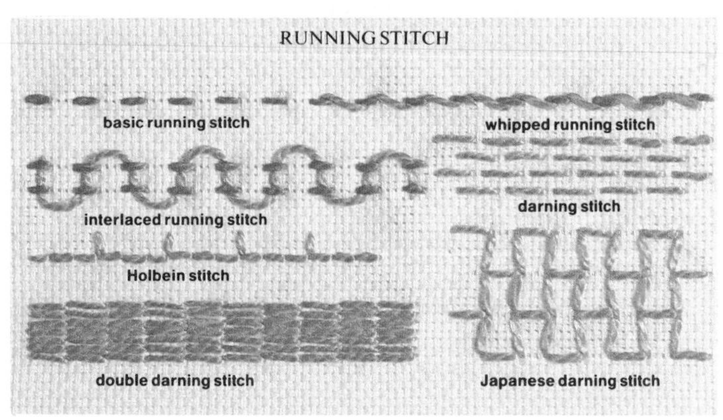

together APPLIQUÉ
– embroidery border adorning clerical vestments ORPHREY
– embroidery frame in the form of two concentric wooden hoops between which the fabric is locked TAMBOUR
– embroidery in which cloth is gathered and stitched into decorative rows SMOCKING
– embroidery in which heavy thread is sewn to a backing with tiny stitches COUCHING
– embroidery of an open pattern done on white cotton or fine linen BRODERIE ANGLAISE
– embroidery or lace edging PURL
– decorative piece of embroidery in which many different stitches are used, often with pictures and mottoes SAMPLER

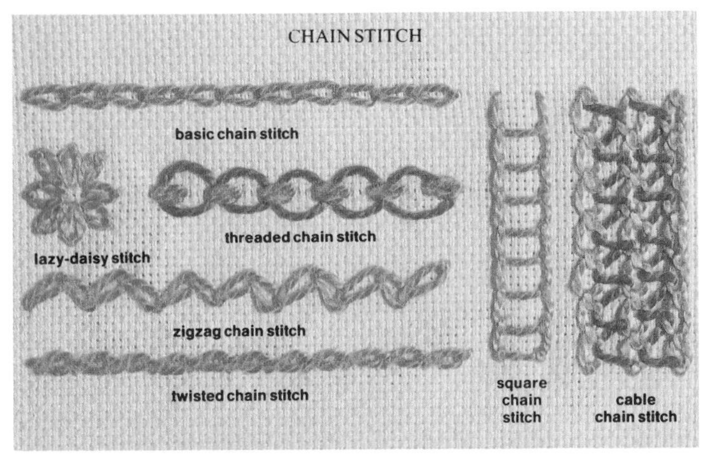

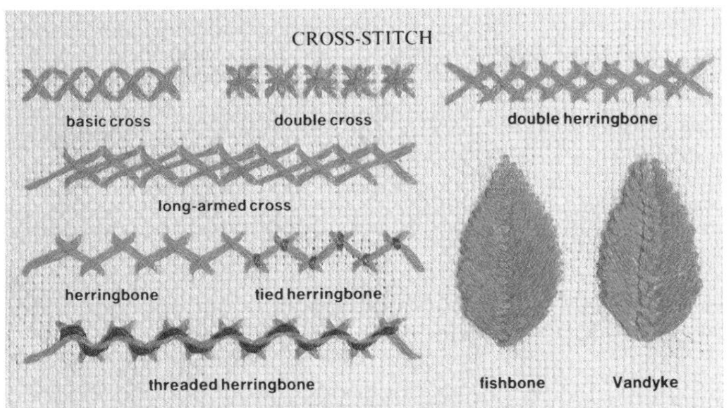

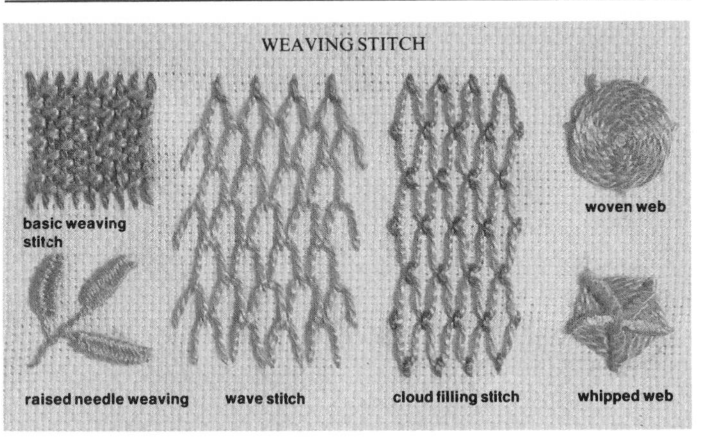

embryo See **egg**, **baby**
-embryo- -BLAST-, BLASTO-
emergency, state of urgent need EXIGENCY
– emergency or critical point beyond which a tense situation will erupt into war or violence FLASHPOINT
– adopted temporarily, often as an emergency measure MAKESHIFT, STOPGAP, EXPEDIENT
– providing for some possible though unlikely future occurrence or emergency, as a fund or plan might CONTINGENCY
emigrant or expatriate living on money sent from home REMITTANCE MAN
emotion of great joy, delight ECSTASY, RAPTURE, TRANSPORT
– assigning of human emotions or characteristics to natural or inanimate objects, as in poetic metaphors PATHETIC FALLACY
– express or release an emotion VENT
– range of emotions, musical notes, or other repertoire or series GAMUT
– relating to emotions and their arousal, rather than to thoughts and ideas AFFECTIVE
– showing or feeling no emotion IMPASSIVE
– sudden rush of emotion SURGE
– understanding of another that is so deep that one seems to enter into or share his or her emotions EMPATHY
emotional and intellectual affinity, sympathetic relationship RAPPORT
– emotional and spontaneous rather than rational and deliberate DIONYSIAC
– emotional behaviour of a wild, neurotic kind HYSTERIA
– emotional fit or outburst, as of rage PAROXYSM
– emotional in an excessive, theatrical way HISTRIONIC
– emotional or nervous disorder, revealed in phobias, obsessions, or the like, that induces anxiety and is mildly disabling NEUROSIS
– emotional or sentimental when drunk MAUDLIN
– emotional outpouring in speech or writing EFFUSION
– emotional poetry, rather than dramatic or narrative LYRIC POETRY

– emotional purification through pity and fear, as when watching a tragic drama CATHARSIS
– emotional reaction of an exaggerated kind to a situation MELODRAMA
– emotional shock, typically having long-lasting psychological effects TRAUMA
– emotionally affecting or distressing POIGNANT
– emotionally charged speech or writing, as in a tribute or literary work RHAPSODY
– emotionally detached and unbiased DISPASSIONATE, OBJECTIVE
– emotionally insecure, oversensitive VULNERABLE
– emotionally sensitive, easily affected SUSCEPTIBLE
– emotionally upset or extremely agitated DISTRAUGHT
– excessively excited, strained, or emotionally worked up OVERWROUGHT
– excessively or unrestrainedly emotional GUSHING, EFFUSIVE
– openly emotional, expressing one's feelings readily DEMONSTRATIVE

-emotional state -THYMIA

emperor of Germany in former times, or of the Holy Roman Empire KAISER
– emperor of Japan MIKADO, TENNO
– emperor of Russia in former times TSAR, CZAR
– like an emperor IMPERIAL

emphasis through contrast, as of colour or shading RELIEF

emphasise, stress, or intensify, draw attention to something emphatically ACCENTUATE, UNDERSCORE
– emphasise a point by constantly repeating it, dwell on, hammer home BELABOUR
– emphasise or bring to people's attention HIGHLIGHT

emphatic, passionate, or intense VEHEMENT
– emphatically and unmistakably noticeable, bold or striking PROMINENT, CONSPICUOUS, SALIENT, GLARING
– state emphatically ASSEVERATE

empire See **dynasties**
– adjective for an empire or emperor IMPERIAL

employ more workers than needed, especially in order to avoid redundancies FEATHERBED

employee in a large organisation, underling MINION
– employee or assistant doing a variety of work FACTOTUM
– employee's extra benefit, in addition to his wages or salary FRINGE BENEFIT
– reduction in the number of employees through redundancy RETRENCHMENT
– reduction in the number of employees through retirement or resignation NATURAL WASTAGE, ATTRITION

empty, clear out, remove the contents or air from EVACUATE, VOID
– empty or discharge, as a river does into a lake or the sea DISEMBOGUE, DEBOUCH
– empty space, emptiness VACUITY

enamel or glossy black lacquer JAPAN
– technique or style of enamelling different coloured panels between strips of metal, or enamelware made in this way CLOISONNÉ
– enamelled, glazed pottery, brightly decorated, of a 16th-century Italian style MAJOLICA
– silver or other metal ornament or object decorated by the insertion of coloured enamel into cut grooves CHAMPLEVÉ

encircling a body part, as nerves, blood vessels, or the like do CORONARY

enclosed building or grounds, as of a church PRECINCT

encore at a concert, or some similar short, pleasant treat BONNE BOUCHE

encourage, give renewed cheer to HEARTEN, REASSURE, BUOY UP
– encourage, help forward, or cultivate something, such as someone's career FOSTER, ADVANCE, NURTURE
– encourage, revive, inspire with renewed strength or determination ANIMATE, EMBOLDEN, INSPIRIT, INVIGORATE
– encourage, support, or give approval for COUNTENANCE, SANCTION, ENDORSE
– encourage or assist, especially in some wrongdoing, be an accessory to ABET, CONNIVE
– encourage or support a cause ADVOCATE, CHAMPION, PROMOTE
– encourage strongly or appeal to urgently EXHORT

encouragement, influence, goad or spur to action INCENTIVE, INDUCEMENT, INCITEMENT, MOTIVATION, STIMULUS
– encouragement of a wrongful act, such as one's spouse's adultery, by ignoring it CONNIVANCE
– encouragement or active support PATRONAGE, CHAMPIONSHIP

encouraging, urging HORTATORY, HORTATIVE

encroach or trespass on INFRINGE

end See also **stop**
– end, edge, furthest point or part EXTREMITY
– end, last part or element of something OMEGA
– end, run out, cease to be effective EXPIRE
– end in a climax, reach a conclusion CULMINATE
– end or conclude something successfully, such as a conflict RESOLVE
– end or crush something firmly, such as a rumour or rebellion SCOTCH, QUASH
– ending of a play with the unwinding or solution of the plot DENOUEMENT
– ending or failure DEMISE
– ending that fails ludicrously after a promising start ANTICLIMAX, BATHOS
– add or attach at the end APPEND, SUFFIX
– complete successfully, reach the end of, fulfil ACCOMPLISH, CONSUMMATE, CROWN
– directed or tending towards a specific end or purpose TELIC

end-, purpose- TEL-, TELE-

end-, tip-, summit- ACRO-

end of the world – branch of theology dealing with the end of the world ESCHATOLOGY
– relating to, prophesying, resembling, or suggesting the end of the world APOCALYPTIC
– setting of the final battle between the forces of good and evil that will herald, according to the Bible, the end of the world ARMAGEDDON

endanger, put at risk IMPERIL, JEOPARDISE

endless, tediously long INTERMINABLE
– endless or inexhaustible supply WIDOW'S CRUSE

endurance, capacity of enduring or withstanding something unpleasant TOLERANCE
– powers of endurance, staying power STAMINA

endure, survive a crisis, danger, or the like WEATHER

enema for washing out the bowels COLONIC
– former term for an enema CLYSTER

enemy, opponent, or rival ADVERSARY, ANTAGONIST
– enemy territory secured by advance troops as a foothold or protection for the main attacking force BRIDGEHEAD, BEACHHEAD, SALIENT
– enemy within, hostile or subversive element within a country at

war or an organisation FIFTH COLUMN, TROJAN HORSE
– adjective for an enemy INIMICAL
– barrier of buffer states guarding a country from potential enemy attack CORDON SANITAIRE
– distraction or deception of an enemy, such as a pretended attack DIVERSION, DECOY
– mixing socially with the people of an occupied or enemy country FRATERNISATION
– policy of agreeing to the demands of a potential enemy for the sake of maintaining peace APPEASEMENT
– preventing of enemy forces or nations from extending their territory or influence CONTAINMENT
– victor's decree or settlement imposed on a defeated enemy DIKTAT

energetic See also **enthusiastic**
– energetic, forceful, vigorous VIRILE, VITAL, VIBRANT
– energetic, hardworking, or forceful person DYNAMO
– energetic, inspiring, and emotional person FIREBALL, FIREBRAND
– energetic and passionate in a creative way DIONYSIAC
– energetic or vigorous, even though elderly SPRY, SPRIGHTLY
– energetic resourcefulness, enterprise INITIATIVE

energy See also **enthusiasm**
– energy, vigour, verve, zest ÉLAN, BRIO, VITALITY, PIZZAZZ
– energy of a system or body based on its actual motion KINETIC ENERGY
– energy of a system or body based on its position rather than its motion POTENTIAL ENERGY
– energy or divine spirit supposedly inhabiting and guiding a person NUMEN
– energy or powers of endurance enabling one to resist fatigue or hardship STAMINA
– energy released in a nuclear explosion, expressed in terms of weight of TNT YIELD
– energy unit of the smallest possible size in physics QUANTUM
– channel or transform a sexual impulse or other instinctual energy into a socially or culturally more acceptable activity SUBLIMATE
– control or direct energy HARNESS
– focusing of psychic or emotional energy on a person, thing, or idea CATHEXIS
– means of displaying or releasing one's talents, energies, or creative ability OUTLET
– referring to an energy source considered never-ending RENEWABLE
– referring to energy derived from heat in the Earth's interior GEOTHERMAL
– requiring or involving great effort or energy STRENUOUS
– running down of the energy in the universe or any other closed system ENTROPY

engaged to be married BETROTHED, AFFIANCED

engine See chart, page 170, and also **internal-combustion engine**, **car**, **motor**, **jet engine**
– engine, usually detachable, fitted externally at the stern of a boat OUTBOARD MOTOR
– engine positioned crossways rather than lengthways in a car TRANSVERSE ENGINE
– engine valve regulating the flow of steam or vaporised fuel to the cylinders THROTTLE
– engine's removable cover, as on a car or aircraft COWLING
– chamber in which vaporised fuel burns, as in the cylinders of an internal-combustion engine COMBUSTION CHAMBER
– clean an engine of its carbon deposits DECOKE, DECARBONISE, DECARBURISE
– cooling system, as in a car engine, through which water or other coolant flows RADIATOR
– device for conveying electric current to the spark plugs in an engine DISTRIBUTOR
– device in the exhaust of an engine, as in a car, for burning off or neutralising harmful fumes AFTERBURNER
– electrical coil used as a relay or switch connecting the battery to the starter motor of an engine SOLENOID
– electrical contact, as in the distributor of a car engine POINTS
– fan or compressor used to increase the air intake in an internal-combustion engine SUPERCHARGER, BOOSTER, BLOWER
– make sharp popping noises, as a poorly tuned engine might KNOCK, PINK
– smooth worn-out engine cylinders by drilling, and fit slightly larger pistons REBORE
– start an engine, as of an early car, by vigorously turning a handle inserted into it CRANK
– system for setting the vaporised fuel burning in an internal-combustion engine IGNITION

engineering – application of biology to engineering and electronics, especially of brain functions to computers BIONICS
– deliberate modification or "engineering" of the gene structure, as in breeding improved plant or animal strains GENETIC ENGINEERING
– study or application of biology and engineering in work and the workplace ERGONOMICS, BIOTECHNOLOGY

England – area in northeast England under Danish law in Anglo-Saxon times DANELAW
– former or literary name for England ANGLIA
– poetic or old-fashioned term for Britain or England ALBION

English of a plain, straightforward, blunt kind, sometimes using swear words ANGLO-SAXON
– English of a simplified spoken form, including elements from other languages, used for basic communication PIDGIN ENGLISH
– English word, or phrase, or idiom occurring in another language ANGLICISM
– English-speaking ANGLOPHONE
– in English, translated into English ANGLICE
– make English in style, form, or the like ANGLICISE

English- ANGLO-

Englishman – derogatory term for an Englishman or -woman, as used by Scots SASSENACH

engraving in relief, typically with the raised design of a different colour from the background CAMEO
– engraving or etching with a sharp pointed instrument STYLOGRAPHY
– engraving or incising to produce a sunken rather than raised design, as for a signet ring INTAGLIO
– engraver's style or technique, or sharp chisel-like tool used in engraving BURIN
– decorate metal by engraving or embossing CHASE, ENCHASE
– relating to carving or engraving, especially on gemstones GLYPTIC

enjoy greatly, take pleasure in, delight in RELISH
– enjoy in an appreciative or leisurely way SAVOUR

enjoyable, delightful, or delicious DELECTABLE
– enjoyable, pleasing, satisfying GRATIFYING

enjoyment, delight, great pleasure DELECTATION
– enjoyment, zest, or vitality GUSTO
– enjoyment of life JOIE DE VIVRE
– enjoyment or merrymaking of a

wild uninhibited kind HILARITY
enlarge See **increase**
enlightened people ILLUMINATI
enlightenment, in Buddhism or Hinduism NIRVANA
enliven, give life or liveliness to ANIMATE, VIVIFY
enormous See **huge**
enslavement, slavery THRALL, THRALDOM
ENT specialist OTORHINOLARYNGOLOGIST
enter a town, country, or the like to attack and conquer it INVADE
– enter gradually or penetrate secretly an enemy country or territory, criminal organisation, or the like INFILTRATE
– enter illegally or unwarrantedly ENCROACH, TRESPASS, IMPINGE, INFRINGE, INTRUDE
– enter suddenly and violently, burst in IRRUPT
enterprise, adventure, exploit, or project UNDERTAKING
– enterprise, energetic resourcefulness INITIATIVE
– enterprise, initiative, pluck GUMPTION
– enterprising businessman undertaking new and risky ventures ENTREPRENEUR
entertain or give pleasure to, as by telling stories REGALE
– entertaining, amusing, or distracting DIVERTING
entertainer, as at a funfair, who bites off the head of a live frog, mouse, chicken, or the like GEEK
– entertainer or acrobat who twists his limbs and body into abnormal positions CONTORTIONIST
– entertainer who breaks free from chains, escapes from locked boxes, and the like ESCAPOLOGIST
– entertainer who "throws his voice", giving the impression that it originates elsewhere, especially in a dummy VENTRILOQUIST
– entertainers in a group, especially a touring group TROUPE
entertainment, literary work, or the like that is elaborate, fanciful, or spectacular EXTRAVAGANZA

ENGINES AND MOTORS

aeolipile	ancient steam engine or simple turbine, consisting of a rotating metal sphere powered by exhaust jets
beam engine	large early steam engine in which a beam or lever transferred the motion from piston rod to crankshaft, as used for pumping out mines
booster	engine or rocket that supplements the main power system of a jet or spacecraft, often as the first stage of a multistage rocket
bypass engine	jet engine or gas turbine in which some of the compressed air is diverted round the combustion zone to join the exhaust gases directly for extra thrust
donkey engine	small auxiliary steam engine used for hoisting or pumping
fuel injection engine	internal combustion engine with a system for spraying vaporised fuel into the cylinders without carburettors
induction motor	electric motor whose rotation is induced by the interaction of magnetic fields
internal combustion engine	standard modern engine in which the fuel is burned internally, rather than externally as in a steam engine
ion engine/ion rocket	rocket engine producing thrust by expelling a high-speed beam of ions
Lenoir's engine	first successful gas-fired, two-stroke internal combustion engine, built in 1860
Newcomen atmospheric engine	early beam engine, invented in 1712
plasma engine	hypothetical engine for use in space, producing thrust by expelling a jet of plasma — or highly ionised gas
radial engine	internal combustion engine with cylinders arranged around the crankshaft like the spokes of a wheel, as formerly used in propeller-driven aircraft
ramjet, athodyd	jet engine with a special duct for air intake and compression, operating only at speed
retrorocket	rocket engine for braking or reversing
sustainer	small rocket motor that sustains the speed of a spacecraft after the booster is jettisoned
synchronous motor	electric motor with a speed directly proportional to the frequency of the current driving it
thermomotor	engine operated by the expansion of heated gas
thruster	small rocket engine for controlling altitude in a spacecraft or aircraft
turbine	rotary engine with a vaned shaft rotated by the pressure of steam, water, exhaust gases or the like
turbojet	jet engine with a turbine-powered compressor feeding compressed air to the combustion chamber
turboprop/prop-jet	turbojet engine used to drive an external propeller
V-engine	engine with cylinders arranged in the shape of a V
vernier rocket/ vernier engine	small secondary rocket engine used for making fine adjustments in speed or direction
Wankel engine	internal combustion engine without pistons, having a triangular rotor forming combustion chambers as it turns

– entertainment given at night, typically outdoors, using sound and light effects in presenting the history of the site SON-ET-LUMIÈRE
– entertainment hall, athletics or sports stadium, large arena, or the like COLISEUM
– entertainment on stage during the interval of an opera or play DIVERTISSEMENT
– entertainment or pleasure based on the suffering of others ROMAN HOLIDAY

enthusiasm combined with style and vigour, zest, flair ÉLAN, VIVACITY, BRIO
– enthusiasm of a passionate, burning kind ARDOUR, FERVOUR
– enthusiasm or devotion that is extreme and often excessive or irrational FANATICISM
– arouse or inspire passion, enthusiasm, or the like KINDLE
– unselfconscious enthusiasm, lack of inhibition ABANDON

enthusiastic See also **emotional**
– enthusiastic, extremely keen and devoted AVID, ARDENT, FERVENT, PERFERVID
– enthusiastic, loyal, or dutiful to an excessive, foolish, or dangerous degree GUNG HO
– enthusiastic enjoyment or vitality GUSTO
– extremely enthusiastic and zealous in promoting a cause EVANGELISTIC
– extremely enthusiastic or excited, full of high spirits EXUBERANT, EBULLIENT, EFFERVESCENT
– passionately enthusiastic, highly delighted, ecstatic RHAPSODIC

entice, lure, or incite, especially into a sinful or illegal act SOLICIT

entire, whole INTEGRAL

entirely- PAN-

entrails See also **digestive system**
– entrails, internal bodily organs VISCERA, INNARDS
– entrails of a chicken or other fowl GIBLETS
– entrails of a deer as formerly used for food NUMBLES, UMBLES
– entrails of animals, especially of pigs, used in cooking HASLET
– priest in ancient Rome who looked into the future by inspecting animals' entrails HARUSPEX

entrance, right to enter, or means of entering ACCESS, INGRESS
– entrance hall or room leading into a larger room ANTECHAMBER, VESTIBULE, ANTEROOM
– entrance hall, waiting room, or reception area FOYER, LOBBY
– entrance hall or offices at a college LODGE, PORTER'S LODGE
– entrance or doorway THRESHOLD
– entrance stairway or porch at a house door STOOP
– entrance to a building, with a roof often supported by columns PORTICO
– entrance to or porch of a temple PROPYLAEUM
– canvas canopy marking the entrance to a theatre, club, or the like in the U.S. MARQUEE
– outside stairway or platform at the entrance of a building PERRON

entry, admittance, right of access ENTRÉE
– certain means of gaining entry or success OPEN SESAME
– impossible to capture or enter forcibly, as a castle might be IMPREGNABLE

envelop, wrap closely, as in furs SWATHE

environment, network, or context in which something develops MATRIX
– environment for an animal or plant HABITAT
– environment or surroundings MILIEU
– adjust to a new environment ACCLIMATISE
– capable of living under more than one set of environmental conditions, as some microorganisms are FACULTATIVE
– environmental influences on the development of an organism, as distinguished from genetic influences NURTURE
– having lost one's bearings, as when in an unfamiliar environment DISORIENTATED
– protection and preservation of the natural environment CONSERVATION
– relationship between people, plants, or animals and their environment ECOLOGY
– theory, opposed by strict Darwinian ideas of evolution, that new characteristics produced environmentally can be inherited LAMARCKISM, LYSENKOISM
– characteristics transmitted by genetic means as opposed to those arising from environmental influences HEREDITY

environment- ECO-

envy and desire to own something owned by someone else COVET
– envy someone for his or her possessions, or envy the possessions BEGRUDGE

-enzyme -ASE

epic poem, or part of one used for recitation, in ancient Greece RHAPSODY

epidemic and deadly disease, especially bubonic plague PESTILENCE
– epidemic over a very wide area PANDEMIC

epilepsy or epileptic fit of a kind involving severe convulsions and lengthy unconsciousness GRAND MAL
– epilepsy or epileptic fit of a mild kind PETIT MAL
– noise, flashing of light, or other sensation occurring just before an attack of epilepsy or migraine AURA

episode of a serial INSTALMENT
– dramatic situation at the end of an episode of a serialised film, radio or television play, or the like CLIFFHANGER

epitaph – "in memory of", as used in epitaphs IN MEMORIAM

equal, person having the same status or ability as another person PEER, COMPEER
– equal in rank, status, or the like COORDINATE
– equal in score, performance, or the like, as two competitors might be LEVEL-PEGGING
– equal in size, range, or duration COMMENSURATE, COTERMINOUS, CO-EXTENSIVE
– equal in value or effect, amounting to, equivalent TANTAMOUNT, CONSTITUTING
– "equal quantities of", referring to ingredients in a prescription ANA
– equality or equivalence, as of amount or status PARITY
– relating to or supporting equality, as of political and legal rights EGALITARIAN
– make or treat as equal or equivalent EQUATE

equal- EQUI-, IS-, ISO-

equation containing an unknown term raised to the power of two QUADRATIC EQUATION

equipment, buildings, and other provisions for an activity FACILITIES
– equipment, clothing, or other distinctive trappings ACCOUTREMENTS
– equipment, furniture, or fittings APPOINTMENTS
– equipment or machinery for a specified purpose, as for drilling or for extracting oil from a well RIG
– equipment or gear needed for an activity PARAPHERNALIA, APPURTENANCES
– equipment or requirements for effectiveness in one's profession or pursuits STOCK IN TRADE
– referring to teaching aids or equipment, such as films, that conveys information to both hearing

and sight AUDIOVISUAL
equipped properly, well-furnished WELL-APPOINTED
equivalence, idea of balance or equality EQUATION
- correspondence, equivalence, or identity between systems or parts of a system SYMMETRY
equivalent, equal in value or effect, amounting to TANTAMOUNT
- equivalent or corresponding person in another team, organisation, or group COUNTERPART, OPPOSITE NUMBER
- item or favour of equivalent value given in exchange or compensation for another QUID PRO QUO
era, historical period EPOCH
erase, rub out, wipe out permanently EFFACE, EXPUNGE
- erase words, computer data, tape recordings, or the like DELETE
erosion – area badly eroded into ridges and gullies BADLANDS
- gully caused by soil erosion in South Africa DONGA
- low wall or fence jutting into the sea to control erosion of a beach GROYNE
erratic or peculiar action or notion WHIM, CAPRICE, VAGARY
erring, liable to err FALLIBLE
error See also **mistake**
- error based on the apparent change in the position of an object when the observer changes position PARALLAX ERROR
- error-free, perfect IMMACULATE, IMPECCABLE
- error in logic or reasoning that invalidates the conclusion FALLACY
- error in printing, typing, or writing TYPOGRAPHICAL ERROR, TYPO
- error of grammar or pronunciation, such as "between you and I", produced by avoiding an imaginary error HYPERCORRECTION
- error or variation in a measurement, judgment, or the like owing to human differences or prejudices PERSONAL EQUATION
- add to or aggravate an error or difficulty COMPOUND
- errors and corrections in a book, as listed on an inserted sheet of paper CORRIGENDA, ERRATA
- glaringly or offensively obvious, as a lie or error might be BLATANT
- supposed source of problems, errors, or mischief GREMLIN
escalator – escalator-like device, consisting of a horizontal rotating belt on corridor floors, for transporting pedestrians MOVING PAVEMENT, TRAVELATOR, WALKWAY
escape See also **depart**
- escape or avoid capture, hunters, or the like, especially by cunning ELUDE, EVADE, BILK
- entertainer who breaks free from chains, escapes from locked boxes, and the like ESCAPOLOGIST
- escaped or fleeing criminal, runaway FUGITIVE
- means of escape, way out of a difficult situation BOLT HOLE
- person who escapes from war or suppression REFUGEE
escapist or sheltered intellectual retreat from everyday life, as a university is sometimes considered to be IVORY TOWER
escort, accompany troops, ships, or vehicles for protection CONVOY
- escort, gentlemanly companion GALLANT, CAVALIER
- escort, guide, or attendant, especially when riding a horse or motorcycle OUTRIDER
- escort, lead, or conduct USHER
- escort or companion for someone, especially a young unmarried woman, for protection and propriety CHAPERONE, DUENNA
- escort ship CONSORT
- escort typically paid for by an older woman GIGOLO
Eskimo boat made of animal skins over a wooden frame UMIAK
- Eskimo boot of sealskin or reindeer hide MUKLUK
- Eskimo canoe KAYAK
- Eskimo from the islands off Alaska ALEUT
- Eskimo of North America or Greenland INUIT
- Eskimo's ice house IGLOO
- Eskimo sledge dog HUSKY, MALAMUTE
especially, extremely, clearly, remarkably SIGNALLY, EMINENTLY, CONSPICUOUSLY
essays and poetry considered as art rather than for their educational or moral value BELLES-LETTRES
- volume of essays by academics or scholars compiled as a tribute to a learned colleague FESTSCHRIFT
essence, embodiment, typical or perfect example of its kind EPITOME, PERSONIFICATION
- essence, foundation, underlying principle SUBSTRATUM, ANLAGE
- essence, fundamental factor, starting point BEDROCK
- essence, or concentrated or pure form of something DISTILLATE
- essence of a speech, plot, or argument, crux, nub, gist TENOR, BURDEN, GRAVAMEN
- essence or basic nature of something HYPOSTASIS, QUINTESSENCE, ELIXIR, QUIDDITY
- essence produced by boiling down a liquid DECOCTION
essential, basic, underlying, fundamental CONSTITUTIVE, SUBSTANTIVE
- essential, inseparable, forming a vital constituent INTEGRAL, INTRINSIC, INHERENT
- essential, required by law or demanded by custom COMPULSORY, STATUTORY, MANDATORY, DE RIGUEUR
- essential as a duty, inescapable, binding INCUMBENT, OBLIGATORY, IMPERATIVE, IRREMISSIBLE
- essential details, basic facts, the quick or core, brass tacks NITTY-GRITTY
- essential element, core, gist PITH
- essential or central component or participant LINCHPIN, CORNERSTONE, ALPHA AND OMEGA
- essential or primary, of basic or underlying importance RUDIMENTARY, PRIMORDIAL
- essential or vital, impossible to leave out, absolutely necessary INDISPENSABLE
- essential thing or condition, a factor without which something cannot occur PREREQUISITE, SINE QUA NON
establish, work out the answer, as by calculating DETERMINE
- establish an argument on certain facts or suppositions PREDICATE
established, firm, inherent, underlying SUBSTANTIVE
- established, fixed, firmly and immovably settled, as opinions or troops might be ENTRENCHED
- established or settled firmly or securely in position ENSCONCED
- person or thing long established and regarded as permanent in a given place or position FIXTURE
estate See also **land**, **property**
- estate, domain, or house of a feudal lord MANOR
- estate manager in Scotland FACTOR
- estate or large landed property DEMESNE
- estate or plantation of a Spanish type HACIENDA
- estate-owner in Scotland LAIRD
- estate returning to a lessor or grantor after the agreed term, or the right to this estate REVERSION
- estate that cannot be disposed of except for a permitted period, or this limitation on it PERPETUITY
- agent legally entitled to control or administer the estate or other property of someone else TRUSTEE
- agent who runs a landowner's estate STEWARD, BAILIFF
- large landed estate, especially in

Latin America or ancient Rome LATIFUNDIUM
– limit the inheritance of an estate to a particular line of heirs ENTAIL
estate agent – U.S. term for an estate agent REALTOR
estate car SHOOTING BRAKE, STATION WAGON
estimate of costs or prices, as for a building job QUOTATION
– estimate or assess the value of EVALUATE, APPRAISE, ASSAY
– estimating of building costs and materials QUANTITY SURVEYING
– rough estimate or calculation APPROXIMATION
etch or inlay metal bearing wavy decorative patterns DAMASCENE, DAMASK
– etching or engraving with a sharp pointed instrument STYLOGRAPHY
– etching technique producing varied tones, or an etching produced by this technique AQUATINT
eternal See **permanent**, **constant**
– eternal damnation, hell PERDITION
eternity, endlessness PERPETUITY
ethics – relating to rights, duties, and similar ethical concepts DEONTIC
etiquette – code of behaviour, especially among diplomats or rulers PROTOCOL
– mistake or improper usage, especially in grammar or etiquette SOLECISM
– over-fussy detail, as of etiquette or protocol PUNCTILIO
Eucharist See **Communion**
euphemism – unpleasant or offensive word or phrase substituted for a neutral or favourable one, the reverse of a euphemism DYSPHEMISM
Europe and America, and the West in general OCCIDENT
European woman in India, especially the wife of a British official during the Raj MEMSAHIB
euthanasia in the form of withholding treatment that would prolong the patient's life PASSIVE EUTHANASIA
evaporating readily at normal temperatures and pressure VOLATILE
– thicken or condense, as by boiling or evaporating INSPISSATE
evasive, avoiding indicating any definite preference or purpose, as by a cautious reply NONCOMMITTAL
– evasiveness, shiftiness, or ambiguous speech or behaviour, as to gain time EQUIVOCATION, TEMPORISING, TERGIVERSATION, PREVARICATION
even temper, psychological stability EQUILIBRIUM, EQUANIMITY
even-tempered See **calm**
evening party or reception SOIRÉE
– evening prayers VESPERS, COMPLINE, VIGILS
– love song, typically sung outside a woman's house in the evening SERENADE
– relating to, appearing in, or occurring in the evening VESPERTINE, CREPUSCULAR
event marking an important stage in history or in one's life MILESTONE, LANDMARK
– projected or possible chain of events SCENARIO
everybody agreeing, of one mind, as in a vote UNANIMOUS
evergreen, cone-bearing tree, such as a pine or fir CONIFER
everlasting, permanent, perpetual PERENNIAL
– "everlasting" plant, which keeps its colour when dried IMMORTELLE
everyday, uninspired, ordinary, commonplace HUMDRUM, MUNDANE, PEDESTRIAN
– everyday speech of the people VERNACULAR, VULGATE, DEMOTIC
everything- PAN-, PANTO-
everywhere at any one time UBIQUITOUS, OMNIPRESENT, IMMANENT
everywhere- OMNI-
evidence, often relating to medical or scientific facts, used in legal cases FORENSIC EVIDENCE
– evidence, proof, demonstration TESTIMONY, TESTAMENT
– evidence based on what others have said HEARSAY
– evidence given on oath DEPOSITION
– evidence or indication of a disease, social condition, or the like SYMPTOM
– evidence that one possesses a specified quality PATENT
– evidence that is indirect, requiring an inference rather than relating directly to the case CIRCUMSTANTIAL EVIDENCE
– evidence that would be considered strong or reliable unless challenged PRIMA-FACIE EVIDENCE
– alter a document, accounts, evidence, or the like in order to deceive FALSIFY
– clearly understandable, substantial, as concrete evidence is TANGIBLE, SUBSTANTIVE
– confirm or back up an opinion or statement, as with additional evidence CORROBORATE, SUBSTANTIATE
– deliberate giving of false evidence by a witness under oath PERJURY
– document, weapon, or other object formally used as evidence in court EXHIBIT
– from a different source, from somewhere else, as evidence might be ALIUNDE
– give evidence of, bear witness to ATTEST, TESTIFY
– indisputable, undeniable, certain, as an overwhelmingly powerful argument or piece of evidence would be INCONTROVERTIBLE
– material evidence or substance of a crime CORPUS DELICTI
– record or report in detail, and support with evidence DOCUMENT
– supporting, as evidence might be CORROBORATIVE, COLLATERAL
evil See also **immoral**
– evil, decay, or corruption, especially when rampant CANKER
– evil, wicked, infamous, as a sinful plot or notorious murderer is NEFARIOUS
– evil, wickedness, baseness, sinfulness INIQUITY, DEPRAVITY, TURPITUDE
– evil in influence or effect, or foreshadowing evil BALEFUL
– evil or evil deed, outrage, monstrous act ENORMITY
– evil or harmful in intention or influence MALEVOLENT, MALICIOUS, MALIGN, MALEFICENT, MALIGNANT, PERNICIOUS
– anxiety, feeling that evil or disaster is to come FOREBODING
– designed to ward off evil, as a ritual ceremony might be APOTROPAIC
– extremely evil, shockingly wicked, vile INFAMOUS, HEINOUS, FLAGITIOUS
evil spirit reputed to have sex with a sleeping man SUCCUBUS
– evil spirit reputed to have sex with a sleeping woman INCUBUS
– drive out an evil spirit, or free a possessed person from evil spirits, as by religious rites EXORCISE
– person supposedly possessed by an evil spirit DEMONIAC, ENERGUMEN
evolution of a species into several different species adapted to different environments ADAPTIVE RADIATION
– evolution or development of a species, genus, race, or the like PHYLOGENY
– evolution or development of an individual ONTOGENY
– theory, opposed by strict Darwinian ideas of evolution, that acquired characteristics can be inherited LAMARCKISM, LYSENKOISM
– theory or classification system based on the view that shared

characteristics indicate species' evolution from a common ancestor CLADISTICS
ex-directory – U.S. term for ex-directory UNLISTED
ex-serviceman – U.S. term for an ex-serviceman VETERAN
exact See also **precise**
– exact description, list of details, plan, or proposal SPECIFICATION
– contained an exact number of times in a larger quantity, as a fraction or part might be ALIQUOT
exaggerate, improve, or enliven a report or story by adding colourful details EMBELLISH, EMBROIDER
– exaggerate one's illness, as to get off work MALINGER
– exaggerated, overstated, or theatrical, as a display of a person's emotions might be HISTRIONIC, MELODRAMATIC
– exaggerated or affected habit or trait IDIOSYNCRASY, ECCENTRICITY, ABERRATION, MANNERISM
– exaggeration AGGRANDISEMENT, HYPERBOLE
exalted, awe-inspiring SUBLIME
examination in the form of an interview rather than written answers ORAL, VIVA VOCE
– examination of a dead body, usually to establish the cause of death POST-MORTEM, AUTOPSY, NECROPSY
– examination of one's feelings or motives HEART-SEARCHING, INTROSPECTION
– examination of tissue from a living body, used in diagnosing disease BIOPSY
– examination or course for a B.A. honours degree at Cambridge University TRIPOS
– examination or instruction-book, particularly one on the basic principles of Christianity CATECHISM
– examination or investigation, such as a judicial inquiry, into a matter of concern INQUISITION
– certificate, pass, or degree awarded when a university student misses part of an examination through illness AEGROTAT
– instructions printed at the head of an examination paper RUBRIC
– outline of a course of study or examination requirements SYLLABUS, CURRICULUM
– revise intensely at the last minute for an examination, swot up CRAM
– supervise and keep watch over students at an examination INVIGILATE
-examination -OPSY
examine See also **test**
– examine accounts, claims, or records as to correct or approve them AUDIT
– examine and discuss a subject thoroughly CANVASS
– examine by touching for the purpose of a preliminary medical diagnosis PALPATE
– examine in order to sort the good from the bad, sift through WINNOW
– examine or analyse in fine detail DISSECT, ANATOMISE
– examine or investigate thoroughly, probe PLUMB
– examine or question intensely INTERROGATE, CROSS-EXAMINE
– examine or study in detail, pore over PERUSE, SCRUTINISE, TRAVERSE, CON
– examine something to assess its value or quality ASSESS, APPRAISE
-examining -SCOPY
example, or perfect or typical representative or embodiment, of an idea or ideal EXEMPLAR, ARCHETYPE, AVATAR, EPITOME, PERSONIFICATION, INCARNATION, TYPE
– example, typical or representative, of a class or quality BYWORD
– example from a classic or standard text that is considered authoritative LOCUS CLASSICUS
– example or model serving as a standard for others PARADIGM
– action or decision used as an example or justification when treating later cases similarly PRECEDENT
– be a typical example or symbol of, exemplify EMBODY, EPITOMISE, TYPIFY
– produce or cite an example, argument, or reason as evidence or proof ADDUCE
– serve as an example of, or demonstrate by example EXEMPLIFY
– "that is", "namely", term introducing examples VIDELICET, VIZ
exceed, as in quantity or degree SURPASS, PREPONDERATE
exceeding- SUPER-, ULTRA-
excellent See also **perfect**
– excellent, incomparable, unequalled or unsurpassed PEERLESS, MATCHLESS, UNPARALLELLED, UNRIVALLED
– excellent, of outstanding quality or reputation BLUE-CHIP
– excellent, outstanding, superior to all others SUPERLATIVE
– excellent, serving as an example or model for others of its kind EXEMPLARY, COPYBOOK
– excellent, wonderful, stunning STUPENDOUS, SUBLIME
– excellent or perfect example or representative EXEMPLAR, PARAGON
– excellent person or thing, a marvel HUMDINGER
– excellent person or thing, without equal NONPAREIL, NONESUCH
excelling others, outstanding PRE-EMINENT, TRANSCENDENT
exceptional, remarkable, extraordinary SURPASSING
excess, overabundance, or surplus GLUT, PLETHORA, SUPERFLUITY, SURFEIT
– excess or redundancy NIMIETY
excessive, beyond the required or regular number SUPERNUMERARY, SUPERFLUOUS, REDUNDANT, SUPEREROGATORY
– excessive, extravagant, unreasonable, as prices or demands might be EXORBITANT, EXTORTIONATE
– excessive, unrestrained, beyond reasonable limits INTEMPERATE, IMMODERATE, DISPROPORTIONATE, UNCONSCIONABLE
– excessive or exaggerated, as ambition might be OVERWEENING, INORDINATE
– excessive or indulgent act, as of violence, drinking, or crime ORGY, RAMPAGE, FRENZY
– excessive or insincere, as overlavish praise might be FULSOME
– excessive praise, emotion, or the like SCHMALTZ
– excessive response to a problem or challenge OVERREACTION, OVERKILL
– excessive talking, sometimes caused by mental illness LOGORRHOEA
– excessively, overly UNDULY
– excessively and monotonously sweet-tasting, devoted, or the like CLOYING
– excessively eager to help or advise OFFICIOUS
– excessively revered object or activity FETISH
– excessively worried, fussy, sensitive, or the like NEUROTIC
excessive- HYPER-, POLY-
-excessive discharge -RRHAGIA
exchange, interchange, give or take mutually RECIPROCATE
– exchange, marketplace, trading centre RIALTO
– exchange goods or services directly, without using money BARTER
– exchange of one thing for something equivalent QUID PRO QUO
– exchange or central distribution point for banking transactions, commodities, information, or the like CLEARING HOUSE

– exchange or substitute COMMUTE

excite, stimulate, stir up, or provoke GALVANISE, ELECTRIFY, ENERGISE, INVIGORATE
– excite by suggestive or suspenseful stimulation TITILLATE
– excite or arouse someone's curiosity, interest, or the like PIQUE
– excitable or nervous, fidgety and restless SKITTISH
– excited or agitated uncontrollably DELIRIOUS, FRENZIED
– be eager for or excited at something SALIVATE
– excitedly active, bustling HECTIC
– excitedly nervous and flustered ATWITTER
– extremely excited or enthusiastic, full of high spirits EXUBERANT, EBULLIENT, EFFERVESCENT
– wildly or uncontrollably excited, frenzied FRANTIC, FRENETIC

excitement, arousal, incentive, or stimulus FILLIP
– feeling of prickling or stinging, as from excitement TINGLING
– substance that supposedly produces a surge of excitement or nervousness ADRENALINE

-excitement -MANIA

exciting, colourful, or noisy display, designed to impress or advertise RAZZLE-DAZZLE, RAZZMATAZZ
– exciting, stimulating, invigorating HEADY, EXHILARATING
– clearly described in vivid or exciting detail GRAPHIC

exclamation, sudden emphatic utterance INTERJECTION, EJACULATION
– exclamation of praise, joy, or surprise HALLELUJAH
– exclamation of praise to God HOSANNA
– exclamation of triumph on finding, solving, or discovering something EUREKA
– exclamation or oath, especially a swearword or profanity EXPLETIVE

exclamation mark combined with a question mark into a single punctuation mark INTERROBANG
– informal term for an exclamation mark SCREAMER, BANG

exclude See also **prevent**
– exclude, cast out, or banish from a group RELEGATE
– exclude, shut out, or prohibit, DEBAR
– exclude from all business dealings, refuse to trade or associate with, typically as a protest BOYCOTT, BLACKLIST
– exclude from membership of a club or society by vetoing or voting against BLACKBALL
– exclude from one's community or social circle, shun OSTRACISE
– exclude officially from religious rights and privileges, membership of a church, or the like EXCOMMUNICATE
– exclude or eliminate after careful sorting, sift out WINNOW OUT
– excluded because, or as if because, blasphemous or cursed TABOO

exclusion, shunning, or banishment from a social group OSTRACISM, PURDAH
– exclusion or deliberate blocking of thoughts, desires, or the like from one's mind SUPPRESSION

exclusive, restricted to a small group SELECT, ESOTERIC, RAREFIED
– exclusive circle of friends or colleagues CLIQUE
– exclusive control or rights, dominance to the exclusion of all others MONOPOLY
– exclusive right or possession, or something claimed to be one PERQUISITE
– exclusiveness and standoffishness ÉLITISM
– divided up into separate and exclusive racial groupings, as a community or country might be SEGREGATED

excommunication – formal pronouncement of excommunication, damning curse ANATHEMA

excrement, dung FAECES, DEJECTA, EXCRETA, EGESTA, ORDURE
– excrement-eating, feeding on dung, as some insects are COPROPHAGOUS, SCATOPHAGOUS
– excrement of a newborn baby MECONIUM
– excrement of insects FRASS
– excrement or droppings of animals, especially those being hunted or trailed SCATS
– excrement or dung of sea birds, as used for fertiliser GUANO
– containing or relating to excrement STERCORACEOUS
– fossilised excrement, as found in archaeological sites COPROLITE
– human excrement for use as a fertiliser NIGHT SOIL
– medical or archaeological study of excrement SCATOLOGY
– soiled with or as if with excrement, extremely dirty FECULENT

excrement- COPRO-, SCATO-

excrete DEFECATE, EVACUATE
– excrete, as birds do MUTE
– coil of earth excreted by an earthworm CAST, CASTING

excusable, easily pardoned or forgiven VENIAL

excuse See also **forgive**, **pardon**
– excuse, specifically a claim that one was somewhere else than at the scene of the crime ALIBI
– excuse, uphold, or justify by means of arguments, evidence, or proof VINDICATE
– excuse or expedient, face-saver SALVO
– excuse or free from responsibility, a duty, or the like EXONERATE, EXEMPT, ACQUIT
– believable or persuasive, as an excuse or politician might be PLAUSIBLE
– lessen or try to lessen the seriousness of a crime, guilt, or the like, as by offering certain excuses EXTENUATE, MITIGATE
– make up or invent an excuse, story, or the like CONCOCT
– pretended or false excuse PRETEXT
– self-deceiving excuse or explanation for one's actions, giving likely reasons but ignoring deeper motives RATIONALISATION
– try to satisfy or appease someone by means of an excuse, trick, or the like FOB OFF

execution, as formerly in Spain, by means of strangling or breaking the neck with an iron collar GARROTTE
– device for executing people by beheading, consisting of a heavy blade running between vertical posts GUILLOTINE
– platform or raised wooden framework, as formerly used for executing criminals SCAFFOLD

exempt, free or excuse from responsibility, blame, or the like EXONERATE

exemption or immunity, as for foreign diplomats, from the jurisdiction of one's country of residence EXTRATERRITORIALITY
– exemption or release from a rule, law, obligation, or the like DISPENSATION

exercise, based on Hindu principles, for physical and mental well-being YOGA, HATHA YOGA
– exercise and stretch, as before beginning a race LIMBER UP
– exercise that stimulates the breathing and blood circulation AEROBICS
– exercise through contracting the muscles without changing their length or moving the limbs ISOMETRIC EXERCISE
– exercises of a simple physical kind done for fitness and muscle tone CALLISTHENICS
– heavy ball used for physical exercise MEDICINE BALL
– system of exercise, therapy, diet, or the like REGIMEN

– wooden bottle-shaped club swung about for physical exercise INDIAN CLUB

exhaust pipe's attachment, purifying the engine's exhaust gases CATALYTIC CONVERTER
– something that is given off, such as radiation or exhaust fumes EMISSION

exhausted, deprived of one's natural force and vitality, as through inbreeding or over-indulgence EFFETE
– exhausted, severely weakened, drained or enfeebled DEBILITATED, DEPLETED, ENERVATED

exhaustion, as through starvation INANITION

exhibit or 3-D scene, as in museums, with models of figures set against a background DIORAMA
– exhibit or parade ostentatiously, show off FLAUNT

exhibition, especially a large industrial exhibition EXPO, EXPOSITION
– exhibition covering many years of an artist's work RETROSPECTIVE
– exhibition hall or display stand PAVILION

exile, banish, forbid, or outlaw PROSCRIBE
– exile or banish DEPORT
– exiled, banished, or living in a country other than one's homeland EXPATRIATE
– place of exile or captivity BABYLON

exist, be current, remain in force, as a custom might PREVAIL, OBTAIN
– exist, continue in existence, or manage to exist SUBSIST
– existing in the real world independently of the mind OBJECTIVE
– existing state of affairs STATUS QUO
– existing still, surviving, not lost or extinct or destroyed EXTANT
– existing thing, independent of other things ENTITY

existence – regard a concept or idea as having a real concrete existence HYPOSTATISE, REIFY

existence- ONTO-

exit, outlet, means of escape VENT
– exit, way out EGRESS
– stage direction indicating the exit of all the characters EXEUNT OMNES

expand See **increase**
– expand and clarify a remark, idea, or the like by adding details AMPLIFY, ELABORATE, DILATE, EXPATIATE
– expand range of activities or interests DIVERSIFY

expatriate or emigrant living on money that has been sent from home REMITTANCE MAN

expect, look forward to ANTICIPATE

expectations, chances or hopes of success, outlook PROSPECTS
– go against expectations CONFOUND

expedition or military advance ANABASIS

expel See **drive**

-expelling -FUGE

expenditure, money or funds paid out DISBURSEMENT

expenses – referring to expenses that are minor and not essential INCIDENTAL

expensive and inefficient gift, project, or possession, requiring more trouble than it is worth WHITE ELEPHANT
– extremely expensive, extravagantly or excessively priced, ruinous EXORBITANT, EXTORTIONATE, PROHIBITIVE

experience in and confident knowledge of society, tact in social situations SAVOIR-FAIRE
– experience involving great effort or suffering ORDEAL
– changes in fortune, experience, or the like VICISSITUDES
– doctrine that all knowledge derives from experience, especially from sense perceptions EMPIRICISM
– relating to intuitive knowledge or supernatural experience TRANSCENDENTAL
– unpleasant or dangerous experience, of short duration MAUVAIS QUART D'HEURE

experienced, sophisticated, even cynical WORLDLY-WISE, WORLDLY
– experienced in, acquainted or familiar with CONVERSANT, AU FAIT
– experienced or enjoyed through the actions or achievements of someone else, as pleasure might be VICARIOUS
– experienced person, as through long service in the army VETERAN
– experienced worker, artiste, or the like TROUPER
– expert, person skilled and experienced at a specified pursuit DAB HAND, PAST MASTER, MAVEN

experiment – experimenting or operating on the body of a living animal, especially for research VIVISECTION
– referring or relating to an experiment in which neither the subjects nor the testers know which test items are real or active and which are just controls DOUBLE-BLIND
– relating to arguments or reasoning based on experiment or experience rather than on theory or internal consistency EMPIRICAL, INDUCTIVE, A POSTERIORI

experimental, incompletely developed, or provisional, as a plan might be TENTATIVE

expert See also **able**, **skilful**
– expert, person skilled and experienced at a specified pursuit DAB HAND, PAST MASTER, MAVEN
– expert in a scientific or technical field, originally one working for the RAF BOFFIN
– expert in fine food and drink GOURMET, CONNOISSEUR
– expert or authority in any field PUNDIT, FUNDI
– expert, especially a master chef CORDON BLEU
– expert or master in any of the arts, especially music MAESTRO
– expert adviser CONSULTANT
– expert source of information, whether human or written AUTHORITY
– experts with specialised knowledge or superior tastes COGNOSCENTI
– group of experts discussing given topics in public, as for a radio broadcast BRAINS TRUST

expertise – acting or speaking out of turn, beyond the range of one's ability or expertise ULTRACREPIDARIAN
– pretended expertise or knowledge, veneer of scholarship SCIOLISM

expiation See **atonement**

explain, make clear, or interpret EXPOUND, EXPLICATE, ELUCIDATE
– explain in a reasonable or apparently reasonable way, often to suit one's convenience RATIONALISE
– explain in lengthy detail, enlarge on DILATE, ELABORATE, AMPLIFY, EXPATIATE
– explainable EXPLICABLE
– explaining, interpreting EXPONENT

explanation EXPLICATION, EXPOSITION
– explanation, as in science, that awaits proof HYPOTHESIS, WORKING HYPOTHESIS
– explanation or critical analysis of a text, especially of the Bible EXEGESIS
– explanation or interpretation of a statement or action CONSTRUCTION
– explanation that is more difficult to understand than the problem IGNOTUM PER IGNOTIUS
– principle that the best explanation for something is the simplest one OCKHAM'S RAZOR

explanatory note, translation, or commentary, as in the margin of a

manuscript or text GLOSS
– explanatory or introductory commentary or instructions RUBRIC
– explanatory phrase or remark within a sentence PARENTHESIS

explode, as a bomb might, or cause to explode DETONATE
– explode, as a mine does when set off SPRING
– explode, burst out violently, as in anger ERUPT

exploitation or intimidation of slum tenants by a ruthless landlord RACHMANISM

exploration, investigation, or survey, as of a stretch of enemy territory RECONNAISSANCE, RECCE

explore an area for gold or other minerals PROSPECT

explorer who travels by ship NAVIGATOR

explosion See also **bomb**
– energy released in a nuclear explosion, expressed in terms of weight of TNT YIELD
– relating to an earthquake, large explosion, or other vibration of the Earth's crust SEISMIC
– small explosion or thudding noise CRUMP
– sudden and violent inward collapse, the opposite process to an explosion IMPLOSION

explosive, unstable VOLATILE
– explosive cap, as used either in a toy pistol or in a firearm PERCUSSION CAP
– explosive charge, rocket fuel etc generating thrust PROPELLANT
– explosive charge in a missile's warhead PAYLOAD
– explosive liquid used in the manufacture of dynamite and gelignite NITROGLYCERIN
– explosive mixture of methane and air, in coal mines FIREDAMP
– explosive place, situation, or person TINDERBOX, POWDER KEG
– explosive powder, as for bullets and shells CORDITE
– explosive power equivalent to one million tons of TNT MEGATON
– explosives, or destruction by explosives, as by military engineers DEMOLITIONS
– cellulose nitrate in a form used as an explosive GUNCOTTON
– potassium nitrate, used in making explosives and preserving meat SALTPETRE

expose See **reveal**

exposures – apparatus giving brief exposures of visual images, as for experiments in memory or perception TACHISTOSCOPE

express a thought or idea in words of a particular style COUCH
– express an emotion or idea in words ARTICULATE, VERBALISE, ENUNCIATE
– express openly, discuss freely, examine publicly VENTILATE
– express or display something clearly, such as surprise EVINCE, MANIFEST
– express or release an emotion VENT

expression See also **emotion**, **figures of speech**, **style**, **phrase**
– expression, bearing, or manner MIEN
– expression of a feeling, or the form it takes MANIFESTATION
– expression in the voice, use of stress and pitch to convey meaning MODULATION
– expression of an indirect, roundabout kind CIRCUMLOCUTION, PERIPHRASIS
– expression of sulkiness POUT, MOUE
– expression of sulkiness or threat, frown SCOWL
– expression or sign of intentions or feelings GESTURE
– expression that is simple, clear, and elegant ATTICISM
– expressions of great delight ECSTASIES, RAPTURES, TRANSPORTS
– choice of words, mode of expression, as of a particular person or group PARLANCE, PHRASEOLOGY
– choice of words or manner of expressing oneself in speech or writing DICTION
– contorted facial expression, as of pain or disgust GRIMACE
– cowardly, ashamed, or downcast, as someone's expression might be SHEEPISH, HANGDOG
– distinctive word, phrase, or expression, especially when typical of a regional or cultural style LOCUTION
– informal word or expression, as used in everyday speech COLLOQUIALISM
– phrase or expression used as a figure of speech TROPE
– showing distaste or cynicism, as one's expression might WRY
– uninterpretable, as a facial expression might be INSCRUTABLE, UNFATHOMABLE, DEAD-PAN, ENIGMATIC

-expression -LOGY

expressionless, unemotional, showing no distinctive attitude or response VACUOUS, IMPASSIVE

expressive, expressing emotions or one's feelings openly DEMONSTRATIVE
– expressive or emotional, as a poem might be EVOCATIVE
– expressive or moving, especially in use of language ELOQUENT

exquisite, elegant, refined, especially in an affected or pretentious way RECHERCHÉ

extend See also **increase**
– extend, prolong, cause to continue PERPETUATE
– extend over, bridge SPAN
– extend range of activities or interests DIVERSIFY

extent, range, or scope, as of a law or one's outlook PURVIEW

exterminate – fill a room or building with poisonous smoke to disinfect it, exterminate insects, and so on FUMIGATE

extermination of a whole racial or social group GENOCIDE

external angle of a wall QUOIN, COIGN
– coming from outside, of foreign or external origin EXTRANEOUS, EXTRINSIC, EXOGENOUS

external- EXO-

extinct See also **dinosaur**
– extinct ox, probably the forebear of today's domestic cattle AUROCH, URUS
– extinct prehistoric bird still retaining some reptile features such as teeth and a long tail ARCHAEOPTERYX
– extinct prehistoric flying reptile PTERODACTYL
– extinct prehistoric horse-like mammal COHIPPUS
– extinct mammal resembling the elephant or mammoth MASTODON
– flightless bird from Mauritius, extinct since the 17th century DODO
– flightless bird from New Zealand, extinct since the 19th century MOA
– still in existence, surviving, not lost or extinct EXTANT
– zebra-like mammal from southern Africa, extinct since the 19th century QUAGGA

extra actor who has a non-speaking role, as in a play or film SUPERNUMARY
– extra, additional SUPPLEMENTARY, SUPERVENIENT
– extra, exceeding the required or regular number, excessive or redundant SUPERFLUOUS, SUPEREROGATORY
– extra charge or cost SURCHARGE
– extra information, added at the end of a book, message, or the like AFTERTHOUGHT, POSTSCRIPT, APPENDIX, ANNEXE, SUPPLEMENT, ADDENDUM
– extra-marital sex, sexual unfaithfulness INFIDELITY, ADULTERY

– extra profit or benefit from one's employment over and above one's salary or wages PERK, PERQUISITE, FRINGE BENEFIT
– extra soldiers or supplies sent to support those that are already in use REINFORCEMENTS
extra- SUPER-
extract an essence from a liquid by boiling DECOCT
– extract from a text, snippet GOBBET
– extract or concentrated essence of something QUINTESSENCE
– extract or selected passage or scene from a book, film, or the like EXCERPT
– extract or separate an essence, idea, or the like DISTIL
– extract something with difficulty, such as information WINKLE OUT, PRISE OUT
– extract the essentials of a book, report, or the like GUT
– extraction of useful substances from waste material RECOVERY, RECYCLING
– evaporate and condense a liquid repeatedly by boiling, as when extracting substances REFLUX
extraordinary, exceptional, remarkable SURPASSING, SINGULAR
– extraordinary, or wonderful PRODIGIOUS
extrasensory perception, such as clairvoyance CRYPTAESTHESIA, TELAESTHESIA
extravagant or generous LAVISH
– extravagant or wasteful PRODIGAL
extreme in political attitudes, favouring basic and far-reaching social and economic changes RADICAL
– extreme or excessive in one's devotion to a cause, irrationally enthusiastic or furious FANATICAL, RABID
– extreme or uncompromising, as in one's political stance INTRANSIGENT
– extreme point or perfect state NE PLUS ULTRA
– divide into two extreme and hostile positions or groups POLARISE
extreme – ULTRA-
extremely, especially, clearly, remarkably SIGNALLY, EMINENTLY, CONSPICUOUSLY
extremist, radical, or revolutionary in politics SANS-CULOTTE, JACOBIN
– extremist and uncompromising revolutionary MAXIMALIST
– extremist revolutionary advocating the destruction of all existing social and political institutions NIHILIST, ANARCHIST
eye See illustration

eye

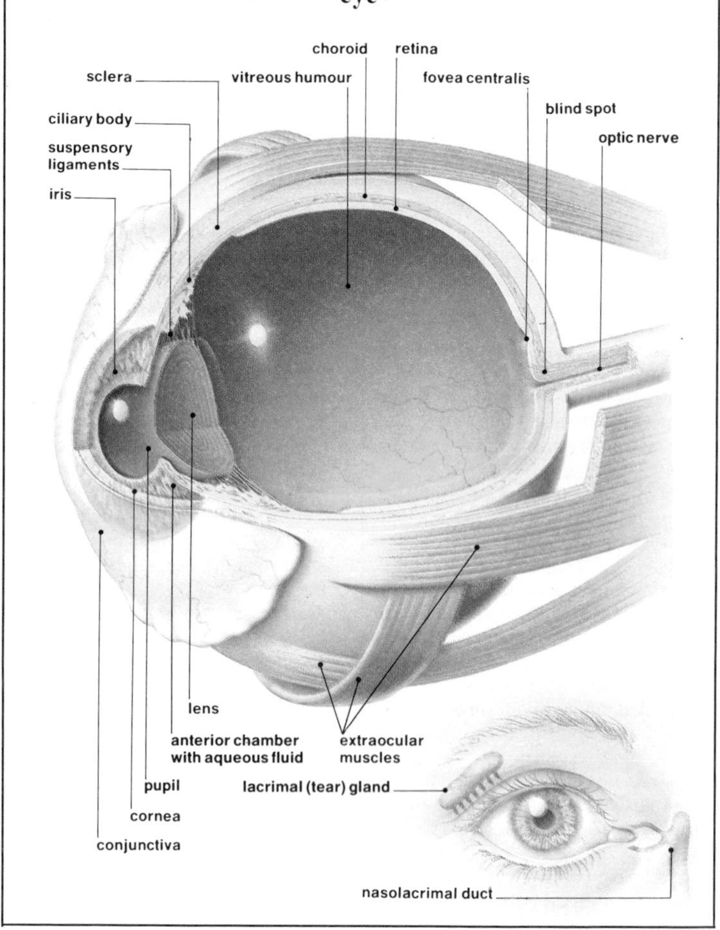

– eye, as of most insects, made up of many separate light-sensitive elements COMPOUND EYE
– eye-bearing stalk, as of a snail or crab OMMATOPHORE
– eye of an elementary kind, as in some insects, or eye-like marking, as on a peacock's tail OCELLUS
– eye socket ORBIT
– eye specialist, medical expert in eye diseases OCULIST, OPHTHALMOLOGIST
– eye specialist, prescribing glasses but not medical treatment OPTOMETRIST, OPHTHALMIC OPTICIAN
– eye's ability to focus by changing the direction of incoming light rays REFRACTION
– eye with a whitish iris, or an outward-turning squint WALL-EYE
– adjective for the eye OCULAR, OPHTHALMIC, OPTICAL
– any of the lenses in a compound eye as of an insect FACET
– clouding of the lens of the eye CATARACT
– corner of the eye, meeting-point of the eyelids CANTHUS, COMMISSURE
– focusing defect caused by an imbalance in the eye muscles, squint STRABISMUS
– focusing of one's eyes or attention firmly on something FIXATION
– fold of skin descending over the inner corner of the eye, characteristic of Mongoloid peoples EPICANTHIC FOLD
– having bulging eyes, specifically as a result of excess thyroid hormone EXOPHTHALMIC
– having eyes dulled by tears or tiredness BLEARY-EYED
– having very dark blue eyes, or slanted eyes SLOE-EYED
– mucous discharge from the eyes RHEUM
– poisonous chemical extract used to dilate the pupil of the eye ATROPINE
– red light-sensitive pigment in the retinal rods of the eye RHODOPSIN

– relating to one eye rather than two MONOCULAR
– relating to the use of both eyes, specifically to their focusing on a single object at one time BINOCULAR
– "spots before the eyes", specks or threads in one's vision caused by defects or impurities in the eyes MUSCAE VOLITANTES
– turn away one's eyes, gaze, or the like AVERT
– turning inwards of the eyes to focus on a nearer object CONVERGENCE
– uncontrolled movement of the eyeball NYSTAGMUS
– violet light-sensitive pigment in the retinal cones of the eye IODOPSIN
– white opaque narrow circle round the cornea of the eye, as found sometimes in elderly people ARCUS SENILIS
– white opaque patch or tissue on the cornea of the eye LEUCOMA
– widen or expand, as the pupil of the eye does in the dark DILATE
– wrinkles at the outer corner of the eye CROW'S-FEET

-eye- OPHTHALMO-, -OCUL-

-eye condition -OPIA
– eye exercises as a method of improving eyesight ORTHOPTICS
– eye-for-an-eye law or punishment, or the system or principle of making the punishment fit the crime TALION, LEX TALIONIS

eye lotion, eyewash COLLYRIUM

eye shadow, as used in Eastern countries KOHL

eye tooth CANINE

eyebrow – relating to or positioned above the eyebrow SUPERCILIARY
– having bushy and prominently projecting eyebrows BEETLE-BROWED

eyelash make-up MASCARA
– eyelashes CILIA

eyelet or ring, as of rope or rubber, for securing a sail, protecting a wire from chafing, or the like GROMMET

eyelid – adjective for the eyelids PALPEBRAL
– having eyelids PALPEBRATE
– inflammation of a sebaceous gland in the eyelid STY
– membrane forming an inner eyelid, as in reptiles, birds, and cats NICTITATING MEMBRANE

eyesight See also **colour blindness**
– eyesight on the outer edge of the normal field of vision PERIPHERAL VISION
– eyesight that is perfect EMMETROPIA, TWENTY-TWENTY VISION
– eyesight that is satisfactory straight ahead but poor or limited on either side TUNNEL VISION
– eyesight that is weak in dim light NYCTALOPIA
– eye exercises as a method of improving eyesight ORTHOPTICS
– long-sightedness HYPERMETROPIA
– relating to eyesight OPTICAL, VISUAL, OCULAR
– sharpness of eyesight, hearing, or mind ACUITY
– short-sightedness, defective distance vision MYOPIA
– very short-sighted or nearly blind PURBLIND

-eyesight -OPIA

F

fable, moral story, or picture in which the characters or scenes symbolise abstractions or ideas and convey a deeper meaning ALLEGORY
- fable or moral story, as used in medieval sermons EXEMPLUM
- fable with a moral message APOLOGUE
- collection, especially in medieval times, of moral fables based on animals BESTIARY
- writer of fables or fantasies FABULIST

fabric See chart, and also **cloth**
- fabric, cloth, material TEXTILE
- fabrics with a wrinkled or crinkly texture CREPE, PLISSÉ, SEERSUCKER
- shimmering or changing in colour, as some fabrics do SHOT, IRIDESCENT
- thin, light, and translucent, as some fine fabrics are SHEER, DIAPHANOUS

face, or expression on a face COUNTENANCE, VISAGE
- face downwards, lying face downwards PRONE, PROSTRATE
- face or front of a building FAÇADE
- face or turn in a specified direction, specifically eastwards as with a church ORIENTATE
- face that is long, gaunt, and sharp-featured HATCHET FACE
- face that reveals nothing about one's thoughts or feelings, an inscrutable face POKER FACE
- face to face, opposite VIS-À-VIS
- contort the face into an expression of pain, contempt, or disgust GRIMACE
- keeping a straight face or being apparently serious, as when telling a joke DEADPAN
- kit or method for creating a picture of a wanted suspect's face IDENTIKIT, PHOTOFIT
- pale face, or pale-faced person WHEY-FACE
- pull a face, especially when competing in a face-pulling contest GIRN
- twitch or spasm, especially in the face TIC
- uninterpretable, as a facial expression might be INSCRUTABLE, UNFATHOMABLE, DEAD-PAN, ENIGMATIC

-face -HEDRON

face value, value printed on the face of a share certificate or bond, as used for assessing dividends PAR VALUE

facelift or similar surgery designed to improve one's physical appearance COSMETIC SURGERY

facial features, especially when regarded as indicating character PHYSIOGNOMY
- facial features or shape LINEAMENTS, COUNTENANCE
- facial pain caused by the fifth cranial nerve TRIGEMINAL NEURALGIA, TIC DOLOUREUX

facilities, conveniences, pleasant and helpful features or services AMENITIES

facing, opposite VIS-À-VIS
- facing the observer OBVERSE

-facing -WARD, -WARDS

fact – by the fact itself, by its very nature, by definition IPSO FACTO
- facts of a case, accepted as evidence in court RES GESTAE
- practical, dealing with or relating to facts and circumstances rather than to theories or ideals PRAGMATIC
- repeat or reproduce facts in an unthinking way REGURGITATE
- set out or arrange the facts in order MARSHAL
- something that is already done and unalterable, an unchangeable fact FAIT ACCOMPLI

factor that makes up or compensates for faults or deficiencies REDEEMING CHARACTERISTIC, MITIGATING FACTOR
- factor that shares in the responsibility for something CONTRIBUTORY FACTOR

factory, farm, or business owned collectively by the workers or users COOPERATIVE
- factory, workshop, or the like where pay and working conditions are very poor SWEATSHOP
- continuous moving belt carrying objects, as on a factory's assembly line CONVEYOR BELT
- deliberate disruption of normal functioning or industrial procedures, as in a factory SABOTAGE
- enclosure, especially in the East, for a factory, rich housing, or the like COMPOUND
- item thrown out as substandard, as in a factory REJECT
- line of workers and equipment operating step by step on a product in a factory ASSEMBLY LINE, PRODUCTION LINE

factual, actual, existing in the real world independently of the mind OBJECTIVE

fade from sight, disappear slowly EVANESCE
- faded or blanched, as grass becomes when shielded constantly from sunlight ETIOLATED

faeces See **excrement**

fail, go wrong, come a cropper MISCARRY, FOUNDER
- fail to honour one's debts, keep one's promises, or the like WELSH, DEFAULT
- complete and usually embarrassing failure, utter disaster FIASCO

failed, unsuccessful, would-be, unfulfilled MANQUÉ
- failed through lacking complete development ABORTIVE

failure, disappointment, or anticlimax following high expectations DAMP SQUIB
- failure, ending, or death DEMISE
- failure or destruction of some magnificent project or person GÖTTERDÄMMERUNG

faint SWOON
- fainting, temporary loss of consciousness SYNCOPE

fair, even-handed, just and reasonable EQUITABLE
- fair, unbiased, and emotionally detached DISPASSIONATE
- fair, unbiased, unprejudiced IMPARTIAL, DISINTERESTED
- fair-haired and fair-skinned XANTHOCHROID
- fair-skinned or white person CAUCASIAN
- charity fair or bazaar, typically held outdoors FÊTE
- large public exhibition, such as a trade fair EXPOSITION

fair play – rules of fair play, specifically those applied in boxing

QUEENSBERRY RULES
fairground See **funfair**
fairness, justice EQUITY
fairy See also **gnome**, **spirit**
– fairy, elf, or pixie FAY
– beautiful fairy-like creature, originally in Persian folklore PERI
– mischievous fairy or elf, in Irish folklore, typically a cobbler with buried treasure LEPRECHAUN
fairy wheel on a child's bicycle OUTRIDER
faith – adopt or support a cause, faith, or ideal ESPOUSE
– complete and unquestioning, as strong faith is IMPLICIT
– creed or profession of faith widely used in churches ATHANASIAN CREED, NICENE CREED
– disbeliever, sceptic, person without faith or beliefs NULLIFIDIAN, AGNOSTIC
– formal statement of religious beliefs, confession of faith, especially in Christianity CREED
– profess one's faith openly TESTIFY
faithful See **loyal**
– faithfulness or loyalty, as to one's spouse, the facts, or one's duty FIDELITY
faithlessness, disloyalty, treachery PERFIDY
fake, cheap imitation, as flashy jewellery might be PINCHBECK, GIMCRACK, BRUMMAGEM
– fake, contrived or insincere, as an emotion might be FACTITIOUS
– fake, forged, as a coin might be SNIDE
– fake, forged, fraudulently imitative, as a document or emotion might be COUNTERFEIT, SPURIOUS
– fake, imitation, artificial, as a synthetic flavouring would be SIMULATED, ERSATZ
– fake, invisibly spoilt or cheapened by deliberate dilution or adding of impurities ADULTERATED
– fake, not genuine, sham BOGUS
– fake, pretend, or falsely display something, such as relief FEIGN, SIMULATE, DISSEMBLE
– fake, substituted fraudulently SUPPOSITITIOUS
– fake identity or similar deception IMPOSTURE
falcon See also **hawk**
– falcon of a small and dark-feathered species MERLIN
– falcon of a small, fast, common species, popular in falconry in former times PEREGRINE FALCON
– falcon or hawk that is still young enough to be trained for falconry EYAS
– falcons released by a falconer in a pair to pursue quarry as a team CAST
– male hawk or falcon TERCEL
– stitch closed the eyes of a falcon to quiet or tame it SEEL
fall See also **lessen**
– fall, as in a series from one level to the next CASCADE
– fall, sink, or settle down GRAVITATE, SUBSIDE
– fall, trip, sprawl on the ground MEASURE ONE'S LENGTH
– fall behind or stray STRAGGLE
– fall in the pitch of the voice, as at the end of a sentence, falling intonation CADENCE
– fall out of place PROLAPSE
– fall straight down and suddenly, hurtle PLUMMET, PRECIPITATE
– fall to someone, be passed on to or conferred on DEVOLVE ON
– fall to the ground, or sprawl or grovel GRABBLE
– falling down, badly built or maintained, shaky, as an old house might be RICKETY, RAMSHACKLE, DILAPIDATED
– falling off or shed at a point of time or growth, as leaves or antlers might be DECIDUOUS
fallacy of assuming in the premise the very conclusion to be proved, begging the question PETITIO PRINCIPII, HYSTERON PROTERON
– fallacy of assuming that an event or situation that follows another in time must also be the result of it POST HOC ERGO PROPTER HOC
– fallacy of proving or disproving an irrelevant conclusion rather than the proposition at issue IGNORATIO ELENCHI
– fallacy or invalid argument, especially when it is unintended PARALOGISM
Fallopian tube SALPINX
fallow – year in which farm land is left to lie fallow, observed every seventh year by the ancient Jews SABBATICAL YEAR
false See also **fake**, **lie**
– false, made-up, concocted, as a charge or accusation might be TRUMPED-UP
– false, sham, pseudo, artificial or inauthentic SPURIOUS, POSTICHE
– false appearance, feigning, pretence SIMULATION, GUISE
– false conclusion, faulty argument, or invalid reasoning, especially when unintended PARALOGISM
– false evidence used to incrimi-

FABRICS

COTTON OR LINEN	WOOLLEN OR WOOL-LIKE	MIXED FIBRE	
buckram	**alpaca**	**barathea**	**nylon**
bunting	**angora**	**bombazine**	**polyester**
calico	**baize**	**Clydella**	**rayon**
cambric	**camel hair**	**linsey-woolsey**	**Terylene**
candlewick	**cashmere**	**Viyella**	SPECIAL WEAVES AND FINISHES
cheesecloth	**Duffel**	JUTE OR HEMP	**astrakhan**
chintz	**grogram**	**burlap/gunny**	**batiste**
corduroy	**Harris tweed**	**canvas**	**bombazine**
cretonne	**hodden**	**hessian**	**bouclé**
denim	**Kendal green**	**hopsack**	**brocade**
dimity	**kersey**	**sackcloth**	**challis**
drill	**melton**	MAN-MADE OR SILK	**chenille**
duck	**merino**	**chiffon**	**ciré**
flannelette	**mohair**	**grosgrain**	**foulard**
gingham	**paisley**	**ninon**	**gaberdine**
lawn	**petersham**	**organza**	**gauze**
lisle	**serge**	**taffeta**	**georgette**
madras	**tweed**	**tulle**	**lamé**
moleskin	**vicuna**	MAN-MADE	**moquette**
muslin	**whipcord**	**acetate**	**mousseline**
nainsook	**worsted**	**acrylic**	**organdie**
nankeen	SILK	**Courtelle**	**poplin**
percale	**crepe de Chine**	**Crimplene**	**rep**
sailcloth	**gossamer**	**Dacron**	**satin**
sateen	**marocain**	**Lurex**	**seersucker**
scrim	**moiré**		**suede cloth**
terry towelling	**organzine**		**twill**
ticking	**shantung**		**velours**
tiffany			**velvet**
velveteen			**voile**
winceyette			

nate an innocent party FRAME-UP
– false idea or misleading opinion, based on misinformation or faulty reasoning FALLACY
– false interpretation or incorrect explanation, misunderstanding MISCONSTRUCTION
– false opinion or faulty understanding MISCONCEPTION, MISAPPREHENSION
– false or artificial outward appearance FAÇADE
– false or deceptive speech or behaviour, deliberate misleading of someone DUPLICITY
– false or highly questionable, as a story might be APOCRYPHAL
– false or insincere claim to have certain feelings or beliefs HYPOCRISY
– false or lying MENDACIOUS
– false or superficial likeness or image of something SIMULACRUM
– false perception MIRAGE, ILLUSION, DELUSION, HALLUCINATION
– false report or accusation, intended as a slighting criticism ASPERSION
– false statement, forgery, or similar deliberately contrived deception FABRICATION
– false statement or charge made knowingly that injures someone's reputation SLANDER, DEFAMATION, LIBEL, CALUMNY
– false story or report, unfounded rumour CANARD
– false though plausible, as an ingenious argument might be SOPHISTIC, SPECIOUS
– falsely reasoned, logically inconsistent, as a conclusion might be INVALID
– apparent or outward, but often false or pretended, as someone's stated reason for an action might be OSTENSIBLE
– deliberate giving of false evidence by a witness under oath PERJURY
– display something falsely, fake or pretend something, such as relief FEIGN, SIMULATE, DISSEMBLE
– prove an argument or statement false CONFUTE, REFUTE, REBUT
– put someone right, rid someone of a mistake or false notion DISABUSE
– represent falsely or show to be false BELIE

false- PSEUD-, PSEUDO-

false identity – person who assumes a false identity IMPOSTOR

false teeth – dental plate with a false tooth or teeth permanently fixed to natural teeth BRIDGE, BRIDGEWORK
– plate or set of false teeth DENTURE

fame, reputation STATURE
– fame or glory resulting from some achievement KUDOS
– fame or great success LUSTRE, ÉCLAT
– fame or high status, typically coupled with considerable influence PRESTIGE

familiar, closely associated, very friendly INTIMATE
– familiar or acquainted with, knowledgeable CONVERSANT, AU FAIT
– familiar theme, idea, or image in literature TOPOS

familiarise, adapt, adjust to new circumstances ORIENTATE

family, relatives KIN, KINSMEN
– family name, surname COGNOMEN
– family of rulers over successive generations DYNASTY
– family unit consisting of parents and children and sometimes grandparents NUCLEAR FAMILY
– family unit including grandparents, cousins, and the like all living together EXTENDED FAMILY
– family's female side or maternal line DISTAFF SIDE, SPINDLE SIDE
– family's male side or paternal line SPEAR SIDE
– descended from the same ancestor, though by different lines, as branches of a family might be COLLATERAL
– within or with one's family EN FAMILLE

family tree, list of ancestors PEDIGREE
– family tree or history, or study of one's ancestors GENEALOGY, LINEAGE
– family tree showing the ancestry of Jesus JESSE TREE

famous, widely known or admired by the public CELEBRATED, NOTED, RENOWNED, ACCLAIMED, ILLUSTRIOUS
– famous for a particular and usually unfavourable quality NOTORIOUS, INFAMOUS
– famous or greatly respected and honoured, especially when old VENERABLE, AUGUST
– famous or highly regarded for outstanding qualities or contributions EMINENT, DISTINGUISHED, PROMINENT
– famous person or VIP, often famous chiefly for being famous CELEBRITY, LUMINARY
– famous to the point of becoming a historical hero, legendary FABLED, STORIED
– be famous, achieve wide publicity RESOUND

fan, as in India, in the form of a large cloth or leaf waved to and fro PUNKA
– fan, vent, or vacuum device for drawing out gas or stale air from a room EXTRACTOR, VENTILATOR
– fan or enthusiastic follower of a specified sport or pastime, buff DEVOTEE, AFICIONADO
– fan-shaped FLABELLATE
– fan used in religious ceremonies FLABELLUM
– fan whose blades form the outer edge of a cylinder SQUIRREL CAGE
– any of the ribs of a fan BRIN

fanatic, extremist ZEALOT, ENERGUMEN

fanciful idea, often combined with mildly eccentric behaviour WHIMSY

fanfare on a trumpet TUCKET
– fanfare or blast on a horn or trumpet TANTARA, TANTIVY
– fanfare or similar dramatic musical passage FLOURISH

fanlight – U.S. term for a fanlight TRANSOM

fantasy, notion typically credited to imagination FIGMENT
– fantasy land of luxury and idleness COCKAIGNE
– fantasy of a playful kind WHIMSY
– fantasy world, impractical realm of the imagination and dreams CLOUD-CUCKOO-LAND
– person who indulges in fantasies to compensate for his inadequacies WALTER MITTY
– relating to dreams or fantasies VISIONARY
– writer or teller of fables or fantasies FABULIST

far away, fairly distant or remote from the centre OUTLYING
– far away and difficult to reach INACCESSIBLE
– far from the joint, centre, or the like, as a bone or limb might be DISTAL

Far Eastern countries or regions ORIENT

far-sighted, prudent PROVIDENT
– far-sightedness, long-sightedness, defective close vision HYPEROPIA, HYPERMETROPIA

faraway or remote region, goal, or ideal ULTIMA THULE

farewell, goodbye, act of leave-taking VALEDICTION, CONGÉ
– farewell or final appearance, act, work, or statement SWAN SONG

farm, factory, or business owned collectively by the workers or users COOPERATIVE
– farm of very small size SMALLHOLDING

– farm or farm buildings GRANGE
– farm or farmhouse of a Spanish type HACIENDA
– farm or settlement collectively administered in Israel KIBBUTZ
– farm or settlement collectively administered in the USSR KOLKHOZ
– farm worker bound to a feudal lord or estate SERF, VILLEIN
– farm worker during the U.S. depression who was impoverished and uprooted OKIE
– farm worker in Scotland renting a cottage and smallholding COTTER
– farm workers or peasants in an Arab country FELLAHIN
– farmhouse and adjoining buildings and land HOMESTEAD
– farming cooperative in Israel, consisting of a group of small farms MOSHAV
– farming estate, especially in Latin America or ancient Rome LATIFUNDIUM
– large farm for sheep or cattle in Australia STATION

farmer, especially a U.S. tenant farmer, who pays rent in the form of crops SHARECROPPER
– farmer holding his own land YEOMAN
– farmer of a smallholding, especially in Scotland CROFTER
– farmer or rancher rearing livestock on grazing land GRAZIER
– farmer who rents his land from another rather than owning it himself TENANT FARMER
– large-scale sheep- or cattle-farmer in Australia PASTORALIST, SQUATTER

farming AGRICULTURE, HUSBANDRY
– farming of a kind in which the farmer and his family consume most of the produce, with little surplus for marketing SUBSISTENCE FARMING
– referring or relating to farming based on large amounts of capital and labour rather than on large stretches of land INTENSIVE
– referring or relating to farming of large stretches of land with little labour or capital expense EXTENSIVE
– referring to the farming of corn or other crops ARABLE
– referring to the farming of livestock, particularly sheep PASTORAL
– relating to farming or farming land AGRARIAN, AGRICULTURAL

farming- AGR-, AGRI-, AGRO-

fascinating, tempting, attractive ALLURING

Fascism – bundle of rods with a projecting axehead, a symbol of Italian Fascism FASCES

fashion – fashion-conscious man, whose chief interest is in clothes and manners BEAU, DANDY, FOP, SWELL, PETIT MAÎTRE
– fashion or popularity VOGUE
– designer, maker, and seller of fashionable clothing for women COUTURIER, MODISTE
– forefront of, or early participants in, an artistic fashion, political movement, or the like VANGUARD
– high fashion, or fashionable clothes HAUTE COUTURE
– latest fashion DERNIER CRI
– person who starts or popularises a fashion or fad TRENDSETTER
– swirl within a current, as of a river or a fashion EDDY

fashionable, elegant, or sophisticated CHIC, SOIGNÉ
– fashionable, in keeping with current style À LA MODE
– fashionable gathering of or a reception for intellectuals, celebrities, or the like SALON
– fashionable man widely seen in public, man-about-town BOULEVARDIER
– fashionable or pretty in a pretentious or affected way CHICHI
– fashionable society BEAU MONDE
– relating to clothing, especially fashionable men's clothing SARTORIAL

fast See **quick**

fast observed by Muslims during the ninth month of their calendar, or the month itself RAMADAN

fast- TACH-, TACHY-, TACHEO-

fasten See **join**

fastener or clasp hinged over a fixed staple, and typically secured with a padlock HASP
– fastener or metal pin with two flexible arms, as for securing a wheel to an axle SPLIT PIN, COTTER PIN
– fastening device, such as a strap or grommet, for securing ropes, spars, or oars on a boat or ship BECKET
– fastening device consisting of a bolt tightened by a peg-like crosspiece TOGGLE BOLT
– fastening device consisting of two strips of fabric with minute interlocking nylon hooks and loops VELCRO
– bent metal bar fastening stones or timbers together, as in a wall CRAMP IRON, AGRAFFE
– clamp, beam, or the like for fastening or steadying something in position BRACE
– double-headed bolt or pin, typically used for fastening metal plates together RIVET

fat See also **fatty**
– fat, bulky yet typically sleek-looking CORPULENT, PORTLY, ROTUND, SONSY
– fat, especially chicken fat, used in cooking SCHMALTZ
– fat, such as butter or lard, as used to make crumbly biscuits or flaky pastry SHORTENING
– fat, well-fed appearance, plumpness, stoutness EMBONPOINT
– fat belly PAUNCH, CORPORATION
– fat in its hard or solidified form STEARIN
– fat in living cells LIPID
– fat of a whale, forming in a layer beneath its skin BLUBBER
– fat-streaks or mottling of fat on high-quality beef MARBLING
– acid found in solid fat, used in making soap and candles STEARIC ACID
– extremely fat, dangerously overweight OBESE, BLOATED
– hard fatty substance extracted from beef or mutton fat, formerly used in making candles TALLOW
– melt, extract, or convert fat by heating RENDER
– purify butter or fat by gentle heating CLARIFY
– short fat person SQUAB, DUMPLING
– slightly fat in an attractive way, as a plump shapely woman is BUXOM
– stale, decomposing, smelling off, as old butter or bacon fat might be RANCID

fat- LIPO-, SEBI-, SEBO-, STEAT-, STEATO-

fate, certain outcome DESTINY, LOT, PORTION
– fate or destiny, especially in Hinduism and Buddhism KARMA
– fate or destiny, in Eastern or Muslim countries KISMET
– fated, certain to happen, as if decreed in advance by providence PREDESTINED, FOREORDAINED, PREDETERMINED, FOREDOOMED
– accept one's fate, submit to destiny DREE ONE'S WEIRD
– appear or occur as an unexpected but important factor, as fate is said to do INTERVENE
– inescapable, unavoidable, as one's fate is INELUCTABLE
– rendezvous, as with one's lover or with fate TRYST
– unpredictable action or twist, as of fate QUIRK

Fates in Roman mythology PARCAE

father, be the parent of BEGET, SIRE
– father, term of address for a Roman Catholic priest PADRE

– father of a family, viewed as the head of the household PATERFAMILIAS
– father or founder of a tribe, tradition, or the like PATRIARCH
– adjective for a father PATERNAL
– informal or mock formal term for a father PATER
– murder of one's father PATRICIDE
– name based on one's father's name PATRONYMIC
– relating or referring to descent traced through the father PATRILINEAL
– reputed or commonly considered, as a child's supposed father might be PUTATIVE

father- PATR-, PATRI-

Father Time – Death viewed as Father Time with his scythe GRIM REAPER

fatherhood, or origin or descent from a father PATERNITY

fatty, oily, greasy PINGUID, SEBACEOUS, UNCTUOUS, OLEAGINOUS
– fatty, relating to animal fat ADIPOSE
– fatty material, as on the thighs and buttocks CELLULITE
– fatty substance formed from oils in a whale's head, used for cosmetics, ointments, and candles SPERMACETI
– fatty substance produced by the skin glands SEBUM, SMEGMA

fault – fault-finding, critical in a petty, nitpicking way CARPING, CAPTIOUS, CAVILLING, NIGGLING
– fault in the Earth's surface DISLOCATION
– fault or impairment, as in a body organ DYSFUNCTION
– fault or sin considered petty or trifling PECCADILLO
– minor personal fault or shortcoming, character flaw or demerit FOIBLE
– person given to petty criticism, quibbler, fault-finder MOMUS, PETTIFOGGER
– technical fault, mechanical breakdown, malfunction GLITCH

faultless, flawless, unblemished IMMACULATE, UNIMPEACHABLE, IMPECCABLE

faulty- DYS-

favour or an equivalent-value item given in exchange or compensation for another QUID PRO QUO
– favour or service for which the recipient is indebted OBLIGATION
– ask favours persistently IMPORTUNE, HECTOR
– curry favour for oneself with others, as by flattery INGRATIATE, FAWN, KOWTOW, TRUCKLE
– given as a favour rather than out of legal obligation, as a payment might be EX GRATIA
– restore oneself to favour REDEEM ONESELF
– trying to gain favour by excessive flattery, humility, or obligingness INGRATIATING, TOADYING, SYCOPHANTIC, SERVILE, FAWNING, UNCTUOUS, OBSEQUIOUS

favourable, advantageous, healthy BENEFICIAL, BENIGN, BENIGNANT
– favourable, promising AUSPICIOUS, PROPITIOUS
– favourable or "cosmetic" presentation of awkward facts or policies, as by their careful selection WINDOW DRESSING

favouring one particular view, especially a controversial one, biased TENDENTIOUS
– favouring or supporting a single cause or party in a prejudiced way PARTISAN

favouring- PRO-

favourite, darling MINION
– favourite place to visit HAUNT

favouritism, such as the giving of political appointments or promotions to relatives, by those in positions of power NEPOTISM

fear See also **phobia, scared**
– fear of or anxiety over the future APPREHENSION
– feared or respected as awesome or very impressive FORMIDABLE, REDOUBTABLE
– back or shy away in fear COWER, CRINGE, FLINCH, WINCE, RECOIL, QUAIL, BLENCH
– calm or reduce someone's fear, anger, or the like ALLAY, LULL
– disguise or hide something, such as one's fear DISSEMBLE
– dispel or lay to rest someone's fears QUELL
– exaggerated, psychologically unhealthy, as a fear might be MORBID
– feeling or situation of sudden dismay, fear, and confusion CONSTERNATION
– irrational, uncontrollable fear or hatred of some particular thing PHOBIA
– object or thought causing persistent but often needless fear BUGBEAR, BUGABOO, BOGEY, CHIMERA, HOBGOBLIN
– shiver or thrill of fear or excitement FRISSON
– state of fear or panic FUNK
– state of nervous fear, dread, alarm TREPIDATION
– sudden feeling of anxiety or fear, misgiving QUALM
– tremble or shake, as with fear PALPITATE
– unconscious, as secret fears or painful memories might be REPRESSED

-fear -PHOBE, -PHOBIA, -PHOBIC

feast See also **holiday**
– feast, holiday, carnival, or celebration FIESTA
– feast that is plentiful or luxurious, but only in appearance or by report BARMECIDAL FEAST
– luxurious or elaborate, as a feast might be LUCULLAN
– relating to a feast, festival, or festivity, especially a joyous one FESTAL
– weekday that is not a feast day FERIA

Feast of Lights, "Feast of Dedication" in the Jewish calendar CHANUKKAH

feat of outstanding skill or strength TOUR DE FORCE
– feat or exploit of note GEST

feather, ribbon, or rosette worn on the hat, especially by soldiers COCKADE
– feather, specifically a flight feather PINION
– feather, wing, fin, or similar projecting body part PINNA
– feather on an arrow VANE
– feather or plume on a helmet or hat PANACHE
– feather or trimming of feathers, as formerly used on women's hats OSPREY
– feather-shaped PINNATE
– feathered cork used in badminton SHUTTLECOCK
– feathered or winged PENNATE
– flat side section of a feather VANE, VEXILLUM, WEB
– hollow main shaft of a feather QUILL, CALAMUS, RACHIS, BARREL, SCAPE
– opening or small hole in the shaft of a feather UMBILICUS
– small parallel filaments, attached to the shaft, forming the flat sides of a feather BARBS

feather- PTERO-

feathers See also **bird**
– feathers PLUMAGE
– feathers, especially an egret's tail feathers, used for a plume, as on a hat AIGRETTE
– feathers in or around a bird's ears, as on the owl AURICULARS
– feathers of a bird's back and wings when of a diffferent colour from the other feathers MANTLE
– feathers or hair projecting from an animal's neck FRILL, RUFF
– feathers or hairs on the back of an animal's neck HACKLES
– any of the large curving feathers on a cock's tail SICKLE FEATHER
– any of the large visible feathers

on a bird's plumage, as opposed to the down feathers PENNA
– any of the small feathers clustered at the base of a main feather on a bird's wing or tail TECTRIX, COVERT
– any of the stiff flight feathers on a bird's wing REMEX
– any of the stiff main feathers, regulating flight, in a bird's tail RECTRIX
– bristly feathers near the beak of an insect-eating bird VIBRISSAE
– clean the feathers with the beak PREEN
– cover with, or develop feathers FLEDGE
– erect the feathers RUFFLE
– outer feathers on a bird's body, determining its characteristic shape CONTOUR FEATHERS
– shed feathers or fur, as many animals do MOULT
– still without feathers, as a young bird might be CALLOW, UNFLEDGED

feature or aspect, as of someone's personality FACET
– feature that makes up or compensates for faults or deficiencies REDEEMING FEATURE, MITIGATING FACTOR
– features, marks, or characteristics of a very distinctive or important kind LINEAMENTS
– bent or twisted out of shape, as a person's features might be CONTORTED

fee, as paid initially to a barrister, or regularly to an occasional consultant RETAINER
– fee, usually small, paid for a service that is technically free HONORARIUM
– fee, wages, or other form of profit from one's job or office EMOLUMENT
– fee or percentage paid to a salesman or agent for successfully completed services COMMISSION
– fee paid for instruction TUITION

feed, nourish NURTURE

feeding by means of a tube down the throat, especially force-feeding GAVAGE
– feeding on all kinds of food, both meat and plant foods OMNIVOROUS
– feeding on ants, as anteaters do MYRMECOPHAGOUS
– feeding on corpses or carrion NECROPHAGOUS
– feeding on dung, as some beetles and flies do COPROPHAGOUS, SCATOPHAGOUS
– feeding on fish PISCIVOROUS
– feeding on fruit, as some bats do FRUGIVOROUS, CARPOPHAGOUS
– feeding on grasses, seeds, or grains GRAMINIVOROUS, GRANIVOROUS
– feeding on insects, as some birds and mammals do ENTOMOPHAGOUS, INSECTIVOROUS
– feeding on leaves, as some insects do PHYLLOPHAGOUS
– feeding on many kinds of food POLYPHAGOUS
– feeding on meat from time to time, or feeding exclusively on meat CARNIVOROUS
– feeding on plants, as an insect might PHYTOPHAGOUS
– feeding on plants only, as many animals do HERBIVOROUS
– feeding on wood, as some insects do XYLOPHAGOUS
– feeding trough in a stable or barn MANGER

-feeding on -VOROUS, -PHAGOUS

feel and return the same emotion as someone feels towards oneself RECIPROCATE
– feel around for or scratch about with the hands, grope GRABBLE
– sensitive to emotion or suffering, able to feel, or sympathise PASSIBLE

feelers on the head of an insect, crustacean, or the like ANTENNAE
– feelers or sensory organs near the mouth, as in some insects and shellfish PALPS, PALPI

feeling See also **emotional**
– feeling, as distinct from thought or perception SENTIENCE
– feeling for language, an "ear" for what is correct or appropriate SPRACHGEFÜHL
– feeling of doubt, social unease, troubled conscience, or the like MISGIVING, SCRUPLE, QUALM
– feeling of great happiness, joy, or delight ECSTASY, RAPTURE, TRANSPORT
– feeling of having undergone previously an experience that one is now having for the first time DÉJÀ VU
– feeling of illness, unease, or depression MALAISE
– feeling of impending disaster or evil FOREBODING
– feeling or emotion in psychology, usually associated with a particular idea or thought AFFECT
– feeling or sense of something about to happen FOREBODING, PREMONITION, PRESENTIMENT
– feeling or showing no emotion IMPASSIVE
– feelings conveyed, often unconsciously, by one person or group to another VIBES
– assigning of human feelings or characteristics to inanimate or natural objects, as in poetic metaphors PATHETIC FALLACY
– depth, as of feeling, meaning, or thinking PROFUNDITY
– examine a part of the body by feeling it with the hands, for a preliminary medical diagnosis PALPATE
– expressing emotions or one's feelings openly DEMONSTRATIVE
– fine feeling, keen power of perception, sensitive openness to emotional influences SENSIBILITY, SUSCEPTIBILITY
– have specific feelings ENTERTAIN, NOURISH, HARBOUR
– hide one's true feelings or intentions by pretending DISSIMULATE
– understanding of another that is so deep that one seems to enter into or share his feelings EMPATHY
– used for feeling and touching, as an insect's antenna is TACTILE
– vague feeling or intuition, hint, inkling INTIMATION
– wound or hurt someone's feelings, as for instance by severe criticism SCARIFY

-feeling -PATHY

feet See also **foot**
– feet or hands EXTREMITIES
– beat with a stick, especially on the soles of the feet BASTINADO
– care of or treatment for the feet and toenails PEDICURE, CHIROPODY
– chains or bands around the ankles or feet FETTERS, SHACKLES
– fettered iron bar, formerly used for shackling prisoners' feet BILBOES
– turned outwards, as feet might be SPLAY
– walking, or one's own legs or feet, as a means of travel SHANKS'S PONY

-feet- -PEDI-, -PEDE, PEDI-, -POD, -PODE

feign See **pretend**

fellow countryman, person from the same country as another person COMPATRIOT
– fellow worker in a joint effort COADJUTANT, COADJUTOR, COLLABORATOR

fellowship, brotherhood, community of feeling or interests FRATERNITY, SODALITY, FREEMASONRY

female behaviour and dress adopted by a man EONISM, TRANSVESTISM
– female club or social group, as at a U.S. university SORORITY
– female demon supposed to have sexual intercourse with a sleeping man SUCCUBUS
– "female hormone" OESTROGEN
– female principle or personality

in a man's unconscious, in Jungian psychology ANIMA
– female side or maternal line of a family DISTAFF SIDE, SPINDLE SIDE
– fastening of the female genitals with clasps or stitches to prevent sexual intercourse INFIBULATION
– related through the female line of a family, especially having the same mother but different fathers UTERINE
– relating to the female line of descent MATRILINEAL

-female- -GYN-, GYNO-, -ESS, -TRESS, -TRIX

femininity or womanhood MULIEBRITY

feminist symbol or emblem, in the form of a double-headed axe LABYRIS

fence, hedge, or row of trees designed to break the force of the wind WINDBREAK
– fence, line, or the like protecting or marking the boundary of an area PERIMETER
– fence-making material of poles interlaced with reeds, sticks, or the like WATTLE
– fence of barbed wire or sharpened stakes FRAISE
– fence of pointed upright stakes PICKET FENCE, PALING
– fence of wood temporarily surrounding a construction site or the like HOARDING
– fence of wooden stakes serving as a fortification PALISADE, STOCKADE
– board forming the top rail of a fence or balustrade LEDGER BOARD

fenced enclosure for cattle or horses in the U.S. CORRAL
– fenced enclosure for cattle or sheep in South Africa KRAAL
– fenced-in field, as for horses and other farm animals PADDOCK

fencing See chart, and also **sword**
– types of sword used in modern fencing competitions SABRE, FOIL, ÉPÉE

fermentation – chemistry of fermentation in brewing ZYMURGY
– fermenting grape juice MUST, STUM

fermentation- ZYMO-

fern leaf FROND
– feathery fern with fan-shaped leaves MAIDENHAIR
– hooked or coiled tip of a young fern frond CROSIER
– large, coarse fern BRACKEN
– primitive seed-bearing plant, resembling a palm, but having fernlike leaves and seed cones CYCAD
– reproductive cell or organ in non-flowering plants such as mosses, ferns, and fungi SPORE
– stalk, as of a mushroom or a frond of fern or seaweed STIPE

ferret, weasel, badger, otter, or related animal MUSTELINE

ferryboat, steamer taking a regular route PACKET

fertile, capable of reproduction PROGENITIVE
– fertile area in a desert OASIS
– fertile or productive, producing many offspring, crops, creative works, or the like FECUND, PROLIFIC

fertilisation of a plant by its own pollen, self-fertilisation AUTOGAMY
– fertilisation of one plant by another, cross-pollination XENOGAMY
– referring to fertilisation induced in an artificial laboratory environment rather than occurring naturally in the womb IN VITRO

fertilise an egg IMPREGNATE
– fertilise by pollen POLLINATE
– fertilise or make pregnant FECUNDATE
– fertilised egg or ovum ZYGOTE
– sperm cell, ovum, or other cell that can combine to form a fertilised cell GAMETE

fertiliser, lime, or the like added to improve soil DRESSING
– fertiliser consisting of human excrement NIGHT SOIL
– fertiliser from coastal deposits of the dried dung of sea birds GUANO
– fertiliser or protective humus for young plants MULCH
– chemical compounds commonly used in fertilisers PHOSPHATE, POTASH, NITRATE
– conversion of nitrogen in the air into a fertiliser or other compound FIXATION
– decayed organic matter that fertilises the soil HUMUS

FENCING TERMS

appel	stamping of the foot as a feint
balestra	attacking movement in the form of a short jump forward
barrage	deciding heat in the event of a draw
coquille	guard at the end of the blade, protecting the hand
en garde	term warning a fencer to take the starting position for a bout
épée	sword with a triangular, fluted, blunt blade and a bell-shaped guard
feint	false attack, intended to create an opening for a final thrust
flèche	running attack, a short quick run forward
foible	weaker half of the blade, nearer the point
foil	light sword, with a blunt point, for competition, practice, and teaching
forte	stronger half of the blade, nearer the handle
parry, parade	defensive action, deflecting the attacker's blade
piste	long rectangular area in which bouts take place
plastron	protective quilted covering for the upper body and armpit
remise	renewed attack, made without returning to the en garde position
reprise	renewed attack, made after returning to the en garde position
riposte	attacking movement following a successful parry
sabre	cut-and-thrust sword, with a slightly flattened blade and a half-circular guard
touché	word used to acknowledge a hit by one's opponent
volt	sudden movement made to dodge a thrust

festival See **holidays**
– festival or religious celebration, as on a saint's day, especially in a Spanish-speaking country FIESTA
– festival parade or costumed procession PAGEANT, CAVALCADE

-festival -MAS

fetch, carry back RETRIEVE

feud, maintained by a cycle of revenge VENDETTA

feudal system See chart

fever See also **disease**
– fever AGUE, PYREXIA
– fever, especially a mild tropical fever CALENTURE

FEUDAL AND MEDIEVAL TERMS

allodium	land held in absolute ownership, rather than subject to feudal restrictions	**hue and cry**	pursuit of a felon with shouts and cries; legal duty to join such pursuit
attainder	forfeiture of land and civil rights imposed upon outlaws and condemned felons	**liege**	lord to whom feudal service is due; vassal, liegeman owing allegiance to a lord
benevolences	"voluntary" payments made to earn the goodwill of the king	**marshal**	senior member of the king's household, especially a judicial adviser
ceorl/churl	lowest-ranking freeman	**mesne lord**	feudal lord holding land from a superior
chamberlain	principal financial officer of the king's household	**moot/gemot**	meeting, assembly or court
commonage	right of pasture on common land	**murage**	tax levied to maintain or build city walls
constable	chief military officer of the king's household	**pannage**	right of a villein to pasture his pigs in woodland; rent paid for this right
corvée	day's unpaid labour owed by a vassal to his lord	**pardoner**	layman commissioned to sell ecclesiastical indulgences
cottar	villein granted a cottage and land in return for work	**quitrent**	rent paid by a freeman in lieu of various feudal services
demesne	lands kept by a feudal lord for his own use	**reeve**	high-ranking local administrative officer; bailiff or steward
droit de seigneur	rights of a feudal lord over his vassals, specifically his supposed right to have sexual intercourse with a vassal's new bride	**scutage**	tax paid in lieu of doing military service
ealdorman/ alderman	chief officer of a shire	**seneschal**	steward, official in charge of servants and domestic arrangements in a noble household
escheat	return of lands to a feudal lord, as when the tenant has no heir	**serf**	peasant bound to the land and its lord in an almost slave-like condition
esquire/ squire	candidate for knighthood in the service of a knight	**socage**	holding of land by a tenant in return for payment or services
fealty	allegiance owed by a vassal or tenant to his feudal lord	**suzerain, seigneur**	feudal lord or overlord
fee/feoff/ fief/feud	feudal land granted by a lord to a vassal in return for homage and service	**thane/thegn**	freeman ranking above a churl but below a noble
franklin	landowning commoner, country gentleman	**tithe**	annual tax of one-tenth of a person's income and produce, paid to support the Church
frankpledge	joint responsibility among members of a tithing for the good conduct of the others	**tithing**	group of ten householders bound together by a system of mutual responsibility for good conduct
geld	tax or tribute paid to the Crown	**vassal**	liegeman or feudal tenant owing allegiance to a lord
glebe	land endowed to a parish church		
grange	farm building in which grain paid as tithes was stored	**vavasor/ vavasour**	knightly vassal ranking just below a baron, and having other vassals subject to him
hide	amount of land adequate to support a peasant family	**villein**	semi-freeman, owing some rents and services to his lord, but not in bondage
homage	formal acknowledgment of allegiance by a vassal to a feudal lord	**witan, witenagemot**	national assembly in Anglo-Saxon England, consisting of noblemen advising the king

– fever or extremely high body temperature HYPERPYREXIA, HYPERTHERMIA
– fever-reducing, as a drug might be ANTIPYRETIC
– chill or shivering attack, as preceding a fever RIGOR
– mentally confused or agitated, as during a high fever DELIRIOUS
– recurring daily, as attacks of a fever might be QUOTIDIAN
– relating to inflammation and fever PHLOGISTIC
– subsiding or ending of a fever, inflammation, or disease RESOLUTION

fever- FEBRI-

feverish, bustling HECTIC
– feverish or relating to fever FEBRILE, PYRETIC

few- OLIGO-

fewness or scarcity PAUCITY

fiancé or fiancée BETHROTHED

fibre See also **fabric**
– thin wire, thread, or the like FILAMENT
– fibre from coconut husks, as used for ropes and matting COIR
– fibre from palm leaves used for weaving baskets or mats RAFFIA
– fibre from which linen is made, or the plant producing it FLAX
– fibre in the diet ROUGHAGE
– fibre of hemp or jute, often treated with tar, used for sealing pipe points and caulking the seams in wooden ships OAKUM
– fibre used in making ropes, or the tropical plant whose leaves yield the fibre SISALL
– fibre used in pillows, for soundproofing, and so on KAPOK
– fibre used in sacking HEMP, JUTE
– fibres, typically in a silky mass, as from cotton, maize, or silkworm cocoons FLOSS
– hard fibre used for making twine MAGUEY, CANTALA
– short, broken fibre, as of flax or hemp, used for yarn, stuffing, or the like TOW
– synthetic fibre ACRYLIC, ORLON
– thin, flexible fibre for transmission of light and telecommunications messages, as round corners OPTICAL FIBRE
– tough tropical fibre, as used for making rope and paper ABACA, MANILA HEMP

fickle, changing constantly or liable to change LABILE, TAFFETA
– fickleness, unsteadiness, inconstancy LEVITY

fictional place or imaginary world or land where things are better than in real life UTOPIA, COCKAIGNE, SHANGRI-LA
– fictional place or imaginary world or land where things are worse than in real life DYSTOPIA, CACOTOPIA

fictitious, imaginary MYTHICAL, CHIMERIC

field, plot of land held by a parson as part of his benefice GLEBE
– field of study, academic subject or speciality DISCIPLINE
– field or province of activity, sphere of operation or expertise PRESERVE, DOMAIN, BAILIWICK
– field or range of possible activity, scope, reach AMBIT, ORBIT, COMPASS
– enclosed field or pasture CROFT
– grassy field or meadow LEA
– ploughed but left unseeded, as a field might be, to regain fertility for a season FALLOW
– relating to open country or uncultivated fields CAMPESTRAL

FIGURES OF SPEECH AND RHETORICAL DEVICES

alliteration	use of words starting with or containing the same letter or sound: *The furrow followed free*
anacoluthon	grammatically inconsistent sentence or phrase, with a shift of construction midway: *My advice is, since time is running out, shouldn't you get started at once?*
anadiplosis	repetition of a word or group of words at the end of one phrase and beginning of the next one, for rhetorical effect: *At dawn — the dawn that would restore hope*
anastrophe	rhetorical inversion of normal word order: *Full many a glorious morning have I seen*
antiphrasis	ironic or playful use of words in an opposite sense: *Eighty years young*
antithesis	expression in which contrasting ideas are carefully balanced: *More haste, less speed*
antonomasia	use of a personal name or proper noun to refer to anyone belonging to a class; for example *an Einstein* to refer to a genius
aposiopesis, ellipsis	omission of words, or sudden breaking off in mid-sentence, for dramatic effect: *The door opened, and ...*
apostrophe	direct address to an absent or dead person or personified thing: *O Freedom! hear my call!*
assonance	repetition of vowel sounds, producing a half-rhyme effect: *Slow progress across the cold plateau*
asyndeton	omission of conjunctions: *I came, I saw, I conquered*
chiasmus	rhetorical device in which the grammatical structure of one phrase is reversed in the second, as in: *As they came out, in went we*
euphemism	use of an inoffensive expression to stand in for a sharper or more explicit one; for example, *passed away* for *died*
hendiadys	use of two nouns joined by *and* to express an idea that would normally be expressed by an adjective and noun; or a similarly expanded phrase; for example, *through storm and weather* instead of *through stormy weather*
hyperbole	exaggeration or overstatement for emphasis: *I could eat a horse*
irony	use of word or words to convey something markedly different from the literal meaning: *I don't suppose you want to hear that you've just won the jackpot*
litotes, meiosis	understatement in which an idea is tellingly conveyed, typically by contradicting its opposite: *He's not exactly sober*

– ridge or bank bordering a river or irrigated field LEVEE
-field- AGR-, AGRI-, AGRO-, -DROME
fierce See **cruel**
fifth QUINARY
– fifth anniversary QUINQUENNIAL
fifty-year-old, or a person who is aged between 50 and 59 inclusive QUINQUAGENARIAN
fig, fruit of the fig tree SYCONIUM
fight See also **attack**, **dispute**, **hostile**
– fight back, attack in revenge RETALIATE
– fight or argument, within a larger conflict, in which outsiders often get caught up CROSSFIRE
– fight or campaign in favour of a cause CRUSADE
– fight or combat between two mounted knights armed with lances JOUST, TILTING MATCH
– fight or oppose TILT AT
– fighting imaginary enemies, "shadow boxing" SCIAMACHY
– angry conflict or disagreement, often with bitter fighting STRIFE, FRICTION, DISSENSION
– angry quarrel or fight, clash ALTERCATION, CONTRETEMPS
– brawl, scuffle, disorderly fight or free-for-all, dust-up FRAY, SHINDY, MÊLÉE, TUSSLE
– deeply involved in a fight, scandal, or the like EMBROILED
– engaged in a fight or running argument, seriously in dispute AT LOGGERHEADS
– given to fighting, easily provoked or antagonised FRACTIOUS, TRUCULENT, PUGNACIOUS
– hostile encounter, fight or conflict CONFRONTATION
– minor fight or conflict, sometimes preliminary to a major battle SKIRMISH
– noisy fight or quarrel, rowdy brawl AFFRAY, BROIL, DONNYBROOK, FRACAS
– person who fights publicly for a cause he supports GLADIATOR
– petty fight or quarrel TIFF, SPAT
– referring to destructive fighting or conflict within a group INTERNECINE
– stir into a fighting mood MAKE ONE'S HACKLES RISE
fighter See **soldier**
figure – shapely and narrow-waisted, as a woman's figure might be HOURGLASS
-figure -GON
figure of speech See chart
– figure of speech, or figurative use of language, as for rhetorical effect TROPE
– based on or using figures of speech, metaphorical FIGURATIVE
– clever and elaborate figure of speech, especially an ingenious metaphor CONCEIT
figurine, usually crouched and grotesque, of Chinese or Japanese carving MAGOT
file, grate, or scrape RASP
– file for wood- or metalworking that is long, thin, and cylindrical RAT'S TAIL
– file or collection of papers giving information on a particular person or subject DOSSIER
– file or similar scraping tool with a curved face RIFFLER
– file with metal rings for holding loose leaves RING BINDER
– shape or enlarge a hole, as in wood, with a special cylindrical file REAM
fill, spread widely, or permeate with something damaging RIDDLE
– fill or resupply something, such

malapropism	word misused through confusion with a similar sounding word, sometimes deliberately for comic effect: *He's being used as a prawn in the game*	**rhetorical question, erotema**	question asked for effect or to convey information rather than to elicit an answer: *Isn't it a lovely day?*
metaphor	description of one thing in terms of another that is related to it by analogy: *She sailed across the room*	**simile**	comparison of two unlike ideas or objects, using the word *like* or *as* to make it explicit: *Lips like rosebuds, kisses like wine*
metonymy	use of a term to refer to some wider idea that it characterises: for example, *the Crown* referring to the monarchy	**syllepsis**	use of a single word to apply to two others, in different ways: *He held his tongue and my hand*
onomatopoeia	use of words whose sound suggests their meaning: for example, *sizzle, splash, ping-pong*	**synecdoche**	use of the name for a part to refer to the whole, or vice versa; for example, *fifty sail* to refer to fifty ships
oxymoron	linking of incongruous or contradictory terms: *The wisest fool in Christendom*	**tautology**	repetition of an idea by needless or emphatic use of words: *Reverse backwards and then do a U-turn to face the other way*
pathetic fallacy	assigning of human feelings or characteristics to natural or inanimate objects: *The trees groaned*	**tmesis**	separation of the parts of a word by the insertion of another word: *Abso-bloody-lutely*
personification, prosopopoeia	representation of an object or idea as human: *The jovial Moon smiling benignly down at us*	**transferred epithet, hypallage**	deliberate misapplication of an adjective to a noun, for a compact or dramatic effect: *A sleepless night; the poisoned cup; the condemned cell*
pleonasm	use of superfluous or redundant words: *How did the story end up?*	**zeugma**	use of a single word to apply to two others, especially when it is appropriate to only one; a faulty syllepsis: *He held his tongue and his promise*
polysyndeton	repetition of conjunctions for rhetorical effect: *Went to Florence and Venice and Rome and Naples*		

as a larder REPLENISH
– fill someone with or feed into someone knowledge, principles, or the like IMBUE, PERMEATE, PERVADE, INCULCATE, INSTIL
– fill something with a substance or introduce it into something, as by soaking IMPREGNATE, INFUSE, SATURATE, SUFFUSE
– filled, as with food or drink, satisfied to the point of excess SATED, SATIATED, REPLETE, GLUTTED, GORGED
– filled to excess with blood or other fluid ENGORGED
– overfilled or overcrowded, as a room might be CONGESTED

filler, glaze, or coating, as for paper or walls, made of wax, clay, glue, resin, or the like SIZE

filling – mercury alloy, such as that used by dentists as a filling for teeth AMALGAM

film See also chart
– film, book, or the like dealing with events earlier than those in the previous one PREQUEL
– film, book, or the like dealing with events following those in the previous one SEQUEL
– film, book, or the like, mixing fact and fiction FACTION
– film buff, cinema enthusiast, creative film-maker or critic CINEASTE
– film camera or projector CINEMATOGRAPH
– film library or repertory cinema CINEMATHEQUE
– film-making as an art or technique CINEMATOGRAPHY
– film or television programme intended as an accurate history or analysis but using actors and dramatic reconstructions DOCUDRAMA
– film or television programme presented as a non-fictional analysis or history DOCUMENTARY
– film projector of an early type BIOSCOPE
– accumulation of a thin film of a substance on the surface of a solid ADSORPTION
– blank length of tape, used for threading, at the beginning or end of a reel of film or tape LEADER
– brief scene in a film, book, or play VIGNETTE
– category of literature, films, or the like GENRE
– early or afternoon screening of a film MATINÉE
– extract or selected passage or scene from a book, film, or the like EXCERPT
– first public presentation of a film, play, or the like PREMIERE
– join two strips of film, rope, or the like at the ends SPLICE
– place something over or on top of something else, such as one film sequence on another SUPERIMPOSE
– pornographic film STAG FILM
– prepare, treat, or rectify something, such as cheese or film, by a special method PROCESS
– review or criticism of a book, film, play, or the like CRITIQUE
– scene or passage in a film, novel, or the like that interrupts the main story line to revert to previous events FLASHBACK
– single exposure on a strip of film FRAME
– toy producing simple film-like images, consisting of a picture-lined cylinder revolving past a viewing slit ZOETROPE
– vegetable matter used in making paper, rayon, and photographic film CELLULOSE

film- CINE-

filter or sift PERCOLATE
– clay used in filtering FULLER'S EARTH
– technique for filtering impurities from the blood of patients with kidney failure DIALYSIS
– pass through a filter or filter-like obstruction INFILTRATE

filthy See **dirty**

fin See also **fish**
– fin, wing, feather, or similar projecting body part PINNA
– fin on a bomb or missile for guiding or stabilising it VANE
– bony spines supporting a fish's fin RAYS

final and decisive, allowing of no refusal or argument, as a command might be PEREMPTORY
– final or farewell appearance, act, work, or statement SWAN SONG
– final or highest point CULMINATION
– final part of a formal speech or written discourse, typically a summing-up PERORATION
– final part of the action in a play or novel, resolving or unravelling the plot DÉNOUEMENT
– final part or element of something OMEGA
– final poem or speech following the end of a play EPILOGUE
– final section, often an afterthought or addition, of a novel, piece of music, or the like CODA
– final terms offered in negotiating, to be accepted "or else" ULTIMATUM
– final touch, finishing act COUP DE GRÂCE
– make something decided or final, such as an argument or bargain CLINCH

final- TEL-, TELEO-

finance See also **economics**
– finance, guarantee against financial failure UNDERWRITE
– finance a project, support an institution, or the like by means of a grant of money SUBSIDISE
– finance office of a college or university BURSARY
– relating to finances, especially those of a country or government department FISCAL

financial centre or powerful financial interests in the British economy THE CITY, LOMBARD STREET
– financial centre or powerful financial interests in the Canadian economy BAY STREET
– financial centre or powerful financial interests in the U.S. economy WALL STREET
– financial director COMPTROLLER
– financial grant, such as an endowment SUBVENTION
– financial obligation LIABILITY
– financial supporter or promoter of a project, sportsman, cultural activity, sport, or the like SPONSOR, PATRON
– financially in a position to meet all debts SOLVENT
– financially restrictive, characterised by a scarcity of loan money STRINGENT

finch, sparrow, or related bird FRINGILLID

find, bring to light, dig up, root out UNEARTH
– find or discover by painstaking research or observation DESCRY
– find out the meaning of, come to understand FATHOM
– find out with difficulty WINKLE OUT, PRISE OUT
– finding one's bearings, socially or spatially ORIENTATION
– exclamation of triumph on finding, solving, or discovering something EUREKA
– tendency to make fortunate finds by chance SERENDIPITY

fine distinction or subtle point or detail NICETY
– fine or damages imposed by a court in former times AMERCEMENT
– fine or similar penalty MULCT
– impose or collect a tax, fine, membership fee, or the like LEVY

fine arts BEAUX-ARTS

finger See also **hand**, **thumb**
– finger, toe, or corresponding part of an animal DIGIT, DACTYL
– finger bones or toe bones PHALANGES

FILMS AND FILMING TERMS

animation	art or process of filming a series of static drawings to give the impression of movement, as for cartoon films
back projection	projection of a film onto the reverse side of a screen, as a background for filming in front of it
best boy	assistant to the gaffer
biopic	biographical film
cameo role	brief but dramatic appearance of a well-known actor
cinéma-vérité	films or filming intended to represent life very realistically
clapperboard	hinged board bearing the take number clapped in front of the camera to synchronise sound and picture prints
commissary	cafeteria in a film studio
compilation film	film using some real-life documentary sequences
continuity	detailed script for ensuring consistency from scene to scene
credits	list of performers and workers in the making of a film
cut-in	inserted shot, typically a still close-up, interrupting a running sequence of film
dissolve	change of scenes, in which one scene fades out as the next appears
dolly	low platform on castors for moving a camera about the set
dub	add a new soundtrack, especially a translation of the dialogue
fade in, fade out	gradual appearance or disappearance of an image or sound
film à clef	apparently fictional film based on facts, but with the names of places and characters changed
footage	sequence or portion of film
freeze frame	repeated single frame, producing the impression of a static picture
gaffer	electrician or lighting technician on a production crew
grip	member of a production crew who adjusts the set and shifts the camera equipment
intercut/ crosscut	insert a shot or scene into a sequence, as for dramatic contrast
klieg light	carbon-arc lamp producing intense light
location	site for filming that is outside the studio
montage	sequence of shots or short scenes depicting the same theme or event in different ways
new wave/ nouvelle vague	French cinema movement of the 1960s that cut down on standard narrative and filming techniques in favour of improvisation, simple settings, and symbolism
opticals	trick techniques such as wipes and dissolves
outtake	series of frames discarded from the finished version of a film
pan	swing the camera sideways, across a scene, to follow a moving object or produce a panoramic effect
rush	first, unedited print of a scene
scenario/ screenplay	script that includes camera directions and scene descriptions
shooting script	script giving details of camera work and the order of shooting
split-screen	referring to the technique in which two or more images appear simultaneously on different parts of the same screen
take	uninterrupted filming of a scene; filmed scene produced in this way, often re-shot several times
time-lapse	referring to the technique of photographing a scene at intervals to give a continuous, accelerated view of a slow process, such as a flower opening
track	move the camera, usually on rails, to follow the action
treatment	full and detailed version of a script
voice-over	commentary of an unseen narrator, or representation on the sound-track of a character's unspoken thoughts
wipe	change of scenes, in which a line moves across to obliterate the old scene and bring in the new
zoom	quick increase or decrease in the size of the image of an object, by means of a special lens

– finger of a glove, or protective sheath for an injured finger or toe STALL
– broad-tipped, as fingers or leaves might be SPATULATE
– fleshy underpart of the top joint of a finger or toe PAD
– flicking of the finger after holding it back with the thumb FILLIP

finger- DACTYL-, DACTYLO-
finger hole as on a flute VENTAGE
fingernail – crescent-shaped mark at the base of a fingernail LUNULA
– strip of hardened skin at the

base of a fingernail CUTICLE

fingerprint See also **hand**
– basic patterns for classifying and identifying fingerprints LOOP, ARCH, WHORL
– informal term for a fingerprint DAB
– scientific study of fingerprints as a technique of identification DACTYLOGRAPHY
– technical term for a fingerprint DACTYLOGRAM

finish See **end**, **stop**
– finish off, dispose of, complete efficiently DISPATCH
– finishing or surface layer, as of fine wood VENEER

finishing point, destination, objective, goal TERMINUS AD QUEM

finishing touch, final action COUP DE GRÂCE

Finnish steam-bath treatment or recreation, typically followed by a cold plunge SAUNA

fir, pine, or related cone-bearing tree CONIFER

fire blazing furiously with hellish flames INFERNO
– fire of a large-scale and destructive kind CONFLAGRATION
– fire sensor that activates an extinguisher or alarm PYROSTAT
– able to cause fire or catch fire INCENDIARY
– attack enemy ground troops with bombs or machine-gun fire from low-flying aircraft STRAFE
– attack or burst of gunfire, rocket fire, or the like SALVO, FUSILLADE
– attack with gunfire from the side, raking the entire length of a troop formation or position ENFILADE
– burning readily, catching fire easily INFLAMMABLE, FLAMMABLE
– catch fire, or set fire to IGNITE
– catching fire without external ignition, as in coal dust or hay self-heated through oxidation SPONTANEOUS COMBUSTION
– cooking pot or large kettle with a hooped handle for hanging over an open fire CAULDRON
– cover a fire with ashes or fresh fuel to keep it burning low BANK
– form of legal trial in the Middle Ages, in which God's judgment was allegedly secured through exposing the accused to fire, immersion in water, or the like ORDEAL
– glowing or smouldering coal or wood, as in a dying fire EMBERS
– great destruction by or as if by fire HOLOCAUST
– hypothetical substance or principle formerly thought to exist in combustible matter and be released in a fire PHLOGISTON
– lizard-like creature in myth, that lived in or withstood fire SALAMANDER
– person who sets fire to property illegally, fire-raiser ARSONIST, INCENDIARY
– put out a fire or flame, extinguish QUENCH, DOUSE
– relating to or resembling fire IGNEOUS
– setting fire to buildings or other property deliberately, for criminal purposes ARSON
– strip or destroy the inside of, as fire might destroy the inside of a building GUT
– three-legged metal stand, as for supporting pots over a fire TRIVET
– twigs, decayed wood, or similar combustible material used to get a fire going TINDER, KINDLING, TOUCHWOOD, SPUNK, PUNK
– twist of paper or sliver of wood for lighting a fire SPILL
– wood pile prepared for a funeral fire on which to cremate a corpse PYRE

fire- PYRO-

fire bomb, bomb designed to start a destructive fire INCENDIARY BOMB
– fire bomb containing highly inflammable jellied petrol NAPALM BOMB
– fire bomb or inflammable substance used in ancient sea warfare GREEK FIRE
– crude fire bomb, such as a petrol bomb, thrown by hand, typically a fuel-filled bottle stoppered with a rag wick MOLOTOV COCKTAIL

fire hose – pavement water pipe for fire hoses HYDRANT

firearm See **gun**

fireball or meteor that is unusually large and bright, and may burn out or explode BOLIDE

fireplace HEARTH
– fireplace frame, often decorated MANTEL
– fireplace rack or stand, as for keeping dishes warm FOOTMAN
– fireplace shelf, as for keeping food warm HOB
– chimney-corner by a fireplace, often with seats facing each other INGLENOOK
– fireguard, metal grid keeping coals or embers within the fireplace FENDER
– metal stand, used in pairs, for logs in a fireplace ANDIRON, FIREDOG
– screen or decorative iron plate at the back of a fireplace REREDOS
– solid residue from a coal-fired furnace or fireplace CLINKER

firework rocket that flies in a winding or spiral path TOURBILLION
– firework that makes a hissing or fizzing sound FIZGIG
– fireworks display or manufacture PYROTECHNICS
– fireworks or jets of water that appear to rotate GIRANDOLE
– loud exploding firework PETARD
– paper casing for the powder in some fireworks CARTOUCHE
– small firework that hisses and then explodes with a bang SQUIB
– smouldering substance, such as knotted rags, used to light fireworks PUNK

firing of guns in a rapid burst FUSILLADE, BARRAGE
– firing platform behind a parapet or in a trench BANQUETTE
– firing simultaneously of all the guns along one side of a warship BROADSIDE
– platform or mound along the wall of a fort, from which cannons are fired over the parapet BARBETTE
– object for firing or throwing, such as a bullet or missile PROJECTILE

firm, established, inherent, or essential SUBSTANTIVE
– firm, loyal, steadfast STAUNCH
– firm, tough, resolute TENACIOUS
– firmly and immovably settled, as opinions or troops might be ENTRENCHED
– firmly fixed or established in position, impossible to release or dislodge INEXTRICABLE

firmness, texture, as of a pudding CONSISTENCY

first, earliest, original PRIMARY, INITIAL, PRIMAL, ARCHETYPAL, PRIMEVAL
– first, second, third, and so on ORDINAL NUMBERS
– first example or model, on which copies or later developments are based PROTOTYPE, ARCHETYPE
– first experience of or exposure to a painful ordeal, especially on the battlefield BAPTISM OF FIRE
– first principle or elementary stage of a skill or subject RUDIMENT
– first public appearance, as of an actor, musician, or the like DEBUT
– first public displaying of a monument, work of art, or the like UNVEILING
– first public presentation of a film, play, or the like PREMIERE
– first success or foothold that opens the way to further achievements BEACHHEAD, BRIDGEHEAD, SALIENT

– ability to take the first step of a plan or project INITIATIVE
– condition of being first PRIMACY
– just beginning to develop, in the first stages of growth EMBRYONIC, SEMINAL, GERMINAL, NASCENT, INCIPIENT, INCHOATE

first- FORE-, PROTO-, UR-

first-aid post near a battlefield DRESSING STATION

first among equals PRIMUS INTER PARES

first-born – state of being the first-born child, or his right to inherit the entire estate or monarchy PRIMOGENITURE

first cousin COUSIN-GERMAN

first-year student of a university or college FRESHER, FRESHMAN

fish See illustration and chart
– fish, such as sharks and rays, whose skeleton is entirely of cartilage rather than hard bone CARTILAGINOUS FISH
– fish, turtles, and other free-swimming animals, in a lake, the sea, or other body of water NEKTON
– fish-eating, feeding on fish PISCIVOROUS
– fish eggs, frog eggs, or the like SPAWN
– fish in lakes or rivers that is not from the salmon family COARSE FISH
– fish pen, turtle enclosure, or the like CRAWL
– fish sperm or testis MILT
– fish tank AQUARIUM
– air bladder of a fish SOUND
– basket used for catching fish COOP

fish

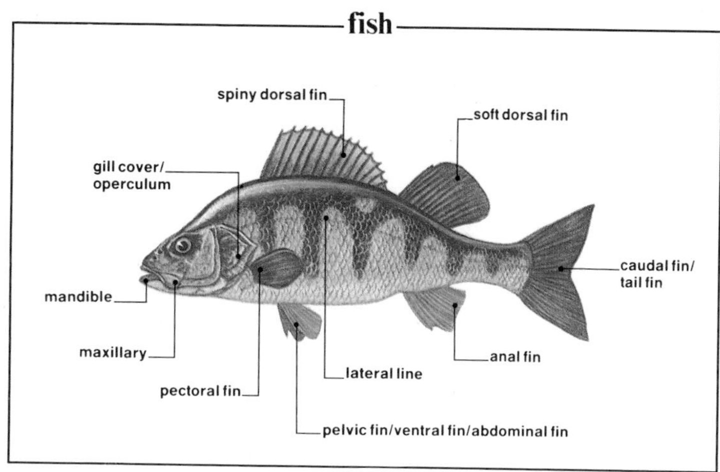

– catch or attempt to catch fish with one's hands GUDDLE
– dive down quickly and deep, as a whale or large fish might SOUND
– gash or score raw meat or fish for crisper cooking CRIMP
– group or school of fish SHOAL, RUN
– having spawned recently, as a food fish might have done, and so of less value as food SHOTTEN
– opening for the digestive and genital tracts in birds, fish, and reptiles CLOACA
– relating to or resembling a fish PISCINE
– steak cut from the side of a halibut or other fish FLITCH
– very small fish TIDDLER
– young or undeveloped fish FRY, FINGERLING

fish- ICHTHY-, ICHTHYO-, PISC-, PISCI-

fishing See chart, page 194
– fishing equipment TACKLE
– fishing spear or set of hooks for impaling fish GIG
– fishing spear with three prongs, used in catching salmon LEISTER
– baggy middle section of a fishing net or square sail BUNT
– relating to fishing or fishermen PISCATORIAL
– remove the hook from a fish after catching it DISGORGE
– time of year when hunting, fishing, shooting of game, or the like is permitted OPEN SEASON
– time of year when hunting, fishing, shooting of game, or the like is prohibited CLOSE SEASON

fit, join, or connect comfortably or harmoniously DOVETAIL

FISH DISHES

Arbroath smokie	small whole haddock hot smoked to a brown colour	**goujons**	strips of plaice or sole, crumbed and fried
bloater	dried, salted and smoked whole herring	**gravadlax**	Scandinavian pickled salmon
Bombay duck	dried and salted bummalo, an Indian fish, eaten as a savoury with curry	**kedgeree**	flaked fish mixed with rice, and sometimes eggs and cream
bouillabaisse	strongly seasoned French stew of several kinds of fish and shellfish	**matelote**	French fish stew with wine
calamari	squid, often served deep fried	**rissoles**	small balls or cakes of minced cooked fish or meat, crumbed and fried
coquilles St Jacques	scallops prepared and served in their own shells	**rollmop**	pickled herring fillet, sometimes wrapped round an onion or gherkin
coulibiac	traditional Russian fish pie	**sole bonne femme**	fillets of sole served with a white wine and button mushroom sauce
gefilte fish	seasoned fishcakes or fishballs bound with meal, and typically boiled in fish stock	**sole meunière**	sole lightly fried in butter, then sprinkled with lemon juice and herbs

FISHING TERMS

capta	pyramid-shaped weight	**ledgerbait**	bait fixed in position, typically on the bottom
coop	basket used for trapping or landing fish	**lure**	spinning bait or artificial fly that does not resemble any natural fly
creel	basket or trap made of wickerwork	**paternoster**	weighted fishing line with one or more shorter lines carrying hooks
dapping	bobbing a fly or baited hook gently on the surface of the water	**priest**	small weighted club for killing fish after landing
disgorger	instrument for removing hook from fish	**seine**	net hanging upright in the water
drail	lead-weighted hook dragged through the water	**setline, trawl line**	long line with several secondary hooked lines, towed by a boat
fancy fly	artificial fly that does not resemble a living fly	**skittering**	skipping or skimming a lure or hook lightly over the water
gaff	hooked pole for hauling large fish aboard or ashore	**spinning**	winding back the bait after casting, so that it simulates a swimming fish
gag	instrument for holding open the jaws of a pike while hooks are extracted	**spoon**	shiny concave lure that spins when drawn through the water
gang hook	compound fishhook made of several hooks joined shank to shank	**squatt**	maggot of the housefly, used as bait
gentle	maggot of the bluebottle, used as bait	**tag**	colourful piece of feather or other material surrounding the shank of the hook in a fishing fly
gillie	one who attends the angler, especially in game fishing	**trace**	connecting line, often of wire, between the hook and the main line
ground bait	unattached bait thrown into the river, sea, or pool to attract fish	**trammel**	net of three layers, set upright in the water
guddling	catching or trying to catch fish with one's hands	**trawl**	bag-shaped net towed along the bottom of the sea
hackle fly	artificial fly with a ruff-like tuft, as of feathers	**trolling**	fishing with a baited hook trailing behind a boat
jig	metal lure with one or more hooks, which lurches about when pulled through the water	**trotting**	angling in fast-moving water, using a float and line that holds the bait near the bottom
keepnet	net placed in the water, into which caught fish are put to keep them alive		

– fit, stroke, or brainstorm ICTUS
– fit, sudden attack, spasm, frenzy PAROXYSM, SEIZURE, APOPLEXY, CONVULSION
– fit of resentment or temper, as from a blow to one's pride PIQUE
– fit or accord comfortably, harmonise MESH
– fit or frenzy of frustrated desire for something unattainable NYMPHOLEPSY

-fit, -seizure -LEPSY

fits and starts – happening in fits and starts, intermittent SPASMODIC

fitted and permanent appliance, item of furnishings, or the like FIXTURE

five children or young born at one birth QUINTUPLETS
– five-lined light humorous verse, rhyming *aabba* LIMERICK
– five-pointed star, formed by five straight lines, sometimes credited with magic powers PENTACLE, PENTANGLE, PENTAGRAM
– five-sided figure PENTAGON
– five-year period QUINQUENNIUM
– group or series of five elements PENTAD
– group or setting of five objects arranged in a rectangle with one in the middle, as with the five on dice QUINCUNX
– multiply by five QUINTUPLE
– the number five, in cards or dice CINQUE

five- PENT-, PENTA-, QUIN-, QUINQU-

five finger, plant with five-lobed compound leaves CINQUEFOIL

five hundred pounds – slang term for £500 MONKEY

five-hundredth anniversary QUINCENTENARY

fix See **repair**, **join**

fixed, established, firmly and immovably settled, as opinions, or troops on a battlefield, might be ENTRENCHED
– fixed, rooted, immovable, as barnacles are SESSILE
– fixed firmly, impossible to eliminate, as incorrigible vices are INERADICABLE
– fixed firmly, impossible to release or to move EMBEDDED, INEXTRICABLE
– fixed idea, preoccupation to the exclusion of everything else OBSESSION, IDÉE FIXE
– fixed or impressed firmly, as in the memory ENGRAVED

– "fixed price" meal, typically offering a narrow range of choices, served in a restaurant or hotel TABLE D'HÔTE, PRIX FIXE

fizzy drink CARBONATED DRINK
– fizzy mineral water, either natural or artificially aerated SELTZER WATER

flabby and limp, drooping, lacking firmness FLACCID
– flabby flesh under the jaw JOWL, DEWLAP

flag See illustration
– flag, especially one of small size, on the bow of a ship to indicate its nationality JACK
– flag, typically triangular or forked, flown from the mast of a ship or yacht BURGEE
– flag or banner, as of a military unit ENSIGN, ANCIENT, STANDARD
– flag or banner, especially on a horizontal bar, as used in church parades GONFALON
– flags, especially those of a boat, or the light cloth used in making them BUNTING
– flags grouped to make a signal HOIST
– ceremonial military parading of flags TROOPING THE COLOUR
– inspiring flag or other symbol, modelled on a traditional red royal French flag ORIFLAME
– long, narrow flag, often forked, as attached to a knight's lance BANDEROLE, BANNEROL, PENCEL, STREAMER, PENNONCEL
– long, narrow flag, often triangular, as used for signalling PENNANT, PENNON
– lower a mast, sail, or flag STRIKE
– relating to flags or ensigns VEXILLARY
– roll up a flag or umbrella FURL
– rope used for hoisting or lowering a flag HALYARD
– side of a flag nearest the flagpole HOIST
– small flag carried as the standard of a military unit GUIDON
– small flag for signalling or indicating wind direction WAFT, WAIF
– study of flags VEXILLOLOGY
– unroll or open out something, such as a flag UNFURL
– wave or flutter proudly, as a flag does FLAUNT

flake- LEPID-, LEPIDO-

flame See also **fire**
– flame hovering over marshy ground WILL-O'-THE-WISP, JACK-O'-LANTERN, IGNIS FATUUS, FRIAR'S LANTERN
– extinguish a lamp, candle, flame, or the like, typically by smothering it SNUFF
– flaming torch FLAMBEAU
– flicker or be on the point of going out, as a candle flame might GUTTER
– flickering or glowing gently, as a flame might be LAMBENT
– gas burner producing a hot flame, used for laboratory experiments BUNSEN BURNER
– gas mixture used for the high-temperature flame in welding OXYACETYLENE
– put out a flame, candle, or the like, extinguish DOUSE, QUENCH
– ring of hot gas around a flame MANTLE

flap, as a sail might when losing wind LUFF
– flap of cloth at the back of a cap, to protect the neck from sunburn HAVELOCK

flare fired from a special pistol, used as a signal or for illumination, especially at sea VERY LIGHT

flash, glitter, sparkle, as a gemstone might CORUSCATE, SCINTILLATE, FULGURATE

flashy See **showy**

flask with a long near-horizontal neck, formerly used for distilling in chemistry MATRASS, ALEMBIC

flat, or block of flats, especially in North America, with individually owned freehold rather than leasehold CONDOMINIUM, CONDO
– flat, having a broad plane surface TABULAR
– flat, level, parallel to the horizon HORIZONTAL
– flat, room, or the like, especially near a city centre, kept for occasional use by someone whose main

flags

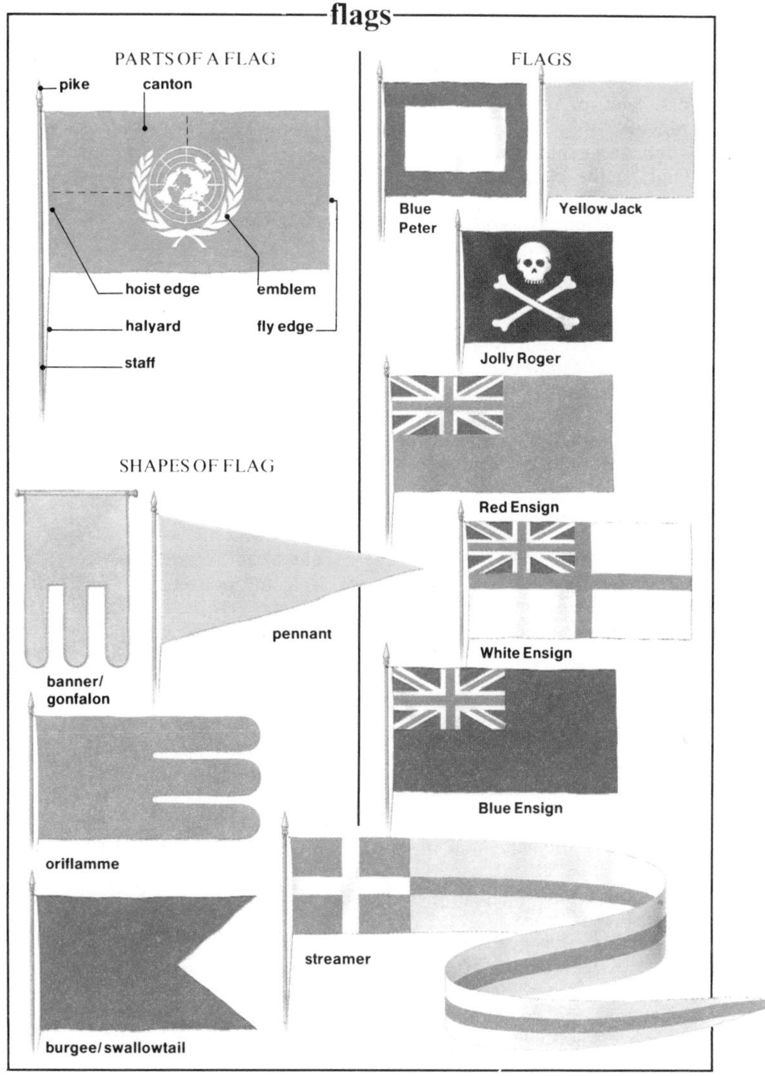

home is elsewhere PIED-À-TERRE
– flat, turned-out foot SPLAYFOOT
– flat and raised stretch of land PLATEAU
– flat on the roof or top floor of a large building PENTHOUSE
– flat on two floors DUPLEX
– flat on two floors, usually having its own outside door MAISONETTE
– flat or even, as two neatly fitting edges are FLUSH
– flat or suite of rooms APARTMENT
– flat shelf cut, usually in a series, into the side of a slope, for cultivation, preventing erosion, or the like TERRACE
– flat stretch of ground for walking along, especially along a sea shore ESPLANADE
– flat-topped hill, with steep sides, as in the arid areas of south-western U.S. MESA
– block of flats owned collectively by the leaseholders COOPERATIVE
– concluding of all legal formalities in the purchase of a house, flat, land, or other property COMPLETION
– full ownership of a house, flat, land, or the like, as distinct from leasing FREEHOLD
– go back on an agreement with someone intending to buy one's house or flat, by raising the price after a rival offer GAZUMP
– large building, often in a slum area, divided into rooms or flats for rent TENEMENT
– lying down flat PROSTRATE, RECUMBENT
– lying flat on one's back SUPINE
– lying flat on one's front PRONE
– lying flat with one's arms and legs spread out SPREADEAGLED
– transferring of the ownership of a house, flat, land or other property CONVEYANCING

flat- PLAN-, PLANO-, PLATY-

flatter See also **praise**
– flatter or deceive with smooth, charming talk BLARNEY, FLANNEL
– flatter with undue respect or admiration, treat as a VIP LIONISE
– flatterer or toady, buttering up influential people as a means of self-advancement SYCOPHANT
– flatterers or self-interested followers of an influential patron CLAQUE
– flattering, temptations, urging or wheedling BLANDISHMENTS
– flattering and over-humble underling, a groveller, toady, or bootlicker APPLE-POLISHER, LICKSPITTLE
– flattering or cooperating over-eagerly, slavishly submissive or yielding, over-eager to please SERVILE, OBSEQUIOUS
– flattery or sentimentality, excessive praise or emotion SCHMALTZ
– coax or persuade, as by means of flattery CAJOLE
– curry favour, as by flattery or excessive humility FAWN, KOWTOW, TRUCKLE
– gushing or excessively demonstrative, as flattering compliments might be EFFUSIVE
– smoothly flattering or obliging in a suspiciously humble way, oily, smarmy UNCTUOUS
– submissive self-humbling follower, flattering and dancing attendance on his patron FLUNKY, LACKEY, MINION, COURTIER

flavour, taste RELISH, SAPOR, SAVOUR
– flavour-enhancer, as used in many Chinese restaurants MONOSODIUM GLUTAMATE, MSG
– sharp smell, taste, or flavour TANG

flavouring for drinks in the form of a bitter tonic ANGOSTURA BITTERS
– flavouring of orange and almond, as used in cocktails ORGEAT
– flavouring of pomegranate or redcurrant syrup GRENADINE

flavourless, dull, unexciting INSIPID

flavoursome, tasty, or agreeable to eat PALATABLE

flawless, faultless IMMACULATE, IMPECCABLE

flax – steel comb for combing flax HACKLE

flecked or dotted, as with paint or natural colours STIPPLED

flee, run away or depart hastily SKEDADDLE, SCARPER, VAMOOSE
– flee secretly, as after committing a theft ABSCOND, ABSQUATULATE, DECAMP, HIGHTAIL
– flee secretly with a lover, typically to get married ELOPE
– fleeing person or escaped criminal FUGITIVE
– emigrant, specifically one who has fled his homeland for political reasons ÉMIGRÉ
– person who flees from war or suppression REFUGEE

fleecy or fluffy mass FLOCCULUS

fleet of merchant ships ARGOSY
– fleet of small ships, or small fleet of ships FLOTILLA
– fleet of warships ARMADA

flesh – flesh-coloured INCARNADINE
– flesh-eating or insect-eating, as lions, dogs, vultures, and pitcher plants are CARNIVOROUS, CREOPHAGOUS
– flesh of a dead and rotting animal CARRION
– discipline one's fleshly appetites and desires by punishment or self-denial MORTIFY
– tear the flesh, as with a knife or whip LACERATE

flesh- SARC-, SARCO-, CARN-, CARNI-

flexible, easily drawn out into threads DUCTILE
– flexible, easily moulded or shaped MALLEABLE, PLIABLE
– flexible, supple, nimble, or agile LITHE, LIMBER, LISSOM

flick of the finger FILLIP

flicker or be on the point of going out, as a candle flame might GUTTER, WAVER
– flickering or glowing gently, as a flame might be LAMBENT

flight from danger HEGIRA
– flight path, often circular, of an aircraft awaiting clearance to land HOLDING PATTERN
– flight path, typically curved, of a missile, ball, or the like TRAJECTORY
– referring to flights over long distances LONG-HAUL

flightless, as the ostrich and related birds are STRUTHIOUS
– flightless bird such as the ostrich, emu, or kiwi RATITE

flint tool with a chisel-like head, from prehistoric times BURIN

flirt, or engage in casual love affairs PHILANDER
– flirt, tease, or toy with TRIFLE, DALLY, COQUET
– flirt or socialise, especially while wandering about GAD ABOUT, GALLIVANT
– flirtation, loveplay DALLIANCE
– flirtatious woman COQUETTE

float attached parallel on one or both sides of a canoe to stabilise it OUTRIGGER
– float filled with air for raising sunken ships CAISSON, CAMEL
– float for raising a sunken vessel or supporting a floating bridge PONTOON
– float in the air, apparently in defiance of gravity LEVITATE
– float in the air, or fly without changing position HOVER
– float or drift gently, as the smell of flowers does in the wind WAFT
– floating or swimming NATANT
– floating wreckage or cargo after a ship has sunk FLOTSAM
– tendency or ability to float BUOYANCY

flock of geese or other wildfowl in flight SKEIN
– flock or herd of animals being driven together DROVE
– living or migrating in a herd, pack, flock, or the like GREGARIOUS

flog, whip, as for religious discip-

line or sexual gratification FLAGELLATE, SCOURGE

flood, downpour DELUGE
- flood, earthquake, or other sudden, ruinous disaster CATACLYSM
- flood, overwhelm INUNDATE
- flood barrier in the form of an embankment along a river LEVEE
- flood barrier in the form of an embankment DYKE
- flood or sudden, violent torrent after heavy rains FLASH FLOOD
- flood that is typically sudden and violent SPATE, DÉBÂCLE
- flooding INUNDATION, ALLUVION
- existing or occurring before the biblical Flood ANTEDILUVIAN
- relating to a flood DILUVIAL
- unrestrained flood of water, passion, or the like TORRENT

floor covering of mosaic wood blocks or strips PARQUET
- floor of a building lying between the ground floor and first floor MEZZANINE, ENTRESOL
- concrete mixture or finish, as on a floor SCREED
- principal floor of a building PIANO NOBILE
- horizontal beam supporting a ceiling or floor JOIST
- varnish used on wooden floors or furniture FRENCH POLISH

Florence – Italian dialect spoken in Florence TUSCAN

flour from a cereal grain FARINA
- floury or starchy FARINACEOUS
- coat food with flour, sugar, or the like, as by sprinkling DREDGE
- protein mixture in wheat flour, used in glues GLUTEN
- wholemeal flour GRAHAM FLOUR
- wholemeal flour mix, with malted wheat and rye, used for bread GRANARY FLOUR

flourish, as in music or handwriting QUIRK
- "flourished", term indicating the most active or creative period of someone whose birth and death dates are uncertain FLORUIT
- flourishing, rich, as vegetation might be VERDANT, VERDUROUS, LUSH, LUXURIANT
- "may it flourish", motto used with the name of a place or institution FLOREAT

flow See also **flowing**
- flow of water, passion, or the like that is turbulent and unrestrained TORRENT
- flow or stream of people or things coming in INFLUX
- flow out of a valley, as a river might DEBOUCH
- flow out or discharge at the mouth of a river DISEMBOGUE
- flow towards, as of blood to the head AFFLUX
- instrument for measuring the rate of flow of a fluid ANEMOMETER

flow- RHEO-

flower See illustration
- flower cluster, in which each flower has its own stem attached to a larger branch THYRSUS

flower

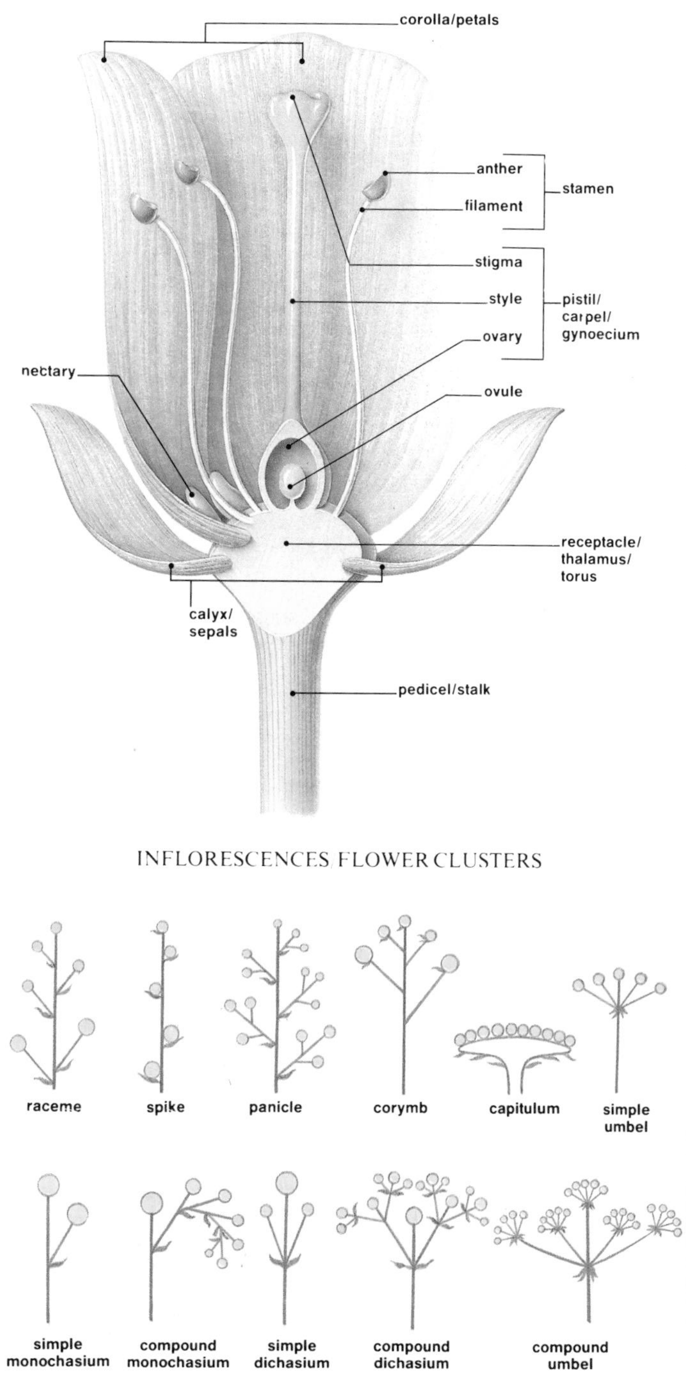

– flower cluster developing outwards, with the central stem and all side stems bearing a single flower CYME
– flower cluster in the form of a compacted head, as in a daisy or thistle GLOMERULE
– flower cluster or flower-bearing stalk, or the arrangement of the flowers on it INFLORESCENCE
– flower cluster or spike, typically dense and drooping, as of the birch or alder CATKIN, AMENT
– flower gardening or cultivation HORTICULTURE
– flower or fruit cluster at the end of a stalk TRUSS
– flower or fruit of a cultivated rather than natural variety CULTIVAR
– flower or plant bred from two different varieties or species HYBRID
– flower or plant that turns to keep facing the sun HELIOTROPE
– flower or small posy of flowers, as pinned to a woman's dress CORSAGE
– flower support, such as a spiked board or pierced sponge in a vase FROG
– flower that, according to legend, never fades or dies AMARANTH
– flower that keeps its colour when dried IMMORTELLE
– flowering plant ANGIOSPERM
– flowering plant living for three or more years PERENNIAL
– flowering plant that develops and dies within a single year ANNUAL
– flowers arranged in a ring, as for decoration or as a memorial WREATH
– flowers cut and arranged in a cluster POSY, BOUQUET, NOSEGAY
– adjective for a flower FLORAL
– attached directly at the base, without a stalk, as a flower might be SESSILE
– bell-shaped, as some flowers are CAMPANULATE
– circular series of leaf-like scales below a flower, fruit, or flower cluster INVOLUCRE
– clustered, formed of tightly packed parts, as a fruit or flower might be AGGREGATE
– crown-like or bell-shaped part of a daffodil or similar flower CORONA
– cut the dead flowers from a plant DEADHEAD
– decorative chain or garland of flowers, ribbons, or the like suspended in a loop FESTOON
– drooping, as some flowers and buds are CERNUOUS
– gather or collect something, such as flowers CULL
– go limp, droop, as a flower might WILT
– having both male and female flowers on the same stalk, as some plants have ANDROGYNOUS
– head-shaped, as some flowers or flower-clusters are CAPITATE
– leaf-like plant part just beneath a flower or cluster of flowers BRACT
– open during the day and closed at night, as many flowers are DIURNAL
– opening in the evening, as some flowers do VESPERTINE
– outer part of a flower, the petals and sepals collectively FLORAL ENVELOPE, PERIANTH
– plant that flowers continuously through the growing season PERPETUAL
– pollinated by insects, as some flowers are ENTOMOPHILOUS
– pollinated by wind-blown pollen, as grass flowers are ANEMOPHILOUS
– relating to flowers and other plants BOTANICAL
– remaining attached to the plant even after withering, as some leaves and flowers do PERSISTENT
– short-lived, dying or falling quickly, as flowers might be FUGACIOUS
– spike of tiny close-packed flowers, as in the cuckoopint SPADIX
– stem supporting a flower, fruit, or flower cluster PEDUNCLE
– sweet liquid secreted by flowers, and gathered by bees for making honey NECTAR
– tiny disc flower or ray flower, usually in a cluster, as in the head of a daisy or other composite flower FLORET
– wreath or crown of flowers worn on the head GARLAND, CHAPLET, CORONAL
– wreath or garland of flowers, worn round the neck in Polynesia, especially in Hawaii LEI

-flower- ANTHO-, -ANTHOUS, -FLOR-

flower arranging as an art, of Japanese origin IKEBANA

flower garden designed with an ornamental pattern of paths between the flowerbeds PARTERRE

flowerbed, typically of perennial plants HERBACEOUS BORDER

flowering, bursting into bloom, blossoming, or the time of flowering FLORESCENCE, EFFLORESCENCE
– flowering process or period in plants ANTHESIS

flowery, fussy, pretentious or overelaborate in style FLORID, CHICHI, CHINTZY, PRECIOUS

flowing, effortless, or graceful FLUENT
– flowing out or something that flows out EFFLUENCE, EFFLUX
– flowing together or meeting point of two or more rivers CONFLUENCE

-flowing -RRHOEA, -RRHAGIA

flu – former term for flu GRIPPE

fluent, effortless FACILE
– fluent or effortless, as in speaking or writing, but typically shallow and insincere GLIB

fluffy mass FLOCCULUS
– fluffy or downy matter, as gathering on fur or a new carpet FLUE

fluid, clear and thick, secreted by membranes in joints, tendon sheaths, and so on SINOVIA
– fluid-containing cavity or sac in the body CISTERNA, CISTERN
– fluid in the body, according to ancient and medieval medicine, determining the personality and health HUMOUR
– fluid surrounding the embryo or foetus, as in the womb AMNIOTIC FLUID
– device to slow down or regulate the flow of a fluid BAFFLE
– operated by or involving fluid pressure HYDRAULIC
– pouch or bag-like part, often filled with fluid, in a plant or animal SAC
– swelling caused by a build-up of fluid in the tissues OEDEMA

fluke, parasitic flatworm TREMATODE

fluorescent lamps – gas used in fluorescent lamps KRYPTON

flute – flute-like instrument, egg-shaped with fingerholes OCARINA
– flute-player FLAUTIST
– finger hole, as on a flute VENTAGE
– referring to the modern flute, with its mouthpiece on the side TRANSVERSE
– trilling of a flute or other wind instrument by a rapid vibration of the tongue FLUTTER TONGUING

fly an aircraft very low, not far above hedges, fences, and so on HEDGE HOP
– fly for fishing, with a tuft of feathers HACKLE FLY
– fly or move rapidly away, as flushed gamebirds do SKIRR
– fly or sail completely around something, such as the Earth CIRCUMNAVIGATE
– fly whisk, as used in East Africa MGWISHO
– fly without changing position HOVER

– flying and navigating by visual observation of beacons and landmarks CONTACT FLYING
– flying or able to fly VOLANT, VOLITANT
– adjective for a fly, especially a housefly MUSCID
– art, science, profession, or pastime of flying aircraft AVIATION
– bloodsucking fly from Africa, transmitting sleeping sickness TSETSE FLY
– disturbed mental and body rhythms owing to long flights across time-zones JET LAG
– still without flight feathers, not yet developed enough to fly UNFLEDGED
– tour the countryside in North America to give theatrical or stunt-flying performances or make election speeches BARNSTORM

flying buttress ARC-BOUTANT

flying saucer or similar mysterious flying object UFO, UNIDENTIFIED FLYING OBJECT

foam gathering at the surface of fermenting beer BARM
– foam occurring during fermentation, as of vinegar or cider WORK
– foam or froth, especially on or from the sea SPUME
– foamy light white synthetic solid substance used as packing and insulating material POLYSTYRENE

focus – apparent focus of light rays, as in the image in a mirror VIRTUAL FOCUS
– sharpness of image in a photograph achieved by sharpness of focusing ACUTANCE

focus of attention, especially an admired or beloved person CYNOSURE

focusing ability of the eye through changing the direction of incoming light rays REFRACTION
– focusing disability resulting from faulty curvature of the lens of the eye ASTIGMATISM

fodder, as made of clover STOVER
– fodder, such as hay, fed to livestock PROVENDER
– fodder of fermented grass, corn, or the like prepared in a pit or silo SILAGE
– fodder trough or rack CRIB, MANGER, CRATCH
– residue of oilseed, used as animal fodder EXPELLERS, EXTRACTIONS
– tall fodder plant with clover-like leaves ALFALFA, LUCERNE
– yellow-flowering crop grown for oilseed and fodder RAPE, COLZA
– yellowish beet used for fodder MANGEL-WURZEL

foetus See **baby**

fog – fog-like polar weather condition producing very low visibility WHITE-OUT
– thick yellow fog or smog, as formerly in London PEA-SOUPER

foil – hammer metal into foil, or coat glass with metal foil FOLIATE

fold, wrinkle, or crease, as when pursing one's lips PUCKER
– fold or curl something tightly, such as hair or dress material CRIMP
– fold or ridge of skin, shell, or the like PLICA
– fold up or collapse in on itself CONCERTINA
– make or press fluted folds in a piece of fabric, as for a ruff QUILL

folded into a series of long parallel ridges, as land or an iron sheet might be CORRUGATED
– folded page or insert in a book or magazine that is larger than other pages GATEFOLD, FOLD-OUT

folk song of a melancholy kind sung in Portuguese FADO

folk tales, traditional stories, local legends MÄRCHEN
– anthology of folk tales from Wales MABINOGION

folksy, quaint ETHNIC

follow a trail, fox, or the like, as hunting hounds do DRAG
– follow directly, come immediately after, often as a direct result SUPERVENE, ENSUE
– follow directly in a job or the like, take over from SUCCEED
– follow persistently HOUND
– development, continuation, something that follows on SEQUEL

follower, imitator, or disciple who is markedly inferior to his master EPIGONE
– follower of or devoted believer in a religion, political leader, or the like VOTARY
– follower of the doctrines of a philosopher, teacher, intellectual movement, or the like DISCIPLE, ACOLYTE, ADHERENT
– follower or companion who is over-eager to please SYCOPHANT, MINION, TOADY
– follower or fan, as of a specified sport or pastime DEVOTEE, AFICIONADO
– follower or trusted supporter, ready to lend physical as well as moral support HENCHMAN, MYRMIDON
– followers or attendants, as of a nobleman RETAINERS, ENTOURAGE, RETINUE
– followers or devoted admirers, typically self-interested and fawning toadies CLAQUE

following, coming after in time SUBSEQUENT
– following as an effect or conclusion, resulting CONSEQUENTIAL
– following in order, as of office-holders or monarchs SUCCESSION
– following in order, successive SEQUENTIAL, CONSECUTIVE
– following in sequence, item by item in series SERIATIM

-fond- PHIL-, -PHILE

fondly devoted to one's wife, especially in an excessive or fawning way UXORIOUS

fondness, loving feelings TENDRESSE

font, basin for holy water at the entrance of a church STOUP

food See also **cooking terms**, **menu terms**, and entries at various types of food
– food COMESTIBLES, VICTUALS, VIANDS
– food, especially sweets and cakes, as eaten by schoolchildren TUCK
– food, nourishment NURTURE, SUSTENANCE, ALIMENT
– food, or food for thought, typically of an insipid and easily digested kind PABULUM
– food, packaged and processed, requiring little preparation before serving CONVENIENCE FOOD
– food additive or flavour-enhancer, as used in Chinese restaurants MONOSODIUM GLUTAMATE, MSG
– food basket HAMPER
– food for animals, especially pigs, consisting of kitchen scraps and liquid SWILL, SLOPS
– food in its partly digested fluid form in the stomach CHYME
– food of the gods, in mythology AMBROSIA, AMRITA
– food or provisions, especially when of poor quality TACK
– food preparation, or the food prepared, of a particular style CUISINE
– food seasoning, such as salt, mustard, or spices CONDIMENT
– food seller or provider, such as a wholesale grocer PROVISIONER, PURVEYOR
– food stand or trolley placed next to a dining table DUMB WAITER
– food storage room PANTRY, BUTTERY
– food store, specialising in fine ready-prepared foods DELICATESSEN
– food that is soft or mashed, as for a baby PAP
– concentrated preparation or essence of a food or other sub-

stance, as for flavouring EXTRACT
– craving for unnatural food, such as mud or chalk PICA
– decorate food, as with cress or a slice of lemon GARNISH
– digest, absorb, or incorporate something, such as food or facts ASSIMILATE
– eating all kinds of food, both meat and plant foods OMNIVOROUS
– expertise in good food or cooking GASTRONOMY
– full to excess, as of food REPLETE, SATIATED, SATED, GLUTTED, GORGED
– informal Australian term for food TUCKER
– item of food, something edible ESCULENT
– liking for good food or abundant eating GOURMANDISE
– nourishing substance, as in food or in the solution absorbed by plant roots NUTRIENT
– officer of a ship, aeroplane, or the like supervising the food and provisions STEWARD
– person who appreciates or is an expert in fine food and drink GOURMET, CONNOISSEUR, EPICURE, GASTRONOME
– person who enjoys food and eats abundantly GOURMAND, TRENCHERMAN
– referring to food considered pure according to Jewish law KOSHER
– referring to food, such as pork, considered impure and forbidden according to Jewish law TREF
– referring to food or cooking of a very high standard CORDON BLEU
– relating to food intake DIETARY
– relating to food, nutrition, or digestion ALIMENTARY
– search through refuse for food or useful objects SCAVENGE
– small, soft lump of matter, particularly of chewed food BOLUS
– small, tasty item of food BONNE BOUCHE
– study of the intake, assimilation, and value of food, especially in the human diet NUTRITION
– substance added to a food to preserve, flavour, colour, or enrich it ADDITIVE
– take in food by or as if by swallowing INGEST
– vomit or bring up partly digested food REGURGITATE

food poisoning PTOMAINE POISONING
– food poisoning caused by a bacterial toxin found in badly tinned or smoked food BOTULISM
– food poisoning caused by rod-shaped bacteria of a kind often found in inadequately cooked meat and eggs SALMONELLA POISONING, SALMONELLOSIS

fool See also **clown**, **cheat**, **victim**
– fool, blunderer, person who tends to get things wrong DUFFER, SCHLEMIEL, DRONGO
– fool, dim-witted and usually clumsy person, dolt BOOBY, IMBECILE, NUDNIK, SCHMUCK, ZOMBIE
– fool, dunce, blockhead, dull-brained person DUNDERHEAD, NUMSKULL, NINCOMPOOP, CRETIN
– fool, simpleton, silly person who is forgetful and easily confused ADDLEPATE, NINNY, MOONCALF
– fool, very talkative scatterbrain BLATHERSKITE, FLIBBERTIGIBBET
– multi-coloured clothing of a court jester or fool MOTLEY
– playing the fool BUFFOONERY
– red cap of a court jester or fool COXCOMB

foolhardiness, reckless disregard of danger TEMERITY

foolish See **stupid**, **silly**

fool's gold IRON PYRITES, PYRITE

foot See also **feet**
– foot, especially a pig's foot, used as food TROTTER
– foot massage as a form of therapy for all parts of the body REFLEXOLOGY
– foot misshapen from birth CLUBFOOT, TALIPES
– foot-operated lever for driving a sewing machine, potter's wheel, or the like TREADLE
– foot soldiers INFANTRY
– foot that is abnormally flat and turned outwards SPLAYFOOT
– on or relating to the sole of the foot PLANTAR
– relating to the sole of the foot VOLAR
– sole of the foot THENAR
– wart or wart-like growth, especially on the foot VERRUCA

-foot- -PEDI-, -PEDE, PEDI-, -POD, -PODE

football or other match between teams from the same area DERBY
– competition in which each participant plays all the others, as in a football league ROUND ROBIN
– demotion to a lower division of the football league RELEGATION
– selection and combination of results on the football pools PERMUTATION, PERM

foothold of a temporary or uncertain kind TOEHOLD
– foothold or early success that makes possible further achievements BEACH-HEAD, BRIDGEHEAD
– military foothold or front-line position projecting into enemy-held territory SALIENT

footlights in a theatre FLOATS

footnote See also **reference**
– footnotes, references, lists of variants, and the like, as in a literary text APPARATUS CRITICUS, CRITICAL APPARATUS
– cross-shaped printing symbol, †, as for indicating footnotes DAGGER, OBELISK, OBELUS
– double cross-shaped printing symbol, ‡, as for indicating footnotes DOUBLE DAGGER, DIESIS
– star-shaped printing symbol, *, indicating footnotes ASTERISK

footprint mould, as taken for evidence in court MOULAGE
– footprints, tracks, trail SPOOR

foot specialist, expert in the treatment of feet and toenails CHIROPODIST, PEDICURE

footstool – padded cushion used as a footstool or leg rest, or for kneeling on in church HASSOCK

for- PRO-

for ever IN PERPETUITY

for example, e.g. EXEMPLI GRATIA

for one's country PRO PATRIA

for the present, for the time being, temporarily FOR THE NONCE, PRO TEM

forbid See **prohibit**, **prevent**

forbidden, prohibited VERBOTEN
– forbidden as food to Jews, non-kosher, as pork is TREF
– forbidden or shunned because, or as if because, blasphemous or cursed TABOO

force, speed, or other quantity having both magnitude and direction VECTOR
– force acting inwards on a rotating or revolving body, towards the centre or axis CENTRIPETAL FORCE
– force acting outwards on a rotating or revolving body, away from the centre or axis CENTRIFUGAL FORCE
– force driving or moving a person or thing onwards PROPULSION
– force-feeding, by means of a tube down the throat GAVAGE
– force or bully someone into a course of action, as by bluster, threats, or violence BLUDGEON, BULLDOZE, STRONG-ARM
– force or compulsion DURESS, COERCION, CONSTRAINT
– force or drive someone to action, spur or goad, incite or prompt IMPEL, ACTUATE
– force or impose a person or thing on someone FOIST, OBTRUDE
– force or occurrence that unavoidably spoils one's plans or prevents the fulfilment of a con-

tract FORCE MAJEURE
- force or power, especially as a result of continuing movement MOMENTUM, IMPETUS
- force or pressure someone into doing something against his will DRAGOON, PRESS-GANG, RAILROAD
- force or trick someone into an undesirable action or situation SHANGHAI
- force out, push, or squeeze EXTRUDE
- force out, remove from office, power, the throne, or the like DEPOSE, OUST
- force out and provide a substitute for SUPPLANT
- force out from a fixed position, hiding place, dwelling, or the like DISLODGE
- force payment, tribute, or the like EXACT, EXTORT
- force produced by lowered pressure SUCTION
- force that overpowers and destroys, or demands self-sacrifice JUGGERNAUT
- force to leave, dismiss, expel, as from a building or rented property EJECT, EVICT
- force under one's control, or crush or put down by force SUPPRESS, SUBDUE, SUBJUGATE, REPRESS
- seize by force and hold illegally the power, rights, throne, or the like of another USURP
- seize or wrench something by force, such as power WREST
- stability, balance of forces EQUILIBRIUM
- tendency of a body to remain at rest or in unchanged motion until it is affected by an external force INERTIA
- twisting force or the technical measurement of it TORQUE

forced, artificial, stiff and unspontaneous CONTRIVED, MANNERED, STILTED, RECHERCHÉ
- forced, done or required against one's will INVOLUNTARY
- forced, embarrassed, or inhibited manner, situation, or the like CONSTRAINT
- forced, striving for effect, strained AGONISTIC, VOULU
- forced labour and imprisonment PENAL SERVITUDE

forceful, aggressively confident, stating and enforcing one's rights and wishes boldly ASSERTIVE
- forceful, clear, and crisp, as a remark or argument might be INCISIVE, TRENCHANT, COMPELLING, COGENT
- forceful, hardworking, and energetic person DYNAMO
- forceful, passionate, or emphatic VEHEMENT
- forceful, vigorous, possessing great energy VIRILE, POTENT
- forceful in an irresponsibly bullying or overbearing way, dictatorial, tyrannical IMPERIOUS, DOMINEERING
- forceful seizing of property, as in wartime PILLAGE, RAPINE

forecast See also **fortune-telling**
- forecast based on the relative positions of planets and signs of the zodiac at a given time HOROSCOPE
- forecast or predict on the basis of signs or symptoms PROGNOSTICATE
- forecast or prediction, especially of the development of a disease PROGNOSIS
- scientific study of the weather, especially for the purpose of making forecasts METEOROLOGY

forefather or ancestor, especially the first or earliest ancestor as of a people PRIMOGENITOR
- forefather or forebear, direct ancestor PROGENITOR
- forefathers, ancestors ANTECEDENTS, FOREBEARS

forefront of, or early participants in, an artistic fashion, political movement, or the like VANGUARD

forehead of a bird or animal FRONTLET
- relating to or of the forehead FRONTAL, METOPIC
- slope backwards, as one's forehead might RECEDE

foreign, coming from outside, of external origin EXTRANEOUS, EXTRINSIC
- foreign, from another part of the world EXOTIC, PEREGRINE
- foreign, growing or living in a new or temporary environment, as a weed might be ADVENTIVE
- foreign or barbarous TRAMONTANE
- foreign resident ALIEN

foreign- XENO-

foreign language – alleged ability of clairvoyants or mediums to speak a foreign language they do not know XENOGLOSSIA

foreign policy based on revenge or regaining of territory REVANCHISM, IRREDENTISM
- foreign policy based uncompromisingly on national self-interest rather than on moral considerations REALPOLITIK

foreigner having certain citizenship rights in his country of residence DENIZEN
- expel a foreigner from a country DEPORT
- hostility to or fear of foreign people and ideas XENOPHOBIA

-foreknowledge -MANCY

forerunner, person or thing signalling the arrival of something HARBINGER, PRESAGER, HERALD
- forerunner, person or thing that came before, such as a previous occupant of a position PREDECESSOR, ANTECEDENT, PRECURSOR

foresee, think of as a future possibility ENVISAGE, ENVISION

foresight – having foresight or great imagination VISIONARY

foreskin PREPUCE
- abnormal tightness of the foreskin, preventing it from being retracted PHIMOSIS
- fatty substance collecting under the foreskin SMEGMA
- removal of the foreskin CIRCUMCISION

forest clearing, open space in a wood GLADE
- forest from prehistoric times, "turned to stone" by the action of mineral-rich water PETRIFIED FOREST
- forest's outskirts or perimeter area PURLIEU
- forests or trees of a particular region SILVA
- officer in charge of the royal forests in former times VERDERER
- relating to woods or forest areas SYLVAN
- top layer, consisting of dead leaves, of a forest floor LITTER

forestry, care and cultivation of trees in forests SILVICULTURE

foretell See also **prophetic**, **fortune-telling**
- foretell or forecast on the basis of signs or symptoms PROGNOSTICATE
- foretell or indicate, be a sign or omen of, point to the future occurrence of FORESHADOW, PREFIGURE, BODE, PRESAGE, BESPEAK, BETOKEN, ADUMBRATE
- foretell or indicate some unfavourable event, serve as a warning sign or omen PORTEND, FOREBODE
- foretell or predict on the basis of signs and omens, prophesy AUGUR, SPAE, VATICINATE
- foretelling events or revealing hidden information, as by observing omens or drawing on supernatural help DIVINATION, SOOTHSAYING
- foretelling things just before they happen, having an advance sense of events PRESENTIENT
- power of foretelling events,

extra-sensory advance knowledge, accurate foresight CLAIRVOYANCE, PRECOGNITION, PRESCIENCE

forever See **permanent**

forge something, especially banknotes, for the purpose of fraud COUNTERFEIT
- forged, fake SPURIOUS
- forged cheque or counterfeit banknote STUMER
- put forged money into circulation UTTER

forget – forgetful, absent-minded, and unaware of one's surroundings OBLIVIOUS, ABSTRACTED, PREOCCUPIED
- forgetfulness, loss of memory OBLIVION, LETHE
- forgetting of one's past, loss of memory, as caused by shock or brain damage AMNESIA
- drug, potion, or technique for forgetting pains and sorrows NEPENTHE

forget-me-not MYOSOTIS
- forget-me-not or related flower HELIOTROPE

forgivable, easily excused or pardoned VENIAL

forgive See also **excuse**, **pardon**
- forgive or overlook an offence readily CONDONE
- forgiveness for sins, or release from punishment or guilt ABSOLUTION, REMISSION
- forgiving attitude, mildness or mercifulness CLEMENCY, LENIENCY, INDULGENCE

forgotten or neglected state, oblivion LIMBO

fork – fork-like bone or body part, such as a chicken's wishbone FURCULA, FOURCHETTE
- fork or branch into two as a road might BISECT
- fork or spear with three prongs, as used by gladiators or carried by Neptune TRIDENT
- forked, branching FURCATE
- forked, branching, divided into two streams or parts BIFURCATE
- prong of a fork or fork-shaped tool TINE

fork-lift – platform supporting cargo or stored goods, typically moved by a fork-lift truck PALLET, SKID

form, shape, or outline CONFIGURATION, CONTOUR, CONFORMATION
- form or structure, as of a plant or animal organism MORPHOLOGY
- form that a god, idea, feeling, or the like may take MANIFESTATION
- capable of existing in different forms, as a chemical element might be ALLOTROPIC
- capable of occurring in different forms, as crystals of a mineral or insects of a single species might be POLYMORPHIC
- give a definite shape or form to something, such as an idea CRYSTALLISE

-form- -GEN, -GENIC, -GENOUS, -MORPH-, MORPHO-, -MORPHIC, -FY

formal See also **stiff**, **old-fashioned**
- formal, traditional, or coldly conventional approach to art ACADEMICISM
- formal academic clothing, worn especially at Oxford University SUBFUSC
- formal and appropriate behaviour, propriety, etiquette CONVENANCE
- formal approval, official confirmation RATIFICATION, SANCTION, VALIDATION
- formal black evening jacket for men TUXEDO, DINNER JACKET, TUX
- formal or extremely polite and proper DECOROUS, CEREMONIOUS
- formal rules of behaviour, code of ceremonial conduct PROTOCOL
- formal title or name, as of a nobleman STYLE, DESIGNATION

formation, as of soldiers or ships, in stepped parallel rows ECHELON
- formation of troops in close array PHALANX

former, one-time ERSTWHILE, QUONDAM

former- EX-

formidable, awesome, very impressive REDOUBTABLE

formless, lacking shape APLASTIC, AMORPHOUS

formula in chemistry detailing the arrangement of atoms and bonds within the molecule STRUCTURAL FORMULA

fort See also **castle**
- fort in the form of a round tower built in ancient times in Scotland BROCH
- fort or small tower formerly guarding the coast MARTELLO TOWER
- fortress or stronghold protecting a town or city CITADEL

forthright See **frank**

fortification See also **castle**
- fortification, such as a trench, within outer walls or defences RETRENCHMENT
- fortification, typically of a temporary kind, of two walls joined at an angle LUNETTE, REDAN
- fortification, usually small and temporary, sometimes within a permanent fortress REDOUBT
- fortification against enemy fire or observation DEFILADE
- fortification in the form of a fence of wooden stakes PALISADE, STOCKADE
- fortification of concrete or wood, with loopholes for observation or weapons BLOCKHOUSE
- fortification or parapet built hastily to about chest height BREASTWORK
- fortified or well-defended place BASTION, FASTNESS, STRONGHOLD
- fortified shelter underground with a bank or gun emplacements above ground BUNKER
- fortified wall about a castle, town, or the like, or the area protected by it ENCEINTE
- fortified wall or bank, as behind a trench, giving protection from the rear PARADOS
- fortified wall or barricade for protection against explosions REVETMENT
- fortified wall or barrier, such as a bank of earth, in front of a trench or rampart TRAVERSE
- building or setting up of fortifications, or an earthwork, wall, or rampart forming part of a fortification VALLATION
- defence or protection, specifically the walls of a fortification RAMPART, BULWARK
- embankment in front of a fortification or castle, making attackers vulnerable to the defenders GLACIS
- flat open area in front of a fortification, exposing the attackers to the defenders' fire ESPLANADE
- half-moon or crescent-shaped object or structure, such as the outwork of a fortification DEMILUNE
- inner side of a ditch in a fortification ESCARP
- opening in fortifications for the passage of troops DÉBOUCHÉ
- outer side of a ditch in a fortification COUNTERSCARP
- part of a fortification, trench system, or the like that projects towards the enemy SALIENT
- passage into an outwork of a fort or fortification GORGE
- platform in a trench or behind the parapet of a fortification, from which firing takes place BANQUETTE
- platform or mound along the wall of a fortification, from which firing takes place over the parapet BARBETTE
- pointed wall or parapet of a fortification projecting outwards towards the enemy FLÈCHE
- small overhanging turret, as on the tower of a fortification BARTIZAN
- two-faced embankment that

projects outwards in front of a fortification RAVELIN
fortune See **fate**, **luck**, **rich**
– accidental developments, such as changes of fortune VICISSITUDES
fortune-telling, telling the future, or revealing hidden information, as by means of visions CLAIRVOYANCE
– fortune-telling based on an ancient Chinese book containing 64 symbolic diagrams I CHING
– fortune-telling based on the pattern of lines in the palm of the hand PALMISTRY, CHIROMANCY
– fortune-telling based on the relative positions of planets and signs of the zodiac at a given time HOROSCOPE
– fortune-telling by means of casting or drawing lots SORTILEGE
– fortune-telling by means of consulting ghosts SCIOMANCY
– fortune-telling by means of communication with the spirits of the dead NECROMANCY
– fortune-telling by means of examining a pack of tarot or playing cards CARTOMANCY
– fortune-telling by means of inspecting the entrails of animals, as practised by priests in ancient Rome HARUSPICATION
– fortune-telling by means of interpreting dreams ONEIROMANCY
– fortune-telling by means of interpreting lines or figures drawn randomly or patterns in the dust GEOMANCY
– fortune-telling by means of interpreting passages chosen at random from the Bible or some other book BIBLIOMANCY
– fortune-telling by means of observing fire or flames PYROMANCY
– fortune-telling by means of observing the feeding or flying patterns of birds AUSPICE, ORNITHOSCOPY
– fortune-telling or revealing hidden information, as by observing omens or drawing on supernatural help DIVINATION, AUGURY, SOOTHSAYING
– fortune-telling or revealing hidden information by gazing into a crystal ball SCRYING
– playing cards of a kind used in fortune-telling TAROT CARDS
forty-five-degree arc OCTANT
forwards- PRO-
fossil – fossilised excrement COPROLITE
– fossilised shell of a type of extinct mollusc AMMONITE
– fine-grained rock-material in which fossils are found MATRIX
– scientific study of fossils PALAEONTOLOGY
foul-smelling, smelly MALODOROUS, FETID, RANCID
foundation, basis, underlying principle SUBSTRATUM
– foundation of a building, typically a solid brickwork platform STEREOBATE
– foundation post or pillar for a building PILE, SPILE
– row of large concrete wedges or pillars used as foundations or stilts for a building PILOTIS
– slab of reinforced concrete laid on soft ground as part of a building's foundations RAFT
founder of a tradition, tribe, trend, or the like PROGENITOR, PRECURSOR, PATRIARCH
– founder or leader of a movement PATRON SAINT
founding member of an organisation CHARTER MEMBER
fountain with rotating jets GIRANDOLE
four children or young born at one birth QUADRUPLETS
– four-dimensional extension of a cube, as a hypothetical mathematical construct TESSERACT
– four-dimensional space in mathematics HYPERSPACE
– four-legged animal QUADRUPED, TETRAPOD
– four-lined stanza or verse of poetry QUATRAIN
– four-sided closed figure QUADRILATERAL, TETRAGON
– four-year period QUADRENNIUM
– multiply by four QUADRUPLE
four- TETR-, TETRA-, QUADR-, QUADRI-, QUADRU-
four-hundredth anniversary QUADRICENTENNIAL, QUATERCENTENARY
fowl See **chicken**
fox, as named in folk tales and fables REYNARD
– fox's lair EARTH
– fox's tail BRUSH, BUSH
– adjective for a fox VULPINE
– female fox VIXEN
foxglove or related plant DIGITALIS
– stem or arrangement of flowers attached singly to a stalk, as in the foxglove, with the youngest at the top RACEME
foxhunter – foxhunter's scarlet coat PINK
foxhunting See **huntsman**
fraction in which both the numerator and denominator are whole numbers, simple fraction, common fraction VULGAR FRACTION
– based on the number ten, as a fraction, number system, or currency might be DECIMAL
– cancelling of common factors in a fraction, or converting a fraction to a decimal REDUCTION
– number or expression positioned above the line in a fraction NUMERATOR, DIVIDEND
– number or expression positioned below the line in a fraction DENOMINATOR, DIVISOR
– related inversely to each other, as fractions might be RECIPROCAL
– simple fraction equal to greater than one IMPROPER FRACTION
– simple fraction that is less than one PROPER FRACTION
fracture See illustration, page 204
– fracture of a bone in surgery in order to reset it or correct a deformity OSTEOCLASIS
– fracture that is very thin and clean HAIRLINE
fragment or chip of stone SPALL
– fragment or splinter of glass, pottery, or other brittle substance SHARD
– fragments, scattered remains, or the like of something broken RUBBLE, DEBRIS, DETRITUS
– fragments, splinters, broken pieces SMITHEREENS
– fragments from a shell, bomb, or mine produced by an explosion SHRAPNEL
fragrant or smelly ODOROUS, ODORIFEROUS
frame for drying or stretching cloth during manufacture TENTER
– frame of two upright bars securing cattle round the neck in a stall, or upright of a goalpost in sports STANCHION
– frame or arch, typically made of crisscrossing sticks, on which vines or creepers are trained to grow TRELLIS
– picture frame with extending sides that cross each other and project outwards OXFORD FRAME
– walking-frame of light metal, as used by the old or disabled ZIMMER, WALKER
framework, structure, or basic pattern FABRIC
– framework of criss-crossed strips of wood or metal, as in a screen or window LATTICE
– framework of guidelines or limits, as of a budget or schedule PARAMETERS, CONSTRAINTS
– framework supporting a travelling crane, railway signals, or the like GANTRY
France- FRANCO-, GALLO-, GALLIC-
Franco – Franco's title as dictator of Spain CAUDILLO
frank, honest and open, straightforward CANDID

fractures

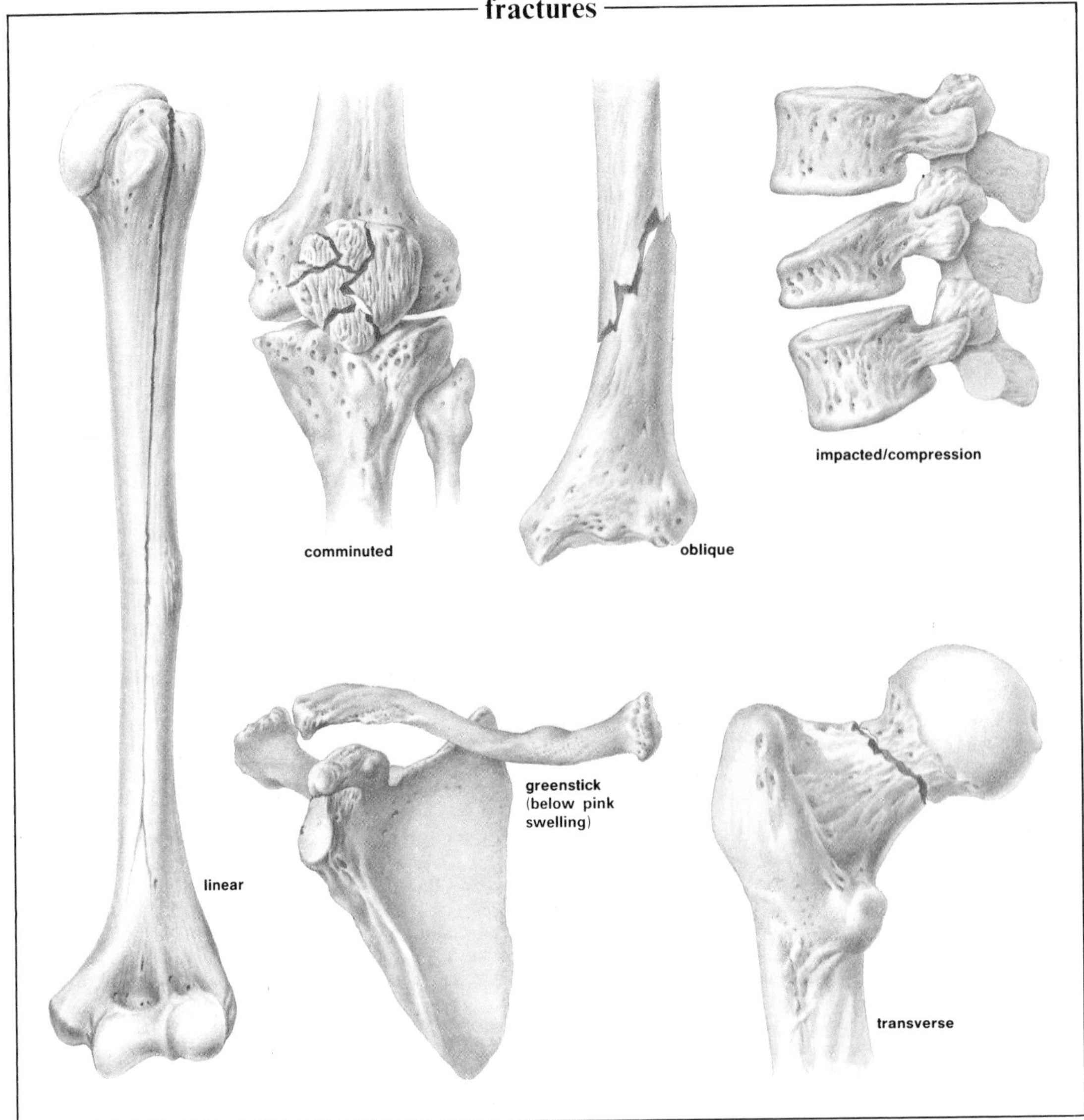

– frank, simple, or naive GUILELESS, ARTLESS, INGENUOUS
– frank and forthright, blunt, no-nonsense BLUFF, FOUR-SQUARE
– frank and open, communicative, informative FORTHCOMING
– frank and unreserved, direct, down-to-earth UP-FRONT, EXPLICIT, OUTSPOKEN, UNCONSTRAINED
– abrupt and gruff, blunt or frank CURT, BRUSQUE

fraud See also **trick**
– fraud, cheating, deception DUPLICITY
– fraud, trickster CHARLATAN, MOUNTEBANK
– fraud or deception, as by assuming a false identity IMPOSTURE
– fraudulent or worthless discovery MARE'S NEST
– fraudulent taking or using for oneself money or property entrusted to one EMBEZZLEMENT, DEFALCATION, PECULATION
– fraudulently substituted SUPPOSITITIOUS, SPURIOUS
– inflate the value of something fraudulently SALT

freak, monster LUSUS NATURAE

freckle LENTIGO
– freckle of large size developing on the skin LIVER SPOT
– freckle, spot, or similar discoloration of the skin MACULA

free See also **release**
– free, release, especially from foreign domination LIBERATE
– free a captive by making a payment REDEEM, RANSOM
– free a prisoner without bail, on certain conditions RELEASE SOMEONE ON HIS OWN RECOGNISANCE
– free a prisoner provisionally before the completion of his sentence PAROLE
– free and unrestricted, unimpeded or unchained UNFETTERED, UNSHACKLED, UNTRAMMELLED
– free from or relieve of a problem or burden DISEMBARRASS, DISENCUMBER
– free from slavery, duties, obligations, or the like ENFRANCHISE, AFFRANCHISE

– free from slavery or oppression EMANCIPATE, MANUMIT
– free hand, freedom to act as one thinks best CARTE BLANCHE
– free of charge GRATIS, GRATUITOUS, BUCKSHEE
– free or excuse from responsibility, a duty, or the like EXEMPT, EXONERATE
– free or reduced goods or similar offer, used as an incentive to purchase PREMIUM
– free or release from difficulties, unfasten or disentangle EXTRICATE
– free, or set loose, as from prison or slavery ENLARGE, SET AT LARGE
– free to do whatever one likes, FOOTLOOSE, UNENCUMBERED
– freeing or rescuing DELIVERANCE
– freely or spontaneously, without preparation AD LIB
– freely or willingly given, generous UNSTINTED, UNGRUDGING
– referring to property owned by the sovereign and let free of charge to a favoured tenant GRACE-AND-FAVOUR

free- UN-

Free Church – minister presiding at an assembly of a Free Church MODERATOR

free house – pub that, unlike a free house, is owned by a brewery and restricted to selling beer made by that brewery TIED HOUSE

free trade, non-interference by governments in commercial activity LAISSEZ FAIRE

free verse VERS LIBRE

free will, free choice VOLITION
– arising from or relating to free choice or an action of one's own free will VOLUNTARY
– attitude of submissiveness to fate, as though lacking free will FATALISM
– belief or philosophy that everything follows inescapably from a cause, and that there is no real free will DETERMINISM

freedom, especially from imperialist rule in Africa UHURU
– freedom, lack of controls LAISSEZ ALLER
– freedom of speech, assembly, and so on CIVIL LIBERTY
– freedom of thought or action, allowing room for movement LATITUDE, LEEWAY

freehold farmer in former times YEOMAN

-freeing- -LYS-, LYSO-, -LYSIS

freemasons' secrets MYSTERIES

freeze See also **frozen**
– freeze, solidify, or jell CONGEAL, COAGULATE
– freezing, solidification through cooling GELATION
– freezing of a corpse, with the intention of reviving it in the future CRYONICS

freezing- CRYO-

French See chart, page 206, and also **menu terms**
– French, relating to France or ancient Gaul GALLIC
– French borough or small administrative district ARRONDISSEMENT
– French café or small shabby bar ESTAMINET
– French containing many English words and elements FRANGLAIS
– French "county", main administrative unit within France DÉPARTEMENT
– French courtly poet-musician in the Middles Ages TROUBADOUR, TROUVÈRE
– French king's eldest son in former times DAUPHIN
– French national anthem MARSEILLAISE
– French policeman GENDARME
– French Protestant of the 16th and 17th centuries HUGUENOT
– French-speaking FRANCOPHONE
– French word, phrase, or idiom in another language GALLICISM
– any of the French provincial dialects PATOIS
– pronunciation of a final consonant that is normally silent, especially in French, when the next word begins with a vowel LIAISON
– French-speaking state academic secondary school LYCÉE

-French- FRANCO-, GALLO-, -GALLIC

French bean HARICOT

French polish or thin varnish used for coating wood SHELLAC

French Revolution – extreme radical republican in the French Revolution SANS-CULOTTE
– old French government and social system that was swept away by the French Revolution in 1789 ANCIEN RÉGIME
– Parisian women who would knit unconcernedly while watching guillotinings during the French Revolution TRICOTEUSES

frenzy of frustrated desire for something unattainable NYMPHOLEPSY
– frenzied, behaving violently or destructively RAMPAGING, ON THE RAMPAGE

frequency of occurrence INCIDENCE
– frequency distribution in statistics OGIVE
– units of measurement of frequency FRESNEL, HERTZ

frequent, common, normal PREVAILING, PREVALENT, PREDOMINANT
– frequent, repeated, continuous PERSISTENT, RECURRENT, HABITUAL
– frequent visitor HABITUÉ

fresh, healthy, and vigorous condition VERDURE
– fresh, striking, bright, or lively VIVID, VIBRANT
– fresh and youthful, spring-like VERNAL
– fresh start, clean slate, need or chance to start again from scratch TABULA RASA
– freshness, originality, newness NOVELTY

Freudian See also **complex**
– Freudian theories, or the practice of psychological treatment based on them PSYCHOANALYSIS
– in Freudian psychology, deathwish or instinct for self-destruction THANATOS
– in Freudian psychology, life-enhancing drive and self-preserving instincts EROS
– in Freudian psychology, mental and emotional energy and sexual drive derived from deep biological urges LIBIDO

friar belonging to an order living on charity MENDICANT FRIAR

friction, as of wheels on a road TRACTION
– oil, grease, or other substance used to reduce friction LUBRICANT
– rubbing down or wearing away, through friction, as by wind-blown sand ATTRITION
– study of friction and lubrication TRIBOLOGY

friction- TRIBO-

fridge – cooling substance, as for operating a fridge REFRIGERANT

fried lightly in butter or fat SAUTÉED

friend or acquaintance with whom one discusses private personal matters CONFIDANT
– friend or companion who is affectionate, reliable, and usually lively BOON COMPANION
– friends extremely devoted to each other DAMON AND PYTHIAS
– exclusive circle of friends or colleagues CLIQUE
– close friend, associate, or hanger-on CRONY, SIDEKICK, FAMILIAR
– extremely close friend, constant companion INTIMATE, ALTER EGO
– loyal friend, faithful companion ACHATES

friendly, sympathetic, sharing one's tastes CONGENIAL, SIMPATICO
– friendly, easy to get along with AFFABLE, CORDIAL, DEBONAIR
– friendly, enjoying the company of others, sociable GREGARIOUS, EXPANSIVE, CONVIVIAL, JOVIAL
– friendly, good-natured AMIABLE

FRENCH TERMS

à la mode	in fashion
amour-propre	self esteem
au fait	familiar or conversant with
avant-garde	ahead of the times, pioneering
beau monde	fashionable society
beaux-arts	fine arts
belle époque	"beautiful period", the era preceding the First World War
belles-lettres	fine literature
bête noire	especially disliked person or thing
billet-doux	love letter
bon mot	pithy witticism
bonne bouche	delectable titbit or item
bon vivant	person who enjoys luxurious living
carte blanche	free hand, unconditional authorisation
cause célèbre	interesting and controversial public issue
c'est la vie	that's life!
comme il faut	proper, in keeping with accepted standards
cordon sanitaire	buffer zone
coup de grâce	conclusive stroke; death blow
coup d'état	sudden overthrow of government
cri de coeur	heartfelt cry or appeal
crime passionel	crime provoked by sexual jealousy
déjà vu	sense of having undergone before something being experienced for the first time now
démodé	out of fashion, out of date
de rigueur	required by fashion or social custom
dernier cri	latest fashion
de trop	unwanted, getting in the way
éminence grise	influential person behind the scenes
enfant terrible	provokingly unconventional person
en passant	by the way
entente cordiale	informal friendly understanding between nations
entre nous	between ourselves
esprit de corps	group spirit, morale
fait accompli	irreversible fact
faute de mieux	for want of anything better
faux pas	blunder
haute couture	high fashion
haute cuisine	high-class cooking
hors de combat	out of action
idée fixe	obsession
idée reçue	conventional opinion
je ne sais quoi	an indefinable but distinctive quality
jeu d'esprit	witty comment
jeunesse dorée	wealthy, fashionable young people
joie de vivre	high spirits
laissez-faire	non-interference
laissez-passer	entry permit, pass
mauvais quart d'heure	brief, nasty experience
mot juste	the exactly appropriate expression
noblesse oblige	obligations imposed by honour or rank
nouveau riche	newly and ostentatiously rich person
par excellence	to the highest degree
parti pris	prejudice
passé	out of date or fashion
pièce de résistance	outstanding item
pied-à-terre	temporary or secondary residence
pis aller	desperate course of action, last resort
plat du jour	dish of the day
porte-cochère	covered entrance to a building
raison d'être	purpose of existence
réchauffé	a rehash
recherché	in great demand, mannered, affected
risqué	indelicate or suggestive, saucy
sang-froid	calm self-control, self-possession
savoir-faire	knowledge of appropriate behaviour
soi-disant	self-styled, so-called
tant mieux	so much the better
tant pis	so much the worse
tête-à-tête	intimate conversation
tour de force	outstanding feat
tout court	plainly and simply
trahison des clercs	betrayal of a cause by intellectuals
vis-à-vis	in relation to, compared with
volte-face	about-turn, policy reversal

– friendly, kindly, or well-disposed in an uncle-like way AVUNCULAR
– friendly, lively, hearty, especially in a facile or gushing way HAIL-FELLOW-WELL-MET
– friendly, outgoing, lively person EXTROVERT
– friendly and sympathetic fellowship, especially among those of similar interests FREEMASONRY
– friendly understanding and trust RAPPORT, CAMARADERIE
– friendly good nature BONHOMIE, GENIALITY
– friendly in tone, characterised by good will AMICABLE
– friendly social relations, as with the people of an occupied or an enemy country FRATERNISATION
– friendly understanding or informal agreement between countries or powers ENTENTE CORDIALE
– be friendly and associated socially HOBNOB
– bubbling with excitement, enthusiasm, or friendliness EBULLIENT, EXUBERANT, EFFERVESCENT
– having a friendly and cosy atmosphere GEMÜTLICH
– relating to utterances or conversation, as about the weather, whose purpose is to express friendliness rather than to convey ideas PHATIC

friendship, peaceful relations, especially between countries AMITY
– referring to love or close friendship between two people that is free of sexual desire PLATONIC
– restore friendship, marital harmony, or the like between people in conflict RECONCILE

frighten or dismay into losing confidence UNNERVE, DISCOMFIT
– frighten so as to silence or deter INTIMIDATE, COW
– frighten to the point of paralysis PETRIFY, GORGONISE

frightened See **scared**, **cowardly**

frightening, fearsome, formidable REDOUBTABLE, FLEYSOME
– frightening, forbidding or repelling REBARBATIVE
– frightening and discouraging, disheartening DAUNTING

frill of lace or fabric, used as a trimming RUCHE, RUFFLE
– frill or ruff of lace or linen formerly worn by women round the neck or shoulders TUCKER
– frills down the front of a blouse or shirt JABOT
– frilly paper adorning the end of a chop or cutlet PAPILLOTE

fringe, border, or edge of a fabric, carpet, or the like finished so as to prevent unravelling SELVAGE
– fringe, edge, or boundary, as of a social group PERIPHERY

frivolity of manner, especially when inappropriate LEVITY

frog, newt, or related animal developing in water but living or able to live on land AMPHIBIAN
– adjective for a frog or toad ANURAN, SALIENTIAN, BATRACHIAN, RANINE

from- EX-

from the beginning AB INITIO, AB OVO

front of a building FACADE, FRONTISPIECE
– front position or troops of an advancing army VANGUARD
– front side of a leaf of printed paper RECTO
– relating to the head end or front part of something ANTERIOR

front- FORE-

front man or cover, apparently but not really in charge of a dubious scheme MAN OF STRAW

frontier See **border**, **boundary**
– frontier settlement OUTPOST

frost, as formed on the windward side of trees, twigs, telegraph wires and the like RIME
– frost of small white ice crystals HOARFROST

frost- CRYO-

frosted glass – allowing the passage of light, as frosted glass does, but only in a diffused form unlike transparent glass TRANSLUCENT

froth See **foam**

frown, look angry, menacing, or sulky SCOWL, LOWER, GLOWER

frozen See also **freeze**
– frozen dessert or starter similar to a sorbet FRAPPÉ
– frozen ground, where subsoil is permanently frozen PERMAFROST
– frozen-subsoil region between the Arctic's perpetual snow and the tree line TUNDRA

frugal, austere, simple SPARTAN, THRIFTY, PARSIMONIOUS

fruit See chart
– fruit having a single hard stone enclosing the seed DRUPE
– fruit produced by the fusing of several flowers or flower ovaries MULTIPLE FRUIT, AGGREGATE FRUIT, COLLECTIVE FRUIT
– fruit whose seeds are in a large central capsule POME
– fruit-bearing FRUCTIFEROUS
– fruit-eating, as some bats are CARPOPHAGOUS, FRUGIVOROUS
– fruit or flower of a cultivated rather than natural variety CULTIVAR
– fruit salad finely diced and sometimes in jelly MACÉDOINE
– fruit stewed and served hot or cold in a syrup COMPOTE

FRUIT

EXOTIC FRUIT	
breadfruit	**kumquat**
cantaloupe, span spek	**mandarin**
cherimoya	**naartjie**
durian	**ortanique**
granadilla, passion fruit	**satsuma**
guava	**shaddock, pomelo**
kiwi fruit, Chinese gooseberry	**tangelo**
longan	**ugli**
loquat	HARD FRUIT
lychee	**bullace**
mangosteen	**crab apple**
naseberry, sapodilla	**damson**
pawpaw, papaya	**greengage**
persimmon	**medlar**
pomegranate	**nectarine**
rambutan	**quince**
Sharon fruit	**sloe**
star apple	SOFT FRUIT
tamarind	**bilberry**
CITRUS FRUIT	**blueberry**
citron	**boysenberry**
clementine	**cranberry**
	loganberry
	mulberry
	whortleberry, blaeberry

– fruit such as oranges, lemons, and grapefruit CITRUS FRUIT
– fruit that has fallen in the wind WINDFALL
– fruit tree or shrub trained to lie flat against a wall, trellis, or the like ESPALIER
– fruit whose stone or pip does not separate easily from the flesh CLINGSTONE
– fruit whose stone or pip separates easily from the flesh FREESTONE
– bear fruit, or make something fruitful or productive FRUCTIFY
– fleshy fruit, or the flesh of such a fruit SARCOCARP
– gel-forming substance found in ripe fruit and used as a setting agent in jams PECTIN
– open tart filled with fruit or cheese FLAN
– person who eats only fruit FRUITARIAN
– pulp remaining after apples, pears, or other fruits have been crushed in order to extract the juice POMACE, MARC
– scientific study and cultivation of fruit POMOLOGY
– softening or near-decay in some fruits BLET
– split or burst open along a seam,

as a pod or fruit might, to release seeds or pollen DEHISCE
– sugar-coated, as preserved fruit might be CRYSTALLISED

-fruit- -CARP-, -CARPY, -FRUCT-, -FRUG-, FRUCTI-, FRUGI-

frustrate and annoy EXASPERATE
– frustrate or torment by parading but withholding something desirable TANTALISE
– frenzy of frustrated desire for something unattainable NYMPHOLEPSY

fry lightly in butter or fat SAUTÉ

frying pan – U.S. term for a frying pan SKILLET

fuel, such as coal or petroleum, found in the Earth's crust, and formed from decomposed living matter FOSSIL FUEL
– fuel in a rocket, explosive charge, or similar agent generating thrust PROPELLANT
– hydrocarbon gas used in fuels such as those in gas canisters BUTANE, PROPANE

fugitive or runaway slave in the West Indies MAROON

fulfil a promise, pledge, or the like REDEEM

full See also **fill**
– full, abounding, swarming TEEMING
– full, as of food or drink, satisfied to the point of excess SATED, SATIATED, REPLETE, GLUTTED, GORGED
– full, as of liquid or happiness BRIMMING
– full amount, number, or the like COMPLEMENT
– full-length, not shortened or condensed UNABRIDGED
– full of emotion, danger, tension, or the like CHARGED, FRAUGHT
– full to excess, blocked or clogged, as the nasal passages might be CONGESTED
– fullness, completeness PLENITUDE, PLENUM

-full -ULENT

full moon that follows the harvest moon HUNTER'S MOON

fully and clearly expressed, as directions might be EXPLICIT
– fully attended or open to all, as a session of a conference might be PLENARY

fumigation chamber for killing insects or fungi FUMATORIUM
– fumigation or deodorising lozenge that is set alight PASTILLE

fun or merrymaking of a wild, noisy, and uninhibited kind HILARITY, REVELRY

function, correspondence, rule associating the members of one set with those of another MAPPING
– functioning properly, in working order OPERATIONAL, OPERATIVE
– functions or processes maintaining life METABOLISM

fund used for bribing and other corrupt activities SLUSH FUND
– providing for some possible though unlikely future occurrence or emergency, as a fund or plan might CONTINGENCY

fundamental See **basic**, **essential**

funds – appeal for or request something earnestly, such as votes or funds SOLICIT
– misuse or theft of property or funds entrusted to one MISAPPROPRIATION, EMBEZZLEMENT, DEFALCATION, PECULATION

funeral, or funeral ceremonies and rites OBSEQUIES, EXEQUIES
– funeral director UNDERTAKER, MORTICIAN
– funeral hymn, lament DIRGE
– funeral procession or other formal or ceremonial procession CORTÈGE
– funeral speech of praise EULOGY
– funeral watch or festivity prior to burial WAKE
– bugle call sounded at military funerals or to signal lights out in a military camp LAST POST
– church gate with a roof, at which the coffin is rested before funerals or burials LICH GATE
– person who carries or accompanies the coffin at a funeral PALLBEARER
– raised platform or table on which a coffin or corpse lies, as during a state funeral CATAFALQUE
– vehicle for carrying a coffin to a funeral HEARSE
– wood pile prepared for a funeral fire on which to cremate a corpse PYRE

funfair attendant who attracts customers to a booth or sideshow by loud sales patter BARKER
– funfair elevated railway, providing a fast exciting ride ROLLER COASTER, SWITCHBACK, BIG DIPPER
– funfair performer who bites off the head of a live frog, mouse, chicken, or the like GEEK
– funfair ride with small, rapidly moving cars WHIP
– small electric car driven and bumped into others on a funfair rink BUMPER CAR, DODGEM
– spiral slide at a funfair HELTER-SKELTER

fungus See also **mushroom**
– fungus, as in plant diseases or on damp walls MILDEW, MOULD
– fungus growing underground and considered a delicacy TRUFFLE
– fungus producing a disease in cereals ERGOT
– fungous skin disease, such as athlete's foot or ringworm TINEA, DERMATOPHYTOSIS
– chemical that destroys fungi FUNGICIDE
– horn-like substance occurring in some fungi and shells CHITIN
– plant body, as in fungi, without distinct parts THALLUS
– reproductive cell or organ in non-flowering plants such as mosses, ferns, and fungi SPORE

-fungus- -MYC-, MYCO-, -MYCETE

funnel – funnel-shaped, as some plant parts are INFUNDIBULIFORM
– funnel-shaped device, such as a sea anchor or a target towed behind an aircraft DROGUE
– slope backwards, as a ship's mast or funnel might RAKE

funny See also **humorous**
– funny, jolly, given to joking JOCULAR, JOCOSE, WAGGISH
– funny in a bizarre or clownish way ZANY
– funny in a coarse way, vulgarly humorous BAWDY, RABELAISIAN
– funny in a peculiar, whimsical, or wry way DROLL
– funny in an unintentional way, laughable, ridiculous LUDICROUS, RISIBLE
– extremely funny, side-splitting, priceless, hysterical HILARIOUS, RIOTOUS, UPROARIOUS
– jesting or lack of earnestness at the wrong time, inappropriate attempt at being funny LEVITY, FRIVOLITY, FLIPPANCY
– mildly funny, pleasantly amusing or entertaining DIVERTING

funny bone OLECRANON
– long bone of the upper arm, ending near the "funny bone" on the elbow HUMERUS

fur, wool, or soft hair PILE
– fur-trimmed cloak PELISSE
– white fur of the stoat, as used to trim peers' or judges' robes ERMINE
– white or light grey fur used to trim medieval robes MINIVER

Furies in Greek mythology EUMENIDES, ERINYES

furnace, as for burning rubbish INCINERATOR
– furnace, as for smelting iron, in which the coke is ignited by a blast of hot air BLAST FURNACE
– furnace, as in a smithy FORGE
– furnace for smelting metal, using reflected heat on the ore REVERBERATORY FURNACE
– furnace or oven for drying or

hardening, as in a pottery KILN
– furnace's waste material after smelting or refining SLAG, SINTER, CINDER, SCORIA
– bottom part of a furnace HEARTH
– container in a furnace that receives the molten metal CRUCIBLE
– heat-resistant material, such as alumina or fireclay, as used to line furnaces REFRACTORY
– metal residue or slag remaining in a furnace SALAMANDER
– movable plate adjusting the airflow in a stove or furnace flue DAMPER
– nozzle or duct through which the air is blown into a blast furnace TUYÈRE

furnished properly, well-equipped WELL-APPOINTED

furniture See chart
– furniture, equipment, or fittings APPOINTMENTS
– furniture, ornaments, curios, and the like, displayed and valued as rare or quaint BRIC-A-BRAC
– furniture leg of an 18th-century style, curving outwards near the top, and inwards to an ornamental foot CABRIOLE
– aged artificially, as some furniture or leather is DISTRESSED
– cane from a tropical Asian palm, as used for wickerwork furniture and walking sticks RATTAN
– fabric, padding, springs, as used in making a soft covering for furniture UPHOLSTERY
– item of furniture or fittings that

FURNITURE

armoire	large ornate cabinet or wardrobe
chaise longue	reclining chair with a long padded seat resembling a settee
chesterfield	large padded sofa, often with button upholstery
cheval glass	long mirror mounted on swivels in a frame
chiffonier	ornamental cabinet with drawers or shelves; high and narrow chest of drawers
club chair	deep, thickly upholstered easy chair with heavy arms and sides, and often a low back
commode	low cabinet or chest of drawers, usually on legs or short feet
console table	table supported by decorative brackets fixed to a wall
credenza	cupboard or sideboard, typically without legs
davenport	small writing desk with side drawers
dos-à-dos	sofa that accommodates two people seated back to back
escritoire	writing desk, typically with a hinged top closing over small drawers
farthingale chair	armless chair with a high seat and low straight back
fauteuil	upholstered armchair
love seat	large chair or small sofa that seats two people
Morris chair	large easy chair with an adjustable back and big loose cushions
ottoman	long upholstered seat, with or without a back
pier table	table designed to stand against a wall between two windows
pouffe	large firm cushion used as a seat; low, soft, backless couch
secretaire	drop-front desk, sometimes with drawers below and a bookcase above
tabouret	low stool or cabinet
tallboy	double chest of drawers, with one section standing on top of the other
teapoy	small tea table, typically with three legs
tête-à-tête	S-shaped sofa allowing two people to face each other when seated
torchère	slender decorative candlestand, often with a tripod base
triclinium	couch or set of couches surrounding three sides of a table
whatnot, étagère	lightweight stand with three or more open shelves
Windsor chair	comfortable wooden chair with arms, a spoked back, and splayed legs

FURNITURE STYLES

Adam	delicate 18th-century English neoclassical style developed by Robert Adam
Biedermeier	conventional 19th-century style developed in Germany
buhl/boule/ boulle	style developed by the French cabinet-maker André C. Boulle (1642-1732), using inlays of metal and tortoiseshell
Chippendale	elegant and ornate mid 18th-century English style developed by Thomas Chippendale
Queen Anne	early 18th-century English style characterised by fine upholstery and wood inlays
Regency	decorative early 19th-century English style
Second Empire	ornate 19th-century French style
Sheraton	late 18th-century English style developed by Thomas Sheraton, characterised by graceful proportions

can be moved about FITMENT
– item of furniture or fittings that is fixed in place and cannot be moved about FIXTURE
– made of rough branches, as some furniture is RUSTIC
– modern style of furniture, typically using metal piping HIGH-TECH
– narrow fabric trimming, used on clothes, curtains, and furniture GIMP, GUIMPE, GUIPURE
– narrow tube of folded material, often enveloping a cord, as used for edging upholstered furniture PIPING
– patterns of inlaid wood, ivory, and the like, as used in decorating furniture MARQUETRY
– ready-made standard unit used in constructing furniture MODULE
– referring to furniture with an indented or scalloped edging or moulding PIECRUST
– small swivelling wheel on each leg of an item of furniture, for easy moving CASTOR

furniture van or warehouse PANTECHNICON

furrow or narrow groove, as on a plant stem or the surface of the brain SULCUS

furthest down, deepest, lowest NETHERMOST
– furthest point or part, end, edge EXTREMITY
– furthest possible stage, greatest possible degree NE PLUS ULTRA

fuse See **join**
– fuse, grow together, merge COALESCE
– fuse consisting of a line of gunpowder laid to explode a charge TRAIN
– fuse metals using heat WELD
– fuse or blend MELD

fusion- ZYG-, ZYGO-

fusion bomb, such as a hydrogen bomb THERMONUCLEAR BOMB

fuss, ado, showy display or stir FANFARE
– fuss or bother, needlessly complicated procedure PALAVER
– fuss or fret over petty details NIGGLE
– fuss over nothing, pointless argument or to-do PRODUCTION, HOO-HA

fussy, choosy, picky CHARY, FADDISH
– fussy, determined, or insistent person, perfectionist PRECISIAN, STICKLER
– fussy, needlessly concerned with minute details, nit-picking PERNICKETY, QUIBBLING, PETTIFOGGING
– fussy attention to small details of knowledge, especially when at the expense of deeper insight and understanding PEDANTRY
– fussy in one's tastes or habits, selective or refined DISCERNING, DISCRIMINATING
– fussy or precise to a fault, painstakingly conscientious or dutiful METICULOUS, FASTIDIOUS, FINICKY, FINICAL
– fussily proper or refined, over-nice PRECIOUS, EXQUISITE, PRISSY
– conscientious, attentive to duty or detail, precise, appropriately fussy PUNCTILIOUS, SCRUPULOUS

future See also **fortune-telling**, **foretell**
– future or future generations POSTERITY
– future time of happiness and prosperity expected or desired MILLENNIUM
– about to happen, due to take place in the very near future, looming IMMINENT, IMPENDING
– advance sense or intuition of something that is to happen in the near future PREMONITION, PRESENTIMENT
– advance sign or intuition of something, especially something evil or dangerous, that is to happen in the near future PORTENT, FOREBODING
– announcer or announcement of a future event HERALD, HARBINGER, PRECURSOR
– impression or overall view of historical events, the future, or the like VISTA, PROSPECT
– likely to happen in the future, probably forthcoming PROSPECTIVE
– possible future occurrence or situation EVENTUALITY, CONTINGENCY
– think of as a future possibility, foresee ENVISAGE, ENVISION

-future -MANCY

G

gable roof with step-like projections or cuts near the top CORBIE GABLE
Gaelic or Celtic, specifically from Ireland or Scotland GOIDELIC
gain an advantage over OUTFLANK
galaxy other than the Milky Way NEBULA
– brightest part of a galaxy NUCLEUS
gall, bitterness WORMWOOD
gall- CHOLE-
gall bladder – surgical removal of the gall bladder or part of the urinary bladder CYSTECTOMY
gallant, chivalrous man CHEVALIER
gallery or verandah along the outside of the upper level of a building LOGGIA
galloping at full speed TANTIVY
gallows GIBBET, SCAFFOLD
– gallows trapdoor DROP
– horizontal beam or crossbar, on a gallows or cross TRANSOM
gallstone, kidney stone, or similar solid mass formed in a body cavity or tissue CALCULUS, CONCRETION, CYSTOLITH
gambling See also **horse-racing**, **bet**, **poker**, **roulette**
– gambling chip JETTON
– gambling game where winning tickets are picked from a revolving container TOMBOLA
– gambling venue CASINO
– gambling technique of raising or doubling the stakes after each loss MARTINGALE
– gamble, risk, expose to danger HAZARD, VENTURE, BRAVE
– gambler on the dealer's right, or the dealer's opponent in two-handed card games PONE
– gambler or better, especially on a horse race PUNTER
– gambler who cannot refrain from gambling COMPULSIVE GAMBLER
– box from which cards are dealt in gambling SHOE, SABOT
– card-dealer or bet-taker at a gambling table CROUPIER
game, match, or the like between two drawn or tied contestants to determine a winner PLAY-OFF
– game animal or animals, prey of hunters QUARRY
– game killed during a day's hunting or shooting BAG
– game or hunting preserve, privately owned but unfenced CHASE
– store and ripen game such as venison or pheasant HANG
gamekeeper WARRENER
games See **sports**, **card games**
– games or sports festival in ancient Greece AGON
– collection, as of games or useful hints COMPENDIUM
gammon See **bacon**
Gandhi – Gandhi's policy of nonviolent resistance in India to press for political reform SATYAGRAHA
gang of young noblemen in 18th-century London, engaging in muggings and vandalism MOHOCKS
– Mafia-like criminal gang in Naples CAMORRA
gangplank – rope handrail on a ship's ladder or gangplank MANROPE
gangrene NECROSIS, MORTIFICATION
gap See also **hole**
– gap between the teeth, especially one that is abnormally wide DIASTEMA
– gap or break caused by splitting, cutting, or the like CLEAVAGE, DISCONTINUITY, VOID
– gap or break in proceedings, such as an interval RECESS, RESPITE, ADJOURNMENT, INTERMISSION
– gap or missing part, interruption, break in continuity HIATUS, LACUNA
– gap or opening in a bone, membrane, or other part of the body FORAMEN
– gap or oversight, as in a law or contract, making evasion possible LOOPHOLE
– gap or point between two nerve cells across which a nerve impulse is transmitted SYNAPSE
– deep gap in the Earth's surface or on a mountain, gorge or gulf ABYSS, CHASM
– narrow gap or gorge, as gouged out by a river or flood waters CANYON, RAVINE, COULOIR, GULLY, GULCH, WADI
– narrow gap or pass, as through mountains DEFILE
– small gap or opening, as in a wall or rock CRANNY, FISSURE, RIFT, CLEFT, CREVICE
– small space, opening, or gap, as between the strands of a net INTERSTICE
garden arch or frame made of criss-crossing sticks, on which climbing plants are trained to grow TRELLIS
– garden designed with an ornamental pattern of paths between the flowerbeds PARTERRE
– garden of formal design, with detailed patterns of flowerbeds KNOT GARDEN
– garden party, picnic, or other outdoor meal or entertainment FÊTE CHAMPÊTRE
– garden pavilion or summerhouse, usually having a fine view GAZEBO, BELVEDERE
– garden shears used for pruning SECATEURS
– garden shelter, often made of trellising BOWER, ARBOUR
– garden walk or tree-lined terrace in ancient Rome XYST
– garden's summerhouse, bower, or other secluded spot ALCOVE
– improved by contouring and planting, as large grounds or gardens might be LANDSCAPED
gardening, especially flower growing HORTICULTURE
– gardening tool for making holes in the soil, as for bulbs or seedlings DIBBER, DIBBLE
– ornamental gardening in which trees or hedges are clipped into designs TOPIARY
garland or wreath CORONAL
garlic, onion, leek, or related plant ALLIUM
– smelling or tasting of onions or garlic ALLIACEOUS
garlic mayonnaise AÏOLI
garment, especially a ceremonial robe VESTMENT
– garment made up in cheap cloth as a basis for alterations or copies TOILE
– triangular insert of material for enlarging or reinforcing a garment, bag, or the like GUSSET
garnish of diced, cooked vegetables JARDINIÈRE
gas See chart, page 212
– gas, smoke, or vapour blown or breathed out EXHALATION
– gas, such as helium or neon, for-

merly considered incapable of chemical reaction INERT GAS, NOBLE GAS, RARE GAS
– gas build-up in the digestive tract, causing breaking of wind FLATULENCE
– gas built up in the digestive tract FLATUS
– gas burner producing a hot flame, used for laboratory experiments BUNSEN BURNER
– gas-like matter of enormously high temperature, as in stars and fusion reactors PLASMA
– gas of a poisonous or bad-smelling kind rising from the ground MEPHITIS
– gas or vapour, as rising from a swamp or rubbish heap, smelly and invisible EFFLUVIUM
– gas produced in radioactive decay EMANATION
– gas used in aerosol sprays PROPELLANT
– gas well or oil well with an abundant natural flow GUSHER
– abdominal pain caused by gas in the intestines COLIC
– able to absorb gas or liquid PERMEABLE, POROUS
– adjective for a gas GASEOUS
– butane gas liquefied in portable cylinders CALOR GAS
– convert into a gas VAPORISE
– expelling or reducing gas in the stomach or intestines, relieving flatulence CARMINATIVE
– hypothetical gas-like substance formerly thought to fill all space and sustain light waves ETHER
– low in density, thin, as the air of the upper atmosphere is or a gas might be RAREFIED
– release air or gas from something, such as a tyre DEFLATE
– resistant to liquids or gases IMPERMEABLE, IMPERVIOUS
– send out or give off something, such as gas or radiation EMIT
– turn directly from a gas into a solid or vice versa without becoming a liquid SUBLIMATE

-gas- -AER-, -AERO-, ATMO-, PNEUM-, PNEUMO-, PNEUMATO-

gas mask – covering for the mouth and nose, resembling a gas mask, to purify or warm the air before breathing RESPIRATOR

gate partially enclosed at the free end, allowing only one person through at a time KISSING GATE
– churchyard's roofed gate, where the coffin is traditionally rested at the start of the burial LICH GATE
– defensive tower or fortification, such as the gate of a castle or town BARBICAN
– revolving door or gate TURNSTILE
– side or back gate POSTERN

gather, collect, store up ACCUMULATE, AMASS
– gather, crowd together, assemble CONGREGATE, FORGATHER
– gather and store, as in a granary GARNER
– gather data, poems, or other items from several sources, for use in a book or survey COMPILE
– gather grain or crops left in a field after harvesting GLEAN
– gather into a mass or whole, come or bring together AGGREGATE, CONGLOMERATE
– gather or bring together helpers, arguments, or the like MARSHAL, MUSTER, MOBILISE, ENLIST, RALLY
– gather or collect something, such as flowers CULL
– gather or summon, as for a for-

GASES

acetylene, ethyne	used for producing a hot flame for welding and cutting metal
ammonia	used in making fertilisers and synthetic fibres, and as a refrigerant
blackdamp, chokedamp	mixture high in carbon dioxide, found in coal mines after a fire or explosion
butane	used in cigarette lighters and domestic fuels
carbon dioxide	used as a refrigerant and in fizzy drinks and aerosols
carbon monoxide	formed by incomplete burning coal, petrol, or the like; known as white damp or afterdamp in coal mines
CS gas	tear gas, used in riot control
cyanogen	used for pest control and as a chemical weapon and rocket propellant
diethyl ether, ethoxyethane	used as an anaesthetic and in many industrial processes
ethylene, ethene	made from natural gas or petroleum, used in making plastics
helium	used in fluorescent lighting tubes, lasers and balloons
hydrogen sulphide	smell of rotten eggs; used in chemical analyses
krypton	used in light bulbs, and in high-speed photography
laughing gas, nitrous oxide	used as a mild anaesthetic
methane, marsh gas, firedamp	main constituent of natural gas, and found in coal mines, marshlands, and the like; used in making chloroform and methyl alcohol
mustard gas, yperite	dichlorodiethyl sulphide, used in chemical warfare to produce burns and eye irritation
neon	used in lasers and illuminated signs, glowing pink or red
ozone	unstable form of oxygen, common in the upper atmosphere; used in bleaches, air-conditioning systems and purification processes
propane	often found in natural gas and petroleum, used as a fuel and refrigerant
radon, niton	formed by the radioactive decay of radium, used in radiotherapy and atomic research
xenon	used in thermionic valves, lamps, and lasers

mal meeting or public assembly CONVENE, CONVOKE
gathering See also **meeting**, **crowd**
– gathering or contracting, as of the brows PURSING, PUCKERING
– gathering and stitching of cloth into tucked patterns SMOCKING
– gather fabric into decorative rows, as on a dress SHIRR
– gathering or pleating of fabric into a frilled trimming or decoration RUFFLING, RUCHING
gaudy, vulgar, tasteless and showy, cheap-looking TAWDRY, GIMCRACK
gauge – metal strip of known thickness used to gauge a narrow gap between two parts FEELER GAUGE
gauze drum or dome that increases the light of a gas lamp MANTLE
gear enabling the driving wheels to turn at different rates, as when cornering DIFFERENTIAL GEAR
– gear higher than the normal range OVERDRIVE
– gear system synchronising the speeds of the moving parts SYNCHROMESH
– gear system in which one or more wheels move round the outside or inside of a fixed-axis wheel EPICYCLIC TRAIN
– gears, clutch, or shaft by which power passes from an engine or pedals to the axle TRANSMISSION
– change gear by pausing in neutral to declutch and pressing the accelerator briefly DOUBLE-DECLUTCH
– conical gear meshing with another to transmit power between shafts at an angle to each other but in the same plane BEVEL GEAR
– device for changing gear on a bicycle, transferring the chain between sprockets DERAILLEUR
– engage or interlock, as gear teeth might MESH
– smaller gearwheel PINION
– toothed bar that meshes with a gearwheel RACK
– toothed gearwheel or bar allowing movement in one direction only RATCHET
– tooth-like projection, as on a gearwheel DENT, DENTATION, DENTICLE
geese – adjective for geese ANSERINE
– flock of geese on land GAGGLE
– flock of geese or other wildfowl in flight SKEIN
gel – gel-forming substance used as a setting agent in jams PECTIN
gelatine made from the air bladders of certain freshwater fish ISINGLASS
gelatine- COLLO-
gemstone See illustration, page 214, and also **jewellery**, **precious stones**
– gemstone, shell, or the like engraved with a raised design CAMEO
– gemstone associated with people born during a given month BIRTHSTONE
– gemstone set by itself, as in a ring SOLITAIRE
– gemstone with a changing lustre or twinkling surface, such as a cat's eye CHATOYANT
– art of carving or engraving on gemstones GLYPTOGRAPHY
– artificial gemstone of quartz or fine glass RHINESTONE
– degree of shine or transparency of a gemstone LUSTRE, WATER
– deep red, rounded, uncut gemstone CARBUNCLE
– fake gemstone, typically consisting of coloured glass with a face of real gemstone DOUBLET
– fine hard glass used in making artificial gemstones PASTE, STRASS
– groove, rim, ring, or the like for clamping a gemstone or watch crystal BEZEL
– metal leaf fixed under a gemstone for added brilliance FOIL
– person who cuts and polishes gemstones LAPIDARY
– relating to carving or engraving, especially on gemstones GLYPTIC
– revolving drum in which gemstones are smoothed and polished by abrasives TUMBLING BARREL, TUMBLER, RUMBLE
– rim securing a gemstone in a piece of jewellery COLLET
– setting for a gemstone OUCH
– support or backing, as for a gemstone MOUNTING
gender, as of *child* or *lawyer*, that may be either masculine or feminine in reference COMMON GENDER
– neither masculine nor feminine in gender NEUTER
gene See **genetics**
general, universal, sweeping, all-embracing CATHOLIC
– general, universal, very widespread, prevalent, EPIDEMIC, PANDEMIC, ENDEMIC
– general, wide-ranging, comprehensive, giving or having a broad view SYNOPTIC, PANORAMIC, MACROSCOPIC
– general agreement CONSENSUS
– general assembly, meeting with all members present PLENUM, PLENARY SESSION
– general assistant or employee doing a variety of work FACTOTUM
– general direction or movement, as of someone's life TENOR
– general idea, or word referring to a general idea rather than to a specific thing ABSTRACTION
– general impression, survey, or description OVERVIEW, CONSPECTUS
– belonging to a higher or larger class or level of generality SUPERORDINATE
– classify or include in a wider category or under a general heading or principle SUBSUME
– generally or widely applicable, talented, or the like VERSATILE
generalness, or generalisation GENERALITY
generator, especially of direct current DYNAMO
– generator in the ignition system of some engines MAGNETO
– device, as on an electric motor or generator, for reversing the direction of a current, or converting alternating current into direct current COMMUTATOR
– electrostatic generator in which the charge accumulates on a hollow metal ball VAN DE GRAAFF GENERATOR
– rotating part of a generator or electric motor ARMATURE
generosity shown in the form of gifts of money or favours LARGESSE
generous, or willingly given UNSTINTED, UNGRUDGING, BOUNTEOUS
– generous and charitable, selfless PHILANTHROPIC, ALTRUISTIC
– generous in forgiving, big-hearted, noble MAGNANIMOUS
– generous or extravagant LAVISH, PRODIGAL, PROFUSE
– generous with gifts, hospitality, or the like, open-handed MUNIFICENT, BOUNTIFUL, LIBERAL
– obligation on noble or noble-minded people to be generous and honourable NOBLESSE OBLIGE
genetics See also **cell**
– genetically deviant organism MUTANT, SPORT
– gene that can produce a particular characteristic in an organism when paired with an identical or dissimilar gene DOMINANT GENE
– gene that can produce a particular characteristic only when it is paired with an identical gene RECESSIVE GENE
– laws of genetics, the basic principles of heredity MENDEL'S LAWS
– plant, animal, or cell genetically identical to another through asexual descent from a common ancestor CLONE
– plant or animal that is a genetic mix CHIMERA
– thread of RNA, DNA, and protein in a cell nucleus, carrying genes with genetic code and responsible for transmitting hereditary characteristics CHROMOSOME

gemstones

GEMSTONE CUTS

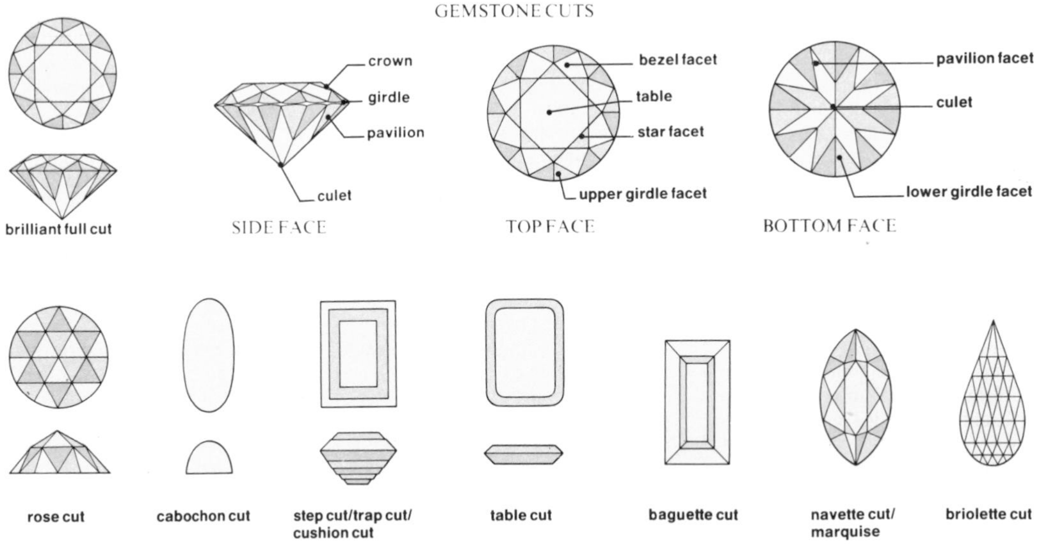

TYPES OF GEMSTONE

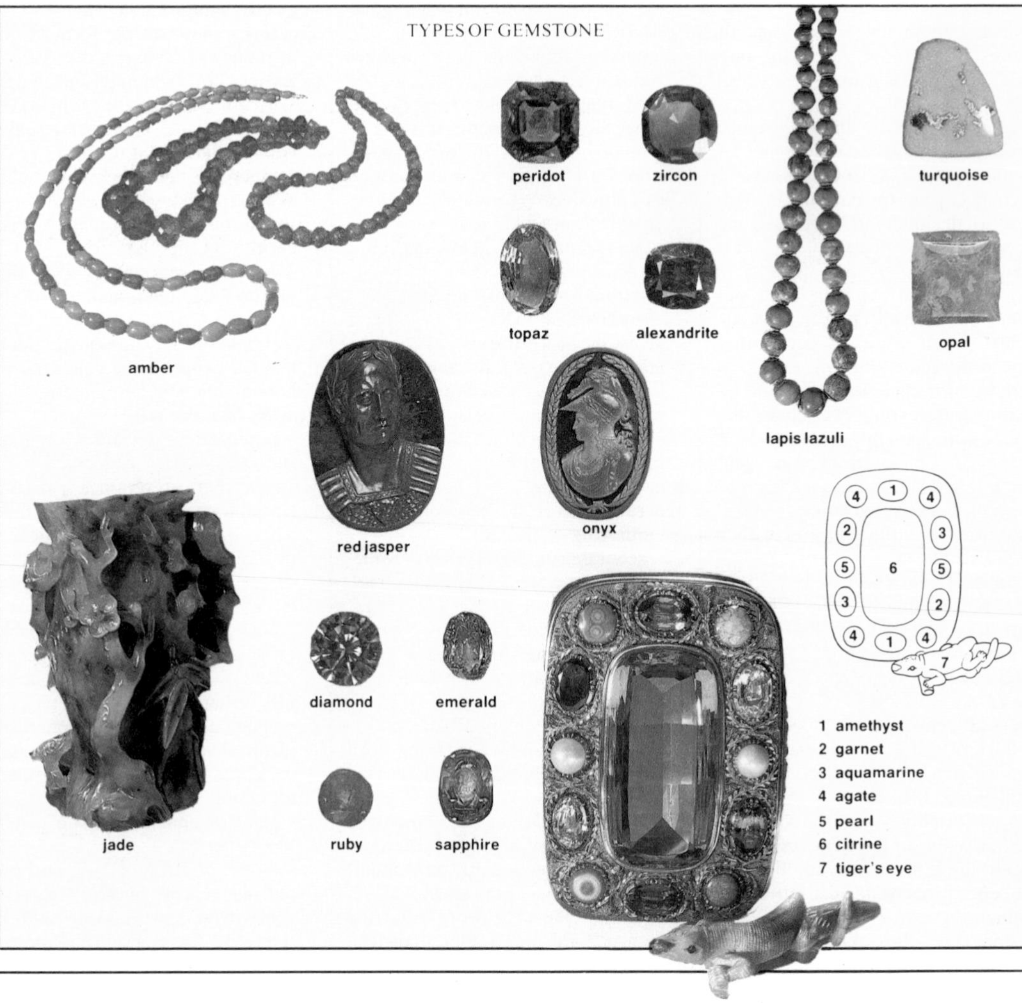

1 amethyst
2 garnet
3 aquamarine
4 agate
5 pearl
6 citrine
7 tiger's eye

– transference of genetic information from DNA to RNA TRANSCRIPTION

genie, spirit taking human form, in Muslim legend JINNI

genitals See also **sex**

– genital, relating to the region around the sex organs PUBIC

– genital area CROTCH, CRUTCH

– genital area in males GROIN

– genital sore or growth, hard and red, indicating syphilis CHANCRE

– genital sore or growth that is soft and non-syphilitic CHANCROID

– area between the anus and genitals in the human body PERINEUM

– external genital organs, especially a woman's PUDENDA

– fastening of the female genitals with clasps or stitches to prevent sexual intercourse INFIBULATION

– opening for the digestive and genital tracts in birds, fish, and reptiles CLOACA

– relating to sex or the genital organs VENEREAL

gentleman, such as an able horseman or a courtly escort CAVALIER

– gentleman in Spanish-speaking countries CABALLERO

– gentlemanly, courteous, especially towards women CHIVALROUS

gentleness, mildness of manner MANSUETUDE

gentry – referring to or resembling the British country gentry TWEEDY

genuine, real, not imaginary or apparent SUBSTANTIVE, VERITABLE

– genuine, real, true, reliable AUTHENTIC, BONA FIDE, ECHT, DINKUM, SIMON-PURE, KOSHER

– genuine, right and proper PUKKA

– genuine or true, in accordance with the facts VERIDICAL

– attractive or plausible but not really true or genuine SPECIOUS

– superficially similar but not corresponding or genuine SPURIOUS

genus – adjective for a genus or similar classification GENERIC

geography See chart, and also **Earth**, **glacier**, **volcano**, **map**, **atmosphere**

– geographical features of a region, as on a map TOPOGRAPHY

– geographical mistake, place-error, positioning something in the wrong locality ANACHORISM

geology See also **Earth**, **earthquake**, **glacier**, **volcano**, **rock**, **mountain**, **continent**

– geological accumulation of rock debris SCREE, TALUS

– geological deposit of dust laid down by the wind LOESS

– geological downfold of rock layers SYNCLINE

– geological fracture along which rock displacement occurs FAULT

– geological mountain-building episode OROGENY

– geological upfold of rock layers ANTICLINE

– geological uplift or subsidence of continental landmasses without folding EPEIROGENY

– divisions of geological time ERA, PERIOD, EPOCH, AGE

– highland between two parallel geological faults HORST

– in geology, a mass of calcite projecting from the floor of a cave STALAGMITE

– in geology, an icicle-like mass of calcite hanging from the roof

GEOGRAPHICAL FEATURES

archipelago	cluster of islands in the sea
atoll	circular coral reef enclosing a lagoon
barrier reef	coral reef running parallel to the coast
bushveld, veld	grassland with low trees in parts of southern Africa
butte	small, prominent, flat-topped hill rising abruptly from the surrounding desert
campo	large, grassy plain with small trees in Brazil
cay	low islet of coral or sand
erg	area of shifting sand dunes, typically in North Africa
fiord/fjord	deep and long inlet of the sea
guyot	flat-topped mountain on the sea bed
inselberg	isolated domed hill in arid regions
isthmus	strip of land connecting two much larger pieces of land
kop/koppie	small prominent hill in southern Africa
llano	treeless grassland in northern South America
massif	large highland region with well-defined boundaries
mesa	flat-topped highland with cliff-like sides in arid regions
oxbow, oxbow lake, mortlake	bow-shaped lake formed when a river cuts across the neck of a U-shaped bend
pamir	high grassland in central Asia
pampas	grasslands in Argentina and Uruguay
playa, salina, shott	flat basin which may periodically become a shallow salt lake
polder	area of low-lying reclaimed land, typically in the Netherlands
prairie	treeless grassland in North America
reg	flat, stony desert, typically in North Africa
ria	indentation where the sea has drowned the lower part of a river valley
savannah	grassland with scattered trees in tropical and subtropical regions
sierra	high range of mountains with jagged peaks
strath	steep-sided, broad, flat-floored valley in Scotland
tundra	area between the area of permanent snow and the treeline in Arctic regions
wadi, donga	rocky desert ravine occasionally carrying a torrent after heavy rain

geometrical shapes

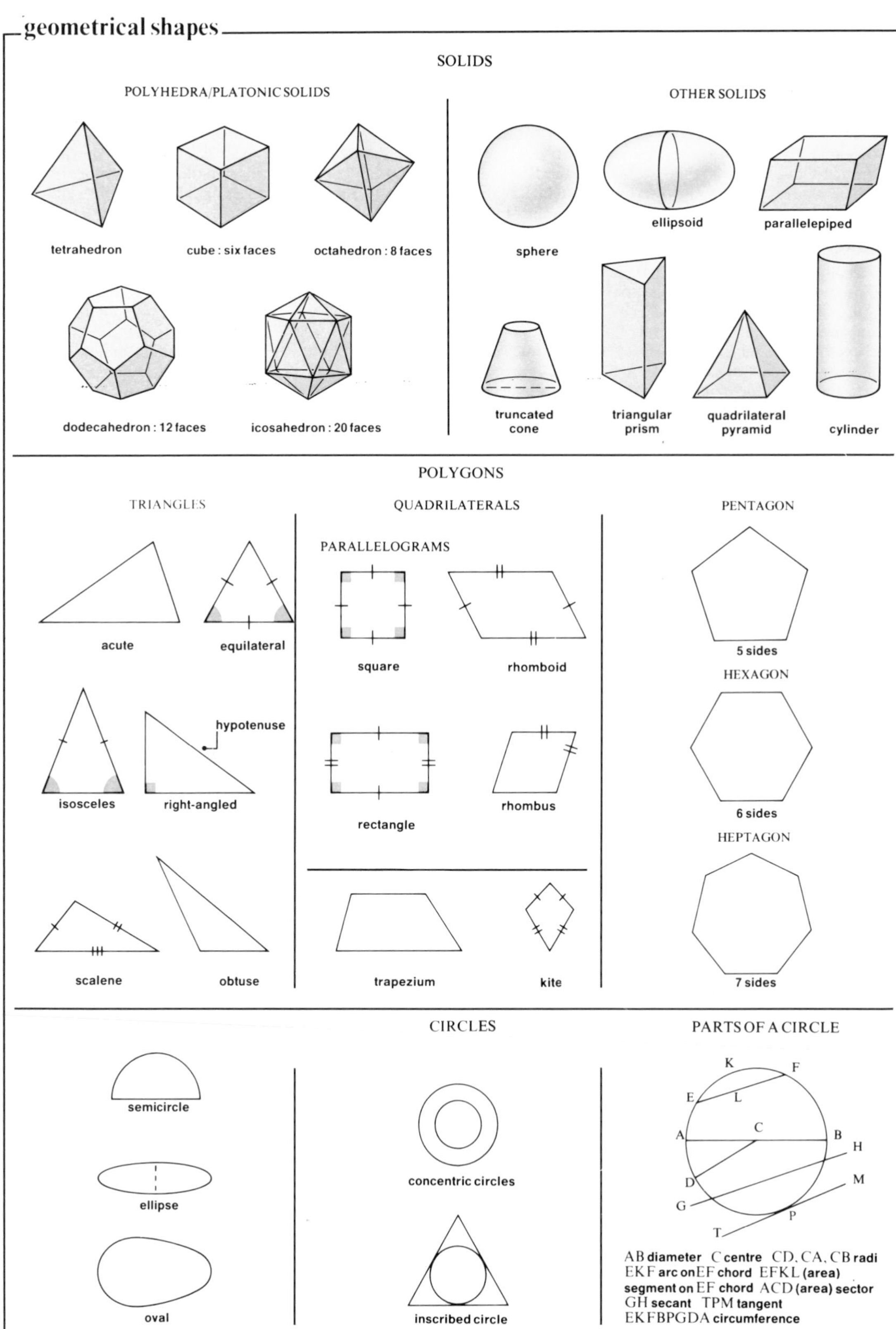
SOLIDS
POLYHEDRA/PLATONIC SOLIDS
tetrahedron
cube : six faces
octahedron : 8 faces
dodecahedron : 12 faces
icosahedron : 20 faces
OTHER SOLIDS
sphere
ellipsoid
parallelepiped
truncated cone
triangular prism
quadrilateral pyramid
cylinder
POLYGONS
TRIANGLES
acute
equilateral
isosceles
hypotenuse
right-angled
scalene
obtuse
QUADRILATERALS
PARALLELOGRAMS
square
rhomboid
rectangle
rhombus
trapezium
kite
PENTAGON
5 sides
HEXAGON
6 sides
HEPTAGON
7 sides
CIRCLES
semicircle
ellipse
oval
concentric circles
inscribed circle
PARTS OF A CIRCLE
K
F
E
L
A
C
B
H
D
M
G
P
T
AB diameter C centre CD, CA, CB radi
EKF arc on EF chord EFKL (area)
segment on EF chord ACD (area) sector
GH secant TPM tangent
EKFBPGDA circumference

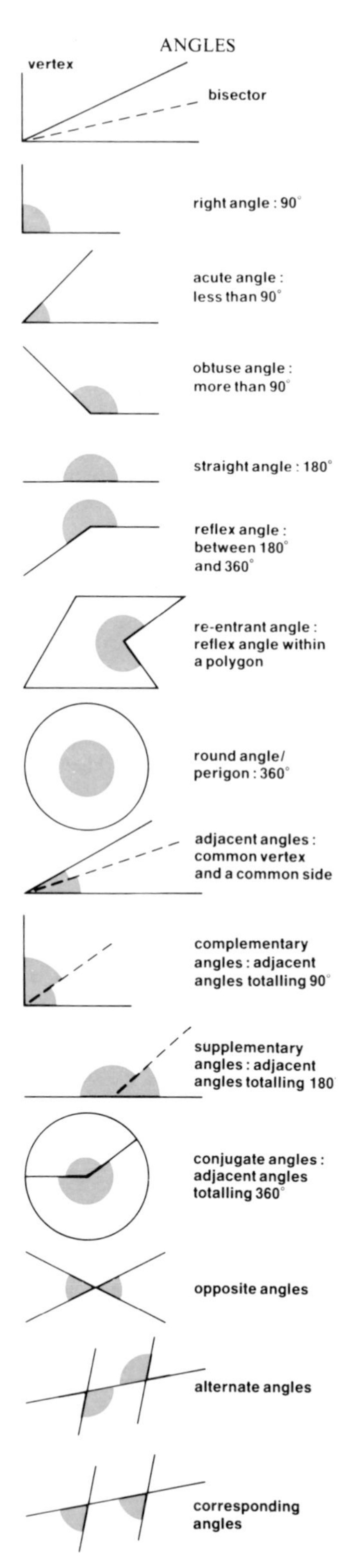

of a cave STALACTITE
– replacement of geological organic matter by minerals, as in fossils PETRIFACTION
– study of rocks in geology PETROLOGY
– trough in the Earth's crust whose floor is subsiding under geological sediments GEOSYNCLINE
– valley between two parallel geological faults GRABEN, RIFT VALLEY

geometry See illustration, and also **mathematics, graph, curve, line**
– geometric figure, line, or angle, as used in solving a problem or proving a theorem CONSTRUCTION
– geometrical measurement MENSURATION
– geometrical puzzle consisting of a one-sided surface made by forming a twisted strip into a ring MÖBIUS STRIP
– instrument used to draw circles, as in geometry COMPASSES
– instrument used to measure and draw angles, as in geometry PROTRACTOR
– problem or supplementary rule arising from a theorem, as in geometry RIDER

geranium PELARGONIUM

germ See also **bacteria**, **virus**
– germ, disease-causing agent PATHOGEN
– germ, poison, or any other harmful substance that prompts the body's immune system to produce antibodies ANTIGEN
– blood protein that is produced to counteract germs or other invading substances ANTIBODY
– insect or other organism that transmits germs VECTOR, CARRIER

-germ- -BLAST-

German See chart, page 218
– German chief minister CHANCELLOR, KANZLER
– German having some Dutch features PLATTDEUTSCH
– German POW camp for captured other ranks STALAG
– German pub or restaurant, originally in the cellars of a town hall RATSKELLER
– German town hall RATHAUS
– Germany's annexation of Austria in 1938 ANSCHLUSS
– derogatory term for a German BOCHE
– member of German guild formed to promote music and poetry MEISTERSINGER
– Rhine siren of German legend LORELEI

German measles RUBELLA, ROSEOLA

germinate or sprout PULLULATE

germination See **seed**

germination- BLASTO-

gesture of greeting SALUTATION
– gesture of greeting or respect, as in India, by placing one's hands out together in front of one and bowing slightly NAMASTE
– gesture of greeting or respect, as in many Muslim societies, by bowing and touching the forehead with the right hand SALAAM
– gesture of humility, as formerly in China, by prostrating oneself or kneeling and touching the ground with one's forehead KOWTOW
– gesture of humility or reverence, by bending or kneeling briefly on one knee GENUFLECTION
– gesture of minimal compliance with a law or custom TOKENISM
– gesture of respect or submission, such as a bow or curtsy OBEISANCE
– gesture of scorn made by thumbing the nose SNOOK
– gesture or action that is noble in appearance, though sometimes empty in effect BEAU GESTE
– gesture vigorously, as to reinforce speech GESTICULATE
– gestures, posture, and similar nonverbal and unconscious communication BODY LANGUAGE
– hostile gesture made when leaving PARTHIAN SHOT
– study of movement, gesture, and expression KINESICS
– supplementing verbal communication, as voice qualities and gestures do PARALINGUISTIC

get, obtain, receive, gain ACQUIRE, SECURE, PROCURE, GARNER

get rid of See also **destroy**, **exclude**
– get rid of, cancel, or withdraw officially a law, decree, or the like REPEAL, REVOKE, RESCIND
– get rid of, put an end to, abolish, or lessen something ABATE
– get rid of, reject, or disown a wife, child, or the like REPUDIATE
– get rid of or abolish formally a law, treaty, or the like ABROGATE, ANNUL, NULLIFY
– get rid of or manage without DISPENSE WITH
– get rid of or throw away something unwanted DISPOSE OF, DISCARD, JETTISON, SLOUGH OFF

geyser – expel hot water and steam forcefully and abundantly, as a geyser does ERUPT

ghost See also **spirit**, **demon**
– ghost, supernatural being, spirit from another world VISITANT
– ghost-like substance supposedly emerging from a spiritualist medium during a seance ECTOPLASM
– ghost or ghostly figure, phantom SPECTRE, APPARITION, PHANTASM,

GERMAN TERMS

Angst	anxiety
auf Wiedersehen	farewell
Bierkeller	beer cellar
Bildungsroman	novel dealing with the early life of one person
Blitzkrieg	lightning attack
Doppelgänger	ghostly double
ersatz	substitute,artificial
Gastarbeiter	immigrant worker
Gasthof	hotel
Gauleiter	Nazi district governor; petty tyrant
gemütlich	comfortable; snug
Gesundheit!	Bless you!
Hausfrau	housewife
Herrenvolk	master race
Junker	reactionary Prussian aristocrat
Kaiser	emperor
Kapellmeister	director of a choir or orchestra
kaput	broken, out of order, useless
Kitsch	bad taste, or sentimentality in the arts
Lebensraum	living space for an expanding population
Lederhosen	man's leather shorts
Lied	song for solo voice and piano
Luftwaffe	German air force
Panzer	army tank
Putsch	attempt to overthrow a government by a sudden rebellion
Realpolitik	harsh policy of national self-interest
Reich	empire or republic
Schadenfreude	delight in others' misfortunes
Schmalz	excessive sentimentality
Stein	earthenware tankard
Sturm und Drang	late 18th-century German romantic literary movement
Weltanschauung	philosophy of life, world view
Weltschmerz	romantic sadness or pessimism; world-weariness
Zeitgeist	the spirit of the times

PRESENCE, EIDOLON
– ghost or spirit, someone returned from the dead in ghostly form SHADE, WRAITH, REVENANT
– ghost or spirit in Caribbean folklore DUPPY
– ghosts or spirits of the dead in ancient Rome MANES, LEMURES
– appearance of a ghost, spirit, angel, or the like VISITATION
– corpse animated by a voodoo spell, body without a spirit, the converse of a ghost ZOMBIE
– forecasting or divination by consulting ghosts SCIOMANCY
– ghostly counterpart or double DOPPELGÄNGER, FETCH
– noisy or mischievous ghost or spirit POLTERGEIST
– take bodily form, become visible, as a ghost might MATERIALISE

giant See also **monster**
– giant TITAN, COLOSSUS
– giant or man-like monster OGRE
– giant or gnome in Scandinavian folklore TROLL

gift, payment, or other expression of respect, submission, homage, or the like TRIBUTE, FAVOUR
– gift, possession, or project requiring more trouble than it is worth WHITE ELEPHANT
– gift or grant, as to a charity CONTRIBUTION, DONATION
– gift or payment in return for a service or favour CONSIDERATION, RECOMPENSE
– gift or small favour offered to appease or bribe SOP
– gift that serves to remind one of the giver KEEPSAKE, MEMENTO
– gifts, money, or favours distributed generously LARGESSE
– small gift or bonus, tip PERK, PERQUISITE

gift of tongues, emotional or ecstatic and largely unintelligible speech GLOSSOLALIA

gifts of the Magi – perfumed resins, among the gifts of the Magi MYRRH, FRANKINCENSE

Gilbert-and-Sullivan fan, performer, or producer SAVOYARD

gilded silver, bronze, or copper VERMEIL

gill – gill cover on a fish OPERCULUM

-gills- -BRANCH-

gin, as sold in stone bottles HOLLANDS, HOLLAND'S GIN, GENEVA
– berries used to flavour gin JUNIPER BERRIES

ginger root RACE

Gipsy See **Gypsy**

giraffe – African forest mammal, related to the giraffe OKAPI
– former term for a giraffe CAMELOPARD

girder supporting the timbers of a floor STRINGER, SUMMER

girl, maiden, young woman DAMSEL
– girl from abroad, working as a nanny or household help in return for board and lodging AU PAIR
– girl of the streets URCHIN, WAIF
– girl or young woman, slim and attractive in a boyish way GAMINE
– girls' or women's club, as at a U.S. university SORORITY
– beautiful girl NYMPH
– group of girls, larks, quail, or roe deer BEVY
– ideal fashionable girl in the U.S. around 1900 GIBSON GIRL
– innocent and naive girl or young women INGÉNUE
– Irish term for a young girl COLLEEN
– small, slim, dainty as a girl might be PETITE

Girl Guides – senior member of the Girl Guides RANGER

give away or sell DISPOSE OF
– give back as much as one has received RECIPROCATE
– give off or discharge slowly or conspicuously EXUDE
– give off something, such as radiation EMIT, EMANATE, EXHALE
– give or apply medication, assistance, or the like ADMINISTER
– give or commit something permanently CONSIGN
– give or contribute DONATE
– give or convey something, such as greetings or respectability EX-

TEND, IMPART
– give or grant something, such as a favour or nod, in a patronising way VOUCHSAFE
– give or grant something, such as an honour or blessing BESTOW, CONFER, ACCORD
– give or provide something, such as assistance or a view AFFORD, FURNISH, RENDER
– give or spend generously and unsparingly, dole out LAVISH
– give or yield formally CEDE
– give out or distribute something, in portions or shares DISPENSE, ALLOCATE, ALLOT, APPORTION
– give reluctantly DISGORGE
– give rise to ELICIT, EVOKE
– give to, provide with, equip or entrust with INVEST WITH, ENDOW WITH, ENDUE WITH
– keep offering or giving something to PLY
– person who gives money for charity or the like DONOR

give in See also **yield**
– give in to or indulge a whim, desire, or the like GRATIFY

give up See also **stop**, **surrender**
– give up a claim or right voluntarily WAIVE
– give up or abandon something desirable FORSAKE, RELINQUISH, ABNEGATE, ABJURE
– give up or abstain from something desirable or promising, such as an opportunity FORGO
– give up or lose something by way of a fine or penalty FORFEIT
– give up or reject all claims to or connection with, disown RENOUNCE, DISCLAIM, REPUDIATE, FORSWEAR
– give up power ABDICATE

given or done in return or exchange RECIPROCAL
– given willingly, unsparing UNSTINTED, UNGRUDGING

giving up or surrender of something, as of land or rights CESSION

glacier See illustration
– ridge of debris deposited by a melting glacier or ice-sheet KAME
– streamlined hill formed by glacial deposits DRUMLIN
– wearing away of a glacier, as by melting ABLATION

gladiator, in ancient Rome, armed with a net and trident RETIARIUS
– gladiator's three-pronged spear TRIDENT

glamour, aura of mystery MYSTIQUE

glance, quick inspection COUP D'OEIL, SHUFTI

gland See chart, page 220
– chemical secretion from glands, modifying the workings of a tissue or organ HORMONE
– oily substance produced by glands SEBUM, SMEGMA
– relating to glands ADENOIDAL
– study of glands ENDOCRINOLOGY
– swelling and inflammation of a lymph gland BUBO

gland- ADEN-, ADENO-

glandular fever INFECTIOUS MONONUCLEOSIS

glare – glare-reducing plastic, as used in some sunglasses POLAROID
– glare shield fitted at the top of a car's windscreen VISOR

glaringly or outrageously wrong or evil FLAGRANT, EGREGIOUS
– glaringly bright in colour GARISH, LURID

glass, goblet, tankard, or the like filled to the brim BUMPER
– glass cover for a watch face LUNETTE
– glass for drinking, especially one having a rounded bottom inside TUMBLER
– glass in a heated lump, ready for

glacier

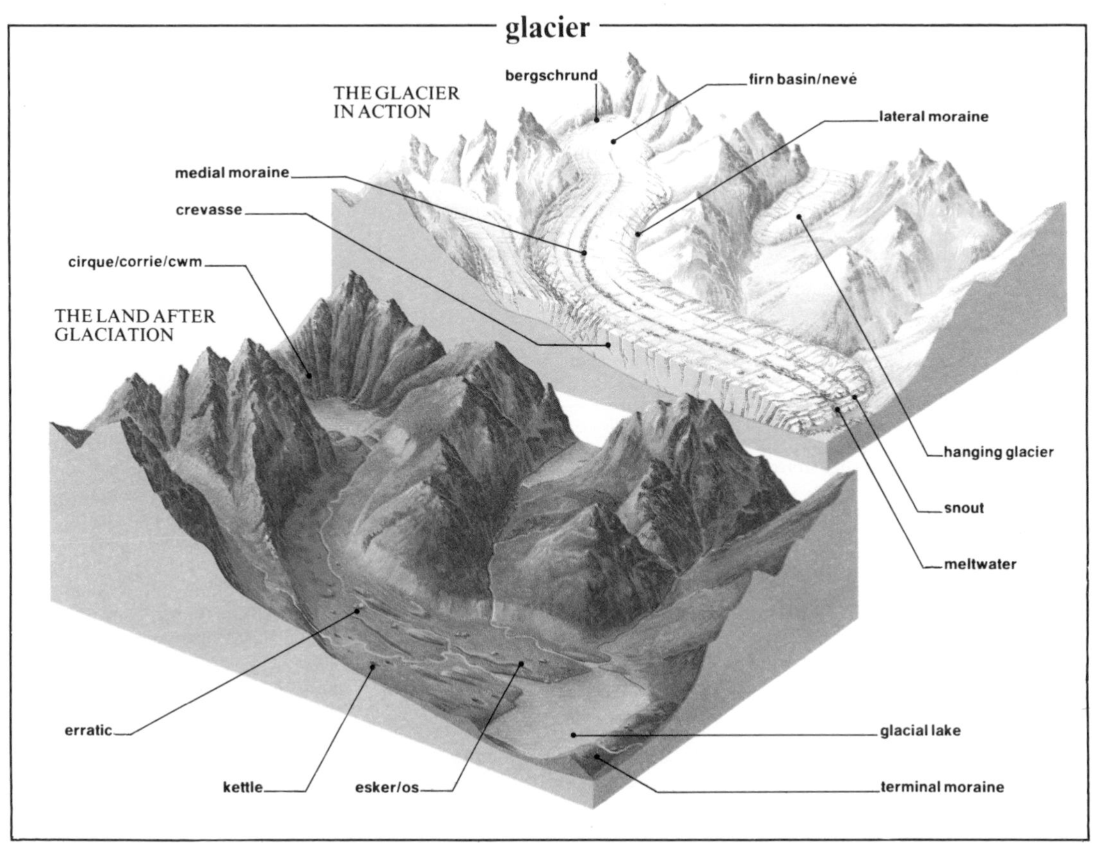

GLANDS

adrenal glands, suprarenal glands	glands located above the kidneys that secret adrenaline and corticosteroid hormones into the bloodstream
apocrine glands	glands, such as mammary glands, in which part of the secreting cell itself goes into the secretion
eccrine glands	glands that secrete externally, specifically the sweat glands
endocrine glands, ductless glands	glands, such as the thyroid and pituitary, that secrete hormones directly into the bloodstream
exocrine glands	glands, such as sweat glands, that secrete through a duct
holocrine glands	glands, such as sebaceous glands, in which cells disintegrate entirely to form the secretion
lachrymal glands	tear glands beneath the upper eyelids
lymph nodes, lymph glands	gland-like masses of tissue that supply certain white blood cells, absorb bacteria, and purify the lymph
mammary glands	milk-producing glands in female mammals
merocrine glands	glands, such as sweat glands, in which the secreting cells remain intact
ovaries	female reproductive glands
pancreas	gland near the stomach, secreting digestive juices into the duodenum, and containing the insulin-producing islets of Langerhans
parathyroid glands	glands that secrete hormones that raise the level of calcium in the blood
parotid glands	largest of the salivary glands below each ear
pineal body, pineal gland, epiphysis	gland-like structure in the brain of vertebrates, possibly regulating the human body's internal clock
pituitary gland, pituitary body, hypophysis	master endocrine gland at the base of the brain, producing hormones that regulate other glands and stimulate bone growth
prostate gland	gland in male mammals, secreting a liquid that forms part of the semen
sebaceous glands	skin glands that secrete an oily substance into the hair follicles and onto the skin
testes	male reproductive glands, the testicles
thymus	gland-like structure producing some white blood cells
thyroid gland	gland in the neck, regulating metabolism and growth

moulding or blowing PARISON
– glass of a decorative multi-coloured type, as used in lamps and ornaments in the early 1900s FAVRILE GLASS, TIFFANY GLASS
– glass of a heat-resistant type, used for ovenware PYREX
– glass of a pale whitish, semi-transparent type OPALINE
– glass or transparent plastic block, triangular in cross-section, as in cameras, for reflecting, refracting, or dispersing light PRISM
– glass tile or disc inset to admit light BULL'S-EYE
– glass tube, open at both ends, into which liquid is sucked to be measured or transferred PIPETTE
– glass vessel with a long drooping neck, as used for distilling RETORT
– glassware decorated with pieces of coloured metal or glass MURRHINE GLASS
– allowing light to pass diffusely, as frosted glass does TRANSLUCENT
– allowing light to pass freely, as clear glass does TRANSPARENT
– chemical compound used in glass and concrete manufacture SILICA, SILICON DIOXIDE, QUARTZ
– clarifying of molten glass by removing gas bubbles FINING
– clear acrylic plastic used as a substitute for glass PERSPEX
– dark glass containing sparkling metal particles AVENTURINE
– darkening or changing colour if exposed to light, as some glass or plastic does PHOTOCHROMIC
– fine hard glass of varying kinds used in making lenses OPTICAL GLASS, CROWN GLASS, FLINT GLASS
– fine hard glass used in making artificial gems PASTE, STRASS
– fine Irish glassware with a bluish tinge WATERFORD GLASS
– former medical technique of attaching a glass cup to the skin by a partial vacuum, in order to draw blood to the surface CUPPING
– heat, then cool, metal or glass to strengthen it TEMPER, ANNEAL
– installer of window glass GLAZIER
– iron rod used for finishing in glassmaking PUNTY, PONTIL
– large drinking glass, usually with a short stem RUMMER
– large glass for sherry or port, or large beer glass SCHOONER
– process discarded glass, paper, and so on for re-use RECYCLE
– relating to glass ground and polished on both sides PATENT
– safety glass containing layers of plastic LAMINATED GLASS
– small glass used for serving or measuring spirits JIGGER
– small mat placed under a glass to protect the table top COASTER
– soluble fusible mineral used in making glass and pottery BORAX
– turn into glass, as by heating or melting VITRIFY
– window glass of former times, with a circular shape and a lump in the centre CROWN GLASS

glass- HYAL-, HYALO-, VITR-, VITRO-

glass fibre, thin and flexible, for transmission of light and telecommunications OPTICAL FIBRE

glasses or pair of opera glasses supported in position by a small handle LORGNETTE, LORGNON
– glasses with compound lenses, correcting for both near and distant vision BIFOCALS
– glasses without sidepieces, held in place by being clipped to the

bridge of the nose PINCE-NEZ
– maker and seller of glasses OPTICIAN
– referring to glasses with frames of horn, tortoiseshell, or plastic HORN-RIMMED, TORTOISESHELL
– single glass lens serving as half of a pair of glasses MONOCLE, QUIZZING GLASS

glasshouse in which plants are cultivated CONSERVATORY

glassy, or relating to or consisting of glass VITREOUS
– glassy rock, black and shiny, of volcanic origin OBSIDIAN

glaze of a shiny metallic kind on pottery LUSTRE
– glazed fish or meat dish, served cold GALANTINE

glide, skim, or skip lightly, as over the surface of water SKITTER
– glide or move smoothly, as clouds might SCUD
– glide without power, as an aircraft might VOLPLANE

glider in the form of a single large cloth wing from which the pilot hangs in a harness HANG-GLIDER

glitter, sparkle, flash, as a gemstone might CORUSCATE, SPANGLE, SCINTILLATE, FULGURATE
– glitter gently, gleam GLISTEN, SHIMMER
– glitter or sheen LUSTRE
– glitter or shine producing a variety of colours IRIDESCENCE
– glittering, as with sequins CLINQUANT
– glittering, decorated with glass, sequins, or jewels to produce a diamond-like effect DIAMANTÉ
– glittering decoration of thin threads or strips TINSEL
– glittering fabric containing silver or golden threads LAMÉ

gloomy, tomb-like SEPULCHRAL
– gloomy in temper, or cold in temperament SATURNINE

glorification by or as if by elevation to the status of a god EXALTATION, DEIFICATION, APOTHEOSIS, TRANSLATION

glorify, exalt TRANSFIGURE

glory, honour LAURELS
– glory or prestige resulting from some achievement KUDOS

glove, as on a suit of armour or for certain sports GAUNTLET
– glove-like fur ring for keeping the hands warm MUFF
– glove or other object formerly thrown down as a challenge GAGE
– finger of a glove, or sheath for an injured finger or toe STALL
– forked strip of material linking the front and back parts of the fingers of a glove FOURCHETTE

glowing, as with self-generated light LUMINOUS
– glowing coals or wood, burning without flame CINDER, EMBERS
– glowing electrical discharge seen on a ship's mast, church spire, or the like during stormy weather ST. ELMO'S FIRE, CORPOSANT
– glowing emitted by some fungi on rotting wood FOXFIRE
– glowing or shimmering with a range of colours OPALESCENT
– glowing produced at low temperatures, as through radioactivity LUMINESCENCE
– glowing produced by high temperature, as in a light bulb INCANDESCENCE
– glowing in living organisms, such as fireflies, some fish, and some fungi BIOLUMINESCENCE
– glowing produced during stimulation by radiation, as in a neon light FLUORESCENCE
– glowing that continues after stimulation by radiation PHOSPHORESCENCE
– glowing or flickering gently, as a flame might LAMBENT

glucose- GLYC-, GLYCO-

glue, paste, or other substance for sticking something to a surface ADHESIVE, MUCILAGE
– resin of a tough synthetic kind used in coatings and glues EPOXY
– spatula or similar device for applying glue, ointment, or the like to a surface APPLICATOR

glue- COLLO-

glue-sniffing SOLVENT ABUSE

gluey, gummy, sticky GLUTINOUS, VISCOUS, VISCID

gluttony, over-eating GOURMANDISE
– eat gluttonously or greedily, gorge GORMANDISE

gnawing mammal, such as the rat or squirrel RODENT

gnome or goblin in German folklore, who lives either underground or secretly among humans KOBOLD
– gnome or giant in Scandinavian folklore, living in caves or on mountains TROLL

gnu WILDEBEEST

go one's way WEND

go along with someone's wishes or ideas HUMOUR, INDULGE

go back on a commitment RENEGE
– go back to an earlier condition RELAPSE, REVERT, REGRESS

go-between, agent or mediator between people INTERMEDIARY, ARBITRATOR, HONEST BROKER
– go-between in a sexual relationship PIMP, PANDER, PANDERER, PROCURER

go off, as a bomb might, or cause to go off DETONATE

goal, aim, desired end, finishing point TERMINUS AD QUEM
– goal, aim, intention OBJECTIVE
– goal of strivings ZION, MECCA
– goal or destination BOURN
– goal or intention, or the fulfilment of it CONSUMMATION
– belief that Nature is directed towards goals TELEOLOGY
– directed or tending towards a specific goal or purpose TELIC
– upright pole or support, such as a goalpost STANCHION

goat – like a goat CAPRINE, HIRCINE
– bear young, as goats do YEAN
– female goat NANNY GOAT
– male goat BILLY GOAT
– rural deity in mythology, part man and part goat FAUN, SATYR
– skin of a young goat, or the leather made from it CHEVRETTE
– young goat, kid YEANLING

goat hair as used in fabrics ANGORA, MOHAIR

goatskin or sheepskin treated for writing or painting on PARCHMENT

goblin – goblin-like creature supposedly causing mechanical failures, especially in aircraft GREMLIN
– goblin or gnome in German folklore, living underground or secretly among humans KOBOLD

god – god-like or godly DIVINE
– god of minor rank, or mythological being who is half mortal and half divine DEMIGOD
– god or goddess DEITY, DIVINITY
– belief in or worship of a single god MONOTHEISM
– belief in or worship of two or more gods POLYTHEISM
– blood of the gods ICHOR
– destruction of the ancient gods in their battle with the forces of evil GÖTTERDÄMMERUNG
– drink of the gods NECTAR
– food of the gods AMBROSIA
– guardian spirit or protective god of a particular person or place TUTELARY
– group of all the gods, or a temple dedicated to them PANTHEON
– household gods in ancient Rome LARES, PENATES
– image of a Chinese god JOSS
– killing or killer of a god DEICIDE
– luminous cloud surrounding a god when visiting Earth NIMBUS
– minor woodland god, half man and half goat SATYR, FAUN
– offering to a god, designed to appease PROPITIATION
– prophecy, shrine, or priest, of a prophetic god ORACLE
– raise to the rank of a god, glorify EXALT, DEIFY, APOTHEOSISE,

GODS AND GODDESSES OF GREECE AND ROME

GREEK	ATTRIBUTE	ROMAN
Apollo	the Sun, poetry, music, prophecy	**Apollo**
Aphrodite	love, beauty	**Venus**
Ares	war, strife	**Mars**
Artemis	hunting, the Moon	**Diana**
Asclepius	healing, medicine	**Aesculapius**
Athena, Athene	wisdom, the arts	**Minerva**
Demeter	corn	**Ceres**
Dionysus	wine, ecstasy	**Bacchus**
Eros	love	**Cupid**
Hades	the underworld	**Pluto**
Hephaestus	fire, metal-working	**Vulcan**
Hera	marriage, motherhood; queen of the gods	**Juno**
Hermes	trade, invention, cunning; messenger of the gods	**Mercury**
Kronos	fertility, the violent powers of nature	**Saturn**
Pan	pastures, forests, flocks, herds	**Faunus**
Persephone	fertility	**Proserpina**
Poseidon	sea, earthquakes	**Neptune**
Zeus	order and justice; king of the gods	**Jupiter, Jove**

TRANSLATE
– relating to the Greek gods OLYMPIAN
– representation of gods in the form of animals ZOOMORPHISM
– representation of gods in the form of humans ANTHROPOMORPHISM

God – God-like being in ancient philosophy, who created or regulates the universe DEMIURGE, PRIME MOVER, PRIMUM MOBILE
– God's name, as assigned at various times or places ANCIENT OF DAYS, ADONAI, ELOHIM, YAHWEH, JEHOVAH, LORD OF HOSTS, LORD OF SABAOTH, THE OMNIPOTENT, DOMINUS, ALLAH
– God's ordering of earthly life and events DISPENSATION, PROVIDENCE
– God's self-revealing thought and will LOGOS
– appearance or manifestation to man of God or a divine influence EPIPHANY, AVATAR, THEOPHANY
– belief in God as being present throughout Nature, or identical with nature PANTHEISM
– belief in God as the creator who at once transcends and yet is present in the world THEISM
– belief in God as the creator who no longer intervenes in the world DEISM
– contemptuous or disrespectful towards God, religion, or sacred things BLASPHEMOUS, PROFANE
– devotion, great respect, awe, as shown to God or a god REVERENCE, VENERATION
– disclosure or realisation of God's will or some religious truth REVELATION
– independent of and outside the created universe, as God is said to be in some views TRANSCENDENT
– philosophical doctrine rejecting belief in God, and elevating scientific or human values instead RATIONALISM, HUMANISM
– philosophical doctrine that one cannot know whether God exists or not AGNOSTICISM
– philosophical doctrine that there is no God ATHEISM
– present throughout the universe, and within nature and people's souls, as God is said to be in some views IMMANENT
– set of four Hebrew letters, corresponding to YHWH, that represents God's name in the Old Testament TETRAGRAMMATON
– study of the nature of God and religious truth THEOLOGY

God- THE-, THEO-

God willing DEO VOLENTE

godliness, saintliness SANCTITY

godparent SPONSOR

going away, especially of a large number of people EXODUS
– going out EGRESS

gold, silver, or other metal that resists corrosion NOBLE METAL
– gold bar or similarly convenient block of metal INGOT
– gold-bearing, as gravel or rocks might be AURIFEROUS
– gold-bearing fragmentary rock found in South Africa BANKET
– gold-like, or covered in gold leaf GILT, GILDED, AUREATE
– gold or silver in bulk BULLION
– gold or silver thread used in embroidery PURL
– gold or silver wire or cord used as a trimming BULLION FRINGE
– gold-plated silver, bronze, or copper, as used in jewellery ROLLED GOLD, VERMEIL
– alchemists' alleged conversion of base metals into silver or gold TRANSMUTATION
– alloy of copper and zinc used as imitation gold PINCHBECK
– alloy with gold colour, made of copper and zinc, used in decorating furniture ORMOLU
– chemical analysis, as of the gold content of a metal object ASSAY
– convert or transform something, such as base metal into gold COMMUTE, TRANSMUTE
– cover with a thin layer of gold or gold leaf, gold-plate GILD
– explore an area for gold or other minerals PROSPECT
– fabric decorated with gold or silver thread LAMÉ
– imitation gold leaf CLINQUANT
– tool for applying gold leaf in bookbinding PALLET
– long, sloping trough, as for washing gold ore SLUICE
– lump of natural gold NUGGET
– mark stamped on gold or silver objects indicating the purity of the metal HALLMARK, PLATEMARK

– ornamental work of twisted gold or silver wire FILIGREE
– pseudo-science in the Middle Ages, seeking a cure-all medicine and a means of turning base metal into gold ALCHEMY
– search for gold, as in rivers or waste dumps FOSSICK
– separate gold from earth or sand by washing PAN
– substance or stone believed by alchemists to have the power of turning base metals into gold PHILOSOPHERS' STONE, ELIXIR
– weighing system for gold, other precious metals, and gems, using a 12-ounce pound TROY WEIGHT

-gold- -CHRYS-, CHRYSO-, AURI-

golden GILDED, AUREATE

golden age, looked forward to in the distant future MILLENNIUM
– belief in the imminent arrival of a golden age MESSIANISM

golf See chart

gondolier – gondolier's song having a rhythm of rowing BARCAROLE

good See also **excellent**, **perfect**
– good, admirable, deserving praise or respect COMMENDABLE, LAUDABLE, ESTIMABLE, CREDITABLE, MERITORIOUS
– good, helpful, useful ADVANTAGEOUS, BENEFICIAL
– good, reliable, honourable REPUTABLE, STERLING
– good, typical or reminiscent of the best from the past VINTAGE
– good, very well-behaved ANGELIC, IRREPROACHABLE, DOCILE
– good for the health, promoting well-being, SALUTARY, SALUBRIOUS
– extremely good or pleasing, champion, capital, corking BONZER, BRAW, COPACETIC, CRACKERJACK, SPIFFING, TOPNOTCH

good- EU-

good appetite, eat well, enjoy your meal BON APPETIT

good faith BONA FIDES

good-luck object, animal, or person, as adopted by a team MASCOT

good-natured, friendly, likable AFFABLE, AMIABLE, CONVIVIAL, GENIAL, CORDIAL
– good-natured, kind or generous BENIGN, HUMANE, BENEFICIENT
– good-natured friendliness BONHOMIE

goodbye, leave-taking VALEDICTION
– goodbye, from other languages ADIEU, AU REVOIR, ARRIVEDERCI, CIAO, AUF WIEDERSEHEN, ADIOS, HASTA LA VISTA, SAYONARA

goodness, virtue, moral uprightness RECTITUDE, INTEGRITY, PROBITY

goods, such as furniture and household appliances, that are long-lasting DURABLES
– goods for carriage, and then delivery or disposal CONSIGNMENT
– goods or property in one's personal possession CHATTELS, CHOSES
– goods or total stock on hand INVENTORY
– anything commercially useful, tradable goods or services COMMODITY
– not ordered or asked for, as some goods delivered by mail might be UNSOLICITED

goodwill, love of one's fellow man and promotion of his welfare PHILANTHROPY, ALTRUISM
– goodwill or similar business asset that has a value but no physical existence INTANGIBLE

goose – goose-like, resembling or characteristic of a goose ANSERINE
– goose-liver paste, typically with truffles PÂTÉ DE FÒIE GRAS

goose flesh HORRIPILATION

gorge, narrow pass DEFILE
– gorge or narrow ravine with a stream in the U.S. FLUME
– gorge or ravine, as gouged out by a river or flood waters CANYON, COULOIR, GULLY, GULCH, WADI

gospels – referring or relating to the first three gospels SYNOPTIC

gossip HEARSAY, ON DIT
– gossip or busybody QUIDNUNC
– gossipy meeting GABFEST

GOLF TERMS

albatross	score of three strokes under par for the hole
apron	section of the fairway leading onto the green
birdie	score of one stroke under par for the hole
bogey	score of one stroke over par for the hole
borrow	slope or undulations of a green, which have to be taken into account when putting
brassie	formerly, a wooden-headed club equivalent to a modern No 2 wood
caddie	person who carries a player's clubs
carry	distance a ball struck from the tee travels through the air until it touches the ground
divot	clump of turf gouged out by a golf club
dormy/ dormie	ahead by as many holes as there are holes left to play
eagle	score of two strokes under par for the hole
fade	veer; cause the ball to veer
fore	warning cry to people in the line of play
golden ferret	holing of a ball directly from a bunker
handicap	allowance corresponding to the number of strokes by which a player is expected to exceed par in a round of golf
links	golf course, especially one by the sea
mashie	formerly, a club for lifting the ball high, especially a No 5 iron
match play	match or competition decided by the number of holes won by each player or side
medal play, stroke play	match decided by the total number of strokes taken by each player or side
niblick	formerly, a club producing a great deal of lift, specifically a No 9 iron
par	number of strokes set as a testing standard for each hole
stableford	system of scoring that awards points for each hole
stymie	obstruction of opponent's ball on the green
wedge	club with very wide angled face, specifically a No 10 iron, as used for bunker shots

– pass or toss something back and forth, such as a person's name in a gossipy conversation, or the like BANDY
Gothic typeface BLACK LETTER
gourd CALABASH
gourmet, connoisseur, person who appreciates fine food and wine EPICURE, GASTRONOME
gout, especially as affecting the big toe PODAGRA
– natural acid in the body that can cause gout when unregulated URIC ACID
governess, chaperone, or elderly female companion of the daughters in a Spanish or Portuguese family DUENNA
governing, ruling, in authority DOMINANT
– governing itself, relatively independent of outside rule or domination AUTONOMOUS
– governing strictly, or favouring strict authority and obedience AUTHORITARIAN
government See chart, and also **feudal**, **leader**
– government action taken to regulate economic factors such as the exchange rate INTERVENTION
– government advisers forming an unofficial yet influential group KITCHEN CABINET
– government departments in Britain, as distinct from Parliament WHITEHALL
– government grant, as of property or exploration rights CONCESSION
– government in which the laws and political principles limit the powers of the rulers CONSTITUTIONALISM
– government made up of a group of officers after a military takeover JUNTA
– government or authority exercised in a fatherly way, typically generous and concerned but restricting individual responsibility PATERNALISM
– government or authority that was formerly in power but has now been replaced ANCIEN RÉGIME
– government or rule, especially when authoritarian or military REGIME
– government policy, especially foreign policy, based uncompromisingly on national self-interest rather than on moral considerations REALPOLITIK
– government policy statement or official report prior to discussion in parliament WHITE PAPER
– government publication in Britain containing proposals for legislation, issued to interested parties for comments and discussion GREEN PAPER
– government publication or official report in Britain BLUEBOOK
– government-sponsored organisation that is independent of government control QUANGO
– government structure of a nation, church, or the like POLITY
– opponent of a government, especially in a one-party state DISSIDENT
– overthrow or attempt to destroy something, especially a government or political system, by means of concerted secret undermining SUBVERT
– period of time between two successive reigns, governments, or the like INTERREGNUM
– power of government, influence, or authority of one state over another HEGEMONY, SUZERAINTY
– power of government, rule, control, authority DOMINION, SOVEREIGNTY, SUPREMACY, JURISDICTION
– power to appoint people to government jobs PATRONAGE
– relating or referring to a form of government or a country in which power is divided between a central authority and various regions FEDERAL
– support for a government's policies, as considered given by an election victory MANDATE
– transfer of power from central government to regional or local authorities DEVOLUTION
-government -CRACY, -OCRACY, -NOMY, -ARCHY
governor See also **leader**
– governor of a colony or country ruling in the name of the sovereign VICEROY
– governor of a country while the king or queen is incapable of ruling REGENT
– relating to a governor, as of a U.S. state GUBERNATORIAL
grace or blessing, as before meals BENEDICITE

GOVERNMENT SYSTEMS

absolutism	all-powerful monarch or dictator	**ochlocracy**	the mob
aristocracy	hereditary ruling class or privileged minority	**oligarchy**	small faction of people or families
autarchy, autocracy, monocracy	all-powerful individual person	**pantisocracy**	all members of a community equally
despotism	all-powerful person or group	**patriarchy**	men, to the exclusion of women
diarchy	two rulers or ruling bodies jointly	**pentarchy**	five rulers or officials jointly
duumvirate	two rulers or officials jointly	**plutocracy**	the wealthy
gerontocracy	elderly men	**stratocracy**	the army
hierocracy	priests or clergymen	**technocracy**	scientific and technical experts
matriarchy	women	**theocracy**	priesthood representing God or a deity
meritocracy	people who have proven skill or intellect	**timocracy**	citizens possessing property
		totalitarianism	all-powerful dictator or party
		triumvirate	three rulers or officials jointly

grace note in music, usually just above the main note APPOGGIATURA
– grace note in music, usually just below the main note ACCIACCATURA

graceful and slim, as a racehorse or elegant woman might be WILLOWY
– graceful or effortless, as a dancer's movements might be FLUENT
– graceful or agile, supple and nimble LITHE, LIMBER, LISSOM
– graceful or sleek, as cats are SLINKY
– graceful, persuasive, or moving in use of language, expression, or the like ELOQUENT

gracious, refined in manner, courtly, polished URBANE, GENTEEL, SUAVE
– gracious in a superior way PATRONISING, CONDESCENDING

graded series according to rank or importance HIERARCHY
– graded series of slight differences, as of form or intensity CONTINUUM, CLINE

gradual absorption or acquisition, as of knowledge OSMOSIS
– gradual development, slow, natural or historical process of change EVOLUTION
– gradual progression, series of tiny stages, as in the change from one colour to another GRADATION

gradually, bit by bit PIECEMEAL

graduate or former student of a school, college, or university ALUMNUS, ALUMNA
– graduates of a university, or an assembly or conference of them CONVOCATION

graduation ceremony at U.S. high schools, colleges, and universities COMMENCEMENT

graft – budded shoot or twig detached and joined to a stock for grafting SCION

grain, especially oats, that is coarsely ground GRITS, GROATS
– grain due for grinding or having been ground GRIST
– grain-eating GRAMINIVOROUS, GRANIVOROUS
– grain fungus or disease ERGOT
– amount of liquid, grain, or the like that evaporates or leaks from a container ULLAGE
– funnel for dispensing fuel or grain HOPPER
– gather leftover grain or other crops after harvesting GLEAN
– particle, pellet or small grain GRANULE
– pile of maize or sheaves of grain gathered in a field to dry STOOK, SHOCK
– resembling or made of grain, especially wheat FRUMENTACEOUS
– separate chaff from grain or seed by means of a wind WINNOW
– separate chaff from grain or seed by means of beating THRESH, FLAIL
– storage tower or pit for grain or fodder SILO
– storehouse for grain, or region producing grain GRANARY

grain- GRANI-

grainy in texture or appearance GRANULAR

grammar See also chart, page 226
– grammatical correctness, or the adherence to traditional rules of grammar PURISM
– grammatical error or improper usage SOLECISM
– grammatical error produced by avoiding an imaginary error, as in the faulty phrase *between you and I* HYPERCORRECTION
– analyse the grammatical structure of a sentence CONSTRUE, PARSE
– any of two or more varying realisations of the same grammatical form VARIANT

gramophone needle or jewel for tracing the groove of a record STYLUS
– U.S. term for a gramophone PHONOGRAPH

grand See also **famous**, **high-falutin**, **large**
– grand, high, majestic as a literary style or social circle might be RAREFIED
– grand, high-ranking, or honoured, especially when elderly AUGUST, VENERABLE
– grand, impressively large or noble, majestic or monumental EXALTED, LOFTY, IMPOSING, SUBLIME
– grand, luxurious, extravagant LAVISH, SUMPTUOUS, EXPANSIVE
– grand, majestically elegant or dignified STATELY, STATUESQUE
– grand, superbly confident or skilful, authoritative MAGISTERIAL
– grand in a showy or pretentious way OSTENTATIOUS

Grand Lama of Tibet DALAI LAMA, PANCHEN LAMA, TASHI LAMA

grandfather clock LONGCASE CLOCK

grandstand in the open air, especially in a U.S. sports stadium BLEACHERS

granite, basalt, or other rock formed directly from cooled molten rock IGNEOUS ROCK

grant by a government, as of property, or exploration or prospecting rights CONCESSION
– grant of money to support some person or institution, finance a project, or the like SUBSIDY
– grant or gift, as to a charity CONTRIBUTION, DONATION

grape cultivation, especially for winemaking VITICULTURE, VINICULTURE
– grape harvest or yield VINTAGE
– grape juice fermenting into wine MUST, STUM
– grape pip or seed, or bunch of grapes ACINUS
– grape skins, pips, and stems left over after the juice has been extracted for winemaking RAPE
– destructive insect, very harmful to grape crops PHYLLOXERA
– fungus on grapeskins producing a sweeter grape, as for dessert wines NOBLE ROT
– having the shape of a bunch of grapes or a raspberry ACINIFORM
– pulp left after fruit, especially grapes, has been pressed to extract the juice MARC

grapefruit or grapefruit-like citrus fruit SHADDOCK, POMELO

graph See also **geometry**, **statistics**, **mathematics**
– graph of a cumulative frequency distribution in statistics OGIVE
– graph or chart in the form of a circle with sectors of varying size representing the units PIE CHART
– graph or chart in the form of a series of columns whose lengths are proportional to the sizes of the quantities concerned BAR GRAPH, BAR CHART
– flattish section of a graph PLATEAU
– line approaching a curve, as on a graph, such that they will meet only at infinity ASYMPTOTE
– loop on a graph or diagram LOBE
– set of numbers or measurements that pinpoint a position, as on a map or graph COORDINATES
– set of values in statistics, often represented by a graph FREQUENCY DISTRIBUTION

graphite PLUMBAGO

grappling irons CRAMPONS

grass border at the roadside VERGE
– grass circle more luxuriant than the surrounding grass, typically caused by fungal growth underground FAIRY RING
– grass-eating, feeding on grasses, seeds, or grains GRAMINIVOROUS
– grass-like marsh plant SEDGE
– grass-like nylon and vinyl surfacing material, as used on sports grounds ASTROTURF
– grass-like or relating to grass GRAMINEOUS
– grass of a Spanish or Algerian species yielding a fibre used in making rope, paper, and the like ESPARTO

GRAMMAR AND LINGUISTIC TERMS

ablative	case of a noun expressing direction from or cause, as in Latin
ablaut, gradation	change of vowels in verb forms, typically indicating different tenses: *sing, sang, sung*
accidence	part of grammar that deals with word inflections
accusative	case of a noun that is the direct object of a verb or preposition
amelioration, elevation	process by which a word acquires a more favourable meaning or tone, as *shrewd* has developed from its earlier sense of "wicked" or "cruel"
apposition	relationship of two nouns or noun phrases set side by side, the one explaining or identifying the other: *Socrates, the philosopher, died after drinking hemlock*
auxiliary verb	verb such as *may* or *will* that accompanies a main verb to form a mood, tense, or the like
back-formation	formation of a new word by mistakenly assuming that is the form from which an existing word derives: *burgle*, from *burglar*
case	form of a word, indicating its relation to other words in a sentence
complement	noun, noun phrase, or clause that follows a verb to complete the predicate
conjugation	inflection or set of inflections of a verb
dangling participle, misrelated participle	participle that has no clear connection with the word it modifies grammatically: *Walking home from work, it started to rain*
dative	case of a noun that is the indirect object of a verb, as in Latin
declension	inflection or set of inflections of a noun, pronoun, or adjective
deterioration, pejoration	process by which a word acquires a less-favourable meaning or tone, the way *surly* has developed from its earlier sense of "lordly, masterful"
determiner	word, such as *the* or *my*, that qualifies a noun or noun phrase and is positioned in front of any other adjective
diachronic	referring or relating to study of languages or a language developing over time
genitive	case of a noun expressing possession, measurement, or source, as in Latin
gerund	verb form, ending in *-ing* in English, that can be used as a noun: *I hate jogging*
imperative	construction or form of a verb expressing a command
indicative	construction or form of a verb indicating that something is a fact
infinitive	basic uninflected form of a verb, often preceded by *to* in English: *to be*
inflection	change in the form of a word to indicate tense, number and so on, as in *sounds, sounding, sounded*
interrogative	construction expressing a question
intransitive	referring or relating to a verb that has no direct object: *The King triumphed*
langue	language regarded as an abstract system available to all speakers
morpheme	word or word-element that cannot be divided into smaller parts: *time* and *-ly*, from *timely*
nominative	case of a noun that is the subject of a verb, as in Latin
parole	language as actually used by individual speakers
participle	form of a verb, typically ending in *-ed* or *-ing* in English, used in forming tenses or as an adjective
predicate	the part of a sentence or clause that expresses something about the subject of the sentence or clause, often consisting of a verb and object
preterite	form of a verb expressing a past or completed action: *walked, ran*
reflexive	referring to a verb or pronoun in a construction expressing an action or relationship affecting the subject itself: *prides himself on his strength*
semantics	study or science of meaning in language
structuralism	study of the internal structure of a language rather than its history or its resemblances to other languages
subjunctive	form of a verb expressing a supposition, purpose, wish, condition, or doubt: *unless I be mistaken*
substantive	word or phrase serving as a noun
synchronic	referring to the study of languages at any one time rather than developing over time
transformational grammar	grammar that studies the ways in which elements of one sentence can be rearranged to produce more complex sentences
transitive	referring or relating to a verb that needs a direct object: *The king defeated his enemy*
vocative	case of a noun used in addressing a person or thing directly, as in Latin

– grass of a genus widely cultivated and used for lawns and pasturage FESCUE
– grass or hay cut by a scythe or mower SWATH
– grass or other vegetation eaten by grazing livestock PASTURE, PASTURAGE, HERBAGE
– grass stem that is hollow and jointed CULM
– clump of thick grass TUSSOCK, HASSOCK, TUFFET
– clump of turf dug from a grass surface,. as by a golf club or horse's hoof DIVOT
– cut or graze on grass CROP
– field plant that is not a grass FORB
– second crop of grass or hay in a single season AFTERMATH, ROWEN
– whitened through lack of sunlight, as grass or other green plants might become ETIOLATED

grasshopper with long horns, and a high-pitched song in the males KATYDID
– grasshopper's shrill grating chirp STRIDULATION

grassland, meadow LEA
– grassland or open country in South Africa VELD
– grassland with scattered shrubs and trees in drier tropical and subtropical regions SAVANNAH
– grasslands, especially in North America PRAIRIE
– grasslands, especially in South America LLANOS, PAMPAS
– vast plain of semiarid grassland, especially in southern Siberia and European USSR STEPPE

grassy lawn or meadow SWARD

grate, file, or scrape RASP
– grating chirp of a cricket or grasshopper STRIDULATION

grateful, thankful OBLIGED, INDEBTED, BEHOLDEN

gratitude – expression of gratitude or appreciation TRIBUTE, TESTIMONIAL

grave See also **burial**
– grave, tomb, or burial vault SEPULCHRE, REPOSITORY
– grave-mound of ancient times TUMULUS, BARROW
– grave robber GHOUL
– dig up or remove from a grave or tomb DISINTER, EXHUME
– gravestone inscription meaning "here lies" HIC JACET
– inscription on a gravestone, tombstone, or monument commemorating the person buried there EPITAPH
– stone slab, as set over a grave LEDGER

graveyard or burial chamber underground CATACOMB, HYPOGEUM

gravity – rise and float in the air, apparently in defiance of gravity LEVITATE

gravy – gravy-soaked piece of bread or toast SIPPET, SOP, BREWIS
– served in its own gravy or juices, as a roast might be AU JUS

graze or rub the skin from something, especially one's shin BARK

grazing land, or the grass or other vegetation on it that is eaten by livestock PASTURE, PASTURAGE, HERBAGE

grease, oil, graphite, or other substance used to reduce friction LUBRICANT

greaseproof paper or foil in which some foods are cooked PAPILLOTE

greasy, oily, fatty, or slippery PINGUID, SEBACEOUS, UNCTUOUS

great See **famous**, **large**, **huge**
– great work of scholarship, research, or artistic creation MAGNUM OPUS
– "greatest happiness for the greatest number is the greatest good" as an ethical theory UTILITARIANISM

greater than- SUPRA-

greatness, fame STATURE, EMINENCE

Greece See **Greek**

greed, powerful desire, especially for money CUPIDITY, AVARICE, MAMMONISM

greed or gluttony GULOSITY

greedy, especially for money or material possessions MERCENARY, ACQUISITIVE
– greedy, excessively demanding, whimsical, self-pitying, or the like SELF-INDULGENT
– greedy, grasping, or hungry to an extreme degree RAVENOUS, VORACIOUS, INSATIABLE, RAPACIOUS
– greedy, hungry, or gluttonous EDACIOUS, ESURIENT
– greedy or grasping person, glutton or moneygrubber CORMORANT
– eat gluttonously or greedily, gorge GORMANDISE

Greek See diagram, and also **menu terms**, **column**, **drama**, **Eastern Orthodox**
– Greek, characteristic of ancient or modern Greece, Greeks, or the Greek language HELLENIC
– Greek and Latin literature CLASSICS
– Greek and Roman culture as a subject of study HUMANITIES
– Greek artistic style, cultural spirit, idiom, or the like GRAECISM
– Greek city-state in ancient times POLIS
– Greek dialect used as a lingua franca that became the standard form, and gave rise to later stages of Greek KOINE
– Greek dialects in ancient times ATTIC-IONIC, ARCADO-CYPRIAN, AEOLIC, DORIC
– Greek drinking party in ancient times, typically with music and intellectual conversation SYMPOSIUM
– Greek kinship grouping, civic class, or tribal subdivision in ancient times PHYLE, PHRATRY
– Greek person in ancient times ARGIVE, ACHAEAN
– Greek restaurant TAVERNA
– Greek string instrument similar to the mandolin BOUZOUKI
– Greek wine flavoured with resin RETSINA
– admirer or student of classical Greek culture HELLENIST

Greek alphabet

FORM	NAME	TRANSLITERATION
Αα	alpha	a
Ββ	beta	b
Γγ	gamma	g
Δδ	delta	d
Εε	epsilon	e
Ζζ	zēta	z
Ηη	ēta	ē
Θθ	thēta	th
Ιι	iota	i
Κκ	kappa	k
Λλ	lambda	l
Μμ	mu	m
Νν	nu	n
Ξξ	xi	x
Οο	omicron	o
Ππ	pi	p
Ρρ	rhō	r, rh
Σσς	sigma	s
Ττ	tau	t
Υυ	upsilon	u
Φφ	phi	ph
Χχ	chi khi	kh
Ψψ	psi	ps
Ωω	ōmega	ō

– assembly of citizens in an ancient Greek state ECCLESIA
– banishment of a citizen, by popular vote, from an ancient Greek city OSTRACISM
– citadel of an ancient Greek city ACROPOLIS
– foreign resident of an ancient Greek city, enjoying some rights of citizenship METIC
– heavily armed foot soldier in ancient Greece HOPLITE
– market-place in ancient Greece, used for meetings of the people's assembly AGORA
– modern Greek in its everyday colloquial form DHIMOTIKI, DEMOTIC
– modern Greek in its literary and official form, patterned on classical usage KATHAREVUSA, PURISTIC
– prostitute, courtesan, or concubine in ancient Greece HETAERA
– referring or relating to ancient Greek or Roman civilisation CLASSICAL
– religious festival held in the spring in ancient Greece ELEUSINIAN MYSTERIES
– serf in ancient Greece, especially Sparta, ranking between a slave and free man HELOT
– short white skirt worn by Greek men at folk festivals and ceremonial occasions FUSTANELLA

Greek- GRAECO-

Greek tragedy See **drama**, **tragedy**

green See also **colours**
– green, especially as growing plants are, or covered with vegetation VIRID, VERDANT
– green mineral, used for jewellery and ornaments VERDITER, MALACHITE
– green pepper, red pepper, or similar vegetable CAPSICUM
– green pigment in leaves that traps energy from sunlight for photosynthesis CHLOROPHYLL
– green vegetation VERDURE
– green wollen fabric used on top of snooker or billiard tables BAIZE
– greenish crust that forms on exposed copper, brass, or bronze objects VERDIGRIS, AERUGO, VERD ANTIQUE
– thin green layer of oxide forming naturally or artificially on a copper or bronze surface PATINA

-green- -CHLOR-, CHLORO-

greenhouse ORANGERY
– greenhouse or glasshouse, typically attached to a house CONSERVATORY

greeting SALUTATION
– greetings, respects, compliments DEVOIRS
– greetings of a formal kind, as on an official letter COMPLIMENTS

grenade – powerful oval-shaped hand grenade MILLS BOMB

grey – grey-haired GRIZZLED
– grey or white, as through old age HOARY
– design, painting, or style of painting using various shades of grey GRISAILLE

grey friar FRANCISCAN

greyhound racing – box-like stall from which a greyhound is released at the start of a race TRAP

grief or sorrow DOLOUR
– enduring pain and grief with unemotional resignation STOICAL
– free one's mind of a worry, grief, anxiety, guilt, or other burden DISBURDEN
– public show of grief or repentance SACKCLOTH AND ASHES
– reduce the severity of pain, grief, or the like ALLAY, ALLEVIATE, ASSUAGE
– waste away, as with grief PINE

grievance – valid or reasonable, as a grievance might be LEGITIMATE

grill, expose to direct heat BROIL
– grilling frame of parallel metal bars GRIDIRON

grin, unnatural gaping expression or smile RICTUS
– grin-like fixed facial expression, as from muscular contraction in tetanus cases RISUS SARDONICUS

grind, crush, or pound into powder or small particles TRITURATE, PULVERISE, BRAY, COMMINUTE
– grind the teeth, as in anger GNASH
– bowl in which a pestle is used to grind something MORTAR

grindstone made of or containing the abrasive mineral aluminium oxide CORUNDUM STONE
– type of silicon carbide, as used in grindstones and the like CARBORUNDUM

grip or stance adopted when shifting or securing something PURCHASE
– any of the ridges on a handle or object to make it easier to grip KNURL
– gripping, sticking, or clinging firmly TENACIOUS
– gripping or grasping device, especially a grapnel GRAPPLE

gristle, tough tissue, as at the joints between bones CARTILAGE

groggy, dazed STUPEFIED, WOOZY

groin – relating to or located in the groin INGUINAL

groove, especially around a bullet CANNELURE
– groove, notch, slot, or decorate by engraving CHASE
– groove or indentation, as in a stone column or pleated ruffle FLUTE
– groove or narrow furrow, as on a plant stem or the surface of the brain SULCUS
– groove or notch, as in a piece of wood CHAMFER
– groove or notch made in wood by chopping or sawing KERF
– groove or notch, or a series of them INDENTATION
– groove or notch that houses an inserted part in a joint or hinge MORTISE, GAIN, RABBET
– groove or ridge linking two planks, shafts, or the like SPLINE
– groove running vertically from the nose to the upper lip PHILTRUM
– grooved, streaked, or ridged STRIATE, STRIGOSE
– grooved beam of wood in which a sliding frame or panel is fitted COULISSE
– grooved or indented like a castle's battlements, as a ridge of hills might be CASTELLATED
– grooves or ridges around the edge of a coin MILLING, FLUTING
– grooves or teeth in a series, as on a saw or the edge of a leaf SERRATION
– square notches or grooves, as on a moulding CRENELLATIONS
– strip or wedge of wood fitting into a groove to make a joint FEATHER, TENON
– vertical groove, as in a decorative band on a Doric column GLYPH

grope, scratch about or feel around for with the hands GRABBLE

grotesque stone figure, as on a cathedral roof, that often serves as a rainwater spout from a gutter GARGOYLE

ground or land, especially in respect of its physical characteristics TERRAIN
– collapse, cave in, as the ground might SUBSIDE
– demolish a building or city, destroy down to the ground RAZE
– level at or below which the ground is saturated with water WATER TABLE
– physical features of ground or land TOPOGRAPHY

grounds – improved by contouring and planting, as large grounds or gardens might be LANDSCAPED

group See also **classification**, **animal terms**, **bird**, **services**
– group, as within a religion or political party, typically dissenting from the larger group FACTION,

CAUCUS, ENCLAVE, SECT
– group of armed men temporarily empowered with law-enforcement powers, as for capturing criminals in the Wild West POSSE
– group of artistic or intellectual people who meet frequently COTERIE
– group of artists, writers, or the like using the most modern or experimental methods or ideas AVANT-GARDE
– group of attendants or assistants accompanying a VIP RETINUE
– group of cars, ships, or the like travelling together CONVOY
– group of famous or glamorous people, as at a public function GALAXY
– group of girls BEVY
– group of individual items massed together AGGREGATE, CONGERIES, ASSEMBLAGE, CONGLOMERATION
– group of jazz musicians, small jazz band COMBO
– group of people, nations, political parties, or the like cooperating in a common cause ALLIANCE, COALITION, BLOC, ALIGNMENT, CONFEDERACY, LEAGUE
– group of people gathered in response to a summons CONVOCATION
– group of people living in the same area or having interests in common COMMUNITY
– group of people living together and sharing their property COMMUNE
– group of people of the same age and status as oneself PEER GROUP
– group of people picturesquely arranged TABLEAU
– group of people with common aims or interests CLIQUE, CORPS, GUILD, LOBBY, COHORT
– group of people with common political aims, usually subversive CABAL, JUNTO, CELL
– group of representatives, such as a group of workers having discussions with the management DELEGATION, DEPUTATION
– group of similar or related items intended for use together BATTERY, SUITE, COMPENDIUM, ENSEMBLE
– group of songs, plays, or the like that an artiste or company can perform REPERTOIRE
– group of undesirable or disreputable people GALÈRE, ROGUE'S GALLERY
– group of voters, supporters, or people whose interests have to be considered CONSTITUENCY
– group or company of touring actors, dancers, or the like TROUPE
– group or society of men, brotherhood FRATERNITY, SODALITY
– group or society of women, sisterhood SORORITY
– group pride or loyalty, fellowship ESPRIT DE CORPS
– group together or arrange in correct order, classify COORDINATE, CODIFY, TABULATE, CATALOGUE, COLLOCATE, COLLATE
– group unity, fellow-feeling and mutual support within a group, especially in the face of opposition SOLIDARITY
– grouping of business interests formed for some joint enterprise CONSORTIUM, SYNDICATE
– grouping of businesses or industries, especially an illegal one, that operates to monopolise manufacture or control prices CARTEL, TRUST
– grouping of citizens or clans, as in ancient Greece PHRATRY, PHYLE
– break up a group or cease to function as a group DISBAND
– large group of people crowded together DROVE, CONCOURSE, RUCK, CONFLUENCE, PHALANX
– large group of people or things BATTALION, HORDE, THRONG, MULTITUDE
– relating to a group, crowd, flock, or the like, or liking to be in a group GREGARIOUS
– relating to a whole group or category, such as a genus in biological classification GENERIC
– relating to all the members of a group jointly, shared, common, as a name or decision might COLLECTIVE, COMMUNAL
– separation into divided racial, religious, or cultural groups SEGREGATION
– small central group of experts or founder members, as in a political movement, forming the nucleus of a larger organisation CADRE
– small group of people or things COVEY
– social coexistence of several racial, religious, or cultural groups PLURALISM

-group -OME

grouse – large, dark, woodland species, wood grouse CAPERCAILLIE
– mountain-dwelling grouse of a species that turns white in winter PTARMIGAN

grove or small thicket of trees COPSE, SPINNEY

grow See also **increase**
– grow, sprout, as seeds do GERMINATE
– grow buds or sprouts, or breed rapidly PULLULATE
– grow crops in a fixed sequence ROTATE
– grow or develop rapidly FLOURISH, BURGEON
– grow or reproduce rapidly PROLIFERATE
– grow or spread abnormally, with fleshy outgrowths, as warts and some tumours do VEGETATE
– grow slowly or gradually, as an idea might, or cause to grow INCUBATE, GESTATE
– grow together, merge, fuse COALESCE, AMALGAMATE, ACCRETE
– develop, help to grow, encourage the advancement of NURTURE, FOSTER
– develop, reproduce, breed, cause to grow PROPAGATE

growing along the ground as a vine or creeper might PROSTRATE
– growing old SENESCENCE
– growing or mounting up by a series of steps or additions CUMULATIVE
– growing or spread out in an untidy, irregular way STRAGGLY
– growing together, fusion, as of plant parts or body organs CONCRESCENCE, CONCRETION, COALESCENCE
– growing vegetation VERDURE
– growing vigorously and widely, as weeds might RANK
– growing wild, especially on cultivated land, as wild flowers or weeds might AGRESTAL

-growing -PLASTIC, -TROPE, -TROPIC

growth, small swelling, or wart-like projection NODULE, TUBERCLE
– growth of a population that is optimal and therefore accelerating EXPONENTIAL GROWTH
– growth on or under a mucous membrane, as in the nose POLYP
– growth or abnormal projection on the body EXCRESCENCE
– growth or evolution of a species, genus, language, custom, or the like PHYLOGENY
– growth or expansion, increase INCREMENT
– growth or increase, as of public feeling or opinion GROUNDSWELL
– growth through slow additions, build-up ACCRETION
– in the earliest stage of growth or development EMBRYONIC, SEMINAL, GERMINAL
– something that nourishes or promotes growth or development NUTRIMENT

-growth- -BLAST-, BLASTO-, -TROPH-, TROPHO-, -TROPHIC, -TROPHY, -PLASIA, -PLASY

grub – grub-like young hatched from the egg of an insect LARVA
grudge – bear a grudge HARBOUR
gruel or thin broth SKILLY
grumble See **complain**
guarantee, assurance, promise WARRANT, WARRANTY, UNDERTAKING, COVENANT
– guarantee, give personal assurance for VOUCH FOR
– guarantee, token, pledge, or promise EARNEST
– guarantee against financial failure UNDERWRITE
– guarantee or guarantor against loss or damage SURETY
– guarantee or promise UNDERTAKING
– guarantee or safeguard of society PALLADIUM
guard, sentry SENTINEL
– guard duty WATCH
– guard of the Roman emperors PRAETORIAN GUARD
– guard one's position of success against rivals LOOK TO ONE'S LAURELS
– guard or watch kept during the hours of sleep VIGIL
– guard or watch stationed as a defence against surprise attack, or in an industrial dispute PICKET
– guard's van on U.S. trains, with eating and sleeping facilities for the crew CABOOSE
– release from guard duty, through the arrival of a replacement RELIEF
guardian of a minor in Roman and Scottish law TUTOR
– guardian spirit of a place GENIUS, GENIUS LOCI
– guardian spirit or guiding genius DAEMON
– relating to or acting as a guardian TUTELARY
guardianship, as of an orphan or prisoner CUSTODY
– guardianship or tutorship, or subjection to it TUTELAGE
guerrilla fighting behind enemy lines or in territory occupied by the enemy PARTISAN
– deliberate damaging or destruction of property, as by guerrillas or dissatisfied workers SABOTAGE
– military action taken by the authorities against rebels or guerrillas COUNTERINSURGENCY, PACIFICATION
guess, opinion based on incomplete evidence SPECULATION, SURMISE, CONJECTURE
– guess or deduce from known information EXTRAPOLATE, INFER
– guess or know by intuition, or predict DIVINE
– guesswork, calculation of a rough-and-ready kind DEAD RECKONING
– offer a guess HAZARD, VENTURE
guest, visitor, or the like who expects or accepts too much hospitality or generosity FREELOADER, SPONGER, SCROUNGER, CADGER, BLUDGER
– frequent guest, as at a club HABITUÉ, FREQUENTER
guide, escort, or attendant, especially when riding a horse or motorcycle OUTRIDER
– guide, warning, or sign BEACON
– guide a pilot, aircraft, missile, or the like by radio instructions VECTOR
– guide for tourists on sightseeing expeditions CICERONE
– guide or attendant of a hunter or angler in Scotland GILLIE
– guide or interpreter in the Middle East in former times DRAGOMAN
– guide or plot the course of a ship, aircraft, or other vehicle NAVIGATE
– guide or wise personal teacher MENTOR, GURU
– guide to conduct, in the form of a short maxim MOTTO
– guiding, helping the learning process HEURISTIC
– guiding principle, belief, or doctrine GOSPEL
– guiding principle, objective, or standard LODESTAR, POLESTAR
– guiding spirit, guardian genius DAEMON
guidebook for tourists BAEDEKER
– guidebook or ready-reference manual VADE MECUM
guidelines or limiting factors, as of a budget or schedule PARAMETERS, CONSTRAINTS
guild or trade association in the City of London LIVERY COMPANY
guillotine – guillotine-like frame used in 16th- and 17th-century Scotland for executions MAIDEN
– cart that carried prisoners off to the guillotine during the French Revolution TUMBREL
– Parisian women who would knit unconcernedly while attending guillotinings as spectators during the French Revolution TRICOTEUSES
guilt – clear of guilt or blame EXCULPATE, EXONERATE
– consider or pronounce free of blame or guilt, or from responsibility or punishment ABSOLVE
– free one's mind of a worry, grief, anxiety, guilt, or other burden DISBURDEN
– lessen or try to lessen the seriousness of a crime, guilt, or the like, as by offering certain excuses EXTENUATE, MITIGATE
– suggest the guilt of someone INCRIMINATE, INCULPATE
guilty feeling, regret or remorse COMPUNCTION
– guilty-looking or ashamed HANGDOG, SHAMEFACED
– guilty of sin PECCANT
– guilty party in a damages case TORTFEASOR
– negotiations between the defence and prosecution prior to a criminal trial, aimed at exchanging a guilty plea in court for a reduced charge PLEA BARGAINING
– person guilty of a crime or responsible for a mistake or accident CULPRIT
guinea pig or related South American rodent CAVY

GUNS

HANDGUNS AND PISTOLS
Beretta
bulldog
Colt
derringer
Luger
magnum
Mauser
six-shooter
Smith and Wesson
Walther
Webley and Scott
zip gun

MACHINE GUNS
Breda
Bren gun
Browning gun
Gatling gun
Hotchkiss gun
Lanchester gun
Lewis gun
Maxim
mitrailleuse
Sten gun
Sterling gun
Thompson gun/ Tommy gun
Uzi
Vickers gun

SHOTGUNS AND RIFLES
Armalite
arquebus/ harquebus/ hackbut
blunderbuss
Browning automatic
carbine
chokebore
Enfield/ Lee-Enfield
flintlock
FN rifle
fowling piece
fusil
Garand rifle
jingal
Kalashnikov/ AK 47
matchlock
musket
petronel
pump gun
punt gun
Springfield
wheel-lock
Winchester

ARTILLERY
ack-ack gun
basilisk
bazooka
Big Bertha
Bofors gun
bombard
carronade
culverin
howitzer
long tom
mortar/trench-mortar
pom-pom
serpentine
stern chaser/ bow chaser
swivel gun

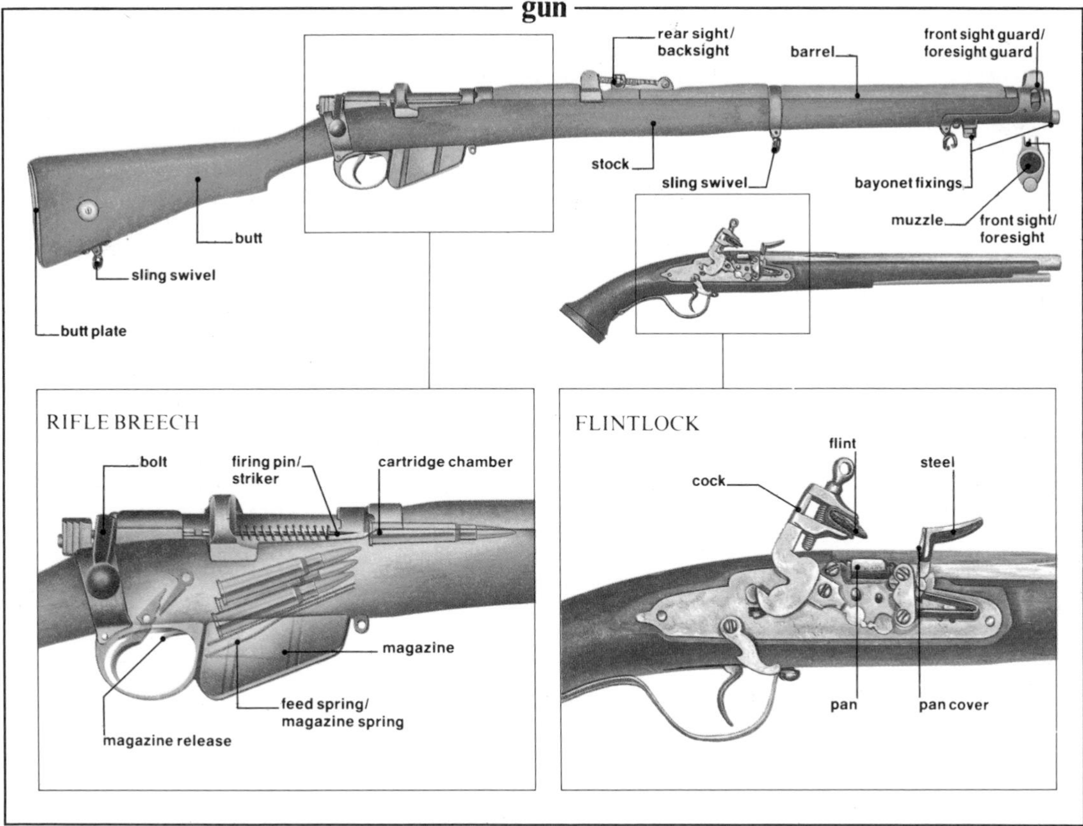

guitar that does not use electric amplification ACOUSTIC GUITAR
– movable bar clamped to the fingerboard of a guitar, lute, or the like to raise the pitch of all the strings CAPO
– placing of the forefinger over some or all of the strings of a guitar, lute, or the like to raise their pitch BARRÉ
– small thin disc or plate, as of plastic, used for plucking the strings of a guitar, lute, or related instrument PLECTRUM, PICK

gullet OESOPHAGUS

gullible person, sucker GREENHORN, DUPE, GULL

gully See **gorge**

gulp, drink or swallow eagerly SWIG, SWILL

gum from the sap of the sapodilla tree, used as the main ingredient of chewing gum CHICLE
– gum in which one's teeth are lodged GINGIVA
– gum inflammation, often causing loosening of the teeth PYORRHOEA
– gum obtained from some plants RESIN, MUCILAGE
– gum or resin used in making perfume MYRRH
– gum resin used in incense FRANKINCENSE, OLIBANUM
– gum or resin used in varnish MASTIC

gummy, gluey, sticky, as some thick liquids are GLUTINOUS, VISCOUS, VISCID

gun See illustration and chart
– gun opening in a wall, tank, or the like PORT
– gun or cannon firing shells at a steep angle HOWITZER
– check the range of a gun CALIBRATE
– guns, ammunition, and other equipment of an army, as distinct from personnel MATÉRIEL
– guns, especially heavy guns, of a military unit ARTILLERY, ORDNANCE
– guns along one side of a warship, or their combined firing simultaneously BROADSIDE
– guns or heavy artillery, as on a warship BATTERY
– guns or missiles grouped in an emplacement NEST
– harness strapped to a soldier for hauling large guns BRICOLE
– low, round concrete building serving as a small fort for guns and gunners PILLBOX
– plug or cover for the muzzle of a gun when not in use TAMPION
– position, such as a platform or mounting, specially prepared for a gun or other weapon EMPLACEMENT
– revolving armoured dome or drum on a tank or warship in which guns are mounted TURRET
– rod for cleaning a rifle or inserting the charge into a muzzle-loading gun RAMROD
– spring back, as a gun may do when fired RECOIL
– sighting lines, at right angles to each other, in the sights of a gun, theodolite, or the like CROSS WIRES, CROSS HAIRS
– study of guns, bullets, shells, and so on BALLISTICS

gunfire, blows, bombing, or the like of a heavy and sustained kind BARRAGE
– gunfire in a rapid burst FUSILLADE, VOLLEY, SALVO
– abrupt, distinct, and jerky in sound, as gunfire might be STACCATO
– troop formation or position subject to gunfire along its entire

length ENFILADE

gunman or marksman shooting, typically at long range and from a well-concealed position, at exposed individuals SNIPER

gunpowder – gunpowder-filled cap, as used either in a toy pistol or in a firearm, that explodes when struck PERCUSSION CAP
– line of gunpowder laid as a fuse to explode a charge TRAIN
– potassium nitrate, as used in making gunpowder and preserving meat SALTPETRE, NITRE

guru, spiritual leader or teacher in Hinduism MAHARISHI
– guru's pupil or disciple CHELA

gushing, emotionally demonstrative EFFUSIVE

gut feeling – instinctive or intuitive, as a "gut feeling" is, rather than rational VISCERAL

gutter on a roof CULLIS

gymnastics – gymnast or acrobat specialising in turning somersaults or cartwheels TUMBLER
– gymnastic exercises designed to improve physical fitness and muscle tone CALLISTHENICS, FLOOR EXERCISES
– apparatus in gymnastics exercises and competitions POMMEL HORSE, PARALLEL BARS, ASYMMETRIC BARS, RINGS, BEAM, VAULTING HORSE
– back handspring in gymnastics, a key tumbling move FLIC-FLAC
– form of dance-like gymnastics for pairs, trios, or groups of four performers SPORTS ACRO, SPORTS ACROBATICS
– form of dance-like gymnastics for women, performed to music with various apparatus such as ribbons or hoops MRG, MODERN RHYTHMIC GYMNASTICS
– handspring vault in gymnastics involving a cartwheel onto the horse and a back somersault in the flight-off TSUKAHARA
– handspring vault in gymnastics involving a tight tucked position in the flight-off from the horse YAMASHITA
– near-horizontal position of a gymnast when supporting himself on his hands and arms alone PLANCHE
– position on the rings in gymnastics in which the body is held upright and the arms stretched out horizontally CROSS, CRUCIFIX
– somersault in gymnastics, taking off from the feet and landing on the feet SALTO
– wooden bottle-shaped club thrown or swung about in juggling and gymnastics INDIAN CLUB

gymshoe PLIMSOLL, DAP

gynaecological smear test PAP TEST

Gypsy, especially an Italian Gypsy ZINGARO
– Gypsy, especially one from Hungary TZIGANE
– Gypsy man or gentleman ROM, RYE
– Gypsy man or woman, or the Gypsy language ROMANY
– person who is not a Gypsy, as referred to by Gypsies GORGIO
– travelling scrap-metal dealer, typically living in a caravan and often taken for a Gypsy DIDICOY, TINKER

H

h – breathy speech sound represented in English by the letter *h* ASPIRATE

habit, custom WONT, USAGE
– habits of a social group, defining it and its values MORES
– exaggerated or affected habit or trait IDIOSYNCRASY, ECCENTRICITY, ABERRATION, MANNERISM

habitual, confirmed, regular, as a persistent liar might be INVETERATE, CHRONIC
– habitual tendency or inclination DISPOSITION
– habitual through irrational compulsion, as a liar might be PATHOLOGICAL

had – past perfect tense of a verb, as in *had climbed* PLUPERFECT

haddock – smoked haddock FINNAN HADDOCK, FINNAN HADDIE

haggle or bargain CHAFFER

hair See also **hairstyle**
– hair dye or tint of a reddish colour HENNA
– hair in a detached tress, worked into a person's own hair in certain hairstyles SWITCH
– hair in the region of the genital organs PUBIC HAIR
– hair-like projection, as on moss or in the small intestine VILLUS
– hair-like threads on a cell or microscopic organism, whose waving produces locomotion CILIA
– hair-like, very slender CAPILLARY
– hair loss or baldness, as caused by a skin disease ALOPECIA
– hair of artificial fibre, used for make-up in the theatre CREPE HAIR
– hair or feathers projecting from an animal's neck FRILL, RUFF
– hair-removing lotion DEPILATORY
– hairs in a tuft on the seed coat of some seeds COMA
– hairs or feathers on the back of an animal's neck HACKLES
– arrange a woman's hair COIF
– auburn or reddish gold colour of a person's hair TITIAN, STRAWBERRY BLONDE
– bleach used to make hair blonde PEROXIDE
– bristling of the hair on the body HORRIPILATION, GOOSE FLESH
– cavity in the skin from which a hair grows FOLLICLE
– comb the hair downwards near the roots in order to bulk it up BACKCOMB, TEASE
– covered with fine greyish hairs or down HOARY
– covered with grey hair GRIZZLED
– covered with soft hairs CRINITE
– covered with tiny barbed hairs or bristles, as some plants and animals are BARBELLATE
– covered with woolly hairs, as leaves might be LANATE
– curl the hair tightly, as with curling tongs CRIMP
– destruction of hair roots or other living tissue by means of an electric current ELECTROLYSIS
– having fair hair and skin XANTHOCHROID
– having tightly-curled hair on the head, as black Africans have ULOTRICHOUS
– headband, typically U-shaped and of stiff plastic, for holding down the hair on the crown of a woman's head ALICE-BAND
– light streak in the hair HIGHLIGHT
– lock or tuft of hair across or rising from the forehead COWLICK
– long, flat, and limp, as some hair is LANK
– long lock of hair on the forehead LOVELOCK
– narrow band, ribbon, velvet strip, or the like, as worn in a woman's hair FILLET, BANDEAU
– natural brown pigment colouring the skin and hair MELANIN
– pale yellow, as hair might be FLAXEN
– remove the hair from DEPILATE
– shear, trim, or cut the hair, wool, or horns of POLL
– shed hair, feathers, or fur, as many animals do MOULT
– short, fine, downy hair, as on a foetus LANUGO
– single curl of hair RINGLET
– small cap or pouch, typically of netting, holding a woman's hair in place at the back SNOOD
– study of hair and its diseases, especially baldness TRICHOLOGY
– tangled mass, as of matted hair SHAG
– taper, thin, and trim the hair by cutting FEATHER
– thick bushy mass, as of hair SHOCK
– tiny lump on the root of a hair PAPILLA, FOLLICLE BULB
– tough protein substance forming the outer layer of hair, nails, horns, and the like KERATIN
– tuft of hair, as on a dog's tail FEATHER
– tuft or lock of hair brushed up from or onto the forehead QUIFF
– uncombed or untidy, as hair might be UNKEMPT, DISHEVELLED, UNGROOMED, RUMPLED, TOUSLED
– whiskers or sensitive hairs, as on either side of a cat's mouth VIBRISSAE
– woman's thick, long, flowing locks of hair TRESSES

-hair- PIL-, PILI-, PILO-, -TRICH-, TRICHO-, -TRICHOUS

hair clip with clamped ends KIRBY GRIP, BOBBY PIN

hair oil, perfumed and sometimes thickened into a gel BRILLIANTINE
– hair oil, or cream for the hair, usually perfumed POMADE, POMATUM
– hair oil popular in the 19th century MACASSAR OIL

hair-slide – U.S. term for a hair-slide BARRETTE

haircut – massage of perfumed lotion into the scalp, as after a haircut FRICTION

hairdresser COIFFEUR, COIFFEUSE

hairdressing parlour, stylish fashion store, or the like SALON
– relating to barbering or hairdressing TONSORIAL

hairless and smooth GLABROUS

hairline forming a V-shape in the centre of the forehead WIDOW'S PEAK
– hairline of a balding man that is moving back increasingly from the forehead RECEDING HAIRLINE

hairpiece covering and hiding a bald spot TOUPEE

hairpin of an old-fashioned ornamented type BODKIN

hairsplitting, nitpicking, needless arguing or drawing of distinctions QUIBBLING, PEDANTRY
– hairsplitting, quibbling, over-precise, pedantic or dogmatic

SCHOLASTIC, SOPHISTIC

hairstyle See chart
– hairstyle, especially of a woman COIFFURE

hairy, having long or thick hair HIRSUTE
– hairy, relating to or consisting of hair PILEOUS
– hairy, covered with fine soft hair PILOSE, CRINITE, LANATE
– hairy or resembling a tuft of hairs COMATE

Haiti – Haiti's irregular police force, established by "Papa Doc" Duvalier TONTON-MACOUTES
– Haitian religious cult of African origin, involving magical practices and spiritualist communication VOODOO

half a sphere, globe, or the Earth HEMISPHERE
– half board DEMI-PENSION
– half-line of verse HEMISTICH
– half or portion MOIETY
– half-way, in the middle, in between INTERMEDIATE
– referring to half-brothers or half-sisters having the same mother but a different father UTERINE

half- SEMI-, DEMI-, HEMI-

half-caste or mixed-race person, as in the Caribbean or Latin America, typically speaking a hybrid language CREOLE
– half-caste or mixed-race person of white and black descent, specifically a person with one black and one white parent MULATTO
– half-caste or mixed-race person who is one-eighth black, specifically a person with one white parent and one quarter-black parent OCTOROON, MUSTEE
– half-caste or mixed-race person who is one-quarter black, specifically a person with one white parent and one half-white parent QUADROON
– half-caste person, especially of mixed French Canadian and American Indian descent MÉTIS, BRULE, BOIS-BRÛLÉ
– half-caste person, especially of mixed Spanish American and American Indian descent MESTIZE
– half-caste person of mixed European and Asian descent, especially formerly in India EURASIAN

half-hearted, unenthusiastic TEPID, LUKEWARM

hall in which an audience sits, as for a meeting or play AUDITORIUM

hall of fame of a particular group or field of endeavour PANTHEON

Hallowe'en lantern made from a pumpkin JACK-O'-LANTERN
– Hallowe'en masquerader or mummer GUISER, GUISARD

hallucinations – producing or relating to hallucinations PSYCHEDELIC
– severe mental disorder, as in some alcoholics, involving tremors and hallucinations DELIRIUM TREMENS, D.T.'s

halo – halo-like area of light, in medieval paintings, surrounding a holy figure MANDORLA, AUREOLE, VESICA, PISCIS
– halo-like radiance or similar sign of sanctity above or behind the head of God, a saint, or a monarch in art NIMBUS, GLORIA, GLORIOLE, GLORY
– halo-like ring of faint light, as around the Moon when viewed through a haze CORONA

ham See **bacon**
– ham cured and spiced in a traditional Italian style PROSCIUTTO

Hamlet – dramatic monologue, as by Shakespeare's Hamlet, typically representing the character's unspoken thoughts SOLILOQUY

hammer, long and heavy, for driving in stakes or pegs MAUL
– hammer having a fork at one end of the head for removing nails CLAW HAMMER
– hammer used by a judge, auctioneer, or chairman, for making a rapping noise GAVEL
– hammer whose head has one rounded end, usually used for beating metal BALL-PEEN HAMMER
– hammer with small rubber head used for testing reflexes and tapping the chest for purposes of diagnosis PLEXOR
– blunt or broad end of a hammer, axe, or the like POLL
– break up stone, especially with a

HAIRSTYLES

Afro	bushy and frizzy	**en brosse**	cut short and standing stiffly upright
bangs	fringe cut straight across the forehead	**Eton crop, shingle**	cropped short in the manner of a schoolboy, popular with women in the 1920s
beehive	piled up by backcombing	**French pleat, French roll**	cylindrical roll gathered at the back
bob	short even cut all round the head	**frizette**	curled fringe across the forehead
bouffant	puffed out through backcombing	**marcel wave**	regular, tight waves set close to the head
chignon	long hair rolled into a knot or bun at the back	**Mohican**	spiky sweep of hair down the centre of an otherwise shaved head
corn rows	tight parallel plaits set close to the head, popular with West Indian and African women	**pageboy**	straight hair with the ends curled gently inwards, typically shoulder-length at the back and with a fringe on the forehead
crimps	tight curls or waves	**pompadour**	brushed up from the forehead and turned back over a pad, as worn by women in the early 18th century
dreadlocks	long twisted locks, typically worn by Rastafarian men	**pouffe**	piled high in rolled puffs, as worn by women in the 18th century
ducktail, duck's arse, DA	hair back-swept at the sides with a high quiff and a curl at the back, resembling a duck's tail, popular among young men in the 1950s		

hammer SPALL
- handle of a hammer HELVE
- handle or binding of shock-absorbing material on a hammer or other tool WITHE
- heavy forge hammer levered up and then dropped TILT HAMMER
- wedge- or ball-shaped head opposite the flat surface of a hammer PANE, PEEN, PEIN

hammock – cords supporting a hammock CLEWS

hand See illustration, and also **bones**
- hand, paw, claw, hoof, or the like MANUS
- hand-shaped PALMATE
- hand-warmer consisting of a large fur or cloth ring MUFF
- hands or feet EXTREMITIES
- able to use both hands equally expertly AMBIDEXTROUS
- adjective for the hands MANUAL
- distance between the tips of the thumb and little finger of a spread hand SPAN
- gesture of greeting or respect, as in India, by placing one's hands together out in front of one and bowing slightly NAMASTE
- pad of muscle on the hand below the thumb HEEL
- palm of the hand, or fleshy base of the thumb THENAR
- skilful or clever, especially with one's hands DEXTEROUS, DEFT, ADROIT
- skill or speed of hand movements, as used in conjuring tricks SLEIGHT OF HAND, LEGERDEMAIN

hand- CHIRO-, MANU-

hand down or pass on to one's children or successors BEQUEATH
- something handed down from the past LEGACY, BEQUEST

hand grenade – powerful oval-shaped hand grenade MILLS BOMB

hand over goods for transporting, delivery, disposal, or the like CONSIGN
- handing over a criminal, fugitive, or the like to the authority or country where he is wanted EXTRADITION

handbag, pouch, or purse, in former times RETICULE
- small case or handbag used by women for carrying cosmetics or

hand

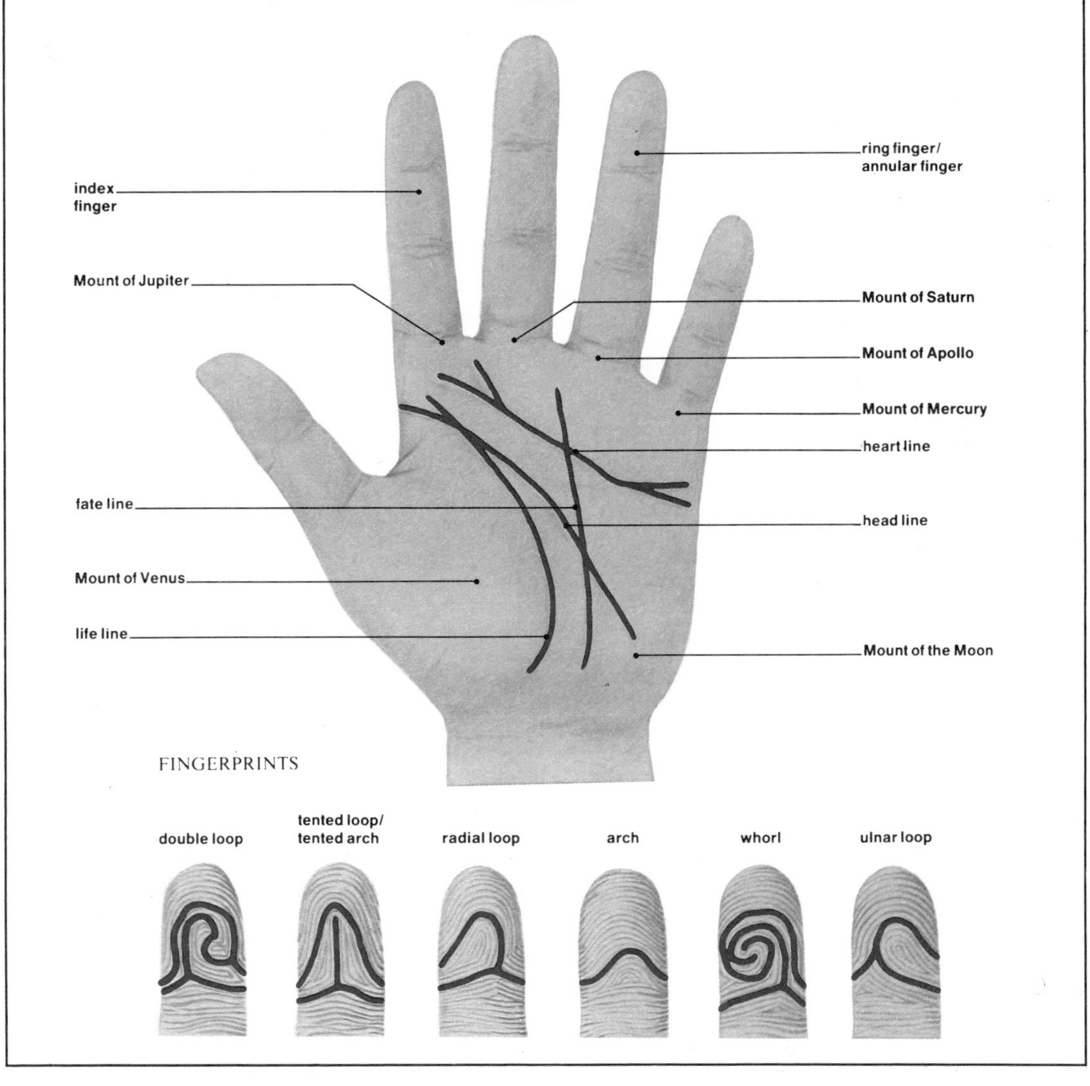

toiletries VANITY CASE, ÉTUI
– U.S. term for a handbag PURSE, POCKETBOOK

handcuffs or similar metal fastening confining the hands and arms or the feet MANACLES, FETTERS, SHACKLES, IRONS
– fettered iron bar, a counterpart of handcuffs, formerly used for shackling prisoners' feet BILBOES
– slang term for handcuffs DARBIES

handicap, burden, or hinder ENCUMBER
– handicap, disadvantage, hindrance LIABILITY
– handicap, put at a disadvantage PENALISE
– handicap weight that a racehorse must carry IMPOST

handkerchief, large and usually brightly coloured, used as a scarf BANDANNA, NECKERCHIEF

handle in the form of a hooped rod, as of a bucket or kettle BAIL
– handle of a sword, knife, or the like HILT, HAFT
– handle of an axe, hammer, or the like HELVE
– handle or binding of shock-absorbing material on a hammer or other tool WITHE
– handle or butt of a whip, fishing rod, or the like STOCK
– any of the ridges on an object to make it easier to grip KNURL
– ear-shaped handle on a machine, jug, or the like LUG
– having a handle or similar extension ANSATE

handrail – handrail's supporting post BALUSTER

handsome in a modest and unspectacular way, pleasing and presentable PERSONABLE, PREPOSSESSING
– handsome young man APOLLO, ADONIS, DEMIGOD

handwriting See also **writing**, **script**
– handwriting, or a handwritten document MANUSCRIPT
– handwriting, or a manuscript in the author's own handwriting AUTOGRAPH
– handwriting or penmanship that is very neat, elegant, or artistic CALLIGRAPHY, CHIROGRAPHY
– handwriting style based on capital letters MAJUSCULE
– handwriting style based on small joined-up letters, as in medieval manuscripts MINUSCULE
– handwriting style using joined-up letters, as distinct from block printing CURSIVE
– handwriting style using large, rounded, separated capital letters, as in early medieval Greek and Roman manuscripts UNCIAL
– handwriting that is poor or illegible, scrawl HIEROGLYPHICS, CACOGRAPHY
– handwriting using full spelling, as distinct from shorthand LONGHAND
– difficult to read, as a cramped handwriting might be CRABBED
– downward stroke of the pen in handwriting MINIM
– readable, as handwriting might be LEGIBLE
– secretary or scribe who takes dictation or makes neat copies of documents in handwriting AMANUENSIS
– showy decoration in handwriting, especially in a signature FLOURISH, QUIRK
– study of handwriting, as for psychological analysis or detection of forgery GRAPHOLOGY
– trembling or caused by trembling, as shaky handwriting might be TREMULOUS

hanger-on, sponger, person living off another PARASITE, FREELOADER, SCROUNGER

hanging, dangling, suspended from above PENDENT, PENDULOUS
– hanging limply, drooping FLACCID
– hanging sculpted ornament on a Gothic ceiling, or hanging item of jewellery PENDANT
– part of a garment hanging down or out, such as a sleeve, hood, or cape TIPPET
– platform or raised wooden framework, as formerly used for hanging or beheading criminals SCAFFOLD
– post for displaying the bodies of hanged criminals GIBBET
– rope for securing a horse or cow, or for a noose in hanging HALTER

hangover remedy of a raw egg usually immersed in Worcester sauce or vinegar PRAIRIE OYSTER
– having a hangover as a result of drunkenness CRAPULENT

happen, occur, take place, come to pass TRANSPIRE
– happen as a result, follow ENSUE, EVENTUATE
– happen as something unexpected, irrelevant, or unnecessary SUPERVENE
– happen at the same time, cause to be simultaneous SYNCHRONISE
– develop into reality, become fact, actually happen MATERIALISE

happening at the same time or place, simultaneously, as two prison sentences might be CONCURRENT
– happening in fits and starts, intermittent SPASMODIC

happiness, joy FELICITY
– happiness or well-being, especially that produced, according to Aristotle's philosophy, by an active and rational life EUDEMONIA
– continual happiness and optimism, enjoyment of life JOIE DE VIVRE
– place or state of perfect happiness ELYSIUM
– state of supreme or blessed happiness BEATITUDE

happy, cheerful, and carefree BLITHE, BUOYANT, DEBONAIR, JAUNTY
– enchanted, extremely happy or delighted ENRAPTURED, TRANSPORTED, RAPTUROUS
– excitedly happy, filled with joy, as after a triumph or success ELATED, EXHILARATED, EXULTANT
– extremely happy, often in a dangerously exaggerated or complacent way EUPHORIC
– extremely happy or pleased, overwhelmed with delight, overjoyed ECSTATIC, DELIRIOUS
– pleased, satisfied, happy and contented GRATIFIED
– supremely and serenely happy, as if blessed BEATIFIC
– very happy, delighted, in high spirits JUBILANT, COCK-A-HOOP, EXUBERANT

happy-go-lucky See **casual**

harass in a bullying way HECTOR, BADGER
– harass or jeer at a speaker with repeated critical comments HECKLE

harbour protected by a massive stone breakwater, or the breakwater itself MOLE
– clean or deepen a harbour, channel, or the like by means of a scooping machine DREDGE
– pier or breakwater to protect a harbour or shore JETTY
– platform or dockside in a harbour for mooring, loading, and unloading ships WHARF, QUAY

hard See also **difficult**
– hard and apparently unbreakable stone or other substance ADAMANT
– hard coating or shell, as of some insects TEST
– hard or unyielding as stone FLINTY, GRANITE

hard- SCLER-, SCLERO-

hard coal ANTHRACITE

hard work, effort, or attention to duty APPLICATION

hard-working, dedicated, conscientious, and persevering ASSIDUOUS, DILIGENT, SEDULOUS
– hardworking, energetic, and forceful person DYNAMO

hardback and cloth-covered, as a book might be CLOTHBOUND, CASED, CASEBOUND

harden, solidify, curdle, or clot, as exposed blood does CONGEAL, COAGULATE
- harden, toughen, or make callous INDURATE
- harden or strengthen rubber by heat-treating with sulphur compounds VULCANISE
- harden or toughen glass, steel, or the like, as by alternate heating and cooling TEMPER, ANNEAL
- hardened, bony SCLEROUS
- hardened emotionally CASE-HARDENED, CALLOUS
- hardening of the arteries SCLEROSIS
- hardening of tissue or other substance through the action of calcium salts CALCIFICATION

hardness – index of the hardness of a metal BRINELL HARDNESS
- scale of hardness of minerals, based on resistance to scratching by a diamond or other mineral MOHS SCALE

hare stew JUGGED HARE
- adjective for a hare LEPORINE
- sport of hunting game, such as hares, with hounds relying on sight rather than scent COURSING
- young hare, especially one in its first year of life LEVERET

harem SERAGLIO
- harem concubine or woman slave ODALISQUE

harm See also **damage**
- harm, damage, disadvantage DETRIMENT, DISSERVICE
- harm, harmful effects, damage RAVAGES
- harm, injury, or wound LESION
- harm the originator, as a hurtful policy might REBOUND, RECOIL, REDOUND

harmful, damaging, poisonous, or corrupting NOXIOUS
- harmful, extremely infectious, or very rapid in effect, as a disease or poison might be VIRULENT
- harmful in a stealthy or secretive way, treacherous INSIDIOUS
- harmful or damaging INJURIOUS, DELETERIOUS, DETRIMENTAL
- harmful or evil in intention or influence MALEVOLENT, MALICIOUS, MALIGN, MALEFICENT, PESTILENT, MISCHIEVOUS, BALEFUL, MALIGNANT, PERNICIOUS
- harmful to something or someone ADVERSE, INIMICAL

harmless or unobjectionable INOFFENSIVE, INNOCUOUS

harmony See also **agree**
- harmony of musical notes CONCORD, CONSONANCE
- harmony or correspondence among parts, claims, or the like, consistency COMPATIBILITY, CONGRUENCE, CONCURRENCE
- harmony or order COSMOS
- harmonious, in agreement, corresponding CONFORMABLE, IN UNISON
- harmonious and balanced arrangement of parts SYMMETRY
- harmonious and effective interaction COORDINATION

harness See illustration, page 238

harpsichord – plucking device or plectrum for the strings of a harpsichord or related instrument QUILL

harsh See also **cruel**, **bitter**, **strict**
- harsh, demanding, or severe, as strict rules or standards are RIGOROUS, STRINGENT
- harsh, dissonant, discordant, or out-of-tune sound, as of a faulty violin or specially tuned piano WOLF
- harsh, very severe, as laws or punishments might be DRACONIAN
- harsh and persistent, relentless or pitiless, unyielding IMPLACABLE, INEXORABLE, UNREMITTING
- harsh or abrupt in manner or speech GRUFF, CURT, BRUSQUE
- harsh or grim, as a bleak, barren landscape is STARK, DESOLATE
- harsh or severe, as a very strict upbringing is SPARTAN, AUSTERE
- harsh-sounding or shrill or hoarse-sounding, grating RAUCOUS, STRIDENT

Harvard – referring to eight old and famous American universities, including Harvard and Yale IVY LEAGUE

harvest of an abundant kind FOISON
- harvesting machine that cuts, threshes, and cleans a crop of grain COMBINE HARVESTER

hasty, rash IMPETUOUS, IMPULSIVE, PRECIPITATE, CURSORY

hat See illustration, page 239
- hat with a high crown and wide brim, popular in the western U.S. STETSON
- black academic hat consisting of a tight cap topped by a stiff square and sometimes a tassel MORTARBOARD, SQUARE, TRENCHER
- hats for women MILLINERY
- Cockney rhyming slang for "hat" TITFER
- feather, ribbon, or rosette worn on the hat, especially by soldiers COCKADE
- huntsman's hat in the form of a round cap with ear-flaps MONTERO
- low brimless Scottish hat or cap with a crease down the crown and often ribbons at the back GLENGARRY
- low brimless Scottish hat or cap, often having a pompom on top TAM-O'-SHANTER
- low-crowned hat with a broad brim projecting at the front, as formerly worn by some clergymen SHOVEL HAT
- maker or seller of women's hats MILLINER
- man's felt hat with a narrow brim and dented crown TRILBY, HOMBURG
- put on one's hat or clothes DON
- small, stiff round hat for a woman PILLBOX
- soft cloth hat with peaks at front and back, and ear-flaps typically tied on top DEERSTALKER
- soft hat with a low crown and very wide brim WIDEAWAKE
- stiff straw hat with a low crown BOATER
- take off one's hat or clothes DOFF
- top hat BEAVER, CASTOR
- trimming of twisted ribbon or cord for a hat TORSADE
- U.S. term for a bowler hat DERBY
- waterproof hat, as worn by sailors, with a broad brim at the back SOU'WESTER
- wide-brimmed hat made of tropical leaves, as worn in Latin America PANAMA
- wide-brimmed Spanish or Mexican hat of felt or straw SOMBRERO

hatch – keep eggs warm prior to hatching INCUBATE, BROOD

hatchway, hinged porthole, or the like on a ship SCUTTLE

hate intensely, loathe, ABOMINATE, EXECRATE, ABHOR

-hate-, -hatred- MIS-, MISO-, -PHOBE, -PHOBIA, -PHOBIC

hated person or thing ANATHEMA

hateful, vile, or appallingly wicked ABOMINABLE, ODIOUS, HEINOUS

hatred, ill will MALIGNITY, MALICE
- hatred of men MISANDRY
- hatred of other people MISANTHROPY
- hatred of women MISOGYNY
- hatred or bitter enmity ANIMUS, ANIMOSITY
- hatred or contempt ODIUM
- hatred or intense feeling of hostility or repulsion AVERSION, ANTIPATHY, REVULSION, REPUGNANCE
- bitterness, deep hostility, feeling of hatred or ill will RANCOUR
- feelings of or remarks indicating intense hatred VITRIOL
- irrational and uncontrollable

harness

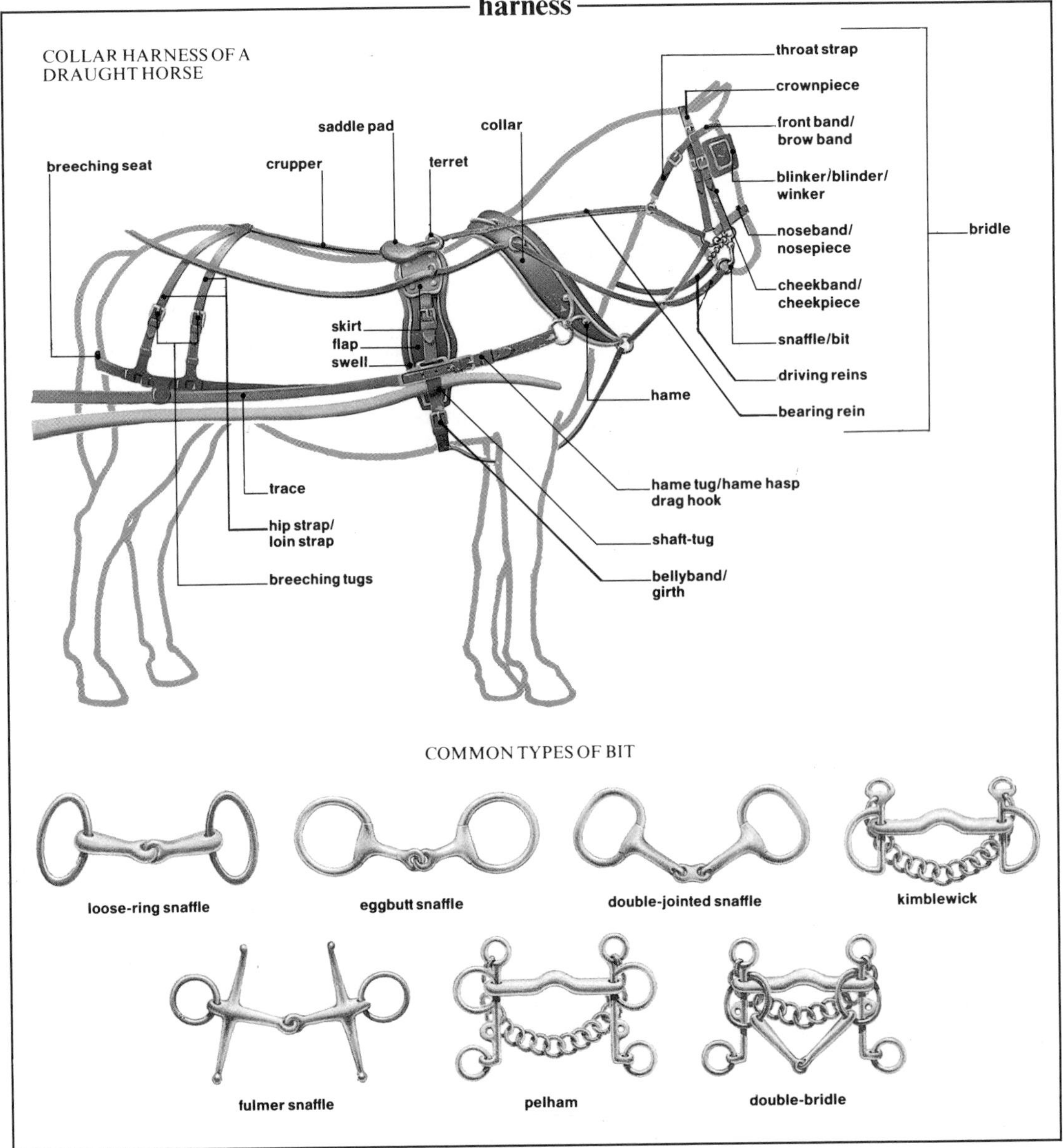

fear or hatred of something specified PHOBIA

haughty, disdainful SUPERCILIOUS
- haughtiness, arrogance HAUTEUR

hauling machine, typically a rope-wound drum WINDLASS, CAPSTAN

haven, refuge, or relief OASIS

-having -OSE

havoc – cause havoc WREAK

Hawaiian dress of a loose, brightly coloured style MUUMUU
- Hawaiian feast LUAU
- Hawaiian greeting or farewell ALOHA
- Hawaiian wreath or garland of flowers, typically worn round the neck LEI

hawk of various kinds, including the sparrowhawk and goshawk ACCIPITER
- hawk or falcon still young enough to be trained for falconry EYAS
- bunch of feathers, sometimes with a bait of meat, attached to a long cord, used by a falconer to recall a hawk LURE
- cage for hawks, especially one to moult in MEW
- feeding rack for a hawk HACK
- female hawk, especially one used in falconry FORMEL
- free a dog, hawk, or the like from its leash or other restraint SLIP
- group of hawks CAST, LEASH
- hawks released by a falconer in a pair to pursue quarry as a team CAST
- jump about and struggle to escape, as a leashed hawk might BATE
- leather strap or leash tied to the leg of a hawk JESS
- male hawk, especially one used in falconry TERCEL
- stitch up the eyes of a hawk or falcon to quieten or tame it SEEL

– untamed adult hawk HAGGARD
hawker, seller of small items who typically roves the streets PEDLAR
hay, grass, or the like for pasturing HERBAGE
– hay or grass cut by a scythe or mower SWATH
– hay or other dry fodder fed to livestock PROVENDER
– rack for hay or other food for farm animals CRATCH, CRIB
– second crop of grass or hay in a single season AFTERMATH, ROWEN
hayfever remedy, reducing the symptoms of allergies ANTI-HISTAMINE
haystack, pile of straw, or the like in the open air RICK
– haystack of a small cone-shaped kind COCK, HAYCOCK
hazelnut FILBERT
hazy, misty, cloudy NEBULOUS
head See also **bones**, **skull**
– head, especially the hairy top of the head POLL
– head, or crown of the head PATE
– head-cloth framing the face, as worn by some nuns WIMPLE
– head-like part, such as the end of a long bone or insect's antenna CAPITULUM
– head-shaped, as some flowers or flower-clusters are CAPITATE
– head swelling caused by a build-up of cerebrospinal fluid HYDROCEPHALUS
– head to foot CAP-À-PIE
– back of the head, rear skull OCCIPUT
– cut the head off, behead DECAPITATE
– front of the head, upper forward part of the skull SINCIPUT
– having a broad, roundish head, relatively short from front to back BRACHYCEPHALIC
– having a long head, with the length of the skull front to back considerably greater than its breadth DOLICHOCEPHALIC
– having a medium-shaped head, neither markedly long nor broad MESOCEPHALIC
– having an enlarged head-like end, as some bones have CAPITATE
– having two heads BICEPHALOUS
– jerking of the head, causing injury to the neck, as in a car accident WHIPLASH
– medallion, on a brooch, ring, or the like, with a head in profile in raised relief CAMEO
– outermost point at the back of the head, used when measuring the skull INION
– relating to the head end or front part of animals, leaves, or the like ANTERIOR

hats

MEN'S HATS

bearskin
bicorn
tricorn
yarmulke
biretta
shako
busby
kaffiyeh
forage cap (popular)
mitre
tarboosh/fez
zucchetto
kepi
sola topi/pith helmet
fedora

WOMEN'S HATS

Dolly Varden
slouch hat
cornet
toque
cloche
mobcap

– relating to the head or the skull CEPHALIC
– shaven head, especially of a monk or priest TONSURE
– system for classifying people or races according to the shape of the skull or head CEPHALIC INDEX
– top of the head, highest point of the skull VERTEX
– top of the head, or other crown-shaped body part CORONA
– wreath or crown of flowers worn on the head GARLAND, CHAPLET

-head- -CEPHAL-, CEPHALO-, -CAPIT-

head cold CORYZA

head waiter MAJOR-DOMO, MAÎTRE D'HÔTEL

headache, often accompanied by nausea and faulty vision MIGRAINE

headband as worn by desert Arabs to hold the kaffiyeh or headdress in place AGAL
– headband, typically U-shaped and of stiff plastic, for holding down the hair on the crown of a woman's head ALICE-BAND
– headband, usually decorated FRONTLET
– headband of a narrow strip of metal, ribbon, or the like worn around the forehead FILLET
– headband or semicircle, typically decorated with diamonds or other jewels, worn by a woman on formal occasions TIARA

headed notepaper, or the heading on it LETTERHEAD

heading or introduction LEMMA
– heading or title under which something is classed RUBRIC
– classify or include in a wider category or under a general heading or principle SUBSUME

headline or title on every page or other page of a book or magazine RUNNING HEAD
– headline running right across the page of a newspaper BANNER HEADLINE, STREAMER

headquarters – group of senior officers responsible for planning at military headquarters GENERAL STAFF

heads face on a coin OBVERSE

headscarf as worn by Russian peasant women BABUSHKA

heal, cure, treat medically PHYSIC
– heal by forming a scar CICATRISE

healing, curing, remedial THERAPEUTIC, SANATIVE
– healing or soothing substance, person, or influence SALVE
– formation of small beads of new tissue on the surface of a wound during healing GRANULATION
– medical, relating to healing AESCULAPIAN

heart

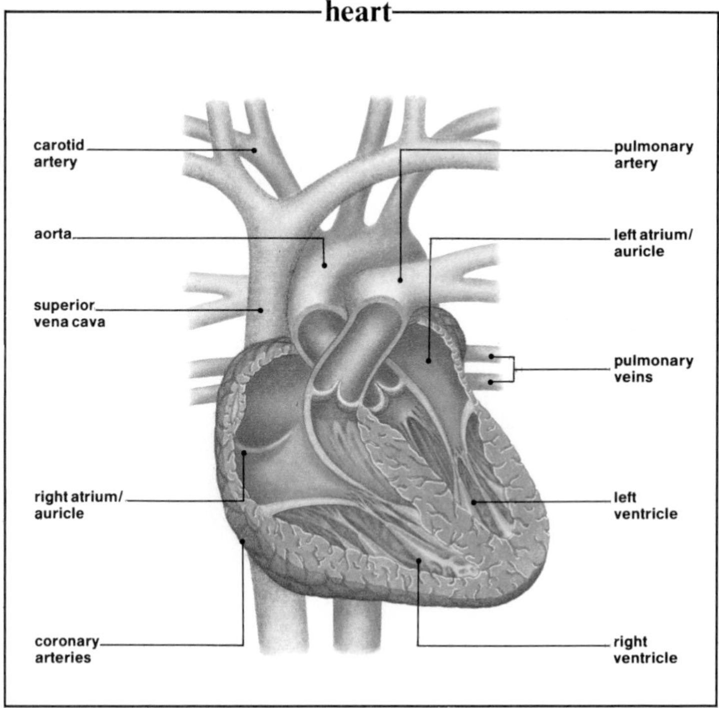

health – health-obsessed person HYPOCHONDRIAC, VALETUDINARIAN
– health-promoting, favourable to well-being SALUBRIOUS, BENEFICIAL
– health-promoting or -preserving, free from infection SANITARY
– general state of health or state of mind CONSTITUTION
– recover strongly, improve quickly, as one's health or spirits might RALLY
– regain one's health or strength, as after an illness RECUPERATE, CONVALESCE
– restoration of one's health through therapy REHABILITATION
– restoring or promoting health, curative SALUTARY

health farm HYDRO

healthy SALUBRIOUS, WHOLESOME, SALUTARY
– healthy, active, and vigorous, typically in spite of being old SPRY, SPRIGHTLY
– healthy, fresh, and vigorous condition VERDURE
– healthy, robust HALE
– healthy and nourishing, as good food is NUTRITIOUS

heap of earth or stones covering an ancient burial site BARROW, MOUND, TUMULUS

hear ye, call for attention by town crier or court official OYEZ

hearing of supposedly superhuman perception or telepathic sensitivity CLAIRAUDIENCE
– perceptible to hearing, loud enough to be heard AUDIBLE
– relating to sound or hearing ACOUSTIC
– relating to the sense or organs of hearing AUDITORY, AURICULAR

hearing- AUDI-, -AUDIO-

heart See illustration
– heart attack or condition caused by a blood clot in the coronary artery CORONARY THROMBOSIS
– heart murmur or other abnormal body sound BRUIT
– heart muscle, muscle tissue of the heart MYOCARDIUM
– heart specialist CARDIOLOGIST
– heart-shaped, as a shell or leaf might be CORDATE, CORDIFORM
– heart wall PARIES
– beat abnormally fast, as the heart might PALPITATE
– beat in a regular rhythm, as the heart does PULSATE
– death of an organ or part of an organ, such as the heart, as due to a blood clot INFARCTION
– instrument recording the electrical impulses in the heart ELECTROCARDIOGRAPH, ECG
– machine used to start the heart beating again, by administering an electric shock DEFIBRILLATOR
– relating to the heart CORONARY, CARDIAC
– rhythmic contraction of the

heart, pumping the blood into the aorta and pulmonary arteries SYSTOLE
– rhythmic relaxation of the heart, drawing blood into its chambers DIASTOLE
– soapy substance found in body tissue, fat, and bile, which may be involved in heart disease CHOLESTEROL
– study of the heart CARDIOLOGY
– twitching of the heart muscle, affecting the normal rhythm of contractions FIBRILLATION

heart- CARDI-

heartbeat irregularity ARRHYTHMIA
– heartbeat regulator, either natural tissue or a small implanted device PACEMAKER
– heartbeat that is abnormally slow BRADYCARDIA
– heartbeat that is abnormally fast TACHYCARDIA
– heartbeat that is irregular or abnormally fast PALPITATION
– rotating cylinder on which a pen records changes in pressure, heartbeat, or the like KYMOGRAPH
– technique for regulating one's own heartbeat, blood pressure, or other apparently involuntary bodily functions BIOFEEDBACK

heartburn BRASH, PYROSIS

hearty and outdoorsy, in the style of the British county gentry TWEEDY
– hearty eater TRENCHERMAN

heat, period of sexual excitement in some female mammals OESTRUS, RUT
– heat and spice wine or ale MULL
– heat given out or absorbed by a substance when it changes state, as during melting LATENT HEAT
– heat-producing CALEFACIENT
– heat-proof, sound-proof, or protect from electricity INSULATE
– heat-treatment of milk, beer, and other consumable liquids to destroy germs and regulate fermentation PASTEURISATION
– measurement of heat, as in chemical reactions CALORIMETRY
– referring to heat from the Earth's interior GEOTHERMAL
– relating to the measuring of heat or calories CALORIC, CALORIFIC
– relating to heat THERMAL
– transfer of heat along or through a static body CONDUCTION
– transfer of heat by rays from a hot object RADIATION
– transfer of heat through the movement of air or other fluid between areas of different temperatures and densities CONVECTION

-heat- -THERM-, THERMO-, -THERMY, CALE-, CALOR-, PYRO-

heat shield of a spacecraft ABLATOR

heated passion or burning enthusiasm ARDOUR

heater essentially consisting of a series of pipes through which hot water or steam flows RADIATOR
– heater typically consisting of an electric element from which warm air gently circulates CONVECTOR
– portable stove or heater, as for drying out a building under construction SALAMANDER

heather HEATH, LING

heating channel under the floor in an ancient Roman house HYPOCAUST
– heating element or coil in a hot-water tank IMMERSION HEATER
– heating of the Earth's atmosphere through increased absorption of solar radiation GREENHOUSE EFFECT

heaven See also **paradise**
– heaven, arching vault of the sky WELKIN, FIRMAMENT
– heaven-like abode of the gods in Greek mythology OLYMPUS
– heavenly, relating to the sky or heavens, sublime SUPERNAL, CELESTIAL, ETHEREAL, EMPYREAL
– heavenly kingdom ZION
– heavens, the skies, space beyond the Earth's atmosphere, according to Greek myth ETHER
– abode of just souls barred from heaven, as through not having been baptised LIMBO
– branch of theology dealing with last things, such as heaven and hell ESCHATOLOGY
– highest level of heaven, formerly thought to be the realm of pure fire or of God and the angels EMPYREAN
– relating to the joys of heaven or sainthood BEATIFIC
– taking up of the Virgin Mary into heaven THE ASSUMPTION
– transporting to heaven of someone who has not yet died TRANSLATION, ASCENSION, APOTHEOSIS

heavens- URAN-, URANO-

heavy See also **big**, **huge**, **fat**
– heavy, starchy, as thick porridge or similar food is STODGY
– heavy and awkward, bulky or lumbering, ungainly PONDEROUS
– "heavy hydrogen" DEUTERIUM
– "heavy water" DEUTERIUM OXIDE
– heavy, as breathing might be LABOURED
– difficult to handle, awkward or unwieldy, as through being too heavy CUMBERSOME
– imposing heavy burdens or responsibilities, oppressive, as a task might be ONEROUS

heavy goods vehicle JUGGERNAUT

Hebrew scholar HEBRAIST
– secret or mystical philosophy, specifically an occult philosophy based on the Hebrew scriptures CABALA

hedge, fence, or row of trees designed to break the force of the wind WINDBREAK
– hedge of plants or cuttings individually planted QUICKSET
– hedged pathways in a puzzling pattern MAZE
– hedging shrub, having dark purple berries PRIVET
– plait or weave branches or bark in making a hedge or arbour PLASH, PLEACH
– sunken hedge, as in a garden HA-HA
– trimming of trees or hedges into ornamental shapes TOPIARY

hedgehog – hedgehog's spines QUILLS
– adjective for a hedgehog ERINACEOUS

heel bone CALCANEUS
– high, tapering, pointed heel on a woman's shoe STILETTO
– high, thick heel on a shoe CUBAN HEEL
– solid tapering heel joined to the sole of a shoe to form a single surface WEDGE HEEL, WEDGIE
– weakness or flaw, as small and apparently unimportant as one's heel, but fatally vulnerable ACHILLES' HEEL

-heel- -CALC-

Hegel – final stage in the dialectical reasoning process of Hegel, through combining thesis and antithesis SYNTHESIS
– process of reaching truth, as in Hegel, by examining and exploiting contradictions DIALECTIC

height, especially of a person when standing upright STATURE
– height, width, or length DIMENSION
– dizziness or sense of confusion, as experienced when looking down from a height VERTIGO
– fear of heights ACROPHOBIA, HYPSOPHOBIA, CREMNOPHOBIA
– instrument measuring the height of an aircraft above the ground ALTIMETER
– instrument measuring height of land above sea level OROMETER

height- ACRO-, HYPS-, HYPSO-

heir or offspring SCION
– heir sharing equally with another PARCENER
– assured and unchallengeable heir HEIR APPARENT
– current and provisional heir, whose claims would be cancelled by the birth of someone with a

prior right HEIR PRESUMPTIVE
– deprive an heir of his inheritance, as by cutting him out of one's will DISINHERIT
– passing or transmitted to an heir HEREDITARY

helicopter CHOPPER, WHIRLYBIRD
– helicopter's control lever that adjusts the angle of attack of all the rotor blades at once, regulating vertical movement COLLECTIVE PITCH LEVER
– helicopter's control lever that adjusts the angle of attack of individual rotor blades, regulating horizontal movement CYCLIC PITCH LEVER
– descend, as from a cliff top or helicopter, by means of a supporting rope fastened around one's body ABSEIL
– runners or struts beneath a helicopter, on which it stands SKIDS
– system of blades supporting a helicopter or similar aircraft in flight ROTOR

helium, neon, or other gaseous element formerly considered incapable of chemical reaction INERT GAS, NOBLE GAS, RARE GAS

hell, eternal damnation PERDITION
– hell, place of punishment for the wicked after death GEHENNA, SHEOL
– hell or the underworld in Greek mythology HADES, ORCUS, TARTARUS
– hell, or a blazing fire suggestive of hell INFERNO
– Jesus's rescue of righteous souls trapped in hell HARROWING OF HELL
– region or state in the afterlife between heaven and hell, in which venial sinners can atone PURGATORY
– relating to hell or the abode of the dead INFERNAL

hellfire preacher HOT-GOSPELLER

helmet, or helmet-like covering or knob, as on the bill of a hornbill CASQUE
– helmet, or the ridge or plume on it CREST
– helmet of light steel often with a visor BASINET
– hinged front part of an armoured helmet, covering the eyes and nose VISOR, BEAVER
– light 15th-century helmet with a neck guard at the rear SALLET
– movable lower front part of a medieval helmet VENTAIL
– plume on a helmet PANACHE
– ridge on the top of a helmet COMB
– scarf or cloth covering a helmet in medieval times LAMBREQUIN

help, especially financial assistance SUBVENTION, SUBSIDY
– help or be of value AVAIL
– help another by begging or pleading on his behalf INTERCEDE
– help or encourage, especially in wrongdoing ABET, CONNIVE
– help or relief in time of distress SUCCOUR
– help or service MINISTRATIONS
– help or support by a grant of money SUBSIDISE
– help to bring about, ease FACILITATE, EXPEDITE
– applying or turning for help to a person or thing, such as the courts RECOURSE
– call upon or appeal to for help INVOKE
– give something, such as help or assistance RENDER
– something that helps or serves a higher cause HANDMAIDEN

helper, especially one who gives financial assistance BENEFACTOR, BENEFACTRESS
– helper offering his services willingly and for free VOLUNTEER
– helper or fellow worker COADJUTANT, COADJUTOR

helping, assisting, supplementing, or supporting AUXILIARY, ADJUVANT, ADJUNCT, SUBSIDIARY, ANCILLARY
– helping, cooperative, or considerate OBLIGING
– helping, promoting, contributing to, or favourable to a given result CONDUCIVE

hem or edging of decorative design PURFLE

hen, especially when less than a year old PULLET
– hen kept in farmyards or fields rather than batteries FREE-RANGE HEN
– hen that has been spayed and fattened for eating POULARD

henchman or follower MYRMIDON
– henchman who does somebody else's dirty work HATCHET MAN

heraldry See illustration, and chart, page 244; also **coat of arms**
– relating to heraldry ARMORIAL

herb having medicinal properties SIMPLE

herb tea INFUSION, TISANE

herbs See chart, page 245

Hercules – snake-like monster with multiplying heads, killed by Hercules HYDRA

herd or flock of animals being driven together DROVE
– herding of cattle, horses, or the like DRIFT
– living or migrating in a herd, or the like GREGARIOUS

here lies, a Latin inscription used on gravestones HIC JACET

hereditary, as some diseases are GENETIC
– hereditary unit in a chromosome that determines an individual's characteristics GENE
– referring to a condition or abnormality existing from birth but not hereditary CONGENITAL

heredity laws in genetics MENDEL'S LAWS

heresy of various kinds in the early Christian church ARIANISM, GNOSTICISM, PELAGIANISM
– heresy of various kinds in the medieval church ALBIGENSIANISM, CATHARISM
– heresy, or doctrines and movement considered heretical, in the Roman Catholic church in the 17th century JANSENISM
– heretical, different from orthodox beliefs HETERODOX
– burning of a heretic at the stake, as ordered by the Inquisition AUTO-DA-FÉ
– investigation or tribunal of the Roman Catholic Church, as for trying suspected witches or heretics in former times INQUISITION

heritage, legacy PATRIMONY

Hermes – staff of Hermes, with wings and two twining snakes, serving as a symbol of the medical profession CADUCEUS

hermit, solitary person, living alone in seclusion RECLUSE
– hermit in early Christian times who lived on top of a high pillar STYLITE
– hermit or recluse, person who has gone into seclusion for religious reasons ANCHORITE, ANCHORESS, EREMITE

hernia in which part of the stomach pushes through the diaphragm HIATUS HERNIA
– belt-like medical device worn to keep a hernia from protruding TRUSS
– press against or obstruct a blood vessel, hernia, or the like so as to prevent natural flow or functioning STRANGULATE

-hernia -CELE

hero or leading character in a play, novel, or other literary work PROTAGONIST
– heroes or list of heroes of a particular group or field of endeavour PANTHEON
– referring to the person, fictional hero, or the like, after whom a city, novel, or the like is named EPONYMOUS
– unhonoured and usually un-

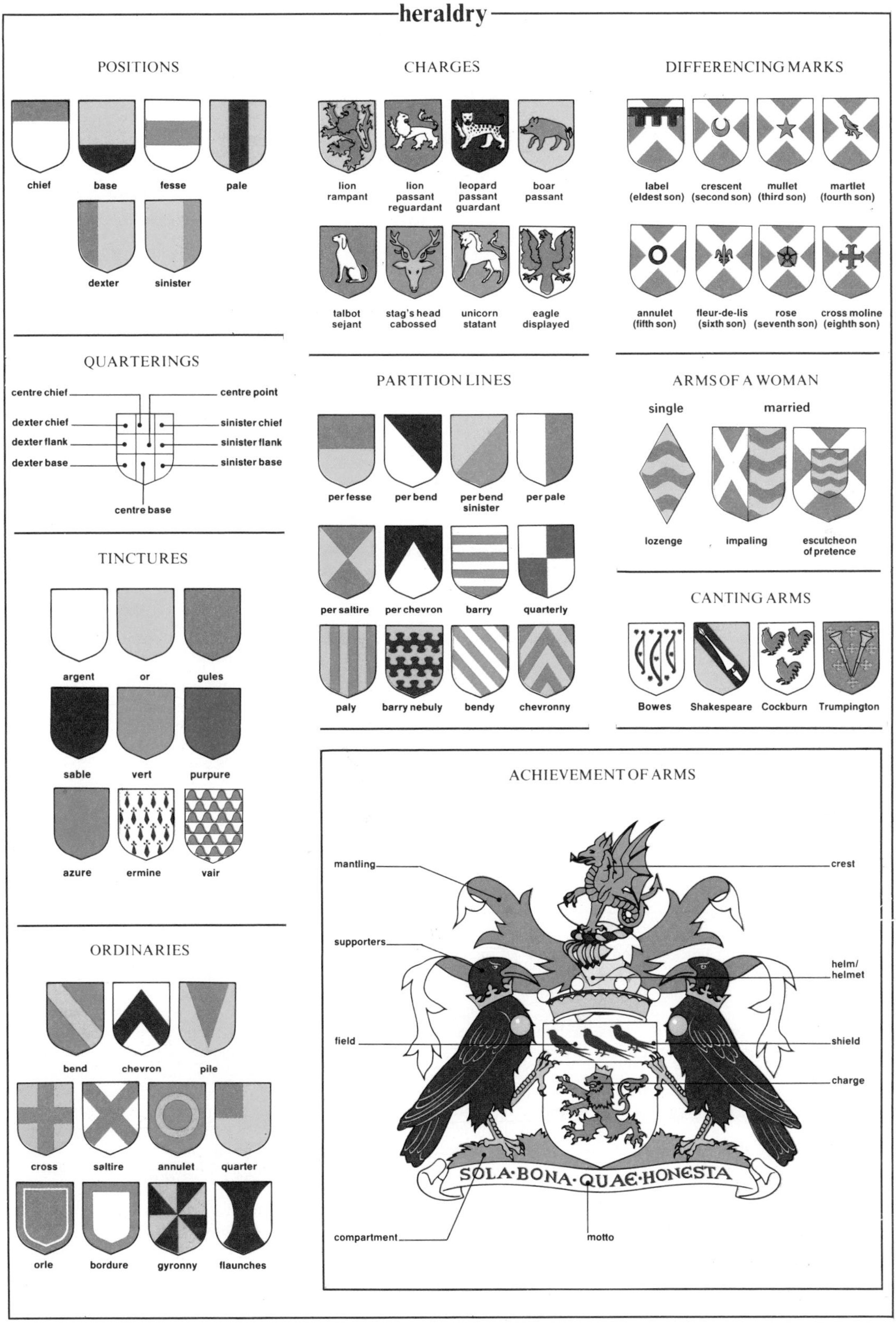

heraldry

POSITIONS

chief · base · fesse · pale

dexter · sinister

CHARGES

lion rampant · lion passant reguardant · leopard passant guardant · boar passant

talbot sejant · stag's head cabossed · unicorn statant · eagle displayed

DIFFERENCING MARKS

label (eldest son) · crescent (second son) · mullet (third son) · martlet (fourth son)

annulet (fifth son) · fleur-de-lis (sixth son) · rose (seventh son) · cross moline (eighth son)

QUARTERINGS

centre chief · centre point

dexter chief · sinister chief

dexter flank · sinister flank

dexter base · sinister base

centre base

PARTITION LINES

per fesse · per bend · per bend sinister · per pale

per saltire · per chevron · barry · quarterly

paly · barry nebuly · bendy · chevronny

ARMS OF A WOMAN

single · married

lozenge · impaling · escutcheon of pretence

TINCTURES

argent · or · gules

sable · vert · purpure

azure · ermine · vair

CANTING ARMS

Bowes · Shakespeare · Cockburn · Trumpington

ACHIEVEMENT OF ARMS

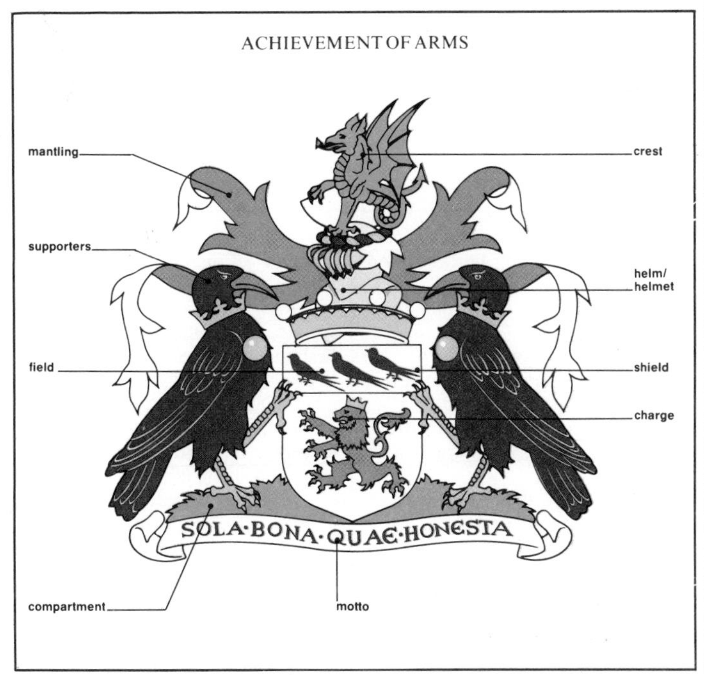

ORDINARIES

bend · chevron · pile

cross · saltire · annulet · quarter

orle · bordure · gyronny · flaunches

HERALDRY TERMS

addorsed	back to back
ambulant	walking
attires	deer's antlers
bearing, device, charge	emblem or figure on a shield
bezant	gold roundel
blazon	written description of armorial bearing
camelopard	giraffe-like creature with horns
canting arms, armes parlantes	punning shield or emblem
canton	small square division on a shield
cinquefoil	five-petalled flower
clarion	horn or trumpet
cockatrice	cockerel with a dragon's wings and tail
cognisance	crest or badge
College of Arms	ruling body of heraldry in England
couchant	lying, with head raised
Court of the Lord Lyon	ruling body of heraldry in Scotland
dormant	lying, with head on paws
embattled	with battlements
ensigned	with official headgear, such as a coronet or mitre, set above the shield
escutcheon	shield
field	surface of a shield
gouttes	droplets
griffin	beast with the front parts of an eagle and the back parts of a lion
hatchment, achievement	diamond-shaped display of a dead person's coat of arms
herald	senior heraldic officer
issuant	emerging
lambrequin, mantling	scarf over a helmet
mound	ball or orb of gold
nowed	knotted
phoenix	eagle-like bird arising from flames
pursuivant	junior heraldic officer
quatrefoil	four-petalled flower
roundel	circular design or symbol
salient	leaping, jumping, or rearing
semé	scattered with small figures
splendour	human-faced Sun surrounded by rays
tierced	divided into three
undé, undy	wavy
urdé	pointed
urinant	with head bowed
voided	with centre empty or cut out
volant	flying
wyvern	two-legged dragon

known, as obscure heroes often are UNSUNG.

heroic knightly or chivalrous hero PALADIN
– heroic deed or exploit GEST

heroin – inject heroin or other drugs directly into a vein MAINLINE

herring, especially from Norway, typically canned like sardines SILD, BRISLING
– herring fillet that is marinated and rolled up ROLLMOP
– herring or mackerel salted in brine and lightly smoked BLOATER
– herring that is smoked and eaten as a delicacy BUCKLING
– having spawned recently, as a herring might have done, and so of less value as food SHOTTEN
– unit of measure for fresh herring, equal to 37.5 gallons CRAN
– young herring or similar fish BRIT, SPRAT, BRISLING

hesitant, undecided VACILLATING, WAVERING, IRRESOLUTE
– hesitant or jerky, as uncertain speech is HALTING

hesitate, be undecided VACILLATE, WAVER, HOVER
– hesitate, dither, avoid committing oneself HAVER, SHILLY-SHALLY, PUSSYFOOT
– hesitate and postpone, delay or put off PROCRASTINATE
– hesitate for reasons of conscience or principle SCRUPLE
– hesitate in speech, walking, operation, or the like FALTER

hi-fi – cabinet of a television set, hi-fi system, or the like, standing on the floor CONSOLE
– referring to a hi-fi or sound reproduction system giving the effect of sounds coming from several directions SURROUND SOUND
– referring or relating to a hi-fi or sound reproduction system using two sources, typically varying in tone or pitch and usually relayed through headphones BINAURAL
– using four separate sound channels, as some hi-fi systems do QUADRAPHONIC
– using two separate sound channels, as some hi-fi systems do STEREOPHONIC

hibernation – sleep or dormancy

HERBS AND SPICES

allspice	spice with a flavour of cinnamon, clove and nutmeg, used in baked fruit	**coriander seeds**	seeds with a flavour of orange peel used in chutneys and cheeses
aniseed	liquorice-flavoured spice used in pie fillings	**cumin**	seeds used in curry
asafetida	yellow-brown resinous spice used in oriental cooking	**dill**	spice with a mild aniseed flavour used in fish dishes, salads and sauces
balm	lemon-scented leaves used in omelettes and fruit drinks	**fennel**	herb with an aniseed flavour used to counteract the richness of oily fish in sauces
basil	clove-flavoured herb used with poultry	**fenugreek**	pungent, aromatic seed used in curries
bay leaf	herb used to flavour sauces and as part of a bouquet garni	**garam masala**	mix of spices used in Indian cooking
borage	cucumber-flavoured leaves used in salads and cold drinks	**lovage**	strongly flavoured, celery-like leaves used to flavour soups, stews and sauces
bouquet garni	mix of herbs tied or wrapped together, as used to flavour soups or stews	**mace**	the husk of nutmeg, used whole or ground
caraway	seeds of a parsley-like plant used to flavour bread and cakes	**marjoram**	spicy leaves similar in flavour to thyme, used in stuffings and meat dishes
cardamom	spice with a flavour similar to eucalyptus, either pods as used in curries, or seeds as used in custards and baked fruits	**nutmeg**	spice used ground for sweet or savoury flavouring
		oregano	herb used in Greek and Italian dishes
cayenne	hot spice used in chutneys and cheese dishes	**paprika**	mild, sweet pepper for spicy meat dishes such as goulash
chervil	delicate, parsley-flavoured herb used in soups	**rosemary**	strongly flavoured leaves used with lamb
chilli	hot spice used in dishes such as chilli con carne	**saffron**	vivid yellow spice for colouring rice and fish dishes
chives	mild onion-flavoured leaves used to season salads	**sage**	strong bitter leaves used in stuffings
		tarragon	herb with sweet leaves used in vinegar and mayonnaise
cinnamon	pungent sweet spice used to flavour cakes and stewed fruit	**thyme**	herb used in stuffings and meat dishes
cloves	pungent spice used whole with baked fruits, and ground in milk puddings	**turmeric**	spice with vivid yellow colour, used in curries for colouring rice

through the summer, rather than through the winter as in hibernation AESTIVATION

hiccup – technical term for a hiccup SINGULTUS

hidden, present but not visible or active, as a tendency might be LATENT
– hidden, remote, shut away from the world SECLUDED, CLOISTERED
– hidden, secret, operating unseen SUBTERRANEAN
– hidden, secret, or secluded places RECESSES
– hidden and secret, often for an illicit purpose CLANDESTINE, FURTIVE, COVERT, SURREPTITIOUS
– hidden or secluded place, hideaway HERMITAGE, RETREAT
– hidden or secret, as knowledge might be OCCULT, ESOTERIC
– hidden store of money, drugs, or the like, or its hiding place STASH
– hidden store of stolen goods, arms, or the like, or its hiding place CACHE
– obscured or half-hidden, scarcely visible UNOBTRUSIVE, INDISTINCT, IMPERCEPTIBLE

hidden- CRYPT-, CRYPTO-

hide See also **leather**
– hide of an animal, removed from the carcass PELT, FELL
– hide of an animal, tanned and entire CROP
– hide on board a departing ship, train, or the like for a free journey STOWAWAY
– hide or cover, as if by draping with a cloth MANTLE, ENSHROUD
– hide or disguise something, such as one's fear DISSEMBLE
– hide or mask something, typically a woman's face VEIL
– hide or lie in wait, typically for a sinister purpose SKULK, LURK
– hide or shut away safely, as for private discussions CLOSET, ENSCONCE
– hide or shut oneself away IMMURE, SECLUDE
– hiding place of an animal LIE, LAIR
– person who hides away or lives in solitude RECLUSE, HERMIT

hideaway, place for seclusion or withdrawal HERMITAGE, RETREAT

– hideaway, shelter, hiding place, or disguise COVERT
hieroglyphics of a kind used by priests in ancient Egypt HIERATIC
– hieroglyphics of a simplified form, used by literate laymen in ancient Egypt DEMOTIC
– oblong frame around names of gods, kings, or queens in Egyptian hieroglyphics CARTOUCHE
– stone tablet providing the key to ancient Egyptian hieroglyphics ROSETTA STONE
high, inaccessible place, fortress, or the like EYRIE
– high and impressive, as a tall building or cliff might be IMPOSING, TOWERING, COMMANDING, SOARING
– high-pitched or shrill, as a voice might be REEDY, CLARION, TREBLE
– high-pitched or squeaky, as a boy's voice might be FALSETTO
– high-ranking or important person DIGNITARY
– high-ranking or noble-looking person MAGNIFICO, GRANDEE
– high up in altitude, rank, intellectual level, or the like ELEVATED, LOFTY
high- ACRO-, ALTI-
high-falutin, exaggeratedly rich or elegant in style, as purple prose is FLORID, TUMID, AUREATE, ROCOCO
– high-falutin, full of windy style or padding but lacking in real content FUSTIAN, FLATULENT, TURGID
– high-falutin or lofty in style and vocabulary SONOROUS, LATINATE, SESQUIPEDALIAN, MANDARIN
– high-falutin, pompous and inflated, inappropriately grand, as a speaker or a speech might be BOMBASTIC, GRANDILOQUENT, ROTUND, MAGNILOQUENT, OROTUND
– high-falutin, speechifying, trying to impress and manipulate rather than inform RHETORICAL, ORATORICAL, DECLAMATORY
– high-falutin and artificially stylish in expression, using very long words and extravagant figures of speech EUPHUISTIC, GONGORISTIC
high-jump technique in which the jumper is face up with back arched at his highest point over the bar FOSBURY FLOP
– high-jump technique in which the jumper is face down and parallel to the bar at his highest point STRADDLE
– high-jump technique in which the jumper is on his side and parallel to the bar at his highest point WESTERN ROLL
high point, final development or achievement, peak ACME, APEX, PINNACLE, ZENITH, MERIDIAN, SUMMIT, APOGEE, VERTEX
– high point, furthest possible stage or degree NE PLUS ULTRA
– high point, time or point of greatest intensity, as of a series of events, story, play, or the like CLIMAX, CULMINATION
– high point or essence, final development or distillation APOTHEOSIS
high-pressure area ANTICYCLONE
high priest in ancient Rome PONTIFEX MAXIMUS
high relief ALTO-RELIEVO
high spirits, mischief, lively prankishness SHENANIGANS, HIGH JINKS
– high spirits, zest for life, enjoyment of living JOIE DE VIVRE
high-wire walker or other performer of balancing feats EQUILIBRIST
higher in status, rank, or value, superior SUPERORDINATE
higher-, higher than- SUPER-, SUPRA-
higher education TERTIARY EDUCATION
highest in pitch ALTISSIMO
– highest or final point CULMINATION, PINNACLE, MERIDIAN
highest- ARCH-
– flat-topped high ground with cliff-like sides MESA
– large highland region with well-defined boundaries MASSIF
Highlands – dagger worn in the stocking of a person wearing traditional Scottish Highland dress SKEAN DHU, DIRK
hijack captive HOSTAGE
hill in North America with a flat top and steep sides MESA, BUTTE
– hill or high ground, rise EMINENCE, ELEVATION
– hill or hillside in Scotland BRAE
– hill or outcrop that is high, rocky, and bare TOR
– hill or ridge formed by glacial deposits DRUMLIN, KAME, ESKER, OS
– hill or ridge with steep eroded sides HOGBACK
– hill that is small, rounded, and often grassy or wooded KNOLL, HUMMOCK, HOLT
– hilly ridge or crest of land CHINE
– heap of rock fragments at the foot of a cliff or hill TALUS, SCREE
– rocky hill standing solitary on a plain KOP, INSELBERG
hillock or mound TUFFET
hills – person who "takes to the hills", living a primitive life, to escape the effects of an expected nuclear war SURVIVALIST
hinder See also **prevent**, **prohibit**, **limit**
– hinder, burden, or handicap ENCUMBER
– hinder, obstruct, or delay as a deliberate strategy, as in cricket or parliamentary debate STONEWALL
– hinder, obstruct, or delay the progress of a parliamentary debate by the use of unnecessarily long speeches FILIBUSTER
– hinder, obstruct, restrict IMPEDE, HAMPER, STIFLE, STRAITJACKET, TRAMMEL, HAMSTRING, HAMSHACKLE
– hinder, thwart the efforts or aims of FOIL, FRUSTRATE, DISCOMFIT, BAFFLE, STYMIE
– hinder or prevent FORECLOSE
– hinder the progress of, delay, slow down RETARD
– hindering rather than helping as intended COUNTER-PRODUCTIVE
Hindi – script, syllabic rather than alphabetic, in which Sanskrit and Hindi are written DEVANAGARI
hindquarters of a horse or other domestic animal RUMP, CROUP, HAUNCHES, CRUPPER
hindrance, handicap LIABILITY
– hindrance, obstruction IMPEDIMENT, TRAMMEL, STUMBLING BLOCK
Hinduism See chart
hinge joining a door to a door frame, consisting of two metal flaps linked with a stout pin BUTT HINGE
– cylindrical edge of a hinge in which the pin is fitted KNUCKLE
– notch or groove that houses an inserted part in a joint or hinge MORTISE, GAIN
– socket, as for a rudder or the pin of a hinge GUDGEON
hinged metal clamp for lifting heavy objects such as building materials GRAPPLING IRONS, CRAMPONS
– measuring instrument consisting of a pair of graduated arms hinged at one end SECTOR
hint, give a useful warning, tip off TIP SOMEONE THE WINK
– hint, make known indirectly or subtly INTIMATE
– hint at, outline ADUMBRATE
– hint or oblique reference, passing mention ALLUSION
– hint or suggestion of a veiled and typically offensive kind INNUENDO, ASPERSION, INSINUATION, IMPUTATION
– hint or unconfirmed suspicion INKLING, INTIMATION
– hint or vague suggestion of something about to happen STRAW IN THE WIND
– hint slyly INSINUATE
– indefinable quality, distinctive feature that can only be hinted at JE NE SAIS QUOI
– tiny amount, trace or hint of

something SMACK, SOUPÇON

hip bone INNOMINATE BONE
 – hip bone or joint COXA
 – hip of an animal HAUNCH, HUCKLE
 – hips and pelvic region LOINS
 – socket of the hip bone, into which the thigh bone fits ACETABULUM

hippopotamus, elephant, or similar thick-skinned mammal PACHYDERM
 – hippopotamus or similar large animal mentioned in the book of Job BEHEMOTH

hire-purchase payment made as part of a series INSTALMENT
 – travelling salesman or debt-collector working for a hire-purchase company TALLYMAN
 – U.S. term for a hire-purchase arrangement INSTALLMENT PLAN

hiring or leasing of a vehicle, especially a ship or aeroplane CHARTER

hissing sound such as /s/ or /z/ SIBILANT

historian – community bard or oral historian in a West African community GRIOT

historical, relating to the development of something through time DIACHRONIC
 – historical development of a language, custom, or the like PHYLOGENY
 – historical period or era EPOCH
 – historical records of events over the years CHRONICLE, ANNALS
 – historical records of an institu-

HINDUISM TERMS

ashram	holy man's hermitage; religious retreat or meeting place
atman	individual essence; universal soul
avatar	descent to Earth of a deity; any of the incarnations of the god Vishnu
Bhagavad-Gita	religious text in the Mahabharata
bhakti	devotion to a particular god as a means of achieving salvation
Brahma	creator god of the divine trinity
Brahman/ Brahmin	member of the highest caste, originally composed of priests
chela	pupil or disciple of a guru
deva	god or divinity
dharma	ultimate principle of all things, cosmic or natural law; behaviour or duty in keeping with this
fakir, sadhu	wandering religious ascetic or preacher
guru	spiritual teacher or leader
harijan	lower-class Hindu, an "untouchable", technically outside the caste system
Juggernaut	form of the god Krishna, or an idol of him drawn on a huge wagon at an annual festival
Kamasutra	ancient text on erotic love
karma	fate; force produced by one's deeds, affecting one's destiny in the next existence
Krishna	main avatar or incarnation of the god Vishnu
Mahabharata, Ramayana	ancient epic Sanskrit poems
maharishi	wise man or great spiritual teacher
mahatma	person revered for his wisdom and virtue, specifically a Brahman sage
mandala	symbol representing the universe, as used in meditation
mandir	Hindu temple
mantra	sacred sound or formula used in prayer and meditation
maya	illusion; the world regarded as unreal or illusory
mudra	set of ritual hand movements and body postures used in sacred dancing
nirvana	state of blessedness or enlightenment, involving release from the cycle of reincarnation, leading to reabsorption into Brahma
pandit/pundit	learned Brahman
Rig-Veda	ancient collection of religious poems
samsara	repeated cycle of birth, suffering, death and rebirth
sannyasi	holy Brahman beggar in his final incarnation, who will not return to Earth again
Sanskrit	ancient language of Hinduism
Siva/Shiva	destroyer god of the divine trinity
suttee	former practice of willing self-cremation by a widow on her husband's funeral pyre; widow who cremates herself in this way
swami	term of address for a religious teacher or ascetic
tantras	various mystical religious texts
Upanishads	various philosophical and theological texts elaborating upon the Vedas
Vedanta	philosophical system dealing with the singleness of reality and the believer's duty of self-transcendence
Vedas	various ancient sacred writings
Vishnu	preserver god of the divine trinity

tion or group, or the place where they are kept ARCHIVES
– historical turning point LANDMARK
– devise a dramatised version of a crime or historical event to gain a vivid idea of what actually took place RECONSTRUCT

history long ago, ancient times ANTIQUITY
– history that is very short and simplified POTTED HISTORY
– calculation of the dates of historical events, or ordering of events according to their dates, or a list of such events CHRONOLOGY
– complete, reliable, and authoritative, as a history or biography might be DEFINITIVE
– dating from or relating to the beginning of time or history PRIMORDIAL
– use of statistics in the study of history CLIOMETRICS

hit See **beat**

Hitler – Adolf Hitler's title as Nazi leader of Germany FÜHRER

hives, nettle rash URTICARIA, UREDO

hoarse and often emotional in sound HUSKY

hoax or worthless discovery MARE'S NEST
– rumour or news report that is false or a deliberate hoax CANARD

hobby, leisure activity AVOCATION
– person who has a specified hobby, especially breeding plants or animals FANCIER

hockey or ice-hockey of an early form BANDY
– Irish ballgame similar to hockey HURLING, HURLEY
– Scottish ballgame similar to hockey SHINTY, SHINNY
– starting procedure formerly in hockey, in which two opposing players would tap each other's sticks and then the ground three times before trying to hit the ball BULLY-OFF

hoe – hoe-like farming or gardening tool MATTOCK

hoist or raise, especially by machine WINCH

hold someone round the arms to restrain him PINION
– holding, sticking, or clinging firmly, clasping, TENACIOUS
– holding or grasping device, especially a grapnel GRAPPLE
– firm hold or grip, as when pushing, climbing, or the like PURCHASE

hole See also **gap**
– hole, slit, or opening, such as the adjustable opening in a camera lens APERTURE
– hole cut with a special tool into a metal sheet, skull bone, or the like TREPAN, TREPHINE
– hole or cavity, such as a honeycomb cell or a tooth socket in the jawbone ALVEOLUS
– hole or opening for fumes, air or liquids to pass through VENT
– hole or opening for the digestive and genital tracts in birds, fish, and reptiles CLOACA
– hole or rectangular slot into which the matching tenon is fitted when joining two pieces of wood, stone, or metal MORTISE
– hole or series of holes made in something PERFORATION
– breathing hole near an insect's neck, blowhole of a whale, or the like SPIRACLE
– hollow or dig out, as to make a hole or tunnel EXCAVATE
– gardening tool for making holes in the soil, as for bulbs or seedlings DIBBER, DIBBLE
– make a hole or row of holes through PERFORATE
– make or enlarge a hole by means of a gimlet or similar tool BROACH
– pierce with many holes RIDDLE
– shape or enlarge a hole, as in wood, with a special cylindrical file REAM
– small bodily hole or opening, especially any of those in a bone through which blood vessels and nerves pass FORAMEN
– small bodily hole or opening, especially that between the middle and inner ear FENESTRA
– small hole, as for a shoelace or hook fastening EYELET
– small mouth-like hole, especially any of those in a sponge OSCULUM

holiday See chart
– holiday arranged and sold as a single unit, with transport, accommodation, and other elements priced jointly PACKAGE HOLIDAY
– holiday hut at a resort CHALET
– holiday organiser accompanying a tour party COURIER
– holiday resort modelled on a ranch, featuring riding and camping DUDE RANCH
– shared ownership of a holiday home TIME SHARING

-holiday -MAS

holier-than-thou SANCTIMONIOUS, CANTING, PIETISTIC, PECKSNIFFIAN

holiness, saintliness SANCTITY

Holland – stretch of low-lying land reclaimed from the sea, especially in Holland POLDER

hollow, area or place sunk below the surrounding ground DEPRESSION
– hollow, cavity, or channel in the body, containing or conveying air, pus, blood, or the like SINUS
– hollow filled with mud SLOUGH
– hollow or dig out, as to make a hole or tunnel EXCAVATE
– hollow or indented space, as set back from the main surface of a wall RECESS, ALCOVE

-hollow- -COEL-, COELO-

hollyhock ALTHAEA

holy, extremely sacred SACROSANCT, INVIOLABLE
– holy, deeply religious, pious DEVOUT, REVERENT
– Holy Communion given to a person in danger of death VIATICUM
– holy in a hypocritical or self-satisfied way, pretending to be pious SANCTIMONIOUS, UNCTUOUS, PIETISTIC
– holy place associated with a saint or other revered person SHRINE
– holy place, or the holiest part of a sacred place SANCTUARY
– authorise to be a clergyman, invest with holy orders ORDAIN
– beggar, often a holy beggar wandering from place to place MENDICANT
– Hindu holy man, preacher or ascetic SADHU
– Hindu or Muslim holy man or ascetic, often wandering and begging from place to place FAKIR
– make or declare something holy, such as a church CONSECRATE, SANCTIFY
– make or treat as holy REVERENCE, HALLOW, VENERATE
– Muslim holy man or ascetic DERVISH, CALENDER
– shrine or container for holy relics RELIQUARY
– spoiling or destruction of the holy quality of a church, graveyard, or other consecrated place, as by blasphemy or vandalism DESECRATION, PROFANATION, VIOLATION, SACRILEGE

holy- HIER-, HIERO-

holy books See **scriptures**

Holy Ghost in the role of comforter, supporter, or counsellor PARACLETE

holy of holies in the Temple in ancient Israel SANCTUM SANCTORUM, ORACLE

holy place- HAGI-, HAGIO-

holy war conducted by Muslims, in particular against unbelievers JIHAD
– holy war or expedition, especially any of those conducted by European Christians in the Holy Land in the Middle Ages CRUSADE

HOLIDAYS AND FESTIVALS

ANZAC Day	April 25, a holiday in Australia and New Zealand commemorating the landing at Gallipoli in 1915
Ascension Day	fortieth day after Easter, a Christian Church feast commemorating the ascension of Christ into heaven
Ash Wednesday	seventh Wednesday before Easter, a day of penitence in the Roman Catholic Church
Assumption Day	August 15, Christian Church feast celebrating the taking up of the Virgin Mary into heaven
Bairam	either of two Muslim festivals, one at the end of Ramadan and the other 70 days later
Bastille Day	July 14, a holiday in France commemorating the storming of the Bastille in 1789
Bon, Feast of Lanterns	in July, a Buddhist festival held in Japan, honouring ancestral spirits
Candlemas	February 2, a Christian Church feast commemorating the purification of the Virgin Mary and the presentation of the infant Christ in the temple
Chanukkah, Feast of Lights	usually in December, an eight-day Jewish festival commemorating the victory of the Maccabees over the Syrians in 165 BC
Columbus Day	October 12, a holiday in the U.S. commemorating the discovery of the Bahamas by Columbus in 1492
Corpus Christi	ten or 14 days after Pentecost, a Roman Catholic festival in honour of the Eucharist
Day of the Vow	December 16, a holiday in South Africa celebrating the victory of the Boers over a Zulu army at Blood River in 1838
Dominion Day, Canada Day	July 1, a holiday in Canada celebrating the anniversary of the founding of the Dominion of Canada in 1867
Fasching	December 31 to Ash Wednesday, pre-Lenten carnivals and feasts in many German and Austrian towns
Halloween	October 31, "All Hallows Eve", the eve of All Saints' Day, when ghosts, witches, and fairies are supposed to walk abroad
Independence Day	July 4, a holiday in the U.S. commemorating the signing of the Declaration of Independence in 1776
Labor Day	first Monday in September, a holiday in the U.S. and Canada
Lady Day	March 25, a Christian Church feast commemorating the Annunciation
Mardi Gras	last day before Lent, celebrated by carnivals, especially in New Orleans
Martinmas	November 11, a Christian Church festival celebrating St Martin's Day
Maundy Thursday	Thursday before Easter, a commemoration of the Last Supper, on which in England the Sovereign gives specially minted coins to selected poor people
Muharram	in July or August, a Muslim festival held during the first ten days of the Muslim year
Orangeman's Day	July 12, a public holiday in Northern Ireland celebrated by Protestants — "Orangemen" after William, Prince of Orange — as the anniversary of the Battle of the Boyne in 1690
Passover, Pesach	in March or April, an eight-day Jewish festival commemorating the escape of the Jews from Egypt
Pentecost	Whit Sunday, the seventh Sunday after Easter, a Christian Church festival commemorating the descent of the Holy Ghost on the followers of Jesus; Jewish Feast of the Weeks, 50 days after the second day of Passover
Ramadan	in March and April, 30 days' fast from sunrise to sunset, observed by Muslims
Rosh Hashanah	Jewish New Year, between late September and early October
St John's Eve	June 23, the eve of the feast of St John the Baptist, a holiday in Portugal
Shrove Tuesday	last day before Lent, seven weeks before Easter, the day when pancakes are traditionally eaten
Tet	Vietnamese New Year, in January or February
Thanksgiving Day	fourth Thursday of November, a holiday in the U.S. commemorating the first harvest of the Pilgrim Fathers in 1621
Twelfth Night, Epiphany	January 6, the twelfth night after Christmas, celebrating the manifestation of the divine nature of Christ to the Magi, the three Wise Men
Waitangi Day	February 6, a national holiday in New Zealand on the anniversary of the Treaty of Waitangi, between the British Government and Maori tribes in 1840
Walpurgisnacht	the eve of May Day, in Germany the supposed occasion of a witches sabbath
Yom Kippur, Day of Atonement	in September or October, a Jewish day of fasting, to pray for the atonement of sins

holy water – basin for holy water at the entrance of a church STOUP, FONT, ASPERSORIUM
– sprinkler for holy water, such as a brush or perforated spoon ASPERGILLUM
home, legal dwelling place or country of residence DOMICILE
– home, one's place of living ABODE
– occasional home, typically a small flat near a city centre, kept by someone whose main home is elsewhere PIED-À-TERRE
homeland – desert one's homeland, political party, or the like, especially to join its opponent DEFECT
– person from the same homeland as another person COMPATRIOT
– person who has left or been driven from his homeland and now lives in another country EXPATRIATE, EXILE
– return someone to his homeland REPATRIATE
homeopathy – conventional medical treatment, as opposed to homeopathy ALLOPATHY
homesickness NOSTALGIA
homosexual INVERT
– homosexual man's boy lover CATAMITE
– homosexual or effeminate CAMP
– homosexual relations, especially between a man and a boy PEDERASTY
– attracted to persons of the opposite sex, as distinct from homosexual HETEROSEXUAL
honest See **frank**
– honest, constantly truthful VERACIOUS
honesty, moral soundness INTEGRITY, PROBITY, RECTITUDE, VERACITY
honey as used in medicines MEL
– honey-based alcoholic drink, common in the Middle Ages MEAD
– sweet liquid secreted by flowers and gathered by bees for making honey NECTAR
– sweetmeat made of honey and crushed sesame seeds HALVA
honey badger RATEL
honeycomb cell or similar deep cavity ALVEOLUS
– honeycombed, pitted with small, deep indentations ALVEOLATE, FAVEOLATE
honorary, awarded as a mark of honour, as a degree might be HONORIS CAUSA
honour See also **praise**
– honour, duty, or respect, granted to someone or to a belief or cause HOMAGE, REVERENCE, TRIBUTE
– honour, expression of gratitude or appreciation, a written or spoken tribute TESTIMONIAL
– honour, glory, or a mark of honour, originally a wreath or crown of laurel or bay leaves LAURELS, BAYS
– honour, moral soundness, virtue INTEGRITY, PROBITY, RECTITUDE
– honour generously or flatteringly, treat as a hero or celebrity FÊTE, LIONISE
– honour or award, such as a medal or honorary degree ACCOLADE
– honour or glorify above all others VENERATE, BEATIFY, HALLOW, REVERENCE, EXALT
– honour the memory, as of a person or event, by means of a ceremony COMMEMORATE
– challenge, attack, or spoil someone's dignity, honour, integrity, or the like IMPUGN, IMPEACH, DISCREDIT
– obligation on noble or noble-minded people to be generous and honourable NOBLESSE OBLIGE
– poet, Nobel prize winner, or other eminent person in the arts or sciences who receives a special honour LAUREATE
– present or bestow a degree or honour CONFER
honourable, chivalrous or gallant man GALAHAD, CHEVALIER
hood-shaped or hooded CUCULLATE
hoof, claw, nail, or similar part UNGUIS
– divided into two, as an animal's or devil's hoof might be CLEFT, CLOVEN, BISULCATE
– hoofed mammal, such as a horse, pig, or deer UNGULATE
– horny wedge in the sole of a horse's hoof FROG
hook on a drying or stretching frame for cloth during manufacture TENTERHOOK
– hook or small hook-like device CROTCHET
– hook-shaped UNCIFORM
– iron device with hooks, attached to a rope, thrown on to a wall, nearby ship, or the like to grip it and create a connection GRAPNEL, GRAPPLING IRON
– remove the hook from a fish after catching it DISGORGE
hooked or coiled tip of a young fern frond CROSIER
– hooked or curved, resembling an eagle's beak, as one's nose might be AQUILINE
– hooked pole used for hauling large fish aboard GAFF
hoop of plastic, swung around the body by hip movements HULA HOOP
– hoop or series of hoops formerly worn under a skirt to support it, or the skirt itself FARTHINGALE
hooter on old cars KLAXON
hope or wish that is fanciful and unrealistic PIPE DREAM
– deprived, as of hope or comfort BEREFT
– ruin or thwart hopes, ambition, or the like BLIGHT
hopeful, cheerful, confident SANGUINE, BUOYANT
– hopeful or optimistic, especially about economic prospects and stock-exchange prices BULLISH
hopeless, beyond remedy IRREDEEMABLE
– hopeless, in an awkward or helpless position IN CHANCERY
– hopeless plan or attempt FORLORN HOPE
hops – kiln for drying hops or malt OAST
horizontal beam or crossbar, as in a window or over a door TRANSOM, LINTEL
– horizontal or diagonal route across a slope, as in skiing TRAVERSE
– horizontal timber beam in a building, as for supporting a floor STRINGER, SUMMER
hormone or drug, based on a ring of carbon atoms, sometimes used by bodybuilders and athletes STEROID
– hormone secreted by the pancreas and regulating the level of blood sugar INSULIN
– hormone secreted during times of stress, and increasing pulse rate and blood pressure ADRENALINE
– hormone used in the treatment of allergies and rheumatoid arthritis CORTISONE
– "female hormone", regulating ovulation and promoting feminine characteristics such as developed breasts OESTROGEN
– "male hormones", promoting masculine characteristics such as facial hair ANDROGEN, TESTOSTERONE
horn – horn-like in shape or texture CERATOID
– horn-like or horn-shaped body part CORNU
– horn-like or horny CORNEOUS
– horn-like substance occurring in some fungi and in the shell of a lobster, crab, or the like CHITIN
– horn of plenty, goat's horn overflowing with fruit and vegetables, symbolising abundance, in paintings and sculptures CORNUCOPIA
– horn on old cars KLAXON
– horn-shaped or having horns CORNUTE

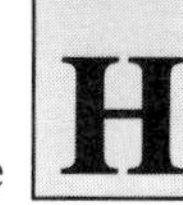

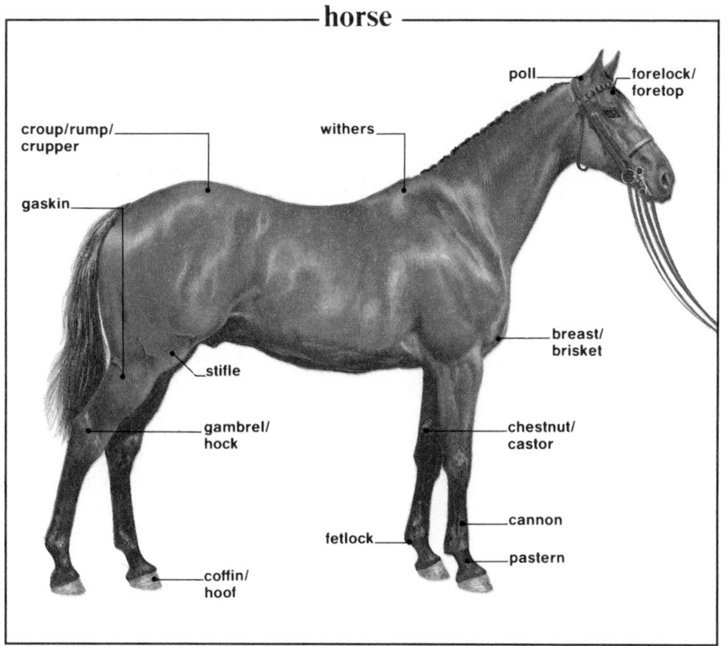

– arched, curved, as horns might be ARCUATE
– fanfare or blast on a horn or trumpet TANTARA, TANTIVY
– having hollow horns rather than antlers CAVICORN
– having horns or horn-like projections CORNICULATE
– hornless goat, ox, sheep, or other usually horned animal POLLARD
– pierce or stab with a horn or tusk, as in bullfighting GORE

hornet – hornets' nest, or colony of wasps or hornets VESPIARY

horny tissue- KERAT-, KERATO-

horrible, dreadful, grim, as a ghastly sight of bloodshed is GRISLY, GRUESOME
– horrible, hideous, terrifyingly hateful LOATHSOME, ABOMINABLE, HORRENDOUS, UNSPEAKABLE
– horrible, sensational, or blood-curdling, often in a deliberately artificial way GRAND-GUIGNOL
– horrible, very upsetting, as an appalling ordeal is HARROWING
– horrible, weird, dealing or obsessed with death, LURID, MORBID, MACABRE

horror – draw back, as in fear or horror RECOIL

hors d'oeuvre, appetiser ANTIPASTO

horse See illustration, and also **harness**, **horse-racing**, **saddle**
– horse, pig, deer, or other hoofed mammal UNGULATE
– horse, or the like regarded as the mother of another DAM
– horse dealer COPER
– horse-like hybrid animal, from a female ass and male horse HINNY
– horse that is old or worn out HACK, NAG, JADE
– horses harnessed one behind the other in a team, or a two-wheeled carriage drawn by such a team TANDEM
– adjective for a horse EQUINE
– attendant for horses at an inn, stableman OSTLER
– brown or black horse with a sprinkling of greyish hairs on its coat ROAN
– brownish, golden-coloured horse SORREL
– brownish horse with a cream-coloured mane and tail PALOMINO
– brush used in grooming a horse DANDY BRUSH
– buyer of old horses for slaughter KNACKER
– castrated male horse GELDING
– drug or disable a racehorse, in order to prevent a win NOBBLE
– enclosure for horses CORRAL, PADDOCK
– extinct horse-like mammal of prehistoric times EOHIPPUS
– groom a horse CURRY
– having different colours, especially blotches of black and white, as a horse might PIEBALD, PINTO
– herding of horses DRIFT
– horny wedge in the sole of a horse's hoof FROG
– infectious bacterial disease in horses, causing ulcers in the lungs and skin GLANDERS, FARCY
– ironsmith who made spurs and bits for horses LORIMER
– jerky, inclined to stop abruptly, as a horse might be BAULKY
– laming inflammation of the sensitive tissue in a horse's hoof LAMINITIS, FOUNDER
– laming swelling or growth on a horse's hock or lower leg SPAVIN
– long hair on the legs or tail of some horses or dogs FEATHERS
– marked with white or grey, brown, or reddish spots, as some horses are SKEWBALD
– monster in Greek mythology having a man's torso, and a horse's body or legs CENTAUR
– ornamental armour or covering for a horse BARD
– ornamental covering and harness for a horse CAPARISON, TRAPPINGS
– person who sells horse-racing information to punters TOUT
– person who shoes horses or treats them for disorders FARRIER
– racehorse, book, or the like that achieves sudden success after an unpromising early phase SLEEPER
– refuse, stop short, as a horse might at a jump JIB, BAULK, SHY
– restrict or prevent a horse's straying, by means of a rope hampering leg movements HOBBLE, HAMSHACKLE
– rider of the left front horse of a coach POSTILION
– rising and falling of the rider in the saddle in time with a horse's trot POST
– rope, chain, or halter restricting a horse to a small range of movement or grazing area TETHER
– saddle or seat for a second rider, as on a horse or motorcycle PILLION
– section of the body of a horse or dog between the forequarters and hindquarters COUPLING
– short-legged, extremely stocky horse SHETLAND PONY, SHELTIE
– short-legged, stocky, compact horse COB
– stable for boarding horses or letting out horses and carriages LIVERY STABLE
– strap or rope to secure a horse by the neck HALTER
– strap that ties a saddle, blanket, pack, or the like around a horse SURCINGLE
– strike a hind foot against a forefoot, as a horse might OVERREACH
– stumble and go lame, as a horse might FOUNDER
– swelling on a horse's back, typically causing stiffness SPAVIN

– thoroughbred horses, especially racehorses BLOODSTOCK
– troops on horses CAVALRY
– uncastrated male horse ENTIRE
– urine of horses STALE
– water spirit in the form of a horse, in Scottish folklore, that would drown its riders KELPIE
– white horse of a breed used in the Spanish Riding School in Vienna LIPIZZANER
– white spot on a horse's forehead STAR
– wild horse of the U.S. plains MUSTANG
– wild or untamed U.S. horse, as used in rodeos BRONCO
– woman's riding horse in former times PALFREY

horse- HIPPO-, EQUIN-

horse-drawn vehicles See chart

horse-racing See chart
– horse race across open country, or over artificial jumps STEEPLECHASE
– horse race or other contest in which the entire prize is awarded to the winner SWEEPSTAKE
– horse-race track HIPPODROME
– horse race with only one starter, which wins by walking or running over the course WALKOVER
– Derby or any of the five major British flat horse races CLASSIC

horseman in former times, especially an armed and mounted gentleman or knight CAVALIER
– horseback rider or performer EQUESTRIAN, EQUESTRIENNE

horsemanship See chart
– relating to horsemanship or mounted troops EQUESTRIAN
– sports competition and display, especially of skills in horsemanship by children GYMKHANA

horseshoe – stud on a horseshoe or shoe to prevent slipping CALK

hospital attendant ORDERLY
– hospital for those suffering from chronic diseases SANATORIUM
– hospital formerly for treating contagious diseases LAZARETTO
– hospital or clinic INFIRMARY
– hospital specialising in care for the dying HOSPICE
– hospital unit specially for the gravely ill INTENSIVE-CARE UNIT
– hospital's medical equipment and supplies ARMAMENTARIUM
– formerly, a hospital social worker or charity worker ALMONER
– place, such as a hospital office, from which medicines and medical supplies are given out DISPENSARY

hostage – tendency of a hostage to help or protect his captor STOCKHOLM SYNDROME

hostile, full of hate or spite, doing or wishing evil to others MALEVOLENT, RANCOROUS
– hostile, quarrelsome, or unruly TRUCULENT
– hostile, ready or eager to argue or fight AGGRESSIVE, COMBATIVE, BELLIGERENT, BELLICOSE
– hostile, uncompromisingly opposed IRRECONCILABLE, IMPLACABLE
– hostile or opposed to something or someone ANTAGONISTIC, INIMICAL, AVERSE, ANTIPATHETIC, OPPUGNANT
– hostile or subversive element within an organisation or country at war FIFTH COLUMN
– hostile reaction, as to an apparent social threat BACKLASH
– divide into two extreme and hostile positions or groups POLARISE
– very bitter or hostile VIRULENT
– extremely hostile, chilling GLACIAL

hostility, open opposition ANTAGONISM
– become liable or subject to something such as debts or someone's hostility INCUR
– deep hostility, intense dislike, enmity ANIMUS, ANIMOSITY
– feeling of intense hostility, dislike, or revulsion ANTIPATHY, AVERSION
– lay to rest the hostility of, win the friendship of DISARM

hot, relating to heat or hot springs THERMAL
– hot and airless, stuffy FROWSTY
– hot and humid, sweltering, as tropical weather can be TORRID, SULTRY, MUGGY

hot- PYRO-, THERM-, THERMO-

hot spring THERMAL SPRING
– hot spring throwing up column of water and steam GEYSER

hot water – deep tray containing hot water, in which deep dishes of food are kept warm, as in a cafeteria BAIN-MARIE

hot-water bottle – forerunner of a hot-water bottle, consisting of a covered metal pan filled with hot water or coals WARMING PAN

hotchpotch, mixture of many widely varying elements MISCELLANY, POTPOURRI, SALMAGUNDI, GALLIMAUFRY

hotel, as at a spa, providing water-based therapy HYDRO
– hotel or inn, with a courtyard, for groups of travellers in the East CARAVANSERAI
– boarding house or small hotel, as in France PENSION
– half board, as at a hotel DEMI-PENSION
– entrance hall of a hotel or other public building LOBBY, VESTIBULE

hothouse ORANGERY

hounds – baying of hounds when pursuing game QUESTING
– hunting of game, such as hares, with hounds relying on sight rather than scent COURSING
– pack of hounds CRY

hour – adjective for an hour HORARY
– hours between 8 a.m. and 6 p.m. during which marriages may be legally conducted in an Anglican church CANONICAL HOURS

house, such as a brothel, where public order or decency is violated DISORDERLY HOUSE
– house, very small and on two floors, contained within a larger building MAISONETTE
– house for a clergyman VICARAGE, RECTORY, MANSE
– house in the centre of a block, not bordering the street, with a long access path or driveway PANHANDLE HOUSE
– house on a Spanish or Latin American ranch or large estate, or the estate as a whole HACIENDA
– house on an island in a lake or marsh, in ancient Ireland and Scotland CRANNOG
– house or hut that is run-down and dirty HOVEL

HORSE-DRAWN VEHICLES

TWO-WHEELED	FOUR-WHEELED
buggy	**barouche**
cabriolet	**berlin**
curricle	**brougham**
désobligeante	**buckboard**
dogcart	**calash**
gig	**clarence**
hansom	**Conestoga wagon**
jaunting car	**coupé**
quadriga	**diligence**
stanhope	**dos-à-dos**
sulky	**droshky**
tilbury	**fiacre**
tonga	**fly**
trap	**four-in-hand**
tumbrel	**growler**
	hackney carriage
	landau
	phaeton
	post chaise
	surrey
	victoria
	vis-à-vis
	wain

VARYING NUMBERS OF WHEELS
break/brake
chaise
dray
gharry
troika

HORSE-RACING AND HORSEMANSHIP TERMS

HORSE-RACING TERMS	
accumulator, parlay	cumulative bet in which winnings from one race form the stake on the next
antepost bet	bet placed at any time up to the day before a race
blind bet	bet made by bookmaker to divert attention from a favourite
double	bet on the winners of two races
each way	bet on a horse to win or be placed
forecast, perfecta, exacta	bet on the first and second finishers in the correct order
handicap	race in which extra weight is carried by some horses to even out the abilities of the field
lay off, hedge	bookmaker's placing of a bet on a horse against which he has accepted many bets, to reduce his losses if the horse wins
long odds	odds offered on a horse considered unlikely to win
maiden	horse that has never won a race
nap	tipster's most fancied horse of the day
nursery stakes	race for two-year-olds
odds on	odds offered on a horse extremely likely to win
pari-mutuel	betting system, used by the tote, in which all bets are pooled and the pool divided among the winners
place	finishing position of a horse, varying from the first two to the first four according to the total number of runners
point-to-point	cross-country race around a course marked by flags
pulling	illegal holding back of a horse by its jockey to stop it winning or doing well
ringer	horse entered in a race under the name of another, usually inferior, horse
short odds	odds offered on a horse considered to have a good chance of winning
show	be placed third, or fourth, in a handicap race with more than 16 runners
silks	jockey's cap and shirt bearing the colours of his horse's owner or stable
starting price	final odds offered at the start of a race
steward	racecourse official
string	group of horses belonging to one owner
ticktack	bookmakers' system of hand signals used to communicate at racecourses
totalisator/tote	organised system of pari-mutuel betting; computer used to record bets and calculate winnings
yankee	stake adding up to 11 bets, laid on four horses each running in a different race

HORSEMANSHIP TERMS	
capriole	upwards jump in dressage, in which the horse kicks back its hind legs
caracole	half-turn movement in dressage
cavaletto	rail for training horses in jumping
cavesson	noseband with a lunging rein, used in training
curvet, gambado	low prancing jump in dressage, launched from the hind legs
dressage	movements performed by a horse responding to the rider's indications
hacking	leisurely riding, usually for pleasure
hand	measure, equal to four inches, of a horse's height
haute école	stiff classical style of riding
jib, baulk	shy or refuse at a jump or obstacle
levade	dressage movement in which the horse balances on its hind legs
lunging rein	long rein used for exercising and training horses
manège	training of riders and horses in dressage techniques; riding school
martingale	strap linking the bit or noseband and the girth, as used in training a horse to keep its head lowered
oxer	obstacle consisting of a hedge and rails, and sometimes a ditch
passage	high-stepping trot in dressage
piaffe	trot very slowly, in dressage, sometimes on the spot
pirouette	turn on the haunches, in dressage
puissance	show-jumping competition involving large obstacles
rack, single-foot	fast, showy walking step in dressage
tittup	prance or caper
volte	movement tracing a 6-metre circle, in dressage

– house or lodge a soldier, especially in a civilian residence BILLET
– house that goes with a particular job TIED HOUSE
– badly built or maintained, shaky, as an old house might be RICKETY, RAMSHACKLE, DILAPIDATED
– built in sections in advance, prior to its assembly, as cheap housing might be PREFABRICATED
– built shoddily and unreliably, as houses sometimes are JERRY-BUILT
– concluding of all legal formalities in the purchase of a house or other property COMPLETION
– country house or farmhouse with its outbuildings GRANGE
– country house or summer villa in Russia DACHA
– Eskimo house, typically domed and made of ice IGLOO
– full ownership of a house, flat, land, or the like, as distinct from leasing FREEHOLD
– go back on an agreement with someone intending to buy one's house, by raising the price after a rival offer GAZUMP
– irregular and spread-out in design, as a large house might be SPRAWLING, RAMBLING
– play house WENDY HOUSE
– repair something, such as a house REFURBISH, RENOVATE
– round house, cottage, or hut with a conical roof, in South Africa RONDAVEL
– transferring of the ownership of a house, flat, land, or other property CONVEYANCING

household MÉNAGE
– household gods in ancient Rome LARES, PENATES
– household implement, especially one used in the kitchen UTENSIL
– father, viewed as head of the household PATERFAMILIAS
– master and mistress of a castle, or a large household CHATELAIN, CHATELAINE
– valued household possessions LARES AND PENATES

houseman – U.S. equivalent of a houseman INTERN

housing built in a line along a road leading out of a town RIBBON DEVELOPMENT
– enclosure, especially in the East, for a factory, rich housing, or the like COMPOUND

howl or wail, as if lamenting ULULATE

hub of a wheel NAVE
– hub of a propeller BOSS

huge, drastic, large enough to cause severe damage or distress, as spending cuts might be SWINGEING
– huge, immense, as someone's appetite might be GARGANTUAN
– huge, immense GIGANTIC, COLOSSAL, BROBDIGNAGIAN
– huge, overwhelmingly or abnormally large or imposing PRODIGIOUS, TITANIC, HERCULEAN
– huge, vast, limitless, incalculable BOUNDLESS, IMMEASURABLE
– huge animal or object LEVIATHAN, BEHEMOTH
– huge column of burning gas rising from the Sun, visible during a total eclipse PROMINENCE
– huge statue, or extremely large or important person or object COLOSSUS

huge- MEGA-, MEGALO-, MACRO-

human, ape, monkey, or related mammal PRIMATE
– human being, regarded as a thinking animal HOMO SAPIENS
– human being identical to another CLONE
– human flesh as eaten by cannibals LONG PIG
– human in form or nature INCARNATE, EMBODIED, PERSONIFIED
– human in shape or appearance ANTHROPOID, ANTHROPOMORPHIC
– human of very small proportions HOMUNCULUS, MANIKIN, PYGMY
– human or human-like extinct mammal HOMINID
– attributing of human form or behaviour to gods, animals, nonliving objects, and so on ANTHROPOMORPHISM, PERSONIFICATION
– crediting of human qualities, as in poetry, to things in nature PATHETIC FALLACY
– representative, in human form, of an ideal, god, or model EMBODIMENT, INCARNATION, AVATAR
– study of or attempts at improving the human race by selective breeding EUGENICS

-human- -ANTHROP-, ANTHROPO-

humanitarian work or feelings, charity PHILANTHROPY

human nature – rational, orderly, and sober, as one side of human nature is APOLLONIAN
– spontaneous, irrational, passionate, and creative, as one side of human nature is DIONYSIAC

humble See also **flatter**, **modest**, **humiliate**
– humble oneself, cringe, bow and scrape GROVEL, TRUCKLE
– humble oneself or make oneself inconspicuous EFFACE
– humbled, subdued, or restrained, as by punishment CHASTENED
– humbly asking or begging SUPPLIANT, SUPPLICANT
– very humble or respectful, as an apology might be ABJECT
– extremely humble or submissive in attitude or behaviour SERVILE

humbug – full of humbug about benevolence and high moral standards SANCTIMONIOUS, PECKSNIFFIAN, PIETISTIC, CANTING

humid – containing as much water vapour as possible, as humid as can be SATURATED

humidity – instrument for measuring relative humidity HYGROMETER, PSYCHROMETER

humiliate See also **insult**, **disgrace**
– humiliate or belittle, as by contemptuous remarks DENIGRATE, DISPARAGE, DEROGATE
– humiliated, disgraced, or dishonoured DEGRADED, DEBASED
– humiliated by the puncturing of one's self-esteem or boasting, as through a rebuff or put-down DEFLATED, CHASTENED
– humiliated or ashamed, as by a failure MORTIFIED
– humiliating of oneself, as through a sense of guilt or inferiority SELF-ABASEMENT

humorous See also **funny**
– humorous action or remark PLEASANTRY
– humorous but disguised so as to appear as if intended seriously TONGUE-IN-CHEEK
– humorous in a coarse, earthy, and robust way RABELAISIAN
– humorous in a dry way WRY
– humorous in a mocking or cynical way SARDONIC
– humorous or mildly sarcastic use of words to express something markedly different from or opposite to their literal sense IRONY
– keeping a straight face as a humorous person might DEADPAN

humour based on the use of words or expressions that seem to have a second, typically saucy meaning DOUBLE ENTENDRE
– humour oneself or someone else by yielding to wishes INDULGE
– something used to soothe or humour someone PLACEBO

humours – character of a person, according to medieval physiology, based on the dominance of one of the four humours TEMPERAMENT
– characterised by one of the four humours in medieval physiology SANGUINE, CHOLERIC, PHLEGMATIC, MELANCHOLIC
– the four humours in medieval physiology BLOOD, YELLOW BILE (CHOLER), PHLEGM, BLACK BILE

hump across a road to limit vehicle speed SLEEPING POLICEMAN

humus forming in soil MULL
hunchback or other visible bodily defect DEFORMITY
– hunchbacked GIBBOUS
hundred – British slang term for 100 as a rate or score TON
hundred- CENT-, CENTI-, HECT-, HECTO-
hundred-year-old, or a person aged 100 or more CENTENARIAN
hundredth anniversary CENTENARY, CENTENNIAL
Hungarian cavalryman HUSSAR
– Hungarian Gypsy TZIGANE
– Hungarian person or language MAGYAR
– traditional Hungarian stew, seasoned with paprika GOULASH
hunger – satisfy or appease someone's hunger, longings, or the like ASSUAGE
– sharp feelings of hunger PANGS
hungry or greedy to an extreme degree RAVENOUS, VORACIOUS, INSATIABLE
– starving, in an extremely hungry state FAMISHED
hunter of dangerous animals or criminals on the offer of a reward BOUNTY HUNTER
– hunter or guide for big-game hunters in India SHIKAREE
– hunter who is extremely keen and skilled NIMROD
– hunter's or fisher's attendant in Scotland GILLIE
– drink taken by fox hunters while mounted STIRRUP CUP
hunting as an art or hobby VENERY
– hunting of game, such as hares, with hounds relying on sight rather than scent COURSING
– hunting or game preserve, privately owned but unfenced CHASE
– animal pursued in hunting, or anything pursued in a conscientious way QUARRY
– relating to hunting VENATIC
– scented bag used in hunting to lay on artificial trail DRAG
– time of year when hunting, fishing, shooting of game, or the like is permitted OPEN SEASON
– time of year when hunting, fishing, shooting of game, or the like is prohibited CLOSE SEASON
huntsman CHASSEUR
– huntsman's assistant who controls the hounds WHIPPER-IN
– huntsman's scarlet coat PINK
– call to the huntsman that a fox has been sighted VIEW HALLOO
– chief huntsman of a fox hunt MASTER OF FOXHOUNDS, MFH
hurry, nag, harass CHIVVY
– hurry along the progress of something EXPEDITE
– hurry away or flee SKEDADDLE, SCARPER, HOTFOOT
– hurry or make a quick escape HIGHTAIL, DECAMP
– hurry the occurrence of something, bring about quickly or prematurely PRECIPITATE
hurt, distressed, or offended by an apparent injustice AGGRIEVED
– hurt or offend, cause a sympathetic or friendly person to become indifferent or hostile ALIENATE, ANTAGONISE, ESTRANGE
– hurt someone's feelings, as by severe criticism SCARIFY
husband and wife who are elderly and devoted DARBY AND JOAN
– husband of a woman who has committed adultery CUCKOLD
– husband or wife, especially of a monarch CONSORT
– common-law husband TALLYMAN
– crime of having two wives or husbands at any one time BIGAMY
– custom or state of having only one husband at a time, as in most cultures MONANDRY
– custom or state of having two or more husbands or male mates at a time, as in some cultures POLYGAMY, POLYANDRY
– excessively devoted to one's wife, as an attentive husband might be UXORIOUS
– legal right to the help, company, and affection of one's husband or wife CONSORTIUM
-husband- -ANDR-
hut – hut-like shelter of arched corrugated iron sheets NISSEN HUT
– hut or shack, typically crudely built and run-down SHANTY
– hut that is run-down and dirty HOVEL
– hut used by hunters, skiers, or the like LODGE
hybrid animal, from a female ass and male horse HINNY
hydrogen isotope, with atomic mass 1 PROTIUM
– hydrogen isotope, with atomic mass 2 DEUTERIUM
– chemical removal of hydrogen from a compound or adding of oxygen to it OXIDATION
– chemical removal of oxygen from a compound or adding of hydrogen to it REDUCTION
hydrogen bomb, extremely powerful bomb produced by the fusion of light atomic nuclei FUSION BOMB, THERMONUCLEAR BOMB
hyena, vulture, insect, or the like that feeds on dead animals, rotting meat, or other decaying organic matter SCAVENGER
hygienic, free of infection SANITARY
hymn See also **prayer**
– hymn, service, or piece of music in honour of a dead person REQUIEM
– hymn, verse, or formula praising God in the liturgy DOXOLOGY
– hymn and frenzied dance for a chorus in ancient Greece, in honour of Dionysus DITHYRAMB
– hymn of praise or adoration sung during the Communion service SANCTUS
– hymn or piece of music at the beginning of a church service, while the choir and clergy are entering PROCESSIONAL
– hymn or piece of music at the end of a church service, while the choir and clergy are leaving RECESSIONAL
– hymn or psalm sung at the beginning of a service INTROIT
– hymn or psalm sung with responses ANTIPHON
– hymn or religious song or poem CANTICLE
– hymn or song of praise LAUD, MAGNIFICAT
– hymn tune, as for singing or for the organ CHORALE
– medieval Latin hymn commemorating the Virgin Mary's grief at the Crucifixion STABAT MATER
– medieval Latin hymn describing the Last Judgment, used in the Mass for the dead DIES IRAE
hypnotic, dream-like state TRANCE
hypnotise MESMERISE
hypochondriac, health-obsessed person VALETUDINARIAN
hypocrisy, pretending HUMBUG
hypocrite, especially a pious hypocrite WHITED SEPULCHRE, PLASTER SAINT, PHARISEE
hypocritical, affecting benevolence and high moral standards SANCTIMONIOUS, PECKSNIFFIAN, PIETISTIC
– hypocritical, insincere, sly rather than forthright DISINGENUOUS
– hypocritical, insincere, or moralising speech or writing CANT
– hypocritical, two-faced JANUS-FACED
– hypocritically self-righteous, puritanically disapproving PHARISAICAL
hypothesis or premise put forward without proof THESIS
hypothetical, assumed SUPPOSITITIOUS, CONJECTURAL, NOTIONAL
hysteria – hysteria-induced symptoms of a non-present disease MIMESIS
– hysteria or depression, supposed in former times to be caused by gases produced within the body THE VAPOURS
hysterical or over-emotional in behaviour MELODRAMATIC

I

ice coating rock, roads, or the like in a thin film VERGLAS
- ice covering a road or path in a thin, transparent layer BLACK ICE, GLAZE ICE
- ice floating in small harmless pieces in the sea DRIFT ICE
- ice-hole used by whales, seals, and so on for taking breath BLOWHOLE
- ice mass or other obstruction blocking a narrow passage GORGE
- ice masses floating in polar seas PACK ICE
- ice sheet or slab floating in the sea FLOE
- breaking up of the ice on the surface of a river, often causing flooding DÉBÂCLE
- controlled slide over ice GLISSADE
- drink, usually alcoholic, poured over crushed ice FRAPPÉ
- house built of ice, as of an Eskimo IGLOO
- mass of porous ice formed from snow, but not yet turned into glacier ice FIRN, NÉVÉ
- metal spikes or spiked plate fastened to a shoe or boot, as for mountaineering or walking across ice CRAMPONS, CLAMPER
- river of ice formed of snow and moving very slowly GLACIER
- slushy ice, as forming on the surface of the sea SLUDGE
- water ice made from fruit SORBET

ice-cream cone CORNET
- ice cream as formerly sold by street vendors HOKEY-POKEY
- ice cream or other delicacy containing candied or fresh diced fruits TUTTI-FRUTTI
- dessert or delicacy of frozen syrup or fruit purée, resembling ice cream, water ice SORBET
- Italian ice cream of various kinds CASSATA, SPUMONE
- served with ice cream, as apple pie might be À LA MODE
- small brick or block of ice cream, charcoal, or other substance BRIQUETTE

ice hockey – hard rubber disc used in ice hockey PUCK
- pass in ice hockey that enables a teammate to score ASSIST

ice-skating See also **skating**
- jumps in ice-skating, taking off on one skate, spinning in the air, and landing on the other skate AXEL, LUTZ, SALCHOW
- turn from one edge of one skate to the other edge of the other skate in ice-skating CHOCTAW

iceberg – small iceberg, presenting a danger to shipping GROWLER

icicle – lime deposit, resembling an icicle, hanging from the roof of a cave STALACTITE

icing in thin tube-like strands squeezed through a nozzle PIPING
- icing of sweet almond paste, as on wedding cakes MARZIPAN
- coated with icing or sugar, as cherries might be GLACÉ
- U.S. term for the icing on a cake FROSTING
- U.S. term for icing sugar CONFECTIONERS' SUGAR

idea, custom, institution, or person considered, unreasonably, to be beyond criticism SACRED COW
- idea based on extracting the qualities from various specific things or examples GENERALISATION, ABSTRACTION
- ideas, principles, or understanding LIGHTS
- idea or deduction based on scanty evidence SURMISE, CONJECTURE
- idea or feeling that dominates all others OBSESSION, PREOCCUPATION, IDÉE FIXE, FIXATION
- idea or hint that is unconfirmed or still not fully formed INKLING, HUNCH, INTUITION, INTIMATION
- idea or logical invention forming part of a theory CONSTRUCT
- idea or opinion based on convention rather than real belief IDÉE REÇUE
- idea or proposition put forward as the basis on which an argument or theory can be built AXIOM, POSTULATE, PREMISE
- idea that, in Jungian psychology, derives from the collective unconscious ARCHETYPE
- based on convention rather than belief, as an idea or practice might be RECEIVED
- develop slowly in the mind, as an idea might do GESTATE
- difference between ideas, opinions, or the like DIVERGENCE
- discussion in which thoughts are swapped or analysed intensely as a means of solving problems or creating new ideas BRAINSTORMING
- existing only as an idea, not in reality HYPOTHETICAL, NOTIONAL
- formed beforehand, without knowledge or experience, as ideas might be PRECONCEIVED
- general idea or understanding CONCEPT, NOTION, APPREHENSION
- give a definite shape or form to something, such as an idea CRYSTALLISE
- gradual absorption or acquisition, as of ideas OSMOSIS
- medium, such as a play, for conveying ideas, expressing talents, or the like VEHICLE
- mix up or confuse ideas, elements, or the like CONFOUND
- odd, fanciful, or impulsive idea or wish WHIM, CAPRICE
- odd or eccentric idea, flight of fancy VAGARY
- odd or fanciful idea, bee in one's bonnet CROTCHET, MAGGOT
- person or group whose reactions serve as a test for new ideas or opinions SOUNDING BOARD
- put one's ideas into words FORMULATE, ARTICULATE
- relating to an idea or concept inherent in the mind rather than learnt INNATE
- similarity of ideas, opinions, or the like CONVERGENCE
- spread or try to circulate ideas or opinions PEDDLE
- treat an idea or abstraction as a real or concrete thing REIFY
- undeveloped though promising, as an idea might be FALLOW

idea- IDEO-

ideal, model, or original that is copied or worth copying, PROTOTYPE, ARCHETYPE, EXEMPLAR
- ideal example or typical representative of a specified virtue or vice PERSONIFICATION, EMBODIMENT, INCARNATION
- ideal or principle expressed by a word or maxim MOTTO
- ideal place, condition of per-

fect justice and happiness or the like UTOPIA

idealise, exalt, treat with awe DEIFY
– idealised image formed in childhood IMAGO

idealist with impractical ambitions DON QUIXOTE
– writer or artist favouring a real-life representation of everyday subject matter rather than an idealised approach REALIST

idealistic, unrealistic, and impractical, especially in wishing to reform society UTOPIAN, VISIONARY
– idealistic in an excessively romantic way, and hence impractical or absent-minded QUIXOTIC
– idealistic belief in the imminent arrival of a golden age of peace MESSIANISM, MILLENARIANISM

identical See **same**, **equal**
– twins MONOZYGOTIC TWINS
– genetically identical organism or group of organisms CLONE
– person almost identical in appearance to another RINGER
– twins that are not identical FRATERNAL TWINS

identical- TAUT-, TAUTO-

identification of a disease, injury, or problem DIAGNOSIS
– close emotional identification with another EMPATHY
– system or equipment for creating a picture of a face, as for police identification, by combining drawings of features IDENTIKIT
– system or equipment for creating a picture of a face, as for police identification, by combining photographs of features PHOTOFIT

identifying sign, as of a current or former disease STIGMA

identity or social role that a person adopts, especially when in public PERSONA
– person who takes another's identity IMPERSONATOR, IMPOSTOR
– sense of rootlessness, confusion, and loss of personal identity, in the absence of a supportive community ALIENATION, ANOMIE

ideology – influence someone into accepting an ideology, belief, or point of view uncritically INDOCTRINATE, BRAINWASH

idiom, way of talking PARLANCE
– idiom of a trade, profession, or other specialised group JARGON, CANT, ARGOT, VERNACULAR

idiot See **fool**, **madman**, **stupid**

idler, aimless loafer FLÂNEUR, FAINÉANT

idol worship, or strong and uncritical admiration IDOLATRY

if, *provided that*, or other conjunction that introduces a supposition SUPPOSITIVE
– clause, typically beginning with *if* or *unless*, stating the condition in a conditional sentence PROTASIS, CONDITIONAL CLAUSE
– main clause in an *if* or conditional sentence APODOSIS
– proposition or premise in the *if*-part of a conditional sentence ANTECEDENT

ignition – generator in the ignition system of some engines MAGNETO

ignorance – vast and deeply bad, as ignorance might be ABYSMAL

ignorant See also **stupid**
– ignorant, unaware UNWITTING
– ignorant, uninformed in moral or cultural matters, unenlightened BENIGHTED, NESCIENT
– ignorant of reading and writing ILLITERATE, UNLETTERED
– ignorant yet behaving as if knowledgeable ULTRACREPIDARIAN

ignore, avoid BYPASS, CIRCUMVENT
– ignore, neglect, overlook, or omit PRETERMIT
– ignore or disregard something irrelevant or unreliable DISCOUNT
– ignore or pretend ignorance of a wrongful act, and thereby encourage it CONNIVE AT, WINK AT
– ignore or snub abruptly or disdainfully REBUFF

ill, unwell, poorly, under the weather AILING, INDISPOSED
– ill-looking, deathly pale CADAVEROUS
– chronically ill person INVALID
– person who is constantly worrying about his health or constantly thinks he is ill HYPOCHONDRIAC, VALETUDINARIAN
– pretend to be ill, as to get off work MALINGER

ill will, bitterness, hostility ACRIMONY, ANIMOSITY, ANIMUS, RANCOUR, MALEFICENCE
– ill will, resentment GRUDGE
– full of ill will, MALICIOUS, MALEVOLENT
– offensive, liable to cause ill will or resentment INVIDIOUS

illegal See **crime**
– illegal, unlawful ILLEGITIMATE, ILLICIT, UNCONSTITUTIONAL
– illegal act, especially by a public official MALFEASANCE, MALVERSATION

illegitimate, bastard MISBEGOTTEN, SPURIOUS
– referring to an illegitimate child, or one falsely represented as the genuine heir SUPPOSITITIOUS, SUPPOSITIOUS
– sign or suggestion of illegitimate birth BAR SINISTER

illicit whiskey, especially in the Southern U.S. MOONSHINE, MOUNTAIN DEW

illiterate or uneducated UNLETTERED
– unable to deal with numbers, as opposed to illiterate INNUMERATE

illness See also **disease**
– illness, disease AILMENT, COMPLAINT, AFFLICTION, MALADY
– illness and its attendant weakness and failing powers INFIRMITY
– illness or fear of illness that is imaginary or self-induced HYPOCHONDRIA
– caused by the doctor or his treatment, as an illness might be IATROGENIC
– decline or regress after apparently recovering from an illness RELAPSE
– gradual return to health after an illness, especially by resting CONVALESCENCE
– pass certificate awarded even when a university student misses part of an examination through illness AEGROTAT
– referring to illness brought on by stress or other psychological factors PSYCHOSOMATIC
– regain one's health or strength, as after an illness RECUPERATE, CONVALESCE
– sudden fit of illness ICTUS

illogical, against reason IRRATIONAL
– illogical or irrelevant conclusion or statement NON SEQUITUR
– illogical reasoning or argument, though not deliberately so PARALOGISM
– illogical reasoning or argument that is knowingly invalid and deliberately misleading SOPHISM
– illogical reasoning or faulty argument that invalidates the conclusion FALLACY

illuminated title, heading, or letter, standing out from the rest of the text in a manuscript or book RUBRIC

illumination, such as a small picture or ornamental letter, in a manuscript MINIATURE

illusion, apparent object that is not real PHANTASM, HALLUCINATION
– illusion or image of an object, such as an oasis MIRAGE
– illusion produced by a disturbed mind, over-active imagination, or the like ABERRATION, CHIMERA, SPECTRE

illusory image, especially mirage FATA MORGANA
– illusory or unrealistic hope or wish PIPE DREAM, FAIRY GOLD
– illusory, seemingly plentiful or lavish BARMECIDAL
– visual illusion, deceptive impres-

sion presented to the eyes OPTICAL ILLUSION

illustration See also **picture**
- illustration at the front of a book, often opposite the title page FRONTISPIECE
- illustration or diagram of a machine or structure showing its parts separately EXPLODED VIEW
- illustration or model, as of an engine or building, with part of the wall or casing omitted or cut away to reveal the interior CUTAWAY
- illustrations accompanying a text GRAPHICS

image, representation, or likeness of something, sometimes misleading or superficial SIMULACRUM
- image or opinion of someone or something that is conventional, unthinking and usually oversimplified STEREOTYPE
- image or symbol ICON
- image that is familiar and recurrent in literature TOPOS, MOTIF
- apparatus giving brief exposures of visual images, as for experiments in memory or perception TACHISTOSCOPE
- apparent image formed by reflected or refracted light rays, such as the image in a mirror VIRTUAL IMAGE
- referring to very vivid yet unreal visual images, as experienced in childhood EIDETIC

imaginary, fictitious, misleading, deceiving ILLUSORY
- imaginary fear, pure fantasy, or the like CHIMERA, SPECTRE
- imaginary land of luxury and idleness COCKAIGNE
- imaginary or self-induced illness or suffering HYPOCHONDRIA
- imaginary or theoretical rather than actual NOTIONAL, HYPOTHETICAL
- imaginary or unreal thing NONENTITY
- imaginary place, as in fiction, where things are worse than in real life DYSTOPIA, CACOTOPIA
- imaginary place or condition of perfect justice, ideal happiness, or the like UTOPIA, SHANGRI-LA

imagination of a lively kind, often combined with mildly eccentric behaviour WHIMSY
- having foresight or great imagination VISIONARY
- inventive cleverness, showing imagination INGENUITY
- notion, fantasy, or invention, typically credited to the imagination FIGMENT
- state of being lost in thought or living briefly in one's imagination REVERIE

imagine, bring to the mind's eye CONJURE UP, FANTASISE
- imagine, form a mental image or vision of VISUALISE, ENVISAGE

imbalance between parts ASYMMETRY
- imbalance or instability DISEQUILIBRIUM

imitate See also **copy**
- imitate another person's voice or mannerisms in a mocking way MIME, MIMIC, APE
- imitate in order to equal or outperform EMULATE
- imitate or pass oneself off as someone else IMPERSONATE
- imitate the form, appearance, or sound of, often in order to deceive SIMULATE
- unique, impossible to imitate successfully MATCHLESS, INIMITABLE

imitation, fake, substitute, or artificial SYNTHETIC, ERSATZ, PINCHBECK, SPURIOUS
- imitation or representation of nature or human nature in literature and art MIMESIS
- imitation or representation that is crudely distorted TRAVESTY, MOCKERY, PARODY
- mocking imitation, satire, or caricature SPOOF, BURLESQUE, LAMPOON
- satirical imitation of a literary, musical, or other artistic work PARODY, PASTICHE

imitator, follower, or disciple who is markedly inferior to his master EPIGONE

immature, underdeveloped, basic, in an early stage RUDIMENTARY, INCHOATE,
- immature, young, childish, unsophisticated JUVENILE, ADOLESCENT, PUERILE, JEJUNE
- immature early work of a composer, writer, artist, or the like JUVENILIA
- immature or inexperienced, unsophisticated CALLOW, VERDANT
- immature or inexperienced person GREENHORN

immaturity NONAGE

immediately, instantly, without hesitation or delay INSTANTANEOUSLY, FORTHWITH, INSTANTER

immigrant group's adjustment to or adoption of a dominant culture ASSIMILATION
- immigrant worker, especially a Turk or Yugoslav in West Germany GASTARBEITER
- limited or specified quantity or number, as of imports, immigrants, or the like QUOTA
- relating to a distinctive racial, religious, or cultural group, such as an immigrant group, within a society ETHNIC

immoral, corrupt, debased DEGENERATE, REPROBATE
- immoral, utterly abandoned or unprincipled, shameless DISSOLUTE, LIBERTINE, LICENTIOUS, PROFLIGATE, WANTON
- immoral and debauched man, rake, especially an ageing one ROUÉ, CORINTHIAN
- immoral behaviour of a base and vile kind DEPRAVITY, TURPITUDE
- immoral over-indulgence in sensual pleasures DISSIPATION, INTEMPERANCE, DEBAUCHERY
- immorally luxurious place or situation BABYLON

immovable See also **fixed**
- immovable and impersonal, as inflexible bureaucracy might be MONOLITHIC

immune to attack, damage, or the like INVULNERABLE

immunise against a disease, dangerous opinion, or the like INOCULATE

immunity from consequences, such as regret or punishment IMPUNITY
- immunity from prosecution, or a period of immunity, enabling offenders to confess without fear AMNESTY
- immunity or exemption, as for foreign diplomats, from the jurisdiction of one's country of residence EXTRATERRITORIALITY
- blood protein produced to counteract germs or other invading substances, and so promote immunity against infection ANTIBODY

impatient, fidgety, on edge RESTIVE
- impatient or restless, as to go travelling FOOTLOOSE
- impatient with curiosity AGOG

imperfect or unsatisfactory item that is thrown out REJECT, DISCARD

impersonal and immovable, as an inflexible bureaucracy might be MONOLITHIC

imply, involve, have as a necessary consequence ENTAIL
- imply slyly INSINUATE
- implied, unspoken, understood, as an informal agreement might be TACIT, IMPLICIT

importance in rank or status, relative greatness MAGNITUDE
- increase in power, importance, or the like AGGRANDISEMENT
- play down, minimise the importance of SOFT-PEDAL
- right of priority, first choice, or the like, as by virtue of greater importance or urgency PRECEDENCE

important, extremely significant, as historic discovery might be EARTH-SHAKING, EPOCH-MAKING, MONUMENTAL
- important, influential, high-ranking CONSEQUENTIAL, CONSIDERABLE, PROMINENT, EXALTED, FORMIDABLE, REDOUBTABLE
- important and genuine, as some issues of concern are SUBSTANTIVE
- important and wealthy man NABOB, MAGNATE, GRANDEE, MAGNIFICO
- important for long-term policy STRATEGIC
- important or high-ranking person DIGNITARY, NAME TO CONJURE WITH, EMINENCE
- important person or personality, leading light CELEBRITY, WORTHY, LUMINARY
- extremely important, crucial, vital PIVOTAL, CARDINAL, SEMINAL, SIGNAL
- extremely important, urgently essential IMPERATIVE
- extremely large or important person or thing COLOSSUS
- having important and far-reaching consequences FATEFUL, MOMENTOUS, PORTENTOUS
- most important, more necessary or urgent than anything else PARAMOUNT, OVERRIDING
- most important or common, basic or customary STAPLE
- most important or striking, as the main point of a talk is SALIENT
- most important or powerful, leading, foremost PREDOMINANT, PREPONDERANT
- most important part, core or essence ALPHA AND OMEGA
- most important work of scholarship or literature MAGNUM OPUS

imports – import duty TARIFF
- limited or specified quantity or number, as of imports QUOTA

impose or collect a tax, fine, membership fee, or the like LEVY

impractical, excessively idealistic or romantic QUIXOTIC
- impractical and absent-minded, daydreaming OTHER-WORLDLY
- impractical and idealistic, especially in wishing to reform society radically UTOPIAN, VISIONARY
- impractical idealist, romantic dreamer DON QUIXOTE
- impractically committed to a theory, dogmatic DOCTRINAIRE

impregnate or fertilise FECUNDATE
- impregnate with semen INSEMINATE

impression, suspicion, hint INKLING, INTIMATION, HUNCH, INTUITION
- impression or overall view of a series of historical events, the future, or the like VISTA
- person who shows off in an attempt to make an impression on others POSEUR
- unforgettable or enduring, as an impression might be INDELIBLE

impressive, respected FORMIDABLE, REDOUBTABLE
- impressive and complete display, defence, or the like PANOPLY
- impressive and dignified, commanding or elegant STATELY, LOFTY, BARONIAL

imprison, jail INCARCERATE
- imprison, shut up within walls IMMURE
- imprison or detain, especially in wartime INTERN

imprisonment DURANCE, CONFINEMENT, DURESS
- imprisonment and forced labour PENAL SERVITUDE
- imprisonment or temporary custody DETENTION
- document in former times under a sovereign's seal, typically authorising imprisonment without trial LETTRE DE CACHET
- legal writ for release from unlawful imprisonment HABEAS CORPUS

improper or distasteful UNSEEMLY, UNBECOMING, INDECOROUS, INDELICATE
- improper usage, especially in grammar or etiquette SOLECISM

improve, become or make better AMELIORATE, MELIORATE, AMEND
- improve, make reparation, or atone for REDRESS, MAKE AMENDS, MAKE RESTITUTION
- improve, reform, revitalise or restore RECLAIM, REGENERATE, REHABILITATE
- improve as much as possible OPTIMISE
- improve by a spectacular change of appearance, attitude, or the like TRANSFORM, TRANSFIGURE
- improve by cleaning or repairing, restore to good condition RENOVATE, REFURBISH, REVAMP
- improve in health after an illness RECUPERATE, CONVALESCE
- improve or enliven a story by adding colourful, often false, details EMBELLISH, EMBROIDER, GARNISH
- improve or increase the value or quality of ENHANCE
- improve the appearance of, usually deceptively GILD, GLOSS
- improvement, instruction, or enlightenment, especially when morally uplifting EDIFICATION

improving, correcting, beneficial, as advice might be SALUTARY

improvised, makeshift, temporary EXTEMPORANEOUS
- improvised, unrehearsed, off-the-cuff, as a speech might be IMPROMPTU, EXTEMPORE

imprudent, ill-advised or incautious, as a rash remark might be INJUDICIOUS, INDISCREET, IMPOLITIC

impudent See **cheeky**

impulsive See **rash**, **reckless**

impure blemished MACULATE
- impure, tainted, CONTAMINATED, POLLUTED, DEFILED
- add impurities to a substance, such as milk or wine ADULTERATE

in- END-, ENDO-, ENTO-, INTRA-, INTRO-

in accordance with PURSUANT TO

in bad faith MALA FIDE

in confidence, just between ourselves ENTRE NOUS

in consequence of PURSUANT TO

in fact, in reality, actually DE FACTO

in front, at the head ANTERIOR

in front- PROS-

in front of- ANTE-, PRE-

in itself, as such PER SE

in labour, about to give birth PARTURIENT

in love ENAMOURED
- passionately in love in an intense but often immature or superficial way INFATUATED, BESOTTED

in memory of, as used in epitaphs IN MEMORIAM

in name only, not actual NOMINAL

in order, proper, acceptable KOSHER
- in order, all right HUNKYDORY
- in order, working OPERATIONAL, OPERATIVE, FUNCTIONAL

in passing, by the way EN PASSANT

in person, live IN PROPRIA PERSONA

in proportion PRO RATA

in relation to, regarding, compared with VIS-À-VIS

in suspense, anxious, tense, nervous ON TENTERHOOKS

in the act RED-HANDED, IN FLAGRANTE DELICTO

in the red OVERDRAWN

in the same place, used as a footnote formula IBIDEM, IBID.

in the way, unwanted SUPERFLUOUS, DE TROP

in two minds, having conflicting feelings or views AMBIVALENT

in vain, useless, futile UNAVAILING, TO NO AVAIL, BOOTLESS

inability to carry out some duty or task INCAPACITY

inactive, chemically unreactive, as some elements are INERT
- inactive, unlikely to erupt, as a volcano might be EXTINCT
- inactive, sluggish TORPID, LETHARGIC

– inactive but capable of being aroused LATENT, DORMANT
– inactive or dormant, as a disease might be QUIESCENT
– temporarily inactive IN ABEYANCE

inactivity, depression, or boredom DOLDRUMS, ENNUI

inadequate, See **mediocre**
– inadequate, scanty, sparse or skimpy MEAGRE, JEJUNE, LENTEN, EXIGUOUS

inanimate, without human understanding or feelings, as a block of wood is INSENSATE, INSENSIBLE

inappropriate, inconvenient, unsuitable, or badly timed INOPPORTUNE, UNSEASONABLE, UNTIMELY
– inappropriate, out of place, as a saucy joke might be INAPPOSITE, MALAPROPOS, INDECOROUS
– inappropriate, strange, out of place INCONGRUOUS
– inappropriate, unsuitable, or unbecoming, as a rash remark might be UNTOWARD, INFELICITOUS

inattentive, absent-minded, or distracted DISTRAIT

inborn INNATE

Inca wind instrument, egg-shaped OCARINA

incarnation or embodiment of an idea, model, or god AVATAR

incense – container for burning incense, especially one that is swung at festivals CENSER, THURIBLE
– resin used in incense FRANKINCENSE, OLIBANUM
– stick of perfumed substance, burnt as incense JOSS STICK

incessant See **constant**

incidental, added in a secondary or helping role rather than essential AUXILIARY, ADJUNCT, ADSCITITIOUS
– incidental, not intended or inherent ADVENTITIOUS, CONTINGENT, FORTUITOUS
– incidental, not relevant MARGINAL, PERIPHERAL, TANGENTIAL
– incidental, of secondary importance, serving a subordinate function ACCESSORY, SUPPLEMENTARY, SUBSIDIARY
– incidental remark, comment made in passing OBITER DICTUM
– something that is incidental to something else CONTINGENCY

incidentally, by the way EN PASSANT, PARENTHETICALLY, APROPOS

incite, entice, or lure, especially into a sinful or illegal act SOLICIT, SUBORN, SEDUCE
– secret agent who joins a political or criminal group and tries to incite it into punishable or discrediting activities AGENT PROVOCATEUR

-inciter -AGOGUE

inclination See **tendency**

include, contain, consist of COMPRISE
– include, take in EMBRACE, COMPREHEND, SUBSUME
– include or contain INCORPORATE, EMBODY, EMBED, ENCOMPASS
– including many things, aspects, or examples OMNIBUS, COMPENDIOUS

income, as from a bequest or trust, or the source of it ENDOWMENT
– income, especially that of a government REVENUE
– income level that is the minimum for providing the necessities of life SUBSISTENCE LEVEL
– income or standard of living that is adequate but modest SUFFICIENCY, COMPETENCE
– income remaining for use after taxes have been deducted, net income DISPOSABLE INCOME

incompatible, as two people or ideas might be IRRECONCILABLE
– incompatible, jarring INCONGRUOUS, DISCORDANT, DISSONANT

incompetence – principle that people tend to get promoted until they reach a position in which they are incompetent PETER PRINCIPLE

incomplete or insufficient DEFICIENT

incomprehensible or inscrutable UNFATHOMABLE

inconsistency or disagreement, as in results, claims, or reports DISCREPANCY, VARIANCE, DISPARITY

inconsistent or apparently self-contradictory phrase, such as *joyous grief*, used as a figure of speech OXYMORON
– inconsistent or apparently self-contradictory statement, often used for effect PARADOX
– inconsistent or clashing, jarring or divergent DISSONANT, DISCORDANT, INCONGRUOUS
– inconsistent or conflicting, as two opposed logical propositions might be INCOMPATIBLE, IRRECONCILABLE

inconspicuous, attracting little attention LOW-PROFILE, UNOBTRUSIVE, UNOSTENTATIOUS

inconvenience, disturb INCOMMODE

inconvenient, inappropriate, or badly timed INOPPORTUNE, UNSEASONABLE, UNTIMELY

incorrect See also **mistake**
– incorrect, making or based on a mistake ERRONEOUS
– incorrect, out of proper order, off course, off beam ADRIFT, AMISS, AWRY
– incorrect conclusion, faulty argument, or invalid reasoning, especially when unintended PARALOGISM
– incorrect idea or misleading opinion, based on misinformation or faulty reasoning FALLACY
– incorrect interpretation or explanation, misunderstanding MISCONSTRUCTION
– incorrect opinion or faulty understanding MISCONCEPTION, MISAPPREHENSION
– incorrect or illogical though plausible, as an argument might be SPECIOUS, SOPHISTIC
– incorrect or inappropriate name MISNOMER
– incorrect use of a word, such as *flaunt* in a context requiring *flout* CATACHRESIS
– incorrect use of words, grammatical error SOLECISM
– prove a statement of argument incorrect REFUTE, REBUT, CONFUTE
– word used incorrectly in place of one which sounds similar MALAPROPISM

incorrect- CACO-

increase, as capital does by the addition of interest ACCRUE
– increase, extend, enlarge, expand AMPLIFY, AUGMENT, WAX
– increase as much as possible MAXIMISE
– increase dramatically, as an animal population might in favourable conditions IRRUPT
– increase greatly or intensify energetically one's efforts REDOUBLE
– increase in intensity or scope, as a war or quarrel might ESCALATE, FLARE UP, INFLAME, SPIRAL
– increase in loudness, as of a passage of music CRESCENDO
– increase in size, swell, expand DILATE, INFLATE, DISTEND
– increase or addition, as to one's salary INCREMENT
– increase or growth, as of public feeling or opinion GROUNDSWELL
– increase or spread, as by reproduction PROPAGATION
– increase or spread rapidly PROLIFERATE, BURGEON
– increase or stimulate, as appetite might be WHET
– increase suddenly, as electric current might SURGE
– increase the intensity or severity of a pain, problem, or the like AGGRAVATE, EXACERBATE
– increase the power, influence, or reputation of ENHANCE, ELEVATE, EXALT, AGGRANDISE
– increase the time or length of, extend PROTRACT
– increase through slow additions ACCUMULATION, ACCRETION
– increasing or mounting up by a series of steps or additions CUMULATIVE

incurable, beyond remedy, hopeless IRREDEEMABLE
– incurable optimist MICAWBER, POLLYANNA

indecent See also **rude**
– indecent, outrageously indelicate or rude SCABROUS

indecisive, hesitant, lacking in confidence or commitment FALTERING
– indecisive, in two minds AMBIVALENT
– indecisive, uncertain, in two minds WAVERING, VACILLATING

indefinable but distinctive characteristic JE NE SAIS QUOI

indefinitely, without a date being set for resumption SINE DIE

indentation See **groove**, **notch**

indented space or hollow, niche, as set back from the main surface of a wall RECESS, ALCOVE

independence, self-government SOVEREIGNTY, AUTONOMY

independent, existing or functioning in its own right rather than as subordinate to something else SUBSTANTIVE
– independent, self-governing, or self-sufficient AUTONOMOUS, SOVEREIGN
– independent-minded politician in the U.S. MUGWUMP
– independent-minded or unorthodox thinker or group member, individualist MAVERICK
– independent of the order of the terms, as an operation such as multiplication is COMMUTATIVE

indescribable, unspeakable INEFFABLE

index in which the keyword is listed with its context KWIC INDEX
– index of all the words in a text, such as the Bible or the works of Shakespeare, listing every occurrence of each word CONCORDANCE

Indian terms See chart, and also **Hinduism terms**, **menu terms**, **clothes**, **American Indian terms**

indicate, point out DESIGNATE, SPECIFY, PARTICULARISE

INDIAN TERMS

ahimsa	doctrine of non-violence towards all living creatures	**nautch**	dance performed by girls
beedi	hand-rolled cigarette, typically a single rolled leaf tied with thread	**nawab, nabob**	governor of a province or state under the Mogul Empire
bhishti	water-carrier in former times	**nizam**	title of the former rulers of the state of Hyderabad
chapatti, roti, nan, puri, paratha	flat bread of various kinds	**pan**	leaf of the betel palm; preparation of this leaf with betel nuts and lime for chewing
charkha	spinning wheel	**punka**	ceiling fan made of a cloth or palm leaf
charpoy	light bedstead	**purdah**	curtain concealing women from public view, or the social system requiring this
crore	ten million	**raga**	conventional music pattern forming the basis of a composition of interpretation
dacoit	member of an armed robber band	**raj**	dominion, sovereignty
dak	post or mail	**rajah, maharajah**	prince, chief, or ruler
dak bungalow	house providing accommodation for travellers	**rani, maharani**	wife of a rajah, princess in her own right
dhobi, dhobi-wallah	man who washes clothes	**sahib**	form of address, as formerly used to Colonial Europeans, equivalent to *sir* or *master*
doolie	stretcher or litter for carrying a person or goods	**satyagraha**	Gandhi's policy of non-violent resistance to British rule
durbar	state reception; reception hall of an Indian prince	**sepoy**	Indian soldier serving under the British in India
gharry	small horse-drawn carriage	**shikaree**	hunter, or guide for big-game hunters
ghat	mountain pass; flight of steps down to a river	**sitar, vina, tamboura, sarod**	stringed musical instruments of various kinds
ghee	clarified butter, as from buffalo milk, used in Indian cooking	**syce**	stableman or groom
lakh	hundred thousand, especially when referring to rupees	**tabla**	pair of small drums
mahout	keeper and driver of an elephant	**tiffin**	light lunch or snack
maidan	open space in or near a town, used for sports or displays	**tonga**	light, two-wheeled horse-drawn vehicle

– indicate, reveal, disclose MANIFEST, EVINCE, EVIDENCE
– indicate, signify, signal, mean DENOTE, BESPEAK, BETOKEN
– indicate, show, exhibit REGISTER
– indicate or signal the approach of something HERALD, HARBINGER, PRESAGE

indication, sign, token INDEX
– indication or evidence of a disease, social condition, or the like SYMPTOM
– indication or evidence that one possesses a specified quality PATENT

indicator, especially of an early kind in the form of a small arm on the side of a car, that would swing out and light up to indicate a change of direction TRAFFICATOR
– indicators on a car, flashing together HAZARD WARNING SIGNAL

indifferent, lukewarm, especially in politics or religion LAODICEAN
– indifferent, unexcitable, not caring greatly NONCHALANT, INSOUCIANT

indigestion DYSPEPSIA
– build-up of gas in the digestive tract, or the feeling of indigestion caused by it FLATULENCE

indirect, evasive, not straightforward OBLIQUE, ABSTRUSE
– indirect, roundabout expression CIRCUMLOCUTION, PERIPHRASIS
– indirect or roundabout route or road DETOUR
– indirect or second-hand, as pleasure is when gained through someone else's achievements or actions VICARIOUS

indispensable or essential thing or condition SINE QUA NON

indisputable, undeniable, certain, as an overwhelmingly powerful argument or evidence would be INCONTROVERTIBLE, IRREFUTABLE

individual, definite, particular, explicit SPECIFIC
– individual, unconnected, separate, distinct DISCRETE, DIVERSE
– individual born singly rather than as a twin or in a litter SINGLETON
– individual detail PARTICULAR
– individual speech pattern of a person IDIOLECT
– relating to or arising from the individual self or mind rather than observable external reality SUBJECTIVE

individual- IDIO-

individually, singly, in the order stated RESPECTIVELY

inducing contractions to bring on childbirth, as some drugs do OXYTOCIC

indulge one's lust, appetites, or the like to the full SATE, SATIATE
– indulge oneself in pleasures, extravagant emotions, or the like LUXURIATE, REVEL, WALLOW
– indulge or yield to a whim, desire, or the like GRATIFY

indulgence in sensual or immoral pursuits DISSIPATION, INTEMPERANCE, DEBAUCHERY, DEPRAVITY, DISSOLUTENESS

indulgent or excessive act, as of violence, drinking, or crime ORGY, RAMPAGE, FRENZY

industrial diamond BORT
– industrial exhibition EXPO
– industrial workers or the working class generally PROLETARIAT
– industrial worker, such as a welder or riveter, in heavy industries such as shipbuilding and the like BOILERMAKER

industrial dispute – deliberate disruption of normal functioning, as in a factory during an industrial dispute SABOTAGE
– harassment of employers by the workers in industrial disputes in India GHERAO
– settlement of an industrial dispute by negotiating through a third party CONCILIATION, MEDIATION
– settlement of an industrial dispute by submitting to the judgment of a third party ARBITRATION, ADJUDICATION

industrialist or businessman of great power and influence MAGNATE, TYCOON

industrious, painstaking, persevering SEDULOUS, ASSIDUOUS, DILIGENT

industry – modernise an industry, process, or the like, and make it more efficient RATIONALISE
– return a nationalised industry to private ownership DENATIONALISE, PRIVATISE

ineffective or powerless as a result of counterbalancing NEUTRALISED
– make ineffective or invalid an argument, contract, or the like NULLIFY, INVALIDATE, VITIATE, VOID

inequality- ANISO-

inescapable, inevitable INELUCTABLE

inessential, suitable for throwing away if necessary EXPENDABLE
– inessential, supplementary, not inherent EXTRANEOUS, EXTRINSIC

inevitable, not to be eluded or escaped INELUCTABLE

inexperienced or immature, unsophisticated CALLOW, UNFLEDGED, VERDANT
– inexperienced person, especially in the armed forces ROOKIE
– inexperienced person, relative newcomer, beginner TENDERFOOT, NOVICE, GREENHORN, TYRO, NEOPHYTE

infallible judgment or utterance ORACLE

infamous, well-known for a particular and usually unfavourable quality NOTORIOUS

infection – blood protein produced to counteract germs or other invading substances, and so promote immunity against infection ANTIBODY
– development or spread of infection, or of an infectious disease ZYMOSIS
– main site of an infection FOCUS, NIDUS

infectious, as a disease might be COMMUNICABLE
– infectious, extremely harmful, or very rapid in effect, as a disease or poison might be VIRULENT
– infectious, spreading disease PESTIFEROUS, PESTILENT
– spread by physical contact, as an infectious disease might be CONTAGIOUS

infer or guess with only scanty evidence to go on SURMISE, CONJECTURE
– infer or work out from given evidence DEDUCE, EXTRAPOLATE

inference of general truths from particular instances, as distinct from strict logical deduction INDUCTION

inferior- INFRA-, SUB-

infidel, non-believer, especially a Christian regarded as an infidel by a Muslim GIAOUR

infidelity – man who tolerates his wife's infidelities WITTOL

inflammation – reducing inflammation, as a drug might ANTIPHLOGISTIC
– relating to inflammation and fever PHLOGISTIC

-inflammation -ITIS

inflatable rubber mattress, as used for floating on in swimming pools LILO

inflation in which an increase in demand or in money supply causes prices to rise DEMAND-PULL INFLATION
– inflation in which wage increases and other increased production costs cause prices to rise COST-PUSH INFLATION
– means of protection, as against inflation HEDGE
– official price index issued each month, used as a guide to inflation RETAIL PRICE INDEX

inflexibility, unadaptability PERSEVERATION

influence, drive, or force VECTOR
- influence, motivation, encouragement INCENTIVE, INCITEMENT, STIMULUS
- influence, power of affecting others' decisions or behaviour, pulling strings, LEVERAGE, MANIPULATION, CLOUT
- influence, serve as evidence, or affect MILITATE
- influence, such as a moral principle, that determines an action or decision SANCTION
- influence or urge legislators to adopt a certain policy LOBBY
- influence someone into accepting something uncritically, as by biased education INDOCTRINATE, BRAINWASH
- influenced, guided, or driven by some motive or force ACTUATED, IMPELLED, INSTIGATED
- easily influenced, readily affected, prone to something SUSCEPTIBLE
- easily led, persuaded, or influenced, cooperative FLEXIBLE, DUCTILE, TRACTABLE, MALLEABLE, PLIABLE, BIDDABLE, DOCILE
- leading position of power, influence, or control DOMINANCE, PRE-EMINENCE, ASCENDANCY
- magnetic personal charm and power of influence or inspiration CHARISMA
- person exerting or trying to exert a sinister influence over another's will SVENGALI

influential and powerful person, typically a rich industrialist MAGNATE, TYCOON
- influential but unofficial group of advisers to a head of government or other leader KITCHEN CABINET
- influential or inspiring person LUMINARY
- influential person wielding power behind the scenes ÉMINENCE GRISE

inform against or accuse DENOUNCE
- inform or advise someone of something, keep someone posted NOTIFY, ALERT, ACQUAINT, APPRISE, FAMILIARISE

informal See **casual**
- informal, conversational, characteristic of casual spoken language COLLOQUIAL
- informally, casually EN FAMILLE

information, news, reports INTELLIGENCE, TIDINGS
- information, often dubious, spread publicly to further a cause PROPAGANDA
- information added at the end of a book, message, or the like AFTERTHOUGHT, POSTSCRIPT, APPENDIX
- information from other people HEARSAY
- information in response to an inquiry, experiment, programme, or the like FEEDBACK
- information or mental stimulation, usually of a dull and pointless kind PABULUM
- information or news as communicated informally GEN, LOWDOWN, SCOOP
- information store, as for a computer DATA BASE
- announcement of some new information, item of news REVELATION, DISCLOSURE
- exchange or central distribution point for banking transactions, commodities, information, or the like CLEARING HOUSE
- file or collection of papers giving information on a particular person or subject DOSSIER
- gather information or knowledge bit by bit GLEAN
- official announcement of information for public attention COMMUNIQUÉ, BULLETIN
- reveal or relate information IMPART, DIVULGE
- secret, as official information might be CLASSIFIED
- study of information flow and control systems in electronics, mechanics, and biology CYBERNETICS
- supply someone with background information BRIEF, PRIME

informed, conscious, having knowledge COGNISANT

informer, decoy, or police spy STOOL PIGEON
- police informer NARK, GRASS

-ing – verb form functioning as a noun, ending in *-ing* in English, as in *They enjoy sailing* GERUND
- verb form used as an adjective or in indicating various tenses, typically ending in *-ing* or *-ed* in English, as in *She was running* or *an invented expression* PARTICIPLE

inhabit or occupy a place TENANT

inhabitant of a place going back to the earliest times ABORIGINAL, AUTOCHTHON
- inhabitant or resident of a place or region DENIZEN

-inhabiting -COLOUS

inhale – medical preparation inhaled with steam to relieve colds or sore throats FRIAR'S BALSAM

inherent in the very structure of the economy, society, or the like, as unemployment might be STRUCTURAL

inheritance, or the right to it or sequence of it, of a title, property, throne, or the like SUCCESSION
- inheritance from one's father or ancestor PATRIMONY
- inheritance or heirship shared by two or more beneficiaries PARCENARY
- inheritance or legacy BEQUEST
- laws of inheritance in genetics MENDEL'S LAWS
- legal limitation on the inheritance or use of an estate, interest, or the like to a specific person or persons TAIL
- limit the inheritance of property to a particular line of heirs ENTAIL
- owned through or passing down by inheritance HEREDITARY
- right of the eldest son to inherit the entire estate, the kingship, or the like PRIMOGENITURE
- right to or expectation of an inheritance REVERSION
- theory, opposed by strict Darwinian ideas of evolution, that acquired characteristics can be inherited LAMARCKISM, LYSENKOISM

inherited, as some diseases are GENETIC, HEREDITARY
- inherited article of value, kept within a family HEIRLOOM
- inherited traditions, customs, or the like HERITAGE

inhuman, without truly human understanding or feelings INSENSATE, INSENSIBLE

initial letter – repeated occurrence of a letter or sound, especially the initial letter, in writing or speech ALLITERATION

initials – design, often of one's initials, as for an emblem MONOGRAM

initiation ceremony or similar ritual marking a change of status in a person's life RITE OF PASSAGE
- initiation into or first experience of a painful ordeal, especially on the battlefield BAPTISM OF FIRE
- initiation or introduction, as into a ritual or profession INDUCTION

initiative, enterprise, pluck GUMPTION
- initiative or step, as in diplomatic matters DÉMARCHE

inject heroin or other drugs directly into a vein MAINLINE

injection made just beneath the skin SUBCUTANEOUS
- injection of blood, plasma, or the like into the blood stream TRANSFUSION
- injection of liquid into the rectum for medication or purging the bowels ENEMA, COLONIC, CLYSTER
- injection of vaccine following the main dose to increase or sustain its effectiveness BOOSTER

– administration of a medicine by slow injection INFUSION
– given or taken by injection rather than by mouth, as a medical drug might be PARENTERAL
– in or into a vein, as an injection might be INTRAVENOUS
– puncturing of a vein, as in injecting medicine VENIPUNCTURE
– referring to an injection beneath the skin HYPODERMIC
– small glass bottle, especially a sealed one containing liquid for injections AMPOULE

injure or wound very severely, causing serious disfigurement or disability MAIM, MUTILATE
– injured or seriously weakened or disabled INCAPACITATED
– anger arising from being injured or wronged GRIEVANCE

injury, wound, or harm LESION
– injury or destruction of a wanton or widespread kind MAYHEM
– injury or wound, as caused by an accident or surgery TRAUMA
– injury to the neck, caused by a sudden jerk WHIPLASH
– susceptible to danger, injury, or attack VULNERABLE

injustice due to inconsistencies, bias, or unfairness, as in a law INEQUITY
– injustice or supposed injustice GRIEVANCE
– outrageous or glaringly wrong, as an injustice might be FLAGRANT

ink that cannot be washed off or erased INDELIBLE INK
– dark brown ink or pigment originally obtained from the inky secretion of the cuttlefish SEPIA

inkblot test, personality test based on the subject's interpretations of various abstract inkblot designs RORSCHACH TEST

inland, without access to the sea, as some countries are LANDLOCKED
– inland region HINTERLAND

inlay, pave, or decorate with a mosaic of tiny tiles TESSELLATE
– inlay or etch metal with wavy decorative patterns DAMASCENE, DAMASK
– inlaid furniture decoration, or an item of furniture so decorated BUHL
– inlaid wood work, as used in decorating furniture MARQUETRY

inn or hostel in Eastern countries, typically built round a large courtyard, for groups of travellers CARAVANSERAI, KHAN
– inn or pub HOSTELRY
– inn or shelter for the needy or travellers HOSPICE
– inn-keeper VICTUALLER
– servant caring for guests' horses at an inn OSTLER

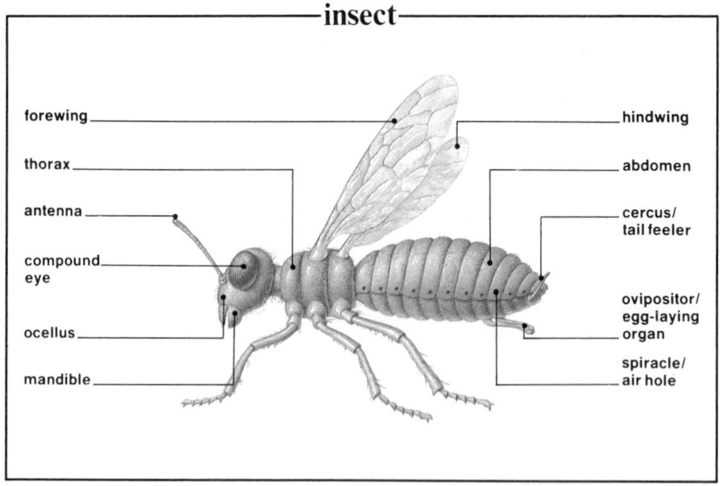

innocent, unsophisticated, simple NAIVE, ARTLESS, GUILELESS, INGENUOUS
– innocent and naive young woman INGÉNUE
– clear of blame, declare innocent EXONERATE, EXCULPATE
– person, typically innocent, who is involved in an incident merely by being present BYSTANDER

Inquisition – burning of a heretic at the stake, as ordered by the Inquisition AUTO-DA-FÉ

inquisitive person, busybody or gossip QUIDNUNC

insane See **mad**
– prove someone to be insane and therefore not legally responsible or liable STULTIFY

insanity See **madness**

inscription or title LEGEND
– scroll-shaped ornamental tablet sometimes bearing an inscription CARTOUCHE

inscriptions – study of ancient inscriptions EPIGRAPHY

insect See **illustration**
– insect, spider, centipede, or related animal having jointed limbs, a horny shell, and a segmented body ARTHROPOD
– insect-eating, feeding on insects INSECTIVOROUS, ENTOMOPHAGOUS
– insect-eating plant having jug-like leaves that attract and trap the insects PITCHER PLANT
– insect-eating plant trapping its prey between hinged leaf blades VENUS'S-FLYTRAP
– insect excrement FRASS
– insect of a kind that feeds on plant juices, often causing serious damage to grape crops PHYLLOXERA
– insect in the adult stage IMAGO
– insect in the non-mobile stage between larva and adult PUPA, CHRYSALIS
– insect larva, as of the mayfly or dragonfly, that develops directly into the adult rather than going through the pupal stage NYMPH
– insect larva of the mayfly or similar insect, living in water NAIAD
– insect of a kind found in hot countries, producing a high-pitched droning sound CICADA
– insect of a kind that feeds on plant juices, often being a serious garden pest APHID
– insect or other organism that transmits germs VECTOR, CARRIER
– insect that rests in a praying position MANTIS
– air bubble surrounding some water-dwelling insects PLASTRON
– back or upper surface of a body segment, as of an insect or lobster TERGUM
– fear of insects ENTOMOPHOBIA
– fumigation chamber for killing insects or fungi FUMATORIUM
– head-like part at the end of an insect's antenna CAPITULUM
– lotion or other substance that keeps insects away REPELLENT
– nest of an insect NIDUS
– projecting or secondary part of a plant or lower animal, such as an insect's leg or feeler APPENDAGE
– shed skin of an insect CAST, CASTING
– sting or egg-laying tube of an insect ACULEUS
– study or student of insects ENTOMOLOGY, ENTOMOLOGIST
– transformation of an insect's structure and properties METAMORPHOSIS
– tube-like feeding structure on some insects PROBOSCIS

insect- ENTOMO-
insecure, risky PRECARIOUS
– insecure, susceptible to danger, injury, or attack VULNERABLE
inseparable, part and parcel, forming an essential part of the whole INTEGRAL, INTRINSIC, INHERENT
– inseparably linked, connected closely and in many complex ways INEXTRICABLY LINKED
insert or introduce between other elements, layers, or the like INTERCALATE, INTERPOLATE, INTERPOSE
inside, existing within as an essence or force IMMANENT, IMPLICIT, INHERENT, INTRINSIC
inside- END-, ENDO-, ENTO-, INTRA-
inside out or upside down INVERTED
– turn a body part or organ inside out EVAGINATE, EVERT
insight INTUITION
– insightful remark or observation APERÇU
insignificant, worthless, trifling NUGATORY, PALTRY, NOMINAL
– insignificant person or thing NONENTITY
insincere, hypocritical, or moralising speech or writing CANT
– insincere, pretending to be ignorant, not candid DISINGENUOUS
– insincere claims to have certain feelings or beliefs HYPOCRISY
– insincere person adapting his actions and opinions to those currently accepted OPPORTUNIST, TIMESERVER, TEMPORISER, VICAR OF BRAY
– effortless or fluent, as in speaking or writing, but typically shallow and insincere GLIB, PAT
– insincerely or over-earnestly charming, or flattering, fawning UNCTUOUS, INGRATIATING
insistent, assertive, or pushy in manner STRIDENT, IMPORTUNATE, VOCIFEROUS
inspect See **examine**, **study**
inspection of the structural state of a building SURVEY
– preliminary inspection of a region, as to assess the terrain or study enemy positions RECONNAISSANCE, RECONNOITRE
inspiration, especially a poetic impulse AFFLATUS
– magnetic personal charm and power of influence or inspiration CHARISMA
inspire with ideas, principles, or the like IMBUE, PERMEATE, PERVADE, INSEMINATE
– inspired new idea or discovery TROUVAILLE
– inspiring or ringing, as a call to action might be CLARION
instability, constant change FLUX
– instability or imbalance DISEQUILIBRIUM
install or introduce, especially with formality INDUCT, INVEST, INAUGURATE, INSTATE
instalments – pay off a debt or mortgage by instalments AMORTISE
instant, moment, very short period of time TRICE
instead of IN LIEU OF
instinct for self-destruction, deathwish in Freudian theory THANATOS
– instinct for self-preservation and pleasure, life-instinct and sexual drive in Freudian theory EROS
– channel or transform a sexual or other instinctual impulse into a socially or culturally more acceptable activity SUBLIMATE
– instinctive drive to achieve, in human or animal behaviour MOTIVATION
– instinctive knowledge INTUITION
– instinctive or intuitive, as a "gut feeling" is, rather than rational VISCERAL
– emotional and mental energy and sexual drive derived from the basic life-instinct in Freudian theory LIBIDO
institution, custom, idea, or person considered, unreasonably, to be beyond criticism SACRED COW
– member of the supervisory board of an institution TRUSTEE
– someone confined in an institution, such as a mental hospital or a prison INMATE
instruction See also **order**
– instruction, enlightenment, or improvement, especially when morally uplifting EDIFICATION
– instruction by question and answer, especially on the basic principles of Christianity CATECHISM, CATECHESIS
– instruction or teaching TUITION
instrument See **laboratory**, **measuring**, **medical**, **scientific**, **percussion**, **keyboard**, **wind**, **electronic**, **string**, **tool**
– instrument, tool IMPLEMENT, UTENSIL
insufficient or incomplete, lacking a necessary quality DEFICIENT
insulation, coating, or facing material on the outside of a building, pipe, tank, or the like CLADDING, LAGGING
– insulation or seed-bed material in the form of lightweight fragments of mica-derived material VERMICULITE
– rubbery latex substance used in electrical insulation and dentistry GUTTA-PERCHA
insulator, non-conductor of electric current DIELECTRIC
insult, address in a rude and contemptuous way ABUSE, REVILE, BLACKGUARD
– insult, taunt, scoff at, sneer at, or despise FLEER, TWIT, FLOUT
– insult, tease, or ridicule repeatedly, torment BAIT
– insult, typically in the form of a false charge, that injure's someone's reputation LIBEL, SMEAR, SLANDER, DEFAMATION, CALUMNY, ASPERSION, SLUR, CHARACTER-ASSASSINATION
– insult in a slanderous way, describe or accuse in a false and demeaning way MALIGN, CALUMNIATE, VILIFY, TRADUCE, STIGMATISE
– insult or contempt directed at God, religion, or anything sacred BLASPHEMY, PROFANITY, SACRILEGE
– insult or criticise with passionate scorn, curse heartily, DENOUNCE, EXECRATE, ANATHEMATISE, VITUPERATE, INVEIGH AGAINST
– insult or slander someone in his absence BACKBITE
– insult to someone's dignity or authority, overstepping the mark LESE MAJESTY
– insulting, rude, or contemptuous behaviour or remark CONTUMELY
– insulting in a deliberate way, intended to offend or belittle DEROGATORY, DISPARAGING
– insulting language, abuse or obscenities BILLINGSGATE
– insulting or offensive statement or act OUTRAGE
– insulting or personally abusive, as criticism of an opponent might be AD HOMINEM
– insultingly haughty or contemptuous DISDAINFUL, SUPERCILIOUS
– criticise in an insulting or diminishing way, belittle and despise DENIGRATE, DISPARAGE, DERIDE, DECRY, DEPRECIATE, DEROGATE, VILIPEND
– disgrace or disrepute after being subjected to insult and abuse OBLOQUY, IGNOMINY
– offend someone, as by a direct insult or rebuff AFFRONT
– offend someone, as by an unintended insult PIQUE
– passionate criticism, accusation, or insulting curse INVECTIVE, DENUNCIATION, VITUPERATION
– resentment, offence, feeling of anger at some supposed insult UMBRAGE
insurance See chart, page 266
insure against loss or legal responsibility INDEMNIFY, UNDERWRITE

integrity – challenge or attack someone's honour or integrity IMPEACH, DISCREDIT
intellectual people regarded as a social class INTELLIGENTSIA
– intellectual or bookish people LITERATI
– intellectual or cultured HIGHBROW
– intellectual person, especially if old or conservative MANDARIN
– intellectual or scholarly woman, especially an austere and unappealing one BLUESTOCKING
– intellectual rather than emotional and instinctual CEREBRAL, APOLLONIAN
– gathering of intellectuals, celebrities, or the like SALON
intelligence – level of intelligence I.Q, INTELLIGENCE QUOTIENT
intended, planned PROJECTED, CONTEMPLATED, PURPOSED
– intended or certain, fated DESTINED, PREDESTINED
intense, passionate, or emphatic as a denial might be VEHEMENT
intention, aim, goal OBJECTIVE
– intention, purpose, or motive ANIMUS, IMPULSION
– intention or goal, or the fulfilment of it CONSUMMATION
– intention or purpose that is concealed, especially so as to deceive ULTERIOR MOTIVE, HIDDEN AGENDA, ARRIÈRE-PENSÉE
– test, sample, or probe opinions or intentions SOUND
interbreeding between people of different races MISCEGENATION
interchange, exchange, give or take mutually RECIPROCATE
intercourse See **sex**
interest greatly, fascinate, rivet the attention of OBSESS, INTRIGUE, PREOCCUPY, HAUNT
– interest in or concern for social institutions, economic policies, or the like that one derives personal benefit from VESTED INTEREST
– interest paid on both the principal and the accumulating interest COMPOUND INTEREST, CUMULATIVE INTEREST
– all-absorbing interest FIXATION
– increase, as capital does by the addition of interest ACCRUE
– lowest rate of interest on bank loans PRIME RATE
– play at some pursuit, take a casual interest in something DABBLE
– similarity, as of people's interests COMMUNITY
– special interest or strong point METIER, FORTE
– wide-ranging, all-embracing, liberal and broad-minded, as one's interests might be CATHOLIC
interested by and deeply engaged in an activity, to the point of losing contact with one's surroundings ABSORBED, IMMERSED, ENGROSSED, INTENT, RAPT, PREOCCUPIED
interesting, colourful, or thought-provoking CHALLENGING, ROUSING, STIMULATING
– interesting or attractive in a slightly disturbing or provocative way PIQUANT, TANTALISING
– extremely interesting, gripping the attention ENTHRALLING, RIVETING, SPELLBINDING, MESMERISING, COMPELLING, ARRESTING
– extremely interesting and very charming BEWITCHING, CAPTIVATING, BEGUILING, ENTRANCING, ENCHANTING, ENGAGING
interfere, as in a nation's internal affairs INTERVENE
– interfere, meddle inappropriately, as in a conversation INTRUDE
interfering, over-attentive, excessively eager to help OFFICIOUS
– interfering person, especially an onlooker at a card game, who gives unwanted advice KIBITZER
– interfering person or intruder INTERLOPER
– warning against touching or interfering NOLI ME TANGERE
interference, unwanted electric signals producing random noise in a radio or a speckled television picture STATIC
– interference in a legal action by someone not directly involved in it MAINTENANCE
intermediate course of action, factor, or the like when there are sup-

INSURANCE TERMS

actuary	statistician whose calculations of risk are the basis of insurance premiums
annuity	fixed annual payment in return for a lump sum, or premiums over a number of years
comprehensive	providing wide-ranging insurance cover, especially for a motor vehicle
endorsement	amendment to a policy
endowment policy	life-insurance policy which matures on the death of the insured or at a set date, whichever is the earlier
loading	extra charge or payment on top of a premium to cover special risks or expenses
maturity	time at which the proceeds of a policy are due to be paid
moral hazard	risk to the insurer resulting from the possible dishonesty or carelessness of the insured
mortality table	table used by insurers to calculate risk, showing life expectancies and death rates of people of varying age and status
personal liability	risk of a person causing death, injury, or loss to other persons by his action
pluvius insurance	insurance against bad weather taken out by organisers of holidays and indoor or outdoor events
reversion	sum of money paid on the death of the holder of a life-insurance policy
surrender value	value of a policy when it is discontinued voluntarily before its maturity
third party	providing cover against liability for accidents to other people or their property
tontine	insurance scheme in which a member's shares or benefits pass to the other members when he dies or defaults
underwriter	company or agent that accepts part of an insurance risk

posed to be only two TERTIUM QUID
– intermediate place or condition, such as an unsatisfactory state of waiting LIMBO

intermittent, irregular, occasional, periodic SPORADIC, FITFUL, EPISODIC, SPASMODIC

internal-combustion engine See illustration, pages 268-269, and also **jet engine**, **engine**

internal in origin, as a body organ might be ENDOGENOUS
– internal or inside, existing within as an essence or force IMPLICIT, IMMANENT, INHERENT, INTRINSIC
– internal to a given institution, as a private inquiry or training course might be INTRAMURAL

internal organs See **intestines**, **digestive system**, **entrails**

international agreement, such as a peace agreement PACT, TREATY
– international conference of top officials SUMMIT
– international language of the sea, used by naval and maritime officers for communication, based on simple English SEASPEAK
– international language of various kinds, based typically on common roots from several European languages ESPERANTO, IDO, INTERGLOSSA, INTERLINGUA, NOVIAL, VOLAPÜK
– international negotiation aimed at gaining an advantage, by pressing a dispute towards a crisis without backing down BRINKMANSHIP
– international or multi-cultural, as a city might be COSMOPOLITAN
– international relations, or skill in conducting them DIPLOMACY

interpret in a reasonable or apparently reasonable way, often to suit one's convenience RATIONALISE
– interpret or clarify a code, obscure text, mystery, or the like DECIPHER, DECRYPT
– interpret or explain EXPOUND, ELUCIDATE, CONSTRUE

interpretation, as of the scriptures, with a mystical emphasis, identifying spiritual symbols ANAGOGY
– interpretation or analysis of a literary work, philosophical theory, or the like EXPLICATION, EXPOSITION
– interpretation or critical analysis of a text, especially of the Bible EXEGESIS
– interpretation or explanation of a statement or action CONSTRUCTION
– interpretation or explanation that is convenient but often misleading GLOSS
– open to two or more interpretations AMBIGUOUS
– permitting or admitting of something, such as an interpretation SUSCEPTIBLE
– study or methods of interpretation, especially of the bible HERMENEUTICS

interpreter, person who explains a theory, cause, or the like EXPONENT
– interpreter or guide in the Middle East in former times DRAGOMAN

interrupt, hinder, or throw into disorder DISRUPT
– interrupt, seize, or stop something, such as a message, in its course INTERCEPT
– interrupt at regular intervals PUNCTUATE
– interrupt by throwing in a comment INTERJECT, INTERPOSE
– interrupt or disturb the peace, someone's privacy, or the like VIOLATE
– interrupt some intended course of action SUPERVENE, INTERVENE
– interrupt with jeering or critical comments HECKLE

interruption, hindrance to concentration DISTRACTION

interval, intervening period or event INTERLUDE
– interval, pause, temporary stop INTERMISSION
– interval, time between two periods or events INTERIM
– interval of peace or inactivity LULL, RESPITE
– interval or discontinuity, specifically between two successive reigns or governments INTERREGNUM
– interval or interval performance in a theatre, such as a short play or dance INTERMEZZO, ENTR'ACTE
– referring to an interval in music that is decreased by a semitone DIMINISHED
– referring to an interval in music that is increased by a semitone AUGMENTED

intervention by an intermediary between disputing people or groups MEDIATION, INTERCESSION, CONCILIATION

intestines See also **digestive system**
– intestines, or the internal organs generally VISCERA, ENTRAILS
– intestines, usually of a pig, prepared as a food CHITTERLINGS
– intestinal pains GRIPES, COLIC
– milky fluid formed in the small intestine during digestion CHYLE
– muscular contractions in the intestine or similar tube-like organ that force the contents onwards PERISTALSIS, VERMICULATION
– sac or pouch formed in the weakened wall of a hollow body part, especially the intestines DIVERTICULUM
– tiny hair-like projection, as on moss or in the small intestine VILLUS

intestine- ENTER-, ENTERO-

into- INTRO-

intolerable, unbearable, unendurable INSUFFERABLE, INSUPPORTABLE

intolerant and prejudiced person, fanatic BIGOT, ZEALOT
– intolerant towards or discriminating against outsiders SECTARIAN

intrigue or plot, or group of plotters CONSPIRACY, CABAL
– devious or complicated, as intrigue often is LABYRINTHINE, BYZANTINE

introduce See also **begin**
– introduce or begin something new, in an inventive way INNOVATE
– introduce or gain acceptance for gradually or cunningly INSINUATE
– introduce or insert between other elements, layers, or the like INTERCALATE, INTERPOSE, INTERPOLATE
– introduce or install, especially through a formal procedure INDUCT, INVEST
– introduce or precede something, or signal its approach HERALD, INAUGURATE, USHER IN, HARBINGER, PRESAGE
– introduce someone into participation in an activity or to new knowledge INITIATE

introduction of themes, intentions, or the like, as in an argument or artistic work EXPOSITION
– introduction or heading LEMMA
– introduction or prior event, period, or the like PRELUDE
– introduction to a book, speech, or the like PREFACE, FOREWORD, PROLOGUE, PROEM
– introduction to a scholarly text or more detailed study PROLEGOMENON, PROLUSION
– introductory, preliminary, or preparing for something to come PREPARATORY, PRECURSORY, PREFATORY
– introductory course to a new setting, as for novice university students FAMILIARISATION, ORIENTATION, INDUCTION
– introductory event, entertainment, or the like, as before the main sports match or play CURTAIN RAISER
– introductory or explanatory

commentary or instructions RUBRIC
– introductory part of a classical drama PROTASIS
– introductory piece of music to an opera, play, or the like OVERTURE
– introductory statement or explanation, as to a formal document, treatise, or speech EXORDIUM, PREAMBLE

introductory- FORE-

intrude on someone's property, privacy, or rights TRESPASS, INFRINGE
– intruder or interfering person INTERLOPER

intuition – perception by means of a sixth sense, supernatural powers, intuition, or the like ESP, EXTRASENSORY PERCEPTION, CRYPTAESTHESIA

invader in search of loot MARAUDER, PLUNDERER, PILLAGER

invalid, chronically weak and sickly person, especially a hypochondriac VALETUDINARIAN
– invalid, inauthentic, false SPURIOUS
– invalid, inoperative, or powerless, as a disregarded law or regulation is NUGATORY
– make invalid, useless or ineffective, deprive of force NULLIFY

invasion of people or things INFLUX

invent or develop something, such as a new machine or technique EVOLVE, PIONEER
– invent or make up a story, deception, or the like FABRICATE, CONCOCT
– invent or produce something using available resources IMPROVISE
– invent or plan DEVISE, CONTRIVE, EXCOGITATE, ORIGINATE

invention or something new INNOVATION
– inventor's right to the exclusive use and development of his invention, or the document granting such a right PATENT
– share of the proceeds paid to an inventor for the use or development of his invention ROYALTY

inventiveness, imagination INGENUITY

inversion of left and right, as in an image seen in a mirror LATERAL INVERSION

investigate, probe SOUND

investigation of a formal or official kind, as into the cause of a death INQUEST, INQUIRY

investigator or questioner, especially one appointed to root out supposed evil INQUISITOR

investment company buying a variety of shares and selling publicly the units from the combined portfolio

internal combustion engine

OVERHEAD-VALVE (OHV) ENGINE

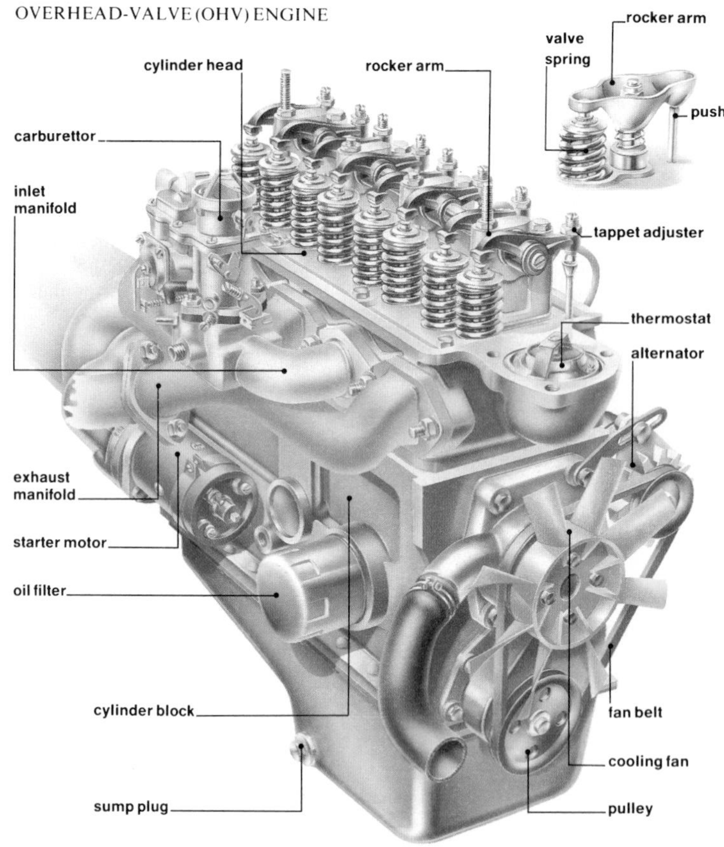

UNIT TRUST, MUTUAL FUND
– investment in a government stock GILT, GILT-EDGED SECURITY
– investment of a risky but potentially very profitable kind SPECULATION
– investments and other assets, in a detailed list PORTFOLIO
– investments in the form of stocks, shares, or bonds SECURITIES
– person whose income is derived chiefly from rents or investments RENTIER

invisible, impossible to see IMPERCEPTIBLE, INDISCERNIBLE
– invisible radiation with a wavelength between those of light and microwaves INFRARED
– invisible radiation with a wavelength between those of light and X-rays ULTRAVIOLET

invitation or offer OVERTURE

invite or approach a potential customer, as a prostitute might IMPORTUNE, SOLICIT, ACCOST
– invite someone in return RECIPROCATE

involuntary, automatic, unstudied, unrehearsed SPONTANEOUS
– involuntary, mechanical, or unconscious, as sneezes, knee-jerks, or similar responses are REFLEX

involve, imply, have as a necessary consequence ENTAIL

involved, as in a robbery IMPLICATED
– involved, entangled ENMESHED
– involved in an argument, scandal, or the like EMBROILED

inward-moving or inward-growing CENTRIPETAL
– inward-tending, especially towards the brain or spinal cord, as some nerves are AFFERENT
– inward-turned alignment of front wheels to improve steering TOE-IN
– having feet that turn inwards PIGEON-TOED

inward- INTRO-

ion with a negative charge ANION
– ion with a positive charge CATION

I.O.U., certificate or voucher acknowledging a debt DEBENTURE
– I.O.U. note, a written promise to pay a specified sum on a

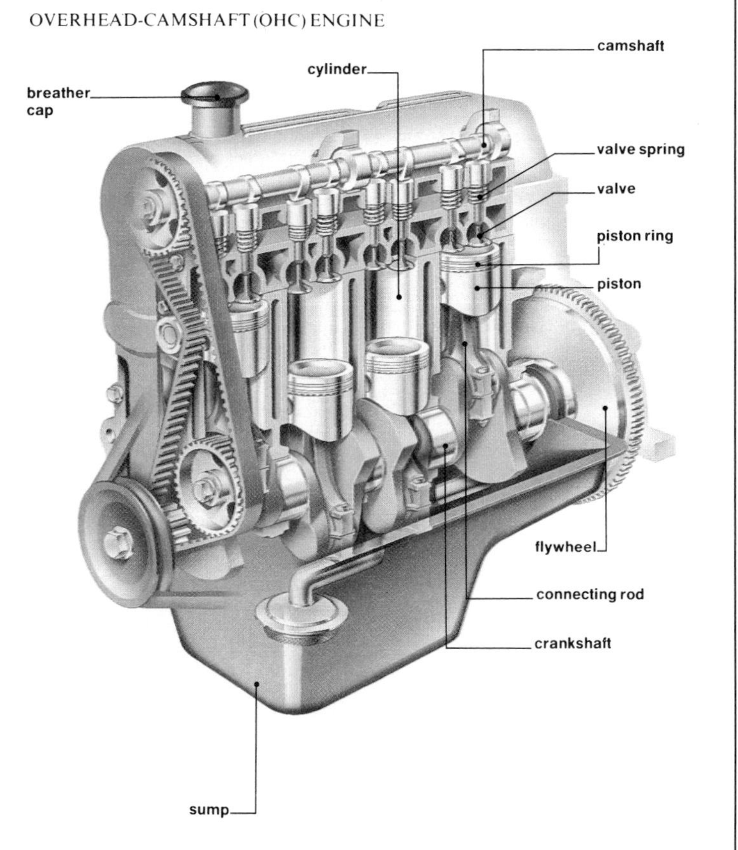

specified date or else on demand PROMISSORY NOTE
– I.O.U. or bond guaranteeing the repayment of a debt after the death of a person whose heir the debtor is POST-OBIT

Iran – garment of a long cloth, usually black, worn by some Muslim women, especially in Iran, to cover the head and shoulders and part of the face CHADOR
– religious leader of the highest rank among Shiite Muslims, as in Iran AYATOLLAH

Ireland See also chart of **Irish terms**
– adjective for Ireland MILESIAN, GAELIC, HIBERNIAN
– Irish accent BROGUE
– Irish Gaelic, the Celtic language of Ireland ERSE
– Irish person, especially an Irish speaker GAEL
– Irish Protestant favouring or stressing links between Northern Ireland and Britain UNIONIST, LOYALIST, ORANGEMAN
– national emblem of Ireland, a clover or similar plant with compound leaves of three leaflets SHAMROCK
– poetic name for Ireland HIBERNIA
– supporter of the republican cause in Northern Ireland FENIAN

iris, especially a white-flowered variety FLEUR-DE-LIS
– iris with a fragrant rootstock ORRIS

iron or steel sheet, as for roofing, folded into a series of parallel ridges and furrows CORRUGATED IRON
– iron ore PYRITE, HAEMATITE, MAGNETITE, LIMONITE
– bundle or load of scrap iron, or the iron box holding it FAGGOT
– coat or rustproof iron with zinc GALVANISE
– containing iron salts, or tasting of iron, as some waters do CHALYBEATE
– crude iron cast in oblong blocks PIG IRON
– made by hammering or shaping with tools rather than by casting, as iron railings might be WROUGHT
– press pleats or ridges into material, especially with a heated iron GOFFER
– relating to or containing iron FERRIC, FERROUS
– undersurface of an iron that presses the cloth or clothes SOLEPLATE

iron- FERR-, FERRI-, FERRO-, SIDER-, SIDERO-

ironic in tone, meant humorously not seriously TONGUE-IN-CHEEK
– ironic or joking at the wrong time or in an inappropriate way FACETIOUS
– ironic use of a word in a very different sense from its usual one ANTIPHRASIS
– bitingly or cruelly ironic SARCASTIC, CAUSTIC, MORDANT

IRISH TERMS

acushla	"O pulse (of my heart)": a term of endearment
banshee	female spirit whose wailing warns of an impending death
céad míle fáilte	"a hundred thousand welcomes"
ceilidh	social gathering
colleen	young girl
coronach	Gaelic funeral dirge
Gaeltacht	region where Gaelic is usually spoken
Garda	the police force
gombeen-man	village money-lender
gossoon	young lad
leprechaun	mischievous elf
machree/ mochree	"my heart": a term of endearment
mavourneen	"my darling"
pishogue	witchcraft or black magic
poteen	illicitly distilled whiskey
shebeen	illegal drinking house
shillelagh	club or cudgel
spalpeen	rascal or young lad

ISLAM TERMS

Allah	God, supreme being of the Muslim faith
ayatollah	Shiite religious leader
azan	summons to prayer, made by the muezzin five times daily
begum	Muslim princess or lady of high rank, especially in India
cadi	judge, intepreting the Muslim law
calender	member of a wandering mystical sect, as in Turkey and India, supported by charity
dervish	member of various ascetic Muslim orders, some of which perform whirling dances to attain ecstasy
emir	Muslim prince, chieftain, governor, or head of state
ghazi	Muslim warrior fighting against infidels in former times
giaor	infidel, non-Muslim, especially a Christian, as formerly referred to by the Turks
hadj	pilgrimage to Mecca, undertaken as a religious duty
hadji	person who has made the hadj
hafiz	Muslim who knows the Koran by heart
hakim	ruler, governor or judge
halal	to kill animals in accordance with Muslim law; meat from such animals
Hegira	the Muslim era, dating from AD 622; Muhammad's flight from Mecca to Medina in that year
houri	nymph or virgin attending the blessed in Paradise
ihram	white robes worn by pilgrims to Mecca
imam	prayer leader in a mosque; scholar or legal expert; ruler, caliph
Imam	Shiite leader considered to be a divinely appointed successor of Muhammad
Ismaili	small Shiite sect, led by the Aga Khan; member of this sect
jihad	holy war or crusade, waged as a religious duty
Juma	Islamic Sabbath, falling on Friday
Kaaba	shrine in Mecca, the goal of Muslim pilgrimage, towards which Muslims turn in praying
Koran/Alcoran/Qur'an	Muslim sacred book, containing Allah's revelations to Muhammad
Mahdi	Muslim messiah, and a leader claiming to be the messiah
marabout	Muslim holy man in North Africa, or a shrine marking his grave
mihrab, kiblah	niche in the wall of a mosque, indicating the direction of Mecca towards which the faithful pray
minaret	tall slender tower of a mosque, from which the faithful are summoned to prayer
moolvi	title of respect, especially in India, for a Muslim scholar, teacher or legal authority
mosque, masjid	house of worship
muezzin	official who summons the faithful to prayer at five fixed times every day, from the minaret or door of the mosque
mufti	expert in and adviser on the laws of the Koran; community leader during the Ottoman Empire
mullah	scholar or teacher of holy law
Ramadan	holy month, during which the faithful fast from dawn to dusk; the fast itself
sherif/sharif	title of respect for a Muslim ruler; governor of Mecca; person claiming descent from Muhammad
Shiite, Shiah	member of the smaller of the two main branches of Islam, believing in a line of succession of spiritual authority from Muhammad's cousin and son-in-law Ali
Sufi	member of a mystical Muslim sect, associated chiefly with Iran
Sunnite, Sunni	member of the larger of the two main branches of Islam, stressing the authority of traditional Islamic law
sura	chapter of the Koran
ulema	group of religious scholars or leaders, or a member of this group
Wahhabi	member of a puritanical sect, observing strictly the wording of the Koran, based mainly in Saudi Arabia

– ironically mocking or disdainful SARDONIC
– ironically or drily humorous WRY
ironsmith who made spurs and bits for horses LORIMER
irrational, distorted or dream-like in a bizarre way SURREAL
– irrational and habitual, compulsive, as an inveterate liar might be PATHOLOGICAL
– irrational or extreme devotion, excessive enthusiasm FANATICISM
– irrational, uncontrollable fear or hatred of something specified PHOBIA
– relating to irrational, mystical, or supernatural experience TRANSCENDENTAL
irregular, departing from the normal or expected DEVIANT, ABERRANT, ANOMALOUS
– irregular, discontinuous, occasional, periodic INTERMITTENT, SPORADIC, FITFUL, EPISODIC, SPASMODIC
– irregular, inconsistent, or unconventional ERRATIC, ECCENTRIC
– irregular, unsystematic, rambling, as a conversation might be DESULTORY
– irregular in design, unbalanced ASYMMETRICAL
– rough-edged, having an irregular or idented surface, jagged SERRATED, CORRUGATED
– irregularly spread out STRAGGLY
irregularity, abnormality ANOMALY, ABERRATION
irrelevant, not of central importance, non-essential MARGINAL, PERIPHERAL, TANGENTIAL, INCIDENTAL
– irrelevant, unimportant, inapplicable IMMATERIAL, IMPERTINENT, EXTRANEOUS
– irrelevant statement NON SEQUITUR
irreligious or extremely disrespectful treatment of something sacred or considered sacred SACRILEGE
irresponsible, dangerously unthinking IMPETUOUS, IMPULSIVE, HARUM-SCARUM, RECKLESS
irreversible, impossible to change or take back, as a decision might be IRREVOCABLE
irrigation device, as along the Nile, consisting of a bucket on a counterweighted pivoted pole SHADOUF
– irrigation device consisting of a wheel rimmed with buckets that dip into a stream or pool NORIA
irritable, easily angered, peevish TETCHY, CHOLERIC, BILIOUS, FRACTIOUS, DYSPEPTIC
– irritable, ill-tempered, easily provoked SPLENETIC, CANTANKEROUS, IRASCIBLE, ATRABILIOUS
– irritable, surly, or gloomy CURMUDGEONLY, QUERULOUS
– irritable or fussy behaviour FANTOD
– irritability, harsh temper ASPERITY
– unreasonably irritable, snappish, shirty PETULANT
irritate See also **anger**, **angry**
– irritate persistently, badger, HECTOR, HARASS, HARRY
– irritated in a snobbish way HOITY-TOITY
– irritating, annoying IRKSOME, VEXATIOUS, PESTIFEROUS, GALLING
– irritating person, pest, nuisance GADFLY
– cause irritation or bitterness over a long period of time FESTER, RANKLE
Islam See chart, and also **clothes**
island in a lake or river HOLM
– island in a river EYOT
– adjective for an island INSULAR
– group of islands, or sea containing such groups ARCHIPELAGO
– ring of coral islands enclosing a lagoon ATOLL
– small low island, typically of coral and sand CAY, KEY
– small rocky island, as off the coast of Scotland SKERRY
Isle of Man – any of the six administrative divisions of the Isle of Man SHEADING
-isms See **philosophy**
isolated, scattered, or occasional SPORADIC
– isolated, withdrawn into seclusion SEQUESTERED
isolation, remoteness, or aloneness SOLITUDE
– isolation of a sick or possibly sick person or animal to prevent the spread of disease QUARANTINE
Israel – political movement to establish or consolidate Israel as the Jewish national state ZIONISM
Israeli communal farm KIBBUTZ
– Israeli cooperative settlement, consisting of a group of small farms MOSHAV
– native-born Israeli SABRA
Israelites – Israelites' tent or sanctuary for the Ark of the Covenant during the Exodus TABERNACLE
issue or originate from a source EMANATE
– genuine and important, as some issues of concern are SUBSTANTIVE
– in honour of the memory of a person or event, as an issue of stamps might be COMMEMORATIVE
Italian See chart, and also **menu terms**, **pasta**
– Italian dialect spoken in Florence TUSCAN
itch to write CACOETHES SCRIBENDI
– itching of the skin PRURITUS
– itching or stinging sensation, typically accompanied by weals on the skin URTICATION
– itching sensation, as though ants were crawling over one's skin FORMICATION
item, individual detail PARTICULAR
ivory or wooden carved toggle formerly used in Japan to fasten a pouch or other object to a kimono sash NETSUKE
– carved or engraved articles of ivory, whalebone, or the like SCRIMSHAW

ITALIAN TERMS

aggiornamento	modernisation
al fresco	in the open air
arrivederci	goodbye
autostrada	motorway
carabiniere	policeman
che sarà sarà	what will be, will be
ciao	informal greeting or goodbye
cicerone	guide who shows visitors round a place
cognoscente	connoisseur
condottieri	mercenary soldiers
dolce far niente	enjoyable idleness
dolce vita	the good life
gran Turismo	high performance touring car
opera buffa	comic opera
padrone	proprietor of an inn or restaurant
palazzo	mansion or palace
piazza	public square; courtyard with a colonnade
prima donna	leading female singer in an opera; temperamental performer
sotto voce	in an undertone
trattoria	restaurant

J

jacket See **clothes**
jade, the less valuable variety, as distinct from jadeite NEPHRITE
jagged, as a coastline might be INDENTED
jail See **prison**, **imprison**
jailer, prison guard WARDER
– jailer who keeps the keys to an old-style prison TURNKEY
jam – gel-forming substance found in ripe fruit and used as a setting agent in jams PECTIN
Jamaican Creole PATOIS
Japanese See chart, and also **menu terms**
– Japanese, Chinese, or person from any of various other East Asian countries ORIENTAL
– Japanese name for Japan NIPPON, NIHON
– Japanese or Chinese figurine, usually in a grotesque, crouched position MAGOT
jar lined inside and out with tin foil, forming an early type of storage device for an electrical charge LEYDEN JAR
– jar or urn used in ancient Egypt for holding a mummy's entrails CANOPIC JAR

JAPANESE TERMS

aikido	martial art, similar to judo
Ainu	aboriginal inhabitant of northern Japan
banzai	"10,000 years", battle cry, or greeting to the emperor
bonsai	cultivation of miniature trees
bunraku	traditional puppet theatre
bushido	Samurai code of ethics
daimio	prince or noble
futon	padded mattress laid on the floor, used as a bed
geisha	young woman trained as a professional entertainer and companion for men
geta	wooden sandal
haiku	poem with 17 syllables
hara-kiri, seppuku	ritual suicide by disembowelling
hibachi	portable charcoal grill
ikebana	art of flower arranging
inro	lacquered box for carrying medicine, fastened to the belt by a netsuke
jujitsu	art of unarmed self-defence from which judo developed
Kabuki	popular traditional stylised theatre, developed from the Noh theatre
kamikaze	suicide pilot or plane of the Second World War
kendo	fencing with bamboo poles or sticks
kimono	long loose robe secured with a wide sash
mikado	Japanese emperor, as referred to by foreigners
netsuke	carved wooden or ivory toggle, as used for fastening a pouch to a kimono sash
Noh/No	stylised classical drama, including music, dancing, and elaborate costumes
obi	wide sash securing a kimono, typically with a large flat bow at the back
origami	art of folding paper into decorative shapes and designs
sake/saki	rice wine
samisen	three-stringed musical instrument
samurai	knight or aristocratic warrior in feudal Japan
sayonara	goodbye
Shinto	Japanese religion involving veneration of nature spirits and ancestors
shogun	hereditary commander-in-chief of the Japanese army until 1867
shoji	translucent sliding door or screen made of paper
Sumo	elaborate and ritualised form of wrestling
tanka	poem of 31 syllables
tenno	Japanese emperor, especially as considered the divinely appointed religious leader
tatami	straw mat or floor covering
torii	gateway of a Shinto temple, essentially two uprights with a crosspiece
zaibatsu	powerful business enterprise or association, in the control of a few leading families

– jar with two handles and a narrow neck, used for wine or oil in ancient Greece and Rome AMPHORA
– large earthenware jar or pot with a wide mouth OLLA
– small ceramic jar formerly used for ointments or medicines GALLIPOT

jargon, specialised language of a group CANT, PATOIS, ARGOT

jarring, inconsistent, discordant INCONGRUOUS

jaundice ICTERUS
– liver disease producing jaundice HEPATITIS
– yellow compound in the bile, causing the yellowish skin in jaundice sufferers BILIRUBIN

Java – orchestra, as in Java, based on chimes and other percussion instruments GAMELAN

jaw, lower jaw, or either part of a beak MANDIBLE
– jaw or cheek of a pig, used as food CHAP
– jaw that is squarish and jutting LANTERN JAW
– jaws, as of a shark or lion MAW
– jaws, or fleshy flaps under the jaw JOWLS
– adjective for the jaw GNATHIC
– corner point on either side of the lower jaw GONION
– having a jutting jaw or jaws PROGNATHOUS
– having correctly positioned jaws ORTHOGNATHOUS
– having or referring to a lower jaw that projects beyond the upper jaw UNDERHUNG, UNDERSHOT
– having or referring to an upper jaw that projects too far beyond the lower jaw OVERSHOT
– paralysis of the jaw muscles LOCKJAW, TETANUS, TRISMUS

-jaw- -GNATH-, -GNATHOUS

jazz based on a traditional New Orleans style, but with more regular melody and rhythm DIXIELAND
– jazz group or other small group of musicians COMBO
– jazz of an early style, involving energetic improvisations BARRELHOUSE
– jazz player or fan HEPCAT

jealously defensive or possessive TERRITORIAL

jeer, shout criticisms or insults at a player, team, or speaker BARRACK
– jeer at, harass and interrupt a public speaker or performer with repeated critical comments or questions HECKLE

Jehovah – set of four Hebrew letters, corresponding to YHWH, and often rendered as Jehovah or Yahweh, representing God's name in the Old Testament TETRAGRAMMATON

jelly – jelly-covered fish or meat dish, served cold GALANTINE
– jelly-like and thick VISCOUS, GELATINOUS
– jelly made from meat or fish stock, used as a garnish or mould ASPIC
– becoming liquid when stirred or shaken, as emulsion paint and some other jelly-like substances do THIXOTROPIC

jellyfish MEDUSA, MEDUSOID
– jellyfish-like sea-creature with long stinging tentacles PORTUGUESE MAN-OF-WAR

jerk – move in a jolting way, jerk along JOUNCE, LURCH
– shake up and down, jerk about JIGGLE, JOGGLE
– uncontrollable muscular jerks or spasms CONVULSIONS, PAROXYSM

jerky, in fits and starts, periodic, occasional INTERMITTENT, SPORADIC, SPASMODIC, FITFUL, EPISODIC
– jerky or hesitant, as uncertain speech is HALTING

jester – jester's cap COCKSCOMB, COXCOMB
– jester's multicoloured clothing MOTLEY
– jester's sceptre, in the form of a stick with a carved head BAUBLE

Jesus See also **Christ**
– Jesus's birth, or a painting, play, or any other representation of it NATIVITY
– Jesus's name or title, as assigned at various times and places THE NAZARENE, PASCHAL LAMB, SACRED HEART, THE REDEEMER, GREAT PHYSICIAN
– Jesus's route from Pilate's judgment hall to the hill of Calvary VIA DOLOROSA
– Jesus's sayings that do not appear in the Gospels AGRAPHA
– Jesus's sufferings prior to and during the Crucifixion PASSION
– ancient Semitic language that was spoken by Jesus ARAMAIC
– family tree showing Jesus's ancestry JESSE TREE
– image of Jesus's face, as on a cloth or badge VERONICA
– picture or sculpture of Jesus wearing the crown of thorns ECCE HOMO
– sores or marks corresponding to Jesus's crucifixion wounds, apparently developing spontaneously in some saintly people STIGMATA
– tableau, as at Christmas, of Jesus's Nativity CRÈCHE, CRIB
– taking down of Jesus from the cross, or a painting or sculpture of this DEPOSITION

jet engine See illustration, page 274, and also **engine**
– device in a jet engine for burning unburnt gas to provide extra power AFTERBURNER
– widening duct in a wind tunnel or jet engine that slows down the flow DIFFUSER

jetty jutting into the sea to control erosion, direct a current, or the like GROYNE, SPUR, BREAKWATER
– jetty or breakwater of stone, protecting a harbour MOLE

Jew See also **Judaism**
– Jew converted nominally to Christianity in medieval Spain or Portugal MARRANO
– Jew in Biblical times, such as Samson, committed by vows to a life of austerity NAZIRITE
– adjective for Jews or Jewish culture JUDAIC
– among Jews, a person who is not a Jew GENTILE, GOY
– homeland of the Jews, symbolic of Jewish aspirations ZION
– hostile towards or prejudiced against Jews ANTI-SEMITIC
– in Nazi doctrine, a Caucasian, especially Nordic, person of non-Jewish descent ARYAN
– Jewish books, art objects, and the like JUDAICA
– mass killing of the Jews by the Nazis THE HOLOCAUST
– massacre, typically organised with official backing, as of Jews in Eastern Europe in former times POGROM
– quarter in European cities inhabited by Jews in former times GHETTO
– temple of the Jews in ancient times TABERNACLE

Jew-, Jewish JUDAEO-

jeweller – jeweller's eyepiece or magnifying glass LOUPE
– jewellers' weighing system for gems, using a 12-ounce pound TROY WEIGHT

jewellery See chart, page 275, and also **gemstone**
– jewellery carried, usually around the neck, as a charm against evil or misfortune AMULET
– jewellery chest or similar small box for valuables CASKET
– jewellery of a delicately worked kind, or a collection of it BIJOUTERIE
– jewellery, especially imitation jewellery, or other goods that are small, cheap, and gaudy BRUMMAGEM, TRINKETS, GEWGAWS, BAUBLES

jet engine

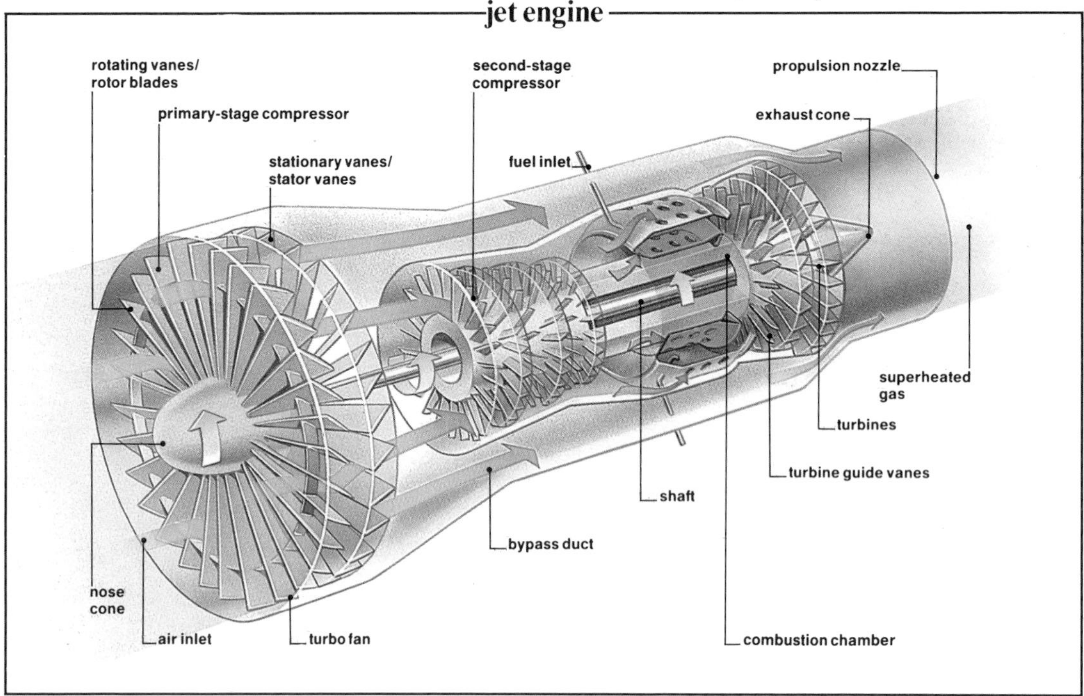

– circular rim securing the gemstone in a ring or other piece of jewellery COLLET
– richly decorated, as with jewels ENCRUSTED

jigsaw – jigsaw-like Chinese puzzle of simple shapes for reassembling into different figures TANGRAM

job, position, or activity particularly suited to a person NICHE
– job at which one is skilled and happy MÉTIER
– job or office that requires little or no work even though providing an income SINECURE, GRAVY TRAIN
– demanding and difficult, as a job might be EXACTING
– easy, comfortable, as a job might be CUSHY
– involving a great deal of sitting, as a job might SEDENTARY
– loss of jobs through their elimination rather than dismissal REDUNDANCY, RETRENCHMENT
– person writing a reference for a job applicant, scholarship candidate, or the like REFEREE
– recruiting of managers or officials from other firms for jobs in a particular firm HEADHUNTING
– report or summary of a person's education and career, as for job applications CURRICULUM VITAE, RÉSUMÉ

jockey – jockey's identifying cap and shirt, typically in bright colours SILKS

join, connect, or fit neatly, tightly, or harmoniously DOVETAIL, FAY
– join, grow or run together, fuse or unify, form a single mass or single unit ACCRETE, AGGLOMERATE, AGGLUTINATE, AGGREGATE, CONGLOMERATE, COALESCE
– join, link, or connect COUPLE
– join, unite, combine, as in business MERGE, AMALGAMATE, CONSOLIDATE, INCORPORATE
– join at a point after approaching from different directions CONVERGE
– join by tying together COLLIGATE, LASH
– join one object to another one, attach, fasten AFFIX, APPOSE
– join or attach by means of a joint or hinge ARTICULATE
– join or attach to something that is larger or more important ANNEX, APPEND
– join or bind together, clamp or connect YOKE, TETHER
– join or blend the versions of a text into a single version CONFLATE
– join or fasten firmly by or as if by bolting together RIVET
– join or hold together, stick or cling COHERE
– join or link into a single group or cluster CONSTELLATE
– join the parts of something together, build up ASSEMBLE
– join two strips of film, wire, rope, or the like together at the ends SPLICE
– joined or grouped together as a pair CONJUGATE, CONJOINT, CONJUNCT
– joined or united into an alliance or league CONFEDERATE
– joined to or associated with a larger grouping or organisation AFFILIATED
– "joined-up writing" CURSIVE
– joining, touching, positioned next to, side by side ABUTTING, CONTIGUOUS, ADJACENT, JUXTAPOSED
– made up of several different components joined together COMPOUND, COMPOSITE, INTEGRATED, SYNTHESISED

joint, consisting of a notch and projection, between items of building material DOWEL, JOGGLE
– joint, formed by a groove, between two pieces of wood, or the groove itself RABBET, REBATE
– joint between two bevelled edges, typically forming a right-angled corner MITRE JOINT
– joint between two surfaces lying flush against each other BUTT JOINT, CARVEL JOINT
– joint in which a rounded edge or knob moves freely within a socket BALL-AND-SOCKET JOINT
– joint in which a strip on the edge of one board fits into a corresponding groove in another TONGUE-AND-GROOVE JOINT

– joint in woodwork, including a wedge-shaped tenon, or the tenon itself DOVETAIL
– joint or branching point on the stem of a plant NODE
– jointed or segmented ARTICULATE
– bending of a joint or limb FLEXION
– clear thick liquid secreted by membranes in joints, tendon sheaths, and similar points in the body SINOVIA
– inflammation of the body's joints, resulting in pain and stiffness ARTHRITIS
– length of tube or bushing for making a pipe joint FERRULE
– notch or groove that houses an inserted part in a joint or hinge MORTISE, GAIN
– projecting end, strip, or wedge on a piece of wood fitting into a corresponding mortise in another piece to form a joint TENON, COG, FEATHER
– small cavity in the body, filled with fluid to reduce friction, as at joints BURSA
– tough fibrous tissue in the joints between bones, gristle CARTILAGE

-joint- -ARTHR-, ARTHRO-

jointly- COM-

joke or drawn-out jokey anecdote whose supposed humour lies in the irrelevance or anticlimax of the punch line SHAGGY-DOG STORY
– joke or humorous antic PLEASANTRY
– joke or teasing remark at someone's expense, taunt GIBE
– joke or prank, gag, jest JAPE
– joking and playful conversation BADINAGE, BANTER, REPARTEE
– joking at the wrong time or in an inappropriate way FACETIOUS
– clever, subtle remark WITTICISM
– clever retort or taunting joke, quip WISECRACK, SALLY
– given to joking, good-humoured, jolly JOCOSE, JOCUND
– intended as a joke, meant in jest JOCULAR
– keeping a straight face or being apparently serious, as when telling a joke DEADPAN
– play a prank or practical joke on, trick COD
– range or stock of jokes, pieces of music, operatic roles, or the like available to a performer REPERTOIRE
– verging on the indelicate or improper, as a joke might be RISQUÉ

jolly See **friendly**, **happy**

journal article printed alone as a separate pamphlet OFFPRINT
– journal or periodical recording the meetings of a learned society, developments in an academic field, or the like ANNALS

journalist, typically one covering the local news in an area, working on a part-time basis STRINGER
– journalist, writer, artist, or the like, who is self-employed and tends to undertake only short-term projects FREELANCE
– journalist doing routine or mediocre work HACK
– journalist or writer SCRIBE

journey, often by foot, that is long and far PEREGRINATION
– journey or short outing, often at a special low fare EXCURSION
– journey that is long and eventful ODYSSEY
– journey's destination or goal BOURN
– long and indirect, as a journey or argument might be CIRCUITOUS
– planned route for a journey ITINERARY
– provisions or allowance for a journey VIATICUM
– requiring a great deal of effort or endurance, as a journey might ARDUOUS, STRENUOUS

joust – aim or thrust a lance in a joust TILT

joy See **delight**

Judaism See chart, page 276

judge in a county court CIRCUIT JUDGE
– judge in a court of law, or his seat or his official position BENCH
– judge of a lower court in Scotland SHERIFF
– judge of lower rank, associate judge PUISNE
– judge or bishop having direct judicial authority ORDINARY
– judge, interpret, or make statements in a priggish or preachy way MORALISE, SERMONISE

JEWELLERY

aigrette	spray of gemstones in the form of a tuft of feathers
cameo	engraved gemstone with a design in relief; medallion with a silhouetted head in relief
carcanet	jewelled necklace or collar, in former times
circlet	ornamental band worn round the head
coronet	crown-shaped headband of precious metal, set with jewels
diadem	royal crown or headband
diamanté	jewellery made from paste, or artificial gemstones, designed to glitter like diamonds
girandole	earring, brooch, or the like with a large gemstone surrounded by smaller ones
intaglio	engraved gemstone with a sunken design
labret	item of jewellery, ornament, or gemstone set into the lip
locket	small, hinged case holding a picture or keepsake, usually worn on a chain round the neck
ouch	jewelled brooch or clasp, in former times
pendant, lavaliere	single ornament, medallion, or item of jewellery worn on a chain round the neck
rivière	necklace of diamonds or other precious stones, typically in a single strand
signet ring	ring bearing a seal or set of initials
solitaire ring	ring with a single gemstone, such as a diamond
tiara	formal semicircular headband of precious metal set with jewels
torque	necklace or collar, typically of twisted metal, in former times

JUDAISM AND JEWISH TERMS

Ashkenazi	Jew of Central or Eastern European descent
bar mitzvah	boy of 13, considered an adult; ceremony marking his attaining adult status
cabala	mystical philosophy based on interpretations of the Old Testament
Chassidim/ Hassidim	sect of extremely orthodox Jews of a mystical tradition
chazan	cantor, chief singer in a synagogue
chutzpah	cheek, effrontery
Diaspora	Jews or Jewish communities living outside Israel; dispersion of the Jews in ancient times
dybbuk	in folklore, evil spirit that enters and controls the body
golem	in folklore, man-made human figure brought to life
goy	gentile, non-Jew
Kaddish	ancient prayer praising God, recited especially by those in mourning
kosher	referring to ritually pure food, prepared and served according to Jewish dietary laws
matzo	unleavened bread, as eaten during Passover
menorah	ceremonial seven-branched candelabrum, symbolising the seven days of the Creation
mezuzah	tiny scroll of parchment inscribed with biblical passages and fixed to doorposts in the homes of observing Jews
minyan	quorum of ten male Jews needed for a fully formal religious service
mitzvah	command imposed by the scriptures; good deed
parev/parve	referring to foods prepared without meat or milk products,.so suitable for any meal
phylacteries/ tefillin	small leather boxes containing parchments inscribed with biblical passages which are tied by leather straps to the head and left arm by devout Jewish men during their morning prayers
Sanhedrin	ancient Jewish high court and council
schlemiel	clumsy, unlucky, or long-suffering person
schmaltz	syrupy sentimentality
schmuck, schnook	foolish or stupid person; person who is easily duped
schnorrer	beggar; sponger
Sephardi	Jew of Spanish or Portuguese descent
shikse	non-Jewish girl; Jewish girl not keeping to Jewish traditions
shofar	ram's horn blown like a trumpet on various holy days
tabernacle	portable sanctuary or tent in which the Ark of the Covenant was carried through the desert by the ancient Jews
tallith	fringed prayer shawl worn by Orthodox Jewish men
Talmud	collection of ancient writings forming the basis of Jewish traditional law and teachings
Torah	the first five books of the Old Testament, the Pentateuch; scroll or parchment containing this text
tref	referring to food considered impure, not in keeping with Jewish dietary laws
yarmulke	skullcap worn by observing Jewish men
yeshiva	school for religious or rabbinical studies
Yiddish	language of Central and Eastern European Jews, based on High German dialects with Hebrew and Slav additions, and written in Hebrew characters

– judge or referee in a dispute ARBITER, ARBITRATOR, ADJUDICATOR, MEDIATOR, MODERATOR
– judge's clerk in the U.S. MARSHAL
– judge's expert assistant or adviser ASSESSOR
– judge's hammer GAVEL
– judge's incidental comment during a case, that is not directly relevant or binding OBITER DICTUM
– judge's minority opinion in a court of law or tribunal DISSENTING JUDGMENT
– judge's order compelling or prohibiting a party from a particular action INJUNCTION
– judge's room for hearing minor cases or conducting private consultations CHAMBERS
– judge's summing-up and address to the jury once all the evidence has been presented in court CHARGE
– judges and law courts collectively JUDICATURE, JUDICIARY
– adjective for judges or justice JUDICIAL, JUDICIARY
– attempt to influence a judge or jury, as by bribes or threats EMBRACERY
– challenge, object to, or reject a judge or juror RECUSE
– experienced lawyer serving as a part-time judge RECORDER
– Muslim judge, or interpreter of Islamic law QADI, CADI
– office, status, or dignity of a judge, king, or nobleman ERMINE
– referring or relating to a judicial system in which the judge in a criminal trial also acts as prosecutor INQUISITORIAL
– referring or relating to a judicial system in which the judge in a criminal trial only considers the case, which is argued by a prosecutor ACCUSATORIAL

– senior civil judge in England, sitting on the Court of Appeal MASTER OF THE ROLLS
– still before a judge or court and therefore not to be discussed in public, as a legal case might be SUB JUDICE
– travelling from place to place, as some circuit judges or preachers do ITINERANT
judgment, good sense DISCRETION
– judgment, legal decision, or the like used as an example or standard justification when treating later cases similarly PRECEDENT
– judgment, opinion ESTIMATION, ASSESSMENT, EVALUATION, VERDICT, APPRAISAL
– adjective for judgment JUDICIAL, JUDICIARY
– having good judgment in practical matters and social situations, tactful DISCREET, PRUDENT, POLITIC, JUDICIOUS
– having good judgment or perception, shrewd or quick-witted ASTUTE, SAGACIOUS
– having good taste or judgment DISCERNING, DISCRIMINATING
– measure or standard used when making a judgment YARDSTICK, CRITERION
– overturning or cancellation as of a law or judgment ANNULMENT, ABROGATION, CASSATION
– place for making judgments, or group who judge or decide TRIBUNAL
– severe in judgment, going strictly by the letter of the law LEGALISTIC, RHADAMANTHINE
judo, karate, kung-fu, and similar self-defence techniques or sports MARTIAL ARTS
– judo expert or one who competes JUDOKA
– judo suit, as worn during contests JUDOGI
– any of the 12 proficiency grades in judo at black-belt level DAN
– full scoring point in a judo bout, resulting in victory directly IPPON
– room or mat for judo practice DOJO
jug, specifically a large two-handled jug PITCHER
– jug, typically large and with a wide mouth EWER
juggling – bottle-shaped wooden club thrown or swung about by persons engaged in juggling and gymnastics INDIAN CLUB
juice of grapes or other fruit before fermentation MUST
– juice of unripe grapes, sour apples, or the like, used in cookery VERJUICE
– squeeze or press out juice or milk EXPRESS, EXTRACT
juicy and usually delicious SUCCULENT, LUSCIOUS, LUSH
jukebox or player piano NICKELODEON
jumble sale – U.S. term for a jumble sale RUMMAGE SALE
jump about, move about playfully FRISK, GAMBOL, FROLIC, ROMP, SPORT, ROLLICK, CAPER, CAVORT
– jump in a sequence, as in a series of logical arguments SALTUS
– jump or bounce back, as after a collision REBOUND
– jump or change of a sudden, dramatic, and vast kind QUANTUM LEAP
– jump or obstacle for a horse, in the form of a hedge and rails, and sometimes a ditch OXER
– jumping, leaping, or dancing SALTATION
– jumping, moving by means of leaping, as frogs and toads usually do SALIENT
– jumping about, disconnected, as conversation might be DESULTORY
– jumping movement of various kinds in ballet ENTRECHAT, JETÉ
– jumping movement of various kinds performed by a horse in dressage CURVET, CAPRIOLE, GAMBADO
– lively jumping movement, as of a spirited horse PRANCE, TITTUP
– pole, with a spring at the base, on which one can bounce or jump along POGO STICK
– relating to or adapted for jumping SALTATORIAL
– springy nylon or canvas sheet used for recreational jumping, acrobatic displays, or the like TRAMPOLINE
Jung – in Jungian psychology, an inherited idea or cast of mind deriving from the collective unconscious ARCHETYPE
– in Jungian psychology, the masculine side of the female personality ANIMAS
– in Jungian psychology, the social mask or front adopted by a person in keeping with his or her outward role in life PERSONA
– in Jungian psychology, the true inner self, or the feminine side of the male personality ANIMA
junior employee in a big organisation MINION
junk, odds and ends, discarded or miscellaneous objects FLOTSAM, JETSAM, BRIC-A-BRAC
– junk dealer, rag-and-bone man TOTTER
Jupiter – adjective for Jupiter JOVIAN
jury, or trial by jury, in Scotland ASSIZE
– jury that is unable to agree on a verdict HUNG JURY
– jury's verdict or similar formal pronouncement DELIVERANCE
– attempt to influence a judge or jury, as by bribes or threats EMBRACERY
– bribe or threaten a jury into reaching a particular verdict SUBORN
– defendant's right to reject certain proposed members of the jury in a criminal trial PEREMPTORY CHALLENGE
– fill a jury, committee, or the like with one's supporters PACK
justice, fairness IMPARTIALITY, EQUITY
– adjective for judges or justice JUDICIAL, JUDICIARY
– deliver or administer justice or the law DISPENSE, RENDER
– distribute or deal out something, especially justice METE OUT, ALLOT
– failure or misapplication of justice MISCARRIAGE
– place or court of justice, or group who judge TRIBUNAL
– power or right to administer laws and justice JURISDICTION
– pretence, caricature, or crudely distorted imitation of something, such as justice TRAVESTY
– the legal system of administering justice JUDICATURE, JUDICIARY
justification, as for a belief WARRANT
– justification, typically a formal defence, as of one's beliefs APOLOGIA
justify, authorise, accept, or permit as rightful LEGITIMATE
– justify, uphold, or excuse by means of arguments, evidence, or proof VINDICATE
– justify in a reasonable or apparently reasonable way, often to suit one's convenience RATIONALISE
jut out, project or overhang PROTRUDE, BEETLE, EXTRUDE

K

kangaroo or other pouch-bearing mammal MARSUPIAL
- kangaroo's pouch MARSUPIUM
- female kangaroo DOE, BLUE FLIER
- male kangaroo BUCK, BOOMER
- young or baby kangaroo JOEY

Kant – thing as it appears, according to Kantian philosophy, as experienced by the senses rather than as understood by reason or intuition PHENOMENON
- thing in itself, according to Kantian philosophy, as understood by reason or intuition rather than as it appears to the senses NOUMENON
- universally applicable moral law, according to Kantian philosophy, that is derived from pure reason CATEGORICAL IMPERATIVE

karate, kung-fu, judo, and similar self-defence techniques or sports MARTIAL ARTS

keel, as on a yacht, that can be raised or lowered CHEESECUTTER

keen See **eager**, **enthusiastic**
- keen and willing, eager SOLICITOUS
- keenness or sharpness of the senses or the mind ACUITY

keep back, hold on to RETAIN
- keep back, keep in good condition, or preserve something, such as food or one's strength CONSERVE
- keep or set aside for future use in long-lasting storage, shelve indefinitely MOTHBALL
- keep safe or secure, protect, as from danger or attack SAFEGUARD
- "keeper" of a magnet ARMATURE
- keeper or caretaker, as of an art collection CUSTODIAN
- keeping, guarding, protection, or imprisonment CUSTODY
- kept temporarily inoperative, set aside, or suspended, as a law might be IN ABEYANCE

kettle – kettle's handle, in the form of a hooped rod BAIL

kettledrum TIMBAL
- percussionist in an orchestra, especially one who plays the kettledrums TIMPANIST
- set of kettledrums TIMPANI

key explaining the symbols used in a map, chart, or the like LEGEND
- key-like tool, typically a small metal bar with a right-angled bend, serving as a spanner or screwdriver for bolts or screws with a special six-sided recess in the head ALLEN KEY, LEX KEY
- key on the keyboard of a piano, organ, or other keyboard instrument DIGITAL
- key or central component or participant LINCHPIN
- key ring consisting of a tight double coil of wire SPLIT RING
- key that fits a variety of locks PASSE-PARTOUT, SKELETON KEY, PASSKEY, MASTER KEY
- key to a simple form of secret code CIPHER
- looped end of a key BOW
- ridge in a lock or keyhole, or corresponding notch on a key WARD
- shield-like plate covering a keyhole, surrounding a door handle, protecting a light switch, or the like ESCUTCHEON
- write or play a musical composition in a different key TRANSPOSE

keyboard instruments See chart

kidnap NOBBLE, ABDUCT
- kidnap, seize RAVISH
- kidnap and press-gang a man, typically after making him drunk or drugging him, for service on a ship SHANGHAI
- tendency of a kidnap victim or other hostage to help or protect his captor STOCKHOLM SYNDROME

kidney – "kidney machine" HAEMODIALYSER, DIALYSER
- kidney pain NEPHRALGIA
- kidney stone, gallstone, or similar solid mass formed in a body cavity or tissue CALCULUS, CONCRETION
- kidney-shaped RENIFORM
- kidneys, liver, and other organs of an animal, especially when regarded as edible OFFAL
- relating to the kidneys RENAL, NEPHRITIC

-kidney- -REN-, RENI-, RENO-

kill, get rid of or destroy utterly, wipe out ANNIHILATE, EXTIRPATE, EXTERMINATE, LIQUIDATE
- kill a prominent politician or public figure ASSASSINATE
- kill an animal, especially a weak one, as to reduce a herd CULL
- kill as a sacrifice, as by burning IMMOLATE
- kill by beheading DECAPITATE
- kill by cutting off the supply of air, strangle, stifle, smother, or suffocate ASPHYXIATE
- kill by strangling, wring the neck of, manhandle SCRAG
- kill or killing by strangulation or by breaking the neck with an iron collar, as used formerly for executions in Spain GARRÓTTE
- kill or destroy a large proportion of DECIMATE
- kill secretively, especially by stifling BURKE
- kill summarily, dispose of promptly DISPATCH
- kill without trial an alleged offender, as an impassioned mob might LYNCH
- killed, ruined, or exhausted FOREDONE
- agent or power that kills, suppresses, or eliminates QUIETUS

killer or killing of a brother or sister FRATRICIDE
- killer or killing of a father PATRICIDE
- killer or killing of a god or goddess DEICIDE
- killer or killing of a human being HOMICIDE
- killer or killing of a king or sovereign REGICIDE
- killer or killing of a mother MATRICIDE
- killer or killing of a parent or other close relative PARRICIDE
- killer or killing of a prophet VATICIDE
- killer or killing of a sister SORORICIDE
- killer or killing of one's wife UXORICIDE
- hired killer HATCHET MAN
- person who kills himself SUICIDE

-killer -CIDE

killing, violence, or bloody fighting, as in films or on television GORE
- killing of a person, as through negligence, that is unlawful though not necessarily murder CULPABLE HOMICIDE

KEYBOARD INSTRUMENTS

accordion	portable instrument with metal reeds controlled by a small keyboard and sounded by a rush of air produced by a pleated bellows
carillon	set of bells, often housed in a tower, still sometimes operated by manual and pedal keyboards
celeste	small, piano-like instrument with a bell-like sound produced by hammers striking metal bars
clavicembalo/ cembalo	"keyed dulcimer", or harpsichord
clavichord	soft-sounding instrument with horizontal strings struck by brass pins
clavier/ klavier	"keyboard", any of various keyboard instruments, such as a piano or harpsichord
Hammond organ	trademark for an electronic organ that sounds like a pipe organ
harmonium	small organ powered by bellows forcing air through the reeds
harpsichord	piano-like instrument with strings plucked by quills or leather plectrums
pedal piano	piano with a pedal keyboard in addition to a manual keyboard, as used for practising the organ
piano accordion	accordion-like instrument with a keyboard for the right hand
Pianola, player piano	piano that plays automatically by means of a mechanism guided by a perforated roll of paper
portative organ	portable medieval organ
regal	small, portable organ of the 16th and 17th centuries
spinet	wing-shaped instrument like a small harpsichord
square piano	box-like piano with horizontal strings
synthesiser, Moog synthesiser	electronic keyboard instrument that can produce a wide range of musical and electronic sounds
virginal	small harpsichord-like instrument
Wurlitzer	trademark for an organ formerly widely used in cinemas

– killing of a person or animal already seriously wounded, as in battle, duel or a bullfight COUP DE GRACE
– killing of a whole racial or social group GENOCIDE
– killing of oneself, or a person who does this SUICIDE
– killing on a huge scale, slaughter, especially in war CARNAGE, MASSACRE, HOLOCAUST
– killing that is unlawful though not deliberate MANSLAUGHTER
– action by one person that provokes another into killing him PROVOCATION
– "mercy killing" EUTHANASIA
– mutually destructive, within a group and ruinous to both sides, as killings within a family or nation are INTERNECINE
– random, wilful, unprovoked, as vandalism or mindless killing is WANTON, GRATUITOUS
– violent, frenzied, and destructive action or behaviour, often involving indiscriminate and wide-scale killing RAMPAGE
– wide-scale killing, typically organised with official backing, as of Jewish communities in Eastern Europe in former times POGROM

-killing -CIDE

kiln for drying hops or malt OAST

kilt worn by Scottish Highlanders FILIBEG
– dagger worn in the stocking of a person dressed in a kilt SKEAN DHU, DIRK
– furry pouch worn in front of the kilt in traditional Highland dress SPORRAN

kimono – wide sash securing a kimono, tied in a large flat bow at the back OBI

kind, charitable, acting or done for the good of others, particularly the poor or distressed ALTRUISTIC, PHILANTHROPIC
– kind and benevolent, as an uncle might be AVUNCULAR
– kind, friendly, good-natured, pleasant to be with AFFABLE, AMIABLE, CORDIAL, GENIAL, WELL-DISPOSED
– kind, generous or charitable, full of goodwill BENEVOLENT, BENEFICENT, BOUNTEOUS
– kind, gentle, mild BENIGN
– kind, sympathetic, agreeable CONGENIAL, SIMPATICO
– kind, sympathetic, merciful, forgiving, full of pity COMPASSIONATE, HUMANE, HUMANITARIAN, MAGNANIMOUS
– kind to a fault, over-lenient, spoiling INDULGENT

kindling in the form of decayed wood or similar dry material TOUCHWOOD, PUNK, TINDER

king – king's assistant or officer who manages the royal household CHAMBERLAIN
– "King's evil", disease of the lymph nodes SCROFULA
– king's wife or queen's husband CONSORT
– attain or ascend the throne, as when a prince becomes king ACCEDE
– attendants or companions of a king or queen RETINUE
– "defender of the faith", one of the titles of the British king or queen FIDEI DEFENSOR
– give up or relinquish the throne formally, as a king or queen might ABDICATE
– killer or killing of a king REGICIDE
– land or other means of support given by a king to a relative, typically a younger son APPANAGE
– office, status, or dignity of a judge, king, or nobleman ERMINE
– relating to a king or queen, royal REGAL
– replacement ruler for a king during his illness, minority, or the like REGENT
– ruling by hereditary right, as a king might LEGITIMATE

– staff carried by a king or queen as a sign of authority SCEPTRE
– title of a king, as used in lawsuits REX
king cobra HAMADRYAD
kingdom REALM
kingfisher in mythology HALCYON
kiss OSCULATE
– kiss, bow, or other gesture of greeting SALUTATION
– kiss of peace at Communion, or the plate used to convey it PAX
– "kissing disease" GLANDULAR FEVER, INFECTIOUS MONONUCLEOSIS
– kiss, pet, and cuddle CANOODLE, NECK
– routine, mechanical, as a kiss might be PERFUNCTORY
kit – standard unit in a kit, as of electronic circuits MODULE
kitchen See also **cooking**
– kitchen implement UTENSIL
– kitchen on a ship, boat, or aircraft GALLEY
– kitchen on the deck of a ship CABOOSE
– kitchen scraps or rubbish SWILL
– menial kitchen servant SCULLION
– relating to cooking or the kitchen CULINARY
– room off or recess in a kitchen for dishwashing, vegetable peeling, and the like SCULLERY
kite – kite-like glider in the form of a single large cloth wing from which the pilot hangs HANG-GLIDER
kitsch – fashionable in an affected or slightly kitschy way CHICHI
– sentimentally or pretentiously quaint or pretty in a slightly kitschy way TWEE
kittens – litter or group of kittens KINDLE
kiwi APTERYX
knave – utter, notorious, as a knave is said to be ARRANT
knee – knee-jerk or similar response performed involuntarily rather than by conscious choice REFLEX, AUTOMATISM
– bounce a child affectionately up and down, especially on one's knees DANDLE
– "housemaid's knee" BURSITIS
– joint corresponding to the knee in the hind leg of a horse or other four-legged mammal STIFLE
kneecap PATELLA
kneel or bend the knees as in worship GENUFLECT
– cushion for kneeling on, especially in church HASSOCK
– cushioned stool for kneeling on during prayer, as by a sovereign at the coronation FALDSTOOL
knick-knack, trinket, or small curio or item of bric-a-brac BIBELOT
knife See chart
– knife blade, cutting part of a tool BIT
– knife handle, hilt HAFT
– knife seller, maker, or repairer CUTLER
– knife sharpener HONE, WHETSTONE
– knives, forks, and spoons CUTLERY
– former term for a dagger or similar knife BODKIN
– sharpen a knife or other cutting tool WHET, HONE
– tongue or prong at the foot of the blade of a knife, tool, or the like for embedding into the handle SHANK, TANG

KNIVES

WORKING KNIVES	
bistoury	**bolo**
cleaver	**bowie knife**
draw-knife	**dagger**
lancet	**dirk**
machete	**dudgeon**
palette knife	**flick knife, switch blade**
panga	**kirpan**
scalpel	**kris**
Stanley knife	**kukri**
Swiss Army knife	**misericord**
WEAPONS	**poniard**
anlace	**shiv**
bayonet	**skean**
	skean dhu
	snickersnee
	stiletto
	trench knife

knight, mounted soldier, or military cadet in France in former times CHEVALIER
– knight commanding men in battle under his own standard or banner BANNERET
– knight of lowest rank in some orders of knighthood COMPANION
– knight wandering about in search of chivalric adventures KNIGHT ERRANT
– knight's expedition, as in search of the Holy Grail QUEST
– knight's page VARLET
– knight's tunic, often bearing his coat of arms and worn over his armour TABARD, SURCOAT
– knights' tournament, involving horse-races and riding displays CAROUSEL
– area set aside for knights to joust LISTS
– attendant and armour-bearer of a knight in medieval times, typically a candidate for knighthood ESQUIRE, ARMIGER
– charge by knights in a medieval tournament COURSE
– duel between knights with lances on horseback JOUST, TILTING MATCH
– perfect, chivalrous and heroic knight PALADIN, GALAHAD
knighthood as a medieval institution, or the qualities of a knight, such as courtesy, honesty and gallantry CHIVALRY
– ceremonial conferring of knighthood, as by a touch of a sword on the shoulder ACCOLADE
– confer knighthood on by ceremonially tapping on the shoulder with a sword DUB
knitted socks, stockings and underwear HOSIERY
– knitted with two kinds of wool, one in the front and one at the back PLATED
knitting See also **sewing**, **embroidery**
– knitting of a long, thin woollen tube, often using a cotton reel for a frame FRENCH KNITTING
– knitting or weaving pattern of diamond shapes in two or more colours ARGYLE
– knitting stitch made by inverting a plain stitch PURL STITCH
– knitting technique for using several differently coloured yarns to produce complex stocking-stitch designs, as for sweaters FAIR ISLE
– knitting technique for using several yarns on the needle at once to produce designs of large stocking-stitch coloured patches INTARSIA
– Parisian women who would continue knitting unconcernedly while attending guillotinings as spectators during the French Revolution TRICOTEUSES
– measure of fineness or density in knitting, as based on the thickness of wool, number of loops per inch, or the like TENSION, GAUGE
knob, as on a shield or ceiling BOSS
– knob, knotty projection, swelling NODE, NODULE
– knob-like growth or projection, as on a legume's root, the skin, or a bone TUBERCLE
– knob-like protuberance, as in the centre of a shield or on a mushroom's cap UMBO
– knob or bump, especially any of the ridges on a handle or object to make it easier to grip KNURL
– knob or head-like part, such as the end of a long bone or insect's antenna CAPITULUM
knobbly – small lump in a yarn or in fabric, producing a knobbly appearance SLUB

knots

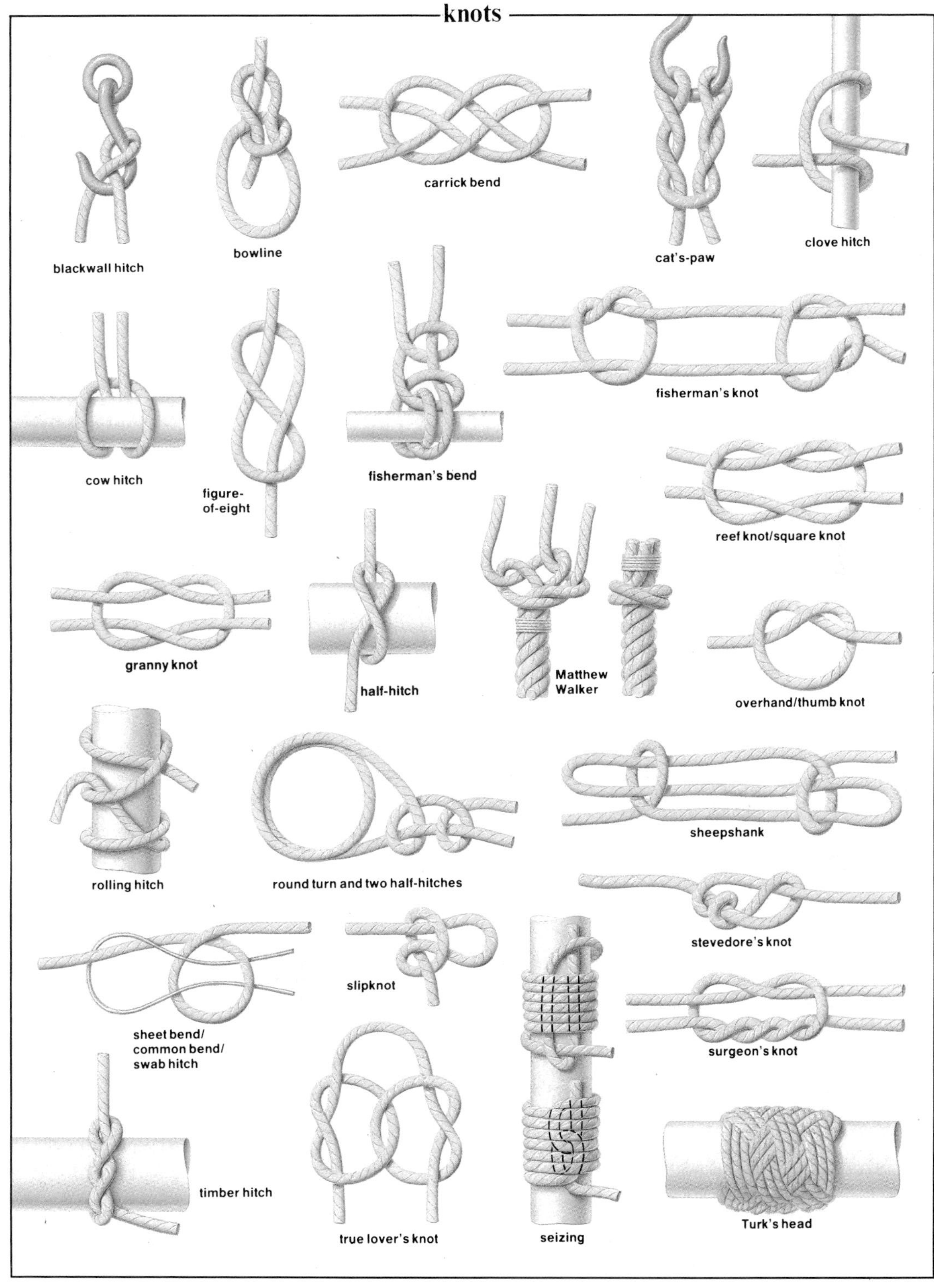

knock down to the ground SPREAD-EAGLE
knock-knees VARUS
knot See illustration
– knot or bump on a tree or timber KNUR
– knot or lump in wool or cloth BURL
– knotted string patterned into ornamental lacework MACRAMÉ
– pin inserted into a knot to stop it slipping TOGGLE

knotty and twisted, as the trunk or branches of a tree might be GNARLED
- knotty problem that can be resolved only by bold or drastic action GORDIAN KNOT
- knotty projection, knob, swelling NODE, NODULE

know See **foretell**
- come to light, become known TRANSPIRE
- know by intuition DIVINE

know-all WISEACRE, WISE GUY

knowledge, or the mental processes used in acquiring it COGNITION
- knowledge after the event HINDSIGHT
- knowledge of a deep or scholarly kind ERUDITION
- knowledge of a formal, unimaginative, drily detailed kind, book-learning PEDANTRY
- knowledge of an instinctive kind INTUITION
- knowledge of appropriate behaviour, especially in social situations SAVOIR-FAIRE
- knowledge of everything, or of a great deal OMNISCIENCE
- knowledge of something before it actually happens PRECOGNITION
- knowledge or learning, as encouraged or represented by the Renaissance HUMANISM
- knowledge or perception by means of a sixth sense, supernatural powers, intuition, telepathy, or the like CLAIRVOYANCE, EXTRASENSORY PERCEPTION, ESP, CRYPTAESTHESIA
- doctrine that all knowledge derives from experience, especially from sense perceptions EMPIRICISM
- doctrine that all knowledge derives from the exercise of reason rather than from experience or perception RATIONALISM
- gather information or knowledge bit by bit GLEAN
- gradual absorption or acquisition, as of knowledge OSMOSIS
- having a deep knowledge of or close acquaintance with INTIMATE
- pretended learning or knowledge, veneer of scholarship SCIOLISM
- relating to intuitive knowledge or supernatural experience TRANSCENDENTAL
- secret, hidden from the uninitiated, as knowledge or understanding of a cult may be ARCANE, OCCULT, ESOTERIC
- slight and fragmented knowledge, as of a foreign language SMATTERING
- spread something widely, such as news or knowledge DISSEMINATE, DIFFUSE, DISPERSE, PROMULGATE
- theory of knowledge, or the philosophical study of the nature of knowledge EPISTEMOLOGY
- traditional knowledge and beliefs LORE

-knowledge -GNOSIS, -NOMY, -SOPHY

knowledgeable, expert or skilful VERSED, WELL-VERSED, AU FAIT
- knowledgeable, made aware, free from prejudice or superstition ENLIGHTENED
- knowledgeable about, or acquainted with CONVERSANT WITH
- knowledgeable person, especially an expert in a particular field of study SAVANT
- conscious, aware, informed, knowledgeable COGNISANT
- person knowledgeable in many subjects POLYMATH, POLYHISTOR

Koran – chapter of the Koran SURA
- Muslim who memorises the entire Koran HAFIZ

kosher – forbidden as food in Judaism, non-kosher, as pork is TREF
- laws concerning kosher food, or the state of being kosher KASHRUTH
- Muslim equivalent of kosher HALAL

kung-fu, karate, judo, and similar self-defence techniques or sports MARTIAL ARTS

L

label or ticket, as fixed on or attached to a parcel DOCKET

laboratory See chart

– laboratory used in establishing scientific or medical facts for use as evidence in legal cases FORENSIC LABORATORY

laborious, troublesome ONEROUS

labour, toil, strenuous physical or mental effort TRAVAIL

– labour carried out by exploited and underpaid workers SWEATED LABOUR

– producing contractions to bring on childbirth, as some labour-inducing medical drugs do OXYTOCIC

– hasten the onset of labour or childbirth, especially by the use of medical drugs INDUCE

– in labour, about to give birth PARTURIENT

labourer, as on a building site NAVVY

– labourer bound by a contract for a specified period INDENTURED LABOURER

– labourer in a slave-like condition, bound to a feudal lord or estate SERF

labyrinth – monster slain by Theseus

LABORATORY EQUIPMENT

alembic	distilling flask or retort used by alchemists in former times
autoclave	chamber for heating substances under high pressure, as in sterilising and cooking
bell jar	bell-shaped cover used to protect delicate instruments or to maintain a controlled environment
Buchner funnel	device for filtering by suction
Bunsen burner	small burner that uses a mixture of gas and air, producing a single concentrated flame
burette	graduated glass tube with a stopcock, used for dispensing known volumes of liquid
centrifuge	machine that separates particles from a suspension by means of high-speed rotation
condenser	device for converting vapour into liquid during distillation
crucible	small ceramic cup used for calcining and melting substances at high temperatures
desiccator	drying chamber, containing chemicals that readily take up water or water vapour
diffusion pump, condensation pump	pump for producing a high vacuum
fractionating column	condenser used to collect the components of a mixture as they boil off at different temperatures
glove box	chamber with protective gloves sealed into the side, in which dangerous radioactive or toxic substances can be handled
Kipp's apparatus	arrangement of three linked glass vessels used for the controlled production of a gas such as hydrogen sulphide by the action of a liquid on a solid
Leyden jar	glass jar whose lower walls are lined inside and outside with tin foil to form an electrostatic capacitor
Liebig condenser	device for condensing a vapour by passing it through a tube inside another tube through which a coolant, usually water, passes
Nicol prism	two prisms cut and cemented together in such a way that waves of light passing through them vibrate in a single plane
Petri dish	shallow, flat, round glass dish with a lid, used especially for culturing microorganisms
pipette	glass tube of known capacity, used for transferring liquid
rectifier	condenser for separating or purifying a liquid
retort	round flask with a bent over, narrowing neck, used especially for distillation
wash bottle	sealed container with two outlet tubes, from which liquid is dispensed by blowing down one tube
Wimshurst machine	demonstration apparatus generating static electricity by the rotation of its two insulating discs in opposite directions
Winchester, Winchester quart	cylindrical, narrow-necked glass bottle with a capacity of about 2 litres ($3\frac{1}{2}$ pints), used for storing and carrying liquids
Woulfe bottle	glass container with two or more necks, used for passing a gas through a liquid

in the Labyrinth, in Greek mythology MINOTAUR

lace – lace-like ornamental metalwork FILIGREE
- lace-like or criss-cross pattern or design TRACERY
- lace made by looping a single thread by means of a small hand shuttle TATTING
- lace made by winding thread around pins stuck into a small cushion in a set pattern BOBBIN LACE, PILLOW LACE
- lace made with a needle on a paper pattern NEEDLEPOINT, POINT LACE
- lace of a heavy, large-patterned kind on a backing of fabric rather than netting GUIPURE
- lace or embroidery edging PURL
- lace or linen formerly worn in a frill by women round the neck or shoulders TUCKER
- background of a design, as in lacework FOND
- background pattern or mesh used in lacemaking RÉSEAU
- coarse lace with a simple geometric pattern TORCHON LACE
- edging of tiny loops, as on ribbon or lace PICOTS
- lacework of knotted string MACRAMÉ
- fine ornamental lace of various kinds BRUSSELS LACE, DUCHESSE LACE, CHANTILLY LACE, MALINES, MECHLIN, HONITON, MIGNONETTE, VALENCIENNES
- metal or plastic tip on a ribbon, shoelace, or the like AGLET
- pleated or gathered strip of lace or fabric, used as a trimming RUCHE, RUFFLE
- thread or loop joining sections of a lace or needlework pattern BRIDE, BAR

lack, insufficiency, shortage, scarcity SPARSITY, DEARTH, PAUCITY, DEFICIENCY
- lack, need, fault, or failure to perform some duty DEFAULT
- lack or loss of basic comforts or of the essentials of life PRIVATION
- extreme poverty, lack of all comforts and essentials PENURY, DESTITUTION

lack- DIS-, MIS-

lacking, incomplete, or insufficient DEFICIENT
- completely lacking, entirely without DESTITUTE OF, DEVOID OF

lacking- AP-, APO-, UN-

lacquer or glossy black varnish JAPAN
- lacquer or similar preservative applied to a drawing, as to prevent smudging FIXATIVE

lacrosse stick, consisting of a racket-like staff bearing a shallow net CROSSE
- keep the ball in the net of the stick in lacrosse while running CRADLE

lad, adolescent boy STRIPLING

ladder on a ship, usually of rope but with rigid rungs JACOB'S LADDER
- ladder or portable staircase on the side of a ship ACCOMMODATION LADDER
- ladder with rope sides and two or three rungs of metal or wood, used in mountaineering ÉTRIER
- any of the rungs of a ladder SPOKE, STAVE
- scaling, by ladders, of a castle wall, rampart, or the like, as during a military attack ESCALADE
- upright post or strut of a ladder, door frame, window sash, or the like STILE

ladybird or related beetle having club-shaped antennae CLAVICORN

lady's fingers OKRA, BHINDI, GUMBO

lag, fall behind or stray STRAGGLE

lake in a hollow in the mountains TARN
- lake in the area formed by a loop in a river OXBOW LAKE
- lake or bay in Ireland LOUGH
- lake or bay in Scotland LOCH
- lake or pond MERE
- adjective for a lake LACUSTRINE
- scientific study of lakes and other bodies of fresh water LIMNOLOGY

Lama – Grand Lama of Tibet DALAI LAMA, PANCHEN LAMA, TASHI LAMA

lamb See illustration
- lamb reared as a pet COSSET
- leg of mutton or lamb GIGOT

Lamb of God, picture of a lamb representing Christ AGNUS DEI

lame or limping HALTING
- lameness, limp CLAUDICATION

lament, funeral hymn, or poem of mourning on the occasion of someone's death DIRGE, ELEGY, THRENODY, MONODY
- lament, poem of grief, usually over lost love COMPLAINT
- lament or mourn for the dead KEEN
- lamentation or elaborate complaint JEREMIAD

lamp See also **light**
- lamp gauze drum or dome that increases the light of a gas lamp when heated MANTLE
- safety lamp formerly used by coal miners DAVY LAMP

lance – aim or thrust a lance in a joust TILT
- duel between mounted knights, with lances JOUST, TILTING MATCH
- lower a lance to the attacking position, as in a joust COUCH

land See also **estate**, **property**
- land, buildings, and other immovable property REAL PROPERTY, REAL ESTATE, REALTY
- land belonging to a church, and typically granted to a clergyman as part of his benefice GLEBE
- land formation, especially by the deposit of sediment from a river ALLUVION
- land that is gained from the sea, a river, or a lake, as by natural tide changes DERELICTION
- land in border areas MARCHLANDS, MARCHES
- land of luxury and idleness in medieval legend COCKAIGNE
- land of perfect peace and happiness, utopia SHANGRI-LA
- land of plenty and contentment GOSHEN
- land or ground, especially in respect of its physical characteristics TERRAIN
- land or other means of support given by a king to a relative, typically a younger son APPANAGE
- land or settlement that is reserved for a minority community, such as the North American Indians RESERVATION
- land owned or the ownership of it DOMAIN
- land reclaimed from the sea or a lake and protected by dykes, especially in Holland POLDER
- land used for camping or grazing animals by ox-wagon travellers OUTSPAN
- absolute ownership of inherited land, allowing the owner to dispose of it as he or she wishes FEE SIMPLE
- appropriation of land, especially common land, by fencing it in ENCLOSURE
- come in to land past the end of the runway, as an aircraft might OVERSHOOT
- come in to land short of the runway, as an aircraft might UNDERSHOOT
- concluding of all legal formalities in the purchase of a house or land COMPLETION
- divide land or property into several small units COMMINUTE
- dry, as land might be ARID
- flood land for irrigation purposes FLOAT
- government's right to take over private land or property for public use, compensation usually being paid EMINENT DOMAIN
- inspect or survey a stretch of

lamb cuts

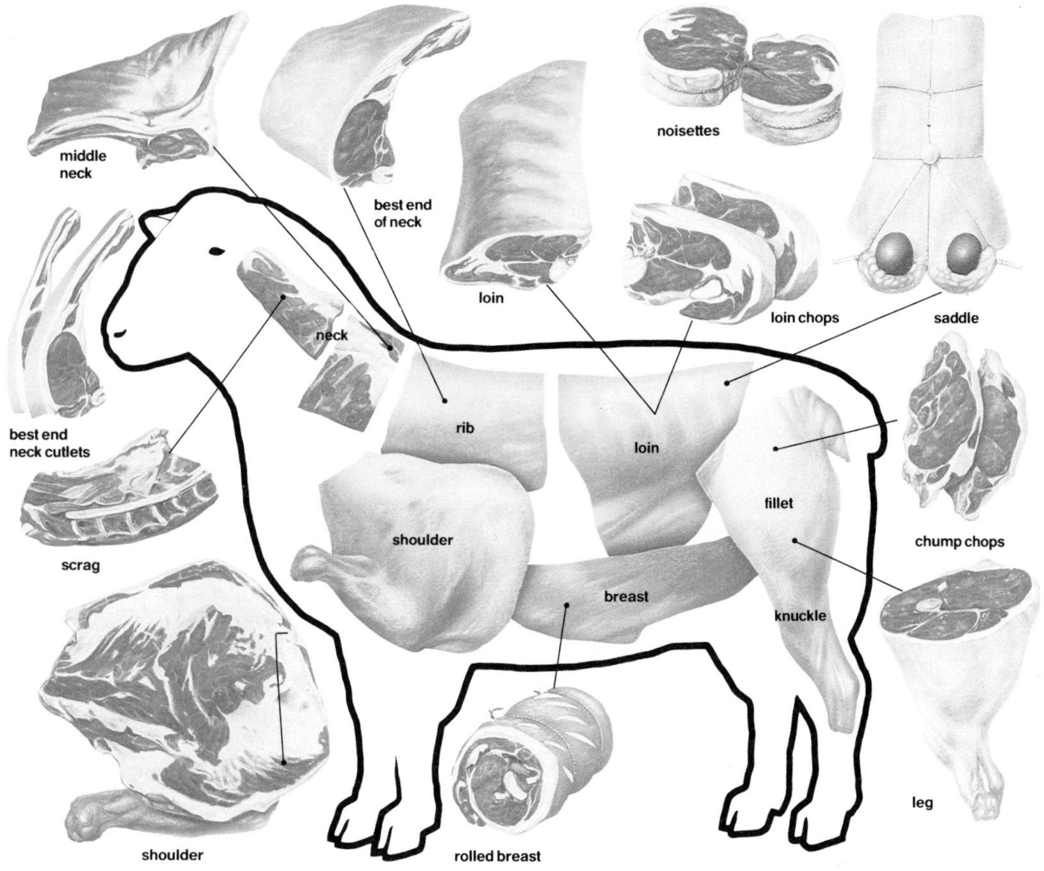

land, an enemy's positions, or the like RECONNOITRE, RECCE
– levelling of land, as by erosion or deposition GRADATION
– measure, or measure and map, the heights and distances of an area of land SURVEY
– narrow strip of land, as for allowing an inland country access to the sea CORRIDOR
– narrow strip of land extending into the sea or a lake from the mainland PENINSULA
– narrow strip of land from one territory, state, or the like projecting into another PANHANDLE
– narrow strip of land joining two larger land areas ISTHMUS
– northern part of the Earth's hypothetical original landmass or supercontinent Pangaea LAURASIA
– outline or shape, as of a stretch of land CONTOUR
– ownership of land, as by churches, that is fixed forever, preventing sale or transfer MORTMAIN, DEAD HAND
– physical features of land or a region TOPOGRAPHY
– ploughable, and suitable for cultivating crops, as land might be ARABLE
– ploughed but left unseeded, as farming land might be, to regain fertility for a season FALLOW
– policy of regaining land that is historically or culturally connected to one's nation but now under foreign control IRREDENTISM
– qualified ownership of inherited land, restricting its disposal to a specified heir or heirs FEE TAIL
– relating to land, farming, or the country AGRARIAN
– relating to or living on dry land TERRESTRIAL
– return of land, in former times, to the Crown or a feudal lord in the absence of legal heirs ESCHEAT
– right of use over another person's land or property for specific purposes SERVITUDE
– right of way or similar legal right over another person's land EASEMENT
– share of the proceeds paid to a landowner for the use or development of his property ROYALTY
– small triangular piece of land GORE
– southern part of the Earth's hypothetical original landmass or supercontinent Pangaea GONDWANALAND
– stretch of land TRACT
– stretch of scrubby open land HEATH
– take away a person's private property or land, especially for public ownership EXPROPRIATE
– touching, adjoining, be positioned next to, as pieces of land might be ABUTTING, ADJACENT, CONTIGUOUS
– turning desert, marshes, sub-

merged land, or the like into useful land fit for living on or farming RECLAMATION
– use and possession of one's own land, in law DEMESNE
– wide, open stretch of land, sea, or sky EXPANSE
– year in which farm land is left to lie fallow, observed every seventh year by the ancient Jews SABBATICAL YEAR

landed gentry class, or government by it SQUIREARCHY

landlord or landlady, person letting property under a lease LESSOR
– landlord or other person whose income is derived chiefly from rents or investments RENTIER
– landlord's agent STEWARD, BAILIFF
– landlord's policy of exploiting and intimidating slum tenants RACHMANISM

landowner in Scotland LAIRD
– landowner's agent STEWARD, BAILIFF
– landowning gentleman in medieval England FRANKLIN

language See also **grammar**, **style**
– language, based on a mix of a colonial and an indigenous language, that has developed into a mother tongue CREOLE
– language, based on a simplified mix of two or more languages, used for basic communication PIDGIN
– language, such as Chinese, that distinguishes words by their pitch or intonation TONE LANGUAGE
– language, typically extinct and reconstructed by scholars, that is the parent language of a group of later languages URSPRACHE
– language as actually used, rather than as an abstract system PAROLE
– language as an abstract system shared by a speech community LANGUE
– language element, word or part of a word, with a fixed meaning and not divisible into smaller elements MORPHEME
– language expert, a speaker of several languages, or person who studies language LINGUIST
– language family to which English belongs, embracing most European languages and many Indian and Iranian languages INDO-EUROPEAN
– language group or sub-family descended from Latin, including French, Italian, and Spanish ROMANCE
– language of a literary, persuasive, or oratorical kind, or the study of its structure and effects RHETORIC
– language of an earlier stage of development, no longer in everyday use ARCHAISM
– language of an elegant rhetorical style PERIODS
– language of an obscene kind BAWDRY
– language of the people, informal everyday speech VERNACULAR, VULGATE
– language or speech exclusive to a profession or other group JARGON, CANT, ARGOT
– language or speech pattern of an individual person IDIOLECT
– language or speech pattern of a particular regional or social group DIALECT
– language spoken between people who have different mother tongues LINGUA FRANCA, KOINE
– language study based on analysis of actual usage rather than on standards of correctness DESCRIPTIVISM
– language study based on ideas of correctness rather than on actual usage PRESCRIPTIVISM, NORMATIVE GRAMMAR
– language style appropriate to a particular social setting or use REGISTER
– language teaching using very little of the pupils' mother tongue or the formal grammar DIRECT METHOD
– language that is ambiguous or deliberately distorted for propaganda purposes NEWSPEAK
– language that is long-winded, indirect, or evasive CIRCUMLOCUTION, PERIPHRASIS, PROLIXITY
– language that is pompous and showy FUSTIAN, BOMBAST, EUPHUISM, GRANDILOQUENCE
– language used in a graceful, moving, or effective way ELOQUENCE
– ability to use and understand spoken language ORACY
– actual forms of expression in a language USAGE
– adherence to traditional standards or rules, as in the use of language PURISM
– adjective for language or languages LINGUISTIC
– adopt a foreign term fully into the language NATURALISE
– ancient Semitic language, that was spoken by Jesus ARAMAIC
– bureaucratic language or official jargon that is wordy and difficult to understand GOBBLEDEGOOK, OFFICIALESE
– collection of texts in a language used for grammatical analysis, compiling dictionaries, and the like CORPUS
– commonly used, popular, as the ordinary form of a language is DEMOTIC, VERNACULAR
– conversational, informal, characteristic of casual spoken language COLLOQUIAL
– feeling for language, an "ear" for what is correct or appropriate SPRACHGEFÜHL
– gradual change in a language DRIFT
– international language of the sea, used by naval and maritime officers for communication, based on simple English SEASPEAK
– international language of various kinds, based typically on common roots from several European languages ESPERANTO, IDO, INTERGLOSSA, INTERLINGUA, NOVIAL, VOLAPÜK
– knowledge or general ability underlying one's use of language, human faculty of using language in general COMPETENCE
– line on a language map linking places using the same distinctive word or pronunciation ISOGLOSS
– perfect or effortless, as one's use of a foreign language might be FLUENT
– referring to a language, such as English or Chinese, using word order or function words rather than inflections to indicate grammatical structure ISOLATING, ANALYTICAL
– referring to a language, such as Latin or Russian, using inflections rather than word order or function words to indicate grammatical structure SYNTHETIC
– referring to a language, such as Turkish or Swahili, in which complex words are formed by the regular addition of unchanging component units AGGLUTINATIVE
– relating to a mix of languages, as in some witty verse MACARONIC
– relating to events or phenomena, such as language usage, at a given point in time without regard to the historical background SYNCHRONIC
– relating to events or phenomena, such as language usage, viewed as a process of historical development DIACHRONIC
– relating to meaning in language SEMANTIC
– slight and fragmented knowledge, as of a foreign language SMATTERING

– speaking, knowing, or involving only one language MONOLINGUAL, MONOGLOT
– speaking, knowing, or involving several languages MULTILINGUAL, POLYGLOT
– speaking, knowing, or involving two languages BILINGUAL
– statistical study of the historical relationship between different languages GLOTTOCHRONOLOGY
– study or science of grammar in language, or the grammar of a sentence, phrase, or the like SYNTAX
– study or science of language LINGUISTICS, PHILOLOGY
– study or science of language meaning SEMANTICS
– study or science of language sounds PHONETICS, PHONOLOGY, PHONEMICS
– study or science of language use, including contexts, behaviour of speakers, and the like PRAGMATICS
– style of expressing oneself in language, way of putting things PHRASEOLOGY, DICTION
– text used by linguists for analysing features of language beyond the level of single sentences DISCOURSE
– using language clearly and effectively ARTICULATE

language- LINGU-, -LINGUA-, -GLOT

-language speaker -PHONE

lantern made from a pumpkin JACK-O'-LANTERN
– lantern with a thick glass lens BULL'S EYE

lapel, turned-back cuff, or other part of clothing showing the reverse side REVERS
– decorative chain or pendant worn on the lapel CHATELAINE

lapse, uncharacteristic piece of behaviour or thinking ABERRATION, BRAINSTORM

large See also **huge**, **fat**
– large, bulky, ungainly and heavy PONDEROUS, HULKING
– large, considerable, as in size or number AMPLE, SUBSTANTIAL
– large, grand, impressive IMPOSING, MONUMENTAL, GRANDIOSE
– large, spacious, roomy, extensive COMMODIOUS, CAPACIOUS, VOLUMINOUS
– large, sturdy and thickset BURLY
– large or long, and disorganised, as a house or speech might be RAMBLING
– large-scale and indiscriminate, as slaughter might be WHOLESALE

large- MACRO-, MAXI-, MEGA-, MEGALO-

larger- SUPER-

larks – flock of larks EXALTATION

larva See also **insect**
– larva, as of the mayfly or dragonfly, that develops directly into the adult rather than going through the pupal stage NYMPH
– larva of an oyster or other bivalve mollusc SPAT
– larva of the mayfly or similar insect, living in water NAIAD

laser – laser-produced 3D photo or pattern HOLOGRAM

lasso – lasso-like device of a rope with weights attached, used in South America for catching cattle or game by snaring the legs BOLA
– lasso used for catching livestock LARIAT

last, final, concluding ULTIMATE
– last but one, second to last PENULTIMATE
– last but two, third from last ANTEPENULTIMATE
– last part of something, the end OMEGA

last-born – right of the last-born son to inherit the estate ULTIMOGENITURE, BOROUGH-ENGLISH

last resort, expedient adopted for want of any alternative PIS ALLER
– last resort, of unsuspected power or effectiveness TRUMP CARD
– as a last resort, if all else fails IN EXTREMIS

Last Supper – cup or platter used, according to medieval legend, by Jesus at the Last Supper GRAIL, HOLY GRAIL, SANGRAAL
– room in which the Last Supper took place CENACLE

last things – branch of theology dealing with last things, such as heaven and hell ESCHATOLOGY

lasting only a short time, short-lived, fleeting EPHEMERAL, TRANSITORY
– lasting throughout the year, as high snows might PERENNIAL

late, after the appropriate time, as thanks or a gift might be BELATED
– late, past the due time of arrival or return, as a train or library book might be OVERDUE
– late-blooming period of contentment or tranquil success, as in the autumn of one's life INDIAN SUMMER
– late in acting, tending to postpone or delay DILATORY
– late in arriving, unpunctual, or slow and reluctant TARDY
– late in paying rent or some other debt IN ARREARS
– delay, be late or slow in doing something TARRY
– delay, put off a duty or the like till later PROCRASTINATE

later SUBSEQUENTLY

later- META-, POST-

latest fashion DERNIER CRI

lathe with a swivelling attachment holding a number of tools for successive operations CAPSTAN LATHE, TURRET LATHE
– rotating shaft, as in a lathe or other machine tool ARBOR, SPINDLE, MANDREL
– vice or clamp used to hold a tool or workpiece, as in a drill or lathe CHUCK

Latin See chart, pages 288-289, and also **legal terms**
– Latin and Greek literature CLASSICS
– Latin as spoken by the common people in ancient Rome, from which the Romance languages developed VULGAR LATIN
– Latin version of the bible by Saint Jerome, authorised by the Roman Catholic Church VULGATE
– relating to writings mixing a modern language with Latin or mock-Latin MACARONIC

Latin America – adjective for Spain and Latin America HISPANIC
– large farming estate, as in Latin America or ancient Rome LATIFUNDIUM
– ranch or ranch-house in Spain or in Latin America HACIENDA

laugh See also **mock**
– laugh, giggle, or smile in a silly, coy, and affected way SIMPER
– laugh in a snide, malicious, or slightly stifled way SNIGGER, SNICKER, TITTER, WHICKER
– laugh inappropriately on stage, as an actor might, or cause another actor to laugh CORPSE
– laugh loudly, make belly laughs GUFFAW, CACHINNATE
– laugh with a throaty chuckle CHORTLE
– loud, unrestrained or coarse laugh HORSE LAUGH, BELLY LAUGH

laughable, absurd LUDICROUS
– laughable, relating to laughter, or inclined to laugh RISIBLE
– laughably inadequate, insultingly small or mean, as a proposed pay increase might be DERISORY

laughing jackass KOOKABURRA

laughter or enjoyment MIRTH, GLEE
– laughter that is loud and uninhibited HILARITY
– fit of uncontrollable laughter CONVULSIONS
– spreading from one person to another easily, as laughter or enthusiasm might INFECTIOUS, CONTAGIOUS

laundry – device for squeezing water from wet laundry by pressing it between rollers WRINGER, MANGLE

LATIN WORDS AND PHRASES

a fortiori	all the more so, with even greater reason
a priori	self-evident, known independently of experience; from the general to the particular, as deductive reasoning is
ab ovo	"from the egg": from the beginning
ad hoc	"for this thing": for a particular purpose or occasion, as a committee might be
ad hominem	"to the man": directed at someone personally, as criticism might be
ad lib, ad libitum	"at pleasure": freely, unscripted, improvised
ad nauseam	to the point of disgust
aegrotat	"he is ill": sickness certificate
alma mater	"nourishing mother": one's old school, college, or university
alumnus	"foster child": former pupil or student, as of an alma mater
annus mirabilis	year of wonders, great achievements or disasters, or the like
bona fide	"in good faith": genuine or sincere
casus belli	"cause of war": justification or cause of a dispute
cave	"beware": look out, be careful
caveat emptor	"let the buyer beware": the principle that a purchaser cannot assume that his purchase will be exactly as hoped
compos mentis	"of sound mind": sane
cum laude	"with praise": referring to a good examination result or degree
curriculum vitae	"course of life": outline or resumé, as on a job application, of one's qualifications and career
de facto	in reality; regardless of legal status
de jure	in accordance with the law, by right, legally
de profundis	"from the depths": in deep despair
deo volente, d.v.	"God willing"
deus ex machina	"god out of a machine": person or thing that suddenly resolves a problem; device providing a contrived resolution in a play
ex gratia	"out of goodness": referring to a payment made as a favour, not an obligation
ex libris	"from the books": phrase used before the owner's name on bookplates
felo de se	"felon of himself": suicide
festina lente	"hasten slowly": more haste, less speed
genius loci	"spirit of the place": atmosphere of a place and its influence on visitors
in loco parentis	"in the place of a parent": having the responsibilities or role of a parent
in medias res	"into the middle of things": the way a story or play might begin
in propria persona	in person, personally

– laundry basket HAMPER
– laundryman in India DHOBI

lava in a solidified sheet COULÉE
– lava rock of a glassy black type OBSIDIAN, BASALT
– molten rock material which flows out as lava on the surface MAGMA
– referring to rocks formed from solidified lava IGNEOUS
– solid lava fragments from a volcano SCORIAE, CINDERS, SLAG

lavatory, especially one in an outhouse PRIVY
– lavatory in which matter is later covered with earth EARTH CLOSET
– lavatory at a military base or camp LATRINE
– lavatory or privy behind a dormitory in an abbey or monastery REREDORTER
– lavatory tank, water tank in the roof, or similar container CISTERN
– communal lavatories and bathroom facilities at a military base or camp ABLUTIONS
– device controlling water levels, as in a lavatory cistern, based on a floating ball connected to a valve BALL COCK
– euphemistic term for a lavatory COMFORT STATION
– old term for a lavatory JAKES
– pipe carrying sewage from a lavatory SOIL PIPE
– ship's lavatory HEAD
– slang term for a lavatory KHAZI, CARZEY, THUNDERBOX, LOO

law See also **legal**, **court**, **trial**
– law, or order that has the force of law DECREE, EDICT, PROCLAMATION, RESCRIPT, FIAT, UKASE
– law, rule, or code of laws CANON
– law as relating to practice and procedure rather than legal principles ADJECTIVE LAW
– law as relating to rights, duties, and legal principles rather than practice and procedure SUBSTANTIVE LAW
– law based on custom and court decisions rather than written codes COMMON LAW
– law based on judgments in earlier cases rather than strictly on statutes CASE LAW
– law courts and judges collectively JUDICATURE, JUDICIARY
– law-enforcement officer in a U.S. county SHERIFF
– law formally enacted and recorded STATUTE
– law giving special powers to a minister, government department, or the like ENABLING ACT
– "law" or mock-scientific prin-

in toto	completely, as a whole, totally	**per se**	"by itself", in itself, as such, intrinsically
infra dig, infra dignitatem	beneath one's dignity	**persona non grata**	"person not acceptable": person, especially a diplomat, whose presence is not welcome
inter alia	among other things		
ipso facto	"by that fact": as an immediate consequence of that fact or act	**pons asinorum**	"bridge of asses": test for beginners; problem that the slow-witted cannot solve
magnum opus	"great work": major work of a writer, composer, or the like	**prima facie**	at first sight; on the face of it
mea culpa	"my fault": acknowledging one's guilt	**pro rata**	in proportion
mirabile dictu	"wonderful to relate": amazingly	**quid pro quo**	"something in return for something else": a favour in return, a substitution or fair exchange
modus operandi	"way of working": method of proceeding with a task		
modus vivendi	"way of living": compromise or living arrangement between people or parties of differing interests	**quod erat demonstrandum, Q.E.D.**	"which was to be demonstrated": as added to the end of a proof to show that the point has been made
mutatis mutandis	with the necessary or appropriate changes having been made	**rara avis**	"rare bird": unusual or exceptional person or thing
ne plus ultra	"no more beyond": the limit; perfection	**sine die**	"without a day": at no set date, indefinitely
nil desperandum	"nothing to be despaired of": don't despair; never say die	**sine qua non**	"without which not": a necessity, something indispensable
non sequitur	"it does not follow": an illogical remark or inapplicable statement	**status quo**	the present position, the existing state of affairs
obiter dictum	"said by the way": an incidental remark	**sub rosa**	"under the rose": secretly, confidentially, privately
pace	"by leave of": as used in front of someone's name as an apology when contradicting him	**sui generis**	"of its own kind": unique
		victor ludorum	"winner of the games": sports champion
per capita	measured "by head" of the population, per person	**vox populi**	"the voice of the people": public opinion

ciple to the effect that if anything can go wrong it will MURPHY'S LAW
– "law" or mock-scientific principle to the effect that employees tend to get promoted from positions they are competent in until they reach their level of incompetence PETER PRINCIPLE
– "law" or mock-scientific principle to the effect that work expands to fill the time available for its completion PARKINSON'S LAW
– law or principle of all things, cosmic or natural law in Hindu philosophy DHARMA
– law or rule no longer enforced though still officially valid DEAD LETTER
– law setting a time limit for enforcing a right or bringing a legal action STATUTE OF LIMITATIONS
– laws framed into a complete system, legal code PANDECTS, CANON
– laws of inheritance of characteristics in genetics MENDEL'S LAWS
– lawful, legal, in accordance with the law LEGITIMATE, LICIT
– lawmaking, or a law or laws made by means of drafting and enacting LEGISLATION
– administer justice or the law DISPENSE
– against the law ILLEGITIMATE, ILLICIT, ILLEGAL
– applying to the past, or taking effect as from a date in the past, as a law might RETROACTIVE, RETROSPECTIVE, EX POST FACTO
– body of legal rules based on natural justice and fairness, supplementing and moderating common and statute law EQUITY
– branch of government authorised to make laws LEGISLATURE
– branch of government responsible for carrying out the laws EXECUTIVE, ADMINISTRATION
– breaking of a law or regulation VIOLATION, BREACH, INFRINGEMENT, TRANSGRESSION, INFRACTION, CONTRAVENTION, FLOUTING
– breaking or violation of civil law, other than breach of contract TORT
– bring a law into operation by official publication of it PROMULGATE
– bringing a lawsuit, pursuing a case in court LITIGATION
– by right, legally, according to law DE JURE
– cancel or invalidate a law RESCIND, REVOKE, REPEAL, ANNUL, QUASH
– civilian who arrogates law-

enforcement and punitive powers to himself VIGILANTE
– collect and arrange laws, rules, principles, or the like into a comprehensive system CODIFY
– confirm a law, ruling, or the like RATIFY, SANCTION
– court case debated as a training exercise by law students MOOT
– draft and enact laws LEGISLATE
– exemption or release from a rule, law, obligation, or the like DISPENSATION
– expert on the law or legal principles JURIST
– full listing of laws or court rulings DIGEST
– gap or oversight, as in a law or contract, making evasion possible LOOPHOLE
– implying or setting standards of acceptability, as a strict law or a prescriptive grammar does NORMATIVE
– in force, as laws might be OPERATIVE
– injustice due to inconsistencies, bias, or unfairness, as in a law INEQUITY
– invalid, inoperative, or powerless, as a disregarded law or regulation is NUGATORY
– making or relating to rules or laws PRESCRIPTIVE
– official doorkeeper in a court of law, parliament, or the like USHER
– overturning or cancellation, as of a law or judgment ANNULMENT, ABROGATION, CASSATION
– person or group that is sued by another, party against which a lawsuit is brought DEFENDANT
– person or group that sues another, party initiating a lawsuit PLAINTIFF
– philosophy or the science of law JURISPRUDENCE
– power or right to administer laws and justice JURISDICTION
– relating to criminal law and court cases FORENSIC
– relating to, permitted, or enforced by the law LEGAL
– sessions of the law courts in English and Welsh counties in former times ASSIZES
– severe and literal in interpreting the law LEGALISTIC, RHADAMANTHINE
– very harsh, as laws or punishments might be DRACONIAN

-laws- -NOM-, NOMO-, -NOMY

lawn or grassy meadow SWARD

lawyer See also **barrister**, **solicitor**
– lawyer in a paid full-time position presiding in a magistrate's court STIPENDIARY MAGISTRATE
– lawyer or group of lawyers giving legal advice, especially a barrister in a court case COUNSEL
– lawyer who pleads a case on behalf of a client in court ADVOCATE
– lawyer who uses unscrupulous and dubious methods PETTIFOGGER
– lawyer contracted to a solicitor as assistant or trainee ARTICLED CLERK
– duty lawyer's consultation with or hiring by the accused in the court building DOCK BRIEF
– government lawyer who argues the case against the accused in a criminal trial PUBLIC PROSECUTOR
– seeking of or meeting for advice, as from a doctor or lawyer CONSULTATION
– U.S. term for a lawyer ATTORNEY

laxative, bowel stimulant CATHARTIC, EVACUANT, PHYSIC, PURGATIVE, APERIENT
– medicinal salts used as a vigorous laxative and for reducing inflammation EPSOM SALTS

lay down as a condition in an agreement or contract STIPULATE

layer, as of folded cloth or paper PLY
– layer, as of rock, archaeological remains, or skin cells STRATUM
– layer of green oxide forming on a copper or bronze surface PATINA, VERDIGRIS, AERUGO
– layer on or near the outside, as of a root or stem, or brain or kidney CORTEX
– layer or thin plate or scale of plant or animal tissue LAMELLA, LAMINA
– having concentric layers such as those of the onion TUNICATE
– split or beat into thin layers, or join several layers together LAMINATE

-layered -FOLIATE

layout or design of a book or magazine FORMAT

laziness IDLENESS, INDOLENCE
– laziness, aversion to work or effort SLOTH, ACCIDIE
– laziness, dullness of mind, indifference, lack of emotion or interest APATHY, HEBETUDE
– laziness, indifference, sluggishness LETHARGY
– laziness, torpor, exhaustion LANGUOR, LASSITUDE

lazy IDLE, INDOLENT
– lazy, careless, unconcerned or slack LAX, REMISS, LACKADAISICAL, INSOUCIANT
– lazy, dull, or sluggish COSTIVE, BOVINE
– lazy, good-for-nothing, habitually avoiding work or commitment SHIFTLESS, WORK-SHY
– lazy, idle, useless, or superfluous OTIOSE
– lazy, incompetent, or ungainly person SLOUCH
– lazy, lacking energy, will, or vitality, sluggish LISTLESS, LETHARGIC, TORPID, LANGUID
– lazy, neglectful, shirking TRUANT
– lazy, sluggish, difficult to arouse, resisting motion or activity INERT
– lazy, timid, or petty person who avoids commitment and shirks work PIKER
– lazy, torpid, sleepy COMATOSE
– lazy and self-indulgent person devoted to pleasure and luxury LOTUS-EATER, SYBARITE, VOLUPTUARY
– lazy by nature, unemotional in temperament, calm, unexcitable PHLEGMATIC, LYMPHATIC
– lazy in a carefree or irresponsible way FAINÉANT
– lazy man who idles away his time in fashionable places LOUNGE LIZARD
– lazy or inactive period of one's life DOG DAYS
– lazy person, addicted to inactive amusements such as watching television COUCH POTATO
– lazy person, aimless idler, loafer FLÂNEUR, WASTREL
– lazy person, idler SLUGGARD
– lazy person, lagging behind LAGGARD, DAWDLER, SLOWCOACH
– be lazy, avoid work, neglect one's duties SHIRK, SCRIMSHANK
– being lazy to the point of harming one's own interests FESTERING

lead See also **order**, **begin**
– lead, arrange, guide, set in order MARSHAL
– lead, conduct, and escort, or precede and introduce USHER
– lead, direct, have authority over a meeting, committee, or the like PRESIDE
– lead, escort and protect on a journey CONVOY
– lead, first step or action, initial impulse THE INITIATIVE
– lead an attack, drive, or the like SPEARHEAD
– leading, foremost, chief, supreme PARAMOUNT, PREDOMINANT, PRE-EMINENT, PREPONDERANT
– leading character, as in a play, novel, or other literary work PROTAGONIST
– leading position of power, influence, or control DOMINANCE, PRE-EMINENCE, ASCENDANCY, PRIMACY, SUPREMACY

lead oxide, red lead, as used formerly in paint MINIUM, CINNABAR

– lead poisoning PLUMBISM, SATURNISM
– lead weight hanging on a cord or line, as used in fishing, depth-sounding, or for determining a truly vertical line PLUMB
– dark grey allotropic form of carbon used for pencil leads and as a lubricant GRAPHITE, PLUMBAGO
lead- PLUMB-, PLUMBO-
leader See chart
– leader in name only, without any real power or true responsibility FIGUREHEAD, FRONT MAN
– leader or founder of a movement PATRON SAINT
– leader or initiator in any field of endeavour TRAILBLAZER, PIONEER,

LEADERS AND RULERS

aga	high-ranking official of the Ottoman Empire	**khan/cham**	medieval emperor or ruler in China or central Asia
Asantehene	paramount chief of the Ashanti people of West Africa	**khedive**	viceroy in Egypt during the period of Ottoman control
ataman/hetman	Cossack chief	**mandarin**	senior civil servant in imperial China; any powerful and relatively independent official
ayatollah	highest ranking religious leader of the Shiite branch of Islam	**mikado, Tenno**	emperor of Japan
bey/beg	provincial governor or other high official in the Ottoman Empire	**nawab**	Muslim prince or ruler in India in former times
cacique	chief of an American Indian tribe in Latin America; local political boss in Latin America	**nizam**	former ruler of Hyderabad
Caesar	Roman emperor; any powerful or dictatorial leader	**pasha**	former provincial governor in the Ottoman Empire
caliph	ruler of a Muslim state	**sachem, sagamore**	North American Indian tribal chief
capo	divisional leader in the Mafia	**satrap**	provincial governor in ancient Persia; any dictatorial minor ruler
caudillo	Spanish military dictator	**sheikh**	leader of an Arab tribe or village; Muslim religious leader
Chogyal	ruler of Sikkim	**shogun**	Japanese military commander, especially any of those who effectively ruled Japan in former times
collector	chief administrative officer of a district of India during British rule	**stadholder**	chief magistrate or provincial governor in the Netherlands in former times
consul	chief official or magistrate in the ancient Roman Republic, ruling in a pair	**sultan**	ruler of a Muslim state, especially under the Ottoman Empire
Dalai Lama	leader of Tibetan Buddhists	**suzerain**	feudal lord
dey	Turkish governor or commander in Algeria in former times	**Taoiseach**	prime minister of the Irish Republic
doge	chief magistrate of the old republics of Venice and of Genoa	**tetrarch**	any of four joint rulers, or ruler of a quarter of a region; prince enjoying limited power in the Roman Empire
duce	leader or ruler in Italy	**tsar**	emperor of Russia in former times
emir	Muslim prince, chieftain, or governor in the Middle East	**tuchun**	military governor of a Chinese province in former times
fugleman	political leader; formerly, a leader or demonstrator in military drill	**viceroy**	governor of a country, colony, or the like, ruling in the name of his sovereign or government
Führer	leader or dictator in Germany	**vizier**	high-ranking official, such as a provincial governor or chief minister, in Muslim countries, especially under the Ottoman Empire
Gauleiter	district governor in Nazi Germany		
kabaka	former ruler of the Baganda people of Uganda		
Kaiser	Holy Roman emperor, Austro-Hungarian emperor, or German emperor		

leaf shapes

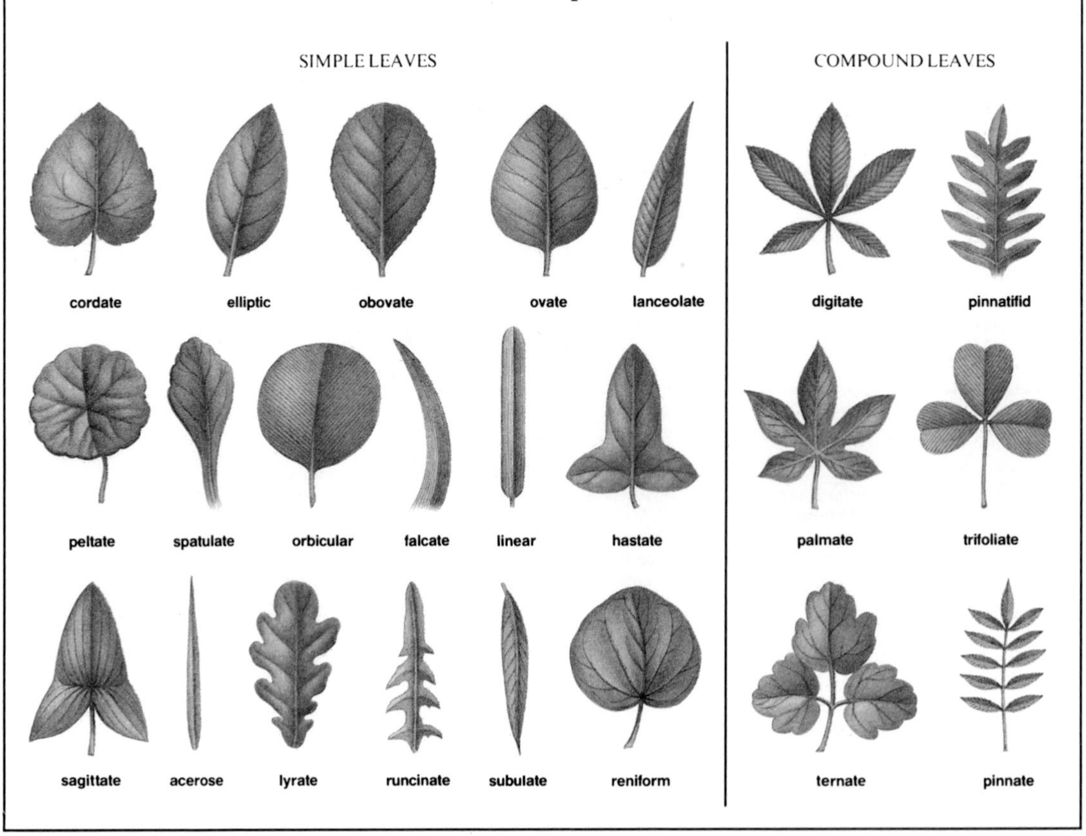

SIMPLE LEAVES

cordate elliptic obovate ovate lanceolate

peltate spatulate orbicular falcate linear hastate

sagittate acerose lyrate runcinate subulate reniform

COMPOUND LEAVES

digitate pinnatifid

palmate trifoliate

ternate pinnate

INNOVATOR, GROUND-BREAKER, TREND-SETTER, PACEMAKER
- leader or representative of a faithful or closely knit group BELL-WETHER
- leaders or those in the most advanced position of a military advance, artistic movement, or the like VANGUARD
- idealistic or visionary, promising deliverance or prosperity, as a charismatic leader might MESSIANIC
- spiritual teacher or leader, as among Hindus or Sikhs GURU

-leader -AGOGUE, -ARCH

leaf See illustration
- leaf-eating, feeding on leaves PHYLLOPHAGOUS
- leaf-like plant part growing in pairs at the base of some leaves STIPULE
- leaf-like plant part just beneath a flower or cluster of flowers BRACT
- leaf-like sheath that encloses a flower spike, as on the cuckoopint SPATHE
- leaf made up of three leaflets TREFOIL
- leaf of a fern or palm FROND
- leaf-patterned carving on the capital of a Corinthian column ACANTHUS
- leaves FOLIAGE
- leaves or petals in a radiating pattern WHORL
- angle between a leafstalk and the stem, between a branch and the trunk, or the like AXIL
- arrangement of leaves on a stem PHYLLOTAXY
- attached at the base, without a stalk, as a leaf might be SESSILE
- blade of a leaf or petal LAMINA
- blistered or wrinkled in appearance, as some leaves are BULLATE
- clover or similar plant with compound leaves of three leaflets SHAMROCK
- cluster of leaves. branches, and the like FASCICLE, FASCICULE
- covered with a sticky substance, as some leaves are VISCID
- covered with stiff bristly hairs, as leaves might be STRIGOSE
- covered with very fine, small, or woolly hairs, as leaves might be LANATE, CILIATE, VILLOUS, HOARY
- curved like a scimitar, as some leaves are ACINACIFORM
- dry, withered, shrivelled, as a dead leaf would be SERE
- falling off or shed at a point of time or growth, as leaves or antlers might be DECIDUOUS
- green pigment in leaves that traps energy from sunlight for photosynthesis CHLOROPHYLL
- having wavy edges, as some leaves have CRENATE, CRENULATE, SINUATE, REPAND
- lose or give off water vapour through pores, as from the surface of a leaf TRANSPIRE
- main axis or stem, as of a flower cluster, compound leaf, or feather RACHIS
- notch or hollow between the lobes of a leaf, petal, or the like SINUS
- plant's use of light energy, absorbed by chlorophyll in the leaves and other plant tissues PHOTOSYNTHESIS
- pointed, tapering to a tip, as some leaves are ACUMINATE, APICULATE, CUSPIDATE
- pore on the surface of a leaf for the passage of gases and water vapour STOMA

– ridged or wrinkled in appearance, as some leaves are RUGOSE
– relating to or resembling a leaf or leaves FOLIACEOUS, FOLIATE
– remaining attached to the plant even after withering, as some leaves and flowers do PERSISTENT
– rounded projecting part, as on the ear or a leaf LOBE
– stalk attaching a leaf to a stem PETIOLE
– strip a tree or other plant of leaves, as by means of a chemical spray in a war zone DEFOLIATE
– tiny leaf or leaflet, as on a fern frond PINNA
– vein or rib of a leaf NERVURE
– veins, or the arrangement of veins, on a leaf, insect's wing, or the like VENATION

-leaf- -PHYLL-, PHYLLO-, -FOLI-

leaflet, advertisement, or notice distributed widely CIRCULAR, FLIER
– leaflet distributed by hand, handout HANDBILL

leafy retreat ARBOUR, BOWER

leakage, oozing SEEPAGE
– amount of liquid, grain, or the like that evaporates or leaks from a container ULLAGE

lean back or lie down RECLINE
– lean or tip over to one side, as a ship or boat might LIST, HEEL OVER, KEEL OVER, CAREEN
– leaning or resting against related tissue, as a bodily organ might RECUMBENT

leap See **jump**

leap year BISSEXTILE
– year with an extra day or month inserted, such as a leap year INTERCALARY YEAR

learn, determine, or discover by examination or experimentation ASCERTAIN
– learn, grasp mentally, understand APPREHEND
– learn and understand something thoroughly ASSIMILATE, DIGEST
– learn off by heart, memorise CON, LEARN BY ROTE
– learn or collect information or the like bit by bit GLEAN

learned, scholarly ERUDITE
– learned in a showy way, as deliberately "literary" terms are INKHORN
– learned person, especially an expert in a particular field of study SAVANT
– learned person who is knowledgeable in many subjects POLYMATH, POLYHISTOR
– learned written study on a particular subject TREATISE

learning, culture HUMANISM
– learning, scholarly knowledge ERUDITION
– learning of a formal, unimaginative, drily detailed kind PEDANTRY
– learning or remembering by repetition rather than through understanding ROTE-LEARNING
– learning or teaching by means of lessons heard during sleep HYPNOPAEDIA
– learning process in young animals IMPRINTING
– learning process, training, or behaviour modification through adjustment of stimuli CONDITIONING
– learning based on step-by-step instruction from a book or computer rather than by classroom lessons PROGRAMMED LEARNING
– helping or encouraging the process of learning or discovery HEURISTIC
– institution for the advancement of learning ATHENAEUM
– strengthening of learning by means of rewards or punishments REINFORCEMENT

lease – a person who grants a lease LESSOR

leaseholder LESSEE

leash – free a dog, hawk, or the like from its leash or any other form of restraint SLIP
– ring on a dog's collar for attaching a leash TERRET

leather See chart

LEATHERS AND HIDES

box calf	calfskin tanned black, with square-shaped markings
buff	thick, soft, undyed leather, cream to light brown in colour, typically made from buffalo, ox, or elk hide
cabretta	soft leather made from the skins of African or South American sheep
capeskin	soft leather made from the skins of lambs or sheep with hair-like wool
chamois	soft leather, as for garments or for polishing, originally from a mountain antelope, now commonly from flesh side of deerskin or sheepskin
chevrette	leather made from the skin of a young goat
cordovan	fine leather, usually made from horsehide, originally made from goatskin in Cordoba, Spain
glacé kid	soft shoe leather with a glossy finish
levant	morocco leather patterned with irregular creases
mocha	soft goatskin or sheepskin with a suede finish, used for gloves
morocco, morocco leather, morocco goat	fine, soft leather made from goatskin treated with sumac, originally made in Morocco, and used mainly for bookbinding and shoes
nappa	soft leather made from kid, lambskin, or sheepskin, used for gloves and garments
patent leather	leather or imitation leather lacquered to give a hard, glossy finish
rawhide	untanned hide
roan	soft, flexible leather with a close, tough grain, made from sheepskin
shagreen	untreated sharkskins, or rayskins, used as abrasives; rough, grainy leather
skiver	soft, thin leather made from hair side of sheepskin
slink, hair calf	skin of a prematurely born calf
wash leather	soft leather, such as chamois, used for cleaning and polishing

– leather, goatskin, or sheepskin treated for writing or painting on PARCHMENT
– leather-like, tough CORIACEOUS
– leather or canvas strip for sharpening a cutthroat razor STROP
– leather strap split into strips at the end, used for beating children, especially in Scotland TAWSE
– leather strip THONG
– aged artificially, as some furniture or leather is DISTRESSED
– bend leather, as in shoemaking CRIMP
– decorate leather or a similar material with a pattern of tiny holes PINK
– dress leather by rubbing DUB
– grainy or crinkled surface, as on leather or paper PEBBLE
– grease of tallow and oil used for waterproofing leather DUBBIN
– person who softens, dyes, or prepares tanned leather CURRIER
– pointed instrument for making holes in leather or cloth BODKIN
– soften, dye, or prepare tanned leather CURRY
– stamped or gilded ornamenting on books or leather TOOLING
– tan hides, as with alum or salt, especially to produce pale leather TAW

leave See also **depart**
– leave behind, abandon, desert or give up FORSAKE, RELINQUISH
– leave granted, as to a soldier, for reasons of personal distress, such as a death in the family COMPASSIONATE LEAVE
– leave of absence, as from school EXEAT
– leave of absence in the U.S. armed forces FURLOUGH
– absence without leave FRENCH LEAVE, AWOL

leave-taking, farewell, goodbye VALEDICTION

leaves See **leaf** and illustration

Lebanese Christian MARONITE

lecherous man SATYR

lecture made by a recently installed professor, president, or the like INAUGURAL LECTURE
– lecture of a boring, moralising kind HOMILY
– lecture or treatise on or formal study of a subject DISQUISITION

lecturer in certain universities LECTOR, DOCENT
– lecturer of senior rank, just below professor READER
– lecturer who looks after and supervises a group of undergraduates TUTOR

leech, earthworm, or other similarly segmented worm ANNELID

leek, onion, garlic, or related plant ALLIUM

leer, stare at lustfully OGLE

left – left-hand page in a book VERSO
– left-handed, on the left, or relating to the left side SINISTRAL
– left-handed and regarded as being clumsy, as phrased in various dialects CACK-HANDED, CUDDY-WIFTED, CORRIE-FLUG, PALLY-KLOOKIT, GAMMY-FISTED
– left-hander, specifically a boxer adopting a left-handed stance SOUTHPAW
– left side of a ship PORT, LARBOARD
– left-winger or extreme radical BOLSHEVIK, BOLSHIE
– both left-handed and right-handed, able to use both hands equally expertly AMBIDEXTROUS

left-, leftwards- LAEV-, LAEVO-, LEVO-

left over, surviving, remaining, continuing RESIDUAL
– leftover part, inferior remnant RUMP
– leftovers or remains of something destroyed REMNANTS, VESTIGES, WRACK
– referring to leftover food that is warmed up before serving RÉCHAUFFÉ

leg, especially the lower leg between knee and foot SHANK, CRUS
– leg coverings, either a long cloth strip for winding or a wide canvas strip for buckling round the leg PUTTEE
– leg coverings, of cloth or leather, buttoned from knee to ankle and strapped under the foot GAITER, LEGGING
– leg covering, of leather, as formerly worn to protect against splashes when riding SPATTERDASH
– leg covering or gaiter, as on the leg of a rider GAMBADO
– leg coverings of leather, worn over the trousers, as by cowboys CHAPS, CHAPAREJOS
– leg of an item of furniture, curving outwards near the top, and then inwards to an ornamental foot CABRIOLE
– leg of mutton or lamb GIGOT
– leg supports consisting of metal rods with straps CALLIPERS
– angle or fork formed by steps, trouser legs, or the like CROTCH
– relating to the leg, shank, or thigh CRURAL
– tendon on the leg, above and behind the knee HAMSTRING
– top of the leg HAUNCH, LOIN
– vein, especially in the legs, that has become abnormally knotted and swollen VARICOSE VEIN, VARIX
– walking, or one's own legs or feet, as a means of travel SHANKS'S PONY

legacy, heritage PATRIMONY
– legacy or inheritance BEQUEST

legal See chart, and also **law**, **court**, **trial**
– legal, proper, conforming with the requirements CANONICAL
– legal authorisation to act as another's agent, or the document conveying it POWER OF ATTORNEY, PROCURATION
– legal case arousing great public interest CAUSE CÉLÈBRE
– legal document, analysing a case and detailing instructions, given by a solicitor to a barrister BRIEF
– legal document certifying a contract or transfer of property DEED
– legal means of ensuring justice REMEDY
– legal philosophy JURISPRUDENCE
– legal right DROIT
– legally acceptable, binding, or in force, as a title or passport might be VALID
– legally qualified ADMISSIBLE, COMPETENT, ELIGIBLE
– legally required LIABLE
– bringing a legal action, pursuing a case in court LITIGATION
– heading in or section of a legal code RUBRIC

legging See **leg**

leisure activity, hobby AVOCATION

lemon or orange rind used as flavouring ZEST
– sliver of lemon to decorate or flavour a drink TWIST

lend a small amount, especially an advance on future payments SUB

length, height, or width DIMENSION
– length of time for which something continues or lasts DURATION
– ancient measure of length, based on the length of the arm from fingertip to elbow CUBIT
– relating to length LONGITUDINAL

lengthen or extend PROLONG, PROTRACT

lenient and unwilling to impose discipline on others INDULGENT

lens, as though from a pair of glasses, for just one eye MONOCLE
– lens covering a watch face LUNETTE, CRYSTAL
– lens defect or the blurred pear-shaped image it causes COMA
– lens of a compound or twofold prescription, correcting for near and distant vision BIFOCAL LENS
– lens or group of lenses forming the image in a camera or projector OBJECTIVE LENS
– lens-shaped surface MENISCUS

– lens or mirror that concentrates light CONDENSER
– lens system on a camera allowing rapid changes in the degree of magnification while retaining the sharpness of an image ZOOM LENS
– adjustable opening controlling the amount of light entering a lens APERTURE
– curved inwards, as a mirror or lens might be CONCAVE
– curved outwards, as a mirror or lens might be CONVEX
– defect in a lens ABERRATION
– faulty image, as caused by an

LEGAL TERMS

affidavit	"he has sworn": a sworn, written statement
ancient lights	right to unobstructed light; windows protected by this right
bind over	order a person to do something, such as keep the peace, or refrain from some action
codicil	supplement or afterthought added to a will
corpus delicti	"body of the crime": material evidence or substance of a crime, such as a corpse
delict	wrongful act, for which the injured party is entitled to compensation
deposition	written statement made under oath, presented as evidence in court
distrain	seize goods as redress or compensation
easement	right of a house-owner or landowner over another's property, as for access
entail	settling of the inheritance of an estate beyond one generation, so that it may not be disposed of by an individual heir
equity	body of legal rules based on natural justice and fairness, supplementing and moderating common and statute law
escrow	goods, money, a contract, or the like that is put in the safekeeping of a third party, to be handed over only when certain conditions are met
estovers	articles such as fallen timber that tenants are legally permitted to remove from their landlord's estate
ex parte	"on behalf of": referring to a court application or injunction made on behalf of one side only
garnishment	court order requiring a trustee or third party holding property of a debtor either to withhold it from the debtor or to hand it over to the creditor
habeas corpus	"you may have the body": writ requiring that a detainee be produced before a court and reasons be given for his detention
in camera	"in the chamber": referring to proceedings that a judge hears with the public excluded from the court
indemnity	legal exemption from penalties or liabilities one may incur or has incurred
indictment	written accusation, read out to the accused at a trial
in flagrante delicto	in the very act of committing a crime; red-handed
injunction	court order to carry out or refrain from an act, such as visiting a person or place
laches	negligence or unreasonable delay in pursuing a legal claim
lien	right to take or hold another's property as security for a debt
malice aforethought, malice prepense	premeditation, plan or conscious intention to commit a crime, especially a murder or a violent crime leading to death
mens rea	criminal intent
nolle prosequi	"to be unwilling to pursue": an entry in court records showing that a case was not proceeded with
parole	"word of honour": release of a prisoner, before the end of a sentence, on condition of good behaviour
piscary	rights of fishing in another's waters
probate	establishing of the validity of a will; document certifying the validity of a will
procurator fiscal	in Scotland, a court officer who acts as public prosecutor and coroner
pupillage	apprenticeship as an advocate or barrister
recognisance	undertaking by a person to pay a debt or return to court on a specific day; money pledged as security for this
sequestration	seizure of goods or assets until conditions laid down in a decree have been met
sub judice	"under a judge": under deliberation by the courts, and therefore not open to public comment or discussion
subpoena	writ requiring a person to appear and give evidence in court
tort	breach or violation of civil law, other than breach of contract
turbary	rights of digging peat or turf on common land or on land owned by another
ultra vires	beyond the legal powers of a person or institution
usufruct	right to use and benefit from another's property, so long as it remains undamaged

imperfect lens DISTORTION
– irregularity in the lens of the eye, or the faulty vision resulting from it ASTIGMATISM
– network of lines or fine wires, as on a lens, used for measuring or locating the observed objects RETICLE, RETICULE, GRATICULE
– very thick lens, with high magnification PEBBLE LENS

lentils or other edible seeds of leguminous plants PULSES

leopard – leopard's spots MACULATIONS

leprosy HANSEN'S DISEASE
– hospital for treating leprosy, plague, or other contagious diseases in former times LAZARETTO
– person afflicted with leprosy, leper LAZAR

lesbian SAPPHIC
– lesbian woman TRIBADE
– lesbian symbol or emblem, of a double-headed axe LABYRIS

lessen, decrease, reduce, or decline DIMINISH
– lessen in size or significance MINIFY
– lessen in size or volume, make smaller CONDENSE, COMPRESS
– lessen or cut back on expenditure, size of the work force, or the like RETRENCH
– lessen or decline dramatically in number or value, fall uncontrollably PLUMMET, SLUMP
– lessen or decline gradually in amount or intensity, wind down, as if coming to an end ABATE, SUBSIDE, TAPER OFF
– lessen or decline gradually in size, number, or strength, usually gradually DWINDLE, WANE, EBB
– lessen or decline in size or number, shrink CONTRACT
– lessen or ease a hardship, pain, fear, or the like, relieve ALLAY, ALLEVIATE, PALLIATE, ASSUAGE
– lessen or limit the scope or freedom of CONSTRICT
– lessen or reduce significantly in amount or number DEPLETE
– lessen or reduce the dignity, importance, or apparent worth of a person or thing BELITTLE, DEBASE, DEMEAN, DISPARAGE, DEPRECIATE, MINIMISE, DEVALUE, DETRACT FROM, DEROGATE
– lessen or reduce the size of a herd or flock by killing selected animals CULL
– lessen or relax the intensity, pace, or the like REMIT, SLACKEN
– lessen or wear down gradually, as if by cutting away with a knife PARE DOWN, WHITTLE DOWN
– lessen or withdraw, usually gradually, as hair might RECEDE
– lessen the apparent severity of a crime or fault, partially excuse EXTENUATE, MITIGATE
– negative or contemptuous, serving to lessen someone's reputation or dignity DEROGATORY, DISPARAGING, PEJORATIVE
– reduce, cut short, lessen the time or extent of ABBREVIATE, CURTAIL, TRUNCATE
– shorten, lessen the time or length of, as by making cuts from a book ABRIDGE
– weaken or thin down, lessen in strength, force, or purity DILUTE, ATTENUATE

lesson or bible passage to be read during a church service LECTION
– drive home a lesson, as by repetition INSTIL, INCULCATE

let See **allow**
– "let it stand", instruction to a typesetter or printer to ignore a correction STET
– "let the buyer beware", principle that the buyer bears the risk CAVEAT EMPTOR

letdown, disappointing ending after a promising build-up ANTICLIMAX, BATHOS

letter See also **scripts**, **typefaces**
– letter, especially a long, formal, or official letter EPISTLE, MISSIVE
– letter, for airmail delivery, without an envelope AEROGRAMME
– letter, symbol, or group of characters that can represent more than one sound, such as the English *g* in *gin* and *gain* POLYPHONE
– letter, usually anonymous, containing abuse, warnings, or the like POISON-PEN LETTER
– letter, written þ, representing the sounds /th/ and /t͟h/, as used in Old and Middle English THORN
– letter, written ð, representing the /t͟h/ sound as in *this*, in old Germanic languages and in modern Icelandic EDH, ETH
– letter, written ʒ, representing various sounds similar to /y/ or the /k͟h/ of *loch*, as used in Old and Middle English YOGH
– letter, written *æ*, representing various vowel sounds including /a/ as in *hat*, used in Old English, modern Icelandic, and other old Germanic languages ASH
– letter from the Pope to bishops in all countries ENCYCLICAL
– letter of a decorative italic design SWASH LETTER
– letter of an early medieval Germanic alphabet, typically used in carved inscriptions RUNE
– letter of recommendation, a reference TESTIMONIAL
– letter of the alphabet, A-G, applied to the Sundays in a given year to determine the church calendar DOMINICAL LETTER
– letter of the alphabet or symbol representing an entire word or phrase LOGOGRAM, LOGOGRAPH
– letter of the alphabet that is a capital letter MAJUSCULE, UPPER-CASE LETTER
– letter of the alphabet that is not a capital letter MINUSCULE, LOWER-CASE LETTER
– letter officially recorded and insured REGISTERED LETTER
– letter or number printed at the foot of some pages in a book, specifying the sequence for binding the sections SIGNATURE
– letter or number written or printed slightly above another, as in ab^2 SUPERSCRIPT, SUPERIOR
– letter or number written or printed slightly below another, as in H_2O SUBSCRIPT
– letter or symbol ŋ, used in dictionaries to represent the /ng/ sound, as in *long* AGMA, ENG
– letter or symbol ə, used in dictionaries to represent the unstressed central vowel sound, as in the first syllable of *about* SCHWA
– letter sent by a woman breaking off her relationship with her boyfriend or fiancé DEAR JOHN LETTER
– letter that is very long and typically dull SCREED
– letter which each recipient in turn is meant to copy and send to several further addresses CHAIN LETTER
– letters run together, such as *æ*, or paired to represent a single speech sound, such as *th* DIGRAPH
– "Dear Sir" or similar conventional opening words of a letter SALUTATION
– design consisting of superimposed letters, as for an emblem MONOGRAM, CIPHER
– humorous term for a love letter BILLET-DOUX
– loss or cutting off of a letter, syllable, or sound at the beginning of a word APHAERESIS, APHESIS
– loss or cutting off of a letter, syllable, or sound from the end of a word APOCOPE
– loss or cutting off of a letter, syllable, or sound in a word or group of words ELISION
– loss or cutting off of a letter, syllable, or sound in the middle of a word SYNCOPE
– mark or stamp a letter or parcel

to indicate payment of postage FRANK
– message or afterthought at the end of a letter, after the writer's signature POSTSCRIPT, P.S.
– old-fashioned term for an official letter or business letter FAVOUR
– part of a small letter, such as *q* or *y*, reaching below the normal letter size, or such a letter DESCENDER
– part of a small letter, such as *b* or *k*, rising above the normal letter size, or such a letter ASCENDER
– phrase used in the address on a letter that is to be kept at a particular post office for collection by the addressee GENERAL DELIVERY, POSTE RESTANTE
– raised part of a piece of printer's type, bearing the letter or character to be printed KERN
– relating to letters or letter writing, or consisting of letters, as some novels do EPISTOLARY
– repeated occurrence of a letter or sound, especially at the start of words, in writing or speech ALLITERATION
– short ornamental line finishing the stroke of a printed letter SERIF
– sign or mark, such as a cedilla or circumflex, added to a letter to indicate a special pronunciation DIACRITIC
– typed or printed character of two or more letters joined together, such as *fi* LIGATURE
– upright stroke of a typeface or letter or musical note STEM
– write or spell in the letters of another alphabet TRANSLITERATE

lettuce with a long head and crisp leaves COS, ROMAINE

level See also **flat**
– level, as of anxiety QUOTIENT
– level, flat, parallel to the horizon HORIZONTAL
– level, such as a class or caste, within a society or series STRATUM
– level at or below which the ground is saturated with water WATER TABLE
– level of authority or responsibility in a hierarchical organisation ECHELON
– level of income that is the minimum for providing the necessities of life SUBSISTENCE LEVEL
– level or condition, as of economic activity, that is relatively stable PLATEAU
– level or flat, having a broad plane surface TABULAR
– level or flat and even, as two neatly fitting edges are FLUSH
– level or row, as of seating in a theatre or stadium, in a rising series TIER, TERRACE
– level stretch of ground for walking along, especially along a sea shore ESPLANADE
– levelling of land, as by erosion or deposition GRADATION
– instrument using an air bubble in a tube of liquid to test if a surface is level SPIRIT LEVEL

lever – hinge, support, or turning point of a lever FULCRUM

lewd, arousing or appealing to sexual lust SALACIOUS, PRURIENT

liability – person who assumes liability for the debts or obligations of another SURETY, GUARANTOR

liable or tending to err FALLIBLE
– liable to be affected by something adverse, such as an illness SUSCEPTIBLE, PRONE, VULNERABLE, EXPOSED, SUBJECT
– liable to or allowing of testing, criticism, or judgment ACCESSIBLE, AMENABLE
– become liable or subject to something such as debts or someone's wrath INCUR

liar See **lie**

liberal, especially in matters of religion LATITUDINARIAN

liberal arts HUMANITIES
– higher division, with four subjects, of the liberal arts studied at a medieval university QUADRIVIUM
– lower or earlier division, with three subjects, of the liberal arts studied at a medieval university TRIVIUM

library book or similar addition to a collection ACCESSION
– library classification system for cataloguing books DEWEY DECIMAL SYSTEM, LIBRARY OF CONGRESS CLASSIFICATION
– library or catalogue of books BIBLIOTHECA
– library reading room, as in an academy ATHENAEUM
– author's right to a fee when his books are borrowed from public libraries PUBLIC LENDING RIGHT, PLR
– bookcase in a library PRESS
– classification or shelf number of a book in a library CALL NUMBER
– double-faced bookcase in a library RANGE
– run out, come to an end, as the loan period of a library book might EXPIRE
– section of shelving, as in a library, usually separated from other shelves by vertical dividing walls STACK
– sheet of microfilm, as used for the pages of library catalogues MICROFICHE, FICHE
– small cubicle in a library for private study CARREL

lice – infestation with lice PEDICULOSIS, PHTHIRIASIS
– relating to lice PEDICULAR

licence fee for certain pursuits, such as sports promotions and operating a casino EXCISE
– licence for the temporary import of a car, or for a motorist to cross certain frontiers CARNET
– licence or authorisation given by a business enterprise to dealers to use its name and products FRANCHISE
– licensed purveyor of alcoholic spirits VICTUALLER

lie See also **lying**
– lie, falsehood, evasion of the truth, deceptive speech or action PREVARICATION, EQUIVOCATION, MENDACITY
– lie, misrepresentation, or deliberate concealment of relevant information SUBREPTION
– lie, or act ambiguously or evasively TERGIVERSATE, EQUIVOCATE, TEMPORISE, PREVARICATE, FUDGE, PALTER
– lie, toss, or writhe about in WELTER, WALLOW
– lie about in a relaxed or apathetic way LANGUISH
– lie illegally before a court, on oath, or the like PERJURE ONESELF
– lie in and enjoy something, such as a bath or favourable publicity BASK
– lie or crawl face downwards, as in self-abasement or fear GROVEL
– glaringly or offensively obvious, as a lie or error might be BLATANT
– habitual or regular, especially in an uncontrolled way, as a persistent liar might be INVETERATE, CHRONIC
– invent or devise evidence, a story, or the like, typically embellished with lies FABRICATE
– outrageously big or glaring lie WHOPPER
– petty lie, fib TARRADIDDLE
– shameless or despicable, as a liar might be ABJECT

lie detector, or any instrument recording changes in pulse, blood pressure, breathing rate, and the like POLYGRAPH

lie down and rest REPOSE
– lie down or lean back RECLINE

lie in wait for and take by surprise WAYLAY, AMBUSH

lieutenant or other commissioned army officer ranking below a captain SUBALTERN

life See also **living**

– life-enhancing, original, or creative PROMETHEAN, DIONYSIAN
– life-expectancy chart as used by insurance companies MORTALITY TABLE
– life-form of a basic single-celled type, typically microscopic, such as an amoeba PROTOZOAN
– life history, story of a person's life, as written by another person BIOGRAPHY
– "life instinct", self-preserving instincts and life-enhancing drive in Freudian theory EROS
– life-like, true to life, as an objective novel or painting would be NATURALISTIC, REALISTIC
– life-supporting regions of the Earth or universe ECOSPHERE
– life-sustaining agent, especially food SUSTENANCE
– adjective for life VITAL
– functions or processes maintaining life METABOLISM
– give life or liveliness to ANIMATE, VIVIFY, ENLIVEN
– give new life and energy to REVIVIFY
– hypothetical emergence of life or living organisms from non-living matter SPONTANEOUS GENERATION, ABIOGENESIS
– length of life LONGEVITY
– liquid mixture of organic chemicals in early times from which life may have developed PRIMORDIAL SOUP
– restore to life or consciousness RESUSCITATE, RESURRECT
– return to life after apparent death RESUSCITATION, ANABIOSIS
– reverence for all life, as in some Indian religions, often with a belief in non-violence and reincarnation AHIMSA
– study of the life processes and the functioning of living matter PHYSIOLOGY
– substance sought by alchemists for prolonging life indefinitely ELIXIR, ELIXIR OF LIFE

life- BIO-

life jacket MAE WEST

lifeboat – ship's crane, typically paired with another, for hoisting lifeboats, cargo, or the like DAVIT

lift consisting of open platforms on a continuous chain, moving round very slowly without stopping PATERNOSTER
– small lift for carrying food, dishes, or the like between floors DUMB WAITER

lifting machine, such as the moving hoist on a crane CRAB
– lifting machine, typically a rope-wound drum WINDLASS
– crane with boom and cables for lifting heavy objects DERRICK

light See also **shine**
– light, extremely delicate, almost insubstantial GOSSAMER, CHIFFON, ETHEREAL
– light and delicate, translucent, as fine silk is DIAPHANOUS
– light, of great intensity, produced by an electric arc crossing a gap ARC LIGHT
– light and shade in drawing and painting CHIAROSCURO
– light emission at low temperatures, through chemical or atomic processes LUMINESCENCE, FLUORESCENCE, PHOSPHORESCENCE
– light emitted as a result of heating INCANDESCENCE
– light emitted in quick intense flashes, producing a jerky or stationary image of moving objects STROBE LIGHT
– light emitted, through a biochemical process, by fireflies, fish, fungi, or other living organisms BIOLUMINESCENCE
– light fitting or chandelier for gas lights GASELIER
– light fitting suspended from the ceiling PENDANT
– light fixture, usually hanging from the ceiling, holding many bulbs or candles CHANDELIER
– light fixture's frosted covering, matt reflector, or the like, designed to reduce glare DIFFUSER
– light hovering over marshy ground, probably produced by flaming methane gas WILL-O'-THE-WISP, IGNIS FATUUS, JACK-O'-LANTERN, FRIAR'S LANTERN
– light inside a car COURTESY LIGHT
– light lunch, snack TIFFIN
– light meal COLLATION
– light or halo, as in a painting, around the head or body of a saint, deity, or the like AUREOLE, NIMBUS
– light produced by heating lime, as formerly used in theatres LIMELIGHT, CALCIUM LIGHT
– light supposedly given off by and surrounding a person, visible to clairvoyants AURA
– light that shines brilliantly, sparkle RADIANCE, LUSTRE, SCINTILLATION
– lights seen flashing in the night sky, especially in polar regions AURORA
– lights used in navigation, either on shore as a guide to ships, or on the masts of ships for identification purposes RANGE LIGHTS
– adjusting of light or other radiation into a particular pattern, especially restricting its vibrations to a single plane POLARISATION
– allowing the passage of light, as frosted glass does, but only in a diffused form TRANSLUCENT
– allowing the passage of light freely, as clear glass does, so that objects on the other side are fully visible TRANSPARENT
– allowing the passage of no light at all, not transmitting light, or not reflecting light OPAQUE
– apparatus that produces a beam of intensely pure light LASER
– apparent movement of a stationary light, such as a candle flame, when observed in a darkened room AUTOKINETIC PHENOMENON
– breaking up of light into the colours of the rainbow, as by a glass surface DIFFRACTION
– bright carbon-arc light used in making films KLIEG LIGHT
– change in direction of a light or sound wave as it changes speed between mediums REFRACTION
– colours of the rainbow, or an image of them, as when a light beam is split up SPECTRUM
– dazzling or harsh, as artificial light might be GARISH
– device, as in a digital clock, that gives off light when electrically stimulated LED
– device launched into the air to produce a bright light, as for illuminating a search area at night or as a distress signal FLARE
– dim or faint, as a weak light is WAN
– electronic device that reacts to changes in light intensity, as used in light meters, burglar alarms, and automatic doors PHOTOELECTRIC CELL, PHOTOCELL, ELECTRIC EYE, MAGIC EYE
– emitting self-generated light, glowing LUMINOUS, FLUORESCENT, PHOSPHORESCENT
– flickering or glowing with a gentle light LAMBENT
– give out heat, light, or the like RADIATE
– having waves of the same frequency or related phases, as light can have COHERENT
– lacking light, or relating to the absence of light APHOTIC
– lamp or light bulb producing light from a heated element or filament INCANDESCENT LAMP
– lamp projecting bright light up to the ceiling to produce pleasant, soft, reflected lighting for a room UPLIGHTER, HALOGEN UPLIGHTER
– neon light or similar lamp based

on the stimulation of atoms or molecules into emitting light FLUORESCENT LAMP
– plant's use of light energy, absorbed by chlorophyll, for forming organic compounds from carbon dioxide and water PHOTOSYNTHESIS
– put out a light or fire EXTINGUISH, DOUSE, SNUFF, QUENCH
– radiation with wavelengths between those of visible light and radio waves INFRARED
– radiation with wavelengths between those of visible light and X-rays ULTRAVIOLET
– relating to light PHOTIC
– ring or disc of faint light, as around the Moon when viewed through a haze CORONA, AUREOLE
– scientific study of vision and light OPTICS
– separate light or other radiation into parts with different wavelengths DISPERSE
– signal flare used in former times, burning with a bright blue light BENGAL LIGHT
– signal or lighting flare fired from a special pistol VERY LIGHT
– substance that emits light when stimulated by radiation PHOSPHOR
– theory that light consists of a stream of tiny particles rather than of waves CORPUSCULAR THEORY
– torch, as of flaming pitch, formerly used to light one's way along dark streets LINK
– triangle of light seen in the sky near sunrise or sunset ZODIACAL LIGHT

-light- LUMIN-, PHOTO-, -PHOS-, -PHOT-

light and dark – belief or religion based on a conflict between the universal forces or principles, as of good and evil, or light and dark MANICHAEISM

light-bulb fitting in which pins fasten into slots BAYONET FITTING
– fine wire in a light bulb, heated by electric current to emit light FILAMENT
– hard metallic element used in light-bulb filaments TUNGSTEN

light switch – shield-like plate covering a keyhole, surrounding a door handle, protecting a light switch, or the like ESCUTCHEON

lighten or liven up something dull or humourless LEAVEN

light-hearted, high-spirited literary work JEU D'ESPRIT

lighthouse PHAROS
– British organisation in charge of lighthouses, buoys, and other safety measures around the coast TRINITY HOUSE

lighting technician or electrician on a film or television crew GAFFER
– assistant lighting technician or electrician on a film or television crew BEST BOY

lightness or frivolity of manner, especially when it is inappropriate LEVITY

lightning in the form of a single well-defined electrical discharge STREAK LIGHTNING
– lightning that appears as a broad sheet-like flicker, owing to reflection by clouds SHEET LIGHTNING
– discharge of ball lightning FIREBALL
– flash with or like lightning FULGURATE
– old word for lightning LEVIN

lights out – bugle call sounded at military funerals or to signal lights out in a military camp LAST POST

likable, agreeable to one's tastes CONGENIAL

like, similar to, or resembling but not really being QUASI-
– like, want, or be fond of in a limited way FANCY
– like and enjoy, or look forward to eagerly RELISH
– like or display a preference for FAVOUR, AFFECT
– like or enjoy something very much, such as praise or glory REVEL IN, BASK IN
– like too much, be foolishly, excessively, and indulgently fond of DOTE ON
– like with a warm and caring affection, hold dear CHERISH

-like- HOMEO-, HOMO-, PARA-, -ESQUE, -OID, -OSE

like it or not WILLY-NILLY, NOLENS VOLENS

likely, believable, possible FEASIBLE
– likely, seemingly true, as an excuse might be COLOURABLE, PLAUSIBLE
– likely to become someone or something specified, in the offing PROSPECTIVE

likeness, representation, or image of something, sometimes misleading or superficial SIMULACRUM

liking See also **tendency**, **love**
– natural personal liking or attraction, affection AFFINITY
– special liking, often for something unusual PARTIALITY, PREDILECTION
– strong and continued liking or inclination PENCHANT

-liking -PHIL-, -PHILE

lilt, rise and fall of the pitch of the voice INTONATION

lily or related water-plant LOTUS
– water lily NENUPHAR

limb – cut or pull off a limb or body part of a person or animal MUTILATE, MAIM, DISMEMBER
– displace a limb or organ, or put a bone out of joint DISLOCATE
– illusory limb, still felt as the source of pain even though the real limb has been amputated PHANTOM LIMB
– replacement of a limb by tissue growth, as of a lizard's tail REGENERATION
– ripping away or sudden amputation of a limb or other body part, either surgically or in an accident AVULSION

lime – pillar or cone of lime deposit hanging from the roof of a cave STALACTITE
– pillar or cone of lime deposit rising from the floor of a cave STALAGMITE

-lime- -CALC-, CALCI-

limestone – chalky, containing or resembling limestone or calcium carbonate CALCAREOUS

limit, or establish the limits or boundaries of CIRCUMSCRIBE, DEMARCATE, DELIMIT
– limit, moderate, restrain TEMPER, QUALIFY, CHASTEN
– limit, outermost boundary, outer surface, or the like PERIPHERY
– limit, restraint, restriction STRICTURE
– limit or boundary level above which something takes place or comes into effect THRESHOLD
– limit or confine something, such as an outbreak of disease to a restricted area LOCALISE
– limit or outer edge, as of the range of one's authority or hearing PERIMETER
– limit or turning point, beyond which there is no going back RUBICON
– limit the amount given, begrudge, be miserly with STINT
– limit the movement or freedom of, as by strict rules or physical restraint STRAITJACKET, TETHER
– limitation or condition, as in an agreement or document PROVISO
– limited or specified quantity or number, as of imports, members of a group, or the like QUOTA
– limited amount or fixed allowance allocated to a person, as during a shortage RATION
– limited in number or amount, liable to end or run out FINITE
– limited in size, growth, or development, as through insufficient food or stimulation STUNTED
– limited severely by rules or prejudices HIDEBOUND, INFLEXIBLE
– limited to a small group, re-

stricted EXCLUSIVE, SELECT, ESOTERIC, RAREFIED
– limits of one's knowledge or experience HORIZONS
– limits or boundaries, as of a budget or schedule PARAMETERS, CONSTRAINTS
– limits or boundaries, as of a restricted space or strict set of rules CONFINES
– degree of variation from a standard without going beyond the limit TOLERANCE, LEEWAY, PLAY
– go beyond a limit TRANSGRESS
– law setting a time limit for enforcing a right or bringing a legal action STATUTE OF LIMITATIONS
– regulation limiting people's movements, especially after a set hour at night CURFEW
– rise above or extend beyond the limits of TRANSCEND

limp, drooping, flabby, lacking firmness FLACCID
– limp, lameness CLAUDICATION
– limp or walk awkwardly HOBBLE
– limping or lame HALTING

line, as of ships or police, surrounding or guarding an area CORDON
– line, curve, or surface touching but not intersecting another TANGENT
– line approaching a curve, as on a graph, such that they will meet only at infinity ASYMPTOTE
– line at the top of a page, stating the title of the chapter, page number, or the like HEADLINE
– line of latitude PARALLEL
– line of longitude MERIDIAN
– line of poetry STICH
– line or cord with a weight on the end, as for determining depth or the true vertical PLUMB LINE
– line or curve enclosing a plane area in geometry PERIMETER
– line or set of lines marked on the side of a cargo ship showing its legal load-level in various conditions PLIMSOLL LINE
– line that is very thin, as in a fracture or typeface HAIRLINE
– line up, arrange in rows ALIGN
– line up in straight ranks, as soldiers do on parade DRESS
– line used for reference, as on a graph or technical drawing AXIS
– lines, as of a poem, in which some letters, usually the first, spell out a name or message ACROSTIC
– lines intersecting to form a pattern or design TRACERY
– lines joining hilltops, church sites, and other prominent points, sometimes apparently corresponding with prehistoric tracks LEY LINES
– lines of fine wire, at right angles to each other, used for sighting on a rifle, theodolite, or the like CROSS WIRES, CROSS HAIRS
– lines or grid of fine wires, as on a lens, used for measuring or locating the objects under observation RETICLE, RETICULE, GRATICULE
– adjective for a line, relating to lines LINEAR
– code of lines and numbers, as on a library book or item of shipping, typically read by a laser optical scanner BAR CODE
– cut or divide a line or space, cross INTERSECT
– decorative line painted along the side of a car or other vehicle COACH LINE, CARRIAGE LINE
– dialogue, as in ancient Greek drama, in which alternate lines of verse are spoken by different characters STICHOMYTHIA
– distance east or west of the prime meridian at Greenwich, measured in degrees and represented typically by vertical lines on a map LONGITUDE
– distance north or south of the equator, measured in degrees and represented by horizontal lines on a map LATITUDE
– fine lines forming the shading in a drawing HATCHING
– having lines written alternately from left to right and from right to left BOUSTROPHEDON
– having or referring to lines of verse that pause at the end, typically with a punctuation mark END-STOPPED
– having or referring to lines of verse that run over into the following line without any pause produced by a sense-break or punctuation ENJAMBED
– lying on the same straight line, as various points might be COLLINEAR, COAXIAL
– meeting at or approaching a common point, as intersecting lines do CONCURRENT, CONVERGENT
– pattern of coloured lines forming squares against a plain background TATTERSALL
– point at which lines intersect or diverge NODE, CUSP, VERTEX
– relating to straight lines RECTILINEAR
– short ornamental line finishing off a stroke of a printed letter SERIF

-line-, -lines- -STICH-, -STICHOUS

linen – chest or wooden trunk, as for linen KIST

linguistics See **language**, **grammar**
– linguistics, language-study PHILOLOGY
– linguistics using a historical approach, studying a language through its development through time DIACHRONIC LINGUISTICS
– linguistics using a non-historical approach, studying a language at one particular point in time SYNCHRONIC LINGUISTICS

lining of a lapel, cuff, or other folded part of clothing REVERS

lining up, as of colour plates in printing colour pictures REGISTER
– lining up three celestial bodies, as of the Earth, Sun, and Moon at full moon or new moon SYZYGY

link, bond, or tie VINCULUM
– link in a series CONCATENATE, CATENATE
– link or bond, or network of connections NEXUS
– linked tightly, in many complex ways INEXTRICABLY LINKED
– linking groove or ridge between two planks, shafts or the like SPLINE

lion, as named in children's stories LEO, SIMBA
– adjective for a lion LEONINE
– group or family of lions PRIDE

lip – adjective for the lips LABIAL
– congenital split in the upper lip, associated with cleft palate HARELIP
– draw in the lips to a tight wrinkled shape PURSE, PUCKER
– ring or ornament inserted in the lip LABRET
– shallow groove running vertically from the nose to the upper lip PHILTRUM
– sulky expression in which lips are pushed outwards POUT

-lips- -LABI-, LABIO-

liqueur See **drinks**

liquid of a kind in between a fine suspension and a solution, containing particles that are larger than molecules COLLOID, COLLOIDAL SOLUTION
– liquid or sauce in which meat or fish is left to soak before cooking MARINADE
– liquid poured out as part of a religious ritual LIBATION
– liquid suspension, in pharmacology MAGMA
– liquid waste, as from a factory or sewage works EFFLUENT
– able to absorb or admit gas or liquid POROUS, PERMEABLE
– amount of liquid, grain, or the like that evaporates or leaks from a container ULLAGE
– become a soft, solidified mass,

as blood, milk, or other liquids might COAGULATE, CLOT, CURDLE
- becoming liquid when stirred or shaken THIXOTROPIC
- change from a liquid into a gas or vapour EVAPORATE
- change from a vapour or gaseous state to a liquid CONDENSE
- clear, thick liquid, secreted by membranes in joints, tendon sheaths, and so on SINOVIA
- clear to whitish, watery liquid from the body tissues LYMPH
- device to slow down or regulate the flow of a liquid BAFFLE
- essence produced by boiling down a liquid DECOCTION
- gluey, thick, and sticky, as some liquids are VISCID, VISCOUS
- injection of liquid into the rectum, as for medication ENEMA
- make a liquid cloudy or muddy by stirring up sediment ROIL
- mixture of solid particles dispersed but not dissolved in a liquid SUSPENSION
- movement of a liquid through a semipermeable membrane such as a cell wall OSMOSIS
- operated by or involving liquid pressure HYDRAULIC
- property of liquids of appearing to form a film across their surface SURFACE TENSION
- raising or lowering of the surface of a liquid in contact with a solid, as a result of surface tension CAPILLARITY, CAPILLARY ACTION
- resistant to liquids or gases IMPERMEABLE, IMPERVIOUS
- sediment or residue at the bottom of liquid LEES, DREGS
- surface forming the boundary between liquids INTERFACE
- surface of a liquid, curved like a lens MENISCUS
- suspension of globules of one liquid inside another EMULSION
- thin layer of liquid LAMELLA, LAMINA
- thin liquid mixture of cement, manure, mud, or the like SLURRY
- unable to blend or mix, as two liquids might be IMMISCIBLE
- watery, yellowish liquid discharged from an ulcer or wound PUS, ICHOR

liquid- HYDR-, HYDRO-

liquid crystal, between liquid and solid or crystal in structure or properties MESOMORPHIC
- referring to the phase of a liquid crystal in which the molecules are arranged in layers with their axes parallel and perpendicular to the plane of the layers SMECTIC
- referring to the phase of a liquid crystal in which the molecules are not arranged in layers but have their axes parallel NEMATIC

liquorice-flavoured seed of the anise plant, used as a flavouring and medicine ANISEED

list, or the items listed INVENTORY
- list items one by one, as on a bill ITEMISE, ENUMERATE
- list of dead people NECROLOGY
- list of duties or of the people to perform them ROSTER, ROTA
- list of items to be dealt with at a meeting AGENDA
- list of people to be murdered, projects to be axed, or the like HIT LIST
- list of plays, skills, or the like that a drama group, or the like can draw on REPERTOIRE
- list of procedures that is pointlessly complicated RIGMAROLE
- list of requirements, described and detailed SPECIFICATIONS
- list item by item TALLY
- list or note in detail PARTICULARISE, SPECIFY
- arrange in lists, tables, or the like TABULATE, CODIFY
- definitive list, as of church laws or an author's works CANON
- listed in the same order as a previous list RESPECTIVELY
- ordered list of people, goods, or the like DIRECTORY, CATALOGUE
- put someone's name on a list to join a club, class, or the like ENROL, REGISTER
- reading out of a list of names of those supposed to be present, as in the army ROLL-CALL, MUSTER

listen closely HEARKEN
- listen secretly to a conversation between others EAVESDROP
- "listen!" call to attention, as when a town crier makes an announcement OYEZ
- listener AUDITOR
- listening, especially when attempting a diagnosis by means of a stethoscope AUSCULTATION
- listening instrument used by doctors to study sounds produced in the body STETHOSCOPE

literacy – ability to use and understand language, though not necessarily to read and write it as in literacy ORACY
- basic skill in arithmetic or competence in numerical calculations, regarded as the counterpart of literacy NUMERACY

literal and unduly fussy about details PEDANTIC
- metaphorical, based on or using figures of speech, not literal FIGURATIVE

literary See chart, page 302, and also **poetry**, **drama**, **high-falutin**
- literary, artistic, or cultural circle COTERIE, CLIQUE, CENACLE
- literary characters, as in a novel or play PERSONAE
- "literary" in a showy way INKHORN
- literary or scientific institution ATHENAEUM
- literary selections from a larger work or group of works DIGEST, ANTHOLOGY, ANALECTS
- literary theft, passing off as one's own the writings or ideas of another PLAGIARISM
- literary work, entertainment, or the like that is elaborate, fanciful, or spectacular EXTRAVAGANZA
- literary work in a light-hearted, high-spirited vein JEU D'ESPRIT
- note of critical commentary or explanation, as on a literary text ANNOTATION, GLOSS
- short literary work, dramatic sketch, or the like CAMEO
- contrast as a literary or artistic technique CHIAROSCURO
- over-refined, excessively rich or precious, as a literary style might be DECADENT
- references, footnotes, and so on in a scholarly edition of a literary text APPARATUS CRITICUS

literature ancient works of literature still admired CLASSICS
- bookish people who parade their knowledge of literature and writers LITERATI
- category of literature, films, or the like GENRE
- fine literature BELLES-LETTRES
- great work of literature OEUVRE
- relating to literature that is refined and classically elegant in style AUGUSTAN
- repeated theme in a work of literature, art or music MOTIF, LEITMOTIF
- selection of passages from literature, used as a text when studying a foreign or ancient language CHRESTOMATHY

litter of piglets FARROW

little See **lack**, **mediocre**, **small**

little'un, someone or something relatively small TIDDLER, RUNT

live See also **living**
- live, continue in existence, or manage to survive SUBSIST
- live, in person IN PROPRIA PERSONA
- live a dull, passive life VEGETATE, STAGNATE
- area where an animal or plant normally lives HABITAT
- place where one lives, legal

LITERARY TERMS

allegory	work in which the characters or events have symbolic meaning and illustrate a moral or spiritual theme
antinovel	work of fiction that rejects the conventional elements of a novel
bathos	sudden descent from the exalted to the ridiculous
belles-lettres	literature considered as art rather than for its educational or moral value
Bildungsroman	novel relating the early development and education of the hero
epigram	short, pithy, and memorable saying making a pointed observation
epistolary novel	novel in the form of a series of letters
euphuism	high-flown rhetorical style of writing
gothic novel	novel popular in the 18th-19th century, characterised by exotic or medieval settings, and macabre or supernatural incidents
leitmotif	recurring theme, as in a novel
mimesis	imitation or realistic representation in literature of nature or human nature
naturalism	true-to-life style of writing
novella	short narrative or novel
passus	section of a story, poem, or the like, especially in medieval literature
pastiche	literary work, often satirical, imitating the style of another writer
pathetic fallacy	representation of inanimate objects in nature as having human qualities and feelings
picaresque novel	episodic novel, popular in the 18th century, relating the adventures of an amiable wandering rogue
roman à clef	novel representing real people, places, and events in a thinly disguised fictional form
roman-fleuve	novel, or series of novels, such as a family saga, chronicling a social group over many years
stream of consciousness, interior monologue	technique of depicting a character's thoughts and feelings as a flow of disjointed or ungrammatical reflections
Sturm und Drang	"storm and stress", late 18th-century German literary movement, highly romantic and inspirational in spirit, often dealing with an individual person's struggle against society or nature
textual criticism	in-depth study and analysis of a text; examination of a literary work, the Bible, or the like in the attempt to establish the original text
topos	stock theme or idea, often forming the basis of early narratives
trilogy	set of three related works by the same author

place of residence DOMICILE

liveliness, spirit, wit ESPIRIT

lively, active, and vigorous SPRY, SPRIGHTLY
– lively, mischievous SKITTISH
– lively, sociable, friendly person EXTROVERT
– lively, sparkling, or spirited ANIMATED, VIVACIOUS, EFFERVESCENT, EXUBERANT
– lively, stimulating, or cheering INVIGORATING, EXHILARATING
– lively, noisy, unruly RUMBUSTIOUS, BOISTEROUS
– lively spirits, enjoyment of life JOIE DE VIVRE

liven up or lighten something dull or humourless LEAVEN

liver, kidneys, and so on of an animal OFFAL
– liver disease or degeneration, often due to alcoholism CIRRHOSIS
– liver disease or inflammation, typically producing jaundice HEPATITIS
– adjective for the liver HEPATIC
– savoury paste of goose liver PÂTÉ DE FOIE GRAS

liver- HEPAT-, HEPATO-

Liverpool – person born or living in Liverpool LIVERPUDLIAN, WACKER, SCOUSE

living See also **live**, **life**
– living, or resembling a living organism, as society or poetry might be considered ORGANIC
– living or able to live both on land and in water AMPHIBIOUS
– living plant or animal ORGANISM
– living together without being legally married COHABITATION, CONCUBINAGE, LIVING TALLY
– living together of two organisms in association, often beneficial, never parasitic COMMENSALISM
– living together of two organisms in close or dependent association, especially when beneficial to both SYMBIOSIS
– capable of living or surviving independently VIABLE
– capable of living, working, or functioning together in a harmonious or efficient way COMPATIBLE
– cutting up or into the body of a living animal, especially when done for research VIVISECTION
– death-like or temporary dormant state of a living organism SUSPENDED ANIMATION

-living -BIOSIS

-living matter -PLAST

-living on -COLOUS

lizard – lizard-like creature in myth, living in or capable of withstanding fire SALAMANDER
– lizard-like SAURIAN

– lizard with the ability to change colour as a means of camouflage CHAMELEON
– Australian monitor lizard GOANNA
– insect-eating lizard with adhesive foot-pads, often seen on walls and ceilings in warm countries GECKO
– large tropical American lizard with a spiny ridge along its back IGUANA
– tropical lizard with very short legs and a scaly body SKINK
– fold of skin hanging from the throat, as of some lizards and birds WATTLE
– replacement of a limb by tissue growth, as of a lizard's tail REGENERATION
– shedding of a body part, such as a lizard's tail, as a means of protection when attacked AUTOTOMY

-lizard- -SAUR-, SAURO-, -SAURUS

llama – South American mammals that are closely related to and very similar to the llama GUANACO, ALPACA, VICUÑA

Lloyd's bell, rung to announce news that an insured ship has gone missing LUTINE BELL

loan agency or moneylender that accepts trade debts as security FACTOR
– loan for a short term made by a bank to a housebuyer still waiting to sell his previous home BRIDGING LOAN
– loan guaranteed by the pledge of property as security COLLATERAL LOAN
– loan of a small amount of money, especially in advance on future payments SUB
– loan repayable immediately on demand CALL LOAN, DEMAND LOAN
– pay off a loan, promissory note, mortgage, or the like REDEEM
– secured loan to a company, bearing interest which is payable prior to any dividends DEBENTURE
– temporary or conditional transfer of title deeds of property as security for a loan MORTGAGE

loan translation, word or phrase translated element by element from another language CALQUE

lobster, crab, prawn, or related ten-legged creature DECAPOD
– lobster, crab, shrimp, or related creature having a segmented body, jointed limbs, and horny shell CRUSTACEAN
– lobster trap or fish basket of wickerwork CREEL
– lobster's claw PINCER, CHELA
– lobster's liver, sometimes regarded as a delicacy TOMALLEY
– lobster's shell MAIL
– roe of a lobster or crab, pink when cooked CORAL

local, native, restricted to a particular area or group, as a disease might be ENDEMIC
– local, native to or originating in a particular region INDIGENOUS, ABORIGINAL, AUTOCHTHONOUS
– local, on or for a particular place, as the application of a medicinal cream might be TOPICAL
– local language or dialect of a particular region VERNACULAR
– local political division in some European countries COMMUNE

lock of the kind almost wholly contained within a cavity in the edge of the door MORTISE LOCK
– lock of the kind having a revolving barrel or cylinder operated by a flat, serrated key YALE LOCK
– lock whose bolt can be drawn back only by means of a key DEADLOCK
– axle, revolving bolt, or the like, as in a lock or between two door handles SPINDLE
– clasp or fastener hinged over a fixed staple, and typically secured with a padlock HASP
– edge of a lock's bolt against which the key presses to drive it home TALON
– edge plate of a lock into which the bolt slots SELVAGE
– metal plate surrounding or covering the keyhole on a lock ESCUTCHEON
– ridge on a lock, or keyhole, or corresponding notch in a key WARD
– section of a lock that obstructs the bolt until moved away by the key TUMBLER

lockjaw TETANUS, TRISMUS

locomotive – frame on the roof of a tram, locomotive, or the like collecting electric current from an overhead wire as it slides along it PANTOGRAPH
– steam-powered locomotive, as for dragging heavy equipment over roads or fields TRACTION ENGINE
– steam-powered locomotive, that carries its own water and coal rather than using a separate tender TANK ENGINE

log – channel for transporting logs SLUICE
– floating barrier, as of logs or empty drums, to confine other logs, protect a harbour, or the like BOOM
– logrolling BIRLING
– metal stand, used in pairs, for logs in a fireplace ANDIRON, FIREDOG
– pole with an adjustable hook used for moving logs PEAVEY, CANT HOOK
– wedge or block placed under a wheel, log, or the like, to immobilise it on a slope SCOTCH, CHOCK

logarithm – decimal part of a logarithm MANTISSA
– integer part of a logarithm CHARACTERISTIC, ARGUMENT

logic See also **argument**, **reasoning**, **fallacy**, **philosophy**
– logic or study of necessity, possibility, and so on MODAL LOGIC
– logic system or method based on deductions using syllogisms ARISTOTELIAN LOGIC
– logic system using mathematical symbols and relationships BOOLEAN ALGEBRA
– logical, based on or showing reason RATIONAL
– logical argument in the form of an extended series of incomplete syllogisms SORITES
– logical coherence or compatibility CONSISTENCY
– logical disproof of a proposition by showing that the inevitable consequences of it are absurd REDUCTIO AD ABSURDUM
– logical element or invented idea forming part of a theory CONSTRUCT
– logical error or faulty argument that invalidates the conclusion FALLACY
– logical or reasonable, as a conclusion might be LEGITIMATE
– logical pattern of deduction in which two premises generate a conclusion SYLLOGISM
– logical reasoning that is based on moving from general premises to particular conclusions that follow from them necessarily DEDUCTION, SYNTHESIS
– logical reasoning RATIOCINATION
– logical reasoning by inferring general truths from particular instances, as distinct from strict logical deduction INDUCTION
– logically inconsistent or conflicting, as two opposed propositions might be INCOMPATIBLE
– logically inconsistent or false, as a conclusion might be INVALID
– logically obvious or self-evident, true by the very nature of its wording or logical form ANALYTIC, TAUTOLOGOUS, A PRIORI, APODICTIC
– logically organised, consistent, and comprehensible COHERENT
– characteristic or attribute that is

affirmed or denied of something in a proposition in logic PREDICATE
– conclusion that is faulty by failing to follow logically from the premises NON SEQUITUR
– diagram of overlapping circles, as for representing relations between the terms of a proposition in logic VENN DIAGRAM
– minor proposition, taken as valid or self-evidently true, and used in proving another proposition LEMMA
– proposition in logic, forming either of the first two parts of a syllogism, from which the conclusion can be deduced PREMISE
– proposition in logic containing two simple statements joined by the word *or* DISJUNCTION
– refuting of an argument in logic by proving that the contrary of its conclusion is true ELENCHUS
– shortened syllogism in logic, in which one of the premises is left unstated ENTHYMEME
– sudden jump in a sequence, as of logical arguments SALTUS
– thinking of an imaginative and free-ranging rather than strictly logical mode, often producing unexpected solutions to problems LATERAL THINKING

London – London's banking and financial world LOMBARD STREET, THE CITY
– cost-of-living allowance in an expensive area such as London WEIGHTING

lonely See also **alone**
– lonely, remote, isolated, solitary, as a place or a life might be SECLUDED
– lonely or miserable through the loss or desertion of a companion or loved one BEREFT, FORLORN, FORSAKEN, DESOLATE
– lonely through being an outcast, withdrawing from society, or losing the sympathy of others ESTRANGED, ALIENATED
– person who is lonely or alone through living independently of society OUTSIDER, LONER
– state of being alone, lonely, or secluded SOLITUDE

long, drawn-out, extended in time, as applause might be PROLONGED, PROTRACTED, SUSTAINED
– long, lengthened, extended, stretched ELONGATED
– long and indirect, as a journey or argument might be CIRCUITOUS
– long and tedious, seemingly endless INTERMINABLE, MARATHON
– long-established, persistent, or deep-rooted, as a tendency might be INVETERATE
– long for something intensely, yearn PINE, HANKER
– long period of time, specifically a thousand million years AEON
– long-range overall view, as in military combat STRATEGY
– long life, age LONGEVITY

long ago, in the old days LANG SYNE

long division or other calculating procedure using a series of steps ALGORITHM

long-lasting See **constant**, **permanent**
– long-lasting, continuing, or regularly recurring, as an illness might be PERSISTENT, CHRONIC
– long-lasting, resistant to decay ABIDING, DURABLE, RESILIENT, ENDURING
– long-lasting in its effect, as poetry might be RESONANT

long-sightedness, defective close-up vision HYPEROPIA, HYPERMETROPIA
– long-sightedness caused by advancing age and the hardening of the lens PRESBYOPIA

long-winded, roundabout, or evasive speech or writing CIRCUMLOCUTION, PROLIXITY, PERIPHRASIS
– long-winded, talkative, chattering in an aimless or boring way GARRULOUS, LOQUACIOUS, MAUNDERING
– long-winded, tedious, or very strained, as a political speech might be LABOURED
– long-winded, wordy in a boring way PROLIX, VERBOSE, DIFFUSE
– long-winded or glib speech, sales talk, or the like SPIEL, PATTER

longing, yearning, sadly reflective over something unobtainable WISTFUL
– longing or sentimental yearning for the past NOSTALGIA

longitude – line of longitude MERIDIAN

look See also **search**, **see**
– look, glance, brief inspection SHUFTI, BUTCHERS, GANDER
– look at someone, especially in a lustful way LEER, OGLE
– look at fixedly and wide-eyed, stare GAPE, GAUP, GOGGLE
– look down on from a height, overlook, tower above DOMINATE
– look for, scratch about, or feel around for with the hands, grope GRABBLE
– look forward to, expect ANTICIPATE
– look or stare angrily or frowningly GLOWER, SCOWL
– look through, grub about, ferret RUMMAGE, FOSSICK
– belittling, causing embarrassment, as sarcasm or a disapproving look might WITHERING
– invite foolishly or unwittingly look for trouble COURT DISASTER
– suspiciously or disapprovingly, the way one might look at a person or suggestion ASKANCE
– take a look, make a preliminary investigation, as of enemy positions RECONNOITRE, RECCE

lookalike, person bearing a striking resemblance to another RINGER

looking back HINDSIGHT, RETROSPECT

loom, of the early 19th century, for mechanical weaving of intricately patterned cloth JACQUARD LOOM

loop on a graph or diagram LOBE
– loop or coil, as of rope HANK
– loops forming an edging on ribbon, lace, or the like PICOTS
– decorative chain or garland of flowers, ribbons, or the like suspended in a loop FESTOON, SWAG
– uncut loop in the pile of towelling or a similar fabric TERRY

loose, sagging, or flabby FLACCID
– loose, supple, nimble, or agile LITHE, LISSOM, LIMBER
– loose, unconnected DETACHED

loosen or slacken a rope or cable SURGE

-loosening- -LYS-, LYSO-, -LYSIS

loot, booty, stolen property PLUNDER, SWAG, HAUL
– raider in search of loot PLUNDERER, MARAUDER, PILLAGER

lord of the manor in Scotland LAIRD
– lord or vassal in feudal times LIEGE
– lord's estate, domain, or house in feudal times MANOR, DEMESNE
– civil, lay, or secular, as most lords are TEMPORAL

Lord See also **God**
– "Lord, have mercy", the Christian prayer or the musical setting for it KYRIE ELEISON
– Lord's prayer, especially in its Latin version PATERNOSTER

Lord Chancellor – Lord Chancellor's office or position, or his official seat in the House of Lords WOOLSACK

lorry in two sections, a tractor and a trailer, pivoted for greater manoeuvrability ARTICULATED LORRY
– lorry used in furniture removals PANTECHNICON
– lorry's or other vehicle's "spy in the cab", device recording the travel times and speeds TACHOGRAPH
– large heavy lorry, used for long-distance transport JUGGERNAUT
– swing out of control into a V-shape, as an articulated lorry might JACKKNIFE
– U.S. lorry driver TEAMSTER
– weight of an unloaded lorry or

goods vehicle TARE
lose MISLAY, MISPLACE
- lose a legal case, sports competition, or the like through failure to appear DEFAULT
- lose confidence momentarily, hesitate WAVER, FALTER
- lose or surrender as punishment for a crime or the like FORFEIT
- lose resistance, yield, submit, or give in to SUCCUMB

loser or likely loser in an election, fight, or other contest UNDERDOG
loss, as through evaporation or leakage, of a substance in a container ULLAGE
- loss, damage, disadvantage DETRIMENT
- loss in value, as of a car, as through age or wear DEPRECIATION
- loss or death of a loved one BEREAVEMENT
- make amends for a loss or injury, as by a payment COMPENSATE
- make good one's losses RECOUP

lost, missing ASTRAY
- lost in thought ABSTRACTED, PREOCCUPIED, ABSORBED
- having lost one's bearings or sense of place DISORIENTATED

lotion for soothing and softening the skin EMOLLIENT
- lotion with soothing or healing properties, rubbed into the skin LINIMENT, EMBROCATION

lots See also **many**, **plenty**
- lots, many, a multitude LEGIONS
- lots, many, loads, tons SLEWS
- lots, much OODLES, REAMS, LASHINGS, SLATHERS

lottery game where winning tickets are picked from a revolving container TOMBOLA
- lottery in which the entire prize is awarded to the winner SWEEPSTAKE

loud See also **noisy**
- loud, booming, deep, and rich in sound SONOROUS, RESONANT
- loud, deep, and resonant, as the sound of waves crashing on the shore is PLANGENT
- loud, harsh or shrill STRIDENT, EAR-PIERCING, BLARING
- loud, having or referring to an extremely loud voice STENTORIAN
- loud, resonant, sustained or repeated noise, din CLANGOUR
- loud and insistent, especially in protest VOCIFEROUS
- loud enough to be heard AUDIBLE
- "loud pedal" on a piano SUSTAINING PEDAL, REVERBERATION PEDAL

loudly, especially in music FORTE, FORTISSIMO
loudness – gradual decrease in loudness, as of a passage of music DECRESCENDO, DIMINUENDO
- gradual increase in loudness, as of a passage of music CRESCENDO
- unit of loudness DECIBEL

loudspeaker reproducing bass frequencies WOOFER
- loudspeaker reproducing high-pitched frequencies TWEETER
- loudspeaker system for public announcements, especially in a large building TANNOY
- sound-regulating device, as in a microphone, or loudspeaker or the like BAFFLE, DIFFUSER

Louisiana – member of a community in Louisiana descended from 18th-century Canadian immigrants, or their French dialect CAJUN
louse See **lice**
love See also **like**, **friendly**, **sex**
- love affair, especially a secret or illicit one AMOUR, LIAISON
- "love feast", meal commemorating the Last Supper, in the early Christian Church AGAPE
- love letter BILLET-DOUX
- love of great intensity, ecstatic love RAPTURE, ARDOUR
- love or passion, typically foolish and short-lived INFATUATION
- love play or flirtation DALLIANCE
- love potion PHILTRE
- love produced or feigned for the sake of some selfish benefit CUPBOARD LOVE
- love song, especially about unrequited love TORCH SONG
- love song, typically sung outside a woman's house in the evening SERENADE
- love too much, adore, be excessively fond of IDOLISE, DOTE ON
- loving devotion, awe, as shown to God REVERENCE, VENERATION
- Christian love, charity, as distinct from erotic love AGAPE
- loving feelings towards someone, fondness TENDRESSE
- loving word, gesture, or the like ENDEARMENT
- engage in casual love affairs PHILANDER
- excessive love, praise, or flattery, worship ADULATION
- in love ENAMOURED, SMITTEN
- not returned or reciprocated, as love might be UNREQUITED
- referring to love between two unrelated people that is free of sexual desire PLATONIC
- relating to love, especially sexual love AMOROUS, AMATORY, EROTIC
- return someone's love REQUITE, RECIPROCATE

-love -PHIL-, PHILO-
lovely See **beautiful**, **attractive**
lovemaking in the form of kissing and cuddling NECKING, CANOODLING
lover, sweetheart PARAMOUR, LEMAN
- lover kept by an older woman GIGOLO
- lover of a promiscuous kind, playboy RAKE, LADYKILLER, CASANOVA, DON JUAN
- lover of his own creation, as an artist might be PYGMALION
- lovers' meeting, or the appointment for it RENDEZVOUS, TRYST, ASSIGNATION
- abandon a lover cruelly JILT
- female lover, mistress, or girlfriend, especially a disreputable one MOLL, FLOOZY, DOXY
- female lover, regular or live-in mistress, or secondary wife CONCUBINE, TALLYWOMAN
- male lover or escort of a married woman, especially in 18th-century Italy CICISBEO
- male suitor, lover, or sweetheart SWAIN, BEAU, INAMORATO
- run away secretly with a lover, especially to marry ELOPE
- self-lover, person in love with himself or herself NARCISSUS

low – low-cut, as a dress or blouse might be, or dressed in such a garment DÉCOLLETÉ
- low part of a cycle, graph, or the like TROUGH

low- HYPO-
low-church in the Church of England EVANGELICAL
lower See **lessen**, **insult**
- lower in rank or status, subordinate, secondary SUBALTERN
- lower or downgrade in status DEMOTE, RELEGATE, DEGRADE

lower- BASI-, CATA-, INFRA-
lower class or working class, especially the class of industrial wage-earners PROLETARIAT
- lower-class person PLEBEIAN, PLEB
- lower classes, considered by Marxists to be uninterested in social change LUMPENPROLETARIAT

lower jaw MANDIBLE
- having or referring to a lower jaw that projects beyond the upper jaw HYPAGNATHOUS, UNDERSHOT, UNDERHUNG
- having or referring to an upper jaw that projects beyond the lower jaw OVERSHOT

lowest, deepest NETHERMOST
- lowest layer or level BEDROCK
- lowest point, as of one's fortunes or of depression NADIR

lowland Scots dialect, especially as

developed as a literary language LALLANS

loyal, dutiful, or enthusiastic to an excessive, foolish, or dangerous degree GUNG HO
- loyal, firm, steadfast STAUNCH
- loyal colleague, advisor or friend TROUPER
- loyal follower or supporter LIEGEMAN
- loyal or supportive in a passionate, often mindless way PARTISAN
- blindly and unthinkingly loyal or imitative of SLAVISH
- loyalty, faithfulness, or steadfastness, as to a spouse, the facts, or one's duty FIDELITY, CONSTANCY
- loyalty, or the duties it demands, to one's country, king, or cause ALLEGIANCE
- loyalty or dutifulness, especially towards one's parents PIETY
- loyalty or fidelity to a party, cause, or set of rules ADHERENCE
- loyalty to and pride in one's group, fellowship ESPRIT DE CORPS
- constant and changeless, as unwavering loyalty is UNSWERVING
- entitled to loyalty, as a lord might be, or bound to give loyalty, as a subject might be LIEGE
- oath or public expression of loyalty by a vassal to his feudal lord HOMAGE, FEALTY

lozenge of a medicated preparation for chewing or sucking PASTILLE, TROCHE

LSD or similar drug producing hallucinations or sensory distortion HALLUCINOGENIC DRUG, PSYCHEDELIC DRUG

lubrication – study of friction and lubrication TRIBOLOGY

luck See also **fate**
- accidental developments, such as changes of luck VICISSITUDES
- depending on or happening by chance or luck ALEATORY
- source of great wealth or luck BONANZA
- tendency to make pleasant discoveries by accident or good luck SERENDIPITY
- unexpected piece of good luck WINDFALL, GODSEND

lucky, boding well, as a day or sign might be considered AUSPICIOUS, PROPITIOUS
- lucky, by a happy accident, by chance FORTUITOUS
- lucky, opportune, happening as if by a miracle PROVIDENTIAL
- lucky accident FLUKE
- lucky charm, magic stone, or the like supposedly with supernatural powers or protection TALISMAN
- lucky charm or piece of jewellery carried about for protection AMULET, PERIAPT
- lucky object, animal, or person, as adopted by a team MASCOT

luggage compartment or folding seat at the rear of a carriage or early motor car DICKEY, RUMBLE SEAT
- conveyer-belt apparatus in the luggage-retrieval hall of an airport CAROUSEL

lukewarm TEPID
- lukewarm, especially in politics or religion LAODICEAN

lullaby or cradle-song BERCEUSE

luminous glow of fungus on rotting wood FOXFIRE

lump, bump, bulge, or similar rounded projection PROTUBERANCE, PROTRUSION
- lump, especially of natural gold NUGGET
- lump in a yarn of fabric, sometimes made deliberately to produce a knobbly appearance SLUB
- lump of soft matter, particularly of chewed food BOLUS
- lump or chunk, as of raw meat GOBBET
- small knob, lump, bump, or swelling NODULE, NODE

lunch – snack or light lunch TIFFIN

lung disease of an infectious bacterial type, characterised by small swellings or lesions TUBERCULOSIS, TB, CONSUMPTION, PHTHISIS
- lung disorder, caused by swelling of the air sacs, involving wheezing and breathlessness EMPHYSEMA
- lungs of a slaughtered pig, sheep, or the like, used especially for pet food LIGHTS
- crackling sound of diseased or fluid-filled lungs RALE
- creak, rattle, or crackle, as diseased lungs or broken bones might CREPITATE
- membrane lining the chest cavity and encasing the lungs PLEURA
- pooling of blood or fluid in the lungs or other organ owing to bad circulation HYPOSTASIS
- relating to the lungs PULMONARY, PNEUMONIC
- small cavity or pit, such as a honeycomb cell or any of the tiny air cells in a lung where oxygen is absorbed by the blood ALVEOLUS
- thick-walled tubes linking the windpipe to the lungs BRONCHI

lung- PNEUM-, PNEUMO-

lure, entice, or incite, especially into a sinful or illegal act SOLICIT
- lure, tempt, attract ENTICE
- bird or other animal, artificial or live, used to lure others into shooting range or capture DECOY

lust See also **sex**
- arousing or appealing to sexual lust, lewd SALACIOUS, PRURIENT, LUBRICIOUS
- indulge one's lust, appetites, or the like to the full SATE, SATIATE
- unsatisfiable, as thirst or lust might be INSATIABLE
- lustful, given to or arousing excessive and uncontrolled lust or sexual desire LASCIVIOUS, LECHEROUS, LIBERTINE, LIBIDINOUS, CONCUPISCENT, RUTTISH
- lustful as a goat HIRCINE
- lustful man, lecher SATYR
- lustful or knowing look LEER

lusty, robust, or coarsely humorous RABELAISIAN

luxurious, grand or ornate, as plush furnishings might be LAVISH, OPULENT, SUMPTUOUS
- luxurious, gratifying to the senses VOLUPTUOUS
- luxurious or elaborate, as a feast might be LUCULLAN
- luxurious or immoral place or situation BABYLON
- luxurious or plentiful only in appearance or by report, as an illusory feast might be BARMECIDAL
- luxuriously sensual or self-indulgent living FLESHPOTS
- indulge oneself luxuriously, as in sensual pleasures or self-pity REVEL, WALLOW

luxury – luxury-loving person, devoted to sensual pleasures SYBARITE, VOLUPTUARY, HEDONIST, EPICUREAN
- luxury-loving, spendthrift, or wasteful person PRODIGAL, PROFLIGATE
- land of luxury and idleness in medieval legend COCKAIGNE
- living in wasteful or immoral luxury CORINTHIAN
- person who enjoys luxurious living BON VIVANT

lying See also **lie**
- lying down, especially face down, as in submission or grief PROSTRATE
- lying down flat RECLINING, DECUMBENT, RECUMBENT
- lying face downwards PRONE
- lying face upwards on one's back SUPINE
- lying next to or alongside ADJACENT, CONTIGUOUS, MARGINAL, TANGENTIAL
- lying or false MENDACIOUS
- lying stretched out on the ground, with arms and legs spread out SPREADEAGLED

lying-in, confinement during childbirth ACCOUCHEMENT

lymph vessel- ANGIO-

lynch mob POSSE, POSSE COMITATUS

M

machine See also **medical**, **scientific**, **measuring**, **laboratory**
- machine-like person, behaving as though not under his own control AUTOMATON, ROBOT
- machine or device, especially an irregular or makeshift one CONTRAPTION
- part attached as an accessory, as to a machine FITMENT
- person opposed to the introduction of machinery or technical advance LUDDITE
- remove useful parts from a car, machine, or the like for repairing a similar model CANNIBALISE
- working model or device reproducing the conditions of a real environment, machine, or the like, used for training or experiment SIMULATOR

machine-gun emplacement in the form of a low round concrete building PILLBOX
- machine-gun or bomb enemy ground troops from low-flying aircraft STRAFE
- machine-guns, missiles, or the like grouped in an emplacement NEST

mackerel or herring salted in brine and lightly smoked BLOATER
- small young mackerel SPIKE

mad, crazy, insane CERTIFIABLE
- mad, frantic, or unbalanced, as through anxiety or grief DEMENTED, DERANGED, DISTRACTED, DISTRAUGHT, UNHINGED
- mad, out of one's mind, and thus not responsible for one's actions NON COMPOS MENTIS
- mad or uncontrollable through the influence of evil spirits or an overpowering emotion POSSESSED
- mad woman in a frenzied and ecstatic state MAENAD
- act with mad, destructive, or frantic violence GO BERSERK, RUN AMOK
- madly enthusiastic, extreme, possessed by excessive or irrational zeal FANATICAL, OBSESSED
- odd, cranky, a little mad, with "bees in one's bonnet" ECCENTRIC, IDIOSYNCRATIC, QUIRKY
- slang terms for mad DOOLALLY, LOCO, MESHUGGA

mad dog – fatal illness caused by the bite of a mad dog RABIES, HYDROPHOBIA

made-to-order, as a suit of clothes might be BESPOKE

made-up, false, fabricated, as a charge or accusation might be TRUMPED-UP

madman – aggressive, violent madman, typically subject to wildly fluctuating moods PSYCHOPATH

madness – mental disorder characterised by delusions of persecution or grandeur and similar signs of apparent madness PARANOIA
- mental illness characterised by emotional instability, delusions, withdrawal from reality, and similar serious signs of apparent madness SCHIZOPHRENIA
- mental illness or apparent madness occurring simultaneously in a married couple or pair of close relatives FOLIE À DEUX
- mental or emotional deterioration to the point of apparent madness DEMENTIA
- fit of madness that is characterised by irrational enthusiasm, rapidly changing ideas, or violence MANIA
- psychological disorder characterised by deep obsessions, hallucinations, severe confusion, and similar serious signs of apparent madness PSYCHOSIS
- temporary madness characterised by confusion, raving, tremors, or the like, as caused by fever, intoxication, or shock DELIRIUM
- wild, violent madness, or a fit of such madness FRENZY

Mafia leader CAPO
- secret society or criminal organisation, similar to the Mafia; based in Naples CAMORRA
- U.S. criminal organisation related to or modelled on the Sicilian Mafia COSA NOSTRA

magazine, review, or periodical with short or summarised articles and reports DIGEST
- magazine for those with a particular hobby or interest, especially a science-fiction magazine FANZINE
- magazine's listing of its owner and staff, often printed prominently on the front page FLAG, MASTHEAD
- magazine's size, shape, layout, or design FORMAT
- magazines or books that are typically cheap and sensational or sentimental PULP
- small stall, as for selling magazines KIOSK
- expensively produced magazine, usually with many colour photographs, on shiny paper GLOSSY
- number of copies distributed or sold of a newspaper or magazine CIRCULATION
- payment or order for an advance purchase, as of concert tickets or issues of a magazine over a period of time SUBSCRIPTION

Magi – names of the three Magi, according to tradition CASPAR, MELCHIOR, BALTHAZAR
- perfumed resins among the gifts of the Magi MYRRH, FRANKINCENSE

magic See also **black magic**
- magic, sorcery SORTILEGE
- magic intended to achieve an effect by some imitative ceremony or symbolic object, as in sticking pins into a doll SYMPATHETIC MAGIC
- magic or supernatural arts and happenings THE OCCULT
- magic potion believed to arouse love or desire PHILTRE
- magic spell cast through ritual chanting INCANTATION
- magic stone, lucky charm, or the like supposedly giving supernatural powers or protection TALISMAN
- magic symbol, inscription, or the like RUNE
- object believed to have magical powers or to house a spirit FETISH, JUJU

magician CONJURER
- magician, astrologer, or soothsayer CHALDEAN
- magician or astrologer of ancient times MAGUS
- magician or miracle-worker THAUMATURGIST, ENCHANTER
- magician or ventriloquist ILLUSIONIST
- magician or wizard SORCERER
- magician's or scholar's attendant in medieval times FAMULUS

– magician's talk HOCUS-POCUS
– great magician or chief wizard ARCHIMAGE
– skill or speed of hand movements, as used in a magician's conjuring tricks SLEIGHT OF HAND, LEGERDEMAIN, PRESTIDIGITATION

magistrate in a Scottish town in former times BAILIE
– magistrate of high rank in ancient Rome PRAETOR
– magistrate who is legally qualified and receives a salary STIPENDIARY MAGISTRATE
– magistrate's court, or a sitting of it PETTY SESSIONS
– chief magistrate of a Scottish burgh PROVOST
– relating to a master or magistrate MAGISTERIAL

magnet – condition of having two opposing physical properties at different points, as a magnet or battery has POLARITY
– soft iron bar linking the two poles of a horseshoe magnet KEEPER, ARMATURE

magnetic force driving two bodies apart REPULSION
– magnetic mineral, used in early compasses LODESTONE
– magnetic personal charm and power of inspiration CHARISMA
– neutralise the magnetic field of something, especially of a ship's hull DEGAUSS
– pair of closely positioned magnetic poles or electric charges that are equal but opposite DIPOLE
– state of maximum magnetisation of a metal SATURATION

magnificent in appearance, splendid RESPLENDENT, DAZZLING

magnifying glass in a jeweller's eyepiece LOUPE

maharajah's wife MAHARANI

mahogany wood ACAJOU

maid – maidservant, nanny, or nursemaid in the tropics AYAH
– young woman, especially a flirtatious lady's maid, in a comic opera SOUBRETTE

maiden name – "born", used before the maiden name of a married woman when identifying her NÉE

maidenhead HYMEN

mail See **letter, post**

main See also **important**
– main, chief, foremost, supreme PARAMOUNT, PREDOMINANT, PREEMINENT, PREPONDERANT
– main axis or stem, as of a flower cluster or feather RACHIS
– main dish of a meal PIÈCE DE RÉSISTANCE
– main part of something, such as a body organ CORPUS
– main part or ingredient STAPLE
– main point of a speech or argument GIST, BURDEN, GRAVAMEN
– main route bearing traffic, messages, or the like ARTERY

main- ARCH-

maintenance payment made to a lover after separation PALIMONY

maisonette – small and tasteful, as a maisonette is sometimes humorously described as being BIJOU

maize INDIAN CORN, SWEETCORN
– maize meal or porridge SAMP
– maize meal, used for a porridge-like food HOMINY GRITS
– maize whiskey BOURBON
– dish of maize kernels and lima beans SUCCATASH

majority, the greater part THE GENERALITY
– majority in an election in which the winner fails to secure more than half of the votes or seats RELATIVE MAJORITY, PLURALITY
– majority in an election in which the winner secures more than half of the total votes or seats ABSOLUTE MAJORITY
– overpowering or irresistible, as an election majority might be OVERWHELMING

make, accomplish, produce according to a prescribed plan EXECUTE
– make, as of a car MARQUE
– make, cause to become RENDER
– make, construct, or put together from separate parts ASSEMBLE
– make, invent, or prepare something artificial or dubious, cook up CONCOCT, FABRICATE
– make, put together, prepare CONFECT
– make, produce, or invent something using readily available resources IMPROVISE
– make again in the original form RECONSTITUTE, RECONSTRUCT
– make by careful planning or inventiveness CONTRIVE, DEVISE, EXCOGITATE
– make by giving shape to FORGE, MOULD, FASHION
– make industrially MANUFACTURE
– make or introduce by developing or inventing PIONEER, ORIGINATE, INNOVATE
– make or invent by gradual development EVOLVE

-make -FY

make good one's losses RECOUP
– making good, compensation, repayment RESTITUTION, AMENDS, REPARATIONS, REDRESS
– making good, release from debt or sin, atonement REDEMPTION, QUITTANCE, EXPIATION, REQUITAL

make-up See **cosmetics**
– make-up used by actors GREASEPAINT
– covered with make-up, as a clown might be FARDED

make up for or counterbalance something OFFSET, COMPENSATE, COUNTERVAIL

makeshift, improvised, temporary EXTEMPORANEOUS
– makeshift, substitute STOPGAP

-making -FACIENT, -FIC, -POIESIS

malaria PALUDISM
– malaria or other disease transmitted by animals ZOONOSIS
– malaria-infested PALUDAL
– malaria or similar fever involving chills and shivering AGUE
– malaria treatment, drug derived from the bark of a South American tree QUININE, CINCHONA, CINCHONINE
– mosquito of the kind that carries malaria ANOPHELES
– recurring daily, as attacks of malaria might QUOTIDIAN

Malay village or compound KAMPONG
– Malay garment in the form of a coloured cloth wrapped round the waist SARONG
– Malay sword or large knife with a wavy double-edged blade KRIS
– Malayan form of polite address, equivalent to *Mr* or *Sir* TUAN
– Malaysian who is an indigenous ethnic Malay BUMIPUTRA

male club or social group FRATERNITY
– male-dominated society PATRIARCHY
– "male hormone" ANDROGEN, TESTOSTERONE
– male menopause CLIMACTERIC
– male pride of a swaggering, exaggerated kind, aggressive masculinity MACHISMO
– male principle or personality in a woman's unconscious, in Jungian philosophy ANIMUS
– abnormal development of male characteristics in a woman VIRILISM
– active male force or principle in eastern philosophy YANG
– having the qualities of an adult male VIRILE
– relating to the male line of descent PATRILINEAL
– sex chromosome in humans and most animals associated with male characteristics Y-CHROMOSOME
– weaken, deprive of initiative and other qualities traditionally regarded as male EMASCULATE

-male- -ANDR-, ANDRO-

malicious, random, unprovoked, as vandalism or wilful destruction is

WANTON, GRATUITOUS
– malicious, spiteful, hate-filled VIRULENT
malnutrition disease, especially among African children, due to lack of protein KWASHIORKOR
– malnutrition disease due to lack of vitamin B BERIBERI
– malnutrition disease due to lack of vitamin C SCURVY
malt vinegar ALEGAR
– frame or floor on which barley is spread for malting COUCH
– kiln for drying hops or malt OAST
mammal of a very large build with a very thick skin, especially the elephant, rhinoceros, and hippopotamus PACHYDERM
– mammal of the group having hooves, including horses and cattle UNGULATE
– mammal of the order having an even number of toes, including cattle, antelope, deer, and pigs ARTIODACTYL
– mammal of the order having an odd number of toes, including horses and rhinoceroses PERISSODACTYL
– mammal of the order having incisor teeth especially adapted for gnawing, including rats and squirrels RODENT
– mammal of the sub-order having four stomachs and chewing the cud, including cattle, sheep and deer RUMINANT
– having a backbone or spinal column, as fish, birds, and mammals have VERTEBRATE
man as a thinking animal HOMO SAPIENS
– man-like, as some of the apes are ANTHROPOID
– man of very small proportions HOMUNCULUS, MANIKIN, PYGMY
– man or man-like extinct mammal HOMINID
– having the qualities of a grown man VIRILE
-man- -ANDR-, ANDRO-, -ANTHROP-, ANTHROPO-
man-about-town, man of fashion BOULEVARDIER
man-made, artificial SYNTHETIC
– man-made object ARTEFACT
man of fashion whose chief interest is in clothes and manners BEAU, BEAU BRUMMELL, DANDY, FOP
manage, supervise, or control ADMINISTER, REGULATE, SUPERINTEND
– manage to do something, especially by means of a trick ENGINEER, CONTRIVE
– manage without or get rid of DISPENSE WITH
manager of property, finances, social arrangements, or the like STEWARD
Manchester – person born or living in Manchester MANCUNIAN
-mancy See **fortune-telling**
Mandarin Chinese GUOYU
manhood, masculine vigour VIRILITY
mania See chart
– compulsive and harmful mania, desire, or urging CACOETHES
-manifestation -PHANY
manipulate the boundaries of an electoral constituency for party advantage GERRYMANDER
– manipulating the bones, as a form of therapy OSTEOPATHY
– person or group manipulated to further the purposes of another PAWN
manner of behaving or conducting oneself DEMEANOUR, DEPORTMENT
– affected, fussily over-elegant as someone's manner or speech might be PRECIOUS
– harsh or curt in speech or manner BRUSQUE, ABRASIVE
-manner -WISE
manners, code of proper behaviour within a given group or society, good form ETIQUETTE, PROTOCOL
– manners of a smooth or perfect kind, polish FINISH
– act, usually unintended, of bad manners or improper behaviour SOLECISM
– good manners or correct behaviour, propriety DECORUM
– over-fussy detail, as of manners or protocol PUNCTILIO
manoeuvrable, steerable DIRIGIBLE
manoeuvre around an enemy unit OUTFLANK
– manoeuvre for position or advantage JOCKEY
– manoeuvre in which deception or surprise is used to outwit the enemy STRATAGEM
manor of a feudal lord SEIGNIORY, DEMESNE
manual worker who is skilled at a craft ARTISAN
– relating to industrial wage earners in manual labouring jobs BLUE-COLLAR
manufacturer – powerful business person, industrialist, or manufacturer TYCOON, MAGNATE
manuscript adorned with painted designs and lettering ILLUMINATED MANUSCRIPT
– manuscript illumination, such as a small picture or ornamental letter MINIATURE
– manuscript in the author's handwriting, AUTOGRAPH, HOLOGRAPH
– manuscript with more than one layer of text visible PALIMPSEST

MANIAS

OBSESSION WITH, OR ADDICTION TO:	
alcohol	**dipsomania**
books	**bibliomania**
bridges	**gephyromania**
cats	**ailuromania**
crowds	**demomania, ochlomania**
dead bodies	**necromania**
death	**thanatomania**
dogs	**cynomania**
drugs	**narcomania**
eating	**phagomania, sitomania**
fire-raising	**pyromania**
flowers	**anthomania**
horses	**hippomania**
lying and exaggerating	**mythomania**
oneself	**egomania**
personal cleanliness	**ablutomania**
pleasure	**hedonomania**
power	**megalomania**
religion	**entheomania, theomania**
riches	**plutomania, chrematomania**
sex	**erotomania, nymphomania, satyromania**
single idea or thing	**monomania**
stealing	**kleptomania**
surgery or undergoing surgery	**tomomania**
talking	**logomania, verbomania**
travelling	**dromomania, hodomania, poriomania**
work	**ergomania**

– compare manuscripts or other texts to see where they differ COLLATE
– containing errors or changes, as the text of a copied manuscript might CORRUPT
– copyist of manuscripts in ancient and medieval times SCRIBE
– correct and style a manuscript in preparation for typesetting COPY-EDIT
– room in a monastery in which scribes could copy records or manuscripts SCRIPTORIUM
– space or missing part in a manuscript LACUNA
– style of script or handwriting in medieval manuscripts MINUSCULE, UNCIAL
– title, heading, or letter, typically illuminated in red in a manuscript or book RUBRIC
– treated sheepskin or goatskin, on which ancient manuscripts are written PARCHMENT
– volume of ancient manuscripts, as of the Scriptures CODEX

Manx emblem of three limbs radiating from a centre TRISKELION

many See also **lots**, **excessive**, **plenty**
– many, several, varied MULTIPLE, MANIFOLD, DIVERSE, SUNDRY, NUMEROUS, MULTIPLEX
– made of many parts or kinds, having great variety MULTIFARIOUS
– very many, countless INNUMERABLE, MYRIAD, MULTITUDINOUS, UMPTEEN, LEGION

many- PLURI-, MULTI-, POLY-

many-headed monster killed by Hercules HYDRA

many-sided, as a problem might be HYDRA-HEADED

Maori See chart

map See illustration
– map projection of the Earth producing straight parallel lines for both latitude and longitude, similar to Mercator's projection GALL'S PROJECTION
– map projection of the Earth showing the various continents in correct proportion to their real size HOMOLOGRAPHIC PROJECTION, HAMMER'S PROJECTION, PETERS PROJECTION
– map showing different altitudes of the land CONTOUR MAP, RELIEF MAP
– map the heights and distances of an area of land by measuring and calculating SURVEY
– mapping of a region, as a skill or technique CHOROGRAPHY
– mapping system, especially the representation of the Earth on a flat surface PROJECTION
– circle, often decorated, printed on a map, showing the points of the compass COMPASS ROSE
– crisscross pattern, as on a map GRID
– description or display of a place's geographical features, as on a map TOPOGRAPHY
– distance east or west of the prime meridian at Greenwich, measured in degrees and often represented by vertical lines on a map LONGITUDE
– distance north or south of the equator, measured in degrees and often represented by horizontal lines on a map LATITUDE
– key explaining the symbols used in a map or chart LEGEND
– line on a language map linking places using the same distinctive word or pronunciation ISOGLOSS
– line on a weather map linking places of equal atmospheric pressure ISOBAR
– numbers or measurements that pinpoint a position, as on a map or graph COORDINATES

mapmaking or chartmaking CARTOGRAPHY
– mapmaking organisation in Britain or Ireland ORDNANCE SURVEY

marathon runners' physical or psychological difficulties often arising after about 20 miles THE WALL

marble, of a fine white variety, as used in ancient statues PARIAN MARBLE
– marble-like ornamental stone ALABASTER, ONYX MARBLE
– marble-like stone that has a glassy finish PURBECK MARBLE
– marble of high quality used in sculpture CARRARA MARBLE
– marble of Italian origin having green streaks CIPOLIN
– marble or similar stone with greenish veins or mottles, as used for interior decoration VERD ANTIQUE
– marble tomb or stone coffin SARCOPHAGUS
– adjective for marble MARMOREAL
– area or pit from which marble is extracted QUARRY

marbles as a game, or a large marble, or the line from which a marble-player shoots TAW
– large playing marble ALLEY

march in single file, as troops might DEFILE
– marching or other military drill on a barrack square SQUARE-BASHING
– marching step, as in Nazi military parades, in which the leg is swung high with the knee locked GOOSE STEP

March – 15 March in the Roman calendar, or a corresponding day in other months IDES

margarine – referring to natural oils, as used in healthy margarines, having many double or triple chemical bonds POLYUNSATURATED

margin of error, shortfall, or variation LEEWAY, LATITUDE
– margin set in at the beginning of a paragraph INDENTATION
– having printed lines set flush with the margins JUSTIFIED
– marginal note or explanation in the bible POSTIL

MAORI TERMS

Aotearoa	"land of the long white cloud": New Zealand
haere mai	"welcome!"
haka	war dance accompanied by chanting
kit, kite	basket, usually of woven flax
kia-ora	"good luck!", "good health!": a greeting
mahi	work
mana	magical power; charismatic personality
marae	meeting-place
moko	tattoo pattern
pa, pah	village, originally fortified
pakeha	white person, as opposed to a Maori
rangatira	chief or noble
taiaha	long, spear-like weapon
tama	youth, boy
tangata	man or husband
tangi	"weeping": mourning, or a funeral
tiki, heitiki	stone figurine of an ancestor, strung on flax and worn around the neck as a talisman
wahine	Polynesian or Maori woman or wife

map projections

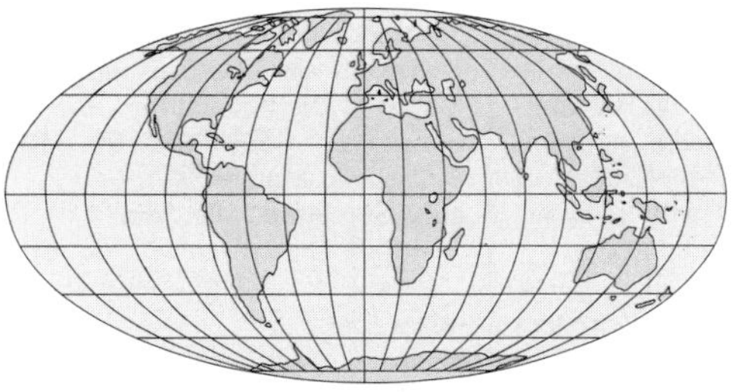

MOLLWEIDE'S HOMOLOGRAPHIC PROJECTION
continents in correct proportion to their actual size

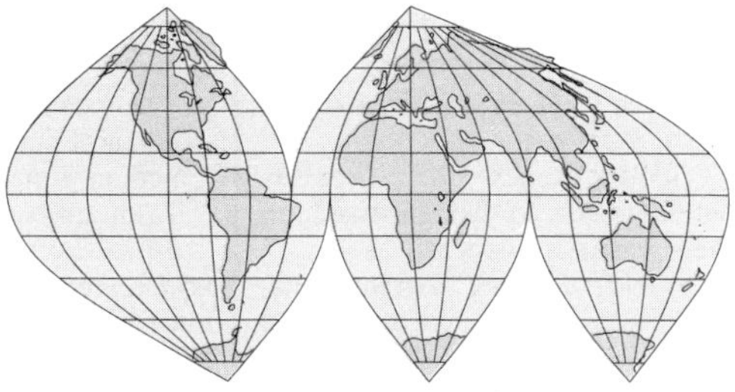

INTERRUPTED PROJECTION
distortion reduced by division into segments

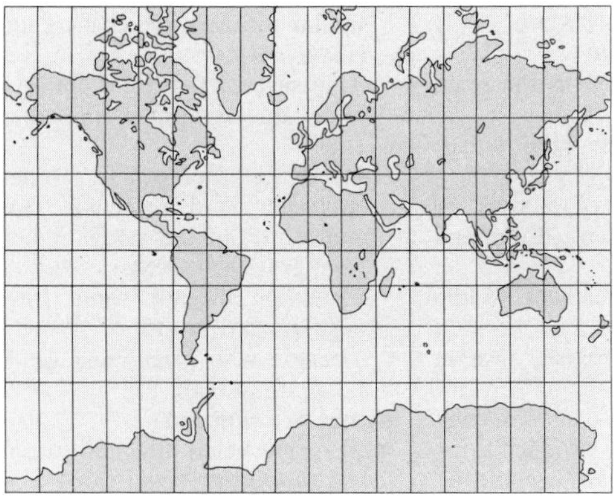

MERCATOR'S PROJECTION
shapes and bearings accurate; high-latitude areas distorted

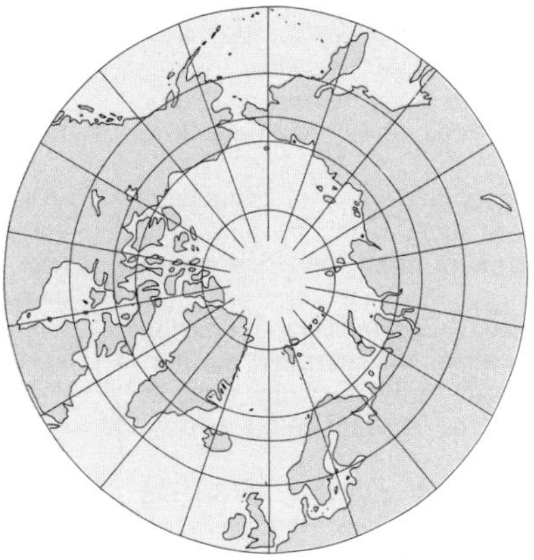

POLAR ZENITHAL PROJECTION
compass bearings accurate from a central point

– set lines of type or print against a specified margin RANGE
marines See **services**
mark of quality or identification, impressed faintly on to paper and visible when held up to the light WATERMARK
– mark or sign of shame or disgrace STIGMA
– mark something, such as a passage in a book, with a tab, symbol, or the like FLAG
– mark stamped on gold or silver objects indicating the purity of the metal HALLMARK, PLATEMARK
– marks, features, or characteristics of a very distinctive or important kind LINEAMENTS
market or covered bazaar in a Muslim country SOUK
– market quarter of a North African town KASBAH
– maximum possible supply of a commodity within a market SATURATION
– seller of food or goods from a barrow or market stall COSTERMONGER
market garden – U.S. term for a market garden TRUCK FARM
marketing and transport of commercial goods DISTRIBUTION
– marketing rights for a particular product in a given area CONCESSION
marketplace, exchange, trading centre RIALTO
– marketplace in an ancient Greek city, in which public meetings took place AGORA
marksman shooting, typically at long range, at exposed individuals or victims SNIPER
marquis's wife, widow, or female counterpart MARCHIONESS
marriage, in keeping with Old Testament law, to the widow of one's brother LEVIRATE
– marriage-announcement, as read out in church on the three Sundays before the wedding BANNS
– marriage between a royal or noble person and a partner of lower rank, with strict limitations on rights of inheritance MORGANATIC MARRIAGE
– marriage between people of different tribes, clans or castes OUTBREEDING, EXOGAMY
– marriage by a man to two or more sisters successively SORORATE
– marriage-like relationship, sometimes recognised as a marriage in law, of a couple who have lived together for several years COMMON-LAW MARRIAGE
– marriage officer in a registry office REGISTRAR
– marriage or sexual relations between people of different races MISCEGENATION
– marriage performed by a registrar or other qualified civil official rather than by a clergyman CIVIL MARRIAGE
– marriage song or poem EPITHALAMIUM, PROTHALAMIUM, HYMENEAL
– marriage state or ceremony MATRIMONY
– marriage that is unsuitable or unsuccessful MISALLIANCE
– marriage with someone from a lower class MÉSALLIANCE
– marriage within one's own tribe, clan, or caste ENDOGAMY

– married SPLICED
– married couple who are elderly and devoted DARBY AND JOAN
– married or engaged ESPOUSED, BETROTHED
– born in wedlock, of married parents LEGITIMATE
– bride's money or property handed over to her husband on their marriage DOWRY
– capable of living together harmoniously, as the partners in a marriage should be COMPATIBLE
– celebrate a marriage, perform a ceremony, or the like with formal or religious rites SOLEMNISE
– clothing, linen, and the like collected by a woman for use after her marriage TROUSSEAU
– crime of being married to two or more people at any one time BIGAMY
– custom or practice of being married to more than one man at a time, as in some cultures POLYANDRY
– custom or practice of having more than one marriage partner, especially more than one wife, at a time, as in some cultures POLYGAMY
– custom or practice of having only one marriage partner at a time, as in most cultures MONOGAMY
– desirable, marriageable, as an attractive young woman is said to be NUBILE
– desirable and worthy for marriage, as a rich bachelor might be considered ELIGIBLE
– end or cancel a legal bond such as marriage ANNUL, DISSOLVE
– in reaction to or during recovery from disappointment, as a marriage might be ON THE REBOUND
– legal completion of a marriage by an act of sexual intercourse CONSUMMATION
– legal right to the help, company, and affection of one's marriage partner CONSORTIUM
– living together and having a sexual relationship without being formally married COHABITATION
– persistent conflict and disharmony in a marriage INCOMPATIBILITY
– person who tries to bring a suitable pair together for marriage MATCHMAKER
– real or fictitious drawer for a trousseau saved by a young woman for use after her marriage, or the goods themselves BOTTOM DRAWER, HOPE CHEST, GLORY BOX
– referring or relating to a spouse's sexual relationship outside marriage EXTRAMARITAL, ADULTEROUS
– relating to marriage MARITAL, MATRIMONIAL, HYMENEAL, NUPTIAL, CONJUGAL, CONNUBIAL
– restoration of harmony or mutual acceptance between the partners in a marriage RECONCILIATION
– run away secretly with a lover, especially to get married ELOPE

-marriage- -GAM-

marrow of a bone or pith of a stem MEDULLA

marrow- MYEL-, MYELO-

Mars – "sea" or dark patch on Mars or the Moon MARE

marsh, swamp, mire or bog QUAGMIRE, SLOUGH, FEN, MUSKEG
– marsh gas METHANE
– marsh plant related to the grass family SEDGE
– marshy stretch of land WASH, MORASS, OOZE, SWALE, VLEI
– marshy tributary of a river or lake, especially in Louisiana BAYOU
– adjective for a marsh or swamp PALUDAL, PALUDINAL
– atmosphere of a marsh, swamp, or the like MIASMA
– light hovering over marshy ground, probably produced by flaming methane gas WILL-O'-THE-WISP, IGNIS FATUUS, JACK-O'-LANTERN, FRIAR'S LANTERN
– smelly and invisible vapour or gas, as rising from a marsh or rubbish dump EFFLUVIUM

marsupials See **Australian terms**

martial arts See **sports**

marvel, outstanding person or thing HUMDINGER
– marvel or extraordinary event, thing, or action PRODIGY, PORTENT

Marxist theory of reality, in which historical change occurs through the resolving of successive contradictions DIALECTICAL MATERIALISM

masculine See **male**

mash or sieve boiled food to produce a pulpy consistency PURÉE

mask, or the hooded robe worn with it, at a masquerade DOMINO
– mask for shielding the eyes, as worn by welders VISOR
– mask over the mouth and nose to purify or warm the air before breathing RESPIRATOR
– masked actor in an old-fashioned masque or mime MUMMER
– masked ball MASQUERADE

masonry See **brickwork**

Mass See also **Communion, church**
– Mass of a traditional Latin form used from 1570 to Vatican II TRIDENTINE MASS
– Mass that is optional or special, as for a wedding, rather than the prescribed Mass of the day VOTIVE MASS
– endowment for the saying of prayers or Mass, usually for the soul of the benefactor CHANTRY
– prayer book for the Roman Catholic Mass MISSAL

mass See **lump, pile, join**
– thick bushy mass, as of hair SHOCK

-mass -OME

massacre, typically organised with official backing, as of Jews in Eastern Europe in former times POGROM

massage, remedial exercises, and similar forms of medical treatment PHYSIOTHERAPY
– massage of perfumed lotion into the scalp, as after a haircut FRICTION
– massage therapy for relieving emotional and muscular tension and adjusting the body to benefit from gravity ROLFING
– massage therapy using fragrant oils AROMATHERAPY
– person who gives massages MASSEUR, MASSEUSE

masses See **common**

mast – crossbeam attached to a mast and supporting a sail YARD
– crosstree on a masthead JACK
– iron rod buttressing a ship's mast FUTTOCK SHROUD
– lower a mast, sail, or flag STRIKE
– lower end of a mast HEEL
– pole used as a mast or boom SPAR
– rope or cable supporting a mast on a ship or boat SHROUDS, GUYS, STAYS
– slope backwards, as a ship's mast or funnel might RAKE
– support frame on deck for a pivoting mast TABERNACLE
– tub-shaped lookout platform near the top of a ship's mast CROW'S-NEST

master of an art, especially a leading musician MAESTRO, VIRTUOSO
– adjective for a master MAGISTERIAL
– title of respect in East Africa, as used for a master or boss BWANA
– title of respect in colonial India, roughly equivalent to "Master" or "Sir" SAHIB

master key or skeleton key PASSKEY, PASSE-PARTOUT

master of ceremonies, as on a radio show COMPERE
– master of ceremonies at a celebration or banquet who proposes toasts and presents speakers TOASTMASTER

masterpiece CHEF D'OEUVRE, TOUR DE FORCE

masturbation ONANISM

mat of lace, paper, or the like, as placed on plates DOILY
– mat of straw used as a floor covering in a Japanese home TATAMI
– mat on the upper part of a chair to protect the fabric from hair oil ANTIMACASSAR
– coconut-husk fibre, as used for ropes and matting COIR

match See also **agree**
– match, correspond TALLY
– match, game, or the like played between tied contestants to determine a winner PLAY-OFF
– match formerly used for lighting cigars VESUVIAN
– match that ignites when struck against any rough surface FRICTION MATCH, LUCIFER
– match with a large head, remaining alight in the wind FUSEE
– chemical element used in safety matches PHOSPHORUS
– short friction match, typically with a wax-coated stick VESTA

matchbox label collector PHILLUMENIST

matching clothes or accessories designed to be worn together CO-ORDINATES
– matching partner, complementary part PENDANT

mate – habit of having only one female mate, as with many male animals MONOGYNY
– habit of having only one male mate, as with many female animals MONANDRY
– habit of having only one mate at a time, as with many animals MONOGAMY
– habit of having several different mates during a single breeding season, as with some animals POLYGAMY
– habit of mating with several different females during a single breeding season, as with some male animals POLYGYNY
– habit of mating with several different males during a single breeding season, as with some female animals POLYANDRY

material See also **cloth**, **fabric**
– material, physical, or actual rather than conceptual or imaginary OBJECTIVE
– material, such as reinforced concrete, made of two or more distinct materials COMPOSITE
– trimming or decoration consisting of different materials pasted or sewn together APPLIQUÉ

materialistic, interested chiefly or only in money and possessions MERCENARY
– materialistic, purely functional or mechanical BANAUSIC

mathematics See chart, page 314, and diagram, and also **geometry**, **graph**, **statistics**
– mathematical representation of a problem, system, or situation SIMULATION
– mathematical study of information flow and control systems in electronics, mechanics, and biology CYBERNETICS
– familiar with mathematical principles or a scientific approach NUMERATE
– first-class honours graduate in the mathematics tripos at Cambridge WRANGLER

mathematical symbols

$\approx$	is approximately equal to
$\equiv$	is identical to
$\sim$	is equivalent/similar to
$\cong$	is congruent to
$\propto$	varies directly as/ is proportional to
$:$	to (in ratios)
$\therefore$	therefore
∞	infinity
$\angle$	angle
$\llcorner$	right angle
$\parallel$	parallel/is parallel to
$\surd$	root/radical/ square root
$\int$	indefinite integral
$\sum$	sum, summation
π	pi
$!$	factorial
$^\circ$	degrees
$'$	minutes; feet
$''$	seconds; inches
$\cup$	union of two sets
$\cap$	intersection of two sets
$\subset$	is included in/ is a subset of
$\supset$	contains as a subset
$\in$	is an element of
$\notin$	is not an element of
$\emptyset$ $\{\}$	empty set, null set

matter- HYL-, HYLO-

Matthew, Mark, Luke, or John, as author of one of the Christian Gospels EVANGELIST
– Gospels of Matthew, Mark, and Luke SYNOPTIC GOSPELS

mattress – hard mattress, typically filled with straw PALLET, PALLIASSE
– strong cloth used to cover a mattress or pillow TICKING
– unsprung mattress of Japanese style FUTON

mature and dignified MELLOW
– maturing or developing unusually early, as a clever or sophisticated child seems to do PRECOCIOUS
– phase in maturing during early adolescence, in which adult reproductive characteristics develop PUBERTY

maximum, as of magnetisation, strength of a solution, or supply in a market SATURATION
– maximum possible speed of a missile, falling object, aircraft, or the like, as determined by such factors as air resistance TERMINAL VELOCITY

May bug COCKCHAFER

mayfly or related short-lived insect EPHEMERID

mayonnaise flavoured with garlic AÏOLI

mayor or chief magistrate in a Dutch- or German-speaking town BURGOMASTER

maze, confusing network of paths or passages LABYRINTH
– maze-like place or thing, such as a crowded neighbourhood WARREN

mead, spiced or medicated, as drunk in former times METHEGLIN

meadow, grassland LEA
– meadow, lawn, or similar grassy stretch of land SWARD

meal See also **menu**, **cooking**, and entries at various types of food
– meal, or the food eaten at a meal REPAST
– meal eaten late in the morning as a combination of breakfast and lunch BRUNCH
– meal in which diners help themselves from dishes of food placed on a counter or table BUFFET
– dish or course served between the main courses of a meal ENTREMETS
– first course of a meal, or appeti-

ser HORS D'OEUVRE
– just after a meal, especially dinner POST-PRANDIAL
– light meal COLLATION
– main course, or course just before the main course, of a meal ENTRÉE
– outdoors, in the open air, as a meal might be ALFRESCO
– referring to a meal, typically with a narrow range of choices, offered at a fixed price in a restaurant or hotel TABLE D'HÔTE, PRIX FIXE
– referring to a meal of separately priced dishes in a restaurant or hotel À LA CARTE
– relating to a meal, especially dinner PRANDIAL
– snack or light meal TIFFIN

mean See also **stingy**
– mean, claim, present an appearance of PROFESS, PURPORT
– mean, imply, represent, give a

MATHEMATICS TERMS

algorithm	method of calculation by the use of a detailed step-by-step procedure
arithmetic progression	sequence in which each number differs from the preceding one by a constant amount, such as *2, 5, 8, 11, 14 ...*
binary	relating to a system of numbers having 2 as its base
calculus	branch of mathematics dealing with continuously changing quantities; method of calculation in which symbols are used
coefficient	numerical factor in an elementary algebraic term, such as 3 in the term $3x$
congruent	referring to geometrical figures that coincide exactly in shape and size
constant	quantity retaining a fixed value throughout a series of calculations
coordinates	set of numbers used to determine the position of a point, line or curve
denominator, divisor	quantity that is divided into another; quantity below the division line in a fraction
equation	mathematical statement in which two expressions or numbers are connected by an equals sign, such as $3x + 2y = 17$
exponent, index, power	symbol indicating the number of times a quantity is to be multiplied by itself, such as the ^{3} in $2^3 = 8$
factor	any of the quantities that can be divided into a given quantity exactly: 7 and 5 are factors of 35
factorial	product of all the whole numbers from a given number down to 1: 4 factorial is $4 \times 3 \times 2 \times 1 = 24$
Fibonacci sequence	infinite series of numbers, each of which is the sum of the preceding two
function	variable connected with another variable in such a way that a change in one produces a corresponding change in the other
geometrical progression	sequence of numbers in which each term is obtained by multiplying the preceding term by a constant factor, such as *2, 6, 18, 54 ...*
integer	any whole number, positive or negative, together with zero
locus	path traced by a point, line or surface that moves under stated conditions
logarithm, log	any one of a system of figures used in calculations, based on the number of times a base number, such as 10, has to be multiplied by itself to produce a given number
multiple	any of the quantities that a given number can be divided into exactly: 21, 35, 49 and so on are all multiples of 7
numerator, dividend	quantity into which another is divided; quantity above the division line in a fraction
permutation	ordered arrangement of the quantities in a set into any of various possible groups
product	result of multiplying one quantity by another
Pythagoras's theorem	theorem relating to the length of the sides of a right-angled triangle
quotient	result of dividing one quantity by another
rational number	number that can be expressed as a real whole number, or as a fraction involving two whole numbers
reciprocal, inverse	number obtained when another number is divided into 1
recurring decimal	decimal number ending in a pattern of one or more digits repeated indefinitely, as 0.878787
secant	straight line intersecting a curve at two or more points
tangent	line, curve, or surface touching but not cutting another
topology	geometry studying the properties of a figure or solid that remain unaffected even when the figure or solid is stretched or twisted
trigonometry	study and application of the relationships involving the sides and angles of triangles, as used in surveying and navigation
variable	quantity that can assume any of various possible values
variance	in statistics, a measure of the spread of a source of numbers or measurements
vertex	point at which two lines or planes meet to form an angle

sign of BETOKEN, SIGNIFY
– mean, indicate, refer to directly, stand for, or specify DENOTE, DESIGNATE, DENOMINATE
– mean, suggest, imply, involve as a consequence CONNOTE

meaning, aim, purpose INTENT
– meaning, sense, general direction PURPORT, TENOR
– meaning, significance IMPORT
– meaning implied by a word's associations, rather than literal meaning CONNOTATION
– meaning or explicit reference of a word DENOTATION
– meaning or message that is implied but not directly expressed, as in a speech or play SUBTEXT
– accepted or usual meaning or sense of a word or phrase ACCEPTATION
– deduce or interpret the meaning of CONSTRUE
– depth of feeling, meaning, or thinking PROFUNDITY
– general meaning or drift, main point, as of a speech GIST, BURDEN, GRAVAMEN
– having a hidden or mysterious meaning CRYPTIC, ENIGMATIC
– having only one meaning UNIVOCAL
– having several different meanings POLYSEMOUS
– having two or more meanings AMBIGUOUS
– object of meaning, the idea or thing referred to by a word, phrase, or sign REFERENT
– referring to a word having full lexical meaning rather than just grammatical function NOTIONAL
– relating to meaning, as of words, gestures, or symbols SEMANTIC
– shade of meaning, subtle distinction NUANCE
– speech or writing surrounding a specified word or passage and refining its meaning CONTEXT
– twist the meaning of, misinterpret PERVERT, DISTORT, MISCONSTRUE
– word in which sound echoes meaning ONOMATOPOEIA
– word meaning the same or nearly the same as another in the same language SYNONYM
– word meaning the opposite or nearly the opposite of another in the same language ANTONYM
– word or phrase that seems to have a second, typically saucy, meaning DOUBLE ENTENDRE

means or medium, such as a play, for conveying ideas, expressing talents, or the like VEHICLE
– means to an end, or device adopted for an urgent purpose EXPEDIENT

meanwhile, in the meantime IN THE INTERIM

measles RUBEOLA, MORBILLI
– German measles RUBELLA
– red skin rash, as in measles ROSEOLA

measurable by the same units or standard COMMENSURABLE, COMMENSURATE

measure See also **weights and measures**
– measure, test, or standard used for judgment or comparison YARDSTICK, CRITERION
– measure or basic property in physics DIMENSION
– measure or map an area of land SURVEY
– measure the depth of, as with a weighted line SOUND, FATHOM
– adjective for measures or measurement MENSURAL, METRICAL

measurement, as in geometry MENSURATION
– measurement around a person's waist or a tree GIRTH

-measurement- -METR-, -METRY

measures – temporary or provisional, as emergency measures might be INTERIM

measuring instrument See chart, page 316
– measuring instrument consisting of a pair of arms hinged at one end, as used in geometry SECTOR, DIVIDERS
– finely adjusted or graduated scale supplementing the main scale of a measuring instrument VERNIER
– mark, adjust, or check the scale of a measuring instrument CALIBRATE

meat See **menu terms**, and also **bacon**, **beef**, **lamb**, **pork**, **cooking**
– meat-eating, feeding on meat or flesh CARNIVOROUS, CREOPHAGOUS
– meat patty or meatball RISSOLE, FAGGOT, FRIKKADEL
– meat substitute made of soya bean protein TEXTURED VEGETABLE PROTEIN, TVP, SPUN PROTEIN
– meat tenderiser consisting of a papaya-derived enzyme PAPAIN
– meat that is dried and salted, especially strips of beef JERKY, CHARQUI, BILTONG
– meatless, as a diet might be, or certain days of religious abstinence MAIGRE
– brown meat by quick frying at high temperature SEAR
– cooking appliance fitted with a rotating spit for roasting meat ROTISSERIE
– highly seasoned smoked meat, prepared from breast or shoulder of beef PASTRAMI
– gash or score raw meat or fish for crisper cooking CRIMP
– lump or chunk, as of raw meat GOBBET
– referring to meat slaughtered in accordance with Jewish law KOSHER
– referring to meat slaughtered in accordance with Muslim law HALAL
– referring to meat that is medium-cooked À POINT
– referring to meat that is underdone SAIGNANT
– referring to meat that is very rare AU BLEU
– referring to meat that is well done BIEN CUIT
– refraining from eating meat, as an act of penance, especially as formerly among Roman Catholics ABSTINENCE
– sausage, ham, and other cold cooked meats CHARCUTERIE
– spicy minced meat or poultry used for stuffing FORCEMEAT
– thin slice of meat, especially veal, typically fried in breadcrumbs ESCALOPE

Mecca – Muslim pilgrimage made to Mecca HAJ

mechanic in the armed forces, especially in the navy ARTIFICER

mechanical, involuntary, or unconscious, as sneezes, knee-jerks, or similar responses are REFLEX
– mechanical, purely functional or materialistic BANAUSIC
– mechanical, routine, indifferent, as a glance or smile might be PERFUNCTORY
– mechanical or electrical device or element forming part of a machine or circuit COMPONENT
– mechanical repetition, unthinking routine ROTE

medal, badge, or similar item awarded as an honour DECORATION
– medal, brooch, or the like worn on the chest PECTORAL
– back of a coin or medal, "tails" VERSO, REVERSE
– French medal or military decoration for bravery in battle CROIX DE GUERRE
– front of a coin or medal, "heads" OBVERSE
– small metal tag, bar, or insignia on a medal ribbon, indicating either a second award or details of the award CLASP
– study of coins, money, or medals NUMISMATICS

MEASURING INSTRUMENTS

actinometer	intensity of radiation	**gaussmeter**	magnetic flux, density	**psychrometer**	humidity
almucantar	bearing and altitude of celestial bodies	**Geiger counter**	radiation	**pycnometer**	relative density of liquids and solids
altimeter	height of an aircraft above the ground	**goniometer**	angles, as of crystals	**pyrheliometer**	solar radiation
anemometer	wind speed; flow rate of a fluid	**gravimeter**	gravitational field	**pyrometer**	high temperatures
atmometer, evaporometer	rate of evaporation	**hydrometer**	relative density of liquids	**radio-micrometer**	heat radiation
baroscope	atmospheric pressure	**hygrometer**	humidity	**saccharometer**	sugar content in a solution
bathometer	depth of water in the sea	**hypsometer**	land elevations	**salimeter**	salt in a solution
Beckmann thermometer	small temperature changes	**interferometer**	wavelengths of light	**scintillation counter**	ionising radiation
callipers	diameters of rods or tubes	**Machmeter**	speeds at and beyond the speed of sound	**sclerometer**	hardness of material
calorimeter	heat	**magnetometer**	strengths of magnetic fields	**seismograph**	earth tremors
cathetometer	distances between fluid levels in vertical tubes	**manometer**	pressures of gases and liquids	**sextant**	altitude of celestial bodies
chronometer	precise time	**micrometer**	precise dimensions of small distances or angles	**spectrometer**	optical spectra
clinometer	angle of an incline	**octant**	altitude of celestial bodies	**spherometer**	curvature of a sphere or cylinder
colorimeter	colours; concentration of solutions, by comparison of colours	**ondometer**	frequency of radio waves	**steelyard**	weight of heavy loads
Crookes radiometer	intensity of radiated light	**optometer**	refraction of the eye	**tacheometer**	distance, elevations, and bearings
cryometer	extremely low temperatures	**orometer**	height above sea level	**tachometer, rev counter**	speed of rotation of a shaft
cyclometer	distance travelled by a wheel	**pedometer**	distance travelled by a walker	**tasimeter**	small temperature changes
densimeter	density	**photometer**	light intensity	**tellurometer**	distances, up to 40 miles
densitometer	optical density, degree of transparency	**piezometer**	high pressures, compressibility	**tensiometer**	tensile strength, stretchability
dilatometer	volume expansion of liquids with temperature	**planimeter**	surface area of a plane figure	**theodolite**	vertical and horizontal angles, and hence distances and elevations
electrometer	potential difference and charge	**pluviometer**	rainfall	**variometer**	rate of climb or descent of an aircraft
electroscope	presence of an electric charge	**polarimeter**	optical rotation of polarised light	**velocimeter**	velocity or speed
		potentiometer	voltages or potential differences	**vinometer**	alcohol content of wine
		protractor	angles		

– U.S. medal or military decoration awarded to those wounded in action PURPLE HEART
mediation in a dispute INTERCESSION, CONCILIATION
mediator in a dispute between two parties ARBITRATOR, GO-BETWEEN, INTERMEDIARY, HONEST BROKER
medical See charts, pages 317, 318, and also **therapies**, **surgical**
– medical equipment and supplies of a doctor or hospital ARMAMENTARIUM
– medical implement inserted into a body canal for dilation, medication, or the like BOUGIE
– medical pad, as of gauze, used to stop bleeding or to reduce pain

MEDICAL AND SURGICAL INSTRUMENTS

aspirator	removing liquids from a body cavity	**kymograph**	recording variations in blood pressure
audiometer	measuring sharpness of hearing	**lancet**	making incisions, in surgery
bistoury	making small surgical incisions	**ophthalmoscope**	examining the interior of the eye
cannula	draining or injecting fluids	**osteoclast**	fracturing a bone, as for resetting to correct a deformity
CAT scanner	creating a three-dimensional image of body tissues by X-ray recordings	**otoscope**	examining the eardrum
colposcope	examining the cervix	**polygraph**	recording changes in heartbeat, breathing rate and blood pressure
defibrillator	restoring heart rhythm by electric shock	**raspatory**	scraping bones
dermatome	cutting skin for grafting	**retinoscope**	examining light refraction in the eye
écraseur	removing tumours by tightening a wire loop	**retractor**	holding open a surgical incision
electrocardiograph	recording heartbeats	**scalpel**	making incisions
electroencephalograph	recording brain activity	**snare**	removing tumours and polyps
electromyograph	recording muscle activity	**speculum**	opening a body passage for inspection
endoscope	examining hollow organs such as the bowel	**sphygmomanometer**	measuring blood pressure
forceps	delivering babies	**sphygmometer**	strength of the pulse
fibrescope	examining tissues and organs	**stethoscope**	listening to body sounds
gastroscope	examining the interior of the stomach	**tenaculum**	lifting and holding blood vessels
gorget	removing stones from the bladder	**trephine/trepan**	removing discs of bone from the skull
iron lung	providing artificial respiration	**xyster**	scraping bones

or inflammation COMPRESS
– medical practitioner, especially a doctor who is not a surgeon PHYSICIAN
– medical records or full case history of a patient ANAMNESIS
– medical, relating to healing AESCULAPIAN
– medical social worker in former times ALMONER
– medical testing for potential sufferers from a disease, carried out on a wide range of the population SCREENING
– medical specialist DIPLOMATE
– combining inefficiently or dangerously, as different medical drugs might INCOMPATIBLE, ANTAGONISTIC
– referring to medical drugs used to prevent rejection of a transplanted organ IMMUNOSUPPRESSIVE
– relating to medical staff, such as therapists, who are not trained doctors PARAMEDICAL
– symbol of the medical profession, a winged staff with two snakes twined around it CADUCEUS

-medical- -IATR-, -IATRO-, -IATRICS, -IATRY

medical drug- PHARMACO-

-medical examination -OPSY

medical student in the U.S. undergoing supervised hospital training INTERN
– advanced medical student or junior doctor continuing training in a hospital HOUSEMAN
– optional period of hospital training undertaken by a medical student ELECTIVE

medical treatment See also **therapies**
– medical treatment, of Chinese origin, in which needles are inserted into the skin or body at given points ACUPUNCTURE
– medical treatment of bone and muscle disorders ORTHOPAEDICS
– medical treatment of children's diseases PAEDIATRICS
– medical treatment of disorders of the nervous system NEUROLOGY
– medical treatment using massage and infrared or ultraviolet rays PHYSIOTHERAPY
– medical treatment of skin diseases DERMATOLOGY
– medical treatment of blood disorders HAEMATOLOGY
– medical treatment of disorders of the bladder UROLOGY
– medical treatment of women's diseases GYNAECOLOGY
– medical treatment, type of therapy MODALITY
– medical treatment based on giving tiny doses of a substance that in larger doses would induce symptoms similar to those of the disease HOMEOPATHY
– medical treatment based on inducing a condition different from

MEDICINES

GROUP OF MEDICINES	WHAT THEY TREAT
analgesic	pain
antacid	stomach and gullet ulcers
antibiotic	bacterial infections
anticoagulant	blood clotting
anticonvulsant	convulsions, epilepsy
antihistamine	hay fever and other allergies
antipyretic	fever
antiscorbutic	scurvy
antitussive	coughs
beta blocker	anxiety, hypertension
bronchodilator	asthma and other breathing difficulties
cathartic	constipation
cytotoxin	tumours
decongestant	blocked nasal passages
demulcent	mouth ulcers
diuretic	water retention
emetic	poisoning, by causing vomiting
expectorant	phlegm in the air passages
hypnotic, soporific	insomnia
laxative	constipation
paregoric	intestinal pain, diarrhoea
purgative	constipation
sedative	anxiety, tension, insomnia
sulphonamide, tetracycline	bacterial infections
tranquilliser	anxiety, stress, insomnia
vasodilator	angina
vermifuge, anthelmintic	intestinal worms

SPECIFIC MEDICINE	WHAT IT TREATS
amitryptiline	depression
amoxycillin	bacterial infections
atropine	peptic ulcers, spasms
calamine	skin inflammation
chloral hydrate	insomnia
codeine	pain, coughing, insomnia
cortisone	arthritis, rheumatism, skin disorders
curare	tetanus
diazepam, Valium	anxiety, tension
digitalis, digoxin	heart disorders
Dimotane	allergies
disulfiram	alcoholism
gentian violet, crystal violet	skin infections
Glauber's salts	constipation
gripe-water	babies' colic
heparin	blood-clotting
insulin	diabetes
L-dopa	Parkinson's disease
nitrazepam, Mogadon	insomnia
noradrenaline	shock
paracetamol	pain, fever
pentobarbitone sodium, Nembutal	insomnia
pethidine	pain
phenacetin	pain
phenelzine	depression
quinine	malaria
valerian	anxiety, tension
Warfarin	blood-clotting

the symptoms of the disease, conventional medicine ALLOPATHY
– medical treatment of an unorthodox kind, opposed to mainstream Western medical techniques ALTERNATIVE MEDICINE
– based on practical experience rather than theory or proof, as medical treatment might be EMPIRICAL
– restoration of one's health through medical treatment REHABILITATION

-medical treatment- -PATH- -PATHY

medication in solid form designed to be inserted into a body cavity, especially the rectum SUPPOSITORY

medicinal, remedial THERAPEUTIC
– medicinal drug PHARMACEUTICAL
– medicinal plant, especially a herb SIMPLE
– medicinal preparation or drug, especially a laxative PHYSIC
– medicinal sweet LOZENGE, PASTILLE, TROCHE
– medicinal tablet or pill of large size BOLUS

medicine See chart
– medicine, medicinal remedy MEDICAMENT
– medicine, method, or device designed to protect against disease PROPHYLACTIC
– medicine as used in establishing facts for evidence in legal cases FORENSIC MEDICINE
– medicine boasting of secret ingredients, typically a quack remedy NOSTRUM
– medicine or remedy for all ailments PANACEA
– medicine intended for a particular disease or disorder SPECIFIC
– medicine or drug that revives or restores one's health or strength RESTORATIVE
– medicine protected by a trademark and typically available without prescription PATENT MEDICINE
– capsule or wafer of an early kind for containing an unpleasant-tasting medicine CACHET
– dose, as of medicine DRAUGHT
– drugs collectively, as used in the preparation of medicine PHARMACOPOEIA
– effect, especially an adverse effect, of a medicine or drug REACTION
– effective, powerful, or still active, as drugs or medicines might be POTENT
– give out in portions, distribute something such as medicines as a chemist does DISPENSE
– given or taken by injection rather than by mouth, as a medi-

cine or medical drug might be PARENTERAL
– inactive substance administered as a medicine, as for humouring a patient or for comparisons in an experiment PLACEBO
– mix medicinal drugs according to a prescription COMPOUND
– oil or other inert medium used for bulking up an active medicine VEHICLE
– place, such as a hospital office, from which medicines and medical supplies are given out DISPENSARY
– referring or relating to a medicine or drug available without prescription OVER-THE-COUNTER, OFFICINAL
– referring or relating to a medicine or drug prepared according to a specific prescription MAGISTRAL
– referring or relating to a medicine or drug sold under a trade name PROPRIETARY
– referring or relating to a prescription medicine or drug ETHICAL
– sign, such as an allergy or dangerous side effect, that argues for the discontinuation of a medicine or treatment CONTRAINDICATION
– small container for medicine, poison, or other liquid, typically a tiny stoppered glass bottle VIAL, PHIAL
– sugar or other inactive substance added to a medical drug to make it more suitable for administering EXCIPIENT
– syrup or similar preparation added to an unpleasant-tasting medicine ELIXIR
– syrupy drink to which medicine can be added JULEP

medicine man or similar priest endowed with apparent magic powers SHAMAN

medieval See also **feudal**
– medieval church music, traditionally chanted unaccompanied PLAINSONG
– medieval European social system in which vassals exchanged homage and service for land and protection from a lord FEUDALISM, FEUDAL SYSTEM
– medieval romance in prose or verse GEST
– medieval tournament, in which knights took part in horseraces and riding displays CAROUSEL
– medieval town, largely self-governing COMMUNE
– medieval trade and mutual-aid association of merchants or craftsmen GUILD, COMPANY
– medieval wandering minstrel JONGLEUR, TROUBADOUR
– higher division, with four subjects, of the liberal arts studied at a medieval university QUADRIVIUM
– lower division, with three subjects, of the liberal arts studied at a medieval university TRIVIUM

mediocre, acceptable, reasonable, merely satisfactory or competent ADEQUATE, PASSABLE, PRESENTABLE, TOLERABLE
– mediocre, average, or uneven in quality MIDDLING, PATCHY
– mediocre, fairly bad, disappointing INDIFFERENT
– mediocre, lacking distinctive character, uninspiring BLAND, INSIPID
– mediocre, ordinary, everyday, uninspired RUN-OF-THE-MILL, UNDISTINGUISHED, UNEXCEPTIONAL, WORKMANLIKE

meditation of a simple westernised form TRANSCENDENTAL MEDITATION, T.M.
– meditation or religious contemplation as a means of experiencing communion with the divine MYSTICISM
– sitting position, with crossed legs and hands resting on knees, as used in yoga and meditation LOTUS POSITION
– word or formula repeated, silently or aloud, in meditation MANTRA

Mediterranean – countries bordering the eastern Mediterranean THE LEVANT

medium or means, such as a play, for conveying ideas, expressing talents, or the like VEHICLE

meek, submissive, and excessively eager to please SERVILE, FAWNING, SYCOPHANTIC
– behave meekly and submissively, yield weakly to someone TRUCKLE

meet and confront or attack someone unexpectedly ACCOST, WAYLAY

meeting, typically casual and unplanned ENCOUNTER
– meeting between lovers or with one's fate, or the appointment for it TRYST, ASSIGNATION
– meeting for a discussion, typically on a specialist academic or professional theme SYMPOSIUM, COLLOQUIUM, SEMINAR
– meeting for a public discussion FORUM
– meeting in which thoughts are swapped or discussed intensely as a means of solving problems or creating new ideas BRAINSTORMING
– meeting of the members of a local political party in the U.S. to decide policy or select candidates for office CAUCUS
– meeting or assembly of a shire's freemen in Anglo-Saxon times MOOT
– meeting or assembly of clergymen to discuss policy CONSISTORY
– meeting or assembly with all members present PLENUM
– meeting or conference session attended by heads of government or other very senior politicians SUMMIT
– meeting or council, especially of church officials SYNOD
– meeting or interview for exchanging views or securing advice CONFERENCE, CONSULTATION, POWWOW
– meeting or local court in Anglo-Saxon England GEMOT
– meeting or meeting place agreed on beforehand RENDEZVOUS
– meeting or reception formerly held by a monarch or VIP when getting up in the morning LEVEE
– meeting or seminar in which problems in a given field are discussed CLINIC, WORKSHOP
– meeting or social gathering, especially for discussion of the arts CONVERSAZIONE
– meeting-point or boundary at which two different theories, groups, or systems communicate or interact INTERFACE
– chairman or presiding officer of a meeting MODERATOR
– decision or statement discussed and voted on at a meeting RESOLUTION, MOTION, BILL
– end and dismiss a meeting, parliament, or the like DISSOLVE
– formal meeting or assembly of representatives or delegates, as to decide policy CONGRESS, CONVENTION
– formal meeting or conference with a VIP, such as the Pope or a monarch AUDIENCE
– interrupt or postpone a meeting until a later time ADJOURN
– minimum number of persons required for a committee meeting, assembly, or the like QUORUM
– public meeting or assembly, usually for a political or religious cause RALLY
– published records or transcripts of a conference, learned society's meetings, or the like PROCEEDINGS, TRANSACTIONS
– record of the points of a meeting MINUTES
– secret meeting, specifically the meeting of cardinals to elect a new Pope CONCLAVE
– secret religious meeting, as among dissenters in 17th-

century England CONVENTICLE
– summary or memorandum of a meeting or agreement AIDE-MÉMOIRE
– summon an assembly, call a meeting, or the like CONVOKE, CONVENE

melody added as counterpoint above a basic melody DESCANT
– combination of two or more distinct melodic parts COUNTERPOINT, POLYPHONY

melon, squash, pumpkin, or related pulpy fruit or vegetable PEPO
– melon with a fragrant orange flesh MUSKMELON, CANTALOUPE, SPANSPEK
– melon with a sweet green flesh HONEYDEW MELON

melt or extract fat from meat by heating RENDER
– melt gradually DELIQUESCE
– extract metal from ore by melting it SMELT
– vessel in which metals are melted CRUCIBLE

member – acquire new members, soldiers, or the like RECRUIT, ENLIST, ENROL
– elect or appoint a new member to a group by a decision of the existing group COOPT
– original or founding member of an organisation CHARTER MEMBER

membership fees SUBSCRIPTIONS, SUBS
– ceremony of admission, as to membership of a group INITIATION
– come to an end, as a contract or membership might EXPIRE
– trial period, as for membership of a profession or religious order PROBATION

membrane, partition, or division separating tissues or cavities, as between the nostrils SEPTUM
– membrane, such as the peritoneum, lining a closed body cavity SEROUS MEMBRANE, SEROSA
– membrane forming an inner eyelid NICTITATING MEMBRANE
– membrane lining the abdominal cavity and covering most of the organs PERITONEUM
– membrane of tissue initially blocking the entrance to the vagina HYMEN
– membrane or similar thin partition DIAPHRAGM
– membrane surrounding an embryo or foetus AMNION, CHORION
– gradual evening out of differently concentrated solutions by transfer through the separating membrane OSMOSIS
– separation of different types of molecule in a solution by means of a membrane DIALYSIS

memorable or long-lasting in its effect, as poetry might be RESONANT

memorandum or summary of a meeting or agreement AIDE-MÉMOIRE

memorial, monument honouring dead people buried elsewhere CENOTAPH

memorial tablet, nameplate, or the like, as mounted on a wall or monument PLAQUE

memory, power of remembering RETENTION, RECALL, RETRIEVAL
– memory-aid, such as a jingle or formula MNEMONIC
– memory disorder in which dreams and fantasies are confused with reality PARAMNESIA
– memory loss, as through shock or brain damage AMNESIA, FUGUE
– memory loss OBLIVION, LETHE
– memory of an event REMINISCENCE, RECOLLECTION, ANAMNESIS
– memory-training system PELMANISM
– push painful memories or thoughts into the unconscious REPRESS

memorise, learn off by heart CON
– memorising by repetition rather than through understanding ROTE
– arouse or summon a memory, answer, or the like EVOKE
– clutching or retentive, as a good memory is TENACIOUS
– fixed firmly, as in the memory INSCRIBED, ENGRAVED
– preserve the memory of EMBALM
– referring to a very strong visual memory that retains perfect or vivid images EIDETIC
– reinforcement, as of a memory CONSOLIDATION
– unconscious, as secret fears or painful memories might be REPRESSED

men – men-only party, held just before a wedding STAG PARTY
– hatred of men MISANDRY
– rule by men PATRIARCHY

mend See **repair**

menopause CLIMACTERIC

menstruation on its first occurrence in a young woman MENARCHE
– menstrual blood MENSES
– abnormal absence of menstruation AMENORRHOEA
– discontinuation of the menstrual cycle in women MENOPAUSE, CLIMACTERIC, CHANGE OF LIFE
– mucous membrane lining the uterus, shed during menstruation or childbirth DECIDUA

mental See also **mad**, **madness**
– mental or illusory image of an object PHANTASM
– mental lapse, sudden eccentric thought or lapse of thought BRAINSTORM, ABERRATION
– official sending of a person to prison or a mental hospital COMMITTAL
– mentally confused or agitated, as during a high fever DELIRIOUS
– mentally deficient, backward RETARDED, IMBECILIC, CRETINOUS

mental- PSYCH-, PSYCHO-

mentality that is rigid, narrow, unsympathetic, and defensive BUNKER MENTALITY, LAAGER MENTALITY

mention, list, or record by way of example, proof, or the like CITE
– mention individually, single out PARTICULARISE, SPECIFY
– mention or refer to indirectly ALLUDE TO

menu See chart, and also **cooking** and entries for various foods
– menu TARIFF, BILL OF FARE

merchant ship, especially a richly laden one ARGOSY
– trade and mutual-aid association, especially of merchants or craftsmen in medieval times GUILD, COMPANY

mercury QUICKSILVER
– mercury as used in alchemy AZOTH
– reddish mineral that is the principal ore of mercury CINNABAR, VERMILION

Mercury – Mercury's staff, with wings and two twining snakes, serving as a symbol of the medical profession CADUCEUS

mercy, mild treatment, or merciful attitude CLEMENCY, LENIENCY
– mercy, pity COMPASSION
– "mercy killing" EUTHANASIA
– "mercy-killing" by withholding treatment that would prolong the patient's life PASSIVE EUTHANASIA

merry See **happy**, **lively**, **friendly**

merry-go-round CAROUSEL

merrymaking See **party**, **celebration**
– merrymaking or noisy celebration or festivity ROISTERING, REVELRY, JOLLIFICATION, CAROUSAL

mesmerise, paralyse, or stupefy, as with fear GORGONISE, PETRIFY

mess See **confusion**, **mixture**, **untidy**
– mess about, treat disrespectfully TRIFLE WITH

message or meaning that is implied but not directly expressed, as in a speech or play SUBTEXT
– interrupt, seize, or stop something, such as a message, in its course INTERCEPT
– pass on a message RELAY

messenger, as for a parcel delivery service, diplomatic service, or spy ring COURIER

MENU TERMS

CHINESE	
dim sum	small sweet or savoury snacks
foo yong	omelette filled with minced pork, chicken, or vegetables
wo mein	egg noodles in meat sauce, with vegetables, prawns, or crab
won ton	deep-fried spicy chicken or pork dumplings
CENTRAL AND EAST EUROPEAN	
blinis	buckwheat pancakes, served with soured cream or caviar
kasha	boiled or baked buckwheat
knish	ball of dough stuffed with meat or vegetables and baked or fried
pirog, pirozhok	pastry with a savoury filling
FRENCH	
à la carte	referring to separately priced dishes, as distinct from a set meal
à la grecque	cooked in olive oil, with herbs, lemon juice, or vinegar
à la normande	cooked with cider and cream
au gratin/ gratiné	browned with breadcrumbs or cheese, butter, and sometimes cream
blanquette	casserole of white meat in a creamy sauce
bouchée	puff pastry case with a savoury or sweet filling
bourguignonne	cooked with red wine
canapé	small piece of bread or toast with a savoury topping
carbonade	beef stew made with beer
cassoulet	stew of meat or poultry, with haricot beans
coq au vin	casserole of chicken in red wine
daube	stew of braised meat and vegetables
en brochette	cut into chunks, and grilled on a skewer
en croûte	encased in pastry, as beef Wellington is
en papillote	baked in a paper case
entrée	main dish; in an elaborate meal, the course following the fish course
filet mignon	small fillet steak
forestière	garnished with mushrooms, bacon, and tiny potatoes
fricandeau	veal braised or roasted with vegetables
fricassée	chicken or veal in white sauce, served with rice
galantine	cold, boned stuffed meat set in jelly
goujon	small strip of fish, usually deep-fried
julienne	garnish of matchstick-thin strips of vegetables
lyonnaise	garnished or cooked with onions
marinière	referring to fish cooked in white wine
meunière	referring to fish cooked in butter and herbs
navarin	lamb or mutton stew, with root vegetables
niçoise	cooked with tomatoes, onions, garlic, and black olives
noisette	small, round piece of meat; made with hazel nuts; nut-sized piece of potato
parmentier	cooked or garnished with potatoes
pâté de foie gras	pâté made from goose or duck liver
paupiette	small, thin slice of meat rolled round a savoury filling
prix fixe	set price for any of a variety of set meals
provençale	cooked with garlic and tomatoes
quenelles	dumplings of fish or meat
roulade	slice or joint of meat rolled up, often round a filling
service compris	service charge included in the price
tournedos	thick, round steak cut from a fillet of beef
Véronique	garnished with white grapes
GREEK	
baklava	dessert made from paper-thin layers of pastry, with chopped nuts and honey
moussaka	pie of minced lamb and aubergines, topped with béchamel or cheese sauce
souvlakia, kebabs	skewers of meat, often with vegetable chunks, grilled over charcoal
stifado	veal or hare stewed with shallots and spices
taramasalata	purée of grey mullet roe or cod roe
tzatziki	cucumber and yoghurt salad or dip with oil, vinegar, and garlic

continued

MENU TERMS *continued*

INDIAN	
bhindi	okra
biriani	highly spiced meat, fish, or vegetables mixed with rice and coloured with saffron or turmeric
chapatti	thin, flat cake of unleavened wholemeal bread
dhal/dal	pea-like pulse often served as a purée
garam masala	mixture of spices
ghee	clarified butter
jalebis, gulab jaman	syrupy fried dumpling
khorma	cooked dry in curd, with spices and vegetables
koftas	spiced balls of meat, fish, or vegetables
mulligatawny	curried meat soup
nan	leavened bread, usually cooked in a clay oven
paratha	puffed wholemeal bread
pilau/pulao/ pilaf	seasoned rice with added meat and vegetables
poppadom/ poppadum	thin crisp-fried pancake made of pulse flour
samosa	deep-fried pastry case with a sweet or savoury filling
tandoori	cooked in a clay oven
vindaloo	cooked in curry sauce with ginger and chilli
INDONESIAN	
bami goreng	savoury spiced dish based on fried noodles
nasi goreng	savoury spiced dish based on fried rice
rijstafel	meal based on rice served with numerous side dishes of meat and vegetables, with sauces and condiments
satay	grilled marinated meat kebabs with peanut sauce
ITALIAN	
antipasto	hors d'oeuvre
gnocchi	small dumplings served with a sauce
lasagne	dish of wide flat noodles layered with spiced mincemeat
napolitana	cooked with tomatoes and basil
osso bucco	shin of veal cooked with wine and tomatoes
parmigiana	prepared with grated cheese from Parma
pizzaiola	cooked in oil with chopped tomatoes, garlic, and herbs
prosciutto	raw, smoked ham
ravioli	small savoury-filled pasta envelopes, served with a sauce
saltimbocca	rolls of veal and ham, cooked in wine
scaloppe/ scaloppine	veal escalope
tournedos Rossini	fillet steak served with a coating of pâté
JAPANESE	
sukiyaki	thin slices of meat, fried with vegetables and seasoning
sushi	small snacks of raw fish and cold rice
tempura	deep-fried pieces of fish and vegetables
teriyaki	skewered and grilled slices of marinated meat or shellfish
MIDDLE EASTERN	
dolmas	vine leaves with a savoury filling
doner kebab	thin lamb slices, flavoured with garlic and herbs, cut from a revolving spit
halvah/halva	confection of honey and crushed sesame seeds
hummus	dip made from puréed chickpeas
pitta	flat, unleavened bread
shashlik	skewer of grilled mutton chunks, with vegetables and peppers
tahina/tahini	sesame paste, as used in hummus and other dips
SPANISH AND LATIN AMERICAN	
enchilada	fried tortilla served with a hot chilli sauce
paella	seasoned rice dish with chicken, shellfish, and often vegetables
taco	tortilla with a meat or cheese filling
tamale	dish of spicy fried mincemeat and crushed maize
tapas	hors d'oeuvres or savoury snacks of sausage, seafood, or the like
tortilla	thin maize-meal pancake, usually served hot with a savoury filling

– messenger or agent sent on a mission ENVOY, EMISSARY
– messenger or envoy delivering news HERALD

Messiah in Islam MAHDI
– relating to the Messiah or a messiah MESSIANIC

metal See also **steel**
– metal, such as gold or silver, that resists corrosion NOBLE METAL
– metal alloy, chiefly of iron and nickel, which hardly expands or contracts, used for measuring rods and the like INVAR
– metal alloy of copper and tin, polished for use in mirrors, reflectors, and the like SPECULUM
– metal alloy of gold and brass, as used for jewellery TALMI GOLD
– metal alloy of gold or nickel and silver, as used for jewellery ELECTRUM
– metal alloy of gold or silver with a base metal such as copper, used for making coins BILLON
– metal alloy of tin and lead, used for making tableware, drinking vessels, and the like PEWTER
– metal bar or block prepared for storage or transport INGOT
– metal-casting factory or workshop FOUNDRY
– metal consisting of a mix of two or more metals, or of metal with other elements such as carbon ALLOY
– metal disc PATEN
– metal filings or shavings removed by a cutting tool SWARF
– metal foil released in strips into the air to thwart an enemy's radar system CHAFF, WINDOW
– metal fragments from a shell, bomb, or mine SHRAPNEL
– metal mesh, as used for reinforcing glass EXPANDED METAL
– metal or alloy, especially brass, produced in thin sheets LATTEN
– metal or mineral deposit in rock VEIN, LODE
– metal plate for reinforcing a corner joist GUSSET
– metal strip used to measure or set a narrow gap between two parts FEELER GAUGE
– metal that is not a precious metal BASE METAL
– metal tool, machine part, stamp, or the like, for cutting, punching, or folding objects DIE
– alloy melted to fuse two metal parts SOLDER
– alloy of various metals, producing very little friction, used in bearings BABBITT METAL
– capable of being drawn or pulled out, stretchable as some metals are TRACTILE, DUCTILE, TENSILE
– capable of being shaped by pressure or blows, workable, as some metals are MALLEABLE
– chemical analysis, as of a sample of metal ASSAY
– chief metal in an alloy MATRIX
– decorate metal by engraving or embossing CHASE, ENCHASE
– dissolving or wearing away, especially of metals CORROSION
– etch or inlay metal with wavy decorative patterns DAMASCENE, DAMASK
– gold-coloured metal alloy of copper, zinc, and sometimes tin used for jewellery, clocks, furniture ornamentation, and the like ORMOLU
– gold-coloured metal alloy of copper and zinc, used in cheap jewellery PINCHBECK
– hammer or cut metal into thin foil FOLIATE
– heat and beat metal into shape FORGE
– heat and then cool metal or glass to strengthen it TEMPER, ANNEAL
– impurities formed on molten metal during smelting DROSS
– join or fuse metals using heat WELD
– made by hammering or shaping rather than by casting, as a metal object might be WROUGHT
– maker of metal accessories, such as bits and spurs, for horses in former times LORIMER
– produce wire, metal or plastic sheeting, or the like by pressing through a nozzle or die EXTRUDE
– refuse from smelted ore or crude metal SLAG, SCORIA
– study of metals, or the extraction and refinement of them METALLURGY
– vessel for heating or melting metals, or floor of a furnace for collecting molten metal CRUCIBLE
– weakness in metal or other solid material caused by stress FATIGUE

metaphor or image of a witty, far-fetched kind CONCEIT
– metaphor replacing a common term in Old Norse and Old English poetry KENNING
– metaphors and symbols, as in poetry IMAGERY
– based on or using figures of speech, metaphorical FIGURATIVE
– image in which the meaning of a metaphor is embodied VEHICLE
– meaning or general drift of a metaphor TENOR

meteor shower's apparent point of origin in the sky RADIANT
– meteor that is large, bright and may explode FIREBALL, BOLIDE

meteorite or stone from a meteorite CHONDRITE

meteorology See **weather**

meter – referring to a watch, clock, or meter indicating readings by changing numbers rather than by moving hands on a dial DIGITAL
– referring to a watch, clock, or meter indicating readings by moving hands on a dial ANALOG

methane – organic compound such as methane, containing only hydrogen and carbon HYDROCARBON

method of operation, way of working MODUS OPERANDI
– method of teaching the violin or other instrument to young children, based on imitation and repetition SUZUKI METHOD
– method or approach, especially a mode of therapy MODALITY
– method or plan based on a long-range or overall view of things STRATEGY
– method or prescribed procedure of operating REGIMEN
– method or style MODE
– methods or plans designed to achieve short-term, local, or immediate objectives TACTICS
– based on or relating to scientific observation or experiment, as a method of investigation might be EMPIRICAL
– referring to the educational method based on independent investigation HEURISTIC

meths – nausea-inducing substance added to meths or ethyl alcohol so as to make it unfit for drinking DENATURANT, PYRIDINE

metre See also **poetry**
– analysis of the metrical or rhythm patterns of verse SCANSION
– unit of poetic metre, corresponding to a bar in music FOOT

Mexican-American CHICANO
– Mexican cowboy or herdsman VAQUERO
– Mexican hors d'oeuvre or dip of puréed avocado GUACAMOLE
– Mexican sun-dried brick ADOBE

Mexico – Spanish conqueror of Mexico and Peru in the 16th century CONQUISTADOR

mice fear of mice MUSOPHOBIA

microchip, tiny electronic circuit based on a semiconductor wafer SILICON CHIP
– electronic circuit formed on a microchip INTEGRATED CIRCUIT
– relating to semiconductors, as in microchips SOLID-STATE

microfilm sheet, as used for library catalogues MICROFICHE, FICHE

microphone – long movable metal arm supporting an overhead microphone BOOM
– return into a system or process of a part of its output, such as microphone noise FEEDBACK
– sound-regulating device, as in a microphone or loudspeaker BAFFLE
– thin disc, as in a telephone or microphone, whose vibrations convert sound to electronic signals or vice versa DIAPHRAGM

microscope in which the specimen is side-lighted to show the particles are bright spots against a dark background DARK-FIELD MICROSCOPE, ULTRAMICROSCOPE
– eyepiece of a microscope OCULAR
– having fine threads for use in measuring, as the eyepiece of a microscope might have FILAR
– lens or set of lenses, nearest to the object being viewed, in a microscope or telescope OBJECTIVE
– place a specimen on a slide for a microscope MOUNT
– thin slice or specimen, as of tissue, for examination by microscope SECTION
– visible to the naked eye, without a microscope MACROSCOPIC

microscopic organism, invisible to the naked eye ANIMALCULE
– microscopic single-celled organism PROTOZOAN

microwaves – device producing microwaves RESONATOR
– electronic valve helping to generate high-power microwaves, as in radar systems MAGNETRON

middle See also **mediocre**
– middle, between extremes INTERMEDIATE
– middle course of action, factor, or the like when there should be only two TERTIUM QUID
– middle ear TYMPANUM
– middle in position, quality, or extent, average MEAN
– middle item or value in an ordered list of numbers MEDIAN
– middle way, policy, or course of action that avoids extremes VIA MEDIA
– adjective for the middle MEDIAL, MEDIAN
– "into the middle of things", straight into the narrative or plot, as a book or play might begin IN MEDIAS RES

middle- MEDI-, MEDIO-, MES-, MESO-

Middle Ages See **feudal**, **medieval**
– adjective for the Middle Ages MEDIEVAL

middle-class BOURGEOIS
– middle-class American man, narrow-minded and self-satisfied BABBITT
– change a working-class area into a middle-class one GENTRIFY

middleman or agent in a business transaction BROKER, FACTOR, JOBBER

middling in quality MEDIOCRE

midsummer or midwinter position of the Sun in relation to the Earth, at its apparently furthest point from the equator SOLSTICE

midwife or obstetrician ACCOUCHEUSE, ACCOUCHEUR

migrate – non-migratory, resident in one area only, as some birds are SEDENTARY

mild in climate TEMPERATE

mildness of manner, gentleness MANSUETUDE

mile – nautical mile per hour KNOT

mileometer ODOMETER

military See also **services**, **soldiers**, **troops**
– military attack or campaign that is quick and intensive BLITZKRIEG
– military attack or manoeuvre to draw an enemy away from the planned main attack DIVERSION
– military attack or raid INCURSION
– military barracks or quarters, especially in a town, in former times CASERN
– military base or camp INSTALLATION
– military base's canteen or shop NAAFI
– military base's shops for U.S. servicemen or their families POST EXCHANGE, PX
– military communications to maintain contact LIAISON
– military court, or a trial conducted by it COURT-MARTIAL
– military demand or request for needed supplies or equipment REQUISITION
– military department in charge of food supplies and equipment COMMISSARIAT
– military detachment protecting the front of an army unit VANGUARD
– military detachment protecting the rear of an army unit, as in retreat REARGUARD
– military disciplinarian or authority demanding strict obedience MARTINET
– military display presented outdoors, usually in the evening TATTOO
– military drill on a barrack square SQUARE-BASHING
– military encampment set up temporarily, as during an expedition BIVOUAC
– military establishment of the U.S. PENTAGON
– military expedition ANABASIS
– military forces or supplies sent to support those already in use REINFORCEMENTS
– military formation, in ancient Greece, of foot soldiers with overlapping shields and long spears PHALANX
– military formation or siege device in ancient Rome, typically of a screen of overlapping shields held above the heads of soldiers approaching the walls TESTUDO, TORTOISE
– military leader of a royal household in the Middle Ages CONSTABLE
– military leave in the U.S. FURLOUGH
– military manoeuvre in which deception or surprise is used to outwit the enemy STRATAGEM
– military manoeuvre of attacking an enemy force or position on two flanks PINCER MOVEMENT
– military officer or official of high rank BRASS HAT
– military officer holding an official appointment COMMISSIONED OFFICER
– military officer responsible for provisions, clothing, and the like QUARTERMASTER
– military officer serving as assistant to the general or other senior officer AIDE-DE-CAMP, ADC
– military officer who assists a senior officer in administrative work ADJUTANT
– military officer's honorary promotion to a higher rank, without the corresponding rise in pay or authority BREVET
– military officers who help to plan and control battle operations GENERAL STAFF
– military operations or techniques designed to achieve short-term, local, or immediate objectives TACTICS
– military or diplomatic planning as an art or science STRATEGY
– military or naval subdivision ECHELON
– military or political grouping that forms the core of a potentially larger unit CADRE
– military parade first thing in the morning REVEILLE
– military persecution, subjection to soldiers DRAGONNADE, DRAGOONING
– military planning, specifically of organising and transporting men and equipment LOGISTICS

– military policy of burning or destroying all crops, food, and anything else likely to be of use to an advancing enemy SCORCHED-EARTH POLICY
– military position or foothold established in enemy territory by advance troops BRIDGEHEAD, SALIENT
– military position set up on an enemy's shoreline in advance of the main invading force BEACHHEAD
– military post, or the soldiers stationed there GARRISON
– military regiment's permanent base and training centre DEPOT
– military scientist or technical expert, originally one working for the RAF BOFFIN
– military serviceman, such as a sergeant, having certain leadership functions but without an official appointment as an officer NON-COMMISSIONED OFFICER, NCO
– military unit, squadron of ships, or the like selected from a larger unit for a special mission DETACHMENT, TASK FORCE
– military unit in ancient Rome, consisting of 3000 to 6000 troops LEGION
– military unit in ancient Rome, forming one-tenth of a legion COHORT
– military unit in ancient Rome, forming one-fiftieth of a legion MANIPLE
– military unit or post far from the main body of the army OUTPOST
– military weapons, ammunition, and related equipment ORDNANCE, MUNITIONS
– acquire new members for military service by force of law CONSCRIPT, LEVY, DRAFT
– acquire new members, sign men on for military service, or the like RECRUIT, ENLIST, ENROL
– assign accommodation to military officers or troops, as in civilian buildings BILLET, QUARTER, CANTON
– braided cord on the left shoulder, as on a military uniform FOURRAGÈRE
– commanding officer of a military post, organisation, or the like COMMANDANT
– discharge from military service DEMOBILISE , DEMOB
– dismiss from a military unit, impose a dishonourable discharge on CASHIER
– equipment used in a military operation or by a military unit MATERIÉL
– extremely heavy concentration of bombing or other military force on an enemy target SATURATION
– force into military service, draft or recruit by violence or threats COMMANDEER, PRESSGANG, PRESS, IMPRESS, CRIMP
– government by the military STRATOCRACY
– lieutenant or other military officer below the rank of captain SUBALTERN
– menial work in a military camp or barracks, often imposed as punishment FATIGUE
– minor or preliminary conflict or military encounter SKIRMISH
– move military forces to a new area REDEPLOY
– official commendation or public statement, as for bravery or outstanding military service CITATION
– part of or group within a conference, military force, or the like CONTINGENT
– people involved in a military operation or employed by a military force PERSONNEL
– person who is not employed in military service CIVILIAN
– person who signs up for military service of his own free will VOLUNTEER
– reduction or removal of military forces and weapons DISARMAMENT
– relating to an unofficial or auxiliary military group PARAMILITARY
– release or exempt from military service, active duty, or the like, on the grounds of illness or disability INVALID
– relating to ordinary public life or work, as distinct from the military or ecclesiastical CIVIL
– remove troops, military equipment, or military control from an area DEMILITARISE
– report sent over a distance, as by a newspaper correspondent or military field officer DISPATCH
– ruling group of officers after a military takeover JUNTA
– section of a military force consisting of foot soldiers fighting with small arms INFANTRY
– section of a military force consisting of troops mounted on horseback CAVALRY
– section of a military force consisting of troops serving on both land and sea MARINES
– section of a military force consisting of troops trained for parachute missions PARATROOPS
– section of a military force consisting of troops using heavy guns ARTILLERY
– small military unit or fighting force specialising in quick destructive raids COMMANDO
– smallest military unit or formation, as for drilling or patrol SQUAD
– trainee officer in the police or military forces CADET
– transfer of a teacher, military officer, or the like for temporary duty elsewhere SECONDMENT
– withdraw military forces from active conflict DISENGAGE

milk containing bacteria that survive in acids, used in treating digestive disorders ACIDOPHILUS MILK
– milk drink, heated, spiced, and sweetened, and curdled with wine or beer POSSET
– milk heated rapidly and then cooled, to allow longer preservation UHT
– milk-protein that forms the basis of cheese CASEIN
– "milk sugar" LACTOSE
– milk that has been concentrated but not sweetened EVAPORATED MILK
– milk that is sour and curdled CLABBER
– milk that is the first produced by a cow or similar mammal directly after giving birth BEESTINGS, COLOSTRUM
– milk that is uniform in consistency, through the emulsification of the fat HOMOGENISED MILK
– milk's watery part that can be separated from the solid curds WHEY, SERUM
– adjective for milk LACTEAL, LACTIC
– become a soft, solidified mass, as blood, milk, or other liquids might COAGULATE, CLOT, CURDLE
– dilute or add impurities to a substance, such as milk ADULTERATE
– get a baby or young animal off mother's milk and on to solid food WEAN
– heat-treatment of milk, beer, and other liquids to destroy germs and regulate fermentation PASTEURISATION
– produce milk, especially when breast-feeding LACTATE
– squeeze or press out juice or milk EXPRESS

milk- GALACT-, GALACTO-, LACT-, LACTO-

milky liquid EMULSION

mill driven by water flowing over the top of the water wheel OVERSHOT MILL
– mill driven by water flowing under the base of the water wheel UNDERSHOT MILL

– mill for grinding grain, turned by hand QUERN
– watercourse directing water into a mill, turbine, or waterwheel HEADRACE
million- MEGA-
million million- TERA-
million million million- EXA-
million million millionth- ATTO-
million millionth- PICO-
millionth- MICRO-
mime artist or actor in an old-fasioned masque MUMMER
mimicry, mocking and satirical, as of a writer's or composer's work PARODY, PASTICHE
– mimicry of one animal by another for protection MIMESIS
mincemeat – spicy mincemeat used for stuffing FORCEMEAT
mind, especially considered in relation to the body PSYCHE
– mind or reason, especially as the governing principle in the universe NOUS, LOGOS
– mind-reading or other form of extrasensory perception CRYPTAESTHESIA, TELEPATHY
– mind regarded as a clean slate, before being formed by outside impressions TABULA RASA
– "of sound mind", sane COMPOS MENTIS
– relating to diseases, disorders, or the like based on an interaction of mind and body PSYCHOSOMATIC
-mind- -PHREN-, PHRENO-, PSYCH-, PSYCHO-
mindless, random, unprovoked, as vandalism or wilful destruction is WANTON, GRATUITOUS
mine See also **bomb**
– mine, oil well, or similar asset whose value diminishes over the years WASTING ASSET
– mine attached to a wall, vehicle, or the like LIMPET MINE
– mine or other source of great wealth GOLCONDA
– mine wagon or basket in former times CORF
– mines connected into a single explosive sequence GIRANDOLE
– mining by means of surface excavation rather than shafts OPENCAST MINING, STRIP MINING
– coal mine COLLIERY
– cut or channel, as for access in mining or excavating GULLET
– drainage pit or pool, as in a mine SUMP, SINK
– excavation in a mine, typically like a set of steps, formed as the ore is extracted from a vein STOPE
– explode a mine SPRING
– explore an area for gold or other minerals worth mining PROSPECT
– horizontal, or almost horizontal shaft into a mine, for access or drainage ADIT
– horizontal passage into a mine, following a mineral vein DRIFT
– introduce valuable ore fraudulently into a mine to inflate its value SALT
– lifting equipment and framework above a mine shaft HEADGEAR
– living quarters for black workers, as in the mines in South Africa COMPOUND
– methane-based gas, explosive when mixed with air, formed in coal mines FIREDAMP
– poisonous gas in a mine after an explosion or fire AFTERDAMP, BLACKDAMP, CHOKEDAMP, WHITEDAMP
– prop supporting the roof of a tunnel in a mine SPRAG, GIB
– rock-boring tool, as used in mining TREPAN
– safety lamp formerly used by coal miners DAVY LAMP
– sawing device at the front edge of a minesweeper used to cut mine cables PARAVANE
– screen of wood or cloth used to control mine ventilation BRATTICE
– sloping or vertical shaft in a mine, as for ventilation between levels WINZE
– thin seam of coal or mineral ore lying above a larger seam in a mine RIDER
– ventilation shaft in a mine DOWNCAST, UPCAST
mineral See **rocks**
– mineral deposit in rock VEIN, LODE, REEF, SEAM
– mineral- or water-divining by means of a stick or wand RHABDOMANCY
– mineral spring SPA
– mineral water, either natural or artificially aerated SELTZER WATER
miniature man HOMUNCULUS, MANIKIN, PYGMY
– miniature representation of the whole universe, as a single person, group, or system might be MICROCOSM
– miniature tree or shrub produced by rigorous pruning, or the traditional Japanese art of producing such plants BONSAI
minimal compliance with a law or a custom through a small gesture TOKENISM
minimise the importance of, play down SOFT-PEDAL
minimum level of intensity for registering or tolerating something, such as pain THRESHOLD
– minimum number of persons required for a committee meeting, assembly, or the like QUORUM
– minimum of food, shelter, or the like necessary to sustain life SUBSISTENCE
minister's post or duty in the government PORTFOLIO
– reorganisation or reassignment of cabinet ministers RESHUFFLE
ministry – clergyman's acceptance into the ministry, or the ceremony of admission ORDINATION
minor, insignificant, as differences might be SUPERFICIAL, TRIVIAL
– minor, unimportant INCIDENTAL
– minor god DEMIGOD
minor- DEMI-
minority, period of being legally under age NONAGE
– minority group's adjustment to or adoption of the dominant culture ASSIMILATION
– relating to a distinctive racial, religious, or cultural group, typically a minority group, within a society ETHNIC
minstrel, specifically a medieval poet-musician of northern France TROUVÈRE
– minstrel, specifically a medieval poet-musician writing in Provençal TROUBADOUR
– minstrel travelling about in medieval times JONGLEUR
mint flavouring MENTHOL
– box in the British mint, in which new coins are kept for testing PYX
– fee charged by the mint for turning bullion into coins SEIGNIORAGE
mint-flavoured cocktail, of U.S. origin JULEP
minutes or business records of an organisation or society PROCEEDINGS
miracle-worker or magician THAUMATURGIST
mirage, false or illusory image FATA MORGANA
mirror or lens that concentrates light CONDENSER
– mirror or reflector in some optical instruments SPECULUM
– curved inwards, as a mirror or lens might be CONCAVE
– curved outwards, as a mirror or lens might be CONVEX
– defect in a mirror ABERRATION
– full-length mirror, hinged to swivel in its frame CHEVAL GLASS
– image apparently formed by reflected or refracted light rays, such as the image in a mirror VIRTUAL IMAGE
– inversion of left and right, as in an image seen in a mirror LATERAL INVERSION
– metal coating behind the glass of a mirror FOIL, TAIN

– relating to mirrors and reflections CATOPTRIC
– signal or signalling device based on mirror-reflected flashes of sunlight HELIOGRAPH
– similarity, balance, mirror-image relationship, or the like between structures or parts of a system SYMMETRY
– tall mirror, especially one hung between two windows PIER GLASS

misbehaviour, misdeed, or minor offence DELINQUENCY

miscarriage SPONTANEOUS ABORTION

mischief, high spirits, hanky-panky SHENANIGANS
– supposed source of problems, errors, or mischief GREMLIN

mischievous, elf-like PUCKISH
– mischievous or wild adventure, caper, prank ESCAPADE

misconduct by someone acting in a professional capacity or as a public official MALVERSATION, MALFEASANCE

miserable or wretched ABJECT

miserly See **stingy**, **thrifty**
– miserly or sour-tempered person CURMUDGEON
– miserly, stingy, and grasping person SKINFLINT, NIGGARD, PINCH-PENNY, TIGHTWAD

misery, lonely wretchedness DESOLATION

misfortune, bad luck AMBSACE

misinterpret, twist the meaning of PERVERT, DISTORT, MISCONSTRUE

mislead See also **deceive**, **deceptive**
– mislead or surprise someone and force him into an embarrassing position WRONG-FOOT
– misleading, deceiving, ILLUSORY, FACTITIOUS
– misleading, especially as a result of deliberate misrepresentation DISTORTED, GARBLED
– misleading or evasive, as an answer might be EQUIVOCAL
– misleading person or thing WILL-O'-THE-WISP, IGNIS FATUUS

misprint or misspelling LITERAL

mispronunciation CACOEPY
– mispronunciation of a word by omission of a syllable HAPLOLOGY

missile See also **bomb**
– missile or other object that is fired or hurled PROJECTILE
– missile guidance by means of instructions radioed to it during its flight COMMAND GUIDANCE
– missile in the form of a shot-filled cylinder or shrapnel shell fired from a cannon CANISTER
– missile system in which a single rocket launches several warheads MIRV
– missile that is powered on its ascent but unpowered and unguided on its descent BALLISTIC MISSILE
– missile's sideways deviation from its intended course AZIMUTH
– missile's warhead or explosive charge PAYLOAD
– bullet-filled or pellet-filled anti-personnel missile exploding above enemy positions SHRAPNEL
– cigar-shaped self-powered underwater missile TORPEDO
– curved flight path of a missile, ball, or the like TRAJECTORY
– explosive guided missile used by the Germans to bombard London in the Second World War BUZZ-BOMB, V-1, DOODLEBUG, FLYING BOMB, ROBOT BOMB
– guided missile tracing the path of a microwave beam BEAM RIDER
– guided missile typically fired from an aircraft at a ship EXOCET
– guiding or stabilising fin on a bomb or missile VANE
– long-range low-flying nuclear missile CRUISE MISSILE
– medium-range ballistic missile of a kind deployed by the U.S. navy POLARIS
– nuclear ballistic missile deployed on U.S. submarines TRIDENT
– section of a bomb, missile, or the like containing the actual explosive or toxic material WARHEAD
– short-range high-speed air-to-air missile SIDEWINDER
– simultaneous or rapid discharge or release of several bombs or missiles SALVO
– Soviet medium-range nuclear ballistic missile SS-20
– spin or wobble in flight, as a missile or aircraft might YAW
– surface-to-air missile SAM
– underground shelter for housing guided missiles SILO
– U.S. intercontinental ballistic missile MINUTEMAN
– U.S. short-range nuclear ballistic missile PERSHING

missing part in a manuscript LACUNA
– missing part or gap in a series HIATUS

mission – messenger or agent sent on a mission, typically by a government or head of state EMISSARY
– report by or questioning of a spy, astronaut, diplomat, or the like on his return from a mission DEBRIEFING
– representative, messenger, or agent sent on a mission ENVOY

missionary work, devoted spreading of the gospel EVANGELISM

misspelling CACOGRAPHY
– misspelling or misprint LITERAL

mist, paint, or other suspension of very fine particles in a consistent medium COLLOID
– mist-like polar weather condition producing very low visibility WHITE-OUT
– disappear slowly, as mist might EVANESCE
– misty, cloudy, hazy NEBULOUS

mistake See also **error**
– mistake, such as a slip of the tongue, that discloses someone's real feelings or unconscious thoughts FREUDIAN SLIP
– mistake made in one's speech, slip of the tongue LAPSUS LINGUAE
– mistake of spelling or typing in a printed text LITERAL
– mistake one thing for another, treat two different things as the same, confuse CONFOUND
– mistake or improper usage in grammar or etiquette SOLECISM
– mistaken, incorrect, off beam ADRIFT, AMISS, AWRY
– mistaken interpretation or explanation, misunderstanding MISCONSTRUCTION
– mistaken interpretation or faulty understanding, delusion MISCONCEPTION, MISAPPREHENSION
– mistaken or faulty reasoning, illogical argument, or invalid conclusion, especially when unintended PARALOGISM
– mistaken or misleading idea or opinion, based on misinformation or faulty reasoning FALLACY
– mistaken though plausible, as a cunning but illogical argument might be SPECIOUS, SOPHISTIC
– mistaken use of a word, such as *flaunt* in a context requiring *flout* CATACHRESIS
– embarrassing mistake or laughable blunder HOWLER, BONER, CLANGER, PRATFALL
– liable or tending to make mistakes FALLIBLE
– person guilty of a crime or responsible for a mistake or accident CULPRIT
– prove a statement or argument to be mistaken REFUTE, REBUT, CONFUTE
– put someone right, rid someone of a mistaken idea DISABUSE
– "so", "thus", term used in a printed text to indicate the deliberate reproduction of a mistaken or surprising wording or fact being quoted SIC
– social mistake or blunder, such as a gauche or tactless remark GAFFE, FAUX PAS
– word used by mistake in place of a similar one, such as *pineapple* for *pinnacle* MALAPROPISM

mistress of a high-ranking man, or a fashionable prostitute COURTESAN
- mistress or sexually promiscuous woman consigned to the fringes of respectable society, as in the 19th century DEMIMONDAINE

mistrusting, disbelieving SCEPTICAL

misunderstand or misinterpret MISCONSTRUE
- misunderstanding, mistaken assumption MISAPPREHENSION, MISCONCEPTION
- misunderstanding, or opposing aims CROSS-PURPOSES

misuse, use for an improper or incorrect purpose PERVERT
- misuse of a word through confusion with a similar-sounding word MALAPROPISM

mite, tick, or similar related creature ACARID
- infestation of the skin or hair with mites or ticks ACARIASIS

mix or counteract and thereby make ineffective NEUTRALISE
- mix or combine BLEND, MELD
- mix a speech, article, or the like with jokes or other extraneous matter INTERLARD, INTERSPERSE
- mix and combine to form a new, complex product or whole SYNTHESISE, HOMOLOGISE
- mix into a crowd or other larger entity so as to become inconspicuous MERGE, MINGLE
- mix socially, come to participate in the life of a group or community INTEGRATE, ASSIMILATE
- mix to an even consistency, make the same in all parts HOMOGENISE
- mix up or confuse ideas, elements, or the like CONFOUND
- mixed, confused, and unruly crowd MELEE
- mixed and varied in ingredients, characteristics, or subject matter MISCELLANEOUS
- mixed in origin or make up, crossed HYBRID, MONGREL
- mixing two reagents in solution so as to measure the concentration of a solute TITRATION
- mixing socially with the people of an occupied or enemy country FRATERNISATION
- containing deliberately mixed or usefully varied parts DIVERSIFIED
- having mixed, dissimilar, or unmatching parts HETEROGENEOUS, PROMISCUOUS, MULTIFARIOUS, OMNIFARIOUS, DIFFUSE
- part or element mixed in, ingredient ADMIXTURE
- unable to blend or mix, as two liquids might be IMMISCIBLE

mixed feelings, conflicting views AMBIVALENCE

mixed race See **half-caste**

mixture, assembly, collection, choice ASSORTMENT, CONGLOMERATION
- mixture of disparate parts or elements, especially an unsuitable or confused one JUMBLE, FARRAGO, GALLIMAUFRY, MOTLEY, MÉLANGE, MISHMASH, PATCHWORK, OMNIUM GATHERUM, HYBRID
- mixture of elements chemically combined COMPOUND
- mixture of many assorted parts HOTCHPOTCH, POTPOURRI, OLLA PODRIDA, OLIO, PASTICCIO, SALMAGUNDI, PASTICHE
- mixture of many widely varying elements MISCELLANY, MEDLEY
- mixture of various kinds, based on fine particles dispersed but not dissolved in a liquid to form a consistent medium COLLOID, EMULSION, SUSPENSION
- mixture or combination of varied but usefully integrated parts ALLOY, AMALGAM
- mixture such as plaster or mortar COMPO
- book, performance, or the like containing a mixture or collection of connected works OMNIBUS, ANTHOLOGY

moat or defensive ditch FOSSE
- moat or protective ditch, as in a garden HA-HA, SUNK FENCE

mob, the masses, common people HOI POLLOI, PLEBS, CANAILLE
- mob rule OCHLOCRACY
- seize and kill without trial an alleged offender, as an impassioned mob might LYNCH

mock, ridicule, make scornful comments at JEER, TWIT, DERIDE, FLEER, SCOFF AT, DEROGATE
- mock or criticise bitterly and mercilessly PILLORY
- mock or make fun of by imitating MIMIC, APE
- mock to expose and ridicule pretensions DEBUNK
- mockery DERISION, RIDICULE
- mocking, light, flippant chat or repartee, teasing BANTER, BADINAGE, PERSIFLAGE, RAILLERY
- mocking and bitingly critical piece of writing SATIRE, LAMPOON, PASQUINADE
- mocking and derisive or hurtful remark GIBE, TAUNT
- mocking imitation of a literary or other artistic work BURLESQUE, PARODY, PASTICHE, SPOOF, TRAVESTY, CARICATURE
- mocking in a disdainful, cynical way SARDONIC
- harsh, shrill call or whistle, indicating disapproval or mockery CATCALL
- ignore someone's authority or wishes to the point of mockery or contempt FLOUT
- interrupt a speaker with mocking comments HECKLE
- rude and contemptuous mockery CONTUMELY

mock trial or legal debate conducted by law students MOOT

model for clothes, whether a woman or a life-size dummy MANNEQUIN
- model of excellence, perfect representative EXEMPLAR, PARAGON
- model of behaviour, standard of acceptability, or the like NORM
- model of the celestial sphere, consisting of solid rings, used by early astronomers ARMILLARY SPHERE
- model of the solar system, used in studying astronomy ORRERY
- model or copy in reduced size MINIATURE
- model or illustration, as of an engine or building, with part of the wall or casing omitted to reveal the interior CUTAWAY
- model or original pattern on which other versions or copies are based ARCHETYPE, PROTOTYPE, BLUEPRINT
- jointed dummy of a human figure, used as an artists' model and by medical students LAY FIGURE, MANNEQUIN, MANIKIN
- person or thing valued as a guide or model LODESTAR
- rough model for a sculpture MAQUETTE, BOZZETTO
- system or item regarded as a model of a larger system of which it is a part MICROCOSM
- three-dimensional scene or tableau, as in museums, with models of figures exhibited against a background DIORAMA

moderation or restraint, especially in drinking alcohol TEMPERANCE
- path of moderation VIA MEDIA

modern, ahead of one's times, with it AVANT-GARDE
- modern, up to date CONTEMPORARY
- modern, using the latest technology or theories STATE-OF-THE-ART
- modern design or style using industrial materials HIGH-TECH
- modern in an extreme or unnecessary way NEWFANGLED
- modern or recent LATTER-DAY
- extremely modern, in advance of current fashion FUTURISTIC
- traditional and conventional in the arts and sciences, as opposed to modern and experimental CLASSICAL

modernising or updating of ideas, especially in the Roman Catholic Church AGGIORNAMENTO

modest See also **mediocre**, **humble**, **shy**
– modest, avoiding all boasting or showiness UNASSUMING
– modest, reserved, sometimes in an affected way DEMURE
– modest and discreet, staying in the background UNOBTRUSIVE, SELF-EFFACING, UNPRETENTIOUS
– modest but adequate income or standard of living SUFFICIENCY
– modest or prim to an excessive degree, especially in sexual matters PRUDISH
– modest or shy, lacking in confidence DIFFIDENT
– modestly playing down one's own achievements or qualities SELF-DEPRECATING
– modestly putting aside one's own claims, rights, or interests SELF-ABNEGATING

Mogul governor in India NABOB

mohair ANGORA

moist- HYGRO-

moisture – containing as much moisture as possible SATURATED
– deprived of water or moisture, dry DEHYDRATED
– helping to retain moisture, as glycerine does HUMECTANT

mole – mole's burrow FORTRESS
– adjective for a mole TALPINE
– group or family of moles LABOUR, MOVEMENT, COMPANY

mole, birthmark, or other congenital skin blemish or growth NAEVUS

molecule molecule-like group of atoms or atom having an electric charge through gaining or losing one or more electrons ION
– compound formed of chains of repeated units of molecules POLYMER
– twin spiral structure of a DNA molecule DOUBLE HELIX

molten rock LAVA, MAGMA

moment, instant, very short period of time TRICE
– moment of sanity or normal consciousness between bouts of coma or insanity LUCID MOMENT

momentary See **short-lived**

Monaco – person born or living in Monaco MONÉGASQUE

monarch See also **king**
– council advising the British monarch PRIVY COUNCIL

monastery See also **monk**, **abbey**
– monastery, convent, or other place of seclusion CLOISTER
– monastery belonging to the Carthusian order CHARTERHOUSE
– monastery church MINSTER
– monastery inn or shelter for the needy or travellers HOSPICE
– monastery or convent PRIORY
– Buddhist monastery LAMASERY
– deputy head of a monastery in former times PROVOST
– dining hall of a monastery REFECTORY, FRATER
– head of a monastery ABBOT
– head of a monastic community SUPERIOR, CUSTOS
– head of a monastery in the Eastern Orthodox Church ARCHIMANDRITE, LEGUMEN
– latrine behind a dormitory in an abbey or monastery RÈREDORTER
– layman living a religious life in a monastery without having taken formal vows OBLATE
– room in a monastery in which scribes could copy records or manuscripts SCRIPTORIUM

money See also **currency**, **coins**
– money, contract, or the like held by a third party until certain conditions are fulfilled ESCROW
– money, currency serving as a legally authorised medium of exchange or payment CIRCULATING MEDIUM, LEGAL TENDER
– money, profits, especially as a temptation to sin LUCRE
– money, wealth as a corrupting influence MAMMON
– money or wealth, especially if acquired in a dubious way PELF
– money bestowed as a gift, especially to an inferior LARGESSE
– money deposited as security or guarantee, as against damage, debt, or non-payment CAUTION MONEY, EARNEST, BOND
– money earned for or spent on non-essential items PIN MONEY
– money given as a tip or reward POURBOIRE, GRATUITY
– money as coinage SPECIE
– money-market dealer, speculator, or specialist CAMBIST
– money-mindedness MATERIALISM
– money or income REVENUE
– money or other resources required for a particular purpose WHEREWITHAL
– money or property left in a will LEGACY, BEQUEST
– money order or bill of exchange DRAFT
– money paid as a bribe to preserve secrecy HUSH MONEY
– money paid by an employer as a compensation, to an employee who has lost his job SEVERANCE PAY, REDUNDANCY PAY, GOLDEN HANDSHAKE
– money paid out, expenditure DISBURSEMENT
– money raised by a charity campaign or sale PROCEEDS
– money set aside for a specific purpose APPROPRIATION
– money store, funds, treasury COFFERS, EXCHEQUER
– money supplement paid as a cost-of-living allowance in an expensive area WEIGHTING
– money used to provide change at the start of a business day FLOAT
– money voted by Parliament for the running of the royal household PRIVY PURSE
– money withdrawn from one's bank account in excess of one's credit balance OVERDRAFT
– amount by which an actual amount, as of money, is lower than the expected or required amount SHORTFALL, DEFICIT
– beads and polished shells formerly used by North American Indians as money WAMPUM, PEAG
– conceal the dubious or illegal origin of a sum of money LAUNDER
– convert property or assets into ready money REALISE, LIQUIDATE
– devoted to gaining money or material possessions MATERIALISTIC, MERCENARY
– economic doctrine that a country's economy is best controlled by means of careful regulation of the money supply MONETARISM
– forge something, especially money COUNTERFEIT
– having money in hand, able to meet all debts SOLVENT
– misuse or steal money that one has control of MISAPPROPRIATE, EMBEZZLE
– obtain money, promises, or the like by threats EXTORT
– principal or capital sum of money, value of an estate, or the like, as distinct from the interest or income CORPUS
– producing much money, profitable REMUNERATIVE, LUCRATIVE
– profitable job requiring little work, or similar easy source of money GRAVY TRAIN, MILCH COW
– reduction by a government in the monetary or exchange value of a currency DEVALUATION
– relating to money MONETARY, PECUNIARY
– relating to money, coins, or currency NUMISMATIC
– relating to paper money not backed by gold FIDUCIARY
– return of part of the money paid REBATE
– seizure of money or property as security against legal claims

SEQUESTRATION
– slang term for money, dough, bread, lolly MOOLAH, SPONDULIKS, GELT, MAZUMA
– slang term for small amounts of money, peanuts DIBS
– tiny, token, insignificant, as a sum of money might be NOMINAL
– trade through direct exchange of goods and services, without using money BARTER
– transfer money REMIT
– unexpected piece of good fortune, especially the sudden acquiring of money WINDFALL
– unit of money used for purposes of accounting UNIT OF ACCOUNT
– very small amount of money, such as a tiny salary PITTANCE

moneylender, especially one who charges an exorbitant rate of interest USURER
– moneylender or loan agency that accepts trade debts as security FACTOR

mongolism DOWN'S SYNDROME

monk See also **monastery**
– monk in the Greek Orthodox Church CALOYER
– monk of a Cistercian order noted for its austerity and vow of silence TRAPPIST
– monk or friar of various orders BENEDICTINE, CARTHUSIAN, CAPUCHIN, CISTERCIAN, DOMINICAN, FRANCISCAN
– monk or nun VOTARY
– monk or nun holding a subordinate office OBEDIENTIARY
– monk or other member of a communal order CENOBITE
– monk wandering about in former times PALMER
– monk's garment consisting of a long band of cloth hanging at the front and back from the shoulders SCAPULA
– monk's hood or hooded cloak or habit COWL, CAPUCHE
– monk's shaven head TONSURE
– Buddhist monk in Tibet or Mongolia LAMA
– candidate monk or nun POSTULANT, NOVICE, NEOPHYTE
– referring to a clergyman who is not a monk SECULAR

monkey, ape, human, or related mammal PRIMATE
– relating to or resembling an ape or monkey SIMIAN
– small Indian macaque monkey widely used in medical research RHESUS MONKEY

monocle QUIZZING GLASS

monopoly – association, often unofficial or illegal, of independent businesses combining to secure a monopoly in a market and control prices CARTEL, TRUST
– regulating business monopolies in the U.S. to ensure fair competition ANTITRUST

monotonous task, routine TREADMILL

monster See chart
– monster, freak LUSUS NATURAE
– monster-like creation or scheme dangerous even to its creator FRANKENSTEIN'S MONSTER
– story or book about monsters or mythical creatures TERATOLOGY

monster- TERAT-, TERATO-, THERI-, THERO-

monstrous deed or behaviour, outrage ENORMITY
– monstrously large animal or thing LEVIATHAN, BEHEMOTH

month – "in or during the next month", as used in business correspondence PROXIMO, PROX.
– "in or during the previous month", as used in business corre-

MONSTERS AND MYTHOLOGICAL CREATURES

abominable snowman, yeti	large, hairy manlike animal said to live in the Himalayas
afreet	powerful evil demon of Arab mythology
basilisk	serpent, lizard, or dragon reputed to kill by its breath or look
behemoth	hippopotamus-like beast described in the Book of Job
bunyip	monster said to live in the swamps and lagoons of central Australia
centaur	creature of Greek mythology having the head, trunk and arms of a man, and the legs of a horse
Cerberus	three-headed watchdog of Hades, the Greek underworld
Chimera/ Chimaera	fire-breathing monster of classical mythology, having a lion's head, a she-goat's body, and a serpent's tail
cockatrice	creature of classical mythology, supposedly hatched from a cock's egg and having a death-dealing glance
cyclops	giants with a single eye in mid-forehead, encountered by Odysseus
dryad, hamadryad	wood nymph of classical mythology
Fafnir	dragon slain by Siegfried, in German mythology
Furies, Eumenides, Erinyes	three winged goddesses of classical mythology, with serpents for hair, who punished evil-doers
Gigantes	giants with a man's torso, and legs in the form of serpents, defeated by the gods and Hercules
golem	man-made human-like creature of Jewish legend
Gorgons	winged female creatures of classical mythology, having serpents for hair
griffin/ gryphon	creature of classical mythology having an eagle's head and wings, and a lion's body
Harpies	ravenous, slimy monsters of classical mythology, having women's heads and birds' bodies
hippocampus	sea horse with a horse's forelegs and the tail of a fish or dolphin, ridden by Neptune
hippogriff/ hippogryph	creature of classical mythology having the head, claws, and wings of a griffin and the body of a horse

spondence ULTIMO, ULT.
– "of the current month", as used in business correspondence INSTANT, INST.
– per month, monthly PER MENSEM

monument, as in ancient Egypt, in the form of a tapering four-sided stone pillar with a pyramidal top OBELISK
– monument commemorating a nation's heroes PANTHEON
– monument honouring soldiers killed in battle or other dead people buried elsewhere CENOTAPH
– ceremony at which a new monument, work of art, or the like is formally displayed to the public for the first time UNVEILING
– wording carved on a statue, monument, or building EPIGRAPH, INSCRIPTION
– sculpture or painting of a person, as on a monument EFFIGY

mood, frame of mind HUMOUR, DISPOSITION, TEMPERAMENT
– suffering from extreme shifts of mood, from overexcitement to deep depression MANIC-DEPRESSIVE

moody See **irritable**

Moon, as personified in poetry CYNTHIA, DIANA, PHOEBE, SELENE
– Moon when between half and full GIBBOUS MOON
– Moon's orbit of the Earth, or similar orbit in which the same face of the satellite is always pointing to the primary CAPTURED ROTATION, SYNCHRONOUS ROTATION
– adjective for the Moon LUNAR
– any of several long channels or valleys on the Moon RILL
– arrangement of three celestial bodies in a straight line, as of the Earth, Sun, and Moon at new moon or during an eclipse SYZYGY
– concave shape, as of a sickle or the Moon in its first or last quarter CRESCENT
– decrease in apparent size or illumination, as the Moon does when approaching new moon WANE
– decreasing, as the waning Moon is DECRESCENT
– either pointed end of a crescent Moon CUSP
– full moon nearest to the autumn equinox HARVEST MOON
– full moon that follows the harvest moon HUNTER'S MOON
– half-moon or crescent-shaped object or structure, such as the outwork of a fort DEMILUNE
– having two points, horns, or cusps, as a crescent moon does BICUSPID
– increase in apparent size or illumination, as the Moon does when approaching full moon WAX
– increasing, as the waxing Moon is INCRESCENT
– period between the old and new moon during which the Moon is invisible INTERLUNATION
– point at which a spacecraft in lunar orbit is closest to the Moon PERICYNTHION, PERILUNE
– point at which a spacecraft in lunar orbit is farthest from the Moon APOCYNTHION, APOLUNE, APOSELENE
– point in its orbit when the Moon or a satellite is farthest from the Earth APOGEE
– point in its orbit when the Moon or a satellite is nearest the Earth PERIGEE
– ring of faint light, as around the Moon when viewed through a haze CORONA, AUREOLE
– scientific study or geography of

Hydra	nine-headed water snake, which sprouted two heads where one was struck off
kelpie	Scottish water spirit, usually a horse that drowned its riders
kraken	sea monster of Norwegian waters
lamia	creature of classical mythology having the head and breasts of a woman and the body of a serpent
leviathan	fiery, scaled, seven-headed sea serpent described in the Book of Job
Lilith	Biblical female demon living in deserted places, said to assault children
Minotaur	eater of human flesh, half man and half bull, confined to the Cretan Labyrinth and killed by Theseus
naiad	freshwater nymph of classical mythology
nereid	sea nymph of classical mythology
orc	monstrous creature of classical mythology
oread	mountain nymph of classical mythology
Pegasus	winged horse, the offspring of the Gorgon Medusa, and the mount of Perseus and Bellerophon
Phoenix	fabulous bird of classical mythology which from time to time destroyed itself on a burning altar, a new bird emerging from the ashes
roc	bird of enormous size and strength in Arabian legend
salamander	lizard or other reptilian monster; creature able to live in fire
satyr, faun	spirit of field and woodland of classical mythology, having a human torso, the hindquarters of a goat, and horns, noted for lechery
Sphinx	creature of classical mythology, having the head of a woman and the body of a lion, that killed all those unable to solve its riddle
unicorn	white, horse-like animal with a long, single horn, able to outwit all captors except virgins
werewolf	monster alternating between the forms of a human being and a wolf
wyvern/ wivern	winged dragon of European mythology, having bird's feet and a serpent's tail

the Moon SELENOGRAPHY
– "sea" or dark patch on Mars or the Moon MARE
Moon- SELEN-, SELENO-, LUN-
Moonies UNIFICATION CHURCH
mooring post on a quay or deck for a ship's ropes or cables BOLLARD
moral baseness or vileness DEPRAVITY, TURPITUDE
– moral considerations or doubts SCRUPLES
– moral disapproval of an excessive kind, narrow-minded propriety GRUNDYISM
– moral duty, promise, contract, or the like OBLIGATION
– moral lesson HOMILY
– moral or intellectual instruction or enlightenment EDIFICATION
– "moral philosophy" ETHICS
– moral principles allowing different behaviour in one person or group from that expected of another DOUBLE STANDARD
– "Moral Rearmament" BUCHMANISM, OXFORD GROUP
– moral soundness, honesty INTEGRITY, PROBITY, RECTITUDE
– moral story or fable, as used in medieval sermons EXEMPLUM
– moralising in a pompous way, especially by means of proverbs and platitudes SENTENTIOUS
– morally corrupting or evil PERNICIOUS, PESTIFEROUS, PESTILENT, NOXIOUS
– morally instructive, designed to convey a moral lesson DIDACTIC
– morally unrestrained DISSOLUTE, LIBERTINE, LICENTIOUS
– absence of clear moral guidelines in a person or society ANOMIE
– declining or decaying in morale DECADENT
– moral customs and conventions of a group MORES
– philosophy of moral duty or responsibility DEONTOLOGY
– rejection of all moral and social values NIHILISM, ANARCHISM
– relating to rights, duties, and similar moral concepts DEONTIC
– unable to distinguish between moral and immoral AMORAL
morale, group spirit ESPRIT DE CORPS
more- PLEO-, PLEIO-, PLIO-, SUPER-, PLURI-, MULTI-
Mormons LATTER-DAY SAINTS
– Mormon priest of high rank PATRIARCH, EVANGELIST
– person who is not a Mormon, as referred to by Mormons GENTILE
morning prayer MATINS
– adjective for the early morning MATUTINAL
– in the morning ANTEMERIDIAN
– poem, song, or tune suited to or dealing with dawn or the early morning AUBADE
morse-code signal or signalling device based on mirror-flashes of sunlight HELIOGRAPH
mortar – mortar-like cannon firing shells at a steep angle HOWITZER
– mortar or cement for filling cracks or seams POINTING
– crush to a powder, as in a mortar BRAY
– small club-shaped implement for crushing or grinding substances in a mortar PESTLE
– thin mortar, as used between tiles GROUT
mortarboard, hard black academic cap TRENCHER, SQUARE
mortgage or other charge or claim on a property ENCUMBRANCE
– mortgage or pledge something as security HYPOTHECATE
– pay off a debt or mortgage by instalments AMORTISE
– repossess mortgaged property FORECLOSE
mortise – projecting end of a piece of wood fitting into a corresponding mortise in another piece to form a joint TENON
mortuary – U.S. term for a mortuary MORGUE
mosaic of inlaid wood INTARSIA
– inlay, pave, or decorate with a mosaic of tiny tiles TESSELLATE
– tiny square tile used in making a mosaic TESSERA
Moscow – person born or living in Moscow MUSCOVITE
Moslem See **Muslim**, **Islam**
mosque in an Arab country MASJID
– mosque official who summons the faithful to prayer MUEZZIN
– niche in a mosque to show the direction of Mecca MIHRAB
– narrow tower of a mosque, from which the faithful are summoned to prayer MINARET
– pulpit in a mosque MIMBAR
mosquito of the kind that transmits malaria ANOPHELES
– mosquito of the kind that transmits yellow fever AEDES
– mosquito or other organism that transmits germs VECTOR, CARRIER
– mosquito or related insect CULICID
– common house mosquito CULEX, CULICINE
– fabric used as mosquito netting MARQUISETTE
– lotion or other substance that keeps mosquitoes away REPELLENT
moss of the kind that forms peat when decomposed SPHAGNUM
– reproductive cell or organ, in non-flowering plants such as mosses, ferns, and fungi SPORE
– study of mosses BRYOLOGY
– tiny hair-like projection, as on moss or in the intestines VILLUS
moss- BRYO-
moth, butterfly, or related insect LEPIDOPTERAN
– pupa of a moth or butterfly, often encased in a cocoon CHRYSALIS
mothballs – sharp-smelling hydrocarbon substance used in mothballs, dyes, and explosives NAPHTHALENE
mother of a family, as the head of the household MATERFAMILIAS
– mother or bearer of a child on behalf of another, usually infertile, woman SURROGATE MOTHER
– mother or founder of a tribe, tradition, or the like MATRIARCH
– adjective for a mother or motherhood MATERNAL
– complex of unconscious emotions, in Freudian theory, including sexual desire in a boy for his mother OEDIPUS COMPLEX
– female sheep, horse, or the like as the mother of another DAM
– having the same mother but a different father UTERINE
– legal term for the womb of a mother VENTER
– mock-formal term for a mother MATER
– murder of one's mother MATRICIDE
– name based on one's mother's name, or that of a female ancestor METRONYMIC, MATRONYMIC
– relating or referring to descent traced through the mother rather than the father MATRILINEAL
mother- MATRI-
motherhood MATERNITY
mother-of-pearl NACRE
– large shellfish providing mother-of-pearl ABALONE
– New Zealand shellfish with a shimmering green shell like mother-of-pearl PAUA
motion – random motion of microscopic particles suspensed in liquid or gas BROWNIAN MOTION
– relating to motion KINETIC
– tendency of a physical body to remain at rest or in unchanged motion unless acted on by external forces INERTIA
motionless, unchanging, or producing no movement or change STATIC, INERT
motivation, encouragement, influence INCENTIVE, INCITEMENT, STIMULUS, INDUCEMENT
motive kept concealed so as to deceive ULTERIOR MOTIVE
motiveless, random, unprovoked, as vandalism or wilful destruction is

WANTON, GRATUITOUS

motor See also **engine**, **car**, **internal-combustion engine**, **jet engine**
- motor, usually detachable, fitted externally at the stern of a boat OUTBOARD MOTOR
- motor-racing assembly area for the cars PADDOCK
- motor-racing over a rough grass track AUTOCROSS
- rotor of an induction motor, having copper bars arranged to form the outer edge of a cylinder SQUIRREL CAGE
- series of tight bends, or a barrier used in forming them, on a motor-racing circuit CHICANE
- stationary part of an electric motor or generator STATOR
- team, or stable, of motor-racing cars ÉCURIE
- turning or rotating part of an electric motor or generator ROTOR

motor car See **car**

motorboat that skims the surface of the water HYDROPLANE

motorcycle escort OUTRIDER
- motorcycle or bicycle with high handlebars CHOPPER
- motorcycle partly propelled by pedals MOPED
- motorcycle-racing arena VELODROME
- seat for a second rider, as on a horse or motorcycle PILLION

motorcyclist carrying official documents or reports DISPATCH RIDER

motorway in a French-speaking country AUTOROUTE
- motorway in a German-speaking country AUTOBAHN
- motorway in Italy or an Italian-speaking region AUTOSTRADA
- motorway verge for emergency stopping HARD SHOULDER

motto, slogan, or principle BANNER
- motto, slogan, or rallying cry, summing up the principles of a group or project WATCHWORD, MAXIM
- motto or quotation, as at the head of a chapter, suggesting its theme EPIGRAPH

mould MUST, MILDEW
- mould, typically reusable, in which objects are cast DIE
- mould taken, especially from a footprint, as for evidence in court MOULAGE
- mouldy-smelling FUSTY, MUSTY
- clay mould around a wax model of a sculpture MANTLE
- hole or channel through which molten material is introduced into a mould SPRUE
- small cup-shaped mould, for jellies, cakes, or the like DARIOLE

moulding See also **column**
- moulding around or above a doorway, window frame, or the like ARCHITRAVE
- moulding in the form of a narrow, protruding, half-cylindrical piping BAGUETTE
- moulding projecting beyond an adjacent panel or frame BOLECTION
- moulding with a zigzag pattern CHEVRON, DANCETTE
- concave moulding CAVETTO, CONGÉ, COVE
- continuous ornamental moulding along a wall CORDEN, STRING COURSE, TABLE, CORNICE
- double-curved moulding CYMA, OGEE, TALON
- groove running lengthways along an architectural moulding QUIRK
- narrow convex moulding BAGUETTE, BEADING, REEDING
- narrow convex moulding, sometimes resembling a string of beads ASTRAGAL, CHAPLET

mound covering an ancient burial site BARROW, TUMULUS
- mound of stones serving as a memorial or landmark CAIRN
- mound on which a fort or castle is sited MOTTE
- mound or hillock TUFFET

mountain See also **hill**
- mountain-dweller or backwoodsman in the U.S. HILLBILLY
- mountain group within a larger chain MASSIF
- mountain lake TARN
- mountain nymph, in Greek mythology OREAD
- mountain pass or chain in India GHAT
- mountain pass or gap COL
- mountain peak PINNACLE
- mountain range or system of parallel ranges CORDILLERA
- mountain range with a rugged outline SIERRA
- mountain ridge with a knife edge ARÊTE
- mountain ridge projecting sideways from the main line or range of mountains SPUR
- flat piece of land surrounded by rising slopes, as in the mountains AMPHITHEATRE
- flat-topped mountain on the sea bed GUYOT
- from or at the other side of the mountains, especially the Alps as viewed from Italy TRAMONTANE
- relating to or inhabiting mountains MONTANE
- rocky needle-shaped mountain peak AIGUILLE
- situated on, or relating to the other side of the mountains, or south of the Alps ULTRAMONTANE
- situated on, living on, or relating to this side of the mountains, or north of the Alps CISMONTANE
- sloping rock surface at the base of a mountain or ridge in an arid region PEDIMENT
- steep or very sharply angled, as the side of a mountain might be PRECIPITOUS
- steep rocky mountain peak CRAG
- steep slope or face of a mountain ridge or plateau ESCARPMENT

mountain- ORO-, MONT-

mountaineering – descend a steep slope or vertical cliff in mountaineering by sliding down a rope around one's body ABSEIL, RAPPEL
- metal ring for fastening to a spike or running a rope through in mountaineering KARABINER, SNAP RING
- metal spikes fitted to boots, as for mountaineering or walking on ice CRAMPONS
- move sideways or diagonally across a slope, as in skiing or mountaineering TRAVERSE
- rock or ice pillar around which a rope can be tied in mountaineering BOLLARD
- secure a mountaineer at the end of a rope, or secure a rope to a rock or post BELAY
- short rope ladder, with a few solid rungs, as used in mountaineering ÉTRIER
- spike driven into rock to secure a rope in mountaineering PITON
- temporary or overnight camp, as set up by explorers or mountaineers BIVOUAC
- vertical crack in a rock or ice wall which a mountaineer can fit into CHIMNEY

mounted sentry stationed ahead of an army's outposts VEDETTE

mounting – mat, typically decorated, on which a photo or picture is mounted PASSE-PARTOUT

mourn with a wailing lament KEEN

mournful, expressing sadness PLAINTIVE, PLANGENT, WISTFUL
- mournful, sorrowful, sad, in style or substance ELEGIAC

mourning band of black material, worn on the sleeve or hat CREPE
- mourning clothing, as worn by a widow WEEDS
- mourning fabric, typically of black silk or crepe CYPRESS
- mourning poem or song on someone's death DIRGE, ELEGY, THRENODY, MONODY
- public showing of mourning or

repentance SACKCLOTH AND ASHES
- vigil and mourning over a dead person before burial WAKE

mouse, rat, squirrel, or related gnawing mammal RODENT
- mouse-like, resembling or relating to a rat or mouse MURINE

moustache of a bushy drooping shape WALRUS MOUSTACHE
- moustache with upward-curling ends HANDLEBAR MOUSTACHE

mouth See illustration
- mouth, as of a shark or lion MAW
- mouth-like opening, as in a sponge or hookworm STOMA
- mouth of a river EMBOUCHURE, ESTUARY
- mouth or other opening in the body ORIFICE
- adjective for the mouth ORAL
- relating to the mouth or cheeks BUCCAL
- split in the roof of the mouth, often occurring in conjunction with harelip CLEFT PALATE
- technical term for a mouth or other opening OS
- width or gap of the open mouth or beak RICTUS

-mouth- OR-, ORO-, STOMATO-, -STOM-, -STOME

mouthpiece of a wind instrument, especially brass EMBOUCHURE

move about playfully, jump about FRISK, GAMBOL, FROLIC, ROMP
- move across TRAVERSE
- move along swiftly and easily, as light clouds might SCUD, FLIT
- move away in different directions from a single starting point, separate DIVERGE
- move back and forth between two positions, swing rhythmically OSCILLATE
- move back, as the tide might RECEDE
- move back to where one started from RETRACE ONE'S STEPS
- move backwards, retreat RETIRE
- move backwards or get worse RETROGRESS
- move clumsily and heavily LUMBER, GALUMPH, TRUNDLE
- move duties or assets elsewhere HIVE OFF
- move easily and effortlessly, as downhill on a bicycle COAST, FREEWHEEL
- move furtively, sneak SLINK, SIDLE, PROWL
- move hurriedly and out of control, as charging cattle might STAMPEDE
- move in a tired, listless way SHAMBLE, SHUFFLE
- move in a winding or undecided way MEANDER, MAUNDER
- move in an aimless, apathetic, or furtive way SKULK, MOOCH
- move in an easy, carefree manner AMBLE, LOPE, MOSEY, SAUNTER, IDLE, WEND ONE'S WAY
- move lightly and rapidly across a surface in a darting motion, as a fishing fly might SKITTER
- move or get going, rouse oneself, become active BESTIR ONESELF
- move or go hurriedly SCURRY, SCAMPER, SCARPER, SKEDADDLE
- move or go to a specified place REPAIR, RESORT, BETAKE ONESELF
- move or march quickly while heavily laden, as soldiers have to YOMP
- move or push vigorously forward SURGE
- move or roam about ROVE
- move or roam about aimlessly, frivolously, or irresponsibly GAD ABOUT, GALLIVANT, TRAIPSE
- move rapidly and erratically, as if out of control CAREER, CAREEN
- move reluctantly and little BUDGE, SHIFT
- move round or avoid SKIRT, CIRCUMVENT
- move slowly, lag behind DAWDLE, LOITER
- move to a later time, postpone ADJOURN
- move to another place RELOCATE
- move towards, as if drawn by an irresistible attraction GRAVITATE
- move towards the same point from different directions CONVERGE
- move with an up-and-down motion UNDULATE
- move with bumps and jolts JOUNCE
- move with exaggerated gestures of displeasure or impatience FLOUNCE, SASHAY
- prevent from moving IMMOBILISE, PARALYSE

moved easily, readily affected, sensitive SUSCEPTIBLE

movement, as by bacteria, in reflex response to light or a similar stimulus TAXIS
- movement, by mystical or mental powers, of distant objects TELEKINESIS, PSYCHOKINESIS
- movement back and forth ALTERNATION, RECIPROCATION
- diminished power of movement, lack of coordination, caused by brain damage or disease APRAXIA
- movement forwards, progress, advance HEADWAY
- movement of the limbs or body to express or reinforce meaning GESTURE
- movement or general direction, as of someone's life TENOR
- movement or transport of goods or people from place to place TRANSIT, CONVEYANCE
- apparent movement of a stationary light, such as a candle flame, when observed in a darkened room AUTOKINETIC PHENOMENON
- force or power resulting from continuing movement MOMENTUM, IMPETUS
- instrument for observing, measuring, or adjusting vibration, rotation, or the like by using light flashes to make the moving object appear stationary STROBOSCOPE
- relating or referring to movement MOTIVE, KINETIC

-movement- -KIN-, KINET-, KINETO-, -KINESIS, -TROP-, TROPO-, -TROPIC, -GRADE, -TACTIC

movie See **film**

moving, affecting, or touching, as a memory might be POIGNANT
- moving, arousing sympathy PATHETIC
- moving easily and gracefully LITHE, LIMBER, SUPPLE, LISSOM, AGILE, FLEXIBLE
- moving from place to place, mobile as opposed to stationary AMBULATORY, AMBULANT
- moving or growing inwards, towards a centre or axis AFFERENT, CENTRIPETAL
- moving or growing outwards, away from a centre or axis EFFERENT, CENTRIFUGAL
- "moving pavement" TRAVELATOR
- moving staircase ESCALATOR
- moving under one's own power, as a microorganism might MOTILE

-moving -DROMOUS

mowing of a second crop of grass in a single season AFTERMATH
- mown grass or hay cut by a scythe or mower SWATH

Mozart – catalogue number of a Mozart composition KÖCHEL NUMBER

MP See also **parliament**
- MP formerly representing a borough, town, or university BURGESS
- MP in France and some other countries DEPUTY
- MP or similar member of a lawmaking body LEGISLATOR
- MP who is neutral or independent, committed neither to the government nor to the opposition CROSSBENCHER
- MP who is not a minister or shadow minister BACKBENCHER
- MP who supervises attendance and voting of his party's other MPs WHIP

mouth, nose and throat

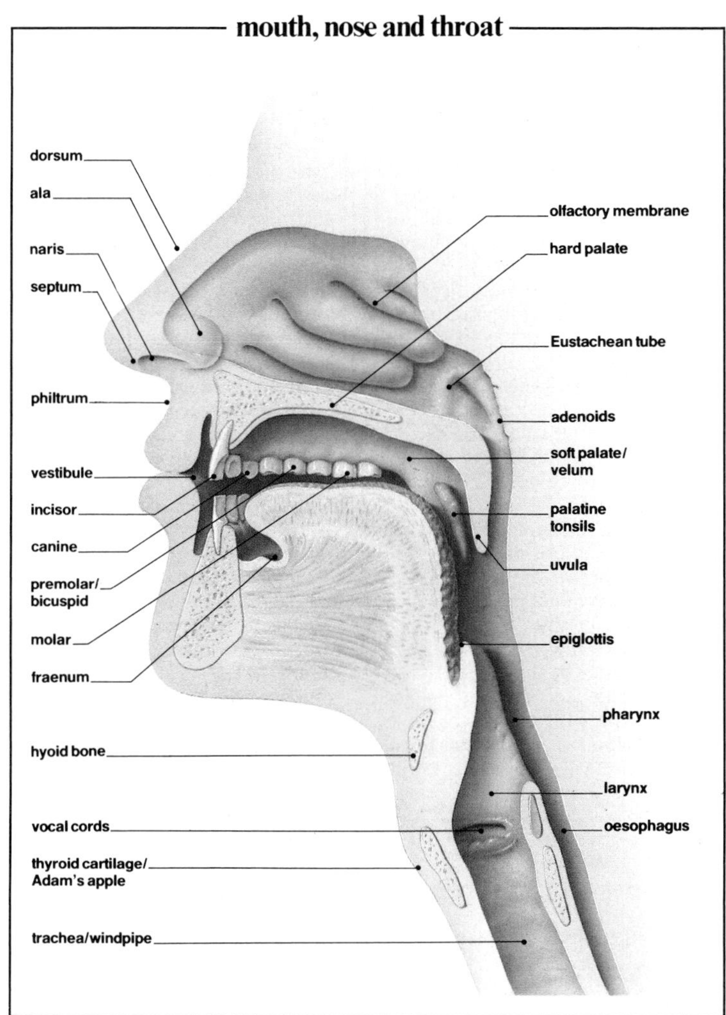

– formal office of the Crown that an MP applies for when relinquishing his seat CHILTERN HUNDREDS
– person represented by an MP, agent, or the like CONSTITUENT
– senior MP who serves as chairman during debates SPEAKER
– withdraw party backing from a candidate, especially a sitting MP, in an election DESELECT

much See **lots**, **many**, **plenty**, **excessive**
– much in a small space MULTUM IN PARVO

much- POLY-, MULTI-

mucus – mucus-like discharge from the eyes or nose RHEUM
– mucus secreted in the breathing passages PHLEGM
– mucous matter coughed up from the lungs and windpipe SPUTUM

mud – mud-filled hollow SLOUGH
– muddied through sediment or foreign particles, as river water might be TURBID
– muddy deposit, as on a river bed or the inside of a boiler SLUDGE
– board or boards laid over wet or muddy ground DUCKBOARD
– building material of interlaced sticks plastered with mud or clay WATTLE AND DAUB
– craving for unnatural food, such as mud or chalk, occurring sometimes during pregnancy PICA
– lie or roll lazily about in mud, a hot bath, or the like WALLOW
– thin, liquid mixture of mud, cement, manure or the like SLURRY
– trapped in mud MIRED

muddle or disorder HAVOC, SHAMBLES, HUGGER-MUGGER
– muddled by many conflicting interests or forces, as political life might be TURBID

mug, tankard, or large cup STOUP
– mug, typically made of pottery and having a lid, holding about a pint of beer STEIN
– mug in the shape of a man wearing a three-cornered hat TOBY JUG
– small mug or cup NOGGIN

Muhammad See also **Islam**
– Muhammad, or any of his various successors IMAM

mule driver MULETEER
– mule-like hybrid animal, from a female ass and male horse HINNY
– group or family of mules PACK, BARREN, RAKE, SPAN

mulled wine BISHOP

multi – multi-coloured PIED, PIEBALD, MOTLEY, PARTI-COLOURED, POLYCHROME, VARICOLOURED, VARIEGATED
– multi-dimensional, having or including many aspects or elements OMNIBUS
– multi-talented VERSATILE

multi- PLURI-, POLY-

multilingual POLYGLOT

multiply by five QUINTUPLE
– multiply by four QUADRUPLE
– multiply plants using graftings and cuttings PROPAGATE
– multiplying by means of buds, shoots, or small bulbs rather than by seeds VIVIPAROUS
– independent of the order of the terms, as an operation such as multiplication is COMMUTATIVE

mummy – jar used in ancient Egypt for holding a mummy's entrails CANOPIC JAR

murder See also **kill**, **killing**
– killing of a person, as through negligence, that is unlawful though not necessarily murder CULPABLE HOMICIDE, MANSLAUGHTER
– list of people to be murdered HIT LIST
– murder a prominent politician or public figure ASSASSINATE
– planned beforehand, deliberate, as a murder may be PREMEDITATED
– plea that mental abnormality at the time of a murder reduces the culprit's responsibility DIMINISHED RESPONSIBILITY

-murder -CIDE

murderer See **killer**

murmuring, whispering, or rustling sound SUSURRATION

muscle, as at the back of the upper arm, having three points of attachment at one of the ends TRICEPS
– muscle, as on the front of the upper arm, having two points of attachment at one of the ends BICEPS
– muscle, typically regulating an internal organ, that cannot be consciously controlled INVOLUNTARY MUSCLE

– muscle cramp or rigid muscular contraction, as in a fever RIGOR
– muscle on the forearm, helping to turn the palm of the hand downwards PRONATOR
– muscle on the forearm, helping to turn the palm of the hand upwards SUPINATOR
– muscle sense, awareness of one's own muscles and bodily movements KINAESTHESIA
– muscles behind the thigh, or tendons behind the knee HAMSTRINGS
– muscular contraction, involuntary and often violent and painful CONVULSION
– muscular contractions in the intestine or similar tube-like organ that force the contents onwards PERISTALSIS
– any of the three buttock muscles GLUTEUS
– circular or ring-like muscle squeezing or relaxing a body passage SPHINCTER, CONSTRICTOR
– cord of fibres connecting the heelbone to the calf muscles ACHILLES TENDON
– either of two large chest muscles, helping to move the shoulder and upper arm PECTORAL MUSCLE
– exercise through contracting the muscles without changing their length or moving the limbs ISOMETRIC EXERCISE
– fibrous tissue beneath the skin and encasing muscles FASCIA
– flat muscle on the shoulder and back, helping to move the shoulder blade TRAPEZIUS
– health or condition of muscle, as shown by its tension and response to stimuli TONE, TONUS
– long muscle extending from the front of the thigh round to behind the knee, helping to bend the knee SARTORIUS
– loss or lack of muscular coordination ATAXIA
– picture of the body, or a section of the body, without the skin, to show the muscle structure ÉCORCHÉ
– sharpness of outline, as of well-developed muscles DEFINITION
– shortening or tensing of a muscle, either voluntary or involuntary CONTRACTION
– sinew attaching a muscle to a bone or other support TENDON
– thick shoulder muscle, helping to raise the arm DELTOID
– tough band of fibrous tissue connecting moving bones or cartilages, or supporting organs or muscles LIGAMENT
– twitching of muscle fibres FIBRILLATION
– wide swelling section of a muscle VENTER

muscle- MY-, MYO-

Muses – relating to the Muses or artistic inspiration PIERIAN

museum director CURATOR
– museum exhibit, with models of figures set against a background DIORAMA
– museum or place of safekeeping REPOSITORY

mushroom See illustration
– mushroom-like fungus growing underground, considered a great delicacy TRUFFLE
– mushroom-lover MYCOPHILE
– mushroom-shaped FUNGIFORM
– cooked or served with a sauce of olive oil, lemon juice, spices, and tomato, as mushrooms might be A LA GRECQUE
– edible mushroom of various types CHAMPIGNON, MOREL, CHANTERELLE
– fungus of the family that includes mushrooms AGARIC
– thin skin or outer covering on the cap of a mushroom PELLICLE

music See chart, page 339
– music, drama, or poetry competition, of Welsh origin EISTEDDFOD
– music based on an untraditional sequence of notes, typically using a twelve-tone scale SERIAL MUSIC, DODECAPHONY
– "music business", popular-music industry in the U.S. in former times TIN PAN ALLEY
– music suggesting a story, scene, or idea PROGRAMME MUSIC
– music-loving PHILHARMONIC
– music of a bland kind providing a background in waiting rooms, airports, and so on MUZAK
– music of a random kind in which the performer is given a great deal of choice by the composer ALEATORY MUSIC
– music played on saloon pianos HONKY-TONK
– music school CONSERVATOIRE
– music stand used by two players in an orchestra, or this pair of players DESK
– music that is purely formal or intellectual, and does not attempt to represent a story, scene, or idea ABSOLUTE MUSIC
– music using short series of notes repeated many times with small variations MINIMALISM
– musical composition, typically numbered in sequence OPUS

mushroom

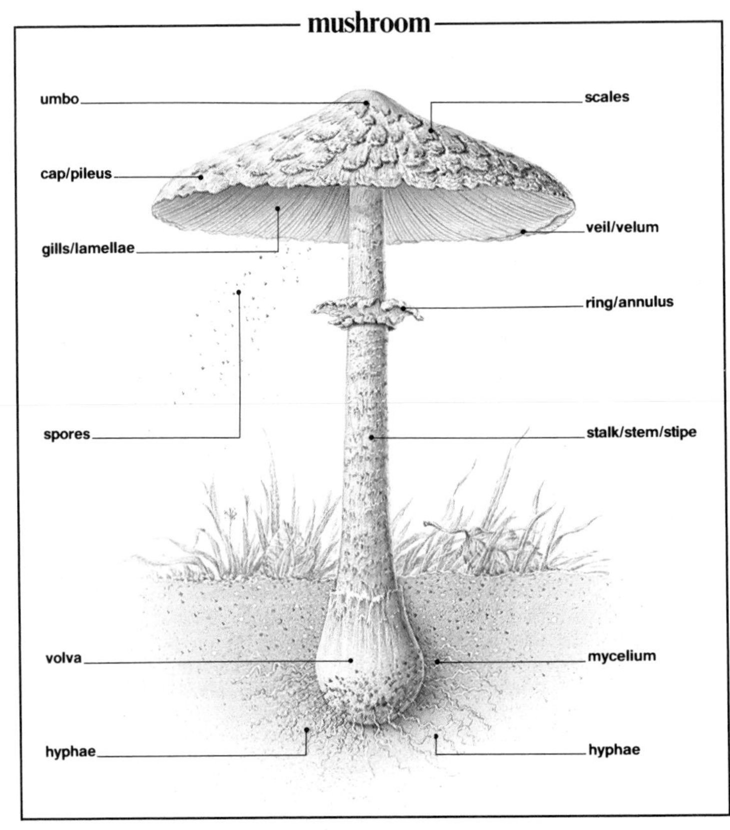

MUSIC

MUSICAL COMPOSITIONS	
arabesque	short, elaborately ornamented piece
aubade	music originally intended for performance in the morning
bagatelle	short, unpretentious composition
barcarole	song with a rhythm resembling that of rowing a gondola
berceuse	cradle song
canon	composition, often choral, where one part is imitated by other parts in the same or a related key
cantata	work for several solo singers and a choir
capriccio	composition that does not follow any strict form
cavatina	short, simple instrumental piece
chaconne, passacaglia	piece incorporating variations on a repeated harmonic pattern
concerto	composition for a solo instrument and an orchestra
concerto grosso	composition for several solo instruments and an orchestra
divertimento	light piece for a chamber orchestra, with several short movements
étude	"study", a piece designed as an exercise to develop or embody a particular point of technique
extravaganza	light orchestral work
fantasia	composition in which form takes second place to the composer's fancy
fugue	composition in which two or more themes are stated separately then developed in counterpoint
humoresque	playful or humorous composition
idyll	calm, pastoral composition
intermezzo	short piece for performance between the acts of an opera or play
nocturne	composition suggestive of the qualities of night
oratorio	composition, usually on a religious theme, for voices and an orchestra
partita	suite consisting of several instrumental pieces
pastorale	orchestral piece suggesting a rural scene
prelude	piece introducing a larger work; showpiece for piano and orchestra
requiem	composition written as a setting of the Mass for the dead
rhapsody	work with no set form, often based on folk tunes
rondo	composition in which a refrain is repeated between separate sections
scherzo	lively piece, often the third movement of a symphony
serenade	music originally intended for performance in the evening
sonata	composition consisting of three or four independent and contrasting movements
symphonic poem, tone poem	orchestral work interpreting a non-musical subject such as a folk tale
toccata	composition, as for the organ, originally a showpiece for the performer
voluntary	piece, sometimes improvised, played by an organist before or during a church service

MUSIC TERMS	
accelerando, stringendo	gradually quickening
acciaccatura	grace note played as quickly as possible before accented main note
accidental	sign indicating a sharp, flat or natural note outside the key signature of a piece
adagio, lento	slowly
ad libitum/ad lib	play as desired
affettuoso	tenderly or passionately
agitato	agitatedly
allargando	becoming slower
allegretto	briskly, but more slowly than allegro
allegro	briskly
amoroso	lovingly
andante	at a moderate tempo
andantino	a little slower or faster than andante
animato	animatedly
appassionato	with passion
appoggiatura	accented grace note taking part of value of main note
arpeggio	notes of a chord played in quick succession

continued

MUSIC *continued*	
cadence	build-up of chords towards a close
cadenza	unaccompanied, sometimes improvised, passage by a soloist in a concerto
cantabile	in a singing manner
capriccioso	in a free and lively manner
chord	group of three or more notes played together
chromatic scale	scale that consists of all 12 semitones in Western music, as distinct from the diatonic scale
coda	short additional passage at the end of a movement or composition
con brio	vigorously
con sordino	with a mute
con spirito	with spirit
continuo, figured bass	bass part with numbered chords
counterpoint	set of two or more melody lines played together and in harmony
crescendo	rising volume and intensity
decrescendo, diminuendo	falling volume and intensity
diatonic scale	scale that consists of varying intervals, as distinct from the chromatic scale of 12 semitones
double stop	two notes played simultaneously on a stringed instrument
forte	loudly
fundamental	lowest note of a chord
glissando	referring to notes blended together in a rising or falling scale
grace note	embellishing note, with no time value
grave	very solemnly
grazioso	gracefully
interval	difference in pitch between two notes
largo	slowly, solemnly
legato	smoothly and evenly
leitmotiv	musical phrase associated with a particular character or situation
ligature	group of notes played as one phrase and indicated by a curved line
maestoso	majestically
major scale	scale with semitones between the third and fourth notes and the seventh and eighth notes
minor scale	scale with semitones between the second and third, fifth and sixth and seventh and eighth notes
natural	note that is neither flat nor sharp
non troppo	"not too much": term moderating an instruction
obbligato	essential, not to be omitted, not optional
octave	eight notes of a diatonic scale
ostinato	repeated phrase
pentatonic scale	five-note scale
piano	softly
pizzicato	referring to the plucking of notes that are normally bowed
presto	fast
recitative	sung narrative in opera or oratorio, in the rhythm of ordinary speech
reprise	repetition of a phrase, or return to an earlier theme
ritardando	gradual slowing of tempo
rubato	to be played with a varying tempo
segue	continue to the next movement without pause
semitone	smallest standard interval in Western music, or a note separated from another by this interval
sforzando	accented strongly
sostenuto	in a sustained or prolonged manner
spiccato	referring to the playing of notes by bouncing the bow
staccato	referring to notes played crisply and sharply
syncopation	accenting of a beat in a bar which would not normally be accented
tempo	speed at which a piece is played
tonic sol-fa, solfeggio, solmisation	musical training through singing the *doh-re-mi* syllables
tutti	all together
vigoroso	vigorously
vivace	briskly

– musical dramatic entertainment in England in the 16th and 17th centuries MASQUE
– musical encore or some similar short, pleasant treat LOLLIPOP, BONNE BOUCHE
– musical fanfare or similar dramatic musical passage FLOURISH
– musical medley, based on popular tunes QUODLIBET
– musical training based on rhythmical free-style dance movements to music EURHYTHMICS
– instrument sounding out the beat, used when practising music METRONOME
– play music, composing as one goes IMPROVISE
– range or stock of pieces of music, available to a performer REPERTOIRE
– short line above or below the staff in a piece of printed music, to indicate the position of a high or low note LEDGER LINE
– study of the physical properties of musical sounds HARMONICS
– style of popular musical entertainment, in which improvised poetry is recited or chanted to a musical accompaniment RAPPING
– text of the songs and dialogue of an opera or musical LIBRETTO

music hall – U.S. term for music hall entertainment VAUDEVILLE

musical instruments See **keyboard**, **percussion**, **string**, **wind**, **electronic**
– musical instrument cranked by hand, such as a barrel organ HURDY-GURDY
– distinctive tone of a musical instrument or singing voice, tone colour TIMBRE
– range of a musical instrument DIAPASON, REGISTER

musician, singer, or any other entertainer performing in public places for money from idlers or passers-by BUSKER
– musician of masterly technical skill or outstanding flair VIRTUOSO
– musician or performing artist, on a specified instrument or in a specified technique EXPONENT
– musician who travelled about in the Middle Ages MINSTREL, TROUBADOUR, JONGLEUR
– musicians playing at public processions or entertainments in former times WAITS
– famous musician MAESTRO
– group of musicians CONSORT
– performance by pop or jazz musicians, as at a club or party GIG

Muslim See **Islam**
– Muslim at the time of the Crusades SARACEN

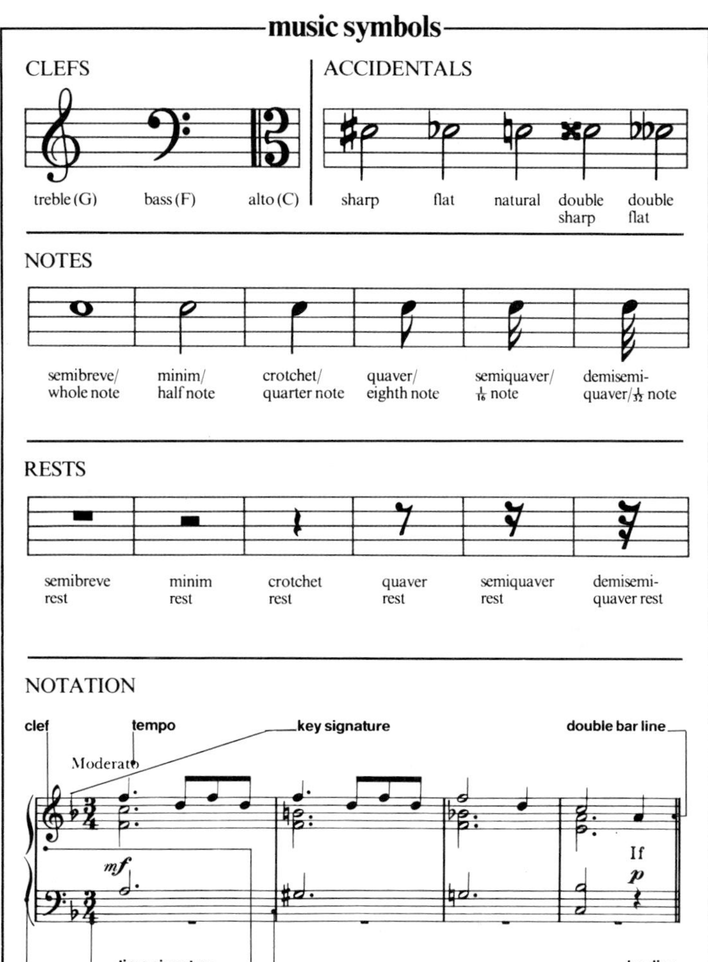

– Muslim or Turkish emblem of power THE CRESCENT
– former term for a Muslim MOHAMMEDAN, MAHOMETAN, MUSSULMAN

Mussolini – Mussolini's title as dictator of Italy IL DUCE

mustard, cress, or related plant having a four-petalled cross-shaped flower CRUCIFER
– mustard, spice, vinegar, or other seasoning CONDIMENT

mustard gas or other blistering agent VESICANT

mutant or genetically deviant organism SPORT

mutation of or abrupt variation within a species SALTATION

mute or damper for a musical instrument SORDINO

mutton See **lamb**

mutual, given or done in return or exchange RECIPROCAL
– mutually destructive or fatal, as civil war is INTERNECINE

mutual- INTER-

my fault MEA CULPA

mysterious, apparently wise but really pompous, as an utterance might be GNOMIC, OBSCURANTIST
– mysterious, awe-inspiring, having a magical aura NUMINOUS
– mysterious, secret, known or understood only by those who have made a special study or been initiated ARCANE, ESOTERIC
– mysterious because uninterpretable, as a facial expression might be INSCRUTABLE, UNFATHOMABLE, DEAD-PAN, ENIGMATIC
– mysterious or puzzling person or thing, riddle ENIGMA

mystical, as rituals might be OCCULT, ESOTERIC, ORPHIC
– mystical or secret philosophy, specifically one based on the Hebrew scriptures CABALA

mythical creatures See **monsters**

N

nag, harass, and dominate one's husband HENPECK
- nag, harass, urge to make haste CHIVVY
- nag, make requests persistently IMPORTUNE, HECTOR
- nagging, insistent IMPORTUNATE

nail, claw, hoof, or similar structure UNGUIS
- nail file in the form of a hard sandpaper-like wooden or cardboard strip EMERY BOARD
- cell tissue from which nails and teeth develop MATRIX
- crescent-shaped mark at the base of a fingernail or toenail LUNULA
- hardened dead skin at the base of a fingernail or toenail CUTICLE
- live sensitive flesh under one's nails QUICK
- painful swelling or abscess around the nail of a finger or toe AGNAIL, WHITLOW
- piece of dead skin around a fingernail HANGNAIL
- secure a nail by bending the projecting pointed end over CLINCH
- short, flat-headed nail, as used for fixing metal sheeting to wood CLOUT
- small, headless wedge-shaped nail or tack used in mending shoes SPARROW-BILL
- thin headless nail SPRIG
- thin or flattish nail with a small or narrow head BRAD

naive, unsophisticated, simple, innocent ARTLESS, GUILELESS, INGENUOUS
- naive and innocent young woman INGÉNUE
- naive and over-optimistic person, especially an innocent young man CANDIDE
- appearing or pretending to be simple and naive FAUX-NAÏF, DISINGENUOUS

naked, nude AU NATUREL, UNCLAD
- naked person running through a public place as a publicity stunt STREAKER

name, give a title, name, or nickname to DESIGNATE, NOMINATE, STYLE, DUB
- name, such as the name of a city or country, derived from a person's name, or the person himself or his name EPONYM
- name adopted as a disguise, especially a false name assumed for a particular purpose or occasion PSEUDONYM, ALIAS, NOM DE GUERRE, INCOGNITO
- name adopted by an author, as to conceal his identity PEN NAME, NOM DE PLUME
- name based on one's mother's name METRONYMIC, MATRONYMIC
- name derived from the first name of one's father or paternal ancestor, typically with an affix such as *-son*, *Mac-*, or *-ovich* PATRONYMIC
- name explicitly, spell out SPECIFY
- name expressing endearment, often a diminutive form HYPOCORISM
- name in common use, rather than the technical Latin name, of a plant or animal, TRIVIAL NAME, VERNACULAR
- name of a category or class RUBRIC
- name of a city or other place used in a foreign language, such as *Florence* for *Firenze* EXONYM
- name of a place or region, or a word derived from it TOPONYM
- name or act of naming DENOMINATION, DESIGNATION
- name or nickname MONIKER
- name or title APPELLATION
- adjective for names ONOMASTIC
- "born", used before the maiden name of a married woman when identifying her NÉE
- having or relating to two names or terms BINOMIAL
- having the same name HOMONYMOUS
- having two parts, as a hyphenated surname such as *Bentley-Smith* has DOUBLE-BARRELLED
- in name only, having the official title but not the real power, as with a figurehead ruler TITULAR, NOMINAL
- legal document involving one person only, especially to change his name DEED POLL
- line under the title of a magazine or newspaper article giving the writer's name BY-LINE
- mark stationery or other goods with the name, initials, or other form of identification of the owner PERSONALISE
- nickname or assumed name SOBRIQUET
- nickname or descriptive term forming part of a person's name or title EPITHET, COGNOMEN
- pass or toss something back and forth, such as a person's name in a gossipy conversation BANDY
- preposition such as *von* or *de* accompanying a title or surname, indicating noble rank NOBILIARY PARTICLE
- publicise a product or service by using one's name to recommend it ENDORSE
- referring to a person of unknown or suppressed name, or to a book, contribution, or the like by such a person ANONYMOUS
- referring to the person, fictional hero, or the like, after whom a city, novel, or the like is named EPONYMOUS
- study and history of names ONOMASTICS
- system of names or terms, for plants or chemicals NOMENCLATURE
- use of a title or epithet, such as *Her Majesty*, in place of a proper name ANTONOMASIA
- wrong or unsuitable name for someone or something MISNOMER

-name- NOMIN-, -ONYM

nameless, unnamed INNOMINATE

namely – "namely", "that is", term introducing examples VIDELICET, VIZ
- "namely", "to wit", "that is to say", used to introduce a synonym, explanation, or missing word SCILICET, SC.

nameplate, memorial tablet, or the like, as mounted on a wall or monument PLAQUE
- nameplate or brand name, as of a car MARQUE
- nameplate or small signboard, as of a doctor or lawyer SHINGLE

nanny, nursemaid, or maidservant in India, East Africa, and elsewhere AYAH
- nanny or wet nurse in the East AMAH

nape of the neck NUCHA

Naples – person born or living in Naples NEAPOLITAN
nappy – U.S. word for a baby's nappy DIAPER
narrow pass or gorge DEFILE
– narrow strip of land joining two larger land areas ISTHMUS
– narrowing towards one end TAPERING
– abnormal narrowing or blocking of a body passage STRICTURE
narrow- STEN-, STENO-
narrow-minded See also **conservative**, **old-fashioned**
– narrow-minded, bigoted, intolerant, prejudiced SECTARIAN, BLINKERED
– narrow-minded, limited in perspective, concerned only with one's immediate surroundings INSULAR, PAROCHIAL, PROVINCIAL, PARISH-PUMP
– narrow-minded, self-satisfied, and arrogant person PRIG
– narrow-minded, set in one's ways, incapable of changing with the times HIDEBOUND
– narrow-minded and bigoted white rural American REDNECK
– narrow-minded and embittered, envious, cynical, prejudiced, and hostile JAUNDICED
– narrow-minded and old-fashioned person, unfamiliar with and uninterested in modern urban life BACKWOODSMAN
– narrow-minded attitudes LAAGER MENTALITY
– narrow-minded person with old-fashioned ideas TROGLODYTE
– narrow-minded propriety and excessive criticism of the unconventional GRUNDYISM
– narrow-mindedly conservative, misinformed, and mindlessly patriotic BLIMPISH
– narrow-mindedness, inability to take a broad view of things TUNNEL VISION
– person typifying narrow-minded prudishness and conservatism MRS GRUNDY
nasal RHINAL
– nasal or constricted in sound ADENOIDAL
– nasal quality of speech, as in certain accents TWANG
-nasal- -RHIN-, -RHINO-
nasturtium or related plant TROPAEOLUM
nasty See **bad**, **spiteful**, **disgusting**
nation that is not allied with a superpower, a neutral nation NON-ALIGNED NATION
– nations recognising and accepting the institutions of one another, or the policy of such acceptance COMITY OF NATIONS
– easing of tension, as between nations DÉTENTE
– newly independent, as a nation might be EMERGENT
national – national anthem of France MARSEILLAISE
– national policy, especially foreign policy, based uncompromisingly on national self-interest rather than on moral considerations REALPOLITIK
nationalism or patriotism of a narrow, militant, fanatical kind CHAUVINISM, JINGOISM
nationality – person having nationality, residence, or citizenship rights in the U.K., especially by virtue of a parent or grandparent born there PATRIAL
native, local, restricted to a particular area or group ENDEMIC
– native language or dialect of a country or region VERNACULAR
– native to or originating in a particular place, ABORIGINAL, INDIGENOUS, AUTOCHTHONOUS
Nativity – tableau, as at Christmas, of Jesus' Nativity CRÈCHE, CRIB
natural, inborn, as some skills or talents are NATIVE, INNATE
– natural, simple, and basic, as one's lifestyle might be ORGANIC
– natural environment or surrounding for an animal or plant HABITAT
– natural in behaviour or origin, unrehearsed, unprompted SPONTANEOUS
– natural in manner, frank and honest ARTLESS, UNSTUDIED, GUILELESS
– natural talent, gift, or characteristic ENDOWMENT
natural gas METHANE
nature or wildlife reserve SANCTUARY
– belief in God as being present throughout Nature, or identical with Nature PANTHEISM
– belief that Nature is directed or determined by an end or purpose TELEOLOGY
– environmental influences on the development of an organism, as distinguished from genetic influences or Nature NURTURE
– imitation or representation of nature or human nature in literature and art MIMESIS
– Nature worship, or belief that natural objects have souls ANIMISM
– protection and preservation of the natural environment CONSERVATION
– relate to closely or communicate intimately with someone or something, such as Nature COMMUNE
– study or theory of the universe or Nature as a whole COSMOGRAPHY
nature- PHYSI-, PHYSIO-
naughty See also **disobedient**
– naughty, cheeky, or mischievous in an engaging way, roguish, scampish ARCH, INCORRIGIBLE, PUCKISH
– naughty, conceited, or cheeky child or young man JACKANAPES
– naughty, racy, verging on the indelicate or improper, as a joke might be RISQUÉ
– naughty behaviour, bad deeds, misconduct MISDEMEANOURS, DELINQUENCY
nautical See **ship**, **sailing**
– nautical mile per hour KNOT
naval See **military**, **services**, **sailing**
– naval mechanic ARTIFICER
– naval or military subdivision ECHELON
– naval petty officer in charge of signalling or clerical duties YEOMAN
– naval petty officer responsible for steering or navigating QUARTERMASTER
– small fleet of ships, or small naval task force FLOTILLA, SQUADRON, ESCADRILLE, DETACHMENT
navel UMBILICUS, OMPHALOS
navigation by means of the stars and planets CELESTIAL NAVIGATION, ASTRONAVIGATION
– navigation by visual observation of beacons and landmarks CONTACT FLYING
– navigation by working out one's position by one's speed and direction rather than by radio or observing the stars DEAD RECKONING
– instrument, used in navigation, for measuring the angles of stars and planets to determine the observer's position SEXTANT, ASTROLABE
navy See **military**, **services**, **sailing**
– recruit forcibly into the navy PRESS, PRESSGANG, CRIMP, IMPRESS, SHANGHAI
Nazi emblem, consisting of a cross with right-angled ends SWASTIKA
– Nazi Germany's annexation of Austria in 1938 ANSCHLUSS
– Nazi storm troopers, the Brown Shirts STURMABTEILUNG
– Hitler's title as Nazi leader of Germany FÜHRER
– marching step, as in Nazi military parades, in which the leg is swung high with the knee locked GOOSE STEP
– person of a northern European gentile racial type, especially Nordic, in Nazi ideology ARYAN

– provincial or district governor in Nazi Germany GAULEITER
– secret police in Nazi Germany GESTAPO
– territory claimed by a nation, as by Nazi Germany, as being necessary for its well-being LEBENSRAUM

NCO – NCO's stripes, worn on the sleeve, indicating rank or length of service CHEVRON

near, touching, bordering, as two plots of land might be ABUTTING, ADJACENT, ADJOINING, CONTIGUOUS
– near, very like, approaching, almost equivalent to VERGING ON
– near enough to be heard WITHIN EARSHOT
– nearby area, local surroundings, neighbourhood VICINITY, ENVIRONS, LOCALITY
– nearness in time or position PROPINQUITY, PROXIMITY
– in the near future, about to happen APPROACHING, IMMINENT, IMPENDING
– place things near to each other or side by side APPOSE
– placed near or next to each other so as to invite comparison JUXTAPOSED

near- EPI-, PARA-, PERI-, -PROS-

nearly, practically, in essence but not in appearance VIRTUALLY
– nearly, roughly, more or less APPROXIMATELY, CIRCA

neat in dress or appearance TRIM, DAPPER, SPRUCE, WELL-GROOMED

necessary, inseparable, forming an essential part of the whole INTEGRAL, INTRINSIC, INHERENT
– necessary, required by law or demanded by custom COMPULSORY, STATUTORY, DE RIGUEUR, MANDATORY
– necessary as a duty, inescapable, binding INCUMBENT, OBLIGATORY, IMPERATIVE, IRREMISSIBLE
– necessary minimum of food, shelter, or the like to sustain life SUBSISTENCE
– necessary thing or condition, factor without which something cannot occur SINE QUA NON, PREREQUISITE
– absolutely necessary, vital, essential, impossible to leave out INDISPENSABLE
– be proper or necessary for BEHOVE
– existing or true or false by reason of chance or fact in the real world rather than by logical necessity CONTINGENT
– involve, have as a necessary consequence ENTAIL

neck See illustration at **mouth, nose, and throat**
– neck or neck-shaped structure in the body, especially the lower part of the uterus CERVIX
– neck or spine injury caused by sudden jerking of the head, as in a car accident WHIPLASH
– adjective for the throat or neck JUGULAR
– back of the neck SCRUFF, NAPE, NUCHA
– bent abnormally, as the neck might be WRY
– chronic enlargement of the thyroid gland, causing a severely swollen neck, often due to iodine deficiency GOITRE, STRUMA
– fold of skin hanging from the neck, as of some birds and lizards WATTLE
– frill or ruff of lace or linen formerly worn by women round the neck or shoulders TUCKER
– loose fold of skin at the neck, as in cattle or old people DEWLAP
– natural collar or ring of hair or feathers round the neck of a mammal or bird RUFF, RUFFLE
– relating to the neck or cervix CERVICAL
– wrench, sprain, or strain one's neck, ankle, or the like RICK

neckerchief, usually of brightly coloured cotton BANDANNA

necklace or collar, typically of twisted metal, worn in ancient times TORQUE
– necklace or jewelled collar in former times CARCANET
– necklace with a medallion, piece of jewellery, or the like hanging freely on it PENDANT
– tight-fitting necklace or band worn round the neck CHOKER

neckline that is low and revealing, or a dress or blouse with such a neckline DÉCOLLETAGE

nectar – food of the gods in classical mythology, corresponding to their drink of nectar AMBROSIA

need – needed thing or necessary quality REQUISITE
– needs that are urgent or pressing EXIGENCIES
– in great danger, distress, or need IN EXTREMITY
– something wished for, needed, or desired DESIDERATUM

needle for pulling ribbon or cord through loops or a hem BODKIN
– needle or jewel in a gramophone pickup for tracing the groove of a record STYLUS
– needle or syringe for injections beneath the skin HYPODERMIC
– needle-shaped, pointed ACERATE, ACEROSE, ACULEATE
– needle-shaped natural object or part, such as a crystal, quill, or bristle ACICULA, ACULEUS
– needle-shaped rock mass or mountain peak AIGUILLE
– moving arm that holds the needle of a record-player TONE ARM
– small case for needles, cosmetics, or the like ÉTUI

needlework See **embroidery**, **sewing**
– needlework frame in the form of two concentric wooden hoops between which the fabric is locked TAMBOUR
– decorative piece of needlework, often with pictures and mottoes SAMPLER
– make a piece of needlework or decorate a fabric using a technique of looping thread with a hooked needle CROCHET
– thread or loop joining sections of a lace or needlework pattern BRIDE, BAR

negligée, light and loose-fitting dressing gown for a woman PEIGNOIR

negotiate, discuss, or debate PARLEY
– negotiate or perform business TRANSACT

negotiation involving hard bargaining and shrewd compromises HORSE-TRADING
– negotiations between explorers and local African chiefs in former times PALAVER
– final terms offered in negotiating, to be accepted "or else" ULTIMATUM

neigh gently or quietly WHINNY, NICKER

neighbourhood, nearby or surrounding area VICINITY, LOCALITY
– neighbourhood with defined boundaries PRECINCTS, ENVIRONS

neon, helium, or other gaseous element formerly considered incapable of chemical reaction INERT GAS, NOBLE GAS, RARE GAS

Neptune – Neptune's three-pronged spear TRIDENT

nerve See illustrations, pages 343, 344
– nerve cell NEURONE
– nerve ending that receives outside stimuli and converts them into nerve impulses RECEPTOR
– nerve ending that stimulates a muscle to contract or a gland to secrete EFFECTOR
– nerve that produces very fine sensitivity to temperature or pressure EPICRITIC NERVE
– nerve that produces only coarse sensitivity to pain or heat PROTOPATHIC NERVE
– bundle or cluster of fibres, espe-

nerve cell

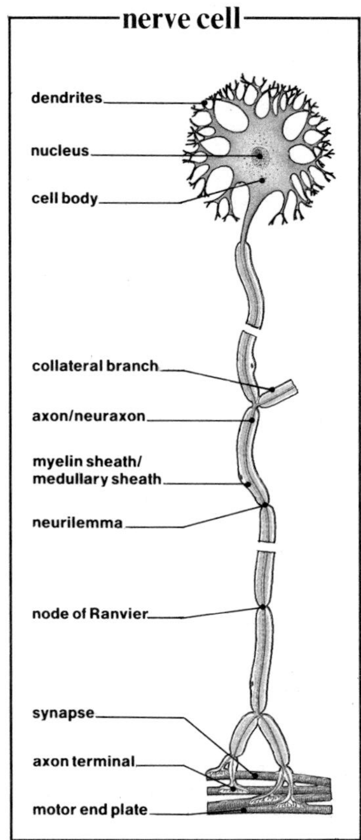

cially nerve fibres FASCICLE, FASCICULUS, FUNICULUS
– either of the fifth pair of cranial nerves TRIGEMINAL NERVE
– either of the tenth pair of cranial nerves VAGUS NERVE
– group of nerve-cell bodies usually outside the brain and spinal cord GANGLION
– network of nerves and blood vessels PLEXUS
– referring to nerves directing impulses inwards towards the brain or spinal cord AFFERENT
– referring to nerves directing impulses outwards from the brain or spinal cord EFFERENT, DEFERENT
– relating to the nerves or nervous system NEURAL
– stalk-like structure, as of nerve fibres PEDUNCLE

nerve- NEUR-, NEURO-

nervous, anxious, tense, in suspense ON TENTERHOOKS
– nervous, or difficult to control SKITTISH
– nervous, on edge, agitated JITTERY, HIGHLY STRUNG, FRETFUL
– nervous, very tense or strained, agitated or perturbed FRAUGHT, OVERWROUGHT
– nervous breakdown or nervous exhaustion NEURASTHENIA
– nervous disorder causing uncontrollable, irregular movements of the limbs and face CHOREA
– nervous or emotional disorder, revealed in phobias, obsessions, or the like, that induces anxiety and is mildly disabling NEUROSIS
– nervous twitch or spasm, especially in the face TIC

nervous system See illustration, page 344
– nervous system consisting of the brain and spinal cord CENTRAL NERVOUS SYSTEM
– nervous system excluding the brain and spinal cord PERIPHERAL NERVOUS SYSTEM
– division of the nervous system that regulates involuntary processes AUTONOMIC NERVOUS SYSTEM
– sub-division of the nervous system that serves to slow down the heartbeat, dilate the blood vessels, and stimulate secretions PARASYMPATHETIC NERVOUS SYSTEM
– sub-division of the nervous system that serves to speed up the heartbeat, contract the blood vessels, and slow down secretions SYMPATHETIC NERVOUS SYSTEM

nervousness, anxiety, uneasiness HEEBIE-JEEBIES, JITTERS
– nervousness, or a stomach upset resulting from it COLLYWOBBLES
– substance that supposedly produces a surge of excitement, nervousness, or power ADRENALINE

-ness -TUDE

nest, especially for insect or spider eggs NIDUS
– nest-building NIDIFICATION
– nest of a bird of prey, built on a cliff or other high place EYRIE
– referring to birds born blind and helpless, and requiring lengthy care in the nest NIDICOLOUS
– referring to birds born fairly well-developed, and able to leave the nest fairly soon NIDIFUGOUS

net in which caught fish are kept alive in the water KEEPNET
– net-like in structure, as with some bones and the vein patterns of some leaves CANCELLATE
– net-like, resembling a network or web RETICULAR, RETICULATE, RETIFORM
– net of three layers for catching birds or fish TRAMMEL
– net or network MESH
– catch or tangle in or as if in a net ENMESH
– large, sheet-like fishing net hanging upright in the water SEINE
– small cap or pouch, typically of netting, holding a woman's hair in place at the back SNOOD
– Roman gladiator armed with a net and trident RETIARIUS
– small space, opening, or gap, as between the strands of a net INTERSTICE

nettles – former medical treatment involving lashing with nettles URTICATION

network, context, or environment in which something develops MATRIX
– network, interwoven complex of parts PLEXUS, NEXUS
– network of lines or fine wires, as on a lens, for measuring or locating objects under observation RETICLE, RETICULE, GRATICULE
– network of lines used as a reference grid in photography and measuring stars RÉSEAU

neurotic psychological attachment to a person or thing, dating back to early development FIXATION

neutral, specifically not allied with a superpower NON-ALIGNED
– neutral mediator in a dispute GO-BETWEEN, ARBITRATOR, INTERMEDIARY, HONEST BROKER
– adoption of a policy of international neutrality together with co-operation, especially towards the USSR FINLANDISATION
– right of a nation at war to use or destroy the property of a neutral nation on condition that full compensation is paid ANGARY

new See also **modern**
– new, up-to-date NEOTERIC
– new wine MUST
– newly coined word or expression NEOLOGISM
– newness or something new INNOVATION
– fresh, clean, pure, or perfectly restored, as if brand new PRISTINE

new- ANA-, NEO-

New Orleans – carnival in New Orleans celebrating the last day before Lent MARDI GRAS

New Testament event or person supposedly foreshadowed or symbolised by a counterpart in the Old Testament ANTITYPE

New York stock-exchange price index DOW JONES AVERAGE
– New York's banking and financial world, including the Stock Exchange WALL STREET

New Zealand See also **Maori**
– New Zealander of European rather than Maori descent PAKEHA
– coniferous New Zealand tree, cultivated for its wood and resin KAURI
– edible New Zealand shellfish, with a shiny greenish shell like mother-of-pearl, used for orna-

nervous system

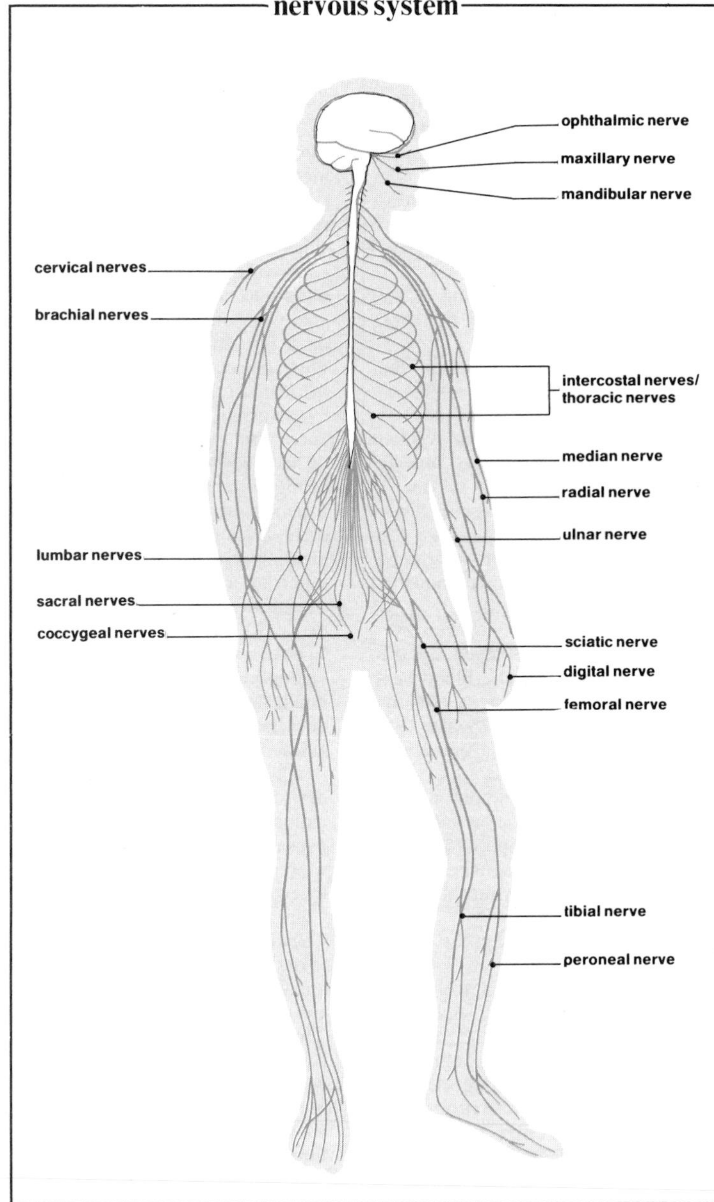

ments and jewellery PAUA
– extinct large flightless New Zealand bird MOA
– Maori name for New Zealand AOTEAROA
– rare flightless New Zealand bird NOTORNIS
– small New Zealand tree, valued for its timber NGAIO

newborn child NEONATE

Newcastle – person born or living in or near Newcastle NOVOCASTRIAN, GEORDIE

newcomer, inexperienced person, as in the armed forces ROOKIE
– newcomer, novice, beginner NEOPHYTE, TYRO
– newcomer who is typically fumbling and inexperienced TENDERFOOT, GREENHORN, FLEDGLING
– newcomer to wealth or social status, johnny-come-lately UPSTART, PARVENU, NOUVEAU RICHE

news, information INTELLIGENCE, TIDINGS
– news item or story reported by only one journalist, newspaper, or the like, unique scoop EXCLUSIVE
– news report or rumour that is false or a deliberate hoax CANARD
– news reporter, typically covering the local news in a specific area, working on a part-time basis STRINGER
– newsworthy and of current interest TOPICAL
– spread gradually, as warmth or news might PERMEATE, DIFFUSE, PERCOLATE
– spread something widely, such as news or knowledge DISSEMINATE, DISPERSE, PROMULGATE

newspaper archives MORGUE
– newspaper of large format, with large wide pages BROADSHEET
– newspaper headline running right across a page BANNER, BANNER HEADLINE, STREAMER
– newspaper of small format, typically having a high proportion of photographs and sensational news reports TABLOID
– newspaper or magazine published in the past, and no longer the current issue BACK NUMBER
– newspaper workers' association or trade-union branch CHAPEL
– newspapers of a cheap and sensationalising kind YELLOW PRESS, GUTTER PRESS
– agency selling cartoons, articles, and the like for simultaneous publication in numerous newspapers or magazines SYNDICATE
– column or space in a newspaper for last-minute reports FUDGE, STOP PRESS
– continuous roll of paper, especially newsprint, for use in a rotary printing press WEB
– number of copies distributed or sold of a newspaper or magazine CIRCULATION
– panel at the top of the front page of a newspaper or magazine, bearing its name, logo, and so on MASTHEAD, FLAG
– reject an article or report, as the editor of a newspaper or magazine might SPIKE
– report sent over a distance, as by a newspaper correspondent or military field officer DISPATCH
– small display box, typically for advertisements, in an upper corner of the front page of a newspaper EAR
– small stall, as for selling newspapers KIOSK

next to, alongside, side by side ADJACENT, ADJOINING, CONTIGUOUS, JUXTAPOSED, TANGENTIAL, ABUTTING

next to- EPI-

ng – symbol ŋ used in phonetics to represent the *ng*-sound, as in *long* ENG, AGMA

nice See **friendly**, **good**, **fussy**
– nice or quaint in an affected or pretentious way TWEE
nickname AGNOMEN
– nickname or assumed name SOBRIQUET
– nickname or descriptive term forming part of a person's name or title EPITHET, COGNOMEN
– nickname or personal name MONIKER
– give a title, name, or nickname to DESIGNATE, NOMINATE, STYLE, DUB
Nietzschean superman ÜBERMENSCH
night – "night blindness", weak vision in dim light NYCTALOPIA
– either of the two times during the year when day and night are of equal length all over the Earth EQUINOX
– official regulation requiring citizens to go home or be indoors by a certain hour of night CURFEW
– painting of a night scene or short lyrical composition, especially for the piano, suggestive of or suitable for the night NOCTURNE
– relating to, occurring in, or active during the night NOCTURNAL
night- NOCT-, NOCTI-, NYCT-, NYCTI-, NYCTO-
nightclub – female singer, as in a nightclub or cabaret CHANTEUSE
nightdress – light, loose-fitting gown, resembling a nightdress, for a woman NEGLIGÉE, PEIGNOIR
– nightdress, underwear, and so on for women LINGERIE
nightingale or similar songbird, mentioned in Persian poetry BULBUL
– poetic name for the nightingale PHILOMEL
nightmare or obsessive worry INCUBUS
– nightmarish, disturbingly weird, surreal KAFKAESQUE
Nile houseboat DAHABEAH
– irrigation device, as along the Nile, consisting of a bucket on a pivoted pole SHADOUF
nimble, agile DEXTROUS, LITHE
– nimble, unpredictable, or changing constantly QUICKSILVER, MERCURIAL
nine- NONA-
nine-day devotion undertaken by Roman Catholics NOVENA
ninety-degree- QUADR-, QUADRI-, QUADRU-
ninety-year-old, or a person aged between 90 and 99 NONAGENARIAN
ninth- NONA-
nipple or nipple-shaped projection MAMILLA
– nipple or teat PAP
– darkish area, on a breast, surrounding the nipple AREOLA
– small round patch covering the nipple on a striptease artist's breast PASTY
nitpicking, hairsplitting, needless arguing or drawing of distinctions QUIBBLING, SOPHISTRY, PEDANTRY, SCHOLASTICISM, CASUISTRY
– nitpickingly critical, fault-finding CARPING, CAPTIOUS, CAVILLING
nitrogen – conversion of nitrogen in the air into a fertiliser or other compound FIXATION
– relating to or containing nitrogen AZOTIC
Noah – relating to Noah or his time, as the seven pre-Mosaic commandments do NOACHIAN
Nobel prize winner, poet, or other eminent person in the arts or sciences who receives a special honour LAUREATE
nobility See chart, and also **rulers**
noble, held in great honour and esteem VENERATED
– noble, majestic, of great spiritual, intellectual, or moral worth SUBLIME
– noble action or gesture, sometimes empty in effect BEAU GESTE
– noble in character, as an ideal or ambition might be EXALTED, ELEVATED, LOFTY
– noble in quality, unstinted, worthy, as someone's assistance or efforts might be STERLING
– noble in spirit, generous and forgiving MAGNANIMOUS
– noble-looking or high-ranking person MAGNIFICO, GRANDEE
– noble or dignified in appearance DISTINGUÉ, MAJESTIC, STATELY
– noble or gallant man GALAHAD
nobleman See chart, and also **rulers**
– nobleman, or person from an old and distinguished family PATRICIAN
– office, status, or dignity of a judge, king, or nobleman ERMINE
– person who is not a nobleman or noblewoman, ordinary person COMMONER
noise See also **sound**
– noise across a wide range of frequencies, able to block out other sounds WHITE NOISE

NOBILITY

aetheling/ atheling	Anglo-Saxon nobleman or prince
banneret	knight who led men into battle
boyar/boyard	Russian aristocrat
burgrave	hereditary lord of medieval Germany
chevalier	knight of a French order
daimio	noble of feudal Japan
dauphin	eldest son of the French king
ealdorman/ alderman	Anglo-Saxon noble, or chief officer of a shire
elector	German prince who took part in the election of the Holy Roman Emperor
eupatrid	noble of ancient Athens
gaekwar	prince of former Indian state of Baroda
graf	German, Austrian, or Swedish count
gräfin	German, Austrian, or Swedish countess
grandee	Spanish or Portuguese nobleman
hidalgo	Spanish nobleman of minor rank
landgrave	medieval German count
margrave	lord of a German border province in former times
margravine	wife of a margrave
marquis/ marquess	nobleman ranking above an earl but below a duke
marquise/ marchioness	wife of a marquis

– noise of boiling or choppy water POPPLE
– continual, confused noise or racket, such as a babble of voices or series of cries CLAMOUR, HUBBUB
– gradual decrease in the volume of a noise or passage of music DECRESCENDO, DIMINUENDO
– gradual increase in the volume of a noise or passage of music CRESCENDO
– harsh creaking or wheezing noise caused by diseased lungs CREPITATION
– harsh whistling or wheezing noise, as caused by congested breathing passages STRIDOR, RHONCHUS
– hold back, cut off, or muffle a scream, noise, or the like STIFLE
– jarring, ugly, unharmonious noise CACOPHONY, DISCORDANCE, DISCORD, DISSONANCE
– light, tinkling noise, as of keys or small bells JANGLE, TINTINNABULATION
– loud, repeated, clanging noise CLANGOUR
– loud, resounding, echoing noise REVERBERATION
– make a great noise, cause trouble or an uproar RAISE CAIN
– murmuring noise, rustling, as of light wind through trees SOUGH, SUSURRATION
– murmuring noise of rippling water PURL
– resounding harmoniously and richly as a noise might RESONANT, SONOROUS
– rustling noise, as of silk FROU-FROU
– shrill and clear, as a noise or call might be CLARION
– shrill, chirping noise, especially that of crickets STRIDULATION
– slapping noise SKELP
– wailing or lamenting noise KEENING, ULULATION

noisy and disorderly crowd TUMULT
– noisy and harsh-sounding, grating or blaring JARRING, RAUCOUS, DISCORDANT
– noisy and insistent, as in protest VOCIFEROUS, STRIDENT, CLAMOROUS, BLUSTERING
– noisy and lively in an excited or unruly way RUMBUSTIOUS, BOISTEROUS
– noisy and very enthusiastic, as applause might be TUMULTUOUS
– noisy confusion or upheaval, rowdy stir COMMOTION, FURORE, HULLABALOO, BROUHAHA, KERFUFFLE, SCHEMOZZLE, BALLYHOO
– noisy disturbance, uproar, din RUCKUS, RUCTION, RUMPUS
– noisy merrymaking or celebration ROISTERING, REVELRY
– noisy mock serenade to a newly-wed couple CHARIVARI
– noisy or showy display, designed to impress or advertise RAZZLE-DAZZLE, RAZZMATAZZ
– noisy place, scene of uproar and disorder BEAR GARDEN, BEDLAM, BABEL
– referring to a very loud or very noisy voice STENTORIAN
– scene of noisy or riotous confusion, utter chaos BEDLAM, PANDEMONIUM, MAYHEM, HAVOC
– screech noisily, especially in argument CATERWAUL

nominal but not real, as a figurehead ruler might be TITULAR

non-believer HEATHEN, PAGAN, INFIDEL, ATHEIST, AGNOSTIC

non-committal, timid, or cautious behaviour PUSSYFOOTING

non-drinker, person who avoids alcohol TEETOTALLER, ABSTAINER, RECHABITE
– non-drinking, abstaining from alcohol TEMPERATE, ABSTINENT

non-existence, nothingness NIHILITY, NONENTITY

non-human, without human understanding, as a block of wood is INSENSATE, INSENSIBLE

non-interference by governments in commercial activity, free trade LAISSEZ-FAIRE

non-military CIVILIAN

non-professional people, those outside a particular profession LAYMEN, LAY PEOPLE

non-religious in form or content PROFANE, SECULAR

non-stick – trademark for a non-stick plastic coating material, as used to line frying pans TEFLON

non-violent opposition, as by fasting and non-cooperation, to a law, policy, colonial authority, or the like PASSIVE RESISTANCE
– non-violent resistance and a refusal to obey laws regarded as unjust, undertaken as a form of political protest CIVIL DISOBEDIENCE
– non-violent resistance, as initiated by Gandhi in India, to press for political reform SATYAGRAHA
– code of non-violence based on reverence for all living things, as practised in Buddhism and Hinduism AHIMSA

Nonconformist chapel, or a chapel for seamen BETHEL

nonsense, foolish speech or writing, rubbish, moonshine, tripe BALDERDASH, CODSWALLOP, DRIVEL, TWADDLE, GUFF, HOGWASH, POPPYCOCK, TOMMYROT
– nonsense, stupid or untruthful speech or writing, bosh BALONEY, BILGE, BUNKUM, FANDANGLE, FLAPDOODLE, GAMMON
– nonsense verse, or a nonsense poem or story AMPHIGORY
– confused or nonsensical speech GIBBERISH, GALIMATIAS, JABBERWOCKY
– high-sounding but obscure official language, bureaucratic nonsense or empty jargon GOBBLEDEGOOK, HOCUS-POCUS, MUMBO-JUMBO
– insincere, foolish, or empty and long-winded talk, nonsense, waffle CLAPTRAP, HOKUM, BLATHERSKITE, DOGGEREL, FLUMMERY, FLIMFLAM, HUMBUG, MALARKEY, TARADIDDLE, RIGMAROLE
– trifling, time-wasting talk or activity, nonsense FIDDLE-FADDLE, FOOTLE, FOLDEROL, TRUMPERY

noodles See **pasta**

noon – in the morning, before noon ANTEMERIDIAN
– in the afternoon POSTMERIDIAN

norm or commonest item in a numerical list MODE
– differ or depart from the norm or standard, as of a policy, a route, or one's behaviour DEVIATE

normal See also **regular**, **mediocre**
– normal, standard, traditional CONVENTIONAL, ORTHODOX
– normal, usual, in keeping with custom or current fashion ESTABLISHED, PREVAILING, WONTED
– normal practice or accepted custom, especially when having legal force CONSUETUDE
– abiding strictly by what is normal or accepted CONFORMIST, ACCORDING TO HOYLE

normal- ORTHO-

Norse bard or minstrel in ancient times SKALD

north – "northern lights", seen flashing in the night sky, especially near the North Pole AURORA BOREALIS
– Northerner who went to the South to profiteer after the U.S. Civil War CARPETBAGGER
– northernmost inhabited land, according to ancient geographers THULE, ULTIMA THULE
– adjective for the north, especially relating to the north wind BOREAL
– of or in the far north, arctic HYPERBOREAN
– region of northwest Africa, between the Sahara Desert and the

Mediterranean MAGHREB
Norwegian herring, typically canned like sardines SILD
– Norwegian sea inlet that is long, deep, and narrow FJORD
nose See illustration at **mouth, nose, and throat**
– nose that is short and slightly turned-up or flattened at the tip SNUB NOSE, PUG NOSE
– nose that turns up slightly at the tip RETROUSSÉ NOSE
– nose with a high, conspicuous, slightly convex bridge ROMAN NOSE
– adjective for the nose NASAL, RHINAL
– blockage of the nose through accumulation of mucus CONGESTION
– bulging and swollen-looking, as a large nose might be BULBOUS
– curved or hooked, resembling an eagle's beak, as a nose might be AQUILINE
– derisive gesture made by thumbing the nose SNOOK
– growth on or under a mucous membrane, as in the nose POLYP
– humorous or slang term for a person's nose, especially a prominent nose PROBOSCIS, SCHNOZZLE
– long, straight nose extending as if in continuation of the line of the forehead GRECIAN NOSE
– relieving congestion, especially in the nose DECONGESTANT
-nose- -RHIN-, -RHINO-, NAS-, NASO-
nostrils NARES
– air-filled cavity in the skull, leading to a nostril SINUS
– membrane, partition, or division separating tissues or cavities, as between the nostrils SEPTUM
nosy, prying, curious INQUISITIVE
not, *non-*, or similar word or word-element indicating the absence or opposite of something positive or real NEGATIVE
not- A-, AN-, DIS-, MAL-, UN-
not-guilty verdict ACQUITTAL
notch See also **groove**
– notch or groove, as in a piece of wood CHAMFER, CHASE
– notch or groove, especially around a bullet CANNELURE
– notch or groove made in wood by chopping or sawing KERF
– notch or groove, or a series of them INDENTATION
– notch or groove that houses an inserted part in a joint or hinge MORTISE, GAIN, RABBET
– notch or ridge linking two planks, shafts, or the like SPLINE
– notched or indented like a castle's battlements, as a cliff top might be CASTELLATED
– notched stick formerly used for keeping accounts or records TALLY
– notches or ridges around the edge of a coin MILLING, FLUTING
– notches or teeth in a series, as on a saw or the edge of a leaf SERRATION
– square notches or indentations, as on a moulding CRENELLATIONS
– strip or wedge of wood fitting into a notch or groove to make a joint FEATHER, TENON
note, as to a colleague in an organisation MEMORANDUM, MINUTE
– note of critical commentary or explanation on a literary text ANNOTATION, GLOSS
– notes or comments written in the margin of a book MARGINALIA
– note or list in detail PARTICULARISE, ENUMERATE, SPECIFY
– note or reference in a text, placed at the end of the text or at the foot of the page FOOTNOTE
– note serving as a reminder MEMORANDUM
notebook containing quotations, comments, poems, and the like that strike one as worth recording COMMONPLACE BOOK
nothing, zero ZILCH
– nothingness, non-existence NIHILITY
– person or thing worth nothing NONENTITY, CIPHER
notice, acknowledge, take official note of TAKE COGNISANCE OF
noticeable, observable, apparent DISCERNIBLE, EVIDENT, MANIFEST, EXPLICIT
– noticeable, possible to feel or distinguish as a difference might be APPRECIABLE, PALPABLE
– noticeable, striking, very marked PROMINENT, CONSPICUOUS, PRONOUNCED
– very noticeable, unmistakable, as an error might be GLARING, PATENT
noughts and crosses – U.S. term for the game of noughts and crosses TICK-TACK-TOE
noun, pronoun, or word or phrase functioning as a noun SUBSTANTIVE
– noun, such as *hatred*, referring to an idea or quality rather than to a material object ABSTRACT NOUN
– noun, such as *pencil*, referring to a material object rather than to an idea or quality CONCRETE NOUN
– noun, such as *pebble* and unlike *soil*, that can easily be used in the plural COUNTABLE NOUN
– noun, such as *table*, that can refer to any member of a class rather than to a particular or unique person or thing COMMON NOUN
– noun, such as *William*, that refers to a particular or unique person or thing PROPER NOUN, PROPER NAME
– change of the form of a noun, pronoun, or adjective to indicate gender, number, or case DECLENSION
– case of a noun expressing direction from or cause, as in Latin ABLATIVE
– case of a noun expressing possession, measurement, or source, as in Latin GENITIVE
– case of a noun that is the direct object of a verb or preposition ACCUSATIVE
– case of a noun that is the indirect object of a verb, as in Latin DATIVE
– case of a noun that is the subject of a verb, as in Latin NOMINATIVE
– case of a noun used in addressing a person or thing, as in Latin VOCATIVE
– referring to a noun, such as *baby* or *doctor* that can apply to either a male or a female person or animal EPICENE
– relating to a noun NOMINAL
– relationship of two nouns or noun phrases set side by side, the one explaining or identifying the other, as in *Socrates, the philosopher, said so* APPOSITION
– use of a name or proper noun, such as *an Einstein*, in place of an idea or common noun ANTONOMASIA
– verb form, ending in *-ing* in English, that can be used as a noun GERUND
nourishing or supporting ALIMENTARY
– nourishing substance, as in food or in the solution absorbed by plant roots NUTRIENT
– process of nourishing or being nourished NUTRITION
– nourishment, food, something that sustains life or promotes growth NURTURE, NUTRIMENT, SUSTENANCE
novel, film, or the like that continues the story and character development of the previous one SEQUEL
– novel, film, or the like that deals with earlier events than those related in the previous one PREQUEL
– novel dealing with the early development and education of a central character BILDUNGSROMAN
– novel depicting real people under fictional names ROMAN À CLEF
– novel in the form of a series of

letters EPISTOLARY NOVEL
– novel of a loose, episodic structure dealing with the travels or adventures of a rogue-hero PICARESQUE NOVEL
– novel or series of novels relating the history of a person, family, or community ROMAN-FLEUVE, SAGA NOVEL
– additional section at the end of a novel, piece of music, or the like CODA
– afterword or postscript, such as an additional chapter at the end of a novel outlining the future of the characters EPILOGUE
– introductory chapter at the beginning of a novel PROLOGUE
– passage of conversation in a play, novel, or the like, or the words spoken DIALOGUE
– scene or passage in a novel, film, or the like that interrupts the main story line to revert to past events FLASHBACK

novice, beginner NEOPHYTE, TYRO
– novice, fumbling or inexperienced newcomer GREENHORN, TENDERFOOT, FLEDGLING
– novice, especially in the armed forces ROOKIE

nuclear arms supply greater than required for victory OVERKILL
– nuclear bomb's explosive power equivalent to one million tons of TNT MEGATON
– nuclear reaction in which heavy atomic nuclei are split FISSION
– nuclear reaction in which light atomic nuclei combine to form a heavy nucleus FUSION
– nuclear reactor PILE
– nuclear reactor for changing one type of fuel to another CONVERTER REACTOR
– nuclear reactor producing more radioactive nuclear fuel than it consumes BREEDER REACTOR
– nuclear weapons or other arms or defence policy designed to discourage enemy attack DETERRENT
– energy released in a nuclear explosion, expressed in terms of weight of TNT YIELD
– great destruction, as might be caused by nuclear war HOLOCAUST
– heavy water, graphite, or the like in a nuclear reactor's core, used to slow down neutrons and promote fission MODERATOR
– overheating and melting of a nuclear reactor's core MELTDOWN
– person reverting to primitive living in open country to escape the effects of an expected nuclear war SURVIVALIST
– point on the ground at, above, or under the centre of a nuclear explosion GROUND ZERO
– radioactive chemical elements used as nuclear fuels and in nuclear weapons URANIUM, PLUTONIUM
– referring to non-nuclear warfare or weapons CONVENTIONAL
– round cloud of hot gas and dust generated by a nuclear explosion FIREBALL
– treaty restricting the production or deployment of nuclear weapons NON-PROLIFERATION TREATY

-nuclear accelerator -TRON

nucleus- KARY-, KARYO-

nudism NATURISM

nuisance or very burdensome task IMPOSITION

numb- NARCO-

number See chart, and also **mathematics**
– number, numeral CIPHER
– number, such as *third* or *tenth*, indicating position in a sequence ORDINAL NUMBER
– number, such as *three* or *ten*, indicating quantity rather than the position in a sequence CARDINAL NUMBER
– number assigned to a library book to classify and locate it CALL NUMBER
– number needed to make up a whole COMPLEMENT
– number or letter printed at the foot of some pages in a book, specifying the sequence for binding the sections SIGNATURE
– number or letter written or printed slightly above another, as in ab^2 SUPERSCRIPT, SUPERIOR
– number or letter written or printed slightly below another, as in H_2O SUBSCRIPT
– number or quantity by which another is divided DIVISOR
– number or quantity into which another is divided DIVIDEND
– number or quantity from which another is subtracted MINUEND
– number or quantity that is added to others in a sum ADDEND
– number or quantity that divides exactly into another FACTOR
– number or quantity that is subtracted from another in a sum SUBTRAHEND
– number that occurs most often in a numerical list MODE

NUMBERS

LARGE NUMBERS

British usage; American usage differs

million	one thousand thousand, 1 followed by 6 zeros
milliard	one thousand million, 1 followed by 9 zeros
billion	one million million, 1 followed by 12 zeros; or, increasingly in Britain, one thousand million, 1 followed by 9 zeros
trillion	1 followed by 18 zeros
quadrillion	1 followed by 24 zeros
quintillion	1 followed by 30 zeros
sextillion	1 followed by 36 zeros
septillion	1 followed by 42 zeros
octillion	1 followed by 48 zeros
nonillion	1 followed by 54 zeros
decillion	1 followed by 60 zeros
googol	1 followed by 100 zeros
centillion	1 followed by 600 zeros

PREFIXES FOR METRIC UNITS

exa-	one trillion
peta-	one thousand million million
tera-	one million million
giga-	one thousand million
mega-	one million
kilo-	one thousand
hecto-	one hundred
deca-	ten
deci-	one tenth
centi-	one hundredth
milli-	one thousandth
micro-	one millionth
nano-	one thousand millionth
pico-	one million millionth
femto-	one thousand million millionth
atto-	one trillionth

– number system using base 10, the Arabic or decimal system ALGORISM
– number system using only the digits 0 and 1 BINARY SYSTEM, BINARY NOTATION
– adjective for a number or numbers NUMERICAL
– act or system of numbering or counting NUMERATION, RECKONING, TALLYING
– amount obtained by adding numbers together SUM, SUM TOTAL
– any written number between 0 and 9 DIGIT, FIGURE
– based on the number ten, as a fraction, number system, or currency might be DECIMAL
– limited or specified quantity or number, as of imports, members of a group, or the like QUOTA
– real number in the form of a whole number or fraction RATIONAL NUMBER
– relating or referring to a number that divides exactly into a larger number ALIQUOT
– relationship between two numbers or quantities RATIO, PROPORTION
– square layout of numbers in which any row produces the same sum MAGIC SQUARE
– study of the mystical influence or significance of numbers NUMEROLOGY
– triangular arrangement of numbers with each being the sum of the two numbers just above PASCAL'S TRIANGLE
– very large but indefinite number MYRIAD, MULTITUDE
– whole number or zero INTEGER

number plates specially designed by the vehicle's owner, often including his initials CHERISHED NUMBER PLATES, VANITY PLATES

numerous See **lots**, **many**, **plenty**, **excessive**

nun of a Roman Catholic teaching order URSULINE
– nun of an austere order, the counterpart of the White Friars CARMELITE
– nun of high rank ABBESS, PRIORESS
– nun or monk VOTARY
– nun or monk holding an office just subordinate to the superior OBEDIENTIARY
– become a nun TAKE THE VEIL
– candidate monk or nun POSTULANT, NOVICE, NEOPHYTE
– dress worn by a nun HABIT
– head-cloth framing the face, as worn by some nuns WIMPLE
– large white headdress worn by some nuns CORNET
– lay nun or sister in a Roman Catholic organisation, especially in Belgium and Holland BEGUINE
– starched cloth, part of a nun's habit, covering the neck and shoulders GUIMPE
– sum of money paid by a woman when joining certain orders of nuns DOWRY
– woman member of a convent or religious community bound by a rule, but not by vows as a nun is CANONESS

nurse, especially a male nurse, supervising a hospital ward CHARGE NURSE
– nurse who makes home visits to the sick and old HEALTH VISITOR

nursemaid, nanny, or maidservant in India, East Africa, and elsewhere AYAH
– nursemaid, nanny, or wet nurse in the East AMAH

nursery for babies or very young children, especially to enable parents to go to work CRÈCHE
– nursery school KINDERGARTEN

nut from an evergreen Australian tree, with a tasty round oily kernel MACADAMIA NUT
– nut-like seed of an Indian palm, used in a popular chewing mixture in south-east Asia BETEL NUT
– nut with a closed end, capping a bolt LUG
– hazelnut FILBERT
– Mexican nut yielding a valuable liquid wax, as used in shampoos JOJOBA NUT
– North American nut, related to the walnut, with a sweetish kernel HICKORY NUT
– small Asian nut with a tasty greenish kernel PISTACHIO NUT
– U.S. nut with a kernel similar to that of the walnut PECAN NUT

-nutrition- -TROPH-, TROPHO-, -TROPHIC, -TROPHY

nymph inhabiting a tree, in classical mythology HAMADRYAD
– nymph of rivers or lakes, in classical mythology NAIAD
– nymph of the mountains, in classical mythology OREAD
– nymph of the sea, in classical mythology NEREID
– nymph of the woods or trees, in classical mythology DRYAD
– nymph or virgin in paradise, according to Islamic belief or folklore HOURI

O

oar – blade of an oar or paddle PALM
– looped rope, strap, or the like, as for holding an oar or sliding rope in position BECKET
– peg, pin, or short rod, as for supporting an oar in the side of a boat THOLE
– swivelling support for an oar on the side of a boat ROWLOCK
– turn an oar horizontal between strokes in rowing FEATHER

oasis – illusion or image of a non-present object, such as an oasis MIRAGE

oath formerly taken by graduating doctors, undertaking to observe professional ethics HIPPOCRATIC OATH
– oath of loyalty by a vassal to his feudal lord HOMAGE, FEALTY
– declaration in writing that is made under oath AFFIDAVIT
– declare under oath, as in a court of law TESTIFY
– formal declaration and undertaking to tell the truth, as in court, in place of an oath AFFIRMATION
– person who makes an affidavit or testifies in writing under oath DEPONENT
– solicitor authorised to administer oaths on sworn statements COMMISSIONER FOR OATHS
– public official, typically a solicitor, authorised to administer oaths, certify documents, and the like NOTARY PUBLIC, NOTARY
– testimony given on oath DEPOSITION
– trial in former times where the accused and 11 of his neighbours offered to swear to his innocence under oath WAGER OF LAW

oats or other coarsely ground grain GRITS, GROATS

obedience or cooperation of a token or insincere kind LIP SERVICE
– demand and obtain obedience, vengeance, or the like EXACT
– show obedience RENDER

obedient, easily controlled, governable BIDDABLE, TRACTABLE, CONFORMABLE
– obedient, easily influenced or manipulated, unresistingly submissive PLIABLE, MALLEABLE
– obedient, submissive, or eager to please in a fawning way SERVILE, SYCOPHANTIC, OBSEQUIOUS, UNCTUOUS
– obedient, unquestioningly submissive, even to oppressive or unreasonable demands and rules DOCILE, ACQUIESCENT
– obedient, willing to listen and follow advice, open to suggestion AMENABLE
– obedient, yielding, submitting to rules or orders easily COMPLIANT
– obedient or submissive in a respectful or humble way OBEISANT, DEFERENTIAL, TOUCHING ONE'S FORELOCK

obey a rule or order, carry out someone's wish or demand, or the like COMPLY WITH
– obey someone's wishes so as to keep the peace HUMOUR, INDULGE, ACQUIESCE IN, DEFER TO
– obey the regulations, respect or observe the conventions, or the like ABIDE BY, ADHERE TO
– obey the rules, toe the line CONFORM
– obey too readily, flatter, humble oneself, or the like, so as to curry favour FAWN, TRUCKLE, KOWTOW
– person who obeys and obliges too readily, groveller, bootlicker APPLE-POLISHER, LICKSPITTLE
– person who obeys unquestioningly, such as a self-humbling follower of a patron FLUNKY, LACKY, MINION

obituary NECROLOGY
– obituary speech or composition commemorating a dead person EPITAPH

object believed to have magical powers or to house a spirit FETISH, JUJU
– object grasped by the intellect or intuition rather than as perceived by the senses, thing-in-itself NOUMENON
– object perceived by or apparently real to the senses, rather than known through reasoning or intuition PHENOMENON
– object or target of scorn BYWORD

objection See also **complain**, **protest**
– objection, disagreement, refusal to comply or conform DISSENT, DISSIDENCE
– objection, especially to the relevance of an argument raised in court DEMURRER
– objection, hesitation, or misgiving, as based on doubt or conscience QUALM, SCRUPLE
– objection or criticism EXCEPTION
– objection that is trivial, trifling, and petty CAVIL, QUIBBLE
– confirm as valid or just, uphold something, such as an objection SUSTAIN

objective, unbiased IMPARTIAL, DISINTERESTED
– objective and emotionally detached DISPASSIONATE
– objective or life-like in its representation, as a painting might be REALISTIC

obligation, debt LIABILITY
– obligation on noble or noble-minded people to be generous and honourable NOBLESSE OBLIGE

oblong or square figure QUADRILATERAL, TETRAGON

obscene or sexually-arousing films, writings, photographs, or the like PORNOGRAPHY
– obscene, coarse sexual language BAWDRY

obscenity – obsessive interest in obscenity, especially in relation to excrement SCATOLOGY

obscure, as with fog or clouds OBNUBILATE
– obscure, confuse, complicate OBFUSCATE
– obscure, known only to experts and connoisseurs RECHERCHÉ
– obscure or ambiguous, as though spoken by an oracle DELPHIC

observable by scientific methods or by disinterested outsiders OBJECTIVE
– readily observable, open for all to see, above-board OVERT

observant and alert VIGILANT, ARGUS-EYED

observation See also **remark**
– observation or close watch, especially on someone or something suspicious SURVEILLANCE
– observation point that allows a particularly good view COIGN OF VANTAGE, RINGSIDE SEAT
– based on or relating to observation or experiment rather than

pure theory EMPIRICAL
observe or inspect carefully and intensely SCRUTINISE
observer, as at a card game, offering uninvited comments or advice KIBITZER
– observer or onlooker at an incident, rather than a participant in it BYSTANDER
-observing -SCOPY
obsess or occupy the thoughts of HAUNT
obsession See **manias**
– obsession or preoccupation FIXATION, IDÉE FIXE
obsessive interest in obscenity, especially in relation to excrement SCATOLOGY
– obsessive worry or nightmare INCUBUS
– obsessively worried, fussy, sensitive, or the like NEUROTIC
obsolete See **old-fashioned**
– replace something outdated or obsolete SUPERSEDE, PENSION OFF
obstacle See **barrier**, **obstruction**
– obstacle, minor problem SNAG
obstruct See also **prevent**, **hinder**
– obstruct, hinder, or delay as a deliberate strategy, as in cricket or parliamentary debate STONEWALL
– obstruct or ward off a blow, fencing thrust, or the like PARRY
– obstructed or clogged, as by blood or mucus CONGESTED
obstruction, hindrance IMPEDIMENT, ENCUMBRANCE, STUMBLING BLOCK
– obstruction of a blood vessel as by an air bubble or blood clot EMBOLISM
– obstruction of legislation by means of delaying tactics such as lengthy speeches FILIBUSTER
– obstruction or blockage in a body passage or opening, as in the bowels STRICTURE, OCCLUSION, OPPILATION
– obstructive or destructive action of an underhand kind SABOTAGE, SUBVERSION
– causing obstruction, especially in the bowels OBSTRUENT
– deadlock or serious obstruction, as in negotiations or an industrial process LOG JAM
– death of a body organ or tissue due to obstruction of the blood supply, as by a blood clot INFARCTION
– delay in a traffic flow, industrial process, or the like due to an obstruction BOTTLENECK
obtain or achieve COMPASS, ENCOMPASS
– obtain or produce from a source DERIVE
obvious, clear, plain to see EVIDENT, PATENT, MANIFEST
– obvious, dull, or trite remark PLATITUDE, COMMONPLACE
– obvious, highly visible, easily noticed CONSPICUOUS
– obvious, self-explanatory, or self-proving SELF-EVIDENT, AXIOMATIC
– obvious, true by the very nature of its wording or logical form ANALYTIC, TAUTOLOGOUS
– obvious or unmistakable, as a lie or error might be BLATANT, GLARING, GROSS, PALPABLE
– dealing with only the most obvious or apparent features of something SUPERFICIAL, TRIVIAL
– outrageously bad in an obvious way EGREGIOUS
– wrong or evil in an obvious or conspicuous way FLAGRANT
obviously, clearly, plainly PATENTLY
occasional, irregular, periodic INTERMITTENT, SPORADIC
occupation, profession VOCATION
– occupation, trade, or profession to which one is particularly well suited MÉTIER
occupy oneself in a pleasurable activity DISPORT
– occupy or conquer territory, and incorporate it into another state or an empire ANNEX
– occupy or inhabit a place, live in TENANT
occur, happen, take place, come to pass TRANSPIRE
– occur as a result, follow ENSUE, EVENTUATE
– occur at the same time, be or make simultaneous SYNCHRONISE
– occur or appear as an unexpected but important factor, as fate is said to do INTERVENE, SUPERVENE
– occurring at the same time or place, simultaneous, as two prison sentences might be CONCURRENT
– occurring in fits and starts, intermittent SPASMODIC
– develop into reality, become fact, actually occur MATERIALISE
occurrence, or the frequency of an occurrence INCIDENCE
ocean, open sea MAIN
– relating to the deep levels or floor of the ocean ABYSSAL
– relating to the deepest levels of the ocean, below about 20,000 ft (6000 metres) HADAL
– relating to the levels of the ocean below about 300 ft (90 metres), where sunlight no longer penetrates APHOTIC
octopus – an octopus's sucker ACETABULUM
– arm-like flexible projection near the mouth of an octopus, jellyfish, or the like TENTACLE
odd, abnormal, not proper or true to type ABERRANT, DEVIANT
– odd, curious, typical of a closed group with special or secret interests ABSTRUSE, ESOTERIC
– odd, inconsistent, discordant, out of place INCONGRUOUS, ANOMALOUS, ERRATIC
– odd, peculiar, unconventional, in a distorted or ludicrous way BIZARRE, GROTESQUE, OUTLANDISH, OUTRÉ
– odd, seemingly random or individual and not governed by a pattern or reason, as a person, idea, or behaviour might be ECCENTRIC, IDIOSYNCRATIC, QUIRKY, WHIMSICAL, SINGULAR, PIXILATED
– odd, without normal or rational explanation INEXPLICABLE, PRETERNATURAL, RUM
– odd habit or piece of behaviour IDIOSYNCRASY, QUIRK, ECCENTRICITY, MANNERISM
– odd or fanciful action or notion WHIM, CAPRICE, VAGARY, FOIBLE
– oddball, person who does not fit into society MISFIT
– amusingly odd, whimsically comical, eccentric in a quaint way ZANY, KOOKY, DROLL
– stubbornly holding to eccentric ideas, odd CROTCHETY, CAPRICIOUS, PERVERSE
– weird, inexplicably worrying and odd UNCANNY, EERIE
odds and ends, junk, discarded or miscellaneous objects FLOTSAM, BRIC-A-BRAC
– odds and ends of one's personal property PARAPHERNALIA
Oedipus complex in a young girl ELECTRA COMPLEX
of one mind, all agreeing UNANIMOUS
of sound mind, sane COMPOS MENTIS
off- AB-, CATA-
off by heart BY ROTE
off the cuff, as a speech or statement might be IMPROMPTU, EXTEMPORE, EXTEMPORANEOUS, SPONTANEOUS
offal, especially of a deer, as formerly used for food NUMBLES, UMBLES
– offal of a chicken or other fowl GIBLETS
– offal of animals, especially of pigs, used in cooking HASLET, FRY, PLUCK, PURTENANCE
– meatball, typically of minced pig's offal FAGGOT
offence See **crime**
offend or hurt, cause a sympathetic or friendly person to become indifferent or hostile ALIENATE, ANTAGONISE, ESTRANGE

– offend someone by a blow to his pride PIQUE
– to be offended, feel resentment, as at a slighting remark TAKE UMBRAGE, TAKE EXCEPTION

offensive See also **disgusting**
– offensive, liable to cause ill will or resentment INVIDIOUS
– offensive and unnecessary, as an undeserved insult would be GRATUITOUS
– offensive in a deliberate way, intended or meant to insult or belittle DEROGATORY
– offensive or revolting, as a foul smell is NOISOME
– offensively gracious, as though dealing with one's subordinate PATRONISING, CONDESCENDING, PATERNALISTIC

offer or invitation APPROACH, OVERTURE
– offer or propose, present formally PROFFER, TENDER
– amount offered for an item at an auction or the like BID
– ridiculously small or inadequate, as a pay offer might be DERISORY

offering of worship, thanksgiving, an altar gift, or the like OBLATION
– offering to a god, designed to appease PROPITIATION
– based on the fulfilment of a vow, as a religious offering might be VOTIVE

office note or letter MEMORANDUM
– office tape recorder for dictation and later typing DICTAPHONE
– appointed to an office or position though not actually installed yet DESIGNATE
– ceremonial installing of a person in office INVESTITURE, INDUCTION
– holding or occupying of a property, office, or the like TENURE
– promotion or advancement to a higher office or post PREFERMENT
– relating to office work or office workers CLERICAL
– remove from office, power, the throne, or the like DEPOSE

officer See **military**, **services**
– officer of a U.S. court MARSHAL
– commanding officer of a military post, organisation, or the like COMMANDANT
– military officer holding an official appointment COMMISSIONED OFFICER
– military officer with an intermediate rank, between commissioned and noncommissioned officer WARRANT OFFICER

official See also **diplomat**
– official, orthodox, authoritative CANONICAL
– official, or person discharging official duties FUNCTIONARY
– official, usually a doctor, conducting inquests into deaths that might not be due to natural causes CORONER
– official announcement made to the press and public COMMUNIQUÉ, PROCLAMATION
– official announcement or report COMPTE RENDU
– official approval, formal confirmation or authorisation, as of a law RATIFICATION, SANCTION, FIAT, VALIDATION
– official authorised to administer oaths, certify documents, and the like NOTARY PUBLIC, NOTARY
– official authorised to investigate citizens' complaints against government departments or other official bodies OMBUDSMAN
– official badges, emblems, distinguishing symbols, or the like INSIGNIA
– official corruption, private profit derived from a public office JOBBERY, GRAFT
– official document or letter certifying a person's creditworthiness, qualifications, authority, or the like CREDENTIALS
– official government report or policy statement prior to discussion in Parliament WHITE PAPER
– official government publication in Britain containing proposals for legislation, issued to interested parties for comments and discussion GREEN PAPER
– official government publication or report in Britain BLUEBOOK
– official in ancient Rome elected by the common people to represent their interests TRIBUNE
– official in the EEC, especially a senior administrator EUROCRAT
– official investigator, especially one who is appointed to root out supposed evil INQUISITOR
– official jargon that is wordy and hard to understand OFFICIALESE, GOBBLEDEGOOK
– official opening ceremony, installation, or beginning INAUGURATION, DEDICATION, COMMENCEMENT, INVESTITURE, INDUCTION
– official or officer who is pompous, complacent, and reactionary COLONEL BLIMP
– official regulation on movement, especially one requiring people to be indoors by a certain hour of night CURFEW
– official responsible for maintaining order in a law court, or the like SERJEANT AT ARMS, USHER
– official status, allowing one to speak at a meeting and enjoy similar rights LOCUS STANDI
– official who is self-important yet inefficient POOH-BAH
– official who is unduly zealous or rigid APPARATCHIK
– officially authorised and recognised, as a diplomat should be ACCREDITED
– officially recognised or legally accepted LEGITIMATE
– charge an official such as a president with an offence committed while in office IMPEACH
– Communist Party official who teaches or enforces party policy COMMISSAR
– court official or sheriff's officer BAILIFF, TIPSTAFF
– government official, or any mean-minded and inflexible official BUREAUCRAT
– objectionable or pompous petty official JACK-IN-OFFICE
– senior official administering a district in British India COLLECTOR
– senior official of a Scottish borough PROVOST
– senior official in local administration in England during the Middle Ages REEVE
– wrongdoing, especially by a public official MALFEASANCE, MALVERSATION

officialdom, bureaucracy, or self-importance in a petty official BUMBLEDOM, BEADLEDOM

offset, compensate for, make up for COUNTERVAIL

offspring or descendant, especially male SCION
– bearing more than one offspring at a time MULTIPAROUS
– produce offspring, reproduce PROCREATE
– producing live offspring rather than laying eggs VIVIPAROUS
– producing many offspring PROLIFIC, PHILOPROGENITIVE
– producing offspring by means of eggs that hatch outside the body OVIPAROUS
– producing offspring by means of eggs that hatch within the female's body, as with some fish and reptiles OVOVIVIPAROUS

-offspring -PAROUS

often, frequently, over and over again RECURRENTLY, REPEATEDLY
– referring to a person who often or repeatedly engages in a dubious practice, such as smoking or lying HABITUAL, INVETERATE

-ographies See chart, pages 354-355

oil, grease, graphite, or other substance used to reduce friction LUBRICANT

– oil from a tropical grass, used in insect repellents and perfume-making CITRONELLA OIL
– oil from flax seeds, used as a drying oil in paints, varnishes, and inks LINSEED OIL
– oil from the rind of a small, sour citrus fruit, used in perfume-making BERGAMOT OIL
– oil-processing plant REFINERY
– oil-refining unit in which petroleum is converted to fuels with lower boiling points CRACKER
– oil used on the hair, popular in the 19th century MACASSAR OIL
– dregs or sediment in a liquid, as in varnish or cooking oil FOOTS
– light yellow oil, used for dressing leather, obtained by boiling the feet and shinbones of cattle NEAT'S-FOOT OIL
– pattern of oil when spread thinly on the surface of water OLEOGRAPH
– place or rub oil or ointment on ANOINT
– reduction or decomposition, as by heat-treating oil CRACKING
– referring to natural oils, as used in healthy margarines, having many of the atoms in its molecules linked by double or triple chemical bonds POLYUNSATURATED
– rod for checking the level of oil in a crankcase DIPSTICK
– sesame-seed oil GINGILI
– therapy using fragrant oils AROMATHERAPY

oil- OLE-, OLEO-

oil well, mine, or similar asset whose value diminishes over the years WASTING ASSET
– oil well or gas well with an abundant natural flow GUSHER
– begin the drilling of an oil well SPUD
– equipment for a specified purpose, as for drilling or for extracting oil from an oil well RIG
– framework over an oil well for supporting pipes or drilling equipment DERRICK, PLATFORM
– uncontrollable flow from a gas well or oil well, as after an explosion BLOWOUT

oilseed and fodder crop, with a distinctive yellow flower RAPE, COLZA
– residue of oilseed, used as animal fodder EXPELLERS, EXTRACTIONS

oily, fatty, greasy PINGUID, SEBACEOUS
– oily, greasy, or fawningly compliant UNCTUOUS, OLEAGINOUS
– oily substance produced by glands SEBUM, SMEGMA

ointment of olive oil and balsam used in sacramental anointing, as at baptism or confirmation CHRISM
– ointment or bandage applied to produce warmth CALEFACIENT
– ointment or lotion with soothing or healing properties, rubbed into the skin LINIMENT, EMBROCATION, SALVE, UNGUENT
– ointment or oil used for soothing or anointing UNCTION
– fat from sheep's wool, used in cosmetics and ointments LANOLIN
– fragrant ointment in ancient times, or the Indian plant it supposedly derived from SPIKENARD

OK, satisfactory, in order HUNKY-DORY

okra, okra pods, or a soup or stew thickened with okra pods GUMBO

old See also **ancient**
– old, former, previous, as one's divorced spouse is ERSTWHILE, QUONDAM
– old, senile person DOTARD
– old, shrivelled, and wrinkled WIZENED
– old, stale, reworked, as material for a comedy act might be RÉCHAUFFÉ
– old and grey HOARY
– old and respected VENERABLE
– old and unsteady, as through senility DODDERING
– old and weak, in a poor state of repair DECREPIT, DILAPIDATED
– old days, bygone times LANG SYNE
– old quarter of a North African town KASBAH
– old woman of status or wealth DOWAGER
– becoming old, of advanced age SENESCENT
– good because old and mature, as wine might be VINTAGE
– healthy, active, and vigorous, typically in spite of being old SPRY, SPRIGHTLY
– possessed by the same family since olden times, as a house or characteristic might be ANCESTRAL
– so old that its origins are forgotten, as those of a tradition might be IMMEMORIAL
– specialist in or lover of old things, especially books ANTIQUARIAN
– very old, ancient, belonging to bygone times SUPERANNUATED, ARCHAIC, ANTIQUATED
– very old man METHUSELAH
– weak and feeble, resembling a frail old woman ANILE

old- PALAEO-, ARCHAEO-

old age, quality of being ancient ANTIQUITY
– feeble-mindedness and loss of faculties through old age SENILITY, DOTAGE
– relating to old age and its medical problems GERIATRIC
– relating to old age, especially showing mental deterioration in old age SENILE

old age- GERONT-, GERONTO-

Old English ANGLO-SAXON
– Old English letter, written þ, and representing the sounds /th/ and /t͟h/ THORN
– Old English letter, written ð, and representing the /t͟h/ sound as in *this* EDH, ETH
– Old English letter, written ȝ, and representing various sounds similar to /y/ or the /k͟h/ of *loch* YOGH
– Old English letter, written *æ*, and representing various sounds including /a/ as in *hat* ASH

old-fashioned, stale FUSTY, MUSTY
– old-fashioned, out of date, dated, having outlasted its usefulness OBSOLETE, SUPERSEDED, ANTIQUATED
– old-fashioned, out of date, not up with the latest trends OUTMODED, PASSÉ, DÉMODÉ
– old-fashioned, shabby, or untidy, as a woman or her clothes might be DOWDY
– old-fashioned and conservative person, seemingly left over from a bygone age ANACHRONISM, RELIC, TROGLODYTE, THROWBACK, ANTEDILUVIAN
– old-fashioned and fussy person FUDDY-DUDDY
– old-fashioned custom, idiom, or the like of a group, now fallen into disuse SHIBBOLETH
– old-fashioned in moral outlook, prudish, square STRAITLACED, VICTORIAN
– completely old-fashioned and incapable of evolving FOSSILISED, OSSIFIED, STAGNATED
– stubbornly old-fashioned person, one resisting all change DIEHARD, TRADITIONALIST

Old Testament See also **bible**
– Old Testament figure or event foreshadowing one in the New Testament TYPE
– Old Testament founder or father of the human race or the Hebrew people PATRIARCH
– interpretation of the Old Testament as an allegory or prefiguring, foreshadowing of the New Testament ANAGOGY

-ologies See chart, pages 354-355

omission of an unstressed vowel or syllable, as in *th' appetite*, commonly in a line of verse ELISION

– omission or loss of a sound or letter at the beginning of a word, as in *phone* for *telephone* or *'bout* for *about* APHAERESIS, APHESIS
– omission or loss of a sound or letter at the end of a word as in *walkin'* APOCOPE
– omission or loss of a sound or letter from the middle of a word, as in *bo's'n* for *boatswain* SYNCOPE
– omission or loss of a sound or syllable when pronouncing a word, as when saying *deteriate* for *deteriorate* HAPLOLOGY
– act of omission or neglect, passing by, disregarding PRETERITION

omnipresent, everywhere UBIQUITOUS

on- EPI-

on and on, in a boring way INTERMINABLE, REPETITIVE

on behalf of PER PRO, PER PROC.

on duty, at work IN HARNESS

on heat OESTROUS

one, two, three, and so on CARDINAL NUMBERS
– one-legged camera support MONOPOD
– "one out of many", the U.S. motto E PLURIBUS UNUM
– one-wheeled vehicle, as pedalled

-OLOGIES AND -OGRAPHIES

TERM	SUBJECT OF STUDY OR PRACTICE
acarology	mites and ticks
aetiology	causes, especially of diseases
anemology	wind
angiology	blood and lymph vessels
anthropology	mankind
astrology	heavenly bodies
bryology	mosses
campanology	bell ringing
cardiology	heart functions and diseases
carpology	fruits and seeds
cetology	aquatic mammals, especially whales
cartography	map-making
choreography	dancing, composing ballets
chorography	mapping of regions
chorology	geographical regions; plant and animal distribution
chronology	dates
conchology	seashells
cosmology	the universe
craniology	skulls
criminology	crimes and criminals
cryptology	codes and ciphers
cytology	plant and animal cells
dactylology	fingerprints
demography	population statistics
dendrology	trees
deontology	moral responsibilities
dermatology	human skin
ecology	relationships between living things and their environment
endocrinology	glands
entomology	insects
epidemiology	incidence and risk of disease
epigraphy	ancient inscriptions
epistemology	nature of knowledge
eschatology	death, destiny
ethnology	cultures, primitive peoples
ethology	animal behaviour
etymology	word origins
futurology	the future
genealogy	ancestry
gerontology	old age
glottochronology	history of language
gynaecology	women's disorders
haematology	blood
helminthology	worms, especially parasitic worms
herpetology	reptiles and amphibians
histology	plant and animal tissue
horology	measurement of time; timepieces
hydrology	water and ice
hypnology	sleep
ichthyology	fish
lexicography	dictionaries
lexicology	vocabulary
limnology	freshwater life
lithology	characteristics of rocks
malacology	molluscs
meteorology	weather
metrology	measurement
mycology	fungi
myology	muscles
myrmecology	ants
nomology	law-making or scientific laws
nosology	classification of diseases
odontology	teeth
oenology	wines
oncology	tumours and cancer
oneirology	dreams
ontology	nature of existence
oology	eggs

by acrobats UNICYCLE
one- MON-, MONO-, UNI-
one-and-a-half- SESQUI-
one-sided, without compensation or benefit in return GRATUITOUS
– one-sided conversation, lengthy and uninterrupted speech by one person MONOLOGUE
– one-sided surface made by forming a once-twisted strip into a ring MÖBIUS STRIP
– one-sided surface made by passing the narrow end of a tapered tube through the tube's side then widening it and fusing it to the other open end KLEIN BOTTLE
oneself, in person, or personally IN PROPRIA PERSONA
onion, leek, garlic, or plant related to them ALLIUM
– onion-like bulb, growing in clusters, used for pickling and cooking SHALLOT, SCALLION
– cooked with onions, as potatoes might be LYONNAISE
– having concentric layers such as those of the onion TUNICATE
– smelling or tasting of onions or garlic ALLIACEOUS
onlooker, as at a card game, offering uninvited comments or advice KIBITZER
– onlooker or observer at an incident, rather than a participant in it BYSTANDER
ooze out, emerge slowly, as through pores EXUDE
– oozing, leakage SEEPAGE
open and start using the contents of something, such as a shipment or box BROACH
– open and unobstructed, as ducts or passages in the body should be PATENT
– open country or grassland in South Africa VELD
– open for all to see, observable, above-board OVERT
– open formally a building, exhibition, or the like DEDICATE, INAUGURATE
– open space for parades, meetings, sport, and so on in India and Southeast Asia MAIDAN
– open stretch of land, sea, or sky EXPANSE
– open to the passage of fluids POROUS, PERMEABLE
– open to view, danger, attack, or the like EXPOSED
– openly acknowledged, candidly admitted, self-confessed AVOWED
– openly expressed, unreserved, outspoken, forthright EXPLICIT
– slightly open, as a door might be AJAR
– wide open, yawning AGAPE
opening See also **hole**, **gap**
– opening in a wall, wider inside than out, for a door or window EMBRASURE
– opening in fortifications for the passage of troops DÉBOUCHÉ
– opening move or manoeuvre, as in negotiations, designed to secure an early advantage GAMBIT
– opening part of a sonata, play, or the like that introduces the themes EXPOSITION
– opening quotation, as at the head of a chapter or the start of a book, suggesting its theme EPIGRAPH
– opening sentence or paragraph of a newspaper or magazine article STANDFIRST
– opening words of a speech or

TERM	SUBJECT OF STUDY OR PRACTICE	TERM	SUBJECT OF STUDY OR PRACTICE
ophiology	snakes	**pteridology**	ferns
ophthalmology	eyes	**radiology**	radiation and radiotherapy
ornithology	birds	**reflexology**	reflexes; healing through foot massage
orography	mapping of relief	**rhinology**	noses
orology	mountains	**scatology**	excrement; obscene language
osteology	bones	**seismology**	earthquakes
otology	ears	**selenology**	the Moon
paedology	children	**semiology**	signs and signalling
palaeography	old manuscripts	**sinology**	China
palaeontology	fossils	**speleology**	caves
palynology	pollen	**stomatology**	mouth disorders
pathology	diseases	**teratology**	monsters; congenital abnormalities
pedology	soil	**topography**	surface features of a region
penology	prisons and treatment of criminals	**topology**	shapes and surfaces
petrology	rocks	**toxicology**	poisons
pharmacology	drugs	**tribology**	friction and lubrication
philology	languages	**trichology**	hair
phrenology	character, by studying skull irregularities	**ufology**	Unidentified Flying Objects
physiology	life processes, functioning of organisms	**uranography**	mapping of stars and galaxies
phytology	plants	**vexillology**	flags
polemology	wars	**zymology**	fermentation
pomology	fruit		
potamology	rivers		
psephology	elections		

letter, such as "Dear friends" SALUTATION
– abnormal opening or channel, from a hollow organ, abscess, or cavity to the skin's surface or to another hollow organ FISTULA
– small space, opening, or gap, as between the strands of a net INTERSTICE

-opening-, -mouth- -STOM-, -STOME, STOMATO-

opera company's chief female singer PRIMA DONNA, DIVA
– opera or ballet performers' coach RÉPÉTITEUR
– opera singer with a strong tenor voice HELDENTENOR
– operatic song for a solo voice ARIA, ARIETTA
– interval entertainment between the acts of an opera or play DIVERTISSEMENT
– interval or interval performance during a play or opera ENTR'ACTE
– text of the songs and dialogue of an opera or operetta LIBRETTO
– translation shown above, as projected above an opera stage SURTITLE

opera glasses supported by a small handle LORGNETTE, LORGNON

operation See **surgical**
– operation or experiment on the body of a living animal, especially for research VIVISECTION
– operation or project to control a tricky situation and limit the damage HOLDING OPERATION

opinion, judgment ESTIMATION
– opinion based on incomplete evidence, guess SPECULATION, CONJECTURE, SURMISE
– opinion differing from the orthodox view HERESY, HETERODOXY
– opinion or belief firmly held CONVICTION, DOGMA, PERSUASION
– opinion or belief that is mistaken or misleading DELUSION
– opinion or decision already formed PARTI PRIS
– opinion or idea based on convention rather than real belief IDÉE REÇUE
– opinion or image of someone or something that is conventional, unthinking and usually oversimplified STEREOTYPE
– opinion poll or similar statistical enquiry SURVEY
– opinion poll taken unofficially or impromptu STRAW POLL
– opinion that is widespread, a general agreement, a majority opinion CONSENSUS
– opinions or prejudices expressing one's outlook SENTIMENTS
– difference, of ideas, opinions, or the like DIVERGENCE
– division or classification into two parts, such as conflicting opinions DICHOTOMY
– established, fixed, firmly and immovably settled, as opinions or troops might be ENTRENCHED
– give an opinion RENDER
– growth or increase, as of public feeling or opinion GROUNDSWELL
– passing of opinions on subjects of which one has little knowledge SCIOLISM, ULTRACREPIDARIANISM
– person or group whose reactions serve as a test for new ideas or opinions SOUNDING BOARD
– similarity of ideas, opinions, or the like CONVERGENCE
– test, sample, or probe opinions or intentions SOUND
– unprincipled person who changes his policies or opinions to serve his interests TIMESERVER, TRIMMER, VICAR OF BRAY, TEMPORISER

opium – medicinal preparation, widely used in former times, based on opium LAUDANUM

opponent, enemy, foe ADVERSARY, ANTAGONIST
– opponent, rival, participant in a contest CONTENDER, CORRIVAL
– opponent of mechanisation or technical advance LUDDITE
– opponent of or objector to the views, policies, and demands of an authoritarian ruling party DISSIDENT

opportunity – make use of an opportunity, turn to advantage EXPLOIT, UTILISE, CAPITALISE ON, CASH IN ON
– place of great wealth or opportunity ELDORADO

oppose, argue against or dispute, contradict or deny GAINSAY, REPUDIATE, OPPUGN, CONTROVERT
– oppose, challenge, stand up to CONFRONT, DEFY
– oppose, offset, or balance with an equal force COUNTERVAIL, COUNTERBALANCE
– oppose or fight vigorously TILT AT
– opposed or hostile to something or someone AVERSE, OPPUGNANT, ANTIPATHETIC
– opposed uncompromisingly, relentlessly hostile IRRECONCILABLE, IMPLACABLE, INEXORABLE
– opposing, conflicting, not in agreement with AT VARIANCE, AT LOGGERHEADS
– opposing or opposite, as winds or criticism might be ADVERSE
– opposing others' wishes or suggestions unreasonably PERVERSE, CONTRARY
– divide into two extreme and opposing positions, groups, opinions, or the like POLARISE
– linking or shared by opposing parties, as an agreement might be RECIPROCAL
– having opposing senses or implications, as conflicting statements or claims have INCOMPATIBLE, INCONSISTENT, CONTRADICTORY

opposed-, opposing- ANTI-, CONTRA-

opposite, face to face VIS-À-VIS
– opposite, word having a sense directly opposed to that of another word ANTONYM
– opposite or absence of something positive or real NEGATION
– completely contrary, as two opposites might be DIAMETRICAL, POLAR
– completely opposite or contrary to one's nature, experience, or principles ABHORRENT, REPUGNANT, ALIEN
– exact or direct opposite or contrast ANTITHESIS, CONVERSE, INVERSE
– part or number opposite to and completing another COMPLEMENT
– place on the opposite side of the Earth, especially Australia and New Zealand ANTIPODES
– use of words to express something markedly different from or opposite to their outward or literal sense IRONY

opposite- A-, ALLO-, ANTI-, COUNTER-, UN-, CATA-

opposite direction- DIA-

opposition, as to government authority or colonial rule, by non-violent methods such as fasting and non-cooperation PASSIVE RESISTANCE
– opposition, disagreement, non-acceptance DISSENT
– opposition, inconsistency, lack of agreement, as between two logically incompatible claims CONTRADICTION, DISPARITY, DISCREPANCY, DISSONANCE, INCONGRUITY
– opposition or conflict between two rules or laws ANTINOMY
– opposition or conflict within a group, nation, or the like FACTION
– strong opposition or hostility ANTAGONISM

oppress or ill-treat, especially for racial, religious, or political differences PERSECUTE
– oppressed, unfortunate, or subordinate person UNDERDOG

oppressive or cruel person in authority TYRANT, DESPOT

optical illusion or image of a non-present object, such as an oasis MIRAGE
– painting or the like giving an optical illusion or appearance of

reality TROMPE L'ŒIL

optimist, especially one who is blindly or excessively optimistic POLLYANNA
- optimist in spite of suffering repeated misfortunes MICAWBER
- optimistic and confident, cheerful SANGUINE
- optimistic and confident spirits, as among soldiers MORALE
- optimistic and naive person, especially an innocent young man CANDIDE

optional or contingent, capable of happening or of not happening FACULTATIVE

or else – final terms offered in negotiating, to be accepted "or else" ULTIMATUM

oracle – ambiguous or obscure, as though spoken by an oracle DELPHIC

orange of a bitter variety, used especially for making marmalade SEVILLE ORANGE
- orange or lemon rind used as flavouring ZEST
- orange stuck with cloves, as for scenting linen POMANDER
- oranges, lemons, grapefruit, or related fruit CITRUS FRUIT
- sour, pear-shaped orange with a rind that yields an aromatic oil BERGAMOT
- spongy white tissue between the rind and pulp of oranges or other citrus fruits PITH

oratory, art of effective and persuasive speech RHETORIC

orbit, as of the Moon around the Earth, in which the same face of the orbiting body is always pointing to the orbited body CAPTURED ROTATION, SYNCHRONOUS ROTATION
- orbit of a satellite timed to keep it apparently fixed over one point on the surface of the Earth SYNCHRONOUS ORBIT, GEOSTATIONARY ORBIT
- orbiting in an opposite direction RETROGRADE
- closest or farthest point in the irregular orbit of a celestial body from the body it is orbiting round APSE, APSIS
- elliptical rather than circular, as a planet's orbit might be ECCENTRIC
- point at which a spacecraft in lunar orbit is farthest from the Moon APOCYNTHION, APOLUNE, APOSELENE
- point at which a spacecraft in lunar orbit is nearest the Moon PERICYNTHION, PERILUNE
- point in its orbit when a planet, comet, or the like is farthest from the Sun APHELION
- point in its orbit when a planet, comet, or the like is nearest the Sun PERIHELION
- point in its orbit when the Moon or a satellite is farthest from the Earth APOGEE
- point in its orbit when the Moon or a satellite is nearest the Earth PERIGEE
- small circle, supposedly followed by a planet, moving in a large orbit around the Earth, according to early astronomers EPICYCLE
- star or other celestial body round which a planet or other satellite orbits PRIMARY

orchestra, as in Java, based on chimes and other such percussion instruments GAMELAN
- orchestra, music society, or a choir PHILHARMONIC
- orchestra or choir leader, as in 18th-century Germany KAPELLMEISTER
- orchestra with only a small number of players, typically performing in a small hall CHAMBER ORCHESTRA
- percussion section of an orchestra BATTERY

orchids of various kinds CALYPSO, CATTLEYA, POGONIA, TWAYBLADE

ordain a bishop CONSECRATE

order See **column**

order, arbitrary command, or law as announced by a ruler, autocrat, or authority EDICT, DECREE, PROCLAMATION, UKASE, RESCRIPT, FIAT, DIKTAT, IRADE, PRONUNCIAMENTO
- order, balance between parts SYMMETRY, PROPORTION
- order, command, or instruction MANDATE, DIRECTIVE
- order, distribution, or arrangement DISPOSAL
- order, law, rule, or regulation STATUTE, ORDINANCE
- order of power or status in a group PECKING ORDER, HIERARCHY
- order or arrange something, as by a decree or guidelines ORDAIN, PRESCRIBE
- order or arrange something in a particular way DISPOSE
- order or cosmic reason in ancient Greek philosophy LOGOS
- order or harmony COSMOS
- order or permission to leave, dismissal NUNC DIMITTIS
- order or rank, as at public ceremonies PRECEDENCE
- order or request, often in writing and official, for needed supplies or equipment REQUISITION
- order or sequence, as of those in line for a title or throne SUCCESSION
- order or urge solemnly, as if under oath ADJURE, ENJOIN, EXHORT
- order something officially, such as a biography or painting COMMISSION
- order warning against a certain action MONITION
- ordered, successive, or serial SEQUENTIAL, CONSECUTIVE
- ordered or requested by AT THE BEHEST OF
- allowing no denial, refusal, or argument, as an order or decree might PEREMPTORY
- arrange something, such as pages, in the correct order COLLATE, COLLOCATE
- cancel or reverse an order or instruction COUNTERMAND
- change or reverse the ordering or relative position of two or more things TRANSPOSE
- court order directed at some lower court, official body, or the like MANDAMUS
- court order requiring a person to appear in court to give evidence SUMMONS, SUBPOENA
- court order requiring an untried prisoner to be brought before a judge, who may order his release HABEAS CORPUS
- court order requiring or banning a certain action WRIT, INJUNCTION
- expressing an order IMPERATIVE
- lacking a planned order or arrangement RANDOM, HAPHAZARD, ARBITRARY
- lay down as an order or condition DICTATE, STIPULATE
- put into order, systematise CODIFY, TABULATE
- rearrangement or reordering PERMUTATION

-order- -TAX-, TAXO-, -TAXY, -TAXIS

orderly, rational, and sober, as one side of human nature is APOLLONIAN

ordinary See also **mediocre**, **dull**
- ordinary, commonplace, day-to-day QUOTIDIAN, WORKADAY
- ordinary, plain, or unstriking INCONSPICUOUS, ANONYMOUS, UNEXCEPTIONAL, PROSAIC
- ordinary, simple, homely, and unpretentious HOMESPUN
- ordinary member of the public, as opposed to a specialist, clergyman, or other professional LAY PERSON, LAYMAN
- in ordinary, everyday language COLLOQUIAL, VERNACULAR

ordinary seaman, sailor of basic rank in certain navies RATING

ordinary shares EQUITIES

ore – separation or refinement of ores or other minerals by skimming off the required particles in bubbles of a liquid FROTH FLOTATION
oregano MARJORAM
organ See illustration, and also **digestive system**
– abnormal change to a body part, organ, or tissue LESION
– abnormal opening or channel, from a hollow organ, abscess, or cavity to the skin's surface or to another hollow organ FISTULA
– abnormal rift or gap in a body part or organ DIASTEMA
– adjust organ pipes or a wind instrument to perfect the tone and pitch VOICE
– air valve in the wind chest of an organ PALLET
– body organs, especially those essential for life VITALS
– death of an organ or part of an organ due to obstruction of its blood supply INFARCTION
– desk-like section of an organ containing the keyboard, pedals, and stops CONSOLE
– displacement of a body part or organ through the wall normally enclosing it HERNIA, RUPTURE
– faulty continuous sounding of an organ pipe even when the key is not being pressed CIPHER
– group of organ pipes producing the same tone colour REGISTER, STOP
– health of body organs, as shown by their tension and response to stimuli TONE
– internal bodily organs ENTRAILS, VISCERA, INNARDS
– internal organs of an animal, especially when regarded as edible OFFAL
– leaning or resting against related tissue, as a bodily organ might RECUMBENT
– main part of something, such as a body organ CORPUS
– organ stop producing low notes BOURDON, BOMBARDON
– person who provides an organ for transplant DONOR
– person who receives a transplanted organ DONEE, RECIPIENT
– principal organ stop or set of pipes, determining the organ's characteristic tone DIAPASON
– relating to the internal organs VISCERAL, SPLANCHNIC
– set of organ pipes controlled by a single stop RANK
– system of organs and tissues that function as a unit TRACT
– turn a body part or organ inside out EVAGINATE, EVERT
– wall of a body organ such as the heart PARIES
organic matter that decays and fertilises the soil HUMUS
organisation sponsored but not controlled by the government QUANGO
organise See **arrange**
organiser of stage shows, concerts, or the like IMPRESARIO
organising of any complicated project, especially one involving transport LOGISTICS
– organising, supervision, direction, sponsorship AUSPICES, AEGIS
organism of a basic single-celled type, typically microscopic, such as an amoeba PROTOZOAN
– living together of two organisms in close or dependent association, especially when beneficial to both SYMBIOSIS
orgy, revelry, unrestrained licentious celebration SATURNALIA
– orgy or drunken, noisy festivity BACCHANAL, BACCHANALIA
-orientation- -TROP-, TROPO-, -TROPIC
origin, beginning, or creation, as of an idea or project GENESIS, CONCEPTION
– origin, parentage, descent LINEAGE, EXTRACTION
– origin or descent DERIVATION
– origin and development of a word, or the study of such origins ETYMOLOGY
– origin and historical development of something PEDIGREE
– origin or authorship PATERNITY
– main source or origin, as of an idea FOUNTAINHEAD
– place of origin, as of a work of art PROVENANCE
– point of origin, starting point, beginning in time TERMINUS A QUO
– point of origin or root of an organ or part RADIX
– scientific study of the origin of mankind or the species of man ANTHROPOGENESIS
– study of origins or causes, as of a disease or in mythology AETIOLOGY
– study of the origins of personal and place names ONOMASTICS
-origin- -GEN, -GENESIS, -GENY, -GON-, GONO-
original, creative, or life-enhancing PROMETHEAN
– original, first, earliest PRIMARY, PRIMAL, ARCHETYPAL, PRIMEVAL
– original and creative, providing a basis for development SEMINAL
– original model or pattern on which other versions or copies are based ARCHETYPE, PROTOTYPE, BLUEPRINT
– original or local, belonging to or relating to a particular place NATIVE, ENDEMIC
– original or special to an individual PATENT
– referring to the original inhabitants of an area ABORIGINAL, AUTOCHTHONOUS, INDIGENOUS
– relating to an original time or condition PRISTINE, PRIMORDIAL
original- UR-, PRIM-, PRIMO-
originality, freshness, or newness NOVELTY
originate See also **begin**
– originate or issue from a source EMANATE
– originating externally, coming from outside EXOGENOUS
– originating in a particular place, native ABORIGINAL, INDIGENOUS, AUTOCHTHONOUS
– originating internally, coming from within ENDOGENOUS
originator of a tradition or trend PROGENITOR, FOUNTAINHEAD, PRECURSOR
Orkneys – person born or living in the Orkneys ORCADIAN
ornament See also **decorate**
– ornament, often carved, in the form or a small figure or statuette FIGURINE
– ornament a surface by embedding decorative pieces in it INLAY
– ornament hanging from a thread, with parts that move when pushed or when blown by the wind MOBILE
– ornament of a showy but worthless kind TRINKET, BAUBLE, GEWGAW, FALLAL, GIMCRACK, KNICKKNACK
– ornament of enamelware in differently coloured panels within a decorative grid of metal strips CLOISONNÉ
– ornament or sculpture in low relief, such as a cameo ANAGLYPH
– ornamentation or decoration, as of buildings or clothing TRIM
– ornamented, ornate, elaborate CORINTHIAN
– ornamented or styled in an elaborate, uninhibited, or exaggerated way ROCOCO
– ornaments, curios, odd items of furniture, and the like, valued as rare or quaint BRIC-A-BRAC
– small, inexpensive ornament or toy NOVELTY
ornamental loop of drapery, flowers, or the like SWAG, FESTOON
– ornamental ridge running along the top of a roof or wall CRESTING
– ornamental strip of wood, metal, or the like, as for trimming or edging BEADING

organ

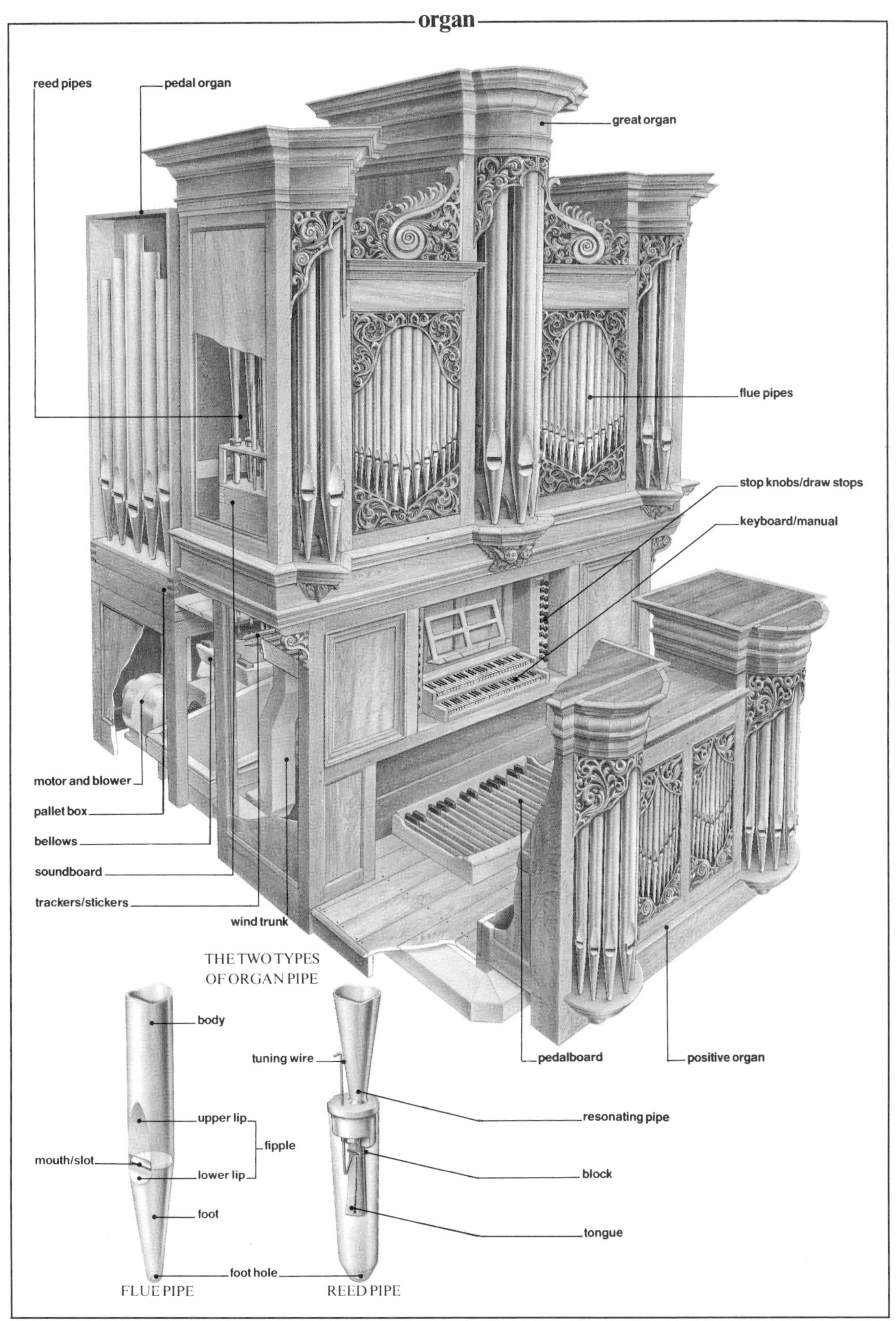
reed pipes
pedal organ
great organ
flue pipes
stop knobs/draw stops
keyboard/manual
motor and blower
pallet box
bellows
soundboard
trackers/stickers
wind trunk
pedalboard
positive organ
THE TWO TYPES OF ORGAN PIPE
body
tuning wire
upper lip
fipple
mouth/slot
lower lip
foot
foot hole
resonating pipe
block
tongue
FLUE PIPE
REED PIPE

orthodox, official, authoritative CANONICAL
Oscar ACADEMY AWARD
– award for work in the New York theatre, the rough equivalent of an Oscar TONY
ostrich, emu, kiwi, or related flightless bird RATITE
– relating to or resembling the ostrich STRUTHIOUS
other – felt or expressed by two people about each other MUTUAL, RECIPROCAL
other- HETER-, HETERO-
otter, badger, ferret, or related mammal MUSTELINE
– otter's den LODGE, HOLT
– rise to the surface to breathe, as beavers and otters do VENT
out-and-out, thoroughgoing, notorious, as a knave is said to be ARRANT
out of- EC-, EX-, E-
out of control, with uncontrolled force HEADLONG
out of date, no longer in everyday use ANTIQUATED, ARCHAIC, OBSOLETE, OUTMODED, SUPERANNUATED
– replace something that is out of date or out of fashion SUPERSEDE
out of order, not working, in need of repair OUT OF KILTER, MALFUNCTIONING, KAPUT
out of place, inappropriate INOPPORTUNE, INAPPOSITE, MALAPROPOS
out-of-tune, harsh, or dissonant sound, as of a faulty violin or specially tuned piano WOLF
outbreak of a disease, civil unrest, or the like after a period of inactivity RECRUDESCENCE
outburst, as of anger, hatred, or violence ERUPTION
– outburst, sudden rush, flood SPATE
– outburst or uncontrollable display of rage, laughter, or the like PAROXYSM
outcast from society PARIAH, ISHMAEL, LEPER
outcome or final result, as of a play DÉNOUEMENT
outdated See **out of date**
outdoor bench, typically curved and made of stone or masonry EXEDRA
– outdoor meal, or entertainment, such as a picnic or garden party FÊTE CHAMPÊTRE
– outdoor skills such as hunting and fishing, mainly in the U.S. WOODCRAFT
– outdoors, in the open air, as a meal might be ALFRESCO
– outdoorsy, in the style of the British county gentry TWEEDY
outer covering, such as a seed's coat or an animal's skin INTEGUMENT
– outer layer of an organ, such as the brain or kidney CORTEX
– outer layer or covering, as of the brain PALLIUM
-outer space- -ASTR-
outermost part, the boundary area PERIPHERY
outgoing, friendly, lively person EXTROVERT
– outgoing or sociable, seeking or enjoying the company of others GREGARIOUS
outgrowth or swelling of an organ or other body part APOPHYSIS
outhouse, lavatory PRIVY
outing or short journey, often at a special low fare EXCURSION
outlaw, banish, or exile PROSCRIBE
– person who hunts outlaws or dangerous animals for a reward BOUNTY HUNTER
outlet, as for goods or troops DÉBOUCHÉ
– outlet, exit, means of escape VENT
outline See also **summary**
– outline, shape, form CONFIGURATION, CONTOUR, CONFORMATION, LINEAMENT
– outline, sketch, describe, or draw DELINEATE
– outline of the plot of a novel, play, or the like SCENARIO
– outline or sketch out something, such as a plan ADUMBRATE
– picture formed from shadows or outlines SCIAGRAM
– shadow image or filled-in outline, typically of solid black against a white background, as of a person's profile SILHOUETTE
outmoded See **old-fashioned**
outpouring of emotion in speech or writing EFFUSION
outrage, monstrous behaviour or deed ENORMITY
outrageous, unconventional, or provocative person ENFANT TERRIBLE
– outrageously bad EGREGIOUS
– outrageously indelicate or rude SCABROUS
– outrageously or glaringly wrong or evil FLAGRANT
outside and independent of the created universe, as God is, according to some views TRANSCENDENT
– outside angle of a wall QUOIN, COIGN
– coming from outside, of foreign or external origin EXTRANEOUS, EXOGENOUS, EXTRINSIC
outside- AB-, ECTO-, EXO-, EXTRA-, SUPER-
outsider, unorthodox thinker or group member MAVERICK
– sense or state of being an outsider, isolated from one's society ALIENATION
outskirts, as of a cathedral close or forest PURLIEUS
– outskirts or suburbs of a town ENVIRONS
outstanding See also **perfect**, **excellent**
– outstanding, excelling others TRANSCENDENT, SUPERLATIVE, PRE-EMINENT
– outstanding, striking, conspicuous, as an argument might be SALIENT
– outstanding dish, work of art, performance, or the like within a set or series of related items PIÈCE DE RÉSISTANCE, SHOWPIECE
– outstanding person or thing, a marvel HUMDINGER
– outstandingly able or beautiful person PARAGON, PHOENIX
outward – outward-moving or -growing CENTRIFUGAL
– outward-tending, especially away from the brain or spinal cord, as some nerves are EFFERENT, DEFERENT
– outward signs, symbolic decorations, or ornamental equipment, as of power TRAPPINGS
– push or jut outwards PROTRUDE
– turned outwards, as feet might be SPLAYED
oval, almond-shaped AMYGDALOID
ovary – ovaries or testes GONADS
– cavity in the ovary, containing an ovum FOLLICLE
– cell in the ovary that later develops into an ovum OOCYTE
– remove the ovaries from a bitch or other female animal SPAY
– small fluid-filled sac in the ovary, containing a developing egg cell GRAAFIAN FOLLICLE
ovary- OOPHOR-
oven or furnace for drying or hardening, as in a pottery KILN
– stove of a large iron make, usually burning coal or wood, with one or more ovens RANGE
over- EPI-, HYPER-, SUPER-, SUPRA-, SUR-, TRANS-
over-abundant See **excessive**
overalls combined with a workman's shirt, or a woman's fashion garment resembling this BOILER SUIT
– overalls or similar clothing for menial work in a military camp or barracks FATIGUES
– baby's garment or child's play suit resembling a pair of overalls ROMPERS
– ski trousers resembling a pair of overalls SALOPETTE
over-attentive, excessively eager to help or advise OFFICIOUS

overbearing, arrogant, as someone's confident manner might be IMPERIOUS, DOMINEERING, PEREMPTORY, OVERWEENING
overboard – throw overboard JETTISON
over-charging, demanding of an excessive price EXTORTION
overcome a difficulty or obstacle SURMOUNT
– impossible to overcome, as a barrier or obstacle might be INSUPERABLE, INSURMOUNTABLE
over-development of a body part or organ, caused by enlargement of cells HYPERTROPHY
overeat and become ill, as cattle might FOUNDER
– illness, often combined with anorexia nervosa, in which compulsive overeating is followed by bouts of self-induced vomiting BULIMIA, BULIMIA NERVOSA
over-elaborate, flowery, pretentious or fussy in style CHINTZY, CHICHI, PRECIOUS
overflow channel, as round the side of a dam SPILLWAY
– overflow or sudden surge in a stream, as after heavy rains FRESHET, SPATE
– overflowing, abounding, swarming TEEMING
overgrown area, thick with shrubs and undergrowth THICKET, BRAKE
over-indulge, surfeit SATIATE, SATE
– over-indulgence in sensual or immoral pursuits INTEMPERANCE, DEBAUCHERY, DISSIPATION, DEPRAVITY
overlap INTERSECT
– overlapping circles, used as a diagram to represent mathematical or logical relations VENN DIAGRAM
– overlapping in a regular pattern, as fish scales or roof tiles tend to IMBRICATE
– built with overlapping rather than edge-to-edge planks, as a ship or boat might be CLINKER-BUILT, LAPSTRAKE
overlook, tower above, look down on DOMINATE, COMMAND
overlord SUZERAIN
overly, excessively UNDULY
overmanning, employing more workers than needed, as to avoid redundancies FEATHERBEDDING
over-much See **excessive**
over-optimistic person POLLYANNA, MICAWBER, CANDIDE
over-precise, pedantic, or dogmatic SCHOLASTIC
over-reacting and seeking confrontation rather than compromise TRIGGER-HAPPY, GUNG-HO
over-refined, excessively rich or precious, as a literary style might be DECADENT
– over-refined, affected, over-elaborate RECHERCHÉ
overrun and inhabit in large numbers, as vermin might a garden or animal INFEST
over-satisfy, provide or gratify in excess PALL
over-sensitive, as to chafing or sunburn IRRITABLE
– over-sensitive, easily offended, touchy UMBRAGEOUS
overshadow, reduce from power or importance to obscurity ECLIPSE
over-simplified or given to over-simplifying REDUCTIONIST
over-subtle or devious arguing or reasoning SOPHISTRY, CASUISTRY, QUIBBLING, SCHOLASTICISM
over-used, and thereby deprived of its liveliness or force, as a phrase or idea might be CLICHÉD, TRITE, HACKNEYED, SHOPWORN, BANAL
– over-used, unoriginal, and predictable remark, phrase, or thought CLICHÉ, PLATITUDE, TRUISM, COMMONPLACE, BROMIDE
– over-used moral lesson, sermon, or proverb HOMILY
– over-used saying, slogan, or belief SHIBBOLETH
overwhelm or swamp, as with requests or work INUNDATE
overwhelming influence or activity, that seems to swallow up its participants VORTEX
ovum See **ovary**
own, or take pride or pleasure in owning something, such as an unusual name REJOICE IN
owned and controlled privately PROPRIETARY
owner with exclusive legal rights to something PROPRIETOR
ownership of land DOMAIN
– absolute ownership of inherited land, allowing the owner to dispose of it as he wishes FEE SIMPLE
– full and unrestricted ownership, of a house, flat, land, or the like FREEHOLD
– qualified ownership of inherited land, restricting its disposal to a specified heir or heirs FEE TAIL
ox – adjective for oxen BOVINE, TAURINE
– domesticated ox of Asia and Africa, with a hump and a large dewlap ZEBU
– encampment for ox-wagons OUTSPAN
– extinct ox, probably the forebear of today's domesticated cattle AUROCHS, URUS
– matching pair of oxen yoked or driven together SPAN
Oxford – Oxford Movement, or the doctrines of this Anglican high-church movement in the 19th century TRACTARIANISM
– Oxford University's commemoration ceremony ENCAENIA
– autumn, spring, and summer terms at Oxford University MICHAELMAS, HILARY, TRINITY
– feast, especially an annual university or college feast, as at Oxford GAUDY
– formal academic wear, especially at Oxford University SUBFUSC
– person born or living in Oxford OXONIAN
– technical term for pronunciation known as "Oxford English" RECEIVED PRONUNCIATION, RP
oxygen in the form O_3, used in bleaching OZONE
– oxygenate blood VENTILATE
– chemical removal of oxygen from a compound or adding of hydrogen to it REDUCTION
oyster, mussel, or similar hinged shellfish MOLLUSC, BIVALVE
– oyster bed or oyster spawn CULCH
– oyster larva SPAT
– large oyster-like shellfish providing mother-of-pearl ABALONE, ORMER
– savoury of oysters wrapped in bacon and served on toast ANGELS-ON-HORSEBACK
– shiny inner surface of the shell of an oyster or related shellfish, used for ornamentation MOTHER-OF-PEARL, NACRE

P

pace, rate, or speed TEMPO
pacify See also **calm**
- pacify, calm down, soothe someone's anger MOLLIFY, PLACATE, APPEASE, PROPITIATE
- pacify, end disputes between CONCILIATE, RECONCILE
- pacify, soothe, make pain or troubles easier to bear ALLAY, ALLEVIATE, PALLIATE

pack down or stamp down tightly tobacco, concrete, or the like by means of light blows TAMP
- pack of hounds CRY

packet – small, sealed packet, typically holding one portion of sugar, shampoo, or the like SACHET
packing and insulating material of a synthetic light white solid foam POLYSTYRENE
- packing, as between lengths of piping, machine parts, or the like, serving as a seal GASKET

pad, as of gauze, used to stop bleeding or to reduce pain or inflammation COMPRESS
padding, fabric, and springs used in making a soft covering for furniture UPHOLSTERY
- padding material used in former times BOMBAST
- silky plant fibre used for padding, soundproofing, and the like KAPOK
- wool or cotton waste used for padding furniture or mattresses FLOCK

paddle – blade of an oar or paddle PALM
- blade on a paddle wheel FLOAT

page or insert in a book or magazine that is larger than other pages and is folded to fit GATEFOLD, FOLDOUT
- page or page-size equal to half a large sheet of paper, or a book with such pages FOLIO
- page or page-size equal to a quarter of a large sheet of paper, or a book with such pages QUARTO
- page or page-size equal to an eighth of a large sheet of paper, or a book with such pages OCTAVO
- page width or column width in printing MEASURE
- arrange pages or sheets in the correct order COLLATE
- having the edges of the pages still unslit or untrimmed, as a book might UNCUT
- headline or title on every page or other page of a book or magazine RUNNING HEAD
- large page printed on one side with news, advertisements, or the like BROADSHEET
- leaf rapidly through files, the pages of a book, or the like RIFFLE
- left-hand page of a book, typically having an even number VERSO
- letter or number printed at the foot of some pages in a book, specifying the sequence for binding the sections SIGNATURE
- number the pages of PAGINATE
- pair of facing pages in a book, magazine, or newspaper, especially when the text or picture stretches across the fold SPREAD
- right-hand page of a book, typically having an odd number RECTO
- separate multiple copies, continuous stationery, or the like into individual pages or documents DECOLLATE
- set of four sheets of paper folded to produce 16 pages QUIRE
- set of printed pages, typically 16 or 32, folded from a single sheet, for binding with others to form a book SIGNATURE, GATHER
- white space between two postage stamps on a sheet, facing pages of a book, or the like GUTTER

-pages, number of pages from a folded sheet -MO
paid regularly or relating to a regular payment STIPENDIARY
pain, suffering, agony, anguish PURGATORY, TRAVAIL
- pain felt in a part of the body different from its place of origin REFERRED PAIN
- pain reliever that is a common alternative to aspirin PARACETAMOL
- pain-relieving or tranquillising substance secreted by the brain ENDORPHIN
- pain spasms shooting along the path of a nerve NEURALGIA
- painful, torturing, agonising EXCRUCIATING
- painful and difficult route or course of action VIA DOLOROSA
- painful experience, or the distress it causes WORMWOOD
- painful spasms, as on approaching death PANGS, THROES
- acute, sudden, or piercing, as a pain might be LANCINATING, FULGURATING, FULMINANT
- causing or suffering pain, distress, or sorrow DOLOROUS
- enduring pain and grief with unemotional resignation STOICAL
- insensitivity or loss of sensitivity to pain ANAESTHESIA, ANALGESIA
- intense, throbbing facial pain in the region of the fifth cranial nerve TRIGEMINAL NEURALGIA, TIC DOLOUREUX
- mildly painful, stinging TINGLING, SMARTING
- minimum level of intensity for registering or tolerating something, such as pain THRESHOLD
- person who enjoys inflicting pain, or is sexually aroused by it SADIST
- person who enjoys undergoing pain, or is sexually aroused by it MASOCHIST
- pull a face or flinch, as from pain WINCE
- relieve pain without getting rid of the cause ALLAY, ALLEVIATE, MITIGATE, PALLIATE
- relieving pain ANALGESIC, LENITIVE, ANODYNE
- sharp and repeated pains in the intestines GRIPES, COLIC

-pain- ALG-, -ALGIA, ALGO-
painful- DYS-
paint, draw, or engrave using dots or flecks STIPPLE
- paint, mist, or other dispersion of very fine particles in a consistent medium COLLOID
- paint containing a rubbery sap or gum to increase its smoothness and adhesive properties LATEX PAINT
- paint in which the colouring is contained in tiny oil droplets suspended in water EMULSION PAINT
- paint ingredient prepared from chalk WHITING
- paint-mixing board of an artist PALETTE
- paint or draw a picture of LIMN

– paint or similar substance that is applied as a sealer or undercoat PRIMER
– paint that dries to a hard, glossy finish ENAMEL
– paint thickly, hastily or crudely DAUB
– paint-thinner made of a thin resinous oil TURPENTINE
– becoming liquid when stirred or shaken, as certain paints and some other jelly-like substances do THIXOTROPIC
– blue paint-colouring made from the crushed particles of a special glass SMALT
– clay or natural earthy substance used as a colouring agent in paints, ink, and the like SIENNA, UMBER, OCHRE
– coloured powder mixed with oil or water to produce a paint PIGMENT
– drying substance added to paints, inks, some medicines, and the like SICCATIVE
– priming layer of varnish or paint, as in a painting COUCH
– producing a dull, unglossy finish, as some paints do MATT
– quick-drying semi-gloss paint based on a synthetic resin ACRYLIC PAINT
– substance added to paint, glue, or the like, as to thicken or dilute it EXTENDER
– thick paint-like sealer, filler, or glaze, as used for coating paper, cloth, or plastered walls SIZE
– water-based paint, including whitewash DISTEMPER

painting See chart, page 364
– painting in different shades of a single colour MONOCHROME, MONOTINT
– painting medium, such as oil, into which the pigments are mixed VEHICLE, BASE
– painting of a saint or holy person ICON
– painting of a very small yet detailed kind MINIATURE
– painting or sculpture of a person, as on a monument EFFIGY
– painting that is pretentious and vulgar KITSCH
– artistic or harmonious arrangement of parts, as in a painting COMPOSITION
– halo-like area of light that in medieval paintings surrounds a holy figure MANDORLA, AUREOLE, VESICA
– plaster of Paris preparation used as a painting surface GESSO
– represent in words or images, as by painting or describing DEPICT
– representation of a scene, painting, or the like by costumed actors who pose silent and motionless TABLEAU VIVANT
– representing a scene objectively as a painting might REALISTIC
– shortening of lines in drawing or painting a scene, for apparent depth or distance PERSPECTIVE, FORESHORTENING
– simplified, abstract, stylised, as a painting or design might be CONVENTIONALISED
– sketch or preliminary drawing, often full-size, for a tapestry, painting, mosaic, or the like CARTOON

pair of similar objects, such as partridges BRACE
– pair of similar things, or one of such a pair DOUBLET
– pair of words differing in only one small respect, helping to identify distinctive sounds or features of the language MINIMAL PAIR
– paired, as compound leaves might be JUGATE
– arrange or occur in pairs GEMINATE

pair- ZYG-, ZYGO-

palace of a sultan SERAGLIO
– adjective for a palace PALATIAL

pale, as through illness, shock, or anger, as someone's complexion might be PALLID, ASHEN, LIVID
– pale and weakened, as through fever or starvation, CADAVEROUS, ETIOLATED
– pale face, or pale-faced person WHEY-FACE
– pale from illness or unhappiness WAN
– pale in complexion, unhealthy-looking, sickly PEAKY, PEELIE-WALLY, PASTY
– pale yellowish in colour or complexion SALLOW
– cause to become white or pale BLANCH, BLEACH

palm See also **hand**
– palm leaf FROND
– palm of the hand, or fleshy base of the thumb THENAR
– palmistry, reading a person's life or future by examining the palm of his hand CHIROMANCY
– any of the seven fleshy pads on the palm of the hand MOUNT
– primitive seed-bearing plant shaped like a palm tree, but having fern-like leaves CYCAD
– relating to the palm of the hand or sole of the food VOLAR

pamphlet distributed by hand, handout HANDBILL
– pamphlet or booklet on some specialist subject MONOGRAPH
– pamphlets, handouts, and other short-lived topical publications EPHEMERA

pan See **cooking utensils**
– pan or small metal cup PANNIKIN

Pan – rural deity in classical mythology, resembling the god Pan, part man and part goat FAUN, SATYR

pancake – pancakes of a savoury Russian style, made of buckwheat flour and typically served with caviar or sour cream BLINI
– flat, round pancake, sometimes containing dried fruit BANNOCK
– thin pancake often folded round a filling CREPE

panel – panelling or facing, typically of wood, fixed to the walls of a room WAINSCOTING, DADO
– pair of painted or carved panels hinged together, as for an altarpiece DIPTYCH
– set of three painted or carved panels hinged together, as for an altarpiece TRIPTYCH

panic-stricken headlong rush, as of horses or a crowd of people STAMPEDE

panpipe SYRINX

pantomime featuring the clown Harlequin HARLEQUINADE

pantry or wine cellar BUTTERY

pants See **clothes**

papacy, papal government or authority VATICAN

papal See also **Pope**
– papal, relating to the Pope considered as the successor of St Peter PETRINE
– papal ambassador NUNCIO
– papal delegate or representative LEGATE, EMISSARY
– papal court and administration of the Roman Catholic Church CURIA
– papal document or letter, in antique handwriting BULL
– papal inability to err in doctrinal matters concerning faith and morals INFALLIBILITY
– papal letter of instructions or judgment, in modern handwriting BRIEF
– papal letter or edict on a point of church law or doctrine DECRETAL
– papal letter sent to bishops in all countries ENCYCLICAL
– papal treasurer, cardinal who handles the Pope's financial affairs CAMERLINGO
– favouring a policy of centralised and absolute papal authority in the Roman Catholic Church ULTRAMONTANE
– favouring a policy of decentralised authority in the Roman Catholic Church, restricting

papal power in the various branches of the church CISALPINE, GALLICAN

paper See chart

– paper fragments thrown at festive occasions, especially weddings CONFETTI

– paper frill adorning the end of a chop or cutlet PAPILLOTE

– paper impregnated with a purple chemical that turns red in acid solutions and blue in alkaline solutions, used as an acid-base indicator LITMUS PAPER

– paper in a continuous roll, for use in a rotary printing press WEB

– paper-like transparent wrapping material CELLOPHANE

– paper made in ancient times from a reed-like plant PAPYRUS

– paper pulp or moistened paper used in moulding PAPIER-MÂCHÉ

– paper screen used in a Japanese house SHOJI

– paper trimmer, or frame for the pulp used in handmade paper DECKLE

– paper-trimming device consisting of a long blade hinged to a frame GUILLOTINE

– paper used to protect areas or edges during painting MASKING PAPER

– cheap paper made from wood pulp or recycled paper, used for newspapers NEWSPRINT

– continuous strip of paper such as that on which stock-exchange reports used to be printed TICKER TAPE

– crinkled tissue paper used for decorations CREPE PAPER

– drying board, blanket, or roller used in papermaking COUCH

– fine quality paper resembling

PAINTING AND RELATED ARTS TERMS

abstract	referring to a style that relies on pure form for its effect, rather than attempting to represent any object
aquarelle	painting made using transparent watercolours
aquatint	etching process producing tonal effects
chiaroscuro	arrangement of strongly contrasting light and shade in a painting
collage	picture composed of a variety of materials pasted onto a surface
craquelure	network of small cracks in the paint or varnish of an old painting
diptych	altarpiece of two panels
fête champêtre, fête galante	18th-century French painting of figures in a pleasant, rural setting
figurative	referring to a style, as of painting, that represents humans, animals or objects, rather than relying purely on abstract forms
fresco	painting on fresh plaster on a wall or ceiling
frieze	decorative horizontal band, as along the top of a wall
frottage	technique of making images by rubbing a soft pencil over paper on a textured surface
genre painting	painting of a scene from everyday life, as in the 17th-century Dutch school
gouache	painting technique using opaque watercolours bound with gum
grisaille	painting in tones of grey, usually striving for an effect of a sculpture or relief
grotesque	decoration combining animal, human, and plant forms
impasto	thick, opaque surface paint in oil painting
mezzotint	engraving process producing tonal effects
minimal art	abstract style using geometric shapes and primary colours
montage	picture composed of a number of individual pictures
mural	painting on a wall or ceiling
Op Art	modern art form using optical illusions to create the impression of movement
pastel	drawing or sketch in delicate colours made by using a chalky crayon
pastoral	painting that portrays rural life, often in an idealised way
paysage	landscape, rural scene
pentimento	reappearance through a painting of traces of an earlier painting from beneath
pieta	representation of the Virgin Mary mourning over the body of Jesus
pointillism	painting technique using closely spaced dots of primary colours
putto	representation of a small boy or angel
secco	painting on dry plaster on a wall or ceiling
sgraffito	design, as on pottery or a wall, scratched through a thin surface layer to reveal the colour beneath
still life	representation of inanimate objects, such as fruit and flowers
tempera	paint made of colour mixed with a substance such as egg white and water
tondo	circular painting, cameo, or medallion
triptych	altarpiece of three panels
trompe l'oeil	technique or style of painting in which a trick effect of three-dimensional reality is produced

PAPER SIZES	
atlas	34 × 26 inches (864 × 660 mm)
crown	20 × 15 inches (508 × 381 mm)
demy	$22\frac{1}{2}$ × $17\frac{1}{2}$ inches (572 × 444 mm)
elephant	28 × 23 inches (711 × 584 mm)
foolscap	17 × $13\frac{1}{2}$ inches (431 × 343 mm)
imperial	30 × 22 inches (762 × 559 mm)
medium	23 × 18 inches (584 × 457 mm)
royal	25 × 20 inches (635 × 508 mm)

thin goatskin VELLUM
– emboss paper with a pattern GOFFER
– file or collection of papers giving information on a particular person or subject DOSSIER
– front side of a sheet of paper, such as the side of a letter that is to be read first RECTO
– give a glossy finish to paper, as by pressing it in rollers PLATE
– grainy or crinkled surface, as on leather or paper PEBBLE
– headed writing paper, or the heading on it LETTERHEAD
– identifying mark impressed faintly on to paper, visible when help up to the light WATERMARK
– large sheet of paper printed on one side with news, advertisements, or the like BROADSHEET
– page or page-size equal to half a large sheet of paper, or a book with such pages FOLIO
– page or page-size equal to quarter of a large sheet of paper, or a book with such pages QUARTO
– page or page-size equal to an eighth of a large sheet of paper, or a book with such pages OCTAVO
– process discarded glass, paper, water, and the like for re-use RECYCLE
– quantity of paper, usually 500 sheets REAM
– quantity of paper, usually 24 or 25 sheets QUIRE
– raised in relief, as words or symbols on specially pressed paper or metal may be EMBOSSED
– reverse side of a sheet of paper, such as the side of a letter that is to be read second VERSO
– rough edge of a sheet of paper, especially handmade paper DECKLE EDGE
– smooth, buff-coloured paper, used for envelopes MANILA PAPER, MANILA
– smooth, heavy paper as used for drawings CARTRIDGE PAPER
– stiff paper resembling thin goatskin PARCHMENT
– strong, brown wrapping paper made from wood pulp treated with sulphate KRAFT
– strong white paper used especially for writing and typing BOND PAPER
– technique of decorating with paper cutouts DÉCOUPAGE
– thin, edible paper used in baking RICE PAPER
– thin paper typically used for carbon copies FLIMSY, BANK
– thin, tough opaque printing paper BIBLE PAPER, INDIA PAPER
– vegetable matter used in making paper, rayon, and photographic film CELLULOSE
– wood-fibre mixture used in making paper PULP

paper-folding as an art or hobby of Japanese origin ORIGAMI, KIRIGAMI

parachute used to slow down an aircraft or spacecraft, or to drag out the main parachute DROGUE PARACHUTE
– parachuting as a sport SKYDIVING
– cord attaching a parachute pack to the aircraft to open the parachute automatically once the jumper is clear STATIC LINE
– cord pulled by a parachute jumper to open the parachute RIPCORD
– ropes or cords connecting the canopy of a parachute to the jumper's harness SHROUDS
– set of straps attaching a parachute to the body HARNESS
– silk or nylon hemisphere forming the main part of a parachute CANOPY
– system of ropes or cords on a parachute, hot-air balloon, or the like RIGGING

parade, such as a ceremonial procession of horses or cars CAVALCADE
– parade and carnival held on Shrove Tuesday MARDI GRAS
– parade ground in India and southeast Asia MAIDAN
– parade or costumed procession in a festival PAGEANT
– parade or exhibit in an ostentatious, showy or vulgar way FLAUNT
– parade or procession of cars or other motor vehicles MOTORCADE
– parading of a flag along the ranks in a military ceremony TROOPING THE COLOUR
– ceremonial parade or procession, especially a funeral procession CORTÈGE
– welcoming parade in which paper strips are thrown jubilantly down from the buildings lining the streets TICKER-TAPE PARADE

-parade -CADE

paradise – paradise-like abode of heroes and virtuous people after death in Arthurian or Celtic mythology AVALON
– paradise-like abode of heroes and virtuous people after death in Greek mythology HESPERIDES, ISLANDS OF THE BLESSED
– paradise-like abode of the blessed after death in Greek mythology ELYSIUM, ELYSIAN FIELDS
– paradise-like hall in Norse mythology, where slain heroic warriors dwell after death VALHALLA
– paradise-like imaginary place of simple and contented country life ARCADIA
– paradise-like place in American Indian folklore HAPPY HUNTING-GROUNDS
– paradise on earth, or idyllic place, especially when purely imaginary SHANGRI-LA, UTOPIA
– nymph or virgin attending the blessed in paradise, according to Islamic belief or folklore HOURI

paradox, contradiction between two equally plausible statements ANTINOMY

paraffin – U.S. term for paraffin KEROSENE

paragraph – set in a paragraph from the margin INDENT

parallel, running side by side COLLATERAL

paralyse IMMOBILISE
– paralyse or pierce with a spear, one's gaze, or the like TRANSFIX, IMPALE
– paralyse or stupefy, as with fear GORGONISE, PETRIFY
– device that allows paralysed patients to type, phone, or the like by blowing through a tube POSSUM

paralysis PALSY, PARESIS
– paralysis from the neck down QUADRIPLEGIA, TETRAPLEGIA
– paralysis from the waist down PARAPLEGIA
– paralysis-like condition together with reduced consciousness, as occurs in schizophrenia and the

like CATALEPSY, CATATONIA
- paralysis of a single limb or group of muscles MONOPLEGIA
- paralysis of one side of the body HEMIPLEGIA
- paralysis of the jaw muscles LOCKJAW, TETANUS, TRISMUS

-paralysis -PLEGIA

paraplegia – paralysis from the neck down, rather than from the waist down as in paraplegia QUADRIPLEGIA, TETRAPLEGIA

parasite, person who takes advantage of another LEECH, SPONGER
- parasitic flatworm such as the fluke TREMATODE
- parasitic worm such as the tapeworm HELMINTH
- intestinal parasite causing dysentery AMOEBA
- inhabit in large numbers, as parasites might their hosts INFEST

parcels – person delivering messages, parcels, smuggled drugs, or the like on behalf of another COURIER

parchment of calfskin, lambskin, or kidskin, as used in bookbinding VELLUM
- parchment or manuscript with one or more earlier layers of text still visible PALIMPSEST

pardon See also **excuse**, **forgive**
- pardon, as of prisoners, granted by a government AMNESTY
- pardon, or declare not guilty ACQUIT
- pardon or release from punishment ABSOLVE, ASSOIL, REMIT
- pardon or overlook an offence readily CONDONE
- corrupt buying and selling of church offices, relics, pardons, and the like SIMONY
- hear the confession of and give a pardon to SHRIVE

pardonable, easily excused or forgiven VENIAL

parent – parent or forbear PROGENITOR
- father, be the parent of BEGET, SIRE
- murder of one's parent or other close relative PARRICIDE
- in place of or with the responsibilities of parents, as a headmaster might be IN LOCO PARENTIS
- influenced by or derived from one's parents HEREDITARY

Paris stock exchange BOURSE
- Parisian borough or administrative district ARRONDISSEMENT

parish meeting of the administrative committee or congregants VESTRY
- relating to a parish PAROCHIAL

parking – post on a traffic island, on a pavement to prevent parking, or the like BOLLARD

parliament See chart, and also **MP**, **government**
- parliament or similar lawmaking body or assembly LEGISLATURE
- parliament without a majority party HUNG PARLIAMENT
- box on a table in the British parliament at which ministers or shadow ministers stand when making a speech DISPATCH BOX
- chairman controlling the debate in a parliament, a similar legislative body, or the like SPEAKER

PARLIAMENTS

Alderney	**States of Alderney**
Austria	**Bundesversammlung**
Bulgaria	**Narodna Subranie**
Denmark	**Folketing**
Ethiopia	**Shergo**
Finland	**Eduskunta**
Greenland	**Landstraad**
Guernsey	**States of Deliberation**
Iceland	**Althing**
India	**Rajya Sabha and Lok Sabha**
Iran	**Majlis**
Ireland	**Oireachtas**
Isle of Man	**Court of Tynwald**
Israel	**Knesset**
Japan	**Diet**
Jersey	**States of Jersey**
Mongolia	**Khural**
Nepal	**National Panchayat**
Netherlands	**Staten-Generaal**
Norway	**Storting**
Sark	**Court of Chief Pleas**
Spain	**Cortes**
Sweden	**Riksdag**
Switzerland	**Bundesversammlung**
West Germany	**Deutscher bundestag**

- close at the end of a session, as the courts and parliament do ADJOURN
- discontinue parliament or a similar body, without actually dissolving it PROROGUE
- end and dismiss a meeting, parliament, or the like DISSOLVE
- ending of a debate, as in parliament, and the immediate voting on the motion CLOSURE, CLOTURE
- having only one chamber or house, as many parliaments have UNICAMERAL
- having two chambers or houses, as many parliaments or legislative bodies have BICAMERAL
- meeting or series of meetings of parliament or a court, or the period during which meetings are held SESSION
- method of limiting a debate in parliament by the imposition of time limits beforehand GUILLOTINE
- obstruct parliamentary proceedings deliberately, as by rambling debate STONEWALL, FILIBUSTER, TALK OUT
- official doorkeeper in a court of law, parliament, or the like USHER
- official who maintains order in a court of law, parliament, or the like SERJEANT-AT-ARMS
- presentation of a bill to parliament at the various stages of its passage READING
- question a minister, in some European parliaments, on a point of policy INTERPELLATE
- representative assembly or lower chamber of the Irish parliament DAIL
- speech read at the opening of parliament in Commonwealth countries, by the Queen, governor, or the like SPEECH FROM THE THRONE, GRACIOUS SPEECH
- seating in parliament for government or opposition MPs who are not ministers or shadow ministers BACKBENCHES
- seating in parliament for neutral or independent MPs, committed neither to the government nor to the opposition CROSSBENCHES
- temporary ending of business, as between court sessions or during the parliamentary holiday RECESS
- transcript or report of British parliamentary debates HANSARD
- unrepresentative parliament that occurs after most of its members have left, died, or been driven out RUMP
- vote by separating into two groups, as in parliament DIVIDE

parody, imitation or representation

that is crudely distorted TRAVESTY, CARICATURE
- parody of the style of an artistic work PASTICHE
- mocking parody or satire SPOOF, LAMPOON, BURLESQUE

parrot – adjective for a parrot PSITTACINE
- virus disease in parrots, producing a pneumonia-like fever in humans PSITTACOSIS

part, subdivision, offshoot, or branch RAMIFICATION
- part attached as an accessory, as to a machine FITMENT
- part cut from a whole, especially that bounded by a chord of a circle SEGMENT
- part into which an area, building, train, or the like is divided COMPARTMENT
- part of a book, TV drama, or the like EPISODE, INSTALMENT
- part of a group within a conference, military force, or the like CONTINGENT, DETACHMENT
- part of a whole, element, or section CONSTITUENT, COMPONENT, INGREDIENT
- part or division, especially that bounded by two radii of a circle SECTOR
- part or portion, especially a half MOIETY
- part or side of an issue, argument, or the like FACET, FACTOR
- part viewed as a fraction of a whole PROPORTION, PERCENTAGE
- break down into small or basic parts, analyse DECOMPOSE, DISINTEGRATE, DECONSTRUCT
- combining of parts or elements to form a whole SYNTHESIS
- corresponding or complementary part COUNTERPART
- distinct stage in the course of an extended process PHASE
- having a uniform structure or similar parts, aspects, or elements throughout HOMOGENEOUS
- having dissimilar parts, aspects, or elements HETEROGENEOUS
- having many and varied aspects or parts MULTIFARIOUS
- having or divided into two parts BIPARTITE
- made up of several parts, compound COMPOSITE
- referring to equal parts, especially when they jointly make up the whole ALIQUOT
- small part, fraction MODICUM
- small part or shred of a conversation, book, or the like SNIPPET
- something that is good in parts, but really of poor quality overall CURATE'S EGG

-part- -MERE, -MER-, -OME, HYPO-, MERO-

part and parcel, inseparable, vital, forming an essential part INTEGRAL, INTRINSIC, INHERENT

part of speech FORM CLASS, WORD CLASS

part song – unaccompanied secular song or part song, developed in Renaissance Italy MADRIGAL

participle incorrectly or inadequately connected to the word it modifies MISRELATED PARTICIPLE, DANGLING PARTICIPLE, HANGING PARTICIPLE

particle See also **subatomic particle**
- particle, pellet, small grain GRANULE
- particle of the smallest possible size, as of energy, in physics QUANTUM
- suspension of particles, as in smog or a colloid DISPERSION
- tiny particle, such as a droplet or electron CORPUSCLE

particular, definite, individual SPECIFIC

parting shot, clinching argument, or hostile remark made when leaving PARTHIAN SHOT

partition dividing up a ship, aircraft, or spacecraft BULKHEAD

partly- QUASI-, SEMI-

partner, comrade, companion COMPEER, YOKEFELLOW
- partner, especially the spouse of a monarch CONSORT
- partner, helper, especially a spouse HELPMATE, HELPMEET
- partner, helper, or fellow worker ASSOCIATE, COLLABORATOR, COLLEAGUE, CONFRERE, CONSOCIATE
- partner, member of a group of fellow students, sportsmen, workers, or the like STABLEMATE
- partner in a friendly contest, rival SPARRING PARTNER
- partner or follower, often one who is willing to do the "dirty business" COHORT, HENCHMAN, SIDEKICK, CRONY
- partner or helper, usually in a dubious enterprise ACCESSORY, ACCOMPLICE, CONFEDERATE
- temporary partner, associate, or companion BEDFELLOW

partner- CO-

partnership – collaborating, in partnership with, especially in some dubious enterprise IN CAHOOTS, COLLUDING

partridges – pair of similar objects, such as partridges BRACE
- small flock or family of partridges COVEY

party See also **celebration**, **political**
- party, banquet, or outing JUNKET
- party attended by men only, typically one held just before the organiser's wedding STAG PARTY
- party or excursion for women only HEN PARTY
- party or festivity that is drunken and noisy, or a reveller at such an event BACCHANAL
- party or gathering for a special occasion, as after a wedding or to welcome visitors RECEPTION
- party or gathering for discussion of the arts SALON, CONVERSAZIONE
- party where gifts are given to a bride-to-be in the U.S. SHOWER
- party with dancing at tea-time in the afternoon THÉ DANSANT
- annual dinner or party provided by a company for its employees BEANFEAST
- formal evening party, often with musical or literary entertainments SOIRÉE
- formal royal reception or party LEVÉE
- move about from person to person, as at a party CIRCULATE
- noisy party or wild celebration SHINDIG, CORROBOREE
- outdoor party or picnic of various kinds BURGOO, CLAMBAKE, COOKOUT, BRAAIVLEIS, FÊTE CHAMPÊTRE
- personally involved or affected, as parties in a dispute would be INTERESTED
- traditional Irish or Scottish party with dances, music, and the like CEILIDH

pass, ooze, or seep slowly through or as if through a filtering substance PERCOLATE, PERMEATE
- pass allowing entry to a specific area LAISSEZ-PASSER
- pass between two mountain peaks COL
- pass beyond or rise above the limits of TRANSCEND
- pass on property, especially land or buildings, by a will DEVISE
- pass on something from one person or point to another RELAY
- passing of the soul into another body after death TRANSMIGRATION, METEMPSYCHOSIS
- passing on of rights or duties, as to a substitute or successor DEVOLUTION
- passing through or across TRANSIT
- passing through, staying only temporarily, as a farmworker or bird might be TRANSIENT
- gain possession of the ball by cutting off a pass, as in soccer or hockey INTERCEPT

passage copied from a text, speech, or the like, as for separate publi-

cation EXTRACT, EXCERPT
– passage of writing that is more striking, elaborate or extravagant than the surrounding text PURPLE PATCH, PURPLE PASSAGE
– passage or extract from a text GOBBET, SNIPPET

passageway, roofed but often without walls, between two buildings BREEZEWAY
– passageway, typically lined with shops, as through a building ARCADE
– passageway to a bank of seats in a stadium or amphitheatre, as in the Colosseum in Rome VOMITORY
– dialect term for a passageway or alley between buildings GINNEL, SNICKET, WYND
– network of hedged or walled passageways in a puzzling pattern MAZE, LABYRINTH
– public passageway or right of passage from one point to another THOROUGHFARE

passenger list MANIFEST

passion, poetic emotion or eloquence, especially among the Welsh HWYL
– passion, typically foolish and short-lived, especially for another person INFATUATION
– passion or burning enthusiasm ARDOUR, RAPTURE, FERVOUR
– not returned or reciprocated, as a person's love or passion for another might be UNREQUITED

passionate, fiery, intense, or emphatic VEHEMENT
– passionate, rabble-rousing orator FIREBRAND, DEMAGOGUE, INCENDIARY
– passionate, stormy, chaotic, as a love affair might be TEMPESTUOUS, TURBULENT, TUMULTUOUS
– passionate and energetic in a creative way DIONYSIAC
– passionate and volatile, easily angered INFLAMMABLE
– passionate choral hymn and dance in ancient Greece, in honour of Dionysus DITHYRAMB
– passionate speech of denunciation TIRADE, DIATRIBE
– passionately angry, infuriated INCENSED
– passionately enthusiastic and zealous in promoting a cause EVANGELISTIC
– passionately enthusiastic or devoted AVID, ARDENT, FERVENT, PERFERVID, IMPASSIONED
– passionately enthusiastic or devoted, to an extreme or excessive and irrational degree FANATICAL, RABID
– passionately enthusiastic or highly delighted ECSTATIC, RHAPSODIC
– passionately in love, though usually only temporarily INFATUATED, BESOTTED

passive, slack, weak-willed SUPINE
– passive resistance, as initiated by Gandhi in India, to press for political reform SATYAGRAHA

Passover PESACH
– Passover feast SEDER
– adjective for Easter or the Passover PASCHAL
– book read at the Passover feast, relating the story of the Exodus HAGGADAH
– flat, crisp bread, eaten by Jews during Passover MATZO
– made of dough without yeast or other fermentation agent, as Passover bread is UNLEAVENED

passport allowing entry to a specific area LAISSEZ-PASSER

password COUNTERSIGN
– password, catchphrase, slogan, or the like that distinguishes a group from others SHIBBOLETH
– password used for identification or recognition among members of a group WATCHWORD

past, early life, or background of a person ANTECEDENTS
– applying to the past, or taking effect as from a date in the past, as a law might RETROACTIVE, RETROSPECTIVE
– calculation of the dates of past events, or ordering of events according to their dates, or a list of such events CHRONOLOGY
– looking back on the past, with hindsight IN RETROSPECT
– scene or passage in a novel, film, or the like that interrupts the main story line to revert to past events FLASHBACK
– something handed down from the past LEGACY, HERITAGE

past perfect tense of a verb, as in *had climbed* PLUPERFECT

pasta See illustration
– pasta in the form of long narrow ribbons FETTUCINE
– pasta in the form of long, thin, flat strands LINGUINI
– pasta in the form of short ribbed noodles, hollow and often slightly curved RIGATONI
– containing or relating to pasta FARINACEOUS
– firm and chewy through being lightly cooked, as pasta might be AL DENTE

paste, semi-solid mixture MAGMA
– art form or work in which many pieces of fabric, cloth, or the like are pasted on a surface COLLAGE
– patchwork, embroidery, or similar decoration consisting of different materials pasted or sewn together APPLIQUÉ

pastille of a medicinal substance, for chewing or sucking TROCHE, LOZENGE

pastry See also **cake, dessert**
– pastry case, filled with a savoury mixture and served hot as an hors d'oeuvre or snack BOUCHÉE
– pastry made with eggs, of a very light consistency, as used for éclairs CHOUX PASTRY
– pastry or pastries PATISSERIE
– pastry shell filled with a savoury mixture of fish, mushrooms, or the like in thick sauce VOL-AU-VENT
– pastry strip sealing the edge of a pie crust LUTING
– crescent or other small ornamental piece of puff pastry used as a garnish in cooking FLEURON
– fat, such as butter or lard, as used to make crumbly biscuits or flaky pastry SHORTENING
– light pastry in paper-thin layers, as in some Greek sweet and savoury dishes FILO
– pinch the edges of pastry for a fluted appearance CRIMP

patch of colour on an animal's coat FLASH
– brown or grey with darker streaks or patches, as a dog, cat, or cow might be BRINDLED
– marked with black and white patches, as some horses are PIEBALD, PINTO
– marked with patches of different colours PIED
– marked with white, grey, brown, or reddish patches, as some horses are SKEWBALD

patchwork, embroidery, or similar decoration consisting of different materials pasted or sewn together APPLIQUÉ

paté TERRINE

patent medicine, especially one boasting of secret ingredients NOSTRUM

path along a canal or river, as still sometimes used by horses pulling boats TOWPATH
– path or promenade made of wooden planks, as beside a beach BOARDWALK
– path or road from one point to another THOROUGHFARE
– path or strip, such as that left behind by a scythe or mower SWATH
– pathway used for horse-riding BRIDLEPATH
– curved flight path of a missile, ball, or the like TRAJECTORY
– dialect term for a path or alley

pasta

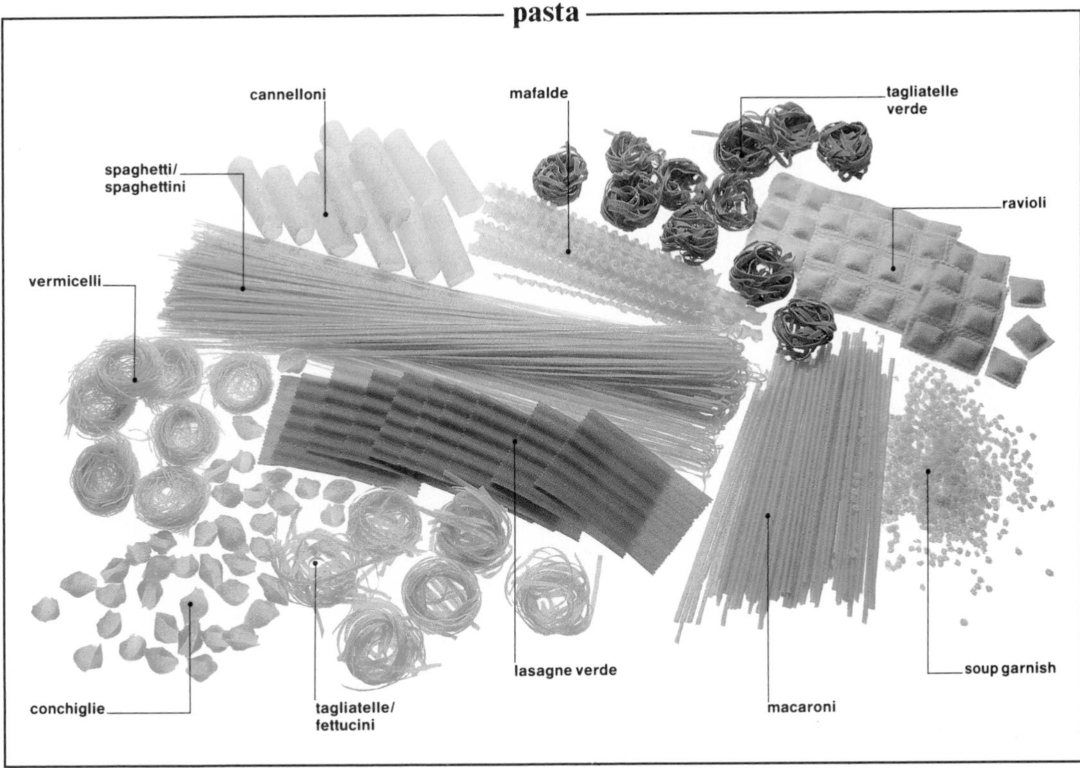

between buildings or fences SNICKET, GINNEL, WYND
- narrow pathway or platform, as along the side of a bridge CATWALK
- paved footpath CAUSEWAY

pathfinder TRAILBLAZER

patience – U.S. name for any patience card game SOLITAIRE

patient, calm and uncomplaining in the face of provocation LONG-SUFFERING, FORBEARING
- patient receiving blood, tissue, a transplanted organ, or the like from a donor RECIPIENT, DONEE
- patient's full case history or medical records ANAMNESIS
- relating to the direct treatment of patients, as in the practical section of medical training CLINICAL
- restraining garment with long sleeves for binding the arms of a violent patient or prisoner STRAITJACKET

patriot of an extreme or uncritical kind CHAUVINIST, JINGO, JINGOIST
- patriotism of a narrow, militant, fanatical kind CHAUVINISM, JINGOISM

patron or sponsor of artists, writers, and the like MAECENAS
- person whose welfare is protected or career advanced by an influential patron PROTÉGÉ

patronising system of government or authority, typically generous and concerned but restricting individual responsibility PATERNALISM

patter, long-winded or slick sales talk or attempt at persuasion SPIEL

pattern See also **design**
- pattern, mould, plate, or similar guide, as in woodwork, for making or reproducing something accurately TEMPLATE
- pattern, routine, or way of operating REGIMEN
- pattern, structure, or framework, as of an argument SCHEMA
- pattern of coloured lines forming squares against a plain background TATTERSALL
- pattern of complicated curved shapes, as on colourful woollen shawls PAISLEY
- pattern of draped or curved strings of leaves, ribbons, or the like FESTOON
- pattern of elements forming an identifiable problem, undesirable condition, behaviour disorder, or the like SYNDROME
- pattern of four leaves or petals, as in heraldry or tracery QUATREFOIL
- pattern of inlaid work, as used in decorating furniture MARQUETRY
- pattern made of multicoloured diamond-shaped areas, as used in knitting ARGYLE
- pattern of overlapping edges, as of roof tiles or fish scales IMBRICATION
- pattern of slanted parallel lines in alternating rows HERRINGBONE
- pattern of superimposed letters, as for making an emblem MONOGRAM, CIPHER
- pattern or arrangement of parts CONFIGURATION, CONFORMATION
- pattern or cycle of one's mental, physical, or emotional condition BIORHYTHM
- pattern or design of three curved or bent branches radiating from a centre TRISKELION
- pattern or design on metal, raised in relief by hammering REPOUSSÉ
- pattern or direction of the fibres in wood, meat, muscle or the like GRAIN
- pattern or distinctive quality of a piece of music, historical period, or the like TEXTURE, ETHOS
- pattern or model on which other versions or copies are based BLUEPRINT, ARCHETYPE, PROTOTYPE
- pattern or symbol, as on a flag or in embroidery DEVICE
- pattern produced by superimpos-

ing one design on another MOIRÉ PATTERN
– patterned fabric produced by shielding various areas with wax before the dyeing stage BATIK
– patterning or artistic arrangement of the elements in a poem, painting, building plan, or the like ORDONNANCE
– complex multicoloured pattern of geometrical shapes, as used in knitting FAIR ISLE
– complex pattern of interlaced leaves, flowers, or geometrical shapes ARABESQUE
– example or model serving as a standard or pattern for others PARADIGM, TOUCHSTONE
– leaf-pattern in architecture, as engraved on Corinthian columns ACANTHUS
– make a design or pattern by embedding decorative pieces in a surface INLAY
– ornamental pattern of interlaced lines or repeated geometrical shapes within a band, as on wall decorations or mouldings FRET, MEANDER
– repeated shape or theme in a pattern, composition, or the like MOTIF
– traditional Chinese blue-on-white design, as on a patterned china plate WILLOW PATTERN

-patterned -TACTIC

pause, interval, temporary stop, as between acts of a play INTERMISSION
– pause, rest, or postponement, typically in the middle of something unpleasant RESPITE
– pause in a line of verse, especially at a natural sense division CAESURA
– pause or break in proceedings or continuity HIATUS
– pause or discontinuity, specifically between two successive reigns, or governments INTERREGNUM
– pause or interval in the sessions of a committee, court, or the like RECESS, ADJOURNMENT

paved footpath CAUSEWAY
– paved outdoor area adjoining a house PATIO

pavement – canvas canopy over the pavement, marking the entrance to a theatre, club, or the like in the U.S. MARQUEE
– glass tile or disc set in a pavement, deck, or the like to admit light BULL'S-EYE

paving block of wood or stone, as formerly used in roadmaking SETT
– paving brick CLINKER
– paving stone FLAGSTONE

pawn – in pawn IN HOCK
– pawned item PLEDGE
– recover or regain something, such as pawned goods, by payment REDEEM

pay, meet the costs or expenses DEFRAY
– pay back REIMBURSE
– pay off a debt or mortgage by instalments AMORTISE
– pay or give what is due RENDER
– pay out, as from a fund DISBURSE
– pay supplementing a salary as a cost-of-living allowance in an expensive area such as London WEIGHTING
– difference in rates of pay for different types of work DIFFERENTIAL
– money paid by an employer as a compensation to an employee who has lost his job SEVERANCE PAY, REDUNDANCY PAY
– ridiculously small or inadequate, as a pay offer might be DERISORY

payment, as made initially to a barrister, or regularly to an occasional consultant RETAINER
– payment, as of dividends or a pension, made once a year ANNUITY
– payment, gift, or other expression of respect, submission, or the like TRIBUTE
– payment, such as an allowance or salary, that is received regularly STIPEND
– payment, usually small, for a service that is technically free HONORARIUM
– payment made in an illicit or underhand way to secure a favour BACKHANDER
– payment made periodically by a divorced person to an ex-spouse MAINTENANCE, ALIMONY
– payment made to a salesman or agent for successfully completed services COMMISSION
– payment made to workers to encourage increased production INCENTIVE, BONUS
– payment or gift in return for a service or favour CONSIDERATION, RECOMPENSE, REMUNERATION
– payment or maintenance settlement made to a lover after separation PALIMONY
– payment or order for an advance purchase, as of concert tickets or issues of a magazine over a specified period of time SUBSCRIPTION
– payment or profit from one's job or office EMOLUMENT
– payment or reward GUERDON
– based on personal decision rather than on regulations, as powers or payments might be DISCRETIONARY
– extra payment made to a barrister during a long legal case REFRESHER
– force payment, tribute, or the like EXACT, EXTORT
– given as a favour rather than out of legal obligation, as a payment might be EX GRATIA
– make amends for a loss or injury, as by a payment COMPENSATE
– reduce or revise a debt, payment, or the like COMMUTE
– return of part of the payment made REBATE
– something, especially money, that is offered as payment TENDER
– system of making wage payments in goods or vouchers rather than cash TRUCK SYSTEM
– without constraint and without payment VOLUNTARY

pea, bean, or related pod-bearing plant LEGUME
– pea-like pickled bud with a pungent flavour used as a condiment CAPER
– small tender green peas PETIT POIS

peace agreement PACT, TREATY
– peace agreement and informal decision to cooperate, as between two countries ENTENTE CORDIALE
– peace established temporarily, agreed suspension of hostilities TRUCE, ARMISTICE
– peace of mind, emotional tranquillity EQUANIMITY, ATARAXIA
– peace or harmony CONCORD
– "peace", "truce", used as an immunity or exemption call, as in children's games PAX, FAINITES, BARLEY, SCRIBS, CREE, SKINCH
– "peace to", "with deference to", used to acknowledge someone when disagreeing with his opinion PACE
– peaceful relations, friendship, especially between countries AMITY
– policy of agreeing to the demands of a potential enemy for the sake of maintaining peace APPEASEMENT
– politician or adviser favouring aggression rather than peace HAWK
– politician or adviser favouring peace DOVE
– promoting peace, reducing conflict IRENIC, PACIFIC, PLACATORY, CONCILIATORY
– resumption of or the approach towards peaceful relations, as between two countries or nations RAPPROCHEMENT, DETENTE

peace pipe CALUMET

peaceful See **calm**

peach or related fruit whose stone or pip tends to cling to the flesh CLINGSTONE
– peach or related fruit whose stone or pip tends to separate easily from the flesh FREESTONE

peacock – eye-like marking, as on a peacock's tail OCELLUS
– flock of peacocks or peafowl MUSTER, PRIDE, OSTENTATION
– relating to or resembling a peacock or peacock's tail PAVONINE

peak, highpoint, final development or achievement PINNACLE, ZENITH, MERIDIAN, SUMMIT

peanuts – poison produced by fungus on peanuts and maize AFLATOXIN

pear – pear-shaped PYRIFORM
– alcoholic drink made from fermented pear juice PERRY

pearl produced through artificial stimulation of an oyster by the insertion into it of a small bead CULTURED PEARL
– pearl that is smooth, round, and very large PARAGON
– pearl that is very small and often imperfect SEED PEARL
– pearl's quality of lustre, or a high-quality pearl ORIENT
– adjective for a pearl MARGARIC
– irregularly shaped, as a pearl might be BAROQUE

pearly, consisting of or resembling mother-of-pearl NACREOUS
– pearly, shiny inner surface of some mollusc shells, used for ornamentation MOTHER-OF-PEARL, NACRE

peasant in a slave-like condition, bound to a feudal lord or estate SERF
– peasant in feudal times who had the status of a freeman but owed services or rent to his lord in return for land VILLEIN
– peasant in feudal times who occupied a cottage and smallholding in return for labour COTTER
– peasant in Russia in tsarist times MUZHIK
– peasant or unskilled worker, especially in Latin America PEON
– peasants or farm-labourers in Arab countries FELLAHIN

peat bog TURBARY
– peat moss SPHAGNUM

peculiar See **odd**

peculiar- IDIO-

peculiarity of behaviour, or odd notion or action QUIRK, MANNERISM, FOIBLE, WHIM, ECCENTRICITY, IDIOSYNCRASY, VAGARY, CAPRICE

pedal on a piano for prolonging a note, the loud pedal SUSTAINING PEDAL, REVERBERATION PEDAL
– pedal or foot-operated lever for driving a sewing machine, potter's wheel, or the like TREADLE

pedantic, dogmatic, excessively precise or subtle SCHOLASTIC, NITPICKING, CASUISTIC

pedestrian crossing at which pedestrians themselves activate the traffic lights PELICAN CROSSING
– pedestrian crossing on which pedestrians have priority over vehicles at all times ZEBRA CROSSING
– pedestrian district of a town, closed to traffic PEDESTRIAN PRECINCT
– area for pedestrians, such as a concourse or wide passageway, lined with shops MALL, ARCADE
– beacon in the form of a flashing orange globe, indicating a pedestrian crossing on British roads BELISHA BEACON

pedigrees – study of pedigrees, coats of arms, precedence, and the like HERALDRY

pedlar, trader, or supplier in former times CHAPMAN

peephole in a door for identifying visitors JUDAS, JUDAS HOLE

peeping Tom VOYEUR

peg, pin, or short rod fitting into holes to fasten adjoining pieces of wood or stone DOWEL
– peg-like crosspiece inserted to fasten a loop or strap, or secure a knot TOGGLE
– peg or pin, especially one used as a rowlock in the side of a boat THOLE

pen – pen-like instrument with a small toothed wheel for perforating wax stencils for copying on an office duplicator CYCLOSTYLE
– pen made of the hollow main shaft of a feather QUILL
– pen or pound for animals, such as stray sheep PINFOLD
– pen with a felt tip, used to pick out printed words by broad coloured strokes HIGHLIGHTER
– pen with a hollow needle instead of a nib for the release of the ink STYLOGRAPH
– downward stroke of the pen in handwriting MINIM

pen-name NOM DE PLUME, NOM DE GUERRE, PSEUDONYM

penalty, especially a fine, imposed at the court's discretion AMERCEMENT
– penalty imposed or threatened, as a means of enforcing a law, standard, or decree SANCTION
– reduce to a lighter sentence, penalty, or the like COMMUTE
– suspend or refrain from enforcing a rule, penalty, or the like WAIVE

pencil – pencil-like stick containing a chemical for stopping the bleeding from small cuts, as after shaving STYPTIC PENCIL
– pencil whose writing cannot be erased INDELIBLE PENCIL
– dark grey allotropic form of carbon used in lead pencils and as a lubricant GRAPHITE, PLUMBAGO

pendulum – long, heavy free-swinging pendulum that demonstrates the rotation of the Earth FOUCAULT PENDULUM

penetrate or spread through DIFFUSE, PERMEATE
– impossible to penetrate, resisting penetration by liquids or gases IMPERMEABLE, IMPERVIOUS

penetrating, cutting, to the point, as a remark might be INCISIVE, TRENCHANT, MORDANT

penicillin or related medicine used in treating or preventing bacterial infections ANTIBIOTIC

penis, or a sculpture or other symbolic representation of it PHALLUS
– penis of an animal, especially of a bull PIZZLE
– penis-symbol or phallic image of the Hindu god Shiva LINGAM
– body canal or opening, as in the ear or at the tip of the penis MEATUS
– canal in the penis for the passage of urine and semen URETHRA
– fatty substance collecting at the end of the penis under the foreskin SMEGMA
– gland between the bladder and penis, secreting seminal fluid PROSTATE
– image or representation of the penis, as in sculpture PRIAPUS
– loose fold of skin covering the tip of the penis FORESKIN, PREPUCE
– referring to a statue, painting, or the like of a man or fertility god with a prominent penis ITHYPHALLIC
– small sensitive organ in the female genitalia, the counterpart of the penis in males CLITORIS
– subsidence of a swelling or swollen organ, especially of the penis DETUMESCENCE
– swollen, as a body organ such as the penis might be TUMESCENT, TUMID
– tip or head section of the penis GLANS

penknife – implement resembling a small penknife, used for cleaning and servicing a pipe SMOKER'S COMPANION

penmanship, fine handwriting CALLIGRAPHY, CHIROGRAPHY

pension, dividends, or the like paid once a year ANNUITY

– pension rights or other benefit enjoyed by an employee, in addition to his wages or salary FRINGE BENEFIT
– pensioned off, retired or discharged because of old age or illness SUPERANNUATED
– rising in keeping with the cost of living, as a salary or pension might INDEX-LINKED

people, the masses POPULACE
– people in the mass, the mob, rabble CANAILLE, HOI POLLOI, RAGTAG, RIFF-RAFF
– people of a nation, regarded as a political group DEMOS
– common people, the lower classes or working people PLEBEIANS, PROLETARIAT
– common people or inhabitants of a place POPULACE, COMMONALTY
– relating to the common people, unsophisticated DEMOTIC

people- DEM-, DEMO-, ETHN-, ETHNO-

pepper – pepper-like condiment with a fierce burning taste, red pepper CAYENNE PEPPER
– pepper shaker, salt cellar, mustard pot, or the like, or a set of such containers CRUET
– sweet pepper, red or green pepper or similar vegetable PIMIENTO, CAPSICUM

peppermint flavouring MENTHOL

per day, daily PER DIEM

per month, monthly PER MENSEM

per person PER CAPITA

per thousand PER MILL

per year, annually PER ANNUM

perception by means of a sixth sense, supernatural powers, intuition, or the like EXTRASENSORY PERCEPTION, ESP, CRYPTAESTHESIA, TELAESTHESIA
– below a person's threshold of consciousness or perception SUBLIMINAL
– fine feeling, keen power of perception, sensitive openness to emotional influences SENSIBILITY
– object grasped by the intellect or intuition rather than known through sense perception, thing-in-itself NOUMENON
– object known through sense perception, rather than known through reasoning or intuition PHENOMENON

percussion See chart
– percussion section of an orchestra BATTERY
– percussionist in an orchestra, especially one who plays the kettledrums TYMPANIST

perfect See also **excellent**
– perfect, free of error or failing IMMACULATE, IMPECCABLE, FLAWLESS, UNBLEMISHED, CONSUMMATE
– perfect, impossible to fault or blame, beyond criticism IRREPROACHABLE, UNIMPEACHABLE
– perfect, inevitably correct, and incapable of making a mistake INFALLIBLE
– perfect example or specimen, serving as a model for others EXEMPLAR, PARAGON
– perfect example or typical representative of a specified vice or

PERCUSSION INSTRUMENTS

bones	pair of small bones, making a clicking sound
bongo drums	pair of small, Cuban hand drums
castanets	concave wooden discs or shells, clicked together in the hand
claves	wooden sticks beaten together rhythmically
conga	tall Cuban hand drum
cymbal	metal plate struck with a drumstick or clashed against another
glockenspiel	set of tuned metal bars struck with a small hammer, sounding like bells
gran cassa	bass drum
kettledrum, timbal	large bowl-shaped drum which can be tuned; used in orchestras and mounted military bands
lithophone	xylophone-like instrument, with tuned stones instead of bars
maraca	seed-filled gourd that rattles when shaken
marimba	large, deep-pitched xylophone-like instrument, usually played with soft-headed hammers
nakers	pair of small, shallow drums, played in medieval times
pedal drum	kettledrum, mechanically tuned by pedals
side drum, snare drum	small, shallow, cylindrical drum with a skin at either end, making a rattling tone
tabla	pair of small Indian hand drums
tabor	small drum beaten by hand rather than with sticks
tambourine	small drum, with jingles or bells set in the frame, that is rattled or struck
tenor drum	drum similar to a side drum, but deeper pitched
timpani	set of two or three kettledrums
tom-tom	oriental drum, often used in pairs
tubular bells, chimes	set of hanging metal tubes, struck with a small hammer
vibraphone	set of tuned metal bars, arranged like a keyboard, with resonators below
washboard	board with a ridged metal or wooden surface, used to make a rattling sound, typically used in skiffle
wood block, Chinese block	resonant, hollow block of wood, struck with wooden sticks
xylophone	set of tuned wooden bars, arranged as a keyboard and struck with small, hard hammers

virtue PERSONIFICATION, EMBODIMENT, INCARNATION
– perfect example, representative, or embodiment of an idea or ideal EPITOME, ARCHETYPE, AVATAR
– perfect place, paradise on earth, especially when imaginary SHANGRI-LA, UTOPIA, ARCADIA
– perfect society, looked forward to in the future MILLENNIUM
– perfect state or extreme point NE PLUS ULTRA
– perfectly, with precision TO A NICETY

perforation between rows of stamps for easy separation ROULETTE

perform or celebrate with formal or religious rites SOLEMNISE
– perform a hoax, commit a crime, or the like PERPETRATE
– perform official duties on a formal occasion OFFICIATE
– perform or devise a poem, play, melody, or the like, composing as one goes IMPROVISE
– perform business TRANSACT
– perform or speak without preparation EXTEMPORISE

performance, as by a musician, that is additional to the scheduled programme, in response to audience applause ENCORE
– performance by a solo musician RECITAL
– performance of a dramatic role or musical composition RENDERING, RENDITION
– performance of a play or show, or screening of a film in the afternoon MATINÉE
– brilliant technically, or showy, as a musical performance might be BRAVURA

performer of considerable experience, veteran performer TROUPER
– performer of miracles, magician THAUMATURGIST
– performer on a specified instrument or in a specified technique EXPONENT
– range of jokes, pieces of music, or the like, available to a performer REPERTOIRE, REPERTORY

perfume box with a perforated lid POUNCET BOX
– perfume fixative based on a waxy cholesterol substance that is secreted by whales AMBERGRIS
– perfume fixative derived from glands under a beaver's tail CASTOR
– perfume made from sandalwood CHYPRE
– perfume made from the oil derived from the leaves of an Asian tree PATCHOULI
– perfume or fragrant oil extracted from petals ATTAR
– perfumed mixture, as of dried petals, in a small packet or box, as for scenting linen POMANDER
– perfumed oil or cream for the hair POMATUM, MACASSAR OIL, POMADE
– perfumed smoke, or the substance producing it INCENSE
– perfumed stick, burnt as incense JOSS STICK
– perfumed toilet water EAU DE COLOGNE
– fragrant glandular secretion from various mammals, used in perfume-making CIVET, MUSK
– gum or resin used in making perfume MYRRH
– jar of dried petals or spices, used to perfume the air POTPOURRI
– oil extracted from a tropical grass, used in insect repellents and perfume-making CITRONELLA
– oil extracted from the rind of a citrus fruit, and used in perfume-making BERGAMOT
– rootstock of a type of iris, used in perfume-making ORRIS
– small bottle for perfume PHIAL, VIAL
– small packet or bag containing perfumed powder, to scent clothes and linen SACHET
– spray device, as for perfume ATOMISER
– substance added to a perfume to reduce evaporation FIXATIVE

period during which a foetus or baby animal is carried in the womb GESTATION PERIOD
– period of greatest strength or success HEYDAY, PRIME
– period of history, era EPOCH
– period of time for which something continues or lasts DURATION
– woman's period, monthly discharge of blood from the uterus MENSTRUATION, MENSES

periodic, stopping and starting at intervals INTERMITTENT

perjury – induce someone to commit a wrongful act, especially perjury SUBORN

perk or other customary benefit attached to a position APPANAGE, PERQUISITE, FRINGE BENEFIT

permafrost region between the Arctic's perpetual snow and the tree line TUNDRA

permanent See also **constant**
– permanent, everlasting ETERNAL, SEMPITERNAL
– permanent, indestructible, or immortal IMPERISHABLE, INDISSOLUBLE, ABIDING, ENDURING
– permanent, lasting indefinitely or forever PERPETUAL, PERENNIAL, PERDURABLE
– permanent, unchangeable, irreversible IRREVOCABLE
– permanent, unchanging IMMUTABLE
– permanent, unerasable INDELIBLE
– permanent and definite, not merely acting or temporary SUBSTANTIVE
– permanent and unbreakable, as a union or contract might be INDISSOLUBLE
– permanent or secure employment status, as enjoyed by some university teachers TENURE
– permanently attached or fixed ENTRENCHED, INGRAINED
– permanently beautiful, everlasting AMARANTHINE
– permanently fitted item of furnishings or the like FIXTURE
– permanently frozen ground, as in the Arctic PERMAFROST
– make permanent or everlasting PERPETUATE

permission, official authorisation FIAT
– permission for an aircraft or ship to proceed, as after a traffic delay, or the like CLEARANCE
– permission for the publication of a book, as granted by a bishop or censor IMPRIMATUR
– permission or order to leave, dismissal NUNC DIMITTIS
– permission or toleration implied by the absence of an explicit prohibition SUFFERANCE
– permission to be absent, as from school EXEAT
– permission to leave CONGÉ

permit, authorise, or approve COUNTENANCE, EMPOWER, WARRANT, SANCTION, RATIFY
– permit allowing entry to a specific area LAISSEZ-PASSER
– permit for the temporary import of a car, or for a motorist to cross certain frontiers CARNET
– permit oneself, in a haughty way, to do something DEIGN, CONDESCEND
– permit oneself to satisfy a whim or craving INDULGE
– permit or accept as rightful, justify LEGITIMATE

permitting, making possible but not obligatory FACULTATIVE
– permitting or admitting of something, such as an interpretation SUSCEPTIBLE

perpendicular, exactly vertical PLUMB

perpendicular- ORTHO-

perpetual See **constant**, **permanent**

persecution complex PARANOIA
– persecution of suspected Communist sympathisers in the U.S.

in the 1950s MCCARTHYISM
persevering, dogged INDEFATIGABLE, UNREMITTING, TENACIOUS, PERTINACIOUS, PERSISTENT
Persia – Persian lamb or the fur prepared from it KARAKUL
– Persian title of respect, placed before the surname of a distinguished man MIRZA
– provincial governor in ancient Persia SATRAP
– title of the king of Persia in ancient times SOPHY
person of Christ, unifying the divine and human natures HYPOSTASIS
personal, and hence often unfounded or biased SUBJECTIVE
– personal, deeply private, secret INTIMATE
– personal belongings PARAPHERNALIA, EFFECTS, CHATTELS
– personal charm and magnetic power of inspiration CHARISMA
– personally, without an intermediary IN PROPRIA PERSONA
– personally involved or affected, as parties in a dispute would be INTERESTED
– report or summary of one's education, career, and other personal details, as for job applications CURRICULUM VITAE, RÉSUMÉ
personality, character HUMOUR, DISPOSITION, TEMPERAMENT
– personality assets or requirements in one's profession or pursuits STOCK IN TRADE
– personality test based on the subject's interpretations of various abstract inkblot designs, "inkblot test" RORSCHACH TEST
– aspect or feature, as of someone's personality FACET, TRAIT
– changeable, as someone's personality might be MERCURIAL, VOLATILE
– harmonious organisation of the psychological and intellectual characteristics into a unitary and effective personality INTEGRATION
– sense of a loss of personality, personal identity, and self-esteem, as among industrial workers in modern society ALIENATION
– sense of rootlessness, confusion, and loss of personality or personal identity, in the absence of a supportive community ANOMIE
personnel – guns, ammunition, and other equipment of an army, as distinct from personnel MATÉRIEL
perspective in a drawing or painting, through shortening of lines FORESHORTENING
perspiration See **sweat**
persuadable, easily led DUCTILE, MALLEABLE, IMPRESSIONABLE
– persuadable, obliging, cooperative FLEXIBLE, TRACTABLE
persuade by craftiness, trickery, and deceit FINAGLE, WANGLE
– persuade or force someone into doing something, as by threats COERCE, DRAGOON
– persuade or pressure someone into doing something INDUCE, PREVAIL UPON
– persuade someone to go along with one by promises or gifts ENTICE
– persuade with deceitful flattery CAJOLE, WHEEDLE, INVEIGLE, COAX, SMOOTH-TALK, SOFT-SOAP, BLARNEY
– persuade with private hints or intrigue EARWIG
– incite or persuade someone to act wrongly SUBORN, SEDUCE
– try to persuade people to support someone or buy from someone specified TOUT, CANVASS
persuasion – long-winded or slick sales talk or attempt at persuasion SPIEL, PATTER
persuasive, forceful, telling, as an argument might be COGENT, TRENCHANT, INCISIVE, COMPELLING, POINTED
– persuasive or believable, as an excuse or politician might be PLAUSIBLE
– possible and defendable, but not really persuasive, as an argument might be TENABLE
perversions See **sex**
pervert, corrupt, or undermine SUBVERT
pessimism – sentimental or romantic pessimism about life in general WELTSCHMERZ
pessimist, warning others of disaster JEREMIAH, CASSANDRA
– pessimistic, doubting, disbelieving SCEPTICAL, CYNICAL
– pessimistic, predicting disaster APOCALYPTIC
pestle – bowl in which something is ground with a pestle MORTAR
pet animal, especially a lamb COSSET
– pet name HYPOCORISM, DIMINUTIVE
– lungs of a slaughtered pig, sheep, or the like, used especially for pet food LIGHTS
– sawdust or similar material, in a tray, for pets to excrete on indoors LITTER, CAT LITTER
petals or leaves in a radiating pattern WHORL
– relating to or having petals and sepals CHLAMYDEOUS
– short-lived, dying or falling quickly, as petals might be FUGACIOUS
petition on which the signatures are arranged in a circle ROUND ROBIN
petrified wood or similar substance hardened by calcium salts CALCIFICATION
petrol bomb or similar crude fire bomb thrown by hand, typically a fuel-filled bottle stoppered with a rag wick MOLOTOV COCKTAIL
– petrol thickened to form a jelly-like substance used in firebombs and flamethrowers NAPALM
– measure of petrol's anti-knock properties OCTANE NUMBER
petroleum – reduction or decomposition by heat, as of petroleum CRACKING
– separation of petroleum and other chemical mixtures into their components, as on the basis of different boiling points FRACTIONATION
petting, kissing and cuddling NECKING, CANOODLING
petty but nagging, as minor doubts or anxiety might be NIGGLING
– petty criticism or fault-finding NITPICKING, CARPING, CAVILLING
phantom pregnancy PSEUDOCYESIS
pharmacist – former term for a chemist or pharmicist APOTHECARY
pheasant – flock, nest, or family of pheasants NYE, NIDE, BOUQUET
– store and ripen venison, pheasant, or other game HANG
philosopher, scholar, or thinker, especially a devious or over-subtle one SOPHIST
– philosopher, wise teacher, or the like, deeply respected for his experience and judgment SAGE
philosophy See chart
– philosophical, abstract, speculative METAPHYSICAL
– philosophical discussion and logical disputing DIALECTIC
– philosophical or theological argument, as attempted by students QUODLIBET
– philosophical principle, devised by Descartes, that the very fact of one's thinking or consciousness is a proof of one's existence COGITO
– philosophical standpoint from which one views and interprets the world WELTANSCHAUUNG
– philosophical work, as by Plato, in the form of a conversation DIALOGUE
– actuality or realisation of a thing, rather than just potentiality, according to Aristotle's philosophy ENTELECHY
– combine or try to reconcile different philosophical, religious, or other beliefs SYNCRETISE
– mind of a newborn baby consid-

ered, as in Locke's philosophy, a clean slate until receiving sense impressions TABULA RASA
– principle of philosophical and scientific investigation that the simpler a theory is and the fewer unproved assumptions it makes the better OCKHAM'S RAZOR
– relating to philosophical thought or pure intellect NOETIC
– relating to the concepts of duty and obligation, in philosophy and logic DEONTIC
– secret or mystical philosophy, specifically occult philosophy based on the Hebrew scriptures CABALA
– thing as it appears, according to Kantian philosophy, as experienced by the senses rather than as understood by reason or intuition PHENOMENON
– thing in itself, according to Kantian philosophy, as understood by reason or intuition rather than as it appears to the senses NOUMENON
– universally applicable moral law derived from pure reason, according to Kantian philosophy CATEGORICAL IMPERATIVE

phobias See chart, page 377
phone See **telephone**
phonetics See **pronunciation**, **sound**, **speech**, **voice**
photocopying process XEROGRAPHY, XEROX
photographer or freelance journalist who badgers celebrities and the like PAPARAZZO
photography See also **camera**, **lens**, **film**
– photograph, engraving, or the like with blurry edges VIGNETTE
– photograph in a brownish tint, especially from earlier times SEPIA
– photograph of a person's face, as of a criminal MUGSHOT
– photograph or photographic process of an early type, based on a silver-coated metal plate DAGUERROTYPE
– photographs, as in magazine advertisements, of handsome or muscular men scantily clothed BEEFCAKE
– photographs, as in magazine advertisements, of sexually attractive women scantily clothed CHEESECAKE
– photographs, particularly aerial photographs, set side by side to form a large composite picture MOSAIC
– photographic film or plate EXPOSURE
– photographic print of the same size as the negative, for prelimi-

PHILOSOPHIES

aestheticism	belief that beauty is the basic principle of chief good in life and underlies morality
antinomianism	rejection of conventional morality; doctrine rejecting moral law on the ground that salvation derives from grace or faith alone
behaviourism	doctrine that behaviour, rather than mind or consciousness, is all that can really be known or studied about human nature
determinism	doctrine that every event happens according to physical laws, is causally determined, and is independent of human will
empiricism	doctrine that knowledge can only be gained through sense perception and experience
Epicureanism	ancient Greek teaching that good was pleasure and evil was pain
epistemology	study of the nature and origin of knowledge
ethics	philosophy of morals and moral choices
existentialism	philosophical doctrine that man has complete free will but no given essence, and has to define himself by his choices in a world without ultimate moral values
Fabianism	political doctrine favouring gradual, non-confrontational social progress and change
fatalism	doctrine that everything is predestined, as by fate, and that human will and action are powerless to affect events
hedonism	belief that pleasure is the basic principle or chief good in life, and underlies morality or determines one's actions
historicism	doctrine that history is governed by inevitable processes; theory that a past age should be judged on its own terms rather than by modern values
humanism	belief that the basic principle of morality is the well-being of man, and in this life rather than the next
idealism	belief that the true reality lies beyond the observable world; theory that consciousness or reason is the true reality, or the only thing really knowable
instrumentalism	doctrine that the value of ideas lies not in their correctness but in their practical success
jurisprudence	philosophy of law
logical positivism	doctrine that the only meaningful statements are either self-evident or scientifically confirmable, and that statements about unobservable things such as God or mental states are therefore meaningless
materialism	doctrine that physical matter is the basic reality and that thoughts and emotions are simply results of it, and that religious and supernatural beliefs are baseless; doctrine that history and social and economic changes have mechanical material causes
metaphysics	study of underlying principles and ultimate reality
millenarianism	belief in a perfect future period or society
nihilism	doctrine that denies the existence of everything; political theory or movement based on the rejection of all authority or any curtailment of individual freedom

continued

PHILOSOPHIES *continued*

nominalism	doctrine that only actual individual objects really exist, and that essences, universals, or abstract concepts exist only as names
ontology	study of the nature of being or existence
perspectivism	doctrine that there can be no absolute knowledge of truth, since rival conceptual systems produce different views; theory that several points of view are needed to understand reality
phenomenalism	doctrine that the only thing knowable for certain is our set of sense perceptions or sensations
phenomenology	study of awareness and of perceived objects rather than of objective reality
positivism	doctrine that knowledge consists of or is derived from actual facts, and that religious or supernatural beliefs are not true knowledge
pragmatism	practical approach to political or personal dealings, rejecting ideological and historical considerations
prescriptivism	theory that statements about good and evil cannot be either true or untrue, but simply reflect and prescribe moral attitudes
rationalism	doctrine that knowledge can only be gained through reason; rejection of religion on the grounds that it is contrary to reason
reductionism	analysis of a subject or problem into its components, often by over-simplifying it
relativism	doctrine that truth is not absolute, but varies from individual to individual, culture or culture, and age to age
scholasticism	medieval Christian philosophy and theology associated with the Church Fathers, sometimes influenced by Aristotle
solipsism	belief that the self is the only thing in existence, or the only thing knowable for certain
stoicism	ancient doctrine that man's only worthwhile aim is virtue, and that this involves submitting to nature and suppressing one's emotions
structuralism	theory or movement in many academic fields based on the view that the subject has various underlying structures, contrasts, and assumptions; study of the structure rather than the history of a language
syndicalism	revolutionary movement or theory supporting government by trades unions or workers' syndicates, to be achieved by radical industrial action
transcendentalism	doctrine that the ultimate reality is in a realm beyond everyday experience; doctrine that knowledge is obtained by intuition or by reflecting on the reasoning process itself
utilitarianism	doctrine that the greatest good is what produces most happiness for the greatest number of people

nary viewing CONTACT PRINT
– photographic print on dull, rough, unshiny paper MATT
– photographic print on smooth, shiny paper GLOSSY
– photographic slide, lit from behind, TRANSPARENCY
– device used in photography for softening the lighting and the shadows, such as a screen of fabric placed in front of a spotlight DIFFUSER
– difference in brightness, as of separate areas of a photograph or television picture CONTRAST
– having poor definition and a speckled appearance, as some photographs have when an inappropriate film is used GRAINY
– improve a photographic negative or print by adjusting details or removing flaws RETOUCH
– laser-produced photograph or pattern producing a powerful 3D effect HOLOGRAM
– light-sensitive coating, on photographic film or paper EMULSION
– prepare photographs for display, as by pasting them onto cardboard MOUNT
– screen or network of fine lines, used in astronomical and colour photography RÉSEAU
– sharpness or clarity of outline, as of a photograph or television image DEFINITION, ACUTANCE
– title or short account of a photograph, illustration, cartoon, or the like CAPTION

phrase in popular use, especially one associated with a particular entertainer CATCH PHRASE
– phrase or clause, group of words forming part of a sentence CONSTRUCTION
– phrase or expression that has been shortened, such as *Morning* for *Good morning* BRACHYLOGY
– phrase or expression that is roundabout or long-winded CIRCUMLOCUTION
– phrase or remark, with independent syntax, within a sentence PARENTHESIS
– phrase or word, recorded only once in a given text or language HAPAX, HAPAX LEGOMENON
– phrase or word used for the first time COINAGE
– phrase or word whose letters are rearranged from or into those of another phrase or word ANAGRAM, TRANSPOSITION

physical, bodily, having a real or material rather than spiritual nature CORPOREAL, TANGIBLE
– physical, fleshly, relating to bodily desires and appetites SENSUAL, CARNAL
– physical, material, or actual rather than conceptual or imaginary OBJECTIVE
– physical exercises done to improve or maintain one's fitness and muscle tone CALLISTHENICS

physics See chart, page 378

piano See illustration, page 379
– piano, or similar stringed keyboard instrument CLAVIER

PHOBIAS

irrational or excessive fear of:	
aeroplanes or flying	**aerophobia, pterophobia**
animals	**zoophobia**
bees	**apiophobia, melissophobia**
birds	**ornithophobia**
blood	**haemophobia, haematophobia**
bridges, or crossing bridges	**gephyrophobia**
burial alive	**taphophobia**
cats	**ailurophobia, gatophobia**
children	**paedophobia**
choking	**pnigophobia**
cold	**psychrophobia, cheimophobia, cryophobia**
confined spaces	**claustrophobia, clithrophobia**
crowds	**ochlophobia, demophobia**
dark	**scotophobia, nyctophobia, achluophobia, lygophobia**
death or dead bodies	**necrophobia, thanatophobia**
depths, deep places	**bathophobia**
deserts, dry places	**xerophobia**
dirt	**rupophobia**
dogs	**cynophobia**
drinking or drunkenness	**dipsophobia**
fear, being alarmed	**phobophobia**
fire	**pyrophobia**
fish	**ichthyophobia**
foreigners	**xenophobia**
fur	**doraphobia**
germs	**microbiophobia**
ghosts	**phasmophobia**
heat	**thermophobia**
heights	**acrophobia, hypsophobia, cremnophobia**
horses	**hippophobia**
illness	**nosophobia, pathophobia**
injury	**traumatophobia**

irrational or excessive fear of:	
insects	**entomophobia**
lightning	**astrapophobia, keraunophobia**
loneliness	**eremiophobia, autophobia, monophobia**
madness	**maniaphobia, lyssophobia**
men and boys	**androphobia**
mice	**musophobia**
name or particular word	**onomatophobia**
night	**nyctophobia**
noise	**phonophobia**
old age	**gerascophobia**
open spaces, or going out in public	**agoraphobia, kenophobia**
pain	**algophobia, odynophobia**
particular place	**topophobia**
poisoning	**toxicophobia, iophobia**
pregnancy	**maieusiophobia**
sea	**thalassophobia**
sharks	**galeophobia**
sleep	**hypnophobia**
snakes	**ophidiophobia**
speaking, public speaking	**lalophobia, glossophobia**
speed	**tacophobia**
spiders	**arachnaphobia**
streets, or crossing streets	**dromophobia**
surgery	**ergasiophobia, tomophobia**
thirteen	**triskaidekaphobia**
thunder	**keraunophobia, brontophobia, tonitrophobia**
trains	**siderodromophobia**
travel	**hodophobia**
water or wetness	**hydrophobia, aquaphobia, hygrophobia**
women or girls	**gynophobia**
worms	**helminthophobia, scoileciphobia**

– piano accompanist assisting at opera rehearsals RÉPETITEUR
– piano having two sets of strings crossing each other OVERSTRUNG PIANO
– piano music as played in saloons, usually on a tinny piano HONKY-TONK
– piano of a fine make BECHSTEIN, STEINWAY
– piano of the largest size CONCERT GRAND
– piano operated mechanically, sounding the notes indicated on a perforated paper roll PLAYER PIANO, PIANOLA
– piano or similar instrument KEYBOARD INSTRUMENT
– any key on a piano or similar instrument DIGITAL

pick See **choose**

– pick-like hoe for farming or gardening MATTOCK
– pick out or select the best or worst specimens CULL

pickle, soak in brine or vinegar in order to pickle SOUSE
– pickle or soak meat or fish in a sauce before cooking MARINATE
– pickled bud with a pungent flavour, used as a condiment CAPER
– pickling sauce in which meat or fish is left to soak before cooking MARINADE
– salty water for pickling BRINE
– small cucumber usually used for pickling GHERKIN

pickpocket – former term for a pickpocket CUTPURSE

picnic, garden party, or other outdoor meal or entertainment FÊTE CHAMPÊTRE

picture See also **painting**
– picture, as of a battle scene, right round the inside wall of a circular room CYCLORAMA
– picture, graphic description or representation TABLEAU
– picture, typically an engraved or photographic portrait, with blurry edges VIGNETTE
– picture at the front of a book FRONTISPIECE
– picture formed from shadows or outlines SCIAGRAM
– picture frame with crossing and projecting edges OXFORD FRAME
– picture-framing method in which the glass and backing are taped together, or the tape used for this purpose PASSE-PARTOUT
– picture made up of many other pictures overlapping or stuck side

PHYSICS TERMS

absolute zero	lowest temperature that theoretically can be reached: 0°Kelvin, – 273.15°C or – 459.67°F
Archimedes' principle	principle that a body's apparent loss of weight when it is immersed in a fluid is equal to the weight of the fluid it displaces
Avogadro's law	law stating that equal volumes of all gases under the same temperature and pressure conditions contain the same number of molecules
Boyle's law	law stating that at constant temperature the volume of a gas varies inversely with its pressure
Brownian motion	random motion of microscopic particles suspended in a liquid or gas
Charles' law	law stating that at constant pressure the volume of a gas varies directly with its absolute temperature
conservation of energy	law stating that in a closed system the total energy remains constant
Doppler effect	apparent change in the frequency of a wave when the observer and the source are moving relative to each other, as in the changing pitch of a train's whistle as it approaches
dynamics	branch of mechanics concerned with the forces that produce or alter the motions of bodies
half-life	time taken for half the nuclei in a sample of radioactive material to decay
Hooke's law	law stating that the strain produced in a solid body is proportional to the stress applied to it
hydraulics, fluid mechanics	branch of mechanics concerned with the flow of liquids
inertia	tendency of a body to remain at rest or in a state of uniform motion unless disturbed by an external force
kinetics	branch of mechanics concerned with all aspects of motion
mechanics	branch of physics concerned with the action of forces on matter
Planck's constant	universal constant relating the frequency of a radiation to its energy
quantum jump, quantum leap	transition of an atomic or molecular system from one distinct energy level to another
quantum theory	theory that light and other forms of energy are emitted not as a continuous wave motion, but in small "packets" or quanta
scalar	quantity, such as time, that has magnitude but no direction
statics	branch of mechanics concerned with the action of forces on bodies at rest
surface tension	property of liquids in which the surface acts like a stretched elastic skin
thermodynamics	branch of physics concerned with the relationship of heat to other forms of energy
torque	turning effect of a force on a body free to rotate about an axis; also known as the moment of a force
vector	quantity such as velocity that has direction as well as magnitude

piano

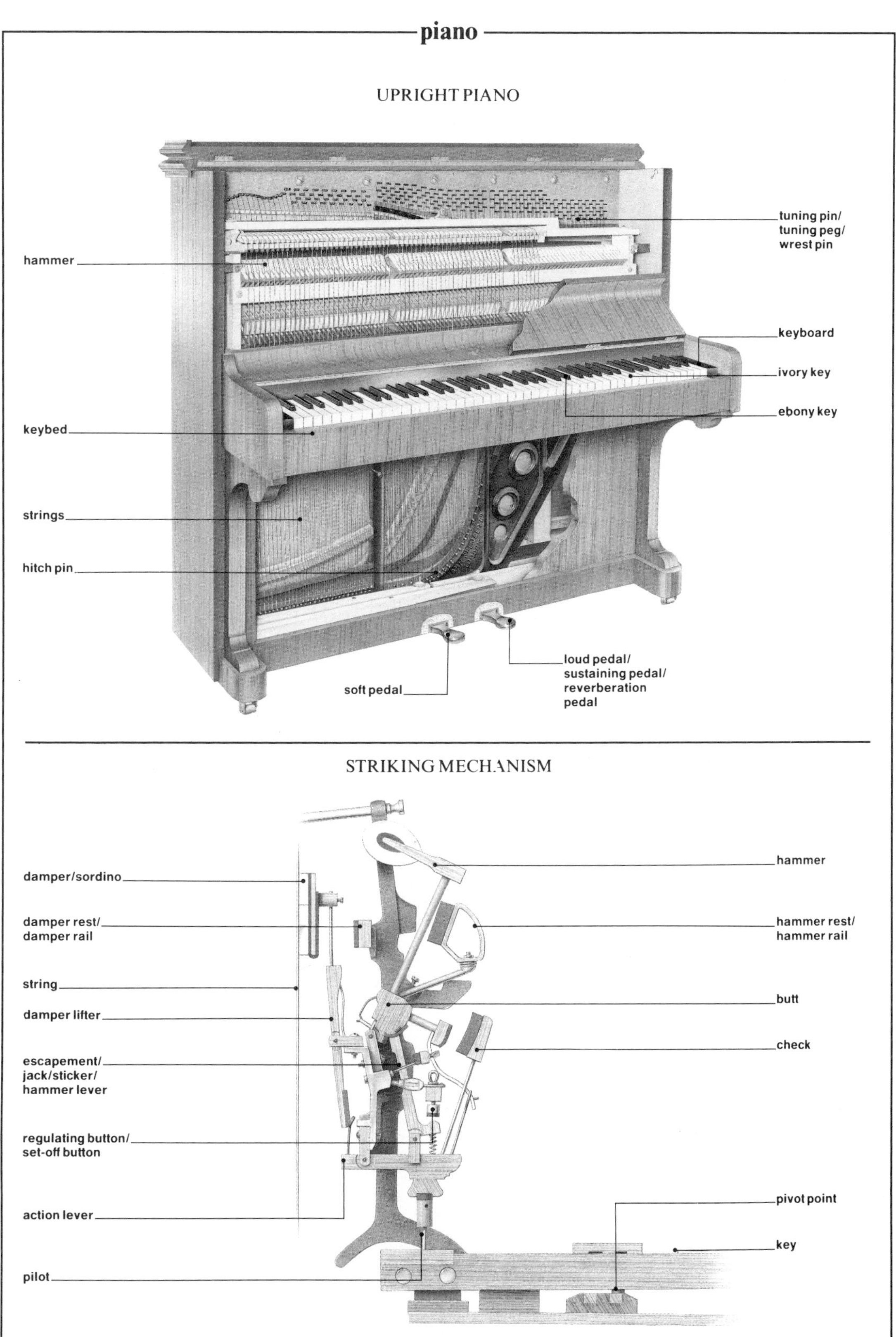
UPRIGHT PIANO
hammer
tuning pin/
tuning peg/
wrest pin
keyboard
ivory key
ebony key
keybed
strings
hitch pin
loud pedal/
sustaining pedal/
reverberation
pedal
soft pedal
STRIKING MECHANISM
damper/sordino
damper rest/
damper rail
string
damper lifter
escapement/
jack/sticker/
hammer lever
regulating button/
set-off button
action lever
pilot
hammer
hammer rest/
hammer rail
butt
check
pivot point
key

by side MONTAGE, COLLAGE
– picture of a memorial plaque made by rubbing graphite or wax on paper pressed against it BRASS RUBBING
– picture or design made up of many small pieces of stone, tile, or glass MOSAIC, TESSELATION
– picture or scene, as viewed through a slit, that is formed on a series of translucent cloth sheets DIORAMA
– picture representing a word or idea, as in ancient writing systems PICTOGRAPH, HIEROGLYPH
– picture writing, as used in ancient Egypt HIEROGLYPHICS
– card or disc that is spun or twirled to produce a merged image of the partial words or pictures on either side THAUMATROPE
– pair of nearly identical pictures that give a 3D effect when viewed through special lenses STEREOGRAPH
– prepare pictures for display, as by pasting them onto cardboard MOUNT
– puzzle in the form of pictures or symbols representing syllables or words REBUS
– relating to pictures PICTORIAL
– represent in words or images, as by painting or describing DEPICT
– title or short account of a photograph, illustration, or other picture CAPTION

picturesque in a simple way IDYLLIC, ARCADIAN

pier or mole to protect a harbour or shore JETTY, GROYNE

pierce or paralyse with a weapon, one's gaze, or the like TRANSFIX, IMPALE
– pierce with many holes RIDDLE

pig See also **bacon**, **pork**
– pig offal used in cooking FRY, HASLET, PLUCK, PURTENANCE
– pig or other male animal castrated after maturity STAG
– pig that has been castrated when young BARROW
– pig's feet, used as food TROTTERS, PETTITOES
– pig's jaw or cheek, used as food CHAP
– piglet newly weaned SHOAT
– piglet or puppy that is the smallest of the litter RUNT
– adjective for a pig PORCINE
– female piglet, or young sow that has not yet produced a litter GILT
– fodder or pasturage for pigs, as in a forest PANNAGE
– food for pigs, consisting of acorns and beech nuts MAST
– food for pigs, consisting of kitchen scraps and liquid SWILL, SLOPS, WASH
– group of piglets produced at a single birth LITTER, FARROW
– small intestines of pigs, prepared as a food CHITTERLINGS
– viral disease of pigs, causing fever and blistering on feet and snout SWINE VESICULAR DISEASE

pigeon loft or a dovecote COLUMBARIUM
– adjective for a pigeon COLUMBINE
– baby pigeon SQUAB
– captive or dummy pigeon used to decoy others STOOL PIGEON
– domestic pigeon that can perform backward somersaults while flying TUMBLER, ROLLER
– domestic pigeon with a large crop that can be puffed out POUTER
– domestic pigeon with a rounded tail than can be spread out like a fan FANTAIL
– person who has a specified hobby, especially breeding roses, pigeons, or the like FANCIER

pigeon-hole, divide into different classes, categories, sections, or the like COMPARTMENTALISE

pigment See also **colour**, **paint**
– pigment consisting of a natural clay or brown earthy substance UMBER, SIENNA, OCHRE
– bright blue pigment made from the crushed particles of a special glass SMALT
– bright red pigment or dye obtained from a tropical cactus insect COCHINEAL, CARMINE
– grey-green pigment used in paints, derived from a greenish sandstone TERRE-VERTE
– yellow-brown pigment made from wood soot BISTRE

pigtail or plait QUEUE

pike – young pike PICKEREL

pile, heap, or mound CUMULUS
– pile or bank of snow or sand, accumulated by wind or water DRIFT

piles, swollen anal tissue HAEMORRHOIDS

pilgrim, especially one in former times who carried a palm branch as an indication of having visited the Holy Land PALMER
– pilgrim to Mecca HAJI
– pilgrimage to Mecca by Muslims HAJ

pill or medicinal tablet of large size BOLUS
– package of pills in which each pill is contained in a separate plastic bubble on a card BLISTER PACK

pillar See also **column**
– pillar, typically rectangular, set into a wall and projecting slightly from it PILASTER
– pillar, typically rectangular, supporting an arch or vault PIER
– pillar carved and painted with kinship symbols, as by certain North American Indians TOTEM POLE
– pillar in classical architecture in the form of a statue of a man TELAMON, ATLAS
– pillar in classical architecture in the form of a statue of a woman CARYATID
– pillar-like stone, large and flat, usually part of a prehistoric monument MEGALITH, MONOLITH, DOLMEN, MENHIR
– pillar of stone, four-sided and tapering up to a pyramidal top, of a kind used as a monument in ancient Egypt OBELISK
– pillar or column on a pavement for the display of advertising posters MORRIS COLUMN
– pillar or other construction supporting the edge of an arch or end of a bridge ABUTMENT
– pillar or slab of stone, with an engraved surface, as used in ancient times as a monument, gravestone, or the like STELE
– pillar with a stone bust on top, used as a boundary marker or architectural ornament in ancient Rome TERM, TERMINUS
– early Christian hermit who lived on top of a pillar STYLITE
– prehistoric monument or chamber formed by stone pillars with a crossbeam DOLMEN, TRILITHON
– ring of stone pillars forming part of a prehistoric monument HENGE, CROMLECH
– row of pillars, columns, or trees that are positioned at regular intervals COLONNADE

-pillar- -STYL-, STYLO-, -STYLAR

pillow or long cushion that is often hard, stiff, and narrow BOLSTER
– silky plant fibre used for stuffing pillows KAPOK
– strong cloth used to cover a mattress or pillow TICKING

pilot of a balloon or lighter-than-air aircraft AERONAUT
– pilot of an aircraft, especially in the early days of flying AVIATOR, AVIATRIX
– seat in a military aircraft that is designed to hurl the pilot or a crew member clear in an emergency EJECTION SEAT, EJECTOR SEAT
– suicide pilot in the Japanese armed forces during the Second World War KAMIKAZE

pimp, or go-between in a sexual relationship PANDER, PANDERER, PROCURER

pimple – pimple-like protuberance, as on the tongue or at the root of a hair PAPILLA
- pimple-like pus-filled skin inflammation PUSTULE, PAPULE, TETTER
- pimple on the eyelid, caused by the inflammation of an oil gland STYE
- break out, appear on the skin, as a pimple or other blemish does ERUPT
- dark oily plug blocking a pore of the skin and forming a pimple, especially on the face BLACKHEAD, COMEDO
- goose pimples, goose flesh, bristling of the body hair, as from fear or cold HORRIPILATION
- hard, lightish, pimple-like mass under the skin, caused by the blockage of the outlet of an oil gland MILIUM
- inflamed area surrounding a pimple AREOLA
- large, oily pimple or cyst, especially on the scalp WEN
- slang term for a pimple, especially in acne ZIT

pin, bolt, revolving axle, or the like, as in a lock or between two door handles SPINDLE
- pin, peg, or short rod fitting into holes to fasten adjoining pieces of wood or stone DOWEL
- pin at the end of an axle, to hold the wheel in place LINCHPIN
- pin for fastening two parts or objects together, either by spreading its split end or by bolting its threaded end COTTER PIN
- pin or fastener with two flexible arms as for securing a wheel to an axle SPLIT PIN
- pin or pierce with a stake or sharp object IMPALE, TRANSFIX

pinball BAGATELLE

pinch into tight curls, folds, or the like CRIMP

pine, fir, or other cone-bearing tree CONIFER

pineal gland EPIPHYSIS

pink, carnation, or related flower DIANTHUS

pinkish, flesh-coloured INCARNADINE

pioneer or leader in any field of endeavour TRAILBLAZER

pious hypocrite TARTUFFE
- pious in a hypocritical or self-satisfied way, pretending to be holy, smug SANCTIMONIOUS, CANTING, HOLIER-THAN-THOU
- piously and narrow-mindedly convinced of the value of one's own virtues SELF-RIGHTEOUS

pip or seed of a grape berry, or the like ACINUS
- peach or related fruit whose stone or pip tends to cling to the flesh CLINGSTONE
- peach or related fruit whose stone or pip tends to separate easily from the flesh FREESTONE

pipe, tube, or canal for the passage of fluids, as in a building, a plant, or the human body DUCT
- pipe carrying sewage from a lavatory SOIL PIPE
- implement for cleaning and servicing tobacco pipes, consisting of several small utensils linked at the base like a penknife SMOKER'S COMPANION
- pipe connecting smaller pipes HEADER
- pipe fitting, typically a U- or S-shaped bend, for holding water as a barrier against the return flow of gases TRAP
- pipe or channel, as for rainwater or an electric cable CULVERT, CONDUIT
- pipe or duct for hot air, smoke, or the like, as in a boiler or chimney FLUE
- pipe rising vertically within a building RISER
- pipe running up a building, for pumping water from street level in the event of a fire DRY RISER
- pipe smoked in the East, in which the smoke is bubbled through water to cool it HOOKAH, HUBBLE-BUBBLE, KALIAN, WATER PIPE, NARGHILE
- pipe with many holes and connections MANIFOLD
- access opening in the side of a pipe for inspection or cleaning FERRULE
- ceremonial pipe with a long stem, used by North American Indians, "peace pipe" CALUMET
- clay pipe with a long stem CHURCHWARDEN
- fibre of hemp or jute, often treated with tar, used for sealing pipe joints and caulking the seams in wooden ships OAKUM
- rubber suction cup on a handle, used for clearing blocked drains and pipes PLUNGER, PLUMBER'S HELPER
- short tobacco pipe made of clay DUDEEN
- small tool for packing tobacco down into the bowl of a pipe TAMPER
- threaded adaptor or linking pipe for two pipes of different diameters BUSHING
- tobacco pipe made of wood, especially from a woody root BRIAR
- tobacco pipe with a bowl made from a light whitish earthy mineral MEERSCHAUM
- tobacco pipe with a short stem CUTTY
- Turkish pipe with a red clay bowl and very long stem CHIBOUK
- upright outdoor water pipe with a tap STANDPIPE

piping or roll of ribbon as used for trimming ROULEAU

pirate, especially along the Barbary Coast of North Africa in former times CORSAIR
- pirate, especially one frequenting the Caribbean in the 17th and 18th centuries BUCCANEER
- pirate, plunderer, military adventurer, or the like in former times FREEBOOTER, FILIBUSTER
- pirate flag JOLLY ROGER, SKULL-AND-CROSSBONES
- pirate or pirate ship ROVER, PICAROON
- pirate's sword, of a short and curved design CUTLASS

pistil or all the pistils of a flower GYNOECIUM

pit or small crater used by soldiers as protection against enemy fire FOXHOLE

pitch – pitch-like bitumen mixture, as used in roofing and roadmaking ASPHALT
- pitch-like, especially in being glossy and blackish PICEOUS
- adjust the pitch of a musical instrument, string, note, or the like TEMPER
- fibres, often treated with pitch, used for sealing the seams in wooden ships OAKUM
- waterproof the hull or seal the seams of a wooden ship, as with tar or pitch PAY, CAULK

pith of a stem or marrow of a bone MEDULLA

pith helmet SOLA TOPI

pituitary gland HYPOPHYSIS

pity, sympathise with, feel sorry for COMMISERATE
- pity, sympathy, mercy COMPASSION
- arousing pity or sympathy, pitiful, piteous PATHETIC

pivot SWIVEL
- pivot pin, as on a rudder, gun carriage, or towing vehicle PINTLE
- pin on either side of a cannon, container, or the like enabling it to be pivoted on a supporting frame TRUNNION

pizza – long-handled shovel used for moving bread, pies, pizza, or the like in and out of an oven PEEL

place See also **position**

– place, setting, or surroundings MILIEU

– place ceremonially in office INSTATE, INSTALL

– place frequently visited HAUNT, PURLIEU

– place in order, arrange, set up ARRAY

– place in society or a profession, prestige STATUS

– place in the care of another, entrust CONSIGN

– place inside something else, such as a new word into a sentence EMBED, INSERT

– place of security or refuge STRONGHOLD

– place or area where some particular event occurred, or where a play or novel is set LOCALE, SETTING, LOCUS

– place or arrange correctly in relation to other things COORDINATE

– place or hide securely ENSCONCE

– place or state of perfect happiness ELYSIUM

– place or way of life considered empty of spiritual values, cultural interest, or the like WASTELAND

– place over or on top of something else, as one film sequence over another SUPERIMPOSE

– place selected or designated for a sports match, concert, or the like VENUE

– place side by side, as for contrast JUXTAPOSE

– place that is perfect and idyllic, especially when purely imaginary SHANGRI-LA, UTOPIA

– place that is very unpleasant, especially when purely imaginary DYSTOPIA, CACOTOPIA

– place where things are stored for safekeeping REPOSITORY

– approximate place or location WHEREABOUTS

– assign to a place, position LODGE, SITUATE, STATION

– distinctive feeling of a place GENIUS LOCI

– find or specify the place of something, as on a map LOCATE, PINPOINT

– listing or dictionary of places GAZETTEER

– neighbourhood, district, places nearby LOCALITY, VICINITY

-place- TOP-, TOPO-, -ORY, -ARIUM, -ORIUM

place-error, geographical mistake, positioning something in the wrong region ANACHORISM

place name, or a word derived from it TOPONYM

plague fever spread by rats' fleas, black death BUBONIC PLAGUE

– plague or other epidemic and deadly disease PESTILENCE

– hospital for treating the plague, leprosy, or other contagious diseases in former times LAZARETTO

plain, as in Russia, that is flat, treeless, and grass-covered STEPPE

– plain, clear, unambiguous, not open to doubt UNEQUIVOCAL

– plain, cooked in a simple way AU NATUREL

– plain, stretch of open, treeless country CHAMPAIGN

– plain to see, obvious EVIDENT, MANIFEST

– plainly and simply, without mincing words TOUT COURT

plainsong GREGORIAN CHANT

– plainsong opening, sung as a solo INTONATION

– music of a single melodic line, as in plainsong MONOPHONY

plait or pigtail QUEUE

– plaited braid, or its metal tag, as on the shoulder of a military uniform AIGUILLETTE

plan See also **plot**

– plan, outline, or arrangement, as for a radio programme FORMAT

– plan, proposal, intended or suggested scheme PROJECT, PROPOSITION

– plan, sketch, or rough drawing of something DRAFT

– plan or arrangement, ordering DISPOSITION

– plan or intend MEDITATE, PURPOSE, CONTEMPLATE, DESTINE

– plan or invent, scheme DEVISE, CONTRIVE, CONCOCT, CAST ABOUT, DESIGN

– plan or method based on a long-range or overall view of things STRATEGY

– plan or model, original and detailed, that forms the basis for subsequent versions PROTOTYPE, BLUEPRINT

– plan or record of a journey ITINERARY

– planned, intended PROJECTED

– planned beforehand, deliberate, as a murder might be PREMEDITATED

– planned or performed together, combined, as an effort might be CONCERTED, COORDINATED

– planning, preparation FORETHOUGHT

– planning of any complicated project, especially one involving transport LOGISTICS

– planning technique for a complex project, based on comparing various combinations of stages CRITICAL-PATH ANALYSIS

– plans or methods designed to achieve short-term, local, or immediate objectives TACTICS

– carry out a plan IMPLEMENT, EXECUTE

– course of action for carrying out a plan, process, or the like PROCEDURE

– delay or difficulty in one's plans HITCH

– draft or specify a plan, ideas, or the like FORMULATE

– precise description, list of details, plan, or proposal SPECIFICATION

– providing for some possible though unlikely future occurrence or emergency, as a fund or plan might CONTINGENCY

– provisional, incompletely developed, or experimental, as a plan might be TENTATIVE

– sketch out or give a rough outline of something, such as a plan ADUMBRATE

– success or realisation of plans or wishes FRUITION

planet, star, or comet CELESTIAL BODY

– planet of very small size, especially in an orbiting belt between Mars and Jupiter PLANETOID, MINOR PLANET, ASTEROID

– planet that is closer to the Sun than Earth is INFERIOR PLANET

– planet that is farther from the Sun than Earth is SUPERIOR PLANET

– chart of the relative positions of planets and signs of the zodiac at a given time HOROSCOPE

– elliptical rather than circular, as a planet's orbit might be ECCENTRIC

– imaginary band around the celestial sphere, as used by astronomers and astrologers, representing the path of the Sun, Moon, and planets ZODIAC

– point in its orbit when a planet, comet, or the like is farthest from the Sun APHELION

– point in its orbit when a planet, comet, or the like is nearest the Sun PERIHELION

plank of wood joined to others to form a beam FLITCH

– plank or ramp, as on a building site, used for crossing a muddy area GANGPLANK, DUCKBOARD

– plank used for strengthening the side of a trench, ship, or the like WALE

– path or promenade made of wooden planks, as beside a beach BOARDWALK

– referring to a ship or boat built with overlapping planks CLINKER-BUILT, LAPSTRAKE
– referring to a ship or boat built with the planks lying edge to edge on the hull, rather than overlapping CARVEL-BUILT
– strip of planking or metal plating stretching the entire length of a ship's hull STRAKE

plant See also **flower**
– plant, such as moss, growing on another plant without being parasitic on it EPIPHYTE
– plant body, as in algae or fungi, without distinct parts THALLUS
– plant cultivation, especially of flowers HORTICULTURE
– plant cultivation without soil, using nutrients dissolved in water HYDROPONICS, AQUICULTURE
– plant cutting, as for grafting SLIP, SCION
– plant disease affecting cereals, caused by various fungi SMUT, ERGOT
– plant disease causing the withering and death of leaves and other parts without rotting BLIGHT
– plant-eating, feeding solely on plants as many animals do HERBIVOROUS, PHYTOPHAGOUS
– plant-life of an area VEGETATION, FLORA
– plant-like animal, such as a sea anemone ZOOPHYTE
– plant-like, relating to plants or plant growth VEGETAL
– plant living for one year or a single season ANNUAL
– plant living for three or more years, typically with new growth or flowering each year PERENNIAL
– plant living for two years BIENNIAL
– plant of a cultivated rather than natural variety CULTIVAR
– plant of the common group including most trees and shrubs, characterised by two embryonic seed leaves DICOTYLEDON, DICOT
– plant of the group including grasses, orchids, and lilies, characterised by a single embryonic seed leaf MONOCOTYLEDON
– plant or animal established in a region although not indigenous to it DENIZEN
– plant or crop growing from seed that was not deliberately sown VOLUNTEER
– plant or flower bred from two different varieties or species HYBRID
– plant or grow crops in a fixed sequence ROTATE
– plant part resembling a leaf, just beneath a flower or cluster of flowers BRACT
– plant-pot of a large, decorated type JARDINIÈRE
– plant that keeps its colour when dried IMMORTELLE
– plant tissue conducting nutrients, made up of sieve tubes PHLOEM, BAST
– plant tissue conducting water and providing support, woody tissue XYLEM
– plant used in making medicines OFFICINAL, SIMPLE
– plants of a primitive water-dwelling kind, ranging from seaweeds to tiny diatoms ALGAE
– bell-shaped cover of plastic or glass, placed over young plants for protection CLOCHE
– box or small case used by botanists for carrying plant specimens collected on their expeditions VASCULUM
– branch, leaf, or other secondary or projecting part of a plant APPENDAGE
– building in which plants are cultivated under controlled conditions PHYTOTRON
– cultivate wild plants or adapt foreign plants to a new environment DOMESTICATE
– enclosure for keeping or breeding animals or plants indoors VIVARIUM
– fleshy part of plants, often edible HERBAGE
– go limp, droop, as a plant might WILT
– green pigment in plants that traps energy from sunlight for photosynthesis CHLOROPHYLL
– primitive seed-bearing plant shaped like a palm tree but having fern-like leaves CYCAD
– protective layer covering the epidermis of a plant CUTICLE
– radiating pattern of leaves or petals around the stem of a plant WHORL
– referring to a plant that is local or native to the region INDIGENOUS
– referring to a plant that is not local or native to the region, but that comes from a foreign region EXOTIC
– relating or referring to a plant's growth or movement in a particular direction through internal rather than external factors NASTIC
– repeated branching or forking of a plant into two equal parts DICHOTOMY
– reproduce, breed, or cause plants or animals to reproduce themselves PROPAGATE
– study of plants BOTANY, PHYTOLOGY
– tendency of a plant to grow in a particular direction TROPISM
– tropical American plant with fleshy leaves, of a family including the pineapple BROMELIAD
– tropical American plant with fleshy leaves, some species yielding fibre such as sisal and alcoholic drinks such as tequila AGAVE
– use of light energy by a plant, absorbed by chlorophyll, for forming organic compounds from carbon dioxide and water PHOTOSYNTHESIS

-plant- ANTHO-, -PHYT-, PHYTO-, -PHYTE

plaster a wall or surface RENDER
– plaster of a coarse, gravelly kind, applied to outside walls ROUGHCAST
– plaster of a smooth kind used for frescoes or mouldings STUCCO
– plaster used as a finishing coating on walls GROUT
– decoratively patterned plasterwork on walls PARGETING
– rough finish for outside walls, produced by small pebbles embedded in the plaster PEBBLE-DASH
– roughen or scratch plaster KEY
– smooth or level plaster FLOAT
– tray with a handle underneath, as for carrying plaster HAWK
– wall painting made on dry plaster SECCO
– wall painting made on damp plaster FRESCO
– wooden or metal strip used as a thickness guide or leveller, as when plastering SCREED

plaster of Paris preparation, used as a painting surface or for bas-relief sculpture GESSO
– white mineral used in fertilisers and plaster of Paris GYPSUM

plastic of a light, foamy consistency, as used for packaging material EXPANDED PLASTIC, POLYSTYRENE
– chemical compound with large molecules containing repeated units, forming the basis of plastics POLYMER
– clear plastic specially treated to reduce glare, as used in sunglasses POLAROID
– clear resilient plastic used as a substitute for glass PERSPEX
– floor-covering of a plastic-like material, produced either in sheets or in tiles LINOLEUM
– glossy plastic sheeting, as used for table-tops FORMICA
– heavy plastic of a hard resistant kind, as used for the casings of early radio sets BAKELITE

– lightweight resilient plastic of various kinds ACRYLIC
– produce wire or plastics, or the like by pressing through a nozzle or die EXTRUDE
– tough, flexible, shiny plastic of various kinds VINYL

plastic surgery ANAPLASTY
– plastic surgery, such as a facelift, designed to improve one's physical appearance COSMETIC SURGERY

plate, protective shell, or similar hard covering, as on some animals or ships CUIRASS
– plate, scale, or similar thin layer of plant or animal tissue LAMELLA, LAMINA
– plate, typically of silver or gold, used for holding the bread at Communion PATEN
– plate of a large shallow design CHARGER, PLATTER
– plate or shield, as worn by fencers, or forming the underside of a tortoise PLASTRON
– plate or tray of wood, used for carving or serving food TRENCHER
– plate set on a hotplate or warmer, used to cook food or keep it warm CHAFING DISH
– plated or scaled, as an armadillo or lobster is MAILED
– plates, saucers, and other flat crockery FLATWARE
– covered in scales or bony plates, as some insects and seeds are SCUTATE, SCUTELLATE
– having a traditional blue-on-white Chinese design, as a china plate might WILLOW-PATTERN

plateau of uplands or a well-defined block of mountains MASSIF

platform, as for a lecturer or conductor DAIS, PODIUM, ROSTRUM
– platform, or the stairway leading to it, outside the entrance of a large building PERRON
– platform or raised wooden framework, as formerly for hanging or beheading criminals SCAFFOLD
– platform supporting cargo or stored goods, typically moved by a fork-lift truck PALLET, SKID
– platform which election candidates formerly used to make speeches HUSTINGS
– raised platform in a public place TRIBUNE

Plato – philosophical work, as by Plato, in the form of a conversation DIALOGUE

platypus or related egg-laying mammal MONOTREME

play See also **drama**, **theatre**
– play about with, treat disrespectfully TRIFLE WITH
– play at some pursuit, take a casual interest in something DABBLE
– play down, minimise the importance of, detract from SOFT-PEDAL
– play for time, evade or postpone commitments TEMPORISE
– play house WENDY HOUSE
– play on words, especially a pun PARANOMASIA
– play or scene in a play in which only two actors have speaking parts DUOLOGUE
– play or write a musical composition in a different key TRANSPOSE
– play's scenery and props MISE EN SCÈNE
– playing or expected to play similar roles continually TYPECAST
– climax, solution, or unravelling of a play DÉNOUEMENT, CATASTROPHE
– closing poem or speech following the end of the action of a play EPILOGUE
– early or afternoon performance of a play MATINÉE
– first public presentation of a film, play, or the like PREMIERE
– interval entertainment between the acts of an opera or play DIVERTISSEMENT, INTERLUDE, ENTR'ACTE
– "into the middle of things", straight into the narrative or plot, as a book or play might begin IN MEDIAS RES
– list of characters in a play DRAMATIS PERSONAE
– outline of the plot of a play, novel, or the like SCENARIO
– passage of conversation in a play, novel, or the like, or the characters' spoken words in such a passage DIALOGUE
– relating to play or games LUDIC
– scene in a play in which the actors freeze in position TABLEAU
– speech addressed only to oneself, such as a character in a play might utter SOLILOQUY
– supporting actors in a play ENSEMBLE
– test for a part in a play, concert, or the like, by giving a sample performance AUDITION
– theatrical company performing a variety of plays during a season REPERTORY COMPANY
– writer of plays, dramatist DRAMATURGE

playboy, lecherous man, or compulsive womaniser RAKE, ROUÉ, PROFLIGATE, SKIRTCHASER, LIBERTINE, DEBAUCHEE
– playboy, sexually promiscuous man, seducer LADYKILLER, CASANOVA, DON JUAN, LOTHARIO

playful, abounding in high spirits FROLICSOME, SPORTIVE
– playful and joking conversation BADINAGE, BANTER, REPARTEE
– move about in a playful way, jump and skip about FRISK, GAMBOL, FROLIC, ROMP, SPORT, ROLLICK, CAPER, CAVORT

playing card See **card**, **card games**

playwright, dramatist DRAMATURGE

plead or beg on behalf of another INTERCEDE

pleasant See **good**, **friendly**
– pleasant, agreeable, or satisfying GRATIFYING
– pleasant-sounding, pleasing to the ear EUPHONIOUS
– pleasantness AMENITY
– having an appropriate and pleasant style, as a writer might FELICITOUS

pleasant- EU-

please or satisfy GRATIFY
– pleased or self-satisfied, to the point of feeling that nothing more needs to be done COMPLACENT
– pleasing, or trying to please or gain favour, as by excessive flattery, humility, or obligingness TOADYING, SYCOPHANTIC, SERVILE, OBSEQUIOUS, UNCTUOUS, FAWNING
– hugely pleased or overwhelmed with delight TRANSPORTED, ENRAPTURED

pleasure, delight, or enjoyment DELECTATION, GRATIFICATION
– pleasure in or satisfaction at the misfortunes of someone else SCHADENFREUDE
– pleasure-loving, devoted to food and drink and other sensual pleasures HEDONISTIC, EPICUREAN
– pleasure-loving person, devoted to luxurious and sensual living SYBARITE, VOLUPTUARY
– pleasure or entertainment based on the suffering of others ROMAN HOLIDAY
– pleasurable and intense emotions RAPTURES, TRANSPORT, ECSTASY
– experienced or enjoyed through the actions or achievements of someone else, as pleasure might be VICARIOUS
– occupy oneself in a pleasurable activity DISPORT
– regard with cruel satisfaction or smug pleasure GLOAT
– relating to or gratifying the pleasures of the senses or the bodily appetites SENSUAL

-pleasure -MANIA

pleat, flute, or crimp material, as with a heated iron GOFFER
– pleated or gathered strip of lace or fabric, used as a trimming RUCHE, RUFFLE
– pleated or gathered strip of

material sewn to the lower edge of a garment or curtain FLOUNCE
pledge or mortgage something as security HYPOTHECATE
– fulfil a promise, pledge, or the like REDEEM
plenty See also **lots**, **many**, **excessive**
– plenty, abundance or fullness AMPLITUDE, PLENITUDE
– plentiful, endless or countless BOTTOMLESS, INEXHAUSTIBLE, UNTOLD
– plentiful, generous, numerous, in good supply ABOUNDING, ABUNDANT, BOUNTEOUS, BOUNTIFUL, OPULENT, PRODIGAL
– plentiful harvest or supply FOISON
– plentiful or generous, as a helping of food might be LAVISH, AMPLE, COPIOUS
– plentiful or luxurious only in appearance or by report, as an illusory feast BARMECIDAL
– plentiful supply, as of wealth or choices, overabundance EMBARASSMENT OF RICHES
– extremely plentiful, excessively abundant or productive, swarming THRONGING, TEEMING, PULLULATING
– full, well-stocked, having a plentiful supply BRIMMING, POPULOUS, FLUSH, REPLETE
– given generously or plentifully UNSTINTED
– "horn of plenty", overflowing store, abundance CORNUCOPIA
– in plenty, in abundance GALORE
– produced or producing plentifully, fertile, fruitful, as an imagination or vegetation might be FECUND, EXUBERANT, LUXURIANT, PROFUSE, PROLIFIC
– too plentiful, over-supplied RIFE, AWASH
pliable, flexible, easily moulded DUCTILE, MALLEABLE, PLASTIC
plot See also **plan**
– plot, conspire, cooperate in a secret or underhand way COLLABORATE, COLLUDE, COLLOGUE, CONNIVE
– plot, intrigue, conspiracy MACHINATIONS, COMPLOT
– plot of land in the centre of a block, not bordering the street PANHANDLE
– plot or group of plotters CONSPIRACY, CABAL, CONFEDERACY
– plot or secret agreement for sinister or illegal purposes COLLUSION, CONNIVANCE
– plot or use of false evidence to incriminate an innocent party FRAME-UP
– criminal plot to cheat, harm, or injure a victim COVIN
– outline of the plot of a novel, play, or the like SCENARIO
– resolution or clarification, as of the plot of a play or a story DÉNOUEMENT
– sinful, wicked, infamous, as an evil plot or notorious murderer is NEFARIOUS
– straight into the plot, as a book or play might begin IN MEDIAS RES
plough – plough-like implement used to level or break up soil HARROW
– plough of an ancient design ARD
– ploughable, and suitable for cultivating crops, as land might be ARABLE
– ploughing at right angles to the slope of the land, in order to reduce erosion CONTOUR PLOUGHING
– blade or cutting wheel at the front of a plough, cutting a preliminary furrow COULTER
– ridge between ploughed furrows LIST
plucking device for the strings of a harpsichord or related instrument QUILL
– played by plucking rather than bowing the strings, as a passage for the violin might be PIZZICATO
– small thin disc or plate, as of plastic, used for plucking the strings of a guitar, lute, or related instrument PLECTRUM, PICK
plug connecting one or more other plugs to an electrical socket ADAPTER
– plug or bung in the vent of a cask SPIGOT, SPILE
– plug or cover for the muzzle of a gun when not in use TAMPION
– plug such as a cork or bung STOPPLE
plum of a small, blue-black variety DAMSON
plum brandy from Eastern Europe SLIVOVITZ
plume on a helmet or hat PANACHE
plump or full-bosomed, and healthy and energetic, as some women are BUXOM
plunder, rob violently PILLAGE
– plunder and destruction DEPREDATION, RAPINE, SPOLIATION
– plundered or stolen goods LOOT, BOOTY, SPOILS
– plundering and destructive, as an advancing army might be RAPACIOUS
– raider in search of plunder MARAUDER, LOOTER, PILLAGER
-plus- -CUM-
plywood or similarly layered sheet of material LAMINATE
– any of the thin layers bonded together to form plywood VENEER
pneumonia – crackling sound in the chest, as of pneumonia patients CREPITUS
poacher's dog LURCHER
pocket, as on a waistcoat, designed for a pocket watch FOB
– slit in a dress, skirt, or the like, as for fitting a fastening or for access to a pocket PLACKET
pod or seed of the pea, bean, or related plant LEGUME
– split or burst open along a seam, as a pod or fruit might, to release seeds or pollen DEHISCE
poem See also **poetry**
– poem about rural life BUCOLIC, GEORGIC, ECLOGUE, IDYLL
– poem in which some letters, usually the first, of the lines spell out a name or message ACROSTIC
– poem of a formal, dignified, and stylistically complex kind ODE
– poem of a simple, musical, and often emotional kind, rather than dramatic or narrative LYRIC
– poem of grief, lament, usually over lost love COMPLAINT
– poem of lament for someone's death ELEGY, THRENODY, MONODY
– poem of recantation PALINODE
– poem or other material spoken from memory in front of an audience RECITATION
– poem or song in celebration of a marriage EPITHALAMIUM
– poem to be sung or recited before a wedding PROTHALAMION
– poem to be sung or recited at dawn AUBADE
– long poem with a heroic narrative EPIC
– narrative poem of simple rhyming stanzas and a repeated refrain BALLAD
– rhymed poem of fourteen lines SONNET
– short poem with a heroic narrative LAY
– verse or stanza of a poem STAVE
poet, bard, or minstrel in ancient Scandinavia SKALD
– poet, bard, or minstrel in Anglo-Saxon England SCOP
– poet, especially an ancient Celtic singing poet, an honoured national poet, or a prizewinning Eisteddfod poet BARD
– poet, Nobel prize winner, or other eminent person in the arts or sciences who receives a special honour LAUREATE
– poet and musician in medieval France TROUBADOUR, TROUVÈRE, JONGLEUR
– poet of poor quality RHYMESTER, POETASTER, VERSIFIER
– poets of the 17th century, such

as Donne and Herbert, using far-fetched metaphors METAPHYSICAL POETS
– poetic inspiration or other creative impulse AFFLATUS

poetry See chart, and also **poem**, **figures of speech**
– book or collection of poetry ANTHOLOGY, CHRESTOMATHY
– complex metaphor used in Old English and Old Norse poetry KENNING
– pair of consecutive and rhyming lines in poetry COUPLET
– passion, as when reciting poetry HWYL
– referring to lines of poetry that continue as a single flowing sentence without pause to the next ENJAMBED
– referring to lines of poetry that end with a distinct pause END-STOPPED
– relating to artistic inspiration, especially poetry PIERIAN
– relating to poetry or drama that is refined and classically elegant in style AUGUSTAN
– relating to the world of poetry PARNASSIAN
– rhymed verse forms common in English poetry OTTAVA RIMA, SPENSERIAN, STANZA
– rhythm or metrical lines in poetry NUMBERS
– rhythmical or metrical stress in a line of poetry ICTUS
– study of the forms and metres of poetry PROSODY

POETRY TERMS

anapaest	metrical foot consisting of two short or unstressed syllables followed by one long or stressed syllable
blank verse	verse form, as in Shakespeare's plays, of unrhymed ten-syllable lines
caesura	pause or break within a line of verse
canto	section or "chapter" of a long poem
clerihew	comic four-line verse, typically about a person named in one of the lines
concrete poetry	poetry in which the shape of the words on the page conveys added meaning
dactyl	metrical foot consisting of one long or stressed syllable followed by two short or unstressed syllables
eclogue	short pastoral poem, often in the form of a dialogue
elegy	poem lamenting a dead person; broadly, any wistful poem
envoi	short, final stanza of certain poems, especially French poems
feminine rhyme	rhyme of two or more syllables, such as *measure* and *treasure*
foot	unit of metre in poetry, corresponding to a bar in music
free verse, vers libre	verse without conventional metre or rhyme
georgic, bucolic	poem about rural, pastoral, or farming life
haiku	Japanese three-line poem of seventeen syllables
heroic couplet	verse form of two rhyming ten-syllabled lines
hexameter	line of six metrical feet
iambic/iambus/iamb	metrical foot consisting of one short or unstressed syllable followed by one long or stressed syllable
idyll	short lyrical poem about everyday life in rural surroundings
internal rhyme	rhyme occurring within a line of verse rather than at the ends of two or more lines
limerick	light witty poem or nonsense verse of a fixed five-line form
macaronic verse	humorous verse written in a jumble of languages
ode	long, usually rhymed, heroic poem
pentameter	line of five metrical feet
quatrain	stanza consisting of four lines rhyming alternately
rondeau, roundel	lyrical poem of French origin using only two rhymes throughout
roundelay	poem or song with a regularly repeated refrain
scansion	rhythmic or metrical pattern of a verse
spondee	metrical foot, as in Latin poetry, consisting of two long syllables
sprung rhythm	heavily accented verse rhythm with an irregular number of unstressed syllables in each foot
stanza	complete verse or "paragraph" of a poem
stich	line of verse
strophe	verse, especially the first of two differently structured verses making up a poem
tanka	Japanese five-line poem of thirty-one syllables
tetrameter	line of verse consisting of four feet
trochee	metrical foot consisting of one long or stressed syllable followed by one short or unstressed one
villanelle	poem of a complex 19-line form of French origin, using much repeated rhyme

– style of popular musical entertainment, in which improvised poetry is recited or chanted to a musical accompaniment RAPPING
– vivid comparisons, metaphors, and the like, that are used in poetry to evoke pictures in the mind IMAGERY

point at which lines intersect or diverge NODE
– point at which three or more lines in geometry intersect CONCURRENCE
– point of crisis beyond which a tense situation will erupt into war or violence FLASHPOINT
– point of greatest intensity, as of a series of events, or in a story, play, or the like CLIMAX
– point of no return, limit beyond which one becomes fully committed to a course of action RUBICON
– point of origin, starting point TERMINUS A QUO
– point of view, attitude PERSPECTIVE, STANDPOINT
– point on the body where an artery can be pressed shut to stop the bleeding of a wound further on PRESSURE POINT
– point or detail based on a strict ruling or literal interpretation of a law TECHNICALITY
– point still in dispute or open to debate MOOT POINT
– pointing or jutting outwards, projecting, as an angle or the like might SALIENT
– acknowledgment of a telling point, argument, or accusation made against one TOUCHÉ
– approach the same point from different directions CONVERGE
– move away from the same point in different directions DIVERGE

-point- ACRO-, -STYL-, STYLO-, -STYLAR

pointed, cutting, or piercing, as a witty retort might be POIGNANT
– pointed, needle-shaped ACERATE, ACEROSE, ACULEATE
– pointed, tapering, narrowing to a point, as a leaf might ACUMINATE
– pointed end or figure CUSP
– pointed writing instrument, as used on wax tablets in ancient times STYLUS

Poiseidon's three-pronged spear TRIDENT

poison, germ, or any other harmful substance that prompts the body's immune system to produce antibodies ANTIGEN
– poison extracted from an Indian tree, much favoured by early crime-writers STRYCHNINE
– poison produced by a fungus on peanuts and maize AFLATOXIN
– poisoning by a cereal fungus, capable of producing itching, gangrene, or convulsions ERGOTISM, ST ANTHONY'S FIRE
– poisonous chemical element, used in insecticides, weed-killers, and the like ARSENIC
– poisonous compound, smelling of almonds, as used for fumigation CYANIDE
– poisonous flowering plant, or the poison derived from it, which Socrates drank when condemned to death HEMLOCK
– poisonous fluid secreted in a snakebite, scorpion sting, or the like VENOM
– poisonous plant of various kinds, of the buttercup and lily families, or the poison extracted from its underground stem HELLEBORE
– poisonous solid compound dissolved for use as a weed-killer PARAQUAT
– poisonous substance, especially of organic origin TOXIN
– poisonous substance extracted from deadly nightshade, used in various medical treatments ATROPINE, BELLADONNA
– affecting the entire body, as a disease or poison might SYSTEMIC
– antidote to poison obtained from the blood or tissue of immunised animals SERUM
– arrow poison used by South American Indians, obtained from the resin of tropical trees CURARE
– chemical compound used to prevent blood-clotting and as a rat poison WARFARIN
– deadly poison BANE
– effective, powerful, or still active, as a drug or poison might be POTENT
– extremely harmful or rapid in effect, as a disease or poison might be VIRULENT
– food poisoning PTOMAINE POISONING
– food poisoning, often fatal, caused by a bacterial toxin found in badly tinned, preserved, or smoked food BOTULISM
– food poisoning caused by rod-shaped bacteria of a kind often found in inadequately cooked meat SALMONELLA POISONING, SALMONELLOSIS
– glass box with protective gloves sealed into the side for handling radioactive or poisonous substances GLOVE BOX
– immunity to poison through habituation to it by taking small doses MITHRIDATISM
– Indian tree with poisonous seeds, the source of strychnine and other poisons NUX VOMICA
– Japanese fish with some poisonous parts that have to be removed before it is eaten FUGU
– medicine, serum, or antibody that counteracts the effects of a poison ANTIDOTE, ANTITOXIN, ANTIVENIN
– small container for medicine, poison, or other liquid, typically a stoppered glass bottle VIAL, PHIAL
– study of poisons and the treatment of poisoning TOXICOLOGY
– supposed antidote against all poisons MITHRIDATE
– tropical American plant with poisonous seeds used in insecticides SABADILLA
– weed-killer or other poison for destroying plants HERBICIDE

-poison- -TOX-, TOXO-, TOXICO-

poisonous TOXIC, VENOMOUS
– poisonous gas remaining in a mine, especially a coal mine, after an explosion or fire AFTERDAMP

poker or other heat-resistant implement used in fire SALAMANDER

poker hand containing five consecutive cards, but not all of the same suit STRAIGHT
– poker hand containing three cards all with the same value, and two cards both with the same value FULL HOUSE
– poker hand in which all five cards are in a single suit FLUSH
– poker hand of five consecutive cards in a single suit STRAIGHT FLUSH
– poker hand of the top five cards of a single suit ROYAL FLUSH
– bet made by a poker player before looking at his cards BLIND
– demand by a poker player to see an opponent's hand, made by matching but not increasing his bet CALL
– drop out of the betting during a hand of poker FOLD
– form of poker in which some cards are dealt face upwards STUD
– increase the bet in a poker game RAISE
– showing of the cards at the end of a poker game SHOWDOWN
– stake put into the pool by a poker player receiving his cards ANTE

polar weather condition producing very low visibility WHITE-OUT

pole for marking positions in surveying RANGING POLE
– pole or pillar carved and painted

with kinship symbols, as by certain North American Indians TOTEM POLE
– pole used as a mast or boom SPAR
– pole used for pushing a punt or similar flat-bottomed boat QUANT
– pole with a bucket on the end for drawing water from a well SWEEP, SWIPE
– pole with a spring at the base, on which one can bounce along POGO STICK
– variation, in 14-month cycles, of the position of the geographical poles CHANDLER WOBBLE

police force of a town or district CONSTABULARY
– police hunt of a widespread and coordinated kind DRAGNET
– police informer GRASS, NARK, STOOL PIGEON
– police kit or method for creating a picture of a wanted criminal IDENTIKIT, PHOTOFIT
– police line, series of ships, or the like, surrounding or guarding an area CORDON
– police officer of fairly senior rank SUPERINTENDENT
– police or military trainee CADET
– police patrol car used in Britain PANDA CAR
– police van for transporting offenders BLACK MARIA
– police van in the U.S. and Australia for transporting offenders PADDY WAGON
– civilian who takes on, without legal right, judicial or police powers for himself VIGILANTE
– detention, being held under arrest or under guard, as by the police CUSTODY
– district of a U.S. city under a particular administrative or police authority PRECINCT
– senior police officer of a metropolitan district COMMANDER
– tricking or luring of someone, as by the police, into danger or self-incrimination ENTRAPMENT

police-state system aiming at total control TOTALITARIANISM

policeman in Canada MOUNTY
– policeman in France GENDARME
– policeman in Ireland GARDA
– policeman under military command in Italy CARABINIERE
– policeman in London in the 18th and early 19th centuries BOW STREET RUNNER
– policeman's short club or truncheon in the U.S. NIGHTSTICK
– slang or informal terms for a policeman FLATFOOT, NARC, OLD BILL, ROZZER, SHAMUS, SWEENEY, WALLOPER, PEELER, BOBBY

policy, plan, or method based on a long-range or overall view of things STRATEGY
– policy of burning or destroying all crops, food, and anything else likely to be of use to an advancing enemy SCORCHED-EARTH POLICY
– declaration of policies, as by a political party MANIFESTO
– reversal or about-turn of attitude or policy VOLTE-FACE

polio INFANTILE PARALYSIS, POLIOMYELITIS
– polio vaccine, formerly injected, based on a weakened or killed virus SALK VACCINE
– polio vaccine, taken orally, based on a live but weakened virus SABIN VACCINE

polish and brighten BURNISH, FURBISH
– polish or gloss LUSTRE
– polish or smoothness, as of speech or manners FINISH
– polish with wax SIMONISE
– polished surface layer or finishing, as of fine wood VENEER

polite, proper, avoiding disrespect and impropriety DEFERENTIAL, DECOROUS
– polite, refined, polished in social behaviour GENTEEL
– polite, socially gracious, and charming, often in a superficial way SUAVE, URBANE
– polite, well-mannered CIVIL, COURTEOUS
– polite or extremely formal CEREMONIOUS
– polite remarks, small talk PLEASANTRIES
– polite social gestures, courtesies CIVILITIES
– accepted or expected forms or standards of polite social behaviour CONVENTIONS, ETIQUETTE, PROTOCOL, CONVENANCES
– referring to polite remarks, as about the weather, made for the sake of social contact rather than true communication PHATIC

political activity, especially foreign policy, based uncompromisingly on national self-interest rather than on moral considerations REALPOLITIK
– political agitation and propaganda, especially that by left-wing radicals AGITPROP
– political agitator provoking civil discontent or strife INCENDIARY
– political and social system that prevailed in former times but has now been replaced ANCIEN RÉGIME
– political campaigning, especially for elections HUSTINGS
– political cooperation between different parties or groups in power COHABITATION
– political cunning or opportunism MACHIAVELLIANISM
– political deals among legislators, such as the swapping of votes and other mutual favours in the U.S. LOGROLLING
– political elimination of opponents or dissidents PURGE
– political extremist in favour of basic and far-reaching social and economic changes RADICAL
– political extremist or revolutionary SANS-CULOTTE, MAXIMALIST, JACOBIN
– political extremist advocating the destruction of all existing social and political institutions NIHILIST, ANARCHIST
– political grouping or agreement ALIGNMENT
– political leader or agitator rallying support by crude emotional speeches DEMAGOGUE
– political manipulation of the boundaries of an electoral constituency for party advantage GERRYMANDER
– political opponent of a government, especially in a one-party state DISSIDENT
– political or military grouping that forms the core of a potentially larger unit CADRE
– political or other group, typically causing dissension, within a larger group FACTION
– political or religious document or pamphlet containing a forceful declaration or rallying call TRACT
– political party's declaration of its policies, as before an election MANIFESTO
– political party's sub-group or policy meeting CAUCUS
– political policies and actions based on the wishes of the majority CONSENSUS POLITICS
– political principles of a country, concerning basic rights and duties, either unwritten or embodied in statutes CONSTITUTION
– political protest in the form of non-violent resistance and a refusal to obey laws regarded as unjust CIVIL DISOBEDIENCE
– political protester or energetic campaigner ACTIVIST, MILITANT
– political reformer or rebel within a particular group or party YOUNG TURK
– political reformer or theorist who is hopelessly idealistic and impractical VISIONARY, UTOPIAN
– political style or presentation

aimed at appealing to ordinary people POPULISM
– political union, league, or association of states with a fairly strong central government FEDERATION
– politically committed, active in promoting a moral or political cause ENGAGÉ
– alliance, typically temporary, of political parties or other groups COALITION
– catchphrase, motto, jingle, or the like used repeatedly, as in political campaigns SLOGAN
– change a person's beliefs or political attitudes by indoctrination or intensive conditioning BRAINWASH
– extreme or uncompromising, as one's political stance might be INTRANSIGENT
– overthrow or attempt to destroy something, especially a government or political system, by means of concerted secret undermining SUBVERT
– place, platform, or occasion for public speeches, especially on political issues STUMP
– relating to a politically corrupt organisation in U.S. city or state government TAMMANY
– secret agent who joins a political or criminal group and tries to entrap it into punishable or discreditable activities AGENT PROVOCATEUR
– small local political division in certain European countries COMMUNE
– sympathiser with the aims and ideals of a political or other group, without being a member of it FELLOW TRAVELLER, CAMP FOLLOWER

politician in the U.S. who is neutral or independent MUGWUMP
– politician responsible for ensuring that fellow party members attend and vote correctly in parliament WHIP
– politician who seeks office in an area that he is not directly associated with CARPETBAGGER
– government-funded project in the U.S. benefiting a particular politician's constituency PORK BARREL

poll that is taken in a cross-section of society, especially to forecast election results GALLUP POLL
– rough-and-ready unofficial opinion poll, especially on an election or political issue STRAW POLL

pollen – pollinated by insects, as many flowering plants are ENTOMOPHILOUS
– pollinated by wind-blown pollen, as grass flowers are ANEMOPHILOUS
– pollination between two flowers on a single plant ENDOGAMY
– pollination from one plant to another plant, cross-fertilisation XENOGAMY
– medical drug used in the treatment of allergic reactions, as to pollen or bee-stings ANTIHISTAMINE
– self-pollination by a flower, self-fertilisation AUTOGAMY

polo stick MALLET
– any of the sessions of play, each lasting about seven minutes, in a polo match CHUKKER

polony BOLOGNA SAUSAGE

Polynesian skirt formed by a wrap-around rectangular cloth LAVA-LAVA, PAREU

pomegranate or redcurrant syrup, used as a cordial or flavouring GRENADINE

pomp and ceremony, grand spectacle PAGEANTRY

pompous See also **high-falutin**, **pride**, **proud**
– pompous, petty, self-important person, such as an office manager or minor bureaucrat HIS NIBS, HIGH MUCKAMUCK, JOBSWORTH, PANJANDRUM, TIN GOD
– pompous, putting on airs, behaving in an artificial way to impress others AFFECTED, PORTENTOUS, PRETENTIOUS
– pompous, self-important, swaggering STRUTTING, BUMPTIOUS, PUSHY, CONSEQUENTIAL, VAINGLORIOUS
– pompous, snobbish, stuck-up ALOOF, HOITY-TOITY, LA-DI-DA, LOFTY, SNIFFY, SNOOTY, SNOTTY, TOFFEE-NOSED, UPPISH
– pompous, standing on ceremony, and bossy OFFICIOUS
– pompous and arrogant, assuming an air of superiority CONDESCENDING, DISDAINFUL, PATRONISING, SUPERCILIOUS
– pompous and reactionary man, especially an officer or bureaucrat COLONEL BLIMP
– pompous official with apparently wide-ranging powers POOH-BAH
– pompous or affected in style, stiff and unnatural MANNERED, STILTED, STARCHY
– pompously moralising, especially by means of proverbs and platitudes SENTENTIOUS, PONTIFICAL, PREACHY
– pompously moralistic, precise, or narrow-minded CANTING, HOLIER-THAN-THOU, PUNCTILIOUS, PIOUS, PRIGGISH, SERMONISING, SANCTIMONIOUS
– pompously self-assured and inflexible, arrogant OPINIONATED, COCKSURE
– pompously self-satisfied COMPLACENT, SMUG
– angry or peevish in a pompous way, as from an affront to one's supposed dignity HUFFISH

pond or small lake MERE

pool – still, filled with motionless water, as a pool or pond might be STAGNANT

poor, down and out, poverty-stricken, having few or no possessions DESTITUTE, PENURIOUS, INDIGENT
– poor, down at heel, deprived of one's former wealth or comforts DISTRESSED, IMPOVERISHED, IN STRAITENED CIRCUMSTANCES, IN REDUCED CIRCUMSTANCES
– poor, penniless, needy IMPECUNIOUS, NECESSITOUS, PINCHED
– poor, underprivileged, lacking most of the advantages in life DEPRIVED, DISADVANTAGED
– poor but refined SHABBY GENTEEL
– poor person, sometimes living on public charity PAUPER

pop music of a black American style, often with blues or gospel rhythms MOTOWN

Pope PONTIFF, VICAR OF CHRIST, VICEGERENT
– Pope's ambassador NUNCIO
– Pope's authority, office, or term of office PAPACY
– Pope's beehive-shaped three-tiered crown or hat TIARA
– Pope's meeting with the cardinals CONSISTORY
– Pope's unfailing correctness in doctrinal matters of faith and of morals INFALLIBILITY
– adjective for the Pope PAPAL
– authorised by the Pope, as a doctrine might be EX CATHEDRA
– cardinal who handles the Pope's financial affairs, papal treasurer CAMERLINGO
– delegate or representative of the Pope EMISSARY, LEGATE
– favouring a policy of centralised authority in the Roman Catholic Church, investing the Pope with absolute power ULTRAMONTANE
– favouring a policy of decentralised authority in the Roman Catholic Church, restricting the Pope's power in the various branches of the church CISALPINE, GALLICAN
– formal agreement, especially between the Pope and a country's government, over religious affairs CONCORDAT

– formal meeting with a monarch, the Pope, or the like AUDIENCE
– letter from the Pope to bishops in all countries ENCYCLICAL
– letter of instructions or judgment, in modern handwriting, issued by the Pope BRIEF
– letter or document, in antique handwriting, issued by the Pope BULL
– letter or edict issued by the Pope on a point of church law or doctrine DECRETAL
– meeting of cardinals to elect the Pope CONCLAVE
– relating to St Peter or to the Pope considered as his successor PETRINE

popular, commonly used, as the ordinary form of a language is DEMOTIC, VERNACULAR
– popular feeling, public opinion VOX POPULI

popularity or fashion VOGUE

population growth that is optimal and therefore accelerating EXPONENTIAL GROWTH
– increase dramatically, as an animal population might in favourable conditions IRRUPT
– referring to the population of an area that seems always to have been there INDIGENOUS, ABORIGINAL, AUTOCHTHONOUS
– sample taken at random, as of the general population, regarded as typical of the whole CROSS-SECTION
– science of population statistics, such as distribution and birth rate DEMOGRAPHY

population- DEM-, DEMO-

porcelain See **pottery**

porch, especially at the entrance to a temple PROPYLAEUM
– porch or corridor used by athletes for exercise in ancient Greece XYST
– porch or entrance stairway at a house door STOOP
– porch with a roof and columns, sometimes surrounding a building PORTICO

porcupine – spines covering the body of a porcupine QUILLS

pork See illustration, and also **bacon**
– forbidden as food in Islam, as pork is HARAM
– forbidden as food in Judaism, non-kosher, as pork is TREF
– salted and cured side of pork FLITCH

pornography, sexually explicit art or writing EROTICA
– pornography of a mild kind SOFT-CORE PORNOGRAPHY
– pornography of a very explicit or deviant kind HARD-CORE PORNOGRAPHY
– pornographic film STAG FILM, BLUE MOVIE
– detailed in describing or representing sexual acts, as some pornographic films are EXPLICIT

porpoise, whale, or similar fish-like aquatic mammal CETACEAN

porridge – porridge-like dish of boiled sweetened wheat FRUMENTY
– thick maize porridge SAMP, POLENTA, PUTU, HOMINY GRITS, GRITS
– thick oatmeal porridge, as served to sailors in former times BURGOO, LOBLOLLY
– thin, watery porridge GRUEL, SKILLY

port side of a ship LARBOARD
– crust forming in bottles of old wine, especially port, or a wine containing this crust BEESWING

porter – porter's office in a college LODGE
– U.S. term for a caretaker or porter SUPERINTENDENT, JANITOR

porthole, hinged hatchway, or the like on a ship SCUTTLE

portion or share specially set aside ALLOCATION, ALLOTMENT

portmanteau word BLEND

portrait, typically an engraving or photograph, in which the edges have been blurred VIGNETTE
– portrait in profile in the form of a shadow image or filled-in outline SILHOUETTE
– portrait of a person, such as a cartoon or written parody, exaggerating his features and qualities for comic or satirical effect CARICATURE
– portrait sculpture of a person, as on a monument EFFIGY
– referring to a statue or portrait in which the subject is depicted on horseback EQUESTRIAN

portray or describe LIMN

Portugal- LUSO-

Portuguese and Spanish IBERIAN
– melancholy Portuguese folk song FADO

position See also **place**
– position, job, or activity particularly suited to a person NICHE
– position accurately, find or specify the position of something, as on a map LOCATE, PINPOINT
– position accurately in relation to something else, especially by placing in a straight line ALIGN
– position in relation to one's surroundings BEARINGS, ORIENTATION
– position or locate in a specified direction, as when facing a church east ORIENTATE

pork cuts

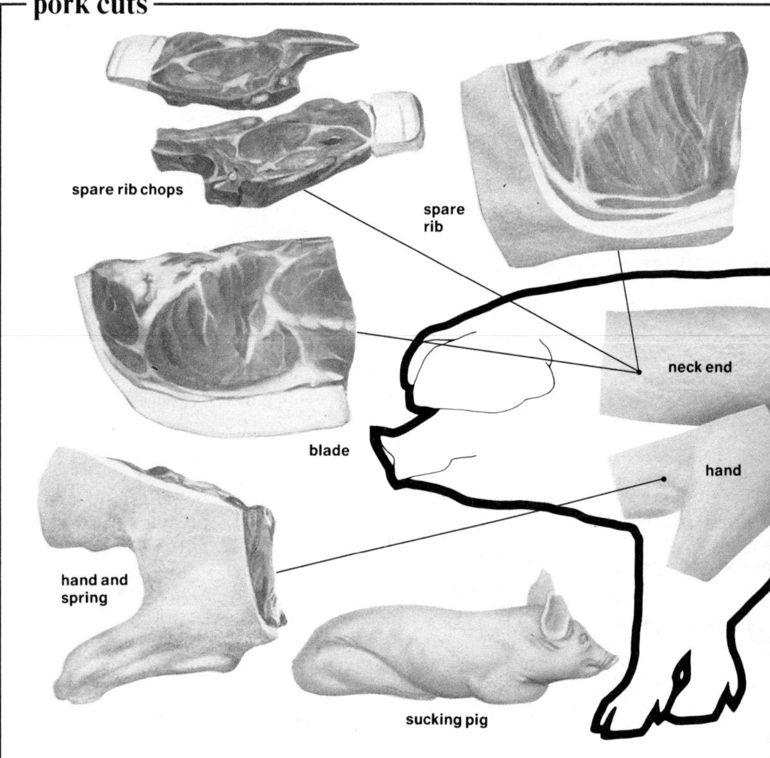

– position or outlook of a house, as in a specified direction EXPOSURE, ASPECT
– position or ranking on a scale RATING
– change in the apparent position of an object when the observer changes position PARALLAX ERROR
– change or reverse the ordering or relative position of two or more things TRANSPOSE
– defensible or maintainable, as a military or philosophical position might be TENABLE
– force out from a fixed position, hiding place, dwelling, or the like DISLODGE
– have the most prominent position, as in a room or landscape DOMINATE
– important or high in status, position, or the like EXALTED
– occupying the same space or position, or identical in size and shape COINCIDENT
– two or more numbers, readings, or measurements that define a position, as on a map or graph COORDINATES

-position -WISE

-positioned -TACTIC

possess, or take pride or pleasure in possessing something, such as an unusual name REJOICE IN

possessed – drive out demons or evil spirits, or free a possessed person from them, as by religious rites EXORCISE
– person possessed or apparently possessed by an evil spirit DEMONIAC, ENERGUMEN

-possessing -OSE

possession, gift, or project, expensive and inefficient, requiring more trouble than it is worth WHITE ELEPHANT
– possession desired or valued as an indicator of wealth or social prestige STATUS SYMBOL
– interest in possessions rather than spiritual or moral values MATERIALISM
– valued household possessions LARES AND PENATES

possible, practicable, or imaginable CONCEIVABLE, FEASIBLE
– possible, uncertain CONTINGENT
– possible, workable, practicable, realistic VIABLE
– possible but not yet actual POTENTIAL, LATENT
– possible occurrence or event CONTINGENCY, EVENTUALITY
– possible or projected course of action or chain of events SCENARIO
– possibly true, apparently valid, as an excuse might be PLAUSIBLE
– enabling, making possible but not obligatory FACULTATIVE

post See also **letter**
– post, stake, pile as for foundations SPILE
– post code in the U.S. ZIP CODE
– post for tethering a horse HITCHING POST
– post officially recorded and insured REGISTERED POST
– post on a traffic island, on a pavement to prevent parking, or the like BOLLARD
– post or pointed stake driven into the ground, as for defence PICKET
– post or target to be tilted at as by horsemen QUINTAIN
– centralised system for banks and post offices to transfer money GIRO
– department of a post office, holding letters for collection by the addressee POSTE RESTANTE, GENERAL DELIVERY
– fortress or defensive barrier made of upright posts or stakes STOCKADE, PALISADE
– mark or stamp a letter or parcel to indicate payment of postage FRANK

post-mortem, medical examination or dissection of a dead body to establish the cause of death AUTOPSY
– post-mortem investigation, as into the cause of a death or failure INQUEST
– medical specialist who conducts a post-mortem examination to establish the cause of death PATHOLOGIST
– public officer presiding at post-mortem investigations CORONER

postcard collector DELTIOLOGIST

poster PLACARD
– unauthorised sticking up of posters in public places FLYPOSTING, BILLSTICKING

postpone, delay doing something until later, waste time PROCRASTINATE
– postpone, put aside temporarily, put off WAIVE, DEFER, REMIT, PUT ON THE BACK BURNER
– postpone, suspend, put aside for later consideration PIGEONHOLE, SHELVE, MOTHBALL, TABLE, HOLD IN ABEYANCE, HANG FIRE
– postpone acceptance of an offer that will remain open TAKE A RAIN CHECK
– postpone decisions or draw out discussions as a way of gaining time TEMPORISE
– postpone discussions, break off a court hearing or meeting temporarily ADJOURN
– postpone or avoid giving direct

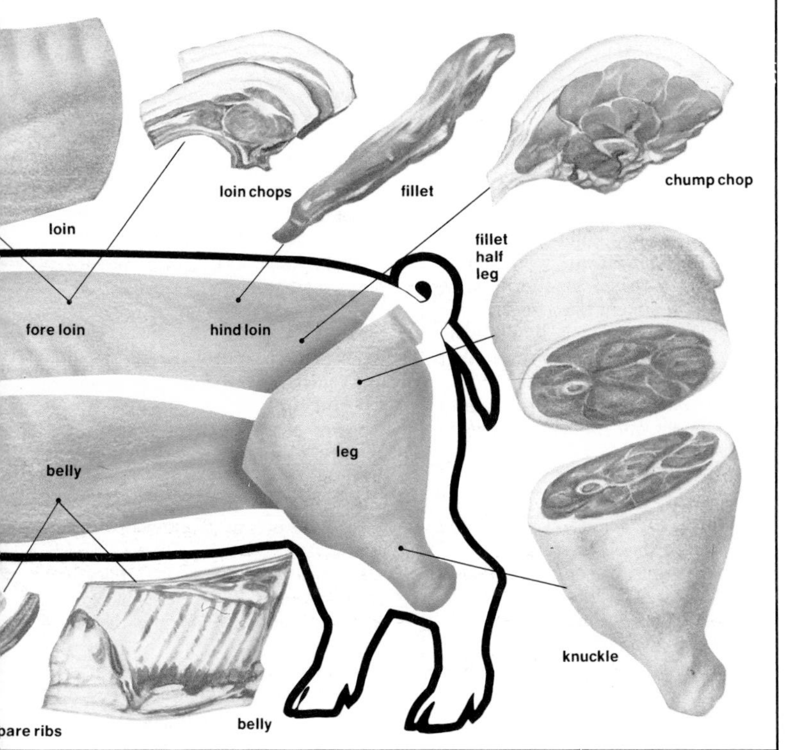

answers, beat about the bush EQUIVOCATE, PREVARICATE
– postpone or discontinue temporarily the sessions of parliament or a similar body PROROGUE
– postponement or delay, as of payments MORATORIUM
– temporary postponement, especially of something unpleasant REPRIEVE, RESPITE

postulate, put forward a proposition or idea for the sake of argument POSIT, PREMISE

posture, way of walking or standing POISE, BEARING, CARRIAGE, GAIT
– woman's fashionable forward-tilting posture in the late 19th century, often enhanced by a bustle GRECIAN BEND

posy, small bunch or bouquet of flowers NOSEGAY

pot See **cooking utensils**
– pot for cooking, covered and often of earthenware CASSEROLE, MARMITE
– pot or large kettle with a hooped handle for hanging over an open fire CAULDRON
– pot or small pan of earthenware PIPKIN
– large, decorated pot or stand for plants JARDINIÈRE

pot marigold CALENDULA

pot plant – tree or shrub of dwarf size, produced by rigorous pruning, and displayed as a pot plant BONSAI

potato SPUD, MURPHY
– potato beetle COLORADO BEETLE
– potato flour or the starch from it FARINA
– potato or similar swollen underground bud-bearing stem or root TUBER
– potato pancake of traditional Jewish style LATKE
– baked cakes of mashed potatoes bound with egg DUCHESSE POTATOES
– cooked with onions, as potatoes might be LYONNAISE
– fried potatoes of traditional Swiss style RÖSTI
– Scottish dish of steamed potatoes STOVIES
– shredded or sliced into narrow strips, as potatoes might be JULIENNE
– sliced thin and baked in a sauce, as potatoes might be SCALLOPED
– thick creamy leek and potato soup, typically served cold VICHYSSOISE

potency, sexual functioning or prowess in an adult male VIRILITY

potential, present but not visible, as a tendency might be LATENT
– potential, unfulfilled MANQUÉ

pottery See chart
– pottery or vessels made of baked clay EARTHENWARE
– potter's wooden spatula used for mixing or moulding clay PALLET
– fragment of pottery, as found in archaeological excavations SHARD, POTSHERD, SHERD, CROCK
– fragment of pottery used in ancient Greece when voting for the banishment of an unpopular citizen OSTRACON
– oven or furnace for drying and hardening pottery KILN
– soluble fusible white mineral used in making glass and pottery BORAX

pouch – pouch-bearing mammal, such as a kangaroo MARSUPIAL
– pouch for sheltering the young, as in the kangaroo MARSUPIUM
– pouch in the body, especially that between the small and large intestines CAECUM
– pouch-like sac or cavity in the body, either normal or abnormal CYST
– pouch of furry leather worn in front of the kilt in traditional Highland dress SPORRAN
– pouch or bag-like part, often filled with fluid, in a plant or animal SAC
– pouch or sac formed in the weakened wall of a hollow body part, especially the intestines DIVERTICULUM

poultry See **chicken**

pound or pen for animals, such as stray sheep PINFOLD

pound – system of weights including the ounce, pound, and ton AVOIRDUPOIS

pounding, crushing, or grinding implement, as in a mill PESTLE

pour a liquid from one container to another, as when separating wine from its sediment DECANT
– pour or transfer a liquid from one container or vessel to another TRANSFUSE
– pour out, emerge, or issue, as a river might DISCHARGE, DISGORGE, DEBOUCH
– pouring of a liquid, as a religious ritual LIBATION
– pouring of water, especially on the head at baptisms AFFUSION
– pouring out, or something that is poured out EFFUSION

pout, sulky expression MOUE

poverty See also **lack**
– poverty, financial embarrassment or seriously reduced circumstances DIRE STRAITS, IMPOVERISHMENT
– poverty, lack of basic comforts or essentials of life PRIVATION
– poverty, complete lack of money, pennilessness IMPECUNIOUSNESS
– poverty, state of want or neediness INDIGENCE
– extreme poverty, lack of all comforts and even necessities, beggary PENURY, DESTITUTION
– miserable, pitiable, grindingly wretched, as poverty might be ABJECT

POW camp – German POW camp for NCOs and privates during the Second World War STALAG
– German POW camp for officers during the Second World War OFLAG

powder – mineral used in cosmetic powder, pills, tablets, and so on TALC, TALCUM
– crush to a powder, as with a mortar and pestle BRAY
– grind, crush, pound, or reduce to powder PULVERISE, COMMINUTE, TRITURATE
– small flat case containing face powder, a mirror, and a powder puff, as carried in a woman's handbag COMPACT

powdery coating, as on plums or new coins BLOOM
– powdery or mealy in texture FARINACEOUS

power See also **authority**, **force**, **government**
– power, authority, or influence of one state over another HEGEMONY, SUZERAINTY
– power, governing control, authority DOMINION, SOVEREIGNTY
– power, influence SWAY, CLOUT
– power, inherent ability, or skill FACULTY, APTITUDE
– power, strength, or vitality THEWS, SINEW
– power, superiority, clear advantage ASCENDANCY, DOMINANCE, PREDOMINANCE, PRE-EMINENCE, SUPREMACY
– power and control, or the legal and territorial extent of power JURISDICTION
– power centre, hub of influence, activity, or interest GANGLION
– power failure OUTAGE
– power-mad person, typically with delusions of grandeur MEGALOMANIAC
– power of a microscope, photographic emulsion, or the like to separate and reveal fine details RESOLUTION
– power of choosing, will VOLITION
– power of jurisdiction that a country has beyond its borders, as over its citizens living abroad

EXTRATERRITORIALITY
– power or ability that is as yet unrealised POTENTIAL
– power or capacity to produce results EFFICACY
– power or force, especially as a result of continuing movement MOMENTUM, IMPETUS, INERTIA
– power or influence, moral authority or prestige MANA
– power or rule of an absolute kind AUTARCHY, AUTOCRACY
– power to make use of something or someone DISPOSAL
– area in someone's power, or sphere of someone's influence FIEFDOM, DOMAIN, REALM, PARISH, BAILIWICK
– assign work, duties, or powers to one's agent or subordinate DELEGATE, DEPUTE
– based on personal decision rather than on regulations, as powers or payments might be DISCRETIONARY
– be superior to in power, importance, influence, or quantity PREDOMINATE
– complete, full, unlimited, as a dictator's powers would be, absolute PLENARY, PLENIPOTENTIARY
– give up or relinquish power or responsibility formally ABDICATE, RENOUNCE
– increase in power, reputation, or the like AGGRANDISEMENT
– level of power or responsibility in a hierarchical organisation ECHELON
– order of power or status in a group PECKING ORDER, HIERARCHY
– outward signs, symbolic decorations, or ornamental equipment, as of power TRAPPINGS
– referring to power derived from heat in the interior of the Earth GEOTHERMAL
– remove from office, power, the throne, or the like, overthrow DEPOSE
– seize by force and hold illegally the power, rights, throne, or the like of another USURP
– seize or wrench something forcibly or unlawfully, such as power WREST
– supposed substance that produces a surge of excitement, or power ADRENALINE
– transfer of power from central government to regional or local authorities DEVOLUTION
– unlimited power to act as one

POTTERY AND CHINA TERMS

argil	clay used by potters
basaltware	black, unglazed pottery
biscuit, bisque	unglazed pottery
blunger	vessel in which pottery ingredients are mixed
bone china	semi-translucent porcelain made of clay mixed with bone ash
cameo ware	pottery with raised white designs on a contrasting background
celadon ware	pottery with a pale grey-green glaze
clair de lune	pale grey-blue glaze applied to certain Chinese porcelain
crackle ware	pottery or porcelain with a network of fine cracks in the glaze
delft ware	blue and white pottery originally made in Delft, Holland
faience	fine pottery with a colourful glaze, named after Faenza, Italy, one of its sources
fairing	pottery of a type sold or given as a prize at travelling fairs
glost	lead glaze used for pottery
ironstone	hard, white pottery
jasper ware	coloured stoneware with raised designs in white, invented by Josiah Wedgwood
lambrequin	scalloped edging decorating the top of an item of porcelain
maiolica/ majolica	brightly decorated pottery in 16th-century Italian style
muffle	kiln in which pottery is fired without direct exposure to the flames
nankeen	Chinese-style porcelain with a blue and white pattern, originally imported into Europe from Nanking
pallet	spatula or paddle-like implement used for mixing or shaping clay
Parian ware	fine white porcelain resembling marble
saggar	casing of fire clay in which delicate ceramic ware is fired
slip	thin clay used by a potter for coating or decorating
stoneware	heavy pottery fired at a high temperature, and often glazed with salt
terracotta	unglazed pottery made of clay and fine sand
throw	shape clay on a potter's wheel
underglaze	pigment or decoration applied to pottery before it is glazed

FAMOUS MAKES OF CHINA AND PORCELAIN

Adams
Belleek
Bow
Bristol
Chelsea
Coalport
Copeland
Crown Staffordshire
Davenport
Dresden
Goss
Limoges
Longton Hall
Meissen
Minton
Rockingham
Rosenthal
Royal Copenhagen
Royal Crown Derby
Royal Doulton
Royal Worcester
Sèvres
Spode
Sunderland
Swansea
Wedgwood

wishes, or a document conferring it CARTE BLANCHE
power- DYNAM-, DYNAMO-
powerful See also **large**, **strong**
– powerful, mighty, strong PUISSANT
– powerful, rich, or important man NABOB, MOGUL, POTENTATE
– powerful and convincing, as someone's reasoning might be COGENT, COMPELLING, TRENCHANT, INCISIVE
– powerful and influential person, typically a rich industrialist MAGNATE
– powerful controlling and constricting force, such as one that is imposed by tradition or custom TYRANNY
– powerful in a wide-ranging and effective way, as a remedy or the like might be SOVEREIGN, EFFICACIOUS, POTENT
– powerful in an irresponsibly bullying or overbearing way IMPERIOUS, DOMINEERING, DICTATORIAL
– powerful in effect, or forceful, arresting, as an advertisement might be PUNCHY
– powerful in or having control over an enterprise IN THE DRIVER'S SEAT
– powerful official or authority OVERLORD
– powerful to a great or excessive degree OMNIPOTENT, OVERWHELMING
– conclusive, with powerful influence, as a textbook might be AUTHORITATIVE, DEFINITIVE
– huge and powerful TITANIC
powerless, inoperative, or invalid, as a disregarded law or regulation is NUGATORY, DEAD-LETTER
practicable, capable of working, realistic VIABLE, FEASIBLE
practical, dealing with, ruled by, or relating to facts and actual circumstances rather than theories or ideals PRAGMATIC, REALISTIC
– practical and purely functional, wholly mechanical or materialistic BANAUSIC
– practical rather than decorative UTILITARIAN, FUNCTIONAL
– practical shrewdness, common sense GUMPTION, NOUS
– based on practical experience rather than theory or proof, as a medical treatment might be EMPIRICAL
practically, nearly, in essence but not in appearance VIRTUALLY
practice or practical side of a profession or field of study as distinct from the theory PRAXIS
– practice or rehearsal DUMMY RUN
– disuse, state of being out of use or practice DESUETUDE
practise or engage in one's trade PLY
praise, acknowledgment of qualities HOMAGE, TRIBUTE
– praise, adore, worship REVERE, VENERATE
– praise, applause, compliment ACCLAIM, ACCOLADE, BOUQUET
– praise, compliment, or express approval of COMMEND
– praise, enthusiastic approval PLAUDITS, APPROBATION
– praise, or a speech of praise or a

PRAYERS

Agnus Dei	"Lamb of God", prayer in three parts spoken or sung in the Mass
Alenu	prayer near the end of a Jewish service
Amidah	main prayer at a Jewish service
Angelus	prayer said morning, noon, and night by Roman Catholics to commemorate the Annunciation
Ave Maria	"Hail Mary", prayer honouring the Virgin Mary, in Roman Catholic worship
canonical hours	prayers or services set for specific times of day in the Roman Catholic Church
collect	brief prayer spoken before the epistle at Mass or Holy Communion
compline	last of the seven canonical hours
Confiteor	prayer including a standardised confession of sins, in Roman Catholic worship
epiclesis	prayer in the Mass calling on the Holy Spirit to transform the bread and wine into the body and blood of Christ
Fatiha	standard prayer and declaration of faith in Islamic worship
Gloria	prayer of praise in Christian worship
intercession	prayer to God on behalf of another
invocation	prayer asking for God's help
Kaddish	daily prayer in praise of God in Jewish services; also recited by those mourning the death of a close relative
Kol Nidre	prayer on the eve of Yom Kippur, the Jewish Day of Atonement
Kyrie eleison	"Lord have mercy", prayer, often sung, in Christian worship
litany	prayer in which the congregation's responses alternate with the leader's invocations
matins	first of the seven canonical hours
Miserere	prayer for mercy, the 51st Psalm, in Christian worship
nones	fifth of the seven canonical hours
Pater Noster	"Our Father", the Lord's Prayer
prime	second of the seven canonical hours
requiescat	prayer for the souls of the dead
rogation	prayer said during the Rogation Days, preceding Ascension Day
sext	fourth of the seven canonical hours
Shema	"Hear, O Israel", the confession of the Jewish faith
terce	third of the seven canonical hours
vespers	sixth of the seven canonical hours

tribute that is written EULOGY, ENCOMIUM, PANEGYRIC
– praise highly, glorify, honour EXALT, EXTOL, LAUD
– praise highly or with suspect enthusiasm TOUT, PUFF
– praise of an excessive kind, idolisation HAGIOGRAPHY, ADULATION
– praise or prestige as a result of achievements or success KUDOS
– praise or recommend, as in an advertisement ENDORSE
– praise or talk in an extremely enthusiastic way RHAPSODISE
– praise publicly and in a conspicuous way, celebrate EMBLAZON, EULOGISE, PROCLAIM
– cry of praise to God HOSANNA
– hymn, verse, or formula praising God in the liturgy DOXOLOGY
– lavish in an excessive way, as praise might be FULSOME
– song or expression of joy and praise PAEAN

praiseworthy LAUDABLE, COMMENDABLE

pram PERAMBULATOR

pranks or high-spirited adventures CAPERS, TOMFOOLERY, HIGH JINKS, SKYLARKING, ESCAPADES, ANTICS, SCRAPES

prawn or lobster or related shellfish CRUSTACEAN
– large prawn, often eaten fried DUBLIN BAY PRAWN, NORWAY LOBSTER, LANGOUSTINE
– large prawns, especially when served fried SCAMPI

pray – desk at which a person may kneel to pray PRIE-DIEU
– "praying" insect MANTIS

prayer See chart, and also **hymn**
– prayer beads ROSARY
– prayer book, especially for the Roman Catholic Mass MISSAL
– prayers or other, usually private, religious observances DEVOTIONS
– endowment for the saying of prayers or Mass, usually for the soul of the benefactor CHANTRY
– expressing or based on a vow or wish, as a prayer might be VOTIVE
– former term for a prayer ORISON
– person in former times who prayed, often for pay, for another's soul or welfare BEADSMAN
– psalm, anthem, or the like sung as an invitation to prayer during a church service INVITATORY
– psalm, prayer, or hymn sung at the beginning of a church service INTROIT

pre-war, especially before the American Civil War ANTEBELLUM

preacher or evangeliser full of enthusiasm HOT-GOSPELLER
– preacher with a loud voice and impassioned delivery BOANERGES
– belonging to the congregation or general public as opposed to the clergy, as a preacher might LAY
– travelling from place to place, as some judges or preachers do ITINERANT

preachy, pompously moralising, as by means of clichéd advice SENTENTIOUS, PONTIFICAL
– preachy or priggish explanations or criticisms MORALISING, CANT, SERMONISING

precautions – taking appropriate precautions CIRCUMSPECT

precede – ANTEDATE

preceding- SUPRA-

precious or high-quality, as a ruby or amethyst might be ORIENTAL
– extremely precious, beyond price INVALUABLE

precious stones See chart, and also **gemstones**

precise description, list of details, plan, or proposal SPECIFICATION
– precise details, sometimes needlessly fussy MINUTIAE, TRIVIA
– precise or careful to a fault, extremely painstaking METICULOUS, FASTIDIOUS, SCRUPULOUS, PUNCTILIOUS
– precise to a fault, oversubtle, pedantic or dogmatic SCHOLASTIC, ACADEMIC, SOPHISTICAL
– adjust so as to make more precise CALIBRATE, FINE-TUNE
– demanding person, insisting on precise accuracy, obedience, and the like STICKLER, PURIST
– quoting precisely, using the identical words, word for word VERBATIM

precision, delicacy, subtlety, as in negotiations NICETY

preconceived opinion, prejudice PARTI PRIS

predict See **forecast**, **foretell**, **prophetic**, **fortune-telling**

predictable or automatic, as a reaction or response may be PAVLOVIAN, KNEE-JERK

pregnancy in which the fertilised egg develops outside the uterus, typically in a Fallopian tube ECTOPIC PREGNANCY
– pregnancy occurring in a female who is already pregnant SUPERFETATION
– pregnancy test by prodding the uterus to feel a rebound from the foetus BALLOTTEMENT
– clawed toad used in pregnancy testing XENOPUS, PLATANNA
– craving for unnatural food, such as mud or chalk, occurring sometimes during pregnancy PICA
– custom in some cultures in which the husband too takes to his bed during the later stages of his wife's pregnancy COUVADE
– developing embryo during the later stages of pregnancy FOETUS
– illusory pregnancy, often including such signs as a swollen abdomen, typically due to an emotional disorder PHANTOM PREGNANCY, PSEUDOCYESIS
– occurring during or relating to pregnancy PRENATAL, ANTENATAL
– premature expulsion of a foetus in mid-pregnancy MISCARRIAGE, SPONTANEOUS ABORTION

PRECIOUS AND SEMI-PRECIOUS STONES

COLOURLESS	PURPLE AND VIOLET
diamond	**almandine**
topaz	**amethyst**
white sapphire	**garnet**
zircon	**spinel**

YELLOW AND ORANGE	BLUE
amber	**lazurite/ lapis lazuli**
chrysoberyl	**sapphire**
citrine	**turquoise**
fire opal/ girasol	**water sapphire**
topaz	**sodalite**

BROWN	GREEN
agate	**alexandrite**
andradite	**amazon stone/ amazonite**
cairngorm/ smoky quartz	**aquamarine**
cat's-eye/ tiger's-eye	**beryl**
jade/ jadeite	**chrysoberyl**
jasper	**chrysoprase**
morganite	**emerald**
sardonyx	**heliotrope/ bloodstone**
	jade/ nephrite/ jadeite
	malachite
	olivine/ peridot
	topaz
	tourmaline
	verdite

RED AND PINK	WHITISH
almandine	**moonstone**
beryl	**onyx**
carbuncle	**opal**
carnelian/ cornelian	
garnet	
red zircon/ hyacinth/ jacinth	
rose quartz	
rubasse	
rubellite	
ruby	
rutile	
spinel	

	BLACK
	jet
	melanite
	rutile

– relating to the care of women during pregnancy and after childbirth OBSTETRIC
– toxic condition, involving convulsions and sometimes coma, during the last three months of pregnancy ECLAMPSIA

pregnant, with child GRAVID, ENCEINTE, EXPECTANT
– be pregnant, carry unborn young GESTATE
– fertilise, make pregnant FECUNDATE, IMPREGNATE, INSEMINATE
– not pregnant, as a mare might be FALLOW
– not pregnant or not calving in a particular year, as a cow might be FARROW
– withdrawal by syringe of some of the fluid in a pregnant woman's womb, to monitor the health of the foetus AMNIOCENTESIS

prehistoric See **archaeology**

prehistoric- EO-, PALAEO-

prehistoric animals See **dinosaur**, **extinct**

prehistoric man known from skeleton remains in Europe, an early form of modern man CRO-MAGNON
– prehistoric man-like creature, of several species PROTOHUMAN
– prehistoric man-like creature of eastern and southern Africa AUSTRALOPITHECINE, PARANTHROPUS, ZINJANTHROPUS
– prehistoric man of Europe, Asia, and North Africa, an early user of tools and early species of Homo sapiens NEANDERTHAL MAN
– ape-like prehistoric man, such as Peking Man or Java Man HOMO ERECTUS, SINANTHROPUS, PITHECANTHROPUS
– supposed species of prehistoric man, later proved to be based on a forgery of various modern bones PILTDOWN MAN

prejudice, pre-formed judgment or preference PREDISPOSITION, PRECONCEPTION, PREDILECTION, PARTI PRIS, PARTIALITY
– prejudice against or hatred of foreigners XENOPHOBIA
– prejudice against or hatred of men MISANDRY
– prejudice against or hatred of people MISANTHROPY
– prejudice against or hatred of women MISOGYNY
– prejudiced, mindlessly devoted or loyal PARTISAN
– prejudiced and intolerant person BIGOT
– prejudiced attitudes or actions, as on the basis of race or sex DISCRIMINATION
– prejudiced by one's fixed beliefs or ideology, not open-minded DOGMATIC, DOCTRINAIRE
– prejudiced favouring of one's own group or country JINGOISM, CHAUVINISM
– prejudiced or biased against something, pessimistic or cynical JAUNDICED
– prejudiced or narrow-minded, blinkered MYOPIC, PAROCHIAL

preliminary See also **introduction**
– preliminary, introductory, or preparing for something to come PREPARATORY, PREFATORY, PRECURSORY
– preliminary draft for a treaty or other document PROTOCOL
– preliminary event, entertainment, or the like, as before the main sports match or play CURTAIN RAISER
– preliminary inspection of a region, as to assess the terrain or study enemy positions RECONNAISSANCE, RECONNOITRE
– preliminary statement or explanation, as in a formal document PREAMBLE

preliminary- FORE-

premature, ill-prepared HALF-COCKED
– give premature birth to a calf SLINK, SLIP
– temperature-controlled hospital container, as for premature babies INCUBATOR

premise – pattern of logical reasoning in which two premises generate a conclusion SYLLOGISM
– put forward as a premise or axiom, as in a geometry theorem POSTULATE, POSIT, HYPOTHESISE

preoccupation or obsession FIXATION, IDÉE FIXE

prepare See **make**
– prepare for something difficult, dangerous, or undesirable MAKE PROVISIONS, GIRD UP ONE'S LOINS, PRIME ONESELF, BATTEN DOWN THE HATCHES
– prepare something, as in cooking, by mixing various elements CONCOCT

prepared, ready POISED, BRACED

prescription – "equal quantities of", referring to the ingredients in a prescription ANA
– referring or relating to a medical drug available only on prescription ETHICAL, MAGISTRAL
– referring or relating to a medical drug available without prescription OVER-THE-COUNTER, OFFICINAL

present See also **gift**
– present, current, happening or existing at the present time, now CONTEMPORARY
– present but not visible, as a tendency might be LATENT
– present or bestow a degree or honour CONFER
– present or offer formally TENDER
– present or submit something, such as a bill RENDER
– for the present, for the time being FOR THE NONCE

present tense of verbs used when narrating events of the past HISTORICAL PRESENT

presenter of a radio or television broadcast who coordinates many reports ANCHORMAN, ANCHORWOMAN
– presenter of a radio or television programme FRONT MAN, FRONT WOMAN

preservative, as of specimens for dissecting FORMALDEHYDE
– preservative or protective substance FIXATIVE
– potassium nitrate, used as a preservative of meat SALTPETRE

preserve See also **keep**, **protect**
– preserve a corpse from decay by means of chemical treatment EMBALM
– preserve food, especially meat, in brine or with salt CORN
– preserve food by drying DESICCATE
– preserve meat, fish, tobacco, rubber, or the like CURE

presidency or government of France ELYSÉE
– presidency or presidential power in the U.S. OVAL OFFICE, WHITE HOUSE

president of the U.S. during his remaining time in office, especially after his successor has been elected LAME-DUCK PRESIDENT
– president or other official currently in office INCUMBENT
– charge a president or other public official with an offence committed while in office IMPEACH
– install someone, such as a president, formally in office INDUCT, INAUGURATE, INVEST

press of a cheap and sensationalising kind YELLOW PRESS
– press through which paper or cloth is rolled for a smooth or glossy finish CALENDER

press stud – U.S. term for a press stud or popper SNAP FASTENER

pressure cooker, or similar sealed vessel for sterilising surgical instruments AUTOCLAVE
– pressure gauge MANOMETER, SPHYGMOMANOMETER
– enclosed space inside which the air or gas pressure is greater than that outside PLENUM

– feeling of tightness or pressure, as in the chest CONSTRICTION
– instrument for measuring the atmospheric pressure, used in calculating altitude and making weather forecasts BAROMETER
– line on a weather map linking places with the same atmospheric pressure ISOBAR
– operated by or involving fluid pressure HYDRAULIC
– painful condition, as in deep-sea divers, following sudden change of pressure THE BENDS, CAISSON DISEASE, DECOMPRESSION SICKNESS, AEROEMBOLISM
– rotating cylinder on which a pen records changes in pressure, heartbeat, or the like KYMOGRAPH
– tube with a narrow throat, as in a pipe or carburettor, for measuring fluid pressure or for providing suction VENTURI
– unit of atmospheric pressure MILLIBAR

pressure- BARO-, PIEZO-

pressure point – artery that can be constricted at the pressure point against the collarbone SUBCLAVIAN ARTERY
– artery that can be constricted at the pressure point at the base of the neck COMMON CAROTID ARTERY
– artery that can be constricted at the pressure point below the jaw FACIAL ARTERY
– artery that can be constricted at the pressure point in front of the ear TEMPORAL ARTERY
– artery that can be constricted at the pressure point in the groin FEMORAL ARTERY
– artery that can be constricted at the pressure point in the inner side of the upper arm BRACHIAL ARTERY

prestige or glory resulting from some achievement KUDOS
– prestige or social distinction CACHET

pretence, caricature, or a crudely distorted imitation TRAVESTY, PARODY
– pretence, false appearance GUISE
– pretence, hypocrisy HUMBUG
– pretence, trickery DECEIT, GUILE, FINESSE
– pretence intended to mislead, especially a misleading movement or feigned attack FEINT
– scheme or trick relying on pretence and deceit ARTIFICE, DODGE, RUSE, STRATEGEM, SUBTERFUGE, WILE

pretend, fake, or falsely display something, such as relief FEIGN, SIMULATE, AFFECT, ASSUME, COUNTERFEIT, SHAM
– pretend, mislead, hide one's true thoughts or feelings DISSEMBLE, DISSIMULATE
– pretend to be dead, asleep, or ignorant PLAY POSSUM
– pretend to be ill, as to get off work MALINGER, SKIVE
– pretend to be someone else IMPERSONATE, MASQUERADE, MIMIC
– pretended, feigned, false, as an emotion might be COLOURABLE, SIMULATED, SHAM, BOGUS
– pretended, merely apparent or outward, as a given reason might be PROFESSED, SPECIOUS, OSTENSIBLE
– pretended reason, apparent purpose or justification PRETEXT
– pretending or appearing to be unsophisticated and naive FAUX-NAÏF
– pretending to be ignorant, insincere DISINGENUOUS

pretending- PSEUD-, PSEUDO-

pretentious See also **pompous**
– pretentious, flowery, affected, fussy, or over-elaborate in style, pretty-pretty CHINTZY, PRECIOUS, CHICHI
– pretentious and typically sentimental art KITSCH
– pretentious newcomer in a social circle, upstart PARVENU, ARRIVISTE
– pretentious things, such as over-ornate clothes FRIPPERY
– pretentiously quaint or pretty TWEE
– socially pretentious, affecting posh manners GENTEEL

pretty See **attractive**, **beautiful**
– pretty girl or woman BELLE

prevent See also **hinder**, **limit**, **prohibit**
– prevent, hold back, or hide laughter, a yawn, or the like STIFLE, SUPPRESS
– prevent, nip in the bud, take advance action against ANTICIPATE, FORESTALL, OBVIATE, PRECLUDE, PRE-EMPT
– prevent, ward off, or deflect a blow, problems, or the like AVERT, FORFEND, PARRY, STAVE OFF
– prevent acceptance of a proposal by exercising one's absolute right to decide VETO
– prevent from continuing, cut short, or end prematurely ABORT, ARREST
– prevent from joining a social group, exclude BLACKBALL, DEBAR, OSTRACISE
– prevent from moving IMMOBILISE, PARALYSE
– prevent from happening or moving, put obstacles in front of, restrain, check BAULK, BILK, CURB, FRUSTRATE, PUT THE KIBOSH ON, SPIKE, THWART
– prevent or discourage someone from doing something, as by threatening DETER
– prevent or restrain oneself from doing something, refrain or desist from FORBEAR
– prevent the free or unregulated publication of a book, newspaper, or the like, as by inspecting and making cuts CENSOR
– preventing or protecting against something, especially against disease PROPHYLACTIC
– preventing or trying to prevent, anticipating PREVENIENT

previous, earlier, being before in time, rank, order or the like PRECEDING
– feeling of having undergone previously an experience that one is only having for the first time DÉJÀ VU
– "in or during the previous month", formerly used in business correspondence ULTIMO, ULT.

previous- EX-, SUPRA-

prey, hunted game QUARRY
– animal that kills and eats prey PREDATOR
– seizing and eating prey, as birds of prey do PREDACIOUS, PREDATORY, RAPACIOUS, RAPTORIAL, RAVENING

price index issued each month, used as a guide to inflation RETAIL PRICE INDEX
– price list TARIFF
– price that is the minimum that the owner will accept at an auction RESERVE PRICE
– excessive, unreasonable, as prices or demands might be EXORBITANT, EXTORTIONATE
– go back on an agreement with the prospective buyer of a property by raising the price previously agreed GAZUMP
– maintain or increase the price of a commodity or service, as by government subsidies, levies or the like VALORISE

prick or stab lightly, as with a sword PINK

prickly bush or shrub, especially a wild rose BRIAR
– prickly husk or seedpod BURR
– prickly shrub or plant such as the blackberry or dog rose BRAMBLE

prickly- ECHINO-

prickly pear OPUNTIA

pride See also **proud**, **boast**, **pompous**

– pride in attitude, arrogance, habit of putting on airs HAUTEUR, GRANDEUR, CONCEIT
– pride in oneself, sense of one's own worth and dignity SELF-ESTEEM, AMOUR-PROPRE
– pride or arrogance, which often leads to downfall HUBRIS
– pride or plume oneself on something, congratulate oneself PIQUE, PREEN
– downfall or undoing, typically just retribution, as following pride or overconfidence NEMESIS
– excessive, out of proportion, as ambitions or pride might be OVERWEENING
– excessive pride in one's appearance or abilities, boastfulness and vanity VAINGLORY
– humble, reduce the pride or confidence of DEFLATE
– please, satisfy, or indulge something, such as one's pride GRATIFY

priest See also **clergyman**, **clerical clothing**
– priest, clergyman ECCLESIASTIC
– priest in ancient Rome, serving a specific deity FLAMEN
– priest-like, relating to priests HIERATIC, SACERDOTAL
– priest of senior status in ancient Rome PONTIFEX
– priest officiating at the Eucharist or other religious ceremony or rite CELEBRANT
– priest or elder in various churches PRESBYTER
– priest's acceptance into the ministry, or the ceremony of admission ORDINATION
– priest's assistant when at the altar ACOLYTE
– priest's official clothing CANONICALS, VESTMENTS
– abstaining from sexual intercourse, as priests do, and others who have taken a vow of chastity CELIBATE
– authorise to be a priest, invest with holy orders ORDAIN
– Buddhist priest or monk in Tibet or Mongolia LAMA
– calling or strong urging or inclination, as to the priesthood VOCATION
– confession heard or absolution granted by a priest SHRIFT
– deprive a priest of his clerical rights and functions UNFROCK, DEFROCK
– residence of a Roman Catholic parish priest PRESBYTERY
– right to nominate a priest to a vacant benefice or to a position ADVOWSON

priestess in ancient Rome tending the sacred fire in the temple of the goddess Vesta VESTAL VIRGIN
– priestess or nun VOTARESS

prim, affectedly delicate or refined MINCING, NIMINY-PIMINY

primitive, original PRIMAL
– person who "takes to the hills", living a primitive life, to escape the effects of an expected nuclear war SURVIVALIST
– relating to a primitive time or condition PRISTINE, PRIMORDIAL
– reversion to a more primitive state ATAVISM

primitive- UR-

primitive man See **prehistoric man**

prince or high nobleman in Anglo-Saxon times ATHELING

princess of a Spanish or Portuguese royal family other than the heir apparent INFANTA

principal See also **main**
– principal, foremost, leading, supreme PARAMOUNT, PREDOMINANT, PRE-EMINENT, PREPONDERANT
– principal of a university VICE-CHANCELLOR
– principal or capital sum of money, value of an estate, or the like, as distinct from the interest or income CORPUS
– principal or governing representative in some colleges WARDEN, PROVOST, RECTOR

principle, body of beliefs, or the like CREDO, CREED, DOGMA, DOCTRINE
– principle, guiding doctrine, or the like, adhered to unwaveringly GOSPEL
– principle, standard, or basis or measure for judgment CRITERION, CANON
– principle or doctrine, as of a religious, political, or professional group TENET
– principle or ideal expressed by a word or maxim, as on a coat of arms MOTTO
– principle or mock-scientific law to the effect that if anything can go wrong it will MURPHY'S LAW
– principle or mock-scientific law to the effect that people tend to get promoted until they reach a position in which they are incompetent PETER PRINCIPLE
– principle or mock-scientific law to the effect that work expands to fill the time available for its completion PARKINSON'S LAW
– principle or rule of conduct, command or maxim PRECEPT
– principle or rule widely accepted AXIOM
– principle underlying something, foundation SUBSTRATUM
– principles allowing different behaviour in one person or group from that expected of another DOUBLE STANDARD
– principles and techniques of a discipline, art, or science METHODOLOGY

-principles -NOMY

print made from a specially carved or etched block or printing plate ENGRAVING

printing See chart, and also **typesetting**, **script**, **paper**, **typefaces**
– printing error or typing error TYPOGRAPHICAL ERROR, TYPO
– printing plate or mould MATRIX
– printing symbol, *, as for referring to a footnote ASTERISK
– printing symbol, †, as for referring to a footnote DAGGER, OBELISK, OBELUS
– printing symbol, ‡, as for referring to a footnote DIESIS, DOUBLE DAGGER
– printing type of a sloping style, as used for emphasis ITALIC
– printing worker who sets type, typesetter COMPOSITOR
– printing workers' association or trade-union branch CHAPEL
– printed character of two or more letters joined together, such as *fi* LIGATURE
– printed pamphlets, handouts, and other short-lived topical publications EPHEMERA
– printer for a word-processor, printing each character in the form of a set of tiny dots DOT-MATRIX PRINTER
– check a printer's copy for mistakes against the original manuscript or typescript PROOFREAD
– short ornamental line finishing off a stroke of a printed letter SERIF
– small wheel-like device supporting the printing characters on a modern typewriter or word-processor printer DAISY WHEEL

priority given according to position or rank PRECEDENCE

prise out, extract something with difficulty, such as information or the like WINKLE OUT

prison for petty offenders in former times BRIDEWELL, HOUSE OF CORRECTION
– prison guard WARDER
– prison-like institution for young offenders BORSTAL, REFORMATORY
– prison or fortress BASTILLE
– prison or place of detention for juvenile offenders awaiting trial REMAND HOME
– prison sentence whose length is not specified when imposed INDETERMINATE SENTENCE

– prison warder who keeps the keys to an old-style jail TURNKEY
– being held in prison, usually while awaiting trial CUSTODY, REMAND, DETENTION
– centre to help people readjust to society after release from prison or a mental hospital REHABILITATION CENTRE, HALFWAY HOUSE
– confinement in isolation within a prison, usually as a punishment SOLITARY CONFINEMENT
– dark cell or prison, usually underground DUNGEON, OUBLIETTE
– early release from a prison, on condition of good behaviour PAROLE
– empty one's chamber pot as a morning routine in prison SLOP OUT
– enclosed area inside a prison or prison camp COMPOUND
– German prison camp for captured enemy NCOs and privates during the Second World War STALAG
– German prison camp for captured enemy officers during the Second World War OFLAG
– labour camp or prison, especially for political prisoners in the USSR GULAG
– legal writ for release from prison or other rights for a prisoner HABEAS CORPUS
– local prison for holding offenders awaiting a court hearing LOCK-UP
– military prison GUARDHOUSE
– military prison enclosure in the U.S. STOCKADE
– official sending of a person to prison or a mental hospital COMMITTAL
– person confined in an institution, such as a prison or a mental hospital INMATE
– reduction of the duration of a prison sentence, as for good behaviour REMISSION
– remain neglected and disheartened, as in prison LANGUISH
– release from prison against payment of a security BAIL
– running simultaneously, as two prison terms might be CONCURRENT
– send to prison CONSIGN
– ship used as a prison HULK
– short-term prison for young offenders DETENTION CENTRE
– slang term for a prison sentence PORRIDGE
– slang term for a prison warder SCREW
– slang term for prison CHOKEY, CLINK, COOLER, NICK, STIR

PRINTING TERMS

bold face	heavy thick-lined type presenting an emphatic black appearance
caret	arrow head mark indicating to the typesetter where material is to be inserted
cast-off	calculation of the amount of space that a manuscript will take when set in type
catchword	word printed at the top of a page or column, as in a dictionary, to indicate its entries
chase	metal frame that holds type for printing or platemaking
composing stick	small, hand-held adjustable tray in which type is set before fitting in the galley
feathering, carding	adjustment of the spacing between lines to fill the column exactly
flong	papier-mâché sheet used for making stereotype moulds; mould made of this
font, fount	set of type characters of a particular design
forme	type assembled in a chase and ready for printing
galley	metal tray in which set type is held before pagination; printer's proof from such type
gutter	white space running down between the facing pages of a book
imposition	arrangement of pages of type in a forme to read consecutively when the printed sheet is folded
impression	printed sheet produced by a letterpress machine; copies of a book printed at one time from a single set of type
indent	set in from the margin, as for the first line of a paragraph
intaglio, gravure	technique of printing from a plate in which the images are incised rather than raised
justification	equal spacing of words to produce a line to the full width of a given column
kern	part of a piece of type that projects beyond the body or shank
leaders	dots or dashes along a line linking separated words, as in an index
leading	spacing between lines
letterpress	technique of printing from raised inked surfaces
Linotype	machine for setting an entire line of type on a single slug or metal bar
lithography	technique of printing from a plate treated so that some areas accept ink while others repel it
logotype	single piece of type bearing two or more characters
lower-case	referring to small letters, the type for which was originally held in the lower frame of a case of type
mackle	blur or double impression on a printed sheet
matrix	metal plate for casting type faces

continued

PRINTING TERMS *continued*

offset	printing process in which ink is transferred from the plate to an offset cylinder and then to the paper
proof	trial sheet of print on which corrections are written
quoin	wedge used to lock type in a chase
range	lie flush at the margin
registration	exact alignment of print on a page
running head	title printed at the top of every page or every alternate page
signature, gather, section	groups of printed pages, usually 16 or 32, folded from a large single sheet and bound with others to make up a book
stereotype, cliché	printing plate cast from a papier-mâché mould
stet	instruction to a typesetter to ignore a correction
upper-case	referring to capital letters, the type for which was originally held in the upper frame of a case of type
widow	word or very short line, especially when ending a paragraph or standing by itself at the top of a column or page

– study of the punishment and treatment of criminals, especially prison management PENOLOGY
– unable to communicate with others, as when detained in prison INCOMMUNICADO
– U.S. prison where short-term sentences are served by manual labour WORKHOUSE
– U.S. slang term for a prison CALABOOSE
– U.S. term for a prison PENITENTIARY

prisoner serving as an informer to the authorities NARK, GRASS, STOOL PIGEON
– prisoner with special privileges, as for good behaviour TRUSTY
– guardianship, as of an orphan or prisoner CUSTODY
– restraining garment with long sleeves for binding the arms of a violent patient or prisoner STRAITJACKET
– separation or isolation of an individual or small group from the group as a whole, as of prisoners SEGREGATION
– tendency of former prisoners to revert to crime RECIDIVISM

privacy – person who values his privacy and lives in solitude RECLUSE, HERMIT

private See also **secret**
– private, deeply personal, secret INTIMATE
– private, hidden, tucked away or sheltered alone SOLITARY, SEQUESTERED, SECLUDED
– private conversation between two people TÊTE-À-TÊTE
– private soldier in the British Army TOMMY ATKINS, SQUADDY
– privately, in confidence SUB ROSA
– privately owned and controlled PROPRIETARY
– in private, especially relating to a court hearing from which the public is excluded IN CAMERA
– knowing something secret or private PRIVY TO
– person to whom one tells one's secrets or with whom one discusses private matters CONFIDANT, CONFIDANTE

private enterprise, non-interference by governments in commercial activity LAISSEZ-FAIRE

privatise assets HIVE OFF

privilege or right, as conferred by rank, the law, or the like PREROGATIVE

prize, award, or some other honour ACCOLADE
– prize for a particular deed PREMIUM
– prize given in a mocking spirit to the contestant who comes last BOOBY PRIZE, WOODEN SPOON
– prize given to a worthy loser CONSOLATION PRIZE
– prize or high distinction CORDON BLEU
– prize winner, poet, or other eminent person in the arts or sciences who receives a special honour LAUREATE
– prizes awarded annually in the U.S. for journalism, literature, and music PULITZER PRIZES
– second prize, or a person who nearly wins an academic prize or other award PROXIME ACCESSIT

probability – having an even probability, not planned to favour any particular outcome RANDOM
– mathematical analysis of data using sampling techniques and probability theory STATISTICS

probable, believable, likely or possible FEASIBLE
– probable, in the offing, likely to become someone or something specified PROSPECTIVE
– probable, seemingly true, as an excuse might be PLAUSIBLE, COLOURABLE

probably, clearly, or obviously EVIDENTLY

problem, behaviour pattern, or the like consisting of several associated elements SYNDROME
– problem, condition of difficulty or distress PLIGHT, PREDICAMENT
– problem, confused or entangled situation IMBROGLIO, MARE'S NEST
– problem, minor obstacle SNAG, HITCH
– problem-solving by means of an imaginative and free-ranging rather than strictly logical mode of thinking LATERAL THINKING
– problem that can be resolved only by bold or drastic action GORDIAN KNOT
– problem that is hard, difficult to solve, puzzle POSER, CONUNDRUM, ENIGMA
– problem that is unresolvable and blocks progress IMPASSE, DEADLOCK, STALEMATE
– problem that is very complicated, with each apparent solution leading only to further difficulties LABYRINTH
– problem that is very demanding and difficult to escape from MORASS, QUAGMIRE, HYDRA
– problem that seems to have no satisfactory solution DILEMMA, QUANDARY
– difficult to solve or deal with, as a knotty problem would be SCABROUS
– having many aspects, as a difficult problem might have HYDRA-HEADED
– having very serious problems IN EXTREMIS
– identification of a disease, injury, or problem DIAGNOSIS

– referring to a problem that cannot be solved INSOLUBLE
– relating to problem-solving techniques based on trial and error HEURISTIC
– supposed source of problems, errors, or mischief GREMLIN
– tackle a problem or risky project boldly GRASP THE NETTLE
procedure that is pointlessly long and complicated RIGMAROLE
– procedure or programme, as of daily exercise REGIMEN
– characteristic procedure, way of operating MODUS OPERANDI
-process -OSIS
processes or functions maintaining life METABOLISM
procession, especially a funeral procession CORTÈGE
– procession, such as a ceremonial parade of horses CAVALCADE
– procession of the choir and clergy out of the chancel at the end of a church service RECESSION
– procession or costumed parade in a festival PAGEANT
– procession or parade of cars or other motor vehicles MOTORCADE
– official who walks ahead of a person of rank in a formal procession USHER
– placard or message carried in a demonstration or procession BANNER
– precedence, or right of priority in a procession PAS
-procession -CADE
produce, give rise to ELICIT, EVOKE
– produce or obtain from a source DERIVE
producer or sponsor of stage shows, concerts, or the like IMPRESARIO
-producer -PHORE, -PHOROUS
producing or about to produce a discovery, inspired idea, or the like PARTURIENT
-producing- -GEN-, -GENIC, -GENOUS, -FER-, -FACIENT, -FIC
product that is the most successful of a business's output FLAGSHIP
– anything commercially useful, such as a farm product, or any tradable goods or services COMMODITY
– crop or product that is the major one of its kind in a region STAPLE
-product- -GEN-
production – prepare a play for production MOUNT
-production- -GON-, GONO-, -POIESIS
profession, occupation to which one is suited VOCATION, CALLING, MÉTIER
– members collectively of the medical, legal, or other learned profession FACULTY
– person who works in a profession, by contrast to a theoretician, or teaches PRACTITIONER
– requirements in one's profession or pursuits STOCK IN TRADE
professional – *y*oung *u*rban *p*rofessional, affluent and trendily chic YUPPY, YUPPIE
professional misconduct, offence or offences committed by a public official MALVERSATION
professor holding a professorship created by royal grant REGIUS PROFESSOR
– retired but retaining an honorary title, as a professor might be EMERITUS
– university lecturer of senior rank, just below professor READER
profile portrait in the form of a shadow image or filled-in outline SILHOUETTE
profit or payment from one's job or office EMOLUMENT
– profits of a business, charity campaign, or the like PROCEEDS
– anything that can be turned to one's profit or advantage GRIST
– referring to the final profit, weight, price, or the like after all deductions have been made NET
– referring to the profit, weight, price, or the like before deductions have been made GROSS
– share of profits or a bankrupt's assets DIVIDEND
profitable, fruitful, producing a great deal of money LUCRATIVE, REMUNERATIVE
– profitable job requiring little work, or similar easy source of income GRAVY TRAIN, MILCH COW
programme See also **radio**, **television**
– programme at the end of a day's broadcasting, typically a short religious programme EPILOGUE
– programme covering a week's episodes of a series that have previously been broadcast separately OMNIBUS PROGRAMME
– programme of events, schedule of activities CURRICULUM, ROSTER
– programme or procedure, as of daily exercise REGIMEN
– programme that has been prerecorded for broadcasting TRANSCRIPTION
– programme that is broadcast simultaneously on radio and television SIMULCAST
– announcements or linking items designed to avoid breaks between broadcast programmes CONTINUITY
– broadcast live a programme via a transmitter RELAY
progress, movement forwards HEADWAY
– progress or general direction, as of someone's life TENOR
– progress to a more important role GRADUATE
-progression -GRADE
progressive or rebellious activist within a political group or party YOUNG TURK
prohibit See also **hinder**, **limit**, **prevent**
– prohibit, forbid, ban DEBAR, OUTLAW, PROSCRIBE, VETO
– prohibit or cut off from membership of a church EXCOMMUNICATE
– prohibit or forbid by force of law ENJOIN, INTERDICT
– prohibited, forbidden VERBOTEN
– prohibited because blasphemous or cursed TABOO
– prohibited goods, obtainable only by smuggling CONTRABAND
– court order prohibiting or enforcing an action INJUNCTION, WRIT
prohibition, as of foreign ships or of arms trading EMBARGO
– make, sell, or transport goods illegally, especially alcohol during the Prohibition era in the U.S. BOOTLEG
project, gift, or possession requiring more trouble than it is worth WHITE ELEPHANT
– project or enterprise, often risky VENTURE, UNDERTAKING
– projected or possible course of action or chain of events SCENARIO
– dark chamber in which the image of an outside view is projected onto a surface by a lens set above or opposite CAMERA OBSCURA
– organising of any complicated project, especially one involving transport LOGISTICS
projecting, jutting out PROTRUDING, EXTRUDING, BEETLING
– projecting, rounded part, as on the ear or a leaf LOBE
– projecting end of a piece of wood fitting into a corresponding mortise in another piece to form a joint TENON
– projecting from the surrounding wall or surface PROUD
– projecting or swelling part, bulge PROTUBERANCE
– projecting pin on either side of a cannon, container, or the like enabling it to be pivoted on a supporting frame TRUNNION
– projecting rim or edge, as on a wheel or beam, for strengthening, attaching, or the like FLANGE
– pointing or jutting outwards, projecting, as an angle might be SALIENT
projector for showing images, as

written or drawn on transparent material such as film, or on opaque material, onto a screen EPIDIASCOPE
- projector or camera for cinematic films CINEMATOGRAPH
- projector or other apparatus giving brief exposures of visual images, as for experiments in memory or perception TACHISTOSCOPE

prolong, extend, cause to continue PERPETUATE, PROTRACT

promise, token, or guarantee EARNEST, PLEDGE, UNDERTAKING
- promise of support and vow of faith by members of a church COVENANT
- promise or obligation, recorded in court BOND, RECOGNISANCE
- promise solemnly to be faithful, especially when getting married PLIGHT ONE'S TROTH
- fail to honour one's debts, promises, or the like WELSH
- fulfil a promise REDEEM
- go back on one's promise or commitment RENEGE, WELSH
- obtain a promise, commitment, or the like by persuasion EXTRACT
- written promise to pay a specified sum IOU, PROMISSORY NOTE

promised land, utopia ZION

promising, developing, up-and-coming BUDDING
- promising, favourable, boding well AUSPICIOUS, PROPITIOUS

promontory in Scotland MULL

promote, move to a new and grander role TRANSLATE, PREFER
- promoting or favourable to a given result CONDUCIVE

promoter or financial supporter of a project, sportsman, cultural activity, or the like SPONSOR, PATRON·

-promoter -MONGER

promotion of a military officer to a higher rank, without the corresponding rise in pay or authority BREVET
- promotion or advancement to a higher office or post PREFERMENT
- lowering of rank or status, as opposed to promotion DEMOTION, RELEGATION

prong of a fork or fork-shaped tool TINE

pronoun, in English ending in *-self*, that refers back to the subject of the verb, such as *herself* in *she hurt herself* REFLEXIVE PRONOUN
- adjective for a pronoun PRONOMINAL
- use of pronouns or similar reference to something previously mentioned ANAPHORA
- word, phrase, or clause to which a pronoun refers ANTECEDENT

pronounce, especially in a clear way ARTICULATE, ENUNCIATE
- name, sentence, or the like that is difficult to pronounce or to say quickly TONGUE-TWISTER

pronouncement – from the source of authority, as an official pronouncement might be EX CATHEDRA

pronunciation See also **sound**, **voice**, **speech**
- pronunciation of a final consonant that is normally silent, especially in French, when the next word begins with a vowel LIAISON
- pronunciation of the sound /r/ as /l/, as by Chinese people speaking English LALLATION
- pronunciation of words, or the study of it ORTHOEPY
- pronunciation or spelling differing slightly from another form of the same word VARIANT
- pronunciation that is incorrect CACOEPY
- pronunciation widely used by the upper-middle classes in England and often considered standard, "BBC English" RECEIVED PRONUNCIATION, RP
- conforming to pronunciation, as spelling in Spanish does PHONETIC
- error in pronunciation or grammar produced by the avoidance of another, often imaginary error HYPERCORRECTION
- excessive or inconsistent use of the *r*-sound in pronunciation RHOTACISM
- insertion of an extra sound into a word to make its pronunciation easier, as when *umbrella* is pronounced as though it were spelt *umbarella* EPENTHESIS
- manner or clarity of one's pronunciation DICTION, ELOCUTION, ENUNCIATION, ARTICULATION
- omitting or slurring of a vowel or syllable in pronunciation, as to make a verse scan ELISION
- study of pronunciation and speech sounds PHONETICS, PHONEMICS, PHONOLOGY
- tendency to change a speech sound for the sake of easier pronunciation EUPHONY
- throaty and harsh, as a person's pronunciation might be GUTTURAL

proof See also **prove**
- proof, evidence, or arguments used in justifying a claim or action VINDICATION
- proof or disproof of a proposition by showing that the logical consequences of it or its opposite are absurd or ridiculous REDUCTIO AD ABSURDUM
- proof or firm evidence or witness TESTAMENT
- proof or process of deduction in mathematics or logic DERIVATION
- additional proposition following from the proof of another proposition COROLLARY
- be evidence or proof of, be a witness for ATTEST, TESTIFY
- establish or confirm by evidence or proof VERIFY, SUBSTANTIATE, CORROBORATE
- responsibility in law to provide proof for one's charge or claim BURDEN OF PROOF
- substantial, as concrete proof is TANGIBLE, SUBSTANTIVE
- supposed or presumed, but without proof, and often doubtful ALLEGED, HYPOTHETICAL
- theory that awaits proof HYPOTHESIS, WORKING HYPOTHESIS
- unquestionable, impossible to dispute or contradict, as a watertight proof is INCONTROVERTIBLE
- "which was to be proved", formula indicating that full proof has been achieved, as in a geometry theorem Q.E.D., QUOD ERAT DEMONSTRANDUM

proofreading mark in the shape of an inverted V or Y, placed in the text to indicate where new material is to be inserted CARET
- word written by a proofreader to reinstate a deleted piece of text or overrule a correction STET

prop See **support**

propaganda or presentation of awkward facts, policies, or the like in a selectively favourable way WINDOW DRESSING
- propaganda and agitation, especially by left-wing radicals AGITPROP
- propaganda pamphlet or book containing a forceful declaration or rallying call TRACT
- influence someone into accepting an ideology, belief, or point of view uncritically, as by propaganda INDOCTRINATE, BRAINWASH

propeller blade VANE
- propeller's hub BOSS
- powerful rush of air or water forced backwards by a propeller SLIPSTREAM, RACE

proper, in keeping with good manners and social conventions SEEMLY, DECOROUS, COMME IL FAUT
- proper, legal, officially approved, conforming with the requirements CANONICAL
- proper or formal behaviour, good manners, observing of the formalities ETIQUETTE, PROTOCOL

– be proper or necessary for BEHOVE, BEFIT

property See also **land**, **estate**
– property, as of a bankrupt, used to pay debts ASSETS
– property abandoned by its owner DERELICT
– property in one's personal possession CHATTELS, CHOSES
– property owned or the ownership of it DOMAIN
– property-owning or landed gentry class, or government by it SQUIREARCHY
– property pledged as security for a loan COLLATERAL
– property returning to a lessor or grantor after the agreed term, or the right to this property REVERSION
– property right retained by the lessor or seller RESERVATION
– property to be left in a will by a husband to his widow JOINTURE
– divide land or property into several small units COMMINUTE
– full ownership of land or property FREEHOLD
– go back on an agreement with someone intending to buy one's property, by raising the price after a rival offer GAZUMP
– government's right to take over private land or property for public use, compensation usually being paid EMINENT DOMAIN
– holding or occupying of a property, office, or the like TENURE
– intrude slowly on the property or rights of someone else, trespass ENCROACH
– large landed property or estate DEMESNE
– legal document certifying a contract or transfer of property DEED
– legal right to the use of benefits from someone else's property USUFRUCT
– legally attested right to a property TITLE
– limit the inheritance of property to a particular line of heirs ENTAIL
– mortgage or other charge or claim on a property ENCUMBRANCE
– repossess mortgaged property when the scheduled payments are not met FORECLOSE
– return of land or property to the Crown or a feudal lord in the absence of legal heirs, in former times ESCHEAT
– right of use over another person's land or property for specific purposes SERVITUDE
– seize or confiscate property temporarily, especially a debtor's goods SEQUESTRATE
– seize property, as to force payment of a debt DISTRAIN, DISTRESS
– share of the proceeds paid to a landowner for the use or development of his property ROYALTY
– strip or deprive of something, such as clothes, rights, or property DIVEST
– take away a person's private property or land, especially for public ownership EXPROPRIATE
– take or use fraudulently for oneself money or property entrusted to one EMBEZZLE, PECULATE, DEFALCATE
– transferrable to another owner, as some inherited property is ALIENABLE
– transferring of the ownership of a house, flat, land, or other property CONVEYANCING
– value of property once all debts are taken into account EQUITY

prophecy See also **fortune-telling**
– prophecy, shrine, or priest of a prophetic god, as in ancient Greece ORACLE
– prophecy, vision, or revelation of a great disaster APOCALYPSE

-prophecy -MANCY

prophesy See also **foretell**, **fortune-telling**
– prophesy or predict on the basis of signs and omens AUGUR, SPAE, VATICINATE

prophet, astrologer, or sorcerer CHALDEAN
– prophet, visionary, or clairvoyant SEER
– prophet of doom whose warnings are ignored CASSANDRA
– prophet who warns of disaster JEREMIAH
– prophetess or sorceress SIBYL

prophetic, able to tell the future MANTIC, ORACULAR, CLAIRVOYANT
– prophetic, relating to a prophet VATIC, FATIDIC, PYTHONIC
– prophetic sign OMEN, PORTENT, PRESAGE, HARBINGER

proportion or correct relationship between things, especially their relative importance PERSPECTIVE

proportionate, corresponding in amount or degree, as one's salary might be with one's qualifications COMMENSURATE
– proportionate or balanced arrangement of parts, harmony SYMMETRY

proposal – precise description, list, or proposal SPECIFICATION

propose or name as a candidate NOMINATE
– propose or put forward for consideration PROPOUND

proposition in logic, forming either of the first two parts of a syllogism, from which the conclusion can be deduced PREMISE
– proposition in logic containing two simple statements joined by the word *or* DISJUNCTION
– logically inconsistent or conflicting, as two opposed propositions might be INCOMPATIBLE
– minor proposition taken as valid and used to prove a more important proposition LEMMA
– referring to a proposition whose truth-value depends entirely on the meanings of its terms rather than on real-life facts ANALYTIC
– referring to a proposition whose truth-value depends on real-life facts rather than on the meanings of its terms SYNTHETIC

props and scenery in a play MISE EN SCÈNE

prostitute, typically with wealthy clients, or the mistress of a high-ranking man COURTESAN, DEMIREP, DEMIMONDAINE, COCOTTE, HETAERA
– prostitute, whore, promiscuous woman CYPRIAN, DOXY, DRAB, FILLE DE JOIE, FLOOZY, HARLOT, MOLL, STRUMPET, TROLLOP, TRULL
– prostitute now reformed MAGDALEN
– prostitute or other civilian who follows an army unit to provide unofficial services CAMP FOLLOWER
– prostitute who makes appointments by telephone CALL GIRL
– prostitute's session with a client TRICK
– approach someone with an offer of sex, as a prostitute might SOLICIT, ACCOST, HUSTLE, IMPORTUNE
– engage someone to act as a prostitute PROCURE
– male prostitute or boy kept for sexual purposes CATAMITE, GANYMEDE, RENT BOY
– man who finds clients for a prostitute or brothel PIMP, PONCE, PANDER, PROCURER
– U.S. slang term for a prostitute or streetwalker HOOKER
– woman kidnapped into prostitution WHITE SLAVE

protect or make immune to attack SECURE
– protect, shield, cushion BUFFER, BUTTRESS
– protect against disease by introducing resistance-building materials into the body IMMUNISE, INOCULATE, VACCINATE
– protect and rear a child FOSTER, NURTURE
– protect one's position or one's success against rivals or competi-

tors LOOK TO ONE'S LAURELS
– protect or exempt from loss or legal responsibility INDEMNIFY
– protect or preserve nature, food, or the like from decay CONSERVE
– protect or shelter HARBOUR, SAFEGUARD
– protect or shield someone from what is considered unsuitable INSULATE
– protected, supported, sponsored, or supervised by UNDER THE AEGIS OF, UNDER THE AUSPICES OF
– protected by a trademark, as a medicine might be PATENT, PROPRIETARY
– over-protect or indulge, spoil by pampering COCOON, MOLLYCODDLE
– person whose welfare is protected or career advanced by an influential patron PROTÉGÉ

protection See also **defence**, **fortification**
– protection, as against inflation HEDGE
– protection, sponsorship, supervision, especially of a young person PATRONAGE, TUTELAGE
– protection and preservation, as of a house UPKEEP, MAINTENANCE
– protection and preservation of the environment CONSERVATION
– protection money, as paid by a vassal nation to a dominant nation TRIBUTE
– protection or defence, specifically the walls of a fortification RAMPART, BULWARK
– protection or guardianship, as granted by a court CUSTODY
– protection or shelter, as from persecution, or a place offering such safety ASYLUM, REFUGE, SANCTUARY, HAVEN
– child, senile person, or the like under the legal protection of a guardian or court of law WARD
– demand protection money EXTORT

protection- PARA-

protective, as a deity is supposed to be towards his shrine TUTELARY
– protective, jealously defensive TERRITORIAL
– protective, on one's guard, watchful VIGILANT
– protective against or preventing something, especially against disease PROPHYLACTIC
– protective charm AMULET, TALISMAN
– protective charm or practice, guarantee, safeguard PALLADIUM
– protective colouring of an animal, by which it resembles an unrelated animal that is unpalatable or poisonous to its predators BATESIAN MIMICRY
– protective or preservative substance FIXATIVE
– protective shell or the outer covering of an animal or plant ARMATURE, INTEGUMENT

protector, in the form of a person, institution, or place, of a cause, attitude, or principle BASTION, OUTPOST, BULWARK, STRONGHOLD
– protector or supporter PATRON, BENEFACTOR, SPONSOR
– outstanding protector or defender of a cause, champion PALADIN
– escort, usually an elder woman, serving as protector of a young woman's reputation CHAPERONE, DUENNA

protein in milk, forming the basis of cheese CASEIN
– protein of various kinds in blood, milk, and the like GLOBULIN
– protein produced by living cells and serving as a biochemical catalyst ENZYME
– protein substance made from soya beans, processed to resemble meat TEXTURED VEGETABLE PROTEIN, TVP, SPUN PROTEIN
– acid forming a basic part of proteins AMINO ACID
– common protein found in blood plasma and egg white ALBUMIN

protest See also **complain**, **criticise**, **objection**
– protest, complaint, or statement, as in diplomatic matters or to the public authorities DÉMARCHE
– protest, raise objections, take exception DEMUR
– protest against, disapprove of, condemn, or discourage DEPRECATE, DEPLORE, REPREHEND, REPROBATE
– protest against bitterly, rail against INVEIGH, LAMBAST
– protest demonstration MANIFESTATION
– protest in the form of nonviolent resistance and a refusal to obey laws regarded as unjust CIVIL DISOBEDIENCE
– protest or complaint, or the injustice giving rise to it GRIEVANCE
– protest or demonstrate outside a place of work, typically during a strike, as to discourage other workers or customers from entering PICKET
– protest or object earnestly REMONSTRATE, EXPOSTULATE
– protest speech that is typically loud, emotional, and rhetorical TIRADE, HARANGUE, PHILIPPIC, DECLAMATION
– protester or devoted and energetic campaigner in pursuing a political aim ACTIVIST, MILITANT
– protesting noisily VOCIFEROUS
– protesting disagreement, refusal to comply or conform DISSENT, DISSIDENCE
– protests or appeals, as to an authority REPRESENTATIONS
– launch or hand in a protest REGISTER, LODGE
– noisy and insistent, as a protest might be VOCIFEROUS
– noisy and insistent pubic protest CLAMOUR, OUTCRY
– refuse to buy, deal with, or the like, as a form of protest or coercion BOYCOTT

Protestant, especially Calvinist or Zwinglian rather than Lutheran REFORMED
– Protestant, especially Low-Church or fundamentalist EVANGELICAL
– Protestant destroyer of religious statues and sacred objects ICONOCLAST
– Protestant from France in the 16th and 17th centuries HUGUENOT
– Protestant in Northern Ireland ORANGEMAN
– Protestant in the early Scottish Presbyterian church COVENANTER
– Protestant or person who refuses to comply with an established church NONCONFORMIST, DISSENTER
– Christian reform movement in 16th-century Europe that gave rise to Protestantism REFORMATION

proud See also **pride**, **pompous**, **boast**
– proud, self-centred, full of oneself EGOCENTRIC
– proud, stately, dignified MAJESTIC, OLYMPIAN
– proud and boastful of one's appearance or abilities, stuck up VAIN, BLOATED, BLUSTERING, INFLATED, SWANKY
– proud and rude INSOLENT
– proud in a scornful way, pompous, presumptuous ARROGANT, ASSUMING, CONCEITED, GRANDIOSE, HAUGHTY, IMPERIOUS, LOFTY, LORDLY, OVERBEARING, OVERWEENING
– proudly distant, reserved, and unfriendly ALOOF, SNIFFY, SNOOTY
– excessively proud in one's appearance, totally taken up in self-admiration NARCISSISTIC

prove See also **proof**
– prove, confirm as genuine or correct VERIFY, AUTHENTICATE, VALIDATE
– prove, establish or confirm by convincing evidence, bear out

CORROBORATE, SUBSTANTIATE
– prove false, disprove, contradict BELIE, CONFUTE, GIVE THE LIE TO, REBUT, REFUTE
– prove or justify, in the face of adverse criticism or evidence VINDICATE
– proving something directly by means of logical argument DEICTIC
– bear witness to or provide evidence for in an attempt to prove or justify VOUCH FOR, TESTIFY TO
– show plainly or prove, demonstrate clearly with convincing examples EVIDENCE, MANIFEST, ATTEST TO
– support or give good reasons for, but without actually proving AFFIRM, SUSTAIN

proven beyond doubt, indisputably certain APODICTIC, INCONTROVERTIBLE, IRREFUTABLE

Provençal courtly poet-musician in the Middle Ages TROUBADOUR
– region of southern France where Provençal is spoken LANGUEDOC

proverb or clichéd moral speech or lesson HOMILY
– proverb or motto MAXIM, ADAGE, APOTHEGM, GNOME, SAW, APHORISM, PRECEPT
– pompously moralising, especially by means of proverbs and platitudes SENTENTIOUS

provide for, make allowance for something LEGISLATE FOR
– provide or supply FURNISH, PURVEY

provisional, incompletely developed, or experimental TENTATIVE
– provisional, temporary INTERIM

provisions or allowance for a journey VIATICUM
– supplier of provisions and food to an army, a ship, or the like VICTUALLER, SUTLER

provoke or arouse discontent, friction, or the like, agitate FOMENT
– provoke something, often something wrong, or provoke someone into doing it INSTIGATE
– provoked or aroused very easily HAIR-TRIGGER
– provoking anger or violence, as a speech might INCENDIARY, INFLAMMATORY

prow of an ancient Roman ship ROSTRUM

prudent, careful or reserved in one's behaviour, wary CIRCUMSPECT, JUDICIOUS, GUARDED
– prudent, tactful, cautious in one's social dealings DISCREET, DIPLOMATIC, POLITIC
– prudent in the circumstances, advisable EXPEDIENT

prunes – savoury dish of prunes stuffed with chutney and wrapped in bacon DEVILS-ON-HORSEBACK

pruning shears SECATEURS

prying into other people's business, nosy INQUISITIVE

psalm See **prayer**, **hymn**
– psalm or hymn sung with responses, or in alternating parts ANTIPHON
– psalms, or a book of psalms, or music for the Psalms PSALTER

pseudonym, pen-name NOM DE PLUME, NOM DE GUERRE

psychiatry See chart, pages 406-407

psychiatrist in the U.S. specialising in legal aspects of mental illness ALIENIST

psychic or supernatural, beyond normal experience or scientific laws PARANORMAL
– study of telepathy and other psychic phenomena PARAPSYCHOLOGY

psychology See chart, pages 406-407, and also **Freud**, **Jung**
– psychologically disordered person, typically aggressive, moody, and lacking in conscience PSYCHOPATH, SOCIOPATH
– psychologically unhealthy or obsessed MORBID
– relating or referring to physical diseases or disorders caused or aggravated by psychological factors such as stress PSYCHOSOMATIC

psychotic condition that involves personality disturbances and a weakened grip on reality SCHIZOPHRENIA

pub or inn HOSTELRY
– pub owned by a brewery and restricted to selling beer made by that brewery TIED HOUSE
– pub-owner, innkeeper, licensed purveyor of alcoholic spirits LICENSED VICTUALLER
– small separate bar or private room in a pub or inn SNUG
– valved tap on an inverted bottle of spirits, as in a pub, releasing an exact tot measure OPTIC

public announcement by a government or official body COMMUNIQUÉ, PROCLAMATION
– public announcement or brief official report, as of the latest news of a battle BULLETIN
– public appearance or presentation, as on television EXPOSURE
– public attention LIMELIGHT
– public baths, especially in ancient Greece and Rome THERMAE
– public building, as for lectures and concerts LYCEUM
– public funds set aside or assigned by vote for a particular purpose APPROPRIATION
– public image or self-projection adopted by a person PERSONA
– public meeting and discussion FORUM
– public meeting or local court in Anglo-Saxon England GEMOT
– public prosecutor and coroner in Scotland PROCURATOR FISCAL
– public record office or archive CHANCERY
– public ridicule or abuse PILLORY
– public right of way THOROUGHFARE
– public service such as water, electricity, or transport UTILITY
– public speaking, or the art or style of a public speaker ORATORY, RHETORIC, ELOCUTION
– public square or open space, especially in a Spanish-speaking town PLAZA
– public square, especially in an Italian town PIAZZA
– public-address system, especially in a large building TANNOY
– belonging to the congregation or general public as opposed to the clergy, as a preacher might LAY, SECULAR
– make public or reveal some private or confidential information DIVULGE

public opinion as a court of appeal or judgment TRIBUNAL
– public opinion or popular feeling VOX POPULI
– survey public opinion on certain topics, as by questionnaires POLL, CANVASS

publication – stop the publication or circulation of SUPPRESS

publicise, announce or proclaim publicly or widely BLAZON ABROAD, BRUIT ABROAD
– publicise a product by using one's name to recommend it ENDORSE

publicity, or a liking for or power to attract publicity RÉCLAME
– publicity or advertising campaign, or publicity in general PROMOTION
– attracting little attention or publicity LOW-PROFILE, UNOBTRUSIVE, UNOSTENTATIOUS, INCONSPICUOUS

publish a law and thereby bring it into operation PROMULGATE
– published after the writer's death POSTHUMOUS
– publisher's list of books still available even though published in the distant past BACKLIST

pudding See **dessert**
– bead-like granules of cassava-root starch, used in milk puddings, and as a thickener in soup and the like TAPIOCA

puff-pastry case that is filled with a savoury mixture and served hot as an hors d'oeuvre or snack BOUCHÉE, VOL-AU-VENT
– puff-pastry cream and jam slice MILLE FEUILLE

puffed or made light by beating or cooking SOUFFLÉ
– puffed out, as a sleeve or hairstyle might be BOUFFANT

puffy, swollen, bloated TURGID
– puffy or swollen condition, or the process leading to it TUMEFACTION

pull a face, especially when competing in a face-pulling contest GIRN
– pull a heavy object on wheels or rollers TRUNDLE
– pull limb from limb DISMEMBER
– pull or drag behind ENTRAIN
– pull or wrench from someone's grasp or control WREST
– pull out something, such as a tooth, by force EXTRACT
– pulling power, as of a locomotive TRACTION, DRAUGHT

pulley of a small wooden kind formerly used on ships BULL'S EYE
– pulley or system of pulleys set in a casing BLOCK
– pulley wheel with a grooved rim SHEAVE
– lower section of a pulley BREECH
– system of ropes and pulleys for hoisting, or the like TACKLE

pulp left over after fruit, especially grapes, has been pressed MARC
– pulp remaining after apples or other fruits have been crushed to extract the juice POMACE

pulpit, used in pairs, in the early Christian church AMBO
– pulpit in a mosque MIMBAR
– pulpit cloth or altar covering ANTEPENDIUM
– pulpit or reading-desk in a synagogue ALMEMAR, BEMA
– roof-like covering over an altar, pulpit, or the like CANOPY, BALDACHIN

pulse – technique for regulating one's own pulse rate, blood pressure, or other apparently involuntary bodily functions BIOFEEDBACK

pulse- SPHYGM-, SPHYGMO-

pulsing, rippling, swaying, or other wave-like movement UNDULATION

pulverise, reduce to a powder by crushing or grinding TRITURATE

pump based on suction, as used in surgery for removing fluids from a body cavity ASPIRATOR
– pump powered by a windmill GIN
– small hand pump whose lower end is placed in a bucket of water, as used in fighting fires STIRRUP PUMP
– type of vacuum pump in which steam is condensed in, and water admitted to two chambers alternately PULSOMETER
– water pump using the momentum of running water to direct some of the water upwards through a pipe HYDRAULIC RAM

pumpkin – lantern made from a pumpkin JACK-O'-LANTERN

pun or play on words PARANOMASIA

punctuation See diagram, page 408
– joining phrases or clauses with conjunctions rather than punctuation HYPOTAXIS
– joining phrases or clauses with punctuation rather than conjunctions PARATAXIS
– sign or mark, as distinct from a punctuation mark, added to a letter to indicate a special pronunciation DIACRITIC

punish See also **criticise**
– punish, as by flogging with a whip SCOURGE
– punish, usually at the court's discretion, as by a fine AMERCE
– punish by demoting, sending away, consigning to an inferior locality, or the like RELEGATE
– punish by subjecting to a penalty PENALISE
– punish or criticise severely CHASTISE, CASTIGATE
– punish or discipline in order to improve CHASTEN

PSYCHOLOGY AND PSYCHIATRY TERMS

abulia/aboulia	chronic inabilty to decide or act independently
alienation	state of estrangement from the real world
amentia	lower than normal mental development
amnesia	loss of memory, as through hysteria or brain damage
behaviourism	school of psychology emphasising the study of behaviour or of stimulus and response, rather than of mental processes
Binet-Simon scale, Stanford-Binet scale	scale in IQ testing, evaluating children's intelligence
classical conditioning, Pavlovian conditioning	learning process of associating two stimuli and eventually securing a response from each of them that was originally elicited only by one of them
compensation	exaggerated action or behaviour intended to make up for real or supposed defects or losses
complex	set of unconscious ideas or urges that continue to influence a person's behaviour
conditioned response, conditioned reflex	reaction to a specially contrived stimulus that replaces the original stimulus
configurationism, Gestalt psychology	school emphasising the indivisibility of various behaviour patterns and psychological experiences
displacement	unconscious redirecting of feelings or urges to a more acceptable person or thing
ego	conscious part of the personality that deals with external reality
Electra complex	Oedipus complex in a young girl
fixation	persistent attachment to a person or thing continuing from childhood
fugue	dream-like state in which a person loses his or her memory and often wanders from home
id	unconscious and deepest part of the personality, the basis for instinctive and biological drives

imago	idealised impression of oneself, a parent, or another person, based on an image formed in childhood
inhibition	restraint of an instinctive impulse
libido	psychic energy derived from deep biological urges, underlying the sex drive
Oedipus complex	set of unconscious emotions affecting a young child, including sexual desire for the parent of the opposite sex
operant conditioning, instrumental learning	simple learning process or training in which a particular action or response to a given stimulus is reinforced by means of reward
paranoia	mental disorder involving delusions, as of persecution or grandeur
persona	social mask or front adopted by a person in keeping with his or her outward role in life
projection	attribution of one's own feelings or urges to others
psychosomatic	showing a link between the physical and the psychological, as in stress-related illness
Rorschach Test	personality test in which the subject offers interpretations of a variety of abstract inkblots
schizophrenia	psychotic condition involving personality disturbances and a weakened grip on reality
sublimation	conversion of instincts or impulses into other usually most socially acceptable urges and activities
subliminal	below the threshold of conscious awareness
superego	partially unconscious part of the personality, based on parental and social standards of morality, and underlying the conscience
transactional analysis	psychotherapy analysing one's social exchanges and relating them to roles, games, and hidden aspects of the personality
transference	unconscious shifting of emotions, thoughts, and wishes regarding one person or object to another

– punish unfairly, bully, or discriminate against VICTIMISE

punishment, as formerly in the army or navy, in which two lines of men beat an offender running between them GAUNTLET

– punishment fitted to the crime, or the system or principle of such retaliatory punishment TALION

– punishment for sailors, consisting of being dragged under the ship KEELHAULING

– punishment in the form of being made to stay in class after the end of the school day DETENTION

– punishment in which the victim is hoisted on a rope attached to his arms tied behind his back, and then dropped with a jerk STRAPPADO

– punishment or adverse result that is well-deserved, one's just deserts COMEUPPANCE

– punishment or affliction, especially when regarded as imposed by God VISITATION

– punishment or other steps taken to correct someone's behaviour and restore discipline DISCIPLINARY ACTION

– punishment or revenge in return for mistreatment or wrongdoing RETRIBUTION

– cancel or reduce a punishment REMIT

– cancellation or postponement of a punishment, such as the death penalty REPRIEVE, RESPITE

– deserved and appropriate, as a punishment might be CONDIGN

– designed to inflict punishment PUNITIVE

– exemption or immunity from punishment IMPUNITY

– former instrument of punishment in Scotland, an iron collar chained to a wall or post JOUGS

– large wheel, as for driving a mill, turned by people walking on steps at the ends of its spokes, formerly used as a punishment TREADMILL

– relating to punishment or legal penalties PENAL

– right or possession that one has to surrender by way of punishment FORFEIT

– send abroad to a penal colony, formerly a punishment for convicts TRANSPORT

– serving as a warning or example to others, as a harsh punishment might EXEMPLARY

– stool to which wrongdoers or suspects were formerly tied as a punishment, as for ducking or public mockery CUCKING STOOL

– study of the punishment and treatment of criminals, especially prison management PENOLOGY

– take away someone's private property by way of punishment CONFISCATE

– very harsh, as laws or punishments might be DRACONIAN

– wooden frame with holes for locking the feet, hands, or head of an offender and exposing him to public abuse as a punishment STOCKS, PILLORY

punt pole QUANT

puny person RUNT

pupa of a moth or butterfly, often encased in a cocoon CHRYSALIS

pupil or disciple of a guru CHELA

– pupil who is top of the class DUX

– relation between pupil and tutor TUTELAGE

puppet leader set up by an occupying foreign power QUISLING

– puppets moved by strings or wires MARIONETTES, FANTOCCINI

– puppet theatre of a traditional Japanese school BUNRAKU

puppy WHELP

– puppy or piglet that is the smallest of the litter RUNT

– group of puppies produced at a single birth LITTER

pure, as in sexual morality CHASTE

– pure, flawless, as perfect behaviour is IRREPROACHABLE, UNIMPEACHABLE, IMPECCABLE

punctuation

( )	brackets, parentheses
⟨ ⟩	angle brackets
[ ]	square brackets
{	brace
.	bullet
†	dagger/obelisk
‡	double dagger/diesis
*	asterisk/star
/	solidus/oblique/slash/virgule
§	section
~	swung dash
. . .	ellipsis /suspension points
¶	paragraph

ACCENTS AND DIACRITICS

´ é	acute
˚ Å	bolle
˘ ŭ	breve
¸ ç	cedilla
^ ê	circumflex
¨ ö	diaeresis/umlaut
` è	grave
ˇ č	háček
¯ ō	macron
/ ø	streg
~ ñ	tilde

– pure, out-and-out, utter, as a downright scoundrel or scandal is UNMITIGATED, VERITABLE
– pure, uncorrupted IMMACULATE, UNBLEMISHED, PRISTINE
– pure, unmixed or undiluted UNALLOYED, UNADULTERATED
– pure and noble man GALAHAD

purely and simply, without mincing words TOUT COURT

purify, cleanse of germs, pollutants, or impurities, disinfect SANITISE, DECONTAMINATE
– purify, make holy, cleanse of sin SANCTIFY, CONSECRATE, HALLOW, LUSTRATE
– "purify" a text by removing objectionable passages from it EXPURGATE, BOWDLERISE
– purify or cleanse something, such as the body DEPURATE
– purify or refine DISTIL
– purify or separate a substance or mixture, such as crushed ore, by washing and then filtering, straining, or the like ELUTRIATE
– purifying or straining by filtering FILTRATION
– purifying power, agent, or device ALEMBIC
– purification of the emotions through pity and fear CATHARSIS
– purification plant, as for crude oil, sugar, or ore REFINERY

purityand brilliance of a diamond or other gemstone WATER

puritanical See **strict**, **old-fashioned**
– puritanical belief in the virtues of hard work WORK ETHIC
– puritanically self-righteous and usually hypocritical PHARISAICAL

purple See also **colours**
– sea creature from which the royal purple dye, Tyrian purple, used to be extracted MUREX

purpose, destination, goal, finishing point TERMINUS AD QUEM
– purpose, intention, or motive ANIMUS, IMPULSION
– purpose in Nature, or the study of or belief in it TELEOLOGY
– purpose or intention that is concealed ULTERIOR MOTIVE, HIDDEN AGENDA, ARRIÈRE-PENSÉE
– pretended purpose PRETEXT

purposeful, directed or tending towards a specific goal TELIC

purse – cord or ribbon running inside a hem, as to tighten a sleeve or close a purse DRAWSTRING
– purse or pouch worn in front of a kilt by Scotsmen SPORRAN

pursue in an irritating and persistent way HARASS, HOUND

pus – pus-filled channel SINUS
– pus-filled skin inflammation resembling a blister PUSTULE
– pus-like liquid from an ulcer or wound ICHOR
– discharge pus, as a wound might SUPPURATE, MATURATE, FESTER
– relating to or containing pus PURULENT

-pus- -PY-, PYO-

push, squeeze, or force out EXTRUDE
– push in or enter uninvited or inappropriately INTRUDE
– push oneself or one's opinions on others OBTRUDE
– push or elbow one's way in a crowd JOSTLE
– push or prod lightly or surreptitiously NUDGE
– set in motion by a push PROPEL

pushchair for a baby STROLLER

pushy, assertive, or insistent in manner STRIDENT, SELF-AGGRANDISING
– pushy, self-important, meddlesome OFFICIOUS, INTRUSIVE
– pushy or aggressive BRASH, BUMPTIOUS, ASSERTIVE, OBTRUSIVE

put aside for a specific use APPROPRIATE
– put forward a proposition or idea for the sake of argument POSTULATE, POSIT
– put forward or propose for consideration PROPOUND
– put into words VERBALISE
– put on an act, show off, try to impress POSE, POSTURE
– put on one's hat or clothes DON

put down a riot or the like QUELL, SUPPRESS

put off doing something until later DEFER, PROCRASTINATE

put out a fire or flame EXTINGUISH, DOUSE, QUENCH

putty – rubbery putty-like filler or sealer MASTIC
– thin mortar used like putty, as for filling cracks GROUTING

puzzle, confront with an insoluble problem STUMP, STYMIE, BAFFLE, CONFOUND, FLUMMOX, NONPLUS
– puzzle, confuse, mystify BEMUSE, BEFUDDLE, BEWILDER, PERPLEX, BAMBOOZLE, OBFUSCATE, STUPEFY
– puzzle, extremely difficult decision, problem with no satisfactory solution DILEMMA, QUANDARY
– puzzle, troublesome problem or embarrassing situation PREDICAMENT, PLIGHT
– puzzle in the form of pictures or symbols representing syllables or words REBUS
– puzzle consisting of a set of simple shapes for reassembling into different figures TANGRAM
– puzzle or poem in which some letters, usually the first, of the lines spell out a name or message ACROSTIC
– puzzle that is difficult to solve POSER, CONUNDRUM, ENIGMA

puzzling, mysterious, as a brief and ambiguous comment might be CRYPTIC, ORACULAR
– puzzling because uninterpretable, as a facial expression might be INSCRUTABLE, UNFATHOMABLE, DEAD-PAN, ENIGMATIC
– puzzling network of hedged or walled pathways MAZE, LABYRINTH
– puzzling or mysterious person or thing, riddle ENIGMA, SPHINX

pyramid – pyramid-shaped temple, as in ancient Babylon ZIGGURAT
– base part or mid-section of a cone, pyramid, or other solid object FRUSTUM

Q

QC, barrister of senior rank SILK
quack doctor or other fraudulent self-proclaimed expert CHARLATAN
- quack remedy, especially one claiming to have secret ingredients NOSTRUM
- seller of quack medicines MOUNTEBANK
quadrangle surrounded by covered corridors GARTH
- covered and colonnaded walk around a quadrangle CLOISTERS
quail – flock or family of quail BEVY
quaint, folksy ETHNIC
- quaint and attractive, visually appealing PICTURESQUE
- quaint idea, eccentric gesture, odd piece of behaviour, or the like WHIMSY
qualifications – letter or certificate of a person's qualifications or rights CREDENTIALS
qualified, authorised, or valid, as a spokesman might be LEGITIMATE
- qualified, worthy, appropriate, as for a task or post ELIGIBLE
qualifying phrase or remark within a sentence PARENTHESIS
quality, degree of excellence or worthiness CALIBRE
- quality, feature, characteristic ATTRIBUTE, TRAIT
- distinctive and characteristic air or quality ACCENT, AURA, ETHOS
- indication of quality HALLMARK, CACHET
quantity See **plenty**
- quantity, size, extent MAGNITUDE, AMPLITUDE, PROPORTIONS
quarantine building or ship in former times LAZARETTO
quarrel, dispute, or difference of opinion DISSENSION, VARIANCE
- quarrel, heated argument or disagreement CONTRETEMPS, ALTERCATION, ARGY-BARGY
- quarrel, wrangle, squabble or something petty BICKER
- quarrel or feud persisting over a long period of time VENDETTA
- quarrel or noisy disturbance, uproar, commotion RUCTION
- quarrel with a statement, call into question, dispute or contradict OPPUGN, GAINSAY, REPUDIATE, CONTROVERT
- quarrelling, disputing, conflicting, at odds AT LOGGERHEADS, AT VARIANCE
- quarrelsome, argumentative DISPUTATIOUS, CONTENTIOUS
- causing quarrels or disputes DIVISIVE
- come forward to try to settle a quarrel or dispute INTERCEDE
- go-between or judge in a quarrel or dispute ARBITRATOR, HONEST BROKER, MEDIATOR, MODERATOR, INTERMEDIARY, ADJUDICATOR
- involved in a quarrel, dispute, scandal, or the like EMBROILED
- resolve or attempt to end a quarrel or dispute between others CONCILIATE
- settle a quarrel, dispute, or differences RECONCILE, COMPOSE, DETERMINE
quarter circle, or quarter of a disc QUADRANT
- quarter or suburb of a city, especially a French-speaking city FAUBOURG
quay – pier or mole to protect a quay or shore JETTY, GROYNE
queasy, seasick, or dizzy WOOZY
queen – queen's husband or king's wife CONSORT
- attain or ascend the throne, as when a princess becomes queen ACCEDE
- attendants or companions of a queen or king RETINUE
- "defender of the faith", one of the titles of the British queen or king FIDEI DEFENSOR
- give up or relinquish the throne formally, as a queen or king might ABDICATE
- relating to a queen or king, royal REGAL
- ruling by hereditary right, as a queen might LEGITIMATE
- staff carried by a queen or king as a sign or royal authority or power SCEPTRE
- title of a queen, as used in lawsuits REGINA
quench one's thirst SLAKE
question a witness who is called to the witness box by the opposing side in a court case CROSS-EXAMINE, CROSS-QUESTION
- question one's own witness in a court case, in trying to establish one's case EXAMINE-IN-CHIEF
- question-and-answer examinations or instruction-book, particularly one on the basic principles of Christianity CATECHISM
- question-and-answer method of instruction, aimed at drawing out the pupil's supposedly inborn knowledge SOCRATIC METHOD
- question closely, intensely, or systematically, sometimes using threats INTERROGATE
- question or examine in a probing way, interrogate CATECHISE
- question such as *isn't it?* added at the end of a remark TAG QUESTION
- question that is fairly difficult to answer POSER
- question that is put for effect or to make a point rather than to secure an answer RHETORICAL QUESTION
- questioning of or report by a spy, astronaut, diplomat, or the like on his return from a mission DEBRIEFING
- always asking questions, in the way a child might INQUISITIVE
- evade or counter a hostile or embarrassing question PARRY
- relating to Socrates' method of eliciting someone's submerged knowledge by means of a series of questions MAIEUTIC
- sustained delivery of punches, questions, words, or the like BARRAGE
question mark combined with an exclamation mark into a single punctuation mark INTERROBANG
questionable, still uncertain or unresolved, as a point under debate would be MOOT
- questionable, widely disputed or earnestly debated CONTROVERSIAL
quibbling, hairsplitting, and oversubtle in argument SOPHISTIC, CASUISTIC
quick, prompt, done speedily and efficiently EXPEDITIOUS
- quick, rapid, swift FLEET
- quick and informal, as an execution might be SUMMARY
- quick cooperation, prompt and eager willingness ALACRITY
- quick glance COUP D'OEIL

– quick movement or action, speed or briskness CELERITY, DISPATCH
– quick or brief, and typically half-hearted, as a routine inspection would be CURSORY, PERFUNCTORY
– quick or brief to the point of rudeness, abrupt, or gruff, as a reply might be CURT
– quick to respond, rashly overreacting TRIGGER-HAPPY
– quicker than normal, speeded up ACCELERATED
– quickly, at a very rapid pace HOTFOOT, LICKETY-SPIT
– dangerously or recklessly quickly, hurtling, hell-for-leather PELL-MELL, HEADLONG, HELTER-SKELTER
– excessively quick, rash, impulsive, as a decision might be PRECIPITATE
– lively, full of vitality, quick and agile SPRIGHTLY
– moving about quickly, nimble, nippy VOLANT, VOLITANT

quick-tempered, easily angered, very touchy, snappish IRASCIBLE, INFLAMMABLE, VOLATILE

quickly or suddenly PRESTO

quiet, avoiding drawing attention to oneself SUBDUED, LOW-KEY, LOW-PROFILE
– quiet, silent, not speaking, as though stunned into silence MUTE, MUMCHANCE, DUMBSTRUCK
– quiet and calm, tranquil SERENE, REPOSEFUL
– quiet and inactive, still QUIESCENT, PASSIVE
– quiet and reserved, not saying as much as one could UNCOMMUNICATIVE, RETICENT, TACITURN
– quiet and thoughtful PENSIVE, REFLECTIVE, MEDITATIVE, CONTEMPLATIVE, INTROSPECTIVE
– quiet place or situation BACKWATER
– quietly-spoken utterance or the subdued sound of it UNDERTONE

quill, hollow, stem-like shaft of a feather CALAMUS
– quill, crystal, bristle, or similar needle-shaped natural object or part ACICULA, ACULEUS

quilt stuffed with down, feathers, or synthetic insulating material, used in place of a sheet and blankets DUVET, CONTINENTAL QUILT
– quilting with a stitched design TRAPUNTO

quinine or related drug, or the bark or tree from which it is derived CINCHONA

quivering, shaking, or trembling movement TREMOR

quotation considered a standard or definitive example LOCUS CLASSICUS
– quotation or reference used as an authority, as for a dictionary or legal argument CITATION
– quotation or statement printed at the start of a book or chapter to indicate its theme MOTTO, EPIGRAPH

quote as an example, authority, or proof CITE
– "so", "thus", term used in a printed text to indicate the deliberate reproduction of a mistaken or surprising wording or fact being quoted SIC

R

r – *r*-sound inserted inappropriately into a word or phrase, as when *drawing* is pronounced as though it were spelt *draw-ring* INTRUSIVE *R*
– excessive or inconsistent use of the *r*-sound in pronunciation RHOTACISM
– pronunciation of the *r*-sound as an *l*-sound, as by Chinese people speaking English LALLATION
– relating to varieties of English in which the *r*-sound is retained before a consonant or pause RHOTIC
– trilling or braying pronunciation of *r*, as in Scotland or Northumbria BURR, ROLL

rabbit colony or breeding area WARREN
– rabbit of a greyish, thick-coated breed CHINCHILLA
– rabbit of a white, long-haired breed ANGORA RABBIT
– rabbit or similar animal CONY
– infectious viral disease of rabbits, producing skin tumours and usually fatal MYXOMATOSIS

rabble-rousing, inciting, as a political speech might be INFLAMMATORY
– rabble-rousing political leader or agitator, rallying support by crude emotional speeches and the like DEMAGOGUE
– rabble-rouser, person causing anger or violent quarrels INCENDIARY, FIREBRAND

rabies HYDROPHOBIA
– rabies, malaria, or any other disease transmitted by animals, insects, or the like ZOONOSIS

race See also **horse-racing**
– race or contest in which the advantages are adjusted to give all the competitors an equal chance of winning HANDICAP
– race or contest forming the basis of a lottery SWEEPSTAKE
– race or series of races for boats REGATTA
– checkpoint in a race such as a car rally where progress is confirmed and assessed CONTROL

race-, racial- ETHN-, ETHNO-

racecourse HIPPODROME
– racecourse enclosure for preparing the horses PADDOCK
– racecourse sign-language used by bookmakers TICKTACK

racehorse See **horse**

racial separation within a society SEGREGATION
– abolish racial separation, as in a school DESEGREGATE
– open a society, a school, or the like to all races INTEGRATE
– prejudiced attitudes or actions, as on the basis of racial or sexual difference DISCRIMINATION
– referring or relating to the racial division including Europeans and most Indians CAUCASOID
– relating to a distinctive racial, religious, or cultural group, typically a minority group, within a society ETHNIC

racing See **horse-racing**

racing car – air deflector, as on an aircraft's wing or a racing car, to increase drag and reduce the tendency to lift SPOILER
– assembly area for racing cars, next to the track PADDOCK
– team of racing cars ÉCURIE

radar antenna's dome-like covering, as in some aircraft RADOME
– radar-like establishing of the position of an object, as in bats or dolphins, by high-frequency sound waves ECHOLOCATION
– radar-like sonar device or system, as used for detecting enemy submarines ASDIC, ECHO SOUNDER
– radar-like system or apparatus for detecting or locating objects underwater by means of sound waves SONAR
– airborne radar system for detecting enemy bombers AWACS
– electronic valve helping to generate high-power microwaves, as in radar systems MAGNETRON
– metal foil released in strips into the air to thwart an enemy's radar system CHAFF, WINDOW

radiant, shining brilliantly RESPLENDENT, EFFULGENT, SCINTILLATING, CORUSCATING

radiation having wavelengths between those of visible light and radio waves INFRARED
– radiation having wavelengths between those of visible light and X-rays ULTRAVIOLET
– allowing the passage of specified radiation, such as X-rays or visible light TRANSPARENT
– apparatus for radiation treatment, directing gamma rays from cobalt-60 COBALT BOMB
– preventing the passage of specified radiation, such as X-rays or visible light OPAQUE
– send out or give off something, such as gas or radiation EMIT

radiation- ACTINO-

radical, extremist, or revolutionary in politics SANS-CULOTTE, JACOBIN, MAXIMALIST
– radical or reforming activist within a political group or party YOUNG TURK
– radical political revolutionary advocating the destruction of all social and political institutions NIHILIST, ANARCHIST

radio frequency band assigned for private radio communication between members of the public, such as motorists CITIZENS' BAND
– radio of an early kind, using a semiconducting crystal to receive signals, and requiring earphones CRYSTAL SET
– radio or television announcements or linking items designed to avoid breaks between programmes CONTINUITY
– radio or television broadcast covering a week's episodes of a series that have previously been broadcast separately OMNIBUS EDITION
– radio or television network GRID
– radio or television programme that has been pre-recorded TRANSCRIPTION
– broadcast live a concert, speech, or the like, as over the radio RELAY
– broadcast of a programme simultaneously on radio and television SIMULCAST
– capable of transmitting or receiving two signals at once over a radio channel DIPLEX
– degree of accurate reproduction, as by a radio or amplifier, of an input signal FIDELITY
– device in or part of a radio, television, telephone, or the like that receives and converts incoming signals RECEIVER

– estimates of the audience figures, and hence popularity, of radio or television programmes RATINGS
– fine wire used for electrical contact in a crystal radio set CAT'S WHISKER
– presenter of a radio or television programme FRONT WOMAN, FRONT MAN
– relating to radio in which members of the general public rather than professionals make the programmes ACCESS
– small, portable radio receiver that sounds a coded alert signal BLEEPER
– unwanted electric signals that produce random noise in a radio STATIC

radioactive, especially when decomposing rapidly UNSTABLE
– radioactive particles in the atmosphere, caused by a nuclear explosion or accident FALLOUT
– radioactive substance, dye, or the like, whose course can be monitored through a system, as used in medical diagnosis TRACER
– chemical elements with radioactive isotopes of various uses CAESIUM, COBALT, PLUTONIUM, RADIUM, STRONTIUM, THORIUM, URANIUM
– dangerous as a result of exposure to radioactivity CONTAMINATED
– gas produced in the process of radioactive decay EMANATION
– glass box with protective gloves sealed into the side in which radioactive substances can be handled GLOVE BOX
– instrument for detecting radioactivity GEIGER COUNTER

radiotherapy apparatus, directing gamma rays from cobalt-60 COBALT BOMB

raft of a light, buoyant kind BALSA
– raft of logs or floats tied together CATAMARAN

rag-and-bone man TOTTER, SCAVENGER

rage – attack or fit, as of rage ACCESS
– fit of rage or hysterics CONNIPTIONS
– outburst or uncontrollable display of rage, laughter, or the like PAROXYSM
– pale or ashen-faced, as through rage LIVID

ragtime music as played on saloon pianos HONKY-TONK

raid See also **attack**
– brief military excursion or attack SORTIE, SALLY, FORAY
– raid an enemy, village, or the like SACK, PILLAGE, MARAUD, FREEBOOT, PLUNDER, HARRY
– raid or invasion INCURSION
– raiding and looting a village, community, or the like PREDATION

rail and its supporting posts, as along the edge of a staircase BALUSTRADE
– rail round the stern of a ship TAFFRAIL
– railing or wall on the edge of a balcony or roof PARAPET
– handrail along the edge of a staircase BANISTER

railway carriage of a comfortable and spacious design PULLMAN
– railway carriage's enclosed entrance area VESTIBULE
– railway carriages, wagons, and locomotives ROLLING STOCK
– railway goods wagon of a low and open design GONDOLA
– railway or road bridge, typically supported by a series of arches, as over a valley VIADUCT
– railway sleeping car, especially on a continental train WAGON-LIT
– railway system, often elevated, in which a single rail supports the trains MONORAIL
– railway truck for transporting rock, coal, or the like BOGIE
– railway truck that unloads through its floor HOPPER
– railway wagon behind a steam locomotive, carrying fuel and water TENDER
– railway yard in which carriages, engines, and so on are joined up MARSHALLING YARD
– bed or folding bunk in a railway carriage COUCHETTE
– bumper or grid in front of a railway locomotive to clear the track FENDER, COWCATCHER
– compartment at the end of a railway carriage, having seats along one side only COUPÉ
– cord or chain in a railway carriage that a passenger can pull in an emergency to stop the train COMMUNICATION CORD
– device for linking any two railway carriages or trucks COUPLING, DRAWBAR
– frame on the roof of a railway train, tram, or trolleybus, collecting electric current from an overhead wire PANTOGRAPH
– gravel, rock chips, or the like used as foundation for a road or railway track BALLAST
– heavy beam supporting the rails of a railway system SLEEPER, TIE
– open, elevated railway in a funfair, providing visitors with a fast exciting ride ROLLER COASTER, SWITCHBACK, BIG DIPPER
– overhead cable of an electric rail, tram, or trolleybus system CATENARY
– overlapping section of railway track, as on a narrow pass GANTLET
– shock-absorbing or cushion-like device, such as the steel springs or pads at the ends of railway lines or carriages BUFFER
– sloping section or incline, as of a road or railway track GRADIENT
– worker who lays and repairs railway track PLATELAYER
– worker who repairs a stretch of railway track or road LENGTHMAN

rain – rain cloud NIMBUS
– rain gauge UDOMETER, PLUVIOMETER
– rainy, or relating to rain or rainy regions HYETAL
– rainy season in south and southeast Asia MONSOON
– formation or fall of rain, snow, dew, or the like PRECIPITATION
– great downpour of rain CATARACT, DELUGE
– pouring or flooding copiously, as heavy rain does TORRENTIAL
– spray dry-ice crystals or sprinkle chemicals onto a cloud to cause condensation and so produce rain SEED

rain- PLUVI-, PLUVIO-

rainbow – having all the colours of the rainbow, multicoloured PRISMATIC
– range or image of the colours of the rainbow SPECTRUM
– shimmering with a rainbow-like effect, as a soap bubble or opal does IRIDESCENT

raise an anchor, as in preparation for sailing WEIGH, TRIP
– raise from obscurity, unearth DREDGE UP
– raise from the dead, revive RESUSCITATE
– raise in rank, status, or the like EXALT, ELEVATE, PROMOTE, PREFER, MAKE UP
– raise or hoist, especially by machine WINCH
– raise or lift up UPREAR
– raise or lift up jerkily HOICK
– raised in relief, as words or symbols on specially pressed paper or metal may be EMBOSSED
– raised platform in a public place TRIBUNE, DAIS, PODIUM, ROSTRUM
– raising agent or fermentation agent added to dough, such as yeast in bread-making LEAVEN
– woven with a raised pattern, as brocade and some other fabrics are BROCHÉ

rajah – wife of a rajah, or a woman

with the rank of rajah RANI
rake, immoral and debauched man, especially an ageing one ROUÉ
– rake-like farm implement used to level or break up soil HARROW
rakish, unconventional RAFFISH, DISREPUTABLE
rally or large gathering, especially of miners in the North of England GALA
– rally or large gathering, especially of Scouts or Guides JAMBOREE
– person accompanying and guiding the driver in a car rally NAVIGATOR
ram, male sheep TUP
– ram that has been gelded WETHER
– ram that leads a flock of sheep BELLWETHER
rambling, as a speech or argument might be DIGRESSIVE, DISCURSIVE
– rambling or disorderly, as a conversation might be DESULTORY, EXCURSIVE
ranch or ranch-house of Spanish style HACIENDA
random, depending on mere chance ALEATORY, HAPHAZARD
– random, done or applied without making any sensitive distinctions INDISCRIMINATE, ARBITRARY
– random, especially in statistics STOCHASTIC
– random, rambling, or casual DESULTORY
– random, wilful, unprovoked, as vandalism or mindless destruction is WANTON, GRATUITOUS
– random or based on personal decision rather than on regulations DISCRETIONARY
– acquired or added at random, not inherent ADVENTITIOUS
– acting randomly or according to whim CAPRICIOUS, FICKLE, IMPULSIVE
– happening at random, usually to one's benefit FORTUITOUS
– occurring irregularly or at random SPORADIC, INTERMITTENT
– tendency to make lucky discoveries at random or by accident SERENDIPITY
range, distribution, or spread, as of colours or radiation SPECTRUM
– range, extent, or scope, as of a law or one's outlook PURVIEW
– range of a musical instrument or singer's voice COMPASS, REGISTER, DIAPASON
– range of one's understanding, perception, or knowledge COGNISANCE
– range or extent of something, from the beginning to the end GAMUT
– range or field of activity, sphere of operation or expertise PRESERVE, DOMAIN, BAILIWICK, PROVINCE
– range or scope of possible activity, reach, extent AMBIT, ORBIT, RADIUS
– range or stock of jokes, pieces of music, operatic roles, or the like available to a performer REPERTOIRE
– acting or speaking beyond the range of one's ability or expertise ULTRACREPIDARIAN
rank – deprivation of rank, status, office, or the like DEGRADATION, CASHIERING
– organisation according to rank or importance HIERARCHY
– priority given according to position or rank PRECEDENCE
ranks See also **services**
– crowded, pressed together, tightly packed, as ranks of troops might be SERRIED
ransom – captive for whose safety a ransom is demanded HOSTAGE
rape RAVISH, VIOLATE
– criminal offence, considered a form of rape, of having sexual intercourse with a girl who is below the age of consent STATUTORY RAPE
rapid See **quick**
rapid- TACH-, TACHY-, TACHEO-
rare, obscure, known only to experts and connoisseurs RECHERCHÉ, ABSTRUSE
– referring to meat served medium-cooked or slightly rare À POINT
– referring to meat served underdone or fairly rare SAIGNANT
– referring to meat served very rare AU BLEU
rash See also **reckless**
– rash, frantic, disorderly, confused HEADLONG, HARUM-SCARUM, HELTER-SKELTER, PELL-MELL
– rash, giddy, wild, unreasonable MADCAP
– rash, out of one's personal control, as passion might be UNBRIDLED
– rash, overhasty, reckless, devil-may-care IMPETUOUS, IMPULSIVE, PRECIPITATE
– rash, scar, birthmark, or spot on the skin STIGMA
– rash in over-reacting TRIGGER-HAPPY, GUNG-HO
– rash or careless, heedless, ill-advised, unthinking IMPROVIDENT, IMPRUDENT, INJUDICIOUS
– rash or ulcerous skin disease LUPUS
– red skin rash, as that which occurs in measles ROSEOLA
raspberry brandy FRAMBOISE
rat, mouse, squirrel, or related gnawing mammal RODENT
– rat-like, resembling or relating to a rat or mouse MURINE
– rats, cockroaches, lice, or similar small animals that are harmful or annoying to humans VERMIN
ratchet – locking hinge or small lever engaging the teeth of a ratchet PAWL, PALLET, DETENT
rate, pace, or speed TEMPO
– rate at which body processes function METABOLISM
– rate of change, action, or the like VELOCITY
– rate or frequency of occurrence INCIDENCE
– currency equivalent, at the official rate of exchange PARITY
ratio, rate, or proportion QUOTIENT
– first term in a ratio ANTECEDENT
– second term in a ratio CONSEQUENT
rational and deliberate rather than emotional and spontaneous, as one side of human nature is APOLLONIAN
rattle or creak as diseased lungs or broken bones might CREPITATE
rattlesnake – tip of a rattlesnake's tail BUTTON
raven – adjective for a raven CORVID
– flock or family of ravens UNKINDNESS
ravine or gorge, as gouged out by a river or flood water CANYON, GULLY, COULÉE, WADI, GULCH, KLOOF
– narrow ravine or gorge in the U.S., usually with a stream flowing through it FLUME
raw material STAPLE
ray – relating to rays, beams, or radii from a common source or point RADIAL
ray- ACTINO-
razor – principle urging the simplest and most sparing use of terms and assumptions to argue or explain something OCKHAM'S RAZOR
– leather or canvas strip for sharpening a cutthroat razor STROP
re-use – process discarded glass, paper, water, and so on for re-use RECYCLE
reach or retrieve something, such as computer data ACCESS
reacting too quickly and seeking confrontation rather than compromise TRIGGER-HAPPY, GUNG-HO
reaction of a violent kind HORNET'S NEST
– reaction of an adverse or hostile kind, as to an apparent social threat BACKLASH

– reaction that is unthinking and automatic KNEE-JERK REACTION
– reactions, speed of response REFLEXES
– person or group whose reactions serve as a test for new ideas or opinions SOUNDING BOARD
– referring to a reflex reaction or conditioned response to a stimulus PAVLOVIAN

read, especially with care and in detail PERUSE, PORE OVER
– read, interpret, or clarify a code, obscure text, mystery, or the like DECIPHER
– read or recite expressively a poem, speech from a play, or the like DECLAIM
– able to read and write LITERATE
– unable to read and write ILLITERATE

readable, as handwriting ought to be LEGIBLE

reader of a draft academic article who advises the editor or publisher on its suitability for publication REFEREE
– reader of lessons from the bible in a church sevice LECTOR
– eager, insatiable, taking in everything available, as some readers are AVID, VORACIOUS, OMNIVOROUS

reading disability caused by brain damage or disease, "word blindness" ALEXIA
– reading disability caused by learning difficulties or a brain disorder DYSLEXIA
– reading of a text to a musical accompaniment DECLAMATION
– reading of printed text by a machine for conversion to computer data OPTICAL CHARACTER RECOGNITION
– reading room, library, or similar institution ATHENAEUM
– reading stand for supporting a book or notes, as in a church or lecture hall LECTERN

ready, prepared POISED, BRACED
– ready, waiting to be called in or activated PRIMED, ON STANDBY, IN THE WINGS

ready-reference manual or guidebook VADE MECUM

real, actual, existing in the real world independently of the mind OBJECTIVE
– real, genuine, not imaginary or merely apparent SUBSTANTIVE, SUBSTANTIAL
– real, genuine, true, reliable, actual AUTHENTIC, VERITABLE, BONA FIDE
– real, physical, material CORPOREAL, TANGIBLE, PALPABLE
– slang terms for real, authentic, or genuine DINKUM, KOSHER, PUKKA, REAL MCCOY

realistic, capable of working, practicable VIABLE
– realistic and lifelike in art or literature NATURALISTIC, REPRESENTATIONAL
– realistic painting that deceives the eye by its striking 3D effect TROMPE L'OEIL

reality – lacking a body or lacking in reality INCORPOREAL, DISEMBODIED
– quality of appearing to be reality or the truth VERISIMILITUDE
– regard a concept as having concrete reality HYPOSTATISE, REIFY

really, actually, in fact DE FACTO

rear end of a horse or other domestic animal CROUP, HAUNCHES, RUMP, CRUPPER
– relating to the rear or tail end of the body of an animal POSTERIOR, CAUDAL
– to the rear of a ship ASTERN

rearing up on the hind legs, as a heraldic animal might be RAMPANT

rearrangement or reordering PERMUTATION

reason for an action MOTIVE
– reason for being, point of or justification for existence RAISON D'ÊTRE
– reason or cosmic order in ancient Greek philosophy LOGOS
– reason or mind, especially as the governing principle in the universe NOUS
– adjective for reason RATIONAL
– against reason, illogical IRRATIONAL
– for an even stronger reason, all the more so A FORTIORI
– pretended, merely apparent or outward, as a given reason might be OSTENSIBLE, PURPORTED, COLOURABLE, SPECIOUS
– pretended or apparent reason PRETEXT
– produce or cite an example, argument, or reason as evidence or proof ADDUCE

reasonable or valid, as a grievance or conclusion might be LEGITIMATE

reasoning See also **logic**, **fallacy**
– reasoning by inferring general truths from particular instances, as distinct from strict logical deduction INDUCTION
– reasoning from the general to the particular, deductive reasoning SYNTHESIS
– reasoning in a logical and systematic way RATIOCINATION
– reasoning or argument that is plausible but over-subtle, faulty, or deliberately deceptive CHOPLOGIC, CASUISTRY, SOPHISTRY
– reasoning that is faulty or illogical and that invalidates the conclusion FALLACY
– reasoning that is faulty or invalid, though not deliberately so PARALOGISM
– based on abstract philosophical reasoning METAPHYSICAL
– conclusion based on strict logical reasoning DEDUCTION
– logical reasoning and disputation DIALECTIC
– pattern of logical reasoning in which two premises generate a conclusion SYLLOGISM
– powerful and convincing, as someone's reasoning might be COGENT, COMPELLING, INCISIVE, TRENCHANT
– relating to reasoning from the general to the particular, from principles or causes to facts or effects DEDUCTIVE, A PRIORI
– relating to reasoning from the particular to the general, from facts or effects to principles and causes EMPIRICAL, INDUCTIVE, A POSTERIORI
– using the premise and conclusion to prove each other, as faulty reasoning might CIRCULAR
– work out or prove by reasoning, deduce, infer DERIVE

rebel against accepted rules, practices, and religious beliefs DISSENTER, NONCONFORMIST, RECUSANT
– rebel against an official church, person holding forbidden religious views HERETIC
– rebel or reformer within a political group or party YOUNG TURK
– military action taken by the authorities against rebels or terrorist groups COUNTERINSURGENCY

rebellion, revolt, uprising INSURGENCE, INSURRECTION
– rebellion by soldiers or sailors against their officers MUTINY
– rebellion leading to the sudden overthrow of a government COUP, COUP D'ÉTÂT, PUTSCH
– put down, crush, or suppress something, such as a rebellion REPRESS, QUELL
– stir up trouble, rebellion, or the like FOMENT, INSTIGATE
– suppression of a rebellion or terrorism in a region PACIFICATION

rebellious MUTINOUS, DISAFFECTED
– rebellious, discontented person MALCONTENT
– rebellious, disobeying orders, behaving badly RESTIVE, UNRULY, INSUBORDINATE, DEFIANT
– rebellious, uncooperative, obstinate, difficult to manage BOLSHIE,

RECALCITRANT, REFRACTORY, CONTUMACIOUS
– rebellious person who stirs up unrest or discontent FIREBRAND, INCENDIARY, AGITATOR, SUBVERSIVE
– rebellious speech or action, incitement to undermine authority SEDITION

rebirth in another body or form REINCARNATION
– rebirth or revival, as of a cultural heritage RENASCENCE, RENAISSANCE

reborn – person, project, or the like that seems to be reborn after destruction or downfall PHOENIX

recantation in the form of a poem or official declaration PALINODE

receiver – person who receives or takes delivery of something RECIPIENT, ADDRESSEE
– receiver and seller of stolen goods FENCE
– person who receives charity, a favour, money from a will, or the like BENEFICIARY

recent- NEO-

recently LATTERLY

reception, as for a VIP LEVEE
– reception office in a college LODGE, PORTER'S LODGE

recess in a wall, as for a statue NICHE

recite expressively a poem, speech from a play, or the like DECLAIM
– recite or chant in a half-musical tone INTONE, CANTILLATE

reckless See also **rash**
– reckless, headlong, as if suddenly sent crazy GADARENE
– reckless, heedless, negligent, slack REMISS
– reckless, thoughtless, without due reflection beforehand UNADVISED, UNCONSIDERED
– reckless disregard of danger TEMERITY
– reckless or rash, without regard for possible dangers or consequences IMPETUOUS, IMPULSIVE, PRECIPITATE
– reckless person TEARAWAY, MADCAP
– recklessly bold and brave, or lacking restraint AUDACIOUS

reckon, count TALLY

recluse or hermit, person who has gone into seclusion for religious reasons ANCHORITE, ANCHORESS, EREMITE
– reclusive person TROGLODYTE

recognised officially, authorised, having acceptable credentials ACCREDITED
– generally recognised, accepted RECEIVED, ACKNOWLEDGED

-recognition -GNOSIS

recommend, approve, give one's backing to SANCTION, ENDORSE
– recommend highly or with suspect enthusiasm TOUT, PUFF
– recommend or argue in favour of a proposal, course of action, or the like ADVOCATE

reconcile, or attempt to reconcile, disputing people or groups MEDIATE, MODERATE, CONCILIATE, ARBITRATE, INTERCEDE

record, list, or check off item by item TALLY
– record an interview, programme, or the like for broadcasting at a later time TRANSCRIBE
– record of ancestral line or purity of breeding PEDIGREE
– record of negotiations used as a first draft for a treaty or similar document PROTOCOL
– record or report in detail, and support with evidence DOCUMENT
– recording on thin, transparent, bendy plastic, usually given away for promotional purposes FLEXIDISC
– recording using separate electronic signals rather than a continuous fluctuating signal DIGITAL RECORDING
– records of an institution, group of people, or the like ARCHIVES
– records of events over the years ANNALS, CHRONICLES
– records or files held on a particular person or subject DOSSIER
– records or published transcripts of a conference, learned society's meetings, or the like ACTS, PROCEEDINGS, TRANSACTIONS
– records stored in a computer ELECTRONIC DATA
– hard plastic-like resin from which old 78 rpm records were made SHELLAC
– official record of events at a meeting MINUTES
– person in charge of official registers and records REGISTRAR
– personal record of one's education and career details, as shown to prospective employers CURRICULUM VITAE, RÉSUMÉ
– places where records or ledgers are stored REGISTRY
– small laser-read metal disc for reproducing music or other recorded sound on a special player COMPACT DISC

-record -GRAM

record player – moving arm of a record player, holding the cartridge and needle TONE ARM, PICKUP ARM
– needle or jewel in a record player pickup for tracing the groove of a record STYLUS
– rapid distortion or variation of pitch, as produced by a faulty record player or tape recorder FLUTTER
– slow distortion or variation of pitch, as produced by a faulty record player or tape recorder WOW
– small shaft or protruberance, on the turntable of a record player, passing through the centre hole of a record CAPSTAN
– U.S. term for a record player PHONOGRAPH

recorder – lip or plug producing the vibration in an organ pipe, the mouthpiece of a recorder, or the like FIPPLE

-recording -GRAPH

recover from a loss or setback, and regain a favourable position RECOUP
– recover or regain something, such as pawned goods, by payment REDEEM
– recover or regain something that was lost, left behind, or confiscated RECLAIM, RETRIEVE
– recover or save property or damaged materials, as from a fire or a sinking ship SALVAGE
– recover strongly, improve rapidly, as one's health or spirits might RALLY
– recovering from illness or injury, trying to return to health CONVALESCENT, RECUPERATING, VALETUDINARIAN
– recovery of one's status, good name, or the like REHABILITATION
– ability to recover quickly from illness or other setbacks RESILIENCE, BUOYANCY
– help to recover, restore to life REVIVE, RESUSCITATE
– legal action to recover personal property REPLEVIN
– medical drug, tonic, or the like that helps in the recovery of health or strength RESTORATIVE

recruit forcibly into military service PRESS, PRESS-GANG, IMPRESS, SHANGHAI
– recruiting of managers or officials from other firms HEADHUNTING

rectangular OBLONG
– rectangular slot into which the matching tenon is fitted when joining two pieces of wood, stone, or metal MORTISE

rectory or similar office having fixed capital assets, or the revenue derived from these BENEFICE

rectum See also **anus**
– injection of liquid into the rectum as for medication or purging the bowels ENEMA

– medication in solid form designed to be inserted into a body cavity, especially the rectum SUPPOSITORY

rectum- PROCT-, PROCTO-

recurring phrase, design, or thematic element in music, art, or literature MOTIF, MOTTO

– recurring regularly CYCLICAL, RECURRENT

red See **colours**

– red-faced and often swollen and coarse-looking BLOWZY

– red-hot or white-hot, glowing with heat INCANDESCENT

– red lead, as used formerly in paint MINIUM, CINNABAR

– red pepper, sweet pepper PIMIENTO, CAPSICUM

– red pepper as a condiment CAYENNE PEPPER

red- ERYTHR-, ERYTHRO-, RHOD-, RHODO-

red-handed, in the very act of committing an offence IN FLAGRANTE DELICTO

Red Indian See **American Indian**

redcurrant or pomegranate syrup, used as a cordial or flavouring GRENADINE

reddening or blushing ERUBESCENCE

reddish in appearance or complexion, rosy, ruddy, flushed FLORID, RUBICUND

reduce See **lessen**

reduction, or the amount lost or wasted in a reduction DECREMENT

redundancy, needless repetition of a single idea in separate sets of words TAUTOLOGY

– redundancy, use of more words than necessary in expressing an idea PLEONASM

– reduction in the work force as through retirement or resignation rather than through redundancies NATURAL WASTAGE, ATTRITION

redundant See **excessive**, **long-winded**

– redundant, purposeless, having no real use OTIOSE

– make something redundant, make unnecessary by anticipating OBVIATE, PRE-EMPT

reed – reed-like, relating to or resembling a reed ARUNDINACEOUS

– reed-like marsh plant related to the grass family SEDGE

– reed-like plant, or the paper once made from its pith PAPYRUS

– metal band securing the reed to the mouthpiece of a clarinet or saxophone LIGATURE

reef of coral, parallel to the coastline and forming a deep, wide lagoon BARRIER REEF

– reef or small rocky island, as off the coast of Scotland SKERRY

– ring of islands around a lagoon, formed of coral reefs ATOLL

– sea water separated from the sea, as by coral reefs LAGOON

reel or spool around which yarn is wound in weaving SPINDLE, BOBBIN, QUILL

– reel used for spinning silk from cocoons, or the place where such spinning is done FILATURE

refectory in a medieval monastery FRATER

refer a case or decision to a lower court, committee, or the like REMIT

– refer to indirectly ALLUDE

– refer to something, call attention or remark ADVERT

reference See also **footnote**

– reference, letter of recommendation TESTIMONIAL

– reference book presenting a specialised vocabulary or selected information THESAURUS

– reference line, as on a graph or technical drawing AXIS

– reference manual or handy guidebook VADE MECUM

– reference or note in a text, placed at the end of the text or at the foot of the page FOOTNOTE

– reference or quotation used as an authority, as for a dictionary or legal argument CITATION

– reference point, starting point, or standard, as in surveying or sociology DATUM LINE

– list of references used in researching or compiling a book or report BIBLIOGRAPHY

– person writing a reference for a job applicant, scholarship candidate, or the like REFEREE

– "and the following", used in references and footnotes to refer to the lines, pages, or the like following the one just listed FF.

– "in the place cited", used in references and footnotes to refer to the work or page previously cited LOC. CIT.

– "in the same place", used in references and footnotes to refer to the chapter, page, or the like cited immediately before IBID., IBIDEM

– "in the text above", used in references and footnotes to refer to a previous passage in the text SUPRA

– "in the text below", used in references and footnotes to refer to a later passage in the text INFRA

– "in the work cited", used in references and footnotes to refer to the book, article, or other work previously cited OP. CIT.

– "see" or "which see", used in references and footnotes to direct the reader's attention to a specified page, work, or the like VIDE, Q.V.

– "the same", used in references and footnotes to indicate a reference already mentioned IDEM

– "throughout", "here and there", used in references and footnotes to indicate the frequent occurrence of an item in a text PASSIM

referring to or relating to, concerning PERTAINING TO, ANENT, APROPOS OF

-referring to -WISE

refined, elegant, exquisite, especially in a pretentious way RECHERCHÉ

– refined, often in an affected way GENTEEL

– refined, sensitive, capable of or based on fine distinctions SUBTLE

– refined, very delicate ETHEREAL

– refined and very well-bred person PATRICIAN

– refined or dainty in an affected way MINCING, NIMINY-PIMINY

– refined or elegant feature NICETY

reflector or mirror in some optical instruments SPECULUM

– reflector set in the road at intervals to indicate traffic lanes at night CAT'S-EYE

reflex, knee-jerk, sleepwalking, or similar involuntary, unthinking action AUTOMATISM

– reflex movement, as by bacteria, in response to light or a similar stimulus TAXIS

– referring to a reflex reaction or conditioned response to a stimulus PAVLOVIAN

– small rubber-headed hammer used for testing reflexes and tapping the chest for purposes of diagnosis PLEXOR

reformer or rebel within a political group or party YOUNG TURK

– reformer or social theorist who is hopelessly idealistic and impractical VISIONARY, UTOPIAN

reforms – superficial, just for show, shallow rather than really effective, as reforms might be COSMETIC, TOKEN

refrigeration- CRYO-

refrigerator – chemical commonly used in refrigerators and air conditioners FREON

– switching or controlling device for regulating temperature, as in a refrigerator or central-heating system THERMOSTAT

refuge, haven, or relief OASIS

– immunity from arrest or punishment, as by taking refuge in a church or embassy SANCTUARY

refugee or emigrant, specifically one

who has fled his homeland for political reasons ÉMIGRÉ

refund of part of a sum paid, as of one's taxes REBATE

refusal, denial, or contradiction NEGATION
– refusal or blunt rejection, as of an offer REBUFF, SNUB, REPULSE

refuse or neglect to carry out the wishes of DISOBLIGE
– refuse or reject a proposal by exercising one's absolute right to decide VETO
– refuse or reject an offer, approach, or the like REPEL, REPULSE
– refuse to acknowledge a debt, authority, claim, or the like REPUDIATE
– refuse to buy, deal with, or the like, as a form of protest or economic pressure BOYCOTT
– refuse to continue, be reluctant, avoid JIB, BAULK, SHRINK
– refuse to do or accept something DECLINE
– refuse to obey, approve, or conform to DISSENT, DEFY, OUTFACE
– refuse to recognise or acknowledge, turn one's back on DISOWN
– refuse to speak to or deal with, exclude, shun OSTRACISE
– refuse with scorn DISDAIN, SPURN

regain a favourable position, as by recovering from a loss RECOUP
– regain one's health, wealth, social standing, or the like RECUPERATE

regard as having a particular quality, consider to be ADJUDGE, DEEM, PRONOUNCE
– regards, greetings, good wishes COMPLIMENTS, SALUTATIONS
– high regard, respect DEFERENCE, REVERENCE

regarding, in relation to, compared with VIS-À-VIS
– regarding, relating to, concerning PERTAINING TO, ANENT, APROPOS OF

regardless of, without reference to, without consideration of IRRESPECTIVE OF

regards, greetings SALUTATIONS

region See also **area**
– region into which a county might be divided in former times HUNDRED, RAPE, WAPENTAKE, RIDING
– region into which French cities and départements are divided ARRONDISSEMENT
– electoral region or police district of a U.S. city PRECINCT
– English county, or regional division of an Australian state SHIRE
– geographical features of a region, or their display on a map TOPOGRAPHY

region- TOP-, TOPO-

register of workers, soldiers, or the like, or the list of duties to be performed by them ROSTER

registration plates that include the initials of the vehicle's owner CHERISHED NUMBER PLATES, VANITY PLATES

regret, feel sorry about RUE
– regretting one's sins or offences REPENTANT, PENITENT, CONTRITE

regular, typical, predictable STATUTORY
– regular, unbroken, and typically unpleasant, as boredom might be UNRELIEVED
– regular, uniform, solid, and impersonal MONOLITHIC
– regular, with little variation, as a climate or personality might be EQUABLE
– regular throughout, predictable, forming a coherent whole CONSISTENT, INTEGRATED, OF A PIECE, UNIFORM
– flowing regularly and rhythmically, as good prose does SEAMLESS, MEASURED
– occurring at regular intervals CYCLICAL, RECURRENT
– system or institution, such as a college, with a regular and reliable output of dull standardised products, graduates, or the like PRODUCTION LINE, SAUSAGE MACHINE

-regulator -STAT

rehearsal or practice DUMMY RUN
– rehearsal or trial run, as of a military attack DRY RUN

reheated before serving, as leftover food might be RÉCHAUFFÉ

reign – reigning or ruling REGNANT
– period of time between two successive reigns, governments, or the like INTERREGNUM
– referring to a particular year of the reign of a named king or queen REGNAL

reincarnation – reverence for all life, as in some Indian religions, often with a belief in nonviolence and reincarnation AHIMSA

reindeer in North America CARIBOU

reinforced concrete FERROCONCRETE

reinforcing triangular metal plate for a corner joist GUSSET

reins See **harness**

reject a proposal by exercising one's absolute powers of refusal VETO
– reject a sweetheart in a cruel way JILT
– reject as being of no further use DISCARD, JETTISON
– reject or abandon a cause, commitment, or the like, turn one's back on, desert DISAVOW, FORSAKE, DISOWN
– reject or cold-shoulder, treat dismissively SLIGHT
– reject or deny a claim or accusation REPUDIATE
– reject or disregard something as irrelevant or unreliable DISCOUNT
– reject or give up solemnly or resolutely ABJURE, FORSWEAR, RENOUNCE
– reject or shun someone utterly from all social dealings in one's community BOYCOTT, OSTRACISE
– reject the authority of a person or group, refuse to obey or conform DISSENT, DEFY, OUTFACE
– reject with scorn DISDAIN, SPURN

rejection of all moral and social values NIHILISM, ANARCHISM
– rejection or blunt refusal of an offer REBUFF, SNUB, REPULSE

relate to, be connected with, or belong to as a rightful part or function APPERTAIN
– relate to closely or communicate intimately with someone or something, such as Nature COMMUNE

related, especially through the father's line AGNATE
– related, especially through the mother's line COGNATE
– related but separated by a specified number of generations, as distant cousins might be REMOVED
– related but subordinate ADJUNCT
– related by blood CONSANGUINEOUS
– related in form, development, or function, as a human arm and a bird's wing are HOMOLOGOUS
– related or resembling AKIN, KINDRED

relating to or referring to PERTAINING, ANENT, APROPOS
– of or relating to a number divided into one RECIPROCAL

relations – resumption of friendly relations, as between two countries RAPPROCHEMENT, DÉTENTE

relationship, especially a sexual relationship LIAISON
– relationship, or quality of relationship, as between business associates FOOTING, STANDING
– relationship between two numbers or quantities RATIO, PROPORTION
– relationship by adoption or marriage, as distinct from a blood relationship AFFINITY
– relationship by blood CONSANGUINITY
– relationship of close and beneficial association, with dependency but without parasitism, as between two different organisms SYMBIOSIS
– relationship of close and beneficial association, without depen-

dency or parasitism, as between two different organisms COMMENSALISM, MUTUALISM
– relationship of correspondence, equivalence, or identity between systems or parts of a system SYMMETRY
– relationship of correspondence between two things CORRELATION
– relationship of equivalent giving and taking on both sides RECIPROCITY, MUTUALITY
– relationship of mutual trust and participating in another's thoughts and feelings RAPPORT, COMMUNION
– relationship or similarity KINSHIP
– capable of living or working together harmoniously, as the partners in a relationship should be COMPATIBLE
– characteristic way of thinking and feeling as a help or hindrance to relationships with others WAVELENGTH
– correct relationship between things, especially their relative importance PERSPECTIVE
– formation of a close relationship, usually between mother and child BONDING
– having the same relationship to each other MUTUAL, RECIPROCAL
– referring to love or a close relationship between two unrelated people that is free of sexual desire PLATONIC
– set of social or psychological factors underlying a relationship DYNAMIC
– value or thing having a close relationship with another, or corresponding to it closely and dependent on it FUNCTION

relative, blood relation KINSMAN, SIB
– relative importance of things, or the ability to see them objectively PERSPECTIVE
– relative or relatives closest to a person NEXT OF KIN
– favouritism, such as political appointments, shown to relatives or friends by those in positions of power NEPOTISM
– murder of one's parent or other close relative PARRICIDE

relative density SPECIFIC GRAVITY
– apparatus to measure the relative density of liquids, as used in beer- and winemaking HYDROMETER
– scale in measuring the relative density of liquids BAUMÉ SCALE

relax See also **calm**
– relax, ease up, cease being tense THAW, UNBEND, UNCLENCH
– relax in a listless or apathetic way LANGUISH, LOLL
– relaxation of or release from a rule, law, obligation, or the like DISPENSATION
– relaxation technique popular in western countries, based on Hindu traditions of meditation TRANSCENDENTAL MEDITATION
– relaxed and friendly MELLOW, GENIAL
– relaxing, calming, soothing, as a medical drug might be SEDATIVE, ANODYNE
– relaxing of tension, as between nations DÉTENTE, RAPPROCHEMENT
– relaxing or sleep-inducing drug NARCOTIC, OPIATE, SOPORIFIC

relay race – last runner or swimmer in a relay race ANCHORMAN, ANCHORWOMAN
– short stick that is passed from one runner to the next in a relay race BATON

release, as from duty, debt, or life QUIETUS
– release a dog, hawk, or the like from its leash or other restraint SLIP
– release of a prisoner before the end of his sentence, on condition of good behaviour PAROLE
– release or discharge from obligation, debt, or penalty QUITTANCE
– release or discharge smoke, steam, or the like VENT
– writ to release a person from unlawful imprisonment, or the right to demand such a writ HABEAS CORPUS

relentless, deaf to all pleas REMORSELESS, INEXORABLE

relevant, applicable, or to the point APPOSITE, APROPOS, AD REM, GERMANE, PERTINENT, APT
– relevant, crucially important MATERIAL
– relevant or well-suited to the occasion OPPORTUNE, SEASONABLE, TIMELY
– relevance, applicability to the matter at hand BEARING
– be suitable, appropriate, or relevant PERTAIN

reliable, expert, and conclusive, as a textbook might be DEFINITIVE
– reliable, honest, as a lawyer or shopkeeper might be REPUTABLE
– reliable, official, based on expert sources AUTHORITATIVE
– reliable, trusty, loyal, and resolute STALWART, STAUNCH, STEADFAST
– reliable all the time and in every case, unfailing, as a remedy might be INFALLIBLE, FOOLPROOF, FAIL-SAFE, DEPENDABLE
– reliable and hardworking YEOMANLY
– reliable colleague or adviser TROUPER
– reliable or believable CREDIBLE

relics – corrupt buying and selling of church offices, relics, pardons, and the like SIMONY

relief in sculpture in which the forms project only very slightly from the background BAS-RELIEF, BASSO-RELIEVO, LOW RELIEF
– relief or assistance in time of distress SUCCOUR

relieve of or free from a problem DISEMBARRASS, DISENCUMBER
– relieve oneself by disclosing the thoughts or feelings that are troubling one UNBOSOM
– relieve or stand in for somebody at work, by taking a turn SPELL

religion See chart, pages 420-421, and also **Buddhism**, **Hinduism**, **Islam**, **Judaism**, **church**, **Communion**, **clergymen**, **prayers**, **Roman Catholic**
– religion based on belief in a single God MONOTHEISM
– religion based on belief in several gods POLYTHEISM
– religion based on belief in two gods or forces, one good and one bad DUALISM
– religion based on the belief that all things have a spirit ANIMISM
– religious act or rite, such as baptism, representing or helping to achieve grace SACRAMENT
– religious annointing UNCTION
– religious belief of a strict or passionate kind FUNDAMENTALISM
– religious beliefs PERSUASION
– religious custom, ceremony, or ritual marking a change of status in a person's life RITE OF PASSAGE
– religious devotion PIETY
– religious doctrine or belief differing from the orthodox view HERESY, HETERODOXY
– religious festival, as on a saint's day, especially in a Spanish-speaking country FIESTA
– religious gift or offering OBLATION
– religious hermit, living in discomfort and solitude for prayer and meditation RECLUSE, ANCHORITE, ANCHORESS, EREMITE, STYLITE
– religious hypocrite TARTUFFE
– religious in a deeply sincere or observant way DEVOUT, PIOUS
– religious in an affected or excessive way PHARISAICAL, RELIGIOSE, HOLIER-THAN-THOU, SANCTIMONIOUS
– religious meditation as a means of experiencing communion with the divine MYSTICISM
– religious meeting, especially

when illegal and held in secret CONVENTICLE
– religious or formal celebration of a rite, performance of a ceremony, or the like SOLEMNISATION, CONSECRATION
– religious or philosophical system holding that knowledge of God comes through mystical intuition THEOSOPHY
– religious or political document or pamphlet containing a forceful declaration or rallying call TRACT
– religious person living a monastic life but without having taken formal vows OBLATE
– religious principle, body of beliefs, or the like DOGMA, DOCTRINE, CREED, CATECHISM, GOSPEL
– religious programme at the end of a day's broadcasting EPILOGUE
– religious rite of removing the foreskin CIRCUMCISION
– religious ritual considered foolish and obscure MUMBO-JUMBO
– religious ritual involving the pouring of a liquid LIBATION
– religious sacrament including confession, absolution, and penalties PENANCE
– religious separation or exclusivity SECTARIANISM, DENOMINATIONALISM
– religious song, poem, or hymn CANTICLE
– religious system or code DISPENSATION
– religious system or group, especially a primitive or dubious one CULT
– religious view that God created the universe and natural laws but no longer directs them DEISM
– religious view that God is both the creator and director of the universe THEISM
– religious view that God is present throughout Nature and is identical with it PANTHEISM
– calling or strong urging or inclination, as to a religious life VOCATION
– combine or try to reconcile different philosophical, religious, or other beliefs SYNCRETISE
– conversion from or abandoning of one's religion or loyalty APOSTASY
– cut off from membership of a church or religion EXCOMMUNICATE
– declare a belief in something, especially in a religion PROFESS
– disclosure or realisation of God's will or some religious truth REVELATION
– lacking religious beliefs, or lacking the beliefs regarded as the correct ones INFIDEL
– lacking religious beliefs, or not belonging to a monotheistic religion PAGAN, HEATHEN
– liberal, especially in matters of religion LATITUDINARIAN
– living a strict, self-denying life, with minimum comforts and pleasures, often for religious reasons ASCETIC, AUSTERE
– movement or doctrine favouring greater unity among the various churches or religions ECUMENISM, ECUMENICALISM
– officiating priest or lay participant in a religious ceremony or rite CELEBRANT
– person enthusiastically following a specified religion, cause, or god VOTARY, DEVOTEE
– person on probation in a religious order, prior to taking vows NOVICE
– place or rub oil or ointment on, as part of a religious ceremony ANOINT
– recent convert to a religion NEOPHYTE, PROSELYTE
– recognition of others' rights to dissenting beliefs, especially in matters of religion TOLERATION
– rejection of religion as lacking a logical basis RATIONALISM
– rejection of religion on the ground that the existence of God is unknowable or at least unprovable AGNOSTICISM
– rejection of religion on the ground that there is no God ATHEISM
– reserve or ceremonially set aside for sacred or religious use CONSECRATE, SANCTIFY, DEDICATE
– spoiling or destruction of the sacred quality of a religious building, graveyard, or the like DESECRATION, PROFANATION, VIOLATION, SACRILEGE, DEFILEMENT
– strict and stiffly correct observer of the rules, a religion, or the like PRECISIAN
– study of religion, especially Christianity THEOLOGY
– relating to worldly rather than spiritual or religious matters SECULAR, TEMPORAL, PROFANE

reluctant, unwilling, forced, involuntary GRUDGING
– be reluctant, refuse to continue JIB, BAULK

remain, continue, or survive, as pain might PERSIST
– remain in or at a place temporarily TARRY, SOJOURN
– remain or hang about aimlessly, or dawdle idly LINGER, LOITER
– remain unmoved or unchanged, especially in the face of outside pressures ABIDE, ENDURE
– remaining only temporarily, passing through, as a labourer or bird might TRANSIENT, ITINERANT, MIGRANT

remains, leftovers, scraps, remainders ODDMENTS, REMNANTS
– remains, traces left by something that has mostly disappeared VESTIGES
– remains from a past age RELICS
– remains of something destroyed WRACK
– remaining quantity or substance at the end of a chemical process, settling of debts, or the like RESIDUE
– amount that remains after part is deducted, as from a bank account BALANCE
– inferior remains, part left over once the best has been removed RUMP
– solid remains or residue of oilseed after processing, used as animal fodder EXPELLERS, EXTRACTIONS
– solid remains settling at the bottom of a liquid DREGS, SEDIMENT
– solid remains settling at the bottom of a liquid, especially coffee GROUNDS, GROUTS
– solid remains settling at the bottom of a liquid, especially wine LEES
– solid remains settling or filtered out when refining oil, distilling liquids, or the like FOOTS

remark, clinching argument, or hostile gesture made when leaving PARTHIAN SHOT
– remark made in passing, incidental comment OBITER DICTUM
– remark or carefully considered observation, usually very critical ANIMADVERSION
– remark or phrase, with independent syntax, within a sentence PARENTHESIS
– remark or statement having no apparent relevance to what came before it NON SEQUITUR
– remark spoken in an undertone, as by a character in a play, so as to be inaudible to others ASIDE
– clear, crisp, and forceful, as a remark or argument might be TRENCHANT, COGENT
– cutting, penetrating, to the point, as a remark might be INCISIVE, MORDANT
– hurtfully direct, cutting, as a remark might be BARBED
– inappropriate or ill-chosen, as a remark, style, or expression might

be INFELICITOUS
– insulting in a deliberate way, intended to offend or belittle, as a slighting remark is DEROGATORY
– perceptive remark, insightful observation APERÇU
– throw in a remark by way of interruption INTERJECT, INTERPOSE

remarkable, exceptional, extraordinary SURPASSING, SINGULAR
– remarkable or wonderful PRODIGIOUS

remedial, curative THERAPEUTIC

remedy for all ailments or problems PANACEA, CATHOLICON
– remedy intended for a particular disease or disorder SPECIFIC
– remedy or scheme, as for social problems, that is considered facile or simplistic NOSTRUM
– effective all the time and in every case, as a remedy might be INFALLIBLE, FOOLPROOF, FAILSAFE
– having wide-ranging and effective power, as a remedy might SOVEREIGN
– powerful or successful, as a remedy might be EFFICACIOUS

remember, bring to mind again RECALL, RECOLLECT, RETRIEVE
– remember and honour a person or event by means of a ceremony COMMEMORATE
– remember and recount past events, especially with nostalgia REMINISCE
– remember by conscious effort, commit to memory, learn by rote MEMORISE, CON
– remember consciously, go back over in one's mind RETRACE
– remember or keep in mind,

RELIGION

RELIGIONS AND BELIEFS

Babism	Persia: religion founded in the 19th century by Ali Muhammad, known as "the Bab", "Gateway", who tried to combine the best of all religions
Bahaism	Persia: religion developed from Babism by the 19th-century religious leader Bahaullah
Buddhism	India, China, southeast Asia: religious and moral system founded in the 6th century BC by the Indian mystic Gautama Siddhartha
Confucianism	ancient China: religious and moral system based on the teachings of Confucius, the 6th-century BC philosopher
Druses	Lebanon: followers of a sect based on Islam, founded in the 11th century by Al-Hakim Bi-Amr Allah
Hinduism	India: traditional religion of the greater part of the Indian subcontinent
Islam	Middle and Far East: religion founded by the 7th-century prophet Muhammad
Jainism	northern India: religion developed from Hinduism by "Jinas" or "conquerors", such as Mahavira, a 6th-century BC sage
Judaism	Israel and worldwide: the religion of the Jewish people
Manichaeism	Persia: religion based on the teachings of the 3rd-century teacher Manes, similar to Mazdaism
Mazdaism, Zoroastrianism	ancient Persia: religion based on the teachings of the 6th-century BC prophet Zoroaster, who regarded the world as a battleground between good and evil
Mithraism	ancient Persia: worship of Mithras, god of light
obeah/obi	West Indies: set of beliefs based on witchcraft and sorcery
Parseeism	western India: surviving form of Zoroastrianism
Rastafarianism	Jamaica: set of beliefs including the veneration of Ras Tafari, or Haile Selassie, the former emperor of Ethiopia, as God
Shamanism	northern Siberia and North America: belief that spirits control life and can be influenced by priests
Shintoism	Japan: traditional religion, involving the worship of numerous gods
Sikhism	Punjab: religion developed from Hinduism in the 16th century by Guru Nanak, incorporating elements of Islam
Sufism	Iran: mystical form of Islam
Taoism	China: religious and philosophical system based on the teachings of the 6th-century BC philosopher Lao-tze
Wahhabism	Saudi Arabia: beliefs of a rigid Islamic sect, strict observers of the Koran
Zen Buddhism	Japan, and formerly China: mystical form of Buddhism, seeking enlightenment through meditation

CHRISTIAN GROUPS

Albigensians	ascetic Catharian sect in 12th and 13th-century France, believing that the material world was purely evil
Amish	U.S. Anabaptist sect that broke away from the Mennonites in the 17th century
Anabaptists	radical Protestant movement that developed in the 1520s, believing in pacifism and adult baptism
antinomians	sect believing that salvation depends on faith alone
Calvinists	followers of the 16th-century Protestant theologian John Calvin, believing in the strict authority of the bible, and in Salvation through God's grace alone

especially after a long time RETAIN
– be remembered, come back to mind, as a dream might RECUR
– things or events that deserve to be remembered MEMORABILIA

remembering, recall, recollection ANAMNESIS
– remembering by repetition rather than through understanding ROTE
– formula, rhyme, or the like used as an aid to remembering MNEMONIC

reminder, usually in the form of a note MEMORANDUM, AIDE-MÉMOIRE
– reminder of inescapable death, such as a skull MEMENTO MORI
– object that reminds one of a person or place SOUVENIR, KEEPSAKE, MEMENTO
– serving as a reminder of, prompting memories, suggestive REMINISCENT, EVOCATIVE, REDOLENT

remorse for one's sins CONTRITION, REPENTANCE, PENITENCE

remote, separated, lonely, as a place or life might be SECLUDED, CLOISTERED, SEQUESTERED, SOLITARY
– remote and difficult to reach INACCESSIBLE
– remote country areas, the sticks, the bush BOONDOCKS, OUTBACK, HINTERLAND, BACKVELD, BACKBLOCKS, GRAMADOELAS, BUNDU
– remote from the centre, far away, fairly distant OUTLYING
– remote region, goal, or ideal ULTIMA THULE

removal or seclusion from public view, as of some women, or as when in disgrace PURDAH

charismatics	followers of a movement seeking to reassert the influence of the Holy Spirit and full freedom of worship, and marked by such practices as spiritual healing and speaking in tongues
Christadelphians	sect founded in the U.S. in the late 1840s, rejecting the Holy Trinity and believing in the complete obliteration of the wicked
Christian Scientists	members of the Church of Christ, Scientist, founded in 1879, emphasising spiritual healing
Copts	members of the Coptic Church centred in Egypt, professing monophysitism
Dunkers	German-American Baptist sect opposed to military service and the taking of oaths
Gnostics	early Christian sect believing that salvation was attainable only by the few with a special knowledge of God
Huguenots	French Protestants of the 16th and 17th centuries
Hussites	followers of the 14th to 15th-century Bohemian reformer John Huss
Illuminati	16th-century Spanish sect claiming special religious enlightenment
Jehovah's Witnesses	sect founded in 1879, active in missionary work, whose dedication to the bible can entail opposition to organised religion and government authority
Lollards	followers of the 14th-century English reformer John Wycliffe
Maronites	members of an ancient Uniat church from Syria, now living mainly in Lebanon
Melchites	members of the Greek Catholic Church in the Middle East
Mennonites	pacifist Protestant sect arising from the Anabaptist movement
Monophysites	believers in the doctrine that Christ had only one nature, being purely divine rather than both human and divine
Moravians	members of the Protestant Moravian Church founded by Hussites in 1722
Mormons	members of the Church of Jesus Christ of Latter Day Saints, founded in the U.S. in 1830, whose book of Mormon supplements the bible as official scripture
Mozarabs	Spaniards who continued to practise modified Christianity under Muslim rule
Plymouth Brethren	puritanical sect founded in 1830 in Plymouth, Devon, holding the bible to be the sole source of truth
Seventh-Day Adventists	sect observing the sabbath on Saturday and believing that Christ's Second Coming and the end of the world are about to happen
Shakers	radical Quaker sect founded in 1747, believing in common ownership of property, named from their former custom of dancing and shaking movements during ceremonies
Swedenborgians	followers of the 18th-century Swedish theologian Emanuel Swedenborg, or members of the New Jerusalem Church, believing in direct mystical communication between the world and the spiritual realm
Tractarians	followers of the 19th-century Oxford Movement, who sought closer ties between the Anglican and Roman Catholic churches
Uniats	members of the Eastern Orthodox churches that acknowledge the Pope but keep their own liturgy
Zwinglians	followers of the 16th-century Swiss Protestant reformer Ulrich Zwingli, holding that Christ's presence in the Communion is symbolic rather than actual

-removal- EX-, -ECTOMY
remove, separate, or isolate from the main group SEGREGATE
– remove a limb, as by surgery AMPUTATE
– remove an organ or other body party by surgery EXCISE
– remove all trace of ERADICATE, OBLITERATE
– remove and set aside a passage from a text for special consideration ABSTRACT, EXTRACT
– remove bad or weak parts or members, weed out CULL
– remove entirely, pull up by the roots DERACINATE, EXTIRPATE, UPROOT
– remove from office, especially by force, overthrow, unseat DEPOSE, DISPLACE, SUPPLANT, OUST
– remove or cut the end from, abbreviate PRUNE, TRUNCATE, CURTAIL
– remove or delete offending parts from a text EXCISE, EXPUNGE, EXPURGATE
– remove or rescue from difficulties EXTRICATE
– remove something from, relieve or deprive of something, such as powers, duties, or problems DISBURDEN, DIVEST, DISEMBARRASS, DISENCUMBER
– remove soluble parts from a substance such as soil, as by flushing with water LEACH
– removed, remote, lonely, solitary, as a place or life might be SECLUDED, CLOISTERED, SEQUESTERED
remove- DE-, DIS-, UN-
rendezvous, especially of lovers or with one's destiny TRYST
renew See also **repair**
– renew, re-establish, repair RESTORE
– renew, start again RESUME
– renew or reform spiritually, morally, or culturally REGENERATE, REVITALISE, REVIVIFY
– renew or revive, return to consciousness or life RESUSCITATE
– renew the social standing of, restore to power or favour REHABILITATE, REINSTATE
– renew the supply of, refill REPLENISH
– renew the vigour of, restore the youth of REJUVENATE
renewal or revival of culture RENASCENCE, RENAISSANCE
renewed bout of ill health after an apparent recovery RELAPSE
– renewed outbreak of disease, civil unrest, or the like after a period of inactivity RECRUDESCENCE
rent, at a lower rate, to reserve accommodation during one's absence RETAINER
– rent-free, referring to property owned by the sovereign and let free of charge to a favoured tenant GRACE-AND-FAVOUR
– rent of a very small, purely nominal amount PEPPERCORN RENT
– rent or some other debt that remains unpaid ARREARS
– rent that is outrageously high RACK-RENT
– person whose income is derived chiefly from rents or investments RENTIER
reordering or rearrangement PERMUTATION
repair See also **renew**
– repair, improve, make better or easier AMEND, AMELIORATE
– repair, patch up, restore to an acceptable or original state REVAMP, RECONDITION
– repair, rebuild, or restore from fragments or original plans RECONSTRUCT, RECONSTITUTE
– repair and restore something, such as a house FURBISH, REFURBISH, RENOVATE
– repair in a desultory or inexpert fashion TINKER
– repair or remedy an injustice or inequality REDRESS
– dismantle, examine, and repair DEBUG, OVERHAUL
– impossible to repair or make good, as devastating damage might be IRREPARABLE
repay REIMBURSE
– repay an injury like for like RETALIATE
– repay for loss or injury COMPENSATE, INDEMNIFY, RECOMPENSE
– repay or reward someone REQUITE
repayment RECOMPENSE, REQUITAL, QUITTANCE
– repayment, compensation, making good RESTITUTION, REPARATIONS, INDEMNIFICATION, AMENDS, REDRESS, ATONEMENT
repeat, say again ITERATE, REITERATE, REAFFIRM, INGEMINATE
– repeat in concise form, sum up RECAP, RECAPITULATE
– repeat or make a copy of REPRODUCE, DUPLICATE
– repeat or reproduce facts in an unthinking way REGURGITATE
– repeat or rework old material without any significant alteration REHASH
repeated phrase, design, or thematic element in music, art, or literature MOTIF, LEITMOTIV, MOTTO
– repeated verse, tune, theme, or the like REFRAIN, CHORUS, BURDEN
repentance for sin based on fear rather than on love of God ATTRITION
– repentance for sin based on love of God rather than fear CONTRITION
– repentant, humbly or sorrowfully regretting one's sins or offences PENITENT, CONTRITE
– act of self-punishment or devotion to demonstrate sorrow or repentance for sin PENANCE
– forgiveness or release from punishment, as after sincere repentance ABSOLUTION
– making good, atonement, reparations or compensation, as after repentance RESTITUTION, REDRESS, AMENDS, EXPIATION, REDEMPTION
– public show of mourning or repentance SACKCLOTH AND ASHES
repetition, at the start of a phrase, of the word or words ending the previous phrase ANADIPLOSIS
– repetition, especially of a phrase or theme in music REPRISE
– repetition, unthinking routine ROTE
– repetition of a single idea in separate sets of words TAUTOLOGY
– repetition of a word or phrase at the start of successive clauses, lines of verse, or the like ANAPHORA
– repetition of conjunctions for stylistic effect, as in *blood and sweat and tears* POLYSYNDETON
– repetition or excess of information, either deliberately, as in telegrams or computer programs, or carelessly, as in tautology REDUNDANCY
– repetition or uncontrollable recurrence of an idea, spoken word, or the like PERSEVERATION
replace a lost or damaged body part by the formation of new tissue REGENERATE
– replace another in a position or office, especially by force or intrigue SUPPLANT, OUST, DISPLACE, DEPOSE
– replace another in a position or office, especially on the death or retirement of the incumbent SUCCEED
– replace something outdated or obsolete SUPERSEDE
– replace temporarily, stand in for DEPUTISE
replacement, stand-in SUBSTITUTE
– replacement doctor, chemist, or clergyman, a temporary stand-in LOCUM, LOCUM TENENS
– person serving as a replacement for another, such as a teacher who

fulfils the emotional role of a parent SURROGATE

reply, quick retaliatory action or retort RIPOSTE, REJOINDER
– deliberately vague, ambiguous, or non-committal, as a reply might be EVASIVE, EQUIVOCAL
– sharp and witty reply in a conversation, piece of clever backchat RETORT, REPARTEE
– witty reply or retort that occurs to one only when it is too late ESPRIT D'ESCALIER

report or record in detail, and support with evidence DOCUMENT
– report or rumour that is false or a deliberate hoax CANARD
– report sent over a distance, as by a newspaper correspondent or military field officer DISPATCH
– official government report in Britain containing proposals for legislation, issued to interested parties for comments and discussion GREEN PAPER
– official government report or policy statement prior to discussion in Parliament WHITE PAPER
– official government report or publication in Britain BLUEBOOK
– revealing of a scandal or crime, or the book, broadcast, or the like in which it is reported EXPOSÉ
– spread a rumour or report BRUIT

reporter, typically covering the local news in a specific area, working on a part-time basis STRINGER
– reporter doing routine or mediocre work HACK
– reporter or freelance photographer who badgers celebrities PAPARAZZO

repossess mortgaged property when the scheduled payments are not met FORECLOSE

represent graphically in pictures or words, describe, portray DEPICT, DELINEATE, REALISE, RENDER, LIMN
– represent perfectly, be a typical example of TYPIFY, EMBODY, PERSONIFY, INCARNATE, EPITOMISE
– representing a scene objectively, lifelike, as a painting might be REALISTIC

representational, not abstract, as a painting might be FIGURATIVE

representative See also **diplomat**
– representative, agent, or deputy, performing duties for someone else PROXY, MINISTER, COMMISSARY, ASSIGNEE
– representative, agent, or messenger sent on a mission, typically by a government or head of state EMISSARY, LEGATE, ENVOY
– representative, agent, or middleman in business dealings BROKER, FACTOR
– representative, as of a university, in business matters SYNDIC
– representative, especially at a conference DELEGATE
– representative, stand-in, or replacement DEPUTY, SUBSTITUTE
– representative or agent in former times, as for collecting tithes or conducting a case in court PROCTOR
– representative or agent legally entitled to control or administer the property or funds of someone else TRUSTEE
– representative or agent legally entitled to control or administer the will of a dead person or the funds that have been bequeathed EXECUTOR, EXECUTRIX
– representative or agent secretly standing in for someone else FRONT, FRONT MAN, DUMMY
– representative or agent who runs a landowner's estate STEWARD, BAILIFF
– representative or assistant performing a wide range of duties, general dogsbody FACTOTUM
– representative or means mediating between people or things, go-between INTERMEDIARY
– representative or perfect example or embodiment of an idea or ideal EXEMPLAR, ARCHETYPE, AVATAR, PERSONIFICATION, EPITOME, INCARNATION
– representative or substitute for another, such as someone fulfilling the emotional role of a parent SURROGATE
– representative trained to replace someone when necessary, as in the theatre UNDERSTUDY
– representative who speaks for someone else, spokesman MOUTHPIECE
– appoint as one's agent, substitute, or representative DEPUTE
– deputy administrative officer or representative assisting a king, magistrate, or the like VICEGERENT
– performed or experienced through a representative or substitute VICARIOUS
– person or group acting as representative, especially on a mission DEPUTATION, DELEGATION
– put into the hands of a representative or those of a subordinate DELEGATE

reprint of an article on its own, after it has appeared in a journal or book OFFPRINT

reproduce, or cause plants or animals to reproduce PROPAGATE
– reproduce or spread rapidly PROLIFERATE

reproducing by means of splitting, as some one-celled plants and animals do FISSIPAROUS
– reproducing or developing without sexual union and fertilisation, asexual AGAMIC, AGAMOGENETIC, PARTHENOGENETIC
– reproducing young by means of eggs that hatch outside the body OVIPAROUS
– reproducing young by means of eggs that hatch within the female's body, as with some fish and reptiles OVOVIVIPAROUS
– reproducing young in the form of live offspring developed within the mother's body VIVIPAROUS

reproduction, producing of offspring PROCREATION
– reproduction that is asexual, in which there is no direct fertilisation of an egg by a sperm APOMIXIS, APOGAMY, PARTHENOGENESIS
– reproduction that is sexual, involving fertilisation of the egg by the sperm AMPHIMIXIS
– barren, incapable of further reproduction, as a plant or animal might be EFFETE

-reproduction- -GON-, GONO- -GEN-, -GENESIS

reproductive gland in female mammals OVARY
– reproductive organs, especially the external sex organs GENITALIA, GENITALS
– reproductive organs, especially those of a man VITALS

reptile- HERPET-, HERPETO-

repulsive, dreadful, grim, as a horrible sight of bloodshed is GRISLY, GRUESOME
– repulsive, hideous, terrifying horrible or hateful LOATHSOME, ABOMINABLE, HORRENDOUS, UNSPEAKABLE
– repulsive, offending one's tastes or senses, causing aversion REPELLENT, REPUGNANT
– repulsive, offensive, disgusting, sickening NAUSEATING

reputation, especially good reputation REPUTE, REGARD, RENOWN
– reputation, status or renown as through success or wealth PRESTIGE, CACHET, KUDOS
– reputation, status, rank, or level of achievement STATURE, STANDING, STOCK
– reputation for evil or wickedness, or an act contributing to such a reputation INFAMY
– damage or spoil someone's reputation, name, or the like SULLY,

DEFILE, TARNISH, PROFANE, DISCREDIT
– disgrace, dishonour, bad reputation DISREPUTE, NOTORIETY
– restore someone to his former status or reputation, as after a counter-revolution REHABILITATE

reputed or commonly considered, as a child's supposed father might be PUTATIVE

request See **ask**
– requested or commanded by AT THE BEHEST OF

require, demand or lay down as a condition in an agreement or contract STIPULATE
– required as a duty INCUMBENT
– required by law or enforced by custom COMPULSORY, OBLIGATORY, MANDATORY

requirements that are listed precisely SPECIFICATIONS

rescue from sin, ignorance, danger, or the like SALVATION, DELIVERANCE
– rescue or save, as from loss, damage, or cancellation SALVAGE
– rescue or save from danger or trouble RETRIEVE
– rescue or save from sin and punishment REDEEM
– rescue or save someone from evil ways by reforming him RECLAIM

research into and analysis of the efficiency of a workforce, machine system, or the like, as an aid to policy-making OPERATIONAL RESEARCH
– research report or treatise, especially for an academic degree THESIS, DISSERTATION

resemble or imitate, often for camouflage MIMIC, SIMULATE
– resembling but not really being QUASI-, BOGUS, ERSATZ

-resembling- PARA-, -INE, -OSE, -OID

resentment, feeling of anger and ill will GRUDGE
– resentment, offence, feeling of anger at some supposed insult UMBRAGE
– resentment or temper, as from a blow to one's pride PIQUE
– offensive, liable to cause ill will or resentment INVIDIOUS

reserve or book, claim or arrange in advance, or order specifically BESPEAK
– reserve strategem or device whereby one may snatch victory from defeat TRUMP CARD
– reserve supply or store accumulated for future use STOCKPILE
– nature or wildlife reserve SANCTUARY

reserved See **shy**
– reserved, silent, uncommunicative TACITURN, RETICENT

resident or inhabitant of a place or region DENIZEN

resin – resin-flavoured Greek wine RETSINA
– resin of various pine trees, used on the bows of stringed instruments ROSIN, COLOPHONY
– resin or gum from various acacia trees, used in ink, glues, and the like GUM ARABIC, GUM ACACIA
– resin or gum used in making perfume MYRRH, BDELLIUM
– resin or gum, as used in varnish MASTIC, GUAIACUM
– resin used in incense FRANKINCENSE, OLIBANUM
– artificial resin used in synthetic rubber, paints, plastics, and the like ACRYLIC RESIN
– artificial resin used in tough adhesives EPOXY
– fragrant, oily resins from various trees, used in lotions, perfumes, and the like BALM, BALSAM, TOLU
– gum resin used as the source of a yellow pigment for paints GAMBOGE
– gum resin with onion-like smell, used in Eastern cooking and formerly in medicines ASAFOETIDA
– purified resin from various insects, used in making French polish, old gramophone records, and the like SHELLAC
– turpentine resin from pine trees GALIPOT

resistance, as to government authority or colonial rule, by non-violent methods such as fasting and non-cooperation PASSIVE RESISTANCE
– resistance, capacity of enduring or withstanding something burdensome or unpleasant TOLERANCE
– deliberate damaging or destruction of property, as by underground resistance groups or dissatisfied workers SABOTAGE
– unit of electrical resistance OHM

resistant to damage, harm, or injury INVULNERABLE, IMMUNE, UNASSAILABLE

resolve or solve a mystery, puzzle, or problem UNRAVEL, DECIPHER

resort area with mineral springs SPA

resources, especially money, required for a particular purpose WHEREWITHAL
– use or spend resources thriftily HUSBAND

respect, courteous or submissive regard DEFERENCE
– respect, great devotion, awe, as shown to God REVERENCE, VENERATION
– respect, honour, or duty, as granted to someone or to a belief or cause HOMAGE
– respect or admire greatly, honour ESTEEM
– gift, payment, or other expression of respect, submission, or the like TRIBUTE

respectable, often in an affected way GENTEEL

respected, especially because of old age VENERABLE
– respected or feared as awesome or very impressive FORMIDABLE, REDOUBTABLE
– made respected or honoured, as by time CONSECRATED, VENERATED

respectful – courteously respectful and compliant DEFERENTIAL, SUBSERVIENT
– excessively respectful and humble, slavish OBSEQUIOUS, SERVILE, FAWNING, UNCTUOUS, SYCOPHANTIC
– submissively respectful and admiring OBEISANT, REVERENTIAL

respects, greetings, compliments DEVOIRS

response See also **reaction**
– response sung during a church service ANTIPHON
– response to a stimulus that does not directly cause it but has come to be associated with it, as through training CONDITIONED RESPONSE
– response to or information resulting from an inquiry, experiment, programme, or the like FEEDBACK
– referring to a reflex reaction or conditioned response to a stimulus PAVLOVIAN

responsibility or burden ONUS
– deny or reject responsibility DISCLAIM
– factor that shares in the responsibility for something CONTRIBUTORY FACTOR
– give up or relinquish responsibility ABDICATE, DEROGATE, RENOUNCE
– plea that mental abnormality at the time of a crime, especially a murder, reduces the culprit's responsibility DIMINISHED RESPONSIBILITY
– relating to or shared by a united body, as responsibility might be COLLECTIVE, CORPORATE

responsible, legally required LIABLE
– responsible and punishable for wrongdoing, blameworthy CULPABLE
– person guilty of a crime or responsible for a mistake or accident CULPRIT

responsive to stimuli, conscious, aware SENTIENT

rest See also **remains**, **pause**, **stop**
- rest, pause, or postponement, typically in the middle of something unpleasant RESPITE
- rest, state of inactivity or relaxation REPOSE
- resting, alive but in a suspended or inactive stage of biological development DORMANT
- allow a brief rest to SPELL
- relating to bodies at rest or to forces in equilibrium STATIC
- tendency of a physical body to remain at rest or in unchanged motion unless acted on by external forces INERTIA

restaurant See also **menu**
- restaurant, typically sharing premises with a bar BRASSERIE
- restaurant, typically small, cosy, and modest BISTRO
- restaurant counter, or a restaurant having such a counter BUFFET
- restaurant dispensing food by means of vending machines AUTOMAT
- restaurant or inn in former times CHOPHOUSE, PORTERHOUSE
- restaurant or shop specialising in roast meat ROTISSERIE, CARVERY
- beer hall or German restaurant, originally in the cellar of a town hall RATSKELLAR
- cheap, unhygienic, and unappetising restaurant GREASY SPOON
- deep tray containing hot water, in which deep dishes of food are kept warm, as in a self-service restaurant BAIN-MARIE
- Greek or Greek-style restaurant TAVERNA
- Italian or Italian-style restaurant TRATTORIA
- table setting in a restaurant, or the cover charge for it COUVERT

restless, agitated TURBULENT
- restless or impatient, as to go travelling FOOTLOOSE
- restlessness or feeling of unease FANTODS

restore oneself to favour REDEEM
- restore or patch up, return to an acceptable or original state RECONDITION, REVAMP
- restore or reform spiritually, morally, or culturally REGENERATE, REVITALISE, REVIVIFY
- restore or repair something, such as a house FURBISH, REFURBISH, RENOVATE
- restore or return to life, revive RESUSCITATE, RESURRECT
- restore something to its natural state, such as dried food or concentrated lemon juice, as by adding water RECONSTITUTE
- restore the social status of, return to power or favour REHABILITATE, REINSTATE
- restore to youth or vigour REJUVENATE
- restoring of property to its rightful owner RESTITUTION

restrain or check a smile, groan, or the like SUPPRESS, STIFLE
- restrain someone by binding his arms PINION
- restraining garment with long sleeves for binding the arms of a violent patient or prisoner STRAITJACKET

restrained, sparing, or disciplined, especially in eating and drinking ABSTEMIOUS, TEMPERATE

restraint, restriction, confining influence SHACKLES, FETTERS
- restraint or moderation, especially in drinking alcohol TEMPERANCE

restrict See also **limit**, **hinder**, **prevent**, **prohibit**
- restrict an animal's movements by tying a rope around its head and one of its legs HAMSHACKLE
- restrict an animal's movements by tying it to a tree, post, or the like TETHER
- restrict an animal's movements by tying its legs together HOBBLE
- restrict someone's movements by holding or tying him round the arms PINION
- restrict the freedom or movement of, as by strict rules or physical restraint STRAITJACKET

restricted by rules or prejudices HIDEBOUND, INFLEXIBLE
- restricted or specified number or quantity, as of imports or immigrants QUOTA
- restricted to a relatively small group EXCLUSIVE, SELECT, ESOTERIC, RAREFIED

restriction, restraint, confining influence FETTERS, SHACKLES
- restriction or condition, as in an agreement or document PROVISO
- restriction or regulation requiring people to go home or be indoors by a certain hour of night CURFEW

result considered definite or inevitable FOREGONE CONCLUSION
- result from or follow from immediately ENSUE, SUPERVENE
- result or final outcome, as of a play DÉNOUEMENT
- result or occur eventually or ultimately EVENTUATE
- resulting, following as an effect or conclusion CONSEQUENTIAL
- resulting state or period, as after a disaster or misfortune AFTERMATH, BACKWASH
- results, often disastrous, of one's actions HANDIWORK
- results, often indirect and harmful, of an action, decision, or event REPERCUSSIONS, REVERBERATIONS
- results, unavoidable but usually undesirable, of an action or decision RAMIFICATIONS
- adverse reaction resulting from a perceived threat BACKLASH
- final result, outcome UPSHOT
- have a favourable or unfavourable result or effect REDOUND
- incidental result or secondary effect, usually desirable BY-PRODUCT, SPIN-OFF
- incidental result or secondary effect, usually undesirable FALL-OUT, SIDE EFFECT
- information or response resulting from an experiment, enquiry, or the like FEEDBACK
- logical result or effect of an action or condition CONSEQUENCE, COROLLARY, SEQUEL

retail – sale of goods in bulk, as to a store, as distinct from retail WHOLESALE

retain See **keep**
- word written to instruct a typesetter or printer to retain deleted text STET

retaining wall REVETMENT

retired but retaining an honorary title, as a professor might be EMERITUS
- retired into seclusion, isolated SEQUESTERED, IMMURED, CLOISTERED
- retired or discharged because of old age or illness SUPERANNUATED

retort or quick retaliatory action RIPOSTE

return an accused person to prison, another court, or the like REMAND
- return feelings, invitations, or the like RECIPROCATE, REQUITE
- return like for like, especially evil for evil, repay in kind RETALIATE
- return of disease, rebellion, or the like after a period of improvement RECRUDESCENCE
- return of like for like, equal exchange QUID PRO QUO
- return of part of the payment made REBATE
- return someone or something to the country of origin REPATRIATE
- return someone to his former power, favour, or fitness for society REHABILITATE, REINSTATE
- return something to a correct, proper, or balanced state RECTIFY, REDRESS
- return to an earlier and less

favourable condition RELAPSE, REVERT, REGRESS, BACKSLIDE
– return to an earlier, more primitive state or pattern of behaviour, throwback ATAVISM
– return to harm the originator, as a hurtful policy might, boomerang REBOUND, RECOIL, REDOUND
– return to life or active use after apparent death RESURRECTION, RESUSCITATION, ANABIOSIS
– returning, strengthening, re-emerging RESURGENT
– returning of property to its rightful owner RESTITUTION
– person who returns, sometimes as a ghost, after an absence REVENANT
– person who returns or relapses into a former habit, especially crime RECIDIVIST

reveal, bring to light, uncover UNEARTH, EXHUME, DISINTER
– reveal, expose, or betray UNMASK
– reveal, introduce, or make public formally or officially, as in announcing plans or dedicating a monument UNVEIL
– reveal, show, make public, be evidence of MANIFEST
– reveal a scandal or the like DISINTER
– reveal or confide one's thoughts or feelings UNBOSOM
– reveal something, such as a secret DISCLOSE, DIVULGE

revelation, vision, or prophecy of a great disaster APOCALYPSE
– revelation or appearance of a god, angel, or the like EPIPHANY, MANIFESTATION, THEOPHANY
– revelation or public exposure of a scandal, corruption, or the like EXPOSÉ

revenge VENGEANCE
– revenge attack, striking back RETALIATION
– revenge by one state or nation upon the citizens of another RETORSION
– revenge or just retribution, or an agent of it NEMESIS
– revenge or punishment in return for mistreatment or wrongdoing RETRIBUTION, REPRISALS
– blood feud, maintained by a cycle of revenge VENDETTA
– clear of an accusation or dishonour, as by legal action or revenge VINDICATE
– fitting repayment, restoring of the balance, or the like, as through revenge REDRESS, REQUITAL
– foreign policy based on revenge or on the regaining of lost territory REVANCHISM
– principle of revenge or retaliation, law of "an eye for an eye" LEX TALIONIS
– relating to or motivated by revenge VINDICTIVE

reversal of direction, policy, attitude, or results TURNROUND, ABOUT-TURN, VOLTE-FACE, U-TURN
– reversal or sudden change in fortunes or the course of events, especially in a play or other literary work PERIPETEIA

reversal- CATA-

reverse, backward, or unprogressive RETROGRADE, REGRESSIVE, RECESSIVE, RETROGRESSIVE
– reverse-charge call in the U.S. COLLECT CALL
– reverse in position, order, or the like INVERT
– reverse or change the ordering or relative position of two or more things TRANSPOSE
– reverse side of a leaf of printed paper, or of a coin or medal, "tails" VERSO
– in a reverse direction, opposite to the movement of the Sun, or anti-clockwise WIDDERSHINS, WITHERSHINS

reverse- DE-, DIS-, UN-

reversed- OB-

review or analysis of a recent event, game, failure, or the like POSTMORTEM
– review or criticism of a book, film, play, or the like CRITIQUE, NOTICE
– review or description for promotional purposes, as on the dust jacket of a book BLURB
– review or short criticism, especially of a book COMPTE RENDU

revise a text, plan, or the like REVAMP
– revise intensely at the last minute for an exam CRAM

revision or critical edition of a text, incorporating the most plausible variant readings RECENSION

revival, return to life after apparent death RESUSCITATION, ANABIOSIS, RESURRECTION
– revival of a disease, civil unrest, or the like after a period of inactivity RECRUDESCENCE
– revival or rebirth, as of a culture RENASCENCE, RENAISSANCE

revive, especially spiritually or morally REGENERATE
– revive, refresh, give new life or vigour to QUICKEN, REANIMATE, REVITALISE, REVIVIFY
– revive, restore or return to life RESUSCITATE, RESURRECT

revolt See **rebel**, **rebellion**

revolution, as of the Moon's around the Earth, in which the same face of the satellite is always pointing to the primary CAPTURED ROTATION, SYNCHRONOUS ROTATION
– revolution in the form of a sudden seizing of power COUP D'ÉTAT, PUTSCH

revolutionary See also **rebellious**
– revolutionary, radical, or extremist in politics SANS-CULOTTE, JACOBIN
– revolutionary believing in or urging the seizure by workers of economic and government control, as through strikes and sabotage SYNDICALIST
– revolutionary of an extreme, uncompromising kind MAXIMALIST
– revolutionary of an extremist tendency, advocating the destruction of all existing social and political institutions NIHILIST, ANARCHIST
– revolutionary or reforming activist within a political group or party YOUNG TURK

revolve round a point or axis GYRATE

revolver – foolhardy risk or betting game in which a person pulls the trigger of a revolver loaded with one bullet and aimed at his head RUSSIAN ROULETTE

revolving, whirling VERTIGINOUS
– revolving circular tray holding food on a dining table DUMB WAITER, LAZY SUSAN
– revolving door or gate that lets people or animals through one by one TURNSTILE
– revolving or rolling movement VOLUTION
– revolving part in a motor, generator, or other machine ROTOR

reward in psychology, or the strengthening of a learned response as by means of rewards REINFORCEMENT
– reward or payment, as for services rendered RECOMPENSE, GUERDON
– reward or payment offered by the authorities in return for helpful service, such as arresting outlaws BOUNTY
– reward or repay someone REQUITE, REIMBURSE

reword a passage to clarify its meaning PARAPHRASE
– rewording or summary of a text ABSTRACT, PRÉCIS

rhetorical See also **high-falutin**, **figures of speech**
– rhetorical figure of speech, such as metaphor TROPE

Rhine siren in German mythology whose singing lured sailors to de-

struction LORELEI
– adjective for the river Rhine RHENISH

rhinoceros – herd or family of rhinoceroses CRASH

rhyme of a rough or approximate kind, as where the stressed vowels are the same but the final consonants differ ASSONANCE
– rhyme of a single stressed syllable MASCULINE RHYME
– rhyme of two or more syllables, of which the first is stressed FEMININE RHYME
– rhyme or tune of a simple, catchy kind, as used in advertisements JINGLE
– false rhyme between words similar in spelling rather than sound, such as *home* and *some* EYE-RHYME
– "initial rhyme", similarity of sounds at the beginning of words ALLITERATION
– word game in which one player or team produces a word or line rhyming with a cue from the other CRAMBO

rhythm in music TEMPO
– rhythm of biological processes in response to environmental changes or internal control mechanisms BIORHYTHM
– rhythm of biological processes that have a regular 24-hour cycle CIRCADIAN RHYTHM
– analysis of the metrical or rhythm patterns of verse SCANSION
– regular in rhythm MEASURED
– study of rhythm and metre in poetry or speech PROSODY

rhythmic flow, as of poetry or tuneful speech CADENCE
– rhythmic irregularity in music, as caused by stressing a weak beat SYNCOPATION
– rhythmic swinging movement OSCILLATION
– rhythmic variation within a phrase or bar of music without changing its length RUBATO
– rhythmical, springy flow or swing, as in a person's voice or walk LILT
– rhythmical free-style dance to music, or a form of musical training using such movement EURHYTHMICS
– rhythmical stress in verse ICTUS

rib, ridge, or large vein, as on a leaf or insect's wing COSTA
– rib or ridge on corduroy or a similar fabric, or the texture of such a fabric WALE
– relating to or located in the space between ribs INTERCOSTAL

ribbon, feather, or rosette worn on the hat, especially by soldiers COCKADE
– ribbon or coloured patch worn on a uniform for purposes of identification FLASH
– ribbon worn on the chest as an honour or sign of rank CORDON
– decorative chain or garland of flowers, ribbons, or the like suspended in a loop FESTOON
– rose-shaped design or structure, such as a pleated ribbon badge ROSETTE
– strip of ribbon, lace, or metal worn in the hair or round the neck FILLET

rice, or rice field PADDY
– rice of a long-grained variety used for savoury dishes PATNA RICE
– dish of eastern origin, consisting of rice cooked in a spicy stock, often with meat or fish added PILAU, PILAF
– Indian dish of spiced rice with meat or fish BIRIANI
– Italian dish of rice cooked in stock, mixed with cheese, vegetables, seafood, or the like RISOTTO
– Spanish dish of rice cooked in stock, mixed with shellfish, chicken, and vegetables PAELLA
– yellow spice, made from crocuses, used to flavour and colour rice SAFFRON

rich See also **money**, **plenty**
– rich, comfortably off, well-to-do AFFLUENT, PROSPEROUS, SUBSTANTIAL, WELL-HEELED
– rich, loaded, especially temporarily FLUSH
– rich, plentiful, or luxurious OPULENT, SUMPTUOUS
– rich, powerful, and important man NABOB, MOGUL, TYCOON, MAGNATE
– rich class of people exercising power in a society PLUTOCRACY
– extremely rich person CROESUS, DIVES
– person who has recently become rich, especially when living in a showy but unrefined style NOUVEAU RICHE, PARVENU

riches, wealth, or money, especially if acquired in a dubious way PELF, LUCRE
– riches regarded as a corrupting influence MAMMON
– mine or other source of great riches GOLCONDA
– place of great riches or opportunity EL DORADO
– source of great riches or good luck BONANZA

rickets RACHITIS
– preventing or curing rickets, as a drug might ANTIRACHITIC

riddle, mysterious or puzzling person or thing ENIGMA
– riddle, typically based on a pun CONUNDRUM
– riddle in the form of pictures or symbols representing syllables or words REBUS
– riddle or brain-teaser in Zen Buddhism, designed to free the mind from the constraints of logic KOAN

rider of the left front horse of a coach POSTILION
– rising and falling of the rider in the saddle in time with a horse's trot POST

ridge, as on corduroy or round a basket or ship's rail WALE
– ridge of land jutting into the sea PROMONTORY, NESS, NAZE, NAB
– ridge of sand or shingle extending from the shore into the sea or across an estuary SPIT
– ridge or arch in the Earth's folded rocks ANTICLINE
– ridge or bank bordering a river or irrigated field LEVEE
– ridge or crest of land CHINE
– ridge or groove linking two planks, shafts, or the like SPLINE
– ridge or hill of streamlined shape formed of glacial deposits DRUMLIN
– ridge or low hill KNOLL, HUMMOCK
– ridge or low mound of sand or gravel left by melting glacial ice ESKER, OS, KAME
– ridge or upland formed by an upthrust between two parallel or two sets of parallel geological faults HORST
– ridge with steep eroded sides HOGBACK, HOG'S BACK
– ridged, grooved, or striped STRIATE, STRIGOSE
– ridges or grooves around the edge of a coin MILLING, FLUTING
– ridges or teeth in a series, as on a saw or the edge of a leaf SERRATION

ridicule See also **mock**
– ridicule, crude parody LAMPOON, BURLESQUE, SPOOF, SQUIB, SKIT, TRAVESTY
– ridicule and expose the falseness or pretentiousness of DEBUNK, DEFLATE
– ridicule or abuse in public, mock or jeer at PILLORY
– ridicule or mock by imitating MIMIC, APE, PASTICHE, SATIRISE, PARODY, CARICATURE
– light ridicule, poking fun in a playful manner BADINAGE, BANTER, CHAFF, PERSIFLAGE, RAILLERY

– object of ridicule or scorn LAUGHING-STOCK, BUTT, BYWORD

ridiculous See also **nonsense**
– ridiculous, laughable, or absurd LUDICROUS, FARCICAL, PREPOSTEROUS, RISIBLE
– ridiculous, senseless, empty and silly, as a remark might be ASININE, FATUOUS, INANE
– ridiculous, strange, incomprehensible BIZARRE, OUTLANDISH, OUTRÉ
– ridiculously impractical or visionary LAPUTAN
– ridiculously small or inadequate, as a pay offer might be DERISORY

riding breeches JODHPURS

riding school MANÈGE

rifle See also **gun**
– carry a rifle diagonally across the body PORT
– rod for cleaning a rifle or inserting the charge into a muzzle-loading firearm RAMROD
– sighting lines, at right angles to each other, in a riflesight, theodolite, or the like CROSS WIRES, CROSS HAIRS

rift valley, trough formed between two roughly parallel geological faults GRABEN

rigging See **sail**

right See also **correct**
– right, granted temporarily, to buy or sell property, shares, or the like exclusively OPTION
– right, power, or authorisation FACULTY
– right and proper, acceptable or satisfactory KOSHER
– right and proper, genuine PUKKA
– right-hand page of a book RECTO
– right-handed, on the right, or relating to the right side DEXTRAL
– right in law DROIT
– right in law, as to a property or claim TITLE
– right of an untried prisoner to appear before a judge or to be released HABEAS CORPUS
– right of the eldest son to inherit the entire estate PRIMOGENITURE
– right of the government to take over private land or property for public use, compensation usually being paid EMINENT DOMAIN
– right of the youngest son to inherit the estate ULTIMOGENITURE, BOROUGH-ENGLISH
– right of use over another person's land or property for specific purposes SERVITUDE
– right or claim considered absolute or God-given DIVINE RIGHT
– right or possession, claimed as one's exclusive own PERQUISITE
– right or privilege, as conferred by rank, the law, or the like PREROGATIVE
– right or status, as of appearing in court, speaking at a meeting, and so on LOCUS STANDI
– right side of a ship STARBOARD
– right to freedom of speech, assembly, and so on CIVIL LIBERTY
– right to market a particular product in a given area CONCESSION
– right to the first offer of something, especially the chance of buying something such as a house FIRST REFUSAL
– right to the help, company, or affection of one's husband or wife CONSORTIUM
– right to the use of benefits from someone else's property USUFRUCT
– right to vote FRANCHISE, SUFFRAGE
– rights of a citizen within society CIVIL RIGHTS
– rights retained by the lessor or seller of a property RESERVATION
– at right angles PERPENDICULAR
– both right-handed and left-handed, able to use both hands equally expertly AMBIDEXTROUS
– champion of rights, especially for the oppressed TRIBUNE
– defend or enforce one's rights ASSERT
– give up a claim or right voluntarily WAIVE, RELINQUISH
– intrude slowly on the property or rights of someone else, trespass ENCROACH
– political principles, of a country, concerning basic rights and duties, either unwritten or embodied in statutes CONSTITUTION
– referring to rights that cannot be withdrawn or transferred INALIENABLE
– relating to rights, duties, and similar ethical concepts DEONTIC
– strip or deprive of something, such as clothes, rights, or property DIVEST

-right- -DEXTR-, DEXTRO-, ORTHO-

right angle- DIA-

right of way THOROUGHFARE
– right of way or similar legal right over another person's land EASEMENT

rightful, in accordance with the law LEGITIMATE

rigidity and temporary insensitivity in reaction to shock RIGOR

rim or projecting edge, as on a wheel or beam, for strengthening, attaching, or the like FLANGE

rind, bark, husk or similar outer layer CORTEX

ring, usually of gold, worn in a pierced ear to prevent the hole from sealing up SLEEPER
– ring engraved with initials or a design, originally for use as a seal SIGNET RING
– ring inserted in the lip LABRET
– ring made of two interlocking rings GIMMAL
– ring of faint light, as around the Moon when viewed through a haze CORONA
– ring of light around the Sun or Moon, as when viewed through mist AUREOLE
– ring of light or halo, especially in art GLORIA, GLORIOLE, GLORY, NIMBUS
– ring of metal, such as a key ring, consisting of a tight double coil of wire SPLIT RING
– ring of muscle constricting or relaxing a body passage, as in the bladder or anus SPHINCTER
– ring of plaited leather used by Scouts and Guides to fasten their neck squares WOGGLE
– ring of stone at the top of a column, directly beneath the capital ANNULET
– ring of stone or wooden pillars, from prehistoric cultures HENGE
– ring of three braided loops of different kinds of gold RUSSIAN WEDDING RING
– ring on a dog's collar for attaching a leash TERRET
– ring on a vehicle, into which a towing hook is inserted LUNETTE
– ring or eyelet, as of rope or rubber, for securing a sail, protecting a wire from chafing, or the like GROMMET
– ring shape, shape of a ring doughnut TORUS
– ring-shaped ANNULAR, TOROID
– ring-shaped figure, space, marking, part, or object ANNULUS
– ring-shaped or coiled, as the frond of a young fern might be CIRCINATE
– ring with an oval-shaped gemstone or oval cluster of stones MARQUISE
– circular rim securing the gemstone in a ring or other piece of jewellery COLLET
– large ring, open at the top, through which a cable or rope is run on shipboard CHOCK
– made of or marked with rings, as an annelid worm might be ANNULATE
– medallion, on a brooch, ring, or the like, with a head in profile in raised relief CAMEO
– study of seals and signet rings SPHRAGISTICS

ring- GYRO-

ringing, loud or repeated metallic noise CLANGOUR
- ringing of bells or chimes using all possible variations CHANGE RINGING

ringworm, athlete's foot, or similar fungal skin disease TINEA, DERMATOPHYTOSIS

rinsing – kitchen utensil for rinsing or draining, consisting of a perforated bowl COLANDER

Rio de Janeiro – person born or living in Rio de Janeiro CARIOCA

riot with much noise and disorder TUMULT
- break up a riot or drive off the rioters DISPERSE
- encourage or provoke unrest, a riot, or the like FOMENT
- suppress something forcibly, such as a riot QUELL

riotous and uninhibited, as a drunken party might be BACCHANALIAN, BACCHANT, BACCHIC

ripe and sweet, as a fruit might be MELLOW

rippling, swaying, pulsing, or other wave-like movement UNDULATION

rise See also **increase**
- rise, climb ASCEND
- rise above or extend beyond the limits of TRANSCEND
- rise above, overcome SURMOUNT
- rise and fall with a strong regular rhythm, as waves do in the open sea SURGE, HEAVE, SWELL
- rise and float in the air, apparently in defiance of gravity LEVITATE
- rise or increase INCREMENT
- rise or increase that is very rapid UPSURGE
- rise steeply or suddenly, as prices might SKYROCKET, SOAR, SPIRAL
- rise up on its hind legs, as a horse might REAR UP
- rising and falling movement, as of waves UNDULATION
- rising again RESURGENT
- very fast, impressive, as a rise to fame might be METEORIC

risk, endanger IMPERIL, JEOPARDISE
- risk, gamble, expose to danger HAZARD, VENTURE, BRAVE
- risk, threat, danger MENACE
- risk-assessor, as for an insurance company UNDERWRITER
- risk everything on a single bet or chance GO NAP
- risk or danger associated with one's job or a specified activity OCCUPATIONAL HAZARD
- risk-taking of a foolhardy kind, reckless and open disregard of danger TEMERITY
- risk to an insurance company based on a policyholder's possible dishonesty or carelessness MORAL HAZARD
- risky, insecure, or unstable PRECARIOUS
- risky buying and selling of a commodity in the hope of a large profit SPECULATION

ritual, custom, or ceremony marking a change of status in a person's life RITE OF PASSAGE
- ritual ban or restriction of something considered either too holy or too unholy TABOO
- ritual chanting of magic sounds or spells INCANTATION
- ritual or ceremony of admission, as to group membership INITIATION
- ritual or religious ceremony that is considered foolish and obscure MUMBO JUMBO
- ritual pouring of a liquid LIBATION
- ritual revel or celebration, typically marked by sexual acts and heavy drinking, in ancient Greek cults ORGY, BACCHANAL
- designed to prevent or turn away evil, as a ritual ceremony might be APOTROPAIC
- mystical and obscure, as rituals might be OCCULT, ESOTERIC, ORPHIC

river channel or stagnant pool or backwater in Australia BILLABONG
- river embankment, or, in the U.S., a landing place or pier LEVEE
- river of ice and snow moving slowly down a valley GLACIER
- river or stream flowing into a larger one TRIBUTARY
- river or stream flowing out of a lake EFFLUENT
- adjective for a river POTAMIC, FLUVIAL
- adjective for a river bank RIPARIAN
- area, typically triangular, at the branching mouth of a river DELTA
- branch of a river, especially in a delta, that flows away from it without returning DISTRIBUTARY
- dam in a river or canal to raise the water or regulate its flow WEIR
- flight of steps beside a river in India GHAT
- flow out of a valley to emerge into a more open area, as a river might DEBOUCH
- flow out or discharge at the mouth of a river DISEMBOGUE
- flowing together or meeting point of two or more rivers CONFLUENCE
- flowing with a violently agitated movement, as a river or stream might TURBULENT
- follow a winding course, as some rivers do MEANDER
- formation of land, especially by deposition in a river ALLUVION
- gorge of a river, typically dry except after heavy rain WADI
- gorge with high walls, cut by a river CANYON, RAVINE, GULCH
- migrating down a river to the sea to breed, as some fishes do CATADROMOUS
- migrating up a river to breed, as salmon do ANADROMOUS
- mouth of a river, outlet for a channel, or the like DEBOUCHURE, EMBOUCHURE
- mouth or wide lower reaches of a river where it approaches or meets the sea ESTUARY
- muddy or cloudy, as a river might be TURBID
- name used formerly for a branch of a river that flows away but rejoins the main stream later ANABRANCH
- path along a canal or river, as still sometimes used by horses pulling boats TOWPATH, BRIDLEPATH
- referring to a river whose direction is directly related to the original main slope of the land CONSEQUENT
- referring to a river that is a tributary of a consequent river SUBSEQUENT
- referring to a tributary river flowing in a direction opposite to a consequent river OBSEQUENT
- rippling or swirling movement in a river EDDY, PURL
- search the bed of a river, lake, or canal by trailing a hook or net along it DRAG, DREDGE
- section of a river where the flow is very strong and rough RAPIDS
- sediment of fine sand deposited in or by a river SILT
- small island, especially in a river AIT, EYOT
- small river or brook RIVULET
- small river or stream, as referred to in various regions BECK, BOURN, BURN, RILL, CREEK, RUNLET, RUNNEL
- small, swift-flowing mountain river or stream GILL
- source of a river HEADWATERS
- source of a river in the form of a spring FOUNTAINHEAD
- uninterrupted stretch of water on a river or canal REACH
- U-shaped bend in a river OXBOW
- usually dry river bed in an arid area of the Americas ARROYO

– valley or pass that no longer holds a river WIND GAP
– wave moving upstream on a river, as caused by tidal currents BORE, EAGRE

road, as across marshy ground, made of logs laid sideways CORDUROY ROAD
– road along the coast, often built into the side of a cliff CORNICHE
– road ascending a steep slope in a winding course SWITCHBACK
– road junction, painted with criss-crossed yellow lines, that vehicles must not enter if their exit is not clear BOX JUNCTION
– road junction with a flyover and four curving access roads CLOVERLEAF
– road-mender, person who maintains roads LENGTHMAN
– road on which cars may not stop except in an emergency CLEARWAY
– road or passage from one point to another THOROUGHFARE
– road or railway bridge, typically supported by a series of arches, as over a valley VIADUCT
– road or route deviating from the standard or direct one DETOUR
– road or similar area lined with shops and closed to motor vehicles MALL, PEDESTRIAN PRECINCT
– road or track used for carrying boats or supplies between waterways PORTAGE
– road passing above another road OVERPASS, FLYOVER
– road surface consisting of small stones, commonly bound with tar MACADAM, TARMAC
– road that leads through traffic around congested areas BYPASS, RELIEF ROAD
– road vehicle's degree of stability, as on wet roads ROADHOLDING
– road with a central barrier or strip of land dividing traffic moving in opposite directions DUAL CARRIAGEWAY, DIVIDED HIGHWAY
– road with no exit, dead-end road CUL-DE-SAC, IMPASSE
– roadway or bridge, hinged near a weighted end so as to be raised or lowered BASCULE
– arched or upwardly curved surface of a road CAMBER
– black, often syrupy, naturally occurring hydrocarbon mixture used in roadmaking and roofing BITUMEN, ASPHALT
– break up and loosen the surface of topsoil, a field, a road, or the like SCARIFY
– broad city road or avenue, especially in Paris BOULEVARD
– broad road or square, especially in a city CONCOURSE
– central or highest part of a cambered road CROWN
– central strip of land, separating the two carriageways of a road RESERVATION, RESERVE
– circular one-way road round a central island at a road junction ROUNDABOUT, ROTARY
– flashing beacon beside a road, marking a zebra crossing BELISHA BEACON
– grassy border of a road VERGE
– gravel, rock chips, or the like used as foundation for a road or railway track BALLAST
– hump built across a road to limit the speed of vehicles SLEEPING POLICEMAN
– junction between a motorway and another road INTERCHANGE
– junction where two or more roads meet CROSSROADS, INTERSECTION
– major road linking towns or cities ARTERY, TRUNK ROAD
– man-made valley carrying a road or railway through high ground CUTTING
– minor or side road BYROAD
– motorway or fast road for motor vehicles only, in various countries AUTOBAHN, AUTOROUTE, AUTOSTRADA, EXPRESSWAY, FREEWAY, PARKWAY
– narrow road, lane, or alley WYND
– narrow road, or lane between walls or hedges TWITTEN
– narrow one-way road connecting a motorway with another road SLIP ROAD, ACCESS ROAD
– parking or waiting strip built as a recess beside a road LAY-BY
– raised roadway, as across water or marshland CAUSEWAY
– reflector set in a road at intervals to indicate traffic lanes at night CAT'S-EYE
– relating to travelling or roads VIATIC
– secondary road linking smaller communities with a trunk road or motorway FEEDER
– sloping section or incline, as of a road or railway track GRADIENT
– small pillar by a road to direct traffic or prevent parking BOLLARD
– small street behind a residential road, formerly containing stables, now usually converted to small houses MEWS
– subsidiary road, leading to a sandbank, built at a corner on a steep slope, to avert accidents if drivers lose control ESCAPE ROAD
– thin coating of ice, as on a road GLAZE ICE, BLACK ICE
– toll road, especially a toll motorway in the U.S. TURNPIKE
– traffic signal in Britain in the form of a green arrow, allowing traffic to turn from a main road but not proceed straight on FILTER
– very sharp bend in a road, as on a mountainside HAIRPIN
– winding or twisting, as a mountain road might be TORTUOUS

roadholding capacity, as of moving wheels TRACTION

roast – moisten roasting meat with melted fat or sauce BASTE

roasting appliance fitted with a rotating spit ROTISSERIE
– roasting spit or skewer BROACH, BROCHETTE

rob See also **steal**
– rob by force, as in wartime PLUNDER, PILLAGE, LOOT, RAVAGE, DESPOIL, RANSACK, MARAUD
– rob or deprive of DISPOSSESS, RELIEVE

robber in an armed band in the hills in India or Burma DACOIT
– rob by plunder PILLAGE
– robber or bandit BRIGAND
– robber who formerly held up coaches or travellers HIGHWAYMAN

robbery and destruction PILLAGE, DEPREDATION, PLUNDER, SPOLIATION
– robbery of public, private, or company funds entrusted to one EMBEZZLEMENT, MALVERSATION, PECULATION
– robbery or large theft HEIST
– robbery or misappropriation of property left in one's care CONVERSION
– involved in a robbery or other crime IMPLICATED
– proceeds of a robbery LOOT, HAUL, BOOTY

robot or robot-like person behaving mechanically as if not under his own control AUTOMATON
– having certain robot-like or electronically enhanced functions, as some science-fiction characters and creatures have BIONIC

robust, lusty, or coarsely humorous RABELAISIAN

rock See chart, and also **geology**, **gemstones**, **precious stones**
– rock, stones, or soil covering a mineral vein or archaeological stratum OVERBURDEN
– rock base lying under topsoil, lose sand or the like BEDROCK
– rock cavity lined with crystals pointing inwards GEODE
– rock containing metal or mineral deposits LODE
– rock-forming mineral of a common kind, consisting of any of

ROCKS AND MINERALS

ROCKS AND ROCK TERMS

agglomerate	rock composed of volcanic fragments
aggregate	rock of mixed minerals or separable fragments
basalt	dark, fine-grained, hard extrusive rock
breccia	rock composed of angular fragments
calcite, calcspar	white calcium mineral that is the main constituent of limestone, chalk, and marble
conglomerate, pudding stone	rock composed of rounded rock fragments cemented together
detritus	mineral particles derived from rocks by weathering and erosion
dolomite	type of limestone found in the Dolomites, in north Italy
erratic	large fragment of rock that is different from surrounding rock types
extrusive rock	fine-grained igneous rock that has cooled and solidified on the Earth's surface or on the seabed
gabbro	coarse-grained igneous rock containing the same minerals as basalt
gneiss	metamorphic rock with alternating bands of light and dark material
igneous rock	rock that has solidified from molten rock
intrusive rock	coarse-grained igneous rock that has solidified in cracks or cavities in existing rocks
lodestone	highly magnetic rock
metamorphic rock	rock that has been altered in chemical composition or texture by high temperatures or pressures, or both
obsidian	hard, black volcanic glass used to make cutting tools in prehistoric times
oolite/oolitic limestone	limestone composed mainly of tiny rounded particles
outcrop	section of a rock formation exposed at the Earth's surface or covered only by a thin layer of soil or the like
plutonic rock	intrusive rock formed at great depth
pumice stone	rock with many small cavities formed from lava
sarsen stone	sandstone block found on the chalk of southern England, and probably a remnant of an eroded sandstone layer
schist	metamorphic rock with minerals arranged in wavy bands, which split easily
sedimentary rock	rock formed from particles of pre-existing rock, or other material, deposited by water, wind, or ice
shale	sedimentary rock formed from clay which has narrow layers and splits easily
tufa	calcium carbonate deposited round a spring
vesicle	small cavity in a rock formed by a bubble of gas in the rock in its molten state

MINERALS AND THEIR USES AND PRODUCTS

alabaster	sculpture, ornaments
albite	glass, ceramics
anhydrite	cement, fertilisers
azurite	copper
bauxite	aluminium
blue john	jewellery and ornaments
calcite, calcspar, Iceland spar	cement, plaster, paint, glass, fertiliser, optical instruments
cassiterite	tin
cinnabar	mercury
corundum	abrasives, gemstones
dolomite	cement, building stone
fluorite	glass, enamel, jewellery
galena	lead
graphite, plumbago	lead pencils
gypsum	plaster of Paris, cement, school chalk
haematite	iron
halite, rock salt	common salt, chlorine, pottery glazes, glass
jet	jewellery
kaolinite	porcelain, coating and filler for paper
malachite	copper, ornaments
microline	glass, ceramics
muscovite mica, isinglass	insulators, lubricants, paints
orthoclase	glass, ceramics
pyrite, fool's gold, iron pyrites	sulphur, iron
quartz	abrasives, cement, glass, gemstones
rutile	titanium
serpentine	ornaments; a variety is known as asbestos
sphalerite	zinc
talc	talcum powder, electrical insulators

ROMAN TERMS

aedile	official responsible for public works
agnomen	additional, usually fourth, name as bestowed on military heroes
atrium	open courtyard within a house or villa
augur, auspex	religious official who interpreted omens, soothsayer
basilica	large public hall or court
calends	first day of the month
censor	either of two officials who were responsible for the public census, and public morals and behaviour
centurion	officer commanding a small military unit
cognomen	third name of a citizen
cohort	subdivision of a legion, numbering 300 to 600 men
consul	either of two chief officials of the republic, elected for one year
curia	senate house
decimate	kill every tenth man in a cowardly or mutinous military unit
denarius	silver coin issued by magistrates
fasces	bundle of rods tied round the handle of an axe, carried before magistrates as a symbol of authority
forum	marketplace, public square and place for political assembly
haruspex	priest who foretold the future by examining animal entrails
ides	13th or 15th day of the month
lares and penates	household gods
legion	basic military unit, numbering 3000 to 6000 men
lemures	unfriendly spirits of the dead
lictor	official who carried the fasces
Lupercalia	fertility festival of the god Lupercus, celebrated in February
manes	friendly spirits of the dead; deified souls of ancestors
maniple	subdivision of a cohort, 60 to 120 men
nomen	second or family name of a citizen
nones	ninth day before the ides of a month
patrician	noble
plebeians, plebs	ordinary citizens, the masses, the common people
pontifex	priest of high status
praenomen	first or personal name of a citizen
praetor	leading magistrate of the republic
Praetorian Guard	elite troops of the emperors
proletarian	citizen of the lowest class
quaestor	financial and administrative official
retiarius	gladiator armed with a net and trident rather than a sword
saturnalia	bawdy festival of the god Saturn, celebrated in December
sesterce	quarter of a denarius
SPQR	slogan or identifying insignia, "Senate and People of Rome"
testudo	siege device formed by interlocking shields held above legionaries' heads to protect them against missiles
thermae	public baths
tribune	official elected by the plebeians to champion their rights against the patricians
triclinium	couch round three sides of a table, on which Romans reclined at meals; a dining room
triumvir	any of three joint rulers

various types of aluminium silicate FELDSPAR
– rock fragment CLAST
– rock fragment of medium size COBBLE
– rock fragments, rubble DEBRIS
– rock fragments or rubble at the foot of a hill or cliff SCREE, TALUS
– rock-hurling weapon of various kinds in ancient warfare CATAPULT, BALLISTA, ONAGER, BRICOLE, MANGONEL, TREBUCHET
– rock layer STRATUM
– rock mass or mountain peak that is steep and pointed AIGUILLE
– rock or pile of stones on a hilltop TOR
– rock painting, carving, or inscription from ancient or prehistoric times PETROGLYPH
– rock projecting beyond a cliff face OVERHANG
– rock shaped in a large, usually upright, block MONOLITH
– rocky cliff or peak CRAG
– rocky plateau with distinct borders, or a distinct mountain group in a chain MASSIF
– rocky ridge of land jutting into the sea PROMONTORY

– basin or layer of porous rock, between layers of hard rock, in which water is trapped ARTESIAN BASIN
– crack in the Earth's crust and resulting shift and discontinuity of the rocks on either side FAULT
– cross-section of the Earth's crust showing rock and soil layers PROFILE
– crust of porous rock formed from mineral deposits around a geyser or hot spring SINTER
– delicate curving decoration of rock fragments or shells, used in rococo design ROCAILLE
– having small bubbles or cavities, as some rocks have POROUS, CELLULAR
– intensely folded rock formation displaced from its site of origin by the forces causing the folding NAPPE
– lacking a crystalline structure, as a rock or chemical might AMORPHOUS
– narrow layer of rock LAMINA
– oval cavity, originally a bubble, in lava rock, often filled with mineral crystals AMYGDULE
– pillar or cone of rocky lime deposit hanging from the roof of a cave STALACTITE
– pillar or cone of rocky lime deposit rising from the floor of a cave STALAGMITE
– rubbing down or wearing away of rock through friction, as by wind-blown sand ATTRITION
– small lump of a mineral or rock, typically found in a different kind of rock NODULE
– wear or rub away, as rock might ABRADE, CORRADE
– splitting or flaking easily, as some rocks do SPATHIC

-rock- -LITE, -LITH-, LITHO-, PETRO-

rocket See also **missile**
– rocket, shell, missile, bullet, or other object fired or hurled PROJECTILE
– rocket engine used to slow down or reverse a missile, spacecraft, or the like BRAKING ROCKET, RETROROCKET, RETRO
– rocket fuel, explosive charge, or similar agent generating thrust PROPELLANT
– rocket propelled by successive firings MULTISTAGE ROCKET, STEP ROCKET
– rocket that supplements the main power system of a jet or spacecraft, often as the first stage of a multistage rocket BOOSTER
– curved flight path of a rocket ball, or the like TRAJECTORY
– spin or wobble in flight, as a rocket or aircraft might YAW
– supporting tower or scaffolding for a rocket on the launching pad GANTRY

rococo – decoration of or resembling rock fragments or shells, used in rococo design ROCAILLE

rod, forked stick, or the like that quivers or dips when held above ground containing water or minerals DIVINING ROD, DOWSING ROD
– rod for cleaning a rifle or inserting the charge into a muzzle-loading firearm RAMROD
– rod for marking positions in surveying RANGING POLE
– rod or pin holding a spool or bobbin, as in a spinning machine SPINDLE
– rod or staff carried as an emblem of authority or office VERGE
– rod or stick from which lengths are cut for fastening adjoining wood or stone parts DOWEL
– rod-shaped BACILLARY, BACILLIFORM, VIRGATE, VIRGULATE
– bundle of rods with an axe, carried as a symbol of the magistrates' authority in ancient Rome FASCES

roe of a lobster or crab, pink when cooked CORAL
– roe of the male fish, "soft roe" MILT

rogue, adventurer PICARO, PICAROON

role or public face that a person adopts in social situations PERSONA
– role or status of a plant or animal within its ecological community NICHE
– brief role or small part played by a famous actor or actress CAMEO ROLE
– playing or expected to play similar roles continually TYPECAST

roll, lie, or toss about in WELTER, WALLOW
– roll heavily or noisily along TRUNDLE
– roll of cloth BOLT
– roll of coins wrapped in paper ROULEAU
– roll of paper, especially newsprint, for use in a rotary printing press WEB
– roll of parchment or paper used for written documents SCROLL
– roll or breadstick made into a long, American-style sandwich HERO, SUBMARINE
– roll up a flag, umbrella, or the like FURL
– rolled up or coiled CONVOLUTE, CONVOLUTED
– rolling or revolving movement VOLUTION

roller of a typewriter PLATEN
– device for squeezing water from wet laundry by pressing it between rollers WRINGER, MANGLE

Roman See chart
– Roman and Greek culture as a subject of study HUMANITIES
– Roman army unit, originally of 100 troops CENTURY
– Roman body-armour LORICA
– Roman building, divided by columns into a long nave and side aisles, used for public assembly and administration BASILICA

Roman Catholic See chart, page 434
– Roman Catholic in 16th- to 18th-century England who defied the law requiring attendance at Church of England services RECUSANT

romance in verse or prose, especially as written in the Middle Ages GEST

romantic idealistic, but impractical or absent-minded QUIXOTIC
– writer or artist favouring a real-life representation of everyday subject matter rather than a romantic approach REALIST

romanticism – style and artistic principles marked by simple and regular form and by restraint in emotions, in contrast to romanticism CLASSICISM

Rome – arch of spears through which the defeated enemies of ancient Rome had to walk as a gesture of submission YOKE
– chief of the seven hills of Rome PALATINE
– relating to the civilisation of ancient Greece and Rome CLASSICAL
– underground galleries and tunnels with niches or ledges for graves, especially those in Rome CATACOMBS

roof See illustration, page 435
– roof, or structure on a roof, in the shape of a dome CUPOLA
– roof at the entrance of a building, providing sheltered access PORTE-COCHÈRE
– roof of the mouth PALATE
– roofing slate with one side left rough RAG
– roof with a ridge, and a gable at each end SADDLE ROOF, SADDLEBACK
– roof with double-sloping sides, the lower slope being steeper in each case CURB ROOF
– roof with two sloping sides of equal angle and size SPAN ROOF
– arched roof or ceiling, typically of stone or masonry VAULT
– beam in the frame of a vaulted roof LAMELLA

ROMAN CATHOLIC TERMS

aggiornamento	modernisation of the ideas and administration of the Church
beatification	official recognition and proclaiming of a dead person to be blessed, usually preliminary to canonisation
breviary	book of hymns, psalms, and prayers to be recited by the clergy at services
bull	edict issued by the Pope often sealed with a bulla or lead seal
canonisation	official recognition and proclaiming of a dead person to be a saint
Codex Juris Canonici	code of law governing the Church since 1918
conclave	meeting of cardinals to elect a new Pope
consistory	meeting of the Pope and cardinals to announce papal acts officially
Curia	papal court and its officials
decretal	papal decree deciding a point of canon law
de fide	referring to a doctrine that is an article of faith
devil's advocate, Promoter of the Faith, Promoter Fidei	official appointed to argue against a proposed beatification or canonisation
Dom	title given to monks of certain orders, especially Benedictines
encyclical	letter sent by the Pope to bishops in all countries
extreme unction, Sacrament of the Sick	ceremony in which a priest anoints and prays for a very ill or dying person
Host/Eucharistic Host	wafer consecrated and consumed during Mass
Index Librorum Prohibitorum/ Index	formerly an official list of books banned by the Church
indulgence	reduction in or cancellation of the punishment, especially in purgatory, for a sin, after it has been forgiven
infallibility	principle of the Pope's unfailingly correct judgment in matters of faith and morals, accepted by the First Vatican Council, in 1870
limbo	eternal home of the souls of unbaptised infants, and of the just who died before the birth of Christ
metropolitan	archbishop with authority over other bishops
Monsignor	title or form of address for certain church officials
mortal sin	sin that is unpardonable, depriving the soul of God's grace
nihil obstat	censor's approval of a book, certifying that it is doctrinally acceptable
novena	nine-day period of prayer
ordo	calendar with details for services for each day of the year
Propaganda Fide/ Propaganda	Vatican department in charge of training, posting, and supervising missionaries
purgatory	condition or temporary home in which the souls of the dead suffer remorse for their venial sins, and are purified for heaven
requiem	Mass for a dead person
Rota	supreme ecclesiastical court
sodality	society or association of lay members of the church for devotional or charitable purposes
transubstantiation	doctrine that the bread and wine used during Mass actually turn into the body and blood of Christ
Tridentine Mass	Mass in the form used from 1570 until recent times
Venerable	title given to a dead person who is at the first level of sainthood
venial sin	sin that is not fully evil, and does not deprive the soul of God's grace
Vulgate	4th-century Latin translation of the bible by St Jerome

– black, sticky, hydrocarbon mixture used in roadmaking and roofing BITUMEN, ASPHALT
– circular or crescent-shaped opening in a roof LUNETTE
– covering of overlapping boards, as for a roof or wall WEATHERBOARDING, CLAPBOARDING
– flat on the roof or top floor of a large building PENTHOUSE
– gutter in the eaves of a roof CULLIS
– horizontal beam forming the ridge of a roof, to which the rafters are attached RIDGEPOLE
– horizontal bracket on the top of a wall, for supporting a roof HAMMERBEAM
– horizontal beams supporting the rafters of a roof PURLINS
– metal strips or similar strong weatherproof material covering the joints and angles of a roof FLASHING
– ornamental ridge running along the top of a roof or wall CRESTING
– pair of sloping wooden beams,

often curved, helping to support a roof CRUCKS
– room just under a pitched roof GARRET, ATTIC
– slanting upper part of a roof or wall COPING
– sloping beam forming part of the framework of a roof RAFTER
– sloping roof PITCHED ROOF
– small turret or spire, as on the roof of a Gothic building PINNACLE
– supporting framework of struts, or the like, as for a roof TRUSS
– triangular upper wall at the edge of a pitched roof GABLE
– upright pole or post, as for supporting a roof STANCHION
– wall or railing on the edge of a balcony or roof PARAPET

rook – adjective for a rook or related bird CORVID
– flock or family of rooks PARLIAMENT, CLAMOUR, BUILDING

room for manoeuvre, margin for error, freedom within limits LEEWAY, LATITUDE, PLAY
– room for play or parties, in the U.S. RUMPUS ROOM
– room in a church for storing sacred vessels and vestments SACRISTY, VESTRY
– room or attic just under a pitched roof GARRET
– room or building where records are stored ARCHIVES
– room or cell in a dungeon, entered only through a trapdoor in the ceiling OUBLIETTE
– room or office in a hospital where medical supplies are issued DISPENSARY
– room or shed built on to the side of a house LEAN-TO
– room or shop in a college, supplying provisions BUTTERY
– room or vault housing the bones or bodies of dead people CHARNEL HOUSE
– room or wardrobe for storing clothes GARDEROBE
– room such as a private study where one can remain undisturbed, den SANCTUM
– "room to live", space to expand, especially as used in Nazi philosophy to justify invasions and genocide LEBENSRAUM
– room with boiler, washing equipment, and the like, often used for storage UTILITY ROOM
– alcove in a larger room for informal meals DINETTE
– circular, often domed, building or room ROTUNDA
– connect, as two rooms might, through a shared door, passage, or the like COMMUNICATE

roof shapes

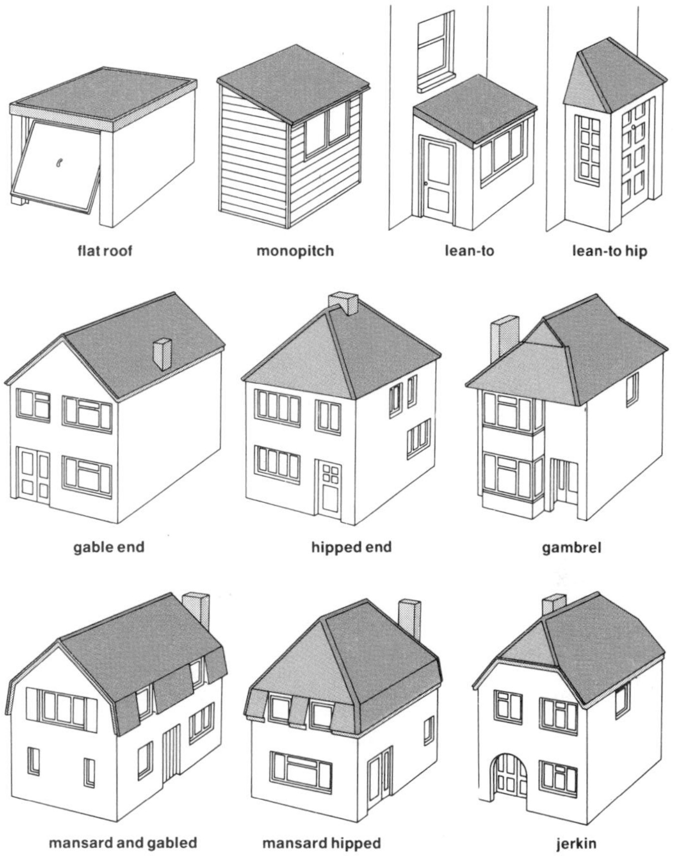

PARTS OF A ROOF

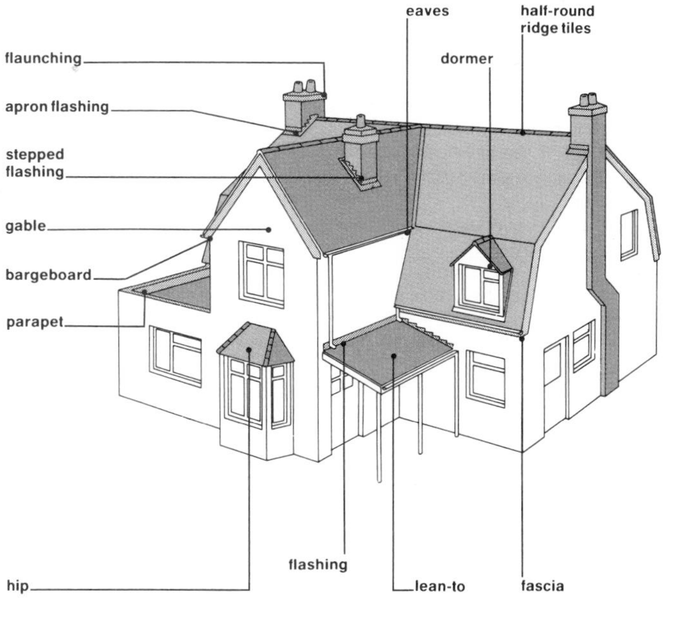

– darkened room into which an image from the outside is projected through an opening or lens CAMERA OBSCURA
– dining room or hall in a college or monastery REFECTORY
– dining room with low tables and couches, especially in ancient Rome TRICLINIUM
– entrance and reception room of a hotel, theatre, or the like LOBBY, FOYER
– fellows' common room at a Cambridge college COMBINATION ROOM
– forming a set, especially of rooms EN SUITE
– furnished accommodation consisting of a single room for both sleeping and living in, bedsitter, bedsit in the U.S. EFFICIENCY
– gatekeeper's room or small building at the entrance to a college PORTER'S LODGE
– glassed-in room or porch for sunning oneself, as in a sanatorium SOLARIUM
– hot-air room for sweat baths, especially in ancient Rome SUDATORIUM
– large drawing room or hall for receiving guests SALON
– meeting room or hall of a guild or corporation in former times GUILDHALL
– open, central room or court of a house, especially in ancient Rome ATRIUM
– private cabin or room on a passenger ship STATEROOM
– reading room, library, or the like ATHENAEUM
– separate room or section, especially of a railway carriage COMPARTMENT
– sleeping room with many beds, in a school or the like DORMITORY
– small dining room, usually on an upper floor CENACLE
– small room, cupboard, or cabin on a ship CUDDY
– small room for storing cases, boxes, and the like BOX-ROOM, GLORY HOLE
– small room off a kitchen, for dishwashing, storing pots and pans, and the like SCULLERY
– small room partitioned off, as for sleeping, changing, or washing CUBICLE
– small room serving as an entrance to a reception room ANTECHAMBER, ANTEROOM, VESTIBULE
– small separate room, especially in a library, used for private study CARREL
– smoking room or coffee house with couches, in former times DIVAN
– snug or cramped room, cupboard, or compartment CUBBY HOLE
– woman's private sitting room, dressing room, or bedroom BOUDOIR, BOWER

room and board, as in a small French hotel PENSION

roomy, large, bulky, or baggy VOLUMINOUS
– roomy, spacious CAPACIOUS, COMMODIOUS

root, especially of ginger RACE
– root-like stem growing under the ground, as in the iris or grasses RHIZOME
– root on some bulbs, serving to draw the bulb downwards in the soil CONTRACTILE ROOT
– root or underground stem that is swollen and bears buds, as of the potato or dahlia TUBER
– root that grows from and supports the stem or trunk of a plant, as in maize or the mangrove tree BUTTRESS ROOT, PROP ROOT
– root valued in the East for its medicinal properties GINSENG
– rootstock of a type of iris, used in perfume-making ORRIS
– adjective for a root RADICAL
– determine the root of a number EXTRACT
– located or active in the air, as some plants' roots are AERIAL
– main root of certain plants, growing straight downwards and giving off small lateral roots TAPROOT
– mathematical extraction of the root of a number or quantity EVOLUTION
– part of a plant embryo that develops into the main root RADICLE
– plant with a forked root, formerly used as a narcotic drug and thought to shriek when pulled from the ground MANDRAKE
– tropical plant whose starchy root is eaten as a vegetable, and used as the basis of tapioca CASSAVA
– uproot, pull up by or as if by the roots DERACINATE

root- -RADIC-, -RAC-, RHIZ-, RHIZO-

rooted, fixed, immobile, as barnacles are SESSILE
– rooted firmly and too deeply to be removed, as incorrigible vices are INERADICABLE, INGRAINED

rootless, separated from one's homeland, social origins, familiar culture, or natural environment DERACINATED, DÉRACINÉ

rope, chain, or the like, as used for steadying a load or mooring an aerial or tent GUY, STAY
– rope, used on ships, of two twisted strands MARLIN
– rope at the front of a boat for tying it up PAINTER
– rope between the top of a boom or gaff and the deck VANG
– rope for raising or lowering a sail or flag HALYARD
– rope for restricting an animal to a small range of movement or grazing area TETHER
– rope for securing a horse or cow, or for a noose in hanging HALTER
– rope for tying together the legs of a horse or cow HOBBLE
– rope handrail on a ship's ladder or gangplank MANROPE
– rope ladder with rigid rungs JACOB'S LADDER
– rope ladder with two or three rungs of metal or wood, used in mountaineering ÉTRIER
– rope or cable for tying up or towing a ship HAWSER, TOWLINE, WARP
– rope or chain attached to and controlling the lower corner or corners of a sail SHEET
– rope or cord used for tying or binding LASHING
– rope passed over a beam, as on a mast, and used for hoisting GANTLINE
– rope sling for sliding or lifting tree trunks, barrels, or the like PARBUCKLE
– rope trailing from a balloon or airship, used for mooring or braking DRAGROPE
– rope with attached weights, used in South America for catching cattle or game by snaring the legs BOLA
– ropes, cables, and the like supporting or controlling the masts, spars, and sails of a sailing ship RIGGING
– ropes across the sail of a ship, forming a rope ladder RATLINE
– ropes in a ship's rigging CORDAGE
– ropes or cables supporting the mast on a ship or boat SHROUDS
– bind a rope-end with twine to stop it fraying WHIP
– coconut-husk fibre, as used for ropes and matting COIR
– descend, as from a cliff top or helicopter, by means of a supporting rope around one's body ABSEIL
– fasten a rope, as on a ship or in mountaineering BELAY
– fibre used in making ropes, or the plant that yields the fibre SISAL, JUTE

– iron device with hooks, attached to a rope, thrown on to a wall, nearby ship, or the like to grip it and create a connection GRAPNEL, GRAPPLING
– join two strips of film, rope, or the like at the ends SPLICE
– lifting machine, typically using ropes for hoisting WINDLASS
– loop in a rope for hitching to a hook, as on shipboard CAT'S-PAW
– loop in a rope, or slack middle part of a rope BIGHT
– loop or coil, as of rope HANK
– peg or crosspiece, attached to a rope, chain, or the like, used for fastening or to prevent slipping TOGGLE
– relating to rope, string, or cable FUNICULAR
– restrict the movement of a horse or farm animal by means of a rope, hobble or tether HAMSHACKLE
– short rope or nautical cord, as for fastening sails LANYARD
– strand twisted with others to make wool, rope, or the like PLY
– thread a rope through a ring, pulley, or the like REEVE
– T-shaped bar or post for securing ropes, as on a ship's deck CLEAT
– willow twig used as a rope WITHE, WITHY

rose of Asian origin with fragrant red or pink petals, used in perfume-making DAMASK ROSE
– "Rose of Sharon" ALTHAEA
– rose-shaped design or structure, such as a pleated ribbon badge ROSETTE
– rose that blooms twice or more during a season REMONTANT ROSE
– climbing or sprawling rose bearing clusters of small flowers RAMBLER
– cultivated hybrid rose bearing abundant clusters of flowers FLORIBUNDA
– having prickles or thorns, as a rose has ACULEATE
– perfume or fragrant oil extracted from petals, especially rose petals ATTAR
– wild rose with pinkish petals and fragrant leaves SWEETBRIER, EGLANTINE

rose- RHOD-, RHODO-

rosy, reddish, ruddy RUBICUND

rot, become gangrenous or ulcerous FESTER, SUPPURATE, MATURATE, PUSTULATE
– rot or decay DECOMPOSE, PUTREFY, PERISH

rotating blade, as on a propeller, windmill, or turbine VANE
– rotating fireworks or jets of water GIRANDOLE
– rotating flow or rush, such as a whirlwind or whirlpool VORTEX

rotation – force, or moment of a force, tending to produce rotation TORQUE
– straight line around which an object rotates, as in geometry AXIS

rotation- GYRO-

rotten, decayed, as bad teeth or bones become CARIOUS
– rotten, full of pus, as a wound might be MATURATING, PURULENT, PUSTULATING, SUPPURATING
– rotten, spoilt by decay PERISHED
– rotten, ulcerous, dying, as a body part might be FESTERING, GANGRENOUS
– rotten and foul-smelling, high, off DECOMPOSED, FECULENT, FETID, PUTRID, PUTRIFIED, RANK
– rotten, off, bitter-tasting or -smelling, as bacon fat might be RANCID

rotting and death of a limb, body tissue, or the like, typically through a failure of blood supply GANGRENE, NECROSIS, MORTIFICATION
– rotting flesh of a dead animal CARRION
– rotting of teeth or bones CARIES
– rotting or decaying smell, as from a swamp or rubbish heap EFFLUVIUM
– hyena, vulture, insect, or the like that feeds on dead animals, rotting meat, or other decaying organic matter SCAVENGER

rotting matter- SAPR-, SAPRO-

rouge – apply rouge to the face coarsely RADDLE

rough, gruff, abrasive, abrupt, discourteously blunt BRUSQUE, CURT, CRUSTY
– rough, harsh, or throaty, as some speech sounds seem GUTTURAL, RASPING
– rough, unrestrained, and noisy, usually in a playful manner BOISTEROUS
– rough and harsh, as sandpaper is or as someone's manner might be ABRASIVE
– rough drawing, plan, or sketch of something DRAFT
– rough edge or bump, as on processed metal, or a burl on a tree trunk BURR
– rough or disturbed, as water might be, CHOPPY, TURBULENT
– rough or grainy surface, as of leather or the like TEXTURE
– rough or jagged projection SNAG
– rough to the touch, horny or scaly, as hard dry skin might be SCABROUS
– roughened with a metal brush, as the plaster on a wall might be KEYED

rough-and-ready temporary device or substitute MAKESHIFT, STOPGAP

roughness or harshness, as of climate, mood, voice, or surface ASPERITY

roulette – bet in roulette made on numbers 1 to 18 MANQUE
– bet in roulette made on numbers 19 to 36 PASSE
– bet in roulette made on any one single number EN PLEIN
– bet in roulette made on two numbers side by side on the layout À CHEVAL
– bet in roulette that the winning number will be an even number PAIR
– bet in roulette that the winning number will be an odd number IMPAIR
– bet in roulette that the winning number will be black NOIR
– bet in roulette that the winning number will be red ROUGE
– call by the croupier to end the placing of bets for any one spin of the wheel RIEN NE VA PLUS
– call by the croupier to roulette-players or other gamblers to place their bets FAITES VOS JEUX
– "doubling up" system in gambling, especially in roulette MARTINGALE
– lay a bet against the bank in roulette, faro, or other gambling games PUNT

round object, ball SPHERE, ORB, GLOBE

round- CYCL-, CYCLO-

roundabout, long and indirect, as a journey or argument might be CIRCUITOUS
– U.S. term for a roundabout on a road ROTARY

rounded, bulging CONVEX, PROTUBERANT, GIBBOUS
– rounded, spherical GLOBULAR
– rounded line or shape, as of a whirlpool SPIRAL, HELIX, VOLUTE, WHORL

rouse to action, as by nagging or irritating GOAD, INCITE

route of principal importance in a transport system TRUNK LINE
– route or road deviating from the standard or direct one DETOUR
– route or road that bears the main flow of traffic, messages, or the like ARTERY
– route planned for a journey ITINERARY
– sail regularly over a particular route PLY

routine, mechanical repetition ROTE

– routine, mechanical, superficial, as a glance or smile might be PERFUNCTORY
– routine, pattern, or way of operating REGIMEN
– routine and boring STULTIFYING
– routine or monotonous task TREADMILL

row of columns or trees positioned at regular intervals COLONNADE
– row or level, as of theatre seating, in a rising series TIER

-row-, -line- STICH-, -STICHOUS

rowing – catch up and touch the boat ahead, in university rowing races BUMP
– covered section at the front or back of a racing boat in rowing CANVAS
– mishandle the oar in rowing, as by striking the water with the blade when recovering from a stroke CATCH A CRAB
– oar or small racing boat used in rowing SCULL
– oarsman nearest the cox at the stern of a racing crew, setting the tempo STROKE
– person who steers the boat or directs the crew in rowing races COXSWAIN, COX
– turn the blade of the oar upright when rowing PEAK
– turn the blade of the oar horizontal between strokes in rowing FEATHER

rowing boat – bracket supporting a rowlock, projecting from the side of a racing or rowing boat RIGGER
– light rowing boat, used in races, for a single oarsman WHERRY
– peg or pin, especially one used as a rowlock in the side of a rowing boat THOLE
– seat extending across a rowing boat, typically for the oarsman THWART
– spaces at the front and back of a rowing boat SHEETS

royal, dignified, or gracious REGAL
– royal attendant, formerly responsible for the horses of the royal household EQUERRY
– royal authority or power, or the symbol or insignia of it SCEPTRE, DIADEM
– royal power, rank, or authority SOVEREIGNTY
– royal reception formerly held by the sovereign just after getting out of bed LEVEE
– royal seal on documents GREAT SEAL, PRIVY SEAL
– funds voted each year by Parliament to maintain members of the royal family CIVIL LIST
– marriage between a royal or noble person and a partner of lower rank, with strict limitations on inheritance rights MORGANATIC MARRIAGE
– money voted by Parliament for the running of the royal household PRIVY PURSE
– regularly and officially employed by the royal family IN ORDINARY

royalty – symbol of royalty in the form of a cross attached to a globe ORB
– symbol of royalty, or royal authority or power SCEPTRE, DIADEM
– symbols or trappings, especially of royalty REGALIA

rub down a horse, groom CURRY
– rub or wear away, as by rust or acid CORRODE
– rub out, wipe out, erase EFFACE
– rub to produce a smooth and polished finish BURNISH, LEVIGATE
– rubbing against another person's body, as in a crowded bus, for sexual satisfaction FROTTAGE
– rubbing between two surfaces in contact, reducing or preventing slipping FRICTION
– rubbing or wearing away, as of rock during erosion ABRASION, CORRASION, ATTRITION
– lotion for rubbing onto the skin EMBROCATION, LINIMENT
– study of friction, rubbing, and lubrication TRIBOLOGY
– taking of a rubbing, as from a rough wooden surface, in art FROTTAGE
– wear away by, or as if by, rubbing ABRADE, CORRADE
– wear away or become tattered or irritated by rubbing CHAFE, FRAY, FRAZZLE

rubbing-, friction- TRIBO-

rubber for removing pencil marks or writing ERASER
– rubber or leather blade, fixed to a handle, for wiping liquid, as in cleaning windows SQUEEGEE
– rubber shoes worn over standard shoes to keep them dry GALOSHES
– rubber suction cup fitted with a handle, used for clearing blocked drains and pipes PLUNGER, PLUMBER'S HELPER
– rubbery latex substance used in electrical insulation and waterproofing GUTTA-PERCHA
– milky sap of certain plants, used in the manufacture of rubber LATEX
– raw or natural rubber INDIA RUBBER, CAOUTCHOUC
– resilient chemical polymer used in paints and varnishes, electrical insulators, as a rubber additive, and in cosmetic surgery SILICONE
– treat rubber with sulphur, heat, and pressure to improve its strength VULCANISE
– whitish or yellowish crinkly, raw rubber, as used on the soles of shoes CREPE RUBBER

rubbish See also **nonsense**
– rubbish, refuse, garbage, litter CULCH
– rubbish, trash, tawdry objects RAFFLE, PUNK
– rubbish consisting of fragments of broken rocks or masonry BRASH, DEBRIS, RUBBLE
– rubbish heap or dunghill MIDDEN
– rubbish or scum produced in cooking, a chemical process, or the like OFFSCOURING
– furnace used for burning rubbish INCINERATOR
– search through rubbish or refuse for food or useful objects SCAVENGE
– waste products or slag from smelting, or stupid and worthless rubbish generally DROSS, RECREMENT

rubble, scattered remains, or the like of something broken DEBRIS, BRASH

rudder – crossbar on a rudder, to which the steering ropes or cables are attached YOKE
– socket, as for the rudder of a boat or the pin of a hinge GUDGEON
– upright pivot pin, as on a rudder or towing vehicle PINTLE

rude, abrupt, gruff, discourteously blunt BRUSQUE, CURT, TERSE, UNCEREMONIOUS, CRUSTY
– rude, abusive, or blasphemous language PROFANITY
– rude, impolite, or discourteous UNCIVIL, UNMANNERLY, ILL-BRED, ILL-MANNERED
– rude, in bad taste, improper, as indelicate behaviour would be INDECOROUS, UNBECOMING, UNSEEMLY
– rude, obsessed with or dealing explicitly with excrement SCATOLOGICAL
– rude, obsessed with sexual matters PRURIENT
– rude, saucy and lively, broadly and lustily humorous BAWDY, RABELAISIAN, RACY, RAUNCHY, SALTY, RIBALD
– rude, uncultured, unpolished or coarse AGRESTIC, CHURLISH, UNCOUTH
– rude in a cheeky, disrespectful way IRREVERENT
– rude in a coarse, unrefined way EARTHY

– rude in a contemptuous, insulting way CONTUMELIOUS, INSOLENT
– rude in a perverted or sick way DEPRAVED
– rude or indecent, especially through being sexually suggestive, as a poem or play might be SALACIOUS, LEWD, LUBRICIOUS, LASCIVIOUS
– rude or profane exclamation or oath EXPLETIVE
– rude sexual language BAWDRY
– cut the rude bits from a book or other text, censor BOWDLERISE, EXPURGATE
– dealing with rude and explicitly sexual material, as a steamy blue film would be PORNOGRAPHIC
– extremely rude, offensively coarse, outrageously vulgar UNPRINTABLE, SCURRILOUS, SCABROUS, OBSCENE, FESCENNINE
– fairly rude, rather dirty or vulgar SMUTTY, UNSAVOURY
– mildly rude, slightly improper, off-colour, as a joke might be RISQUÉ
– mildly rude, hinting at sexual matters, as a saucy remark might be SUGGESTIVE

rudeness or insult CONTUMELY

rug See also **carpet**
– rug of Asian origin, typically with a black-and-white pattern on a reddish background BUKHARA RUG
– Persian rug with an ornate border KIRMAN
– tapestry-woven rug of Asian origin KILIM

rugby – kick in rugby that sends the ball bouncing along the ground GRUBBER
– loose informal scrum in rugby MAUL, RUCK
– player of position in rugby providing the link between the scrum half and the other backs FLY HALF, STAND-OFF HALF, OUTSIDE HALF
– pretended pass in rugby to deceive an opponent DUMMY
– swerve suddenly when running in rugby, to evade an opponent JINK

ruin See also **destroy**, **destruction**, **damage**
– ruin, as caused by war HAVOC, DEVASTATION, DESPOLIATION, DESOLATION
– ruin, damage extensively, spoil or destroy, as grief or fire might RAVAGE, DEVASTATE, DESOLATE
– ruin, decay, extremely run-down condition, as in a slum area BLIGHT
– ruin, destroy, or damage something, such as a plan or ship SCUPPER, SCUTTLE
– ruin, destruction, or doom, often self-inflicted UNDOING, DOWNFALL
– ruin, loss of everything, utter impoverishment DESTITUTION
– ruin, wreck, cause the downfall or loss of reputation of WRACK
– ruin or destroy personal or public property wantonly VANDALISE
– ruin or spoil, make imperfect VITIATE
– ruined, beyond saving or repair IRREPARABLE, IRREMEDIABLE
– ruined or completely destroyed FOREDONE
– ruined or deserted, as a dilapidated old house or the like might be DERELICT
– sudden and violent change, upheaval, or ruin CATACLYSM

ruins – archaeological diggings, or the hollow formed or the ruins revealed by them EXCAVATION

rule See also **authority**, **power**, **government**, **order**
– rule, authority, or influence of one state over another HEGEMONY, SUZERAINTY
– rule, control, or authority DOMINION, SOVEREIGNTY, SUPREMACY
– rule, doctrine, or a principle widely accepted AXIOM, TENET, PRECEPT, CREED
– rule, law, or code of laws CANON
– rule, order, regulation, or an authoritative ruling or pronouncement DECREE, DICTUM, ORDINANCE, PRESCRIPT
– rule, test, or standard on which a judgment or decision is based CRITERION, NORM, YARDSTICK, TOUCHSTONE
– rule of behaviour, as expressed in a brief saying MAXIM
– rule or custom, as for the conducting of a church ceremony RUBRIC
– rule or law no longer enforced though still officially valid DEAD LETTER
– rules, customs, or code of proper behaviour within a given group or society ETIQUETTE
– rules formally and permanently guiding the internal affairs of a club, university, or the like STATUTES, ARTICLES
– rules governing grammatical correctness, formulas in logic, computer programming, and the like SYNTAX
– rules of behaviour and etiquette, especially among diplomats and rulers PROTOCOL
– rules of fair play QUEENSBERRY RULES
– breaking of a law or rule VIOLATION, BREACH, TRANSGRESSION, INFRINGEMENT, INFRACTION
– breaking or ignoring a rule PECCANT
– exemption or release from a rule, law, obligation, or the like DISPENSATION
– making or relating to rules or laws PRESCRIPTIVE, NORMATIVE
– mathematical statement of a rule, proof, principle, or the like FORMULA, THEOREM
– obey a rule or order, carry out someone's wish or demand, or the like COMPLY WITH
– obeying the rules needlessly closely HIDEBOUND, FASTIDIOUS
– put forward as a rule or guide PRESCRIBE
– referring to extremely harsh laws, rules, or penalties DRACONIAN
– referring to or enforcing strict rules, demanding standards, or the like STRINGENT
– rough rules or principles on which to base actions or judgments GUIDELINES
– strict and stiffly correct observer of the rules, a religion, or the like PRECISIAN
– strict or rigorous, as a rigid rule is IRONCLAD
– suspend a rule, penalty, or the like, or refrain from enforcing it WAIVE
– unbreakable, as a sacred rule should be INVIOLABLE

-rule -ARCHY, -CRACY, -OCRACY

ruler See also **leader**
– ruler, hereditary lord DYNAST
– ruler, stick, or the like for beating children, especially on the hand FERULE
– ruler during the absence, illness, or minority of the monarch PROTECTOR, REGENT
– ruler who is harsh, absolute, and arbitrary TYRANT, DESPOT
– ruler's staff carried as a sign of royal authority or power SCEPTRE
– remove a ruler or other high office-holder from his position of power DEPOSE
– subordinate ruler or dictator SATRAP

-ruler -ARCH

ruling, governing, in authority DOMINANT
– ruling by hereditary right, as a monarch might LEGITIMATE
– ruling group of officers after a military takeover JUNTA
– ruling in a fatherly way, typically generous and concerned but restricting individual responsibility PATERNALISTIC

RUSSIAN TERMS

apparat	Communist Party machine or administrative system; bureaucracy	**Menshevik**	moderate socialist, at the time of the Russian Revolution
apparatchik	bureaucrat	**mir**	pre-Revolutionary peasant community; the world; peace
artel	workers' cooperative	**muzhik/moujik**	pre-Revolutionary peasant
babushka	grandmother; old woman; headscarf	**oblast**	local administrative division
balalaika	three-stringed guitar-like instrument	**perestroika**	policy of "restructuring" the Soviet system
blini	buckwheat pancakes	**pirog, pirozhok**	small pie or pasty
Bolshevik	member of the Communist party; formerly, supporter of Lenin	**pogrom**	massacre or persecution
borscht	beetroot or cabbage soup	**Politburo**	Communist Party's ruling committee
boyar	aristocrat in former times	**Pravda**	"Truth", used as the title of a newspaper
commissar	Communist Party official supervising party loyalty and education	**Presidium**	highest policy-making committee of the Supreme Soviet, the legislature
Cossack	member of a southern Russian people, formerly famous as cavalrymen	**refusenik**	Soviet citizen refused permission to emigrate
dacha	country house	**rouble**	monetary unit, equal to 100 kopecks
droshky	open horse-drawn carriage	**samizdat**	underground publishing unit or press
Duma	pre-Revolutionary parliament	**samovar**	tea urn
glasnost	policy of "openness" in government	**soviet**	national, regional, or local council
gospodin	title used as a polite form of address to foreign men	**sovkhoz**	state farm
guberniya	administrative division or region	**sputnik**	orbiting spaceship, satellite
gulag	forced-labour camp	**Stakhanovite**	outstanding industrial worker
Izvestia	"News", used as the title of a newspaper	**steppe**	wide, grassy plain of southern USSR
kibitka	covered cart or sled	**taiga**	subarctic pine forest of Siberia
kolkhoz	collective farm	**tovarisch**	comrade, used as a polite form of address
Komsomol	Communist youth organisation	**troika**	three-horse carriage or sledge
kopeck/kopek	smallest unit of currency	**tsarevitch**	son of the tsar
kremlin	citadel	**tsarina/czarina**	empress; wife of the tsar
Kremlin	chief government building in Moscow; Soviet government	**ukase**	command or edict, as issued by the tsars
kulak	formerly, a prosperous peasant or usurer	**verst**	measure of distance, just over a kilometre, about two-thirds of a mile
kvass	beer-like drink	**volost**	pre-Revolutionary local council in a rural area
matrioshka	traditional set of hollow wooden dolls, encased one inside another	**zemstvo**	pre-Revolutionary district council

– ruling itself, relatively independent of outside control, government, or domination AUTONOMOUS
– ruling or reigning REGNANT

rumbling in the abdomen, caused by intestinal fluids and gas BORBORYGMUS

rumour, idle talk, gossip SCUTTLEBUTT, TITTLE-TATTLE
– rumour or news report that is false or a deliberate hoax CANARD
– rumour or unconfirmed report HEARSAY
– crush or put an end to something, such as a rumour, plan,

or rebellion SCOTCH
– informal or secret means of passing on rumours or information BUSH TELEGRAPH, GRAPEVINE
– long-lasting, continuing despite discouragement, as a rumour might be PERSISTENT
– spread a rumour or report widely BRUIT, DISSEMINATE, CIRCULATE

run or walk awkwardly LOLLOP
– running naked through a public place as a stunt STREAKING
– adapted for running, as some birds or bones are CURSORIAL

run away, depart hastily, flee SCARPER, SKEDADDLE, VAMOOSE
– run away, especially when leaving unpaid debts behind LEVANT, DO A MOONLIGHT FLIT
– run away secretly, as after committing a theft ABSCOND, DECAMP, ABSQUATULATE, HIGHTAIL
– run away secretly with a lover, especially to marry ELOPE

run-down, abnormally weak and tired DEBILITATED, ENERVATED
– run-down, worn out, or untidy, as through debauchery RADDLED

runaway, fleeing or escaped criminal FUGITIVE
– runaway or fugitive slave in the West Indies in former times MAROON

rung of a ladder SPOKE, STAVE

runic alphabet FUTHARK
– runic letter æ, representing the sound /a/ as in *cat*, as used in Old English ASH
– runic letter ð, representing the sounds /th/ and /th̲/, as used in Old and Middle English ETH, EDH
– runic letter þ, representing the sounds /th/ and /th̲/, as used in Old and Middle English THORN

runner, creeping stem or branch, as of the strawberry STOLON, STOLE
– runner or long whip-like shoot of a primitive plant FLAGELLUM

-running -DROMOUS

running down of the energy in the universe or any other closed system ENTROPY

runway – land or run past the end of the runway, as an aircraft might OVERSHOOT
– land short of the runway, as an aircraft might UNDERSHOOT

rupture, displacement of a body organ through the wall that normally contains it HERNIA

rural scene or event of simple charm IDYLL
– idealistically rural, peaceful, and simple ARCADIAN, PASTORAL
– old-fashioned, rural, and unspoilt RUSTIC

rush, sudden flood, outburst SPATE
– rush about wildly, as a frenzied animal might RAMPAGE
– rush in violently IRRUPT
– panic-stricken headlong rush, as of horses or a crowd of people STAMPEDE

Russian See chart, and also **menu terms**
– Russian alphabet CYRILLIC
– traditional liturgical language of the Russian Orthodox Church OLD CHURCH SLAVONIC
– Russian-style picture of a saint or holy person ICON

rusting, eating away, or dissolving of metals CORROSION

rustling, whispering, or murmuring sound, as of wind or surf SOUGH, SUSURRATION

rustproof iron or steel by coating it with zinc GALVANISE

rye bread – aromatic seeds, as sometimes used in rye bread CARAWAY

S

s, z, or related hissing sound SIBILANT

S-shaped SIGMOID
- S-shaped curve in architecture OGEE

Sabbath – person who observes the Sabbath strictly SABBATARIAN

sacking, or the plant or its fibre used in making sacks JUTE
- sacking made of jute HESSIAN

sacred, very holy HALLOWED, SACROSANCT, INVIOLABLE, VENERATED
- sacred and not to be mentioned or described INEFFABLE
- sacred object reputedly protecting a city or state PALLADIUM
- sacred place, or a place treated as sacred HOLY OF HOLIES, SANCTUM SANCTORUM
- sacred place, or the holiest part of a church SANCTUARY, SACRARIUM
- sacred place associated with a saint or revered person SHRINE
- anything seen as sacred, or the quality of being sacred SANCTITY
- make or declare something sacred CONSECRATE, SANCTIFY
- relating to everyday earthly matters rather than to anything sacred SECULAR, PROFANE
- shrine or container for sacred relics RELIQUARY
- spoiling of the sacred quality of a church, as by blasphemy or vandalism DESECRATION, PROFANATION, VIOLATION, SACRILEGE
- treat as sacred, cherish ENSHRINE

sacred- HIER-, HIERO-

sacred books See **scriptures**

sacrifice or slaughter on a large scale HECATOMB
- sacrificial offering burnt in flames HOLOCAUST
- atoning or expiatory, as a sacrifice might be PIACULAR
- kill as a sacrifice IMMOLATE
- pouring of a liquid as a religious sacrifice LIBATION

sad See also **unhappy**
- sad, depressing, or dreary, CHEERLESS, BLEAK, MELANCHOLY, DISMAL
- sad, gloomy, or threatening, as a look might be BALEFUL
- sad, gloomy, quietly mournful DOLEFUL, LUGUBRIOUS
- sad, mournful, expressing sorrow, as some poems are ELEGIAC
- sad, sorrowful, mourning TRISTFUL, DOLOROUS
- sad and subdued, melancholy or gloomy, as a mournful atmosphere is FUNEREAL, SOMBRE
- sad and tearful, as through grief or depression LACHRYMOSE
- sad or discouraged, depressed DEJECTED, DESPONDENT, DOWNCAST, DISCONSOLATE, DISPIRITED, CRESTFALLEN, CHAPFALLEN
- sad or ill-humoured, quietly gloomy or resentful DYSPEPTIC, GLUM, MOROSE, SULLEN, DOUR
- sad or mournful, expressing sorrow or yearning, as a song might PLAINTIVE, PLANGENT, WISTFUL
- sad or mournful in appearance, sorrowful WOEBEGONE
- sad or suffering through frustrated love LOVELORN
- sad yearning pessimism about life, typically sentimental or romantic WELTSCHMERZ
- extremely sad, heartbroken, INCONSOLABLE, PROSTRATE
- extremely sad, as a tragic play might be HEART-RENDING

saddle

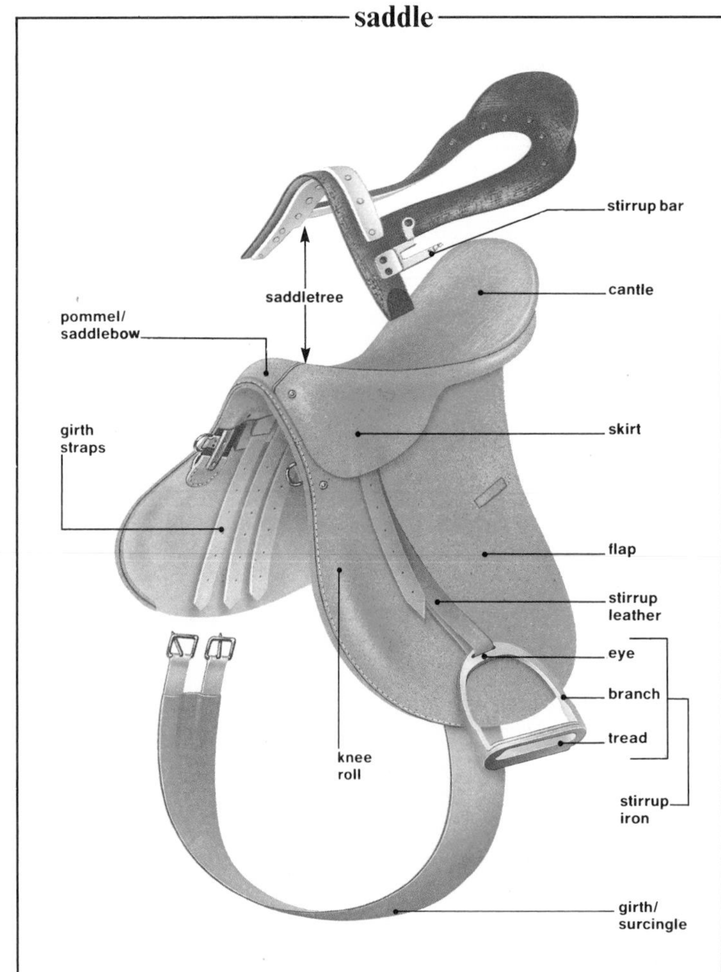

– extremely sad as a result of loss, as on the death of a loved one BEREFT, DESOLATE, FORLORN
– sorry for one's misdeeds, sad at what one has done CONTRITE, RUEFUL, REMORSEFUL
– tending to be sad or melancholy ATRABILIOUS
– thoughtful in a sad, quiet way, brooding PENSIVE

saddle See illustration
– saddle, as for a mule, to which loads can be fastened PACKSADDLE
– saddle or canopied seat on an elephant's back HOWDAH
– saddle or seat for a second rider, as on a motorcycle PILLION
– leather gaiters attached to a saddle GAMBADOES
– ornamental covering, especially for a horse's saddle or harness CAPARISON
– soft, flexible saddle made without a frame PAD

sadism or masochism, any sexual pleasure derived from pain ALGOLAGNIA

safe, reliable, almost risk-free, as secure investments are COPPER-BOTTOMED, BLUE-CHIP
– safe and sound, unhurt despite the dangers UNSCATHED
– safe place or retreat HAVEN, REFUGE, SANCTUARY
– place of safekeeping REPOSITORY
– utterly safe or secure, impossible to overcome UNASSAILABLE, INVULNERABLE, IMPREGNABLE

safebreaker, burglar skilled in opening safes PETERMAN

safeguard, insurance measure against harm SAFETY NET, BACKSTOP, BACK-UP
– safeguard or guarantee of society PALLADIUM

safekeeping – person entrusted with something for safekeeping DEPOSITORY, TRUSTEE

safety or shelter, as from persecution, or a place offering such protection ASYLUM, REFUGE, SANCTUARY
– safety precaution, person or thing that double-checks for safety SAFEGUARD, LONGSTOP, SAFETY NET
– safety switch or lever, as on a train, that causes mechanical shutdown if released by the operator DEAD MAN'S HANDLE

Sahara – region of northwest Africa, between the Sahara and the Mediterranean MAGHREB
– semi-desert region just south of the Sahara SAHEL

sail See chart, illustration, pages 444-445, and also **ship**

SAILING TERMS

belaying pin	pin fitted to a rail to secure a rope
Bermuda rig, Marconi rig	rig with a triangular mainsail, as used on cruising and racing vessels
broaching	turning dangerously sideways on to the wind and waves
careening	turning a boat on its side for cleaning and repairs
carvel-built	constructed with planks lying flush
clinker-built	constructed with overlapping planks
close	sailing as nearly as possible into the wind
crabbing	sailing slightly sideways to offset the drift caused by a current
davits	cranes on deck for hoisting or lowering lifeboats
dogwatch	short spell of duty, from 4pm to 6pm or 6pm to 8pm
fiddle	rail around a table to prevent objects from sliding off
fo'c's'le	forecastle, the short raised deck near the front of a ship
fore-and-aft	referring to a sail that lies along a vessel, not across it
Genoa jib	large triangular sail, as used on racing yachts
gunwale	upper section or top plank of the side of a vessel
gybing/jibing	causing a fore-and-aft sail to swing to the other side of the vessel when sailing before the wind
heaving to	bringing a ship to a standstill by heading into the wind and trimming the sails
heeling	leaning or tilting when sailing into the wind
kite	small sail, set high on a mast, used in a light wind
lateen	triangular sail slung from a long diagonal spar attached to the top of a mast
luffing	turning into the wind, making the sails flap
lugsail	four-sided sail, widest at the bottom, on a diagonal yard
painter	rope attached to the bow of a boat
reaching	sailing with the wind blowing from the side
reefing	tucking or rolling in part of a sail
running	sailing with the wind blowing from directly behind
spar	wooden or metal pole used to support rigging or sails
spinnaker	billowing, triangular sail, as used on racing yachts
tacking	sailing into the wind on a zigzag course
thwart	seat across a small boat, as for the oarsman
trimming	adjusting the sails so that they catch the wind
warp	mooring line; to move a small boat by pulling at this line
yawing	deviating temporarily from a straight course

– sail, travel on water NAVIGATE
– sail on the lowest yard on a square-rigged ship COURSE
– sail successfully, as round a tight bend NEGOTIATE
– sail or fly completely around something CIRCUMNAVIGATE
– sail regularly on a route PLY
– sails, ropes, and other equipment of a sailing ship GEAR
– adjust sails to catch the wind better TRIM
– baggy middle section of a fishing net or square sail BUNT
– bulging section of a sail BAG
– corner of a sail CLEW
– crossbeam attached to a mast and supporting a sail YARD
– fasten a sail securely LASH, FRAP
– gather in and fasten a sail FURL
– let the wind out of a sail SPILL
– lower a boat's mast, sail, or flag STRIKE
– number, shape, and pattern of masts and sails on a vessel RIG
– rope for raising or lowering a sail or flag HALYARD
– rope or chain attached to and controlling the lower corner or corners of a sail SHEET
– rope or strap attaching a furled sail to a crossbeam GASKET
– ropes across a ship's sail, forming a rope ladder RATLINE
– ropes, cables, and the like supporting or controlling the masts and sails of a sailing ship RIGGING
– small ring of rope or metal on the edge of a sail CRINGLE

sailor See also **services**
– sailor, soldier or army servant from the East Indies LASCAR
– sailor or seaman MARINER
– sailor who is not an officer RATING, DECKHAND
– sailors' chapel BETHEL
– sailors' rebellion MUTINY
– sailors' work song SHANTY
– bed of canvas or string, suspended at both ends, as formerly used by sailors HAMMOCK
– biscuit or bread eaten by sailors HARDTACK, SHIP'S BISCUIT
– carved or engraved articles of ivory, whalebone, or the like, typically made by sailors SCRIMSHAW
– clothing and bedding issued to sailors from a ship's stores SLOPS
– gruel or thick porridge eaten by sailors in former times LOBLOLLY, BURGOO
– informal term for a sailor MATELOT, TAR
– person considered by sailors to be inexperienced LANDLUBBER
– punishment for sailors in former times, involving being dragged under the ship KEELHAULING
– stew of meat, vegetables, and ship's biscuit, as formerly eaten by sailors LOBSCOUSE
– trick or force men into serving as sailors or soldiers PRESS, IMPRESS, COMMANDEER, PRESSGANG, CRIMP, SHANGHAI

saint considered the special protector of a person, group, city, or the like PATRON SAINT
– biography of a saint or saints HAGIOGRAPHY
– declare a person to be a saint CANONISE
– honour a deceased person as blessed, as a first step towards declaring him or her a saint BEATIFY
– list or calendar of the saints that are recognised by the Roman Catholic Church CANON
– picture of a saint or holy person ICON
– relating to Saint Peter PETRINE
– revered object, associated with a saint or martyr RELIC
– ring of light around a saint's head in a painting HALO, MANDORLA, AUREOLE
– Roman Catholic official who argued the case against accepting a deceased person as a saint DEVIL'S ADVOCATE, PROMOTER OF THE FAITH, PROMOTOR FIDEI
– Roman Catholic official who argues the case in favour of accepting a deceased person as a saint POSTULATOR
– title given to a deceased Roman Catholic at the first level of sainthood VENERABLE

saint- HAGI-, HAGIO-
saintliness, holiness SANCTITY
saintly, joyful BEATIFIC
sal volatile HARTSHORN
salad See **menu terms**, **vegetables**
salad – oil-and-vinegar salad dressing FRENCH DRESSING, VINAIGRETTE
– small toasted or fried square of

sailing boats and sailing ships

PARTS OF A SAILING BOAT

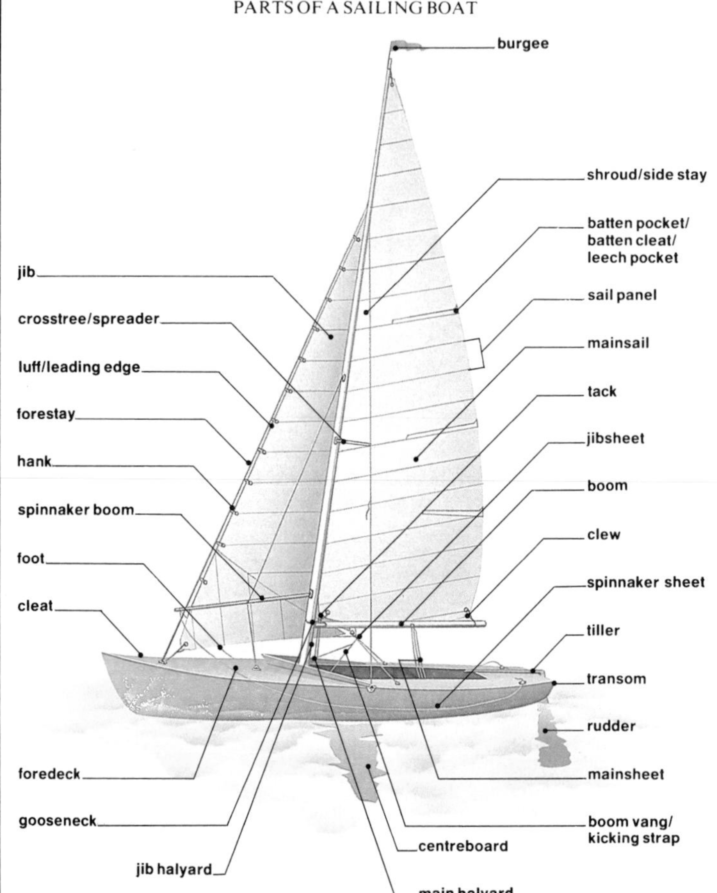

bread served in soups and salads CROUTON

salary, allowance, or similar regular payment STIPEND
- salary, wages, or profit from one's job or office EMOLUMENT
- salary scale formerly used for teachers in English and Welsh state schools BURNHAM SCALE
- salary supplement paid as a cost-of-living allowance in an expensive area WEIGHTING
- deduct a part from someone's salary or wages DOCK
- rising in keeping with the cost of living, as a salary or pension might INDEX-LINKED

sale item offered very cheaply as an inducement LOSS LEADER
- collection of varied items for sale as a single lot JOB LOT
- slick sales talk, patter SPIEL

salesman using dishonest or aggressive selling techniques HUCKSTER

saliva, spittle SPUTUM
- dribble saliva from the mouth SLOBBER, DROOL, SLAVER

salmon after spawning, usually in an exhausted condition KELT
- salmon in the freshwater phase of its life PARR
- salmon of about two years old, when it turns silvery and begins to migrate to the sea SMOLT
- salmon of between two and three years old MORT
- female salmon that has recently spawned BLACKFISH
- male salmon that has recently spawned REDFISH
- migrating from the sea to breed, as salmon do ANADROMOUS
- Scandinavian pickled salmon GRAVADLAX
- U.S. term for smoked salmon LOX
- young salmon or trout ALEVIN
- young salmon returning from the sea to inland waters for the first time to spawn GRILSE

salt, pepper, mustard, or other sauce or seasoning CONDIMENT
- salt cellar, pepper shaker, mustard pot, or the like, or a set of such containers CRUET
- salt deposit frequented by animals to lick minerals LICK
- salt-like flavour-enhancer MONOSODIUM GLUTAMATE, MSG
- remove salt, as from sea water DESALINATE
- turn into, treat with, or mix with salt or a salt SALIFY

salt- SALI-, HAL-, HALO-

salts – chemical salts used in paper- and glassmaking, and as a laxative GLAUBER'S SALTS
- medicinal salts used as a vigorous laxative, and for reducing inflammation EPSOM SALTS

salty, as water might be BRACKISH, BRINY
- salty, relating to salt, or mineral salts SALINE
- salty or spicy to the taste, rather

FULL-RIGGED SAILING SHIP

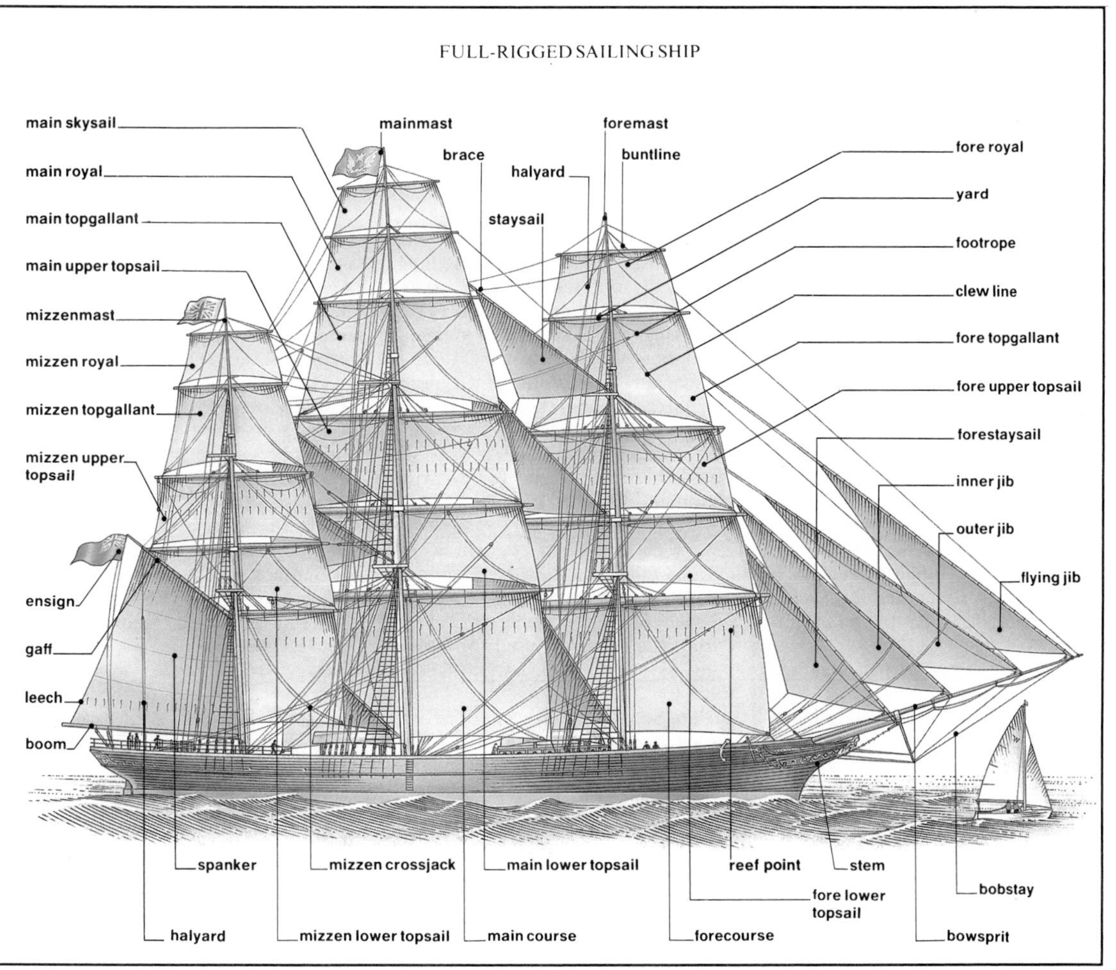

than sweet SAVOURY
– salty water, as used for pickling BRINE
salvation from sin through Christ's death on the Cross REDEMPTION, DELIVERANCE
– chosen by God's will for salvation ELECT
Salvation Army meeting-hall CITADEL
same in age, duration, or period CONTEMPORARY, COETANEOUS, COEVAL
– same in size or duration COMMENSURATE
– same in status, type, or the like COORDINATE
– same or coinciding in meaning, range, proportions, or the like COTERMINOUS, CO-EXTENSIVE
– sameness or equivalence, as of amount PARITY
– amounting to, the same as, equivalent to TANTAMOUNT TO
– be the same as or equivalent to CONSTITUTE
– coinciding in shape, having exactly the same proportions, as with two identical geometrical figures CONGRUENT
– having the same meaning SYNONYMOUS
– having the same shape or form about a given axis, point, line, or plane SYMMETRICAL
– having the same structure, force, or the like, such that an exchange of positions or roles is possible INTERCHANGEABLE
– make equal or treat as the same EQUATE
– person or thing exactly the same as another, perfect copy DUPLICATE, CLONE
same- AUT-, AUTO-, HOM-, HOMO-, IS-, ISO-, SYN-, SYM-, TAUT-, TAUTO-
sample piece of fabric SWATCH
– sample taken at random, as of the general population, regarded as typical of the whole CROSS-SECTION
Samson – Jew in Biblical times, such as Samson, committed by sacred vows to a life of purity and austerity NAZIRITE
sanctuary or sacred part of a church SACRARIUM
sand or other sediment deposited in a tidal estuary WARP
– chemical compound that is a major constituent of sand and is used in the manufacture of glass SILICA, SILICON DIOXIDE, QUARTZ
– fine light sand or clay particles deposited by the wind LOESS
– growing or living in sand ARENACEOUS, ARENICOLOUS
– rock particles finer than sand but coarser than clay, deposited by rivers and streams SILT
– strip of sand or shingle extending from a shore SPIT
sandbags, stones, concrete, or other covering supporting a wall or embankment REVETMENT
sandbank, mudbank, or the like, often dangerous to shipping, sometimes exposed at low tide SHOAL
sandpaper – abrasive mineral or mixture, as on sandpaper, for grinding and polishing CORUNDUM, EMERY
sandwich of an American style, made of a long roll or breadstick HERO, SUBMARINE
– snack or appetiser in the form of a small open sandwich CANAPÉ
sandy in composition, texture, or appearance ARENACEOUS
sane, coherent, conscious and reasonable LUCID, RATIONAL
– sane, of sound mind COMPOS MENTIS
Sanskrit – syllabic script used for Sanskrit and Hindi DEVANAGARI
sap – milky sap of certain plants, used in making rubber LATEX
sarcasm – belittling, causing embarrassment, as sarcasm or a disapproving look might WITHERING
– sarcastic, biting CAUSTIC, MORDANT
– sarcastic in a sneering or insulting way, as a cruel remark might be SNIDE
– humorous or mildly sarcastic use of words to express something markedly different from or opposite to their literal sense IRONY
– joking in a sarcastic or inappropriate way FACETIOUS
– mocking or scornful in a cynical or sarcastic way SARDONIC
sardines – Norwegian herring, typically canned like sardines SILD
Sark – hereditary head of the government of the island of Sark when male SEIGNEUR
sash, wide and often pleated, worn round the waist with a dinner jacket CUMMERBUND
– sash or belt crossing the chest from the shoulder, used for carrying a sword or bugle BALDRIC
Satan LUCIFER
satellite See **spacecraft**
– satellite orbiting in a fixed position relative to a point on the equator GEOSTATIONARY SATELLITE, GEOSYNCHRONOUS SATELLITE
satire, send-up, take-off SKIT, SPOOF
– satirical portrait CARICATURE
– satirical literary work, usually treating a subject in an inappropriate style BURLESQUE
– satirical literary work treating a lowly or comic subject in a heroic or high literary style MOCK-HEROIC
– satirical mimicry, as of a writer's or composer's work PARODY, PASTICHE
– satirical work in the form of a grotesque imitation of an original work TRAVESTY
– satirise or mock by imitating MIMIC, APE
– mocking satire of another work LAMPOON, PASQUINADE, SQUIB
satisfaction – experienced or enjoyed through the actions or achievements of someone else, as satisfaction might be VICARIOUS
satisfactory See **mediocre**
satisfied or self-satisfied to the point of feeling that nothing more needs to be done COMPLACENT
– satisfied with or complacent about one's past achievements RESTING ON ONE'S LAURELS
satisfy a whim or craving INDULGE, GRATIFY
– satisfy one's lust, appetites, or the like to the full SATE, SATIATE
– satisfy one's thirst QUENCH, SLAKE
– satisfy someone's whims or wishes, especially unworthy wishes PANDER TO
Saturday – one who observes Saturday as the Sabbath SABBATARIAN
sauces See chart
– sauce in which meat or fish is soaked before cooking MARINADE
saucepan, typically with legs and a long handle, for cooking on a hearth SKILLET
sausage, ham, and other cold cooked meats CHARCUTERIE
– sausage made with pig's blood, blood sausage BLACK PUDDING
– sausage-shaped, as a plant part might be ALLANTOID
– Australian informal term for sausages SNAGS
– British informal term for sausages BANGERS
– German sausages of various kinds BRATWURST, KNACKWURST
– highly seasoned smoked pork sausage SAVELOY
– large, mild sausage sliced and eaten cold in salads or sandwiches POLONY, BOLOGNA, MORTADELLA
– mild smoked sausage FRANKFURTER, WIENER, WIENERWURST
– smoked Polish sausage KIELBASA
– Spanish sausage of very spicy pork CHORIZO
– spicy sausage of various kinds, as used in sandwiches CERVELAT, SALAMI
– spicy South African sausage BOEREWORS

– very small spicy sausage, served as a snack or side dish CHIPOLATA
– very spicy Italian sausage, eaten cold PEPPERONI
savage, untamed, wild FERAL
save, keep in existence SUSTAIN
– save, use economically, budget HUSBAND
– save from loss, damage, or cancellation SALVAGE
– save or protect from harm, loss, or decay CONSERVE
– save or rescue from danger or trouble RETRIEVE
– save or rescue from sin and punishment REDEEM
– save someone from evil ways by reforming him RECLAIM
– saving or rescue from sin, ignorance, danger, or the like SALVATION, DELIVERANCE, REDEMPTION
– gather, store, and save, accumulate a reserve AMASS, GARNER, STOCKPILE
saving grace REDEEMING CHARACTERISTIC, MITIGATING FACTOR
saw – groove or notch made in wood by an axe or saw KERF
– having small notches or teeth, as the edge of a saw has SERRATED
say See **speak**, **speech**, **state**, **conversation**
– say, put into words, give voice to VOCALISE, ARTICULATE, PRONOUNCE, UTTER, VERBALISE
– say something deliberately or formally DELIVER ONESELF OF
– say something impulsively and suddenly BLURT OUT
– say something that one should not, give away secret or private information DIVULGE, DISCLOSE,
– say emphatically ASSEVERATE
saying expressing a deep truth or principle in an elegant or witty way APHORISM
– saying or proverb expressing a general truth ADAGE, AXIOM, APOPHTHEGM, DICTUM
– insight or sharp observation, or a saying expressing it APERÇU
– overused, unoriginal, or obvious saying CLICHÉ, COMMONPLACE, TRUISM, PLATITUDE, BROMIDE
– proverb or similar short saying, typically overused or outdated SAW, BYWORD
– rule of conduct, or a saying summing it up PRECEPT
– short saying that sums up a guiding principle MAXIM, MOTTO, SLOGAN
– short witty saying, often with a paradoxical twist EPIGRAM, MOT, GNOME
scab or layer of dead skin, as caused by a burn ESCHAR

SAUCES

aïoli	garlic mayonnaise
béarnaise	sauce of egg yolk, butter, lemon juice or vinegar, and herbs
béchamel	white sauce made with milk, butter, and flour, flavoured with herbs
chasseur	brown sauce with shallots, mushrooms, and tomatoes, for hot meat
espagnole	brown sauce made with stock, bacon, and vegetables
hollandaise	sauce of butter, egg yolk, and lemon juice or vinegar, for fish or vegetable dishes
matelote	wine sauce for fish
mornay	béchamel sauce with added cheese
pesto	Italian sauce of basil and pine kernels
pistou	Provençal sauce of crushed basil leaves, tomatoes, Parmesan cheese, garlic, and olive oil
ravigote	oil and vinegar sauce with herbs, for boiled meat or fish
rémoulade	mayonnaise with herbs and chopped capers and gherkins, for cold shellfish and egg dishes
sambal	vinegary chutney used as a relish for curries, or in Malay cooking
satay	spicy peanut and coconut sauce, served with Indonesian dishes
soubise	white sauce with puréed onions
suprême	white sauce made with veal or chicken stock, with added cream and egg yolk, for eggs, poultry, and vegetables
Tabasco	pungent pepper sauce
tartare	mayonnaise with chopped gherkins, chives, and cream, for hot fish
velouté	white sauce made with veal, chicken, or fish stock, with added cream and egg yolk
vinaigrette	oil, vinegar, and seasoning sauce, as served with salads and the like

scabbard – metal tip or trimming on a scabbard CHAPE
scaffolding – horizontal pole or timber on scaffolding LEDGER
– short wooden beam supporting the planks of a platform on scaffolding PUTLOG
scale, flake of skin, or similar structure SQUAMA
– scale, plate, or similar thin layer of plant or animal tissue LAMELLA, LAMINA
– scale balance consisting of a pivoted bar STEELYARD
– scale for comparison, as for the cost of living INDEX
– scale indicating one's weight by a pointer shifted along a marked bar PLATFORM SCALE
– scale of colours, based on equal changes of hue MUNSELL SCALE
– scale of hardness of metals, based on resistance to indentation from the pressure of a standard steel ball BRINELL SCALE
– scale of hardness of minerals, based on resistance to scratching MOHS SCALE
– scale of magnitude of earthquakes RICHTER SCALE
– scale of mental ability or IQ in children BINET-SIMON SCALE, STANFORD-BINET SCALE
– scale of relative density of liquids BAUMÉ SCALE, TWADDELL SCALE
– scale of wind velocities BEAUFORT SCALE
– scale or series of steps, stages, or degrees, a gradual progression GRADATION
– scale systems in music, such as

major and minor MODES
– scaly dry skin, as in dandruff SCURF
– scaly or rough to the touch, as hard dry skin might be SCABROUS
– covered in scales or bony plates MAILED, SCUTATE, SCUTELLATE
– drawing made to scale PROTRACTION
– drawing made to scale of an outside face of a building or structure ELEVATION
– finely marked scale supplementing the main scale of a measuring instrument VERNIER
– mark, adjust, or check the scale of a measuring instrument CALIBRATE
– position or ranking, as on a scale RATING
– relating to a musical scale consisting of all twelve semitones of an octave CHROMATIC, DODECAPHONIC
– relating to the basic Western major or minor musical scale, without modifications DIATONIC
– system or practice of using the *doh-re-mi* syllables to correspond to notes of the scale SOLMISATION, TONIC SOL-FA, SOLFEGGIO

scale- LEPID-, LEPIDO-

scalpel – long, narrow scalpel for delicate surgery BISTOURY
– surgical cut, as made by a scalpel INCISION

scaly anteater PANGOLIN

scandal or controversy arousing public interest CAUSE CÉLÈBRE
– revealing of a scandal or crime, or the book, broadcast, or the like in which it is reported EXPOSÉ

Scandinavian NORSE
– Scandinavian in ethnic grouping or appearance NORDIC
– Scandinavian-style buffet meal SMORGASBORD

scapegoat, target for insults or criticism AUNT SALLY, WHIPPING BOY

scar formed by the stitching up of a wound SUTURE
– scar or mark from branding, as formerly on the skin of a slave or criminal STIGMA
– scar resulting from a flesh wound CICATRIX, CICATRICE
– hard pink scar tissue KELOID

scarcity See **lack**

scared See also **frighten**, **cowardly**, **fear**
– scared, timid, fearful TIMOROUS, TREMULOUS
– scared in a base or cowardly way CRAVEN, LILY-LIVERED
– scared into silence or inaction, as by threats INTIMIDATED, UNNERVED
– scared or suspicious to an unreasonable degree PARANOID
– extremely scared, paralysed with fear PETRIFIED
– extremely scared, to the point of loss of self-control PANIC-STRICKEN
– nervous, scared, ill at ease JITTERY, FRETFUL, APPREHENSIVE

scarf – scarf-like neckband, arranged like a very wide tie CRAVAT
– scarf of wool COMFORTER
– scarf or large handkerchief, usually of brightly coloured cotton BANDANNA, NECKERCHIEF
– scarf worn over the head and tied under the chin, as worn by Russian peasant women BABUSHKA

scarlet fever SCARLATINA

scatter, break up, as troops of a defeated army might DISBAND, DISPERSE
– scatter in a squandering or irresponsible way DISSIPATE
– scatter or drive off rioters or enemy troops ROUT, DISPEL
– scatter or spread something widely, such as news DISSEMINATE
– scatter randomly or untidily STREW
– scatter throughout a speech, text, or the like, interlace INTERLARD, INTERSPERSE
– scattered, isolated, occasional, intermittent SPORADIC
– scattered or spread out in an untidy, irregular way STRAGGLY
– scattered widely, widespread, widely distributed BROADCAST, DIFFUSE, DISPERSED
– scattering of a nation's people, especially of the Jews DIASPORA
– scattering of people or things DISPERSION

scene in a play in which the actors freeze briefly in position TABLEAU
– scene of a crime VENUE
– scene or setting, as in museums, with models of figures exhibited against a background DIORAMA
– scene or view, especially through a frame such as an avenue of trees VISTA, PROSPECT
– representation of a historical scene, painting, or the like by costumed actors posing silent and motionless TABLEAU VIVANT

-scene -SCAPE

scenery See **theatre**
– scenery and props in a play MISE EN SCÈNE

scent See also **perfume**
– scented mixture, as of dried petals, in a sachet or box, as for scenting linen POMANDER
– scented oil or cream for the hair POMADE, POMATUM, MACASSAR OIL
– scented toilet water EAU DE COLOGNE, EAU DE TOILETTE
– jar of dried petals or spices, used to scent the air POTPOURRI
– small packet or bag containing perfumed powder, for scenting clothes and linen SACHET

schedule or diagram explaining a series of operations, as in a computer program or industrial process FLOW CHART

scheme involving bonuses to workers for increased production INCENTIVE SCHEME
– scheme or solution, as for social problems, that is considered facile or simplistic NOSTRUM

scheming, crafty CALCULATING, CONNIVING

scholar of or expert in Sanskrit or Hinduism PUNDIT
– scholar or religious leader in Islam IMAM, AYATOLLAH
– scholar who shows off his knowledge PEDANT
– servant of a scholar or magician in medieval times FAMULUS

scholarly comments, footnotes, variant readings, and the like in an edition of a text APPARATUS CRITICUS, CRITICAL APPARATUS
– scholarly edition of a writer's works, together with notes by various commentators VARIORUM
– scholarly knowledge, deep learning ERUDITION

scholarship or allowance awarded to a student at a British public school or university EXHIBITION
– scholarship or grant awarded to a student, as at a Scottish university BURSARY
– student who is not on a scholarship COMMONER

school, university, or college that one used to attend as a student ALMA MATER
– school ceremony in North America, as for presenting prizes COMMENCEMENT
– school classes specially designed for pupils with learning difficulties REMEDIAL CLASSES
– school elementary textbook PRIMER
– school for very young children KINDERGARTEN
– school of music CONSERVATOIRE
– school offering intensive preparation for exams CRAMMER
– school pupil who is top of the class DUX
– school pupil who stays away from school without permission TRUANT
– school to which juvenile offenders were sent REFORMATORY

– school training corps in military techniques and discipline CADET CORPS
– schoolmaster in Scotland DOMINIE
– abolish racial separation, as in a school DESEGREGATE
– academic high school in European countries such as Germany, especially in former times GYMNASIUM
– area that is served by a particular school, hospital, or the like CATCHMENT AREA
– class intermediate between two regular classes in a school REMOVE
– divided along racial lines or restricted to certain racial groups, as some schools or buses might be SEGREGATED
– evaluating the work of a student or school pupil throughout the course rather than simply on the basis of a final exam CONTINUOUS ASSESSMENT
– free school for poor children in former times RAGGED SCHOOL
– leave of absence, as from school EXEAT
– occurring outside the normal course of studies or timetable, as in a school or university EXTRACURRICULAR, EXTRAMURAL
– principal of a school, college, or university RECTOR
– secondary school in France, or similar school elsewhere LYCÉE
– traditional Jewish school emphasising religious studies YESHIVA

science See **chemistry**, **physics**
– science as used in establishing facts for evidence in legal cases FORENSIC SCIENCE
– misguided form of science in the Middle Ages, seeking a cure-all medicine and a means of turning base metal into gold ALCHEMY

-science -GRAPHY, -LOGY, -NOMY, -SOPHY

science-fiction magazine or other magazine for those with a particular hobby or interest FANZINE
– having certain robot-like or electronically enhanced body functions, as some characters and creatures of science-fiction BIONIC

scientific and rigorously objective, accurate and thorough in detail CLINICAL
– scientific or technical expert, originally such an expert working for the RAF BOFFIN
– based on or relating to scientific observation or experiment rather than theory EMPIRICAL

scientific instruments See chart, and also **electrical**, **laboratory**, **measuring**, **medical**

scientology, or the therapy based on it DIANETICS

scimitar – scimitar-shaped, curved, as some leaves are ACINACIFORM

scissors with toothed blades for cutting a zigzag edge on cloth to prevent fraying PINKING SHEARS

scold See also **criticise**
– scold, dress down, take to task CHIDE, REPROVE
– scold, punish, or criticise severely CASTIGATE, CHASTISE, KEELHAUL
– scold or blame for a failing or misdeed REPROACH
– scold or criticise sharply REBUKE, REPRIMAND, OBJURGATE
– scold or warn gently but firmly ADMONISH
– scold sternly or severely BERATE, UPBRAID
– scolding by a wife of her hus-

SCIENTIFIC INSTRUMENTS

barostat	maintains constant pressure
chronograph	records short time intervals
dephlegmator	condenses the constituents having high boiling points of a mixed vapour
electromyograph	records electrical activity in a muscle
hodoscope	traces the paths of high-energy particles
hydrophone	detects and monitors sounds underwater
hydroscope	views objects deep underwater
hydrostat	detects the presence or absence of water
hygrograph	records variations in the humidity of the atmosphere
hygrostat, humidistat	controls the relative humidity of the air
image converter, image tube	converts X-rays or other radiation into a visual image
microtome	cuts very thin slices for examination by microscope
nephograph	photographs cloud patterns
optical character reader	converts printed characters into digital form, as for computers
oscillograph	records electric currents as a graph
pantograph	copies pictures and diagrams to scale
radarscope	displays radar signals
radiosonde	transmits meteorological data from a balloon at high altitudes
spectroscope	observes optical spectra
stauroscope	helps in the study of the crystal structure of minerals
stroboscope	helps in the adjustment of moving machine parts by making them appear stationary while operating
tachistoscope	tests perception and memory by displaying visual images very rapidly
tachograph	records speeds and times of use of vehicles
telethermoscope	indicates the temperatures of remote locations
thermostat	maintains a constant temperature
transponder	transmits information in response to a radio signal
zymoscope	monitors fermentation by recording the amount of carbon dioxide produced

SCOTTISH TERMS

ashet	serving dish	**peelie-wally**	sickly
bairn	child	**pibroch**	bagpipe dirge or war song
bawbee	halfpenny	**policy**	park of a large house
brae	hillside	**procurator fiscal**	coroner and public prosecutor
bubbly jock	turkey	**quaich**	drinking cup
burgh	town or borough	**sark**	shirt, short shift, or petticoat
burn	stream	**Sassenach**	English person; lowland Scot
ceilidh	social gathering	**shieling**	shepherd's hut
cotter, crofter	cottager and smallholder	**skean dhu**	dagger, worn in the stocking
dominie	schoolmaster	**skelp**	spank
gang	go	**sleekit**	crafty, sly
gillie/ ghillie	attendant of a hunter or angler	**sonsy**	plump
glaikit	stupid, bemused	**sporran**	pouch worn with a kilt
greet	weep	**stramash**	commotion
jo	sweetheart	**strath**	long, steep-sided, flat-bottomed valley, wider than a glen
jougs	iron collar for punishing offenders	**tawse**	leather strap
kelpie	malicious water sprite	**teuchter**	person from north-west Scotland; country bumpkin
ken	know	**thole**	endure, bear
kyle	narrow sea channel	**unco**	very; unusual
laird	landowner, owner of a country estate	**wheen**	a few
Lallans	lowland dialect	**wynd**	narrow lane
lum	chimney		
mod	cultural festival		

band in private, or similar private reproach CURTAIN LECTURE
– scolding, telling off REPROOF, WIGGING
– bridle with an iron bit formerly used to silence scolding women BRANKS

scope, extent, or range, as of a law or one's outlook PURVIEW, COMPASS
– scope for freedom of thought or action LATITUDE, LEEWAY
– scope of one's understanding, perception, or knowledge COGNISANCE
– scope or field of activity, sphere of expertise PRESERVE, DOMAIN, BAILIWICK, PROVINCE
– scope or range, reach, extent AMBIT, ORBIT, RADIUS
– acting or speaking beyond the scope of one's ability or expertise ULTRACREPIDARIAN

score – score-keeper in various sports MARKER
– score or reckoning, as in a game or account TALLY

scorn See **mock**, **ridicule**
– scorn or despise DISDAIN
– object or target of scorn LAUGHING-STOCK, BUTT, BYWORD

scornful, contemptuous, and reproachful, as a remark might be OPPROBRIOUS
– scornful, belittling, causing embarrassment, as a look or sarcasm might WITHERING
– scornful in a haughty way SUPERCILIOUS, DISDAINFUL
– scornful in a dismissive, belittling, or mocking way DISPARAGING, DERISIVE
– scornful in a mocking or cynical way SARDONIC
– scornful in an arrogant and overbearing way OVERWEENING; IMPERIOUS

scorpion – pincer-like claw of a scorpion CHELA

Scottish, relating to Scotland CALEDONIAN
– Scottish Highlander GAEL

scourge, flog, or whip, as for religious discipline or sexual gratification FLAGELLATE

scouring or cleansing, as a cleaning powder might be ABSTERGENT
– scouring substance for smoothing or cleaning ABRASIVE

scout or advance patroller OUTRIDER
– scout or sentry on horseback stationed ahead of an army's outposts VEDETTE
– scout out or survey a stretch of land, an enemy's positions, or the like RECONNOITRE, RECCE

Scout aged 16 to 20 belonging to the senior branch of the Scouts VENTURE SCOUT
– large gathering, especially of Scouts or Guides JAMBOREE
– ring of plaited leather used by Scouts and Guides to fasten their neck squares WOGGLE

scowl, frown, stare angrily GLOWER

scrape, grate, or file RASP
– scraping instrument used by ancient Greeks and Romans for cleaning the skin STRIGIL
– scraping or scouring substance, such as emery, used for cleaning or smoothing ABRASIVE

scraps or fragments, as of fabric ODDMENTS, OFFCUTS, REMNANTS

scratch about or feel around for with the hands, grope GRABBLE
– scratch or cut the skin slightly, as for vaccination SCARIFY
– scratch or graze something, such as a shoe SCUFF
– scratch or wear away, rub off, as by chafing ABRADE
– scratch the flesh deeply and jaggedly, tear roughly LACERATE

scream or howl in a loud, lamenting way, wail ULULATE
– scream shrilly, shriek like a cat in heat CATERWAUL
– hold back, cut off, or muffle a

scream, noise, or the like STIFLE

screech or cry, as of a cat in heat CATERWAUL

screen of rice-paper used as a sliding door or partition in a Japanese house SHOJI
- screen or shutter protecting a window from the sun in hot countries BRISE-SOLEIL
- screen used to conceal women, especially in India PURDAH

screenplay or shooting script for a film SCENARIO

screw – screw-like device within a tube, used in ancient times for raising water ARCHIMEDES' SCREW
- screw that is sunk so deep that its head lies flush with or below the surface COUNTERSUNK SCREW
- screw with a cross-shaped groove in the head PHILLIPS SCREW, CROSSHEAD SCREW, POZIDRIV SCREW
- screw with holes through the head, turned by a bar inserted through one of the holes CAPSTAN SCREW
- cut or finish the thread of a screw CHASE
- hollow plug, as of plastic, typically inserted into a hole in the wall as a mooring for a nail or screw RAWLPLUG
- hollow tool with an internal thread with cutting edges, used for cutting threads on screws DIE
- tool for cutting internal screw threads on nuts, pipes, sockets, and the like TAP
- width of the thread of a screw, or distance advanced by a screw in one full turn PITCH

screwdriver – sloping surface leading to the tip or cutting edge of a chisel, screwdriver, or other tool BEZEL
- tool serving as a screwdriver, consisting of a small bent metal bar whose tip fits into the six-sided recess in the head of special screws or bolts ALLEN KEY

scribbled messages or drawings, often witty or obscene, in public places, typically on walls GRAFFITI

scribe or copyist in former times SCRIVENER

script See diagram, page 452, and also **alphabets**

scriptural interpretation with a mystical emphasis, identifying spiritual symbols ANAGOGY

scriptures See also **bible**
- scriptures of Islam, containing Allah's revelations to Muhammad KORAN, QUR'AN, ALCORAN
- scriptures of the Sikh religion GRANTH
- scriptures of the Zoroastrian religion ZEND-AVESTA
- body of ancient rabbinical writings or scriptures, forming the basis of religious authority in orthodox Judaism TALMUD
- epic poems in Sanskrit, forming Hindu scriptures RAMAYANA, MAHABHARATA
- Hindu and Buddhist mystical scriptures, written in Sanskrit TANTRAS
- Hindu scriptures and holy verses from ancient times, gathered in four collections VEDAS
- Hindu scriptures that comment and build upon the four Vedas UPANISHADS
- first five books of the Old Testament, or the scroll used in a synagogue on which these scriptures are written TORAH

scroll – scroll-like or spiral shell, architectural ornament, or the like VOLUTE
- scroll-shaped TURBINAL
- scroll-shaped ornamental tablet of stone, plaster, or the like, sometimes carrying an inscription CARTOUCHE

scrubbing – sponge-like, fibrous interior of the dishcloth gourd, used for scrubbing the skin LOOFAH

sculpture See chart, page 453

scurvy – relating to scurvy, scurvy-like, or suffering from scurvy SCORBUTIC
- preventing or curing scurvy, as a medical drug might ANTISCORBUTIC

scythe – Death viewed as Father Time with his scythe GRIM REAPER
- path or strip, such as that left behind by a scythe or mower SWATH

sea See also **ship**
- sea, open ocean MAIN
- sea floor, especially when regarded as the grave of those who died at sea DAVY JONES'S LOCKER
- sea foam or froth SPUME
- sea inlet at the mouth of a river ESTUARY, FIRTH
- sea inlet that is long and narrow FJORD
- sea inlet, long and wide SOUND
- sea mist or cold fog as off the east coast of Scotland HAAR
- "sea" on the Moon MARE
- sea-wall or jetty jutting into the water to control erosion, direct a current, or the like BREAKWATER, GROYNE, MOLE, BULWARK
- sea water BRINE
- sea water separated from the sea, as by coral reefs LAGOON
- adjective for the sea MARINE, NAUTICAL, MARITIME
- backward pull in the sea caused by receding waves after breaking on the shore UNDERTOW
- bottom of the sea or of a deep lake BENTHOS
- cargo or wreckage floating on the sea after a ship has sunk FLOTSAM
- cargo thrown overboard at sea and washed ashore JETSAM
- cargo thrown overboard at sea but marked by buoys to locate it later LAGAN
- flat stretch of ground for walking along, especially along a sea shore ESPLANADE
- floating or drifting mass of tiny animal or plant organisms at or near the surface of the sea or a lake PLANKTON
- fresh, invigorating sea air OZONE
- humorously informal term for the sea THE BRINY, BRINY DEEP
- large expanse of sea partially enclosed by land GULF
- narrow strip of land, as for allowing an inland country access to the sea CORRIDOR
- narrow strip of land extending into the sea from the mainland PENINSULA
- narrow waterway linking two seas or other large bodies of water STRAIT
- pebbles or coarse gravel along a seashore SHINGLE
- person inexperienced at sailing or unsuited to life at sea LANDLUBBER
- relating to or inhabiting the sea MARINE, PELAGIC, THALASSIC
- remove salt, as from sea water DESALINATE
- ridge of land, usually with cliffs, jutting into the sea PROMONTORY
- rise and fall with a strong regular rhythm, as waves do in the open sea SURGE, HEAVE, SWELL
- without access to the sea, as some countries are LANDLOCKED

sea- HAL-, HALO-

sea anemone coral, or related creature, typically tube-like and with tentacles POLYP
- sea anemone, sponge, or similar plant-like animal ZOOPHYTE, ANTHOZOAN
- arm-like flexible projection near the mouth of a squid, sea anemone, or the like TENTACLE

sea horse in mythology, having a horse's front legs and a fish's tail HIPPOCAMPUS

seafood See **fish**

seal a boat, pipe, or the like by packing the seams or cracks with a filler CAULK

scripts

INTERUOS CON
DENS UNUS DE

uncial

insular half uncial

cursive minuscule

Ceteraq: librorum nonparuam
tiam. quandointerfedicuntur
etricesimo anno temporib; pro

Caroline minuscule/Carolingian minuscule

Gothic/black letter

cauit interualla ramorum amplitudinis ratio
umbrę cuiusque arboris quoniam has quoque

humanistic

secretary

Governor, Deputy-Governor, and Directors
Of the Bank of England.

copperplate

– seal between lengths of piping, machine parts, or the like, to prevent the escape of gas or liquid GASKET
– seal-like mammal with small paddle-like forelimbs MANATEE
– seal on a document in former times CACHET
– seal on a papal bull BULLA
– seal the seams of a wooden ship, as with tar or pitch PAY
– seal or enclose an area, as with a line of troops CORDON OFF
– seal or sealed impression as used on official documents SIGNET
– sealed, air-tight HERMETIC
– sealing material of cement and clay LUTE, LUTING
– adjective for a seal or related animal PHOCINE
– document under a sovereign's seal in former times, typically authorising imprisonment without trial LETTRE DE CACHET
– group of female seals that are the mates of an individual male seal HAREM
– group or colony of seals, or their breeding ground ROOKERY
– group or school of seals POD
– royal seal on documents GREAT SEAL, PRIVY SEAL
– strip a whale, seal, or the like of its skin or blubber FLENCH, FLENSE
– study of seals and signet rings SPHRAGISTICS

seam or joint-line, as on a seedpod or between the bones of the skull SUTURE
– double seam with the raw edges inside it FRENCH SEAM
– finish a seam by stitching on a strip of material WELT
– fold in and stitch flat the raw edges of a seam FELL

seaplane or its broad float HYDROPLANE
– float supporting a seaplane PONTOON

search a person, as for concealed weapons, typically using quick hand movements FRISK
– search for food or provisions, as by scouring the country FORAGE
– search for something, such as an explanation, without much hope CAST ABOUT FOR
– search for something in an unmethodical way RUMMAGE, FOSSICK
– search intensely and thoroughly, inquire deeply DELVE, PROBE
– search the bed of a river, lake, or canal by trailing a grappling hook or net along it DRAG
– search through and examine closely to separate the good from the bad, sift WINNOW

– search through rubbish for food or useful objects SCAVENGE
– search for senior employees from other firms HEADHUNTING
– close examination or search, as by careful reading PERUSAL, SCRUTINY
– expedition made in search of something FORAY
– judicial writ, as for authorising a search or arrest WARRANT
– make a preliminary search or survey of an area RECONNOITRE
– object of a long search GRAIL
– solve a problem, penetrate a mystery, or the like, by painstaking searching or research FATHOM

seasick, queasy, or dizzy WOOZY
– seasickness MAL DE MER
– seasickness or similar queasy feeling preceding vomiting NAUSEA

season or time of year when hunting, fishing, shooting of game, or the like is permitted OPEN SEASON
– season or time of year when hunting, fishing, or the like is prohibited CLOSE SEASON

seasonings See **herbs**

seat extending across a small boat, typically for an oarsman THWART
– seat in a military aircraft designed to hurl the pilot or crew member clear in an emergency EJECTION SEAT, EJECTOR SEAT
– seat or saddle for a second rider, as on a horse or motorcycle PILLION
– seat that folds down, as in a taxi or aircraft JUMP SEAT
– seats facing each other by or beside a large fireplace INGLENOOK
– open-air and inexpensive rows of seats, especially in a U.S. sports stadium BLEACHERS
– luggage compartment or folding seat at the rear of some early motor cars DICKEY, RUMBLE SEAT
– row of seats in a rising series TIER

seat belt that allows free movement except when jerked suddenly INERTIA-REEL SEAT BELT
– tape or strong woven strip of cotton or nylon, as used for seat belts WEBBING

seaweed ash used as a source of iodine and potash KELP, VAREC
– seaweeds and other primitive water-dwelling plants ALGAE
– brown seaweed of various kinds, whose ash is a source of iodine KELP, OARWEED, TANGLE, FUCOID, FUCUS
– brownish seaweed floating in large masses in tropical Atlantic waters GULFWEED, SARGASSO
– edible seaweed of various kinds LAVER, BADDERLOCKS, DULSE
– fried seaweed dish eaten in Wales LAVER BREAD
– jelly-like substance prepared from certain seaweeds, used as a laxative, food thickener, and medium for bacteria cultures AGAR
– mass of seaweed on the shore or floating on the sea WRACK
– plant body, as of seaweeds, that is not differentiated into stem, branches, and roots THALLUS
– purple seaweed yielding a carbohydrate extract used in making ice-cream, jellies, and soft drinks CARRAGEEN, IRISH MOSS
– stalk, as of a mushroom or a

SCULPTURE TERMS

alabaster	marble-like stone, usually white
anaglyph	carving or ornament in basrelief
armature	frame used to support clay, wax, or plaster in modelling
atlas, telamon	male statue used as a column, as in an ancient Greek temple
banker	sculptor's workbench
basrelief, basso-relievo, low relief	sculpture in which the figures project only slightly from the background
calvary	representation of the Crucifixion
cameo	small basrelief carving in stone, glass, or shell, the design in relief being a different colour from the background
caryatid	female statue used as a column, as in an ancient Greek temple
chryselephantine	made or decorated with gold and ivory, as ancient Greek statues were
cire perdue, lost-wax process	technique in bronze casting in which the wax layer between core and mould is melted away and replaced by bronze
corbeil	sculpture of a basket of fruit or flowers, used as an architectural ornament
diaglyph	carving or ornament in intaglio
gesso	mixture of plaster of Paris or gypsum and glue, used as a base for basrelief or to prepare a painting surface
intaglio	carving in which the design is cut into the surface, the opposite of relief
kore	ancient Greek female statue, usually draped
kouros	ancient Greek male statue, usually nude
mantle	clay mould around a wax model
maquette, bozzetto	preliminary model for a sculpture
mobile	abstract construction with parts that move when pushed or blown
pietà	representation of Mary with the body of Jesus
putto, amorino	figure of a small child or cherub
relief, relievo	sculpture in which the figures half project from a flat background
restrike	impression taken from a sculptor's mould at some time after the original edition
spall	chip broken from a stone carving
stabile	construction resembling a mobile in appearance, but partly stationary

frond of fern or seaweed STIPE

second – second hand on a watch or clock SWEEP-SECOND HAND
– second prize, or person who nearly wins an academic prize or other award PROXIME ACCESSIT
– second self, another side to oneself ALTER EGO

second- DEUT-, DEUTO-, DEUTERO-

second-hand or indirect, as pleasure is when gained through someone else's achievements or actions VICARIOUS

second-last, last but one PENULTIMATE

second-year student at a U.S. university, college, or high school SOPHOMORE

secondary, accompanying or associated rather than central AFFILIATED, APPENDANT, ATTENDANT, ACCESSORY, APPURTENANT, CONCOMITANT
– secondary, having a helping or enabling rather than central function AUXILIARY, ANCILLARY
– secondary, less important SUBORDINATE, COLLATERAL, INCIDENTAL
– secondary or lower in rank or status SUBSIDIARY, SUBSERVIENT, SUBALTERN
– secondary remark or action AFTERTHOUGHT, FOOTNOTE, POSTSCRIPT

secondary- BY-, SUB-

secret, as official information or documents might be CLASSIFIED
– secret, hidden SUBTERRANEAN, COVERT
– secret, hidden, or secluded places RECESSES, FASTNESSES
– secret, mysterious, known or understood only by those who have made a special study or been initiated ARCANE, ESOTERIC, OCCULT, CRYPTIC
– secret, private, very personal INTIMATE
– secret agent who joins a political or criminal group and tries to incite it into punishable or discrediting activities AGENT PROVOCATEUR
– secret agreement for sinister or illegal purposes COLLUSION, CONNIVANCE
– secret and hidden, and often probably illegal CLANDESTINE, FURTIVE, BACKSTAIR, HOLE-AND-CORNER
– secret and stealthy, as political manoeuvring might be SURREPTITIOUS, HUGGER-MUGGER
– secret entry into or establishment in an organisation, region, or the like, as by spies or enemy troops INFILTRATION
– secret group or committee as of plotters CABAL, JUNTO
– secret information, especially about an enemy, as obtained by spies INTELLIGENCE
– secret meeting or appointment, especially between lovers ASSIGNATION
– secret or in private, especially relating to a court hearing from which the public has been excluded IN CAMERA
– secret or mystical philosophy, specifically one based on the Hebrew scriptures CABALA
– secret store of money, drugs, or the like STASH
– secret thought or intention that is deliberately held back ARRIÈRE-PENSÉE
– secret weapon to pull out when all else has failed TRUMP CARD
– secret writing system or code in which letters are substituted according to a key CIPHER
– secretive, done or carried out in a stealthy or underhand manner SURREPTITIOUS, FURTIVE
– secretly, in confidence SUB ROSA
– secretly, in disguise or under an assumed name, to avoid being recognised INCOGNITO
– secretly or stealthily harmful, treacherous INSIDIOUS
– announcement of some new information or secret fact REVELATION, DISCLOSURE
– bring a secret or obscure information to light DISINTER
– done or acting in secret UNDERCOVER
– done or told in secret, private, hush-hush CONFIDENTIAL
– knowing something secret or private PRIVY
– person to whom one tells one's secrets or private worries CONFIDANT, CONFIDANTE
– place for depositing secret letters, stolen goods, or the like for collection DROP
– reveal some private or secret information DISCLOSE, DIVULGE
– security classification for documents, less tight than secret RESTRICTED
– uncommunicative, keeping or appearing to be keeping secrets TACITURN, CLOSE

secret- CRYPT-, CRYPTO-

secret service, secret police, or intelligence agency of the USSR, in its various forms prior to the KGB CHEKA, GPU, OGPU, NKVD, MVD
– secret service and private police force under the former Duvalier dictatorship in the Caribbean state of Haiti TONTONS MACOUTE
– secret service department of the KGB, used to eliminate spies overseas SMERSH
– secret service of France SDECE, SERVICE DE DOCUMENTATION EXTERIEURE ET CONTRE-ESPIONAGE
– secret service of Israel MOSSAD
– secret service or security police in Nazi Germany GESTAPO
– military secret service in the USSR, covering international intelligence GRU

secret society of French settlers in Algeria opposed to Algerian independence OAS, ORGANISATION DE L'ARMÉE SECRÈTE
– secret society in China at the turn of the century that sought to drive out foreigners BOXERS
– secret society of prominent Afrikaners in South Africa, promoting Afrikaner interests BROEDERBOND
– body of people joined in a religious order, guild, secret society, or the like FRATERNITY
– Chinese secret society, often engaged in criminal activities TONG
– criminal secret society in the U.S., probably closely linked with the Mafia COSA NOSTRA
– fanatical Muslim secret society that preyed upon Christian Crusaders ASSASSINS
– French secret society that organised underground resistance to the Germans during the Second World War MAQUIS
– international charitable and quasi-religious secret society FREEMASONS, MASONS
– international Chinese secret society, often engaged in drug trafficking TRIAD
– Kenyan secret society of Kikuyu tribesmen that used terrorism in the 1950s to end white colonial rule MAU MAU
– liberal and republican German secret society of the 18th century ILLUMINATI, ILLUMINATEN
– member of a Japanese secret society similar to the Mafia YAKUZA
– members of a 17th-18th century religious secret society, claiming to have mystical knowledge, or of a modern society descended from it ROSICRUCIANS
– Neapolitan secret society, similar to the Mafia CAMORRA
– notorious secret society of racist white supremacists in the U.S. KU KLUX KLAN
– Sicilian criminal secret society active in the U.S. in the early 20th century BLACK HAND

secretary or official clerk SCRIBE

– secretary or scribe who takes dictation or makes neat copies of documents AMANUENSIS
– secretary to a king or nobleman in former times CHANCELLOR
section See **part**
– section, as of a text or recital, that is more striking or elaborate than the rest PURPLE PATCH, PURPLE PASSAGE
– section of a document, contract, law, or the like CLAUSE
secular, lay, or civil rather than spiritual or religious TEMPORAL
secure See **safe**, **tight**, **join**
security classification for documents, less tight than secret RESTRICTED
– security in the form of a deposit or pledge GAGE
– security issued by a government and considered a safe investment GILT, GILT-EDGED SECURITY
– security or guarantor against loss or damage SURETY
– security pledged for a loan COLLATERAL
– pledge or mortgage something as security HYPOTHECATE
– something giving security or emotional stability MOORING
sediment of fine sand deposited in or by a river SILT
– sediment of wine, cider, or the like DREGS, LEES
seduce or corrupt someone, especially someone young and innocent DEBAUCH
– man who pursues and seduces women regularly, playboy DON JUAN, CASANOVA, LADYKILLER, LOTHARIO
see See also **look**
– see, catch sight of, especially when on the lookout DETECT, DISCERN, DESCRY
– "see above", term directing a reader to consult an earlier passage VIDE SUPRA
– "see below", term directing a reader to consult a later passage VIDE INFRA
– see clearly, make out, notice distinctly DISTINGUISH
– see in the mind's eye, imagine, fancy VISUALISE, ENVISION
– see or glimpse something elusive or far away, catch sight of ESPY
– see or hear, observe clearly PERCEIVE, REMARK, WITNESS
– see the point of, understand, grasp APPREHEND, PENETRATE
seed See also **flower**
– seed coat, animal skin, or similar natural covering INTEGUMENT
– seed-eating, feeding on seeds or grain GRANIVOROUS
– seed-eating, feeding on seeds or grass GRAMINIVOROUS
– seed leaf, a simple food-storing leaf in some sprouting seeds COTYLEDON
– seed or pip of a grape or berry ACINUS
– seed or pod of the pea, bean, or related plant LEGUME
– seed pod of cotton, flax, or similar plants BOLL
– seed used as an aromatic flavouring in cooking and baking, as in rye bread CARAWAY
– seeds of a leguminous plant such as lentils PULSES
– begin to grow, as seeds do GERMINATE
– casing of a seed or seeds of a fruit, developed from the plant's ovary PERICARP
– cut or soften the coat of a hard seed to speed up germination SCARIFY
– embryonic seed of a plant, prior to fertilisation OVULE
– furrow or implement for planting seeds DRILL
– having two wing-like projections, as some seeds have DIPTEROUS
– lightweight fragments of mica-derived material used in seed-beds and for insulation VERMICULITE
– part of a seedling plant between the cotyledons and the radical HYPOCOTYL
– part of the seed that develops into the main root RADICLE
– part of the seed that develops into the shoot or stem PLUMULE
– referring to or producing seeds that germinate while still attached to the parent plant VIVIPAROUS
– relating to seeds SEMINAL
– reproductive cell or organ, the counterpart of a seed, in non-flowering plants such as mosses, ferns, and fungi SPORE
– scar on the coat of a bean or other seed, marking the point where it was joined to the stalk HILUM, UMBILICUS
– seam or joint-line, as on a seed-pod or between the bones of the skull SUTURE
– seam or raised ridge on the coat of some seeds RAPHE
– small, flattish seed used for flavouring food, often sprinkled on bread rolls SESAME, BENNE
– sow seed over a wide area, typically by hand BROADCAST
– split or burst open along a seam, as a pod or fruit might, to release seeds or pollen DEHISCE
– stalk connecting a seed to the wall of the ovary FUNICLE
– swelling or fleshy outgrowth on the coat of a seed CARUNCLE
– thick hard outer coat of a seed TESTA
– thin delicate inner coat of a seed TEGMEN
– thin membrane covering a seed or other plant part TUNIC
– tiny opening in a plant ovule through which the pollen tube can enter to produce a fertilised seed MICROPYLE
– tissue surrounding and feeding the embryo in the seed of a flowering plant ENDOSPERM
– tray of soil in which seeds or cuttings are grown PROPAGATOR
– tuft of hairs on the seed coat of some seeds COMA
-seed- -SPERM-, -GON-, GONO-, GRANI-
seed vessel- ANGIO-
seeing or knowing things by supposedly superhuman or telepathic means CLAIRVOYANCE
– seeing or showing everything PANOPTIC
seek See **search**
-seeking -PETAL
seem, *be*, *feel*, or similar verb that identifies the predicate of a verb with the subject COPULA
seeming, apparent, but usually just pretended, as someone's alleged purpose might be PURPORTED, PROFESSED
– seeming, apparent, outward, as a given reason might be OSTENSIBLE
– seeming change in the position of an object when the observer changes position PARALLAX
– seemingly, apparently, supposedly REPUTEDLY
– seemingly attractive, genuine, or sound, but not really so SPECIOUS
– seemingly but not really, in name only NOMINALLY
seemingly- QUASI-
seesaw, balance precariously TEETER
– seesaw-like bridge or roadway, hinged near a weighted end so as to be raised or lowered BASCULE
– arm of a seesaw, or other extension from a fulcrum CANTILEVER
seize, conquer, or occupy territory, and incorporate it into another state or an empire ANNEX
– seize, interrupt, or stop something, such as a message, in its course INTERCEPT
– seize and kill without trial an alleged offender, as an impassioned mob might LYNCH
– seize at customs IMPOUND, EMBARGO
– seize by force and hold illegally the power, rights, throne, or the like of another USURP

– seize or take possession, especially under wartime regulations COMMANDEER
– seize or take temporary possession of someone's property, as to force payment of a debt DISTRAIN, DISTRESS, SEQUESTRATE
– seize someone's property as an official penalty APPROPRIATE, CONFISCATE
– seizing property by force PILLAGE, RAPINE
– seizure of a neutral ship in wartime SPOLIATION

-seizure, -fit -LEPSY

select See **choose**

selection of literary passages, as used for studying a foreign language CHRESTOMATHY
– selections from a literary work or works ANALECTS

self – another side to oneself, a second self ALTER EGO
– relating to or arising from the individual self or mind rather than external reality SUBJECTIVE
– theory that the self is the only knowable reality SOLIPSISM

self- – self-assured, poised, not embarrassed UNABASHED
– self-confessed, openly acknowledged by oneself, candidly admitted AVOWED, PROFESSED
– self-confidence, assured manner COMPOSURE, POISE, APLOMB
– self-confident and self-assertive, pushy BUMPTIOUS
– self-contradictory or apparently absurd statement that is not necessarily untrue PARADOX
– self-control, ability to keep one's temper COUNTENANCE, COMPOSURE
– self-control or restraint, such as sexual restraint CONTINENCE
– self-defence techniques, such as kung-fu and karate MARTIAL ARTS
– self-denial, especially restraint in eating and drinking ABSTINENCE, ABSTEMIOUSNESS, TEMPERANCE
– self-denying, living a strict life, with minimum comforts and pleasures, often for religious reasons ASCETIC
– self-destructive or suicidal person, especially when part of a larger group LEMMING
– self-evident, obvious AXIOMATIC
– self-evident or self-confirming, as a proposition in logic might be ANALYTIC, A PRIORI
– self-examination, reflection on one's feelings or motives HEART-SEARCHING, INTROSPECTION
– self-generated, apparently uncaused SPONTANEOUS
– self-government, independence SOVEREIGNTY, AUTONOMY
– self-importance in a minor official OFFICIOUSNESS, BUMBLEDOM
– self-indulgence in immoral or sensual pursuits DISSIPATION, DISSOLUTION, INTEMPERANCE, DEBAUCHERY, DEPRAVITY
– self-indulgent or luxuriously sensual living FLESHPOTS
– self-indulgent, decadent, self-absorbed EFFETE
– self-interest, advantageous rather than fair behaviour EXPEDIENCY
– self-love or excessive admiration of oneself NARCISSISM
– self-opinionated and reactionary man, especially an officer or bureaucrat COLONEL BLIMP
– self-persuasion, either conscious or unconscious AUTOSUGGESTION
– self-reflecting, turned back upon the source, as thoughts might be REFLEXIVE
– self-reliance as a government policy, or a self-sufficient territory or country AUTARKY
– self-respect, appropriate pride in oneself, sense of one's own worth and dignity AMOUR-PROPRE
– self-righteous, holier-than-thou MORALISTIC, SANCTIMONIOUS
– self-righteous or puritanically disapproving, usually in a hypocritical way PHARISAICAL
– self-sacrifice or self-denial ABNEGATION
– self-taught person AUTODIDACT
– self-satisfied, narrow-minded, and arrogant person PRIG
– self-satisfied or smug, to the point of feeling that nothing more needs to be done COMPLACENT
– self-seeking, largely or purely self-interested EGOISTIC
– self-service meal in which the dishes are all placed on a counter or table BUFFET, SMORGASBORD
– having great self-discipline, fortitude, and endurance SPARTAN
– indulge oneself luxuriously, as in sensual pleasures or self-pity REVEL, WALLOW
– universal life-enhancing drive or instinct for self-preservation, in Freudian theory EROS
– universal death-wish or instinct for self-destruction, in Freudian theory THANATOS

self- AUT-, AUTO-

self-important See **pompous**

selfish, self-centred EGOCENTRIC
– selfish, self-seeking, intent only on increasing one's own power or status SELF-AGGRANDISING
– selfishly advantageous rather than fair or moral EXPEDIENT

selfless, concerned for others' welfare ALTRUISTIC

sell assets for cash, as to pay off debts LIQUIDATE
– sell goods in the street or while travelling from place to place VEND, PEDDLE, HAWK
– sell in a forceful way HUSTLE
– sell or give away DISPOSE OF
– sell or transfer the ownership of documents, shares, or the like NEGOTIATE
– selling and buying, especially of disreputable goods such as drugs TRAFFICKING
– selling of goods in a foreign country cheaply, often at below cost price DUMPING
– selling of unsolicited goods by demanding payment from those recipients who fail to send them back INERTIA SELLING
– selling system in which the goods are sold in turn to several agents or distributors before going on retail sale PYRAMID SELLING
– selling through advertising, exhibitions, and other techniques MERCHANDISING
– do business, buy, sell TRANSACT
– foil a would-be buyer by raising the price of a property between agreeing to sell and signing the contract GAZUMP

seller, specifically the seller of a house or flat VENDOR
– seller of bibles, sermons, and the like in former times COLPORTEUR
– seller of cloth and sewing materials DRAPER
– seller of food or goods from a barrow or market stall COSTERMONGER
– seller of goods in the street or door-to-door HAWKER, PEDLAR, HUCKSTER
– seller of provisions who accompanied an army in former times SUTLER
– seller of quack remedies, as in the Wild West MOUNTEBANK
– seller of sewing and dressmaking accessories HABERDASHER
– seller or manufacturer of candles CHANDLER
– seller or manufacturer of socks and knitted underwear HOSIER
– seller or provider of food, such as a wholesale grocer PURVEYOR, PROVISIONER

-seller -MONGER

semen – glandular tissue at the base of the bladder in men, secreting the fluid for semen PROSTATE
– impregnate with semen INSEMINATE
– person or animal that provides semen for artificial insemination DONOR

- sudden discharge of semen EJACULATION

semi-consciousness, especially as a result of anaesthetics TWILIGHT SLEEP

semi-precious stones See **precious and semi-precious stones**

send away or withdraw troops or inhabitants from a place of danger EVACUATE
- send money, as through the post REMIT
- send out or give off something, such as radiation EMIT, EMANATE
- send to a particular destination DISPATCH
- hand over goods to someone to send or deliver CONSIGN

senile person DOTARD
- senility DOTAGE

senior or eldest member of a group, society, diplomatic circle, or the like DOYEN, DOYENNE

sensation in one part of the body produced by stimulation in another SYNAESTHESIA

sensational, macabre, or gruesome, often in a deliberately artificial way GRAND-GUIGNOL
- sensationalising journals and newspapers YELLOW PRESS

sense See **meaning**

senseless and irresponsible, as a wild spree might be INSENSATE

senses, such as sight, smell, and touch MODALITIES
- sensing cell, nerve, organ, or the like RECEPTOR
- sensing or perceiving by means of a sixth sense TELAESTHESIA
- detectable by any of the senses PERCEPTIBLE
- doctrine that all true knowledge derives from experience, especially from sense perceptions EMPIRICISM
- object or experience perceived by or apparently real to the senses, rather than known through reasoning or intuition PHENOMENON
- object or experience that is known through reasoning or intuition rather than perceived by the senses, thing in itself NOUMENON

sensitive, delicate, capable of or based on fine distinctions SUBTLE
- sensitive emotionally, easily affected SUSCEPTIBLE, VULNERABLE, THIN-SKINNED
- sensitive part, as of one's nails or emotions QUICK
- sensitive to emotion or suffering, able to feel PASSIBLE

sensory organs or feelers near the mouth, as in some insects and shellfish PALPS, PALPI
- sensory organs or feelers on the head of an insect, shellfish, or the like ANTENNAE
- sensory organs or feelers on the head of the catfish and some other fishes BARBELS

sensual, luxurious, and self-indulgent living FLESHPOTS
- sensual over-indulgence, especially in immoral pursuits DISSIPATION, INTEMPERANCE, DISSOLUTION, DEBAUCHERY, DEPRAVITY
- sensualist, person devoted to luxurious living and the sensual pleasures VOLUPTUARY, SYBARITE, HEDONIST

sentence, name, or the like that is difficult to pronounce or to say quickly TONGUE-TWISTER
- sentence containing every letter of the alphabet, such as *The quick brown fox jumps over the lazy dog* PANGRAM
- sentence-formation through joining phrases or clauses with punctuation rather than conjunctions PARATAXIS
- sentence-formation in which subordinating clauses are joined by conjunctions HYPOTAXIS
- sentence in which the completion of the main clause comes right at the end PERIODIC SENTENCE
- sentence in which there is a sudden change to a second, inconsistent grammatical pattern ANACOLUTHON
- sentence or utterance that is very short or curt, specifically one of a single syllable MONOSYLLABLE
- sentence stating the main idea in a paragraph, often placed at the beginning TOPIC SENTENCE
- sentence with several carefully arranged clauses PERIOD
- being or referring to a subordinate clause within a sentence EMBEDDED
- break down a sentence into its component parts of speech and give a grammatical explanation of these PARSE
- breaking off speech or writing in mid-sentence, for dramatic effect APOSIOPESIS
- phrase or clause, group of words forming part of a sentence CONSTRUCTION
- prison sentence or detention order, imposed by a court CUSTODIAL SENTENCE
- prison sentence that is served only in the event of a subsequent conviction SUSPENDED SENTENCE
- prison sentence whose length is not specified at the time it is imposed INDETERMINATE SENTENCE
- reduction of the length of a prison sentence, as for good behaviour REMISSION
- reduce to a lighter prison sentence, penalty, or the like COMMUTE
- release of a prisoner before the full completion of his sentence, on condition of good behaviour PAROLE
- running simultaneously, as two prison sentences might be CONCURRENT
- suspending of an offender's prison sentence subject to good behaviour and submission to supervision PROBATION

sentimental, excessively romantic, gushing or soppy NOVELETTISH
- sentimental about things of the past, especially about a previous home NOSTALGIC
- sentimental and clichéd material, as in a film or play HOKUM
- sentimental and pretentious art KITSCH
- sentimental in a cheap or vulgar way, mushy MAUDLIN, MAWKISH
- sentimental in a weak, affected way, as manners or poetry might be NAMBY-PAMBY
- sentimentality, as in art and music SCHMALTZ
- sentimentally affecting or touching POIGNANT
- sentimentally or excessively sweet, polite, or friendly SACCHARINE, CLOYING
- sentimentally or pretentiously quaint or pretty TWEE

sentry, guard SENTINEL
- sentry on horseback stationed ahead of an army or formation on the move VEDETTE

separate See also **divide**
- separate, disconnect, remove without breaking DETACH, DISJOIN, DISLODGE
- separate, distinct, or individual DIVERSE
- separate, remove, or distance, as when distancing oneself from a decision DISSOCIATE
- separate, unconnected, individual, distinct DISCRETE
- separate and move in different directions from a point DIVERGE, DIVARICATE
- separate from the surrounding environment INSULATE, ISOLATE, CORDON OFF
- separate grain or seed from the stems and husks by means of wind WINNOW
- separate grain or seed from the stems and husks by means of beating THRESH, FLAIL

– separate into sections, divide up PARTITION, DISMEMBER, FRAGMENT, SEGMENT
– separate into small or basic parts DECOMPOSE, DISINTEGRATE
– separate multiple copies, continuous stationery, or the like into individual documents DECOLLATE
– separate or divide into branches, fork BIFURCATE, RAMIFY
– separate or divide into different classes, categories, or the like PIGEON-HOLE, COMPARTMENTALISE
– separate or extract an essence, idea, or the like DISTIL
– separate, remove, or take out as for special attention or treatment PRESCIND
– separate or remove from others or from an entire group SEGREGATE
– separate or scatter, as troops might after a defeat DISBAND
– separate someone from his environment, especially to prevent spread of a disease QUARANTINE
– separated, divided, split CLEFT, CLOVEN, ASUNDER
– separated, remote, lonely, solitary, as a place or life might be SECLUDED, SEQUESTERED, CLOISTERED
– separated or unfriendly through having been offended or antagonised ESTRANGED, ALIENATED
– come between, as to separate people fighting INTERPOSE, INTERVENE

-separate- DIA-, -SECT

separately, apart, in pieces PIECEMEAL
– separately or severally, in the order stated RESPECTIVELY

separation into constituent parts or elements RESOLUTION
– separation of a chemical mixture into its components, as on the basis of different boiling points FRACTIONATION
– separation or classification into two parts, such as conflicting opinions DICHOTOMY

separation- AP-, APO-

sequence of those in line for a title or throne SUCCESSION
– sequence or order of priority, based on rank, as at public ceremonies PRECEDENCE
– arrange something, such as pages, in the correct sequence COLLATE, COLLOCATE
– change or reverse the sequence or relative positioning of two or more things TRANSPOSE
– lacking an orderly arrangement or sequence HAPHAZARD, RANDOM, ARBITRARY
– ordered, in sequence, successive, serial SEQUENTIAL, CONSECUTIVE
– put into sequence, systematise CODIFY, TABULATE
– rearrangment, shuffling, change of sequence PERMUTATION

serf See **peasant**
– serf in ancient Sparta HELOT
– serf in Russia in tsarist times MUZHIK

sergeant, corporal, or other serviceman with some authority but without an official appointment NON-COMMISSIONED OFFICER

serial, successive, ordered SEQUENTIAL, CONSECUTIVE
– broadcast of a week's episodes of a serial previously broadcast separately OMNIBUS EDITION
– episode of a serial INSTALMENT

series, as of electrical components CASCADE
– series, full range or extent, from the beginning to the end, as of musical notes GAMUT
– series, unbroken chain of events, office-holders, or the like SUCCESSION, PROGRESSION, SEQUENCE
– series graded according to rank or importance HIERARCHY
– series of changes without any obvious divisions CONTINUUM, SPECTRUM, CLINE
– series of events in which each causes or influences the one following CHAIN REACTION
– series of linked events, ideas, terms, or the like CONCATENATION, CATENATION
– series of steps, stages, degrees, or the like, a gradual progression GRADATION
– series of things occurring or used together and forming a unit SUITE
– series of tunes played as a single piece of music MEDLEY
– one after another in sequence, item by item in series SERIATIM

serious, deep, and sincere, as desires might be FERVENT, HEARTFELT
– serious, critically important MOMENTOUS, CONSEQUENTIAL
– serious, determined, meaning business RESOLUTE, INTENT
– serious, dignified, earnest, sober in manner STAID, SEDATE
– serious, grim, grave, unsmiling, solemn SOMBRE, POKER-FACED
– serious, intense, very dangerous, as a hardship or shortage might be DRASTIC, ACUTE, GRIEVOUS
– serious and dutiful hard work DILIGENCE, ASSIDUITY, CONSCIENTIOUSNESS, APPLICATION
– serious or solemn manner, bearing, or quality GRAVITAS, GRAVITY
– intensify, make something more serious, such as an error or anxiety COMPOUND
– keeping a straight face or being apparently serious, as when telling a joke DEADPAN
– lightness or frivolity of manner, especially when seriousness would be more appropriate LEVITY
– make something more serious or severe, such as a pain or difficulty EXACERBATE
– represent a crime, fault, or the like as less serious or blameworthy, as by making certain excuses EXTENUATE, MITIGATE
– thoughtful, serious, or reflective PENSIVE, INTROSPECTIVE

sermon making practical suggestions HOMILY
– sermon or similar formal discussion of a topic DISCOURSE
– fable or moral story, as used in medieval sermons EXEMPLUM

servant, assistant, or private secretary of a scholar, magician, or the like in former times FAMULUS
– servant, attendant, or disciple ACOLYTE, VARLET
– servant, attendant, or minor official in a royal or noble household in former times YEOMAN
– servant, employee, or assistant with varied duties FACTOTUM
– servant, usually a young foreign girl, employed to help with children and domestic chores AU PAIR
– servant acting as a steward or administrator of a landed estate BAILIFF, FACTOR, REEVE
– servant employed as a driver CHAUFFEUR, CHAUFFEUSE
– servant employed to breast-feed her employer's baby WET NURSE
– servant of long-standing service with a particular family or household RETAINER
– servant or official formerly employed to carry out the orders of a magistrate or judge APPARITOR
– servant or porter carrying baggage or supplies, especially on an arduous journey BEARER, SHERPA
– servant or stableman in former times who took care of horses, as at a coaching inn OSTLER
– servant who cares for or supervises the horses GROOM
– servant who supervised the serving of meals in medieval times SEWER
– servant whose work is within a house rather than in the gardens, stables, or the like DOMESTIC
– adjective for a servant MENIAL
– boy or young man employed at a hotel, club, or the like as a messenger or general junior servant

PAGE, BUTTONS, BELLHOP
– boy servant at an inn in former times POT BOY
– boy servant in former times who cleaned shoes BOOTBLACK, BOOTS
– boy servant in Ireland GOSSOON
– castrated male servant in a harem EUNUCH
– college servant in some British universities, looking after students' rooms GYP, SCOUT, BEDDER, SKIP
– devil or spirit acting as servant to a witch or magician FAMILIAR
– female attendant or servant in former times HANDMAID
– female servant in the East, especially a nursemaid AMAH
– female servant who cleans, makes beds, and the like in a hotel or similar establishment CHAMBER MAID, FEMME DE CHAMBRE
– group of servants or employees in attendance upon a person or household RETINUE, TRAIN, SUITE
– high-ranking servant or steward in a royal or noble household in former times CHAMBERLAIN, SENESCHAL
– highest-ranking male servant in a household BUTLER, MAJOR DOMO
– Indian male domestic servant WALLAH
– Indian male servant acting as stableman or groom SYCE
– Indian nursemaid or female domestic servant AYAH
– Indian or Chinese labourer or outdoor servant, especially in former times COOLIE
– junior employee or low-ranking servant in a large organisation MINION, VASSAL
– junior schoolboy who acts as servant to a senior boy in some public schools FAG
– knight's attendant or personal servant in former times SQUIRE, ESQUIRE, VARLET
– lady's maid, personal servant of a woman ABIGAIL, FEMME DE CHAMBRE, TIREWOMAN
– liveried servant in former times who ran messages and accompanied his employer on outings FOOTMAN, CHASSEUR
– low-ranking servant of various kinds, performing menial kitchen tasks or lowly domestic duties SCULLION, SKIVVY, SLAVEY, DOGSBODY, TWEENY
– man's personal servant VALET, VALET DE CHAMBRE
– male servant or employee with numerous duties and responsibilities MAN FRIDAY, FACTOTUM
– male servant such as a footman, especially one dressed in a uniform FLUNKY, LACKEY
– person who fetches and carries, runs errands, and is generally treated as a servant GOFER
– personal servant of a military officer BATMAN
– personal servant or employee performing various secretarial tasks AMANUENSIS
– trusted female servant who acts as governess or chaperone to the daughters of the family, especially as formerly in Spanish-speaking countries DUENNA

service or assistance MINISTRATIONS
– services or features of a place that are convenient and helpful FACILITIES, AMENITIES

service industry TERTIARY INDUSTRY

services See chart

SERVICES RANKS AND APPOINTMENTS

COMMISSIONED OFFICERS

ROYAL NAVY	ARMY	ROYAL AIR FORCE	ROYAL MARINES
admiral of the fleet	**field marshal**	**marshal of the RAF**	—
admiral	**general**	**air chief marshal**	**general**
vice admiral	**lieutenant general**	**air marshal**	**lieutenant general**
rear admiral	**major general**	**air vice marshal**	**major general**
commodore	**brigadier**	**air commodore**	**brigadier**
captain	**colonel**	**group captain**	**colonel, lieutenant colonel**
commander	**lieutenant colonel**	**wing commander**	**major**
lieutenant commander	**major**	**squadron leader**	**captain**
lieutenant	**captain**	**flight lieutenant**	**lieutenant**
sub-lieutenant	**lieutenant**	**flying officer**	**acting lieutenant**
acting sub-lieutenant	**2nd lieutenant**	**pilot officer**	**2nd lieutenant**

NON-COMMISSIONED OFFICERS AND OTHER RANKS

ROYAL NAVY	ARMY	ROYAL AIR FORCE	ROYAL MARINES
midshipman **warrant officer** **chief petty officer** **petty officer** **leading rating/seaman** **able rating/ seaman** **ordinary rating/seaman**	**warrant officer I** **warrant officer II** **company sergeant major** **staff sergeant** **sergeant** **corporal, bombardier** **lance corporal, lance bombardier** **private, gunner, trooper, sapper** **guardsman** **signalman**	**warrant officer** **flight sergeant** **chief technician** **sergeant** **corporal** **junior technician** **senior aircraftman** **leading aircraftman** **aircraftman**	**warrant officer I (regimental sergeant major)** **warrant officer II** **colour sergeant** **sergeant** **corporal** **marine I** **marine II**

– services units in the army GROUP, CORPS, DIVISION, BRIGADE, REGIMENT, BATTALION, COMPANY, BATTERY, TROOP, PLATOON, SQUAD
– services units in the air force COMMAND, GROUP, WING, SQUADRON, FLIGHT

serving as host, priest, or other official for the occasion OFFICIATING
– serving only as a means to an end, purely instrumental SUBSERVIENT
– serving stand or trolley next to a dining table DUMB WAITER
– something serving a higher cause HANDMAIDEN

sesame seed or oil BENNE
– sesame-seed oil GINGILI
– sesame-seed paste TAHINA
– sweetmeat made of honey and crushed sesame seeds HALVA

session – fully attended or open to all, as a session of a conference might be PLENARY

set, as of matching clothes or furniture ENSEMBLE
– set in motion, start ACTUATE
– set in one's ways, refusing to change mind or course IMPLACABLE, INTRACTABLE, INEXORABLE
– set in one's ways, unyielding or blinkered RIGID, INFLEXIBLE, OSSIFIED, FOSSILISED
– set up or establish a court, institution, or the like CONSTITUTE
– setting forth of information, intentions, or the like EXPOSITION
– associating the members of one set with those of another MAPPING
– person who sets type, in preparation for printing COMPOSITOR
– forming a set, especially of rooms EN SUITE

set fire to IGNITE, KINDLE

setting for a jewel, or a jewelled brooch or clasp OUCH
– setting of a play or novel LOCALE
– setting or surroundings MILIEU

settle a debt or claim LIQUIDATE
– settle an argument or differences COMPOSE, RECONCILE, DETERMINE
– settle or attempt to settle a dispute between other people or groups MEDIATE, ARBITRATE, CONCILIATE, MODERATE
– settle or sink, as the sediment in a liquid does SUBSIDE
– settling of a bill or account RECKONING

settled or established firmly or securely in a position ENSCONCED, ENTRENCHED

settler or colonist in a new region in former times PLANTER

seven – relating to or based on the number seven, or having seven parts SEPTENARY
– seven deadly sins CARDINAL SINS
– lasting for seven years, or occurring once every seven years SEPTENNIAL
– meeting or occurring every seven days, as a weekly committee would HEBDOMADAL

-seven- -SEPT-, SEPTI-, HEBDO-, HEPT-, HEPTA-

seventy-year-old, or aged between 70 and 79 SEPTUAGENARIAN

several See **many**
– several, various MISCELLANEOUS, SUNDRY, DIVERS, MYRIAD

several- PLURI-, MULTI-, POLY-

severe, demanding, strict, as a law might be EXACTING, IRONCLAD
– severe, grim, stern, unfriendly in appearance PO-FACED
– severe, strict, moralistic, and self-denying, especially from religious considerations ASCETIC, PURITANICAL
– severe, strict, rigid, demanding RIGOROUS
– severe, strict, stern, and serious in life-style and morality AUSTERE
– severe, tough, very disciplined, as an upbringing might be SPARTAN
– severe, very harsh, as a law or punishment might be DRACONIAN
– severe, very harsh, as scornful criticism might be SCATHING
– severe and stiff in discipline, allowing little individualism PRUSSIAN, TEUTONIC
– severe disciplinarian or strict authoritarian MARTINET, RAMROD
– reduce the severity of a crime, pain, or the like MITIGATE, PALLIATE, EXTENUATE, ALLEVIATE

sewing See chart, pages 462-463, and also **embroidery**
– sewing kit, as issued to soldiers HOUSEWIFE
– sewing or stitching together of edges of a wound SUTURE
– foot-operated lever for driving a sewing machine, potter's wheel, or the like TREADLE
– tapered tuck made when sewing an item of clothing DART

sewage, chemical waste, or other waste liquid EFFLUENT
– sewage enriched by air and added to untreated sewage to encourage bacterial action and speed up purification ACTIVATED SLUDGE
– sewage tank in which solid waste is decomposed by bacteria SEPTIC TANK
– pit or hole for sewage or waste from household drains CESSPOOL
– solid deposit produced during the early stages of sewage treatment SLUDGE

sewer CLOACA
– sewer or drain, as under a road CULVERT, CONDUIT

sex attractant, warning chemical, or other substance secreted by certain animals and affecting others of the same species PHEROMONE
– sex between closely related people INCEST
– sex classification GENDER
– sex gland, specifically an ovary or testis GONAD
– sex party, or gathering involving unrestrained promiscuity ORGY
– sexual activity, typically in short casual relationships, with a number of partners PROMISCUITY
– sexual arousal by or obsession with inanimate objects, such as shoes, or parts of the body other than the sexual organs FETISHISM
– sexual capability in the male POTENCY, VIRILITY
– sexual drive LIBIDO, EROS
– sexual excitement in female animals HEAT, OESTRUS
– sexual excitement or frenzy in male camels, elephants, and other large mammals MUSTH
– sexual harassment, abuse, or assault MOLESTATION
– sexual intercourse, copulation, as referred to in formal contexts or in former times COITUS, COITION, CONGRESS, CARNAL KNOWLEDGE, CONVERSATION
– sexual intercourse, especially when adulterous or immoral FORNICATION
– sexual intercourse between a man and a boy or youth PEDERASTY
– sexual intercourse cut short before ejaculation, as a means of contraception COITUS INTERRUPTUS
– sexual intercourse or intimacy involving three people, typically a man and two women TROILISM
– sexual interest in or attraction towards children PAEDOPHILIA
– sexual intimacy between women, of a kind mimicking sexual intercourse between men and women TRIBADISM
– sexual language of an obscene kind BAWDRY
– sexual or emotional attachment, typically immature and neurotic, to a person or thing FIXATION
– sexual organs GENITALS, GENITALIA
– sexual organs, especially those of men VITALS
– sexual organs, especially those of women PUDENDA
– sexual perversions of various kinds ALGOLAGNIA, BESTIALITY,

BONDAGE, COPROPHILIA, EXHIBITIONISM, FROTTAGE, MASOCHISM, NECROPHILIA, PAEDOPHILIA, SADISM, SCOPOPHILIA, VOYEURISM
– sexual relations or marriage between people of different races MISCEGENATION
– sexual relationship, an affair LIAISON
– sexual relationship of three people living together MÉNAGE À TROIS
– sexual reproduction of the true kind, involving fertilisation of the egg by the sperm AMPHIMIXIS
– sexual restraint, abstinence, or self-control CONTINENCE
– sexual unfaithfulness, especially adultery INFIDELITY
– sexually abnormal behaviour DEVIANCE, PERVERSION
– sexually active woman who remains a virgin nevertheless DEMI-VIERGE
– sexually appealing VOLUPTUOUS
– sexually arousing or arousable, as a part of the body might be EROGENOUS
– sexually arousing or tantalising TITILLATING, PROVOCATIVE
– sexually arousing writings, films, photographs, or the like PORNOGRAPHY, EROTICA
– sexually attracted to other women, as homosexual women are LESBIAN, SAPPHIC
– sexually attracted to people of one's own sex HOMOSEXUAL
– sexually attracted to people of the opposite sex HETEROSEXUAL
– sexually attractive, as a young marriageable woman is said to be NUBILE
– sexually inactive period in female mammals METOESTRUS, ANOESTRUS
– sexually promiscuous man, stud, playboy RAKE, LADYKILLER, CASANOVA, DON JUAN, PHILANDERER, LOTHARIO, LIBERTINE
– sexually promiscuous or immoral WANTON
– sexually promiscuous woman living on the fringes of respectable society, especially in the 19th century DEMIMONDAINE
– sexually uninhibited person, especially one who enjoys swapping sexual partners SWINGER
– abnormally strong sexual desire in a man SATYRIASIS
– abnormally strong sexual desire in a woman NYMPHOMANIA
– abstaining from or uninterested in sexual intercourse CELIBATE, MONASTIC, ASCETIC
– abstaining from unlawful or all sexual activity CHASTE, CONTINENT
– annual state of heat or sexual excitement, as in male deer RUT
– approach someone with an offer of sex, as a prostitute might SOLICIT, ACCOST, PROPOSITION
– broad-minded or tolerant, especially in matters of sexual conduct PERMISSIVE
– characteristic of or resembling both male and female sexes HERMAPHRODITIC, EPICENE, ANDROGYNOUS, MONOECIOUS
– channel or transform a sexual or other instinctual impulse into some socially or culturally more acceptable activity SUBLIMATE
– detailed in describing or representing sexual acts EXPLICIT
– developing or reproducing without sexual union and fertilisation, asexual AGAMIC, AGAMOGENETIC, PARTHENOGENETIC
– devil or spirit adopting female form to have sexual intercourse with a sleeping man SUCCUBUS
– devil or spirit adopting male form to have sexual intercourse with a sleeping woman INCUBUS
– early phase of adolescence in which adult sexual characteristics begin to develop PUBERTY
– feudal lord's right to sexual intercourse with the bride of a vassal on her wedding night DROIT DE SEIGNEUR
– go-between in a sexual relationship PIMP, PANDER, PANDERER, PROCURER
– having an obsessive interest in sexual matters PRURIENT
– in the very act of having sexual intercourse, especially when illicit IN FLAGRANTE DELICTO
– legal right to sexual intercourse with one's husband or wife CONJUGAL RIGHTS
– living together and having a sexual relationship but without being formally married COHABITATION, LIVING TALLY
– lustful or lewd, given to or arousing sexual desires LASCIVIOUS, LECHEROUS, DEBAUCHED, LIBERTINE, LIBIDINOUS, SALACIOUS, CONCUPISCENT, LUBRICIOUS
– man deriving sexual pleasure from secretly watching courting couples, women undressing, or the like VOYEUR, PEEPING TOM
– person who feels an urge to belong to the opposite sex, or one who has undergone a sex-change operation TRANSSEXUAL
– phase in the life of a middle-aged man marked by loss of interest in sexual activity MALE MENOPAUSE, CLIMACTERIC, MID-LIFE CRISIS
– practice of habitually dressing in clothing intended for people of the opposite sex TRANSVESTISM, EONISM, CROSS-DRESSING
– referring to love or a close relationship between two unrelated people that is free of sexual desire PLATONIC
– referring to or suitable for people of either sex UNISEX
– relating to the region above or around the sexual organs PUBIC
– relating to or transmitted by sexual intercourse VENEREAL
– relating to sexual and other physical desires and appetites, sexually suggestive SENSUAL, CARNAL
– relating to sexual love or desire EROTIC, AMATORY
– stimulating or increasing sexual desire, as certain drugs or foods allegedly do APHRODISIAC
– unable to achieve full sexual satisfaction, as some women may be FRIGID
– unable to have sexual intercourse, as some men are IMPOTENT
– unconscious or unacknowledged, as secret fears or sexual feelings might be REPRESSED
– whip, flog, or scourge, as for religious discipline or sexual gratification FLAGELLATE

sexless, neither male nor female NEUTER, EPICENE

sexton of a synagogue BEADLE, SHAMMES

-sexual- -GON-, GONO-

sexual desire- EROT-, EROTO-

-sexual union- -GAM-

sexy, as a shapely and sensual woman would be CURVACEOUS, VOLUPTUOUS

shabby, frayed, scruffy, or mangy THREADBARE

shackles, restraint, restriction, chains FETTERS

shade a drawing or map with intersecting sets of parallel lines CROSS-HATCH
– shade of meaning, subtle distinction NUANCE
– shading of fine lines in a drawing or map HATCHING
– shady, or covered by trees or shrubs BOSKY
– shady, providing shade UMBRAGEOUS
– shady garden shelter, nook, or retreat, often made of trellising BOWER, ARBOUR

shadow image or filled-in outline, typically of solid black against a white background, as of a person's profile SILHOUETTE

– shadow-picture SCIAGRAM
– shadow play, using small paper figures GALANTY SHOW
– darkest part of a shadow UMBRA
– object, such as the arm of a sundial, that casts a shadow to indicate the time GNOMON
– partial shadow, as during an eclipse, lying between the areas of full shadow and full illumination PENUMBRA

shadow boxing, fighting imaginary enemies SCIAMACHY

shaft that rotates, as in a machine tool ARBOR, SPINDLE, MANDREL

shake, quiver, tremble, or vibrate PALPITATE, QUAVER, PULSATE
– shake, quiver, or tremble, as with rage or from shock QUAKE
– shake a patient vigorously to listen for abnormal pockets of body fluid SUCCUSS
– shake or flap rapidly and irregularly FLUTTER
– shake or move in a smooth, wavy rhythm, ripple UNDULATE
– shake or swing regularly back and forth OSCILLATE, VACILLATE, FLUCTUATE
– shake or twitch VELLICATE
– shake or waggle the body rapidly, as if dancing vigorously SHIMMY
– shake or vibrate abnormally, as when changing gear JUDDER
– shake or wave something energetically, such as a weapon or flag BRANDISH, FLOURISH
– shake something vigorously AGITATE, CONVULSE
– shaking, quivering, trembling, or vibrating TREMULOUS
– shaking, quivering, or trembling movement, as due to illness or fear TREMOR, TREPIDATION

Shakespeare – excessive enthusiasm for Shakespeare's works BARDOLATRY
– index of all the words in a text, such as the works of Shakespeare, listing every occurrence of each word CONCORDANCE

shaky, badly built or maintained, as a house might be RICKETY, RAMSHACKLE, DILAPIDATED, DECREPIT
– walk in a shaky, unsteady way TEETER, TOTTER

shallow, lacking in depth, interest, or originality SUPERFICIAL, FACILE
– shallow, merely for show, decorative rather than effective, as reforms might be COSMETIC
– shallow stretch of water SHOAL
– shallow stretch of water where the depth can be measured by a weighted line SOUNDING
– effortless or fluent, as in speaking or writing, but typically shallow and insincere GLIB

sham compliance with a law or custom by means of a small gesture TOKENISM

shame, modesty, or prudishness PUDENCY
– shame, dishonour or disgrace HUMILIATION, DEGRADATION, IGNOMINY, INFAMY
– mark or sign of shame or disgrace STIGMA

shampoo – reddish dye often added to shampoo HENNA
– waxy plant extract used in shampoos, polishes, and the like JOJOBA

shape See chart, page 464, and also **geometry**
– shape, form, outline CONFIGURATION, CONFORMATION
– shape of a person or thing when set against a lighter background SILHOUETTE
– shape or outline, as of a stretch of land CONTOUR
– shape or view of something from the side PROFILE
– shaped wrongly or abnormally MALFORMED, DEFORMED
– ability to revert to an earlier shape or condition RESILIENCE
– change of a spectacular kind in shape, appearance, or attitude METAMORPHOSIS, TRANSFIGURATION, TRANSMOGRIFICATION
– distinctive shape or outline of something, especially of the face LINEAMENTS
– general shape or plan, as of a complicated project FORMAT
– shadow image or shape of something, filled-in outline SILHOUETTE
– twisted out of its natural shape DISTORTED

-shape- -MORPH-, MORPHO-, -FORM, -MORPHIC

shapeless, lacking a distinct form AMORPHOUS, APLASTIC

share, as of work, given to or required by a participant QUOTA

SEWING AND DRESSMAKING TERMS

appliqué	decorative finish made by stitching shapes of one material onto a different material
basting, tacking	temporary stitching to hold pieces of fabric together during making-up
bias	line diagonal to the selvedge of a fabric
bias binding	strip of fabric, cut on the bias, used for binding edges
Binca	even-weave fabric with four groups of intersecting threads to the centimetre
blackwork	embroidery with a repetitive pattern
blocking board	board used to stretch and straighten pieces of embroidery
bobbin	small spool holding the lower thread supply of a sewing machine
bodkin	tool shaped like a long, blunt needle, used to thread elastic or piping cord through a casing
broderie anglaise	embroidery of perforated shapes on fine white linen, cotton, or the like
couching	stitching with two threads, the couching thread being used to stitch a laid thread to the fabric
crewel needle	standard embroidery needle
curve square	instrument for measuring curves, seam allowances, and buttonholes
gusset	piece of fabric, usually triangular, inserted to enlarge or strengthen a garment
Hardanger work	openwork embroidery on even-weave fabric, with nine pairs of intersecting threads to the centimetre

– share of profits or a bankrupt's assets DIVIDEND
– share of the proceeds paid to a writer, composer, or the like from sales or performances of his work ROYALTY
– share or portion specially set aside ALLOCATION, ALLOTMENT
– shared, common, joint MUTUAL
– shared, common, relating to all members of a group COMMUNAL
– shared ownership of a holiday home TIME-SHARING
– sharer, equal heir PARCENER
– sharing, through an illegal agreement, in the money won in a lawsuit by an outside party who is financing it CHAMPERTY
– sharing in or being an accomplice to a criminal act, cruel deed, or the like COMPLICITY

shares, stocks, or bonds SECURITIES
– shares and other assets and investments, in a detailed list PORTFOLIO
– shares bearing the name of the owner or original purchaser NOMINAL SHARES
– share-buying for quick resale at a higher price ARBITRAGE
– share certificate or other document of entitlement SCRIP
– share considered safe and profitable through having a long record of reliability BLUE CHIP
– share dealing, stockbroking, or financial speculation AGIOTAGE
– agree to buy or guarantee the purchase of a share issue UNDERWRITE
– application to purchase newly issued shares SUBSCRIPTION
– convert shares into cash, paper money into bullion, or the like REDEEM
– daily average of various share prices on the London Stock Exchange FT INDEX
– daily average of various share prices on the New York Stock Exchange DOW JONES INDEX
– face value, value printed on the face of a share certificate or bond, as used for assessing dividends PAR VALUE
– finance and investment company buying a variety of shares, and selling units from the combined portfolio to the public UNIT TRUST, MUTUAL FUND
– formal statement or brochure giving details of a forthcoming share issue PROSPECTUS
– issue of new shares at a discount price to current shareholders RIGHTS ISSUE
– issue of new shares free to current shareholders SCRIP ISSUE, BONUS ISSUE
– launching or financing of a business venture by means of a share issue FLOTATION
– middleman formerly dealing in stocks and shares JOBBER
– offer shares, bonds, or the like for sale FLOAT
– ordinary shares EQUITIES, COMMON STOCK
– referring to stocks and shares not quoted on the stock exchange UNLISTED
– special shares with fixed dividends, which will be paid before those of ordinary shares PREFERENCE SHARES
– speculator who anticipates falling prices, and sells shares hoping to buy them back later at a lower price BEAR
– speculator who anticipates rising prices, and buys shares hoping to sell them later at a profit BULL
– speculator who buys newly issued shares in the hope of selling them quickly for a large profit STAG
– total value of a business's shares CAPITALISATION

shark, ray, or similar fish whose skeleton is of cartilage rather than hard bone CARTILAGINOUS FISH
– shark with a flattened head, with the eyes at the ends of the bulging sides HAMMERHEAD
– large shark that often floats near the surface of the water BASKING SHARK, SAILFISH
– relating to sharks or rays SELACHIAN
– small shark with a pointed nose and a crescent-shaped tail PORBEAGLE, MACKEREL SHARK

sharkskin with a rough surface, used as a leather and as an abrasive SHAGREEN

sharp, cutting, or sarcastic, as wit might be CAUSTIC, MORDANT

interfacing	crisp, fibrous backing material giving shape and body
interlining	insulating lining sewn between the outer garment or curtain and the lining
lettuce edge	decorative finish giving a frilly effect to knitted fabrics
mercerised	referring to a cotton or linen fabric or thread that has been pre-shrunk and treated to give it greater lustre and strength
mitring	diagonal joining of two edges at a corner
nap	raised fabric surface, as in velvet and corduroy
piping	rounded strip of cloth, sometimes covering a cord, used for trimming furniture covers or garments
placket	slit in a garment, such as a cuff or zip opening, to make it easier to put on and take off
quilting	embroidery dividing padded material into decorative shapes
rickrack braid	wavy braid used for decorative trimming
selvedge	ribbon-like, non-fraying edge running lengthways along each side of a woven fabric
shirring	decorative, multiple gathering of a fabric, often with elastic thread, to control fullness, especially at the waist and cuffs
slate frame	frame on which fabric is stretched between rollers
smocking	decorative stitching of evenly gathered material to give a regular, patterned effect
tambour, hoop, tabouret	round embroidery frame
trapunto	quilting made by filling stitched areas with padding

– sharp, harsh, or irritating, as a smell or taste might be ACRID, PUNGENT
– sharp fragment, splinter SLIVER
– sharp or penetrating, as a comment might be TRENCHANT, INCISIVE
– sharp-sighted LYNX-EYED
– sharp smell or taste TANG
– sharply tipped, narrowing to a point, as a leaf might be ACUMINATE, APICULATE

sharp- OXY-

sharpen a blade or the like, as on a grindstone HONE, WHET

SHAPES

IN THE SHAPE OF	DESCRIPTION
almond	**amygdaloid**
arrowhead	**sagittate**
bell	**campanulate**
berry	**bacciform**
boat	**navicular, scaphoid**
bow, arch	**arcuate**
bristle	**setiform, acicular, styliform**
bunch of grapes	**botryoidal, aciniform**
club	**clavate, claviform**
coil	**circinate**
coin	**nummular**
comb	**pectinate**
cone	**fastigiate**
crescent	**bicorn, lunular**
cross, X	**decussate, cruciform, cruciate**
cup	**cotyloid, cupulate**
diamond	**rhomboidal**
dish, pan	**patelliform**
doughnut, ring	**toroid**
droplet	**guttate, stilliform, globular**
eagle's beak	**aquiline**
ear	**auriculate**
eel	**anguilliform**
egg	**oval, ovoid**
fan	**flabellate**
feather	**pinnate**
fingers	**digitate**
fish	**pisciform**
foot	**pediform**
fork	**furcate, bifurcate**
funnel	**infundibular**
hand	**palmate**
head	**capitate**
heart	**cordate**
helmet	**galeate**
hood, cowl	**cucullate**
hook	**uncinate, unciform**
horn	**cornual**
keel	**carinate**
kidney	**reniform**
knife blade	**cultrate**
ladder	**scalariform**
lance	**lanceolate**
lens, lentil seed	**lenticular**
lyre	**lyrate**
needle	**acerose**
pear	**pyriform**
pine cone	**strobilaceous**
pouch, sac	**bursiform, saccate**
ribbon	**cestoid**
ring	**annular, toroid**
rod	**bacillary, bacilliform, virgate, virgulate**
S, the letter	**sigmoid**
sausage	**allantoid**
saw, teeth of a saw	**runcinate, serrate**
scimitar	**acinaciform**
shield	**scutate, scutellate, peltate, clypeate**
sickle	**falcate**
slipper	**calceolate**
snail's shell	**cochleate**
snake	**anguiform**
spearhead	**hastate**
spiral	**helical, turbinal, volute**
spokes of a wheel	**rotate**
star	**stellate**
strap	**ligulate**
string of beads	**moniliform**
sword	**ensiform, gladiate, xiphoid**
tongue	**lingulate**
tooth	**dentiform**
tree	**dendriform, dendroid**
triangle	**deltoid**
urn	**urceolate**
violin	**pandurate**
wand, rod	**virgate**
wedge	**cuneal, sphenic**
wheel	**trochal**
whip	**flagellate**
wing, wings	**alary, aliform**
worm	**vermicular, vermiform, lumbricoid**

– sharpen a cutthroat razor on a leather or canvas strip STROP
– sharpening wheel, an abrasive wheel CARBORUNDUM WHEEL
– stone for sharpening knives and other cutting tools WHETSTONE, GRINDSTONE

sharpness or clarity of outline, as of a photograph or television image DEFINITION, ACUTANCE
– sharpness or keenness of the senses or the mind ACUITY

shaven head, or top part of the head, especially of a monk or priest TONSURE

shaving – stick of chemical for stopping bleeding from small cuts, as after shaving STYPTIC PENCIL

shears used for pruning SECATEURS
– shears with toothed blades for cutting a zigzag edge on cloth to prevent fraying PINKING SHEARS

sheath of leaf-like bracts enclosing a flower spike, as on the cuckoopint SPATHE
– clear thick liquid secreted by membranes in joints, tendon sheathes, and the like SINOVIA
– forming a sheath or enclosed in a sheath VAGINATE
– metal tip or trimming for a sheath or scabbard CHAPE

sheaves of grain piled together in a field to dry SHOCKS, STOOKS

shed, typically with a sloping roof, against the side of a building PENTHOUSE, LEAN-TO
– shed feathers or fur MOULT
– shedding of a body part, such as a lizard's tail, as a means of protection when attacked AUTOTOMY
– shedding of the outer layer, shell, or skin, as in insects and snakes SLOUGHING, ECDYSIS
– shedding all their leaves at a particular time each year, as some trees do DECIDUOUS

sheen on a surface produced by age or handling PATINA
– sheen or wavy finish, as given to silk WATER

sheep, horse, or the like regarded as the mother of another DAM
– sheep between one and two years old TEG
– sheep disease caused by a tapeworm larva in the brain, leading to staggering and often fatal GID, STURDY, WATERBRAIN
– sheep disease caused by a virus, causing intense itching and tremors, and often fatal SCRAPIE
– sheep of a breed originally from Spain, producing a soft fine wool MERINO
– sheep of a central Asian breed, whose young have a curled glossy coat yielding Persian lamb fur KARAKUL, BROADTAIL
– sheep of a wild variety in North Africa BARBARY SHEEP, AOUDAD
– sheep of a wild variety in Sardinia and Corsica MOUFLON
– sheep that resists shearing and is often left till last COBBLER
– adjective for a sheep OVINE
– bear young, as sheep do YEAN
– gelded male sheep WETHER
– male sheep, ram TUP
– male sheep that leads the flock BELLWETHER
– person who herds and drives cattle or sheep DROVER
– relating to shepherds and their flocks of sheep BUCOLIC, PASTORAL
– young sheep, lamb YEANLING

sheet, as of folded paper or wooden boarding PLY
– sheet for wrapping a corpse SHROUD, WINDING SHEET
– sheet of natural or artificial tissue through which fluids can pass slowly MEMBRANE
– split or beat into thin sheets, or join several parallel sheets together LAMINATE

shelf, as above a fireplace MANTELPIECE, MANTEL
– open free-standing display shelf, as in a supermarket GONDOLA
– ornamental bracket, as for supporting a shelf CONSOLE

shell See also **bomb**
– shell, bullet, missile, rocket, or other object fired or hurled PROJECTILE
– shell, protective plate, or similar hard covering, as on some animals or ships CUIRASS
– shell beads formerly used as currency by North American Indians WAMPUM, PEAG
– shell fragments produced by an explosion SHRAPNEL
– shell-like protective horny covering on some insects, crustaceans, and the like CUTICLE
– shell of a tortoise, crab, lobster, or the like CARAPACE
– shell of various sea molluscs, used as money in some cultures COWRIE
– shell or hard coating, as of some insects TEST
– shell or protective outer covering of an animal or plant ARMATURE
– shell-producing or -containing CONCHIFEROUS
– shelling or heavy bombardment by artillery STONK
– coil or single turn, as of a spiral shell VOLUTE, WHORL, VOLUTION
– delicate curving decoration of rock fragments or shells, used in rococo design ROCAILLE
– diameter of the inside of a tube, the bore of a gun, or a bullet or shell CALIBRE
– fossil shell of a common, flat, coiled type, from various extinct squid-like creatures AMMONITE
– horn-like substance occurring in some fungi and in the shell of a lobster, crab, or the like CHITIN
– knob-like protruberance, as in the centre of a shield or at the top of a clam's shell UMBO
– opening or hollow at the base of a mollusc's shell UMBILICUS
– shiny inner surface of some mollusc shells, used for ornamentation MOTHER-OF-PEARL, NACRE
– single turn or spiral on a shell WHORL
– scallop, oyster, or similar mollusc having a pair of hinged shells BIVALVE
– snail, whelk, or similar mollusc having a single shell UNIVALVE
– spiralling and cone-shaped, as some shells are TURBINATE
– top section of a coiled shell, including the apex SPIRE

-shell- -CONCH-, CONCHO-

shellfish See also **fish**
– shellfish such as a lobster or prawn CRUSTACEAN
– shellfish such as an oyster or whelk MOLLUSC
– shellfish such as a shrimp or lobster, or any insect, spider, or the like, having a horny, segmented covering and jointed limbs ARTHROPOD
– shellfish, such as a whelk or limpet, having a single shell and a foot-like muscle used for crawling about UNIVALVE, GASTROPOD
– shellfish, such as an oyster or mussel, having a pair of hinged shells BIVALVE
– shellfish of the kind clinging to ships' hulls BARNACLE
– shellfish resembling a small lobster CRAYFISH, LANGOUSTE
– shellfish with a ridged, fan-shaped shell SCALLOP
– shellfish with a spiralled shell, related to the squid NAUTILUS
– large edible shellfish with a large ear-shaped shell yielding mother-of-pearl ABALONE, ORMER
– New Zealand shellfish with a shimmering greenish shell resembling mother-of-pearl PAUA
– small shrimp-like shellfish forming the principal food of some whales KRILL
– squid-like shellfish, whose internal shell is sometimes placed in

bird cages to supplement the bird's diet CUTTLEFISH

shelter of arched corrugated iron sheets NISSEN HUT
- shelter or cover providing protection against the wind LEE
- shelter or inn for the needy or travellers HOSPICE
- shelter or protect HARBOUR
- shelter or protection, as from persecution, or a place offering such safety ASYLUM, HAVEN, REFUGE, SANCTUARY
- sheltered, private, or hidden SECLUDED, SEQUESTERED, CLOISTERED
- sheltered place, especially a small bay COVE

shepherds – relating to shepherds BUCOLIC, PASTORAL

sheriff or similar officer in the U.S. MARSHAL
- sheriff's office, term of office, or authority SHRIEVALTY
- sheriff's officer in medieval times who arrested debtors CATCHPOLE
- sheriff's officer who serves writs and carries out a court's orders BAILIFF
- group of men assembled by a U.S. sheriff, as to pursue a fugitive POSSE, POSSE COMITATUS

sherry, port, or other strengthened wine FORTIFIED WINE
- sherry glass, traditionally tulip-shaped COPITA
- sherry of a pale dry variety from Spain MANZANILLA
- large glass for sherry or port SCHOONER

shield, as in heraldry, bearing a coat of arms ESCUTCHEON
- shield large enough to protect the whole body, used in medieval times PAVIS
- shield-like plate covering a keyhole, surrounding a door handle, protecting a light switch, or the like ESCUTCHEON
- shield-shaped SCUTATE, SCUTELLATE, PELTATE, CLYPEATE
- ornamental knob in the centre of a shield BOSS, UMBO
- overhead cover, of an overlapping roof of shields, protecting an ancient Roman military unit TESTUDO, TORTOISE
- small, round shield worn or carried on the arm in former times BUCKLER, TARGET, TARGE

shift of duty on guard or on shipboard WATCH
- shift or session of duty, as at the helm of a ship TRICK

shimmering, changing in brightness, twinkling, as a cat's eye or similar gemstone does CHATOYANT

SHIPS

POWERED BY OARS	POWERED BY ENGINE
bireme	**collier**
bucentaur	**container ship**
galley	**freighter**
galliot	**liner**
longship	**motorised fishing vessel/ MFV**
quinquereme	**packet**
trireme	**paddle steamer**
	stern-wheeler
	tanker
	trawler
	tug
	whaleback

POWERED BY SAIL	WARSHIPS
argosy	**aircraft carrier, ASW carrier**
barque	**battle cruiser**
barquentine	**battleship**
bilander	**corvette**
brig	**cruiser**
brigantine	**destroyer**
caravel	**dreadnought**
carrack	**escort carrier**
clipper	**frigate**
cutter	**man-of-war**
dandy	**minelayer**
dromond	**minesweeper**
galleass	**monitor**
galleon	**Q ship**
Indiaman	**submarine**
ketch	
knockabout	
schooner	
sloop	
square-rigger	
tartan	
windjammer	
xebec	
yawl	

- shimmering with a rainbow-like effect, as a soap bubble or opal does IRIDESCENT, OPALESCENT

shin – graze one's shin BARK

shinbone TIBIA

shine, smooth polished finish LUSTRE, GLOSS, BURNISH, SHEEN
- shining brightly RELUCENT
- shining brilliantly, radiantly illuminated, dazzling RESPLENDENT, EFFULGENT, REFULGENT
- shining or flickering gently, shimmering or glistening LAMBENT
- shining or glittering brilliantly, sparkling, as a person's wit or a gemstone might be SCINTILLATING, CORUSCATING
- shining or glowing intensely, brilliantly bright INCANDESCENT

shiny, flaky mineral MICA
- shiny, glossy LUSTROUS
- shiny disc or button, used to ornament clothing, handbags, or the like SEQUIN
- shiny in a shimmery way IRIDESCENT, OPALESCENT
- shiny surface layer or finishing, as of fine wood or plastic VENEER

ship See chart, and also **boat, sailing**
- ship abandoned at sea DERELICT
- ship escorting another CONSORT
- ship of a heavy and awkward design HULK
- ship's bearing calculated from a fixed reference, such as due north on the horizon, typically measured clockwise in degrees AZIMUTH
- ship's boat or lifeboat, typically a small rowing boat YAWL, JOLLY BOAT
- ship's cabin, especially a large, comfortable private cabin STATEROOM
- ship's officer in charge of equipment, maintenance, and deck crew BOATSWAIN, BO'S'N
- ship's officer in charge of finances and passenger welfare PURSER
- ship's officer supervising the food and provisions STEWARD
- ship's officers' living quarters WARDROOM
- ship's rigging TACKLE
- ship's steering equipment, tiller, or wheel HELM
- ship's storeroom between decks LAZARETTO
- ship's supplier or other dealer in a specified trade or commodity CHANDLER
- ships travelling in a group, especially when protected by an escort of warships CONVOY
- armoured pilot house on a ship, or the superstructure of a submarine CONNING TOWER
- cargo or wreckage found floating after a ship has sunk FLOTSAM
- cargo thrown overboard from a ship or washed ashore JETSAM
- cargo thrown from a ship but marked by buoys for later recovery LAGAN
- carved bust or full figure in the prow of some sailing ships FIGUREHEAD
- complete staff of officers and crew of a ship COMPLEMENT, COMPANY
- curved wooden rib forming part of a ship's frame FUTTOCK
- deep, wide, and safe enough for ships or boats to sail on or through NAVIGABLE
- depth below the water line of the keel of a loaded ship DRAUGHT
- device dragged through the water from a ship's stern to determine the speed or distance covered PATENT LOG, SCREW LOG, TAFFRAIL LOG
- dock-worker who boards ships to load and unload them STEVEDORE
- document recording details of

goods for shipment, especially in foreign trade BILL OF LADING, WAYBILL, MANIFEST
– easily overturned, top-heavy, unstable, as a sailing ship might be TENDER, CRANK
– equip and check a ship for active service COMMISSION
– fibre of hemp or jute, often treated with tar, used for sealing pipe joints and caulking the seams in wooden ships OAKUM
– fleet of small ships, or small fleet of ships FLOTILLA
– force a person, by trickery or threats, into service on a ship SHANGHAI, PRESS, PRESSGANG, CRIMP
– raised frame of windows on a ship's upper deck, affording light below COMPANION
– heavy material, such as sandbags, helping to stabilise a ship or balloon BALLAST
– inside of the lowest part of a ship's hull, or the water collecting there BILGE
– kitchen on the deck of a ship CABOOSE
– ladder, usually of rope but with rigid rungs, used on a ship JACOB'S LADDER
– ladder or portable staircase that can be hung over the side of a ship for access ACCOMMODATION LADDER
– large section of a passenger ship for those paying the cheapest fares STEERAGE
– large spike on the prow of an ancient warship for puncturing an enemy ship's hull ROSTRUM, RAM, BEAK
– line of plates or planking running the length of a ship's hull STRAKE
– line or set of lines marked on the side of a cargo ship, showing its legal load-level in various conditions PLIMSOLL LINE
– lookout platform near the top of a mast of a sailing ship CROW'S NEST
– main body or shell of a ship HULL
– modernise and re-equip a ship REFIT
– person who hides on board a departing ship, train, or the like for a free journey STOWAWAY
– pier, docking platform, or the like at which ships can moor for loading or unloading WHARF
– plate or place on the stern of a ship or boat bearing the vessel's name ESCUTCHEON
– platform above the main deck on a ship, housing the controls BRIDGE
– porthole, hinged hatchway, or the like on a ship SCUTTLE
– prohibition, as of foreign ships or of arms trading EMBARGO
– protective plate, shell, or similar hard covering, as on some animals or ships CUIRASS
– rail round the stern of a boat or ship TAFFRAIL
– ramp sloping into the water, supporting a ship being built or repaired SLIPWAY
– relating to ships or seafaring NAUTICAL, MARITIME
– rescue of a ship, cargo, or crew SALVAGE
– rope or cable used in mooring or towing a ship HAWSER
– ropes or cables supporting the mast on a ship or boat SHROUDS
– rotating drum on the deck of a ship around which ropes or cables are wound CAPSTAN
– run before a gale, as a ship might even when carrying little sail SCUD
– seaworthy or strongly built, as a wooden ship might be SNUG
– section of a ship's structure situated above the main deck SUPERSTRUCTURE
– seizure of a neutral ship in wartime SPOLIATION
– senior captain of a shipping line, merchant fleet, or naval squadron COMMODORE
– shellfish with hard shells that often cling to and foul the bottoms of ships BARNACLES
– shelter against rain or spray on a yacht or ship's bridge DODGER
– shift or session of duty, as at the helm of a ship TRICK
– shift or session of duty as on guard or on shipboard WATCH
– side of a ship to the left when facing the bow or front LARBOARD, PORT
– side of a ship to the right when facing the bow or front STARBOARD
– small selected unit of troops or ships sent on an assignment DETACHMENT
– small squadron of ships ESCADRILLE, FLOTILLA
– stairway from a ship's upper deck to the cabins or deck below COMPANIONWAY
– steer or direct a ship CON
– supplier of provisions or equipment, as for a ship CHANDLER
– track of visible foam or waves in water, as left by a ship WAKE
– T-shaped bar or post for securing ropes, as on a ship's deck CLEAT
– vertical exhaust pipe or "chimney" on a steamship STACK
– waterproof the hull or seal the seams of a wooden ship, as with tar or pitch PAY, CAULK
– window, usually circular, in the side of a ship PORTHOLE
– wooden frame supporting a ship during construction STOCKS
– wooden strip or plank forming part of a barrel, ship's hull, or the like STAVE
– wreckage from a shipwrecked ship WRACK

shipping and sailing within a country's territorial waters CABOTAGE
– adjective for shipping MARITIME, MARINE

shirk work or duty SCRIMSHANK

shirt See **clothes**
– false front of a dress shirt DICKY, PLASTRON
– frills down the front of a blouse or shirt JABOT, RUFFLE

shiver or thrill of fear or excitement FRISSON
– shivering attack and chills, as in malaria AGUE, RIGOR

shock See also **surprise**
– shock having long-lasting psychological effects TRAUMA
– shock or violent jarring, especially to the brain, typically producing temporary loss of bearings and alertness CONCUSSION
– shocked or amazed STUPEFIED
– shocked or amazed by something horrible AGHAST, APPALLED
– temporary rigidity and insensitivity in reaction to shock RIGOR
– therapy for treating psychiatric patients, involving an electric shock to the brain ELECTROCONVULSIVE THERAPY, ECT

shock-absorbing system in motor vehicles, based on pistons in fluid-filled cylinders rather than with springs HYDRAULIC SUSPENSION
– shock-absorbing handle or binding, as on a hammer WITHE
– shock-absorbing or cushion-like device, such as the steel springs or dampers at the ends of railway lines or carriages BUFFER

shocking, sensational, or gruesome, often in a deliberately artificial way GRAND-GUIGNOL
– shocking or startling, outrageously unconventional ÉPATANT
– shockingly or glaringly wrong or evil FLAGRANT
– shockingly unjust or unreasonable UNCONSCIONABLE

shoddy and cheap GIMCRACK, BRUMMAGEM, TAWDRY

shoe See illustration and chart
- covering or gaiter of cloth or leather protecting the upper shoe and ankle SPAT
- large, heavy, and ugly shoes or boots CLODHOPPERS
- layers forming the heel of a shoe LIFTS
- men's shoes made with two differently coloured leathers CO-RESPONDENT SHOES
- men's thick-soled suede shoes BROTHEL CREEPERS
- protective iron plate on the sole of a shoe, as for prodding a spade into the ground TRAMP
- small protective metal plate attached to the sole or heel of a shoe TAP
- spiked plate on the sole of a shoe to prevent slipping on ice CLAMPER
- spikes fastened to a shoe or boot, as for mountaineering or walking across ice CRAMPONS
- strip of iron, rubber, or leather attached to the sole of a shoe to reduce wear or prevent slipping CLEAT
- strip of leather fitted to the base of a shoe before the heel is attached RAND
- stud on the heel or sole of a shoe to prevent slipping CALK

-shoe- -CALC-

shoelace – metal or plastic tip on a shoelace, to prevent fraying and make threading easier AGLET, TAG

shoemaker or -mender COBBLER
- shoemaker's block, shaped like a foot, supporting the shoe being shaped or mended LAST

shoot from the roots or lower stem of a plant SUCKER
- shoot-like twining part, as on a grapevine, serving to attach a climbing plant to its support, trellis, or the like TENDRIL
- shoot or long thin runner of a plant FLAGELLUM
- shoot or twig cut for planting or grafting SLIP, SCION
- shoots, as of willow, used in basketwork WICKER

shooting – clay disc hurled into the air for use as a shooting target CLAY PIGEON
- hidden marksman shooting at exposed individuals SNIPER
- time of year when hunting or shooting is permitted OPEN SEASON
- time of year when hunting or shooting is prohibited CLOSE SEASON

shop, typically small and fashionable, selling clothes, gifts, or the like BOUTIQUE
- shop in a remote area, as in pioneering times, in which goods were often bartered TRADING POST
- shop-lined roofed passageway, as through a building ARCADE
- shop-lined street for pedestrians only MALL
- shop or canteen for military personnel or their families NAAFI
- shop restricted to military personnel, diplomats, or the like COMMISSARY
- shop selling goods at prices lower than the manufacturers' recommended prices DISCOUNT HOUSE
- shop specialising in ham, sausage, and other cold cooked meats CHARCUTERIE
- shopping district of a town, especially when closed to traffic SHOPPING PRECINCT
- shops on a U.S. military base POST EXCHANGE, PX
- code of lines and numbers, as on a library book or item of shopping, typically read by a laser optical scanner BAR CODE

shoe

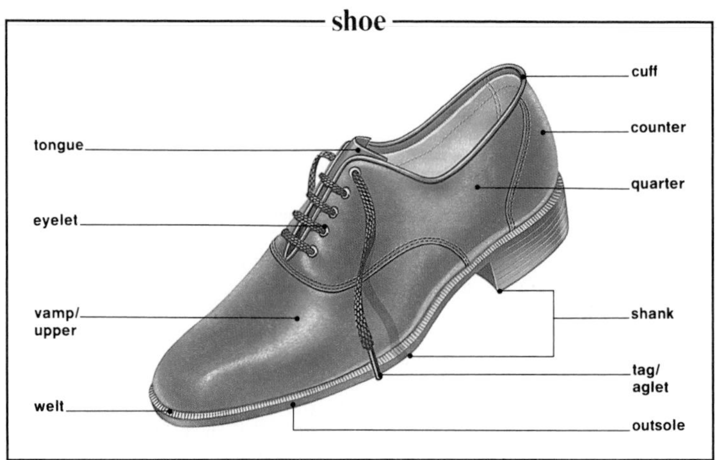

- display board or sign above the door or window of a shop FASCIA
- large retail shop selling a wide range of goods EMPORIUM

shop-window – life-size model used for displaying clothes in shop windows MANNEQUIN

shoplifting – loss of goods from a shop or supermarket, as through shoplifting SHRINKAGE

shore or beach STRAND
- shore or beach covered with pebbles or stony gravel SHINGLE
- adjective for a shore LITTORAL

short See also **brief**, **concise**, **summary**
- short and abrupt CURT
- short and heavily built PYKNIC, ENDOMORPHIC
- short and mysterious, pithy, as an utterance might be GNOMIC
- short literary work, scene, or the like VIGNETTE, CAMEO

short- BRACHY-

short-lived, lasting only a short time EPHEMERAL, TRANSITORY, VOLATILE
- short-lived, passing quickly, brief FLEETING, FUGITIVE, FUGACIOUS, TRANSIENT
- short-lived, vanishing rapidly EVANESCENT

shortage See **lack**

shorten, abbreviate TRUNCATE, CURTAIL
- shorten, cut, or summarise a text ABRIDGE, CONDENSE
- shortened version of a text, summary ABSTRACT, SYNOPSIS, DIGEST, ABRIDGMENT, EPITOME, PRÉCIS

shortening of a word by dropping one or more letters or sounds from the end, as with *prof* from *professor* APOCOPE
- shortening of a word by dropping one or more letters or sounds from the middle, as with *fo'c's'le* from *forecastle* SYNCOPATION, SYNCOPE
- shortening of a word by omission of a syllable, as when saying *deteriate* for *deteriorate* HAPLOLOGY
- shortening of a word by the loss of a letter or sound from the beginning, as with *squire* from *esquire* APHAERESIS, APHESIS
- shortening of a word or words by combining or leaving out some of the sounds or letters, as with *shan't* CONTRACTION

shortfall, amount by which an actual amount is lower than the expected or required amount DEFICIT

shorthand of a kind using the letters of the alphabet STENOTYPY
- shorthand writing STENOGRAPHY

SHOES AND BOOTS

Balmoral	heavy walking boot	**mukluk**	Eskimo boot of soft reindeer skin or sealskin
brogan	ankle-high work shoe	**mule**	loose, backless, strapless slipper
brogue	stout walking shoe with decorative punch-marks	**oxford**	stout shoe with a low heel
buckskin	shoe made from deerskin or sheepskin	**pantoffle**	slipper
buskin, cothurnus/ cothurn	thick-soled, calf-length or knee-length boot, as worn by ancient Greek actors	**patten**	wooden overshoe or clog on a raised wooden sole or metal platform
chappal	Indian leather sandal	**peeptoe**	shoe with the toe cut away
chukka	suede ankle-boot, usually with two eyelets	**plimsoll, dap, gymshoe, tacky**	light rubber-soled shoe with a cloth upper, usually laced
court shoe	woman's plain high-heeled shoe without fastenings	**pump**	light, flat or low-heeled shoe, without fastenings, often worn for dancing
espadrille	rope-soled shoe with canvas or fabric upper	**sabot**	clog, made from a single piece of wood
galosh	waterproof overshoe	**sneaker**	soft-soled shoe
geta	Japanese wooden-soled sandal	**stiletto**	woman's shoe with a narrow, tapering high heel
ghillie	shoe with fringed laces	**velskoen/ veldskoen**	South African shoe or boot of untanned hide
gumshoe	rubber shoe or overshoe; sneaker	**wader**	very high waterproof boot, as used by anglers
Hessian boot	high, tasselled man's boot	**Wellington**	unlaced rubber boot for wet conditions; high leather riding boot
larrigan	moccasin with knee-length leggings	**winkle-picker**	man's shoe with a very pointed toe
loafer	casual shoe resembling a moccasin		
moccasin	soft, heel-less, slip-on leather shoe with a stitched upper		

– U.S. term for a shorthand typist STENOGRAPHER

short-sightedness, defective distance vision MYOPIA

shoulder – shoulder belt fitted with cartridge pockets, worn across the chest BANDOLEER
– shoulder blade SCAPULA
– shoulder socket GLENOID CAVITY
– braid, fringed strap, or the like worn on the shoulder, as on a military uniform EPAULETTE
– garment worn by monks, consisting of a long band of cloth hanging at the front and back from the shoulders SCAPULA

shout criticisms or insults at a player, team, or speaker BARRACK
– shout or cry out loudly, especially in protest VOCIFERATE
– shout or yell HOLLER
– shouting, noisy outcry CLAMOUR, HUBBUB

shovel – shovel-like implement, typically with a long handle, used for moving bread, pies, pizza, or the like in and out an oven PEEL

show, demonstrate plainly MANIFEST
– show, display, activity, or the like that is elaborate, fanciful, or spectacular EXTRAVAGANZA
– show, prove, or suggest strongly EVIDENCE
– show a feeling clearly, such as surprise REGISTER, EVINCE
– afternoon performance of a play, film, or other show MATINÉE
– first or opening performance of a play, film, or other show PREMIERE
– master of ceremonies of a show COMPERE
– producer or organiser of stage shows, concerts, or the like IMPRESARIO

show off, parade or exhibit ostentatiously FLAUNT
– show off, put on an act, parade, try to impress POSE, POSTURE, ATTITUDINISE, MASQUERADE
– showing off, drawing attention to oneself, as by rowdy behaviour EXHIBITIONISM
– person who puts on an act, shows off, or assumes a role in an attempt to impress others POSEUR

showing or demonstrating directly OSTENSIVE, DEICTIC
– showing or seeing everything PANOPTIC

showmanship, liking for or power to attract publicity RÉCLAME

showpiece, outstanding item in a group PIÈCE DE RÉSISTANCE

showy, artificially spectacular, garishly brilliant TECHNICOLOR
– showy, demonstrative, gushing EFFUSIVE
– showy, drawing attention to oneself OSTENTATIOUS, OBTRUSIVE
– showy, elaborately decorated or unrestrained FLAMBOYANT, FLORID, ROCOCO
– showy, flashy, ornate or brightly coloured in a tasteless way GAUDY, GARISH, TAWDRY, TINSELLY
– showy, swanky, swish, luxurious RITZY, GLITZY
– showy, trifling ornament TRINKET, FALLAL
– showy and brightly coloured EMBLAZONED

– showy but brilliant, as a musical performance might be BRAVURA
– showy but worthless TRUMPERY
– showy clothing or decoration FROU-FROU, FRIPPERY, FURBELOWS
– showy display or public ceremony FANFARE
– showy in a vulgar way RAFFISH
– showy or colourful display or symbol BLAZON
– showy or dramatic gesture, movement, or action FLOURISH
– showy or noisy display, designed to impress or advertise RAZZLE-DAZZLE, RAZZMATAZZ

shredded or finely sliced, as vegetables are in some dishes JULIENNE

shriek – "shrieking root", plant with a forked root, formerly used for a narcotic drug, and thought to shriek when pulled from the ground MANDRAKE

shrill grating chirp of a cricket or grasshopper STRIDULATION
– shrill or high-pitched TREBLE

shrimp, crab, lobster, or related creature having a segmented body, jointed limbs, and horny shell CRUSTACEAN
– shrimp-like, small marine creatures, forming the main food of some whales KRILL

shrine or container for sacred relics RELIQUARY
– canopied niche or recess used as a shrine TABERNACLE

shrivelled and wrinkled, as an old person's face might be WIZENED

shroud – wax-coated cloth formerly used as a shroud CERECLOTH, CEREMENT

Shrove Tuesday or its carnival celebrations MARDI GRAS

shrunk – referring to a kind of pre-shrunk fabric used for clothing SANFORIZED

shun – shunned person or social outcast ISHMAEL, PARIAH, LEPER
– shunning, exclusion from society OSTRACISM, PURDAH

shut away from the world, confine or hide SECLUDE, CLOISTER, SEQUESTER, IMMURE
– shut oneself away, as for a private discussion CLOSET

shut out See **exclude**

shutter or blind with adjustable horizontal slats JALOUSIE
– shutter or screen protecting a window from the sun in hot countries BRISE-SOLEIL

shy, avoiding public exposure, not drawing attention to oneself RETIRING, RESERVED, UNDEMONSTRATIVE
– shy, hesitant, or uncertain, as a smile might be TENTATIVE
– shy, inward-looking, socially withdrawn INTROVERTED
– shy, self-conscious, and easily embarrassed BASHFUL
– shy, timid, lacking in confidence or self-assertiveness DIFFIDENT
– shy, unassertive, or unattractive person who is left out of social activities, as at a dance WALLFLOWER
– shy, uncommunicative, saying less than one could RETICENT, TACITURN, UNFORTHCOMING
– shy away, draw back RECOIL, FLINCH, QUAIL, BLENCH
– shy or embarrassed to the point of being speechless TONGUE-TIED
– shy or modest, often in a way suggesting flirtatiousness COY, DEMURE, SKITTISH
– shy or socially awkward and ill at ease GAUCHE, FAROUCHE
– shy or timid, very nervous TREMULOUS, TIMOROUS
– shy or wary, as of meeting people CHARY
– shy person, very reluctant to come forward SHRINKING VIOLET
– shyly or sheepishly guilt-stricken SHAMEFACED, RUEFUL
– distant or stand-offish out of a sense of superiority rather than shyness ALOOF
– embarrassed and too shy to speak out CONSTRAINED
– excessively modest, as through shyness, about one's own qualities, running oneself down SELF-EFFACING, SELF-ABNEGATING

sick See **ill**, **illness**, **disease**
– sick, vomiting or feeling as if about to vomit NAUSEOUS, BILIOUS, QUEASY

sick bay, especially in a boarding school SANATORIUM

sickeningly often, regularly or repeatedly to a tiresome extent AD NAUSEAM

sickle – sickle-shaped, as some leaves are FALCATE

sickly and chronically weak person INVALID, VALETUDINARIAN
– sickly in appearance, pale PEAKY
– sickly yellowish in colour or complexion SALLOW

side of a ship above the water, or the guns along the side BROADSIDE
– side view, especially of a human head PROFILE
– side with a contestant, opinion, political party, or the like ALIGN
– having sides of equal length, as a triangle might EQUILATERAL
– place or be placed on both sides of a divide STRADDLE
– relating to or situated on the side or flank LATERAL

side by side, often for the sake of contrast JUXTAPOSED
– side by side, running parallel COLLATERAL

side effects – signs, such as allergies or dangerous side effects, that argue for the discontinuation of a medicine or treatment CONTRA-INDICATIONS

-sided -GON, GONAL

sideways, glancingly, obliquely, the way one might look at a person ASKANCE
– sideways on BROADSIDE

siege – catapult-like launcher of rocks or other missiles, as used in ancient siege warfare ONAGER, BRICOLE, BALLISTA
– lay siege to, besiege, surround with soldiers BELEAGUER
– lifting of a siege RELIEF
– protective cover against overhead attack, often in the form of overlapping shields, as used by ancient Roman soldiers when attacking the walls of a city under siege TESTUDO, TORTOISE
– raid against the enemy by those under siege SORTIE
– tall wheeled wooden frame used to scale fortress walls during a siege in ancient times TURRET

sieve or mash boiled food to produce a pulpy consistency PURÉE
– coarse sieve, as for sifting grain or gravel RIDDLE

sift grain, gravel, or the like RIDDLE
– sift or filter PERCOLATE

sigh or breathe SUSPIRE
– sighing or rustling sound, as of wind or surf SOUGH, SUSURRATION

sight See **eyesight**
– sudden or unusual sight APPARITION

sighting lines, at right angles to each other, in the sight of a rifle, theodolite, or the like CROSS WIRES, CROSS HAIRS

sign See also **symbol**
– sign, indication, token INDEX
– sign, symbol, or letter standing for an entire word, such as £ for *pound* LOGOGRAM, LOGOGRAPH
– sign a document that already bears a signature, to ratify or authenticate it COUNTERSIGN
– sign of illness, deterioration, or the like SYMPTOM
– sign one's name at the foot of a document as a witness or contracting party SUBSCRIBE
– sign or character representing an entire idea, as in Chinese writing IDEOGRAM
– sign or design made up of initial letters MONOGRAM
– sign or emblem of a company or corporation LOGO, LOGOTYPE
– sign or endorse a document or

the like UNDERWRITE
– sign or evidence that one possesses a specified quality PATENT
– sign or indication of the reality or existence of something, such as envy MANIFESTATION
– sign or mark of shame or disgrace STIGMA
– sign or nameplate, as of a doctor or lawyer SHINGLE
– sign or pictorial character used in ancient Egyptian writing HIEROGLYPH
– sign or signal of the approach of something HARBINGER, HERALD
– sign or symbol, or its intended meaning or reference DENOTATION
– sign or warning of a coming event OMEN, AUGURY, AUSPICE, PORTENT, PRODIGY, PRESAGE
– signs, such as allergies or dangerous side effects, that argue for the discontinuation of a medicine or treatment CONTRAINDICATION
– make signs or signals by gesturing vigorously GESTICULATE
– person, party, government, or the like that has signed and is bound to a convention or treaty SIGNATORY
– promising, favourable, as a sign or outlook might be AUSPICIOUS
– publisher's sign or emblem on a book COLOPHON
– science or study of signs and symbols SEMIOTICS

sign language used at racecourses by bookmakers TICK-TACK
– sign language with the hands, as used by deaf and dumb people DACTYLOLOGY

sign of the zodiac See **astrology**, **zodiac**

signal flare fired from a special pistol, especially at sea VERY LIGHT
– signal or call to action TOCSIN
– signal or signalling device based on flashes of sunlight from a mirror HELIOGRAPH
– signalling system or apparatus, as on a railway line, using lights, flags, or pivoted arms SEMAPHORE

signature written on behalf of another person ALLOGRAPH
– petition or protest on which the signatures are arranged in a circle ROUND ROBIN
– place one's signature on a document, the back of a cheque, or the like, as to indicate agreement, receipt, or transfer ENDORSE
– showy decoration or squiggle under a signature FLOURISH, PARAPH, CURLICUE

signboard or band of wall above the door or window of a shop FASCIA
– signboard or name plate, as of a doctor or lawyer SHINGLE

signet rings – study of seals and signet rings SPHRAGISTICS

Sikh scriptures GRANTH
– short sword traditionally carried by Sikh men as a symbol of loyalty KIRPAN

Sikkim – title of the ruler of Sikkim CHOGYAL

silence – bridle with an iron bit, formerly used to silence scolding women BRANKS
– monk of a Cistercian order noted for its austerity and vow of silence TRAPPIST

silencer or other sound-reducing device BAFFLE, MUFFLER

silent, not speaking, as though stunned into silence MUTE, DUMBSTRUCK, MUMCHANCE
– silent, reserved, not saying as much as one could RETICENT, UNCOMMUNICATIVE, TACITURN
– silent and inactive, still QUIESCENT, PASSIVE
– silent and thoughtful PENSIVE, REFLECTIVE, MEDITATIVE, CONTEMPLATIVE, INTROSPECTIVE

silk or gauze fabric of very fine texture GOSSAMER
– silk production by rearing silkworms SERICULTURE
– silk-screen print SERIGRAPH
– allowing some light through, as silk or a similar fine fabric does DIAPHANOUS
– spinning of silk from cocoons, or the reel used for it, or the place where such spinning is done FILATURE
– swishing or rustling sound, as of silk FROU-FROU

silky fibre used in pillows, for soundproofing, and so on KAPOK
– silky mass of fibres, as from cotton, or silkworm cocoons FLOSS
– silky protective capsule spun by worms, larvae, or the like, to house the developing pupa COCOON

silly See also **stupid**, **fool**
– silly, ass-like, as a remark might be ASININE
– silly, goose-like ANSERINE
– silly, inappropriately joky or lightweight, as a response to a serious inquiry might be FACETIOUS, FLIPPANT, FRIVOLOUS, TRIVIALISING
– silly, ridiculous, laughable, as an absurd suggestion would be RISIBLE, LUDICROUS
– silly, senseless, empty of thought or purpose, as a speech might be VACUOUS
– silly, talkative person, especially a scatterbrained girl or woman FLIBBERTIGIBBET
– silly, thoughtless, showing poor judgment INJUDICIOUS
– silly, trifling, foolish, as an objection might be FOOTLING
– silly, unrealistic, whimsical, as a scheme might be FANCIFUL
– silly, vain, pretentious person COCKSCOMB
– silly in a childish way PUERILE
– extremely silly, utterly foolish or thoughtless, as a comment might be INANE

silver as referred to in alchemy LUNA
– silver or gold thread used in embroidery PURL
– silver or silvery ornament or object decorated by the insertion of coloured enamel into cut grooves CHAMPLEVÉ
– silver that is 92.5 per cent pure STERLING SILVER
– silver tray or platter for serving food, presenting visiting cards, or the like SALVER
– silvery ARGENTINE
– silvery decoration of thin strips, as on a Christmas tree TINSEL
– mark stamped on gold or silver objects, indicating the purity of the metal HALLMARK, PLATEMARK
– work of twisted wire, especially of gold or silver FILIGREE

silver- ARGENT-

similar, corresponding, consistent, or harmonious CONGRUOUS
– similar or corresponding, especially in shape, as two triangles might be CONGRUENT
– similar or corresponding, especially in sound CONSONANT
– similar or equivalent in certain respects, close enough to be compared COMPARABLE, ANALOGOUS, AKIN, COGNATE
– similar or related KINDRED
– similar or uniform in kind or structure HOMOGENEOUS
– person or thing very similar in appearance to another RINGER
– very similar, impossible to tell apart IDENTICAL, INDISTINGUISHABLE

-similar- HOMEO-, HOMO-, IS-, ISO-, PARA-, SYN-, SYM-, -OSE

-similar substance -PHANE

similarity, as of people's interests COMMUNITY
– similarity between things, such as languages, based on a relationship or causal connection AFFINITY
– similarity of a rough or approximate kind ASSONANCE
– similarity of shape or form about a given axis, point, line, or plane SYMMETRY
– similarity, correspondence or agreement between otherwise dif-

fering elements ANALOGY
- similarity or relationship KINSHIP
- figure of speech pointing directly to a similarity between two things, as in *a wind like a whetted knife* SIMILE
- figure of speech pointing indirectly to a similarity between two things, as in *a razor-sharp wind* METAPHOR
- person or thing having a similar or related form, function, job, or the like COUNTERPART

simple, austere, frugal SPARTAN
- simple, charming, or picturesque event or scene IDYLL
- simple, cooked in a plain way AU NATUREL
- simple, plain, without decoration or fussy additions UNADORNED, UNEMBELLISHED
- simple, relating to basic knowledge, elementary RUDIMENTARY
- simple, unadorned, austere, as furniture might be CLINICAL
- simple, unsophisticated, innocent, as through inexperience NAIVE, INGENUOUS
- simple, unsophisticated, or unpretentious HOMESPUN
- simple and forthright, unscheming, frank ARTLESS, GUILELESS, UNCONTRIVED
- simple and modest in manner, lifestyle, or the like UNASSUMING, UNPRETENTIOUS, UNOSTENTATIOUS
- simple and unsophisticated in a charming way RUSTIC
- simple habits and living conditions, as wartime policy might impose AUSTERITY
- simple to follow or grasp, understandable COMPREHENSIBLE, INTELLIGIBLE, ACCESSIBLE
- simple to understand, very clearly expressed LUCID, PERSPICUOUS, TRANSPARENT

simplified, abstract, stylised, as a painting or design might be CONVENTIONALISED
- simplified and often prejudiced image or opinion of someone or something STEREOTYPE

simplify by drawing conclusions, on the basis of evidence that is not or cannot be exhaustive GENERALISE
- simplify or clarify a passage by rewording it PARAPHRASE
- simplifying of complex information, plans, or the like, especially in an unsophisticated and misleading way REDUCTIONISM

simply, without mincing words TOUT COURT

simultaneous, happening or existing at the same time CONTEMPORARY, CONTEMPORANEOUS, CONCURRENT, COINCIDENT
- simultaneous occurrence, coinciding CONJUNCTION
- simultaneously IN UNISON
- happen at the same time, be simultaneous SYNCHRONISE

simultaneous- SYN-, SYM-

sin or crime TRESPASS, TRANSGRESSION
- sin or fault considered petty or trifling PECCADILLO
- sin so grave that it leads to the forfeiting of God's grace MORTAL SIN
- sin that is relatively minor and excusable, and does not cut the soul off from God's grace VENIAL SIN
- act of self-punishment or devotion to demonstrate sorrow or repentance for sin PENANCE
- cancelling of or release from punishment for a sin, after pardoning, in the Roman Catholic Church INDULGENCE
- liable to sin, open to temptation PECCABLE
- pardon or forgive for a sin ABSOLVE, REMIT
- remorse for one's sins CONTRITION, REPENTANCE, PENITENCE
- rescue or save from sin REDEEM
- seven deadly sins CARDINAL SINS

sincere, deeply or truly felt HEARTFELT
- sincere, genuine, whole-hearted, without pretending UNFEIGNED, FOUR-SQUARE
- sincere and modest, not making any false claims for oneself UNAFFECTED, UNPRETENTIOUS
- sincere or devoted in one's affections, religious duties, or the like DEVOUT

sinew attaching a muscle to a bone or other support TENDON
- sinews, muscles THEWS

sinful See **evil**, **immoral**

sing a love song to one's sweetheart SERENADE
- sing a part-song, such as a carol or round TROLL
- sing in a voice wavering between normal and falsetto, as among folk-singers in the Alps YODEL
- sing or recite in a half-musical tone, chant INTONE, CANTILLATE
- sing with trills, as a thrush does WARBLE
- singing or chanting that involves responses or alternating parts ANTIPHONY
- singing training through the use of the *doh-re-mi* syllables TONIC SOL-FA, SOLFEGGIO, SOLMISATION
- singing voice, typically male, when forced into an unnatural register much higher than the normal range FALSETTO
- director of singing in a church PRECENTOR
- highest singing part in a choral song, or a decorative air sung above a melody DESCANT
- operatic singing of a pure, rich, unstrained, even-toned style BEL CANTO
- referring or relating to singing or compositions based on the harmonising of two or more different melodic lines POLYPHONIC
- referring to male voices singing unaccompanied in four-part harmony BARBERSHOP
- referring to singing performed without instrumental accompaniment À CAPELLA

singer, as in a band or pop group VOCALIST
- singer, especially a soprano, who specialises in ornamental trills and runs COLORATURA
- singer, musician, or other entertainer performing in public places for money from idlers or passersby BUSKER
- singer in the role of a young woman, especially a flirtatious lady's maid, in a comic opera SOUBRETTE
- singer or poet in 15th- to 16th-century German guilds MEISTERSINGER
- singer-poet and storyteller in medieval times MINSTREL, JONGLEUR, TROUBADOUR
- singer's range of notes from high to low COMPASS, REGISTER
- boy singer performing the highest voice part TREBLE
- choir-leader, lead singer, or soloist, as in a church or synagogue CANTOR, PRECENTOR
- female singer, as in a nightclub or cabaret CHANTEUSE
- female singer or boy singer with the highest natural range SOPRANO
- female singer with a medium high natural range MEZZO-SOPRANO
- female singer with a relatively low natural range CONTRALTO, ALTO
- group of singers in the U.S., typically performing choral music GLEE CLUB
- group of singers or musicians CONSORT
- leading female opera singer PRIMA DONNA, DIVA
- male singer, usually a bass, performing comic opera roles BUFFO
- male singer castrated in boyhood in former times, to keep his high-pitched voice CASTRATO
- male singer with a strong high

voice, especially suited to Wagnerian opera HELDENTENOR
- male singer with an extremely high natural range COUNTERTENOR, ALTO
- male singer with a high natural range TENOR
- male singer with a medium low natural range BARITONE
- male singer with the lowest natural range BASS
- male singer with an extremely low natural range BASSO PROFUNDO
- melodic rather than dramatic, as a singer might be LYRIC

single, sole SOLITARY
- single, undivided UNITARY
- single-celled organism MONAD
- single out, mention individually PARTICULARISE, SPECIFY

single- UNI-, MONO-

single file INDIAN FILE
- single file, as of troops marching DEFILE

singly, individually, in the order stated RESPECTIVELY

sinister – person exerting or trying to exert a sinister influence over another's will SVENGALI

sink, as a ship might FOUNDER
- sink one's ship, accidentally or deliberately SCUPPER, SCUTTLE
- sink or settle SUBSIDE

sinning, guilty PECCANT

sir – respectful term of address to one's boss or employer in East Africa, roughly equivalent to "Master" or "Sir" BWANA
- title of respect in colonial India, roughly equivalent to "Master" or "Sir" SAHIB

siren in German myth whose singing lured sailors to destruction along the Rhine LORELEI
- change in pitch of sound, as of a siren, as the source approaches or moves away from the listener DOPPLER EFFECT

sister or brother SIBLING
- custom in some societies by which a man marries two or more sisters successively SORORATE
- male or female nurse, the equivalent of a nursing sister, supervising a hospital ward CHARGE NURSE
- murder of one's sister SORORICIDE

sisterhood, state of being sisters or sisterly SORORITY

sitting a great deal, or requiring much sitting, as a job might SEDENTARY
- upright, cross-legged sitting position, as in yoga and meditation, with the hands resting on the knees LOTUS POSITION

situation requiring a choice between two equal and typically undesirable alternatives DILEMMA, DOUBLE BIND
- situation that is difficult, embarrassing, or unpleasant PREDICAMENT

six children or young born at one birth SEXTUPLETS
- six-pointed star, such as the Star of David HEXAGRAM
- group of six people or things, especially musicians SEXTET
- lasting for six years, or occurring once every six years SEXENNIAL
- relating to or based on the number six, or having six parts SENARY

six- HEX-, HEXA-, SEX-

sixteenth century in Italian art and architecture CINQUECENTO

sixth sense – perception by means of a sixth sense, supernatural powers, intuition, or the like EXTRASENSORY PERCEPTION, ESP, CRYPTAESTHESIA, TELAESTHESIA

sixty – sixty-year-old, or a person aged between 60 and 69 SEXAGENARIAN
- relating to or based on the number 60 SEXAGESIMAL

size or extent DIMENSIONS, PROPORTIONS, MAGNITUDE, AMPLITUDE

skating – blade of a skate or sledge RUNNER
- jump of various kinds in ice-skating, in which the skater takes off on one foot, spins in the air, and lands on the other foot AXEL, LUTZ, SALCHOW
- notched section on the front of the blade of a skate, used for braking TOE RAKE, TOE PICKS
- position in ice-skating in which the feet are splayed outwards with the heels together SPREADEAGLE
- turn of various kinds in ice-skating, in which the skater switches from skating forwards to skating backwards, or vice versa, while changing from one foot to the other MOHAWK, CHOCTAW

skeleton key or master key PASSKEY, PASSE-PARTOUT

sketch, outline, draw or describe DELINEATE
- sketch, plan, or rough drawing of something DRAFT
- sketch or brief incident or scene in a book, film, or play VIGNETTE, CAMEO
- sketch or preliminary drawing, often full-size, for a tapestry, painting, or the like CARTOON
- sketch out or give a rough outline of something, such as a plan ADUMBRATE

skewer of grilled meat KEBAB, SHASHLIK
- skewer or small spit for grilling or roasting, or the food cooked on this BROCHETTE

ski See chart, page 474
- ski-lift cable-car typically for one or two skiers GONDOLA
- ski-lift for a single skier, who is dragged uphill by a plastic disc on the end of a bar placed between the legs BUTTON LIFT, POMA LIFT
- ski-like blade on the hull of a boat that raises it when speeding HYDROFOIL
- block or plastic arch fitted on the tip of a ski to prevent the skis from crossing PARABLOCK
- device on a ski for securing the boot firmly but releasing it when strain arises, as during an accident RELEASE BINDING, SAFETY BINDING
- disc near the tip of a ski pole to stop it from sinking into the snow BASKET
- dungaree-style ski trousers SALOPETTE
- machine for packing down the snow on the ski slopes RATRAC
- season ticket or pass for ski lifts ABONNEMENT

skid, slide, or slither, as a car might on a wet road AQUAPLANE

skilful, very able in a confident way PROFICIENT, ACCOMPLISHED
- skilful at, expert in AU FAIT, ADEPT
- skilful craftsman or manual worker ARTISAN, ARTIFICER
- skilful or clever, especially with one's hands DEXTEROUS, DEFT, ADROIT, HABILE
- skilful or knowledgeable VERSED
- skilful or talented in a wide variety of ways VERSATILE
- reasonably skilful COMPETENT

skill, power, or ability FACULTY, APTITUDE
- skill at conjuring or card tricks, involving deceptive hand movements LEGERDEMAIN, SLEIGHT OF HAND
- skill displaying outstanding technical ability, especially in playing a musical instrument VIRTUOSITY
- skill of a delicate or subtle kind, as in painting style, negotiations or tennis strokes FINESSE
- skill of an effortless kind FACILITY
- skill or sensitivity, as in one's dealings with other people, social know-how TACT, SAVOIR FAIRE
- inventive skill or cleverness INGENUITY, ARTIFICE
- outstanding skill PROWESS
- strong point, major skill, speciality FORTE, MÉTIER

skim, glide, or skip lightly SKITTER

– skim or glide in the wind, as clouds do SCUD

skin See illustration

– skin, membrane, seed coat, or similar natural outer covering INTEGUMENT

– skin, strip the skin of, as by whipping FLAY

– skin blemish, scar, birthmark, or rash STIGMA

– skin blemish or growth, such as a mole or strawberry mark, present from birth NAEVUS

– skin blemish or spot MACULA

– skin cancer of a slow-growing type CANCROID

– skin condition marked by a horny patch or growth, such as a wart KERATOSIS

– skin condition or allergy involving itching and bumps HIVES, NETTLE RASH, URTICARIA, UREDO

– skin grafting in plastic surgery DERMATOPLASTY

– skin inflammation in the form of a pus-filled blister or pimple PUSTULE

– skin irritation caused by the wind WINDBURN

– skin-like sheet of natural or artificial tissue through which fluids can pass slowly MEMBRANE

– skin-like sheet of tissue covering or lining all body parts EPITHELIUM

– skin lotion for relieving pain or stiffness LINIMENT, EMBROCATION, UNGUENT

– skin lotion for soothing and softening EMOLLIENT

– skin of a sheep or goat, treated for writing or painting on PARCHMENT

– skin of an animal, hide PELT, FELL

– skin pigment MELANIN

– skin rash, as in measles ROSEOLA

– break out, appear on the skin, as a pimple or other blemish does ERUPT

– brownish patches on the skin, as occurring during pregnancy CHLOASMA

– cold and clammy, as the skin of malaria patients is ALGID

– curved blunt blade used by ancient Greeks and Romans for scraping the skin STRIGIL

– fibrous tissue beneath the skin and encasing muscles FASCIA

– fold of skin hanging from the throat, as of some birds and lizards WATTLE

– fold or flap of skin, such as that under the tongue FRAENUM

– former medical technique of attaching a glass cup to the skin by a partial vacuum, in order to draw blood to the surface CUPPING

– itching sensation, as though ants were crawling all over one's skin FORMICATION

– large freckle or discoloration developing on the skin of elderly people LIVER SPOT, LENTIGO

– located or made just beneath the skin, as fat or an injection might be SUBCUTANEOUS

– oil secreted by small glands in the skin SEBUM, SMEGMA

– outgrowth on an animal, seed, the skin, or the like, such as a cock's comb CARUNCLE

– piece of skin pulled away but partially attached beside a fingernail HANGNAIL

– relating to the region just beneath the skin HYPODERMIC

– relating to the skin CUTANEOUS, DERMAL

– rough to the touch, horny or scaly, as hard dry skin might be SCABROUS, SQUAMOUS

– rub or tear away the skin of EXCORIATE

– scab or layer of dead skin, as caused by a burn ESCHAR

– scaly dry skin, as in dandruff SCURF, FURFURES

– shedding of the outer layer,

SKIING TERMS

Term	Definition	Term	Definition
Alpine	referring to downhill and slalom racing	**schuss**	fast, straight downhill run
biathlon	winter-sports contest involving cross-country skiing and target shooting	**skibob**	bicycle-like vehicle that has short skis in place of wheels
christiania/ christy	medium-fast turn with the skis kept parallel	**skijoring**	skiing behind a towing horse or vehicle
fall-line	most direct line of descent	**slalom**	zigzag downhill race between poles or posts
geländesprung	jump launched from a crouching position during a downhill run	**snowploughing**	slowing by turning the tips of the skis inwards to form a V
herringboning	climbing uphill by turning skis outwards to form a V	**stem turn**	turn made by pushing the heel of one or both skis outwards
hot-dogging	spectacular freestyle skiing	**swing**	high-speed turn with the skis kept parallel
kick turn	pivot while stationary by raising and reversing the skis one by one	**telemark**	turn across the fall line made by pushing one ski well forward and round; possible only with bindings that leave the heel free, as in cross-country skiing
langlauf	cross-country skiing		
mogul, bosse	mound or hillock of compacted snow	**traversing**	skiing diagonally or almost horizontally across the slope
Nordic	referring to cross-country racing and related events	**vorlage**	position in which the skier or ski jumper leans forward from the ankles
off-piste	referring to skiing on unmarked slopes	**wedeln**	series of short zigzag turns down the fall-line
piste	marked ski run		

shell, or skin, as in insects and snakes SLOUGHING, ECDYSIS
– slit or scratch the skin slightly, as for vaccination SCARIFY
– strip of hardened skin at the base of a fingernail or toenail CUTICLE
– technical name for the skin DERMIS, CUTIS
– thickened or horny patch of skin, caused by pressure or friction, as on the hand or foot CALLUS, CALLOSITY
– tiny hole in the skin for perspiration to pass through PORE

-skin- -DERM-, DERMO-, DERMATO-

skin diseases See **diseases**

skip, glide, or skim lightly SKITTER
– skip or jump about playfully FROLIC, CAVORT, FRISK, GAMBOL, SPORT, ROLLICK, CAPER, ROMP

skirt See also **clothes**
– skirt of an old style, very tight below the knees HOBBLE SKIRT
– skirt that is bell-shaped, being draped over a structure of hoops HOOP SKIRT
– skirt worn as folk costume by Greek men, as on ceremonial occasions FUSTANELLA
– ballerina's very short skirt TUTU
– frame or pad formerly worn under a woman's skirt to expand it at the rear BUSTLE
– hoop or series of hoops formerly worn under a skirt to support it, or the skirt itself FARTHINGALE
– support, as of wire, spreading a skirt at the hips PANNIER

skull See also **bones**, **head**
– skull CRANIUM
– skull or a picture of it, representing mortality or death DEATH'S-HEAD
– cut a hole in or remove a disc of bone from the skull, using a special instrument TREPAN, TREPHINE
– former practice of studying the shape and irregularities of a person's skull as a supposed indication of his character and mental powers PHRENOLOGY
– front upper part of the skull, the forehead area SINCIPUT
– furthermost point at the back of the skull INION
– opening at the base of the skull, through which the spinal cord passes FORAMEN MAGNUM
– relating to the head or skull CEPHALIC
– reminder of inescapable death, such as a skull MEMENTO MORI
– seam or joint-line, as on a seedpod or between the bones of the skull SUTURE
– spongy bone between the hard inner and outer bone layers of the skull DIPLOË
– top of the head, highest point of the skull VERTEX
– top part of the skull, skullcap CALVARIA

-skull- -CEPHAL-, CEPHALO-

skull-and-crossbones, pirate flag JOLLY ROGER

skullcap worn by religious male Jews YARMULKE, KIPA, KOPPEL
– skullcap worn by some male Muslims TAQIA, GHOL-TOPI
– skullcap worn by some Roman Catholic clergymen CALOTTE, ZUCCHETTO

sky, arching vault of the heavens WELKIN, FIRMAMENT
– look menacing and dark, as the sky or weather might LOWER
– relating to the sky or heavens SUPERNAL, CELESTIAL, EMPYREAL

sky- URAN-, URANO-

sky-blue AZURE, CERULEAN

slander, insult in a false or unfairly demeaning way DEFAME, MALIGN, VILIFY, CALUMNIATE, SMEAR
– slander, knowingly false statement that injures someone's reputation CALUMNY, DEFAMATION
– slander, malicious injury or damage to someone's reputation

skin

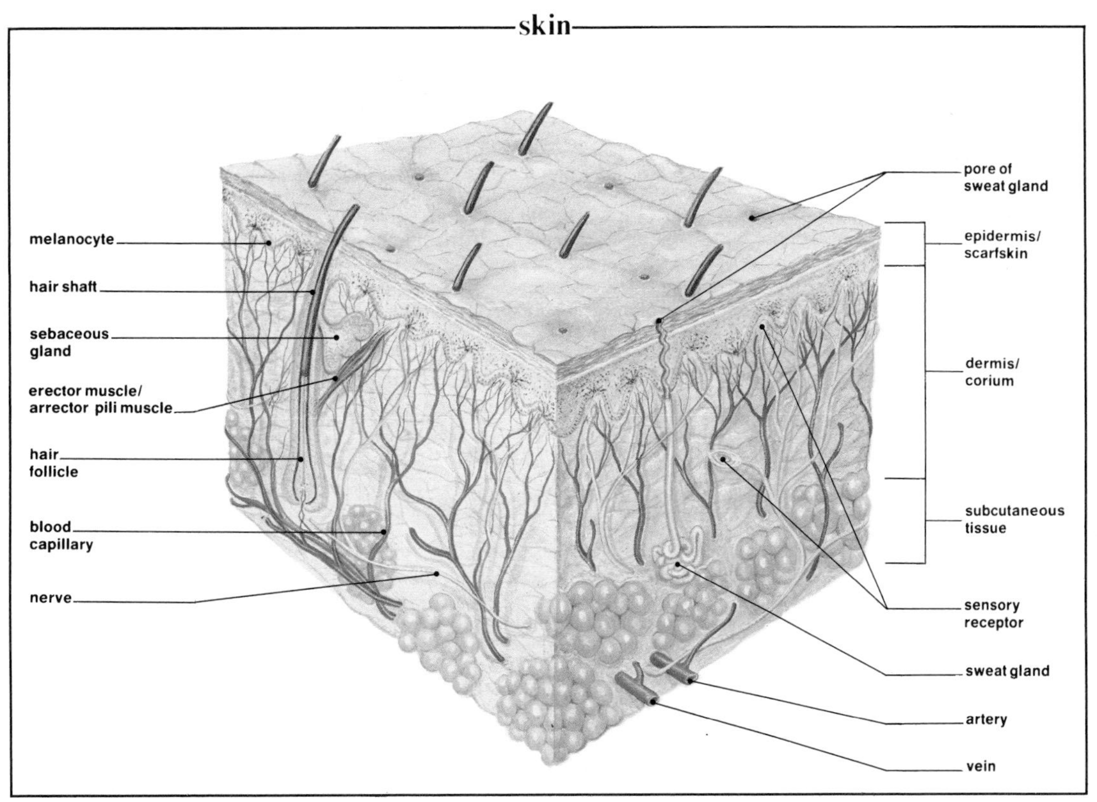

CHARACTER ASSASSINATION
– slander or betray TRADUCE
– circulate slander openly UTTER
– defamation that is permanent, not spoken as slander is LIBEL

slang or jargon of a group ARGOT, CANT, PATOIS
– informal, slightly slangy word or phrase COLLOQUIALISM

slant See **slope**

-slant- -CLIN-, CLINO-

slanting- PLAGI-, PLAGIO-

slash, punctuation mark as in *and/or* SOLIDUS, VIRGULE, OBLIQUE, SHILLING MARK

slat or strip of wood or metal used in sheets as a backing for plaster, slates, tiles, or the like LATH
– slatted shutter or blind that can be adjusted to regulate the air or light admitted JALOUSIE
– slatted window or door, or any of the slats LOUVRE

slaughter or massacre, especially in war CARNAGE
– slaughter or sacrifice on a large scale HECATOMB
– without making any distinctions, as among the victims of wholesale slaughter INDISCRIMINATE

slaughterhouse ABATTOIR, SHAMBLES

slave in Muslim countries in former times MAMELUKE
– slave-like, relating to a slave SERVILE
– slave-like labourer, bound to a lord or estate SERF, BONDSERVANT, HELOT
– slave on the run, in the West Indies MAROON
– slave or concubine forming part of a harem ODALISQUE
– slave owned by a specific person CHATTEL
– slave who escaped or was freed during the American Civil War CONTRABAND
– supervisor of a gang of slaves OVERSEER, TASKMASTER
– temporary barracks for slaves or convicts in former times BARRACOON

slavery or enslavement BONDAGE, SERVITUDE, THRALL
– ending of slavery and the slave trade ABOLITION
– free from slavery EMANCIPATE, MANUMIT, ENFRANCHISE

sledge with an upturned front, used for transport or sliding downhill TOBOGGAN
– blade of metal or wood on a skate or sledge RUNNER
– command to sledge dogs to speed up MUSH

sleep LAND OF NOD
– sleep-inducing NARCOTIC, SOPORIFIC, HYPNOTIC, HYPNAGOGIC, SOMNIFEROUS, SOPORIFEROUS, SOMNOLENT
– "sleep-learning" HYPNOPAEDIA
– sleep of the commonest kind, involving deep relaxation and no dreaming ORTHODOX SLEEP
– sleep of the kind involving dreaming and eye movements, occurring in phases during the sleep cycle PARADOXICAL SLEEP
– sleep or remain in a dormant state throughout the winter, as some animals do HIBERNATE
– sleep or remain in a dormant state throughout the summer, as some animals do AESTIVATE
– sleep or rest taken in the afternoon, especially in hot southern countries SIESTA
– sleep personified, or the god of sleep MORPHEUS
– calm someone to sleep LULL
– movement of the eyeballs behind closed lids during the dreaming phase of sleep REM, RAPID EYE MOVEMENT

sleep- HYPN-, HYPNO-, SOMN-, SOMNO-

sleeper – U.S. term for a railway sleeper CROSSTIE, TIE

sleeping, inactive DORMANT
– sleeping car, especially on a European train WAGON-LIT
– sleeping quarters, as in a boarding school DORMITORY

sleeping pill or potion HYPNOTIC, SOPORIFIC, NARCOTIC, SEDATIVE, OPIATE
– sleeping pill of a common synthetic type NITRAZEPAM, DIAZEPAM

sleeping sickness ENCEPHALITIS LETHARGICA, TRYPANOSOMIASIS
– bloodsucking fly in Africa that causes sleeping sickness TSETSE FLY

sleeplessness INSOMNIA

sleepwalking SOMNAMBULISM, NOCTAMBULISM
– sleepwalking, knee-jerk, or similar involuntary, unthinking action AUTOMATISM

sleepy DROWSY
– sleepy feeling, sluggishness TORPOR, SOMNOLENCE
– sleepy or yawning OSCITANT
– sleepy semi-consciousness induced by anaesthetics TWILIGHT SLEEP

sleepy- NARCO-

sleeve extending all the way to the collar RAGLAN SLEEVE
– sleeve that is wide at the armhole and tapers to a narrow wrist DOLMAN SLEEVE
– full at one end and tapering at the other, as a sleeve might be LEG-OF-MUTTON
– loose-fitting sleeve cut in one piece with the bodice MAGYAR SLEEVE
– puffed out, as a sleeve or hairstyle might be BOUFFANT

sleight of hand, as of a magician in performing tricks PRESTIDIGITATION, LEGERDEMAIN

slice of bacon or ham RASHER
– slice of veal coated in egg and breadcrumbs and fried lightly in butter WIENER SCHNITZEL
– sliced or finely shredded, as vegetables might be JULIENNE

slide, slip, or skid, as on a wet road SLITHER, SLEW
– slide, sloping channel or duct down which water, coal, parcels, or the like can be conveyed CHUTE
– slide, X-ray photograph, or the like TRANSPARENCY
– projector for slides, diagrams on transparent plates, or the like DIASCOPE
– spiral slide at a funfair HELTER-SKELTER

slide rule – sliding transparent indicator on a slide rule CURSOR

slimming – high-class French cooking that cuts down on rich ingredients, favoured by diners who are slimming CUISINE MINCEUR

sling for sliding or lifting tree trunks, barrels, or the like PARBUCKLE
– giant sling or catapult, as for hurling rocks, used in medieval warfare TREBUCHET

slip of the tongue, verbal blunder LAPSUS LINGUAE
– slip of the tongue or similar lapse that discloses someone's real feelings or unconscious thoughts FREUDIAN SLIP, PARAPRAXIS

slipper PANTOFFLE
– slipper-shaped, as some orchids are CALCEOLATE

slippery, difficult to catch or pin down ELUSIVE
– slippery and smooth LUBRICOUS

slit in a dress, skirt, or the like, as for fitting a fastening or for access to a pocket PLACKET

slope, slant, be at an angle BEVEL, SPLAY
– slope, slant, tilt INCLINATION, DEVIATION, CANT
– slope backwards, as someone's forehead might RECEDE
– slope of a roof PITCH
– slope or angle, as of a mast, theatre stage, aircraft's wings, or cutting edge of a tool RAKE
– slope or gentle incline GLACIS
– sloping or slanting, at an angle INCLINED, OBLIQUE
– sloping section or incline, as of a road or railway track GRADIENT

– sloping typeface, as used for emphasis ITALIC
– diagonal or crosswise route across a slope, as in skiing TRAVERSE
– downward slope or tendency DECLENSION, DECLINATION, DECLINE, DECLIVITY
– flat shelf cut, usually as part of a series, into the side of a slope, for cultivation, preventing erosion, or the like TERRACE
– less steep, sloping rock surface at the base of a mountain in dry areas PEDIMENT
– long, steep slope, as from a plateau or in front of a castle ESCARPMENT
– upward slope ACCLIVITY

-slope- -CLIN-, CLINO-

sloping- PLAGI-, PLAGIO-

slot, groove, or notch CHASE
– slot into which a matching tenon is fitted when joining two pieces of wood, stone, or metal MORTISE

sloth – two-toed sloth UNAU

slow, causing delays DILATORY
– slow, unhurried, at a comfortable pace LEISURELY
– slow absorption or acquisition, as of knowledge OSMOSIS
– slow and unhurried, thinking out each move DELIBERATE
– slow down DECELERATE, RETARD
– slow down or reduce in intensity or volume, peter out, dwindle SUBSIDE, RECEDE, TAPER OFF
– slow-motion balletic body movements performed in a series as part of a Chinese form of exercise and mental training TAI CHI
– slow-moving, sluggish TARDY
– slow or sluggish, as though constipated COSTIVE
– slow person, lagging behind LAGGARD, DAWDLER, SLOWCOACH
– slow through lacking energy or interest LANGUID, LACKADAISICAL
– slow to finish, long and drawn out PROLONGED, INTERMINABLE, PROTRACTED
– delay, be late or slow in doing something TARRY, PROCRASTINATE
– emerge or discharge slowly, as through pores EXUDE

slow- BRADY-

slowing or stoppage of blood flow, digestion, or the like STASIS

-slowing -STASIS, -STAT

sluggish, inactive TORPID, LETHARGIC

slum clearance URBAN RENEWAL
– slum area or old area of a city, inhabited by a poor minority group GHETTO
– exploitation or intimidation of slum tenants by a ruthless landlord RACHMANISM
– large building, often in a slum area, divided into rooms or flats for rent TENEMENT

slur or slight of an oblique or veiled kind INNUENDO, ASPERSION, INSINUATION

sly, cunning, crafty, full of tricks ARTFUL, INGENIOUS, WILY
– sly, shifty, calculating, or sneaky DEVIOUS, GUILEFUL
– sly, shrewd ASTUTE
– sly or knowing look LEER
– sly or secret, as a rendezvous might be CLANDESTINE
– sly or stealthy in a secretive or underhand way FURTIVE, SURREPTITIOUS
– slyly feigning ignorance or innocence, insincere DISINGENUOUS
– slyly imply, hint, or introduce something INSINUATE

small, charming, and delicate trinket or other object BIJOU
– small, puny person RUNT, MINNOW, PIPSQUEAK
– small, ungenerous, skimpy, as an allowance might be BEGGARLY, MEAGRE, PALTRY
– small allowance, salary, or the like PITTANCE
– small amount, especially a slight knowledge of a language SMATTERING
– small amount, modest quantity SEMBLANCE, MODICUM
– small and quaint DINKY, ELFIN
– small and trim, dainty, compact, as a woman might be PETITE
– small but self-important man COCKALORUM
– small or ridiculously inadequate, as a pay offer might be DERISORY
– smallest possible, as in amount or degree MINIMAL
– extremely small, microscopic, insignificant INFINITESIMAL
– so small as to pass unnoticed IMPERCEPTIBLE
– very small, barely noticeable, as a slight difference or increase might be MARGINAL
– very small amount, merest hint or trace SOUPÇON, TINCTURE, VESTIGE
– very small amount, tiny bit SLIVER, IOTA, SCINTILLA, SMIDGEN
– very small in size or stature, miniature DIMINUTIVE, MIDGET, LILLIPUTIAN, MINUSCULE

-small- -CLE, -CULE, -KIN, -ULE, -Y, -EY, -IE, MICRO-, NANO-

small ad CLASSIFIED ADVERTISEMENT

small letters, as distinct from capital letters LOWER CASE, MINUSCULE LETTERS

small talk, polite remarks PLEASANTRIES

-small version -LING

smaller- MINI-

smallness See **lack**

smallpox VARIOLA

smart, well-groomed, elegant SOIGNÉ
– smart in a cheeky way, jaunty, as the angle of a hat might be RAKISH
– smartly dressed, neat and trim, spruce DAPPER

smarten up in appearance as by adornment or refurbishment TITIVATE

smash or crush inwards STAVE

smear or spread roughly a substance such as mud, plaster, or grease DAUB

smear test in gynaecology PAP TEST

smell, or smelly gas or vapour, as from a swamp or rubbish heap EFFLUVIUM
– smell of a wine, brandy, or liqueur BOUQUET
– bad smell, stink, stench, as of rotting organic material FETOR, MEPHITIS, HUM
– carry lightly, as the wind carries the smell of flowers WAFT
– loss of the sense of smell ANOSMIA
– pleasant smell, as of food AROMA, SAVOUR
– pleasant smell, as of perfume or flowers FRAGRANCE, INCENSE
– relating to the sense of smell OLFACTORY, OSMATIC
– sharp or harsh, as a smell or taste might be ACRID, PUNGENT
– spray, liquid, or other substance used to suppress or mask smells such as those of sweat or cooking DEODORANT

smelling, especially pleasant-smelling FRAGRANT, REDOLENT, AROMATIC
– smelling, especially unpleasant-smelling ODOROUS, ODORIFEROUS
– smelling mouldy FUSTY, MUSTY, FROWZY
– smelling of decay, foul-smelling MEPHITIC
– smelling off, stale, decomposing, as old butter or bacon fat might be RANCID, RANK
– smelling or tasting bad or rotten RANK, GAMY
– smelly, stinking FETID, MALODOROUS, REEKING, NOISOME
– smelly as a goat HIRCINE

smelling salts containing ammonium carbonate SAL VOLATILE
– bottle for smelling salts VINAIGRETTE

smelting – solid waste material from a furnace after smelting or refining SLAG, SINTER, CINDER, SCORIA

smile in an irritatingly shy or affected way SIMPER

– smile in an irritatingly smug or knowing way SMIRK
– smiling expression on the face of early Greek statues ARCHAIC SMILE
– apologetic or regretful, in a slightly cynical way, as a wry smile might be RUEFUL
– joyful in a serene or saintly way, as a smile might be BEATIFIC
– puzzling or mysterious, as a smile might be ENIGMATIC
– shy, hesitant, or uncertain, as a smile might be TENTATIVE
– unnatural gaping expression or smile RICTUS

smoke, vapour, or gas that is blown or breathed out EXHALATION
– dark and oppressive covering, as of smoke PALL, SHROUD
– fill a room or building with poisonous smoke to disinfect it or rid it of vermin FUMIGATE
– relating to smoke FUMATORY
– wood used for smoking food in North America HICKORY

smoked haddock FINNAN HADDOCK, FINNAN HADDIE

smoked herring BUCKLING

smoked salmon LOX

smoking – inhaling by non-smokers of other people's tobacco smoke, now confirmed as a health hazard PASSIVE SMOKING

smoky or sooty FULIGINOUS

smooth, socially gracious and charming, often in a superficial way SUAVE, URBANE
– smooth and bald GLABROUS
– smooth and charming but often deceiving talk BLARNEY
– smooth and polished, as leather might be GLACÉ
– smooth and shiny, having a satiny finish SLEEK
– smooth and sweet, as a voice might be MELLIFLUOUS
– smooth surface on a bone or tooth FACET
– smoothly charming in an insincere, over-earnest way UNCTUOUS, INGRATIATING
– smoothly or easily done FACILE
– make plaster or a similar surface smooth or level FLOAT
– speaking or writing in a smooth and effortless but sometimes shallow way FLUENT, GLIB

smuggling, or smuggled goods CONTRABAND
– smuggled or illicitly manufactured goods, especially alcohol during the Prohibition era in the U.S. BOOTLEG
– official who prevented smuggling in former times EXCISEMAN

snack or appetiser of a small open sandwich or spread biscuit CANAPÉ
– snack or light luncheon TIFFIN

snail or related land creature HELIX
– snail or related shell-covered land or sea creature MOLLUSC
– edible snail, especially when cooked ESCARGOT
– shaped like a snail shell, twisted spirally COCHLEATE

snake, such as the anaconda, python, or boa, that coils round and crushes its prey CONSTRICTOR
– snake-like monster with multiplying heads, killed by Hercules HYDRA
– snake's long, pointed tooth FANG
– adjective for a snake ANGUINE, COLUBRINE, OPHIDIAN
– curving gracefully, as a winding road or the movements of a snake might be SINUOUS
– poisonous snake, probably a small cobra, that killed Cleopatra ASP
– shedding of the outer layer, shell, or skin, as in insects and snakes SLOUGHING, ECDYSIS
– staff with wings and two twining snakes, serving as a symbol of the medical profession CADUCEUS
– weasel-like mammal noted for its skill in killing snakes MONGOOSE

snakebite antidote obtained from the blood or tissue of immunised animals SERUM
– poisonous fluid secreted in a snakebite, scorpion sting, or the like VENOM

snapdragon or related plant ANTIRRHINUM

snare See **trap**

sneeze, or the act or noise of sneezing STERNUTATION
– German equivalent of "Bless you!", said to someone who has sneezed GESUNDHEIT

snipe – flock of snipe WISP

snobbish, haughty, or pretentious HOITY-TOITY
– snobbish, stuck-up TOFFEE-NOSED
– snobbishness, exclusiveness, and standoffishness ÉLITISM

snooker – fabric, usually green and woollen, used on top of snooker or billiard tables BAIZE
– snooker support or rest on legs for a cue during a difficult or inaccessible shot SPIDER
– shot in snooker in which the red ball struck by the cue ball goes on to strike another red ball PLANT
– shot made with a near-upright cue in snooker or billiards, designed to curve the cue ball around an obstructing ball to hit another MASSÉ

snoring heavily, or relating to a heavy snoring noise STERTOROUS

snow – snow-like NIVEOUS
– snow pellets, soft hail GRAUPEL
– ledge of snow overhanging a cliff or mountain top CORNICE
– mass of porous ice formed from snow but not yet turned into glacier ice FIRN, NÉVÉ

snowshoe consisting of a stringed loop RACKET

snowstorm that is heavy and cold, with high winds BLIZZARD

snuff made from a strong tobacco RAPPEE

so – "so", "thus", term used in a printed text to indicate the deliberate reproduction of a mistaken or surprising wording or fact being quoted SIC

so-called, self-styled SOI-DISANT

so much the better TANT MIEUX

so much the worse TANT PIS

soak, cover completely in a liquid IMMERSE, SUBMERGE
– soak, wet, or fill with a substance IMPREGNATE, SATURATE, INFUSE, IMBUE
– soak or pickle meat or fish in a sauce before cooking MARINATE
– soak or steep herbs, tea, or the like without boiling INFUSE
– soften, separate, or disintegrate by means of soaking MACERATE

soap – soap-like or soapy PINGUID, SAPONACEOUS
– fine hard white soap containing olive oil CASTILE SOAP
– referring to soap containing a pungent disinfectant acid derived from coal tar CARBOLIC

soccer – player in soccer who defends from a position near his own goal SWEEPER
– player in soccer who is usually positioned in the opponent's half to exploit scoring opportunities STRIKER
– pretended pass or swerve, as in soccer or rugby, to deceive an opposing player DUMMY

sociable See also **friendly**
– sociable, enjoying the company of others GREGARIOUS
– sociable, friendly, lively person EXTROVERT
– sociable, jolly, or festive, as a party atmosphere or companion might be JOVIAL, CONVIVIAL

social distinction or prestige CACHET
– social disturbance or agitation of a violent kind UPHEAVAL, CONVULSION
– social event or sports match, or the date of it FIXTURE
– social group of the same age and status as oneself PEER GROUP
– social group or clique, such as a

literary discussion group CENACLE
– social institutions or ideas that are, according to Marxist theory, really based on economic and labour relations SUPERSTRUCTURE
– social mixing or friendly relations, as with the people of an enemy country FRATERNISATION
– social or artistic group consigned to the fringes of respectable society, as in the 19th century DEMIMONDE
– social outcast ISHMAEL, PARIAH, LEPER
– social reformer or theorist who is hopelessly idealistic and impractical VISIONARY, UTOPIAN
– social role or self-projection adopted by a person when in the company of others PERSONA
– social self-assurance and adeptness, tact SAVOIR-FAIRE
– social success, acclaim, or distinction ÉCLAT
– social system in medieval Europe, in which vassals exchanged homage and service for land and protection from a lord FEUDALISM, FEUDAL SYSTEM
– social worker responsible to a court for supervising offenders with suspended sentences PROBATION OFFICER
– grand, lofty, or exalted, as a literary style or social circle might be RAREFIED
– possession desired or valued as an indicator of wealth or social prestige STATUS SYMBOL
– raising one's social status UPWARDLY MOBILE
– rejection of all moral and social values NIHILISM
– treat someone as a social idol or celebrity LIONISE

social blunder GAFFE, FAUX PAS

social climber, upstart, johnny-come-lately ARRIVISTE, PARVENU, NOUVEAU RICHE

socialise or associate in a familiar way HOBNOB, CONSORT
– socialise or flirt, especially while wandering about GAD ABOUT, GALLIVANT

socialism of a non-revolutionary, democratic, gradually developing kind FABIANISM

socially acceptable and polite remarks, small talk PLEASANTRIES, CIVILITIES
– socially awkward or ill-at-ease teenager or young man or woman HOBBLEDEHOY
– socially correct and acceptable, proper COMME IL FAUT
– socially exclusive and cultivated person, intellectual snob, in the U.S. BRAHMIN
– socially gracious and charming, often in a superficial way SUAVE
– socially humbled, reduced in social status or class DÉCLASSÉ
– socially skilful, tactful, or sensitive DIPLOMATIC

society or association, specifically a charitable society of lay Roman Catholics SODALITY
– society's basic structures and institutions, such as transport and education INFRASTRUCTURE
– divided according to castes or classes, as a nation or society might be STRATIFIED
– influential conservative group of people, subtly directing political trends, artistic activity, or the like within society ESTABLISHMENT
– level, such as a class or caste, within a society or series STRATUM
– local branch of a society or club CHAPTER, LODGE
– referring to a society in which several racial, religious, or cultural groups coexist freely and harmoniously PLURALISTIC
– sense or state of being an outsider, isolated from one's society ALIENATION
– young upper-class lady undergoing a formal presentation to society, as at a ball DEBUTANTE

socket, as for the rudder of a boat or the pin of a hinge GUDGEON

socks or stockings HOSE, HOSIERY
– socks with a diamond-shaped pattern of two or more colours ARGYLE SOCKS
– embroidered or woven design on the side of a sock CLOCK

Socrates – poison drunk by Socrates in accordance with his death sentence HEMLOCK
– process of reaching the truth, as in Hegel or Socrates, by examining contradictions DIALECTIC
– relating to Socrates' method of eliciting someone's submerged knowledge by means of a series of questions MAIEUTIC

soda water, sparkling water CARBONATED WATER, CLUB SODA, SELTZER WATER
– emitting small bubbles of gas, as soda water does EFFERVESCENT

sofa See **furniture**
– sofa or couch SQUAB

soft and crumbly, as soil might be FRIABLE
– soft and flexible enough to be bent or shaped, as some metals are PLIABLE, DUCTILE, MALLEABLE
– soft and limp, drooping, flabby, lacking firmness FLACCID
– soft or mashed food, as for a baby or sick person PAP
– soft sighing sound, as of the wind SOUGH, SUSURRATION

soft- MALACO-

soft coal BITUMINOUS COAL

soft hail, snow pellets GRAUPEL

soft roe MILT

soften, ease, make gentler, or pacify MOLLIFY
– soften, separate, or disintegrate by means of soaking MACERATE
– soften or reduce the intensity of something, such as anger MITIGATE, MODERATE, TEMPER
– soften the sound of a trumpet or other instrument MUTE, MUFFLE

softly and privately, in a subdued voice, under one's breath SOTTO VOCE
– softly-spoken utterance or the subdued sound of it UNDERTONE

soil consisting of a fertile mix of clay, sand, and silt LOAM
– soil formed from crumbled limestone MALM
– soil of very fine rock particles SILT
– soil or other sediment deposited by a river or flood ALLUVIUM
– break up and loosen the surface of topsoil, a field, a road, or the like SCARIFY
– crumbly, as soil might be FRIABLE
– crumbly clay soil MARL
– dark, fertile soil, rich in humus CHERNOZEM
– harrow used for crushing clods or levelling the soil DRAG
– layer of humus in soil MULL
– loose, crumbly soil, rich in organic matter MOULD
– referring to rich, fertile, workable, soil UNCTUOUS, PINGUID
– remove soluble parts from a substance such as soil, as by flushing with water LEACH
– scientific study of soil PEDOLOGY
– any soluble mineral salt found in natural water and arid soils ALKALI
– sudden shifting of soil from one property to another, as through flooding AVULSION
– wearing away or washing away, as of the soil cover EROSION

soil- AGR-, AGRI-, AGRO-, PED-, PEDO-

solar system – model of the solar system, used in studying astronomy ORRERY

solder – join or fuse two metal surfaces with a hard solder BRAZE

soldier See chart, page 480, and also **services**, **military**, **troops**
– soldier assisting a duty officer ORDERLY
– soldier in a small irregular military unit carrying out sabotage

and harassment operations GUERRILLA, PARTISAN
– soldier or soldiers assigned to a particular duty DETAIL
– soldier serving in a foreign army or organisation for payment MERCENARY
– soldier who is enrolled compulsorily for military service CONSCRIPT, RECRUIT
– soldier who signs up for military service of his own free will VOLUNTEER
– soldier's equipment in addition to his uniform and his weapons ACCOUTREMENTS
– soldiers' lodgings in a civilian building BILLET
– soldiers' quarters, building or group of buildings for housing soldiers BARRACKS
– soldiers' quarters, especially in a town, in former times CASERN
– soldiers' quarters or housing, especially temporary quarters CANTONMENT
– acquire new members, soldiers, or the like RECRUIT, ENLIST, ENROL
– acquire new soldiers for service by force of law CONSCRIPT, LEVY, DRAFT
– adjective for a soldier MILITARY, MARTIAL
– band of soldiers, strikers, protesters, or the like COHORT
– dismiss a soldier from a military unit, impose a dishonourable discharge on CASHIER, DRUM OUT
– ordinary soldier in the British Army, private TOMMY, TOMMY ATKINS, PONGO
– persecution by soldiers, military subjection or bullying DRAGONNADE, DRAGOONING
– person who is not a soldier or other military employee CIVILIAN
– person who, on moral grounds, refuses to serve as a soldier CONSCIENTIOUS OBJECTOR
– pit or crater serving as protection for soldiers against enemy fire FOXHOLE
– release or discharge soldiers from military service DEMOBILISE, DEMOB, DISBAND
– release or exempt a soldier from military service or active duty, on the grounds of illness or disability INVALID OUT
– straighten ranks, align as soldiers do on parade DRESS
– trick or force men into serving as sailors or soldiers PRESS, IMPRESS, COMMANDEER, PRESSGANG, CRIMP
– unit of part-time or civilian

SOLDIERS

askari	East African soldier	**hussar**	Hungarian light cavalryman of the 15th century; light cavalry soldier
bashibazouk	irregular 19th-century Turkish cavalryman	**Ironside**	Puritan cavalryman in Cromwell's army in the English Civil War
berserker	Norse warrior fighting in a drugged frenzy	**janissary**	Turkish soldier of an elite guard, between the 14th and 19th centuries
carabineer	soldier armed with a carbine, or short rifle	**kern**	medieval Irish foot soldier
centurion	Roman officer in command of a century, which originally consisted of 100 men	**Landsknecht**	German 16th to 17th-century mercenary
chasseur	light cavalryman or infantryman in the French army	**lascar**	soldier, sailor, or army servant from the East Indies
Chetnik	Serbian nationalist guerrilla, especially of the Second World War	**legionary**	Roman soldier belonging to a legion
Chindit	member of the Allied commando force in Burma during the Second World War	**legionnaire**	soldier of the French Foreign Legion
condottiere	mercenary in Europe between the 14th and 16th centuries	**Minuteman**	American militiaman during the War of Independence
doughboy	U.S. infantryman of the First World War	**Myrmidon**	Greek warrior at the siege of Troy
dragoon	European mounted infantryman or heavy cavalryman of the 17th and 18th centuries	**peltast**	lightly armed foot soldier of ancient Greece
fusilier	soldier armed with a fusil, or light musket	**poilu**	French infantryman, especially one in the front line during the First World War
ghazi	Turkish or Muslim warrior of high rank	**rapparee**	Irish freebooting soldier of the 17th century
Gurkha	Nepalese soldier serving in the British or Indian army	**sepoy**	Indian soldier formerly serving under British command
halberdier	medieval soldier armed with a halberd, or axe-like weapon on a long shaft	**sowar**	mounted soldier or policeman in India
Hessian	German mercenary in the British army during the American War of Independence and Napoleonic Wars	**spahi**	Turkish cavalryman; Algerian cavalryman in the French army
		vexillary	ancient Roman veteran; standard-bearer
hoplite	heavily armed foot soldier in ancient Greece	**Zouave**	Algerian infantryman in the French army

soldiers MILITIA
sole – relating to the sole of the foot PLANTAR, THENAR, VOLAR
solicitor authorised to certify sworn statements COMMISSIONER FOR OATHS
– solicitor's document, analysing a case and detailing instructions, given to a barrister BRIEF
– contracted period of training or apprenticeship undertaken by a trainee solicitor ARTICLES
solid ground, dry land TERRA FIRMA
solid- STERE-, STEREO-
solidify CONSOLIDATE
– solidify into a soft mass, as liquids might COAGULATE, CLOT, CURDLE, CONGEAL
– solid mass, such as a kidney stone CALCULUS, CONCRETION
solitary person who has withdrawn from society, as for religious reasons HERMIT, RECLUSE
solo song, as in an opera or oratorio ARIA, ARIETTA
solution or final result, as of a play DÉNOUEMENT
– solution or molten material that conducts electricity ELECTROLYTE
– solution or scheme, as for social problems, that is considered facile or simplistic NOSTRUM
– containing as much dissolved substance as possible, as a solution might SATURATED
– gradual evening out of differently concentrated solutions by the transfer of molecules through the separating membrane OSMOSIS
– separation of different types of molecule in a solution by means of a membrane DIALYSIS
– solid substance separated out from a solution PRECIPITATE
solve or interpret something puzzling or obscure DECIPHER
– solve or penetrate to the meaning of a mystery or puzzle FATHOM, UNRAVEL
– capable of being solved, resolved, or dissolved SOLUBLE
– impossible to solve, resolve, or dissolve INSOLUBLE
– triumphant exclamation on finding, solving, or discovering something EUREKA
solvent supposedly capable of dissolving anything, as sought by the alchemists ALKAHEST
sometimes, now and then, occasionally, from time to time INTERMITTENTLY, PERIODICALLY
son – adjective for a son or daughter FILIAL
sonar device or system used for detecting enemy submarines ASDIC, ECHO SOUNDER
song, hymn, or religious poem CANTICLE
– song about unrequited or passionate love TORCH SONG
– song business or popular-music industry in the U.S. in former times TIN PAN ALLEY
– song for a solo voice, as in an opera or oratorio ARIA, ARIETTA
– song of a simple kind DITTY
– song of lamentation, mourning song THRENODY
– song of a Venetian gondolier BARCAROLE
– song of West Indian origin with a syncopated rhythm and lyrics, typically improvised on a humorous or topical theme CALYPSO
– song or expression of joy and praise PAEAN
– song or round for three or more voices, popular in the 17th and 18th centuries CATCH
– song sung by sailors, typically in rhythm with their work SHANTY
– song to celebrate a wedding PROTHALAMION, EPITHALAMIUM
– chorus or bass accompaniment of a song BURDEN
– chorus or repeated section of a song REFRAIN
– cradle song, lullaby BERCEUSE
– formal song or poem honouring and praising someone PANEGYRIC
– German song, especially in the form of a poem set to music for solo voice and piano LIED
– range or stock of jokes, songs, operatic roles, plays, or the like REPERTOIRE
– sung without instrumental accompaniment, as some choral songs are A CAPPELLA
– text of the songs and dialogue of an opera, musical, or other musical work LIBRETTO
– unaccompanied secular song or part song, developed in Renaissance Italy MADRIGAL
– words of a song LYRICS
songbird PASSERINE
songwriter LYRICIST
sonnet of a form of Italian origin PETRARCHAN SONNET
– sonnet's first eight lines OCTET
– sonnet's last six lines SESTET
soon to happen IMMINENT, IMPENDING
– soon, tomorrow MAÑANA
soot particle SMUT
– relating to or resembling soot FULIGINOUS
soothe See **calm**
soothing, comforting, relaxing ANODYNE, LENITIVE
– soothing, relaxing, or sleep-inducing substance SEDATIVE, NARCOTIC, OPIATE, SOPORIFIC
– soothing and softening, as a skin lotion should be EMOLLIENT
– soothing ointment or lotion LINIMENT, EMBROCATION, UNGUENT
– soothing or healing substance, person, or influence SALVE
– soothing potion or drug, or technique for forgetting one's pains and sorrows NEPENTHE
– something, such as an idle promise or excuse, used to soothe or humour someone PLACEBO
soothsayer See also **prophet**
– soothsayer in ancient Rome HARUSPEX, AUGUR
sophisticated, elegant, or fashionable SOIGNÉ
– sophisticated, very cultured or learned HIGHBROW, CULTIVATED
– sophisticated and broad-minded, as through being familiar with a variety of cultures COSMOPOLITAN
– sophisticated and charming in company, socially refined SUAVE, URBANE, DEBONAIR
– sophisticated or clever beyond his years, as an advanced child seems to be PRECOCIOUS
– stylish or fashionable in a pretentious way, over-sophisticated or over-elaborate CHICHI
soprano specialising in ornamental trills and runs COLORATURA
sorcery See **magic**, **black magic**, **prophet**
sore, blister, or blotch on the skin BLAIN
– sore, broken or scraped skin ABRASION, EXCORIATION
– sore, raised patch or stripe on the skin, as caused by a blow or an insect bite WEAL, WELT
– sore, wound, or injury LESION
– sore in the form of a hard, infected, pus-filled swelling, boil FURUNCLE
– sore in the form of a hard, pale mass under the skin, caused by a blocked oil gland MILIUM
– sore in the form of a pocket of pus in inflamed tissue ABSCESS
– sore or cyst in the eyelid, caused by a blocked oil gland CHALAZION
– sore or cyst under the tongue, caused by a blocked salivary gland or duct RANULA
– sore or itchy inflammation on the hands, feet, or ears, caused by exposure to the cold and damp CHILBLAIN
– sore or pus-filled inflammation near a fingernail or toenail WHITLOW
– sore or scab formed by a burn, chafing, or the like ESCHAR
– sore or ulcer in the mouth or on the lips CANKER

– sore resembling a large boil, caused by bacterial infection CARBUNCLE
– sore swelling of the first joint of the big toe BUNION
– sore swelling under the hide of cattle or horses WARBLE
– bedsore, pressure sore DECUBITUS ULCER
– hard reddish sore that is an early indication of syphilis CHANCRE
– oily sore or cyst, especially on the scalp WEN
– small, pus-producing sore or ulcer FESTER, GATHERING
– small sore on the skin or a mucous membrane, caused by a tiny haemorrhage PETECHIA
– swollen pimple, blister, or sore, typically filled with pus PUSTULE, WHELK, BLEB, BULLA
– wart-like sore in the rectal or genital area CONDYLOMA

sore throat caused by a common bacterial infection STREP THROAT

sorrowful See also **sad**

sorry for one's sins, or regretting one's misdeeds REPENTANT, PENITENT, REMORSEFUL, CONTRITE
– be sorry about, lament REGRET, DEPLORE, RUE
– feel sorry for or sympathise with someone COMMISERATE

SOS, distress call MAYDAY

soul, in Hindu philosophy ATMAN
– soul, vital spirit PNEUMA
– soul or spirit, as distinct from the body PSYCHE
– soul or true inner self in Jungian psychology ANIMA
– soul's migration, after a person's death, into another body or cycle of existence TRANSMIGRATION, REINCARNATION, METEMPSYCHOSIS, PALINGENESIS
– abode, in Christian theology, of just souls barred from heaven, as through not having been baptised LIMBO
– belief among certain peoples that each thing, both living and nonliving, has its own individual soul ANIMISM
– condition or place in which souls are purified of their sins before admission to heaven PURGATORY
– damnation, loss of the soul PERDITION

sound See also **noise**, **pronunciation**, **speech**, **voice**
– sound, effective, or acceptable, as an argument, title, or passport might be VALID
– sound, especially in speech, that is pleasant to listen to EUPHONY
– sound across a wide range of frequencies, capable of blocking out other noises WHITE NOISE
– sound or sound reproduction, as of a television or hi-fi set AUDIO
– sound-proof, heat-proof, or prevent the transfer of electricity INSULATE
– sound quality produced by overtones rather than volume and pitch TIMBRE
– sound-regulating device, as in a microphone or loudspeaker BAFFLE
– sound reproduction that creates the effect in the listener of being bombarded with sound from all sides SURROUND-SOUND
– sound-system of a particular language PHONOLOGY
– sound that is ugly and jarring CACOPHONY, DISCORDANCE, DISSONANCE
– sounding harsh or hoarse RAUCOUS
– sounding of a final consonant that is normally silent, especially in French, when the next word begins with a vowel LIAISON
– sounding of the *r* after vowels, as in *card*, in keeping with the spelling, as in Irish and American English RHOTACISM
– sounding pleasant, pleasing to the ear EUPHONIOUS
– sounding pleasantly melodious DULCET
– sounding rich, deep, or impressively loud SONOROUS, RESONANT
– sounds of prolonged vibration or echoing REVERBERATIONS
– alter or insert the soundtrack of a film or tape DUB
– change in pitch of sound, as of a siren, as the source approaches or moves away from the listener DOPPLER EFFECT
– change in the sound of a consonant because of the influence of another consonant, as in pronouncing *incline* as though it were *ing-cline* ASSIMILATION
– change in the vowel sound of a verb, as in *sing*, *song*, *sung* ABLAUT, GRADATION
– change in the vowel sound of a word, especially of a verb, originally due to the influence of a nearby vowel UMLAUT, MUTATION
– deaden a sound MUFFLE, MUTE
– disconnected or distinct in sound, as sharply played musical notes are STACCATO
– fall in the sound level or pitch of the voice, as at the end of a sentence CADENCE
– glorious or harmonious burst of musical sound DIAPASON
– gradual decrease in the volume of sound, as in a passage of music DIMINUENDO, DECRESCENDO
– gradual increase in the volume of sound, as in a passage of music CRESCENDO
– hissing sound, as of *s* or *z* SIBILANT
– increase in volume or length of a sound, as by an echo or vibration RESONANCE
– insertion of an extra sound into a word to make its pronunciation easier, as when *umbrella* is pronounced as though it were spelt *umbarella* EPENTHESIS
– letter, symbol, or group of characters that can represent more than one sound, such as the English *g* in *gin* and *gain* POLYPHONE
– loss or cutting off of a letter, syllable, or sound at the beginning of a word, as with *squire* from *esquire* APHAERESIS, APHESIS
– loss or cutting off of a letter, syllable, or sound from the end of a word, as with *prof* from *professor* APOCOPE
– loss or cutting off of a letter, syllable, or sound from the middle of a word, as with *fo'c's'le* from *forecastle* SYNCOPATION, SYNCOPE
– loss or cutting off of a syllable or sound from the middle of a word, as when *deteriorate* is pronounced as though it were spelt *deteriate* HAPLOLOGY
– omitting or slurring of a vowel sound or syllable, as to make a line of verse scan ELISION
– pronunciation of the sound /r/ as /l/, as by Chinese people speaking English LALLATION
– quality of sound reproduction in a hall, auditorium, stadium, or the like ACOUSTICS
– recording or transmitting sound by means of only one channel MONOPHONIC, MONAURAL, MONO
– recording or transmitting sound by means of two separate channels STEREOPHONIC, BINAURAL, STEREO
– relating to sound or hearing ACOUSTIC
– relating to sound, sound waves, audible sound, or the speed of sound SONIC
– relating to speech sounds PHONETIC
– relating to speed greater than the speed of sound SUPERSONIC
– repeated occurrence of a letter or sound, especially at the start of words, in writing or speech ALLITERATION
– repeated occurrence of sounds, especially vowels, as in poetry ASSONANCE
– sensation of colour evoked by a

sound, or similar sensation of a sense different from the one stimulated SYNAESTHESIA
– speech sound identified as significant in a given language through serving to distinguish one word from another PHONEME
– speech sound of a breathy kind, such as the *h*-sound in English ASPIRATE
– speech sound of a throaty kind, such as the Parisian *r*-sound UVULAR
– speech sound of an unstressed mid-central vowel, as at the end of *Anna*, or the symbol ə that represents it SCHWA
– speech sound produced in the throat GUTTURAL
– speech sound such as the *i*-sound in *side*, in which a vowel changes in quality during the syllable DIPHTHONG
– speech sound such as /ch/ or /j/, produced by the sudden release of the breath AFFRICATE
– speech sound such as /d/ or /t/, formed with the tip of the tongue just behind the upper teeth ALVEOLAR
– speech sound such as /f/ or /z/, formed by partially blocking the flow of breath FRICATIVE, SPIRANT
– speech sound such as /j/ or /k/, formed with the back of the tongue near or against the soft palate VELAR
– speech sound such as /m/ or /p/, involving the use of the lips LABIAL
– speech sound such as the /p/ in *top*, involving the brief blocking of the breath PLOSIVE
– study of pronunciation and speech sounds PHONETICS, PHONEMICS, PHONOLOGY
– switching, usually unintended, of the initial sounds of two or more words, as when *red hat* comes out as *head rat* SPOONERISM
– system or apparatus for detecting or locating objects underwater by means of sound waves SONAR, ASDIC, ECHO SOUNDER
– tendency to change a sound for the sake of easier pronunciation EUPHONY
– unit for measuring the loudness of a sound DECIBEL
– word in which sound echoes meaning ONOMATOPOEIA

-sound- -PHON-, PHONO-, -PHONE, -PHONY, -AUDI-, -AUDIO-

sound-and-light entertainment given at night, typically outdoors, presenting the history of the site SON-ET-LUMIÈRE

soup See chart
– soup-like mixture of organic chemicals in early times from which life may have developed PRIMORDIAL SOUP
– broad deep bowl, as used for serving soup TUREEN
– small toasted or fried square of bread, served in soups or salads CROUTON
– thin soup, oatmeal gruel, or the like SKILLY

sour, tart, bitter to the taste ACERBIC, ACETOUS, ACIDULOUS

source See also **origin**
– source in the form of a spring FOUNTAINHEAD
– source of a river HEADWATERS
– source of easy money or help MILCH COW
– source of supply, as of raw materials LODE
– selecting or selected from several different sources ECLECTIC

south, southerly MERIDIONAL
– "southern lights", seen flashing in the night sky, especially near the South Pole AURORA AUSTRALIS
– southern U.S. states DIXIE
– alliance of the southern U.S. during the American Civil War CONFEDERACY
– adjective for the south AUSTRAL

south- AUSTR-, AUSTRO-, NOT-, NOTO-

South Africa See chart, page 484

South America – blanket-like cloak with a hole in the centre for the head, originally from South America PONCHO
– cowboy on the South American grassland plains GAUCHO
– grassland plains of South America PAMPAS
– large South American rodents CAPYBARA, COYPU
– mammals from South America that are closely related to the llama ALPACA, GUANACO, VICUÑA
– tea-like drink popular in South America MATÉ, YERBA MATÉ, PARAGUAY TEA

souvenir, especially a gift that serves as a reminder KEEPSAKE, MEMENTO

sovereign See **king**

Soviet See **Russian**

space allowing access or free play, as between a vehicle and an overhead bridge or between two parts of a machine CLEARANCE
– space of four dimensions in mathematics HYPERSPACE
– space or heavens beyond the Earth's atmosphere, according to Greek myth ETHER
– space or missing part, as in a bone or manuscript LACUNA
– creature from another world or from outer space ALIEN, EXTRATERRESTRIAL

SOUPS

avgolemono	Greek chicken-and-lemon soup thickened with beaten egg
bisque	thick French shellfish soup
borscht	Russian beetroot soup
chowder	thick U.S. soup or stew made with shellfish or fish
cock-a-leekie	Scottish soup of chicken and leek
consommé	clear, stock-based soup
gazpacho	spicy Spanish vegetable soup, usually served chilled
gumbo	African, Caribbean, and U.S. soup or stew thickened with okra
madrilène	French tomato-flavoured consommé, usually served chilled
minestrone	Italian vegetable soup with bacon and rice or pasta
mulligatawny	curry-flavoured soup of Anglo-Indian origin
potage	thick soup
pot-au-feu	thick French soup of vegetables and meat, sometimes with pasta or rice
vichyssoise	thick soup of leek and potato, usually served chilled

– depth appearance of various objects in different spatial relationships PERSPECTIVE
– relating to outer space COSMIC
– small space or gap, as between the strands of a net INTERSTICE
– unsuccessful or prematurely ended, as a space flight might be ABORTIVE

spacecraft that was the first to orbit the Earth, launched by the USSR SPUTNIK I
– spacecraft's heat shield ABLATOR
– activity, such as spacewalking, by an astronaut outside the spacecraft while away from Earth EXTRAVEHICULAR ACTIVITY
– load of equipment or cargo on a spacecraft PAYLOAD
– minimum speed needed by a spacecraft to overcome the gravitational field ESCAPE VELOCITY
– pilot or crew member of a spacecraft ASTRONAUT, COSMONAUT
– point at which a spacecraft in lunar orbit is farthest from the Moon APOCYNTHION, APOLUNE, APOSELENE
– point at which a spacecraft in lunar orbit is nearest to the Moon PERICYNTHION, PERILUNE
– point in its orbit when the Moon or a spacecraft is farthest from the Earth APOGEE
– point in its orbit when the Moon or a spacecraft is nearest to the Earth PERIGEE
– rocket supplementing the main power system of a jet or spacecraft BOOSTER
– self-contained unit, sometimes separable, of a spacecraft MODULE
– Soviet spacecraft SALYUT, SOYUZ, VOSTOK, COSMOS
– supply tube to a spacecraft prior to launching UMBILICAL CORD
– supporting tower or scaffolding for a spacecraft on the launching pad GANTRY
– U.S. spacecraft APOLLO, SKYLAB, TELSTAR, CHALLENGER, MARINER, VIKING

spacious, large, bulky, or baggy VOLUMINOUS
– spacious or roomy, as an office might be COMMODIOUS, CAPACIOUS

spade – small narrow spade SPUD

spaghetti See **pasta**
– firm and chewy through being lightly cooked, as spaghetti might be AL DENTE

Spain – adjective for Spain and Latin America HISPANIC

Spanish See chart, and also **menu terms, bullfighting**
– Spanish and Portuguese IBERIAN
– Spanish conqueror of Mexico and Peru in the 16th century CONQUISTADOR
– Spanish dancer's small wooden shells clicked in the hand in time to the music CASTANETS
– Spanish dialect spoken by Sephardic Jews, as formerly in the Balkans LADINO, JUDAEO-SPANISH
– Spanish dialect that is now the standard and official form of Spanish in Spain CASTILIAN
– Spanish fascist organisation that became the ruling party in Spain under General Franco FALANGE
– Spanish-speaking neighbourhood or community, as in a U.S. city BARRIO
– elderly woman employed by Spanish or Portuguese families as governess and chaperone for the daughters DUENNA
– group of confidential advisers, as formerly to the Spanish kings CAMARILLA
– powerful politician in a Spanish-speaking country CACIQUE

Spanish- HISPANO-

Spanish fly CANTHARIDES

SOUTH AFRICAN TERMS

amandla!	power! used as a black power slogan	**kraal**	fenced village of huts; cattle fold
apartheid	racial segregation	**krans**	steep rock face
biltong	sun-dried strips of salted meat	**laager**	encampment protected by a circle of wagons
boerewors	spicy sausage	**lekker**	delicious; pleasing
bonsella	small tip, gift, or reward	**morgen**	former measure of land, about 2 acres
braaivleis	barbecue	**naartjie**	tangerine or mandarin orange
bundu, gramadoelas	remote country area, back of beyond	**sjambok**	taut whip, especially of rhinoceros or hippopotamus hide
donga	wet or dry gully	**skelm**	rascal or lawbreaker
dorp	village or small country town	**skokiaan**	potent home-brewed alcoholic drink
drift	ford across a river	**sloot**	ditch or channel
gogga	insect, creepy-crawly	**stoep**	raised verandah
indaba	meeting or conference, as of headmen	**tacky**	plimsoll, tennis shoe
kaross	cloak of animal skins	**velskoen**	hide shoe
kloof	deep ravine	**verkrampte**	person of ultra-conservative views
knobkerrie	short club with a knobbed end	**verligte**	person of relatively liberal views
koppie	small, prominent, isolated hill	**voetsek!**	shoo! go away! push off!

spanner – tool serving as a spanner or screwdriver, consisting of a small bent bar whose tip fits into the six-sided recess in the head of special screws or bolts ALLEN KEY
sparing, restrained, in eating and drinking ABSTEMIOUS, TEMPERATE
spark, excite, or inspire KINDLE, INFLAME
– spark or flash SCINTILLATION
– sparking system in an engine IGNITION
– device in an internal-combustion engine for supplying current in the correct sequence to the spark plugs DISTRIBUTOR
sparkle, flash, or shine SCINTILLATE, CORUSCATE, SPANGLE, FULGURATE
– sparkle gently, gleam GLISTEN, SHIMMER
– sparkle or sheen LUSTRE
– sparkle or shine producing a variety of colours IRIDESCENCE
– sparkling, as with sequins CLINQUANT
– sparkling, decorated with sequins, powdered glass, or artificial jewels to produce a diamond-like effect DIAMANTÉ
– sparkling decoration of thin threads or strips, as on a Christmas tree TINSEL
– sparkling fabric containing silver or golden threads LAMÉ
sparrow – relating to sparrows, finches, and related birds FRINGILLID
spasm, fit PAROXYSM, CONVULSION
– spasm or twitch, especially in the face TIC
– spasms of facial pain caused by the trigeminal nerve TIC DOLOUREUX
– impaired control of the muscles and limbs, sometimes including spasms or convulsions, resulting from brain damage before or during birth CEREBRAL PALSY
speak See also **spoken**, **speech**, **say**, **state**, **conversation**, **talkative**
– speak about business matters or private concerns, discuss, exchange views CONFER, CONSULT
– speak about familiar things in a relaxed way, chat or gossip CHEW THE FAT, CONFABULATE, HAVE A CHINWAG, SHMOOZE
– speak about openly, bring into public discussion VENTILATE
– speak aimlessly and at tedious length WITTER, RABBIT, MAUNDER, PRATE
– speak cautiously and in a noncommittal way HEDGE
– speak evasively, hedge EQUIVOCATE, PREVARICATE, QUIBBLE
– speak in a long-winded, lengthy, pompous, and rhetorical way PERORATE, DECLAIM, SPEECHIFY
– speak in a lazy, drawn-out way DRAWL
– speak in a monotonous or boring way DRONE
– speak in a preachy or moralising way SERMONISE
– speak in an extremely enthusiastic way, as in praising something over-eagerly RHAPSODISE
– speak in an incoherent or stammering way, as when very angry SPLUTTER, STUTTER
– speak in an over-confident and opinionated way PONTIFICATE, DOGMATISE
– speak incoherently or nonsensically, as after a shock GIBBER
– speak long and often irrelevantly in a debate as a delaying tactic to obstruct legislation FILIBUSTER

SPANISH TERMS

alcalde	mayor or chief magistrate
alcazar	palace or fortress, as built by the Moors
bodega	wineshop or wine store
caballero	gentleman
cantina	bar or wine shop
caudillo	military leader, dictator
Cortes	Parliament
fiesta	holiday, religious festival, or saint's day
grandee	gentleman of the highest rank
Guardia Civil	national police force
hacienda	ranch or ranch-house
hidalgo	minor nobleman
hostería	restaurant
infanta	princess
mañana	tomorrow, shortly
parador	state-supervised country house hotel
plaza	public square
posada	inn
siesta	afternoon sleep or rest

– speak loudly in a boastful or threatening way BLUSTER
– speak or perform without preparation EXTEMPORISE
– speak or write about formally DISCOURSE
– speak or write lengthy detail on a subject ELABORATE, EXPATIATE, ENLARGE, DILATE, EXPOUND
– speak out, as in open protest CLAMOUR, YAMMER
– speak rapidly and casually or aimlessly, chatter, jabber BLABBER, GABBLE, TATTLE, PALAVER, CLACK, BABBLE, PRATTLE, NATTER
– speak to a gathering, in a passionate, ranting, or argumentative way HARANGUE
– speak with an irritatingly shy or affected smile SIMPER
– speaking clearly and effectively, expressive ARTICULATE
– speaking disability or writing disability caused by brain damage or disease APHASIA
– speaking in a hesitant or devious way MEALY-MOUTHED
– speaking or chanting improvised poetry to a musical accompaniment RAPPING
– speaking or writing effortlessly FLUENT
– speaking or writing in an effortless but shallow manner GLIB
– speaking style or delivery, especially in public ELOCUTION
– excessive or uncontrollable speaking, sometimes due to mental illness LOGORRHOEA
– person speaking to another COLLOCUTOR, INTERLOCUTOR
speaker who is impressive and persuasive or else excessively high-flown RHETORICIAN
– speakers' platform, as in a lecture hall DAIS, ROSTRUM
– jeer at a speaker with repeated critical comments HECKLE
-speaker -PHONE
spear, as used formerly by warriors in southern Africa ASSEGAI
– spear used in sporting competitions or formerly as a weapon JAVELIN
– spear with three prongs, as used by gladiators or carried by Neptune TRIDENT
– spear with three prongs, used in salmon fishing LEISTER
– arch of spears through which the defeated enemies of ancient Rome had to walk as a gesture of submission YOKE
– shaped like a spearhead, as some leaves are HASTATE
specialised or technical vocabulary TERMINOLOGY, NOMENCLATURE

specialist adviser CONSULTANT
- person with wide-ranging knowledge or interests, as distinct from a specialist GENERALIST

-specialist -ICIAN

species name following the genus name in biological classification TRIVIAL NAME, SPECIFIC EPITHET
- species to which humans belong HOMO SAPIENS
- continuous variation in form among members of a widespread species or population CLINE
- development by slow or natural means, as of species, art, or social systems EVOLUTION
- development of a species into several different species adapted to different environments ADAPTIVE RADIATION
- evolution or development of a species, genus, or the like PHYLOGENY
- mutation of or abrupt variation within a species SALTATION
- protective or cooperative instinct or behaviour among animals, serving to benefit the species as a whole ALTRUISM
- still in existence, not extinct, as surviving species are EXTANT
- system of classifying and naming animals or plants using two Latin names, indicating the genus and then the species BINOMIAL NOMENCLATURE

specific gravity RELATIVE DENSITY
- apparatus to measure the specific gravity of liquids, as used in beer- and winemaking HYDROMETER
- scale in measuring the specific gravity of liquids BAUMÉ SCALE

specify, require, or lay down as a condition in an agreement or contract STIPULATE

speckled or dotted, as with paint or natural colours STIPPLED

spectacles See **glasses**

spectacular, elaborate, or fanciful entertainment, display, or the like EXTRAVAGANZA

spectrum or other unbroken series of changes without any obvious divisions CONTINUUM

speech See also **conversation**, **speak**, **sound**, **voice**, **pronunciation**, **style**
- speech, as to a party conference, stating important plans or principles KEYNOTE SPEECH
- speech, story, sales talk, or the like that is glib or long-winded SPIEL, PATTER
- speech, way of talking, specific or personal language or style PARLANCE, IDIOM
- speech addressed only to oneself, such as a character in a play might utter SOLILOQUY
- speech coloured by a nasal quality, often suggesting a regional accent TWANG
- speech defect, such as a stammer IMPEDIMENT
- speech made by a recently installed professor, president, or the like INAUGURAL SPEECH
- speech of an elegant rhetorical style PERIODS
- speech of denunciation that is long and passionate TIRADE, DIATRIBE, HARANGUE, PHILIPPIC
- speech of farewell VALEDICTION, VALEDICTORY
- speech of lamentation that is long and passionate JEREMIAD
- speech of praise or a written tribute, as for someone recently dead EULOGY
- speech of praise that is long, elaborate, and formal ENCOMIUM, PANEGYRIC
- speech of some length, dominating a conversation or addressed only to oneself MONOLOGUE
- speech of the people, informal everyday language VERNACULAR, VULGATE, DEMOTIC
- speech of urgent appeal or encouragement EXHORTATION
- speech or formal address, as at a ceremony or funeral ORATION
- speech or formal address or explanation, lecture DISQUISITION
- speech or language exclusive to a profession or other group CANT, JARGON, ARGOT
- speech or language pattern of a particular regional or social group DIALECT, PATOIS
- speech or language pattern of an individual person IDIOLECT
- speech or other sound that is pleasant to listen to EUPHONY
- speech or writing, especially of a formal kind DISCOURSE
- speech or writing of a light, teasing style PERSIFLAGE, BANTER, BADINAGE, RAILLERY
- speech or writing that is graceful, moving, or effective ELOQUENCE
- speech or writing that is high-flown, showy, and also pompous BOMBAST, FUSTIAN, FLATULENCE, GRANDILOQUENCE, EUPHUISM
- speech or writing that is hypocritically moralising CANT
- speech or writing that is impressively high-flown but may be empty of real meaning RHETORIC
- speech or writing that is long-winded, roundabout, or evasive CIRCUMLOCUTION, PROLIXITY, PERIPHRASIS, EQUIVOCATION
- speech that is charming and smooth but often deceiving BLARNEY
- speech that is deliberately emotional or rhetorical ORATORY, DECLAMATION
- speech that is ecstatic and unintelligible, as in some religious services, "gift of tongues" GLOSSOLALIA
- speech that is long and tedious LITANY, HOMILY
- speech that is pleasant in sound EUPHONY
- speech that is ugly and jarring in sound CACOPHONY
- speech with another or others, conversation, especially of a formal or literary kind COLLOQUY
- speeches or discussions, especially between enemies over terms of a truce PARLEY
- ability to use and understand speech ORACY
- bureaucratic speech or writing that is pretentiously wordy and difficult to understand GOBBLEDEGOOK, OFFICIALESE
- capable of logical thought, comprehensible speech, and so on COHERENT
- capable of speech ARTICULATE
- concluding part of a long speech, often recapitulating its main themes PERORATION
- conversational or informal in style, characteristic of casual everyday speech COLLOQUIAL
- decorate speech and writing with quotations, anecdotes, or the like LARD
- degree of clarity of one's speech DICTION, ELOCUTION, ENUNCIATION, ARTICULATION
- deliver a speech without having prepared it IMPROVISE, AD-LIB, EXTEMPORISE
- digression in a speech for rhetorical effect, especially to address an imaginary or absent person APOSTROPHE
- distinctive type, style, or level of speech and language, varying according to profession, social environment, or the like REGISTER
- harsh or curt in speech or manner BRUSQUE, ABRASIVE
- harsh or cutting in speech or manner ACERBIC, CAUSTIC, ACIDULOUS, ACRID
- heavily accented speech, especially Irish BROGUE
- hesitant or jerky, as uncertain speech is HALTING
- impressive, grand, or highfalutin in style or speech SONOROUS

– "ladies and gentlemen", or similar conventional opening words of a speech SALUTATION
– line on a language map linking places using the same distinctive form of speech ISOGLOSS
– loss of one's powers of speech, as by injury or disease APHONIA
– observation, as in a conversation or speech, that departs briefly from the main subject DIGRESSION, ASIDE, PARENTHESIS
– obstruction of legislation by means of delaying tactics such as lengthy speeches FILIBUSTER
– outpouring of emotion in speech or writing EFFUSION
– place, platform, or occasion for public speeches, especially on political issues STUMP
– political leader or agitator rallying support by crude, emotional speeches DEMAGOGUE, RABBLE-ROUSER
– produce speech sounds VOCALISE
– quick counter or reply in speech or action RIPOSTE, RETORT
– rabble-rousing, inciting, as a political speech might be INFLAMMATORY
– referring to speech that is disorganised or unconnected INCOHERENT
– relating to or representing speech sounds PHONETIC
– relating to speech ORAL
– scattered throughout a speech, text, or the like INTERSPERSED, INTERLARDED
– showing effortless ease in speech or writing, flowing and graceful FLUENT
– study or science of speech sounds PHONETICS, PHONOLOGY, PHONEMICS
– style of speech or writing, way of putting things PHRASEOLOGY, DICTION
– unrehearsed, off-the-cuff, as a spontaneous, unprepared speech EXTEMPORANEOUS, IMPROMPTU
– wandering or digression from the main topic or course, as in a speech EXCURSION, EXCURSUS

-speech- -LOG-, -LOGUE, LOGO-, -PHON-, PHONO-, -PHONE, -PHONY

-speech disorder -PHASIA

speech therapy LOGOPAEDICS

speed See also **quick**
– speed, eager promptness ALACRITY
– speed, especially in a given direction VELOCITY
– speed, force, or other quantity having both magnitude and direction VECTOR
– speed, haste or promptness DISPATCH, EXPEDITION
– speed, swiftness CELERITY
– speed at which a piece of music is or should be played TEMPO
– speed needed by a spacecraft to overcome the Earth's gravitational field ESCAPE VELOCITY
– speed of one nautical mile per hour KNOT
– speed up the progress of something, such as a business matter EXPEDITE
– maximum possible speed of a missile, falling object, aircraft, or the like, as determined by such factors as air resistance TERMINAL VELOCITY
– relating to speed greater than the speed of sound SUPERSONIC
– "spy in the cab", device recording the travel times and speeds of a vehicle TACHOGRAPH

speed- TACH-, TACHO-

speedboat that skims the surface of the water HYDROPLANE

spell, charm, or sorcerer in a Haitian religious cult VOODOO
– spell cast through ritual chanting INCANTATION

spelling, or the study of spelling ORTHOGRAPHY
– spelling change produced by the transposing of letters within a word METATHESIS
– spelling or pronunciation differing slightly from another form of the same word VARIANT
– spelling or writing in the letters of another alphabet TRANSLITERATION
– spelling words in keeping with their pronunciation, as a language such as Spanish does PHONETIC
– change in the form or spelling of a word through a mistaken association with some other word POPULAR ETYMOLOGY, FOLK ETYMOLOGY

spend, lay out EXPEND, DISBURSE
– spend extravagantly or use up wastefully SQUANDER, DISSIPATE
– spend or give something generously, such as affection or money LAVISH

spending in a showy and extravagant way, especially to impress others CONSPICUOUS CONSUMPTION

spendthrift PRODIGAL, PROFLIGATE, WASTREL

sperm cell, male reproductive cell SPERMATOZOAN
– sperm cell, ovum, or other cell that can combine to form a fertilised cell GAMETE
– sperm or testis of fish MILT

sphere imagined as surrounding the Earth at a great distance, and housing the stars and planets on its surface CELESTIAL SPHERE
– sphere of operation or expertise, field of activity PROVINCE, PRESERVE, DOMAIN, BAILIWICK
– sphere or range of possible activity, scope, reach AMBIT, ORBIT, COMPASS
– elongated sphere, like a rugby ball SPHEROID
– model of the universe, with solid rings within a sphere to represent planetary paths ORRERY, ARMILLARY SPHERE

spice See also **herbs**
– spice, mustard, vinegar, or other seasoning CONDIMENT
– spice and heat wine or ale MULL
– spice mill QUERN

spicy or pleasantly sharp to the taste PIQUANT
– spicy or salty to the taste, rather than sweet SAVOURY
– spicy sauce RELISH, CHUTNEY
– spicy sauce in which meat or fish is left to soak before cooking MARINADE

spider See also **insect**
– spider, insect, crustacean, centipede, or related creature having jointed limbs, a horny shell, and a segmented body ARTHROPOD
– spider, tick, or related creature ARACHNID
– spider's nest NIDUS
– large hairy spider with a painful bite TARANTULA
– organ on a spider, caterpillar, or the like for producing silky threads for a web or cocoon SPINNERET

spike or peg, usually with an eye or ring for a rope, driven into a rock or ice surface for support in mountaineering PITON
– spike-tipped walking stick PIKESTAFF
– spike used in ropemaking on ships MARLINSPIKE, FID
– spiked frame used as a defensive obstacle against enemy troops or horses CHEVAL-DE-FRISE
– spiked heel, high and tapering, on a woman's shoe STILETTO
– spiked iron ball, formerly used to slow down enemy troops, as by laming horses CALTROP, CROWFOOT
– spiked plate on the sole of a shoe to prevent slipping on ice, as used in mountaineering CRAMPON, CLAMPER
– heavy war club with a spiked metal head, used to crush armour MACE

spike- ACANTH-, ACANTHO-

spiky- ECHINO-

spin See also **turn**, **twist**

– spin on tip-toe or on the ball of a foot, as in ballet PIROUETTE
– spin or turn on an axis ROTATE
– spin or wobble in flight, as a missile or aircraft might YAW
– spin round and round, whirl, twirl REEL, TRUNDLE
– spin round a point or axis GYRATE, REVOLVE
– spinning flywheel maintaining a stable angle or direction in a frame of pivoted supports GYROSCOPE
– rod, hinge, or axis around which something fixed spins PIVOT
spin- GYRO-
spinal cord- MYEL-, MYELO-
spinach – cooked or served with spinach, as an egg dish might be FLORENTINE
spine See also **nerve**
– spine, or the second vertebra from the top of the spine AXIS
– spine manipulation as a form of therapy OSTEOPATHY, CHIROPRACTIC
– abnormal curving or bending, as of the spine CURVATURE
– abnormal sideways curvature of the spine SCOLIOSIS
– having a backbone or spinal column VERTEBRATE
– having no backbone or spinal column INVERTEBRATE
– insertion of a syringe needle into the lower spine to inject drugs or withdraw spinal fluid LUMBAR PUNCTURE
– relating to or located on the same side of the body as the spinal cord DORSAL, NEURAL
– small bone at the base of the spine COCCYX
– surgeon specialising in spinal and joint disorders ORTHOPAEDIC SURGEON
– triangular bone near the base of the spine, consisting of five fused vertebrae SACRUM
– top vertebra of the spine, supporting the skull ATLAS
spines covering a porcupine or hedgehog QUILLS
spinning machine of an early design SPINNING JENNY, MULE, THROSTLE
– spinning or twisting of silk, cotton, or the like into threads FILATURE
– cleft stick for holding raw flax or wool prior to spinning DISTAFF
– spool or reel, for the yarn in spinning or for the wire in an electromagnetic buzzer BOBBIN
– stick or pin on which thread is twisted in spinning SPINDLE
spiny- ECHINO-
spiny anteater ECHIDNA
spiny lobster LANGOUSTE
spiral device within a tube, as used in ancient times for raising water ARCHIMEDES' SCREW
– spiral round a point or axis, revolve GYRATE
– spiral slide at a funfair HELTER-SKELTER
– spiral structure or shape HELIX, VOLUTE, WHORL
– spiralling and cone-shaped, as some shells are TURBINATE
– spiralling flow or rush, such as a whirlwind or whirlpool VORTEX
– spiralling shoot-like part, as on a grape vine, serving to attach a plant to its support TENDRIL
– shaped like a spiral or snail shell COCHLEATE
spiral- GYRO-, HELIC-, HELICO-
spire or turret, as on the roof of a Gothic building PINNACLE
spirit, soul PNEUMA
spirit, soul PNEUMA
– spirit, wit, liveliness ESPRIT
– spirit in Scottish legend, in the form of a horse that drowns its rider KELPIE
– "spirit matter" or spectre allegedly conjured up by a medium during a spiritualism session ECTOPLASM
– spirit of enterprise or adventure, initiative or pluck GUMPTION
– spirit of optimism and confidence, as among soldiers MORALE
– spirit of the times ZEITGEIST
– spirit or atmosphere, or its guardian deity of a place GENIUS LOCI
– spirit or divine force supposedly guarding a place, inhabiting a natural object, or guiding a person NUMEN
– spirit or divinity of forests and trees in classical mythology, wood nymph DRYAD, HAMADRYAD
– spirit or divinity of the fields and woodlands in classical mythology, with a human head and goats' legs, noted for its lechery FAUN, SATYR
– spirit or divinity of the mountains in classical mythology, a mountain nymph OREAD
– spirit or elf-like creature, such as a water nymph SPRITE
– spirit or ghost in the West Indies DUPPY
– spirit or ghost that is noisy or mischievous POLTERGEIST
– spirit or imaginary creature living in the air SYLPH
– spirit or soul, as distinct from the body PSYCHE
– spirit taking human form, in Muslim legend GENIE, JINNI
– spirit that supposedly acts through a spiritualist medium, especially at a seance CONTROL
– appear or become visible, as a spirit might MANIFEST
– arrival or visit of a ghost, spirit, angel, or the like VISITATION
– beautiful fairy-like creature or spirit, especially in Persian folklore PERI
– belief in the presence and power of spirits ANIMISM
– benevolent spirit or demon EUDEMON
– calling up spirits of the dead, as in black magic NECROMANCY
– drive out an evil spirit, or free a possessed person from evil spirits, as by religious rites EXORCISE
– emergence or appearance of a spirit, as at a seance, in visible bodily form MATERIALISATION, PRECIPITATION
– evil spirit in the shape of a man that has sex with sleeping women INCUBUS
– evil spirit in the shape of a woman that has sex with sleeping men SUCCUBUS
– female spirit in Irish folklore, whose wailing foretells a death in the household BANSHEE
– guiding spirit, guardian genius DAEMON
– malicious spirit in Jewish folklore, usually the soul of a dead sinner, that enters a person's body DYBBUK
– malicious spirit in German mythology, who carries children away to death ERLKING
– migration of a spirit, after a person's death, into another body or a new cycle of existence TRANSMIGRATION, METEMPSYCHOSIS, PALINGENESIS, REINCARNATION
– mischievous or wicked spirit or elf PUCK, BOGY, HOBGOBLIN
– person allegedly able to communicate with the spirits of dead people MEDIUM
– person supposedly possessed by an evil spirit DEMONIAC, ENERGUMEN
– summon up a spirit by means of spells or incantations CONJURE, INVOKE
– water spirit in Germanic folklore, usually hostile to humans NIX
– water spirit or nymph UNDINE
spirit- PNEUMAT-, PNEUMATO-
spirits See **alcohol**, **drinks**
spiritual divine, heavenly CELESTIAL
– spiritual, referring to the spirit or vital spark PNEUMATIC
– spiritual, unearthly, impalpable ETHEREAL
– spiritual, without material substance INCORPOREAL, INTANGIBLE,

INSUBSTANTIAL, IMMATERIAL
– spiritual contemplation or meditation as a means of experiencing communion with the divine MYSTICISM
– spiritual damnation, loss of the soul PERDITION
– spiritual leader or teacher in Hinduism GURU, MAHARISHI
– spiritual lethargy, despairing indifference ACCIDIE
– spiritually uplifting NUMINOUS
– civil, lay, or secular rather than spiritual or religious TEMPORAL
– symbol, relationship, or the like considered to have sacred or spiritual significance SACRAMENT

spiritualist and magical religious cult of African origin, practised in Haiti VOODOO
– spiritualist meeting in which people try to communicate with the dead SEANCE
– spiritualist religious and medical practices, as among North American Indians, in which the priest's spirit leaves his body during drumming or dancing SHAMANISM
– spiritualist's trick or the act of conjuring up or transporting a physical object APPORT
– alleged ability of spiritualists or clairvoyants to speak a foreign language they do not know XENOGLOSSIA
– board displaying the alphabet, used in spiritualism sessions to register messages OUIJA BOARD
– ghost-like substance supposedly emerging from a spiritualist medium during a seance ECTOPLASM
– mobile board with a pencil, used in spiritualism sessions to write or spell out messages from the spirit world PLANCHETTE

spit, saliva SPUTUM
– spit for roasting meat BROACH
– spit or small skewer for grilling or roasting, or the food cooked on it BROCHETTE
– spit or spit out EXPECTORATE
– helping the flow of spit, easing the production and expulsion of phlegm or sputum EXPECTORANT
– produce or secrete spit or saliva SALIVATE
– thick mucus or spit PHLEGM

spiteful, bitter, vengeful VINDICTIVE
– spiteful, bitterly hostile, hate-filled VIRULENT, MALIGNANT
– spiteful, ill-willed, intending to hurt MALEVOLENT, MALICIOUS
– spiteful, vicious, hurtful, as a comment might be VENOMOUS, VIPEROUS

spittoon CUSPIDOR

spiv WIDE BOY
– spiv, street-trader, hawker, or the like, specialising in the hard sell HUCKSTER, HUSTLER
– spiv who resells sports tickets, theatre tickets, or the like at an inflated price TOUT

splendid in appearance, magnificent, dazzling RESPLENDENT

splendour of achievement, appearance, or the like LUSTRE

splinter, chip, or break stone, especially with a hammer SPALL
– splinter, a thin and sharp fragment SLIVER

split, separated, divided CLEFT
– split or burst open along a seam, as a pod or fruit might, to release seeds or pollen DEHISCE
– split or cut, as by chopping with an axe CLEAVE

split- FISSI-, SCHIZ-, SCHIZO-

splitting, cutting SCISSION
– splitting, especially of heavy atomic nuclei in a nuclear reaction FISSION
– splitting into opposing factions, as within a church SCHISM
– splitting or flaking easily, as some minerals do SPATHIC
– splitting up of a word by an expression put between its parts, as in *abso-blooming-lutely* or *a-whole-nother problem* TMESIS

spoil, bungle, botch, damage during work or repair BODGE
– spoil, corrupt, lower in moral or intellectual character BASTARDISE, DEGRADE
– spoil, make crude or savage BARBARISE
– spoil by drying up, shrinking, or fading SHRIVEL, WITHER, WIZEN
– spoil by making impure or dirty DEFILE, FOUL, POLLUTE, SOIL, SULLY
– spoil one's chances or plans QUEER ONE'S PITCH
– spoil oneself or someone else by yielding to wishes INDULGE, PAMPER, GRATIFY, PANDER TO
– spoil or corrupt morally DEPRAVE, PERVERT
– spoil or degrade oneself for money or an unworthy cause PROSTITUTE
– spoil or frustrate something, especially someone's hopes or opportunities BLIGHT
– spoil or make dangerous, impure, or poisonous CONTAMINATE
– spoil or reduce the importance, quality, or value of DEVALUE, IMPAIR, VITIATE
– spoil or reduce the purity of something valuable by adding inferior material ADULTERATE, ALLOY, DEBASE
– spoil or ruin, by harassment BEDEVIL
– spoil or stain something, such as a person's reputation BLEMISH, BESMIRCH, TAINT, TARNISH
– spoil someone, especially a child, through excessive affection and compliance CODDLE, MOLLYCODDLE, COSSET, COSHER
– spoil the appearance of, damage, harm, injure DISFIGURE, DEFACE, MAR, MUTILATE

spoils, booty, loot, as from a plundering expedition PILLAGE
– spoils of victory, including captured weapons TROPHY

spoilt, excessively demanding, whimsical, self-pitying, or the like SELF-INDULGENT
– spoilt, overprotected, as a child might be CODDLED, COSHERED, COSSETED, INDULGED, MOLLYCODDLED, PAMPERED, SPOONFED
– spoilt by over-familiarity or over-indulgence, hence bored and unenthusiastic BLASÉ, JADED

spoken, by word of mouth ORAL, VIVA VOCE, VERBAL
– spoken clearly and distinctly ARTICULATE
– conversational, informal, characteristic of casual spoken language COLLOQUIAL
– passage of conversation in a play, novel, or the like, or the characters' spoken words DIALOGUE

sponge, sea anemone, or similar plant-like animal ZOOPHYTE
– sponge-like, fibrous interior of the dishcloth gourd, used for scrubbing the skin LOOFAH
– opening in a sponge, for the passage of water OSCULUM, OSTIUM, STOMA

sponsor or benefactor PATRON
– sponsor or patron of artists MAECENAS

spontaneous, automatic, involuntary or unthinking, as a reaction might be REFLEX, KNEE-JERK
– spontaneous, off the cuff, without prior preparation, as a speech might be IMPROMPTU, EXTEMPORE, AD LIB, IMPROVISED
– spontaneous, without forethought, spur-of-the-moment UNPREMEDITATED
– spontaneous and emotional rather than rational and deliberate DIONYSIAN
– devised spontaneously as a temporary measure MAKESHIFT
– knowing or acting spontaneously, insightful INTUITIVE
– offered or given freely or spontaneously, without being asked

GRATUITOUS, UNPROMPTED
– rational and deliberate rather than spontaneous and emotional APOLLONIAN
spool or reel, as for yarn in spinning or wire for an electromagnetic buzzer BOBBIN
spoon – spoon-like piece of cutlery with prongs and a sharp edge, combining the features of knife, fork, and spoon RUNCIBLE SPOON
– spoon of silver, with an ornamental handle and knob in the form of one of Jesus's disciples APOSTLE SPOON
– spoon whose handle continues as a tail-like ridge under the bowl RAT-TAIL SPOON
sports See chart
– sports arena, hall, or the like, with seating all the way round AMPHITHEATRE
– sports arena, stadium, or large entertainment hall COLISEUM
– sports car or similar sleek high-speed car GRAN TURISMO, GT
– sports car with two doors COUPÉ
– sports competition and display, especially of horse-riding skills by children GYMKHANA
– sports match between two teams from the same area DERBY
– sports match in the U.S. in which one of the sides fails to score SHUTOUT
– sports match or social event, or the date of it FIXTURE
– sports or games festival in ancient Greece AGON
– sports stadium's open-air grandstand in the U.S. BLEACHERS
– fail to appear in a sports match, thereby forfeiting it DEFAULT
– fan or enthusiastic follower of a specified sport or pastime DEVOTEE, AFICIONADO
– grass-like nylon or vinyl surfacing material, as used on sports grounds ASTROTURF
– make clear to an opponent in various sports, without meaning to, a move or pass that one is about to make TELEGRAPH
– score-keeper in various sports MARKER
sportsman in an American college or university JOCK
– sportsman or -woman who is officially an amateur but who receives payment for participating SHAMATEUR
– amateur sportsman, especially from the intellectual or upper classes CORINTHIAN
– artificial male sex hormone increasing muscle and bone growth, sometimes illegally used by sportsmen ANABOLIC STEROID
– promoter or financial supporter of a project, sportsman, cultural activity, or the like SPONSOR
spot, scar, birthmark, blemish, or rash on the skin STIGMA, MACULA
– spotted, as a horse's coat might be DAPPLE, MOTTLED
– spotted, dotted, pockmarked, or the like PUNCTATE
– spotted patterning, as on a leaf or a leopard's coat MACULATIONS
– spotted with or as if with drops GUTTATE
– brown or grey with darker streaks or spots, as a dog, cat, or cow might be BRINDLED
– marked with white and grey, brown, or reddish spots, as some horses are SKEWBALD
spotless, pure, free of stains or sins IMMACULATE, UNBLEMISHED, UNSULLIED
spouse See **husband**, **wife**
sprain, wrench, or strain one's back, ankle, or the like RICK
sprat BRISLING
spray device, as for perfume or deodorant ATOMISER
– convert a liquid to a fine spray, as by an atomiser NEBULISE
spread, distribution, or range, as of colours or radiation SPECTRUM
– spread a rumour or report BRUIT
– spread across or through, as an idea or a colour might SUFFUSE, INFUSE, INTERFUSE, IMBUE
– spread by physical contact, as a disease might be CONTAGIOUS
– spread from one person to another, as some diseases are COMMUNICABLE, INFECTIOUS
– spread gradually, as warmth or news might PERMEATE, PERVADE, DIFFUSE, PERCOLATE
– spread information, doctrines, rumours, or the like widely CIRCULATE, PROMULGATE, PROPAGATE, DISSEMINATE
– spread or increase rapidly PROLIFERATE
– spread or pass on rumours, words, or the like frivolously or indiscriminately BANDY ABOUT
– spread or smear roughly a substance such as mud, plaster, or grease DAUB
– spread or throw here and there, sprinkle, scatter STREW
– spread or try to circulate ideas or opinions PEDDLE
– spread out, unroll, or unfold something, such as a flag UNFURL
– spread out and irregular in design, as a large house might be SPRAWLING, RAMBLING
– spread out in an untidy or irregular way STRAGGLY
– spread out like rays from a common source or point RADIATE
– spread out or apart, as limbs might be SPLAYED
– spread through or introduce gradually, implant, teach INSTIL
– spread widely, scattered, widespread DIFFUSE, DISPERSED
– ordered and impressive spread, selection, or arrangement, as of clothes, facts, or troops ARRAY
spreading freely, unchecked, as vegetation might be RAMPANT
– spreading from one person to another easily, as laughter or enthusiasm might INFECTIOUS, CONTAGIOUS
– spreading implement having a wide-tipped and flexible blade, as for icing SPATULA
– spreading of a cancer, bacteria, or the like from the original site to other parts of the body METASTASIS
– spreading of information, often dubious, to further a cause, or the information itself PROPAGANDA
– spreading or gradual widening, as of a trouser leg FLARE
– spreading rapidly throughout an area, as an infectious disease might EPIDEMIC
spring, as on a lorry's back axle, consisting of a set of layered metal strips LEAF SPRING
– spring, daybreak, or similar early part or beginning of something PRIME
– spring from a source, originate DERIVE
– spring of mineral water SPA
– spring that forms the source of a river FOUNTAINHEAD
– spring throwing up column of hot water and steam GEYSER
– springs, padding, and fabric, as used in making a soft covering for furniture UPHOLSTERY
– springs, shock absorbers, and the like to help a vehicle to run more smoothly SUSPENSION
– adjective for the spring VERNAL
– crust of porous mineral deposit formed around a geyser or hot spring SINTER
– hot spring THERMAL SPRING
spring onion, shallot, or young undeveloped onion SCALLION
sprout or germinate PULLULATE
-sprout- -BLAST-
spruce tree from North America HEMLOCK
spur See also **stimulate**
– spur into action, startle GALVANISE
– spur or jutting part, as on a

chicken's leg or a flower's corolla CALCAR
– spur to action INCENTIVE, GOAD, INCITEMENT, STIMULUS
– ironsmith who made spurs and bits for horses LORIMER
– small toothed wheel on the end of a cowboy's spur ROWEL

spy, intelligence officer, or secret agent who joins a political or criminal group and tries to incite it into punishable or discrediting activities AGENT PROVOCATEUR
– "spy in the cab", device recording the travel times and speeds of a vehicle TACHOGRAPH
– spy planted for future use rather than current activity SLEEPER
– spy who is given a mission only after he has established himself in a foreign organisation MOLE
– spying, intelligence gathering ESPIONAGE
– informer, decoy, or police spy STOOL PIGEON, NARK, GRASS
– report by or questioning of a spy, astronaut, diplomat, or the like on his return from a mission DEBRIEFING
– secret entry into or establishment in an organisation, region, or the like, as by spies or enemy troops, for the purpose of subversion INFILTRATION
– woman spy MATA HARI

square or oblong figure RECTANGLE, QUADRILATERAL, TETRAGON
– large public square, wide street, or open space where crowds can gather CONCOURSE
– large public square or open space, especially in a Spanish-speaking town PLAZA
– large public square or open space, especially in an Italian town PIAZZA
– layout of numbers in the form of a square, in which any of the rows produces the same sum MAGIC SQUARE

square- QUADR-, QUADRI-, QUADRU-

square dance, or the music or a party for it in the U.S. HOE-DOWN

square root or other root of a quantity as indicated by the sign √ RADICAL

squash – session in a squash game throughout which one player retains the service by winning rallies HAND
– shot in squash played so as to rebound off a side wall before hitting the front wall BOAST

squeaky, unnaturally high-pitched, as a teenage boy's voice might be FALSETTO

squeeze, push, or force out EXTRUDE

SPORTS AND GAMES

TRACK AND FIELD EVENTS, AND RELATED SPORTS

decathlon
fell running
heptathlon
orienteering
pentathlon
tossing the caber
trampoline

WINTER SPORTS

biathlon
bobsleighing/ bobsledding
curling
langlauf, cross-country skiing
luging, tobogganing
skibobbing
skijoring
slalom
sled-dog racing

INDOOR GAMES

backgammon, acey-deucy, sheshbesh
charades
consequences
crambo
forfeits
go
halma
jacks, knucklebones
mah-jong/ mah-jongg
pachisi/ Parcheesi
pinball, bagatelle
reversi
shove-halfpenny
spillikins, jackstraws

MARTIAL ARTS AND SPORTS

aikido
bujutsu
cireum
Cumberland and Westmorland style wrestling
Greco-Roman wrestling
Jidokwan
jujitsu
karate
kendo
kung fu
Sumo
Tae Kwon Do

MOTOR, MOTORCYCLE, AND CYCLE SPORTS

autocross
cyclo-cross
drag racing
go-karting/ karting
Grand Prix, Formula One
GT/grand touring
motocross, scrambling
rally cross
stock car
TT/Tourist Trophy

SHOOTING AND BOWLING SPORTS

archery, toxophily
biathlon
boules, pétanque
clay-pigeon shooting, skeet shooting, trapshooting
pall mall
quoits

TEAM AND BALL GAMES

bandy
croquet
Eton wall game
fives, Eton fives
Gaelic football
hurling/hurley
jai alai, pelota
korfball
lacrosse
pushball
rackets/ racquets
real tennis/ royal tennis, court tennis
rounders
shinty/shinny
stoolball
volleyball

– rubber blade or roller used in printing or photography, as for squeezing water from wet prints SQUEEGEE

squid, cuttlefish, or related ten-tentacled creature DECAPOD
– squid, octopus, nautilus, or related mollusc CEPHALOPOD
– long horny internal shell of a squid PEN

squint caused by a malfunction of the eye muscles STRABISMUS
– slight squint of the eye CAST

squire for a knight, armour-bearer ARMIGER

squirrel – squirrel-like, or relating to squirrels SCIURINE
– squirrel-like rodent living in burrows MARMOT
– squirrel's nest DREY

Sri Lankan belonging to the majority ethnic community SINHALESE

stab lightly or prick, as with a sword PINK

-stabilisation -STASIS

stabilising material or device, such as an electrical resistor, or sandbags in a ship's hold BALLAST

stability, state of balance of forces EQUILIBRIUM
– road vehicle's degree of stability, as at high speeds or on wet roads ROADHOLDING
– something giving security or emotional stability MOORINGS

stable condition or period, as of economic activity PLATEAU
– stable for boarding horses or letting out horses and carriages LIVERY STABLE

stableman at an inn OSTLER

stadium, as for chariot races, in ancient Greece and Rome HIPPODROME
– stadium, sports arena, or large entertainment hall COLISEUM
– passageway to a bank of seats in a stadium, as in the Colosseum in Rome VOMITORY

staff See also **stick**
– staff, typically decorated with leaves and tipped with a pine cone, carried by Dionysus and his followers THYRSUS
– staff carried by a bishop or abbot, having a crook or cross at the top CROSIER
– staff of office carried as a symbol of authority VERGE, SCEPTRE, MACE
– staff or wand decorated with wings and two twining snakes, serving as a symbol of the medical profession CADUCEUS
– long wooden staff, often with a metal point or blade, used as a weapon in former times QUARTER-

STAFF, PIKESTAFF, PARTISAN, HALBERD

stage See also **drama**, **theatre**
– stage, step, or degree in a gradual progression GRADATION
– stage or platform, as for a public speaker or music conductor ROSTRUM, PODIUM, DAIS
– passing down from stage to stage DEVOLUTION

stage direction indicating a speech or the start of a speech by a character LOQUITUR
– stage direction indicating the exit of all the characters EXEUNT OMNES

stage setting in a play MISE EN SCÈNE

stain DISCOLORATION
– stained blood-red INCARNADINE
– stained or discoloured, as old books might be FOXED

stained glass – thin lead strip securing the panes in latticework or stained-glass windows CAME

stairs See illustration
– stair in a straight rather than winding staircase FLIER
– stair in a winding rather than straight staircase WINDER
– stair post, table leg or the like, typically turned and decorated SPINDLE
– central pillar, typically of stone, about which a spiral staircase winds NEWEL
– skirting board along the side of a staircase STRINGBOARD, STRINGER
– underside of an arch, staircase, or other overhang SOFFIT

stairway or platform outside the entrance of a large building PERRON
– stairway or small porch at the entrance to a house STOOP
– moving stairway between floors, consisting of steps on a conveyor belt ESCALATOR

stake or heavy post, as of timber SPILE
– stake or pointed post driven into the ground, as for defence PICKET, PALING, PALE
– stake placed in the pool by a poker player ANTE
– defensive barrier made of upright posts or stakes STOCKADE, PALISADE

stale, reworked, as material for a comedy act might be RÉCHAUFFÉ
– stale, unoriginal, or predictable remark, phrase, or thought CLICHÉ, PLATITUDE, COMMONPLACE, BROMIDE
– stale, unoriginal and overused, theadbare and uninspiring, as a boring remark might be HACKNEYED, TRITE, BANAL, SHOPWORN
– stale and usually over-simplified image or opinion of someone or something STEREOTYPE
– stale joke, old story, or the like CHESTNUT
– stale-smelling MUSTY, FUSTY, FROWZY

stalemate or unresolvable difficulty blocking progress IMPASSE, DEADLOCK

stalk See also **stem**
– stalk, as of a mushroom or a frond of fern or seaweed STIPE
– stalk attaching a leaf to a stem PETIOLE
– stalk bearing a flower, fruit, or entire flower cluster PEDUNCLE
– stalk bearing flowers, or the arrangement of flowers on it INFLORESCENCE
– stalk creeping from the base of a plant, such as the strawberry, and producing new roots and buds STOLON, RUNNER
– stalk or arrangement of flowers attached singly to a main stem, with the youngest at the top RACEME
– stalk supporting a flower in a flower cluster PEDICEL
– stalkless, attached directly at the base, as a leaf or flower might be SESSILE
– stalks of plants used for thatching or animal litter HAULM

stamen- ANDRO-

stamens of a flower ANDROECIUM

stammer or hesitate in speaking FALTER, STUTTER

stamp collector PHILATELIST
– stamps in a rectangular sheet,

stairs

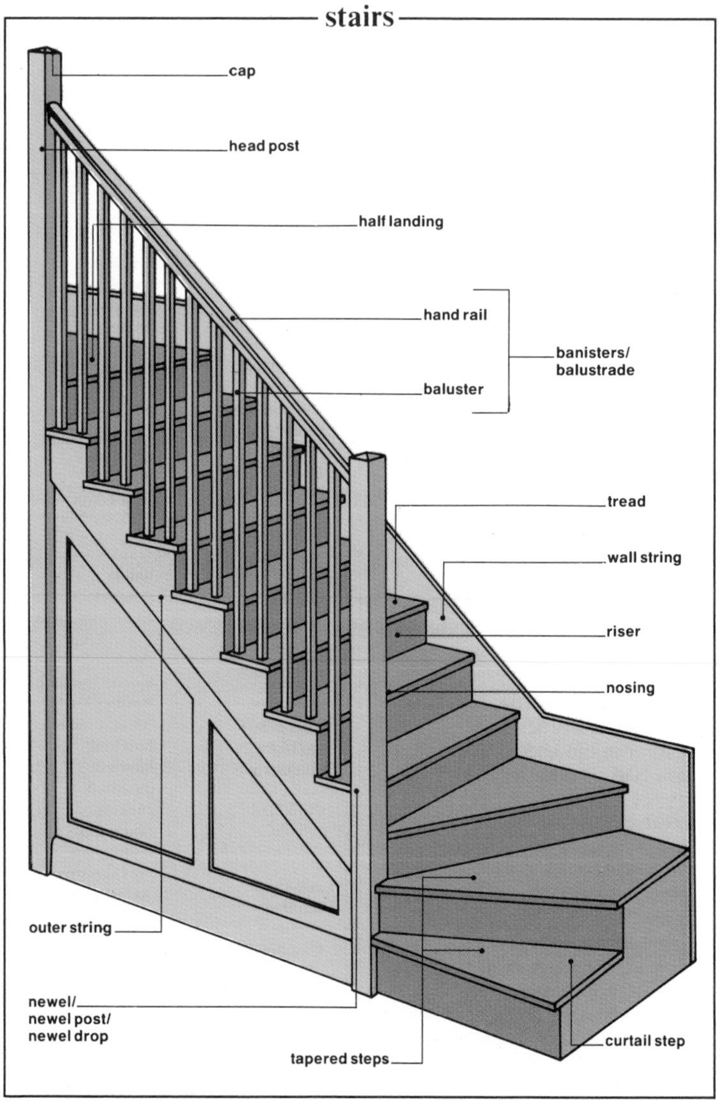

as a page of a stamp book PANE
– cancel a stamp by means of a postmark FRANK
– design stamped on an envelope to commemorate a postal event CACHET
– issued in honour of the memory of a person or event, as stamps or coins might be COMMEMORATIVE
– picture in a postage stamp, as distinct from the frame and lettering VIGNETTE
– referring to a pair of postage stamps in which one is upside-down in relation to the other TÊTE-BÊCHE
– series of holes, or of ridges and indentations, around postage stamps PERFORATION
– series of tiny slits between rows of stamps for easy separation ROULETTE
– white space between two postage stamps on a sheet, facing pages of a book, or the like GUTTER

stamped mark on gold or silver objects indicating the purity of the metal HALLMARK, PLATEMARK

stand, often with three legs, as used to support pots during cooking TRIVET
– stand for supporting a book or notes, as in a church or lecture hall LECTERN
– stand or sit astride BESTRIDE, STRADDLE
– stand or support having just one leg, as for a camera MONOPOD
– stand or support having three legs, as for a camera TRIPOD

stand-in See **agent**, **substitute**

stand in for or relieve somebody at work, by taking a turn SPELL
– stand in for temporarily, replace, serve as a substitute DEPUTISE, UNDERSTUDY

standard, guiding principle POLESTAR, LODESTAR
– standard, principle, or basis or measure for judgment CRITERION, CANON
– standard, reference point, or starting point, as in surveying or sociology DATUM LINE
– standard, unoriginal, or oversimplified image of someone or something STEREOTYPE
– standard-bearer, flag-bearer VEXILLARY
– standard example or measurement used as a reference for comparisons BENCHMARK, TOUCHSTONE, YARDSTICK, LITMUS PAPER
– standard of acceptability, model of behaviour, or the like NORM
– standard of comparison as used in a statistical analysis, scientific experiment, or the like CONTROL
– standard of living that is adequate but modest SUFFICIENCY
– standard of living that is the minimum for reasonable survival SUBSISTENCE LEVEL
– standard that is arbitrary but is rigidly enforced PROCRUSTEAN BED
– differ or depart from the norm or standard, as of a policy, a route, or one's behaviour DEVIATE
– meet the required standards PASS MUSTER

standard- ORTHO-

standing stones See **pillar**

standpoint, point of view PERSPECTIVE

stanza of a poem, verse STAVE, STROPHE

star See also **astronomy, astrology, zodiac**
– star, especially the North Star, used as a guide by sailors and astronomers LODESTAR
– star, planet, or comet CELESTIAL BODY
– star cluster ASTERISM
– star grouping, consisting of most of the known stars including the Sun MAIN SEQUENCE
– star of a large, cool, and old type RED GIANT
– star of a small, cool type RED DWARF
– star of a small, hot, dense type WHITE DWARF
– Star of David MAGEN DAVID
– star-shaped ASTEROID, ACTINOID
– star-shaped printing symbol, *, as for referring to a footnote ASTERISK
– star system, any of the millions of groups of stars held together by gravity GALAXY
– star system, any of the 88 groupings of stars as viewed from the Earth CONSTELLATION
– star that, from a given viewing point, never dips below the horizon CIRCUMPOLAR STAR
– star that is the brightest or largest in its constellation ALPHA
– star with five points, formed by five straight lines, and sometimes credited with magic powers PENTACLE, PENTANGLE, PENTAGRAM
– adjective for a star or stars STELLAR, ASTRAL, SIDEREAL
– brightness of a star MAGNITUDE
– building housing telescopes for observing the stars OBSERVATORY
– fainter of the two units of a double star COMPANION
– instrument for measuring the angles of stars and planets to determine the observer's position on Earth SEXTANT, ASTROLABE
– network of lines used as a reference grid, as in photography and in measuring stars RÉSEAU
– North Star POLESTAR, POLARIS
– pair of stars circling each other BINARY STAR
– projector of images of the stars and planets, or the domed room or building in which it operates PLANETARIUM
– scientific study of the stars and planets, and outer space generally ASTRONOMY
– study of the stars and planets for their supposed effects on human life and destiny ASTROLOGY

-star- -ASTR-, -ASTRO-, STELL-

starch, sugar, or a related compound CARBOHYDRATE
– starch from potato flour FARINA
– starch from the root of a tropical plant, as used for making tapioca CASSAVA
– starch used in cooking, or the tropical American plant from which it is extracted ARROWROOT
– starchy, heavy and filling, as thick porridge or similar food is STODGY
– starchy or floury FARINACEOUS

starch- AMYL-, AMYLO-

stare at, especially in a lustful way LEER, OGLE
– stare down, outstare OUTFACE
– stare or look angrily or frowningly GLOWER, SCOWL

starfish, sea urchin, or related sea creature ECHINODERM
– arm of a starfish RAY
– technical name for a starfish ASTEROID

starling – flock or family of starlings MURMURATION

start See **begin**, **beginning**
– start a car by means of cables connected to another car's battery JUMP-START
– start a car by pushing or rolling it before engaging the clutch BUMP-START

starter course to a meal HORS D'OEUVRE, ANTIPASTO

starting from scratch, clean slate, need or chance to have a fresh start TABULA RASA
– starting point, outset THRESHOLD
– starting handle, as on an early car or aeroplane CRANK
– starting point, point of origin TERMINUS A QUO
– starting point, reference point, or standard, as in surveying or sociology DATUM LINE

-starting -ESCENT

starvation – exhaustion, often fatal, as caused by starvation INANITION

starve – starved and extremely thin

EMACIATED, MACERATED, CADAVEROUS, ANOREXIC
– starving, or extremely hungry RAVENOUS, FAMISHED
– condition of extreme thinness and weakness, as among starving people MALNUTRITION

state See also **government**
– state economically or politically dependent on a more powerful country CLIENT STATE
– state or zone, usually small and neutral, lying between two enemy forces or rival powers BUFFER STATE, BUFFER ZONE
– state that exercises control or dominion over a dependent state, especially over its foreign affairs SUZERAIN
– state's authority or power of jurisdiction beyond its borders, as over its citizens living abroad EXTRATERRITORIALITY
– narrow strip of land, as for allowing an inland state access to the sea CORRIDOR
– part of a state that is isolated within a nearby foreign state's territory EXCLAVE
– part of a foreign state lying entirely within a state's territory ENCLAVE
– relating to a governor, as of a U.S. state GUBERNATORIAL
– rule, authority, or influence of one state over another HEGEMONY

state See also **speak**
– state, put into words, or say ARTICULATE, PRONOUNCE, UTTER, VERBALISE
– state explicitly or in detail, spell out SPECIFY
– state in detail, set forth or explain fully EXPOUND, PROPOUND
– state openly, or under oath TESTIFY
– state or announce publicly and officially PROCLAIM
– state or claim, typically without proving ALLEGE
– state or declare, claim MAINTAIN, ASSERT, CONTEND, SUBMIT
– state or declare, confidently or forcefully AFFIRM, AVER, AVOUCH, AVOW, WARRANT, PROFESS
– state formally ENUNCIATE
– state or declare to be true or existing, assume or put forward, as for the sake of argument POSTULATE, PREMISE, POSIT
– state or declare to be true, back up, confirm ATTEST, CORROBORATE
– state or declare as belonging to or characteristic of someone or something PREDICATE
– state emphatically ASSEVERATE

-state -OSIS, -TUDE

state of affairs as it currently exists STATUS QUO

state of mind, spirit of optimism and confidence, as among soldiers MORALE

-state of mind -THYMIA

statement, complaint, or protest, as in diplomatic matters or to the public authorities DÉMARCHE
– statement based on evidence that is not or cannot ever be exhaustive GENERALISATION
– statement or remark having no apparent relevance to what came before it NON SEQUITUR
– statement that is apparently self-contradictory or absurd though not necessarily untrue PARADOX
– statement that is arbitrary and unsupported DICTUM, IPSE DIXIT
– referring to a statement whose truth-value depends on real-life facts rather than on the meanings of its terms SYNTHETIC
– referring to a statement whose truth-value depends on the meaning of its terms rather than on real-life facts ANALYTIC

static or balanced condition, as in body chemistry and functions, or within a society or personality HOMEOSTASIS

station – open space for crowds, at an airport, station, or other public place CONCOURSE

stationary, fixed, unmoving STATIC, STABILE
– moving from place to place, mobile, as opposed to stationary AMBULATORY, AMBULANT

-stationary -STASIS, -STAT

stationery box PAPETERIE
– mark stationery or other goods with the name, initials, or other form of identification of the owner PERSONALISE

statistician in an insurance company who calculates risks, premiums, and the like ACTUARY

statistics – statistical chart in the form of a circle with sectors of varying size PIE CHART
– statistical chart in the form of a set of upright rectangles HISTOGRAM
– statistical chart or diagram presented in the form of a picture PICTOGRAPH
– statistical variation, difference between any one number and the average DEVIATION
– statistically random STOCHASTIC
– interdependence in statistics of two random variables, increasing or decreasing simultaneously CORRELATION
– set of statistical data showing how often the various values of a variable occur FREQUENCY DISTRIBUTION, OGIVE
– use of statistics in the study of history CLIOMETRICS

statue See also **sculpture**
– statue of a discus-thrower, as in ancient Greece and Rome DISCOBOLUS
– statue of huge size COLOSSUS
– base block or slab, as of a column, statue, or trophy PLINTH
– destroyer of religious statues and sacred objects ICONOCLAST
– inscription on a statue, monument, or building EPIGRAPH
– referring to a statue or portrait in which the subject is depicted on horseback EQUESTRIAN
– referring to ancient statues of a conventional or stiff style ICONIC

statuette or small ornamental figure FIGURINE

status, reputation, or renown, as through success or wealth PRESTIGE, KUDOS, CACHET
– status or right, as of appearing in court, speaking at a meeting, and the like LOCUS STANDI
– status or role of a plant or animal within its ecological community NICHE
– important or high in status, position, or the like EXALTED
– order of power or status in a group PECKING ORDER, HIERARCHY

stay about, hang around aimlessly, or dawdle idly LOITER, LINGER
– stay in or at a place temporarily TARRY, SOJOURN
– stay unmoved or unchanged, especially in the face of outside pressures ABIDE, ENDURE, PERSIST
– staying only temporarily, passing through, as a farmworker might TRANSIENT, ITINERANT, MIGRANT

staying power, endurance STAMINA

steady, hardworking, and reliable YEOMANLY, STALWART
– steady, unchanging, and unpleasant UNRELIEVED
– steady, unhesitating, exhibiting no sign of doubt UNFALTERING, UNWAVERING
– steady, uniform, consistent INVARIABLE, UNDEVIATING

steak See **beef**, **meat**
– raw minced steak with chopped onion, herbs, and raw egg STEAK TARTARE

steal See also **rob**, **robbery**
– steal, remove illegally, or use for one's own purposes without permission MISAPPROPRIATE, APPROPRIATE, CONVERT
– steal another person's ideas, writ-

ings, tunes, or the like and pass them off as one's own PLAGIARISE
– steal back, or steal something to which one considers one has a right LIBERATE
– steal cattle or other livestock RUSTLE
– steal money or goods entrusted to one EMBEZZLE, PECULATE, DEFALCATE
– steal or use illegally, especially by publishing a work protected by another's copyright PIRATE
– steal something small or cheap, often in a sneaky way, swipe, nick FILCH, NOBBLE, PILFER, PURLOIN
– steal the show from, draw attention away from UPSTAGE
– compulsive urge to steal things KLEPTOMANIA
– flee and hide, often after stealing goods ABSCOND
– ransack with intent to steal, loot RIFLE

stealthy, done or carried out in a secretive or underhand manner SURREPTITIOUS, CLANDESTINE, FURTIVE
– stealthily or secretly harmful, treacherous INSIDIOUS

steam-bath treatment or recreation of Finnish origin, typically followed by a cold plunge SAUNA

steam engine or locomotive that carries its water supply in tanks around the boiler TANK ENGINE
– steam engine or locomotive with two large rear wheels, formerly used for hauling heavy loads TRACTION ENGINE
– steam engine or turbine of an ancient, simple design AEOLIPILE

steam organ – U.S. term for a steam organ CALLIOPE

steel of high quality, typically made by melting and fusing iron and charcoal CRUCIBLE STEEL
– steelmaking furnace in which fuel and ore are separated and heat reflected off the roof onto the ore REVERBERATORY FURNACE, OPEN-HEARTH FURNACE
– steelmaking process in which air is blown through molten iron BESSEMER PROCESS
– chemical elements used in conjunction with iron to make various kinds of steel COBALT, CHROMIUM, MANGANESE, VANADIUM, NIOBIUM, TITANIUM, MOLYBDENUM, TUNGSTEN
– coat steel with zinc to rustproof it GALVANISE
– harden or toughen steel or other metal, as by alternate heating and cooling TEMPER
– harden the surface of iron or steel by heat and carbon treatment CASE-HARDEN
– turn iron into steel ACIERATE

steep – rather steep, sloping, inclined DECLIVITOUS
– very steep ABRUPT, PRECIPITOUS
– vertical or very steep PERPENDICULAR, SHEER

stem bearing a flower, fruit, or entire flower cluster PEDUNCLE
– stem bearing flowers, or the arrangement of flowers on it INFLORESCENCE
– stem creeping from the base of a plant, such as the strawberry, and producing new roots and buds STOLON, RUNNER
– stem growing on or under the ground, as in the iris or grasses RHIZOME, ROOTSTOCK
– stem growing under the soil, like a bulb but with papery scale leaves, such as that of the gladiolus CORM
– stem growing under the soil, swollen and bearing buds, such as that of the potato or dahlia TUBER
– stem of a twining plant or creeper, or the plant itself BINE
– stem or arrangement of flowers attached singly to a stalk, with the youngest at the top RACEME
– stem or main axis, as of a flower cluster, compound leaf, or feather RACHIS
– stem or stalk, as of a mushroom or a fern or seaweed frond STIPE
– stem supporting a flower in a flower cluster PEDICEL
– grow into a long, thin stalk or stem, as a plant might SPINDLE
– joint or branching point on a stem NODE
– spongy core running through stems and branches PITH, MEDULLA
– stalk attaching a leaf to a stem PETIOLE

stencil having many curves, used by draughtsmen and dressmakers FRENCH CURVE
– stencil-like pattern, mould, plate, or the like, as in woodwork, for making or reproducing something accurately TEMPLATE
– pen-like instrument with a small toothed wheel used to perforate wax stencils for copying on an office duplicator CYCLOSTYLE

step See also **stairs**
– step, stage, or degree in a gradual progression GRADATION
– step in a straight staircase FLIER
– step in a winding staircase WINDER
– step taken by placing one foot ahead of and touching the other PIGEON STEP
– stepped formation, as of soldiers or ships, in offset parallel rows ECHELON
– stepping on the toes only while walking, as horses do DIGITIGRADE
– stepping on the whole foot while walking, as humans do PLANTIGRADE
– steps leading to river in India GHAT
– backward, unprogressive, as a step or decision might be RETROGRADE

step in, as to mediate or prevent INTERVENE

stepmother – adjective for a stepmother NOVERCAL

stereo, recording or transmitting sound by means of two separate channels BINAURAL
– using four separate sound channels, rather than two as in stereo QUADRAPHONIC
– using only one sound channel, rather than two as in stereo MONOPHONIC, MONAURAL, MONO

sterilise a bitch or other female animal by removing the ovaries SPAY
– sterilisation of a man, especially as a form of permanent contraception, by cutting the sperm-carrying ducts VASECTOMY

sterilising vessel, using steam under pressure, much like a pressure cooker AUTOCLAVE

stethoscope – blowing or whispering sound heard through a stethoscope, typically due to the flowing of the blood SOUFFLE
– crackling sound of diseased or fluid-filled lungs, as heard through a stethoscope RALE
– listening to body sounds, as through a stethoscope, for purposes of diagnosis AUSCULTATION

stew See also **menu terms**
– stew or casserole of game in a rich brown sauce, often containing wine SALMI, SALMIS
– stew or casserole of meat or fish with vegetables MULLIGAN
– stew or casserole of meat or poultry with vegetables RAGOUT
– rich meat stew, of Hungarian origin, strongly seasoned with paprika GOULASH
– rich Spanish or Latin American stew containing several different meats and vegetables OLIO, OLLA PODRIDA
– rich spicy seafood stew or soup containing several different types of seafood, often flavoured with saffron BOUILLABAISSE
– traditional French stew of beef and vegetables POT-AU-FEU

steward of a medieval royal house-

hold or manor SENESCHAL, CHAMBERLAIN, REEVE
– steward or chief butler MAÎTRE D'HÔTEL, MAJOR-DOMO
– steward who buys provisions in a college or monastery MANCIPLE

stick See also **join**, **club**, **staff**
– stick, forked twig, or the like that quivers or dips when held above ground containing water or minerals DIVINING ROD, DOWSING ROD
– stick, ruler, or the like for beating children, especially on the hand FERULE
– stick fast, cling ADHERE, CLEAVE
– stick of perfumed substance, burnt as incense JOSS STICK
– stick on which notches are cut, formerly used for keeping accounts or records TALLY
– stick or baton formerly used by a king or military commander to signal orders WARDER
– stick or pole with a fork on the end, or the fork itself CROTCH
– stick or pole, with a spring at the base, on which one can bounce along POGO STICK
– stick or rod from which lengths are cut for fastening adjoining wood or stone parts, or the fastener itself DOWEL
– stick or short cane carried by army officers SWAGGER STICK
– stick or short staff used as a police weapon, symbol of official authority, or the like BATON
– stick out, jut, project PROTRUDE
– stick together COHERE
– stick used for beating, or a beating with a stick, especially on the soles of the feet BASTINADO
– stick with a pointed or electrified tip for prodding animals GOAD
– sticking, holding, or clinging firmly TENACIOUS
– fence of pointed sticks forming a defensive barrier PALISADE, STOCKADE
– long, iron-tipped stick, used by hikers in the mountains ALPENSTOCK
– long stick with a curved blade used for rough pruning and harvesting fruit BILLHOOK
– small stick or wand used as a pointer, as by teachers FESCUE
– small thin stick for stirring or removing bubbles from a drink SWIZZLE STICK
– spiked walking stick whose handle opens into a flat seat SHOOTING STICK
– upright pointed stick forming part of a fence or the like PALE, PALING, PICKET

sticks, branches, or twigs tied in a bundle FAGGOT
– building material of poles interlaced with reeds, sticks, or the like WATTLE
– bundle of sticks with an axe, carried as a symbol of the magistrates' authority in ancient Rome FASCES

sticky ADHESIVE
– sticky, gummy, gluey GLUTINOUS, VISCOUS, VISCID
– sticky gum obtained from some plants RESIN, MUCILAGE

stiff, frosty, unfriendly, scornful or haughty ALOOF, DISDAINFUL, STANDOFFISH
– stiff, inelegant, and forced, as a strained way of speaking is STILTED
– stiff, starchy, conservative, prudish STRAITLACED
– stiff, strict, severe, as a law might be EXACTING, STRINGENT
– stiff, unbending, unwilling or unable to change UNADAPTABLE, INFLEXIBLE, INELASTIC, UNWAVERING, UNYIELDING
– stiff and inflexible person, strict disciplinarian MARTINET, RAMROD
– stiff and very strict in matters of discipline PRUSSIAN, TEUTONIC
– stiffly and hypocritically self-righteous, holier-than-thou PHARISAICAL
– stiffly and pompously authoritative DOCTRINAIRE, OPINIONATED, PONTIFICAL
– stiffly austere and self-denying, especially in the cause of religious devotion ASCETIC, PURITANICAL
– stiffly committed to one's opinions or beliefs, unwilling to change or adapt one's views DOGMATIC, UNSHAKABLE
– stiffly correct and strict observer of the rules, a religion, or the like PRECISIAN, FORMALIST, STICKLER, PURIST
– stiffly or excessively correct and hard to please, picky, choosy, fussy FASTIDIOUS, FINICKY, HYPERCRITICAL, PEDANTIC, PERNICKETY
– thin strip of wood, whalebone, or the like for stiffening a corset BUSK

stiffness, cramp, or rigid muscular contraction, as in a fever RIGOR
– stiffness in artistic technique or criticism, overconcentration on form rather than meaning FORMALISM, STYLISATION
– inflammation of the joints that results in pain, stiffness, and often deformity ARTHRITIS

still See also **calm**, **quiet**
– still, motionless, as a sailing ship is when there is no wind or current BECALMED
– still, not flowing, as pond water is STAGNANT
– still, stationary, unmoving or incapable of moving IMMOBILE
– still, unchanging, making no progress STATIC
– still, unmoving, very sluggish or passive INERT
– temporarily still or inactive DORMANT

still in existence, surviving, not lost or extinct or destroyed EXTANT

stimulate, agitate, or stir up discontent, riot, or the like FOMENT
– stimulate, arouse, inspire, startle, or spur into action GALVANISE
– stimulate, inflame, or excite interest, love, or the like KINDLE
– stimulate, put life or energy into ANIMATE, INVIGORATE, VIVIFY
– stimulate, set in motion or action, prompt ACTIVATE, ACTUATE
– stimulate, urge on, spur, prod into action or movement GOAD, EGG ON
– stimulate, whip up, provoke, or take the initiative in something, especially wrongdoing or riot INCITE, INSTIGATE
– stimulate or increase appetite, desire, or interest WHET
– stimulate or inspire, provide an incentive MOTIVATE
– stimulating, lively, or cheering INVIGORATING, EXHILARATING

stimulus, "come-on", promise of reward, threat, or the like to secure cooperation INCENTIVE, INDUCEMENT
– stimulus, impelling force, initial spur or drive to action IMPETUS, IMPULSE, MOMENTUM
– stimulus, slight goad or incentive, especially one providing a boost FILLIP

sting – having a sting, as a bee has ACULEATE

stinging or itching sensation, typically accompanied by weals on the skin URTICATION, HIVES, UREDO

stingy, miserly, grasping, cheap CHEESE-PARING, COSTIVE, CLOSE-FISTED, NIGGARDLY, MINGY, PARSIMONIOUS, PENNY-PINCHING
– stingy, miserly, and grasping person CHEAPSKATE, PINCHPENNY, NIGGARD, SKINFLINT, TIGHTWAD, CURMUDGEON
– stingy, over-anxious about finances CARKING
– stingy and miserly, or very poor PENURIOUS
– stingy or unduly thrifty, unwilling to spend sufficient money, time, or effort SKIMPY

stinking, foul-smelling FETID, RANK, MALODOROUS, REEKING, NOISOME
stir up, disturb ROIL
– stir up trouble, rebellion, or the like FOMENT, INSTIGATE, PROVOKE, INCITE
stitch See **sewing**, **embroidery**
– stitching of cloth with a decorative honeycomb pattern of tucks SMOCKING
– stitching or sewing together of the edges of a wound SUTURE
– fastening of the female genitals with clasps or stitches to prevent sexual intercourse INFIBULATION
stock or broth from stewed beef or chicken BOUILLON
– stock or range of jokes, pieces of music, roles, or the like to a performer REPERTOIRE
– stock or total quantity of goods on hand INVENTORY
– add new stocks or supplies, as in refilling a larder REPLENISH
stock exchange See also **shares**, **economics**
– stock exchange, especially that of Paris BOURSE
– stock-exchange average in London FT INDEX
– stock-exchange average in New York DOW JONES AVERAGE
– continuous strip of paper such as that on which stock-exchange reports used to be printed TICKER TAPE
– middleman formerly dealing in stocks and shares on the stock exchange JOBBER
– referring to stocks and shares not quoted on the stock exchange UNLISTED
– short-term speculation on the stock exchange ARBITRAGE, STAGGING
stockings – embroidered or woven design on the side of a sock or stocking CLOCK
– thin, light, and translucent, as some stockings are SHEER
stocky, heavily built PYKNIC, ENDOMORPHIC
stole with long front ends of the types worn by women or Anglican vicars TIPPET
stolen goods or property SWAG, LOOT, BOOTY, PLUNDER, SPOILS
– person who knowingly buys or stores stolen goods RECEIVER
– person who receives and sells stolen goods FENCE
stomach area MIDRIFF
– stomach lining of calves, or an extract of it used in cheesemaking RENNET
– stomach of an animal, or crop of a bird CRAW
– stomach or intestinal pains, especially in infants, due to a build-up of gas COLIC, MULLIGRUBS, GRIPE
– stomach pain or upset, especially resulting from nervousness COLLYWOBBLES
– stomach rumbling BORBORYGMUS
– stomach section in birds, often containing grit, for breaking down food GIZZARD
– stomach upset, indigestion DYSPEPSIA
– adjective for the stomach GASTRIC
– contents of the stomach GORGE
– displacement of a part of the stomach through the diaphragm HIATUS HERNIA
– first stomach of a cow or other cud-chewing mammal, in which food is partly digested before returning to the mouth RUMEN
– fourth stomach of a cow or other cud-chewing mammal, where true digestion takes place ABOMASUM
– lower opening of the stomach for food to pass into the duodenum PYLORUS
– membrane lining the abdominal cavity and covering most of the stomach and other organs PERITONEUM
– part of the body containing the stomach and intestines ABDOMEN
– "pit of the stomach" SOLAR PLEXUS
– second stomach of a cow or other cud-chewing mammal RETICULUM
– third stomach of a cow or other cud-chewing mammal MANYPLIES, OMASUM, PSALTERIUM
– tube through which food passes from the pharynx to the stomach OESOPHAGUS, GULLET
– whitish chemical substance swallowed by a patient to make the stomach and intestines visible for X-ray photographs BARIUM MEAL
-stomach- -GASTR-, -GASTRO-
stone See also **rock**, **gemstones**, **precious stones**
– stone band or moulding along a wall, as an architectural ornament CORDON, STRING COURSE
– stone breakwater or jetty, protecting a harbour MOLE
– stone coffin or marble tomb, typically having a sculpture or inscriptions SARCOPHAGUS
– stone figure of grotesque appearance as on a cathedral roof, often serving as a rainwater spout from a gutter GARGOYLE
– stone fragment or chip SPALL
– stone-like mass of mineral salts in the body, such as a gallstone or kidney stone CALCULUS
– stone or brick used in the top, usually sloping, section of a wall or roof COPESTONE, COPING STONE, CAPSTONE
– stone or light volcanic rock used for scrubbing and polishing PUMICE
– stone or rock formation that protrudes sharply above the soil level, as on a plain OUTCROP
– stone or slab of stone used for paving FLAGSTONE
– stone or substance believed by alchemists to have the power of turning base metals into gold PHILOSOPHERS' STONE, ELIXIR
– stone pillar, four-sided and tapering up to a pyramidal top, of a kind used as a monument in ancient Egypt OBELISK
– stone slab, as laid flat over a grave LEDGER
– stone slab on top of a pillar, for supporting an arch or lintel SUMMER
– stone slab or pillar, with an engraved surface, as used in ancient times as a monument, gravestone, or the like STELE
– stone tablet that provided the key to ancient Egyptian hieroglyphics ROSETTA STONE
– stone tool used during the later Stone Age NEOLITH
– adjective for stone LITHIC
– area or pit from which stone is extracted QUARRY
– cavity in a stone or rock lined with crystals GEODE
– engraved in stone LAPIDARIAN, LAPIDARY
– game in which flat stones are bounced across water DUCKS AND DRAKES
– large standing stone, usually part of a prehistoric monument MEGALITH, MONOLITH, MENHIR
– metal clamp or cramping iron for fastening blocks of stone together AGRAFFE
– metal pin for fastening blocks of stone together GUDGEON
– mound of stones serving as a memorial or landmark CAIRN
– person who shapes building-stone, or is skilled at building with it MASON
– prehistoric monument or chamber formed by stone pillars with a crossbeam DOLMEN, TRILITHON
– ring of stone pillars forming part of a prehistoric monument HENGE, CROMLECH
– shape or dress stone roughly with a broad chisel BOAST
– turn into stone LAPIDIFY, PETRIFY

– unbreakable stone, according to legend ADAMANT
-stone- -LITE, -LITH-, LITHO-, LAPID-, PETR-, PETRI-, PETRO-
Stone Age – middle Stone Age MESOLITHIC
– new Stone Age NEOLITHIC
– old Stone Age PALAEOLITHIC
Stonehenge – prehistoric pillar-like stone, as at Stonehenge, probably erected for religious purposes MEGALITH, MONOLITH, MENHIR
stonemason's chisel DROVE
stonework in a building MASONRY
– stonework prepared for mouldings, sills, or the like DRESSINGS
– lacy ornamental pattern or stonework, as at the top of a Gothic window TRACERY
stool to which wrongdoers or suspects were formerly tied, as for ducking or public mockery CUCKING STOOL
– folding stool or desk for kneeling at during prayer, as by the English sovereign at the coronation FALDSTOOL
stoop, agree in a haughty or patronising way to do or give something DEIGN, CONDESCEND, VOUCHSAFE
stop See also **end**, **prevent**, **hinder**, **obstruct**
– stop, cease, quit doing, discontinue DESIST, PRETERMIT
– stop, seize, or interrupt something, such as a message, in its course INTERCEPT
– stop, stoppage, immobility STASIS
– stop and confront someone unexpectedly ACCOST, WAYLAY
– stop doing or participating in, refrain or abstain FORBEAR
– stop or check the movement, development, or spread of ARREST
– stop or suspend a meeting, court proceedings, or the like temporarily ADJOURN, RECESS
– stop short, refuse, as a horse might at a jump JIB, BAULK, SHY
– stopping, ceasing, termination CESSATION, SURCEASE
– stopping and starting at intervals, periodic INTERMITTENT
– come to a stop, or bring a ship to a stop HEAVE TO
– complete stop in progress or activity STANDSTILL
– old shipboard command to stop AVAST!
– suspended, or stopped temporarily, as a project might be IN ABEYANCE
stop- PARA-
stop-press space in a newspaper, for last-minute reports FUDGE
stop watch or other instrument for measuring time very accurately CHRONOGRAPH
-stoppage -STASIS
stopping place for rest or refuelling during a long journey STAGING POST
store, as in a granary GARNER
– store of hidden arms, stolen goods, or the like, or its hiding place CACHE
– store or supply accumulated for future use STOCKPILE
– funnel-shaped dispenser for bulk materials, as at a storage place for fuel or grain HOPPER
– storage place, warehouse DEPOSITORY, DEPOT, ENTREPÔT
– storeroom for cuttings and files in a newspaper office MORGUE
– secret store of money, drugs, or the like STASH
storey between ground and first floor MEZZANINE, ENTRESOL
– storey or gallery that has windows, as in a Gothic church CLERESTORY
– storey or gallery that lacks windows, as in a Gothic church BLINDSTOREY
– storey within a double-sloped roof MANSARD
stork – large African stork MARABOU
– large Asian stork ADJUTANT BIRD
storm – interval of calm during a storm LULL
– lessen in intensity, decline or die down, as a storm or a feeling might SUBSIDE, ABATE
– still area at the centre of a cyclonic storm EYE
stormy, as the weather, sea, or a meeting or person might be BOISTEROUS, TURBULENT, TEMPESTUOUS, TUMULTUOUS
– stormy and wild, unpleasant, as weather might be INCLEMENT
story, especially a tale of adventure CONTE
– story, speech, sales talk, or the like that is glib or long-winded SPIEL
– story from one's past, usually related with nostalgia REMINISCENCE
– story of a person's life or experiences, as written by another person BIOGRAPHY
– story of a person's life or experiences, as written by himself AUTOBIOGRAPHY, MEMOIRS
– story or drawn-out joky anecdote whose supposed humour lies in the irrelevance or anticlimax of the punch line SHAGGY-DOG STORY
– story or picture in which the characters or scenes symbolise abstractions or ideas and convey a deeper meaning ALLEGORY
– story or rumour that is false or a deliberate hoax CANARD
– story with a moral, usually a beast fable APOLOGUE
– storytelling, or the story told NARRATION
– collection of poems, stories, or the like ANTHOLOGY
– doubtful, of very questionable authenticity, as an extraordinary story or anecdote might be APOCRYPHAL
– entertain or give pleasure to, as by telling stories REGALE
– events of a story as opposed to its dialogue, descriptions, and the like PLOT
– improve or enliven a report or story by adding colourful, often false, details EMBELLISH, EMBROIDER
– incoherent, disconnected, or disordered, as a report or story might be DISJOINTED
– make up or invent an excuse, story, or the like CONCOCT
– medieval verse story with comic, satirical, or ribald themes FABLIAU
– short story relating some interesting or humorous incident ANECDOTE
– simple story which, usually indirectly, points a moral or religious lesson PARABLE
– skilled teller of witty stories or anecdotes RACONTEUR
stove of a large iron make, usually burning coal or wood, with one or more ovens RANGE
– stove top HOB
– movable plate adjusting the airflow in a stove DAMPER
– portable stove or heater, as for drying out a building under construction SALAMANDER
– small portable stove, burning paraffin or oil PRIMUS
straight LINEAR
– straight, arrow-like SAGITTAL
– relating to straight lines RECTILINEAR
straight- ORTHO-
strain, wrench, or sprain one's back, ankle, or the like RICK
– straining or purifying by use of a filter FILTRATION
– reduce food to a pulpy consistency by mashing it or pressing it through a strainer PURÉE
strained, long-winded, or tedious, as a speech might be LABOURED
– strained, striving for effect, or forced AGONISTIC, VOULU
– strained, tense, or nervy OVERWROUGHT, AGITATED
strait-jacket – confine or bind with a tight-fitting garment such as a corset or strait-jacket TRUSS

strand twisted with others to make wool, rope, or the like PLY

strange, abnormal, irregular, inconsistent with or deviating from the norm ANOMALOUS
– strange, beyond normal nature, supernatural PRETERNATURAL, UNCANNY
– strange, inexplicable, conspicuously odd or very unconventional FANTASTIC, FREAKISH, BIZARRE, OUTRÉ, OUTLANDISH
– strange, odd, peculiar, especially in an interesting or amusing way ECCENTRIC, RUM
– strange, "one-off", unique, or remarkable and rare SINGULAR, SUI GENERIS
– strange, quirky, "a rule unto itself" IDIOSYNCRATIC
– strange, unfamiliar, foreign to one's experience or nature ALIEN
– strange and fascinating through being unfamiliar or foreign EXOTIC

strange- XENO-

strangers – person who is hostile to or scared of strangers and unfamiliar ideas XENOPHOBE

strangle, as with wire, typically in order to commit robbery or as a means of execution GARROTTE
– strangle or choke THROTTLE
– strangle or stifle secretly, so as to leave the body unmarked BURKE

strap around an animal's body as to hold a saddle in place GIRTH, SURCINGLE
– straps for tying together the legs of a horse or cow HOBBLE
– leather strap, split into strips at the end, used for beating children, especially in Scotland TAWSE
– system of elastic straps used for tying down loads, as on a car roof SPIDER, OCTOPUS

straw bedding for cattle LITTER
– straw mat used as a floor covering in a Japanese home TATAMI
– haystack, pile of straw, or the like in the open air RICK

strawberry basket, typically small and rectangular, as sold at fruit stalls PUNNET
– runner on a strawberry plant STOLON
– leafy cup-like base in which the strawberry nestles HULL

stray and homeless child or animal WAIF
– stray, fall behind STRAGGLE, LAG
– stray from the main subject of one's speech or writing DIGRESS
– straying from the proper moral course, erring, wayward ERRANT

streak – streaked, grooved, or ridged STRIATE, STRIGOSE
– streaked or marked with several different colours VARIEGATED, PIED, BRINDLED

stream See also **river**
– stream flowing out of a lake, dam, or the like EFFLUENT
– stream of air or water forced backwards by a propeller SLIPSTREAM, RACE
– stream of water or air directed at or into a part of the body for cleansing or healing DOUCHE
– stream or flow of people or things coming in, such as tourists arriving INFLUX
– stream or small river RIVULET, BROOK
– stream or small river, as referred to in various regions BECK, BOURN, BURN, RILL, RUNLET, RUNNEL
– clear stream, or a sudden river flood due to heavy rains or melting snow FRESHET
– narrow gorge or ravine in the U.S., usually with a stream flowing through it FLUME
– small stream in the U.S., or a narrow tidal inlet CREEK
– swift-flowing mountain stream GILL

stream- RHEO-

streamlined to reduce air resistance, as the design of a car might be AERODYNAMIC

street See **road**
– street entertainer or musician performing for money from idlers or passers-by BUSKER
– street urchin GUTTERSNIPE
– mechanical instrument played in the street, such as a barrel organ HURDY-GURDY

strength See also **strong**
– strength, power, or vitality THEW, SINEW
– strength of a metal or similar solid material to withstand a pulling force or longitudinal stress TENSILE STRENGTH
– strength of character, determination BACKBONE, SPUNK
– strength of mind, courage, and hardiness, especially in battle or against adversity FORTITUDE, VALOUR, PROWESS
– strength to endure or resist, staying power, vigour STAMINA
– brute strength, muscular power BRAWN
– rest and regain one's strength after illness CONVALESCE, RECUPERATE

strengthen See also **support**
– strengthen, back up, or confirm an argument, proof, or the like CORROBORATE, SUBSTANTIATE, VERIFY, UNDERPIN
– strengthen, revive, enliven, impart new vitality to INVIGORATE, REVITALISE
– strengthen, stabilise, secure CONSOLIDATE
– strengthen against danger, attack, or impact, prop up BOLSTER, BRACE, BUTTRESS
– strengthen or harden steel by heating and cooling TEMPER
– strengthen or increase the effectiveness of a drug, hormone, or the like by administering another POTENTIATE
– strengthen or reinforce a defensive position, wine, a decision, or the like FORTIFY
– strengthen the will or determination ANNEAL
– strengthening, returning, flowing strongly again, re-emerging RESURGENT
– strengthening of a learned response, as by means of rewards REINFORCEMENT

stress, emphasise, or intensify, draw attention to in an emphatic way ACCENTUATE, UNDERSCORE, HIGHLIGHT
– stress for rhythm or metre in verse ICTUS
– stress or emphasise a point by constantly repeating it, dwell on, hammer home BELABOUR
– referring to the syllable carrying the principal stress or accent in a sentence or word-group TONIC, NUCLEAR

stretch, widen, expand DILATE, DISTEND
– stretch and exercise, as before beginning a race LIMBER UP
– stretch of a river REACH
– stretch of land, water, or sky EXPANSE
– stretch out or into PROTRUDE, OBTRUDE
– stretch over, bridge SPAN
– stretchable, capable of being drawn out without breaking, as some metals are TENSILE, EXTENSILE, DUCTILE, TRACTILE
– stretched out on the ground, with arms and legs spread out SPREADEAGLED
– continuous stretching of a compressed or injured body part as a medical treatment TRACTION

stretcher for the wounded or sick LITTER

strict See also **stiff**
– strict, austere, moralistic, and self-denying, especially from religious considerations ASCETIC, PURITANICAL
– strict, demanding, severe, as a law, rule, or the like might be EX-

ACTING, STRINGENT, IRON-CLAD
– strict, grim, stern, unfriendly in appearance PO-FACED
– strict, relentless, not yielding to entreaty, not making allowances INEXORABLE, UNCOMPROMISING
– strict, rigid, severe, demanding RIGOROUS
– strict, severe, stern, and serious in life-style and morality AUSTERE
– strict, unyielding, rigorous, unshakable, stubborn ADAMANT, INFLEXIBLE, UNBENDING, OBDURATE, UNSWERVING
– strict and harsh, extremely severe, or cruel, as a law might be DRACONIAN
– strict and literal-minded believer in the Bible or other unalterable religious doctrine FUNDAMENTALIST
– strict and stiff in discipline, allowing little individualism PRUSSIAN, TEUTONIC
– strict and stiffly correct observer of the rules, a religion, or the like PRECISIAN, FORMALIST, PURIST
– strict disciplinarian or authority MARTINET, RAMROD
– strict ruler, or a person favouring strict authority and obedience AUTHORITARIAN
– person who is strict in matters of correctness, as in use of words PURIST, STICKLER

strife – referring to destructive conflict or strife within a group INTERNECINE

strike See also **beat**
– strike or boycott in India, as for political protest HARTAL
– striker or group of protesters positioned outside a place of work, as to discourage other workers or customers from entering PICKET
– anticipating and thwarting an opponent's moves, as a military strike might PRE-EMPTIVE
– harassment of employers by the workers during strikes in India GHERAO
– settlement of a strike or dispute by negotiating through a third party CONCILIATION, MEDIATION
– settlement of a strike or dispute by submitting to the judgment of a third party ARBITRATION, ADJUDICATION

strikebreaker BLACKLEG, SCAB

striking, outstanding, conspicuous, as arguments might be SALIENT
– striking of a surface, as by sound on the ear or by a stick on a drum PERCUSSION

string, cord, or ribbon running inside a hem, as to tighten a sleeve or close a purse DRAWSTRING
– string worn round the neck, as for carrying a whistle LANYARD
– pad in a piano or other keyboard instrument that deadens a string's vibrations DAMPER
– plucking device for the

STRING INSTRUMENTS

aeolian harp, wind harp	small box-like instrument that sounds when blown by the wind	**mandolin**	plucked instrument, related to the lute, with four pairs of strings
balalaika	plucked three-stringed, guitar-like, triangular Russian folk instrument	**oud**	lute-like instrument of northern Africa and western Asia
bouzouki	mandolin-like Greek folk instrument	**pandoura**	long-necked Persian lute
cimbalom	large Hungarian dulcimer	**psaltery**	ancient and medieval instrument like a dulcimer, but plucked instead of struck
cithara/kithara	ancient Greek lyre, with a box-shaped frame	**rebec/rebeck, ribible**	medieval three-stringed bowed instrument, shaped like a half-pear
cittern	lute-like 16th-century instrument	**samisen**	three-stringed, guitar-like Japanese instrument
clarsach/ clairschach	ancient Irish harp	**sarod**	Indian instrument with two sets of strings, one plucked and the other acting as a drone
crowd/crwth	ancient Celtic lyre-shaped instrument, played with a bow		
dulcimer	instrument with strings stretched over a soundboard and struck with hammers	**sitar**	long-necked Indian instrument made of gourds and wood
gittern	medieval four-stringed guitar	**theorbo, archlute**	long-necked lute with extra bass strings
hurdy-gurdy	medieval mechanical lute-shaped instrument in which a wheel, turned by a handle, acted as the bow	**ukulele**	small, four-stringed guitar of Hawaiian origin, often strummed
kit, pochette	miniature violin, formerly used by dancing masters	**viol**	any of a family of early violin-like instruments, with a fretted fingerboard, and usually six strings
koto	box-shaped, 13-stringed Japanese instrument	**viola da gamba, bass viol**	large viol, played between the legs like a cello
lute	medieval plucked instrument, usually shaped like a half-pear, a bent neck, and a fretted fingerboard	**viola d'amore**	tenor viol
lyre	harp-like ancient instrument	**zither/zithern**	plucked, many-stringed Central European folk instrument, placed on the knees when played

strings of a harpsichord or related instrument QUILL
- relating to rope, string, or cable FUNICULAR
- small thin disc or plate, as of plastic, used for plucking the strings of a guitar, lute, or related instrument PLECTRUM, PICK
- strand making up string, rope, or thread PLY

string instruments See chart, and also **guitar**, **violin**
- string instrument, keyboard instrument, or any other instrument producing sound by means of vibrating strings CHORDOPHONE

strip, as of paper, that is twisted and formed into a ring to create a one-sided surface MÖBIUS STRIP
- strip of leather THONG
- strip or deprive of something, such as clothes or rights DIVEST
- strip or path, such as that left behind by a scythe SWATH
- strip or slat of wood or metal, used especially in sheets as a backing for plaster, slates, tiles, or the like LATH

stripe or line of colour LIST
- striped, grooved, or ridged STRIATE, STRIGOSE
- stripes on an NCO's sleeve, indicating rank or length of service CHEVRON

striptease – humorous word for a stripper or striptease artist ECDYSIAST
- small round patch covering the nipple on a striptease artist's breast PASTY

stroke, fit, or brainstorm ICTUS
- stroke, often followed by paralysis, resulting from the bursting or blocking of a blood vessel in the brain CEREBRAL HAEMORRHAGE, APOPLEXY

strong See also **strength**
- strong, clumsy, and unwieldy HULKING
- strong, sturdy, steadfast, as a supporter might be STALWART, STAUNCH
- strong, tough, long-lasting DURABLE
- strong against adversity or attack, quick to recover RESILIENT, RESISTANT
- strong and effective, as a medicine or alcoholic drink might be POTENT
- strong and healthy, surviving easily HARDY, ROBUST, RUGGED, VIGOROUS
- strong and large, awesome, impressive FORMIDABLE, REDOUBTABLE, HERCULEAN
- strong and undeniable, as a legal case or an argument might be AIRTIGHT, CAST-IRON, IRREFUTABLE
- strong in a masculine way, manly, or sexually potent VIRILE
- strong or clearly noticeable, as an accent might be PRONOUNCED
- strong or forceful, emphatic, vigorous, as a denial or objection might be STRENUOUS, VEHEMENT
- strongest or most widespread, having the greatest importance, authority, or force PREDOMINANT
- physically strong, stocky, muscular, thickset BURLY, BRAWNY
- so strong as to be unbeatable INVINCIBLE

strong point, one's special talent FORTE, MÉTIER

structure, framework, or pattern FABRIC
- structure, system, organisation, or the like that is elaborate and complex EDIFICE
- structure or form, as of a plant or animal organism MORPHOLOGY
- structured, systematic, classified, as a body of knowledge might be ARCHITECTONIC

struggle See **fight**
- struggle, agonising effort THROES
- struggle for superiority, especially hand-to-hand GRAPPLE
- relating to contests or struggles AGONISTIC
- relating to infighting or destructive struggles within a group INTERNECINE

stubborn, bloody-minded, pigheaded, opposing things just for the sake of it CONTRARY, PERVERSE, CROSS-GRAINED, CUSSED, MULISH
- stubborn, hardened, habitual, or deep-rooted, as a criminal or vice might be INVETERATE
- stubborn, inflexible, unshakable, holding fast to opinions or refusing to make allowances INTRANSIGENT, UNCOMPROMISING, UNSWERVING, DIEHARD
- stubborn, obstinate, unyielding, wanting one's own way HEADSTRONG, WILFUL, STIFF-NECKED
- stubborn and disobedient, as a spoilt child might be FROWARD
- stubborn or relentless, refusing to go away, as pain or rain might be UNREMITTING, INEXORABLE
- stubbornly disobedient or rebellious, insubordinate, unmanageable CONTUMACIOUS, REFRACTORY, INTRACTABLE, RECALCITRANT, UNRULY
- stubbornly persistent in the face of adversity, persevering, refusing to give up DOGGED, PERTINACIOUS, TENACIOUS
- stubbornly prejudiced, refusing to accept new social attitudes, ultra-conservative UNREGENERATE, UNRECONSTRUCTED
- stubbornly refusing to forgive, modify, or back down IMPLACABLE
- stubbornly refusing to mend one's ways, hardened against good or moral influence INDURATE, OBDURATE, IMPENITENT, UNREPENTANT
- fast and immovable, as a stubborn stain is INERADICABLE, INGRAINED, PERSISTENT

stuck-up See **proud**
- stuck-up, snobbish, high and mighty, haughty TOFFEE-NOSED, DISDAINFUL
- stuck-up and acting in a superior manner SUPERCILIOUS, PATRONISING, CONDESCENDING

student about to receive a degree GRADUAND
- student in the first year of study at university or college FRESHER
- student in the last year of study at a university or college FINALIST
- student in the second year at a U.S. university, college, or high school SOPHOMORE
- student who is not on a scholarship COMMONER, PENSIONER
- students' social organisation in the U.S. FRATERNITY, SORORITY
- attend a course or class without receiving academic credit, as a U.S. student might AUDIT
- graduate or former student of a school, college, or university in the U.S. ALUMNUS, ALUMNA
- put a student back or down a year or more, or allow a student leave of absence DEGRADE
- supervise and keep watch over students at an examination INVIGILATE
- suspend a student from college or university RUSTICATE

studio or workshop of an artist or craftsman ATELIER

study See also **analysis**, **examine**
- study, deep reflection, laborious meditation LUCUBRATION, EXCOGITATION
- study, office, or other private room where one can remain undisturbed SANCTUM
- study course offered by a university or college to part-time students EXTENSION COURSE
- study group or meeting SEMINAR
- study intensely at the last minute for an exam CRAM, GEN UP, MUG UP
- study leave for a term or year granted to a teacher after a number of years' work SABBATICAL

– study leave of several weeks or months given to trainees or apprentices BLOCK RELEASE
– study leave on a day-to-day basis given to trainees or apprentices DAY RELEASE
– study of or formal lecture or treatise on a subject DISQUISITION
– study or examine in detail CON, ANATOMISE, DISSECT, SCRUTINISE, PERUSE, TRAVERSE
– occurring outside the normal course of studies or timetable, as in a school or college EXTRACURRICULAR, EXTRAMURAL
– outline of a course of study or exam requirements CURRICULUM, SYLLABUS
– relating to two or more academic subjects or fields of study INTERDISCIPLINARY
– subject of study, branch of knowledge DISCIPLINE
– systematic account or written study of a particular subject MONOGRAPH, TREATISE, DISSERTATION

-study -GRAPHY, -ISTICS, -LOGY, -OLOGY, -ICS

stuffed, as mushrooms or a roast chicken might be FARCI

stuffing, fabric, and springs used in making a soft covering for furniture UPHOLSTERY
– stuffing and preparing the skins of dead animals for exhibiting TAXIDERMY
– stuffing of seasoned mincemeat or chopped poultry FORCEMEAT
– stuffing of wool or cotton waste for furniture or mattresses FLOCK
– stuffing or padding material used in former times BOMBAST
– silky plant fibre used for stuffing cushions, for soundproofing, and the like KAPOK

stuffy, hot, and airless FROWSTY
– stuffy, hot, and humid MUGGY
– stuffy, hot, and usually smoke-laden atmosphere FUG

stumble, trip, lose one's footing FALTER
– stumble and go lame, as a horse might FOUNDER

stunned, confused STUPEFIED

stupid See also **silly**, **fool**
– stupid, dull-witted, awkward and clueless GORMLESS
– stupid, foolish, lacking understanding and human sensitivity INSENSATE
– stupid, muddled, confused ADDLE-PATED
– stupid, slow-witted or insensitive OBTUSE, LUMPEN, PURBLIND
– stupidly and boringly routine STULTIFYING
– stupidly and boringly routine work CONVEYOR BELT, GRINDSTONE, TREADMILL
– stupidly insensitive, gross, unthinking, as a needlessly clumsy remark would be CRASS
– extremely stupid or foolish, senseless, as an impulsive blunder might be IMBECILIC, MORONIC, CRETINOUS

style, enthusiasm, vigour, vivacity BRIO, DASH, FLAIR, PANACHE, ÉLAN, VERVE
– style of a graceful, moving, or effective kind in speech or writing ELOQUENCE
– style of a light, bantering kind in speech or writing PERSIFLAGE, BADINAGE, RAILLERY
– style of language appropriate to a particular social setting or use REGISTER
– style of modern design, using industrial materials HIGH-TECH
– style of speech or writing, way of putting things in words PHRASEOLOGY, DICTION
– style of speech or writing that is pompous, high-flown, and showy FUSTIAN, GRANDILOQUENCE, BOMBAST, EUPHUISM, GONGORISM
– agreeable or appropriate in style FELICITOUS
– characterised more by style than by content, as showy language is RHETORICAL
– clear and easy to understand, as a prose style might be LIMPID, LUCID
– commonly used, popular, as the informal everyday local style of speech is DEMOTIC, VERNACULAR
– concise, often to the point of obscurity, as a literary style might be ELLIPTICAL
– concise and elegant, as a prose style might be LAPIDARY
– conversational or informal in style, characteristic of casual everyday speech COLLOQUIAL
– deliberately emotional or stirring in style, as a high-flown speech of protest would be ORATORICAL, DECLAMATORY
– effortless ease of style, flowing gracefulness, as in speech or movement FLUENCY
– excessively ornate or high-flown, as a literary style might be FLORID, AUREATE, TUMID, BAROQUE, ROCOCO, EUPHUISTIC, MANDARIN
– grand, lofty, or exalted, as a literary style or social circle might be RAREFIED
– impressive, grand, or highfalutin in style or speech ROTUND, SONOROUS, OROTUND
– inappropriate or ill-chosen, as a remark, style, or expression might be INFELICITOUS
– language of an elegant rhetorical style PERIODS
– language or speech of a distinctive style, exclusive to a profession or other group JARGON, ARGOT, CANT
– long-winded, indirect, or roundabout in style, as a speech might be PERIPHRASTIC, CIRCUMLOCUTORY, PROLIX
– old-fashioned or outdated in style or idiom, no longer in common use ARCHAIC
– overrefined, excessively rich or precious, as a literary style might be DECADENT
– pompously ornate or windy in style, but lacking any real content TURGID, FLATULENT
– simple and long-lasting in style, rising above changing fashions CLASSIC
– tending to use or characterised by very long words, as a writer's style might be SESQUIPEDALIAN, INKHORN
– writing of a more striking or elaborate style than the surrounding text PURPLE PATCH, PURPLE PASSAGE

subatomic particle forming part of an atom's nucleus, and having a positive electric charge PROTON
– subatomic particle forming part of an atom's nucleus, and without any electric charge NEUTRON
– subatomic particle having half-integral spin FERMION
– subatomic particle having integral spin BOSON
– subatomic particle of various kinds participating in strong interactions HADRON, BARYON, PROTON, MESON, PION, NEUTRON, KAON
– subatomic particle of various kinds participating in weak actions LEPTON, ELECTRON, MUON, TAU, NEUTRINO
– subatomic particle properties that are described by quantum numbers STRANGENESS; TOP, TRUTH; BOTTOM, BEAUTY; COLOUR; SPIN; CHARM
– subatomic particle revolving around an atom's nucleus, and having a negative electric charge ELECTRON
– hypothetical subatomic particle thought to be the fundamental unit of known elementary particles QUARK

subconscious, as secret fears or painful memories might be REPRESSED

subdue or discipline one's body by self-denial or punishment MORTIFY

subject case in grammar NOMINATIVE
– subject of study, branch of knowledge DISCIPLINE
– subject that is remote or only vaguely understood HINTERLAND
– begin to discuss a subject BROACH
– relating to two or more academic subjects or fields of study INTERDISCIPLINARY
-subject, -LOGY, -OLOGY, -GRAPHY, -ICS, -ISTICS, -NOMY
submarine observation vessel for manned scientific research in deep-sea waters BATHYSCAPH, BATHYSPHERE
– submarine's rudder on a horizontal axis HYDROPLANE
– device or system used for detecting enemy submarines ASDIC, ECHO SOUNDER, SONAR
– optical instrument, as on a submarine, containing mirrors or prisms for viewing objects that are not in the direct line of sight PERISCOPE
– raised observation post or bridge on a submarine, usually housing the entrance CONNING TOWER, SAIL
– wake made by a submarine's periscope above the water FEATHER
submerge, cover completely in a liquid IMMERSE
submissive attitude, or respect DEFERENCE, HOMAGE, OBEISANCE
submit over-respectfully to another's wishes or decisions KOWTOW
– submit to or respect the wishes or opinion of someone else DEFER
– submitting, as to misfortune or to unfair treatment ACQUIESCENT, RESIGNED
subordinate See also **secondary**, **servant**
subordinate- PARA-
subordination of a clause in grammar by means of a conjunction HYPOTAXIS
– linking of clauses in grammar by means of punctuation rather than by conjunctions or subordination PARATAXIS
subsidy, financial grant, such as an endowment SUBVENTION
-substance -PHANE
substitute See also **agent**
– substitute, imitation ERSATZ
– substitute or agent, deputy, stand-in VICAR, PROXY, SURROGATE
– substitute or exchange COMMUTE
– substituted fraudulently SUPPOSITITIOUS; SPURIOUS
– relating to, serving as, performed or suffered by, or experienced through a substitute VICARIOUS
subtitle – translation shown above the stage or screen, rather than as a subtitle at its foot SURTITLE
subtle shade of meaning NUANCE
– subtle to a fault, over-precise, pedantic or dogmatic SCHOLASTIC, SOPHISTICAL
– subtly harmful, treacherous, or seductive INSIDIOUS
– making needless or oversubtle distinctions, nitpicking QUIBBLING, HAIRSPLITTING
subtlety, delicacy, precision, as in negotiations NICETY
subtraction – number or quantity from which another number is subtracted MINUEND
– number or quantity that is to be subtracted SUBTRAHEND
suburb from which many people commute to their place of work DORMITORY SUBURB
– suburb or quarter of a city, especially a French city FAUBOURG
– suburbs or outskirts of a town ENVIRONS, PRECINCTS
succeed, bear fruit, work out well, as a plan might FRUCTIFY
– succeed, meet the required standards PASS MUSTER
– succeed in doing, manage, as by scheming CONTRIVE
– succeed in life, thrive, do well, make out FLOURISH, PROSPER
– succeed in the face of opposition, win through PREVAIL
– succeed or replace somebody in a position or office SUPERSEDE
– succeed or thrive, typically by exploiting others BATTEN
– succeed to a throne, title, or the like, inherit ACCEDE TO
success of a book, film, or the like with the reviewers, but not with the public at large SUCCÈS D'ESTIME
– success of a book, play, or the like, due mostly to its shock value SUCCÈS DE SCANDALE
– success or achievement of a brilliant kind ÉCLAT
– success or realisation of plans or wishes FRUITION
– definite, indisputable, widely acknowledged, as a victory or success might be RESOUNDING
– desire or striving for success and recognition, ambition ASPIRATION
successful, bearing results, as an idea or project might be FRUITFUL
– successful, thriving, doing well FLOURISHING
– successful or extremely brilliant person of very young age WHIZZ KID, WUNDERKIND, CHILD PRODIGY
– successful or powerful, as a remedy might be EFFICACIOUS, POTENT
successive, ordered, following in a series SEQUENTIAL, CONSECUTIVE
sucker, as of a leech or octopus ACETABULUM
suction – relating to breathing or suction ASPIRATORY
sudden See also **surprise**
– sudden, brilliant, and fast, as a rise to fame might be METEORIC
– sudden, rapid, and uncontrolled, without due care or planning HEADLONG, PRECIPITATE
– sudden, spontaneous, without planning, as a snap decision would be SPUR-OF-THE-MOMENT
– sudden and artificial development or device introduced to resolve a tricky situation or plot DEUS EX MACHINA
– sudden and powerful, as a disease might be FOUDROYANT
– sudden and entirely unexpected UNFORESEEN, UNANNOUNCED
– sudden and unexpected piece of good fortune, especially the sudden acquiring of money WINDFALL
– sudden and violent change or destruction CATACLYSM
– sudden and violent disruption, radical change UPHEAVAL
– sudden change of opinion or policy, U-turn VOLTE-FACE
– sudden decision or change of mood WHIM, CAPRICE, HUMOUR
– sudden emphatic utterance, exclamation EJACULATION
– sudden insight or recognition, such as a mystical experience of the essence of an event EPIPHANY, REVELATION
– sudden jump in a sequence, as in a set of logical arguments SALTUS
– sudden or surprising event or development COUP DE FOUDRE
– sudden pain PANG
– sudden reversal in fortunes or the course of events, especially in a tragic play PERIPETEIA
– suddenly lift or shift someone, as to stardom CATAPULT
– suddenly or quickly PRESTO
– acting suddenly, on whim rather than by planning IMPULSIVE, IMPETUOUS
sue – person or group that is sued by another or against whom a court action is brought DEFENDANT
– person or group that sues another or brings a civil action in court PLAINTIFF
suffering, agony TRAVAIL, ANGUISH
– suffering, as from a disease or disaster STRICKEN
– suffering, hardship, distress, or misfortune ADVERSITY, AFFLICTION
– suffering, tyrannised, or persecuted DOWNTRODDEN, OPPRESSED, MALTREATED

– suffering, under great strain or anguish ON THE RACK
– suffering and death for one's faith or cause MARTYRDOM
– suffering or great distress, especially from persecution TRIBULATION
– suffering or spiritual torment or ordeal CALVARY, PURGATORY
– sufferings of Jesus prior to and during the Crucifixion PASSION
– cause or means of severe or widespread suffering SCOURGE
– exist in a state of depression, weakness, or suffering LANGUISH
– occasion or place of great suffering GETHSEMANE
– unflinching steadfastness in the face of suffering STOICISM

-suffering -OTIC

suffocate STIFLE, SMOTHER, ASPHYXIATE

suffocation ASPHYXIATION, ASPHYXIA

sugar, starch, or a related compound CARBOHYDRATE
– sugar-coated and shiny, as cherries sometimes are GLACÉ
– sugar-coated, as preserved fruit might be CRYSTALLISED
– sugar deficiency in the blood HYPOGLYCAEMIA
– sugar excess in the blood, as in diabetes HYPERGLYCAEMIA
– sugar of a brown, sticky, raw type MUSCOVADO
– sugar of a powdery consistency ICING SUGAR, CASTOR SUGAR
– sugar or other substance added to a drug to make it more suitable for administering EXCIPIENT
– sugar-processing plant REFINERY
– sugar sprinkler CASTOR
– sugar substitute, artificial sweetener SACCHARIN, CYCLAMATE
– sugar syrup MOLASSES, TREACLE
– sugary, sweet, often excessively so SACCHARINE
– brown crystallised sugar DEMERARA
– cane sugar, common edible sugar SUCROSE, SACCHAROSE
– coat food with flour, sugar, or the like, as by sprinkling DREDGE
– common sugar forming the basic energy source in plants and animals GLUCOSE
– corn or grape sugar DEXTROSE
– disease characterised by excess sugar in the blood and urine DIABETES MELLITUS
– fruit sugar, used in medicinal drips and as a preservative FRUCTOSE, LAEVULOSE
– hormone secreted by the pancreas and regulating the blood-sugar level INSULIN
– milk sugar, used in baby foods and confectionery LACTOSE
– wood sugar, used in dyeing and tanning and in foods for diabetics XYLOSE

-sugar- GLYC-, GLYCO-, -SACCHAR-, SACCHARO-, -OSE

suggest, hint, imply, let something be known indirectly INSINUATE, INTIMATE
– suggest, propose, or put forward a theory for consideration PROPOUND, PREDICATE, ADVANCE
– suggest, recommend, or support ADVOCATE, COMMEND
– suggest, refer to indirectly, hint at ALLUDE TO
– suggest strongly, prove, or indicate EVIDENCE

suggestion or association that is evoked by a word or thing, rather than its literal meaning CONNOTATION, OVERTONE
– suggestion or hint, something implied but not said directly IMPLICATION
– suggestion or hint of a veiled and typically offensive kind INNUENDO, ASPERSION, INSINUATION, IMPUTATION
– advance or seek support for a scheme, project, or suggestion FLOAT
– underlying suggestion or implied tendency or meaning UNDERTONE, UNDERCURRENT

suggestive, atmospheric, or arousing memories, as an idea or story might be EVOCATIVE
– suggestive of sexual impropriety RISQUÉ, TITILLATING, INDELICATE
– suggestive or naughty pun, double meaning DOUBLE ENTENDRE

suicide attempt by a person who does not really want to die PARASUICIDE
– suicide by a Hindu widow who would cremate herself on her late husband's funeral pyre SUTTEE
– suicide or person who commits suicide FELO DE SE
– suicidal or self-destructive person, especially one who is part of a larger group LEMMING
– suicidally risky venture RUSSIAN ROULETTE
– Japanese ritual suicide by disembowelment HARA-KIRI, SEPPUKU
– Japanese suicide pilot during the Second World War KAMIKAZE

suitable, appropriate, corresponding to what is right or needed FITTING, BEFITTING, BEHOVING, MEET
– suitable, appropriate, relevant, as a comment might be APPOSITE, APROPOS, APT
– suitable, proper, conforming to good manners or taste BECOMING, DECOROUS, SEEMLY
– suitable for marriage, and typically very attractive, as a young woman might be NUBILE
– suitable or corresponding in character or type CONGRUENT, CONGRUOUS
– suitable or qualified for office, marriage, or the like ELIGIBLE
– suitable, harsh, deserved, or adequate, as a punishment might be CONDIGN
– be suitable, appropriate, or relevant PERTAIN, APPERTAIN, BEAR UPON
– occurring at a suitable or helpful time OPPORTUNE, PROPITIOUS

suitcase See also **case**, **bag**
– large suitcase with two hinged compartments PORTMANTEAU
– small bag or suitcase used as hand luggage VALISE

suitor – male suitor, lover, or sweetheart SWAIN

sulky expression POUT, MOUE

sulphur – old term for sulphur BRIMSTONE

sulphur- THION-

sulphuric acid VITRIOL

sultan – sultan's palace SERAGLIO
– group of wives and concubines in a Muslim household, such as that of a sultan HAREM

sum of many parts, whole, sum total AGGREGATE
– tiny, token, insignificant, as a sum of money might be NOMINAL

summary, list of main points, brief statement or outline of a subject ABSTRACT, APERÇU, EPITOME, SYNOPSIS
– summary, shortened or condensed version, as of a book ABRIDGEMENT, COMPENDIUM, CONDENSATION, DIGEST
– summary at the beginning of a speech, book, or the like, listing the main points CONSPECTUS
– summary at the end of a speech, book, or the like, repeating the main points RECAPITULATION, RÉSUMÉ, SUMMATION, WRAP-UP
– summary of the contents of an academic course SYLLABUS
– summary or skeleton account of the plot of a dramatic or literary work SCENARIO
– summary that is very short but captures the main points ENCAPSULATION, OVERVIEW, PARAPHRASE, PRÉCIS
– summarised account of one's education, work experience, and the like, as for a prospective employer CURRICULUM VITAE, C.V., RÉSUMÉ
– summarised biography, a brief

account of someone's life and character PROFILE
– summarised record of the proceedings of a law court DOCKET
– summarised statement, as of the terms of an agreement, used in drafting a formal document AIDE-MÉMOIRE
– diagrammatic summary or outline SCHEMA
– formal summary of a proposed commercial, literary, or other venture PROSPECTUS

summer days from mid-July to September DOG DAYS
– summer term at some British universities TRINITY TERM
– period of summery weather when summer is over INDIAN SUMMER, ST. LUKE'S SUMMER, ST. MARTIN'S SUMMER
– sleep or remain in a dormant state throughout the summer, as some animals do AESTIVATE

summerhouse, bower, or other secluded spot in a garden ALCOVE
– summerhouse or garden pavilion, usually having a fine view GAZEBO, BELVEDERE

summon an assembly, call a meeting, or the like CONVOKE, CONVENE
– summon up a spirit by means of spells or incantations CONJURE, INVOKE
– summoning of a prisoner or accused before a court of law ARRAIGNMENT

summons to appear in court CITATION, SUBPOENA
– urgent, demanding, as a summons might be PEREMPTORY, IMPERIOUS

Sun personified SOL
– adjective for the Sun SOLAR
– brief flaming eruption of radiation from the Sun FLARE
– bright surface layer of gases on the Sun or other star PHOTOSPHERE
– flower or plant that turns, or is believed to turn, with the Sun HELIOTROPE, TURNSOLE
– highest point of the Sun ZENITH
– huge column of burning gas rising from the surface of the Sun, as is visible during a total eclipse PROMINENCE
– layer of hydrogen and other gases, thousands of miles thick, around the Sun or a star CHROMOSPHERE
– layer of ionised gases outside the Sun's chromosphere, visible as a halo during an eclipse CORONA
– point furthest from the Sun in the orbit of a planet or comet around the Sun APHELION
– point nearest to the Sun in the orbit of a planet or comet around the Sun PERIHELION
– ring of light around the Sun or Moon, as when viewed through mist AUREOLE

Sun- HELI-, HELIO-, SOL-

sunburn – skin condition induced by sunburn MELANOSIS

sunburnt or dark-skinned in appearance SWARTHY

Sundays – any of the letters A-G, applied to the Sundays in a given year to determine the church calendar DOMINICAL LETTER

sundial – arm of a sundial, or similar object that casts a shadow to indicate the time GNOMON, STYLE

sunflower or related plant HELIANTHUS

sunglasses – darkening or changing colour when exposed to light, as some sunglasses do PHOTOCHROMIC
– glare-reducing plastic, as used in some sunglasses POLAROID

sunroom, as for therapy SOLARIUM

sunshade shield fitted at the top of a car's windscreen VISOR

sunspot MACULA
– darkest central area of a sunspot UMBRA
– lighter outer area of a sunspot PENUMBRA

sunstroke INSOLATION

superficial, routine, indifferent, as a quick inspection might be PERFUNCTORY, CURSORY
– superficial effort or merely symbolic gesture towards a goal or legal requirement TOKENISM
– superficially impressive or deceptively attractive outward appearance VENEER, GLOSS
– superficially or vulgarly attractive MERETRICIOUS
– person whose interest in the arts, antiques, or the like is an amateurish or superficial one DABBLER, DILETTANTE

superfluous See **excessive**

superior See **excellent**, **perfect**
– superior, outstanding, excelling others PRE-EMINENT, TRANSCENDENT
– superior in status, rank, or value SUPERORDINATE
– superior position or condition giving one an advantage over an opponent VANTAGE GROUND

superiority, as of power, number, or weight PREPONDERANCE
– superiority, power, clear advantage ASCENDANCY, DOMINANCE

superman in the philosophy of Nietzsche ÜBERMENSCH

supermarket item offered very cheap as an inducement to customers LOSS LEADER
– open free-standing display shelf or rack, as in a supermarket GONDOLA

supernatural See also **spirit**
– supernatural force in an object, in South Pacific religions MANA
– supernatural or magical arts and happenings THE OCCULT
– supernatural or psychic, beyond normal experience or scientific laws PARANORMAL
– supernatural power of a magical object, according to superstition FETISH, JUJU
– appearance or manifestation of a god or supernatural force EPIPHANY, THEOPHANY, REVELATION, VISITATION
– having supernatural powers, or in touch with the supernatural VISIONARY, CLAIRVOYANT, FEY, PSYCHIC
– perception by means of a sixth sense, supernatural powers, intuition, or the like EXTRASENSORY PERCEPTION, ESP, CLAIRVOYANCE, CRYPTAESTHESIA
– relating to irrational, mystical, or supernatural experience TRANSCENDENTAL
– study of telepathy and other supernatural phenomena PARAPSYCHOLOGY

superstition – object invested with superstition and used, carried, or worn for its magical powers FETISH, JUJU, AMULET
– plant, animal, or object invested with superstition in some societies, involved in various rituals and functioning as a symbol of a particular tribe, clan, or family TOTEM

supervisor of slaves or workers OVERSEER

supple, agile, loose-limbed, and nimble LITHE, LIMBER, LISSOM

supply See also **give**
– supply or provide FURNISH, PURVEY
– supply or source, as of raw materials LODE
– supply or store accumulated for future use STOCKPILE
– supply ship, provisioning vessel VICTUALLER, SUTLER
– supply that seems to be endless WIDOW'S CRUSE, CORNUCOPIA
– add new stocks or supplies, as in refilling a larder REPLENISH

support See also **strengthen**
– support, approve, or encourage COUNTENANCE, ENDORSE, SANCTION
– support, as for scaffolding or a table top, consisting of a horizontal bar on two pairs of splayed legs TRESTLE

– support, especially financial assistance SUBVENTION, SUBSIDY
– support a new cause enthusiastically; preach PROSELYTISE
– support, propose, or recommend ADVOCATE, COMMEND, PROPOUND
– support, protection, sponsorship PATRONAGE, AEGIS, AUSPICES
– support or prove with convincing evidence VERIFY, SUBSTANTIATE, CORROBORATE, VOUCH FOR
– support, usually with three legs, for a pot during cooking TRIVET
– support against danger, attack, or impact BOLSTER, BUTTRESS, BRACE, REINFORCE
– support at or for the back of something BACKSTAY
– support from below, hold up SUSTAIN, UNDERGIRD, UNDERPIN
– support or adopt a cause ESPOUSE, CHAMPION, ADVANCE
– support or base, as for a statue or column PEDESTAL, PLINTH
– support or principal sponsor of something or someone MAINSTAY
– support or stand with one leg, as for a camera MONOPOD
– support or stand with three legs, as for a camera TRIPOD
– support with money, finance SUBSIDISE, PATRONISE, SPONSOR
– supporting, as evidence might be CORROBORATIVE, COLLATERAL
– supporting beam in a building, placed horizontally, as between floors STRINGER, SUMMER
– supporting beam or bracket, as for a balcony CANTILEVER
– supporting framework of beams, struts, or the like for a bridge or roof TRUSS
– supporting or helping AUXILIARY
– supporting or stabilising structure attached by spars, as to a vehicle or building OUTRIGGER
– supporting structure or pillar, as for an arch or bridge PIER
– appeal to in support of something INVOKE
– "athletic support" JOCKSTRAP
– heavy beam driven vertically into the ground as a foundation or support for a building PILE
– hinge or support on which a lever turns PIVOT, FULCRUM
– incapable or unworthy of being supported or believed INSUPPORTABLE, INDEFENSIBLE
– legally enforced financial support ALIMONY, MAINTENANCE
– mutual support, unity, and fellow-feeling in a group SOLIDARITY
– obtain or seek support RECRUIT, CANVASS, SOLICIT
– person who relies on someone else for financial support DEPENDANT, CLIENT
– stone or brick structure built for support against a wall, or anything that supports or sustains BUTTRESS
– "surgical support", belt worn to restrain a hernia TRUSS
– upright pole used as a support STANCHION

supporter who is reliable and hardworking STALWART
– supporter, follower, or champion, as of a cause or theory EXPONENT, ADHERENT, PROPONENT
– supporter who argues in defence of a cause or another person ADVOCATE, APOLOGIST
– supporter of a group, without being a member of it FELLOW TRAVELLER, CAMP FOLLOWER
– supporter or helper in some dubious or criminal activity ACCOMPLICE, ACCESSORY, CONFEDERATE
– supporter or promoter, especially with money SPONSOR, PATRON
– supporter or trusted follower, often willing to do "the dirty work" HENCHMAN, MYRMIDON
– supporters of a person or organisation whose wishes have to be taken into account CONSTITUENCY
– aggressively active supporter of a political cause MILITANT
– early supporter of a new religion or cause, disciple APOSTLE
– enthusiastic supporter, fan, or follower, as of a particular sport DEVOTEE, AFICIONADO
– enthusiastic supporter of a political party or a cause PARTISAN
– enthusiastic supporter of a religion, leader, or doctrine VOTARY

supporting- PRO-

supposed, assumed, conjectural HYPOTHETICAL, SUPPOSITITIOUS
– supposed, unproved and often doubtful ALLEGED
– reputed as a child's supposed father might be PUTATIVE

suppository – medicated vaginal suppository PESSARY

suppress comments, argument, or the like MUZZLE, GAG, STIFLE
– suppress something forcibly, such as a riot QUELL, QUASH
– medicinal drug that calms or suppresses emotion BROMIDE

sure See **certain**, **confident**

surface appearance, gloss, or lustre, especially one acquired by age or association PATINA, BURNISH
– surface curve of a liquid in a tube or container MENISCUS
– surface features, feel, or appearance TEXTURE
– surface forming the boundary between liquids INTERFACE
– surface layer or finishing, as of fine wood VENEER
– surface of a suspension bridge DECK
– surface of the body or a body part PERIPHERY
– grainy or crinkled surface, as on leather or paper PEBBLE
– having a dull, unglossy finish, as a painted surface might MATT
– on or near the surface, as a wound might be SUPERFICIAL
– process by which a thin film of substance accumulates on the surface of a solid ADSORPTION
– smooth surface on a bone or tooth FACET

-surface, -sided -HEDRON

surface tension – distortion or tendency to rise of a liquid in a pipe, due to surface tension CAPILLARITY, CAPILLARY ACTION

surgical See chart, and also **medical**
– surgical cut INCISION
– surgical cutting instruments BISTOURY, LANCET, SCALPEL
– surgical cutting or separating of tissue SECTION
– surgical removal of an organ or other body part EXCISION, ABLATION, AMPUTATION, EXTIRPATION
– surgical replacement of a limb, tooth, eye, or the like, or the artificial device used PROSTHESIS
– surgical rod, long and flexible, as for removing obstructions from the throat PROBANG
– surgical scraping or scooping instrument, as for removing dead tissue from the uterus CURETTE
– surgical stitching together of the edges of a wound SUTURE
– surgical thread LIGATURE
– surgery for bone and joint disorders ORTHOPAEDIC SURGERY
– surgery, such as a facelift, designed to improve one's physical appearance COSMETIC SURGERY
– surgery in which unwanted tissue is destroyed by sudden freezing CRYOSURGERY
– surgical transplant of animal tissue to man ZOOPLASTY

-surgical cut- -TOM-, -TOME, -TOMY, -OTOMY

-surgical opening -STOMY

-surgical removal -ECTOMY

surname, family name COGNOMEN
– having two parts, as a surname such as *Bentley-Smith* has DOUBLE-BARRELLED

surplus See **excessive**

surprise See also **sudden**
– surprise, astonish, amaze ASTOUND, STAGGER
– surprise, bewilder, confuse CONFOUND, BAFFLE, PERPLEX

– surprise, take aback, disturb the composure or calm of DISCONCERT, PERTURB, RUFFLE
– surprise, thrill, and startle, make people sit up and take notice ELECTRIFY, RIVET
– surprise attack on an enemy COUP DE MAIN
– surprise find, or bright new idea TROUVAILLE
– surprise someone and force him into an embarrassing position WRONG-FOOT
– surprised and disbelieving, taken aback INCREDULOUS

SURGICAL OPERATIONS

amniocentesis	piercing, through the abdominal wall, of the membrane surrounding a foetus, in order to withdraw a sample of fluid for testing for such conditions as Down's syndrome and spina bifida
apicectomy	removal of part of the root of a tooth
appendicectomy/ appendectomy	removal of the appendix
arterioplasty	reconstruction of an artery
autograft, autoplasty	replacement or repair of damaged tissue with sound tissue taken from the same person
Caesarean section	delivering of a baby through an incision in the abdominal wall
cholecystectomy	removal of the gall bladder
cholelithotomy	removal of gallstones
colostomy	formation in the abdominal wall of an opening for part of the colon, to drain the intestine
cordotomy	severing of nerve fibres in the neck to relieve chronic pain
craniotomy	removal of part of the skull
cryosurgery	freezing of small areas to destroy damaged or unwanted tissue, such as cataracts
cystectomy	removal of the bladder
D and C/dilatation and curettage	expansion of the neck of the womb and scraping away of its lining
débridement	removal of dead tissue and foreign matter from a wound
episiotomy	incision into the tissues surrounding the vagina to ease delivery of a baby
fenestration	creation of a new opening in the labyrinth of the inner ear, to relieve deafness
gastrectomy	removal of all or part of the stomach
goniopuncture	draining of fluid from the eye, as a treatment for glaucoma
hepatectomy	removal of all or part of the liver
homograft, allograft, homoplasty	replacement or repair of damaged tissue or organs with tissue or organs taken from another person
hysterectomy	removal of the womb
ileostomy	formation in the abdominal wall of an opening for the ileum, to drain the intestine
iridectomy	removal of part of the iris of the eye, usually to create an artificial pupil
labioplasty	repair or reconstruction of damaged or deformed lips
laparotomy	incision into the abdominal cavity, usually as part of an exploratory operation
laryngectomy	removal of the larynx
leucotomy, lobotomy	cutting of nerve fibres in the brain to relieve emotional disorders
lithonephrotomy	removal of a kidney stone
mastectomy	removal of a breast
necrotomy	removal of dead tissue, especially a dead piece of bone
nephrectomy	removal of a kidney
neurotomy	severing of a nerve
oophorectomy, ovariectomy	removal of an ovary
orchidectomy	removal of a testicle
ostectomy	removal of a bone or piece of bone
otoplasty	repair or reconstruction of the ears
phlebotomy, venesection	opening or piercing of a vein
pneumonectomy	removal of all or part of a lung
rhinoplasty	repair or reconstruction of the nose
rhizotomy	cutting of nerve roots where they leave the spinal cord, in order to relieve chronic pain
salpingectomy	removal or severing of a Fallopian tube, usually as part of sterilisation
thoractomy	opening of the chest cavity
tracheostomy/ tracheotomy	cutting into and opening of the windpipe, as to assist breathing
vasectomy	cutting of a sperm-carrying duct, usually as part of sterilisation

– surprised and horrified, shocked, appalled AGHAST
– surprised and worried RATTLED, UNNERVED, FLUSTERED
– surprising and artificial development or device introduced to resolve a tricky situation or plot DEUS EX MACHINA
– by surprise, as when caught committing an offence RED-HANDED, IN FLAGRANTE DELICTO
– left speechless with surprise DUMBFOUNDED, NONPLUSSED
– show a feeling, especially surprise, clearly EVINCE
– sudden and shocking surprise, piece of unexpected bad news BOMBSHELL, BOLT FROM THE BLUE, THUNDERCLAP, COUP DE FOUDRE
– take by surprise, ambush WAYLAY
– taken by surprise, confronted unexpectedly CAUGHT UNAWARES, CAUGHT NAPPING
– utterly surprised, stunned FLABBERGASTED, BANJAXED, STUPEFIED, THUNDERSTRUCK
– wide-eyed or open-mouthed with surprise AGAPE

surrender See also **give up**
– surrender, accept or assent meekly ACQUIESCE, KOWTOW
– surrender, or admit CONCEDE
– surrender or give in, yield on agreed terms CAPITULATE
– surrender or giving up of something, as of land, territory, or rights CESSION
– surrender or hand over formally rights, territory, or the like CEDE
– surrender or voluntary relinquishing of a claim, privilege, or right WAIVER
– surrender to a superior force, temptation, or the like SUCCUMB
– surrender to another's authority, yield, bend the knee SUBMIT
– complete, absolute, unlimited, as the surrender of a warring nation might be UNCONDITIONAL

surround, encircle, hem in CINCTURE, COMPASS, ENVIRON
– surround completely, enfold, or swallow up ENGULF, ENVELOP
– surround or enclose protectively EMBOSOM, EMBOWER
– surround or include within its scope, take in COMPRISE, EMBRACE, ENCOMPASS
– surround with troops, besiege, lay siege to BELEAGUER
– surrounded, as an island is by water GIRDED

surrounding See also **boundary**
– surrounding, in the immediate vicinity, as the air is AMBIENT
– surrounding area, neighbourhood ENVIRONS, VICINITY, PRECINCTS, PURLIEUS
– surrounding area, scope, sphere of operation or influence AMBIT, COMPASS, MILIEU, ORBIT
– surrounding band, as around the base of a tooth CINGULUM
– adjust or grow accustomed to new surroundings ACCLIMATISE

surrounding- AMPH-, AMPHI-, PERI-, CIRCUM-

survey or inspect a stretch of land, an enemy's positions, or the like RECONNOITRE, RECCE
– survey or view that is wide-ranging PANORAMA

surveyor – surveyor's instrument, essentially a small moving telescope, for measuring horizontal and vertical angles THEODOLITE
– surveyor's instrument, essentially a telescope and spirit level, for measuring relative heights LEVEL
– surveyor's mark on a known object, used as a reference point for other measurements BENCHMARK
– surveyor's theodolite adapted to measure distances rapidly or directly TACHEOMETER
– electronic device used by surveyors for measuring fairly large distances by timing radio waves transmitted between the two points TELLUROMETER
– horizontal angle of a bearing in surveying, measured clockwise from a standard direction, especially north AZIMUTH
– moving marker on a surveyor's levelling rod VANE, TARGET
– striped pole used as a marker in surveying RANGING ROD

survival of the fittest NATURAL SELECTION

survive a crisis, danger, or the like WEATHER
– survive or continue in existence SUBSIST

surviving, left over, remaining, continuing RESIDUAL, VESTIGIAL
– surviving, still in existence, not lost or extinct EXTANT
– surviving species from an earlier age RELICT
– capable of living or surviving independently VIABLE
– object surviving from a bygone civilisation RELIC

suspend or refrain from enforcing a rule, penalty, or the like WAIVE
– suspend or transfer proceedings ADJOURN

suspense – episode of a serial, as on the radio, that ends in suspense CLIFFHANGER
– nervous, anxious, tense, in suspense ON TENTERHOOKS

suspension of an operation or activity for a time ABEYANCE
– suspension or delay, as of payments MORATORIUM
– suspension spring, as on a lorry's back axle, consisting of a set of layered metal strips LEAF SPRING
– suspension that is based on fluid-filled cylinders rather than springs HYDRAULIC SUSPENSION
– suspension of very fine particles in a fluid medium, as in mist or paint COLLOID
– suspension of small globules of one liquid within another, as in homogenised milk EMULSION
– pharmacological term for a paste or suspension of solid particles in a liquid MAGMA
– scattering of particles, as in a colloid or suspension DISPERSION

suspicion – calm or dispel someone's suspicions LULL, ALLAY
– clear of blame or suspicion VINDICATE
– lay to rest the suspicion or hostility of, win round DISARM

suspicious, doubtful EQUIVOCAL
– suspicious, doubting, unwilling to trust or believe SCEPTICAL
– suspicious, wary, distrustful LEERY, CHARY
– suspicious or scared to an alarmingly unreasonable degree PARANOID
– suspiciously or disapprovingly, the way one might look at a person or suggestion ASKANCE
– referring to behaviour which is suspicious, stealthy, or secretive FURTIVE
– steal about, move in a suspicious way SKULK, SLINK, SIDLE, PROWL

swagger, bluster, or brag ROISTER
– swagger, boasting BRAGGADOCIO
– swagger, walk in a pompously affected way STRUT
– swaggering swordsman or adventurer SWASHBUCKLER

swallow or drink eagerly, gulp SWIG, SWILL
– swallow or take in food as if by swallowing INGEST
– swallowing or act of drinking, or the amount taken in DRAUGHT
– act of swallowing DEGLUTITION
– adjective for a swallow or related bird HIRUNDINE
– difficulty in swallowing, or refusal or inability to swallow APHAGIA
– inflammation of the tonsils that makes swallowing difficult QUINSY

swamp, bog, or marsh SLOUGH, MIRE, QUAGMIRE
– swamp atmosphere MIASMA
– swamp gas METHANE
– swampy grassland area in the

U.S., especially Florida EVERGLADE
– swampy hollow, often filled with decaying plant matter, in the far north of Canada MUSKEG
– swampy stretch of land WASH, FEN, MORASS, SWALE
– swampy stretch of land or shallow lake in South Africa VLEI
– swampy tributary or sluggish backwater, especially in Louisiana BAYOU
– adjective for a swamp or marsh PALUDAL, PALUDINAL
– earliest, first, or original, as an ancient swamp might be PRIMEVAL
– light hovering over swampy ground, probably produced by flaming methane gas WILL-O'-THE-WISP, IGNIS FATUUS, JACK-O'-LANTERN, FRIAR'S LANTERN
– smelly and invisible vapour or gas, as rising from a swamp or rubbish heap EFFLUVIUM
– tree or shrub with aerial roots, flourishing in tropical coastal swamps MANGROVE

swan – female swan PEN
– male swan COB
– young swan CYGNET

swarm, as vermin might in a garden or on an animal INFEST
– swarm or teem, as if with ants FORMICATE
– swarming, abounding, full TEEMING, THRONGING

swastika-like design GAMMADION, FYLFOT

sway, swing from side to side FLUCTUATE, OSCILLATE, VACILLATE
– swaying, rippling, or other wave-like movement UNDULATION

swear-word or profanity used as an exclamation EXPLETIVE
– swear-word or term of abuse EPITHET
– swear-word or vulgar language PROFANITY

sweat, especially when abundant or excessive DIAPHORESIS, HIDROSIS
– sweat gland ECCRINE GLAND
– sweat-inducing or -increasing SUDORIFIC, DIAPHORETIC
– spray, liquid, or other substance used to suppress or mask smells such as those of sweat or cooking DEODORANT

sweater See **clothes**

Swedish – Swedish-style buffet meal SMORGASBORD

sweet, creamy paste used in sweets and icings FONDANT
– sweet, typically with a soft centre, and often coated with chocolate BONBON
– sweet delicacy or crushed sesame seeds with honey HALVA
– sweet delicacy or icing of ground almonds and sugar MARZIPAN
– sweet in the form of a soft liquorice disc POMFRET CAKE, PONTEFRACT CAKE
– sweet in the form of an iced nut, raisin, or the like DRAGÉE
– sweet liquid in flowers, gathered by bees for making honey NECTAR
– sweet or charming, especially in a pretentious way FAY
– sweet or rich to an excessive degree CLOYING, SACCHARINE
– sweets, cakes, preserves, and other sweet items of prepared food CONFECTIONERY
– sweet-voiced MELLIFLUOUS
– crisp sweet or delicacy of nuts browned in boiling sugar PRALINE
– large round sweet for sucking, with differently coloured layers GOBSTOPPER
– pastille that is sucked to sweeten the breath CACHOU
– rich, round sweet made of chocolate, egg, butter, and sometimes liqueur TRUFFLE
– sugar-coated sweet COMFIT

sweet pepper, red pepper PIMIENTO

sweetcorn INDIAN CORN, MAIZE

sweetener – sugar substitute, artificial sweetener SACCHARIN, CYCLAMATE

sweetheart See **lover**

swell See also **increase**
– swell, bulge BILGE
– swell or expand by pressure from inside DISTEND, DILATE
– swell out, as sails might BILLOW
– swelling, becoming swollen or bloated TUMESCENT
– swelling, knob, knotty projection, or small growth NODE, NODULE, TUBERCLE
– swelling and inflammation of a lymph gland, especially in the armpit or groin BUBO
– swelling caused by a build-up of fluid in the tissues OEDEMA
– swelling of the head, caused by a build-up of cerebrospinal fluid HYDROCEPHALUS
– swelling on a horse's back, typically causing stiffness SPAVIN
– swelling or bulging out TUMID, TURGID
– swelling or outgrowth of an organ or other body part APOPHYSIS
– swelling outwards, bulging, as eyes might be PROTUBERANT
– subsidence of a swelling or swollen organ DETUMESCENCE

swerve or deviate from a path SHEER, VEER
– swerve or quick turn by a rugby player JINK

swimming kick in which the legs move up and down alternately, as in the crawl FLUTTER KICK
– swimming or floating NATANT
– swimming race in which the four strokes are swum in succession MEDLEY
– swimming stroke similar to the crawl but with a slower kick TRUDGEN
– art or action of swimming NATATION
– dance-like swimming to music, often for pairs of swimmers SYNCHRONISED SWIMMING
– relating to or adapted for swimming NATATORIAL
– stretching the arm forward in swimming prior to taking another stroke RECOVERY
– topless swimming costume, worn by a woman MONOKINI

swimming pool – inflatable rubber mattress, as used for floating on in swimming pools LI-LO
– primitive, water-dwelling plants, ranging from seaweeds to the tiny diatoms that flourish in swimming pools ALGAE

swindle, fraudulent act or business scheme RAMP, SCAM
– swindle in the form of taking for oneself money or property entrusted to one EMBEZZLEMENT, DEFALCATION, PECULATION

swing from branch to branch, as some apes and monkeys do BRACHIATE
– swing from side to side, sway FLUCTUATE, OSCILLATE, VACILLATE
– swinging, hanging loosely PENDULOUS

Swiss HELVETIAN
– Swiss breakfast food of cereals, nuts, raisins, and the like MUESLI
– Swiss state or a similar small regional unit CANTON
– sing in a voice wavering between normal and falsetto, as among Swiss folk-singers YODEL

switch – switching, usually unintended, of the initial sounds of two or more words, as when one accidentally pronounces *red hat* as *head rat* SPOONERISM
– switching device in an electric circuit RELAY
– activate a mechanism by releasing a catch, trigger, or switch TRIP
– electrical coil producing a magnetic field, as used for activating switches SOLENOID

swollen, as a body part might be TUMESCENT, TUMID
– swollen, as through overeating or filling with water BLOATED, DISTENDED
– swollen area around a wound that is healing PROUD FLESH,

GRANULATION TISSUE
– swollen, fat, puffy PURSY
– swollen or bulging TURGID
– swollen or puffy condition, or the process leading to it TUMEFACTION

swoop down, as a bird of prey does on its victim STOOP

sword See illustration, and also **fencing**
– sword handle, hilt HAFT
– sword-shaped, long and narrow and pointed, as a leaf might be ENSIFORM, GLADIATE, XIPHOID
– sword-thrust or -lunge FOIN
– belt or sash crossing the chest from the shoulder, used for carrying a sword or bugle BALDRIC
– broad sword with only one cutting edge BACKSWORD
– carry a sword diagonally across the body PORT
– combatant, typically with a sword, in an arena in ancient Rome GLADIATOR
– former term for a sword of various kinds BRAND, BILBO, GLAIVE
– knob on a sword hilt POMMEL
– Malay sword or dagger with a wavy double-edged blade KRIS
– pierce or stab lightly, as with a sword PINK
– stick used instead of a sword in fencing BACKSWORD, SINGLESTICK
– stronger section of a sword blade, near the hilt FORTE
– weaker section of a sword blade, from the middle to the tip FOIBLE

sword- XIPH-, XIPHI-

sworn statement made in writing before a notary public or similar officer AFFIDAVIT
– sworn statement of a witness absent from court DEPOSITION

syllable – alphabet-like system of writing in which each symbol represents a whole syllable, as in Sinhalese SYLLABARY
– contraction of two syllables into one by fusing two adjacent vowel sounds SYNAERESIS, SYNIZESIS
– omission of an unstressed vowel or syllable, as in verse ELISION
– second-last syllable in a word PENULT
– stressed, carrying the principal accent in a word, as a syllable might be TONIC, NUCLEAR

syllogism See **logic**

symbol See also **punctuation**, **letter**, **mathematical symbols**, **Greek alphabet**
– symbol, as on a road sign GLYPH
– symbol, emblem, or trademark of a company LOGO, LOGOTYPE
– symbol, number, or letter, often of miniature size, written just above the level of another as in xy^2 SUPERSCRIPT
– symbol, number, or letter, often of miniature size, written just below the level of another as in H_2O SUBSCRIPT
– symbol, sign, or letter representing an entire word or phrase such as £ for *pounds* LOGOGRAM, LOGOGRAPH
– symbol, picture, or object representing an abstract idea EMBLEM
– symbol or character in a writing system, such as Chinese, that represents a thing or idea rather than the sound IDEOGRAM
– symbol or design, as on a flag or embroidery DEVICE
– symbol or image ICON
– symbol or kinship emblem, often a plant or animal, of a tribe, clan, or family TOTEM
– symbol or motif, as in literature, that keeps recurring ARCHETYPE
– symbol or pictorial character used in ancient Egyptian writing HIEROGLYPH
– symbol or sign, or its intended meaning or reference DENOTATION
– symbols, figures, or the like used systematically, as in music or mathematics, to represent elements or quantities NOTATION
– symbols and metaphors, as in poetry IMAGERY
– alphabet in which each symbol represents a whole syllable, as in Sinhalese SYLLABARY
– feminist or lesbian symbol of strength or solidarity, in the form of a double-headed axe LABYRIS
– printing symbol, †, as for indica-

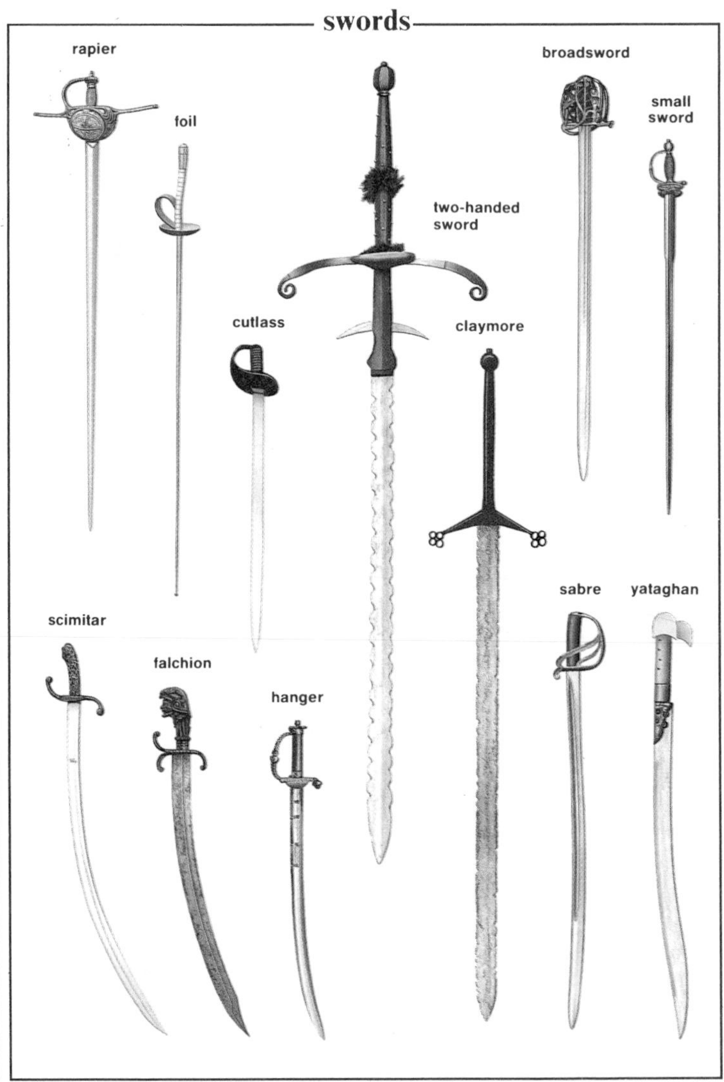

ting footnotes DAGGER, OBELISK, OBELUS
– printing symbol, ‡, as for indicating footnotes DOUBLE DAGGER, DIESIS
– printing symbol, *, as for indicating footnotes ASTERISK
– printing symbol, &, representing the word *and* AMPERSAND
– printing symbol, ☞, used to alert the reader to the passage following FIST, HAND, INDEX
– printing symbol of three stars, ⁂ or ⁂, used to alert the reader to the passage following ASTERISM
– printing symbol, §, used to indicate a footnote or mark off a section SECTION MARK
– proofreading symbol, resembling an inverted *V* or *Y*, indicating the position for an insert in a text CARET
– publisher's symbol or emblem on a book COLOPHON
– puzzle in the form of pictures or symbols representing syllables or words, such as *I8LN£*, meaning *I hate Ellen Pound* REBUS
– relating to meaning, as of words, gestures, or symbols SEMANTIC
– science or study of signs and symbols SEMIOTICS

symbolic, emblematic FIGURATIVE
– symbolic clothes, decorations, or characteristics, as of power or an official post TRAPPINGS, REGALIA
– symbolic story or picture in which the characters or scenes symbolise ideas and illustrate a deeper meaning ALLEGORY
– merely symbolic and superficial effort or gesture towards compliance with a law or social requirement TOKENISM

symbolise, be a typical example of EMBODY, TYPIFY
– symbolise or represent an idea as something concrete or human PERSONIFY, HYPOSTATISE, REIFY
– character, event, or thing in the New Testament that is supposedly foreshadowed or symbolised by a corresponding one in the Old Testament ANTITYPE
– character, event, or thing in the Old Testament that is supposedly foreshadowing or symbolising a corresponding one in the New Testament TYPE

symmetry in a plant, animal, or organ, such that the two halves are mirror images of each other, though only when cut along one plane BILATERAL SYMMETRY
– symmetry in a plant, animal, or organ, such that the two halves are mirror images of each other when cut along any of two or more planes RADIAL SYMMETRY

sympathetic See also **kind**
– sympathetic, thinking along similar lines, sharing attitudes ON THE SAME WAVELENGTH
– sympathetic relationship of mutual trust and emotional understanding RAPPORT

sympathise with, pity, feel sorry for COMMISERATE, CONDOLE

sympathiser or comforter who causes only distress JOB'S COMFORTER

sympathy, pity, mercy COMPASSION
– sympathy and understanding so deep that one seems to share the other person's feelings EMPATHY, FELLOW FEELING
– sympathy for someone in distress or mourning COMMISERATION, CONDOLENCE
– arousing pity or sympathy PATHETIC

symptoms of a non-present disease in a hysterical patient MIMESIS
– symptoms or signs jointly indicating or characterising a disease, abnormality, or the like SYNDROME
– relating to the early stage of an infection or disease, before the symptoms appear SUBCLINICAL
– study of disease symptoms SYMPTOMATOLOGY, SEMIOTICS

synagogue sexton BEADLE, SHAMMES

synod delegate who represents the clergy PROCTOR
– presiding officer of a synod MODERATOR

synonym – word-finder book, classifying synonyms systematically THESAURUS

syphilis LUES
– hard, red, knotty growth or sore that is an early indication of syphilis CHANCRE

syringe – syringe-like device with a flexible wire used to operate a camera's shutter from a distance so as to avoid shaking the camera CABLE RELEASE
– syringe or needle for injections beneath the skin HYPODERMIC
– syringe or similar instrument for directing a stream of air or water at or into a part of the body for cleansing or healing DOUCHE

syrup from sugar MOLASSES, TREACLE
– syrupy drink to which medicine can be added JULEP
– syrupy medicine for coughs and sore throats LINCTUS
– medicinal paste formed by mixing the drug with honey or syrup ELECTUARY

system, structure, organisation, or the like that is elaborate and complex EDIFICE
– system of channels transporting watery body fluid between the tissues and the blood system or organs LYMPHATIC SYSTEM
– system of exercise, therapy, diet, or the like REGIMEN
– system of principles, methods, and techniques of a discipline or science METHODOLOGY
– system or framework of scientific theories and concepts at any time, within which a scientist works PARADIGM
– systematic, structured, classified, as a body of knowledge might be ARCHITECTONIC
– systematic arrangement of parts CONFIGURATION
– medieval social system in Europe, in which vassals exchanged homage and service for land and protection from a lord FEUDALISM, FEUDAL SYSTEM
– political and economic system in Europe after the feudal system, based on increased trade MERCANTILISM, MERCANTILE SYSTEM
– running down of the energy in the universe or any other closed system ENTROPY

-system -NOMY

T

table See also **furniture**
- table consisting of a board or boards on top of hurdle-like supports TRESTLE TABLE
- table in church for the Communion bread and wine CREDENCE TABLE
- table leg, stair post, or the like, typically turned and decorated SPINDLE
- table of numbers for calculating discounts, interest, and the like READY RECKONER
- table of the chemical elements arranged according to their atomic properties PERIODIC TABLE
- table with hinged leaves supported by movable pairs of legs GATE-LEG TABLE
- arranged in both rows and columns TABULAR
- hinged flap that can be raised and supported to increase the size of the table DROP LEAF
- set of objects, such as small tables, designed for stacking one inside the other NEST

table wine VIN DE TABLE, TAFELWEIN

tablecloth – long narrow carpet or tablecloth RUNNER

tablet of a medicated preparation for chewing or sucking LOZENGE, PASTILLE, TROCHE

tact, knowledge of appropriate behaviour, especially in various social situations SAVOIR-FAIRE

tactful, sensitive to the situation, carefully weighed-up POLITIC, DIPLOMATIC, JUDICIOUS
- tactful in a quiet, wise, practical way PRUDENT, DISCREET

tactic or trick, as in a game, to secure an advantage STRATAGEM, PLOY

tadpole POLLIWOG

tail, short and often erect, of a rabbit, hare, or deer SCUT
- tail assembly of an aeroplane EMPENNAGE
- tail of a fox BRUSH, BUSH
- tail with a distinctive shape or marking, as on a deer and certain dogs FLAG
- adapted for grasping, as a monkey's tail is PREHENSILE
- bony part or the solid part of an animal's tail DOCK
- bushy tip of the tail of a cow or other animal SWITCH
- having a tail CAUDATE
- relating to the tail, posterior, or hind parts of the body CAUDAL

-tail- CAUD-, -UR-, URO-, -UROUS

tailor – tailors's adjustable pattern, for cutting different sizes DELINEATOR
- made-to-order, as clothes made by a tailor might be, or dealing in such items BESPOKE
- relating to a tailor SARTORIAL

tails, back of a coin or medal VERSO, REVERSE

take apart DISASSEMBLE, DISMANTLE, DISMEMBER, DISMOUNT
- take away from, cause to seem inferior DEROGATE, DETRACT, BELITTLE
- take away someone's property, by an official decree CONFISCATE, SEQUESTRATE
- take back, often publicly, a belief, accusation, or claim RECANT, RETRACT, DISAVOW, REVOKE
- take for oneself, typically without the owner's permission APPROPRIATE, ARROGATE
- take off one's hat or clothes DOFF
- take turns, alternate, proceed in a given order or sequence ROTATE

take advantage of, use selfishly and unjustly EXPLOIT
- person who takes advantage, often unfairly, of an opportunity OPPORTUNIST

take-off of a person, especially a celebrity IMPERSONATION, MIMICRY

talent, natural gift, speciality, strong point MÉTIER, FORTE
- talent, skill, knack, or fluency derived from practice or familiarity FACILITY, FLAIR
- talent or ability resulting from a special interest or leaning BENT, PENCHANT
- talented or skilled in a wide variety of ways VERSATILE
- inborn talent, quality, or gift ENDOWMENT, APTITUDE, ATTRIBUTE
- person with exceptional powers or talents PRODIGY

talk See **conversation**, **speak**, **speech**, **say**, **state**

talkative, extravagant in speech, compliments, and endearments GUSHY, EFFUSIVE, PROFUSE
- talkative, glib-tongued, willing to speak at length EXPANSIVE, LOQUACIOUS, VOLUBLE
- talkative, long-winded, and disorganised in speech or in writing DIFFUSE, MAUNDERING, PROLIX, RAMBLING
- talkative, open, responsive COMMUNICATIVE, FORTHCOMING
- talkative, wordy, windy, speaking more than is necessary VERBOSE, GARRULOUS
- talkative and silly person, especially a scatterbrained girl or woman FLIBBERTIGIBBET
- talkative person, liable to blurt out secrets BLABBERMOUTH
- person who is talkative, boastful, and vain, windbag POPINJAY

tall See **high**
- tall and thin, and usually clumsy or ungainly LANKY, GANGLING
- tall and well-built, sturdy STRAPPING

tame, train, or breed animals to live with and be of use to man DOMESTICATE

tan hides, as with alum or salt, especially to produce pale leather TAW

tangle, coil SKEIN
- tangle or catch in a net ENMESH
- tangled mass, as of matted hair SHAG

tank for water, as in the roof or attached to a lavatory CISTERN
- tank in which solid waste is decomposed by bacteria SEPTIC TANK
- tank or other vehicle that moves on a caterpillar, a continuous circular belt TRACK-LAYING VEHICLE
- main body or shell of a ship or military tank HULL
- opening in a wall, tank, or the like, through which a gun is fired PORT
- revolving armoured dome or drum on a tank or warship in which guns are mounted TURRET
- wheel or roller within a tractor-track, as on a tank BOGIE

tap, as in a barrel FAUCET, SPIGOT
- tap, valve in a pipe regulating the flow of liquid or gas STOPCOCK
- tap on an inverted bottle that releases a tot measure OPTIC

– tap with a downturned nozzle BIBCOCK, BIBB
– tapping the chest or back and attempting a diagnosis from the sound produced PERCUSSION

tape or strip of cotton or nylon, as used for safety belts WEBBING
– tape used to protect areas during painting MASKING TAPE

tape recorder for office dictation and later typing DICTAPHONE
– tape recorder in which the tape passes between separate reels REEL-TO-REEL TAPE RECORDER
– tape recorder system that reduces tape hiss DOLBY
– tape recording using separate electronic signals rather than a continuous fluctuating signal DIGITAL RECORDING
– distortion or rapid variation of pitch, as produced by a faulty tape recorder FLUTTER
– distortion or slow variation of pitch, as produced by a faulty tape recorder WOW
– pulley or rotating shaft of a tape recorder regulating the movement of the magnetic tape CAPSTAN

tapestry of a rich pictorial design GOBELINS
– tapestry, sculpture or other decoration behind an altar REREDOS
– hanging for a wall, especially a tapestry ARRAS

tapeworm or other parasitic worm HELMINTH

tapioca – starch from the root of a tropical plant, as used for making tapioca CASSAVA

tar – tar-based liquid applied to wood as a preservative CREOSOTE
– black tar-like hydrocarbon used in roadmaking and roofing BITUMEN, ASPHALT

target for insults or criticism, scapegoat AUNT SALLY, WHIPPING BOY
– target in archery, or its centre CLOUT
– target in throwing games and contests COCKSHY
– target or post to be tilted at, as by horsemen QUINTAIN
– bull's eye on a target, the white centre circle BLANK
– outermost ring but one on a target MAGPIE

tarot – fortune-telling with tarot or playing cards CARTOMANCY
– section of a tarot pack, the major or minor division ARCANA
– suits found in many tarot packs, corresponding to spades, hearts, diamonds, and clubs DISKS, CUPS, PENTACLES, WANDS

tartan, cloth or pattern or strip of tartan worn over the left shoulder in traditional Scottish Highland dress PLAID

task or project UNDERTAKING
– difficult, laborious, or very straining, as a task might be HERCULEAN, ONEROUS

taste, act of tasting GUSTATION
– taste, flavour SAPOR
– taste carefully or appreciatively SAVOUR, DEGUST
– tasty, flavoursome, or agreeable to eat PALATABLE
– common or crude, having vulgar tastes PLEBEIAN
– having good taste or judgment DISCERNING, DISCRIMINATING
– lacking taste, flat, stale VAPID
– person considered a judge, as in matters of taste ARBITER
– relating to the sense of taste GUSTATORY
– salty or spicy to the taste, rather than sweet SAVOURY
– sharp or harsh, as a smell or taste might be ACRID, PUNGENT
– sharp smell or taste TANG
– spicy and sharp, as a taste might be TART, PIQUANT
– wide-ranging, all-embracing, liberal and broad-minded, as one's tastes might be CATHOLIC

tasteless See **showing**

tax, levy, or duty IMPOST
– tax-collecting department in the U.K. INLAND REVENUE
– tax-collecting department in the U.S. INTERNAL REVENUE
– tax estimate ASSESSMENT
– tax in the U.S. corresponding to P.A.Y.E. WITHHOLDING TAX
– tax levied in Anglo-Saxon England for opposing or placating the Viking invaders DANEGELD
– tax levied in former times for the building or repair of city walls MURAGE
– tax of a fixed amount for each member of a household CAPITATION, POLL TAX
– tax levied by a feudal lord on his vassals TALLAGE
– tax official in India in former times ZAMINDAR
– tax on money or property received as a gift or inheritance INHERITANCE TAX
– tax on tobacco, spirits, and certain other goods EXCISE
– tax paid by a feudal vassal in lieu of military service SCUTAGE
– tax paid by landowners to the king in medieval England GELD
– tax schedule or system of duties, especially on imports TARIFF
– annual tax equivalent to one-tenth of a person's income and produce, paid to the Church TITHE
– avoidance of tax by cunning or illegal means EVASION
– free or excuse from a tax, duty, or the like EXEMPT
– impose or collect a tax, fine, membership fee, or the like LEVY
– in proportion to the value of the goods, as a tax or duty might be AD VALOREM
– referring to a tax system in which the taxation rate decreases as the amount to be taxed increases REGRESSIVE
– referring to a tax system in which the taxation rate increases as the amount to be taxed increases PROGRESSIVE
– refund of part of a sum paid, as of one's taxes REBATE
– relating to a country's treasury, finances, or tax matters FISCAL

taxi – mock-serious term for a taxi HACKNEY CARRIAGE
– seat that folds down from a recess, as in a taxi JUMP SEAT

taxonomy See **classification**

TB, tuberculosis of the lungs CONSUMPTION, PHTHISIS

tea, carbonated drink, spirits, or any drink other than water BEVERAGE
– tea, coffee, or other drink, food, or drug that temporarily increases activity or efficiency STIMULANT
– tea-box CADDY
– tea-like beverage from South America MATÉ, YERBA MATÉ, PARAGUAY TEA
– tea-like beverage made from wild flowers, leaves, or the like HERB TEA, TISANE
– tea-like drink made from the root of an Asian plant GINSENG
– teatime dance popular in the 1920s and 1930s THÉ DANSANT
– black China tea of various types BOHEA, CONGGOU, OOLONG, PEKOE, SOUCHONG
– fine variety of black tea from India DARJEELING
– orange whose rind yields a fragrant oil used in perfume-making and in flavouring tea BERGAMOT
– Russian tea urn SAMOVAR
– steep tea or herbs in preparing a drink or extract INFUSE

teach forcefully, as by repetition INSTIL, INCULCATE
– teach or instruct, especially in an uplifting way EDIFY, ENLIGHTEN
– teach someone to accept something uncritically INDOCTRINATE, BRAINWASH

teacher employed by two or more schools, constantly travelling from one to the other PERIPATETIC
– teacher, especially a private teacher TUTOR

– teacher or educator, especially a rather fussy and dogmatic one PEDAGOGUE
– teacher or instructor PRECEPTOR
– teacher or schoolmaster in Scotland DOMINIE
– teacher or wise adviser MENTOR
– teachers' salary scale in English and Welsh state schools BURNHAM SCALE, BAKER SCALE
– spiritual teacher or leader, as among Hindus or Sikhs GURU
– university teacher, lecturer, or reader DON, DOSENT, LECTOR

teaching designed to instruct, often in an excessively dull or moralising way DIDACTICS
– teaching or instruction TUITION
– teaching or learning by lessons heard during sleep HYPNOPAEDIA
– teaching specially designed for slow learners REMEDIAL TEACHING

teal – flock of teal SPRING

team's lucky object, animal, or person MASCOT

tear See also **break**
– tear down or demolish a building or city, destroy down to the ground RAZE
– tear or catch clothing on a nail, wooden stump, or the like SNAG
– tear the flesh, as with a knife or whip LACERATE
– tearing away or sudden amputation of a limb or other body part, either surgically or in an accident AVULSION
– apart or into pieces, as one might tear something ASUNDER

tear gas CS GAS

tearful, tending to weep, weepy LACHRYMOSE
– tearful or sentimental, as when drunk MAUDLIN

tears – adjective for tears LACHRYMAL
– small vase formerly used to hold mourners' tears LACHRYMATORY

tease a public speaker with interruptions HECKLE
– tease good-humouredly, kid, pull someone's leg BANTER, JOSH, RALLY, RIB, COD, RAG
– tease in a mocking or scoffing way, taunt GIBE, TWIT
– tease in a way that ridicules exaggerated claims, bring down a peg or two DEBUNK, DEFLATE
– tease or torment by withholding something desirable TANTALISE

teasing, frivolous style, speech, or the like PERSIFLAGE
– teasing, playful conversation BANTER, BADINAGE, RAILLERY

teat or nipple PAP
– teat or a projection that is nipple-shaped MAMILLA

technical or specialised vocabulary TERMINOLOGY, NOMENCLATURE, JARGON

-technique -URGY

technology – person opposed to new technology LUDDITE

-technology -URGY

teens – beginning of sexual maturing, as in one's early teens PUBERTY
– phase of physical and psychological maturing, typically during one's teens ADOLESCENCE

teeth See also **tooth**
– teeth having sharp edges for tearing flesh, as in meat-eating animals CARNASSIAL TEETH
– teeth or notches in a series, as on a saw or leaf SERRATION
– arrangement, number, and type of teeth in an animal DENTITION
– dental plate with a false tooth or teeth permanently fixed to natural teeth BRIDGE, BRIDGEWORK
– dentist specialising in correcting the positioning of teeth ORTHODONTIST
– film or crust, containing bacteria and other matter, formed on the teeth PLAQUE
– fit of the teeth when the jaws are closed, "bite" OCCLUSION
– grind the teeth, as in anger GNASH
– growing continuously throughout life, as rodents' teeth do PERSISTENT
– gum inflammation, often causing loosening of the teeth PYORRHOEA
– having two successive sets of teeth, as humans and most other mammals have DIPHYODONT
– mercury alloy, as used by dentists as a filling for teeth AMALGAM
– plate or set of false teeth DENTURE
– relating to the tissues surrounding the teeth PERIODONTAL
– tablet used to show the plaque on the teeth by temporarily staining it red DISCLOSING TABLET
– thin strong thread used to clean between the teeth DENTAL FLOSS
– wide gap between the teeth DIASTEMA
– yellowish, limey deposit building up on the teeth TARTAR, CALCULUS

-teeth- DENT-, DENTI-, -ODON, -ODONT

teetotal, non-drinking TEMPERATE, ABSTINENT
– teetotaller ABSTAINER, RECHABITE

telegraphic system for transmitting copies of documents by photoelectric scanning and reproduction FACSIMILE, FAX

telepathy See also **fortune-telling**
– ability to foretell the future, as through telepathy FORESIGHT, PRECOGNITION, PRESCIENCE
– perception by means of a sixth sense, telepathy, intuition, or the like EXTRASENSORY PERCEPTION, ESP, CRYPTAESTHESIA, TELAESTHESIA
– person with telepathic powers, especially one able to predict future events CLAIRVOYANT
– study of telepathy and other psychic phenomena PARAPSYCHOLOGY

telephone attachment that records conversations DICTOGRAPH
– telephone box KIOSK
– telephone coupled with a television set, allowing the people to see as well as talk to each other over a distance VIDEOPHONE, VIEWPHONE
– telephone line connecting two distant exchanges TRUNK LINE
– telephone link between computers MODEM
– telephone link between heads of state for emergencies HOT LINE
– telephone system allowing direct dialling for long-distance calls SUBSCRIBER TRUNK DIALLING, STD
– contribute or pledge a sum of money, as to a charity or for a telephone service SUBSCRIBE
– device in or part of a radio, television, telephone, or the like that takes in and converts incoming signals RECEIVER
– thin disc, as in a telephone earpiece or mouthpiece, whose vibrations are made to produce electric signals or vice versa DIAPHRAGM, TYMPANUM
– unlisted, by request, in a telephone directory, and unavailable to enquirers EX-DIRECTORY
– whining device in a telephone to indicate when the receiver has not been replaced HOWLER

telescope for viewing objects on land or on water rather than in space TERRESTRIAL TELESCOPE
– telescope-like toy producing varied symmetrical coloured patterns when one looks through and rotates it KALEIDOSCOPE
– building housing telescopes for observing the stars OBSERVATORY
– eyepiece of a telescope, microscope, or the like OCULAR
– having fine threads for use in measuring, as the eyepiece of a telescope might have FILAR
– lens or set of lenses, nearest to the object being viewed, in a telescope or microscope OBJECTIVE
– sliding tube within another, as in a telescope DRAWTUBE
– small telescope SPYGLASS

– small telescope attached to a larger one and used for locating the object to be observed FINDER
– surveyor's instrument, essentially a small telescope, for measuring angles THEODOLITE

television award in the U.S., the equivalent of an Oscar EMMY
– television or radio announcements or linking items designed to avoid breaks between programmes CONTINUITY
– television or radio broadcast covering an entire week's episodes of a series OMNIBUS EDITION
– television or radio network GRID
– television or radio programme that has been pre-recorded TRANSCRIPTION
– television programme or film intended as an accurate history or analysis but using actors and dramatic reconstructions DOCUDRAMA
– television programme or film presented as a non-fictional analysis or history DOCUMENTARY
– television-programme presenter FRONT MAN, FRONT WOMAN
– television system, as for security in shops, using cable or telephone links rather than broadcasting CLOSED-CIRCUIT TELEVISION
– television tube, oscilloscope tube, or similar electron-generating and -focusing vacuum tube CATHODE-RAY TUBE
– broadcast live a concert, speech, or the like, as on television RELAY
– cabinet of a television set, hi-fi system, or the like, standing on the floor CONSOLE
– cuing device producing a magnified script for someone speaking before television cameras TELEPROMPTER, AUTOCUE
– current information in printed form receivable on a specially adapted television set TELETEXT, VIEWDATA, ORACLE, CEEFAX
– difference in brightness, as of a television picture CONTRAST
– estimates of the audience figures of a radio or television programme RATINGS
– pattern of horizontal lines traced by a scanning electron beam, as on a television screen RASTER
– public appearance or presentation, as on television EXPOSURE
– ratio of a television picture's width to its height ASPECT RATIO
– referring to television in which members of the general public rather than professionals make the programmes ACCESS
– sharpness or clarity of outline, as of a photograph or television image DEFINITION

tell, inform, make familiar ACQUAINT
– tell, report, or repeat, especially a story or an account of a past event NARRATE, RECITE, RECOUNT, REHEARSE, RELATE
– tell a secret, reveal DISCLOSE, DIVULGE
– tell things apart, see or show the differences DIFFERENTIATE, DISTINGUISH, DISCRIMINATE
– entertain, especially by telling stories REGALE

teller of witty anecdotes or stories RACONTEUR

telling the future See **fortune-telling**, **foretell**
– telling the future, prophetic MANTIC

-telling the future -MANCY

temper, irritability ASPERITY
– temper metal or glass ANNEAL
– temper or resentment, huff or pet, as from a blow to one's pride PIQUE
– bad temper, ill humour SPLEEN, IRASCIBILITY, BILE
– easily provoked, as someone's temper might be HAIR-TRIGGER
– fit of temper PADDY, PADDYWHACK, TANTRUM
– quick-tempered, easily angered IRASCIBLE, INFLAMMABLE, VOLATILE

temperament, personality, or mood DISPOSITION
– changeable, as someone's temperament might be MERCURIAL
– gloomy, cold and sluggish in temperament SATURNINE

temperature – temperature-controlled container, as for premature babies INCUBATOR
– temperature scales of various kinds CELSIUS, CENTIGRADE, RÉAUMUR, FAHRENHEIT, KELVIN, RANKINE
– abnormally high body temperature, as produced by fever HYPERPYREXIA, HYPERTHERMIA
– abnormally low body temperature HYPOTHERMIA
– cooling power of the air based on both wind speed and air temperature WIND-CHILL FACTOR
– surrounding, in the immediate vicinity, as the air or temperature might be AMBIENT
– switching or controlling device for regulating temperature, as in a refrigerator THERMOSTAT

temple See also **column**
– temple, as in Rome, for all the gods PANTHEON
– temple or shrine in Chinese communities JOSS HOUSE
– temple or shrine, typically a tapering tower with many storeys PAGODA
– temple tower, in the shape of a steep pyramid, as in ancient Babylon ZIGGURAT
– entrance or porch of a temple PROPYLAEUM
– innermost chamber in the Temple in ancient Israel, which housed the Ark of the Covenant HOLY OF HOLIES, SANCTUM SANCTORUM, ORACLE

tempo – instrument indicating musical tempo by sounding out the beat METRONOME

temporarily, for the time being PRO TEM

temporary See also **short-lived**
– temporary, improvised, often as an emergency measure EXTEMPORANEOUS, EXPEDIENT, MAKESHIFT
– temporary or conditional, subject to change when permanent arrangements can be made STOPGAP, PROVISIONAL, INTERIM
– temporary stay or residence in a place SOJOURN
– temporary stop, pause RESPITE
– temporary suspending of operation or activity ABEYANCE
– temporary transfer of a teacher, military officer, or the like for duty elsewhere SECONDMENT

tempt, lure, attract ENTICE, INVEIGLE
– temptations, wheedling, or flattering BLANDISHMENTS
– tempting, fascinating ALLURING

ten – ten-legged crustacean such as a lobster, or ten-tentacled mollusc such as a squid DECAPOD
– ten times, tenfold DECUPLE
– ten-year period DECADE, DECENNARY, DECENNIUM
– based on the number ten, as a fraction, number system, or currency might be DECIMAL, DENARY

ten- DEC-, DECA-, DEK-

Ten Commandments DECALOGUE
– chest that contained the stone tablets with the Ten Commandments ARK OF THE COVENANT

ten-gallon hat – hat with a high crown and wide brim, resembling a ten-gallon hat STETSON

tend, care for MINISTER TO
– tend or drift towards, as if irresistibly attracted GRAVITATE

tendency, preference, leaning, liking APPETENCE, PREDISPOSITION, PROCLIVITY, PROPENSITY
– tendency of a physical body to remain at rest or in unchanged motion unless acted on by external forces INERTIA
– tendency of the energy in the universe or any other closed system to run down ENTROPY

– tendency or calling, as to a religious life VOCATION
– individual and habitual tendency or leaning, trend or bias of character BENT, DISPOSITION, INCLINATION
– liable to or showing a tendency for SUSCEPTIBLE TO
– strong tendency or inclination, definite and continued liking or favouring AFFINITY, PARTIALITY, PENCHANT, PREDILECTION

-tendency towards- -PHIL-, -PHILIA

tendon above and behind the knee HAMSTRING

tennis – early forms of tennis SPHAIRISTIKE, BANDY
– free point allowed a weaker player at times in a handicap tennis match BISQUE

tenon – slot into which a tenon is fitted when joining two pieces of wood, stone, or metal MORTISE

tenor with a strong voice, especially one suited to Wagnerian opera HELDENTENOR

tense, anxious, nervous, in suspense ON TENTERHOOKS
– tense, nervy, or strained OVERWROUGHT, AGITATED
– past perfect tense of a verb, as in *had climbed* PLUPERFECT

tension – remove the tension or danger from a situation DEFUSE

tent of a conical shape, as used by North American Indians TEPEE
– tent of a large ornate kind, as used by medieval knights at tournaments or at war PAVILION
– tent of a very large and airy design, for balls, wedding parties, and the like MARQUEE
– tent or booth as used by the Israelites during the Exodus TABERNACLE
– tent or house used by North American Indians, or a play tent for children WIGWAM
– flap forming an entrance or extended roof for a tent FLY
– hooped rod supporting a canopy, as of a tent or covered wagon BAIL
– horizontal pole forming the ridge of a tent RIDGEPOLE
– put up a tent PITCH
– rope used to secure a tent GUY
– wooden block or strip with holes for securing and adjusting ropes, as of a tent or on a ship EUPHROE

tentacled- ACTINO-

tenth of one's yearly income or production donated to the church or other good cause TITHE

tenth- DECI-

tequila – tropical plant from which tequila is produced AGAVE

term in a U.S. or German university, typically forming half an academic year SEMESTER
– term of endearment HYPOCORISM
– term that is less general than another and is embraced by it, as *dog* is by *animal* HYPONYM
– term that is more general than another and embraces it, as *animal* does *dog* SUPERORDINATE
– terms used in a particular science, art, profession, or the like NOMENCLATURE, TERMINOLOGY
– learned in a showy sort of way, as deliberately "literary" terms are INKHORN
– spring term at some British universities HILARY, LENT
– summer term at some British universities TRINITY
– winter or autumn term at some British universities MICHAELMAS

terrace or tree-lined garden walk in ancient Rome XYST

terrify See **scared**, **fear**
– terrify, paralyse with fear GORGONISE, PETRIFY
– terrifying, thrilling book, film, or the like SPINE-CHILLER

territory administered by a country authorised by the League of Nations MANDATE
– territory needed for expansion, such as that claimed by Germany in the 1930s LEBENSRAUM
– divide a territory into small warring states BALKANISE
– foreign policy based on revenge or regaining of territory REVANCHISM
– incorporate territory into another state or an empire ANNEX
– policy of regaining territory that is historically or culturally connected to one's nation but now under foreign control IRREDENTISM

-terror -PHOBE, -PHOBIA, -PHOBIC

terrorists – deliberate damaging or destruction of property, as by terrorists SABOTAGE
– military action taken against rebels or terrorist groups COUNTERINSURGENCY, PACIFICATION

test See also **examine**
– test, measure, or standard used for judgment or comparison YARDSTICK, CRITERION, TOUCHSTONE
– test for a part in a play, concert, or the like, by giving a sample performance AUDITION
– test for cancer of the cervix in women PAP TEST, SMEAR TEST
– test identifying a person's skills and potential, often used as an aid in career guidance APTITUDE TEST
– test in which a choice of possible answers is provided MULTIPLE-CHOICE TEST
– test something to assess its value or quality ASSAY, APPRAISE
– test that will decide the effectiveness of something LITMUS TEST
– "inkblot test", personality test based on the subject's interpretations of various abstract inkblot designs RORSCHACH TEST
– person or group whose reactions serve as a test for new ideas or opinions SOUNDING BOARD
– rigorous or decisive test, "the crunch" ACID TEST

test-tube baby – referring to fertilisation induced in an artificial laboratory environment, as when producing a "test-tube baby" IN VITRO

testicle- ORCH-, ORCHID-

testicles or ovaries GONADS
– area around and including the testicles GROIN
– condition in which the testicles have not descended into the scrotum CRYPTORCHIDISM
– external pouch of the male genital organs, containing the testicles SCROTUM
– long, coiled tube forming part of the sperm-bearing system attached to the testicles EPIDIDYMIS
– region of the body just behind the testicles in a male PERINEUM
– sperm-bearing duct connected by a tube to either of the testicles VAS DEFERENS
– surgical cutting of the sperm-bearing ducts near the testicles, used for sterilising a man VASECTOMY

testify falsely in court PERJURE ONESELF
– person who makes an affidavit or testifies in writing under oath DEPONENT

testimony given on oath DEPOSITION

tetanus – grin-like expression, as from muscular contraction in tetanus RISUS SARDONICUS
– lockjaw, as in tetanus TRISMUS

text edited or revised critically to include the most plausible variant readings RECENSION, REDACTION
– text of a writer's works, together with collected notes and comments by scholars VARIORUM
– text of the songs and dialogue of an opera or operetta LIBRETTO
– text or passage from a classic or standard work that is considered authoritative LOCUS CLASSICUS
– text used by linguists for analysing features of language beyond single sentences DISCOURSE
– change or corrupt a text by inserting material INTERPOLATE
– commonly accepted text or version of a work VULGATE
– compare texts in order to see

where they differ COLLATE
– containing errors or changes, as the text of a copied manuscript might CORRUPT, GARBLED
– correct and improve a text by critical editing EMEND
– critical analysis or explanation of a text, especially of the Bible EXEGESIS
– cut or delete a passage from a text EXCISE
– devise a version of a text, art object, or the like, on the basis of surviving fragments and other evidence RECONSTRUCT
– edit or revise a text for publication REDACT
– extract from a text GOBBET
– fuse or blend two versions of a text to produce a full or reliable version CONFLATE
– insert or patch together a text in a strained and inharmonious way SPATCHCOCK
– note of critical commentary or explanation on a literary text ANNOTATION, GLOSS
– original text of a literary or musical work UR-TEXT, ARCHETYPE
– presenting texts or data in columns side by side for comparison SYNOPTIC
– scholarly comments, footnotes, variant readings, and so on in an edition of a text APPARATUS CRITICUS, CRITICAL APPARATUS
– variant reading in a particular edition of a text LECTION

textile See **fabric**, **cloth**

texture, firmness, as of a pudding CONSISTENCY

th – runic letter ð, representing the sounds /th/ and /t͟h/, as used in Old and Middle English EDH, ETH
– runic letter þ, representing the sounds /th/ and /t͟h/, as used in Old and Middle English THORN

thanks – "thanks be to God" DEO GRATIAS
– in debt to, owing thanks to, grateful OBLIGED, INDEBTED, BEHOLDEN

that is, "namely", term introducing examples VIDELICET, VIZ

thatching – stalks of long grass, beans, peas, and other plants used for thatching HAULM

the or equivalent word in other languages, identifying specifically the noun or noun phrase that follows it DEFINITE ARTICLE

the end, word that was used formerly to indicate the end of a book or manuscript EXPLICIT

the same, term used in references and footnotes to indicate a passage already referred to IDEM, ID.

theatre See chart, illustration on pages 518-519, and also **drama**
– theatre as a profession, the stage FOOTLIGHTS
– theatre as an art DRAMATURGY
– theatre award in New York, that is the theatrical equivalent of an Oscar prize TONY
– theatre company performing a variety of plays during a season REPERTORY COMPANY
– theatre for circus acts or music-hall entertainments HIPPODROME
– theatre that is unofficial, unorthodox, or away from the main theatre areas FRINGE THEATRE

THEATRE TERMS

amphitheatre	outdoor auditorium, particularly in ancient Rome
apron	section of a conventional stage extending beyond the curtains into the auditorium
auditorium	seating area for the audience, as distinct from the stage
box set	three flat pieces of scenery representing three walls of a room
coulisse	flat piece of scenery in the wings
décor	stage setting or scenery
drop scene	painted cloth behind which scenery is changed and in front of which short scenes are acted
fourth wall	apparent wall of a room represented by the proscenium arch, so that the audience appears to eavesdrop on the play's action
green room	backstage restroom for actors, especially in former times
grip	stagehand, helping to shift scenery
Kensington gore	imitation blood
loge	box, or upper section of seats
loggia	open balcony for seating
logum	stage provided by the flat roof of the proscenium, in an ancient Greek theatre
mezzanine	floor or room under the stage
odeum	theatre or concert building in ancient Greece or Rome
orchestra	circular area in front of the stage, used by the chorus, in an ancient Greek theatre
picture-frame stage	stage lying almost entirely behind the proscenium arch
platform stage	Elizabethan stage which projected into the central area, with the audience on three sides
proscenium	front part of a stage, or the arch framing it; performing area in front of the stage in an ancient Greek theatre
rake	upward slope of the stage away from the audience
skene	two-storey building in an ancient Greek theatre, providing changing and storage rooms
tableau curtain	curtain that draws up and outwards from centre stage
theatre-in-the-round, arena theatre	theatre in which the stage is almost entirely surrounded by the audience

– theatrical touring company or group TROUPE
– serious drama, as opposed to comedies, musicals, and the like LEGITIMATE THEATRE
theatrical or over-emotional behaviour HISTRIONICS
– theatrically affected or effeminate CAMP
theft of another person's writings, ideas, or the like, passing them off as one's own PLAGIARISM
– theft of another's property LARCENY
– theft of cattle or sheep, typically by driving them away RUSTLING
– theft of something small or cheap, minor thievery, filching PILFERAGE, PURLOINING
– theft or illegal use, especially by publishing a work protected by another's copyright PIRACY
– theft or misuse of property or funds that have been entrusted to one MISAPPROPRIATION, EMBEZZLEMENT, PECULATION, DEFALCATION, CONVERSION
– flee and hide, as after committing a theft ABSCOND
theme in music SUBJECT
– theme, motif, or commonplace image in literature TOPOS
– theme, repeated idea, recurring verse, or the like REFRAIN, CHORUS, BURDEN
– theme or recurrent idea or symbol in a book, symphony, or the like MOTIF, LEITMOTIV, MOTTO
– musical theme SUBJECT
theology as a subject of academic study DIVINITY
– theological study of first things, such as creation AETIOLOGY
– theological study of last things, such as heaven ESCHATOLOGY
– theological training school for clergymen SEMINARY
theorem – problem or supplementary rule arising from a theorem, as in geometry RIDER
theoretical, in name only, not actual NOMINAL
– theoretical or imaginary rather than actual NOTIONAL
– theoretical rather than realistic or provable SPECULATIVE, CONJECTURAL
theory See also **philosophy**
– theory, as the basis of scientific experiments HYPOTHESIS
– theory, religious principle, body of beliefs, or the like DOGMA, DOCTRINE, CREED
– theory differing from the orthodox view HERESY, HETERODOXY
– theory or proposition put forward for argument THESIS
– theory that the universe came gradually rather than suddenly into being, by the regular creation of matter CONTINUOUS-CREATION THEORY, STEADY-STATE THEORY
– theory that the universe originated by an explosion of a small dense mass and is still expanding BIG BANG THEORY, SUPERDENSE THEORY
– accepted, generally believed, as a theory might be RECEIVED
– assent to or believe in a theory, doctrine, or the like SUBSCRIBE, ADHERE
– blindly committed to a theory, dogmatic DOCTRINAIRE
– formulation or explanation of a theory EXPLICATION
-theory -LOGY, -OLOGY, -ISM
therapy See chart, page 520
– therapy, form of medical treatment MODALITY
– therapy for treating psychiatric patients, involving an electric shock to the brain ELECTROCONVULSIVE THERAPY, ECT
– therapy through engaging in crafts or creative hobbies OCCUPATIONAL THERAPY
– untraditional or unorthodox, as a lifestyle or therapy might be ALTERNATIVE
therefore, consequently ERGO
thermometer for measuring very low temperatures CRYOMETER
– thermometer that records temperatures THERMOGRAPH
– electrical thermometer for measuring very high temperatures PYROMETER
– instrument consisting of two thermometers, one with a dampened bulb, whose differing readings produce a measure of the humidity in the air PSYCHROMETER, WET-AND-DRY-BULB THERMOMETER, WET-AND-DRY BULB HYGROMETER
– mercury thermometer registering very small changes in temperature BECKMANN THERMOMETER
thesis or treatise, as for a higher academic degree DISSERTATION
thick and sticky, as some liquids are VISCID, VISCOUS
– thick-skinned mammal, such as the elephant or hippopotamus PACHYDERM
thicken, clot, or solidify, as blood might CONGEAL
– thicken, curdle, or jell into a semi-solid mass COAGULATE
– thicken or condense, as by boiling or evaporation INSPISSATE
– thicken or curdle, as milk does CLABBER
– thickened at one end, club-shaped CLAVATE, CLAVIFORM
– thickener or starch used in cooking ARROWROOT
– thickening agent, such as cream or egg yolks, for soups, sauces, or

theatre

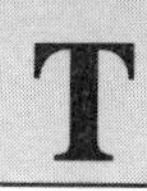

the like LIAISON

thickness or width, as of a circle, piping, or wire DIAMETER

thief or rascal GANEF
- thieves' vocabulary or similar half-secret language CANT, ARGOT

thigh or thighbone FEMUR
- thighs and pelvic region LOINS
- join of the inner thighs and trunk GROIN
- relating to the thigh CRURAL
- side of the body or thigh FLANK

thin, lean SPARE, MEAGRE
- thin, lean, slender, but tough SINEWY, STRINGY, WIRY, WITHY

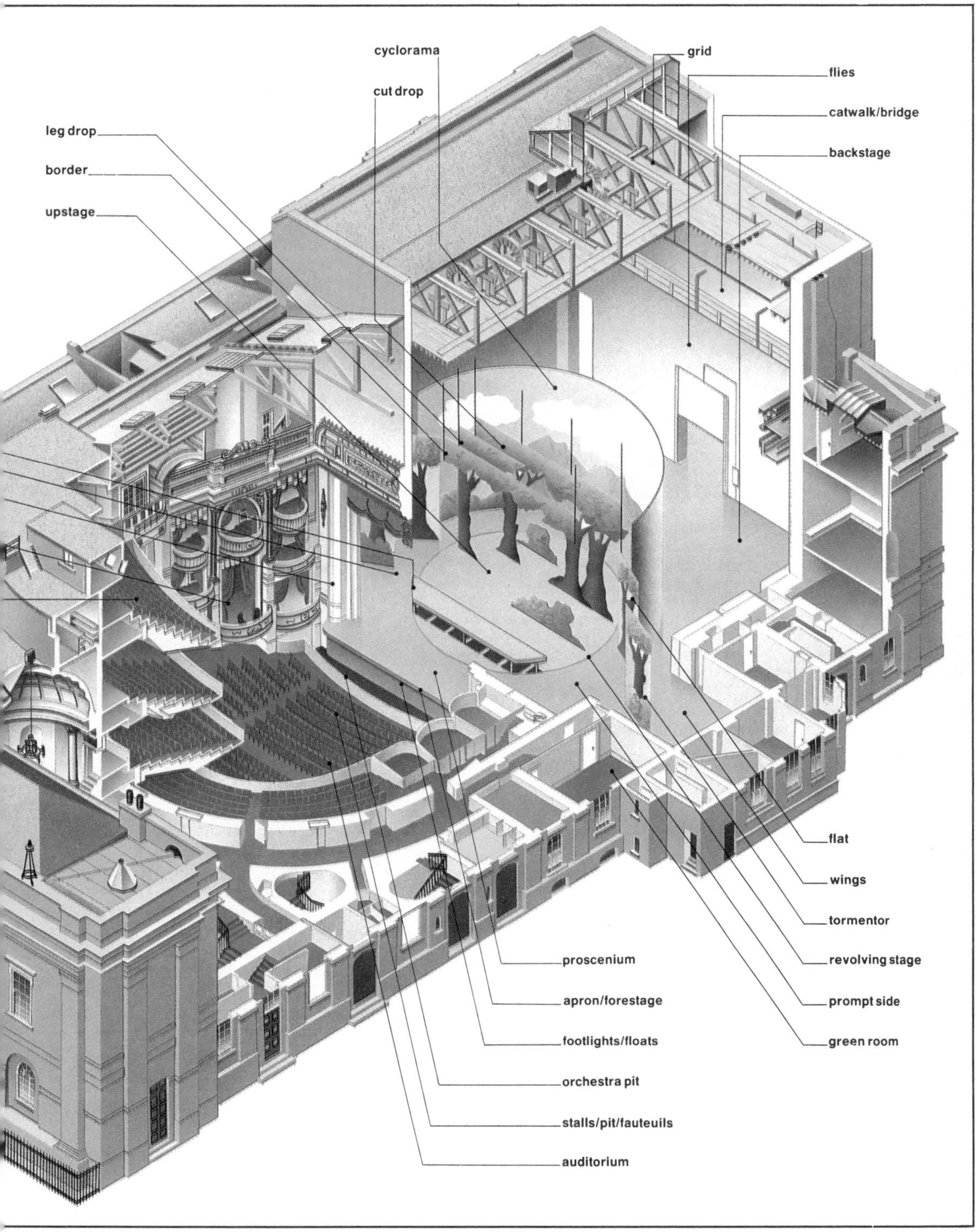

cyclorama
grid
flies
cut drop
catwalk/bridge
leg drop
backstage
border
upstage
flat
wings
tormentor
proscenium
revolving stage
apron/forestage
prompt side
green room
footlights/floats
orchestra pit
stalls/pit/fauteuils
auditorium

– thin, light, and partially see-through, as a fabric might be DIAPHANOUS, SHEER, TRANSLUCENT, GOSSAMER, CHIFFON
– thin, pale, sickly person WRAITH
– thin, sharp fragment, splinter, as of glass or stone SLIVER
– thin, slender, slim and graceful, trim GRACILE, LITHE, SVELTE, SYLPH-LIKE, WILLOWY
– thin and bony, especially in an awkward way, lean, skinny, weedy ANGULAR, SCRAGGY, SCRAWNY, ECTOMORPHIC
– thin and exhausted-looking, pinched, peaky HAGGARD, GAUNT
– thin and fine, as hair might be WISPY
– thin and gaunt LANK
– thin and long-limbed ASTHENIC, RANGY
– thin and shrivelled, withered SERE, WIZENED
– thin and tall, and usually clumsy or ungainly LANKY, GANGLING, SPINDLY
– thin and untidy, as handwriting might be SPIDERY
– thin in consistency or density, diluted, weakened, as a gas or liquid might be RAREFIED, TENUOUS, ATTENUATED
– thin or weaken a cordial, concentrate, or other liquid, as by adding water DILUTE
– thin out, make or become less dense or compact RAREFY
– thin thread, fibre, wire, or the like FILAMENT
– thinner or narrow towards one end TAPERING
– abnormally thin and weak, especially from nervous self-starvation ANOREXIC
– abnormally thin, as through starvation, undernourished SKELETAL, EMACIATED, MACERATED, CADAVEROUS

thing as it appears to the mind or senses, according to Kantian philosophy, regardless of its underlying nature PHENOMENON
– thing in itself, according to Kantian philosophy, rather than as it appears to the mind or senses NOUMENON
– thing that exists in its own right, independently of other things ENTITY
– "things done", deeds, achievements RES GESTAE
– treat an idea or abstraction as a real or concrete thing REIFY

thingummy, thingummy-jig, whatsitsname JIGGER, DINGBAT, GISMO, DINGUS, DOODAH, DISTING

think See also **thought**
– think, consider, judge, reckon, have an opinion DEEM, OPINE
– think, hold thoughts, illusions, or the like ENTERTAIN
– think, suppose, take for granted or accept PRESUME, ASSUME
– think, work out, conclude DEDUCE, FIGURE
– think about or study something laboriously LUCUBRATE
– think and make rough calculations about something, form a theory CONJECTURE, ESTIMATE, SPECULATE, THEORISE

THERAPIES

acupuncture	insertion of needles into the skin to relieve pain or treat disease
Alexander Technique	training in good posture
aromatherapy	use of sweet-smelling oils to influence mood and treat disease
aversion therapy	eradication of harmful habits by associating them with something unpleasant
biofeedback	use of measuring instruments to monitor bodily responses and thereby help a patient to control them
chemotherapy	use of chemicals to treat mental illness, cancer, and some other conditions
chiropractic	spinal manipulation to relieve various ailments
herbalism	use of herbal extracts to treat various ailments
homeopathy	use of minute amounts of drugs or natural remedies which in larger quantities would reproduce the effects of the disease being treated
hydrotherapy	use of water, usually in remedial swimming pools, to relieve pain in the muscles and joints, and treat disease
hypnotherapy	use of hypnosis to treat physical and mental disorders
irradiation, radiation therapy	use of radiation to control disease, especially cancer
moxibustion	burning of mugwort, or moxa, leaves at particular points on the skin, often in association with acupuncture
naturopathy	use of natural remedies and healthy living habits to restore or improve well-being
osteopathy	manipulation of bones and joints to treat backache and muscle problems
phototherapy	use of light, including infrared and ultraviolet rays, to treat disease, especially tumours
physiotherapy	use of exercise, heat, or massage to treat injury or disability
primal therapy	treatment for neurotic behaviour in which a patient is encouraged to "relive" painful experiences in early childhood, or even at birth
reflexology, zone therapy	use of foot massage to treat ailments elsewhere in the body
rolfing	use of deep massage to relieve muscular and emotional tension
shiatsu, acupressure	use of finger pressure at specific points on the body, and of massage, to relieve pain or treat disease

– think deeply and at length, turn over in the mind MULL OVER, MUSE, RUMINATE, BROOD ON
– think hard, ponder deeply CEREBRATE, CUDGEL ONE'S BRAINS
– think logically, reason RATIOCINATE
– think of or imagine something, especially some future possibility ENVISAGE
– think or consider carefully, reflect COGITATE, DELIBERATE, PERPEND
– think or consider deeply, ponder CONTEMPLATE, MEDITATE
– think or know by special insight, sense INTUIT
– think or ponder moodily BROOD
– think or reflect to oneself, search one's mind INTROSPECT
– think or work out in great detail EXCOGITATE
– think through, form an opinion APPRAISE, TAKE STOCK
– think up or invent something, especially in a devious way CONTRIVE, CONCOCT, FABRICATE
– think up or invent something, such as a plan CONCEIVE, DEVISE, FORMULATE, FASHION

thinker, scholar, or philosopher, especially an over-subtle or devious one SOPHIST, CASUIST

thinking, thought CEREBRATION
– thinking of an imaginative and free-ranging rather than a strictly logical kind, often producing unexpected solutions to problems LATERAL THINKING

third course of action, factor, or the like when there are supposed to be only two TERTIUM QUID
– third last, last but two ANTEPENULTIMATE
– third-ranking or third-level TERTIARY
– occuring every third year or lasting for three years TRIENNIAL

third- TER-

thirst – satisfy one's thirst QUENCH, SLAKE
– unsatisfiable, as thirst or lust might be INSATIABLE

thirsty PARCHED

this, *those*, or similar word pointing out the person or thing referred to DEMONSTRATIVE, DEICTIC

this side- CIS-

thistle – thistle-like shrub with spikes of flowers ACANTHUS
– tuft of feathery bristles on a thistle or the like, helping to disperse the seeds PAPPUS

thorn, prickle, or spine, as on a rose ACULEUS
– thorny bush or shrub BRIAR, BRAMBLE

thorn- ACANTH-, ACANTHO-

thorough, covering all aspects COMPREHENSIVE, EXHAUSTIVE, ALL-ENCOMPASSING
– thorough, painstaking, diligent, or hard-working CONSCIENTIOUS, INDUSTRIOUS, SEDULOUS, ASSIDUOUS
– thorough, very careful or precise, paying close attention to detail METICULOUS, PUNCTILIOUS, SCRUPULOUS
– thorough, wide-ranging, sweeping EXTENSIVE

thoroughbred PEDIGREE
– thoroughbred horses, especially racehorses BLOODSTOCK

thoroughgoing, out-and-out ARRANT

thoroughly- CATA-

thought See also **think**, **thinking**
– thought, idea, mental image CONCEPTION
– thought, thinking, contemplation CEREBRATION, COGITATION
– thought, thinking, the mental faculty by which things become known or recognised COGNITION
– thought or intention that is deliberately held back and remains unrevealed ARRIÈRE-PENSÉE
– thought or study, deep reflection, laborious meditation LUCUBRATION
– thought transference TELEPATHY
– arrange one's thoughts in order MARSHAL
– period or state of deep thought BROWN STUDY, REVERIE
– put one's thoughts into words, express FORMULATE
– referring to thought that is very disorganised INCOHERENT

thoughtful, absorbed, fully occupied mentally ENGROSSED, IMMERSED, INTENT
– thoughtful, attentive, and concerned, considerate SOLICITOUS
– thoughtful, reflective, meditative RUMINANT, PENSIVE, CONTEMPLATIVE, COGITATIVE
– thoughtful and careful in behaviour, avoiding trouble CIRCUMSPECT, DISCREET, PRUDENT
– thoughtful and sensitive, carefully considered JUDICIOUS, POLITIC
– thoughtful and withdrawn, self-examining INTROSPECTIVE
– deeply thoughtful, lost in thought, distracted ABSTRACTED, PREOCCUPIED

thousand – thousand-year period MILLENNIUM
– thousand years, or group of 1000 elements CHILIAD
– adjective for a thousand MILLENARIAN, MILLENARY

thousand- KILO-

thousand million, billion MILLIARD
– thousand-million-year period in geology AEON

thousand million- GIGA-

thousand-millionth- NANO-

thousandth MILLESIMAL

thousandth- MILLI-

thread, thin wire, fibre, or the like FILAMENT
– thread, wire, or cord used in surgery, as for closing a blood vessel LIGATURE
– thread-like or relating to thread FILAR
– thread of gold or silver wire used in embroidery PURL
– thread that has separated from a fabric RAVELLING
– threads running across the width in weaving or a fabric WOOF, WEFT
– threads running lengthways in weaving or a fabric WARP
– ball of twine or thread CLEW
– cone-shaped roll of thread wound on a spindle COP
– loose coil of thread, wool, or the like SKEIN, HANK
– small lump in a thread or fabric, sometimes made deliberately for a knobbly appearance SLUB
– loosely twisted thread, as used in embroidery FLOSS
– spinning or twisting of silk, cotton, or the like into threads FILATURE
– tool for cutting an internal screw thread TAP
– tool parts with an internal thread used for cutting threads on screws, pipes, and the like DIE

thread- NEMAT-, NEMATO-

threat, risk, or danger MENACE, PERIL, JEOPARDY, HAZARD
– threat in the form of a perceived warning of future calamity OMEN, PORTENT, PRESAGE
– threat of disaster, causing constant anxiety SWORD OF DAMOCLES
– threat of punishment or revenge, denunciation COMMINATION
– threat or warning CAVEAT
– threats by means of a display of military power SABRE RATTLING
– final terms offered in negotiating, carrying a threat of breakdown if rejected ULTIMATUM
– force or compulsion, as by means of threats DURESS, COERCION, CONSTRAINT

threaten, attack verbally, or denounce with great force BLUSTER, FULMINATE, INVEIGH
– threaten, endanger, put at risk JEOPARDISE, HAZARD, IMPERIL
– threaten, look menacing, as the sky or weather might LOWER
– threaten or bribe someone into

committing a wrongful act, especially perjury SUBORN
– threaten so as to silence or dissuade, INTIMIDATE, DETER

threatening MENACING, MINATORY, MINACIOUS
– threatening, overhanging, unpleasant and likely to occur soon IMMINENT, IMPENDING
– threatening and prophetic, warning of some future calamity FOREBODING, OMINOUS, PORTENTOUS
– threatening or gloomy, as the expression on someone's face might be BALEFUL
– threatening or sulky frown SCOWL

three bent or curved branches constituting a pattern radiating from a centre TRISKELION
– three in cards or dice TREY
– three-in-one TRIUNE
– three-leafed or having three leaflets, as clover has TRIFOLIATE
– three-legged stand or support TRIPOD, TRIVET
– three-legged table, typically used for serving tea TEAPOY
– three-monthly or three-month TRIMESTRIAL
– three-ness, or group of three TRINITY
– three-part painting or carving, typically on three panels TRIPTYCH
– three people living together in a sexual relationship MÉNAGE À TROIS
– three-pronged fork or spear, as used by gladiators or carried by Neptune TRIDENT
– three-tiered Greek or Roman ship rowed with three banks of oars TRIREME
– three times, threefold TRIPLE, TREBLE, TRIPLICATE
– Three Wise Men MAGI
– division or separation into three parts TRICHOTOMY
– group of three TRIAD, TRIO, TROIKA
– group of three people TRIUMVIRATE
– leaf made up of three leaflets, or a design, symbol, or architectural ornament resembling this TREFOIL
– occurring once every three years or lasting for three years TRIENNIAL

three- TER-, TRI-

three-dimensional appearance, or a technique for representing it, in a drawing or painting PERSPECTIVE
– three-dimensional laser-produced photo or pattern HOLOGRAM
– three-dimensional picture or process based on images viewed through glasses with one green and one red lens ANAGLYPH
– three-dimensional scene or tableau, as in museums, with models of figures exhibited against a background DIORAMA
– design, painting, or style of painting using shades of grey and aiming at a 3D effect GRISAILLE
– optical instrument with twin lenses, producing a 3D effect when used to view two similar photographs STEREOSCOPE
– pair of similar pictures that give a 3D effect when viewed through special lenses STEREOGRAPH
– realistic painting that deceives the eye by its striking 3D effect TROMPE L'OEIL

three-dimensional- STERE-, STEREO-

threshold at which a stimulus begins to evoke a response LIMEN
– below the threshold of perception or consciousness SUBLIMINAL

thrifty See also **miserly**
– thrifty, economical, unwasteful, prudent in spending CANNY, FRUGAL, PROVIDENT, SPARING
– thrifty or economical to the point of meanness PARSIMONIOUS
– thrifty or penny-pinching SCRIMPING, SKIMPING
– thrifty use and spending of resources HUSBANDRY, CONSERVATION
– aimed at thrift, regulating or limiting expenses, as a rule might be SUMPTUARY

thrill or shiver of fear or excitement FRISSON

-thriving on -PHILE, -PHILIC

throat See illustration at **mouth, nose, and throat**
– throat and chest area THORAX
– throat or oesophagus GULLET, GORGE
– throaty, relating to or pronounced in the throat GUTTURAL
– adjective for the throat or neck JUGULAR, GULAR
– band of colour on the throat of a bird or other animal GORGET
– clear the throat loudly HAWK
– fold of skin hanging from the throat, as of some birds and lizards WATTLE
– loose fold of skin at the throat, as in cattle or old people DEWLAP
– surgical cut or opening through the throat to help breathing TRACHEOTOMY
– surgical rod used for removing obstructions from the throat PROBANG

throne – attain the throne or other high office ACCEDE
– give up or relinquish the throne formally ABDICATE
– remove from office, power, the throne, or the like DEPOSE
– right of a person or line to inherit a title, property, throne, or the like SUCCESSION
– seize by force and hold illegally the power, rights, throne, or the like of another USURP

through- DIA-, PER-

throughout, "here and there", used in references and footnotes to indicate the frequent occurrence of an item in a text PASSIM

throw away, get rid of, reject DISPOSE OF, DISCARD
– throw forward, launch or lob IMPEL, PROJECT, PROPEL
– throw from a great height, hurl down PRECIPITATE
– throw hard, fling, shower PELT
– throw or thrust into a position suddenly or unceremoniously PITCHFORK
– throw out, drive out, force out EJECT, EXPEL
– throw out of a window DEFENESTRATE
– throw overboard, or discard something burdensome JETTISON
– throw sticks, as at birds or fruit SQUAIL
– throw stones at, stone to death LAPIDATE
– "throwback", characteristic or individual affected by reversion to a more primitive state ATAVISM
– "throwing the voice" VENTRILOQUISM
– curved flight path through the air taken by something thrown, shot, or the like TRAJECTORY

thrush – flock or family of thrushes MUTATION
– poetic or regional term for a thrush THROSTLE

thumb or corresponding digit in an animal POLLEX
– thumb that can be placed against the fingertips, as in humans OPPOSABLE THUMB
– thumb the nose COCK A SNOOK
– fleshy underpart of the top joint of a finger or the thumb PAD
– pad of muscle on the hand below the thumb HEEL, THENAR

thus, "so", term used in a printed text to indicate the deliberate reproduction of a mistaken or surprising wording or fact being quoted SIC

Tibetan Buddhist monastery LAMASERY

tick, mite, or related small creature ACARID
– tick off item by item TALLY
– infestation of the skin or hair with mites or ticks ACARIASIS

ticket or label, as might be tied on a parcel DOCKET
– book of tickets or travel vouchers CARNET
– person using a free ticket, as for a theatre or train DEADHEAD
– person who resells tickets at an inflated price TOUT

tidal flood BORE, EAGRE
– wave like a tidal wave, but due to an underwater earthquake or volcanic eruption TSUNAMI

tide of maximum rise, occurring at the new or full moon of each month SPRING TIDE
– tide of minimum rise, occurring during the first and third quarter of the Moon NEAP TIDE
– falling or receding tide EBB TIDE
– rising or incoming tide FLOOD TIDE
– seashore, specifically the area between high- and low-tide marks of the spring tide LITTORAL

tidy, careful, and systematic in work or behaviour METHODICAL, ORDERLY, PAINSTAKING
– tidy or dress oneself very neatly PRIMP, PRINK
– neat and tidy in dress or appearance TRIM, DAPPER, SPRUCE, WELL-GROOMED
– neat and tidy, orderly SHIPSHAPE

tie See also **join**
– tie, bond, connection LIGATURE, VINCULUM
– scarf-like neckband, arranged to resemble a very wide tie CRAVAT
– U.S. term for a draw, tie, or deadlock, especially in a sports event STANDOFF
– wide triangular tie knot, made with an extra turn WINDSOR KNOT

tie up, as by binding the arms, wings, or legs TRUSS
– sexual perversion in which one partner is tied up BONDAGE

tight – tightly closed, as a fist or teeth might be CLENCHED
– tightly fixed in place CRAMMED IN, IMMOVABLE, WEDGED IN
– tightly pressed down, as trodden earth might be COMPACTED
– tightly pressed together, very crowded, as ranks of troops might be SERRIED
– feeling of tightness or pressure, as in the chest CONSTRICTION
– pulled or stretched tight, as a rope might be TAUT

tightrope or slack-rope walker FUNAMBULIST
– tightrope walker or other performer of balancing feats EQUILIBRIST

tile, especially of wood, laid in overlapping rows on a roof SHINGLE
– curving roof tile overlapping or interlocking with the adjoining tiles PANTILE
– decorate, inlay, or pave with a mosaic of tiny tiles TESSELLATE
– thin mortar, as used between tiles GROUT

tilt, slope, slant INCLINATION, DEVIATION, CANT
– tilt or sway, as a ship might when sailing into the wind LIST, CANT, HEEL, CAREEN

tilting, or a post or target tilted at by horsemen QUINTAIN

timber beam between walls supporting a ceiling or roof JOIST
– timber beam placed horizontally in a building, as for supporting a floor STRINGER, SUMMER
– timber stake or heavy post SPILE
– horizontal timber beam over a window or doorway LINTEL

time between two periods or events, interval INTERIM
– time-error, dating mistake, placing a person, thing, or event in the incorrect historical period ANACHRONISM
– time of greatest strength or success HEYDAY, PRIME
– time or distance between two limits SPAN
– time period, or continuation through time DURATION
– timekeeping instrument used when practising music METRONOME
– times gone by, the old days LANG SYNE
– timing or pace, especially in music TEMPO
– adjective for time TEMPORAL
– arrange in slightly different but overlapping positions or time periods STAGGER
– dominant outlook and spirit of the times ZEITGEIST
– happening or existing at the same time SIMULTANEOUS, COINCIDENT, CONTEMPORANEOUS, CONTEMPORARY
– immediately before or after in time CONTIGUOUS
– instrument for measuring tiny intervals of time CHRONOGRAPH
– ordered according to time of occurrence CHRONOLOGICAL
– pass by, as time does ELAPSE
– period or point of time, especially when critical JUNCTURE
– referring to time going back to the distant past IMMEMORIAL
– science of measuring time, or the study of timepieces HOROLOGY
– scientific measurement or calculation of time CHRONOMETRY
– system allowing variable working hours to employees each day either side of the obligatory core time FLEXITIME
– very long time, specifically a thousand million years AEON

time- CHRON-, CHRONO-, TEMP-, TEMPOR-

-times -FOLD

time limit – law setting a time limit for prosecuting a crime or bringing a legal action STATUTE OF LIMITATIONS

tin works, or tin-mining centre or region STANNARY
– relating to or containing tin STANNIC, STANNOUS

tinder in the form of decayed wood or similar dry material TOUCHWOOD, PUNK

tinker or scrap-metal dealer, typically living in a caravan, and often taken for a Gypsy DIDICOY

tiny See **small**

-tiny- MICRO-, NANO-, -ULE

tip, gift of money in return for a service POURBOIRE, GRATUITY
– tip, small bribe, or charity, given in Eastern countries BAKSHEESH
– tip, small gift, or bonus PERQUISITE, BUCKSHEE
– tip or small bribe or gift DOUCEUR
– tip or small bribe or gift in West Africa DASH
– metal ring or cap on the tip of a walking stick or umbrella to protect it against wear FERRULE

tip- ACRO-

tip-toe, walking with only the toes touching the ground, as with dogs and horses DIGITIGRADE
– spin on tip-toe or on the ball of a foot, as in ballet PIROUETTE

tired FATIGUED, WEARY
– tired, run-down, drained, abnormally weak or feeble DEBILITATED, ENERVATED
– tired and lazy LANGUID, LETHARGIC, LISTLESS
– tired and sleepy, drooping, drowsy SOMNOLENT, SOPORIFIC
– tired and stale, dulled, having lost interest JADED, BLASÉ
– tired and worried in appearance CAREWORN, HAGGARD
– tired-eyed, as from lack of sleep BLEARY-EYED
– tired out, exhausted, shattered, done in DEAD-BEAT, FORSPENT, FORWORN, PROSTRATE
– tired through being drained of strength or energy DEPLETED, FLAGGING
– tired through overwork, or excessive effort OVEREXTENDED, OVERTASKED, OVERTAXED
– feeling of being tired of life, desperate boredom ENNUI, TAEDIUM VITAE, WELTSCHMERZ

– slang terms for tired or exhausted TUCKERED OUT, STONKERED, BUSHED, FRAZZLED, KNACKERED, WHACKED
– spiritually tired and feeble, drained of moral force or vitality DECADENT, EFFETE
tired- NARCO-
tiredness, lack of energy LANGUOR, LASSITUDE, LETHARGY, LISTLESSNESS, SLUGGISHNESS
– tiredness, lack of interest, mental dullness APATHY, HEBETUDE
– tending to cause tiredness or induce sleep SOMNOLENT, SOPORIFIC
tireless, untiring INDEFATIGABLE
tiring, demanding TAXING, GRUELLING, EXACTING
– tiring or boring work DRUDGERY
tissue, in fibrous sheets, beneath the skin and encasing muscles FASCIA
– tissue of a single layer of tightly packed cells, covering body organs and surfaces EPITHELIUM
– tissue from which nails and teeth develop MATRIX
– tissue in a plant containing channels for conducting fluids VASCULAR TISSUE
– tissue of natural or synthetic material through which fluids can pass slowly MEMBRANE
– tissue structure, or the scientific study of it HISTOLOGY
– body tissue in which fat is stored ADIPOSE TISSUE
– wasting away of tissue, as through disease ATROPHY
– watery liquid from the body tissues LYMPH
tissue- HIST-, HISTO-
tit-for-tat injury, raid, punishment, or the like RETALIATION, REPRISAL, REQUITAL
title, formal name, or description STYLE, DESIGNATION, APPELLATION
– title given to a dead person placed at the first level on the way to sainthood in the Roman Catholic Church VENERABLE
– title of a category RUBRIC
– title of a work, stating its argument or theme LEMMA
– title of respect used for a man in Turkey and the Middle East EFFENDI
– title of respect in addressing an employer in East Africa BWANA
– title of respect for someone of superior status HONORIFIC
– title or inscription, as on a coin or coat of arms LEGEND
– adjective for a title TITULAR
– "defender of the faith", one of the titles of the British sovereign FIDEI DEFENSOR
– use of a title or epithet, such as *Her Majesty*, in place of a proper name ANTONOMASIA
TNT – explosive power equivalent to one million tons of TNT MEGATON
to – uninflected verb form that in English often follows *to*, or the combination of *to* with that verb form, as in *to dream* INFINITIVE
to- AD-, EPI-
to wit, "namely", "that is to say", used to introduce a synonym, explanation, or missing word SCILICET, SC.
– "to wit", "namely", used to introduce examples, lists, or explanations VIDELICET, VIZ.
toad of southern Africa, used in pregnancy testing XENOPUS, PLATANNA
– toad or frog, or adjective for a toad or frog ANURAN, SALIENTIAN, BATRACHIAN
– European toad whose fertilised eggs are carried on the hind legs of the male MIDWIFE TOAD
– European "running toad" with a yellow-striped back, that swells up when alarmed NATTERJACK
toadstool See **fungus**, **mushroom**
toady See **flatter**
toast See chart
– toast, drinking someone's health PLEDGE
– toast, or salute formerly given on drinking someone's health WASSAIL
– toast on which a savoury mixture is served CROUTE
– toast that is very thin and crisp MELBA TOAST
– toasted or fried square of bread, served in soups or salads CROUTON
– wedge of toast or fried bread, typically served as a garnish SIPPET
tobacco case in which the humidity can be kept constant HUMIDOR
– tobacco leaf around a cigar WRAPPER
– tobacco of a strong coarse type, cut into shreds SHAG
– tobacco plug left in a pipe after smoking DOTTLE
– coarse, broken dried tobacco leaves CANASTER
– light Kentucky tobacco BURLEY
– pack down or stamp down tightly tobacco, concrete, or the like by means of light blows TAMP
– poisonous addictive chemical compound in tobacco NICOTINE
– strong, dark tobacco, of various kinds CAPORAL, PERIQUE, LATAKIA
– sweetened tobacco moulded into oblong cakes CAVENDISH
– twisted roll of tobacco PIGTAIL
– wad of tobacco for chewing QUID
toboggan for one person LUGE
toe, finger, or corresponding part in other animals DIGIT
– toe bones PHALANGES
– big toe HALLUX
– fleshy underpart of the top joint of a finger or toe PAD
– hoofed mammal, such as a deer or cow, having two or four toes on each foot ARTIODACTYL
– painful condition in the joints, especially those of the big toe, caused by an excess of uric acid GOUT
– painful swelling of the lower joint of the big toe BUNION
– spin on tip-toe or on the ball of a foot, as in ballet PIROUETTE
toe- DACTYL-, DACTYLO-
toenails – care of the feet and toenails PEDICURE
together, joined to form a whole INTEGRATED
– together with, associated with, accompanying CONCOMITANT, COROLLARY
together- CO-, COM-, SYN-, SYM-
-together with- -CUM-
toilet See **lavatory**
toilet water EAU DE COLOGNE
toiletries – small case for needles, toiletries, or the like ÉTUI
token, tiny, insignificant, as a sum of money might be NOMINAL
tolerant, broad-minded, as in matters of sexual conduct PERMISSIVE
– tolerant, long-suffering, putting up patiently with provocation FORBEARING
– tolerant, mild, and forgiving of others' faults or crimes LENIENT
– tolerant, undogmatic, and liberal, especially in matters of church doctrine and ritual, broad-church LATITUDINARIAN
– tolerant, unvengeful, willing to forgive and forget MAGNANIMOUS
– tolerant and obliging, yielding to others' wishes COMPLAISANT
– tolerant of other people's whims, desires, or faults INDULGENT
tolerate, allow, or approve COUNTENANCE, SANCTION
– tolerate, endure, put up with BROOK, STOMACH, WITHSTAND
– tolerate, forgive, or overlook an offence CONDONE
toleration or permission implied by the absence of an explicit prohibition SUFFERANCE
tolling of a bell, as at a funeral KNELL
tomb, burial vault SEPULCHRE
– tomb, or impressive building housing a tomb MAUSOLEUM
– tomb cover of dark material, often velvet PALL
– tomb in ancient Egypt, of ob-

long shape with sloping sides and a flat roof MASTABA
– tomb of marble, typically decorated with a sculpture or inscriptions SARCOPHAGUS
– inscription on a gravestone, tombstone, or monument commemorating the person buried there EPITAPH
tomboy, young woman or girl attractive in a boyish way GAMINE
tomorrow, or shortly MAÑANA
tone colour, sound quality produced by overtones rather than volume and pitch TIMBRE
– distinction or variation of a very fine or subtle kind, as of tone, colour, or meaning NUANCE
tongs or long tweezers used by a surgeon FORCEPS
– hinged metal bars resembling tongs, used for lifting heavy objects such as building materials CRAMPONS
tongue See also **mouth**
– tongue-shaped, as some leaves are LINGULATE
– adjective for the tongue GLOSSAL, LINGUAL
– any of the tiny pimple-like bumps on the tongue PAPILLA
– fold or flap of skin, such as that under the tongue FRAENUM
– implement having a wide-tipped or flexible blade, as for pressing down the tongue when examining the throat SPATULA
– sore or cyst under the tongue, caused by a blocked salivary gland or duct RANULA
– trilling of a flute or other wind instrument by a rapid vibration of the tongue FLUTTER TONGUING
– U-shaped bone at the base of the tongue HYOID BONE
-tongue- -GLOSS-, GLOSSO-
tonic RESTORATIVE
– tonic with a bitter taste, used to flavour drinks ANGOSTURA BITTERS
tool See chart, page 526
– tool, instrument IMPLEMENT, UTENSIL
– handle or binding of shock-absorbing material on a hammer or other tool WITHE
– shaft of a tool, such as the mounting of a dentist's drill MANDREL
– sharp part of a tool, such as the blade of a knife or plane BIT
– tongue or prong at the foot of the blade of a knife, tool, or the like for embedding into the handle SHANK, TANG
tooth See illustration, page 527, and also **teeth**, **mouth**
– tooth-like projection, as on a gearwheel DENT, DENTATION, DENTICLE
– tooth or notch, as on a saw or the edge of a leaf SERRATION
– tooth-shaped DENTIFORM
– tooth socket in the jawbone ALVEOLUS
– tooth that is broken, protruding, or out of line SNAGGLETOOTH
– appear by breaking through the gum, as an emerging tooth does ERUPT
– belt-like band or surrounding structure, such as the ridge around the base of a tooth CINGULUM
– broad, flat back tooth, for grinding MOLAR
– long, pointed tooth, as of a snake or bat FANG
– pointed tooth beside a front tooth, for biting and tearing CANINE, EYETOOTH, LANIARY
– pull out something, such as a tooth, by force EXTRACT
– referring to a tooth jammed against another tooth, and unable to emerge normally IMPACTED
– sharp front tooth, for biting off INCISOR
– side tooth, for grinding, having two crests BICUSPID, PREMOLAR
-tooth- DENT-, DENTI-, -ODON-
tooth decay DENTAL CARIES
– addition of fluorine compounds to the public water supply as a measure to reduce tooth decay FLUORIDATION
toothed bar that meshes with a gearwheel RACK
– toothed metal wheel or disc, as used for perforating sheets of stamps or pressing dots onto an engraving plate ROULETTE
– toothed projection on a wheel or cylinder, as to engage a bicycle chain or the perforations on a film SPROCKET
– toothed wheel COG, COGWHEEL
– toothed wheel or bar engaged by a hinged catch to allow movement in one direction only RATCHET
toothpaste or tooth powder DENTIFRICE
top See also **best**, **good**
– top-to-toe CAP-À-PIE
– top up, refill REPLENISH
– topmost point, peak, or best or final development or achievement PINNACLE, ZENITH, APEX, APOGEE, MERIDIAN, SUMMIT, VERTEX, CREST, CROWN
– extreme, utmost, or top point, point of highest achievement ACME, NE PLUS ULTRA
– place something on top of something else, such as one film sequence over another SUPERIMPOSE

TOASTS

"Cheers!" around the world

Albania	**Gëzuar!**
Austria	**Prost!**
Belgium	**A votre santé! Gezondheid!**
Bulgaria	**Nazdrave!**
China	**Gun-bei!**
Denmark	**Skål!**
Finland	**Kippis! Skål! Hölkyn kölkyn!**
France	**A votre santé!**
Germany	**Prosit! Prost! Zum wohl!**
Greece	**Stin yia ssas!**
Hong Kong	**Yum-sing!**
Ireland	**Slàinte!**
Israel	**L'chaim!**
Italy	**Salute! Ciao!**
Japan	**Kam pai!**
Mexico	**Salud!**
Netherlands	**Proost! Santjes!**
Norway	**Skål!**
Poland	**Na zdrowie!**
Portugal	**Saúde!**
Romania	**Noroc!**
Scotland	**Slàinte mhath!**
South Africa	**Geluk! Gesondheid!**
Spain	**Salud!**
Sweden	**Skål!**
Switzerland	**Prost! Zum wohl! Santé! Salute!**
Thailand	**Chokdee!**
Turkey	**Şerefe!**
USSR	**Na zdorovye!**
Wales	**Iechyd da!**
Yugoslavia	**Zieili!**

– reach or be at the top of SURMOUNT
– spinning top, shaped like an hourglass, that is thrown and caught on a cord held between the hands DIABOLO
– spinning top spun with the fingers, sometimes having four sides with letters or numbers on for use in games TEETOTUM

top- ACRO-

torch formerly used to light the way in dark streets LINK
– torch of former times, in the form of a pole-mounted cup burning oil or pitch CRESSET
– flaming torch FLAMBEAU

torment See also **tease**
– torment or tease by parading but withholding something desirable TANTALISE
– torment or treat cruelly HARROW

tortoise – tortoise-like reptile living in fresh water TERRAPIN
– tortoise's shell CARAPACE
– adjective for a tortoise or turtle CHELONIAN, TESTUDINAL
– bony plate covering the chest of a tortoise or turtle BREASTPLATE, PLASTRON

torture in which the victim is beaten on the soles of the feet BASTINADO
– torture in which the victim is hoisted on a rope and then dropped with a jerk STRAPPADO
– instrument of torture consisting of a coffin-like case lined with iron spikes, into which the victim was locked IRON MAIDEN
– instrument of torture for squeezing the fingers and thumbs PILLIWINKS
– instruments of torture of various kinds RACK, WHEEL, BOOT, THUMBSCREW

tot, small quantity of whisky or other drink DRAM, NIP, SLUG
– valved tap on an inverted bottle, releasing a tot measure OPTIC

total, or the addition process by which it is reached SUMMATION
– total, whole amount, sum of many parts AGGREGATE

total- HOL-, HOLO-

totally, altogether, entirely IN TOTO

tote – U.S. term for the tote or a totalisator machine PARI-MUTUEL

touch, join, be positioned next to, as pieces of land might ABUT
– touch, without intersecting, as two curves in geometry might OSCULATE
– touch or enter where one should not IMPINGE
– touch or handle a body part as an aid to diagnosis or as a therapy MANIPULATE, PALPATE
– touch or stroke lovingly or affectionately CARESS, FONDLE
– apparent ability to know facts about people or events by touching objects associated with them PSYCHOMETRY
– perceptible to the touch, capable of being felt PALPABLE, TANGIBLE
– relating to the sense of touch TACTILE, TACTUAL

touching, bordering, neighbouring, alongside CONTIGUOUS, ADJACENT, ABUTTING, JUXTAPOSED
– touching or affecting POIGNANT
– touching without intersecting, as a line in geometry might TANGENT

touchy, easily offended UMBRAGEOUS

tough, austerely self-disciplined, having great fortitude SPARTAN
– tough, bold, and stout-hearted, as a warrior might be DOUGHTY
– tough, buoyant, able to recover quickly from misfortune or illness RESILIENT
– tough, spirited, and frisky, as a terrier might be FEISTY
– tough, unyielding, and inflexible, or firm of purpose or opinion ADAMANT, ADAMANTINE
– tough and firm against pressure or attack RESISTANT
– tough and hard to chew, as meat might be FIBROUS
– tough and long-lasting DURABLE, ENDURING
– tough and uncompromising, unsentimentally practical HARD-BITTEN, HARD-NOSED
– tough-minded and able to withstand grief, disappointment, or pain STOICAL
– tough-minded and impassive, showing little emotion STOLID

tour guide on sightseeing expeditions CICERONE
– tour guide or interpreter in the Middle East formerly DRAGOMAN
– tour in which an electioneering politician briefly visits a series of small towns WHISTLE-STOP TOUR
– tour organiser accompanying a holiday party COURIER

TOOLS

AGRICULTURAL AND GARDENING TOOLS

billhook
cant hook
croze
dibber
draw hoe
Dutch hoe
flail
grub hoe
mattock
maul
pitchfork
sickle

BLACKSMITH'S TOOLS

anvil
drift
flatter
fuller
hardy
leaf hammer
mandrel
sett hammer
swage

DRILLING TOOLS

auger
broach
countersink bit
gimlet
reamer
twist drill
wimble

CUTTING TOOLS

boaster
bolster chisel
cold chisel
cleaver
firmer chisel
gouge
paring chisel
router
scorper
waster

HAMMERS AND MALLETS

ball-pein hammer
beetle mallet
bush hammer
claw hammer
club hammer
cross-pein hammer
joiner's mallet
sledgehammer
soft-faced hammer
soft-faced mallet
tack hammer

MARKING AND MEASURING TOOLS

callipers
centre punch
mitre box
mitre square
mortise gauge
pinking wheel
plumb rule
scriber
T-square

SAWS

backsaw, tenon saw
band saw
bucksaw
chain saw
circular saw
compass saw
coping saw
flooring saw
fret saw
gent's saw, dovetail saw
hacksaw
jigsaw
log saw
padsaw
panel saw
pitsaw
ripsaw
scroll saw

SHAPING TOOLS

adze
block plane
file
jack plane
rasp
spokeshave
smoothing plane

SPANNERS AND WRENCHES

Allen key
box spanner
bulldogs
pipe wrench
ring spanner
socket spanner
stillson wrench
strap wrench
torque wrench
molegrip wrench

THATCHER'S TOOLS

eaves hook
eaves knife
long straw rake
reed knife
reed leggett
shearing hook
spar hook
yoke

WHEELWRIGHT'S TOOLS

auger
bruzz
boxing engine
felloe pattern
jarvis
samson
traveller

– touring group of entertainers TROUPE
– "touring car", such as a sports car GRAN TURISMO, GT

tourist – dialect term for a tourist GROCKLE

tournament arena, as for chivalric combat LISTS
– tournament in medieval times, in which knights took part in horseraces and riding displays CAROUSEL
– tournament of duels between knights, with lances on horseback JOUSTS, TILTING MATCH

tow – ring on a vehicle, into which a towing hook is inserted LUNETTE
– upright pivot pin, as on a rudder or towing vehicle PINTLE

-towards- AD-, EPI-, -PROS-, -PETAL

towelling or similar absorbent fabric with uncut loops on both sides TERRY

tower, mobile or makeshift, used in attacking castle walls TURRET, BELFRY
– tower formerly guarding the coast in various European countries MARTELLO TOWER
– tower or parapet in a medieval fortification BRATTICE
– freestanding bell tower CAMPANILE
– pyramid-shaped temple tower in ancient Babylon ZIGGURAT
– round, fortified tower built in ancient times in Scotland BROCH
– small tower TURRET
– small turret jutting from a wall or tower BARTIZAN
– tall cylindrical tower for storing grain or fodder SILO
– tall slender tower of a mosque, from which the muezzin summons the faithful to prayer MINARET

town See also **city**
– town, city, or self-governing community MUNICIPALITY
– town, outside a larger city, from which many people commute to work DORMITORY TOWN
– town area, often closed to traffic, set apart for pedestrians and shopping PRECINCT
– town crier's call for attention OYEZ
– town-dweller OPPIDAN, BURGESS
– town hall in Germany RATHAUS
– town or borough in Scotland BURGH
– adjective for a town MUNICIPAL, URBAN
– senior member of a town council ALDERMAN

township in South Africa for black or coloured residents LOCATION

toy consisting of a card or disc that is spun or twirled to produce a merged image of the partial words or pictures on either side THAUMATROPE
– toy consisting of an hourglass-shaped spinning top that is thrown and caught on a cord held between the hands DIABOLO
– toy-like ornament with moving parts, usually of shiny metal, as found on office desktops EXECUTIVE TOY
– toy spinning top spun with the fingers TEETOTUM
– toy with a rounded weighted base that always rights itself after being rocked or pushed down TUMBLER
– popular toys of various kinds for entertainment or exercise HULA-HOOP, FRISBEE, KALEIDOSCOPE, KAZOO, RUBIK'S CUBE, POGO STICK
– spinning toy of various kinds WHIRLIGIG

trace, small amount SEMBLANCE, MODICUM, SCINTILLA, IOTA, JOT, TITTLE
– traces left by something that has disappeared VESTIGES

track of visible foam or waves in water, as left by a ship WAKE
– track or trail, especially of a wild animal SPOOR, SLOT

trade, occupation, career VOCATION
– trade and mutual-aid association, especially of merchants or craftsmen in medieval times GUILD
– trade association or guild in the City of London LIVERY COMPANY
– trade restrictions imposed to protect a country's industries against competition from abroad PROTECTIONISM
– trade restrictions or similar measures imposed on a nation to put pressure on it to change its policies SANCTIONS
– trade through direct exchange of goods and services, without using money BARTER
– adjective for trade or commerce MERCANTILE
– practise or engage in one's trade PLY
– prohibition, as of foreign merchant ships, of arms trading, or of all trade EMBARGO

trade union federation in the U.S. AFL-CIO
– trade-union member elected by

tooth

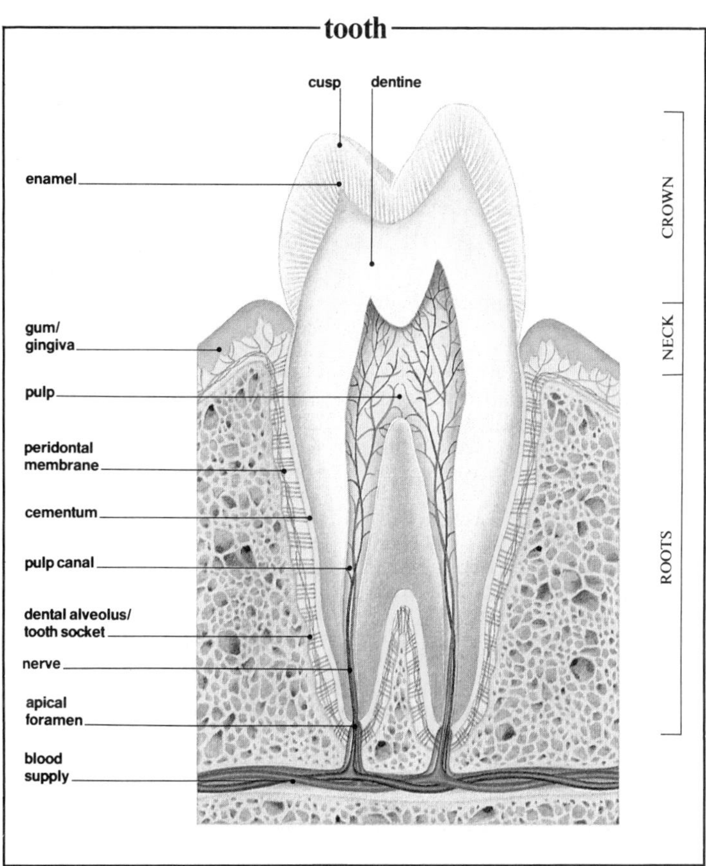

fellow workers, typically in a factory, as their spokesman and representative SHOP STEWARD
– trade union open to all the different types of workers in an industry INDUSTRIAL UNION, VERTICAL UNION
– trade union restricted to people engaged in the same trade or work CRAFT UNION, HORIZONTAL UNION
– business or factory contracted to employ only members of a particular trade union CLOSED SHOP
– business or factory employing workers without regard to trade union membership OPEN SHOP
– business or factory whose employees are required to join a specific trade union after being hired UNION SHOP
– clearly defined separation of the tasks done by various trade union members DEMARCATION
– employee who works on while his trade union has ordered a strike BLACKLEG, SCAB

trademark, emblem, or symbol of a company LOGO, LOGOTYPE
– protected by a trademark, as a medicine might be PROPRIETARY, PATENT

trader, pedlar, or supplier in former times CHAPMAN, CHANDLER

trading centre where goods are held for re-export ENTREPÔT
– trading centre, marketplace, exchange RIALTO

traffic detour DIVERSION
– traffic hold-up caused by an obstruction or narrow stretch of road, or the point of this hold-up BOTTLENECK
– traffic island REFUGE
– traffic jam CONGESTION, GRIDLOCK
– traffic junction, painted with criss-crossed yellow lines, that vehicles must not enter if their exit is not clear BOX JUNCTION
– post on a traffic island, on the pavement to prevent parking, or the like BOLLARD
– road system or sectioned-off area, permitting traffic to move in both directions along one carriageway of a motorway, as during road repairs CONTRAFLOW

tragedy See also **drama**
– avenging justice, as in Greek tragedy NEMESIS
– excessive pride leading to downfalls, as in Greek tragedy HUBRIS
– "fatal flaw" in the character of a hero, which leads to his downfall, as in Greek tragedy HAMARTIA
– moment of recognition or insight by the hero, as at the climax of a Greek tragedy ANAGNORISIS
– purgation of the emotions through pity and fear, as when watching a tragic drama CATHARSIS
– sudden change of fortune, usually from prosperity to ruin, as at the climax of a Greek tragedy PERIPETEIA

trail or tracks, especially of a wild animal SPOOR, SLOT

trailer – link bolt or hook, as at the back of a car, to which a trailer, caravan, or the like is attached PINTLE

train, aeroplane, or the like carrying no passengers DEADHEAD
– train carriage of a comfortable and spacious design PULLMAN
– train carriage's enclosed entrance area VESTIBULE
– train carriages, wagons, and locomotives ROLLING STOCK
– train compartment at the end of a continental railway carriage, with seats on one side only COUPÉ
– train depot in which carriages, engines, and so on are joined up MARSHALLING YARD
– train running on a single rail, often on an elevated track MONORAIL TRAIN
– train's undercarriage with swivelling wheels for negotiating bends BOGIE
– bed or folding bunk in a train carriage COUCHETTE
– bumper or grid in front of a train to clear the track FENDER, COWCATCHER
– cord or chain in a railway carriage that a passenger can pull in an emergency to stop the train COMMUNICATION CORD
– device for linking any two carriages or trucks of a train COUPLING, DRAWBAR
– frame on the roof of an electric train engine, tram, or trolleybus, collecting current from an overhead wire PANTOGRAPH
– goods truck on a train, that unloads through its floor HOPPER
– guard's van on U.S. trains, with eating and sleeping facilities for the crew CABOOSE
– low, open goods wagon pulled by a train GONDOLA
– overhead cable for an electric train or trolleybus CATENARY
– safety switch or lever, as on a train, that causes mechanical shutdown if released by the operator DEAD MAN'S HANDLE
– shock-absorbing or cushion-like device, such as the steel pads between train carriages BUFFER
– sleeping car, especially on a continental train WAGON-LIT
– truck for transporting rock, coal, or the like, pulled by a train BOGIE
– wagon behind a steam-train's locomotive, carrying fuel and water TENDER

trainee, contracted worker receiving instruction in a trade APPRENTICE
– trainee officer in the police or armed forces CADET
– contracted as a trainee, apprenticed ARTICLED

training, upbringing NURTURE
– training device consisting of a model, machine, or system reproducing actual conditions, such as a model flight deck for training pilots SIMULATOR
– training in a particular trade or skill that is to be the basis of a career VOCATIONAL TRAINING

traitor, deserter, faithless or disloyal person RECREANT, TURNCOAT
– traitor, especially one serving as the puppet leader of an occupying foreign power QUISLING
– traitor, person who abandons his religion, allegiances, or loyalties RENEGADE, APOSTATE
– traitor, person who betrays a partner DOUBLE-CROSSER
– traitor cooperating with enemy forces occupying his country COLLABORATIONIST, COLLABORATOR
– traitor or rebel who works secretly to undermine the government SUBVERSIVE
– traitor or refugee who abandons his country for that of an enemy DEFECTOR
– traitor or secret agent who deliberately incites people to illegal acts to entrap them AGENT PROVOCATEUR
– traitor or spy who infiltrates an organisation to betray its secrets MOLE, PLANT
– traitorous, treacherous, faithless PERFIDIOUS
– informer, police spy, traitor in the criminal world who betrays associates to the police GRASS, NARK, STOOL PIGEON
– person considered a traitor or collaborator through his undue acceptance of or cooperation with his oppressors UNCLE TOM

tram – device collecting electric current transmitted to a tram, as from an overhead wire TROLLEY
– frame on the roof of an electric train engine, tram, or trolleybus, collecting current from an overhead wire PANTOGRAPH
– overhead cable for a tram, electric railway, or the like CATENARY
– U.S. term for a tram TROLLEY,

TROLLEY CAR, STREETCAR
tramp, down-and-out, bum DERELICT
– tramp, rogue, thief, or adventurer PICARO, PICAROON
– tramp or drifter, especially in the U.S. HOBO
– tramp or itinerant labourer in Australia SWAGMAN
– tramp who begs for money on U.S. streets PANHANDLER
– former Scottish term for a tramp or beggar GANGREL
– wandering tramp or beggar, drifter VAGRANT, VAGABOND
tranquilliser, medical drug with a soothing or calming effect SEDATIVE, ATARACTIC
– tranquilliser or sleeping pill of a common synthetic make NITRAZEPAM, DIAZEPAM
– tranquillising or pain-killing substance secreted by the brain ENDORPHIN
transfer a design by loosely shading or colouring its reverse side, and then tracing it onto a surface or paper underneath CALK
– transfer an estate, sovereignty, or the like, as by a will DEMISE
– transfer of a teacher, military officer, or the like for temporary duty elsewhere SECONDMENT
– transfer of property, interests, or rights in law ASSIGNMENT
– transfer of the ownership of property by means of a legal document CONVEYANCE
– U.S. term for a transfer, the sticky design rubbed onto paper or tiles by children DECAL, DECALCOMANIA
transform See **change**, **turn**
transformation, as of a caterpillar into a butterfly METAMORPHOSIS
– transformation or change of a spectacular kind TRANSFIGURATION, TRANSMOGRIFICATION
translate, as formerly from a Latin text, usually aloud, as a classroom exercise CONSTRUE
– translate in another language or form RENDER
translation, explanatory note, or commentary, as in the margin of a manuscript or text GLOSS
– translation shown above the stage or screen SURTITLE
– insert a new soundtrack into a film, especially a translation of the dialogue DUB
– word for word, as a translation might be LITERAL, VERBATIM
translucent, as some fine fabrics are DIAPHANOUS, SHEER, GOSSAMER
transmigration of the soul METEMPSYCHOSIS
transmit something, such as a radio-wave, through a given medium PROPAGATE
transparent, very clear or pure CRYSTALLINE, PELLUCID, LIMPID
– transparent or translucent, as some fine fabrics are DIAPHANOUS, SHEER, GOSSAMER
– transparent paper like wrapping material CELLOPHANE
– allowing the passage of light, as frosted glass does, but only in a diffused form, unlike transparent glass TRANSLUCENT
– preventing the passage of light, not transparent OPAQUE
transplant of animal tissue to man ZOOPLASTY
– fail to accept a tissue graft or transplanted organ REJECT
– person who provides an organ for transplant DONOR
– person who receives a transplanted organ DONEE, RECIPIENT
– referring to medical drugs used to prevent rejection of a transplanted organ IMMUNOSUPPRESSIVE
transport or movement of goods or people from place to place TRANSIT, CONVEYANCE
– transportation or carrying, as of heavy supplies, or the cost of it PORTAGE
– transporting of goods as a business, or the charge for it HAULAGE
– organising of any complicated project, especially one involving transport LOGISTICS
transposing of letters within a word, as in the development of *bird* from Old English *brid* METATHESIS
transvestism and female behaviour by a man EONISM
trap See also **trick**
– trap, capture by trickery ENSNARE
– trap, enclosure, or the like, into which birds or game can be lured DECOY
– trap, entice, tempt or lead astray by flattery or promises INVEIGLE
– trap, trick, dodge, devious scheme to gain the upper hand STRATAGEM, SUBTERFUGE
– trap birds by means of a sticky substance spread on branches or twigs LIME
– trap for catching animals GIN
– trap for large animals, in which a heavy weight crushes the quarry DEADFALL
– trap for small animals or birds, typically a noose attached to a bent twig or branch SPRINGE
– intended as a trap, treacherous, as a sneaky argument might be INSIDIOUS
– things in which one is trapped, caught, or confined TOILS
trappings or symbols, especially of royalty REGALIA
travel across or through TRAVERSE
– travel in stages or relays POST
– travel or wander far and wide, usually on foot PEREGRINATE
– travel slowly and laboriously, specifically by ox-wagon TREK
– travels, typically long and far, and often by foot PEREGRINATIONS, PILGRIMAGE
– person who regularly travels a considerable distance between home and work COMMUTER
– planned route for one's travels ITINERARY
– yearning for travel or urge to travel, especially in foreign countries WANDERLUST
travel agent that sells cut-price air tickets BUCKET SHOP
traveller, usually on foot WAYFARER
– traveller who journeys far and wide and frequently JETSETTER, GLOBETROTTER
– travellers in a group or convoy across a desert CARAVAN
travelling, caravan-dwelling scrap-metal dealer, often taken for a Gypsy DIDICOY, TINKER
– travelling from place to place, as some judges, labourers, or preachers ITINERANT, MIGRANT
– travelling in disguise or under a false name INCOGNITO
– travelling musician in the Middle Ages MINSTREL, TROUBADOUR, TROUVÈRE, JONGLEUR
– travelling salesman who regularly collects payments for a hire-purchase company TALLYMAN
– travelling scholar or student in the Middle Ages GOLIARD
– employed in a number of places, especially schools, and travelling between them PERIPATETIC
– relating to travelling VIATIC
tray, with a handle underneath, for carrying cement or plaster HAWK
– tray for bricks or mortar, carried over the shoulder on a pole HOD
– tray or platter, often made of silver, for serving food, presenting visiting cards, or the like SALVER, WAITER
– circular, revolving tray, used to hold food on a dining table DUMB WAITER, LAZY SUSAN
– small tray, sometimes on wheels, for a wine bottle, decanter, or the like COASTER
treacherous See **traitor**
– treacherous, disloyal, faithless TREASONOUS, PERFIDIOUS
– treacherously and subtly harmful INSIDIOUS

treachery, disloyalty, breach of trust PERFIDY
treason See also **traitor**
- treason or other offence committed against a sovereign power LESE MAJESTY
- accuse of treason IMPEACH
treasure ship ARGOSY
- place where treasure is put for safekeeping REPOSITORY
treasurer, as of a municipality CHAMBERLAIN
treasury, government department that is in charge of funds or revenue EXCHEQUER
- relating to a country's treasury, finances, or tax matters FISCAL
treatment See **therapy**, **medical**, **surgical**
treaty See also **agreement**
- treaty or peace agreement CONCORD, ACCORD
- treaty restricting the increased production or deployment of nuclear weapons NON-PROLIFERATION TREATY
- acceptance of an agreement or treaty ACCESSION
- affecting or undertaken by two parties, as a treaty might be BILATERAL, BIPARTITE
- amendment to, draft for, or supplement to a treaty or other document PROTOCOL
- announce formally the rejection of a treaty DENOUNCE
- give formal approval to a treaty and thereby confirm it RATIFY
- person, party, government, or the like that has signed and is bound to a treaty SIGNATORY
tree – tree-lined terrace or garden walk in ancient Rome XYST
- tree of a cone-bearing, usually evergreen type, such as a pine or fir CONIFER
- tree or shrub of dwarf size, produced by rigorous pruning, or the traditional Japanese art of producing such plants BONSAI
- tree-shaped, resembling a tree DENDROID, DENDRIFORM, ARBORESCENT
- tree spirit, or divinity of the woods and trees, in mythology DRYAD, HAMADRYAD
- tree such as a conifer or yew, that produces naked seeds not enclosed in an ovary GYMNOSPERM
- tree trunk BOLE
- tree whose branches are cut back to the trunk to encourage new foliage POLLARD
- trees, hedge, or fence breaking the force of the wind WINDBREAK
- trees or forests of a particular region SILVA
- trees or shrubs in a thicket BOSK, BOSCAGE
- avenue or row of trees placed at regular intervals COLONNADE
- covered or shaded by trees or shrubs BOSKY
- cut a ring of bark from a tree trunk or branch to kill it or slow its growth RING-BARK, GIRDLE
- grove or small thicket of trees COPSE, SPINNEY, COPPICE
- having spread-out branches arranged in pairs, as some trees have BRACHIATE
- high, overhead cover, as of the foliage on treetops CANOPY
- knotty and twisted, as the trunk of a tree might be GNARLED
- large roundish outgrowth of wood in a tree's trunk, branches, or roots BURL
- leafy upper part of a tree CROWN
- notch made in a tree being felled, or the cut end of a felled tree KERF
- place where trees and shrubs are cultivated for exhibition or study ARBORETUM
- plant of the common group including most trees and shrubs, characterised by two embryonic seed leaves DICOTYLEDON, DICOT
- relating to, resembling , or living in trees ARBOREAL
- retaining their leaves through winter, as most coniferous trees do EVERGREEN
- shedding all their leaves at a particular time each year, as some trees do DECIDUOUS
- study or cultivation of trees ARBORICULTURE, SILVICULTURE
- trimming of trees or hedges into ornamental shapes TOPIARY
tree- DENDR-, DENDRI-, DENDRO-, ARBOR-, SILV-
trellis or frame against which a shrub or fruit tree is trained to lie flat ESPALIER
- trellis or other framework carrying climbing plants and forming a covered walk PERGOLA
trench, channel, or groove, as for drainpipes or electric wires CHASE
- defensive bank, as behind a trench, giving protection from the rear PARADOS
- platform behind a parapet or in a trench, on which soldiers stand when firing BANQUETTE
trespass, intrude slowly on the property or rights of someone else ENCROACH, INFRINGE
trial See also **court**
- trial by combat in former times WAGER OF BATTLE
- trial in the Middle Ages, in which God's judgment was allegedly secured through exposing the accused to fire, immersion in water, or the like ORDEAL
- trial or acquittal in former times in which a number of people swore to the innocence of the accused COMPURGATION
- trial or inquest in England in former times ASSIZE
- trial period, as for membership of a profession or religious order PROBATION
- held in secret or behind closed doors, as a trial or hearing might be IN CAMERA
- negotiations between the defence and prosecution prior to a criminal trial, aimed at exchanging a guilty plea in court for a reduced charge PLEA BARGAINING
- preliminary trial or inquest HEARING
- privilege of clergymen in the Middle Ages to undergo trial in a church court rather than a secular court BENEFIT OF CLERGY
- relating or referring to a judicial system where the judge in a criminal trial also acts as prosecutor INQUISITORIAL
- relating or referring to a judicial system where the judge in a criminal trial considers the case argued by a prosecutor ACCUSATORIAL
trial and error – relating to problem-solving techniques based on trial and error HEURISTIC
triangle See **geometrical shapes**
- triangle with all three sides having different lengths SCALENE TRIANGLE
- triangle with three sides of equal length EQUILATERAL TRIANGLE
- triangle with two equal sides ISOSCELES TRIANGLE
- point of intersection of the altitudes of a triangle ORTHOCENTRE
- rule relating the lengths of the sides of a right-angled triangle PYTHAGORAS' THEOREM
- side of a right-angled triangle opposite the right angle HYPOTENUSE
triangular arrangement of numbers with each number being the sum of the two numbers just above it PASCAL'S TRIANGLE
- triangular in shape DELTOID
- triangular insert of material for enlarging or reinforcing a garment, bag, or the like GUSSET
- triangular section of wall or gable above the facade of a Grecian-style building PEDIMENT
- triangular sheet of wood, metal, or plastic, used to construct cer-

tain angles and lines quickly in geometry or technical drawing SET SQUARE
tribal family group's symbol or kinship emblem, often a plant or animal TOTEM
– tribal grouping of related or intermarried clans PHRATRY
tribe- ETHN-, ETHNO-
tribute, expression of gratitude or appreciation TESTIMONIAL
trick See also **cheat**, **trap**
– trick, cheat, or defraud COZEN
– trick, crafty scheme, or the like, as to conceal or escape something SUBTERFUGE, EVASION, SHIFT
– trick, swindle, deception FLIMFLAM
– trick or ruse, especially where one appears to decline an advantage FINESSE
– trick or ruse in various sports, in which one pretends to make a particular move in order to deceive an opponent FEINT
– trick or swindle in which the victim is defrauded after his trust has been won CONFIDENCE TRICK
– trick or tactic, as in a game, to secure an advantage by deceit STRATAGEM, PLOY, ARTIFICE, MANOEUVRE
– tricking or luring of someone as by the police, into crime, danger, or the like ENTRAPMENT
– tricks, either deceitful or playful WILES
– tricks, either mischievous or fraudulent SHENANIGANS
– easily deceived, tricked, or duped CREDULOUS, GULLIBLE
– magician's manual skill and speed in performing tricks SLEIGHT OF HAND, PRESTIDIGITATION, LEGERDEMAIN
– playful or clever trick or idea, prank DODGE, STUNT, WHEEZE, WRINKLE
– victim of a trick, person fooled or used CAT'S PAW, FALL GUY, PAWN
trickery, cunning, ingenuity GUILE
– trickery, underhand or devious action SKULDUGGERY, CHICANERY, JIGGERY-POKERY
– trickery and plotting, deviousness, secret and hostile schemes MACHINATIONS
– secure or achieve by trickery or craftiness FINAGLE
trickster or con-man MOUNTEBANK, CHARLATAN
tricky, crafty, cunning FOXY, SLY, WILY
– tricky, untrustworthy DEVIOUS, SHIFTY
– ruthlessly tricky, sly, or opportunistic, especially in politics MACHIAVELLIAN
trifling or hairsplitting distinction QUIBBLE, QUIDDITY
– trifling or utterly unimportant thing BAGATELLE
trillionth- ATTO-
trimming See also **edge**
– trimming for hats, of twisted ribbon or cord TORSADE
– trimming of a flat, narrow braid forming zigzags RICKRACK
– trimming of lace or embroidery PURL
– trimming or edging, as for upholstery, consisting of a narrow tube of folded cloth, usually enveloping a cord PIPING
– trimming or fancy edging consisting of lace, braid, beadwork, or the like PASSEMENTERIE
– band of braid, lace, or embroidery forming a decorative border or trimming GALLOON
– gold or silver wire or cord used as a trimming, as on military uniforms BULLION FRINGE
– narrow and sometimes stiffened trimming used on clothes, curtains, and furniture GIMP, GUIPURE
– pleated or gathered lace or fabric used as a frilly trimming RUCHE, RUFFLE, FLOUNCE, FURBELOW
– richly embroidered border or trimming, as on clerical vestments ORPHREY
trinity – any of the three persons of the Holy Trinity HYPOSTASIS
– God's word, regarded as the second person of the Trinity LOGOS
– identical in essence or substance, as the three persons of the Trinity are sometimes interpreted as being CONSUBSTANTIAL
– relating to a trinity with an underlying unity TRIUNE
trinket, small, cheap, and flashy article or ornament BAUBLE, GEWGAW, FURBELOW
– trinket, small inexpensive ornament or toy KNICK-KNACK, NOVELTY, FOLDEROL, TSATSKE
– trinket or small curio BIBELOT
– trinkets, showy or flashy objects or oddments BRIC-A-BRAC, FRIPPERY, GAUDERY
trip or stumble FALTER
– trip or pleasure outing, especially by public officials using public funds JUNKET
– coach or large bus hired for a trip CHARABANC
– printers' annual trip, outing, or picnic, formerly on Maundy Thursday WAYZGOOSE
– roam aimlessly or go on frivolous trips GAD ABOUT, GALLIVANT
– short trip, outing, usually to a designated destination EXCURSION
– short trip, outing, spree JAUNT
trite See **cliché**
triumphant, joyous, elated JUBILANT, EXULTANT
trombone – U-shaped section of tubing in a trombone that is moved outwards and back to produce different notes SLIDE, GLIDE
troop formation of infantry in ancient Greece bearing overlapping shields PHALANX
– troop formation of stepped or offset parallel rows ECHELON
– troop formation or position subject to gunfire along its entire length ENFILADE
troops See also **soldiers**, **services**, **military**
– troops or supplies sent to support those that are already in use REINFORCEMENTS
– troops protecting the front of an army unit VANGUARD
– troops stationed as a guard in case of surprise attack PICKET
– troops stationed at a military post or outpost GARRISON
– arrangement or orderly display, as of troops ARRAY
– assemble and prepare troops, as for an emergency MOBILISE, MARSHAL, MUSTER
– assign accommodation to military officers or troops BILLET, QUARTER, CANTON
– dismiss or discharge troops from military service DEMOBILISE, DEMOB, DISBAND
– march or emerge into a more open space, as a column of troops might DEBOUCH
– reassemble troops for a renewed attack RALLY
– remove troops or military control from an area DEMILITARISE
– small selected unit of troops or ships sent on an assignment DETACHMENT
– station troops or weapons in an area, or make them ready for action DEPLOY
– withdraw troops from active conflict DISENGAGE
trophy – base block or slab, as of a column, statue, vase, or trophy PLINTH
troubadour or poet-musician of northern France in medieval times TROUVÈRE
trouble spot or explosive situation or person TINDERBOX, POWDER KEG
– make trouble, cause an uproar or disturbance RAISE CAIN
troublemaker, person who causes or

heralds trouble STORMY PETREL
troublesome, burdensome ONEROUS, TOILSOME
– troublesome, unruly, given to fighting FRACTIOUS, BELLIGERENT
trousers See **clothes**
– trousers with very narrow legs DRAINPIPES
– angle or fork formed by branches, steps, trouser legs, or the like CROTCH
– remove someone's trousers by force, as a joke, initiation rite, or the like DEBAG
– spreading or gradual widening, as of a trouser leg FLARE
truce between warring factions or armies ARMISTICE
truck See **lorry**
true, genuine, real, reliable AUTHENTIC, VERIDICAL, PUKKA, KOSHER
– true beyond question, indisputably certain VERITABLE, APODICTIC
– true by virtue of correspondence to facts in the real world rather than by the meaning of its words, as a proposition in logic might be SYNTHETIC, A POSTERIORI
– true by virtue of the meaning of its words rather than by correspondence to facts in the real world, as a proposition in logic might be ANALYTIC, A PRIORI
– true or indisputably accurate statement, belief, principle, or the like VERITY
– true to life, life-like, as a very realistic novel or painting would be NATURALISTIC
– confirm as existent, true, correct, or genuine ATTEST, CORROBORATE, SUBSTANTIATE, VALIDATE, VERIFY
trump – play a trump in card games RUFF
trumpet fanfare TUCKET
– trumpet of an early kind with a high pitch CLARION
– trumpet's high register CLARINO
– blast or flourish on a horn or trumpet TANTARA, TANTIVY
– flourish, short ceremonial tune, or the like played on trumpets or other brass instruments FANFARE
– mute for a musical instrument, as on a trumpet SORDINO
trumpeter or proclaimer at royal announcements HERALD
truncheon – U.S. term for a truncheon or bludgeon BLACKJACK, NIGHT STICK
trunk of a tree BOLE
– trunk of the body, or a sculpture of it TORSO
– elephant's trunk, or similar long flexible snout PROBOSCIS
trust – held in trust, or relating to a trust or trustee FIDUCIARY
– steal or misuse funds held in trust EMBEZZLE, DEFALCATE, PECULATE
trustee, person entrusted with something for safekeeping DEPOSITORY
truth, accurate correspondence to the facts VERACITY, FIDELITY
– truth that is universally acknowledged or self-evident AXIOM
– process of reaching the truth, as in Hegel or Socrates, by examining and exploiting contradictions DIALECTIC
– quality of appearing to be the truth VERISIMILITUDE
– straightforward, without any softening or decoration, as the plain truth is UNVARNISHED
truthful or genuine VERIDICAL
try, put to the test, evaluate or assess ASSAY
– try hard, make a conscious and earnest attempt ENDEAVOUR
– try or strive for superiority against, take on CONTEND WITH, VIE WITH
– try or try out, especially in a careful or tentative way ESSAY
– trying something out, taking a chance ON SPEC
– first try, initial venture or attempt FORAY
tube, open at both ends, into which liquid is sucked to be measured or transferred PIPETTE
– tube, pipe, or canal for the passage of fluids, as in a building, a plant, or the human body DUCT
– tube inserted into a body cavity or channel for draining or introducing fluid CATHETER, CANNULA
– tube through which an ovum passes from the ovary FALLOPIAN TUBE, OVIDUCT
– tube with a narrow throat, used for measuring fluid flow rates, or to provide suction, as in a carburettor VENTURI
– tube with a very narrow bore CAPILLARY
– tube with internal mirrors producing an endless variety of symmetrical coloured patterns when one looks through it and rotates it KALEIDOSCOPE
– diameter of the inside of a tube, the bore of a gun, or a bullet or shell CALIBRE
– sliding tube within another, as in a telescope DRAWTUBE
tuberculosis of the lungs, TB CONSUMPTION, PHTHISIS
tuck – tapered tuck made in dressmaking DART
tummy rumbling BORBORYGMUS
tumour that is dark in colour and malignant MELANOMA
– grow or spread abnormally, with fleshy outgrowths, as warts and some tumours do VEGETATE
– hard, slow-growing cancer tumour, as in the breast SCIRRHUS
– malignant cancer tumour of various kinds SARCOMA, CARCINOMA
– malignant tumour of the face, that eats away at the bone and muscle behind the lips and nose RODENT ULCER
– referring to a tumour that does not seriously threaten a person's health BENIGN
– referring to a tumour that is spreading out of control and is resistant to treatment MALIGNANT
– small growth or tumour projecting from a mucous membrane, as in the nose POLYP
– soft tumour or swelling on the lower leg of a horse WINDGALL
– wart, corn, or similar benign growth or tumour PAPILLOMA
-tumour- ONCO-, -CELE, -OMA
tuna or tunny, commonly eaten as tinned tunafish ALBACORE
tune, musical passage STRAIN, ARIA, MEASURE, AIR
– tune accompanying and identifying a particular programme or performer SIGNATURE TUNE
– tune added as counterpoint above a basic theme DESCANT
– tune added as counterpoint below a basic musical theme, usually played on a keyboard instrument, with the chords being indicated but the notes being left to the performer CONTINUO, FIGURED BASS
– tune or rhyme of a simple, catchy kind, as used in advertisements JINGLE
– tune or verse repeated regularly REFRAIN, CHORUS, BURDEN
– tunes played in succession as a single piece of music MEDLEY
– tuning fork or pitch pipe DIAPASON
– musical medley based on popular tunes QUODLIBET
tungsten WOLFRAM
tunic of chain mail HAUBERK, HABERGEON
– tunic worn by a medieval knight over his armour SURCOAT
tunnel – digging of a trench or tunnel towards or under an enemy position, fort, or the like SAP
– form a tunnel by digging EXCAVATE
turban, sash, skirt, or loincloth of cotton worn by Indian men LUNGI
turbine blade VANE
turf – legal right to dig peat or turf TURBARY

Turkish elite soldier or bodyguard in former times JANISSARY
– Turkish empire and dynasty from 1300 to 1922 OTTOMAN
– Turkish irregular cavalryman of a notoriously brutal band in the 19th century BASHIBAZOUK
– Turkish language as written in Arabic script until 1930 OSMANLI
– Turkish or Balkan brandy or plum spirits, flavoured with aniseed RAKI
– Turkish or Muslim emblem of power THE CRESCENT
– Turkish soldier, especially in the 19th century NIZAM
– Turkish viceroy in Egypt in former times KHEDIVE
– respectful term of address in Turkey, corresponding to *Mr* or *Sir* BEY, EFFENDI

turn See also **change**, **twist**
– turn, curve, bend, or fold, as of a body part FLEXURE
– turn, whirl around, spin GYRATE, ROTATE, REVOLVE
– turn aside a fencing thrust, hostile question, or the like PARRY, WARD OFF
– turn aside, differ, or depart from the norm or standard, as of a policy or route DEVIATE
– turn aside from the main route, go by a roundabout way DETOUR
– turn aside or stray from the main subject DIGRESS
– turn aside or swerve away DEFLECT, DIVERT
– turn away one's eyes, gaze, or the like AVERT
– turn in the order assigned by rotation rather than merit, or the system of assigning turns in this way BUGGINS' TURN
– turn into a new form, or the next phase, as from a caterpillar to a butterfly METAMORPHOSE
– turn into a new form, especially one that is fantastic or bizarre TRANSMOGRIFY
– turn into a new sequence or order, rearrange PERMUTE
– turn into something radically new or better, change the appearance of TRANSFIGURE
– turn or change into a new form, convert TRANSFORM, TRANSMUTE, MUTATE
– turn or direct inwards upon itself INTROVERT
– turn or fold a body part inside out or outwards EVERT
– turn or fold a body part inwards INTUSSUSCEPT, INVAGINATE
– turn or quick swerve by a rugby player JINK
– turn or rotate while fastened or linked to another part or surface PIVOT, SWIVEL
– turn or swirl, as currents might in a stream EDDY
– turn out, come to pass TRANSPIRE
– turn to bone OSSIFY
– turn to salt SALIFY
– turn to stone PETRIFY
– turn upside down or inside out INVERT
– in turn, by turns ALTERNATING
– relieve or stand in for somebody at work, by taking a turn SPELL

-turn- -TROP-, TROPO-, -TROPIC

turnabout, U-turn, reversal of attitude or policy VOLTE-FACE

turning, act of twisting, or stress produced by it TORSION
– turning, twisting, winding CONTORTED, TORTUOUS, ANFRACTUOUS
– turning, whirling, revolving VERTIGINOUS
– turning force or the technical measurement of it TORQUE
– turning or applying for help to a person or thing, such as the courts RECOURSE

turning point, beyond which there is no going back RUBICON
– turning point, crucial time or event WATERSHED
– turning point or critical point in time JUNCTURE

turnip – shaped like a turnip, as some roots are NAPIFORM

turtle – turtle's shell MAIL
– adjective for a turtle or tortoise CHELONIAN, TESTUDINAL
– bony plate on the chest of a turtle BREASTPLATE, PLASTRON
– fresh-water turtle TERRAPIN

tutorship or guardianship, or subjection to it TUTELAGE

TV See **television**

twelfth night EPIPHANY

twelve – relating to the number 12 or to a twelfth DUODECIMAL, DUODENARY

twelve- DODECA-

twelve-tone – referring or relating to the twelve-tone system of music SERIAL, DODECAPHONIC

twenty – occurring once every 20 years, or lasting or existing for 20 years VICENNIAL
– relating to or based on the number 20 VICENARY, VIGESIMAL

twenty-five pounds – slang term for £25 PONY

twice a year BIANNUAL

twice- BI-, DUO-, DI-, SEMI-

twig, flexible rod, whip, or the like SWITCH
– twig from a willow, as used in basketmaking OSIER
– twig or rope made of twigs, used for tying things together WITHE, WITHY
– twig or shoot cut for planting or grafting SLIP, SCION

twilight, dusk GLOAMING
– "twilight of the gods", destruction of the ancient gods in their battle with the forces of evil GÖTTERDÄMMERUNG
– relating to or resembling twilight, dim CREPUSCULAR

twin – twin-hulled boat CATAMARAN
– individual born singly, not as a twin or in a litter SINGLETON

twin- ZYG-, ZYGO-

twining shoot-like part serving to attach a climbing plant to its support TENDRIL

twinkling, as a cat's eye or similar gemstone is CHATOYANT
– twinkling or luminosity of a diamond or other precious stone FIRE

twins – referring to identical twins, derived from a single ovum MONOZYGOTIC
– referring to non-identical twins, derived from quite separate ova DIZYGOTIC

twist See also **turn**
– twist, interweave, or intertwine ribbons, hair, or the like BRAID, PLAIT
– twist, turn, or veer off course or to the side SLEW, SHEER
– twist, unpredictable action, as of fate QUIRK
– twist and turn as a river might MEANDER
– twist around, about, or together ENTWINE
– twist as if in pain or struggle WRITHE
– twist or curl, especially in a fingerprint WHORL
– twist or curl, such as a flourish under a signature CURLICUE
– twist or spiral shape HELIX, VOLUTE
– twist or spin on one's toe or ball of the foot PIROUETTE
– twist or weave branches or twigs, as in hedgelaying PLEACH
– twist strands, as of wool or rope, together PLY

twisted and knotty, as the trunk of a tree might be GNARLED
– twisted facial expression, as of pain or disgust GRIMACE
– twisted or bent out of shape, as a person's features might be CONTORTED, DISTORTED
– twisted or corrupted, as a sick sense of humour is PERVERTED
– twisted to one side, out of true, amiss AWRY, ASKEW
– very twisted, involved, and confused CONVOLUTED

twisting, act of turning, or stress produced by it TORSION
- twisting force or the technical measurement of it TORQUE
- twisting, spiralling water current, whirlpool MAELSTROM, VORTEX
- twisting or winding, as a mountain road might be TORTUOUS, ANFRACTUOUS

twitch or spasm, especially in the face TIC

two aces or ones at dice AMBSACE
- two-chambered, as many legislative systems are BICAMERAL
- two dots placed above a vowel, as in *naïve* DIAERESIS, UMLAUT
- two-footed animal BIPED
- two-headed BICEPHALOUS
- two in card games or dice DEUCE
- two-sided BILATERAL
- two-year period BIENNIUM
- cut or divide into two equal parts BISECT
- divided into or having two parts BIPARTITE
- division or classification into two parts, such as conflicting opinions DICHOTOMY
- in two minds AMBIVALENT
- lasting or living for two years, or occurring once every two years BIENNIAL

two- AMBI-, BI-, DI-, DUO-, ZYG-, ZYGO-

two parts- DICH-, DICHO-

twofold, double, having two separate parts BINARY, DIPLOID, DUAL

tying or binding together LIGATURE

Tynesider, or his accent or dialect GEORDIE

type See illustration
- type data or text, as onto a word processor KEYBOARD
- type or category of art, films, or the like GENRE
- complete set of printer's type of any one style FONT, FOUNT
- flat top of the shaft of a piece of printer's type, forming the base for the raised letter or character SHOULDER
- having both edges of a column of type set flush with the margins JUSTIFIED
- part of a letter or character on a piece of printer's type that extends beyond or overhangs the main shaft KERN
- printer's unit of type size, equal to one seventy-second of an inch POINT
- printer's unit of type size, equal to one sixth of an inch PICA
- raised part of a piece of printer's type, bearing the letter or character to be printed BEVEL

typeface See illustration, this page,

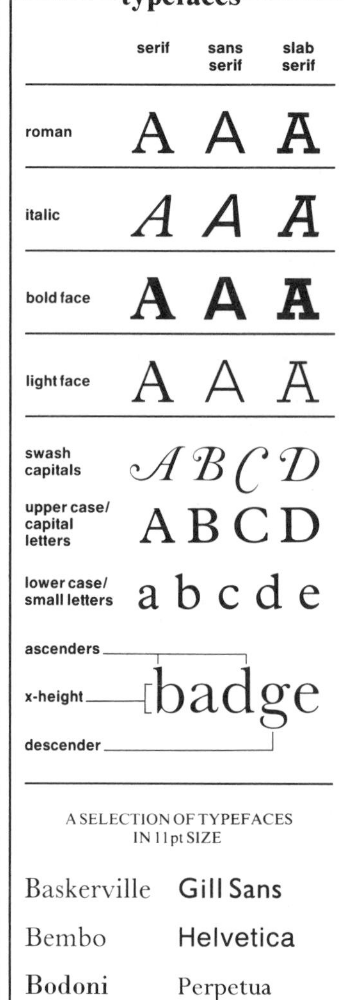

and also **scripts**

typesetter COMPOSITOR

typesetting COMPOSITION
- typesetting machine in which each letter is cast individually from hot metal MONOTYPE
- typesetting machine that casts a full line of type on a single metal slug LINOTYPE

typewriter device allowing paralysed patients to type by blowing through a tube POSSUM
- typewriter type size with 10 characters to the inch PICA
- typewriter type size with 12 characters to the inch ÉLITE
- typewriter used, as in U.S. courts, to record speech in a form of shorthand STENOTYPE
- device on a typewriter for setting automatic stops or column margins TABULATOR, TAB
- hinged bar on a typewriter for holding the paper down against the cylinder BAIL
- key on a typewriter that adjusts the mechanism to allow typing of capital letters SHIFT KEY
- roller on a typewriter CYLINDER, PLATEN
- small wheel-like device supporting the printing characters on a modern typewriter or word-processor printer DAISY WHEEL

typical, characteristic, providing good evidence of a state or event SYMPTOMATIC
- typical, conformist, or orthodox STEREOTYPICAL, IDENTIKIT
- typical, original, or perfect example or model, on which all others are or seem to be based ARCHETYPE, PROTOTYPE
- typical, regular, and predictable STATUTORY
- typical, standard, everyday, in no way special STOCK, COMMONPLACE, UNIFORM
- typical, standard, serving as an illustration EXEMPLARY, REPRESENTATIVE, TEXTBOOK, PARADIGMATIC
- typical or purest example or representative of its kind, essence EMBODIMENT, QUINTESSENCE, PERSONIFICATION, INCARNATION
- typical or representative example of a class or quality BYWORD, EPITOME, PARADIGM, TYPE
- typical pattern, standard of acceptability, or the like NORM
- typical person or thing, conforming to the standard image or attitude STEREOTYPE

typist who can type material from a tape recorder or dictating machine AUDIOTYPIST
- typist who types pre-written material COPY TYPIST
- U.S. term for a shorthand typist STENOGRAPHER

tyrant or dictator AUTOCRAT, DESPOT

tyre or ring-doughnut shape TORUS
- tyre with fabric cords running diagonally to stiffen the sidewalls CROSS-PLY TYRE
- tyre with fabric cords spread at right angles from the circumference to provide for flexible sidewalls RADIAL-PLY TYRE
- filled with or run by compressed air, as most tyres are PNEUMATIC
- release air or gas from something, such as a tyre DEFLATE
- system of cords in a tyre WARP

U

U-shaped lake formed from a river meander OXBOW, OXBOW LAKE, OXBOW CUT-OFF, MORTLAKE

U-turn, about-turn, reversal of attitude or policy VOLTE-FACE

udder, breast, or teat DUG

ugly, deformed or monstrous GROTESQUE MISBEGOTTEN, MISSHAPEN
- ugly, displeasing to one's artistic sensibilities UNAESTHETIC
- ugly, grotesquely deformed person QUASIMODO
- ugly, plain, and shabby, as a girl might be DOWDY, FRUMPISH
- ugly, short, fat, and comic-looking man PUNCHINELLO
- ugly, unattractive ILL-FAVOURED, UNSIGHTLY
- ugly feature on something BLOT, BLEMISH
- ugly through injury, deformed, or badly damaged DISFIGURED, MUTILATED
- ugly or plain, but attractive, woman or girl JOLIE LAIDE
- building, piece of furniture, or the like, noticeable because of its ugliness EYESORE, ABOMINATION
- coarsely ugly, red-faced, and bloated BLOWZY
- frighteningly ugly GRISLY, GRUESOME
- grotesquely ugly person GARGOYLE
- plain rather than actually ugly, as a woman might be HOMELY
- unattractive rather than actually ugly UNPREPOSSESSING
- very ugly, hideous, offensive to look at REPULSIVE, REPELLENT

ulcer, as in the lining of the stomach, caused or irritated by digestive juices PEPTIC ULCER
- ulcer in the first part of the intestine DUODENAL ULCER
- ulcer in the lining of the stomach GASTRIC ULCER
- form an ulcer FESTER

ultimate point, furthest possible stage or degree NE PLUS ULTRA

umbrella – informal or humorous term for a large umbrella GAMP
- light and portable sunshade or umbrella PARASOL
- metal ring or cap on the tip of a walking stick or umbrella to protect it against wear FERRULE
- roll up a flag, umbrella, or the like FURL

unable or unwilling to move INERT
- unable to act effectively, unfit for a particular task UNEQUAL
- powerless, prevented from taking action, unable to act as desired IMPOTENT

unacceptable or unwelcome person PERSONA NON GRATA

unadaptability, inflexibility PERSEVERATION

unaffected, uninfluenced IMPERVIOUS, OBLIVIOUS

unambiguous, clear, plain, not open to doubt UNEQUIVOCAL

unanimous – without any dissenting votes, with no one contradicting, virtually unanimously NEM CON

unarmed combat or self-defence techniques, such as kung-fu and karate MARTIAL ARTS

unavoidable, certain to happen, inescapable INEVITABLE, INELUCTABLE

unaware, ignorant UNWITTING

unbalanced, not perfectly regular in pattern ASYMMETRIC

unbearable, intolerable, unendurable INSUFFERABLE, INSUPPORTABLE

unbeliever, or believer in another religion INFIDEL

unbiased, fair, unprejudiced IMPARTIAL
- unbiased, uninfluenced by any emotion or personal prejudice OBJECTIVE, DISPASSIONATE, DISINTERESTED

unbreakable, as a sacred rule should be INVIOLABLE, IRREFRANGIBLE
- unbreakable, as a union or agreement might be INDISSOLUBLE

unbroken or continuous belief, course of action, or the like, usually in the face of discouragement PERSEVERANCE, STEADFASTNESS

uncalled-for, unjustified, without cause GRATUITOUS

uncaring or unfeeling INDURATE, OBDURATE

uncertain, hesitant, or shy, as a smile might be TENTATIVE
- uncertain, hesitant, stumbling, as someone's speech might be FALTERING
- uncertain, in two minds, unable to make firm decisions INDECISIVE, IRRESOLUTE
- uncertain, in two minds, undecided UNRESOLVED, VACILLATING, WAVERING
- uncertain, questionable, still unresolved, as a point under debate would be MOOT
- uncertain, questionable, widely disputed CONTROVERSIAL
- uncertain, uncommitted, lukewarm, sitting on the fence LAODICEAN
- uncertain, undecided, sceptical, or doubtful DUBIOUS
- uncertain in attitude, holding simultaneously opposing views about one thing AMBIVALENT
- of uncertain length, size, or number, open-ended INDEFINITE, INDETERMINATE
- of uncertain meaning, open to various interpretations, as a puzzling answer might be AMBIGUOUS, EQUIVOCAL
- of uncertain size or number, usually because very large or numerous INCALCULABLE
- of uncertain outcome, failing to settle an issue decisively, as a battle might be INCONCLUSIVE

uncertainty – state of uncertainty or perplexity DILEMMA, QUANDARY

unchanging See also **stubborn**, **regular**
- unchanging, addicted by long use, as a drinker or liar might be CHRONIC, COMPULSIVE, HABITUAL, CONFIRMED, INVETERATE
- unchanging, always the same, constant INVARIABLE
- unchanging, immobile, stable, not fluctuating or decomposing readily STABILE
- unchanging, inflexible, thoroughgoing, especially in political views DYED-IN-THE-WOOL
- unchanging, motionless, or producing no movement or change STATIC, STATIONARY
- unchanging, reliable, persevering, and firm of purpose STEADFAST, STAUNCH, UNFALTERING, UNDEVIATING, RESOLUTE
- unchanging, unageing, fixed forever IMMUTABLE
- unchanging, unbroken and unpleasant, as boredom might be UNRELIEVED

– unchanging, unrepentantly or obstinately prejudiced in social attitudes UNREGENERATE, UNRECONSTRUCTED, UNREFORMED
uncle – relating to or resembling an uncle AVUNCULAR
unclear, imprecise, vague ELUSIVE, INTANGIBLE
uncoded, in ordinary language, not put in code EN CLAIR
uncombed or untidy, as hair might be UNKEMPT, DISHEVELLED, UNGROOMED, TOUSLED
uncomfortable, forced, or inhibited manner or situation CONSTRAINT
uncommunicative, reserved, silent TACITURN
unconcerned about problems, carefree NONCHALANT, INSOUCIANT, DEBONAIR
unconnected, separate, individual, distinct DISCRETE
unconquerable INDOMITABLE
unconscious, as secret fears or painful memories might be REPRESSED
– unconscious, as through injury or disease COMATOSE
– unconscious, having no feeling INSENSATE, INSENSIBLE
– unconscious, mechanical, or spontaneous as sneezes, knee-jerks, or similar responses are REFLEX, INVOLUNTARY
– unconscious or unaware OBLIVIOUS, UNMINDFUL
unconsciousness or stupor induced by drugs NARCOSIS
– unconsciousness together with a rigid bodily posture, as sometimes occurs in schizophrenia CATALEPSY, CATATONIA
– state or period of deep unconsciousness, as through injury COMA
uncontrollable See **disobedient**, **stubborn**
uncontrolled in one's sexual activity or bodily functions INCONTINENT
unconventional, rakish RAFFISH, DISREPUTABLE, OUTRÉ
– unconventional or provocative person ENFANT TERRIBLE
– unconventional or unorthodox, as a lifestyle or therapy might be ALTERNATIVE
– unconventional person with artistic interests BOHEMIAN
uncooperative See **disobedient**, **stubborn**
– uncooperative, opposing others' wishes or suggestions unreasonably PERVERSE, CONTRARY, BOLSHIE
uncorrectable, unimprovable INCORRIGIBLE, IRREDEEMABLE
uncover, reveal, bring to light UNEARTH, EXHUME, DISINTER, EXPOSE
uncultivated, ploughed but left unseeded, as a field might be, to regain fertility for a season FALLOW
undecided See also **uncertain**
– undecided, still before a judge or court, and therefore not to be discussed in public SUB JUDICE
– undecided, still not settled or finished PENDING
under, below, especially beneath the Earth's surface NETHER
under- HYPO-, INFRA-, SUB-
undercarriage – capable of being drawn in or pulled back, as an aerial or aeroplane's undercarriage might be RETRACTABLE
undercoat – paint a surface with a sealer or undercoat PRIME
underdeveloped, immature, at a very early stage of development RUDIMENTARY, INCHOATE, EMBRYONIC
underground SUBTERRANEAN
– underground chamber, such as a church vault CRYPT, UNDERCROFT
– underground defensive shelter with a bank of gun emplacements above ground BUNKER
– underground galleries and tunnels with niches or ledges for graves, especially those in Rome CATACOMBS
– underground railway system, as in New York SUBWAY
– underground railway system, as in Paris MÉTRO
undergrowth, or an area covered by it BRUSHWOOD, BRUSH, MAQUIS
– overgrown area, thick with shrubs and undergrowth THICKET, BRAKE
underhand, done or carried out in a secretive or stealthy manner SURREPTITIOUS, CLANDESTINE, SUBVERSIVE, FURTIVE
– underhand, or devious action, trickery SKULDUGGERY
underlying layer, support, or principle SUBSTRATUM
– underlying motive kept concealed so as to deceive ULTERIOR MOTIVE
undermine a castle wall or other fortification, as by tunnelling beneath it SAP
– enter secretly in order to destroy or undermine INFILTRATE
– secret undermining or the attempted destruction of a government or political system SUBVERSION
underside of an arch, staircase, or other overhang SOFFIT
understand, comprehend, take in APPREHEND, COMPASS, ENCOMPASS
– understand, form a mental picture of, be able to grasp CONCEIVE, PERCEIVE, DISCERN
– absorb mentally, take in, come to understand DIGEST
– penetrate to the meaning of, come to understand FATHOM
understandable INTELLIGIBLE, COMPREHENSIBLE
– understandable, easy to follow, straightforward ACCESSIBLE
– easily understandable, very clear LUCID, LUMINOUS
understanding, acute, INSIGHTFUL, DISCERNING, PERSPICACIOUS, PERCEPTIVE, SAGACIOUS
– understanding, opinions, or principles LIGHTS
– understanding of another that is so deep that one seems to enter into or share his feelings EMPATHY
– understanding or awareness PERCEPTION, COGNISANCE, DISCERNMENT, SAVVY
– understanding or informal agreement between countries or powers ENTENTE CORDIALE
– understanding relationship of mutual trust and emotional sympathy RAPPORT
understood, implied, unspoken, as an informal agreement might be TACIT, IMPLICIT
undertaker, funeral director in the U.S. MORTICIAN
– undertaker's room where bodies are kept prior to burial CHAPEL OF REST
undertaking or project that may be risky or dangerous VENTURE, ENTERPRISE
undertone – softly, in an undertone, under one's breath SOTTO VOCE
underwater breathing apparatus, using compressed air cylinders AQUALUNG, SCUBA
– underwater chamber from which construction or repair work is done CAISSON
– underwater research vessel for deep-sea exploration, in the form of a submarine with a large round observation cabin on the underside BATHYSCAPH
– underwater vessel, open at the bottom, supplied with pressurised air DIVING BELL
– person living and working in an underwater building AQUANAUT
underwear and nightwear for women LINGERIE
underworld in classical mythology HADES, DIS
– relating or referring to the underworld and its spirits and gods CHTHONIC
undeveloped, immature, at a very early stage of development RUDIMENTARY, EMBRYONIC, INCHOATE
undignified, unsuitable, or unbecoming INFRA DIG
undisciplined, rebellious, extremely

disobedient DISAFFECTED, UNRULY, MUTINOUS, INTRACTABLE, REFRACTORY, RECALCITRANT
undo- DE-
undoubtedly INDUBITABLY
undress DISROBE, DOFF
- undressed or partially dressed DISHABILLE, DÉSHABILLÉ

unease or depression MALAISE, ANGST
uneasy, forced, or inhibited manner or situation CONSTRAINT
uneatable INEDIBLE
uneducated or illiterate UNLETTERED
unemotional See **calm**
- unemotional, detached, and unbiased DISPASSIONATE, OBJECTIVE, IMPARTIAL, DISINTERESTED
- unemotional, expressionless, unexcitable PHLEGMATIC, IMPASSIVE, INSCRUTABLE, UNDEMONSTRATIVE, APATHETIC
- unemotional, unaffected by either pleasure or pain STOICAL, STOLID, IMPERVIOUS

unemployed as a result of the elimination of one's job REDUNDANT, RETRENCHED
unenthusiastic, half-hearted TEPID, LUKEWARM, LAODICEAN
- unenthusiastic, lazy, indifferent LACKADAISICAL, LANGUID

unequal- ANISO-
unerasable, permanent INDELIBLE, INERADICABLE, INGRAINED
unexcitable See **calm**
unexciting See **dull**
unexpected See also **surprise**
- unexpected, chance, accidental ADVENTITIOUS, FORTUITOUS
- unexpected, inappropriate, out of place INCONGRUOUS, DISCORDANT, DISPARATE
- unexpected discovery or bright new idea TROUVAILLE
- unexpectedly, unplanned UNAWARES
- appear, occur, or interrupt unexpectedly INTERVENE
- occur as something unexpected or unnecessary SUPERVENE
- sudden and unexpected UNFORESEEN, UNANNOUNCED
- tendency to make lucky discoveries unexpectedly or by accident SERENDIPITY

unexplored country or subject matter TERRA INCOGNITA
unfair, unjustified, as a conclusion might be UNWARRANTED
- unfair and prejudiced attitudes or actions, as on the basis of race or sex DISCRIMINATION
- unfair in a thoughtless or arrogant way HIGH-HANDED
- unfair or offensive, as a discriminatory comparison would be INVIDIOUS
- unfairly distributed or allocated, out of proportion, as a share might be DISPROPORTIONATE
- unfairly favouring one side over another, biased PARTIAL
- unfairness, as due to a biased or inconsistent law INEQUITY

unfaithful husband PHILANDERER
- unfaithful or wayward, as a husband or wife might be ERRANT
- unfaithfulness, especially adultery INFIDELITY
- husband of an unfaithful woman CUCKOLD
- husband of an unfaithful woman, who knows about and accepts her infidelity WITTOL

unfavourable or disapproving, as a particular sense or use of a word might be PEJORATIVE, DISPARAGING, DEPRECIATORY
- unfavourable to something or someone ADVERSE, INIMICAL

unfavourable- DYS-
unfeeling or uncaring INDURATE
unfinished, still not settled or confirmed PENDING
unfold, unroll, spread out UNFURL
unforced, unprompted, as laughter might be SPONTANEOUS
unforgettable or enduring, as an impression might be INDELIBLE, INERADICABLE, INGRAINED
unfortunate See **unlucky**
- unfortunate, inappropriate, or unsuitable INFELICITOUS

unfriendly, distant, or stand-offish ALOOF, UNAPPROACHABLE
- unfriendly, threatening, or discouraging access or progress FORBIDDING
- unfriendly or hostile to something or someone ANTAGONISTIC, INIMICAL
- unfriendly or separated through having been antagonised ALIENATED, ESTRANGED
- unfriendly to outsiders, forming closed groups CLANNISH, EXCLUSIVE, CLIQUISH

ungrammatical or incorrect use of a word, phrase, or construction BARBARISM, SOLECISM, CATACHRESIS
ungrateful person INGRATE
unhappy See also **sad**
- unhappy, depressed, pessimistic IN THE DOLDRUMS
- unhappy, discontented, driven to a feeling of disloyalty DISAFFECTED, ALIENATED, ANTAGONISED, ESTRANGED
- unhappy, discontented, or moody as a result of being thwarted DISGRUNTLED
- unhappy, ill-chosen, inappropriate, as a flippant remark might be INEPT, INFELICITOUS
- unhappy or distressed at some development, uneasy, disturbed DISQUIETED, DISMAYED
- be unhappy, fret REPINE, RUE, BEMOAN, LAMENT

unharmed, completely uninjured UNSCATHED
unhealthy condition MALADY, MORBIDITY, MALAISE
uniform and unbudgeable, as a large bureaucracy might be MONOLITHIC
- uniform of a group of servants, guild members, or the like LIVERY
- uniform or similar in kind or structure HOMOGENEOUS
- braid, fringed strap, or the like worn on the shoulder, as on a military uniform EPAULETTE, AIGUILLETTE
- civilian clothing, as distinct from one's uniform MUFTI, CIVVIES
- identifying emblem, marking, or the like on a military uniform or vehicle FLASH
- looped braid or cord used as a fastening, as formerly on a military uniform FROG

unify See **join**
- unifying, or promoting or relating to unity, specifically among the world's various churches ECUMENICAL
- unified pattern or structure that is more than the sum of its parts GESTALT

unimportant See also **secondary**
- unimportant, inapplicable, or unrelated IRRELEVANT, IMMATERIAL
- unimportant, lightweight, having little effect INCONSEQUENTIAL, INSIGNIFICANT
- unimportant, minor, beside the point, not central to the issue at hand MARGINAL, INCIDENTAL, PERIPHERAL
- unimportant, not crucial or needed DISPENSABLE, EXPENDABLE
- unimportant, small-time, of secondary status MINOR-LEAGUE, SUBORDINATE
- unimportant, trifling, and petty, or foolish and silly FIDDLING, FOOTLING, PIDDLING, PIFFLING
- unimportant, unworthy of serious attention, as an argument might be FRIVOLOUS, TRIVIAL
- unimportant, very small, not worth considering, as a sum of money might be MINIMAL, NEGLIGIBLE, PALTRY, PICAYUNE
- unimportant and playful small talk, chitchat BADINAGE, BANTER, PERSIFLAGE
- unimportant and triflingly small, or invalid or inoperative, as a law might be NUGATORY
- unimportant but impertinent

person WHIPPERSNAPPER
- unimportant or worthless thing, trifle BAGATELLE
- unimportant person or thing NONENTITY, CIPHER, SMALL BEER
- unimportant person or thing taken up to make good a lack MAKEWEIGHT, PASSENGER
- event that turns out to be unimportant or disappointing after expectations have been raised NON-EVENT, DAMP SQUIB

unimpressive, disappointing, failing to come up to expectations UNDERWHELMING

uninhabited, deserted DESOLATE

uninjured, completely unharmed UNSCATHED

unintended, unconscious, reflex INVOLUNTARY

unintentionally accidentally, without meaning to INADVERTENTLY, UNWITTINGLY

uninvolved, unprejudiced, uninfluenced by emotion or personal preference DISINTERESTED, DISPASSIONATE, OBJECTIVE, IMPARTIAL, DETACHED

union See also **trade union**, **join**
- union, especially of independent political parties forming a joint government COALITION
- union, league, or association of states, companies, or the like united for a common purpose CONFEDERATION, ALLIANCE, BLOC, CONFEDERACY
- union, league, or association of states, or a country formed by it, with a fairly strong central government FEDERATION
- union, often temporary, especially of political parties with common policies ALIGNMENT
- union between countries, specifically that imposed on Austria by Nazi Germany in 1938 ANSCHLUSS
- union of business companies to finance and carry out projects jointly CONSORTIUM, SYNDICATE
- union of traders, companies, or the like to monopolise and regulate business to their common advantage CARTEL, TRUST
- union of traders, especially antique dealers, to hold auction prices down and share the profits amongst themselves RING
- complete union or fusion, as of companies or political parties, to form a new, single entity AMALGAMATION, MERGER
- secret union of subversives or conspirators CABAL

-union- -GAM-, PAN-, SYN-, SYM-, ZYG-, ZYGO-

unique, beyond comparison or without rival INCOMPARABLE, UNRIVALLED, UNPARALLELED
- unique, excelling all others PRE-EMINENT, TRANSCENDENT
- unique, impossible to equal or imitate successfully MATCHLESS, INIMITABLE, PEERLESS, NONPAREIL
- unique, individual, being the only one of its kind SUI GENERIS
- unique, unheard-of, never having happened before UNPRECEDENTED
- unique person or thing RARA AVIS
- uniquely able or beautiful person PARAGON, PHOENIX

unique- IDIO-

unit See **weights and measures**
- unit or grade in a classification system, such as a coin of a specified value DENOMINATION

unit trust – U.S. term for a unit trust MUTUAL FUND

unite See **join**

United Nations – administrative department of a large public or international organisation such as the United Nations SECRETARIAT

unity of and mutual support within a group, especially in the face of opposition SOLIDARITY

universal, general, all-embracing CATHOLIC, ECUMENICAL
- universal, general, very widespread, as a disease might be EPIDEMIC, PANDEMIC
- universal remedy, cure-all, as sought by alchemists PANACEA, ELIXIR, CATHOLICON, AZOTH
- universal solvent believed by alchemists to be possible and discoverable ALKAHEST

universe See also **astronomy**
- universe or society regarded as a single complex whole MACROCOSM
- universe or world regarded as an orderly system COSMOS
- belief that life and the universe have a purpose and guiding principle TELEOLOGY
- hypothetical elemental matter, probably neutrons, according to the big-bang theory of the creation of the universe YLEM
- person, group, or system regarded as a small representation of the whole universe MICROCOSM
- relating to the whole universe, especially as distinct from the Earth COSMIC
- running down of the energy in the universe or any other closed system ENTROPY
- study or theory of the origin and development of the universe COSMOGONY, COSMOLOGY
- theory that the universe came gradually rather than suddenly into being, by the regular creation of matter CONTINUOUS-CREATION THEORY, STEADY-STATE THEORY
- theory that the universe originated by an explosion of a small, dense mass, and is still expanding BIG BANG THEORY, SUPERDENSE THEORY

-universe- -COSM-, COSMO-

university See also **college**
- university, school, or college that one used to attend ALMA MATER
- university brochure detailing courses, charges, and the like PROSPECTUS
- university ceremony in the U.S. for conferring degrees COMMENCEMENT
- university class given by a teacher to an individual student or a very small number of students TUTORIAL, SUPERVISION
- university college's annual feast GAUDY
- university degree of the basic level, such as B.A. or B.Sc. BACCALAUREATE
- university degree ranking below a doctorate in some European countries LICENTIATE
- university department or its teaching staff FACULTY
- university education and the world of scholarship ACADEMIA
- university fraternity for academically gifted students and graduates in the U.S. PHI BETA KAPPA
- university gathering, or body of the senior members CONGREGATION
- university governor or trustee in the U.S. REGENT
- university lecturer of senior rank, just below professor READER
- university lecturer or fellow of a college DON
- university official in charge of discipline and the supervision of exams PROCTOR
- university official in charge of finances BURSAR
- university official in charge of student records REGISTRAR
- university official who organises and leads the formal processions BEADLE
- university or college admission or enrolment MATRICULATION
- university or college course of study offered to part-time students EXTENSION COURSE
- university or college education TERTIARY EDUCATION
- university or college grounds CAMPUS

– university principal or administrator VICE-CHANCELLOR, RECTOR
– university professor holding a professorship created by a royal grant REGIUS PROFESSOR
– university's graduates collectively, or an assembly or conference of them CONVOCATION
– university's representative in business matters SYNDIC
– university term, in the U.S. or Germany, typically forming half an academic year SEMESTER
– any of eight old and famous American universities, including Harvard and Yale IVY LEAGUE UNIVERSITY
– B.A. honours exam or course at Cambridge University TRIPOS
– challenge a fellow student, at Oxford or Cambridge University, to drink a large amount of beer without stopping SCONCE
– complete and be awarded a degree at a university GRADUATE
– formal academic dress, especially at Oxford University SUBFUSC
– governing body of some universities SENATE
– graduate or former student of a school, college, or university in the U.S. ALUMNUS, ALUMNA
– higher division, with four subjects, of the liberal arts studied at a medieval university QUADRIVIUM
– honorary head of a university CHANCELLOR
– lower division, with three subjects, of the liberal arts studied at a medieval university TRIVIUM
– men's club, as at a U.S. university FRATERNITY
– period of paid leave, especially for university teachers, for research or travel SABBATICAL
– permanent or secure employment status, as enjoyed by some university teachers TENURE
– put a student back a year or more at a university, as by reason of ill-health DEGRADE
– referring to non-resident students or to studies or activities outside the normal courses of a university or college EXTRAMURAL
– room in a college or university where students can purchase food BUTTERY
– send down, suspend, or expel a student temporarily from a university RUSTICATE
– sheltered intellectual retreat from everyday life, as a university is sometimes considered to be IVORY TOWER
– student in the first year at a university FRESHMAN, FRESHER
– student in the second year at a U.S. university, college, or high school SOPHOMORE
– women's or girls' club, as at a U.S. university SORORITY

unjust in a shameful way INIQUITOUS
– unjust or unfair, not even-handed INEQUITABLE
– unjustly treated by a court or official ruling AGGRIEVED

unjustified, uncalled-for, needless, as an insult might be GRATUITOUS

unknowing, unaware UNWITTING

unknown, not famous or prominent OBSCURE, INCONSPICUOUS
– unknown and unhonoured, as obscure heroes are UNSUNG
– unknown or unnamed, as an author or contributor might be ANONYMOUS, INNOMINATE
– unknown territory, unexplored country or subject-matter TERRA INCOGNITA

unlawful, illegal, against the law ILLEGITIMATE, ILLICIT

unleavened bread, eaten by Jews during the Passover MATZO

unless – taking effect, as a divorce decree might, on a specificed date unless the court is shown cause why it should not NISI

unlucky, unfortunate HAPLESS, STAR-CROSSED
– unlucky, unpromising, threatening disaster, as a sign might be FOREBODING, UNPROPITIOUS, PORTENTOUS, INAUSPICIOUS, OMINOUS
– unlucky person, thing, or force, bringing misfortune JINX

unmanly, woman-like EFFEMINATE

unmarried person, especially one who has taken a religious vow of chastity CELIBATE
– live together as an unmarried couple LIVE TALLY, COHABIT
– man or woman that someone lives with and who has some of the rights of a spouse even though not legally married COMMON-LAW HUSBAND, COMMON-LAW WIFE

unmoving See **still**

unnamed, nameless or unknown, as an author or contributor might be ANONYMOUS, INNOMINATE

unnatural See **artificial**

unnecessary, excessive, beyond the required or regular number SUPERNUMERARY, SUPERFLUOUS, REDUNDANT
– unnecessary, inessential, capable of being left out DISPENSABLE, EXPENDABLE
– unnecessary, inessential, or irrelevant, as remarks might be EXTRANEOUS
– unnecessary, undeserved, or unjustified, as some criticism might be UNCALLED FOR, UNWARRANTED, GRATUITOUS
– unnecessarily conscientious or observant, beyond the call of duty SUPEREROGATORY
– make unnecessary, as by anticipating OBVIATE, FORESTALL, PRE-EMPT

unnoticed – spreading or progressing almost unnoticed, as a disease might INSIDIOUS

unoriginal, conventional, and usually oversimplified image or opinion of someone or something STEREOTYPE
– unoriginal, copied from or based on an earlier example DERIVATIVE, IMITATIVE
– unoriginal, dull, or obvious remark PLATITUDE, COMMONPLACE, CLICHÉ, BROMIDE
– unoriginal, dull, stale, antiquated, overused HACKNEYED, TRITE, SHOPWORN, MUSTY, THREADBARE, FLOGGED TO DEATH
– unoriginal, everyday, obvious, boring PREDICTABLE, TIMEWORN

unorthodox HETERODOX
– unorthodox opinion in religion, politics, or the like HERESY, HETERODOXY
– unorthodox or independent-minded thinker or group member MAVERICK

unpaid, as a job or position might be HONORARY
– unpaid rent, subscription, or other debt ARREARS
– unpaid work willingly undertaken VOLUNTARY WORK

unplanned, by chance, accidental FORTUITOUS, ADVENTITIOUS
– unplanned, not asked for or suggested, as a compliment might be SPONTANEOUS, UNPROMPTED, UNSOLICITED
– unplanned, thrown together as a temporary expedient or substitute AD HOC, MAKESHIFT
– unplanned, unexpectedly, by surprise UNAWARES
– unplanned, without forethought, or unintentional, as manslaughter is UNPREMEDITATED
– unplanned or unprepared, as a speech might be IMPROMPTU, IMPROVISED, UNREHEARSED, EXTEMPORE, EXTEMPORANEOUS

unpleasant See also **disgusting**, **horrible**, **rude**, **spiteful**
– unpleasant, disagreeable, causing dislike or antipathy ABHORRENT, REBARBATIVE, REPUGNANT, OFFPUTTING
– unpleasant, not to one's taste INSUFFERABLE, UNPALATABLE
– unpleasant and annoying, irk-

some, disturbing VEXATIOUS
– unpleasant and unhealthy UNWHOLESOME
– unpleasant or unfavourable, as a particular sense or use of a word might be PEJORATIVE, DISPARAGING, DEPRECIATORY
unpleasant- CACO-
unpractical, impracticable, or idealistic VISIONARY, UTOPIAN
unpredictable, changing constantly QUICKSILVER, MERCURIAL
– unpredictable, or changeable in affections, wants, or aims FICKLE
– unpredictable, unstable, liable to changes VOLATILE
unprejudiced, open-minded, open to suggestion, prepared to change RECEPTIVE, AMENABLE
– unprejudiced, uninfluenced by emotion or personal preference OBJECTIVE, IMPARTIAL, DISINTERESTED, DETACHED, DISPASSIONATE
unprepared See **unplanned**
unprincipled, unscrupulous, not guided or restrained by conscience UNCONSCIONABLE
– unprincipled person changing his policies or opinions to serve his interests TRIMMER, TIMESERVER, OPPORTUNIST, VICAR OF BRAY
unpromising, unlucky, threatening disaster, as a sign might be OMINOUS, INAUSPICIOUS, UNPROPITIOUS, PORTENTOUS
unprotected, open to danger or attack VULNERABLE, SUSCEPTIBLE
unqualified or unworthy to be chosen INELIGIBLE
unreadable ILLEGIBLE, INDECIPHERABLE
unreal, imagined, fanciful, or given to fantasising CHIMERICAL
– unreal or imaginary object, illusion PHANTASM, FIGMENT OF THE IMAGINATION
unrealistic, excessively idealistic or romantic QUIXOTIC
– unrealistic, idealistic, impracticable or unpractical VISIONARY, UTOPIAN
unreasonable, excessive UNCONSCIONABLE
– unreasonable, quite illogical IRRATIONAL
unreciprocated, as a person's love or passion for another might be UNREQUITED
unreformable, untamable, uncorrectable INCORRIGIBLE
unreformed, unreconciled to social changes UNRECONSTRUCTED, UNREGENERATE
unrehearsed See **unplanned**
unreliable, changeable in mood or opinion, hard to pin down MERCURIAL, VOLATILE, QUICKSILVER
– unreliable, dangerous, as thin ice might be, dodgy TREACHEROUS
– unreliable, incapable of being defended, as a belief might be UNTENABLE
– unreliable, not following any particular rule or pattern ARBITRARY, RANDOM, HAPHAZARD
– unreliable, occurring irregularly ERRATIC, FITFUL
– unreliable, rash, spontaneous, tending to be governed by emotion rather than reason IMPETUOUS, IMPULSIVE
– unreliable, unpredictable, inconstant, undependable SKITTISH, CAPRICIOUS, FICKLE, FLIGHTY, WHIMSICAL
– unreliable and untrustworthy, as a trader might be DISREPUTABLE, FLY-BY-NIGHT
unrequested, without being ordered or asked for, as goods delivered by mail might be UNSOLICITED
unresponsive, as a disease might be to treatment, or a nerve to stimulation REFRACTORY
unrest See **rebellion**
unrestrained, excessive, beyond all reasonable limits INORDINATE, IMMODERATE
– unrestrained, immoral WANTON
– unrestrained or unchecked, as vegetation might be RAMPANT
unrewarded, without compensation or benefit in return GRATUITOUS, GRATIS, COMPLIMENTARY
unroll or open out something, such as a flag UNFURL
unsatisfiable, as one's appetite might be INSATIABLE
unselective in a way that suggests lack of ability to choose or interest in choosing INDISCRIMINATE
unselfish, concerned for others' welfare ALTRUISTIC
unsettled, aimless, drifting person VAGABOND, VAGRANT
unshiny finish or surface, as of a non-glossy paint MATT
unskilled labourer, as on a building site NAVVY
– unskilled work, such as domestic cleaning, that is considered undignified MENIAL WORK
unsophisticated, modest and unpretentious HOMESPUN
– unsophisticated, straightforward, honest, simple, innocent NAIVE, UNWORLDLY, GUILELESS, ARTLESS, INGENUOUS
– unsophisticated, unenlightened, ignorant BENIGHTED
– unsophisticated, unrefined, or unused to urban life RUSTIC
– unsophisticated, unrefined, unpolished, oafish BOORISH, PHILISTINE, UNCOUTH
– unsophisticated and rough people, the masses, the herd HOI POLLOI, PLEBS, RAGGLE-TAGGLE, RIFF-RAFF
– unsophisticated and unrefined person, boor, yob PHILISTINE YAHOO
– unsophisticated country person or out-of-towner BUMPKIN, HICK, RUSTIC, YOKEL, HAYSEED
– unsophisticated opinion, taste, or group of people LOWEST COMMON DENOMINATOR
– unsophisticated or uninformed, typical of village-store conversation in the U.S. CRACKER-BARREL
unspeakable, indescribable UNUTTERABLE, INEFFABLE
unspoken, implied, understood, as an informal agreement might be TACIT, IMPLICIT
unstable See also **unreliable**
– unstable, changing, inconstant TURBULENT, VERTIGINOUS
– unstable, risky, or insecure PRECARIOUS
– unstable chemically or temperamentally LABILE, VOLATILE
– unstable person, typically aggressive, moody, and lacking in conscience PSYCHOPATH, SOCIOPATH
unstated though understood, inferred TACIT, IMPLICIT
unsteady See also **unstable**, **unreliable**
– unsteady, constantly changing, as prices might be FLUCTUATING
– unsteady, tottery, wobbly, unbalanced, liable to fall PRECARIOUS, TEETERING
– unsteady, unreliable, unpredictable, undependable, inconstant CAPRICIOUS, ERRATIC, FICKLE, FLIGHTY, SKITTISH
– unsteady, winding from side to side or up and down FLUXUOUS, SINUOUS, UNDULATING
unsuccessful, failed, would-be MANQUÉ
– unsuccessful through lacking complete development ABORTIVE
unsuitable, inappropriate, or inopportune INFELICITOUS
unsure See **uncertain**
unsympathetic, impolite OFFHAND, IMPERSONAL
– unsympathetic treatment, curt consideration and dismissal SHORT SHRIFT
unsystematic, lacking a systematic order or arrangement RANDOM, HAPHAZARD, ARBITRARY
untangle, disentangle UNSNARL
unthrifty or wasteful IMPROVIDENT, PRODIGAL, SPENDTHRIFT

untidy, and typically wet or limp BEDRAGGLED
– untidy, run down, or worn out, as through debauchery RADDLED
– untidy, scruffy SCRAGGLY
– untidy, shabby, lazy and careless in appearance or work SLOVENLY
– untidy, shabby, or old-fashioned, as a woman or her clothes might be DOWDY, FROWZY
– untidy, sloppy, careless SLIPSHOD, HAPHAZARD
– untidy handwriting SCRAWL
– untidy in appearance as hair might be UNKEMPT, DISHEVELLED, TOUSLED, UNGROOMED
– untidy or sluttish SLATTERNLY, BLOWZY
– untidily or irregularly spread out STRAGGLY
until, awaiting PENDING
untiring, tireless INDEFATIGABLE
untouchable, imperceptible to the touch IMPALPABLE, INTANGIBLE
– "untouchable", member of the lowest classes in Hindu society, technically outside the caste system HARIJAN
untransferrable, as rights or property might be INALIENABLE
untrue or untruthful MENDACIOUS
untrustworthy See **unreliable**
unusual See **unique**, **strange**, **odd**
– unusual, out of the ordinary UNWONTED, UNORTHODOX
– unusual and hence valued person or thing RARITY, RARA AVIS
– unusually skilful or gifted EXCEPTIONAL
unutterable, unspeakable, indescribable INEFFABLE
unwanted, in the way SUPERFLUOUS, DE TROP, REDUNDANT
unwelcome or unacceptable person PERSONA NON GRATA
– unwelcome or uninvited INTRUSIVE
unwilling RELUCTANT
– unwilling, enforced, or compelled INVOLUNTARY
– unwilling, reluctant, opposed LOATH, AVERSE, DISINCLINED
– unwilling, reluctant, or forced, as admiration or a compliment might be GRUDGING
– unwilling to act, hesitant, shy BACKWARD
– unwilling to say much, somewhat secretive or withdrawn TACITURN, RETICENT, UNFORTHCOMING
unworthy of being chosen, or unqualified to be chosen INELIGIBLE
unyielding, unbudging, deaf to all pleas REMORSELESS, INEXORABLE, ADAMANT
up- ANA-
up-to-date, informed, knowledgeable about current affairs AU COURANT, AU FAIT
upbringing, training NURTURE
upgrade an area socially, as when middle class residents move in GENTRIFY
upheaval, sudden and very violent change or disruption CATACLYSM
uphold, justify, or excuse by means of arguments or proof VINDICATE
upon- EPI-
upper surface of a body segment, as of an insect or lobster TERGUM
upper-class, as an accent might be PUKKA
– upper-class language, as *scent* rather than *perfume* is said to be U
– upper-class person, or someone affecting upper-class habits and mannerisms NOB, TOFF, SWELL
– upper or upper-middle class collectively GENTRY
– person who has acquired upper-class wealth and pretensions but is not fully accepted socially UPSTART, PARVENU, NOUVEAU RICHE, ARRIVISTE, JOHNNY-COME-LATELY
upright VERTICAL, PERPENDICULAR, PLUMB
– upright pole or post, as for supporting a roof STANCHION
– upright post or strut of a ladder, door frame, window sash, or the like STILE
– upright, rib, or strip of a window, screen, or rock face MULLION
uprising See **rebellion**
uproot, pull up by or as if by the roots DERACINATE
– uprooted, rootless, separated from one's homeland, social origins, familiar culture, or natural environment DERACINATED, DÉRACINÉ, LUMPEN
upset, agitated, worried DISQUIETED, PERTURBED
– upset, flustered, at a loss DISCONCERTED, DISCOMPOSED
– upset, sudden and violent disruption, radical change UPHEAVAL
– upsetting, extremely distressing HARROWING
upside down or inside out INVERTED
upstart, person of lowly background who is newly invested with wealth, power, or advanced social status PARVENU, ARRIVISTE, JOHNNY-COME-LATELY, NOUVEAU RICHE
upstream – migrating upstream from the sea to breed, as salmon do ANADROMOUS
upward slope ACCLIVITY
uranium ore PITCHBLENDE
urban sprawl formed by the fusion of many towns CONURBATION
urchin, waif, boy roaming the streets GAMIN, STREET ARAB, GUTTERSNIPE
urge See also **tendency**
– urge, appeal for, apply for SOLICIT, SUPPLICATE
– urge, prod, get someone to do something by pressure or persuasion IMPEL, INDUCE
– urge, propose, or recommend a policy, view, or course of action ADVOCATE, CHAMPION, COMMEND, PROMOTE
– urge or arouse unrest or rebelliousness, stir up trouble FOMENT, INSTIGATE, INCITE
– urge or encourage, reassure, inspire, or egg on HEARTEN, EMBOLDEN, MOTIVATE
– urge or try to influence legislators to adopt a policy LOBBY
– urge strongly or appeal to earnestly EXHORT, ENTREAT, IMPORTUNE, BESEECH, ADJURE
– urge to hurry, nag, harass, goad CHIVVY
– urging, encouraging HORTATORY
– channel or transform a sexual urge or other instinctual energy into a socially or culturally more acceptable activity SUBLIMATE
– irresistible and often irrational urge to perform a certain action COMPULSION
– pressure, promise of reward, goal, or the like that urges one to act STIMULUS, INCENTIVE
urgent, demanding, as a summons might be PEREMPTORY, IMPERIOUS
– urgent, essential, important IMPERATIVE, IMPELLING
– urgent, requiring immediate attention EXIGENT, PRESSING, COMPELLING
– urgently insistent in requests or demands, pestering IMPORTUNATE, CLAMANT, CLAMOROUS
urinal – public urinal, especially, as formerly found in the streets of Paris and other European cities PISSOIR
urine of horses or camels STALE
– causing increased urine or urination DIURETIC
– lacking control of one's urinary or other bodily functions INCONTINENT
– pass urine, urinate MICTURATE
– thin, flexible tube inserted into a body channel, as for draining urine or introducing medication CATHETER
– tube or canal that conveys urine from the bladder out of the body URETHRA
– tube or duct that conveys urine from a kidney to the bladder URETER
urn of Russian origin, used for making tea SAMOVAR

– urn-shaped, shaped like a pitcher or urn, as some plants are URCEOLATE

U.S. See also **American English**

– U.S. motto, "one out of many" E PLURIBUS UNUM

– U.S. nation or government personified UNCLE SAM

– U.S. presidency, the President and his government OVAL OFFICE, WHITE HOUSE

– U.S. southern states as a region or grouping during the American Civil War DIXIE

– alliance of U.S. northern states during the American Civil War THE UNION

– alliance of U.S. southern states during the American Civil War THE CONFEDERACY

– easing of tensions between nations, especially between the U.S. and the USSR DÉTENTE

– relating or referring to the central government of the U.S. or Canada FEDERAL

use, make specific or practical use of UTILISE, EMPLOY

– use an opportunity, take advantage of, turn to advantage EXPLOIT, UTILISE, CAPITALISE ON, PARLAY

– use in an irresponsible way, misuse, abuse PROSTITUTE, PERVERT

– use of and benefits from someone else's property, or the legal right to them USUFRUCT

– use up, consume EXPEND, EXHAUST

– use up, reduce greatly in quantity DEPLETE

– use up wastefully SQUANDER

– available for one's use AT ONE'S DISPOSAL

– disuse, state of being out of use or practice DESUETUDE

– make use of or turn to when forced to do so by difficulties HAVE RECOURSE TO, RESORT TO

– obtain and make use of AVAIL ONESELF OF

– practical or specific use for something APPLICATION

used to, accustomed to, familiar with ORIENTATED, ATTUNED TO

– used to, accustomed to, hardened to INURED, HABITUATED, ACCLIMATISED

– used to, accustomed to, in the habit of doing something WONT TO

– get used to, adapt or adjust to ACCOMMODATE ONESELF TO

useful, advantageous, or favourable in enabling something to happen CONDUCIVE

– useful and practical rather than just decorative UTILITARIAN, FUNCTIONAL

– useful only in furtherance of some other purpose SUBSERVIENT, INSTRUMENTAL

– useful or applicable in a wide variety of ways VERSATILE

– useful or usable, appropriate, giving good service SERVICEABLE

usefulness or useful thing UTILITY

useless, of no benefit or advantage, in vain TO NO AVAIL, UNAVAILING, BOOTLESS

– useless, producing no worthwhile result, as unsuccessful efforts are FUTILE, FRUITLESS, VAIN

– useless, purposeless, serving no real purpose, as merely decorative language is OTIOSE

– useless, unsuccessful, or inadequate, failing to produce the desired effect INEFFECTUAL

– useless and expensive gift, project, or possession, requiring more trouble than it is worth WHITE ELEPHANT

– useless because of old age or illness SUPERANNUATED

– useless or unused because out of date OUTMODED, OBSOLETE

– deprive of force, make useless or ineffective, enfeeble NULLIFY

USSR See also **Russian terms**

– adoption of a policy of international neutrality together with cooperation, especially towards the USSR FINLANDISATION

– easing of tensions between nations, especially between the U.S. and the USSR DÉTENTE

usual, current, common or widespread PREVAILING, PREVALENT

– usual, expected, matter-of-course, or habitual CUSTOMARY, WONTED, PREDICTABLE

– usual, in line with customs or standards CONVENTIONAL, PRESCRIBED, CONSUETUDINARY

– usual, standard, stock, as the everyday diet of a region is STAPLE

uterus – abnormal positioning of a body organ, especially the uterus VERSION

– either of the pair of narrow tubes along which the eggs pass from the ovaries to the uterus FALLOPIAN TUBE, OVIDUCT, SALPINX

– emptying of the uterus, especially for an abortion, by means of suction through a tube VACUUM ASPIRATION

– legal term for the uterus of a mother VENTER

– mass of tissue linking the foetus to the uterus lining PLACENTA

– mucous membrane lining the uterus, shed during menstruation or childbirth DECIDUA

– slipping out of position of a body part or organ, such as the uterus PROLAPSE

– surgical operation involving opening the cervix and scraping the uterus DILATATION AND CURETTAGE, D AND C

– surgical removal of the uterus HYSTERECTOMY

– surgical scraping or scooping instrument, as for removing dead tissue from the uterus CURETTE

– testing for the presence or position of a foetus by prodding the uterus BALLOTTEMENT

– withdrawal by syringe of fluid from a pregnant woman's uterus, to monitor the health of the foetus AMNIOCENTESIS

uterus- HYSTER-, HYSTERO-, METR-, METRO-

utopia – fictional place or imaginary world where things are worse than in real life, the reverse of a utopia DYSTOPIA, CACOTOPIA

utter, complete, absolute RANK

– utter, out-and-out, notorious, as a knave is said to be ARRANT

utterance – short and mysterious, pithy, as an utterance might be GNOMIC

V

V-shaped pattern, as on a heraldic shield or an NCO's stripes of rank CHEVRON
vaccination – slit or scratch the skin slightly, as for vaccination SCARIFY
vaccine dose following the main dose to increase or sustain its effectiveness BOOSTER
- vaccine for polio, formerly injected, based on a weakened or killed virus SALK VACCINE
- vaccine for polio, taken orally, based on a weakened but live virus SABIN VACCINE
- give a vaccine to, as by injection INOCULATE

vacuum formed at the top of an upright, sealed, inverted mercury-filled tube, as in a barometer TORRICELLIAN VACUUM
- referring to an incomplete vacuum PARTIAL

-vacuum tube -TRON
vagina – vaginal insert, as for contraception or as a medicated suppository PESSARY
- entrance to or chamber leading to a bodily cavity or canal, such as the vagina VESTIBULE
- external female genitals, including the labia and the entrance to the vagina VULVA
- fold of skin lying behind the entrance to the vagina FOURCHETTE
- folds of tissue surrounding the opening of the vagina LABIA
- instrument inserted into the vagina or other body passage for examination or treatment SPECULUM
- membrane sometimes partially blocking the entrance to the vagina, as before loss of virginity HYMEN
- raised mass of fatty tissue over the pubic bones, which lie in front of the vagina MONS, MONS VENERIS, MONS PUBIS
- sensitive external genital organ in a woman, situated in front of the vagina CLITORIS
- surgical cut into the tissues around the vagina during childbirth to make the delivery easier EPISIOTOMY

vague, imprecise or indistinct ELUSIVE, INTANGIBLE
- vague, indecisive, hesitant SHILLY-SHALLYING, VACILLATING
- vague, uncertain, unclear, still not finally decided INDETERMINATE, INCONCLUSIVE
- vague, undecided, having conflicting feelings AMBIVALENT
- vague notion, hint that is unconfirmed or still not fully formed INKLING, INTIMATION
- vague or evasive, as an answer might be EQUIVOCAL, AMBIGUOUS

valid or reasonable, as a grievance might be LEGITIMATE
- approve something formally, such as a treaty, thereby making it valid and operative RATIFY

valley, between parallel faults in the Earth's crust RIFT VALLEY
- valley, typically narrow and wooded DENE, DEAN, DINGLE
- valley, typically small, steep, and near the coast COOMB
- valley, wide and open, typically in Yorkshire DALE, VALE
- valley or hollow, sunken area of land DEPRESSION
- ditch or small valley cut by rain- or floodwater GULLY
- high-lying steep-walled basin-like valley, often containing the head of a glacier or a small lake CIRQUE, CORRIE, CWM, COIRE, KAR
- narrow, flat-bottomed, and steep-sided valley in Scotland or Ireland GLEN
- mouth of a valley as it opens out onto a plain EMBOUCHURE
- ravine, deep mountain pass, or steep-sided valley GORGE, CANYON, COULÉE, DEFILE, GULCH
- vast, steep-sided valley CHASM, ABYSS, GULF
- wide, flat-bottomed, and steep-sided valley or the grassland lying in it, especially in Scotland STRATH

valuable possession kept within a family by inheritance HEIRLOOM
- valuable possession, talent, or the like ASSET
- extremely valuable, impossible to replace IRREPLACEABLE
- highly valued and energetically competed for, as an award might be COVETED
- highly valued by its owner, often for sentimental reasons, as a treasured childhood possession or memory would be CHERISHED
- highly valued or respected, well-regarded ESTEEMED

value indicated on a cheque, share certificate, or the like, as distinct from the real market value, NOMINAL VALUE, PAR VALUE, FACE VALUE
- value of a property or business once all debts are taken into account EQUITY
- value of an insurance policy that is voluntarily discontinued before it matures SURRENDER VALUE
- value or high regard placed on something PREMIUM
- in proportion to the value of the goods, as a tax or duty might be AD VALOREM
- loss in value, as of a car, as through age or wear DEPRECIATION
- rejection of all moral and social values NIHILISM, ANARCHISM
- rise in value of property ACCESSION, APPRECIATION
- traditional customs and values of a social group MORES

value-system and beliefs of a society, as expressed in its arts MYTHOS
- value-system or distinctive character of a particular people, artistic movement, or the like ETHOS

valve in a pipe for regulating the flow of liquid or gas STOPCOCK
- valve regulating the flow of vapour in an engine THROTTLE
- electronic valve helping to generate high-power microwaves, as in radar systems MAGNETRON
- heart valve regulating the flow of blood from the left atrium to the left ventricle MITRAL VALVE, BICUSPID VALVE
- mushroom-shaped valve, as in the exhaust or inlet system in an internal combustion engine POPPET VALVE
- simple valve, using either a ball or a hinged flap, allowing fluid flow in only one direction CLACK VALVE

vampire or witch LAMIA
vanish See **disappear**
vanishing See **short-lived**
vaporiser ATOMISER
vapour, smoke, or gas that is blown or breathed out EXHALATION

– vaporising readily VOLATILE
– change into or produce vapour EVAPORATE
– smelly and invisible vapour or gas, as rising from a swamp or rubbish heap EFFLUVIUM
– turn directly from solid to vapour, or vice versa, without becoming liquid SUBLIMATE

vapour- ATMO-

vapour trail CONTRAIL

variable or adaptable, as working hours might be FLEXIBLE

variation from a standard without going beyond a certain limit, leeway TOLERANCE, PLAY
– variation or distinction of a very fine or subtle kind, such as a shade of meaning NUANCE
– variation or possible combination of elements PERMUTATION
– mutation of or abrupt variation within a species SALTATION

varied, assorted, various DIVERSE, MISCELLANEOUS, SUNDRY
– varied, having many different aspects or parts MULTIFARIOUS, DIVERSIFIED, MULTIFORM, VARIEGATED
– varied, several, many MULTIPLE, MANIFOLD, MYRIAD

variety of talents, uses, or the like VERSATILITY

-variety- -TROP-, TROPO-, -TROPIC

varnish for wooden floors or furniture FRENCH POLISH, SHELLAC
– varnish or glossy black lacquer JAPAN

vase, especially one used for storing the ashes of the dead after cremation URN
– support for stems in a flower arrangement, such as a spiked board or pierced sponge in a vase FROG

vat in which clay or a similar substance is mixed with water when making pottery BLUNGER

Vatican See **Pope**

vault, underground chamber, especially when under a church or cathedral UNDERCROFT, CRYPT
– vaulted or arched structure, cave, room, or the like FORNIX
– curved line at the intersection of two vaults GROIN

veal See illustration
– thin slice of meat, especially veal ESCALOPE, SCHNITZEL

vegetable See charts, pages 545 and 546
– vegetables that are typically diced and cooked as a side dish JARDINIÈRE
– finely sliced or shredded, as vegetables may be JULIENNE

vegetarian, feeding on plants only, as many animals do HERBIVOROUS
– vegetarian who avoids all animal products, including milk VEGAN
– vegetarian who eats only fruit FRUITARIAN

vegetation growing healthily VERDURE, HERBAGE
– vegetation of a region FLORA

vehicle See chart, page 547, and

veal cuts

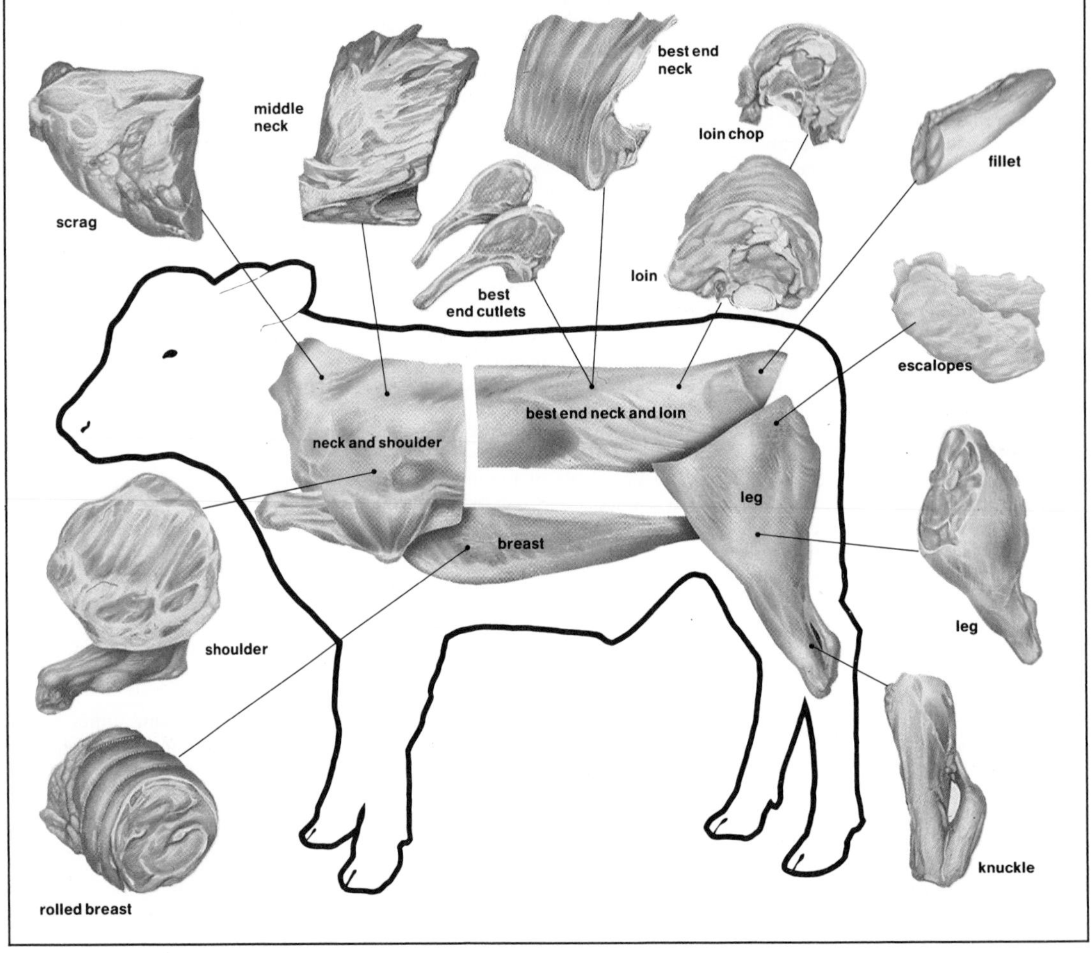

scrag
middle neck
best end neck
loin chop
fillet
best end cutlets
loin
escalopes
best end neck and loin
neck and shoulder
leg
breast
shoulder
leg
knuckle
rolled breast

VEGETABLES

FLOWERS, LEAVES, STALKS, AND SHOOTS

Batavian endive, scarole
borecole, kale
broccoli, calabrese
cardoon
chard, leaf beet
chicory
Chinese cabbage, pe-tsai
Chinese leaves, pak-choi
collard, colewort
corn salad, lamb's lettuce, mâche
finochio, Florence fennel, sweet fennel
globe artichoke
kohlrabi, turnip cabbage
marsh samphire, glasswort
mung beanshoots
radicchio
romaine, cos
salad burnet
sea kale
sorrel

FRUITS

aubergine, eggplant, brinjal
breadfruit
breadnut
chayote
squash
zucchini, courgette

PODS AND PULSES

adzuki bean, red bean
capsicum, pimiento, sweet pepper
chickpea, garbanzo
cowpea, black-eyed pea
dal, dahl, pigeon pea
fava bean, broad bean
flageolet, haricot bean
gram
gumbo, okra, bhindi, lady's fingers
lima bean
mangetout, sugar pea
St John's bread, carob, algarroba, locust

ROOTS AND TUBERS

cassava, manioc
celeriac
Chinese water chestnut
earthnut, pignut
Jerusalem artichoke
ramson
rutabaga, swede
salsify, oyster plant
scallion, shallot
scorzonera, black salsify
succory
sweet potato
taro, cocoyam, eddoe, dasheen
yam

also **horse-drawn vehicles**
– vehicle, means of transport CONVEYANCE
– vehicle that is old and broken-down JALOPY, RATTLETRAP, BONESHAKER, BANGER
– vehicle's degree of stability, as on wet roads ROADHOLDING
– vehicles travelling together in a group CONVOY

-vehicle -MOBILE

veil covering the face of some Arabic Muslim women in public as a gesture of modesty YASHMAK

vein, especially in the legs, that has become abnormally knotted and swollen VARICOSE VEIN, VARIX
– vein, ridge, or rib, as on a leaf or insect's wing COSTA
– vein conducting blood directly from one organ to another, especially that between the digestive organs and the liver PORTAL VEIN
– vein in the neck JUGULAR VEIN
– vein just beneath the collarbone SUBCLAVIAN VEIN
– either of two large veins returning blood to the upper right chamber of the heart VENA CAVA
– in or into a vein, as an injection or drip might be INTRAVENOUS
– opening a vein for drawing or letting blood PHLEBOTOMY, VENESECTION
– patterning or system of veins, as on a leaf or insect's wing VENATION
– puncturing of a vein, as when injecting medicine VENIPUNCTURE
– relating to or containing veins VENOUS
– space surrounded by lines or veins, as on a leaf or insect's wing AREOLA
– tiny blood vessel between an artery and a vein CAPILLARY
– tiny vein, as in the blood system or on a leaf VENULE
– vertical, cylindrical vein of ore PIPE

vein- PHLEB- PHLEBO-, VEN-, VENI-, VENO-

velvet – velvety or fuzzy surface of raised fibres on a fabric NAP
– surface of soft loops or threads, as on velvet or a carpet PILE

vending machine DISPENSER
– vending machine, or room or restaurant dispensing food through vending machines AUTOMAT

vengeance See **revenge**
– inflict or obtain vengeance EXACT, WREAK
– means of vengeance, criticism, or punishment SCOURGE

Venice – chief magistrate in Venice and Genoa in former times DOGE
– narrow boat, propelled by a single oar at the stern, on the canals of Venice GONDOLA
– nobleman of Venice in former times MAGNIFICO
– song of gondoliers in Venice, having a rhythm of rowing BARCAROLE
– steam-powered bus-boat along the canals of Venice VAPORETTO

Venus – relating to the Roman goddess Venus PAPHIAN

verandah or balcony along the outside of the upper level of a building LOGGIA
– verandah or entrance stairway at a house door STOOP
– verandah or paved outdoor area adjoining a house PATIO

verb, as in Latin or Greek, that is passive in form but active in meaning DEPONENT
– verb, especially the verb *be*, expressing or relating to existence SUBSTANTIVE VERB
– verb, such as *be*, *feel*, or *seem*, that identifies the complement with the subject COPULA
– verb, such as *be* or *sing*, that does not follow the usual pattern of inflections IRREGULAR VERB
– verb, such as *must*, *will*, and *can*, that usually occurs with another verb to express possibility, probability, or the like MODAL AUXILIARY, MODAL VERB
– verb, such as *have*, *is*, or *can*, used together with a main verb to indicate its tense, mood, voice or aspect AUXILIARY VERB
– verb, such as *rise*, that does not need or does not take a direct object INTRANSITIVE VERB
– verb, such as *risk*, that takes or needs a direct object TRANSITIVE VERB
– verb derived from a noun, such as *to jackknife* DENOMINATIVE
– verb form or construction used to indicate a fact or neutral attitude, as in *He was there* INDICATIVE MOOD
– verb form or construction used to indicate a hypothesis or imaginary situation, as in *if he were there* SUBJUNCTIVE MOOD
– verb form that does not show person, number, or tense, and in English often follows *to* INFINITIVE
– verb whose past tense or participle is formed from a different root from the present tense, as in *go* and *went* SUPPLETIVE VERB
– verbal idiom consisting of a verb and adverb, as in *turn it on* PHRASAL VERB
– verbal idiom consisting of a verb and preposition, as in *turn on him* PREPOSITIONAL VERB
– changes in the form of verbs, nouns, adjectives, and the like, as

by adding suffixes, as with *take, takes, taking* INFLECTION
– form of a verb, ending in *-ing* in English, used like a noun, as in *Cooking is fun* GERUND
– form of a verb, usually ending in *-ing* or *-ed* in English, as used in forming tenses or as an adjective PARTICIPLE
– past perfect tense of a verb, as in *had climbed* PLUPERFECT
– referring to verb forms using auxiliary words rather than inflections, as in *She did walk* rather than *She walked* PERIPHRASTIC
– vowel changes especially in strong verbs, as in *sing-sang-sung* ABLAUT, GRADATION

verdict of a jury, or similar formal pronouncement DELIVERANCE
– verdict of not guilty ACQUITTAL
– added clause, amendment, or qualification to a verdict, parliamentary bill, or the like RIDER
– deliver a verdict RENDER

verse See also **poem**, **poetry**
– verse of a poem STROPHE, STANZA, STAVE
– verse, line of poetry STICH
– verse mixing words from two or

VEGETABLE AND GRAIN DISHES

baba ganoush	Middle Eastern dish of puréed aubergine, garlic, tahini, lemon juice, and herbs
bhajia/bhagi	Indian dish of deep-fried, spiced, chopped vegetables
bubble and squeak	English dish of fried left-over mashed potato and vegetables
caesar salad	Mexican salad of lettuce, garlic, cheese, croutons, and sometimes anchovies, in an egg, lemon juice, and oil dressing
champ	Irish dish of mashed potato and spring onions, served with lumps of butter
colcannon	Irish dish of mashed potato and green vegetables, usually cabbage
couscous	North African dish of cracked wheat, steamed and served with spiced vegetables, fish, or meat
crudités	French hors d'oeuvre, consisting of fingers of raw vegetables served with a dip; crudely grated raw vegetables with a dressing
dhal/dal	Indian dish of puréed spiced "pigeon peas", or other pulses, onions, and ghee
dolmas/ dolmades	Greek or Middle Eastern dish of stuffed vine leaves
duchesse potatoes	small baked cakes of mashed potatoes bound with egg
falafel/felafel	Middle Eastern dish of deep-fried balls of mashed chickpeas, onion, parsley, and coriander
fasolia	Greek bean salad in a garlic dressing
gado-gado	Indonesian vegetable salad with peanut sauce
gnocchi	Italian dumplings of semolina or potato
guacamole	Mexican dip or salad of mashed avocado, lemon juice, garlic, and olive oil
hummus/ hummous	Middle Eastern dish of puréed chickpeas, often with olive oil, lemon, garlic, and tahini
imam bayildi	Turkish dish of aubergines, onions, tomatoes, and garlic
latke	potato pancake of traditional Jewish style
macedoine	mixture of diced vegetables
paella	Spanish dish of rice cooked in oil and stock with seafood, chicken, and vegetables
pakora	Indian fritters of chickpea flour
pease pudding	British dish of a thick purée of cooked dried peas
peperonata	Italian dish of peppers, tomatoes, onions, garlic, and olive oil
pilau/pulao	Middle Eastern dish of savoury rice and vegetables
pissaladière	French yeast tart of tomato, onion, anchovies, olives, and garlic
polenta	Italian maize porridge
raita	Indian dish of chopped cucumber, onion, or the like in yoghurt
ratatouille	French stew of aubergines, onions, peppers, courgettes, and tomatoes
risotto	Italian dish of rice cooked in oil and stock with onions and Parmesan cheese, often served with fish, poultry, or meat
rösti/roesti	Swiss dish of grated, fried potatoes
salade niçoise	French hors d'oeuvre of lettuce, tomatoes, olives, boiled eggs, and anchovies in a garlic dressing
sauerkraut	German dish of shredded, salted cabbage fermented in its own juice
stovies	Scottish dish of stewed potatoes
succotash	U.S. dish of lima beans and maize kernels
tabbouleh/ tabbouli	Middle Eastern salad of cracked wheat and vegetables in an oil and lemon juice dressing
tahini/tahina	Middle Eastern sesame seed paste
tsatsiki	Greek dish of cucumber, garlic, and yoghurt
Waldorf salad	U.S. salad of apple, celery, and chopped walnuts in mayonnaise

more languages MACARONIC VERSE
– verse or saying inscribed in a locket POSY
– verse repeated at regular intervals REFRAIN, CHORUS, BURDEN
– analysis of the metrical or rhythm patterns of verse SCANSION
– light verse, rhyming *aabba* LIMERICK
– pause in a line of verse, especially at a natural sense division CAESURA
– rhythmical stress in verse ICTUS
– study of verse forms and metres PROSODY
– trivial or predictably rhythmical verse DOGGEREL, CRAMBO

version – commonly accepted text or version of a work VULGATE

-version-, -variant- -TROP-, TROPO-, -TROPIC

vertebra See also **bones**
– bony spur at the side of a vertebra TRANSVERSE PROCESS
– insertion of a syringe needle between the lower vertebrae to inject drugs or withdraw spinal fluid LUMBAR PUNCTURE
– second vertebra from the top AXIS
– top vertebra, supporting the skull ATLAS

vertebrate animal, including humans, or animal having a backbone-like supporting structure CHORDATE

vertical See **upright**

very, extremely, to a great degree EXCEEDINGLY, EXCEPTIONALLY

very- PER-

vessel See **ship**, **boat**, **sailing**, **glass**, **drinking**, **kitchen**, **laboratory**
– vessel or channel in the body DUCT, VAS
– relating to or containing vessels for conveying blood, sap, or other biological fluids VASCULAR

vessel- ANGIO-

vest, sleeveless undershirt SINGLET

vestry, room in a church in which the sacred objects and vestments are stored SACRISTY, SACRARIUM

veteran performer TROUPER

vibrate and produce a corresponding sound when stimulated RESONATE
– vibrate or swing from one extreme to the other OSCILLATE
– vibrating element in a loudspeaker, buzzer, or the like ARMATURE

vibration, shaking and quivering movement TREMOR
– vibration in a string or other body caused by vibrations of the same frequency in a nearby body SYMPATHETIC VIBRATION
– point or region, as on a violin string, of minimum vibration NODE

vice See **immoral**

vice or clamp used to hold a tool or workpiece, as in a drill or lathe CHUCK

viceroy – wife of a viceroy VICEREINE

vicious See **cruel**, **spiteful**, **immoral**

victim of someone's exploitation STOOGE, PAWN, PUPPET, TOOL, CAT'S-PAW
– victim of someone's joke, plot, swindle, or the like, dupe or sucker BUTT, GULL, MARK, GUDGEON, PATSY, PIGEON
– person or group victimised for the faults or distresses of others SCAPEGOAT, WHIPPING-BOY, FALL-GUY, AUNT SALLY

victimise, discriminate against and oppress or ill-treat PERSECUTE

victory achieved very easily against a weak opponent, or as a formality through the withdrawal or absence of the opponent WALKOVER
– victory in which the victor too suffers great losses PYRRHIC VICTORY, CADMEAN VICTORY
– victory parade or ceremony in ancient Rome TRIUMPH, OVATION
– victory spoils, including captured weapons TROPHY
– victory symbol in ancient times LAURELS, BAYS
– definite, indisputable, widely acknowledged, as a victory or success might be RESOUNDING

view, illustration, or diagram of a machine or structure showing its parts separately EXPLODED VIEW
– view, typically covering a wide area PROSPECT, VISTA, PERSPECTIVE
– view or impression that is broad or general OVERVIEW, PANORAMA
– view revealing everything PANOPTIC VIEW
– accepted, generally believed, as a theory or view might be RECEIVED
– balcony, window, or tower offering a wide view MIRADOR
– dark chamber in which the image of an outside view is projected onto a surface by a lens above CAMERA OBSCURA
– giving a general view of a whole subject SYNOPTIC
– overlooking, having a view from above COMMANDING, DOMINANT
– place or point that allows a particularly good overall view COIGN OF VANTAGE, RINGSIDE SEAT, VANTAGE POINT
– summerhouse or gallery having a fine view BELVEDERE

-view -SCAPE

viewing instrument with twin lenses, producing a 3D effect when used to view two nearly identical photographs STEREOSCOPE

-viewing -SCOPY

vigour combined with style FLAIR, ÉLAN, BRIO, PANACHE

Viking NORSEMAN
– Viking boat LONGSHIP
– tax levied in Anglo-Saxon England for opposing or placating the Viking invaders DANEGELD

villa or country house in Russia DACHA

village or compound in Malaysia KAMPONG
– small or remote village HAMLET
– traditional fenced African village in southern Africa KRAAL

villain, criminal, or wrongdoer MISCREANT
– villain, petty criminal, person who behaves in an anti-social way DELINQUENT
– villain, quack, person using bogus claims to cheat others CHARLATAN, MOUNTEBANK
– villain, rascal, scoundrel, good-for-nothing, especially one with some lovable qualities SCAMP,

VEHICLES

MOTOR VEHICLES

amphibian
bendibus
berlin
Black Maria
bowser
cabriolet
camion
convertible
coupé
crawler
dodgem car
dragster
duck, DUKW
fastback
float
juggernaut
limousine
moon buggy
moped
paddy wagon
pantechnicon
rig
roadster
scrambler
sedan
streetcar
utility
victoria

SNOW AND ICE VEHICLES

bobsleigh
drag
kibitka
luge
pung
Skidoo
skibob
skimobile
snowmobile, Snocat
toboggan
troika
weasel

RAILWAY VEHICLES

caboose
bogie truck
dandy cart
fly coach
freightliner
pony engine
Pullman
tender
wagon-lit

MAN-POWERED VEHICLES

hobby horse
litter
palanquin
pedicab
penny-farthing
quadricycle
rickshaw, jinricksha
sedan chair, jampan
tandem
trishaw
unicycle, monocycle
velocipede

RAPSCALLION, SCALLYWAG, SCAPEGRACE
- villain, rogue, knave, treacherous or morally unprincipled man BLACKGUARD, RECREANT, REPROBATE
- villain, wretch, especially a base, mean, sneaking coward CAITIFF, DASTARD
- former term for a villain or knave VARLET

vine – arch or frame of crisscrossing sticks, on which vines or creepers are trained to grow TRELLIS
- common woody vine of tropical rain forests LIANA
- covered walk or arbour with a latticework roof covered with roses, vines, or the like PERGOLA
- growing along the ground, as a vine or creeper might PROSTRATE
- twining shoot-like part, as on a grape vine, serving to attach a plant to its support TENDRIL

vinegar made from ale, malt vinegar ALEGAR
- relating to vinegar ACETIC
- small bottle for oil or vinegar, as used at table CRUET
- turn into vinegar ACETIFY

vineyard, estate DOMAINE

violence, killing, or bloody fighting, as in films or on television GORE
- critical point beyond which a tense situation will erupt into war or violence FLASHPOINT
- referring to violence or conflict between neighbouring or rival communities SECTARIAN
- uncalled-for, unjustified, without need or cause, as violence in a film might be GRATUITOUS

violent, frenzied, or destructive in behaviour RAMPAGING, ON THE RAMPAGE, BERSERK, AMOK
- violent, sensational, or gruesome, often in a deliberately artificial way GRAND-GUIGNOL
- violent and sudden change, upheaval, or destruction CATACLYSM
- violent destruction, vandalism, confusion or injury of a wanton or widespread kind MAYHEM
- violent or cruel act OUTRAGE
- violent social disturbance UPHEAVAL, CONVULSION

violin See illustration
- violin or related instrument made in the 17th or 18th century by various outstanding craftsmen in Cremona, Italy GUARNERIUS, STRADIVARIUS, AMATI
- violin-shaped, as some leaves are PANDURATE
- violin-teaching method for young children, based on imitation and repetition SUZUKI METHOD
- bouncing the bow lightly off the strings of a violin or related instrument SPICCATO, JETÉ
- harsh sound sometimes produced by a violin or related instrument, due to faulty vibration WOLF
- played by plucking rather than bowing the strings, as a passage for the violin might be PIZZICATO
- small violin of a kind once used by dancing masters KIT, POCHETTE

violin

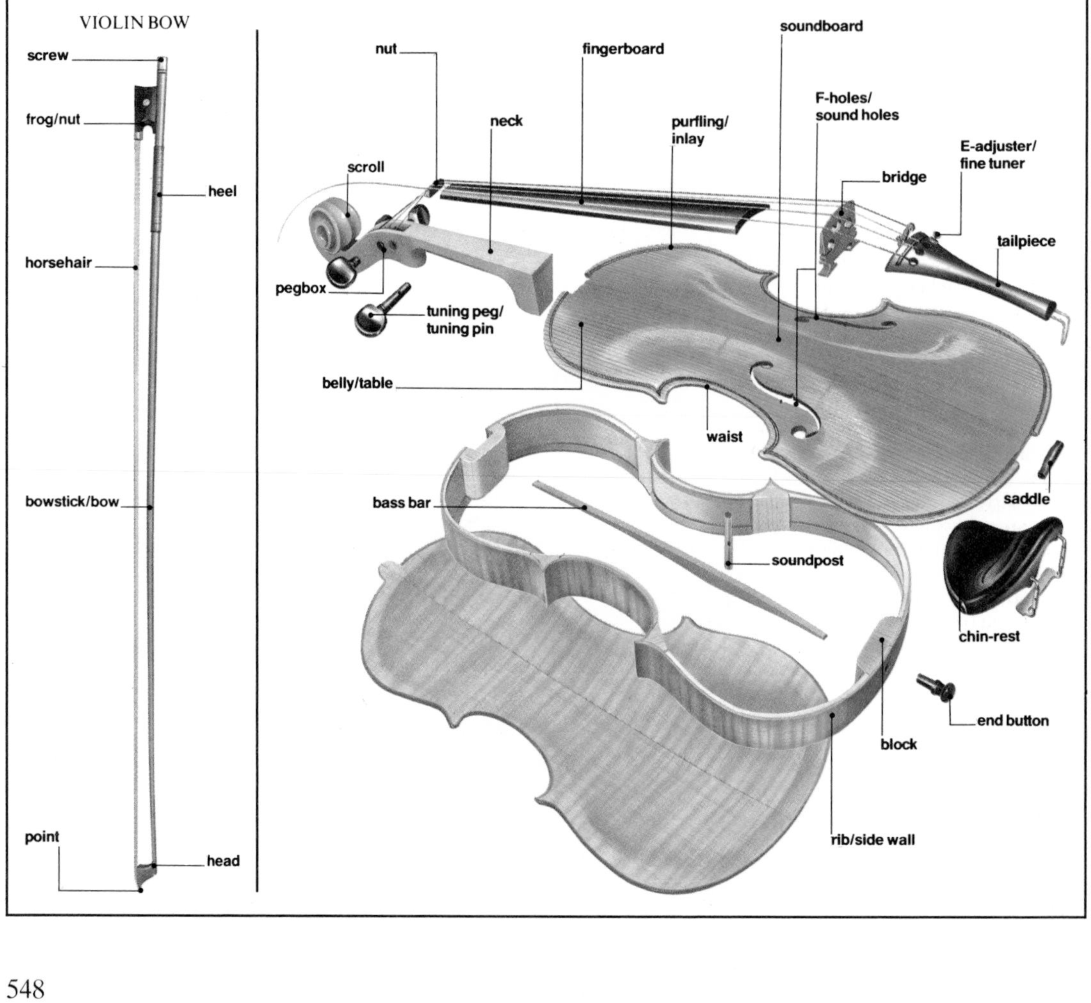

VIP or famous person CELEBRITY, PERSONAGE
– VIP or high-ranking person BIGWIG, DIGNITARY, GRANDEE
virgin birth, reproduction without fertilisation PARTHENOGENESIS
– virgin or nymph in paradise, according to the Koran HOURI
– virgin priestess tending the sacred fire in the temple of the Roman goddess Vesta VESTAL VIRGIN
– virgin who is nevertheless sexually active DEMIVIERGE
Virgin Mary – taking up of the Virgin Mary into heaven, or the feast day commemorating it, August 15, in the Roman Catholic Church THE ASSUMPTION
virginity CHASTITY
– deprive of virginity DEFLOWER
virtue, goodness, moral uprightness RECTITUDE
– virtues, traditionally the basic moral qualities, of justice, prudence, fortitude, and temperance CARDINAL VIRTUES
– piously and narrow-mindedly convinced of one's own virtues SELF-RIGHTEOUS, SANCTIMONIOUS, HOLIER-THAN-THOU
virus See also chart at **diseases**
– virus in its complete inert form prior to its invasion and infection of a cell VIRION
– virus of a group that multiplies in the stomach or intestines, causing gastrointestinal diseases, polio and meningitis ENTEROVIRUS
– virus of a harmless kind in the respiratory and digestive systems REOVIRUS
– virus of various groups causing respiratory infections that produce symptoms like those of the common cold ADENOVIRUS, RHINOVIRUS
– insect-borne virus, causing diseases such as yellow fever ARBOVIRUS
– weaken a virus, as for use in a vaccine ATTENUATE
visible, easily noticed, obvious CONSPICUOUS
– visible, or detectable by any of the senses PERCEPTIBLE
– visible to the naked eye, without a microscope MACROSCOPIC
vision, See also **eyesight**
– vision, prophecy, or revelation of a great disaster APOCALYPSE
– vision on the outer edge of the field of vision PERIPHERAL VISION
visit a place regularly FREQUENT, HAUNT
visitor, guest, or the like who expects or accepts too much hospitality or generosity FREELOADER, SPONGER, SCROUNGER, CADGER, BLUDGER
– frequent visitor, as to a club HABITUÉ, FREQUENTER
visual or visible OCULAR
-visual defect -OPIA
vital See **essential**
vitamin A, as found in eggs and fish liver oils, essential for normal vision RETINOL
– vitamin B_c, as found in leaf vegetables, essential for the normal production of red blood cells FOLIC ACID
– vitamin B_1, as found in meat, essential for breaking down and absorbing carbohydrates THIAMINE
– vitamin B_2, or vitamin G, as found in milk and egg yolks, essential for breaking down carbohydrates RIBOFLAVIN
– vitamin B_{12}, as found in liver, essential for red blood cell formation CYANOCOBALAMIN
– vitamin C, as found in fruit and vegetables, essential in avoiding scurvy ASCORBIC ACID
– vitamin D, as found in milk, fish, and eggs, essential for normal bone growth CALCIFEROL
– vitamin of the vitamin B complex, as found in milk, essential for growth and energy NICOTINIC ACID, NIACIN
– vitamin preparation taken to improve the diet SUPPLEMENT
viva – "may it flourish", motto similar to "viva", used with the name of a place or institution FLOREAT
vocabulary exclusive to a profession or other group JARGON, CANT, ARGOT
– vocabulary of a particular language, person, profession, subject, or the like LEXICON, LEXIS
– vocabulary of technical or very specialised terms TERMINOLOGY, NOMENCLATURE
– vocabulary or small specialised dictionary often accompanying or supplementing a difficult or technical text GLOSSARY
– relating to the words or vocabulary of a language LEXICAL
voice See also **mouth**, **pronunciation**, **sound**
– voice, put into words VOCALISE
– voice-amplifying device consisting of a wide tapering tube, as used at protest demonstrations MEGAPHONE
– voice-amplifying device with a built-in microphone and loudspeaker LOUD-HAILER
– voice-production, especially by an entertainer, giving the impression that the sound originates elsewhere, as from a dummy VENTRILOQUISM
– voice training through singing the *doh-re-mi* syllables TONIC SOL-FA, SOLFEGGIO, SOLMISATION
– adjective for the voice VOCAL
– adjust the pitch or tone of one's voice MODULATE, INFLECT
– having many voices, often with different melodic parts, as a piece of music might POLYPHONIC
– having or referring to a voice that is deep, full-throated, or loud BOOMING, SONOROUS, OROTUND, RESONANT
– having or referring to a voice that is high-pitched and shrill REEDY
– having or referring to a voice that is hoarse, deep, and often emotional HUSKY
– having or referring to a voice that is nasal or choky ADENOIDAL
– having or referring to a voice that is rich and full-toned MELLOW, FRUITY
– having or referring to a voice that is unpleasantly loud STRIDENT, STENTORIAN
– having or referring to a voice that is very smooth and sweet MELLIFLUOUS
– light rhythmical, springy flow or swing, as in a person's voice or walk LILT
– loss of one's voice through injury or disease APHONIA
– range of the voice REGISTER, DIAPASON
– rise and fall of the pitch of the voice INTONATION, MODULATION, CADENCE, INFLECTION
– trembling or caused by trembling, as the voice of a frightened person might be TREMULOUS
-voice- -PHON-, PHONO-, -PHONE, -PHONY
volcanic and other rocks such as granite, produced from cooled magma IGNEOUS ROCKS
– volcanic glass that is black and shiny OBSIDIAN, PITCHSTONE
– volcanic lava fragments SCORIA, SLAG, CINDERS
– volcanic rock, light and porous, used for scrubbing and polishing PUMICE
– volcanic rock that can be ground for making cement TRASS
– destructive flowing cloud of burning gas emitted in certain volcanic eruptions NUÉE ARDENTE
– jet of steam, gases, and smoke issuing from the ground in volcanic regions SOFFIONE, FUMAROLE
– oval cavity, originally a bubble, in volcanic rock, filled with quartz

or similar mineral AMYGDULE
– vent in the ground in an otherwise extinct volcanic region, emitting carbon dioxide MOFETTE

volcano See illustration
– expel fumes violently, as a rumbling volcano might ERUCT
– expel lava forcefully and abundantly, as a volcano might ERUPT
– inactive but not extinct, as a volcano might be DORMANT
– matter thrown out of an erupting volcano EJECTA
– relating to a volcano or volcanic eruption VULCANIAN
– small cone or exposed rock-filled vent of an extinct volcano PUY
– still active, not extinct, still in danger of erupting, as a volcano might be EXTANT
– vent in or near a volcano, emitting sulphurous gases and often water vapour SOLFATURA

voluntary, unforced, unprompted, as laughter might be SPONTANEOUS

vomit, often without bringing up anything HEAVE, RETCH
– vomit or bring up partly digested food REGURGITATE
– vomit or spew out DISGORGE
– causing vomiting, as a medicine might EMETIC
– illness, often combined with anorexia nervosa, in which compulsive eating is followed by bouts of self-induced vomiting BULIMIA, BULIMIA NERVOSA
– sick feeling, urge to vomit NAUSEA

von, *de*, or similar preposition accompanying a title or surname, indicating noble rank NOBILIARY PARTICLE

vote See also **election**
– vote against or veto someone, especially from membership of a club BLACKBALL
– vote by the electorate on a proposal or issue of public importance REFERENDUM
– vote by the electorate to accept or refuse a proposal, programme, or government PLEBISCITE
– vote cast in the U.S. for someone not listed on a ballot paper, by writing his name on it WRITE-IN
– vote in parliament DIVISION
– vote of approval at a meeting, expressed by cheering rather than by a formal ballot ACCLAMATION
– vote of the chairman or the presiding officer that decides the outcome when the votes in an assembly are tied CASTING VOTE
– vote or right to vote SUFFRAGE, FRANCHISE
– vote that may be transferred to another candidate if the first choice is eliminated from the ballot TRANSFERABLE VOTE
– appeal for or request something earnestly, such as votes or funds SOLICIT
– campaign for votes from people or a region in an election campaign CANVASS
– decision or statement discussed and voted on at a meeting RESOLUTION, MOTION
– electoral system in which parties are represented according to the proportion of votes that they win PROPORTIONAL REPRESENTATION
– give voting rights or full citizenship rights to ENFRANCHISE
– informally and by consensus rather than by formal discussion and voting ON THE NOD
– majority in an election in which the winner fails to secure more than half of the total votes or seats RELATIVE MAJORITY, PLURALITY
– majority in an election in which the winner secures more than half of the total votes or seats ABSOLUTE MAJORITY
– officer, who announces the number of votes and the result of an

volcano

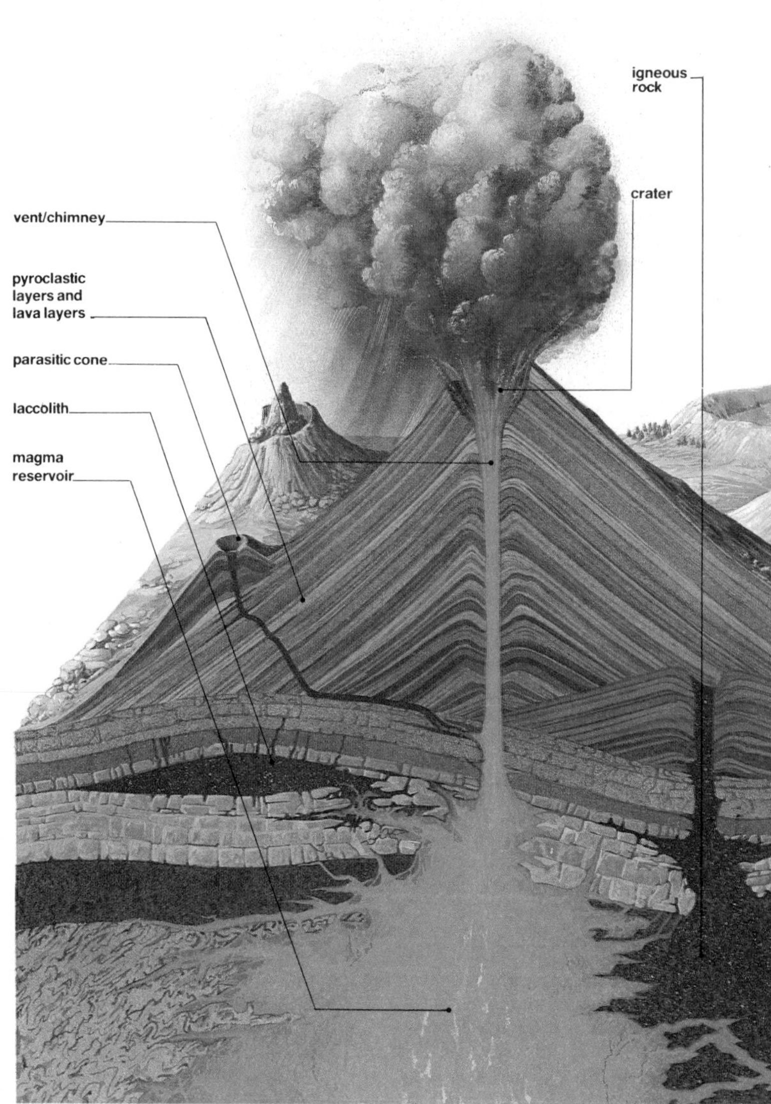

election RETURNING OFFICER
– person casting a vote on behalf of another PROXY
– person who checks or counts votes at an election SCRUTINEER
– person who counts the votes in an election, assembly, parliament, or the like TELLER
– refrain from voting ABSTAIN
– without any dissenting votes, with no one contradicting, virtually unanimously NEM CON

voter who remains uncommitted and readily votes differently at successive elections FLOATING VOTER
– group of voters electing a representative, or the area in which they live CONSTITUENCY

voting district in the U.S. PRECINCT
– voting for the candidate most likely to defeat a candidate one dislikes, rather than for the candidate one positively favours TACTICAL VOTING
– voting rights, the vote SUFFRAGE, FRANCHISE
– voting system in which each voter is allowed as many votes as there are candidates, to be distributed as he wishes CUMULATIVE VOTING
– voting system in which the voter indicates his choices in order of preference PREFERENTIAL VOTING
– study of voting patterns and electoral systems PSEPHOLOGY

voucher, certificate, or other formal document DOCKET
– exchange coupons, vouchers, or the like for goods REDEEM

vow of faith and promise of support by members of a church COVENANT
– relating to a vow or wish, as a prayer or religious offering might be VOTIVE

vowel sound that changes in quality during the syllable, such as the *ay*-sound in *pain* DIPHTHONG
– change in the vowel sound of a verb, as in *sing-sang-sung* GRADATION, ABLAUT
– omitting or slurring of an unstressed vowel or syllable, as to make a line of verse scan ELISION
– pair of vowels run together as *æ* or *œ* in Latin LIGATURE, DIGRAPH, DIPHTHONG
– repetition or similarity of the vowels in a series of words, as for poetic effect ASSONANCE
– two dots placed above a vowel, as in *naïve* DIAERESIS, UMLAUT
– unstressed mid-central vowel sound, as at the end of *Anna*, or the symbol ə that represents it SCHWA

voyage, long journey or wanderings PEREGRINATIONS

vulgar See also **rude**, **showy**
– vulgar, unrefined, coarse, oafish BOORISH, UNCOUTH, PHILISTINE
– vulgar and showy, flashy or cheap-looking TAWDRY, TINSELLY, GAUDY, GARISH, RAFFISH, BRASH
– vulgar and unrefined person, lout, yob PHILISTINE, YAHOO
– vulgar language or swearword PROFANITY
– vulgar opinion, taste, or group of people LOWEST COMMON DENOMINATOR
– vulgar or crude, having common or coarse tastes PLEBEIAN
– vulgar or rough people, the masses, the herd HOI POLLOI, RAGGLE-TAGGLE, RIFFRAFF, PLEBS
– "vulgar tongue", the ordinary spoken language rather than the refined or written form of a language VERNACULAR
– vulgarly or superficially attractive MERETRICIOUS, SPECIOUS
– vulgarly sentimental MAUDLIN, MAWKISH

vulture, hyena, insect, or the like that feeds on dead animals, rotting meat, or other decaying organic matter SCAVENGER

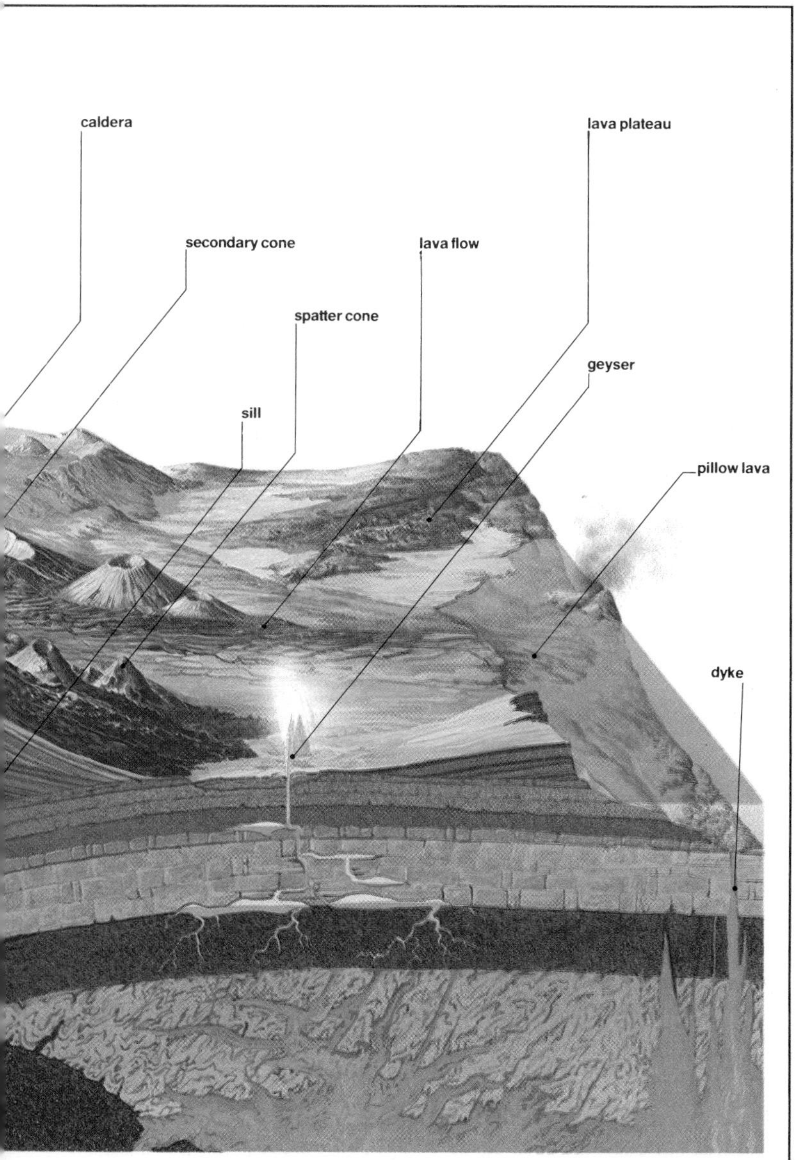

W

wafer See **Communion**
wage earners – relating to industrial wage earners in manual-labour jobs BLUE-COLLAR
wages, fees, or other form of profit from one's job or office EMOLUMENT
– system of paying wages in the form of goods TRUCK SYSTEM
wagon See also **horse-drawn vehicles**
– wagon-builder WAINWRIGHT
– canvas-covered wagon, used by North American pioneers PRAIRIE SCHOONER, CONESTOGA WAGON
– defensive camp formed by a circle of covered wagons CORRAL, LAAGER
– hooped rod supporting the canopy of a covered wagon BAIL
– old-fashioned or regional term for a farm wagon WAIN
– open wagon used to transport condemned prisoners to the place of execution, as during the French Revolution TUMBREL
– pivoted bar linking a wagon, plough, or the like to the side straps or traces of the horse's harness SWINGLETREE, WHIFFLETREE
wail, lament for the dead KEEN
– wail as if lamenting ULULATE
– wail weakly, whimper, whine MEWL, PULE
waist or bodice of a dress CORSAGE
– waistline, particularly when large GIRTH
waistcoat for a woman GILET
– waistcoat pocket, originally designed for a pocket watch FOB
wait, linger TARRY, LOITER, LAG
waiter in France or a French restaurant GARÇON
waiting state, intermediate or transitional condition LIMBO
waiting room, entrance hall, or reception area FOYER, VESTIBULE, LOBBY
wakefulness VIGILANCE
waking signal, usually by bugle, in the armed forces REVEILLE
Wales See **Welsh**
walk See also **move**
– walk about casually, usually for pleasure, stroll, stretch one's legs AMBLE, DANDER, PERAMBULATE
– walk aimlessly from place to place RAMBLE, ROAM
– walk along without apparent worry or care SWAN
– walk at a leisurely pace, typically in a public place PROMENADE
– walk casually or furtively SIDLE, SLINK
– walk casually or wearily TRAIPSE
– walk determinedly, brushing all aside WADE
– walk heavily, march long distances, plod FOOTSLOG, TRUDGE
– walk in an affected or prim way, with very short steps MINCE
– walk in an idle or leisurely way, stroll SAUNTER, MOSEY, SASHAY
– walk in a proud or pompously affected way STRUT, SWAGGER
– walk or move haltingly HOBBLE
– walk or run awkwardly LOLLOP, WADDLE, GALUMPH
– walk slowly, lag behind DAWDLE, LOITER
– walk swiftly with long steps STRIDE, PACE
– walk taken for the good of one's health CONSTITUTIONAL
– walk unsteadily or clumsily, shuffle SHAMBLE
– walk with conspicuous movements to express impatience, anger, or the like FLOUNCE
– walk with short, unsteady steps, as very young children do TODDLE
walking, or one's own legs or feet, as a means of travel SHANKS'S PONY
– walking about, able to walk AMBULATORY, AMBULANT
– walking area, typically covered, such as an aisle or cloister AMBULATORY
– walking-frame of light metal for the elderly or disabled ZIMMER, WALKER
– walking or moving from place to place, as in the course of one's business ITINERANT, PERIPATETIC
– walking with both heel and toes touching the ground, as humans do PLANTIGRADE
– walking with only the toes touching the ground, as cats do DIGITIGRADE
– flat stretch of ground for walking along, especially along a sea shore ESPLANADE, PROMENADE
– instrument gauging the distance covered while walking, by recording the number of steps taken PEDOMETER
– style of walking or carrying oneself, bearing GAIT, CARRIAGE, DEPORTMENT
-walking -GRADE
walking stick made from the stem of the rattan palm MALACCA CANE
– walking stick whose handle opens into a flat seat SHOOTING STICK
– walking stick with a spike at the tip PIKESTAFF
– metal ring or cap on the tip of a walking stick FERRULE
wall See also **brickwork**, **fortification**, **castle**
– wall consisting of two layers with a small space between them for insulation CAVITY WALL
– wall hanging made from a heavy woven textile TAPESTRY, ARRAS
– wall-like partition dividing up a ship, aircraft, or spacecraft BULKHEAD
– wall of a bodily cavity or organ PARIES
– wall or roof covering of overlapping boards WEATHERBOARDING, CLAPBOARDING
– wall painting MURAL
– wall painting made on dry plaster SECCO
– wall painting made on fresh damp plaster FRESCO
– adjective for a wall MURAL
– boarding running along the foot of an interior wall SKIRTING, SKIRTING BOARD
– bricks jutting out from a wall CORBELLING
– circular wall, especially one supporting a dome TAMBOUR
– coating of cement, plaster, or the like covering a wall or other surface RENDERING
– coating of cement, sand, and lime forming a hard finish on outside walls STUCCO
– construction or prop pressing against a wall to strengthen it BUTTRESS, PIER
– decorative slab, memorial tablet, or the like, as mounted on a wall or monument PLAQUE
– decoratively patterned plasterwork on walls PARGETING

– exterior angle of a wall QUOIN, COIGN
– facing of rectangular tiles fixed on an external wall in imitation of stone blocks STONE-CLADDING
– fortified wall surrounding a castle, town, or the like, or the area protected by it ENCEINTE
– gluey glaze, filler, or coating, as for paper or walls, made of wax, clay, resin, or the like SIZE
– hole or niche in a wall for supporting a beam COLUMBARIUM
– hollow plug, as of plastic, typically inserted into a hole in the wall as a mooring for a nail or screw RAWLPLUG
– imprison, shut up within walls IMMURE
– inward-curving surface between a ceiling and wall, or a concave moulding COVE, COVING
– lower section of a wall, distinguished by different decoration such as panelling DADO, WAINSCOT
– moulding running along the top of a building or wall CORNICE
– opening in a wall, wider inside than out, for a door or window EMBRASURE
– ornamental ridge running along the top of a roof or wall CRESTING
– outside the walls or boundaries, as of a castle, city, or university EXTRAMURAL
– plaster of a coarse, gravelly kind applied to outside walls ROUGHCAST, SLAPDASH
– plaster used as a finishing coating on walls GROUT
– projecting from the surrounding wall or surface PROUD
– protective row of spikes or broken glass fitted to the top of a wall CHEVAL-DE-FRISE
– rough finish for outside walls, produced by small pebbles embedded in the plaster PEBBLE-DASH
– roughened with a metal brush, as a wall might be KEYED
– scaling, by ladders, of a castle wall, rampart, or the like, as during a military attack ESCALADE
– section or space set back from the main surface of a wall, as for a statue or bookcase ALCOVE, RECESS, NICHE
– strip of ornamental plasterwork, stone, wood, or the like on a building or wall MOULDING
– tall frame used to scale fortress walls during a siege in ancient times TURRET, BELFRY
– top layer of bricks, tiles, or the like, usually sloping, of a wall COPING
– triangular section at the top of a wall, supporting a roof GABLE

wallet – U.S. term for a wallet BILLFOLD

wallpaper that is thick and textured ANAGLYPTA
– tufts of wool or other fibre forming a raised pattern on wallpaper or fabrics FLOCK

wander about aimlessly MAUNDER, MEANDER, RAMBLE, ROAM
– wander about, especially in an enjoyable and sociable way GAD ABOUT, GALLIVANT
– wander from the main subject of one's speech or writing DIGRESS, DEVIATE

wandering See also **travelling**
– wandering, erratic PLANETARY
– wandering about, drifting, homeless VAGABOND, VAGRANT
– wandering from the main topic or course, as in a speech DIGRESSION, EXCURSION, EXCURSUS
– wandering in search of adventure, as medieval knights were ERRANT
– wandering medieval musician MINSTREL, TROUBADOUR, JONGLEUR
– wandering or travelling from place to place, as in search of work ITINERANT, MIGRANT
– wandering scholar or student in the Middle Ages GOLIARD

wanderer, specifically a member of a pastoral people moving about in search of food or grazing land NOMAD, BEDOUIN, TUAREG

waning, as the Moon might be DECRESCENT

war See also **military**
– war memorial or other monument honouring a dead person or dead people buried elsewhere CENOTAPH
– war or phase of a war in which little fighting is done or little change in the military balance occurs SITZKRIEG, STAND-OFF
– war waged by the giants against the gods in Greek mythology GIGANTOMACHY
– adjective for war MARTIAL
– aggressive, hostile, war-like BELLIGERENT, BELLICOSE, HAWKISH, MILITANT
– arms or other goods that a neutral nation cannot legally supply to a warring nation CONTRABAND OF WAR
– display of military power or threatening of war by one country in its dealings with another SABRE RATTLING, GUN-BOAT DIPLOMACY
– murderous, marked by widespread slaughter, as a bloody war is INTERNECINE
– payments demanded as compensation from the losing side in a war REPARATIONS
– person forced from his home or homeland, especially by a war, refugee DISPLACED PERSON, DP
– person moved from a war zone to a safe area EVACUEE
– politician or adviser favouring aggression or war HAWK
– politician or adviser favouring conciliation or avoidance of war DOVE
– prepare for war, as troops might MOBILISE
– provocative act or event that prompts or justifies a war CASUS BELLI
– referring to non-nuclear warfare or weapons CONVENTIONAL
– referring to the period after a war, especially the American Civil War POST-BELLUM
– referring to the period before a war, especially the American Civil War ANTE-BELLUM
– right of a nation at war to use or destroy the property of a neutral nation on condition that full compensation is paid ANGARY
– simple living conditions, as imposed in wartime AUSTERITY
– slaughter or massacre, especially in war CARNAGE
– victor's decree or settlement imposed on a defeated enemy after a war DIKTAT
– wearing down or slow exhaustion of enemy forces during a war ATTRITION

-war -MACHY, -MACHIA

ward – relation between ward and guardian TUTELAGE

wardrobe or large, heavy cabinet ARMOIRE
– wardrobe or small room for hanging clothes GARDEROBE
– wardrobe specially prepared by a bride TROUSSEAU

warehouse for storing goods prior to payment of duty or prior to export BONDED WAREHOUSE
– warehouse or similar place for storage DEPOSITORY, DEPOT, ENTREPÔT, REPOSITORY, REPERTORY

warm a wine to room temperature after opening it CHAMBRÉ
– warm-blooded, as mammals are HOMOIOTHERMIC, HOMEOTHERMIC
– warm up by stretching and exercising, as before a race LIMBER UP
– warmed up before serving, as leftover food might be RÉCHAUFFÉ
– warming dish CHAFING DISH
– warming rack or stand, next to a fireplace FOOTMAN
– warmish, lukewarm TEPID

– warmth-producing CALEFACIENT
warn, give a useful hint TIP SOMEONE THE WINK, TIP OFF
– warn or advise against a particular action, caution ADMONISH
– warn or indicate that something is about to happen PRESAGE, HARBINGER, HERALD
warning, guide, or sign BEACON
– warning against touching or interfering NOLI-ME-TANGERE
– warning of an event before it occurs PREMONITION
– warning or caution CAVEAT
– warning or elaborate complaint JEREMIAD, DENUNCIATION
– warning signal or alarm, typically on a bell TOCSIN
– "beware", word used by schoolchildren as a warning that a teacher is coming CAVE
– gentle warning or scolding ADMONITION
– Latin maxim warning the buyer to beware CAVEAT EMPTOR
– remedial, improving, as advice or a warning might be SALUTARY
– sign or warning of a coming event AUGURY, AUSPICE, PORTENT, OMEN, PRODIGY, PRESAGE
warrior – full equipment of weapons and armour belonging to a warrior PANOPLY
warship See **ships**
– armoured cylinder protecting the turret of a warship BARBETTE
– fleet or grouping of warships ARMADA, SQUADRON, FLOTILLA
– revolving armoured dome or drum on a tank or warship, in which guns are mounted TURRET
wart, corn, or other small benign growth PAPILLOMA
– wart-like growth or projection, as on a legume's root, the skin, or a bone TUBERCLE
– wart on the sole of the foot PLANTAR WART
– wart or any similar horny growth on the skin KERATOSIS
– wart or wart-like growth, usually on the foot VERRUCA
– destruction of warts or other unwanted tissue by means of electric sparks FULGURATION
– grow or spread abnormally, with fleshy outgrowths, as warts and some tumours do VEGETATE
wash by flushing out or flooding with water SWILL OUT, SLUICE, DOUSE
– wash or purify ceremonially LUSTRATE
– wash out a wound, the eye, or the like with water or a medicinal solution IRRIGATE
– washing of the body, as in religious ceremonies ABLUTION
– washing out of an organ, such as the stomach LAVAGE
– washing substance as used for industrial and household cleaning DETERGENT
– low basin-like bathroom fixture on which one sits to wash one's private parts BIDET
– purify, separate, or remove a substance, such as ore, by washing and straining it ELUTRIATE
– remove soluble parts from a substance such as soil by washing it out with water LEACH, LIXIVIATE, ELUVIATE
washbowl – bedside table, movable stand, or the like containing a washbowl COMMODE
washer for a rivet BURR
wasp – wasp's nest, or colony of wasps or hornets VESPIARY
– adjective for a wasp VESPINE
waste, spend or use extravagantly SQUANDER
– waste, spend or use up in an inefficient or wasteful way DISSIPATE
– waste liquid, as from a factory or sewage works EFFLUENT
– waste material from a furnace after smelting or refining SLAG, SINTER, CINDER, SCORIA
– waste matter discharged from the body EXCREMENT, EXCRETA, FAECES, EGESTA, ORDURE, DEJECTA
– waste time DAWDLE, DALLY, TARRY
– waste time, money, or the like FRITTER AWAY, FRIVOL AWAY
– wasting away of the body or part of the body PHTHISIS, ATROPHY, EMACIATION, MACERATION
– wasting disease, especially tuberculosis of the lungs CONSUMPTION
– wasting of the body or of an organ as a result of lengthy disease TABES
– wasting time, or causing a delay DILATORY, PROCRASTINATING
– extraction of useful substances from waste material RECOVERY, RECYCLING
wasteful, excessive, unrestrained WANTON, IMMODERATE
– wasteful or unthrifty IMPROVIDENT, SPENDTHRIFT
– irresponsibly and recklessly wasteful or extravagant PRODIGAL, PROFLIGATE
wasteland DEVASTATION, DESOLATION
watch See also **clock**
– watch or clock of a very precise kind, especially one used at sea CHRONOMETER
– watch or clock that can be primed to strike the hour or quarter-hour REPEATER
– watch or guard kept during the hours of sleep VIGIL
– watch that is wound by a small attached knob projecting outside the casing STEM-WINDER
– watch with a hinged metal lid protecting the face HUNTER
– watch with a sweep-second hand CHRONOGRAPH
– adjust watches to register the identical time SYNCHRONISE
– art of making watches or clocks, or the study of them HOROLOGY
– display of symbols, as on a quartz watch, produced by liquid crystals LCD
– fine coiled spring helping to regulate the movement of a watch HAIRSPRING
– glass or plastic cover of a watch face LUNETTE, CRYSTAL
– referring to a watch, clock, or meter that indicates readings by changing numbers rather than by moving hands on a dial DIGITAL
– referring to a watch, clock, or meter with traditional hands and dial to indicate readings ANALOG
– second hand of a watch SWEEP-SECOND HAND
– small, notched winding knob on an old-fashioned watch CROWN
– waistcoat pocket, originally designed for a pocket watch FOB
watchful, alert, on the lookout for danger VIGILANT, ON THE QUI VIVE, ARGUS-EYED
watchtower of a fortress BARBICAN
water – water-borne barrier, as of logs or empty drums BOOM
– water cask or drinking fountain on a ship SCUTTLEBUTT
– water channel or canal that is man-made AQUEDUCT
– water channel or ditch in South Africa SLOOT
– water channel or small dam, or the gate or valve holding back or regulating the water SLUICE
– water channel such as a ravine or gully GULLET
– water collecting in a ship's hull BILGE WATER
– water-cooled smoking pipe, used in the East HOOKAH, NARGHILE, HUBBLE-BUBBLE, KALIAN
– water-divining by means of a rod or wand RHABDOMANCY, DOWSING
– water drops formed on surfaces from cooling air CONDENSATION
– water-dwelling, as some plants are HYDROPHILOUS, HYDROPHYTIC, AQUATIC
– water-heater, usually operated by gas, in one's home GEYSER
– water nymph in classical mythology NAIAD
– water or air stream directed at

or into a part of the body for cleansing or healing DOUCHE
– water pipe on a pavement, with nozzles for hoses HYDRANT
– water pipe or channel CONDUIT, CULVERT
– water-raising apparatus, as used in ancient times, typically a spiral device within a tube ARCHIMEDES' SCREW
– water-raising apparatus, as used in Egypt, consisting of a pivoted pole with a bucket and a counterweight on the end SHADOOF
– water-spirit in Germanic folklore, usually hostile to humans NIX
– water-spirit in Scottish folklore, in the form of a horse that would drown its riders KELPIE
– water-spirit or nymph UNDINE
– water tank, as in the roof or attached to a lavatory CISTERN
– addition of fluorine compounds to the public water supply as a measure to reduce tooth decay FLUORIDATION
– artificial water channel, as for providing power or transporting logs FLUME
– backward flow of air or water, as from a propeller or a wave on the beach BACKWASH
– channel for excess water, as round the side of a dam SPILLWAY
– channel or bay through which water flows inland INLET, ESTUARY
– cover with water, flood INUNDATE
– cultivation of plants without soil, using nutrients dissolved in water HYDROPONICS, AQUICULTURE
– curved surface of water or other liquid held in a tube or container MENISCUS
– deprived of water or moisture, dry DEHYDRATED, DESICCATED
– dip lightly into the water, as a bird might DAP
– fit for drinking, as uncontaminated water is POTABLE
– fizzy mineral water that is either natural or artificially aerated SELTZER WATER
– floating mass of tiny animal or plant organisms on a large body of water PLANKTON
– flowing with a violently agitated movement, as river water might TURBULENT
– legal trial in the Middle Ages, in which God's judgment was allegedly secured through exposing the accused to fire, immersion in water, or the like ORDEAL
– level at which the ground is saturated by water WATER TABLE
– living, growing, or occurring in or on water AQUATIC
– living both on land and in water, or relating to both land and water AMPHIBIOUS
– measure the depth of water, as with a weighted line SOUND, FATHOM, PLUMB
– muddied through sediment or foreign particles, as river water might be TURBID
– operated by or involving water pressure HYDRAULIC
– plunge beneath the water, soak completely IMMERSE, SUBMERGE
– process discarded glass, water, and so on for re-use RECYCLE
– remove salt, as from sea water DESALINATE
– rippling movement in water EDDY, PURL
– rising, lowering, or distortion of the surface of water or other liquid, as when held in a tube, due to surface tension CAPILLARITY, CAPILLARY ACTION
– shallow stretch of water SHOAL
– sheet of water flowing over a weir or dam wall NAPPE
– slightly salty, as water might be BRACKISH, BRINY
– stick, forked twig, or the like that quivers or dips when held above ground containing water or minerals DIVINING ROD, DOWSING ROD
– stretch of land intermittently covered by water WASH, FLOOD PLAIN
– strong swift current of water, or its channel RACE
– supply water to a region, farmland, or the like IRRIGATE
– thin or weaken a cordial, concentrate, or other liquid, as by adding water DILUTE
– track of visible foam or waves in water, as left by a ship WAKE
– uninterrupted stretch of water along a river or canal REACH
– unmoving, not flowing, as pond water is STAGNANT
– upright outdoor water pipe with a tap STANDPIPE
– very clear, as pure water is LIMPID, PELLUCID

-water- -AQU-, AQUA-, AQUI-, HYDR-, HYDRO-

water buffalo CARABAO

water clock CLEPSYDRA

water ice SORBET

water lily or related plant LOTUS, NENUPHAR, NYMPHAEA

water on the brain HYDROCEPHALUS

water ski consisting of a single board AQUAPLANE

water vapour – containing as much water vapour as possible, as a humid atmosphere might SATURATED
– containing large amounts of water vapour, as moist air does HUMID, MUGGY, CLOSE
– lose or give off water vapour through pores, as from the surface of a leaf TRANSPIRE

water wheel See illustration at **windmill**
– water wheel rimmed with buckets that dip into a stream or pool, used in irrigation systems NORIA
– referring to a water wheel driven by water flowing beneath UNDERSHOT
– referring to a water wheel driven by water flowing over its top OVERSHOT
– watercourse directing water into a mill, turbine, or water wheel HEADRACE

watercolour painting or wash AQUARELLE
– watercolour pigment mixed with gum to make it opaque, or a painting or the method using such pigments GOUACHE

waterfall CHUTE
– waterfall, or series of small waterfalls CASCADE, CATARACT

watering place, resort area with mineral springs SPA

waterproof IMPERMEABLE
– waterproof rubber shoes worn over standard shoes GALOSHES
– waterproof sheet of canvas used as a covering TARPAULIN
– pitch or tarry mixture, as used in waterproofing BITUMEN, ASPHALT

watershed – area bounded by watersheds, in which all water drains into one river system CATCHMENT AREA, DRAINAGE BASIN

watertight chamber from which underwater construction or repair work is done CAISSON
– watertight enclosure or compartment, as for construction on a riverbed COFFER
– make a boat watertight by sealing or packing the seams, as with tar CAULK, PAY

waterway linking two larger bodies of water STRAIT, SOUND
– clean or deepen a harbour or waterway by means of a scooping machine DREDGE

watery, containing, relating to, or dissolved in water AQUEOUS
– watery chemical solution used as a disinfectant and bleaching agent JAVELLE WATER
– watery liquid from the body tissues LYMPH

wave formation in the form of apparently motionless waves, as near a breakwater or sea wall CLAPOTIS

– wave-like, wavy UNDULANT
– wave moving upstream in a river estuary, as caused by tidal currents BORE, EAGRE
– wave or reveal a weapon or similar object openly or defiantly BRANDISH, FLOURISH
– wave or swell of the sea, smoke, sound, or the like BILLOW
– wave the arms about to convey meaning GESTICULATE
– backward pull of waves towards the sea when receding after breaking on the shore UNDERTOW
– broken wave of the sea, as on a shore COMBER, BREAKER, ROLLER
– huge wave due to an earthquake or volcanic eruption on the seabed TSUNAMI
– loud, deep, and resonant, as the sound of waves crashing on the shore is PLANGENT
– relating to waves, such as light waves, of the same frequency or related phases COHERENT
– rise and fall as waves do in the open sea SURGE, HEAVE, SWELL
– transmit a wave through a medium, in physics PROPAGATE

wavelength – invisible radiation having wavelengths between those of visible light and microwaves INFRARED
– invisible radiation having wavelengths between those of visible light and X-rays ULTRAVIOLET

wavy, having winding lines, movements, decorations, or the like VERMICULATE, UNDULATE

wax modelling CEROPLASTICS
– wax or polish something, such as a car SIMONISE
– wax polish or similar polishing agent LUSTRE
– bronze-casting technique in which a mould is formed around a wax model, which is then melted and drained off LOST-WAX PROCESS, CIRE PERDUE
– pointed writing instrument, as used on wax tablets in ancient times STYLUS

wax- CERO-

waxing, as the Moon might be INCRESCENT

waxy or wax-like CERACEOUS
– waxy substance formed from oils in a whale's head, as used for cosmetics and candles SPERMACETI
– waxy substance secreted by the ear, earwax CERUMEN
– waxy substance secreted by whales, used as a fixative in perfume-making AMBERGRIS

way in which something works or is used MODUS OPERANDI
– way of working or living together MODUS VIVENDI
– go one's way WEND

weak, bland, lacking all real force, as a character or comment might be ANODYNE, ANAEMIC, INSIPID
– weak, feeble, frail, doddering like an old woman ANILE
– weak, limp, lacking energy and vitality LETHARGIC, LANGUID
– weak, powerless, lacking force or competence, as a king might be IMPOTENT, INEFFECTUAL
– weak, unaccented, as a syllable might be ATONIC
– weak and small PUNY
– weak and unconvincing, as an excuse or argument might be TENUOUS, FLIMSY, UNTENABLE
– weak area or vulnerable aspect SOFT UNDERBELLY, ACHILLES' HEEL
– weak or ineffectual, drained of energy and vitality, as through self-indulgence EFFETE, DEGENERATE, DECADENT
– weak through age, illness, overuse, or the like DECREPIT, INFIRM
– weak-willed, indecisive, lacking purpose or perseverance IRRESOLUTE
– weak-willed, lacking courage or strength of character SPINELESS, LILY-LIVERED
– weak-willed, passive, slack, wishy-washy SUPINE, FECKLESS
– weakly built, liable to collapse, as a building might be RICKETY
– weakly defended, open to attack PREGNABLE, VULNERABLE
– weakly sentimental and affected, as someone's manner or poetry might be NAMBY-PAMBY, TWEE, MAWKISH, MAUDLIN
– chronically weak and sickly VALETUDINARIAN

weak person, especially one lacking courage or determination, sissy MILKSOP, WIMP, NINNY
– weak person, ineffectual or powerless man EUNUCH, MEDIOCRITY
– weak person, once strong or honourable but now spineless or feeble BROKEN REED
– weak person, over-protected and pampered MOLLYCODDLE
– weak person, team, or the like, easily defeated PUSHOVER
– weak person, timid and retiring man in the U.S. MILQUETOAST

weaken, deprive of initiative, energy, and other qualities traditionally regarded as masculine EMASCULATE
– weaken, go limp, as a flower might WILT
– weaken, grow feeble or disheartened FLAG, SAG, LANGUISH
– weaken, make useless STULTIFY
– weaken, tire out or wear down by sapping energy or vigour ENERVATE, ENFEEBLE, DEBILITATE, DEVITALISE
– weaken in a stealthy way, as in preparing to overthrow a regime UNDERMINE, SUBVERT
– weaken or make thin, as disease or dilution might ATTENUATE
– weaken or thin a cordial, concentrate, or other liquid, as by adding water DILUTE
– weaken or wither, waste away, as a body part might ATROPHY
– weaken the reputation or position of, as by scandal COMPROMISE
– weakened and pale, as through fever or starvation ETIOLATED
– weakened or seriously injured or disabled INCAPACITATED
– weakened to the point of exhaustion, drained of strength or resources DEPLETED

weakness, chronic loss or lack of strength, as through disease DEBILITY, ASTHENIA, CACHEXIA
– weakness, flaw, small but fatally vulnerable spot ACHILLES' HEEL
– weakness, minor personal failing, small fault of character FOIBLE
– weakness and failing powers due to illness or old age INFIRMITY

-weakness- -ASTHEN-

wealth, riches, or money, especially if acquired in a dubious way PELF, LUCRE
– wealth regarded as a corrupting influence MAMMON
– mine or other source of great wealth GOLCONDA, EL DORADO
– source of great wealth or good luck BONANZA

wealthy See **rich**

weapons See chart, and also **bomb**, **missile**, **knives**, **gun**, **club**, **sword**
– weapons or arms, especially heavy guns ORDNANCE
– weapons and ammunition MUNITIONS
– weapons manufacturer or repairer ARMOURER
– weapons or defence policy designed to discourage enemy attack DETERRENT
– weapons supply greater than required for victory OVERKILL
– referring to a weapon or bomb that produces a violent fire INCENDIARY
– referring to non-nuclear warfare or weapons CONVENTIONAL
– remove weapons from a person or group DISARM
– search a person, as for concealed weapons, using quick hand movements FRISK
– station troops or weapons in an

area, or make them ready for action DEPLOY
– store of hidden weapons, stolen goods, or the like, or its hiding place CACHE
– storehouse or factory for weapons ARMOURY, ARSENAL
– wave a weapon or similar object about in a threatening, boastful, or showy way BRANDISH, FLOURISH

wear away, wear down, as through the action of wind or water ERODE, CORRADE
– wearing away by chemical action, as of rusting metals CORROSION
– gradual wearing down, as of rock or enemy forces ATTRITION

weasel, ferret, badger, otter, or related mammal MUSTELINE
– tree-dwelling mammal resembling the weasel PINE MARTEN

weather See chart, pages 558-559, and also **wind**
– balloon-borne instrument used to collect and transmit weather information RADIOSONDE
– dangerous lack of protection from the weather EXPOSURE
– look menacing and dark, as the sky or weather might LOWER
– mild, as the weather or one's temper might be CLEMENT, TEMPERATE, EQUABLE
– period of settled weather around the winter solstice HALCYON DAYS
– science of weather conditions and forecasting METEOROLOGY
– stormy and wild, as weather might be INCLEMENT
– unfavourable, as winds or weather might be ADVERSE, CONTRARY

weathercock VANE, WEATHER VANE

weaving – boat-shaped device holding the bobbin in weaving, and used for passing the weft threads through the warp threads SHUTTLE
– device on a loom that keeps the cloth stretched during weaving TEMPLE
– heavy decorative weaving used as a wall hanging TAPESTRY, ARRAS
– loom, invented in the early 19th century, for mechanical pattern-weaving JACQUARD LOOM
– parallel cords or wires in a loom, separating the warp threads for the shuttle HEDDLES
– reel around which yarn is wound in weaving SPINDLE, BOBBIN, QUILL
– threads running crosswise in weaving or in a woven fabric WOOF, WEFT, FILLING, PICKS
– threads running lengthways in weaving or in a woven fabric WARP

webbed, as a duck's feet are PALMATE

wedding See **marriage**
– wedding ceremony NUPTIALS
– noisy mock serenade, as with pots and pans, made to a newly married couple at their wedding CHARIVARI

wedge, as for locking printing type, raising a cannon, or the like QUOIN, COIGN
– wedge or wooden block stopping a barrel, wheel, or boat from rolling or sliding CHOCK, SCOTCH
– wedge-shaped CUNEAL, CUNEATE, SPHENIC
– ancient writing system in the Middle East, using wedge-shaped characters CUNEIFORM

weedkiller HERBICIDE
– weedkiller chemical PARAQUAT

weed with fleshy leaves, sometimes eaten as a salad PURSLANE
– weeding spade SPUD, HOE
– weeds growing in cornfields TARES
– clinging bristly seed pod of various weeds, such as burdock BUR
– growing vigorously and widely, as weeds might RANK
– growing wild, especially on cultivated land, as wild flowers or weeds might AGRESTAL

weekday that is not a feast day FERIA

weekly HEBDOMADAL

weeping continually, tearful LACHRYMOSE

weigh down, burden, or hinder ENCUMBER

weight hanging on a cord, as

WEAPONS

arbalest	large crossbow used to fire arrows, stones, and other missiles
assegai	light spear used by tribesmen of southern Africa
ballista, onager	ancient catapult-like device used to hurl missiles
belfry	movable siege tower used to attack enemy walls
caltrop	spiked ball placed in the path of troops
flail	swinging bar attached to a long handle, used in close combat
gladius	short double-edged sword of ancient Rome
Greek fire	flaming chemical substance, used as a kind of fire-bomb, mainly by the Byzantine navy
halberd, gisarme	pikestaff topped by an axe-like blade and a spike
javelin, lance	long, pointed spear
mace	club with a spiked metal head
parazonium	ancient Greek dagger
partisan	pikestaff topped by a long double-edged blade
pilum	long spear of ancient Rome
quarterstaff	long wooden staff, tipped with iron
spatha	long single-edged sword of ancient Rome
spontoon	pikestaff topped by a pointed metal head and cross-bar
trebuchet, mangonel	medieval catapult-like device used to hurl missiles
trident	three-pronged weapon used by Roman gladiators
twibil	battle-axe with two cutting edges
waddy	straight stick used by Australian Aborigines as a club or missile
woomera	notched stick used by Australian Aborigines to throw a spear

used in fishing, depth-sounding, or determining a vertical line PLUMB
– weight lifted for exercise, typically consisting of a small bar with a fixed metal ball at each end DUMBBELL
– weight lifted for exercise or in competitions, consisting of a metal bar with heavy removable metal discs at both ends BARBELL
– weight of a person, especially of a heavy person AVOIRDUPOIS
– weight of an unladen vehicle, or of the container or wrapping material of goods TARE

weight- BARO-

weightlifting – lifts of various kinds in weightlifting, to raise the weight above the head PRESS, SNATCH, JERK
– lift in weightlifting in which the weight is raised to shoulder height, and held there CLEAN

weights and measures See chart, pages 560-561

weird See **odd**
– weird, nightmarish or surreal KAFKAESQUE

weld or unite two metal parts by means of melted alloy SOLDER
– welder or other metal worker in heavy industry BOILERMAKER
– gas mixture used for the high-temperature flame in welding OXYACETYLENE
– mask for shielding the eyes, as worn by welders VISOR

welfare work or humanitarian feelings, charity PHILANTHROPY

well drilled through impermeable rocks to reach water that is under pressure ARTESIAN WELL
– bucket used in wells or mine shafts KIBBLE
– pivoted pole with a bucket on the end for drawing water from a well SWEEP, SWIPE

well- EU-

well-bred and cultivated person PATRICIAN

Welsh, or a Welshman CAMBRIAN
– Welsh art of singing poetry to a harp accompaniment PENILLION
– Welsh emotional enthusiasm, as in the reciting of poetry HWYL
– Welsh language CYMRIC
– Welsh name for Wales CYMRU
– Welsh people CYMRY
– Welsh terms of endearment, as in addressing a child DEL, BACH
– annual Welsh gathering or competition for musicians and poets EISTEDDFOD
– British group of Celtic languages, including Welsh and Cornish BRYTHONIC LANGUAGES
– ice-gouged, steep-walled hollow on a Welsh mountain CWM
– medieval anthology of Welsh legends MABINOGION

werewolf LOUP-GAROU, LYCANTHROPE

West Indies – form of religion in the West Indies, of a kind involving magic rituals and witchcraft OBEAH
– heavily rhythmical form of popular music originating in the West Indies REGGAE
– light rhythmical form of popular music originating in the West Indies SKA
– religious and political movement among black West Indians, involving veneration of the late Haile Selassie, former Ethiopian emperor RASTAFARIANISM
– slave on the run in the West Indies in former times, or a descendant of such a slave MAROON
– song from the West Indies, with a syncopated rhythm, and lyrics typically improvised on a humorous or topical theme CALYPSO

Western countries or regions THE OCCIDENT

wet, fill, soak completely SATURATE
– wet, soggy, marshy PLASHY
– wet and sticky, as the air might be HUMID, MUGGY
– wet and untidy, as one's hair or clothes might be BEDRAGGLED
– wet or wash with a flow of water SLUICE, SWILL
– wet thoroughly, drench DOUSE
– wet through, sopping SODDEN
– wetting, helping to retain moisture, as glycerin does HUMECTANT
– unpleasantly cold and wet, chilly and damp DANK, CLAMMY

wet- HYGRO-

wet-and-dry-bulb thermometer PSYCHROMETER

whale, porpoise, or similar fish-like aquatic mammal CETACEAN
– whale-like mammal with small paddle-like forelimbs MANATEE,

WEATHER AND CLIMATE TERMS

anticyclone	area of high atmospheric pressure, with winds spiralling outwards
backing	referring to a change of wind direction anticlockwise, as from south to south-east to east, at a particular place
Beaufort scale	scale of wind force, ranging from 0 for calm to 12 for hurricane
col	area of intermediate pressure separating two anticyclones or two depressions
convection	transfer of heat by massive movement within the atmosphere, typically upwards
cyclone	tropical storm with violently rotating winds around a low-pressure centre
depression, low	area of low atmospheric pressure in temperate latitudes, with winds spiralling inwards
dust devil	rapidly moving column of dust whipped up by a swirling of wind round an intense low-pressure area
front, discontinuity	boundary between air masses of different temperature and humidity
glazed frost, black ice	thin coating of transparent ice
greenhouse effect	heating of the Earth's surface by retention of infrared radiation, caused by increasing carbon dioxide in the atmosphere
haar	cold sea-mist or fog on Britain's north-east coast
hoar frost	powdery, white coating of small ice crystals
hurricane	intense, tropical disturbance – force 12 on the Beaufort Scale – in the West Indies and Gulf of Mexico
inversion, inversion layer	increase of temperature with height, or the layer of the atmosphere where this occurs

DUGONG, SEA COW
– whale's fat forming in a layer beneath its skin BLUBBER
– whale's air hole on the top of its head BLOWHOLE, SPIRACLE
– arctic whale with teeth and, in the male, a long spiral tusk NARWHAL
– dive down quickly and deep, as a whale or large fish might SOUND
– either of the flaps of the tail of a whale or related animal FLUKE
– herd or school of whales GAM, POD
– hunting black-and-white toothed whale, the killer whale ORC, GRAMPUS
– large toothed whale, hunted for its valuable oil, the sperm whale CACHALOT
– shrimp-like sea creatures forming the principal food of some whales KRILL
– small pale whale of northern seas, the white whale BELUGA
– spear-like instrument used to kill whales HARPOON
– strip a whale, seal, or the like of its skin or blubber FLENCH, FLENSE
– surface or leap from the water, as a whale might BREACH
– toothless, plankton eating whale of various kinds, the whalebone whale MYSTICETE, BALEEN WHALE
– waxy cholesterol substance, secreted by whales, used as a fixative in perfume-making AMBERGRIS
– waxy substance formed from oils in a whale's head, used for cosmetics and candles SPERMACETI
– whalebone whale with a furrowed throat and chest, and a dorsal fin COMMON RORQUAL, FINBACK, RAZORBACK

whalebone, flexible horn-like material from the upper jaw of certain whales, as formerly used for making corset stays BALEEN
– carved or engraved articles of ivory, whalebone, or the like SCRIMSHAW

wheat – cereal food produced by boiling and then drying coarsely ground wheat BULGUR WHEAT, CRACKED WHEAT
– dish of hulled wheat, boiled in milk, sweetened, and spiced FRUMENTY
– hard wheat granules left over after the grinding of flour, used in milk puddings SEMOLINA
– hard wheat whose flour is used in making pasta DURUM WHEAT
– North African dish of crushed steamed wheat granules served with various meats or vegetables COUSCOUS
– protein mixture in wheat flour, used in glues GLUTEN
– resembling or made of grain, especially wheat FRUMENTACEOUS
– species of wheat with reddish grains, widely cultivated in ancient times SPELT

wheel – wheel-like cage that spins when a pet mouse or hamster runs along inside it for exercise SQUIRREL CAGE
– wheel or cylinder with a toothed rim, as to engage a bicycle chain or film perforations SPROCKET
– wheel or disc whose axis is off-centre and which converts rotary to reciprocating motion ECCENTRIC
– wheel or roller within a tractor-tread, as on a tank BOGIE
– wheel rotated by the tread of a prisoner, pet mouse, or the like TREADMILL
– wheel-shaped, or resembling a wheel TROCHAL
– wheel used by a potter LATHE
– wheel with a grooved rim, as on a pulley SHEAVE
– wheel's spindle, as in a watch or clock ARBOR
– wheels slanting towards each other at the bottom DISHED WHEELS
– abrasive wheel for sharpening knives CARBORUNDUM WHEEL
– "big wheel", giant fairground wheel FERRIS WHEEL
– centre of a wheel, through which the axle passes HUB, NAVE
– curved metal plate on the rim of a wooden wheel STRAKE
– heavy or noisy rolling movement of a wheel TRUNDLE
– inward-turned alignment of front wheels to improve steering TOE-IN
– one-wheeled vehicle, as pedalled by acrobats UNICYCLE
– outward tilt of a vehicle's front wheels CAMBER

isobar	line on a weather map linking places that have the same atmospheric pressure
isohyet	line on a weather map linking places that have the same rainfall
isotherm	line on a weather map linking places that have the same temperature
jet stream	narrow, fast-moving, generally westerly airstream at high altitude
monsoon	major pressure and wind system that reverses direction with the seasons, as in south and south-east Asia
occluded front/occlusion	front formed in a depression when the cold front overtakes the warm front
ridge	elongated area of high pressure between two depressions
rime, frost feathers	frost in the form of granular ice crystals on the windward side of objects
thermal	vertically rising current of warm air, used by glider pilots
tornado	intense cyclone with winds whirling at more than 200 miles (320 km) per hour
trough	elongated area of low atmospheric pressure between two areas of higher pressure
typhoon	intense cyclone in the China Sea, with winds whirling at more than 100 miles (160 km) per hour
veering	referring to a change of wind direction clockwise, as from south to south-west to west, at a particular place
waterspout	rapidly moving column of cloud and water whipped up by a small, intense, short-lived low-pressure area over the sea
wedge	area of high pressure between two depressions, narrower than a ridge

– pivot of metal at the end of a wooden shaft or axle, as for a wheel to turn on GUDGEON
– projecting rim or edge, as on a wheel or beam, for strengthening, attaching, or the like FLANGE
– small flywheel on a spinning wheel WHORL
– small stabilising wheel attached on each side of the back wheel of a child's bicycle FAIRY WHEEL, OUTRIDER
– small swivelling wheel on each leg of an item of furniture, for easy moving CASTOR
– small toothed wheel on the spur on a cowboy's boot ROWEL
– spinning flywheel maintaining a stable angle or direction in a frame of pivoted supports GYROSCOPE
– wedge or block placed under a wheel, log, or the like, to immobilise it on a slope SCOTCH, CHOCK

wheelchair with a hood BATH CHAIR

wheezing or whistling sound from the chest, caused by partial blocking of the air channels RHONCHUS

whether you like it or not, willy-nilly NOLENS VOLENS

whey, watery part of milk SERUM

whimsical or peculiar action or notion CAPRICE, VAGARY, QUIRK

whip, flexible rod, twig, or the like SWITCH
– whip, flog, or scourge, as for religious discipline or sexual gratification FLAGELLATE
– whip-like leather strap split into strips at the end, formerly used for beating children, especially in Scotland TAWSE
– whip made of bull's penis PIZZLE
– whip mark on the flesh WEAL, WALE
– whip of stiff leather, especially of rhinoceros or hippopotamus hide, in South Africa SJAMBOK
– whip to the point of stripping the skin from FLAY
– whip used for punishment SCOURGE
– whip used formerly in Russia for flogging KNOUT
– whip with a leather loop at the tip, used by horseriders CROP
– handle of a whip, fishing rod, or

WEIGHTS AND MEASURES

UNIT	WHAT IT MEASURES
ENERGY AND MOTION	
bar, barye, pascal	pressure
dyne, newton, poundal	force
erg, joule, kilowatt-hour	work or energy
knot, mach	speed
watt	power
HEAT, LIGHT, AND SOUND	
angstrom	formerly wavelength of light
calorie, therm	heat
candela	luminous intensity
decibel, phon	loudness
fresnel, hertz	frequency
kelvin	temperature
lumen	luminous flux, the rate of flow of luminous energy
ELECTRICITY AND MAGNETISM	
ampere	electric current
coulomb	electric charge
farad	electrical capacitance, the capacity to store an electric charge
gauss, tesla	magnetic flux density, the direction and magnitude of magnetic force
henry	electrical inductance, the property of enabling an electromagnetic force to be generated
maxwell, weber	magnetic flux, the strength of a magnetic field through an area
oersted	magnetic field strength
ohm	electrical resistance
siemens	electrical conductance
volt	electric potential and electromotive force
ATOMIC PHYSICS	
becquerel, curie	radioactivity
dalton, atomic mass unit	mass of an isotope
rad, gray	energy absorbed from radiation
rem/REM	radiation dose
roentgen	X-rays or gamma rays

UNIT	VALUE
METRIC UNITS	
grade	one-hundredth of a right angle
gram	about 0.002 pound avoirdupois
hectare	100 ares, or 2.47 acres
micrometre, micron	10^{-6} metres, about $^{1}/_{25,000}$ inch
quintal	100 kilograms, or about 220 pounds avoirdupois
tonne or metric ton	10 quintals, or 0.98421 long tons
IMPERIAL UNITS: LINEAR MEASURE	
1 cable	about 608 feet
1 chain	4 rods, or 22 yards

the like STOCK, BUTT
whirling, revolving VERTIGINOUS
– Muslim ascetic, sometimes engaging in ecstatic, whirling dancing DERVISH
whirlpool, whirlwind, or similar fast-rotating flow VORTEX
– whirlpool-like shape or line SPIRAL, HELIX, VOLUTE, WHORL
– whirlpool or dangerous swirl in the sea MAELSTROM
– current or swirl moving against the main current, often creating a miniature whirlpool EDDY, GULF
whirlwind TOURBILLION
– whirlwind in an arid area, that draws up a column of dust DUST DEVIL
– whirlwind in the southern U.S. TORNADO, TWISTER
– whirlwind or hurricane in the China Sea TYPHOON
– whirlwind or hurricane in tropical areas CYCLONE
– whirlwind that forms over the sea and draws up a column of water WATERSPOUT
whiskers or sensitive hairs, as either side of a cat's mouth VIBRISSAE
– whiskers spreading in a roughly triangular shape down the side of the face MUTTON-CHOP WHISKERS
– feeler or "whisker" on a fish such as the catfish BARBEL
whiskey distilled illicitly, especially in the Southern U.S. MOONSHINE, MOUNTAIN DEW
– whiskey that is distilled illicitly in Ireland POTEEN
whisky, brandy, or other strong spirits AQUA VITAE, EAU DE VIE
– whisky factory DISTILLERY
– blend or dilute whisky or other alcoholic spirits RECTIFY
– Irish or Scottish term for whisky USQUEBAUGH
– leftover impure spirits from the distillation of alcoholic drinks, especially whisky FEINTS
– tot or small quantity of whisky or other drink DRAM
whispering or rustling, as of the wind, or surf SOUGH, SUSURRATION
whist See **bridge**
whistle – whistling noise produced when loudspeaker noise re-enters a microphone FEEDBACK

UNIT	VALUE
1 fathom	6 feet
1 furlong	10 chains, or 220 yards
1 hand	4 inches
1 league	3 nautical miles
1 rod, pole, or perch	$5^1/_2$ yards
IMPERIAL UNITS: LIQUID MEASURE	
1 barrel	$31^1/_2$-35 gallons
1 firkin	9 gallons
1 fluid drachm	60 minims, or $^1/_8$ fluid ounce
1 gill, noggin	5 fluid ounces, or $^1/_4$ pint
1 hogshead	2 barrels
1 minim	$^1/_{480}$ fluid ounce
IMPERIAL UNITS: DRY MEASURE	
1 bushel	4 pecks
1 peck	8 quarts
IMPERIAL UNITS: JEWELLERS' WEIGHTS	
1 carat	$^1/_{24}$ (4.2%) gold
1 grain	$^1/_{480}$ ounce Troy
1 ounce Troy	$^1/_{12}$ pound Troy, or 1.097 ounces avoirdupois
IMPERIAL UNITS: AVOIRDUPOIS WEIGHTS	
1 dram	$27\ ^{11}/_{32}$ grains, or $^1/_{16}$ ounce
1 drachm	3 scruples
1 scruple	20 grains

UNIT	VALUE
ARCHAIC AND FOREIGN UNITS	
barleycorn	$^1/_3$ inch (length of a barley grain)
catty/kati	about $1^1/_3$ pounds (China)
crore	10 million (India)
cubit	18 inches
ell	45 inches (cloth)
hide	100 to 120 acres
kilderkin	about 18 gallons
lakh	100,000 (India)
maund	about 82 pounds (India)
morgen	2.12 acres (South Africa)
mutchkin	about 1 pint (Scotland)
picul	133 pounds (China)
pipe	105 gallons (wine)
pood	about 36 pounds (Russia)
rood	$^1/_4$ acre; 40 square rods
shekel	about $^1/_2$ ounce (ancient Hebrew)
span	9 inches (tip of thumb to tip of little finger of an extended hand)
tael	$1^1/_3$ ounces (Asia)
tierce, terce	42 wine gallons; about 33 gallons
verst	about $^2/_3$ mile, or just over 1 kilometre (Russia)
virgate	about 30 acres

– cord worn round the neck, as for carrying a whistle LANYARD

white See also **colours**

– white, cold, and smooth or hard, like marble MARMOREAL

– white of an egg ALBUMEN

– white or grey, as through old age HOARY

– white person CAUCASIAN

– white person in New Zealand, as distinct from a Maori PAKEHA

– derogatory term for a white person, as sometimes used by black people BUCKRA, HONKY, WHITEY

– person or animal having abnormally white skin and hair through lacking normal pigmentation ALBINO

white- LEUC-, LEUCO-, LEUKO-

white ant TERMITE

White Friar CARMELITE

white whale BELUGA

whiten, as by cutting off light or soaking in acid BLANCH

– whitened through lack of sunlight, as grass or other green plants might become ETIOLATED

whole, entire INTEGRAL

– whole, sum total, sum of many parts AGGREGATE

– whole, unbroken, still in one piece, having all its parts INTACT

– whole, undivided UNITARY

– whole, unified pattern or structure that is more than the sum of its parts GESTALT

– whole number or zero INTEGER

– wholeness, fullness, completeness PLENITUDE, PLENUM

– wholeness, unity, undivided or unbroken condition INTEGRITY

– breaking down a whole into its component parts in order to examine it ANALYSIS

– combining of parts or elements to form a whole SYNTHESIS

– form into a whole, make solid or united CONSOLIDATE

– set of well-matching parts, such as garments, effecting a unified whole ENSEMBLE

– something that completes a whole COMPLEMENT

– universe or society regarded as a single, complex whole MACROCOSM

whole- HOL-, HOLO-

whooping cough PERTUSSIS

wick – charred end of a candle's wick SNUFF

wicked See **evil, immoral**

– wicked, vile, hateful ABOMINABLE, ODIOUS, HEINOUS

wickerwork – cane from a tropical Asian palm, as used for wickerwork furniture RATTAN

wide, open stretch of land, sea, or sky EXPANSE

– wide-ranging, all-embracing, liberal and broad-minded, as one's interests might be CATHOLIC

– wide-ranging, general, comprehensive, giving or having a broad view SYNOPTIC

– wide-tipped and flexible blade, as for spreading paint SPATULA

– widely applicable, talented, or the like VERSATILE

– person with wide-ranging knowledge or interests, as distinct from a specialist GENERALIST, POLYMATH

widen, expand DILATE, DISTEND

widespread, as a disease might be EPIDEMIC, PANDEMIC

– widespread, common, or deeply rooted within a particular region or group ENDEMIC

– widespread, occurring in quite separate regions, as some species are ALLOPATRIC

– widespread, scattered widely DIFFUSE, DISPERSED, BROADCAST

– widespread, very common or frequent PREDOMINANT, RIFE

– widespread, wide-ranging, embracing many aspects or a wide area EXTENSIVE, COMPREHENSIVE

– widespread or current PREVAILING, PREVALENT, REGNANT

widow having a title or property derived from her late husband DOWAGER

– widow's clothing while in mourning WEEDS

– widow's share, during her lifetime, of her late husband's property or the interest on it DOWER

– formal or old-fashioned term for a widow RELICT

– former Hindu custom in which a widow cremated herself on her late husband's funeral pyre SUTTEE

– practice, in keeping with Old Testament law, of marrying one's brother's widow LEVIRATE

width, height, or length DIMENSION

– width or thickness, as of piping or wire DIAMETER

wife and husband who are elderly and devoted DARBY AND JOAN

– wife or husband SPOUSE

– wife or husband, especially of a monarch CONSORT

– wife or husband, regarded as a helper HELPMATE, HELPMEET

– wife's scolding of her husband in private, or similar private reproach CURTAIN LECTURE

– adjective for a wife UXORIAL

– common-law wife TALLYWOMAN

– crime or state of having two wives or husbands at any one time BIGAMY

– custom or state of having only one wife at a time, as in most cultures MONOGAMY, MONOGYNY

– custom or state of having two or more wives or female mates at a time, as in some cultures POLYGAMY, POLYGYNY

– dominated by a nagging or wilful wife HENPECKED

– group of wives and concubines in a Muslim household HAREM

– killing of a wife UXORICIDE

– legal right to the help, company, and affection of one's husband or wife CONSORTIUM

– man who has had several wives BLUEBEARD

– man whose wife has committed adultery CUCKOLD

– relating to an excessive devotion to one's wife UXORIOUS

– secondary wife in some societies CONCUBINE

wife-swapping SWINGING

wig, especially a long curly wig PERIWIG, PERUKE

– wig for the genital area MERKIN

– wig or hairpiece covering a bald spot TOUPEE

– wig that is long at the back FULL-BOTTOMED WIG

– decorative wig or hairpiece, especially for a woman POSTICHE

wild, intemperate, or overindulgent behaviour EXCESSES

– wild, savage, especially when formerly domesticated FERAL

– wild, untamed, living in the wild UNDOMESTICATED

– wild, violently out of control, ranting and raving, as in a fit of madness HYSTERICAL, BERSERK, RUNNING AMOK, RAMPAGEOUS, FRENZIED, FRENETIC, FRANTIC

– wild, without any order, pattern, or control ANARCHIC, CHAOTIC

– wild headlong rush, as of startled cattle or horses or of a panic-stricken crowd STAMPEDE

– wild or mischievous adventure, caper, prank ESCAPADE

– referring to or engaging in wild and ecstatic revels or orgies, in the style of an ancient Greek cult CORYBANTIC, CYPRIAN, DIONYSIAC

– uncontrolled, irresponsibly uninhibited, as wild behaviour is EXTRAVAGANT, UNBRIDLED, MADCAP

wild ass ONAGER

wild boar or male elephant with impressive tusks TUSKER

wild cherry GEAN

wild duck MALLARD

wild flowers – growing wild, especially on cultivated land, as wild flowers or weeds might AGRESTAL

wildlife reserve SANCTUARY

wilful, based on or acting on perso-

nal whim or prejudice CAPRICIOUS, ARBITRARY
– wilful, stubbornly self-willed, unwilling to cooperate or back down PERVERSE, CONTRARY

will – addition to a will CODICIL
– deprive an heir of his inheritance, as by cutting him out of one's will DISINHERIT
– estate to be left in a will by a husband to his widow JOINTURE
– leave money or property to someone in a will BEQUEATH
– leaving a valid will when dying TESTATE
– leaving no valid will when dying INTESTATE
– legal proof of the validity of a will PROBATE
– liable to alteration or cancellation, as a will might be AMBULATORY
– lowest level of will or desire, typically without any action taken to fulfil it VELLEITY
– money or property left in a will LEGACY
– pass on property, especially land or buildings, by a will DEVISE
– person appointed by a testator to carry out the requirements of his will EXECUTOR, EXECUTRIX
– person exerting or trying to exert a sinister influence over another's will SVENGALI
– person who makes a will LEGATOR, TESTATOR
– person who receives charity, a favour, money from a will, or the like BENEFICIARY
– transfer an estate, sovereignty, or the like, as by a will DEMISE

will-o'-the-wisp, flickering light sometimes seen over marshy ground IGNIS FATUUS, JACK-O'-LANTERN, FRIAR'S LANTERN

willing, act of choosing VOLITION
– willing, eager to please, cooperative OBLIGING, COMPLIANT, COMPLAISANT
– willing, without constraint and without payment VOLUNTARY
– willingly or freely given, generous UNSTINTED, UNGRUDGING
– willing or inclined, prepared to do a particular job DISPOSED
– willingness or promptness ALACRITY

willow shoots or similar flexible twigs used to make baskets WICKER
– willow twig, or rope made of such twigs, used for tying things together WITHE, WITHY
– willow with long twigs used in basket making OSIER

willy-nilly, whether you like it or not NOLENS VOLENS

wimple – scarf-like or collar-like part of a wimple, covering the throat and shoulders GORGET

win, triumph or overcome through greater power or ability PREVAIL, PREDOMINATE
– win achieved very easily against a weak opponent, or as a formality through the withdrawal or absence of the opponent WALKOVER

Winchester College – pupil or former pupil of Winchester College WYKEHAMIST

wind See chart, and also **weather**

WINDS	
austral wind	south wind
berg wind	warm, dry wind blowing down from the South African plateau to the coast
bise	cold, dry, northerly wind in Switzerland, France, and Italy
bora	cold, squally, dry wind blowing from the mountains of central Europe to the northern Adriatic area in winter
boreal wind	north wind
chinook, snow eater	warm, dry wind blowing down the eastern side of the Rocky Mountains in Canada and the U.S.
chinook, wet chinook	warm, wet wind blowing from the Pacific onto the coasts of Oregon and Washington in the U.S.
Doctor	any local wind that offsets unpleasant weather
favonian wind	west wind
föhn/foehn	warm, dry wind blowing down the northern sides of the Alps
harmattan	dry, dusty, north-easterly wind blowing from the Sahara to the West African coasts
helm wind	strong easterly wind on the northern Pennines, England
khamsin	hot, southerly wind blowing from the Sahara to the eastern Mediterranean from March to May
levanter	easterly wind in the extreme westernmost Mediterranean
libeccio	strong south-westerly wind in central Italy
mistral	violent, cold, dry, generally northerly wind blowing down the Rhône valley in France
pampero	violent, cold, south-westerly wind on the pampas of Argentina
Santa Ana	hot, dry, north-easterly wind blowing down from the mountains in southern California in the U.S.
simoom, samiel	swirling, burning, sand-laden wind in the deserts of Arabia and North Africa in summer
sirocco	southerly wind blowing in spring from the Sahara, being hot, dry, and dusty in North Africa, but humid in southern Europe
trade wind	tropical wind that blows from the north-east in the Northern Hemisphere, or from the south-east in the Southern Hemisphere
tramontana	cold, dry, north wind blowing down from the mountains in Italy and Spain
willy-willy	desert whirlwind in Australia; intense tropical storm in north-west Australia
zonda	warm, humid, northerly wind in South America

– wind-blown, dispersed as by wind, fanned WINNOWED
– wind caused by the Earth's rotation GEOSTROPHIC WIND
– wind or airstream moving very fast at high altitudes JET STREAM
– wind or windstorm that is snowy and very violent BLIZZARD
– belt of calm or light winds at sea along the equator DOLDRUMS
– blowing down from the mountains, as a wind might TRAMONTANE
– blowing or gusting fast and noisily, as the wind might BLUSTERY
– build-up of gas in the digestive tract, causing belching and breaking of wind FLATULENCE
– carry lightly, as the wind carries the smell of flowers WAFT
– diagram showing wind directions and frequency WIND ROSE
– facing or moving in the direction towards which the wind is blowing LEEWARD
– gentle wind or breeze, especially the west wind ZEPHYR
– gust of wind, or wind-driven shower or snow flurry SCUD
– instrument for measuring windspeed ANEMOMETER
– plant, such as the dandelion, whose fruits or seeds are spread by the wind ANEMOCHORE
– referring to a downward wind or air current, especially one flowing down a slope KATABATIC
– referring to a rising wind or air current, especially one rising along a slope ANABATIC
– relating to the wind AEOLIAN
– scale of wind velocities BEAUFORT SCALE
– sighing sound, as the wind might make SUSURRATION, SOUGH
– sudden, violent burst of wind, typically with rain or snow SQUALL
– tapering cloth tube fixed to a pole to indicate wind direction, as at airfields WINDSOCK, WIND CORE, WIND SLEEVE, AIR SOCK, DROGUE

WIND INSTRUMENTS

alphorn/ alpenhorn	long wooden tube producing a single powerful note	**hautbois/ hautboy/hoboy**	early form of oboe
aulos	ancient Greek oboe-like instrument	**helicon, sousaphone**	large spiral brass instrument that coils round the player's body
bassoon	low-pitched woodwind instrument, with a double wooden tube, and a double-reed mouthpiece	**hunting horn, cor de chasse, waldhorn**	simple early form of the French horn
bombardon	large low-pitched tuba-like instrument used in brass and military bands	**kazoo**	children's instrument with a paper membrane that turns the player's hum into a buzzing sound
clarion	shrill, medieval trumpet	**musette**	small French bagpipe
cor anglais, English horn	double-reed woodwind instrument, similar to an oboe but lower pitched	**oboe**	woodwind with a double reed and a cone-shaped tube, pitched between a flute and clarinet
cornet	valved instrument, very like a trumpet, used chiefly in brass bands	**ocarina**	small, simple egg-shaped metal or clay instrument with finger holes
crumhorn/ krummhorn	deep-pitched medieval instrument, with a double reed	**panpipes, syrinx**	set of short vertical pipes or reeds, played by blowing over their tops
didgeridoo	Aboriginal Australian instrument, consisting of a long pipe that produces a droning noise	**piccolo**	small, high-pitched flute
double bassoon, contrabassoon	woodwind pitched one octave lower than an ordinary bassoon	**post horn, coaching horn**	simple brass instrument with no valves, having a limited range of notes
euphonium, bombarda	tenor tuba, used especially in brass and military bands	**sackbut**	trombone-like instrument used in the middle ages
fife	high-pitched flute in former times; flute in a modern "fife and drum" band	**sarrusophone**	bassoon-like brass instrument, with a double reed
flageolet	six-holed woodwind instrument, similar to a flute, but blown at the end rather than the side	**serpent**	deep-toned, S-shaped wind instrument, used mainly in the 18th century
flügelhorn	valved instrument, similar to a trumpet, used chiefly in brass bands	**shawm/shaum, pommer**	early double-reed woodwind, forerunner of the oboe
French horn, horn	circular, coiled brass instrument with a wide bell	**trombone**	brass instrument, bent back twice on itself, with a U-shaped slide
harmonica, mouth organ	small, box-shaped instrument played by sucking and blowing through metal reeds	**tuba**	large valved brass instrument, with a bass pitch

– unfavourable, blowing in an inconvenient direction, as winds might be ADVERSE, CONTRARY
– upright pivoting plate, typically of metal and shaped like a cock or arrow, used to indicate wind direction VANE, WEATHERCOCK
wind- ANEMO-
wind instruments See chart
– band of metal fastening the reed to the mouthpiece of a wind instrument such as a clarinet or saxophone LIGATURE
– device to reduce or muffle sound, especially of a wind instrument MUTE, SORDINO
– flared end of a wind instrument such as a clarinet or trumpet BELL
– lip, wooden plug, or other obstruction serving in place of a reed to initiate the vibration in certain organ pipes and wind instruments FIPPLE
– mouthpiece of a wind instrument, especially a brass one, or the position and use of the lips in playing it EMBOUCHURE
winding, twisting and turning CONTORTED, TORTUOUS, ANFRACTUOUS
– winding knob of a watch CROWN
– winding or curving gracefully, as the movements of a snake might be SINUOUS
– winding or twisting path, as of a river MEANDER
windmill See illustration
– windmill-operated pump GIN
– arm of a windmill, carrying a sail WHIP
– blade of a windmill, catching the wind SAIL, SWEEP, VANE
window See illustration, page 566
– window above a door, as to admit light from one room to another FANLIGHT, TRANSOM
– window blinds that can be raised and lowered, and whose horizontal slats can be angled VENETIAN BLINDS
– window-cleaners' movable platform on the outside walls of a building GONDOLA, CRADLE
– window consisting of two sliding frames set in grooves in a fixed frame SASH WINDOW
– window frame with hinges along one side CASEMENT
– window glass of former times, circular in shape, with a lump in the centre from the worker's rod CROWN GLASS
– window pane of a small and typically diamond-shaped kind QUARREL, QUARRY
– window with horizontal adjustable glass slats JALOUSIE, LOUVRE WINDOW
– windows formed by small pieces of glass fastened by lead strips LEAD LIGHTS
– circular or semi-circular window, panel, or the like ROUNDEL
– crescent-shaped recess or additional window above a main window LUNETTE
– crisscrossed strips of wood or metal, as in a screen or window LATTICE
– decorative frame or moulding around a door, window, or recess ARCHITRAVE
– horizontal dividing bar or strip in a window TRANSOM
– lacy ornamental pattern or

windmills and watermills

sail
vane
gallery
SMOCK MILL

body
post/main post
POST MILL

TOWER MILL

paddles
axletree
WATERMILL: UNDERSHOT WHEEL

water supply
WATERMILL: OVERSHOT WHEEL

window

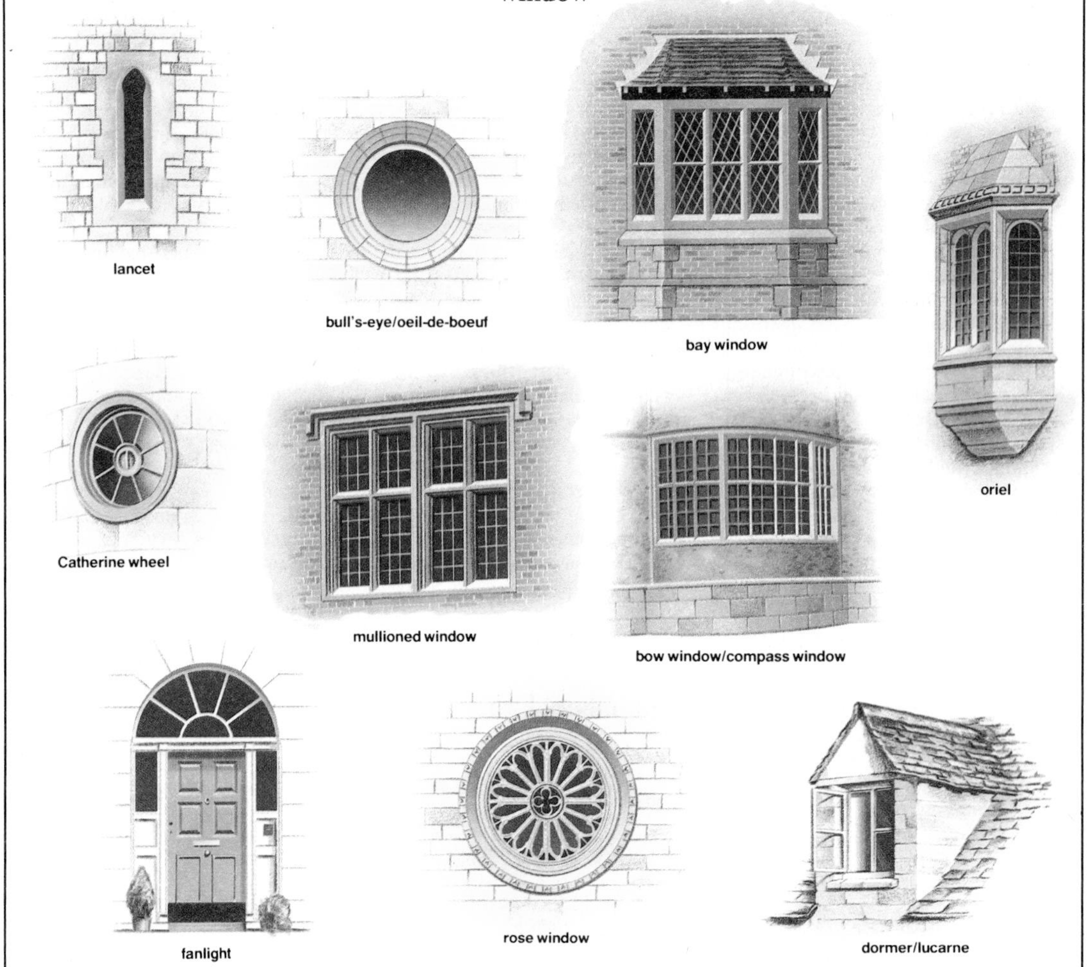

lancet

bull's-eye/oeil-de-boeuf

bay window

oriel

Catherine wheel

mullioned window

bow window/compass window

fanlight

rose window

dormer/lucarne

stonework, as at the top of a Gothic window TRACERY
– leaf-like shape in the tracery of Gothic windows FOIL
– legal right to unobstructed light through an old window ANCIENT LIGHTS
– length of board or fabric along the top of a window, used to hide the curtain rod PELMET
– opening in a wall, wider inside than out, for a door or window EMBRASURE
– person who installs window glass GLAZIER
– rubber or leather blade, fixed to a handle, for wiping liquid, as in cleaning windows SQUEEGEE
– section of a wall, as between windows TRUMEAU, PIER
– short decorative skirt of drapery hung along the top of a window, shelf, or the like VALENCE
– small triangular window in the front door of a car QUARTERLIGHT
– small window FENESTELLA
– small window, usually circular, in the side of a ship PORTHOLE
– thin lead strip securing the panes in stained-glass windows CAME
– throwing a thing or person out of the window DEFENESTRATION
– triangular moulding or recess, usually decorated, above a door or window PEDIMENT, FRONTISPIECE, GABLE
– upper horizontal beam or support, as of a window LINTEL
– upright dividing bar or strip in a window MULLION
– upright post or strut of a ladder, door frame, window sash, or the like STILE
– upright side of a door post or window frame JAMB
– wall or panel with windows, designed for light or ventilation CLERESTORY
– wooden bar or strip securing the panes in a window or door GLAZING BAR, MUNTIN, MUNTING

windpipe TRACHEA
– tubes that carry air from the windpipe to the lungs BRONCHI, BRONCHIAL TUBES

windscreen – glare shield fitted at the top of a car's windscreen VISOR

wine See chart
– wine of high quality, identified by year and region VINTAGE
– wine cask or beer barrel of large capacity TUN
– wine cellar or pantry BUTTERY
– wine cup used at Mass CHALICE
– wine expert OENOLOGIST
– wine glass with a stem GOBLET
– wine-loving BACCHANT
– wine merchant VINTNER
– wine of low quality PLONK
– wine or water bottle at table CARAFE, DECANTER
– wine that is sugared, spiced,

and then heated MULLED WINE
– wine that is still fermenting MUST, STUM
– wine vessel of silver, with handles, that is drunk from in turn, as by guests at a banquet LOVING CUP
– wine waiter SOMMELIER
– wine's fragrance BOUQUET
– winery or wine cellars of a French vineyard CAVE
– wineshop, sometimes selling groceries too, in Spanish-speaking countries BODEGA
– basic local wine VIN ORDINAIRE, TAFELWEIN
– bring a wine to room temperature after opening it CHAMBRÉ
– clarifying of wine, beer, or the like, as by adding isinglass FINING
– clear wine, beer, or cider of its dregs RACK
– crust forming in bottles of old wine, especially port, or a wine containing this crust BEESWING
– dilute or add impurities to a substance, such as wine ADULTERATE
– expert in wine, art, or the like, or a person of refined tastes CONNOISSEUR
– fee or price charged at a restaurant for serving wine brought in by the customer CORKAGE
– fine wine, certified quality wine APPELLATION CONTRÔLÉE, QUALITÄTSWEIN
– finest wine of its type in France PREMIER CRU
– grape skins, pips, and stems left over after the juice has been extracted for winemaking RAPES
– mature and rich, not acidic, as a good wine is MELLOW
– person who drinks excessive amounts of wine WINE BIBBER
– pour a liquid from one container to another, as when separating wine from its sediment DECANT
– reddish substance in grape juice deposited as a crust in wine vats TARTAR, ARGOL
– referring to dry wine SEC
– referring to extremely dry wine, especially champagne BRUT
– referring to sweet wine DOUX
– relating to wine, wine-drinking, or excessive wine-drinking VINOUS
– sediment or residue in wine, coffee, or other liquid LEES, DREGS

wine- VIN-, VINI-, VINO-

winemaking or grape-growing VINICULTURE, VITICULTURE

wing See also **bird**
– wing, feather, fin, or similar projecting body part PINNA
– wing, tailplane, flap, or other surface of an aircraft affecting lift or stability in flight AEROFOIL
– wing-like, winged, or wing-shaped ALAR
– wing-like membrane between the fore and hind limb of a bat or flying squirrel PATAGIUM
– wing of a bird, specifically the rear section holding the flight feathers PINION
– winged or feathered PENNATE
– feathered part of a bird's wing in the position corresponding to the thumb ALULA, BASTARD WING
– having wings or wing-like projections ALATE, ALAR
– underside of a wing, corresponding to the human armpit AXILLA

-wing- -PTER-, PTERO-

wink or blink NICTITATE
– wink or blink repeatedly or involuntarily PALPEBRATE
– suggesting a plot or secret, as a knowing wink or nudge might CONSPIRATORIAL

winter – adjective for winter HIBERNAL, HIEMAL
– pass the winter in a very inactive, semi-sleeping state, as some animals do HIBERNATE

wipe out, rub out, erase EFFACE

wiper – rubber or leather blade resembling a windscreen wiper, fixed to a handle and used for wiping liquid, as in cleaning windows SQUEEGEE

wire, thin thread, fibre, or the like FILAMENT
– wire coil producing a magnetic field when carrying an electric current, as used for activating switches SOLENOID
– wire used for electrical contact, as in a crystal radio set CAT'S WHISKER
– ornamental work consisting of fine, twisted wire, especially of gold or silver wire FILIGREE
– plate with tapering holes through which wire is drawn to reduce its thickness DRAWPLATE
– produce wire, metal or plastic sheeting, or the like by pressing through a nozzle or die EXTRUDE
– unit of measure of the diameter of wire MIL

wisdom – widely accepted wisdom or belief, often of a hackneyed, standard, and unquestioned kind RECEIVED WISDOM

-wisdom -SOPHY

wise, having wisdom SAPIENT
– wise, showing or having good judgment, well-advised DISCERNING, SAGACIOUS, JUDICIOUS
– wise adviser or prophet, apparently infallible authority ORACLE
– wise and respected leader or adviser SOLON, NESTOR
– wise or learned person, expert PUNDIT, LUMINARY
– wise teacher, judge, philosopher, or the like SAGE

wish or hope that is fanciful and unrealistic PIPE DREAM, CASTLE IN THE AIR, CASTLE IN SPAIN
– wish or tendency, without any action taken to fulfil it VELLEITY
– help to attain someone's wishes, often unworthy wishes GRATIFY, PANDER TO
– obey a rule or order, carry out someone's wish or demand, or the like COMPLY
– respect or submit to the wishes or opinion of someone else DEFER

wishbone or similar forked bone or body part FURCULA

wit, spirit, liveliness ESPRIT
– wit of a wry, delicate, but pointed kind ATTIC SALT
– biting or cutting, as wit can be

WINES

FRANCE

Alsace
Beaujolais
Bergerac
Bordeaux, claret
Bourgogne/ Burgundy
Chablis
Champagne
Côtes-du-Rhône
Entre-deux-Mers
Graves
Mâcon
Médoc
Muscadet
Muscat/ Muscatel
Sancerre
Sauternes

GERMANY

hock
Liebfraumilch
Mosel
Nierstein
Riesling
Sekt
Silvaner

GREECE

retsina

ITALY

Asti spumante
Barbera
Bardolino
Barolo
Chianti
Dolcetto
Frascati
Lacrima Christi
Lambrusco
Marsala
Orvieto
Soave
Sylvaner
Tocai
Valpolicella

PORTUGAL

Aveleda
Dão
Douro
Madeira
Mateus Rosé
vinho verde

SPAIN

Málaga
Navarra
Rioja
Valdepeñas

CAUSTIC, TRENCHANT, PUNGENT, MORDANT
– sparkling or brilliant, as a person's wit might be LAMBENT, CORUSCATING, SCINTILLATING
– sparkling or brilliant, reminiscent of fireworks, as a person's wit might be PYROTECHNIC

witch SORCERESS, SIBYL
– witch, wizard, sorcerer, or male witch WARLOCK
– witch or female vampire LAMIA
– witch's attendant spirit, often assuming animal form FAMILIAR
– witches' gathering, or a group of 13 witches COVEN

witch doctor, as among some North American Indians MEDICINE MAN, SHAMAN
– witch doctor among Australian Aboriginals BOYLA, BONE-POINTER

witch hunt against suspected communist sympathisers in the U.S. in the 1950s MCCARTHYISM
– witch-hunter who questions suspects INQUISITOR

witchcraft, black magic, devil worship, or the like DIABOLISM
– witchcraft, use of supernatural power, as with the help of evil spirits SORCERY, SORTILEGE
– witchcraft and other supernatural arts THE OCCULT
– witchcraft or black magic practised in Haiti, or the religious cult using it VOODOO
– witchcraft or magic practised in the West Indies, or the religious belief incorporating it OBEAH, OBI

-with- -CUM-, CO-, COM-, SYN-, SYM-

with a pinch of salt, not too seriously CUM GRANO SALIS

withdraw, often publicly, a former belief or claim RECANT, RETRACT, DISAVOW
– withdraw as a member, break away from an alliance, or the like SECEDE, DISSOCIATE, DISAFFILIATE
– withdraw from or go back on a promise or deal RENEGE
– withdraw from or leave a fortress, infected area, or the like EVACUATE
– withdraw or annul officially a law, regulation, or the like RESCIND, REVOKE, REPEAL
– withdraw or cancel an order or command COUNTERMAND

withdrawn into seclusion, isolated CLOISTERED, SEQUESTERED
– withdrawn person, living alone as for religious reasons HERMIT, RECLUSE

withered, dry, shrivelled, as a dead leaf would be SERE

within or internal, existing inside as a force or essence IMPLICIT, IMMANENT, INHERENT, INTRINSIC

within- END-, ENDO-, ENTO-, INTRA-, INTRO-

without- A-, AN-

without meaning to, without realising INADVERTENTLY

without reference to, without consideration of, regardless of IRRESPECTIVE OF

witness in court considered unfairly biased HOSTILE WITNESS
– witness who testifies in writing under oath DEPONENT
– witness's evidence or declaration given in court TESTIMONY
– witness's sworn statement, used when he is absent from court DEPOSITION
– be evidence or proof of, be a witness for ATTEST, TESTIFY
– deliberate giving of false evidence by a witness under oath PERJURY

witty, brilliant, or vivacious SCINTILLATING
– witty, high-spirited literary work JEU D'ESPRIT
– witty or fanciful thought or expression CONCEIT
– witty or humorous in a dry, ironical way WRY
– witty reply in a conversation BACKCHAT, RETORT, REPARTEE
– witty saying, clever remark MOT, BON MOT, WITTICISM

wives See **wife**

wizard, witch doctor MEDICINE MAN, SHAMAN
– wizard in ancient times MAGUS
– wizard or magician SORCERER
– wizard or male witch WARLOCK
– wizard's attendant spirit, often assuming animal form FAMILIAR

wobble or spin in flight, as a missile or aircraft might YAW

wolf – wolfman, person who thinks he is a wolf LYCANTHROPE
– adjective for a wolf LUPINE
– group or pack of wolves ROUT

woman leader of a tribe or large family MATRIARCH
– woman-like, unmanly EFFEMINATE
– woman living with and supported by a man without being married to him CONCUBINE
– woman or girl who acts in a frivolous or scatterbrained way FIZGIG, FLIBBERTIGIBBET, FEATHERHEAD
– woman or girl who behaves like, or is, a prostitute COCOTTE, TART, FILLE DE JOIE, HARLOT, HUSSY, JADE, FLOOZY, SCRUBBER, TROLLOP
– woman or girl who indulges in flighty or flirtatious behaviour SOUBRETTE, COQUETTE
– woman or girl who is attractive though not pretty JOLIE LAIDE
– woman or girl whose charm or attractiveness make her a favourite BELLE
– woman or sweetheart who is idealised, as Don Quixote's sweetheart was DULCINEA
– woman or wife in Polynesian or Maori cultures WAHINE
– woman oracle, prophetess SIBYL
– woman urging the extension of voting rights to women, especially one campaigning in Britain in the early 20th century SUFFRAGETTE
– woman who behaves in a conceited or dominating way, as a temperamental leading actress or singer might PRIMA DONNA
– woman who intimidates people, through her ugliness or her behaviour GORGON, DRAGON
– woman who is aggressive, spiteful, quarrelsome, and scolding HARRIDAN, HARPY, SHREW, HELLCAT, TERMAGANT, VIRAGO, VIXEN
– woman whose husband is frequently absent GRASS WIDOW
– woman whose sexual charms or scheming can lead her admirers into danger FEMME FATALE, MATA HARI, JEZEBEL, SIREN, VAMP
– woman with an excessive sexual appetite NYMPHOMANIAC
– woman with scholarly or literary interests BLUESTOCKING
– woman's dressing room, bedroom, or private sitting room BOUDOIR, BOWER
– womanly, characteristic of or appropriate to a woman FEMININE
– women-only party HEN PARTY
– women with contrived sex appeal, or photographs of them, as in advertising CHEESECAKE
– women's clothes worn by a man DRAG
– women's hats MILLINERY
– women's movement, "women's liberation" FEMINISM
– women's or girls' club, as at a U.S. university SORORITY
– women's quarters in an Asian house ZENANA
– women's work or preoccupations DISTAFF
– abnormal development of male traits in a woman VIRILISM
– bust, waist, and hip measurements of a woman VITAL STATISTICS
– column in an ancient Greek building, in the form of a sculpture of a loosely robed woman CARYATID
– cross old woman GRIMALKIN
– dirty, untidy, or sluttish woman

SLATTERN, DRAB
– dull and old-fashioned, as a woman's clothing or appearance might be DOWDY, FRUMPISH
– elderly and dignified or wealthy woman, often a widow DOWAGER
– elderly woman, especially a grandmother GRANDAM
– elderly woman, typically unattractive BELDAME, HAG, CRONE
– external sexual organs of a woman PUDENDA
– girl or very young woman who, though sexually immature, is attractive to men NYMPHET, LOLITA
– graceful and slender woman or girl SYLPH
– group of women, usually wives, concubines, or female family of a Muslim man HAREM
– hatred of women MISOGYNY
– mistress or sexually promiscuous woman living on the fringes of respectable society, as in the 19th century DEMIMONDAINE, DEMIREP
– money or property handed over by a woman to her husband on their marriage DOWRY
– old-fashioned term for a young woman WENCH
– outstandingly attractive woman STUNNER, STOTTER
– plump or full-bosomed, as some women are BUXOM
– respectable older woman, who accompanies or supervises a young or unmarried woman in public CHAPERONE, DUENNA
– scolding, nagging woman or wife XANTHIPPE
– seclusion of women from view, especially in India PURDAH
– sensually built, with a very shapely figure, as a woman might be VOLUPTUOUS, LUSCIOUS, BUSTY, PNEUMATIC
– small and slim in build, trim, dainty as a woman or girl might be PETITE
– suitable and ready for marriage, as an attractive young woman is said to be NUBILE
– terrifying woman, evil female demon LAMIA
– uninhibited, unrestrained by social conventions, as a liberated woman is EMANCIPATED
– warrior-like woman VALKYRIE, AMAZON, BATTLEAXE
– young French working woman GRISETTE
– young woman, especially in the 1920s, who enjoyed defying the conventions of society FLAPPER
– young woman in a harem ODALISQUE
– young woman or girl who acts in a high-spirited and cheeky or tomboyish way HOYDEN
– young woman or girl who is naive or innocent INGENUE
– young woman or maiden DAMSEL, DEMOISELLE

-woman- -GYN-, GYNO-, GYNAECO-

womanhood or femininity MULIEBRITY

womaniser, seducer LOTHARIO, DON JUAN, CASANOVA, LADYKILLER, RAKE, PHILANDERER

womb See **uterus**
– mass of tissue linking the foetus to the womb lining PLACENTA
– surgical removal of the womb HYSTERECTOMY

womb- HYSTER-, HYSTERO-, METR-, METRO-

wonder See **think**
– year of wonders ANNUS MIRABILIS

wonderful, extraordinary PHENOMENAL, STUPENDOUS, PRODIGIOUS

wonderful to relate MIRABILE DICTU

wood from which Noah's ark was made GOPHERWOOD
– wood-eating XYLOPHAGOUS
– wood engraving, wood-block printing XYLOGRAPHY
– wood-fibre mixture from which paper is made PULP
– wood floating on or washed up by the sea, a river, or a lake DRIFTWOOD
– wood from newly felled trees TIMBER, LUMBER
– wood used for smoking food and making walking sticks in North America HICKORY
– boarding made of thin sheets of wood glued together PLYWOOD
– coat wood with varnish SHELLAC, FRENCH-POLISH, JAPAN
– cut small shavings from wood WHITTLE
– dry wood, used for starting fires TINDER, PUNK, TOUCHWOOD
– hard brown wood from a south Asian tree TEAK
– inlaid work, as in wood MARQUETRY
– mosaic of inlaid wood INTARSIA
– relating to, consisting of, or resembling wood LIGNEOUS
– shiny surface layer or finish, as of fine wood VENEER
– sliding front of a rolltop desk, or similar covering consisting of strips of wood pasted on a stretch of canvas TAMBOUR
– strip of wood cut lengthways from a tree trunk FLITCH
– strip of wood trimmed from a plank LIST
– tar-based liquid applied to wood as a preservative CREOSOTE
– utensils made of wood TREEN
– very dark wood, as used in making black piano keys EBONY
– very lightweight wood, from a tropical American tree, as used for making model boats BALSA

wood- LIGN-, LIGNI-, LIGNO-, XYL-, XYLO-

wood alcohol CARBINOL, METHANOL, METHYL ALCOHOL

wood grouse CAPERCAILLIE

wooded, having many trees ARBOREOUS

wooden defensive barrier of upright posts or stakes STOCKADE
– wooden frame for confining an offender and exposing him to public abuse PILLORY, STOCKS
– wooden or wood-like XYLOID
– wooden panelling fixed to the walls of a room WAINSCOTING
– wooden strip or plank forming part of a barrel, ship's hull, or the like STAVE
– wooden strip used in flooring, for supporting roof tiles, securing sails, or the like BATTEN
– wooden strips in a mosaic pattern, as used on floors PARQUET
– wooden table leg, handrail support, or the like, typically turned and decorated SPINDLE
– wooden tray or plate for carving or serving food TRENCHER

woods, small stretch of trees COPPICE, THICKET, COPSE, SPINNEY, HOLT
– woods, woodland, or undergrowth sheltering game COVERT
– woods or woodland area BOSCAGE, BOSK
– wood nymph, spirit or deity of the woods and trees, in Greek mythology DRYAD, HAMADRYAD
– open area in the woods or other overgrown land CLEARING
– relating to woods SYLVAN

woodwinds See **wind instruments**

woody tissue of plants XYLEM

wool See also **fabric**
– wool-bearing, or covered in woolly hair LANIFEROUS
– wool-like or fluffy in appearance or texture FLOCCULENT
– wool or cotton wadding used as stuffing BATTING, FLOCK
– wool recycled from unfelted cloth SHODDY
– fat from sheep's wool, used in cosmetics and ointments LANOLIN
– long woolly nap, as on coarse cloth or a carpet SHAG
– lump in wool or cloth BURL
– loose coil of thread, wool, or other yarn SKEIN, HANK
– open and clean raw cotton or wool fibres by means of a spiked drum WILLOW

– produce or become covered with small balls of wool PILL
– shear, trim, or cut the hair, wool, or horns of POLL
– silky wool from a llama-like South American mammal ALPACA
– soft downy wool from a Himalayan goat CASHMERE
– strand twisted with others to make wool, rope, or the like PLY
– unravel and straighten wool or similar fibre by combing it TEASE

woolly, covered with woolly hairs, as leaves might be LANATE
– woolly-haired, as black Africans are ULOTRICHOUS

word See also **verb**, **noun**
– word, expression, idea, or action that is overused CLICHÉ
– word in which sound echoes meaning ONOMATOPOEIA
– word, name, or phrase forming a main heading and fully explained in a dictionary or encyclopaedia HEADWORD, LEMMA
– word, name, or phrase spelt out by the first letters of the lines of a poem or message ACROSTIC
– word, phrase, or construction used incorrectly or ungrammatically BARBARISM, SOLECISM
– word, phrase, or form indicating respect HONORIFIC
– word, such as a noun or verb, having reference to the real world rather than just to relationships within a sentence CONTENT WORD, NOTIONAL WORD
– word, such as a pronoun, conjunction, or article, indicating a grammatical, logical, or textual relationship FUNCTION WORD
– word, such as *and*, indicating equal alternatives CONJUNCTIVE
– word, such as *but*, expressing contrast or opposition DISJUNCTIVE
– word, such as *sociology*, with elements from two or more languages HYBRID
– word, such as *this* or *those*, pointing out the person or thing referred to DEMONSTRATIVE, DEICTIC
– word as regarded as a series of sounds or letters rather than as a unit of meaning VOCABLE
– word at the top of a page of a dictionary, telephone directory, or the like, indicating the alphabetical entries of that page RUNNING HEAD, CATCHWORD, GUIDE WORD
– word borrowed from another language, such as *cul-de-sac* LOAN WORD
– word coined specially for a single occasion and not intended for use anywhere else NONCE WORD
– word-element, such as *en-* or *un-*, added at the beginning of a word or stem PREFIX
– word-element, such as *-ing* or *-ness*, added at the end of a word or stem SUFFIX
– word-element, such as *-ing* or *un-*, added to a word or stem either before or after AFFIX
– word-element, such as *micro-* or *-graphy*, that occurs as part of a compound word COMBINING FORM
– word-formation, or a word so formed, from a supposed derivative, such as *laze* from *lazy* BACK-FORMATION
– word formed by fusing parts of two or more other words, such as *chortle* from *chuckle* and *snort* BLEND, PORTMANTEAU WORD
– word formed from a more basic word, as through the addition of a prefix or suffix such as *indecisive* from *decide* DERIVATIVE
– word formed from the initial letters or syllables of other words, such as *NATO* ACRONYM
– word having the opposite meaning from another, such as *refuse* in relation to *accept* ANTONYM
– word having the same meaning as another such as *refuse* in relation to *decline* SYNONYM
– word having the same pronunciation and sometimes spelling as another, but differing in meaning and origin, such as *maroon* the verb in relation to *maroon* the colour HOMONYM
– word having the same pronunciation as another, but a different spelling, meaning, and origin, such as *sale/sail* HOMOPHONE
– word having the same spelling as another, but a different meaning and origin and sometimes pronunciation, such as *sow* the verb in relation to *sow* the noun HOMOGRAPH
– word in a foreign language, closely resembling a word in one's own language but differing from it in meaning, such as the French *actuel*, which means 'present-day, current' FALSE FRIEND, FAUX AMI
– word in fashionable use that suggests one is knowledgeable in a particular field BUZZ WORD
– word-list, specialised dictionary LEXICON, GLOSSARY, VOCABULARY
– word misused through confusion with a similar-sounding word, such as *pineapple* for *pinnacle* MALAPROPISM
– word now obsolete except in certain idioms or phrases, such as *fro* in *to and fro* FOSSIL
– word of a kind serving as a noun or pronoun, such as *hat*, *me*, or *the rich* SUBSTANTIVE
– word of a kind that can stand alone, typically expressing emotion, such as *alas!* INTERJECTION
– word of a kind that is usually positioned before a noun or noun phrase, and indicates relationships in position, time, or the like, such as *to*, *of*, and *despite* PREPOSITION
– word of a kind that joins words, clauses, or phrases, such as *and*, *or*, and *while* CONJUNCTION
– word of a kind that limits or specifies a noun and is placed before descriptive adjectives, such as *the*, *your*, or *many* DETERMINER
– word or expression no longer in everyday use, such as *yonder* ARCHAISM
– word or expression that fits the context appropriately MOT JUSTE
– word or formula repeated in meditation MANTRA
– word or phrase as an expression of style LOCUTION
– word or phrase borrowed from another language by a literal translation of each element, such as *superman* from the German *Übermensch* CALQUE, LOAN TRANSLATION
– word or phrase intended to characterise a person or thing, often part of a name or title, as in *Richard the Lionheart* EPITHET
– word or phrase that is neutral or acceptable, substituted for one that is blunt or offensive, such as *passed away* for *died* EUPHEMISM
– word or phrase that is unpleasant or offensive, substituted for a neutral or favourable one, the reverse of a euphemism DYSPHEMISM
– word or phrase that seems to have a second, typically saucy meaning DOUBLE ENTENDRE
– word or phrase used for identification or recognition, as among members of a group WATCHWORD, SHIBBOLETH
– word or phrase whose letters are rearranged from or into another word or phrase, as with *stop* and *spot* ANAGRAM, TRANSPOSITION
– word or proposition that is less general than another and is embraced by it, as *poodle* is by *dog* HYPONYM
– word or proposition that is more general than another and embraces it, as *furniture* does *chair* SUPERORDINATE
– word or word-element, such as *'em*, lacking an independent accent and typically linked with a preceding word ENCLITIC
– word or word-element, such as

piglet or *-let*, indicating small size, unimportance, youth, affection, or the like DIMINUTIVE
– word or word-element, such as *superstar* or *super-*, indicating increase in size or intensity AUGMENTATIVE
– word or word-element with a fixed meaning and not divisible into smaller elements MORPHEME
– word or words reading the same backwards as forwards, such as *madam* PALINDROME
– word printed or typed separately at the foot of a page to indicate the first word of the following page CATCHWORD
– word recorded only once in a text, ancient language, or the like HAPAX LEGOMENON, HAPAX
– word related in origin to another word, through sharing a root, as *sing* is to *song* PARONYM, COGNATE
– word-structure of a given language, including inflections and derivatives MORPHOLOGY
– words and phrases exclusive to a profession or other group JARGON, ARGOT, CANT
– words suggesting yet evading a promise or commitment WEASEL WORDS
– words used by or available to a person, group, or entire language VOCABULARY, LEXIS
– adjective for a word or words VERBAL
– adopt a foreign word or phrase fully into the language NATURALISE
– alteration of a borrowed word or expression to make it fit familiar patterns of the language, as when *asparagus* is called *sparrow-grass* FOLK ETYMOLOGY, POPULAR ETYMOLOGY, HOBSON-JOBSON
– altered form of a word, differing from the original or correct form CORRUPTION
– change in the form of a word, especially a noun or pronoun, showing its function in a sentence, as with *he* and *him* CASE
– change in the form of a word to indicate tense, gender, and the like as in *cry*, *crying*, *cries* INFLECTION, ACCIDENCE
– change in the sense or tone of a word to a less favourable one, as with *lewd*, which once meant 'ignorant' DETERIORATION, PEJORATION
– change in the sense or tone of a word to a more favourable one, as with *shrewd*, which once meant 'wicked' AMELIORATION, MELIORATION, ELEVATION
– change of a word's sound or spelling by the transposing of sounds or letters within the word, as in the development of *bird* from Old English *brid* METATHESIS
– choice of words, mode of expression, as of a particular person or group PHRASEOLOGY, PARLANCE, DICTION
– code or puzzle in which a word or phrase is represented by pictures, symbols, or numerals, as in representing the phrase *I hate Ellen Pound* by a picture of an eye followed by *H8 LN £* REBUS
– combination or arrangement, especially of words typically occurring together, as of *juvenile* with *delinquent* COLLOCATION
– core part of a word to which endings such as *-ing* or *-ed* can be added STEM
– describe fully the grammar of a word in its context PARSE
– earliest known form of a word or word-element ETYMON
– express one's ideas in words FORMULATE, VERBALISE
– game in which one player or team produces a word or line rhyming with a cue from the other CRAMBO
– game in which one player or team represents in mime, syllable by syllable, a word or phrase for the others to guess CHARADES
– incorrect use of words, choice of the wrong word for the context CATACHRESIS
– index of all the words in a text, such as the works of Shakespeare, listing every occurrence of each word CONCORDANCE
– invent or make up a new word COIN
– loss or accidental omission of words or letters in a piece of writing LIPOGRAPHY
– loss or cutting off of a letter, syllable, or sound at the beginning of a word, as with *squire* from *esquire* APHAERESIS, APHESIS
– loss or cutting off of a letter, syllable, or sound from the end of a word, as with *prof* from *professor* APOCOPE
– loss or cutting off of a letter, syllable or sound from the middle of a word, as with *fo'c's'le* from forecastle SYNCOPATION, SYNCOPE
– loss or cutting off of a syllable or sound from the middle of a word, as when pronouncing *deteriorate* as though it were spelt *deteriate* HAPLOLOGY
– meaning of a word in normal use ACCEPTATION
– meaning or explicit reference of a word DENOTATION
– newly invented word or expression NEOLOGISM, COINAGE
– object of meaning, the idea or thing referred to by a word, phrase, or sign REFERENT
– omission of a word or words from a sentence, as for compression or dramatic effect ELLIPSIS
– origin and development of a word, or the study of such origins ETYMOLOGY, DERIVATION
– pair of words, or one of the pair, deriving via different routes from a single source, as with *royal* and *regal* DOUBLET
– pair of words differing in only one small respect, helping to identify a language's distinctive sounds or features MINIMAL PAIR
– pass or toss something back and forth, such as words in an argument BANDY
– piece of writing that deliberately excludes any word containing a particular letter of the alphabet LIPOGRAM
– piece of writing that is deliberately composed entirely of words containing only one particular vowel UNIVOCALIC
– pronounce words unclearly, as by running them together SLUR
– provide evidence for or prove the use of a word, especially its first recorded use ATTEST
– referring to very long words POLYSYLLABIC, SESQUIPEDALIAN, INKHORN
– relating to meaning, as of words, gestures, or symbols SEMANTIC
– relating to the words or vocabulary of a language LEXICAL
– shorten a word or words by combining or leaving out some of the sounds or letters, as in *can't* CONTRACT
– spelling or pronunciation differing slightly from another form of the same word VARIANT
– splitting up of a word by an expression put between its parts, as in *abso-flaming-lutely* or *a whole nother problem* TMESIS
– study or science of the meaning of words, or of meaning in general SEMANTICS
– study or science of the way words are built or change in use MORPHOLOGY
– study or science of the way words link into sentences, grammar SYNTAX
– surrounding speech or writing of a specified word or passage refining its meaning CONTEXT
– switching, usually unintended, of

the initial sounds of two or more words, as when *red hat* comes out as *head rat* SPOONERISM
– symbol representing an entire word or phrase, such as % for *per cent* LOGOGRAM
– write or engrave words, as in a gift book or by incision into a hard surface INSCRIBE
-word- -LOG-, -LOGUE, LOGO-, LEX-, LEXIC-, -ONYM
word blindness, reading difficulties ALEXIA, DYSLEXIA
word-for-word, as a translation might be LITERAL
– word-for-word, using the very same words VERBATIM, AD VERBUM
word processor – designed specifically and exclusively for one purpose, as a word processor might be DEDICATED
– flickering point of light indicating the position on a VDU, as on a word processor CURSOR
wordiness, longwindedness VERBIAGE, VERBOSITY, PROLIXITY
– wordiness, roundabout or evasive speech or writing CIRCUMLOCUTION, PERIPHRASIS
wordy in a boring way, long-winded PROLIX, VERBOSE
– wordy or talkative LOQUACIOUS, VOLUBLE, GARRULOUS
work, occupation, career VOCATION
– work, such as domestic cleaning, that is routine and unskilled or undignified MENIAL WORK
– work, typically numbered in sequence, of a composer OPUS
– work at which one is skilled and happy MÉTIER, FORTE, VOCATION
– work done without pressure and without any payment VOLUNTARY WORK
– work or operate in harmony or at the same time SYNCHRONISE
– work regarded as a pointless waste of time in the U.S. BOONDOGGLE
– work that is boring and often tiring and unpleasant DRUDGERY
– work that is very easy but yields a high income GRAVY TRAIN
– work together, as on a scholarly or artistic project COLLABORATE
– work together harmoniously COORDINATE
– working hard and dutifully DILIGENT, ASSIDUOUS, CONSCIENTIOUS, SEDULOUS
– working in conjunction, cooperating IN TANDEM
– working properly, in working order OPERATIONAL, FUNCTIONAL, OPERATIVE
– assign work, duties, or powers to one's agent, subordinate, or the like DELEGATE, DEPUTE
– belief in the virtues of hard work WORK ETHIC
– fixed amount or spell of work or duty STINT, SHIFT
– hard or dirty domestic work in a military camp or barracks, often imposed as punishment FATIGUE
– "law" or mock-scientific principle to the effect that work expands to fill the time available for its completion PARKINSON'S LAW
– paying job or position that requires little or no work SINECURE
– person doing a specified type of work WALLAH
– person who cannot stop working WORKAHOLIC
– person who regularly travels a considerable distance between home and work COMMUTER
– relieve or stand in for somebody at work, by taking a turn SPELL
– share of work given to or required by a participant QUOTA
– shirk work or duty SCRIMSHANK, SKIVE
– study or application of biology and engineering in work and the workplace BIOTECHNOLOGY, ERGONOMICS
– task allotted to a person or group, job of work ASSIGNMENT, COMMISSION
work- ERG-, ERGO-
work of art, usually fairly small OBJET D'ART
– work of art or literature OEUVRE
work out, deduce, or guess at from known information EXTRAPOLATE
– work out an answer, as by calculating DETERMINE
– work out or prove by reasoning, deduce, infer DERIVE
workable, possible, practicable, realistic VIABLE
worker See also **servant**
– worker, especially a skilled industrial worker OPERATIVE
– worker from another country, especially a Turk or Yugoslav in West Germany GASTARBEITER
– worker in the USSR regarded as especially zealous or productive STAKHANOVITE
– worker opposed to mechanisation or technical advance LUDDITE
– worker qualified at his craft but still employed by someone else JOURNEYMAN
– worker receiving instruction in a trade, trainee APPRENTICE
– worker who defies a strike by continuing to work or replaces a worker on strike BLACKLEG, SCAB
– worker who performs tasks, often unpleasant tasks, purely for the money HIRELING
– worker's supervisor OVERSEER
– assign new tasks to workers REDEPLOY
– metal-worker, such as a welder, in heavy industries such as shipbuilding BOILERMAKER
– peasant or unskilled worker, especially in Latin America PEON
– reduction in the number of workers, through retirement or resignation rather than through redundancies NATURAL WASTAGE, ATTRITION
– relating to industrial wage earners or workers in manual labour jobs BLUE-COLLAR
– relating to office workers and other non-manual workers WHITE-COLLAR
– wandering or travelling from place to place, as a farmworker or casual labourer might ITINERANT, MIGRANT
working class or lower class, especially the class of industrial wage-earners PROLETARIAT
working hours – adaptable or variable, as working hours might be FLEXIBLE
– system allowing variable working hours to employees each day either side of the obligatory core time FLEXITIME
works – collection or full list of works, especially by a particular writer CORPUS, OEUVRE, CANON
workshop, factory, or the like where pay and working conditions are very poor SWEATSHOP
– workshop or studio of an artist or craftsman ATELIER
world See also **Earth**
– world of fashion, high society BEAU MONDE, HAUT MONDE
– world of the dead, the underworld NETHERWORLD
– fictional place or imaginary world where things are better than in real life UTOPIA
– fictional place or imaginary world where things are worse than in real life DYSTOPIA, CACOTOPIA
– person, group, or system regarded as a small representation of the whole world MICROCOSM
– regarding the world as the centre of the universe, as in early astronomy GEOCENTRIC
-world- -COSM-, COSMO-
world languages See **international**
world view, philosophical standpoint WELTANSCHAUUNG
worldly, earthly, of this life SUBLUNARY
– worldly, ordinary TERRESTRIAL, MUNDANE

– worldly rather than spiritual or religious SECULAR, TEMPORAL
worldwide, universal ECUMENICAL
worm – worm-eaten or worm-infested VERMICULATE
– worm in the intestines, tapeworm HELMINTH
– worm-like, relating to worms, or caused by worms VERMICULAR
– worm-like creature having one pair of legs on each body segment CENTIPEDE
– worm-like creature having two pairs of legs on each body segment MILLIPEDE
– worm-like young hatched from the egg of an insect LARVA
– worm of a type having segmented bodies, including the earthworms and leeches ANNELID
– worm of a type having long, unsegmented bodies, often parasitic, including the hookworm NEMATODE, ROUNDWORM
– worm remedy, expelling or destroying intestinal worms VERMIFUGE, ANTHELMINTIC, VERMICIDE
– parasitic flatworm of various kinds, including the flukes, having suckers and a tough skin TREMATODE
– resembling or relating to an earthworm LUMBRICOID
– shaped like a worm VERMIFORM
– silky protective capsule spun by larvae such as silkworms, to house the pupa COCOON
worm- VERMI-
worn out, drained of one's natural force and vitality, as through inbreeding or indulgence EFFETE
– worn out, exhausted, strained HAGGARD
– worn out, run down, or untidy, as through debauchery RADDLED
– worn out, severely weakened, exhausted or enfeebled DEBILITATED, DEPLETED, ENERVATED
– worn out or broken down through age or overuse DECREPIT, DILAPIDATED
– worn out or degraded, as through over-sophistication or debauchery DECADENT, DEGENERATE
worried, distressed, very nervous FRAUGHT, PERTURBED, AGITATED, DISQUIETED, EXERCISED
– worried, fretful, very tense, in suspense ON TENTERHOOKS
– worried, nervous, or concerned SOLICITOUS
– worried or troubled repeatedly, plagued by problems BESET, BEDEVILLED, BELEAGUERED
– very worried or emotionally upset UNNERVED, UNSTRUNG, DISCOMPOSED, DISTRAIT, DISTRAUGHT, OVERWROUGHT
worry, annoy repeatedly, pester, badger HARASS, HECTOR
– worry or burden, such as a debt MILLSTONE
– worry or uneasiness, anxious state DISQUIETUDE, CARK, APPREHENSIVENESS
– worry or vague unease, feeling of unspecific but powerful anxiety ANGST
– worry over petty details, fuss NIGGLE
– worrying or dangerous experience, of short duration MAUVAIS QUART D'HEURE
– free one's mind of a worry, grief, anxiety, guilt, or other burden DISBURDEN
– object or thought causing persistent but often needless worry BUGBEAR, BUGABOO
– sudden worry or dismay that throws everything into confusion CONSTERNATION
worsen, complicate, or intensify something, such as an injury or difficulty AGGRAVATE, EXACERBATE, COMPOUND
– worsen, decline in value, quality, health, or the like DETERIORATE, DEGENERATE
– worsen, return to an earlier and inferior stage or condition, take a step backwards REGRESS, RETROGRESS, RELAPSE
– worsen, weaken or cheapen, reduce in quality, corrupt or devalue DEBASE, DEGRADE, DEMEAN
– gradual worsening in the sense of a word with time, as with *lewd*, which once meant 'ignorant' DETERIORATION, PEJORATION
worship of the dead NECROLATRY
– offering of worship, thanksgiving, or the like OBLATION
– relating to worship DEVOTIONAL
-worship -LATRY
worthless, insignificant, trifling PALTRY, NUGATORY
– worthless but showy TRUMPERY
– worthless or unimportant thing BAGATELLE, TRIFLE
worthy, qualified, appropriate, as for a job or post ELIGIBLE
would-be, unsuccessful MANQUÉ
wound, injury LESION
– wound or hurt someone's feelings, as by insults or severe criticism SCARIFY, LACERATE
– wound or injure very severely, causing serious disfigurement or disability MAIM, MUTILATE
– wound or injury, as caused by an accident or surgery TRAUMA
– burn flesh or tissue with a corrosive chemical or a very hot or very cold instrument, as in treating wounds CAUTERISE
– discharge pus, as a wound might SUPPURATE, MATURATE, FESTER
– formation of small beads of new tissue on the surface of a wound during healing GRANULATION
– joining of broken bones, the edges of a wound, or the like COAPTATION
– on or near the surface, as a wound might be SUPERFICIAL
– sewing or stitching together of the edges of a wound SUTURE
– swollen area around a healing wound PROUD FLESH, GRANULATION TISSUE
woven See **weaving**, **fabrics**
wrap a newborn baby tightly with clothes or strips of cloth SWADDLE
– wrap closely, envelop, as in furs SWATHE
– wrap up in a scarf or blanket, as for warmth or disguise MUFFLE
wrath – become liable or subject to something such as debts or someone's wrath INCUR
wreath or crown of flowers worn on the head GARLAND, CHAPLET, CORONAL
– wreath or crown of leaves and branches, presented as an award or token of honour in ancient times BAYS, LAURELS
wreckage from a shipwrecked ship WRACK
– wreckage or cargo remaining afloat after a ship has sunk FLOTSAM
wrestle or come to grips GRAPPLE
wrestling – held in a headlock in wrestling IN CHANCERY
– holds of various kinds in wrestling SUPLEX, NELSON,
– Japanese style of wrestling, in which one tries to force one's opponent out of the ring or to the ground SUMO
– referring to a wrestling contest in which the usual weight divisions are disregarded CATCHWEIGHT
– style of wrestling in which holds are restricted to the upper body GRAECO-ROMAN WRESTLING
– throws of various kinds in wrestling FLYING MARE, CROSS-BUTTOCK
– wrestling contest involving two pairs of wrestlers TAG WRESTLING
wrinkle, crease, fold up RUCK, RUMPLE, PURSE, PUCKER
– wrinkled and shrivelled, as an elderly person's face might be WIZENED
wrist bone CARPAL, CARPUS
write, set down in writing, as one might a poem INDITE
– write hastily and untidily

SCRAWL, SCRIBBLE
– write or engrave words, as in a gift book or by incision into a hard surface INSCRIBE
– write or play a musical composition in a different key TRANSPOSE
– write or spell in the letters of another alphabet TRANSLITERATE
– write or talk at length and in detail on a subject ELABORATE, EXPATIATE, ENLARGE, DILATE
– write or type out a copy of a recording, shorthand notes, or the like TRANSCRIBE
– able to read and write LITERATE
– itch or urge to write CACOETHES SCRIBENDI
– unable to read or write ILLITERATE

write off an asset gradually, or prepare for its replacement by paying into a sinking fund AMORTISE

writer See also **author**
– writer, artist, or the like living in an unconventional way BOHEMIAN
– writer, journalist, artist, or the like who is self-employed and tends to undertake only short-term projects FREELANCE
– writer of fables or fantasies FABULIST
– writer or artist who favours a real-life representation of everyday subject matter REALIST, NATURALIST
– writer or journalist SCRIBE
– writer who writes a memoir or book on behalf of somebody else GHOST WRITER
– writer's complete works or output OEUVRE, CORPUS, CANON
– writers, artists, or other grouping whose aims or methods seem experimental, very daring, and ahead of their times AVANT-GARDE
– line under the title of a magazine or newspaper article giving the writer's name BY-LINE
– list of works by or about a particular writer BIBLIOGRAPHY
– relating to or written by an unnamed writer ANONYMOUS
– share of the proceeds paid by a publisher to a writer from sales of his work ROYALTY
– world of hack writers and mediocre journalists GRUB STREET

writing See also **handwriting**, **scripts**, **style**, **alphabets**, **speech**, **highfalutin**
– writing desk, typically with a hinged top closing over small drawers ESCRITOIRE, SECRETAIRE
– writing disability caused by brain disease AGRAPHIA, DYSGRAPHIA, APHASIA
– writing instrument, as used on wax tablets in ancient times STYLUS
– writing or copying room in a monastery SCRIPTORIUM
– writing or speaking effortlessly in a graceful, flowing way FLUENT
– writing or speech of an elegant, high-flown style PERIODS
– writing or speech that is pompous, high-flown, and showy FUSTIAN, BOMBAST, EUPHUISM, GRANDILOQUENCE
– writing or speech that is roundabout or evasive CIRCUMLOCUTION, PROLIXITY, PERIPHRASIS
– writing system, as in Chinese, in which each word is represented by a single character or symbol LEXIGRAPHY
– writing system, especially one based on an alphabet ORTHOGRAPHY
– writing that is more striking or elaborate than the surrounding text, often in an overblown way PURPLE PATCH, PURPLE PASSAGE
– bureaucratic speech or writing that is wordy and often empty GOBBLEDEGOOK, OFFICIALESE
– long and typically dull speech or piece of writing SCREED
– outpouring of emotion in speech or writing EFFUSION
– person employed in writing, either by taking dictation or by making neat copies of handwritten documents AMANUENSIS
– picture representing a word or idea, as in a writing system such as hieroglyphics PICTOGRAM
– piece of writing that deliberately excludes throughout a particular letter of the alphabet LIPOGRAM
– piece of writing that deliberately permits the use of only one of the vowels UNIVOCALIC
– scientific study of writing systems GRAMMATOLOGY
– study of handwriting, as for psychological analysis or detection of forgery GRAPHOLOGY
– symbol or character in a writing system, such as Chinese, that represents a thing or idea rather than the sound IDEOGRAM

-writing -GRAM, -GRAPH

writings of a deep, scholarly, often dry kind LUCUBRATIONS
– writings of doubtful authorship or reliability APOCRYPHA
– writings or drawings, often witty or obscene, scribbled typically on walls in public places GRAFFITI
– writings produced by a writer in his earlier years before reaching his mature style JUVENILIA
– complete collection of writings by a particular writer CORPUS, OEUVRE, CANON
– passing off as one's own the writings, tunes, ideas, or the like of another PLAGIARISM

written study or systematic examination of a particular subject TREATISE, DISSERTATION, THESIS
– having lines written alternately left to right and right to left BOUSTROPHEDON

wrong See also **mistake**, **false**, **incorrect**
– wrong, erring, straying from the moral course, wayward ERRANT
– wrong or unjust in a shameful way INIQUITOUS
– distress or anger arising from a sense of being injured or wronged GRIEVANCE
– prove a statement or argument wrong REFUTE, REBUT, CONFUTE
– provoke something, often something wrong, or provoke someone into doing it INSTIGATE

wrong- CACO-, MAL-, MIS-, PARA-

wrongdoer, criminal, or villain MISCREANT

wrongdoing, especially by a public official MALFEASANCE, MALVERSATION

wrongful act in civil law, other than breach of contract TORT

wrongly- CATA-

X, Y, Z

X-ray ROENTGEN RAY
– X-ray or gamma-ray examination, or the technique involved RADIOGRAPHY
– X-ray technique in which brain tissue or other soft tissue is scanned and a computer provides a 3-D image COMPUTERISED AXIAL TOMOGRAPHY, CAT SCAN
– X-ray technique that shows up only the section of tissue wanted TOMOGRAPHY
– medical treatment, particularly of cancer, by means of X-rays or similar radiation, or radioactive chemicals RADIOTHERAPY
– reveal or make visible an internal body part by means of surgery or X-rays VISUALISE
– whitish preparation containing barium sulphate, eaten prior to an X-ray examination of the alimentary canal BARIUM MEAL

-X-ray -GRAM

X-shaped, crossing, intersecting DECUSSATE

xylophone of Latin American style MARIMBA

yacht See illustration at **sailing**, and also **boat**, **sailing terms**
– yacht's keel that can be raised when not in use CHEESECUTTER
– chairman of a yacht club COMMODORE
– dinghy or small service boat towed or carried by a yacht or ship TENDER
– docking basin or mooring area for yachts MARINA
– shelter against rain or spray on a yacht or ship's bridge DODGER

yard in which railway carriages, engines, and so on are collected and then joined up to form new trains MARSHALLING YARD

yarn or fabric made from recycled wool SHODDY
– ball of twine, yarn, or thread CLEW
– bundle or measure of yarn HANK
– knot or lump in yarn or cloth BURL
– loose coil of thread, wool, or other yarn SKEIN
– loosely twisted yarn used in embroidery and tapestries CREWEL
– small lump in yarn or a fabric, sometimes made deliberately to produce a knobbly appearance SLUB
– smooth yarn used in making braids and fringes GENAPPE
– tightly twisted woollen yarn made from long fibres WORSTED

yawning or sleepy OSCITANT

year in which farm land is left to lie fallow, observed every seventh year by the ancient Jews SABBATICAL YEAR
– year of origin, especially of a wine VINTAGE
– year of remarkable events ANNUS MIRABILIS
– year of rest, restitution, or celebration JUBILEE
– years important to one's development, especially in childhood FORMATIVE YEARS
– adjective for a year ANNUAL

yearly, annually PER ANNUM
– yearly payment of an allowance, dividends, or the like ANNUITY

yearn or long for something intensely PINE, HANKER
– yearning or sentimental longing for something in the past, especially one's childhood home NOSTALGIA

yeast or similar substance added to dough to aid fermentation LEAVEN

yell or shout HOLLER

yellow See **colours**
– yellow-flowering crop producing a valuable oilseed and used for fodder RAPE, COLZA
– pale sickly yellowish in colour or complexion SALLOW

yellow- XANTHO-

yellowing of the skin and eyes, or an illness producing it JAUNDICE, ICTERUS

yes – answering yes, expressing assent or agreement AFFIRMATIVE

yes-man, servile follower LACKEY, FLUNKY, MINION, TOADY, SYCOPHANT, LICKSPITTLE

yield See also **give up**
– yield control or possession of, release or abandon RELINQUISH
– yield or hand over formally rights, territory, or the like CEDE
– yield or give up a claim or right voluntarily, as to a trial by jury WAIVE
– yield or surrender, end one's resistance CAPITULATE
– yield out of pity, withhold a planned punishment or victory blow RELENT
– yield over-respectfully to another person's wishes or decisions KOWTOW, TRUCKLE
– yield reluctantly DISGORGE
– yield to a superior force, temptation, or the like SUCCUMB
– yield to a whim or craving INDULGE, GRATIFY
– yield to or comply with another's decision or opinion DEFER TO
– yield to someone's authority, bend the knee SUBMIT
– yield to someone's urging, consent or agree to a request ACCEDE, CONCEDE, ACQUIESCE

yielding or giving up of something, as of territory or rights CESSION
– yielding or voluntary relinquishing of a claim, right, or privilege WAIVER
– yielding over-eagerly, slavishly submissive SERVILE, OBSEQUIOUS, FAWNING

yoga of a form emphasising exercises HATHA YOGA
– sitting position, with crossed legs and hands resting on knees, as used in yoga and meditation LOTUS POSITION

yoke- ZYG-, ZYGO-

yolk of an egg VITELLUS

young See also **animal terms**
– young and immature JUVENILE, ADOLESCENT, PUERILE
– young and immature or inexperienced CALLOW
– young and inexperienced person or organisation FLEDGLING, STRIPLING
– young child, youngster SPROG
– young child or animal that is still unweaned SUCKLING
– young person who is extremely clever or successful for his age WHIZZ KID, WUNDERKIND, CHILD PRODIGY
– make young again, restore to youthful appearance or energy REJUVENATE

-young -LING

young man kept as a lover by an

older woman GIGOLO, TOYBOY
– young man who is very good-looking APOLLO, ADONIS
young woman, girl, maiden DAMSEL
– young woman or girl, who is slim and attractive in a boyish way GAMINE
– young woman undergoing a formal presentation to society, as at a ball DEBUTANTE
youth, adolescent boy STRIPLING
– give renewed youth or vitality to REJUVENATE
– time of one's youth or immaturity, especially the time of one's minority, during which one is legally under age NONAGE
youthful, young, fresh, spring-like VERNAL
Yugoslavia – the main official language in Yugoslavia SERBO-CROAT
z, s, or related hissing sound SIBILANT
zebra-like mammal, now extinct, of southern Africa QUAGGA
Zen riddle or brain-teaser, designed to free the mind from the constraints of logic KOAN
zenith – point in the heavens directly beneath the observer, diametrically opposite the zenith NADIR
zero, nothing ZILCH
– zero, the symbol 0 CIPHER
zest, enthusiasm, dash, vigour FLAIR, ÉLAN, PIZZAZZ
– zest, hearty enjoyment of life JOIE DE VIVRE
– zest, vitality or enjoyment, liveliness ANIMATION, VIVACITY, GUSTO
zigzag braid, flat and narrow, as used to trim clothing RICKRACK
– zigzag course, especially in sailing when trying to progress into the wind TACK
– zigzag path, as taken by a sailing ship TRAVERSE
– cut a zigzag or scalloped edge on PINK
zinc – coat or rustproof steel or iron with zinc GALVANISE
zodiac See chart, and also **astrology**
– chart of the relative positions of planets and signs of the zodiac at a given time HOROSCOPE
zone on the Earth's surface lying between the tropics TORRID ZONE
– zones on the Earth's surface lying between the polar regions and the tropics TEMPERATE ZONES
– zones on the Earth's surface lying within the polar regions FRIGID ZONES
– sensitive to sexual stimulation, as certain zones of the body are EROGENOUS
zoo – small zoo or display enclosure of wild animals MENAGERIE

ZODIACAL SIGNS

SIGNS	DATES	SIGNS	DATES
Capricorn: the Goat	Dec 23-Jan 19	**Cancer: the Crab**	June 23-July 23
Aquarius: the Water Carrier	Jan 20-Feb 19	**Leo: the Lion**	July 24-Aug 23
Pisces: the Fishes	Feb 20-Mar 21	**Virgo: the Virgin**	Aug 24-Sept 23
Aries: the Ram	Mar 22-Apr 20	**Libra: the Scales/ the Balance**	Sept 24-Oct 23
Taurus: the Bull	Apr 21-May 21	**Scorpio: the Scorpion**	Oct 24-Nov 22
Gemini: the Twins	May 22-June 22	**Sagittarius: the Archer**	Nov 23-Dec 22

Part Two

LEXICON OF DIFFICULT WORDS

The 10,000 words brought together in this lexicon form a central phalanx in the ranks of the English vocabulary – that array of tricky or reasonably difficult terms that speakers and writers are most likely to look up for confirmation or for information.

This is in keeping with the dual purpose of the lexicon. First, it serves as a quick-check reference for your intuitions. Suppose you need the technical term for a kneecap, and you have an inkling that it is SCAPULA. Simply look up **scapula** in this lexicon, and put your inkling to the test. The lexicon, in other words, is there to confirm your suspicions. It's when your suspicions are *not* confirmed (the word *scapula*, it turns out, refers to the shoulder blade, not to the kneecap), or when you cannot even hazard a suspicion in the first place, that you turn to Part One, the reverse dictionary proper (where the cue word **kneecap**, or the illustration at **bones**, leads you at once to the target word you need – PATELLA). In short, look up the lexicon when you think you know the word; look up the reverse dictionary when you don't know the word or can't remember it.

The second function of the lexicon is as a supplement to Part One. The definitions are expanded, pronunciations given, and related word-forms and points of usage noted where necessary. In addition, the history or origin of a word is traced when it is especially interesting or memorable, or helps to fix the meaning of the word in your mind. Suppose that a particular word for "carefree" or "casual" has been eluding you. You turn to Part One, and it reveals that the word you are seeking is *nonchalant*. But further questions might now arise. Does the word really answer your purpose? How is it pronounced exactly? Look up *nonchalant* in the lexicon, and your questions are answered. You'll find a set of definitions carefully distinguishing various shades of meaning; there's an easy-to-follow pronunciation guide to reassure or enlighten you; and there's an interesting etymology that might prove a useful memory aid – pointing out that the word's Latin roots embody the concept "not warm", and that the word *scalding* is related in origin.

To provide for maximum information and efficiency, the entries have been kept as economical as possible. The definitions at any particular headword will cover only those senses that are at the appropriate level of difficulty. Most of the senses of the word *sheet*, for instance, are far too obvious to need defining here: the only sense that you might want to check is the nautical sense, and that's the one sense entered – "rope or chain attached to and controlling the lower corner of a sail".

Similarly, pronunciations are given only where appropriate. Often they are perfectly familiar or else easily deduced. Even where there may be doubt over various possible pronunciations, there is usually little point in entering them if they are all acceptable. The word *gratis*, for instance, can be pronounced /graáa-tiss/ or /gráy-tiss/ or even /gráttiss/. And the word *surmise* can take the stress on either syllable: /sur-mīz/ or /súr-mīz/. Where the pronunciations are omitted, as in both these cases, you can trust your intuition.

GUIDE TO PRONUNCIATION

The pronunciation guide in this dictionary is based on a simple re-spelling system that uses for the most part familiar combinations of letters of the alphabet. The only symbol taken from outside the alphabet is (ə) which conveys the sound represented by the er in matter or the a in approve. The symbols used are listed below:

a	as in *trap* /trap/
aa	as in *calm* /kaam/
air	as in *scarce* /skairss/
ar, aar	as in *cart* /kart/ *carnation* /kaar/náysh'n/
aw	as in *thought* /thawt/
awr	as in *warm* /wawrm/
ay	as in *face* /fayss/
b, bb	as in *stab* /stab/, *rubber* /rúbbər/
ch	as in *church* /church/, *nature* /náychər/
ck	as in *pocket* /póckit/
d, dd	as in *dead* /ded/, *ladder* /láddər/
e	as in *ten* /ten/
ee	as in *meat* /meet/
eer	as in *fierce* /feerss/
er	as in *term* /term/
ew	as in *few* /few/
ewr	as in *pure* /pwer/
ə	as in *about* /ə-bówt/, *cannon* /kánnən/
ər	as in *persist* /pər-síst/, *celery* /séllәri/
f, ff	as in *sofa* /sṓfə/, *suffer* /súffər/
g, gg	as in *stag* /stag/, *giggle* /gigg'l/
h	as in *hat* /hat/
i	as in *grid* /grid/
ī	as in *price* /prīss/
īr	as in fire /fīr/
j	as in *judge* /juj/
k	as in *kick* /kik/
<u>kh</u>	as in *loch* /lo<u>kh</u>/
l, ll	as in *fill* /fil/, *colour* /kúllər/
'l	as in *channel* /chánn'l/
m, mm	as in *man* /man/, *summer* /súmmər/
'm	as in *blossom* /blóss'm/
n, nn	as in *fan* /fan/, *honour* /ónnər/
'n	as in *sudden* /súdd'n/
ng	as in *tank* /tangk/, *finger* /fíng-gər/
o	as in *rod* /rod/
ō	as in *goat* /gōt/
ŏŏ	as in *would* /wŏŏd/
o͞o	as in *shoe* /sho͞o/
oor	as in *poor* /poor/
or	as in *north* /north/
ow	as in *stout* /stowt/
owr	as in *sour* /sowr/
oy	as in *boy* /boy/
p, pp	as in *crop* /krop/, *pepper* /peppər/
r, rr	as in *red* /red/, *terror*, /térrər/
s, ss	as in *sauce* /sawss/, *fussy* /fússi/
sh	as in *ship* /ship/
t, tt	as in *state* /stayt/, *totter* /tóttər/
th	as in *thick* /thik/
<u>th</u>	as in *this* /<u>th</u>iss/, *smooth* /smo͞o<u>th</u>/
u	as in *cut* /kut/
ur	as in *turn* /turn/
v, vv	as in *valve* /valv/, *cover* /kúvvər/
w	as in *wet* /wet/
y	as in *yes* /yess/
z, zz	as in *zoo* /zo͞o/, *scissors* /sízzərz/
<u>zh</u>	as in *vision* /ví<u>zh</u>'n/

FOREIGN SOUNDS

Words and names from other languages are shown with an English-style pronunciation, if they have one. Otherwise, an approximation to the foreign-language pronunciation is shown wherever possible. The symbols used are as follows:

aN	nasalised, as in French *demain* /də-máN/
<u>kh</u>	as in German *Achtung* /á<u>kh</u>-tŏŏng/
ö	as in French *boeuf* /böf/, German *schön* /shön/
ON	nasalised, as in French *enfant* /ON-fÓN/
ü	as in French *lune* /lün/, German *Führer* /fǘr-ər/

STRESS

Stress in words of more than one syllable is shown by the mark ´ over the stressed vowel symbol.

ín-sīt	insight
in-sīt	incite

ABBREVIATIONS KEY

adj.	adjective	*n.*	noun
adv.	adverb	*pl.n.*	plural noun
comb.form	combining form	*prep.*	preposition
conj.	conjunction	*pron.*	pronoun
interj.	interjection	*tr.*	transitive
intr.	intransitive	*v.*	verb

abacus *n.* calculating device, as used in Asia, operated by moving beads on rods [Latin, from Greek *abax*, a slab, an arithmetic table, a dust-covered drawing board, from Hebrew *'abhaq*, dust]

abalone (ábbə-lṓni)) *n.* large edible shellfish providing mother-of-pearl, especially one found off the Pacific coast of North America

abate *intr.v.* to lessen in intensity, decline or die down: *the storm/pain abated* — **-ment** *n.*

abattoir *chiefly British. n.* slaughterhouse

abdicate *v.* to give up or relinquish power or responsibility formally

abduct *tr.v.* to kidnap; to draw away from a bone, muscle, or the like — **-tor**, **-tion** *n.*

aberrant (ab-érrənt) *adj.* abnormal — **-ration** *n.*

abeyance (ə-báy-ənss) *formal. n.* — **in abeyance** temporarily suspended or inactive

abhorrent (əb-hórrənt) *adj.* loathsome or disgusting [related to *horrid*] — **abhor** *tr.v.* — **-rence** *n.*

abject *adj.* miserable, grindingly wretched: *abject poverty*; extremely humble or respectful: *an abject apology*; shameless or despicable: *an abject liar*

abjure (ab-jóor) *formal. tr.v.* to take back or renounce formally or under oath, recant, forswear; to avoid, give up, or abstain from — **-ration** *n.*

ablution *n.* washing of the body, as in religious ceremonies

ablutions *pl.n. British.* bathroom or lavatory facilities at a military base, latrines — **perform one's ablutions** to wash oneself (humorously pompous)

abnegation *n.* self-sacrifice or self-denial

abolition *n.* ending or getting rid of something, especially of slavery and the death penalty — **-ist**, **-ism** *n.*

abominable (ə-bómm'nəb'l) *adj.* causing revulsion or disgust; of extremely poor quality — **-ination** *n.*

abominate *tr.v.* detest, abhor

aboriginal *adj.* native to a region, local, indigenous

abrade *v.* to wear or rub away — **abrasion** *n.*

abrasive *adj.* causing abrasion; harsh or curt in speech or manner ~ *n.* something that abrades, especially a cleaning or smoothing substance that scours and scrapes, such as pumice or emery

abscess (áb-sess) *n.* pus-filled blister, boil, or inflammation [Latin, *abscedere*, to go away; referring to the departure of supposed bad humours from a wound by means of pus]

abscond (ab-skónd) *intr.v.* to flee and hide, especially in order to escape detection or punishment: *abscond with stolen goods*

abseil (áb-sayl) *intr.v.* to descend, as from a cliff top or helicopter, by means of a supporting rope around one's body — **abseil** *n.*

absolutism *n.* authoritarian form of government, such as a dictatorship or absolute monarchy — **-ist** *n.*, *adj.*

absolve *tr.v.* to consider or pronounce free of blame or guilt, or free from responsibility or punishment; to pardon or remit (a sin) — **absolution** *n.*

abstemious *adj.* sparing, restrained, or disciplined, especially in eating and drinking; characteristic of an abstemious person [Latin, *ab-*, away from + *temetum*, wine, mead, or an alcoholic drink]

abstinence *n.* self-denial, especially restraint in eating and drinking; refraining from eating meat, as an act of penance, especially formerly among Roman Catholics — **-ent** *adj.* — **abstain** *intr.v.*

abstract (ábstrakt) *n.* summary, list of the main points; work of art that does not represent objects or beings

abstracted *adj.* lost in thought

abstraction *n.* general idea, or word referring to a general idea rather than to a specific thing

abstruse (ab-stróoss) *adj.* intellectually difficult: *abstruse arguments*

abut (ə-bút) *formal. v.* to touch, join, be adjacent to: *Their property abuts on mine/abuts mine*

abysmal *adj.* deeply, profoundly bad: *abysmal ignorance/poverty* [related to *abyss*]

academia *n.* university education and the world of scholarship (also "academe") — **-mic** *n.*, *adj.* — **-micism** *n.* [from Greek *Akademia*, Platonic philosophy, originally, the place in Athens where Plato taught]

acanthus (ə-kán-thəss) *n.*, *pl.* **-thuses** or **-thi** thistle-like shrub with spikes of flowers; leaf-patterned carving on the capital of a Corinthian column

a cappella (áa kə-péllə) *adv.*, *adj.* without instrumental accompaniment, in the manner of some choral music [Italian, literally, in the style of a chapel]

acceptation *formal. n.* meaning of a word or phrase

access *n.* entrance, right to enter, or means of entering; attack of rage, disease, or the like ~ *adj.* referring to broadcasting in which members of the general public rather than professionals make the programmes ~ *tr.v.* reach or retrieve (something, such as computer data) — **-ible** *adj.*

accession *n.* addition or newly acquired possession, as in a library or other collection; act of acceding: *accession to the throne/to a treaty*; *formal.* rise in value of property ~ *tr.v.* to enter in a list of accessions

accessory *n.* additional, supplementary, or accompanying item, as to a motor car or a woman's clothing; person who encourages or helps another in the committing of a crime though not directly involved in it (in this sense, also "accessary")

accidie (áksidi) *formal. n.* spiritual lethargy, despairing indifference (also "acedia")

acclamation *n.* acclaiming or being acclaimed — **by acclamation** by a vote of approval at a meeting, expressed by cheering rather than by a formal ballot — **-tory** *adj.*

acclimatise *v.* to adjust to a new climate or surroundings — **-tisation** *n.*

accolade (áckə-layd) *formal. n.* an expression of praise, as by words or an award; ceremonial confer-

ring of knighthood, as by a touch of a sword on the shoulder

accomplice *n.* person who helps another to commit a crime

accost *formal. tr.v.* to approach in order to speak to or accuse; to invite or entice sexually

accouchement (ə-kōōsh-moN) *formal. n.* period of confinement of a woman at the time of giving birth, lying-in [French, from *couche*, a bed]

accoucheuse (ákoo-shérz) *formal. n.* woman, such as a midwife or obstetrician, who helps a woman to give birth (masculine counterpart "accoucheur")

accoutred (ə-kōōtərd) *formal. adj.* dressed, ornamented, or equipped in a specified way

accoutrements (ə-kōōtrəmənts) *formal. pl.n.* soldier's equipment in addition to his uniform and weapons

accretion *n.* growth through slow additions, build-up; unearned or unexpected increase in land, property, an inheritance, or the like

accrue *intr.v.* to be added in addition to what is already present: *Interest accrued at 6%* — **accrual** *n.*

accumulator *n.* calculator's circuit where figures are stored and computed; *chiefly British.* storage battery, as in a car; *chiefly British.* bet on four or more successive races, the winnings each time becoming the stake on the next

acerbic (ə-sérbik) *adj.* harsh or cutting in speech or manner

acetic (ə-seétik) *formal. adj.* relating to vinegar: *acetic acid*

acetylene (ə-sétt'l-een) *n.* gas whose flame is used for cutting and welding metal

Achilles' heel *n.* weakness or flaw, small and apparently unimportant, but fatally vulnerable [after *Achilles*, the hero in Greek mythology who was invulnerable except in the heel]

achromatic *adj.* colourless, or of neutral colour, such as black, white, or grey

acinus (ássi-nəss) *formal. n., pl.* **-ni** small segment or division of an aggregate fruit such as the raspberry; pip or seed of a fruit such as the raspberry or grape

ack-ack *n.* anti-aircraft gun or fire [signalling code for *AA*, abbreviation for *anti-aircraft*]

acme (ákmi) *n.* highest point or summit of attainment

acolyte *formal. n.* follower, disciple; altar boy, priest's assistant at the altar

acoustic *adj.* relating to sound or hearing; referring to a musical instrument that does not use electric amplification of its sound: *an acoustic guitar* — **-ics** *n., pl.n.*

acquiesce (áckwi-éss) *intr.v.* to accept, agree, or cooperate meekly: *acquiesce in the shameful policy* [related to *quiet*] — **-scent** *adj.* — **-scence** *n.*

acquit *tr.v.* to clear (someone) of a crime, declare to be not guilty; *formal.* to conduct (oneself) as specified in facing a challenge: *acquitted themselves well on the field of honour* — **acquittal** *n.*

acrid (áckrid) *adj.* sharp or harsh, as a smell or taste might be; harsh and irritating, bitter: *acrid wit*

acrimonious (áckri-mōni-əss) *adj.* bitter or acerbic, as in speech, manner, or tone — **-mony** *n.*

acronym (áckrə-nim) *n.* word formed from the initial letters or syllables of a group of words, such as *NATO* or *Comintern.* Compare INITIALISM

acrophobia *n.* excessive or irrational fear of heights or of being in high places — **bic** *adj., n.*

acropolis (ə-krópp'l-iss) *n.* citadel in ancient Greece

acrostic *n.* lines, as of a poem, in which some letters, usually the first, spell out a name or message — **acrostic** *adj.*

acrylic *n.* synthetic resin used in making plastics, fibres, and paints (also "acrylic resin")

actuary *n.* insurance company's statistician who calculates risks, premiums, and the like — **-arial** *adj.*

actuate *tr.v.* to cause to act, impel: *actuated by self-interest*; *formal.* to cause to operate, activate: *actuate a mechanism*

acuity *formal. n.* sharpness or keenness of the senses or the mind, acuteness: *visual acuity*

acumen (áckew-mən) *n.* ability to make shrewd decisions or judgments; insight, perceptiveness

acupuncture *n.* Chinese-style "alternative" therapy in which needles are inserted into the skin or body at given points

adage (áddij) *n.* short proverb or maxim

adagio (ə-daá-ji-ō) *n., pl.* **-os** musical composition or movement played at a slow tempo — **adagio** *adv., adj.*

adamant (áddə-mənt) *n.* legendary unbreakable stone ~ *adj.* unbreakable or unyielding in spirit

adaptive radiation *n.* evolution of a species into several different species adapted to different environments

addendum (ə-dén-dəm) *n., pl.* **-da** added material, as in a book

additive *n.* something added to food or drink to preserve, flavour, or otherwise alter it

addled *adj.* rotten: *an addled egg*; muddled and confused

adduce *tr.v.* to produce or cite (an example, argument, or reason) as evidence or proof

adenoidal *adj.* nasal or choky in sound; breathing with difficulty owing to swollen adenoids; relating to glands

adept *adj.* very skilful, expert ~ *n.* highly skilled person, expert

adherent *n.* supporter or follower of a policy, person, or faith

adhesive *n.* glue, paste, or other substance for sticking something to a surface — **adhesive** *adj.*

ad hoc (ád hók) *adj., adv.* for a particular purpose: *an ad hoc committee*; in response to particular circumstances: *took the decision ad hoc*; *an ad hoc decision* [Latin, literally, towards this]

ad hominem (ád hómminem) *adj., adv.* based less on reason than on references to one's opponent's personal affairs or qualities: *an ad hominem argument*; *arguing ad hominem* [Latin, literally, to the man]

adieu (ə-déw) *formal. n., interj.* farewell [French, literally, to God]

ad infinitum (ád ínfi-nī́təm) *adv.* to infinity; without an end

adipose (áddi-pōss) *formal. adj.* fatty, relating to animal fat: *adipose tissue* — **-posity** *n.*

adit (áddit) *n.* shaft, horizontal or nearly so, cut into the side of a hill, for drainage or mining

adjacent *adj.* next to or close to

adjourn (ə-júrn) *intr.v.* to suspend or transfer proceedings: *The council adjourned until Monday/to another room* ~ *tr.v.* to cause to adjourn

adjudicate *v.* to judge or act as a judge, as in a court case or dispute — **-cation**, **-cator** *n.*

adjunct (ájungkt) *n.* person or thing that is associated with another in a subordinate or temporary way —

adjunct *adj.*
adjure (ə-jo͝or) *formal. tr.v.* to order or enjoin solemnly; to beg or entreat earnestly — **-ration** *n.*
adjutant (ájoo-tənt) *n.* officer who assists a more senior officer in administrative work
ad-lib *informal. v.* to improvise (typically, something spoken) ~ *n.* something ad-libbed ~ *adj.* improvised, ad-libbed [shortened from *ad libitum*, Latin, literally, to the desire] — **ad lib** *adv.*
admonish *formal. tr.v.* to scold gently but firmly; to warn or advise against something, caution — **-monition** *n.*
ad nauseam *formal. adv.* sickeningly often, regularly or repeatedly to a tiresome extent [Latin, literally, to nausea]
adobe (ə-dṓbi) *n.* clay, or a sun-dried brick made from it, as in Mexico
Adonis (ə-dṓniss) *n.* beautiful young man [after *Adonis*, a beautiful young man in Greek mythology with whom Aphrodite fell in love]
adrenaline (ə-drénnə-lin) *informal. n.* supposed substance that produces a surge of excitement, nervousness, or power (also "adrenalin") [after the substance secreted by the *adrenal glands*]
adroit (ə-dróyt) *adj.* dexterous or skilful; resourceful [French, *à droit*, literally, to the right]
adscititious (ádsi-tíshəss) *formal. adj.* added, supplementary, incidental rather than essential
adulation *n.* flattery, excessive praise, admiration to the point of hero-worship
adulterate *tr.v.* to dilute or add impurities to (a substance, such as milk or wine) — **-terant** *adj.*, *n.*
adumbrate (áddəm-brayt) *formal. tr.v.* to sketch out or give a rough outline of; to hint — **-tion** *n.*
adventitious (ádvən-tíshəss) *formal. adj.* accidental, by chance, unexpected; occurring or positioned abnormally or unusually: *adventitious plant roots*
adverse *adj.* against one's interests, unfavourable — **-sity** *n.*
advert (əd-vért) *formal. intr.v.* to refer to something, call attention or remark: *adverted to those baseless allegations*
advocaat (ádvō-kaa, -kaat) *n.* sweet liqueur made of raw egg yolks and brandy
advocate *tr.v.* (ádvə-kayt) to recommend, favour, support, or champion ~ *n.* (-kət) supporter or champion of some idea or person; barrister — **-cacy** *n.*
advowson (əd-vówz'n) *n.* right to nominate a priest to a vacant benefice or position
adze (adz) *n.* tool with a cutting blade at right angles to the handle, used for dressing wood (also *U.S.* "adz")
aegis (éejiss) *n.* — **under the aegis of** under the sponsorship, patronage, or supervision of [after the *aigis*, Zeus's shield in Greek mythology]
aegrotat (ī́-grə-tat) *British. n.* certificate, pass, degree, or subsequent examination when a university student misses part of an examination through illness [Latin, literally, he is ill, from *aeger*, ill]
aeolian (ee-ṓli-ən) *adj.* relating to or caused by the wind [after *Aeolus* or *Aiolos*, god of the winds in classical mythology]
aeon (ée-ən) *n.* very long period of time; specifically, in geology, 1,000,000,000 years (also *chiefly U.S.* "eon")
aerobics *n.* system of exercises to stimulate breathing and oxygenate the blood — **-bic** *adj.*
aeronaut *n.* balloon pilot, or person flying in a lighter-than-air aircraft — **-nautic** *adj.* — **-nautics** *n.*
Aesculapian (éeskew-láypi-ən) *formal. adj.* medical, relating to healing [after *Aesculapius*, the god of medicine or healing in Roman mythology]
aesthete (éess-theet) *n.* art lover, person who is sensitive to beauty — **-thetic** *adj.*, *n.* — **-thetics** *n.*, *pl.n.* — **-icism** *n.*
aestival (eess-tī́v'l, ess-) *formal. adj.* relating to the summer
aetiology (éeti-ólləji) *n.* origin or cause, as of a disease or social problem (also *U.S.* "etiology") — **-logical** *adj.*
affable *adj.* easy to get on with; friendly — **-bility** *n.*
affaire d'honneur (ə-fáir don-ér, -ṓr) *n.* question of honour or matter of honour, serious enough to provoke a duel [French]
affect (áffekt) *n.* feeling or emotion in psychology, usually associated with a particular idea or thought
affectation *n.* artificial way of speaking, dressing, or behaving, in order to impress others — **affected** *adj.* — **affect** *tr.v.*
affidavit (áffi-dáyvit) *n.* declaration in writing that is made under oath [Medieval Latin, literally, he has stated on oath]
affiliate *v.* — *tr.* to adopt or accept as an associate member or subordinate partner — *intr.* to join a large grouping as an associate: *to affiliate to the TUC* — **affiliate**, **-tion** *n.*
affinity *n.* attraction, as between people or molecules; similarity suggesting a common origin; relationship by adoption or marriage, as distinct from a blood relationship
afflatus (ə-fláytəss) *formal. n.* poetic inspiration or other creative impulse: *a divine afflatus*
affluence (áffloo-ənss) *n.* abundance of material goods; wealth — **-ent** *adj.*
affray (ə-fráy) *n.* in law, a rowdy public quarrel or brawl
affront *tr.v.* to insult or offend ~ *n.* insult, slight, anything that causes offence
aficionado (ə-físh-yə-náado) *n.*, *pl.* **-dos** fan or devotee: *an aficionado of real ale*; specifically, bullfighting aficionado [Spanish; related to *affection*]
a fortiori (áy fórti-áwrī) *adv.* for an even stronger reason, all the more so: *If I can't lift it, then a fortiori neither can my brother* [Latin, from the stronger (reason)]
aftermath *n.* period following or state resulting from an event, especially a disaster; second crop of grass or hay in a single season
agape (ággə-pee) *n.*, *pl.* **-pae** loving kindness, Christian love, charity, as distinct from erotic love; "love feast", meal commemorating the Last Supper, in the early Christian Church
agenda (ə-jéndə) *n.* list of items to be dealt with, especially at a meeting
agent provocateur (ázhoN-prə-vóckə-tér) *n.*, *pl.* **-s -s** secret agent who joins a political or criminal group and tries to incite it into punishable or discrediting activities [French, literally, provocative agent]
agglomerate *v.* to form or gather into a rounded mass — **-ration** *n.*
aggrandisement (ə-grándiz-mənt) *n.* increase in power, reputation, or the like; especially, excessive or unwarranted aggrandisement [related to *grand*] — **aggrandise** *tr.v.*

aggrieved *adj.* hurt, distressed, or offended by an apparent injustice

aghast *adj.* shocked or amazed by something horrible, appalled

agitprop (ájit-prop) *n.* political agitation and propaganda, especially by left-wing radicals [shortened from Russian *Agitpropbyuro*, a propaganda department of the Communist Party, from *agitatsya-propaganda*, agitation propaganda]

aglet (ágglit) *n.* metal or plastic tip on a shoelace; pendant, hanging brooch or other jewellery

agnostic *n.* person who is uncertain whether God exists or who doubts whether we can know one way or the other; *formal.* person who is uncertain or uncommitted: *an agnostic on the question of tax cuts* — **agnostic** *adj.* — **-ticism** *n.*

agog *informal. adj.* expectant, excited or impatient with curiosity or surprise

agora (ággərə) *n., pl.* **-rae** or **-ras** marketplace in an ancient Greek city in which public meetings took place; public meeting held in an agora

agoraphobia *n.* excessive or irrational fear of open spaces or going out in public — **-bic** *adj., n.*

agraffe (ə-gráf) *n.* stonemason's clamp or cramp iron; fastening consisting of a hook and loop, as formerly used on armour

agrarian *adj.* relating to land, farming, or the country

ague (áygew) *archaic.n.* malaria or similar fever involving chills and shivering [from Medieval Latin *febris acuta*, an acute fever, from Latin *acus*, a needle]

aide-de-camp (áyd-de-koN) *n., pl.* **aides-de-camp** officer serving as assistant to a general or other senior officer (abbreviation "ADC") [French, literally, camp assistant]

aide-mémoire (áyd-mem-wáar) *n., pl.* **aides-mémoire** summary or memorandum of a meeting or agreement, used as the basis of a fully detailed text [French, literally, help memory]

aigrette (áy-gret) *n.* plume, especially of an egret's tail feathers, as used on a hat; object, such as piece of jewellery, in the shape of a spray, resembling an aigrette [related to *egret*]

aiguillette (áygwi-lét) *n.* metallic plaited braid or cord, or its metal tag, as on the shoulder of a military uniform

aikido (ī-kéedō) *n.* Japanese martial art that resembles judo

Akela (ə-káylə) *British. n.* adult supervisor of a pack of Cub Scouts (U.S. female equivalent "den mother") [after *Akela*, the chief wolf in Kipling's *Jungle Book*]

akimbo *adj., adv.* — **with arms akimbo** with hands on hips and elbows outwards

akin *adj.* related by blood; similar, resembling

alabaster *n.* marble-like rock used for sculpture ~ *adj.* of or like alabaster, smooth and white

à la carte *adj.* having each item priced separately (said of a menu or part of one) [French, literally, by the menu] — **à la carte** *adv.*

alacrity *formal. n.* quick cooperation, prompt and eager willingness

à la mode *adj.* fashionable, in keeping with current style, trendy; *chiefly U.S.* served with ice cream: *pie à la mode* [French, literally, according to the fashion]

alb (alb) *n.* long white robe for a priest, as worn during Mass

albino (al-béenō) *n., pl.* **-nos** person or animal having abnormally pale skin and light hair through lacking normal pigmentation — **albino** *adj.* — **-nism** *n.*

Albion *archaic or formal. n.* England or Britain (literary)

albumen (ál-bew-min) *n.* white of an egg

alchemy *n.* pseudo-science in the Middle Ages, seeking a cure-all medicine and a means of turning base metal into gold; a medieval forerunner of chemistry — **-mical** *adj.*

alcove *n.* recess or niche in a room or wall; summerhouse, bower, or other secluded spot in a garden

al dente (al dénti) *adj.* firm and chewy through being lightly cooked: *al dente spaghetti* [Italian, literally, to the tooth] — **al dente** *adv.*

alderman *n.* senior member of a town council, especially in former times (female equivalent sometimes "alderwoman")

aleatory (áyli-ə-tri) *adj. formal.* depending on or happening by chance or luck; relating or referring to music of a random kind in which the performer is given a great deal of choice by the composer (also "aleatoric") [Latin, *alea*, a dice]

alembic (ə-lémbik) *n.* distilling flask as used by alchemists, an early form of retort; *formal.* transforming or purifying power, agent, or device

alfalfa (al-fál-fə) *n.* perennial forage or fodder plant, having three leaflets (also "lucerne")

alfresco *adj., adv.* out of doors, in the open: *an alfresco meal* [Italian, literally, in the fresh (air), in the cool]

algorithm *n.* computation or discovery procedure using a series of steps, such as long division — **-rithmic** *adj.*

alias (áyli-əss) *n.* name assumed for a particular purpose or occasion ~ *adv.* "also known as", under the assumed name of [Latin, otherwise]

alibi (ál-i-bī) *n., pl.* **-bis** legal defence in the form of a claim by an accused person that he was not present at the scene of the crime in question; *informal.* excuse [Latin, elsewhere] — **alibi** *tr.v.*

alienate *tr.v.* in law, to transfer alienable property to; to cause to turn hostile or indifferent: *alienated their friends/their friends' affections*

alienation *n.* action or result of alienating; sense or state of being an outsider, isolated from one's society; sense of a loss of personal identity and self-esteem, as among industrial workers in modern society

alimentary *formal. adj.* relating to food, nutrition, or digestion: *the alimentary canal*

alimony *now chiefly U.S. n.* maintenance due after a divorce

aliquot *adj.* referring to equal parts, especially when they jointly make up the whole; relating or referring to a number that can be divided exactly into another number: *aliquot parts of an old pound*

alkali *n.* soluble base that can neutralise an acid; soluble mineral salt found in natural water and in soils — **-line** *adj.*

allegiance *n.* loyalty or the duty of loyalty, as to one's country; obligations of duty and service of a feudal vassal to his lord

allegory *n.* story or picture in which the characters or scenes symbolise abstractions or ideas and convey a deeper meaning — **-gorical** *adj.*

allegro *n., pl.* **-os** musical composition or movement played at a rapid tempo — **allegro** *adv., adj.*

allergy *n.* excessive sensitivity or adverse reaction to something, such as pollen or various types of food — **-gic** *adj.*
alleviate *tr.v.* to reduce (pain, grief, or the like), make more bearable — **-tion** *n.*
alliteration *n.* repeated occurrence of a letter or sound, especially the initial letter, as in poetry. Compare ASSONANCE — **-tive** *adj.*
allotrope *n.* any of the different physical forms, such as crystals, that an element may take: *Diamonds and graphite are allotropes of carbon* — **-tropic** *adj.* — **-tropy** *n.*
alloy *n.* metal consisting of a mix of two or more metals, or of one metal with another element such as carbon
allude *intr.v.* — **allude to** to refer to indirectly — **allusion** *n.* — **allusive** *adj.*
allure *n.* appeal, attraction, or fascination — **-luring** *adj.*
alluvium *n., pl.* **-viums** or **-via** soil or other sediment deposited by a river or flood (also "alluvion") — **-vial** *adj.*
alma mater *n.* university, school, or college that one used to attend [Latin, literally, caring mother]
almanac *n.* annual book, magazine, or calendar listing information such as tide patterns and weather records
aloof *adj.* reserved, distant, slightly haughty
alopecia (ál-ə-péeshə) *n.* hairlessness or hair loss, especially as caused by skin disease
alpaca *n.* llama-like South American pack animal, valued for its fine wool; alpaca wool
alpenstock *n.* long, iron-tipped stick used by hikers in the mountains [German, literally, Alps staff]
alpha *n.* star that is the brightest or largest in its constellation
alpha rhythm *n.* brain-wave pattern that is typical of a resting or drowsy adult (also "alpha wave"). Compare BETA RHYTHM
altercation *n.* heated argument or quarrel — **-cate** *intr.v.*
alter ego (áltər éegō) *n., pl.* **alter egos** second self, another side to oneself; intimate friend or confidant [Latin, literally, other I]
alto *n.* in music, low female or high male singing voice; range between soprano and tenor; singer or instrument that produces sounds within the alto range — **alto** *adj.*
altruistic *adj.* unselfish, concerned for others' welfare — **-ism, -ist** *n.*
alumnus (ə-lúm-nəss) *chiefly U.S. n., pl.* **-ni** male graduate or former student of a school, college, or university (feminine form "alumna")
alveolus (al-vée-ə-ləss, ál-vi-ṓ-) *n., pl.* **-li** honeycomb cell or similar deep cavity; tooth socket in the jawbone — **-late** *adj.*
Alzheimer's disease (álts-hīmərz) *n.* genetic brain disease causing premature senility (also "presenile dementia") [after Alois *Alzheimer*, a 19th-20th-century German physician who studied the disease]
amalgam (ə-mál-gəm) *n.* combination, mixture; specifically, mercury alloy, as used by dentists as a filling for teeth — **-mate** *v.*
amanuensis (ə-mánnew-én-siss) *n., pl.* **-ses** secretary or scribe who takes dictation or makes neat copies of handwritten documents; broadly, writer's personal assistant [Latin, from the phrase *servus a manu*, a slave at hand(writing); related to *manual*]
amazon *n.* tall, very well-built woman (often used humorously) [after the *Amazons*, a nation of female warriors in Greek mythology]
ambergris (ámbər-greess, -griss) *n.* waxy cholesterol substance from sperm whale intestines that may be found floating on the sea and is used as a fixative in perfume-making [Old French *ambre gris*, grey amber]
ambiance (ámbi-ONSS, -ənss) *n.* atmosphere of a place, as of a restaurant or night-club (also "ambience")
ambidextrous *adj.* able to use both hands equally expertly
ambient (ámbi-ənt) *formal.adj.* surrounding, in the immediate vicinity: *the ambient air temperature*
ambiguous *adj.* open to two or more interpretations; broadly, of doubtful or vague meaning — **-guity** *n.*
ambit *n.* scope or range of something; boundary or circuit
ambivalent *adj.* in two minds, having conflicting feelings or views — **-lence** *n.*
ambrosia *n.* food of the gods in classical mythology, corresponding to their drink of nectar; delicious food [from Greek, literally, immortality, since the food was supposed to bestow immortality] — **-ial, -ian** *adj.*
ambulatory (ámbew-lətri, -láytəri) *formal. adj.* able to walk; walking about; used or adapted for walking; liable to alteration or cancellation, as a will might be while its maker is still alive ~ *n.* walking area, typically covered, such as an aisle or cloister
ameliorate *formal. v.* to improve — **-tion** *n.*
amenable *adj.* cooperative or obedient, open to suggestion or criticism
amenity *n. formal.* agreeable or pleasing quality of something; something that has or provides this quality: *the amenities of a luxury hotel* — **the amenities** the forms of polite society: *One was brought up to observe the amenities at all times*
amiable *adj.* friendly, likable: *an amiable fellow/grin*; hospitable, cordial, or reassuring: *an amiable atmosphere*
amicable *adj.* characterised by good will, harmonious: *an amicable settlement of the dispute*
amino acid (ə-mī́nō, ə-méenō) *n.* acid forming a basic part of proteins
amity (ámməti) *n.* friendship, peaceful relations, especially between countries
amnesia *n.* memory loss, as through shock or brain damage — **-siac** *adj., n.*
amnesty *n.* pardon, as of fugitives or political prisoners, granted by a government; immunity from prosecution, or a period of immunity, enabling offenders to confess without fear — **amnesty** *tr.v.*
amniocentesis (ámni-ō-sen-tée-siss) *n., pl.* **-ses** withdrawal by syringe of some of the fluid in a pregnant woman's womb, to monitor the health of the foetus
amoeba (ə-méebə) *n., pl.* **-bae** or **-bas** tiny creature of various kinds, sometimes harmful, in water or soil or as an internal parasite in animals or humans — **-bic** *adj.*
amoral (ay-mórrəl) *adj.* non-moral; unable to distinguish between right and wrong — **-ity** *n.*
amorous (ámmə-rəss) *formal. adj.* relating to love
amorphous *adj.* formless, shapeless; lacking a crystalline structure, as a rock or chemical might
amortise (ə-mór-tīz) *tr.v.* to pay off (a debt or mortgage) by instalments; to write off (an asset) gradu-

ally; to prepare for the replacement of (an asset) by paying into a sinking fund — **-sation** *n.*

amour (ə-mo͝or) *formal. n.* love affair, especially a secret or illicit one [French, love]

amour-propre (ámmoor-própr) *formal. n.* self-respect, appropriate pride in oneself, sense of one's own worth and dignity [French, literally, self-love]

ampersand (ámpər-sand) *n.* the sign "&", representing the word *and* [shortened from the phrase *& per se and*, literally, & by itself (represents) and, an explanation of the symbol]

amphetamine *n.* stimulant drug, sometimes causing addiction

amphibious *adj.* living or able to live both on land and in water; moving on or relating to both land and water: *amphibious vehicles* [Greek *amphibios*, literally, having a double life] — **-ian** *n.*

amphitheatre *n.* arena, sports hall, or the like, with seating all the way round; gallery, or the first seating tier in the gallery, of a theatre; hall with a fan-shaped gallery of seats; flat stretch of land surrounded by rising slopes, as in the mountains

amphora (ámfə-rə) *n., pl.* **-rae** or **-ras** jar with two handles and a narrow neck, used for wine or oil in ancient Greece and Rome

amplify *v.* to expand and clarify (a remark, idea, or the like) by adding details ~ *tr.v.* to increase the volume or size of (sound, voltage, current, or the like) — **-fier**, **-fication** *n.*

ampoule (ám-po͞ol) *n.* small glass bottle, especially a sealed one containing liquid for injections (also "ampule")

amputate *tr.v.* to cut off (a part of the body), as by surgery — **-tation**, **-tee** *n.*

amulet (ámmew-lət) *n.* charm carried, usually around the neck, as a protection against evil or misfortune

anabolic steroid (ánnə-bóllik) *n.* artificial hormone increasing muscle and bone growth, sometimes used by athletes

anachronism (ə-náckrə-niz'm) *n.* time-error, historical mistake, placing a person, thing, or event in the wrong historical period

anacoluthon (ánnəkə-lo͞othon) *n., pl.* **-tha** sentence in which there is a sudden change to a second, inconsistent grammatical pattern, as in *I asked him why did he do it* instead of *I asked him why he had done it*; process by which an anacoluthon is produced

anaemic (ə-ne͞emik) *adj.* relating or suffering from anaemia, a blood deficiency that reduces its oxygen-carrying capacity; weak, tired, or feeble

anaglyph *n.* cameo or other ornament or sculpture in low relief; three-dimensional picture or process based on superimposed images viewed through glasses with one green and one red lens — **-ic** *adj.*

anaglypta *n.* wallpaper that is thick and textured

anagram *n.* word or phrase whose letters are rearranged from or into those of another word or phrase: *"Tan" is an anagram of "ant"* — **-grammatic** *adj.*

analects *pl.n.* selections from a literary work or works

analgesia *n.* absence or reduction of pain without unconsciousness or numbness — **-sic** *adj., n.*

analog *adj.* referring to a watch, clock, or meter indicating readings by moving hands on a dial rather than by changing numbers. Compare DIGITAL

analogy *n.* similarity in at least one respect, which may suggest similarities in other respects; comparison based on analogy — **-gous** *adj.*

analytic *adj.* referring to a statement, such as *Bachelors are unmarried*, that is true or false by virtue of the meaning of its words rather than by correspondence to facts in the real world, as in a synthetic statement such as *Bachelors are mortal.* Compare SYNTHETIC

anaphora (ə-náffərə) *n.* repetition of a word or phrase at the start of successive clauses, lines of verse, or the like; reference to something previously mentioned, as through pronouns — **-phoric** *adj.*

anarchy *n.* lack of all political control, lawlessness; state of confusion or disorder, chaos: *artistic anarchy/classroom anarchy* — **-chic**, **-chical** *adj.* — **-chist** *n.*

anathema (ə-náthəmə) *n.* curse of excommunication or damnation ~ *adj.* detestable, abhorrent: *Hypocrisy was anathema to them* — **-matise** *tr.v.*

anchorite (áng-kə-rīt) *n.* hermit or recluse, person who has gone into seclusion for religious reasons (feminine form "anchoress")

ancien régime (ON-si-ÁN re-zhe͞em) *n.* the old French government and social system that was swept away by the French Revolution in 1789; broadly, superseded system of authority [French, literally, old regime]

ancient lights *n.* in English law, right to continued unobstructed access to light through a window that has admitted it for at least 20 years

ancillary (an-síllәri) *adj.* secondary, subordinate; helping auxiliary: *ancillary staff* — **ancillary** *n.*

andiron (ánd-ī-ərn) *n.* metal stand, used in pairs, for logs in a fireplace (also "firedog")

androgynous (an-drójі-nəss) *adj.* having characteristics of both male and female sexes; having both male and female flowers on the same stalk, as some plants have

aneroid barometer *n.* barometer based on displacements of the lid or sides of a partial-vacuum drum, according to variations in atmospheric pressure

aneurysm (ánnewr-iz'm) *n.* sac, bulge, or pouch in the weakened wall of a blood vessel (also "aneurism") — **-rysmal** *adj.*

anfractuous *formal. adj.* turning, twisting, winding — **-tuosity** *n.*

angiosperm (ánji-ō-sperm) *formal. n.* flowering plant — **-spermous** *adj.*

Anglicise *tr.v.* to make English in style, form, or the like

Anglicism *n.* English or English-based word or phrase

Anglophone *n.* English speaker — **Anglophone** *adj.*

angora (ang-gáwrə) *n.* mohair [earlier form of *Ankara*, now capital of Turkey]

Angostura bitters (áng-gə-stéwr-ə) *chiefly British. pl.n.* trademark for a bitter tonic mixture used to flavour drinks [after *Angostura bark*, the bark of certain Brazilian trees, from which the bitter flavouring is extracted, from *Angostura*, a former name for Ciudad Bolívar, a city in Venezuela]

angst *n.* anxiety of a strong but unspecific kind

anguine (áng-gwīn) *formal. adj.* snake-like

anima *n.* in Jungian psychology: soul or true inner personality; female principle or personality in a man's unconscious. Compare ANIMUS

animadversion *formal. n.* comment or carefully considered observation, usually very critical — **animadvert** *intr.v.*

animism *n.* belief among certain peoples that each thing, both living and non-living, has its own individual soul; belief in the presence and power of spirits; belief that the universe is given life by some immaterial force
animosity *n.* hostility, open dislike
animus *n.* animosity; in Jungian psychology, male principle or personality in a woman's unconscious. Compare ANIMA
ankh (angk) *n.* ansate cross
annals *pl.n.* historical records of events over the years: *It will live in the annals of time*; records of proceedings or transactions, such as those published annually by a learned society [Latin, *annus*, a year; related to *annual*]
anneal (ə-néel) *tr.v.* to strengthen (metal or glass) by heating followed by cooling; to temper; *formal.* to strengthen (will or resolve)
annex *tr.v.* to gather in or append (typically something smaller) to something typically larger; specifically, to incorporate (territory) into a larger political unit — **-ation** *n.*
annihilate (ə-nī́-ə-layt) *tr.v.* to destroy completely, wipe out; *informal.* to defeat, crush, overwhelm — **-lation** *n.*
annotation *n.* note of critical commentary or explanation on a text — **annotate** *v.*
annuity *n.* annual payment of an allowance, dividend, or the like; right to an annuity, as through membership of a pension plan
annul *tr.v.* to cancel or invalidate (a law, marriage, or the like), make null and void
annular *adj.* ring-shaped
annus mirabilis (ánnəss mi-raábi-liss) *n., pl.* **anni mirabiles** year of remarkable events [New Latin, literally, a year of wonders, a marvellous year]
anodyne *adj.* bland and uncontroversial: *an anodyne speech*; *archaic.* soothing, comforting, relaxing; *archaic.* relieving pain
anoint *tr.v.* to place or rub oil or ointment on; specifically, to anoint as part of a religious ceremony
anomaly (ə-nómmə-li) *n.* irregularity, abnormality, deviation — **-lous** *adj.*
anomie (ánnō-mi) *formal. n.* feeling of rootlessness, confusion, or loss of personal identity, typically caused by or accompanied by the loss of involvement with a supportive community; absence of clear moral guidelines in a person or society — **-mic** *adj.*
anonymous *adj.* unnamed or unknown, as an author or contributor might be — **anonymity** *n.*
anorexia *n.* psychological disorder characterised by a refusal to eat and a fear of putting on weight (also "anorexia nervosa"). Compare BULIMIA — **-rectic, rexic** *n., adj.*
ansate cross *n.* T-shaped cross whose top arm consists of a loop, considered a symbol of life especially in ancient Egypt (also "ankh")
Anschluss (án-shlŏŏss) *n.* union between countries, specifically that imposed on Austria by Nazi Germany in 1938 [German]
anserine (ánsə-rīn) *formal. adj.* goose-like, resembling or characteristic of a goose; silly
antagonism *n.* opposing force, active resistance, or strong dislike; counteracting or neutralising effect of one drug, muscle, or the like on another — **-nist** *n.*
antebellum *adj.* pre-war, especially before the American Civil War
antecedent (ánti-séed'nt) *adj. formal.* occurring before and related to something ~ *n. formal.* something antecedent to something else; subordinate clause, stating the actual condition, in a conditional sentence or proposition, typically beginning with *if* or *unless* (also "protasis"). Compare CONSEQUENT, APODOSIS; first term in a ratio. Compare CONSEQUENT; word, phrase, or clause that a pronoun refers to
antecedents *formal. pl.n.* ancestry or background: *of humble antecedents*
antedate *tr.v.* to come earlier in time than, precede; to discover or claim an earlier date for (an era, event, or the like); to put an earlier date on (a cheque or document) than when actually signed (opposite "postdate")
antediluvian *adj.* existing or occurring before the biblical Flood; hopelessly old-fashioned
antenatal *adj.* before birth; during pregnancy: *an antenatal clinic*
antenna *n., pl.* **-ae** feeler, found in pairs, on the head of an insect, crustacean, or the like; *pl.* **-as** aerial
antepenultimate (ánti-pen-últimət) *adj.* third from the last, last but two
anterior *adj.* earlier; relating to the head end or front part of animals, leaves, or the like; forward, at the head (opposite "posterior") — **-ority** *n.*
anthelmintic (án-thel-mín-tik) *n.* worm remedy, expelling or destroying intestinal worms, vermifuge — **anthelmintic** *adj.*
anther *n.* pollen-producing tip of the stamen of a flower
anthology *n.* collection of poems, stories, or the like; especially, anthology of items previously published [from Greek *anthologia*, literally, flower gathering]
anthracite *n.* hard, heavy coal, burning slowly with a hot, clear flame, "hard coal". Compare BITUMINOUS COAL
anthrax (án-thraks) *n.* infectious disease of cattle and sheep, causing severe ulceration
anthropoid *adj.* human in shape, form, or appearance; especially, man-like, as some of the apes are; *informal.* ape-like in appearance or behaviour (usually derogatory) — **anthropoid** *n.*
anthropomorphism *n.* attributing of human form or behaviour to gods, animals, and non-living objects — **-morphise** *tr.v.*
anthropology *n.* scientific study of mankind, in his physical, social, and cultural aspects — **-logical** *adj.* — **-ologist** *n.*
anthropophagi (ánthrə-póffə-jī, -gī) *archaic. pl.n.*, cannibals (singular "anthropophagus")
antibody *n.* blood protein produced by the body's immune system that counteracts pathogens and so promotes resistance to infection
anticipate *tr.v.* to foresee, expect; to anticipate and act in advance of: *anticipated the fall in prices by selling beforehand*; to anticipate and act prematurely — **-pation** *n.* — **-patory** *adj.*
anticyclone *n.* weather system that is a high-pressure area — **-lonic** *adj.*
antidote *n.* substance counteracting the effect of a poison; remedy for any unwanted condition
antihistamine (ánti-hístə-meen) *n.* anti-allergy drug, as for hay fever — **antihistamine** *adj.*
antimacassar (ánti-mə-kássər) *n.* coverlet for the top of the back of an armchair or sofa, as for protection

against staining by hair oil [*anti-* + *Macassar* oil, a perfumed hair oil popular in former times, after *Makassar*, a port and region now in Indonesia, the reputed source of the ingredients]

antinomy (an-tínnəmi) *n.* contradiction between two equally plausible statements, paradox; conflict between two rules or laws

antipasto *n., pl.* **-tos** or **-ti** appetiser, hors d'oeuvre [Italian]

antipathy (an-típpəthi) *n.* strong dislike, distaste — **antipathetic** *adj.*

antiphon (ánti-fən, -fon) *n.* plainsong setting of a religious text, sung as a response during a church service — **-al** *adj.* — **-ny** *n.*

Antipodes (an-típpə-deez) *pl.n.* — **the Antipodes** Australia and New Zealand viewed as being on the other side of the Earth from a point of reference such as Britain (often humorous)

antiquarian *adj.* relating to antiques, antiquities, or old and rare books: *an antiquarian bookseller*

antiquary (ánti-kwəri) *n.* collector of, dealer in, or expert on antiques and other old objects

antiquities *pl.n.* ancient objects

antiquity *n.* ancient times, history long ago: *classical antiquity*; old age, quality of being ancient

antirrhinum (ánti-rīnəm) *n.* snapdragon, or other plant of its genus [from Greek *antirrhinon*, from *anti-*, imitating + *rhis*, a nose; referring to the flower's resemblance to an animal's snout]

anti-Semite *n.* person who is prejudiced against or hostile to Jews — **-mitic** *adj.*

antithesis (an-títhə-siss) *n., pl.* **-ses** contrast or opposite — **-thetic**, **-thetical** *adj.*

antonomasia (ántə-nə-máyzi-ə) *n.* use of a title or epithet, such as *Her Majesty*, in place of a proper name; use of a name or proper noun, such as *an Einstein*, in place of an idea or common noun — **-mastic** *adj.*

antonym *n.* word opposite in meaning to another word in the same language (opposite "synonym") — **-nymic** *adj.*

anuran (ə-néwr-ən) *formal. n.* frog or toad (also "salientian") — **anuran** *adj.*

aorta (ay-ór-tə) *n.* main artery carrying blood from the heart to all parts of the body except the lungs

apatetic (áppə-téttik) *formal. adj.* referring or relating to protective or camouflaging colouring of an animal. Compare APOSEMATIC

apathy *n.* lack of interest, concern, enthusiasm, excitement, or the like, indifference — **apathetic** *adj.*

aperçu (áppər-séw, -sóō) *formal. n., pl.* **-çus** insightful perception, observation, or remark; brief summary or synopsis [French, literally, perceived]

aperient (ə-péer-i-ənt) *formal. adj., n.* laxative

aperture *n.* opening, especially adjustable opening controlling the amount of light entering a lens

aphasia *n.* speaking or writing disability caused by brain damage or disease — **-sic** *adj.*

aphelion (ap-héeli-ən, ə-féel-) *n., pl.* **-helia** point furthest from the Sun in an orbit round it. Compare APOGEE, APOLUNE, PERIHELION

aphonia *n.* loss of one's voice through injury or disease — **-nic** *adj.*

aphorism (áffə-riz'm) *n.* short, pointed saying that expresses a truth or opinion succinctly

aphrodisiac (áffrə-dízzi-ak) *n.* something that stimulates or increases sexual desire [Greek, from *Aphrodite*, the Greek goddess of love] — **aphrodisiac** *adj.*

apian *formal. adj.* relating to bees

apiarist (áyp-yə-rist) *formal. n.* beekeeper

apiary (áyp-yəri) *n.* beehive or group of beehives

aplomb (ə-plóm) *n.* great self-confidence or self-assurance, poise

apocalypse *n.* event, such as the end of the world, involving great destruction or disruption, disaster; prophecy, vision, or revelation of an apocalypse — **-lyptic** *adj.*

apocope (ə-póckəpi) *n.* clipping of a word by omission of a final segment, as when *professor* yields *prof.* Compare HAPLOLOGY, SYNCOPE

Apocrypha *pl.n.* — **the Apocrypha** the non-canonical books of the bible collectively — **-phal** *adj.*

apocryphal *adj.* of doubtful authenticity: *an apocryphal anecdote about Samuel Goldwyn*

apodictic (áppə-díktik) *formal. adj.* proven beyond doubt, indisputably certain

apodosis (ə-póddə-siss) *n., pl.* **-ses** main clause, stating the conclusion or consequence, in a conditional sentence or proposition (also "consequent"). Compare PROTASIS, ANTECEDENT

apogee (áppə-jee) *n.* point furthest from the Earth in an orbit round it. Compare APOLUNE, APHELION, PERIGEE; high point, height: *the apogee of her fame*

Apollonian *formal. adj.* rational, orderly, and sober, as one side of human nature is. Compare DIONYSIAC [coined, in German form, by Nietzsche, after the cult of *Apollo*, the Greek god of the Sun and music]

apologetics *n.* theology devoted to defending the truth and authority of Christianity ~ *n., pl.n.* systematic arguments in defence of a doctrine: *Marxist apologetics* (often derogatory)

apologia (áppə-lṓji-ə) *n.* defence or formal justification, as of one's beliefs

apologist *n.* defender or champion of a cause, especially an unworthy cause

apolune *n.* furthest point from the Moon of a spacecraft orbiting it (also "apocynthion"). Compare PERILUNE

apophthegm (áppə-them) *n.* witty instructive saying, maxim (also *U.S.* "apothegm")

apoplectic *adj. archaic.* relating to or undergoing an apoplexy; *informal.* extremely angry or annoyed

apoplexy *archaic or informal. n.* fit or stroke

aposematic *adj.* referring or relating to the colouring of an animal that warns off predators by suggesting that it is poisonous or bad-tasting. Compare APATETIC

aposiopesis (áppō-sī́-ə-pée-siss) *n., pl.* **-ses** breaking off speech or writing in mid-sentence, for dramatic effect — **-petic** *adj.*

apostasy (ə-pósstəssi) *n.* conversion from or abandoning of one's religion or loyalty — **apostate** *n.* — **-tatise** *intr.v.*

a posteriori (áy poss-térri-áwrī) *adj.* relating to reasoning from the particular to the general, from facts or effects to principles and causes, empirical, inductive; relating to arguments or reasoning based on external evidence rather than on theory or internal consistency. Compare A PRIORI [Latin, literally, from the latter, that is, from effect to cause]

apostrophe *n.* digression in a speech for rhetorical effect, especially to address an imaginary or absent person — **-phise** *tr.v.*

apothecary *archaic. n.* pharmacist

apotheosis (ə-póthi-ō-siss) *n.*, *pl.* **-ses** glorification of someone or something, by or as if by elevation to the status of a god; high-point, quintessence, apogee: *the apotheosis of her career* — **-sise** *tr.v.*

appanage (áppənij) *n.* land or other means of support given by a king to a relative, typically a younger son; *formal.* perk or other customary benefit attached to a position

apparatchik (áppə-rát-chik) *informal. n.*, *pl.* **-chiks** or **-chiki** functionary in the administrative system of an organisation, specifically the Communist bureaucracy (usually derogatory)

apparel *formal. n.* clothing — **apparel** *tr.v.*

apparition *n.* sudden or unusual sight; *formal.* ghost or spectre

appeasement *n.* policy of agreeing to the demands of a potential enemy for the sake of maintaining peace — **appease** *tr.v.*

appellant (ə-péllənt) *n.* person or party that appeals to a higher court to reverse a lower court's decision

appellate court (ə-péllət) *n.* court of appeal

appellation *formal. n.* name or title

appellation contrôlée (áppel-áss-yoN koN-trō-láy) *n.* certification of the quality and region of a French wine, as printed on the labels on bottles

append *tr.v.* add or attach (something extra) — **-age** *n.*

appendix *n.*, *pl.* **-dices** supplement or extra information at the back of a book

appertain *formal. intr.v.* to relate to, be connected with, or belong to as a rightful part or function: ... *and everything appertaining thereto*

appliqué (ə-pleékay) *n.* trimming or decoration consisting of different materials pasted or sewn together — **appliqué** *tr.v.*

appoggiatura (ə-pójə-tóorə) *n.*, *pl.* **-ture** or **-turas** grace note in music, usually just above the main note

appointments *formal. pl.n.* equipment, furniture, or fittings collectively

apposite (áppə-zit) *formal. adj.* suitable, appropriate

apposition *n.* grammatical construction in which a word or phrase is placed immediately after another to explain it, as in *Cicero, the famous orator, then spoke*; relationship between such pairs of words or phrases

appraise *tr.v* to estimate the value of; to give an expert opinion on — **appraisal** *n.*

apprehend *formal. tr.v.* to arrest, seize, take into custody; to perceive and begin to understand; to expect with foreboding — **-hension** *n.* — **-hensive** *adj.*

apprise *formal. tr.v.* to tell, inform: *I apprised him of my whereabouts*

approbation *formal. n.* approval, especially official; praise, good opinion

appropriate (ə-prōpri-ayt) *tr.v.* to take for oneself, typically without permission; to set aside for a specific use

appurtenance (ə-púrt-inənss) *formal. n.* less important part, accessory — **appurtenances** equipment used for a particular purpose

a priori (áy prī-áwrī) *adj.* relating to reasoning from the general to the particular, from principles or causes to facts or effects, deductive; relating to arguments or reasoning based on theory, tradition, or internal consistency rather than on experiment, experience, or other external evidence; true by virtue of internal consistency, self-verifying, without the need for experimental proof. Compare A POSTERIORI [Latin, literally, from the former, that is, from cause to effect]

apron stage *n.* stage extending into the auditorium

apropos (áppr̥ə-pō) *adj.* appropriate, relevant ~ *adv.* appropriately, relevantly; by the way, incidentally ~ *prep.* with regard to

apse *n.* semicircular or polygonal part that projects from a building, especially at the east end of a church, and is often domed or vaulted

apteryx *formal. n.* kiwi

aptitude *n.* talent or skill, usually of a specified kind: *an aptitude for maths*

aquamarine *n.* blue-green colour or gemstone — aquamarine *adj.*

aquaplane *n.* water ski consisting of a single board ~ *intr.v.* to use an aquaplane; *chiefly British.* to skid, as a car might on a wet road

aquarelle (ákwə-rél) *formal. n.* watercolour wash or painting; painting using watercolour washes

aquatic (ə-kwáttik) *adj.* living, growing, or occurring in or on water

aquatint *n.* etching technique producing varied tones, or an etching produced by this technique

aqua vitae (ákwə veétī, vítee) *n.* distilled spirits, such as whisky or brandy [Medieval Latin, literally, water of life, used by alchemists to refer to alcohol]

aqueduct *n.* man-made water channel or canal; arched, bridge-like structure supporting an aqueduct

aqueous (áykwi-əss, ákwi-) *adj.* resembling, containing, relating to, or dissolved in water, watery

aquiline *adj.* eagle-like; especially, suggestive of an eagle's hooked beak or profile: *an aquiline nose*

arabesque (árrə-bésk) *n.* intricate design, typically of intertwined flowers, leaves, or the like; ballet position in which the dancer stands on one leg with one arm stretched in front, and the other arm and leg extending backwards [from Italian *arabesco*, in Arab style]

arable (árrəb'l) *adj.* suitable for cultivating crops: *arable land*

arachnid (ə-rák-nid) *n.* eight-legged insect-like arthropod, such as a spider or tick

arbalest (árbə-lest) *adj.* large medieval crossbow designed to fire arrows, stones, and other missiles

arbiter (árbi-tər) *formal. n.* person who settles disputes, arbitrator; an authority who sets standards for others: *an arbiter of elegance*

arbitrage (árbi-traazh) *n.* buying of currencies, shares, or the like for quick resale at a higher price, stagging (now sometimes used also as a euphemism for "insider trading") — **-trageur** *n.*

arbitrary *adj.* random, by chance; based on whim or prejudice; absolute, despotic, above the law: *arbitrary powers*

arbitration *n.* settlement of a dispute by an impartial third party — **-trate** *v.* — **-trator** *n.*

arboreal (aar-báwri-əl) *formal. adj.* relating to, resembling, or living in trees: *arboreal animals*

arboretum (árbə-reétəm) *n.*, *pl.* **-tums** or **-ta** place where trees and shrubs are cultivated for exhibition or study

arbour *n.* shady garden shelter, often made of trellising, bower

arcade *n.* series of linked arches; shop-lined roofed passageway, as through a building; arched building or passageway

Arcadia *n.* paradise-like imaginary place of simple and contented country life [after *Arcadia*, an idyllic rural region of Greece] — **-ian** *adj.*

arcane (aar-káyn) *adj.* highly specialised or technical and rather mysterious to the layman, esoteric: *arcane knowledge*

archaic (aar-káy-ik) *adj.* ancient, dating to an earlier era; out of date, no longer in everyday use

archaism (ár-kay-iz'm, -ki-) *n.* archaic quality; word or expression, such as *yonder* or *goodly*, characteristic of an earlier stage of a language, and no longer in everyday use

archetype (árki-tīp) *n.* model or original pattern on which other versions or copies are based, prototype; perfect or typical example or model; in Jungian psychology, idea that derives from the collective unconscious — **-typical**, **-typal** *adj.*

archimandrite (árki-mándrīt) *n.* in the Eastern Orthodox Church: clergyman ranking below a bishop; specifically, head of a large monastery or group of monasteries

archipelago (árki-péllǝgō) *n., pl.* **-goes** or **-gos** island group, or sea containing such groups — **-pelagic** *adj.*

architectonics (árki-tek-tónniks) *n.* architecture or other science of design ~ *pl.n.* features of design or structure, as in architecture or music

architrave *n.* base of an entablature, resting on top of a column in a classical building, epistyle; moulding around a doorway or window

archives (ár-kīvz) *pl.n.* historical records of an institution, group of people, or the like; place where such records are stored — **archival** *adj.* — **-vist** *n.*

ard *n.* plough of an ancient design

ardour *n.* burning passion or enthusiasm — **ardent** *adj.*

arduous *formal. adj.* requiring great effort or endurance

arenaceous (árri-náyshǝss) *formal. adj.* sandy, sandlike; growing in sandy areas

areola (ǝ-rée-ǝ-lǝ) *n., pl.* **-lae** or **-las** space surrounded by lines or veins, as on a leaf or insect's wing; inflamed area surrounding a pimple; darkish area, on a breast, surrounding the nipple [from Latin, a little area]

argent (árjǝnt) *n., adj.* silver (in poetry and heraldry)

argil (árjil) *n.* clay as used in pottery

argol (árg'l) *n.* crusty tartar deposit building up on vats during winemaking (also "argal")

argosy *formal. n.* fleet of merchant ships; merchant ship, especially a richly laden one; abundant supply [from Italian *nave ragusea*, a ship of *Ragusa*, the former name of the port of Dubrovnik, in Yugoslavia]

argot (ár-gō) *n.* vocabulary peculiar to a group, especially when considered jargon or slang

Argus-eyed *formal. adj.* observant and alert [after *Argus*, the giant watchman in Greek mythology, who had 100 eyes]

argyle (aar-gīl) *n.* knitting or weaving pattern of diamond shapes in two or more colours [after the tartan of the clan Campbell of *Argyle*]

aria *n.* song for a solo voice, as in an opera or oratorio

arid *adj.* dry and therefore infertile: *arid land/theorising*

armada *formal. n.* fleet of warships

armadillo *n., pl.* **-los** burrowing American mammal covered in bony, armour-like plates [Spanish, literally, little armour-plated man, from Latin, *arma*, arms]

Armageddon *n.* final battle between good and evil, as in the bible; *formal.* battle or great conflict causing disaster and destruction [from Hebrew *har megiddon*, the mountain area of *Megiddo*, the site of various Old Testament battles]

armature *n.* vibrating element in a loudspeaker, buzzer, or the like; soft iron bar linking the two poles of a horseshoe magnet; protective shell or covering of an animal or plant; framework or core supporting the clay or other modelling material in sculpture

armiger (ármijǝr) *n.* squire for a knight, armourbearer; person entitled to a coat of arms — **armigerous** *adj.*

armistice *n.* truce

armorial *adj.* relating to heraldry or coats of arms

armoury *n.* weapons store, arsenal; weapons factory

aromatherapy *n.* massage with fragrant oils, practised as an "alternative" therapy

arpeggio (aar-péji-ō) *n., pl.* **-os** chord played note by note in quick succession rather than simultaneously

arrack (árrǝk) *n.* strong Eastern alcoholic drink, distilled typically from rice (also "arak")

arraign (ǝ-ráyn) *tr.v.* to accuse or charge, as before a court of law — **-ment** *n.*

arrant (árrǝnt) *formal. adj.* thoroughgoing, out-and-out, notorious: *an arrant knave* [variant of *errant*, wandering; the pejorative sense developed through association with vagabonds]

arras (árrǝss) *archaic. n.* wall hanging, typically of tapestry [after *Arras*, a French town formerly famous for its tapestries]

arrhythmia *n.* irregularity in the heartbeat

arrière-pensée (árri-air póN-say, poN-sáy) *n., pl.* **-sées** thought or intention that is deliberately held back and remains unrevealed [French, literally, behind thought]

arrivederci (ǝ-reévǝ-dérchi) *informal. interj.* goodbye till we meet again, au revoir, auf Wiedersehen [Italian]

arriviste (árree-veést) *formal. n.* person who has recently "arrived", in a social, economic, or cultural sense, newcomer or upstart [French]

arrogate *formal. tr.v.* to claim as one's own without any right to do so

arsenal *n.* weapons store, armoury

arson *n.* setting fire to buildings or other property deliberately, for criminal purposes — **-ist** *n.*

Art Deco *n.* decorative style of the 1920s and 1930s that used man-made materials and bold geometrical lines (also "art deco")

artefact *n.* man-made object; by-product of a process (also *chiefly U.S.* "artifact")

artesian well *n.* well drilled through impermeable rocks to reach water that is under pressure [French *puits artésien*, a well of *Artois*, formerly a French province, where such wells were commonly drilled]

arthropod *n.* insect, spider, crustacean, centipede, or related animal having jointed limbs, a horny shell, and a segmented body

articulate *v.* to express (an emotion or idea) in words; *formal.* to pronounce ~ *adj.* articulating well; well-articulated; capable of speech; *formal.* having joints or segments

artifice (árti-fiss) *n.* cunning technique or device, stratagem; *formal.* trickery, clever deception; *formal.* skill, ingenuity

artificer (aar-tíffi-sǝr) *n. formal.* person who crafts or

devises skilfully; in Britain, mechanic in the armed forces, especially in the navy

artisan *formal. n.* manual worker who is skilled at a craft — **-al** *adj.* — **-ship** *n.*

Art Nouveau (ár nōō-vṓ) *n.* decorative style of the 1890s using motifs from nature and curved flowing lines (also "art nouveau") [French, literally, new art]

Aryan (aír-i-ən) *n. archaic.* member of an Indo-European people; in Nazi doctrine, a Caucasian, especially Nordic, person of non-Jewish descent — **Aryan** *adj.*

ascendancy *n.* superiority, power, clear advantage; period or quality of ascendency or group having ascendency: *the Anglo-Irish ascendancy*

ascertain (ássər-táyn) *formal. tr.v.* to discover, find out

ascetic (ə-séttik) *adj.* self-denying, living a strict life, with minimum comforts and pleasures, often for religious reasons — **ascetic**, **-icism** *n.*

ascribe *tr.v.* to assign or attribute to a specified cause, source, or origin: *He ascribed the poem to Dryden* — **ascription** *n.*

Ashkenazi (áshkə-náazi) *n., pl.* **-nazim** Jew of Central or East European origin or descent; especially, Yiddish-speaking Ashkenazi or descendant of one. Compare SEPHARDI [Hebrew *Ashkenaz*, a descendant of Noah through Japheth, associated in medieval times with the Germans] — **Ashkenazi**, **-zic** *adj.*

ashlar *n.* building stone, either a square block for walls or a thin slab for facings (also "ashler")

ashram *n.* Hindu religious retreat, specifically that of a Hindu holy man

asinine (ássi-nīn) *formal. adj.* stupid, idiotic, ass-like

aspergillum (ásper-jílləm) *n., pl.* **-la** or **-lums** sprinkler for holy water, such as a brush or spoon

asperity *formal. n.* irritability, harsh temper; roughness or harshness, as of climate, mood, voice, or surface

aspersion *formal. n.* — **cast aspersions on** to criticise or cast doubt on, especially without providing convincing evidence — **asperse** *tr.v.*

asphyxiate *v.* to suffocate; to smother — **-iation**, **asphyxia** *n.*

aspirate *tr.v.* to drain (a body cavity) of (fluid) by means of a suction device, as in surgery; to pronounce with an *h*-sound; to pronounce (a stop consonant such as *p*, *b*, or *g*) with a following puff of breath, as English-speakers do in *pin* but not in *spin* ~ *n.* fluid drained off by aspirating; breathy speech sound represented in English by the letter *h*; aspirated consonant — **-ator** *n.*

aspiration *n.* act or result of aspirating or aspiring; ambition, desire or striving for success and recognition

aspire *intr.v.* to aim at or strive towards some goal, have an ambition

assail *tr.v.* to attack physically or verbally; to trouble, plague: *assailed by fresh doubts* — **-ant** *n.*

assay *tr.v.* to test or assess; to make a chemical analysis of, especially to establish the proportion of gold or silver *formal.* to attempt — **assay** *n.*

assegai (ássi-gī) *n.* light spear used by southern African tribesmen

assent *formal. intr.v.* to agree: *he assented to the proposal* ~ *n.* agreement

assert *tr.v.* to state or claim; to defend or enforce (a right); to present (oneself) forcefully in a way that cannot be brushed aside

assertive *adj.* forceful, aggressively confident, stating and enforcing one's rights and wishes boldly

assessor *n.* judge's expert assistant or adviser

assets *pl.n.* property, as of a bankrupt, used to pay debts

asset-stripping *n.* business practice of buying a struggling company and selling off its assets bit by bit

asseverate (ə-sévvə-rayt) *formal. tr.v.* to state firmly or earnestly

assiduous (ə-síddew-əss) *formal. adj.* diligent, dedicated, persevering — **-duity** *n.*

assignation *n.* meeting between lovers, or the appointment for it, especially when the meeting is secret

assignment *n.* task or duty that one has been specifically set to perform; transfer of property, interests, or rights in law — **assign** *tr.v.*

assimilate *tr.v.* to digest, absorb, or incorporate (something, such as food or facts); to make, or present as, similar; to make, or allow to become, part of a larger pre-existing culture or community: *assimilate the newcomers* ~ *intr.v.* to become assimilated — **-lation** *n.*

assizes *pl.n.* formerly, sessions of the law courts in English and Welsh counties

assonance (ássə-nənss) *n.* resemblance of sounds, especially of vowel sounds; rhyme of a rough or approximate kind, as where the stressed vowels are the same but the final consonants differ. Compare ALLITERATION

assuage (ə-swáyj) *formal. tr.v.* to reduce, satisfy, or appease: *assuaged my hunger/grief* — **-ment** *n.*

Assumption *n.* — **the Assumption** taking up of the Virgin Mary into heaven; religious celebration of the Assumption, as by Roman Catholics on 15 August

asterisk *n.* star-shaped printing symbol, *, as for referring to a footnote

asteroid *n.* very small planet, especially in an orbiting belt between Mars and Jupiter (also "minor planet", "planetoid"); *formal.* starfish

astigmatism *n.* focusing disability resulting from faulty curvature of the lens of the eye — **-matic** *adj., n.*

astrakhan (ástrə-káan) *n.* black or grey fur made from the curly wool of young lambs from the Astrakhan region in the USSR; fabric resembling this

astringent (ə-strín-jənt) *adj. formal.* harsh or acidic, as in smell, manner, or effect; contracting tissue and stanching blood flow, styptic — **astringent**, **-gency** *n.*

astral *adj.* of, like, or consisting of stars

astrolabe *n.* astronomical instrument, used in medieval times for measuring the altitude of the Sun, planets, and stars, and also for navigation

astute *adj.* shrewd, admirably clever, having good judgment

asylum *n.* shelter or protection, as from persecution, or a place offering such safety; formerly, institution caring for the insane, or for the blind, the deaf, or orphans

asymmetry *n.* lack of symmetry — **-metric**, **-metrical** *adj.*

asymptote (ássimp-tōt) *n.* line, as on a graph, associated with a curve in such a way that if both are extended they will approach each other ever more closely without meeting — **-totic** *adj.*

asyndeton (a-síndətən) *n., pl.* **-tons** or **-ta** in grammar, absence of conjunctions, typically *and*, especially where they could occur, as in *apples, peaches, pears* or *It rained; I got wet*. Compare PARATAXIS, HYPOTAXIS — **-detic** *adj*.

ataman (áttə-mən) *n., pl.* **-mans** Cossack chief (also "hetman")

ataraxia *formal. n.* tranquillity, peace of mind — **-ractic, -raxic** *adj*.

atavism (áttə-viz'm) *n.* "throwback", characteristic or individual affected by reversion to a more primitive state; appearance of such a characteristic in an individual or group — **-vistic** *adj*.

atelier (a-télli-ay, áttel-yay) *n.* studio or workshop of an artist or craftsman

Athanasian Creed *n.* creed or profession of faith widely used in Western churches. Compare NICENE CREED [after Saint *Athanasius*, a 4th-century patriarch of Alexandria, formerly thought to have devised the creed]

atheling (áthə-ling) *n.* prince or high nobleman in Anglo-Saxon times

atlas *n., pl.* **atlantes** column, in the form of a sculpture of a man, supporting a roof or storey in an ancient Greek or Greek-style building (also "telamon"). Compare CARYATID [the column represents or resembles *Atlas*, the Titan in Greek mythology who was condemned by Zeus to supporting the heavens on his shoulders]

atoll (áttol) *n.* coral reef or small chain of coral islands, typically circular and forming a lagoon

atrabilious *formal. adj.* melancholic; peevish, bad-tempered [Latin *atra bilis*, black bile, loan translation of Greek *melankholia*, melancholy]

atrium (áytri-əm) *n., pl.* **-ums** or **atria** courtyard, in front of a church or within an ancient Roman house; either of the heart's two upper chambers (also "auricle")

atrocious (ə-trṓshəss) *adj.* horrific, appalling; *informal.* very bad: *atrocious weather conditions*

atrocity (ə-tróssəti) *n.* atrociousness; barbaric act, especially one committed in wartime (often plural)

atrophy (áttrə-fi) *n.* wasting away, especially of body tissue — **atrophy** *v*.

attaché (a-táshay) *n.* person assigned to an embassy or diplomatic mission for a specified task: *naval attaché* [French, literally, attached]

attaché case *n.* briefcase in the form of a small hinged suitcase

attar (áttər) *n.* perfume or fragrant oil extracted from petals, especially rose petals

attenuate *tr.v.* to dilute, thin, or weaken (a solution or other substance); to weaken (a virus), as for use in a vaccine — **-ation** *n*.

attest *tr.v.* to confirm as existent, true, correct, or genuine: *a word attested since at least 1925*; to confirm by oath; to put under oath — **attest to** to be evidence of; to vouch for — **-ation** *n*.

Atticism (átti-siz'm) *n.* expression that is simple, clear, and elegant [after the idiom of *Attica*, the region around Athens in ancient Greece]

Attic wit *n.* wit of a wry, delicate, but pointed kind (also "Attic salt")

attire *formal. n.* clothing, especially ornate or ceremonial clothing — **attire** *tr.v*.

attributive *adj.* referring or relating to an adjective directly in front of, or sometimes after, a noun, as in *the dark hall*, rather than separated from it by a verb. Compare PREDICATIVE

attrition *n.* wearing down of a gradual kind, as of rock or enemy forces; reduction of a work force through retirement, resignation, and the like rather than by dismissal and redundancy, "natural wastage"; repentance based on fear rather than, as in contrition, on love of God

au courant (ṓ-ko͞o-róɴ) *adj.* informed of the latest news, up-to-date, au fait: *au courant with all the office gossip* [French, literally, in the current]

auctorial (áwk-táwri-əl) *formal. adj.* authorial

audacious (aw-dáyshəss) *adj.* bold to the point of recklessness or impudence — **audacity** *n*.

audible *adj.* hearable — **-bility** *n*.

audit *tr.v.* to examine, adjust, or certify (accounts or other records); in the U.S., to register for and attend (a course, class, or the like) without receiving academic credit towards a degree or diploma — **-or** *n*.

auditorium *n., pl.* **-ums** or **-ria** part of a theatre or hall where the audience sits; large building for meetings, concerts, or the like

auditory *adj.* relating to the sense or organs of hearing

au fait (ō fáy) *adj.* skilled, expert; familiar, conversant: *au fait with all the latest proposals* [French, literally, to the fact]

au fond (ō fóɴ) *formal. adv.* basically, fundamentally [French, literally, at the bottom]

Augean stables (aw-jée-ən) *formal. pl.n.* dirty or corrupt place or situation: *cleaning the Augean stables of a deposed bureaucracy* [after one of the labours of Hercules, cleaning the stables of king *Augeus*]

auger (áwgər) *n.* boring or drilling tool with a corkscrew-shaped bit

augment *formal. v.* to increase, enlarge

au gratin (ō grattáɴ) *adj.* coated with breadcrumbs and sometimes cheese, and then grilled or browned: *cauliflower au gratin* [French, literally, with the grating or crust]

augur (áwgər) *v.* — *tr.* to predict or foretell, especially from omens; to be an omen of, presage — *intr.* to serve as an omen or indication: *This augurs well/ill* ~ *n.* official in ancient Rome responsible for interpreting omens; soothsayer — **augury** *n*.

august (aw-gúst) *formal. adj.* grand, dignified, imposing

Augustan *adj.* relating to poetry or drama that is refined and classically elegant in style

au jus (ō zho͞o) *adj.* served in the natural gravy or juices: *roast beef au jus* [French, literally, with the juice]

au naturel (ō nátto͞o-rél) *adj. formal.* naked, nude (usually humorous); cooked simply [French, in a natural state]

Aunt Sally *British. informal. n.* target for insults or criticism, whipping boy [after the name for a fairground target, in the form of a woman's head, often with a clay pipe]

aura *n.* light supposedly given off by and surrounding a person, visible to clairvoyants; air or special quality: *projected an aura of professional competence*; noise, flashing of light, or other sensation preceding an attack of epilepsy, migraine, or the like

aural (áw-rəl) *adj.* relating to the ear or the sense of hearing

aureole (áwri-ōl) *n.* halo of light, as in a painting, around the head or body of a saint, deity, or the like; ring of light around the Sun or Moon, as when viewed through mist

auricle (áwrik'l) *n.* external ear, pinna; ear-shaped

part or extension on a body organ; atrium of the heart — **auricular** *adj.*

aurora australis (o-stráyliss) *n.* "southern lights", sometimes seen in the night sky, especially near the South Pole

aurora borealis (báwri-áyliss) *n.* "northern lights", sometimes seen in the night sky, especially near the North Pole

auscultation (áwsskəl-táysh'n) *n.* listening to body sounds, as through a stethoscope, for purposes of diagnosis — **-tate** *v.*

auspices (áwsspissiz) *pl.n.* — **under the auspices of** under the patronage or sponsorship of

auspicious *adj.* favourable, promising

austere *adj.* without luxury or adornment, simple and rigorous; humourlessly serious — **austerity** *n.*

austral (áwstrəl) *formal. adj.* relating to the south, southern, southerly; relating to Australasia: *Austral English*

autarky *archaic. n.* economic self-sufficiency as a government policy; autarkic area — **-kic** *adj.*

authentic *adj.* genuine, of reliable origin: *an authentic account/antique* — **-ticate** *tr.v.* — **-ticity** *n.*

autism *n.* disorder, as in some children, characterised by a severe inability to relate to other people — **autistic** *adj.*

autochthonous (aw-tók-thənəss) *formal. adj.* originating in a particular place, native, aboriginal, indigenous

autochthon (aw-tók-thən) *formal. n., pl.* **-thons** or **-thones** earliest or original indigenous human, animal, or plant in an area

autocracy *n.* absolute, arbitrary, non-democratic rule; area ruled in this way — **-crat** *n.* — **-cratic** *adj.*

autocross *n.* motorcar-racing over a rough grass track

Autocue *trademark. n.* cuing device allowing a television newsreader or other speaker to read his script inconspicuously while looking straight at the camera (also *U.S.* "Teleprompter")

auto-da-fé (áwtō-də-fáy) *n., pl.* **autos-da-fé** burning of a heretic at the stake, as ordered by the Inquisition [Portuguese, literally, act of the faith]

autodidact *n.* self-taught person — **-ic** *adj.*

autograph manuscript *n.* manuscript in its author's own handwriting

automaton (aw-tómmə-tən) *n., pl.* **-matons** or **-mata** robot, or robot-like person behaving mechanically as if not under his own control

autonomous *adj.* independent, self-governing, or self-sufficient — **-omy** *n.*

autopsy (áwtopsi) *n.* post-mortem examination to determine the cause of death (also "post-mortem")

autosuggestion *n.* self-persuasion, either conscious or subconscious

autotomy (aw-tóttəmi) *n.* shedding of a body part, such as a lizard's tail, as a means of protection when attacked

auxiliary *adj.* helping or supporting — **auxiliary** *n.*

auxiliary verb *n.* verb, such as *be*, *will*, or *can*, used together with a main verb to indicate its tense, mood, voice, or aspect

avail *formal. v.* to be of help, value, or advantage to (someone) — **avail oneself of** to make use of ~ *n.* — **of/to no avail** of no use, in vain: *They worked long and hard, but to no avail*

avant-garde (ávvoN-gárd) *n.* writers, artists, or other grouping whose aims or methods seem experimental, very daring, and ahead of their times; intellectual or artistic vanguard [French, literally, fore-guard, vanguard] — **avant-garde** *adj.*

avarice (ávvəriss) *n.* greed for wealth — **avaricious** *adj.*

avatar (ávvə-taar) *n.* manifestation or incarnation of a Hindu deity; *formal.* perfect example, representative, or embodiment of an idea or ideal

aver (ə-vér) *formal. tr.v.* to declare, affirm; in law, to state as a fact

averse *adj.* opposed; unwilling, reluctant *not averse to the idea* — **aversion** *n.*

aversion therapy *n.* therapy based on breaking a bad habit or addiction by associating it with something unpleasant

avert *tr.v.* to prevent or ward off (danger, disaster, or the like); *formal.* to turn away (one's eyes, gaze, or the like)

avian (áyv-yən) *formal. adj.* relating to birds

aviator *n.* pilot of an aircraft, especially in the early days of flying (feminine form "aviatrix")

avid (ávvid) *adj.* eager in a greedy way: *avid for news*; enthusiastic, keen — **avidity** *n.*

avionics *n.* electronics applied to aeronautics and space travel

avocation (ávvō-káysh'n) *n.* hobby, leisure activity

avoirdupois (ávwaar-dew-pwáa, ávvər-də-póyz) *n.* system of weights including the ounce, pound, and ton; weight of a person, especially of a heavy person (usually humorous)

avow *formal. tr.v.* to admit, confess, acknowledge openly — **-al** *n.* — **avowed** *adj.*

avuncular *formal. adj.* relating to or resembling an uncle, especially a benevolent uncle [related to *uncle*]

awry (ə-rī́) *adv.* squint, askew; wrong, amiss

axiom *n.* rule or principle that is widely accepted or seems self-evident; unproved assertion that is typically one of a set from which other propositions can be derived logically by using rules of inference — **-matic** *adj.*

ayah (ī́-ə) *n.* nanny, nursemaid, or maidservant in India, East Africa, and elsewhere

ayatolla (ī́-ə-tóllə) *n.* Shi'ite Muslim religious leader of the highest rank

azimuth (ázziməth) *n.* angle, as of a star, from a fixed reference, usually due south to the horizon, and typically measured clockwise in degrees; horizontal bearing measured clockwise from a given direction; sideways deviation, as of a missile, from an intended course — **-al** *adj.*

azoth (áz-oth) *n.* in alchemy, mercury; Paracelsus's panacea or universal remedy

azure (ázh-ər, ázzewr) *adj., n.* sky-blue; in heraldry, blue [related to *lapis lazuli*]

B

babushka (bə-bo͞osh-kə) *n.* headscarf, tied under the chin, as worn by Russian peasant women; grandmotherly Russian peasant woman [Russian, a grandmother, a little old woman]

baccalaureate (báckə-láwri-ət) *n. formal.* bachelor's degree, such as B.A. or B.Sc.; qualification awarded, especially in France, on successfully completing secondary education and often ensuring a university place

bacchanalia (báckə-náyl-i-ə) *formal. n., pl.n.* orgy or drunken, noisy festivity [after *Bacchus*, the Roman god of wine and pleasure] — **-nalian** *adj., n.*

bacchant (báckənt) *formal. adj.* wine-bibbing; revelling

bacciferous (bak-síffərəss) *formal. adj.* producing or bearing berries

baccillus (bə-sílləss) *n., pl.* **-li** any of various rod-shaped bacteria

back formation *n.* word formed on the mistaken assumption that it is the basis of an existing word, such as *laze* from *lazy*

backlist *n.* publisher's list of previously published works still in print

Bactrian camel *n.* camel with two humps. Compare DROMEDARY [after *Bactria*, an ancient country, now part of Afghanistan]

badinage (báddi-naazh) *n.* joking, playful banter

Baedeker (báydikər) *n.* guidebook for tourists [after Karl *Baedeker*, a 19th-century German publisher of guidebooks for travellers]

baffle *n.* device to control sound or the flow of a fluid

bagatelle *n.* unimportant thing, trifle: short piece of light music or light verse; pinball or bar billiards or similar game

bagel (báyg'l) *n.* chewy ring-shaped roll, typical of Jewish cookery (also "beigel")

bagnio (bán-yō) *archaic. n., pl.* **-nios** brothel [Italian, literally, a bath, a bathhouse]

baguette (ba-gét) *n.* moulding in the form of a narrow, protruding, half-cylindrical piping; gemstone cut into a narrow rectangular shape; shape of a baguette; long rod-shaped loaf, as of French bread

bail *n.* handle in the form of a hooped rod, as of a bucket or kettle; hooped rod supporting the canopy of a covered wagon

Bailey bridge *n.* bridge for temporary use assembled rapidly from prefabricated steel parts [after Sir Donald *Bailey*, the 20th-century English engineer who designed it]

bailie *n.* formerly, a magistrate in a Scottish town

bailiff *n.* officer who serves writs and carries out a court's orders, such as confiscating the property of a bankrupt; landowner's steward

bailiwick *n. informal.* sphere of a person's skills or interests; *archaic.* bailiff's area of jurisdiction

bain-marie (báɴ-mə-rée) *n., pl.* **bains-marie** pan containing hot water, into which a smaller pan is placed, as for slow cooking or making sauces; trough of hot water for keeping trays of food warm at a buffet [French, from Medieval Latin *balneum Mariae*, literally, the bath of Mary, mistranslation of Medieval Greek *kaminos Marios*, furnace of Miriam, Moses's sister who according to legend wrote a treatise on alchemy]

baize (bayz) *n.* fabric, usually green and woollen, used on top of snooker or billiard tables

baklava (báckla-vaa) *n.* Greek or Turkish dessert of flaky layered pastry filled with chopped nuts and honey

baksheesh *n.* money given, specifically in Eastern countries, as a tip or small bribe

balaclava (bál-ə-kláavə) *n.* woollen hood covering the head and neck (also "balaclava helmet") [after *Balaklava*, a small port in the USSR, site of a major battle during the Crimean War]

balalaika (bál-ə-lī́kə) *n.* Russian string instrument, played by plucking, with three strings and a triangular body

baldachin (báwl-də-kin) *n.* canopy placed over an altar or dais, or used in church processions [Italian, *Baldacco*, Baghdad, formerly famous for its rich fabrics]

balderdash *n.* nonsense

baldric (báwl-drik) *n.* belt or sash crossing the chest from the shoulder, used for carrying a sword or bugle

baleen (bə-léen) *n.* whalebone

baleful *formal. adj.* harmful, dangerous; threatening evil

balkanise (báwl-kənīz) *tr.v.* to divide (a territory) into small warring or ineffectual states [after the *Balkan* countries, divided by the Great Powers in the early 20th century]

ballast *n.* heavy material, such as sandbags, helping to stabilise a ship or balloon; gravel, rock chips, or the like used as foundation for a road or railway track; coarse gravel used in making concrete; underlying source of personal stability: *the ballast of her moral convictions*; stabilising device, such as an electrical resistor

balletomane (bál-it-ō-mayn) *n.* keen ballet-lover

ballista (bə-lístə) *n., pl.* **-tae** giant catapult or war engine used to hurl rocks or other missiles in earlier times

ballistic *adj.* relating to missiles or projectiles

ballottement (bə-lótmənt) *n.* testing for the presence or position of a foetus by prodding the uterus

ball-pein hammer *n.* hammer whose head has one rounded end, usually used for beating metal (also "ball-pane hammer")

balneal (bál-ni-əl) *formal. adj.* relating to baths or bathing

balsa (báwl-sə, ból-) *n.* light-weight wood of a South American tree used to make model boats or aircraft;

raft of a light, buoyant kind [Spanish, a raft]
balsam (báwl-səm, ból-) *n.* aromatic medicinal oil or resin, or an ointment based on or resembling it [related to *balm*]
baluster (bál-əstər) *n.* any of the upright posts supporting a banister or handrail
balustrade *n.* structure, such as a banister, consisting of a handrail and its supporting balusters
banausic (bə-náwzik) *formal. adj.* strictly functional or materialistic, boringly practical, mechanical, utilitarian
bandanna *n.* large neckerchief or handkerchief, often patterned or brightly coloured
bandeau (bán-dō, -dṓ) *n., pl.* **-deaus** or **-deaux** narrow band, ribbon, velvet strip, or the like, worn in a woman's hair
bandoleer (bándə-léer) *n.* bullet-belt worn across the chest from the shoulder
banker *n.* workbench, especially of a sculptor, craftsman, or bricklayer
banshee *n.* in Gaelic folklore, female spirit whose wailing is believed to warn of approaching death
barbel (bárb'l) *n.* any of the feelers or slender hair-like sensory organs on the mouth of the catfish or similar fish
barbican *n.* defensive tower or fortification, as the gate of a castle or town
barbiturate *n.* sleep-inducing or calming medical drug or drug of addiction
barcarole *n.* song of a Venetian gondolier; musical composition imitating such a song
[1]**bard** *n.* poet, especially an ancient Celtic singing poet, an honoured national poet, or a prizewinning Eisteddfod poet — **the Bard** Shakespeare — **-ic** *adj.*
[2]**bard** *n.* piece of bacon or pork fat roasted with game or lean meat to keep it moist; armour or ornamental covering on a horse — **bard** *tr.v.*
bardolatry (baar-dóllətri) *n.* excessive enthusiasm for the works of Shakespeare (usually humorous) — **-dolater** *n.*
barker *n.* attendant who attracts customers to a booth or sideshow by loud sales patter [from the barking voice used]
barm *n.* yeasty froth gathering at the surface of fermenting beer or other malt liquors
Barmecidal (bármi-sī́d'l) *adj.* seemingly plentiful or lavish but not really so, illusory: *a Barmecidal feast* (also "Barmecide") [after *Barmecide*, a wealthy Persian nobleman who in *The Arabian Nights* served a beggar a feast of imaginary food]
bar mitzvah (baar míts-və) *n.* Jewish boy 13 years old, admitted to adult status and religious responsibilities; ceremony conferring this status [Hebrew, literally, son of the commandment]
barometer *n.* instrument for measuring atmospheric pressure, as used in weather forecasting; any indicator of changes: *barometer of public opinion*
baroque (bə-rók) *adj.* styled or ornamented in an elaborate, uninhibited, or exaggerated way, especially in relation to a chiefly 17th-century European style in art and architecture. Compare ROCOCO; irregularly shaped: *baroque pearls* — **baroque** *n.*
barracoon (bárrə-kṓōn) *n.* barracks used in former times as temporary housing for slaves and convicts [Spanish, related to *barracks*]
barre (bar) *n.* bar on a studio wall at hip height used for ballet practice
barré (bárray) *n.* technique in guitar- and lute-playing of laying the forefinger over some or all of the strings to raise the pitch [French, literally, barred]
[1]**barrow** *n.* large heap of earth or stones covering an ancient burial site (also "mound")
[2]**barrow** *n.* male pig that has been castrated when young
bar sinister *n.* illegitimacy, or a sign or suggestion of illegitimate birth [from a supposed design in heraldry indicating bastardy]
bartizan *n.* small turret jutting from a wall or tower
bascule *n.* seesaw-like bridge or roadway, hinged near a weighted end so as to be raised or lowered
basilica (bə-zíllikə) *n.* Roman Catholic church or cathedral with special rights or functions
basilisk *n.* mythical serpent that could kill by its look or breath
basinet (bássi-net) *n.* close-fitting helmet of light steel, often with a visor, used in medieval times
bas-relief (báa-ri-léef, báss-) *n.* sculptural relief in which the figures project only very slightly from the background; a sculpture made in bas-relief (also "basso-relievo", "low relief")
bastille (ba-stéel) *formal. n.* prison or fortress [French, after the *Bastille*, formerly a fortress in Paris used as a prison, from Provençal, *bastir*, to build]
bastinado (básti-náydō, -náadō) *n., pl.* **-does** beating administered with a stick as punishment, especially on the soles of the feet; stick used for beating — **bastinado** *tr.v.*
bastion *n.* projecting part of a fortification; strongly defended position; any person or thing considered a defender or stronghold: *the last bastion of civilisation*
Batesian mimicry (báyts-i-ən) *n.* in zoology, the phenomenon whereby an animal takes on the appearance of another poisonous or unpalatable species to protect itself against predators [after Henry W. *Bates*, a 19th-century English naturalist who identified the phenomenon]
bathos (báythoss) *n.* sudden ludicrous shift from the sophisticated to the commonplace in speech or writing; let-down, anticlimax; sentimentality or triteness, false pathos — **bathetic** *adj.*
bathysphere *n.* manned spherical diving vessel for deep-sea exploration and research, typically lowered by a cable
batik (báttik) *n.* dyeing technique in which wax is used to keep areas of the fabric undyed; design or fabric produced by batik (also "battik")
batrachian (bə-tráyki-ən) *adj.* relating to frogs and toads ~ *formal. n.* frog or toad
battledore *n.* early form of badminton (also "battledore and shuttlecock"); light racket used in playing battledore
bawdry *n.* obscene or coarse sexual language
bawdyhouse *archaic. n.* brothel
bayou (bī́-ōō) *n., pl.* **-ous** swampy tributary of a river or lake, especially in Louisiana
beading *n.* ornamental strip of wood, metal, or the like, as for trimming or edging
beadle *n.* church official in former times, with caretaking and ushering duties; caretaker or sexton of a synagogue (also "shammes"); university official who organises and leads formal processions
beatific (bée-ə-tíffik) *adj.* relating to the joys of heaven or sainthood; joyful in a serene or saintly way: *a beatific smile*

beatify (bee-átti-fī) *tr.v.* to honour above all others; in the Roman Catholic Church, to honour (a deceased person) as blessed, as a first step towards a declaration of sainthood. Compare CANONISE — **-fication** *n.*

beatitude (bee-átti-tewd) *formal. n.* blessedness or a state of serene, joyful happiness

Beau Brummell *n.* man of fashion, whose chief interest is in clothes and manners, dandy, fop [originally a celebrated dandy in 18th-19th-century English society]

Beaufort scale (bṓ-fərt) *n.* scale indicating wind velocities, using numbers from 0 to 12 [after Sir Francis *Beaufort*, the 19th-century English admiral who devised it]

bedizen *formal or archaic. tr.v.* to dress or decorate in a showy or tasteless way — **-ment** *n.*

bedlam (bédləm) *n.* place, scene, or condition of uproar or disorder [originally a madhouse, from Middle English *Bedlem* or *Bethlem*, Bethlehem, referring to the Hospital of St Mary of *Bethlehem*, in London, once used as a mental hospital]

beebread *n.* mixture of nectar and pollen fed by the worker bees to the larvae (also "ambrosia")

beedi *n.* cigarette of Indian origin, consisting of a rolled leaf secured with thread

beestings *n.*, *pl.n.* milk that is the first produced by a cow or similar mammal directly after giving birth (also "colostrum")

beeswing (beéz-wing) *n.* thin crust forming in bottles of old wine, especially port; wine containing this crust

beget *archaic. tr.v.* to be the father of, sire; to create, give rise to — **-getter** *n.*

beguile (bi-gī́l) *formal. tr.v.* to deceive or cheat by trickery; to fascinate or attract

begum (beégəm) *n.* woman of high rank in Pakistan and other Muslim countries

behemoth (bi-heé-moth) *n.* hippopotamus or similar large animal mentioned in the book of Job; *formal.* huge or powerful person or thing [Hebrew, *behemah*, a beast, Job 40:15-24]

behest (bi-hést) *formal. n.* — **at the behest of** commanded or requested by: *surrendered at his ally's behest*

behove *formal. tr.v.* to be necessary or fitting for: *It ill behoves you to complain*

belabour *formal. tr.v.* to beat or thrash, attack with blows or criticism

beleaguer (bi-leégər) *tr.v.* to lay siege to by surrounding with troops; *formal.* to harass, beset, pester: *beleaguered with problems*

belie *tr.v.* to represent falsely or show to be false: *Her easygoing manner belied her true ambition*

Belisha beacon (bi-leéshə) *n.* beacon in the form of a flashing orange globe, indicating a pedestrian crossing on British roads [after Leslie Hore-*Belisha*, the 20th-century British politician who as Minister of Transport oversaw the introduction of the beacons in the 1930s]

bellicose *formal. adj* inclined to fighting, war-like — **-cosity** *n.*

belligerent *adj.* showing hostility or aggression; engaged in war, or legally recognised as such ~ *formal. n.* belligerent state or nation — **-ence** *n.*

bellwether *n.* ram that leads a flock of sheep; leader or representative of a faithful or closely knit group, especially one that is followed blindly [from the practice of belling the leading ram or *wether*]

beluga (bə-lōōgə) *n.* small whale that is white when adult, found chiefly in northern seas (also "white whale"); large white sturgeon of the Caspian and Black seas, whose roe is valued as caviar

belvedere (bél-və-deer) *n.* summerhouse or gallery having a fine view [Italian, literally, beautiful view]

bench mark *n.* surveyor's mark on a known object, used as a reference point for other measurements; standard example or measurement used as a reference for comparisons, touchstone

benedicite (bénni-dī́-səti) *n.* blessing or grace, especially as said before meals

benediction *n.* act of blessing; invocation of God's blessing, typically at the end of a Christian service; state of being blessed — **-dictory** *adj.*

benefactor *n.* person who gives aid or charity — **-faction** *n.*

benefice *n.* church office, such as a rectory, carrying an assured income; land granted by a feudal lord to his vassal — **benefice** *tr.v.*

beneficence (bi-néffi-sənss) *formal. n.* kindness, charitableness; charitable act or gift. Compare MALEFICENCE — **-cent** *adj.*

beneficial *adj.* promoting health or well-being, favourable

beneficiary (bénni-físh-əri) *n.* person who receives charity, a favour, money from a will, or the like; person who receives, or will receive, funds or other compensation under an insurance policy — **beneficiary** *adj.*

benefit of clergy *n.* privilege of clergymen in the Middle Ages to be tried by a church court rather than a secular court

benighted *formal. adj.* uninformed in moral or cultural matters, unenlightened

benign (bi-nī́n) *adj.* mild or gentle: *benign weather*; referring to a tumour that is not malignant or seriously threatening to health — **-ity** *n.*

benignant (bi-níg-nənt) *adj.* favourable, advantageous; kindly, benign

benison (bénni-zən) *formal. n.* blessing, benediction

bequeath *tr.v.* to leave (money or property) to someone in a will; to pass on or hand down to one's children or successors — **bequest** *n.*

berate *tr.v.* to scold or rebuke

berceuse (bair-sérz) *formal. n.* lullaby

bereaved *formal. adj.* having suffered the sad loss or death of a loved one

bereft *formal. adj.* deprived

bergamot *n.* sour, pear-shaped orange whose rind yields an aromatic oil used in perfume-making

berserk *adj.* wildly violent, uncontrollable — **berserk** *adv.*

beseech *formal. tr.v.* to appeal to urgently, implore; to beg for

besotted *adj.* in love or obsessed in an intense but often immature or superficial way

bespeak *formal. tr.v.* to reserve or book specifically, claim or arrange in advance; to be evidence of, indicate

bespoke *adj.* made-to-order: *a bespoke overcoat*; making or selling made-to-order clothes: *a bespoke tailor*

Bessemer process (béssimər) *n.* steelmaking process in which hot air or oxygen is blown through molten iron [after Sir Henry *Bessemer*, the 19th-century British engineer who invented the process]

bestiary (bésti-əri) *n.* book or collection, especially medieval, of moral fables based on animals
bestride *formal. tr.v.* to step over or stand or sit astride
beta rhythm (beétə) *n.* brain-wave pattern that is typical of a normal waking state in adults (also "beta wave"). Compare ALPHA RHYTHM
bête noire (bét nwár) *n., pl.* **-s -s** person or thing that one particularly dislikes [French, literally, black beast]
bethel *n.* chapel for seamen; Nonconformist chapel [Hebrew *bēth 'Ēl*, literally a house of God]
betrothed *formal. adj.* engaged to be married — **betrothed** *n., pl.n.* — **betrothal** *n.*
bevel (bévv'l) *v.* — *intr.* to form an angle other than a right angle; to slope, incline — *tr.* to cause to bevel by shaping or cutting ~ *n.* angle between lines or surfaces other than a right angle; such a line or surface ~ *adj.* oblique, slanting
bey (bay) *n.* Ottoman governor; former title of rulers of Tunis; Turkish male title of honour and respect, equivalent to *Mr*
bezant (bézzn't) *n.* disc used as an ornament in architecture [from Latin *Byzantius*, of Byzantium, referring to the gold coins that used to be issued there]
bezel (bézz'l) *n.* sloping surface leading to the tip or cutting edge of a chisel, screwdriver, or other tool; groove, rim, ring, or the like for clamping a jewel or watch crystal
bias *n.* line cutting diagonally across the grain of a fabric: *a skirt cut on the bias*
biathlon (bī-áth-lon) *n.* skiing competition involving both cross-country ski-racing and target-shooting — **biathlete** *n.*
bibcock *n.* tap with a downturned nozzle (also "bibb")
bibelot (bíbblō) *n.* knick-knack, trinket, or small curio
bibliography (bíbbli-óggrəfi) *n.* list of works by or about a particular writer; list of references on a particular topic; study of texts — **-pher** *n.* — **-graphic, -graphical** *adj.*
bibliophile (bíbbli-ə-fīl) *n.* book-lover; book collector
bibulous (bíbbew-ləss) *formal. adj.* habitually drinking alcohol, and showing the effects of doing so (often humorous)
bicameral (bī-kámmərəl) *adj.* having two legislative chambers or houses: *a bicameral parliament*
bicuspid (bī-kúspid) *adj.* having two points, horns, or cusps: *a bicuspid moon/tooth*
bidet (beéday) *n.* bathroom fixture in the form of a low basin, for washing one's private parts [French, originally a small horse, alluding to the user's striding posture]
biennial (bī-énni-əl) *n.* plant with a two-year life-cycle ~ *adj.* lasting or living for two years; occurring once every two years
biennium (bī-énni-əm) *formal. n., pl.* **-ums** or **-ennia** two-year period
bier (beer) *n.* platform or stand for a corpse or coffin, prior to burial or cremation
bifocals *pl.n.* glasses in which each lens is divided into two sections, correcting for both near and distant vision
bifurcate (bī-fər-kayt) *formal. adj.* divided into two branches or parts, forked — **bifurcate** *v.* — **-cation** *n.*
bigamy *n.* crime of getting married to a person while still married to another — **-mous** *adj.*
bight *n.* loop in a rope; slack middle part of a rope; bay, or the wide curve in the shoreline that forms it
bigot (bíggət) *n.* prejudiced and intolerant person — **-ed** *adj.* — **-ry** *n.*
bijou (beé-zhōō) *n., pl.* **-jous** or **-joux** small, delicate, and charming trinket or other object ~ *adj.* small and tasteful: *a bijou residence* (usually humorous)
bijouterie (bee-zhōōtəri) *n.* jewellery of a delicately worked kind; collection of bijoux
bilateral (bī-láttrəl) *adj.* involving two sides, factions, or the like; undertaken by or affecting both parties: *a bilateral treaty* — **-ism**, **-ist** *n.*
bilboes *pl.n.* iron bar with fetters, formerly used for shackling prisoners' feet
Bildungsroman (bíldoŏngz-rō-maán) *n.* novel dealing with the personality and views of its central character [German, literally, education novel]
bilingual *adj.* speaking, written in, or relating to two languages — **-ism** *n.*
bilious (bíl-yəss) *adj.* vomiting or feeling as if about to vomit; bad-tempered, splenetic; unpleasantly suggestive of vomit: *a bilious shade of green*
billet *n.* lodgings for soldiers in civilian quarters; *informal.* any temporary lodgings; *informal.* job, especially a temporary job — **billet** *v.*
billet-doux (bílli-dōō) *n., pl.* **billets-doux** love letter (usually humorous) [French, literally, sweet note]
billingsgate *n.* obscene or abusive language (now outdated in use) [referring to the language traditionally heard at *Billingsgate* fish market, London]
bill of lading *n.* document recording details of goods received for shipment, especially in foreign trade
biltong *South African. n.* strips of meat salted and dried in the sun
binary (bīnəri) *adj.* double, having two separate parts: *a binary star*
binary system *n.* number system using only the digits 0 and 1 (also "binary notation")
binaural (bīn-áwrəl) *adj.* relating to both ears; recording or transmitting sound by means of two separate channels
bine *n.* twining plant or creeper, or its stem
binnacle *n.* stand supporting a ship's compass
binocular (bī-nóckew-lər) *adj.* relating to the use of both eyes, and specifically to their focusing on a single object at one time. Compare MONOCULAR — **-larity** *n.*
biodegradable *adj.* capable of being broken down by bacteria or by other natural processes
biofeedback *n.* technique, learnt with the aid of monitoring instruments, for regulating one's own heartbeat, blood pressure, or other apparently involuntary bodily functions
biography (bi-óggrəfi) *n.* story of a person's life, as written by another person — **-pher** *n.* — **-graphical** *adj.*
bioluminescence (bī-o-lōōmi-néss'nss) *n.* light emitted, through a biochemical process, by fireflies, fish, fungi, and some other living organisms — **-ent** *adj.*
bionic (bī-ónnik) *adj.* having certain robot-like or electronically enhanced body parts or functions (not in technical use)
biopsy (bī-opsi) *n.* removal and examination of tissue from a living body, used in diagnosing disease
biorhythm *n.* pattern or cycle of one's mental, physical, or emotional condition (usually plural) — **-rhythmic** *adj.*
bipartite *adj.* having or being divided into two parts

biped (bī́-ped) *n.* any two-footed animal. Compare QUADRUPED — **biped, -al** *adj.*

biretta *n.* stiff squarish clerical cap worn by Roman Catholic priests (also "beretta") [related to *beret*]

bisect *tr.v.* to cut or divide into two equal parts — **-section** *n.* — **-sectional** *adj.*

bisque (bisk, beesk) *n.* thick rich soup: *lobster bisque*

bissextile (bi-séks-tīl) *formal. n.* leap year — **bissextile** *adj.*

bistoury (bíss-tŏŏ-ri) *n.* long, narrow scalpel for making delicate incisions in surgery

bitumen (bíttew-mən) *n.* black, usually syrupy, naturally occurring hydrocarbon mixture, used in road-making and roofing — **-minous** *adj.*

bituminous coal *n.* soft, rich coal, burning with a smoky yellow flame. Compare ANTHRACITE

bivalve *n.* oyster, mussel, or similar hinged mollusc. Compare UNIVALVE — **bivalve** *adj.*

bivouac (bívvōō-ak) *n.* encampment of a rough and temporary kind, as set up during a military or mountaineering expedition [probably from Swiss German *Beiwacht*, supplementary night watch] — **bivouac** *intr.v.*

blackball (blák-bawl) *informal. tr.v.* to vote or decide secretly against (an applicant), as for club membership [referring to the small black ball used as a negative vote in some forms of ballot] — **blackball** *n.*

blackjack *U.S. n.* cosh, truncheon, small club — **blackjack** *tr.v.*

blandishments *pl.n.* temptations, flattering, or wheedling — **blandish** *tr.v.*

blasé (blaázay) *adj.* unenthusiastic or bored, through being over-exposed to something or excessively sophisticated; world-weary

blasphemy *n.* extreme disrespect towards God or the sacred — **-pheme** *v.* — **-phemous** *adj.*

blatant (bláyt'nt) *adj.* glaringly and obviously offensive, outright and undisguised: *a blatant lie/error* — **-ancy** *n.*

blazon *formal. n.* colourful or showy display or symbol — **blazon forth/abroad** to announce or proclaim publicly, publicise — **-ry** *n.*

bleachers *U.S. informal. pl.n.* upper tiers of uncovered cheap seats, specifically at a baseball stadium [referring to the bleaching effect of exposure to the sun]

blend *n.* word formed by combining the beginning of one word with the end of another, as *brunch* is formed from *breakfast* and *lunch* (also "portmanteau word")

blet *n.* softening of some fruits to the point of near-decay

blimp *n.* barrage balloon or other non-rigid airship

blimpish *informal. n.* pompously conservative or reactionary [after *Colonel Blimp*, a character in the cartoons of David Low] — **blimp** *n.*

blini (bleéni) *n., pl.n.* thin pancake or pancakes of Eastern European origin, typically of buckwheat, folded round a savoury filling; dish of blini

blithe *adj.* cheerful, especially in a carefree way: *a blithe disregard for convention*

blitz *informal. n.* intense effort of short duration: *a media information blitz on Aids*; blitzkrieg — **blitz** *tr.v.*

blitzkrieg *n.* concentrated massive offensive intended to overwhelm and subdue an enemy; blitz [German, *Blitz*, lightning + *Krieg*, a war]

bloat *v.* to swell ~ *tr.v.* to cure (fish, such as herring or mackerel) by pickling or salting and smoking — **-ed** *adj.*

bloater *n.* fish cured by bloating

blockhouse *n.* fortification, of wood or concrete, with loopholes for observation or weapons

bloom *n.* powdery coating, as on plums or new coins

blowzy (blówzi) *adj.* red-faced and often swollen and coarse-looking: *a blowzy slattern* (also "blowsy")

bludgeon *n.* short, heavy club, usually of wood, with a thickened or weighted striking end ~ *tr.v.* to hit or subdue with or as if with a bludgeon: *bludgeoned them into submission*

blue chip *n.* stock or share considered safe and profitable through having a long record of reliability [after blue gambling chips, traditionally of high value] — **blue-chip** *adj.*

blue-pencil *tr.v.* to mark (a passage) for deletion; to edit or censor (a text) by blue-pencilling

bluestocking *n.* intellectual or scholarly woman, especially an austere and unappealing one [after the *Blue Stocking Society*, the satirical name given to an 18th-century literary group which met in the houses of society hostesses; some of the men wore blue stockings instead of the customary black] — **bluestocking** *adj.*

blunderbuss *n.* wide-muzzled gun or musket; *informal.* clumsy clot, dolt

blurb *informal. n.* description or review for promotional purposes, as on the dust jacket of a book [coined by Gelett Burgess, a 19th-20th century U.S. humorist]

Boanerges (bō-ə-nérjeez) *formal. n.* speaker or preacher with a loud voice and impassioned delivery [after the name given by Jesus to John and James, in Mark 3:17, from Hebrew *b'ne reghesh*, literally, sons of thunder]

Boche (bosh) *archaic. slang. n., pl.* **Boche** or **Boches** German person, especially a German soldier during the First World War (derogatory) [French]

bodega (bōdeé-gə) *n. U.S.* shop selling Hispanic groceries; shop or storehouse for wine in Spanish-speaking countries

bodkin *n.* pointed instrument for making holes in leather or cloth; blunt needle for pulling ribbon or cord through loops or a hem; hairpin of an old-fashioned ornamented type; *archaic.* dagger

boffin *British. informal. n.* scientific or technical expert or consultant, originally one working with the RAF

bogie *n.* undercarriage, as on a railway coach, having swivelling wheels; any of the wheels or rollers inside the track of a tank or tractor (also "bogy")

Bohemian *archaic. n.* artistic or literary person living in an unconventional way (also "bohemian") [probably by association with Gypsies, sometimes considered, as in France, to have come from *Bohemia* in Czechoslovakia] — **Bohemian** *adj.* — **-ism** *n.*

boisterous *adj.* rowdy, noisy, uncontrolled; *formal.* stormy, turbulent: *boisterous seas*

bole *n.* tree trunk

bolero *n., pl.* **-ros** (bə-láir-ō) Spanish dance, or the music for it; (bóllərō, bə-láir-ō) short, open-fronted jacket or waistcoat for women

bolide (bṓlīd) *n.* meteor that is unusually large and bright, and may burn out or explode, fireball

boll (bōl) *n.* rounded seed pod of cotton, flax, or similar plant

bolshevik *n.* communist or extreme radical (often derogatory) [after the *Bolsheviks*, Lenin's majority faction of the Russian Social Democratic Party, which became the Communist Party of the USSR, from *bol'shoi*, large] — **bolshevik** *adj.*

bolster *n.* long, narrow, stiff cushion; structural support, as in a building ~ *tr.v.* support or strengthen, prop up: *bolstered our determination*

bolus *formal. n., pl.* **boluses** small soft lump, as of chewed food; large pill or tablet of medicine

bombast *n.* padding material of former times; speech or writing that is high-flown and pompous — **-ic** *adj.*

bona fide (bṓnə fī́di) *formal. adj.* genuine, sincere: *a bona fide antique/promise*

bona fides (bṓnə fī́deez) *formal. n.* good faith, good intentions (used with a singular verb) [Latin, literally, good faith]

bonanza *n.* source of great wealth or luck

bonhomie (bónnə-mi, -mée) *formal. n.* good-natured friendliness, sociability [French, from *bon*, good + *homme*, a man]

bon mot (bóɴ mṓ) *n., pl.* **-s -s** witty saying, usually short, clever remark (also "mot") [French, literally, good word]

bonsai (bón-sī) *n., pl.* **bonsai** dwarf tree or shrub produced by rigorous pruning and displayed as a pot plant, or the traditional Japanese art of producing such plants [Japanese, literally, potted plant]

bon vivant (bóɴ vee-vóɴ) *n., pl.* **-s -s** person who goes in for luxurious living (also "bon viveur") [French, literally, good living]

bookplate *n.* ornamental label, with the owner's name, pasted on the inside cover of a book

boom (bōōm) *n.* spar attached to a mast, used to secure or extend the foot of a sail; long movable arm or spar supporting an overhead microphone, forming part of a crane, or the like; water-borne barrier, as of logs or empty drums, to confine other logs, protect a harbour, or the like

boondocks *U.S. informal. pl.n.* remote country areas, the sticks (also "boonies")

boondoggle *U.S. informal. n.* work regarded as a pointless waste of time — **boondoggle** *intr.v.*

bootleg *v.* to make, sell, or transport goods illegally; specifically, to bootleg alcohol during the Prohibition era in the U.S. [from the old practice of hiding bottles of liquor in tall boots] — **bootleg** *adj., n.* — **-legger** *n.*

borborygmus (bórbə-rígməss) *formal. n.* tummy rumbling (often humorous)

bordello (bawr-déllō) *formal. n., pl.* **-os** brothel

bore *n.* large wave moving upstream in a river estuary, as caused by tidal currents (also "eagre")

boreal (báwri-əl) *formal. adj.* relating to the north or the north wind

borstal *n.* formerly, a reformatory or detention school in England, for offenders aged 15 to 21 [after *Borstal*, a village in Kent where the first institution was set up in 1901]

bosky *formal or archaic. adj.* thickly covered with trees or bushes: *a bosky wood*; tree-shaded (both now sometimes humorous)

boss *n.* knob, as on a shield or ceiling; hub of a propeller

botulism (bóttew-liz'm) *n.* food poisoning, often fatal, caused by a bacterial toxin found in badly tinned or smoked food

boudoir (bōō-dwaar) *n.* dressing room, bedroom, or private sitting room of a woman (often humorous)

bouffant (bōō-foɴ) *adj.* puffed out, full: *a bouffant hairstyle/sleeve*

bouillabaisse (bṓō-yə-béss, -báys) *n.* rich French stew or thick soup made with several kinds of fish or shellfish

bouillon (bṓō-yoɴ) *n.* stock or broth from stewed beef or chicken.

boules (bōōl) *n.* bowls-like game played in France, in which small metal balls are thrown at a target ball

boulevardier (bōōl-várd-yay) *n.* fashionable man widely seen in public, man-about-town

bounteous *formal. adj.* generous, giving freely; plentiful, abundant

bouquet (bōō-káy, bō-, bōō-) *n.* flowers cut and arranged in a cluster, posy, nosegay; characteristic fragrance or "nose" of wine or other alcoholic beverage; compliment, praise

bouquet garni (gaar-née) *n., pl.* **-s -s** herbs tied or wrapped together for immersion in a soup, stew, or the like as seasoning [French, literally, garnished bouquet]

bourbon (búr-bən) *n.* American whiskey distilled from maize, plus malt and rye [after *Bourbon* County, Kentucky, where it was commonly produced]

bourgeois (bóor-zhwaa) *n., pl.* **bourgeois** middle-class urban person as distinct from an aristocrat, a peasant, or a proletarian; upholder of supposedly middle-class values (often disparaging) — **bourgeois** *adj.* — **bourgeoisie** *n.*

Bourse (boorss) *n.* stock exchange, especially that of Paris

bovine *adj.* relating to a cow or ox; dull, stolid, unexcitable

bowdlerise (bówd-lər-īz) *tr.v.* to censor, remove from (a text) the parts considered indecent, expurgate [after Thomas *Bowdler*, the 18th-19th-century British editor, who produced expurgated editions of Shakespeare's plays and other famous literary texts] — **-ism**, **-isation** *n.*

boycott *tr.v.* to refuse to buy, deal with, or the like, as a form of protest or coercion: *boycott the goods/shop/shopkeeper* [after Captain Charles *Boycott*, a 19th-century English land agent in Ireland, who was shunned for refusing to lower tenants' rents] — **boycott** *n.*

braaivleis (brī́-flayss) *South African. n.* barbecue

brace *formal. n., pl.* **brace** pair: *a brace of partridges*

brachial (bráyki-əl) *formal. adj.* relating to the arm; arm-like

bract *n.* leaf-like plant part usually at the base of a flower

brad *n.* thin tapering nail with a narrow head

bradycardia (bráddi-kárdi-ə) *formal. n.* abnormally slow heartbeat (opposite "tachycardia") — **-cardic** *adj.*

braggadocio (brággə-dṓchi-ō) *n.* swaggering boastfulness or bragging [after *Braggadocchio*, the character personifying boastfulness in the 16th-century poem *The Faerie Queene* by Edmund Spenser]

braggart *n.* person who boasts and brags — **braggart** *adj.*

Brahman *n.* in Hinduism, member of the highest caste traditionally made up only of priests; Brahmin — **-ism** *n.*

Brahmin *n.* Brahman; *chiefly U.S.* socially exclusive

and cultivated person, especially from an old New England family
Braille (brayl) *n.* reading or printing system for the blind, based on raised dots interpreted by touch. Compare MOON TYPE [after Louis *Braille*, the blind 19th-century French inventor of the system] — **Braille** *adj.*
brainstorming *n.* free production, exchange, or discussion of ideas as a technique of generating further ideas or solving problems
brake *n.* thicket, typically with dense undergrowth, briars, or ferns
branks *n.*, *pl.n.* bridle with an iron bit formerly used to silence scolding women
brassard (brássaard, bra-sárd) *n.* armband or identifying badge worn on the upper arm; piece of armour protecting the arm
brasserie (brássə-ri, -rée) *n.* French-style restaurant-cum-bar serving beer as well as wine and open till late [French, literally, brewery]
brattice (bráttiss) *n.* screen of wood or cloth used to control ventilation in a mine; tower or parapet in a medieval fortification — **brattice** *tr.v.*
bravado (brə-vaádō) *n.* bravery that is confident or swaggering but probably false
bravura (brə-véwrə) *adj.* brilliant in technique, flamboyantly virtuoso: *a bravura performance of "The Flight of the Bumblebee"* — **bravura** *n.*
breach *n.* violation or breaking of a law, contract, relationship, or the like; gap or rift, as in a castle wall; leaping or surfacing of a whale from under the water [related to *break*] — **breach** *v.*
breech *n.* bottom of the human torso, specifically the buttocks; lower section of a pulley; rear section of a gun, behind the barrel ~ *adj.* relating or referring to the emergence of a new-born baby feet or buttocks first rather than head first: *a breech birth/delivery*
brevet (brévvit) *n.* honorary promotion of a military officer to a higher rank, without the corresponding rise in pay or authority — **brevet** *tr.v.*
breviary *n.* in the Roman Catholic Church, book of the psalms, hymns, prayers, and readings to be recited during divine office
brevity *n.* briefness, shortness, conciseness [related to *brief*]
brewis *regional. n.* sop, bread soaked or dunked in gravy, soup, milk, or the like
bric-a-brac *n.* variety of small ornamental objects or trinkets displayed in a room
brickbat *informal. n.* criticism or a blunt critical remark
bridgehead *n.* military position or foothold established in enemy territory by advance troops
brief *n.* legal document, analysing a case and detailing instructions given by a solicitor to a barrister; broadly, set of instructions, guidelines; papal letter of instructions or judgment, in modern handwriting. Compare BULL ~ *tr.v.* to instruct in or inform about what is relevant to a task or mission; specifically, to brief (a barrister); *British.* to hire the services of or retain (a barrister)
brigand (bríggənd) *formal. n.* bandit or robber, outlaw — **-age** *n.*
brilliantine (bríl-yən-teen) *n.* hair oil, perfumed and sometimes thickened into a gel — **brilliantine** *tr.v.*
brimstone *archaic. n.* sulphur
brindled *adj.* brown or grey with darker streaks or spots: *a brindled cat/cow*
brine *n.* salty water, as used for pickling; sea water — **briny** *adj.* — **brine** *tr.v.*
brio (brée-ō) *n.* vivacity, verve [Italian]
brisling *n.* sprat, small herring typically preserved and canned
broach *n.* spit for roasting meat; any of various chisel- or gimlet-like tools ~ *tr.v.* to make or enlarge (a hole) by means of a piercing tool, such as a gimlet; to open (a keg, barrel, or the like) by piercing; to open and start using the contents of (a box, shipment, or the like); to begin discussing (a topic)
broadsheet *n.* large sheet of paper printed on one side with news, advertisements, or the like; newspaper having large pages. Compare TABLOID
broadside *n.* guns along one side of a warship, or their combined firing simultaneously; scathing criticism or verbal attack ~ *adv.* sideways on
Brobdingnagian (bróbding-nággi-ən) *formal. adj.* enormous, huge (humorously pompous) [after *Brobdingnag*, the land of the giants in Swift's *Gulliver's Travels*]
brocade (brə-káyd) *n.* heavy fabric with a raised design woven into it — **brocade** *tr.v.*
brochette (bro-shét) *n.* small skewer or spit for roasting or grilling meat, fish, or vegetables; dish cooked or served on a brochette
brock *n.* badger, or traditional name for a badger
broderie anglaise (brṓdəri ON-gléz) *n.* embroidery of an open pattern done on white cotton or fine linen [French, literally, English embroidery]
brogue (brōg) *n.* broad regional accent; specifically, Irish brogue [after *brogues*, rough heavy shoes, as formerly worn by Irish peasants]
bromide *n.* calming medicinal drug, sedative; clichéd, moralistic, and commonplace saying or idea
brouhaha (brōō-haa-haa) *n.* uproar, commotion, noisy confusion
bruit (brōōt) *formal. n.* heart murmur or other abnormal body sound — **bruit about/abroad** to noise or spread about: *Rumour was bruited about*
brummagem (brúmmə-jəm) *British. informal. n.* cheap and gaudy goods, especially imitation jewellery [dialect form of *Birmingham*, formerly noted for its cheap manufactured goods] — **brummagem** *adj.*
brusque (brŏŏsk) *adj.* abrupt or curt, gruffly blunt: *a brusque manner/greeting* — **-erie** *n.*
brut (brōōt, brüt) *adj.* very dry, as a wine, especially champagne, might be. Compare SEC [French, literally, raw, rough]
bruxism (brúks-iz'm) *formal. n.* habit of grinding the teeth, especially unconsciously, as during sleep
Brythonic (bri-thónnik) *adj.* referring or relating to the Celtic languages of Cornwall, Wales, Brittany, and ancient Cumbria. Compare GOIDELIC [related to *Briton*, *Breton*] — **Brythonic**, **Brython** *n.*
buccaneer *n.* pirate, especially in the Caribbean in the 17th and 18th centuries [French *boucanier*, a pirate, originally a French woodsman in the Caribbean, from *boucaner*, to cure meat over a fire, from Tupi *mukem*, a roasting frame]
buckler *n.* small round shield worn or carried on the arm
buckling *n.* smoked herring
buckram *n.* coarse cotton fabric treated with glue, as used in bookbinding or for stiffening collars [after *Bukhara*, an Asian textile centre now in the USSR]

buckshee *British. informal. n.* lucky break, windfall; bonus or extra ration; tip, as given to a waiter or helper ~ *adj.* free, without charge

bucolic (bew-kóllik) *formal. adj.* relating to idealised country life, pastoral

buffo (bo͝of-ō) *n., pl.* **buffi** male, usually bass, singer of comic opera roles [Italian, literally, puff]

Buggins' turn *British. informal. n.* turn at a task assigned by rotation rather than merit, or the practice or system of assigning turns in this way

buhl (bo͞ol) *n.* ornate inlaid furniture decoration, or an item of furniture so decorated (also "boulle") [after André *Boulle*, a 17th-18th-century French cabinet-maker] — **-work** *n.*

bulbous *adj.* bulb-like, bulging and swollen-looking: *a bulbous nose*

bulimia *n.* pathologically insatiable hunger, often involving compulsive eating and self-induced vomiting, and thereby linked with anorexia nervosa (also "bulimia nervosa"). Compare ANOREXIA — **-mic** *n., adj.*

bulkhead *n.* partition wall dividing a ship or aircraft into compartments

bull *n.* papal document or letter, written in archaic lettering and specially sealed. Compare BRIEF

bulla (bo͝olə) *n., pl.* **bullae** seal on a papal bull; *formal.* blister

bullion fringe *n.* heavy gold or silver wire or cord used as a trimming, as on military uniforms

bull's-eye *n.* glass tile or disc set in a pavement, deck, or the like to admit light, lamp or lantern with a thick lens to concentrate the light; small wooden pulley formerly used on ships

bulwark (bo͝ol-wərk) *n.* wall used for fortification, rampart; person or thing regarded as a steadfast defence; breakwater in the sea, as on the edge of a harbour — **bulwark** *tr.v.*

Bumiputra (bo͞omi-po͞otrə) *n.* Malaysian who is an ethnic Malay

bumptious *informal. adj.* brashly, unselfconsciously, and often loudly self-assertive

bunraku (bo͝on-ráakoo͞) *n.* traditional Japanese puppet theatre

bunting *n.* flags, especially those of a boat, or the light cloth used in making them; cloth strips or colourful streamers strung on a line for decoration

buoyant (bóy-ənt) *adj.* able to float; resisting decline, as if remaining easily afloat: *a buoyant economy*; cheerful or high-spirited — **-ancy** *n.*

burden *n.* chorus or bass accompaniment of a song; drone of bagpipes; theme or recurrent idea or symbol in a book, speech, symphony, or the like, motif

burette *n.* glass tube with markings and a tap, used in a laboratory for dispensing or measuring liquid accurately

burgee (búr-jee) *n.* small identifying flag, usually triangular, flown by a ship or yacht

burgeon (búr-jən) *formal. n.* bud, sprout, or shoot of a plant ~ *intr.v.* to blossom, bud, sprout, begin to grow; to develop or grow rapidly, flourish

burgh (búrrə) *n.* town or borough in Scotland

burgher (búrgər) *n.* citizen: *respectable burghers*; specifically, middle-class citizen of a medieval town

burgoo *n.* porridge or oatmeal gruel formerly served to sailors

burin (béwr-in) *n.* engraver's style or technique, or sharp chisel-like tool; prehistoric flint tool with a chisel-like head

burke *British. tr.v.* to murder, typically by suffocation, so as to leave the body unbruised and unwounded for dissection; *informal.* to suppress or avoid with little publicity: *burke a scandal/question* [after William *Burke*, a 19th-century Irish murderer executed in Scotland for such murders]

burlap *n.* coarse fabric woven from jute, hemp, or the like, sacking

burlesque (bur-lésk) *n.* mocking or satirical imitation, as of a literary work; *U.S.* music-hall entertainment, often including striptease — **burlesque** *v., adj.*

burnish *tr.v.* to rub to produce a smooth, polished finish ~ *n.* burnished appearance

bursa *n., pl.* **-sae** or **-sas** pouch or cavity in the body, filled with fluid to reduce friction, as at joints — **-sal** *adj.*

bursar *n.* university or college official in charge of finances; student with a bursary

bursary *n.* scholarship or grant awarded to a student, as at a Scottish university; office of a bursar

bushwacker *informal. n.* uncultivated person living in remote country areas, such as a hunter or trapper, backwoodsman — **-whack** *intr.v.*

buskin *n.* laced boot reaching to mid-calf; boot worn by actors in classical times

bustle *n.* frame or pad formerly worn under a woman's skirt to expand it at the rear

buttery *chiefly British. n.* pantry or wine cellar; room in a college or university where students can buy food [from Late Latin *buttis*, a cask, wine butt; related to *butt, bottle*]

buttress *n.* construction or prop against a wall to strengthen it; something serving as a support or reinforcement; horny growth on the heel of a horse's hoof ~ *tr.v.* to support or reinforce with or as if with a buttress: *buttressed their argument with facts*

butyraceous (béwti-ráyshəss) *formal. adj.* buttery or butter-like

buxom *adj.* attractively plump (used of women)

buzz word *informal. n.* word in fashionable use, such as *parameters* or *traumatic*, that suggests the user's sophistication or expertise in a particular field

bwana (bwáanə) *n.* boss, master; sir (used in East Africa as a respectful title for a superior)

by-line *n.* line under the title of a magazine or newspaper article giving the writer's name

byre *British. regional. n.* cowshed or barn

byword *n.* target or object of scorn; typical example of a specified quality: *products that have become a byword for excellence*; proverb

Byzantine (bī-zán-tīn, bi-, bízz'n-, -teen) *formal. adj.* devious, ponderous, and complicated: *Byzantine intrigues*; rigid and inflexible: *the Byzantine attitudes of the bureaucracy* [after the *Byzantine Empire* in Asia Minor and the Balkans, between the 4th and 15th centuries, alluding to its artistic sophistication and its political or bureaucratic structure]

C

cabal (kə-baál) *n.* plot or group of plotters; secret or semi-secret faction bent on power or influence [from *cabala*; popularised during the reign of Charles II, when it was applied to the ministry of *C*lifford, *A*rlington, *B*uckingham, *A*shley, and *L*auderdale]
cabala (ka-baálə, kə-) *n.* secret or mystical philosophy, specifically based on the Hebrew scriptures (also "Cabala", "kabala") — **-list** *n.* — **-listic** *adj.*
caballero (kábbəl-aír-ō, -yaír-) *n.*, *pl.* **-ros** gentleman in Spanish-speaking countries
cable release *n.* syringe-like flexible wire used to operate a camera's shutter from a distance
caboose *n.* deckhouse, galley, or kitchen of a ship; *U.S.* guard's van
cabotage (kábbə-taázh) *n.* coastal shipping and sailing, especially within a country's territorial waters; exclusive right of a country to assign internal air traffic to its own carriers
cabriole *n.* chair leg of an 18th-century style, curving outwards near the top, and then inwards to an ornamental foot [French, literally, caper, from its resemblance to the foreleg of a capering animal]
cabriolet (kábbri-ə-láy) *n.* two-seater one-horse vehicle with a folding top; two-door convertible car (old-fashioned)
cache (kash) *n.* hidden store of stolen goods, arms, or the like, or its hiding place — **cache** *tr.v.*
cachet (káshay) *n.* distinguishing mark or stamp; design, other than a postmark, stamped on an envelope for commemorative purposes; prestige or social distinction; capsule or wafer formerly used to contain unpleasant-tasting medicine and make it easier to swallow.
cachinnate (káckinayt) *archaic. intr.v.* to laugh loudly or uncontrollably, guffaw
cachou (ká-shōō) *n.* lozenge or pastille sucked in order to sweeten the breath
cacique (ka-séek) *n.* Indian chief in Latin America
cacoethes scribendi (káckō-éetheez) *n.* urge or itch to write (humorous) [Latin]
cacography (ka-kóggrəfi) *n.* bad handwriting. Compare CALLIGRAPHY; bad spelling (opposite "orthography")
cacophony (kə-kóffəni) *n.* sound or noise that is ugly or jarring. Compare EUPHONY — **-nous** *adj.*
cadaver (kə-dáv-ər, -daáv-) *n.* corpse, especially used for medical research, such as dissection
cadaverous *adj.* corpse-like; gaunt, haggard, and deathly pale in appearance
cadence (káyd'nss) *n.* rhythmic flow, as of poetry or speech; modulation of the voice; falling intonation of the voice, at the end of a declarative sentence; progression of musical chords towards a resolution or rest
cadenza *n.* elaborate flourish occurring in classical music, usually as a solo in part of a song or towards the end of a concerto movement
cadre (kaádər) *n.* activist core of an organisation or movement; member of a cadre
caduceus (kə-déwssi-əss) *n.*, *pl.* **-cei** winged staff with two serpents coiled round it so as to form a double helix, used as a symbol of the medical profession, or of the messenger god Hermes or Mercury; herald's identifying staff or wand in ancient times
caecum (sée-kəm) *n.*, *pl.* **-ca** body pouch, specifically that between the small and large intestines (also "blind gut")
caesarean (si-zaír-i-ən) *n.* surgical incision into the uterus to deliver a baby (also "Caesarian section", "Caesarian") [after the tradition that Julius *Caesar* himself was born in this way, and that his name was based on *caesus*, having been cut, from Latin *caedere*, to cut]
caesura (si-zéwr-ə) *n.*, *pl.* **-ras** or **-rae** pause or break within a line of verse
cairn *n.* mound of stones serving as a memorial or landmark
caisson (kə-sōōn, káyss'n) *n.* watertight chamber for underwater construction or repair work; float for raising sunken vessels; large box for military ammunition, especially one mounted on two wheels and horse-drawn
cajole (kə-jṓl) *tr.v.* to persuade by flattery, coax, wheedle — **-ry** *n.*
calabash *n.* vine or hard fruit of the bottle gourd
calamari *n.*, *pl.n.* squid, served as food
calamus *formal. n.*, *pl.* **-mi** quill of a feather
calcaneus (kal-káy-ni-əss) *formal. n.*, *pl.*, **-nei** heel bone — **-neal** *adj.*
calcareous (kal-kaír-i-əss) *adj.* chalky, containing or resembling limestone or calcium carbonate
calculus *n.*, *pl.* **-li** stone-like object formed in the body from mineral salts, such as a gallstone or kidney stone; *pl.* **-luses** any branch of mathematics using symbolic notation [Latin, a small stone, as used in counting]
Caledonian *formal. adj.* Scottish — **Caledonian** *n.*
calefacient (kál-i-fáysh'nt) *formal. adj.* producing warmth or heat — **calefacient** *n.*
calender *n.* press through which paper or cloth is rolled for a smooth or glossy finish [related to *cylinder*]
calends *n.*, *pl.n.* first day of the month in the Roman calendar (also "kalends")
calendula (kə-léndewlə) *n.* pot marigold
calibrate *tr.v.* to determine the measurement, capacity, or calibre of; to adjust so as to make more accurate, fine-tune, hone
calibre *n.* diameter of the inside of a tube, the bore of a gun, or a bullet or shell; quality, degree of excellence or worthiness: *a boy of his calibre*
caliph (kaál-if, kál-, káyl-) *n.* Islamic religious and secular ruler in former times (also "kalif") — **-ate** *n.*
calk (kawk, kalk) *tr.v.* to transfer (a drawing) by light-

ly shading or colouring its reverse side, and then tracing it onto a surface or paper underneath

calligraphy *n.* fine handwriting. Compare CACOGRAPHY; art of handwriting — **-pher**, **-phist** *n.*

calliope (kə-lī́-əpi) *U.S. n.* steam organ [after *Kalliope*, the Greek Muse of singing]

callipers *pl.n.* measuring instrument consisting of a pair of adjustable curved hinged legs; leg supports consisting of metal rods with straps

callipygian (kál-i-píji-ən) *formal. adj.* having beautiful buttocks (usually humorous; also "callipygous")

callisthenics *n.*, *pl.n.* gymnastic keep-fit exercises — **-ic** *adj.*

callous *adj.* tough, insensitive, and unsympathetic; brutal [related to *callus*]

callow *adj.* immature or inexperienced

callus *n.* thickened or horny patch of skin, caused by pressure or friction, as on the hand or foot; hardened tissue growing over a wound or fracture (also *formal.* "callosity") — **-ed** *adj.*

calotte (kə-lót) *n.* skull cap worn by Roman Catholic clergymen

caloyer (kál-oy-ər) *n.* Greek Orthodox monk

calque *n.* word or phrase translated element by element from another language, such as *superman* from German *Übermensch* (also "loan translation") — **calque** *tr.v.*

caltrop (kál-trəp) *n.* ball of iron with four spikes, placed on the ground and used formerly to slow down advancing enemy troops (also "caltrap")

calumet (kál-yŏŏ-met) *formal. n.* peace pipe

calumny (kál-əm-ni) *formal. n.* strong slander or libel intended to defame — **-lumnious** *adj.* — **-lumniate** *tr.v.*

Calvados (kál-və-doss) *n.* French apple brandy [after *Calvados*, a region in Normandy where it was originally produced]

calvary *n.* artistic representation of the crucifixion of Jesus; gruelling physical or mental ordeal or torment [after *Calvary*, the hill outside ancient Jerusalem, where Jesus was crucified]

camaraderie (kámmə-ráadə-ree) *n.* sense of comradeship; jolly group atmosphere

camber *chiefly British. n.* arching of a surface such as a road or aircraft wing; setting of a vehicle's front wheels to be farther apart at the bottom than at the top

cambist *n.* manual showing exchange rates or weights and measures; money-market dealer, speculator, or specialist

Cambrian *formal. adj.* Welsh — **Cambrian** *n.*

came *n.* thin lead strip securing the panes in latticework or stained-glass windows

camelopard (kámmilə-paard, kə-méllə-) *archaic. n.* giraffe; heraldic beast resembling a horned giraffe

cameo *n.*, *pl.* **-eos** engraving in relief, typically with the raised design of a different colour from the background. Compare INTAGLIO; object with cameo engraving on it; brief literary work; brief appearance or role by a well-known actor

cameo ware *n.* pottery with raised design, typically classical figures

camera *n.* — **in camera** in private, with the public excluded

camera obscura *n.* dark chamber in which the image of an object outside is projected onto a flat surface

campanile (kámpa-née-li) *n.*, *pl.* **-niles** or **-nili** bell-tower, especially one that is freestanding rather than part of a church building [from Late Latin *campana*, a bell, after *Campania*, a region in southern Italy where bell-metal was manufactured]

campanology *formal. n.* bell-ringing, especially the art of musical ringing of church bells — **-gist** *n.*

campanula (kam-pánnew-lə) *n.* bellflower

campestral (kam-péstrəl) *formal. adj.* relating to the open country or uncultivated fields

campus *chiefly U.S. n.* university or college grounds

canaille (ka-nī́) *formal. n.* the vulgar herd, the mob, the rabble [French; related to *canine*]

canapé (kánnə-pay) *n.* snack or hors d'oeuvre consisting of a small open sandwich or spread biscuit [French, literally, a couch, referring to a base for the relish]

canard (kə-nárd, kánnaard) *n.* hoax or false report [French, literally, a duck, from the expression *vendre des canards à moitié*, literally to half-sell ducks, hence to swindle]

cancroid *formal. adj.* crab-like; cancer-like ~ *n.* skin cancer

candelabrum (kándi-láa-brəm) *n.*, *pl.* **-bra** candlestick with several arms (also "candelabra"). Compare CHANDELIER

Candide (kóN-déed, kán-) *formal. n.* naive and over-optimistic person, especially an innocent young man [after the hero of Voltaire's satire of 1759, *Candide*]

candour *formal. n.* truthfulness, frankness — **-did** *adj.*

canine *adj.* relating to or resembling a dog ~ *n.* eye tooth; *formal.* dog or related animal

canker *n.* ulcerous sore of the mouth or lips; diseased condition of plant or animal tissue characterised by decay or inflammation; evil, decay, or corruption, especially when spreading and flourishing [related to *cancer*] — **canker** *v.*

cannelure *n.* groove, especially around a bullet

cannibalise *informal. tr.v.* to use components from something to fit out something else of the same or similar type

cannikin *n.* cup or small can

cannonade *n.* artillery bombardment — **cannonade** *v.*

cannula (kánnew-lə) *n.*, *pl.* **-las** or **-lae** tube inserted into a body cavity for draining or introducing fluid (also "canula")

canon *n.* basis for judgment, criterion; church law; definitive or official list, as of church laws, books of the Bible, Roman Catholic saints, or works of an author, artist, or composer; part of the Tridentine Mass between the Sanctus and the Lord's Prayer; musical form consisting of contrapuntal overlapping repetition of a theme; member of a chapter of priests attached to a cathedral or collegiate church — **-ical** *adj.* — **-ist** *n.*

canoness *n.* woman member of a religious community bound by a rule but not by vows as a nun is

canonical hours *pl.n.* times prescribed in the Roman Catholic Church for certain set prayers; these prayers themselves, such as matins, vespers, and compline; hours between 8 a.m. and 6 p.m. during which marriages may be legally conducted in an Anglican church

canonicals *pl.n.* official priestly clothing

canonise *tr.v.* to declare officially to be a saint. Compare BEATIFY

canoodle *now chiefly British. intr.v.* to neck or pet in lovemaking

canopy *n.* awning-like or roof-like covering or projection; transparent bubble-like cover of the cockpit of an aircraft; silk or nylon hemisphere of a parachute — **canopy** *tr.v.*

[1]**cant** *n.* slant, slope, tilt; outer corner of a building — **cant** *v.*

[2]**cant** *n.* insincere, hypocritical, or moralising speech or writing; special vocabulary of a fringe group, such as thieves, or of a professional group, such as lawyers — **cant** *intr.v.*

Cantabrigian *formal. adj.* of or from Cambridge, or associated with its university (abbreviation "Cantab."). Compare OXONIAN — **Cantabrigian** *n.*

cantankerous *adj.* irritable, bad-tempered, or quarrelsome

cantharides (kan-tháridez) *n., pl.n.* substance prepared from the crushed and dried bodies of a beetle, toxic but used formerly as a counterirritant and aphrodisiac (also "Spanish fly")

canthus *n.* either corner of the eye, where the upper and lower eyelids meet

canticle *n.* religious or liturgical chant, such as the Magnificat, with a biblical text

cantilever (kánti-leevər) *n.* beam or similar projection fixed at only one end; arm of a seesaw or similar extension from a fulcrum; bracket or similar support, as for a balcony — **cantilever** *v.*

cantillate (kánti-layt) *v.* to intone half-musically or murmuringly, as in certain religious rituals

cantle *n.* upward-sloping rear part of a saddle

canto *n., pl.* **-tos** major section of a long poem in classical literature, similar in function to a chapter in a novel

canton *n.* Swiss state or similar small regional unit; section or quarter of a flag or shield in the upper left corner ~ *tr.v.* to quarter or billet (military personnel) — **-ment** *n.* — **-al** *adj.*

cantor *n.* male chief singer or soloist in a synagogue; choir leader or singing leader in church, precentor

canvass *v.* to poll, survey public opinion; to drum up (public support, votes, or the like), solicit; to examine carefully, scrutinise — **canvass** *n.*

caoutchouc (ków-cho͝ok, -cho͞o) *n.* natural rubber

capacious (ka-páyshəss) *formal. adj.* roomy, spacious

cap-à-pie (káppə-pée) *formal. adv.* from head to foot as specified, completely

caparison (kə-párriss'n) *n.* decorative trappings covering a horse; *formal.* finery, regalia — *formal. tr.v.* to cover with decorations, bedeck

caper *n.* pea-like pickled bud with a pungent flavour, used as a condiment

capercaillie (káppər-káyli) *chiefly Scottish. n.* wood grouse

capias *n.* arrest warrant or writ

capillarity (káppi-lárrəti) *n.* distortion of the surface of a liquid in contact with a solid, as a result of surface tension (also "capillary action"); movement of a fluid, as of water upwards through soil, due to capillarity

capillary (kə-píllәri) *formal. adj.* hair-like, very slender; relating to capillarity ~ *n.* blood vessel of a very fine, thin-walled kind

capitulate *intr.v.* to surrender, admit defeat, give in — **-ation**, **-ant** *n.*

capitulum *formal. n., pl.* **-la** flower cluster in the form of a dense disc, as in the daisy; head-like part, such as the end of a long bone or insect's antenna — **-ulate**, **-ulary**, **capitate** *adj.*

[1]**capo** (káypō, káppō) *n., pl.* **-pos** movable bar clamped to the fingerboard of a guitar, lute, or the like to raise the pitch of all the strings

[2]**capo** (káapō) *n., pl.* **-pi** or **-pos** Mafia leader

capon (káypən) *n.* castrated cock bird reared for meat

cappuccino (káppoo-chéenō) *n., pl.* **-nos** or **-ini** coffee with frothed milk [Italian, literally, a Capuchin monk, alluding to the resemblance between the monk's white hood and the coffee's froth]

caprice (kə-préess) *n.* sudden whimsical change of behaviour — **-pricious** *adj.*

caprine (kápprīn) *formal. adj.* relating to or resembling a goat

capsicum (kápsikəm) *n.* red pepper, green pepper, or similar vegetable

capstan *n.* rotating drum on the deck of a ship around which ropes or cables are wound; pulley or rotating shaft in a tape recorder regulating the movement of the magnetic tape

capsule *n.* aircraft's cockpit that can be ejected as a unit in an emergency

captious *adj.* nitpickingly critical, carping; *formal.* tending or intended to entrap or embarrass

captivate *formal. tr.v.* to fascinate, charm — **-ation** *n.*

capuche (ka-po͞osh) *n.* monk's hood or cowl

capuchin (káppew-chin, -shin) *n.* woman's hooded cloak

carabiniere (kárrəbin-yáiri) *n., pl.* **-nieri** Italian national policeman

caracul (kárrə-kul) *n.* Persian lamb fur [after the broadtail sheep originally bred near Kara Kul, a lake in the southern USSR]

carafe (kə-ráf) *n.* open-topped wine or water bottle at table

carapace (kárrə-payss) *n.* shell of a tortoise, crab, lobster, or the like; inflexible protective shell: *shielded by a carapace of cynicism*

caravan *n.* desert travellers in a group or convoy

caravanserai (kárrə-ván-sə-rī) *n.* camp-site and inn for desert caravans

carbine *n.* light, short-barrelled rifle, originally used by cavalrymen (also "carabin") — **carabineer** *n.*

carbohydrate *n.* sugar, starch, or a related compound

carbonated *adj.* fizzy: *carbonated water*

carboniferous *formal. adj.* producing coal or carbon

Carborundum *trademark. n.* abrasive substance containing carbon

carboy *n.* bottle, often in a protective box or basket, for acids or other corrosive liquids

carbuncle *n.* large spreading boil with multiple openings; deep red, rounded, uncut precious stone, especially the garnet

carcanet (kárkənet) *n.* jewelled necklace or collar in former times

carcass *n.* dead body of an animal or bird; *informal.* corpse; ruins, wreckage, or remains from which an original structure may be inferred (also "carcase")

carcinogen (kár-sinnə-jən) *n.* cancer-causing substance — **-ic** *adj.*

carcinoma (kársi-nṓmə) *n., pl.* **-mas** or **-mata** cancer or malignant tumour

cardiac *adj.* relating to the heart

cardinal number *n.* number, such as *4* rather than *4th*, used to indicate magnitude or quantity rather than order in a series. Compare ORDINAL NUMBER

cardinal points *pl.n.* the compass points north, south, east, and west, in terms of which the other 28 compass points, such as south-south-east, are expressed
cardinal sins *pl.n.* the seven deadly sins
cardiologist *n.* heart specialist — **-ology** *n.*
careen *intr.v.* to lean or sway, as a ship might when sailing into the wind; to move very fast, career
caret (kárrət) *n.* proofreading symbol in the form of an inverted Y or V, indicating where an insertion is to be made in a text
caribou (kárri-boo) *n.* North American reindeer
caricature *n.* portrait of a person, such as a cartoon or written parody, exaggerating his features and qualities for comic or satirical effect; copy or imitation that is ridiculously inadequate — **caricature** *tr.v.*
caries (kaír-eez, -i-eez) *n.* decay of teeth or bones — **carious, cariogenic** *adj.*
carillon (kə-ríl-yən) *n.* the pealing of bells, as in a tower; tune on such bells; bell-like organ stop — **-lonneur** *n.*
carminative *formal. adj.* anti-flatulent, reducing or expelling internal gas — **carminative** *n.*
carmine (kár-mīn) *n.* deep red colour; crimson pigment from cochineal — **carmine** *adj.*
carnage *n.* large-scale bloodshed and slaughter
carnal *adj.* fleshly; sexual
carnal knowledge *formal. n.* sexual intercourse
carnet (kár-nay) *n.* book of tickets, vouchers, or the like; customs permit for the temporary import of a car or other vehicle [French, literally, a notebook]
carnivore *n.* flesh-eating animal; insect-eating plant — **-vorous** *adj.*
carob (kárrəb) *n.* chocolate-like substance or flavouring, made from an edible pod
carotid (kə-róttid) *n.* either of the two main arteries in the neck, carrying blood to the head — **carotid** *adj.*
carouse (kərówz) *intr.v.* to revel, especially while drinking heavily — **-sal** *n.*
carousel (kárrə-sél,-zél) *n.* merry-go-round; medieval tournament in which knights took part in horse races and riding displays; conveyor-belt apparatus in the luggage-retrieval hall of an airport
carpetbagger *n.* politician who seeks office in an area with which he is not directly associated (derogatory); Northerner seeking political or financial advantage in the South after the U.S. Civil War (derogatory)
carpus *formal. n., pl.* **-pi** wrist; joint similar to the wrist — **-pal** *adj.*
Carrara marble (kə-raárə) *n.* high-grade white Italian marble prized for sculpture [after *Carrara*, the Italian city where the marble is quarried]
carrel *n.* small cubicle in a library for private study
carrion *n.* rotting flesh of dead animals
carrion crow *n.* crow, both scavenging and predatory, with a black bill
carte blanche (kárt-blóɴsh) *n.* unrestricted power to act, a free hand [French, literally, a blank card]
cartel (kaar-tél) *n.* business association or grouping of companies, especially an illegal one, to monopolise manufacture or control prices (also *chiefly U.S.* "trust")
cartilage *n.* gristle, tough fibrous tissue, as at the joints between bones — **-laginous** *adj.*
cartography *n.* mapmaking or chartmaking — **-pher** *n.* — **-graphic** *adj.*
cartomancy (kártə-mansi) *formal. n.* fortune-telling by means of a pack of tarot or playing cards — **-mancer** *n.*
cartoon *n.* sketch or preliminary drawing, often full-size, for a tapestry, painting, mosaic, or the like
cartouche (kaar-toosh) *n.* scroll-shaped ornamental tablet of stone, plaster, or the like, sometimes bearing an inscription; oblong frame surrounding names of gods, kings, or queens in ancient Egyptian hieroglyphics; paper casing for the powder in some fireworks; former term for a cartridge, bullet, or box of cartridges
caruncle *n.* comb of a cock; similar outgrowth, normal or abnormal, as on an animal, seed, or the skin
carvel joint (kárv'l) *n.* joint between planks lying flush edge to edge rather than overlapping
caryatid (kárri-áttid) *n., pl.* **-ids** or **-ides** column, in the form of a sculpture of a loosely robed woman, supporting a roof or storey in an ancient Greek or Greek-style building. Compare ATLAS [from Greek *Karuatides*, priestesses of Artemis at *Karuai*, a village in ancient Greece]
carzey *British. slang. n.* lavatory (also "carsey", "khazi") [perhaps from Italian *casa*, a house]
Casanova *n.* man who fancies himself as a great lover [after Giovanni *Casanova*, an 18th-century Italian writer who published erotic memoirs]
cascade *n.* waterfall or series of small waterfalls; shower, flood: *a cascade of manuscripts*; series, as of electrical components — **cascade** *intr.v.*
casein (káysee-in) *n.* milk protein, extracted from milk by rennin, that forms the basis of cheese
casement *n.* window frame with hinges along one side
casern (ka-zérn) *n.* military barracks or quarters, especially in a town, in former times (also "caserne")
cashier *tr.v.* to dismiss from a position of authority, as in the military
casino (kə-seénō) *n., pl.* **-nos** room or building used for gambling
casque (kask) *formal. n.* helmet or similar item of armour for the head
cassata (kə-saátə) *n.* ice-cream of Italian origin, typically containing nuts and candied fruit
cassation *formal. n.* overturning or cancellation: *cassation of a law/judgment*
cassava (kə-saávə) *n.* tropical plant whose starchy root is eaten as a vegetable, and used as the basis of tapioca
cassis (ka-seés) *n.* blackcurrant syrup, cordial, or liqueur
cassock *n.* simple, long black robe worn under other vestments by clergymen and choristers in church
cast *n.* coil of earth excreted by an earthworm (also "casting"); pellet or mass of undigested food, including bones, fur, and feathers, ejected by an owl or other bird of prey; shed or moulted skin, as of an insect; pair of hawks released by a falconer to pursue quarry as a team; pale shade or tinge of colour; squint of the eye
castanets *pl.n.* pair of wooden shells cupped in the hand and clicked together rhythmically, as by a Spanish dancer [related to *chestnut*]
caste (kaast) *n.* rigid social class with membership based on birth and sometimes occupation; any of the major social divisions among Hindus, such as the Brahmans
castellated *n.* castle-like; having turrets and battlements like a castle, or indentations resembling these
caster *n.* sugar sprinkler (also "castor")

castigate *formal. tr.v.* to punish or criticise harshly and relentlessly — **-gation**, **-gator** *n.*
castor *n.* perfume fixative derived from glands in a beaver's groin; beaver hat
castrato (kass-tra͡a-tō) *n., pl.* **-ti** or **-tos** male singer castrated in boyhood in former times to keep his high-pitched voice
casuistry (kázzew-istri, káz͟hōō-) *n.* solving of moral dilemmas by applying general principles of ethics; reasoning or argument that is often persuasive but is over-clever or false, sophistry — **casuist** *n.* — **-istic** *adj.*
casus belli (káy-səss béllī) *n., pl.* **casus belli** provocative act or event that provokes or justifies a war [Latin, literally, the occasion of war]
catachresis (káttə-kre͡esiss) *n., pl.* **-ses** strained or paradoxical use of words for rhetorical effect; incorrect use of words as when referring to a divorced couple as *incomparable* instead of as *incompatible* — **-chrestic** *adj.*
cataclysm *n.* sudden violent large-scale upheaval or disastrous change — **-ic** *adj.*
catacombs (káttə-kōōmz, -kōmz) *pl.n.* series of underground chambers and tunnels, especially those in Rome used as a worship and burial area by persecuted early Christians
catafalque (káttə-falk) *n.* raised platform or table on which a coffin or corpse lies, as during a state funeral
catalepsy *n.* abnormal condition of unresponsiveness and rigid muscles, as sometimes occurs in hysteria — **-leptic** *adj.*
catalyst *n.* chemical that affects or speeds up a chemical reaction without itself being changed; person or thing that provokes a change or event: *the catalyst of the mutiny* — **-lyse** *v.* — **-lysis** *n.* — **-lytic** *adj.*
catalytic converter *n.* attachment to an exhaust pipe, purifying the engine's exhaust gases
catalytic cracker *n.* oil-refining unit in which petroleum is converted to fuels with lower boiling points
catamaran *n.* raft of logs or floats tied together; twin-hulled boat
catamite *formal. n.* boy lover kept by a man [Latin, *Catamitus*, Ganymede, the cupbearer of the gods in Greek mythology, loved by Zeus]
cataract *n.* large, steep, fast-flowing waterfall; flood, deluge; clouding of the eye that may lead to partial or total blindness
catarrh (kə-tár) *n.* inflammation of the mucous lining of the nose and throat
catastrophe (kə-tástrəfi) *n.* great disaster with grave consequences for those affected by it; final outcome of a classical tragedy in which the protagonist's fatal flaw leads to his downfall — **-trophic** *adj.*
catatonia *n.* catalepsy as a symptom of schizophrenia — **-tonic** *adj.*
catch *n.* round song for three or more voices, popular in the 17th and 18th centuries
catchment area *n.* drainage basin; area served by an institution such as a school or hospital
catchpole *n.* sheriff's officer in medieval times who arrested debtors; *archaic.* unimportant minor official (also "catchpoll")
catchword *n.* word at the top of a page of a dictionary, telephone directory, or the like, indicating the alphabetical entries of that page; word printed or typed separately at the foot of a page to indicate the first word of the following page; actor's cue to enter
catechise (káttikīz) *tr.v.* to instruct by question-and-answer, as in preparing a boy or girl for confirmation; to question searchingly and intensively — **-chist**, **-chesis** *n.* — **-chistic** *adj.*
catechism (káttikiz'm) *n.* process of catechising; book of questions and answers, especially about Christian doctrine
catechumen (kátti-kéwmen) *n.* person receiving Christian instruction, as prior to confirmation
categorical *adj.* without doubt or reservations: *a categorical denial*
catenary (kə-te͡enəri) *n.* curve hypothetically formed by a uniform cable suspended from two points; overhead cable of an electric railway, tram, or the like — **catenery** *adj.*
catenate *tr.v.* to form into a chain; to link in a series
caterwaul (káttər-wawl) *n.* shrill screech or cry, as of an excited cat — **caterwaul** *v.*
catharsis (kə-thársiss) *n., pl.* **-ses** purging of one's own emotions, especially the emotions of pity and terror, through experiencing other people's feelings, as when watching a classical tragic drama; in psychology, release of emotional tension through acting out repressed anxieties
cathartic *adj.* relating or referring to catharsis; powerfully stimulating the evacuation of the bowels ~ *n.* strong laxative
cathedra (kə-thée-drə, -thé-) *n.* bishop's official chair or throne; bishop's area of authority, see, diocese
catheter (káthitər) *n.* thin and flexible tube inserted into a body channel, such as a vein or the urethra, for draining or introducing fluid — **-ise** *tr.v.*
cathode-ray tube *n.* television tube, oscilloscope tube, or similar electron-generating and focusing vacuum tube
catholic *adj.* universal, general, all-embracing; wide-ranging: *catholic tastes* — **-ity** *n.*
catholicon (kə-thólli-kən) *formal. n.* universal remedy, panacea
catkin *n.* flower cluster or spike, typically dense and drooping, as of the birch or alder (also "ament")
catoptric (kə-tóptrik) *formal. adj.* relating to mirrors and reflections
CAT scanner *n.* X-ray machine taking cross-section images of the brain or other soft tissue, which are then formed into a three-dimensional image by computer [*c*omputerised *a*xial *t*omography] — **CAT scan** *n.* — **CAT-scan** *tr.v.*
cat's-paw *n., pl.* **cat's-paws** person used as a tool by other people for their own scheming purposes [alluding to the proverbial image of a monkey grasping a cat by the paw to scrape roasting nuts from the fire]
Caucasian *n.* person of white European descent [after the *Caucasus*, historic region now in the south-western USSR] — **Caucasian** *adj.*
caucus *n.* sub-group or policy meeting of a political party, especially in the U.S. — **caucus** *intr.v.*
caudal *formal. adj.* relating to the tail, posterior, or hind parts of the body
caudillo (kow-díllō, -díl-yō) *n.*, charismatic political leader of a Spanish-speaking country, especially one who aspires to or has achieved autocratic rule
caul *n.* piece of the membrane surrounding a foetus, sometimes covering a baby's head at birth
caulk (kawk) *tr.v.* to seal or make watertight, especially to pack the seams of a ship with tar or oakum (also "calk")

cause célèbre (kṓz se-lébr) *n.*, *pl.* **causes célèbres** notorious, controversial court case or other event that is hotly debated by the public and the press [French, literally, famous case]
causerie (kṓzəri) *formal. n.* informal conversation; piece of writing in conversational style [French]
caustic *adj.* burning, dissolving, or corrosive through chemical action; biting, cutting, or sarcastic: *caustic wit* ~ *n.* caustic chemical
cautery *n.* something caustic, very hot, or very cold used to destroy abnormal tissue or prevent infection, especially in the treatment of wounds; treatment with a cautery — **-erise** *tr.v.*
cavalcade *n.* a ceremonial parade of horses or cars; any colourful procession
cavalier *n.* gentleman, such as an able horseman or a courtly escort (old-fashioned) ~ *adj.* offhand, disregarding the feelings of others, arrogant
Cavalier *n.* royalist supporter of Charles I in the English Civil War
cave (káyvi) *British. slang. interj.* Beware! (used by schoolchildren) — **keep cave** to keep watch, be on the lookout [Latin, beware!]
caveat (kávvi-at, káyvi-) *formal. n.* warning or proviso, caution [Latin, literally, let him beware]
caveat emptor *formal. interj.* Let the buyer beware (used to remind buyers that without a guarantee they may have no legal remedy if their purchase proves disappointing)
cavil (cávv'l) *formal. n.* objection or criticism that is petty and trifling — **cavil** *intr.v.*
cavort *intr.v.* to skip or caper about in a lively way
cay *n.* small, low island, typically of coral and sand (also "key")
cayenne pepper (kay-én) *n.* hot red-pepper powder
cayman *n.* alligator-like crocodile of tropical America
cedilla (si-díllə) *n.* comma-like diacritic or accent mark placed below the letter *c* in French and Portuguese to indicate that it is to be pronounced as an *s*, as in *soupçon*
ceilidh (káyli) *n.* Scottish or Irish social and cultural get-together featuring folk music, folk dancing, story-telling, and poetry
celebrant *formal. n.* someone who officiates at or participates in a ceremony or rite, especially a religious one
celerity *formal. n.* speed
celestial *formal. adj.* relating to the heavens or sky, heavenly
celestial sphere *n.* imaginary sphere surrounding the Earth at a great distance, and housing the stars and planets on its surface, useful for locating the positions of celestial bodies
celibate *adj.* unmarried; abstaining from sexual intercourse, chaste — **celibate, -bacy** *n.*
cellarer *n.* monk responsible for food and drink supplied in a monastery
cellular *adj.* referring to, relating to, or having cells, openings, or a porous texture: *cellular structure/ rock/blankets*
cellulite *n.* lumpy layer of fat, as on the thighs and buttocks
cellulose *n.* vegetable matter used in making paper, rayon, and photographic film
Celsius *adj.* centrigrade [after Anders *Celsius*, the 18th-century Swedish astronomer who invented the scale]
Celtic cross *n.* upright cross with a circle in the centre
cenacle (sénnək'l) *n.* literary salon or discussion group; similar social group or clique (rare)
cenobite (seén-ə-bīt) *n.* monk or other member of a communal religious order (also "coenobite")
cenotaph (sénnə-taaf) *n.* monument honouring soldiers killed in battle or other dead people buried elsewhere [from Greek, *kenos*, empty + *taphos*, a tomb]
censer (sén-sər) *n.* container in which incense is burned, typically swung back and forth at religious ceremonies (also "thurible") [related to *incense*]
censorious *adj.* very critical; judgmental in a hostile way
censure (sénshər) *formal. tr.v.* to criticise, scold, or blame — **censure** *n.*
census *n.* regular official counting of the population of a country, usually including the collection of statistics about employment, family relationships, and other data
centaur (sén-tawr) *n.* creature in Greek mythology having the head, arms, and trunk of a human, typically a man, and a horse's body and legs
centenarian *n.* person aged 100 or more — **centenarian** *adj.*
centenary *n.* hundredth anniversary (also *chiefly U.S.* "centennial") — **centenary** *adj.*
centillion *n.* in British and German usage, number equivalent to one followed by 600 zeros, usually written 10^{600}; in U.S. and French usage, number equivalent to one followed by 303 zeros, usually written 10^{303}
centrifugal (sen-tríffewg'l) *adj.* directed away from a centre or axis; referring or relating to a force directed outwards in this way; moving away from centralised authority or unity. Compare CENTRIPETAL
centripetal (sen-tríppit'l) *adj.* directed towards a centre or axis; referring or relating to a force directed inwards in this way; favouring centralised authority or unity. Compare CENTRIFUGAL
cephalic (si-fál-ik, ki-, ke-) *formal. adj.* relating or referring to the head or skull; on, in, or near the head
cephalopod (séffələ-pod) *n.* mollusc, such as the octopus, squid, or nautilus, with foot-like tentacles growing around or out of its head
ceraceous (si-ráyshəss) *formal. adj.* waxy; wax-like
ceramic *n.* material, such as pottery or porcelain, made by baking or firing clay or a similar substance — **ceramic** *adj.* — **-mics** *n.*
ceratoid (sérrətoyd) *formal. adj.* horn-like in shape or texture
Cerberus (sér-bərəss) *n.* in Greek mythology, three-headed dog guarding the entrance to the underworld
cerebellum (sérri-bélləm) *n.*, *pl.* **-lums** or **-la** structure within the brain that regulates and co-ordinates complex voluntary movement
cerebral (sérri-brəl) *adj.* relating to the intelligence rather than to the emotions or instincts; relating to the brain or cerebrum — **-bration** *n.*
cerebral palsy *n.* impaired control and loss of strength in the muscles and limbs, typically marked by spasticity, usually caused by brain damage occurring at or before birth
cerebrum (sérri-brəm) *n.*, *pl.* **-brums** or **-bra** large rounded structure of the brain
cerecloth (seér-kloth) *n.* wax-coated cloth in which corpses were formerly wrapped (also *archaic* "cerements")

ceremonious *adj.* polite or extremely formal
cerise (sə-réez, -réess) *n.* purple-pink [related to *cherry*] — **cerise** *adj.*
certitude *formal. n.* certainty, confident assurance
cerulean (sə-rōōli-ən) *formal. adj.* sky-blue, azure
cerumen (si-rōō-men) *formal. n.* earwax
cervical (sér-vīk'l, sérvik'l) *adj.* relating to the neck or cervix
cervine (sérvīn) *formal. adj.* relating to a deer
cervix *n.*, *pl.* **-vixes** or **-vices** neck or neck-shaped structure in the body; lower part of the uterus
cessation *formal. n.* ceasing, discontinuance, ending: *cessation of hostilities*
cession *formal. n.* ceding, yielding, giving up a claim — **-ary** *n.*
cesspool (séss-pōōl) *n.* covered pit for household waste and sewage; filthy, corrupt, or disgusting place or situation (also "cesspit")
[1]**cestus** (séstəss) *n.*, *pl.* **-ti** belt or girdle, as formerly worn by a bride
[2]**cestus** *n.*, *pl.* **-tuses** boxing glove or hand-covering of leather studded with metal, worn by boxers in ancient Rome
cetacean (si-táysh'n) *formal. n.* whale, porpoise, or similar fish-like aquatic mammal — **cetacean**, **-aceous** *adj.*
cete (seet) *n.* group of badgers
ceteris paribus (kéttə-riss páari-bəss, séttə-) *formal. adv.* all other things being equal [Latin]
chador (cháa-dawr) *n.* woman's garment in Iran and some other Islamic countries, consisting of a long black cloth covering the head, upper body, and part of the face
chaff *n.* metal foil released in strips into the air to thwart an enemy's radar system (also "window")
chaffer *intr.v.* to bargain, haggle
chafing dish *n.* dish set on a hotplate or warmer, used to cook food or keep it warm
chagrin (shággrin, shə-grín) *n.* feeling of embarrassed annoyance or irritation, due to failure or frustration — **chagrin** *tr.v.*
chaise longue (sháyz lóNG) *n.*, *pl.* **chaise longues** or **-s -s** reclining chair with a long seat on which one can stretch one's legs [French, literally, long chair]
chalcedony (kal-séddəni) *n.* milky or greyish quartz with distinctive bands of crystals, used as a semiprecious stone — **chalcedony** *adj.*
chaldean (kal-dée-ən, kawl-) *archaic. n.* astrologer, sorcerer, or soothsayer [after the *Chaldeans*, an ancient Semitic people who ruled in Babylonia]
chalice (chál-iss) *n.* cup for the consecrated wine at Communion; *archaic.* goblet; cup-shaped flower; goblet-shaped instrument for inhaling marijuana
chalybeate (kə-líbbi-ət) *formal. adj.* containing iron salts, or tasting of iron: *chalybeate water* — **chalybeate** *n.*
chamberlain *n.* steward of a nobleman or wealthy landowner; treasurer of a municipality
chambers *n.*, *pl.n.* judge's room for hearing minor cases or conducting private consultations; barrister's set of rooms, especially in the Inns of Court
chambré (shómbray) *tr.v.* to prepare (wine) for serving by allowing the opened bottle to stand until reaching room temperature [French, literally, put into a room]
chameleon (kə-méeli-ən) *n.* changeable or fickle person [after the colour-changing lizard]
chamfer (chámfər) *tr.v.* to cut off the corner or edge of, bevel; to make a groove in, flute — **chamfer** *n.*
champaign (shám-páyn) *archaic. n.* open country, stretch of plain (literary)
champignon (sham-pín-yən, shámpin-yóN) *n.* common type of edible mushroom
champlevé (shoN-lə-váy) *n.* silver or other metal ornament or object decorated by the insertion of enamel colours into cut grooves; technique used in such decoration — **champlevé** *adj.*
chancel *n.* space round the altar of a church for the clergy and choir
chancellor *n.* secretary to a king or nobleman in former times; chief secretary at an embassy; bishop's chief administrative officer, dealing with legal secular matters in the diocese; prime minister of any of several European countries, such as West Germany; honorary head of a British university; administrative head of a university in any of several countries, such as the U.S. — **-lory**, **-lery** *n.*
chancery (cháan-səri) *n.* one of the three divisions of the High Court of Justice, concerned mainly with the law of trusts and equity; political section of an embassy or diplomatic mission; church office or department dealing with legal matters, church records, and archives; public record office or archive — **in chancery** *British. informal.* hopeless; in an awkward or helpless position — **chancery** *adj.*
chancre (shángkər) *n.* genital sore or growth that is either soft and non-syphilitic or hard and syphilitic [related to *cancer*] — **-crous** *adj.*
chandelier *n.* large, branched light fixture, usually hanging from the ceiling, holding many bulbs or candles. Compare CANDELABRUM [related to *candle*]
chandelle (shan-dél) *n.* sudden, steep-climbing turn made by an aircraft in order to fly higher and change direction at the same time
chandler *n.* ship's supplier, or other dealer in a specified trade or commodity; candle-maker or seller — **-lery** *n.* [related to *candle*]
Chandler wobble *n.* variation, in 14-month cycles, of the position of the Earth's geographical poles [after S.C. *Chandler*, a U.S. astronomer]
changeling *n.* child secretly substituted for another in infancy
change ringing *n.* ringing of bells or chimes using all possible variations
chanter (cháantər) *n.* pipe on a set of bagpipes on which the tune is played. Compare DRONE
chanteuse (sháan-terz) *n.* female singer, as in a nightclub or cabaret (often humorous)
chanticleer (sháan-tikleer) *n.* name of a cockerel in fables or poetry
chantry (cháantri) *n.* endowment for the saying of prayers or Mass, usually for the soul of the benefactor; altar or chapel maintained by such an endowment
chap *n.* jaw or cheek of a pig, used as food
chaparral (sháppə-rál) *n.* dry scrub vegetation in the southwestern U.S. and Mexico
chapatti (chə-pátti) *n.* thin, flat, unleavened Indian bread (also "chapati")
chapbook *n.* booklet or pamphlet of former times, containing popular poems, ballads, religious homilies, or the like
chape *n.* metal tip or trimming of a scabbard or sheath; metal tongue of a buckle

chapel *n.* non-Anglican, non-Catholic church, especially a Methodist church in Wales or Cornwall; *British.* trade-union branch in printing, publishing, or journalism
chapel of ease *n.* church serving those living too far away to attend the parish church
chapel of rest *chiefly British. n.* undertaker's room where the body is kept prior to burial
chaperone (sháppər-ōn) *n.* someone, usually an older woman, who accompanies an unmarried woman to supervise or protect her — **chaperone** *tr.v.*
chaplet *n.* wreath or crown of flowers worn on the head; string of beads, especially a small string of prayer beads — **-ed** *adj.*
chapman *n.* pedlar, trader, or supplier in former times
chaps *pl.n.* wide sturdy leggings worn by cowboys over their trousers to protect their legs when in the saddle (also "chaparejos")
chapter *n.* group of priests serving in a cathedral, or a meeting of them; *chiefly U.S.* local branch of a club or society
charabanc (shárrə-bang) *n.* bus or large coach, used for group outings (old-fashioned or humorous) [French, literally, carriage with benches]
characteristic *n.* part of a logarithm consisting of a whole number. Compare MANTISSA
charade (shə-ráad) *informal. n.* travesty, farce, ridiculous pretence
charcuterie (shaar-kéwtəri) *n.* French-style cold meats and meat products, especially pork; French-style delicatessen specialising in such meats
charge *n.* judge's final address to the jury before they consider their verdict, reminding them of relevant points of law, procedure, or evidence — **charge** *tr.v.*
chargé d'affaires (shár-zhay da-fáir) *n., pl.* **chargés d'affaires** diplomat or official who stands in for an ambassador [French, literally, entrusted with business]
charger *n.* large shallow dish, platter
charisma (kə-rízmə) *n.* personal charm and magnetic power; influence or inspiration — **-matic** *adj.*
charivari (sháari-váari) *archaic. n.* noisy mock serenade, as with pots and pans, made to a newly-married couple at their wedding
charlatan (shárlə-tən) *n.* person who claims to be an expert but is in fact a fake
charnel house *n.* formerly, building or room in which the bodies or bones of the dead were stored
charpoy *n.* bed of a simple, stretcher-like construction, widely used in India
charter *n.* public document, deed; constitution or statement of aims; licence to do wrong: *The new Act, far from tightening up the law, was a thieves' charter*; hiring or leasing of a vehicle, especially a ship or aeroplane — **-erer** *n.* — **-age** *n.* — **charter** *tr.v.*
charterhouse *n.* monastery belonging to the Carthusian order
charter member *chiefly U.S. n.* founder member
chase *n.* groove, channel, or trench; part of a gun that contains the bore; *archaic.* private unfenced game preserve ~ *tr.v.* to groove or indent, flute; to cut or finish the thread of a screw; to decorate (metal) by engraving or embossing
chaser *n.* weaker drink, such as water or beer, taken after a drink of spirits
chasm (kázz'm) *n.* deep gorge or abyss; gaping hole, glaring lack or gap
chaste *adj.* abstaining from sexual activity; pure: *chaste prose* (literary) — **chastity** *n.*
chasten (cháyss'n) *tr.v.* to punish, discipline; to humiliate, teach a lesson to; *formal.* to purify, refine
chastise *tr.v.* to punish by beating; to criticise or scold severely, reprimand — **-ment** *n.*
chasuble (cházzew-b'l) *n.* long sleeveless vestment worn by a priest at Mass
château (shăttō) *n., pl.* **-eaux** French-style castle or stately home
chateaubriand (shátt-ō-bree-ón) *n.* double-thick steak cut from the fillet, served typically with sauce béarnaise and often in a portion large enough for two [probably devised by the chef of the Vicomte de *Chateaubriand*, an 18th-19th-century French writer and diplomat]
chatelaine (sháttə-layn) *n.* mistress of a castle or a large or fashionable household (male equivalent "chatelain"); chain or clasp formerly worn by women at the waist, and used for holding keys, a handkerchief, or the like; decorative chain or pendant worn on the lapel [related to *castle*]
chatoyant (shə-tóy-ənt) *adj.* changing in lustre, twinkling, as a cat's-eye or similar gemstone does ~ *n.* chatoyant gemstone [related to *cat*]
chattel *archaic. n.* slave
chattels *formal. pl.n.* items of property in one's personal possession: *goods and chattels*
chausses (shōss) *pl.n.* medieval mail armour for the legs and feet
chauvinism *n.* (shṓvin-iz'm) *n.* blinkered patriotism; prejudice and favouritism shown towards one's own social group [after Nicolas *Chauvin*, a legendary French soldier of Napoleon's, noted for his patriotic fervour] — **-ist** *n.* — **-istic** *adj.*
cheese cutter *n.* keel, as on a yacht, that can be raised when not in use
chef-d'oeuvre (sháy-dérvr) *n., pl.* **chefs-d'oeuvre** masterpiece [French, literally, chief work]
[1]**chela** (cháy-lə) *n.* guru's disciple
[2]**chela** (kée-lə) *n., pl.* **-ae** claw or pincer of an arthropod, such as a lobster, crab, or scorpion — **chelate, cheliform** *adj.*
chelonian (ki-lṓni-ən) *n.* turtle, tortoise, or related reptile — **chelonian** *adj.*
chemise (shə-méez) *n.* woman's loose shirt, shift, or petticoat — **-ette** *n.*
chemotherapy *n.* medical treatment, as of cancer, using chemicals, especially man-made drugs — **-therapist** *n.* — **-therapeutic** *adj.*
cheongsam (chóng-sám) *n.* tight Chinese-style dress, with a slit skirt and high collar
cheroot (shə-rōōt) *n.* cigar, typically with both ends cut square
chessel (chéss'l) *n.* container or mould for cheese-making
chesterfield *n.* overcoat, usually with concealed buttons and a velvet collar; large, overstuffed sofa with armrests of the same height as the back [after an Earl of *Chesterfield* in the 19th century]
chestnut *n.* small, hard callus on the inside foreleg of a horse
cheval-de-frise (shə-vál-də-fréez) *n., pl.* **chevaux-de-frise** defensive obstacle, made of a frame with spikes or barbed wire, used against enemy troops or horses; protective row of spikes or broken glass fitted to the

top of a wall [French, literally, Frisian horse: the military device was first used in Friesland]
cheval glass (shə-vál) *n.* full-length mirror, hinged so to swivel in its frame [from French, a horse, hence a support]
chevalier (shévvə-léer) *n.* knight, mounted soldier, or military cadet in France in former times; *formal.* chivalrous or gallant man
chevrette (shəv-rét) *n.* skin of a young goat, or the leather made from it
chevron (shévvrən) *n.* V-shaped pattern or object, as on a heraldic shield or an NCO's stripes of rank
chiaroscuro (ki-áarə-skóor-ō) *n., pl.* **-os** light and shade in drawing and painting; contrast as a literary or artistic technique [Italian: related to *clear* and *obscure*]
chiasma (kī-áz-mə) *n., pl.* **-mas** or **-mata** crossing-over of two structures in the body, such as the optic nerve fibres in the brain
chiasmus (kī-áz-məss) *n., pl.* **-mi** rhetorical figure of speech in which the grammatical structure of one phrase is reversed in the second, as in *As they came out, in went we*
chicanery (shi-káynəri) *n.* trickery, deception, double-dealing — **chicane** *v.*
Chicano (chi-káanō) *chiefly U.S. n., pl.* **-os** Mexican-American (feminine form "Chicana") [American Spanish, *Mejicano*, Mexican] — **Chicano** *adj.*
chichi (shée-shee) *adj.* pretty or fashionable in a pretentious or affected way
chicle (chíck'l) *n.* basic ingredient of chewing gum, gum from the sapodilla
chicory *n.* root product used as a coffee additive or substitute
chide *formal. tr.v.* to scold, rebuke, reprimand
chiffonier (shíffə-néer) *n.* ornamental cabinet with a mirror attached
chignon (shéen-yoN) *n.* small elegant roll of hair or bun worn by women at the back of the head
chiliad (kílli-ad) *formal. n.* thousand years, or group of one thousand elements
chiliastic (kílli-ástik) *formal. adj.* believing in the millennium, the holy thousand-year period either prior to or following Christ's Second Coming — **-asm, -ast** *n.*
Chiltern Hundreds *pl.n.* formal office of the Crown that an MP applies for when wishing to give up his or her seat in the House of Commons, a formal gesture required because elected MPs may not resign
chimera (kī-méerə) *n.* imaginary fear, pure fantasy, or the like; plant or animal that is a genetic mix, as through grafting or genetic engineering [after the *Chimaera*, a fire breathing female monster in Greek mythology] — **-merical** *adj.*
chine *n.* backbone, spine, or a cut of meat containing it; ridge or crest of land; line or edge at which the bottom and side of a boat meet
chinoiserie (sheen-wáazə-ri,-rée) *n.* Chinese-style pottery, ornaments, and decorative design generally (sometimes derogatory, implying that the objects have only a superficial resemblance to real Chinese styles)
chintzy *adj.* fussy, flowery, or over-elaborate in style
chip *n.* dried leaves, straw, or the like prepared for weaving or basket-making
chipolata *n.* very small, often spicy sausage
chirography *n.* handwriting; beautiful handwriting, calligraphy — **-grapher** *n.* — **-graphic** *adj.*
chiromancy *formal. n.* palm-reading, palmistry — **-mancer** *n.*
chiropody (ki-róppədi, shi-) *n.* health treatment of the feet and their ailments, such as corns (also *U.S.* "podiatry") — **-podist** *n.*
chiropractic (kī́r-ə-práktik) *n.* massage and physical manipulation, especially of the spine, with the principal aim of correcting nerve disorders — **-practor** *n.*
chiropteran (kīr-óptərən) *n.* flying mammal, such as a bat (also "chiropter") — **chiropteran** *adj.*
chitin (kī́tin) *n.* horn-like substance that is the chief component of the shells of lobsters, crabs, or the like
chiton (kī́t'n) *n.* tunic worn in ancient Greece
chitterlings *pl.n.* pigs' small intestines, prepared as a food
chivalrous *adj.* knight-like or knightly; gentlemanly — **-ry** *n.*
chloroform *n.* liquid chemical, formerly used as an anaesthetic ~ *tr.v.* to anaesthetise or kill with chloroform
chlorophyll *n.* green pigment in plants that traps energy from sunlight for photosynthesis
chock *n.* wooden block, cradle, or wedge used to stop a barrel, wheel, or boat from rolling or sliding; large ring with an opening at the top through which a cable or rope is run on shipboard
chogyal (chóg-yaal) *n.* ruler of Sikkim
choir *n.* any of the nine orders of angels
chokey *British. informal. n.* prison
cholecystectomy (kólli-sist-éktəmi) *formal. n.* surgical removal of the gall bladder
choler (kóllər) *n.* one of the four humours of the body, according to medieval physiology, and thought to cause irritability and anger when present in excess *formal.* anger — **-ic** *formal. adj.*
cholesterol *n.* soapy substance found in body tissue, fat, and bile, involved in causing heart disease
chondrify (kóndri-fī) *v.* to turn into cartilage — **-fication** *n.*
chondrite *n.* type of stone occurring in meteorites
choplogic *n.* argument or reasoning that is quick and clever but faulty
choragus (kaw-ráy-gəss) *n., pl.* **-gi** leader of a chorus in ancient Greek drama; *formal.* leader of a choir
chorale (ko-ráal) *n.* Christian hymn or psalm for choral singing in church; German Protestant hymn; *chiefly U.S.* choir, chorus
chordate (kórd-ayt) *n.* creature with a backbone or similar supporting structure — **chordate** *adj.*
chordophone *formal. n.* musical instrument, such as a stringed or piano-like instrument, that produces sound by means of vibrating strings
chorea (ko-rée-ə) *n.* nervous disorder of various kinds, including St Vitus' dance, causing uncontrollable, irregular movements of the limbs and face
choreography *n.* creation, arrangement, direction, or notation of a dance, especially for ballet on stage — **-graph** *tr.v.* — **-pher** *n.*
choux pastry (shoo) *n.* éclair-type pastry, made with eggs
chrestomathy (kress-tómməthi) *formal. n.* anthology of literary extracts, as used for studying a foreign language
chrism *n.* mixture of oil and balsam used in sacramental anointing, as at baptism or confirmation in the Orthodox and Roman Catholic churches

chrisom (krízz'm) *n.* baptismal robe worn by a baby
chromatic *adj. formal.* relating to colour or colours; relating to the chromatic scale in music — **-tics** *n., pl.n.* — **-ticity** *n.*
chromatic scale *n.* musical scale consisting of twelve successive semitones
chromosome *n.* thread-like structure within plant and animal cells carrying genetic information that determines and transmits hereditary characteristics
chronic *adj.* long-lasting, continuing, or regularly recurring: *a chronic disease*, *chronic unemployment*; habitual: *a chronic thief* — **-ity** *formal. n.*
chronicle *n.* narrative; record of events, especially in the order in which they occurred — **chronicle** *tr.v.*
chronograph *n.* instrument for measuring tiny intervals of time very accurately
chronology *n.* calculation of the dates of past events; ordering of events according to their dates; list of such events — **-logical** *adj.*
chronometer *n.* clock or watch of a very precise kind, especially one used at sea
chronometry *n.* scientific measurement or calculation of time — **-metric**, **-metrical** *adj.*
chrysalis *n., pl.* **-alises** or **-alides** pupa of a moth or butterfly, often encased in a cocoon
chryselephantine (kríss-elli-fántīn) *formal. adj.* made of or covered with gold and ivory, as an ancient Greek statue might originally have been
chthonic (kthónnik, thónnik) *formal. adj.* relating or referring to the underworld and its spirits and gods
chuck *n.* vice or clamp used to hold a tool or workpiece, as in a drill or lathe; cut of beef going from neck to ribs and including the shoulder blade
churchwarden *n.* long-stemmed clay pipe
churl *n.* rude, surly, ill-educated person (very old-fashioned); medieval English peasant
churlish *adj.* rude, surly, unkind or uncooperative; stingy or miserly
chutzpah (k̲h̲ŏŏtspə) *informal. n.* nerve, gall, cheek, audacity (not necessarily pejorative: often used approvingly) [Yiddish]
chyle (kīl) *n.* milky fluid formed in the small intestine during digestion — **-lous**, **-lacious** *adj.*
chyme (kīm) *n.* food in its partly-digested fluid form in the stomach — **-mous** *adj.*
ciborium (si-báwri-əm) *n., pl.* **-ria** covered container for the consecrated Communion wafers; cover or canopy over a high altar, supported on four pillars
cicada (si-kaádə) *n., pl.* **-das** or **-dae** cricket-like insect, the male producing a high-pitched droning sound
cicatrice (síckətriss) *formal. n.* scar; scar tissue (also "cicatrix") — **-trise** *v.* — **-trical**, **-tricose** *adj.*
cicerone (chichə-rṓni, sissə-) *n., pl.* **-nes** or **-ni** sightseers' guide [Italian, originally, a learned man, after the Roman orator and statesman, *Cicero*]
cicisbeo (chíchiz-báy-ō) *formal. n., pl.* **-bei** male lover or escort of a married woman, especially in 18th-century Italy
cilia (sílli-ə) *pl.n.* hair-like threads on a cell or microscopic organism, whose waving produces locomotion; *formal.* eyelashes (singular "cilium")
cimex (sī́meks) *formal. n., pl.* **-mices** bedbug or related insect
Cimmerian (si-meéri-ən) *formal. adj.* dark, very gloomy [after a mythical people inhabiting a perpetually dark land, according to Homer]
cinchona (sing-kṓnə) *n.* quinine or related drug, or the bark or tree from which it is derived [after the Countess of *Chinchón*, vicereine of Peru in the early 18th century, who introduced it into Europe after recovering from a fever with the help of cinchona bark]
cincture (síngk-chər) *formal. n.* something encircling, such as a belt ~ *tr.v.* to encircle, surround
cineaste (sínni-ast) *n.* cinema enthusiast or expert, film buff; creative film-maker or film critic
cinematheque (sínni-mə-ték) *n.* repertory cinema; film library, especially one that also gives film showings
cinematography *n.* film-making as an art or technique; cinema photography — **-graphic** *adj.* — **-grapher** *n.*
cinéma-vérité (sínni-mə-vérri-tay) *n.* films or film-making using techniques associated with or suggestive of documentary films or rough-and-ready, home-made films [French, literally, cinema truth]
cinerarium (sínnə-ráir-i-əm) *formal. n., pl.* **-ia** place for keeping the ashes of a cremated body
cinereous (si-neér-i-əss) *formal. adj.* consisting of ashes; resembling ash in texture or colour
cingulum (síng-gew-ləm) *formal. n., pl.* **-la** girdle-like structure or band; ridge around the base of a tooth; stripe of colour on an animal's coat
cinnabar (sínnə-baar) *n.* reddish mineral used as the principal ore of mercury; colour of this mineral (both also "vermilion")
cinquecento (chíngkway-chéntō) *n.* 16th-century period of Italian art, literature, and culture
cinquefoil (sángk-foyl, síngk-) *n.* "five finger", plant with five-lobed compound leaves; architectural design resembling this
cipher *n. formal.* number, numeral; zero, the symbol 0; *formal.* insignificant person or thing; code used to conceal information; coded message; key to a code; design of initials, monogram ~ *v.* to write in code; *archaic.* to calculate or solve by arithmetic (all also "cypher")
circa (súr-kə) *prep.* at approximately (a date), round about (a date) (abbreviations "ca.", "c.")
circadian rhythm (sur-káydi-ən) *adj.* cycle or rhythm of body processes lasting about 24 hours [Latin *circa*, about + *dies*, a day]
Circean (sur-seé-ən) *formal. adj.* relating or referring to a dangerously bewitching woman [after *Circe*, an enchantress in Greek mythology]
circinate (súr-si-nayt) *formal. adj.* coiled; ring-shaped
circuitous (sər-kéw-itəss) *adj.* roundabout, long and indirect: *a circuitous journey/argument*
circumcision *n.* removal of the foreskin of the penis, often in a religious ceremony — **circumcise** *tr.v.*
circumference (sər-kúm-fərənss) *n.* line round the edge of a shape or plane figure, specifically a circle; distance round the edge of a shape
circumflex *n.* diacritic or accent mark shaped like a small inverted *v*, placed above vowels, as in *fête*
circumlocution *formal. n.* long-winded, roundabout language; attempt to avoid embarassment by using euphemisms or otherwise beating about the bush in what one says — **-locutory** *adj.*
circumnavigate *formal. tr.v.* to go completely round and return to the starting point, especially by sailing or flying — **-gation** *n.*
circumscribe *tr.v.* to draw or form a line or circle round; to establish the limits or boundaries of

circumscription *n.* circular inscription on a coin or medal
circumspect (súrkəm-spekt) *adj.* having or showing awareness of all possibilities, very careful or prudent
circumstantial *adj.* detailed, complete, thorough; *a circumstantial report*
circumstantial evidence *n.* evidence that is indirect, requiring an inference to be made rather than relating directly to the case: *The keyring they found is only circumstantial evidence that she was there*
circumvent *tr.v.* to get round, avoid, bypass: *circumvent an obstacle* — **-vention** *n.*
circus *n.* unroofed oval arena used in ancient times for public spectacles
cire perdue (séer pair-dŏŏ) *n.* bronze-casting technique, involving the use of a wax model to make a mould, which is then melted and drained off (also "lost wax process") [French, literally, lost wax]
cirrhosis (si-rṓ-siss) *n.*, *pl.* **-ses** chronic inflammation or fibrosis, especially of the liver, often due to alcoholism or hepatitis — **-rhotic** *adj.*
cirrus *n.* tentacle or filament, as on a barnacle; high-altitude wispy cloud — **-rate**, **-rose**, **-rous** *adj.*
citadel *n.* castle, fortress or stronghold protecting a town or city; stronghold, bastion
citation *n.* quotation or reference used as an authority, as in a dictionary or legal argument; official summons to appear in court — **cite** *tr.v.*
cithara (síthərə, kíthərə) *n.* lyre-like musical instrument used in ancient times
civics *n.* study of citizens' rights and duties
civil *adj.* relating to ordinary public life or work, as distinct from the military or religious; polite in a socially acceptable way — **-ity** *n.*
civilian *n.* person who is not a soldier or member of a military or police force — **civilian** *adj.*
civil list *n.* list of members of the royal family and their households entitled to annual maintenance payments voted by Parliament
civvies *informal. pl.n.* civilian clothes rather than military uniform (also "mufti")
cladding *n.* facing material, coating, or insulation, as on a building
clade *n.* group of plants or animals all descended from a common ancestor
cladistics *n.* biological classification using the number and type of shared features as evidence of closeness of relationship — **-distic** *adj.*
clair de lune (kláir də lŏŏn, léwn) *n.* misty-blue glaze on Chinese porcelain [French, literally, moonlight] — **clair-de-lune** *adj.*
clairvoyance (klair-vóy-ənss) *n.* seeing or knowing things by supernatural or telepathic means — **-ant** *adj.*, *n.*
clamour *n.* shouting, noisy outcry: *the clamour of children/bells* — **-morous** *adj.* — **clamour** *intr.v.*
clamper *n.* spiked plate attached to the sole of a shoe to prevent slipping on ice
clandestine (klan-déss-tin, -tīn, klándiss-) *adj.* hidden and secret, and often for an illegal purpose
clangour (cláng-gər, -ər) *n.* loud or repeated discordant metallic ringing (literary) — **-gorous** *adj.*
clapperboard *n.* hinged pair of boards used in film-making, bearing the scene and take number and clapped together in front of the camera before a scene is shot, to help to synchronise sound and picture prints
claque (klak) *n.* group of people hired, especially in former times, to applaud a play, concert, or the like
claret (klárrit) *n.* red Bordeaux wine; dark purplish red — **claret** *adj.*
clarify *tr.v.* to make clear or comprehensible, elucidate ~ *v.* to make or become pure by gentle heating: *clarified butter*
clarion *n.* trumpet of an early kind with a high pitch; *formal.* inspiring and insistent call to action: *heed the clarion call*
clarsach (klár-shəkh, kláir-) *n.* Celtic harp, smaller than a concert harp and having no pedals, originally used in medieval Scotland and Ireland and today revived as a folk instrument (also "clairshach")
clasp *n.* small metal tag, bar, or insignia on a medal ribbon, indicating either a second award or details of the award
classic *adj.* simple and long-lasting in style, rising above changing fashions ~ *n.* Derby or any other of the five major British flat horse-races
classical conditioning *n.* conditioning or altering of behaviour by associating two stimuli so that the response, originally elicited by the first, can now be elicited by the second on its own
classics *pl.n.* ancient works of literature still admired and used as a model for modern writing; specifically, in the West, the writings of ancient Greek and Roman authors — **-icist** *n.* — **-ical** *adj.*
classified *adj.* not available for general circulation for security reasons: *classified documents/information*
classis (klás-iss) *n.*, *pl.* **-ses** governing body of elders and pastors in some Reformed churches
clast *formal. n.* rock fragment
claustrophobia *n.* excessive or irrational fear of enclosed spaces; *informal.* sense of being hemmed in or trapped by people, events, or feelings — **-phobic** *adj.*, *n.*
clavate (kláyv-ayt, -it) *formal. adj.* club-shaped, thickened at one end (also "claviform")
clavichord (klávvi-kawrd) *n.* early musical keyboard instrument with a soft, harpsichord-like sound
clavicle *formal. n.* collarbone, or corresponding bone in animals
clavier *n.* (klávvi-ər) keyboard, as of a piano or harpsichord; (klávvi-ər, klə-véer) musical instrument, such as a piano or harpsichord, with a keyboard
claymore *n.* large heavy two-edged sword, used by Scottish Highlanders in former times
clearance *n.* permission for an aircraft, ship, or the like to proceed, as after a weather check, customs inspection, traffic delay, or the like; getting rid of a stock of goods, as by sale at reduced prices; clearing away of unwanted things or people
clearing *n.* open area in woods or other overgrown land; banks' exchanging and cancelling of cheques, drafts, and the like, or the settling of remaining debts
clearing-house *n.* exchange or central distribution point for banking transactions, commodities, information, or the like
cleat *n.* reinforcing attachment, as on a mast or the sole of a shoe; T-shaped bar or post for security ropes, as on a ship's deck; wedge, usually of wood, fastened to a structure for support
[1]**cleave** *v.* to split, separate, or cut through or nearly through ~ *tr.v.* to make or do by cleaving — **-vage**, **-ver** *n.*

2cleave *archaic. intr.v.* to stick fast, cling: *cleave together/to each other*
clef *n.* musical symbol indicating the pitch or register of the notes shown
cleft palate *n.* congenital cleft of the roof of the mouth, often occurring in conjunction with harelip
cleidoic egg (klī-dṓ-ik) *n.* egg with a tough shell, typical of birds, insects, and reptiles
clemency *formal. n.* mercy, leniency; mildness of weather — **clement** *adj.*
clepsydra (klépsidrə, klep-sídrə) *n.*, *pl.* **-dras** or **-drae** ancient water clock
clerestory (kleér-stəri) *n.* wall with high windows, specifically the windowed upper part of the nave of a church
cleric *n.* member of the clergy — **-al** *adj.* — **-alism** *n.*
clerihew (klérri-hew) *n.* joke rhyme in four lines about a person whose name usually provides one of the rhymes [after Edmund *Clerihew* Bentley, the 20th-century British writer who invented the style]
clerisy (klérri-si) *formal. n.* educated people, considered as a social grouping
clew *n.* ball of twine, yarn, or thread; corner of a sail
clews *pl.n.* cords supporting a hammock
cliché (kleé-shay) *n.* overused phrase, idea, or expression, such as *raining cats and dogs*
climacteric *n. formal.* menopause; *archaic.* period of sudden great change — **climacteric** *adj.*
clime *n.* climate or region (poetic)
cline *formal. n.* continuous variation in form among the members of a widespread species of plant or animal; broadly, any continuous, gradually changing line or whole, such as a spectrum of colours, continuum
clingstone *n.* peach or related fruit in which the stone tends to cling to the flesh — **clingstone** *adj.*
clinical *adj.* relating or referring to the observation and treatment of patients as if in a clinic: *clinical trials of a new drug*; rigorously scientific or objective, though perhaps uncaring or unfeeling; unadorned, austere, and merely functional: *clinical furniture/reports*
clinician *n.* medical practitioner or therapist working with patients rather than as a researcher or theoretician
clinker *n.* ash and other residue from burnt coal
clinquant (klíngkənt) *formal. adj.* glittering, as with tinsel ~ *n.* tinsel or imitation gold leaf
cliometrics (klī́-ə-méttriks) *formal. n.* use of statistics in the study of history [after *Clio*, the Muse of history in Greek mythology] — **-metric** *adj.*
clique (kleek) *n.* gang or circle of friends or colleagues that is close-knit and unwelcoming to outsiders — **-quey**, **-quish** *adj.*
cloaca (klō-áy-kə) *n.*, *pl.* **-cae** or **-cas** *formal.* sewer; single excretory and reproductive passage, as in birds and fish — **-cal** *adj.*
cloche (klosh) *n.* bell-shaped cover, usually of glass, placed over young plants for protection; woman's close-fitting bell-shaped hat, popular in the 1920s and 1930s [French, a bell]
clock *n.* small individual embroidered or woven design on the side of a sock or stocking
cloisonné (klwaá-zonnay, klóy-, -zə-náy) *n.* technique or style of enamelling different coloured panels in a decorative wire grid; enamelware made in this way [French, literally, partitioned]
cloister *n.* monastery, convent, or other place of seclusion ~ *tr.v.* to confine, shut away from the world — **-tral** *adj.*
cloisters *pl.n.* covered walk around a quadrangle
clone *n.* exact genetic copy or duplicate, or group of genetically identical organisms, such as plants produced from cuttings; *informal.* "carbon copy", lookalike — **clone** *tr.v.*
close (klōss) *n.* enclosed place, especially the grounds around a cathedral; *British.* cul-de-sac
cloud seeding *n.* rainmaking by spraying dry-ice crystals or chemicals on clouds
clout *n.* short, flat-headed nail, as used for fixing metal sheeting to wood
cloying *adj.* sweet or rich to an excessive degree — **cloy** *v.*
clunch *n.* tough clay; hard chalk formerly used in building
coach line *n.* decorative line painted along the side of a car or other vehicle
coachwork *n.* bodywork of a motor vehicle
coadjutant (kō-ájoōtənt) *formal. n.* helper or fellow worker (also "coadjutor") — **coadjutant** *adj.*
coadjutor *n.* assistant bishop; *formal.* coadjutant
coagulate (kō-ággew-layt) *v.* to clot or curdle, solidify — **-lation**, **-lator** *n.*
coalesce (kō-ə-léss) *v.* to fuse, merge, or unite — **-lescent** *adj.* — **-lescence** *n.*
coalition *n.* alliance of people or groups that have different interests but are cooperating temporarily for a shared goal
coaptation *formal. n.* joining or fitting together of parts, especially of broken bones, the edges of a wound, or the like
coarse fish *n.* freshwater fish other than salmon, trout, or related fish
coaster *n.* small mat or disc placed under a drink to protect the table top; small tray, sometimes on wheels, for a wine bottle, decanter, or the like
cob *n.* male swan. Compare PEN
cobalt bomb *n.* radiation-treatment apparatus, directing gamma rays from the radioactive metal cobalt-60; "dirty" nuclear bomb that could release large amounts of radioactive cobalt-60 into the atmosphere
coccyx (kók-siks) *n.* small bone at the base of the spinal column in humans and some apes
cochineal (kóchi-neél) *n.* bright red dye, used in cooking; cactus insect from which the dye is derived
cochleate (kóckli-ət) *formal. adj.* spiralled in shape; shaped like a snail shell
cockade (kok-áyd) *n.* feather, ribbon, or rosette worn on the hat, especially by soldiers
Cockaigne (ko-káyn) *n.* fantasy land of luxury and idleness (also "Cockayne")
cockalorum *informal. n.* self-important little man, diminutive "cock of the walk"; boasting talk, bragging (old-fashioned)
cockatrice *n.* mythical serpent hatched from a cock's egg and able to kill with a glance
cockchafer *n.* common beetle, the May bug
cockscomb *n.* jester's cap; vain, fashion-obsessed man, dandy, fop (old-fashioned)
cocotte (kə-kót) *n.* small dish for baking and serving individual portions, especially of egg dishes; mistress paid as a prostitute, especially in 19th-century France
coda *n.* final section, as of a literary or musical work, that is often an afterthought or addition

coddle *tr.v.* to cook (food, especially eggs) in water at just below boiling point
codex *n.*, *pl.* **-dices** volume of ancient manuscripts, as of the Scriptures
codicil (kṓdi-sil) *n.* addition or afterthought, as to a will — **-cillary** *adj.*
codify *tr.v.* to collect and arrange (laws, notes, principles, or the like) into a comprehensive system, such as a code of practice or of laws — **-fication** *n.*
codpiece *n.* pouch at the crotch of tight-fitting breeches or suits of armour in former times
coeliac (se͞eli-ak) *formal. adj.* relating to the abdomen
coerce (kō-érss) *formal. tr.v.* to compel, force, oblige — **-ercion** *n.* — **-ercive** *adj.*
coetaneous (kṓ-ee-táyni-əss) *formal. adj.* contemporary, coeval
coeval (kō-e͞ev'l) *formal. adj.* existing or lasting throughout the same period of time — **coeval** *n.*
coextensive *formal. adj.* lasting or extending over the same period of time or space, having the same limits
coffer *n.* container such as a chest or strongbox; ornamental sunken panel in a ceiling, dome, or the like
cofferdam *n.* watertight enclosure or compartment, as for construction on a riverbed or serving as a safety barrier between sections of a ship (also "coffer")
cogent (kṓ-jənt) *adj.* well-organised and convincing: *a cogent argument*
cogitate (kóji-tayt) *formal. intr.v.* to meditate, ponder, think deeply — **-tation** *n.* — **-tative** *adj.*
cognate *adj.* related by descent, having a common origin: *English "hound" is cognate with/to German "Hund"*; *formal.* related through the maternal line
cognisance (kóg-niz'nss) *formal. n.* process or result of conscious awareness; range or scope of conscious awareness; court's powers, duties, or knowledge in a case — **take cognisance of** to take account of
cognisant (kóg-niz'nt) *formal. adj.* conscious, informed, aware
cognition *formal. n.* mental process of turning one's perceptions into knowledge; knowledge acquired in this way
cognomen (kog-nṓmən) *n. formal.* surname; *formal.* nickname; ancient Roman's third name, originally his nickname, later his family name
cognoscenti (kón-yə-shéntee) *formal. pl.n.* those "in the know", specialists and connoisseurs (singular "cognoscente")
cohabit *intr.v.* to live together, or with another, especially in a sexual relationship without marriage
cohabitation *n.* state or process of cohabiting; political coexistence or cooperation or interests of different parties
cohere *formal. intr.v.* to stick or fit together, so as to form a whole
coherent *formal. adj.* logically organised, consistent, and comprehensible (also "cohesive") — **-herence**, **-hesion** *n.*
cohort *n.* Roman military unit of 300 to 600 men, one tenth of a legion; band of warriors, protesters, or the like; group characterised by at least one shared factor, such as similar age or background, to be compared with other groups in a statistical study
coif (kwof, koyf) *formal. tr.v.* to set, style, or arrange a woman's hair, set in a coiffure (rare)
coiffeur (kwaa-fér) *formal. n.* male hairdresser of women's hair
coiffeuse (kwa-férz) *formal. n.* female hairdresser of women's hair
coiffure (kwaa-féwr) *formal. n.* woman's hairstyle or hairdo — **-fured** *adj.*
coign of vantage (koyn) *formal. n.* ringside seat (old-fashioned)
coinage *n.* act of devising or coining a word or phrase; coined word or phrase
coir (koyr) *n.* coconut-husk fibre, as used for ropes and matting
coitus (kṓ-itəss) *formal. n.* sexual intercourse (also "coition") — **-ital** *adj.*
col *n.* mountain pass or gap
colander (kúl-in-dər, kól-) *n.* bowl-like kitchen utensil with holes in the base for rinsing or draining
cold turkey *informal. n.* immediate and total abstention from an addiction or habit, especially to cure an addiction to drugs [originally, a blunt statement, straight talking, referring to the simple, straightforward dish of cold meat; hence a straightforward, unassisted withdrawal from drugs]
colic (kóllik) *n.* abdominal spasm or pain; specifically, abdominal pain in babies, as caused by gas in the intestines [related to *colon*, a section of the large intestine]
coliseum *chiefly U.S. n.* stadium, sports arena, large entertainment hall, or the like [after the *Colosseum*, the huge amphitheatre in Rome]
collaborate *intr.v.* to work jointly or together; to cooperate in a shameful or treasonable way with an occupying power, especially in wartime [related to *labour*] — **-rator**, **-rationist** *n.* — **-ration** *n.* — **-rative** *adj.*
collage (kə-la͡azh, kóllaazh) *n.* art form or work in which many pieces of fabric, cloth, or the like are pasted onto a surface; assemblage or random collection of images, sound, or ideas
collapsar *n.* star that has collapsed in on itself, black hole
collate *tr.v.* to compare (texts) to note where they differ; to put together in an ordered fashion; to check and gather in order (pages of books for binding); to appoint (a clergyman) to a benefice — **-ation** *n.*
collateral *formal. adj.* parallel to or consistent with something, but typically secondary, subordinate, or incidental; legally corroborating or supporting: *collateral evidence*; accompanying, concomitant: *collateral circumstances*; descended from the same ancestor, though by different lines: *collateral branches of a family* ~ *n.* security, such as property, for a loan
collation *n.* description of the physical and technical features of a book; light meal [second sense, originally referring to a light meal permitted on fast days in the Roman Catholic Church, from the old custom in Benedictine monasteries of preceding such a meal with readings from a book called *Collationes Patrum*, Lives of the Fathers]
collect (kóllikt) *n.* brief formal prayer in a church service
collect call *U.S. n.* reverse-charge telephone call
collective *adj.* relating to all the members of a group jointly: *a collective name/decision*, *collective responsibility* ~ *n.* joint profit-sharing business enterprise: *a workers' collective* — **-ivise** *tr.v.* — **-ivism** *n.*
collegiate church *n.* church having more than one clergyman
collet (kóllit) *n.* circular rim securing the gemstone in

a ring or other piece of jewellery — **collet** *tr.v.*
collier *British. n.* coal miner; coal ship
colliery *British. n.* coal mine
collimator (kólli-maytər) *n.* telescope attached to a larger one, used to adjust the line of sight; instrument for producing a fine, straight beam of light, particles, or the like
collinear (ko-línni-ər) *formal. adj.* lying on the same straight line: *collinear points*
collocate *v.* — *tr. formal.* to arrange or place; to put together or with another — *intr.* to form a collocation: *Does "bath" collocate with "have" or "take"?* ~ *n.* something, such as a word, that can form a collocation with another
collocation *n.* combination or arrangement; typical joining or co-occurrence of words, especially in a single grammatical construction: *the collocation of "interested" with "in", and "depend" with "on"*
collocutor (kə-lóckew-tər) *formal. n.* person taking part in a conversation, interlocutor
colloid *n.* suspension of very fine particles in a consistent medium, as in mist or paint; gelatinous translucent substance found in decaying tissue — **colloid**, **-al** *adj.*
colloquial *adj.* conversational, informal, characteristic of casual spoken language — **-ism** *n.*
colloquium *n., pl.* **-iums** or **-ia** academic meeting or gathering, a large seminar or small conference
colloquy *formal. n.* conversation; dialogue
collusion *n.* plot or secret agreement for sinister or illegal purposes — **-lusive** *adj.* — **-lude** *intr.v.*
collyrium *formal. n., pl.* **-ums** or **-ia** eyewash
colon *n.* final section of the large intestine, extending to the rectum
Colonel Blimp *informal. n.* self-important, ultra-conservative elderly man, often an army officer or civil servant [after a character in the cartoons of David Low]
colonnade (kóllə-náyd) *n.* row of columns or trees positioned at regular intervals [related to *column*]
colophon (kóllə-fon) *n.* inscription giving publishing details at the end of an old book; *formal.* publisher's logo or emblem on the title page of a book
colophony (kə-lóffəni) *archaic. n.* rosin, resin [after *Colophon*, a city in ancient Greece where it was made]
coloratura (kóllərə-téwr-ə) *n.* music, especially singing, characterised by ornamental trills and runs; singer or voice specialising in such a style, specifically a soprano [related to *colour*]
colossus *n., pl.* **-si** or **-suses** huge statue; extremely large or important person or thing — **colossal** *adj.*
colostomy (kə-lóstəmi) *n.* surgical formation of an artificial channel from the colon to the abdomen, in order to allow excretion to take place when normal excretion is impossible
colostrum (kə-lóstrəm) *n.* breast secretion of serum and white blood cells, lasting a few days after childbirth before the flow of milk begins
colourable *adj.* pretended, feigned: *a colourable emotion*; seemingly true, likely, plausible: *a colourable excuse* (both old-fashioned)
colubrine (kóllew-brīn) *formal. adj.* snake-like or snaky
columbarium *n., pl.* **-ia** dovecote; vault with niches in the wall for funeral urns; niche in such a vault; hole or niche in a wall for supporting a beam
columbine (kólləm-bīn) *formal. adj.* relating to a dove or pigeon
comatose (kṓmə-tōz) *formal. adj.* in a coma; unconscious, dead to the world
combative *formal. adj.* aggressive, eager to quarrel or fight
combust *v.* to set alight or burn up, usually in a sudden or wholesale way — **-ion** *n.* — **-ive**, **-ible** *adj.*
comedo (kómmi-dō) *formal. n., pl.* **-dos** or **-dones** blackhead
comestible *formal. adj.* edible or eatable — **-s** *pl.n.*
comfit (kúm-fit) *n.* sugar-coated sweet
comforter *n. chiefly British.* woollen scarf; *U.S.* baby's dummy; *U.S.* quilted bedspread, often resembling a duvet
comity (kómməti) *formal. n.* courtesy, politeness, civility
comity of nations *formal. n.* nations recognising one another and courteously accepting each other's differences in laws and customs, or the policy of such acceptance
commandeer *tr.v.* to seize or confiscate, especially under wartime regulations; to pressgang, force into military service
comme il faut (kóm eel fṓ) *formal. adj.* proper, correct, in keeping with accepted standards [French, literally, as it should be]
commemorate *tr.v.* to show honour to the memory of [related to *memory*] — **-rative** *adj.* — **-ration** *n.*
commencement *U.S. n.* graduation in many American secondary and higher educational institutions; ceremonies and activities associated with graduation day
commend *formal. tr.v.* to put into the care of someone, hand over to someone for looking after, consign
commendation *n.* award of honour, as for bravery
commensalism *n.* relationship of close association between organisms of different types, with or without benefit to those involved, but without harm to any. Compare SYMBIOSIS — **-mensal** *adj.*
commensurate *adj.* measurable by the same units or standard and equal or appropriate: *a salary commensurate with one's responsibilities* [related to *measure*]
commination *formal. n.* threat of punishment or revenge; recital of God's judgments on sinners, read in the Church of England on Ash Wednesday
comminute *formal. tr.v.* to crush to powder, pulverise, triturate; to break (a bone) into many pieces; to divide (land or property) into several small units — **-ution** *n*
commiserate *intr.v.* to feel sorry for or sympathise with someone, condole — **-ation** *n.*
commissar (kómmi-saar) *n.* Communist Party official in charge of political education and party loyalty; Communist or authoritarian official (derogatory); formerly, head of a USSR commissariat
commissariat (kómmi-sáiri-ət) *n.* army department in charge of food and other supplies; formerly, major government department of the USSR
commissary *n. formal.* representative, agent, deputy, proxy; bishop's official representative; *chiefly U.S.* shop restricted to military personnel, diplomats, or the like; *chiefly U.S.* works canteen, especially for a film, television, or radio studio
commission *tr.v.* to equip and check (a ship) for active service; to order or authorise officially ~ *n.* percentage or fee paid to a salesman or agent for successfully completed services; doing or committing,

perpetration: *commission of a crime*
commissionaire *British. n.* uniformed doorman at a hotel, theatre, or the like
committal *n.* official act of committing someone to prison, mental hospital, burial, or the like
commode *n.* chest of drawers or low cabinet, typically on short legs and richly ornamented; bedside table, movable stand, or the like containing a washbowl; chair containing a concealed chamber pot
commodious *formal. adj.* spacious or roomy
commodity *n.* something intended to be sold at a profit; raw material, such as a product of farming or mining, treated as a commodity
commodore *n.* boat club's chairman; senior captain of a shipping line, merchant fleet, or naval squadron
commonage *n.* right to pasture animals on common land
common denominator *n.* common feature or belief characterising a group
commoner *British. n.* student who is not on a scholarship; person who is not of the nobility
commonplace book *n.* notebook containing quotations, comments, poems, and the like that strike one as worth recording
communal *adj.* shared, common, relating to all the members of a group; relating to communities or ethnic groups, inter-community: *communal strife*
[1]**commune** (kə-méwn) *intr.v.* to relate to closely or communicate intimately with someone or something: *commune with nature*
[2]**commune** (kóm-ewn) *n.* local political division in some European countries; medieval town, largely self-governing; small community of like-minded people who share the ownership of all their property: *a hippie commune* — **-munal** *adj.*
communicable *adj.* contagious or infectious
communicative *adj.* talkative, articulate
communiqué (kə-méwni-kay) *n.* official announcement made to the press and the public [French, literally, communicated]
community *n.* sharedness, commonness: *a community of interests*
commutative *adj.* independent of the order of terms, as an operation such as multiplication is
commute *v.* — *tr. formal.* to exchange or substitute; *formal.* to transmute: *commute base metal into gold*; to reduce, lessen, or lighten: *commute a penalty/a debt* — *intr.* to travel as a commuter
commuter *n.* someone who shuttles to and fro between the same two places, especially between home and work
compact (kóm-pakt), *n.* agreement or contract, covenant
companion *n.* knight of lowest rank in some orders of knighthood; fainter of the two units of a double star; frame of windows on a ship's upper deck, affording light to the cabins or deck below
companionway *n.* stairway from a ship's upper deck to the cabins or deck below
company *n.* medieval guild: *the Worshipful Company of Apothecaries*
compartmentalise *tr.v.* to separate or divide into different classes, categories, sections, or the like, pigeon-hole
compass *n. formal.* boundary, circumference: *within the compass of one's interests*; range of a musical instrument or singer's voice, register
compassion *n.* kind-hearted pity, deep sympathy — **-ate** *adj.*
compass rose *n.* circle, often decorated, printed on a map to show the points of the compass
compatible *adj.* capable of living, surviving, co-existing, working, or functioning appropriately together or with another — **-ibility** *n.*
compatriot (kəm-páttri-ət) *n.* fellow countryman or countrywoman
compeer *n.* equal, peer; companion, associate (both old-fashioned)
compelling *adj.* powerful, persuasive, inducing belief or support: *a compelling argument*
compendium *n.* collection; concise summary — **-pendious** *adj.*
compensate *v.* to make up for, counterbalance, or offset; to reimburse or recompense — **-sation** *n.* — **-satory** *adj.*
compere (kóm-pair) *British. n.* master of ceremonies [Old French, literally, godfather] — **compere** *v.*
competence *formal. n.* income or revenue sufficient to live on (also *old-fashioned* "competency"); concept of the innate human capacity to pick up a language — **-tent** *adj.*
compile *tr.v.* to gather material for use in preparing a text: *compile data/a dictionary/an anthology* — **-pilation** *n.* — **-piler** *n.*
complacent *adj.* pleased or self-satisfied, to the point of feeling that nothing more needs to be done — **-cency** *n.*
complaint *n.* ailment; poem expressing grief, usually over lost or unrequited love, lament (old-fashioned)
complaisant (kəm-pláyz'nt) *formal. adj.* eager to please, especially by not resisting the wishes or behaviour of others — **-sance** *n.*
complement *n.* complete amount, number, or the like: *the full complement*; angle related to another so that the sum of the two is 90°; person or thing that completes or enhances another [related to *complete*] — **-ary** *adj.* — **complement** *tr.v.*
compliant *adj.* complying; cooperative, going along with what others want — **-pliance** *n.*
complicity *n.* state or act of being an accomplice in something illegal or bad
compline (kóm-plin) *n.* late evening prayer, as the last of the seven canonical hours [related to *complete*]
comply *intr.v.* to obey or act in accordance with the orders or desires of another
compo *n.* mixture, as of plaster or mortar [short for *composition*]
component *n.* part of a whole, constituent
comport *formal. v.* — **comport oneself** to behave or conduct oneself as specified — **comport with** *archaic.* to correspond to, agree or harmonise with
compose *formal. tr.v.* to settle: *compose differences*; to calm down, make quiet or tranquil — **-posed** *adj.*
composite *adj.* made up of several parts, compound ~ *n.* daisy, dandelion, or similar plant having compound flower heads; material, such as reinforced concrete, made of two or more distinct materials
composition *n.* artistic or harmonious arrangement of parts, as in a painting; *formal.* settlement by which creditors accept partial payment from a debtor about to go bankrupt; typesetting
compositor *n.* typesetter
compos mentis *adj.* sane, of sound mind (often humorous)

composure *formal. n.* self-possession; calm appearance and behaviour
compote (kóm-pōt) *n.* fruit stewed in a syrup and served hot or cold
[1]**compound** *tr.v.* (kəm-pównd) to mix (medicinal drugs) according to a prescription; to make worse or harder to resolve: *compound a difficulty*; to compose: *compound a dispute*; to adjust (a debt) and settle for a smaller amount than the claim; to agree not to prosecute (an offence) in return for a payment or other favour: *compound a felony*; to form (a linguistic compound) ~ *n.* (kóm-pownd) word, such as *flowerbed* or *Sino-Japanese* formed from two or more other words or combining forms
[2]**compound** (kóm-pownd) *n.* enclosed area for living, working, or confining people: *prison compound*
comprehend *formal. tr.v.* to understand, grasp; to take in, include, embrace — **-hensive** *adj* — **-hensible** *adj.*
compress *n.* pad, as of medicated gauze, used to stop bleeding or to reduce pain or inflammation
comprise *tr.v.* to consist of, be composed of: *The league comprises 23 teams*
compromise *tr.v.* to make liable or expose to discredit, suspicion, or scandal — **-ising** *adj.*
compte rendu (KONT-RON-do͞o) *formal. n., pl.* **-s -s** review or short criticism, especially of a book; official announcement or report [French, literally, account rendered]
comptroller (kən-trṓlər, *chiefly U.S.* kəmp-) *n.* financial controller or auditor, as in certain areas of government — **-ship** *n.*
compunction *formal. n.* remorse or regret: *felt no compunction about betraying us* — **-punctious** *adj.*
compurgation *n.* acquittal in a medieval trial on the basis that the defendant must be innocent if a number of people were prepared to swear solemnly to that effect [related to *purge*]
con *archaic. tr.v.* to study or examine closely; to learn off by heart, memorise
conation *formal. n.* mental process or faculty of desire or volition, as distinguished technically from *cognition*, "knowing", and *affection*, "feeling" — **-ative** *adj.* — **-atus** *n.*
con brio (kon brée-ō) *adv.* with vigour and brilliance; in a lively way (used as a musical direction) [Italian, literally, with vigour]
concatenation *formal. n.* linked series or collection, grouping, coming together: *a concatenation of circumstances* — **concatenate** *v., adj.*
concave *adj.* curved inwards: *a concave mirror*. Compare CONVEX — **-cavity** *n.*
concede *v.* — *tr.* to admit, acknowledge as true or fair; to yield or allow: *concede a point/goal* — *intr.* to admit defeat, as in an election
conceit *formal. n.* metaphor or image of a witty, far-fetched kind
concentric *adj.* having the same centre: *concentric circles/gearwheels*. Compare ECCENTRIC — **-tricity** *n.*
conception *n.* initial formulation of an idea or plan; starting of pregnancy through fertilisation of an egg cell by a sperm
conceptual *adj.* referring or relating to ways of thinking or framing ideas — **-ise** *v.*
concerted effort *n.* joint effort
concertina *v.* to fold up or collapse in on itself
concession *n.* grant by a government, as of property or exploration rights; right to market a particular product in a given area — **-ary** *adj.* — **-aire** *n.*
concessive *adj.* expressing a yielding or granting of a point or a possibility, as adverbs such as *although* do — **concessive** *n.*
concha (kóng-kə) *formal. n., pl.* **-chae** shell-like body part or organ, such as the outer ear; half-dome over a church apse
concierge (kón-si-airzh) *n.* doorkeeper and caretaker of a building, especially a block of flats [French]
conciliar *adj.* relating to a council, especially a church council
conciliation *n.* mediation to secure settlement of an argument or conflict, such as an industrial dispute — **conciliate** *tr.v.* — **-ative** *adj.*
conciliatory (kən-sílli-ətri) *adj.* pacifying, appeasing, eager to make up or be reconciled — **conciliate** *formal. tr.v.*
conclave *n.* meeting of cardinals to elect the Pope
concoct *informal. tr.v.* to prepare in an inventive or off-hand way: *concoct a meal/plan*; to make up, fabricate: *concoct an alibi*
concomitant *formal. adj.* accompanying: *fatigue and all its concomitant symptoms* — **-itance** *n.*
concord *formal. n.* harmony, agreement, or peaceful relations — **-ant** *adj.* — **-ance** *n.*
concordance *n.* list or index of all the word-forms in a text or corpus, often giving a context for each instance: *a concordance of/to the works of Shakespeare*
concordat (kon-kór-dat) *n.* formal agreement, especially an agreement between a government and the Roman Catholic Church to regulate church-state relations
concourse *n. formal.* multitude; *formal.* coming together, confluence; large open space within a public building, such as an airport or station, where crowds of people can move about
concretion *formal. n* gallstone, kidney stone, or similar solid mass formed in a body cavity or tissue, calculus — **-tionary** *adj.*
concubine (kóng-kew-bīn) *n.* secondary wife in a polygamous marriage; woman who lives with a man as if she were his wife, and is supported by him but not married to him — **-inage** *n.*
concupiscence (kən-kéwpiss'nss) *formal. n.* strong desire, especially sexual desire — **-scent** *adj.*
concur *formal. intr.v.* to agree, have the same opinion; to occur at the same time, coincide — **-currence** *n.* — **-current** *adj.*
condescend *intr.v.* to do or behave as if doing something beneath one's dignity, deign: *condescended to greet us*; to behave in a patronising way — **-ing** *adj.* — **-cension** *n.*
condign (kən-dī́n) *formal. adj.* deserved and appropriate: *condign punishment*
condiment *n.* a seasoning for food, such as pepper or vinegar
conditioned response *n.* response to a stimulus that does not directly cause it but has come to be associated with it, as through training (also "conditioned reflex")
conditioning *n.* behaviour modification, training, or learning process through adjustment of stimuli
condolence (kən-dṓ-lənss) *n.* expression of sympathy for someone in distress or in mourning — **condole** *v.*
condominium *n.* joint ownership or government: *the Anglo-French condominium of the New Hebrides*;

block of flats each of which is owned freehold rather than leasehold, especially in North America; flat in such a block (also *informal* "condo")
condone *tr.v.* to pardon or overlook (an offence), often in a weak or irresponsible way — **-donation** *n.*
conducive *adj.* helping, promoting, contributing to or favourable to a given result: *hardly conducive to our morale* — **conduce** *formal. intr.v.*
conduit (kón-dit, kún) *n.* channel, such as a pipe or tube, through which something is conveyed [related to *conduct*]
confabulation *informal. n.* discussion or negotiation; informal conversation, chat — **confabulate** *intr.v.*
confederacy *n.* union, alliance; conspiracy, unlawful plotting, collusion — **confederate** *n.*
confederation *n.* joint organisation, typically allowing more independence to its component units or members than a federation
confer *formal. tr.v.* to give, grant, or bestow
confidant (kón-fi-dánt, -dóɴ) *n.* person to whom one confides private or secret information (feminine form "confidante")
configuration *formal. n.* arrangement of parts, pattern — **-ative** *adj.*
confinement *n.* bed-rest for a woman just before or during childbirth (old-fashioned)
conflagration *formal. n.* large, fierce, destructive fire
conflate *tr.v.* to fuse or blend (two versions of a text) into a single whole — **-tion** *n.*
confluence *n.* flowing together, as of two rivers, or the point at which they meet; *formal.* crowd or large gathering — **-fluent** *adj.*
confute *formal. tr.v.* to prove wrong
congenial *adj.* appealingly familiar, sympathetic, agreeable: *a congenial companion/atmosphere*
congenital *adj.* existing at birth though not hereditary: *congenital heart defects*; *informal.* habitual, natural, regular: a *congenital liar*
congeries (kon-jeér-eez) *formal. n.* random collection or heap of things
conglomeration *n.* massing or clustering; collection or heap of varied items — **-merate** *v.*
congruent (kóng-groo-ənt) *adj.* having identical dimensions, coinciding exactly *congruent triangles* — **-ence**, **-uity** *n.*
conifer (kónni-fər, kōni-) *n.* tree of a cone-bearing, usually evergreen type, such as a pine or fir — **-ous** *adj.*
conjecture (kən-jékchər) *n.* guess, opinion based on incomplete evidence, speculation ~ *v.* to make a conjecture or suggest as a conjecture — **-tural** *adj.*
conjugal (kón-jŏog'l) *formal. adj.* relating to marriage, connubial
conjugal rights *pl.n.* legal right to sexual intercourse with one's husband or wife
conjugation *n.* in grammar, change of the form of a verb to indicate tense, plural, person, or the like; complete class of words having the same set of such forms. Compare DECLENSION — **conjugate** *v.*
conjunction *n. formal.* coinciding, simultaneous occurrence; form or word, such as *and*, *but*, or *or*, that links words or larger linguistic units
conjunctivitis *n.* inflammation of the mucous membranes covering the outer surface of the eye and inner surface of the eyelid
conjure (kún-jər) *v.* — *tr.* to summon or command (a devil or spirit) by incantation or spell; (kən-jŏor) *formal.* to beg or entreat, typically by an oath — *intr.* to summon a devil or spirit by conjuring; to perform magic tricks, typically using sleight of hand — **conjure up** to bring into being, as if by magic; to evoke in the imagination or memory, bring to the mind's eye — **-jurer**, **-juror**, **-juration** *n.*
conning tower *n.* superstructure on a submarine, serving as an observation post and entrance; armoured control centre on a warship
connive *intr.v.* to ignore or pretend ignorance of a wrongful act or crime, and thereby encourage it: *connived at the fraud by failing to report it*; to cooperate secretly, be secretly sympathetic or indulgent; to conspire or intrigue: *conniving with our enemies* — **-vance** *n.*
connoisseur (kónnə-sér) *n.* expert in wine, art, or the like, or a person of refined tastes — **-ship** *n.*
connotation *n.* suggested or implied meaning and associations of a word or thing, rather than its literal meaning. Compare DENOTATION — **connote** *tr.v.* — **-tative** *adj.*
connubial *formal. adj.* relating to marriage or the married state, conjugal
conquistador (kon-kwístə-dawr, -keéstə-dór) *n., pl.* **-dors** or **-dores** Spanish conqueror of the New World in the 16th century
consanguineous (kón-sang-gwínni-əss) *formal. adj.* related by blood — **-guinity** *n.*
conscript *n.* (kón-skript) person who is enrolled for compulsory military service ~ *tr.v.* (kən-scrípt) to enlist or enrol for compulsory military service; to force into service — **-scription** *n.*
consecrate *formal. tr.v.* to make or declare sacred: *consecrate a cathedral*; to prepare or convert (bread and wine) for Communion; to ordain (a priest) into the position of bishop; to devote (one's life or time) to a specific cause or purpose; to honour, make venerable: *a custom consecrated by tradition* [related to *sacred*] — **-cration** *n.*
consecutive (kən-séckew-tiv) *adj.* following in uninterrupted sequence
consensus *n.* general or widespread agreement, majority opinion [related to *consent*]
consequent *adj.* following as a natural result or logical conclusion ~ *n. formal.* something consequent to something else; main clause, stating the conclusion or consequence, in a conditional sentence or proposition (also "apodosis"). Compare ANTECEDENT, PROTASIS; second term in ratio. Compare ANTECEDENT
conservatoire (kən-sérvə-twaar, -saírvə-) *n.* institution or school for specialised training in music or other fine art (also *U.S.* "conservatory")
consign (kən-sígn) *formal. tr.v.* to put into the care of someone, hand over, as for safekeeping or transporting; to give or commit irrevocably or permanently: *consigned her letters to the flames*; to send to prison — **-ment** *n.*
consistency *n.* firmness, texture, as of a pudding; logical coherence or compatibility; agreement or harmony among parts, claims, or the like, congruence — **-tent** *adj.*
consistory (kən-sístəri) *n.* church court or governing body, or a meeting of it; meeting of cardinals with the Pope — **-torial** *adj.*
consolation *n.* comforting of someone in distress; person or thing providing such comforting — **-console** *tr.v.*

console (kón-sōl) *n.* ornamental bracket on a wall supporting a shelf, sculpture, or the like; desk containing the keyboards, pedals, and stops of an organ, or the controls of an electronic system such as a computer; cabinet for a television set, hi-fi system, or the like [French, from *consolateur*, a carved figure serving as a bracket supporting a cornice, from Latin *consolator*, a consoler, hence a support]
consolidate *v.* to solidify, form into a tight mass; to strengthen, make or become strong or secure; to unite, merge. combine [related to *solid*] — **-ation** *n.*
consols (kón-solz, kən-sólz) *pl.n.* interest-bearing government bonds that can be cashed on call rather than redeemed on a fixed date (also "bank annuities") [short for *consolidated annuities*]
consommé (kən-sómmay) *n.* clear soup typically made from meat or fish stock [French, literally, concentrated]
consonance *n.* harmony or accord; similarity of sounds — **-nant** *adj.*
consort *n.* (kón-sawrt) husband or wife, especially of a monarch; *formal.* partner or companion; group of singers or musicians, especially one performing early music; ship escorting another ~ *formal. intr.v.* (kən-sórt) to keep company or associate, especially with undesirable companions
consortium *n., pl.* **-ums** or **-tia** association of businesses for the joint financing or undertaking of a very large project; *formal.* legal right to the help, company, and affection of one's marriage partner
conspectus *formal. n.* general survey of a subject; summary, brief synopsis
conspicuous *adj.* easily noticed, glaring, obvious, sometimes by deliberately drawing attention
conspiratorial *adj.* suggesting a plot or shared secret: *a conspiratorial wink* — **-ator**, **-acy** *n.*
constable *n.* keeper of a royal castle or fortification; military leader of a royal household in the Middle Ages [from Latin, *comes*, a companion or count + *stabulum*, a stable]
consternation *n.* sudden dismay, or confusion
constituency *n.* group of voters entitled to elect a representative, especially to a legislative body; area in which such a group is resident; supporters of a person or organisation whose wishes have to be taken into account
constituent *n.* part that makes up a whole, ingredient; person represented by an agent, MP, or the like ~ *adj.* having the authority to frame or alter a constitution: *a constituent assembly*
constitutional *n.* walk taken for the good of one's health, especially regularly (old-fashioned)
constrain *tr.v.* to force, compel, oblige; to restrict the movements of, restrain or detain
constraint *n.* embarrassed, forced, or inhibited feeling, manner, or situation — **constrained** *adj.*
constriction *n.* feeling of tightness or pressure, as in the chest — **constrict** *tr.v.*
construct (kón-strukt) *n.* logical element or invented idea forming part of a theory
construction *n. formal.* interpretation or explanation of a statement or action: *putting the best possible construction on his conduct*; meaningful group of words forming part of a sentence; geometric figure, line, or angle, as used in solving a problem or proving a theorem; a sculpture having an abstract design
construe *formal. tr.v.* to translate, usually aloud, as a classroom exercise; to analyse the grammatical structure of (a sentence); to deduce or interpret the meaning of
consubstantial *formal. adj.* identical in essence or substance, as the three persons of the Trinity are sometimes considered to be — **-tiation** *n.*
consul *n.* official representing a government in a foreign city; in ancient Rome, either of the two chief ministers elected annually — **-ate** *n.*
consummate *tr.v.* (kón-sə-mayt, -sew-) to complete (a marriage) by an act of sexual intercourse; *formal.* to fulfil, perfect, or achieve (an ambition, deal, or the like) ~ *adj.* (kən-súmmət, kónsəmət) extremely skilful or accomplished: *a consummate hypocrite*; perfect, of highest quality: *consummate skill* — **-tion** *n.*
consumption *n.* wasting disease, especially tuberculosis of the lungs (old-fashioned) — **-tive** *adj.*
contagious (kən-táyjəss) *adj.* transmitted by physical contact: *a contagious disease*; tending to produce a similar reaction in others: *contagious mirth* [related to *contact*] — **contagion** *n.*
containment *n.* preventing of enemy forces or nations from extending their territory or influence
contaminated *adj.* radioactive to a dangerous degree as a result of exposure to radioactivity — **contaminate** *tr.v.* — **-tion** *n.*
contemplative *adj.* devoted to religious meditation: *a contemplative order of monks* — **contemplative** *n.*
contemporaneous *adj.* simultaneous, happening or existing at the same time — **-neity** *n.*
contemporary (kən-témp-ərəri) *adj.* simultaneous, contemporaneous; occurring or existing at the present time; following the most recent styles, ideas, tastes, or the like ~ *n.* person of the same age as another
contentious *adj.* tending to or causing controversy; quarrelsome — **-tion** *n.* — **contend** *v.*
contiguous (kən-tíggew-əss) *adj.* sharing a border or boundary, adjacent; coming immediately before or after in time — **-guity** *n.*
continence *n.* self-control or restraint, specifically sexual restraint or control over one's urination and defecation — **-nent** *adj.*
contingency *n.* possible event, especially one to make provision for: *a fund for various contingencies*
contingent *adj.* likely to happen but not certain; conditional, dependent: *success contingent on good management*; occurring randomly or by chance; in philosophy, existing or true or false by reason of chance or facts in the real world rather than by logical necessity ~ *n.* supply or quota, as of troops; group within a larger body or gathering: *the Yorkshire contingent at the conference*
continuity *n.* film or broadcast script with details to ensure consistency from scene to scene; radio or television announcements or linking items designed to avoid breaks between programmes
continuum (kən-tínnew-əm) *n., pl.* **-ums** or **-tinua** unbroken series of variations with no obvious divisions; continuous and gradually changing line or whole, such as a spectrum
contorted *adj.* twisted or strained out of the normal shape: *a face contorted with pain* — **contort** *v.*
contortionist *n.* entertainer or acrobat who twists his limbs and body into abnormal positions
contour (kón-toor) *n.* outline or shape, as of a stretch of land; line on a map that joins points of the same

altitude (in this sense, also "contour line") ~ *tr.v.* to represent in outline; to build so as to follow the outline of the land — **contour** *adj.*

contraband *n.* goods banned from import and export; illegal traffic in such goods; smuggled goods; slave who escaped or was freed during the American Civil War — **contraband** *adj.*

contract (kən-trákt) *tr.v.* to become liable for (a debt); to catch (a disease); to shorten (a word or words) by combining or leaving out some of the sounds or letters — **-ion** *n.*

contraction *n.* shortening or tensing of a muscle or organ, either voluntarily or, as in childbirth, involuntarily

contraflow *n.* system or sectioned-off area allowing traffic to move in both directions along one carriageway of a motorway, as during road repairs

contrail *n.* visible trail of condensed water vapour from the engine exhaust of an aircraft flying at high altitude (also "vapour trail") [*con*densation + *trail*]

contralto *n.*, *pl.* **-tos** or **-ti** in music, the lowest female singing voice; singer with such a voice

contravene *tr.v.* to break (a law or regulation) — **-vention** *n.*

contretemps (kón-trə-toN, kóN-) *formal. n., pl.* **contretemps** awkward or embarrassing situation or occurrence; argument or confrontation

contrition *n.* repentance for sin; specifically, contrition inspired by love of God rather than fear of retribution — **contrite** *adj.*

contrive *tr.v.* to bring about, make, or manage; especially, to contrive by scheming or ingenuity: *somehow contrived to get them to agree* — **-vance** *n.*

contrived *adj.* artificial, strained, unspontaneous

control *n.* standard of comparison in a statistical analysis or scientific experiment; checkpoint in a race such as a car rally where progress is confirmed and assessed; spirit that supposedly acts through a spiritualist medium

contumacious *formal. adj.* wilfully disobedient; rebellious — **-macy** *n.*

contumely (kón-tewm-li) *formal. n.* contemptuous behaviour, especially when arising from a sense of one's own superiority — **-melious** *adj.*

contusion *formal. n.* bruise — **contuse** *tr.v.*

conundrum (kə-nún-drəm) *n.* puzzle or problem that seems insoluble

conurbation *n.* extensive urban area formed by the fusion of several towns or cities [related to *urban*]

convalescence *n.* gradual return to health after an illness, especially by resting — **-scent** *adj., n.* — **convalesce** *intr.v.*

convection *n.* transfer of heat through the movement of air or other fluid between areas of different temperatures and densities — **convect** *tr.v.*

convene *formal. v.* to come or bring together as a meeting or assembly — **-vention** *n.*

conventional *adj.* referring to non-nuclear warfare or weapons

conventionalised *adj.* abstract, stylised, as a painting or design might be

converge *intr.v.* to come together or towards another (opposite "diverge") — **-gent** *adj.* — **-gence** *n.*

conversant *adj.* — **conversant with** familiar with, knowledgeable about

convertible *n.* car whose roof can be folded back or removed

convex *adj.* curved outwards: *a convex mirror*. Compare CONCAVE — **-ity** *n.*

conveyance *formal. n.* land vehicle, especially a public vehicle such as a bus

conveyancing *chiefly British. n.* transferring of the ownership of a house, flat, land, or other property

conviction *n.* quality of being convincing; belief or opinion that is firmly held

convivial *adj.* sociable, jolly, or festive: *a convivial atmosphere/companion*

convocation *n.* church conference, or assembly of churchmen; *chiefly British.* university's graduates collectively, or an assembly or conference of them

convoke *formal. tr.v.* to summon or call together as a formal assembly

convoluted *adj.* tortuously complicated

convolution *n.* complication, tangle, confusing factor

convoy *tr.v.* to escort or accompany, especially for protection ~ *n.* ships travelling in a group, especially when protected by an escort of warships; broadly, any vehicles travelling together in a group

convulsion *n.* muscular contraction, involuntary and often violent and painful; profound social disturbance often leading to upheaval — **convulse** *v.* — **-sive** *adj.*

cony *archaic. n.* rabbit or similar animal

coomb (ko͞om) *British. n.* small valley, especially a short steep valley running down to the coast

cooper *n.* barrel-maker (also "hooper")

co-opt *tr.v.* to elect or appoint (a new member) to a group by a decision of the existing group — **-tion**, **-tation** *n.*

coordinate *adj.* equal in rank, status, or the like ~ *tr.v.* to ensure the appropriate state or functioning of (a complex whole) by regulating the arrangement or interaction of component parts — **-nation** *n.*

coordinates *pl.n.* two or more numbers or measurements that pinpoint a location, as on a map or graph; clothes or accessories designed to be worn together

cope *n.* long flowing cloak worn by churchmen

coper *British. n.* horse-dealer (old-fashioned).

coping *n.* slanting upper part of a wall or roof

coppice *chiefly British. n.* small stretch of trees or bush (also "copse")

copra *n.* dried coconut, the source of coconut oil

coprophagous (kop-róffə-gəss) *formal. adj.* dung-eating, as some insects are — **-phagy** *n.*

copse *n.* thicket of shrubs or small trees

copula (kóppew-lə) *n., pl.* **-las** or **-lae** linking verb, such as *be* or *seem,* that introduces a predicate complement referring to its own subject

coquette (ko-két) *n.* vain and flirtatious woman — **coquetry** *n.* — **coquettish** *adj.* — **coquet** *intr.v.*

coracle *n.* small, roundish boat, made by stretching animals skins or tarpaulin over a frame of branches (also "currach")

coral *n.* lobster's or crab's roe, pink when cooked

corbeil (kórb'l) *n.* carved architectural ornament in the form of a basket of fruit

corbel *n.* bracket, usually of stone or brick, supporting a cornice, arch, or the like [Old French, *corp*, a raven: early corbels were wedge-shaped, like ravens' beaks] — **-belling** *n.*

cordate *formal. adj.* heart-shaped: *cordate leaves/shells*

cordial *adj.* hearty, warm and friendly: *a cordial welcome*

cordillera (kórdil-yáir-ə) *n.* mountain range or system of parallel mountain ranges [Spanish; related to *cord*]
cordite *n.* smokeless explosive powder, as used in bullets and shells
cordon *n.* defensive line, as of ships or police — **cordon off** to seal or enclose (an area), as with a line of troops
cordon bleu (kór-doN blúr, blő) *n., pl.* **-s -s** excellent quality or class of cuisine [French, literally, blue ribbon] — **cordon bleu** *adj.*
cordon sanitaire (kór-doN sánni-táir) *n., pl.* **-s -s** boundary area, such as a buffer zone to prevent contact between nations [French, literally, quarantine line]
co-respondent *n.* person cited in a divorce case as having committed adultery with the partner being divorced
Corinthian *adj.* referring or relating to the most ornate style or order of classical Greek architecture. Compare DORIC, IONIC; *formal.* elegantly ornamented, ornate
corkage *n.* fee or price charged at a restaurant for opening and serving wine brought in by the customer
corm *n.* bulb-like underground stem, as of the gladiolus
corn *tr.v.* to preserve in brine or with salt
cornea *n.* transparent outer coating of the eye — **-neal** *adj.*
corneous *formal. adj.* horn-like or horny
cornet *n.* cone-shaped starched headdress worn by women in the late Middle Ages; large white headdress worn by some nuns
cornice *n.* moulding running along the top of a building or wall; snow ledge overhanging a cliff or mountain top
corniche (kór-neesh, -nish) *n.* coast road, often built into the side of a cliff
cornucopia (kór-new-kṓpi-ə) *n.* horn of plenty, depicted as a curly goat's horn overflowing with fruit and vegetables, symbolising abundance, in paintings, sculptures, and the like [from Latin *cornu*, a horn + *copia*, plenty]
corollary (kə-róllәri) *n.* additional proposition following from the proof of another proposition; deduction, obvious conclusion or inference; result, natural consequence
corona (kə-rṓnə) *n., pl.* **-nae** or **-nas** ring of faint light, as around the Moon when viewed through a haze; top of the head, or other crown-shaped body part; crown-shaped part of the daffodil or similar flower; large circular chandelier, hanging from a church ceiling; long tapering cigar with blunt ends — **-nal** *adj.*
coronary (kórrən-ri) *adj.* relating to the heart ~ *informal. n.* heart attack; coronary thrombosis
coroner (kórrə-nər) *n.* public official, usually a doctor, conducting inquests with a jury into deaths that may not have resulted from natural causes
coronet *n.* small crown, as worn by princes or noblemen as a sign of rank
corporation *n.* body of people acting as a group, as for business purposes; city authorities: *the Corporation of the City of London; informal.* paunch, potbelly (old-fashioned) — **-rate** *adj.*
corporeal (kawr-páwri-əl) *formal. adj.* bodily, physical, having a material rather than spiritual nature
corps (kor) *n., pl.* **corps** military unit for ground combat; branch of department of the armed forces
corpse *British. informal. v.* — *intr.* in acting, to laugh by mistake on stage — *tr.* to cause (an actor) to corpse
corpulent (kórpәw-lənt) *formal. adj.* having a fat body, between portly and stout — **-lence** *n.*
corpus *n., pl.* **-pora** or **-puses** main part of something, such as a body organ; principal or capital sum of money, value of an estate, or the like, as distinct from the interest or income; body of texts, especially for study or research
corpuscle *n.* tiny particle, such as a droplet or electron; blood cell: *white corpuscle* — **corpuscular** *adj.*
corral (kə-ráal) *n.* enclosure for cattle or horses; defensive circle of covered wagons — **corral** *tr.v.*
correlate *v.* to arrange or be arranged in a corresponding or parallel relationship — **-lative** *adj.* — **-lation** *n.*
corrida (ko-réedə, -réethə) *n., pl.* **-das** bullfight [Spanish]
corrigenda *pl.n.* errors and corrections in a book, as listed on an inserted sheet of paper (singular "corrigendum") [related to *correct*]
corroborate *tr.v.* to confirm or back up (an opinion or statement), as with additional evidence — **-tive** *adj.* — **-tion** *n.*
corrode *v.* to destroy or be destroyed gradually, as by chemical action — **-osive** *adj., n.* — **-osion** *n.*
corrugated *adj.* folded into a series of long parallel ridges: *corrugated roofs*.
corsage (kawr-sáazh) *n.* flower or small posy of flowers, as pinned to a woman's dress; waist or bodice of a dress
corsair (kór-sair) *n.* pirate, especially along the Barbary Coast of North Africa in former times; pirate ship
cortège (kawr-tézh) *n.* procession, especially at a funeral
cortex *n., pl.* **-tices** or **-texes** layer on or near the outside, as of a root or stem, or the brain or kidney — **-tical** *adj.*
corundum (kə-rúndəm) *n.* abrasive mineral, aluminium oxide, occurring as rubies, sapphires, and the like, and used in sandpaper
coruscate (kórrə-skayt) *formal. intr.v.* to sparkle and flash, as a gemstone or someone's wit might
corvine *formal. adj.* relating to crows, ravens, or related birds
coryza (kə-rī́zə) *formal. n.* head cold
cos *n.* lettuce with a long head and crisp leaves (also *chiefly U.S.* "romaine") [after *Cos*, the Greek island where it originated]
cosmic *adj.* relating to the whole universe, especially as distinct from the Earth; occurring or originating in outer space: *cosmic dust*; appearing to be in touch with supernatural forces, or having extraordinary psychic powers
cosmology *n.* branch of astronomy concerned with the origin and structure of the universe
cosmonaut *n.* Soviet astronaut
cosmopolitan *adj.* international or multi-cultural: *a cosmopolitan city*; common to much of the world, widely distributed: *cosmopolitan flowers* ~ *n.* person who has lived or travelled in many countries and is free of national prejudices
cosmos *n.* universe or world regarded as an orderly system; system that is orderly, harmonious, and self-sufficient
costermonger *n.* stallholder, seller of food or goods

from a barrow or market stall [originally *costard monger*, literally, apple-seller]
costive *formal. adj.* constipated or causing constipation
coterie (kōtəri) *n.* artistic, literary, or cultural circle, clique
coterminous *adj.* sharing a boundary, or having the same boundaries; same or coinciding in range, size, meaning, or the like, co-extensive
cotyledon (kótti-léed'n) *n.* simple food-storing leaf in some sprouting seeds
couchette (ko͞o-shét) *n.* bed or folding bunk in a train carriage [related to *couch*]
coulisse (ko͞o-léess) *n.* grooved beam of wood in which a sliding frame or panel is fitted; flat piece of stage scenery in the wings of a theatre
countenance *formal. n.* features or expression of the face; self-control, composure: *keep one's countenance*; moral support, sanction ~ *tr.v.* to support, approve, or encourage; to tolerate or allow: *I cannot countenance such behaviour*
counterfeit *tr.v.* to copy or forge for the purpose of fraud — **counterfeit** *n., adj.*
counterfoil *n.* cheque stub or similar detachable record of a transaction, as on a postal order
counterinsurgency *n.* military action taken by the authorities against rebels or terrorist groups
countermand *tr.v.* to cancel or reverse (an order or instruction) — **countermand** *n.*
counterpane *n.* coverlet for a bed, bedspread
counterpoint *n.* interweaving or harmonising of elements, such as simultaneous melodies; use of a contrasting but related element as a foil, as for emphasis — **contrapuntal** *adj.*
countersign *tr.v.* to sign (a document that already bears a signature) so as to ratify or authenticate it — **-signature** *n.*
countersunk screw *n.* screw that is sunk so deep that its head lies flush with or below the surface
countervail *formal. tr.v.* to balance or oppose with equal force; to offset, make up for
coup (ko͞o) *n., pl.* **coups** brilliantly successful act or decision, masterstroke; coup d'état
coup de grâce (ko͞o də gráass) *n., pl.* **coups de grâce** final touch, finishing act; killing of a person or animal already seriously wounded, as in a battle or a bullfight [French, literally, stroke of mercy]
coup d'état (ko͞o day-táa) *n., pl.* **coups d'état** revolution in the form of a sudden seizing of power (also "coup") [French, literally, stroke of state]
coupé (ko͞o-pay) *n.* two-doored sports car; train compartment at the end of a railway carriage, having seats along one side only [French, literally, cut off]
courgette (koor-zhét) *n.* small vegetable marrow (also "zucchini")
courier (ko͝ori-ər) *n.* messenger, as for a parcel delivery service, diplomatic service, or spy; tour organiser accompanying a holiday party
coursing *n.* sport of hunting game, such as hares, with hounds relying on sight rather than scent
courtesan (kórti-zán) *n.* prostitute, typically with wealthy clients, or the mistress of a high-ranking man (old-fashioned)
court-martial *n., pl.* **courts-martial** military court or trial — **court-martial** *tr.v.*
couscous (ko͞oss-ko͞oss) *n.* North African dish of cracked wheat steamed and served with various spicy meats or vegetables
couture (ko͞o-téwr) *n.* high-quality, fashionable dress-making or designing for women — **-turier, -turière** *n.*
couvade (ko͞ováad) *n.* custom in some cultures in which the husband too is put to bed while his wife is in labour or giving birth [French, literally, hatching of eggs]
couvert (ko͞o-vaír) *formal. n.* table setting in a restaurant, or the cover charge for it [French, literally, cover]
coven (kúvv'n) *n.* witches' gathering, or a group of 13 witches
covenant *n.* contract, binding agreement, treaty, or a clause in it; formal agreement or pledge, as to pay a specified sum each year to a charity; God's promises to humankind, as revealed in the bible; promise of support and vow of faith by members of a church — **covenant** *v.*
covert (kúvvərt) *adj.* secret, hidden, not obvious (opposite "overt") ~ *n.* disguise, shelter, or hiding place; especially, woodland, thicket, or undergrowth sheltering game
cowl *n.* monk's hood or hooded cloak or habit; hood-like cover on a chimney to control ventilation
cowrie *n.* shell of various sea molluscs, used as money in some cultures
coxcomb *n.* jester's cap; *formal.* foolish fop
cozen (kúzz'n) *formal. tr.v.* to cheat, trick, or defraud — **-er, -age** *n.*
crampons *pl.n.* grappling irons, as for raising heavy stones; metal spikes fastened to a shoe or boot, as for mountaineering or walking across ice
cranium *formal. n., pl.* **-ums** or **-nia** skull — **-nial** *adj.*
crapulent *formal. adj.* drunken, or having a hangover as a result of drunkenness; broadly, overeating or drinking — **-lence** *n.*
craquelure (kráckə-loor) *n.* network of small cracks in the paint or varnish of an old painting
cravat (krə-vát) *n.* scarf-like item of clothing, worn instead of a tie by men [French, *Cravate*, a Croatian: Croatian mercenaries in France used to wear such neckbands]
craven *formal. adj.* despicably cowardly
craw *n.* stomach of an animal, or crop of a bird
crèche (kresh, kraysh) *n.* tableau, as at Christmas, of Jesus' Nativity; day nursery for babies or very young children, especially to enable parents to go to work
credence *formal. n.* belief, faith, or trust: *gave no credence to their testimony*
credentials *pl. n.* pieces of evidence testifying to someone's qualifications or rights
credo *n., pl.* **-dos** personal creed or statement of beliefs or principles
credulous *adj.* believing something too easily, without sufficient evidence, gullible — **-ulity** *n.*
creel *n.* basket or trap for fish, lobsters, or the like, made of wickerwork
crème de la crème (krém, kráym) *n., pl.n.* best of the best, very best [French, literally, cream of the cream]
crenellations *pl.n.* indented battlements, as on a castle; square notches or indentations, as on a moulding — **crenellated** *adj.*
creole *n.* pidgin or hybrid language that has developed into a mother tongue — **creole** *adj.* — **creolise** *v.*
creosote *n.* tar-based liquid applied to wood as a preservative
crepe (krayp, krep) *n.* thin pancake, often folded

round a filling; mourning band of black material, worn on the sleeve or hat (also "crêpe")

crepitate *formal. intr.v.* to creak, rattle, or crackle, as diseased lungs or broken bones might — **-itation, -itus** *n.*

crepuscular (kri-púskewlər) *formal. adj.* relating to or resembling twilight, dim; active at twilight or before dawn: *crepuscular songbirds*

crescendo (kri-shén-dō) *n., pl.* **-dos** or **-di** gradual increase in the volume of a noise or passage of music: *rose in a crescendo* (opposite "diminuendo"); climax: *rose to a crescendo, reached a crescendo* [Italian, literally, increasing] — **crescendo** *adv., adj., intr.v.*

cretin (kréttin) *n.* person suffering from dwarfish and mental retardation owing to a hormone deficiency from birth; *informal.* fool, idiot [from Swiss French *crestin*, a Christian, hence a human being, referring to the humanity of such people despite their handicaps] — **-ism** *n.*

crevasse (kri-váss) *n.* deep chasm or crevice in a glacier

cri de coeur (krée də kér, kőr) *n., pl.* **cris de coeur** earnest appeal or passionate protest [French, literally, cry from the heart]

criterion (krī-téer-i-ən) *n., pl.* **-teria** standard, test, or rule on which a judgment or decision is based

critique (kri-téek) *n.* review or discussion incorporating criticism — **critique** *tr.v.*

Croesus (krée-səss) *n.* extremely rich person [after *Croesus*, a rich king in ancient Greece]

croft *n.* field or small enclosed pasture; smallholding, especially in Scotland — **-er** *n.*

croissant (krwáa-SON) *n.* sweet, crescent-shaped, puffy bread roll [French, literally, crescent]

cromlech (króm-lek, -lekh) *n.* prehistoric monument or burial site of standing stones

crosier (krṓ-zhər) *n.* staff of a bishop or abbot; hooked or coiled tip of a young fern frond

crossfire *n.* conflict or argument in which outsiders, often against their will, become involved

cross-ply *n.* tyre with fabric cords running diagonally to stiffen the sidewalls. Compare RADIAL-PLY — **cross-ply** *adj.*

crotch *n.* angle or fork formed by branches, steps, trouser legs, or the like; human genital area (also *chiefly British* "crutch")

crotchet *n.* hook or small hook-like device; odd whimsical notion; musical note with the time value of half a minim

croup (kroop) *n.* rump or rear end of a horse or other domestic animal

croupier (kroopi-ay, -ər) *n.* dealer or bet-taker at a gambling table

crouton (kroo-ton, -TON) *n.* small toasted or fried square of bread, served in soups or salads [related to *crust*]

crown *n.* small notched winding knob on an old-fashioned watch

crucible *n.* vessel in which metals or other substances are melted or made very hot; container in a furnace that receives the molten metal; test or trial of a painful or intense kind

cruciform *formal. adj.* cross-shaped (also "cruciate")

cruet *n.* salt cellar, pepper shaker, mustard pot, or the like, or a set of such containers; bottle or small dispenser for oil or vinegar as used at table; small container for wine or water at Communion

crural *formal. adj.* relating to the leg, shank, or thigh

crustacean *n.* shellfish such as a lobster or shrimp, or related animal having a segmented body, jointed limbs, and horny shell. Compare MOLLUSC [related to *crust*]

cryonics (krī-ónniks) *n., pl.n.* investigation or application of techniques of deep-freezing of a corpse, with the intention of reviving it in the future

cryosurgery *n.* surgery in which unwanted tissue is destroyed by sudden freezing

crypt *n.* burial vault or similar underground chamber, especially in a church; *formal.* body cavity, recess, sac, follicle, or the like

cryptanalysis *n.* deciphering of codes, secret writings, and the like. Compare CRYPTOGRAPHY

cryptic *adj.* hard to understand, especially because of insufficient clues to the real meaning

cryptography *n.* study of codes; technique, process, or system of putting messages into code. Compare CRYPTANALYSIS

crystalline *adj.* transparent, very clear

crystallise *v.* to give or get a definite shape or form: *The plan finally crystallised*

cubit *n.* ancient measure of length, based on the length of the arm from fingertip to elbow

cucking stool *n.* chair to which offenders were tied as a punishment in former times, either for ducking in a pond or for exposure to public abuse

cuckold *n.* husband of an adulteress, man with an unfaithful wife, ~ *tr.v.* to commit adultery with the wife of (a man) — **-ry, -er** *n.* [related to *cuckoo*, probably referring to the cuckoo's practice of leaving its eggs in other birds' nests]

cuirass (kwi-ráss) *n.* breastplate or item of armour protecting both the chest and back; shell, protective plate, or similar hard covering, as on some animals or ships

cuisine (kwi-zéen) *n.* preparation of food, or the food prepared, typically of a specified style

cul-de-sac (kúl-də-sak) *n., pl.* **-sacs** or **culs-de-sac** dead end, blind alley; body cavity, tube, or pouch blocked at one end [French, literally, bottom of the bag]

culinary (kúlli-nəry) *formal. adj.* relating to cooking or the kitchen

cull *tr.v* to pick out or select (the best or worst specimens); to gather or collect (something, such as flowers); to reduce (an animal population) by selective killing [related to *collect*] — **cull** *n.*

cullis *n.* gutter on a roof

culmination *n.* highest or final point, climax — **culminate** *v.*

culottes *pl.n.* short, full woman's trousers cut to resemble a skirt

culpable *formal. adj.* blameworthy, responsible for and punishable for wrongdoing — **-ability** *n.*

culpable homicide *n.* killing of a person that is unlawful though not necessarily murderous, as in cases of negligence

culprit *n.* person guilty of a fault or crime

culvert *n.* sewer or drain, as under a road; channel or pipe, as for rain water or an electric cable

cumbersome *adj.* awkward to carry or handle, unwieldy; clumsy and inelegant: *a cumbersome sentence*

cum laude (kŏom lówday) *adv., adj.* with honour, with distinction; referring or relating to an undergraduate degree, especially in the U.S., of relatively high quality [New Latin, literally, with praise]

cummerbund *n.* belt-like sash, wide and often pleated, worn with a dinner jacket
cumulative (kéw-mew-lətiv) *adj.* accumulating by a series of steps or additions
cumulus (kéw-mew-ləss) *n.*, *pl.* **-muli** large, white, bulky cloud with a flat base and rounded top
cuneiform (kéwni-fawrm) *formal. adj.* wedge-shaped (also "cuneal", "cuneate") ~ *n.* writing system using wedge-shaped characters; specifically, ancient Mesopotamian cuneiform as inscribed by a stylus on clay tablets
cupidity *formal. n.* greed, powerful desire, especially for money
cupola (kéwpələ) *n.* dome-shaped roof or ceiling, or dome on a roof or larger dome; dome or dome-like object, such as a rock outcrop or the metal cap protecting a warship's gun
cupping *n.* former medical technique of attaching a glass cup to the skin by means of a partial vacuum, in order to draw blood to the surface
cupreous (kéwpri-əss) *formal. adj.* relating to, containing, or resembling copper [related to *copper*]
cupule *n.* cup-like base of an acorn, or other cup-shaped part or structure
curator (kewr-áytər) *n.* director or keeper of a museum or public art gallery, or of a department of it; *chiefly U.S.* director or keeper of a library, zoo, or other place of public exhibition, or of a section of it
curette *n.* surgical scraping or scooping instrument, as for removing dead tissue from the uterus — **curettage** *n.*
curfew *n.* official regulation requiring people to go home or be indoors by a certain hour of night, or the times of or bell signalling this restriction [Old French *cuevrefeu*, literally, a covering of the fire]
curlicue *n.* twist or curl, such as a flourish made with a pen under a signature
curmudgeon (kər-mújən) *formal. n.* miserly or sour-tempered person — **-ly** *adj.*
curriculum *n.*, *pl.* **-la** or **-lums** course of study; broadly, programme of events, schedule of activities
curriculum vitae *n.*, *pl.* **curricula vitae** summary of one's education, career, and other personal details, as for a job application (abbreviation "c.v.") [Latin, literally, the course of life]
curry *tr.v.* to groom (a horse) by combing; to soften, dye, or prepare (tanned leather) — **currier**, **-iery** *n.*
cursive *adj.* referring or relating to joined-up handwriting by contrast with block printing — **cursive** *n.*
cursor *n.* movable point of light indicating the position on a VDU, as on a word processor; sliding transparent indicator on a slide rule
cursory *formal. adj.* hasty and brief: *a cursory glance*
curtail (kur-táyl) *formal. tr.v.* to reduce or cut short — **-ment** *n.*
cusp *n.* point or pointed end; point of intersection of two arcs of a geometrical curve; either pointed end of a crescent moon; point of transition between one astrological "house" and another; projection on the surface of a tooth; fold or flap of a heart valve; point of transition: *on the cusp between classicism and romanticism* — **-ate** *adj.*
cuspidor *chiefly U.S. n.* spittoon
custody *n.* right of guardianship or supervision: *joint custody of their child after the divorce*; right or power to arrest or to keep in detention or under guard; state of being under guard, under arrest, or in detention; *held in custody* — **-todial** *adj.* — **-todian** *n.*
cutaneous *formal. adj.* relating to the skin, especially by contrast with deeper layers
cutaway *n.* diagram or model, as of an engine or building, with part of the wall or casing omitted or cut away to reveal the interior — **cutaway** *adj.*
cuticle *n.* hardened dead skin at the base of a fingernail or toenail; protective layer covering the epidermis of a plant; shell-like protective horny covering on some insects, shellfish, and the like
cutlass *n.* short, curved sword, as formerly used by sailors or pirates
cutler *archaic. n.* knife seller, maker, or repairer
cuttlebone *n.* dry internal shell of a squid-like shellfish, used in polishes and as a mineral supplement for cage birds' diet
cwm (kōōm, kōōm) *n.* high-lying steep-walled glacial hollow in Wales, often containing a lake (also "cirque" in France, "corrie" in Scotland)
cyan (sī́-ən) *n.* greenish-blue — **cyan** *adj.*
cybernetics (sī́bər-néttiks) *n.* study of information flow and control in electronic, mechanical, and biological systems [akin to *govern*] — **cybernetic** *adj.* — **cybernetician** *n.*
cycad (sī́-kad) *n.* palm-like primitive seed-bearing plant, having fern-like leaves and seed cones — **-aceous** *adj.*
cyclamate (sícklə-mayt) *n.* chemical substance of which some types are used as artificial sweeteners or sugar substitutes. Compare SACCHARINE
cyclorama *n.* picture, as of a battle scene, right round the inside wall of a circular room; curving curtain, wall, or scenery at the back and sides of a theatre stage
cyclone *n.* low-pressure area with violent rotating winds in the tropics
cyclostyle *n.* pen-like instrument with a small toothed wheel to perforate wax stencils for use on an office duplicator; duplicator or simple office copying machine, using specially perforated wax stencils — **cyclostyle** *tr.v.*
cygnet (síg-nit) *n.* young swan
cynosure (sī́nə-sewer) *formal. n.* focus of attention or admiration
Cyrillic (si-ríllik) *n.* alphabet used for Russian, Bulgarian, Serbian, and some other Slavonic languages [after St *Cyril*, a 9th-century missionary who allegedly devised the alphabet]
cyst (sist) *n.* blister-like sac or cavity in the body, either normal or abnormal
cystolith *formal. n.* gallstone or bladderstone
cytology (sī-tólləji) *n.* cell biology — **-gist** *n.* — **-logical** *adj.*

D

dab *informal. n.* fingerprint
dacha (dáchə) *n.* villa or country house in Russia
dacoit (də-kóyt) *n.* robber in an armed band in the hills of India and Burma — **dacoity** *n.*
dactylogram *chiefly U.S. n.* fingerprint — **-graphy** *n.*
dactylology *chiefly U.S. n.* communication by the use of fingers and hands, as by deaf or dumb people
Dadaism *n.* art movement, after the First World War, mocking traditional art (also "Dada") [French *dada*, a hobbyhorse, from baby talk] — **-ist** *n., adj.*
daemon (dée-mən) *n.* demigod; guiding spirit, guardian genius
daguerrotype (də-gérrə-tīp) *n.* early photograph made on a metal plate; process used in making such photographs [after the 19th-century French inventor Louis *Daguerre*]
dais (dáy-iss, dayss) *n.* speakers' platform, as in a lecture hall
daisy wheel *n.* small wheel-like device supporting the printing characters on a modern typewriter or word-processor printer
dale *n.* wide open valley, typically among low hills: *the Yorkshire dales* — **dalesman** *n.*
dalliance *archaic. n.* loveplay, flirtation — dally *intr.v.*
daltonism *n.* colour blindness, especially the kind in which red and green are confused [after John *Dalton*, an 18th-19th-century British chemist, who was himself colour blind]
damascene (dámmə-seen) *tr.v.* to etch or inlay (metal) with wavy decorative patterns (also "damask") [Old French *damasquiner*, to decorate in the style of Damascus steel] — **damascene** *adj.*
damask (dámməsk) *n.* richly patterned fabric [originally from the city of *Damascus*]
Damon and Pythias *formal. pl.n.* friends extremely devoted to each other [after two loyal friends in Greek legend]
damsel *archaic. n.* young woman, girl, maiden
damson *n.* plum of a small, blue-black variety [Latin *prunum Damascenum*, a plum of Damascus]
dandle *tr.v.* to bounce (a child) affectionately up and down, especially on one's knees
daphnia *n.* tiny crustacean used as food for aquarium fish
dapper *adj.* neat in dress or appearance, spruce
dapple *adj.* spotted, as a horse's coat might be, mottled (also "dappled") ~ *n.* dapple horse
Darby and Joan *pl.n.* devoted elderly married couple [after a couple in an 18th-century English ballad]
dariole (dárri-ōl) *n.* cup-shaped mould for jellies, small cakes, or the like
dart *n.* tapered tuck made in dressmaking
dastardly *adj.* cowardly, base — **dastard** *n.*
data base *n.* computer's information store
dauphin (dáwfin, dṓ-faɴ) *n.* French king's eldest son, crown prince of France
davenport (dávv'n-port) *n. chiefly British.* desk with side drawers and a small hinged writing surface; *U.S.* sofa or large sofabed [after Mr *Davenport*, the supposed original maker of the desk]
davit (dávvit) *n.* crane on a ship, typically paired with another, for hoisting lifeboats, cargo, or the like
dead letter *n.* law or rule no longer enforced though still officially valid
dead man's handle *n.* safety switch or lever, as on a train, that causes mechanical shutdown if the operator becomes unable to keep it in position
dead reckoning *n.* calculation of a rough-and-ready kind, based largely on guesswork; in navigation, technique of estimating one's position by one's speed and direction rather than by radio or observing the stars
dearth (derth) *n.* lack, scarcity, shortage
débâcle (day-báak'l) *n.* disastrous collapse or defeat (also "debacle")
debar *tr.v.* to exclude or ban; to prevent or hinder
debauch *tr.v.* to seduce or corrupt (especially someone young and innocent) — **debauch**, **-ee**, **-ery** *n.*
debenture (di-bénchər) *n.* bond, typically long-term and unsecured, issued by a company or government organisation; I.O.U., certificate, or voucher acknowledging a debt; customs certificate authorising repayment of duty [Latin *debentur*, literally, they are owed]
debilitated *adj.* abnormally weak and tired, run-down — **debility** *n.* — **-itate** *tr.v.*
debit *n.* debt as recorded in the left-hand side of an account or bookkeeping ledger [related to *debt*]
debonair (débbə-náir) *adj.* carefree, nonchalant [Old French *de bon aire*, literally, of good temper]
debouch *formal or archaic. intr.v.* to come or flow out, emerge, as from a valley into a plain
debriefing *n.* taking of information from a spy, astronaut, diplomat, or the like on his return from a mission — **debrief** *tr.v.*
débris (dáy-bree, dé) *n.* broken fragments, scattered remains, rubble; accumulated rock fragments (also "debris")
debunk *informal. tr.v.* to expose the falseness or pretentiousness of, by means of ridicule
debut (débbew) *n.* first public appearance, as of an actor
debutante *n.* young upper-class lady undergoing a formal presentation to society, as at a ball
decadent (dékkə-dənt) *adj.* declining or decaying, as in morals or culture [related to *decay*] — **-ence** *n.*
Decalogue *n.* — **the Decalogue** the Ten Commandments
decamp *formal. intr.v.* to run away, depart quickly or unexpectedly
decanal (di-káyn'l) *adj.* relating to a dean
decant *tr.v.* to pour (a liquid) from one container to another, as when separating wine from its sediment — **-er** *n.*

decapitate *tr.v.* to behead
decapod *n.* lobster, crab, prawn, or related ten-legged crustacean; squid, cuttlefish, or related ten-tentacled mollusc
decathlon (di-káthlon) *n.* athletic contest involving ten different track-and-field events for each competitor
deceased *formal. adj.* dead — **the deceased** dead person or people
decibel (déssi-bel) *n.* unit for measuring the loudness of a sound
deciduous *adj.* falling off or shed from time to time: *deciduous leaves/antlers*; shedding all the leaves each year: *deciduous trees*
decimate *tr.v.* to kill or destroy a large proportion of; in ancient Rome, to kill every tenth man in (a mutinous or cowardly military unit)
decipher *tr.v.* to interpret (a code), decode (also "decrypt"); to read and interpret: *simply cannot decipher his handwriting*
deckle edge *n.* rough edge of a sheet of paper, especially handmade paper (also "deckled edge")
declaim *v.* to speak or recite rhetorically or pompously — **declamation** *n.* — **declamatory** *adj.*
déclassé (day-klássay) *adj.* reduced in social status or class
declension *n.* in grammar, change of the form of a noun, pronoun, or adjective to indicate gender, number, or case; complete class of words having the same set of such forms. Compare CONJUGATION; *formal.* downward slope, declivity; *formal.* deterioration — **decline** *v.*, *n.*
declination *formal. n.* downward slope, declivity; deterioration, decline; angle of a star, planet, or the like, measured in degrees from the celestial equator
declivity *formal. n.* downward slope or sloping tendency — **-vitous** *adj.*
decoction *formal. n.* essence produced by boiling down a liquid — **decoct** *tr.v.*
décolletage (dáy-kol-ta̋azh) *n.* low, revealing neckline [French; related to *collar*] — **décolleté** *adj.*
decongestant *adj.* relieving congestion, especially in the nose — **decongestant** *n.*
décor (dáy-kawr) *n.* decorations and furniture of a place, or the style of decoration; stage setting or scenery in a theatre (also "decor")
decorum (di-káwr-əm) *n.* good manners, conventional behaviour, propriety — **-rous** *adj.*
découpage (dáy-kōō-páazh) *n.* technique of decorating a surface with paper cutouts.
decoy *n.* trap, enclosure, or the like, into which birds or game can be lured; bird or other animal, live or artificial, used to lure others into shooting range or captivity; distraction of an enemy, ~ *tr.v.* to lure by means of a decoy
decree absolute *n.* final court ruling granting a divorce
decree nisi (ní-sī) *n.* preliminary and provisional court ruling, especially in a divorce case [Latin *nisi*, unless]
decrepit (di-kréppit) *adj.* weak through age, illness, overuse, or the like; worn out or broken down through age or overuse, dilapidated
decretal (di-kre̋et'l) *n.* papal letter or edict on a point of church law or doctrine
decry *tr.v.* to speak out against, belittle or criticise
decubitus ulcer (di-kéwbitəss) *formal. n.* bedsore
deed poll *n.* legal document involving one person only, especially to change his name
de facto *adv.* really, actually, in fact. Compare DE JURE [Latin, literally, from the fact] — **de facto** *adj.*
defalcation *formal. n.* misuse or theft of funds or property entrusted to one, embezzlement — **-cate** *intr.v.*
defamation *n.* slander or libel, damage to a person's good name — **defame** *tr.v.*
default *n.* failure to carry out a task or duty, especially to pay a debt or to appear in court — **in default of** through the lack or in the absence of — **default** *v.*
defect (di-fékt) *intr.v.* to desert one's country, political party, or the like, especially to join its opponent
defenestration *formal. n.* throwing of a thing or person out of the window
defer *v.* — *tr.* to put off until later, postpone — *intr.* to submit to the wishes or opinion of someone else: *I defer to your judgment* — **-ence** *n.* — **-ential** *adj.*
deferent (déffərənt) *adj.* carrying something down or away from a centre, as some nerves and blood vessels do (also "efferent")
defibrillate *tr.v.* to restore normal beating and rhythm of (a heart), by administering an electric shock to the patient's chest — **-lation, -lator** *n.*
deficient *adj.* incomplete or insufficient — **-ency** *n.*
deficit *n.* amount by which an actual amount, as of money, is lower than the expected or required amount, shortfall
defilade (déffi-láyd) *formal. n.* fortification against enemy fire or observation — **defilade** *tr.v.*
[1]**defile** *tr.v.* to damage or tarnish (someone's reputation, name, or the like); to make (something such as a church) unfit for religious or ceremonial use, desecrate
[2]**defile** *n.* narrow pass or gorge; single file, as of troops marching ~ *v.* to march or cause (troops) to march in single file
definiendum *n.*, *pl.* **-enda** word or phrase to be given a dictionary definition
definiens *n.*, *pl.* **-entes** dictionary definition of a word or phrase
definite article *n.* the word *the* or equivalent form in other languages, identifying specifically its noun or phrase. Compare INDEFINITE ARTICLE
definition *n.* sharpness or clarity of outline, as of a photograph or television image
definitive *adj.* reliable and authoritative, as a history or biography might be, impossible to improve or supersede
deflect *v.* to turn or cause to turn aside or swerve away — **-tion** *n.*
deflection, *n.* light beam's change of direction as it passes from one medium to another
deflower *tr.v.* to end the virginity of by having intercourse with — **defloration** *n.*
defoliate *tr.v.* to strip (a plant) of leaves, as by a chemical spray in a war zone — **-foliant** *adj.*, *n.*
defray *formal. tr.v.* to pay (costs, expenses)
defrock *tr.v.* to strip (a clergyman) of status and rights in the church, unfrock
defunct *adj.* dead, invalid, or inoperative
deglutition *formal. n.* act of swallowing
degust *formal. tr.v.* to taste with care or relish, savour — **-ation** *n.*
dehisce (di-híss) *intr.v.* to split or burst open along a seam, as a pod or fruit might, to release seeds or pollen — **-hiscent** *adj.*
dehydrated *adj.* dry, deprived of water or moisture — **-ate** *v.*

deictic (dī́k-tik) *adj.* in grammar, referring to a word such as *this* or *those* that points out directly what is referred to; in logic, proving something directly by means of argument — **deictic** *n.*

deify (dáy-i-fī, dée-) *tr.v.* to raise to the status of a god, or honour as a god; to treat with awe, idealise — **-fication** *n.*

deign (dayn) *intr.v.* to agree haughtily or condescend: *barely deigned to reply* [related to *dignity*]

deipnosophist (dīp-nóssəfist) *formal. n.* person who excels in conversations at the dinner table

deity (dée-əti, dáy-) *n.* god or goddess

déjà vu (dáy-zhaa vóo) *n.* feeling of having undergone an experience before that one is now having for the first time [French, literally, already seen]

de jure (dáy-jóor-i) *adv.* by right, legally. Compare DE FACTO [Latin, literally, according to the law] — **de jure** *adj.*

delectable *formal. adj.* enjoyable, delightful, or delicious

delegate *n.* agent or representative, as at a conference ~ *v.* — *tr.* to assign (work, duties, or powers); to appoint as one's agent or representative — *intr.* to assign parts of one's work to other people — **-tion** *n.*

delete *tr.v.* to cross out, erase, or cancel (words, computer data, tape recordings, or the like) — **-tion** *n.*

deleterious (délli-téeri-əss) *formal. adj.* harmful, injurious

delicatessen *n.* shop specialising in fine ready-prepared foods

delineate *formal. tr.v.* to sketch, outline; to portray in words — **-tion** *n.*

delinquency *n.* crime or offence of a minor kind, misdeed; failure or neglect in the performing of one's duty, negligence — **-quent** *adj.*

deliquesce (délli-kwéss) *intr.v.* to dissolve gradually, as some chemicals do, by absorbing water vapour from the air; to divide into several branches, as a plant stem might [related to *liquid*] — **-ence** *n.* — **-ent** *adj.*

delirious *adj.* mentally confused or agitated, as during a high fever; uncontrollably agitated, frenzied — **delirium** *n.*

delirium tremens *n.* severe mental disorder, as in some alcoholics, involving tremors and hallucinations (also *informal* "D.T.'s") [New Latin, literally, trembling madness]

dell *n.* small, usually wooded hollow or valley (chiefly poetic)

delphic *adj.* ambiguous or obscure, as though spoken by an oracle: *delphic utterances* [after the oracle of Apollo at *Delphi* in Greece, famous in myth for its obscure predictions]

delta *n.* area, typically triangular, at the branching mouth of a river [after *delta*, the fourth letter of the Greek alphabet, shaped like a triangle when a capital letter]

deluge *formal. n.* flood — **deluge** *tr.v.*

delusion *n.* mistaken or misleading opinion — **delude** *tr.v.*

demagogue (démmə-gog) *n.* political leader or agitator rallying support by crude emotional speeches — **-gogy, -goguery** *n.*

demarcation *n.* setting of boundaries between areas, tasks, ideas, or the like, especially between the kinds of work done by various trade-union members

démarche (dáy-maarsh) *n.* initiative or step, as in diplomatic matters; protest or statement to the public authorities

demeanour *n.* outward behaviour and appearance (also *U.S.* "demeanor")

demented *adj.* insane; wild or distracted, as through grief [related to *mental*]

demesne (di-máyn, -méen) *n.* large landed property or estate; in law, use and possession of one's own land

demigod *n.* god of minor rank, or mythological being who is half mortal and half divine

demimondaine (démmi-món-dayn) *n.* mistress or sexually promiscuous woman consigned to the fringes of respectable society, as in the 19th century

demimonde *n.* demimondaines as a group; any social or artistic group considered not quite respectable [French, literally, half-world]

demi-pension (démmi-póNss-yoN) *n.* half board, as at a hotel

demise *formal. n.* death, ending, or failure ~ *tr.v.* in law, to transfer (an estate, sovereignty, or the like)

demitasse (démmi-tass) *n.* small coffee cup, or the strong black coffee drunk from it [French, literally, half-cup]

demiurge *n.* creative force in Platonic or Gnostic philosophy, often personified and considered the creator of the material world

demivierge (démmi-vi-aírzh) *n.* sexually active woman who nevertheless remains a virgin [French, literally, half-virgin]

demobilise *tr.v.* to discharge (troops) from military service (also *British informal* "demob")

demography *n.* science of population statistics, such as distribution and birth rate — **-pher** *n.* — **-graphic** *adj.*

demolish *tr.v.* to wreck or tear down (a building); to do away with, destroy, or crush: *demolished their arguments* — **-lition** *n.*

demonstrative *adj.* expressing emotions or one's feelings openly; in grammar, referring to the words *this*, *that*, *these*, and *those* or equivalent specifying forms in other languages: *demonstrative pronouns* — **demonstrative** *n.*

demoralise *tr.v.* to deprive of confidence, dishearten

demotic *adj.* commonly used, popular, as the ordinary form of a language is: *demotic Greek*; relating to the masses of the common people, unsophisticated ~ *n.* Egyptian hieroglyphics of a simplified form

demur (di-múr) *formal. intr.v.* to object, take exception — **demur**, **-murral** *n.*

demure *adj.* reserved, modest; mock-modest, coy

demurrer (di-múrrər) *n.* in law, objection, especially to the relevance of an argument raised in court

denizen (dénniz'n) *n. formal.* inhabitant or resident of a place or region; foreigner having certain citizenship rights in his country of residence; animal or plant established in a region although not indigenous to it

denomination *n.* name or act of naming, designation; grade or unit in a classification system, such as a coin of a specified value; religious grouping with a distinct identity

denominative *n.* word derived from a noun, such as the verb *to jackknife* — **denominative** *adj.*

denominator *n.* number below the line in a fraction, divisor. Compare NUMERATOR

denotation *n.* sign or term that refers or names directly, designation; explicit meaning or reference of a word or thing, rather than its implied meaning or associations. Compare CONNOTATION — **denote** *tr.v.* — **-tative** *adj.*

dénouement (day-nóo-MON) *n.* resolution or clarification, as of the plot of a play or story [French, literally, an untying]

denounce *tr.v.* to criticise vigorously, condemn; to accuse or inform against — **denunciation** *n.*

dentifrice (dénti-friss) *formal. n.* toothpaste or tooth powder

dentition *n.* process of teething; arrangement, number, and type of teeth in a given animal

deontic *adj.* in logic, relating to rights, duties, and similar ethical concepts

deontology *n.* philosophy of moral duty or responsibility

depict *tr.v.* to represent in words or images, as by painting or describing, portray — **-tion** *n.*

depilate (déppi-layt) *tr.v.* to remove the hair from — **-latory** *n., adj.* — **-tion** *n.*

deplete *tr.v.* to reduce severely, exhaust; to empty or drain, wholly or partly — **-tion** *n.*

deplore *tr.v.* to disapprove of or criticise strongly, censure, *formal.* to be sorry about, lament

deploy *tr.v.* to station (troops or weapons) in an area, or make them ready for action; broadly, to position ready for action — **-ment** *n.*

deport *tr.v.* to conduct (oneself) in a specified way, behave; to expel from a country, banish — **-ation** *n.*

deportment *n.* posture and bearing; *chiefly U.S.* behaviour, conduct

depose *v.* — *tr.* to remove from office, power, the throne, or the like — *intr.* in law, to make a deposition

deposition *n.* in law, testimony given on oath, or the sworn statement of a witness absent from court — **deponent** *n.*

Deposition *n.* taking down of Jesus from the cross, or a painting or sculpture of this

depository *n.* person entrusted with something for safekeeping, trustee (also "depositary"); warehouse or similar place for safe storage, depot

depraved *adj.* morally corrupt, perverted — **deprave** *tr.v.* — **depravity** *n.*

deprecate *tr.v.* to disapprove of, protest against, or discourage — **-catory** *adj.* — **-ation** *n.*

depreciation *n.* loss in value, as of a car, as through age or wear and tear (opposite "appreciation") — **depreciate** *v.*

depredation *formal. n.* act of plundering, pillage

deputation *n.* group or person chosen to represent others, delegation

depute *tr.v.* to appoint as one's deputy; to assign (work, duties, or powers) to one's deputy

deputy *n.* assistant standing in temporarily for a superior, as in emergencies; MP in France and some other countries; mining safety officer or fireman — **deputise** *v.* — **deputy** *adj.*

deracinate *formal. tr.v.* to uproot, pull up by or as if by the roots

déraciné (day-rássinay) *formal. adj.* rootless, separated from one's origins (also "deracinated") [French]

derailleur (di-ráylər, -yər) *n.* gear-changing device on a bicycle, transferring the chain from one sprocket wheel to another [French, related to *derail*]

deranged *adj.* insane, mentally unstable — **derange** *tr.v.*

derby *n.* (dárbi) *British.* football or other sports match between two teams from the same area; (dérbi) *U.S.* bowler hat [after the 12th Earl of *Derby*]

derelict *adj.* deserted and falling into ruins: *a derelict old building*; remiss in one's duties ~ *n.* property abandoned by its owner, such as a ship abandoned at sea — **-tion** *n.*

deride *tr.v.* mock, scoff at — **derision** *n.* — **derisive** *adj.*

de rigueur (də ri-gér) *formal. adj.* required as a matter of good form by fashion or etiquette [French, literally, of strictness]

derisory (di-rísəri) *formal. adj.* mocking, deriding; laughably small or inadequate: *a derisory pay offer*

derivation *n.* origin and development of a word

derivative *adj.* derived from an earlier example, and hence unoriginal ~ *n.* something derived from something else, such as: chemical compound obtained from other substances; word formed from a more basic word, as by the addition of a prefix or suffix

derive *v.* — *intr.* to originate, spring from a source: *"Beef" derives from French "boeuf"* — *tr.* to obtain or trace from a source; to work out or prove by reasoning, deduce or infer

dermal *formal. adj.* relating to the skin

dermatitis *n.* skin inflammation

dermatology *n.* medical study of skin diseases and treatments — **-gist** *n.* — **-logical** *adj.*

dernier cri (dérn-yay krée) *formal. n., pl.* **-s -s** latest thing, trend, or fashion [French, literally, last cry]

derogate *formal. v.* to belittle, make fun of, or detract from — **-gation** *n.*

derogatory *adj.* deliberately offensive or belittling, disparaging: *derogatory remarks*

derrick *n.* crane with a boom and cables for lifting heavy objects; framework over an oil well for supporting pipes or drilling equipment [originally, a hangman or gallows, after a well-known Tyburn hangman called *Derick* in about 1600]

derrière (dérri-áir, -air) *n.* buttocks, backside (euphemistic) [French, literally, behind, at the rear]

derv *British. n.* diesel oil used as fuel for road vehicles [from *d*iesel *e*ngine *r*oad *v*ehicle]

dervish *n.* member of an ascetic Muslim sect, sometimes engaging in ecstatic, whirling dancing

desalinate *tr.v.* to remove salt from: *desalinate sea water* — **-nation** *n.*

descant *n.* (déss-kant) highest singing part in a choral song; melody added as counterpoint above a basic line ~ *formal. intr.v.* (dess-kánt) to comment on something at length

describe *tr.v.* to move so as to form (a shape or outline): *The missile described a parabola*

descriptivism *n.* study of language based on analysis of actual usage rather than on standards of correctness. Compare PRESCRIPTIVISM — **-ist** *n., adj.*

descry *formal. tr.v.* to catch sight of, discern, notice at a distance; to find out or discover

desecration *n.* spoiling or destruction of the sacred quality of a religious building, graveyard, or the like, as by blasphemy or vandalism — **desecrate** *tr.v.*

deselect *chiefly British. tr.v.* to withdraw constituency-party support from (a previously selected candidate)

desiccate (déssi-kayt) *tr.v.* to preserve food by drying: *desiccated coconut*; to cause to lose enthusiasm or vitality: *a desiccated old curmudgeon* — **-cative** *adj.* — **-tion**, **-tor**, **-cant** *n.*

desideratum *formal. n., pl.* **-ata** something wished for, needed, or desired [related to *desire*]
designate *tr.v.* to name or give a title to; to point out, indicate; to appoint ~ *adj.* appointed to an office or position though not actually installed yet: *the provost designate* — **-nation** *n.*
desist *formal. intr.v.* to stop, cease
desolation *n.* ruin, wasteland; lonely misery, wretchedness — **desolate** *tr.v., adj.*
desperado *formal. n., pl.* **-dos** or **-does** reckless and desperate criminal [related to *desperate*]
despondent *adj.* downhearted, dejected, lacking in hope or confidence — **-ency** *n.* — **despond** *intr.v.*
despot *n.* authoritarian ruler, autocrat, tyrant; overpowering, domineering, or bullying person: *a petty despot ruling the typing pool* — **-ic** *adj.* — **-ism** *n.*
destitute *adj.* impoverished; totally lacking — **-ution** *n.*
desuetude (di-séw-i-tewd, désswi-) *formal. n.* state of being no longer used, practised, or followed, disuse: *words fallen into desuetude*
desultory (déss'l-tri) *formal. adj.* proceeding by fits and starts, especially in a haphazard way: *a desultory conversation*
détente (day-tóNT) *n.* easing of tension, as between nations
deter *tr.v.* to prevent or discourage, as by threats — **deterrent** *adj., n.* — **deterrence** *n.*
deteriorate *v.* to worsen — **-tion** *n.*
determiner *n.* word such as *both*, *a*, *this*, *six*, or *your* that determines the reference of a noun phrase, and is usually positioned before ordinary descriptive adjectives, as in *both the yellow books*
determinism *n.* belief or philosophy that everything follows inescapably from a cause or series of causes, and that there is no real free will
detonate *v.* to explode, typically with a thunderously loud noise — **-tor**, **-tion** *n.*
detour *n.* route or road deviating from the standard or direct one — **detour** *intr.v.*
detract *v.* — **detract from** to belittle, devalue, make light of
detriment *formal. n.* damage, harm, disadvantage — **-mental** *adj.*
detritus (di-trī́təss) *formal. n.* rock fragments; debris
de trop (də trṓ) *adj.* unnecessary or unwanted, superfluous [French, literally, of too much]
deuce *n.* two in card games or dice games
deus ex machina (mácki-nə) *formal. n., pl.* **dei ex machina** person or thing that changes the outcome unexpectedly at the last moment [New Latin, literally, god from a machine, referring to the arrival of a god by stage machinery in an ancient Greek or Latin drama to resolve a difficulty]
Devanagari (dáyvə-náagəri) *n.* syllabic script used for writing Sanskrit, as well as Hindi and other modern Indian languages
devastate *tr.v.* lay waste, damage terribly — **-tation** *n.*
deviance *n.* departure from the norm, as in sexual behaviour — **deviant** *adj., n.*
deviate *intr.v.* to differ or depart from the norm or standard, as of a policy, a route, or one's behaviour — **-iation** *n.*
device *n.* pattern or symbol, as on a flag or embroidery; *formal.* statagem, ploy, ruse: *deceived by a cunning device*
devil's advocate *n.* Roman Catholic official appointed to argue the case against a candidate for sainthood; person who puts forward a contrary or unpopular view, for the sake of argument or provocation
devious *adj.* roundabout, indirect; sneaky, shifty, underhand: *a devious scheme*
devise *tr.v.* to invent or plan; *formal.* to pass on (property, especially land or buildings) by a will
devoid *adj.* totally without, lacking: *devoid of shame*
devoirs (də-vwárz, dé-vwaarz) *formal. pl.n.* personal courtesies, such as greetings or conventional compliments: *paid their devoirs to the hostess and took their leave*
devolution *n.* transfer of power from central government to regional or local authorities; passing down or on of something by stages or steps; biological degeneration, as opposed to evolution
devolve *formal. v.* — **devolve on** to fall to someone, be passed on to or conferred on
devotee (dévvə-tée) *n.* enthusiastic follower of a particular religion or activity
devotions *pl.n.* prayers or other, usually private, acts of religious observance — **-votional** *adj.*
devout *adj.* fervently or deeply religious
dewlap *n.* loose fold of skin at the neck, as in cattle or old people
dexterous *adj.* deft or skilful, especially with the hands, adroit (also "dextrous") — **dexterity** *n.*
dextral *formal. adj.* right, right-handed, or on the right. Compare SINISTRAL — **-ity** *n.*
dhobi (dṓbi) *n.* laundryman in India
dhoti (dṓti) *n.* loincloth worn by some male Hindus
dhow *n.* single-masted Arabian ship with a lateen sail
diabolism *n.* witchcraft, black magic, devil worship, or the like [akin to *devil*] — **-bolic**, **-bolical** *adj.* — **diablerie** *n.*
diachronic *adj.* through the course of time
diachronic linguistics *n.* linguistics using a historical approach, studying a language's development through time, historical linguistics. Compare SYNCHRONIC LINGUISTICS
diaconal (dī-áckən'l) *formal. adj.* relating to a deacon
diaconate (dī-áckonit) *n.* deacon's office or rank; deacons collectively
diacritic (dī́-ə-kríttik) *n.* mark added to a letter to indicate or modify its pronunciation, as in *façade*, *Brontë*, or *cañon* (also "diacritical mark") — **diacritic**, **-al** *adj.*
diadem *formal. n.* crown, typically light and jewelled; diadem as a symbol of royalty or supremacy
diaeresis (dī-éer-ə-siss) *n., pl.* **-ses** diacritic or accent mark, ¨, placed over a vowel, as in *coöp* or *Brontë*, to show that it is pronounced in or as a separate syllable (also "umlaut")
diagnosis *n., pl.* **-ses** identification of a disease, injury, or problem — **diagnose** *v.* — **-nostic** *adj.* — **-nostician** *n.*
dialect *n.* variety of a language characteristic of a particular group of users: *regional dialects*, *social dialects* — **-al** *adj.*
dialectic *n.* process of reaching the truth by examining and exploiting contradictions; philosophical discussion and logical disputation — **-tics** *n.* — **-tical** *adj.*
dialogue *n.* conversation, especially between two people or groups; passage of conversation in a play, novel, or the like; exchange of views, especially between groups with conflicting interests; philosophical work, as by Plato, in the form of a conversation — **dialogue** *v.*

dialysis (dī-ál-ə-siss) *n., pl.* **-ses** separation of different types of molecule in a solution by means of a membrane; technique using dialysis for filtering impurities from the blood of patients with kidney failure — **-lyse** *v.* — **-lyser** *n.*

diamanté (deé-ə-món-tay) *adj.* decorated with powdered glass or artificial jewels to produce a glittery diamond-like appearance — **diamanté** *n.*

diametric (dī́-ə-méttrik) *formal. adj.* opposed, completely contrary — **-cally** *adv.*

dianetics (dī́-ə-néttiks) *n.* scientology, or the therapy based on it

dianthus *n.* carnation, pink, or related flower

diapason (dī́-ə-páy-z'n) *n.* musical range of a voice or instrument; tuning fork or pitch pipe; glorious or harmonious burst of musical sound

diaper (dī́pər) *U.S. n.* nappy

diaphanous (dī-áffənəss) *adj.* so fine as to allow light partially through: *diaphanous silk*

diaphoresis (dī-əfə-reé-siss) *formal. n.* perspiration, sweating — **-phoretic** *n., adj.*

diaphragm (dī́-ə-fram) *n.* membrane or similar thin partition, specifically the one between chest and stomach; thin disc, as in a telephone or microphone, whose vibrations convert sound to electric signals or vice versa; contraceptive device in the form of a flexible cap placed over the cervix

diaphysis (dī-áffi-siss) *n., pl.* **-ses** shaft of a long bone

diaspora (dī-áss-pərə) *n.* migration or scattering of a nation's people, especially of the Jews

diastema (dī́-ə-steémə) *n., pl.* **-mata** abnormal split or gap in a body part or organ; wide gap between the teeth

diastole (dī-ástəli) *n.* rhythmic expanding of the chambers of the heart, during which phase they fill with blood. Compare SYSTOLE — **-lic** *adj.*

diatonic (dī́-ə-tónnik) *adj.* referring to the basic Western major or minor musical scale, consisting of eight notes

diatribe (dī́-ə-trīb) *n.* bitter criticism, scathing denunciation

dibble *n.* pointed gardening tool for making holes in the soil, as for bulbs or seedlings (also "dibber") — **dibble** *tr.v.*

dichotomy (dī-kóttəmi) *n.* division or separation into two parts, especially opposing or contrasting parts; loosely, disagreement or conflict — **-mise** *v.* — **-mous** *adj.*

dickey seat *n.* front seat of a carriage for the driver or rear seat for a servant (also "dicky"); *British.* seat that folded out at the back of some early motor cars (in this sense, also "dicky", *chiefly U.S.* "rumble seat")

dicky *n.* false shirt or blouse front, as worn under a jacket; *British.* dickey seat

dicotyledon (dī́-kotti-leéd'n) *n.* plant of the common group including most trees and shrubs, characterised by two embryonic seed leaves (also "dicot") — **-ous** *adj.*

diction *n.* manner or clarity of one's pronunciation; choice of words or manner of expressing oneself in speech or writing

dictum *n., pl.* **-tums** or **-ta** authoritative statement on a topic; proverbial saying or popular maxim or rule

didactic (dī-dáktik) *adj.* designed to teach, often in a heavy-handed or moralising way; morally instructive; concentrating on a moral or political message rather than artistry: *didactic poetry* — **-icism** *n.*

didicoy (díddi-koy) *British. n.* scrap-metal dealer or tinker, typically living in a caravan, not considered nowadays to be a true Gypsy

differential gear *n.* gear in motor vehicles enabling the driving wheels to turn at different rates, as when cornering ("differential")

differentiate *v.* — *tr.* to see or show the difference between; to make distinct — *intr.* to make distinctions; to become distinct

diffident *adj.* lacking in confidence or assertiveness — **-dence** *n.*

diffraction *n.* change in direction or intensity of a wave hitting an obstacle, as when light is broken up by a glass surface — **diffract** *v.*

diffuse *adj.* (di-féwss) scattered, widespread; wordy, lacking conciseness ~ *v.* (di-féwz) to spread out or pour out — **-sion** *n.* — **-sive** *adj.*

digit *n.* finger, toe, or corresponding part in other animals; any of the Arabic numerals between 0 and 9

digital (díjit'l) *adj.* referring to a watch, clock, or meter indicating readings by changing numbers rather than by moving hands. Compare ANALOG

digitalis (díji-táyl-iss) *n.* foxglove or related plant, from which a drug used as a heart stimulant is obtained [from Latin, *digitus*, a finger, referring to the finger-shaped foxglove flower]

digital recording *n.* method of tape-recording using separate electronic signals

dignitary *n.* important or high-ranking person [related to *dignity*]

digraph *n.* pair of letters used together, such as *th* or *æ*, to represent a single speech sound

digress *intr.v.* to turn aside or stray from the main subject of one's speech or writing — **-gression** *n.* — **-gressive** *adj.*

diktat *n.* victor's decree or settlement imposed on a defeated enemy; dogmatic statement [German, related to *dictate*]

dilapidated *adj.* in a state of disrepair — **-date** *v.*

dilapidations *pl.n.* damage or disrepair to a property caused by the tenant's neglect

dilate *v.* to widen, stretch, or expand; *formal. intr.v.* to write or speak on a subject in lengthy detail — **-lation, dilatation** *n.*

dilatory (díllə-tri) *formal. adj.* causing delay; having a tendency to delay or waste time

dilemma *n.* situation requiring a choice between two usually undesirable alternatives

dilettante (dílli-tánti) *n., pl.* **-tantes** or **-tanti** person whose interest in something, such as the arts, is amateurish or superficial [akin to *delight*] — **dilettante, -tantish** *adj.* — **-tantism** *n.*

diligence *n.* hard work and careful attention to the task in hand — **-gent** *adj.*

diminuendo (dimínnew-éndō) *n., pl.* **-dos** or **-does** decrescendo in music, gradual decrease in loudness (opposite "crescendo") [related to *diminish*] — **diminuendo** *adj., adv.*

diminutive *n.* word or word-element, such as *piglet* or *-let*, indicating small size, unimportance, youth, affection, or the like ~ *adj.* of small size

diocese (dī́-ə-siss) *n.* area over which a bishop has authority — **diocesan** *adj., n.*

Dionysiac (dī́-ə-nízzi-ək) *formal. adj.* energetic, passionate, or ecstatic; irrational, creative, spontaneous, and emotional, as one side of human nature is (also

"Dionysian"). Compare APOLLONIAN [coined, in German form, by Nietzsche, after the cult of *Dionysus*, the Greek god of wine and ecstasy

diorama *n.* three-dimensional scene or tableau, as in museums, with models of figures exhibited against a painted background

diphthong (dif-thong) *n.* vowel sound that changes in quality during the syllable, such as the *i*-sound in *sigh*; digraph such as *œ* or *æ* in Latin

dipsomania *formal. n.* craving for alcoholic drink, alcoholism — **-iac** *n., adj.*

diptych (díptik) *n.* painting or decorative work in the form of two panels hinged together

dirge *n.* funeral hymn or lament; mournful piece of music, as for a funeral

dirigible (dírrij-ib'l) *n.* airship of an early type, capable of being steered [akin to *direct*] — **dirigible** *adj.*

disabuse *tr.v.* to rid (someone) of a mistaken idea or impression

disaffected *adj.* no longer feeling affection or loyalty, as to someone in authority — **-fection** *n.*

disambiguate *tr.v.* to make clear and unambiguous

disapprobation *formal. n.* disapproval, censure

disarm *tr.v.* to lay to rest the suspicion or hostility of; to win the confidence of, charm — **-ing** *adj.*

disavow *tr.v.* reject, disclaim, disown, deny knowledge of or responsibility for

disbar *tr.v.* to expel (a lawyer) from the Bar, thereby preventing him from practising as a barrister

disburden *tr.v.* to free (oneself or one's mind) of worry, grief, guilt, or a similar burden — **-ment** *n.*

disburse *formal. tr.v.* to pay out, as from a fund — **-ment** *n.*

discerning (di-sérn-ing) *adj.* having good taste or judgment — **discernment** *n.*

discipline *n.* subject of study, branch of knowledge

disclaim *tr.v.* to deny or reject (knowledge or responsibility) — **-er** *n.*

discobolus (diss-kóbbə-ləs) *n., pl.* **-li** discus-thrower, or a statue of one, in ancient Greece or Rome

discombobulate *chiefly U.S. tr.v.* to confuse utterly, bamboozle

discomfit (diss-kúmfit) *formal. tr.v.* to puzzle, embarrass, or make uneasy; to thwart, frustrate, foil the plans of — **-ure** *n.*

discommode *formal. tr.v.* to disturb or inconvenience

disconcert *tr.v.* to upset, frustrate, or throw into disorder — **-ed, -ing** *adj.*

disconsolate *adj.* extremely unhappy, beyond consolation, hopeless [related to *console*]

discourse *n.* (díss-kawrss) speech or writing, especially of a formal kind; conversation; formal discussion of a topic ~ *intr.v* (diss-kō̆rss) to talk, converse; to speak or write formally and at some length

discovery *n.* compulsory revealing of relevant documents by one party to the other in a civil lawsuit

discreet *adj.* tactful or diplomatic, able to avoid embarrassment, as by keeping secrets — **-cretion** *n.*

discrepancy (diss-kréppən-si) *n.* disagreement or variation between results, claims, reports, or the like

discrete *informal. adj.* separate, individual, and distinct *three discrete strands* — **-ness** *n.*

discretionary *adj.* based on personal decision rather than on regulations: *discretionary powers/payments*

discriminate *v.* — *intr.* to differentiate, distinguish; to be selective or discerning; to show favour or disfavour on the basis of race, sex, or the like — *tr.* to tell apart — **-natory, -nating** *adj.* — **-nation** *n.*

discursive *adj.* based on reason and logical argument rather than on intuition; tending to digress or ramble

disdain *n.* contempt and scorn ~ *tr.v.* to reject or hold back from out of disdain, not deign: *She disdained to argue*; to treat or regard with disdain — **-ful** *adj.*

disembodied *adj.* lacking or apparently lacking a body or substance

disembogue (díssim-bō̆g) *formal. v.* to flow out, discharge, or empty, as at a river mouth

disenchanted *adj.* suffering from disappointment or disillusionment — **disenchant** *tr.v.* — **-ment** *n.*

disequilibrium *n.* imbalance or instability

disgorge *tr.v.* to yield (something kept back, such as information) reluctantly ~ *v.* to discharge violently, spew out — **-ment** *n.*

disgruntled *adj.* discontented, peeved, irritable — **disgruntle** *tr.v.*

dishabille (díss-ə-beél) *formal. n.* state of being undressed or partially dressed (also "déshabillé") — **dishabille** *adj.*

dishevelled (di-shévv'ld) *adj.* very untidy, in disarray: *dishevelled hair/appearance*

disingenuous (díss-in-jénnew-əss) *adj.* pretending to be naive, ignorant, or straightforward

disinter (díss-in-térr) *tr.v.* to dig up or remove from a grave or tomb; to bring (a secret or obscure information) to light — **-ment** *n.*

disinterested (diss-íntrəstid) *adj.* impartial, objective: *disinterested advice* — **disinterest** *n.*

disjointed *adj.* disconnected, lacking a proper order, not coherent: *disjointed speech*

disjunctive (diss-júngktiv) *n.* word, such as *but*, expressing contrast or opposition — **disjunctive** *adj.*

dislodge *tr.v.* to force out from a fixed position, hiding place, dwelling, or the like

dismantle *tr.v.* to take to pieces: *Stagehands dismantled the set*

dismember *tr.v.* to pull or cut the limbs from; to divide or break up into parts or sections

disorderly house *formal. n.* house, such as a brothel, where public order or decency is violated

disorientated *adj.* having lost one's sense of direction or bearings, as when in an unfamiliar environment; confused and bewildered — **-tate** *tr.v.* — **-tation** *n.*

disparage *tr.v.* to imply criticism or disapproval of, belittle — **-ing** *adj.* — **-ment** *n.*

disparate (díss-pər-ət) *adj.* utterly different or distinct, so that no comparison is possible — **-parity** *n.*

dispassionate *adj.* unemotional, detached, and unbiased

dispatch *n.* report sent over a distance, as by a newspaper correspondent or military field officer; due promptness (also *British* "despatch")

dispatch rider *n.* motorcyclist carrying official documents or reports

dispensary *n.* place, as in a hospital or chemist's shop, from which medicines and medical supplies are given out

dispensation *n.* relaxation of or release from a rule, law, vow, obligation, or the like; system or code, especially a religious one; God's ordering of earthly life and events

dispense *tr.v*, to give out in portions; to prepare and distribute (prescribed medication); to administer (justice or the law) — **dispense with** to get rid of or manage without — **-er** *n.*

disperse *v.* — *tr.* to spread (news, knowledge, or the like) widely; to break up (a riot) or drive off (rioters); to separate (light or other radiation) into parts with different wavelengths; to cause (fog) to vanish — *intr.* to become dispersed — **-persal**, **-persion** *n.*
disport *formal. v.* — *tr.* to amuse or occupy (oneself) in a pleasurable activity — *intr.* to frolic, jump about playfully
disposition *n.* personality, temperament; habitual tendency or inclination
disputation *formal. n.* a debate, especially a formal and learned debate
disquisition *formal. n.* lecture or treatise on or formal study of a subject
disrepute *formal. n.* loss of good reputation, disgrace: *bring/fall into disrepute* — **-table** *adj.*
disrobe *formal. tr.v.* to undress
dissect (di-sékt, dī-) *tr.v.* to cut or open, as in surgery or laboratory examination; to examine or analyse in fine detail — **-section** *n.*
dissemble *v.* — *tr.* to disguise or conceal (one's feelings, character, or the like); to fake, pretend, or display falsely: *dissembled friendship* — *intr.* to engage in dissembling
disseminate *tr.v.* to spread widely: *disseminating information* — **-tion** *n.*
dissent *intr.v.* to disagree, differ; to refuse to obey, approve, or conform to ~ *n.* disagreement, especially non-compliance with the doctrines of an established church or political regime — **-sension** *n.*
dissertation *n.* academic treatise or thesis, as for a higher academic degree
dissident *n.* political opponent of a government, especially in a one-party state — **dissident** *adj.*
dissimulate *formal.v.* — *intr.* to disguise one's true feelings or intentions by pretending — *tr.* to pretend, feign
dissipate *v.* — *tr.* to drive away, dispel, scatter; to use up, squander, exhaust — *intr.* to become dissipated, vanish or scatter — **-tion** *n.*
dissipated *adj.* immorally or excessively given to sensual pleasures, indulgent, dissolute
dissolute *adj.* morally unrestrained, overindulgent in sensual pleasures, debauched
dissolve *tr.v.* to end and dismiss (a meeting, Parliament, or the like); to end or cancel (a legal bond such as marriage) — **dissolution** *n.*
dissonance *n.* harsh combination of sounds, discord: disagreement or inconsistency — **-nant** *adj.*
distaff *n.* cleft stick for holding raw flax or wool prior to spinning; *archaic.* women's work
distil *tr.v.* to separate or extract (an essence, idea, or the like); to purify or refine (also *U.S.* "distill") — **-tillery** *n.*
distillate (dístil-ət) *n.* concentrated or pure form of something, essence (also "distillation")
distingué (di-stáng-gay, deéss-taN-gáy) *formal. adj.* dignified, elegant, or noble in appearance [French]
distrain *formal. tr.v.* to seize (property), as to force payment of a debt
distrait (dístray, di-stráy) *formal. adj.* absent-minded, inattentive; worried, distracted
distraught (di-stráwt) *adj.* very anxious or agitated, frantic with worry [related to *distracted*]
distressed *adj.* treated so as to give an artificial appearance of age: *distressed leather/furniture* — **distress** *tr.v.*
diuretic (dī-yoor-éttik) *adj.* causing increased urine or urination: *a diuretic drug* — **diuretic** *n.*
diurnal (dī-úrnəl) *formal. adj.* occurring during the day or daily; active or open during the day rather than at night: *diurnal animals/flowers*
diva (deé-və) *n.* leading female opera singer [Italian, literally, goddess]
divan *n.* coffee house or smoking room in former times
divers (dívərz) *archaic or formal. adj.* various or several
diverse (dī-vérss, dí-verss) *adj.* distinct, individual; varied, assorted — **-versity** *n.* — **-versify** *v.*
diverticulum (dí-ver-tíckew-ləm) *n.*, *pl.* **-la** sac or pouch formed in the weakened wall of a hollow body part, especially the intestines — **-lar** *adj.*
divertissement (deévair-teéss-moN) *n.* short entertainment given on stage between the acts of an opera or play; any amusement or entertainment
Dives (dí-veez) *n.* rich man [after the rich man in Jesus's parable of Lazarus, Luke 16:19-31]
divest (dī-vést) *tr.v.* to strip or deprive of something, such as clothes, rights, or property — **-ment** *n.*
divide *intr.v.* to vote in Parliament by separating into opposing groups
dividend *n.* number or quantity that is divided by another; share of profits or a bankrupt's assets; bonus or benefit (usually plural)
divine *adj.* relating to a deity ~ *formal. n.* clergyman; theologian ~ *formal. tr.v.* to guess, predict, or infer, as by intuition, surmise — **divination**, **divinity** *n.*
divining rod *n.* rod, forked stick, or the like that quivers or dips when held above ground containing water or minerals (also "dowsing rod")
divisor *n.* number or quantity by which another is divided
divot (dívvət) *n.* clump of turf dug from a grass surface, as by a golf club or horse's hoof
divulge *tr.v.* to reveal (a confidence, secret, or the like)
docile *adj.* cooperative, obedient, mild, submissive and yielding
docket *n.* ticket or label, as on a parcel; customs label or receipt; document such as an official voucher or certificate; summary of a court case
doctrinaire *adj.* blindly committed to a doctrine, dogmatic and impractical
doctrine *n.* theory, religious principle, body of beliefs, or the like — **-nal** *adj.*
document *tr.v.* to support with evidence or references, prove by recording details — **document**, **-tation** *n.*
documentary *n.* presentation, especially in film, radio, or television, about real events or conditions, that uses wholly or mostly non-fictional material
doge (dōj) *n.* head of state of the former republics of Venice or Genoa
doggerel *n.* comic or poor-quality verse whose metre is typically either loose and irregular or monotonously regular
dogma *n.* belief or opinion proclaimed with authority or held with tenacity — **-matic** *adj.* — **-matism**, **-matist** *n.* — **-matise** *intr.v.*
Dolby *trademark.*, *n.* system or device to reduce unwanted noise on recorded or broadcast sound
doldrums *pl.n.* boredom, depression, or inactivity; stagnation or recession; belt of calm or light winds and sea along the equator

doleful *adj.* sad, mournful, grieving
dolmen *n.* prehistoric structure consisting of a horizontal stone slab supported by several large standing stones, thought to have been a tomb (also "cromlech"). Compare MENHIR
dolour (dóllər) *formal. n.* grief or sorrow — **dolorous** *adj.*
domesticate *tr.v.* to adapt (an animal or plant) for association with and use to humans
domicile *formal. n.* home, legal dwelling place or country of residence — **domicile** *tr.v.* — **domiciliary** *adj.*
dominate *tr.v.* to have or exercise power or authority over; to have a very prominent or overlooking position with respect to: *a hill dominating the countryside* — **-nant** *adj.* — **-nance** *n.*
domineering *adj.* bullying, tyrannical, dominating arrogantly — **-eer** *v.*
dominie (dómmi-ni) *n. Scottish.* schoolmaster; formerly, a clergyman
dominion *n.* power or control, over a group or region, rule, sovereignty; territory under another's sovereignty
domino *n., pl.* **-nos** or **-noes** masquerade mask covering the top half of the face; hooded robe typically worn with a domino, during the Carnival in Venice
donor *n.* person who makes a donation; person or animal from whom organic material, such as blood, semen, or an organ, is or may be taken for transfer to another
Doppelgänger (dópp'l-gang-ər, -geng-) *n.* double or ghostly counterpart, sometimes haunting a person in legend [German, literally, double-goer]
Doppler effect *n.* change in pitch of sound, as of a siren, as the source approaches or moves away from the listener [after Christian *Doppler*, a 19th-century Austrian physicist who studied the effect]
Doric *adj.* referring or relating to the oldest and simplest style or order of classical Greek architecture. Compare IONIC, CORINTHIAN; referring or relating to a dialect of ancient Greek — **Doric** *n.*
dormant *adj.* inactive but not dead or extinct, able to be aroused or become active — **-mancy** *n.*
dormer *n.* upright window in a gable on a sloping roof (also "dormer window"); gable projecting from the roof in this way
dorsal *formal. adj.* relating to the back or upper surface of the body. Compare VENTRAL
dossier (dóssi-ay) *n.* file or collection of documents on a particular person or subject
dotage *formal. n.* senility
dotard *formal. n.* senile person
dottle *n.* tobacco plug left in a pipe after smoking
double-blind *adj.* referring or relating to a rigorous type of experiment with an experimental group and a control group, in which neither subjects nor experimenters know which group is which until the experiment is over
double entendre (dōōb'l ON-tóNdrə) *n.* word or phrase that seems to have a second, typically saucy, meaning; humour based on double-entendres [obsolete French, literally, double meaning]
doublet *n.* false gemstone, typically consisting of coloured glass with a face of real gemstone; pair of similar things, or one of such a pair, especially a pair of words, or one of the pair, deriving via different routes from a single source, as with *royal* and *regal*; tight jacket worn by men from the 15th to 17th century
douceur (dōō-sér) *formal. n.* money payment given as a tip or bribe [French, literally, sweetness]
douche (dōōsh) *n.* water or air stream directed at or into a part of the body for cleansing or healing; syringe or similar instrument for administering a douche — **douche** *v.*
dovetail *n.* carpentry joint including a wedge-shaped tenon, or the tenon itself ~ *v.* to connect, join, or fit neatly or harmoniously
dowager (dów-əjər) *n.* widow with property or a title of nobility from her late husband; dignified or haughty elderly woman
dowel (dów-əl) *n.* peg, pin, or short rod fitting into holes to fasten adjoining pieces of wood or stone
dowse *tr.v.* to use a divining rod, pendulum, or other device or technique to detect unseen water, mineral deposits, or other phenomena, such as signs of disease — **dowsing rod** *n.*
doxology *n.* hymn, verse, or formula praising God in the liturgy
doyen (dóy-en, dwī́-) *n.* eldest or senior member of a group, society, diplomatic corps, or the like (also *U.S.* "dean"; feminine equivalent "doyenne")
draconian *adj.* harsh, very severe *draconian laws* [after *Draco*, a very harsh ancient Greek lawgiver]
draft *n.* preliminary version of a picture, text, or the like; money order or bill of exchange: *a bank draft*; *U.S.* military conscription: *dodging the draft* (also *U.S.* "draught")
drag *tr.v.* to follow (a trail, fox, or the like), as hunting hounds do; to search the bed of (a river, lake, or canal) by trailing a hook or net along it: *dragged the lake in search of the body* ~ *n.* harrow used for crushing clods or levelling the soil; brake on a wagon or carriage; *informal.* women's clothes worn by a man: *a man in drag*
dragoman (drág-ə-man) *n., pl.* **-mans** or **-men** formerly, interpreter in Arabic-, Turkish-, or Persian-speaking countries
dragoon *tr.v.* to compel or pressurise: *dragooned us into participating*
dram *n.* tot, small quantity of whisky or other spirits
dramatis personae (drámmə-tiss per-sṓnī) *pl.n.* participants in a play, whether as characters or actors ~ *n.* list of dramatis personae [New Latin, literally, characters of the drama]
dramaturge (drámmə-turj) *formal. n.* dramatist; theatrical consultant
drapes *U.S. pl.n.* curtains
draught *n.* pulling power, as of a locomotive; depth of the keel of a loaded ship below the water line; act of swallowing a liquid; amount swallowed in one draught: *a draught of medicine* (old-fashioned) ~ *adj.* drawn or served from a container such as a barrel or keg, rather than bottled: *draught ale*
draughtsman *n.* person skilled at drawing: *an architectural draughtsman* (also *U.S.* "draftsman") — **-ship** *n.*
drawtube *n.* sliding tube within another, as in a telescope
dredge *tr.v.* to clean or deepen (a harbour, channel, or the like) by means of a scooping machine
dressage (dré-saazh) *n.* precision manoeuvring by a well-trained horse in response to slight signals from its rider

drift *n.* pile or bank of snow or sand, accumulated by wind or water; herding of cattle, horses, or the like; gradual change in a language; *informal.* gist, general meaning: *the drift of his argument*

drill *n.* implement for planting seeds, or a furrow or row of planted seeds

drogue (drōg) *n.* funnel-shaped device, such as a sea anchor or a target towed behind an aircraft; funnel at the end of the refuelling hose of a tanker aircraft; windsock, tapering tube of cloth indicating wind direction

droit de seigneur (drwáa də sayn-yér) *n., pl.* **droits de seigneur** feudal lord's supposed right to sexual intercourse with a vassal's bride on her wedding night (also "droit du seigneur", "jus primae noctis") [Old French, literally, right of the lord]

dromedary (drómmə-dri) *n.* one-humped camel of North Africa and western Asia. Compare BACTRIAN CAMEL

drone *n.* male bee, doing no work except to fertilise the queen bee; *informal.* person doing no work but living off others, sponger, parasite; aircraft without a pilot, operated by remote control; droning sound; pipe on a set of bagpipes producing a single continuous droning note. Compare CHANTER ~ *v.* to speak in a monotonous or boring way

dross *n.* impurities formed on molten metal during smelting; worthless part of something

drove *n.* flock or herd of animals being driven together — **drover** *n.*

drumlin *n.* streamlined hill or ridge formed by glacial deposit

drupe *n.* fruit, such as a cherry or peach, having a single hard stone enclosing the seed — **drupaceous** *adj.*

dryad *n.*, **-ads** or **-ades** wood nymph in Greek mythology. Compare HAMADRYAD, NAIAD, OREAD, NEREID

dualism *n.* theory of various kinds that the world is divided into two different substances, such as mind and matter, or ruled by two different forces, such as good and evil — **-ist** *n.* — **-istic** *adj.*

[1]**dub** *tr.v.* to confer knighthood or damehood on by ceremonially tapping on the shoulder with a sword; *informal.* to give a nickname or characterising description to: *dubbed her "The Kingmaker"*

[2]**dub** *tr.v.* to alter or insert (the soundtrack) of (a film or tape)

[3]**dub** *n.* drumbeat

dubbin *n.* grease of tallow and oil for softening and waterproofing leather

ducal *formal. adj.* relating to a duke, dukedom, or duchy

Duce (dōōchay) *n.* Mussolini's title as leader of Fascist Italy [Italian, a leader]

duchy *n.* territory of a duke or duchess

duckboard *n.* board or boards laid to form a path over wet or muddy ground

duct *n.* tube, pipe, or canal for the passage of fluids, as in a building, a plant, or the human body; pipe or channel for electric wires or cables; air-conditioning pipe or channel

ductile *adj.* relatively soft and workable, as some metals are, and able to be hammered thin and drawn into wire; *formal.* flexible, pliable, easily moulded

dudgeon *n.* — **in high dudgeon** angrily, indignantly

duenna (dew-énnə) *n.* chaperone, especially an elderly woman, who accompanies and protects a young or unmarried woman, especially in Spanish-speaking countries

dug *archaic or regional. n.* breast, udder, or teat

dulcet (dúl-sit) *archaic or formal. adj.* sounding pleasantly melodious

dulcimer (dúl-simər) *n.* string instrument played with light hammers

dumdum bullet *n.* bullet with a soft or hollow nose that spreads on impact to produce a gaping wound [after *Dum Dum*, an arsenal near Calcutta in India, where such bullets were first made in about 1897]

dumping *n.* marketing of goods in a foreign country at below cost price — **dump** *tr.v.*

dun *n.* debt collector, or his insistent demand for payment — **dun** *tr.v.*

dundrearies *pl.n.* long side whiskers [after Lord *Dundreary*, a character in a mid-19th-century play]

duodenum (déw-ō-déé-nəm) *n., pl.* **-na** or **-nums** upper section of the small intestine, linked to the stomach] — **-denal** *adj.*

duplex *n.* flat on two floors — **duplex** *adj.*

duplicity *n.* deception, cheating, fraud — **-tous** *adj.*

durable *adj.* tough and long-lasting — **-ability** *n.*

duress (dewr-éss) *formal. n.* — **under duress** under compulsion, unwillingly

Dutch auction *n.* auction in which the asking price is progressively lowered until a buyer accepts

dux (duks) *chiefly Scottish. n.* school pupil who is top of the class [Latin, a leader]

dynamo *n., pl.* **-nos** electricity generator, especially of direct current; dynamic person

dynasty (dínnə-sti) *n.* series of related rulers or powerful leaders that is dominant over successive generations — **dynast** *n.* — **dynastic** *adj.*

dyslexia *n.* learning disorder involving poor reading ability (also *informal* "word blindness") — **-lexic** *adj., n.*

dyspepsia *formal. n.* indigestion; grumpiness, irritability — **-peptic** *adj.*

dysphemism (díss-fə-miz'm) *n.* substitution of an unpleasant or offensive word or phrase for a neutral or favourable one, the reverse of a euphemism; word or phrase used in this way

dystopia (diss-tōpi-ə) *n.* imaginary place, as in fiction, where things are worse than in real life, the reverse of utopia (also "cacotopia")

dystrophy (dístrəfi) *n.* wasting away of bodily tissue — **-phic** *adj.*

E

eagre (áy-gər) *n.* large wave moving upstream in a river estuary, as caused by tidal currents (also "bore")
ear *n.* small display box, typically for advertisements, in an upper corner of the front page of a newspaper or magazine
earnest *n.* money paid as a deposit or guarantee to clinch a deal (also "earnest money"); promise, token, or assurance: *an earnest of goodwill*
eau de vie (ṓ də vée) *n.* brandy [French, literally, water of life]
ebullient (i-búl-i ənt) *adj.* bubbling with excitement, enthusiasm, or friendliness, exuberant — **-ience** *n.*
eccentric *adj.* abnormal, departing from the norm or convention; elliptical rather than circular: *the planet's eccentric orbit*; not positioned in or not sharing a centre: *eccentric gearwheels*. Compare CONCENTRIC ~ *n.* odd, whimsical, but typically harmless and engaging person, book, or the like; disc or wheel whose axis is off-centre and which converts rotary to reciprocating motion — **-tricity** *n.*
ecclesiastic *formal. n.* clergyman, priest, especially a Christian clergyman
ecclesiastical *adj.* relating to a church, clerical
eccrine gland *n.* sweat gland
ecdysiast (ek-dízzi-ast) *n.* stripper or striptease artist (humorously pompous) [from ECDYSIS]
ecdysis (ékdi-siss) *formal. n., pl.* **-ses** sloughing, shedding of the outer layer, shell, or skin, as in insects and snakes
echelon (ésha-lon) *n.* level of authority or responsibility in a hierarchical organisation: *the upper echelons of the civil service*; formation, as of troops or ships, in stepped or offset parallel rows; military or naval subdivision: *rear/command echelon* [French *échelon*, literally, a rung on a ladder] — **echelon** *v.*
éclat (ay-kláa) *n.* dazzling display; showiness: *perform with éclat*; brilliant success or achievement; social success or distinction: *a certain éclat*; acclaim or applause [French, literally, burst]
eclectic (i-kléktik) *adj.* selecting or selected from a range of different sources: *an eclectic thinker/poem* — **-ticism** *n.*
eclipse *tr.v.* to overshadow or obscure completely; to reduce from power or importance to obscurity
ecology *n.* relationship between people, plants, or animals and their environment; science or study of this relationship
écorché (áy-kor-sháy) *n.* anatomical picture of the body, or a section of the body, without the skin, to show the muscle structure [French, literally, skinned]
ectomorph *n.* person with a lean, slightly muscular body build. Compare ENDOMORPH, MESOMORPH — **-morphic** *adj.*
-ectomy *n. comb.form.* -surgical removal: *tonsillectomy*
ectopic pregnancy *n.* pregnancy in which the fertilised egg develops outside the uterus, typically in a Fallopian tube
ectoplasm *n.* ghost-like substance supposedly emerging from a spiritualist medium during a seance
ecumenical *adj.* relating to the world's various Christian churches: *an ecumenical council*; promoting or relating to unity among the world's Christian churches; *formal or archaic.* universal, worldwide — **-ism, ecumenism** *n.*
eczema (ék-simə) *n.* skin inflammation marked by itching and oozing sores
eddy *n.* current or swirl moving against the main current, often creating a miniature whirlwind or whirlpool; trend or movement against the prevailing tendency ~ *intr.v.* to move in an eddy
edh (eth) *n.* old runic letter, written ð, representing the /th/ sound in old Germanic languages and in modern Icelandic (also "eth")
edible *adj.* eatable, fit to eat, non-poisonous ~ *n.* something edible, food (usually plural)
edict (éedikt) *n.* official or authoritative decree or command
edifice *formal. n.* building, especially one that is large and imposing; elaborate and complex structure, system, or organisation: *a philosophical edifice*
edify *tr.v.* to teach or enlighten, especially in a morally uplifting way — **-fication** *n.*
efface *tr.v.* to dim, make faded, or obliterate; to rub out, wipe out, erase; to humble (oneself) or make (oneself) inconspicuous, as through modesty
effeminate *adj.* weak and unmanly, or like a woman: *an effeminate man/manner* [related to *feminine*] — **-inacy** *n.*
effendi (e-féndi) *n.* title of respect used in addressing a man in Turkey and the Middle East
effervescent *adj.* carbonated, emitting small bubbles of gas: *effervescent drinks*; high-spirited, very lively and cheerful — **-vescence** *n.* — **-vesce** *intr.v.*
effete *adj.* weak, ineffectual, or worn out, as through decadence or self-indulgence: *effete aristocrats/novelettes*; *formal.* referring to a plant or animal that is incapable of further reproduction
efficacious *formal. adj.* powerful or successful: *an efficacious remedy* — **efficacy** *n.*
effigy (éffiji) *n.* dummy or crude image of a person, intended as an object of scorn or hatred, and sometimes burnt in public; painting or sculpture of a person, as on a monument
efflorescence *n.* flowering, bursting into bloom, blossoming; *formal.* developing and reaching of prominence or success: *an efflorescence of culture/his career* — **-escent** *adj.* — **-resce** *intr.v.*
effluent *n.* liquid waste, as from a factory or sewage works; radioactive liquid waste from a nuclear power station; stream flowing out of a lake, dam, or other body of water — **effluent** *adj.*
effluvium *n., pl.* **-via** or **-viums** smelly and usually invisible gas or vapour rising from a swamp, rubbish

heap, or the like
effrontery *n.* cheeky boldness, insolence
effulgent (i-fúlgənt) *formal. n.* brilliantly shining, radiant, resplendent — **-gence** *n.*
effusive *adj.* expressing feeling or emotion in a forthright or uncontrolled way, gushing: *effusive grandparents/praise* — **effusion** *n.*
egalitarian *adj.* relating to or supporting equality, as of political and legal rights ~ *n.* person holding or promoting egalitarian views [akin to *equality*]
egoistic *adj.* self-seeking, self-interested
egotistic *adj.* self-important, boastful
egregious (i-greé-jəss) *formal. adj.* outrageously and glaringly bad: *an egregious act/bore*
egress (eé-gress) *formal. n.* act of going out; permission or right to go out; exit, way out (opposite "ingress")
eidetic (ī-déttik) *adj.* referring to a very strong visual recall that retains vivid images: *eidetic memory*; referring to very vivid yet unreal visual impressions, as experienced in childhood: *eidetic images*
eisteddfod (ī-stéd-fəd, -steth-, -vod, ay-) *n., pl.* **-fods** or **-fodau** annual gathering, for a conference or contest, of Welsh poets and musicians; competition for young musicians, actors, or the like [Welsh, literally, a sitting]
ejaculation *n.* sudden discharge of semen at orgasm; *formal.* sudden exclamation or utterance — **-late** *v., n.* — **-latory** *adj.*
eject *tr.v.* to throw out, drive out, to force out: *eject lava*; force to leave, dismiss, expel — **-tion** *n.*
elaborate *v.* — *intr.* to explain more fully, give more information — *tr.* to develop in more detail, enrich, add details to, make more complex; to devise or produce painstakingly — **elaborate** *adj.*
élan (ay-lóɴ, -lán) *n.* enthusiasm and vigour combined with stylishness, flair
elapse *intr.v.* to pass: *several hours elapsed before she returned*
elated *adj.* joyful, high-spirited or very pleased — **elate** *tr.v.* — **elation** *n.*
eldorado (éldə-raádō) *n.* place thought to offer great wealth or opportunity [after *El Dorado*, a legendary South American city or country sought by 16th-century treasure hunters, perhaps after the gilded king of this region, from Spanish, literally, the gilded one]
elective *adj.* relating to voting: *elective offices*; optional, open to choice: *an elective course* ~ *chiefly U.S. n.* elective course, subject, or period of training, as for medical students
Electra complex *n.* Oedipus complex in a young girl [after *Electra* in Greek mythology, who avenged the death of her father Agamemnon by helping to kill her mother Clytemnestra]
electrocardiograph *n.* instrument recording the electrical impulses in the heart, used for diagnosis (also "ECG") — **-ography** *n.*
electroencephalograph *n.* instrument recording the electrical impulses in the brain, used for diagnosis (also "EEG") — **-ography** *n.*
electrolysis (eélek-tróllə-siss) *n.* destruction of hair roots or other living tissue by means of an electric current
electrolyte *n.* solution or molten material that conducts electricity — **-lytic** *adj.*
eleemosynary (élli-ee-móssin-əri) *formal. adj.* relating to charity [akin to *alms*]
elegiac (élli-jī-ək) *adj.* relating to elegies; *formal.* expressing sorrow or sadness, mournful: *elegiac tones/music*
elegy (élliji) *n.* lament for the dead, especially a mournful poem or musical composition — **-gise** *v.* — **-gist** *n.*
elevation *n.* scale drawing of an outside face of a building or structure
elicit *formal. tr.v.* to draw out or bring to light: *elicit the truth*; to produce or give rise to, evoke: *elicit a response* — **-tation** *n.*
eligible *adj.* qualified, appropriate, or entitled: *eligible for retirement/the job*; considered desirable and worthy for marriage: *an eligible bachelor* — **-ibility** *n.*
elision *n.* omission of an unstressed vowel or syllable, as in a line of verse or a contraction, such as *he's* for *he is* — **elide** *tr.v.*
elite (i-leét, ay-) *n.* best, most skilled, or most intelligent people within a given group; small group controlling power, wealth, or privilege — **-tism** *n.* — **-tist** *n., adj.*
elixir (i-líksər) *n.* syrup or similar preparation added to an unpleasant-tasting medicine; substance sought by alchemists for transmuting base metals to gold (also "philosopher's stone"); cure-all, universal remedy, as sought by alchemists (also "panacea"); substance sought by alchemists for prolonging life indefinitely (also "elixir of life")
ellipse *n.* shape like a flattened circle
ellipsis (i-líp-siss) *n., pl.* **-ses** in grammar, omission of a word or words from a sentence where syntax requires them but understanding does not, such as *And you?* for *And how are you?*; omission of a word or words for dramatic effect, such as *Stop it, or else ...*; mark such as an asterisk or series of dots used to indicate such omission
elliptical *adj.* shaped like an ellipse; containing or relating to ellipsis, having a word or words omitted; concise or compressed in expression, often to the point of obscurity: *an elliptical style/poem*
elocution *n.* art of public speaking; *formal.* style of speaking, especially public speaking; training for or acquiring of effective speaking style
elope *intr.v.* to run away secretly with a lover, especially in order to marry
eloquent (élləkwənt) *adj.* graceful, persuasive, or moving in use of language, expression, or the like — **-quence** *n.*
elucidate (i-lo͞osi-dayt) *v.* to explain, make clear — **-dation** *n.*
elude *tr.v.* to avoid or escape (capture, hunters, or the like), especially by cunning; to baffle, escape (understanding, notice, detection, or the like) — **elusive** *adj.*
elver *n.* young eel
Elysium (i-lízzi-əm) *formal. n.* place or state of perfect happiness, paradise [after the home of the blessed dead in Greek mythology] — **Elysian** *adj.*
emaciated (i-máysi-aytid) *adj.* abnormally thin, as through starvation or disease — **-ciation** *n.* — **-ciate** *tr.v.*
emanate *v.* — *intr.* to originate or issue from a source — *tr.* to give off, send out, emit — **-nation** *n.*
emancipate *tr.v.* to free, as from oppression, convention, or inhibition — **-pation** *n.*

emasculate *tr.v.* to castrate or geld; to weaken, deprive of initiative, energy, and other qualities traditionally regarded as male characteristics [related to *masculine*] — **emasculate** *adj.* — **-lation** *n.*

embalm *tr.v.* to preserve from decay by chemical treatment; to preserve the memory of

embargo *n., pl.* **-goes** government order prohibiting the movement of ships or cargo, or the trading of arms or some other commodity; any prohibition or suspension: *place an embargo on free speech/cultural relations* ~ *tr.v.* to impose an embargo on; to seize for state use, especially in wartime, commandeer

embarras de richesses (ON-bará də ree-shéss) *n.* range of choices so wide as to make a decision very difficult (also "embarras de choix") [French, literally, an embarrassment of riches]

embellish *tr.v.* to beautify or adorn (a work of art, piece of music, or the like) by adding ornamentation or detail; to improve or enliven (a report or story) by adding colourful, often false, details — **-ment** *n.*

embezzle *v.* to take or use fraudulently for oneself (money or property entrusted to one) — **-ment** *n.*

emblazon (im-bláyz'n) *formal. tr.v.* to brighten or beautify with colours, flowers, or the like; to glorify or celebrate splendidly and showily

embolism (émbə-liz'm) *n.* blocking of a blood vessel by a clot or air bubble; air bubble, clot, or the like circulating in the blood stream and liable to cause an embolism (also "embolus")

embonpoint (ON-boN-pwáN) *formal. n.* plumpness, appearance of being well-fed [French, *en bon point*, in good condition]

embossed *adj.* raised in relief, projecting ornamentally: *embossed lettering*; decorated with embossed designs or lettering: *embossed leather/notepaper* — **emboss** *tr.v.*

embouchure (óm-bŏŏ-shŏŏr, -shoor) *n.* mouth of a river or valley; mouthpiece of a wind instrument, especially a brass instrument; use and position of the lips and tongue when playing a wind instrument

embrasure *n.* opening in a wall, wider inside than out, for a door or window; opening, as in a castle wall, through which cannonballs or arrows can be fired

embrocation *formal. n.* lotion with soothing or healing properties, rubbed into the skin, liniment — **-cate** *tr.v.*

embroider *tr.v.* to embellish or exaggerate, improve or enliven (a report or story) by adding colourful, often false, details — **-dery** *n.*

embroiled *adj.* deeply involved in an argument, scandal, or the like — **embroil** *tr.v.*

embryo (émbri-ō) *n., pl.* **-os** organism in a very early stage of its development, such as a fertilised egg; undeveloped or rudimentary state or stage, or anything at such a stage: *the plot in embryo* — **-onic** *adj.*

emend *tr.v.* to correct and improve by critical editing — **-ation** *n.*

emeritus (i-mérri-təss) *adj.* retired but retaining an honorary title: *professor emeritus* (typically positioned after the noun; changes to *emeriti* when plural) — **emeritus, -ta** *n.*

emery *n.* fine, hard corundum-based mineral, used as a sandpaper or for nail-filing boards, for grinding, smoothing, or polishing

emetic (i-méttik) *adj. formal.* causing or inducing vomiting: *emetic liquids* ~ *n.* emetic medicine — **emesis** *n.*

émigré (émmi-gray) *n.* emigrant, specifically one who has fled his homeland for political reasons

eminence *n.* outstanding or superior position, rank, or the like; *formal.* hill or high ground — **eminent** *adj.*

éminence grise (áymi-noNSS gréez) *n., pl.* **-s -s** influential person wielding power behind the scenes (also "grey eminence") [French, literally, grey eminence, hence, a cardinal in a grey habit, a nickname of the 17th-century French monk and diplomat Père Joseph, who was Richelieu's secretary]

eminent domain *n.* in law, the government's right to take over private land or property for public use, usually with compensation being paid

eminently *adv.* extremely, especially, outstandingly: *eminently qualified*

emissary (émmi-səri) *n.* agent or messenger sent on a mission, typically by a government or head of state; spy or agent on a secret mission

emit *tr.v.* to give off or send out (something such as gas or radiation) — **emission** *n.*

emmetropia (émmi-trṓpi-ə) *formal. n.* perfect eyesight, normal vision — **-tropic** *adj.*

Emmy *n.* annual television award in the U.S. for outstanding performance or production; statuette presented for such an award. Compare TONY [alteration of *Immy*, informal name for an *image orthicon*, a television camera tube]

emollient *n.* lotion for soothing and softening the skin; *formal.* anything that soothes or pacifies: *political promises as emollients to his rivals* — **emollient** *adj.*

emolument (i-móllew-mənt) *formal. n.* fees, wages, or other form of profit from one's job or office

empathy *n.* close emotional identification with another that is so deep that one seems to enter into or share his feelings; crediting an object with the feelings it arouses in oneself, typically as a technique in art appreciation — **-thetic** *adj.* — **-thise** *intr.v.*

empennage *n.* tail assembly of an aircraft, including the rudder [French, originally, the feathers of an arrow]

emphysema (émfi-séemə) *n.* abnormal presence of air in body tissues or parts, or the resulting swelling or condition; specifically, lung disorder involving wheezing or breathlessness — **-sematous** *adj.*

empirical (em-pírrik'l) *adj.* based on or relating to observation or experiment rather than theory: *an empirical investigation*; based on practical experience rather than on theory or proof: *an empirical medical treatment*

empiricism *n.* theory that all knowledge derives from experience, especially from sense perceptions — **-cist** *n., adj.*

emplacement *n.* position, such as a platform or mounting, specially prepared for a gun or other military equipment

emporium (em-páwri-əm) *n., pl.* **-ums** or **-ria** department store or large retail shop selling a wide range of goods (usually humorously pompous); *formal.* trading or commercial centre

empyreal (émpī-rée-əl) *formal. adj.* relating to the sky or heaven, celestial

empyrean (ém-pī-rée-ən) *n.* in religious belief or myth, the highest level of heaven; *formal.* the sky, heavens, outer space — **empyrean** *adj.*

emulate (émmew-layt) *n.* try to equal or rival, especially by imitating, compete — **-tion** *n.*

emulsion *n.* suspension of globules of one liquid inside

another, as of cream within milk; paint in the form of an emulsion (also "emulsion paint"); light-sensitive coating, typically of silver bromide grains in gelatine, on photographic film or paper — **emulsify** *v.* — **emulsifier** *n.*

enactment *n.* law, statute, or regulation

enamoured (in-ámmərd) *formal. adj.* in love, fond: *enamoured with/of himself* — **enamour** *tr.v.*

en bloc (ON blók) *adv., adj.* all together, as a whole, in a group: *examined the claims en bloc rather than individually* [French, literally, in a block]

en brochette (ON bro-shét) *adv., adj.* roasted or grilled on a skewer [French, literally, on a skewer]

encaenia (en-séeni-ə) *n.* annual ceremony at universities, especially Oxford, honouring founders and benefactors

[1]**enceinte** (on-sánt, ON-SÁNT) *formal. adj.* pregnant

[2]**enceinte** *n.* fortified wall surrounding a castle, town, or the like, or the area protected by it

encephalitis (en-séffə-lítiss) *n.* inflammation of the brain tissue, typically caused by infection, "brain fever"

encipher *tr.v.* to put (a message or text) into code

en clair (ON kláir) *adj., adv.* uncoded, in plain language rather than in code [French, literally, in clear]

enclave (én-klayv, ón-) *n.* part of a foreign country entirely within a country's territory. Compare EXCLAVE; any area entirely within a larger area; minority group or community of people, plants, or the like

enclitic *n.* in linguistics, word or word element, such as *'em*, lacking an independent accent and typically linked with a preceding word in a sentence ~ *adj.* referring or relating to such a word

encomium *formal. n., pl.* **-ums** or **-mia** formal or ceremonial speech or article of warm praise, tribute, eulogy — **-iast** *n.* — **-iastic** *adj.*

encore (óng-kawr, -kór) *n.* performance, as by a musician, additional to the scheduled programme, in response to audience applause; audience's demand for an encore [French, literally, again] — **encore** *v., interj.*

encroach *intr.v.* to intrude slowly on the property or rights of someone else, trespass: *encroach on my domain/time*; to go or advance beyond proper limits — **-ment** *n.*

encrusted *formal. adj.* richly decorated, as with jewels — **encrust** *tr.v.*

encumber *tr.v.* to weigh down or burden, hinder or impede, as with clutter; to burden or handicap: *encumbering him with financial demands* — **-brance** *n.*

encyclical (en-sík-lik'l) *adj. formal.* addressed to everyone in a group, intended for wide circulation ~ *n.* letter from the Pope to bishops in all countries

endearment *n.* loving word, gesture, or the like

endemic *adj.* deeply rooted or common within a particular area or group: *endemic prejudices*; local, native, restricted to a particular area or group: *endemic diseases/trees* — **endemic** *n.*

endocrine gland (éndō-krīn, -krin) *n.* ductless gland, such as the pituitary or adrenal, that secretes hormones directly into the bloodstream (also "endocrine", "ductless gland"). Compare EXOCRINE GLAND

endogamy (en-dóggəmi) *n.* in anthropology, marriage within one's own tribe, clan, or caste. Compare EXOGAMY; pollination between the flowers on a single plant — **-gamous** *adj.*

endogenous (en-dójinəss) *adj.* originating internally, as within a cell or within the body; lacking any obvious external cause: *endogenous depression* — **-geny** *n.*

endomorph *n.* person with a heavy, rounded body build, often flabby or fat. Compare ECTOMORPH, MESOMORPH — **-morphic** *adj.*

endorphin (en-dórfin) *n.* pain-killing or tranquillising substance secreted by the brain

endorse *tr.v.* to approve or support: *endorse your candidature*; to place (one's signature) on (a document, the back of a cheque, or the like), as to indicate agreement, receipt, or transfer; to publicise or advertise (a product or service) by using one's name to recommend it; to qualify (a driving licence) by an endorsement

endorsement *n.* record of a motoring offence on a driving licence; amendment to an insurance policy or other contract

endowment *n.* donation such as a bequest or trust, or the income derived from it; natural talent, gift, or characteristic ~ *adj.* relating to a form of life assurance that expires at a specified date and pays out a given sum if the assured is still alive — **endow** *tr.v.*

endue *formal. tr.v.* to provide with a specified quality: *endued with good sense*

energumen (énnər-géw-men) *formal. n.* person supposedly possessed by an evil spirit; fanatic or zealot

enervated *adj.* drained of strength or vigour, weakened or exhausted [related to *nerve*] — **-vate** *tr.v.*

en famille (ON fa-mée) *formal. adv.* within or with one's family, at home; informally, casually [French]

enfant terrible (ON-FÓN te-réebl) *n., pl.* **-s -s** outrageous, unconventional, or provocative person, typically causing embarrassment and yet often secretly admired [French, literally, terrible child]

enfilade (énfi-láyd) *n.* gunfire directed from the side, raking the entire length of a troop formation or position; troop formation or position subjected to enfilade — **enfilade** *tr.v.*

enfranchise *tr.v.* to give voting rights or full citizenship rights to; *formal.* to free, as from slavery

eng *n.* symbol ŋ used in phonetics to represent the *ng*-sound, as in *long* (also "agma")

engagé (ON-ga-zháy) *formal. adj.* committed to and actively promoting a moral or political cause [French]

engender *formal. tr.v.* to give rise to, produce, bring into existence [related to *generate*]

engorged *adj.* filled to excess or congested with blood or other fluid: *an engorged mosquito* — **engorge** *tr.v.*

enhance *tr.v.* to increase or improve, as in quality or reputation

enigma (i-nígmə) *n.* mysterious or puzzling person or thing, riddle — **-matic** *adj.*

enjoin *tr.v.* to urge or command; to prohibit: *enjoined by the court from harassing his neighbour*

enlarge *archaic. tr.v.* to free or liberate, as from prison or slavery

en masse (ON máss) *adv.* in a group, as a whole, all together: *walked out en masse* [French]

enmesh *tr.v.* to tangle or catch in or as if in a net; to involve or entangle, as in a scandal — **enmeshed** *adj.*

ennui (ÓN-nwée) *formal. n.* state of boredom or listlessness through lack of activity or stimulation

enormity *n.* monstrous wickedness or wicked deed, outrage

en passant (ON pa-són, pá-SON) *formal. adv.* by the way, in passing [French]

ensconce *tr.v.* to settle or establish (oneself) firmly or snugly in position: *ensconced herself in an armchair/helpless widowhood*; to place or hide securely

ensemble (on-sómb'l, ON-sóNbl) *n.* coordinated grouping or set, as of matching clothes or furniture; group of musicians, dancers, or other performers; supporting actors in a play; unity and precision of the performance of a group of musicians [French, literally, together]

enshrine *formal. tr.v.* to treat as sacred, cherish; to contain or enclose (something considered sacred): *The constitution enshrines American values*

ensnare *formal. tr.v.* to trap, catch in or as if in a snare

ensue *intr.v.* to follow in time, occur afterwards; to occur as a result

en suite (ON swéet) *adv., adj.* in a set or series, especially so as to form a set of rooms: *with bathroom en suite* [French, literally, in sequence]

entail *tr.v.* to imply, involve, have as a necessary consequence; to limit the inheritance of (an estate or other property) to a particular line of heirs — **entail, -ment** *n.*

entasis (éntə-siss) *n., pl.* **-ses** in architecture, the slight bulge that makes a column appear straight when viewed from below

entente (on-tónt, ON-tóNt) *n.* friendly understanding or informal agreement between countries or powers (also "entente cordiale") [French]

entice *tr.v.* to tempt, lure, attract — **-ment** *n.*

entity *n.* thing existing in its own right, independently of other things; separate self-contained unit or object of discussion; being or existence

entomb *tr.v.* to bury or imprison in or as if in a tomb; to serve as the tomb for — **-ment** *n.* — **entombed** *adj.*

entomology *n.* scientific study of insects — **-gist** *n.* — **-logical** *adj.*

entourage (ón-toor-áazh, -aazh) *n.* retinue, group of followers or associates, typically attending a person of high rank; *formal.* surroundings or environment [French; related to *tour*]

entr'acte (ón-trakt, -trákt) *n.* interval or interval performance in a theatre [French, literally, between act]

entrails *pl.n.* internal organs, especially the intestines; inner reaches of something, interior, core

entrapment *n.* tricking or luring of someone, as by the police, into crime, danger, or the like — **entrap** *tr.v.*

entrecôte (ón-trə-kōt, óN-), *n.* steak cut from between the ribs [French, literally, between rib]

entrée (ón-tray, óN-) *n.* access, right of admittance; *chiefly British.* main course, or dish just before the main course, of a meal [French, literally, entry]

entremets (ón-trə-may, ON-trə-mé) *n.* course or dish served between the main courses of a meal; side dish; dessert, or light dish just before the dessert [French, earlier *entremes*, literally, between dish]

entrenched *adj.* fixed, established, firmly and immovably settled in or as if in a trench: *entrenched troops/opinions* — **entrench** *v.* — **entrenchment** *n.*

entre nous (ón-trə nōō, ON-) *formal. adv.* confidentially, between ourselves, in confidence [French, literally, between us]

entrepôt (ón-trə-pō, ON-) *n.* warehouse or storage depot; trading centre, especially a duty-free port

entrepreneur (óntrə-prə-núr) *n.* businessman undertaking ventures involving risk and initiative [related to *enterprise*] — **-ial** *adj.*

entresol (óntrə-sol) *n.* storey of a building lying between ground floor and first floor (also "mezzanine")

entropy (éntrəpi) *n.* tendency of the energy in the universe or any other closed system to run down; loosely, randomness, disorder, lack of organisation — **entropic** *adj.*

enumerate *formal. tr.v.* to count off or list one by one; to count, establish the number of — **-tion** *n.* — **-tive** *adj.*

enumerator *British. n.* person who delivers and collects census forms

enunciate *v.* to pronounce, especially in a clear and distinct way ~ *tr.v.* to state or declare formally: *enunciated his ideology in a sermon* — **-ation** *n.*

environs (in-vīr-ənz) *pl.n.* surrounding area, as of a town, suburbs or outskirts; neighbourhood, surroundings or environment

envisage (in-vízzij) *tr.v.* to think of or have a mental image of, especially of something expected or possible in the future (also *chiefly U.S.* "envision")

envoy *n.* representative, messenger, or agent sent on a mission, especially a government agent sent on diplomatic business

enzyme (énzīm) *n.* protein produced by living cells and serving as a biochemical catalyst — **-matic, -mic** *adj.*

eonism *formal. n.* adoption of female dress and behaviour by a man, transvestism [after Charles *Eon* de Beaumont, an 18th-19th-century French transvestite] — **eonist** *n., adj.*

epaulette (ép-ə-let, -aw-, -lét) *n.* braid, fringed strap, or the like worn on the shoulder, as on a military uniform; five-sided gemstone cut

epenthesis (e-pénthə-siss) *n., pl.* **-ses** insertion of an extra sound or letter into a word to make its pronunciation easier, as when pronouncing *umbrella* as (úmbə-réllə); sound or letter inserted in this way — **-thetic** *adj.*

ephemera (i-fém-ərə, -féem-) *pl.n.* printed pamphlets, handouts, and other short-lived topical publications; short-lived things (singular "ephemeron")

ephemeral *adj.* short-lived, lasting only a short time, transitory; living or lasting for a single day only: *ephemeral blossoms/insects* — **-ality** *n.*

epicene (éppi-seen) *adj.* characteristic of or resembling both male and female sexes, hermaphrodite: *epicene statues*; sexless, neuter, belonging to neither sex; effeminate

epicentre *n.* area on the Earth's surface directly above the point of origin of an earthquake; any central or focal point — **-tral** *adj.*

epicure (éppi-kewr) *n.* gourmet, connoisseur, person appreciating fine food and wine [after the ancient Greek philosopher *Epicurus*, misrepresented as exalting luxury and sensuous pleasure] — **-curean** *n., adj.*

epidemiology *n.* study of epidemics and of the causes and spread of diseases — **-gist** *n.* — **-logical** *adj.*

epidermis *n.* outer layer of skin — **-dermal, -mic** *adj.*

epidiascope *n.* projector for showing images, as written or drawn on paper or on transparent film, onto a screen

epidural *n.* injection of anaesthetic into the lining of the spinal cord, especially as a local anaesthetic during childbirth — **epidural** *adj.*

epigone (éppi-gōn) *formal. n.* follower, imitator, or

disciple who is markedly inferior to his master, especially in philosophy or the arts — **-gonic** *adj.*

epigram *n.* short witty poem, remark, or saying — **-grammatic** *adj.*

epigraph *n.* opening quotation, as at the head of a chapter or start of a book, suggesting its theme; inscription on a statue, monument, or building — **-graphic** *adj.*

epigraphy (i-píggrəfi) *n.* inscriptions collectively, especially ancient inscriptions; study of ancient inscriptions — **-pher**, **-phist** *n.*

epilogue *n.* closing poem or speech following the end of the action of a play; concluding section or postscript of a book

epiphany (i-píffəni) *n.* sudden appearance or revelation of God or a divine being or reality; insight or sudden recognition, such as a mystical experience of the essence of an event; story, poem, or the like representing such an experience

episcopal *adj.* relating to a bishop or bishops, or to church government by bishops — **-pate**, **-pacy** *n.*

epistemology *n.* theory of knowledge, or the philosophical study of the nature of knowledge — **-gist** *n.* — **-logical** *adj.*

epistle *n.* letter, especially a long, formal letter (often humorously pompous); poem, dedication, or the like in the form of a letter — **epistolary** *adj.*

epitaph *n.* inscription on a gravestone, tombstone, or monument commemorating the person buried there; speech or written obituary commemorating a dead person; final judgment on a person or thing: *an epitaph on her collected poems*

epithalamium (éppi-thə-láymi-əm) *formal. n., pl.* **-ums** or **-mia** song or poem celebrating a marriage

epithet *n.* adjective or descriptive term, often a scornful or disparaging one; word or phrase intended to characterise a person or thing, often used as part of a person's name or title, as in *Ethelred the Unready*; *informal.* swear word or term of abuse

epitome (i-píttəmi) *n.* typical example or representative of its kind, essence, embodiment: *hardly the epitome of a fairy godmother!* — **-mise** *tr.v.*

epoch (ée-pok) *n.* historical period, era; division of a geological period; turning point or milestone, point in time marking an epoch — **-al** *adj.*

eponymous (i-pónni-məss) *adj.* referring to the person, fictional hero, or the like, after whom a city, novel, or the like is named: *the eponymous heroine of the "Martha Quest" series* — **-nym**, **-nymy** *n.*

equable (ékwə-b'l) *adj.* unvarying, even, especially in a pleasant way: *an equable climate*; calm, even-tempered, placid — **-bility** *n.*

equanimity *n.* even-temperedness, calmness, composure

equerry (i-kwérri, ékwəri) *n.* royal attendant, formerly responsible for the horses of the royal household

equestrian *adj.* relating to horsemanship or mounted troops; referring to a statue or portrait in which the subject is depicted on horseback ~ *formal. n.* horseback rider or performer, as in a circus (feminine form "equestrienne")

equilateral *adj.* having all sides of equal length: *equilateral triangles* ~ *n.* equilateral figure, or any of its sides

equilibrist (i-kwílli-brist) *formal. n.* tightrope walker or other performer of balancing feats

equilibrium (éekwi-líbri-əm) *n.* state of balance or stability, as of one's body or of forces in physics; even temper, psychological stability

equine *adj.* relating to a horse or horses ~ *n.* mammal of the horse family

equinox *n.* either of the two times during the year, about 20 March and 23 September, when the Sun crosses the celestial equator, and day and night are of equal length all over the Earth — **-noctial** *adj.*

equitable (ék-witəb'l) *formal. adj.* fair, just, even-handed: *an equitable division of the spoils*

equities *pl.n.* ordinary shares

equity *n.* fairness, justice, impartiality; anything that is fair or just; body of legal rules based on natural justice and fairness, supplementing and moderating common and statute law; net or residual value of a property, business interest, or share issue

equivocal (i-kwívvək'l) *formal. adj.* ambiguous, having more than one possible meaning or interpretation: *equivocal advice*; misleading or evasive: *an equivocal reply*; uncertain, unclear, vague

equivocate (i-kwívvə-kayt) *intr.v.* to speak evasively, hedge — **-cation** *n.*

ergo *formal. adv., conj.* consequently, therefore

ergonomics *n.* study or application of biology and engineering in work and the workplace (also *chiefly U.S.* "biotechnology") — **-nomic** *adj.* — **-nomist** *n.*

erinaceous *formal. adj.* relating to or resembling hedgehogs

eristic *formal. adj.* relating or given to argument, controversy, or logical dispute, typically of an over-subtle or manipulative kind ~ *n.* art or practice of debate; person engaging in or expert in eristic

erogenous (i-rójə-nəss) *adj.* sexually arousing or arousable, sensitive to sexual stimulation: *erogenous zones*

erotic *adj.* relating to sexual desires or love — **-cism** *n.*

erotica *n., pl.n.* literature or art with an erotic or sexually arousing content or effect

errant *formal or archaic. adj.* wandering in search of adventure: *knights errant*; straying from the proper moral course, erring; wayward, unfaithful: *an errant wife* — **-try**, **errancy** *n.*

errata *pl.n.* errors in a book, manuscript, or the like, or a list noting them (singular "erratum")

erratic *adj.* unconventional, irregular, or eccentric; *formal.* wandering, roundabout, deviating: *an erratic route*

ersatz (áir-zats, ér-) *adj.* artificial, substitute, or imitation, typically of inferior quality: *ersatz champagne/Picasso* — **ersatz** *n.*

erubescence (érroo-béss'nss) *formal. n.* blushing or reddening — **-scent** *adj.*

eruct *formal. v.* — *intr.* to belch or burp — *tr.* to expel (fumes or solid matter), as a rumbling volcano might — **-tation** *n.*

erudition *n.* scholarly knowledge, deep learning — **erudite** *adj.*

escadrille (éskə-dril) *n.* small squadron of ships [related to *squadron*]

escalade (éskə-layd) *n.* act of scaling, by ladders, of a castle wall, rampart, or the like, as during a military attack — **escalade** *tr.v.*

escargot (éskaar-gō) *n., pl.* **-gots** edible snail, especially when cooked and ready for eating

escarpment *n.* long steep slope, as from a plateau or in front of a castle

eschar (éss-kaar) *formal. n.* scab or layer of dead skin, as caused by a burn

eschatology (éskə-tólleji) *n.* branch of theology dealing with last things, such as heaven and hell — **-logical** *adj.*
eschew (iss-chōō) *formal. tr.v.* to avoid or abstain from
escritoire (éskri-twáar) *n.* writing desk, typically with a hinged top closing over small drawers
escrow (éskrō, ess-krṓ) *n.* money, contract, or the like held by a third party until certain conditions are fulfilled
esculent *formal. adj.* edible, suitable for eating ~ *n.* food, something edible
escutcheon *n.* shield, as in heraldry, bearing a coat of arms (also "scutcheon"); plate or shield covering a keyhole, surrounding a door handle or light switch, or the like; plate or place on the stern of a ship or boat bearing the vessel's name — **-ed** *adj.*
esoteric *adj.* difficult to understand; limited to or comprehensible to only a small group: *esoteric knowledge*
espalier *n.* shrub or fruit tree trained to lie flat against a wall, trellis, or the like; such a wall or trellis — **espalier** *tr.v.*
espionage (éspi-ə-naazh) *n.* spying [French; akin to *spy*]
esplanade *n.* paved stretch of ground for walking along, especially along a shore
espouse *formal. tr.v.* to adopt or support (a cause); *archaic.* to marry — **-sal** *n.*
esprit (e-spreé) *n.* wit, spirit, liveliness
esprit de corps (də kór) *n.* spirit of fellowship, loyalty to and pride in one's group [French, literally, spirit of the body]
esprit d'escalier (dess-kal-yáy) *n.* tendency to think of a forceful reply or witty retort only when it is too late [French, literally, staircase wit, referring to wit that seems to operate only when one is taking the stairs on leaving the scene of a confrontation]
estranged *adj.* hostile or indifferent following antagonism; separated or alienated from one's spouse: *estranged from his wife* — **estrange** *tr.v.* — **estrangement** *n.*
estuary *n.* wide lower reaches of a river where it approaches or meets the sea; sea inlet, especially at the mouth of a river
ether *n.* light inflammable liquid used as a solvent and anaesthetic; in ancient belief, the space or heavens beyond the Earth's atmosphere, or the thin gas-like element filling it (also "aether") — **-ise** *tr.v.*
ethereal *adj.* airy, light as air; delicate, very refined; unearthly, spiritual, immaterial; relating to the ether or the heavens, celestial — **-ise** *tr.v.*
ethnic *adj.* relating or referring to a distinctive racial, religious, or cultural group, typically a minority group, within a society; relating to a traditional, especially peasant, culture: *ethnic costume*; *informal.* quaint, folksy ~ *chiefly U.S. n.* member of an ethnic group, especially a distinctive minority or immigrant group — **-nicity** *n.*
ethnology *n.* study of the culture of peoples, especially primitive peoples — **-logical** *adj.* — **-gist** *n.*
ethology *n.* study of animal behaviour — **-logical** *adj.* — **-gist** *n.*
ethos *n.* character, distinctive spirit, or value system of a particular culture, people, artistic movement, or the like
etiolated (eéti-ə-laytid) *adj.* whitened through lack of sunlight: *etiolated grass within the tent*; *formal.* pale and weakened, enfeebled — **-late** *v.* — **-lation** *n.*
etiquette *n.* manners, code of proper behaviour within a given group or society: *courtroom etiquette*
etymology *n.* origin and development of a word, or an account of such an origin, or the study of such origins — **-gist** *n.* — **-logical** *adj.*
etymon (étti-mon) *n., pl.* **-mons** or **-ma** earliest known form of a word or word-element
Eucharist (yōōkə-rist) *n.* bread and wine consecrated and consumed in commemoration of Jesus; the Christian sacrament involved (in this sense, also "Communion", "Holy Communion") — **-istic** *adj.*
eugenics (yoo-jénniks) *n.* study of or attempts at improving the human race by selective breeding — **-nic** *adj.*
eulogy (yōōlə-ji) *n.* speech of praise or a written tribute; eulogy for someone who has recently died — **-gise** *tr.v.* — **-gistic** *adj.*
eunuch (yṓō-nək) *n.* castrated man, especially in former times, serving as a harem guard, court attendant, or the like; *informal.* ineffective, unmanly, or weak man
euphemism *n.* substitution of a word or phrase considered neutral or acceptable for one that is blunt or offensive (opposite "dysphemism"); word or phrase used in this way — **-mise** *v.* — **-mistic** *adj.*
euphony *n.* sound, especially in speech, that is pleasant to listen to. Compare CACOPHONY — **-nious** *adj.*
euphoric *formal. adj.* extremely happy or optimistic, sometimes dangerously so — **euphoria** *n.*
euphuism (yōō-few-iz'm) *n.* style of speech or writing that is over-ornate or affected, specifically in English prose around the end of the 16th century [after *Euphues*, a character in the prose works of the 16th-century English writer John Lyly] — **-istic** *adj.*
eurhythmics *n., pl.n.* art of rhythmical free-style dance to music, or a form of musical training using such movement
euthanasia *n.* deliberate causing of a painless death of a person in order to relieve suffering, as from an incurable illness (also "mercy killing")
evacuate *v.* — *tr.* to empty or remove (the contents) from (something); to create a vacuum in; to send away or withdraw (troops, inhabitants, or the like) from (a military zone, infected neighbourhood, or the like) — *intr.* to withdraw from a dangerous building, military zone, or the like — **-uation**, **-uee** *n.*
evanescent *formal. adj.* vanishing, fading, or short-lived: *evanescent anger/mist* — **-escence** *n.* — **-esce** *intr.v.*
evangelist *n.* preacher or missionary of the Protestant faith, dedicated to spreading the gospel; energetic promoter of a cause, crusading enthusiast, zealot — **-lical**, **-listic** *adj.* — **-ism** *n.* — **-ise** *v.*
evasion *n.* act of avoiding or escaping, specifically avoiding a duty, such as paying tax, by cunning or illegal means — **evade** *v.*
evasive *n.* vague, ambiguous, non-committal: *an evasive answer*; referring to action taken in advance to avoid likely trouble or problems
evict *tr.v.* to force out or expel, as from rented property — **-tion** *n.*
evince *tr.v.* to show or reveal clearly: *to evince surprise*
eviscerate (i-víssə-rayt) *tr.v.* to remove the bowels or internal organs of, disembowel (also "exenterate"); to remove surgically the contents of (an organ, eye socket, or the like) — **-ation** *n.*

evoke *tr.v.* to arouse or summon (a memory, emotion, answer, or the like); to conjure up (a spirit) — **evocation** *n.* — **evocative** *adj.*

evolution *n.* development by slow or natural means, as of species, art, or social systems; biological theory, especially Darwin's, that species can over many generations change into different species (also "evolutionism") — **-ary** *adj.* — **evolve** *v.*

ewer (yōō-ər) *n.* large, typically wide-mouthed jug

exacerbate (ig-zássər-bayt) *tr.v.* to make more severe or intense, aggravate: *exacerbated the problem/pain/grief* — **-bation** *n.*

exalt *tr.v.* to raise in rank, status, or the like: *heroes who were exalted to the rank of demigods*; to intensify or stimulate: *exalted our imagination* — **-tation** *n.*

ex cathedra (éks kə-théedrə) *adj.*, *adv.* with authority, from the source of or in the performance of official authority: *ex cathedra pronouncements*; specifically, as authorised by the Pope: *ex cathedra doctrines* [Latin, literally, from the chair, referring to the papal throne or other official seat of an authority]

excerpt *n.* (ék-serpt) extract or selected passage or scene from a book, film, or the like ~ *tr.v.* (ig-zérpt) to choose (an excerpt) for quoting, copying, or the like; to take excerpts from

exchequer *n.* treasury, government department in charge of funds or revenue [Old French *eschequier*, a chessboard, hence a counting table (probably from the chequered table cloth, used perhaps as an aid to calculating); related to *chess*, *check*]

excise *tr.v.* to delete (a passage) from a text; to remove by or as if by cutting out: *excised the tumour/whim* — **excision** *n.*

exclave *n.* part of a country lying entirely within a foreign country's territory. Compare ENCLAVE

excommunicate *tr.v.* to exclude from or deprive officially of membership of a church or religion — **excommunicate** *adj.*, *n.* — **-tion** *n.*

excoriate *formal. tr.v.* to criticise scathingly or scold very severely; to rub or tear away the skin of — **-ation** *n.*

excrescence *formal. n.* outgrowth or projection on the body, especially an abnormal or excessive one such as a bunion

excruciating *adj.* extremely painful, torturing, agonising; *informal.* very poor in quality, inferior: *excruciating jokes* — **excruciate** *tr.v.*

exculpate *formal. tr.v.* to clear of guilt or blame, exonerate — **-pation** *n.* — **-patory** *adj.*

exeat (éksi-ət) *British. n.* leave of absence, as from school; bishop's permission for a clergyman to leave the diocese to work elsewhere

execrable (éksi-krəb'l) *formal. adj.* extremely bad, inferior; appalling, detestable

execration *formal. n.* denunciation, scathing criticism; curse or condemnation; loathing, detestation, abhorrence [related to *sacred*] — **execrate** *tr.v.*

executor *n.* person appointed by a testator to carry out the requirements of his will (feminine form "executrix")

exegesis (éksi-jée-siss) *n.*, *pl.* **-ses** critical analysis or explanation of a text, especially of the bible — **exegete, exegetics** *n.* — **exegetic** *adj.*

exemplar *n.* ideal, model, or original that is worth copying; example, representative

exemplary *adj.* typical, serving as an illustration; admirable, worthy of imitation: *exemplary behaviour*; serving as a warning to others: *exemplary damages/sentencing*

exempli gratia *formal. adv.* for example, e.g. [Latin, for the sake of an example]

exemplum *n.*, *pl.* **-pla** moral story or fable, as used in medieval sermons; *formal.* example, model

ex gratia (eks gráy-shə) *adj.*, *adv.* without legal compulsion, as a favour: *ex gratia payments* [Latin, literally, from favour]

exhibition *n.* scholarship or allowance to a student at a British public school or university — **-er** *n.*

exhort *tr.v.* to encourage strongly or appeal to urgently: *exhorted him to confess* — **-tation** *n.* — **-tative, -tatory** *adj.*

exhume *formal. tr.v.* to dig up and remove (a dead body) from a grave, disinter; to uncover, bring to light, unearth: *exhumed an old scandal* — **-mation** *n.*

exigency *formal. n.* emergency, state of urgent need

exigent (éksi-jənt) *formal. adj.* urgent, pressing, requiring immediate attention; demanding, exacting

exiguous *formal. adj.* scanty, inadequate, meagre

exocrine gland *n.* gland, such as a sweat or salivary gland, that secretes through a duct (also "exocrine"). Compare ENDOCRINE GLAND

exodus *n.* emigration or departure, especially of a large number of people

exogamy (ek-sóggəmi) *n.* in anthropology, marriage outside one's own tribe, clan, or caste. Compare ENDOGAMY — **-gamous** *adj.*

exonerate *tr.v.* to clear of blame, free from a charge, exculpate; to release from a duty or responsibility, exempt

exonym (éksə-nim) *formal. n.* name of a city or other place used in a foreign language, such as English *Florence* for the Italian city of *Firenze*

exophthalmic (éksof-thálmik) *adj.* having bulging eyes, specifically as a result of excess thyroid hormone

exorbitant *adj.* excessive, unreasonably extravagant: *exorbitant prices/demands* — **-tance** *n.*

exorcise *tr.v.* to drive out (an evil spirit or demons), or free (a possessed person) from them, as by religious rites — **-cism** *n.*

exordium *formal. n.*, *pl.* **-ums** or **-dia** beginning or introductory section, as to a speech or treatise

exotic *adj.* foreign, from another part of the world; strange and fascinating through being unfamiliar or foreign ~ *n.* exotic person or thing, such as a nonindigenous plant — **-icism** *n.* — **-ica** *pl.n.*

expatiate (ek-spáyshi-ayt) *intr.v.* to talk or write at length and in detail on a subject, dilate, elaborate: *expatiated on that theme*

expatriate *n.* person who has left or been driven from his homeland and now lives in another country — **expatriate** *v.*, *adj.*

expectorate *formal. intr.v.* to spit or spit out; to clear the chest by coughing up and spitting out phlegm or sputum, hawk — **-rant** *n.*, *adj.* — **-ration** *n.*

expedient *adj.* convenient, selfishly advantageous rather than fair or moral; suitable, appropriate ~ *n.* means to an end, or device adopted for an urgent purpose — **-ency** *n.*

expedite *formal. tr.v.* to speed up the progress of (something such as a business matter); to do or perform with speed and efficiency — **-ditious** *adj.*

expend *formal. tr.v.* to spend, lay out, disburse; to use

up, consume
expendable *adj.* not absolutely essential, possible to do without, sacrificeable
expiate *v.* atone or make amends for [related to *pious*] — **-tion** *n.*
expletive *formal. n.* exclamation or oath, especially a swearword or profanity — **expletive** *adj.*
explication *n.* explanation; formulation or explanation of a theory; critical analysis or interpretation of a literary work, philosophical theory, or the like — **explicate** *tr.v.*
explicit *adj.* clear, detailed, and fully expressed: *explicit directions*; outspoken, forthright; detailed in describing or representing sexual acts
exponent *n.* person who expounds, explains, interprets, or advocates; number placed above and to the right of another number indicating how many times it is to be multiplied by itself
exponential growth *n.* growing at a rate that doubles, trebles, or the like, by contrast with growth through the addition of a specific amount each time; loosely, rapid growth by leaps and bounds
exposé (ek-spṓzay) *n.* revealing of a scandal or crime, or the book, broadcast, or the like in which it is reported
exposition *n.* commentary, precise statement, detailed explanation; setting forth of information, intentions, or the like; introduction of themes, intentions, or the like, as in an argument or artistic work; large public exhibition, as of industrial products — **-sitor** *n.*
ex post facto *adj., adv.* after the events, with retrospective effect: *an ex post facto law* [Latin, from the thing done afterwards]
expostulate *formal. intr.v.* to argue or reason with, especially to dissuade someone — **-lation** *n.*
expound *v.* to comment on in detail; to explain or interpret
express *formal. tr.v.* to squeeze or press out (juice or milk)
expropriate *tr.v.* to take away (a person's private property or land), especially for public ownership — **-ation** *n.*
expunge *formal. tr.v.* to delete, erase, or obliterate: *a remark to be expunged from the records*; to destroy, eliminate
expurgate *tr.v.* to censor or alter a (book or other text) by removing objectionable or obscene passages [related to *purge*] — **-gation** *n.*
extant *adj.* surviving, still in existence, not lost or extinct or destroyed: *extant reptiles/documents*
extemporaneous, *adj.* unprepared, unrehearsed, off-the-cuff: *an extemporaneous speech*; improvised, makeshift, temporary — **extempore** *adj., adv.* — **extemporise** *v.*
extenuate *formal. tr.v.* to make (a crime, fault, or the like) seem less serious or blameworthy, as by making excuses: *extenuating circumstances* — **-uation** *n.*
extirpate *formal. tr.v.* to root up or root out; destroy, exterminate — **-pation** *n.*
extol *formal. tr.v.* to praise highly, laud
extort *tr.v.* to obtain (money, promises, or the like) by threats, corruption, or force — **-tion** *n.*
extortionate *adj.* excessive, over-priced, exorbitant
extracurricular *adj.* occurring outside the normal course of studies or timetable, as in a college
extradition *n.* handing over of a criminal, fugitive, or the like to the authority or country where he is wanted — **-dite** *tr.v.* — **-ditable** *adj.*
extramural *adj.* referring to non-resident students or to studies or activities outside the normal courses of a university or college
extraneous (ek-stráyni-əss) *adj.* non-essential, supplementary; irrelevant or inapplicable; coming from outside, of foreign or external origin
extrapolate (ek-stráppə-layt) *v.* to guess or infer from known information — **-lation** *n.*
extrasensory perception *n.* perception by means of a sixth sense, supernatural powers, intuition, or the like (also "ESP")
extravaganza *n.* spectacular, elaborate, or fanciful entertainment, display, or the like
extricate *formal. tr.v.* to release from a difficult situation, disentangle — **-cation** *n.*
extrovert *n.* sociable, friendly, outgoing person (also "extravert"). Compare INTROVERT — **extrovert, -ed** *adj.* — **-version** *n.*
extrude *v.* — *tr.* to produce (wire, metal or plastic sheeting, or the like) by pressing through a nozzle or die; *formal.* to push, squeeze, or force out — *formal. intr.* to project, jut out, or protrude
exuberant *adj.* joyful, high-spirited — **-ance** *n.*
exude *formal. v.* — *intr.* to ooze out, emerge slowly, as through pores: *sweat/sap exuded* — *tr.* to give off or discharge slowly or clearly: *exude sweat/smugness* — **-dation** *n.*
exultant *formal. adj.* joyous, triumphant, elated, jubilant — **exult** *intr.v.* — **-tation** *n.*
eyas (ī́-əss) *n.* young hawk or falcon, especially when reared for falconry
eyot (ayt, áy-ət) *British. n.* small island, especially in a river (also "ait")
eyrie *n.* nest of an eagle or other bird of prey, built on a cliff or other high place; *formal.* high inaccessible place, fortress, or the like (also "aerie")

Fabergé (fábber-zhay) *adj.* referring to ornate jewelled ornaments, such as golden gift eggs, as made for Russian and other European royalty around the turn of the century [after Peter Carl *Fabergé*, the Russian goldsmith who crafted such objects]

fabricate *tr.v.* to make or construct; to make up (a story or deception) — **-cation** *n.*

fabulist *n.* writer, such as Aesop, of fables or fantasies; liar (used humorously or euphemistically)

facade (fə-sáad) *n.* face or front of a building; outward appearance, especially a person's deceptive or suspect outward appearance: *a facade of spurious goodwill* (also "façade") [related to *face*]

facetious *formal. adj.* inappropriately humorous or joky, flippant

facile *adj.* shallow, superficial, lacking depth, interest, or thoroughness: *a facile theory/writer*; effortless, fluent: *a facile speaker*

facilitate *formal. tr.v.* to ease, help to bring about — **facility, -tator** *n.*

facsimile (fak-símmili) *n.* exact copy, as of a document [related to *similar*] — **facsimile** *adj., tr.v.*

factitious *formal. adj.* artificial, not natural, contrived: *factitious share prices/sympathy*

factotum (fak-tṓtəm) *n., pl.* **-tums** employee or assistant doing a variety of work [from Latin *fac totum!*, do everything!]

fado (fáa-dōō) *n., pl.* **-dos** Portuguese melancholy popular song [Portuguese, literally, fate]

faience (fī-áaNSS, fay-) *n.* pottery with a fine colourful glaze [French, literally, *Faenza*, the Italian town where the type of pottery originated]

fainéant (fáy-ni-ənt, -nay-ON) *formal. adj.* lazy, given to doing nothing ~ *n.* loafer, idler

fait accompli (féttə-kómplee) *formal. n., pl.* **-s -s** something that is already done and unalterable, unchangeable fact [French, literally, accomplished fact]

fakir (fáy-keer, fə-kéer) *n.* Hindu or Muslim holy man, living austerely and usually travelling about living off alms

fallacy *n.* illogical argument; false belief — **-lacious** *adj.*

fallal (fal-lál) *formal. n.* showy but trifling ornament or piece of clothing

fallible *adj.* capable of error, not perfect — **-ibility** *n.*

fallow *adj.* ploughed but left unseeded, as a field might be for a season to regain fertility; not productive; not pregnant: *a fallow mare.*

false friend *n.* word in a foreign language closely resembling a word in one's own language but differing from it in meaning, such as the French *sympathique* meaning "likeable" (also "faux ami")

falsetto *n., pl.* **-os** singing voice unnaturally in the upper register, usually produced by male singers, well above normal range; the use of such a voice [Italian; related to *false*] —**falsetto** *adj., adv.*

familiar *n.* spirit, often assuming animal form, attending and helping a witch or wizard; bishop's household helper or servant; *formal.* close friend or companion

famulus (fámmew-ləss) *n., pl.* **-li** servant or attendant of a magician or scholar in medieval times

fantoccini (fántə-chéeni) *pl.n.* puppets moved by strings or wires, marionettes; puppet shows in which fantoccini are used (singular "fantoccino") [Italian, related to *infant*]

farci (faar-sée) *adj.* stuffed: *roast chicken/mushrooms farci* [French]

farded *archaic or formal. adj.* covered with make-up, especially white cosmetic paint, as a clown might be

farina (fə-réenə) *n.* flour or meal from any cereal grain; potato flour or the starch from it

farinaceous *formal. adj.* floury or starchy; powdery or mealy in texture; containing or relating to pasta

farrago (fə-ráa-gō, -ráy-) *formal. n., pl.* **-gos** mixture, medley, collection: *a farrago of nonsense*

farrier *chiefly British. n.* person who shoes horses or treats them for disorders

[1]**farrow** *n.* litter of piglets — **farrow** *v.*

[2]**farrow** *adj.* not pregnant or not calving in a particular year: *a farrow cow*

farthingale *n.* hoop or series of hoops formerly worn under a skirt to support it; skirt supported by a farthingale

fasces (fásseez) *pl.n.* bundle of rods with an axe, carried as a symbol of the magistrates' authority in ancient Rome, and later of Italian Fascism [Latin, literally, bundles]

fascia (fáy-shə) *n., pl.* **fasciae** fibrous tissue beneath the skin and encasing muscles; band or flat surface in architecture, as on a cornice; band of colour on an insect or plant; signboard or band of wall just above the door or window of a shop; dashboard — **-ial, -iate** *adj.*

fascicle (fássi-k'l) *n.* small bundle; instalment of a book (also "fascicule"); in botany, bundle or cluster of leaves, roots, or the like [see FASCES] — **-ciculate** *adj.*

fastidious *adj.* extremely thorough and careful, meticulous or fussy; over-critical, nitpicking

fastness *formal. n.* fortress, fortified place, stronghold; secret, distant, or inaccessible place

fatalism *n.* belief or theory that all events are fated or predetermined, and that one is powerless to change them; attitude of submissiveness to fate, as though lacking free will — **-ist** *n.* — **-istic** *adj.*

fata morgana (fáatə mawr-gáanə) *formal. n.* mirage, illusory image [Italian, after a sorceress in legend, who was held to have caused a mirage in the Strait of Messina]

fathom *formal. tr.v.* to measure the depth of (water); to succeed in understanding, determine the meaning of: *cannot fathom his motives*

fatuous *adj.* foolish, inane: *a fatuous remark/speaker*

— **fatuity** *n.*
faubourg (fṓ-boorg, fō-bóor) *n.* suburb or quarter of a city, especially a French-speaking city
faucet (fáw-sit) *n.* tap, especially in a barrel; *U.S.* tap
fault *n.* crack in the Earth's crust and resulting shift and discontinuity of the rocks on either side
faun (fawn) *n.* rural deity in Roman mythology, part man and part goat in form [from Latin *Faunus*, the Roman god of nature and fertility, and counterpart of the Greek god Pan]
fauna (fáwnə) *n.*, *pl.* **-s** or **-nae** animals collectively, especially of a given place or time; list of fauna. Compare FLORA [from Latin *Fauna*, the sister of the Roman nature god *Faunus*; see FAUN]
fauteuil (fṓ-tö-i, -turl, fō-tṓ-i) *formal. n.* theatre stall; armchair
faux-naïf (fṓ-nī-éef) *adj.* appearing or pretending to be simple and naive ~ *n.* faux-naïf person [French, literally, false naive]
fava bean (fáavə) *n.* broad bean
faux pas (fṓ páa) *n.*, *pl.* **faux pas** blunder in manners or etiquette [French, literally, false step]
faveolate (fávvi-ə-layt) *formal. adj.* pitted with small cells or cavities, honeycombed
fax *n.* telegraphic system for transmitting facsimiles; document or image sent or produced by fax [from *facsimile* or the trade name *Photofax*] —**fax** *tr.v.*
fay *adj.* fairy-like; *informal.* sweet or charming, especially in a pretentious way, precious, arch ~ *n.* fairy or elf
fealty *n.* vassal's obligation of loyalty to his feudal lord [related to *fidelity*]
feasible (féezə-b'l) *adj.* possible, practicable: *Your plan is simply not feasible*; likely, believable: *a feasible excuse* — **-ibility** *n.*
feather *n.* tuft of hair, as on a dog's tail; strip or wedge of wood fitting into a groove to make a joint; wake made by a submarine's periscope above the water ~ *tr.v.* to taper, thin, and trim (the hair); to turn (an oar) horizontal between strokes in rowing
featherbed *v.* — *intr.* to employ more workers than needed, as to avoid redundancies — *tr.* to spoil, pamper, mollycoddle
febrile (fée-brīl) *formal. adj.* relating to fever; feverish
feckless *adj.* careless, negligent, irresponsibly clumsy; feeble, useless [related to *ineffective*]
feculent (féckew-lənt) *formal. adj.* filthy, foul, covered with or full of impurities or excrement [related to *faeces*] — **-lence** *n.*
fecund (féek-ənd, fék-) *formal. adj.* fertile, fruitful; productive: *a fecund imagination* — **-ate** *tr.v.* — **-ity** *n.*
feints (faynts) *pl.n.* leftover impure spirits from the distillation of alcoholic drinks, especially whisky
feisty (fīsti) *informal. adj.* tough, spirited, or frisky: *a feisty little wrestler*
felicitations *formal. pl.n.* congratulations — **-tate** *tr.v.*
felicitous *formal. adj.* having an agreeable or appropriate style: *a felicitous writer/essay*; appropriate, apt, well-chosen: *a felicitous remark/compliment*; producing or marked by happiness or good fortune: *a felicitous life*
feline (fée-līn) *adj.* belonging or relating to the cat family; cat-like — **feline** *n.*
[1]**fell** *tr.v.* to fold in and stitch flat (a seam)
[2]**fell** *formal. n.* skin of an animal, hide, pelt
fellahin (féllə-héen) *pl.n.* farmworkers or peasants in an Arab country (also "fellaheen"; singular "fellah")
felo de se (féelō-di-sée, féllō, -sáy) *n.*, *pl.* **felones de se** or **felos de se** suicide or person who commits suicide [Medieval Latin, literally, felon of oneself]
felony (félləni) *n.* formerly, crime of a serious kind — **felon, -ry** *n.* — **felonious** *adj.*
feminine rhyme *n.* rhyme of two or more syllables, of which the first is stressed, such as *pencilling* and *stencilling*. Compare MASCULINE RHYME
femme fatale (fám fə-táal) *formal. n.*, *pl.* **-s -s** dangerously attractive or seductive woman [French, literally, disastrous, woman]
femur (féemər) *formal. n.*, *pl.* **-s** or **femora** thigh or thighbone — **femoral** *adj.*
fenestra (fi-néstrə) *n.*, *pl.* **-trae** small opening in the body, especially in the middle ear; *formal.* window-like opening; transparent spot or marking, as on a moth's wing — **-trated** *adj.* — **-tration** *n.*
feral (féerəl, férrəl) *adj.* wild, untamed, especially when of a domesticated breed: *feral cats*; *formal.* savage, cruel — **ferity** *n.*
feria (féeri-ə, férri-) *n.* weekday that is not a feast day, especially in the Roman Catholic church
ferric *adj.* relating to or containing iron (also "ferrous")
Ferris wheel (férriss) *chiefly U.S. n.* "big wheel", giant fairground wheel (also "ferris wheel") [designed by George *Ferris*, a 19th-century U.S. engineer]
ferrule (férrōōl) *n.* protective metal ring or cap on the tip of a walking stick, umbrella, or the like; access opening in the side of a pipe for inspection or cleaning; length of tube for making a pipe joint (also "ferule")
ferule (férrōōl) *n.* stick, ruler, or the like for beating children, especially on the hand; ferrule
fervent *adj.* passionate, very enthusiastic, ardent — **-ency, fervour** *n.* — **fervid** *adj.*
festal *formal. adj.* relating to a feast, festival, or festivity, especially a joyous one
fester *intr.v.* to produce pus; to form an ulcer; to decay or rot; to cause lingering irritation or bitterness
festoon *n.* decorative string of flowers, ribbons, or the like suspended in a loop; looped or scalloped pattern ~ *tr.v.* to decorate with or as if with festoons
festschrift (fést-shrift) *n.*, *pl.* **-s** or **-en** collection of essays by academics or scholars compiled as a tribute to a learned colleague [German, literally, celebration writing]
fête champêtre (fet shoN-péttr) *n.*, *pl.* **-s -s** picnic, garden party, or other outdoor meal or entertainment (also "fête galante"); painting, popular in 18th-century France, of figures in a pastoral setting, or the genre of such painting [French, literally, rural festival]
fetid *formal. adj.* stinking, foul (also *old-fashioned* "foetid") — **fetor** *n.*
fetish *n.* object believed, in some primitive cultures, to have magical powers or to house a spirit; excessively revered object or activity: *make a fetish of punctuality*; object or part of the body producing sexual arousal — **-ism** *n.*
fetlock *n.* joint or projection above and behind a horse's hoof, or the tuft of hair on it
fetters *pl. n.* chains or bands around the ankles; *formal.* shackles, restraint, restriction — **fetter** *tr.v.*
feudalism (féwd'l-iz'm) *n.* medieval European social

system in which vassals exchanged homage and service for land and protection from a lord (also "feudal system") — **feudal**, **feudatory**, **feudalistic** *adj.*
fey (fay) *adj.* having supernatural powers, in touch with the supernatural, visionary, clairvoyant
fiasco *n.*, *pl.* **-cos** or **-coes** embarrassing failure or letdown
fiat (fí-ət, fée-) *formal.* *n.* decree, arbitrary command or order; official permission or authorisation [Latin, literally, let it be done]
fibrillation *n.* twitching of muscle fibres affecting the normal rhythm of contractions; especially, fibrillation of the heart muscle [related to *fibre*]
fidelity *formal.* *n.* faithfulness or loyalty, as to a spouse, the facts, or one's duty; accuracy, correspondence to the facts, adherence to the truth; degree of accurate reproduction, as by a radio or amplifier, of an input signal
fiefdom (féef-dəm) *n.* feudal estate or piece of property; area under a person's authority, or sphere of a person's influence
figurative *adj.* metaphorical, based on or using figures of speech, not literal: *figurative language*; symbolic, emblematic; in art, representational, not abstract: *figurative paintings*
figurehead *n.* leader in name only, without any real power or responsibility; carved bust or full figure in the prow of some sailing ships
filature (fíllə-chər, -tewr) *n.* spinning or twisting of silk cotton, or the like into threads; reel used for spinning of silk from cocoons, or the place where such spinning is done
filial (fílli-əl) *formal.* *adj.* relating to or appropriate for a son or daughter
filibeg (fílli-beg) *n.* kilt worn by Scottish Highlanders
filibuster (fílli-bustər) *n.* obstruction of legislation by means of delaying tactics such as lengthy speeches; *archaic.* military adventurer or irregular mercenary or revolutionary, especially in a foreign country [akin to *booty* and *freebooter*] — **filibuster** *v.*
filigree (fílli-gree) *n.* delicate, lace-like work of twisted wire, especially of gold or silver — **filigree** *adj.*, *tr.v.*
fillet *n.* strip of ribbon, lace, or metal worn in the hair or round the neck; narrow, decorative line pressed into a book cover, or the wheeled tool used
fillip (fíllip) *n.* stimulus, incentive, arousal, or excitement; flicking of the finger after holding it back with the thumb — **fillip** *v.*
finesse (fi-néss) *n.* delicacy or subtlety, as of painting style, negotiation technique, or tennis strokes; winning of a trick by a strategem that induces an opponent to play a relatively high card fruitlessly — **finesse** *v.*
Finlandisation *n.* preservation of national sovereignty while not offending a powerful neighbour, such as the USSR [after *Finland*'s neutralist policy] — **Finlandise** *v.*
fipple *n.* lip, wooden plug, or other obstruction serving in place of a reed to initiate the vibration in certain organ pipes and wind instruments
firkin *n.* small wooden barrel, especially for storing butter or cheese
firmament *formal. or archaic.* *n.* expanse of the sky, the heavens
firth *n.* estuary or sea inlet, especially in Scotland [akin to *ford*, *fjord*]
fiscal (físk'l) *adj.* relating to a country's treasury, finances, or tax matters
fissile *adj.* *formal.* splittable, possible to split; capable of undergoing nuclear fission
fissiparous (fi-síppərəss) *adj.* reproducing by means of splitting, as some one-celled plants and animals do; *formal.* encouraging splits rather than unity
fissure (físhər) *n.* narrow crack or deep groove, as in a rock — **fissure** *v.*
fistula (físs-tewlə) *n.*, *pl.* **-las** or **-lae** abnormal opening or channel between a hollow organ or other body part, and the skin or another hollow organ, as caused by an abscess
fixation *n.* state of being stationary, permanent, or in arrested development; state of being set in one's ways; obsession or preoccupation; in psychology, sexual or emotional attachment, typically immature and neurotic, to a person or thing; focussing of one's gaze or attention firmly on something; conversion of nitrogen in the air into a fertiliser or other compound — **fixate** *v.*
fjord (fyord) *n.* long, narrow, and deep inlet of the sea, typically with high cliffs either side, as in Norway (also "fiord") [Norwegian; akin to *ford*, *firth*]
flabbergasted *adj.* astonished, overwhelmed with surprise — **flabbergast** *tr.v.*
flaccid (flássid, flák-sid) *adj.* limp, drooping, flabby, lacking firmness — **-ity** *n.*
flag *n.* panel at the top of the front page of a newspaper or magazine, bearing its name, logo, and the like (also "masthead"); tail with a distinctive shape or marking, as on a deer and certain dogs ~ *tr.v.* to mark (a text, an entry, or the like) with a tab or symbol
flagellate (flájə-layt) *tr.v.* to whip, flog, or scourge, as for religious discipline or sexual gratification ~ *adj.* (also -lət) whip-like or whip-shaped — **-lation** *n.* — **-lant** *n.*, *adj.*
flagitious (flə-jíshəss) *formal.* *adj.* outrageously criminal or wicked, scandalously villainous
flagon *n.* old-fashioned vessel, with a handle and spout, for wine or other liquid; large bottle, as for cider [related to *flask*]
flagrant (fláy-grənt) *adj.* outrageous, glaring, or conspicuous in its wrongness: *a flagrant injustice*
flail *n.* threshing implement of two hinged sticks ~ *v.* — *tr.* to thresh with a flail; to beat with or as if with a flail — *intr.* to move jerkily, thresh about: *flailing arms*
flambé (flaám-bay, floN-báy) *adj.* served in flaming brandy or other spirits: *a crêpe flambé* [French, literally, flamed or singed] — **flambé** *tr.v.*
flambeau (flám-bō) *n.*, *pl.* **-beaus** or **-beaux** flaming torch; large ornamental candlestick [related to *flame*]
flamboyant *adj.* showy, ornate and ostentatious, dashing [related to *flame*] — **-boyance** *n.*
flan *n.* *chiefly British.* open pastry or sponge tart filled with a fruit or cheese filling; blank metal disc ready for stamping into a coin (in this sense, also "planchet")
flange *n.* projecting rim or edge, as on a wheel or beam, as for strengthening or attaching
flash *n.* identifying emblem, marking, or the like on a military uniform or vehicle; light or coloured marking on an animal's coat
flashing *n.* metal strips or similar strong weatherproof material covering the joints and angles of a roof
flashpoint *n.* critical point at which a tense situation

flares up into serious disruption, disorder, violence, or war

flatulence (fláttew-lənss) *n.* build-up of gas in the digestive tract, causing breaking of wind; *formal.* pompous, high-flown speech or writing — **-lent** *adj.*

flaunt *v.* to show off, parade or exhibit ostentatiously ~ *intr.v.* to wave or flutter proudly, as a flag does

flaxen *adj.* pale yellow: *flaxen hair*

flay *tr.v.* to strip the skin of, as by whipping; to criticise very severely

fledge *v.* — *tr.* to feed and care for (a baby bird) until it is ready to fly; to cover or decorate with feathers; to fit (an arrow) with a feather (in this sense, also "fletch") — *intr.* to grow feathers, as a young bird does

fledgling *n.* bird that has just grown the feathers necessary for flying; young and inexperienced person or organisation —**fledgling** *adj.*

fleer *v.* to mock, scorn, or taunt, sneer or smirk at contemptuously — **fleer** *n.*

flense *tr.v.* to strip (a whale, seal, or the like) of (its skin or blubber) (also "flench")

fleshpots *pl.n.* self-indulgent or luxuriously sensual living; places where such living can be indulged [from its use in Exodus 16:3, referring to Egypt]

fletcher *n.* person who makes arrows

fleuron (flér-on, flōroN) *n.* crescent or other small ornamental piece of puff pastry used as a garnish in cooking

flews *pl.n.* fleshy drooping upper lip of the bloodhound or similar dog

flibbertigibbet *n.* silly, talkative person, especially a girl or young woman

flies *pl.n.* area above a theatre stage for lights, curtains, and the like

flippant *adj.* inappropriately light-hearted or joking, lacking in respectful seriousness — **flippancy** *n.*

flitch *n.* salted and cured side of pork; steak cut from the side of a halibut or other fish; strip of wood cut lengthways from a tree trunk; plank of wood joined to others to form a beam

flocculent *adj.* gathered in woolly masses: *flocculent clouds formal.* wool-like or fluffy in appearance or texture —**flocculate** *v.* — **-lence** *n.*

flock *n.* tuft of fibre or hair; wool or cotton waste, as used for stuffing furniture or mattresses; tufts of wool or other fibre forming a raised pattern on wallpaper or fabrics ~*tr.v.* to fill, decorate, or cover with flock

floe (flō) *n.* sheet or slab of ice floating on the sea

flora *n.*, *pl.* **-ras** or **-rae** plants collectively, especially of a given place or time; list of flora. Compare FAUNA [from Latin *Flora*, the Roman goddess of flowers, from *flos*, a flower]

florescence (flaw-réss'nss) *formal. n.* flowering or the time of flowering

floret (flórrit) *n.* tiny flower, usually in a cluster, as in the head of a daisy or other composite flower

florid (flórrid) *adj.* reddish or flushed, rosy, ruddy: *a florid complexion*; flowery, over-elaborate, too ornate in style: *florid prose*

flotilla (flə-tíllə) *n.* fleet of small ships or small fleet of ships [Spanish; akin to *float, fleet*]

flotsam *n.* floating wreckage or cargo from a ship that has sunk. Compare JETSAM; odds and ends, discarded or miscellaneous objects or junk; tramps or drifters

¹flounce *n.* gathered strip of material or ornamental pleated ruffle sewn to a garment or curtain

²flounce *intr.v.* to walk with conspicuous movements to express anger, impatience, or the like

flounder *intr.v.* to move or act in a clumsy, uncertain, or unbalanced way

flout *tr.v.* to scorn, defy in a contemptuous way: *flout convention/the laws*

fluctuate *intr.v.* to change or swing irregularly; to shilly-shally, waver, keep changing one's mind — **-uation** *n.*

flue (floo) *n.* pipe or duct for hot air, smoke, or the like, as in a boiler or chimney; organ pipe in which the air strikes a projection rather than a reed to initiate the vibrations and sound (in this sense, also "flue pipe")

fluent *adj.* smooth and effortless: *a fluent speaker, in fluent French*; flowing and graceful: fluent *strides/curves* — **fluency** *n.*

fluke (flook) *n.* barb or barbed head on an arrow, harpoon, or anchor arm; either of the flaps of the tail of a whale or related animal

flume (floom) *n. chiefly U.S.* narrow gorge or ravine with a stream flowing through it; artificial water channel, as for providing power or transporting logs

flummox *informal. tr.v.* to puzzle or confuse, perplex, bamboozle

fluorescence (floor-éss'nss) *n.* emitting of light or other radiation by atoms or molecules stimulated from an outside source, as by radiation; light or radiation emitted in this way — **-escent** *adj.* — **-esce** *v.*

fluoridation *n.* addition of fluorine compounds, especially to the public water supply as a measure held to reduce tooth decay — **-date** *tr.v.*

flute *n.* groove or indentation, as in a stone column or pleated ruffle or pastry — **fluted** *adj.* — **fluting** *n.*

fluvial (flóovi-əl) *formal. adj.* relating to or inhabiting a river

fly *n.* flap forming an entrance or extended roof for a tent; outer edge of a flag, or the length from there to the staff; light one-horse carriage

flyleaf *n.* blank leaf at the front or back of a book, especially when forming the other half of the sheet pasted to the inside cover

fob *n.* pocket, as on a waistcoat, designed for a pocket watch; chain, strap, or ribbon attaching a watch to a fob

foetus (féetəss) *n.*, *pl.* **foetuses** embryo at a relatively advanced stage of development before birth (also "fetus") — **foetal** *adj.*

foible *n.* small weakness of character; weaker section of a sword blade, near the tip. Compare FORTE [related to *feeble*]

¹foil *n.* contrasting person or thing; backing, typically of metal or metal leaf, as on a mirror or gemstone; leaflike shape in the tracery of Gothic windows

²foil *n.* fencing sword for thrusting rather than cutting, with a flat handguard

foist *tr.v.* to represent as genuine or valuable, palm off; to force on someone, especially by trickery, fob off: *foisted his aunt/chores onto me* [akin to *fist*]

foliate (fōli-ət) *formal. adj.* having leaves, leafy, relating to leaves

folio *n.*, *pl.* **-os** large page or page-size equal to half a large sheet of paper; book with folio-sized pages: *the 1623 first Folio of Shakespeare*

follicle *n.* cavity in the skin from which a hair grows; cavity in the ovary containing an ovum

foment (fə-mént, fō-) *formal. tr.v.* to encourage or

provoke (unrest, a riot, or the like)
fomentation *n.* act or instance of fomenting; warm, damp medicinal compress, poultice, as for bruises
fondue *n.* hot melted cheese dish; dish of beef slices cooked in hot oil at the table
[1]**font** *n.* container of baptismal water, stoup [related to *fountain*]
[2]**font** *chiefly U.S. n.* fount or set of printing type of any one style
foots *pl.n.* dregs or sediment in a liquid, as in varnish or cooking oil
fop *archaic. n.* vain, affected dandy — **-pish** *adj.* — **-pery** *n.*
forage *n.* fodder for cattle, horses, or sheep ~ *intr.v.* to hunt or search about, or to make a raid, especially for provisions
foray (fórray) *n.* sudden military raid or attack; preliminary attempt — **-foray** *v.*
forbearance *formal. n.* patience or tolerance, restraint when provoked; act of refraining or abstaining — **forbear** *v.* — **forbearing** *adj.*
force majeure (fórss ma-zhőr) *n.* circumstances beyond someone's control, which spoil plans or prevent the fulfilment of obligations [French, literally, greater force]
forcemeat *n.* stuffing or garnish of seasoned minced meat or poultry
foreboding *n.* feeling of forthcoming evil or disaster — **foreboding** *adj.*
forecastle (fők-səl) *n.* deck, or section of the upper deck, near the front of a ship (also "fo'c's'le")
foreclose *v.* to end (a mortgage) when the scheduled payments are not met, and thus repossess a mortgaged property — **-closure** *n.*
forensic *formal. adj.* relating to criminal law and court cases: *forensic science*
foreshortening *n.* shortening of lines in drawing or painting to create an impression of perspective
forestall *tr.v.* to prevent or delay by anticipating and taking precautions
formaldehyde (fawr-máldi-hīd) *n.* colourless gaseous compound, which, in aqueous solution as formalin, is used in fertilisers and in dyeing, and as a preservative, as of specimens for dissecting (also "methanal")
format *n.* plan, outline, or arrangement, as for a radio or television programme; layout or design of printed matter; arrangement of data in a computer ~ *tr.v.* to put into a format, provide a format for
formic *formal. adj.* relating to ants
formicary (fórmi-kəri) *formal. n.* anthill, or ant-farm or colony kept in a glass box
formicate *formal. intr.v.* to swarm or teem with or as if with ants — **-cation** *n.*
formidable *adj.* very impressive or admirable, awe-inspiring; very difficut to defeat, solve, perform, or the like — **-ability** *n.*
forswear *formal. tr.v.* to give up or reject firmly, renounce or forsake
[1]**forte** (fór-tay) *n.* strong point, special talent; stronger section of a sword blade, near the hilt. Compare FOIBLE
[2]**forte** *adj., adv.* in music, loud or loudly ~ *n.* in music, a forte passage
fortuitous *adj.* unplanned, chance: *a fortuitous encounter* — **-tuity** *n.*
forum *n.* ancient Roman marketplace, public square, and assembly place; public discussion, or a meeting or opportunity for public discussion *formal.* court of law, tribunal
fosse (foss) *formal. n.* ditch or defensive moat
fossick *informal. intr.v.* to search for gold, as in rivers or waste dumps; broadly, to rummage about in search of something
founder *intr.v.* to stumble and go lame, as a horse might; to overeat and become ill, as cattle might; to sink, as a ship might; to fail utterly, as a plan might
foxed *adj.* stained or discoloured, as old books might be
foxfire *n.* glow or luminescence of fungus on rotting wood
fracas (fráckaa) *n., pl.* **fracas** uproar, noisy quarrel or fight
fractious *formal. adj.* troublesome, unruly, given to fighting
fraenum (frée-nəm) *formal. n., pl.* **-nums** or **-na** fold or flap of skin or membrane, such as that under the tongue, that restricts movement (also "frenulum")
franchise *n.* right to vote, suffrage; authorisation given by a business enterprise to dealers to use its name and sell its products
Francophone *formal. adj.* French-speaking: *the Francophone nations* — **Francophone** *n.*
Franglais (fróng-glay) *n.* French containing many English words, forms, and elements (often derogatory)
frank *tr.v* to put a stamp or postmark on (a letter or parcel) to show payment of postage
frankincense *n.* gum resin used in incense
franklin *n.* landowning gentleman in medieval England
frappé (fráppay) *n.* sorbet-like frozen dessert or starter; beverage, typically alcoholic, poured over crushed ice — **frappé** *adj.*
frass *n.* excrement of insects
fraternal *formal. adj.* brotherly relating to a brother. Compare SORORAL
fraternise *intr.v.* to mix socially with people; especially, to have unauthorised social contacts with enemy troops or with the people of an occupied or conquered territory
fraternity *n.* brotherhood as a state or condition; U.S. social organisation for male students. Compare SORORITY; group with a specified shared interest: *the hunting fraternity*; brotherliness, fellow-feeling — **-cidal** *adj.*
fratricide *n.* killing or killer of one's brother or sister
fraught *adj.* loaded with something ominous: *fraught with peril*; *informal* anxious, very nervous
freehold *n.* full ownership of a house, flat, land, or the like, by contrast with ownership for the length of time specified in a lease
freemasonry *formal. n.* instinctive sympathy or sense of fellowship among a group of people
French curve *n.* draughtsman's plastic stencil having many curves
French leave *n.* abrupt or unauthorised departure
frenetic (frə-néttik) *formal. adj.* frantic, wildly busy or overexcited, frenzied
frequent (fri-kwént) *tr.v.* to visit (a place) regularly
fresco *n., pl.* **-coes** or **-cos** painting done on fresh damp plaster on a wall. Compare SECCO [Italian, literally, fresh]
freshet (fréshit *n.* sudden surge in a stream, as after heavy rains; stream of clear water
Freudian slip (fróydi-ən) *n.* slip of the tongue or

similar lapse that discloses someone's real feelings or unconscious thoughts [after Sigmund *Freud*, the psychoanalyst, who studied such lapses]
friable (frī́-əb'l) *adj.* soft and crumbly: *friable soil*
fricassee (fríckə-see) *n.* dish of meat or poultry, cut up and stewed, usually served with a white sauce — **fricassee** *tr.v.*
frieze (freez) *n.* band of decoration, as along the top of a wall in a room [ultimately, after *Phrygia* an ancient kingdom in Asia Minor, famous for its embroidery]
frippery *informal. n.* pretentious things, such as clothes that are too expensive or ornate; trivial or inconsequential things
frisson (frée-sON) *n.* shiver or thrill of fear or excitement [French, a shiver]
frivolous *adj.* silly, inappropriately joking, flippant; trivial, unimportant: *a frivolous objection* — **frivolity** *n.*
¹frog *n.* looped braid or cord used as a fastening, as formerly on military uniforms (also "frogging")
²frog *n.* horny wedge in the sole of a horse's hoof
frolicsome *adj.* playful, high-spirited, full of fun — **frolic** *n., intr.v.*
frond *n.* leaf of a fern or a palm; leaf-like part of a seaweed or lichen
frontispiece *n.* illustration at the front of a book, often opposite the title page; facade of a building, especially when ornamented; small ornamented gable-like part, as above a window or door
frontlet *n.* forehead of a bird or animal; headband, especially one that is decorated or of religious significance
frottage (fróttaazh, fro-táazh) *n.* taking of a rubbing, as from a rough wooden surface, in art; rubbing against another person's body, as in a crowded bus, for sexual satisfaction
froward (frṓ-wərd) *formal. or archaic. adj.* stubbornly uncooperative, wilfully disobedient, contrary
frowsty (frów-sti) *chiefly British. informal. adj.* stuffy, hot and airless — **frowst** *n.*
frowzy *adj.* untidy, unkempt, slovenly; stale-smelling, musty (also "frowsy")
fructify *intr.v.* to bear fruit, or make something fruitful or productive — **-ification** *n.*
frugal *adj.* spending little, thrifty — **-ity** *n.*
frugivorous (froo͞-jívvərəss) *formal. adj.* fruit-eating, feeding chiefly on fruit: *frugivorous bats*
fruition *n.* success or realisation of plans or wishes: *to come to fruition*
frumentaceous *formal. adj.* resembling or made of grain, especially wheat
frustum frúss-təm) *n., pl.* **-tums** or **-ta** base part or mid-section of a cone, pyramid, or other solid object
fugacious *formal. adj.* vanishing, fleeting, passing quickly away — **-gacity** *n.*
Führer (féwr-ər, fű-rər) *n.* Hitler's title as leader of Nazi Germany [German, a leader]
fulcrum (fo͝ol-krəm) *n., pl.* **-crums** or **-cra** hinge, support, or turning point of a lever; *formal.* critical or decisive factor
fulgurate (fúl-gewrayt) *formal. v.* — *intr.* to flash with or like lightning; to come on with great and sudden severity: *fulgurating pain* — *tr.* to destroy (tissue, such as warts) by using electric sparks
fuliginous (few-líjinəss) *formal. adj.* soot-like, sooty
fuller *n.* blacksmith's hammer
fuller's earth *n.* clay used in chemical reactions, filters, and the like
fulmination (fúlmi-náysh'n) *formal. n.* thunderous verbal attack, loud and fierce criticism; *archaic.* violent explosion — **fulminate** *v.* — **fulminant** *adj.*
fulsome *adj.* lavish in an excessive and distasteful way: *fulsome praise*
fumarole *n.* hole or vent for volcanic gases and steam (also "soffione") [related to *fumes*]
fumigate *tr.v.* to fill (a room or building) with poisonous smoke, as to disinfect it or exterminate insects
funambulist (few-námbew-list) *formal. n.* tight-rope or slack-rope walker (humorously pompous) — **-ism** *n.*
function word *n.* word, such as a pronoun, conjunction, or article, indicating a grammatical, logical, or textual relationship
fundamentalism *n.* literal belief in the bible as a divinely inspired and accurate historical account; strict and passionate belief, especially in a religious or ideological system
funicular (fə-níckew-lər) *n.* cable railway, typically up a mountainside — **funicular** *adj.*
furbelow *n.* pleated or gathered piece of fabric, especially a flounce or ruffle; small, showy, ornamental object
furcula (fúrkew-lə) *formal. n., pl.* **-lae** forked bone or body part, such as the wishbone
furfures (fúr-fəreez) *formal. pl.n.* scales of skin, as in dandruff (singular "furfur") — **furfuraceous** *adj.*
furlough (fúrlō) *n.* leave of absence in the U.S. armed forces
furore (fewr-ráwri) *n.* uproar, commotion, noisy disturbance; *formal.* furious activity or anger (also *chiefly U.S.* "furor") [related to *fury*]
furtive *adj.* stealthy, secretive; shifty, suspicious
furuncule (féwr-ungk'l) *formal. n.* pus-filled sore or swelling, boil
fusain (few-záyn) *formal. n.* charcoal stick or drawing
fusillade (féwzi-láyd) *n.* gunfire in a rapid burst, barrage; something resembling a burst of gunfire in rapidity, loudness, and aggressiveness: *a fusillade of curses* — **fusillade** *tr.v.*
fustanella *n.* short, stiff, white skirt forming part of a folk costume of Greek and Albanian men [related to *fustian*]
fustian *formal. n.* speech or writing that is full of pompous and needlessly long or difficult words [primary sense, twilled cotton fabric, probably after *Fostat*, a section of Cairo]
fustigate *formal. tr.v.* to beat with a club, cudgel
fusty *adj.* smelling mouldy, musty
futon (fo͞o-ton) *n.* unsprung mattress of Japanese style
futtock *n.* curved wooden rib forming part of a ship's frame
fylfot (fíl-fot) *n.* swastika-like design

G

gaberdine (gábbər-deen) *n.* worsted fabric; raincoat; long cloak worn in the Middle Ages — **gaberdine** *adj.*
gable *n.* triangular upper wall at the edge of a pitched roof
gaff *n.* hooked pole used for landing or hauling large fish; metal spur on a gamecock's leg in cockfighting; metal spur for extending the top edge of a fore-and-aft sail
gaffe (gaf) *n.* faux pas, social blunder such as a tactless remark
gaffer *n.* old man, especially in the country; *British. informal.* boss, supervisor; electrician supervising the lighting on a film set [contraction of *godfather*]
gain *n.* notch or groove that houses an inserted part in a joint or hinge
gainsay *formal. tr.v.* to deny, declare to be false; to contradict, oppose
gaiter *n.* cloth or leather legging buttoned from knee to ankle and strapped under the foot
Galahad *n.* pure, noble, and gallant man (typically ironic) [after *Galahad*, the most virtuous Knight of the Round Table in Arthurian legend]
galantine (gál-ən-teen) *n.* dish of fish or meat glazed with aspic or jelly and served cold [related to *gelatine*]
galanty show (gə-lánti) *archaic. n.* shadow play, using small paper figures
Gallicism *n.* typically French quality or trait; typically French word or construction, especially one used in another language
galligaskins *pl.n. informal.* loose, and baggy trousers (humorous); long, loose breeches worn in the 16th or 17th century
gallimaufrey *formal. n.* mix, jumble, hotchpotch
gallinaceous (gál-i-náyshəss) *formal. adj.* relating to chickens or turkeys or game birds such as pheasants and grouse
gallivant *intr. v.* to gad about, wander about in search of pleasure
Gallup poll (gál-əp) *n.* poll of public opinion, as prior to elections, by careful sampling of a representative cross-section of the population [after George H. *Gallup*, the 20th-century U.S. statistician and pioneer of opinion polls]
galoshes *pl.n.* rubber overshoes (also "goloshes") [from Latin *gallica solea*, Gaulish sandal]
galumph *informal. intr.v.* to walk or move in a clumsy, ungainly way [coined by Lewis Carroll, possibly as a blend of *gallop* + *triumph*]
galvanise *tr.v.* to stimulate or excite, as if by an electric shock; to make rustproof by coating with zinc: *galvanised iron* [after Luigi *Galvani*, an 18th-century doctor and experimenter with electricity] — **-ism** *n.*
gambado (gam-báydō) *n.*, *pl.* **-does** or **-dos** legging or gaiter, as on the leg of a rider
gambit *n.* chess stratagem in which a piece is sacrificed for the sake of a positional advantage; specifically, opening gambit at the beginning of a game; *informal.* opening ploy, as in conversation or negotiations
gambol *intr.v.* to leap about in a playful way, skip or frolic — **gambol** *n.*
gambrel *n.* butcher's frame from which animal carcasses are suspended
gamelan (gámmi-lan) *n.* orchestra, as in Indonesia, based on percussion instruments, especially of the xylophone type
gamete *n.* in genetics, sperm or egg, capable of participating in fertilisation
gamine (ga-meén) *n.* girl roaming the streets (male equivalent "gamin"); young woman or girl, slim and attractive in a boyish way
gammadion (ga-máydi-ən) *n.* swastika-like design in the shape of a cross formed of four capital Greek gammas
gamp *British. informal. n.* big, baggy umbrella [after Sarah *Gamp*, a nurse in Dickens's novel *Martin Chuzzlewit*, who carried a large umbrella]
gamut (gámmət) *n.* full range, originally of musical notes: *the whole gamut of emotions* [from Medieval Latin *gamma ut*, names of musical notes in the medieval scale]
gangling *adj.* tall and gawky
ganglion (gáng-gli-ən) *n.*, *pl.* **-ions** or **-glia** group of nerve cells outside the brain or spinal cord
gangrene *n.* decay and death of body tissue, usually through a failure of blood supply — **-grenous** *adj.*
gantlet *n.* overlapping section of railway track, as on a narrow pass
gantline *n.* rope passed over a beam, as on a mast, and used for hoisting
gantry *n.* supporting frame, such as: bridge-like frame supporting a travelling crane, railway signals, or the like; space rocket's supporting tower or scaffolding on the launching pad; frame supporting a barrel that is lying on its side
garbanzo (gaar-bánzō) *n.*, *pl.* **-zos** chickpea
garçon (gaar-sóɴ) *n.* waiter in France or in a French restaurant [French, literally, boy]
garda (gárdə) *n.*, *pl.* **gardai** policeman in the Republic of Ireland — **the Garda** police force in the Republic of Ireland
garderobe (gárd-rōb) *formal. n.* wardrobe or small room for hanging clothes
gargantuan *formal. adj.* enormous, huge, gigantic [after *Gargantua*, the giant king in Rabelais's satirical novels]
gargoyle *n.* rainwater spout, in the form of a very ugly human or animal figure or head in stone, projecting from a gutter; grotesquely ugly person
garish (gáirish) *adj.* vulgarly or excessively decorated or brightly coloured, flashy, loud; dazzling or harsh: *garish lighting*
garner *formal. tr.v.* gather and store, in or as if in a

granary [related to *grain*]
garnish *tr.v.* to decorate, especially to decorate (food), as with parsley or lemon slices ~ *n.* something used for garnishing
garnishee *formal. tr.v.* to withhold (money or property) from a debtor, usually in order to help to pay off a debt
garret *n.* attic, room just under a pitched roof
garrison *n.* military post, or the troops stationed there [related to *guard*] — **garrison** *tr.v.*
garrotte (gə-rót) *tr.v.* to strangle with an implement such as a cord, wire, or iron collar — **garrotte** *n.*
garrulous *adj.* very talkative — **garrulity** *n.*
garth *n.* courtyard surrounded by cloisters; *archaic.* enclosed area, such as a garden or yard
gascon *archaic. n.* boaster, braggart [French, after the traditional boastfulness of the people of *Gascony* in southwestern France] — **-ade** *n.*
gaselier (gássə-léer) *n.* chandelier with gas lights [*gas + (chand)elier*]
gasket *n.* seal between lengths of piping, machine parts, or the like, to prevent the escape of gas or liquid; rope or strap attaching a furled sail to a crossbeam
Gastarbeiter (gást-aar-bītər) *n., pl.* **-arbeiter** or **-arbeiters** immigrant alien worker; specifically, one in West Germany [German, literally, guest worker]
gastric *adj.* relating to the stomach
gastric ulcer *n.* ulcer of the stomach lining
gastronome *formal. n.* food expert — **-nomic** *adj.* — **-nomy** *n.*
gâteau (gátto) *n., pl.* **-teaux** or **-teaus** large rich cream cake [French, a cake]
gatefold *n.* page that folds out beyond a normal book or magazine page, typically to form a double-sized page
gauche (gōsh) *adj.* awkward, socially ill at ease, tactless [French, left] — **gaucherie** *n.*
gaucho (gówchō) *n., pl.* **-os** Argentine cowboy
gaudy (gáwdi) *British. n.* celebration, typically an annual feast, at some schools and colleges
gaunt *adj.* thin and bony, scrawny
[1]**gauntlet** *n.* glove, as on a suit of armour or for certain sports — **throw down the gauntlet** to challenge someone to or as if to a duel
[2]**gauntlet** *n.* — **run the gauntlet** to have to run as a punishment between two lines of people, such as soldiers, who hit you as you run between them; to undergo severe criticism
gavage (gáv-aazh) *n.* force-feeding by means of a tube down the throat
gavel (gávv'l) *n.* small wooden hammer used by a judge, auctioneeer, or chairman
gazebo (gə-zée-bō) *n., pl.* **-bos** or **-boes** small ornamental summerhouse, belvedere, or other outbuilding, typically having a scenic view
gazetteer *n.* listing or dictionary of places, basic geographical dictionary
gazump (gə-zúmp) *British. v.* to raise the previously agreed price of a property and thereby frustrate (a prospective buyer)
gean (geen) *n.* wild cherry tree or fruit
geek *chiefly U.S. n.* performer at a fairground who bites off the head of a live bird, rat, or the like
Geiger counter (gī́-gər) *n.* instrument for detecting radioactivity [after Hans *Geiger*, a 20th-century German physicist]
geisha (gay-shə) *n.* young Japanese woman trained to work as an entertaining companion for men [Japanese, literally, an artist]
gelatinous *adj.* jelly-like and thick, viscous
gelation *formal. n.* freezing, solidification through cooling (also "congelation")
geld *n.* tax paid by landowners to the king in England during the Middle Ages
geminate (jémmi-nayt) *formal. v.* to arrange or occur in pairs or doubled — **geminate** *adj.*
gemot (gi-mṓt) *n.* public meeting or local court in Anglo-Saxon England
gemütlich (gə-mű́t-likh) *informal. adj.* snug, cosy and cheerful; friendly, sociable [German] — **-keit** *n.*
gendarme (zhón-daarm) *n.* French policeman — **-merie** *n.*
gene *n.* unit in a chromosome whereby an inherited characteristic is transmitted from parent to offspring — **genetic** *adj.*
genealogy *n.* person's family tree, showing ancestors, descendants, and usually other relatives; study of genealogies — **-alogical** *adj.*
generalist *n.* someone with a comparatively wide range of knowledge or interests, by contrast with a specialist
generality *n.* generalness; a generalisation, especially a vague one — **the generality** *formal.* the majority, the greater part or number
general staff *n.* senior army officers collectively
generic (jə-nérrik) *adj.* relating to a genus; general though perhaps not universal; in medicine, referring to a drug sold or prescribed under its general chemical name rather than under a brand name; in social work, referring to a practitioner who works with all categories of client rather than specialising in one field
genesis *n., pl.* **-ses** origin or beginning, especially of something general or abstract
genetic engineering *n.* deliberate modification of genetic structure, in order to change the physical qualities of plants or animals
genetics *n.* study of genes; broadly, study of heredity ~ *pl.n.* genetic characteristics
Geneva bands *pl.n.* two tabs of white cloth worn at the neck, especially by some Protestant clergymen
[1]**genial** (jéeni-əl) *adj.* cheerful and even-tempered — **-ity** *n.*
[2]**genial** (jə-née-əl) *formal. adj.* relating to the chin (also "mental")
genitalia (jénni-táyli-ə) *formal. pl.n.* genitals, reproductive organs
genius *formal. n.* special characteristics collectively: *phrases that violate the genius of the language* [Latin, a god of birth, a guardian spirit]
genocide *n.* extermination of a whole racial, national, or social group — **-cidal** *adj.*
genre (zhóNrə) *n.* type, sort; specifically, genre of an imaginative work in literature, art, or music: *The Western is a popular genre*
genteel *adj.* respectable and refined, or affectedly so, or striving to appear so — **gentility** *n.*
Gentile *n.* non-Jew; in early Christian Europe, a pagan or heathen; in Mormon circles, a non-Mormon — **Gentile** *adj.*
gentrify *informal. tr.v.* to make (an area) more fashionable by middle-class settlement or acquisition — **-fication** *n.*

genuflect *formal. intr.v.* to kneel or bend one's knees, in a respectful or servile way — **-flection** *n.*

genus (jéenəs, jénnəss) *n., pl.* **genera** in biology, category ranking below a family and above a species; *formal.* any class, group, or kind

geode *n.* cavity inside a rock that is lined with crystals

geodesic dome (jée-ō-dessik) *n.* dome formed from interlocking polygons

Geordie *informal.n.* person from Tyneside; language of Geordies — **Geordie** *adj.*

georgic *formal. n.* pastoral poem relating to farming and country life — **georgic** *adj.*

geostationary satellite *n.* satellite whose movement in space is adjusted so as to keep it constantly above one point on the Earth's surface (also "geosynchronous satellite")

geostrophic *adj.* relating to or caused by the Earth's rotation: *geostrophic force*

geothermal *adj.* referring or relating to heat from the Earth's interior, especially when used as a source of energy

geriatric (jérri-áttrik) *adj.* relating to old age and its medical problems — **geriatric, -ics, -ician** *n.*

germane (jer-máyn) *formal. adj.* highly relevant or topical

germinate *v.* to begin to or cause to grow or sprout — **-nation** *n.*

gerontology *n.* study of old age, and the processes, problems, and disorders associated with it — **-gist** *n.* — **-logical** *adj.*

gerrymander (jérri-mándər) *informal. tr.v.* to divide into electoral or other districts in order to gain an unfair advantage; to stipulate the boundaries of (an electoral district or other area) in order to gain an unfair advantage ~ *n.* instance of gerrymandering [after Elbridge *Gerry*, an 18th-19th-century U.S. politician + *(sala)mander*, referring to the shape of an election district formed in Massachusetts while he was governor]

gerund (jérrund) *n.* the *-ing* form of a verb, used as a noun, as in *Skating is my hobby*; equivalent form in other languages

gesso (jéssō) *n.* preparation containing plaster of Paris and used as a surface for painting or a foundation for bas-relief

gest (jest) *archaic. n.* deed or exploit of note or valour; tale in verse or prose, typically written in the Middle Ages, recounting gests

gestalt (gə-shtáalt) *n.* unified structure or pattern that is more than the sum of its parts; school of psychology based on the theory that the personality is made of gestalts [German, a form or shape] — **gestalt** *adj.*

gestate (je-stáyt) *intr.v.* to develop in the uterus before being born; to develop before being put into practice or coming to fruition: *an idea gestating in one's mind* — **-tation** *n.*

gesticulate (je-stíckew-layt) *intr.v.* to make gestures; especially, to move one's hands in a rapid, excited manner — **-lation** *n.*

Gesundheit *U.S. interj.* Health! (said, like "Bless you!", to someone who has just sneezed) [German, literally, health]

gewgaw *n.* decorative trinket, cheap bauble

geyser *n.* hot spring that throws up jets of water and steam; *British.* domestic hot-water heater [Icelandic *Geysir*, literally, gusher, the name of a hot spring in Iceland, from *geysa*, to gush]

ghat (gaat) *n.* in India, mountain pass or chain; flight of steps leading down to a river

ghee (gee) *n.* clarified butter used typically in Indian cooking; specifically, ghee made from buffalo milk

gherao (ge-rów) *n.* harassment of an employer by workers, used as a tactic in industrial disputes, typically in India; especially, a gherao in which the workers surround and detain the employer

gherkin *n.* small cucumber used especially for pickling

ghetto *n., pl.* **-tos** or **-toes** part of a town where people are compelled to live by poverty or discrimination; specifically, in former times, Jewish ghetto; area, institution, or the like that is isolated from the life of the larger community: *a cultural ghetto* — **ghetto** *adj.* — **ghettoise** *v.*

ghost word *n.* word that enters the language as a result of a mistake in writing, printing, or pronunciation, such as *Ye* in *Ye Olde Teashoppe*

ghost writer *n.* writer who is hired by a famous person to write a book, typically a biography or set of memoirs, which is then published as if written by the famous person himself or herself — **ghost-write** *tr.v.* — **ghost-written** *adj.*

ghoul (gōōl) *n.* person who enjoys gruesome or horrible sights or events; *formal.* grave robber; spiteful ghost — **-ish** *adj.*

gibbet (jíbbit) *n.* gallows; structure on which the bodies of executed criminals were displayed to the public — **gibbet** *tr.v.*

gibbous (gíbbəss, jíbbəss) *formal. adj.* rounded, convex, protuberant; hunchbacked — **gibbous moon** moon when between half and full — **-bosity** *n.*

giblets (jíb-lits) *pl.n.* edible offal of a fowl

Gideon bible *n.* bible placed in hotels, hospitals, and other public places by the Gideons, a Christian organisation [after Gideon, a judge and warrior in ancient Israel, Judges 6-8]

gig *n.* fishing spear or set of hooks for impaling fish

gigolo (zhíggə-lō)*n.* paid male lover, escort, or dancing partner

gigot (jíggət) *chiefly Scottish. n.* leg of mutton or lamb; leg-of-mutton sleeve

gild *tr.v.* to cover with a thin layer of gold or gold leaf; to give a superficially better appearance to — **-ed** *adj.*

gilet (ji-láy) *n.* waistcoat for a woman

gillie *n.* in Scotland, guide or attendant to someone going shooting or fishing for sport (also "ghillie")

gilts *pl.n.* government securities, typically considered safe to invest in (also "gilt-edged securities")

gimbals (jím-b'lz, gím-) *pl.n.* device to keep a ship's compass horizontal

gimcrack (jím-krak) *informal. adj.* cheap and shoddy

gimmal (gímm'l) *n.* ring made of two interlocking rings [from Latin *geminus*, a twin]

gimp *n.* braid or cord of fabric used as trimming on clothes, curtains, and furniture (also "guimpe", "guipure")

gingili (jínjili) *n.* sesame-seed oil; sesame plant

gingiva (jín-jivvə) *formal. n., pl* **-givae** gum of the teeth — **-val** *adj.* — **-vitis** *n.*

ginnel (gínn'l, jínn'l) *Northern British. n.* narrow alley or passage between buildings [related to *channel*]

ginseng (jín-seng) *n.* forked root believed, especially in the East, to have medicinal properties; plant with the ginseng root

girandole (jírrən-dōl) *n.* set of rotating fireworks or jets of water, as in an ornamental fountain; piece of jewellery, such as an earring with a large stone surrounded by smaller ones; candlestick with many branches that is typically attached to a wall or mirror; group of military mines connected into a single explosive sequence [related to *gyrate*]

giro (jīr-ó) *n.* centralised system of settling debts or making payments by transfers between accounts, operated by banks and post offices — **giro** *adj.*

girth *formal. n.* distance round something (sometimes humorous); strap round the body of a draught animal, such as a horse, used to fasten a saddle or load

gismo *chiefly U.S. slang. n., pl.* **-mos** gadget, small mechanical device; thingummy, object whose name is unknown or temporarily forgotten (also "gizmo")

gizzard *n.* bird's digestive organ that helps to break down hard food and often contains grit to assist in the process

glabrous (gláy-brəss) *formal. adj.* hairless and smooth, bald: *glabrous skin*

glacé (glássay) *adj.* glazed and glossy; shiny with sugar-coating: *glacé cherries*

glacial *adj.* relating to a glacier or ice-sheet; icy or ice-like, extremely cold; hostile or chilling: *a glacial stare* — **glaciation** *n.*

glacis (glássis) *n.* incline; gentle slope; natural or artificial slope in front of a fortification, on which attackers are exposed to defenders' fire

glade *n.* clearing or open space in a wood or forest

gladiate *formal. adj.* sword-shaped: *a gladiate leaf*

gladiator *n.* combatant, typically with a sword, in an arena in ancient Rome; person who fights publicly for a cause he supports

glasnost *n.* policy of openness in administrative and political matters, recently adopted in the USSR

glaucoma (glaw-kṓmə) *n.* eye disease marked by high pressure in the eyeball — **-matous** *adj.*

glaucous (gláwkəss) *adj.* greyish or bluish green; in botany, referring to plants covered with a fine, whitish, powdery coating

glaze ice *n.* thin coating of ice, as on a road; black ice

glazier (gláyzi-ər) *n.* person who installs window glass [related to *glass*] — **-ery** *n.* — **glaze** *tr.v.*

glebe *n.* church land, typically granted to a clergyman as part of his benefice

glenoid cavity (glée-noyd) *n.* socket of the shoulder joint

glib *adj.* smooth-talking or writing effortlessly, but insincere or superficial

glide *n.* sliding section of tubing on a trombone

glissade (gli-saád, -sáyd) *n.* in ballet, gliding step; controlled slide over ice — **glissade** *intr.v.*

glissando *n.* method of moving from one note of music to another by sliding over every intervening note, as heard typically in harp music — **glissando** *adj., adv.*

gloaming *archaic or poetic. n.* twilight, dusk [akin to *gloom, glow*]

gloat *intr.v.* to regard or think about something with smug satisfaction or malicious delight: *gloating over his rival's embarrassment*

globular (glóbbewlər) *adj.* rounded, spherical, globe-shaped; consisting of globules

globule (glóbbəwl) *n.* tiny droplet of liquid

glockenspiel *n.* xylophone-like percussion instrument [German, literally, play of bells]

glomerule (glómmə-rōōl) *n.* flower cluster, tightly packed on a single stem — **-ulate** *adj.*

gloria *n.* halo or nimbus, especially in art (also "glorìole", "glory")

gloss *n.* translation, explanatory note, or commentary, as in the margin of a manuscript or text; interpretation or explanation that is convenient but misleading — **gloss** *v.*

glossa *n. formal.* the tongue; tongue-like organ, as in an insect — **glossal** *adj.*

glossary *n.* vocabulary or small specialised lexicon, often accompanying or supplementing a difficult or technical text

glossolalia (glóssō-láyli-ə) *n.* "gift of tongues", unintelligible ecstatic speech, thought to be inspired by the Holy Ghost, practised in some Christian churches

glottal stop *n.* speech sound produced just before a vowel, by the sudden release of breath after a brief closure of the glottis, or space between the vocal cords, as in the Cockney pronunciation of *bottle* roughly as /bó-əl)/

glottochronology *n.* statistical study of the historical relationship between different languages

glove box *n.* glass box in which dangerous radioactive or toxic substances can be handled with protective gloves sealed in to the side

glut *n.* excess, over-supply ~ *v.* — *tr.* to over-fill, satiate — *intr.* to overeat

gluten (glṓō-t'n) *n.* sticky protein mixture in wheat flour which is used in glues and sometimes causes an allergic reaction [Latin, glue]

gluteus *n. pl.* **-tei** any of the three buttock muscles

glutinous *adj.* gummy, gluey, sticky, viscous

glyph (glif) *n.* vertical groove, as seen in decorative bands on a Doric column; symbol, as on a road sign — **-ic** *adj.*

glyptography *n.* art of carving or engraving pictures, symbols, or inscriptions on gemstones — **-graph, -grapher** *n.*, — **-graphic, glyptic** *adj.*

gnathic (náthik) *formal. adj.* relating to the jaw

gnomic (nṓmik) *formal. adj.* short and mysterious, pithy or aphoristic, sometimes in a pretentious way: *gnomic utterances*

gnomon (nṓ-mon, -mən) *n.* arm of a sundial or similar object that casts a shadow to indicate the time

gnostic (nósstik) *formal. adj.* relating to or possessing knowledge, especially spiritual or mystical knowledge

gobbet *n.* extract or short passage from a text; chunk or piece, as of raw meat

Gobelins (gṓbə-lin, góbbə-, gō-bláN) *n.* tapestry with a rich pictorial design, of a kind originally woven in the Gobelins works in Paris — **Gobelins** *adj.*

gobo (gṓbō) *n., pl.* **-bos** or **-boes** shield or screen, as round a microphone or camera lens, for excluding unwanted sound or light

goffer (gṓfər) *tr.v.* to pleat, crimp, or press ridges into (material, a lace frill, or the like), especially with a heated iron; to emboss (paper) with a pattern ~ *n.* iron heated and used for goffering; pattern or ornamentation produced by goffering

Goidelic (goy-déllik) *adj.* referring or relating to the Celtic language group comprising Irish Gaelic, Scottish Gaelic, and Manx (also "Goidhelic"). Compare BRYTHONIC [related to *Gaelic*] — **Goidelic, Goidel** *n.*

goitre (góytər) *n.* chronic enlargement of the thyroid gland, causing a severely swollen neck, often due to iodine deficiency (also *formal* "struma") — **goitrous** *adj.*

Golconda (gol-kóndə) *formal. n.* mine or other source of great wealth [after *Golconda*, the capital city of a former Indian kingdom rich in diamond mines]
goliard (gṓl-yərd) *n.* member of a group of wandering students in medieval Europe, living riotously and composing Latin songs — **-ic** *adj.*
gonad (gṓnad) *n.* sex gland, specifically an ovary or testis
-gonal *adj. comb.form.* -sided, -angled: *polygonal, hexagonal.* Compare -HEDRAL — **-gon** *n. comb. form.*
gondola (góndələ) *n.* narrow boat, propelled by a single oar at the stern, used on the canals of Venice; basket or cabin under a balloon or airship; seat or cabin on a cable-car system, as on a ski lift; movable platform on the outside walls of a building, as used by window cleaners; open free-standing display shelf or rack, as in a supermarket; *U.S.* low, open railway wagon for goods — **-dolier** *n.*
gonfalon (gónfələn) *n.* flag or banner, especially on a horizontal bar, as used in church parades; banner or ensign as the emblem of a medieval Italian republic — **-nier** *n.*
Gongoristic (góng-gə-rístik) *formal. adj.* affected, florid, and artificial, as a literary style might be [after Luis de *Góngora y Argote*, a 16th-17th-century Spanish poet who used such a style] — **-rism** *n.*
goniometer (gṓni-ommitər) *n.* radio system for determining the direction of incoming signals; instrument for measuring angles, as between the faces of a crystal — **-metry** *n.*
googly *n.* in cricket, a deceptive off-break bowled to look as if it is a leg-break; *informal.* difficult or tricky question: *bowled the chairman a googly at the meeting*
googol (gṑo-gol) *n.* the number 10 raised to the power of 100, the number 1 followed by 100 zeros
Gordian knot *n.* deadlock or problem that can be resolved only by bold or drastic action (used especially in the phrase *to cut the Gordian knot*) [after the intricate knot, tied by King *Gordius* of Phrygia, which according to legend could be untied only by the future ruler of Asia, and which Alexander the Great simply severed with his sword]
gore *n.* triangle or wedge of cloth, as in a skirt, umbrella, or sail; small triangular piece of land
gorget (górjit) *n.* collar-like piece of armour protecting the throat; part of a wimple covering the throat and shoulders; band or distinctive patch of colour on the throat of a bird or other animal
gorgonise *tr.v.* to paralyse or stupefy, as with fear, petrify, mesmerise [after the *Gorgons*, three terrifying sisters in Greek mythology who would turn to stone anyone who looked into their eyes, from Greek *gorgos*, terrible]
gormandise (górmən-dīz) *v.* to eat gluttonously or greedily, gorge
Goshen (gṓsh'n) *formal. n.* comfortable place, land of plenty and contentment [after the biblical *Goshen* in Egypt, where the Israelites dwelt, Genesis 45:10]
gossamer *n.* cobwebs; soft, sheer fabric, anything very light and delicate — **gossamer** *adj.*
Götterdämmerung (gṓtər-démmərŏong) *n.* in Germanic mythology, the slow defeat and destruction of the gods by the forces of evil; *formal.* heroic failure, destruction of some magnificent project or person [German, literally, twilight of the gods]
gouache (gŏo-áash, gwaash) *n.* painting technique using opaque water colours bound with gum; paint used in gouache; painting done by gouache
gougère (gōō-zhaír) *n.* cheese puff of choux pastry
gourmand (góormənd, gōōr-móN) *n.* person who enjoys good or excessive eating [Old French, a glutton]
gourmandise (goormən-déez) *n.* liking for good food; gluttony, excessive eating
gourmet (góor-may) *n.* person who appreciates or is an expert in fine food and drink, connoisseur
grabble *intr.v.* to grope, scratch about, or feel around for with the hands; to fall to the ground, sprawl, or grovel
graben (graáb'n) *n.* trench between two parallel faults in the Earth's crust, rift valley [German, a ditch or trench]
grace-and-favour *adj.* referring to property owned by the sovereign and let free to a favoured tenant
gracile (grássīl) *formal. adj.* slender, thin and graceful
gradation *n.* series of steps, stages, or degrees, a gradual process; such a step, stage, or degree; passing or advancing by degrees or stages, as from one tone or colour to the next; levelling of land, as by erosion or deposition; in linguistics, a patterned change of the root vowels of a verb, as in *sing, sang, sung* (in this sense, also "ablaut") — **gradate** *v.*
grade *n.* angle of 0.9°, one-hundredth of a right angle
grader *n.* machine for levelling a surface of land, as in road-building
gradient (gráydi-ənt) *n.* sloping section or incline, as of a road or railway track; angle or degree of slope, inclination
gradin (gráydin) *n.* any of a set of steps or tiered seats on a slope; ledge near an altar where candles or ornaments are placed
graffiti (grə-fée-tee) *pl.n.* writings or drawings, often witty or obscene, scribbled typically on walls in public places; in archaeology, drawings or inscriptions scratched or carved on rock, pottery, or the like (singular "graffito") [Italian; akin to *graphic*]
grail *n.* object of a long or difficult quest; cup or platter used, according to medieval legend, by Jesus at the Last Supper (also "Holy Grail", "Sangraal")
grain *n.* pattern or direction of fibres, markings, or the like, as of wood, meat, or leather; outer side of a piece of leather or hide from which the hair or wool is removed ~ *tr.v.* to remove the hair or wool from (skins or hides)
grains *n.* harpoon with barbed prongs used for spearing fish (used with a singular verb)
gram *n.* chickpea, mung bean, or related plant grown in India for its edible seeds; gram seeds used as food
gramineous (grə-mínni-əss) *adj.* grass-like or relating to grass
graminivorous (grámmi-nívvərəss) *adj.* feeding on grasses, seeds, or grains
grammatology *n.* scientific study of systems of writing — **-logical** *adj.* — **-gist** *n.*
grampus *n.* dolphin-like sea mammal with a blunt snout; killer whale or other small whale; *informal.* person who breathes heavily and noisily
gran cassa *formal. n., pl.* **gran casse** bass drum [Italian, literally, great drum]
grandee (gran-deé) *n.* Spanish or Portuguese nobleman of the highest rank; important or high-ranking person, sometimes pompous and self-important
Grand Guignol (gróN geen-yól) *n.* gruesome horror

plays as a theatrical genre [after *Le Grand Guignol*, a small Parisian theatre formerly noted for presenting such plays: the name means, literally, the big puppet] — **Grand-Guignol** *adj.*

grandiloquent (gran-díllə-kwənt) *formal. adj.* pompous or high-falutin in style — **-quence** *n.*

grand mal (gróN mál) *n.* epilepsy of a kind involving severe convulsions and lengthy periods of unconsciousness; severe epileptic fit. Compare PETIT MAL [French, literally, great illness, large harm]

grand seigneur (groN say-nyőr) *n.* man of very dignified or aristocratic manner (sometimes ironic)

grange *n.* farm or farm buildings [akin to *grain*]

granivorous (gra-nívvərəss) *formal. adj.* grain-eating, feeding on grain or seeds

granular (grránnəw-lər) *adj.* grainy in texture or appearance

granulation *n.* formation of small beads of new tissue on the surface of a wound during healing — **-late** *intr.v.*

granule *n.* particle, pellet, small grain; small bright spot briefly mottling the surface of the Sun

grapeshot *n.* cluster of pellets or small projectiles fired from cannons [from the resemblance between the shot and a bunch of grapes]

graphic (gráffik) *adj.* clearly described in vivid or exciting detail: *a graphic account of the accident*

graphics *n.* art or process of technical drawing, as in architecture or engineering ~ *pl.n.* artwork illustrating a text

graphite *n.* dark grey form of carbon used in lead pencils and as a lubricant (also "plumbago")

graphology *n.* study of handwriting, especially as an indication of character; study of writing systems — **-logical** *adj.* — **-gist** *n.*

grapnel *n.* iron device with hooks, attached to a rope, thrown on to a wall, nearby ship, or the like to grip it and create a connection (also "grappling", "grappling hook", "grappling iron"); anchor with several flukes, for mooring a small boat

gratify *tr.v.* to please or satisfy; to give in to, indulge: *gratify a whim* — **-ing** *adj.* — **-fication** *n.*

gratis *adv.* without charge, for free — **gratis** *adj.*

gratuitous (grə-téw-i-təss) *adj.* uncalled-for, unjustified, without cause: *gratuitous violence in the film*; *formal.* free, without charge or obligation

gratuity *n.* tip or bonus, gift payment in return for a favour

graupel (grówp'l) *n.* "soft hail", snow-like pellets of hail

gravamen (grə-váymən) *n., pl.* **-vamina** essential or most telling part of an accusation, charge, or complaint

gravid (grávvid) *formal. adj.* pregnant; full of eggs or roe

gravitate *intr.v.* to move towards a person or thing involuntarily, to be irresistibly attracted [related to *gravity*] — **-tation** *n.*

gravity *n.* solemnity, dignity, grave manner, earnestness

Grecian bend *n.* posture, adopted by fashionable women in the late 19th century, of pressing the chest forward and the buttocks back, often enhanced by a bustle

Grecian nose *n.* nose, long and straight, extending as if in continuation of the line of the forehead

greenhorn *chiefly U.S. informal. n.* inexperienced, immature, or gullible person [formerly, a young animal with new horns]

greenhouse effect *n.* heating of the Earth's atmosphere through increased absorption of solar radiation

gregarious (gri-gáiri-əss) *adj.* enjoying the company of others, sociable; relating to or living in a group, crowd, flock, or the like

Gregorian calendar (gri-gáwri-ən) *n.* calendar, with its system of leap years, introduced in 1582 to replace the Julian calendar, and now in general use [after Pope *Gregory* XIII, who introduced it]

Gregorian chant *n.* chant or liturgical plainsong in the Roman Catholic Church [formalised in about AD 600 in the time of Pope *Gregory* I]

gremlin *informal. n.* puzzling and supposedly mischievous cause of problems, especially in machinery

grenadine (grénnə-deen, -déen) *n.* pomegranate or redcurrant syrup, used as a cordial or flavouring [related to *pomegranate*]

grievance *n.* real or apparent injustice; complaint or feeling of resentment arising from such an injustice

griffin *n.* monster in Greek mythology, with a lion's body and the head and wings of an eagle (also "gryphon")

grilse (grilss) *n., pl.* **grilse** young salmon returning from the sea to inland waters for the first time to spawn

grimace (grímməss, gri-máyss) *n.* twisting of the facial features, as in pain or disgust [akin to *grim*] — **grimace** *intr.v.*

grimalkin (gri-mál-kin, -máwl-) *archaic. n.* cat, especially an old female cat, or the name of such a cat, as in folk tales; spiteful, shrewish old woman [from *grey* + dialectal *malkin*, a female cat or slovenly woman, from the name *Maud* or *Matilda*]

gringo *n., pl.* **-gos** foreigner, especially an American or English person, in Latin America

griot (grée-ot) *n.* oral historian or bard in a West African community

grippe (grip, greep) *archaic. n.* flu

grisaille (gri-záyl, -zíl, -zí) *n.* design, painting, or style of painting using shades of grey and aiming at a three-dimensional effect. Compare TROMPE L'OEIL

grist *n.* grain due for grinding or having been ground; amount of grist in a single grinding

groats *pl.n.* grain, especially oats, that is coarsely ground or crushed; porridge made of groats

groin *n.* join of the inner thighs and trunk, or the region around it; in architecture, curved line at the intersection of two vaults

grommet *n.* ring or eyelet, as of rope or rubber, for securing a sail, protecting a wire from chafing, or the like (also "grummet")

grotesque (grō-tésk) *adj.* bizarre, extravagant or weirdly distorted in style or appearance [from Old Italian *grottesca*, literally, grotto-like, referring to the kind of extravagant painting used to decorate artificial garden grottos] — **grotesque**, **-querie** *n.*

grotto (gróttō) *n., pl.* **-toes** or **-tos** small picturesque cave; decorative artificial cave, as in an 18th-century landscaped garden [Italian; related to *crypt*]

groundswell *n.* sea swell or rolling wave; growth or increase, as of public feeling or opinion

ground zero *n.* point at, above, or under the centre of a nuclear explosion

grout *n.* thin mortar, as used between tiles; plaster

used as a finishing coating on walls; coarse meal or oats, or a porridge made from it — **grout** *tr.v.*
grouts *pl.n.* dregs or sediment, such as coffee grounds [akin to *grit*]
groyne *n.* low wall or fence jutting into the sea to control erosion of a beach
Grub Street *n.* world of hack writers and mediocre or luckless journalists [after a former London street once inhabited by hack writers] — **grubstreet** *adj.*
grudging *adj.* reluctant, unwilling, forced: *a very grudging compliment*
gruel *n.* thin, watery porridge
gruesome *adj.* frightful, shocking, ghastly, causing horror
Grundyism (grúndi-iz'm) *n.* moral disapproval of an excessive kind, narrow-minded propriety and criticism of the unconventional [after Mrs *Grundy*, a prudish offstage character in the play *Speed the Plough* of 1798, by Thomas Morton] — **Grundy, Mrs Grundy** *n.* — **Grundyish** *adj.*
GT *adj.* referring or relating to a luxury sports or touring car (also "Gran Turismo" [abbreviation of Italian or Spanish *Gran Turismo*, grand tourism or grand touring] — **GT** *n.*
guacamole (gwáakə-mṓli) *n.* avocado dip, salad, or hors d'oeuvre, of Mexican origin
guano (gwáa-nō) *n.* substance consisting chiefly of the dried dung of sea birds, collected from deposits along the coast for use as a fertiliser
gubernatorial (gŏŏ-bər-nə-táwri-əl, géw-) *adj.* relating to a governor, as of a U.S. state [related to *govern*]
guddle *chiefly Scottish.v.* to catch fish with one's hands
gudgeon *n.* pivot of metal at the end of a wooden shaft or axle, as for a wheel to turn on; socket, as for the rudder of a boat or the pin of a hinge; metal pin for fastening blocks of stone to each other [related to *gouge*]
guerdon (gérd'n) *archaic or poetic. n.* reward or payment ~ *tr.v.* to reward
guerrilla *n.* irregular soldier, typically in a liberation movement, carrying out sabotage and harassment operations (also "guerilla") [Spanish, literally, small war; akin to *war*]
guidon (gī́d'n) *n.* small, often forked, flag carried as the standard of a military unit; soldier or vehicle bearing a guidon [related to *guide*]
guild *n.* trade and mutual-aid association, especially of merchants or craftsmen in medieval times (also "gild") — **guildsman, -woman** *n.*
guileless (gī́l-ləss) *adj.* simple, artless, unscheming
guimpe (gimp, gamp) *n.* blouse worn under a jumper or pinafore dress; insert or fill-in at the front of a low-cut dress; starched cloth, part of a nun's habit, covering the neck and shoulders; gimp [akin to *wimple*]
guipure (gi-péwr) *n.* lace of a heavy, large-patterned kind on a backing of fabric rather than netting; gimp
guiro (gwéer-ō, wéer-ō) *n., pl.* **-os** percussion instrument of Latin American origin, consisting of a serrated gourd that rattles when scraped with a stick
gular (gŏŏ-lər, géw-) *formal. adj.* relating to the throat
gulch *chiefly U.S. n.* ravine, especially one containing a narrow river
gullet *n.* throat or oesophagus; cut or channel in the ground, as for access in mining or excavating; *chiefly U.S.* ravine, gully, or other water channel
gullible *adj.* easily tricked, possible to deceive, believing things too readily — **gull** *n., tr.v.*
gully *n.* ditch or channel cut in the ground by rainwater or a stream [probably altered from *gullet*]
gumption *informal. n.* common sense, and ability to be practical; courageous initiative, nerve
gung ho *chiefly U.S. slang. adj.* loyal, dutiful, or enthusiastic to an excessive, foolish, or dangerous degree [motto, supposed to mean "work together", of certain U.S. marines in the Second World War, from Mandarin Chinese]
gunwale (gúnn'l) *n.* upper edge of the side of a ship or boat (also "gunnel")
Guoyu (gwō-yǘ) *n.* Mandarin Chinese developed to serve as the national standard language of China [Mandarin Chinese, *guo*, national + *yu*, a language]
guru *n.* spiritual teacher or leader, as among Hindus or Sikhs; personal guide or mentor; *informal.* champion, leading advocate or supporter, as of a cult or doctrine: *the guru of monetarism*
gusset *n.* triangular insert of material for enlarging or reinforcing a garment, bag, or the like; triangular metal plate for reinforcing a corner joist — **-ed** *adj.*
gustatory (gústə-tri) *formal. adj.* relating to the sense of taste — **gustation** *n.*
gusto *n.* zest, vitality, enthusiastic enjoyment
gutta-percha (gúttə-pérchə) *n.* tough, rubbery latex substance used in electrical insulation and dentistry; tree yielding gutta-percha as sap
guttate (góttayt) *formal. adj.* shaped like a drop; containing or covered with drops or drop-like markings — **-ation** *n.*
gutter *n.* perforation between postage stamps on a sheet; white space between facing pages of a book
guttural (gúttərəl) *adj.* throaty, relating to the throat, or pronounced in the throat
guy *n.* rope, chain, or the like, as for steadying a load or mooring an aerial ~ *tr.v.* to moor, fasten, steady, or guide with a guy
gymkhana (jim-káanə) *chiefly British. n.* sports event; specifically, competition and display of horse-riding skills, especially by children; place where a gymkhana is held [alteration, influenced by *gymnasium*, of Hindi *gend-khana*, a racket court, literally, a ball house]
gynaecology *n.* medical study and treatment of diseases affecting the reproductive system of women — **-logical** *adj.* — **-gist** *n.*
gynaecomastia (gī́ni-kō-másti-ə) *formal. n.* abnormal enlargement of breasts in a man, as through hormone imbalance
gynoecium (jī-née-si-əm, gī-) *n., pl.* **-ia** female parts of a flower, pistil or pistils (also "gynaecium")
gypsum (jípsəm) *n.* white mineral used in fertilisers and plaster of Paris — **-seous, -siferous** *adj.*
gyrate *v.* to revolve or spin — **-ration** *n.*
gyroscope (jī́r-ə-skōp) *n.* spinning flywheel maintaining a stable angle or direction in a frame of pivoted supports (also "gyro") — **-scopic** *adj.*

H

habeas corpus (háybi-əs kórpəss) *n.* legal writ to bring an unconvicted prisoner before a judge or to release him [Latin, literally, you may have the body (the opening words of the document)]
haberdasher *n.* seller of sewing or dressmaking materials, or of men's gloves, hats, and the like — **-ery** *n.*
habergeon (hábber-jən) *n.* sleeveless coat of mail
habile *formal. adj.* skilful with the hands, dexterous, adroit
habiliments *formal or archaic. pl.n.* clothes, especially a ceremonial uniform
habitat *n.* natural area or environment for an animal or plant; typical location for a person or thing
habitué (hə-bíttew-ay) *n.* frequent guest of a place, such as pub or club
háček (háa-chek) *n.* diacritic or accent mark, ˇ, as sometimes placed over a *c* in Czech words to modify the sound
hacienda (háassi-éndə) *n.* Spanish-style ranch, estate, or ranch-house
hacker *n.* computer enthusiast, especially one who gains access to private programs
hackles *pl.n.* upright feathers or hairs on the back of an animal's neck — *get one's hackles up/make one's hackles rise* to anger, stir into a fighting mood
hackneyed *adj.* trite, overused, and stale
haematology (héemə-tólləji) *n.* medical or scientific study of the blood — **-gist** *n.* — **-logical** *adj.*
haemophilia (héemə-fílli-ə) *n.* blood disorder, involving excessive bleeding through failure of the blood to clot — **-iac** *n., adj.*
haemorrhage (hémmə-rij) *n.* sudden rush of bleeding — **haemorrhage** *intr.v.*
haemorrhoid (hémmə-royd) *n.* mass of swollen veins in anal tissue — **haemorrhoids** medical condition involving this, piles
haft *n.* handle or hilt, as of a sword — **haft** *tr.v.*
haggard *adj.* exhausted-looking, gaunt; wild, uncontrollable ~ *n.* adult hawk in training
hagiography (hággi-óggrəfi) *n.* biography of saints; over-admiring biography; excessive praise
hagridden *formal or archaic. adj.* pursued or tormented by or as if by a witch; troubled by nightmares, deep fears, or the like
ha-ha *n.* ditch, moat, or sunken hedge, as in a garden [French, probably from an expression of surprise on noticing the hidden obstruction]
haiku (hī-ko͞o) *n., pl.* **haiku** Japanese poem of 17 syllables (also "hokku") [Japanese, *hai*, amusement + *ku*, a sentence or verse]
hair-trigger *adj.* easily aroused or provoked
Haj (haj) *n.* Muslim pilgrimage to Mecca
haji (hájee) *n.* Muslim who has made a Haj or pilgrimage to Mecca
haka (háakə) *n.* Maori war dance
halal (haa-láal) *adj.* referring to meat slaughtered according to Muslim law and ritual (also "hallal") [Arabic, literally, lawful] — **halal** *n., tr.v.*
halberd *n.* weapon of the 15th or 16th century, consisting of a long shaft topped with an axe-like blade and steel spike — **-dier** *n.*
halcyon (hál-si-ən) *n.* kingfisher in mythology ~ *adj.* calm; contented or prosperous: *halcyon days*
halitosis (hál-i-tṓ-siss) *formal. n.* bad breath
hallmark *n.* stamped mark on a gold, silver, or platinum object to indicate the purity of the metal (also "platemark"); indication of quality or of the nature of something
hallow *tr.v.* to make, mark, or honour as holy (old-fashioned) — **-ed** *adj.*
hallucination *n.* false or dream-like perception, sometimes drug-induced; wrong idea or delusion — **-cinate** *v.* — **-cinatory** *adj.*
hallucinogen (hə-lo͞o-si-nə-jən) *n.* drug, such as LSD, that causes hallucinations — **-genic** *adj.*
hallux (hál-əks) *formal. n., pl.* **-luces** the big toe, or equivalent digit in animals
halter *n.* straps for securing a horse or cow by the neck; noosed rope for hanging people; blouse having shoulder straps that tie round the neck, leaving the back bare
halting *adj.* limping, lame; faulty, imperfect: *a halting argument*; jerky, wavering: *halting speech*
halva *n.* oriental sweetmeat of crushed sesame seeds and honey
halyard *n.* rope for raising or lowering a sail or flag
hamadryad (hámmə-drī́-əd) *n., pl.* **-ads** or **-ades** in classical mythology, a female wood nymph, who is the spirit of the tree she lives in. Compare DRYAD; king cobra
hamlet *n.* small village
hamshackle *tr.v.* to hobble or restrict the movement of (a horse or cow) by means of a rope tied to its head and one leg; hinder or hold back [probably from *hamper* + *shackle*]
hamstring *n.* tendon behind the knee ~ *tr.v.* to cut the hamstrings of; to hinder or impede
handbill *n.* pamphlet or advertisement distributed by hand
handmaiden *n.* woman servant or attendant (also "handmaid"); *formal.* person or thing with a useful but secondary function: *Language is the handmaiden of thought*
hand-to-mouth *adj.* precariously poor, with nothing to spare: *a hand-to-mouth existence* — **hand to mouth** *adv.*
hang-dog *adj.* looking ashamed or downcast [originally, a worthless person fit only to hang a dog]
hanger *n.* small sword worn hanging from the waist
hank *n.* coil or loop, bundle or measure of yarn or fabric
Hansard *n.* printed record of parliamentary debates [after Luke *Hansard*, who first printed it in London in the 18th century]

Hansen's disease *n.* leprosy [after G.A. *Hansen*, the 19th-century Norwegian doctor who discovered the bacillus]
haphazard *adj.* planless, disorderly; random, chance
hapless *adj.* unfortunate, luckless, miserable (old-fashioned)
haplology *n.* clipping of a word by omission of a segment in pronunciation, as in pronouncing *February* as if it were spelt *Febry*. Compare SYNCOPE, APOCOPE
hara-kiri *n.* Japanese ritual suicide by disembowelment (also "seppuku") [Japanese, *hara*, the stomach + *kiri*, cutting]
harangue (hə-ráng) *n.* long speech that is passionate, pompous, or argumentative, tirade — **harangue** *v.*
harbinger (hárbinjər) *n.* signal or sign of something to come: *harbingers of autumn* — **harbinger** *tr.v.*
hard tack *n.* hard bread or biscuit formerly eaten by sailors on shipboard (also "ship's biscuit")
hardy *adj.* brave, strong, and able to endure; referring to a cultivated plant that can survive in unfavourable conditions
harem *n.* group of wives, concubines, and female relatives of a Muslim man; place where a harem lives
haricot (hárri-kō) *n.* seed or pod of certain beans, especially the French bean
harijan (húrri-jən, hárri-) *n.* Hindu of the lowest status, technically outside the caste system, formerly called "Untouchable" [introduced by Mahatma Gandhi to replace "Untouchable", from Sanskrit, a devotee of Vishnu]
harlequin *n.* clown or buffoon, from traditional Italian comedy, wearing a mask and chequered tights — **-ade** *n.*
harlot *n.* slut, sexually promiscuous woman, or prostitute (old-fashioned)
harmonics *n.* study of the physical properties of musical sounds
harpy *n.* cruel and greedy person; bad-tempered woman [winged monster in Greek mythology]
harridan *n.* bad-tempered woman
harrier *n.* small hound used originally when hunting hares; member of a cross-country running team [from *hare*]
harrow *n.* plough-like farm implement used to level or break up soil
harrowing *adj.* very upsetting, deeply distressing
harry *tr.v.* to raid repeatedly or destructively; to force (someone) to keep moving; to torment or harrass: *harried housewives with small children*
harum-scarum (háir-əm skáir-əm) *adj.* irresponsible, reckless, rash [perhaps from *hare* + *scare*]
haruspex (hə-rúspeks, hárrə-speks) *n., pl.* **-spices** soothsayer or diviner in ancient Rome who interpreted the entrails of animals
haslet *n.* offal of an animal, especially a pig, or a meatloaf made of it
hasp *n.* hinged metal flap fitting over a staple that is locked by a padlock or pin, as for fastening a door — **hasp** *tr.v.*
hassock *n.* firm, flat cushion for kneeling or sitting on in church; tussock of grass
hatchet face *informal. n.* face that is long, gaunt, and sharp-featured — **hatchet-faced** *adj.*
hatchet job *informal. n.* criticism intended to harm someone's reputation
hatchet man *informal. n.* henchman who is hired to perform a distasteful task, such as dismissing staff
hatching *n.* shading of fine lines in a drawing
hatha yoga *n.* yoga of a kind emphasising breathing exercises
hauberk (háwberk) *n.* tunic of chain mail
haulm (hawm) *chiefly British. n.* plant stalks or long grass used for thatching (also "halm")
haute couture (ṓt koo-téwr) *n.* high fashion in women's clothing [French]
haute cuisine (ṓt kwi-zéen) *n.* cooking of high quality
hauteur (ō-túr) *formal. n.* haughtiness, proud or arrogant attitude
havelock (háv-lok) *n.* cloth flap at the back of a cap, to protect the neck from sunburn [after Sir Henry *Havelock*, a 19th-century British general in India]
haver (háyvər) *British. intr.v.* to hesitate, dither, vacillate
[1]hawk *n.* war-like politician or adviser (opposite "dove")
[2]hawk *intr.v.* to clear the throat loudly ~ *tr.v.* to spit out while hawking
[3]hawk *n.* tray with a handle underneath, for carrying cement or plaster
hawse (hawz) *n.* opening in a ship's bow for the anchor rope (also "hawsehole" or "hawsepipe")
hawser (háwzər) *n.* rope for anchoring or towing a ship
hazard *formal. tr.v.* to risk — **hazard** *n.* — **-ous** *adj.*
headwaters *pl.n.* source of a river
hearing *n.* preliminary trial or inquest
hearken *formal. intr.v.* listen closely or hear
hearsay *n.* information or evidence derived from others rather than based on direct experience
hearse *n.* vehicle for carrying a coffin to a funeral
heat *n.* sexual excitement in female animals, oestrus
heathen *n.* person who believes in many gods or in mysterious natural forces, as among primitive peoples, rather than in one God; person regarded as irreligious or ungodly [related to *heath*, referring to savage, heath-dwelling people] — **-dom, -ry, -ism** *n.* — **heathen, -ish** *adj.*
heave-ho *informal. n.* dismissal from a job, the sack [nautical expression originally used when raising an anchor]
hebdomadal (heb-dómmәd'l) *formal. adj.* weekly [from Greek, *hepta*, seven]
hebetude (hébbi-tewd) *formal. n.* mental dullness or laziness — **-tudinous** *adj.*
Hebraist *n.* scholar of or specialist in the Hebrew language — **-raic** *adj.* — **-raism** *n.*
hecatomb (héckə-tōōm, -tōm) *n.* sacrifice or slaughter on a large scale [from Greek, *hekaton*, a hundred + *bous*, an ox]
hectare (hék-tair) *n.* metric unit of area equal to 10,000 square metres or 2.471 acres
hectic *adj.* feverishly busy, bustling, or active; feverish (old-fashioned)
hector *tr.v.* to bully, intimidate, or harass, as by shouting or nagging [after *Hector*, the swaggering Trojan prince in Greek legend]
hedgehop *intr.v.* to fly an aircraft very low, rising to avoid hedges, fences, and other obstacles, as when spraying crops
hedonism (héed'n-iz'm) *n.* devotion to sensual pleasure, love of luxury — **-istic** *adj.* — **-ist** *n.*
-hedral *adj. comb.form.* -surfaced, -faced: *polyhedral*, *hexahedral*. Compare -GONAL — **-hedron** *n. comb.form.*

[1]heel *n.* crusty end of a loaf or roll; pad of muscle on the hand below the thumb; lower end of a ship's mast

[2]heel *intr.v.* to list or tilt over to one side, as a ship might

hegemony (hee-gémməni, héjiməni) *formal. n.* rule, authority, or dominant influence — **-monic** *adj.*

heifer (héffər) *n.* young cow that has not yet given birth to calves

heinous (háynəss) *formal. adj.* extremely wicked, vile, hateful, or blameworthy

heist (hīst) *U.S. informal. n.* robbery or large theft: *a bank heist*

Heldentenor (héldən-te-nór) *n., pl.* **-tenöre** singer with a strong tenor voice, especially suitable in Wagnerian opera [German, literally, hero tenor]

helianthus *n.* sunflower or related plant

heliograph *n.* signal or signalling device based on mirror-flashes of sunlight — **-gram** *n.*

heliotrope *n.* flower or plant that turns to keep facing the Sun

helix *n., pl.* **-es** or **-lices** shape of a spiral or whirlpool; flap of cartilage and skin around the ear — **-lical**, **-licoid** *adj.*

hellebore (hélli-bawr) *n.* evergreen flowering plant such as the Christmas rose

Hellenic *adj.* characteristic of ancient or modern Greece, Greeks, or the Greek language

Hellenist *n.* admirer or student of classical Greek culture

Hellenistic *adj.* relating to post-classical Greek culture, between the death of Alexander the Great and the rise of the Roman Empire

helm *n.* ship's steering equipment, wheel, or tiller — **helmsman** *n.*

helminth *formal. n.* tapeworm or other parasitic worm — **-ic** *adj.*

helot (héllət) *n.* serf, originally in ancient Sparta — **-ism**, **-ry** *n.*

helpmate *n.* spouse regarded as a helper or companion

helve *n.* handle of an axe, hammer, or the like

Helvetian *formal. adj., n.* Swiss

hemeralopia *formal. n.* difficulty in seeing in bright light, "day blindness". Compare NYCTALOPIA — **-opic** *adj.*

hemiplegia *n.* paralysis of one side of the body — **-gic** *adj., n.*

hemisphere *n.* half a sphere or globe, as of the Earth

hemlock *n.* tall poisonous plant with purple-spotted stems and small white flowers; poison derived from this plant

hemp *n.* fibre used in sacking; cannabis

henge *n.* circle of stone or wooden pillars, as at Stonehenge, built by people from prehistoric cultures

henna *n.* hair dye producing a reddish colour — **henna** *tr.v.*

hepatic *adj.* relating to the liver

hepatitis *n.* liver disease or inflammation, one symptom of which is jaundice

Heptateuch (héptə-təwk) *n.* first seven books of the bible

heraldry *n.* study of pedigrees, coats of arms, insignia, and the like — **-aldic** *adj.* — **herald**, **-aldist** *n.*

herbaceous border *chiefly British. n.* flowerbed, typically of perennial plants

herbage *n.* fleshy part of plants, often edible; hay or similar food for pasturing

herbivorous (her-bívərəss) *adj.* plant-eating, feeding only on plant matter — **-vore** *n.*

herculean *formal. adj.* of enormous size or monumental proportions; difficult or very straining: *a herculean task* [after *Hercules*, the hero in Greek and Roman mythology with superhuman strength]

hereditary (hə-réddi-tri) *adj.* relating to inheritance or heredity

heredity *n.* inheritance or transmission of characteristics by genetic means rather than by environmental inferences

heresy *n.* unorthodox belief or doctrine, typically in religion, that is condemned by the orthodox — **heretic** *n.* — **heretical** *adj.*

heritage *n.* culture or traditions passed down over the generations

hermaphrodite *n.* person or animal having both male and female sex organs or characteristics [after *Hermaphroditos*, the son of Hermes and Aphrodite in Greek mythology, who fused into one body with the nymph Salmacis] — **-ditic** *adj.* — **-ditism** *n.*

hermeneutics (hérmi-néwtiks) *n.* study or technique of interpretation, especially of scriptural texts (used with a singular verb) — **hermeneutic** *adj.*

hermetic *adj.* sealed, air-tight; cut off from outside influences [after *Hermes* Trismegistus, a legendary alchemist who is said to have invented a magic seal to make vessels air-tight]

hernia *n.* displacement of a body part or organ through its lining or wall; result of hernia, rupture

hero *n., pl.* **-roes** large American sandwich made of a long roll (also "hero sandwich", "submarine")

herpetology *n.* scientific study of reptiles and amphibians — **-gist** *n.* — **-logical** *adj.*

herringbone *n.* pattern of parallel lines slanted in rows — **herringbone** *adj.*

hessian (héssi-ən) *chiefly British. n.* sacking material made of jute (also *chiefly U.S.* "burlap") [after the German town of *Hesse*, where it was first made] **hessian** — *adj.*

heterodox *formal. adj.* unorthodox — **-doxy** *n.*

heterogeneous *adj.* having dissimilar parts or elements (opposite "homogeneous") — **-geneity** *n.*

heterosexual *adj.* attracted to the opposite sex — **heterosexual** *n.*

hetman *n., pl.* **-mans** Cossack chief (also "ataman")

heuristic (hewr-rístik) *adj.* relating or referring to learning by problem-solving, experiment, trial-and-error, and the evaluation of feedback — **heuristics** *n.*

hexameter (hek-sámmitər) *n.* line of verse with six stresses

Hexateuch (héksə-tewk) *n.* first six books of the bible

hiatus (hī-áytəss) *n., pl.* **hiatuses** or **hiatus** gap or missing part, lacuna; break in continuity

hiatus hernia *n.* hernia in which part of the stomach pushes through the diaphragm

hibachi (hi-ba̋achi) *n.* portable Japanese charcoal grill, sometimes used for cooking at table [Japanese, *hi*, fire + *bachi*, a bowl]

hibernal *formal. adj.* relating to winter

hibernate *intr.v.* to spend the winter in a sleep-like state; to stay quiet and inactive — **-nation** *n*

hic jacet (hik yácket) here lies (used on tombstones to identify the person buried) [Latin]

hidalgo *n. pl.* **-gos** minor nobleman in Spain; Spaniard or Spanish American man of aristocratic bearing (female counterpart "hidalga")

hidebound *adj.* unimaginative, prejudiced, and inflexible

hidrosis *formal. n.* abnormal or excessive sweating — **-drotic** *adj.*

hierarchy *n.* classification or organisation by rank or importance; group organised or classified in this way; clergy of the rank of bishop and above — **-chical, -chic** *adj.*

hieratic (hīr-áttik) *adj. formal.* relating to priests and their functions, sacerdotal; referring to simplified hieroglyphics, or various art styles and conventions, developed by priests in ancient Egypt

hieroglyphics *pl.n.* writing, as in ancient Egypt, that uses symbols which resemble pictures; illegible writing (humorous) — **-glyph** *n.* — **-glyphic** *adj., n.*

high-tech *n.* style of design using or suggesting ultramodern industrial products or methods — **high-tech** *adj.*

hi-hat *n.* pair of cymbals operated by a foot-pedal in a drumkit

hilarity *n.* unrestrained enjoyment, noisy merriment — **hilarious** *adj.*

hilum (hī́-ləm) *n., pl.* **-la** scar on a bean or other seed at the point where it was attached to the stalk

hinny *n.* hybrid animal, similar to a mule, that is the offspring of a female ass and a male horse

hinterland *n.* inland region; remote country region, back country

Hippocratic oath *n.* oath of allegiance to medical ethics sometimes taken by newly qualified doctors [after *Hippocrates*, the 5th-4th-century B.C. Greek physician known as the Father of Medicine]

hippodrome *n.* open-air oval stadium for horse and chariot races in ancient Greece and Rome; arena or theatre for spectacles such as circuses and tattoos

hircine (húr-sīn) *formal. adj.* goat-like, especially in smell or lustfulness

hirsute (húr-sewt, hur-séwt) *formal. adj.* hairy

Hispanic *adj.* relating to the culture, language, and peoples of Spain and areas influenced by Spain, especially Latin America — **Hispanic** *chiefly U.S. n.*

histamine *n.* chemical compound released by the body in allergic reactions

histogram *n.* statistical bar graph, conveying information by means of a series of columns

histology *n.* study of organic tissue; microscopic structure of organic tissue

historical present *n.* present tense of verbs used when narrating events of the past, as in *Yesterday he comes up to me and he says ...* — **historical present** *adj.*

histrionic *adj. archaic.* relating to acting; emotional in an excessive, theatrical way — **-ics** *pl. n.*

hives *n.* skin condition or allergy involving itching and bumps (also "urticaria", "nettle rash", "uredo")

hoar frost *n.* frost of small white ice crystals

hoary *adj.* grey or white, as through old age; very old or too old: *a hoary anecdote*; covered with fine greyish hair or down: *hoary leaves*

hobble *n.* device of ropes or straps for tying together the legs of a horse or cow ~ *v.* — *tr.* to restrict the movements of (a horse or cow) with a hobble — *intr.* to limp, walk, or move awkwardly

hobbledehoy (hóbb'l-di-hoy) *n.* awkward or gawky adolescent, especially a boy

hobnob *intr.v.* to socialise, associate with on friendly terms: *hobnobbing with the top brass*

Hobson-Jobson *n.* process of altering by folk-etymology an expression borrowed from another language to make it fit into the borrowing language [Anglo-Indian alteration, by this very process, of Arabic *ya Hasan, ya Husayn!*, a ritual cry of mourning for the martyred Shi'ite imams Hasan and Husain, grandsons of Muhammad]

Hobson's choice *n.* choice forced upon one, choice when there is no real alternative [after Thomas *Hobson*, a 17th-century Cambridge stable-owner, who hired out horses on the basis that each customer could choose the horse nearest the stable door — or no horse at all]

hock *n.* joint midway up the hind leg of a horse or similar animal, corresponding to the human ankle

hocus-pocus *n.* nonsense formulas or mystifying jargon, as used by a conjuror; trickery or deception; [related to *hoax*; from a mock-Latin conjuror's formula, probably based on an irreverent parody of part of the Roman Catholic Mass — *Hoc est corpus*, This is the body]

hod *n.* tray attached to a pole and carried against the shoulder, used for transporting bricks or mortar

hoe-down *chiefly U.S. n.* square dance; music for a square dance; party with square dancing

hog back *n.* crested ridge of land with steep eroded sides (also "hog's back") [from the resemblance of such a ridge to the arching back of a wild pig]

hogshead *n.* large barrel for liquids; liquid measure based on the size of a hogshead

hoi polloi (hóy pə-lóy) *pl.n.* the common people, the masses (usually humorous) [Greek, literally, the many]

hoity-toity *informal. adj.* snobbish or haughty; irritable as a result of an offence to one's supposed dignity

hokum *chiefly U.S. n. informal.* nonsense; clichéd showbiz material, often sentimental, introduced to get a sure-fire audience response

holism *n.* doctrine that things should be viewed as wholes greater than the sum of their parts — **holistic** *adj.*

holm (hōm) *n.* small island in an estuary or river; stretch of low-lying land near a river (also "holme")

holocaust *n.* great destruction by or as if by fire: *a nuclear holocaust*; burnt offering — **the Holocaust** the mass killing of Jews by order of the Nazis in the 1940s

hologram (hóllə-gram) *n.* three-dimensional picture or pattern produced, typically by a laser, on a photographic film or plate — **-graphy** *n.* — **-graphic** *adj.*

holograph *n.* manuscript in the handwriting of its author; handwriting of a holograph; hologram — **-graphic** *adj.*

holt *archaic. n.* wooded hill; small woods or grove

homage *n.* under feudalism, ceremonial acknowledgment by an inferior of loyalty to a superior; publicly expressed respect or tribute: *paid homage to a great woman scientist*

homeopathy *n.* treatment of disease by tiny doses of substances that in larger doses would produce symptoms like those of the diseases treated (also *British* "homoeopathy") — **-path** *n.* — **-pathic** *adj.*

homicide *n.* unlawful killing of one person by another, in the form of murder or manslaughter; *formal.* person who has committed homicide — **-cidal** *adj.*

homily (hómmili) *n.* sermon, especially one exploring the practical rather than the theological implications of a part of the bible; boring moralising lecture; catchphrase, proverb, or clichéd formula, especially one intended to sum up good advice — **-letic** *adj.*

hominid *n.* member of a group of mammals that includes human beings and prehistoric man

hominy *chiefly U.S. n.* hulled maize kernels dried for food

homogeneous *adj.* similar or uniform in kind, texture, or structure (also "homogenous"; opposite "heterogeneous") — **-geneity** *n.* — **-genise** *tr.v.*

homograph *n.* word that is spelt the same as another: *The verb "record" and the noun "record" are homographs* — **ic** *adj.*

homologous (ho-mólla-gəss) *adj.* similar in structure or evolutionary history, sometimes in function: *Arms and wings are homologous* — **-logy** *n.* — **-logue** *n.*

homonym *n.* word that is spelt and pronounced the same as another: *The verb "bear" and the noun "bear" are homonyms.* — **-mous** *adj.* — **-my** *n.*

homophone *n.* word that is pronounced the same as another: *The words "son" and "sun" are homophones* — **-phonic** *adj.*

Homo sapiens *n.* species to which all human beings belong; human beings as rational creatures, by contrast with earlier hominids and other animals [New Latin, literally, wise man]

homunculus (ho-múng-kew-ləss) *formal. n., pl.* **-li** miniature man, manikin

hone *n.* fine-grained whetstone for sharpening or smoothing a cutting edge ~ *tr.v.* to make sharper, smoother, or more precise with or as if with a hone: *to hone a blade*; *finely honed wit*

honorarium *n., pl.* **-riums** or **-ria** fee paid for services for which no fee is legally required: *an honorarium for adjudicating the competition*

honorary *adj.* unpaid: *honorary secretary*; awarded as an honour rather than on the basis of paper qualifications: *an honorary degree*; included in a group by general acceptance rather than by standard rights of membership: *His female friends treat him as an honorary woman*

honorific *n.* word, phrase, title, or the like used to express respect or subservience — **honorific** *adj.*

honoris causa (o-náwr-iss ków-zaa) *formal. adj., adv.*, awarded as an honour: *a degree honoris causa*; referring to an honorary university degree [Latin, for the sake of honour]

hoodoo *informal. n.* bad luck, or a bringer or cause of bad luck

hookah *n.* pipe smoked in the East, in which the smoke is cooled by being drawn through an urn of water (also "hubble-bubble", "kalian", "narghile", "water pipe")

hoopla *chiefly U.S. n.* excited bustle, commotion; bewildering or misleading language, as in advertising or publicity

hopper *n.* funnel-shaped apparatus for dispensing solid fuel, grain, or the like; railway truck that unloads through an opening in its floor

hormone *n.* product of living animal or plant cells that circulates in blood or sap and can affect other, remote cells; synthetic hormone — **-monal** *adj.*

horology *n.* science of measuring time; craft of making clocks and watches — **-gist** *n.* — **-logical** *adj.*

horripilation *formal. n.* bristling of body hair, as from great fear or cold

hors d'oeuvre (awr-dérv, -dőrv) *n., pl.* **hors d'oeuvres** or **hors d'oeuvre** any of various small savoury dishes served as an appetiser or the first course of a meal [French, literally, outside of work]

hortatory *formal. adj.* encouraging, urging on (also "hortative")

horticulture *n.* science or art of plant cultivation, as in a garden — **-tural** *adj.* — **-turalist** *n.*

hosanna *formal or archaic. n.* cry of praise to God — **hosanna** *interj.*

hose *archaic. or formal. n.* socks, stockings, or tights — **hosier** *n.* — **hosiery** *n.*

hospice *n.* inn or shelter for the needy or travellers; institution specialising in caring for the dying

hotchpotch *n.* jumble or confused mixture (also *U.S.* "hodgepodge"); thick soup or stew

howdah (hów-də) *n.* seat, often canopied, mounted on an elephant's back

howitzer (hów-itsər) *n.* medium-range cannon for firing shells at a steep angle

howler *n. informal.* comical blunder; device in a telephone that whines when the receiver is not replaced

hoyden *n.* cheeky, high-spirited girl or woman (old-fashioned) — **hoyden** *adj.*

hubble-bubble *n.* pipe smoked in the East, in which the smoke is cooled by being drawn through an urn of water (also "hookah", "kalian", "narghile", "water pipe")

hubbub *n.* noisy bustle, din; confusion or turmoil, disorder, tumult

hubris (héw-briss) *formal. n.* arrogance and insolence, especially when leading to ruin or retribution — **-bristic** *adj.*

huckster *n.* person who sells goods in the streets, as from a market stall; salesman who uses aggressive or dishonest sales techniques — **huckster** *v.*

hugger-mugger *adj.* muddled, jumbled, in confusion; secret or stealthy: *hugger-mugger negotiations* (old-fashioned) — **hugger-mugger** *n., v., adv.*

hull *n.* main body of a ship, aircraft, or tank; leafy part where the fruit of the strawberry, raspberry, or the like joins the stem; outer covering of a nut, fruit, or seed — **hull** *tr.v.*

hullabaloo *n.* loud and confused noise, din, uproar

humanism *n.* cultural movement during the Renaissance emphasising classical learning and secularism; culture, learning; doctrine or philosophy that emphasises the human capacity for self-fulfilment without religion — **-ist** *n., adj.* — **-istic** *adj.*

humanities *pl.n.* study of the languages and literature of ancient Greece and Rome; the arts as contrasted with the sciences

humanoid *n.* in science fiction, creature or robot resembling a human — **-oid** *adj.*

humdinger *informal. n.* excellent or outstanding person or thing

humdrum *adj.* dull, commonplace, unoriginal and often tedious: *humdrum sermons/chores*

humectant *formal. n.* moistening substance — **humectant** *adj.*

humerus *n.* long bone of the upper arm, between the shoulder and the elbow

humid *adj.* damp, moist, having a high water-vapour content: *humid sea air* — **-ity** *n.* — **-ify** *tr.v.*

humidor (héwmi-dawr) *n.* case for tobacco, especially cigars, in which humidity can be kept constant

humiliate *tr.v.* to cause to lose self-respect or status, humble to the point of disgrace — **-ation** *n.*

hummock *n.* low mound or ridge

hummous (hóom-ōoss) *n.* puree of chickpeas and oil, often with sesame paste, usually eaten as an appetiser (also "hummus")

humoresque *n.* lively, playful musical composition

humour *n.* in medieval medicine, any of four body fluids thought to determine a person's health and personality

humus (héw-məss) *n.* decayed organic matter that fertilises the soil

hunky-dory *chiefly U.S. informal. adj.* all right, in good order, very satisfactory

hurdy-gurdy *n.* musical instrument operated by turning a crank; barrel organ

hurling *n.* Irish game similar to lacrosse and hockey, with 15 players to a team (also "hurley")

husbandry *n.* farming; scientific control of farming, especially of livestock breeding; economical use of resources — **husband** *tr.v.*

hussar (hŏo-zár) *n.* 15th-century Hungarian cavalryman; member of a cavalry regiment with an elaborate uniform of Hungarian design [related to *corsair*]

hustings *pl.n.* platform from which election speeches were made in former times; any place where political campaigning is carried out; political campaigning, especially for an election

hustle *v.* to push roughly, jostle; to move, act, or carry hastily; *informal.* to sell, obtain, or earn by forceful and often dishonest means; *chiefly U.S. informal.* to seek clients as or on behalf of a prostitute

hwyl (hōō-il) *n.* poetic fervour, passionate eloquence, as of a Welsh poet

hybrid *adj.* combining different elements, or having a variety of sources — **hybrid**, **-isation** *n.* — **-ise** *v.*

hydra *n.* in Greek mythology, monster with many heads that grew again when cut off; an evil that is difficult to eradicate

hydrant *n.* upright pipe, as for fire hoses, providing an outlet from a water main

hydraulic *adj.* relating to or powered by fluid pressure: *hydraulic brakes* — **hydraulics** *n.*

hydro *British. n.* spa resort or health centre providing water-based therapy

hydrocephalus (hīdrō-séffə-ləss) *n.* accumulation of fluid in the brain that causes an enlarged head (also "water on the brain") — **-cephalic** *adj.*

hydrofoil *n.* blade fixed to the hull of a boat that raises it out of the water when travelling at speed; boat fitted with hydrofoils

hydrology *n.* scientific study of water and ice on or in the earth and in the atmosphere — **-gist** *n.*

hydropathy (hī-dróppəthi) *n.* therapy based on water, whether by drinking or bathing, as at a spa (also "water cure") — **-pathic** *adj.*

hydrophobia *n.* abnormal fear of water; rabies — **-phobic** *adj.*

hydroponics *n.* growing of plants in a soilless substance using plant food dissolved in water (also "aquiculture") — **-ponic** *adj.*

hygrometer *n.* instrument for measuring atmospheric relative humidity — **-metric** *adj.*

hymeneal (hī-me-née-əl) *archaic. adj.* relating to marriage or a wedding [after *Hymen*, the Greek god of marriage]

hyperbola (hī-pérbələ) *n.*, *pl.* **-las** or **-lae** geometrical curve with two branches

hyperbole (hī-pérbəli) *n.* exaggeration used as a figure of speech — **-bolic** *adj.*

hyperborean (hīpər-baw-rée-ən) *formal. adj.* relating to the far north or arctic; freezing cold

hypercorrection *n.* mistake in grammar or pronunciation, such as *between you and I*, made in an effort to avoid an imagined error — **-correct** *adj.*

hyperglycaemia (hīpər-glī-séemi-ə) *n.* abnormally high blood-sugar level, as in diabetes — **-caemic** *adj.*

hypermetropia (hīpər-me-trṓpi-ə) *n.* defect in eyesight, in which close objects appear blurred, longsightedness (also *chiefly U.S.* "hyperopia"). Compare MYOPIA — **-pic** *adj.*

hypertension *n.* abnormally high blood pressure — **-tensive** *adj.*

hypnagogic (hípnə-gójik) *formal. adj.* sleep-inducing; relating to the drowsy state preceding sleep

hypnopaedia (hípnō-péedi-ə) *n.* learning method by which information is absorbed during sleep — **-paedic** *adj.*

hypocaust (hīpō-kawst) *n.* underfloor heating system used by the ancient Romans

hypochondria *n.* neurotic belief that one is ill or about to become ill — **-driac** *n.*, *adj.*

hypocorism (hī-póckə-riz'm) *n.* pet name, term of endearment; use of such names — **-ristic** *adj.*

hypodermic *adj.* relating to the area just beneath the skin: *a hypodermic injection/syringe/needle* — **hypodermic** *n.*

hypoglycaemia (hīpō-glī-séemi-ə) *n.* abnormally low blood-sugar level — **-caemic** *adj.*

hyponym *n.* relatively specific word that includes the meaning of a more general word: *The word "blue" is a hyponym of "colour"* — **-nymy** *n.*

hypostasis (hī-póstə-siss) *n.* essential nature of something; concept or idea treated as though it were a physically real object, as by personification; any of the three persons of the Holy Trinity; person of Christ combining his human and divine aspects; accumulation of blood in a body part, caused by poor circulation — **-statise** *tr.v.* — **-static** *adj.*

hypotaxis *n.* in grammar, the subordination of one clause to another, typically by a conjunction, as in *He'll go when she arrives*. Compare PARATAXIS, ASYNDETON — **-tactic** *adj.*

hypotension *n.* abnormally low blood pressure — **-tensive** *adj.*

hypotenuse (hī-póttə-newz) *n.* in geometry, the side of a right-angled triangle that lies opposite the right angle

hypothecate *formal. tr.v.* to pledge as security without transfer of title or ownership, mortgage — **-cation** *n.*

hypothermia *n.* abnormally low body temperature caused by cold — **-thermal** *adj.*

hypothesis (hī-póthə-siss) *n.* proposition used as a basis of argument, deduction, further investigation, or action; theory put forward as a possible explanation, as in science — **-esise** *v.*

hypothetical (hīp-ə-théttik'l) *adj.* conjectural, supposed; conditional, depending; theoretically possible but not actual

hysterectomy *n.* surgical removal of the uterus

I

iatrogenic (ī-áttrō-jénnik) *adj.* referring to symptoms or illnesses induced in the patient by a doctor's actions or words

Iberian *adj.* relating to Spain and Portugal, or their people or languages — **Iberian** *n.*

ibidem *adv.* in the same place (referring to the same page, book, or the like, as in footnotes; also "ibid.") [Latin]

ichor (ī-kawr) *n.* in Greek mythology, the thin blood in the gods' veins; pus-like liquid from an ulcer or wound — **-ous** *adj.*

ichthyology (íkthi-óllәji) *n.* scientific study of fishes — **-gist** *n.* — **-logical** *adj.*

icon *n.* representation or image; stylised picture of a saint or holy person, as in Eastern Churches (also "ikon") — **-ic** *adj.*

iconoclast *n.* breaker or opponent of sacred images, as during the Reformation; enemy of traditional institutions or ideas — **-ic** *adj.* — **-clasm** *n.*

ictus *formal. n., pl.* **ictus** or **ictuses** beat in the rhythm or metre of poetry; sudden fit or attack of illness [Latin, blow, stroke]

id *n.* basic, instinctive part of the psyche, seeking immediate gratification [Latin, it]

idée fixe (ée-day feeks) *n., pl.* **-s -s** obsessive idea, fixed idea

idée reçue (ée-day rә-séw) *n., pl.* **-s -s** belief that is uncritically accepted, received idea

idem *pron.* the same as previously referred to (used in footnotes; also "id.") [Latin, the same]

ideogram *n.* symbol that represents an idea, a thing, or, as in Chinese writing, a whole word (also "ideograph")

ides *n., pl.n.* in the ancient Roman calendar, the 15th of March, May, July, or October, or the 13th in other months

idiolect *n.* particular way in which an individual uses a language, considered as if it were a dialect — **-al** *adj.*

idiosyncrasy *n.* piece of behaviour characteristic of a particular individual, especially a habit considered curious — **-cratic** *adj.*

idolatry *n.* idol worship; strong and uncritical admiration — **-ter** *n.* — **-trise** *tr.v.* — **-trous** *adj.*

idyll (íddil) *n.* simple and charming event or country scene; short poem or piece of music depicting or reminiscent of such a scene — **-ic** *adj.*

igneous *adj.* relating to fire; referring to rock formed from solidified lava or molten rock

ignis fatuus (íg-nәss fáttew-әss) *formal. n., pl.* **ignes fatui** glowing light seen above marshy ground at night, caused by the burning of natural methane gas; something that proves to be a delusion (also "will-o'-the wisp", "jack-o'-lantern") [Latin, literally, foolish fire]

ignominy (ígnә-minni) *formal. n.* shame, dishonour — **-minious** *adj.*

ikebana (íckә-báanә) *n.* flower arranging as an art, as practised originally in Japan [Japanese, literally, living flowers]

illicit (i-líssit) *adj.* illegal, unlawful

illuminated manuscript *n.* manuscript, as from the Middle Ages, adorned with designs and lettering of bright paint, gold leaf, or the like — **illumination** *n.*

illuminati (i-lo͞omi-náati) *pl.n.* people who claim to be especially or uncommonly enlightened

illusionist *n.* magician or conjuror using elaborate special effects

illustrious *adj.* famous, renowned

imagery *n.* use of symbols or comparisons, as in poetry, to evoke mental images

imago (i-máygō) *n., pl.* **-goes** or **gines** insect that has reached its adult state; in psychology, idealised image of the self or another person, such as a parent, that a child may carry into adult life

imam (i-máam) *n.* Muslim scholar or authority, or leader of prayers; Muhammad, or any of his various successors (also "Imam")

imbecile (ímbә-seel) *n.* fool, idiot — **-cility** *n.* — **imbecile**, **-cilic** *adj.*

imbibe *formal. v.* to drink (especially alcohol)

imbricate *formal. adj.* overlapping in a regular pattern, as fish scales or roof tiles might — **imbricate** *v.*

imbroglio (im-brṓl-yō) *n., pl.* **-os** confused or troubled situation, predicament

imbue *tr.v.* to fill as if by soaking, inspire or permeate: *imbued the pupils with enthusiasm*

immaculate *adj.* free from any flaw, fault, or error; without blemish; perfectly clean — **-lacy** *n.*

immanent *formal. adj.* present throughout the universe (said of God or other divine powers). Compare TRANSCENDENT; existing strictly within something, inherent — **-nence** *n.*

immaterial *adj.* unimportant, irrelevant; lacking material form

immemorial *adj.* going back to the distant past: *from time immemorial*

immerse *tr.v.* to submerge in a liquid; to baptise by submerging; to interest (oneself) deeply in a book, activity, cause, or the like — **-mersed** *adj.* — **-mersion** *n.*

imminent *adj.* just about to happen — **-nence** *n.*

immiscible *formal. adj.* unable to blend or mix, as oil and water are — **-ibility** *n.*

immolate *formal. tr.v.* to kill or offer as a sacrifice — **-lation** *n.*

immortelle (ímmawr-tél) *n.* plant with flowers that keep their colour when dried (also "everlasting")

immunosuppressive *adj.* referring to a drug that suppresses the body's immune response, as used to prevent rejection of a transplanted organ — **-pressant** *adj., n.*

immure *formal. tr.v.* to imprison; to shut up within walls; to shut (oneself) away

immutable *formal. adj.* unchangeable — **-ability** *n.*

impacted *adj.* referring to a tooth that is wedged in the gum socket and unable to emerge from the gum normally; referring to a fracture in which the broken ends of the bones are wedged together
impale *tr.v.* to pierce or pin down, as with a sharp stake; to torture, immobilise, or kill in this way: *impaled on a spear*
impalpable *adj.* impossible to feel or sense by touch, intangible; not easily understood
impart *formal. tr.v.* to give or share; to tell or reveal: *imparted the secret to me*
impartial *adj.* fair, even-handed, unbiased — **-iality** *n.*
impasse (am-paáss) *n.* difficult situation in which no progress can be made; road with no exit
impassive *adj.* showing or feeling no emotion — **-ivity** *n.*
impeach *tr.v.* to accuse of a crime, especially treason; to charge (someone in high office) with misconduct; *formal.* to challenge or attack the integrity of, impugn: *impeached the official's motives* — **-ment** *n.*
impeccable *adj.* flawless, faultless; reliable
impecunious *formal. adj.* without money, penniless — **-iosity** *n.*
impediment *n.* something that hinders or obstructs; speech defect — **impede** *tr.v.*
impending *adj.* about to happen, imminent
imperative *adj.* expressing an order, especially an urgent one; urgent or essential
impersonate *tr.v.* to copy, imitate or pass oneself off as (a person), as for comic or criminal purposes — **-ation**, **-ator** *n.*
imperious *adj.* overbearing, bullying, domineering
impermeable *adj.* not allowing liquids to pass through easily
impervious *adj.* not affected or influenced by something: *impervious to sarcasm*; not penetrable, as by water, impermeable
impetuous *adj.* impulsive and hasty, rash; rushing energetically — **-uosity** *n.*
impetus (ímpitəss) *n.*, *pl.* **-uses** force or factor that incites or encourages, stimulus; forward-driving power, impulsion, as of a blow
impinge *intr.v.* to have an effect, make an impression or impact; to make inroads, encroach: *impinging on our rights*
implacable *adj.* impossible to placate, stubborn, inflexible: *implacable hostility* — **-ability** *n.*
implement *n.* (ímpli-mənt) tool or utensil, or means ~ *tr.v.* (-ment) to fulfil, carry out
implicate *tr.v.* to involve or suggest the involvement of (a person or thing), especially in something unpleasant: *implicated in the crime* — **-ation** *n.*
implicit *adj.* implied or understood but not directly stated; necessarily contained in something, inherent; showing no doubts: *implicit faith*
implode *v.* to collapse inwards, crumple — **-plosion** *n.*
imponderable *n.* aspect of something that cannot be predicted, evaluated, or analysed — **imponderable** *adj.*
importune *formal. tr.v.* to make constant, irritating, bothersome requests to; to accost or solicit, as a prostitute might — **-tunity** *n.* — **-tunate** *adj.*
impost *n.* tax or duty; weight carried as a handicap by a racehorse
impostor (im-póstər) *n.* deceiver or fraudster, especially a person claiming to be someone else — **imposture** *n.*
impound *tr.v.* to confiscate, as a customs officer might; to shut up in a pound
imprecation *formal. n.* curse — **-cate** *tr.v.* — **-catory** *adj.*
impregnable *adj.* impossible to capture: *an impregnable castle*; impossible to shake or destroy: *impregnable arguments* — **-bility** *n.*
impregnate *tr.v.* to saturate, fill, or permeate; to make pregnant; to fertilise (an egg) — **-nation** *n.*
impresario *n.*, *pl.* **-os** person who organises shows or concerts
imprimatur (ímpri-maátər) *n. formal.* authorisation, permission, go-ahead; approval from church authorities to publish something [Latin, let it be printed]
imprinting *n.* learning process of young animals, in which they recognise and imitate their parents
impromptu *adj.* unplanned or unprepared: *an impromptu speech* — **impromptu** *adv.*, *n.*
improvident *formal. adj.* not making provision for the future; imprudent or rash
improvise *v.* to recite, compose, or the like without planning or preparation ~ *tr.v.* to make in a rough-and-ready way, using any materials available — **-sation** *n.*
impugn (im-péwn) *tr.v.* to attack or criticise as false
impunity *n.* exemption from punishment or unpleasant consequences
impute *tr.v.* to attribute (a crime) to somebody; to attribute to a specified cause — **-putation** *n.*
in absentia *adv.* while absent, even though absent [Latin, in absence]
inadvertently *adv.* accidentally, unintentionally; negligently, without due care — **-tent** *adj.* — **-tence** *n.*
inalienable *adj.* not transferable, impossible to withdraw: *inalienable rights* — **-ability** *n.*
inamorata (in-ámmə-raátə) *n.* woman with whom a person is in love (male equivalent "inamorato")
inane *formal. adj.* silly, senseless, insubstantial — **inanity** *n.*
inanition *formal. n.* exhaustion or weakness through hunger; mental or spiritual hollowness
inaugurate *tr.v.* to begin or open officially; to instal formally in office — **-ration** *n.* — **-ral** *adj.*
in camera *adv.* held in secret; in a closed rather than public court; in private in a judge's chambers [Latin, literally, in the chamber]
incandescent *adj.* glowing through being heated: *incandescent/light bulbs* — **-desce** *v.* — **-cence** *n.*
incantation *n.* ritual chanting or casting of spells; formulas or spells so used [related to *enchant*] — **-tatory** *adj.*
incarcerate (in-kár-sə-rayt) *formal. tr.v.* to shut in, especially in jail — **-ation** *n.*
incarnadine (in-kárnə-dīn) *formal or archaic. tr.v.* to stain or turn blood-red or flesh-pink — **incarnadine** *adj.*, *n.*
incarnate *adj.* in bodily form: *the devil incarnate*; personified, being the essence of — **-nate** *tr.v.* — **-nation** *n.*
incendiary (in-séndi-əri) *formal. adj.* causing or producing fire; relating to arson; provoking anger or violence ~ *n.* arsonist; fire bomb; person who stirs up ill feeling or violence, firebrand, rabble-rouser
incense (in-sénss) *formal. tr.v.* to infuriate or outrage — **incensed** *adj.*
incentive (in-séntiv) *n.* influencing or encouraging factor, such as fear or hope of reward — **incentive** *adj.*

inception *formal. n.* beginning, start, outset — **-ceptive** *adj.*
inchoate (in-kṓ-ayt) *adj.* still in the early stages, just beginning; immature, imperfectly developed
incidence *n.* occurrence, or the rate of frequency of occurrence: *the incidence of absenteeism among farmworkers*
incinerate *v.* to burn to ashes — **-tor** *n.*
incipient (in-síppi-ənt) *adj.* still in the early stages, just beginning, about to happen — **-ence**, **-ency** *n.*
incision *n.* delicate cut, as in surgery; notch, as on the edge of a leaf — **incise** *tr.v.*
incisive (in-sī́ss-iv) *adj.* clear and effective in a cutting, sharp, biting way: *incisive criticism*
incisor *n.* sharp tooth at the front of the mouth
inclement (in-klémmənt) *formal. adj.* stormy, wild: *inclement weather* — **-ency** *n.*
incognito (ín-kog-neétō) *adv.* in disguise or in an unofficial capacity, in order to avoid publicity or recognition ~ *n., pl.* **-tos** disguise or false name used when travelling (feminine form "incognita")
incommode *formal. tr.v.* to inconvenience, disturb — **-modious** *adj.*
incommunicado *adv., adj.* out of communication with others, typically against one's will: *to hold/keep a prisoner incommunicado* [Spanish, related to *communicate*]
incongruous *adj.* incompatible; not harmonious; inappropriate; glaringly odd — **-gruity** *n.*
inconsequential *adj.* petty, unimportant
incontinent *adj.* lacking self-restraint; lacking voluntary control of urination or defecation — **-nence** *n.*
incorrigible *formal. adj.* not able or willing to be reformed, hopelessly bad: *an incorrigible liar* [related to *incorrect*] — **-ibility** *n.*
incredulous *formal. adj.* disbelieving — **-ulity** *n.*
increment (íng-kri-mənt) *n.* process or amount of increase, especially regular and gradual increase: *annual increments in salary* [related to *increase*] — **increment** *v.* — **-al** *adj.*
incriminate *tr.v.* to suggest or show the guilt of: *incriminating evidence* — **-nation** *n.* — **-natory** *adj.*
incubate *tr.v.* to warm (eggs) for hatching; to help or cause to develop: *incubating a cold* — **-bation**, **-bator** *n.*
incubus (íng-kew-bəss) *n., pl.* **-bi** demon that lies heavily on sleeping people, specifically one that has sexual intercourse with sleeping women. Compare SUCCUBUS; disturbing recurrent dream or thought; oppressive and inescapable person or thing, worrying burden
inculcate (íng-kul-kayt) *tr.v.* to teach insistently and persistently: *inculcated certain values into them* — **-ation** *n.*
inculpate *formal. tr.v.* to incriminate — **-ation** *n.*
incumbent *formal. adj.* having the character of an obligation: *It is incumbent upon you to comply with the regulations*; referring to a current office-holder: *the incumbent vicar* — **incumbent**, **-bency** *n.*
incunabulum (íng-kew-nábbew-ləm) *n., pl.* **-la** early printed book, specifically one printed before 1501
incur *tr.v.* to become liable, exposed, or subject to (something serious or unpleasant): *to incur debts/hostility/responsibilities*
incursion *n.* raid or attack, as by an enemy; *formal.* entry, especially into an unfamiliar area: *their first incursions into politics*
indefatigable (índi-fátti-gəb'l) *formal. adj.* untiring, tireless: *indefatigable efforts*
indefinite article *n.* the word *a* or *an* or equivalent form in other languages, indicating but not specifically identifying its noun or phrase. Compare DEFINITE ARTICLE
indelible *adj.* impossible to remove by washing or erasing; leaving permanent marks: *indelible pencil/ink*; enduring; unforgettable: *made an indelible impression on me* [related to *delete*]
indemnity *n.* insurance against or compensation for injury, damage, or loss; pre-arranged exemption from a penalty — **indemnify** *tr.v.*
indent *v.* to begin (a line of print) away from the margin; to indent the first line of (a paragraph)
indentation *n.* dent, notch, or groove, or a series of them; blank space left by indenting
indentured *adj.* contractually obliged in former times to work for someone for a specific period, typically in return for passage and maintenance: *an indentured servant/labourer*
indeterminate *adj.* not determined or definite; not determinable or definable — **-nacy** *n.*
Indian summer *n.* period of summery weather when summer is over; late-blooming period of contentment or tranquil success
indict (in-dī́t) *tr.v.* to charge officially with an offence or crime — **-able** *adj.* — **-ment** *n.*
indigenous (in-díjinəss) *adj.* native to an area, not introduced from elsewhere: *The turkey is indigenous to the New World; the indigenous population of an area*
indigent (índijənt) *formal. adj.* poor, needy — **-gence** *n.*
indigo (ín-digō) *n.* blue dye; plant producing this dye; bluish-black colour [from Greek *indikon pharmakon*, Indian dye] — **indigo** *adj.*
indiscriminate (indi-skrímmi-nət) *adj.* random, without distinction or exemption: *indiscriminate slaughter*
indispensable *adj.* impossible to do without, absolutely necessary, essential
indisposed *formal. adj.* slightly unwell — **-position** *n.*
indissoluble *formal. adj.* unbreakable, impossible to dissolve: *an indissoluble union/agreement*
indite *archaic. tr.v.* to write, or set down in writing
indoctrinate *tr.v.* to instruct, typically in an ideology or biased ideas, in a way that leads to uncritical acceptance — **-nation** *n.*
indolence (índə-lənss) *formal. n.* laziness, idleness — **-lent** *adj.*
indomitable (in-dómmitəb'l) *adj.* unconquerable, unsubduable, impossible to dominate
indubitably *formal. adv.* undoubtedly, without question
induce *formal. tr.v.* to infer, conclude by generalisation rather than by strict logical deduction; to influence or persuade; to hasten artificially, as by the use of drugs: *induce sleep/childbirth/an abortion* — **-ment**, **induction** *n.*
induct *tr.v.* to initiate or instal, especially through a formal or official procedure: *inducted us into the army* — **-tion** *n.*
indulgence *n.* remission in this world or in purgatory of the punishment for a sin, after the sin has been pardoned: *The selling of indulgences by church authorities was a cause of the Reformation*
indulgent *adj.* very tolerant or lenient, prone to yielding to other people's whims or desires

indurate *formal. v.* (ín-dewr-ayt) to harden ~ *adj.* (-ət) hardened, unfeeling, uncaring

inebriated *formal. adj.* drunk, intoxicated; exhilarated or befuddled, as if by alcohol — **inebriate** *n., adj., tr.v.* — **-ation** *n.*

inedible (in-éddib'l) *adj.* uneatable — **-ability** *n.*

ineffable *formal. adj.* indescribable, unutterable; sacred and not to be mentioned or described — **-ability** *n.*

ineluctable *formal. adj.* unavoidable, inevitable, inescapable: *an ineluctable necessity* — **-ability** *n.*

inept *adj.* clumsy or awkward in speech or behaviour; not suitable or appropriate — **-itude** *n.*

inequity (in-ékwəti) *formal. n.* unfairness, as due to a biased or inconsistent law — **-table** *adj.*

inertia (in-érshə) *n.* motionlessness, sluggishness; tendency of a physical body to remain at rest or in unchanged motion unless acted on by external forces — **inert** *adj.*

inevitable *adj.* unavoidable, unpreventable; predictable because invariable or certain to take place: *their inevitable reaction when criticised* — **-ability** *n.*

inexorable (in-éksərəb'l) *adj.* relentless despite all pleas or counter-measures, unyielding, remorseless: *the inexorable advance of time* — **-ability** *n.*

inexplicable *adj.* impossible to explain or to account for

in extremis (in ik-stréé-miss) *formal. adv.* in extreme difficulties or circumstances: *heroic measures to be adopted only in extremis*; at the point of death [Latin, in the last]

inextricably (in-ékstrik-ə-bli, -ik-strík-) *adv.* inseparably, in many complex ways: *inextricably linked* — **-ability** *n.*

infallible (in-fál-əb'l) *adj.* unfailingly correct or effective, unable to fail or err

infallibility *n.* infallibleness, specifically that of the *Pope* when pronouncing on questions of faith or morals

infamy (ínfəmi) *n.* great notoriety, extremely bad reputation; disgrace; evil or disgraceful act — **-mous** *adj.*

infanta (in-fán-tə) *n.* Spanish or Portuguese princess other than the heir apparent (male equivalent "infante") [Spanish, literally, infant]

infarction *n.* tissue death, or dead tissue, resulting from an obstruction to the circulation, such as a blood clot

infatuation *n.* love or passion for another person, typically foolish and short-lived — **-ated** *adj.*

infelicitous (ínfi-líssitəss) *formal. adj.* inappropriate, unfortunate, or unsuitable: *an infelicitous style/remark* — **-city** *n.*

inference (ínfə-rənss) *n.* process of reasoning from specific evidence to general conclusions; conclusion reached through inference — **infer** *v.*

inferno (in-férnō) *n., pl.* **-nos** hell; blazing fire suggestive of hellish flames — **-nal** *adj.*

infibulation *n.* fastening of the female genitals with clasps or stitches to prevent sexual intercourse — **infibulate** *tr.v.*

infidel (ínfi-d'l, -del) *formal. n.* unbeliever, especially one who does not accept a particular religion — **infidel** *adj.*

infidelity *n.* unfaithfulness, especially sexual unfaithfulness in the form of adultery

infiltrate (ín-fil-trayt) *tr.v.* to pass through a filter or filter-like obstruction; to enter secretly in order to undermine or subvert — **-tration** *n.*

infinitesimal (ínfini-téssi-m'l) *adj.* minutely or incalculably small

infinitive *n.* basic verb form that typically does not show person, number, or tense and in English often follows *to* — **infinitive** *adj.*

infirmary *n.* hospital or similar place for treatment of the ill; dispensary [related to *infirm*]

infirmity *formal. n.* weakness and failing powers due to illness or old age — **infirm** *adj.*

in flagrante delicto (in flə-gránti di-líktō) *formal. adv.* in the very act of committing an offence, red-handed; in the very act of having sexual intercourse, especially when illicit (also *informal* "in flagrante") [Latin, literally, in blazing crime, with the crime still blazing]

inflammable *adj.* burning readily or catching fire easily (also "flammable"); passionate and easily excited or angered

inflammatory *adj.* arousing strong feelings quickly, especially feelings of anger, typically in a crude or unjustified way; rabble-rousing, inciting: *an inflammatory speech*

inflection *n.* change of form in a word to indicate gender, tense, or other grammatical distinctions; form or element involved in such change; change in the pitch or tone of the voice, or the pattern of such changes — **inflect** *v.*

inflorescence *n.* flower cluster or flower-bearing stalk, or the arrangement of flowers on it

influx (ín-fluks) *n.* inward flow of people or things: *the annual influx of summer tourists*

infra *formal. adv.* below or later in the text (used in footnotes). Compare SUPRA

infraction *n.* breaking of a law or rule — **infract** *tr.v.*

infra dig *informal. adj.* beneath one's dignity, undignified, unsuitable, or unbecoming [contraction of Latin *infra dignitatem*, beneath one's dignity]

infrastructure *n.* network of basic services such as transport, public utilities, education, and health care, forming the hidden foundations of a society

infringement *n.* breaking of a law, agreement, or the like; trespassing on a right, privilege, or the like — **infringe** *v.*

infuse *v.* — *tr.* to add or fill as if by pouring, instil, imbue: *infused enthusiasm into the pupils*; to steep (tea or herbs) in preparing a drink or extract; to administer (a medicine) by slow injection — *intr.* to steep or draw: *Let the tea infuse for four minutes* — **infusion** *n.*

ingenious (in-jééni-əss) *adj.* clever in an imaginative or cunning way: *an ingenious inventor/invention* — **ingenuity** *n.*

ingénue (áN-zhay-new) *n.* naive or innocent young woman; actress playing an ingénue [French, literally, innocent, naive]

ingenuous (in-jénnew-əss) *adj.* unsophisticated, naive, guileless; open and honest, frank

ingest (in-jést) *formal. tr.v.* to take in or absorb by or as if by swallowing — **-tion** *n.*

inglenook *n.* chimney-corner by a fireplace, often with seats facing each other

ingot *n.* bar or block of gold or other metal prepared for storage or transport

ingrate (ín-grayt) *formal. n.* ungrateful person [related to *ungrateful*]

ingratiate (in-gráyshi-ayt) *tr.v.* — **ingratiate oneself** to curry favour with somebody, as by flattery or charm [related to *grace*] — **-tion** *n.* — **-ing** *adj.*
ingress (ín-gress) *formal. n.* act of entering; entry or entrance; permission or right to enter (opposite "egress")
inguinal (ín-gwin'l) *formal. adj.* relating to or located in the groin
inherent *adj.* being part of the very nature of something, intrinsic, essential: *rights inherent in citizenship* — **inhere** *intr.v.*
inimical (i-nímmik'l) *formal. adj.* unfriendly, hostile; unfavourable, adverse, harmful: *policies inimical to peace* [related to *enemy*]
inimitable (i-nímmitəb'l) *adj.* impossible to imitate successfully, unique, matchless
iniquitous (i-níkwitəss) *formal. adj.* wickedly wrong or unjust [related to *unequal*] — **iniquity** *n.*
initialism *n.* abbreviation, such as *B.B.C.*, that uses the initial letters of a phrase and is pronounced as a series of letters. Compare ACRONYM
initiate *tr.v.* to introduce or admit to membership, participation in an activity, or new knowledge — **initiate** *n.* — **-ation** *n.*
initiative *n.* ability to take the first step of a plan or project, energetic resourcefulness or enterprise; right of citizens to petition for a new law and get it voted on
injunction *n.* court order compelling or prohibiting a particular action — **-tive** *adj.*
inkhorn *adj.* learned in a showy way, pretentiously literary: *inkhorn terms* [formerly, an ink bottle of horn, as used by supposedly pedantic scholars]
in loco parentis (in lṓkō pə-réntiss) *formal. adv.* in place of or with the responsibilities of parents: *The headmaster was acting in loco parentis* [Latin]
in medias res (ráyss, ráyz) *formal. adv.* straight into the plot, without preamble [Latin, literally, into the middle of things, from the description by the Roman poet Horace of the good poet's approach]
in memoriam *formal. prep.* in memory of (used in epitaphs) [Latin]
innate *adj.* inborn, present from birth: *innate ideas/characteristics*
innocuous (i-nóckew-əss) *adj.* not harmful; not causing offence, bland, unobjectionable
innominate *formal. adj.* nameless, unnamed
innominate bone *formal. n.* hip bone
innovation *n.* change that results in something new; something new — **-vate** *v.* — **-vative** *adj.*
innuendo (ínnew-éndō) *n., pl.* **-dos** or **-does** hint or suggestion of a sly or offensive kind, insinuation
innumerate *adj.* lacking an understanding of arithmetic or mathematics — **-acy** *n.*
inoculate (i-nóckew-layt) *tr.v.* to introduce micro-organisms into, as by injection; to immunise against a disease by inoculating or vaccinating — **-tion** *n.*
inopportune *adj.* inconvenient, inappropriate, or badly timed
inordinate *formal. adj.* excessive, unrestrained, beyond reasonable limits, unnecessary: *inordinate haste*
in propria persona *formal. adv.* personally, not through an intermediary; in person, "live" [Latin, in one's own person]
inquisition *n.* investigation or tribunal, as for trying heretics or dissidents; intensive and often brutal questioning — **-itor** *n.* — **-torial** *adj.*
inquisitorial *adj.* relating to an inquisitor or an inquisition; referring or relating to a legal process in which the judge is an active investigator rather than just an umpire
insatiable *adj.* unsatisfiable: *insatiable demands*; *an insatiable lover* — **-ability** *n.*
inscribe *formal. tr.v.* to write or engrave; to fix firmly, as in one's memory — **inscription** *n.*
inscrutable *adj.* mysterious because uninterpretable, unfathomable, enigmatic: *an inscrutable face/woman* — **-ability** *n.*
inseminate *tr.v.* to impregnate with semen; to inspire, fill with ideas — **-tion** *n.*
insensate *formal. adj.* foolish and irresponsible, senseless; inanimate or without understanding or feelings: *an insensate block of wood*
insidious *adj.* harmful or spreading in a stealthy or slowly accumulating way: *an insidious disease*; intended as a trap, sneaky: *insidious arguments*
insignia (in-síg-ni-ə) *n., pl.* **-nia** or **-nias** signs or emblems: *the insignia of office/rank* [related to *sign*]
insinuate *tr.v.* to hint or imply slyly; to introduce or gain acceptance for gradually or cunningly: *insinuated herself into the coterie* — **-tion** *n.* — **-ting** *adj.*
insipid (in-síppid) *adj.* bland, flavourless, or dull: *insipid food/comedians* — **-ity** *n.*
insoluble *adj.* unsolvable; undissolvable — **-bility** *n.*
insolvent *adj.* unable to meet outstanding financial obligations, bankrupt — **insolvent**, **-vency** *n.*
insomnia *formal. n.* sleeplessness — **-iac** *adj.*, *n.*
insouciant (in-soo͞-si-ənt, ᴀɴ-soo͞ss-yóɴ) *adj.* carefree and light-hearted (literary) — **-ance** *n.*
inspissate *formal. v.* to thicken or condense, as by boiling or evaporation — **-tion** *n.*
installment plan *U.S. n.* hire-purchase arrangement
instigate (ín-sti-gayt) *tr.v.* to provoke or provide an impetus for or to: *instigate a rebellion; instigated them to rebel* — **-tion**, **-tor** *n.*
insubordinate *adj.* disobedient, rebellious — **insubordinate** *n.* — **-nation** *n.*
insufferable *formal. adj.* unbearable, intolerable, unendurable
insular *adj. formal.* relating to an island; narrow-minded, parochial
insulate *tr.v.* to shield from the passage of electricity, heat, sound, or the like; to detach or keep separated from the surrounding environment; to shield or protect from what is considered unsuitable — **-tion** *n.*
insulin (ín-sew-lin) *n.* hormone secreted by the pancreas and regulating the blood-sugar level; preparation of animal insulin used in treating diabetes [Latin *insula*, an island, referring to the islets of Langerhans, the cells in the pancreas that secrete the hormone]
insuperable *adj.* impossible to overcome: *insuperable difficulties/barriers* — **-ability** *n.*
insupportable *adj.* impossible to tolerate, unbearable; incapable or unworthy of being supported: *an insupportable claim*
insurgence (in-súr-jənss) *formal. n.* uprising, revolt, rebellion (also "insurgency") — **-gent** *n.*, *adj.*
insurmountable *adj.* impossible to overcome
insurrection (ín-sə-réksh'n) *n.* revolt against an established government or civil authority
intaglio (in-táali-ō) *n., pl.* **-glios** or **-glii** design cut into the surface of a hard material such as a semi-precious stone. Compare CAMEO; art or process of

making intaglios; seal, gem, or the like carved with an intaglio; printing process in which the image to be printed is etched into the plate

intangible (in-tánji-b'l) *adj.* imperceptible by touch; too delicate, vague, or elusive to be characterised precisely: *an intangible air of mystery* ~ *n.* business asset, such as goodwill, that has a value but no physical existence (often plural; also "intangible asset")

intarsia *n.* mosaic of inlaid wood; art or craft of making intarsias; knitting pattern or technique involving large patches of colour

integer (íntijər) *n.* whole number or zero

integral (íntigrəl) *adj.* forming an essential part of the whole; whole, entire

integrate *v.* — *tr.* to blend into a whole; to make part of a whole or group; to open (society, a school, or the like) to all races, desegregate — *intr.* to become integrated; to mix socially, participate in the social life of a group or community — **-tion** *n.*

integrated circuit *n.* electronic circuit formed on a microchip (abbreviation "IC")

integrity (in-téggrəti) *n.* strict abiding by a code of moral or artistic values, uncompromising honesty

integument (in-téggew-mənt) *formal. n.* outer covering, such as a seed's coat or an animal's skin

intelligentsia (in-télli-jéntsi-ə) *pl.n.* educated, cultured, or intellectual people regarded as a social class

intelligible (in-téllij-ib'l) *adj.* understandable, comprehensible

intemperate *adj.* lacking in restraint, not moderate: *an intemperate drinker*; impulsive, rash, over-hasty: *an intemperate decision* — **-ance** *n.*

inter (in-tér) *formal. tr.v.* to bury, place in a grave — **-ment** *n.*

inter alia (íntər áyli-ə) *formal. adv.* among other things [Latin]

intercalary (ín-térkə-ləri, íntər-kál-əri) *formal. adj.* referring or relating to a day or month inserted into the calendar to regularise it, as in leap years — **-calate** *tr.v.*

intercede *intr.v.* to intervene, as in a dispute or so as to beg or plead on behalf of another — **-cession** *n.*

intercept *tr.v.* to cut off, interrupt, stop, or keep back (something directed elsewhere: *intercept a message/a pass in football* — **intercept**, **-tion** *n.*

interdict (ínterdikt) *formal. n.* official prohibition, as by a legal or church authority, typically for a limited time or a specific purpose: *under an interdict* — **interdict** *tr.v.* — **-tion** *n.*

interface *n.* boundary between liquids, systems, phases, or the like; meeting-point or boundary at which two different theories, groups, or systems communicate or interact; interaction or communication at such a boundary — **interface** *v.*

interim *n.* interval between two events, eras, or the like: *in the interim* ~ *adj.* temporary, conditional, or partial: *interim measures/payments*

interject *tr.v.* to throw in (a remark) as an interruption

interjection *n.* exclamation, such as *Oh!*, *Gosh!*, or *For goodness' sake!*, that expresses emotion or a strong reaction

interlard *tr.v.* to insert (something foreign or irrelevant, such as anecdotes) throughout (something standard, such as a speech or academic text) [Old French *entrelarder*, to make alternating layers of meat and fat; related to *lard*]

interlocutor (íntər-lóckewtər) *formal. n.* person taking part in a conversation or dialogue — **-cution** *n.* — **-cutory** *adj.*

interloper *n.* interfering person, meddler or intruder — **-lope** *intr.v.*

intermediary *n.* go-between, agent or means mediating between persons or things — **intermediary** *adj.*

intermezzo (íntər-mét-sō) *n.*, *pl.* **-zos** or **-zi** musical composition performed between sections of a longer work; musical composition in this style

interminable (in-términəb'l) *adj.* tedious and seemingly never-ending: *interminable complaints*

intermittent *adj.* stopping and starting at intervals, periodic; irregular, discontinuous — **-ly** *adv.*

intern *n.* (ín-tern) person who is completing or has recently completed professional studies and is having supervised professional experience; *U.S.* trainee hospital doctor, houseman ~ *tr.v.* (in-térn) to detain or imprison, especially in wartime — **-ment**, **-ee** *n.*

internecine (íntər-neésīn) *formal. adj.* relating to infighting or destructive conflict within a group: *internecine disputes*

interpolate (in-tér-pə-layt) *tr.v.* to insert, or change by insertions; to insert (words) into (a text) — **interpolate** *intr.v* — **-tion** *n.*

interregnum *n.*, *pl.* **-nums** or **-na** period of time between two successive reigns, governments, or the like; pause, interval, or discontinuity — **-nal** *adj.*

intersect *v.* — *tr.* to cut or divide (a line or space), cross — *intr.* to cross; to overlap — **-tion** *n.*

interstice (in-tér-stiss) *formal. n.* small space, opening, or gap, as between the strands of a net (usually plural) — **-stitial** *adj.*

intestate (in-téss-tayt) *adj.* without leaving a will: *died intestate* ~ *n.* person who dies intestate — **-stacy** *n.*

intimate (ínti-mayt) *formal. tr.v.* to announce or make known, often by subtle hints — **intimate** *adj.* — **-mation** *n.*

intimidate *tr.v.* to threaten so as to silence or deter [related to *timid*] — **-ation** *n.*

intonation *n.* rise and fall of the pitch of the voice; plainsong opening, sung as a solo; chanting, reciting in a sing-song voice — **intone** *v.*

in toto (in tṓtō) *formal. adv.* totally, altogether, entirely [Latin]

intoxicated *formal. adj.* drunk; extremely excited, stimulated, or enchanted — **-cate** *tr.v.* — **-cation** *n.*

intractable *adj.* difficult to persuade or control, stubborn; difficult to solve or handle: *an intractable problem* — **-bility** *n.*

intransigent *adj.* uncompromising or unyielding, as in one's political stance — **intransigent**, **-gence**, **-gency** *n.*

intransitive verb *n.* verb, such as *rise*, that does not need or take a direct object (abbreviated in this dictionary to *intr.v.*). Compare TRANSITIVE VERB

intravenous (íntrə-veénəss) *adj.* in or into a vein: *an intravenous drip/injection* ~ *n.* intravenous drip, injection, or transfusion (abbreviation "IV")

intrepid *adj.* bold, fearless — **-ity** *n.*

intricate (íntri-kət) *adj.* having many parts in a complex arrangement; difficult to understand, complicated — **-cacy** *n.*

intrinsic *adj.* being an essential part of something or following from the essential nature of something, inherent: *qualities intrinsic to/in a statesman*; originating within the body, or situated in a particular part

of the body
introspection *n.* examination of one's own thoughts and feelings — **introspect** *intr.v.* — **-tive** *adj.*
introvert *n.* inward-looking, reserved, or unsociable person. Compare EXTROVERT — **introvert**, **-ed** *adj.* — **-version** *n.*
inundate (ínnun-dayt) *tr.v.* to overwhelm or submerge by or as if by flooding — **-tion** *n.*
inured (i-néwrd) *adj.* accustomed or used to something unpleasant: *inured to hardship* — **inure** *v.*
invalid *tr.v.* to release from active service for reasons of injury or illness: *He was invalided out of the marines in January*
invective *n.* bitter or abusive criticism or accusation
inveigh *formal. intr.v.* to attack with violent or abusive language, rail: *inveigh against hypocrisy*
inveigle (in-váyg'l, -veég'l) *tr.v.* to persuade by flattering, cajoling, or deceiving: *inveigled me into helping*
inventory (ín-vən-tri) *n.* list of items; stock or total quantity of goods on hand — **inventory** *tr.v.*
invertebrate *adj.* lacking a spine or backbone, not vertebrate — **invertebrate** *n.*
investiture *n.* ceremonial conferring of an office, award, or honour on a person — **invest** *tr.v.*
inveterate (in-véttə-rət) *formal. adj.* of long standing and unlikely to change, habitual: *an inveterate liar* — **-acy** *n.*
invidious (in-víddi-əss) *formal. adj.* offensive or unfair, and likely to cause ill-will or resentment: *invidious comparisons* — **-ness** *n.*
invigilate (in-víji-layt) *v.* to supervise (an exam, or the students taking it) — **-lation**, **-lator** *n.*
invincible (in-vín-si-b'l) *adj.* incapable of being defeated or overcome, unconquerable — **-ibility** *n.*
inviolable *adj.* impossible or forbidden to attack, infringe, or undermine: *an inviolable right/principle* — **-ability** *n.*
in vitro *adv.*, *adj.* in an artificial environment, outside the body: *in vitro fertilisation* [Latin, in glass]
invoke *tr.v.* to call upon or appeal to for help; to appeal to as support or authority: *invoked the previous good behaviour of the accused*; to conjure or summon up (a spirit) by means of spells or incantations — **-vocation** *n.*
invulnerable *adj.* easily withstanding attack, criticism, or the like — **-ability** *n.*
ion (ī-ən) *n.* atom or group of atoms having an electric charge through gaining or losing one or more electrons — **-ic** *adj.* — **-ise** *v.*
Ionic (ī-ónnik) *adj.* referring or relating to a style or order of classical Greek architecture characterised by fluted columns and scroll-like ornamentation. Compare DORIC, CORINTHIAN; referring or relating to a dialect of ancient Greek — **Ionic** *n.*
ipse dixit (íp-si díksit, -say) *formal. n.* dogmatic pronouncement based only on one's own authority [Latin, literally, he himself said, from a Greek phrase referring to the authoritative sayings of Pythagoras]
ipso facto *formal. adv.* by the fact itself, by its very nature, by definition: *Is a genetic illness ipso facto incurable?* [Latin]
irascible (i-rássi-b'l) *adj.* quick-tempered, easily angered — **-ibility** *n.*
irate *formal. adj.* angry, enraged
iridescent (írri-déss'nt) *adj.* shimmering with a rainbow-like effect, as a soap bubble or opal does [Latin and Greek *iris*, a rainbow] — **-ence** *n.*
irreconcilable *adj.* conflicting, incompatible: *irreconcilable claims*; hostile, uncompromisingly opposed: *an irreconcilable foe/husband* — **-bility** *n.*
irredeemable *adj.* hopeless, beyond remedy
irredentism *formal. n.* policy of regaining territory that is historically or culturally connected to one's nation but now under foreign control [Italian, *Italia irredenta*, unredeemed Italy, referring to Italian-speaking territory under foreign control] — **-tist** *n.*, *adj.*
irrefutable *adj.* impossible to disprove or refute: *irrefutable arguments* — **-bility** *n.*
irreparable (i-réppərəb'l) *adj.* impossible to make reparations for, repair, or put right: *an irreparable loss to the nation*
irrespective *adv.* regardless, nevertheless: *and went ahead irrespective* — **irrespective of** regardless of, without heeding
irreverent *adj.* disrespectful; flippant or facetious, inappropriately lacking in seriousness — **-rence** *n.*
irrevocable (i-révvəkəb'l) *adj.* impossible to change or take back: *an irrevocable decision* — **-ability** *n.*
irrigate *tr.v.* to supply water to (a region, farmland, or the like); *formal.* to wash out (a wound, the eye, or the like) with water or a medicinal solution — **-tion** *n.*
irrupt *intr.v.* to rush or burst in suddenly, and typically forcefully or violently; *formal.* to increase dramatically, as an animal population might in favourable conditions — **-ion** *n.* — **-ive** *n.*
ISBN number *n.* number assigned to a newly published book in keeping with an international book classification system [*I*nternational *S*tandard *B*ook *N*umber]
isinglass (īzing-glaass) *n.* gelatine made from the air bladders of certain freshwater fish; a mica, musocvite
isobar *n.* line on a weather chart linking places of equal barometric pressure
isogloss *n.* linguistic boundary line, in the form of a line on a map linking those places where a particular linguistic feature occurs, such as a dialect word or pronunciation
isometric exercise *n.* physical exercise, such as pressing one's hands forcefully against each other, that produces muscle tension with minimal movement at the joints (also "isometrics")
isomorphic *adj.* similar or equivalent in form or structure — **-ism** *n.* — **isomorph** *n.*
isosceles triangle (ī-sóssi-leez) *n.* triangle with two sides equal
isotope *n.* atom whose nucleus has the same number of protons as another of the same element, but a different number of neutrons
isthmus *n.*, *pl.* **-mi** or **-muses** narrow strip of land joining two larger land masses — **-mian** *adj.*
iterate *formal. v.* to repeat, reiterate
itinerant *adj.* travelling from place to place, especially as a normal part of one's work ~*n.* traveller
itinerary *n.* planned route for a journey

J

jabberwocky *n.* nonsense verse; incomprehensible speech or writing, gibberish, nonsense [after the title of a poem by Lewis Carroll in *Through the Looking Glass*]

jabot (zhábbō) *n.* pleated frill down the front of a woman's blouse or dress, or, formerly, a man's shirt

jack *n.* small flag especially on the bow of a ship to show its nationality; small white ball used as the target in bowls

jackanapes *n.* insolent or conceited young man; mischievous or cheeky child (old-fashioned)

Jacob's ladder *n.* ship's ladder typically of rope or chain, and rungs of wood or iron [after the ladder seen by the patriarch *Jacob* in a dream: Genesis, 28:12]

jaded *adj.* drained by fatigue, weary; dulled by excess, sated

jalopy *informal. n.* rickety old car, truck, or other vehicle, rattletrap

jalousie (zháloo-zee) *n.* blind or window consisting of adjustable horizontal slats, so as to admit light and air while protecting against the elements [French, literally, jealousy probably because one can look through it without being seen]

janissary (jánni-səri) *n.* Turkish elite soldier or bodyguard of a group lasting from the 14th to the 19th century

janitor *chiefly U.S. and Scottish n.* caretaker or porter of a building

Janus-faced *formal. adj.* two-faced, hypocritical [after *Janus*, the Roman god of doors and gates, usually represented with two faces looking in opposite directions]

japan *n.* glossy black lacquer or varnish [after *Japan*, where the technique originated] — **japan** *adj., tr.v.*

jardinière (zhárdin-yáir) *n.* large decorative stand or trough for plants; garnish of diced cooked vegetables served with meat or in soup

jargon *n.* specialised or technical language of a particular profession, trade, or other group

jaundice *n.* yellowing of body fluids or tissues, such as the skin, caused by disease, especially of the liver; disease, such as hepatitis, that causes jaundice [Old French *jaune*, yellow]

jaundiced *adj.* embittered, cynical; biased, prejudiced

jejune (ji-jo͞on) *formal. adj.* lacking in substance or originality: *jejune phrases*

je ne sais quoi (zhən-say-kwaá) *n.* indefinable but distinctive feature: *a certain je ne sais quoi that makes them unforgettable* [French, literally, I don't know what]

jeopardy (jéppərdi) *formal. n.* peril, danger, the risk of losing something; the defendant's chance of conviction in a trial [from Old French *jeu parti*, literally, divided play, even chance] — **-dise** *tr.v.*

jeremiad (jérri-mī́-əd) *n.* long elaborate lamentation, complaint, or denunciation [after *Jeremiah*, the biblical prophet of doom]

jerkin *n.* sleeveless, collarless jacket; tight short leather jacket worn in former times

jerry-built *adj.* built shoddily and unreliably

jetsam *n.* cargo or equipment thrown overboard from a ship in distress, especially when found washed ashore. Compare FLOTSAM

jettison *tr.v.* to throw from a ship or other vehicle so as to lighten the load carried; to discard

jeu d'esprit (zhér dess-preé) *formal. n., pl.* **jeux d'esprit** short display of cleverness or wit in speech or writing, often in the course of a longer text [French, literally, play of wit]

jigger *n.* small measure for alcoholic drinks, especially spirits, as used in pubs

jihad (ji-háad) *n.* Islamic holy war; fanatical crusade on behalf of a principle

Jim-Crow *adj.* relating to segregation of and discrimination against blacks, specifically as practised formerly in the American South [after *Jim Crow*, a character in an act by Thomas D. Rice, a 19th-century U.S. entertainer, who based it on an anonymous song called *Jim Crow*]

jingoism *n.* chauvinistic patriotism combined with support of an aggressive foreign policy [from the refrain of a music-hall song sung by supporters of Disraeli's 1878 anti-Russian policy: "We don't want to fight, yet by Jingo! if we do, We've got the ships, we've got the men, and got the money too"] — **-ist** *n. adj.* — **-istic** *adj.*

jobber *n.* middleman; person who buys from wholesalers and sells to retailers; *British.* formerly, middleman in transactions among stockbrokers — **-bery** *n.*

Job's comforter (jōbz) *n.* person who, while seeming or trying to comfort or console, in fact creates increased gloom and despondency [after the biblical *Job*, whose friends treated him in this way]

jocose (jə-kṓss, jō-) *formal. adj.* heartily jolly; full of jokes (also "jocular", "jocund") — **-osity** *n.*

jodhpurs (jód-pərz) *pl.n.* tight riding breeches with loose-fitting hips [after *Jodhpur*, a city in India]

joie de vivre (zhwaá də veévr) *n.* enjoyment of life, vivacity [French, literally, joy of living]

jointure *n.* in law, the estate to be left by a husband to his widow; the arrangement, at the time of the marriage, providing for this

joist *n.* horizontal beam supporting a ceiling or floor boards — **joist** *tr.v.*

jojoba (hə-hṓbə) *n.* flowering American shrub with seeds containing a valuable liquid wax; wax oil extracted from these seeds for use in pharmaceuticals, cosmetics, and polishes — **jojoba** *adj.*

jolie laide (zhóllee láyd, léd) *n., pl.* **-s -s** woman or girl who is attractive though not pretty [French, literally, pretty ugly] — **jolie-laide** *adj.*

Jonah *n.* person believed to bring bad luck [after *Jonah*, the Old Testament prophet, who was thrown

overboard by sailors when they suspected that his presence was causing stormy weather]
jongleur (zhoN-glúr) *n.* minstrel travelling about in medieval times [related to *juggler*]
joss stick *n.* stick of perfumed substance, burnt as incense [from Pidgin English *joss*, a Chinese idol, from Portuguese *deos*, a god, from Latin *deus*]
journeyman *n.* capable workman; craftsman who has fully qualified after serving his apprenticeship, but is still employed by someone else [Middle English dialect *journey*, a day's work, from French *journée*, a day, from Latin *dies*]
joust *n.* combat between mounted lancers — **joust** *intr.v.*
jovial *adj.* hearty, jolly, good-humoured [originally, born under the planet Jupiter, regarded in astrology as the source of happiness] — **-iality** *n.*
Jovian *adj.* relating to Jove the god, or to Jupiter the god or the planet
jubilation *n.* joy at some triumph or success, exaltation — **jubilant** *adj.*
judicature (jóodikə-chər) *formal. n.* administration of legal justice; judge's term of office; judges and law courts collectively, judiciary
judicial *adj.* relating to judges and law courts
judiciary *n.* judges and law courts collectively; the judicial branch of a government — **judiciary** *adj.*
judicious *adj.* having or showing sound judgment, prudent
jugate (jóo-gayt, -git) *formal. adj.* having paired parts; relating to compound leaves
juggernaut *n.* irresistible force that destroys or overcomes everything in its path; *British informal.* very large articulated lorry [after *Jagganath*, a title of the Hindu deity Krishna, whose idol is carried on a huge car or wagon during processions in Puri, India]
jugular *formal. adj.* relating to or positioned near the neck or throat — **jugular vein** *n.*
juju *n.* object used, carried, or worn, especially in West Africa, for its magical powers; magical power of a juju
julep *n.* sweet syrupy drink to which medicine can be added; mint-flavoured cocktail of U.S. origin, made typically with whisky or brandy
julienne (jóo-li-én, zhóo-) *adj.* sliced into very thin strips; garnished with julienne vegetables
juncture *n.* point or short period of time, especially a potential turning-point
juniper *n.* evergreen coniferous tree or shrub, whose berries yield an oil used to flavour gin
junta (júntə, jóontə, hóontə) *n.* ruling group holding power after a coup d'état; especially, military junta
jurisdiction *n.* power or right to administer laws and justice, as over a specified area; area of authority of a person or group
jurisprudence *n.* philosophy or academic study of law; system or body of laws
jurist *n.* expert on the law; especially, one who writes on or expounds legal principles
justify *tr.v.* to set (a line of type) so that one or both ends are exactly above or below the corresponding end or ends of the other lines in the same group
jute *n.* plant that yields a fibre used for sacking, coarse rope, and the like; jute fibre
juvenilia *formal. pl.n.* youthful early works, especially of an artistic or literary kind, typically produced before their creator has formed a mature style
juxtapose *tr.v.* to put or consider side by side or next to each other, especially for the sake of contrast or comparison — **-position** *n.*

K

kabuki (kə-bóoki) *n.* traditional Japanese drama with elaborate costumes, stylised acting, singing, and dancing, and male actors playing male and female roles [Japanese, literally, the art of singing and dancing]
kaffiyeh (kə-fée-yə) *n.* Arab headscarf held in position by a cord (also "keffiyeh")
Kafkaesque *adj.* suggestive of or referring to a surrealistic nightmarish world, especially one in which the individual is prey to a complex and mysterious bureaucracy [after Franz *Kafka*, the 20th-century Czech writer, who described such a world in some of his works]
kaleidoscope *n.* ever-changing series of events [after the child's toy] — **-scopic** *adj.*
kamikaze (kámmi-káazi) *adj.* referring to Japanese suicide pilots of the Second World War; *informal.* suicidally reckless: *kamikaze driving* (often used humorously) [Japanese, literally, divine wind]
kampong *n.* traditional village or settlement in a Malay-speaking area
kanga *n.* strip of brightly-coloured cloth worn as a women's garment in East Africa
Kapellmeister (kə-pél-mīstər) *n.* director of a choir or orchestra, and sometimes official composer, as at an 18th-century German-speaking court [German, literally, choir master]
kapok (káypok) *n.* light silky plant fibre used as stuffing in pillows and lifebelts, and for insulation — **kapok** *adj.*
kaput (kə-póot) *informal. adj.* out of order, useless; destroyed, wrecked [German]
karma *n.* in Hinduism and Buddhism, the force produced by a person's actions, determining his future existence; loosely, fate or destiny [Sanskrit, literally, work] — **karmic** *adj.*
kayak (kī́-ak) *n.* watertight Inuit (Eskimo) canoe

made of animal hides; modern canvas-covered canoe based on the kayak

kazoo *n.* toy musical instrument consisting of a tube with a vibrating membrane that buzzes when the player hums into the mouthpiece

kedge *v.* to move (a boat) or be moved by pulling on a rope attached to an anchor lowered some distance away ~ *n.* light anchor used for kedging

keelhaul *tr.v.* to punish or torture (a sailor) by hauling him under the keel of a ship; *informal.* to scold severely

keen *n.* loud high-pitched wail of lament for the dead; sound like a keen ~ *intr.v.* to make a keen

keepnet *n.* anglers' net placed in the water, into which caught fish are put to keep them alive

keloid (keé-loyd) *n.* mass of thick scar tissue — **keloid** (also "cheloid") **keloidal** *adj.*

kelp *n.* any of various types of large brown seaweed; mass of large seaweed (also "oarweed")

kelpie *n.* water sprite in Scottish folklore, typically in the shape of a horse, that drowns its riders

kelt *n.* salmon that has spawned, and is typically in an exhausted state

kendo *n.* Japanese martial art of fencing, practised as a sport with two-handed bamboo staves [Japanese, literally, the art of fencing]

kenning *n.* metaphorical phrase used in Old English and Old Norse poetry such as *storm of swords* for "battle"

kente (kén-ti) *n.* brightly-coloured Ghanaian cloth; Ghanaian men's garment made from strips of kente and worn like a toga

kepi (káypi) *n.* peaked, pillbox-shaped French military cap [related to *cap*]

kerf *n.* groove or notch made, as in wood, by chopping or sawing; cut end of a felled tree

kerfuffle *chiefly British. informal. n.* uproar, fuss, commotion

kern *n.* raised part of a piece of printers' type that contains the letter or character to be printed

keystone *n.* top or central stone of an arch that wedges the others into place

khedive (ke-deév) *n.* Ottoman Turkish viceroy of Egypt, during the period 1867-1914

kia-ora *interj.* good health or good luck [Maori greeting]

kibbutz (ki-bóots) *n., pl.* **-zim** collective farm or cooperative settlement in Israel — **-nik** *n.*

kibitzer (kíbbitsər) *chiefly U.S. informal. n.* meddler, busybody giving unwanted advice, especially as an onlooker at a card game — **kibitz** *intr.v.*

kilderkin *n.* cask that can hold half a barrelful; amount a kilderkin can hold, used formerly as a unit of quantity and equal to about 18 gallons

kilim (ki-leém) *n.* Eastern tapestry-woven rug or wall hanging (also "kelim")

killick *n.* small anchor, especially one consisting of a stone in a wooden frame

kimono (ki-mṓ-nō) *n.* long, loose Japanese robe secured by a wide sash; dressing gown modelled on a kimono

kinaesthesia (kī́n-ees-theézi-ə) *n.* awareness of one's body and its movements, body sense, muscle sense — **-thetic** *adj.* — **-thetics** *n.*

kinesics (kī-neéz-iks, -néess-) *n.* study of movement, gesture, and expression, and what it communicates

kinetic (kī-néttik, ki-) *formal. adj.* relating to motion or the energy associated with motion — **kinetics** *n.*

kismet *n.* fate or destiny of a person, specifically in Islam

kist *chiefly Scottish or South African. n.* chest or wooden trunk, as for linen [related to *chest*]

kitchen cabinet *n.* group of unofficial yet powerful advisers to a government or business leader; sub-group of official advisers with privileged access to a leader even outside normal working hours

kitsch *n.* sentimentality or empty, showy effects in the arts — **kitsch, -y** *adj.*

klaxon *n.* horn on an old car

kleptomania *n.* compulsive urge to steal things, for psychological rather than economic reasons — **-niac** *adj., n.*

knacker *British. n.* person who buys old horses or their carcasses for use as pet food, in gluemaking, or the like

knell *n.* slow solemn tolling of a bell, as for a funeral; signal or omen of failure or ruin

knickerbockers *pl.n.* breeches or baggy trousers gathered just below the knee

knight errant *n., pl.* **knights errant** knight wandering about in search of chivalric adventures — **-ry** *n.*

knobkerrie *n.* wooden club with a heavy knob at one end, used formerly as a weapon by South African tribesmen, especially Zulus (also "knobkierie")

knoll *n.* small, rounded, often wooded or grassy hill

knot garden *n.* garden of formal design, with detailed patterns of flower beds

knout *n.* whip used formerly in Russia for flogging

koan (kṓ-an) *n.* in Zen Buddhism, brain-teaser or paradox, such as "What is the sound of one hand clapping?", that helps the mind to transcend reason

kohl *n.* preparation used as eyeliner, especially in the Near and Middle East

kosher (kṓ-shər) *adj.* approved by Jewish dietary laws; *informal.* right and proper, above-board: *not exactly a kosher transaction* — **kashruth** *n.*

kowtow (ków-tów) *n.* traditional Chinese act of respect in which one kneels and touches the ground with one's forehead; *informal.* any act of obsequious homage or respect — **kowtow** *intr.v.*

krill *pl.n.* tiny shrimp-like sea creatures forming the main food of some whales

kris *n.* Malay sword or large dagger with a wavy, double-edged blade

kudos (kéw-doss) *n.* fame, status, and prestige as the result of an act or achievement

kukri (kóokri) *n.* broad-bladed Gurkha knife

kwashiorkor (kwáshi-ór-kər) *n.* severe malnutrition caused by a diet high in carbohydrates but low in protein, and found especially among some infants and children in Africa

kwic *adj.* referring to a computer-generated concordance to one or more texts, in which words are printed out in alphabetical order, accompanied in each case by a part of its context [*k*ey*w*ord *i*n *c*ontext]

kymograph *n.* rotating cylinder on which a pen records changes in pressure, especially blood pressure — **-ic** *adj.*

Kyrie eleison (kírri-ay i-láy-i-son) *n.* short prayer for divine mercy used in some Christian churches, as at the beginning of the Mass; musical setting of this prayer, as for a choral Mass (also "Kyrie") [Greek, literally, Lord, have Mercy]

L

laager *n.* defensive camp, such as those existing formerly in South Africa, protected by a circle of wagons

labia (láybi-ə) *pl.n.* folds of flesh surrounding the entrance to the vagina (singular "labium") [Latin, lips]

labial *adj.* relating to the lips or labia; specifically, sounded using one or both lips, as the letters *f* and *b* are ~ *n.* labial sound, such as that of *b* or *v*

labile *formal. adj.* emotionally unstable; specifically, undergoing or showing rapid and continual changes of mood — **-bility** *n.*

laboured *adj.* showing signs of effort: *laboured breathing*; embarrassingly artificial and unduly complicated: *a laboured witticism*

labret *n.* lip-ring or ornament inserted in the lip

labyrinth *n.* maze; specifically, in Greek mythology, the one in which Theseus found and slew the Minotaur; the inner ear, with its complex internal structure — **-ine** *adj.*

labyris (lábbi-riss) *n.* double-headed axe of symbolic significance in the ancient Minoan civilisation of Crete; labyris as a feminist or lesbian symbol

lacerate *tr.v.* to tear (typically flesh); to wound, as with criticism — **-ation** *n.*

lachrymal (láckrim'l) *adj.* relating to tears: *the lachrymal glands*

lachrymatory (láckri-máy-təri) *n.* small vase used formerly to hold mourners' tears ~ *formal. adj.* relating to, causing, or producing tears

lachrymose *formal. adj.* causing or given to tears; tearfully self-pitying — **-osity** *n.*

lackadaisical *adj.* lacking energy or enthusiasm, as through laziness or indifference [from the interjection *lackaday*]

lackey *n. archaic.* liveried servant, such as a footman; servile follower or henchman

lacklustre *adj.* dull, uninspiring: *a lacklustre recital*

laconic (lə-kónnik) *adj.* using few words, gruff, terse [from Greek *Lakonikos*, relating to the Spartans, who were men of action and few words]

lactate *intr.v.* to produce milk — **-ation** *n.*

lactic *adj.* relating to milk: *lactic acid*

lacuna (lə-ko͞onə) *formal. n., pl.* **-as** or **-ae** gap, especially in writing or a person's knowledge; cavity or depression in organic tissue [Latin, a pool; related to *lagoon*]

lacustrine (lə-kúss-trīn) *formal. adj.* relating to a lake or lake shore: *lacustrine vegetation*

lagan (lággən) *n.* cargo or equipment thrown into the sea from a ship in distress, often attached to a buoy for later recovery (also "ligan")

laggard *n.* someone who lags behind, dawdler — **laggard** *adj.*

lagging *n.* insulating material, as round a boiler

laissez-aller (léssay-ál-lay) *n.* freedom from constraints, sometimes to an excessive degree [French, literally, allow to go]

laissez-faire (léssay-fáir) *n.* unrestricted free enterprise, policy of not restricting or being indifferent to what somebody does [French, literally, allow to do]

laissez-passer *n.* permit, pass; specifically, one allowing passage into or out of an area [French, literally, allow to pass]

laity (láy-əti) *n., pl.n.* ordinary lay members of a congregation by contrast with the clergy or members of religious orders; ordinary lay members of the public by contrast with professionals or specialists — **laicise** *tr.v.*

Lallans *n.* Lowland Scots dialect, especially that form of it which has been developed as a literary language — **Lallans** *adj.*

lallation *n.* pronunciation of the sound /r/ as /l/

lama *n.* Buddhist monk in Tibet or Mongolia

Lamarckism *n.* theory that acquired characteristics can be inherited [after Chevalier de *Lamarck* the 18th-19th-century French naturalist who developed the theory] — **-ian** *adj., n.*

lamasery *n.* Buddhist lamas' monastery, as in Tibet

lambast (lam-bást, -báyst) *informal. tr.v.* to give someone a good thrashing or telling-off (slightly old-fashioned)

lambent *formal. adj.* illuminating by flickering over an area; gently or luminously glowing; lightly or effortlessly brilliant — **-bency** *n.*

lamella (lə-méllə) *n., pl.* **-ae** or **-as** thin scale, ring, layer, or plate of organic or inorganic material; thin layer of liquid; beam in the frame of a vaulted roof — **-lar, -late** *adj.*

lamia (láymi-ə) *n., pl.* **-mias** or **-miae** evil enchantress, or female demon or vampire, *formal.* terrifying woman [after the *lamia* in Greek mythology, a bloodsucking monster half-snake half-woman]

lamina *n., pl.* **-ae** or **-as** lamella; blade of a leaf or petal; thin or narrow layer of rock — **-nar, -nal, -nate** *adj.*

laminate *v.* (lámmi-nayt) — *tr.* to make or divide into one or more thin sheets or layers; to cover with thin sheets or layers — *intr.* to split into thin sheets or layers ~ *n.* (lámmi-nit, -nayt) something, such as plywood, composed of thin sheets or layers; laminated substance used as a covering or coating — **laminate** *adj.*

lampoon *n.* bitingly satirical piece of writing that verges on a personal attack against someone [French, from *lampons*, let us drink (used as a refrain in 17th-century poetry)] — **lampoon** *tr.v.* — **-ist** *n.*

lamprey *n.* eel-like fish of fresh and salt water that has typically a sucking mouth without jaws

lanate (láy-nayt) *formal. adj.* covered with or consisting of woolly hairs: *a lanate leaf*

lancet *n.* surgical or dental knife with a double-edged pointed blade

lancinating *formal. adj.* stabbing, piercing

langlauf (laang-lowf) *n.* cross-country skiing by contrast with downhill skiing [German, literally, long run, long race]

langue (laangg, loNg) *n.* language as an abstract system shared by a speech community. Compare PAROLE

languid *adj.* lacking energy, listless or sluggish — **languor** *n.*

languish *formal. intr.v.* to be in a state of unsatisfied longing, especially because of confinement, neglect, or depletion of vital energy (often humorous)

lanolin *n.* fatty substance derived from wool and used in cosmetics and ointments — **lanolin** *adj.*

lanugo (lə-néw-gō) *n.* short fine downy hair, as on a foetus or new-born baby — **-ginous** *adj.*

lanyard *n.* piece of rope used for fastening sails; piece of cord worn round the neck, on which a useful object, such as a whistle or a key, is carried

laodicean (láy-ōdi-sée-ən) *formal. adj.* apathetic or indifferent with respect to a matter of vital importance, such as a question of politics or religion [after *Laodicea ad Lycum*, whose early church is condemned in Revelation 3: 14-16 for being "lukewarm, and neither hot nor cold"] — **laodicean** *n.*

lapidary (láppi-dəri) *formal. adj.* relating to stones, especially gemstones; elegant and concise, as though engraved on a classical stone monument: *a lapidary prose style* ~ *formal. n.* cutter and polisher of gemstones

lapsus linguae (láp-səss líng-gwī) *formal. n., pl.* **lapsus linguae** slip of the tongue, verbal blunder (also *formal* "parapraxis") [Latin]

larboard *n.* left or port side of a boat or ship — **larboard** *adj.*

larceny *formal. n.* theft of another's property — **-nous** *adj.*

lares et penates (láa-rayz et pe-náatayz) *formal. pl.n.* valued personal or household possessions or domestic comforts [after the ancient Roman household gods]

largesse (laar-jéss, -zhéss) *formal. n.* generosity shown in the form of gifts of money or favours, especially to an inferior

largo (lárgō) *adv.* at a calm, slow, steady pace (used as a musical direction) — **largo** *n., adj.*

lariat (lárri-ət) *n.* lasso used for catching or tethering livestock

larva *n., pl.* **-vae** or **-vas** grub-like young, hatched from the egg of an insect — **-val** *adj.*

lascivious (lə-sívvi-əss) *formal. adj.* indulging in or arousing excessive or uncontrolled sexual desire; lewd

laser *n.* apparatus producing a sharp beam of intensely bright light [*l*ight *a*mplification by *s*timulated *e*mission of *r*adiation] — **laser** *adj.*

lashing *n.* rope or cord used for tying or binding [related to *lace*] — **lash** *tr.v.*

lassitude *formal. n.* deep fatigue, sluggishness, or exhaustion

last *n.* shoemaker's block, shaped like a foot, to support shoes being shaped or mended

lateen (lə-téen) *adj.* referring to a rig or its triangular sail slung from a long spar attached to the end of the mast ~ *n.* lateen-rigged boat [from French *voile Latine*, literally, Latin sail, referring to its use in the Mediterranean]

latent (láyt'nt) *adj.* present and potential though not yet noticeable or manifest: *latent tendencies* — **latency** *n.*

latent heat *n.* heat given out or absorbed by a substance when it changes its physical state or phase, as during melting

lateral (láttərəl) *adj.* relating to or situated on the side or sides

lateral thinking *n.* thinking done in an imaginative and free-ranging rather than strictly logical manner, often producing unexpectedly simple solutions to problems

latex (láy-teks) *n.* milky sap of certain plants, used in the manufacture of rubber — **latex** *adj.*

lath (laath) *n.* strip or slat of wood or metal used, especially in the form of sheets, as a backing for plaster, slates, tiles, or the like; laths collectively — **lath** *adj.*

latifundium (látti-fúndi-əm) *formal. n., pl.* **-dia** large landed estate, especially in Latin America or ancient Rome [Latin, *latus*, broad + *fundus*, an estate]

latitude *n.* distance north or south of the equator, measured in degrees and often represented by horizontal lines on a map. Compare LONGITUDE; freedom of thought or action, leeway, scope — **-tudinal** *adj.*

latitudinarian *formal. adj.* liberal, especially in matters of religion — **latitudinarian, -ism** *n.*

latterly *formal. adv.* recently, lately; subsequently, later

lattice *n.* framework of crisscrossed strips of wood or metal, as in a screen or window; regular geometric arrangement, as of the molecules in a crystal — **lattice** *tr.v.* — **latticed** *adj.*

laudable (láwdə-b'l) *formal. adj.* praiseworthy, commendable, admirable — **laud** *tr.v.*

laudanum (lód-nəm, láwd'n-əm) *n.* opium-based medicinal preparation, widely used in former times

launder *informal. tr.v.* to provide an apparently respectable source for (money obtained dubiously or illegally), as by passing it through a bank

laureate (láwri-ət, lórri-) *formal. n.* poet, Nobel prize winner, or other eminent person in the arts or sciences who receives a special honour [Latin, *laureatus*, crowned with laurel] — **laureate** *adj.*

laurels *pl.n.* token or symbol of honour or eminence — **look to one's laurels** to guard against the overtaking of one's achievements or eclipsing of one's fame — **rest on one's laurels** to be satisfied with one's past achievements

lavabo *n., pl.* **-boes** ceremonial washing of the hands at Mass; basin or towel used in this ceremony [Latin, literally, I shall wash, from Psalm 26]

lavage (lávvij, la-váazh) *n.* washing out of an organ, such as the stomach

laver bread (láavər) *n.* Welsh dish of fried, oatmeal-coated seaweed

lavish *adj.* expensive and luxurious: *a lavish opera production* ~ *tr.v.* to spend or give generously: *lavished gifts on his host*

lay *adj.* belonging or relating to the general unqualified public, non-professional, non-specialist, non-clerical: *a lay preacher* — **-man, -woman, laity** *n.*

layette (lay-ét) *n.* clothing and accessories for a new-born baby

lay figure *n.* jointed dummy of a human figure, used as an artist's model (also "mannequin")

lazaretto (lázzə-réttō) *n., pl.* **-os** hospital for treating contagious diseases in former times (also "lazar house"); quarantine building or ship; ship's store-room between decks (also "lazaret") [Italian, partly from *lazzaro*, a beggar or leper, from *Lazarus*, the beggar in Jesus' parable of the rich man and the poor man; partly from earlier *nazareto*, from *Santa Maria de Nazaret*, a church hospital in Venice]

LCD *n.* display of symbols, as on a digital watch, produced by electrical stimulation of liquid crystals [*l*iquid crystal *d*isplay]

lea *n.* meadow, grassland (poetic)

leach *v.* — *tr.* to remove (soluble parts) from (a substance such as soil), as by flushing with water (also "leach out") — *intr.* to lose soluble parts by leaching; to pass out or wash away by leaching — **leach** *n.*

leather *n.* flap of a dog's ear

leaven (lévv'n) *n.* raising or fermenting agent, such as yeast, added to dough in breadmaking; *informal.* enlivening or energising agent, catalyst — **leaven** *tr.v.*

Lebensraum (láybənz-rowm) *n.* living-space or breathing space; territory needed for expansion, specifically that claimed by the Nazis for German economic self-sufficiency prior to the Second World War [German, literally, living space]

lechery *adj.* excessive sexual activity or cravings — **lecher** *n.* — **-rous** *adj.*

lectern *n.* stand for supporting a book or notes, as in a church or lecture hall

lector *formal. n.* reader of lessons from the bible in a church service; lecturer in certain universities — **-ship** *n.*

LED *n.* device, as in a digital clock, that gives off light when electrically stimulated [*l*ight-*e*mitting *d*iode]

Lederhosen (láydər-hōz'n) *pl.n.* traditional leather Tyrolean or Bavarian men's shorts with braces [German, literally, leather trousers]

ledger *n.* book in which accounts are recorded in bookkeeping; horizontal pole or timber on scaffolding

ledger board *n.* board forming the top rail of a fence or balustrade

lee *n.* position affording shelter from the wind; position downwind — **lee** *adj.*

leech *informal. n.* clinging or dependent person; person who persistently takes advantage of another, parasite [after *leech*, the bloodsucking worm] — **leech** *v.*

lees *pl.n.* sediment of wine, cider, or the like; dregs (poetic)

leeway *n.* room for manoeuvre, freedom of action or thought within limits, latitude; margin of error, variation, or shortfall

legacy *n.* money or property left in a will, inheritance; something surviving or handed down from the past, heritage

legal tender *formal. n.* legally valid money or currency that has to be accepted in payment of a financial debt

legate (léggət) *n.* representative or delegate: *a papal legate*

legation *n.* diplomatic mission ranking below an embassy in status, and headed typically by a minister rather than by an ambassador

legato (li-gáatō) *adv.* at a smooth, slowish, flowing pace (used as a musical direction) — **legato** *n.*, *adj.*

legend *formal. n.* title or inscription, as on a coin or coat of arms; key explaining the symbols used on a map

legerdemain (léjərdə-máyn) *n.* deceptive movements of the hands, as in conjuring, sleight of hand; trickery [Old French *leger de main*, literally, light of hand]

legible (léji-b'l) *adj.* readable: *legible handwriting* — **-ibility** *n.*

legion *formal. adj.* abundant, present in very large numbers: *Her enemies were legion but her friends were few*

legislate *intr.v.* to draft and enact a law through an authorised body, such as a parliament; to allow for, make provision for ~ *tr.v.* to bring about by legislating — **-lative** *adj.* — **-lator**, **-lation** *n.*

legislature (léji-sləchər) *n.* political body authorised to make laws for a nation, state, or the like

legitimate (li-jítti-mət) *adj.* within the limits of what is allowed by law, tradition, or accepted authority; having a legal right to the specified position; born in wedlock of married parents; reasonable, valid — **legitimate**, **-mise** *tr.v.* — **-macy**, **-mation** *n.*

legume *n.* bean, pea, or related pod-bearing plant; pod of such a plant, especially as used for food — **-minous** *adj.*

lei (lay, láy-ee) *n.* garland of flowers, typically worn round the neck, especially in Hawaii

leister (léestər) *n.* fishing spear with three or more prongs, used in catching salmon — **leister** *tr.v.*

leitmotif (lī́t-mōteef) *n.* recurring dominant theme or image in a piece of music or literature

lemma *n.*, *pl.* **-mas** or **-mata** proposition used to prove a more important proposition; argument or theme of a work, especially when used as the title; heading or introduction; word or phrase annotated or explained in a text, glossary, or the like — **-tise** *tr.v.*

lemming *n.* self-destructive or suicidal person, especially when acting as part of a larger group [after the rodents that tend to drown in large numbers during mass migrations]

lenient *adj.* generous; forgiving; kind — **-ency** *n.*

lenitive (lénnitiv) *formal. adj.* soothing or alleviating pain, discord, or harshness: *lenitive potions/words* — **lenitive** *n.*

lentigo (len-tī́gō) *formal. n.*, *pl.* **-tigines** freckle or mole [Latin, *lens*, a lentil seed] — **-tiginous** *adj.*

lento *adv.* at a slow pace (used as a musical direction) — **lento** *n.*, *adj.*

leonine *formal. adj.* lion-like, relating to or resembling a lion

leotard (lée-ə-tard) *n.* one-piece close-fitting garment worn by dancers, gymnasts, acrobats, and the like [after Jules *Léotard*, a 19th-century French trapeze artist who popularised it]

lepidopterist (léppi-dóptə-rist) *formal. n.* expert in or collector of butterflies and moths

leporine (léppə-rīn) *formal. adj.* hare-like, relating to or resembling a hare

lese majesty (léez) *formal. n.* treason or other offence committed against a sovereign or sovereign power; serious affront to dignity or authority (also "lèse majesté")

lesion (léezh'n) *n.* abnormal change, wound, or injury to a body part, organ, or tissue

lessee (le-sée) *n.* person or group to whom a lease is granted, leaseholder

lessor *n.* person or group that grants a lease, landlord or landlady

lethal *adj.* causing, able to cause, or relating to death: *a lethal weapon*

lethargy (léthər-ji) *n.* sluggishness, laziness, or fatigue — **-gic** *adj.*
lethe (le͞ethi) *n.* forgetfulness, loss of memory; realm of oblivion (poetic; also "Lethe") [after *Lethe*, the river of forgetfulness in Greek mythology] — **lethean** *adj.*
letterhead *n.* headed notepaper, or the heading on it
letters of credence *pl.n.* documentation authorising a diplomat to act on behalf of his government (also "letters credential")
lettre de cachet (léttrə də ka-sháy) *n.*, *pl.* **lettres de cachet** document under a sovereign's seal, in former times, typically authorising imprisonment without trial [French, literally, letter with a seal]
leucoma (lo͞o-kṓmə, lyo͞o-) *n.*, *pl.* **-mas** or **-mata** white opaque patch of tissue on the cornea of the eye
levant (li-vánt) *British. informal. intr.v.* to run away or abscond, especially when leaving unpaid debts behind [probably from *Levant*] — **-er** *n.*
Levant *n.* region of the Middle East bordering the Eastern Mediterranean (old-fashioned) [from Old French, rising (of the sun), hence the Orient] — **-tine** *n.*, *adj.*
[1]**levee** (lévvi) *chiefly U.S. n.* river embankment, landing place, or quay
[2]**levee** (lévvi, lévvay) *n.* royal reception formerly held by a sovereign just after getting out of bed; reception, as for a VIP
leveret (lévvərit) *n.* young hare, especially one in its first year of life
leviathan (li-vī́-əthən) *n.* huge animal, especially a sea-creature; anything huge and formidable [after the biblical sea monster described in Job 41:1]
levitate *v.* — *intr.* to rise and float in the air, apparently in defiance of gravity — *tr.* to cause to levitate; to support (a severely burnt patient) on a cushion of air — **-tation** *n.*
levity (lévviti) *formal. n.* lightness or frivolity of manner, especially when seriousness would be more appropriate; changeableness, unsteadiness, inconstancy
levy (lévvi) *tr.v.* to impose or collect (a tax, fine, membership fee, or the like); to confiscate (property), typically in accordance with a court order; to declare, prepare for, or wage (war); to register or recruit for military service or membership of an organisation — **levy** *n.*
lexical *adj.* relating to the words or vocabulary of a language
lexicographer *n.* dictionary compiler, editor, or expert — **-graphy** *n.* — **-graphic** *adj.*
lexicon *n.* dictionary, especially of an ancient language; vocabulary of a particular language, person, profession, subject, or the like
lexigraphy (lek-síggrəfi) *n.* writing, as in Chinese, in which each word is represented by a single character or symbol
lex talionis (tál-i-ṓ-niss) *formal. n.* principle of revenge or retaliation, law of "an eye for an eye" [Latin, law of retaliation]
Leyden jar (lī́d'n) *n.* jar lined inside and out with tin foil, forming an early type of storage device for electrical charge [after the Dutch city of *Leiden*, where it was developed in the 18th century]
ley lines (lay) *pl.n.* imaginary lines joining hilltops, church sites, and other prominent points, sometimes apparently corresponding with prehistoric tracks [from *lea*, a meadow or grassland, since the lines are thought to mark the boundaries of ancient meadows]
liability *n.* financial obligation, debt; handicap, disadvantage, hindrance
liaison (li-áy-z'n, -ZON) *n.* communication, contact, or cooperation; relationship, especially a sexual relationship; thickening agent, such as cream or egg yolk, for soups, sauces, or the like; pronunciation of a final consonant that is normally silent, when the next word begins with a vowel, as with the *t* in the French phrase *est-il* — **liaise** *intr.v.*
libation (lī-báysh'n) *formal. n.* pouring of a liquid as a religious sacrifice or ritual; liquid poured in a libation; alcoholic drink (in this sense, humorous)
libertine (líbbər-teen) *n.* person, typically a man, who is not restrained by traditional morality, especially in sexual matters (now usually derogatory) — **libertine** *adj.* — **-tinism** *n.*
libidinous (li-bíddinəss) *formal. adj.* lustful, given to or arousing excessive or uncontrolled sexual desire
libido (li-be͞edō) *n.*, *pl.* **-os** emotional energy that, according to psychoanalytic theory, comes to be directed towards goals and relationships unless blocked by neurotic repression; *informal.* sexual drive or desire — **-dinal** *adj.*
libretto *n.*, *pl.* **-tos** or **-retti** text of the songs and dialogue of an opera or operetta [Italian, literally, little book] — **-rettist** *n.*
licensed victualler (vítt'lər) *British. formal. n.* pubkeeper, publican
licentiate (lī-sénshi-ət) *n.* person with a licence, such as a licence to preach or to practise a profession; university degree ranking below a doctorate in some European countries; person having such a degree
licentious (lī-sénshəss) *adj.* relating to unbridled licence or excessive liberty; unrestrained in sexual activity, lewd
lich-gate (lích-gayt) *n.* roofed gate of a churchyard, where the coffin is traditionally rested at the start of the burial service (also "lych-gate") [Middle English, *lich*, a body or corpse]
lidar (lī́-daar) *n.* radar-like device using light pulses from a laser rather than radio waves [*light* + ra*dar*]
lido (lī́dō, le͞edō) *chiefly British. n.*, *pl.* **-os** bathing beach; open-air public swimming area, sometimes with a recreational centre [Italian, after *Lido*, a lagoon resort near Venice, from Latin *litus*, a shore]
lie *n.* lair, haunt, or hiding place of an animal
lied (le͞ed) *n.*, *pl.* **-er** German song, especially in the form of a ballad or poem set to music for solo voice and piano
liege (le͞ej, le͞ezh) *n.* lord or his vassal in feudal times — **liege** *adj.*
liegeman *n.*, *pl.* **-men** male feudal vassal (also "liege"); loyal follower or supporter
lien (le͞e-ən) *n.* legal right to a debtor's property until he settles the debt [related to *liable*]
lieu (lew, lo͞o) *n.* — **in lieu** instead — **in lieu of** instead of, in place of
lieutenant *n.* deputy, representative of a superior official [Old French, literally, holding a place]
ligament (líggə-mənt) *n.* tough band of fibrous tissue, especially one connecting a bone to a joint or supporting a body organ; connecting tie or bond
ligature (líggə-chər) *n.* act of binding or tying together; something that binds or ties together, specifically surgical thread, as used to constrict or close a blood vessel; metal band securing the reed to the

mouthpiece of a clarinet or saxophone; typed or printed character of two or more letters joined together, such as *fi* — **ligate** *formal. tr.v.*

[1]lights *pl.n.* offal consisting of the lungs of a slaughtered pig, sheep, or the like, used especially for pet food

[2]lights *pl.n.* ideas, principles, or understanding: *proclaimed the truth according to her lights*

ligneous (líg-ni-əss) *formal. adj.* woody; wood-like

lignite *n.* woody coal, typically brownish-black and of poor quality, that is intermediate between peat and bituminous coal (also "brown coal")

Lilliputian *formal. adj.* tiny, diminutive; petty, insignificant, trivial [after Lilliput, the land of the tiny people in Swift's *Gulliver's Travels*] — **Lilliputian** *n.*

limber (lím-bər) *adj.* supple and ready for physical action — **limber up** *v.*

limbo *n., pl.* **-os** in traditional Roman Catholic theology, abode of just souls barred from Heaven, as through being unbaptised; unsatisfactory intermediate or transitional state; state of being forgotten, ignored, or neglected

lime *n.* sticky substance spread on twigs or branches to trap birds (also "birdlime") — **lime** *tr.v.*

limerick (límmərick) *n.* light or nonsense verse of five lines [probably from the use of the name of *Limerick*, the Irish town or county, in an old song of similar form]

limn (lim) *formal. tr.v.* to draw or paint; to describe concisely or in outline

limousine (límmə-zeen, zeén) *n.* very large and luxurious car

limpid *adj.* relating or referring to water that is clear and still; suggesting inner calm and purity; clear and graceful — **-ity** *n.*

linchpin *n.* pin stuck through the end of a shaft of an axle, as to keep a wheel in position; person or thing that holds together the elements of a complex whole (also "lynchpin")

linctus *n.* syrupy medicine for coughs and sore throats

lineage (línni-ij) *n.* direct descent from the same ancestor or ancestors; group of people of the same lineage; descent, derivation — **lineal** *adj.*

lineaments *formal. pl.n.* distinctive outlines, features, or characteristics, as of a face or a building

linear *adj.* relating to a line or a sequence; straight (also "lineal")

ling *n.* heather

lingam (líng-gəm) *n.* in Hinduism, phallic image symbolising the god Shiva or the male principle of the universe

lingerie (láɴ-zhə-ri, lóɴ-) *n.* underwear or nightwear for women [French, literally, linen things]

lingua franca *n.* language widely understood, or a special language made up of elements of two other languages, as used for trading [Italian, literally, the Frankish tongue]

lingual *formal. adj.* relating to, resembling, or near the tongue

linguist *n.* person who knows several languages, or is good at learning languages; specialist in linguistics

linguistic *adj.* relating to language or linguistics

linguistics *n.* study of human language

liniment *formal. n.* lotion, ointment, or the like applied to the skin to relieve pain or stiffness

link *n.* torch formerly used in dark streets

Linotype *trademark. n.* keyboard-operated typesetting machine that casts a full line of type on a single metal slug. Compare MONOTYPE

lintel *n.* beam or support along the top of a window-frame or door-frame

lionise *tr.v.* to treat as or like a celebrity

lipid (líppid) *n.* any of various organic fats or fat-related substances that are an important constituent of living cells

liquidate *tr.v.* to settle (a debt or claim), typically by payment; to settle the financial affairs of (a business or bankrupt business); to convert (assets or property) into ready cash; to get rid of; *informal* to murder — **-dation, -dator** *n.*

liquidity *n.* possession of sufficient cash or ready assets to pay debts or take on financial obligations

lissom *adj.* moving or bending easily, supple or nimble; graceful in movement (also "lissome")

listless *adj.* sluggish, tired, or lazy

lists *pl.n.* area set aside for use in combats of chivalry, such as jousting; area of competition or controversy

litany (líttəni) *n.* prayer in which the congregation's responses alternate with the leader's invocations; presentation that is lengthy, tedious, or repetitive

literal *n.* small typographical or printing error, trivial misprint of one or two letters

literati (líttə-raáti) *pl.n.* people with active intellectual interests; bookish people who parade their knowledge of literature or their acquaintance with writers

lithe *adj.* moving or bending easily, supple; graceful in movement

lithic *adj. formal.* relating to stone; relating to the element lithium

lithography (li-thóggrəfi) *n.* printing process in which a flat surface, originally of stone, is treated so that some areas repel the ink — **-graph** *n., tr.v.*

litigation *n.* legal action, especially when involving lawsuits — **-gate** *v.* — **-gant** *n.* — **-igious** *adj.*

litmus paper *n.* paper treated chemically so that it turns red in an acid solution and blue in an alkaline solution

litotes (lī-tṓ-teez, lítə-) *n., pl.* **litotes** figure of speech in the form of an understatement based on a negative, as in *no mean achievement*

litter *n.* covered seat mounted on poles and used for carrying someone, especially in former times

littoral *formal. adj.* relating to the shore or coast ~ *n.* area on a shore or coast between high- and low-tide marks of the spring tide

liturgy *n.* form or system of public worship in a religious service; rite of the Eucharist — **-urgical** *adj.*

liver spot *n.* brown freckle-like spot on the skin, seen especially on elderly people

livery *n.* uniform or distinctive clothing of a group of servants, guild members, or the like; distinctive colour scheme on vehicles, aircraft, or the like owned by a particular company

livery company *n.* guild or trade association in the City of London

livery stable *n.* stable for boarding horses or letting out horses and carriages

livid *adj.* bluish or black-and-blue, as a bruised skin might be; reddish; pale and ashen, as through illness or anger; furiously angry — **-idity** *n.*

loading *n.* extra payment on top of an insurance premium to cover special risks or expenses

loam *n.* rich, fertile soil; clayey mixture bound with straw, as used in making bricks — **-y** *adj.*

loan translation *n.* word or phrase translated element by element from another language, such as *superman* from German *Übermensch* (also "calque")
lobby *n.* entrance hall or waiting area, as in a hotel; either of two side rooms in the British and some other parliaments, into which MPs walk to indicate their vote during a division; pressure group ~ *v.* to attempt to influence (an official, MP, or the like), as in private meetings; to exert political pressure in this way — **lobbyist** *n.*
loblolly *n.* sailors' gruel or thick porridge
lobotomy (lə-bóttəmi) *n.* surgical cutting of nerve fibres in the front part of the brain, as formerly for treating certain mental disorders
locale (lə-kaál, lō-) *n.* place where an event occurs or where a musical or literary work is set
locum *chiefly British. n.* person who replaces another and does his work until he returns; especially, locum who is a clergyman, pharmacist, or member of the dental, medical, or paramedical professions (also *formal* "locum tenens") [Medieval Latin, *locum tenens*, holding the place]
locus classicus *n., pl.* **loci classici** standard or definitive example or text [Latin, literally, classical place]
locus standi *n.* right, as to appear in court or participate in a meeting; officially recognised status [Latin, literally, place of standing]
locution *formal. n.* word or phrase as an expression or example of style
lode *n.* deposit of a metal or mineral, as in rock; rich supply of something
lodestar *n.* star used as a guide or point of reference by sailors or astronomers, specifically the North Star; guiding principle or objective; person or thing valued as a guide or model
lodestone *n.* magnetic mineral used in early compasses; person or thing that is strongly attractive
loge (lōzh) *n.* box in a theatre; first rows of the upper block of seats in a continental or U.S. theatre
loggerheads *pl.n.* — **at loggerheads** in conflict, in open or complete disagreement
loggia (lōj-ə) *n.* balcony or verandah along the outside of the upper level of a building
logistics *n.* military planning, specifically of the movement of people, equipment, and supplies ~ *pl.n.* details of the organisation of a project, especially those to ensure that people and things are in the right place at the right time — **logistic**, **-ical** *adj.*
logo *n., pl.* **-gos** emblem or symbol of a company or firm, used for identification and publicity
logogram *n.* symbol that, like many Chinese characters, represents a whole word (also "logograph")
logorrhoea (lóg-ə-reé-ə) *n.* excessive talking, often incoherent, which may be due to mental illness
Logos *n.* God's word regarded as a manifestation of the divine will and often associated with Christ as the Second Person of the Trinity; cosmic reason considered in ancient Greek philosophy to be the underlying principle of universal order
logrolling *chiefly U.S. informal. n.* exchanging of favours or concessions, especially in the form of legislators' agreeing to vote for each other's proposals
loins *pl.n.* the thighs, hips, and pelvic region; the small of the back plus the buttocks; groin — **gird (up) one's loins** to prepare for something that requires great effort
lollop *intr.v.* to walk or run in a jerkily bouncy way
longevity (lon-jévviti) *n.* long life; length of life; *formal.* length of time in a state or activity
longitude *n.* distance east or west of the prime meridian at Greenwich, measured in degrees and often represented by vertical lines on a map. Compare LATITUDE
longitudinal *adj.* relating to longitude or length; positioned or going lengthways; referring or relating to studies of change over a period of time
long pig *n.* human flesh as eaten by cannibals
longshoreman *U.S. n.* docker, dockworker
longueurs (lon-gérs, lON-) *formal. pl.n.* boring periods or parts (also "longeurs") [French *longueur*, length]
loofah *n.* dried, fibrous interior of a tropical gourd, used as a bath sponge
loquacious *formal. adj.* talkative — **-acity** *n.*
Lorelei (lórrə-lī) *n.* Rhine siren of German legend whose singing lured sailors to destruction
lorgnette (lor-nyét) *n.* spectacles or opera glasses supported by a small handle (also "lorgnon")
lorimer (lórri-mər) *n.* maker of metal accessories, such as bits and spurs, for horses in former times
loss leader *n.* item, as in a supermarket, offered for sale at a very cheap rate in the hope that people who come to buy it will also buy other things
Lothario *n., pl.* **-os** male seducer of women, especially one who operates in a crude and obvious way [name of a seducer in *The Fair Penitent*, a play of 1703 by Nicholas Rowe]
lotus position *n.* sitting position, as in yoga, with legs crossed and hands resting on the knees
louche (lo͞osh) *adj.* seeming disreputable, unsavoury, or shady [French, literally, squinting]
lough (lokh) *n.* lake or arm of the sea in Ireland, similar to a loch in Scotland
loupe (lo͞op) *n.* small magnifying eyepiece as used by jewellers, watchmakers, and philatelists
loup-garou (lo͞o-ga-ro͞o) *n., pl.* **loups-garous** werewolf, especially in a French-speaking region [French]
louvre (lo͞ovər) *n.* slatted window or door; slat in a louvre; lantern-shaped cupola to let in air and let out smoke, found especially in the roofs of medieval buildings — **-vred** *adj.*
lovelock *n.* curl of hair over the forehead; long lock of hair worn over the shoulder by fashionable men in the 17th and 18th centuries
lower (lów-ər, lowr) *intr.v.* to be gloomily dark and overcast, as if threatening to rain; to look sullenly threatening
lower case *n.* small letters as distinct from capital letters. Compare UPPER CASE [small type used to be stored in the lower of two cases in the days of manual typesetting] — **-lower-case** *adj.*
lox *chiefly U.S. n.* smoked salmon
lozenge *n.* diamond-like shape; lozenge-shaped heraldic device; sweet that dissolves slowly in the mouth; medicinal substance in the form of such a sweet
luau (lo͞o-ow) *n.* Hawaiian feast
lubricant *n.* substance such as oil or graphite, used to reduce friction; something that helps to smooth over or ease strife or difficulty — **-cate** *tr.v.* — **-ricity** *n.*
lubricious *formal. adj.* smooth and slippery; sexually suggestive, saucy; lustful or lewd — **-ricity** *n.*
lucid *adj.* clear and intelligible, typically because well-ordered and coherent: *lucid prose*; sane or rational: *lucid moments* — **-ity** *n.*

lucifer (lo͞osi-fər) *n.* friction match of a kind used in former times [after *Lucifer*, Satan; Latin, literally, light-bringer]
lucrative *formal. adj.* profitable, wealth-producing
lucre (lo͞o-kər) *formal. n.* money, profit
lucubration *formal. n.* complex or deep thought or study — **-brate** *intr.v.*
lucubrations *pl.n.* pompous or pretentious ideas expressed on some subject
Lucullan (lo͞o-kúllən) *formal. adj.* referring or relating to a lavish feast — (also "Lucullian") [after Lucius *Lucullus*, 1st-century B.C. Roman general noted for his luxurious banquets]
Luddite *n.* any of a group of British textile workers who destroyed new machinery in 1811-16 as a social protest; person opposed to mechanisation or technological change [after Ned *Ludd*, a deranged Leicestershire workman who destroyed some stocking frames in about 1779] — **Luddite** *adj.*
ludic *formal. adj.* relating to play or games
ludicrous *adj.* laughable, ridiculous
luff *n.* forward part of a fore-and-aft sail; fullest part of a ship's bow; act of luffing ~ *v.* — *intr.* to flap while losing wind: *a luffing sail*; to sail closer to the wind or into the wind, typically with sails luffing; to move the arm of a crane or derrick — *tr.* to cause to luff
luge (lo͞ozh) *n.* one-person toboggan
lugubrious (lo͝o-go͞obri-əss, lə-) *formal. adj.* mournful, extremely glum or pessimistic
lumbago *n.* pain, as from rheumatism, in the lumbar region of the back
lumbar *adj.* relating to the small of the back or the part of the spine and other organs that it covers
lumbar puncture *n.* medical puncture of the spine in the lumbar region, typically to withdraw spinal fluid for examination or to inject drugs
luminary *formal. n.* well-known person; person of brilliant achievement who is an inspiration to others — **luminary** *adj.*
luminescence *n.* emission of light, or the light emitted, as by glowworms, through chemical action or radioactivity rather than through heat — **-nescent** *adj.* — **-nesce** *intr.v.*
lump *n.* — **the lump** *British. informal.* casual building workers or subcontractors collectively
lumpectomy *n.* surgical removal of a breast tumour without removal of the whole breast. Compare MASTECTOMY
lumpenproletariat *n.* in Marxist sociology, underclass consisting chiefly of the most alienated and degraded sections of the working class, who lack class-consciousness and are hard to organise [German, literally, ragged proletariat]
lunar *adj.* relating to the Moon; *formal.* crescent-shaped (in this sense, also "lunate")
lunette *n.* crescent-shaped space or opening, as over a door or window, which may be filled, as by another window or a decoration; glass covering of a watch (also "watchglass"); ring on a vehicle into which a hook may be inserted when the vehicle is to be towed; fieldwork fortification, usually temporary, with two projecting faces and two parallel flanks
lungi (lo͝ong-gee) *n.* long piece of cloth used to make turbans, scarves, or loincloths worn by men in India; garment made from a lungi
lunula (lo͞o-new-lə) *n., pl.* **-lae** small crescent-shaped mark, at the base of a fingernail (also "lunule", "half-moon") — **-lar**, **-late** *adj.*
lupine *formal. adj.* relating to a wolf, wolf-like; resembling or suggesting a wolf, as in cruelty
lurid *adj.* suggesting the colour of fire seen through a haze; glaringly bright, especially so as to create a spectacular but vulgar effect: *lurid disco lights*; melodramatic and shocking, especially because of emphasis on violence or sex: *a lurid film*
lush *chiefly U.S. informal. n.* drunkard, heavy drinker
lustrate *tr.v.* to purify ceremonially — **-tion** *n.* — **-tive** *adj.*
lustre *n.* shine, sheen; glass pendant of a chandelier; chandelier; wax polish or other polish; pottery glaze that is shiny and metallic
lusus naturae (lo͞o-səss nə-téwr-ee) *formal. n., pl.* **lusus naturae** freak of nature [Latin, literally, joke of nature]
Lutine bell (lo͞o-téen) *n.* bell at Lloyd's of London rung to announce news of an insured ship that has been missing [the bell was salvaged from the *Lutine*, a ship wrecked in 1799]
luting *n.* sealing material of clay or cement (also "lute"); pastry strip sealing the edge of a pie crust
luxuriant *adj.* growing abundantly: *luxuriant vegetation*; very fertile or productive; zestfully decorated, ornate, florid — **-ance** *n.*
luxuriate *intr.v.* to grow or reproduce abundantly; to enjoy in an indulgent way: *luxuriating in a hot bath*
lycanthrope *n. formal.* werewolf; person under a delusion that he has turned into a wolf — **-thropy** *n.*
lycée (lée-say) *n.* state academic secondary school that is in a French-speaking country or region or is run on similar lines elsewhere [see *lyceum*]
lyceum *n.* large public hall for lectures or discussions (now used chiefly in names, including names of theatres and cinemas) [Latin *Lyceum*, the garden near the temple of Apollo where Aristotle taught, from Greek *Lukeios*, an epithet of Apollo]
lymph *n.* watery liquid that circulates through the body, purifies body tissues, and produces antibodies — **-atic** *adj.*
lynch *tr.v.* to execute (a suspect), especially by hanging, without a proper trial, typically by the action of a mob [probably after William *Lynch*, an 18th-19th-century Virginia farmer who organised irregular trials of suspects]
lyonnaise (lée-ə-náyz, -néz) *adj.* cooked with onions [French, literally, in the manner of *Lyon*, a city in southern France]
lyric poetry *n.* poetry that is simple in form, musical, and often emotional, rather than reflective, dramatic, narrative, or epic
lysis *formal. n., pl.* **-ses** gradual dissolution, elimination, destruction, or decomposition; gradual lessening of the severity of a symptom or disease; gradual destruction of bacteria by an antibody

M

macabre (mə-kaábrə) *adj.* relating to death and its physically horrifying aspects [from Old French *Danse Macabre*, the Dance of Death, originally *Danse Macabé*, the Maccabean Dance, probably referring to a representation of the slaughter of the Maccabees in a medieval miracle play]

macaronic *adj.* referring or relating to a mixture of languages, specifically to a mixture of a modern language with Latin or mock-Latin: *macaronic verse* [New Latin *macaronius*, like macaroni, probably suggesting a mixed dish]

macédoine (mássi-dwaán) *n.* salad or garnish of diced mixed fruits or vegetables, sometimes jellied [French, literally, Macedonian, alluding to the mixture of peoples living together in Macedonia]

macerate (mássə-rayt) *v.* to make or become soft or separated into constituent parts by or as if by immersion in liquid

machiavellian (mácki-ə-vélli-ən) *formal. adj.* deviously cunning, sneaky; politically unscrupulous or opportunistic [after the political theories of Niccolò *Machiaveli*, the 15th-16th-century Italian diplomat and writer]

machicolation *n.* ledge or projecting gallery, as on a castle wall, having openings through which stones, hot oil, or the like could be dropped on to attackers; any of these openings; arching bracket such as any of those supporting such a ledge or gallery — **-lated** *adj.*

machinations (máshi-náysh'nz, mácki-) *pl.n.* devious means intended to further a wicked end

machismo (ma-chíz-mō, mə-, -kíz-) *n.* male aggressiveness, unwillingness to compromise, and a striving to dominate others [Spanish, from Latin *masculus*, male] — **macho** *adj.*, *n.*

mackle *n.* fault in the appearance of printed matter caused by a slippage of type or a wrinkle in the paper — **mackle** *intr.v.*

macramé *n.* ornamental lacework made by knotting string

macro- *comb.form.* large size-; excessively or abnormally large size-

macrobiotics *n.* doctrine that long life and good health can be promoted by a balanced diet of health foods — **macrobiotic** *adj.*

macrocosm *n.* the universe; system reflecting the same general structure as smaller subsystems within it: *Society as a whole is just a macrocosm of the classroom.* Compare MICROCOSM

macroeconomic *adj.* relating to the economics of large and complex systems, such as a whole country or region — **-ics** *n.*

macron *n.* diacritic or accent mark, ¯, sometimes placed above a vowel, as to indicate a long sound

macroscopic *adj.* large enough to be seen without the aid of a microscope; taking account of "the big picture", focusing on large units or long-term considerations

macula (máckew-lə) *formal. n., pl.* **lae** or **-las** blemish or spot on the skin

maculations *formal. pl.n.* spots or analogous markings on the skin of an animal, such as a leopard, or the leaves of a plant — **maculate** *adj.*

Madison Avenue *chiefly U.S. n.* the world of advertising and public relations, taken as being glossily glamorous but unscrupulous in its commercialism [after a street in Manhattan, New York City, the centre of the American advertising business]

madrigal *n.* unaccompanied vocal part song on a secular theme, especially of a type developed in the 16th and 17th centuries

Maecenas (mí-seé-nass) *formal. n.* generous patron, especially of the arts [after Gaius *Maecenas*, the 1st-century B.C. Roman statesman, patron of the poets Horace and Virgil]

maelstrom (máyl-strom) *n.* whirlpool, powerful and dangerous current; condition, centre, or focus of turbulence and disorder

maestro (mī́ss-trō) *n., pl.* — **-tros** or **-tri** master of an art, especially music, such as a famous conductor or teacher [Italian, related to *master*]

magenta (mə-jéntə) *n.* purplish red; red dye [after the bloodshed of the battle of *Magenta* of 1859, the year in which the dye was discovered] — **magenta** *adj.*

magisterial *formal. adj.* relating to a master or magistrate; worthy of a master, especially in being authoritative; overbearing or condescending

magma *n.* molten rock within the Earth, which may form igneous rock when cooled

magnanimous *adj.* noble and generous, especially in readiness to forgive — **-nimity** *n.*

magnate *n.* powerful and influential person, especially in industry or commerce

magneto *n., pl.* **-os** generator in the ignition system of some internal-combustion engines

magnetron *n.* electronic valve helping to generate high-power microwaves, as in radar systems

magnifico *n., pl.* **-coes** person of rank, importance, or distinguished appearance (often humorous)

magnum *n.* bottle, as of champagne, of twice the normal size

magnum opus *n., pl.* **magna opera** work of scholarship, research, or artistic creation that is of large size or great importance; someone's largest or greatest single work (now usually ironic) [Latin, literally, great work]

magot (maa-gṓ) *n.* Chinese or Japanese figurine, typically in a grotesque, crouched position

Magus (máy-gəss) *n., pl.* **-gi** any of the Magi, the Three Wise Men; sorcerer or astrologer of ancient times

maharani *n.* female Hindu ruler or princess ranking above a rani; wife of a maharajah

maharishi *n.* Hindu teacher of spiritual knowledge and spiritual development

mahout (mə-hówt) *n.* elephant driver and keeper in India and the East Indies
maidan (mī-da̋an) *n.* open space for parades, meetings, and sport in south and southeast Asia
maieutic (may-ōōtik) *adj.* referring or relating to Socrates' method of eliciting latent knowledge by means of a series of questions
maigre (máygər) *formal or archaic. adj.* meatless: *maigre diet/days*
maiolica (mī-óllikə) *n.* enamelled glazed pottery, originally decorated, of a 16th-century Italian style [from *Majolica*, medieval form of *Mallorca*, where the ceramic style originated]
maître d'hôtel (méttrə-dō-tél) *formal. n., pl.* **maîtres d'hôtel** head waiter; chief steward or butler, major-domo ~ *adj.* referring to a sauce of melted butter flavoured with parsley and lemon juice [French, literally, master of hotel]
major-domo *n., pl.* **-mos** steward or butler, specifically the chief steward or butler
majuscule (májə-skewl) *formal. adj.* relating to or referring to capital letter. Compare MINUSCULE ~ *n.* capital letter
malacca (mə-láckə) *n.* stem of an Asian rattan palm; walking stick made of malacca
malachite (mál-ə-kīt) *n.* green mineral used for jewellery and ornaments, and as a source of copper
maladroit *formal. adj.* clumsy, awkward
malady *n.* illness or disorder (old-fashioned)
malaise *n.* ill-defined feeling of illness, depression, or unease; state of affairs that is unwholesome or undesirable
malapropism *n.* misuse of a word through confusion with a similar-sounding word, such as *pineapple* instead of *pinnacle* [after Mrs *Malaprop* in Sheridan's play *The Rivals* (1775), from *malapropos*]
malapropos (mál-áppṛə-pō) *formal. adj.* inappropriate, out of place [French *mal á propos*, ill-suited for the purpose] — **malapropos** *adv.*
malcontent *formal. n.* rebellious, discontented person — **malcontent** *adj.*
mal de mer (mál-də-ma̋ir) *formal. n.* seasickness
malediction *formal. n.* curse or slander; uttering of a curse or slander
malefactor *formal. n.* criminal or evildoer
maleficence (mə-léffi-sənss) *formal. n.* evil or harmful intention, influence, or result. Compare BENEFICENCE — **-cent** *adj.*
malevolent *formal. adj.* spiteful, full of ill will, malicious
malfeasance *formal. n.* misconduct or wrongdoing, especially on the part of someone with official responsibilities and powers
malign (mə-lī́n) *tr.v.* to say unpleasant and untrue things about (a person) ~ *formal. adj.* wicked, evil — **-ity** *n.*
malignant *adj.* very dangerous or life-threatening; cancerous — **-nancy** *n.*
malinger *intr.v.* to avoid work by feigning or exaggerating illness or injury — **-gerer** *n.*
malleable (mál-i-əb'l) *adj.* bendable, workable, capable of being shaped by pressure or blows: *malleable metals*; easily influenced, weak-willed — **-ability**
malodorous *formal. adj.* bad-smelling (often humorous)
malpractice *n.* in health care, professional negligence or inappropriate treatment; misconduct by an official
malversation *formal. n.* misconduct, especially by a public official
mamilla (mə-míllə) *formal. n., pl.* **-lae** nipple or teat; projecting part shaped like a mamilla — **-late, -lary** *adj.*
mammogram *n.* breast X-ray — **-graphy** *n.*
Mammon *n.* spirit of worldly gain or success regarded as incompatible with virtue or spiritual development: *They must choose between God and Mammon* [after *Mammon* in the New Testament, the personification or false god of greed, riches, and materialistic values]
mana (ma̋anə) *n.* in South Pacific religions, supernatural quality in gods, rulers, and sacred objects; broadly, personal magnetism, prestige, or influence
manacles *pl.n.* handcuffs, metal rings, chains, or the like, that restrain or fetter the hands — **manacle** *tr.v.*
mañana (man-ya̋anə) *informal. adv.* tomorrow; at an unspecified and perhaps indefinitely postponed future time [Spanish]
manciple *n.* in Britain, steward who buys provisions for an institution, such as a college or an Inn of Court
Mancunian *n.* person born or living in Manchester — **Mancunian** *adj.*
mandala (mándələ, man-da̋alə) *n.* in Hindu and Buddhist art, symbolic design that is typically circular in form and represents the universe
mandarin *n.* Chinese public official in imperial times; senior civil servant believed to wield great political influence; ivory-tower intellectual
mandate (mándayt) *n.* order, command, or instruction; right to carry out policies, conferred by victory in an election; League of Nations' authorisation of a country to administer the affairs of another country or territory; country or territory whose affairs were administered in this way — **mandate** *tr.v.*
mandatory (mánde-tri, man-dáytəri) *adj.* obligatory, required by law or custom
mandible *n.* jaw; upper or lower part of beak; mouthpart of an insect
mandorla (man-dórlə) *n.* halo-like area of light surrounding a holy figure in a medieval painting [Italian, an almond]
mandrake *n.* plant with a forked root, formerly used as a narcotic drug and thought to shriek when pulled from the ground
mandrel *n.* mounting for a tool such as a dentist's drill; axle-like spindle supporting wood on a lathe (also "mandril")
manège (ma-náyzh, -nézh) *n.* art of training horses and riders for dressage exercises; riding school [related to *manage*]
manes (ma̋anayz) *pl.n.* spirits of the dead, especially as revered in ancient Rome
mangel-wurzel *n.* beetroot of a large yellowish variety, used mainly as cattle fodder
mangonel (máng-gə-nel) *n.* large medieval catapult or war engine for hurling projectiles
mangrove *n.* tree or shrub with aerial roots, flourishing in the coastal swamps of tropical regions
mania *n.* abnormal excitement or intensity of mood; *informal.* intense enthusiasm for something, craze — **manic** *adj.*
Manichaeism (mánni-ke̋e-iz'm) *n.* Persian religious philosophy of about the 3rd century A.D., regarding God and Satan as equal forces; any point of view that polarises everything into good and bad with

nothing in between [after *Manichaios*, the Persian founder of the sect] — **-aean** *n.*, *adj.*

manifest *adj.* obvious, clear, plain to see ~ *v.* — *tr.* to show, demonstrate plainly — *intr.* to appear or be revealed: *latent problems manifesting as misbehaviour* ~ *n.* commercial list, as of cargo or passengers — **-ation** *n.*

manifesto *n.*, *pl.* **-tos** or **-toes** public official declaration of principles or policies: *an election manifesto*

manifold (mánnifōld) *adj.* varied; multiple, having several parts ~ *n.* pipe with many holes and connections

mannequin (mánni-kin) *n.* model for the fitting or display of clothes, either a real woman or a life-size dummy; jointed dummy of a human figure, used as an artist's model (in this sense, also "lay figure")

mannered *adj.* artificial, contrived, or affected: *a mannered way of speaking*

mannerism *n.* distinctive item of behaviour, especially one that is exaggerated or affected

manometer *n.* pressure gauge for gases and liquids

manqué (móng-kay, -káy, móN-) *adj.* having failed to achieve the position, condition, or status wished for, would-be: *an artist manqué*

mansard *n.* roof with a flat or flattish upper section supported by four steeply sloping sides; space within the four sides of a mansard, used as an upper storey [originally designed by François *Mansart*, a 17th-century French classical architect]

manse *n.* house of a Presbyterian or Nonconformist clergyman

manslaughter *n.* homicide or unlawful killing that is unpremeditated or unintentional

mansuetude (mán-swi-tewd) *formal or archaic. n.* gentleness or mildness of manner

mantissa *n.* fractional or decimal part of a logarithm. Compare CHARACTERISTIC

mantle *n.* layer of the Earth between the crust and the core; outer layer of the brain; gauze drum or dome that increases the light of a gas lamp when heated; ring of hot gas round a flame ~ *v.* — *tr.* to cover with or as if with a mantle, cloak — *intr.* to be or become covered with or as if with a darker layer

mantra *n.* word or formula repeated, silently or aloud, in some types of meditation

manual *n.* organ keyboard

manumit (mánnew-mit) *tr.v.* to free (a slave), emancipate — **-mission** *n.*

maquette (ma-két) *n.* sketch or rough model for a sculpture

maquillage (máckee-aázh) *formal. n.* cosmetics, make-up; application of make-up

marc (mark, mar) *n.* pulp left over after fruit, especially grapes, has been pressed for juice; brandy distilled from marc

marches *pl.n.* borderlands: *the Welsh Marches*

marchioness (mársh'n-iss, -éss) *n.* wife, widow, or female counterpart of a marquis or marquess

Mardi gras (márdi graá) *n.* Shrove Tuesday in an area of French cultural influence, such as New Orleans; Mardi gras carnival [French, literally, fat Tuesday]

mare (maá-ray) *n.*, *pl.* **-ria** large dark area on the Moon or Mars, once thought to be a sea

mare's nest *n.*, *pl.* **mare's nests** or **mares' nests** hoax, fraud; discovery that turns out to be worthless; situation of great complexity or disorder

margaric (maar-gárrik) *formal. adj.* relating to a pearl (also "margaritic")

marginalia (márji-náyli-ə) *formal. pl.n.* notes on the margin of printed matter

margrave *n.* German nobleman corresponding in rank to a British marquess; military governor or lord of a medieval German border province

marimba *n.* xylophone of southern African or Central American origin with resonators beneath each bar

marina (mə-reénə) *n.* dock or basin for yachts and motorboats

marinade (márri-náyd) *n.* spicy liquid in which food is soaked before cooking — **-ade**, **-ate** *tr.v.*

mariner *formal. n.* sailor, seaman

marionette *n.* puppet moved by strings or wires

maritime *adj.* bordering the sea: *maritime provinces*; relating to navigation, sailors, or commerce on the sea, marine

marlinspike *n.* pointed spike used on shipboard to separate strands of rope or wire, as for splicing

marmite (már-mīt, -meet) *n.* large covered cooking pot of earthenware or metal; small covered earthenware casserole dish holding a single portion; broth cooked or served in a marmite [French, literally, pot]

marmoreal (már-máwr-i-əl) *formal. adj.* relating to marble, as in respect of whiteness, coldness, smoothness, or hardness: *marmoreal pallor* [related to *marble*]

marque *n.* brand or make, especially of something fashionable and expensive, such as a sports car; nameplate or insignia signifying a marque

marquetry (márkətri) *n.* inlaid work, as in wood or ivory, used as decoration

marrons glacés (ma-róN gla-sáy) *pl.n.* sweet chestnuts cooked and coated in syrup [French]

marsupial *n.* mammal, such as the kangaroo, whose young complete their gestation period in a marsupium, or abdominal pouch — **marsupial** *adj.*

Martello tower *British. n.* small, circular fort near the sea built for coastal defence [after Cape *Mortella*, Corsica, where a fort of this type held out against the British in 1794]

martial *formal. n.* relating to war or combat [after *Mars*, the Roman god of war]

martinet (márti-nét) *n.* military officer or other person who demands strict discipline and adherence to rules and regulations [after Jean *Martinet*, a 17th-century French general]

martingale *n.* part of the harness that keeps a horse's head steady and checks its movement upwards; gambling technique of doubling the stakes after each loss in the hope of coming out ahead after one win

mascara *n.* make-up used to darken or thicken the eyelashes

masculine rhyme *n.* rhyme on a stressed final syllable, as with *cat* and *hat*, or *believe* and *deceive*. Compare FEMININE RHYME

masochist (mássə-kist) *n.* person who gets pleasure or sexual arousal from undergoing a painful or unpleasant experience. Compare SADIST [after Leopold von Sacher-*Masoch*, a 19th-century Austrian novelist who wrote about sexual masochists] — **-chism** *n.* — **-chistic** *adj.*

masque *n.* allegorical dramatic entertainment performed by masked actors and often involving music, popular in the 16th and early 17th centuries

masquerade *n.* masked ball; false appearance, dis-

guise, pretence — **masquerade** *intr.v.*
masseur (ma-súr) *n.* man who gives massages professionally, sometimes providing various forms of physiotherapy as well (female equivalent "masseuse")
massif (ma-séef) *n.* large section of a mountain range; displaced block of the Earth's crust forming a large plateau-like region
mast *n.* nuts, such as acorns or beechnuts, that have fallen from trees to the forest floor and are used as fodder for animals, such as pigs
mastectomy (mast-éktəmi) *n.* surgical removal of a breast. Compare LUMPECTOMY
masthead *n.* place on the first page of a publication, especially a newspaper, where its name is prominently displayed
mastic *n.* gum or resin, as used in varnish
masticate *formal.* *v.* to chew, grind, crush, or knead — **-cation** *n.*
maté (máttay) *n.* herbal tea-like drink from South America (also "yerba maté", "Paraguay tea")
matelot (mát-lo) *British. informal.* *n.* sailor [French]
matériel (mə-téer-i-él) *n.* guns, ammunition, and other military equipment, as distinct from personnel
maternity *formal.* *n.* motherhood; motherliness — **maternal** *adj.*
matinée (máttin-ay) *n.* afternoon presentation of a play, film, or the like (also "matinee") [French, literally, morning]
matins (máttinz) *n.*, *pl.n.* in the Roman Catholic Church, night-time or dawn prayers and worship according to prescribed forms; in the Anglican Church, Morning Prayer (also "mattins")
matrass (máttrəss) *n.* distilling flask with a long neck, formerly used in chemistry
matriarch (máytri-aark) *n.* woman who rules, leads, or dominates, specifically one who heads her family and their descendants — **-archal** *adj.* — **-archy** *n.*
matriculate *v.* to enrol as a member of a university or similar institution — **-lation**, **-lant**
matrilineal *adj.* relating or referring to descent traced through the mother rather than the father. Compare PATRILINEAL
matrimonial *formal.* *adj.* relating to marriage — **-mony** *n.*
matrix (máy-triks) *n.*, *pl.* **-ices** or **-ixes** context, network, or environment in which something develops; cell tissue from which nails and teeth develop; substance in which something, such as a fossil or a tissue cell, is embedded; cement or other binding agent; chief metal in an alloy; plate or mould used in printing; array of elements, as in mathematics, that can itself be treated as a single element
mattock *n.* hoe-like digging tool, as for farming or gardening
matutinal *formal.* *adj.* relating to the morning
matzo *n.*, *pl.* **-zos**, **-zoth**, or **-zot** unleavened bread of the sort eaten by Jews during the Passover (also "matzoh")
maudlin *adj.* weepily sentimental [after *Maudlin*, Mary *Magdalene*, the repentant prostitute who became a follower of Jesus, often represented in paintings as weeping]
maul *n.* long heavy hammer for driving in stakes or pegs
maunder *intr.v.* to wander slowly and aimlessly; to speak incoherently and ramblingly
mausoleum *n.*, *pl.* **-leums** or **-lea** large and impressive tomb; building with places for the bodies or ashes of several dead people to be interred above ground; large gloomy funereal building [from Greek, originally, the tomb of *Mausolos*, a 4th-century B.C. ruler in Asia Minor
mauvais quart d'heure (mṓ-vay kaar dér, dốr) *formal.* *n.* nasty or nerve-racking brief experience [French, literally, bad quarter of an hour]
maverick *informal.* *n.* person reluctant to join a group; group member who cannot be counted on automatically to support the group [after Samuel A. *Maverick*, a 19th-century Texas rancher who refused to brand his calves] — **maverick** *adj.*
maw *n.* stomach, mouth, jaws, or gullet of an insatiable, ravenous, or predatory eater; something, such as a hole or gap, that appears bottomless or threatening
mawkish *adj.* vulgarly sentimental
maxim *n.* general or fundamental principle; concise, pointed statement
mayhem *n.* utter confusion or disorder, havoc [related to *maim*]
mea culpa (máy-ə kŏŏl-pə) *interj.* my fault (used to acknowledge that the speaker or writer has been at fault) [Latin]
meander *intr.v.* to follow a winding course without apparent purpose ~ *n.* winding route; bend in a river [after the winding river *Maeander* in Turkey]
meatus (mi-áytəss) *formal.* *n.*, *pl.* **-tuses** or **meatus** passage or opening in the body, such as the opening of the ear
mecca *n.* place where people wish to go to because it is the high point of a journey or the most important centre of an activity [after *Mecca*, the holiest city of Islam and a goal for pilgrims]
meconium *formal.* *n.* dark greenish mass of excrement that accumulates in the bowel of a foetus and comes out soon after birth
medial *formal.* *adj.* in, into, or towards the middle
median *n.* the value in an ordered set of values above which and below which there are an equal number of values (compare "mode"); line from an angle of a triangle to the middle of the side opposite the angle — **median** *adj.*
mediate *v.* to settle (a dispute) by reconciling opposed parties; to bring about (a settlement) by mediating; to be a means or agency for the creation, production, or transmission of — **-ator**, **-ation** *n.*
medicament *formal.* *n.* medicine
mediocre *adj.* average or below average in quality — **-crity** *n.*
meditation *n.* concentration of the mind on one point, idea, or the like, for the sake of spiritual development or mental health; serious and sustained thought on a specified subject; thoughtful essay, sermon, or the like — **-tate** *v.* — **-tative** *adj.*
medium *n.* person reputedly able to communicate with the spirits of the dead, as in a seance
medley *n.* mixture, assortment; specifically, series of short pieces of music, typically popular, played in succession without pauses; swimming race in which the four main strokes are swum in succession
medulla *n.*, *pl.* **-las** or **-lae** pith of a plant part; marrow of a bone — **-ry** *adj.*
meerschaum (méer-shəm, -showm) *n.* hard white mineral; pipe made from meerschaum [German, literally, sea foam, loan translation of a Persian

term, referring to its frothy appearance]

meet *formal or archaic. adj.* appropriate or suitable

megalith *n.* large standing stone of the sort used in prehistoric monuments such as Stonehenge — **-ic** *adj.*

megalomania *n.* delusions of grandeur or power — **-maniac** *n., adj.*

megalopolis *n.* city that is very large or too large

megaton *n.* explosive force of 1,000,000 tons of TNT

meistersinger (mī́-stər-sing-ər, -zing-) *n., pl.* **-er** or **-ers** member of any of various German guilds, especially of the 15th and 16th centuries, formed to promote music and poetry [German, literally, master singer]

melancholia *archaic. n.* psychological depression

mélange (may-lóNzh) *n.* mixture, especially an unsuitable or confused one [French]

melanin (méllə-nin) *n.* dark natural pigment, as in the hair or skin

melanosis *n.* abnormally dark pigmentation, as caused by sunburn or disease — **-notic** *adj.*

Melba toast *n.* very thin crisp toast [after Dame Nellie *Melba*, the 19th-20th-century Australian soprano]

mêlée (méllay) *n.* confused, disorderly throng, struggle, or fight (also "melee") [French, a mixture]

meliorate *formal. v.* to improve, ameliorate — **-ration** *n.*

mellifluous *adj.* having a smooth, sweet, rich flow of sound

melodrama *n.* drama with exaggeratedly sensational or romantic content; over-emotional behaviour — **-matic** *adj.* — **-matics** *pl.n.*

memento *n., pl.* **-tos** or **-toes** reminder of a person or past event

memento mori *n., pl.* **memente mori** reminder, such as a skull, of inescapable death [Latin, literally, remember you must die]

memoirs *pl.n.* account, usually personal, of past events

memorabilia *pl.n.* things that are worth remembering or that keep a memory alive

memsahib (mém-saab) *n.* European woman in India, especially the wife of a British official during the Raj

ménage (may-naázh) *formal. n., pl.* **-s** household (also "menage") [French]

ménage à trois (aa trwaá) *n., pl.* **ménages à trois** sexual relationship involving three people, especially when all three live together [French, household of three]

menagerie (mi-nájəri) *n.* collection or enclosure of wild animals for exhibition, small zoo

menarche (me-nárki, ménnarki) *formal. n.* first menstruation

mendacious *formal. adj.* lying, dishonest; untrue, false — **-dacity** *n.*

mendicant *formal. n.* beggar; mendicant friar — **mendicant** *adj.* — **-cancy** *n.*

mendicant friar *n.* friar, such as a Franciscan, belonging to a religious order that originally owned no property (also "mendicant")

menhir (mén-heer) *n.* prehistoric monument in the form of a single upright standing stone. Compare DOLMEN

menial *adj.* referring to a lowly domestic servant or to his low-status manual work — **menial** *n.*

meniscus *n., pl.* **-ci** or **-cuses** concavo-convex lens; crescent-shaped object or design; curved upper surface of liquid held in a tube or container

menopause *n.* ceasing of menstruation that occurs naturally after a certain age (also "climacteric", *informal* "change of life") — **-sal** *adj.*

menses *formal. pl.n.* flow of blood and other organic matter during menstruation

mens rea (ménz reé-ə, ráy-) *n.* in law, criminal intent [Latin, literally, guilty mind]

mensuration *formal. n.* measurement; geometry used in making measurements — **-sural** *adj.*

mental *formal. adj.* relating to the chin (also "genial")

mentor *formal. n.* teacher or wise adviser [after *Mentor*, who in Greek mythology was Odysseus' trusted counsellor]

mephitis (me-fī́tiss) *formal. n.* foul smell, as of rotting organic matter — **-tic** *adj.*

mercantile *formal. adj.* relating to trade and commerce

mercenary *adj.* motivated merely by the desire of economic gain, venal, money-minded

mercer *British. n.* dealer in textiles and fabrics, especially those of high price and quality — **-cery** *n.*

mercerise *tr.v.* to strengthen and improve (cotton thread) by chemical treatment [after John *Mercer*, an 18th-19th-century English textile-maker]

mercurial *adj.* marked by frequent, unpredictable, and extreme changes of mood [after the Roman god *Mercury*, who served as messenger to the other gods and was renowned for his fast travel]

meretricious *formal. adj.* vulgarly, superficially, or deceitfully attractive; insincere, affected [from Latin *meretrix*, a prostitute]

meridian *n.* imaginary half-circle joining the poles on the Earth's surface; line of longitude; high point of achievement, pinnacle, zenith

mesa (máy-sə) *n.* flat-topped and steep-sided hill or upland, as in the southwestern USA

mésalliance (may-zál-i-ənss) *formal. n.* marriage to a person from a lower class [French]

mesmerise *tr.v.* to rivet the attention of, enthral; to hypnotise [after Franz Anton *Mesmer*, an 18th-19th-century German doctor who pioneered hypnotism] — **-ism** *n.*

mesomorph *n.* person with a broad, powerful, muscular body build. Compare ECTOMORPH, ENDOMORPH — **-morphic** *adj.*

messianic (méssī-ánnik, méssi-) *adj.* relating to the Messiah; relating to a messiah; relating or referring to quasi-religious zeal and fervour inspired by desire to attain an ideal [from Greek *Messias*, the Messiah, from Hebrew *mashiaḥ*, the anointed] — **-nism** *n.*

mestizo (me-steé-zō) *n., pl.* **-zos** or **zoes** Latin American man of mixed European and American Indian descent (feminine form "mestiza")

metabolism *n.* in biology, all the life-sustaining chemical processes in an organism — **-olic** *adj.* — **-olise** *v.*

metallurgy *n.* scientific study of metals; technology of metals — **-gist** *n.* — **-lurgic**, **-ical** *adj.*

metamorphosis *n., pl.* **-ses** striking or complete change or transformation; change from one stage of development to others in the life cycle of an organism, as when a caterpillar changes into a butterfly — **-phic** *adj.* — **-phose** *intr.v.*

metaphor *n.* figure of speech involving an indirect comparison, as in *She sailed into the room.* Compare SIMILE — **-phoric** *adj.*

metaphysics *n.* branch of philosophy concerned with first principles and ultimate reality; subtle or specula-

tive philosophy of any kind — **-physician** *n.* — **-sical** *adj.*

metastasis (me-táss-tə-sis) *n., pl.* **-ses** spread of a disease, especially cancer, from one part of the body to another — **-static** *adj.* — **-tasise** *intr.v.*

metathesis (mi-táthə-sis) *n., pl.* **-ses** transposition or switching of parts or sounds, within a word, as when *pretty* becomes *purty* — **-thetic** *adj.* — **-thesise** *v.*

metempsychosis *formal. n.* passing of a soul after death into another body or cycle of existence, transmigration of souls

meteorology *n.* study of atmospheric phenomena; specifically, study and forecasting of the weather — **-gist** *n.* — **-logical** *adj.*

metheglin (me-théglin) *n.* alcoholic drink fermented from honey, mead; especially, spiced mead [Welsh, related to *medicine*]

methuselah (mi-théw-zə-lə) *n.* extremely old man; champagne bottle of eight times the normal capacity [after *Methuselah*, a biblical patriarch said to have lived for 969 years: Genesis 5:27]

meticulous *adj.* very careful and precise: *explained everything in meticulous detail*; excessively tidy, fussy about details

métier (máyti-ay) *n.* activity for which someone is especially suited or in which he is especially interested

métis (may-te̋ess, -te̋e) *n., pl.* **métis** person of mixed French Canadian and American Indian ancestry (feminine form "metisse")

metonymy *n.* figure of speech in which something is referred to by the name of something else associated with it, as when a cricketer is referred to as a *good bat.* Compare SYNECDOCHE — **-mical** *adj.*

metopic (mi-tóppik) *formal. adj.* relating to the forehead

metronome *n.* instrument used to mark a steady rhythmical beat, especially when practising music — **-nomic** *adj.*

metropolis *n.* chief city, or very large and important city — **-politan** *adj.*

metropolitan *n.* bishop or archbishop with authority over other bishops or over a major ecclesiastical district

meunière (mən-yáir) *adj.* coated lightly with flour, sautéed in butter, and served typically with a lemon-and-butter sauce: *sole meunière* [French *(à la) meunière*, (in the manner of the) miller's wife]

mezzanine (mét-sə-neen, -ne̋en) *n.* storey of a building lying between ground floor and first floor, or between two other storeys (also "entresol"); *British.* floor under the stage of a theatre; *U.S.* lowest balcony in a theatre or its first few rows of seats

miasma (mi-ázmə) *n.* swampy vapour once considered a cause of disease; *formal.* unhealthy atmosphere or influence — **-mal**, **-mic** *adj.*

mica (mī́kə) *n.* shiny flaky mineral

micawber *informal. n.* incurable optimist who does little to better himself [after Wilkins *Micawber*, a character in Dickens's novel *David Copperfield*]

Mickey Finn *slang. n.* alcoholic drink laced with knockout drops or some other disabling substance

microcosm *n.* system or item reflecting the same general structure as a larger system of which it is a part: *The classroom is a microcosm of society as a whole.* Compare MACROCOSM

microfiche (mī́krō-feesh) *n.* sheet of microfilm used for storing information, such as printed matter (also "fiche")

micrometer (mī-krómmitər) *n.* measuring instrument for tiny widths or distances

micturate *formal. intr.v.* to urinate — **-ation** *n.*

midden *n.* rubbish heap or dunghill

mien (me̋en) *formal. n.* appearance and expression, especially of the face; general bearing and behaviour

mil *n.* unit of measure of the diameter of wire, equal to one thousandth of an inch

milch cow *n.* cow that yields milk for human use; *informal.* someone or something taken for granted as an unfailing source of easy money or help

milieu (me̋el-yer, meel-yő) *formal. n., pl.* **-s** or **-x** environment, surroundings [French]

militant *adj.* aggressively supporting a cause, as a political activist would be — **militant**, **-tancy** *n.*

militate *formal. intr.v.* to be evidence or a factor: *conditions militating against recovery*

millefeuille (me̋el-fő-i) *adj.* referring to puff pastry that comes in very thin flaky layers ~ *n.* type of patisserie consisting of layers of millefeuille pastry with jam and custard or cream between them [French, literally, thousand-leaf]

millenarian *adj.* relating to the biblical millennium; relating to the millennium as a golden age — **-ianism** *n.*

millennial *adj.* relating to a millennium as a period of 1000 years or a 1000th anniversary; *formal.* very old: *millennial forests*

millennium *n., pl.* **-ums** or **-ia** period of 1000 years; according to the bible, millennium of Christ's righteous and holy reign on Earth after Armageddon and His Second Coming; golden age envisaged in the future rather than the past; 1000th anniversary of something

milliner *n.* maker or seller of women's hats [variant of obsolete *Milaner*, importer of women's clothes from *Milan*] — **-nery** *n.*

milling *n.* ridges round the edge of a coin

milt *n.* spleen-like organ of a bird or animal; fish sperm and seminal fluid; reproductive glands of male fish when filled with milt

mimeograph *n.* duplicating machine producing copies from a waxed stencil fitted to an inked drum; such a copy — **mimeograph** *v.*

mimesis (mi-me̋e-siss, mī-) *n., pl.* **-ses** representation or imitation of reality in literature and art; imitation or mimicry, as by animals for protection, or by hysterical patients — **-metic** *adj.*

minaret *n.* tower associated with a mosque, from which the muezzin summons the faithful to prayer

miniature *n.* painting that is very small, yet detailed; manuscript illumination, especially in the form of a picture

minim *n.* musical note equal to half a semibreve; downward stroke of the pen in handwriting

minion *formal. n.* favourite, darling; follower or companion who is too eager to please, sycophant; subordinate employee in a big, typically bureaucratic, organisation [French, *mignon*, darling]

ministrations *formal. pl.n.* acts of service or assistance — **minister** *intr.v.*

minium *n.* red lead, a type of lead oxide, used as a paint pigment and having various industrial uses

minster *n.* monastery church; any of various British abbeys or cathedrals: *York Minster*

minuend *n.* in subtraction, the number from which the subtrahend is to be subtracted

minuscule *adj.* very small; *formal.* relating or referring to a lower-case letter. Compare MAJUSCULE; relating or referring to a style of ancient and medieval handwriting ~ *n.* minuscule letter or handwriting

minute *n.* memorandum, especially of an official nature

minutiae (mī-néw-shi-ee) *formal. pl.n.* precise details including even minor points

mirabile dictu (mi-ráabili dík-tōō) *formal. adv.* wonderful to relate, strange to say [Latin]

mirador (mírrə-dawr) *n.* balcony, window, or tower offering a wide view

MIRV (murv) *adj.* referring or relating to a missile system in which a single rocket launches several warheads that can be directed to different targets [*M*ultiple *I*ndependently targeted *R*e-entry *V*ehicles]

misadventure *n.* in law, a fatal accident not due to negligence or criminal intent

misalliance *n.* bad or unsuitable marriage

misandry (mi-sándri) *n.* dislike of men — **-ist** *n., adj.*

misanthrope (míss'n-thrōp) *formal. n.* person who dislikes people in general (also "misanthropist") — **-thropy** *n.* — **-thropic** *adj.*

misapprehension *n.* incorrect assumption, misunderstanding

misappropriate *tr.v.* to take and use (funds or other resources) for one's own purposes without the right to do so — **-ation** *n.*

misbegotten *adj. formal.* born out of wedlock, illegitimate; ill-conceived, mistaken: *misbegotten ideas*; *informal.* contemptible, despicable

miscegenation (míssigi-náysh'n) *n.* marriage, sexual relations, or interbreeding between people of different races

miscellaneous *adj.* relating or referring to a mixture of quite different things

miscellany (mi-séllәni) *formal. n.* miscellaneous collection; specifically, a miscellany of writings on diverse subjects — **-anist** *n.*

misconstrue *formal. tr.v.* to misinterpret

miscreant *formal. n.* wrongdoer

misdemeanour *n.* formerly, a relatively minor illegal act; *archaic.* misdeed: *impeached for high crimes and misdemeanours*

mise en scène (meéz-on-sáyn) *n., pl.* **mise en scènes** stage setting of a play [French, literally, placing on stage]

misericord (mi-zérri-kawrd) *formal. n.* something, such as a carved figure, that projects from the underside of a hinged seat in a church pew so that people can lean on it when the seat is raised and they are standing

misnomer *formal. n.* incorrect or inappropriate name or description; use of a misnomer

misogyny (mi-sójәni) *n.* dislike of women — **-nist** *n., adj.* — **-nistic** *adj.*

missal *n.* prayer book, specifically one for the Roman Catholic Mass

missive *formal. n.* letter or other written message (often used humorously)

mithridate *n.* supposed antidote against all poisons

mithridatism *n.* immunity to poison, gained by taking gradually increasing doses of it [after *Mithridates* VI, a 1st-century B.C. king in Asia Minor, who reputedly developed immunity in this way]

mitigate *tr.v.* to lessen the severity of (pain, anger, or the like); to make (a crime) seem less serious or blameworthy, and therefore deserving of a lighter punishment: *mitigating circumstances* — **-tion** *n.*

mitre (mītәr) *n.* pointed ceremonial hat of a bishop or abbot — **mitred** *adj.*

mnemonic (ni-mónnik) *formal. adj.* relating to memory ~ *n.* aid to memory, often a jingle or mental picture, such as the rhyme beginning *Thirty days hath September*

Möbius strip *n.* one-sided surface made by forming a twisted strip into a ring, an interesting phenomenon in geometry [after its inventor August *Möbius*, an 18th-19th-century German mathematician]

mocha (móckә) *n.* Arabian coffee of high quality; broadly, coffee of high quality; flavouring made with coffee, often mixed with chocolate or cocoa; dark olive brown colour [originally exported from *Mocha*, a port now in Yemen]

modal *adj.* relating or referring to assessments of possibility, contingency, or necessity, typically by contrast with simple factuality: *modal logic* ~ *n.* verb, such as *must*, *will*, or *can*, that can precede another verb, as in *must go*, and expresses mood or tense (also "modal auxiliary", "modal verb")

modality *n.* quality or state of being modal; any of the senses, such as sight or hearing, considered as means of perceiving reality; *formal.* way of doing something, mode, especially a mode of therapy

mode *n.* method, fashion, or style; musical scale such as major or minor; norm, number or value that occurs most often in a numerical list. Compare MEDIAN

modem *n.* device to convert signals from one form into another for transmitting, especially a telephone link between computers [*mo*dulator *dem*odulator]

moderator *n.* chairman or presiding officer of a meeting; specifically, one who presides over an assembly of a Free Church (also "Moderator"); graphite, heavy water, or other material in the core of a nuclear reactor, used to slow down fast neutrons and promote fission

modicum (móddi-kәm) *formal. n., pl.* **-cums** or **-ca** small amount: *without even a modicum of sense*

modifier *n.* expression, such as an adjective, that specifies or restricts the meaning of another — **modify** *tr.v.*

modiste (mō-deést) *formal. n.* producer, designer, or seller of fashionable women's clothing [French]

modulate *v.* — *tr.* to adjust the pitch or tone of (one's voice); to cause (music) to pass from one key or scale to another; to adapt or regulate carefully or slightly, temper — *intr.* to modulate something or be modulated — **-lation** *n.*

module *n.* ready-made standard unit used in constructing something such as a building or furniture; ready-assembled set of electronic components for use in combination with other such sets; relatively self-contained unit of course-work or instruction that can be combined with other such units to form a more complete course — **-ular** *adj.*

modus operandi *n.* way of operating or working, characteristic procedure [Latin]

modus vivendi *n.* way of living; way of living together, especially one based on compromise [Latin]

[1]**mogul** *n. informal.* very influential person, usually also rich; steam locomotive with six driving wheels and two leading wheels [after the *Moguls*, the people

of a Muslim empire in India between the 16th and 19th centuries]
2mogul *n.* small mound of packed snow formed on a ski slope
Mohs scale *n.* scale of the hardness of minerals based on resistance to scratching [after Friedrich *Mohs*, the 18th-19th-century German mineralogist who devised it]
moiety (móy-əti) *formal or archaic. n.* part or portion of something, especially half
moiré (mwáa-ray) *n.* wavy pattern produced by superimposing one pattern on another; watered, shiny pattern or finish pressed on to a fabric by heated rollers (also "water") cloth, especially silk, decorated with this finish [related to *mohair*] — **moiré** *adj.*
mole *n.* stone breakwater or jetty protecting a harbour; harbour protected in this way
molest *tr.v.* to annoy or torment, harass; to harass sexually — **-tation** *n.*
mollify *tr.v.* to soothe the (hurt or angry feelings) of (a person)
mollusc *n.* soft-bodied, shell-covered animal such as a snail or oyster. Compare CRUSTACEAN
Molotov cocktail *n.* petrol bomb, typically a bottle filled with petrol and ignited by setting light to a wick just before throwing [after V.M. *Molotov*, the 20th-century Soviet politician]
momentous *adj.* of great importance, very significant in influence or consequences — **moment** *n.*
momentum *n.* force of continuing movement (also "impetus"); driving power, force, or strength: *The campaign gathered momentum*
Monégasque (mónni-gask, mónnay-) *n.* person born or living in Monaco — **Monégasque** *adj.*
monetarism *n.* economic theory or practices based on the advantages of government control of the supply of money in circulation — **-ist** *adj.*, *n.*
moniker (mónnikər) *informal. n.* person's name or nickname
monition *formal. n.* warning of danger; advice; mild criticism or rebuke — **-nitory** *adj.*
monochrome *adj.* relating to a single colour or its shades; referring or relating to a black-and-white television set or photograph — **monochrome** *n.* — **-matic** *adj.*
monocoque (món-ə-kok, -ō-) *n.* design, as of an aircraft fuselage or car body, in which the stress is taken mainly by the outer casing; design, as of a racing car, in which body and chassis are fused into a single casing
monocular *adj.* relating to the use of one eye rather than two: *monocular vision*. Compare BINOCULAR
monogamy *n.* system of marriage, as in Europe, that limits a person to only one husband or wife at any one time. Compare BIGAMY, POLYGAMY; practice of certain animals to have only one mate — **-mous** *adj.*
monogram *n.* design, as for an emblem, based on a letter or letters, often part of a name
monograph *n.* learned treatise, such as a short book or a long article, on a single subject
monolingual *adj.* knowing or involving only one language (also "unilingual") ~ *n.* monolingual person
monolith *n.* large, usually upright, stone block, typically in prehistoric monuments; something, such as a structure or an organisation, that resembles a monolith in being huge, uniform, powerful, impersonal, and unbudgeable — **-lithic** *adj.*
monologue *n.* long speech by an actor, soliloquy; lengthy and often boring talk by one person; conversation monopolised by one speaker
monomania *n.* obsession with a single idea or subject — **-niac** *adj.*, *n.*
mononucleosis *chiefly U.S. n.* glandular fever
monorail *n.* railway system, often elevated, in which the trains use one single track; rail or train of a monorail — **monorail** *adj.*
monosodium glutamate *n.* crystalline salt used as a food additive to enhance flavour (abbreviation "MSG")
monosyllable *n.* word or utterance of one syllable — **-labic** *adj.*
monotheism *n.* belief in only one God. Compare POLYTHEISM
monotreme *n.* egg-laying mammal such as the duck-billed platypus or the echidna
Monotype *trademark. n.* typesetting machine in which each letter is cast separately from hot metal. Compare LINOTYPE
monozygotic twins *formal. pl.n.* identical twins
monsoon *n.* weather system that produces alternate rainy and dry seasons in India and southeast Asia; periodic wind associated with the monsoon; heavy rainfall associated with the monsoon — **-soonal** *adj.*
monstrance *n.* vessel for exhibiting the consecrated Host, as during a Roman Catholic Mass
montage (mon-táazh) *formal. n.* picture, design, or filmed sequence made up of juxtaposed pictures, designs, objects, or sequences; process or use of montage [French, literally, mounting]
Montessori method (mónti-sáwri) *n.* educational technique for young children based on learning through play-like activities and on encouraging self-expression and initiative [after Maria *Montessori*, the 20th-century Italian educationalist]
Moon type *n.* reading or printing system for the blind that uses raised letters. Compare BRAILLE [after William *Moon*, a 19th-century British inventor]
moot *n.* meeting or assembly of the freemen of a shire, especially in Anglo-Saxon times; debate or mock court case conducted by law students as a training exercise ~ *tr.v.* to suggest or bring up for discussion: *mooting a new strategy* ~ *adj.* still in dispute or open to discussion: *a moot point*
morass (mə-ráss) *n.* marsh, bog, swamp; disorderly or puzzling situation through which progress is difficult [akin to *marsh*]
moratorium (mórrə-táwri-əm) *n.* officially approved suspension or delay, as of payment of a debt
morbid *adj. formal.* relating to disease; psychologically unwholesome, obsessively gloomy; preoccupied or fascinated by death or pain — **-bidity** *n.*
mordant *adj.* referring or relating to wit or criticism that is biting and effective in damaging or deflating its object ~ *n.* chemical substance used as a fixative for dyeing; acid or similar substance used in etching — **-dancy** *n.*
mores (máwreez) *pl.n.* customs, habits, or conventions of a social group, especially those regulating moral conduct
morganatic marriage *n.* marriage between a noble and a commoner in which the commoner is not ennobled and their children do not succeed to the title or property rights of the noble parent
morgue *n. chiefly U.S.* mortuary; *informal.* collection

of archives, reference material, past issues, and cuttings in the offices of a newspaper or magazine

moribund *formal. adj.* on the brink of death, about to die; likely to be terminated without being completed: *a moribund project*

morose *adj.* sullen, glum, gloomy, ill-tempered

morpheme *n.* smallest meaningful unit of a language, whether a word or part of a word such as the *-est* of *smallest* — **-phemic** *adj.*

Morpheus *formal. n.* sleep personified: *fell gratefully into the arms of Morpheus* [after *Morpheus*, the Greek god of sleep and dreams]

morphology *n.* form or structure, or the study of it; especially, patterning and structure of vocabulary — **-ological** *adj.*

morris column *British. n.* cylindrical pillar for the public display of advertisements or announcements

mortal sin *n.* deadly sin, grave sin that deprives the soul of God's grace. Compare VENIAL SIN

mortarboard *n.* academic cap topped with a flat square, usually black and tasselled (also "trencher cap")

mortician *U.S. n.* funeral director, undertaker

mortify *v.* — *tr.* to subdue or dominate (the body or its appetites) by self-denial or self-inflicted discomfort; to cause extreme embarrassment to — *intr.* to become mortified — **-fication** *n.*

mortise *n.* hole or indentation, especially a rectangular slot in a piece of wood, made to receive the end of another part to form a joint. Compare TENON; hole cut in a printing plate to accommodate type or another plate

mortmain (mórt-mayn) *formal. n.* right, as of ownership, that cannot be transferred or sold (also "dead hand") [Old French, literally, dead hand]

mortuary *adj. formal.* relating to the dead, and especially to their burial ~ *n.* place where dead bodies are kept either prior to identification and arrangements for their disposal, or until the funeral is held

moshav (mō-shaáv) *n., pl.* **-vim** cooperative settlement in Israel, consisting of a group of small farms. Compare KIBBUTZ

mot (mō) *n.* cleverly appropriate or pithy, witty remark [French, literally, word]

motet *n.* polyphonic choral composition on a religious text, typically without instrumental accompaniment

motif (mō-teéf) *n.* phrase, design, or thematic element repeated or developed in a work of music, art, or literature

motile *formal. adj.* mobile or able to move under one's own power: *a motile micro-organism* — **-tility** *n.*

mot juste (mṓ zhǘst) *n., pl.* **-s -s** word or verbal expression that is exactly appropriate [French, literally, exact word]

motley *adj.* of many colours; of many disparate elements or ingredients ~ *n.* jester's multicoloured clothing; motley mixture or collection

motte (mot) *n.* mound on which a fort or castle is sited [related to *moat*]

moue (mo͞o) *n.* sulky expression, pout

moulage (mo͞olaázh) *n.* mould made from a mark, such as a footprint, or an object and used as evidence, especially in a court; process of taking a moulage [French, related to *mould*]

mount *n.* in palmistry, any of the seven fleshy pads on the palm of the hand

mountebank (mównti-bangk) *formal. n.* person who uses unscrupulous and self-publicising methods, especially to sell something; charlatan or fraudster

moxibustion *n.* burning of a herbal mixture at one or more selected points, such as acupuncture points, on the skin, held to be a treatment for some diseases

mucilage (méwssi-lij) *n.* gum obtained from some plants such as seaweeds; sticky substance used as glue [related to *mucus*] — **-laginous** *adj.*

muezzin (mo͞o-ézzin) *n.* Muslim whose role is to summon the faithful to prayer by public invitation five times a day, typically from the minaret of a mosque

¹mufti *n.* expert in Islamic religious law

²mufti *n.* civilian clothing by contrast with a uniform

mugwump *archaic. informal. n.* politician not aligned, or no longer aligned, with a political party; specifically, such a politician in the U.S.

mukluk (múk-luk) *n.* Eskimo boot of sealskin or reindeer hide; boot resembling a mukluk and big enough to be worn over thick socks

mulatto (mə-láttō) *n., pl.* **-tos** or **-toes** person of mixed white and black descent, specifically person with one white and one black parent — **mulatto** *adj.*

mulch *n.* covering of peat or compost spread on the ground or round plants for protection or as fertiliser — **mulch** *tr.v.*

mulct *formal or archaic. n.* fine, or a similar penalty ~ *tr.v.* to impose a mulct on; *informal.* to swindle

mule *n.* machine for making yarn or thread from fibre (also "spinning mule")

muliebrity (méwli-ébbrəti) *formal. n.* womanhood; womanliness

mullah (mo͝ollə, múllə) *n.* Muslim religious teacher or leader (sometimes used as a title)

mulligatawny *n.* curry-flavoured meat soup of Anglo-Indian origin

mullion *n.* vertical rib or strip on a window, screen, or rock face — **-ed** *adj.*

multifarious *formal. adj.* very numerous and varied: *multifarious activities*

multilateral *adj.* involving several sides, such as nations or factions, typically with divergent interests: *multilateral disarmament* — **-ism, -ist** *n.*

multipara (mul-típpərə) *formal. n., pl.* **-rae** woman who has given birth at least twice; woman who is giving birth for the second time — **-parous** *adj.*

mumchance *archaic. adj.* silent, not speaking; dumbstruck

mummer *n.* performer in an old-fashioned masque or dumb show, especially one wearing a mask; *informal.* actor or actress

mundane *adj.* relating to or dealing with ordinary, everyday concerns rather than loftier ones — **-danity** *n.*

mung bean *n.* Asian bean producing bean sprouts used in salads and cooking

municipality *n.* self-governing community, especially a town or city — **-pal** *adj.*

munificent *formal. adj.* nobly generous in giving or donating — **-cence** *n.*

munitions *formal. pl.n.*, military equipment, weapons, and ammunition

Munsell scale (múnss'l) *n.* scale for ranking colours based on their hue [after A.H. *Munsell*, the 19th-20th-century U.S. scientist who devised it]

murex *n.* sea creature from which the royal purple dye, Tyrian purple, used to be extracted

murine *formal. adj.* relating to rats or mice, specifically of the common domestic kind

Muscovite *n.* person born or living in Moscow; *archaic or informal.* Russian — **Muscovite** *adj.*

mush (mo͝osh) *intr.v.* to travel across the snow using a dog-drawn sledge ~ *n.* journey across the snow using a dog-drawn sledge [Canadian French, *mouche!*, run!, from French *mouche*, a fly] — **mush** *interj.*

Mussulman (múss'l-mən) *archaic. n., pl.* **-men** or **-mans** Muslim

¹must *n.* grape juice being made into wine; pulp and skins of grapes that have yielded must

²must *n.* mustiness; mould

³must *n.* musth

muster *n.* official list of military or naval personnel in a group (also "muster roll"); any group gathered or collected together; flock of peacocks

musth (must) *n.* rut, or state of sexual excitement in the male of certain animals such as the elephant or camel (also "must")

mutable *formal. adj.* changeable or changing by nature; inconstant, fickle — **-ability** *n.*

mutation *n.* change, alteration, specifically a permanent and inheritable change in genetic structure — **mutate** *v.* — **mutant** *n.*

mutatis mutandis (mew-táatiss mew-tándiss) *adv.* when the necessary changes or adjustments have been made or considered [Latin]

mute *v.* to excrete, as a bird does

mutual *adj.* having or showing the same relationship to each other: *mutual suspicion* — **-ality** *n.*

mutual fund *U.S. n.* unit trust

muzhik *n., pl.* **-zhiks** or **-zhiki** Russian peasant in tsarist times (also "moujik")

mycophile *formal. n.* person who likes mushrooms; specifically, one who goes out looking for wild edible mushrooms

mycosis *n., pl.* **-oses** fungal disease or infection

myopia (mī-ṓ-pi-ə) *formal. n.* defect in eyesight in which distant objects appear blurred, shortsightedness. Compare HYPERMETROPIA; lack of foresight or planning — **-pic** *adj.*

myosotis (mī́-ə-sṓtiss) *n.* forget-me-not, or related plant

myriad (mírri-əd) *formal. n.* very large and varied number of things (often used in the plural: *myriads of flowers*) — **myriad** *adj.*

myrmidon (múrmi-don) *formal. n.* follower or henchman [after the *Myrmidons*, an ancient Greek people, loyal followers of their king Achilles during the Trojan war]

myrrh (mur) *n.* aromatic gum resin used in incense and perfume

mystique *n.* aura of mysterious power or glamour; mystifying aura, perhaps created artificially in order to mislead

mythos (mī́thoss) *n.* value-system and beliefs of a group, especially as expressed in its myths, art, and traditions

N

Naafi (náffi) *British n.* military shop or canteen (also NAAFI) [*N*avy, *A*rmy, and *A*ir *F*orce *I*nstitutes]

nabob (náy-bob) *n.* Mogul governor in India in former times (also "nawab"); *informal.* powerful, rich, or important man

nacre (náy-kər) *formal. n.* mother-of-pearl ~ *adj.* pearly, consisting of or resembling mother-of-pearl — **-creous** *adj.*

nadir (náy-deer) *n. formal.* lowest point, as of one's fortunes or of depression; point in the heavens directly beneath the observer, diametrically opposite the zenith

naevus (néevəss) *formal. n., pl.* **-vi** birthmark, mole, or other skin blemish or growth present from birth

naiad (nī́-ad) *n., pl.* **-ads** or **-ades** water nymph in Greek mythology. Compare DRYAD, NEREID, OREAD; larva of the mayfly or similar insect, living in water

namby-pamby *adj.* feeble or indecisive, spineless; sentimental, prim, or flavourless: *namby-pamby poetry* [after the mocking nickname given to *Ambrose Philips*, a 17th-18th-century English writer of sentimental verse]

¹nap *n.* downy or fuzzy surface of raised fibres, as on velvet

²nap *n.* — **go nap** *informal.* to risk everything on a single bet or chance [from *nap*, a card game named after Napoleon]

napalm (náy-paam) *n.* jellied petrol-based substance used in firebombs and flamethrowers [*na*phthenate + *palm*itic acid] — **napalm** *tr.v.*

naphthalene (náf-thə-leen) *n.* sharp-smelling hydrocarbon substance used in mothballs, dyes, and explosives

nappe (nap) *n.* sheet of water flowing over a weir or dam wall

narcissism *n.* self-love or excessive admiration of oneself [after *Narcissus*, a youth in Greek mythology who pined away for love of his own reflection in a pool] — **-ist** *n.* — **-istic** *adj.*

narcissus *n., pl.* **-si** daffodil or related flower

narcolepsy *n.* illness or condition in which the sufferer is frequently overcome by sudden bouts of deep sleep — **-leptic** *adj., n.*

narcosis *formal. n., pl.* **-ses** drug-induced stupor or unconsciousness

narcotic *n.* drug, often addictive and illegal, that typically dulls the senses or induces a deep sleep — **narcotic** *adj.* — **-tise** *tr.v.*

nasal *adj.* relating to or affected by the nose: *a nasal whine* — **-lise** *tr.v.*

nascent (náss'nt) *formal. adj.* coming into being, about to be born — **-cence** *n.*

nastic (nástik) *formal. adj.* relating or referring to a plant's growth or movement in a particular direction through internal rather than external stimulus

natal (náyt'l) *formal. adj.* relating to birth — **-ity** *n.*

natation *formal. n.* swimming — **-tant, -tatorial** *adj.*

naturalise *v.* to grant or acquire citizenship ~ *tr.v.* to establish (a plant, custom, foreign word, or the like) in a new environment, community, or language

naturism *n.* nudism (old-fashioned) — **-ist** *n., adj.*

navvy *British. informal. n.* labourer, as on a building site [slang shortening of *navigator*, used to describe labourers who built the navigation canals of England in the 18th and 19th centuries]

nawab (nə-waáb) *n.* nabob

Nazirite *n.* Jew in biblical times, committed by vows to a life of purity and austerity: *Samson the Nazarite* (also "Nazarite")

Neapolitan (née-ə-póllitən) *n.* person born or living in Naples — **Neapolitan** *adj.*

neap tide *n.* tide of minimum range, occurring at the first and third quarter of the Moon (opposite "spring tide")

nebula (nébbew-lə) *n., pl.* **-las** or **-lae** cloud of dust or gas in outer space; galaxy other than the Milky Way — **-lar** *adj.*

nebulous *formal. adj.* vague, indistinct, undefined — **-losity** *n.*

necessitous *formal. adj.* needy, poverty-stricken

necrology *n.* list of dead people, especially those who have died recently; *formal.* obituary

necromancy *n.* conjuring up of the spirits of the dead in the hope of predicting or influencing the future — **-mancer** *n.* — **-mantic** *adj.*

necropolis (ne-króppə-liss) *n.* ancient cemetery, typically of a large and elaborate design

nectar *n.* drink of the gods in classical mythology. Compare AMBROSIA; delicious drink; sweet liquid secreted by flowers and gathered by bees for making honey

née (nay) *adv., prep.* born with the surname: *Mrs Browning, née Barrett*; broadly, having had the original or former name: *Ho Chi Minh City, née Saigon* (masculine form sometimes "né") [French, born]

nefarious (ni-fáiri-əss) *formal. adj.* wicked, villainous

negate *tr.v.* to deny, contradict, or nullify — **-tion** *n.* — **-tive** *adj., n., tr.v.*

negligée (néggli-zhay) *n.* light and delicate dressing gown for a woman (also "peignoir") [French, literally, neglected, hence casual]

negligent *adj.* careless, in an easygoing or sometimes criminally irresponsible way; *formal.* neglectful, inattentive: *negligent at her attire* [related to *neglect*] — **-gence** *n.*

negligible *adj.* unimportant, not worth considering, trivial; *a negligible sum of money*

negotiate *v.* to discuss in order to reach agreement ~ *tr.v.* to achieve by negotiating; to sell or transfer ownership of (documents, shares, or the like); to manage to get past: *negotiated the rapids* — **-ation** *n.* — **-able** *adj.*

negritude *formal. n.* black cultural pride or racial self-esteem

nem con *chiefly British. informal. adv.* without any dissenting votes, with nobody contradicting, virtually unanimously [abbreviation of Latin *nemine contradicente*, with nobody opposing]

nemesis (némmə-siss) *n., pl.* **-ses** powerful avenger or agent of destruction; ruin or destruction; justified punishment or retribution for arrogance. Compare HUBRIS [after Nemesis, the goddess of vengeance in Greek mythology]

nenuphar (nénnew-faar) *formal. n.* water lily

neologism (nee-óllə-jiz'm) *n.* newly coined word or expression; use or formation of neologisms — **-gise** *intr.v.* — **-gistic** *adj.*

neophyte *n. formal.* beginner, novice; novice nun or monk

nepenthe (ni-pénthi) *formal. n.* drug, potion, or technique for forgetting pains and sorrows — **-ean** *adj.*

ne plus ultra *formal. n.* high point, furthest possible stage, greatest possible degree [Latin, literally, (sail) no more beyond (this point): the phrase was inscribed, according to legend, on rocks at the Strait of Gibraltar, as a warning to sailors]

nepotism *n.* favouritism, such as political appointments or promotions, shown to relatives or friends by those in positions of power — **-ist** *n.*

nereid (néeri-əd) *n., pl.* **-ads** or **-des** sea nymph in Greek mythology. Compare DRYAD, NAIAD, OREAD

Nestor *n.* wise old man [after Nestor, the wise and aged counsellor in Homer's epics]

nether (néthər) *formal or archaic. adj.* being under or below — **-most** *adj.*

netherworld *formal. n.* world of the dead, underworld

netsuke (nét-sŏoki) *n.* ivory or wooden carved toggle formerly used in Japan to fasten a pouch or other object to a kimono sash

neural *adj.* relating to the nerves or nervous system

neuralgia *n.* pain spasms shooting along the path of a nerve — **-gic** *adj.*

neurasthenia *archaic. n.* nervous breakdown; neurotic weakness or exhaustion — **-nic** *adj., n.*

neurology *n.* medical or scientific study of the nervous system and its disorders — **-gist** *n.* — **-logical** *adj.*

neuter *adj.* sexless, neither male nor female; neither masculine nor feminine in grammatical gender ~ *tr.v.* to castrate or spay [Latin, neither]

newel *n.* central pillar, typically of stone, around which a spiral staircase winds

newel post *n.* post supporting the handrail at either end of a flight of stairs

nexus *n., pl.* **nexus** or **-uses** bond or link among members of a group, set, or series; connecting factor; linked series or group

Nicene creed *n.* creed or profession of faith adopted by various churches for use in their liturgy. Compare ATHANASIAN CREED [formulated at the Council of *Nicaea* in A.D. 325]

nicety *n.* distinction or detail of a fine, subtle kind — **to a nicety** perfectly, with precision

niche (neesh) *n.* recess in a wall, as for a statue; job, position, or activity particularly suited to a person; status or role of a plant or animal within its ecological community

nickelodeon *n.* jukebox or player piano in former times; cinema of an early kind in the U.S. charging five cents — a nickel — for admission

nicker *intr.v.* to neigh or whinny quietly — **nicker** *n.*

nictitate *formal. intr.v.* to wink or blink — **-tation** *n.*

nidicolous (ni-díckələss) *formal. adj.* referring or relating to birds born blind and helpless, and remaining a relatively long time in the nest after hatching

nidifugous (ni-díffew-gəss) *formal. adj.* referring to birds born relatively well-developed, and able to leave the nest shortly after hatching

nidify *formal. intr.v.* to build a nest — **-fication** *n.*

nidus (nídəss) *formal. n., pl.* **-duses** or **-di** nest, as for insect or spider eggs; breeding place of bacteria, focus of an infection; cavity in which plant spores develop

niggard *n.* miser, stingy and grasping person — **-ly** *adj.*

night soil *n.* human excrement, especially for use as a fertiliser (old-fashioned)

nightstick *U.S. n.* policeman's truncheon or club

nihilism (nī́-i-liz'm, ní-hi-) *n.* rejection of all authority and all moral and social values; destructiveness of an unselective, all-embracing kind — **-ist** *n., adj.*

nihil obstat *n.* official approval, as of a book, especially certified approval from a Roman Catholic censor [Latin, nothing hinders]

nimbus *n., pl.* **-bi** or **-buses** halo-like radiance or similar sign of sanctity above or behind the head of God, a saint, or a monarch in art; *formal.* aura or atmosphere, typically romantic or splendid, surrounding a person or thing; rain cloud

nimiety (ni-mī́-əti) *formal. n.* excess or redundancy

Nirvana *n.* goal of Buddhism or Hinduism, when craving ceases, the self is extinguished, and no rebirth takes place; *informal.* carefree state of bliss

Nissen hut *chiefly British. n.* hut-like prefabricated semi-cylindrical shelter of arched corrugated iron sheets [after Peter N. *Nissen*, a 19th-20th-century British engineer]

niveous *formal. adj.* snow-like; snowy

nobiliary particle *formal. n.* preposition such as *von*, *de*, or *of*, accompanying a title or surname and indicating noble rank [related to *noble*]

noble gas *n.* inert gas

noble metal *n.* metal, such as gold or silver, that resists corrosion

noble rot *n.* fungus on grapeskins producing a sweeter grape, as for dessert wines

noblesse oblige (nṓ-bléss ō-bléezh) *formal. n., interj.* obligation on noble or noble-minded people to be generous and honourable [French, literally, nobility obliges]

nock *n.* groove at either end of a bow for holding the string; notch in an arrow into which the bowstring fits

nocturnal *adj.* relating to or occurring during the night; active or open at night: *nocturnal animals/flowers*. Compare DIURNAL

nocturne *n.* painting of a night scene, or short lyrical composition, especially for the piano, suggestive of or suitable for the night

node *n.* knob, knotty projection, swelling; joint or branching point on a stem; point at which lines intersect or diverge; point or region, as on a violin string, of minimum vibration — **nodal, nodose** *adj.*

nogging *n.* brickwork or masonry in a wooden framework; wooden beam running horizontally between two upright posts as a support in the framework of a wall

Noh (nō) *n.* classical Japanese drama, performed with music and dancing in a highly stylised manner on an almost bare stage (also "Nō") [Japanese, literally, skill or talent]

noisette (nwaa-zét, nwə-) *n.* small round piece of meat ~ *adj.* made or flavoured with hazelnuts [French, *noix*, a nut]

noisome *formal. adj.* disgusting, foul: *a noisome stench* [related to *annoy*]

nolens volens *formal. adv.* willy-nilly, whether you like it or not [Latin, not wishing, wishing]

nomad *n.* wanderer; specifically, member of a pastoral people moving about in search of food or grazing land — **-ic** *adj.*

nom de guerre (nóm də gáir, nóɴ) *formal. n.* pseudonym or pen-name [French, literally, war name]

nom de plume (nóm də plóóm, nóɴ, plū́m) *n.* pseudonym or pen-name [French, pen name]

nomenclature (nō-méng-kləchər, nə-) *n.* system of names or terms, such as the standard international system of names for plants or chemicals; terms used in a particular science, art, profession, or the like [Latin, *nomenclator*, literally, name-caller, referring to a slave who would accompany his master, as during election campaigns, to remind him of the names of people he met]

nominal *adj.* relating to a name; theoretical, in name only, not actual; tiny, token, insignificant: *a nominal sum*

nominalism *n.* philosophical theory that only actual individual objects really exist, and that abstract general concepts such as "beauty" or the class "dogs" exist only as names — **-ist** *n., adj.*

nominal value *n.* stated or face value of a bond or share certificate, as distinct from its actual market value

nominate *tr.v.* (nómmi-nayt) to propose or name as a candidate, as for an election or award; to appoint to or recommend for an office, responsibility, or the like; *formal.* to give a name or title to, designate ~ *adj.* (-nət, -nit, -nayt) *formal or archaic.* having a specified name — **-nator, -nation, nominee** *n.*

nominative (nómmi-nətiv, nóm-) *adj.* in grammar, relating or referring to the subject of a verb, such as *They* in *They sent us a letter* — **nominative** *n.*

-nomy *n. comb.form.* -science, -laws, -knowledge: *astronomy*, *economy* [Latin, Greek: *nomos*, a law]

non-aligned *adj.* neutral, not allied with a superpower: *the non-aligned nations*

nonce *n.* — **for the nonce** for the present, for the time being (old-fashioned) [from a mistaken division of the Middle English phrase *for then anes*, for the once]

nonce word *n.* word coined specially for a single occasion and not intended for use anywhere else, as in *the sloeblack ... fishingboat-bobbing sea* from Dylan Thomas's *Under Milk Wood*

nonchalant (nónshələnt) *adj.* appearing unconcerned or coolly indifferent; casual or debonair; apparently easygoing or uninvolved in a way that suggests unconcern or indifference: *a nonchalant greeting that masked her vague anxiety* [French, from Latin *non-*, not + *calere*, to be warm, hence to be concerned; akin to *scalding*]

noncommittal *adj.* avoiding indicating any definite preference or purpose: *a noncommittal reply*

non compos mentis *adj.* of unsound mind, and therefore not responsible for one's actions [Latin, literally, not in control of one's mind]

nondescript *adj.* lacking individual features, uninteresting and therefore hard to describe

nonentity *n.* insignificant person or thing

nonpareil (nón-pə-rəl, -ráyl) *formal. adj.* without a rival, matchless, peerless, unequalled — **nonpareil** *n.*
nonplussed *adj.* confused, perplexed, baffled [Latin *non plus*, no more (can be said)] — **nonplus** *tr.v.*
non-proliferation *n.* limitation of the production or spread of something, especially nuclear weapons
non sequitur (nón sékwi-tər) *n.* conclusion that is wrongly or illogically derived from the argument preceding it; statement or remark having no apparent relevance to what came before it [Latin, it does not follow]
non-U *British. informal. adj.* not appropriate to or characteristic of upper-class behaviour or language usage; vulgarly genteel or pretentious, considered unacceptable by snobs. Compare U
Nordic *adj.* blond and blue-eyed, and typically tall and long-headed in appearance, characteristic of northern Europe; relating to northern Europe and especially to Scandinavia [akin to *north*]
noria (náwri-ə) *n.* irrigation device consisting of a wheel rimmed with buckets that dip into a stream or pool
norm *n.* typical pattern, model of behaviour, standard of acceptability, or the like; average
normative *adj.* implying or setting standards of acceptability, as a strict law or a popular fashion does
Norseman *n., pl.* **-men** Viking
nosegay *formal. n.* small bunch of flowers, posy
nosing *n.* horizontal edge, often rounded, projecting at the front of a stair
nosology (no-sólləji, nō-) *formal. n.* branch of medicine dealing with the classification of diseases — **-gist** *n.* — **-logical** *adj.*
nostalgia *n.* yearning or sentimental longing for something in the past — **-gic** *adj.*
nostrum *n.* patent medicine, especially one boasting secret ingredients; remedy or scheme, as for social problems, typically ill-thought-out or simplistic
notary *n.* clerk or secretary in former times, especially one licensed to draft legal documents — **-arial** *adj.*
notary public *U.S. n.* commissioner for oaths
notation *n.* symbols, figures, or the like used systematically, as in music or mathematics, to represent elements or quantities — **-al** *adj.*
notifiable disease *n.* disease of a serious infectious kind, such as cholera or tuberculosis, that has to be reported to the health authorities when diagnosed
notional *adj.* theoretical or imaginary rather than actual
notorious *adj.* famous for a particular quality or act, typically an unfavourable one — **-riety** *n.*
noumenon (nŏŏmi-non) *formal. n., pl.* **-mena** thing in itself, rather than as it appears to the mind or senses, according to Kantian philosophy (also "Ding an sich"). Compare PHENOMENON — **-menal** *adj.*
nous (nowss) *British. informal. n.* common sense
nouveau riche (nŏŏvō réesh) *n., pl.* **nouveaux riches** person who has recently become rich, especially when living and behaving in a showy but vulgar way [French, literally, new rich]
novena (nō-vée-nə) *n., pl.* **-nae** or **-nas** nine-day devotion undertaken by Roman Catholics
novice *n.* person on probation in a religious order, prior to taking vows; beginner
Novocastrian *formal. n.* person born or living in Newcastle — **Novocastrian** *adj.*
noxious *formal. adj.* harmful, damaging, or corrupting
nuance (néw-ONSS) *n.* distinction or variation of a very fine or subtle kind, as of tone, colour, or meaning
nubile *adj.* sexually attractive (used to describe young women and girls); *archaic.* marriageable (used of women)
nuclear family *n.* family unit consisting of parents and children, and sometimes grandparents
nucleus *n., pl.* **-lei** central or fundamental part around which others are grouped or from which development takes place
nugatory (néwgə-tri) *formal. adj.* insignificant, worthless, trifling; invalid, inoperative, or powerless: *nugatory laws/regulations*
nullify *tr.v.* to make invalid, ineffective, or null and void
numen *formal. n., pl.* **-mina** spirit or divine force seen as guarding a place, inhabiting a natural object, or guiding a person
numeracy *n.* basic skill in arithmetic or competence in number calculations, regarded as the counterpart of literacy — **-rate** *adj.*
numeration *n.* act or system of numbering or counting — **-rate** *tr.v.*
numerator *n.* number above the line in a fraction, dividend. Compare DENOMINATOR
numerical *adj.* relating to numbers or numeration
numerology *n.* study of the mystical influence or significance of numbers — **-gist** *n.* — **-logical** *adj.*
numinous *formal. adj.* mysterious, awe-inspiring; spiritually uplifting; divine, filled with a sense of divine influence or energy — **-nosity** *n.*
numismatics *n.* study or collecting of coins, money, or medals — **-matic** *adj.* — **-matist** *n.*
nuncio (núnsi-ō) *n., pl.* **-os** ambassador from the Pope
nuptial *adj.* relating to the ceremonies or rituals of marriage or mating — **nuptials** *pl.n.*
nurture *n.* training, upbringing; broadly, environment contrasted with heredity: *nature versus nurture* ~ *tr.v.* to nourish, foster, or help to develop: *talent that needs nurturing*
nutrient *n.* nourishing substance, as in food or in the solution absorbed by plant roots — **nutrient** *adj.*
nutriment *formal. n.* something that nourishes or promotes growth or development
nyctalopia *formal. n.* difficulty in seeing in dim light, "night blindness". Compare HEMERALOPIA — **-opic** *adj.*
nymph *n.* minor female spirit in classical mythology; *formal.* beautiful young woman or girl; insect larva, as of the mayfly or dragonfly, that develops directly into the adult without going through the pupal stage
nympholepsy *formal. n.* frenzy of frustrated desire for something unattainable — **-leptic** *adj.*
nymphomania *n.* excessive sexual desire in a woman. Compare SATYRIASIS — **-maniac** *adj., n.*

O

oakum (ṓkəm) *n.* fibre of hemp or jute, often treated with tar, used for sealing pipe joints and waterproofing the seams in wooden ships — **oakum** *adj.*

oast *n.* kiln for drying hops or malt; building housing an oast (in this sense, also "oasthouse")

obdurate *formal. adj.* persistently harsh or hard-hearted, unyielding; stubbornly wicked or uncooperative, impenitent — **-racy** *n.*

obeah (ṓbi-ə) *n.* magic or witchcraft, as practised in the West Indies, or the religious belief incorporating it; charm, fetish, or amulet used in obeah (also "obi") — **obeah** *adj.*

obedientiary *n.* monk or nun holding an office subordinate to the superior [related to *obedient*]

obeisance (ō-báyss'nss) *formal. n.* gesture of respect or submission, such as a bow or curtsy; attitude of respect or homage — **-ant** *adj.*

obelisk (óbbə-lisk) *n.* tapering four-sided stone pillar with a pyramidal top, of a kind used as a monument in ancient Egypt; reference sign, †, typically used to indicate footnotes (in this sense, also "obelus", "dagger")

obese *adj.* extremely fat, grossly overweight — **obesity** *n.*

obfuscate (ób-fəss-kayt) *tr.v.* to confuse or bewilder; to obscure, complicate, make difficult to understand *formal.* to darken, blur, make indistinct or dim — **-cation** *n.*

obi (ṓbi) *n.* wide Japanese sash securing a kimono, tied in a large flat bow at the back

obiit (ṓbi-it) "he (or she) died", formal term used before the date of death of the person specified

obiter dictum (óbbitər díktəm, ṓbitər) *n., pl.* **obiter dicta** incidental comment, made by a judge during a case, that is not directly relevant or binding; remark made in passing, incidental comment [Latin, literally, something said in passing]

obituary (ō-bíttew-əri) *n.* death notice, as in a newspaper, often with a short biography of the deceased — **obituary** *adj.*

objective *adj.* real, actual, existing in the real world independently of the mind; observable by scientific methods or by disinterested outsiders; unprejudiced and uninvolved, uninfluenced by emotion or personal preference, disinterested or impartial. Compare SUBJECTIVE ~ *n.* something striven for, goal, aim, intention — **-tivity**, **-tivism** *n.* — **-tify** *tr.v.*

objet d'art (ób-zhay dár) *n., pl.* **objets d'art** artistically impressive object, usually fairly small [French, literally, object of art]

objet trouvé (ób-zhay trōō-vay, trōō-váy) *n., pl.* **-s -s** artistically impressive object that was not intended as a work of art [French, literally, found object]

[1]**oblate** *adj.* spherical but compressed or flattened at the poles, as the Earth is

[2]**oblate** *n.* layman living a religious life in a monastery but without having taken formal vows

oblation *n.* offering of worship, thanksgiving, an altar gift, or the like — **Oblation** offering to God of the bread and wine of Communion — **-latory** *adj.*

obliged *formal. adj.* grateful, indebted

obliterate *tr.v.* destroy, erase, or get rid of completely — **-tion** *n.*

oblique (ō-bléek) *adj.* sloping, slanting, at an angle; not having or being a right angle; indirect, not straightforward: *oblique insults* — **-quity** *n.*

oblivious *adj.* unaware, unmindful: *oblivious of the danger* — **-vion** *n.*

obloquy (óbbləkwi) *formal. n.* abusive verbal attack or condemnation; disgrace suffered by a victim of such an attack

obnoxious *adj.* extremely unleasant or objectionable

obscurantist *n.* opponent of enlightenment and progress; deliberate mystifier — **-ism** *n.* — **-ist** *adj.*

obscure *adj.* difficult through being vague or cryptic; not obvious; little-known, not famous or prominent; *formal.* dark or gloomy ~ *tr.v.* to make or keep obscure — **-scurity** *n.*

obsequies (óbsi-kweez) *formal. pl.n.* funeral, or funeral rites

obsequious *adj.* over-helpful or over-attentive in a self-demeaning way, servile, fawning

observatory *n.* building housing telescopes for astronomical observation

obsession *n.* fixed idea, preoccupation to the exclusion of everything else (also "idée fixe") — **-sional**, **-sive** *adj.* — **obsess** *tr.v.*

obsolete *adj.* no longer current or in use — **-lescent** *adj.* — **-lesce** *intr.v.* — **-lescence** *n.*

obstetric *adj.* relating to the care of women before, during, and after childbirth — **-rician**, **-rics** *n.*

obstreperous *adj.* noisily rude and rebellious

obtain *formal. intr.v.* to prevail, be customary, continue to exist, be in practice: *Such customs no longer obtain*

obtrude *formal. v.* to force (oneself or one's opinions) on others — **-trusive** *adj.* — **-trusion** *n.*

obtuse *adj.* blunt or rounded at the tip: *an obtuse leaf*; greater than 90° but less than 180°: *an obtuse angle*; slow in perception or understanding, stupid

obverse *adj.* referring to that side of a coin, banknote, medal, stamp, or the like which bears the principal motif, such as the head of a monarch (opposite "reverse"); having a top broader than the base: *an obverse leaf*; serving as a counterpart or complement: *one obverse result of inflation* — **obverse**, **-version** *n.* — **-vert** *v.*

obviate *formal. tr.v.* to make unnecessary: *obviated the need for change* — **-viation** *n.*

ocarina (óckə-réenə) *n.* simple egg-shaped wind instrument with finger holes along the side, as used in Andean folk music [Italian, little goose, referring to its shape]

Occident (óksi-dənt) *n.* Europe and America, and the

West in general. Compare ORIENT — **-tal** *adj.*, *n.*
occlude *formal. tr.v.* to block or obstruct: *an occluded blood vessel* ~ *intr.v.* to become occluded; to come into contact, as upper and lower teeth do — **-clusion** *n.* — **-clusive** *adj.*
occult *adj.* supernatural; relating to witchcraft; mysterious, incomprehensible; known only to the initiated, secret: *occult lore* — **occult**, **-ism** *n.*
occultation *n.* eclipse, or disappearance of a heavenly body during an eclipse — **occult** *v.*
ocellus (ō-séllәss) *n.*, *pl.* **-li** eye of an elementary kind, as in some insects; eye-like marking, as on a peacock's tail
oche (ócki) *n.* line from which a darts player throws darts at the board
ochlocracy (ok-lóckrә-si) *formal. n.* mob rule — **-cratic** *adj.*
ochre (ṓkәr) *n.* orange-yellow; clayey mineral used in pigments — **ochre** *adj.*
Ockham's razor *n.* philosophical principle urging the simplest and most sparing use of terms and assumptions in arguing or explaining something (also "Occam's razor") [after William of *Ockham*, the 14th-century English philosopher]
octane number *n.* measure of the anti-knock properties of petrol (also "octane rating")
octant *n.* forty-five-degree arc
octet *n.* group of eight; eight singers or musicians, or a composition for such a group; first eight lines of a sonnet. Compare SESTET
ocular (óckewlәr) *adj.* relating to the eye or to eyesight
odalisque (ṓdәlisk) *n.* harem concubine or female slave
odious *adj.* hateful, loathsome, offensive
odium *formal. n.* hatred or contempt; disgrace, ill repute
odometer (ō-dómmitәr) *chiefly U.S. n.* mileometer
odorous *adj.* fragrant; smelly
odyssey (óddisi) *formal. n.* long and eventful journey [after Homer's epic, dealing with the wanderings of *Odysseus*, after the Trojan War]
oedema (ee-deémә) *n.*, *pl.* **-mas** or **-mata** swelling caused by a build-up of fluid in the body tissues — **-matous** *adj.*
Oedipus complex (eédi-pәss) *n.* in psychoanalytic theory, unconscious complex of emotions in a young child, including sexual desire for one's parent of the opposite sex (in girls also called "Electra complex") [after *Oedipus* in Greek mythology, who unwittingly killed his father and married his mother] — **Oedipal** *adj.*
oenologist (ee-nóllәjist) *formal. n.* wine expert — **-ology** *n.* — **-logical** *adj.*
oesophagus (ee-sóffә-gәss) *n.*, *pl.* **-phagi** gullet, muscular tube from throat to stomach
oestrogen (eéstrә-jәn) *n.* any of several hormones associated with female behaviour and characteristics
oestrus (eéstrәss) *n.* recurrent period of ovulation and sexual excitement in some female mammals (also "heat", "rut") — **oestrous** *adj.*
oeuvre (ṓv-rә) *formal. n.*, *pl.* **oeuvres** great work of art or literature; works of an artist or writer when viewed as a whole [French, literally, work]
offal *chiefly British. n.* internal organs of an animal, such as liver and kidneys, especially when regarded as edible
officiate *intr.v.* to perform official duties on a formal occasion, as a host or priest would — **-iant** *n.*
officinal (óffi-sī́n'l, o-físsin'l) *formal. adj.* available without prescription, over-the-counter: *officinal medicines*; used in making medicines: *officinal plants* ~ *n.* officinal medicine or plant
officious *adj.* over-attentive, excessively eager to help or advise
offprint *n.* extra copy of a part of a larger printed text, as of an article printed in a journal
ogive (ṓ-jīv) *n.* graph of a frequency distribution in statistics
ogle *v.* to stare or leer at in a lecherous way — **ogle** *n.*
oleaginous (ṓli-ájinәss) *formal. adj.* oily or oil-like
olfactory *formal. adj.* relating to the sense of smell — **-faction** *n.*
oligarchy *n.* government by a small group of people — **oligarch** *n.* — **-archic**, **-archical** *adj.*
ombudsman (óm-bŏŏdz-mәn) *n.*, *pl.* **-men** official who investigates citizens' complaints into government incompetence or unfairness [Swedish]
ominous (ómmi-nәss) *adj.* threatening; being or suggesting a bad omen
omni- *comb. form.* all-: *omnivorous*
omnibus (óm-ni-bәss, -buss) *n.* book assembling many related studies, or varied writings by one author ~ *adj.* including many things, aspects, or examples [Latin, for all]
omnipotent (om-níppә-tәnt) *formal. adj.* all-powerful **-potence** *n.*
omniscient (om-níssi-әnt) *formal. adj.* all-knowing — **-ence** *n.*
omnivorous (om-nívvәrәss) *adj.* devouring or able to consume everything: *omnivorous insects/readers* — **omnivore** *n.*
onager (ónnә-jәr, -gәr) *n.* ass living wild in central Asia; siege engine or giant catapult used in ancient warfare
onanism (ṓ-nan-iz'm) *formal. n.* masturbation [after *Onan*, who "spilled [his seed] on the ground", Genesis 38:9] — **-ist** *n.* — **-istic** *adj.*
oncology *n.* medical or scientific study of tumours or cancer — **-gist** *n.* — **-logical** *adj.*
on dit (óɴ-deé) *formal. n.*, *pl.* **on dits** rumour, piece of gossip [French, literally, it is said]
oneiric (o-nī́rik) *formal. adj.* relating to dreams
oneiromancy (o-nī́rәmansi) *formal. n.* fortune-telling or divination by interpreting dreams — **-mancer** *n.*
onerous (ṓnә-ress, ónnә) *formal. adj.* laborious or burdensome: *onerous tasks*
onomastics *n.* study of the origins of people's names and place names — **-mastic** *adj.*
onomatopoeia (ónnә-máttә-peé-ә) *n.* word that sounds rather like what it refers to, as with *click* or *cackle*; formation or use of such words, as for poetic effect — **-poeic** *adj.*
ontogeny (on-tójәni) *n.* development or evolution of an individual animal or plant. Compare PHYLOGENY — **-genic** *adj.*
ontology *n.* philosophical study of first principles and the nature of being — **-gist** *n.* — **-logical** *adj.*
onus *n.* burden or responsibility: *The onus is on him to apologise*
opalescent *adj.* having a pale rainbow-like shimmer or sheen — **-cence** *n.* — **-lesce** *intr.v.*
opaque (ō-payk) *adj.* not penetrable by or reflecting light, not transparent or even translucent; not pene-

trable by radio waves or other specified form of energy; hard to grasp or understand — **opacity** *n.*

ophidian (ō-fíddi-ən) *formal. adj.* relating to snakes, snake-like

ophthalmic (of-thál-mik) *adj.* relating to the eye and its disorders

ophthalmology *n.* branch of medicine dealing with eye diseases, disorders, and treatments — **-gist** *n.* — **-logical** *adj.*

opiate (ṓpi-ət) *formal. n.* relaxing or sleep-inducing drug or other substance — **opiate** *adj.*

opine *formal. tr.v.* to state as one's opinion; consider (often humorous)

oppidan (óppidən) *formal. n.* town-dweller — **oppidan** *adj.*

opportune *adj.* convenient, occurring at a suitable time; suitable for the purpose, handy

opportunist *n.* person who takes advantage, often unfairly, of an opportunity — **opportunist, -istic** *adj.* — **-ism** *n.*

opposable thumb *n.* thumb, as in humans, that can be placed facing any of the fingers, thus enabling the hand to perform delicate manipulations

opprobrium *formal. n.* strong condemnation and disgust, shocked criticism; disgrace in or from shameful behaviour — **-brious** *adj.*

oppugn (ə-péwn) *formal. tr.v.* to contradict, dispute, or call into question — **-nant** *adj.*

Optic *British. trademark. n.* valved top on an inverted bottle of spirits, as in a pub, that releases an exact tot measure when pressed

optical *adj.* relating to vision or eyesight

optical character recognition *n.* reading of printed text by a machine for conversion to computer data (also "optical scanning")

optical fibre *n.* thin and flexible glass fibre for transmission of light and telecommunications messages, enabling them to be transmitted round corners

optics *n.* scientific study of light and vision — **optic** *adj.*

optimise *tr.v.* to plan or use in the most efficient way possible — **-sation** *n.*

optimum *formal. adj.* best or most favourable possible (also "optimal") — **optimum** *n.*

option *n.* choice; exclusive but temporary right to buy or sell property, shares, or the like — **-al** *adj.*

opulent (óppewlənt) *adj.* luxurious, lavish *formal.* very rich, wealthy — **-lence** *n.*

opus *n., pl.* **opuses** or **opera** musical composition by a particular composer, typically numbered in sequence

oracle (órrək'l) *n.* shrine, priest, or message of a prophetic god; holy of holies, innermost chamber within the Temple in ancient Israel, where the Ark of the Covenant was enshrined; pronouncement that seems prophetic or authoritative but is often mysterious or hard to interpret — **oracular** *adj.*

oracy (áwrə-si, órrə-) *n.* ability to use and understand spoken language (usually contrasted with "literacy") — **orate** *adj.*

oral (áwrəl) *adj.* relating to the mouth; spoken as distinct from written ~ *n.* exam in the form of an interview rather than a written paper

orangery *n.* greenhouse or hothouse; specifically, one used, especially in former times, to grow oranges in northern climates

oratory *n.* public speaking, or the art or style of a public speaker — **-torical** *adj.* — **-orator, oration** *n.* — **orate** *intr.v.*

orb *n.* jewelled sphere or globe with a cross mounted on it, carried or displayed as a symbol of royal power or judgment

orchestrate *tr.v.* to arrange, organise, or construct with some overall effect in mind — **-tion** *n.*

ordain *tr.v.* to confer holy orders or clerical status on; to establish, decree, or order by due authority — **ordination** *n.*

ordeal *n.* extremely difficult and testing experience; method of legal trial in former times, in which the accused underwent dangerous tests, such as ducking or exposure to fire, supposedly to establish God's judgment

order *n.* style of classical architecture based on the type of column used

orderly *n.* soldier assisting a duty officer; hospital attendant

ordinal number *n.* number, such as *4th* rather than *I*, used to indicate position in a series. Compare CARDINAL NUMBER

ordinance *n.* command, order, or regulation issued by an authority

ordinand *n.* priest or clergyman about to be ordained

ordinary *n.* judge or bishop having direct judicial authority; clergyman who visited condemned convicts in the death cell; Mass, especially the part that stays the same from day to day; simple or common heraldic device, such as a cross — **in ordinary** regularly and officially employed by the royal family

ordnance *n.* military weapons, especially heavy guns, ammunition, and related equipment

ordonnance (órdənənss) *formal. n.* arrangement or artistic organisation of the elements in a poem, painting, building plan, or the like

ordure *formal. n.* excrement; something offensive or disgusting [related to *horrid*]

oread *n., pl.* **ads** or **ades** mountain nymph in Greek mythology. Compare DRYAD, NAIAD, NEREID

orectic *formal. adj.* relating to appetites or desires

oriel (áwri-əl) *n.* projecting window, bay window, especially on an upper floor (also "oriel window")

orient *formal. n.* quality of lustre in a pearl; or a high-quality pearl — **-tal** *adj.*

Orient *n.* Asian countries, and the East in general. Compare OCCIDENT — **-tal** *adj., n.* — **-talist** *adj., n.*

orientate *tr.v.* to position or locate in a specified direction, as when building a church to face east; to familiarise, adapt, adjust to new circumstances (also *chiefly U.S.* "orient") — **-tation** *n.*

orienteering *n.* cross-country racing involving the use of a compass and map-reading skills

orifice (órri-fiss) *formal. n.* mouth or other opening in the body (often humorous)

oriflamme (órri-flam) *n.* red national French flag in medieval times; flag or other symbol of encouragement, idealism, or inspiration

origami (órri-gáami) *n.* art or hobby of ornamental paper-folding of Japanese origin

orison (órriz'n) *archaic or formal. n.* prayer

ormolu (ór-mə-lōō) *n.* gold-coloured metal alloy, as used in decorating furniture, clocks, and the like [French *or moulu*, literally, ground gold]

ornate *adj.* highly or excessively decorated; showy, florid

ornithology *n.* scientific study of birds — **-gist** *n.* —

-logical *adj.*
orotund (ó-rōtund) *formal. adj.* deep, full-throated, or loud: pompous, high-falutin [Latin *ore rotundo*, literally, with a rounded mouth] — **-ity** *n.*
orphic *adj.* mystical, occult: *orphic rituals* [after *Orpheus*, a poet and musician in Greek mythology, and reputedly the founder of the ancient mystery cult of Orphism]
orphrey *n.* elaborate embroidery, especially when worked in gold; band of embroidery on church vestments [from Latin *aurum*, gold + *Phrygius*, Phrygian: the ancient kingdom of Phrygia was famous for its embroidery]
orrery (órrəri) *n.* model of the solar system, used in studying astronomy [after Charles Boyle, the fourth Earl of *Orrery*, who commissioned one in the early 18th century]
orthodontist *n.* dentist specialising in correcting the positioning of the teeth or jaws — **-tics** *n.*
orthography (awr-thóggrəfi) *n.* spelling or the study of spelling; writing system, especially one based on an alphabet — **-graphic** *adj.*
orthopaedic surgeon (ór-thə-péedik) *n.* surgeon who specialises in bone and joint disorders — **orthopaedic** *adj.* — **orthopaedics** *n.*
oscillate (óssi-layt) *v.* to swing rhythmically; to vibrate; to move back and forth between one position and another — **-tion** *n.*
oscitant (óssi-tənt) *formal. adj.* yawning; sleepy and inattentive — **-tance**, **-tancy** *n.*
osculate (óskew-layt) *v.* to kiss (humorous) ~ *intr.v.* to touch without crossing, as two curves in geometry might — **-latory** *adj.*
osier (ṓziər) *n.* willow with long twigs used in basket-making; willow twig or twigs collectively — **osier** *adj.*
osmatic *formal. adj.* having or relating to the sense of smell (also "osmic")
osmosis (oz-mṓ-siss) *n.* gradual evening out of differently concentrated solutions by the transfer of dissolved molecules through a separating membrane; gradual spread or acquisition of something through continued exposure to or contact with it rather than through deliberate effort — **osmotic** *adj.* — **osmose** *v.*
osseous *formal. adj.* containing or consisting of bone; bone-like
ossify *v.* to turn to bone; to make or become hard or bony, or rigid and inflexible — **-fication** *n.*
ossuary *n.* container, such as an urn or vault, for the bones of a corpse
osteal *formal. adj.* relating to bone
ostensible *adj.* apparent or declared, but perhaps not true or genuine: *his ostensible reasons*
ostensive *formal. adj.* relating or referring to definition by showing or demonstrating rather than by explaining in words
ostentatious *adj.* showing off in a pushy, irritating, or vulgar manner; vain, pretentious — **-tation** *n.*
osteopathy (osti-óppəthi) *n.* manipulation of bones as a way of treating disease or disorders — **osteopath** *n.* — **-pathic** *adj.*
ostler *n.* stableman, especially one at an inn (also "hostler") [related to *hostel, hotel*]
ostracise *formal. tr.v.* to exclude, banish, or shun [from Greek *ostrakon*, a shell or potsherd, from the practice in ancient Athens of using fragments of pottery when voting for a citizen to be banished] — **-cism** *n.*
otiose (ṓti-ōss, ṓshi-, -ōz) *formal. adj.* useless, purposeless, unnecessary, superfluous — **-osity** *n.*
otorhinolaryngologist (ṓtō-rī́no-lárring-góllәjist) *formal. n.* ENT specialist — **-ology** *n.*
ottoman *n.* upholstered divan without arms or a back
oubliette (o͞obli-ét) *n.* dungeon cell, especially an underground cell with access only through a trapdoor in its ceiling
outlandish *adj.* extremely unconventional or absurd, bizarre
outré (o͞o-tray, o͞o-tráy) *formal. adj.* eccentric, unconventional, extremely unusual [French, literally, taken to excess]
outrigger *n.* float attached by a frame to the side of a canoe to stabilise it; boat with such a stabiliser; projecting, supporting, or stabilising structure attached to a vehicle, building, or machine
ovation *n.* victory parade or ceremony in ancient Rome; prolonged and enthusiastic applause
overt *adj.* open for all to see, observable, aboveboard, not hidden (opposite "covert")
overture *n.* introductory piece of music to an opera, play, or the like; free-standing piece of music resembling an overture; offer, invitation, or similar opening move intended to elicit a response: *made renewed overtures to their rivals*; anything that introduces something else
overweening *formal. adj.* excessive and unjustified: *overweening pride*; arrogant, overbearing
ovine *formal. adj.* relating to or resembling a sheep
oviparous (ō-vípparəss) *formal. adj.* egg-laying, bearing young by means of eggs that hatch outside the body. Compare OVOVIVIPAROUS, VIVIPAROUS
ovipositor *n.* egg-laying tube in most insects and some fish
ovoviviparous (ṓvō-vī-vípparəss) *formal. adj.* egg-laying, bearing young by means of eggs hatching within the female's body, as with some fish and reptiles. Compare OVIPAROUS, VIVIPAROUS
ovulate *intr.v.* to produce an egg cell or ovum
ovum *n.*, *pl.* **ova** unfertilised reproductive cell in female animals, egg cell
oxbow *n.* U-shaped bend in a river; lake formed from such a bend (in this sense, also "oxbow lake", "oxbow cut-off", "mortlake")
Oxonian *formal. adj.* of or from Oxford, or associated with its university (abbreviation "Oxon."). Compare CANTABRIGIAN — **Oxonian** *n.*
oxymoron (óksi-máwron) *n.*, *pl.* **-rons** or **-ra** figure of speech, such as *a friendly foe*, in which apparently contradictory or incongruous terms are linked for effect
oxytocic (óksi-tōsik) *formal. adj.* inducing childbirth: *oxytocic drugs*
oyez (ṓ-yess, ō-yáy) *interj.* listen! (used three times, as to order silence in court, or for a town crier to make an announcement) [Anglo-French]
ozone *n. informal.* fresh, pure air, as at the seaside; oxygen in the form O_3, used in bleaching

P

pabulum (pábbewləm) *formal. n.* food, especially when it is easy to eat and digest; mental fodder of a dull and insipid kind
pace (paá-chay, páy-si) *formal. prep.* despite the views of (used in polite or ironic acknowledgment of someone disagreed with): *Pace Professor Lightbody, the text of 1624 is more reliable than that of 1618.* [Latin, with peace]
pacemaker *n.* heartbeat regulator, either of natural tissue or a small implanted device, based on electrical impulses
pachyderm (pácki-derm) *formal. n.* large thick-skinned four-footed mammal, such as an elephant or rhinoceros; specifically, elephant (sometimes humorous) — **-atous** *adj.*
pacific *formal. adj.* peaceful; peacemaking
pacification *n.* maintenance or restoration of an established order through suppression of rebels, terrorists, or the like (often euphemistic)
pacifier *chiefly U.S. n.* baby's dummy or teething ring
pacifism *n.* belief that violence, and especially war, is deeply wrong; refusal to participate in military action, conscientious objection — **-ist** *n., adj.*
packet *n.* boat following a regular, usually coastal, route and carrying passengers as well as cargo and sometimes mail
paddock *n.* motor-racing assembly area for cars, next to the track
paddy wagon *U.S. slang. n.* police van [after *Paddy*, derogatory name for an Irishman]
padre (paá-dray) *informal. n.* chaplain or clergyman, especially one who works with the military
paean (peé-ən) *n.* song or expression of joy and praise (poetic or literary)
paediatrics (peédi-áttriks) *n.* medical treatment specifically concerned with babies and children — **-atric** *adj.* — **-atrician** *n.*
paedophilia (peé-də-fílli-ə) *n.* sexual attraction felt by certain adults towards children — **-philic**, **-philiac** *adj.* — **-philiac**, **-phile** *n.*
pagan *adj.* person who does not believe in God, or who has no religion; relating or referring to ancient or current religions that have more than one god — **pagan** *n.* — **-ism** *n.*
pageant *n.* colourful procession or dramatic presentation: *the pageant of British history* — **-ry** *n.*
paginate *tr.v.* to number the pages of (a book, manuscript, or the like) — **-ation** *n.*
pagoda *n.* eastern temple or shrine, typically a multi-storeyed tapering tower with a series of projecting eaves; ornamental garden pavilion modelled on a pagoda
painter *n.* rope at the front of a boat for tying it up
paladin (pál-ə-din) *formal. n.* heroic knight or chivalric hero
palaeontology (pál-i-ontólləji) *n.* study of fossils — **-gist** *n.* — **-logical** *adj.*
palanquin (pál-ən-keén) *n.* vehicle in East Asia, especially in former times, consisting of a covered couch or litter carried on poles on the shoulders of four men (also 'palankeen")
palatable *adj.* acceptable to one's taste or ideas
palate (pál-it) *n.* roof of the mouth — **-tal** *adj.*
palatial *adj.* palace-like; fit for a palace
palatinate (pə-látti-nayt, -nit) *n.* country or colony in former times whose ruler had royal powers or privileges
palaver (pə-laávər) *n.* conversation or parley, as between Europeans and non-Europeans in a pidgin or lingua franca; *informal.* tiresome or frivolous talk; tedious fuss or bothersome procedure
palette (pál-ət) *n.* artist's paint-mixing board; colour range, as of a painting or painter
palfrey (páwl-fri) *archaic. n.* light horse for leisurely riding by a woman
palimony *informal. n.* alimony-like maintenance payment to an ex-lover
palimpsest (pál-imp-sest) *n.* re-used writing surface, such as parchment, on which earlier text can still be seen through the later text superimposed on it
palindrome (pál-in-drōm) *n.* word, such as *reviver*, or phrase, such as *Madam, I'm Adam*, that reads the same backwards or forwards — **-dromic** *adj.*
palingenesis (pál-in-jénni-siss) *formal. n.* reincarnation
palinode (pál-i-nōd) *formal. n.* recantation or withdrawal of a claim in the form of a poem or official declaration
palisade *n.* fence of sharpened stakes forming a fortification; any of these stakes or pickets (in that sense, also "pale")
palisades *chiefly U.S. pl.n.* line of cliffs along a river
pall *n.* cover, usually of velvet, for a coffin or tomb; dark and oppressive covering: *a pall of smoke*; gloomy atmosphere: *cast a pall over the festivities*
palladium (pə-láydi-əm) *formal. n., pl.* **-ia** or **-iums** sacred object reputedly protecting a city or state; guarantee or safeguard of society [from Greek *Palladion*, the statue of the goddess *Pallas* Athene that would guarantee Troy's safety so long as it survived]
pallbearer *n.* person who carries or accompanies the coffin at a funeral
pallet *n.* lip or small lever for engaging ratchets in machinery; potter's wooden spatula used for mixing or moulding clay; tool for applying gold leaf in book-binding; platform supporting cargo or stored goods, typically moved by a fork-lift truck
palliasse (pál-i-ass) *formal. n.* thin mattress or bed filled with straw or sawdust (also "pallet")
palliate *tr.v.* to make easier, lighter, or more bearable without curing — **-ative** *n., adj.*
pallid *adj.* pale in complexion; second-rate, lacklustre — **pallor** *n.*
pallium *n., pl.* **-iums** or **-ia** outer layer or covering of

an anatomical structure, such as the cerebral cortex of the brain (also mantle)

palmer *archaic. n.* pilgrim, specifically one entitled to bear a palm branch to show that he has visited the Holy Land

palmistry *n.* fortune-telling by reading people's palms (also *formal* "chiromancy") — **palmist** *n.*

palooka *U.S. slang. n.* second-rate boxer; second-rate athlete (becoming outdated)

palpable *adj.* very real, plain, or obvious: *That's a palpable lie*; *formal.* possible to feel or handle, tangible — **-ibility** *n.*

palpate (pal-páyt) *tr.v.* to examine medically by feeling or touching — **-tion** *n.*

palpebral (pálpibrəl) *formal. adj.* relating to eyelids

palpebrate *formal. adj.* having eyelids ~ *intr.v.* to blink or wink, especially frequently or involuntarily

palpitation *n.* tremor or shake of a body organ; irregular or abnormally fast heartbeat — **-tate** *intr.v.* — **-tant** *adj.*

palps *pl.n.* feelers or sensory organs near the mouth, as in some insects and shellfish (also "palpi") — **palpate** *adj.*

palsy *archaic. n.* paralysis; loss of bodily power or control [related to *paralysis*] — **-sied** *adj.*

palter (páwl-tər) *intr.v.* to speak or behave evasively or deceptively; to haggle

paltry (páwl-tri) *adj.* petty, unimportant; mean, base, despicable

paludal (pə-léwd'l) *formal. adj.* relating to swamps and marshes; malarial

pampas (pám-pəz) *pl.n.* bare grassland plains in Argentina (singular "pampa")

[1]pan *v.* to sweep a film or television camera across a scene, as to follow a moving object [short for *panorama*] — **pan** *n.*

[2]pan *n.* Asian chewing mixture of betel nuts and leaves

panacea (pánnə-sée-ə) *n.* cure-all, universal remedy

panache (pə-násh) *n.* ornamental plume on headgear; stylishness of manner, verve, dash

panatella *n.* long thin cigar

pandects *formal. pl.n.* codified legal system, such as Justinian's

pandemic *n.* wide-ranging epidemic — **pandemic** *adj.*

pandemonium *n.* uproar, noisy disorder, chaos, or the place of such disorder [after *Pandaemonium*, the capital of Hell in Milton's *Paradise Lost*, from Greek *pan-*, all + *daimon*, a demon]

pander *n.* person who acts as a procurer or go-between in a sexual relationship ~ *intr.v.* to indulge someone's wishes or satisfy his unworthy desires: *pandered to my cruel appetites* [after *Pandare*, a character in Chaucer's *Troilus and Criseyde*, who contrives to bring the lovers together] — **pander** *intr.v.*

Pandora's box *n.* source of many problems or great suffering [after *Pandora*, a woman in Greek mythology who was sent a box by Zeus and on opening it in defiance of his warnings, released all the evils into the world]

pane *n.* rectangular section of a sheet of stamps; sheet of stamps divided into panes

panegyric (pánni-jírrik) *n.* formal song or poem honouring and praising a person; speech, article, or the like of lavish praise — **-al** *adj.* — **-gyrise** *v.*

Pangaea (pán-jée-ə) *n.* original single landmass that split up into the continents of today

pannage (pánnij) *archaic. n.* pigs' fodder or pasturage, as in a forest; feudal right of pannage for one's pigs; fee for pannage

pannier *n.* basket or similar carrier, as on a pack animal or bicycle; support, usually of wire, spreading a skirt at the hips

panoply (pánnə-pli) *n.* armour, weapons, and full equipment of a warrior; *formal.* complete and impressive display

panoptic *formal. adj.* all-embracing: *a panoptic view/survey*

pantechnicon *British. n. archaic.* furniture warehouse or store; large furniture lorry, removal van (also *chiefly U.S.* "moving van")

pantheism *n.* belief in God as being present throughout nature, or identical to nature — **-theist** *n., adj.* — **-theistic** *adj.*

pantheon *n.* whole group of gods; famous people collectively; building such as a temple, dedicated to a pantheon

pantoffle (pan-tóff'l) *archaic. n.* slipper

pantograph *n.* copying instrument for transferring a diagram or picture by means of a lever system that will reproduce the original to any scale; frame on the roof of a vehicle, such as a train engine, tram, or trolleybus, that collects current from an overhead wire as the vehicle moves along

papacy (páypə-si) *n.* Pope's authority, office, or term of office — **papal** *adj.*

paparazzo (páppə-rát-so) *n., pl.* **-razzi** photographer or freelance journalist who badgers celebrities

papeterie (páppətri) *n.* ornamental box for stationery and writing equipment [related to *paper*]

papier-mâché (páppi-ay-máshay) *n.* paper pulp or sheets used in model-making or moulding [French, literally, chewed paper] — **papier-mâché** *adj.*

papilla *formal. n., pl.* **-lae** bump or tiny rounded protuberance, as on the tongue or the root of a hair

papilloma (páppi-lṓ-mə) *n., pl.* **-mata** or **-mas** wart, corn, or other small benign growth

papillote (páppi-lōt) *n.* paper frill adorning the end of a chop or cutlet; cooking foil or greaseproof paper [French, from *papillon*, a butterfly]

Pap test *n.* smear test for cancer of the cervix [after George *Papanicolaou*, the 20th-century U.S. medical scientist who invented it]

papule *formal. n.* pimple

papyrus (pə-pī́r-əss) *n., pl.* **-ri** or **-ruses** reed-like plant, or the paper once made from its pith; ancient text written on papyrus

parabola (pə-rábbələ) *n., pl.* **-las** or **-lae** geometric curve with symmetrical arms — **-bolic** *adj.*

Paraclete *n.* Holy Ghost, in the role of comforter, supporter, or counsellor

paradigm (párrə-dīm) *n.* example or model used as a standard for the whole group; framework of theories and concepts forming the background to a scientist's approach — **-atic** *adj.*

parados (párrə-dos) *n.* defensive bank, as behind a trench, giving protection from the rear

paradox *n.* statement that is apparently self-contradictory or absurd though not necessarily untrue — **-ical** *adj.*

paragon (párrə-gən) *n.* excellent or perfect example or representative, exemplar; large diamond or pearl of high quality

parallax *n.* apparent change in the position of an object when the observer changes position; measure of

this apparent change — **-lactic** *adj*.
paralogism (pə-rál-ə-jiz'm) *formal. n.* logically ill-formed argument, especially when unintentional — **-logistic** *adj*.
paramedical *adj*. referring or relating to professions allied to or serving the medical profession, such as those of radiographers or laboratory technicians
parameters (pə-rámmitərz) *pl.n.* guidelines or factors that limit, influence, or define something
paramount *adj*. foremost, primary: *of paramount importance*; most important, vital: *Secrecy is paramount*; supreme, leading: *the paramount chieftain*
paramour (párrə-moor) *n*. lover; sweetheart (poetic or humorous) [Old French, literally, by way of love]
paranoia *n*. mental illness or psychosis characterised typically by delusions of grandeur or persecution; *informal*. excessive distrust or suspicion — **-noid**, **-noiac**, **-noic** *adj*., *n*.
paranormal *adj*. inexplicable by science or normal common sense — **the paranormal** the supernatural
parapet *n*. wall or railing on the edge of a balcony, roof, tower, or the like; defensive earthworks or stoneworks
paraph *formal. n.* characteristic flourish or squiggle under a signature
paraphernalia *n*., *pl.n.* equipment or gear needed for an activity; belongings or personal property; any odds and ends
paraphrase *tr.v.* to reword, especially in order to simplify, clarify, or summarise — **paraphrase** *n*. — **-phrastic** *adj*.
paraplegia *n*. paralysis from the waist down. Compare QUADRIPLEGIA, TETRAPLEGIA — **-plegic** *adj*., *n*.
parapsychology *n*. study of paranormal and supernatural phenomena, such as extrasensory perception — **-ologist** *n*.
parasol *n*. light umbrella for protection against the sun
parasuicide *formal. n.* attempted suicide not meant to succeed; person who attempts this — **-cidal** *adj*.
parataxis *formal. n.* in grammar, listing of related clauses without using conjunctions, as in *I came, I saw, I conquered*. Compare HYPOTAXIS ASYNDETON — **-tactic** *adj*.
paravane *n*. device towed by a ship, such as a minesweeper, to cut the cables holding mines in place in the water
par avion (par avyóɴ) *adv*. by airmail [French, literally, by aircraft]
parbuckle *n*. sling or loop of rope for sliding or lifting tree trunks, barrels, or the like
parchment *n*. sheepskin or goatskin prepared as a writing surface; text or drawing on a sheet of parchment; stiff high-quality paper [after *Parthia*, an ancient kingdom now in Iran, a source of leather, and *Pergamum*, an ancient city, kingdom, and Roman province, now in Turkey, where parchment was first widely used to replace papyrus]
pard *archaic. n.* leopard or other big cat [see *leopard*]
paregoric (párrə-górrik) *n*. former medicine containing camphor and opium, used for relieving coughing and diarrhoea
parenthesis *n*., *pl*. **-theses** grammatically separated phrase within a sentence, typically set off from the surrounding text by dashes or brackets; either of the pair of round brackets used to set off a parenthesis (in this sense, also "bracket"); interval or pause that interrupts a sequence of events — **-thetical** *adj*. — **-thesise** *v*.
paresis (pə-rée-siss, párrə-) *formal. n.* partial paralysis — **-etic** *adj*.
par excellence (paár éksə-lonss, -lónss) *adv*. superbly ~ *adj*. of the best possible type [French, literally, by excellence]
parget (párjit) *n*. plaster or other wall coating; ornamental plasterwork — **parget** *tr.v.*
pariah (pə-rí-ə) *n*. social outcast
Parian (paír-i-ən) *adj*. referring to fine white marble, as used in ancient statues, or fine white porcelain [after *Paros*, a Greek island in the Aegean Sea]
paries (paír-i-eez) *formal. n.*, *pl*. **-ietes** wall of a bodily cavity or organ, such as the heart — **-rietal** *adj*.
pari-mutuel (párri-méwchoo-əl) *chiefly U.S. n.* totalisator betting system or machine at horse races [French, mutual stake]
pari passu (párri pássoo) *formal. adv.* with equal pace, speed, or progress [Latin, with equal step]
parity *formal. n.* equality or equivalence: *parity of income/status*
parlance *formal. n.* spoken language of the specified kind: *in medical/common parlance* (sometimes humorous)
parley *informal. n.* discussion, especially to resolve a disagreement, informal negotiation
parlous *archaic or formal. adj.* perilous, dangerous [variant of *perilous*]
Parnassian *adj*. relating to the world of poetry [after Mount *Parnassus*, the site of the Delphic oracle in ancient Greece]
parochial (pə-róki-əl) *adj*. relating to a parish; unconcerned with wider issues and implications, blinkered, narrow in outlook, provincial — **-ism** *n*.
parody *n*. satirical mimicry, as of a writer's or composer's work — **parody** *tr.v.* — **-odic** *adj*. — **-odist** *n*.
parole *n*. early release from prison, on condition of good behaviour; *formal*. language as actually used by a speech community, by contrast with the abstract linguistic system shared by the speech community. Compare LANGUE ~ *tr.v.* to release (a prisoner) on parole
paronomasia (párrə-nō-máyzi-ə) *formal. n.* pun or play on words — **-omastic** *adj*.
parousia (pə-roo-si-ə) *formal. n.* second coming of Christ
paroxysm *n*. sudden outburst, spasm, convulsion, or expression of strong feeling — **-al** *adj*.
parquet (pár-kay) *n*. floor covering of mosaic wood strips — **parquet** *tr.v.* — **-ry** *n*.
parr *n*. salmon in its freshwater phase, during its first two years of life
parricide *formal. n.* killing or killer of a parent or other close relative — **-cidal** *adj*.
parry *v*. to evade or counter (a hostile or embarrassing question); to ward off (a blow, fencing thrust, or the like)
parse (parz) *tr.v.* to break down (a sentence) into the parts of speech that make it up, and give a grammatical explanation of these; to give a full grammatical description of (a word in its context)
parsimonious *formal. adj.* frugal, sparing, or thrifty; stingy, mean — **-mony** *n*.
parterre (paar-taír) *n*. garden designed with an ornamental pattern of paths between the flower beds [from Old French *par terre*, on the ground]

parthenogenesis (párthinō-jénni-siss) *n.* reproduction without fertilisation, as in lower plants and animals; human reproduction without apparent male participation, "virgin birth" — **-genetic** *adj.*

Parthian shot *formal. n.* argument, clinching remark, or hostile gesture made when leaving, "parting shot" [after the soldiers of *Parthia*, an ancient region of Persia, who adopted a battle technique of pretending to flee and then firing arrows at the pursuing enemy]

participle (pártisi-p'l, párti-sipp'l) *n.* grammatical form of a verb, typically ending in *-ed* or *-ing* in English, used when forming verb tenses or as an adjective or noun — **-cipial** *adj.*

parti-coloured *formal. adj.* having differently coloured parts or sections, pied

particular *formal. n.* detail, individual fact or item — **-ise** *v.*

parti pris (párti prée) *formal. n., pl.* **partis pris** opinion or decision that has already been arrived at, prejudice or preconception [French, literally, side taken]

partisan *n.* passionate or militant supporter of a doctrine, faction, or the like; guerrilla fighting behind enemy lines or in occupied territory ~ *adj.* relating to partisans; favouring or supporting a single cause, person, or party in a prejudiced way

partition *n.* division, separation; part or section into which something has been divided; thin wall dividing a larger area, as into small offices ~ *tr.v.* to divide up; to separate off: *partition off a first-aid room*

parturient (paar-téwr-i-ənt) *formal. adj.* relating to childbirth; in labour, about to give birth; producing or about to produce a discovery, inspired idea, or the like — **-ency** *n.*

parturition *formal. n.* act or process of giving birth

par value *n.* value printed on the face of a share certificate or bond, as used for assessing dividends

parvenu (párvə-new) *n.* upstart, person of lowly background who has recently achieved wealth, power, or advanced social status [French, literally, arrived] — **parvenu** *adj.*

parvis (párviss) *n.* courtyard or colonnade in front of a church or palace [from Late Latin *paradisus*, paradise, an enclosed garden]

pas (paa) *n., pl.* **pas** dance step; dance; precedence or right of priority, as in a procession

Pascal's triangle (pass-kálz) *n.* triangular arrangement of numbers with each number being the sum of the two numbers just above it [after Blaise *Pascal*, the 17th-century French philosopher and mathematician who devised it]

paschal (paásk'l, pásk'l) *formal. adj.* relating to the Passover or to Easter [from Hebrew *pesach*, Passover]

pasquinade (páskwi-náyd) *n.* satirical piece of writing, lampoon, especially on a poster in a public place — **pasquinade** *tr.v.*

passé *adj.* old-fashioned, out-of-date, obsolete [French, passed]

passementerie (pass-méntri, -MON-trée) *n.* edging or fancy trimming for a garment, consisting of lace, braid, beadwork, or the like

passe-partout (páss paar-tōō) *n.* something, especially a master key, enabling one to go anywhere; picture-framing method in which the glass and backing are taped together, or the adhesive tape used for this purpose; mat, typically decorated, on which a photograph or picture is mounted [French, literally, pass everywhere]

passerine *adj.* relating or referring to the largest order of birds, the perching birds and songbirds — **passerine** *n.*

passible (pássib'l) *formal. adj.* sensitive to emotion or suffering, able to feel — **-ibility** *n.*

passim (pássim) *adv.* throughout, here and there, (used in references and footnotes to indicate the frequent occurrence of an item in a text)

Passion *n.* the sufferings of Jesus prior to and during the Crucifixion; representation of these, as in the Gospels or a musical composition

passive *adj.* receiving or being subjected to an action rather than being active or taking the initiative; submissive, unassertive, accepting; referring to a verb form, voice, or construction in which the grammatical subject is the logical object of the action or effect of the verb, as in *The warrior was killed by an arrow* (opposite "active"); chemically inactive, inert — **passive** *n.*

passive euthanasia *n.* mercy-killing by withholding treatment that would prolong the patient's life

passive resistance *n.* non-violent opposition, as by fasting and non-cooperation, to a law, policy, colonial authority, or the like

passive smoking *n.* inhaling by non-smokers of other people's tobacco smoke

paste *n.* moist clay used in making pottery or porcelain (also "pâte"); fine hard glass used in making artificial gems, or a gem or gems made of such glass (in this sense, also "strass")

pastel *n.* crayon made from ground pigment mixed with gum; picture made with such crayons — **pastel** *adj.*

pastern *n.* part of a horse's foot just above the hoof, or either of the bones forming this part

pasteurisation *n.* heat-treatment of milk, beer, and other liquids to destroy germs and regulate fermentation [after Louis *Pasteur*, the 19th-century French microbiologist who devised it] — **-ise** *tr.v.*

pasticcio (pa-stích-ō) *n., pl.* **-ticci** work, as of music, compiled by borrowing fragments or ideas from elsewhere (also "pastiche") [Italian, literally, a pasty or hotchpotch]

pastiche (pa-stéesh) *n.* imitation, often satirical, of an earlier work of music, drama, fiction, or the like; pasticcio

pastille *n.* medicated lozenge for chewing or sucking; air-freshener or fumigating substance in the form of a small cone or an aromatic preparation that is set alight; pastel crayon

pastoral *adj.* relating to country life, rural; relating to shepherds or herdsmen; used for pasture; relating to an artistic work that depicts country life in an idealised way; relating to spiritual care and guidance ~ *n.* artistic work depicting country life, typically in an idealised way; letter from a pastor, especially a bishop, to the people of his diocese — **-ist** *n.*

pasty (páysti) *adj.* pale in complexion, unhealthy-looking

patagium (pə-táy-ji-əm) *n., pl.* **-gia** wing-like membrane between the fore and hind limb of a bat, flying squirrel, or the like; fold of skin between the wing and body of a bird

pate *n. archaic or formal.* head, or crown of the head; *informal.* brains or intelligence

pâte (paat) *n.* moist clay used in making pottery or porcelain (also "paste")

pâté de foie gras (paa-táy də fwáa gráa, páttay) *n.* rich savoury paste made from the livers of specially fattened geese (also "foie gras") [French, literally, paste of fat liver]

patella (pə-téllə) *n., pl.* **-tellae** kneecap [Latin, literally, a small dish]

paten (patt'n) *n.* thin metal disc; plate, typically of silver or gold, used for holding the bread at Communion (also "patin")

patent *n.* (pátt'nt) inventor's right to the exclusive use and development of his invention, or the document granting such a right; (páyt'nt) sign or evidence that one possesses a specified quality ~ *adj.* (páyt'nt) obvious, plain to see; (pátt'nt) original or special to an individual; protected by a trademark ~ *tr.v.* (pátt'nt) to secure a patent for (an invention) or grant a patent to (an inventor) — **-ly** *adv.*

paterfamilias (páytər-fə-mílli-ass) *formal. n., pl.* **patresfamilias** father of a family, viewed as head of the household [Latin]

paternalism *n.* patronising system of government or authority, typically generous and concerned but restricting individual responsibility — **-istic** *adj.*

paternity *formal. n.* fatherhood, or origin or descent from a father; authorship or origin; fatherliness — **paternal** *adj.*

paternoster *n.* the Lord's Prayer, especially in its Latin version (also "Paternoster"); bead at the end of each decade on a rosary, marking the point at which the Lord's Prayer is said; fixed formula of words recited as a prayer or charm; lift consisting of open platforms on a continuous chain, moving slowly round without stopping; fishing line with a series of hooks [Latin *pater noster*, our father]

pathetic *adj.* relating to, expressing, or arousing pity or sympathy; *informal.* feeble, hopelessly inadequate: *a pathetic excuse* — **pathos** *n.*

pathetic fallacy *n.* granting or ascribing of human qualities, as in poetry, to things in nature, especially plants and non-living objects

pathogen *formal. n.* disease-causing agent, such as a germ or fungus — **-genic** *adj.*

pathological *adj.* relating to pathology or disease; irrational and habitual, compulsive: *a pathological liar*

pathologist *n.* scientific expert in the nature of diseases; medical specialist who conducts post-mortem examinations to establish the cause of death

pathology *n.* scientific study of disease; abnormal changes, as in tissues or behaviour, that are the signs of a disease

patina (páttinə) *n.* surface appearance, especially a sheen acquired by age or association; layer of oxide, usually green, formed naturally or artificially on a copper or bronze surface, similar to verdigris

patio (pátti-ō) *n., pl.* **-os** courtyard, open to the air, within a house; verandah or similar paved outdoor area adjoining a house

patisserie (pə-téessəri) *n.* bakery specialising in fine cakes and pastries; pastry or pastries

patois (pátwaa, pa-twáa) *n., pl.* **patois** regional dialect; any of the French or Swiss provincial dialects; Creole, especially Jamaican Creole; cant, jargon, specialised language of a group

patrial (páytri-əl) *n.* person having nationality, residence, or citizenship rights in the U.K., especially by virtue of a parent or grandparent born there — **-ity** *n.*

patriarch (páytri-aark) *n.* father or founder of a tribe, tradition, or the like; Old Testament father or founder of the human race or Hebrew people; venerable old man, elder; bishop of senior rank in the early Christian Church, or the Roman Catholic and various Orthodox Churches today; Pope; Mormon priest of high rank (in this sense, also "evangelist") — **-al** *adj.* — **-ate**, **-y** *n.*

patrician *n.* person of noble birth, especially in ancient Rome or various medieval free cities; well-bred person of cultivated tastes — **patrician** *adj.*

patricide *formal. n.* killing or killer of one's father — **-cidal** *adj.*

patrilineal *adj.* relating or referring to the male line of descent. Compare MATRILINEAL

patrimony (páttri-məni) *formal. n.* inheritance from one's father or ancestor; legacy or heritage; longstanding estate or endowment of a church

patristics *n.* study of the lives and writings of the Fathers of the early Christian Church (also "patrology") — **patristic** *adj.*

patron *n.* sponsor or benefactor: *patron of the arts*; protector or supporter; regular customer — **-ess** *n.*

patronage (páttrə-nij) *n.* encouragement or support from a patron; customers, clients, or patrons collectively, or the trade that they provide; patronising treatment or manner; power of bestowing favours, appointing people to jobs, or the like, especially: power to allocate government jobs, or the right to nominate a clergyman to a benefice

patronise (páttrə-nīz) *tr.v.* to be a patron of or to; to treat in an offensively gracious way as though dealing with a subordinate, condescend — **-ising** *adj.*

patronymic (páttrə-nímmik) *n.* name derived from the first name of one's father or paternal ancestor, typically with an affix such as *-son*, *Mac-*, or *-ovich*

paucity (páwssiti) *formal. n.* smallness in number or quantity, fewness or scarcity

pauper *n.* extremely poor person, sometimes living on public charity — **pauper**, **-ise** *tr.v.*

pavis (pávviss) *n.* large medieval shield to protect the whole body (also "pavise") [after *Pavia*, a city in northern Italy where pavises used to be made]

Pavlovian *adj.* referring to a reflex reaction or conditioned response to a stimulus; *informal.* automatic, predictable [after Ivan *Pavlov*, a 19th-20th-century Russian physiologist and psychologist]

pavonine (pávvə-nīn) *formal. adj.* relating to or resembling a peacock or peacock's tail [related to *peacock*]

pawl *n.* hinged bolt or tongue of metal slotting into a notch of a ratchet wheel to produce or ensure movement in one direction only (also "detent")

pawn *n.* unimportant person or group used as a tool to further the purposes of another [after *pawn*, the weakest chesspiece, from Medieval Latin *pedo*, a foot soldier]

pax *n.* kiss of peace at a Christian Communion, or the plate formerly used to convey it ~ *British slang. interj.* truce, peace (used as an immunity or exemption call in children's games)

pay *tr.v.* to waterproof or seal (the seams or hull of a wooden ship), as with tar or pitch

payload *n.* cargo, passengers, bombs, or the like in an aircraft; extra equipment or cargo in a spacecraft;

weight of such a payload; explosive charge in a missile's warhead

payola (pay-ṓlə) *chiefly U.S. slang. n.* bribery, as of disc jockeys, to promote a product [*pay* + Victr*ola*, a record player]

peaky *adj.* pale or sickly in appearance

pebble *n.* grainy or crinkled surface, as on leather or paper ~ *adj.* referring to very thick spectacle lenses — **pebble** *tr.v.*

pebbledash *British. n.* mortar or plaster containing tiny pebbles applied to outside walls, or the rough finish produced by it — **pebbledash** *tr.v.*

peccadillo *formal. n., pl.* **-loes** or **-los** sin or fault considered petty or trifling

peccant *formal. adj.* sinning, guilty; breaking or ignoring a rule — **-cancy** *n.*

peccavi (pe-kaávee, -káyvī) *formal. n.* confession of guilt or acknowledgment of sin [Latin, literally, I have sinned]

pecking order *informal. n.* hierarchy, order of power or status in a group

Pecksniffian *adj.* pretending to be benevolent and have high moral standards, typically by hypocritical conversation about virtue [after Seth *Pecksniff*, a pious hypocrite in Dickens's novel *Martin Chuzzlewit*] — **Pecksniff** *n.*

pectin *n.* gel-forming substance found in ripe fruit and used as a setting agent in jams

pectoral (péktərəl) *formal. adj.* relating to or worn on the chest or breast ~ *n.* pectoral muscle or fin; medicine for chest ailments; medal, brooch, or the like worn on the chest

peculate (péckew-layt) *formal. v.* to steal money or goods entrusted to one, embezzle — **-lation** *n.*

pecuniary (pi-kéwni-əri) *formal. adj.* relating to money, monetary

pedagogue (péddə-gog) *formal. n.* teacher or educator, especially a fussy and dogmatic one — **-gogic, -gogical** *adj.* — **-gogics, -gogy** *n.*

pedant (pédd'nt) *n.* person who is learned without being wise, having formal, bookish, and drily detailed knowledge; scholar who shows off his knowledge; critical fusspot, nitpicker — **-ry** *n.* — **-ic** *adj.*

peddle *v.* to sell goods while travelling from place to place, hawk; to sell narcotic drugs illegally, typically to drug addicts; to spread or try to circulate ideas or opinions — **pedlar** *n.*

pederasty (péddə-rasti) *formal. n.* homosexual relations between a man and a boy — **-rast** *n.*

pedestal (péddist'l) *n.* support or base, as for a statue or column

pedicel (péddi-sel) *n.* small stalk, biological organ, or the like serving as a support, such as a stalk supporting a flower in a flower cluster

pedicular (pi-díckewlər) *formal. adj.* relating to or caused by lice

pediculosis *formal. n.* infestation by lice — **-culous** *adj.*

pedicure *n.* care of or treatment session for the feet and toenails; expert in the treatment of feet and toenails, chiropodist (rare) — **pedicure** *tr.v.*

pedigree *n.* ancestry, lineage; family tree, list of ancestors; breeding record of a thoroughbred horse, dog, or other animal; source and historical development of something [from Old French *pie de grue*, literally, foot of a crane, referring to the appearance of the three-line mark, ╱│╲, used to indicate descent in a pedigree chart] — **pedigree, -greed** *adj.*

pediment *n.* wide, low gable above the façade of a Grecian-style building; similar triangular structure or decoration, as above a window; sloping rock surface at the base of a desert mountain [probably a distortion of *pyramid*]

pedology *n.* scientific study of soil — **-gist** *n.* — **-logical** *adj.*

pedometer (pi-dómmitər) *n.* instrument gauging a distance walked by recording the number of steps

peduncle (pi-dúngk'l) *n.* stalk bearing a flower, fruit, or entire flower cluster; stalk-like structure, as of nerve fibres — **-cular, -culate** *adj.*

peel *n.* long-handled shovel used for moving bread, pies, pizza, or the like in and out of an oven

peen *n.* wedge- or ball-shaped head on a hammer, opposite the flat surface (also "pane"). Compare POLL

peer group *n.* group of people of the same age and status as oneself

peignoir (páyn-waar, payn-waár) *n.* negligée, light and delicate dressing gown for a woman [French]

pejoration (péjə-ráysh'n) *n.formal.* worsening, deterioration; in linguistics, the process by which a word gradually acquires an unfavourable sense or tone, as with *pathetic*, which formerly had only the sense of 'pitiable or touching' (also "deterioration"; opposite "amelioration") — **-rate** *tr.v.*

pejorative (pi-jórrətiv, peéjə-rətiv) *adj.* disapproving or unfavourable, as a particular sense or use of a word might be, disparaging ~ *n.* a disapproving word or expression

pelf *formal. n.* wealth, riches, money, especially if acquired in a dubious way (often humorous) [related to *pilfer*]

pelican crossing *British. n.* pedestrian crossing at which pedestrians themselves activate the traffic lights on the roadside [from *pe*destrian *li*ght *con*trolled crossing]

pelisse (pe-leéss) *n.* long coat or cloak, originally of fur or fur-lined

pellucid (pe-léw-sid) *formal. n.* transparent or translucent; very clearly expressed, easy to understand

Pelmanism *n.* memory-training system; card game testing memory skills to form matching pairs [after the *Pelman* Institute in London]

pelmet *chiefly British. n.* length of board or fabric along the top of a window, used to hide the curtain rod [probably from French *palmette*, a palm-leaf decoration, as used on classical mouldings]

pelt *n.* animal skin or hide removed from the carcass — **-ry** *n.*

pemmican *n.* traditional North American Indian food of pounded dried meat pressed with fat and sometimes fruit into small cakes; similar foodstuff used as emergency rations

¹pen *n.* long horny internal shell of a squid

²pen *n.* female swan. Compare COB

penal *adj.* relating to punishment: *penal actions/code/colony*

penalise *tr.v.* to subject to a penalty or punishment; to handicap or put at a disadvantage

penance (pénnənss) *n.* act of self-punishment or devotion to demonstrate sorrow or repentance for sin; religious sacrament including confession, absolution, and penalties; feeling of sorrow for one's misdeeds

penchant (póN-shoN, pénchənt) *n.* strong tendency or liking, inclination, leaning: *a penchant for* *exaggerating/cigars*

pendant *n. formal.* complement, additional or matching part; medallion, piece of jewellery, or the like hanging freely, as on a necklace; hanging lamp or chandelier; hanging sculpted ornament on a Gothic ceiling

pending *formal. prep.* until, awaiting, or during ~ *adj.* not yet decided or settled; imminent

pendulous (péndewləss) *formal. adj.* swinging or hanging loosely

peninsula *n.* narrow strip of land extending into the sea or a lake from the mainland

penitent *adj.* repentant, contrite, humbly or sorrowfully regretting one's sins or offences ~ *n.* penitent person; person who confesses his sins to a priest and submits to penance — **-tence** *n.* — **-tential** *adj.*

penitentiary *U.S. n.* prison, especially for serious offenders (also *slang* "pen")

pennant *n.* long narrow flag (also "pennon")

pennate *formal. adj.* feathered or winged

penology (pee-nólləji) *n.* study of the punishment and treatment of criminals, especially prison management — **-gist** *n.* — **-logical** *adj.*

pension (póNSS-yoN, poNSS-yóN) *n.* boarding house or small hotel, as in France — **en pension** referring to a fixed-rate board-and-lodging system of hotel charges

pensive *adj.* thoughtful, meditative

pentacle *n.* five-pointed star, formed by five straight lines, sometimes credited with magic powers (also "pentangle", "pentagram")

pentad *formal. n.* group or series of five elements; five-year period

pentagon *n.* five-sided polygon — **the Pentagon** U.S. Department of Defense, or the five-sided building in Arlington, Virginia, that houses it; U.S. military leadership or establishment — **-gonal** *adj.*

Pentateuch (péntə-tewk) *n.* first five books of the bible

pentathlon (pen-táth-lən) *n.* sports contest with five different events for each competitor, consisting of running, riding, fencing, swimming, and pistol shooting

penthouse *n.* flat or shed on the roof or top floor of a large building; shed, typically with a sloping roof, against the side of a building

pentimento *n.* reappearance through a painting of an earlier image or design originally drawn or painted beneath; underlying image revealed in this way [Italian, literally, repentance, hence a correction]

penultimate *formal. adj., n.* second-last, last but one

penumbra *n., pl.* **-brae** or **-bras** partial shadow, as during an eclipse, between areas of full shadow and full illumination; lighter outer area of a sunspot — **-bral, -brous** *adj.*

penury (pénnewr-i) *formal. n.* extreme poverty or need, destitution; great lack, insufficiency — **-urious** *adj.*

peon (pée-ən, -on) *n.* peasant or unskilled worker, especially in Latin America — **-age** *n.*

peppercorn rent *n.* rent of a very small, purely nominal amount [from the traditional representation of a peppercorn as something trifling or worthless]

peptic *adj. formal.* relating to digestion or the promotion of it; referring to an ulcer in the stomach or oesophagus caused by digestive juices

perambulate *formal or archaic. intr.v.* to walk about, stroll (humorously pompous) — **-lation** *n.*

perambulator *chiefly British. formal. n.* pram

per annum *formal. adv.* yearly, annually

per capita (per káppitə) *formal. adv.* per person: *income per capita* [Latin, literally, by heads] — **per capita** *adj.*

percolate *v.* to pass, ooze, or seep slowly through or as if through a filtering substance — *tr.* to make (coffee) in a percolator — *intr. informal.* to pass or spread gradually: *the rumours/warmth percolated through to her* — **percolate, -lation** *n.*

percolator *n.* coffee pot in which hot water, typically rising through a tube, filters through ground coffee held in a small perforated tray

percussion *n.* section of the orchestra containing drums, xylophones, cymbals, and other instruments played by being struck; such instruments collectively; beating or striking on a surface, as by sound on the ear or by a stick on a drum; tapping the chest, back, or the like and attempting a diagnosis on the basis of the sound produced — **percuss** *tr.v.* — **-cussive** *adj.*

percussion cap *n.* gunpowder-filled cap, as used either in a toy pistol or in an ancient firearm, that explodes when struck

per diem (per dī-em, dée-) *formal. adv.* per day, daily ~ *n.* allowance for a day's expenses [Latin]

perdition *formal. n.* eternal spiritual damnation, loss of the soul; hell

peregrination *formal. n.* journey, typically long and far, and often by foot; *plural.* travels, wanderings (often humorous) — **-rinate** *v.*

peremptory (pə-rémp-təri, pérrəmp-) *formal. adj.* urgent or demanding; decisive and final, allowing no argument or refusal; overbearingly self-confident, dogmatic and arrogant: *a peremptory manner*

perennial *adj.* lasting throughout the year, or from year to year; *formal.* permanent, everlasting, perpetual; *formal.* constantly recurring, continual; referring to a plant living for three or more years, typically with new growth or flowering each year ~ *n.* perennial plant

perfidy (pérfidi) *formal. n.* treachery, breach of trust — **-fidious** *adj.*

perforation *n.* hole or series of holes made in something, specifically a sheet of postage stamps — **perforate** *tr.v.*

perfunctory (pər-fúngk-təri) *formal. adj.* routine, superficial, indifferent, mechanical: *gave him a perfunctory kiss*

pergola (pérgələ) *n.* covered walk or arbour formed by a trellised roof carrying climbing plants

periapt (pérri-apt) *formal. n.* charm or amulet, worn to ward off harm or disease

perigee (pérri-jee) *n.* point nearest the Earth in an orbit round it. Compare PERIHELION, PERILUNE, APOGEE

perihelion *n., pl.* **-helia** point nearest the Sun in an orbit round it. Compare APHELION

perilune *n.* nearest point to the Moon of a spacecraft orbiting it (also "pericynthion"). Compare APOLUNE

perimeter (pə-rímmitər) *n.* closed curve or line enclosing a plane area in geometry; length of such a line; boundary, as of a sports field or military position; fence, line, patrol, or the like protecting or marking such a boundary; limit or outer edge, as of the range of one's authority or hearing

perinatal (pérri-náyt'l) *adj.* occurring or relating to the time just before or after birth: *perinatal risks/clinic*

perineum (pérri-née-əm) *n., pl.* **-nea** area between

the anus and genitals in the human body — **-neal** *adj.*

periodic sentence *n.* sentence in which the main clause comes at the end

periodic table *n.* table of the chemical elements arranged according to their atomic number and other properties [elements with similar properties appear at regular periodic intervals in the numerical listing]

periodontal (pérri-ə-dónt'l) *adj.* relating to the tissues or area surrounding the teeth: *periodontal disease* — **-dontics, -dontia, -dontist** *n.*

peripatetic (pérripə-téttik) *formal. adj.* walking or moving from place to place, as in the course of one's business ~ *n.* teacher, coach, or the like employed by two or more schools, and constantly travelling from one to the other

peripeteia (pérripə-tī́-ə, -tée-) *n.* reversal or sudden change in fortunes or the course of events, especially in a play or other literary work (also "peripety")

peripheral (pə-ríffərəl) *formal. adj.* on or relating to the periphery; unimportant, incidental

peripheral nervous system *n.* nervous system excluding the brain and spinal cord

periphery (pə-ríffəri) *formal. n.* outermost part, boundary area; fringe, edge, or boundary, as of a social group; surface of the body or a body part

periphrasis (pə-ríffrə-siss) *formal. n., pl.* **-ses** expression of an indirect, roundabout kind; use of such expressions, circumlocution

periscope *n.* optical instrument, as on a submarine, containing mirrors or prisms for viewing objects that are not in the direct line of sight

peristalsis (pérri-stál-siss) *n.* waves of regular involuntary muscular contractions in the intestine or similar tube-like organ that force the contents onwards — **-staltic** *adj.*

peristyle *n.* in architecture, row of columns surrounding a building or courtyard, or the area surrounded — **-stylar** *adj.*

peritoneum (pérritə-née-əm) *n., pl.* **-nea** membrane lining the abdominal cavity and covering most of the organs — **-neal** *adj.*

periwig *formal. n.* wig, especially a long curly wig [related to *peruke*]

perjury (pérjəri) *n.* violation of an oath, especially, deliberate giving of false evidence by a witness under oath — **perjure** *tr.v.* — **-jurer** *n.* — **-jurious** *adj.*

permafrost *n.* frozen ground, as in the Arctic, that never thaws [*perma*nent + *frost*]

permeate (pérmi-ayt) *v.* to pass through, spread through, or penetrate — **-meable** *adj.* — **-meability, -meation, -meance** *n.*

per mensem *formal. adv.* per month, monthly [Latin]

permissive *adj.* tolerant, lenient, or broad-minded, especially in matters of sexual conduct

permutation *n. formal.* complete change, especially the rearrangement or reordering of elements in a group; in mathematics, any combination or arrangement of the elements of a set; variation or possible combination of elements, as in a detailed plan; *British.* selection and combination of results on the football pools (in this sense, also "perm") — **permute** *tr.v.*

pernicious *formal. adj.* extremely harmful, deadly, destructive: *a pernicious influence*

peroration *formal. n.* concluding part of a formal speech or written discourse, typically a rhetorical summing-up; speech of a long-winded, pompous, and rhetorical kind — **perorate** *intr.v.*

perpendicular *adj.* forming or standing at right angles; vertical, upright ~ *n.* perpendicular line, plane, surface, or position — **-ity** *n.*

perpetrate *formal. tr.v.* to commit, perform, or be guilty of: *perpetrate a crime/hoax/blunder* — **-trator, -tration** *n.*

perpetual *adj.* lasting indefinitely; flowering continuously through the growing season ~ *n.* perpetual plant

perpetuate *tr.v.* to make permanent or everlasting; to extend, prolong, or cause to continue — **-ation** *n.*

perpetuity *n. formal.* eternity, endlessness; in law, an estate that cannot be disposed of except for a permitted period; limitation on or condition of such an estate — **in perpetuity** for ever

perquisite (pérkwizit) *formal. n.* perk, extra benefit; tip, small gift or bonus, gratuity; exclusive right or possession, or something claimed to be one

perron (pérrən) *n.* stairway or platform outside the entrance of a large building

perry *n.* alcoholic drink made from fermented pear juice

per se (per sáy, sée) *formal. adv.* as such, in itself [Latin]

persecute *tr.v.* to oppress or ill-treat, especially because of racial, religious, or political differences; to pester constantly, harass — **-cution, -cutor** *n.*

perseveration *n. formal.* unadaptability, inability to change behaviour, working pattern, or the like; in psychology, repetition or uncontrollable recurrence of an idea, spoken word, or the like — **-rate** *intr.v.*

persiflage (pérsi-flaazh) *formal. n.* speech or writing of a light, bantering style; such a style

persistent *adj.* long-lasting, continuing despite discouragement; remaining attached to the plant even after withering; growing continuously throughout life, as rodents' teeth tend to do — **persist** *intr.v.* — **-ence** *n.*

persona (pər-sṓnə) *n., pl.* **-nae** identity or social role that a person adopts, especially when in public; character in a novel, play, or other literary work [Latin, a mask, especially an actor's mask]

personable *adj.* attractive in appearance or personality, engaging

personage (pérss'n-ij) *n.* celebrity, VIP; character in history or fiction; *formal.* person

personal equation *n.* variation or error in a measurement, judgment, or the like owing to human differences or prejudices; allowance or correction made for such a variation or error

personalise *tr.v.* to mark (stationery or other goods) with the owner's name, initials, or other form of identification — **-isation** *n.*

persona non grata (non graatə) *n., pl.* **personae non gratae** diplomat who is unacceptable to a foreign government; *formal.* unacceptable or unwelcome person, especially as a guest [Latin, literally, person not acceptable] — **persona non grata** *adj.*

personification *n.* ideal example or typical representative of a specified vice or virtue, embodiment, incarnation: *She's the personification of generosity*; figure of speech or artistic representation in which objects or abstract qualities are assigned human characteristics — **personify** *tr.v.*

perspicacious *formal. adj.* shrewd, acute, discerning — **-cacity** *n.*

perspicuous *formal. adj.* easy to understand, clearly expressed, lucid — **-cuity** *n.*
persuasion *n.* belief or confident opinion: set of religious beliefs; sect holding such beliefs
pertain *formal. intr.v.* to belong as a necessary or rightful part; to relate to, concern, deal with; to be suitable, appropriate, or relevant
pertinacity *formal. n.* stubborn persistence or determination, perseverance — **-nacious** *adj.*
pertinent *formal. adj.* relevant — **-ence** *n.*
perturb *tr.v.* to agitate, cause anxiety to, disturb seriously; to throw into confusion or disorder — **-bation** *n.*
pertussis (pər-tússiss) *formal. n.* whooping cough
peruke (pə-ro͞ok) *n.* wig of long, curly locks, as worn by men in the 17th and 18th centuries
peruse (pə-ro͞oz) *formal. tr.v.* to read, especially with care and in detail; to study or examine in detail — **-usal** *n.*
pervade *tr.v.* to spread through, permeate — **-vasion** *n.* — **-vasive** *adj.*
perverse (pər-vérss) *adj.* uncooperative, opposing others' wishes or suggestions unreasonably; based on such a quality, contrary: *a perverse decision*; stubborn — **-sity** *n.*
pervert *tr.v.* (pər-vért) to corrupt, twist from what is correct or proper; to distort, misinterpret, twist the meaning of; to misuse, use for an improper or incorrect purpose ~ *n.* (pér-vert) person who engages in sexual behaviour considered abnormal — **-version** *n.* — **-ed** *adj.*
pessary *n.* vaginal insert as for support or contraception, or medicated vaginal suppository
pestilence *n.* epidemic and deadly disease, especially bubonic plague; outbreak or epidemic of such a disease; evil or corrupting influence or source; *informal.* irritation, source of annoyance — **-lent, -lential** *adj.*
pestle (péss'l) *n.* small club-shaped implement for crushing or grinding substances in a mortar; pounding, crushing, or grinding implement, as in a mill — **pestle** *v.*
pétanque (pay-tóɴk) *n.* bowls-like game, a form of boules, played especially in the south of France
petard (pe-tárd) *n.* bell-shaped bomb used in former times to break into a fortification
peterman *chiefly British. slang. n., pl.* **-men** safe-breaker, burglar skilled in opening safes [from *peter*, a former slang term for a safe or till, after the name *Peter*]
petiole (pétti-ōl) *n.* stalk attaching a leaf to a stem; similar structure, as between the abdomen and the thorax of a wasp — **-olar, -olate** *adj.*
petite (pə-teét) *adj.* small and slim in build, trim (said of a girl or woman) [French]
petit mal (pétti mál) *n.* epilepsy or epileptic fit of a mild kind. Compare GRAND MAL [French, literally, small illness, little harm]
petits pois (pétti pwáa) *pl.n.* small tender green peas (sometimes also "petit pois")
Petrarchan sonnet (pe-trárkən) *n.* sonnet of Italian origin, with a tightly knit rhyme pattern [after Francesco Petrarca or *Petrarch*, the 14th-century Italian poet]
Petri dish (peétri) *n.* dish, typically of glass and fitted with a loose cover, as used in laboratories for growing bacteria cultures [after Julius R. *Petri*, a 19th-20th-century German bacteriologist]
petrify *v.* — *tr.* to turn (wood or other organic matter) to stone, as by the age-long fossilising action of mineral-rich water; to deaden or dull, make stiff or stone-like; to paralyse with fear or shock — *intr.* to become stone or stone-like — **-faction, -fication** *n.*
Petrine (peétrīn) *adj.* relating to St Peter, or to the Pope considered as his successor: *the Petrine succession/doctrines*
petroglyph (péttrə-glif) *n.* rock painting, carving, or inscription from ancient or prehistoric times — **-glyphic** *adj.*
pettifogger *n.* lawyer who uses unscrupulous and dubious methods; person who quibbles over small details, fusspot — **-fog** *intr.v.* — **-fogging** *adj.*
pettitoes *pl.n.* pig's trotters used as food
petty sessions *n.* magistrate's court, or a sitting of it
petulant *adj.* irritable, peevish — **-lance** *n.*
phalanx (fál-angks) *n., pl.* **-lanxes** or **-langes** battle formation of troops in close array, originally in ancient Greece; close-knit ranks, crowd of people, herd of animals, or the like; *formal.* finger bone or toe bone, or a corresponding bone in an animal
phallus (fál-əss) *n., pl.* **-li** or **-luses** *formal.* penis; sculpture or other symbolic representation of the penis and sometimes testicles, typically as a primitive symbol of fertility or generative power — **phallic** *adj.*
phantasm *formal. n.* illusion, apparent object that is not real; mental image of an object
phantasmagoria *n.* changing succession of confusing images, as experienced in a fever or dream; scene presenting such images [after the name of a 19th-century magic-lantern system] — **-goric, -gorical** *adj.*
pharisee *formal. n.* hypocritically self-righteous, puritanically disapproving person [after the *Pharisees*, a strict ancient Jewish sect] — **-saic, -saical** *adj.* — **-saism** *n.*
pharmaceutical (fármə-séwtik'l) *formal. n.* medical drug — **pharmaceutical** *adj.* — **-ceutics** *n.*
pharmacopoeia (fármə-kə-peé-ə) *n.* drugs collectively, as used in the preparation of medicine; stock of medical drugs; book listing medical drugs and detailing their preparation and recommended dosages
pharos (fáir-oss) *formal or archaic. n.* lighthouse [after the ancient Greek lighthouse on the small island of *Pharos*, off Alexandria in Egypt]
phatic (fáttik) *adj.* relating to utterances or conversation, as about the weather, whose purpose is to express friendly feelings rather than to convey ideas
phenomenon *n., pl.* **-mena** observable event or fact, especially a striking or unusual one; in philosophy, object or experience perceived by or apparently real to the senses rather than as it actually is. Compare NOUMENON — **-menal** *adj.* — **-menalism** *n.*
pheromone (férrə-mōn) *n.* sex attractant, warning chemical, or other substance secreted by certain animals and affecting others of the same species — **-monal** *adj.*
phial (fí-əl) *n.* small bottle, usually stoppered, as for perfume or poison (also "vial")
philander (fi-lándər) *formal. intr.v.* to flirt, or engage in casual love affairs (used of a man) [after *Philander*, name of a stock lover in traditional romances, from Greek *phil-*, love- + *aner*, a man] — **-derer** *n.*
philanthropy *n.* charity, love of one's fellow man and promotion of his welfare — **-thropic** *adj.* — **-pist** *n.*
philately (fi-láttə-li) *n.* study and collecting of stamps

or related items such as postmarks — **-telic** *adj.* — **-list** *n.*

philharmonic *formal. n.* orchestra, choir, or music society ~ *adj.* referring or relating to such a music-loving organisation

philippic (fi-líppik) *formal. n.* passionate, bitter, or abusive speech of criticism, tirade [from Greek *philippikoi logoi*, literally, the speeches relating to Philip, referring to the speeches of the Athenian orator Demosthenes, denouncing the political ambitions of *Philip* of Macedon]

philistine *adj.* lacking in or hostile to cultural interests and values ~ *n.* philistine person [after the ancient *Philistines*, regarded as barbarians] — **-tinism** *n.*

Phillips Screw *trademark. n.* screw with a cross-shaped groove in the head

phillumeny (fi-léwməni) *n.* study and collecting of matchboxes, matchbox labels, and books of matches — **-nist** *n.*

philology *n.* language study, especially comparison of languages or study of the historical development of a language — **-gist** *n.* — **-logical** *adj.*

philomel *n.* name of a nightingale in legend or poetry (also "Philomel", "Philomela") [after *Philomele*, a princess in Greek legend who was turned into a nightingale]

philoprogenitive *formal. adj.* producing many children or offspring, prolific; relating to love of children, especially one's own

philosophers' stone *n.* substance or stone believed by alchemists to have the power of turning base metals into gold

philtre (fíltər) *n.* magic potion believed to arouse love or desire, love potion (also *U.S.* "philter")

philtrum *formal. n.* shallow groove running vertically from the nose to the upper lip (rare)

phlebotomy (fli-bóttəmi) *n.* opening of a vein for drawing or letting blood, as for diagnosis or treatment (also "venesection") — **-mise** *tr.v.*

phlegm (flem) *n.* mucus secreted in the breathing passages; one of the four humours in ancient and medieval physiology, believed to cause sluggishness

phlegmatic (fleg-máttik) *formal. adj.* calmly indifferent, emotionally sluggish, unexcitable

phlogiston (flə-jísston) *n.* hypothetical substance or principle formerly thought to exist in combustible matter and to be released in fire — **-tic** *adj.*

phobia *n.* irrational, uncontrollable, and excessive fear or hatred of something — **phobic** *adj.*, *n.*

phocine (fṓ-sīn) *formal. adj.* relating to a seal or related creature

phoenix (féeniks) *n.* mythological bird that would burn itself up every 500 years and rise rejuvenated from the ashes; person, project, or the like that seems to be reborn after destruction or downfall

phoneme (fṓneem) *n.* in linguistics, speech sound identified as significant in a given language because it serves to distinguish one word from another: */l/ and /r/ are phonemes in English but not in Japanese* — **-emic** *adj.*

phonetic *adj.* relating to or representing speech sounds; conforming to pronunciation, as spelling in Spanish does — **-etics** *n.*

phonetic alphabet *n.* set of symbols used in transcribing speech; code, as used by radio operators, for identifying letters of the alphabet, such as *Tango* standing for *T*

phonograph *n.* early recording and sound-reproducing machine, using wax cylinders; *U.S.* record player — **-graphic** *adj.*

phonology *n.* sound system of a particular language; study of the sound system of a language or languages — **-gist** *n.* — **-logical** *adj.*

phosphor (fóss-fər) *n.* substance that emits light when stimulated by radiation

phosphorescence *n.* glowing or sustained emission of light following stimulation by radiation — **-escent** *adj.* — **-esce** *intr.v.*

photochromic *adj.* darkening or changing colour when exposed to light, as the glass or plastic in some sunglasses does — **-mism** *n.*

photosynthesis *n.* use by green plants of light energy, absorbed by chlorophyll in the leaves and other plant tissues, for the making of complex organic compounds from carbon dioxide and water; similar process in some bacteria — **-thetic** *adj.*

phrasal verb *n.* verb combined with an adverb and/or preposition, such as *put up with*, typically having a meaning different from the simple sum of its parts

phraseology *n.* style in speech or writing, way of putting things in words; choice of words, mode of expression, as of a particular person or group

phratry (fráytri) *n.* group of related clans within a tribe; small kinship grouping or civic or tribal subdivision in ancient Greece

phrenology *n.* former practice of studying the skull's shape and irregularities as a supposed indication of a person's character and mental powers — **-gist** *n.* — **-logical** *n.*

phthisis (thī́-siss, fthī́-, tī́-) *n.* TB, tuberculosis of the lungs; progressive wasting away of the body or part of the body — **-sic** *adj.*

phylacteries (fi-láktəri) *pl.n.* pair of small leather boxes containing biblical inscriptions, carried by religious Jewish men during weekday morning worship

phyle (fī́-li) *n.*, *pl.* **-lae** large kinship grouping or civic or tribal subdivision in ancient Greece

phylogeny (fī-lójəni) *n.* development or evolution of a species, genus, race, or the like; historical development of a language, custom, or the like. Compare ONTOGENY — **-genic**

phylum (fī́-ləm) *n.*, *pl.* **-la** in biological classification, category ranking above a class

physic *archaic. n.* medicinal preparation or drug, especially a laxative ~ *tr.v.* to heal, cure, treat medically

physiognomy (fízzi-ónnə-mi) *n.* art of judging character from external appearance, especially from facial features; *formal.* facial features, especially when regarded as indicating character (sometimes humorous) — **-nomic** *adj.* — **-nomist** *n.*

physiology *n.* study of the life processes and functioning of living matter; all these processes and functions themselves — **-gist** *n.* — **-logical** *adj.*

physiotherapy *n.* treatment of disease or disorders by physical or mechanical means, such as massage, exercises, and light rays — **-pist** *n.*

physique (fi-zéek) *n.* structure or appearance of the body, including shape, size, and muscular development

phytology (fī-tólləji) *n.* botany, study of plants — **-gist** *n.* — **-logical** *adj.*

phytotron (fī́tō-tron) *n.* building in which plants are cultivated under controlled conditions

piacular (pī-áckewlər) *formal. adj.* atoning or expi-

atory, especially for sacrilege; calling for or requiring expiation, wicked, sacrilegious
Pianola (peé-ə-nṓlə) *trademark. n.* type of player piano, a mechanically operated piano
piazza (pi-átsə) *n., pl.* **-zas** or **-ze** large public square or open space, especially in an Italian town
pibroch (peé-brok, -brokh) *n.* set of martial or funeral variations for highland bagpipes
¹pica (pī́kə) *n.* printer's unit of type sizes, lines, or page measurement, of 0.42 cm
²pica *n.* craving for unnatural food, such as mud or chalk, occurring sometimes in hysteria or during pregnancy [from Latin *pica*, a magpie, referring to the bird's wide-ranging appetite]
picador *n.* horseman in a bullfight, who lances the bull in the neck
picaresque (píckə-résk) *adj.* relating or referring to a novel of a loose, episodic structure dealing with the travels or adventures of a rogue-hero ~ *n.* picaresque novel
picaro (píckə-rō) *formal or archaic. n., pl.* **-ros** rogue, adventurer (also "picaroon")
piceous (pī́-si-əss) *adj.* relating to or resembling pitch, especially in being glossy and black
picker *n.* person or part of a loom that threads or throws the shuttle in weaving [related to *pitch*, to throw]
pickerel *n.* young pike
picket *n.* striker or group of protesters positioned outside a place of work, to discourage other workers or customers from entering; stake or pointed post driven into the ground, as for defence; military guard or watch stationed as a defence against surprise attack — **picket** *v.*
picot (peé-kō, pee-kṓ) *n.* any of the tiny loops forming an edging on ribbon, lace, or the like — **picot** *tr.v.*
pidgin (píjin) *n.* simplified speech or language, typically a mix of two or more languages used for basic communication, as for trade, between people having no natural language in common [from *pidgin English*, probably from a Chinese pronunciation of *business English*] — **pidgin** *adj.*
piebald *adj.* having different colours; blotched with black and white: *piebald horses.* Compare SKEWBALD; varied in incongruous ways, motley ~ *n.* piebald animal, especially a horse (also *U.S.* "pinto") [see PIED]
pièce de résistance (pyéss də ráyzi-stoNSS) *formal. n.* main dish of a meal; showpiece, outstanding work of art, performance, or the like within a set or series of related items
piecemeal *adv.* gradually, bit by bit; apart, separately, in pieces — **piecemeal** *adj.*
pie chart *n.* graph or statistical chart in the form of a circle with sectors of varying size representing the units (also "pie graph")
piecrust *adj.* referring to furniture with an edging or moulding of an indented or scalloped design
pied *adj.* having patches of different colours, piebald [from Latin *pica*, a magpie, referring to the bird's patched colouring]
pied-à-terre (pyéd-aa-táir) *n., pl.* **pieds-à-terre** flat, room, or the like, especially near a city centre, kept for occasional use by a person whose main home is elsewhere [French, literally, foot to the ground]
pier *n.* supporting structure or pillar, as for an arch or the spans of a bridge; narrow section of a wall between windows or other openings
pier glass *n.* tall mirror, especially one hung in former times on the wall between the windows
Pierian (pī-eéri-ən) *formal or archaic. adj.* relating to artistic inspiration, especially poetry; relating to learning; relating to the Muses [after the *Pierian Spring*, a fountain in Pieria in ancient Macedonia, a shrine for worshippers of the Muses]
piety *n.* religious devotion; dutifulness, especially towards one's parents; pure or outwardly pure act — **pious** *adj.*
piggin *n.* bucket of wood with one stave extended above the rim as a handle (also "pipkin")
pigment *n.* coloured powder mixed with water or oil to produce a paint; any substance producing or used as a colouring, as in petals or ink — **pigment** *tr.v.* — **-ation** *n.*
pikelet *British regional. n.* small, flat crumpet
pikestaff *n.* shaft of a pike or similar spear-like weapon; walking stick with a spike at the tip
pilaf *n.* dish of eastern origin, consisting of rice cooked in a spicy stock, often with meat or fish added (also "pilaff", "pilau", "pilaw")
pilaster (pi-lástər) *n.* pillar or column, typically rectangular, set into a wall and projecting slightly from it
pilfer *v.* to steal (a small item or amount) — **-age** *n.*
pill *intr.v.* to produce or become covered with small balls of fibre, as a woollen jumper might
pillage *v.* to steal or rob violently, plunder ~ *n.* plunder, spoils — **-lager** *n.*
pillbox *n.* cannon or machine-gun emplacement in the form of a low, circular, concrete building
pillion *n.* saddle or seat for a second rider, as on a horse or motorcycle — **pillion** *adv.*
pillory *n.* wooden frame with holes for locking in the head and hands of an offender in former times, and exposing him to public ridicule, scorn, or abuse — **pillory** *tr.v.*
pilose (pī́-lōz) *adj.* in biology, covered with fine soft hair — **-losity** *n.*
pimiento (pi-myéntō) *n.* sweet pepper, vegetable pepper (also "pimento", "capsicum") [Spanish, related to *pigment*]
pimp *n.* man who finds clients for a prostitute or brothel (also "ponce") — **pimp** *intr.v.*
pinafore *n.* apron, typically including a bib [originally *pinned afore* one's dress to protect it]
pince-nez (páNss-náy) *n., pl.* **pince-nez** glasses without sidepieces, held in place by being clipped to the bridge of the nose [French, literally, pinch-nose]
pincer *n.* claw of a lobster or crab (also "chela")
pincer movement *n.* military manoeuvre of attacking an enemy force on two flanks, like a claw closing
pinchbeck *n.* alloy of copper and zinc used in jewellery as imitation gold; cheap imitation, fake [after its inventor, Christopher *Pinchbeck*, a 17th-18th-century English watchmaker] — **pinchbeck** *adj.*
pinfold *n.* pen or pound for animals, such as stray sheep ~ *tr.v.* to pen in or as if in a pinfold
pinguid (píng-gwid) *formal. adj.* fatty, oily, or greasy; referring to rich, fertile soil — **-ity** *n.*
¹pinion *n.* bird's wing, specifically the end rear section holding the flight feathers; flight feather ~ *tr.v.* to restrain (a bird) by binding or plucking its flight feathers; to cut or bind (a bird's wings); to restrain (a person) by binding or holding him round the arms; to confine, shackle, make fast
²pinion *n.* smaller cogwheel or gearwheel

¹pink *n.* fox hunter's scarlet coat
²pink *tr.v.* to stab or prick lightly, as with a sword; to cut a zigzag or scalloped edge on; to decorate (leather or a similar material) with a pattern of tiny holes
³pink *intr.v.* to make sharp popping noises, as a poorly tuned car engine might (also "knock")
pinna *formal. n., pl.* **-nas** or **-nae** small leaf, as on a fern frond; feather, wing, fin, or similar projecting body part; external visible section of the ear (in this sense, also "auricle") — **pinnate** *adj.*
pinnacle *n.* topmost point, heights: *the pinnacle of success*; small turret or spire; mountain peak
pintle *n.* upright pivot pin, as on a rudder, gun carriage, or towing vehicle
pinyin (pín-yín) *n.* system of transcribing Chinese in the Roman alphabet, introduced by China in 1957 and now widely adopted in the West [Chinese, literally, spell sound]
pipe dream *n.* illusory or unrealistic hope or wish [referring to the fantasies produced by smoking an opium pipe]
pipette (pi-pét) *n.* glass tube, open at both ends, into which liquid is sucked to be measured or transferred, especially in chemistry experiments
piping *n.* icing in thin tube-like strands produced by squeezing through a nozzle; narrow tube of folded cloth, often enveloping a cord, as used for edging upholstery or clothes
pipkin *n.* cooking pot or small pan of earthenware; small bucket, piggin
piquant (peék-ənt, -ON) *adj.* tasting pleasantly spicy or savoury; interesting or attractive in a slightly disturbing or provocative way — **-ancy** *n.*
pique (peek) *n.* feeling of anger or resentment, as from a blow to one's pride ~ *tr.v.* to offend (someone), as by an unintended insult or blow to his pride; to provoke or arouse (someone's curiosity, interest, or the like); to pride (oneself) on something, congratulate (oneself) — **piqued** *adj.*
piracy (pír-ə-si) *n.* unauthorised use of someone else's idea, patent, copyright material, or the like
pirouette (pírroo-ét) *n.* rapid spinning of the body, especially a full turn on tip-toe or on the ball of a foot in ballet [French, from Old French *pirouet*, a toy spinning top] — **pirouette** *intr.v.*
pis aller (peéz-állay) *n., pl.* **pis allers** last resort, course of action taken for want of any alternative [French, literally, worst to go]
piscatorial (pískə-táwri-əl) *formal. adj.* relating to fishing or fishermen
piscina (pi-seé-nə, -sí-, -sheé-) *n., pl.* **-nas** or **-nae** stone basin, typically set in the wall of a church, for draining away the water used in ceremonial washing (also "sacrarium") [Latin, a fishpond]
piscine (píssīn) *formal. adj.* relating to or resembling a fish
pismire (píss-mīr) *archaic or dialect. n.* ant [Middle English, *pisse*, urine + *mire*, an ant; referring to the smell of an anthill]
piste (peest) *n.* ski slope or run; long rectangular area for fencing bouts
pitch *n.* width of the thread of a screw, or distance advanced by a screw in one full turn
pith *n.* spongy core running through stems and branches (also "medulla"); spongy white tissue between the rind and pulp of oranges or other citrus fruits; essential element, core, gist — **pith** *tr.v.*
piton (peé-ton, pee-tóN) *n.* spike or peg, usually with an eye or ring for a rope, driven into a rock or ice surface for support in mountaineering
pittance (pítt'nss) *n.* very small amount of money, such as a tiny living allowance or salary [from Vulgar Latin *pietantia*, a charitable donation, as of food given to itinerant monks, from Latin, *pietas*, piety or pity]
pizzicato (pítsi-kaátō) *adv.* played by plucking rather than bowing the strings, as a passage for the violin might be — **pizzicato** *n., adj.*
pizzle *n.* penis of an animal, especially of a bull; whip made of a bull's pizzle
placard *n.* large notice or poster, as for advertisements or carried at protest demonstrations — **placard** *tr.v.*
placate *tr.v.* to soothe or pacify, especially by making concessions, appease — **-catory** *adj.*
placebo (plə-seé-bō) *n., pl.* **-bos** or **-boes** inactive substance administered as a medicine, in order to humour a patient or to make comparisons in an experiment; something, such as an idle promise or excuse, used to soothe or humour someone [Latin, I shall please or pacify]
placenta (plə-séntə) *n., pl.* **-tas** or **-tae** organ connecting a foetus to its mother; afterbirth — **-cental**, **-centate** *adj.*
placket *n.* slit in a dress, shirt, or the like, as for fitting a fastening or for access to a pocket
plafond (plə-fón, pla-fóN) *formal. n.* ceiling, especially one decorated with paintings
plagiarism (pláyjə-riz'm) *n.* adoption or theft of another person's ideas, writings, tunes, or the like and passing them off as one's own — **-ist** *n.* — **-istic** *adj.* — **-ise** *v.*
plaid (plad) *n.* tartan cloth or pattern; strip of tartan worn over the left shoulder in traditional Scottish Highland dress — **plaid** *adj.*
plainsong *n.* Gregorian chant or similar simple medieval church music, traditionally unaccompanied
plaintiff *n.* person or group that sues another or brings a civil action in court (opposite "defendant")
plaintive *formal. adj.* sorrowful, mournful, expressing sadness [related to *complaint*]
planchet (plánchit) *n.* coin blank, plain metal disc ready for stamping as a coin [related to *plank*]
planchette (plaan-shét, ploN-) *n.* mobile board, typically heart-shaped and mounted on casters, that allegedly writes or spells out messages from the spirit world while the medium is touching it lightly
planetarium *n., pl.* **-iums** or **-ia** projector of images of the stars and planets, or the domed room or building in which it operates
plangent *formal. adj.* mournful, expressing sadness, plaintive; loud and deep or resonant [related to *complaint*] — **-gency** *n.*
plankton *n.* floating mass of tiny animal and plant organisms on or near the surface of the sea or a lake
plantain *n.* banana-like starchy fruit used in cooking in tropical areas; tree bearing plantains
plantar (plán-tər) *formal. adj.* on or relating to the sole of the foot: *plantar warts*
planter *n.* settler or colonist in a new region in former times
plaque (plak, plaak) *n.* flat nameplate, memorial tablet, or the like, as mounted on a wall or monument; brooch worn as a membership badge; coating of bac-

terial and other materials on teeth

plashy *adj.* splashing; marshy, wet

plasma *n.* yellowish liquid part of blood, lymph, or the like, in which the cells are suspended; watery part of milk, whey; in physics, gas-like matter of enormously high temperature, as in stars and fusion reactors — **plasmic**, **plasmatic** *adj.*

plastic arts *pl.n.* arts such as film, painting, and sculpture, dealing with three-dimensional representation; visual arts, such as painting and sculpture, as distinct from performing arts

plastron *n.* breastplate as formerly worn under a coat of mail; quilted pad worn to protect the upper body in fencing; false front of a dress shirt; breastbone and its associated cartilages; shell on the underside of a tortoise or turtle — **plastral** *adj.*

plateau (pla-tṓ) *n.*, *pl.* **-s** or **-x** tableland, high and level stretch of land; flattish section of a graph; relatively stable condition or period, as of economic activity — **plateau** *intr.v.*

platelayer *British. n.* worker who lays and repairs railway track

platen (plátt'n) *n.* metal plate, especially one holding the paper as it is printed in a press; roller of a typewriter

plate tectonics *n.* study of the Earth's crust, based on the theory that it consists of giant sliding sections or plates

platitude (plátti-tewd) *n.* unoriginal, dull, or obvious remark, commonplace [French, literally, flatness] — **-tudinous** *adj.* — **-tudinise** *intr.v.*

platonic (plə-tónnik) *adj.* referring to love or a close relationship between two unrelated people that is free of sexual desire [discussed in the writings of the ancient Greek philosopher *Plato*]

plaudits (pláwdits) *pl.n.* praise, enthusiastic approval [related to *applause*]

plausible *adj.* believable, convincing, or likely: *a plausible argument*; seemingly reliable, acceptable, or valid, though often suspect: *a plausible politician/excuse* [related to *applause*]

plaza (plaázə) *n.* large public square or open space, especially in a Spanish-speaking town

plea bargaining *n.* negotiations between the defence and prosecution prior to a criminal trial, aimed at exchanging a guilty plea in court for a reduced charge — **plea bargain** *intr.v.*

pleach *tr.v.* to plait or weave (branches or bark), as in making a hedge or arbour (also "plash")

pleasantry *formal. n.* joking or humorous action or remark — **pleasantries** socially acceptable and polite remarks, small talk

plebeian (pli-beé-ən) *formal. adj.* relating to or characteristic of the masses or of common people, vulgar and crude, having coarse tastes; relating to the Roman plebs — **pleb**, **plebeian** *n.*

plebiscite (plébbi-sīt, -sit) *n.* referendum or vote by an entire electorate on some question of national or regional importance

plebs *n.* masses or class of common people in ancient Rome

plectrum *n.*, *pl.* **-trums** or **-tra** small thin disc or plate, as of plastic, used for plucking the strings of a guitar, lute, or related instrument (also "pick")

pledge *n.* promise or guarantee; item placed in pawn; toast, drinking someone's health — **pledge** *tr.v.*

plenary (pleén-əri, plén-) *formal. adj.* complete, full, absolute: *the plenary powers of our leader*; fully attended, or open to all: *a plenary session* ~ *n.* plenary meeting or session (also "plenum")

plenipotentiary (plénni-pə-tén-shəri) *formal. adj.* full, absolute, plenary: *plenipotentiary powers*; having or granting full powers ~ *n.* ambassador or other diplomat or agent fully authorised to represent a foreign government

plenitude (plénni-tewd) *formal. n.* fullness, completeness; abundance, plentifulness

plenum (pleé-nəm) *n.*, *pl.* **-nums** or **-na** enclosed space inside which the air or gas pressure is greater than that outside; general assembly, meeting with all members present; *formal.* fullness, completeness

pleonasm (pleé-ə-naz'm) *n.* redundancy, use of more words than necessary in expressing an idea — **-nastic** *adj.*

plethora (pléthərə) *formal. n.* excess, overabundance, superfluity: *a plethora of blood/rules* — **-thoric** *adj.*

plexor *n.* small rubber-headed hammer used for testing reflexes and tapping the chest for the purpose of diagnosis (also "plessor")

plexus *n.*, *pl.* **plexus** or **-uses** network, interwoven complex of parts, specifically of nerves or blood vessels

pliable *adj.* flexible, easy to bend, supple; changing easily to new conditions, adaptable; easily persuaded or influenced, compliant, yielding

plight *n.* difficult situation, condition of difficulty or distress, predicament

plimsoll (plím-səl) *British. n.* light canvas rubber-soled sports shoe (also "gym shoe") [probably from the similarity of the surrounding rubber rim to the *Plimsoll line*]

Plimsoll line *n.* line or set of lines marked on the side of a cargo ship to indicate its legal load-level in various conditions (also "Plimsoll mark", "load line") [after Samuel *Plimsoll*, a 19th-century British MP and campaigner for safer shipping]

plinth *n.* base block or slab, as of a column, statue, vase, or trophy; strip of stonework serving as the base or foundation of a wall

plonk *chiefly British. informal. n.* wine of poor quality [probably from a distortion of French *blanc*, white, referring to white wine]

ploy *n.* trick or tactic, as in a game, to secure an advantage, stratagem

plumage *n.* bird's feathers collectively; *informal.* smart clothing, finery

plumb (plum) *n.* lead weight hanging on a cord, as used in fishing, depth-sounding, or determining a vertical line (also "plummet") — **out of plumb** not precisely vertical ~ *adj.* vertical, exactly upright, perpendicular ~ *tr.v.* to check with a plumb line; to establish the depth of, sound; to investigate or examine carefully; to connect or install as part of a plumbing system ~ *informal. adv.* exactly

plumbism (plúm-biz'm) *formal. n.* lead poisoning

pluperfect *adj.* relating or referring to the past perfect tense of a verb, as in *had climbed* — **pluperfect** *n.*

pluralism *n.* social coexistence of several racial, religious, or cultural groups; holding of two or more posts or offices, especially in the church, at one time — **-ist** *n.* — **-istic** *adj.*

plurality *U.S. n.* relative majority in an election

plutocracy (ploō-tóckrə-si) *n.* class of wealthy people wielding power in a society; government by such a

class; country or society under such government — **-crat** *n.* — **-cratic** *adj.*
pluviometer (plōōvi-ómmitər) *n.* rain gauge — **-metric** *adj.* — **-metry** *n.*
ply *v.* — *tr.* to wield skilfully or use regularly (a weapon or tool); to practise or engage in (one's trade); to cover or travel over or on regularly, especially by sailing; to keep offering or giving something to: *plied us with cakes* — *intr.* to travel or sail regularly over a particular route
pneuma (néwmə) *formal. n.* soul, spirit
pneumatic (new-máttik) *adj.* driven by or filled with compressed air: *pneumatic drills/tyres*; relating to the pneuma, spiritual; *informal.* having or relating to full shapely breasts, busty
pocketbook *U.S. n.* wallet or small bag
pococurante (pōkō-kōō-ránti) *formal. adj.* uninterested or uncaring, indifferent, apathetic ~ *n.* an uncaring or uninterested person [Italian, literally, little caring]
[1]**pod** *n.* streamlined compartment, as for fuel or guns, on an aircraft
[2]**pod** *n.* small close-packed group of seals, whales, or the like; small flock of birds
[3]**pod** *n.* socket of a drill or other boring tool, in which the bit is held
podium (pōdi-əm) *n., pl.* **-iums** or **-ia** small platform, as for a lecturer or conductor, dais
poetaster (pō-i-táss-tər) *n.* poet of poor quality, rhymester
pogoniate (pə-gōni-ət) *adj.* in biology, bearded; *formal.* unshaven or bearded (humorously pompous)
pogrom (pə-gróm, póg-rəm, -rom) *n.* massacre, as of Jews in Eastern Europe in former times, typically organised with official backing
poignant (póyn-yənt) *adj.* emotionally affecting or touching; sharp, pointed — **-nance, -nancy** *n.*
pointing *n.* cement or mortar for filling joints, cracks, or seams, as in brickwork
polarise *tr.v.* to adjust light or other radiation into a particular pattern, especially when restricting its vibrations to a single plane; to divide into two extreme and hostile positions or groups — **-ised** *adj.* — **-isation** *n.*
polarity *n.* condition of having two opposing physical properties at different points, as a magnet or battery has; condition of having either a positive or a negative electrical charge; separation into or possession of opposing groups, characteristics, or the like
Polaroid *trademark. n.* camera that produces a print a few seconds after taking the photograph; specially treated, light-polarising, glare-reducing plastic, as used in some sunglasses
polder *n.* stretch of land reclaimed from the sea or a lake and protected by dykes, especially in Holland
polemic (pə-lémmik) *formal. n.* attack on the opinions or beliefs of another; dispute, controversy, argument, especially over a principle or belief; severe criticism — **polemic, -ical** *adj.* — **-icist, -ics** *n.*
polestar *n.* guiding principle, standard
polis (pól-iss) *n., pl.* **-leis** city-state in ancient Greece
polity (póllәti) *formal. n.* government structure of a nation, church, or the like; politically organised unit, such as a nation, having a particular form of government
poll (pōl) *n.* head, especially the hairy top of the head; blunt or broad end of a hammer, axe, or the like. Compare PEEN ~ *tr.v.* to shear, trim, cut, or crop: *poll horns/sheep*
pollard (póllərd) *n.* tree whose branches are cut back to the trunk to encourage a dense growth of new foliage; hornless goat, ox, sheep, or other usually horned animal
pollex *formal. n., pl.* **-lices** thumb, or corresponding digit in an animal — **-lical** *adj.*
Pollyanna *n.* optimist, especially one who is blindly or excessively optimistic [after the heroine of the novel *Pollyanna* of 1913, by Eleanor Porter]
poltergeist (pól-tər-gīst, pōl-) *n.* noisy mischievous ghost or spirit, held responsible for unexplained household noises and damage
poltroon (pol-trōōn) *archaic. n.* cowardly wretch
polygamy (pə-líggəmi) *n.* system of marriage in which a person can have more than one wife or husband at any one time. Compare MONOGAMY; practice of certain mammals to have more than one mate — **-mous** *adj.*
polyglot (pólli-glot) *formal. adj.* speaking, written in, or relating to several languages — **polyglot** *n.*
polygon *n.* any closed geometric figure having three or more straight sides — **-gonal** *adj.*
polygraph *n.* instrument recording changes in pulse, blood pressure, breathing rate, and the like; lie detector — **-ic** *adj.*
polymath *n.* learned person knowledgeable in many subjects (also *formal.* "polyhistor") — **polymath, -ic** *adj.*
polyp (póllip) *n.* sea anemone, coral, or related creature, typically tube-like and tentacled; growth on or under a mucous membrane, as in the nose — **-ous, -oid** *adj.*
polyphony (pə-líffəni) *n.* combination of two or more distinct melodic parts, counterpoint — **-phonic** *adj.*
polysemy (pə-líssəmi, pólli-seemi) *formal. n.* ambiguity or multiple meaning in individual words — **-semous** *adj.*
polystyrene (pólli-stīr-een) *n.* rigid light white synthetic substance used as packing and insulating material
polysyndeton (pólli-síndi-tən) *formal. n.* repetition of conjunctions for stylistic effect, as in *blood and sweat and tears*
polytheism *n.* belief in two or more gods. Compare MONOTHEISM — **-istic** *adj.*
polyunsaturated *adj.* referring to fats or oils which in the human diet inhibit the production of cholesterol, a major factor in heart disease
polyzoan (pólli-zō-ən) *n.* sea creature consisting of a colony of individual polyps (also "bryozoan") — **polyzoan** *adj.*
pomace (púmmiss) *n.* pulp remaining after apples or other fruits have been crushed to extract the juice
pomade (po-maád, pə-, -máyd) *n.* perfumed oil or cream for the hair (also "pomatum") — **pomade** *tr.v.*
pomander (pə-mándər) *n.* fragrant mixture, as of dried petals, for scenting linen; box or bag containing the pomander; orange stuck with cloves
pome *n.* fleshy fruit, such as the apple or pear, whose seeds are in a large central capsule
pomelo (pómmi-lō) *n., pl.* **-los** grapefruit
pommel (púmm'l, pómm'l) *n.* knob on the hilt of a sword; raised section at the front of a saddle ~ *tr.v.* to beat, pummel
pompadour (pómpə-dōōr) *n.* woman's hairstyle; popular in the 18th century, with a high, swept-back roll;

man's high, swept-back hairstyle [after Madame de *Pompadour*, mistress of King Louis XV of France, who popularised it]

ponce *chiefly British. n.* man who controls the trade or lives off the earnings of a prostitute; pimp

poncho *n., pl.* **-chos** blanket-like cloak with a hole or slit in the middle for the head, originally a South American garment

ponderous *adj.* dull and strained, laborious: *a ponderous speech*; large and awkward, ungainly; very heavy, massive

pongid (póng-gid, pónjid) *n.* anthropoid ape — **pongid** *adj.*

poniard (pón-yərd, -yaard) *formal or archaic. n.* dagger

Pontic *formal. adj.* relating to the Black Sea

pontifex (pónti-feks) *n., pl.* **-fices** priest of senior status in ancient Rome

pontiff *adj.* Pope

pontificate *intr.v.* to speak in a dogmatic, overconfident way; to lay down the law — **-ation** *n.* — **-ifical** *adj.*

pontine *formal. adj.* relating to bridges

pontoon *n.* float for supporting a bridge or a vehicle, such as a raft or seaplane

Pooh-Bah *informal. n.* pompous official with seemingly unlimited powers (literary) [after the name of the Lord-High-Everything-Else in W.S. Gilbert's *Mikado* of 1885]

poop deck *n.* deck or platform above the main deck near the back of a ship (also "poop")

populace *formal. n.* inhabitants of a place; population as a whole

populism *n.* political theory, style, or policies based on the needs or interests of the common people — **-list** *adj., n.*

porcine (pór-sīn) *formal. adj.* pig-like; piggish

porous *adj.* having pores; able to absorb gas or liquid through small openings, such as pores — **-osity** *n.*

porringer *n.* shallow bowl or small cup, often with a handle

port *tr.v.* to carry a military weapon diagonally across the body, with its muzzle or blade near one's left shoulder — **port** *n.*

portage (pórt-ij) *n.* act of carrying, transport; cost of transport; carrying of boats and cargo overland between waterways — **portage** *v.*

portals *formal. pl.n.* entrance, gateway: *the portals of the cathedral/knowledge*

porte-cochère (pórt-kō-sháir) *n.* carriage entrance into the courtyard of a large house; roofed structure by a building entrance, at which vehicles take on or let off passengers [French, literally, coach-door]

portend (pawr-ténd) *formal. tr.v.* to be a grave sign or omen of — **-tent** *n.*

portentous *formal. adj.* pompous or pretentiously earnest: *a portentous sermon*; portending, warning of something significant about to happen: *portentous clouds*

portfolio *n., pl.* **-os** case for holding loose papers or official documents; area of responsibility of a government official, such as a cabinet minister; list or collection of investments

portico (pór-tikō) *n., pl.* **-cos** or **-coes** porch with a roof and columns, sometimes surrounding a building

portière *n.* (pór-ti-air) *n.* curtain over a doorway or door

portion *n.* part of an estate received by an heir; *archaic.* dowry; *archaic.* one's lot or fate

portmanteau word (pórt-mán-tō) *n.* word formed by combining parts of two separate words, such as *ginormous* from *gigantic* and *enormous* (also "blend") [coined by Lewis Carroll, referring to the two hinged sections of a *portmanteau*, or traveller's trunk]

poser *chiefly British. informal. n.* question that is difficult to answer

poseur (pō-zér, -zőr) *n.* person who pretends to have great sophistication or experience in order to impress others

posit (pózzit) *formal. tr.v.* to assume for the sake of argument, postulate

posset *n.* heated, spiced, and sweetened milk drink, curdled with wine or beer, sometimes used as a remedy for colds

possum *n.* — **play possum** *chiefly U.S. informal.* to pretend to be dead or asleep [after the American *possum* or *opossum*, a tree-dwelling marsupial that reputedly deters predators by pretending to be dead]

Possum *trademark. n.* device allowing paralysed patients to operate machines such as typewriters by blowing or light touching

post *intr.v. archaic.* to hasten or speed to the specified place or for the specified purpose; to rise and fall in the saddle in time with a horse's trot — **post** *adv.*

post-bellum *adj.* post-war, especially after the American Civil War

poste restante (pṓst réstONT, ri-stÓNT) *interj.* to be collected (written on posted items to request that they should be held at the specified post office until collected by the addressee; also *U.S.* "general delivery") [French, literally, remaining post]

posterior *formal. adj.* behind, at the rear ~ *n.* bottom, buttocks (euphemistic or humorous)

posterity *formal. n.* person's descendants; future generations

postern *archaic. n.* back or side gate, especially to a fortification or castle

posthumous (póstewməss) *adj.* happening, born, published, or continuing after a person's death

postilion *n.* rider of the left front horse of a coach, who helps to guide the coach (also "postillion")

postmeridian *formal. adj.* afternoon

post-mortem *formal. adj.* after death ~ *n.* post-mortem examination, autopsy; *informal.* after-the-fact review or analysis of something, especially something unsuccessful

post-prandial *formal. adj.* after a meal, especially after dinner (often humorously pompous)

postscript *n.* text added after the signature of a letter and typically preceded by the abbreviation "P.S."; extra information added at the end of a text

postulant *formal. n.* person asking for something; person seeking membership of a religious order

postulate *tr.v.* to assume for the sake of argument, posit, hypothesise; *formal.* to put forward for appointment, promotion, or canonisation ~ *n.* basic assumption, premise, axiom — **-lator**, **-lation** *n.*

posture *n.* position of a person's body or of its parts in relation to one another; general position or attitude ~ *intr.v.* to adopt exaggerated attitudes or behaviour for effect

potable (pṓtə-b'l) *formal. adj.* drinkable, usually because uncontaminated — **potables** *pl.n.*

potage (po-táazh) *n.* thick soup

potamic (pə-támmik) *formal. adj.* relating to a river or stream
potation *formal. n.* drink, or the act of drinking (often humorous) — **-atory** *adj.*
poteen (po-téen, -chéen) *n.* whiskey distilled illicitly in Ireland (also "potheen")
potent *formal. adj.* very strong or powerful; forceful — **potency** *n.*
potentate *formal. n.* monarch; person who dominates and rules over a group or enterprise
potential *adj.* possible but not yet present or actual ~ *n.* likely talent or ability that has still not proved itself in actual successes — **-ity** *n.*
potlatch *n.* ceremonial feast among northwestern American Indians marked by the host's lavish presentation of gifts
potpourri (pṓ-pŏŏrri) *n. formal.* varied mixture or collection; jar of dried flower petals and spices, used to scent the air [French, *pot*, pot + *pourri*, rotten; related to *putrid*]
potsherd (pót-sherd) *n.* pottery fragment, as in an archaeological excavation (also "potshard", "shard", "sherd")
poulard (pōō-laard) *n.* hen that has been spayed and fattened for eating [French]
poult (pōlt) *n.* chick, young of a domestic fowl or related bird
poultice (pṓl-tiss) *n.* dressing, often made of moist bread or meal heated and spread on a cloth, applied to ease pain or inflammation (also, old-fashioned, "cataplasm")
pounce *formal. n.* talon of a bird of prey
pouncet box *n.* old-fashioned perfume box with a perforated lid
pound *n.* stretch of canal between two adjoining locks
pourboire (páwr-bwaar, pōōr-bwár) *formal. n.* tip, gratuity (literary) [French, literally, for drinking]
poussin (pōō-sáN) *n.* very young chicken bred for eating [French]
power of attorney *n.* legal authorisation to act as another's agent, or the document conveying it
practitioner *n.* person who works in a profession, by contrast to a theoretician, academic, or teacher
Praetorian guard *n.* Roman emperors' military guard; any corps of bodyguards
pragmatic *adj.* practical, dealing with or relating to facts and actual circumstances rather than theories or ideals — **-tism**, **-tist** *n.*
prairie *n.* grassland, especially in North America
prandial *formal. adj.* relating to a meal, especially dinner (usually humorous)
prate *formal or archaic. v.* to say or speak in a chatty, idle way, chatter
praxis *n.* practical application of a theory or area of study; habitual practice, custom
preamble *n.* preliminary statement or explanation, as in a formal document
prebendary (prébbən-dri) *n.* clergyman attached to a cathedral or large church who receives an allowance, or prebend, from its funds (also "prebend")
precarious *adj.* insecure and uncertain, and therefore risky
precede *v.* to go or come before in time or order
precedence (préssi-d'nss) *n.* priority given according to position or rank: *Should quality take/have precedence over quantity?*
precedent (préssi-d'nt) something earlier than and similar to something else; action or decision used as a justification for treating later cases similarly
precentor (pri-séntər) *n.* director or lead singer of a choir, especially in a church — **-ial** *adj.*
precept *formal. n.* rule, principle, or order that imposes duties or standards — **-ive** *adj.*
precinct *n.* area or neighbourhood with defined boundaries; surroundings or grounds, enclosed by a wall or other boundary; district of a U.S. city under a particular administrative or police authority; electoral district or constituency in the U.S., ward; district in a town, often closed to traffic, set apart for the specified purpose: *a shopping precinct*
precincts *pl.n.* surrounding area or district
preciosity *formal. n.* over-elegance, as of manner or language — **precious** *adj.*
precipice *n.* very steep place, such as a cliff or cliff face — **-cipitous** *adj.*
precipitate *formal. tr.v.* to cause to fall suddenly or steeply; to cause (typically something bad) to happen suddenly; to separate, condense, or deposit (a substance) from a chemical solution ~ *n.* something precipitated, as from a chemical solution ~ *formal. adj.* hasty and typically ill-considered [related to *precipice*]
precipitation *formal. n.* formation and fall or deposit of rain, snow, or dew; quality of being precipitate
précis (práy-see) *n.*, *pl.* **précis** concise summary of a longer account or text [French, literally, precise] — **précis** *tr.v.*
precisian *formal. n.* person who is very precise and strict in the observance of rules, a religion, or the like (old-fashioned)
preclude *formal. tr.v.* to prevent or exclude, especially by previous action — **-clusion** *n.* — **-clusive** *adj.*
precocious *adj.* developing or maturing unusually early: *a precocious child with a precocious interest in science* — **-cocity** *n.*
precognition *formal. n.* clairvoyance in the form of knowledge of something before it actually happens — **-nitive** *adj.*
preconceived *adj.* formed beforehand, without knowledge or experience: *preconceived ideas* (usually derogatory) — **preconception** *n.*
precursor *formal. adj.* forerunner; predecessor
precursory *formal. adj.* introductory; suggesting or warning that something is to follow — **-cursory** *adj.*
predator (préddə-tər) *n.* creature that kills and eats prey; person capable of destroying others or using them ruthlessly — **-tory**, **-dacious** *adj.* — **-dation** *n.*
predecease *formal. tr.v.* to die before (someone else) — **predecease** *n.*
predecessor *n.* someone who precedes another, as in a position or function
predetermined *adj.* already determined, decided in advance, foreordained, predestined
predicament *n.* difficult, embarrassing, or unpleasant situation
predicate *formal. tr.v.* to attribute, ascribe: *predicated sophistication of the Druids*; to base or ground: *a hypothesis predicated on empirical evidence* ~ *n.* the part of a clause or sentence, typically including a verb, that expresses something about the subject — **-ation** *n.*
predicative *adj.* relating to the predicate of a clause; referring or relating to an adjective that is separated from the noun by a linking verb, as in *The hall was*

dark, and functions as a complement. Compare ATTRIBUTIVE

predilection *formal. n.* preference; partiality, taste, liking: *a predilection for sleazy bars*

predisposition *n.* pre-existing inclination or susceptibility to something — **predispose** *tr.v.*

predominate *intr.v.* to be superior in power, importance, influence, or quantity — **-nance** *n.* — **-nant** *adj.*

pre-empt *tr.v.* to prevent, thwart, or counteract by taking precautions or advance action: *pre-empted the attack/his rival/our plans* — **-emption** *n.* — **-emptive** *adj.*

prefabricate *tr.v.* to construct in advance, for later use or assembly; to build in sections prior to on-site assembly — **-ation** *n.* — **-cated** *adj.*

prefer *formal. tr.v.* to bring (legal charges) against someone

preferment *formal. n.* promotion or advancement to a higher office

prehensile (pri-hén-sīl) *adj.* referring or relating to a tail adapted for grasping and holding

prelate (préllət) *n.* bishop, abbot, or other clergyman of similar standing — **-lacy** *n.*

prelude *n.* anything that comes before or serves as an introduction

premedication *n.* sedative given to a patient before a general anaesthetic

premeditated *adj.* deliberately planned beforehand: *premeditated murder* — **-ation** *n.*

première (prémmi-áir) *n.* first public presentation of a film, play, or the like (also "premiere") [French, literally, first] — **première** *v.*

premise (prémmiss) *n.* proposition on which an argument is based or from which a conclusion can be drawn (also *chiefly British* "premiss") ~ *tr.v.* to postulate, assume, hypothesise

premium *n.* something given away free, or sold at a reduced price, to the buyer of something else; bonus or similar additional sum of money added to a regular price, salary, or the like; value or high regard placed on something; insurance policy payment

premonition *n.* sense of something about to happen, presentiment, especially of something bad; feeling of foreboding

preoccupied *formal. adj.* engrossed in thought, absent-minded; too busy to pay attention — **-pation** *n.*

preponderance *formal. n.* superiority, as of power, number, or weight — **-ant** *adj.* — **-ation** *n.* — **-ate** *intr.v.*

prepossessing *formal. adj.* pleasing, attractive: *not a very prepossessing young man* — **prepossess** *tr.v.*

preposterous *adj.* absurd, ridiculous, contrary to all reason and common sense

prepuce *formal. n.* foreskin

prequel *informal. n.* sequel dealing with earlier events

prerequisite *n.* prior requirement, something that is a necessary condition — **prerequisite** *adj.*

prerogative *n.* right or privilege conferred by rank, the law, or other authority — **prerogative** *adj.*

presage (préssij) *tr.v.* to foretell, predict; to portend, be an omen of — **presage** *n.*

presbyopia (prézbi-ṓpi-ə) *n.* focusing disability and longsightedness that develop as one grows older — **-opic** *adj.*

presbyter (prézbi-tər) *formal. n.* priest or elder in various churches — **-ery** *n.*

prescient (préssi-ənt, préshi-) *formal. adj.* having foresight, knowing about events before they happen — **-ence** *n.*

prescribe *tr.v.* to set down as a rule, order or advise ~ *v.* to order or advise a remedy or treatment — **-scription** *n.*

prescriptivism *n.* study of language based on or setting standards of correctness, rather than confining itself to analysing actual usage. Compare DESCRIPTIVISM — **-ist** *n.*, *adj.*

presentiment *n.* sense of something about to happen, feeling of foreboding

prestidigitation *formal. n.* conjuring, or deft hand movements in conjuring, sleight of hand (often humorous)

presto *adv.* suddenly or quickly (used as a musical direction) — **presto** *adj.*, *n.*

presumption *n.* cheek, insolence; accepting something as true — **-tive** *adj.*

presumptuous *formal. adj.* cheeky, insolent; assuming or demanding rights, intimacy, or other status or relationships that one is not entitled to

pretensions *pl.n.* claims, usually false or unproven, to some right, title, skill, or the like

pretentious *adj.* having airs and graces, acting above one's station or in a false, superficial, flashy manner

preterite (préttərit) *adj.* relating or referring to the past tense of a verb, indicating completed actions, as in *I gave* or *She helped* — **preterite** *n.*

preternatural *formal. adj.* supernatural; abnormal

pretext *n.* false but convincing reason or excuse, given publicly to conceal one's real reason or motive

prevailing *adj.* having or showing greater or more widespread force, influence, frequency, or currency — **prevail** *intr.v.*

prevalent *adj.* current or widespread — **-lence** *n.*

prevarication *formal. n.* evasion of the truth, deceptive speech or action — **-cate** *intr.v.*

prie-dieu (prée-dyṓ) *n.*, *pl.* **-x** or **-s** prayer desk, with a knee-support attached to a framework surmounted by a small lectern [French, literally, pray-God]

primacy *n.* condition of being first

prima donna (prée-mə dónnə) *n.*, *pl.* **prima donnas** chief female singer, especially of an opera company; *informal.* temperamental and demanding person [Italian, literally, first lady]

prima facie (prīmə fáy-shee, -see) *adj.* at first sight, likely; apparently true or plausible on the basis of a preliminary impression [Latin] — **prima facie** *adv.*

primal *adj.* first; first in time, primordial; first in importance, prime, primary

primate *n.* bishop or archbishop of the highest rank in a region; monkey, ape, human, or related mammal

primer *n.* elementary or introductory textbook or manual

primeval *adj.* existing since the beginning or the earliest stage: *primeval forest*

primigravida (prīmi-grávvi-də) *formal. n.*, *pl.* **-das** or **-dae** girl or woman who is pregnant for the first time

primogeniture (prīmō-jénnichər) *n.* state of being the first-born; right of the first-born or the eldest to inherit a deceased person's entire estate — **-genitary**, **-genital** *adj.*

primordial *adj.* existing at or relating to the beginning or the earliest stage; *formal.* basic, fundamental, primary — **primordial** *n.*

primordial soup *n.* liquid mixture of organic chemicals in early times from which life may have originally developed
Primus *trademark. n.* small and portable cooking stove, burning paraffin or oil
prior *n.* monk second in rank to an abbot — **-ate, -ship** *n.*
prioress *n.* nun second in rank to an abbess
priory *n.* monastery headed by a prior; convent headed by a prioress
prism *n.* glass or transparent plastic slab, as in cameras and binoculars, for reflecting, refracting, or dispersing light — **-matic** *adj.*
pristine (príss-teen) *adj.* in its original condition; unsullied or uncontaminated
privation *n.* deprivation, especially of basic amenities or essentials
privet (prívvit) *n.* hedging shrub, having dark purple berries
privy (prívvi) *n.* lavatory or latrine, especially in an outhouse ~ *formal. adj.* — **privy to** given access to information that is not generally available
Privy Council *n.* council appointed to advise the British king or queen — **Privy Councillor** *n.*
privy purse *n.* money voted by Parliament for the running of the royal household
probang *n.* long and flexible surgical rod, as for removing obstructions from the throat
probate *n.* legal proof of the validity of wills — **probate** *tr.v.*
probation *n.* trial period on a job or in an organisation; suspension of a convicted criminal's sentence subject to good behaviour and supervision by a probation officer — **-ary** *adj.* — **-er** *n.*
probation officer *n.* social worker responsible to a court for supervising offenders on probation
probity *formal. n.* integrity, honesty, decency, uprightness
proboscis (prə-bóssiss) *formal. n., pl.* **-cises** or **-cides** trunk of an elephant or similar long flexible snout; big long nose (usually humorous)
proceedings *pl.n.* legal action; activities of a meeting or conference; record of a meeting; collection of papers given at a conference
proclamation *n.* official public declaration — **proclaim** *tr.v.*
proclivity *formal. n.* natural inclination or leaning, liking, tendency
procrastinate *formal. intr.v.* to go in for delay or postponement — **-ation** *n.*
procreation *n.* reproduction, producing of offspring — **procreate** *v.*
Procrustean bed (prō-krústi-ən, prə-) *n.* rigid, arbitrary standard imposed on all, regardless of individual differences or circumstances [after *Procrustes*, a robber in Greek mythology, who stretched or shortened his captives to fit an iron bed] — **procrustean** *adj.*
proctology *n.* branch of medicine dealing with the rectum or anus — **-gist** *n.* — **-logical** *adj.*
proctor *n.* university official in charge of discipline; invigilator or supervisor of examinations; agent, as for collecting tithes or conducting a case in court; synod delegate representing the clergy
procurator fiscal *n.* public prosecutor and coroner in Scotland
procure *tr.v.* to obtain; to bring about, cause to happen; to provide (a prostitute) for a client — **-curation, -curement** *n.*
prodigal *adj.* wasteful or extravagant, profligate; generous or lavish ~ *n.* spendthrift; person who has gone astray, as by adopting a disreputable life-style — **-ity** *n.*
prodigious *formal. adj.* extraordinary or wonderful (old-fashioned)
prodigy *n.* person with amazing powers or talents; *informal.* something amazing
proem (prṓ-em) *formal. n.* short introduction or preface to a literary work — **-ial** *adj.*
profane *adj.* not sacred; irreverent, blasphemous, or obscene; secular or worldly, not religious; *formal.* referring or relating to lay people as opposed to experts, professionals, and other specialists ~ *tr.v.* to desecrate, defile — **-fanation** *n.* — **-fanatory** *adj.*
profanity *n.* swearing or coarse language, especially when the swearwords used refer to religion or sex; swearword
profess *formal. tr.v.* to claim by asserting or declaring; to pretend agreement with or belief in
professed *adj.* avowed, self-proclaimed
proffer *formal. tr.v.* to offer or propose
proficiency *formal. n.* skill, competence, expertise — **proficient** *adj.*
profile *n.* side view, especially of a human head; outline survey or biography — **profile** *tr.v.*
profligate (próffli-gət) *formal. adj.* spendthrift; given over to loose living — **-gacy** *n.*
pro forma *formal. adj.* having a set form or following set formalities; referring or relating to an invoice sent before rather than after payment — **pro forma** *adv.*
profound *adj.* deep, deep-thinking, deeply felt, or the like: profound *thoughts/philosophers/contempt* — **profundity** *n.*
profuse *formal. adj.* plentiful, abundant — **-fusion** *n.*
progenitor *formal. n.* begetter of offspring, parent or forebear; originator or forerunner
progeny (prójəni) *formal. pl.n.* offspring or descendants; creations
prognathous *formal. adj.* having jaws that jut out beyond the upper part of the face
prognosis *n., pl.* **-noses** prospect of recovery or improvement; forecast based on a diagnosis — **-nostic** *adj.*
prognosticate *formal. tr.v.* to predict, forecast, foretell — **-cation** *n.*
projectile *n.* bullet, shell, missile, rocket, or other object fired or hurled
projection *n.* in mapping, a system for the representation of the Earth as a flat surface (also "map projection")
prolapse *formal. n.* slipping out of position of a body part or organ, such as the uterus — **prolapse** *intr.v.*
prolegomenon (prṓ-le-gómmi-non) *formal. n., pl.* **-mena** critical introduction to a scholarly text
prolepsis *formal. n., pl.* **-lepses** anticipation and answering of an argument or objection before it has been stated — **-leptic** *adj.*
proletariat *formal. n.* lower class or working class; especially, industrial working class — **-tarian** *adj.*
proliferate *v.* to increase, spread, grow, or produce in ever-increasing amounts — **-ation** *n.*
prolific *adj.* very fertile or productive
prolix *formal. adj.* long-winded, or wordy and tedious

— **-ity** *n.*

prologue *n.* first part of a literary work, serving as an introduction to what follows; *archaic.* actor or character who delivers the prologue to a play; something that sets the stage for what happens subsequently

promenade (prómmə-náad, -naad) *v.* walk along in a leisurely way ~ *n.* leisurely walk; public walking area, as along a seafront; *U.S.* formal dance or ball as at a high school or college

prominent *adj.* noticeable or conspicuous; well-known, leading, or eminent — **-ence** *n.*

promiscuity *n.* sexual activity with a number of partners, usually in short casual relationships — **-cuous** *adj.*

promissory note *formal. n.* written promise to pay a specified sum on a specified date or on demand; written IOU

promontory (prómmən-tri) *n.* ridge of land jutting into the sea, headland, cape

promotion *n.* publicity or advertising campaign

promulgate (prómm'l-gayt) *formal. tr.v.* to proclaim or publicise: *a widely promulgated doctrine*; to make public (a new law) and thereby bring it into effect — **-ation**, **-ator** *n.*

prone *adj.* lying face downwards. Compare SUPINE

propagate *v.* to breed; to transmit or travel through a medium (used of energy waves) ~ *tr.v.* to spread, disseminate; to produce (new plants) using graftings, cuttings, or the like — **-ation** *n.*

propagator *n.* tray of soil in which seeds or cuttings are grown

propensity *formal. n.* natural inclination or leaning, liking, tendency: *a marked propensity towards the sciences*

prophylactic (próffi-láktik) *formal. adj.* preventing or protecting against something, especially disease ~ *n.* protective substance or device, especially a condom — **-laxis** *n.*

propinquity *formal. n.* nearness, proximity

propitiate *formal. tr.v.* to calm or appease (a god or other superior), as by offerings — **-ation** *n.* — **-atory**, **-ative** *adj.*

propitious *formal. adj.* promising, favourable, implying or appearing as if luck or success will come one's way

proponent *n.* champion or proposer, person who argues in favour of another person, a thing, or an idea (opposite "opponent")

propound *formal. tr.v.* to propose or put forward for consideration

proprietor *n.* owner with exclusive legal rights to something; owner or owner-manager of a business; *British.* publisher of a newspaper or magazine — **-ietary** *adj.*

pro rata (prō̃ ráatə, ráytə) *adv.* in proportion, proportionately — **pro-rata** *adj.*

prorogue (prə-rṓg) *formal. tr.v.* to discontinue the meetings of, but without ordering the dissolution of (a legislative assembly such as a parliament) — **-rogation** *n.*

prosaic (prə-záy-ik) *adj.* matter-of-fact, straightforward; drab, dull, commonplace

proscenium (prə-séeni-əm) *n.*, *pl.* **-nia** front part of a theatre stage, or the arch framing it [related to *scene*]

proscribe *formal. tr.v.* to prohibit; to outlaw, banish, or exile — **-scriptive** *adj.* — **-scription** *n.*

proselyte (próssə-līt) *formal. n.* person converted to a religion or ideology — **-lytise** *v.* — **-ism** *n.*

prosody (próssə-di) *n.* study of metrical forms, as in the analysis or writing of poetry; *formal.* writing of poetry — **-sodic** *adj.*

prospect *n.* (próspekt) view, typically covering a wide area, vista ~ *v.* (prə-spékt) to explore in search of gold or other minerals

prospective *n.* likely to become, having prospects of becoming: *a prospective medal-winner*

prospectus *n.* informational brochure issued by an institution, such as a university, describing its activities; formal statement or brochure giving details of a forthcoming share issue

prostate *n.* gland secreting liquid that forms most of the semen (also "prostate gland")

prosthesis *n.* surgical replacement of a leg, tooth, eye, or other body part, or the artificial device used — **-thetic** *adj.* — **-thetics** *n.*

prostrate *formal. tr.v.* (prə-stráyt) to bow, kneel, or lay (oneself) down, as in worship or submission ~ *adj.* (prós-trayt) lying down, especially face down, as in submission or grief; exhausted or defeated; growing along the ground: *a prostrate vine/creeper* — **-ation** *n.*

protagonist *n.* leading character, as in a play, novel, or other literary work

protasis (próttə-siss) *formal. n.*, *pl.* **-ses** subordinate clause, stating the actual condition, in a conditional sentence or proposition, typically beginning with *if* or *unless* (also "antecedent"). Compare CONSEQUENT, APODOSIS; introductory part of a classical drama

protean (prō-tée-ən) *formal. adj.* changeable, variable; shifting in shape, form, character, or mood [after *Proteus*, a sea god in Greek mythology who could change his shape at will]

protégé (próttə-zhay) *n.* person who is protected, trained, encouraged, and promoted by a person of experience, influence, or prestige (feminine equivalent "protégée")

pro tem *adv.* temporarily, for the time being (also "pro tempore") [Latin *pro tempore*, literally, for the time]

prothalamion *formal. n.*, *pl.* **-mia** song or poem celebrating a marriage, wedding song (also "prothalamium", "epithalamium")

protocol *n.* rules of behaviour or etiquette, especially among diplomats or rulers; amendment to, draft for, or supplement to a treaty or other document; record made by a participant of his activities and procedures during a process

protoplasm *n.* basic living matter in a plant or animal cell — **-mic** *adj.*

prototype *n.* forerunner, model, or original example on which copies or later developments are based — **-typical** *adj.*

protozoan *n.*, *pl.* **-zoa** amoeba or similar tiny single-celled creature — **protozoan** *adj.*

protract *tr.v.* to lengthen, extend, or prolong, especially unnecessarily

protractor *n.* instrument used to measure and draw angles

protrude *v.* to push or jut outwards — **-trusion** *n.* — **-trusive** *adj.*

protuberant *adj.* swelling, bulging, or jutting outwards — **-ance** *n.*

proud flesh *n.* swollen area around a healing wound

provenance (próvvə-nənss) *formal. n.* place of origin;

derivation of a word
provender *n.* dry fodder for livestock, such as hay
providence *n.* foresight, advance preparation; care and control on the part of a god who watches over human life; fate — **-dent**, **-dential** *adj.*
provisional *adj.* temporary or conditional, and subject to change when permanent arrangements can be made
proviso (prə-vīzō) *n.*, *pl.* **-sos** or **-soes** condition or restriction, as in an agreement or document
provocative *adj.* arousing anger, lust, or other strong emotion; thought-provoking — **-vocation** *n.*
provost *n.* senior official of various cathedrals and university colleges
prowess (prów-iss) *formal. n.* bravery, strength, or skill, as shown in battle; extraordinary skill or ability [related to *proud*]
proxime accessit (próksi-may ak-séssit, -mi) *formal. n.* second prize or second place [Latin, literally, he/she came very near]
proximity *formal. n.* closeness, nearness in space or time — **-mate**, **-mal** *adj.*
proxy *n.* agent or substitute, person acting on behalf of another; voting right given to such an agent [related to *procure*]
prurient *adj.* having or showing an obsessive interest in sexual matters — **-ence** *n.*
pruritus (proor-rítəss) *formal. n.* itching — **-itic** *adj.*
psalter (sáwl-tər) *n.* psalms, book of psalms, or music for the Psalms
psephology (si-fóllə-ji, se-) *formal. n.* branch of political science concerned with the study of elections and voting patterns [from Greek *psephos*, a pebble, hence a vote, from the use of pebbles to cast votes in ancient Greece] — **-gist** *n.* — **-logical** *adj.*
pseudocyesis (séwdō-sī-ée-siss) *formal. n.*, *pl.* **-cyeses** phantom pregnancy
pseudonym *n.* false name adopted to conceal one's true identity
psittacine (síttə-sīn, -sin) *formal. adj.* relating to parrots
psyche (sī́-ki) *formal. n.* soul or spirit, as distinct from the body
psychedelic *adj.* relating to or producing hallucinations or sensory distortion: *LSD and other psychedelic drugs* — **psychedelia** *n.*
psychic *adj.* having or relating to extrasensory powers such as telepathy or clairvoyance — **psychic** *n.*
psychokinesis *n.* movement of an object by, or apparently by, the use of mental powers alone — **-etic** *adj.*
psychopath *n.* psychologically disordered person, typically anti-social, aggressive, moody, and lacking a sense of morality or conscience (also "sociopath") — **-ic** *adj.* — **-y** *n.*
psychosomatic *adj.* relating or referring to physical diseases or disorders caused or aggravated by psychological factors such as stress
psychotropic *formal. adj.* acting on or affecting the mind (also "psychoactive"): *psychotropic drugs*
psychrometer *n.* wet-and-dry-bulb thermometer, used for measuring the relative humidity of the atmosphere
ptomaine poisoning (tṓ-mayn) *n.* food poisoning (old-fashioned)
puberty *n.* sexual maturing, typically in one's early teens — **-tal** *adj.*
puce *n.* murky red or greyish purple — **puce** *adj.*
puck *n.* hard rubber disc used in ice hockey
puckish *adj.* mischievous, impish [after *Puck*, a mischievous sprite in English folklore]
pudenda (pew-déndə) *formal. pl.n.* external sexual organs, especially a woman's
puerile (péwr-īl) *adj.* childish or immature; silly in a childish way — **-lity** *n.*
puerperal (pew-érpərəl) *formal. adj.* relating to childbirth: *puerperal fever*
pugilist (péwjil-ist) *formal. n.* boxer, fist-fighter (often humorous) — **-ism** *n.*
pugnacious *formal. adj.* quarrelsome, quick to fight; aggressive — **-nacity** *n.*
puisne (péwni) *chiefly British. formal. adj.* referring to a judge of lower rank or associate judge [Old French, born later] — **puisne** *n.*
pukka *adj.* right and proper: *a pukka accent*; genuine
pulchritude (púlkri-tewd) *formal. n.* beauty (humorously pompous) — **-tudinous** *adj.*
pullet *n.* hen, especially when less than a year old
Pullman *n.* comfortable and spacious railway carriage, specifically one with sleeping compartments [after George *Pullman*, a 19th-century U.S. inventor and industrialist]
pullulate (púl-ew-layt) *formal. intr.v.* to germinate or sprout; to breed rapidly or in great numbers; to teem or swarm [related to *pullet*]
pulmonary (púl-mənri) *formal. adj.* relating to the lungs
pulses *pl.n.* peas, beans, lentils, or similar edible legumes
pulverise *tr.v.* to grind to a powder or dust; *informal.* to beat or defeat completely, overwhelmingly, or mercilessly
pumice (púmmiss) *n.* volcanic rock, light and porous, used for scrubbing and polishing — **pumice** *tr.v.*, *adj.*
[1]**puncheon** *n.* wooden beam placed upright as a prop or strut; tool for shaping or punching, as used by a goldsmith
[2]**puncheon** *n.* barrel holding about 100 gallons
punctate *formal. adj.* spotted, dotted, pock-marked, or speckled
punctilio (pungk-tílli-ō) *n.* over-fussy attention to details, as of etiquette or protocol
punctilious *adj.* very thorough or precise, attentive to detail
punctuate *tr.v.* to interrupt
pundit *n* scholar of Sanskrit or Hinduism; *informal.* expert, knowledgeable person — **-ry** *n.*
pungent *adj.* strong and sharp: *pungent smells/flavours/wit* — **-gency** *n.*
Punic *adj.* relating to ancient Carthage [related to *Phoenician*: the Phoenicians founded Carthage]
punitive *adj.* intended to inflict punishment
punk *n.* smouldering substance, such as rags, used to light fireworks; dry and decayed firewood or tinder
punka *n.* fan, as in India, in the form of a large cloth or leaf
punnet *British. n.* small rectangular basket in which soft fruit, such as strawberries, may be displayed for retail sale
punty *n.* iron rod used in glassmaking (also "pontil")
pupillage *British. n.* legal training given to a trainee barrister in the chambers of an established barrister
purchase *n.* stance or hold adopted when moving, lifting, or securing something
purdah *n.* screen used to conceal women, especially in

India; seclusion of women from view, especially in India; *informal.* exclusion from society, shunning, ostracism (humorous)

purée (péwr-ay) *n.* semi-solid food that has been strained or sieved ~ *tr.v.* to make a purée of

purfle *tr.v.* to border, edge, or hem decoratively ~ *n.* purfled border, edge, or hem

purgative *formal or archaic. n.* strong laxative, cathartic [related to *purge*]

purgatory *n.* in Roman Catholic tradition, region or state in the afterlife where minor sinners can atone prior to being admitted to heaven; place, state, or time of intense but temporary discomfort or suffering [related to *purge*] — **-gatorial** *adj.*

purism *n.* strict adherence to traditional standards or rules, as in the use of language — **-ist** *n.* — **-istic** *adj.*

purl *v.* to border or finish with lace or embroidery ~ *n.* purled border or finish; embroidery thread of gold or silver

purlieus (púr-lewz) *formal. pl.n.* outskirts, area surrounding something

purloin *tr.v.* to steal, gain possession of (old-fashioned)

purport *formal. tr.v.* (pər-pórt) to claim or appear to be someone or do something ~*n.* (púr-pawrt) apparent meaning or purpose — **-edly** *adv.*

purser *n.* ship's officer in charge of finances and passenger welfare

pursuant to (pər-séw-ənt) *formal. prep.* in consequence of and in accordance with

pursuit *n.* cycling race in which two riders or teams try to overtake each other on a circular track

purulent (péwr-ŏŏ-lənt) *formal. adj.* relating to or containing pus — **-lence** *n.*

purvey (pər-váy) *formal. tr.v.* to make available, supply, provide — **-or** *n.*

purview (púr-vew) *formal. n.* range, extent, or scope, as of a law or one's outlook

pusillanimous (péwsi-lánniməss) *formal. adj.* cowardly — **-animity** *n.*

pustule *n.* blister-like pus-filled skin inflammation — **-ulant**, **-ular** *adj.*

putative (péw-tətiv) *formal. adj.* supposed or reputed, with no strong evidence to the contrary: *Jack's putative father was her third husband*

putlog *n.* short wooden beam supporting the planks on scaffolding

putrefy (péwtri-fī) *v.* to make or become putrid or gangrenous — **-faction** *n.*

putrid (péwtrid) *adj.* rotten; foul-smelling; *informal.* disgusting, pathetic, or feeble

putsch (pŏŏch) *n.* sudden attempt by a political group or faction to overthrow a government [German, from Swiss German, a thrust]

puttee (pútti) *n.* sock-like leg covering, either a long cloth strip for winding or a wide canvas strip for buckling round the leg, worn especially by soldiers

putto (pŏŏt-ō) *n., pl.* **putti** angelic small boy, cupid, or cherub in baroque paintings, sculptures, or reliefs

puy (pwee) *n.* cone of a small extinct volcano

pyaemia (pī-éemi-ə) *n.* blood poisoning caused by pus-forming bacteria — **-mic** *adj.*

pye dog *n.* half-wild or stray dog in Asia (also "pariah dog")

pyknic (pík-nik) *formal. adj.* having a stocky and strong build, endomorphic

pyorrhoea (pī-ə-rée-ə) *n.* inflammation of the gums that can extend to the tooth sockets and loosen teeth — **-al** *adj.*

pyre *n.* woodpile prepared for a funeral fire on which to cremate a corpse

pyrexia *formal. n.* fever — **-rexial**, **-rexic**, **-retic** *adj.*

pyrite (pī́r-īt) *n.* type of iron ore resembling gold ore in colour (also "iron pyrites", "fool's gold")

pyrosis *formal. n.* heartburn — **-rotic** *adj.*

pyrostat *n.* fire sensor that activates an extinguisher or alarm; high-temperature thermostat

pyrotechnics *n., pl.n.* firework-making; fireworks display; dazzlingly brilliant display of virtuosity: *verbal pyrotechnics* — **pyrotechnic** *adj.*

Pyrrhic victory (pírrik) *n.* victory achieved with great loss to the victors, hollow victory [after *Pyrrhus*, a third-century B.C. Greek king who suffered heavy losses in his early victories against the Romans]

pyx *n.* container for the Communion wafers; box in the British mint, in which new coins are kept for testing

qua (kway, kwaa) *formal. prep.* as, by virtue of being: *Citizens qua citizens have certain rights*

quadrant (kwódrənt) *n.* quarter of the circumference of a circle, or quarter of a disc

quadrennium *n., pl.* **-iums** or **-ia** four-year period or fourth anniversary — **-ial** *adj., n.*

quadrilateral *n.* four-sided geometrical figure, such as a square or parallelogram — **quadrilateral** *adj.*

quadriplegia *n.* paralysis from the neck down, paralysis of the arms and legs (also "tetraplegia"). Compare PARAPLEGIA — **-plegic** *adj., n.*

quadrivium (kwod-rívvi-əm) *n., pl.* **-iums** or **-ia** in a medieval university, higher division of the seven liberal arts, comprising the four subjects of arithmetic, geometry, astronomy, and music. Compare TRIVIUM [Latin, place where four ways meet]

quadroon *n.* person who is descended from three white grandparents and one black one

quadruped *n.* any four-footed animal. Compare BIPED — **-al** *adj.*

quadruple *v.* to multiply by four, increase four-fold — **quadruple** *adj.*, *n.*

quagmire (kwŏ́g-mīr, kwág-) *n.* bog or swamp; difficult situation, morass

qualm (kwaam) *n.* doubt, misgiving, hesitation prompted by conscience

quandary *n.* state of uncertainty or perplexity

quango *British. informal. n., pl.* **-os** government-sponsored organisation with a large degree of administrative independence [*q*uasi-*a*utonomous *n*on-*g*overnmental *o*rganisation]

quant *n.* pole used for pushing a punt or similar flat-bottomed boat — **quant** *v.*

quantity surveying *n.* estimating of building costs and materials

quantum *n., pl.* **-ta** energy unit of the smallest possible size in physics

quantum leap *informal. n.* qualitative change, typically very sudden (also "quantum jump")

quarantine (kwórrən-teen) *n.* detention or isolation of a sick or possibly sick person or animal, to prevent the spread of disease [from Italian *quarantina*, period of forty days] — **quarantine** *tr.v.*

quarrel *n.* crossbow bolt or arrow; small and often diamond-shaped window pane

quarter day *chiefly British. n.* day beginning a new season or payment quarter

quartermaster *n.* officer responsible for provisions, clothing, and the like; naval petty officer responsible for steering or navigating

quasar (kwáy-zaar) *n.* star-like celestial object having great energy and speed [*quas*i-stell*ar*]

quash *tr.v.* to reverse or invalidate (a law or a legal procedure); to suppress without more ado, subdue: *quash a rebellion*

quasi- *comb.form.* almost- or apparently-: *a quasi-stellar object* [Latin, as if]

quatrain *n.* four-lined stanza or verse

quatrefoil (káttrə-foyl) *n.* flower shape with four leaflets or petals

quattrocento (kwóttrō-chéntō, kwáttrō-) *n.* 15th-century period of Italian art, literature, and culture

quaver *n.* musical note equal to an eighth of a semibreve

quenelle (kə-nél) *n.* soft dumpling into which meat, fish, or poultry has been mixed, served typically in a cream sauce

quern *n.* hand-turned mill for grinding grain

querulous *formal. adj.* complaining or grumbling in a whiny way: *a querulous old man*

queue *n.* pigtail or plait

quibble *intr.v.* to nitpick, make petty distinctions or objections — **quibble** *n.*

quick *n.* sensitive, live part, as at the base of one's nails or in one's deepest emotions: *hurt to the quick*

quicksilver *n.* mercury (old-fashioned) ~ *adj.* mercurial, quick-changing

quid *n.* wad of chewing tobacco [related to *cud*]

quiddity *n.* real nature or essence of a thing; quibble, hair-splitting distinction (both rare)

quidnunc *archaic. informal. n.* inquisitive person, busybody or gossip [Latin *quid nunc?*, what now?]

quid pro quo *n., pl.* **quid pro quos** value, item, or favour given in exchange or compensation for another [Latin, something for something]

quiescent (kwi-éss'nt) *adj.* dormant or inactive, at least for the moment — **-scence** *n.*

quietus (kwī-áy-təss, -ée-) *formal. n.* release, as from duty, debt, or life; deathblow, coup de grace

quiff *British. n.* tuft or lock of hair brushed up from or on to the forehead [related to *coif*]

quill *n.* prickly spine of a porcupine or hedgehog; reel around which yarn is wound in weaving, bobbin; plucking device or plectrum for the strings of a clavichord or related instrument; cinnamon stick ~ *tr.v.* to make or press a ridge in or into a piece of fabric, as for a ruff

quinary (kwī́nəri) *formal. adj.* fifth

quinine *n.* substance derived from cinchona bark, and used to treat malaria

quinquagenarian (kwín-kwə-ji-naír-i-ən) *formal. n.* person aged between 50 and 59

quinquennium *n., pl.* **-niums** or **-nia** five-year period or fifth anniversary — **-ial** *adj.*, *n.*

quinquereme (kwín-kwi-reém) *n.* ancient Greek or Roman ship, typically a galley, with five tiers of oars

quinsy *n.* inflammation of the tonsils, commonly forming an abscess that makes swallowing difficult

quintain (kwíntin) *n.* target or post to be tilted at, by horsemen, used for military exercises or as entertainment

quintessence (kwin-téss'nss) *formal. n.* purest or most concentrated essence, example, or embodiment of something [from Medieval Latin *quinta essentia*, the fifth essence] — **-essential** *adj.*

quintuple *v.* to multiply by five, increase five-fold — **quintuple** *adj.*, *n.*

quire *n.* set of all the leaves of a book before binding; set of four sheets of paper folded to produce 16 pages; set of 24 or 25 sheets of paper of the same stock and size

quirk *n.* peculiarity of behaviour, idiosyncrasy; unpredictable twist: *quirk of fate*; groove running lengthways along an architectural moulding — **-y** *adj.*

quisling *n.* traitor, especially one serving as the puppet leader of an occupying foreign power [after Vidkun *Quisling*, a 20th-century Norwegian politician who formed a fascist party under the Nazi occupation, and was later tried and executed for treason]

quittance *formal or archaic. n.* release or discharge from an obligation, debt, or penalty

qui vive (keé veév) *formal. n.* — **on the qui vive** alert, watchful, vigilant [French, who lives?, sentinel's cry to a stranger]

quixotic (kwik-sóttik) *adj.* romantically idealistic, but impractical or absent-minded [after *Don Quixote*, the hero of Cervantes' books of 1605-15]

quizzing glass *archaic. informal. n.* monocle

quodlibet (kwódli-bet) *n.* argument of a subtle philosophical or theological kind, as attempted by students; *formal.* musical medley, based on popular tunes [Latin, what you please]

quoin (koyn, kwoyn) *n.* cornerstone of a building; exterior angle of a wall; wedge, as for locking printing type, raising a cannon, or the like (also "coign")

quorum (kwáw-rəm) *n.* minimum number of people required for a valid committee meeting, assembly, or the like — **quorate** *adj.*

quotidian (kwō-tíddi-ən) *formal. adj.* recurring daily: *quotidian attacks of fever*; everyday: *his quotidian round of petty chores*

quotient (kwṓsh'nt) *n.* result of mathematical division; ratio, rate, or proportion; level, as of anxiety or intelligence

R

rabbet *n.* groove at the end of a piece of wood designed to form a joint with a matching piece; joint formed in this way — **rabbet** *v.*
Rabelaisian (rábbə-láyzi-ən) *adj.* robust, bawdy, and coarsely humorous [after the comic writings of François *Rabelais*, the 16th-century French satirist]
rabid (rábbid) *adj.* extreme, fanatical: *a rabid nationalist*; *formal.* suffering from rabies — **-ity** *n.*
[1]**race** *n.* strong swift current of water, or the channel it flows in
[2]**race** *n.* root of ginger or similar plant
raceme (rə-séem) *n.* stem or arrangement of flowers attached singly to a main stalk, with the youngest at the tip, as in wisteria — **-mose** *adj.*
rachis (ráy-kiss) *n.*, *pl.* **-ises** or **-ides** main axis or stem, as of a flower cluster, compound leaf, or feather; spinal column
rachitis (ra-kī́tiss) *formal. n.* rickets — **-itic** *adj.*
Rachmanism (rákmə-niz'm) *n.* exploitation or intimidation of slum tenants by a ruthless landlord [after Perec *Rachman*, a notorious 20th-century London landlord] — **-ist** *adj.*, *n.*
[1]**rack** *n.* toothed bar that meshes with a gearwheel
[2]**rack** *n.* clouds broken and driven by high winds
[3]**rack** *tr.v.* to clear (wine, beer, or cider) of its dregs; to fill a container with (wine, beer, or cider)
rack-rent *n.* outrageously high rent — **rack-rent** *tr.v.*
raconteur (ráckon-túr) *n.* person who is good at telling jokes, witty stories, and anecdotes [French; related to *recount*]
raddled *adj.* worn-out or drained, as by over-indulgence
radial *adj.* relating to rays, beams, or radii from a common source or point
radial-ply *n.* tyre with fabric cords spread at right angles from the circumference to provide for flexible sidewalls. Compare CROSS-PLY — **radial-ply** *adj.*
radical *n.* group of atoms that function as a single unit in chemical combinations and reactions; root, such as the square root, of a number, indicated by the sign $\sqrt{}$
radicle *n.* part of a plant embryo that develops into the main root
radiography *n.* X-ray or gamma-ray examination — **-grapher** *n.*
radiosonde (ráydi-ō-sond) *n.* balloon-borne instrument used to collect and transmit information used for weather forecasting
radiotherapy *n.* medical treatment, particularly of cancer, by means of X-rays, injection of radioactive chemicals, or the like — **-therapist** *n.*
radix (ráydiks) *formal. n.*, *pl.* **-dixes** or **-dices** point of origin or root of an organ or part
radome (ráydōm) *n.* radar antenna's dome-like covering, as in some aircraft [*ra*dar + *dome*]
raffia (ráffi-ə) *n.* fibre from palm leaves used in weaving mats, making baskets, and the like (also "raphia")
raffish *adj.* looking dashing or jaunty in a somewhat disreputable way
raft *n.* slab of reinforced concrete laid on soft ground as part of a building's foundations
rag *n.* roofing slate with one side left rough
ragout (rággōō, ra-gōō) *n.* stew of meat and vegetables
raillery *n.* friendly teasing or banter, back-chat
raiment (ráy-mənt) *archaic. n.* clothing or garments
raison d'être (ráy-zON déttr) *n.*, *pl.* **raisons d'être** reason for being, justification for or point of existence [French]
rake *intr.v.* to slope backwards, as a ship's mast or funnel might ~ *n.* slope or angle, as of a mast, theatre stage, aircraft wing, or cutting edge of a tool
rakish *adj.* dashing, smart, jaunty: *Her hat was tilted at a rakish angle*
rale (raal) *n.* crackling sound from diseased or fluid-filled lungs
Ramadan (rámmə-dán) *n.* sunrise-to-sunset fasting during the holy ninth month of the Muslim year
ramate (ráymayt) *formal. adj.* branched, branching (also "ramose")
ramification *formal. n.* branch, arrangement of branches, or branching process — **ramify** *intr.v.*
ramifications *pl.n.* complications; unavoidable but usually undesirable consequences of an action or decision
rampage (ram-páyj) *intr.v.* to rush about in a violent frenzy, rage ~ *n.* destructive rage, violent frenzy — **-pageous** *adj.*
rampant *adj.* unrestrained or unchecked: *rampant vegetation*; *running rampant*; in heraldry, rearing up on the hind legs: *a unicorn rampant on a field argent*; *formal.* supported from a higher point on one side than on the other: *a rampant arch*
rampart *n.* raised fortification, such as an embankment or the parapeted upper section of a castle wall; anything that protects or defends: *a rampart against declining standards*
ramrod *n.* rod for cleaning a rifle or inserting the charge into a muzzle-loading firearm
rancid (rán-sid) *adj.* sour, gone off: *rancid butter/bacon* — **-ity** *n.*
rancour *n.* bitter feelings, spite, or ill will — **-corous** *adj.*
range *n.* large cooking stove comprising at least an oven and a hob, especially one that uses solid fuel; bookcase with shelves on both sides, as in a library or bookshop
Ranger *n.* senior member of the Girl Guides
rani (ráa-nee) *n.* female Hindu ruler or queen; rajah's wife; woman with the rank of a rajah
[1]**rank** *n.* set of organ pipes controlled by a single stop
[2]**rank** *adj.* growing vigorously and widely, in an unwelcome way: *rank weeds*; smelling or tasting bad or rotten; utter, complete, absolute: *a rank outsider*

rankle *intr.v.* to irritate persistently, or cause continuing resentment: *His defeat rankled for years* [akin to *dragon*]
ransack *tr.v.* to search (a room, box, or the like) very thoroughly, typically causing a mess; to plunder, loot
ranunculus (rə-núngkew-ləss) *formal. n., pl.* **-luses** or **-li** buttercup or related plant
rapacious *formal. adj.* eager to take and capture; greedy — **-acity** *n.*
[1]**rape** *n.* yellow-flowering crop producing an oil seed and fodder (also "colza", "oilseed rape")
[2]**rape** *n.* grape skins, pips, and stems left over after the juice has been pressed for wine making
rapine (ráp-īn, -in) *formal. n.* plundering, pillage
rapport (ra-pór) *n.* sense of immediate intimacy; mutual emotional understanding [French]
rapprochement (ra-prósh-moN) *n.* process of coming together or reconciliation of two people or parties, especially after a dispute [French; related to *approach*]
rapt *adj.* having or showing rapture or intense interest and concentration
raptor *formal. n.* bird of prey — **-ial** *adj.*
rapture *n.* ecstasy, great joy, bliss; expression or outburst of delight — **-turous** *adj.*
rarefied *adj.* lofty or remote, and apparently protected or isolated from everyday concerns (often mildly derogatory) — **rarefy** *v.*
raster *n.* pattern of lines produced by a scanning electron beam, as on a television screen
ratafia (ráttə-fée-ə) *n.* almond essence, flavouring, or liqueur
ratatouille (ráttə-tōō-i) *n.* French vegetable casserole, including tomatoes, peppers, and aubergine
ratchet *n.* toothed wheel or bar engaged by a hinged catch, for allowing movement in one direction only
Rathaus (rát-howss) *n.* town hall in Germany
ratify (rátti-fī) *tr.v.* to approve or permit formally, confirm officially: *ratify a treaty* — **-fication** *n.*
rating *chiefly British. n.* ordinary seaman, sailor who is not an officer (also "naval rating")
ratings *pl.n.* estimate of the audience figures, and hence popularity, of radio or television programmes
ratio (ráy-shi-ō) *n., pl.* **-os** mathematical relation between two amounts or sizes, proportion
ratiocination (rátti-óssi-náysh'n) *formal. n.* reasoning in a logical and systematic way, sometimes to the point of nitpicking or obsessiveness — **-nate** *intr.v.*
rational *adj.* relating to reason; logical, based on reason; sane, coherent, lucid — **-ity** *n.*
rationale (ráshə-náal) *n.* reason or basis for an action, policy, or belief; statement of reasons or principles
rationalise *v.* — *tr.* to cause to be or seem rational; to make (an industry, process, or the like) more efficient through eliminating what is unnecessary; to interpret (behaviour) — *intr.* to interpret one's behaviour in a way favourable to one's self-esteem — **-isation** *n.*
rationalism *n.* belief in or commitment to reason as the principal or sole source of knowledge or rules of conduct; rejection of revelation as a source of religious knowledge and authority; rejection of commonsense observation in favour of abstract theory — **-list** *adj., n.* — **-listic** *adj.*
ratite (rát-īt) *formal. n.* flightless non-aquatic bird, such as the ostrich, kiwi, or emu
ratline *n.* ropes across the sail of a ship, forming a rope ladder
Ratskeller (ráts-kellər) *n.* beer hall or German restaurant, originally in the cellar of a town hall
rat's tail *n.* file for wood or metalworking that is long, thin, and cylindrical
rattan *n.* cane from a tropical Asian palm, as used for wickerwork furniture and walking sticks; furniture made of this material
raucous *adj.* sounding loud and discordant and typically strident, harsh or hoarse
ravage *tr.v.* to damage extensively or destroy
ravages *pl.n.* destructive effects, damage
rave *n.* upright rail or framework on the side of a cart
ravelin (ráv-lin) *n.* two-faced embankment projecting outwards in front of a fortification
ravening (rávv'n-ing) *formal. adj.* relating to the seizing of prey; greedy
ravenous (rávv'n-əss) *adj. formal.* seizing and eating prey; *informal.* extremely hungry
ravish *archaic. tr.v.* to seize and carry off, kidnap; to rape
ravished *adj.* enraptured, entranced
ravishing *adj.* delightful, enchanting, entrancing; *informal.* breathtakingly beautiful, gorgeous
Rawlplug *British. trademark. n.* hollow plug, often made of plastic, to be inserted into a hole in the wall as a mooring for a nail or screw
raze *formal. tr.v.* to tear down or demolish: *razed the palace to the ground*
razzmatazz *chiefly U.S. n.* noisy, showy, bustling display, designed to impress, as in an election or advertising campaign
reach *n.* uninterrupted stretch of water on a river or canal
reaction *n.* chemical process, change, combination, or the like; effect, especially adverse, of a medicine or drug; allergic response to a medicine, pollen, or other substance — **reactant** *n.*
reactionary *adj.* anti-progressive; very politically conservative and resistant to liberal or socialist ideology — **reactionary** *n.*
reader *British. n.* university lecturer of senior rank, just below professor — **-ship** *n.*
reading *n.* presentation of a Bill to Parliament at various stages of its passage before it becomes an Act
ready reckoner *n.* aid to calculations, especially in the form of a table or list
reagent (ree-áyjənt) *n.* chemical used in analysing, measuring, or changing other substances in a chemical reaction
realise *tr.v.* to convert (property or assets) into ready money — **-isation** *n.*
realist *n.* writer or artist favouring a real-life representation of everyday subject-matter rather than an idealised, formalised, or romantic approach — **-ism** *n.* — **-istic** *adj.*
Realpolitik (ray-ál-polli-teek) *n.* national policy, especially a foreign policy, based uncompromisingly on national self-interest rather than on moral considerations [German, literally, realistic politics]
Realtor (rée-əl-tər) *n.* member of a U.S. professional association of estate agents — **Realty** *n.*
[1]**ream** *n.* quantity of paper, usually 500 sheets
[2]**ream** *tr.v.* to shape or enlarge (a hole, as in wood), with a special cylindrical file — **-er** *n.*
rearguard *n.* rear position, or troops defending the rear, of a military force; conservative element or

grouping, as in the arts or a political party. Compare VANGUARD

rearguard action *n.* action aimed at resisting change or warding off likely defeat

rebarbative *formal. adj.* disgusting, off-putting, repulsive

rebate *n.* discount or partial refund — **rebate** *tr.v.*

rebato (rə-báatō) *n., pl.* **-tos** collar, often of lace, stiffened by wire or starch and worn high at the back and sides, popular in the 17th century (also "rabato")

rebound *intr.v.* to jump or bounce back, as after a collision; to return to harm the originator, as a hurtful policy might ~ *n.* — **on the rebound** during a period of vulnerability after a recent unhappy experience: *married him on the rebound*

rebuff (ri-búf) *tr.v.* to reject or snub abruptly or disdainfully; to repulse: *rebuffed the infantry assault* — **rebuff** *n.*

rebuke *formal. tr.v.* to criticise or scold — **rebuke** *n.*

rebus (réebəss) *n., pl.* **-buses** puzzle or text coded in the form of pictures, letters, or symbols representing syllables or words, such as *I8LN£* meaning *I hate Ellen Pound* [Latin, by things]

rebut (ri-bút) *v.* to argue powerfully or convincingly against, disprove — **-buttal** *n.*

recalcitrant (ri-kálsi-trənt) *formal. adj.* stubbornly resistant to orders or suggestions, disobedient — **recalcitrant, -trance** *n.*

recant (ri-kánt) *v.* to withdraw (a former belief or claim), especially publicly

recapitulate *v.* to summarise in a few short points, repeat the main points already made, sum up (also *informal* "recap") — **-lation** *n.*

recce (récki) *British. informal. v.* to explore one's surroundings, reconnoitre (old-fashioned) — **recce** *n.*

recede (ri-séed) *intr.v.* to move backwards: *a receding tide/hairline*; to seem to move backwards: *a horizon rapidly receding into the distance*; to slope backwards: *a receding forehead/chin*

received *adj.* generally believed or accepted because of tradition or authority rather than through people's own experience or investigation: *the received view*

Received Pronunciation *n.* pronunciation or way of speaking that is considered most neutral and socially acceptable, such as BBC English in Britain (abbreviation "R.P.")

receiver *n.* official appointed by a court to take over and manage the property of a bankrupt, minor, defendant, or the like; person who knowingly buys or stores stolen goods (also *slang* "fence"); device in or part of a radio, television, telephone, or the like, that receives and converts incoming signals

recension *formal. n.* revision or critical edition of a text, incorporating the best variant readings

receptacle *formal. n.* container

receptor *n.* sensing cell, nerve, organ, or the like

recess *n.* break in proceedings or temporary ending of business, as between court sessions or during the Parliamentary vacation; hollow or indented space, such as an alcove

recesses *pl.n.* hidden, secret, or secluded places: *in the dark recesses of his mind*

recession *n.* economic decline or slowing down; procession of the choir and clergy out of the chancel at the end of a church service — **-al** *adj.*

recessional *n.* hymn at the end of a church service

recessive *adj.* receding; giving way to a dominant gene: *a recessive trait*

réchauffé (ray-shō-fáy) *formal. adj.* re-heated before being served; re-used even though presented as fresh [French, literally, re-warmed]

recherché (rə-sháir-shay) *formal. adj.* affected, over-refined, over-elaborate; obscure and difficult to follow, known only to experts [related to *research*]

recidivism (ri-síddi-viz'm) *n.* tendency of convicted criminals to revert to crime — **-ist** *n., adj.* — **-istic** *adj.*

recipient *n.* person or thing that receives; patient receiving blood, tissue, a transplanted organ, or the like from a donor

reciprocal *adj.* to, towards, by, or of each other, mutual: *reciprocal antagonism* ~ *n.* fraction, such as 1/2 or 4/3, derived from another, such as 2/1 or 3/4, by reversing the numerator and denominator

reciprocate *v.* — *tr.* to return in kind: *reciprocates their helpfulness* — *intr.* to do something similar in return: *After their invitation to dinner, we had to reciprocate*; *formal.* to swing back and forth — **-cation, -procity** *n.*

recital *n.* public performance of music, especially classical music, by a soloist or small group — **-ist** *n.*

recite *formal. tr.v.* to list or detail (also "rehearse")

reckoning *n.* settling of a bill or account — **day of reckoning** moment when one is finally judged for past mistakes and wrongdoings

reclamation *n.* conversion or turning of desert, marshes, submerged land, or the like into useful land fit for living on or farming

réclame (ray-klaám, re-) *formal. n.* public acclaim; publicity [French]

recline *formal. v.* to lean back or cause to lean back or lie down

recluse (ri-kloóss) *n.* person who shuns society, loner — **-lusive** *adj.* — **-lusion** *n.*

recognisance (ri-kónni-z'nss, -kóg-ni-) *formal. n.* specific legal obligation or undertaking to a court or magistrate; sum of money pledged as bail — **release someone on his own recognisance** to set someone free without bail, conditional on his abiding by an undertaking

recoil *intr.v.* to spring back, as a gun does when fired; to draw back, as in fear, horror, or disgust; to return to harm the originator, as a hurtful policy might — **recoil** *n.*

recollect (récka-lékt) *formal. v.* to remember — **-lection** *n.*

recompense *formal. n.* payment or reward: *recompense for services rendered*; compensation — **recompense** *tr.v.*

reconcile *tr.v.* to bring into harmony: *reconcile the contradictions/married couple*; settle or resolve (a dispute) — **reconcile oneself to** to come to accept as inevitable — **-ciliation** *n.*

recondite *formal. adj.* not easily understood, abstruse, known only to experts

reconnaissance (ri-kónni-s'nss) *n.* exploration, investigation, or survey, as of a stretch of enemy territory (also *British informal* "recce")

reconnoitre (réckə-nóytər) *v.* to make a preliminary inspection or survey of a stretch of land, an enemy's positions, or the like (also *British informal* "recce")

reconstitute *tr.v.* to re-create, reconstruct, or restore to the original form

reconstruct *tr.v.* to rebuild, re-create — **-struction** *n.*
recorder *n.* experienced lawyer serving as a part-time judge
recoup (ri-ko͞op) *tr.v.* to regain, recover: *recouped his losses*
recourse (ri-kórss) *n.* source of help; effort to seek help: *have recourse to law*
recover *formal. tr.v.* to obtain the award (something, such as damages) in a civil suit — **-ery** *n.*
recreant (réckri-ənt) *formal. n.* faithless or cowardly person (literary) — **recreant** *adj.* — **-ance** *n.*
recriminations *pl.n.* bitter mutual accusations
recrudescence (réckro͞o-déss'nss) *formal. n.* recurrence of a disease, civil unrest, or other trouble after a period of inactivity — **recrudesce** *intr.v.*
rectify *tr.v.* to make right, correct; to refine, separate, or purify in chemistry, usually by distillation; to convert alternating current into direct current; to blend or dilute whisky or other alcoholic spirits — **-fiable** *adj.* — **-fication** *n.*
rectilinear (rékti-línni-ər) *formal. adj.* relating to straight lines — **-ity** *n.*
rectitude *formal. n.* goodness, virtue, moral uprightness
recto *n., pl.* **-tos** right-hand odd-numbered page of a book; front side of a sheet of paper, such as the side of a letter that is to be read first. Compare VERSO [Latin *recto folio*, on the right-hand side of a page]
rector *n.* college, school, or university principal; chancellor of a Scottish university — **-orial** *adj.* — **-ate** *n.*
rectrix *n., pl.* **-trices** any of the stiff main feathers in a bird's tail, serving to regulate flight
recumbent *formal. adj.* reclining; tending to lean or rest against related tissue or the ground *a recumbent organ/vine*
recuperate *v.* — *intr.* to recover health, or financial or social standing — *tr. formal.* to recover: *recuperate a debt* — **-ation** *n.* — **-ative** *adj.*
recurrent *adj.* returning or reappearing regularly: *a recurrent dream* — **recur** *intr.v.*
recusant (réckewz'nt) *n.* Roman Catholic in 16th- to 18th-century England who defied the law requiring attendance at Church of England services; any nonconformist or dissenter — **recusant** *adj.* — **-ancy** *n.*
recuse (ri-kéwz) *formal. tr.v.* to challenge and seek the withdrawal of (a judge or juror)
recycle *tr.v.* to use again, re-use; to extract useful material or substances from (waste): *recycle waste paper*
redact (ri-dákt) *formal. tr.v.* to draft, edit, or revise for publication — **-tion**, **-tor** *n.*
redan (ri-dán) *n.* fortification of two walls joined at an angle
redeem *tr.v.* to recover or regain (something, such as pawned goods) by payment; to pay off (a loan, promissory note, or the like); to exchange (an official certificate such as a note, share, or coupon) for the equivalent value (as of cash or goods); to free (a captive or hostage) by making a payment, as of ransom; to restore (oneself) to favour; to rescue or save from sin and punishment; to fulfil (a promise or pledge) — **-demption** *n.* — **-demptive** *adj.*
redeeming *adj.* making up for or compensating for faults and deficiencies: *her one redeeming feature*
redeploy *tr.v.* to assign new tasks to (workers); to move (military forces) to new positions — **-ment** *n.*
redolent (réddələnt) *formal. adj.* — **redolent of** smelling of; reminiscent of — **redolent with** filled with associations of, evocative of — **-lence** *n.*
redoubt (ri-dówt) *n.* defensive stronghold, usually a small and temporary fortification
redoubtable *adj.* respected or feared as awesome or very impressive (often humorous)
redound (ri-dównd) *formal. intr.v.* to have a specified effect: *policies redounding to their advantage*
redress (ri-dréss) *tr.v.* to set right, adjust, remedy, or restore: *redress a grievance/the balance* — **redress** *n.*
reductio ad absurdum *n.* taking an argument or idea to a logical extreme that turns out to be absurd or counter-productive; disproof of a proposition by this method; proof of a proposition by demonstrating that its opposite is absurd [Latin, literally, reduction to absurdity]
reduction *n.* conversion of a fraction into a more basic form, or into an equivalent decimal; chemical removal of oxygen from a compound or addition of hydrogen to it — **reduce** *tr.v.*
reductionism *n.* analysis of complex phenomena or data using techniques developed for the analysis of simpler ones, especially where this involves oversimplification — **-ist** *adj., n.*
redundant *adj.* excessive and therefore not needed, superfluous; *chiefly British.* unemployed as a result of the elimination of one's job — **-dancy** *n.*
reedy *adj.* sounding thin and high-pitched
reef *n.* section of a sail tucked in or rolled up when reducing the area of the sail
reeve *tr.v.*, to thread (a rope) through a ring, pulley, or the like, as on a ship; to fasten by reeving
refectory *n.* dining hall of an institution such as a college or monastery
referee *n.* expert who advises on the suitability of a paper for publication, especially in a learned journal; *chiefly British.* person who provides a reference as to the suitability of a candidate for employment
referendum *n., pl.* **-dums** or **-da** special vote by the electorate on a proposal or issue of public importance [Latin, literally, it must be referred]
referent *formal. n.* thing or concept referred to by a word, phrase, or sign (also "signifié")
referred pain *n.* pain felt in a part of the body different from its place of origin
refinery *n.* factory or plant for the purification or separation of products or materials, such as crude oil, sugar, or ore
reflective *adj.* thoughtful, pensive
reflex *n.* involuntary response, such as a knee-jerk or sneeze — **reflex** *adj.*
reflexes *pl.n.* automatic physical responses: *the champion's quick reflexes*
reflexive *adj.* referring to a verb or pronoun, as in *betrayed myself*, in a phrase in which the subject or source of the action is itself affected by the action — **reflexive**, **-ivity** *n.*
reflexology (reé-flek-sólləji) *n.* study of the bodily reflexes; foot massage believed to have therapeutic effects elsewhere in the body, especially on the internal organs — **-ologist**
reflux *n.* act of flowing back; ebb ~ *tr.v.* to boil, evaporate, and condense (a liquid) repeatedly, as when extracting substances
refraction *n.* change in direction of a light or sound wave as it changes speed between mediums; ability of the eye to focus by deflecting light rays — **refract** *v.* — **-fractive**, **-fringent**, **-frangible** *adj.*

refractory *formal. adj.* obstinate or disobedient; resistant to medical treatment, or a process such as stimulation or heating
refrain *n.* repeated verse, tune, theme, or the like
refresher *British. n.* barrister's additional fee, paid when a case takes more than one day in court
refulgent (ri-fúljənt) *formal. adj.* shining or flashing brilliantly — **-gence** *n.*
refurbish *tr.v.* to clean, repair, and restore: *refurbish a house* — **-ment** *n.*
refusenik *n.* Soviet citizen, especially a Jew, refused a visa to emigrate
refute *tr.v.* to deny and disprove: *refuted the accusation*; to deny and disprove the claim of: *refuted their accusers* — **-futation** *n.*
regal *adj.* royal in appearance, behaviour, or bearing
regale *tr.v.* to entertain with great generosity or verve: *regaled us with anecdotes/champagne*
regalia *n., pl.n.* showy clothes or trappings of high status or group membership
regatta *n.* boat-race or series of boat-races
regeneration *n.* regrowth of tissue to replace lost or destroyed tissue — **-ate** *v.*
regent *n.* appointed ruler, who acts on behalf of the official ruler such as an under-age or mentally incompetent king; member of a body governing or supervising a U.S. educational institution or system — **-gency** *n.*
regicide (réji-sīd) *n.* killing or killer of a sovereign
regime (ray-zhéem) *n.* government or social system, especially if it is authoritarian; *informal.* regimen
regimen (réji-mən) *formal. n.* prescribed system of rules and regulations; system of therapy (also "regime")
régisseur (réji-súr) *n.* director of a ballet
register *n.* range of notes of a musical instrument or voice; organ stop; variation of language according to use; variety of language characteristic of a specified use: *legal register*
registrar *n.* person in charge of official records and registers; person in charge of a registry office; *British.* hospital doctor ranking above a houseman but below a consultant
Regius professor (réej-əss) *n.* professor at a British university whose chair was established by royal grant
regnant *formal. adj.* reigning, ruling: *a Prince regnant, not a Prince consort*; dominant or prevalent: *customs regnant in that epoch*
regress *intr.v.* to revert to an earlier and less advanced or desirable condition — **-ion** *n.* — **-ive** *adj.*
regurgitate (ri-gúrji-tayt) *v.* to have (partially digested food) come back up into the mouth, as in vomiting; to repeat or reproduce (what has been learnt) parrot-fashion — **-tation** *n.*
rehabilitate *tr.v.* to restore partially or completely to a former or better condition, such as good health or reputation — **-tative** *adj.* — **-tation** *n.*
rehearse *tr.v.* to recite or repeat; to list in detail
reify (rée-i-fī, ráy-) *tr.v.* to regard (something subjective, such as an idea) as objective or real — **-fication** *n.*
reimburse *tr.v.* to compensate by payment: *reimburse them for their efforts*; to compensate someone for, by payment: *reimbursed their travel expenses* [related to *purse*] — **-ment** *n.*
reincarnation *n.* rebirth of one's soul in another body — **reincarnate** *v., adj.*
reinforcements *pl.n.* military forces or supplies sent to support those already in use; psychological rewards, or the strengthening of a learned response by means of psychological rewards
reiterate (ree-íttə-rayt) *formal. tr.v.* to repeat — **-ation** *n.* — **-ative** *adj.*
rejoinder *n.* reply or retort — **rejoin** *v.*
rejuvenate *tr.v.* to cause to become, seem, or feel younger or newer — **-ation** *n.*
relapse *intr.v.* to revert to an earlier and worse condition — **relapse** *n.*
relay *tr.v.* to pass on from one person to another; to receive and then re-broadcast onwards (a programme or signal); to broadcast a concert, performance, or the like from the place where it is in progress ~ *n.* switching device in an electrical circuit
relegation *n.* demotion, as to a lower division of a football league — **relegate** *tr.v.*
relent *intr.v.* to soften in attitude, become less harsh
relict *n.* species surviving as a relic of an earlier age; *formal or archaic.* widow
relief *n.* half-projection of carved or sculpted figures from a flat background (also "relievo"); lifting of a siege
relief map *n.* map showing variations in height as by modelling, shading, colours, or contour lines
religiosity *n.* self-important or affected piety or religious zeal — **religiose** *adj.*
relinquish *formal. tr.v.* to give up, let go, put aside, release — **-ment** *n.*
reliquary (rélli-kwəri) *n.* container for a sacred relic
remainder *tr.v.* to offer (the last unsold copies, as of a book) for sale at a reduced price ~ *n.* item offered for sale in this way
remand (ri-maánd) *tr.v.* to send back or adjourn (a legal case) for further action (also "remit"); to send back (a suspect) for further custody prior to a trial ~ *n.* — **on remand** remanded for further custody
remedial *adj.* intended to remedy defects or deficiencies; intended to help slow learners: *remedial classes*
remedy *n.* legal means of ensuring justice
reminiscence *n.* pleasant or nostalgic remembering; pleasant or nostalgic memory — **reminisce** *intr.v.*
reminiscent *adj.* evocative or suggestive of the past; reminding one of something else
remiss (ri-míss) *formal. adj.* forgetful, negligent
remission *n.* reduction of the length of a prison sentence, as for good behaviour; lessening or disappearance, lasting for a limited or uncertain time, of the signs or symptoms of an illness
remit *v.* (ri-mít) — *tr.* to send or transfer (money), as by post; to cancel or reduce (a punishment); to defer or postpone; to remand (a legal case) — *intr.* to undergo remission ~ *n. chiefly British.* (rée-mit) area of responsibility or authority
remittance man *n.* man living abroad on funds supplied by people at home, typically on condition that he should not return
remnant *n.* something remaining or left over, such as a piece of material
remonstrate (rémmən-strayt) *v.* to make objections or plead against some course of action — **-strance**, **-stration** *n.* — **-strative**, **-strant** *adj.*
remontant (ri-móntənt) *formal. adj.* blooming twice or more during a season — **remontant** *n.*
remove *n.* imaginary unit of distance or separation, step: *at one remove from the facts*; intermediate form

in some British schools
removed *adj.* separated by a specified number of generations: *first cousin twice removed*
remuneration *formal. n.* payment for services rendered; compensation — **-ative** *adj.* — **-ate** *tr.v.*
renaissance *n.* rebirth or revival: *renaissance of a cultural heritage* (also "renascence")
renal *formal. adj.* relating to the kidneys
render *tr.v.* to give, deliver, or perform: *render assistance/a bill/a trumpet solo/a verdict*; to cause to become, make: *rendered unconscious*; to translate: *rendered "j'ai vu" as "I saw"*; to treat (fat) with heat; to coat with plaster or cement
rendezvous (róɴ-di-voo͞, ron-) *n., pl.* **rendezvous** meeting or meeting place agreed on beforehand [Old French, *rendez vous*, literally, present yourselves!]
rendition *formal. n.* performance or interpretation
renegade (rénni-gáyd) *n.* deserter or turncoat, person who deserts a cause or movement; rebel or outlaw
renege (ri-néeg, -nég, -náyg) *formal. intr.v.* to go back on, fail to fulfil: *renege on a promise*
rennet *n.* stomach lining of certain young mammals, such as calves; rennet extract, used in cheesemaking
renounce *formal. tr.v.* to give up, abandon; to reject, disown — **renunciation** *n.*
renovate *tr.v.* to renew, revive, or restore; to restore (a building) to a former or better condition — **-vation** *n.*
rentier (rónti-ay) *n.* person whose income is derived chiefly from rents or investments
repair *formal or archaic. intr.v.* to go, proceed, betake oneself: *repaired to the club*
reparations *pl.n.* payments demanded as compensation from the losing side in a war
repartee (rép-aar-tée) *n.* conversation passing to and fro between people, full of sharp and witty retorts; witty reply or retort
repast *formal or archaic. n.* meal
repatriate *tr.v.* to return (a person) to his or her country of birth or citizenship — **-ation** *n.*
repeal *tr.v.* to cancel (a law) officially — **repeal** *n.*
repercussions *pl.n.* series of results, often harmful, of an action, decision, or event
repertoire (réppər-twaar) *n.* range or stock of jokes, pieces of music, operatic roles, or the like available to a performer
repertory (réppər-tri) *n.* repertoire; set of plays, operas, films, or the like, produced or shown in alternation, as by a repertory company or a cinema — **in repertory** performed or shown as part of a repertory (also *informal* "in rep")
répétiteur (ray-pétti-tér, -tőr) *n.* coach or piano accompanist for opera singers, ballet dancers, or other performers [French, literally, repeater]
repine *formal. intr.v.* to be unhappy, fret
replenish *formal. tr.v.* to refill, restock, top up
replete *formal. adj.* full to overflowing or to excess: *replete after a hearty dinner* — **-tion** *n.*
replica (réppli-kə) *n.* copy, sometimes on a smaller scale, especially of a work of art — **replicate** *tr.v.*
repose *formal. n.* rest, state of inactivity or relaxation; calm, tranquillity ~ *intr.v.* to lie down and rest; to be placed on something specified — **-ful** *adj.*
repository *formal. n.* museum or place of safekeeping; burial vault, tomb
reprehensible *formal. adj.* deserving blame or criticism, unacceptably bad — **reprehend** *tr.v.*
representational *adj.* intended to represent a person, scene, or object in art; realistic, life-like — **-ism** *n.* — **-ist** *adj., n.*
representations *formal. pl.n.* — **make representations to** to lodge a protest with or make one's views known to (an appropriate authority) — **represent** *tr.v.*
repress *tr.v.* to put down, crush, or suppress (something such as a rebellion), quell; to push (painful memories or thoughts) into the unconscious — **-ed, -ive** *adj.* — **-ion** *n.*
reprieve *tr.v.* to bring at least temporary relief to; to postpone or cancel the punishment of: *was reprieved just as the hangman was getting ready* — **reprieve** *n.*
reprimand *formal. tr.v.* to criticise or scold harshly — **reprimand** *n.*
reprisal *n.* harmful or bad deed done in response to a similar deed, act of retaliating
reprise (ri-préez) *n.* repetition, especially of a phrase or theme in music [Old French, literally, a taking back] — **reprise** *tr.v.*
reprobate (rép-rəbayt) *n.* unreformable rogue, scoundrel (often humorous); person doomed to damnation ~ *adj.* rejected by God, damned; *formal.* immoral, shameless ~ *formal. tr.v.* to disapprove of strongly, condemn — **-bation** *n.*
reprove *formal. tr.v.* to criticise or scold — **reproof** *n.*
repudiate *formal. tr.v.* to refuse to acknowledge, disown; to reject or deny — **-ation** *n.*
repugnant *formal. adj.* offensive, disgusting, repulsive; inconsistent, contradictory — **-nance** *n.*
repulse *tr.v.* to repel; to rebuff, spurn ~ *n.* act of repulsing
repulsion *n.* strong aversion or dislike — **-sive** *adj.*
reputable (réppew-təb'l) *adj.* of good repute or reputation, trustworthy, honourable
reputedly *adj.* according to reports or rumours, supposedly
requiem (réckwi-əm, -em) *n.* hymn, service, or piece of music for a dead person
requisite (réck-wizit) *formal. adj.* required, necessary ~ *n.* something needed
requisition *n.* official request or demand, made in writing, for supplies or equipment needed ~ *tr.v.* to take or demand by requisition
requite *formal. tr.v.* to repay or reward; to return or reciprocate; to avenge [related to *quit* and *quiet*] — **-ital** *n.*
reredos (réer-doss) *n.* tapestry, sculpture, or other decoration behind an altar; screen or decorative iron plate at the back of a fireplace
rescind (ri-sínd) *tr.v.* to cancel or repeal (a law or legal document, such as a contract) — **rescission** *n.*
reservation *n.* doubt, misgiving; land or settlement for a minority or suppressed community, such as the North American Indians; property rights retained by a lessor or seller
reserve price *n.* lowest price that the owner will accept at an auction
resident *n.* British colonial representative, as formerly in a protected Indian state; in the U.S., doctor doing a term of specialised hospital training
residue *n.* something remaining or left over, especially if small — **-dual** *adj.*
resigned *adj.* accepting, or showing submission to, what seems unavoidable — **resignation** *n.*
resilient (ri-zílli-ənt) *adj.* able to recover a previous

position or shape; able to recover readily from misfortunes or setbacks, tough — **-ence**, **-ency** *n.*
resolute *adj.* firm, determined, purposeful
resolution *n.* courage, firmness of purpose; solution of a problem; decision or statement discussed and voted on at a meeting; subsiding or ending of a fever, inflammation, or disease; separation into constituent parts or elements; power of a microscope, photographic emulsion, or the like to separate and reveal fine details — **resolve** *n.*, *v.*
resonance (rézzə-nənss) *n.* loudening or lengthening of a sound by sympathetic vibration; sound, as heard by a doctor tapping a patient's chest; long-lasting memorable effect — **-nant** *adj.* — **-nate** *intr.v.*
resonator *n.* microwave-producing device
resound *intr.v.* to echo or ring with noise; to produce excited commentary, publicity, or long-lasting memorable effect
resounding *adj.* reverberating or resonating, as if echoing or ringing; definite, indisputable, widely acknowledged: *resounding success*
respective *adj.* relating to two or more people or things, regarded singly: *their respective birthdays* — **-ly** *adv.*
respiration *n.* breathing, or the related process in plants — **-atory** *adj.* — **respire** *v.*
respirator (réspi-raytər) *n.* device to aid breathing; mask over the mouth and nose to purify or warm the air before breathing
respite (réss-pit) *formal. n.* temporary pause providing relief or protection
resplendent (ri-splénd-ənt) *formal. adj.* splendid in appearance, magnificent, dazzling [related to *splendid*] — **-dence**, **-dency** *n.*
respondent *n.* person called to answer a petition, specifically in a divorce action (opposite "petitioner") or in a higher court of appeal (opposite "appellant")
restitution *formal. n.* restoring of property or compensation to the rightful owner — **-tive**, **-tory** *adj.*
restive *formal. adj.* impatient, misbehaving, or disobedient
restorative (ri-stórrə-tiv) *adj.* restoring, especially restoring health or strength — **restorative** *n.*
résumé (réz-yoo͞-may) *n.* summary; *U.S.* curriculum vitae
resurgent *formal. adj.* surging back or onwards despite setbacks or obstacles — **-gence** *n.*
resurrect (rézzə-rékt) *tr.v.* to bring back to life, raise from the dead; to revive — **-tion** *n.*
resuscitate (ri-sússi-tayt) *formal. tr.v* to revive or revitalise from near-death or near-extinction — **-tation** *n.*
retainer *n.* preliminary or regular fee for professional services, especially those of a lawyer or specialist consultant; money paid to retain the use of accommodation during one's absence; servant of long standing in a particular household
retaliate *intr.v.* to pay back an injury like for like; to launch a revenge attack or reprisal — **-ation** *n.* — **-atory** *adj.*
retard *tr.v.* to slow down — **-ation** *n.* — **-ed** *adj.*
retentive *adj.* good at retaining: *a retentive memory*
retiarius (réeti-áiri-əss) *n.*, *pl.* **-rii** Roman gladiator armed with a net and trident
reticent *formal. adj.* shy, timid; quiet, taciturn; secretive, uninformative — **-cence** *n.*
reticle (réttik'l) *n.* network of lines or fine wires, as on a lens, used for measuring or locating the objects under observation (also "reticule", "graticule")
reticular *formal. adj.* net-like, web-like (also "reticulate", "retiform")
reticule *n.* woman's handbag or purse, typically made of net-like material and closed with a drawstring (old-fashioned)
retinue *n.* formal gathering or group of attendants, companions, or subordinates [related to *retain*, *retainer*]
[1]retort *n.* effective and pointed reply or counter-argument ~ *v.* to make such a reply
[2]retort *n.* laboratory vessel with a long bent-over neck, used typically for distilling
retract *tr.v.* to take back: *retracted his statement*; to draw back or in: *retracted its horns* — **-able**, **-ile** *adj.*
retreat *n.* military bugle call at sunset when the flag is lowered
retrench *intr.v.* to cut back on costs, economise
retrenchment *n.* act or result of retrenching; fortification, such as a trench, within outer walls or defences
retribution *n.* justified punishment or revenge — **-tive** *adj.*
retrieve *tr.v.* to get or fetch back, regain; *formal.* to restore to a favourable position — **-val** *n.*
retroactive *adj.* applying to or from the past, retrospective: *retroactive laws/salary rise* — **-action** *n.*
retrograde *adj.* backward, reverse, unprogressive: *a retrograde step in public policy*; moving or appearing to move backwards or in a direction opposite to what might be expected: *retrograde motion/orbits* — **-gress** *intr.v.* — **-gression** *n.*
retrospect *n.* — **in retrospect** looking back on the past — **-ion** *n.*
retrospective *adj.* retroactive; looking back at the past or past work ~ *n.* retrospective exhibition of an artist's work
retroussé (rə-troo͞-say) *adj.* referring to a nose turned up at the end [French]
retsina (ret-séenə, rétsinə) *n.* resin-flavoured Greek wine
returning officer *n.* officer in charge of an election, who announces the number of votes and the result of voting
revamp *tr.v.* to patch up, restore; to revise (a text or manuscript) extensively — **revamp** *n.*
revanchism (ri-vánch-iz'm, -vóɴsh-) *n.* foreign policy based on revenge or the regaining of territory [related to *revenge*] — **-ist** *adj.*, *n.*
reveille (ri-vál-i, -vél-) *n.* bugle call or military formation first thing in the morning; any signal to wake up or get up in the morning [French, *réveillez*, wake up!]
revel (révv'l) *intr.v.* take pleasure or delight: *revelled in dancing/nostalgia*; *formal.* make merry, celebrate noisily, carouse ~ *n.* noisy merrymaking or festivity (often plural)
revelation *n.* disclosure of surprising or important information that might never otherwise have become known; in religion, sudden realisation of divine truth; something disclosed in a revelation — **-atory** *adj.*
revenant (révvənənt) *formal. n.* person who returns, sometimes as a ghost, after an absence
revenue *n.* income, especially that of a government
reverberation pedal *n.* "loud pedal" on a piano
reverberations *pl.n.* sounds of prolonged vibration; *formal.* consequences — **-rate** *v.* — **-rant** *adj.*

revere *tr.v.* to admire and look up to, respect or worship — **reverence** *n.* — **-rent**, **-rential** *adj.*
reverie (révvə-ri) *n.* daydreaming, musing; daydream
revers (ri-véer, -vaír) *n., pl.* **revers** lapel, turned-back cuff, or other part of clothing showing the reverse side; lining of a turned-back part of clothing, such as a lapel or cuff [French, reverse]
reverse *n.* back or secondary (opposite "obverse") side of a coin, banknote, medal, or the like
reversion *n.* return to an earlier state or pattern of behaviour: *reversion to type*; property, or the right to property, returning to a lessor or grantor after the agreed term; right to or expectation of an inheritance; sum of money paid on the death of a life-assurance policy-holder — **-ary**, **-ist** *adj.* — **revert** *intr.v.*
revetment (ri-vétmənt) *n.* wall or bank of earth serving as a barricade, or its protective covering of stones, concrete, or the like — **revet** *v.*
revile *tr.v.* to criticise, scold, or abuse with harsh language
revivify (ri-vívvi-fī) *formal. tr.v.* to give new life and energy to, revive — **-ficatory** *adj.* — **-fication** *n.*
revoke *tr.v.* to cancel, withdraw, or reverse, annul: *revoked the harsh regulation* — **revocation** *n.*
revulsion *n.* sudden reaction or withdrawal, as through loathing or disgust
Reynard (rén-ərd, -aard, ráynaard) name of a fox in fables or poetry, nickname for a fox (also "Renard") [after the fox who is the hero in a 13th-century French poem *Roman de Renart*]
rhabdomancy (ráb-dō-man-si) *formal. n.* divining for water or mineral ores by means of a wand or rod, dowsing — **-mancer** *n.*
Rhadamanthine (ráddə-mán-thīn, -thin) *formal. adj.* judging severely, going strictly by the letter of the law [after *Rhadamanthus*, one of the underworld judges of the dead in Greek mythology]
rhapsody (rápsədi) *n.* extravagant expression of feeling, as in a speech of praise or literary work; poem or other literary composition written in high-flown emotional language; epic poem, or part of one used for recitation, in ancient Greece; musical composition of irregular form, suggesting improvisation, often based on folk tunes [from Greek *rhapsoidos*, literally, a weaver of songs, hence a reciter of rhapsodies] — **-dise** *v.* — **-dic** *adj.* — **-dist** *n.*
Rhenish (rénnish, réenish) *formal. adj.* relating to the river Rhine
rhesus baby (rée-səss) *n.* baby born with a blood disease in which its blood cells are destroyed by antibodies in the mother's blood [after *rhesus* monkeys, used in experiments in which the condition was identified]
rhetoric (réttərik) *n.* literary, political, or oratorical language, or the study of its structure and effects; speech or writing that is impressively high-flown but may be empty of real meaning — **-al** *adj.* — **rhetor**, **-ician** *n.*
rhetorical question *n.* question that is put for effect or to make a point rather than to secure an answer
rheum (rōōm) *n.* mucus-like discharge from the eyes or nose — **-y** *adj.*
rhinal (rī́n'l) *formal. adj.* relating to the nose, nasal
rhizome (rī́-zōm) *n.* root-like stem growing on or under the ground, as in the iris or grasses (also "rootstock", "rootstalk") — **-omatous** *adj.*
rhombus (róm-bəss) *n., pl.* **-bi** or **-buses** parallelogram with all four sides equal in length (also "rhomb")
rhonchus (róng-kəss) *n., pl.* **-chi** snoring or whistling sound from the chest, as in asthma, caused by partial blocking of the air channels — **-chal**, **-chial** *adj.*
rhotacism (rṓtə-siz'm) *n.* excessive or inconsistent use of the *r*-sound in pronunciation, often including the use of the intrusive *r*, as when pronouncing *drawing* as /dráw-ring/ — **-cist** *adj., n.* — **-cise** *tr.v.*
rhotic (rṓtik) *adj.* relating to, referring to, or speaking a variety of English, such as Scottish English, in which the *r*-sound is retained before a consonant or pause — **-ism** *n.*
rialto (ri-áltō) *chiefly U.S. formal. n., pl.* **-tos** market-place, exchange, trading centre [after *Rialto*, an island and commercial centre in Venice]
ribald (ríbb'ld) *adj.* marked by coarse or indecent joking, humorous in a lewd, vulgar, way — **-ry** *n.*
Richter scale (rík-tər, ríkh-) *n.* scale registering the magnitude of an earthquake, ranging from 0 to about 8.9 [devised by Charles F. *Richter*, the 20th-century U.S. seismologist]
rickets *n.* disease resulting from lack of vitamin D, characterised by defective bone growth, and suffered mainly by children (also "rachitis")
rickrack *n.* braid, flat and narrow and forming zigzags, as used to trim clothing (also "ricrac")
ricochet (ríckə-shay) *intr.v.* to rebound or be deflected once or more than once from a hard surface, as a bullet might ~ *n.* instance or sound of such rebounding
rictus (ríktəss) *formal. n., pl.* **-tus** or **-tuses** width or gap of the open mouth or beak; unnatural gaping expression or grin — **-tal** *adj.*
riddle *n.* coarse sieve, as for grain or gravel ~ *tr.v.* to sift with a riddle; to pierce with many holes; to fill, spread widely, or permeate with something damaging: *riddled with gangrene*
rider *n.* clause, amendment, or qualification added to a legal document, verdict, parliamentary bill, or the like; problem or supplementary rule arising from a theorem, as in geometry; thin seam of coal or ore lying above a larger seam in a mine
ridgepole *n.* horizontal beam forming the ridge of a roof, to which the rafters are attached; horizontal pole forming the ridge of a tent (also "ridgepiece")
riffler *n.* file or similar scraping tool, typically with a curved face
rig *n.* distinctive number and pattern of masts and sails on a sailing vessel; equipment or gear for a specified purpose
rigger *n.* bracket supporting a rowlock, projecting from the side of a racing or rowing boat
rigging *n.* ropes, cables, and the like supporting or controlling the masts, spars, and sails of a sailing ship; system of cords on a parachute, balloon, or the like
rigmarole (rígmə-rōl) *n.* procedure or list of procedures that is pointlessly long and complicated; confused or nonsensical speech or writing [originally *rag-man roll*, a long list or catalogue]
rigor (ríggər, rī́gawr) *n.* chill or shivering attack, as preceding a fever; muscle cramp or rigid muscular contraction, as in fever; temporary rigidity and insensitivity to stimuli in some animals, or in human tissue or organs, in reaction to shock
rigor mortis *n.* temporary rigidity, due to chemical

changes, of the muscles and joints of a dead body [Latin, literally, the stiffness of death]

rill *n.* small stream, brook, or rivulet: long channel or valley on the Moon (in this sense, also "rille")

rime *n.* frost or granular ice formed by frozen fog on the windward side of trees, telegraph wires, and the like (also "frost feathers") ~ *tr.v.* to cover with or as if with rime — **rimy** *adj.*

ringbark *tr.v.* to cut a ring of bark from a tree trunk or branch in order to kill it or slow its growth (also "ring", "girdle")

ringer *informal. n.* person very similar in appearance to another

riparian (rī-páiri-ən, ri-) *formal. adj.* relating to or inhabiting a river bank: *riparian rights/reeds*

riposte (ri-póst) *n.* quick retaliatory action or retort; in fencing, a return thrust made after parrying an opponent's lunge (also "ripost") — **riposte** *intr.v.*

riser *n.* upright part of a stair. Compare TREAD; pipe rising vertically within a building

risible (ríz-ib'l) *formal. adj.* laughable or ridiculous; funny; relating to laughter — **-ibility** *n.*

risotto (ri-zóttō, -sóttō) *n.*, *pl.* **-tos** Italian dish of rice mixed with cheese, vegetables, seafood, or meat

risqué (ríss-kay) *formal. adj.* saucy, naughty, racy, verging on the indelicate or improper

roadholding *n.* road vehicle's degree of stability, as at high speeds or on wet roads

roborant (rṓbə-rənt, róbbə-) *formal. adj.* strengthening, fortifying, invigorating ~ *n.* fortifying medicine or drug, tonic

roc *n.* huge and powerful bird of prey in Arabian legend

rocaille (ro-kī́, rō-) *n.* delicate curving decoration consisting of or resembling rock fragments or shells, used in rococo design [French; related to *rock*]

rococo (rə-kṓkō) *adj.* styled or ornamented in an elaborate but delicate way, especially in relation to an 18th-century European style in art and architecture. Compare BAROQUE; over-ornate, florid, overdone: *rococo prose* — **rococo** *n.*

rodent *n.* mammal, such as the rat or squirrel, with incisor teeth specially adapted for gnawing

rodeo (rō-dáy-ō) *n.* display or contest of cowboy skills, such as lassoing and bronco riding; cattle roundup, as for branding or counting; enclosure for such cattle

rodomontade (róddə-mon-táyd, rṓdə-, -MON-, -taád) *formal. n.* boasting, bragging, bluster; boast or boastful speech (literary) [after *Rodomonte*, the boastful king of Algiers in the late 15th-century Italian epic poem *Orlando Innamorato* by Matteo Boiardo] — **rodomontade** *adj.*, *intr.v.*

Roentgen ray (rónt-gən, rṓnt-, -jən) *n.* X-ray (also "Röntgen ray") [after Wilhelm Konrad *Röntgen*, the German physicist who discovered X-rays in 1895]

roil *tr.v.* to make (a liquid) cloudy or muddy by stirring up sediment; to stir up, disturb; to irritate, annoy, vex

roister *intr.v.* to celebrate noisily, make merry, revel; to swagger, bluster, or brag (old-fashioned) — **-ous** *adj.*

rolling stock *n.* railway carriages, wagons, and locomotives

rollmop *n.* herring fillet, marinated and rolled up, often around a slice of onion

roman à clef (rō-món a kláy, -MÓN aa) *n.*, *pl.* **romans à clef** novel depicting real people under fictional names [French, literally, novel with a key]

roman-fleuve (rō-MÓN flőv) *n.*, *pl.* **romans-fleuves** long novel or series of novels chronicling a family or community over many generations (also "saga novel") [French, literally, river-novel, referring to its slow, flowing movement]

Roman holiday *n.* pleasure or entertainment based on the suffering of others [after the gory gladiator contests enjoyed by the public in ancient Rome]

Roman nose *n.* nose with a high, conspicuous, slightly convex bridge

Romany (rómməni, rṓməni) *n.* Gypsy; language of the Gypsies — **Romany** *adj.*

rood *n. archaic or formal.* cross or crucifix representing the cross on which Jesus died; large cross on a beam or screen at the entrance to the chancel or choir of a church

rookie *chiefly U.S. informal. n.* new recruit in the armed forces; novice, newcomer, or inexperienced person, as in a sports team [probably altered from *recruit*]

Rorschach test (rór-shaak, -shak, -shakh) *n.* personality test based on the subject's interpretations of various abstract inkblot designs [after Hermann *Rorschach*, the early 20th-century Swiss psychiatrist who devised the test]

rosary (rṓzəri) *n.* string of beads used as an aid in counting prayers, especially by Roman Catholics in a lengthy series of devotions

roseola (rō-zeé-ələ) *n.* red skin rash, as in measles or German measles; rubeola, measles — **-lar** *adj.*

roster *n.* register of workers, soldiers, or the like, or the list of duties to be performed by them (also "rota"); people listed on a roster ~ *tr.v.* to place on a roster [Dutch *rooster*, a roasting grid, hence a list on a ruled sheet; akin to *roast*]

rostrum (róss-trəm) *n.*, *pl.* **-trums** or **-tra** platform or raised stage, as for a public speaker or music conductor; bird's beak, insect's snout, or the like; large spike on an ancient warship for puncturing an enemy ship's hull (in this sense, also "ram", "beak"); prow of an ancient Roman ship [Latin *rostra*, an orator's platform, from the speaker's stage in the Roman forum, which was decorated with the prows of captured ships; plural of *rostrum*, a beak, hence a beak-like prow]

rota *chiefly British. n.* list of duties to be done in rotation, or register of people to perform them (also "roster")

rotate *v.* (rō-táyt) — *intr.* to turn or spin on an axis, as the Earth does; to take turns, alternate, proceed in a given order or sequence — *tr.* to cause to rotate; to plant or grow (crops) in a fixed sequence ~ *adj.* (rṓ-tayt) having or referring to parts that spread or radiate like the spokes of a wheel — **rotation** *n.* — **rotary, -tative, -tational** *adj.*

rote *n.* memorising by heart, learning by repetition rather than through understanding; mechanical repetition, unthinking routine

rotisserie (rō-tíssəri) *n.* cooking appliance fitted with a rotating spit for roasting meat; restaurant or shop specialising in roast meat

rotor *n.* revolving part in a motor, generator, or other machine; system of blades supporting a helicopter or similar aircraft in flight [shortened from *rotator*]

rotund (rō-túnd) *formal. adj.* plump, rounded (usually humorous); impressively high-flown or high-falutin in speech — **-ity** *n.*

rotunda (rō-túndə) *n.* circular, often domed, building or room

roué (ro͞o-ay) *formal. n.* rake, immoral and debauched man, especially an ageing one [French, literally, man broken on the wheel, from *rouer*, to punish or torture by breaking on the wheel, referring either to the exhausted appearance of such a man or to the fate that he deserves]

roughage *n.* bulky food, such as bran, rich in fibre and low in digestible elements, assisting bowel regularity

rouleau (ro͞o-lō, ro͞o-lṓ) *n., pl.* **-s** or **-x** piping or roll of ribbon as used for trimming; roll of coins wrapped in paper [related to *roll*]

roulette (ro͞o-lét) *n.* gambling game in which bets are placed on the colour (red or black) or number of the slot where a small ball comes to rest in a rotating wheel; toothed metal wheel or disc, as used for perforating sheets of stamps or pressing dots onto an engraving plate; perforation of tiny slits between rows of stamps for easy separation ~ *tr.v.* to mark or perforate with a roulette

round robin *n.* petition or protest on which the signatures are arranged in a circle to conceal the order in which it was signed; document or letter circulated among a group for comments or consideration; tournament, such as a chess competition, in which each contestant competes against every other contestant

roux (ro͞o) *n., pl.* **roux** heated mixture of flour and butter or other fat, used as a base for sauces

rowel (rów-əl) *n.* small toothed wheel on the end of a cowboy's spur ~ *tr.v.* to spur or goad (a horse) with or as if with a rowel

rowen (rów-ən) second crop of hay in a season (also "aftermath")

rowlock (róllək) *n.* swivelling support for an oar on the side of a boat (also *U.S.* "oarlock")

royalty *n.* share of the proceeds paid to a writer, composer, or the like from sales or performances of his work, or to an inventor or landowner for the use of his invention or property

rubella (ro͞o-béllə) *formal. n.* German measles

rubeola (ro͞o-bée-ə-lə) *formal. n.* measles (also "roseola") — **-olar** *adj.*

Rubicon (ro͞obi-kən) *formal. n.* point of no return, limit beyond which one becomes fully committed to a course of action [after the river in northern Italy, in ancient times part of the boundary between Gaul and Italy: Julius Caesar, in crossing it without prior authorisation in 49 B.C., was in effect declaring civil war on the senatorial party in Rome]

rubicund (ro͞obi-kənd) *formal. adj.* reddish, rosy, or ruddy (often humorous) — **-ity** *n.*

rubric (ro͞o-brik) *n.* heading or title under which something is classed, category; title, heading, or letter, typically illuminated in red, standing out from the rest of the text in a manuscript or book; heading in or section of a legal code; rule or custom, as for the conducting of a church ceremony; explanatory or introductory commentary or instructions; instructions printed at the head of an examination paper [from Latin *rubrica terra*, red earth, red ochre: red ochre was used for illuminating the rubrics in manuscripts] — **-cate** *tr.v.*

ruche (ro͞osh) *n.* pleated or gathered strip of lace or fabric, used as a trimming (also "rouche") — **ruched** *adj.* — **ruching** *n.* — **ruche** *tr.v.*

ruction *informal. n.* noisy disturbance or quarrel

rudiments (ro͞odi-məntss) *pl.n.* basic principles or elementary stages of a skill or subject; beginnings, embryonic or undeveloped stages or forms — **-tary** *adj.*

rue *formal. tr.v.* to regret, feel sorry about — **rueful** *adj.*

ruffle *n.* pleated or gathered strip of lace or fabric, used as a trimming or decoration; low and continuous drumbeat, quieter than a drumroll ~ *tr.v.* to beat a ruffle on (a drum)

rumbustious *chiefly British. informal. adj.* lively and noisy, in an excited or unruly way

ruminate (ro͞omi-nayt) *formal. v.* to chew cud; to consider deeply, ponder — **-native** *adj.* — **-nant** *n., adj.*

rump *n.* unrepresentative parliament after most of its members have left or been driven out

rumpus *n.* noisy disturbance, commotion

runcible spoon (rúnssib'l) *n.* spoon-like piece of cutlery with prongs and a sharp edge, combining the features of spoon, knife, and fork [a nonsense word coined by Edward Lear]

rune *n.* letter of an early Germanic alphabet, used in carved inscriptions; mysterious symbol having supposed magic powers — **runic** *adj.*

runner *n.* blade of a skate or sledge; either of the supporting struts along which a drawer slides; long narrow carpet or tablecloth; stem creeping from the base of a plant and producing new roots and buds (in this sense, also "stolon")

running board *n.* footboard at the side of some old cars

running head *n.* headline or title on every page or every other page of a book or magazine

rupture *n.* breaking or tearing; break in good relations, rift; hernia, as in the groin — **rupture** *v.*

rush *n.* first, unedited print of a film scene

rushlight *n.* candle consisting of a reed wick coated in tallow

Russian roulette *n.* foolhardy risk or betting game in which a person aims a revolver, after spinning the cylinder loaded with one bullet, at his head and pulls the trigger; any suicidally risky venture

rustic *adj.* relating to country life or country people, rural; crude, unrefined, or uncouth; charmingly simple and unsophisticated; made of rough branches: *rustic benches* ~ *formal. n.* rustic person; coarse or simple person — **-ity** *n.*

rusticate *formal. tr.v.* to suspend (a student) from college or university; to send or banish to the country — **-cation** *n.*

rut *n.* annual period or state of sexual excitement or heat as in male deer; recurrent period of ovulation and sexual excitement in some female mammals, heat, oestrus ~ *intr.v.* to be in rut

S

Sabbatarian *n.* person who observes the Sabbath strictly, as by avoiding work and pleasurable activity; person who observes Saturday as the Sabbath — **-ism** *n.*
sabbatical (sə-báttik'l) *n.* period of paid leave, especially for university lecturers, for research or travel ~ *adj.* relating or referring to a sabbatical; *formal.* relating or appropriate to the Sabbath (also "Sabbatical") [the leave is typically granted every seventh year; see *sabbatical* year]
sabbatical year *n.* year in which farm land is left to lie fallow, observed every seventh year by the ancient Jews [the seventh year corresponds to the seventh day of the week, the *Sabbath*, from Hebrew, *shabhath*, to rest]
sable *formal. adj.* black; dark, sombre (literary)
sabot (sábbō) *n.* French clog
sabotage (sábbə-taazh, -taaj) *n.* deliberate damaging or destruction of property, as by enemy agents or dissatisfied workers; any underhand or destructive action designed to thwart a plan or project, subversion [French, from *saboter*, literally, to clatter with one's *sabots* or clogs, hence to work clumsily, hence to botch deliberately] — **sabotage** *tr.v.* — **-boteur** *n.*
sabre rattling *n.* display of military power or threatening of war by one country in its dealings with another (usually derogatory) — **sabre-rattling** *adj.*
sabulous *formal. adj.* sandy in texture, gritty
sac *n.* pouch or bag-like part, often filled with fluid, in a plant or animal — **saccate** *adj.*
saccharin (sáckə-rin, -reen) *n.* artificial sweetener, made from a petroleum or coal-tar extract
saccharine (sáckə-rin, -reen) *adj.* sugary, sweet, often excessively so; sentimentally or cloyingly sweet, polite, or friendly — **-inity** *n.*
sacerdotal (sássər-dṓt'l, sáckər-) *formal. adj.* priestly, relating to priests or priesthood — **-ism** *n.* — **-ist** *n.*
sachet (sáshay) *n.* small sealed packet typically holding one portion of sugar, shampoo, or other products; small packet or bag containing perfumed powder, placed in drawers or cupboards to scent clothes and linen [related to *sac*]
sacrament *n.* religious act or rite, such as baptism or the Eucharist, representing or helping to achieve grace; Eucharist or its elements, especially the consecrated bread; symbol, relationship, or the like considered to have sacred or spiritual significance — **-mental** *adj.*
sacrarium (sa-kráiri-əm) *n.*, *pl.* **-ums** or **-ia** sanctuary of a church; vestry, room in a church in which the sacred objects and vestments are stored, sacristy; ceremonial water basin in a church, piscina
sacred cow *n.* idea, custom, institution, or person considered, unreasonably, to be beyond criticism [alluding to the veneration of cows in Hinduism]
sacrilege (sáckri-lij) *n.* misuse, desecration, or blasphemously disrespectful treatment of a person or thing regarded as sacred — **-legious** *adj.*
sacristan (sáckristən) *n.* church officer in charge of the sacred vessels, vestments, and the like
sacristy (sáckristi) *n.* room in a church in which the sacred vessels and vestments are stored, vestry
sacrosanct (sáckrə-sangkt) *adj.* sacred, very holy, or inviolable — **-ity** *n.*
sadist *n.* person who gets pleasure or sexual arousal from inflicting pain on someone else. Compare *masochist* [after the Marquis de *Sade*, an 18th-century French novelist, who wrote about sexual sadists] — **-dism** *n.* — **-distic** *adj.*
sagacious *formal. adj.* very wise, knowing, shrewd (usually humorous) — **-gacity** *n.*
sage *n.* wise teacher, philosopher, or the like, especially an elderly man, who is deeply respected for his experience and judgment — **sage** *adj.*
sagitate (sáji-tayt) *adj.* shaped like an arrowhead: *sagitate leaves* (also "sagittiform")
sahib (saab, sáa-hib) *n.* title of respect in colonial India, roughly equivalent to "Sir", used to address or refer to a European man
sail *n.* windmill's blade, designed to catch the wind
salaam (sə-láam) *n.* Muslim ceremonial greeting or bow [Arabic, peace] — **salaam** *v.*
salacious (sə-láyshəss) *formal. adj.* arousing or appealing to sexual lust, lewd; lustful, lecherous
salamander (sál-ə-mandər) *n.* lizard-like amphibian; mythical lizard-like creature, living in or withstanding fire; poker or other heat-resistant implement used in fire; portable stove or heater, as for drying out a building under construction; metal plate heated for browning puddings or other food; residue metal and slag remaining in a furnace
salicylism (sál-i-síl-iz'm) *formal. n.* aspirin poisoning
salient (sáyli-ənt) *formal. adj.* outstanding, striking, relating to the most relevant or vital aspects of a subject: *a salient point*; jutting, projecting: *a salient angle* ~ *n.* projecting part of a fortification, battle array, or the like — **-ence** *n.*
salientian (sáyli-énshi-ən) *formal. n.* toad or frog (also "anuran")
salify (sál-i-fī) *v.* to turn into, treat with, or mix with salt or a mineral salt — **-fication** *n.*
saline (sáy-līn) *adj.* salty, relating to salt or mineral salts ~ *n.* saline solution of a concentration similar to that in the blood, as used in a medical drip — **-linity** *n.*
salivate (sáll-i-vayt) *intr.v.* to produce or secrete spit or saliva, sometimes in excess; to be eager for or excited at something, sometimes excessively so — **-vation** *n.*
sallow *adj.* pale-looking, having a sickly yellowish complexion
sally *n.* military attack made from a defensive position, sortie; quick retort or teasing remark — **sally** *intr.v.*
salmagundi (sál-mə-gúndi) *n.* salad including chopped

meat, anchovies, and eggs; *formal.* mixture of many widely varying elements, miscellany, potpourri

salmonellosis (sál-mə-nel-ṓ-siss) *n.* food poisoning caused by the salmonella bacterium (also "salmonella poisoning") [from *salmonella*, the bacterium, after Daniel E. *Salmon*, a 19th-20th-century U.S. veterinary surgeon]

salon (sál-ON, -on) *n.* drawing room, as in a large French house, for receiving guests; gathering of or reception for artists, celebrities, or the like, as in 18th-century France; art gallery or exhibition hall; beauty parlour, stylish fashion store, or the like

salt *tr.v.* to enrich or inflate the value of something in a fraudulent way; to place valuable ore in (a mine) fraudulently

saltation *formal. n.* mutation of or abrupt variation within a species; abrupt, discontinuous development or transition; leaping, jumping, or dancing — **saltant, -tatory** *adj.*

saltatorial (sál-tə-táwri-əl, sáwl-) *formal. adj.* relating to or adapted for leaping: *the flea's saltatorial legs*

saltpetre (sáwlt-péetər, -peetər) *n.* potassium nitrate, used in making explosives and preserving meat (also "nitre")

salubrious (sə-lóo-bri-əss) *formal. adj.* promoting or favourable to health or well-being: *a salubrious climate*; respectable, wholesome: *not the most salubrious part of town* (in this sense, typically used humorously and in the negative) — **-brity** *n.*

salutary (sál-yoo-tri) *formal. adj.* beneficial, improving, or remedial; restoring or promoting health, curative

salutation *formal. n.* expression of greeting or courtesy, by words or gesture; conventional opening words of a speech or letter, such as "Dear friends" — **salute** *v.*

salvage (sál-vij) *tr.v.* to save from loss, damage, or cancellation ~ *n.* rescue of a ship, cargo, or crew; ship, cargo, or anything else that is salvaged

salve (salv, saav) *n.* soothing medicinal ointment; *formal.* healing or soothing substance, person, or influence ~ *tr.v.* to apply a salve to; *formal.* to soothe, calm, or appease

salver *n.* tray or platter, often made of silver, for serving food, presenting visiting cards, or the like [from Spanish *salva*, originally, a sampling of food by a taster to detect poison, from *salvar*, literally, to save]

salvo *n., pl.* **-os** or **-oes** simultaneous or rapid firing of two or more guns, release of several bombs, or the like; sudden burst of cheering, applause, or the like

sal volatile (sál və-láttəli) *n.* smelling salts containing ammonium carbonate (also "spirits of ammonia", formerly "hartshorn") [New Latin, volatile salt]

samara (sə-máarə) *n.* winged, non-splitting, one-seeded fruit, as of the ash or sycamore (also "key fruit")

Sam Browne belt *n.* military officer's wide belt supported by a diagonal strap passing over the right shoulder [after Sir *Sam*uel James *Browne*, a 19th-century British general who after losing his left arm devised such a belt to support his sword]

samizdat (sámmiz-dát) *n.*, underground publishing of banned writings in the USSR; such writings or publications

samovar (sámmə-vaar) *n.* Russiani-style tea urn, originally with an inner container for hot charcoal

samp *chiefly U.S. n.* maize meal or porridge

sampler *n.* decorative piece of needlework, using a variety of stitches and often embroidered with pictures and mottoes [it provides a *sample* of stitches or of the sewer's skill; related to *example*]

samurai (sámmoo-rī) *n., pl.* **samurai** warrior of a military aristocratic order in Japan in former times

sanative (sánnətiv) *formal. adj.* curing, healing

sanatorium (sánnə-táwri-əm) *n., pl.* **-riums** or **-ria** hospital for those suffering from chronic diseases such as tuberculosis, or convalescent home for those recovering (also *U.S.* "sanitarium"); health resort; sick bay, especially in a boarding school

sanctify *tr.v.* to reserve for sacred purposes or religious use, consecrate; to purify ritually, make holy, cleanse of sin; *formal.* to make morally binding — **-ification** *n.*

sanctimonious *adj.* holy in a hypocritical or self-satisfied way, pretending to be pious; self-righteous

sanction *tr.v.* to authorise or permit; to support or encourage; to confirm or ratify (a law, ruling, or the like) — **sanction** *n.*

sanctions *pl.n.* measures imposed on a nation, often by international agreement, to force it to change its policies: *bowed to the threat of trade sanctions*

sanctity *n.* saintliness, holiness, godliness; anything considered sacred; quality of being sacred

sanctuary *n.* sacred place, or the holiest part of a sacred place, such as the chancel of a church; church or other place affording protection or refuge; immunity from arrest or punishment, as conferred by taking refuge in a church or embassy; nature or wildlife reserve

sanctum (sángk-təm) *n., pl.* **-tums** or **-ta** sacred place; study, office, or other private room where one can remain undisturbed

Sanforized (sán-fər-īzd) *trademark. adj.* referring to a kind of pre-shrunk fabric used for clothing

sang froid (sÓN-frwaa, sáng-) *n.* calmness, coolness, self-possession, ability to remain unruffled when in danger or under stress [French, literally, cold blood]

sanguinary (sáng-gwin-əri) *formal. adj.* bloodthirsty, bloodstained, bloody, characterised by blood or bloodshed (also "sanguineous")

sanguine *formal. adj.* cheerful, confident, or optimistic; referring to or having a reddish, florid complexion — **-inity** *n.*

sanitary *adj.* hygienic, free of infection; health-promoting or health-preserving — **-itation** *n.* — **-itise** *tr.v.*

sans-culotte (sánz-kew-lót, SÓN-) *n., pl.* **sans-culottes** extreme radical republican in the French Revolution; extremist, radical, or revolutionary in politics [French, literally, without breeches: the revolutionaries wore pantaloons instead of the typically aristocratic knee-breeches]

sap *tr.v.* to undermine a castle wall or other fortification by tunnelling beneath it — **sap, sapper** *n.*

sapient (sáy-pi-ənt) *formal. adj.* clever, knowing, wise — **-ience** *n.*

saponaceous *formal. adj.* soap-like, soapy

sapor (sáy-pər) *formal. n.* taste, flavour — **-pid** *adj.* **-pidity** *n.*

sapphic (sáffik) *formal. adj.* lesbian (literary) [after *Sappho*, the ancient Greek poet who lived on the island of Lesbos and is considered by scholars to have been a lesbian] — **-phism** *n.* — **-phist** *n.*

Saracen *n.* Muslim at the time of the medieval Crusades — **Saracen** *adj.*

sarcoma (saar-kṓmə) *n., pl.* **-mas** or **-mata** malignant tumour in muscles, tendons, or the like

sarcophagus (saár-kóffə-gəss) *n., pl.* **-gi** coffin of stone, typically having a sculpture or inscription [from Greek (*lithos*) *sarkophagos*, literally, a flesh-eating (stone)]

sardonic *adj.* humorous in a mocking or cynical way [from Latin *Sardonius (risus)*, a bitter (laugh), influenced by *herba Sardonia*, the Sardinian herb, a poisonous plant supposed to distort the face of the eater]

sari *n.* traditional Hindu dress for women, consisting of a length of light cloth wound round the waist and draped over the head or shoulder

sarong *n.* Malay garment for both men and women, consisting of a length of brightly coloured cloth wrapped round the waist or under the armpits

sartorial *formal. adj.* relating to a tailor or tailoring, especially for men: *sartorial elegance*

Sassenach (sássə-nakh) *n.* English person (used chiefly by Scots and Irish and often derogatory) [related to *Saxon*] — **Sassenach** *adj.*

satay (sáttay) *n.* Indonesian or Malaysian dish of small meat kebabs served in a spicy peanut sauce

sate *formal. tr.v.* to satiate — **satiety** *n.*

satiate *tr.v.* to indulge (desires, lusts, or appetites) to the full or to excess (also *formal* "sate") — **-ation** *n.* — **satiable** *adj.*

satrap (sáttrap) *n.* provincial governor in ancient Persia; subordinate ruler or dictator — **-y** *n.*

saturate *tr.v.* to fill or wet completely — **-ation** *n.*

saturnalia (sáttər-náyli-ə) *n., pl.* **-alia** or **-alias** orgy, revelry, unrestrained or riotous celebration [after the festival of *Saturn*, the Roman god of agriculture, celebrated in December in ancient Rome]

saturnine (sáttər-nīn) *formal. adj.* gloomy in temper, or cold and sluggish in temperament [referring to characteristics supposed by astrologers to be typical of those born under the planet *Saturn*]

satyagraha (sət-yáagrə-hə) *n.* Gandhi's policy of non-violent resistance in India to press for political and other reforms [Sanskrit, insistence on truth]

satyr (sáttər, sáytər) *n.* minor woodland god or demon in Greek mythology, half man and half goat; man obsessed with sex (literary)

satyriasis (sáttə-rī́-ə-siss) *formal. n.* abnormally strong or excessive sexual desire in a man (also "satyromania"). Compare NYMPHOMANIA

sauerkraut (sówr-krowt) *n.* shredded or chopped cabbage salted and fermented in its own juice [German, literally, sour cabbage]

saunter *intr.v.* to stroll, walk at a leisurely or slow pace — **saunter** *n.*

saurian *formal. adj.* lizard-like, or relating to lizards — **saurian** *n.*

sauté (sṓ-tay) *tr.v.* to fry lightly in butter or fat: *sautéed potatoes* — **sauté** *n., adj*

savannah *n.* grassland with scattered shrubs and trees in drier tropical and subtropical regions

savant (sávv'nt, sa-vóɴ) *formal. n.* learned or scholarly person (feminine form "savante") [French, literally, knowing]

savoir-faire (sávwaar fáir) *n.* know-how; knowledge of appropriate behaviour, especially in social situations [French, literally, knowing how to do]

savour *formal. n.* taste or smell, flavour; distinctive quality, typical characteristic ~ *v.* — *intr.* to have the taste, smell, flavour, or suggestion of: *savours of ginger/corruption* — *tr.* to flavour or scent; to enjoy the taste, smell, or experience of, relish: *savoured his victory* (also *U.S.* "savor")

savoury *adj.* tasting or smelling pleasant; salty or seasoned rather than sweet-tasting; *formal.* pleasing, agreeable: *a savoury anthology*; morally upright, respectable: *hardly a savoury character* ~ *n.* tasty, seasoned dish, such as Welsh rabbit, served as an hors d'oeuvre or at the end of a meal (also *U.S.* "savory")

Savoyard (sávvoy-árd) *n.* Gilbert-and-Sullivan fan, performer, or producer [after the *Savoy* theatre in London, where the operas of Gilbert and Sullivan were first staged]

saw *n.* familiar old proverb or saying

scabrous (skáybrəss) *adj.* indecent, outrageously indelicate or rude; *formal.* rough to the touch, horny or scaly: *scabrous skin*; *formal.* difficult to solve or deal with: *a scabrous problem*

scaffold *n.* platform or raised wooden framework, as formerly for hanging or beheading criminals

scalene triangle *n.* triangle with all three sides having different lengths

scallion *n.* spring onion or shallot [from Latin *Ascalonia* (*caepa*), an Ascalonian (onion), after the ancient port of *Ascalon* in southern Palestine]

scalloped *adj.* ornamented or bordered with a wavy design, edged with curved or semicircular projections: *scalloped lace*

scallywag *n.* rascal, good-for-nothing [originally, a white Republican southerner after the American Civil War]

scansion *n.* rhythm or metre of verse — **scan** *v.*

scapula (skáppew-lə) *formal. n., pl.* **-las** or **-lae** shoulder blade

scapular *n.* feather on a bird's shoulder; monk's sleeveless outer garment

scarab *n.* beetle of a family including the dung beetles, treated as sacred in ancient Egypt; ancient Egyptian charm or talisman in the shape of a beetle

scarify (skárri-fī) *tr.v.* to slit or scratch (the skin) slightly, as for vaccination or for skin decoration; to cut or soften (the coat of a hard seed) to speed up germination; to break up and loosen the surface of (topsoil, a road, or the like); to wound or hurt the feelings of, as by harsh criticism — **-ification** *n.*

scarlatina *n.* scarlet fever

scarper *British. informal. intr.v.* to run away, depart in haste, flee

scathing *adj.* very harsh: *scathing criticism*

scatology *n.* medical or archaeological study of excrement; obscenity or obsessive interest in obscenity, especially in relation to excrement — **-logical** *adj.*

scatophagous (ska-tóffəgəss) *formal. adj.* dung-eating, feeding on excrement: *scatophagous beetles/flies*

scats *pl.n.* dung or droppings, especially of animals being trailed or hunted

scavenge *v.* to sort through rubbish or refuse for food or useful objects

scavenger *n.* hyena, vulture, insect, or other creature that feeds on dead animals, rotting meat, or decaying organic matter; rag-and-bone man

scenario (si-naár-i-ō) *n., pl.* **-os** outline of the plot of a play, novel, or the like; screenplay or shooting script for a film; *informal.* projected or possible course of

action or chain of events
sceptical (sképtik'l) *n.* doubting, disbelieving, mistrusting (also *U.S.* "skeptical") — **sceptic**, **-icism** *n.*
sceptre (séptər) *n.* ruler's staff carried as a sign of royal authority or power (also *U.S.* "septer")
Schadenfreude (shaád'n-froydə) *formal. n.* pleasure in or satisfaction at others' misfortunes, gloating [German, *Schade*, harm + *Freude*, joy]
schema (skeé-mə) *n.*, *pl.* **-mata** brief representation of something, such as an outline, diagram, or summary; pattern or structure, especially in logic — **-matic** *adj.* — **-matise** *tr.v.*
schism (síz'm, skíz'm) *n.* splitting into opposing factions, as within a religion — **-matic** *adj.*, *n.*
schizophrenia (skíts-ə-freéni-ə) *n.* psychosis involving severe personality disturbances and weakened sense of reality (also formerly "dementia praecox"); *informal.* display or possession of inconsistent or incompatible types of behaviour or ideas [New Latin, literally, split mind] — **-phrenic** *adj.*, *n.*
schlock *chiefly U.S. slang. n.* manufactured goods, ornaments, entertainments, or the like of inferior quality or poor value, junk — **schlock** *adj.*
schmaltz (shmolts, schmawlts) *informal. n.* excessive sentimentality, as in art and music; excessive praise, emotion, or the like [German, literally, melted fat] — **-y** *adj.*
schnapps (shnaps) *informal. n.* strong distilled alcoholic drink
scholastic (skə-lástik) *formal. adj.* relating to schools; pedantic, scholarly in a dry or nitpicking way
scholium *n.*, *pl.* **-ums** or **-lia** scholarly note or marginal comment, as on a Greek or Latin text; incidental note supplementing a train of reasoning, mathematical proof, or the like [related to *scholarly*] — **scholiast** *n.*
schooner (skōōnər) *n. British.* large glass for sherry or port; *Australian or U.S.* large beer glass; large sailing ship
schwa (shwaa) *n.* unstressed mid-central vowel sound, as at the end of *Anna*; symbol ə representing this sound
sciagram (sī́-ə-gram, skī́-) *formal. n.* picture formed from shadows or outlines — **-graphy** *n.*
sciamachy (sī-ámməki, skī-) *formal. n.* fighting imaginary enemies, shadow boxing, tilting at windmills
scilicet (sī́li-set, sílli-, skeéli-ket) *formal. adv.* namely, to wit, that is to say (used to introduce a synonym, explanation, or missing word) [Latin, short for *scire licet*, it is permitted to know]
scintilla (sin-tíllə) *formal. n.*, *pl.* **-las** least amount, iota, trace
scintillate *formal. intr.v.* to sparkle, flash, or give off sparks — **-lant**, **-lating** *adj.* — **-lation** *n.*
sciolism (sī́-ə-liz'm) *formal. n.* pretentious behaviour by which someone tries to appear far more knowledgeable or learned than he or she really is — **-ist** *n.* — **-istic** *adj.*
sciomancy (sī́-ə-mansi) *formal. n.* forecasting or divination by consulting ghosts — **-mantic** *adj.* — **-cer** *n.*
scion (sī́-ən) *n.* budded shoot or twig detached and joined to a stock for grafting, slip; *formal.* descendant or offspring, especially male
scission (sízh'n, sísh'n) *formal. n.* cutting, splitting, dividing — **scissile** *adj.*
sciurine (sī́-yōōr-īn, -in) *formal. adj.* relating to or resembling a squirrel — **sciurine** *n.*
sclerosis (sklə-rṓ-siss) *n.*, *pl.* **-roses** hardening or thickening of the arteries, spinal cord, or other body part, with impaired functioning — **-otic** *adj.*
¹sconce *n.* bracket on a wall for holding a candle, torch, or the like; candlestick attached to a handle or bracket
²sconce *tr.v.* to challenge (a fellow Oxbridge student) to drink a large glass of beer non-stop, specifically as a penalty for infringing table etiquette
scorbutic *formal. adj.* scurvy-like, relating to scurvy, or suffering from scurvy
scoria *n.* rough, heavy, solidified lava with many cavities; slag, refuse from smelted ore or metal
¹scotch *tr.v.* to crush or put an end to (something, such as a rumour or rebellion)
²scotch *n.* wedge or block placed under a wheel, log, or the like to immobilise it on a slope (also "chock") — **scotch** *tr.v.*
scourge (skurj) *n.* whip used for punishment; cause or means of severe or widespread suffering; means of vengeance, criticism, or punishment ~ *tr.v.* to punish with or as if with a scourge; to devastate, afflict severely
scouse *informal. n.* person born or living in Liverpool, or the English dialect spoken in Liverpool (also "Scouse", "scouser") [shortened from *lobscouse*, a meat stew popular in Liverpool] — **scouse** *adj.*
screamer *informal. n.* exclamation mark
scree *n.* rock debris, typically in a sloping heap at the foot of a hill or cliff (also "talus")
screed *n.* long and typically dull speech or piece of writing, especially a letter; concrete mixture or finish, as on a floor; wooden or metal strip used as a thickness guide or leveller, as when plastering
scrimshank *British. informal. intr.v.* to shirk work or duty, skive
scrimshaw *n.* carved or engraved articles of ivory, whalebone, or the like, typically made by sailors
scrip *n.* documentation showing entitlement to something such as stocks and shares [short for *subscription (receipt)*]
scriptorium *n.*, *pl.* **-iums** or **-ia** room in a monastery in which scribes could copy records or manuscripts
scrivener (skriv-nər) *n.* copyist or scribe in former times
scrotum *n.*, *pl.* **-ums** or **-ta** sac of skin containing the testicles — **-tal** *adj.*
scrumptious *informal. adj.* delicious
scrumpy *British. n.* strong rough cider typically from the south-west of England
scruples *pl.n.* moral uncertainties or twinges of conscience giving rise to hesitation ~ *intr.v.* — **not scruple to** to do or act without hesitation
scrupulous *adj.* strictly observing moral principles, having scruples: *scrupulous in all their dealings*; careful or conscientious in a rigorous, painstaking way
scrutineer *British. n.* person who checks or counts votes at an election
scrutinise *tr.v.* to examine or inspect carefully and intensely — **scrutiny** *n.*
scry *formal. intr.v.* to see the future or discover facts by gazing into a crystal ball [variant of *descry*]
scuba *n.* underwater breathing apparatus such as an aqualung [*s*elf-*c*ontained *u*nderwater *b*reathing *a*pparatus] — **scuba** *adj.*
scud *intr.v.* to skim or glide: *clouds scudding across the sky*; to run before a gale, as a ship might even when

carrying little sail ~ *n.* thin broken cloud driven by the wind, below the main rain clouds; gust of wind or wind-driven shower [variant of *scut*, originally, a hare]
scullery *n.* room off or recess in a kitchen for dish-washing, vegetable peeling, and the like
scullion *archaic. n.* kitchen servant, usually a man or boy doing menial chores; vile or despicable person
[1]**scupper** *n.* opening, especially at the side of a deck for draining water away
[2]**scupper** *chiefly British. slang. n.* to rain, spoil utterly: *scuppered our plans*
scurf *informal. n.* scaly dry skin, as in dandruff
scurrilous (skúrri-ləss) *adj.* using obscene or abusive language; slanderously abusive — **-ility** *n.*
scurvy *n.* disease caused by lack of vitamin C, as formerly among sailors, characterised by bleeding gums, and causing physical weakness ~ *adj.* despicable, low-down: *the scurvy dog!* (old-fashioned)
scut *n.* tail, short and often erect, of a rabbit, hare, or deer
scutage (skéwtij) *n.* tax paid by a feudal vassal in place of military service
scutate (skéwtayt) *formal. adj.* covered in scales (also "scutellate"); shaped like a shield: *scutate leaves* (in this sense, also "scutiform")
scuttle *n.* porthole, hinged hatchway, or the like on a ship ~ *tr.v.* to sink (a ship) accidentally or on purpose
scuttlebutt *n.* drinking fountain or cask on a ship; *chiefly U.S. slang.* gossip, rumours
Scylla and Charybdis (sílla; kə-ríbdiss) *formal. n.* — **between Scylla and Charybdis** between the devil and the deep blue sea, facing a choice of two equal dangers [after *Scylla*, a rock on the Italian side of the Strait of Messina, and *Charybdis*, the whirlpool opposite: as hazards to sailors, they were personified as sea monsters in ancient Greek mythology]
séance (sáy-ONSS) *n.* spiritualist meeting in which people try to communicate with the dead [French, literally, a sitting]
sebaceous (si-báyshəss) *formal. adj.* fatty, oily, greasy; secreting oil: *sebaceous glands*
sebum (séebəm) *formal. n.* oily substance secreted by small glands in the skin to keep skin and hair from getting too dry
sec *adj.* dry rather than sweet, as some wines are; dry rather than very dry, as a champagne might be. Compare BRUT [French, literally, dry]
secateurs (séckətérz) *chiefly British. pl.n.* garden shears used for pruning
secco *n., pl.* **-os** painting done on dry plaster on a wall. Compare FRESCO [Italian, literally, dry]
secede *intr.v.* to withdraw as a member; to break away from an alliance or other grouping — **-cession** *n.*
secluded *adj.* removed, remote, lonely, solitary — **-clusion** *n.* — **-clusive** *adj.*
secondment (si-kóndmənt) *chiefly British. n.* temporary release of a person from a post for service elsewhere: *on secondment from her firm to work for the U.N.* — **second** *tr.v.*
secretaire (sekrə-táir) *n.* writing desk, typically with a hinged top closing over small drawers
secretariat *n.* administrative department of a large public or international organisation such as the United Nations
sectarian *adj.* relating to a sect, faction, or narrow grouping: *sectarian violence* — **sectarian** *n.*
section *n.* surgical cutting or separating of tissue; *formal.* thin slice or specimen, as of tissue, for examination by microscope
sector *n.* section of a circle formed by two radii and the arc; section or division, as of a military front or the economy; measuring instrument with two rulers or graduated arms hinged together at one end
secular *adj.* relating to worldly rather than spiritual or religious matters, temporal; referring to a priest who does not belong to a monastic order (opposite "regular") — **-ise** *tr.v.* — **-ism**, **-ity** *n.*
sedan chair *n.* portable chair, usually covered, with poles for two bearers, used for transporting one person, especially in Britain in the 17th and 18th centuries (also "sedan")
[1]**sedate** *adj.* calm and even-tempered, even to the point of dullness
[2]**sedate** *tr.v.* to administer a sedative to — **-tion** *n.*
sedative (séddə-tiv) *n.* medical drug that induces calmness, tranquillity, or sleep — **sedative** *adj.*
sedentary (sédd'n-tri) *formal. adj.* sitting a great deal, or requiring much sitting: *a sedentary job*; non-migratory: *sedentary birds*
sediment *n.* dregs or other matter that settles at the bottom of a liquid; deposit of rock fragments or similar debris left by wind, water, or glaciers — **-ation** *n.* — **-ary** *adj.*
sedition *n.* rebellious speech or action, incitement to undermine authority — **-itious** *adj.*
sedulous (séddew-ləss) *formal. adj.* conscientious, diligent, persevering in one's duty, assiduous — **-lity** *n.*
see *n.* bishop's seat of authority or diocese
seed *tr.v.* to add a small crystal to (a liquid) to cause crystallisation; to sprinkle silver iodide or a similar chemical in (a cloud) to cause condensation and produce rain — **seeding** *n.*
seel *formal. tr.v.* to seal the eyes of a hawk or falcon by stitching them shut
seemly *formal. adj.* suitable, tasteful, or proper, in line with accepted standards
seepage *n.* leakage, oozing — **seep** *intr.v.*
segment *n.* any part, section, or division of something; in geometry, any portion of a curve, or any part of a circle formed by a chord cutting it ~ *v.* to divide into segments — **-mental**, **-mentary** *adj.*
segregate *tr.v.* to separate or isolate from others or from an entire group; to divide (an institution, entire society, or the like) along racial lines (opposite "integrate", "desegregate") — **-tion** *n.*
seicento (say-chéntō) *n.* 17th-century period of Italian art, literature, and culture
seigneur (senyúr, seen-, sen-yór) *n.* feudal lord or large landowner in a French-speaking area; hereditary male head of the government of the island of Sark — **-y**, **seigniory** *n.*
seigniorage (sáyn-yərij) *n.* government revenue from the minting of coins, after the cost of metal and production has been subtracted
seine (sayn) *n.* large fishing net hanging upright in the water
seismic (sízmik) *formal. adj.* relating to, caused by, or subject to earthquakes
seismology *n.* scientific study of earthquakes — **-gist** *n.* — **-logical** *adj.*
selachian (si-láyki-ən) *formal. adj.* relating to sharks or rays — **selachian** *n.*

self-abnegation *n.* self-sacrifice or self-denial

self-aggrandising (sélf-ə-grándīzing) *adj.* aggressively or ruthlessly seeking to increase one's own influence, wealth, or other power [related to *grand*] — **-disement** *n.*

self-deprecating (sélf-déppri-kayting) *adj.* modest or humble to a fault — **-cation** *n.*

seltzer *chiefly U.S. n.* natural sparkling spring water with a high mineral content; artificially carbonated mineral water (also "seltzer water") [after *Nieder Selters*, a spa district in West Germany]

selvage *n.* edge, border, or fringe of a fabric, carpet, or the like finished so as to prevent unravelling; edge plate of a lock into which the bolt slots (also "selvedge")

semantic *adj.* relating to meaning, such as the meaning of words — **-tics** *n., pl.n.* — **-ticist** *n.*

semaphore (sémmə-fawr) *n.* signalling system or apparatus using railway signals, pivoted arms, or the like; signalling system based on the manipulation of two flags held at arm's length, as formerly used at sea — **semaphore** *v.*

semblance *formal. n.* appearance or outward presentation, often deceptive; least trace, tiniest amount: *without even a semblance of concern for others* [related to *resemblance*]

semester *n.* term typically forming half an academic year, as in the U.S. or German universities

semibreve *n.* longest note in ordinary musical notation, equal to two minims

seminal (sémmin'l) *adj.* relating to seeds or semen; creative and original, providing a basis for development: *a seminal work in biophysics*

seminar *n.* study group or meeting; conference or meeting for the exchange of information

seminary *n.* theological school; training school for clergymen or priests — **-arian, -arist** *n.*

semiotics *n.* science or study of signs and symbols — **semiotic** *adj.*

semitone *n.* smallest interval used between notes in Western music, equal to half a tone in the standard diatonic scale

sempiternal *formal. adj.* eternal, perpetual (literary) — **-ternity** *n.*

seneschal (sénnish'l) *n.* steward in charge of the domestic arrangements of a medieval royal or noble household

senile *adj. formal.* relating to old age; showing mental deterioration in old age — **-ility** *n.*

sensibility *n.* fine feelings, keen power of perception, sensitive openness to emotional influences

sensory *adj.* relating or referring to the five senses: *sensory perception/deprivation*

sensual *adj.* relating to gratifying the pleasures of the senses or bodily appetites; sexually suggestive or appealing — **-ity, -ism, -ist** *n.*

sensuous *adj.* relating to or attractive to the senses; delighting in the pleasures of sense perception

sententious *formal. adj.* pompously moralising, especially by means of proverbs or platitudes

sentient *formal. adj.* conscious, aware, responsive to stimuli — **-tience** *n.*

sentinel *formal. n.* guard, sentry — **sentinel** *v.*

Sephardi (se-fár-di) *n., pl.* **-dim** Jew of Spanish or eastern origin or descent. Compare ASHKENAZI [from Modern Hebrew *Sapharadh*, Spain] — **Sephardi, -dic** adj.

sepia (séepi-ə) *n.* dark-brown colour, ink, or pigment; drawing or photograph in a brown tint — **sepia** *adj.*

sepoy (sée-poy) *n.* Indian soldier serving under European, especially British, command in former times

seppuku (sep-o͞okoo͞) *n.* Japanese ritual suicide by disembowelment (also "hara-kiri") [Japanese, literally, to cut open the stomach]

sepsis *n.* process of becoming septic

septicaemia (sépti-séemi-ə) *formal. n.* blood poisoning

septic tank *n.* sewage tank or pit in which solid waste is decomposed by bacteria

septum *n., pl.* **-ta** division, partition, or membrane separating tissues or cavities, as between the nostrils

sepulchral (si-púlkrəl) *adj.* gloomy, tomb-like

sepulchre (sépp'l-kər) *formal. n.* burial vault, tomb, or grave — **sepulchre** *tr.v.*

sequel *n.* development, continuation, something following, such as a novel, film, or the like that continues the story of a previous one

sequela (si-kwéelə) *formal. n., pl.* **-lae** aftereffect, complication, or condition following a disease (usually plural)

sequential *adj.* in order, successive, serial — **-ity** *n.*

sequester *formal. tr.v.* to separate or set apart, especially so as to impede discovery or communication — **sequestered** *adj.*

sequestrate (sée-kwiss-trayt) *tr.v.* to seize or confiscate (property) temporarily, especially that of a debtor — **-ation** *n.*

seraglio (si-ráali-ō) *n., pl.* **-os** sultan's palace; large harem

seraph (serrəf) *n., pl.* **-s** or **-phim** angel of the highest rank, according to the medieval classification

sere (seer) *formal or archaic. adj.* dry, withered, shrivelled, as a dead leaf would be (also "sear")

serenade *n.* love song, typically sung outside a woman's house in the evening — **serenade** *tr.v.*

serendipity (sérrən-díppiti) *formal. n.* tendency or ability to make lucky discoveries by accident [coined in 1754 by Horace Walpole, after the heroes of the Persian fairy tale *The Three Princes of Serendip*, who made such discoveries, *Serendip* being an ancient name for Sri Lanka — **-tous** *adj.*

serf *n.* farm worker bound to a feudal lord or estate; oppressed or enslaved person — **-dom** *n.*

serial music *n.* music based on an untraditional sequence of notes, typically a twelve-tone scale

seriatim (séer-i-áytim, sérri-áatim)) *formal. adv.* one after another in sequence, item by item in a series

sericulture *formal. n.* silk-production by rearing silkworms — **-tural** *adj.* — **-ist** *n.*

serif (sérrif) *n.* short ornamental line finishing off a stroke of a printed letter

serigraph *formal. n.* silk-screen print

serjeant at arms *n., pl.* **serjeants at arms** parliamentary officer who maintains order (also "sergeant at arms")

serjeant at law *n.* British barrister of high rank in former times

serpentine *formal. adj.* resembling a snake in movement or appearance; sly and treacherous

serration *n.* teeth or notches in a series, as on a saw or leaf edge — **serrate** *adj., tr.v.* — **-ated** *adj.*

serried *formal. adj.* crowded, pressed together, tightly packed: *serried ranks of troops*

serum *n., pl.* **-rums** or **-ra** blood plasma; watery part of milk, whey; clear watery fluid produced by tissue,

as in a blister; antidote to poison obtained from the blood or tissue of immunised animals — **serous** *adj.*
servile *adj.* slavish, slave-like; meek, submissive, or eager to please in a fawning way — **-vility** *n.*
servitude *formal. n.* enforced obedience involving loss of freedom, slavery or near-slavery, bondage
sesquipedalian (séskwi-pi-dáyli-ən) *formal. adj.* referring to very long words, polysyllabic; tending to use or characterised by very long words (usually derogatory) [Latin *sesquipedalis*, a foot-and-a-half long: *sesqui-*, one and a half + *pes*, a foot]
sessile *formal. adj.* stalkless, attached at the base: *a sessible leaf/flower*; fixed, rooted, immobile, as barnacles are
sestet *n.* poem or stanza of six lines, especially the last six lines of a Petrarchan sonnet. Compare OCTET
setaceous *formal. adj.* bristly; bristle-like (also "setose")
set square *n.* triangular sheet of wood, metal, or plastic, used to construct certain angles and lines quickly in geometry or technical drawing
sett *n.* badger's burrow; stone or wooden block used for paving roads (also "set")
settle *n.* old-fashioned high-backed bench, typically with arms at the sides and a storage chest beneath
sextant *n.* instrument used in navigation, for measuring the angles of stars and planets
sexton *n.* church caretaker, often acting as bellringer and gravedigger as well [variant of *sacristan*]
shaddock *n.* grapefruit-like citrus fruit (also *chiefly U.S.* "pomelo") [after Captain *Shaddock*, a sea captain who took the seed from the East Indies to Jamaica in 1676]
shadoof (shə-dŏŏf) *n.* water-raising apparatus, as used in Egypt, consisting of a pivoted pole with a bucket on one end and a counterweight on the other (also "shaduf", "shadouf")
shag *n.* tangled mass, as of matted hair; long woolly nap, as on coarse cloth or a carpet; tobacco of a strong coarse type cut into shreds
shaggy-dog story *n.* story or drawn-out anecdote whose humour is supposed to lie in the irrelevance or anticlimax of the punch line [an early anecdote of this kind dealt with a shaggy dog]
shagreen (shə-gréen) *n.* sharkskin with a rough surface, used as an abrasive; rough animal hide used as leather [from French *chagrin*, literally, rough hide]
shallot (shə-lót) *n.* onion-like bulb, growing in clusters, used for pickling and cooking [see SCALLION]
shaman (shámən) *n., pl.* **-mans** cult priest; medicine man, witch doctor
shamanism *n.* spiritualist religious practices, as in northern Asia or among North American Indians, in which priests act as mediums — **-ist** *n.* — **-istic** *adj.*
shamateur (shámmə-ter) *informal. n.* sportsman or sportswoman who is officially an amateur but who receives payment for participating (humorous) [blend of *sham* + *amateur*]
shambolic *informal. adj.* in a hopeless mess [from *shambles*]
shamus (sháy-məss, sháa) *U.S. slang. n.* policeman or private detective
shanghai (sháng-hī́) *informal. tr.v.* to press-gang into naval service [after *Shanghai*, from the former custom of kidnapping sailors to man ships sailing to eastern ports such as *Shanghai*]
Shangri-la *informal. n.* remote imaginary earthly paradise, especially in unspoilt natural surroundings [after the name of the imaginary land in James Hilton's novel *Lost Horizon* of 1933]
shanks's pony *informal. n.* walking, or one's legs or feet, as a means of travel (also *U.S.* "shank's mare")
¹shanty *n.* shack or hut, typically crudely built and run-down
²shanty *n.* sailors' song, sung in rhythm with their work [from French *chanter*, to sing; related to *chant*]
shard *n.* pottery fragment, as in an archaeological excavation (also "sherd", "potsherd", "potshard")
sheading (shéeding) *n.* any of the six administrative divisions of the Isle of Man
sheave *n.* pulley wheel with a groove
shebeen (shi-béen) *chiefly Irish or South African. n.* place where alcohol is sold or drunk illegally
¹sheer *intr.v.* to turn off from a chosen or straight course or path, deviate: *suddenly sheered off at a sharp angle*
²sheer *adj.* thin, light, and transparent or translucent: *sheer fine fabrics*
sheet *n.* rope or chain attached to and controlling the lower corner of a sail
sheets *pl.n.* spaces at the front and back of a rowing boat that are not occupied by rowers
shellac (shéllak, shə-lák) *n.* resin or thin varnish used for coating wood — **shellac** *tr.v.*
shenanigans (shi-nánni-g'nz) *informal. pl.n.* tricks, either mischievous or fraudulent
shibboleth (shíbbə-leth) *n.* word, phrase, social custom, or the like that has become a sign of group solidarity; cliché, commonplace unoriginal remark [Hebrew, a stream: this was the password used by the Gileadites, Judges 12:6]
shillelagh (shi-láyli) *n.* club or heavy oak stick in Ireland [after *Shillelagh*, a town in County Wicklow in the Republic of Ireland, where such clubs were made in former times]
shilly-shally *intr.v.* to delay or hesitate; to dawdle, lag behind, or idle [from *shill I, shall I?*, a question that someone undecided would ask himself in former times] — **shilly-shally** *adj., adv., n.*
shindy *slang. n.* uproar or confusion, commotion; rowdy party or noisy celebration (also "shindig")
shingle *n.* wooden tile, as laid in overlapping rows on a roof or outer wall; *U.S.* small signboard or name plate, as of a doctor or a lawyer
shirr *tr.v.* to gather (fabric) into decorative rows, as on a dress, often using elastic thread — **shirr** *n.*
shive *n.* cork or flat bung for a wide-mouthed bottle
shoal *n.* shallow stretch of water; sandbank, mudbank, or the like, often dangerous to shipping, sometimes exposed at low tide
shoat *n.* piglet newly weaned (also "shote")
shock *n.* thick bushy mass: *a shock of hair*; pile of maize, or sheaves of grain gathered in a field to dry
shoddy *n.* wool or cloth recycled from unfelted old or waste cloth
shoji (shṓji) *n., pl.* **-jis** or **-ji** paper screen used as a sliding door or partition in a Japanese house
shooting brake *British. n.* estate car (old-fashioned)
shooting stick *n.* spiked walking stick whose handle opens into a flat seat
short shrift *n.* brief and unsympathetic treatment, curt consideration and dismissal
shot *adj.* shimmering or changing in colour: *shot silk*
shotten *adj.* recently spawned and so of less value as

food: *a shotten herring*

shrievalty (shréev'lti) *British. formal. n.* office or authority of a sheriff

shrift *archaic. n.* confession heard by a priest, or the penance and forgiveness granted by him — **shrive** *v.*

shrine *n.* tomb of or sacred place associated with a saint, holy being, or other revered person; place or container in which sacred relics are kept; place considered sacred or extremely valuable because of its historical or other associations

shrinkage *informal. n.* loss of goods from a shop or supermarket caused by shoplifting

shroud *n.* cloth used to wrap a dead body for burial ~ *tr.v.* to screen or hide from view; to obscure, disguise; to wrap in a shroud for burial

shrouds *pl.n.* ropes or cables supporting the mast on a ship or boat; ropes connecting the harness of a parachute to the canopy

shufti (shŏŏfti) *British. informal. n.* look, glance, brief inspection

sibilant (síbbi-lənt) *n.* consonant such as *s* or *z*, producing a hissing sound, or the sound itself — **sibilant** *adj.* — **-lance** *n.* — **-late** *v.*

sibling *formal. n.* brother or sister

sibyl *n.* in the ancient world, prophetess or woman oracle; witch or sorceress — **sibylline** *adj.*

sic *adv.* so, thus (used in a printed text to indicate the deliberate reproduction of a mistaken or surprising word or fact being quoted)

siccative (síckətiv) *formal. n.* drying substance, as added to paints, inks, and some medicines — **siccative** *adj.*

sidereal (sī-déer-i-əl) *formal. adj.* of or relating to a star or stars

sidle *intr.v.* to move sideways, or in a nervous, suspicious way [probably from *sidelong*]

sienna (si-énnə) *n.* brownish yellow; clayey mineral used in pigments [from Italian *terra di Sienna*, earth from the town of *Siena*] — **sienna** *adj.*

sierra (si-érrə) *n.* mountain range with a jagged outline [Spanish, saw-edge; related to *serrated*]

siesta *n.* sleep or rest taken in the afternoon, especially in hot southern countries [Spanish, from Latin *sexta (hora)*, the sixth (hour after sunrise), noon]

sigmoid *formal. adj.* S-shaped

signal *formal. adj.* extraordinary, remarkable, important: *a signal victory for the party*

signally *formal. adv.* especially, noticeably

signatory (síg-nə-tri) *n.* person, party, government, or the like that has signed and is therefore bound to abide by a convention or treaty

signature *n.* set of printed pages, typically 16 or 32, folded from a single sheet, for binding with others to form a book; letter or number printed at the foot of some pages in a book, specifying the sequence for binding the sections

signet (síg-nit) *n.* seal as used on official documents; impression made by this

silage (sīlij) *n.* fodder of fermented grass, corn, or the like prepared in a pit or silo

silhouette (sílloo-ét) *n.* shadow image or filled-in outline, typically of solid black against a white background, as of a person's profile; shape of a person or thing when set against a lighter background ~ *tr.v.* to represent or cause to appear as a silhouette: *a figure silhouetted against the dawn sky* [French, after Etienne de *Silhouette*, an 18th-century French finance official, probably referring obscurely to his strict economic measures]

silicone *n.* resilient chemical substance of various kinds, used in paints and plastics, electrical insulators, breast implants, and other products

silk *n.* barrister of senior rank, a QC or KC — **take silk** to become a QC or KC [after the silk gown worn by such a senior barrister]

silks *pl.n.* jockey's identifying cap and shirt, typically in bright colours

silo *n., pl.* **-los** cylindrical tower for storing grain or fodder; underground shelter for housing guided missiles

silt *n.* rock particles finer than sand but coarser than clay; fine soil; deposit of fine sandy sediment in or from a river — **silt up** *v.*

silva *formal. n.* forests or trees of a particular region (also "sylva")

simian (símmi-ən) *formal. adj.* relating to or resembling an ape or monkey

simile (sím-i-li) *n.* figure of speech involving a direct comparison, as in *She entered the room like a ship in full sail.* Compare METAPHOR

similitude (si-mílli-tewd) *formal. n.* similarity, likeness

simony (sīməni) *n.* corrupt buying and selling of church offices, relics, pardons, and the like [after *Simon* Magus, a Samaritan who tried to buy spiritual powers from Jesus's disciples Peter and John, Acts 8:18] — **-monist, -moniac** *n., adj.* — **-moniacal** *adj.*

simpatico (sim-pátti-kō) *informal. adj.* compatible, easy to get on with, like-minded, attractive, likeable (often humorous) [Italian]

simper *v.* — *intr.* to smile in an irritatingly coy or self-conscious way — *tr.* to say with a simper — **simper** *n.*

simple *archaic. n.* medicinal plant or herb

simplistic *adj.* over-simplifying, ignoring important complications: *a simplistic solution*

simulacrum (símmew-láy-krəm, -lá-) *formal. n., pl.* **-acra** image, representation, or likeness of something, sometimes misleading or superficial

simulate *tr.v.* to imitate the form, appearance, or sound of, often in order to deceive — **-ation** *n.*

simulator *n.* apparatus or model providing test conditions that imitate the real thing: *a flight simulator for trainee pilots*

simulcast (símm'l-kaast) *n.* simultaneous broadcast of a programme on radio and television [*simul*taneous + broad*cast*] — **simulcast** *tr.v.*

sinecure (sīni-kewr, sínni-) *formal. n.* job or office that requires little or no work even though providing an income; cushy job or post [Medieval Latin (*beneficium*) *sine cūrā;* (benefice) without care (of souls)]

sine die (sīni dī-ee, sínni dée-ay) *formal. adv.* indefinitely: *petitioned the court for an adjournment sine die* [Latin, without a (specified) day]

sine qua non (sīni kway non, sinni kwaa nōn) *formal. n.* indispensable element, necessary condition, prerequisite [Latin, literally, without which not]

singlet *chiefly British. n.* vest, sleeveless undershirt [made of a single layer of material, unlined]

singultus (sing-gúl-təss) *formal. n., pl.* **-ti** hiccup [Latin, a sob]

sinistral (sínnistrəl) *formal. adj.* left, left-handed, or on the left. Compare DEXTRAL — **-ity** *n.*

Sinology (sī-nólləji) *n.* study of the language, culture, and history of China — **gist** *n.* — **-logical** *adj.*

sinuous *adj.* bending or curving gracefully; supple and lithe: *the sinuous movements of a ballet dancer*; complex or devious: *a sinuous argument* — **-uosity** *n.*

sinus *n.* cavity, hollow, or channel in the body, containing or conveying air, pus, blood, or the like; air-filled cavity in the skull, connecting with the nostrils

siphon *n.* pipe or tube, typically curved upwards, for draining liquid by using atmospheric pressure (also "syphon") — **siphon** *v.*

sippet *n.* wedge of toast or fried bread, soaked in gravy or juice, or served as a garnish

siren *n.* sea nymph in Greek mythology who lured sailors to death by her sweet song; *formal.* dangerously attractive woman (old-fashioned and literary) — **siren** *adj.*

sirocco (si-róckō) *n., pl.* **-cos** hot wind from the Sahara blowing in southern Italy and Sicily

sisal (sī́s'l) *n.* fibre used in making ropes; tropical agave plant whose leaves yield sisal

size *n.* glue, glaze, filler, or coating, as for paper or walls, made of wax, clay, resin, or the like (also "sizing")

sjambok (shámbok) *n.* South African whip of stiff leather, especially of rhinoceros or hippopotamus hide

skald (skaald, skawld) *n.* bard or minstrel in ancient Scandinavia

skean dhu (skeé-ən-dōō, shkeé-) *n.* dagger worn in a man's stocking as part of traditional Scottish Highland dress

skedaddle *British. informal. intr.v.* to run away, depart in haste, flee

skeet *n.* clay-pigeon shooting in which the targets are thrown at varying speeds and angles from traps on either side of the range [akin to *shoot*]

skein (skayn, skeen) *n.* loose coil of thread, wool, or yarn; *formal.* flock of geese or other wildfowl in flight

skep *n.* beehive, typically in the form of a straw dome

skerry *chiefly Scottish. n.* reef or small rocky island, as off the coast of Scotland

skewbald *adj.* having a coat with patches of white and grey, brown, or red: *skewbald horses.* Compare PIEBALD ~ *n.* skewbald horse

skillet *n. chiefly British.* saucepan, often with legs and a long handle, for cooking on a hearth; *chiefly U.S.* frying pan

skilly *British. n.* oatmeal gruel or thin broth

skirl *n.* shrill piercing sound of the bagpipes — **skirl** *v.*

skirmish *n.* minor or preliminary conflict, dispute, or military encounter — **skirmish** *intr.v.*

skirr *intr.v.* to fly or move rapidly away, as flushed gamebirds do

skitter *intr.v.* to skim, glide, or skip lightly; to skim a fishing lure or baited hook lightly over the water

skittish *adj.* lively, frisky, frivolous; unreliable or unpredictable; shy or coy

skulduggery *informal. n.* underhand or devious action, trickery (often humorous)

skulk *informal. intr.v.* to steal about, move in a sneaky or suspicious way; to hide or lie in wait, lurk, typically for a sinister purpose

slag *n.* waste material deposited during the smelting of metal ore in a furnace, cinder; rough fragments of dark lava, scoria; waste rocks and minerals from a coal mine

slake *formal. tr.v.* to satisfy (a desire) partly or wholly: *slake one's thirst; gossip to slake their curiosity* [related to *slack*]

slalom (slaá-ləm) *n.* moving speedily, especially in skiing, through a zigzag course; race or speed contest over such a course

slapstick *n.* comedy of an unsubtle, energetic, farcical kind

slattern *n.* woman who is untidy in appearance, habits, or housekeeping — **-ly** *adj.*

slaver (slávvər) *intr.v.* to dribble saliva, slobber; *informal.* to appreciate or desire to excess, drool: *slavering over the prospect of victory*

sleight of hand (slīt) *n.* skill or speed of hand movements, as used in conjuring tricks (also "legerdemain", *formal.* "prestidigitation"); trickery or clever deception

slide *n.* U-shaped section of tubing in a trombone that is moved outwards and back to produce different notes

slink *tr.v.* to give birth to (a calf) prematurely ~ *n.* young farm or domestic animal that is born prematurely, especially a calf

slipper bath *n.* bath covered at one end

slipstream *n.* stream of air or water behind a fast-moving vehicle

slipway *n.* ramp sloping into the water, supporting a ship being built or repaired

slivovitz (sleévə-vits) *n.* plum brandy from Eastern Europe

sloe-eyed *adj.* having very dark blue-black eyes, usually slanted (used especially of women and children)

slop *v.* — **slop out** to empty one's chamber pot as a morning routine in prison

slops *pl.n.* sailor's clothing and bedding issued from a ship's stores

slot *n.* track or trail of an animal, especially of a deer

[1]**slough** (slow) *n.* swamp, bog, or mire

[2]**slough** (sluf) *tr.v.* to shed (a dead outer skin), as snakes do ~ *n.* sloughed skin of a snake

sloven (slúvv'n) *n.* person, especially a man, who is careless, messy, or sloppy (old-fashioned) — **-ly** *adj.*

slub *n.* small lump in a thread or fabric, sometimes made deliberately to produce a knobbly texture

sludge *n.* dirty or muddy deposit of sediment, as on a river-bed or sewage-treatment tank; slushy ice on the surface of the sea — **sludgy** *adj.*

sluice *n.* water channel or small dam, or the gate or valve holding back or regulating the water; long, sloping trough, as for washing gold ore ~ *tr.v.* to pour or splash water on someone or something

slurry *n.* thin liquid mixture of mud, cement, manure, or the like

slush fund *chiefly U.S. informal. n.* money kept for bribing public officials and other corrupt activities

smallholding *n.* small farm

smattering *n.* slight and fragmented knowledge: *a smattering of French*

smegma *n.* oily substance that collects under the foreskin

smelt *tr.v.* to extract metal from ore by melting it — **-er** *n.*

smocking *n.* needlework in which cloth is gathered into decorative diamond-shaped tucks

smolt *n.* salmon of about two years old, at the stage when it turns silvery and begins to migrate to the sea

smorgasbord (smór-gəss-bawrd) *n.* Scandinavian-style

meal or hors d'oeuvres of savoury dishes such as salads, cheeses, and paté

snaffle *n.* bit, usually jointed in the middle, on a horse's bridle — **snaffle** *tr.v.*

snap fastener *U.S. n.* press-stud

snare *n.* string, typically of wire-wound catgut, stretched over the lower skin of a cylindrical drum to increase reverberation and produce a rattling sound

snide *adj.* cutting or sarcastic in a spiteful or humiliating way: *snide remarks*; *archaic.* counterfeit, fake: *a snide shilling*

snifter *n.* small drink of alcoholic spirits, snort

snood *n.* small cap or pouch, typically of coarse netting, holding a woman's hair in place at the back

snook *n.* — **cock a snook at** *British. informal.* to show contempt or disrespect for, by one's actions or by specific gestures of scorn

snuff *tr.v.* to extinguish (a lamp, candle, flame, or the like), typically by smothering; to trim the charred end of (a wick) — **-er** *n.*

snug *adj.* seaworthy or strongly built, as a wooden ship might be ~ *British. n.* small separate bar or private room in a pub or inn

sobriety (sə-brī́-əti) *formal. n.* state of being sober; gravity, serious behaviour

sobriquet (sóbrikay) *formal. n.* nickname or assumed name (also "soubriquet")

sodality *n.* society or association, specifically a charitable society of lay Roman Catholics; *formal.* brotherhood, fellowship, sense of community

soffit *n.* underside of an arch, staircase, or other overhead structure

soi-disant (swáa-dee-zóɴ) *formal. adj.* self-styled, so-called: *the soi-disant chef* [French, literally, saying oneself]

soigné (swáan-yay) *formal. adj.* sophisticated, elegant, or fashionable; well-groomed, smart (feminine form "soignée") [French, literally, taken care of]

soirée (swáa-ray, swó-) *formal. n.* evening party or reception [French]

sojourn (sójərn) *formal. n.* temporary stay or residence in a place — **sojourn** *intr.v.*

solace (sól-əss) *formal. n.* comfort, consolation — **solace** *tr.v.*

solar *adj.* relating to the Sun

solarium *n., pl.* **-iums** or **-ia** sun-room, as for therapy or artificial suntanning

solar plexus *n.* network of nerves in the abdomen, spreading to the intestines and liver [from the resemblance of the radiating nerve fibres to the Sun's rays]

sola topi *n.* topi or sun hat made from the pith of the East Indian sola reed (also "pith helmet")

solder (sól-dər, sṓl-) *n.* alloy melted to fuse two metal parts — **solder** *tr.v.*

solecism (sólli-siz'm) *formal. n.* error of grammar or usage; social blunder, gaffe, embarrassing breach of etiquette [from Greek, *soloikos*, speaking incorrectly, literally, a person from *Soloi*, a city in Asia Minor where the ancient Athenian colonists spoke a corrupt form of Attic Greek] — **-cistic** *adj.*

solenoid *n.* electrical coil producing a magnetic field, as used for activating switches

solfeggio (sol-féji-ō) *n., pl.* **-os** or **-gi** singing exercise or training system based on the *doh-re-mi* syllables (also "solfège", "tonic sol-fa") [Italian, from the syllables *sol* and *fa*]

solicit *formal. tr.v.* to appeal or apply to or for: *solicited support/the mayor* — **-tation** *n.*

soliciting *n.* offence of approaching someone with an illicit offer of sex, especially in exchange for money: *prostitutes arrested for soliciting*

solicitous *formal. adj.* caring and concerned, as for another's welfare — **-citude** *n.*

solidarity *n.* unity and mutual support within a group, especially in the face of opposition: *showed solidarity with the oppressed*

solidus (sólli-dəss) *n., pl.* **-di** diagonal punctuation mark, slash, as in *and/or* (also "virgule", "oblique", "shilling mark")

soliloquy (sə-lílləkwi) *n.* dramatic monologue typically addressed by a character to himself and often taken to represent his unspoken thoughts — **-loquise** *intr.v.*

solipsism *n.* theory that the self is the only knowable reality or the only thing that really exists — **-ist** *n.* — **-istic** *adj.*

solitaire *n.* gemstone set by itself, as in a ring; *U.S.* card game for one player, patience

solitary *adj.* alone or preferring to remain alone; single, sole

solitude *n.* isolation, remoteness, or aloneness

solmisation *n.* use of the *doh-re-mi* syllables to name the notes of a musical scale [from the syllables *sol* and *mi*]

solstice (sól-stiss) *n.* either of the two days of the year, typically the 21st or 22nd of June and December, when the difference is greatest between the length of daytime and the length of night-time; position of the Sun in relation to the Earth at this time — **-stitial** *adj.*

soluble *adj.* possible to dissolve or solve: *soluble problems/salts* — **-bility** *n.*

solute *n.* substance dissolved in a solution

solvent *n.* substance that dissolves a solute in a solution ~ *adj.* financially in a position to meet all debts — **-vency** *n.*

somatic *formal. adj.* bodily, physical

sombre (sóm-bər) *formal. adj.* dim, gloomy; dark or subdued in colour; melancholy, depressing: *a sombre atmosphere* (also *U.S.* "somber")

somnambulism *formal. n.* sleep-walking — **-ist** *n.*

somniferous *formal. adj.* sleep-inducing, soporific

somnolent *formal. adj.* sleepy, lethargic; sleep-inducing, soporific — **-nolence** *n.*

sonar *n.* radar-like system or apparatus for detecting or locating objects underwater by means of sound waves [*so*und *na*vigation *r*anging]

son-et-lumière (sóɴ ay lo͞om-i-air) *n.* entertainment given at night, typically outdoors, using sound and light effects in presenting the history of a site [French, sound and light]

sonic (sónnik) *adj.* relating to sound waves, audible sound, or the speed of sound

sonorous *adj.* sounding rich, deep, or loud; impressive or high-falutin in style, grandiloquent, rhetorical — **-ority** *n.*

sop *n.* piece of bread or other food soaked in a liquid such as gravy; small gift or favour offered as a bribe or to appease someone

sophist *n.* philosopher, scholar, or thinker, especially an over-subtle or devious one — **-ry**, **sophism** *n.* — **-ic** *adj.*

sophomore *U.S. n.* second-year undergraduate — **sophomore** *adj.*

soporific *formal. adj.* sleep-inducing (also "soporiferous", "somniferous"); drowsy or sluggish

sorbet (sór-bay, -bit) *n.* water ice made from fruit (also *chiefly U.S.* "sherbet")

sordid *adj.* dirty; wretchedly poor and squalid or sleazy; despicable, vilely immoral: *a sordid deception*

sordino (sawr-dée-nō) *n.*, *pl.* **-ni** mute for a musical instrument, as on a trumpet [Italian]

sorites (sə-rí̄teez) *n.*, *pl.* **sorites** logical argument in the form of a series of linked premises leading to a single conclusion, as in *Socrates is a man, All men are mortal, All mortals are fallible, Therefore Socrates is fallible*

sororal (sə-ráw-rəl) *formal. adj.* sisterly, relating to a sister. Compare FRATERNAL

sororicide *formal. n.* killing or killer of one's sister (also "fratricide") — **-cidal** *adj.*

sorority *n.* sisterhood as a state or condition; U.S. social organisation for female students. Compare FRATERNITY

sortie *n.* raid or sudden attack against the enemy by those under siege; single raid or mission by a combat aircraft

sortilege (sórtilij) *formal. n.* fortune-telling by means of casting or drawing lots; magic, sorcery

sotto voce (sóttō vṓchi) *adv.* softly and privately, in an undertone, under one's breath — **sotto-voce** *adj.*

soubrette (soo-brét) *n.* young woman; actress playing the role of a young woman, especially a flirtatious lady's maid in a comedy or comic opera

souffle (sóo-f'l) *n.* blowing or whispering sound heard through a stethoscope, typically due to the flowing of the blood

soufflé (sóo-flay) *n.* fluffy baked egg dish, either savoury or sweet ~ *adj.* puffed or made light by beating or cooking [French, literally, blown, puffed up]

sough (sow, suf) *intr.v.* to make a sighing or rustling sound, as the wind or surf might — **sough** *n.*

souk (sook) *n.* market or covered bazaar in a Muslim country

[1]**sound** *n.* passage of water connecting two seas or separating an island from the mainland; air bladder of a fish

[2]**sound** *tr.v.* to measure the depth of, as with a weighted line; to investigate, probe; to dive down quickly and deep, as a whale or large fish might

sounding board *n.* person or group whose reactions serve as a test for new ideas or opinions

souse *tr.v.* to pickle

soutane (soo-tán, -táan) *n.* long dress-like garment worn by Roman Catholic priests, cassock

southpaw *informal. n.* left-handed person, especially a boxer who defends with his left hand and leads with his right

sovereignty *n.* authority of a sovereign; power to act independently of outside intervention or control

spa *n.* mineral spring; watering place, resort area with mineral springs [after *Spa*, a resort town in Belgium]

spadix (spáy-diks) *n.*, *pl.* **-dices** spike of tiny close-packed flowers, as in the cuckoopint

spall *n.* stone fragment or chip — **spall** *v.*

[1]**span** *n.* distance or time between two limits; distance between the tips of the thumb and little finger of a spread hand ~ *tr.v.* to bridge, extend or stretch over

[2]**span** *n. chiefly U.S.* matched yoke of draught animals

spangle *n.* sequin, sparkling plastic or metal disc as used for decorating clothing — **spangle** *tr.v.*

spartan *adj.* tough, austerely self-disciplined, having great fortitude and endurance; simple, austere, frugal: *spartan rations* [after the *Spartans* of ancient Greece, a people renowned for such qualities] — **Spartan** *n.*

spasmodic *formal. adj.* intermittent, fitful, by fits and starts; jerky

[1]**spat** *n.* larva of an oyster or other bivalve mollusc

[2]**spat** *n.* covering or gaiter of cloth or leather protecting the upper shoe and ankle [short for *spatterdash*]

spatchcock *n.* fowl that is dressed, split open, and fried or grilled soon after slaughter (old-fashioned) ~ *informal. tr.v.* to insert or patch together (a text) in a strained or unsuitable way

spate *n.* flood, sudden rush, outburst: *a spate of muggings*

spathe *n.* leaf-like bract enclosing a flower spike, as on the cuckoopint

spathic (spáthik) *formal. adj.* splitting or flaking easily, as some minerals do

spatiotemporal (spáyshi-ō-tém-pərəl) *formal. adj.* relating to both space and time: *spatiotemporal coordinates*

spatterdash *n.* leather legging formerly worn to protect against splashes when riding

spatula *n.* spreading implement having a wide, round-tipped, flexible blade, as for icing; medical tongue depressor

spatulate *formal. adj.* flattish and broad-tipped: *spatulate fingers/leaves*

spavin (spávvin) *n.* swelling on a horse's hock, typically causing stiffness — **-ed** *adj.*

spawn *n.* eggs of a fish or frog; offspring (derogatory) ~ *v.* — *intr.* to produce spawn or young — *tr.* to give birth to (young); *informal.* to give rise to: *spawned a nightmare* [related to *expand*]

spay *tr.v.* to sterilise by removing the ovaries of (a bitch or other female animal)

speakeasy *U.S. informal. n.* bar for the illicit sale of alcoholic drinks, especially during the Prohibition period

spec *informal. n.* — **on spec** taking a risk in the hope of success [short for on *speculation*]

special pleading *n.* biased or selective arguing

specie (spéeshee) *formal. n.* money in the form of coins rather than notes

species *formal. n.* consecrated Communion bread and wine

specific *formal. n.* medicine or remedy intended for a particular disease or disorder

specious (spéeshəss) *formal. adj.* deceptive; apparently attractive, genuine, or sound, but not really so: *a specious argument* — **-iosity** *n.*

spectral *formal. adj.* ghostly

spectrum *n.*, *pl.* **-trums** or **-tra** range, distribution, or spread: *the whole spectrum of colours/opinions*

speculate *intr.v.* to think about a subject idly, reflect, meditate; to engage in risky financial dealings, especially to buy and sell shares or commodities fairly recklessly in the hope of making high profits — **-lation**, **-lator** *n.* — **-lative** *adj.*

speculum *n.*, *pl.* **-lums** or **-la** mirror or reflector in some optical instruments; medical instrument inserted into a body passage for examination or treatment; *formal.* bright coloured patch on a bird's wing

speleology *formal. n.* study or exploration of caves (also *U.S. informal.* "spelunking") — **-gist** *n.* — **-logical** *adj.*

spell *tr.v.* to stand in for, as at work, and relieve temporarily

spermaceti (spérmə-séeti) *n.* fatty substance formed from oils in a whale's head, used for cosmetics, ointments, and candles

sphagnum (sfág-nəm) *n.* moss of the kind that forms peat when decomposed — **-nous** *adj.*

sphincter *n.* circular or ring-like muscle having the function of constricting or relaxing a body passage, as in the bladder or anus

sphinx *formal. n.* puzzling or mysterious person [after the monster in Greek mythology that posed a riddle for passers-by, and killed those who failed to answer it]

sphragistics (sfrə-jístiks) *formal. n.* study of seals and signet rings

sphygmomanometer (sfíg-mō-mə-nómmitər) *formal. n.* instrument for measuring blood pressure, especially in the arteries

spica (spīkə) *n.* bandage tied in a figure-of-eight pattern to immobilise a limb

spider *n.* system of elastic cords joined at the centre, used for strapping down loads, as on a car roof (also "octopus")

spiel (shpeel, speel) *slang. n.* story, speech, sales talk, or the like that is glib or long-winded [German, literally, play]

spigot (spíggət) *n.* plug or bung in the vent of a cask (also "spile", "spill"); tap, especially a wooden tap placed in the bunghole of a cask

¹spike *n.* mackerel when still small and young ~ *informal. tr.v.* to add alcohol to (a drink); to suppress (a news story or report), as an editor might

²spike *n.* cluster of stalkless flowers along a stem, as in the foxglove

spikenard (spīk-naard) *n.* fragrant ointment in ancient times, or the Indian plant from which it is supposed to have derived (also "nard")

spile *n.* post, stake, pile, as for foundations; bung, spigot

spill *n.* twist of paper or sliver of wood for lighting a fire

spillway *n.* channel for excess water, as round the side of a dam (also "spill")

spindle *n.* stick or pin on which thread is twisted in spinning; rod or pin holding a spool or bobbin, as in a spinning machine; axle, revolving bolt, or the like, as in a lock or between two door handles; table leg, upright stair post, or the like, typically turned and decorated

spindrift *n.* wind-blown seaspray

spinnaker (spínnəkər, spáng-kər) *n.* large triangular sail in front of the mainsail on a yacht, used when sailing with the wind [probably after *Sphinx*, the yacht that first used the sail in the 1860s]

spinney *British. n.* small wood or grove, copse

spiracle (spīr-ək'l) *formal. n.* vent for air or gas, such as a whale's blowhole — **-acular**, **-aculate** *adj.*

spirit level *n.* instrument using an air bubble in a tube of liquid to test if a surface is level

spitchcock *n.* eel that is split and then grilled or fried

spiv *British. slang. n.* slick, flashy man living by petty fraud, black marketeering, or the like

splanchnic (splánk-nik) *formal. adj.* relating to the internal organs, visceral

splat *n.* single wooden slat, often decorated, as in the middle of the back of a chair

splayed *adj.* widened or flattened, especially more at one end than the other

spleen *n.* blood-purifying organ below the stomach; this organ considered as the seat of mirth or melancholy, according to medieval beliefs; *formal.* spite or bad temper

splenetic (spli-néttik) *formal. adj.* having a spiteful or irritable character or personality; *archaic.* having a melancholy personality — **splenetic** *n.*

splice *tr.v.* to join (strips of rope, film, or the like) together at the ends

spliced *informal. adj.* married, hitched

spline *n.* ridge that mates with a corresponding groove to join two strips, planks, shafts, or the like

split pin *n.* pin or fastener with two flexible arms, as for securing a wheel to an axle

split ring *n.* ring of metal, such as a key ring, consisting of a tight double coil of wire

spoils *pl.n.* stolen or captured goods, as gained by the victors in a war

spoiler *n.* air deflector, as on an aircraft's wing or a racing car, to increase drag and reduce the tendency to lift

spoliation *formal. n.* plundering; seizure of a neutral ship in wartime; deliberate alteration or mutilation of a document so as to invalidate it

spondulix (spon-déw-liks) *slang. n.* money, ready cash (old-fashioned)

spontaneous *adj.* prompted by natural feeling or an internal tendency rather than by an outside cause; impulsive or voluntary, unforced or unconsidered: *spontaneous cheering*; natural and uncalculating in behaviour, candid: *a friendly, spontaneous young man*

spoonerism *n.* switching, usually unintended, of the initial sounds of two or more words in speech, as in *Take the town drain* for *Take the down train* [after William A. *Spooner*, a 19th-20th-century Oxford clergyman and scholar, who had a habit of making such slips]

spoor *n.*, *pl.n.* animal tracks or footprints ~ *v.* to track an animal by following its spoor

sporadic (spə-ráddik) *formal. adj.* occasional, irregular, intermittent: *sporadic bursts of gunfire*

spore *n.* reproductive cell or organ, the counterpart of a seed, in non-flowering plants such as mosses, ferns, and fungi — **sporaceous** *adj.*

sporran *n.* pouch of leather or fur worn hanging in front of a kilt in traditional Highland dress

sportive *formal. adj.* playful, frolicsome

spouse *formal. n.* husband or wife

Sprachgefühl (shpraákh-gə-fewl, -fül) *n.* instinct for what is idiomatically correct or appropriate in a language [German, literally, language feeling]

spread *n.* pair of facing pages in a book, magazine, or newspaper, especially when the text or picture stretches across the fold

sprightly *adj.* energetic, lively

spring *formal. v.* — *intr.* to explode, as a mine does when set off — *tr.* to cause (a mine) to explode ~ *n.* flock of teal

springe *n.* snare for small game or birds, in the form of a noose attached to a branch that is bent back — **springe** *v.*

springer *n.* cow about to calve

spring-form mould *n.* baking tin with a high rim that can be removed by releasing a clip

sprocket *n.* toothed projection on a wheel or cylinder, designed to engage a moving part, such as a bicycle chain or film with perforations; wheel or cylinder with sprockets
sprog *chiefly British. informal. n.* child, youngster
sprue *n.* hole or channel through which molten material is introduced into a mould
spry *adj.* active, energetic, and healthy (used of the elderly)
spud *n.* small, narrow spade, weeding spade ~ *tr.v.* to begin to drill (an oil well)
spume *formal. n.* foam or froth, especially on or from the sea — **-mous**, **-my** *adj.*
spunk *n.* touchwood or tinder, fungus used in lighting or kindling a fire
spunky *chiefly U.S. informal. adj.* lively or energetic; plucky, spirited
spur *n.* mountain ridge projecting sideways
spurious *formal. adj.* false, fake, invalid: *a spurious resemblance*
sputum (spéw-təm) *formal. n.* saliva, spittle; mucous matter coughed up from the lungs and windpipe
squab (skwob) *n.* fledgling bird, especially a young pigeon of about four weeks old
squamous (skwáy-məss) *formal. adj.* scaly: *dry, squamous skin*
squeegee *n.* wiper-like rubber or leather blade, fixed to a handle, as for washing windows; rubber blade or roller used in printing or photography, as for squeezing water from wet prints [possibly related to *squeeze*]
squirearchy *n.* landed-gentry class, or government by it (often either humorous or derogatory)
stabile *n.* sculpture or abstract construction similar to a mobile in appearance and materials, but stationary ~ *formal. adj.* non-mobile, stationary, unchanging
staccato (stə-kaátō) *adv.* played crisply, so that each note or chord is separated from the next (used as a musical direction) ~ *adj.* clear and disconnected within a series, rather than flowing or continuous: *staccato gunfire*; disjointed, abrupt, and emphatic: *a staccato voice* — **staccato** *n.*
stack *tr.v.* to cheat by arranging (playing cards) secretly in a favourable order
stag *British. n.* person who buys newly issued shares in the hope of selling them quickly for a large profit
stagger *tr.v.* to arrange in slightly different but overlapping positions or time periods; to divide into a series of stages
staging area *n.* soldiers' assembly point prior to posting on a mission or operation
staging post *n.* stopping place for rest or refuelling during a long journey
stagnant *adj.* not moving, changing, flowing, or developing: *stagnant water/economy/pond* — **-nate** *intr.v.* — **-nation** *n.*
stag party *informal. n.* men-only party held for a man about to be married
staid *adj.* steady, old-fashioned, sober, restrained: *a staid manner/design* [related to *stay*]
Stakhanovite (sta-kánnə-vīt, -k̲h̲aánə-) *n.* Soviet industrial worker who is admired or rewarded for being especially zealous or productive; *informal.* workaholic [after Alexei *Stakhanov*, a Russian miner who set a productivity record in 1935, which was treated as a model for other workers] — **Stakhanovite** *adj.*
stalactite *n.* icicle-like lime deposit hanging down from the roof of a cave. Compare STALAGMITE
stalag *n.* German prison camp for captured enemy NCOs and privates during the Second World War [German, short for *Stammlager*, a base camp]
stalagmite *n.* pillar or cone of lime deposit rising from the floor of a cave. Compare STALACTITE
stale *formal or archaic. n.* urine of horses or camels
stalemate *n.* drawn position in chess, based on a player's being unable to move without putting his own king in check; deadlock, drawn contest, immobilised or paralysed state — **stalemate** *tr.v.*
stall *n.* finger of a glove, or protective sheath for an injured finger or toe
stalwart (stáwl-wərt) *adj.* reliable or loyal, staunch, resolute and steadfast ~ *n.* resolute, steadfast person; supporter, as of a political party, who is reliable and hardworking (often humorous)
stamina *n.* staying power, endurance
stampede *n.* headlong rush, as of a startled herd of animals or a panic-stricken crowd; impetuous group movement: *a stampede to buy the new shares* — **stampede** *v.*
stanch (staanch) *tr.* to check or stop (an outflow, as of blood or funds); to stop blood flowing from (a wound) (also "staunch")
stanchion (staán-sh'n) *n.* upright pole or post, as for supporting a roof; frame of two upright bars securing cattle round the neck in a stall — **stanchion** *tr.v.*
standard *formal. n.* flag or banner regarded as an emblem or rallying-point: *raised the standard of revolt*
standfirst *n.* preliminary text or opening sentence or paragraph of a newspaper or magazine article
standoff *U.S. informal. n.* draw or deadlock, as in a sports match
standpipe *n.* upright outdoor water pipe with a tap, as in a garden or street
stannary *British. formal. n.* tin works, or tin-mining
stannic *formal. adj.* relating to or containing tin
stanza *formal. n.* verse or short section of a poem — **-aic** *adj.*
staple *n.* crop or commodity that is the major product of its kind in a region; standard, common, or constantly needed commodity, such as salt or flour; raw material; main part or ingredient ~ *adj.* principal, standard, or regular: *a staple topic of conversation*
star *n.* white spot on a horse's forehead
starboard *n.* right-hand side of a ship or aircraft when facing forwards (opposite "port", "larboard") — **starboard** *adj.*
stateroom *n.* large and comfortable private cabin on a ship
static *adj.* motionless, unchanging, or producing no movement or change; relating or referring to bodies at rest or forces in equilibrium (opposite "dynamic") — **stasis** *n.*
station wagon *chiefly U.S. n.* estate car
statuesque *adj.* statue-like; well-proportioned and tall (used especially of women)
stature *n. formal.* height, especially of a person when standing upright; reputation, status, rank, or level of achievement, eminence
status quo *n.* existing state of affairs [Latin, the state in which]
statute *n.* law or rule formally enacted and recorded
statute of limitations *n.* law setting a time limit for bringing a legal action

statutory *adj.* relating to a statute; *informal.* compulsory, obligatory, though perhaps only because expected or traditional: *the statutory woman on the panel*

statutory rape *U.S. n.* criminal offence of sexual intercourse with a girl below the legally defined age of consent

stave *n.* wooden strip or plank forming part of a barrel, ship's hull, or the like; long thick stick, staff; rung of a ladder; crosspiece securing the legs of a chair; set of five lines on which music is written or printed (in this sense, also "staff")

stay *n.* rope or cable supporting a mast, radio tower, or the like, guy; strip of firm material used to stiffen a corset (usually plural)

steadfast *adj.* steady, unchanging: *steadfast adherence to the rules*; loyal, unwaveringly firm: *a steadfast friend* (old-fashioned)

steatopygia (steé-ə-tō-pī́ji-ə) *formal. n.* development of large fatty deposits in the buttocks, as among the Bushmen — **-gic**, **-gous** *adj.*

steelyard *n.* scale or balance consisting of a pivoted bar, with the counterbalance adjusted along the longer arm

steerage *n.* large section of a passenger ship for those paying the cheapest fares, especially in former times

stein (stīn) *n.* beer mug, typically made of pottery and having a lid, holding about a pint [German, short for *Steingut*, stoneware]

stele (steé-li) *n.*, *pl.* **-les** or **-lae** upright stone or slab with an inscribed surface, marking graves or monuments in ancient times

stellar *adj.* relating to a star

stellate *adj.* star-shaped (also "stelliform")

St Elmo's fire *n.* flame-like electrical glow seen on a ship's mast, church spire, or the like during stormy weather (also "corposant") [after *St Elmo*, the patron saint of sailors]

stem *n.* base of a word to which inflections, such as *-s* or *-ing* are added

stemwinder *n.* watch that is wound by a small attached knob projecting outside the casing

stenography *chiefly U.S. n.* shorthand — **-ographic** *adj.* — **-ographer** *n.*

Stenotype *trademark. n.* typewriter used, as in U.S. courts, to record speech in a form of shorthand

stentorian *formal. adj.* referring or relating to a very loud voice [after *Stentor*, a loud-voiced herald in Homer's *Iliad*]

steppe (step) *n.* grassy plain, as in Siberia, that is flat and treeless

stercoraceous *formal. adj.* relating to excrement, dungy

stereobate *n.* foundation of a building, typically a solid masonry platform

stereograph *n.* pair of nearly identical pictures, sometimes superimposed, that give a three-dimensional effect when viewed through special lenses (also "stereogram")

stereoscope *n.* twin-lensed optical instrument for viewing a stereograph — **-scopic** *adj.*

stereotype *n.* conventional, unoriginal, and usually over-simplified image or opinion of a person or thing; person or thing that fits a stereotype; printing plate cast from a papier-mâché or similar mould — **stereotype** *adj.*, *tr.v.*

sterling silver *n.* silver 92.5% pure [from Middle English *starling*, a small star, referring to the star-like sign stamped on silver pennies]

sternum *formal. n.*, *pl.* **-nums** or **-na** breastbone — **-nal** *adj.*

sternutation *formal. n.* sneeze, or the act or noise of sneezing — **-tatory** *adj.*

steroid *n.* any of a large group of chemical substances having four fused rings of carbon atoms; synthetic steroid of various kinds used, often illegally, by athletes and bodybuilders to increase their strength and stamina (in this sense, also "anabolic steroid")

stertorous *formal. adj.* breathing with or relating to a heavy snoring noise — **stertor** *n.*

stet *interj.* let it stand (used as an instruction to a typesetter or printer to retain a deleted piece of text or ignore a correction) [Latin] — **stet** *tr.v.*

stethoscope *n.* doctor's instrument for listening to sounds produced within the body — **-scopic** *adj.* — **-scopy** *n.*

stevedore (steév-ə-dawr) *n.* worker loading and unloading ships

steward *n.* manager of property, finances, social arrangements, or the like; person supervising food and provisions; waiter on a ship or aircraft, or in a mess; official supervisor at a public event, especially a horse race

stich (stik) *formal. n.* line of verse

stichomythia *n.* dramatic dialogue, as in ancient Greek drama, in which alternate lines of verse are spoken by different characters — **-mythic** *adj.*

stiff *slang. n.* corpse

stifle *n.* joint corresponding to the knee in the hind leg of a horse, dog, or other four-legged mammal

stigma *formal. n.* mark or sign of shame or disgrace: *a lingering stigma attached to divorce* — **-tise** *tr.v.*

stigmata *pl.n.* sores or marks corresponding to Jesus's crucifixion wounds, believed to develop spontaneously in some saintly people

stiletto *n.*, *pl.* **-os** high, tapering, pointed heel on a woman's shoe; small, narrow dagger

stimulant *n.* substance, such as the caffeine in coffee, that has a stimulating physical effect (opposite "depressant") — **stimulant** *adj.*

stint *n. informal.* fixed amount or spell of work or duty ~ *v.* to hold back, stop, or restrain: *Don't stint yourself/the rations/on the gravy*

stipe *n.* stalk, as of a mushroom, fern, or frond of seaweed

stipend (stī́-pend) *n.* salary, allowance, or similar regular payment — **-iary** *adj.*

stipendiary magistrate *n.* magistrate who is legally qualified and receives a salary (also *informal* "stipe")

stippled *adj.* dotted or flecked, as with paint or natural colours; roughened with a metal brush while freshly coated: *a stippled wall* — **stipple** *tr.v.*

stipulate *tr.v.* to require or lay down as a condition in an agreement or contract; to specify rigorously: *stipulated that there be no interruptions* — **-ation** *n.*

stipule *n.* leaf-like projection, occurring in pairs, at the base of a leaf in some plants, such as roses

stirk *n.* bullock or heifer between one and two years old, yearling

stirps *n.*, *pl.* **stirpes** branch of a family, lineage, stock; stable variety of cultivated plants; in biological classification, a category ranking above a family and below an order (in this sense, also "superfamily")

stoa *n.*, *pl.* **-as** or **-ae** covered walk with columns on one or both sides, as in ancient Greek buildings

stochastic (sto-kástik) *adj.* statistically random

stock *n.* handle or butt of a whip, fishing rod, or the like; wooden block from which a bell hangs; cards that are not dealt from the pack but may be drawn during the game

stockade *n.* fortress or defensive barrier made of upright posts or stakes; *U.S.* military prison enclosure

Stockholm syndrome *n.* tendency of a victim, such as a hostage, to identify with and adopt the point of view of his victimiser [referring to the compliance of hostages held in a *Stockholm* bank robbery in 1973]

stocking frame *n.* knitting machine (old-fashioned)

stock-in-trade *n.* standard equipment, skills, or resources used in a business or in any other activity

stockpile *n.* reserve supply or store accumulated for future use — **stockpile** *tr.v.*

stocks *pl.n.* wooden frame supporting a ship during construction; wooden frame in which an offender was formerly locked by the ankles, and sometimes also the wrists, and exposed to public abuse

stogy (stṓgi) *chiefly U.S. n.* long thin cheap cigar (old-fashioned) [after *Conestoga*, a town in Pennsylvania]

stoical (stṓ-ik'l) *adj.* unemotional, unaffected by or apparently indifferent to pleasure or pain [after the *Stoics*, members of an ancient Greek school of philosophy teaching the value of emotional calm and submission, from Greek *stoa*, a portico, referring to the porch where the founder Zeno used to teach] — **stoic** *n., adj.* — **stoicism** *n.*

stolid (stóllid) *adj.* unemotional — **-ity** *n.*

stolon (stṓlon) *formal. n.* runner, stem or branch, as of the strawberry, extending along the ground and taking root to form new plants — **-ate** *adj.*

stoma *n., pl.* **-mata** or **-mas.** mouth-like opening, as in a sponge or hookworm; pore on the surface of a leaf for the passage of gases and water vapour — **-matal**, **-matic** *adj.*

stonewall *v.* to obstruct, hinder, or delay as a deliberate strategy, as in parliamentary debate ~ *intr.v.* to bat very defensively, as in cricket

stook *chiefly British. n.* group of sheaves, as set in a field to dry (also "shock")

stool pigeon *slang.* police informer, or any informer to the authorities (also "stoolie") [referring to a decoy pigeon, of the kind once tied to a stool]

[1]stoop *formal. intr.v.* to swoop down, as a bird of prey does on its victim

[2]stoop *U.S. n.* stairway with a landing at the top of it at the entrance of a house

stopcock *n.* tap, valve in a pipe for regulating the flow of liquid or gas

stopgap *n.* temporary rough-and-ready device or substitute — **stopgap** *adj.*

stopple *n.* plug such as a cork or bung

stormy petrel *n.* person who is a centre, cause, or herald of trouble (old-fashioned) [after the sea bird, believed in folklore to herald or delight in stormy weather]

stoup (stoop) *n.* basin for holy water in a church; *British regional.* bucket, or large drinking vessel (also "stoop")

stover *n.* animal fodder

stowaway *n.* person who hides on board a departing ship, aircraft, train, or the like for a free journey — **stow away** *v.*

strabismus strə-bízməss) *formal. n.* squint — **-mal**, **-mic** *adj.*

Stradivarius *n.* valuable 17th- or 18th-century stringed instrument, especially a violin, made in the workshop of Antonio Stradivari in Cremona, Italy (also *informal* "Strad")

strafe *tr.v.* to attack (enemy ground troops), with bombs or machine-gun fire from low-flying aircraft [adapted ironically from the German slogan during the First World War, *Gott strafe England*, God punish England] — **strafe** *n.*

straggle *intr.v.* lag, fall behind or stray; to grow, spread out, or be arranged in an irregular or untidy way — **straggle** *n.* — **straggly** *adj.*

strain *formal or archaic. n.* tune, musical passage

straitened circumstances *formal. pl.n.* — **in straitened circumstances** in financial distress, with less money than previously

straits *pl.n.* natural waterway linking two larger bodies of water (also "strait"); difficulties, distress: *in dire straits*

straitjacket *n.* restraining garment with long sleeves for binding the arms of a violent patient or prisoner; something that severely limits freedom of expression or movement: *the straitjacket of censorship*

strake *n.* line of plates or planking running the length of a ship's hull; curved metal plate on the rim of a wooden wheel

strand *n.* beach or shore

strangulated hernia *n.* hernia with blood circulation reduced through constriction of the protruding part

straphanger *informal. n.* standing passenger on a crowded bus, underground train, or the like

strappado (strə-páa-dō) *n., pl.* **-does** punishment or torture in which the victim is hoisted on a rope, usually by his hands tied behind his back, and then dropped part of the way with a jerk

stratagem (stráttə-jəm) *n.* piece of strategy, such as a surprise military manoeuvre, or a cunning trick

strategy *n.* long-term policies and techniques, such as a military plan designed to achieve a large objective in due course. Compare TACTICS — **-tegic** *adj.* — **-tegist** *n.*

strath *n.* fairly wide and flat-bottomed valley, especially in Scotland; grassland lying in a strath

stratified *adj.* divided according to castes, classes, or the like, as a nation or society might be — **-ify** *v.* — **-fication** *n.*

stratosphere (stráttə-sfeer) *n.* one of the upper layers of the atmosphere; *informal.* high or exalted region of society, success, or the like: *a concert tour that launched her into the stratosphere of megastardom* — **-spheric** *adj.*

stratum (stráa-təm, stráy-) *n., pl.* **-ta** layer, level: *rock strata, social strata*

stratus (stráy-təss, stráa-) *n., pl.* **-ti** low, fog-like cloud

streaker *n.* person who runs naked through a public place as a stunt — **streaking** *n., adj.*

strenuous *adj.* requiring or involving great effort or energy

striated muscle (strī-áytid) *n.* muscle tissue consisting of long diagonally striped fibres, as in the voluntary muscles attached to the human skeleton (also "striped muscle"; opposite "smooth muscle")

stricken *formal or archaic. adj.* suffering from or affected by a disease or disaster: *grief-stricken* [past participle form of *strike*]

stricture *formal. n.* criticism, censure [related to *strict*]

strident *formal. adj.* loud and harsh or shrill: *a strident voice*; pushy, assertive, or insistent in manner: *strident demands* — **-dency** *n.*
stridor *formal. n.* harsh vibrating sound heard in laboured breathing
stridulation *n.* shrill grating chirp of a cricket — **-late** *intr.v.* — **-lous** *adj.*
strigil (stíjil) *n.* curved blunt blade used by ancient Greeks and Romans for scraping the skin after bathing or exercising
strigose (strī́-gōz, -gōss) *adj.* in botany, covered in stiff, tightly packed hairs or bristles: *strigose leaves*
strike *tr.v.* to lower (a mast, sail, or flag) (opposite "hoist")
Strine *informal. n.* Australian English of a broadly accented or deliberately colourful kind [extreme version of the Strine pronunciation of *Australian*] — **Strine** *adj.*
stringboard *n.* skirting board along the side of a staircase, covering the edges of the steps (also "stringer")
stringent (strínjənt) *formal. adj.* referring to or enforcing strict rules or demanding standards [related to *strict*] — **-gency** *n.*
stringer *n. informal.* part-time news reporter, typically covering the local news in a specific area; beam, girder, or the like, as for reinforcing the body of a ship or aircraft, or for supporting a floor when laid horizontally in a building; stringboard
stripling *formal. n.* youth, adolescent boy
strobe light *n.* electric light producing quick intense flashes to give a stationary image of moving objects (also *informal* "strobe")
stroboscope *n.* instrument for observing, measuring, or adjusting vibration, rotation, or the like by using a strobe light to make the moving object appear stationary
stroller *chiefly U.S. n.* pushchair
stronghold *n.* fortified place; place of security or refuge; person or thing considered a defender or bastion: *a stronghold of conservatism*
strop *n.* strap for sharpening a "cutthroat" razor ~ *tr.v.* to sharpen on a strop
strophe (strṓfi) *n.* verse or stanza of a poem, especially the first of two stanzas — **-phic** *adj.*
struma *formal. n., pl.* **-mae** or **-mas** goitre
strumpet *n.* prostitute (literary or humorous)
struthious (stro͞othi-əss) *adj.* relating to or resembling the ostrich; *formal.* ostrich-like in evading disagreeable truths, "burying one's head in the sand"
strychnine (strík-neen) *n.* poisonous chemical, formally also used as a medical stimulant
stucco (stúckō) *n.* plaster of a smooth, fine kind used for frescoes or mouldings; ornamentation of stucco — **stucco** *tr.v.*
stud *n.* male animal kept for breeding, especially a stallion; group of studs; establishment where studs are kept (also "stud farm"); *informal.* sexually energetic man
stultify *formal. tr.v.* make useless, enfeeble: *the stultifying atmosphere of the suburbs* — **-fication** *n.*
stum *n.* must, grape juice that is still fermenting
stumer (stéw-mər) *British. slang. n.* forged cheque or banknote, or other worthless object or fraud
stump *n.* soft roll of leather, felt, or paper rubbed on a drawing to produce shading effects
stupa (sto͞opə) *n.* Buddhist shrine, typically dome-shaped (also "tope")
stupefy *tr.v.* to stun or shock with amazement, astonishment, or wonder — **-faction** *n.*
stupor *n.* near-unconsciousness, as through drink drugs, or shock — **stupefacient** *adj., n.*
sty *n.* swelling produced by inflammation of a sebaceous gland in the eyelid (also "stye")
stygian (stíji-ən) *formal. adj.* very dark or gloomy (literary) [after the river *Styx*, the underworld boundary river in Greek mythology]
style *n.* arm of a sundial that casts the shadow (also "gnomon"); slender part of the pistil of a flower, supporting the stigma
stylised *adj.* designed for aesthetic rather than realistic effect, conventional or artificial
stylite (stī́līt) *n.* early Christian hermit or ascetic, such as St Simeon Stylites, who lived on top of a pillar
stylograph *n.* pen with a hollow needle instead of a nib for the release of the ink
stylus *n., pl.* **-luses** or **-li** needle or jewel in a gramophone pickup for following the groove of a record; writing or etching instrument, as used on wax tablets in ancient times
stymie *n.* formerly in golf, obstruction of a ball by another ball on the putting green; *informal.* obstacle or predicament, insoluble problem *informal. tr.v.* to stand in the way of, obstruct or thwart (also "stymy")
styptic pencil *n.* pencil-like stick containing a chemical for stopping the bleeding from small cuts, as after shaving — **styptic** *adj.*
suave (swaav) *adj.* socially gracious and charming, often in a superficial way — **-vity** *n.*
subaltern (súbb'l-tərn) *British. n.* commissioned officer in the army ranking below a captain, usually a lieutenant; anyone of subordinate position or rank
subclinical *adj.* referring or relating to symptoms or signs of a disease that are not yet detectable
subcutaneous *adj.* located or made just beneath the skin: *subcutaneous fat/injections*
suberose (séwbə-rōz) *formal. adj.* corky, relating to or consisting of cork tissue
subfusc *formal. adj.* drab, dusky, dull-coloured ~ *n.* formal, dark, academic clothing, especially at Oxford University
subjective *adj.* relating to or arising from the individual self or mind rather than observable external reality; influenced by emotion or personal preference or involvement, and hence often unfounded or biased. Compare OBJECTIVE — **-tivity**, **-tivism** *n.*
sub judice (súb jo͞odi-si) *adj.* still before a judge or court, and therefore not to be discussed in public
subjugate (súb-jo͝o-gayt) *tr.v.* to subdue, as by conquering or taming — **-gation** *n.*
subjunctive *adj.* referring to a verb form indicating a conditional or hypothetical state, as in *I wish I were at home* — **subjunctive** *n.*
sublimate *tr.v.* to channel or transform (a sexual or other instinctual impulse) into something more socially or culturally acceptable ~ *v.* to change from a gas into a solid or from a solid into a gas directly, bypassing the liquid phase — **sublimate**, **-ation** *n.*
sublime *formal. adj.* exalted, noble, awe-inspiring — **-limity** *n.*
subliminal (sub-límmin'l) *formal. adj.* lying or occurring below the threshold of consciousness or perception: *subliminal stimuli*
sublunary (sub-lo͞onəri) *formal. adj.* earthly, worldly,

of this life
submerged *adj.* underwater; hidden as if under water
submission *n.* something, such as a document or argument, submitted for consideration
suborn *tr.v.* to force or persuade, as by bribery, to commit a wrongful act: *tried to suborn the jury* — **-ation** *n.*
subpoena (sub-pééna) *n.* summons to appear in court ~ *tr.v.* to summon to court by a subpoena
subreption *formal. n.* lie, misrepresentation, or the deliberate concealment of relevant information; deduction drawn from such a misrepresentation — **-reptitious** *adj.*
subrogation *formal. n.* substitution of one person for another, especially the substitution of one creditor for another — **-rogate** *tr.v.*
sub rosa *formal. adv.* secretly, privately, in confidence [Latin, literally, under the rose, from a traditional association of roses with secrecy] — **sub-rosa** *adj.*
subscribe *tr.v.* to sign (one's name) at the end of a document, as a witness, contracting party, or the like — **subscribe to** to agree with, approve of, or assent to a belief, opinion, or the like; to take out a subscription for
subscript *n.* letter, number or symbol, often of miniature size, written or printed next to and just below another number, as in H_2O. Compare SUPERSCRIPT
subscription *n.* arrangement to buy a series of things, such as concert tickets or issues of a magazine, and pay for them in advance; application to purchase newly issued shares
subsequent *adj.*, next, following, succeeding
subsequently *adv.* later, afterwards
subservient *adj.* serving a secondary function; functional, instrumental, serving some higher purpose; excessively cooperative, obedient, or eager to please, obsequious — **-ence**, **-ency** *n.*
subside *intr.v.* to sink or settle down; to become less intense or active: *The storm soon subsided*
subsidence (səb-sí́d'nss, súb-sidənss) *n.* sinking of the ground or of a building
subsidiary *adj.* secondary, less important, subordinate ~ *n.* company that is under the control of another company
subsidy *n.* grant of money, as from a government or council, to support a person or institution, finance a project, or the like (also *formal* "subvention") — **-sidise** *tr.v.*
subsist *intr.v.* to live, continue in existence, or manage to survive
subsistence *n.* minimum of food, shelter, and the like necessary to sustain life
subsistence farming *n.* farming of a kind in which the farmer and his family consume most of the produce, with little surplus for marketing
substantiate *formal. tr.v.* to establish or confirm by evidence or proof: *substantiate a charge*
substantive *formal. adj.* (súb-stən-tiv) independent, existing or functioning in its own right rather than as subordinate to something else; relating to the substance or essence of something; genuine, real, not imaginary or merely apparent; genuine and important, having substance: *substantive issues of concern*; *chiefly British.* permanent and definite, not merely acting or temporary ~ *n.* (səb-stántiv) in grammar, word or group of words serving as a noun
substantive law *n.* law as relating to rights, duties, and legal principles rather than to practice and procedure
substratum *n.*, *pl.* **-tums** or **-ta** underlying layer, support, or principle (also "substrate")
subsume *tr.v.* to include as part of a larger or more general class: *The class of rectangles subsumes the class of squares* — **-sumption** *n.*
subtend *tr.v.* to be opposite to (an angle): *The hypotenuse subtends a right angle*
subterfuge (súb-tər-fewj) *n.* deception, crafty scheme, or the like, as to conceal, evade, or escape something
subterranean *formal. adj.* underground; secret, hidden: *subterranean murmurs of discontent*
subtext *n.* meaning or message that is implied but not directly expressed, as in a speech or play
subtle (sútt'l) *adj.* delicate, sensitive, or refined: *a subtle flavour/joke*; capable of or based on fine distinctions: *a subtle mind/difference* — **subtlety** *n.*
subtrahend (súb-trə-hend) *n.* in subtraction, the number that is subtracted from the minuend
subvention *formal. n.* help, support, or subsidy
subvert *tr.v.* to undermine, destabilise, ruin, or try to ruin: *subvert democracy/our plans* — **-version** *n.* — **-versive** *adj.*, *n.*
succedaneum (súksi-dáyni-əm) *formal. n.*, *pl.* **-nea** substitute, replacement [related to *succeeding*]
succès de scandale (sŏŏk-sáy də skon-daál) *n.*, *pl.* **succès de scandale** popularity or success of a book, painting, or the like, due to its shock value rather than its merits; work that enjoys such a success [French, literally, success of scandal]
succès d'estime (sŏŏk-sáy des-téém) *n.*, *pl.* **succès d'estime** success of a book, film, or the like with the critics and reviewers, but not with the public at large; work that enjoys such a success [French, literally, success of respect]
succès fou (sŏŏk-sáy fóó) *n.*, *pl.* **succès fous** tremendous success, as of a book or show; work that enjoys such a success [French, literally, mad success]
successive *adj.* following in sequence, following uninterruptedly — **succession** *n.* — **succeed** *v.*
succinct (sək-síngkt) *adj.* clearly and economically expressed, concise
succour (súcker) *formal. n.* help or relief in time of distress (also *U.S.* "succor") — **succour** *tr.v.*
succubus (súckew-bəss) *n.*, *pl.* **-bi** demon adopting female form to have sexual intercourse with sleeping men. Compare INCUBUS
succulent *n.* cactus or similar plant with fleshy sap-conserving stems or leaves ~ *adj.* relating to a succulent; juicy; *informal.* attractive or desirable (usually said of a woman)
succumb (sə-kúm) *intr.v.* to yield or give in to something more powerful: *succumbed to the enemy/temptation*; *formal.* to be killed: *succumbed to smallpox*
succuss (se-kúss) *formal. tr.v.* to shake (a patient) vigorously to listen for abnormal pockets of body fluid — **-cussion** *n.*
suckling *archaic. n.* young child or animal that is still unweaned: *babes and sucklings*
sudorific *formal. adj.* sweat-inducing or -increasing (also "diaphoretic") ~ *n.* sudorific medicine
sufferance *formal. n.* toleration or permission implied by the absence of an explicit prohibition — **on sufferance** with limited or grudging toleration

sufficiency *formal. n.* adequate but modest amount, income, or standard of living
suffragan (súffrəgən) *n.* bishop assisting or subordinate to another bishop (also "suffragan bishop")
suffrage (súffrij) *formal. n.* right to vote, electoral franchise
suffragette *n.* female supporter of female suffrage, especially in the early 20th century
suffuse *formal. v.* to spread across or through: *suffused with warmth/colour* — **-fusion** *n.*
sui generis (sōō-ee jénnəriss, sōō-ī) *formal. adj.* unique [Latin, of its own kind]
sulcus (súl-kəss) *formal. n., pl.* **-ci** deep groove or furrow, as on the brain — **sulcate** *adj.*
sullen *adj.* gloomy and silently resentful, dismal, sulky; overcast or sombre: *a sullen sky*
sully *formal. tr.v.* to soil, make impure, tarnish: *sullied his reputation* [probably related to *soil*]
sultry *adj.* very hot and humid, sweltering; very sexy or passionate: *a sultry sigh* [related to *sweltering*]
summation *n.* addition or the total reached by it; summary, summing-up
summer *n.* horizontal supporting beam in a building, as between floors; stone slab, as on top of a pillar, supporting an arch or lintel
sump *n.* crankcase or oil reservoir in an engine; drainage pit or pool, as in a mine
sumptuous *formal. adj.* luxurious or splendid, lavishly decorated, spacious, or the like
sunder *formal or archaic. v.* to break apart, divide
sundry *formal. adj.* various, several — **all and sundry** each and every one — **sundries** *pl.n.*
superannuated *formal. adj.* old-fashioned, out-of-date, obsolete; retired or discharged because of old age or illness
superannuation *British. formal. n.* old-age or retirement pension
supercilious *formal. adj.* haughty, disdainful, scornful
supererogatory (sōōpər-ə-róggə-tri) *formal. adj.* beyond what is needed, beyond the call of duty; excessive, superfluous, not essential — **-gation** *n.*
superfetation *n.* presence in the womb of more than one embryo, due to further fertilisation during pregnancy — **-fetate** *intr.v.*
superficial *adj.* on or relating to the surface: *a superficial wound*; shallow, brief, or trivial: *a superficial essay/inspection/mind*; apparent rather than real: *superficial charm/similarities*
superfluous (sōō-pérfloo-əss) *adj.* extra; excessive, redundant, too much — **-fluity** *n.*
superimpose *tr.v.* to place on top of or above
superintendent *U.S. n.* caretaker of a building, especially a block of flats (also *U.S. informal* "super", *U.S. or Scottish* "janitor")
superior *n.* head of a convent, abbey, or other religious community
superlative (sōō-pérlətiv) *adj. formal.* of very high quality, superb; referring or relating to a form of adjective or adverb, such as *biggest* or *best*, that expresses the extreme degree of a quality — **superlative** *n.*
supernal (sōō-pérn'l) *formal. adj.* relating to the sky or heavens
supernumerary *formal. adj.* exceeding a fixed or normal number: *He had a supernumerary nipple* ~ *n.* actor with a walk-on, non-speaking part: *supernumeraries for the crowd scene*
superordinate *adj.* belonging to a higher or larger class or level of generality — **superordinate** *n.*
superscript *n.* letter, number, or symbol, often of miniature size, written or printed next to and just above another, as in mc^2. Compare SUBSCRIPT
supersede *tr.v.* to replace, especially with something better or newer — **-sedence**, **-session** *n.*
supersonic *adj.* faster than the speed of sound
supervene *formal. intr.v.* to happen or interfere unexpectedly, especially so as to disrupt previous arrangements or expected developments — **-venient** *adj.* — **-venience**, **-vention** *n.*
supine *adj.* lying on one's back, face upwards. Compare PRONE; *formal.* passive, slack, weak-willed, over-submissive
supplant *tr.v.* to replace, especially suddenly and completely
supplement *n.* something added, as to strengthen the whole or make good a lack: *vitamin supplement*; angle related to another so that the sum of the two is 180° [related to *supply*] — **-ary**, **-al** *adj.* — **supplement** *tr.v.*
suppliant (súppli-ənt) *formal. adj.* asking or begging humbly (also "supplicant") — **suppliant**, **-ance** *n.*
supplicate *formal. v.* to ask or beg humbly and earnestly, beseech — **-cation** *n.* — **-cant**, **-catory** *adj.*
supposititious *formal. adj.* supposed, hypothetical; counterfeit, fraudulently substituted for the genuine article; *archaic.* referring to an illegitimate child, or one falsely represented as the genuine heir (also "suppositious")
suppository *n.* solid medication designed to melt when inserted into the vagina or rectum
suppress *tr.v.* to subdue or quell, especially by force: *suppress a mutiny*; to keep from growing, developing, or circulating fully or freely: *suppress a smile/a thought/a book* — **-ion** *n.* — **-ive** *adj.*
suppurate (súppewr-ayt) *formal. intr.v.* to discharge pus, as a wound might, fester — **-ation** *n.*
supra *formal. adv.* above or earlier in the text (used in footnotes). Compare INFRA
surcharge *n.* extra charge — **surcharge** *tr.v.*
surcingle (súrsing-g'l) *n.* strap that ties a saddle, blanket, or the like around a horse
surcoat *n.* tunic worn by a medieval knight over his armour
surety (shóor-əti) *n.* guarantee or guarantor against loss or damage, or a debt or obligation
surfeit (súr-fit) *formal. n.* excessive amount of something, especially food and drink — **surfeit** *v.*
surly *adj.* irritable, grumpy, gruff [originally, masterful or lordly, literally, sir-like]
surmise *tr.v.* to infer or suppose on only scanty evidence, conjecture — **surmise** *n.*
surmount *tr.v.* to overcome (a difficulty or obstacle) — **-able** *adj.*
surpass *tr.v.* to exceed in quantity or degree
surplice (súr-pliss) *n.* loose white gown with wide sleeves, sometimes worn over a cassock by a clergyman or chorister
surreal *adj.* dream-like, distorted, or irrational in a bizarre way — **-ism**, **-ist** *n.* — **-istic** *adj.*
surreptitious *formal. adj.* secret, sneaky, covert
surrogate (súrrə-gət) *formal. n.* substitute, something that replaces or functions in place of another — **surrogate** *adj.*, *tr.v.*
surround *n.* border, especially the area of floor bordering a carpet, doorway, fireplace, or the like

surveillance (sur-váylənss) *n.* observation or close watch, especially on someone or something suspicious [related to *vigilant*] — **surveillant** *adj.*, *n.*
susceptible *adj.* easily influenced or affected: *susceptible to flattery/colds*; *formal.* permitting or open to: *a theory susceptible of proof* — **-ibility** *n.*
suspended animation *n.* death-like or temporary dormant state of a living organism, as during hibernation
suspended sentence *n.* prison sentence that is served only in the event of another subsequent conviction
suspension *n.* mixture of solid particles dispersed but not dissolved in a liquid
suspire *formal. v.* to breathe or sigh — **-piration** *n.*
sustain *tr.v.* to support, maintain, or provide for: *sustained our courage/the joke; sustained himself by eating roots*; to suffer or endure: *sustained hardships/losses*; to uphold or confirm as valid: *The judge sustained my objection*
sustaining pedal *n.* right-hand pedal on a piano that increases volume (also "reverberation pedal", *informal* "loud pedal")
sustenance *n.* sustaining or being sustained; food or nourishment
susurration (séw-sə-ráysh'n) *formal. n.* whispering or rustling sound, as of the wind — **-rate** *intr.v.* — **-rous**, **-rant** *adj.*
sutler *n.* person who followed an army and sold provisions to soldiers in former times
suttee *n.* former Hindu custom whereby a widow would cremate herself on her late husband's funeral pyre; widow who has committed suicide in this way
suture (sóo-chər) *n.* strand of thread, gut, or wire used to stitch together parts of a living body; stitching using this material; line and mark produced by such stitching; seam or furrow where body or plant parts are joined, as on a seedpod or between the bones of the skull — **suture** *tr.v.*
suzerain (sóozə-rayn) *n.* feudal lord; dominant nation that controls the foreign affairs though usually not the internal affairs of another country [related to *sovereign*] — **suzerain** *adj.* — **-ty** *n.*
Suzuki method *trademark n.* method of teaching the violin or other musical instruments by imitation and repetition rather than reading the music, especially as used with young children [after S. *Suzuki*, the 20th-century Japanese music teacher who developed it]
svelte (sfelt) *adj.* slim and graceful in build or movement (used mainly of women)
Svengali (sfeng-gáali) *informal. n.* a man who exerts a sinister influence over the will of someone else, usually a woman [after the wicked hypnotist in George Du Maurier's novel *Trilby* of 1894]
swab *n.* cotton-wool ball or similar piece of absorbent material used for cleaning, applying a lotion, or the like; specimen of bodily secretion obtained using a swab; *informal.* mop (also "swob") — **swab** *tr.v.*
swaddling clothes *pl.n.* cloth strips formerly wound around a newborn baby — **swaddle** *tr.v.*
swagger stick *n.* cane or short stick carried by army officers
swain *formal or archaic. n.* male suitor, lover, or sweetheart (humorous)
swale *chiefly U.S. n.* low-lying stretch of land, often wet or marshy (also "swail")
swami *n.* Hindu title of respect for a man; Hindu religious teacher; mystic, yogi
sward (swawrd) *formal or archaic. n.* grassy area, such as a meadow or lawn
swarf (swarf) *n.* filings or shavings of metal, plastic, or the like removed by a cutting tool
swarthy (swáwr-thi) *adj.* having a sunburnt or darkish complexion
swashbuckling *adj.* energetic and flamboyant, adventurous, daredevil — **-buckler** *n.*
swash letter *n.* italic letter with decorative flourishes
swastika *n.* Nazi emblem, consisting of a cross with right-angled ends; ancient Hindu religious symbol from which the Nazis derived their emblem
swatch *n.* sample piece of fabric
swath (swawth, swoth) *n.* strip or path left by a scythe or mower; path of progress: *cut a swath through London society*; mown grass or hay cut by a scythe or mower (also "swathe")
swathe *tr.v.* to bind, wrap, or bandage: *swathed in furs*
sweatshop *n.* workshop, factory, or the like where pay and working conditions are very poor
sweep *n.* pivoted pole with a bucket on the end for drawing water from a well (also "swipe"); windmill sail
sweep-second hand *n.* second-hand on a watch or clock that sweeps round the same dial as the hour and minute hands
sweepstake *n.* horse race or other contest in which the contestants' stakes go to make up the prize awarded to the winner; lottery or prize involved in such a contest
sweetbread *n.* pancreas or thymus gland of a lamb or calf, used as food
sweetmeat *formal or archaic. n.* candied nut, crystallised fruit, or other sugary delicacy
swill *informal. v.* to drink grossly or excessively — **swill out** to wash by flushing or flooding with water ~ *n.* kitchen scraps or rubbish; pigs' food consisting of kitchen scraps and liquid (also "pigswill")
swingletree *n.* pivoted bar linking a cart, plough, or the like to the harness traces of a horse or ox (also "singletree", "whippletree", "whiffletree")
swipes *British. pl.n.* beer, especially beer of poor quality
switch *n.* twig, flexible rod, whip, or the like; bushy tip of the tail of a cow or other animal; hair in a detached tress, worked into a person's own hair in certain hairstyles
swizzle stick *n.* small thin stick for stirring a drink or removing bubbles from it
swoon *intr.v., formal or archaic.* to faint; *informal.* to become enraptured or ecstatic: *still swoons over Cliff Richard*
sword of Damocles *n.* disaster about to happen, or constant threat of disaster causing constant anxiety [after *Damocles*, a courtier of Dionysius the Elder of Syracuse, who forced him to sit at a banquet under a sword suspended by a single hair, to demonstrate the anxieties and insecurity of kingship]
sybarite (síbbə-rīt) *n.* person who loves luxuries and sensual pleasures [after the Greek colony of *Sybaris* in prosperous ancient Italy, whose inhabitants had a reputation for pleasure-seeking and luxury] — **-itic** *adj.*
sycophant (síckə-fant) *n.* toady, flatterer, or smarmy self-seeker — **-phantic** *adj.* — **-phancy** *n.*
syllabary (síllə-bəri) *n.* writing system in which each

symbol represents a complete syllable

syllabub *n.* cold sweetened dessert or drink made of cream with wine or spirits

syllabus *n.*, *pl.* **-buses** or **-bi** outline of a course of study or exam requirements, curriculum

syllepsis (si-le͞ep-siss, -lép-) *n.*, *pl.* **-lepses** use of a single word to apply to two or more other words in different ways or senses, as in *He kept his tongue and my hand.* Compare ZEUGMA

syllogism (sílla-jiz'm) *n.* pattern of logical reasoning in which two premises generate a conclusion — **-istic** *adj.* — **-ise** *v.*

sylph *n.* airy spirit, fairy-like being without a soul; graceful, slender girl or woman — **sylph-like** *adj.*

sylvan *formal. adj.* relating to woods or forest areas (also "silvan")

symbiosis *n.*, *pl.* **-oses** living together of two organisms in close or dependent association, especially when beneficial to both — **-biotic** *adj.*

symmetry *n.* relationship of correspondence, equivalence, or identity between systems or parts of a system; similarity of shape or form around a given axis, point, line, or plane; balanced and harmonious arrangement of parts — **-metrical** *adj.*

sympathetic magic *n.* magic intended to achieve an effect by some imitative ceremony or symbolic object, as when pins are stuck into a doll

symposium *n.*, *pl.* **-iums** or **-ia** conference or discussion, typically on a specialist academic or professional theme, colloquium; Greek drinking party in ancient times, typically with music and intellectual conversation

symptom *n.* indication or evidence of a disease, social condition, or the like — **-atic** *adj.*

synaeresis *n.*, *pl.* **-reses** contraction in which adjacent vowels merge into a single vowel or diphthong, as when *doeth* becomes *doth*

synaesthesia *n.* sensation in one part of the body that is produced by stimulation in another; sensation that is registered by a sense different from the one stimulated, as when a sensation of colour is evoked by a sound — **-aesthetic** *adj.*

synapse (sí-naps) *n.* gap or point across which a nerve impulse is transmitted — **-naptic** *adj.*

synchromesh *n.* gear system allowing smooth changes of gear by synchronising the speeds of the moving parts before they engage

synchronic linguistics *n.* linguistics that ignores the historical approach, and instead studies a language as it exists at one particular time. Compare DIACHRONIC LINGUISTICS

synchronicity *n.* state of being synchronic; coincidence considered to be of a significant kind, especially in Jungian philosophy

synchronise *v.* to happen or cause to happen at the same time, or in harmony ~ *tr.v.* to set (watches or clocks) to show the same time — **-isation** *n.*

syncopation *n.* rhythmic irregularity in music, as caused by stressing a weak beat; syncope of a word — **syncopate** *v.*

syncope (síng-kəpi) *n.* clipping of a word by omission of a middle segment, as in *o'er* for *over* (also "syncopation"). Compare APOCOPE, HAPLOLOGY; *formal.* temporary loss of consciousness, faint — **-copal** *adj.*

syncretism (síng-kri-tiz'm) *n.* attempt or tendency to reconcile differing beliefs or religious value systems [from Greek *sunkretismos*, a union or federation, originally of the cities of *Crete*] — **-cretise** *v.* — **-cretist** *n.* — **-cretistic** *adj.*

syndetic *formal. adj.* serving to connect, as a conjunction does; joined by a conjunction (also "syndetical")

syndic *n.* British university's representative in business matters

syndicate *n.* business association of various interests formed for some joint enterprise; agency selling cartoons, articles, and the like for simultaneous publication in numerous newspapers or magazines; *slang.* criminal association in charge of organised crime — **syndicate** *v.*

syndrome *n.* set of symptoms or signs jointly indicating or characterising a disease, abnormality, or the like; *informal.* pattern of elements forming an identifiable problem, behaviour disorder, or the like: *the Stockholm syndrome*

synecdoche (si-nék-dəki) *n.* figure of speech in which the name of a part of something is used to refer to the whole of it, or vice versa, as in *forty head* to denote forty cattle. Compare METONYMY — **-dochic** *adj.*

synergism *n.* cooperative action, as of medicines or muscles, producing a greater effect than the sum of the individual effects — **-gistic, -gic, -getic** *adj.*

synod *n.* assembly or council, specifically of church officials — **-ic** *adj.*

synonym *n.* word or phrase identical or very similar in meaning to another in the same language (opposite "antonym"); symbolic substitute, equivalent, byword: *a name that has become a synonym for quality* — **-y** *n.* — **-ous** *adj.*

synopsis *n.* summary; brief outline or overview, especially of a book, play, film, or the like — **-optic** *adj.*

Synoptic Gospels *pl.n.* the Gospels of Matthew, Mark, and Luke, which have similarities setting them apart from the Gospel of John

synovia (si-nṓvi-ə) *n.* clear thick liquid secreted by membranes in joints and tendon sheaths (also "synovial fluid") — **-ial** *adj.*

syntax *n.* combination of words into phrases, clauses, and sentences; branch of grammar dealing with this; combination of symbols into well-formed strings, as in logic — **-tactic** *adj.*

synthesis *n.*, *pl.* **-theses** combining of parts or elements to form a whole — **-thesise** *v.*

synthetic *adj.* relating to synthesis; referring to a statement, such as *Bachelors are mortal*, that is true or false by virtue of correspondence to facts in the real world rather than simply of the meanings of its words alone, as in an analytic statement such as *Bachelors are unmarried.* Compare ANALYTIC; artificial, man-made: *synthetic hormones*

syrinx *n.*, *pl.* **-inxes** or **-inges** panpipe; vocal organ in the lower part of a bird's windpipe

systemic *adj.* affecting the entire body: *a systemic disease/poison*; relating to systems and their interdependence

systole (sístəli) *n.* rhythmic contracting of the chambers of the heart, during which phase they pump blood outwards. Compare DIASTOLE; *formal.* intense or energetic phase of a process — **-lic, -taltic** *adj.*

syzygy (sízziji) *n.* arrangement of three celestial bodies in a straight line, as of the Earth, Sun, and Moon at full moon or during an eclipse — **-gial** *adj.*

T

tabard (tábbərd) *n.* knight's tunic bearing his coat of arms and worn over his armour; herald's cape or tunic bearing his lord's coat of arms
tabernacle *n.* tent or booth as used by the Israelites during the Exodus, especially the Israelites' tent sanctuary for the Ark of the Covenant; ornamental box or case for storing the Communion bread and wine; place of worship of certain Protestant denominations
tabes (táybeez) *n.* wasting of the body or of an organ as a result of lengthy disease — **-betic** *adj.*
tableau (táb-lō) *n.*, *pl.* **-x** or **-s** picture, graphic description, or representation; group of people picturesquely arranged; stage scene or pause in which the actors freeze briefly in position
tableau vivant (vee-vóɴ) *n.*, *pl.* **tableaux vivants** representation of a scene, painting, or the like by costumed actors posing silent and motionless
table d'hôte (ta̋ab'l dṓt) *n.*, *pl.* **tables d'hôte** fixed-price meal or menu, typically offering a limited choice of items (also "prix fixe") — **table d'hôte** *adj.*, *adv.*
tabloid *n.* newspaper having small pages, especially a downmarket one. Compare BROADSHEET [from *Tabloid*, trademark for a tablet of medicine] — **tabloid** *adj.*
taboo *n.* prohibition or restriction through fear of divine punishment or of becoming a social outcast (also "tabu") — **taboo** *adj.*, *tr.v.*
tabor (táybər) *n.* small drum accompanying the fife (also "tabour")
tabouret (tábbə-rit) *n.* round embroidery frame
tabular *adj.* flat, having a broad plane surface; relating to tables or columns
tabulate *tr.v.* to arrange in the form of a table or chart (also "tabularise") — **-lation** *n.*
tabulator *n.* typewriter key that sets, and makes automatic stops for, columns and margins (also "tab")
tachistoscope (tə-kístə-skōp) *n.* projector or other apparatus giving brief exposures of visual images, as for experiments in memory or perception
tachograph (táckə-graaf) *n.* "spy in the cab", device recording the travel time and speeds of a lorry or other vehicle
tachycardia *formal. n.* abnormally rapid heartbeat (opposite "bradycardia") — **-cardic** *adj.*
tacit (tássit) *adj.* unspoken, implied, understood: *tacit agreements*
taciturn *adj.* silent, reserved, or habitually uncommunicative — **-ity** *n.*
tack *intr.v.* to sail a zigzag course in order to advance into the wind — **tack** *n.*
tact *n.* sensitivity or delicacy in one's dealings with other people — **-ful**, **-less** *adj.*
tactical voting *n.* voting for the candidate most likely to defeat a candidate one dislikes, rather than for the candidate one positively favours
tactics *pl.n.* short-term policies and techniques, such as military operations designed to achieve local or immediate objectives. Compare STRATEGY — **tactical** *adj.* — **-ician** *n.*
tactile *formal. adj.* relating to touch or the sense of touch
taedium vitae (te̋edi-əm vī́-tee, tī́di-əm ve̋e-tī) *formal. n.* feeling or being tired of life, world-weariness [Latin, literally, weariness of life]
taffeta (táffitə) *n.* stiff glossy fabric, used for women's clothes ~ *formal. adj.* changeable or fickle, resembling shot taffeta
taffrail *n.* rail round the stern of a ship
tag question *n.* question such as *isn't it?* added at the end of a remark
tahina (tə-he̋enə) *n.* sesame-seed paste (also "tahini")
Tai chi (tī́ jee) *n.* Chinese form of exercise and mental training in which a series of balletic body movements is performed very slowly and deliberately
taiga (tī́gə, tī-ga̋a) *n.* subarctic coniferous forest, as in Siberia
tailgate *chiefly U.S. informal. tr.v.* to drive dangerously closely behind (another vehicle)
tain *n.* tin foil that forms the backing of a mirror
talisman *n.*, *pl.* **-mans** magic stone, lucky charm, or the like supposedly giving its bearer supernatural powers or protection — **-ic** *adj.*
tallow *n.* hard, whitish, fatty substance extracted from beef or mutton fat, used in making candles or soap
tally *v.* — *tr.* to list or check off item by item; to reckon, count — *intr.* to agree, correspond, match, be alike ~ *n.* score or reckoning, as in a game or account; notched stick formerly used for keeping accounts or records
tallyman *British. informal. n.* travelling salesman or instalment-collector working for a hire-purchase company
talon *n.* claw of a bird of prey (also "pounce"); edge of a lock's bolt against which the key presses to drive it home; stack of playing cards not dealt out at the beginning of a game
[1]**talus** (táyləss) *formal. n.*, *pl.* **-li** anklebone, ankle
[2]**talus** *n.*, *pl.* **-luses** rock debris at the foot of a cliff, or the slope formed by such debris (also "scree"); sloping side of a fortification or rampart
tambour (tám-bər) *n.* drum; embroidery frame in the form of two concentric wooden hoops between which the fabric is locked; rolltop desk's sliding front or similar covering consisting of wooden strips pasted on a stretch of canvas; circular wall, especially one supporting a dome
tamper *intr.v.* interfere or meddle in a dangerous, damaging, or illegal way: *tampered with the lock/ contract*
tampion (támpi-ən) *n.* plug or cover for keeping moisture or dust out of the muzzle of a gun when not in use

tandem *n.* bicycle or tricycle for two or more riders seated one behind the other; horses harnessed one behind the other in a team, or a two-wheeled carriage drawn by such a team — **in tandem** in conjunction or partnership — tandem *adj.*, *adv.*
tang *n.* sharp smell, taste, or flavour; tongue or prong at the base of the blade of a knife, tool, or the like for embedding into the handle (also "shank")
tangent *n.* line touching a curve or surface at one point only — **go off on/at a tangent** to depart suddenly from the expected direction of thought, speech, or action — **-gency** *n.*
tangential *adj.* only slightly relevant or connected; relating to a tangent
tangible *adj.* capable of being touched, felt, grasped, or handled physically or mentally: *tangible proof of guilt* — **-ibility** *n.*
tangram *n.* jigsaw-like Chinese puzzle consisting of a square cut into simple geometrical shapes for reassembling into different figures
tankard *n.* large mug, typically of pewter or silver, with a handle and often a hinged cover, as used for beer
tannin *n.* staining substance, used in tanning, dyeing, and inks, and found in bark
Tannoy *trademark. n.* public-address system, especially throughout a large building
tantalise *tr.v.* to tease, torment, or excite by showing but withholding something desirable [see TANTALUS] — **-sation** *n.* — **-lising** *adj.*
tantalus *British. n., pl.* **-luses** lockable cage-like container for displaying bottles or decanters of wine or spirits [after *Tantalus*, an evil king in Greek mythology who was condemned in Hades to stand in water that withdrew whenever he tried to drink it, with boughs of fruit dangling temptingly just out of his reach]
tantamount *formal. adj.* — **tantamount to** virtually the same as or equivalent to, amounting to: *Taxation without representation is tantamount to tyranny*
tantivy (tan-tívvi) *n.* blast on the horn; fast and furious gallop ~ *adv.* at full gallop, at top speed
tant mieux (tóɴ myő) *adv.* so much the better, all the better [French]
tant pis (tóɴ peé) *adv.* so much the worse [French]
taper *n.* very small or thin candle [related to *paper*]
tapering *adj.* narrowing or thinning towards one end
tapioca (táppi-ṓkə) *n.* bead-like granules of cassava-root starch, used in milk puddings and as a thickener in soup
tardy *formal. adj.* late, delayed; slow-moving, sluggish
tare (tair) *n.* weight of the container or wrapping material of goods; weight of an unladen lorry or goods vehicle
targe (tarj) *n.* small round buckler shield, as worn on the arm in former times (also "target")
tariff *n.* tax schedule or system of duties, especially for imports; *chiefly British.* price list, as on a menu
tarn *n.* lake in a hollow in the mountains
tarot cards (tárrō) *pl.n.* playing cards of a kind used in fortune-telling, bearing symbolic picture cards
tarpaulin *n.* canvas used as a waterproof covering
tarry *formal. intr.v.* to delay, wait, or linger
tarsus *formal. n., pl.* **-si** ankle — **-sal** *adj.*
[1]**tartar** *n.* reddish substance in grape juice deposited as a crust in wine vats (also "argol"); yellowish deposit building up on the teeth
[2]**tartar** *n.* ferocious, aggressive person [after the *Tatars* or *Tartars*, Genghis Khan's fierce Mongol hordes]
tatami (tə-taámi) *n., pl.* **-mi** or **-mis** straw mat used as a floor covering in a Japanese home
tattersall *n.* checked pattern of coloured lines forming squares against a plain background [after the pattern on blankets formerly used at *Tattersall's* horse market in London]
tattoo *n.* drumbeat in a regular rhythm; bugle call or drumbeat formerly signalling soldiers to return to their quarters in the evening; military display presented outdoors, usually in the evening, as an entertainment [from Dutch *taptoe*, shutting off of taps, signalling the closing of taverns at the end of the day]
taurine (táw-rīn) *formal. adj.* bull-like, relating to a bull; relating to the astrological sign Taurus
tautology *n.* in logic or mathematics, a formula or statement that is self-evidently true or self-proving; unnecessary repetition of a single idea, in different words, amounting to linguistic redundancy, as in *Pair off in twos* — **-logous**, **-logical** *adj.*
taw *n.* marbles as a game, or a large shooting marble, or the line from which a marbles-player shoots
tawdry *adj.* gaudy but vulgar and cheap-looking; tatty, seedy [from *tawdry lace*, short for *Seynt Audries lace*, a cheap and gaudy lace sold at fairs in honour of St *Audrey* or Etheldrida, a 7th-century queen of Northumbria, who died of a throat tumour, supposedly a punishment for her fondness for laces]
tawse (tawz) *n.* whip-like leather strap split into strips at the end, formerly used for beating children, especially in Scotland
tax *tr.v.* — **tax with** *formal.* to accuse of or criticise for: *taxed them with all their misdemeanours*
taxi dancer *n.* dancer employed by a nightclub or dance hall to dance with the patrons for a fee each time
taxidermy *n.* stuffing and preparing the skins of dead animals for exhibiting — **-dermist** *n.*
taxing *adj.* burdensome, troublesome, stressful
taxonomy *formal. n.* theory or principles of classification — **-nomist** *n.* — **-nomic** *adj.*
teamster *U.S. n.* member of a trade union of transport workers that includes lorry drivers
tease *tr.v.* to backcomb one's hair; to unravel and straighten wool or similar fibre by combing it
technicality *n.* petty formal detail or point of procedure: *The defendant was let off on a technicality*
tectonic *formal. adj.* relating to building or construction; relating to the deformation of the Earth's crust. Compare PLATE TECTONICS — **-ics** *n., pl.n.*
tectrix *n., pl.* **-trices** any of the small feathers at the base of larger feathers on the wings or tail of a bird (also "covert")
tedious *adj.* boringly slow or monotonous, tiresome — **tedium** *n.*
tegestology (tégges-tólləji) *n.* study and collecting of beermats — **-gist** *n.*
telaesthesia (tél-eess-theé-zi-ə) *formal. n.* psychic or extrasensory perception involving awareness of something remote in space or time — **-thetic** *adj.*
telamon *n., pl.* **-mons** or **-mones** column, in the form of a sculpture of a man, supporting a roof or storey in an ancient Greek or Greek-style building (also "atlas"). Compare CARYATID
telekinesis (télli-kī-neé-siss) *n.* movement, by mystical

or mental powers, of objects some distance away (also "psychokinesis") — **-etic** *adj.*

teleology *n.* belief that Nature is directed or determined by a plan or purpose — **-gist** *n.* — **-logical** *adj.*

telepathy *n.* mind-reading, thought transference — **-pathic** *adj.*

Teleprompter *chiefly U.S. trademark. n.* cuing device allowing a television newsreader or other speaker to read his script inconspicuously while looking straight at the camera (also "Autocue")

telex *n.* communication system sending telegrams through automatic exchanges [*tele*typewriter + *ex*change]

teller *n.* person who counts the votes in an assembly, parliament, or the like; bank clerk

telluric (te-léwr-ik) *formal. adj.* earthly, terrestrial (also "tellurian")

telpher *formal. n.* cable car, or transport system using such cars (also "telfer")

temerity *formal. n.* risk-taking of a foolhardy kind, reckless disregard of danger; cheek, rudeness, effrontery

temper *tr.v.* to harden or toughen (glass, steel, or the like) as by alternate heating and cooling; to bring to a state of maturity, consistency, or balance: *a character tempered by years of experience*; to moderate with an addition or mixture: *justice tempered with mercy*; to adjust the pitch of (a musical instrument, string, note, or the like)

tempera (témpərə) *n.* painting medium in which the pigment is mixed with glue, egg yolk, or another thick medium rather than oil

temperamental *adj.* moody or irritable, *informal.* erratic or unreliable: *a temperamental steam engine*

temperance *formal. n.* moderation or restraint, especially in drinking alcohol

temperate *adj.* moderate, not extreme: *a temperate climate/speaker*

tempestuous *formal. adj.* stormy: *tempestuous weather/arguments*

template *n.* guiding pattern, mould, plate, or the like, as in woodwork, for making or reproducing something accurately; horizontal beam, block, stone slab, or the like set in a wall to distribute pressure, as over a door frame

tempo *n., pl.* **-pos** or **-pi** rate, pace, or speed; speed at which a piece of music is or should be played

temporal *formal. adj.* relating to time; lay, secular; relating to or situated near the temples of the skull

temporise *formal. intr.v.* to play for time, evade or postpone commitments; to compromise, adapt oneself, or submit temporarily, so as to fit in with current conditions — **-isation** *n.*

tenable *formal. adj.* defensible or maintainable: *a tenable military position/argument* — **-ability** *n.*

tenacious *adj.* holding, sticking, or clinging firmly; persevering, dogged, stubborn — **-acity** *n.*

tendentious *formal. adj.* favouring or having a tendency towards one particular view, especially a controversial one

[1]**tender** *v.* — *tr.* to offer or present formally: *tender one's resignation* — *intr.* to bid, offer to supply goods or labour at a specific rate or price: *tender for a contract* ~ *n.* formal bid or bidding: *put a contract up for tender*; something, especially money, that is offered as payment: *legal tender*

[2]**tender** *n.* wagon behind a steam-train's locomotive, carrying fuel and water; dinghy or small service boat towed or carried by a yacht or ship

tendresse (toN-dréss) *formal. n.* loving feelings towards someone, fondness

tendril *n.* twining shoot-like part attaching a climbing plant to its support

tenebrous (ténni-brəss) *formal. adj.* dark, gloomy, shady (literary) — **-osity** *n.*

tenement *chiefly Scottish and U.S. n.* block flats, especially an older, inner-city block

tenet (ténnət) *formal. n.* firm belief or doctrine, article of faith [Latin, he holds]

tenon *n.* projection, especially a rectangular projection in the end of a piece of wood, made to fit into a corresponding slot in another piece to form a joint. Compare MORTISE

tenor *n.* sense, general meaning, drift, purport; course or general direction: *the quiet tenor of her life*; in music, highest natural adult male singing voice; singer or instrument that produces sounds within the tenor range — **tenor** *adj.*

tensile *adj.* ductile, capable of being stretched or drawn out

tentacle *n.* arm-like flexible projection near the mouth of an octopus, squid, or the like — **-acular** *adj.*

tentative *adj.* incompletely developed, provisional, or experimental: *a tentative agreement*; shy, hesitant, or uncertain: *a tentative suggestion*

tenter *n.* frame for drying or stretching cloth during manufacture

tenuous *formal. adj.* feeble, flimsy, lacking strength or substance: *a tenuous argument*

tenure (tén-yər) *n.* holding or occupying of a property, office, or the like; permanent or secure employment status, as enjoyed by some university teachers

tepee (tée-pee) *n.* tent of a conical shape traditionally used by North American Indians (also "teepee")

tepid (téppid) *adj.* warmish, lukewarm; half-hearted, unenthusiastic — **-ity** *n.*

teratology *n.* study of the causes and development of abnormalities in foetuses — **-gist** *n.* — **-logical** *adj.*

tercel (térss'l) *n.* male hawk, especially one used in falconry (also "tiercel") [from Latin *tertius*, third, from the ancient belief that the third egg of a clutch would always produce a male chick]

tergiversate (térji-ver-sayt) *formal. intr.v.* to lie, or act ambiguously or evasively; to change sides, defect, become a renegade — **-ation** *n.*

tergum *n., pl.* **-ga** back or upper surface of a body segment of an insect, lobster, or the like

term *n.* short pillar with a stone bust on top, used as a boundary marker or architectural ornament in ancient Rome (also "terminus")

termagant (térməgənt) *n.* quarrelsome or nagging woman (humorous) [Middle English *Tervagaunt*, a spiteful Muslim deity in medieval mystery plays] — **termagant** *adj.*

terminal *adj.* referring or relating to fatal illness or its final stages; *informal.* impossible to overcome, and having serious consequences *terminal shyness*

termination *formal. n.* abortion

terminology *n.* technical or specialised vocabulary; study of such vocabulary — **-gist** *n.* — **-logical** *adj.*

terminus ad quem *formal. n., pl.* **termini ad quem** goal, aim, desired end, finishing point. Compare TERMINUS A QUO [Latin, boundary to which]

terminus a quo *formal. n., pl.* **termini a quo** starting point, point of origin. Compare TERMINUS AD QUEM [Latin, boundary from which]

termitarium *formal. n., pl.* **-ria** anthill-like mound built by a colony of termites as their nest

ternary *formal. adj.* composed of three or arranged in threes (also "ternate") — **ternary** *n.*

terpsichorean (térpsi-kə-reé-ən) *formal. adj.* relating to dancing as an art [after *Terpsichore*, the muse of dancing and choral singing in Greek mythology]

terrace *n.* flat shelf cut, usually in a series, into the side of a slope, for cultivation, preventing erosion, or the like

terra-cotta *n.* brownish orange; clayey mineral used in pottery; brown, unglazed pottery [Italian, literally, baked earth] — **terra-cotta** *adj.*

terra firma *n.* dry land, solid ground (often humorous) [Latin, firm ground]

terrain *n.* ground or a stretch of land, especially in respect of its physical characteristics; area, territory, or environment: *unexplored terrain at the frontier of computer technology*

terra incognita (in-kóg-nittə) *formal. n., pl.* **terrae incognitae** unknown territory, unexplored country or subject-matter [Latin, unknown ground]

terrarium *n., pl.* **-iums** or **-ia** cage or closed container for small plants or animals

terrestrial *formal. adj.* relating to the Earth by contrast with other heavenly bodies; relating to or living on land as distinct from water or air (in this sense, also "terricolous")

terret (térrit) *n.* ring on an animal's harness or collar for reins or a lead (also "territ")

terrine (terreén) *n.* baking dish, typically oval-shaped and made of earthenware, in which patés are cooked and served; type of coarse paté

territorial *adj.* defensive, jealously protective of one's territory or possessions — **-ity** *n.*

terry cloth *n.* towelling

terse *adj.* concise, economically and elegantly worded; curt, very brief

tertiary (tér-shəri) *adj.* third-ranking or third-level

tertium quid *formal. n.* third course of action, factor, or the like when there are supposed to be only two [Latin, third something]

tessellate *tr.v.* to inlay, pave, or decorate with a mosaic of tiny tiles — **-ation** *n.*

tessera (téssə-rə) *n., pl.* **-rae** small square or tile of stone or glass used in a mosaic

tesseract *n.* four-dimensional extension of a cube, as a hypothetical mathematical construct

test *n.* shell or hard coating, as of some insects — **-aceous** *adj.*

testa *n., pl.* **-tae** seed's thick hard outer coating

testament *n.* statement of belief; statement of intention, as with regard to one's property after death: *last will and testament*; proof or firm evidence: *symphonies constituting a testament of/to the composer's genius*

testate *adj.* having left a valid will: *died testate* — **testacy**, **-tator**, **-tatrix** *n.*

testimonial *n.* expression or sign of gratitude or appreciation; statement serving as a reference or recommendation — **testimonial** *adj.*

testimony *n.* evidence, proof, demonstration: *Our survival is testimony to his courage*; evidence given in court: *The witness's testimony was harrowing*

testis *formal. n., pl.* **-tes** testicle

testudo *n., pl.* **-dines** overhead covering, made either of a large portable screen or of an overlapping roof of shields, protecting an ancient Roman military unit [Latin, literally, a tortoise, from *testa*, a shell]

tetanus *n.* lockjaw, or other form of prolonged muscle contraction

tête-à-tête (tét-aa-tét, táyt-aa-táyt) *n., pl.* **tête-à-têtes** private conversation, especially when there are only two people present [French, literally, head-to-head]

tether *n.* rope, chain, or halter restricting an animal to a small range of movement or grazing area — **tether** *tr.v.*

Tetragrammaton (téttrə-grámmətən) *n.* set of four Hebrew letters, corresponding to YHWH, and often rendered as Jehovah or Yahweh, representing God's name in the Old Testament

tetraplegia *n.* paralysis from the neck down, paralysis of the arms and legs (also "quadriplegia"). Compare PARAPLEGIA — **-plegic** *adj., n.*

textile *n.* cloth, fabric

texture *n.* rough or grainy surface; surface features, feel, or appearance of a fabric, painting, or the like; pattern or distinctive quality of a piece of music, historical period, or the like — **texture** *tr.v.* — **-tural** *adj.*

thalassic *formal. adj.* relating to or inhabiting the sea

thallus *n., pl.* **-li** or **-luses** plant body, as in algae or fungi, without distinct parts

Thanatos (thánnə-toss) *n.* death as personified in Greek mythology; death-wish or urge for self-destruction in Freudian theory

thaumatrope (tháwmə-trōp) *n.* toy consisting of a card or disc that is spun or twirled to produce a merged image of the partial words or pictures on each side

thaumaturge (tháwmə-turj) *formal. n.* magician or miracle-worker — **-turgy** *n.* — **-turgic**, **-turgical** *adj.*

thé dansant (táy doN-sóN) *n., pl.* **-s -s** tea dance [French, literally, dancing tea]

thenar (theé-naar) *formal. n.* fleshy mound at the inner base of the thumb

theodolite (thi-óddə-līt) *n.* surveyor's instrument, essentially a small mounted telescope, for measuring horizontal and vertical angles

theology *n.* study of the nature of God and religious truth — **-logian** *n.* — **-logical** *adj.*

theophany (thi-óff'n-i) *formal. n.* appearance or revelation of God or a god to man

theorem *n.* mathematical or logical proposition or formula that can be proved using the rules and stated assumptions of the system

therapeutic *formal. adj.* healing, providing mental or physical therapy

thermae (thérmee) *pl.n.* public baths in ancient Greece and Rome

thermal *adj. formal.* relating to heat; naturally hot: *thermal springs*; made of material specially designed to retain heat: *thermal underwear* ~ *n.* rising current of warm air, as exploited by gliders

thermonuclear *adj.* relating to atomic fusion at high temperatures, as in a hydrogen bomb

thermostat *n.* switching or controlling device for regulating temperature, as in a refrigerator or central-heating system — **-static** *adj.*

thesaurus (thi-sáwrəss) *n., pl.* **-ri** or **-ruses** book of carefully classified synonyms; book of classified items in a specialised vocabulary [Latin, treasure; related to *treasure*]

thesis *n.*, *pl.* **theses** idea, hypothesis, or premise put forward without proof; research report or study for an academic degree or diploma
thespian *formal. n.* actor or actress (now usually humorous) [after *Thespis*, a 6th-century B.C. poet, regarded in tradition as the founder of acting] — **thespian** *adj.*
thews *formal. pl.n.* muscles or sinews
thole (thōl) *n.* peg or pin, especially one used as a rowlock in the side of a boat
thorax *n.*, *pl.* **-races** or **-raxes** chest, area of the body between the neck and abdomen; mid-section of an insect's body, bearing the legs and wings — **-racic** *adj.*
thorn *n.* old runic letter, written þ, representing the sounds /th/ and /th̲/, as used in Old and Middle English
thoroughfare *formal. n.* path or road; public right of way
thorp *archaic. n.* village
thrall *archaic n.* slave, bondsman, serf — **in thrall** enslaved, captive: *in thrall to drink* — **thraldom** *n.*
thrasonical *formal. adj.* boastful, swaggering [after *Thraso*, a boastful character in the comedy *Eunuchus* by the ancient Roman playwright Terence]
threnody *formal. n.* song of lamentation, mourning song — **-odial, -odic** *adj.* — **-odist** *n.*
thresh *tr.v.* to separate grain or seed from the stems and husks by beating, as with a flail
threshold *n.* plank or stone lying under a door; doorway or entrance; starting point; boundary level above which something takes place, comes into effect, or is perceived: *The lower the pain threshold, the greater one's sensitivity to pain*
throes *formal. pl.n.* painful spasms, as on approaching death — **in the throes of** in the hard and painful phase of: *in the throes of creation*
thrombus *formal. n.*, *pl.* **-bi** blood clot formed in a blood vessel or in the heart, and remaining fixed in position — **-bosis** *n.*
throttle *tr.v.* to strangle or choke; to suppress vigorously or ruthlessly: *throttle a scream/a rebellion* ~ *n.* engine valve regulating the flow of steam or vaporised fuel
thurible (théwrib'l) *n.* container in which incense is burned, typically swung back and forth at religious ceremonies, censer
thwart *tr.v.* (thwort) to block or frustrate ~ *n.* (thwort, thort) seat extending across a rowing boat, typically for the oarsman
thyrsus (thúr-səss) *n.*, *pl.* **-si** staff, typically decorated with leaves and tipped with a pine cone, carried by the god Bacchus, or Dionysus, and his followers; flower cluster, as of the lilac, in which each flower has its own stem attached to a larger branch (also "thyrse")
tiara (ti-áarə) *n.* jewelled headband or semicircular crown worn by a woman on formal occasions; Pope's beehive-shaped three-tiered crown or hat
tibia *formal. n.*, *pl.* **-as** or **-ae** shinbone
tic *n.* muscular twitch or spasm, especially in the face: *a nervous tic*
tic douloureux (dōōlə-rúr, -rṓ) *n.* acute facial pain, trigeminal neuralgia [French, literally, painful tic]
ticker tape *n.* continuous strip of paper on which a machine prints information, especially stock-exchange reports formerly
ticking *n.* strong cloth of cotton or linen used to cover a mattress or pillow (also "tick")
tick-tack *British. n.* racecourse sign language used by bookmakers
tick-tack-toe *U.S. n.* noughts and crosses
tie *U.S. n.* railway sleeper
tier (teer) *n.* level, row, or stratum: *the highest tiers of seating/government*
tiffin *British. informal. n.* snack or light meal, especially around lunchtime, as formerly in India
tilde (tild, -i, -ə) *n.* accent mark, ~, placed above a letter to indicate a modified sound, as in Spanish *cañon*
tiller *n.* steering lever that operates the rudder of a boat; position of command or control
tilt *intr.v.* to aim or thrust a lance during a joist — **tilt at** to fight or oppose vigorously
tilt hammer *n.* heavy forge hammer levered up and then dropped
timbal (tímb'l) *formal. n.* kettledrum (also "tymbal")
timbre (támbər, taNbr) *n.* tone colour, sound quality produced by overtones rather than volume and pitch
timeserver *n.* opportunist, insincere person adapting his actions and opinions to those currently accepted
timorous (tímmərəss) *formal. adj.* shy, timid
timpani *formal. pl.n.* set of kettledrums (also "tympani")
tincture *n. formal.* colour or tint; solution of a medicinal substance in alcohol: *tincture of iodine*; *informal.* alcoholic drink (humorous) — **tincture** *tr.v.*
tinder *n.* material that burns easily, such as twigs, used to get a fire going
tinderbox *n.* trouble spot, or explosive situation or person
tine *n.* branch of a deer's antler; prong of a fork or fork-shaped tool
tinea (tínni-ə) *formal. n.* fungous skin disease, such as athlete's foot or ringworm (also "dermatophytosis")
tinnitus *n.* buzzing, whistling, or ringing sound in the ear, caused by disease, nerve defects, or drugs
tintinnabulation *formal. n.* ringing or jingling of bells
tippet *n.* stole with long front ends of the types worn by women or Anglican vicars; hanging part of a garment, such as a sleeve, hood, or cape
tirade *n.* long passionate outburst of speech, typically attacking or denouncing someone or something
tisane (ti-zán, -záan) *formal. n.* tea-like beverage made from wild flowers, medicinal leaves, or the like (also "ptisan")
titan (tīt'n) *formal. n.* person or thing of enormous size or importance [after the *Titans* in Greek mythology, a family of terrifying older gods whose power was overthrown by their children, the gods of Mount Olympus] — **-ic** *adj.*
titfer *British. slang. n.* hat [rhyming slang, from *tit for tat*]
tithe *n.* tenth part of one's yearly income or production, donated to the church or some other good cause — **tithe** *tr.v.*
titian (tísh'n) *n.* auburn or reddish gold hair colour, especially of a woman [after the portraits of the 16th-century Venetian painter *Titian*, who often used this colour for women's hair] — **titian** *adj.*
titillate *tr.v.* to arouse or excite, especially by being sexually suggestive — **-ation** *n.*
titivate *formal. v.* to smarten up in appearance [possibly a blend of *tidy* + *cultivate*] — **-ation** *n.*

title *n.* legal right, as to a property, status, or claim
titration (tī-tráysh'n) *n.* measurement of the concentration of a solution by adding another, standard solution to it bit by bit until the chemical reaction between them is complete — **titrate** *v.*
titular (títtew-lər) *formal. adj.* relating to a title; in name only, nominal but not real: *a titular king*
tmesis (tmée-siss) *n.* separation of the parts of a word by a word or words interposed, as in *abso-bloominglutely* or *a-whole-nother*
toastmaster *n.* master of ceremonies at a celebration or banquet, who proposes toasts and introduces the speakers
Toby jug *n.* mug or jug in the shape of a man wearing a three-cornered hat
tocsin *formal or archaic. n.* alarm bell or other warning sound; warning signal, omen
toggle *n.* peg-like crosspiece inserted to fasten a loop or strap, as on a duffle coat, or to secure a knot or bolt — **toggle** *tr.v.*
toile (twaal) *n.* sheer linen or cotton cloth; garment made up in cheap cloth as a basis for design alterations
toils *formal or archaic. pl.n.* things that entrap or ensnare: *in the toils of passion*
toilsome *adj.* troublesome and hard to do
token *adj.* merely symbolic, serving only for show: *a token gesture, a token woman on the board*
tokenism *n.* minimal or sham compliance with a law or custom
tolerance *n.* endurance, capacity to bear or withstand something unpleasant; degree of variation from a standard without going beyond the limit — **-ant** *adj.*
tomalley (tóm-a-li, tə-mál-i) *n.* lobster's fat as food
tombola (tom-bṓlə) *chiefly British. n.* gambling game where winning tickets are picked from a revolving container [related to *tumble*]
tome (tōm) *formal or archaic. n.* book, especially a large, impressive, scholarly book (often humorous)
tomography *n.* X-ray technique that shows up only the plane section wanted — **tomogram** *n.* — **-graphic** *adj.*
tondo *n., pl.* **-dos** or **-di** circular painting, cameo, or medallion
tonic *n.* syllable carrying the main stress, as of a word — **tonic** *adj.*
tonsorial *formal. adj.* relating to hair-cutting or hairdressing (now usually humorous)
tonsure (tón-shər, -sewr) *n.* complete or partial shaving of the head, especially of a monk or priest; part of the head, typically the top, that has been shaved
tontine *n.* insurance plan or other financial scheme involving a group of participants, each share becoming larger as each participant dies, until the final survivor is left with the full benefit [after Lorenzo *Tonti*, a Neapolitan banker who developed this scheme in the mid-17th century]
tonus *formal. n.* muscle tone
Tony *n.* annual award for outstanding work in the U.S. theatre; medallion presented for such an award. Compare EMMY [after *Antoinette* Perry, a U.S. actress
tooling *n.* stamped or gilded ornamenting on books or leather
toper *formal or archaic. n.* heavy drinker, drunkard (now often humorous) — **tope** *v.*
topi *n.* lightweight tropical sun helmet, made of pith or cork (also "topee")
topiary (tṓpi-əri) *n.* trimming or clipping of trees or hedges into ornamental designs — **topiary** *adj.* — **-rist** *n.*
topical *adj.* current and interesting or important: *topical news*; local, on or for a particular place: *topical application of a medicinal cream*
topography *n.* physical features of a region or their display on a map — **-graphic**, **-graphical** *adj.*
toponym *n.* name, such as *Arcadia*, of a place or region; word, such as *Arcadian*, derived from such a name — **-nomy** *n.*
topos *n., pl.* **-poi** basic or commonplace theme, idea, or image in literature
toque (tōk) *n.* small, brimless woman's hat
tor *n.* rock or pile of stones on a hilltop; high, rocky, and bare hill
torchère (tawr-sháir) *n.* stand or table for supporting torches or candlesticks
torch song *informal. n.* sentimental popular song, usually about love
torpid *formal. adj.* sluggish or lazy — **-ity**, **torpor** *n.* — **torpefy** *v.*
torque (tork) *n.* twisting force; collar or necklace, typically of twisted metal, worn in ancient times
torrent *n.* turbulent and unrestrained flow: *a torrent of rain/passion/words* — **-ial** *adj.*
torrid *formal. adj.* baking hot; full of heated passion — **-ity** *n.*
torsade (tawr-sáyd, -sáad) *n.* hat trimming of twisted ribbon or cord
torsion *formal. n.* act of turning or twisting, or stress produced by it
torso *n., pl.* **-sos** trunk of the body, or a sculpture of it
tort *n.* violation of civil law other than breach of contract, such as an act of trespass, or negligence (also *Scottish or South African* "delict") — **-ious** *adj.*
tortfeasor (tórt-féezər) *formal. n.* person who is guilty of tort
tortuous *adj.* winding or twisting: *a tortuous mountain road* — **-uosity** *n.*
torturous *adj.* excruciatingly painful, agonising
torus (táw-rəss) *formal. n., pl.* **-ruses** or **-ri** shape of a ring doughnut or of a tyre
totalisator *n.* race-course betting system in which the winners receive a share of the total amount bet (also *informal* "tote", chiefly *U.S.* "pari-mutuel")
totalitarianism *n.* dictatorial system of government aiming at total control — **totalitarian** *n., adj.* — **-istic** *adj.*
totem *n.* symbol or kinship emblem, often a plant or animal, of a tribal family group — **-ic** *adj.* — **-ism** *n.*
totter *British. slang. n.* rag-and-bone man
touché (too͞-sháy) *interj.* well done, nice one (said to acknowledge a touch or hit made against one in fencing, or a telling point scored against one in conversation) [French, literally, touched]
touchstone *n.* criterion or standard of judgment, especially of excellence
touchwood *n.* tinder in the form of decayed wood or similar dry material
toupee (too͞-pay) *n.* hairpiece covering a man's bald patch [akin to *top*]
tour de force (to͝or də fórss) *n., pl.* **tours de force** outstanding feat of skill or strength; brilliant performance or achievement [French, literally, turn of force]

tournedos (tóor-nə-dō) *n.*, *pl.* **tournedos** small but choice beefsteak from the centre of the fillet or sirloin

tourniquet (tóor-ni-kay) *n.* bandage or other device wound tightly round a limb to stanch heavy bleeding

tousled *adj.* disarranged, rumpled: *tousled hair* — **tousle** *tr.v.*

tout (towt) *informal. v.* — *intr.* to try to persuade people to support you or buy from you: *touting for clients* — *tr.* advertise or promote energetically, hype: *touting the new musical to the skies* ~ *n.* person who sells racing information to punters; person who resells tickets at an inflated price

tout court (tōō kóor) *formal. adv.* without mincing words, plainly and simply: *He's not an underachiever: he's a failure tout court* [French, literally, completely short]

towpath *n.* path along a canal or river, as still sometimes used by horses pulling barges

toxaemia (tok-séemi-ə) *formal. n.* blood poisoning — **-aemic** *adj.*

toxin *n.* poisonous substance, especially one of organic origin — **toxic** *adj.* — **toxicity** *n.*

toxophilite (tok-sóffi-līt) *formal. n.* archer or fan of archery (now chiefly humorous) — **-philic** *adj.*

tracer *n.* radioactive substance, dye, or the like whose course can be traced through a system and thereby be used in medical diagnosis

tracer bullet *n.* bullet leaving a trail of smoke or light that allows its path to be monitored

tracery *n.* lacy ornamental pattern, as in the stonework at the top of a Gothic window — **-eried** *adj.*

trachea (trə-kée-ə) *formal. n.*, *pl.* **-as** or **-ae** windpipe

tracheotomy *n.* surgical cut or opening through the throat into the trachea to help breathing

[1]**tract** *n.* stretch of land; anatomical system of organs and tissues that function as a unit: *the digestive tract*

[2]**tract** *n.* document or pamphlet putting a point of view strongly and often appealing for support

tractable *formal. adj.* obedient, easy to handle or persuade, acquiescent — **-ability** *n.*

traction *n.* pulling of a load; pulling power, as of a locomotive; friction, as of wheels on a road; road-holding capacity, as of moving wheels; continuous stretching of a compressed or injured body part as a medical treatment

traduce *formal. tr.v.* to betray, accuse falsely, or slander — **-ment** *n.*

trafficator *n.* turn indicator on the side of a car, especially of an early kind in the form of a small arm that would swing out and light up [*traffic* + indic*ator*]

trailblazer *n.* innovative leader who creates a path that others follow, pioneer — **-blazing** *adj.*

train *n.* part of a dress or gown trailing behind the wearer; line of gunpowder laid as a fuse to explode a charge

traipse *informal. intr.v.* to walk casually or wearily, stroll or trudge — **traipse** *n.*

trait (tray, trayt) *n.* personality feature, characteristic

trajectory (trə-jéktəri, trájik-tri) *n.* flight path, typically curved, of a missile, ball, or the like; path or course of development that moves upwards at least part of the time: *the trajectory of her career*

trammel *n. formal.* restriction or hindrance (often plural); fishing or bird-trapping net, especially one with three layers; compass for drawing large circles, or similar instrument for drawing ellipses ~ *formal. tr.v.* to hinder, impede; to capture or trap

tramontane *formal. adj.* blowing down from the mountains, as a wind might; foreign or barbarous

tramp *n.* protective iron plate on the sole of a shoe, as for prodding a spade into the ground

transact *tr.v.* to carry out or perform (especially scheduled business) — **-ion** *n.* — **-ional** *adj.*

transactions *pl.n.* published records of scheduled meetings, especially meetings of a learned society where papers are presented

transcend *formal. tr.v.* to rise above or extend beyond the limits of

transcendent *adj.* transcending; beyond ordinary experience: *transcendent knowledge* (also "transcendental"); superior and perhaps unique: *of transcendent importance* (also "transcendental"); independent of and outside the created universe (said of God or divine powers). Compare IMMANENT — **-dence** *n.*

transcendental meditation *n.* westernised Hindu-derived meditation based on silently repeating a personal mantra (abbreviation "T.M.")

transcribe *tr.v.* to write or type out a copy of (a recording, shorthand notes, or the like); to adapt or arrange (a piece of music) for different instruments or voices — **-scription** *n.*

transcript *n.* copy in writing or typescript of court proceedings, a student's academic record, or the like

transept (trán-sept) *n.* shorter division of a cross-shaped church, or either of its arms

transfiguration *n.* spectacular change or transformation, especially to a superior form — **transfigure** *tr.v.*

transfix *formal. tr.v.* to immobilise with terror or enchantment, cause to be motionless as if pinned to the spot: *transfixed by the beauty of her singing*

transfusion *n.* transfer by injection of blood, plasma, or the like into the bloodstream — **transfuse** *tr.v.*

transgress *formal. v.* to overstep a set limit or boundary; to break a law or rule — **-or** *n.* — **-ion** *n.*

transient *formal. adj.* passing, temporary; passing through or staying only temporarily, as at a non-residential hotel — **transient** *n.*

transit *n.* passing through or across: *in transit from London to Tokyo*; transport, especially local — **transit** *v.*

transition *n.* change from one state to another, as of historical eras, musical keys, or energy levels — **-al** *adj.*

transit lounge *n.* airport hall for passengers stopping temporarily, as for changing flights

transitive verb *n.* verb, such as *praise*, that needs a direct object to form a predicate (abbreviated in this dictionary to *tr.v.*) Compare INTRANSITIVE VERB

transitory *formal. adj.* short-lived, lasting for only a short while

translate *formal. tr.v.* to promote, move to a new and grander role; to transfer (a bishop) to another diocese; to transport to heaven (someone who has not yet died) — **-lation** *n.* — **-lator** *n.*

transliterate *tr.v.* to write or spell in the letters of another alphabet — **-ation** *n.*

translucent *adj.* allowing the passage of light, as frosted glass does, but only in a diffused form unlike transparent glass — **-cence, -cency** *n.*

transmigration *n.* passing of a person's soul into another body after death, resulting in reincarnation — **-migrate** *intr.v.*

transmission *n.* system of gears, clutch, and shaft by

which power passes from an engine or pedals to the axle of a vehicle; broadcasting, as of radio or television programmes — **transmit** *v.*
transmogrification *formal. n.* remarkable change or transformation, especially to a grotesque or fantastic form (often humorous) — **transmogrify** *intr.v.*
transmutation *formal. n.* change or transformation to a different form; alleged or attempted conversion of base metals into silver or gold by alchemists — **transmute** *intr.v.*
transom *n.* horizontal crosspiece, as of a cross or gallows, in a window, or above a door; *U.S.* fanlight
transparency *n.* photographic slide, X-ray, photograph, or the like
transparent *adj.* allowing the clear passage of light or other radiation; *transparent to X-rays*; clearly revealing ideas, intentions, or structure, whether deliberately or unintentionally: *a transparent literary style, transparent hypocrisy*
transpire *v.* to lose or give off water vapour through pores, as from the surface of a leaf; *formal.* to come to light, become known: *What transpired about the summit meeting was astonishing*; *informal.* to occur, happen, take place: *What transpired at the summit meeting is unknown* — **-spiration** *n.*
transport *tr.v.* (trən-spáwrt) to ship (a convict) overseas to a penal colony ~ *n.* (trán-sport) state in which one experiences intense or ecstatic emotions: *in a transport of delight* — **-ation** *n.*
transpose *tr.v.* to change or reverse the ordering or relative position of two or more items; to write or play (a musical composition) in a different key; to change (the key of a musical composition) — **-position** *n.*
transsexual *n.* person who feels an urge to belong to the opposite sex, or one who has undergone a sex-change operation. Compare TRANSVESTITE — **transsexual** *adj.* — **-ity** *n.*
transverse *adj.* crosswise, lying across or athwart
transvestite *n.* person who enjoys wearing clothes designed for the opposite sex (also "cross-dresser", *formal.* "Eonist"). Compare TRANSSEXUAL — **transvestite** *adj.* — **-vestism** *n.*
trap *n.* box-like stall from which a greyhound is released at the start of a race; pipe fitting, typically a U- or S-shaped bend, for holding water as a barrier against the return flow of gases
trapezium *n.* four-sided geometrical figure with two parallel sides
trappings *pl.n.* ornamental covering and harness of a horse; symbolic clothes, decorations, or characteristics, as of power or an official post
Trappist *n.* Christian monk of a Cistercian order noted for its austerity and vow of silence [named after *La Trappe*, a monastery in Normandy, where the order was founded in 1664] — **Trappist** *adj.*
trapshooting *n.* clay-pigeon shooting
trapunto (trə-pόontō) *n.* quilting in which padding is fitted into a stitched design
trass *n.* variety of volcanic rock that can be ground for making cement
trauma (tráw-mə, trów-) *formal. n., pl.* **-mas** or **-mata** wound or injury, whether physical or psychological — **-tic** *adj.* — **-tise** *tr.v.*
travail (tráv-ayl) *formal. n.* effort, exertion; agony, suffering ~ *intr.v.* to labour or struggle (literary)
traverse *v.* to travel across in a crosswise, diagonal, or zigzag path; ~ *formal. tr.v.* to examine carefully, inspect *n.* crosswise, diagonal, or zigzag path, movement, barrier, or the like; *formal.* denial of an allegation in a lawsuit
travesty (trávvəsti) *n.* crude and distorted imitation, pretence, or caricature: *The verdict was a travesty of justice* — **travesty** *tr.v.*
trawl *n.* large, cone-shaped fishing net towed along the bottom of the sea ~ *v.* to catch (fish) with a trawl — **trawler** *n.*
tread *n.* horizontal part of a stair. Compare RISER
treadle (trédd'l) *n.* foot-operated lever for driving a sewing machine, potter's wheel, or the like [related to *tread*]
treadmill *n.* wheel or belt that is kept moving by walking or running on it, either by people or by animals, as for exercise, punishment, or research; monotonous routine
treatise (trée-tiz, -tiss) *n.* learned written study, especially a systematic examination of a particular subject
treble *adj.* threefold, triple; high-pitched; soprano; in the upper half of the pitch range (opposite "bass") — **treble** *n., v.*
trebuchet (trébbew-shét, -chét) *n.* large catapult-like war machine as used for hurling rocks, in medieval warfare
trefoil (tréf-oyl, tri-fóyl) *n.* clover or similar plant whose leaves are made up of three leaflets; design or ornament in this shape
trellis *n.* garden arch or frame made of crisscrossing sticks, on which climbing plants are trained to grow
trematode (trémmətōd) *n.* fluke or related parasitic flatworm — **trematode** *adj.*
tremolo (trémmə-lō) *n., pl.* **-los** rapid repetition of one or two musical notes, usually performed on a string instrument or as part of a singing style
tremor *n.* shaking, quivering, or trembling movement
tremulous *formal. adj.* trembling, as from fear or weakness; suggesting or resembling such trembling: *a tremulous voice*
trenchant *adj.* relevant, forceful, and to the point: *a trenchant comment* — **-ancy** *n.*
trencher *n.* wooden tray or plate for carving or serving food; academic cap, mortarboard
trencherman *informal. n.* hearty eater
trepan (tri-pán) *n.* rock-boring tool, as used in mining; surgical instrument formerly used for cutting out circular sections, especially of the skull bone (also "trephine") — **trepan** *tr.v.*
trepidation *formal. n.* alarm, dread, terror (often humorous)
trespass *intr.v.* to go where one should not, intrude on someone's property, privacy, or rights ~ *n.* offence or sin of trespassing; sin — **-er** *n.*
tresses *pl.n.* woman's long, thick, flowing locks of hair (old-fashioned)
trestle *n.* supporting framework of a bridge; support, as for scaffolding or a table top, consisting of a horizontal bar on two pairs of splayed legs
triad *n.* group of three
triage (trī́-ij, trée-aazh) *formal. n.* choosing, sorting, or sifting by quality, as to allocate scarce resources
tribade (tríbbəd) *formal. n.* lesbian — **-dism** *n.*
tribulation *formal. n.* great distress or suffering
tribunal *n.* group that judges, decides, or arbitrates, or place where such a group meets
tribune *n.* ancient Roman official representing the plebs or masses; unofficial defender or champion of

the rights of ordinary people; *formal.* raised platform or dais for a speaker
tributary *n.* smaller stream or river flowing into a larger one ~ *formal. adj.* relating to tribute
tribute *n.* acknowledgment or expression of respect or submission: *paid tribute to her genius*; payment made as tribute; protection money, as paid by a vassal nation to a dominant nation; something that reflects well on the specified person or thing: *The survival of an institution is a tribute to its soundness*
trice *n.* — **in a trice** in a very short time
trichology (tri-kólləji) *formal. n.* study of hair and its diseases, especially baldness — **-gist** *n.* — **-logical** *adj.*
trident *n.* three-pronged spear, as used by some gladiators
Tridentine Mass *n.* traditional Latin Mass used officially in the Roman Catholic Church from 1570 to 1965
trigeminal neuralgia (trī-jémmin'l) *n.* severe pain in the head or face involving the fifth cranial nerve (also "tic douloureux")
trilby *n.* man's felt hat, with a narrow brim and dented crown [after *Trilby*, the heroine of George du Maurier's novel of 1894, who wore such a hat in the London stage version]
trilogy (tríllə-ji) *n.* set of three related plays, novels, or the like
trim *tr.v.* to adjust (sails and yards) to catch the wind better ~ *n.* decoration or ornamentation, as of buildings or clothing
trimmer *chiefly British. n.* unprincipled person who changes his policies or opinions to serve his interests
trip *tr.v.* to activate (a switch or other mechanism) by releasing a catch or trigger; to raise (an anchor)
tripod *n.* stand or support with three legs, as for a camera
tripos (trī́-poss) *n.* examination or course for a B.A. honours degree at Cambridge University [Latin *tripus*, a tripod, referring originally to the stool on which a graduate sat at the degree ceremony]
triptych (tríp-tik) *n.* painting or carving on three panels, usually hinged together, and often used as an altarpiece
trireme *n.* ancient Greek or Roman ship, typically a galley or warship, with three tiers of oars
triskelion (trī-skélli-ən) *n.* pattern or design of three curved or bent lines or bars radiating from a centre; Manx emblem of three limbs radiating from a centre
trismus *formal. n.* lockjaw
trite *adj.* unoriginal, overused, hackneyed, stale: *a few trite remarks*
triturate *formal. tr.v.* to grind or pound to a powder, as in making a medicinal drug — **-ation** *n.*
triumvirate (trī-úmvərət) *formal. n.* group of three joint rulers
triune (trī́-yōōn) *formal. adj.* relating to a trinity with an underlying unity, three-in-one
trivet (trívvit) *n.* three-legged stand or support, especially for cooking pots or hot dishes
trivium (trívvi-əm) *n., pl.* **-iums** or **-ia** in a medieval university, lower division of the seven liberal arts, comprising the three subjects of grammar, logic, and rhetoric. Compare QUADRIVIUM [Latin, place where three roads meet]
troche (trōsh) *formal. n.* medicinal lozenge or pastille
troglodyte (tróg-lə-dīt) *n. formal.* caveman, cave dweller; *formal.* reclusive person, hermit; *informal.* narrow-minded person with old-fashioned ideas — **-dytic** *adj.*
troll *v.* to sing energetically; to fish by trailing a line behind a boat
trolley *n.* device collecting electric current transmitted to an electric tram, as from an overhead wire; *U.S.* tram (also "trolley car")
trompe l'oeil (trónp lő-i) *n.* artistic technique that makes objects in paintings look real or three-dimensional. Compare GRISAILLE [French, literally, deceive the eye]
trope *formal. n.* rhetorical figure of speech
tropism *n.* plant's tendency to grow in a particular direction
troubadour (trōōbə-dawr, -dōōr) *n.* minstrel, specifically a medieval poet-musician of Provence. Compare TROUVÈRE
trounce *tr.v.* to defeat overwhelmingly
troupe (trōōp) *n.* touring group of entertainers
trouper *n.* veteran performer; *informal.* reliable and experienced colleague or adviser
trousseau (trōō-sō) *n., pl* **-x** bride's special wardrobe assembled before her wedding
trouvaille (trōō-vī́) *formal. n.* inspired new idea or discovery [French]
trouvère (trōō-váir) *n.* minstrel, specifically a medieval poet-musician of northern France. Compare TROUBADOUR
Troy weight *n.* system of weights, as for precious metals and gems, using a 12-ounce pound
truant *n.* absentee, especially from school — **-ancy** *n.* — **truant** *adj.*
truck farm *U.S. n.* market garden
truckle *intr.v.* to humble oneself and behave submissively to someone
truckle bed *n.* bed on casters that is low enough to be stored under another bed (also "trundle bed")
truculent (trúckew-lənt) *formal. adj.* aggressive or defiant, eager to quarrel or disobey — **-ence** *n.*
truffle *n.* mushroom-like fungus that grows underground and is considered a delicacy
truism *n.* boringly obvious statement or remark, commonplace or cliché
trumeau (trōō-mo) *n., pl.* **-x** wall, pillar, or the like between two windows, arches, or other openings
trumpery *n.* bric-a-brac, showy but cheap finery — **trumpery** *adj.*
truncate *tr.v.* to cut short, abbreviate, or lop
truncheon *chiefly British. n.* short cudgel or club used by a policeman; *formal.* staff carried as a symbol of office
trundle *v.* to roll heavily or noisily along
trunnion *n.* projecting pin on either side of a cannon, container, or the like enabling it to pivot on a supporting frame; supporting frame from which trunnions project
truss *n.* belt-like medical device worn to keep a hernia from protruding; supporting framework for a bridge or roof, consisting of beams, struts, or the like; cluster of fruit or flowers at the end of a stalk ~ *tr.v.* to tie up, as by binding the arms, wings, or legs
trustee *n.* agent legally entitled to control or administer the property or funds of someone else; member of the supervisory board of an institution
trusty *informal. n.* prisoner with special privileges, as for good behaviour

tryst *formal. n.* rendezvous or secret appointment, especially of lovers or with one's destiny
tsunami (tsōō-naámi) *n.* huge wave due to an underwater earthquake or volcanic eruption [Japanese]
tuber *n.* swollen root or underground stem, as of the potato or dahlia
tubercle *n.* growth, small swelling, or wart-like projection, as on a legume's root, the skin, a bone, or a lung
tucker *n.* frill or ruff of lace or linen formerly worn by women round the neck or shoulders
tucket *n.* trumpet fanfare
tuffet *n.* tuft or clump, as of grass; mound or hillock
tuition *n.* teaching or instruction, especially of a formally organised kind; teaching fee
tumbler *n.* drinking glass, section of a lock that obstructs the bolt until moved away by the key; breed of pigeon that somersaults in flight
tumbrel *n.* cart that carried prisoners to the guillotine during the French Revolution; *formal.* dung cart (also "tumbril")
tumescent *formal. adj.* swelling, bulging out, distending — **-scence** *n.*
tumid *formal. adj.* swollen, bulged out, distended; *informal.* high-falutin, over-ornate — **-ity** *n.*
tumult (téw-mult) *n.* noisy riot; noise and disorder of a tumult, commotion; agitation of mind or feelings — **-tuous** *adj.*
tumulus (téw-mew-ləss) *n., pl.* **-li** burial mound of ancient times (also "barrow") — **-mular** *adj.*
tun *n.* large cask or barrel, especially for beer or wine
tundra *n.* permafrost region between the perpetual snow of the Arctic and the tree line
tunicate *formal. adj.* having concentric layers such as those of the onion
tup *n. chiefly British.* male sheep, ram; heavy metal object, typically the head of a power hammer ~ *tr.v.* to copulate with (a ewe)
turbary (túrbəri) *n.* section of a peat bog where peat is dug; *formal.* legal right to dig peat or turf
turbid *formal. adj.* muddied through sediment or foreign particles, as river water might be; muddled by many conflicting interests or forces: *turbid political life* — **-ity** *n.*
turbinate *formal. adj.* cone-shaped, resembling a cone on its tip
turbulent *adj.* disturbed, restless, agitated — **-lence** *n.*
tureen *n.* broad deep bowl, as for serving soup
turgid (túrjid) *formal. adj.* pompous in style, ornate and slow-moving — **-ity** *n.*
turmoil *n.* wild disorder, great confusion
turnkey *n.* jailer who keeps the keys to an old-style prison
turnover *n.* volume of business activity in a given period
turnround *n.* completion time required for a process, especially in manufacturing or transport; reversal of direction, policy, or results
turnspit *n.* dog formerly placed in a treadmill to turn a roasting spit
turnstile *n.* revolving door, gate, or similar apparatus that lets people or animals through one by one, to control admission
turpitude *formal. n.* moral baseness or vileness, wickedness, depravity
turret *n.* small tower or tower-like ornamental projection on the side of a building; revolving armoured dome or drum on a tank or warship in which guns are mounted; tall wheeled wooden frame used to scale fortress walls during a siege in ancient times — **-ed** *adj.*
tussis *formal. n.* cough
tussock *n.* clump or tuft, as of grass or hair
tutelage *formal. n.* relation between ward and guardian, or pupil and tutor
tutelary (téwti-ləri) *formal. adj.* relating to tutelage; protective, as a deity is supposed to be towards his shrine
tutorial *n.* class given by a teacher to an individual student or a very small number of students
tutu *n.* ballerina's skirt, either short and projecting or reaching to below the knee
tuxedo *pl.* **-dos** *chiefly U.S. n.* dinner jacket [after *Tuxedo* Park, a resort in New York State]
twang *n.* nasal quality of speech, as in certain accents
twee *informal.adj.* pretty or quaint in an affected or pretentious way [childish or pretentious distortion of *sweet*]
tweeter *n.* loudspeaker specially adapted for high-pitched sounds. Compare WOOFER
twilight sleep *n.* drowsy semi-consciousness induced by anaesthetics
twit *tr.v.* to tease or ridicule: *twitted me with my blundering* ~ *n.* critical gibe, taunt
twitcher *British. informal. n.* birdwatcher, especially an extremely enthusiastic or clumsy one
tycoon *informal. n.* powerful business person or industrialist, magnate
tymbal *formal. n.* kettledrum (also "timbal")
tympani (tímpəni) *pl.n.* set of kettledrums (also "timpani")
tympanum (tímpə-nəm) *formal. n., pl.* **-nums** or **-na** eardrum, resonating membrane in the ear (also "tympanic membrane"); middle ear; arched recessed space, sometimes decorated with sculpture, above a doorway, as at the entrance of a medieval cathedral
tympanist *n.* orchestral musician who plays the kettledrums and other percussion instruments
type *n.* Old Testament figure or event foreshadowing one in the New Testament: *Elijah is held to be a type of John the Baptist*
typecast *adj.* referring or relating to an actor always cast in the same type of role; stereotyped, always assigned the same task or function — **typecast** *tr.v.*
typhoon *n.* small but violent tropical whirlwind or cyclone occurring in the western Pacific and China Sea
typify *tr.v.* to be a typical example or symbol of
typography *n.* process or technique of setting type and printing from it — **-pher** *n.*
tyranny *n.* absolute power or control, especially when exercised cruelly or unjustly; government enjoying such power — **tyrant** *n.* — **tyrannical** *adj.*
tyro (tīr-ō) *n., pl.* **-ros** inexperienced person, greenhorn, beginner (also "tiro")
Tzigane (tsi-gaán) *n.* Gypsy, especially a Hungarian Gypsy

U

U *British. informal. adj.* appropriate to or characteristic of upper-class behaviour or language usage; posh, considered acceptable by snobs. Compare NON-U [abbreviation of *u*pper-class]

Übermensch (űbər-mensh) *n., pl.* **-en** superhuman or superior type of person, in the philosophy of Nietzsche [German, literally, over-man]

ubiquitous (yoo-bíkwitəss) *formal. adj.* being everywhere, omnipresent — **-ity** *n.*

udometer (yoo-dómmitər) *n.* device for measuring rainfall, rain gauge

UFO *n., pl.* **-s** Unidentified Flying Object, such as a flying saucer — **ufology**, **-gist** *n.* — **ufological** *adj.*

UHT *adj.* referring or relating to milk that has been heated quickly and then cooled to make it stay usable longer in an unopened container [*u*ltra-*h*eat *t*reated]

uhuru (oo-hoorоо) *n.* freedom, especially from imperialist rule in Africa (used as an African nationalist rallying cry) [Swahili]

ukase (yoo-káyz) *n.* order, edict, or fiat of the former Russian tsar or other authoritarian power

ulcerous *formal. adj.* corrupting, having a bad influence

ullage *n.* loss, as through evaporation or leakage, of a substance in a container; amount lost through this leakage

ulotrichous (yoo-lóttrikəss) *formal. adj.* having tightly curled hair on the head, as black Africans have

ulterior motive *n.* intention or purpose that is concealed, especially so as to deceive

Ultima Thule (théw-li) *n.* most remote region, goal, or ideal [Latin, farthest Thule, the most northerly habitable region of the ancient world, conceived by early geographers as an island north of Britain]

ultimatum *n., pl.* **-tums** or **-ta** final, non-negotiable demand or requirement, especially when it is accompanied by the threat of a penalty or termination of negotiations

ultra- *prefix.* beyond-, exceeding-; extreme-

ultracrepidarian (últrə-kreppi-dáiri-ən) *formal. adj.* acting or speaking outside one's ability or knowledge [Latin, *ultra crepidam*, beyond the sole of a shoe, referring to the story of the ancient Greek painter Apelles, who accepted criticism from a cobbler about the figure's slipper in a painting but not about the figure's leg, warning him against judging "beyond the sole"] — **ultracrepidarian**, **-ism** *n.*

ultra vires (últrə vīreez, ooltraa véerayz) *formal. adv.* beyond the legal authority of a person or company [Latin, literally, beyond power] — **ultra-vires** *adj.*

ululate (yoolew-layt) *formal. intr.v.* to howl or wail, as if lamenting — **-ation** *n.*

umbel *n.* flat-topped or rounded flower cluster resembling an umbrella, as in the carrot family — **-bellate** *adj.*

umber *n.* yellowish brown; clayey mineral used as a pigment [Old French, *terre d'Umbre*, earth from the region of Umbria, in Italy] — **umber** *adj.*

umbilical cord *n.* cord or tube from the navel, linking a foetus to the mother's placenta; tube or line connecting a base or main structure to a dependent structure or person, such as that linking a spacewalking astronaut to the spacecraft; *informal.* bond, lifeline

umbilicus (um-bíllikəss, úmbi-līkəss) *n., pl.* **-ci** navel; opening or hollow at the base of a mollusc's shell

umbles *archaic. pl.n.* entrails, especially of a deer, used for food (also "numbles")

umbo *formal. n., pl.* **-bones** boss of a shield; knob-like protuberance, as on the cap of a mushroom or the top of a clamshell — **-nate** *adj.*

umbra *formal. n., pl.* **-bras** or **-brae** dark area, especially the darkest part of a shadow; area on the Earth's surface in total shadow during an eclipse; central darkest area of a sunspot

umbrage *formal. n.* — **take umbrage** to take offence

umbrageous *formal. adj.* giving shade; inclined to take umbrage

umlaut (óom-lowt) *n.* diacritic or accent mark, ¨, placed over a vowel, as in *coöp* or *Brontë*, to show that it is to be pronounced in or as a separate syllable (also "diaeresis")

unabashed *adj.* not humbled or disconcerted

unadulterated *adj.* pure, not mixed with impure or extraneous matter; *informal.* absolute, utter: *unadulterated rubbish*

unanimous *adj.* of one mind, without any disagreement — **-imity** *n.*

unassailable *adj.* able to withstand attack: *unassailable arguments* — **-ability** *n.*

unavailing *adj.* useless, futile, in vain

unbosom *formal. tr.v.* — **unbosom oneself** to reveal, unburden oneself: *unbosomed themselves of their secret fears*

unbridled *formal. adj.* uncontrolled, unrestrained: *unbridled lust*

uncanny *adj.* extremely strange or surprising, as if contrary to nature: *an uncanny resemblance*; *an uncanny coincidence*

unciform (únsi-fawrm) *formal. adj.* hook-shaped

Uncle Tom *informal. n.* black person, especially a man, considered excessively servile to whites; any person considered a traitor by over-cooperating with the oppressor [after the slave in Harriet Beecher Stowe's novel *Uncle Tom's Cabin* of 1851-52]

unconscionable *formal. adj.* impossible to forgive or condone, excessive: *an unconscionable delay*

uncouth (un-kooth) *adj.* rude or crude, uncultivated, boorish; clumsy, graceless

unction *formal. n.* anointing for ritual or healing purposes; ointment or oil used for anointing

unctuous *formal. adj.* oily, greasy, or slippery; referring to fertile, workable, organically rich soil; charming in an insincere and over-earnest way, smarmy

uncut *adj.* having the edges of the pages still unslit or untrimmed: *an uncut book*

undaunted *adj.* fearless, not discouraged, determined, in good heart (old-fashioned)

undercroft *n.* underground chamber, such as a church vault or crypt

undercut *v.* to charge less than or outmanoeuvre a competitor

understudy *n.* performer kept in reserve to take over in an emergency from the scheduled performer of a role — **understudy** *tr.v.*

undertaking *n.* task, assignment, or project; guarantee or promise; business, commercial venture — **undertake** *tr.v.*

undertow *n.* current or backward pull of receding waves after they have broken on the shore

underwhelm *informal. tr.v.* to fail dismally to overwhelm, impress, or overpower: *a distinctly underwhelming performance* (humorous)

underwrite *tr.v.* to agree to or subscribe to (a decision or policy); to agree to buy or guarantee the purchase of (a share issue); to finance, guarantee against financial failure: *underwrote the new venture*

underwriter *n.* risk-assessor, who guarantees against financial embarrassment by lending cash in an emergency, as for an insurance company

undulate *v.* to wave or sway rhythmically or smoothly — **-lation** *n.* — **undulate, -latory, -lant** *adj.*

unduly *adv.* in an excessive way: *unduly concerned with trifles*

unequivocal *adj.* unambiguous, not open to misinterpretation: *an unequivocal denial*

unfathomable *formal. adj.* too deep to be measured: *unfathomable silence/hatred*

unfledged *adj.* not fledged, still without flight feathers, and so not yet developed enough to fly

unfrock *tr.v.* to deprive (a priest) of his clerical rights and functions

unfurl *tr.v.* to unfold, unroll, spread out: *with flags unfurled*

ungainly *adj.* awkward, clumsy, graceless; unwieldy, difficult to move

unguent (úng-gwənt) *formal. n.* ointment, healing or soothing salve

ungulate (úng-gew-lət) *formal. n.* hoofed mammal, such as a horse, pig, or deer — **ungulate** *adj.*

unicycle *n.* bicycle-like vehicle with a single wheel (also "monocycle")

unilateral *adj.* involving only one side or party: *a unilateral decision* — **-ist, -ism** *n.*

unimpeachable *adj.* beyond doubt, unquestionable; blameless, beyond reproach

uniparous (yo͞o-níppərəss) *formal. adj.* producing only one offspring at a time

unison *n.* — **in unison** simultaneously; all together; in harmony or in agreement

unitary *formal. adj.* whole, undivided, single

unit trust *British. n.* investment company, owning shares in a variety of enterprises (also *U.S.* "mutual fund")

univalve *n.* snail, whelk, or similar mollusc having a single shell. Compare BIVALVE — **univalve** *adj.*

univocal (yo͞o-nívvək'l) *formal. adj.* having only one meaning

unkempt *adj.* uncombed or untidy in appearance

unleavened (un-lévv'nd) *adj.* made without a raising agent such as yeast: *unleavened bread*

unlettered *formal. or archaic. adj.* illiterate, uneducated

unlisted *adj.* not publicly quoted on the Stock Exchange; *U.S.* ex-directory

unmitigated *informal. adj.* absolute, utter: *unmitigated rubbish*

unprecedented *adj.* unheard of, unique, never having happened before

unreconstructed *chiefly U.S. adj.* stubbornly holding to outmoded views, unchanging or diehard: *an unreconstructed Nazi*

unregenerate *formal. adj.* unrepentant or unreformed, unchanging, unconverted, stubbornly persisting in old prejudices

unremitting *formal. adj.* persistent, unceasing, relentless: *unremitting anxiety*

unrequited *formal. adj.* not returned or reciprocated: *unrequited love*

unruly *adj.* undisciplined or ungovernable, out of control: *unruly hair/schoolchildren* [related to *rule*]

unscathed *formal. adj.* unharmed, completely uninjured

unseemly *formal. adj.* impolite, improper, unbecoming

unsolicited *adj.* not requested or invited: *rejected the unsolicited manuscript*

unstable *adj.* radioactive, especially when decomposing rapidly

unstinting *adj.* without being mean, miserly, or economical: *unstinting generosity* — **unstinted** *adj.*

unsung *formal or archaic. adj.* uncelebrated and often unknown: *unsung heroes*

untimely *adj.* occurring at an inappropriate time, especially, premature: *Keats' untimely death at 26*

unveiling *n.* ceremony at which a new monument, work of art, or the like is formally displayed to the public for the first time

unwitting *adj.* unaware, unknowing: *became the unwitting accomplice of a master con-man*

unwonted (un-wṓntid) *formal. adj.* not habitual or ordinary, unusual

upbraid *formal. tr.v.* to scold or criticise sharply

upcast *n.* ventilation shaft in a mine

upheaval *n.* sudden social disruption, violent change, or the like

upholstery *n.* fabric, padding, springs, and the like, as used in making soft coverings for chairs — **upholster** *tr.v.*

upper case *n.* capital letters. Compare LOWER CASE [the type for capital letters used to be stored in the upper of two cases in the days of manual typesetting] — **upper-case** *adj.*

upstage *informal. tr.v.* to draw attention away from, steal the show from: *She keeps upstaging him*

Ur- *formal. prefix.* primitive-, basic-, first-, original-

urban *adj.* relating to or located in a town or city — **-ite** *n.* — **-ise** *v.*

urbane *adj.* smoothly polite and refined, gracious, suave — **-banity** *n.*

urchin *formal. n.* poor and ragged child

ureter (yoor-réetər) *n.* duct for conveying urine from a kidney to the bladder

urethra (yoor-rée-thrə) *n., pl.* **-ras** or **-rae** duct through which urine is discharged from the bladder and which serves as the genital duct in males — **-ral** *adj.*

ursine *formal. adj.* relating to a bear; bear-like

Ur-text *n.* original text of a literary or musical work, especially a lost text reconstructed by scholars on the basis of later versions
urticaria *formal. n.* skin condition or allergy involving itching and bumps (also "hives", "nettle rash", "uredo")
urtication *n. formal.* itching or stinging sensation, typically accompanied by weals on the skin; former treatment for paralysis or itching, consisting of lashing the body with nettles — **urticate** *v.*
usage *n.* custom or habit; actual forms of expression in a language
usher *n.* official doorkeeper in a court of law, parliament, or the like; official who walks ahead of a person of rank in a formal procession ~ *tr.v.* to escort, lead, or conduct: *ushered us into the antechamber* — **usher in** to introduce, inaugurate, herald: *The A-bomb ushered in a new age*
usquebaugh (úskibaw) *Irish or Scottish. n.* whisky (often humorous) [Gaelic *uisge beatha*, literally, water of life]
usufruct (yo͞os-yo͝ofrukt, yo͞oz-) *formal. n.* use of and benefits from someone else's property, or the legal right to them — **-tuary** *adj., n.*
usurer *n.* moneylender who charges an exorbitant rate of interest, loan shark — **-ury** *n.* — **-urious** *adj.*
usurp *tr.v.* to seize by force and hold illegally (another's power, property, rights, throne, or the like) — **-ation** *n.*
uterine *adj.* relating to the womb or uterus; *formal.* having the same mother but a different father, as half-sisters or half-brothers might
uterus *n.* womb
utilise *formal. tr.v.* to use, make use of — **-isation** *n.*
utilitarian *adj.* practical rather than decorative; relating to serviceability and standardisation, as in wartime: *utilitarian furniture*
utilitarianism *n.* belief in or doctrine of "the greatest happiness for the greatest number", or theory that usefulness is the measure of goodness — **-ist** *n., adj.*
utility *n.* usefulness; something useful; public service such as water, electricity, gas, or transport
utopia *n.* ideal place or condition, especially in the future or in an alternative present rather than in an idealised past (opposite "dystopia", "cacotopia") [after *Utopia*, an ideal island commonwealth in the book *Utopia* of 1516 by Sir Thomas More, from Greek *ou*, no + *topos*, a place] — **-ian** *n., adj.* — **-ianism** *n.*
uvula (yo͞ovew-lə) *formal. n.* small fleshy flap hanging from the soft palate above the back of the tongue — **-lar** *adj.*
uxorial (uk-sáw-ri-əl) *formal. adj.* relating to a wife, wifely
uxoricide *formal. n.* killing or killer of one's wife — **-cidal** *adj.*
uxorious *formal. adj.* relating or referring to devotion to one's own wife: *an uxorious husband*

vaccinia (vak-sínni-ə) *formal. n.* cowpox
vacillate (vássi-layt) *intr.v.* to swing back and forth in feelings or beliefs so as to be hesitant or indecisive — **-ation** *n.*
vacuous *adj.* empty, without real content or substance: *vacuous remarks* — **-cuity** *n.*
vacuum aspiration *n.* emptying of a body cavity or organ by suction through a tube, especially in order to abort a foetus in the womb
vade mecum (vaá-di máy-ko͝om, váy-, mée-) *formal. n., pl.* **vade mecums** guidebook or ready-reference manual [Latin, go with me]
vagabond *adj.* roaming or wandering about — **vagabond** *n.*
vagary (váygəri, və-gáiri) *n.* peculiar or erratic action or notion: *the capricious vagaries of fortune*
vagrant (váyg-rənt) *n.* tramp or vagabond — **vagrant** *adj.* — **-rancy** *n.*
valance (vál-ənss, váyl-) *n.* short decorative curtain hung along a pelmet, shelf, edge of the bed, or the like; pelmet
valediction (vál-i-díksh'n) *formal. n.* goodbye, farewell, leave-taking; farewell speech — **-dictory** *adj., n.*
valency (váylən-si) *n.* combining property or capacity to combine, especially that of an atom, element, or chemical group (also *U.S.* "valence")
valet (vál-it, -ay) *n.* personal manservant of a man; attendant, as at a hotel, helping with personal chores such as parking [related to *vassal*] — **valet** *v.*
valetudinarian (vál-i-téw-di-náir-i-ən) *formal. n.* chronic invalid or hypochondriac — **valetudinarian** *adj.* — **-ism** *n.*
validate *tr.v.* to confirm, prove true or accurate, verify; to make or declare valid or legally sound: *validate a will*
valise (və-léez) *n.* small suitcase or overnight bag (old-fashioned)
vallation *formal. n.* fortifications, or a wall or rampart forming part of a fortification
valorise *tr.v.* to maintain or increase the price of a commodity, as by government subsidies or levies — **-isation** *n.*
vamp *n.* toecap or front upper part of a shoe or boot
Van de Graaff generator *n.* electrostatic generator in which the electric charge accumulates on a large hollow metal ball [after Robert *Van de Graaff*, the 20th-century U.S. physicist who devised it]
vandyke *tr.v.* to cut (cloth) to form a deeply indented edging [see *Vandyke*]

Vandyke *n.* beard that is short and pointed; collar of a wide, deeply indented design [after the styles often depicted by Sir Anthony *Van Dyck*, the 17th-century Flemish painter]

vane *n.* weathercock; blade of a turbine, propeller, windmill, or the like; feather on an arrow; stabilising fin on a bomb or missile; moving marker on a surveyor's levelling rod, or the sights on a surveyor's compass or quadrant

vang *n.* rope between the top of a boom or gaff and the deck

vanguard *n.* front position or troops of an advancing military force; forefront of, early participants in, or progressive grouping in an artistic trend, political movement, or the like. Compare REARGUARD

vanquish *formal. tr.v.* to conquer; to suppress or quell

vantage point *n.* viewing position giving a helpful overall image of a scene or situation

vapid (váppid) *adj.* dull, drab, flat, insipid; *formal.* lacking taste, flat, stale — **-ity** *n.*

vaporetto *n., pl.* **-ti** or **-tos** Venetian water-bus

vaporise *v.* to change into a gas — **-isation** *n.*

vapours *archaic. pl.n.* — **the vapours** female depression or hysteria, supposed in former times to be caused by gases produced within the body

vapour trail *n.* visible trail of condensed vapour produced by a high-flying aircraft (also "condensation trail","contrail")

vaquero (va-káirō) *n., pl.* **-os** Mexican cowboy or herdsman

variance *n.* — **at variance** in disagreement, in conflict

variant *n.* any of two or more versions of the same thing; any of two or more varying realisations, such as *burnt/burned*, of the same grammatical form — **variant** *adj.*

varicella (várri-séllə) *formal. n.* chickenpox

varicose vein *n.* vein, especially in the legs, that has become abnormally knotted and swollen (also "varix")

variegated (váiri-gaytid) *adj.* multi-coloured; characterised by variety, varied: *a richly variegated plot* — **-gation** *n.*

variola (və-rī́-ələ) *formal. n.* smallpox — **-late** *adj.*

variorum edition *n.* edition of a text, together with notes by various commentators [related to *various*]

varlet *n.* knight's page in former times; *archaic.* despicable scoundrel [variant of *valet*] — **-ry** *n.*

vas (vass, vaass) *formal. n., pl.* **vasa** bodily channel or duct

vascular *adj.* relating to or containing vessels for conveying blood, sap, or other biological fluids: *cardiovascular disease, vascular plant tissue*

vasectomy *n.* surgical sterilisation of a man by cutting either or both of the sperm-carrying ducts

vassal *n.* person, such as a serf, who owed a feudal lord allegiance in exchange for renting his land; subordinate, henchman, dependant — **-age** *n.*

vatic *formal. adj.* relating to a prophet or bard

vaudeville *chiefly U.S. n.* music-hall entertainment — **-villian** *n., adj.*

vault *n.* arched ceiling or roof, typically of stone or masonry; *formal.* over-arching expanse: *the starry vault of the heavens*; burial chamber; secure place of storage such as a safe or large strong-box built into a wall

vaunt *tr.v.* to show off, brag about something [related to *vain*] — **vaunt** *n.*

vector *n.* force, speed, or other quantity having both magnitude and direction; influence, drive, or force; *formal.* insect, rat, or other organism that transmits disease-causing microorganisms (also "carrier")

vedette *n.* scout or sentry on horseback stationed ahead of an army's outposts; *formal.* media star, especially a woman

vegan *n.* vegetarian who avoids all animal products, including milk and eggs [shortened from *vegetarian*] — **vegan** *adj.* — **-ism** *n.*

vegetate *informal. intr.v.* to lead a dull, passive life

vehement (vée-i-mənt) *adj.* forceful, passionate, or emphatic — **-mence**, **-mency** *n.*

vehicle *n.* substance or means, such as a play, for conveying ideas, expressing talents, or the like; painting medium, such as oil, into which the pigments are mixed (also "base"); oil or other inert substance used for bulking up an active medicine

veil *n.* — **take the veil** *formal.* to become a nun

Velcro *trademark. n.* fastening device consisting of two strips of fabric with minute interlocking nylon hooks and loops

velleity (ve-lée-əti, -láy-) *formal. n.* wish or slight tendency, without any action taken to fulfil it

vellum *n.* fine parchment of calfskin, lambskin, or kidskin, as used in bookbinding [related to *veal*]

velocipede *n.* old-fashioned bicycle propelled by pushing the feet along the ground or by front-wheel pedals

velocity *formal. n.* speed

velodrome *n.* cycle-racing arena, typically with a banked track

venal (vée'n'l) *adj.* corrupt; open to or marked by bribery — **-ity** *n.*

venatic (vee-náttik) *formal. adj.* relating to hunting

venation *n.* patterning or system of veins on a leaf, an insect's wing, or the like

vendetta *n.*, blood feud, maintained by a cycle of revenge; quarrel or feud persisting over a long period of time; campaign of vindictive slander or obstructiveness

veneer *n.* shiny surface layer or finishing, as of fine wood or plastic; superficially impressive or deceptively attractive outward appearance; any of the thin layers bonded together to form plywood — **veneer** *tr.v.*

Venerable *n.* title of respect for an Anglican archdeacon; title given to a deceased Roman Catholic at a preliminary level of sainthood

venerate *tr.v.* to revere, respect highly; to worship, adore — **-ation** *n.*

venereal *adj.* relating to sex

venial *adj.* excusable, easily pardoned or forgiven, especially by God — **-ity** *n.*

venial sin *n.* sin that is relatively minor and excusable, and does not deprive the soul of God's grace. Compare MORTAL SIN

Venn diagram *n.* set of circles, typically overlapping, used as a diagram representing mathematical or logical relations [after John *Venn*, the 19th to 20th-century British logician who devised the idea]

venous *adj.* relating to veins: *venous blood* — **-nosity** *n.*

ventage *n.* finger hole, as on a flute

ventail *n.* movable lower front part of a medieval helmet [related to *vent*]

ventilate *tr.v.* to pass fresh air through (a room, mine,

or other area); to express openly, discuss freely, examine publicly: *ventilated their grievances* — **-lator, -lation** *n.*

ventral *formal. adj.* relating to the front or lower surface of the body. Compare DORSAL

ventricle *n.* small anatomical cavity or chamber, especially in the brain or heart

ventriloquism (ven-tríllə-kwiz'm) *n.* throwing or projecting the voice, as an entertainer does who appears to make a dummy speak — **-ist** *n.* — **-ise** *intr.v.*

venturi (ven-téwr-i, -tŏŏr-) *n.* tube with a narrow throat, as in a pipe or carburettor, for measuring fluid pressure or providing suction [after G.B. *Venturi*, the 18th-19th-century Italian physicist whose research led to its invention]

venue (vénnew) *chiefly British. n.* site of a planned event, such as a match, conference, or concert

veracity *formal. n.* truthfulness, honesty, or accuracy — **-acious** *adj.*

verbatim (ver-báy-tim) *adj.* word-for-word, using the very same words — **verbatim** *adv.*

verbiage *n.* wordiness, excess of words

verbosity *n.* tendency to use too many words, especially in speech — **verbose** *adj.*

verdant *formal. adj.* green with growing vegetation, flourishing — **-dure** *n.*

verderer *n.* officer in charge of the royal forests in former times

verdigris (vérdi-griss, -gree) *n.* greenish crust forming on copper, brass, or bronze surfaces (also "aerugo", "verd antique") [Old French *vert-de-Grice*, literally, green of Greece]

verdure *formal. n.* rich, green, flourishing vegetation — **-durous** *adj.*

verge *n.* rod or staff carried as an emblem of authority or office

verger *n.* church usher and attendant

verglas (váir-glaa) *chiefly British. formal. n.* thin layer of ice or sleet

veridical (ve-rīddik'l) *formal. adj.* truthful, honest; genuine — **-ity** *n.*

verification *n.* proof or proving that a theory or statement is true — **verify** *tr.v.* — **-fiable** *adj.*

verisimilitude *formal. n.* appearance of truth, likeness to reality

veritable *formal. adj.* actual, real; out-and-out, utter, exactly as specified: *She's a veritable saint*

verity *formal. n.* true or indisputably accurate statement, belief, principle, or the like: *the eternal verities*

verjuice *n.* juice of unripe grapes, sour apples, or the like, formerly used in cookery

vermeil (vér-mayl) *formal. n.* gilded silver, bronze, or copper; *archaic.* vermilion

vermicide *n.* worm remedy, medicine used to destroy or expel worms, especially parasitic intestinal worms (also "vermifuge", "anthelmintic")

vermicular *formal. adj.* worm-like, relating to worms, or caused by worms

vermiculate *formal. adj.* wavy, having winding worm-like lines, movements, decorations, or the like; worm-eaten or worm-infested

vermiculite *n.* insulation or seed-bed material in the form of lightweight fragments of mica-derived minerals

vermiform appendix *n.* appendix (organ in the body)

vermilion *n.* vivid red colour (also "vermillion", "cinnabar") — **vermilion** *adj.*

vernacular *n.* language used for ordinary communication within a speech-community, by contrast with a language that has greater prestige, official status, or international currency: *increasing use of English and other vernaculars at the expense of Latin*; specialised sub-language of a trade, profession, or other group: *in the vernacular of physics*; *informal.* swearing, bad language (humorous) — **vernacular** *adj.* — **-ism** *n.*

vernal *formal. adj.* relating to the spring; fresh and youthful

vernier (vérni-ər) *n.* finely calibrated scale supplementing the main scale of a measuring instrument [after Pierre *Vernier*, a 17th-century French mathematician]

verruca (ve-rŏŏkə) *n., pl.* **-cas** or **-cae** wart or wart-like growth, especially on the foot — **-cose** *adj.*

versatile *adj.* capable of doing or being used for a wide variety of things — **-tility** *n.*

vers libre (vaír léebr) *n.* free verse [French]

verso *n., pl.* **-sos** left-hand even-numbered page of a book; reverse side of a sheet of paper, such as the side of a letter that is to be read second. Compare RECTO [from Latin *verso folio*, when the page has been turned]

vertebrate *adj.* having a spine or backbone, as fish, birds, and mammals do — **vertebrate** *n.*

vertex *n., pl.* **-texes** or **-tices** highest point, apex; point of intersection of two lines in geometry; highest point of the skull; *formal.* crown of the head

vertigo (vérti-gō) *n.* dizziness — **-tiginous** *adj.*

vesica *formal. n., pl.* **-cae** bladder, especially the urinary bladder — **-ical** *adj.*

vesicant *formal. n.* blistering agent, such as mustard gas — **vesicant** *adj.* — **-cate** *v.* — **-cation** *n.*

vesicle *n.* cavity filled with air or fluid, as in the body, plant tissue, or volcanic rock; *formal.* blister — **-sicular** *adj.*

vespers *pl.n.* church service in the late afternoon or evening

vespertine *formal. adj.* relating to, appearing in, or occurring in the evening; open or active in the evening, as some flowers and insects are

vespiary *formal. n.* wasps' nest; colony of wasps or hornets

vested interest *n.* interest or involvement in something, based on having a stake in its outcome

vestibule *n.* entrance hall or lobby; body cavity serving as an entrance, as in the inner ear — **-bular** *adj.*

vestige *n.* remnant, trace: *of all that glory not a vestige remains* — **-tigial** *adj.*

vestments *formal. pl.n.* ceremonial garments, such as those of an officiating priest

vestry *n.* small room in a church for storing vestments; parish meeting or meeting place of the administrative committee of a parish or congregation

veteran car *n.* motor car made before 1919. Compare VINTAGE CAR

veterinary *adj.* relating to animal diseases or injuries and their treatment

veto (vée-tō) *n., pl.* **-oes** right to reject or block a course of action, especially a proposed piece of legislation; vote or action taken in exercising this right [Latin *veto*, I forbid] — **veto** *tr.v.*

vexatious *adj.* annoying, irritating; *formal.* referring or relating to a legal action, claim, or suit that is started with the sole intention of harassing the other party: *vexatious litigants*

vexillary *formal. adj.* relating to flags, banners, or standards ~ *n.* standard-bearer

vexillology *formal. n.* study of flags — **-ologist** *n.*

viable *adj.* capable of living or surviving independently: *a viable foetus*; feasible, possible: *viable plans*

viaduct (vī-ə-dukt) *n.* bridge, typically supported by a series of arches, carrying a road or railway over a valley

vial *n.* small container for medicine, poison, or other liquid, typically a tiny stoppered glass bottle (also "phial")

via media *formal. n., pl.* **viae mediae** path of moderation that avoids extremes [Latin, middle way]

viands (vī́-əndz) *formal or archaic. pl.n.* food, provisions (now often humorous)

viatic *formal. adj.* relating to travelling or roads (also "viatical")

viaticum (vī-átti-kəm) *n., pl.* **-cums** or **-ca** holy communion given to a person in danger of death

vibrant (vī́-brənt) *adj.* extremely lively, as if vibrating with life or energy: *vibrant drawings* — **-brancy** *n.*

vibrato (vi-bráa-tō) *n., pl.* **-tos** richly trembling or vibrating sound, especially as heard in violin music — **vibrato** *adv., adj.*

vibrissae (vī-bríssee) *pl.n.* bristly feathers near the beak of an insect-eating bird; whiskers or sensitive hairs, as at either side of a cat's mouth (singular "vibrissa")

vicarious (vi-káiri-əss) *adj.* indirect or second-hand, experienced through someone else's feelings or actions: *his vicarious enjoyment of her success*

vice-chancellor *n.* chief administrator of a university

vicegerent (vī́ss-jérrənt) *n.* official deputy of a sovereign or magistrate — **vicegerent** *adj.*

vicereine (vī́ss-rayn) *n.* viceroy's wife; female viceroy

viceroy (vī́ss-roy) *n.* governor of a country or colony ruling in the name of the sovereign: *viceroy of India* — **viceregal** *adj.*

vicissitudes (vi-sissi-tewdz) *formal. pl.n.* changes, variations, fluctuations, especially when unplanned, and sometimes for the worse

victualler (vítt'l-ər) *n. chiefly British.* pub-owner, innkeeper, licensed purveyor of alcoholic spirits; provisioner, supplier of food to an army, ship, or the like

victuals (vítt'lz) *archaic or formal. pl.n.* food (now humorous) — **victual** *v.*

vicuña (vi-kéwn-ə, -kōōn-yə) *n.* llama-like mammal of the Andes, with a fine silky fleece; vicuña wool

vide infra (vī́-dee ínfrə, vídday) *interj.* see below (used, as in footnotes, to direct a reader to consult a later passage). Compare VIDE SUPRA [Latin]

videlicet (vi-deéli-set, -dáyli-ket) *interj.* that is, namely (used in a text to introduce examples; also "viz.") [Latin, it is easy to see]

vide supra (sōō-prə) *interj.* see above (used, as in footnotes, to direct a reader to consult an earlier passage). Compare VIDE INFRA [Latin]

vie *intr.v.* to compete or strive for victory or superiority

vigil (víjil) *formal. n.* state or period of remaining awake at night, as for guard duty or prayers

vigilant *adj.* alert, watchful, on the lookout for danger — **-lance** *n.*

vigilante (víji-lánti) *informal. n.* member of the public who joins a gang to avenge crimes instead of getting the police involved; zealous but unauthorised person always on the lookout for deviant behaviour in the community — **vigilante** *adj.*

vignette (vin-yét) *n.* sketch or brief incident in a book, film, or play; decorative picture, vine-leaf design, or the like, as on a book's title page; picture on a postage stamp, as distinct from the frame and lettering [French, literally, young vine]

vilify (vílli-fī) *formal. tr.v.* to slander, defame; to insult or abuse vigorously — **-fication** *n.*

villein (víl-ən, -ayn) *n.* feudal peasant who was relatively free but owed rents or services to his lord in return for his land — **-age** *n.*

villus *formal. n., pl.* **-li** tiny hair-like projection, as on moss or in the small intestine — **-lous** *adj.*

vinaigrette (vínni-grét) *n.* oil-and-vinegar salad dressing (also "French dressing") — **vinaigrette** *adj.*

vinculum *n., pl.* **-la** line drawn above two or more terms in algebra, linking them for treatment as a single unit; *formal.* tie, bond, or link

vindicate *tr.v.* to justify, uphold, or excuse by means of argument, evidence, or proof; to clear of blame or suspicion, dispel an accusation against — **-ation** *n.*

vindictive *adj.* spiteful, bitter, vengeful

viniculture *formal. n.* wine-making or grape-growing (also "viticulture") — **-turist** *n.* — **-tural** *adj.*

vin ordinaire (váN órdi-náir) *n., pl.* **-s -s** unpretentious or inexpensive table wine often used as the house wine in a restaurant

vinous *formal. adj.* relating to wine or wine-drinking; wine-coloured

vintage *n.* grape harvest or yield; year of origin of a wine; time of origin ~ *adj.* typical of the best of its kind or source: *a vintage Hollywood musical*

vintage car *n.* motor car made between 1919 and 1930. Compare VETERAN CAR

vintner *n.* wine merchant

violate *tr.v.* to break or disregard (a rule or regulation); to harm, profane, or disturb: *violate the peace/grave*; *formal or archaic* to rape — **-ation** *n.*

virago (vi-ráagō) *n., pl.* **-goes** or **-gos** overbearing, scolding woman

virid *formal. adj.* green, especially with growing plants (also "verdant") — **virescent** *adj.* — **virescence**, **viridity** *n.*

virile *adj.* having or showing the qualities of a grown man, manly; relating to male sexual ability or prowess; energetic, forceful, vigorous — **-ility** *n.*

virilism *n.* abnormal development of male characteristics in a woman

virtu (vur-tōō) *formal. n.* antiques, curios, and objets d'art, or a cultivated liking for them

virtuoso *n., pl.* **-sos** or **-si** person with dazzling mastery of technique: *a virtuoso on the violin* — **virtuoso** *adj.* — **-osity** *n.*

virulent (vírrew-lənt) *adj.* extremely harmful and rapid in effect: *a virulent disease*; bitterly hostile, spiteful, hate-filled — **-lence** *n.*

visage (vízzij) *formal. n.* face, or expression on a face

vis-à-vis (veéz-ə-veé) *prep.* regarding, in relation to, compared with [French, literally, face to face]

viscera (víssərə) *pl.n.* intestines and other internal organs (singular "viscus")

visceral *adj.* relating to the viscera; instinctive or intuitive, as a gut feeling is, rather than rational: *a visceral reaction*

viscid (víssid) *formal. adj.* covered with a sticky substance: *viscid leaves*; viscous — **-ity** *n.*

viscous *formal. adj.* gluey, thick and sticky, as some

liquids are (also "viscid") — **-cosity** *n.*

visionary *adj.* having or showing foresight or great imagination; idealistic, unrealistic, impracticable, or unpractical: *visionary schemes/inventors*; relating to dreams or fantasies — **visionary** *n.*

visitation *n.* official visit, as for purposes of inspection; appearance of a ghost, spirit, angel, or the like; punishment or affliction, especially when regarded as imposed by God — **visitant** *n.*

visor *n.* front part of a helmet; shield or protective mask for the eyes, as worn by welders; glare shield fitted at the top of a car's windscreen

vista *n.* distant view, as through an avenue of trees; broad awareness or mental view: *a vista of his past life*

visualise *tr.v.* to imagine, form a mental picture of — **-sation** *n.*

vitals *informal. pl.n.* organs of the body, especially those essential for maintaining life

vitellus *formal. n., pl.* **-elli** egg yolk — **-elline** *adj.*

vitiate (víshi-ayt) *formal. tr.v.* to reduce the value or effectiveness of: *an argument vitiated by cheap appeals to emotion* — **-ation** *n.*

vitreous *formal. adj.* glassy; glass-like — **-eosity** *n.*

vitrify *v.* to turn into glass, by or as if by heating or melting — **-ification** *n.*

vitriol *n.* sulphuric acid (old-fashioned)

vitriolic *adj.* bitterly critical or condemnatory; relating to vitriol

vituperative (vī-téw-pə-rətiv) *formal. adj.* bitterly critical or abusive — **vituperate** *tr.v.* — **-ation** *n.*

vivacious *adj.* lively, sparkling, spirited — **-vacity** *n.*

vivarium (vi-váiri-əm) *n., pl.* **-ia** or **-iums** enclosure for keeping or breeding animals or plants indoors

viva voce (vīvə vṓsī, -chi) *n.* exam in the form of an interview, rather than as a written paper or practical test (also "viva") [Latin, with the living voice] — **viva voce** *adv.* — **viva** *tr.v.*

viviparous (vi-vípparəss, vī-) *formal. adj.* giving birth to live offspring, as most mammals do, rather than laying eggs. Compare OVIPAROUS, OVOVIVIPAROUS

vivisection *n.* cutting up or into the body of a living animal, especially for research; experimentation on living animals — **-ist** *n.*

vizier (vi-zeér) *n.* high officer in a Muslim government — **-ate** *n.*

vocalise *v.* to voice, put into words, say — **-isation** *n.*

vocalist *informal. n.* singer of commercial popular music

vocation *n.* one's principal or most fitting occupation in life, calling; strong inclination or prompting to a religious life

vocational *adj.* relating to the skills needed for a job, especially a technical rather than a professional or academic job: *vocational training*

vociferous (vō-síffərəss) *formal. adj.* loud and insistent, especially in protest — **-ferate** *v.*

voice *tr.v.* to adjust (organ pipes or a wind instrument) in order to perfect the tone and pitch

volar *formal. adj.* relating to the palm of the hand or sole of the foot

volatile *adj.* evaporating or vaporising readily at normal temperature and pressure; liable to sudden, unpredictable changes of mood or attitude: *a volatile temperament/political situation/electorate* — **-tility** *n.*

vol-au-vent (vól-ə-von, -ō-VÓN) *n., pl.* **vol-au-vents** pastry shell filled with a savoury mixture in a thick sauce, typically served before the main course or as a snack [French, literally, flight in the wind]

volition *n.* power or ability to choose, will; exercise of choice: *They returned of their own volition*

volplane *intr.v.* to glide without power, as an aircraft might

voltaic *adj.* relating or referring to electric current produced by chemical action, as in a battery (also "galvanic") [after Alessandro *Volta*, an 18th-19th-century Italian physicist who pioneered the study of electricity]

volte-face (vólt-fáss) *formal. n.* about-turn in attitude or policy, U-turn

voluble *adj.* fluent, speaking easily, able to chat away (sometimes mildly derogatory) — **-ubility** *n.*

voluminous *formal. adj.* having a large volume, or size; extensive, as if filling volumes: *voluminous writings/output*

voluptuary *formal. n.* person devoted to luxurious living and sensual pleasures — **voluptuary** *adj.*

voluptuous *adj.* curvy and sexually appealing; *formal.* relating to sensual pleasure or desire

volute (və-léwt) *n.* spiral or scroll-like form, shell, architectural ornament, or the like — **volute** *adj.*

volution *formal. n.* rolling or revolving movement; coil or whorl of a spiral shell

vomitory *n.* passageway to a bank of seats in a stadium or amphitheatre, as in the Colosseum in Rome

voodoo *n.* cult or religion of West African origin, practised mainly in Haiti, involving sorcery with some Christian elements — **voodoo** *adj.*

voracious *adj.* having or showing great eagerness to devour: *a voracious appetite/reader* — **voracity** *n.*

vortex *n., pl.* **-texes** or **-tices** rotating flow or rush, as of a whirlwind or whirlpool; overwhelming influence or activity that seems to swallow up its participants

votary *n.* follower of or devoted believer in a religion, political leader, or the like, devotee, enthusiast — **votary** *adj.*

votive *formal. adj.* based on the fulfilment of a vow: *a votive prayer/offering* (also "ex-voto")

vouch *intr.v.* — **vouch for** to provide or serve as support for or a guarantee of

vouchsafe *formal. tr.v.* to give or bestow (an answer, favour, or the like) in a grudging or condescending way

voussoir (vōō-swáar) *n.* wedge-shaped stone in the curved section of an arch or vault

vox populi (vóks póppew-lī) *n.* public opinion, popular feeling (also *British informal* "vox pop") [Latin, the voice of the people]

voyeur (vwī-yúr) *n.* peeping Tom [French, literally, watcher] — **-ism** *n.* — **-istic** *adj.*

vulcanise *tr.v.* to improve (rubber or a similar material) by chemical treatment, especially with sulphur compounds [after *Vulcan*, the Roman god of fire and craftsmanship] — **-isation** *n.*

vulgar fraction *n.* simple fraction, in which both the numerator and the denominator are whole numbers

Vulgate *n.* Latin version of the bible, dating from the 4th century A.D., used in a revised form by Roman Catholics

vulnerable *adj.* in danger of harm, injury, or attack; emotionally insecure, oversensitive — **-ability** *n.*

vulpine *formal. adj.* relating to a fox; foxy, fox-like

W

wacker *British. slang. n.* person born or living in Liverpool, Liverpudlian. Compare SCOUSE

wadi (wóddi) *n.* dry rocky ravine in a desert or semi-desert area, especially Arabia and North Africa, sometimes the channel for a short-lived torrent after heavy rain

wagon-lit (vág-ON-leé) *n., pl.* **wagons-lits** or **wagon-lits** sleeping car, especially on a continental train [French, from *wagon*, a railway carriage + *lit*, a bed]

waif (wayf) *n.* orphaned or forsaken child; stray animal wandering about homeless

wainscot (wáyn-skət) *n.* lower part of a wall covered in wooden panelling or a similar covering; such panelling or facing (also "wainscoting") — **wainscot** *tr.v.*

wainwright *n.* wagon-builder or -repairer

waiter *formal. n.* tray or salver, as for teacups

waits *British. pl.n.* band of musicians formerly playing at public processions or entertainments; tunes typically played by such a band; Christmas buskers or carol-singers

waive *tr.v.* to give up (a claim or right) voluntarily; to suspend or refrain from enforcing (a rule, penalty, or the like); to postpone, or put aside temporarily — **-er** *n.*

wake *n.* funeral watch or festivity prior to burial

Waldorf salad (wáwl-dawrf) *n.* salad of diced walnuts, celery, and apple dressed with mayonnaise [after the *Waldorf*-Astoria Hotel in New York, where it was first served]

wale *n.* rib or ridge on corduroy or a similar fabric; texture of such a fabric; ridge, as round a basket or ship's rail, for strengthening or support; plank used for strengthening the side of a trench, ship, or the like; whip mark, weal

wall *n.* — **the wall** marathon runners' physical or psychological difficulties often arising after about 20 miles

wallah (wóllə) *Indian or British. informal. n.* person doing a specified type of work: *the post-room wallah*

Walter Mitty person who indulges in fantasies to compensate for his inadequacies; daydreamer [after the hero of the short story "The Secret Life of Walter Mitty" of 1932 by James Thurber]

wampum (wómpəm) *n.* shell beads formerly used as currency by North American Indians (also "peag")

wanderlust (wóndər-lust, vaándər-loost) *n.* yearning for travel or urge to travel, especially abroad

wanton (wóntən) *adj.* immoral, unrestrained, licentious; sexually promiscuous; unprovoked, pointless, or arbitrary, especially in a malicious way; wasteful, excessive, or uncontrolled

ward *n.* ridge on a lock or keyhole, or corresponding notch in a key [related to *guard*]

warlock *n.* man practising black magic, sorcerer, male witch

warp (worp) *n.* abnormal twist or curve; threads running lengthways in weaving or in a fabric. Compare WEFT, WOOF; network of cords in a tyre; rope for pulling or tying up a ship; deposit of sediment, as from a river — **warp** *v.*

wash *n.* air turbulence caused by an aircraft; stretch of land intermittently covered by water; kitchen refuse fed to pigs, swill

wasp *chiefly U.S. informal. n.* white Anglo-Saxon Protestant (sometimes derogatory; also "WASP", "Wasp") [taken from the first letters] — **wasp** *adj.*

wassail (wóss-ayl) *n.* toast or salute formerly given on drinking someone's health; drink used in such a toast, typically spiced ale or wine served with baked apples; *archaic.* celebration or festivity marked by heavy drinking and revelry, carousal — **wassail** *v., adj.*

water *n.* purity and brilliance of a diamond or other gemstone; shiny wavy finish, as given to silk

watershed *n.* ridge or other boundary between two areas drained by different river systems; *U.S.* either of such areas; crucial time or event, turning point: *a watershed in the search for peace*

water table *n.* level at and below which the ground is saturated by water

wattle (wótt'l) *n.* fence-making or building material of poles interlaced with reeds, branches, or the like; fold of skin hanging from the throat, as of some birds and lizards; any of several types of Australian acacia tree — **wattle** *tr.v., adj.*

wattle and daub *n.* building material of interlaced sticks plastered with mud or clay, as in old cottages or huts; framework made of such material — **wattle-and-daub** *adj.*

waver *intr.v.* to become uncertain or hesitant: *My trust in him began to waver*; to hesitate, show indecision; to sway, quaver, flicker, or the like

wax *intr.v.* to increase gradually; to increase in apparent size or illumination, as the Moon does when approaching full moon (opposite "wane"); *formal or archaic.* to become or grow: *wax lyrical*

waybill *n.* document listing a ship's goods or passengers, and detailing instructions concerning their transport

wayfarer *formal or archaic. n.* wanderer or traveller, especially on foot — **-faring** *adj.*

waylay (way-láy) *tr.v.* to ambush, lie in wait for and take by surprise; to stop and confront unexpectedly, accost

weal *n.* whip mark or similar ridge raised on the flesh (also "wale", "welt")

wean *tr.v.* to accustom (a child or other young mammal) to food other than its mother's milk; to detach (a person) from old habits and pastimes and thereby encourage independence; to bring up with a specified crucial influence: *weaned on television chat shows*

weasel words *pl.n.* unreliable words or expressions, as in *We will use our best endeavours*, suggesting yet evading a promise or commitment [referring to eggs that when sucked dry by weasels keep their shape but are drained of their content]

web *n.* continuous roll of paper, especially newsprint, for use in a rotary printing press

webbing *n.* tape or strong woven strip of cotton or nylon, as used for straps or safety belts

weeds *formal. pl.n.* mourning clothes, as of a widow

weft *n.* threads running crosswise or horizontally in weaving or in a fabric (also "woof"). Compare WARP

weir (weer) *n.* dam in a river or canal designed to raise the water or regulate its flow

weird *Scottish. n.* — **dree one's weird** to accept one's fate, submit to destiny

welkin *archaic. n.* heaven, arching vault of the sky; upper atmosphere

well *British. n.* open central space in front of the judge's bench in a courtroom, where the lawyers sit

welsh *informal. intr.v.* to fail to honour one's debts, keep one's promises, or fulfil other commitments: *welshed on their undertaking*

Weltanschauung (véltan-shów-o͝ong) *n., pl.* **-ungs** or **-ungen** world view, philosophical standpoint [German, literally, world view]

welter *intr.v.* to lie, roll about, or wallow, as in a mudbath; to be soaked in or covered with blood; to be deeply involved in or absorbed by ~ *n.* mess, jumble: *a welter of paperwork*; turmoil, disorder

Weltschmerz (vélt-shmairts) *n.* sorrowful yearning pessimism about life, typically sentimental or romantic [German, literally, world pain]

wen *n.* oily cyst or sore, especially on the scalp

wench *n.* young and usually attractive woman or peasant girl (humorous)

wend *archaic or formal. tr.v.* — **wend one's way** to proceed, go one's way

wether *n.* gelded ram

wheedle *tr.v.* to try to persuade, as by flattery, coax; to obtain by wheedling

whet *tr.v.* to sharpen (a knife or other cutting tool), hone; to stimulate or increase (appetite, desire, or interest) — **-stone** *n.*

whey (way, hway) *n.* watery part of milk that can be separated from the solid curds, as in cheesemaking (also "serum")

whimsy *n.* lively, playful imagination often combined with mildly eccentric behaviour; quaint idea, eccentric gesture, odd piece of behaviour, or the like — **-sical** *adj.*

whip *tr.v.* to wrap with a protective material (such as twine) in order to prevent fraying

whiplash injury *n.* neck or spine injury caused by sudden jerking of the head (also "whiplash")

whistle-stop *U.S. informal. adj.* relating to a political electioneering campaign featuring a series of brief appearances at small towns

whited sepulchre *formal. n.* hypocrite, wolf in sheep's clothing (literary) [from Jesus's description of the scribes and Pharisees, in Matthew 23:27]

whiting *n.* chalk that is ground for use in paint, polish, or putty

whitlow *n.* sore or abscess near the nail of a finger or toe

whorl (wurl, hwurl) *n.* small flywheel on the spindle of a spinning wheel; something tightly curled or curved; radiating pattern of leaves or petals around a stem; single turn or spiral on a shell; one of the characteristic patterns of ridges on a fingerprint

widow's peak *n.* hairline having a marked V-shaped dip at the centre of the forehead [from its resemblance to the front of the hood that widows used to wear]

wiles *pl.n.* deceitful charms used to influence others

willy-nilly *adv.* whether willingly or unwillingly; haphazardly and excitedly [Middle English *will I nill I*, whether I be willing or unwilling]

wilt *v.* to make or become limp, drooping, or weak

wily *adj.* sly, calculating, full of wiles

wimple *n.* head-cloth framing the face, as worn by some nuns and by women in medieval Europe

winch *tr.v.* to hoist or raise, typically using a winding apparatus — **winch** *n.*

winder *n.* step in a winding staircase

windfall *n.* something, such as a fruit, that has fallen in the wind; stroke of unexpected good fortune

winding sheet *n.* shroud, sheet for wrapping a corpse (old-fashioned)

windlass *n.* winding apparatus, winch

windmill *n.* — **tilt at windmills** to attack something that to the attacker seems powerful and threatening, but that onlookers or observers can see is really harmless [referring to Don Quixote, who charged at windmills, thinking they were monsters]

window *n.* metal foil released in strips into the air to thwart an enemy's radar system (also "chaff")

window dressing *n.* presentation of awkward features or policies in a selectively favourable way

wind rose *n.* diagram with radiating lines showing the frequency and strength of winds from each direction at a certain place

windsock *n.* tapering cloth tube fixed to a pole to indicate wind direction, as at airfields (also "wind sleeve", "air sock", "wind cone", "drogue")

Windsor knot *n.* tie knot, wide and triangular, produced by making an extra turn

winnow *tr.v.* to blow the chaff away in order to separate the grain; to examine with the aim of separating good from bad — **winnow out** to remove something unwanted from a collection or mixture

winsome *adj.* charming, in a youthful or innocent way

winze *n.* sloping or vertical shaft in a mine, as for ventilation between levels

wiseacre *chiefly U.S. informal. n.* wise guy, clever Dick, know-all, smart aleck (also *U.S.* "wisenheimer")

wistful *adj.* sad and thoughtful; full of unfulfilled desires or sad longings

withe *n.* tough, flexible twig or rope made of twigs, used for tying things together (also "withy")

withering *adj.* belittling, causing embarrassment, scornful: *withering sarcasm*

withers *pl.n.* highest point of a horse's back, situated behind the neck, between the shoulder blades

withershins *archaic or Scottish. adv.* in a reverse direction, especially one opposite to that of the Sun; anticlockwise (also "widdershins")

wittol *archaic. n.* man who knows about and tolerates his wife's sexual infidelity. Compare CUCKOLD

wizened (wízz'nd) *adj.* dried up, shrivelled, or wrinkled, as through old age: *wizened features*

woad *n.* blue dye, used by ancient Britons to colour their skin

woggle *n.* leather band used to fasten the neck square of a Scout or Guide

wok *n.* large metal bowl used for frying in Chinese cooking

wont (wōnt, wont) *formal. n.* custom, habit: *worked quickly, as was her wont* ~ *adj.* accustomed, used: *worked quickly, as she was wont to do* — **-ed** *adj.*

woof *n.* threads running crosswise or horizontally in weaving or in a fabric (also "weft"). Compare WARP

woofer *n.* loudspeaker specially adapted for low-pitched sounds. Compare TWEETER

woolgathering *n.* absent-minded daydreaming

woolsack *n.* Lord Chancellor's ceremonial seat in the House of Lords, taken to represent the office itself [from the sack of wool representing Britain's economic wealth in medieval times]

woozy *informal. adj.* dizzy and dazed, as if seasick or slightly drunk

wormwood *n.* plant yielding a bitter oil used in flavouring absinthe and some other drinks; *formal.* bitterness, or some distressing cause of it: *All life was but gall and wormwood to them* [related to *vermouth*]

wow *n.* distortion or variation of pitch, as produced by a faulty record player or tape recorder

wrack *n. formal.* remnant or remains of something, especially a shipwreck; mass of seaweed entangled with driftwood and cast ashore

wraith *n.* ghost; apparition of a person supposedly appearing just before his death (literary)

wrangler *n.* first-class honours graduate in the mathematics tripos at Cambridge; *U.S.* cowboy, or rancher, one tending horses

wreak (reek) *tr.v.* to inflict or cause something: *wreak vengeance on one's enemies; wrought havoc with my make-up box*

wrest *formal. tr.v.* to seize after grappling for: *wrested power from the rulers* [related to *wrist*]

writ *n.* written court order; explicit authority: *My writ doesn't run that far*

wrong-foot *informal. tr.v.* to cause (an opponent) to move into an awkward, embarrassing, or losing position by feinting or pretending to dodge

wrought *adj.* worked by hammering or shaping with tools rather than by cutting: *wrought silver*

wry *adj.* twisted from cynicism or distaste: *a wry smile*; humorous in a dry ironic way: *wry wit*; *formal.* bent abnormally: *a wry neck*

Wunderkind (wúndər-kind, vóóndər-kint) *n., pl.* **-kinds** or **-kinder** child prodigy, infant prodigy; person who gains great success at an unusually early age, whizz kid [German, literally, wonder child]

wurst (wurst, vurst, voorst) *n.* large German sausage

Wykehamist (wíckəmist) *n.* pupil or ex-pupil of Winchester College [after William of *Wykeham*, a 14th-century bishop who founded the school at Winchester] — **Wykehamist** *adj.*

wyvern (wī́vərn) *archaic. n.* dragon with wings and a serpent's tail, as in heraldry (also "wivern") [related to *viper*]

X, Y, Z

Xanthippe (zan-típpi) *formal. n.* overbearing, shrewish, scolding woman [after *Xanthippe* the wife of the ancient Greek philosopher Socrates]

xanthochroid (zán-thə-kroyd) *formal. adj.* having a light complexion and fair hair — **xanthochroid** *n.*

xanthous (zánthəss) *formal. adj.* yellow; having light brown or sallow skin

X-chromosome *n.* larger of the two types of sex chromosome in humans and most animals, associated with female characteristics. Compare Y-CHROMOSOME

xenogamy (ze-nóggəmi, zee-) *formal. n.* cross-pollination, cross-fertilisation — **-gamous** *adj.*

xenoglossia (zé-nō-glóssi-ə, zée-) *formal. n.* speaking in a language unknown to the speaker, believed by some to be possible in a trance

xenophobia (zé-nə-fṓbi-ə, zée-) *n.* excessive or irrational fear of foreigners; prejudice against or hatred of foreigners — **-bic** *adj., n.* — **-phobe** *n.*

xenopus (zénnəpəss) *n.* clawed toad of South African origin, formerly used in pregnancy testing (also *South African* "platanna")

xeric (zé-rik, zée-) *formal. adj.* relating to an extremely dry habitat, such as a desert

xeroderma (zéer-ō-dérmə) *formal. n.* abnormally dry skin or skin condition — **-matic** *adj.*

xerography (ze-róggrəfi, zeer-) *n.* dry photocopying process, using a resinous powder rather than ink — **-graphic** *adj.*

xerophyte (zéer-ō-fīt) *n.* cactus or other plant that grows in very dry conditions — **-phytic** *adj.*

xiphoid (zíffoyd, zī́-foyd) *formal. adj.* shaped like a sword

xylem (zī́-ləm) *n.* woody tissue of plants, which provides support and conducts water

xylograph (zī́lə-graaf) *formal. n.* wood engraving; print made from a wood block — **xylograph** *tr.v.* — **-er, -y** *n.*

xyloid (zī́-loyd) *formal. adj.* woody, wood-like, or wooden

xylophagous (zī-lóffəgəss) *formal. adj.* wood-eating, as some insects are — **-phagy** *n.*

xyst (zist) *n.* portico used by athletes for exercise in ancient Greece; tree-lined terrace or garden walk in ancient Rome (also "xystus")

xyster (zístər) *n.* surgical instrument for scraping bones

yagi (yáagi, yaggi) *n.* directional aerial with several parallel elements, as used in radio, astronomy, and